Glencoe

Literature

LOG ON Literature Online

Textbook Internet resources are just a click away!

STEP 1 Go to glencoe.com

STEP 2 Connect to resources by entering QuickPass™ codes.

LOG ON Literature Online

GL49855u1T — Enter this code with appropriate unit numbers.

STEP 3 Access your Online Student Edition, teaching resources, and more:

Literature and Reading Resources

- Author Search
- Literature Classics
- Big Idea Web Quests
- Literary Elements eFlashcards and Games
- Interactive Reading Practice

Selection Resources

- Audio Summaries
- Selection Quizzes
- Selection Vocabulary eFlashcards and Games
- Reading-Writing Connection Activities

Vocabulary Resources

- Academic and Selection Vocabulary eFlashcards and Games
- Multi-Language Glossaries

Writing, Grammar, and Research Resources

- Interactive Writing Models
- Writing and Research Handbook
- Graphic Organizers
- Sentence-Combining Activities
- Publishing Options

Media Literacy, Speaking, Listening, and Viewing Resources

- Media Analysis Guides
- Project Ideas and Templates
- Presentation Tips and Strategies

Assessment Resources

- End-of-Unit Assessment
- ACT/SAT Vocabulary eFlashcards and Games
- Test-Taking Tips and Strategies

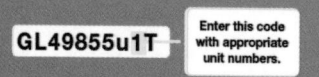

On the Cover:

Arsenault, David (20th C. American)

Outside the Box

Oil on Canvas.

TEACHER EDITION

Program Consultants

Jeffrey D. Wilhelm, Ph.D.
Douglas Fisher, Ph.D.
Beverly Ann Chin, Ph.D.
Jacqueline Jones Royster, DA

McGraw Hill Glencoe

Acknowledgments

Grateful acknowledgment is given authors, publishers, photographers, museums, and agents for permission to reprint the following copyrighted material. Every effort has been made to determine copyright owners. In case of any omissions, the Publisher will be pleased to make suitable acknowledgments in future editions.

Acknowledgments continued on page R103.

COVER (inset)David Arsenault/Private Collection/The Bridgeman Art Library, (bkgd)Jules Frazier/Getty Images; **T6** (t)Images.com, (b)Erich Lessing/Art Resource, NY; **T7** Royalty-Free/CORBIS; **T8** Private Collection/Bridgeman Art Library; **T9** Edward Hopper/Indianapolis Museum of Art/Bridgeman Art Library; **T10** Seamas Culligan/ZUMA/CORBIS; **T13** Mary Evans Picture Library/The Image Works; **T15** Images.com/CORBIS; **T18** Private Collection/Bridgeman Art Library; **T19** Courtesy of Julian Hartnoll/Bridgeman Art Library; **T21** Scala/Art Resource, NY; **T23** Sean Sexton Collection/CORBIS; **T26** CNAC/MNAM/Dist. Réunion des Musées Nationaux/Art Resource, NY; **T27** SuperStock; **T28** CORBIS; **T30** T. F. Chen Cultural Center/SuperStock; **T37** Digital Vision/Getty Images; **T58** David Schmidt/Masterfile.

Glencoe

The McGraw-Hill Companies

Send all inquiries to:
Glencoe/McGraw-Hill
8787 Orion Place
Columbus, OH 43240-4027

ISBN (student edition): 978-0-07-877978-7
MHID (student edition): 0-07-877978-2
ISBN (teacher edition): 978-0-07-877985-5
MHID (teacher edition): 0-07-877985-5

Printed in the United States of America.

1 2 3 4 5 6 7 8 9 10 027/055 13 12 11 10 09 08

Consultants

Senior Program Consultants

Jeffrey D. Wilhelm, PhD, a former middle and secondary school English and reading teacher, is currently Professor of Education at Boise State University. He is the author or coauthor of numerous articles and several books on the teaching of reading and literacy, including award-winning titles such as *You Gotta BE the Book* and *Reading Don't Fix No Chevys.* He also works with local schools as part of the Adolescent Literacy Project and recently helped establish the National Writing Project site at Boise State University.

Douglas Fisher, PhD, is Professor of Language and Literacy Education and Director of Professional Development at San Diego State University, where he teaches English language development and literacy. He also serves as Director of City Heights Educational Pilot, which won the Christa McAuliffe Award from the American Association of State Colleges and Universities. He has published numerous articles on reading and literacy, differentiated instruction, and curriculum design. He is coauthor of the book *Improving Adolescent Literacies: Strategies That Work* and coeditor of the book *Inclusive Urban Schools.*

Program Consultants

Beverly Ann Chin, PhD, is Professor of English, Director of the English Teaching Program, former Director of the Montana Writing Project, and former Director of Composition at the University of Montana in Missoula. She currently serves as a Member at Large of the Conference of English Leadership. Dr. Chin is a nationally recognized leader in English language arts standards, curriculum, and assessment. Formerly a high school teacher and an adult education reading teacher, Dr. Chin has taught in English language arts education at several universities and has received awards for her teaching and service.

Jacqueline Jones Royster, DA, is Professor of English and Senior Vice Provost and Executive Dean of the Colleges of Arts and Sciences at The Ohio State University. She is currently on the Writing Advisory Committee of the National Commission on Writing and serves as chair for both the Columbus Literacy Council and the Ohioana Library Association. In addition to the teaching of writing, Dr. Royster's professional interests include the rhetorical history of African American women and the social and cultural implications of literate practices. She has contributed to and helped to edit numerous books, anthologies, and journals.

Advisory Board

Special Consultants

Donald R. Bear, PhD
Professor, Department of Curriculum and Instruction
Director, E. L. Cord Foundation Center for Learning and Literacy at the University of Nevada, Reno. Author of ***Words Their Way*** and ***Words Their Way with English Learners.***

The Writers' Express
Immediate Impact. Lasting Transformation. wex.org

Jana Echevarria, PhD
Professor, Educational Psychology, California State University, Long Beach.
Author of ***Making Content Comprehensible for English Learners: the SIOP Model.***

FOLDABLES **Dinah Zike, MEd,** was a classroom teacher and a consultant for many years before she began to develop Foldables®—a variety of easily created graphic organizers. Zike has written and developed more than 150 supplemental books and materials used in classrooms worldwide. Her *Big Book of Books and Activities* won the Teachers' Choice Award.

Glencoe National Reading and Language Arts Advisory Council

Mary A. Avalos, PhD
Assistant Department Chair, Department of Teaching and Learning
Research Assistant Professor, Department of Teaching and Learning
University of Miami
Coral Gables, Florida

Wanda J. Blanchett, PhD
Associate Dean for Academic Affairs and Associate Professor of Exceptional Education
School of Education
University of Wisconsin–Milwaukee
Milwaukee, Wisconsin

William G. Brozo, PhD
Professor of Literacy
Graduate School of Education
College of Education and Human Development
George Mason University
Fairfax, Virginia

Nancy Drew, EdD
LaPointe Educational Consultants
Corpus Christi, Texas

Susan Florio-Ruane, EdD
Professor
College of Education
Michigan State University
East Lansing, Michigan

Sharon Fontenot O'Neal, PhD
Associate Professor
Texas State University
San Marcos, Texas

Nancy Frey, PhD
Associate Professor of Literacy in Teacher Education
School of Teacher Education
San Diego State University
San Diego, California

Victoria Ridgeway Gillis, PhD
Associate Professor
Reading Education
Clemson University
Clemson, South Carolina

Kimberly Lawless, PhD
Associate Professor
Curriculum, Instruction and Evaluation
College of Education
University of Illinois at Chicago
Chicago, Illinois

William Ray, MA
Lincoln-Sudbury Regional High School
Sudbury, Massachusetts

Janet Saito-Furukawa, MEd
English Language Arts Specialist
District 4
Los Angeles, California

Bonnie Valdes, MEd
Independent Reading Consultant
CRISS Master Trainer
Largo, Florida

Teacher Reviewers

The following teachers contributed to the review of *Glencoe Literature*.

Bridget M. Agnew
St. Michael School
Chicago, Illinois

Monica Anzaldua Araiza
Dr. Juliet V. Garcia Middle School
Brownsville, Texas

Katherine R. Baer
Howard County Public Schools
Ellicott City, Maryland

Tanya Baxter
Roald Amundsen High School
Chicago, Illinois

Danielle R. Brain
Thomas R. Proctor Senior High School
Utica, New York

Yolanda Conder
Owasso Mid-High School
Owasso, Oklahoma

Gwenn de Mauriac
The Wiscasset Schools
Wiscasset, Maine

Courtney Doan
Bloomington High School
Bloomington, Illinois

Susan M. Griffin
Edison Preparatory School
Tulsa, Oklahoma

Cindi Davis Harris
Helix Charter High School
La Mesa, California

Joseph F. Hutchinson
Toledo Public Schools
Toledo, Ohio

Ginger Jordan
Florien High School
Florien, Louisiana

Dianne Konkel
Cypress Lake Middle School
Fort Myers, Florida

Melanie A. LaFleur
Many High School
Many, Louisiana

Patricia Lee
Radnor Middle School
Wayne, Pennsylvania

Linda Copley Lemons
Cleveland High School
Cleveland, Tennessee

Heather S. Lewis
Waverly Middle School
Lansing, Michigan

Sandra C. Lott
Aiken Optional School
Alexandria, Louisiana

Connie M. Malacarne
O'Fallon Township High School
O'Fallon, Illinois

Lori Howton Means
Edward A. Fulton Junior High School
O'Fallon, Illinois

Claire C. Meitl
Howard County Public Schools
Ellicott City, Maryland

Patricia P. Mitcham
Mohawk High School (Retired)
New Castle, Pennsylvania

Lisa Morefield
South-Western Career Academy
Grove City, Ohio

Kevin M. Morrison
Hazelwood East High School
St. Louis, Missouri

Jenine M. Pokorak
School Without Walls Senior High School
Washington, DC

Susan Winslow Putnam
Butler High School
Matthews, North Carolina

Paul C. Putnoki
Torrington Middle School
Torrington, Connecticut

Jane Thompson Rae
Cab Calloway High School of the Arts
Wilmington, Delaware

Stephanie L. Robin
N. P. Moss Middle School
Lafayette, Louisiana

Ann C. Ryan
Lindenwold High School
Lindenwold, New Jersey

Pamela Schoen
Hopkins High School
Minnetonka, Minnesota

Megan Schumacher
Friends' Central School
Wynnewood, Pennsylvania

Fareeda J. Shabazz
Paul Revere Elementary School
Chicago, Illinois

Molly Steinlage
Brookpark Middle School
Grove City, Ohio

Barry Stevenson
Garnet Valley Middle School
Glen Mills, Pennsylvania

Paul Stevenson
Edison Preparatory School
Tulsa, Oklahoma

Kathy Thompson
Owasso Mid-High School
Owasso, Oklahoma

Book Overview

Stepping into the American Dream. Xavier Cortada. Acrylic on canvas, 243.8 x 248.3 cm. Private collection.

Hotel Lobby, 1943. Edward Hopper. Oil on canvas, 32¼ x 40¾ in. Indianapolis Museum of Art, IN.

Reference Section

Contents

UNIT ONE

The Short Story

Skills and Standards

"Its walls had been lined with human remains . . ."

—Edgar Allan Poe

UNIT TWO

NONFICTION

"Mr. Booth, President Lincoln has been shot! . . . And—oh, Mr. Booth—they say your brother John has done it!"

—James Cross Giblin

PART TWO

ON THE MOVE

PART THREE

FINDING COMMON GROUND

"Begin with that most terrifying of all things, a clean slate."

—Anna Quindlen

UNIT THREE

Poetry

Part One

Nature Inspires

Part Two

Life Lessons

Part Three

The Strength of Family

"I can read regret in her fingers untangling snarls . . ."

—Chitra Banerjee Divakaruni

UNIT FOUR

Drama

Part One

The Power of Love

"O, that I were a glove upon that hand,
That I might touch that cheek!"

—William Shakespeare

Part Two

Awkward Encounters 755

UNIT FIVE

Epic and Myth

Part One

Journeys

"The gods have tried me in a thousand ways."
—Homer

Part Two

Courage and Cleverness ...931

UNIT SIX

Genre Fiction

"There had, after all, been a lunar civilization—and I was the first to find it."

—Arthur C. Clarke

UNIT SEVEN

CONSUMER AND WORKPLACE DOCUMENTS

Reference Section

Selections by Genre

Fiction

Short Story

The Game of Chess, 1943. Maria Helena Vieira da Silva. Oil on canvas, 81 x 100 cm. Musee National d'Art Modern, Centre Georges Pompidou, Paris. ©ARS, NY.

Modern Fable/Parable

Myth

Novel Excerpt

Poetry

El Pan Nuestro, 1923–1928. Diego Rivera. Fresco. Ministry of Education, Mexico City, Mexico.

Ballad

Epic

Graphic Novel

Drama

Tragedy

Comedy

Farce

Modern Drama

Nonfiction and Informational Text

Biography, Autobiography, or Memoir

Essay

Article

Editorial

Interview

Letter

Movie Review

Opinion

Speech

Features

Perspectives

Award-winning nonfiction book excerpts and primary source documents

TIME

High-interest, informative magazine articles

Comparing Literature

Across Genres

UNIT ONE

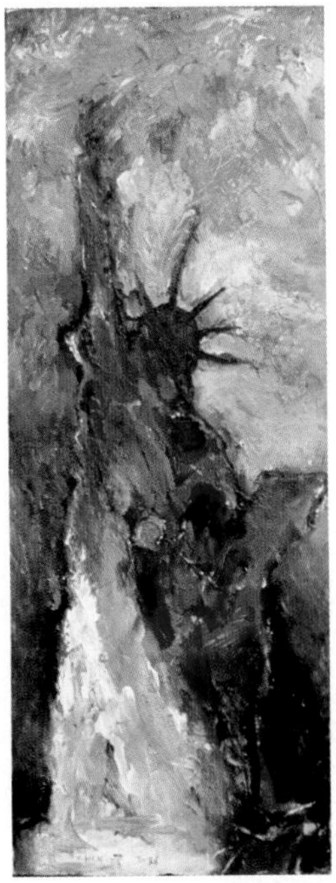

The Burning Passion. Tsing-Fang Chen.

Comparing Literature

Different Viewpoints

UNIT TWO

Features

Comparing Literature

Across Genres

Comparing Literature

Across Genres

Comparing Literature

Across Genres

Comparing Literature

Across Genres

LITERARY FOCUS

Literary History

Independent Reading

Assessment

Skills Workshops

Writing Workshops

Speaking, Listening, and Viewing Workshops

Media Workshop

Grammar Workshops

Vocabulary Workshops

How to Use *Glencoe Literature*

Organization

The literature you will read is organized by literary element and genre into six units: The Short Story, Nonfiction, Poetry, Drama, Epic and Myth, and Genre Fiction.

Each unit contains the following:

A **UNIT INTRODUCTION** provides you with the background information to help make your reading experience more meaningful.

- **GENRE FOCUS** defines the literary elements that make up a unit.

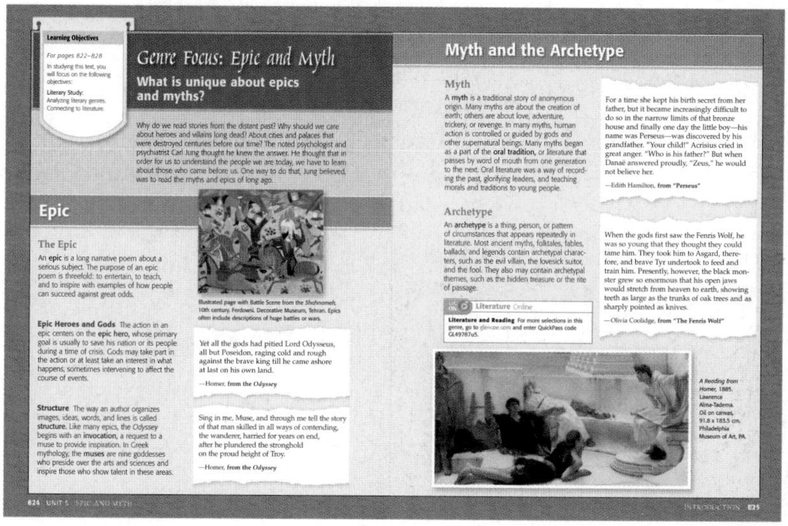

Learning Objectives

For pages 822–828

In studying this text, you will focus on the following objectives:

Literary Study:
Analyzing literary genres.
Connecting to literature.

Genre Focus: Epic and Myth

What is unique about epics and myths?

Why do we read stories from the distant past? Why should we care about heroes and villains long dead? About cities and palaces that were destroyed centuries before our time? The noted psychologist and psychiatrist Carl Jung thought he knew the answer. He thought that in order for us to understand the people we are today, we have to learn about those who came before us. One way to do that, Jung believed, was to read the myths and epics of long ago.

Epic

The Epic

An **epic** is a long narrative poem about a serious subject. The purpose of an epic poem is threefold: to entertain, to teach, and to inspire with examples of how people can succeed against great odds.

Epic Heroes and Gods The action in an epic centers on the **epic hero,** whose primary goal is usually to save his nation or its people during a time of crisis. Gods may take part in the action or at least take an interest in what happens, sometimes intervening to affect the course of events.

Structure The way an author organizes images, ideas, words, and lines is called **structure.** Like many epics, the *Odyssey* begins with an **invocation,** a request to a muse to provide inspiration. In Greek mythology, the **muses** are nine goddesses who preside over the arts and sciences and inspire those who show talent in these areas.

Illustrated page with Battle Scene from the *Shahnameh*, 10th century. Ferdowsi. Decorative Museum, Tehran. Epics often include descriptions of huge battles or wars.

Yet all the gods had pitied Lord Odysseus,
all but Poseidon, raging cold and rough
against the brave king till he came ashore
at last on his own land.

—Homer, from the *Odyssey*

Sing in me, Muse, and through me tell the story
of that man skilled in all ways of contending,
the wanderer, harried for years on end,
after he plundered the stronghold
on the proud height of Troy.

—Homer, from the *Odyssey*

824 UNIT 5 EPIC AND MYTH

Myth and the Archetype

Myth

A **myth** is a traditional story of anonymous origin. Many myths are about the creation of earth; others are about love, adventure, trickery, or revenge. In many myths, human action is controlled or guided by gods and other supernatural beings. Many myths began as a part of the **oral tradition,** or literature that passes by word of mouth from one generation to the next. Oral literature was a way of recording the past, glorifying leaders, and teaching morals and traditions to young people.

For a time she kept his birth secret from her father, but it became increasingly difficult to do so in the narrow limits of that bronze house and finally one day the little boy—his name was Perseus—was discovered by his grandfather. "Your child!" Acrisius cried in great anger. "Who is his father?" But when Danaë answered proudly, "Zeus," he would not believe her.

—Edith Hamilton, from "Perseus"

Archetype

An **archetype** is a thing, person, or pattern of circumstances that appears repeatedly in literature. Most ancient myths, folktales, fables, ballads, and legends contain archetypal characters, such as the evil villain, the lovesick suitor, and the fool. They also may contain archetypal themes, such as the hidden treasure or the rite of passage.

When the gods first saw the Fenris Wolf, he was so young that they thought they could tame him. They took him to Asgard, therefore, and brave Tyr undertook to feed and train him. Presently, however, the black monster grew so enormous that his open jaws would stretch from heaven to earth, showing teeth as large as the trunks of oak trees and as sharply pointed as knives.

—Olivia Coolidge, from "The Fenris Wolf"

Literature Online

Literature and Reading For more selections in this genre, go to glencoe.com and enter QuickPass code GL49787u5.

A Reading from Homer, 1885. Lawrence Alma-Tadema. Oil on canvas, 91.8 x 183.5 cm. Philadelphia Museum of Art, PA.

INTRODUCTION 825

- **THE LITERARY ANALYSIS MODEL** uses an example to help you identify different literary elements and analyze their use within the text.

LITERARY WORKS follow each Part Introduction. The selections are organized as follows.

Why do I need this book?

Glencoe Literature is more than just a collection of stories, poems, nonfiction articles, and other literary works. Every part is built around **Big Ideas,** concepts that you will want to think about, talk about, and maybe even argue about. Big Ideas help you become part of an important conversation. You can join in lively discussions about who we are, where we have been, and where we are going.

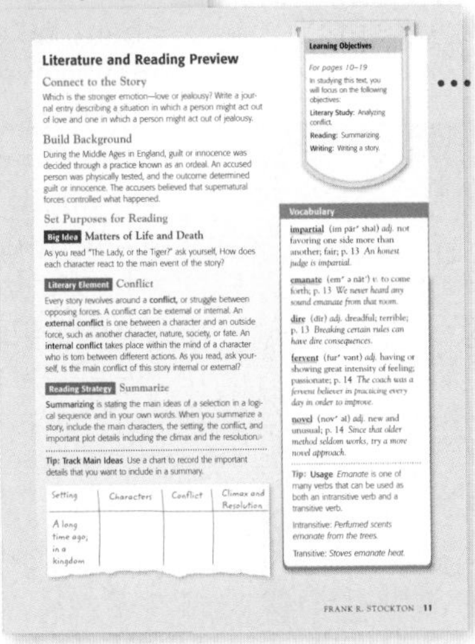

Reading and Thinking

The main literary works in your textbook are arranged in three parts.

- Start with **BEFORE YOU READ**. Learn valuable background information about the literature and preview the skills and strategies that will guide your reading.

MEET THE AUTHOR presents a detailed biography of the writer whose work you will read and analyze.

LITERATURE AND READING PREVIEW lists the basic tools you will use to read and analyze the literary work.

- Next, read the **LITERATURE SELECTION**. As you flip through the selections, you will notice that parts of the text are highlighted in different colors. At the bottom of the page are color-coded questions that relate to the highlighted text. Yellow represents a *Big Idea,* magenta represents a *Literary Element,* and blue represents a *Reading Strategy.* These questions will help you gain a better understanding of the text.

- Wrap up the literature selections with **AFTER YOU READ**. Explore what you have learned through a wide range of reading, thinking, vocabulary, and writing activities.

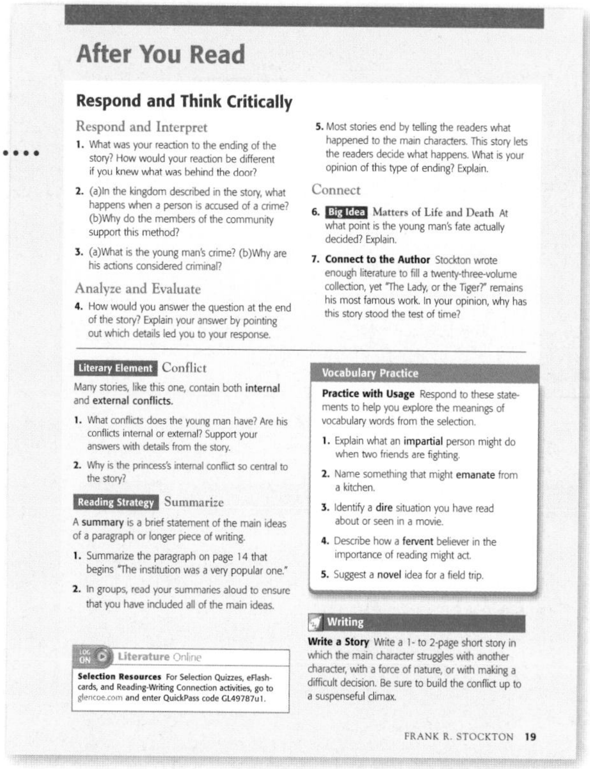

After You Read

Respond and Think Critically

Respond and Interpret

1. What was your reaction to the ending of the story? How would your reaction be different if you knew what was behind the door?
2. (a)In the kingdom described in the story, what happens when a person is accused of a crime? (b)Why do the members of the community support this method?
3. (a)What is the young man's crime? (b)Why are his actions considered criminal?

Analyze and Evaluate

4. How would you answer the question at the end of the story? Explain your answer by pointing out which details led you to your response.
5. Most stories end by telling the readers what happened to the main characters. This story lets the readers decide what happens. What is your opinion of this type of ending? Explain.

Connect

6. **Big Idea** Matters of Life and Death At what point is the young man's fate actually decided? Explain.
7. **Connect to the Author** Stockton wrote enough literature to fill a twenty-three-volume collection, yet "The Lady, or the Tiger?" remains his most famous work. In your opinion, why has this story stood the test of time?

Literary Element Conflict

Many stories, like this one, contain both **internal** and **external conflicts.**

1. What conflicts does the young man have? Are his conflicts internal or external? Support your answers with details from the story.
2. Why is the princess's internal conflict so central to the story?

Reading Strategy Summarize

A **summary** is a brief statement of the main ideas of a paragraph or longer piece of writing.

1. Summarize the paragraph on page 14 that begins "The institution was a very popular one."
2. In groups, read your summaries aloud to ensure that you have included all of the main ideas.

LOG ON Literature Online

Selection Resources For Selection Quizzes, eFlashcards, and Reading-Writing Connection activities, go to glencoe.com and enter QuickPass code GL49787u1.

Vocabulary Practice

Practice with Usage Respond to these statements to help you explore the meanings of vocabulary words from the selection.

1. Explain what an **impartial** person might do when two friends are fighting.
2. Name something that might **emanate** from a kitchen.
3. Identify a **dire** situation you have read about or seen in a movie.
4. Describe how a **fervent** believer in the importance of reading might act.
5. Suggest a **novel** idea for a field trip.

Writing

Write a Story Write a 1- to 2-page short story in which the main character struggles with another character, with a force of nature, or with making a difficult decision. Be sure to build the conflict up to a suspenseful climax.

FRANK R. STOCKTON 19

Vocabulary

VOCABULARY WORDS that may be new or difficult are chosen from most selections. They are introduced on the **BEFORE YOU READ** page. Each word is accompanied by its pronunciation, its part of speech, its definition, and the page number on which it appears. The vocabulary word is also used in a sample sentence. Vocabulary words are underlined in the literary work.

VOCABULARY PRACTICE On the **AFTER YOU READ** pages, you will be able to practice using the vocabulary words in an exercise. This exercise will show you how to apply a vocabulary strategy to understand new or difficult words.

ACADEMIC VOCABULARY Many of the **AFTER YOU READ** pages will also introduce you to a word that is frequently used in academic work. You will be prompted to complete an activity based on that word.

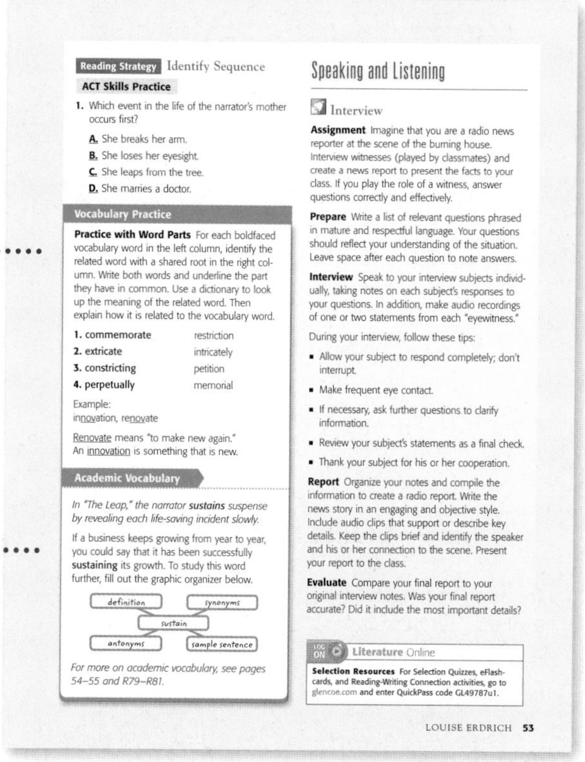

Reading Strategy Identify Sequence

ACT Skills Practice

1. Which event in the life of the narrator's mother occurs first?

   A. She breaks her arm.
   B. She loses her eyesight.
   C. She leaps from the tree.
   D. She marries a doctor.

Vocabulary Practice

Practice with Word Parts For each boldfaced vocabulary word in the left column, identify the related word with a shared root in the right column. Write both words and underline the part they have in common. Use a dictionary to look up the meaning of the related word. Then explain how it is related to the vocabulary word.

1. commemorate	restriction
2. extricate	intricately
3. constricting	petition
4. perpetually	memorial

Example:
innovation, renovate

Renovate means "to make new again."
An innovation is something that is new.

Academic Vocabulary

In "The Leap," the narrator ***sustains*** *suspense by revealing each life-saving incident slowly.*

If a business keeps growing from year to year, you could say that it has been successfully **sustaining** its growth. To study this word further, fill out the graphic organizer below.

definition — synonyms — sustain — antonyms — sample sentence

For more on academic vocabulary, see pages 54–55 and R79–R81.

Speaking and Listening

Interview

Assignment Imagine that you are a radio news reporter at the scene of the burning house. Interview witnesses (played by classmates) and create a news report to present the facts to your class. If you play the role of a witness, answer questions correctly and effectively.

Prepare Write a list of relevant questions phrased in mature and respectful language. Your questions should reflect your understanding of the situation. Leave space after each question to note answers.

Interview Speak to your interview subjects individually, taking notes on each subject's responses to your questions. In addition, make audio recordings of one or two statements from each "eyewitness."

During your interview, follow these tips:

- Allow your subject to respond completely; don't interrupt.
- Make frequent eye contact.
- If necessary, ask further questions to clarify information.
- Review your subject's statements as a final check.
- Thank your subject for his or her cooperation.

Report Organize your notes and compile the information to create a radio report. Write the news story in an engaging and objective style. Include audio clips that support or describe key details. Keep the clips brief and identify the speaker and his or her connection to the scene. Present your report to the class.

Evaluate Compare your final report to your original interview notes. Was your final report accurate? Did it include the most important details?

LOG ON Literature Online

Selection Resources For Selection Quizzes, eFlashcards, and Reading-Writing Connection activities, go to glencoe.com and enter QuickPass code GL49787u1.

LOUISE ERDRICH 53

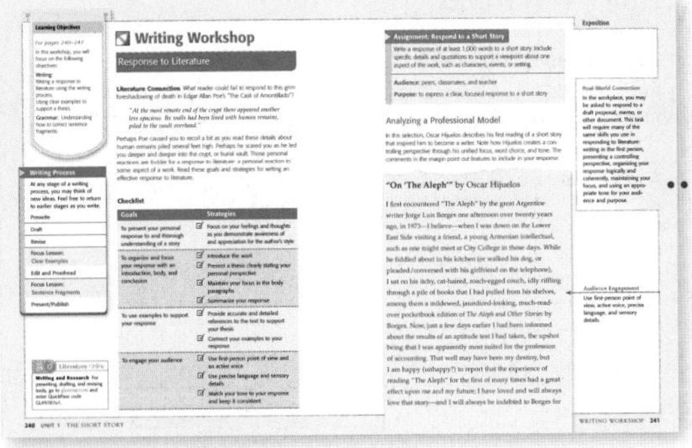

Writing Workshops

Each unit in ***Glencoe Literature*** includes a Writing Workshop. The workshop walks you through the writing process as you work on an extended piece of writing related to the unit.

- You will create writing goals and apply strategies to meet them.
- You will pick up tips and polish your critical skills as you analyze professional and workshop models.
- You will focus on mastering specific aspects of writing, including organization, grammar, and vocabulary.
- You will use a checklist to evaluate your own writing.

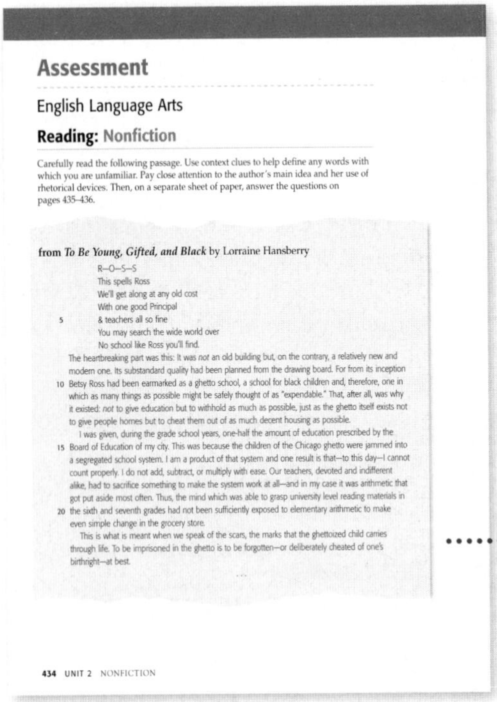

Assessment

English Language Arts

Reading: Nonfiction

Carefully read the following passage. Use context clues to help define any words with which you are unfamiliar. Pay close attention to the author's main idea and her use of rhetorical devices. Then, on a separate sheet of paper, answer the questions on pages 435–436.

from *To Be Young, Gifted, and Black* by Lorraine Hansberry

R—O—S—S
This spells Ross
We'll get along at any old cost
With one good Principal
& teachers all so fine
You may search the wide world over
No school like Ross you'll find.

The heartbreaking part was this: It was *not* an old building but, on the contrary, a relatively new and modern one. Its substandard quality had been planned from the drawing board. For from its inception Betsy Ross had been earmarked as a ghetto school, a school for black children and, therefore, one in which as many things as possible might be safely thought of as "expendable." That, after all, was why it existed: *not* to give education but to withhold as much as possible, just as the ghetto itself exists not to give people homes but to cheat them out of as much decent housing as possible.

I was given, during the grade school years, one-half the amount of education prescribed by the Board of Education of my city. This was because the children of the Chicago ghetto were jammed into a segregated school system. I am a product of that system and one result is that—to this day—I cannot count properly. I do not add, subtract, or multiply with ease. Our teachers, devoted and indifferent alike, had to sacrifice something to make the system work at all—and in my case it was arithmetic that got put aside most often. Thus, the mind which was able to grasp university level reading materials in the sixth and seventh grades had not been sufficiently exposed to elementary arithmetic to make even simple change in the grocery store.

This is what is meant when we speak of the scars, the marks that the ghettoized child carries through life. To be imprisoned in the ghetto is to be forgotten—or deliberately cheated of one's birthright—at best.

. . .

434 UNIT 2 NONFICTION

Assessment

At the end of each unit, you will be tested on the literature, reading, and vocabulary skills you have just learned. Designed to simulate standardized tests, this test will give you the practice you need to succeed while providing an assessment of how well you have met the unit objectives.

FOLDABLES® Study Organizer

BOUND BOOK

Try using this organizer to explore your personal responses to the poetry, play and nonfiction.

Organizing Information

Graphic organizers—such as Foldables®, diagrams, and charts—help you keep your information and ideas organized.

Be Cyber Safe and Smart

Cyber Safety

As you explore the *Glencoe Literature* program, you will have many opportunities to go online. When you use the Internet at school or home, you enter a kind of community—the cyber world. In this online world, you need to follow safety rules and protect yourself. Here are some tips to keep in mind:

Words to Know

cyber world the world of computers and high-tech communications
cyber safety actions that protect Internet users from harm
cyber ethics responsible code of conduct for using the Internet
cyber bully a person who uses technology to frighten, bother, or harm someone else
cyber citizen a person who uses the Internet to communicate

- ☑ Be a responsible cyber citizen. Use the Internet to share knowledge that makes people's lives better. Respect other people's feelings and do not break any laws.
- ☑ Beware of cyber bullying. People can be hurt and embarrassed by comments that have been made public. You should immediately tell your teacher or counselor if you feel threatened by another student's computer postings.
- ☑ Do not give out personal information, such as your address and telephone number, without your parents' or guardians' permission.
- ☑ Tell your teacher, parent, or guardian right away if you find or read any information that makes you feel uneasy or afraid.
- ☑ Do not e-mail your picture to anyone.
- ☑ Do not open e-mail or text messages from strangers.
- ☑ Do not tell anyone your Internet password.
- ☑ Do not make illegal copies of computer games and programs, or software CDs.

LOG ON Literature Online

For more about internet safety and responsibility, go to glencoe.com.

SCOPE AND SEQUENCE

This chart provides an overview of the scope and sequence for *Glencoe Literature—Course 4*. For a detailed scope and sequence of skills, see the chart at the beginning of each unit in the Teacher Edition. Refer also to the Index of Skills in the Reference Section in the back of the book for a comprehensive listing of all skills and concepts taught in Course 4.

✔ = Introduced ✓ = Reviewed

	UNIT ONE	UNIT TWO	UNIT THREE	UNIT FOUR	UNIT FIVE	UNIT SIX
Literary Criticism						
Analyzing Literature in Context						
Historical Approach	✔	✓	✓	✓	✓	✓
Artistic Approach		✔	✓		✓	
Biographical Approach		✔		✓		
Literary Genres						
Oral Tradition Forms						
Myth, Folklore, and Legend					✔	✓
Fiction						
Short Story	✔	✓			✓	✓
Novel Excerpt		✔		✓		
Nonfiction						
Autobiography or Memoir		✔	✓			
Biography	✔	✓				
Magazine Article	✔	✓	✓	✓	✓	✓
Newspaper Article		✔				
Speech		✔				
Informational Text	✔	✓	✓	✓	✓	✓
Public or Functional Document		✔				
Letter		✔				
Graphic Novel		✔	✓		✓	
Poetry						
Narrative Poem	✔	✓	✓	✓	✓	✓
Ballad					✔	
Epic					✔	
Drama						
Comedy				✔		
Tragedy				✔		

	UNIT ONE	UNIT TWO	UNIT THREE	UNIT FOUR	UNIT FIVE	UNIT SIX
Literary Elements						
Literary Structure						
Plot	✔				✔	✔
Setting	✔	✔	✔	✔	✔	
Characters	✔			✔	✔	✔
Point of View	✔	✔				✔
Theme	✔	✔	✔	✔	✔	
Voice and Tone	✔	✔	✔		✔	✔
Author's Purpose	✔	✔	✔	✔	✔	✔
Literary Language						
Imagery	✔		✔		✔	✔
Symbolism	✔		✔		✔	
Figures of Speech			✔	✔	✔	✔
Sound Devices			✔	✔		
Diction	✔		✔	✔	✔	
Rhetorical Strategies		✔	✔			

SCOPE AND SEQUENCE

✔ = Introduced ✓ = Reviewed

	UNIT ONE	UNIT TWO	UNIT THREE	UNIT FOUR	UNIT FIVE	UNIT SIX
Reading Skills						
Strategies						
Analyzing	✔	✓	✓	✓	✓	✓
Clarifying		✔	✓			
Drawing Conclusions		✔	✓	✓		
Making Inferences	✔		✓	✓	✓	✓
Making Predictions	✔			✓		
Monitoring Comprehension		✔	✓			
Paraphrasing	✔					
Previewing	✔	✓	✓	✓	✓	✓
Questioning	✔		✓	✓		
Recognizing Bias	✔	✓				
Summarizing	✔	✓		✓		✓
Synthesizing	✔	✓	✓	✓	✓	✓

	UNIT ONE	UNIT TWO	UNIT THREE	UNIT FOUR	UNIT FIVE	UNIT SIX
Vocabulary Development						
Analogies	✔	✓	✓	✓	✓	✓
Antonyms				✔	✓	✓
Context Clues	✔	✓	✓	✓	✓	✓
Denotation and Connotation			✔	✓		✓
Multiple-Meaning Words	✔					
Prefixes and Suffixes	✔	✓	✓	✓	✓	
Synonyms	✔	✓	✓	✓	✓	✓
Word Roots and Origins	✔	✓	✓		✓	

	UNIT ONE	UNIT TWO	UNIT THREE	UNIT FOUR	UNIT FIVE	UNIT SIX
Writing and Grammar						
Types of Writing						
Response to Literature	✔	✔	✔	✔	✔	✔
Autobiographical Narrative		✔				
Essay	✔	✔	✔			✔
Literary Analysis	✔	✔		✔		✔
Research Report	✔	✔	✔		✔	✔
Editorial				✔		✔
Writing Process						
Prewriting, Drafting, Revising, Editing and Proofreading, Presenting	✔	✔	✔	✔	✔	✔
Traits of Strong Writing	✔	✔	✔	✔	✔	✔
Grammar, Usage, and Mechanics						
Parts of Speech	✔	✔	✔	✔	✔	
Capitalization and Punctuation	✔				✔	✔
Sentence Structure	✔	✔	✔	✔	✔	✔
Speaking, Listening, and Viewing						
Oral Response to Literature	✔	✔	✔	✔	✔	
Narrative Presentation		✔			✔	
Reflective Presentation			✔			
Literary Analysis		✔		✔		
Multimedia Presentation					✔	
Persuasive Presentation						✔

Teaching the Standards: Grade 9

The following abbreviated curriculum is a suggestion for addressing those objectives that students commonly encounter on standardized tests. You may use it as a guide for prioritizing instruction in preparation for the tests.

Unit 1

Selections/Lessons	Pacing/Days	Genre	Where to Find Instruction	Commonly Tested Objectives
The Cask of Amontillado	2–6	Short Story	SE, p. 58 RW, RW-APP, pp. 1–14 RW-EL, pp. 1–14, 324	**Literary Study:** Analyzing mood. [RW, RW-APP, RW-EL] **Reading:** Paraphrasing. [RW, RW-APP, RW-EL] **Reading:** Determining the main idea. [RW, RW-APP, RW-EL]
Comparing Literature: Liberty AND The Struggle to Be an All-American Girl AND Legal Alien	3–8	Short Story AND Memoir AND Poetry	SE, p. 129 RW, RW-APP, pp. 15–32, 324 RW-EL, pp. 15–32, 325–326	**Literary Study:** Analyzing motivation. [RW, RW-APP, RW-EL] **Reading:** Responding to characters. [RW, RW-APP, RW-EL] **Reading:** Comparing and contrasting theme. [RW, RW-APP, RW-EL]
American History	2–8	Short Story	SE, p. 210 RW, RW-APP, pp. 33–48 RW-EL, pp. 33–48, 327	**Literary Study:** Analyzing first-person point of view. [RW, RW-APP, RW-EL] **Literary Study:** Using information from the text. [RW, RW-APP, RW-EL] **Reading:** Making inferences about characters. [RW, RW-APP, RW-EL]

Unit 2

Selections/Lessons	Pacing/Days	Genre	Where to Find Instruction	Commonly Tested Objectives
Of Dry Goods and Black Bow Ties	2–6	Memoir	SE, p. 270 RW, RW-APP, pp. 49–60, 325 RW-EL, pp. 49–60, 328–329	**Literary Study:** Analyzing author's purpose. [RW, RW-APP, RW-EL] **Reading:** Analyzing cause-and-effect relationships. [RW, RW-APP, RW-EL]
from Black Boy	1–5	Autobiography	SE, p . 299 RW, RW-APP, pp. 61–72 RW-EL, pp. 61–72, 330	**Literary Study:** Analyzing anecdote. [RW, RW-APP, RW-EL] **Reading:** Connecting to personal experience. [RW, RW-APP, RW-EL]

[Note: SE= Student Edition; **RW=** *Read and Write;* **RW-APP=** Approaching Level; **RW-EL=** English Learner**]**

TIME: Adventure to Antarctica	3–9	Essay	SE, p. 369 RW, RW-APP, pp. 73–90, 326 RW-EL, pp. 73–90, 331–332	**Reading:** Analyzing text structure. [RW, RW-APP, RW-EL] **Reading:** Preparing a bibliography. [RW, RW-APP] **Reading:** Generating questions. [RW, RW-APP, RW-EL] **Literary Study:** Using information from the text. [RW, RW-APP, RW-EL]
That One Man's Profit Is Another's Loss	2–5	Essay	SE, p. 388 RW, RW-APP, pp. 91–98, 327–328 RW-EL, pp. 91–98, 333–335	**Literary Study:** Analyzing antithesis.[RW, RW-APP, RW-EL] **Reading:** Analyzing argument. [RW, RW-APP, RW-EL] **Reading:** Applying knowledge of word origins. [RW-EL]

Unit 3

Selections/Lessons	Pacing/Days	Genre	Where to Find Instruction	Commonly Tested Objectives
I Wandered Lonely as a Cloud	1–3	Poetry	SE, p. 452 RW, RW-APP, pp. 99–106 RW-EL, pp. 99–106, 336	**Literary Study:** Analyzing rhyme and rhyme scheme. [RW, RW-APP, RW-EL] **Reading:** Previewing the text. [RW, RW-APP, RW-EL] **Reading:** Applying knowledge of word origins. [RW, RW-APP]
Comparing Literature: An Indian Summer Day on the Prairie AND On Summer AND Monument	2–6	Poetry AND Essay	SE, p. 477 RW, RW-APP, pp. 107–118, 329 RW-EL, pp. 107–118, 337–338	**Literary Study:** Comparing structure. [RW, RW-APP, RW-EL] **Literary Study:** Comparing author's ideas. [RW, RW-APP, RW-EL] **Literary Study:** Analyzing line and stanza. [RW, RW-APP, RW-EL] **Reading:** Comparing and contrasting imagery. [RW, RW-APP, RW-EL] **Reading:** Comparing and contrasting theme. [RW, RW-APP, RW-EL]
I Was a Skinny Tomboy Kid	1–3	Poetry	SE, p. 512 RW, RW-APP, pp. 119–126 RW-EL, pp. 119–126, 339	**Literary Study:** Analyzing free verse. [RW, RW-APP, RW-EL] **Reading:** Analyzing sensory details. [RW, RW-APP, RW-EL] **Reading:** Distinguishing between denotative and connotative meanings. [RW-EL]
Remember	1–3	Poetry	SE, p. 538 RW, RW-APP, pp. 127–132, 330 RW-EL, pp. 127–132, 340–341	**Literary Study:** Analyzing repetition. [RW, RW-APP, RW-EL] **Reading:** Drawing conclusions about author's beliefs. [RW, RW-APP, RW-EL]

The Road Not Taken	1–3	Poetry	SE, p. 542 RW, RW-APP, pp. 133–140 RW-EL, pp. 133–140, 342	**Literary Study:** Analyzing lyric poetry. [RW, RW-APP, RW-EL] **Reading:** Making inferences about theme. [RW, RW-APP, RW-EL]
Time	1–3	Poetry	SE, p. 548 RW, RW-APP, pp. 141–146 RW-EL, pp. 141–146, 343	**Literary Study:** Analyzing personification. [RW, RW-APP, RW-EL] **Reading:** Identifying irony. [RW, RW-APP, RW-EL]
Theme for English B	1–3	Poetry	SE, p. 552 RW, RW-APP, pp. 147–152, 331 RW-EL, pp. 147–152, 344–345	**Literary Study:** Analyzing voice. [RW, RW-APP, RW-EL] **Reading:** Analyzing style. [RW, RW-APP, RW-EL]
My Mother Combs My Hair	1–3	Poetry	SE, p. 582 RW, RW-APP, pp. 153–160 RW-EL, pp. 153–160, 346	**Literary Study:** Analyzing similes. [RW, RW-APP, RW-EL] **Reading:** Visualizing. [RW, RW-APP, RW-EL]
Lineage	1–3	Poetry	SE, p. 592 RW, RW-APP, pp. 161–166, 332 RW-EL, pp. 161–166, 347–348	**Literary Study:** Analyzing alliteration. [RW, RW-APP, RW-EL] **Reading:** Analyzing rhythm. [RW, RW-APP, RW-EL]

Unit 4

Selections/Lessons	Pacing/Days	Genre	Where to Find Instruction	Commonly Tested Objectives
Romeo and Juliet, Act 1, Scene 5	3–9	Drama	SE, p. 626 RW, RW-APP, pp. 167–186 RW-EL, pp. 167–186, 349	**Literary Study:** Analyzing foil. [RW, RW-APP, RW-EL] **Reading:** Summarizing. [RW, RW-APP, RW-EL]
Romeo and Juliet, Act 2, Scene 5	3–9	Drama	SE, p. 626 RW, RW-APP, pp. 187–206 RW-EL, pp. 187–206, 350	**Literary Study:** Analyzing figurative language. [RW, RW-APP, RW-EL] **Reading:** Making inferences about characters.
The Bear	3–10	Drama	SE, p. 760 RW, RW-APP, pp. 207–226, 333 RW-EL, pp. 207–226, 351–352	**Literary Study:** Analyzing farce. [RW, RW-APP, RW-EL] **Reading:** Analyzing cause-and-effect relationships. [RW, RW-APP, RW-EL]

[Note: SE= Student Edition; **RW=** *Read and Write;* **RW-APP=** Approaching Level; **RW-EL=** English Learner**]**

Unit 5

Selections/Lessons	Pacing/Days	Genre	Where to Find Instruction	Commonly Tested Objectives
***from* the Odyssey, Part 1**	4–17	Epic Poem	SE, p. 836 RW, RW-APP, pp. 227–266 RW-EL, pp. 227–266, 353	**Literary Study:** Analyzing epic and epic hero. [RW, RW-APP, RW-EL] **Reading:** Analyzing figurative language. [RW, RW-APP, RW-EL] **Reading:** Identifying and using literal and figurative meanings of words. [RW, RW-APP, RW-EL] **Reading:** Distinguishing between denotative and connotative meanings. **Reading:** Identifying mythology. [RW, RW-APP]
Perseus	2–7	Myth	SE, p. 936 RW, RW-APP, pp. 267–280, 334 RW-EL, pp. 267–280, 354–355	**Literary Study:** Analyzing plot pattern archetype. [RW, RW-APP, RW-EL] **Reading:** Identifying genre. [RW, RW-APP, RW-EL] **Reading:** Identifying mythology. [RW-EL]
Coyote and Crow	1–3	Myth	SE, p. 955 RW, RW-APP, pp. 281–286, 335 RW-EL, pp. 281–286, 356–357	**Literary Study:** Analyzing character archetype. [RW, RW-APP, RW-EL] **Reading:** Activating prior knowledge. [RW, RW-APP, RW-EL]

Unit 6

Selections/Lessons	Pacing/Days	Genre	Where to Find Instruction	Commonly Tested Objectives
The Sentinel	2–8	Short Story	SE, p. 996 RW, RW-APP, pp. 287–302, 336 RW-EL, pp. 287–302, 358–359	**Literary Study:** Analyzing suspense. [RW, RW-APP, RW-EL] **Reading:** Analyzing motivations. [RW, RW-APP, RW-EL]
He—y, Come on Ou—t!	2–5	Short Story	SE, p. 1014 RW, RW-APP, pp. 303–312, 337 RW-EL, pp. 303–312, 360–361	**Literary Study:** Analyzing moral. [RW, RW-APP, RW-EL] **Reading:** Connecting to contemporary issues. [RW, RW-APP, RW-EL]
Functional Documents	2–5	Functional Docu-ments	SE, p. 1102 RW, RW-APP, pp. 313–323 RW-EL, pp. 313–323, 362	**Reading:** Identifying sequence. [RW, RW-APP, RW-EL] **Reading:** Summarizing. [RW, RW-APP, RW-EL] **Reading:** Following technical directions. [RW, RW-APP, RW-EL] **Reading:** Demonstrating use of sophisticated learning tools. [RW, RW-APP, RW-EL] **Reading:** Critiquing logic of functional documents. [RW, RW-APP, RW-EL] **Reading:** Preparing a bibliography. [RW-EL]
	Total: 47–150 days			

To Teachers

Welcome to the Teacher Edition of *Glencoe Literature*. We have created this teacher edition based on the standards developed by experienced teachers and educational consultants. Teaching suggestions, additional resources, and leveled activities for differentiated instruction are all labeled and wrapped around the student text for your convenience.

Unit Scope and Sequence

Every unit of *Glencoe Literature* is organized around a carefully researched scope and sequence that includes the reading skills and strategies, literary elements, writing skills, and listening, speaking and viewing skills that students need in order to successfully progress through the program.

UNIT ONE

Skills Scope and Sequence

Readability Scores Key: Dale-Chall/DRP/Lexile

PART 1: Matters of Life and Death

Selections and Features	Literary Elements
Unit Introduction pp. 1–6	Short Story Elements **SE** pp. 2–3 Setting **SE** p. 4 Character **SE** p. 4 Narrator **SE** p. 5 Plot **SE** p. 5 Theme **SE** p. 5
Literary Focus pp. 8–9	Setting **SE** p. 8 Plot **SE** p. 9 Conflict **TE** p. 8
Short Story The Lady, or the Tiger?, by Frank R. Stockton **10.1/68/1260** pp. 10–19	Conflict **SE** p. 11
Short Story The Most Dangerous Game, by Richard Connell **6.2/50/740** pp. 20–42	Suspense **SE** p. 21 Foil **TE** p. 22 Characterization **TE** pp. 26, 30 Figurative Language **TE** p. 36 Conflict (review) **SE** p. 41
Short Story The Leap, by Louise Erdrich **6.4/64/1260** pp. 43–53	
Vocabulary Workshop pp. 54–55	
Short Story The Cask of Amontillado, b **9.8/55/790** pp. 56–67	
Vocabulary Workshop p. 68	
Short Story Blues Ain't No Mockin' Bir **6.8/53/960** pp. 69–76	

1A

Reading Skills and Strategies	Vocabulary	Writing Grammar	Speaking, Listening, and Viewing
Visualize **TE** p. 4 Evaluate **SE** p. 5 Identify Problem and Solution **TE** p. 6		Keep a Reading Journal **TE** p. 2 Write a News Report **TE** p. 4	
Draw Conclusions **TE** p. 9			
Summarize **SE** p. 11 Paraphrase **TE** p. 12	Word Usage **SE** p. 19	Write a Response to Literature **TE** p. 14 Semicolons **TE** p. 18 Write a Story **SE** p. 19	Discussion **TE** p. 16
Make and Verify Predictions About Plot **SE** p. 21 Identify Sequence **TE** p. 28 Visualize **TE** p. 32	Word Origins **SE** p. 41 Academic Vocabulary **SE** p. 41	Write a Journal Entry **TE** p. 26 Punctuation and Dialogue **TE** p. 30 Write a Summary **SE** p. 42 Present-Tense Verbs **SE** p. 42 Revise **TE** p. 42	
Identify Sequence **SE** p. 44	Word Parts **SE** p. 53 Academic Vocabulary **SE** p. 53	Write a Comparison-Contrast Essay **TE** p. 46 Subordinate Clauses **TE** p. 50	Interview **SE** p. 53
	Academic Vocabulary **SE** pp. 54–55		
Paraphrase **SE** p. 57 Compare and Contrast **TE** p. 62	Context Clues **SE** p. 66 Academic Vocabulary **SE** p. 66	Write Dialogue **TE** p. 60 Dashes **TE** p. 64 Write a Research Report **SE** p. 67 Colons **SE** p. 67	
	Homonyms and Homophones **SE** p. 68		
Analyze Concrete Details **SE** p. 70	Analogies **SE** p. 78 Academic Vocabulary **SE** p. 78	Write Dialect **TE** p. 70 Apply Description **SE** p. 78	Analyze Art **TE** p. 72 Discussion **TE** p. 74

1B

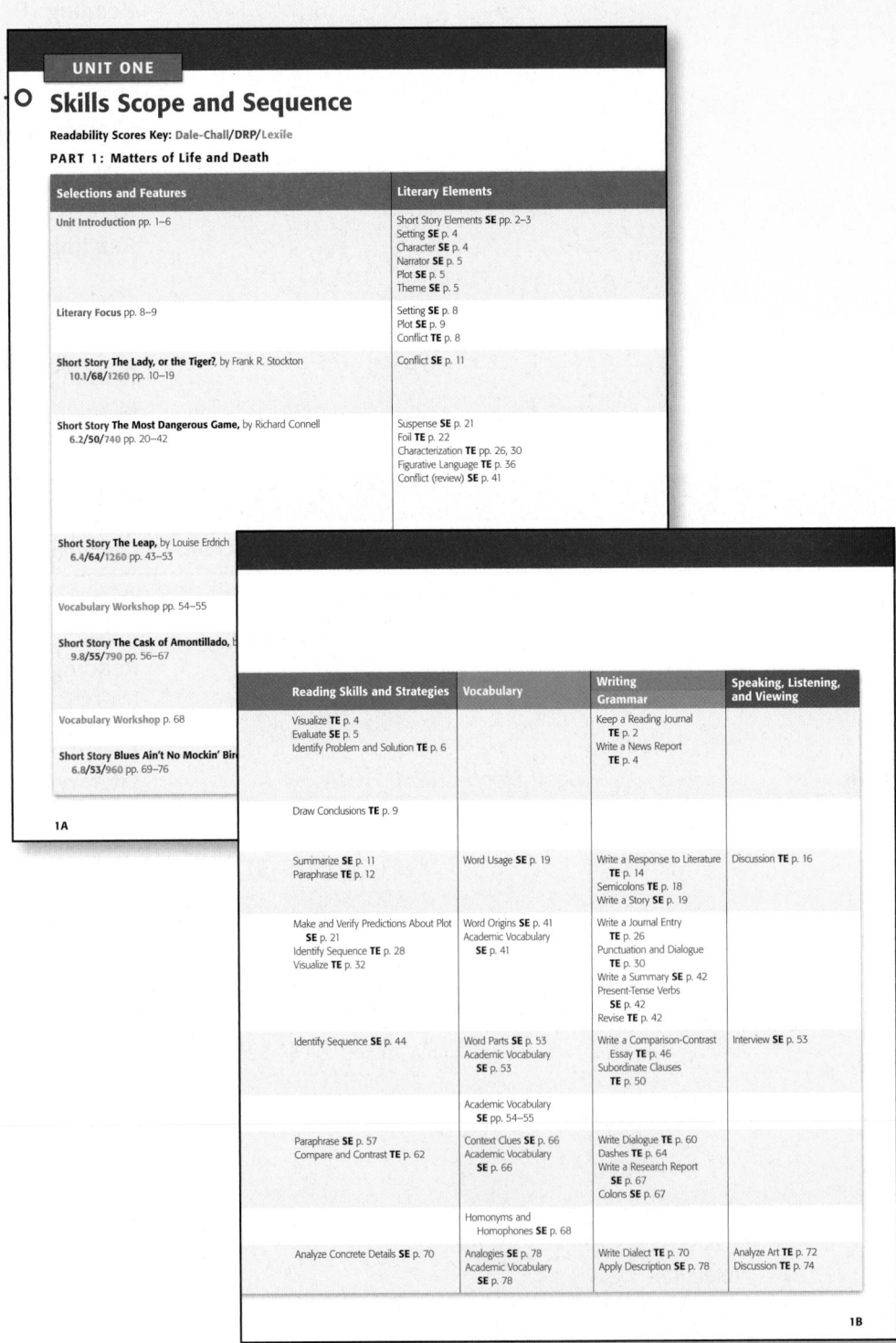

UNIT ONE

Focus

Bellringer Options

Literature Launcher
Pre-Reading Video
Daily Language Practice Transparency 1

Or say: Identify some reasons why people tell and retell stories. *(Students may suggest that stories help us make sense of the world and allow us to go places we could never actually go to or experience things we could not normally do.)*

For school-to-home activities, see Unit 1 Teaching Resource Book, pp. 5–11.

For students who would profit from independent novel study, see Novel Companion pp. 7–74.

Toyota Taxi, 2005. P. J. Crook. Acrylic on canvas, 116.8 x 152.4 cm.
View the Art P. J. Crook is known for her highly detailed paintings. How do the details in this painting suggest that several stories are unfolding in this neighborhood? ★

Unit Introduction Skills

Reading Skills
- Read the Short Story (SE p. 2)
- Problems and Solutions (TE p. 6)

Listening/Speaking
- Create a Timeline (S

UNIT ONE

The Short Story

Looking Ahead

A short story is a little, well-polished stone in a vast quarry of fiction. As with other genres, at the foundation of the short story is a set of key literary elements—setting, character, plot, and theme—that the writer manages to introduce, develop, and display in just a few pages. A large part of a reader's enjoyment is seeing how the author lays this foundation and envisioning what it will become.

Each part in Unit One focuses on a Big Idea that can help you connect to the selections.

PREVIEW	Big Ideas	Literary Focus
PART 1	Matters of Life and Death	Plot and Setting
PART 2	Rewards and Sacrifices	Character and Theme
PART 3	Dreams and Reality	Narrator and Voice

1

UNIT ONE

Focus

Summary

The unit begins with definitions of the short story genre and its main literary elements. It provides insights from professional fiction writers. A story by Leo Tolstoy is used to show examples of short story literary elements. The introduction concludes with review activities.

View the Art ★

Answer: *Students may say that the details suggest several story lines because there is no focus on one person, place, or thing. The people in the painting are doing different things.*

The large, highly detailed canvases of British painter Pamela (P. J.) Crook (1945–) often depict subtle human dramas in busy urban landscapes.

For diagnostic and end-of-unit assessment, see Assessment Resources, pp. 1–6, 225–226.

Unit Resources

Print Materials
- Unit 1 Teaching Resources, pp. 1–307
- Interactive Read and Write (On Level/ Approaching, EL), pp. 1–48
- Novel Companion, pp. 7–74
- Bellringer Option Transparencies: Selection Focus 1–15; Daily Language Practice 1–21
- Literary Element Transparencies 21, 67, 78, 91, 103, 107
- Assessment Resources, Unit Assessment, pp. 1–6
- Assessment Resources, Selection Assessment, pp. 41–78

Technology
- TeacherWorks Plus CD
- StudentWorks Plus CD
- Literature Launchers: Pre-Reading Videos DVD, Unit 1
- Literature Online
- Interactive Vocabulary CD-ROM
- Listening Library CD-ROM
- ExamView CD-ROM
- Skill Level Up! CD-ROM

1

Big Idea

The three Big Ideas from a literary period or movement help your students focus on key concepts that they can trace through the reading selections in each unit.

Unit Introduction Skills

The Web diagram summarizes the skills of a major literary genre taught in the Student Edition and Teacher Edition.

Summary

Each unit begins with an engaging piece of literature chosen to engage students in thinking about the Big Idea.

View the Art

Every unit opener features art that relates to the unit's genre. View the Art gives you information and insight to share with students about the art.

Unit Resources

Glencoe Literature provides a wealth of materials to support your teaching. The Unit Resources box gives you a list of program materials that you can use during the course of the unit.

Three Part Lesson Plan

The Teacher Edition of *Glencoe Literature* is organized in a three-part structure: **Focus, Teach,** and **Assess.**

Focus

Focus activities help you prepare students for the day's lessons. The **Bellringer Activity** provides a choice of transparencies and other teaching strategies that engage students and focus their attention.

Before You Read

Focus

Bellringer Options

Selection Focus Transparency 1
Daily Language Practice Transparency 3

Or ask students to share examples of difficult decisions they have made or have read about.

Ask: What made the decision difficult? *(Students may mention lack of good options, too many good options, or another reason.)* What factors did you consider? *(Possible answers: likely advantages and disadvantages)* Have students consider as they read how the king, the princess, and the young man make their decisions.

Before You Read

The Lady, or the Tiger?

Meet **Frank R. Stockton**
(1834–1902)

At the height of his success, Frank R. Stockton was considered a major literary figure in the United States; writer William Dean Howells considered Stockton to be second in importance only to Mark Twain. Stockton's body of work fills twenty-three volumes and includes stories, novels, and nonfiction. Yet today, this writer is known primarily for one story.

Launching a Career Stockton enjoyed writing during his school days; however, his father hoped that he would become a doctor. Stockton chose another path entirely: wood engraving, a popular way to illustrate stories and articles at the time. Still, Stockton continued to write and began to publish his short stories.

As the wood engraving business gave way to other types of illustrations, Stockton focused his attention on writing and publishing. His early works were mainly written for children. In 1867, he published a short story called "Ting-a-Ling," which he later turned into a book. A fanciful tale about an elf-like character, "Ting-a-Ling" captured the attention of Mary Mapes Dodge, an author and editor of the time. After she was named editor of *St. Nicholas*, a new magazine for children, Dodge invited Stockton to join her staff.

Courtesy St. Nicholas Center

St. Nicholas was a new type of children's magazine. Earlier children's publications were blandly moralistic, but *St. Nicholas* was realistic and literary. Within a few years, it became one of the most successful children's magazines of its time.

The Story That Created a Stir In 1878, Stockton left the magazine because of his failing eyesight, but he continued to write. Within a few years, he published several more books. Still, Stockton's novels never earned attention equal to that which he gained in 1882, when he published a short story in *Century Magazine*. That story was "The Lady, or the Tiger?"

The story not only created a stir at the time but for years afterward. It was later turned into an operetta, a play, a movie, and a recording. The story's unusual ending created a flurry of letters to the author that continued throughout his life. Poet Robert Browning wrote a poem about the ending, and scholars debated the issue. Stockton, however, kept quiet, leaving the debate to continue long after his death.

Literature Online

Author Search For more about Frank R. Stockton, go to glencoe.com and enter QuickPass code GL49787u1.

Listening/Speaking/Viewing Skills
- Analyzing Art (SE p. 15)
- Group Discussion (TE p. 17)

Writing Skills/Grammar
- Write a Short Story (SE p. 19)
- Respond to Literature (TE p. 14)
- Use Semicolons (TE p. 18)

Teach

In these sections, you will find leveled activities that correspond to and extend instruction in the Student Edition. Here you will also find information that enriches students' appreciation of art, photos, culture, or history as they apply to the selections being taught.

Teach

Big Idea 1

Matters of Life and Death

Say: Keep this question in mind as you read: Why does a life-or-death trial appeal to the king? *(The king enjoys putting people at the mercy of a heartless and whimsical fate and uses this cruel spectacle to teach his subjects a lesson.)*

APPROACHING **Ask:** Why do the king's subjects enjoy the life-or-death trial? *(The uncertainty is exciting.)*

Literary Element 2

Conflict **Answer:** *The king is a tyrant who expects the whole world to bend to his will.*

For an audio recording of this selection, use Listening Library Audio CD-ROM.

Readability Scores
Dale-Chall: 10.1
DRP: 68
Lexile: 1260

Frank R. Stockton

1 In the very olden time, there lived a semibarbaric king, whose ideas, though somewhat polished and sharpened by the progressiveness of distant Latin neighbors, were still large, florid, and untrammeled,[1] as became the half of him which was barbaric. He was a man of exuberant fancy, and, withal, of an authority so irresistible that, at his will, he turned his varied fancies into facts. He was greatly given to self-communing; and, when he and himself agreed upon any thing, the thing was done. When every member of his domestic and political systems moved smoothly in its appointed course, his nature was bland and genial;[2] but whenever there was a little hitch, and some of his orbs got out of their orbits, he was blander and more genial still, for nothing pleased him so much as to make the crooked straight, and crush down uneven places.

Among the borrowed notions by which his barbarism had become semified[3] was that of the public arena, in which, by exhibitions of manly and beastly valor, the minds of his subjects were refined and cultured.

But even here the exuberant and barbaric fancy asserted itself.[4] The arena of the king was built, not to give the people an opportunity of hearing the rhapsodies[5] of dying gladiators, nor to enable them to view the inevitable conclusion of a conflict between religious opinions and hungry jaws, but for purposes far better adapted to widen and

1. The king's ideas are somewhat uncivilized (*semibarbaric*); they are very showy (*florid*) and unrestrained (*untrammeled*).
2. The king himself is generally agreeable and mild (*bland*) and pleasantly cheerful (*genial*).
3. *Semified* is a made-up word meaning "reduced in half or made partial."
4. Here, *asserted itself* means "exercised its influence; insisted on being recognized."
5. *Rhapsodies* are enthusiastic expressions of emotion.

Conflict *How does this passage suggest a future conflict?* 2

12 UNIT 1 THE SHORT STORY

Reading Practice

SPIRAL REVIEW SMALL GROUP **Paraphrase Meaning** Explain that this story uses elaborate language, which may be difficult to understand at first. Explain that paraphrasing passages from the story may help students understand information. Remind students that paraphrasing is restating the text in their own words.

Break students into small groups. Model paraphrasing by reading aloud the first sentence from the story. Read aloud these words, which paraphrase the meaning of the first sentence: "Many years ago there was a king, who was somewhat primitive and crude. While the king's ideas were influenced by others who were more modern in their thinking, they were still showy and uncivilized. This pleased the part of him that was wild." Have students work together to paraphrase passages from the story.

12

Brackets and Numbers

When students are asked to think about the text, you will see brackets that are color-coded and numbered so that the corresponding teacher information is readily identifiable.

develop the mental energies of the people. This vast amphitheater,[6] with its encircling galleries, its mysterious vaults, and its unseen passages, was an agent of poetic justice, in which crime was punished, or virtue rewarded, by the decrees of an **impartial** and incorruptible chance.

When a subject was accused of a crime of sufficient importance to interest the king, public notice was given that on an appointed day the fate of the accused person would be decided in the king's arena,—a structure which well deserved its name; for, although its form and plan were borrowed from afar, its purpose **emanated** solely from the brain of this man, who, every barleycorn[7] a king, knew no tradition to which he owed more allegiance than pleased his fancy, and who ingrafted on every adopted form of human thought and action the rich growth of his barbaric idealism.

When all the people had assembled in the galleries, and the king, surrounded by his court, sat high up on his throne of royal state on one side of the arena, he gave a signal, a door beneath him opened, and the accused subject stepped out into the amphitheater. Directly opposite him, on the other side of the enclosed space, were two doors, exactly alike and side by side. It was the duty and the privilege of the person on trial, to walk directly to these doors and open one of them. He could open either door he pleased: he was subject to no guidance or influence but that of the aforementioned impartial and incorruptible chance. If he opened the one, there came out of it a hungry tiger, the fiercest and most cruel that could be procured, which immediately sprang upon him, and tore him to pieces, as a punishment for his guilt. The moment that the case of the criminal was thus decided, doleful iron bells were clanged, great wails went up from the hired mourners posted on the outer rim of the arena, and the vast audience, with bowed heads and downcast hearts, wended slowly their homeward way, mourning greatly that one so young and fair, or so old and respected, should have merited so **dire** a fate.

But, if the accused person opened the other door, there came forth from it a lady, the most suitable to his years and station that his majesty could select among his fair subjects; and to this lady he was immediately married, as a reward of his innocence. It mattered not that he might already possess a wife and family, or that his affections might be engaged upon an object of his own selection: the king allowed no such subordinate arrangements to interfere with his great scheme of retribution and reward.[8] The exercises, as in the other instance, took place immediately, and in the arena. Another door opened beneath the king, and a priest, followed by a band of choristers, and dancing maidens blowing joyous airs on golden horns and treading an epithalamic measure, advanced to

6. An *amphitheater* is a circular structure with rising tiers of seats around a central open space.

7. The *barleycorn* is an old unit of measure equal to the width of one grain of barley—about a third of an inch. This phrase is similar to "every inch a king" and means that he was kingly in every way and in every part, top to bottom.

8. The king's plan for giving out punishment (*retribution*) and reward was of primary importance, and everything else was less important (*subordinate*), including family values.

3 Conflict *Based on this passage, what do you think the main conflict will be?*

Matters of Life and Death *What do these details suggest about the people's view of death and mourning?* 4

Vocabulary

impartial (im pär′ shəl) *adj.* not favoring one side more than another; fair

emanate (em′ ə nāt′) *v.* to come forth

Vocabulary

dire (dīr) *adj.* dreadful; terrible

FRANK R. STOCKTON 13

Teach

Literary Element 3

Conflict **Answer:** *A person on trial will have to choose between the two doors.*

Big Idea 4

Matters of Life and Death **Answer:** *They put on a great show of emotion they did not really feel ("hired mourners").*

Cultural History ☆

Roman Times The author may be alluding to the Romans, the "distant Latin neighbors" named on page 12. During the early years of Christianity, the Romans had a practice of putting Christians in the arena with lions, where they were mauled to death for their beliefs.

Approaching Level

DIFFERENTIATED INSTRUCTION

Established Make sure students understand the historical context of the amphitheater. Explain that in Ancient Rome, people built amphitheaters as places for entertainment. The most famous amphitheater was the Colosseum in Rome, which could accommodate 50,000 people. The Colosseum was four stories high, and the most prominent citizens sat on the lowest level, so they were closest to the action.

People who came to the Colosseum watched fights to the death between wild animals, gladiators and animals, and gladiators themselves. Sometimes spectators even joined in on the action.

Ask: How is the entertainment at the king's amphitheater different from the entertainment at the Colosseum in Rome? *(People who came to the Colosseum watched fights. People who came to the king's amphitheater watched trials*

in which men chose one of two doors to

Color Coding

Teacher information is color coded to match information in the Student Edition.

After You Read

Assess

1. The circus event (the risky trapeze act and fierce storm); the rescue (deadly fire, amazing leap)
2. (a) Lightning hit the pole, sending Harry to his death. Anna saved herself. (b) She wanted to forget the death of her husband and baby.
3. (a) She was trapped inside her burning house. (b) Their lives seemed miraculous and dramatic; both survived deadly events.
4. (a) The mother's first leap to save herself and the one to save her daughter (b) A leap of faith, such as the mother's courage in starting a new life and the daughter's faith that her mother would save her
5. Its unusual details stimulate the reader's interest.
6. (a) The sister seems unreal at first but later becomes a more definite presence. (b) As people age, they can visualize death more clearly.
7. Their calm attitude was realistic. The mother was trained to take great risks; a child might not appreciate the danger she faced or the finality of death.
8. Students may mention the mother's courage in times of danger, her ability to move on after tragedy, the daughter's ability to stay calm during the fire, and her faith in her mother.

Progress Check

Can students explain flashback?

If No → See Unit 1 Teaching Resources Book, p. 54.

52

After You Read

Respond and Think Critically

Respond and Interpret

1. What do you think is the most dramatic event in this story? Give details to explain your choice.
2. (a)What caused the disaster at the circus, and what happened to the Flying Avalons? (b)In your opinion, why didn't the mother save her costume or anything related to this period in her life?
3. (a)What happened to the narrator when she was seven? (b)What comparisons do you think the narrator would make between her life and her mother's? Provide evidence from the story to substantiate your claims.
4. (a)What specific event or events in this story does the title refer to? (b)What else might the title refer to?

Analyze and Evaluate

5. How effective is the author at capturing the reader's attention with the opening passage of this story? Explain.
6. (a)How does the narrator's attitude toward her dead half-sister change? (b)What does information about this sibling add to the story?

Connect

7. **Big Idea** Matters of Life and Death Both the narrator and her mother reacted to matters of life and death in this story. Did you find their reactions realistic? Explain.
8. **Connect to the Author** Louise Erdrich often writes about the personal power or strength of women. How do the narrator and her mother each show their personal strengths in this story?

Literary Element Flashback

A **flashback** can take the form of an earlier event, a prior conversation, or a complete episode. Flashbacks help the reader understand characters as well as events. Often presented as a memory of the narrator, a flashback may be sparked by one or more cues, such as a sound or odor associated with a prior experience or a visit to a related setting.

1. How do a sound, an odor, and a certain setting work together to spark the narrator's memory at the beginning of "The Leap"?
2. What other sensory details help to reveal the similarities between the two main flashbacks in the story?
3. Which of her mother's character traits were displayed throughout the narrator's flashbacks? How did the author's choice to use flashbacks help to better portray these traits? Give reasons for your opinion.

Review: Setting

As you learned on pages 8–9, **setting** is the time and place in which the events of a literary work occur. Setting includes not only the physical surroundings, but also the ideas, customs, values, and beliefs of a particular time and place.

Partner Activity Work with a classmate to record details of the setting. Create a chart like the one below and complete it with details from the story.

	Time	Place
Past	June, years ago	circus tent in a small New Hampshire town
Present		

52 UNIT 1 THE SHORT STORY

Literary Element

1. They remind the narrator of her rescue from the fire.
2. The stitches that burn the narrator's fingers, the mother's burned hands; the mother's grace in the circus, her rescue of the narrator; the falls of the unborn child and the narrator, both held by the mother
3. Resilience, strength, grace, intuitiveness, balance, devotion; The reader sees the traits in action so they seem more real.

Review: Setting

Past: Time: Unnamed past—narrator's childhood and before; **Place:** Hospital; Cemetery; Burning house **Present: Time:** Unnamed present—narrator's adulthood; **Place:** New Hampshire farmhouse—sewing room

Assess

Students are assessed at regular points throughout instruction: after reading selections and at the end of units. The Teacher Edition provides answers to Student Edition questions.

Progress Check

IF a student needs help (based on a quick and informal assessment), THEN we provide a suggestion for reteaching.

Teaching Support

Big Idea Connection

Thought-provoking statements prompt students to explore the Big Idea in context to the reading selection.

Readability Scores

Dale-Chall, DRP, and Lexiles are provided for every selection

Teaching Notes

These notes give you extra teaching hintsand information.

Spiral Review

Because repetition and reinforcement are important for students' learning, we indicate when a skill is being reviewed.

Skills Support

Glencoe Literature provides addition support with the skills, such as reading, writing, literature, listening, speaking, and viewing, research, that provide the framework for all academic success.

Teach

Big Idea 1

Matters of Life and Death
Answer: *For the hunted, it is not sport, but a matter of life and death.*

APPROACHING For approaching-level students, **say:** Keep this question in mind as you read: How does the desire to stay alive affect Rainsford's actions? *(It keeps him pushing the limits of his endurance.)* **Ask:** How does the life-or-death outcome affect the readers' experience? *(It heightens the suspense.)*

View the Art ★

Belgian artist Henri Cleenewerck (1818–1901) was influenced by the Flemish old masters. His painting *A Hunter in the Cuban Jungle* reflects this. In addition to scenes in Cuba, Cleenewerck landscapes included locations in California and Europe.

For an audio recording of this selection, use Listening Library Audio CD-ROM.

Readability Scores
Dale-Chall: 6.2
DRP: 50
Lexile: 740

A Hunter in the Cuban Jungle, Sunrise, 1869. Henri Cleenewerck. Oil on canvas, 96.8 x 82.5 cm. Private collection. ★

THE Most Dangerous GAME

Richard Connell

Off there to the right—somewhere—is a large island," said Whitney. "It's rather a mystery—"

"What island is it?" Rainsford asked.

"The old charts call it 'Ship-Trap Island'," Whitney replied. "A suggestive name, isn't it? Sailors have a curious dread of the place. I don't know why. Some superstition—"

"Can't see it," remarked Rainsford, trying to peer through the dank tropical night that was palpable as it pressed its thick warm blackness in upon the yacht.

"You've good eyes," said Whitney, with a laugh, "and I've seen you pick off a moose moving in the brown fall bush at four hundred yards, but even you can't see four miles or so through a moonless Caribbean night."

"Nor four yards," admitted Rainsford. "Ugh! It's like moist black velvet."

"It will be light enough in Rio," promised Whitney. "We should make it in a few days. I hope the jaguar guns have come from Purdey's. We should have some good hunting up the Amazon. Great sport, hunting."

"The best sport in the world," agreed Rainsford.

"For the hunter," amended Whitney. "Not for the jaguar."

"Don't talk rot, Whitney," said Rainsford. "You're a big-game hunter, not a philosopher. Who cares how a jaguar feels?"

Matters of Life and Death *What does Whitney's statement suggest about his view of hunting?* **1**

22 UNIT 1 THE SHORT STORY

Literary Element

SPIRAL REVIEW PARTNERS **Foils** Tell students that a foil is a minor character whose character traits highlight those of the main character. To practice *reading fluency*, have students read the conversation between Whitney and Rainsford that begins on this page and ends on the fourth paragraph of page 23. **Ask:** What can you tell about Whitney from this conversation? *(He thinks Rainsford has good vision and is a great hunter; he feels for the jaguar; he is not tough like Rainsford.)* **Ask:** What can you tell about Rainsford? *(He has no compassion for a jaguar; he considers himself a hunter and not a huntee.)*

With a partn... Whitney is a... should take... and later sh... class.

22

Teach

Reading Strategy 1

Make and Verify Predictions About Plot
Answer: *He will swim to the island, since the boat is out of reach. He will be stranded there.*

Big Idea 2

Matters of Life and Death
Answer: *Most students will infer that the animal was killed.*

Writer's Technique ☆

Setting The Caribbean Sea, a part of the Atlantic Ocean, is several degrees warmer than the waters farther north. Connell's use of the term *blood-warm* to describe a temperature that would usually seem inviting helps readers imagine Rainsford's fear.

Rainsford sprang up and moved quickly to the rail, mystified. He strained his eyes in the direction from which the reports had come, but it was like trying to see through a blanket. He leaped upon the rail and balanced himself there, to get greater elevation; his pipe, striking a rope, was knocked from his mouth. He lunged for it; a short, hoarse cry came from his lips as he realized he had reached too far and had lost his balance. The cry was pinched off short as the ☆ blood-warm waters of the Caribbean Sea closed over his head.

He struggled up to the surface and tried to cry out, but the wash from the speeding yacht slapped him in the face and the salt water in his open mouth made him gag and strangle. Desperately he struck out with strong strokes after the receding lights of the yacht, but he stopped before he had swum fifty feet. A certain coolheadedness had come to him; it was not the first time he had been in a tight place. There was a chance that his cries could be heard by someone aboard the yacht, but that chance was slender, and grew more slender as the yacht raced on. He wrestled himself out of his clothes, and shouted with all his power. The lights of the yacht became faint and ever-vanishing fireflies; then they were blotted out entirely by the night.

Rainsford remembered the shots. They had come from the right, and doggedly he swam in that direction, swimming with slow, deliberate strokes, conserving his strength. For a seemingly endless time he fought the sea. He began to count his strokes; he could do possibly a hundred more and then—

Rainsford heard a sound. It came out of the darkness, a high screaming sound, the sound of an animal in an extremity of anguish and terror.

He did not recognize the animal that made the sound; he did not try to; with fresh vitality he swam toward the sound. He heard it again; then it was cut short by another noise, crisp, staccato.

"Pistol shot," muttered Rainsford, swimming on.

Ten minutes of determined effort brought another sound to his ears—the most welcome he had ever heard—the muttering and growling of the sea breaking on a rocky shore. He was almost on the rocks before he saw them; on a night less calm he would have been shattered against them. With his remaining strength he dragged himself from the swirling waters. Jagged crags appeared to jut up into the opaqueness;[3] he forced himself upward, hand over hand. Gasping, his hands raw, he reached a flat place at the top. Dense jungle came down to the very edge of the cliffs. What perils that tangle of trees and underbrush might hold for him did not concern Rainsford just then. All he knew was that he was safe from his enemy, the sea, and that utter weariness was upon him. He flung himself down at the jungle edge and tumbled headlong into the deepest sleep of his life.

When he opened his eyes he knew from the position of the sun that it was late in the afternoon. Sleep had given him new vigor; a sharp hunger was picking at him. He looked about him, almost cheerfully.

"Where there are pistol shots, there are men. Where there are men, there is food," he thought. But what kind of men, he

3. *Crags* are steep, rugged, protruding rocks or cliffs. Here, the crags jut up into the darkness *(opaqueness)* of the night.

1 Make and Verify Predictions About Plot *What do you think will happen to Rainsford?*

Matters of Life and Death *Why does the pistol shot stop the sound?* **2**

24 UNIT 1 THE SHORT STORY

Vocabulary Skills Practice

SPIRAL REVIEW SMALL GROUP **Unfamiliar Vocabulary** Have students work in small groups to create a list of five to ten unfamiliar words found on pages 24 and 25. Students should then use a dictionary to define each word, and then use each word in a sentence. After students have finished, a representative from each group should share words and sentences from his or her list.

You may choose to allow students to write words from their list on the board, along with their sentences. Encourage students to add new words to their list as each group responds.

24

Teach

Reading Strategy 1

Identify Sequence **Answer:** *The narrator is going to describe the three events in chronological order. The phrase "the first time" is a clue.*

For additional practice using the reading skill or strategy, see Unit 1 Teaching Resources Book, p. 55.

Literary Element 2

Flashback **Answer:** *She describes what she now thinks the day in the past was like. This gives a smooth link from present to past.*

Cultural History ☆

United States Climate People in the western United States can see storms coming because flat, open spaces make the sky visible. In the East, hills, trees, and buildings block views of the sky.

She has never upset an object or as much as brushed a magazine onto the floor. She has never lost her balance or bumped into a closet door left carelessly open.

It has occurred to me that the catlike precision of her movements in old age might be the result of her early training, but she shows so little of the drama or flair one might expect from a performer that I tend to forget the Flying Avalons. She has kept no sequined costume, no photographs, no fliers or posters from that part of her youth. I would, in fact, tend to think that all memory of double somersaults and heart-stopping catches had left her arms and legs were it not for the fact that sometimes, as I sit sewing in the room of the rebuilt house in which I slept as a child, I hear the crackle, catch a whiff of smoke from the stove downstairs, and suddenly the room goes dark, the stitches burn beneath my fingers, and I am sewing with a needle of hot silver, a thread of fire.

I owe her my existence three times. The first was when she saved herself. In the town square a replica tent pole, cracked and splintered, now stands cast in concrete. It **commemorates** the disaster that put our town smack on the front page of the Boston and New York tabloids.[1] It is from those old newspapers, now historical records, that I get my information. Not from my mother, Anna of the Flying Avalons, nor from any of her in-laws, nor certainly from the other half of her particular act, Harold Avalon, her first husband. In one news account it says, "The day was mildly overcast, but nothing in the air or temperature gave any hint of the sudden force with which the deadly gale would strike."

I have lived in the West, where you can see the weather coming for miles, and it is ☆ true that out here we are at something of a disadvantage. When extremes of temperature collide, a hot and cold front, winds generate instantaneously behind a hill and crash upon you without warning. That, I think, was the likely situation on that day in June. People probably commented on the pleasant air, grateful that no hot sun beat upon the striped tent that stretched over the entire center green. They bought their tickets and surrendered them in anticipation. They sat. They ate caramelized popcorn and roasted peanuts. There was time, before the storm, for three acts. The White Arabians of Ali-Khazar rose on their hind legs and waltzed. The Mysterious Bernie folded himself into a painted cracker tin, and the Lady of the Mists made herself appear and disappear in surprising places. As the clouds gathered outside, unnoticed, the ringmaster cracked his whip, shouted his introduction, and pointed to the ceiling of the tent, where the Flying Avalons were perched.

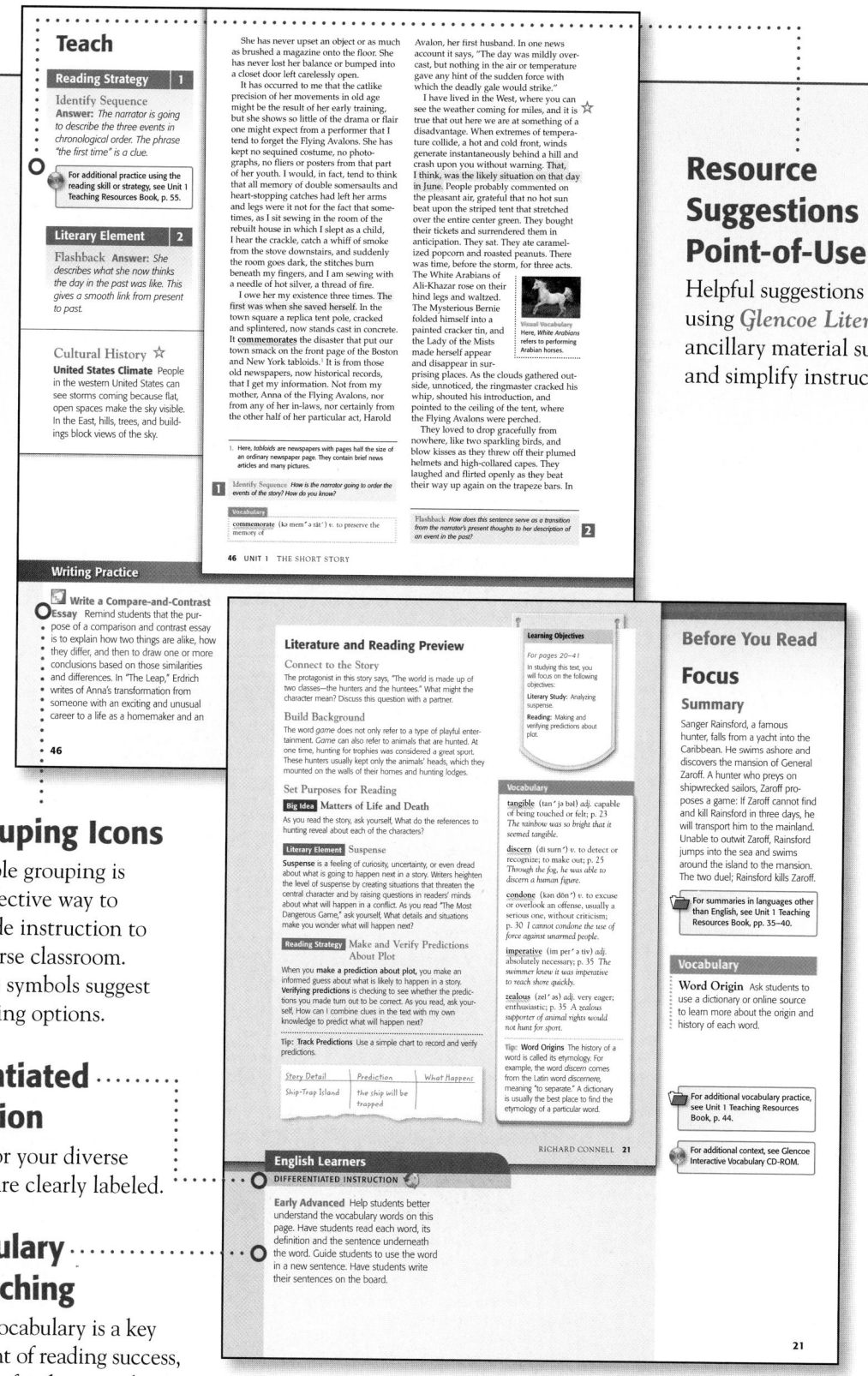

Visual Vocabulary Here, *White Arabians* refers to performing Arabian horses.

They loved to drop gracefully from nowhere, like two sparkling birds, and blow kisses as they threw off their plumed helmets and high-collared capes. They laughed and flirted openly as they beat their way up again on the trapeze bars. In

1. Here, *tabloids* are newspapers with pages half the size of an ordinary newspaper page. They contain brief news articles and many pictures.

1 Identify Sequence *How is the narrator going to order the events of the story? How do you know?*

Vocabulary

commemorate (kə mem′ ə rāt′) *v.* to preserve the memory of

Flashback *How does this sentence serve as a transition from the narrator's present thoughts to her description of an event in the past?* 2

46 UNIT 1 THE SHORT STORY

Writing Practice

Write a Compare-and-Contrast Essay Remind students that the purpose of a comparison and contrast essay is to explain how two things are alike, how they differ, and then to draw one or more conclusions based on those similarities and differences. In "The Leap," Erdrich writes of Anna's transformation from someone with an exciting and unusual career to a life as a homemaker and an

46

Resource Suggestions at Point-of-Use

Helpful suggestions for using *Glencoe Literature* ancillary material support and simplify instruction.

Literature and Reading Preview

Connect to the Story

The protagonist in this story says, "The world is made up of two classes—the hunters and the huntees." What might the character mean? Discuss this question with a partner.

Build Background

The word *game* does not only refer to a type of playful entertainment. *Game* can also refer to animals that are hunted. At one time, hunting for trophies was considered a great sport. These hunters usually kept only the animals' heads, which they mounted on the walls of their homes and hunting lodges.

Set Purposes for Reading

Big Idea Matters of Life and Death

As you read the story, ask yourself, What do the references to hunting reveal about each of the characters?

Literary Element Suspense

Suspense is a feeling of curiosity, uncertainty, or even dread about what is going to happen next in a story. Writers heighten the level of suspense by creating situations that threaten the central character and by raising questions in readers' minds about what will happen in a conflict. As you read "The Most Dangerous Game," ask yourself, What details and situations make you wonder what will happen next?

Reading Strategy Make and Verify Predictions About Plot

When you **make a prediction about plot,** you make an informed guess about what is likely to happen in a story. **Verifying predictions** is checking to see whether the predictions you made turn out to be correct. As you read, ask yourself, How can I combine clues in the text with my own knowledge to predict what will happen next?

Tip: Track Predictions Use a simple chart to record and verify predictions.

Story Detail	Prediction	What Happens
Ship-Trap Island	the ship will be trapped	

Learning Objectives

For pages 20–41

In studying this text, you will focus on the following objectives:

Literary Study: Analyzing suspense.

Reading: Making and verifying predictions about plot.

Vocabulary

tangible (tan′ jə bəl) *adj.* capable of being touched or felt; p. 23 *The rainbow was so bright that it seemed tangible.*

discern (di surn′) *v.* to detect or recognize; to make out; p. 25 *Through the fog, he was able to discern a human figure.*

condone (kən dōn′) *v.* to excuse or overlook an offense, usually a serious one, without criticism; p. 30 *I cannot condone the use of force against unarmed people.*

imperative (im per′ ə tiv) *adj.* absolutely necessary; p. 35 *The swimmer knew it was imperative to reach shore quickly.*

zealous (zel′ əs) *adj.* very eager; enthusiastic; p. 35 *A zealous supporter of animal rights would not hunt for sport.*

Tip: Word Origins The history of a word is called its etymology. For example, the word *discern* comes from the Latin word *discernere,* meaning "to separate." A dictionary is usually the best place to find the etymology of a particular word.

RICHARD CONNELL 21

Before You Read

Focus

Summary

Sanger Rainsford, a famous hunter, falls from a yacht into the Caribbean. He swims ashore and discovers the mansion of General Zaroff. A hunter who preys on shipwrecked sailors, Zaroff proposes a game: If Zaroff cannot find and kill Rainsford in three days, he will transport him to the mainland. Unable to outwit Zaroff, Rainsford jumps into the sea and swims around the island to the mansion. The two duel; Rainsford kills Zaroff.

For summaries in languages other than English, see Unit 1 Teaching Resources Book, pp. 35–40.

Vocabulary

Word Origin Ask students to use a dictionary or online source to learn more about the origin and history of each word.

For additional vocabulary practice, see Unit 1 Teaching Resources Book, p. 44.

For additional context, see Glencoe Interactive Vocabulary CD-ROM.

English Learners

DIFFERENTIATED INSTRUCTION

Early Advanced Help students better understand the vocabulary words on this page. Have students read each word, its definition and the sentence underneath the word. Guide students to use the word in a new sentence. Have students write their sentences on the board.

21

Grouping Icons

Flexible grouping is an effective way to provide instruction to a diverse classroom. These symbols suggest grouping options.

Differentiated Instruction

Activities for your diverse classrooms are clearly labeled.

Vocabulary Preteaching

Because vocabulary is a key component of reading success, we provide for the struggling students and English Learners in your classroom additional vocabulary preteaching activities.

Informational Text

The wide range of informational text in *Glencoe Literature* broadens the students' reading to include more than just poetry, short stories, and plays.

Perspectives

Award-winning book excerpts provide students with the in-depth information they need to explore the cultural, political, historical, and literary contexts of a reading selection.

Historical Perspective
on *American History*

Focus

Summary

This passage from *A Thousand Days* begins with the author hearing the news that President Kennedy was shot. The author then lists the responses of many people in America and around the world to the death of an American President.

Teach

Big Idea 1

Dreams and Reality Many people saw the young, energetic President as a source of hope. His assassination left some feeling that the American dream had been damaged if not altogether destroyed.

Ask: Why would Kennedy's assassination demoralize so many people across the country? *(People hoped Kennedy would improve their lives. Also, the reality of violence is shocking to many.)*

ENGLISH LEARNERS To help English learners identify with President Kennedy ask them to name a well-known and admired leader from their native country who has influenced the lives of others. Have students explain why he or she is admired by others.

For an audio recording of this selection, use Listening Library Audio CD-ROM.

Readability Scores

Dale-Chall: 8.4
DRP: 61
Lexile: 1020

220

Historical Perspective
on *American History*

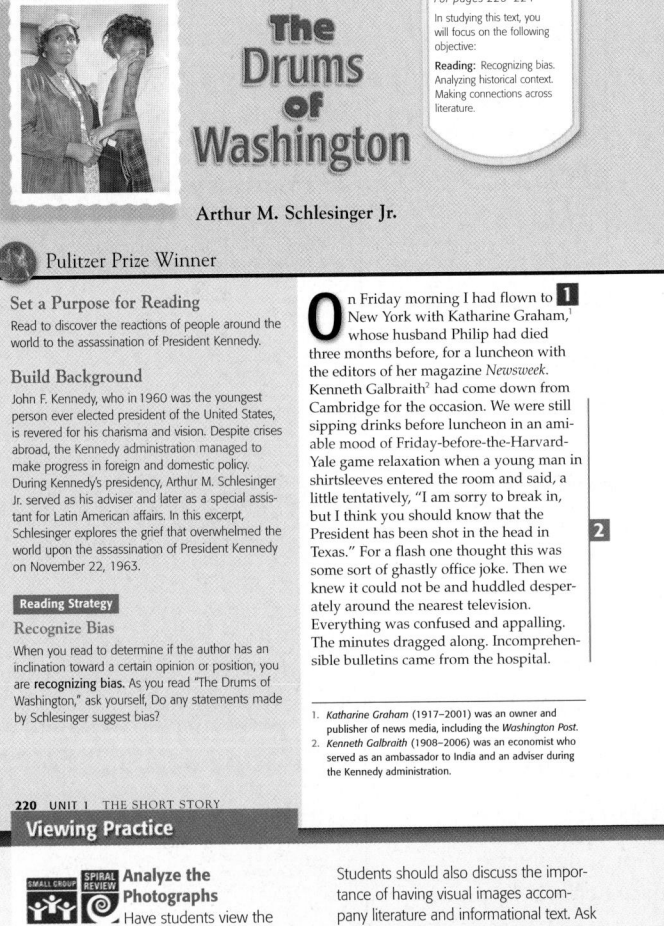

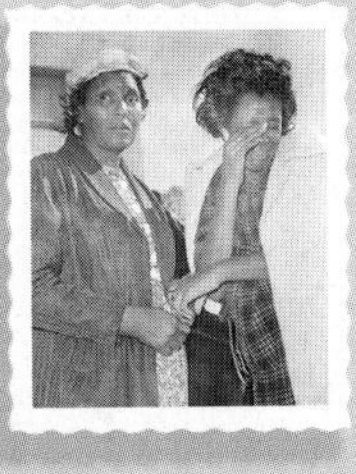

The Drums of Washington

Arthur M. Schlesinger Jr.

Pulitzer Prize Winner

Learning Objectives

For pages 220–224

In studying this text, you will focus on the following objective:

Reading: Recognizing bias. Analyzing historical context. Making connections across literature.

Set a Purpose for Reading

Read to discover the reactions of people around the world to the assassination of President Kennedy.

Build Background

John F. Kennedy, who in 1960 was the youngest person ever elected president of the United States, is revered for his charisma and vision. Despite crises abroad, the Kennedy administration managed to make progress in foreign and domestic policy. During Kennedy's presidency, Arthur M. Schlesinger Jr. served as his adviser and later as a special assistant for Latin American affairs. In this excerpt, Schlesinger explores the grief that overwhelmed the world upon the assassination of President Kennedy on November 22, 1963.

Reading Strategy

Recognize Bias

When you read to determine if the author has an inclination toward a certain opinion or position, you are **recognizing bias.** As you read "The Drums of Washington," ask yourself, Do any statements made by Schlesinger suggest bias?

On Friday morning I had flown to New York with Katharine Graham,[1] whose husband Philip had died three months before, for a luncheon with the editors of her magazine *Newsweek.* Kenneth Galbraith[2] had come down from Cambridge for the occasion. We were still sipping drinks before luncheon in an amiable mood of Friday-before-the-Harvard-Yale game relaxation when a young man in shirtsleeves entered the room and said, a little tentatively, "I am sorry to break in, but I think you should know that the President has been shot in the head in Texas." For a flash one thought this was some sort of ghastly office joke. Then we knew it could not be and huddled desperately around the nearest television. Everything was confused and appalling. The minutes dragged along. Incomprehensible bulletins came from the hospital.

1. *Katharine Graham* (1917–2001) was an owner and publisher of news media, including the *Washington Post.*
2. *Kenneth Galbraith* (1908–2006) was an economist who served as an ambassador to India and an adviser during the Kennedy administration.

220 UNIT 1 THE SHORT STORY

Viewing Practice

SMALL GROUP SPIRAL REVIEW **Analyze the Photographs** Have students view the photographs that appear with this selection. In small groups, students should take notes while answering the following questions:

- What ideas come to mind when you view each photograph?
- Why do you think the photographer felt it necessary to capture this image?

Students should also discuss the importance of having visual images accompany literature and informational text. Ask students to share points of their discussion with the rest of the class. They can use their notes to present information to the class.

TIME Articles

Linked to the Big Idea, an author, or a reading selection, these articles deliver the facts on topical issues.

TIME

Focus

Summary

John Beiler and his friends, Mike and Tom, go hunting on Alaska's Afognak Island. While alone, John breaks his leg. Stranded, he spends the night battling hypothermia, dehydration, and pain. At dawn, ravens overhead reveal his location. A helicopter flies John to a hospital. Although he spends Thanksgiving there, John is grateful to have survived his ordeal.

Teach

Preview the Article

Answers:

1. Excitement and a sense of danger
2. The final subhead is "Just in Time," which indicates that the outcome is probably positive.

Readability Scores

Dale-Chall: 7.1
DRP: 56
Lexile: 900

Learning Objectives

For pages 90–94

In studying this text, you will focus on the following objective:

Reading: Identifying problem and solution.

Set a Purpose for Reading

Read to learn about one man's struggle in a life-or-death situation.

Preview the Article

1. Read the *deck,* or the sentence that appears underneath the title. What emotions do you think the writer wants the reader to feel while reading this article?
2. Skim the boldfaced subheadings that appear in the article. Based on these, what do you think will be the outcome of the article?

Reading Strategy Identify Problem and Solution

Identifying problem and solution involves asking these questions:

- What is the main problem?
- What solutions are tried?
- What happens as a result?

As you read, ask yourself, What steps are taken to solve each problem? Use a chart like the one below.

Problem	Possible Solutions

TIME

Shattered

A terrible fall leaves a lone deer hunter with a shattered leg in the middle of brown-bear country. Now night is falling and nobody knows where he is.

By CHRISTOPHER BATIN

JOHN BEILER LIKED HUNTING SITKA BLACKTAIL DEER ON Alaska's Afognak Island. He loved the otter-filled bays, the scenic rock cliffs, the salmon streams, and just about all of the island's many natural wonders. Except one.

Afognak Island has a dark side. Typhoon winds can hammer the coastline without mercy for days at a time. Huge coastal brown bears roam the dark rain forests and salmon streams. Even hunters who are prepared for disasters often die or get seriously injured. For John Beiler, misfortune happened to others but not to him. Or so he thought.

At daybreak, Beiler and his hunting buddies Mike and Tom eyed the steep slopes of Mount Paramanof, rising 2,100 feet above their tidewater base camp. It was Thanksgiving week, and they were looking forward to blacktail steaks and mashed potatoes smothered in gravy. The hunters planned a several-hour climb to an alpine meadow where big bucks lived.

Beiler, who liked to hunt hillsides alone, left his buddies and crossed a marsh near the base of a steep cliff. He was a muscular, big-boned man, well suited to hunting the mountains. Although his rubber boots with tread soles didn't offer the best traction going uphill, they kept his feet dry as he crossed creeks and swamps.

By late afternoon, a light rain had filled the alpine landscape with the pungent-sweet smell of wet tundra. The approaching ☆ storm had caused the deer to hole up in thickets, and the dark outline of the beach below would take an hour to reach. Beiler walked faster so he could meet up with his friends before dark.

Reading Practice

SMALL GROUP SPIRAL REVIEW **Cause and Effect** Point out to students that the author builds the story through cause and effect. Remind students that what happens is the effect, and the reason it happens is the cause.

Ask: What is the main cause and effect of the story? *(Students may say that Beiler goes off on his own—cause—thereby causing him to break his leg and fight for his lfe—effect.)*

Break students into groups and have them find other causes and effects on page 90 and 91. *(Groups might note that his rubber boots, the approaching storm, and the slick grass and rotting plants may have caused him to fall.)* Ask students to design a cause-and-effect graphic organizer for the story. Have students continue to fill in their cause-and-effect organizer as they read.

Guide to Readability

Throughout the teacher materials in your Teacher Edition, you will encounter DRP readability measures assigned to the reading selections in *Glencoe Literature*. You will also find readability scores based on the Lexile Framework® for Reading and the Dale-Chall Readability Formula. You can use these scores to select reading materials that are suitable for your entire class or for individual students.

Degrees of Reading Power® (DRP)

DRP values indicate the readability of prose text. The higher the value, the more difficult the text. The scale ranges from 1 to 100; commonly encountered English text tends to fall somewhere between 25 and 85. Although middle school texts have an average difficulty of 56, and high school texts have an average difficulty of 62, no single readability level is appropriate for each grade level. Rather, a typical classroom has materials with a range of readability levels available for use—some intended for less proficient readers, some for average readers, and some for stronger readers. The following chart shows the average DRP readability range for materials widely available for use at each grade. Some materials you might use, however, will certainly fall outside of the range for your particular grade.

Grade	DRP Readability Ranges
6	51–61
7	52–62
8	53–64
9	53–65
10	51–68
11	56–67
12	57–68

The Lexile® Framework

A Lexile measure assigned to a text is the specific number that describes the reading demands of the text. The typical Lexile Scale ranges from 200 to 1700 Lexiles. As with the DRP measures, there is not a direct translation from a specific Lexile measure to a specific grade level. Within any classroom, there will be a range of readers and a range of materials to be read. The levels shown on the following chart indicate the approximate range of Lexile scores for 50 percent of the materials found in a typical grade-level classroom. For example, the middle half of the instructional materials typically found in a sixth-grade classroom ranges in difficulty from about 850L to 1050L.

Grade	Text Measures (from Lexile Framework Map)
6	850L to 1050L
7	950L to 1075L
8	1000L to 1100L
9	1050L to 1150L
10	1100L to 1200L
11 and 12	1100L to 1300L

Dale-Chall Readability Formula

The Dale-Chall Formula is based on the average sentence length and the number of unfamiliar words in a passage. The idea behind this formula is that readers typically find it easier to read, process, and recall a passage if the words and sentences are familiar and grade appropriate. The Dale-Chall Formula assesses the difficulty of a passage by computing two different values from the text. The first measure is the average number of words per sentence. The second measure is the percentage of words in the passage not found on the grade appropriate Dale Word List. The following chart shows the average Dale-Chall readability scores for grades 5 thru 12.

Grade	Dale-Chall Readability Score
5-6th Grade	5.0 to 5.9
7-8th Grade	6.0 to 6.9
9-10th Grade	7.0 to 7.9
11-12th Grade	8.0 to 8.9

African American Vernacular English (AAVE)

Some of your students will be speakers of African American Vernacular English (AAVE). AAVE is a language system with well-formed rules for sounds, grammar, and meanings. Throughout the year you will help these students learn standard academic English by focusing on those places where AAVE differs from the standard and on those patterns that will have the most immediate impact on the students' reading and writing development.

These students will need help in understanding that what is appropriate in one setting is not appropriate in another, so they can shift easily and competently between varieties in different social contexts. Instruction will be more effective if it identifies nonstandard varieties of English as different, rather than inferior. All students should be taught standard English in a way that respects their home language.

Use the charts that follow to identify AAVE linguistic differences and instructional modifications that can help students as they learn to successfully and fluently speak, read, and write standard English. The modifications focus on the following:

- Providing students with clear enunciation examples during phonics and phonemic awareness lessons targeting difficult sounds. Then additional pronunciation practice is provided during small group phonics lessons.
- Using contrastive analysis during whole group and small group time in which students code switch between AAVE and standard English. The difference in each grammatical structure is highlighted and students are provided ample opportunities to practice standard English in speaking and writing. They are also taught the proper context for each usage.
- Using Discrimination Drills in which two sentences are read aloud or written on the board. One is standard English, the other reflects common AAVE structures. Students must determine which is standard English.
- Using Translation Drills in which students change an AAVE sentence into standard English.

Phonics Differences

English/Language Arts Skill	Linguistic Differences and Instructional Modifications
Digraph *th* as in bathroom	For many speakers of African American Vernacular English, the initial /th/ sound in function words such as *this* and *then* is often produced as a /d/ sound. In some words, such as *thing* and *through,* the /th/ sound is produced as a /t/ sound. At the ends of words and syllables, such as *bathroom* and *death,* the /th/ sound is replaced by the /f/ sound. This will affect students' spelling and speaking. Students will need additional articulation support prior to spelling these words.
Final Consonant *r*	Many speakers of African American Vernacular English drop the /r/ sound in words. For example, these students will say *sto'* for *store* or *do'* for *door.* Clearly pronounce these words, emphasizing the /r/ sound. Have students repeat several times, exaggerating the sound before spelling these words.
***r*-Blends**	Many speakers of African American Vernacular English drop the /r/ in words with *r*-Blends. For example, these students will say *th'ow* for *throw.* Clearly pronounce these words in the lesson, emphasizing the sounds of the *r*-Blend. Have students repeat several times, exaggerating the sound.

Final Consonant / and Final *l*-Blends	Many speakers of African American Vernacular English drop the */l/* sound in words, particularly in words with *-ool* and *-oal* spelling patterns, such as *cool* and *coal*, and when the letter *l* precedes the consonants *p, t,* or *k* as in *help, belt,* and *milk.* These students will drop the *l* when spelling these words, as well. Provide additional articulation support prior to reading and spelling these words.
Final Consonant Blends	Many speakers of African American Vernacular English drop the final letter in a consonant blend *(e.g., mp, nt, nk, lo, lt, lk).* For example, they will say des' for *desk.* Clearly pronounce the final sound in these words and have students repeat several times, exaggerating the sound.
Plurals	When the letter *-s* is added to a word ending in a consonant blend, such as *test (tests)*, many speakers of African American Vernacular English will drop the final sounds. Therefore they will say *tes' or tesses.* These students will need additional articulation support.
Contractions	Many speakers of African American Vernacular English drop the */t/* sound when pronouncing the common words *it's, that's,* and *what's.* These words sound more like *i's, tha's*, and *wha's.* These students will need additional articulation support in order to pronounce and spell these words.
Short Vowels *i* and *e*	When the /i/ and /e/ sounds appear before the consonants m or n in words, such as *pen/pin* and *him/hem,* many speakers of African American Vernacular English won't pronounce or hear the difference. Focus on articulation, such as mouth position for each vowel sound, during the lesson.
Inflectional Ending *-ing*	Many speakers of African American Vernacular English will pronounce words with *-ing* as /ang/. For example, they will say *thang* for *thing.* Emphasize the /i/ sound in these words to help students correctly spell and pronounce them.

Grammar, Usage, Mechanics Differences

English/Language Arts Skill	Linguistic Differences and Instructional Modifications
Subject-Verb Agreement *(he is , he goes)*	To acquire standard academic English speech and writing, speakers of African American Vernacular English need to learn to use -s with a verb and the third person and only there, as in *he is* and *he goes.* Many speakers of AAVE will leave out the -s or place it elsewhere, as in *he go* or *we goes.* Write a sentence from students' speech or writing. Then provide contrastive analysis work. Write the standard English form above that sentence. Discuss the key differences.
Subject-Verb Agreement *(do/does, have/has, was/were)*	Many speakers of African American Vernacular English have difficulties with subject-verb agreement when the verbs *do/does, have/has,* and *was/were* are used. Additional grammar instruction and practice will be needed. Write a sentence from students' speech or writing. Then provide contrastive analysis work. Write the standard English form above that sentence. Discuss the key differences.
Past Tense *(-ed)*	Many speakers of African American Vernacular English understand the use of *-ed* to form the past tense but leave it out or add sounds when pronouncing the word, as in *pick* or *pickted* for *picked.* Students will need additional work during small group time with *-ed* in order to know when and where to use it in writing.

Past Tense (simple past tense vs. past perfect tense)	Many speakers of African American Vernacular English will add *had* to the simple past tense, saying *We had picked* for *We picked.* The use of *had* indicates the past perfect tense in standard academic English. Other common nonstandard forms of irregular past-tense verbs include *He seen that* and *He had ran over there.*
The Verb "to be" (pronunciation)	In the first person present tense, many speakers of African American Vernacular English will properly use *I am* or *I'm*, but say it more like *"uhm."* Focus on pronunciation.
The Verb "to be" (writing)	To learn standard academic English, many speakers of African American Vernacular English will need to learn not to delete *is* and *are* when speaking and writing. For example, students might say *He my brother* or *She goin' over there.* Additional grammar instruction and practice will be needed. Use Discrimination and Translation Drills.
The Verb "to be" (speaking)	Many speakers of African American Vernacular English will use *was* in the singular and plural forms, as in *He was* and *They was.* Additional grammar instruction and practice will be needed.
The Verb "to be"	To learn standard academic English, many speakers of African American Vernacular English will need to learn to avoid using nonstandard forms, such as *He always be doing this,* in favor of *am, are,* and *is.* Also, additional instruction and practice will be needed to show the proper placement of the adverbs *always, never,* and *others.* For example, *He is always doing this* rather than *He always is doing this.* Write a sentence from students' speech or writing. Then provide contrastive analysis work. Write the standard English form above that sentence. Discuss the key differences.
Possessives ('s)	In standard academic English, *'s* is added to a noun to show possession. For many speakers of African American Vernacular English, the *'s* is absent. However, the *'s* is regularly added to mine, as in *This is mines.*
Possessive (whose)	The possessive pronoun whose is often not used by many speakers of African American Vernacular English. For example, students will say *I don't know who book this was.* Students will need additional instruction and practice to acquire this skill.
There is/There are	Many speakers of African American Vernacular English will need help in pronouncing *its* in standard academic English and in properly using the patterns *there is* and *there are.* In AAVE it is common to replace the word there with *it,* as in *It's a man at the door* rather than *There's a man at the door.* Use Discrimination and Translation Drills.
Plurals (nouns of measure)	Most speakers of African American Vernacular English correctly use the plural, except when it involves "nouns of measure," as in *It cost five dollars* or *She owe me five dollars*. However, the plural /s/ is often absent in writing, and students will need additional instruction and practice during small group time.
Negatives	Many speakers of African American Vernacular English will use several negatives in a sentence when only one is required, as in *Nobody never said nothing.* To master standard academic English, speakers of AAVE will need considerable practice to gain control of any, ever, and either after a negative word. Write a sentence from students' speech or writing. Then provide contrastive analysis work. Write the standard English form above that sentence. Discuss the key differences. In addition, use Discrimination and Translation Drills.

The Interaction Between English and Students' Primary Languages

By Jana Echevarria, PhD
California State University, Long Beach

Donald Bear, PhD
University of Nevada, Reno

It is important for teachers to understand why English Learners (ELs) use alternative pronunciations for some English words. Many English sounds do not exist or transfer to other languages, so English Learners may lack the auditory acuity to "hear" these English sounds and have difficulty pronouncing them. These students are not accustomed to positioning their mouth in a way the sound requires. The charts that appear on the following pages show that there is variation among languages, with some languages having more sounds in common and thus greater transfer to English than others.

For example, an English speaker may be able to pronounce the /r/ in the Spanish word pero ("but"), but not the /rr/ trill in perro ("dog"). The English speaker may also lack the auditory acuity to detect and the ability to replicate the tonal sounds of some Chinese words. Similarly, a Vietnamese speaker may have difficulty pronouncing /th/ in words such as thin or thanks.

Further, English Learners make grammatical errors due to interference from their native languages. In Spanish, the adjective follows the noun, so often English Learners say "the girl pretty" instead of "the pretty girl." While English changes the verb form with a change of subject (I walk. She walks.), some Asian languages keep the verb form constant across subjects. Adding /s/ to the third person may be difficult for some English Learners. Students may know the grammatical rule, but applying it consistently may be difficult, especially in spoken English.

When working with English Learners, you should also be aware of sociocultural factors that affect pronunciation. Students may retain an accent because it marks their social identity. Speakers of other languages may feel at a social distance from members of the dominant English-speaking culture.

English Learners improve their pronunciation in a nonthreatening atmosphere in which participation is encouraged. Opportunities to interact with native English speakers provide easy access to language models and give English Learners practice using English. However, students should not be forced to participate. Pressure to perform—or to perform in a certain way—can inhibit participation. In any classroom, teacher sensitivity to pronunciation differences contributes to a more productive learning environment.

Phonics, word recognition, and spelling are influenced by what students know about the sounds, word structure, and spelling in their primary languages. For example, beginning readers who speak Spanish and are familiar with its spelling will often spell short o with an a, a letter that in Spanish makes the short o sound. Similarly, English Learners who are unaccustomed to English consonant digraphs and blends (e.g., /ch/ and s-blends) spell /ch/ as sh because /sh/ is the sound they know that is closest to /ch/. Students learn about the way pronunciation influences their reading and spelling, beginning with large contrasts among sounds, then they study the finer discriminations. As vocabulary advances, the meaning of words leads students to the sound contrasts. For example, shoe and chew may sound alike initially, but meaning indicates otherwise. Students' reading and discussions of what they read advances their word knowledge as well as their knowledge in all language and literacy systems, including phonics, pronunciation, grammar, and vocabulary.

Phonics Transfers: Sound Transfers

This chart indicates areas where a positive transfer of sounds and symbols occurs for English Learners from their native languages into English. This symbol (✔) identifies a positive transfer. "Approximate" indicates that the sound is similar.

Consonants

Sound Transfers	Spanish	Cantonese	Vietnamese	Hmong	Korean	Khmer
/b/ as in bat	✔	approximate	approximate	approximate	approximate	✔
/k/ as in cake, kitten, peck	✔	✔	✔	✔	✔	✔
/d/ as in dog	✔	approximate	approximate	✔	approximate	✔
/f/ as in farm	✔	✔	✔	✔		
/g/ as in girl	✔	approximate	✔	approximate	approximate	
/h/ as in ham	✔	✔	✔	✔	✔	approximate
/j/ as in jet, page, ledge		approximate	approximate		approximate	
/l/ as in lion	✔	✔	✔	✔	✔	
/m/ as in mat	✔	✔	✔	✔	✔	✔
/n/ as in night	✔	✔	✔	✔	✔	✔
/p/ as in pen	✔	✔	✔	approximate	✔	✔
/kw/ as in queen	✔	approximate	✔		✔	✔
/r/ as in rope	approximate					✔
/s/ as in sink, city	✔	✔	✔	✔	✔	approximate
/t/ as in ton	✔	✔	approximate	approximate	✔	✔
/v/ as in vine	✔		✔	✔		
/w/ as in wind	✔	✔			✔	✔
/ks/ as in six	✔				✔	✔
/y/ as in yak	✔	✔		✔	✔	✔
/z/ as in zebra			✔			

Diagraphs

Sound Transfers	Spanish	Cantonese	Vietnamese	Hmong	Korean	Khmer
/ch/ as in cheek, patch	✔	approximate		✔	✔	✔
/sh/ as in shadow			✔	✔	✔	
/hw/ as in whistle					✔	✔
/th/ as in path	approximate		approximate			
/TH/ as in that	approximate					

Diagraphs (continued)						
Sound Transfers	**Spanish**	**Cantonese**	**Vietnamese**	**Hmong**	**Korean**	**Khmer**
/ng/ as in sting	✔	✔	✔	✔	✔	approximate
Short Vowels						
/a/ as in cat	approximate		approximate	✔	✔	
/e/ as in net	✔	approximate	approximate		✔	
/i/ as in kid	approximate	approximate			✔	
/o/ as in spot	approximate	approximate	approximate	approximate	approximate	✔
/u/ as in cup	approximate	approximate	✔		✔	✔
Long Vowels						
/ā/ as in lake, nail, bay	✔	approximate	approximate	approximate	✔	✔
/ē/ as in bee, meat, cranky	✔	approximate	✔	✔	✔	✔
/ī/ as in kite, tie, light, dry	✔	approximate	✔	✔	✔	✔
/ō/ as in home, road, row	✔	approximate	approximate		✔	
/ū/ as in dune, fruit, blue	✔	approximate	✔	✔	✔	✔
/yü/ as in mule, cue	✔	approximate			✔	
***r*-Controlled Vowels**						
/är/ as in far	approximate	approximate				
/ôr/ as in corn	approximate	approximate				
/ûr/ as in stern, bird, suburb	approximate	approximate				
/âr/ as in air, bear						
/îr/ as in deer, ear						
Variant Vowels						
/oi/ as in boil, toy	✔	approximate	approximate		✔	✔
/ou/ as in loud, down	✔	approximate	✔	approximate	✔	✔
/ô/ as in law	approximate	✔	✔	approximate	approximate	✔
/ô/ as in laundry	approximate	approximate	✔	approximate	approximate	✔
/ôl/ as in salt, call	approximate	approximate			approximate	✔
/o͞o/ as in moon, drew	✔	approximate	approximate	✔	✔	✔
/oo/ as in look		approximate	approximate		approximate	✔
/ə/ as in askew			approximate		✔	

Phonics Transfers: Sound Symbol Match

Consonants

Sound Transfers	Spanish	Cantonese	Vietnamese	Hmong	Korean	Khmer
/b/ as in bat	✔		✔			
/k/ as in cake	✔		✔			
/k/ as in kitten	✔		✔	✔		
/k/ as in peck						
/d/ as in dog	✔		✔	✔		
/f/ as in farm	✔			✔		
/g/ as in girl	✔		✔			
/h/ as in ham			✔	✔		
/j/ as in jet, page, ledge						
/l/ as in lion	✔		✔	✔		
/m/ as in mat	✔		✔	✔		
/n/ as in night	✔		✔	✔		
/p/ as in pen	✔		✔	✔		
/kw/ as in queen			✔			
/r/ as in rope	approximate					
/s/ as in sink, city	✔		✔			
/t/ as in ton	✔		✔	✔		
/v/ as in vine	✔		✔	✔		
/w/ as in wind	✔					
/ks/ as in six	✔					
/y/ as in yak	✔			✔		
/z/ as in zebra						

Sound Transfers	Spanish	Cantonese	Vietnamese	Hmong	Korean	Khmer
Diagraphs						
/ch/ as in cheek, patch	✔					
/sh/ as in shadow						
/hw/ as in whistle						
/th/ as in path			✔			
/TH/ as in that						
/ng/ as in sting	✔		✔			
Short Vowels						
/a/ as in cat			✔	✔		
/e/ as in net	✔		✔			
/i/ as in kid						
/o/ as in spot			✔	✔		
/u/ as in cup						
Long Vowels						
/ā/ as in lake						
/ā/ as in nail						
/ā/as in bay						
/ē/ as in bee						
/ē/ as in meat						
/ē/ as in cranky						
/ī/ as in kite, tie, light, dry						
/ō/ as in home, road, row						
/ū/ as in dune			✔	✔		
/ū/ as in fruit, blue						
/yü/ as in mule, cue						

r-Controlled Vowels

Sound Transfers	Spanish	Cantonese	Vietnamese	Hmong	Korean	Khmer
/är/ as in far	✔					
/ôr/ as in corn	✔					
/ûr/ as in stern	✔					
/ûr/ as in bird, suburb						
/âr/ as in air, bear						
/îr/ as in deer, ear						

Variant Vowels

Sound Transfers	Spanish	Cantonese	Vietnamese	Hmong	Korean	Khmer
/oi/ as in boil	✔		✔			
/oi/ as in toy	✔					
/ou/ as in loud						
/ou/ as in down						
/ô/ as in law						
/ô/ as in laundry						
/ôl/ as in salt	✔					
/ôl/ as in call						
/o͞o/ as in moon, drew						
/o͝o/ as in look						
/ə/ as in askew						

Grammar Transfers: Grammatical Form

This chart can be used to address common mistakes that some English Learners make when they transfer grammatical forms from their native languages into English.

Nouns

Grammatical Form	Transfer Mistakes in English	Native Language	Cause of Difficulty
Plural Marker -s	Forgets plural marker -s *I have 3 sister.*	Cantonese, Haitian Creole, Hmong, Korean, Vietnamese, Khmer	Native language does not use a plural marker.
Countable and Uncountable Nouns	Confuses countable and uncountable nouns *the homeworks* or *the informations*	Haitian Creole, Spanish	Countable and uncountable nouns are different in English and native language.
Possessives	Uses prepositions to describe possessives *the book of my brother* as opposed to *my brother's book*	Haitian Creole, Hmong, Spanish, Vietnamese	Possession is often described using a prepositional phrase.
	Avoids using 's *dog my father* as opposed to *my father's dog*	Haitian Creole, Vietnamese, Khmer	A noun follows the object in the native language.

Articles

	Consistently omits articles *He has book. They want dog not cat.*	Cantonese, Haitian Creole, Hmong, Korean, Vietnamese, Khmer	There is no article in the native language or no difference between the and a.
	Overuses articles *The English is difficult. The soccer is popular in the Europe.*	Haitian Creole, Hmong, Spanish	Some languages use articles that are omitted in English.
a/an	Mistakes *one* for *a/an* *She is one nurse.*	Haitian Creole, Hmong, Vietnamese	The native language either does not use articles or uses articles differently.

Pronouns

Gender-Specific Pronouns	Uses pronouns with the inappropriate gender *He is my sister.*	Cantonese, Haitian Creole, Hmong, Korean, Spanish, Khmer	The third person pronoun in the native language is gender free, or the personal pronoun is omitted.
	Uses inappropriate gender, particularly with neutral nouns *The day is sunny. She is beautiful.*	Spanish	Nouns have feminine or masculine gender in the native language, and the gender may be carried over into English.

Pronouns

Grammatical Form	Transfer Mistakes in English	Native Language	Cause of Difficulty
Object Pronouns	**Confuses subject and object pronouns** *Her talks to me.*	Cantonese, Hmong, Khmer	The same pronoun form is used for subject and object in the native language.
	Omits object pronouns *That girl is very rude, so nobody likes.*	Korean, Vietnamese	The native language does not use direct objects.
Pronoun and Number Agreement	**Uses the wrong number for pronouns** *I saw many red birds. It was pretty.*	Cantonese, Korean	The native language does not require number agreement.
Subject Pronouns	**Omits subject pronouns** *Mom isn't home. Is at work.*	Korean, Spanish	Subject pronouns may be dropped because in the native language the verb ending gives information about the number and/or gender.
Pronouns in Clauses	**Omits pronouns in clauses** *If don't do homework, they will not learn.*	Cantonese, Vietnamese	The native language does not need a subject in the subordinate clause.
Pronouns and Nouns	**Overuses pronouns with nouns** *This school, it very good.*	Hmong, Vietnamese	This is popular in speech in some languages. The speaker mentions a topic, then makes a comment about it.
	Avoids pronouns and repeats nouns *Carla visits her sister every Sunday, and Carla makes a meal.*	Korean, Vietnamese	In the native language, the speaker repeats nouns and does not use pronouns.
Pronoun one	**Omits the pronoun one** *I saw two dogs, and I like the small.*	Spanish	Adjectives can stand alone in the native language, but English requires a ***noun*** or ***one***.
Possessive Forms	**Confuses possessive forms** *The book is my.*	Cantonese, Hmong, Vietnamese	Cantonese and Hmong speakers tend to omit the final ***n*** sound, which may create confusion between my and mine.

Verbs

Grammatical Form	Transfer Mistakes in English	Native Language	Cause of Difficulty
Present Tense	**Omits -s in present tense, third person agreement** *He like pizza.*	Cantonese, Haitian Creole, Hmong, Korean, Vietnamese, Khmer	Subject-verb agreement is not used in the native language.
Irregular Verbs	**Has problems with irregular subject-verb agreement** *Tom and Sue has a new car.*	Cantonese, Hmong, Korean, Khmer	Verbs' forms do not change to show the number of the subject in the native language.
Inflectional Endings	**Omits tense markers** *I study English yesterday.*	Cantonese, Haitian Creole, Hmong, Korean, Vietnamese, Khmer	The native language does not use inflectional endings to change verb tense.
Present and Future Tenses	**Incorrectly uses the present tense for the future tense** *I go next week.*	Cantonese, Korean	The native language may use the present tense to imply the future tense.
Negative Statements	**Omits helping verbs in negative statements** *Sue no coming to school.*	Cantonese, Korean, Spanish	The native language does not use helping verbs in negative statements.
Present-Perfect Tense	**Avoids the present-perfect tense** *Marcos live here for three months.*	Haitian Creole, Vietnamese	The native language does not use the present-perfect verb form.
Past-Continuous Tense	**Uses the past-continuous tense for recurring action in the past** *When I was young, I was talking a lot.*	Korean, Spanish	In the native language, the past-continuous tense is used but in English the expression used to or the simple past tense is used.
Main Verb	**Omits the main verb** *Talk in class not good.*	Cantonese	Cantonese does not require an infinitive marker when using a verb as a noun. Speakers may confuse the infinitive for the main verb.
Main Verbs in Clauses	**Uses two or more main verbs in one clause without any connectors** *I took a book went studied at the library.*	Hmong	In Hmong, verbs can be used consecutively without conjunctions or punctuation.
Linking Verbs	**Omits the linking verb** *He hungry.*	Cantonese, Haitian Creole, Hmong, Vietnamese, Khmer	In some languages, be is implied in the adjective form. In other languages, the concept is expressed with a verb.
Helping Verb in Passive Voice	**Omits the helping verb in the passive voice** *The homework done.*	Cantonese, Vietnamese	In Cantonese and Vietnamese, the passive voice does not require a helping verb.

Verbs

Grammatical Form	Transfer Mistakes in English	Native Language	Cause of Difficulty
Passive Voice	**Avoids the passive voice** *They speak English here.* *One speaks English here.* **English is spoken here.**	Haitian Creole	The passive voice does not exist in the native language.
Transitive Verbs	**Confuses transitive and intransitive verbs** *The child broke. The child broke <u>the plate</u>.*	Cantonese, Korean, Spanish	Verbs that require a direct object differ between English and the native language.
Phrasal Verbs	**Confuses related phrasal verbs** *I ate at the apple.* *I ate up the apple.*	Korean, Spanish	Phrasal verbs are not used in the native language, and there is often confusion over their meaning.
Have **and** *be*	**Uses have instead of be** *I have thirst. He has right.*	Spanish	Spanish and English have different uses for ***have*** and ***be.***

Adjectives

Grammatical Form	Transfer Mistakes in English	Native Language	Cause of Difficulty
Word Order	**Places adjectives after nouns** *I saw a car red.*	Haitian Creole, Hmong, Spanish, Vietnamese, Khmer	Nouns often precede adjectives in the native language.
	Consistently places adjectives after nouns **This is a lesson new.**	Cantonese, Korean	Adjectives always follow nouns in the native language.
-er **and** *-est* **Endings**	**Avoids** *-er* **and** *-est* **endings** *I am more old than you.*	Hmong, Korean, Spanish, Khmer	The native language shows comparative and superlative forms with separate words.
-ing **and** *ed* **Endings**	**Confuses -ing and -ed forms** *Math is bored.*	Cantonese, Korean, Spanish, Khmer	Adjectives in the native language do not have active and passive meanings.

Adverbs

Grammatical Form	Transfer Mistakes in English	Native Language	Cause of Difficulty
Adjectives and Adverbs	**Uses an adjective where an adverb is needed** *Talk quiet.*	Haitian Creole, Hmong, Khmer	Adjectives and adverb forms are interchangeable in the native language.
Word Order	**Places adverbs before verbs** *He quickly ran.* *He ran quickly.*	Cantonese, Korean	Adverbs usually come before verbs in the native language, and this tendency is carried over into English.

Prepositions

Grammatical Form	Transfer Mistakes in English	Native Language	Cause of Difficulty
	Omits prepositions *I like come school.*	Cantonese	Cantonese does not use prepositions the way that English does.

How to Use the Grammar Transfer Charts

The grammar of many languages differs widely from English. For example, a student's primary language may use a different word order than English, may not use parts of speech in the same way, or may use different verb tenses. The Grammar Transfer Charts are designed to help you anticipate and understand possible student errors in speaking and writing standard English. With all grammar exercises, the emphasis is on oral communication, both as a speaker and listener.

1. Highlight Transferrable Skills

If the grammar skill transfers from the student's primary language to English, state that during the lesson. In many lessons an English Learner feature will indicate which skills do and do not transfer.

2. Preteach Non-Transferrable Skills

Prior to teaching a grammar lesson, check the chart to determine if the skill transfers from the student's primary language into English. If it does not, preteach the skill. Provide sentence frames and ample structured opportunities to use the skill in spoken English. Students need to talk, talk, and talk some more to master these skills.

3. Provide Additional Practice and Time

If the skill does NOT transfer from the student's primary language into English, the student will require more time and practice mastering it. Continue to review the skill using additional resources, such as the grammar lessons in the **Grammar and Language Workbook** in upcoming weeks.

4. Use Contrastive Analysis

Tell students when a skill does not transfer and include contrastive analysis work to make the student aware of how to correct their speaking and writing for standard English. For example, when a student uses an incorrect grammatical form, write the student sentence, then write the correct English form underneath. Explain the difference between the student's primary language and English. Have the student correct several other sentences using this skill.

5. Increase Writing and Speaking Opportunities

Increase the amount of structured writing and speaking opportunities for students needing work on specific grammatical forms. Sentence starters and paragraph frames, such as those found in the lessons, are ideal for both written and oral exercises.

6. Focus on Meaning

Always focus on the meanings of sentences in all exercises. As they improve and fine-tune their English speaking and writing skills, work with students on basic comprehension of spoken and written English.

To help students move to the next level of language acquisition and master English grammatical forms, recast their responses during classroom discussions or provide additional language for them to use as they respond further. Provide leveled-language sentence frames orally or in writing for students to use as they respond to questions and prompts. Below are samples.

English Learner Response Chart

Beginning (will respond by pointing or saying one word answers)	**Sample Frames** (simple, short sentences) *I see a ______.* *This is a ______.* *I like the ______.*
Early Intermediate (will respond with phrases or simple sentences)	**Sample Frames** (simple sentences with adjectives and adverbs added, and compound subjects or predicates) *I see a ______ ______.* *The ______ animal is ______.* *There are ______ and ______.*
Intermediate (will respond with simple sentences and limited academic language)	**Sample Frames** (harder sentences with simple phrases in consistent patterns; some academic language included) *The animal's prey is ______ because ______.* *The main idea is ______ because ______.* *He roamed the park so that ______.*
Early Advanced (will begin to use more sophisticated sentences and some academic language)	**Sample Frames** (complex sentences with increased academic language, beginning phrases and clauses, and multiple-meaning words) *When the violent storm hit, ______.* *As a result of the revolution, the army______.* *Since most endangered animals are ______, they ______.*
Advanced (will have mastered some more complex sentence structures and is increasing the amount of academic language used)	Use the questions and prompts provided in the lessons for the whole group. Provide additional support learning and using academic language. These words are boldfaced throughout the lessons and sentence starters are often provided.

Classroom Resources: Print

Blackline Masters

Unit Teaching Resources

These blackline master booklets provide all the teaching materials you need to reinforce the content in each unit of *Glencoe Literature.* Worksheets include the following:

Unit Introduction
Big Idea Foldable
Big Idea School-to-Home Connection
- English
- Spanish
- Vietnamese
- Tagalog
- Cantonese
- Haitian Creole
- Hmong

Challenge Planner
Academic Vocabulary Development
Part Opener
Literary Focus
English Language Coach
Comparing Literature Graphic Organizer
Grammar Workshop Practice
Media Workshop Practice
Selection Summaries
- English
- Spanish
- Vietnamese
- Tagalog
- Cantonese
- Haitian Creole
- Hmong

Literary Element
Reading Strategy
Selection Vocabulary Practice
Grammar Practice
Vocabulary Strategy
Selection Quick Check
- English
- Spanish

Spelling Practice
Writing Workshop Graphic Organizer
Writing Workshop Rubric
Speaking, Listening, and Viewing Activities
Speaking, Listening, and Viewing Workshop Rubric

Practice Books

Read and Write

INTERACTIVE These leveled consumable worktexts provide structured instruction and practice with selected readings from the anthology.

- On-Level provides fast-track instruction for on-level students.
- Approaching provides scaffolding for struggling or reluctant readers.
- English Learners helps students whose primary language is not English read and comprehend selection.

The Novel Companion

This worktext provides accelerated instruction for advanced students through novel study. With the tools for a detailed analysis of a novel and related reading for every unit of the anthology, students explore in more depth the Big Ideas around which the anthology is organized.

Spelling Power Workbook

Provides additional support for practice and mastery of spelling.

Writing

Glencoe Language Arts Writing Resources

This writing resource contains the following transparencies:

Writing Process Strategies Transparencies provide graphic organizers to help you guide your students through the various stages of the writing process.

Writing Practice Transparencies provide opportunities for students to practice writing in modes that are appropriate for their grade level including Narrative, Expository, and Persuasive Writing and Responding to Literary Texts.

Process of Revision Transparencies use base transparencies and corresponding overlays to show and explain actual revisions and edits. The set of revision transparencies guides students through the process of improving a sample essay. A blank Student Revision transparency is included so student volunteers can make their own revisions to improve the quality of an essay.

Writing Constructed Responses

This sourcebook with blackline masters helps students respond effectively to short essay questions.

Success in Writing: Research and Reports

These blackline masters reinforce and extend the coverage of research presented in the student edition.

Grammar and Language Workbook

This workbook provides full coverage of grammar, usage, and mechanics rules, examples, and practice exercises.

Grammar and Composition Handbook

This handbook is a handy desk reference tool providing full coverage of the writing process as well as rules and practice exercises for grammar, usage, and mechanics.

Grammar and Writing Transparencies

Help reinforce the skills taught in the grammar links and writing workshops.

Classroom Resources: Print

Assessment

Assessment Resources

This assessment tool provides three types of tests:

- Diagnostic assessment by learning objectives
- Formative tests and answer keys for selections
- Summative unit tests and answer keys

Standardized Test Prep and Practice

These materials feature exercises and activities that get students ready for standardized exams.

Fluency Practice and Assessment

English Language Development

English Language Coach

These worksheets provide extra support for English Learners.

Independent Reading

Ethnic Anthologies

The following anthologies offer students introductions to the richness and variety of literature written by African, Asian, Hispanic, and Native Americans. A Teacher's Guide for each anthology suggests answers to questions accompanying each selection to help further student discussion.

- *Glencoe African American Literature*
- *Glencoe Asian American Literature*
- *Glencoe Hispanic American Literature*
- *Glencoe Native American Literature*

InTIME Magazines

This lively collection of articles drawn from TIME helps students develop skills for reading informational text.

Transparencies

Bellringer Transparencies

include warm-up exercises to engage students and to provide a quick review of previously taught skills.

Fine Art Transparencies

enhance visual literacy and provide a strong humanities approach to literature.

Literary Elements Transparencies

help reinforce literary elements that are the focus of each lesson.

Read Aloud, Think Aloud Transparencies

model active reading

Classroom Resources: Technology

Classroom Planning, Management, and Instruction

TeacherWorks Plus CD-ROM

- Plan and manage daily lessons and activities
- Access all program resources
- Edit lesson plans and worksheets
- Track the standards taught in your classroom

Classroom Presentation Toolkit CD-ROM or DVD-ROM

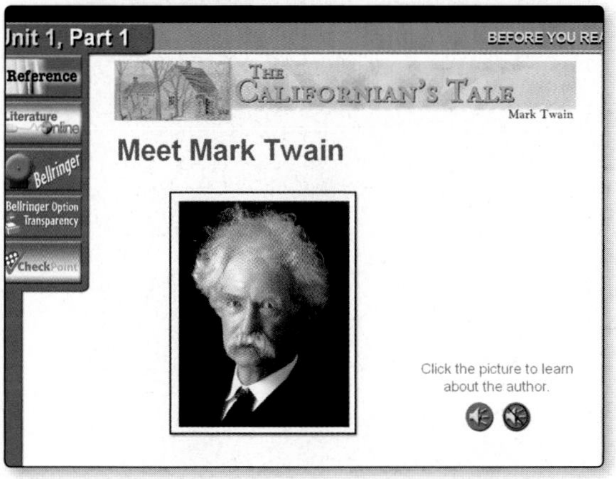

- Present customizable lessons via PowerPoint
- Launch transparencies, audio, video, and software at point-of-use during instruction

Digital Learning

Online Student Edition and StudentWorks Plus CD-ROM or DVD-ROM

- Full-text synced-audio selection read support
- Audio summaries in multiple languages
- Search, highlighting, and notes tools
- Multimedia links to video, activities, animations, and graphic graphic organizers
- Access student workbooks, Student Media Toolkit, and Student Presentation Builder
- Daily Assignments and Grade Log

Assessment and Progress Monitoring

ExamView Assessment Suite CD-ROM

- Administer ready-made diagnostic, formative, and summative assessments in English or Spanish
- Edit assessment items or create new items as needed
- Monitor student progress through a variety of reporting options
- Provides real assessment-driven remediation options

Progress Reporter Online Assessment

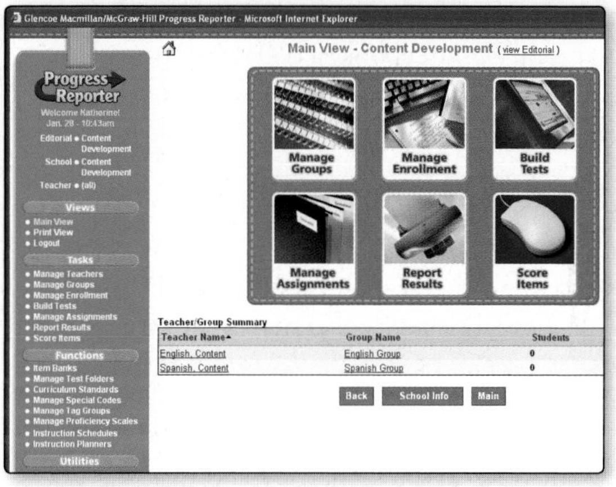

- Administer ready-made diagnostic, formative, and summative assessments online in English or Spanish
- Edit assessment items or create new items as needed
- Assessments administered online are scored automatically
- Essay questions are scored automatically
- Ready-made exams provide students with item rationales, explaining why each answer choice is correct or incorrect
- Automatically assigns reteaching and remediation based on student performance
- Monitor student progress by standard or by standard strand or through a variety of other reporting options

Literature Online: Assessment Resources

- End-of-Unit Assessment
- Test-taking Tips and Strategies

Literature and Reading

Literature Classics

- Choose from over 1,100 additional classic literature selections
- Search selections by author, title, date, genre, country, course/grade level, and Big Question or Big Idea
- Reinforce instruction with Genre Focus Lesson Plans and blackline masters
- Available on CD-ROM and access via glencoe.com

Classroom Resources: Technology

Listening Library CD

- Help students improve overall comprehension and reading fluency with engaging recordings of the selections in *Glencoe Literature*
- Assist English Learners with audio selection summaries in their native language
- Use the Listening Library CDs in conjunction with the Listening Library Sourcebook, a collection of standards-based strategies and activities, found on your TeacherWorks™ Plus CD-ROM

Literature Launchers: Pre-Reading Videos DVD

- Each of the engaging video segments on this DVD brings the literature to life, providing a visual context for every Unit and key selections
- Use this DVD in conjunction with the Literature Launchers Teacher Guide, found on your TeacherWorks™ Plus CD-ROM, which provides teaching strategies and video-specific blackline masters.
- English and Spanish subtitles

Literature Library Teacher Resources CD-ROM

- Access all Glencoe Literature Library Study Guides
- Develop vocabulary with Vocabulary Puzzlemaker
- Assess with ExamView Assessment Suite

BookLink K-12 CD-ROM

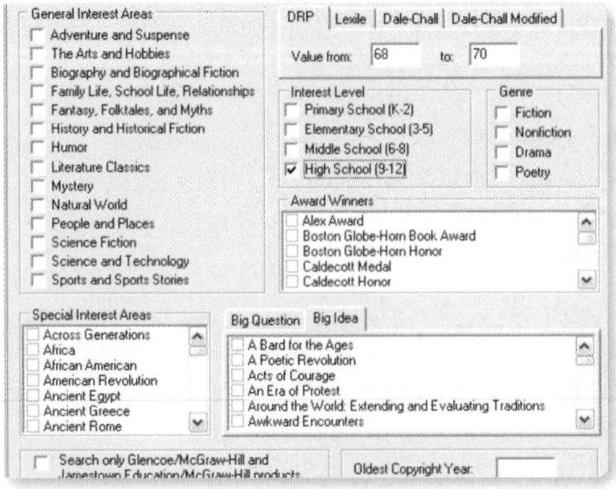

- Create customized reading lists for your students from a database of over 30,000 titles
- Search for award-winning titles and for books on state recommended reading lists
- Organize reading lists by students' reading level, author, genre, theme, or area of interest
- Find Degrees of Reading Power™ (DRP), Lexile™, and Dale-Chall scores for all selections in the Glencoe Literature program

Skill Level Up! A Skills-Based Language Arts Game CD-ROM

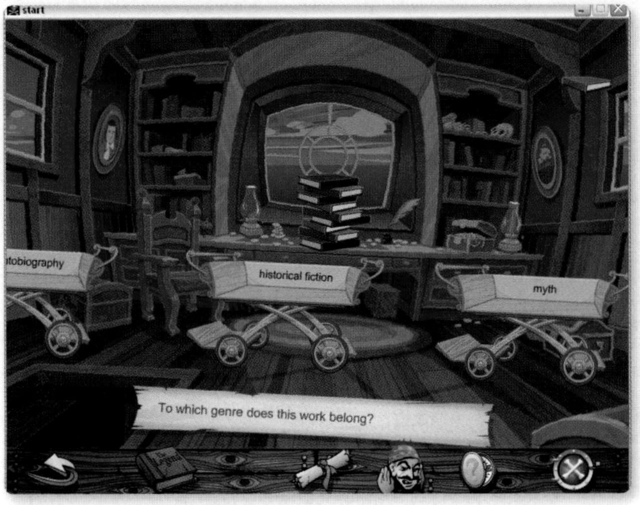

- Offers an innovative approach to Language Arts and Reading skills practice, assessment and remediation
- Skill Level Up!'s networkable game environment provides a context and purpose for learning by immersing students in an engaging adventure
- Features two access modes: the immersive story mode, which covers all the skills in the context of the adventure game play, or the skill-based assignment mode, which allows teachers to assign discrete activities according to their curriculum plan
- Adapts to each student's performance by offering remediation when necessary or enrichment activities when applicable
- Manage and track student performance using convenient assignment, tracking, and reporting functions featured in the program's management system
- Covers the following Reading Skills and Literary Elements:
  - Connecting
  - Questioning
  - Predicting
  - Point of View
  - Visualizing

- Rhyme
- Dialog
- Main Idea and Supporting Details/Paraphrasing and Summarizing
- Plot
- Conflict
- Interpreting
- Drawing Conclusions
- Setting
- Fact and Opinion
- Theme
- Author's Purpose and Perspective
- Voice, Style, Tone, Narrator
- Description, Imagery, Sensory Details
- Symbolism
- Inferring
- Figurative Language
- Analyzing Text Structure
- Meter and Rhythm
- Character and Characterization
- Sound Devices
- Genre
- Synthesizing

Literature Online: Literature, Reading, and Selection Resources (glencoe.com)

- Author and Artist Search
- Web Quest
- Selection Quizzes
- Selection Vocabulary eFlashcards
- Selection Reading-Writing Connection activities
- Reading Skills Review
- Interactive Reading Practice
- Literary Elements eFlashcards
- Fluency Practice
- Games

Vocabulary Development

Glencoe Interactive Vocabulary CD-ROM

- Generate flashcard sets from a visual glossary of selection, academic, content area, and social vocabulary terms
- Includes audio support in multiple languages for all terms
- Provides instructional modules and practice via an engaging game environment:
  - signal words
  - cognates/false cognates
  - multiple meaning words
  - synonyms and antonyms
  - idioms
  - analogies
  - figures of speech
  - context clues
  - etymology
  - troublesome words
  - text features
  - compound words
  - homonyms

Vocabulary PuzzleMaker

- Create crossword puzzles, word search puzzles, and jumble puzzles in an instant
- Choose from selection and academic vocabulary (in both English and Spanish) and literary terms
- Available on CD-ROM and for download via glencoe.com

Skill Level Up! A Skills-Based Language Arts Game CD-ROM

- Using Context Clues
- Multiple Meaning Words
- Examining Words Origins
- Words with Special Meanings
- Denotation and Connotation
- Using Analogies
- Synonyms
- Antonyms
- Homonyms
- Word Parts/Structural Analysis: Base Words
- Word Parts/Structural Analysis: Prefixes
- Word Parts/Structural Analysis: Suffixes

Classroom Resources: Technology

Literature Online: Vocabulary and Spelling Resources (glencoe.com)

- Multi-Language Glossary
- Selection Vocabulary eFlashcards
- Academic Vocabulary eFlashcards
- Vocabulary Games
- Spelling Lessons
- Spelling Games

Writing

Glencoe Online Essay Grader powered by Bookette SkillWriter™ (glencoewriting.com)

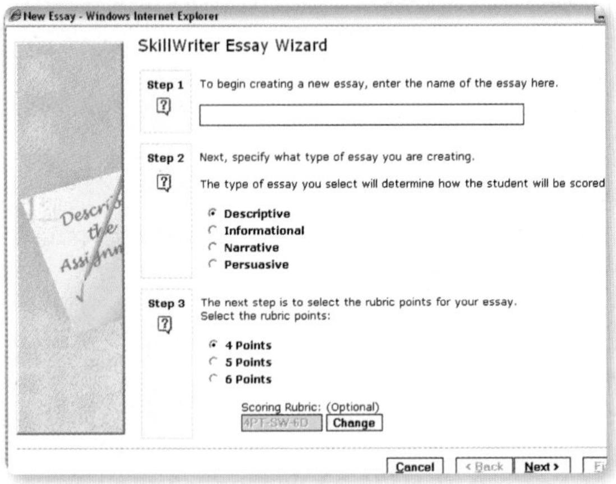

- Score student writing assignments and provide individualized feedback to each student automatically
- Assign prompts from Glencoe Literature Writing Workshops or create your own prompts!
- Manage demographic data, assign tests and run a variety of progress monitoring reports using the program's management system.

Literature Online: Writing and Research Resources (glencoe.com)

- Annotated Writing Models
- Interactive Writing Models
- Writing and Research Handbook
- Research Tips and Strategies
- Graphic Organizers
- Transition Bank
- Grammar Troubleshooter
- Sentence-Combining Practice
- Editing and Proofreading Marks
- Publishing Options

Speaking, Listening and Viewing

Skill Level Up! A Skills-Based Language Arts Game CD-ROM

- Analyzing Persuasive Techniques
- Listening Critically
- Examining Visuals in Literature and Media: Maps, Charts, Graphs
- Examining Visuals in Literature and Media: Visual Techniques

Student Presentation Builder

- Assign additional Unit-based multimedia presentation projects
- Includes a PowerPoint™ tutorial, a PowerPoint™ presentation template, and an image bank
- Available on StudentWorks Plus or via the Online Student Edition
- Teacher Guide is available on TeacherWorks Plus

Literature Online: Speaking, Listening, and Viewing Resources (glencoe.com)

- Project Ideas and Templates
- Presentation Tips and Strategies

Media Literacy

Glencoe Media Workshop DVD

- Engage students in the study and critical review of media from film footage of important events in history to analysis of commercials
- English and Spanish subtitles

Student Media Toolkit

- Provides additional interactive media analysis activities
- Includes media generator tools

Literature Online: Media Literacy Resources (glencoe.com)

- Media Analysis Guides
- Project Ideas

Library Resources

Glencoe Literature Library

Each *Glencoe Literature* Library volume consists of at least one complete extended-length reading accompanied by several related readings from a broad range of genres. A separate Study Guide for each book provides teaching notes and reproducible activity pages for students. Students may also find these activity pages at glencoe.com.

The Adventures of Huckleberry Finn by Mark Twain **DRP 54***

All Quiet on the Western Front by Erich Maria Remarque **DRP 52**

. . . And the Earth Did Not Devour Him by Tomas Rivera **DRP 52**

Animal Farm by George Orwell **DRP 60**

The Autobiography of Benjamin Franklin by Benjamin Franklin **DRP 64**

The Autobiography of Miss Jane Pittman by Ernest J. Gaines **DRP 49**

The Awakening by Kate Chopin **DRP 58**

Beowulf

Billy Budd by Herman Melville **DRP 68**

The Bridge of San Luis Rey by Thornton Wilder **DRP 55**

The Brothers Karamazov by Fyodor Dostoevsky **DRP 55**

The Canterbury Tales by Geoffrey Chaucer **DRP 59**

The Chosen by Chaim Potok **DRP 56**

A Country Doctor by Sarah Orne Jewett **DRP 59**

Cyrano de Bergerac by Edmond Rostand

Ethan Frome by Edith Wharton **DRP 59**

Fallen Angels by Walter Dean Myers **DRP 47**

Frankenstein by Mary Shelley **DRP 64**

Great Expectations by Charles Dickens **DRP 60**

Gulliver's Travels by Jonathan Swift **DRP 67**

Hamlet by William Shakespeare

Heart of Darkness and *The Secret Sharer* by Joseph Conrad **DRP 58**

A House for Mr Biswas by V. S. Naipaul **DRP 58**

The House of the Seven Gables by Nathaniel Hawthorne **DRP 65**

The Importance of Being Earnest by Oscar Wilde

Invisible Man by Ralph Ellison **DRP 57**

Jane Eyre by Charlotte Brontë **DRP 61**

Julius Caesar by William Shakespeare

The Jungle by Upton Sinclair **DRP 59**

The Mayor of Casterbridge by Thomas Hardy **DRP 60**

The Metamorphosis by Franz Kafka **DRP 57**

A Midsummer Night's Dream by William Shakespeare

My Ántonia by Willa Cather **DRP 57**

Narrative of the Life of Frederick Douglass by Frederick Douglass **DRP 62**

Nectar in a Sieve by Kamala Markandaya **DRP 56**

Night by Elie Wiesel **DRP 51**

One Day in the Life of Ivan Denisovich by Aleksandr Solzhenitsyn **DRP 56**

Our Town by Thornton Wilder

Picture Bride by Yoshiko Uchida **DRP 55**

Pride and Prejudice by Jane Austen **DRP 61**

A Raisin in the Sun by Lorraine Hansberry

The Red Badge of Courage by Stephen Crane **DRP 60**

The Return of the Native by Thomas Hardy **DRP 61**

The Scarlet Letter by Nathaniel Hawthorne **DRP 67**

Sense and Sensibility by Jane Austen **DRP 63**

A Separate Peace by John Knowles **DRP 59**

Silas Marner by George Eliot **DRP 55**

The Souls of Black Folk by W. E. B. Du Bois **DRP 66**

The Story of My Life by Helen Keller **DRP 59**

The Strange Case of Dr Jekyll and Mr Hyde by Robert Louis Stevenson **DRP 63**

A Tale of Two Cities by Charles Dickens **DRP 62**

The Tempest by William Shakespeare

Things Fall Apart by Chinua Achebe **DRP 56**

The Time Machine and *The War of the Worlds* by H. G. Wells **DRP 59**

To Kill a Mockingbird by Harper Lee **DRP 51**

Walden by Henry David Thoreau **DRP 62**

The Way to Rainy Mountain by N. Scott Momaday **DRP 55**

Wuthering Heights by Emily Brontë **DRP 61**

The Yearling by Marjorie Kinnan Rawlings **DRP 53**

***Degrees of Reading Power®** DRP values indicate the readability of prose text. The higher the value, the more difficult the text. Though the scale ranges from 0 to 100, texts widely available for use at grades nine through twelve typically range from 53 to 68. Some materials, however, may certainly fall outside of this range.

Skills Scope and Sequence

Readability Scores Key: Dale-Chall/DRP/Lexile

PART 1: Matters of Life and Death

Selections and Features	Literary Elements
Unit Introduction pp. 1–6	Short Story Elements **SE** pp. 2–3 Setting **SE** p. 4 Character **SE** p. 4 Narrator **SE** p. 5 Plot **SE** p. 5 Theme **SE** p. 5
Literary Focus pp. 8–9	Setting **SE** p. 8 Plot **SE** p. 9 Conflict **TE** p. 8
Short Story The Lady, or the Tiger?, by Frank R. Stockton **10.1/68/1260** pp. 10–19	Conflict **SE** p. 11
Short Story The Most Dangerous Game, by Richard Connell **6.2/50/740** pp. 20–42	Suspense **SE** p. 21 Foil **TE** p. 22 Characterization **TE** pp. 26, 30 Figurative Language **TE** p. 36 Conflict (review) **SE** p. 41
Short Story The Leap, by Louise Erdrich **6.4/64/1260** pp. 43–53	Flashback **SE** p. 44 Characterization **TE** p. 48 Character **TE** p. 49 Setting (review) **SE** p. 52
Vocabulary Workshop pp. 54–55	
Short Story The Cask of Amontillado, by Edgar Allan Poe **9.8/55/790** pp. 56–67	Mood **SE** p. 57 Irony **TE** p. 59 Dialogue **TE** p. 63 Suspense (review) **SE** p. 66
Vocabulary Workshop p. 68	
Short Story Blues Ain't No Mockin' Bird, by Toni Cade Bambara **6.8/53/960** pp. 69–76	Description **SE** p. 70 Figurative Language **TE** p. 76 Setting (review) **SE** p. 77

Reading Skills and Strategies	Vocabulary	Writing / Grammar	Speaking, Listening, and Viewing
Visualize **TE** p. 4 Evaluate **SE** p. 5 Identify Problem and Solution **TE** p. 6		Keep a Reading Journal **TE** p. 2 Write a News Report **TE** p. 4	
Draw Conclusions **TE** p. 9			
Summarize **SE** p. 11 Paraphrase **TE** p. 12	Word Usage **SE** p. 19	Write a Response to Literature **TE** p. 14 Semicolons **TE** p. 18 Write a Story **SE** p. 19	Discussion **TE** p. 16
Make and Verify Predictions About Plot **SE** p. 21 Identify Sequence **TE** p. 28 Visualize **TE** p. 32	Word Origins **SE** p. 41 Academic Vocabulary **SE** p. 41	Write a Journal Entry **TE** p. 26 Punctuation and Dialogue **TE** p. 30 Write a Summary **SE** p. 42 Present-Tense Verbs **SE** p. 42 Revise **TE** p. 42	
Identify Sequence **SE** p. 44	Word Parts **SE** p. 53 Academic Vocabulary **SE** p. 53	Write a Comparison-Contrast Essay **TE** p. 46 Subordinate Clauses **TE** p. 50	Interview **SE** p. 53
	Academic Vocabulary **SE** pp. 54–55		
Paraphrase **SE** p. 57 Compare and Contrast **TE** p. 62	Context Clues **SE** p. 66 Academic Vocabulary **SE** p. 66	Write Dialogue **TE** p. 60 Dashes **TE** p. 64 Write a Research Report **SE** p. 67 Colons **SE** p. 67	
	Homonyms and Homophones **SE** p. 68		
Analyze Concrete Details **SE** p. 70	Analogies **SE** p. 78 Academic Vocabulary **SE** p. 78	Write Dialect **TE** p. 70 Apply Description **SE** p. 78	Analyze Art **TE** p. 72 Discussion **TE** p. 74

Readability Scores Key: **Dale-Chall/DRP/Lexile**

PART 1: Matters of Life and Death *(continued)*

Selections and Features	Literary Elements
Short Story The Interlopers, by Saki **14.4/65/1230** pp. 79–89	Irony **SE** p. 80 Imagery **TE** p. 82 Mood (review) **SE** p. 86
Informational Text TIME: Shattered, by Christopher Batin **7.1/56/900** pp. 90–94	Mood **TE** p. 92

PART 2: Rewards and Sacrifices

Literary Focus pp. 96–97	Character and Theme **SE** p. 96
Short Story Rules of the Game, by Amy Tan **7.3/60/990** pp. 98–111	Protagonist and Antagonist **SE** p. 99 Character (review) **SE** p. 110
Grammar Workshop pp. 112–113	
Short Story The Gift of the Magi, by O. Henry **8.0/55/910** pp. 114–124	Characterization **SE** p. 115 Plot (review) **SE** p. 123
Vocabulary Workshop p. 125	
Comparing Literature **Liberty** (short story), by Julia Alvarez **4.5/50/840** **The Struggle to Be an All-American Girl** (short story), by Elizabeth Wong **4.5/50/840** **Legal Alien** (poem), by Pat Mora pp. 126–140	Motivation **SE** p. 128
Short Story Sweet Potato Pie, by Eugenia Collier **6.7/60/970** pp. 141–153	Theme **SE** p. 142 Figurative Language **TE** p. 142 Character (review) **SE** p. 152

Reading Skills and Strategies	Vocabulary	Writing Grammar	Speaking, Listening, and Viewing
Analyze Cause-and-Effect Relationships **SE** p. 80	Synonyms **SE** p. 86 Academic Vocabulary **SE** p. 86	Write an Expository Essay **SE** p. 87 Commas and Adverb Clauses **SE** p. 87	
Identify Problem and Solution **SE** p. 90 Preview **SE** p. 90 Identify Cause-and-Effect Relationships **TE** p. 90		Write a Summary **SE** p. 94	

Analyze Character **SE** p. 97		Write Flashcards **TE** p. 96	
Make Inferences About Characters **SE** p. 99 Analyze Historical Context **TE** p. 100 Compare Characters **TE** p. 106	Word Parts **SE** p. 111	Write a Description **TE** p. 102 Semicolons **TE** p. 104 Write a Research Report **SE** p. 111	Discussion **TE** p. 108
		Sentence Combining **SE** p. 112	
Analyze Description **SE** p. 115 Make Connections **TE** p. 116 Analyze Irony **TE** p. 118	Synonyms **SE** p. 123	Write a Scene **TE** p. 120 Write a Reflective Essay **SE** p. 124 Transitional Phrases **SE** p. 124	
	Dictionary Use **SE** p. 125		
Compare and Contrast **SE** p. 126, **TE** p. 136 Respond to Characters **SE** p. 128 Monitor Comprehension **TE** p. 128 Analyze Wordplay **TE** p. 134	Word Usage **SE** p. 135	Write a Research Report **TE** p. 130 Dashes **TE** p. 132 Write a Summary **TE** p. 138 Write an Expository Essay **SE** p. 140	Discussion **SE** p. 140 Oral Presentation **SE** p. 140
Question **SE** p. 142 Analyze Repetition **TE** p. 148	Word Parts **SE** p. 153	Write a Literary Analysis **TE** p. 146 Write a Research Report **TE** p. 150 Write an Informative Pamphlet **SE** p. 153	Discussion **TE** p. 144

Readability Scores Key: Dale-Chall/DRP/Lexile

PART 2: Rewards and Sacrifices *(continued)*

Selections and Features	Literary Elements
Grammar Workshop p. 154	
Short Story **The Scarlet Ibis,** by James Hurst **6.5/57/1070** pp. 155–170	Symbol **SE** p. 156 Voice **TE** p. 166 Setting (review) **SE** p. 169
Vocabulary Workshop p. 171	
Short Story **The Bass, the River, and Sheila Mant,** by W. D. Wetherell **9.4/62/1110** pp. 172–182	Dialogue **SE** p. 173 Plot (review) **SE** p. 181

PART 3: Dreams and Reality

Literary Focus pp. 184–185	Narrator **SE** p. 184 Point of View **TE** p. 184, **SE** p. 185 Voice **SE** p. 185
Short Story **The Secret Life of Walter Mitty,** by James Thurber **3.3/52/700** pp. 186–194	Diction **SE** p. 187 Narrator (review) **SE** p. 193
Grammar Workshop p. 195	
Short Story **The Necklace,** by Guy de Maupassant **6.9/61/950** pp. 196–207	Point of View **SE** p. 197 Symbol (review) **SE** p. 206
Short Story **American History,** by Judith Ortiz Cofer **5.6/55/990** pp. 208–219	Point of View **SE** p. 209 Setting (review) **SE** p. 218
Historical Perspective **The Drums of Washington *from* One Thousand Days,** by Arthur M. Schlesinger Jr. **8.4/61/1020** pp. 220–224	

Reading Skills and Strategies	Vocabulary	Writing / Grammar	Speaking, Listening, and Viewing
		Misplaced Modifiers **SE** p. 154	
Compare and Contrast Characters **SE** p. 156 Paraphrase **TE** p. 156 Identify Subtleties **TE** p. 164	Word Origins **SE** p. 169	Write a Reflective Essay **TE** p. 160 Write a Literary Analysis **TE** p. 162 Write a Persuasive Essay **SE** p. 170 Semicolons **SE** p. 170	Discussion **SE** p. 168
	Multiple-Meaning Words **SE** p. 171		
Connect to Personal Experience **SE** p. 173 Make Predictions **TE** p. 176 Analyze Dialogue **TE** p. 178	Analogies **SE** p. 182 Academic Vocabulary **SE** p. 182	Write a Research Report **TE** p. 174 Write a Reflective Essay **TE** p. 180 Apply Dialogue **SE** p. 182	
Make Generalizations **TE** p. 185		Write a Description **SE** p. 185	
Visualize **SE** p. 187 Compare and Contrast **TE** p. 188 Analyze Voice **TE** p. 192	Synonyms **SE** p. 194 Academic Vocabulary **SE** p. 194	Write a Character Analysis **TE** p. 190	Oral Interpretation **SE** p. 194
		Run-on Sentences **SE** p. 195	
Analyze Cause-and-Effect Relationships **SE** p. 197 Analyze Characterization **TE** p. 198	Word Usage **SE** p. 206 Academic Vocabulary **SE** p. 206	Write a Monologue **TE** p. 202	Active Note Taking **TE** p. 204 Discussion **SE** p. 205 Write a Short Story **SE** p. 207
Make Inferences About Characters **SE** p. 209	Analogies **SE** p. 219 Academic Vocabulary **SE** p. 219	Write a Research Report **TE** pp. 210, 212 Adverbs **TE** p. 216	Oral Presentation **TE** p. 214 Literature Group **SE** p. 219
Recognize Bias **SE** p. 220 Analyze Historical Context **SE** p. 220	Negative Prefixes **TE** p. 222	Write a Summary **SE** p. 224	Analyze Photographs **TE** p. 220

Readability Scores Key: Dale-Chall/DRP/Lexile

PART 3: Dreams and Reality *(continued)*

Selections and Features	Literary Elements
Short Story Mrs. James, by Alice Childress **4.2/56/880** pp. 225–228	Persona **SE** p. 226
Short Story The Son from America, by Isaac Bashevis Singer **3.8/54/760** pp. 229–239	Style **SE** p. 230 Voice (review) **SE** p. 238
Writing Workshop pp. 240–247	
Speaking, Listening, and Viewing Workshop pp. 248–249	
Independent Reading pp. 250–251	
Assessment pp. 252–257	

Reading Skills and Strategies	Vocabulary	Writing Grammar	Speaking, Listening, and Viewing
Analyze Language **SE** p. 226	Context Clues **SE** p. 228	Write a Letter **SE** p. 228	
Make Inferences About Theme **SE** p. 230 Predict **TE** p. 232 Infer **TE** p. 234	Word Origins **SE** p. 239 Academic Vocabulary **SE** p. 239	Verb Tense **TE** p. 230 Apply Tone **SE** p. 239	Discussion **TE** p. 236
		Note Taking **TE** p. 242 Prewrite **SE** p. 243 Draft **SE** p. 244 Active Voice **TE** p. 244 Revise **SE** p. 246 Sentence Structure **TE** p. 246 Write a Response to Literature **SE** p. 247	
		Note Taking **TE** p. 248 Use a Graphic Organizer **SE** p. 249	Discussion **SE** p. 248
		Write a Review **SE** p. 251	Adapt a Scene **TE** p. 250
		Write an Essay **SE** p. 257	

Focus

Bellringer Options

Literature Launcher
Pre-Reading Video
Daily Language Practice Transparency 1

Or say: Identify some reasons why people tell and retell stories. *(Students may suggest that stories help us make sense of the world and allow us to go places we could never actually go to or experience things we could not normally do.)*

For school-to-home activities, see Unit 1 Teaching Resource Book, pp. 5–11.

For students who would profit from independent novel study, see Novel Companion pp. 7–74.

Toyota Taxi, 2005. P. J. Crook. Acrylic on canvas, 116.8 x 152.4 cm.

View the Art P. J. Crook is known for her highly detailed paintings. How do the details in this painting suggest that several stories are unfolding in this neighborhood?

Unit Introduction Skills

The Short Story

Reading Skills
- Read the Short Story (SE p. 2)
- Problems and Solutions (TE p. 6)

Literary Elements
- Plot and Setting (SE p. 2)
- Character and Theme (SE pp. 2–3)
- Narrator and Voice (SE p. 3)

Listening/Speaking/Viewing Skills
- Create a Timeline (SE p. 6)

Writing Skills/Grammar
- Create a Dictionary (SE p. 6)
- Write a Journal (TE p. 2)

UNIT ONE

The Short Story

Looking Ahead

A short story is a little, well-polished stone in a vast quarry of fiction. As with other genres, at the foundation of the short story is a set of key literary elements—setting, character, plot, and theme—that the writer manages to introduce, develop, and display in just a few pages. A large part of a reader's enjoyment is seeing how the author lays this foundation and envisioning what it will become.

Each part in Unit One focuses on a Big Idea that can help you connect to the selections.

PREVIEW	Big Ideas	Literary Focus
PART 1	Matters of Life and Death	Plot and Setting
PART 2	Rewards and Sacrifices	Character and Theme
PART 3	Dreams and Reality	Narrator and Voice

1

UNIT ONE

Focus

Summary

The unit begins with definitions of the short story genre and its main literary elements. It provides insights from professional fiction writers. A story by Leo Tolstoy is used to show examples of short story literary elements. The introduction concludes with review activities.

View the Art ★

Answer: *Students may say that the details suggest several story lines because there is no focus on one person, place, or thing. The people in the painting are doing different things.*

The large, highly detailed canvases of British painter Pamela (P. J.) Crook (1945–) often depict subtle human dramas in busy urban landscapes.

For diagnostic and end-of-unit assessment, see Assessment Resources, pp. 1–6, 225–226.

Unit Resources

Print Materials

- Unit 1 Teaching Resources, pp. 1–307
- Interactive Read and Write (On Level/ Approaching, EL), pp. 1–48
- Novel Companion, pp. 7–74
- Bellringer Option Transparencies: Selection Focus 1–15; Daily Language Practice 1–21
- Literary Element Transparencies 21, 67, 78, 91, 103, 107
- Assessment Resources, Unit Assessment, pp. 1–6
- Assessment Resources, Selection Assessment, pp. 41–78

Technology

- TeacherWorks Plus CD
- StudentWorks Plus CD
- Literature Launchers: Pre-Reading Videos DVD, Unit 1
- Literature Online
- Interactive Vocabulary CD-ROM
- Listening Library CD-ROM
- ExamView CD-ROM
- Skill Level Up! CD-ROM

UNIT ONE

Teach

- Point out that there are six literary elements students should know before they read the selections in Unit One. An excerpt from a story from the unit illustrates each literary element.
- Help students improve their **reading fluency** skills. Invite volunteers to read aloud the explanation of each literary term and then the literary example beside it. Take time to point out how the excerpt illustrates the literary element.

Language History ☆

Plot *Plot* is a word with many meanings, including "a scheme or plan," "a piece of land," and "a graph." The literary meaning—"the sequence of events in a story"—was first used in the seventeenth century. The word's origin as a literary term is unknown.

Learning Objectives

For pages 1–6

In studying this text, you will focus on the following objectives:

Literary Study:
Analyzing plot and setting.
Analyzing character and theme.
Analyzing narrator and voice.

Genre Focus: Short Story

What are the elements that shape a short story?

African author Chinua Achebe describes perfectly the give-take-give relationship between reader and writer by saying, "people create stories create people; or rather stories create people create stories." Literary elements like plot, setting, and voice help strengthen this link between author and audience and sharpen the reading experience.

Plot and Setting

Sequence of Events

Plot is the sequence of events that ties the ☆ beginning of a story to its end. An important part of any plot is **conflict:** the struggle between two or more forces that must be resolved by the end of the narrative.

Time and Place

Setting is a story's time and place. It includes concrete aspects of a story, such as the location, the weather, and the time of year. Setting can also include abstractions such as the ideas, customs, values, and beliefs of a particular time and place.

At the most remote end of the crypt there appeared another less spacious. Its walls had been lined with human remains, piled to the vault overhead, in the fashion of the great catacombs of Paris. Three sides of this interior crypt were still ornamented in this manner.

—Edgar Allan Poe, **from "The Cask of Amontillado"**

Character and Theme

Individuals

Characters are the people, animals, and other individuals in a story. Authors reveal the personality of each character through **characterization,** or by describing the character's physical appearance, thoughts, spoken words, and actions.

My mother's face, usually sternly set, changed with the varying nuances of her emotion, its planes shifting, shaped by the soft highlights of the sanctuary, as she progressed from a subdued "amen" to a loud "Help me, Jesus" wrung from the depths of her gaunt frame.

—Eugenia Collier, **from "Sweet Potato Pie"**

Writing Practice

SPIRAL REVIEW **Keep a Reading Journal** Encourage students to keep a journal for recording their responses as they read. Explain that a turning point in a story is a moment when a character decides or does something that has a major effect on the outcome of the story. Suggest students note such turning points in their journals and record their responses to them under the following headings: Pros and Cons of Decision/Action; What I Would Have Done; How the Story Would Change.

Message

The **theme** is the main idea, or message, in a literary work. Theme is not the subject of a story but is an insight about life or human nature. Sometimes stories have a **stated theme,** which is expressed directly. More often, however, a story has an **implied theme,** which the author reveals through setting, point of view, and the actions of the characters.

"It will be light enough in Rio," promised Whitney. "We should make it in a few days. I hope the jaguar guns have come from Purdey's. We should have some good hunting up the Amazon. Great sport, hunting."

"The best sport in the world," agreed Rainsford.

"For the hunter," amended Whitney. "Not for the jaguar."

—Richard Connell, **from "The Most Dangerous Game"**

Narrator and Voice

Point of View

A **narrator** is the person who tells a story. The relationship of the narrator to the story is called **point of view.** In a story with **first-person point of view,** the narrator is a character in the story, referred to as "I." In a story with **third-person point of view,** the narrator is outside the story and uses "he" or "she" to tell the story.

He looked at his wife, in the seat beside him, with shocked astonishment. She seemed grossly unfamiliar, like a strange woman who had yelled at him in a crowd.

—James Thurber, **from "The Secret Life of Walter Mitty"**

Language Choices

Voice is the distinctive use of language that conveys the author's or narrator's personality to the reader. Sometimes voice is determined by word choices. In other cases, voice is determined by tone, an author's attitude toward his or her subject matter or audience, and mood, the emotional quality of a literary work.

The light through the large kitchen window of his house told me that El Building blocked the sun to such an extent that they had to turn lights on in the middle of the day. I felt ashamed about it. But the white kitchen table with the lamp hanging just above it looked cozy and inviting. I would soon sit there, across from Eugene.

—Judith Ortiz Cofer, **from "American History"**

LOG ON **Literature** Online

Literature and Reading For more selections in this genre, go to glencoe.com and enter QuickPass code GL49787u1.

Teach

Literary Element

Theme Help students identify themes by comparing them to the morals of Aesop's fables. Ask students to recall a fable such as "The City Mouse and the Country Mouse." Briefly discuss its moral.

Say: Like the moral of a fable, the theme of a story is its main idea or message and provides insight into human nature.

Approaching Level

DIFFERENTIATED INSTRUCTION

Emerging Explain that reading is more useful when students set a purpose for reading. Encourage students to set a purpose for reading by giving them a purpose or having them set their own purpose. Some common purposes for reading are:

- looking for the main idea.
- summarizing the selection.
- learning about a character.

Suggest that students note their purpose for reading on a piece of paper. They can refer to their paper to remind themselves why they are reading. After they have finished reading, have them check their comprehension by asking a question based on their reading purpose; for instance: What is the main idea of the story?

Teach

Reading Strategy 1

Visualize Explain that Tolstoy uses specific details to help readers picture the setting and the action.

Ask: What details help you imagine the monkey? *(The words and phrases* large, capering, silly faces, *and* aped *create a vivid picture)* Encourage students to jot down details that help them visualize as they read.

Writer's Technique ☆

Tolstoy's Sentence Structure

Note that most of Tolstoy's sentences in the first half of the story begin with a subject and verb, rather than with introductory phrases or clauses. The emphasis of the sentences is on the story's action. As a result, the story resembles a news report or a sportscaster's play-by-play. The sentences in the last four paragraphs are more complex. They begin with dependent clauses that are descriptive, slowing the action of the story.

Literary Analysis Model

How do literary elements function in a short story?

The Russian writer Leo Tolstoy (1828–1910) is considered one of the world's greatest authors. Although he is best known for his epic novels *War and Peace* and *Anna Karenina,* Tolstoy also wrote essays, plays, and short stories. "The Jump" is considered one of his finest short stories.

APPLYING Literary Elements

Setting
The first lines offer information about place: aboard a ship.

Character
Notice the contrast between the playful, amusing monkey and the angry, threatening boy.

The Jump

by Leo Tolstoy

translated from the Russian by Miriam Morton

A ship had sailed around the world and was on its homeward journey. The weather was calm and everyone was on deck. A large monkey was capering about amidst the crowd, amusing everybody. She tumbled here and there, made silly faces, and aped the people. It was clear that she knew that she was funny and therefore carried on even more. 1

She jumped over to a twelve-year-old boy, the son of the ship's captain, and snatched his hat from his head, put it on her own, and quickly scampered up the mast. Everyone laughed, and the boy didn't know whether to laugh or be angry.

The monkey perched on the bottom crossbeam of the mast, took off the hat and began to tear it with her teeth and paws. She seemed to be doing it to spite the boy. She pointed at him and made funny faces.

The boy shouted at her and threatened her with his fist, but she kept tearing the hat, doing it even harder. The sailors laughed louder, the boy flushed with anger, threw off his jacket, and went after the monkey on the mast. In an instant he had climbed the rope ladder to the first crossbeam. But just as the boy was about to grab his hat from her, the monkey quickly climbed even higher. ☆

"You won't get away with this," the boy cried out, and climbed after the monkey. The animal lured him on, scrambling still higher, to the top of the high mast.

Up there, holding fast to a rope with one foot, the monkey stretched out her body, extended her long arm, and hung the torn cap on the end of the highest crossbeam. Then she reached the very tip of the mast and sat there making faces, baring her teeth, and enjoying her victory.

Writing Practice

Write a News Report

Review the structure of news reports. Note that the first paragraph always answers the most important questions—*Who? What? When? Where?* Later paragraphs discuss why and how the event happened. Challenge students to use details from Tolstoy's story as the basis of a news report. Students may quote from the story and write a headline. Ask volunteers to read their reports to the class.

There was a space of about six feet between the boy and the end of the crossbeam where his hat was hanging now. To reach it, he would have to let go of both the rope and the mast. He was so upset by now that, forgetting all danger, he stepped onto this highest crossbeam, balancing himself the best he could with his arms.

All the people on deck had been watching the chase between the captain's son and the monkey. But when they saw the son let go of the rope and step out on the crossbeam, they froze with terror. If he lost his balance and fell to the deck, he would be killed. Or even if he somehow reached the end of the crossbeam and got his hat, it would be hard for him to turn around and get back to the mast.

They were looking on in silence, waiting to see what would happen, when someone in the crowd suddenly cried out in panic. The boy heard the cry, looked down, and teetered.

Just then the captain of the ship, the boy's father, came out of his cabin. He was holding a rifle for shooting seagulls. When he saw his son teetering on the uppermost crossbeam, he at once aimed the gun at him, shouting, "Jump! Jump into the water! Or I'll shoot!"

The boy hesitated, not understanding.

"Jump! One, two . . ."

As soon as his father cried "three," the boy stepped out and dived into the sea.

Like a cannonball his body hit the water, but before the waves could cover him, twenty brave seamen had jumped from the ship into the sea. Within forty seconds—they seemed like eternity—the body of the boy came to the surface. The seamen grabbed him and brought him back on board.

After a few long minutes water began to come from his mouth and nose, and he began to breathe.

When the captain saw this, he uttered a choked cry, and he hurried away to his cabin so that no one would see him weep.

Narrator

Tolstoy's narrator is an unbiased observer, which adds a sense of realism to the story.

Plot

As a way of building tension and excitement, the narrator tells the events of the story in the order in which they occurred.

Theme 2

On the surface, the father's order to jump seems heartless. Only after the boy has recovered does the reader understand the extent of the father's love. Then the theme—sometimes drastic measures are necessary—becomes clear.

Leo Tolstoy with his grandchildren. ☆

Reading Check

Evaluate What is the most memorable part of this story? Why?

UNIT ONE

Teach

Reading Check

Answer: *Students should support their answers with details from the story.*

Literary Element 2

Theme Remind students that a theme expresses an idea about the world or human nature.

Ask: What is the theme of the story? *(Guide students to see how the story illustrates the complexity of a father's intense feelings for his son—he unselfconsciously explodes in rage yet seems ashamed of his deep tenderness.)*

Literary History ☆

Leo Tolstoy Tolstoy was one of Russian literature's great realists. His novels and stories depict both the internal and external worlds of a broad range of characters—from aristocrats and soldiers to peasants—in precise detail. As Tolstoy grew older, his interest in worldly affairs waned. He became a pacifist and renounced his possessions.

Approaching Level

DIFFERENTIATED INSTRUCTION

Emerging Ask for volunteers to read passages from the story using expression to suggest mood and emphasis. Have the class point out two areas where the reader did well and two areas where the reader needs improvement. Students should then evaluate the reader's reading technique and offer constructive comments.

Some areas the students can evaluate are:

- pronunciation
- how expressive the reader is
- whether the reading is rushed or too slow
- whether the student pauses when appropriate

Assess

Guide to Reading a Short Story

Remind students to be active readers—to ask questions, make connections, and consider their own reactions as they read.

Elements of a Short Story

Encourage students to focus on the six literary elements described in the introduction as they read.

Activities

1. **Visual Literacy** Remind students that the plot events occur over the course of a few minutes.
2. **Writing** Invite students to illustrate their definitions. Remind them to refer to the *Literary Terms Handbook* on page R1.
3. **Note Taking** Remind students that note taking improves comprehension.

Wrap-up

Guide to Reading a Short Story

- Preview a short story before you begin reading. Read the first sentence carefully, and then skim for key words and phrases.
- Watch for clues about character, setting, and theme as you read.
- Think about the chief conflict of the plot.
- Understand how the conflict is resolved.
- Think about what the story reminds you of in your own life or consider what it is that makes the story memorable.

Elements of a Short Story

- **Plot** is the sequence of events in a story.
- **Setting** is the time and place in which the action of a story occurs.
- **Theme** is the author's message, or insight about life or human nature.
- A **character** is an individual in a literary work.
- The **narrator** is the person who tells the story.
- **Voice** is the distinctive use of language that helps the reader understand the narrator's personality.

LOG ON **Literature** Online

Unit Resources For additional skills practice, go to glencoe.com and enter QuickPass code GL49787u1.

Activities

Use what you have learned about reading and analyzing short stories to do one of the following activities.

1. **Visual Literacy** Create a timeline showing the major plot events in "The Jump." Label the event that marks the climax, or the point of highest emotion, of the story.
2. **Writing** Create a dictionary of literary terms that you can add to over the course of the year. Begin with the six you learned in this unit: plot, setting, theme, character, narrator, and voice. Define each term and provide examples from the unit or your own reading.
3. **Note Taking** Try using the study organizer shown at right to explore your personal responses to the selections you read in Unit 1. See pages R20–R21 for folding instructions.

FOLDABLES Study Organizer **BOUND BOOK**

Reading Practice

SMALL GROUP **Identify Problems and Solutions** Explain that one strategy for reading stories is to think of them as a series of problems and solutions. A character has a problem and may or may not be able to solve it. Have groups of students reread "The Jump" and write down at least two problems and two attempted solutions from the story.

PART 1

Matters of Life and Death

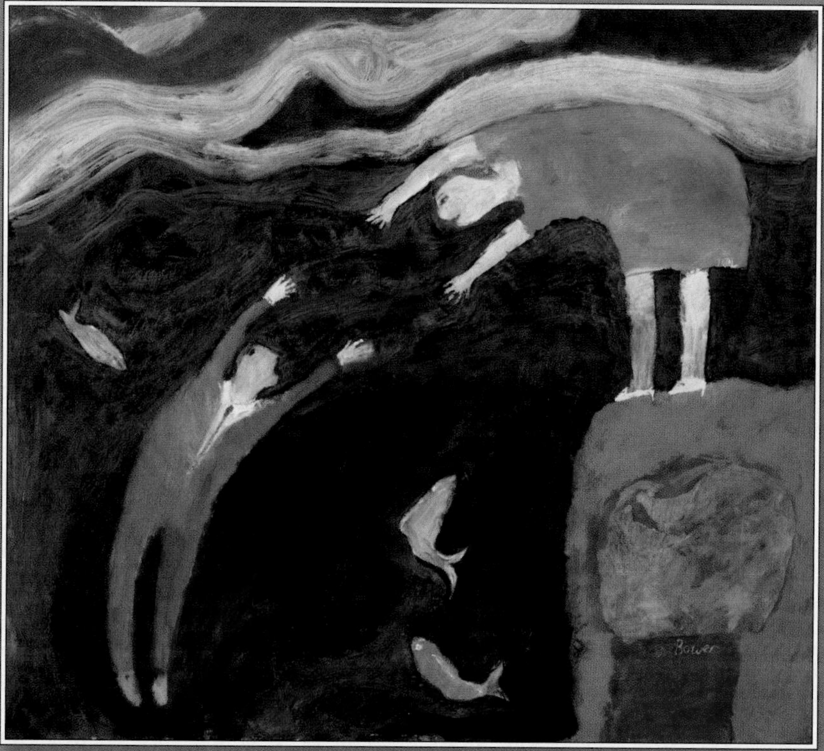

Saving the Man from the Sea, 2003. Susan Bower. Oil on board, 48.2 x 41.9 cm. Private collection.

View the Art This painting shows a woman saving a man from the sea. What is the effect of the painter's style? For example, does the style add meaning to the painting or distract the viewer from the life-or-death scene pictured? Explain. ★

BIG IDEA

Danger can threaten us in many ways. Our pride, our happiness, our safety, even our lives can be at stake. In the short stories in Part 1, you will read about people who face life-and-death challenges, both real and imagined. As you read the short stories, ask yourself, What are effective ways to deal with danger?

7

Approaching Level

DIFFERENTIATED INSTRUCTION

Established Have students name stories or movies in which danger is a key element. Discuss how danger increases suspense and makes readers pay attention to the plot in order to find out what happens.

English Learners

DIFFERENTIATED INSTRUCTION

Beginning/Early Intermediate Ask students to identify the word in their native language that means "danger." Discuss various kinds of danger and how attitudes toward it may differ. Some enjoy danger and others avoid it at all costs. Encourage students to answer the question on page 7.

UNIT ONE

PART 1

Analyze and Extend

Big Idea

Matters of Life and Death

Direct students to read the text under the Big Idea heading.

Ask: What are effective ways to deal with danger? Return to this question after students have read selections and have them reconsider their answers.

ENGLISH LEARNERS To aid English learners, explain that *caution* and *warning* are synonyms of danger. Ask English learners to share words or phrases from their language used to warn people of danger.

View the Art ★

Answer: *Many students may say the whimsical style of the painting is contrary to its subject matter. Others may argue that the style reflects the confusion and surreal quality of facing a life-or-death situation.*

Susan Bower (1953–) lives in Yorkshire, England, where she began painting in 1985. She paints chiefly in oil and uses a carefree and whimsical style to portray a variety of people.

For additional support for English Learners, see Unit 1 Teaching Resources Book, p. 21.

Focus

Bellringer Options

Daily Language Practice Transparency 2

Or display images of various settings—the jungle, a beach, a farm, a city street, and a crowded concert hall.

Ask: How important is a setting in a story? How does the setting affect what happens in a story?

As they read Part 1, have students consider why setting is important.

Teach

Reading Strategy 1

Draw Conclusions **Ask:** Why is it important for a story to have both a setting and a plot? *(Without a setting, readers will not be able to picture where and when events take place. Without a plot, the story will have no action.)* Challenge students to think of a story they have read or seen in movies or on television that lacked either setting or plot. Ask for their reactions.

Learning Objectives

For pages 7–9

In studying this text, you will focus on the following objective:

Literary Study: Analyzing plot and setting.

LITERARY FOCUS

Plot and Setting

How do plot and setting contribute to a story's meaning?

The events of a story and the way they unfold create both the author's meaning and the reader's pleasure. The specific time and place of those events can enhance the meaning and give added realism to the story.

from *The Leap*

by Louise Erdrich

I have lived in the West, where you can see the weather coming for miles, and it is true that out here we are at something of a disadvantage. When extremes of temperature collide, a hot and cold front, winds generate instantaneously behind a hill and crash upon you without warning. That, I think, was the likely situation on that day in June.

Purple Bluff. Frank Reed Whiteside. David David Gallery, PA.

Setting

1 Setting is a story's time and place. It includes simple attributes, like the location, the climate, and the time of year. Setting may also include more complex attributes, such as the historical context of the story and the ideas, customs, values, and beliefs of a particular time and place.

Description Authors create a strong image of a place through the use of clear and vibrant **description.** Good descriptive writing helps readers to see, hear, smell, taste, or feel the person, place, or thing the author is describing.

Rainsford heard a sound. It came out of the darkness, a high screaming sound, the sound of an animal in an extremity of anguish and terror.

—Richard Connell, **from "The Most Dangerous Game"**

Writing Practice

SPIRAL REVIEW **Reading the Text** Note that skimming means looking quickly through a text to find specific information. Remind students to use keywords, headings, and graphics as guides. Have them skim the story to answer these questions in writing:

- What is setting? (The time and place of a story)
- What are the five parts of a plot? (exposition, rising action, climax, falling action, resolution)

Mood Setting can contribute to the **mood,** or emotional quality, of a literary work. For example, a story set in dark, dank catacombs will likely have an eerie and tense mood.

> I passed down a long and winding staircase, requesting him to be cautious as he followed. We came at length to the foot of the descent, and stood together on the damp ground of the catacombs of the Montresors.
>
> —Edgar Allan Poe, **from "The Cask of Amontillado"**

Plot

Plot is the sequence of events in a story. Each event causes or leads to the next. Most plots develop in five stages: exposition, rising action, climax, falling action, and resolution. The events that make up the plot of the classic children's tale "Little Red Riding Hood" are shown in the diagram below.

Most plots develop in five stages.

- **Exposition** introduces the story's characters, setting, and conflict.
- **Rising action** occurs as complications, twists, or intensifications of the conflict occur.
- **Climax** is the story's most dramatic moment.
- **Falling action** is the logical result of the climax.
- **Resolution** presents the final outcome of the story.

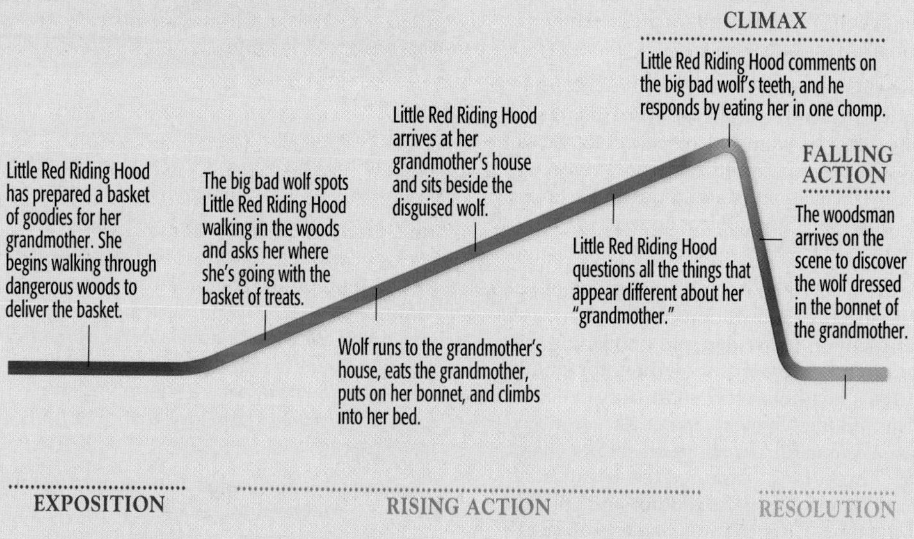

CLIMAX
Little Red Riding Hood comments on the big bad wolf's teeth, and he responds by eating her in one chomp.
Little Red Riding Hood arrives at her grandmother's house and sits beside the disguised wolf.
FALLING ACTION
Little Red Riding Hood has prepared a basket of goodies for her grandmother. She begins walking through dangerous woods to deliver the basket.
The big bad wolf spots Little Red Riding Hood walking in the woods and asks her where she's going with the basket of treats.
Little Red Riding Hood questions all the things that appear different about her "grandmother."
The woodsman arrives on the scene to discover the wolf dressed in the bonnet of the grandmother.
Wolf runs to the grandmother's house, eats the grandmother, puts on her bonnet, and climbs into her bed.
EXPOSITION
RISING ACTION
RESOLUTION

2 **Conflict** Conflict is the struggle between opposing forces. An **external conflict** is one between a character and an outside force, such as another character, nature, society, or fate. An **internal conflict** takes place within the mind of a character.

LOG ON Literature Online

Literature and Reading For more about literary elements, go to glencoe.com and enter QuickPass code GL49787u1.

Quickwrite

A New Setting Think of your favorite fairy tale. Write a new version of the story in a different setting. Use one of these ideas or come up with one of your own.

1. "Little Red Riding Hood" in New York City
2. "Hansel and Gretel" in Hawaii
3. "Beauty and the Beast" on Mars

Teach

Literary Element 2

Conflict Explain that conflict is essential to a good story. It creates the problem that a character has to solve. **Say:** Think of a story you heard as a child, such as "Cinderella." **Ask:** What was the conflict in that story? *(Cinderella longs to go to the ball but her stepmother forbids it.)*

Assess

Quickwrite

Students' responses should identify which elements of a plot might be affected by the change in setting. For example, if "Little Red Riding Hood" were set in a large city, the main character might encounter a stray dog rather than a wolf.

English Learners

DIFFERENTIATED INSTRUCTION

Beginning/Early Intermediate
Help English language learners comprehend the elements of setting and plot. Have them think of a story they have read or heard in their native language and then answer the following questions: *Where and when does the story take place? What happens in the story?*

Advanced Learners

DIFFERENTIATED INSTRUCTION

Plot Diagram Advanced learners may enjoy applying the plot diagram to a favorite story. Have them create a diagram like the one on page 9 and then fill in the appropriate information. Ask volunteers to share their diagrams with the class.

Before You Read

Focus

Bellringer Options

Selection Focus Transparency 1

Daily Language Practice Transparency 3

Or ask students to share examples of difficult decisions they have made or have read about.

Ask: What made the decision difficult? *(Students may mention lack of good options, too many good options, or another reason.)* What factors did you consider? *(Possible answers: likely advantages and disadvantages)* Have students consider as they read how the king, the princess, and the young man make their decisions.

Before You Read

The Lady, or the Tiger?

Meet **Frank R. Stockton**
(1834–1902)

At the height of his success, Frank R. Stockton was considered a major literary figure in the United States; writer William Dean Howells considered Stockton to be second in importance only to Mark Twain. Stockton's body of work fills twenty-three volumes and includes stories, novels, and nonfiction. Yet today, this writer is known primarily for one story.

Launching a Career Stockton enjoyed writing during his school days; however, his father hoped that he would become a doctor. Stockton chose another path entirely: wood engraving, a popular way to illustrate stories and articles at the time. Still, Stockton continued to write and began to publish his short stories.

As the wood engraving business gave way to other types of illustrations, Stockton focused his attention on writing and publishing. His early works were mainly written for children. In 1867, he published a short story called "Ting-a-Ling," which he later turned into a book. A fanciful tale about an elf-like character, "Ting-a-Ling" captured the attention of Mary Mapes Dodge, an author and editor of the time. After she was named editor of *St. Nicholas*, a new magazine for children, Dodge invited Stockton to join her staff.

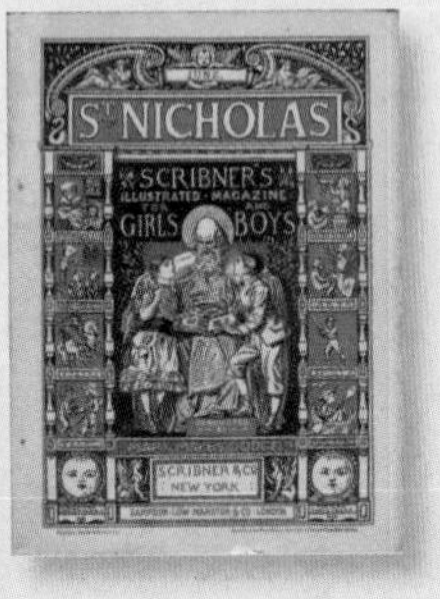

Courtesy St. Nicholas Center

St. Nicholas was a new type of children's magazine. Earlier children's publications were blandly moralistic, but *St. Nicholas* was realistic and literary. Within a few years, it became one of the most successful children's magazines of its time.

The Story That Created a Stir In 1878, Stockton left the magazine because of his failing eyesight, but he continued to write. Within a few years, he published several more books. Still, Stockton's novels never earned attention equal to that which he gained in 1882, when he published a short story in *Century Magazine*. That story was "The Lady, or the Tiger?"

The story not only created a stir at the time but for years afterward. It was later turned into an operetta, a play, a movie, and a recording. The story's unusual ending created a flurry of letters to the author that continued throughout his life. Poet Robert Browning wrote a poem about the ending, and scholars debated the issue. Stockton, however, kept quiet, leaving the debate to continue long after his death.

LOG ON **Literature** Online

Author Search For more about Frank R. Stockton, go to glencoe.com and enter QuickPass code GL49787u1.

Selection Skills

The Lady, or the Tiger?

Literary Elements
- Conflict (SE pp. 11–13, 17, 19)

Listening/Speaking/Viewing Skills
- Analyzing Art (SE p. 15)
- Group Discussion (TE p. 17)

Reading Skills
- Summarize (SE pp. 11, 14, 17, 19)
- Paraphrase (TE p. 12)

Vocabulary Skills
- Usage (SE pp. 11, 19)

Writing Skills/Grammar
- Write a Short Story (SE p. 19)
- Respond to Literature (TE p. 14)
- Use Semicolons (TE p. 18)

Literature and Reading Preview

Connect to the Story

Which is the stronger emotion—love or jealousy? Write a journal entry describing a situation in which a person might act out of love and one in which a person might act out of jealousy.

Build Background

During the Middle Ages in England, guilt or innocence was decided through a practice known as an ordeal. An accused person was physically tested, and the outcome determined guilt or innocence. The accusers believed that supernatural forces controlled what happened.

Set Purposes for Reading

Big Idea Matters of Life and Death

As you read "The Lady, or the Tiger?" ask yourself, How does each character react to the main event of the story?

Literary Element Conflict

Every story revolves around a **conflict,** or struggle between opposing forces. A conflict can be external or internal. An **external conflict** is one between a character and an outside force, such as another character, nature, society, or fate. An **internal conflict** takes place within the mind of a character who is torn between different actions. As you read, ask yourself, Is the main conflict of this story internal or external?

Reading Strategy Summarize

Summarizing is stating the main ideas of a selection in a logical sequence and in your own words. When you summarize a story, include the main characters, the setting, the conflict, and important plot details including the climax and the resolution.

Tip: Track Main Ideas Use a chart to record the important details that you want to include in a summary.

Setting	Characters	Conflict	Climax and Resolution
A long time ago; in a kingdom			

Learning Objectives

For pages 10–19

In studying this text, you will focus on the following objectives:

Literary Study: Analyzing conflict.

Reading: Summarizing.

Writing: Writing a story.

Vocabulary

impartial (im pär′ shəl) *adj.* not favoring one side more than another; fair; p. 13 *An honest judge is impartial.*

emanate (em′ ə nāt′) *v.* to come forth; p. 13 *We never heard any sound emanate from that room.*

dire (dīr) *adj.* dreadful; terrible; p. 13 *Breaking certain rules can have dire consequences.*

fervent (fur′ vənt) *adj.* having or showing great intensity of feeling; passionate; p. 14 *The coach was a fervent believer in practicing every day in order to improve.*

novel (nov′ əl) *adj.* new and unusual; p. 14 *Since that older method seldom works, try a more novel approach.*

Tip: Usage *Emanate* is one of many verbs that can be used as both an intransitive verb and a transitive verb.

Intransitive: *Perfumed scents emanate from the trees.*

Transitive: *Stoves emanate heat.*

Approaching Level

DIFFERENTIATED INSTRUCTION

Emerging Help students better understand the difference between internal and external conflict. Tell them that a character faces an external conflict when an obstacle gets in the way of reaching a goal. An internal conflict, on the other hand, is a struggle in a character's mind between what the character wants to do and what he or she must do.

Ask students to think of a time when they faced an external conflict. For example, maybe they tried to study for a test but could not concentrate because of noise in their home. Have students analyze internal and external conflicts while reading.

Before You Read

Focus

Summary

The king's daughter is in love, but her father does not like her young man and sentences him to the arena. There, he must choose between two doors. Behind one is a man-eating tiger. Behind the other is a lady whom he will marry. The princess is jealous of the maiden behind the door, and she finds out which door conceals her. When the young man enters the arena, the princess gives him a signal. He opens the door she indicates. The reader is left to decide. Does the lady or the tiger emerge?

For summaries in languages other than English, see Unit 1 Teaching Resources Book, pp. 22–27.

Vocabulary

Word Games On the board, write each of the vocabulary words. Have a student define the first word, *impartial*. Tell students they have one minute to list things that are impartial (e.g., judges). When time runs out, allow students to share what they've written. Then move onto the next word.

For additional vocabulary practice, see Unit 1 Teaching Resources Book, p. 30.

For additional context, see Glencoe Interactive Vocabulary CD-ROM.

Teach

Big Idea 1

Matters of Life and Death
Say: Keep this question in mind as you read: Why does a life-or-death trial appeal to the king? *(The king enjoys putting people at the mercy of a heartless and whimsical fate and uses this cruel spectacle to teach his subjects a lesson.)*

APPROACHING **Ask:** Why do the king's subjects enjoy the life-or-death trial? *(The uncertainty is exciting.)*

Literary Element 2

Conflict **Answer:** *The king is a tyrant who expects the whole world to bend to his will.*

For an audio recording of this selection, use Listening Library Audio CD-ROM.

Readability Scores
Dale-Chall: 10.1
DRP: 68
Lexile: 1260

THE LADY, OR THE TIGER?

Frank R. Stockton

1 In the very olden time, there lived a semibarbaric king, whose ideas, though somewhat polished and sharpened by ☆ the progressiveness of distant Latin neighbors, were still large, florid, and untrammeled,[1] as became the half of him which was barbaric. He was a man of exuberant fancy, and, withal, of an authority so irresistible that, at his will, he turned his varied fancies into facts. He was greatly given to self-communing; and, when he and himself agreed upon any thing, the thing was done. When every member of his domestic and political systems moved smoothly in its appointed course, his nature was bland and genial;[2] but whenever there was a little hitch, and some of his orbs got out of their orbits, he was blander and more genial still, for nothing pleased him so much as to make the crooked straight, and crush down uneven places.

Among the borrowed notions by which his barbarism had become semified[3] was that of the public arena, in which, by exhibitions of manly and beastly valor, the minds of his subjects were refined and cultured.

But even here the exuberant and barbaric fancy asserted itself.[4] The arena of the king was built, not to give the people an opportunity of hearing the rhapsodies[5] of dying gladiators, nor to enable them to view the inevitable conclusion of a conflict between religious opinions and hungry jaws, but for purposes far better adapted to widen and

1. The king's ideas are somewhat uncivilized (*semibarbaric*); they are very showy (*florid*) and unrestrained (*untrammeled*).
2. The king himself is generally agreeable and mild (*bland*) and pleasantly cheerful (*genial*).
3. *Semified* is a made-up word meaning "reduced in half or made partial."
4. Here, *asserted itself* means "exercised its influence; insisted on being recognized."
5. *Rhapsodies* are enthusiastic expressions of emotion.

Conflict *How does this passage suggest a future conflict?* **2**

Reading Practice

SPIRAL REVIEW SMALL GROUP **Paraphrase Meaning** Explain that this story uses elaborate language, which may be difficult to understand at first. Explain that paraphrasing passages from the story may help students understand information. Remind students that paraphrasing is restating the text in their own words. Break students into small groups. Model paraphrasing by reading aloud the first sentence from the story. Read aloud these words, which paraphrase the meaning of the first sentence: "Many years ago there was a king, who was somewhat primitive and crude. While the king's ideas were influenced by others who were more modern in their thinking, they were still showy and uncivilized. This pleased the part of him that was wild." Have students work together to paraphrase passages from the story.

develop the mental energies of the people. This vast amphitheater,[6] with its encircling galleries, its mysterious vaults, and its unseen passages, was an agent of poetic justice, in which crime was punished, or virtue rewarded, by the decrees of an **impartial** and incorruptible chance.

When a subject was accused of a crime of sufficient importance to interest the king, public notice was given that on an appointed day the fate of the accused person would be decided in the king's arena,—a structure which well deserved its name; for, although its form and plan were borrowed from afar, its purpose **emanated** solely from the brain of this man, who, every barleycorn[7] a king, knew no tradition to which he owed more allegiance than pleased his fancy, and who ingrafted on every adopted form of human thought and action the rich growth of his barbaric idealism.

When all the people had assembled in the galleries, and the king, surrounded by his court, sat high up on his throne of royal state on one side of the arena, he gave a signal, a door beneath him opened, and the accused subject stepped out into the amphitheater. Directly opposite him, on the other side of the enclosed space, were two doors, exactly alike and side by side. It was the duty and the privilege of the person on trial, to walk directly to these doors and open one of them. He could open either door he pleased: he was subject to no guidance or influence but that of the aforementioned impartial and incorruptible chance. If he opened the one, there came out of it a hungry tiger, the fiercest and most cruel that could be procured, which immediately sprang upon him, and tore him to pieces, as a punishment for his guilt. The moment that the case of the criminal was thus decided, doleful iron bells were clanged, great wails went up from the hired mourners posted on the outer rim of the arena, and the vast audience, with bowed heads and downcast hearts, wended slowly their homeward way, mourning greatly that one so young and fair, or so old and respected, should have merited so **dire** a fate.

But, if the accused person opened the other door, there came forth from it a lady, the most suitable to his years and station that his majesty could select among his fair subjects; and to this lady he was immediately married, as a reward of his innocence. It mattered not that he might already possess a wife and family, or that his affections might be engaged upon an object of his own selection: the king allowed no such subordinate arrangements to interfere with his great scheme of retribution and reward.[8] The exercises, as in the other instance, took place immediately, and in the arena. Another door opened beneath the king, and a priest, followed by a band of choristers, and dancing maidens blowing joyous airs on golden horns and treading an epithalamic measure, advanced to

6. An *amphitheater* is a circular structure with rising tiers of seats around a central open space.
7. The *barleycorn* is an old unit of measure equal to the width of one grain of barley—about a third of an inch. This phrase is similar to "every inch a king" and means that he was kingly in every way and in every part, top to bottom.
8. The king's plan for giving out punishment (*retribution*) and reward was of primary importance, and everything else was less important (*subordinate*), including family values.

3 Conflict *Based on this passage, what do you think the main conflict will be?*

Vocabulary

impartial (im pär′ shəl) *adj.* not favoring one side more than another; fair

emanate (em′ ə nāt′) *v.* to come forth

Matters of Life and Death *What do these details suggest about the people's view of death and mourning?* **4**

Vocabulary

dire (dīr) *adj.* dreadful; terrible

Teach

Literary Element 3

Conflict **Answer:** *A person on trial will have to choose between the two doors.*

Big Idea 4

Matters of Life and Death

Answer: *They put on a great show of emotion they did not really feel ("hired mourners").*

Cultural History ☆

Roman Times The author may be alluding to the Romans, the "distant Latin neighbors" named on page 12. During the early years of Christianity, the Romans had a practice of putting Christians in the arena with lions, where they were mauled to death for their beliefs.

Approaching Level

DIFFERENTIATED INSTRUCTION

Established Make sure students understand the historical context of the amphitheater. Explain that in Ancient Rome, people built amphitheaters as places for entertainment. The most famous amphitheater was the Colosseum in Rome, which could accommodate 50,000 people. The Colosseum was four stories high, and the most prominent citizens sat on the lowest level, so they were closest to the action. People who came to the Colosseum watched fights to the death between wild animals, gladiators and animals, and gladiators themselves. Sometimes spectators even joined in on the action.

Ask: How is the entertainment at the king's amphitheater different from the entertainment at the Colosseum in Rome? *(People who came to the Colosseum watched fights. People who came to the king's amphitheater watched trials in which men chose one of two doors to open; if they chose the door with a fair maiden behind it, it meant that they were innocent of the crime they were charged with. If they chose the door with the ferocious tiger behind it, it meant that they were guilty of committing the crime.)*

Teach

Reading Strategy

Summarize Answer: *A person accused of a crime comes into an arena with two doors. Behind one is a tiger and behind the other is a woman. The accused will either be devoured or married, depending on the door he chooses.*

For additional practice using the reading skill or strategy, see Unit 1 Teaching Resources Book, p. 29.

Literary History ☆

Fables/Fairy Tales The author uses phrases such as "as is usual in such cases" and "common to the conventional heroes of romance." These phrases reflect the style of fables and fairy tales, which have conventions such as the beautiful young maiden and the handsome young hero.

Ask: What other fairy tale conventions can you name? *(Possible answers: "Once upon a time" at the beginning; "They lived happily ever after" at the end.)*

where the pair stood, side by side; and the wedding was promptly and cheerily solemnized.[9] Then the gay brass bells rang forth their merry peals, the people shouted glad hurrahs, and the innocent man, preceded by children strewing flowers on his path, led his bride to his home.

This was the king's semibarbaric method of administering justice. Its perfect fairness is obvious. The criminal could not know out of which door would come the lady: he opened either he pleased, without having the slightest idea whether, in the next instant, he was to be devoured or married. On some occasions the tiger came out of one door, and on some out of the other. The decisions of this tribunal were not only fair, they were positively determinate:[10] the accused person was instantly punished if he found himself guilty; and, if innocent, he was rewarded on the spot, whether he liked it or not. There was no escape from the judgments of the king's arena.

The institution was a very popular one. When the people gathered together on one of the great trial days, they never knew whether they were to witness a bloody slaughter or a hilarious wedding. This element of uncertainty lent an interest to the occasion which it could not otherwise have attained. Thus, the masses were entertained and pleased, and the thinking part of the community could bring no charge of unfairness against this plan; for did not the accused person have the whole matter in his own hands?

This semibarbaric king had a daughter as blooming as his most florid fancies, and with a soul as **fervent** and imperious[11] as his own. As is usual in such cases, she was ☆ the apple of his eye, and was loved by him above all humanity. Among his courtiers was a young man of that fineness of blood and lowness of station common to the conventional heroes of romance who love royal maidens. This royal maiden was well satisfied with her lover, for he was handsome and brave to a degree unsurpassed in all this kingdom; and she loved him with an ardor[12] that had enough of barbarism in it to make it exceedingly warm and strong. This love affair moved on happily for many months, until one day the king happened to discover its existence. He did not hesitate nor waver in regard to his duty in the premises. The youth was immediately cast into prison, and a day was appointed for his trial in the king's arena. This, of course, was an especially important occasion; and his majesty, as well as all the people, was greatly interested in the workings and development of this trial. Never before had such a case occurred; never before had a subject dared to love the daughter of a king. In after-years such things became commonplace enough; but then they were, in no slight degree, **novel** and startling.

The tiger-cages of the kingdom were searched for the most savage and relentless beasts, from which the fiercest monster might be selected for the arena; and the ranks of maiden youth and beauty throughout the land were carefully surveyed by

9. *Epithalamic* (ep′ ə thə lā′ mik) refers to a song in honor of a bride and groom. When a wedding is *solemnized,* it is celebrated with a formal ceremony.
10. Usually, *tribunal* refers to a group of judges or a place of judgment. Here, it is "the king's semibarbaric method of administering justice," and its outcome is absolutely final (*determinate*).

11. To be *imperious* is to be extremely proud and controlling.
12. *Ardor* means intense passion.

1 Summarize *What is the king's "semibarbaric method of administering justice"?*

Vocabulary

fervent (fur′ vənt) *adj.* having or showing great intensity of feeling; passionate

novel (nov′ əl) *adj.* new and unusual

Writing Practice

Respond to Literature Tell students that when you respond to literature, you communicate what you have read. Read aloud the two paragraphs in the second column on this page. Have students write a paragraph in response to this question: Why is this trial "an especially important occasion"?

Remind students to prewrite, draft, and revise. Suggest that they begin by rereading the second column of the page and jotting down details about why this trial is important. They should then write a topic sentence stating what their paragraph is about. Next students should draft their paragraph and revise it so that it is well written and grammatically correct.

Mona Vanna, 1866. Dante Gabriel Rossetti. Oil on canvas, 88.9 x 86.4 cm. Tate Gallery, London.

View the Art How would you describe this woman's personality? Does she match your idea of what the princess would look like? ★

Teach

View the Art ★

Answer: *She appears to be haughty, rather cold and cunning, and someone who loves luxury. Students may say that the princess in the story also seems cold.*

Dante Gabriel Rossetti (1828–1882) was a poet and an artist, who had little formal training in painting. Rossetti's paintings are better known for their brilliant colors than for their technical expertise.

English Learners

DIFFERENTIATED INSTRUCTION

Intermediate Have students work with a partner and discuss the meaning of these lines from the story: "No matter how the affair turned out, the youth would be disposed of; and the king would take an aesthetic pleasure in watching the course of events . . ." Ask a volunteer to explain the meaning of these lines to the class.

Early Advanced Students may be confused by the most familiar senses of multiple-meaning words. Ask students to think of two ways in which the word *fixed* can be used (one meaning is "repaired"; and one is "locked," as in the story).

Have students identify multiple-meaning words on page 14 and determine their meaning in the story (e.g., *fair, interest, duty*).

Teach

View the Art ★

Rosa Bonheur (1822–1899), a French painter and sculptor, was both trained and encouraged by her father. She first exhibited her work in 1841, when she was not yet twenty. Much of her work reflects her love of animals and her skill at observing nature.

Stalking Tiger, Rosa Bonheur. Private collection, ©Gavin Graham Gallery, London. ★

competent judges, in order that the young man might have a fitting bride in case fate did not determine for him a different destiny. Of course, everybody knew that the deed with which the accused was charged had been done. He had loved the princess, and neither he, she, nor any one else thought of denying the fact; but the king would not think of allowing any fact of this kind to interfere with the workings of the tribunal, in which he took such great delight and satisfaction. No matter how the affair turned out, the youth would be disposed of; and the king would take an aesthetic pleasure in watching the course of events, which would determine whether or not the young man had done wrong in allowing himself to love the princess.

The appointed day arrived. From far and near the people gathered, and thronged the great galleries of the arena; and crowds, unable to gain admittance, massed themselves against its outside walls. The king and his court were in their places, opposite the twin doors,—those fateful portals, so terrible in their similarity.

All was ready. The signal was given. A door beneath the royal party opened, and the lover of the princess walked into the arena. Tall, beautiful, fair, his appearance was greeted with a low hum of admiration and anxiety. Half the audience had not known so grand a youth had lived among them. No wonder the princess loved him! What a terrible thing for him to be there!

As the youth advanced into the arena, he turned, as the custom was, to bow to the king: but he did not think at all of that royal personage; his eyes were fixed upon the princess, who sat to the right of her father.

Listening and Speaking Practice

SMALL GROUP

Group Discussion After reading the story, explain that since the author does not tell readers the end of the story, readers often debate which door the princess told her lover to open. Some readers seem sure that the princess told him to open the door with the tiger behind it, and others contend that she loved him too much to do this. **Ask:** Who thinks the princess told her lover to open the door with the tiger behind it? **Then ask:** Who thinks the princess told her lover to open the door with the maiden behind it? Break students into groups based on how they answered the question. Have them reread the story and jot down details that support their position. Ask students to work together to prepare a short persuasive speech based on their findings. Ask a volunteer from each group to present the speech to the class.

Had it not been for the moiety[13] of barbarism in her nature, it is probable that lady would not have been there; but her intense and fervid soul would not allow her to be absent on an occasion in which she was so terribly interested. From the moment that the decree had gone forth, that her lover should decide his fate in the king's arena, she had thought of nothing, night or day, but this great event and the various subjects connected with it. Possessed of more power, influence, and force of character than any one who had ever before been interested in such a case, she had done what no other person had done—she had possessed herself of the secret of the doors. She knew in which of the two rooms, that lay behind those doors, stood the cage of the tiger, with its open front, and in which waited the lady. Through these thick doors, heavily curtained with skins on the inside, it was impossible that any noise or suggestion should come from within to the person who should approach to raise the latch of one of them; but gold, and the power of a woman's will, had brought the secret to the princess.

And not only did she know in which room stood the lady ready to emerge, all blushing and radiant, should her door be opened, but she knew who the lady was. It was one of the fairest and loveliest of the damsels of the court who had been selected as the reward of the accused youth, should he be proved innocent of the crime of aspiring to one so far above him; and the princess hated her. Often had she seen, or imagined that she had seen, this fair creature throwing glances of admiration upon the person of her lover, and sometimes she thought these glances were perceived and even returned. Now and then she had seen them talking together; it was but for a moment or two, but much can be said in a brief space; it may have been on most unimportant topics, but how could she know that? The girl was lovely, but she had dared to raise her eyes to the loved one of the princess; and, with all the intensity of the savage blood transmitted to her through long lines of wholly barbaric ancestors, she hated the woman who blushed and trembled behind that silent door.

When her lover turned and looked at her, and his eye met hers as she sat there paler and whiter than any one in the vast ocean of anxious faces about her, he saw, by that power of quick perception which is given to those whose souls are one, that she knew behind which door crouched the tiger, and behind which stood the lady. He had expected her to know it. He understood her nature, and his soul was assured that she would never rest until she had made plain to herself this thing, hidden to all other lookers-on, even to the king. The only hope for the youth in which there was any element of certainty was based upon the success of the princess in discovering this mystery; and the moment he looked upon her, he saw she had succeeded, as in his soul he knew she would succeed.

Then it was that his quick and anxious glance asked the question: "Which?" It was as plain to her as if he shouted it from where he stood. There was not an instant to be lost. The question was asked in a flash; it must be answered in another.

Her right arm lay on the cushioned parapet[14] before her. She raised her hand, and made a slight, quick movement toward the

13. *Moiety* (moi′ ə tē) means "half."

14. Here, the *parapet* is a low wall or railing around the royal "box seats."

1 Conflict *How does this passage advance the central conflict of the story?*

Summarize *Based on this passage, how would you summarize the relationship between the lovers?* **2**

Teach

Literary Element 1

Conflict Answer: *The princess knows which door the tiger is behind, so she could use that information to save the young man.*

Reading Strategy 2

Summarize Answer: *The youth knows the princess very well; he foresaw that she would seek knowledge of what lay behind the door.*

ENGLISH LEARNERS To help English learners understand word meaning, have a student define *assured* using a dictionary. Ask students to use the word in a sentence.

Advanced Learners

DIFFERENTIATED INSTRUCTION

Analyze Character Explain that readers determine what characters are like from what the narrator says about them and from what characters say and do. In this part of the story, the narrator tells how the princess feels about the maiden.

Ask: What can you tell about the princess from what the narrator says on this page? *(Students may say that the princess is very jealous.)* Expand on the Reading Strategy by having students write a character sketch of the princess based on the details in the story. Tell them that a character sketch is a written description of a character in a story.

Teach

Big Idea 1

Matters of Life and Death

Answer: *Her shriek of protest upon imagining her lover married to another woman is "drowned" by the joyous shouts of the crowd, suggesting that seeing her lover with another woman would feel like dying.*

Writer's Technique ☆

Imagery Stockton uses imagery related to fire throughout the final passage of his story. Words such as "hot-blooded," "white heat," "fires of despair," "burned in agony," and "kindled" work together to create the emotional intensity the author seeks. **Ask:** What does fire imagery suggest about emotions? *(The emotions are fierce and consuming.)*

Progress Check

Can students explain the Literary Element conflict?

If No → See Unit 1 Teaching Resources Book, p. 28.

To check students' understanding of the selection, see Unit 1 Teaching Resources Book, pp. 33 and 34.

right. No one but her lover saw her. Every eye but his was fixed on the man in the arena.

He turned, and with a firm and rapid step he walked across the empty space. Every heart stopped beating, every breath was held, every eye was fixed immovably upon that man. Without the slightest hesitation, he went to the door on the right, and opened it.

Now, the point of the story is this: Did the tiger come out of that door, or did the lady?

The more we reflect upon this question, the harder it is to answer. It involves a study of the human heart which leads us through devious mazes of passion, out of which it is difficult to find our way. Think of it, fair reader, not as if the decision of the question depended upon yourself, but ☆ upon that hot-blooded, semibarbaric princess, her soul at a white heat beneath the combined fires of despair and jealousy. She had lost him, but who should have him?

How often, in her waking hours and in her dreams, had she started in wild horror, and covered her face with her hands as she thought of her lover opening the door on the other side of which waited the cruel fangs of the tiger!

But how much oftener had she seen him at the other door! How in her grievous reveries[15] had she gnashed her teeth, and torn her hair, when she saw his start of rapturous delight as he opened the door of the lady! How her soul had burned in agony when she had seen him rush to meet that woman, with her flushing cheek and sparkling eye of triumph; when she had seen him lead her forth, his whole frame kindled with the joy of recovered life; when she had heard the glad shouts from the multitude, and the wild ringing of the happy bells; when she had seen the priest, with his joyous followers, advance to the couple, and make them man and wife before her very eyes; and when she had seen them walk away together upon their path of flowers, followed by the tremendous shouts of the hilarious multitude, in which her one despairing shriek was lost and drowned!

Would it not be better for him to die at once, and go to wait for her in the blessed regions of semibarbaric futurity?

And yet, that awful tiger, those shrieks, that blood.

Her decision had been indicated in an instant, but it had been made after days and nights of anguished deliberation. She had known she would be asked, she had decided what she would answer, and, without the slightest hesitation, she had moved her hand to the right.

The question of her decision is one not to be lightly considered, and it is not for me to presume[16] to set myself up as the one person able to answer it. And so I leave it with all of you: Which came out of the opened door— the lady, or the tiger? ❧

15. Something that is *grievous* causes great grief or worry; *reveries* are daydreams.

16. *Presume* means "to take upon oneself without permission" or "to dare."

Matters of Life and Death *How does this passage suggest that the trial feels like a matter of life and death for the princess?* 1

Grammar Practice

SPIRAL REVIEW **Use Semicolons** On the board, write the sentence "Never before had such a case occurred; never before had a subject dared to love the daughter of a king." Explain the use of a semicolon to join independent clauses. Have students find other examples in the story. Post these on the board and discuss them together. Then ask students to write their own sentences that contain two independent clauses joined by a semicolon.

After You Read

Respond and Think Critically

Respond and Interpret

1. What was your reaction to the ending of the story? How would your reaction be different if you knew what was behind the door?
2. (a)In the kingdom described in the story, what happens when a person is accused of a crime? (b)Why do the members of the community support this method?
3. (a)What is the young man's crime? (b)Why are his actions considered criminal?

Analyze and Evaluate

4. How would you answer the question at the end of the story? Explain your answer by pointing out which details led you to your response.
5. Most stories end by telling the readers what happened to the main characters. This story lets the readers decide what happens. What is your opinion of this type of ending? Explain.

Connect

6. **Big Idea** Matters of Life and Death At what point is the young man's fate actually decided? Explain.
7. **Connect to the Author** Stockton wrote enough literature to fill a twenty-three-volume collection, yet "The Lady, or the Tiger?" remains his most famous work. In your opinion, why has this story stood the test of time?

Literary Element Conflict

Many stories, like this one, contain both **internal** and **external conflicts.**

1. What conflicts does the young man have? Are his conflicts internal or external? Support your answers with details from the story.
2. Why is the princess's internal conflict so central to the story?

Reading Strategy Summarize

A **summary** is a brief statement of the main ideas of a paragraph or longer piece of writing.

1. Summarize the paragraph on page 14 that begins "The institution was a very popular one."
2. In groups, read your summaries aloud to ensure that you have included all of the main ideas.

LOG ON Literature Online

Selection Resources For Selection Quizzes, eFlashcards, and Reading-Writing Connection activities, go to glencoe.com and enter QuickPass code GL49787u1.

Vocabulary Practice

Practice with Usage Respond to these statements to help you explore the meanings of vocabulary words from the selection.

1. Explain what an **impartial** person might do when two friends are fighting.
2. Name something that might **emanate** from a kitchen.
3. Identify a **dire** situation you have read about or seen in a movie.
4. Describe how a **fervent** believer in the importance of reading might act.
5. Suggest a **novel** idea for a field trip.

Writing

Write a Story Write a 1- to 2-page short story in which the main character struggles with another character, with a force of nature, or with making a difficult decision. Be sure to build the conflict up to a suspenseful climax.

After You Read

Assess

1. Answers will vary.
2. (a) The accused person must choose between two doors concealing either a tiger that will kill him or a woman who will marry him. (b) They find the trials exciting and entertaining, as well as fair, since the accused made the choice.
3. (a) He is in love with the king's daughter (b) His low position in society makes him an unworthy suitor.
4. Students should include clear references to passages and details from the text that support their answer.
5. Students should support their opinions with reasons.
6. Possible answers: when the princess makes her decision; only after the door opens. Students should give reasons.
7. Answers will vary.

Literary Element

1. External: which door to open
   Internal: whether to believe the princess
2. Her decision governs if the young man lives or dies. Readers' view of her will affect their choice of resolution.

Reading Strategy

1. Summaries should contain the main ideas of the story.
2. Students should distinguish main ideas from supporting details.

Vocabulary Practice

Answers will vary. Sample responses:

1. The impartial person would refuse to take sides and might negotiate a truce.
2. the smell of a pie baking in the oven
3. One of the characters was trapped on a falling balcony.
4. He or she would probably do a lot of reading and try to convince others to read.
5. We could volunteer at a food pantry for a day.

Writing

Students' stories should

- include a clear central conflict
- build suspense around that conflict

Before You Read

Focus

Bellringer Options

Selection Focus Transparency 2

Daily Language Practice Transparency 4

Or obtain a copy of the painting *The Hungry Lion* by Henri Rousseau. Have students study it and then discuss these questions.

Ask: What hidden dangers do you see in the painting? *(There is a panther in the trees and other animals partially visible.)* How do dangers that you cannot see differ from those you can see? *(They add a component of the unknown, which heightens tension.)*

Before You Read

The Most Dangerous Game

Meet **Richard Connell**

(1893–1949)

Once asked when he began writing, Richard Connell said he could not remember a time when he did not write. His father edited the *Poughkeepsie News Press* in Poughkeepsie, New York, and young Richard began reporting on baseball games when he was only ten years old. For this, he was paid ten cents a game.

Early Career When his father was elected to Congress in 1910, seventeen-year-old Richard worked as his secretary. He went on to attend Harvard University, where he was an editor for both the *Harvard Lampoon,* a humor magazine, and the *Crimson*, a student-run newspaper.

While working at the newspaper, he wrote an editorial that criticized a publisher. That editorial had unexpected effects: the publisher sued the *Crimson* but also offered Connell a job at a New York City newspaper. From there, he moved to a job in advertising. When World War I began, Connell enlisted. He continued to write during his enlistment, editing the camp weekly newspaper, *Gas Attack*.

> *"There is no greater bore than perfection."*
>
> —Richard Connell
> from "The Most Dangerous Game"

After the war, Connell returned to advertising, but only for a very brief period, until a short story that he wrote was published. His career in advertising ended, and his career as a literary writer began.

A Writer's Life Connell was a prolific short-story writer, producing hundreds of stories for various U.S. and British magazines. These included the *Saturday Evening Post* and *Collier's*, both of which had a broad readership. Many of his stories, including "The Most Dangerous Game," were later turned into movies.

In 1925 Connell moved to California to focus on writing film scripts. He worked on a variety of films for several different studios. His film credits include *Meet John Doe, Presenting Lily Mars,* and *Seven Faces*. At the time of his death, he was working on a play.

Despite a varied career, Connell is best remembered for the story "The Most Dangerous Game," which has been the basis for more than half a dozen films. As a testament to the story's enduring popularity, a movie version was filmed in the late 1980s, decades after Connell's death. The story was also adapted for a Halloween episode of the television show *The Simpsons.*

LOG ON **Literature** Online

Author Search For more about Richard Connell, go to glencoe.com and enter QuickPass code GL49787u1.

Selection Skills

The Most Dangerous Game

Literary Elements
- Suspense (SE pp. 21–41)
- Conflict (SE p. 41)

Reading Skills
- Predictions About Plot (SE pp. 21–41)

Vocabulary Skills
- Word Origins (SE pp. 21, 41)
- Academic Vocabulary (SE p. 41)

Writing Skills/Grammar
- Respond Through Writing (SE p. 42)
- Write a Journal Entry (TE p. 26)
- Punctuation and Dialogue (TE p. 30)

Listening/Speaking/Viewing Skills
- Analyzing Art (SE pp. 26, 32)

Literature and Reading Preview

Connect to the Story

The protagonist in this story says, "The world is made up of two classes—the hunters and the huntees." What might the character mean? Discuss this question with a partner.

Build Background

The word *game* does not only refer to a type of playful entertainment. *Game* can also refer to animals that are hunted. At one time, hunting for trophies was considered a great sport. These hunters usually kept only the animals' heads, which they mounted on the walls of their homes and hunting lodges.

Set Purposes for Reading

Big Idea Matters of Life and Death

As you read the story, ask yourself, What do the references to hunting reveal about each of the characters?

Literary Element Suspense

Suspense is a feeling of curiosity, uncertainty, or even dread about what is going to happen next in a story. Writers heighten the level of suspense by creating situations that threaten the central character and by raising questions in readers' minds about what will happen in a conflict. As you read "The Most Dangerous Game," ask yourself, What details and situations make you wonder what will happen next?

Reading Strategy Make and Verify Predictions About Plot

When you **make a prediction about plot,** you make an informed guess about what is likely to happen in a story. **Verifying predictions** is checking to see whether the predictions you made turn out to be correct. As you read, ask yourself, How can I combine clues in the text with my own knowledge to predict what will happen next?

Tip: Track Predictions Use a simple chart to record and verify predictions.

Story Detail	Prediction	What Happens
Ship-Trap Island	the ship will be trapped	

Learning Objectives

For pages 20–41

In studying this text, you will focus on the following objectives:

Literary Study: Analyzing suspense.

Reading: Making and verifying predictions about plot.

Vocabulary

tangible (tan′ jə bəl) *adj.* capable of being touched or felt; p. 23 *The rainbow was so bright that it seemed tangible.*

discern (di surn′) *v.* to detect or recognize; to make out; p. 25 *Through the fog, he was able to discern a human figure.*

condone (kən dōn′) *v.* to excuse or overlook an offense, usually a serious one, without criticism; p. 30 *I cannot condone the use of force against unarmed people.*

imperative (im per′ ə tiv) *adj.* absolutely necessary; p. 35 *The swimmer knew it was imperative to reach shore quickly.*

zealous (zel′ əs) *adj.* very eager; enthusiastic; p. 35 *A zealous supporter of animal rights would not hunt for sport.*

Tip: Word Origins The history of a word is called its etymology. For example, the word *discern* comes from the Latin word *discernere,* meaning "to separate." A dictionary is usually the best place to find the etymology of a particular word.

English Learners

DIFFERENTIATED INSTRUCTION

Early Advanced Help students better understand the vocabulary words on this page. Have students read each word, its definition and the sentence underneath the word. Guide students to use the word in a new sentence. Have students write their sentences on the board.

Before You Read

Focus

Summary

Sanger Rainsford, a famous hunter, falls from a yacht into the Caribbean. He swims ashore and discovers the mansion of General Zaroff. A hunter who preys on shipwrecked sailors, Zaroff proposes a game: If Zaroff cannot find and kill Rainsford in three days, he will transport him to the mainland. Unable to outwit Zaroff, Rainsford jumps into the sea and swims around the island to the mansion. The two duel; Rainsford kills Zaroff.

For summaries in languages other than English, see Unit 1 Teaching Resources Book, pp. 35–40.

Vocabulary

Word Origin Ask students to use a dictionary or online source to learn more about the origin and history of each word.

For additional vocabulary practice, see Unit 1 Teaching Resources Book, p. 44.

For additional context, see Glencoe Interactive Vocabulary CD-ROM.

Teach

Big Idea 1

Matters of Life and Death

Answer: *For the hunted, it is not sport, but a matter of life and death.*

APPROACHING For approaching-level students, **say:** Keep this question in mind as you read: How does the desire to stay alive affect Rainsford's actions? *(It keeps him pushing the limits of his endurance.)* **Ask:** How does the life-or-death outcome affect the readers' experience? *(It heightens the suspense.)*

View the Art ★

Belgian artist Henri Cleenewerck (1818–1901) was influenced by the Flemish old masters. His painting *A Hunter in the Cuban Jungle* reflects this. In addition to scenes in Cuba, Cleenewerck landscapes included locations in California and Europe.

For an audio recording of this selection, use Listening Library Audio CD-ROM.

Readability Scores

Dale-Chall: 6.2
DRP: 50
Lexile: 740

A Hunter in the Cuban Jungle, Sunrise, 1869. Henri Cleenewerck. Oil on canvas, 96.8 x 82.5 cm. Private collection. ★

THE Most Dangerous GAME

Richard Connell

Off there to the right—somewhere—is a large island," said Whitney. "It's rather a mystery—"

"What island is it?" Rainsford asked.

"The old charts call it 'Ship-Trap Island'," Whitney replied. "A suggestive name, isn't it? Sailors have a curious dread of the place. I don't know why. Some superstition—"

"Can't see it," remarked Rainsford, trying to peer through the dank tropical night that was palpable as it pressed its thick warm blackness in upon the yacht.

"You've good eyes," said Whitney, with a laugh, "and I've seen you pick off a moose moving in the brown fall bush at four hundred yards, but even you can't see four miles or so through a moonless Caribbean night."

"Nor four yards," admitted Rainsford. "Ugh! It's like moist black velvet."

"It will be light enough in Rio," promised Whitney. "We should make it in a few days. I hope the jaguar guns have come from Purdey's. We should have some good hunting up the Amazon. Great sport, hunting."

"The best sport in the world," agreed Rainsford.

"For the hunter," amended Whitney. "Not for the jaguar."

"Don't talk rot, Whitney," said Rainsford. "You're a big-game hunter, not a philosopher. Who cares how a jaguar feels?"

Matters of Life and Death *What does Whitney's statement suggest about his view of hunting?* **1**

Literary Element

SPIRAL REVIEW PARTNERS **Foils** Tell students that a foil is a minor character whose character traits highlight those of the main character. To practice ***reading fluency***, have students read the conversation between Whitney and Rainsford that begins on this page and ends on the fourth paragraph of page 23. **Ask:** What can you tell about Whitney from this conversation? *(He thinks Rainsford has good vision and is a great hunter; he feels for the jaguar; he is not tough like Rainsford.)* **Ask:** What can you tell about Rainsford? *(He has no compassion for a jaguar; he considers himself a hunter and not a huntee.)*

With a partner, have students discuss how Whitney is a foil to Rainsford. Students should take notes during their discussion and later share their responses with the class.

"Perhaps the jaguar does," observed Whitney.

"Bah! They've no understanding."

"Even so, I rather think they understand one thing—fear. The fear of pain and the fear of death."

"Nonsense," laughed Rainsford. "This hot weather is making you soft, Whitney. Be a realist. The world is made up of two classes—the hunters and the huntees. Luckily, you and I are hunters. Do you think we've passed that island yet?"

"I can't tell in the dark. I hope so."

"Why?" asked Rainsford.

"The place has a reputation—a bad one."

"Cannibals?" suggested Rainsford.

"Hardly. Even cannibals wouldn't live in such a God-forsaken place. But it's gotten into sailor lore,[1] somehow. Didn't you notice that the crew's nerves seemed a bit jumpy today?"

"They were a bit strange, now you mention it. Even Captain Nielsen—"

"Yes, even that tough-minded old Swede, who'd go up to the devil himself and ask him for a light. Those fishy blue eyes held a look I never saw there before. All I could get out of him was: 'This place has an evil name among seafaring men, sir.' Then he said to me, very gravely: 'Don't you feel anything?'—as if the air about us was actually poisonous. Now, you mustn't laugh when I tell you this—I did feel something like a sudden chill.

"There was no breeze. The sea was as flat as a plate-glass window. We were drawing near the island then. What I felt was a—a mental chill; a sort of sudden dread."

"Pure imagination," said Rainsford. "One superstitious sailor can taint the whole ship's company with his fear."

"Maybe. But sometimes I think sailors have an extra sense that tells them when they are in danger. Sometimes I think evil is a **tangible** thing—with wave lengths, just as sound and light have. An evil place can, so to speak, broadcast vibrations of evil. Anyhow, I'm glad we're getting out of this zone. Well, I think I'll turn in now, Rainsford."

"I'm not sleepy," said Rainsford. "I'm going to smoke another pipe up on the afterdeck."

"Good night, then, Rainsford. See you at breakfast."

"Right. Good night, Whitney."

There was no sound in the night as Rainsford sat there but the muffled throb of the engine that drove the yacht swiftly through the darkness, and the swish and ripple of the wash of the propeller.

Rainsford, reclining in a steamer chair, indolently puffed on his favorite briar.[2] The sensuous drowsiness of the night was upon him. "It's so dark," he thought, "that I could sleep without closing my eyes; the night would be my eyelids—"

An abrupt sound startled him. Off to the right he heard it, and his ears, expert in such matters, could not be mistaken. Again he heard the sound, and again. Somewhere, off in the blackness, someone had fired a gun three times.

1. Traditions and beliefs that have grown over time about a particular subject are called *lore*.

2. *Indolently* means "lazily"; a *briar* is a tobacco pipe made from the fine-grained wood of the root of a Mediterranean shrub.

2 Make and Verify Predictions About Plot *What do you think will happen, and what clues help you make this prediction?*

3 Suspense *How does this statement generate suspense?*

Vocabulary

tangible (tan′ jə bəl) *adj.* capable of being touched or felt

Teach

Reading Strategy 2

Make and Verify Predictions About Plot

Answer: *The story will involve hunting and the island. Clues include mentions of hunting, the title, and the island's name.*

For additional practice using the reading skill or strategy, see Unit 1 Teaching Resources Book p. 42.

Literary Element 3

Suspense **Answer:** *The reader wonders why the place has an evil name.*

Approaching Level

DIFFERENTIATED INSTRUCTION

Established Rainsford and Whitney discuss superstitions about Ship-Trap Island. Superstitions are unscientific beliefs based on fear or ignorance. Sailors in the past had many superstitions to explain things that they did not understand. For example, they believed that whistling while on board a ship would cause a storm.

Share these superstitions with students: Sailors believed it was unlucky to

- change the name of a boat.
- see rats leaving a ship.
- sail on a Friday.
- lose a bucket at sea.
- sail on a green boat.
- sail on the first Monday in April.

Ask students to think of superstitions they might have heard or read about. Have volunteers to share their answers with the class.

Teach

Reading Strategy 1

Make and Verify Predictions About Plot

Answer: *He will swim to the island, since the boat is out of reach. He will be stranded there.*

Big Idea 2

Matters of Life and Death

Answer: *Most students will infer that the animal was killed.*

Writer's Technique ☆

Setting The Caribbean Sea, a part of the Atlantic Ocean, is several degrees warmer than the waters farther north. Connell's use of the term *blood-warm* to describe a temperature that would usually seem inviting helps readers imagine Rainsford's fear.

Rainsford sprang up and moved quickly to the rail, mystified. He strained his eyes in the direction from which the reports had come, but it was like trying to see through a blanket. He leaped upon the rail and balanced himself there, to get greater elevation; his pipe, striking a rope, was knocked from his mouth. He lunged for it; a short, hoarse cry came from his lips as he realized he had reached too far and had lost his balance. The cry was pinched off short as the ☆ blood-warm waters of the Caribbean Sea closed over his head.

He struggled up to the surface and tried to cry out, but the wash from the speeding yacht slapped him in the face and the salt water in his open mouth made him gag and strangle. Desperately he struck out with strong strokes after the receding lights of the yacht, but he stopped before he had swum fifty feet. A certain coolheadedness had come to him; it was not the first time he had been in a tight place. There was a chance that his cries could be heard by someone aboard the yacht, but that chance was slender, and grew more slender as the yacht raced on. He wrestled himself out of his clothes, and shouted with all his power. The lights of the yacht became faint and ever-vanishing fireflies; then they were blotted out entirely by the night.

Rainsford remembered the shots. They had come from the right, and doggedly he swam in that direction, swimming with slow, deliberate strokes, conserving his strength. For a seemingly endless time he fought the sea. He began to count his strokes; he could do possibly a hundred more and then—

Rainsford heard a sound. It came out of the darkness, a high screaming sound, the sound of an animal in an extremity of anguish and terror.

He did not recognize the animal that made the sound; he did not try to; with fresh vitality he swam toward the sound. He heard it again; then it was cut short by another noise, crisp, staccato.

"Pistol shot," muttered Rainsford, swimming on.

Ten minutes of determined effort brought another sound to his ears—the most welcome he had ever heard—the muttering and growling of the sea breaking on a rocky shore. He was almost on the rocks before he saw them; on a night less calm he would have been shattered against them. With his remaining strength he dragged himself from the swirling waters. Jagged crags appeared to jut up into the opaqueness;[3] he forced himself upward, hand over hand. Gasping, his hands raw, he reached a flat place at the top. Dense jungle came down to the very edge of the cliffs. What perils that tangle of trees and underbrush might hold for him did not concern Rainsford just then. All he knew was that he was safe from his enemy, the sea, and that utter weariness was upon him. He flung himself down at the jungle edge and tumbled headlong into the deepest sleep of his life.

When he opened his eyes he knew from the position of the sun that it was late in the afternoon. Sleep had given him new vigor; a sharp hunger was picking at him. He looked about him, almost cheerfully.

"Where there are pistol shots, there are men. Where there are men, there is food," he thought. But what kind of men, he

3. *Crags* are steep, rugged, protruding rocks or cliffs. Here, the crags jut up into the darkness *(opaqueness)* of the night.

1 Make and Verify Predictions About Plot *What do you think will happen to Rainsford?*

Matters of Life and Death *Why does the pistol shot stop the sound?* **2**

Vocabulary Skills Practice

SPIRAL REVIEW SMALL GROUP

Unfamiliar Vocabulary Have students work in small groups to create a list of five to ten unfamiliar words found on pages 24 and 25. Students should then use a dictionary to define each word, and then use each word in a sentence. After students have finished, a representative from each group should share words and sentences from his or her list.

You may choose to allow students to write words from their list on the board, along with their sentences. Encourage students to add new words to their list as each group responds.

wondered, in so forbidding a place? An unbroken front of snarled and ragged jungle fringed the shore.

He saw no sign of a trail through the closely knit web of weeds and trees; it was easier to go along the shore, and Rainsford floundered along by the water. Not far from where he had landed, he stopped.

Some wounded thing, by the evidence, a large animal, had thrashed about in the underbrush; the jungle weeds were crushed down and the moss was lacerated; one patch of weeds was stained crimson. A small, glittering object not far away caught Rainsford's eye and he picked it up. It was an empty cartridge.

☆ "A twenty-two," he remarked. "That's odd. It must have been a fairly large animal, too. The hunter had his nerve with him to tackle it with a light gun. It's clear that the brute put up a fight. I suppose the first three shots I heard was when the hunter flushed his quarry[4] and wounded it. The last shot was when he trailed it here and finished it."

He examined the ground closely and found what he had hoped to find—the print of hunting boots. They pointed along the cliff in the direction he had been going. Eagerly he hurried along, now slipping on a rotten log or a loose stone, but making headway; night was beginning to settle down on the island.

Bleak darkness was blacking out the sea and jungle when Rainsford sighted the lights. He came upon them as he turned a crook in the coast line, and his first thought was that he had come upon a village, for there were many lights. But as he forged along he saw to his great astonishment that all the lights were in one enormous building—a lofty structure with pointed towers plunging upward into the gloom. His eyes made out the shadowy outlines of a palatial chateau;[5] it was set on a high bluff, and on three sides of it cliffs dived down to where the sea licked greedy lips in the shadows.

"Mirage," thought Rainsford. But it was no mirage, he found, when he opened the tall spiked iron gate. The stone steps were real enough; the massive door with a leering gargoyle for a knocker was real enough; yet above it all hung an air of unreality.

Visual Vocabulary
A *gargoyle* is an outlandish or grotesque carved figure.

He lifted the knocker, and it creaked up stiffly, as if it had never before been used. He let it fall, and it startled him with its booming loudness. He thought he heard steps within; the door remained closed. Again Rainsford lifted the heavy knocker, and let it fall. The door opened then, opened as suddenly as if it were on a spring, and Rainsford stood blinking in the river of glaring gold light that poured out. The first thing Rainsford's eyes **discerned** was the largest man Rainsford had ever seen—a gigantic creature, solidly made and black-bearded to the waist. In his hand the man held a long-barreled revolver, and he was pointing it straight at Rainsford's heart.

Out of the snarl of beard two small eyes regarded Rainsford.

"Don't be alarmed," said Rainsford, with a smile which he hoped was disarming.[6]

---

4. *Quarry* is anything that is hunted or pursued, especially an animal.

5. A *palatial chateau* (sha tō′) is a magnificent, palace-like mansion.

6. *Disarming* means "tending to remove fear or suspicion; charming."

3 Suspense *How does the author's word choice add suspense in this passage?*

Vocabulary

discern (di surn′) *v.* to detect or recognize; to make out

Teach

Literary Element 3

Suspense Answer: Crushed, lacerated, *and* stained crimson *suggest physical violence.*

ENGLISH LEARNERS Ask an English learner to look up *lacerated* in the dictionary and read the definition aloud.

Cultural History ☆

Hunting Guns Rainsford's reference to a "twenty-two" describes the caliber, or approximate size, of the cartridge, or shell case, used in a 22-caliber gun. The caliber of a gun is the inside diameter of its barrel measured in hundredths of an inch. Rainsford thinks only a bold hunter would use such a lightweight gun against big game.

English Learners

DIFFERENTIATED INSTRUCTION

Intermediate Some of the words in the story will be unfamiliar to students. Tell students to jot down unfamiliar words on pages 24 and 25 as they read. When they finish reading, **Ask:** What new words did you find in the story? Write students' responses on the chalkboard. *(Students responses might include* staccato, crags, forbidding, floundered, lacerated, crook, lofty, mirage, booming, *and* menacing.*)* Lead a discussion in which students use context clues to determine synonyms for these words. Then have students use a dictionary to look up the correct meaning for themselves.

Teach

Literary Element 1

Characterization Define *foil* as a character that strongly contrasts with another character.

Ask: How does the man with the gun function as a foil for General Zaroff? *(He is rough, primitive-looking, and menacing. Zaroff is well-groomed, cultivated, and sophisticated.)*

View the Art ★

Answer: *Accept all reasonable answers.*

Paul Cézanne (1839–1906) strongly influenced modern painting. He developed his own unique brushstrokes. Although Cézanne borrowed from Impressionist elements, his work was too realistic to be considered Impressionist.

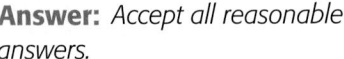

Le Château Noir, 1904–1906. Paul Cézanne. Oil on canvas, 29 x 36¾ in. Gift of Mrs. David M. Levy. The Museum of Modern Art, NY.

View the Art This painting depicts a real building that was owned by a man who manufactured black paint. Locals believed he was involved in black magic and so called the building "the black chateau." Compare and contrast this chateau with the chateau described in the story. ★

"I'm no robber. I fell off a yacht. My name is Sanger Rainsford of New York City."

The menacing look in the eyes did not change. The revolver pointed as rigidly as if the giant were a statue. He gave no sign that he understood Rainsford's words, or that he had even heard them. He was dressed in uniform, a black uniform trimmed with gray astrakhan.[7]

"I'm Sanger Rainsford of New York," Rainsford began again. "I fell off a yacht. I am hungry."

The man's only answer was to raise with his thumb the hammer of his revolver. Then Rainsford saw the man's free hand go to his forehead in a military salute, and he saw him click his heels together and stand at attention. Another man was coming down the broad marble steps, an erect, slender man in evening clothes. He advanced to Rainsford and held out his hand.

In a cultivated voice marked by a slight accent that gave it added precision and deliberateness, he said: "It is a very great pleasure and honor to welcome Mr. Sanger Rainsford, the celebrated hunter, to my home." 1

7. *Astrakhan* is the woolly skin of young lambs and is named after a region in Russia.

Writing Skills

Write a Journal Entry Remind students that one way to gain a deeper understanding of a work of literature is to project themselves into it. Ask students to imagine they are Rainsford, and they have just retired to their room after dinner with General Zaroff. Have them write a journal entry in which they describe General Zaroff, speculate about Ivan, and express their feelings about Zaroff's grisly pastime and what they imagine will take place the next day. Encourage students to use sensory details and vivid descriptions.

Automatically Rainsford shook the man's hand.

"I've read your book about hunting snow leopards in Tibet, you see," explained the man. "I am General Zaroff."

Rainsford's first impression was that the man was singularly handsome; his second was that there was an original, almost bizarre quality about the general's face. He was a tall man past middle age, for his hair was a vivid white; but his thick eyebrows and pointed military mustache were as black as the night from which Rainsford had come. His eyes, too, were black and very bright. He had high cheek bones, a sharp-cut nose, a spare, dark face, the face of a man used to giving orders, the face of an aristocrat. Turning to the giant in uniform, the general made a sign. The giant put away his pistol, saluted, withdrew.

"Ivan is an incredibly strong fellow," remarked the general, "but he has the misfortune to be deaf and dumb. A simple fellow, but, I'm afraid, like all his race, a bit of a savage."

"Is he Russian?"

"He is a Cossack,"[8] said the general, and his smile showed red lips and pointed teeth. "So am I."

"Come," he said, "we shouldn't be chatting here. We can talk later. Now you want clothes, food, rest. You shall have them. This is a most restful spot."

Ivan had reappeared, and the general spoke to him with lips that moved but gave forth no sound.

"Follow Ivan, if you please, Mr. Rainsford," said the general. "I was about to have my dinner when you came. I'll wait for you. You'll find that my clothes will fit you, I think."

It was to a huge, beam-ceilinged bedroom with a canopied bed big enough for six men that Rainsford followed the silent giant. Ivan laid out an evening suit, and Rainsford, as he put it on, noticed that it came from a London tailor who ordinarily cut and sewed for none below the rank of duke.

The dining room to which Ivan conducted them was in many ways remarkable. There was a medieval magnificence about it; it suggested a baronial hall of feudal times with its oaken panels, its high ceiling, its vast refectory tables where twoscore men could sit down to eat.[9] About the hall were the mounted heads of many animals—lions, tigers, elephants, moose, bears; larger or more perfect specimens Rainsford had never seen. At the great table the general was sitting, alone.

"You'll have a cocktail, Mr. Rainsford," he suggested. The cocktail was surpassingly good; and, Rainsford noticed, the table appointments were of the finest—the linen, the crystal, the silver, the china.

They were eating *borscht,* the rich, red soup with whipped cream so dear to Russian palates. Half apologetically General Zaroff said: "We do our best to preserve the amenities of civilization here.[10] Please forgive any lapses. We are well off the beaten track, you know. Do you think the champagne has suffered from its long ocean trip?"

8. The *Cossacks* are a people of southern Russia (and, now, Kazakhstan). During czarist times, Cossack men were famous as horsemen in the Russian cavalry.

9. The words *medieval, baronial,* and *feudal* all relate to the Middle Ages. A *refectory table* might be found in a baron's castle; it is a long, wooden table with straight, heavy legs.

10. *Borscht* (bôrsht) is a soup made from beets. Here, *palates* means "tastes" or "likings," and *amenities* means "agreeable features" or "niceties."

2 Make and Verify Predictions About Plot *What do you predict will happen between Rainsford and General Zaroff?*

Matters of Life and Death *What do all the mounted heads tell you about Zaroff?* **3**

Teach

Reading Strategy 2

Make and Verify Predictions About Plot

Answer: *Students may say the two will get along well.*

Big Idea 3

Matters of Life and Death

Answer: *Zaroff hunts and kills for sport. He likes to have trophies made from the animals he kills, which means he is proud of his kills.*

Approaching Level

DIFFERENTIATED INSTRUCTION

Emerging Make sure students understand the author's emphasis on General Zaroff's polished appearance and demeanor. **Ask:** What details does the author give about General Zaroff on pages 26 and 27?

Established Tell students that when authors give hints of something to come, it is called foreshadowing. **Ask:** How does the author foreshadow that General Zaroff may have a dark side? *(Zaroff tells Rainsford that Ivan is "a bit of a savage" because he is a Cossack, and then Zaroff says that he, too, is a Cossack. The author says Zaroff's smile showed red lips and pointed teeth.)*

Teach

Literary Element 1

Suspense **Answer:** *Readers wonder what game is more dangerous than that mentioned and how this game will affect Rainsford.*

Cultural History ☆

Russian Revolution After the revolution of 1917, many wealthy Russian aristocrats lost their money. Often they were forced to move to other countries and live in humble circumstances.

"Not in the least," declared Rainsford. He was finding the general a most thoughtful and affable host, a true cosmopolite.[11] But there was one small trait of the general's that made Rainsford uncomfortable. Whenever he looked up from his plate he found the general studying him, appraising him narrowly.

"Perhaps," said General Zaroff, "you were surprised that I recognized your name. You see, I read all books on hunting published in English, French, and Russian. I have but one passion in my life, Mr. Rainsford, and it is the hunt."

Visual Vocabulary
The African *Cape buffalo* is a large, often fierce buffalo with heavy curving horns.

"You have some wonderful heads here," said Rainsford as he ate a particularly well cooked *filet mignon.* "That Cape buffalo is the largest I ever saw."

"Oh, that fellow. Yes, he was a monster."

"Did he charge you?"

"Hurled me against a tree," said the general. "Fractured my skull. But I got the brute."

"I've always thought," said Rainsford, "that the Cape buffalo is the most dangerous of all big game."

For a moment the general did not reply; he was smiling his curious red-lipped smile. Then he said slowly: "No. You are wrong, sir. The Cape buffalo is not the most dangerous big game." He sipped his wine. "Here in my preserve on this island," he said in the same slow tone, "I hunt more dangerous game."

Rainsford expressed his surprise. "Is there big game on this island?"

The general nodded. "The biggest."

"Really?"

"Oh, it isn't here naturally, of course. I have to stock the island."

"What have you imported, general?" Rainsford asked. "Tigers?"

The general smiled. "No," he said. "Hunting tigers ceased to interest me some years ago. I exhausted their possibilities, you see. No thrill left in tigers, no real danger. I live for danger, Mr. Rainsford."

The general took from his pocket a gold cigarette case and offered his guest a long black cigarette with a silver tip; it was perfumed and gave off a smell like incense.

"We will have some capital hunting, you and I," said the general. "I shall be most glad to have your society."

"But what game—" began Rainsford.

"I'll tell you," said the general. "You will be amused, I know. I think I may say, in all modesty, that I have done a rare thing. I have invented a new sensation. May I pour you another glass of port?"

"Thank you, general."

The general filled both glasses, and said: "God makes some men poets. Some He makes kings, some beggars. Me He made a hunter. My hand was made for the trigger, my father said. He was a very rich man with a quarter of a million acres in the Crimea, and he was an ardent sportsman. When I was only five years old he gave me a little gun, specially made in Moscow for me, to shoot sparrows with. When I shot some of his prize turkeys with it, he did not punish me; he complimented me on my marksmanship. I killed my first bear in the Caucasus[12] when I

11. *Affable* means "friendly and gracious." A *cosmopolite* (koz mop′ ə līt′) is a gracious and sophisticated person.

12. *Crimea* (krī mē′ ə) is a region in the southern part of the former Russian empire near the Black Sea. *Caucasus* (kô′ kə səs) refers to both a region and a mountain range between the Black and Caspian Seas.

1 Suspense *Why do phrases about dangerous game heighten the suspense?*

Reading Practice

SPIRAL REVIEW **Sequence of Events** Have students create a chain-of-events graphic organizer to show the sequence of events in General Zaroff's life as he explains them to Rainsford on this page. Students graphic organizer should show major events of Zaroff's life from the time he was five to the present time in the story. Allow volunteers to present their graphic organizers to the class. *(He hunted prize turkeys with his father. He went into the army; left Russia; hunted grizzlies in the Rockies; hunted crocodiles in the Ganges; hunted rhinos in East Africa; was injured by a Cape Buffalo; hunted jaguars.)*

was ten. My whole life has been one prolonged hunt. I went into the army—it was expected of noblemen's sons—and for a time commanded a division of Cossack cavalry, but my real interest was always the hunt. I have hunted every kind of game in every land. It would be impossible for me to tell you how many animals I have killed."

The general puffed at his cigarette.

☆ "After the debacle in Russia I left the country, for it was imprudent for an officer of the Czar to stay there.[13] Many noble Russians lost everything. I, luckily, had invested heavily in American securities, so I shall never have to open a tearoom in Monte Carlo or drive a taxi in Paris. Naturally, I continued to hunt—grizzlies in your Rockies, crocodile in the Ganges, rhinoceroses in East Africa. It was in Africa that the Cape buffalo hit me and laid me up for six months. As soon as I recovered I started for the Amazon to hunt jaguars, for I had heard they were unusually cunning. They weren't." The Cossack sighed. "They were no match at all for a hunter with his wits about him, and a high-powered rifle. I was bitterly disappointed. I was lying in my tent with a splitting headache one night when a terrible thought pushed its way into my mind. Hunting was beginning to bore me! And hunting, remember, had been my life. I have heard that in America business men often go to pieces when they give up the business that has been their life."

"Instinct is no match for reason."

"Yes, that's so," said Rainsford.

The general smiled. "I had no wish to go to pieces," he said. "I must do something. Now, mine is an analytical mind, Mr. Rainsford. Doubtless that is why I enjoy the problems of the chase."

"No doubt, General Zaroff."

"So," continued the general, "I asked myself why the hunt no longer fascinated me. You are much younger than I am, Mr. Rainsford, and have not hunted as much, but you perhaps can guess the answer."

"What was it?"

"Simply this: hunting had ceased to be what you call 'a sporting proposition.' It had become too easy. I always got my quarry. Always. There is no greater bore than perfection."

The general lit a fresh cigarette.

"No animal had a chance with me any more. That is no **4** boast; it is a mathematical certainty. The animal had nothing but his legs and his instinct. Instinct is no match for reason. When I thought of this it was a tragic moment for me, I can tell you."

Rainsford leaned across the table, absorbed in what his host was saying.

"It came to me as an inspiration what I must do," the general went on.

"And that was?"

The general smiled the quiet smile of one who has faced an obstacle and surmounted it with success. "I had to invent a new animal to hunt," he said.

"A new animal? You're joking."

"Not at all," said the general. "I never joke about hunting. I needed a new animal. I found one. So I bought this island, built this house, and here I do my hunting. The

13. A *debacle* (di bä′ kəl) is a disastrous defeat. Zaroff refers to the 1917 revolution that overthrew the Czar, an event that made it unwise *(imprudent)* for him to stay in Russia.

2 Matters of Life and Death *What general statement could you make about General Zaroff's life goals?*

Suspense *How does General Zaroff build suspense in the telling of his story?* **3**

Teach

Big Idea 2

Matters of Life and Death
Answer: *He thinks of life as a game or a hunt. His goals are related to achieving hunting success.*

Literary Element 3

Suspense **Answer:** *The reader is waiting to find out what the most dangerous game is and is chilled by Zaroff's boredom with hunting jaguars. This passage builds suspense by making the reader wonder what animal could possibly challenge this man.*

Vocabulary 4

Clarify Meaning *Instinct* describes behavior that is inborn. For example, a baby animal knows without being taught to stay close to its mother. *Reason* refers to thinking and judgment. Humans, like animals, are often driven by instincts but have superior reasoning ability.

English Learners

DIFFERENTIATED INSTRUCTION

Early Intermediate Help students better understand Zaroff's travels by using a globe. Show them Russia, America, the Ganges River in India, East Africa, and the Caribbean Islands where Zaroff now lives. Then have students find information about one of the locations and write two paragraphs to summarize their findings. Students should edit their writings for grammatical errors.

Approaching Level

DIFFERENTIATED INSTRUCTION

African American Vernacular English Approaching-level students who use African American vernacular English (AAVE) may have difficulty recognizing the /r/ sound in consonant clusters at the beginning of words such as "throw," "through," and "brought." As students are rereading the passages about the medals, stop at the word "through" and discuss its pronunciation and spelling. Compare its pronunciation and meaning to *though,* used earlier in the same paragraph.

Teach

Reading Strategy 1

Make and Verify Predictions About Plot
Answer: *Zaroff will name humans.*

Literary Element 2

Characterization **Ask:** What do readers learn about General Zaroff through his dialogue? *(He is cruel and unfeeling; he discriminates among different ethnic and social classes of people. In general, he has no respect for human life.)*

Cultural History ☆

Social Darwinism "Life is for the strong" recalls the ideas of the nineteenth-century naturalist Charles Darwin. His theory of natural selection, or survival of the fittest, proposed that evolution tended to favor strength over weakness. Social Darwinism applied this theory to human society, proposing that it should weed out the unfit.

island is perfect for my purposes—there are jungles with a maze of trails in them, hills, swamps—"

"But the animal, General Zaroff?"

"Oh," said the general, "it supplies me with the most exciting hunting in the world. No other hunting compares with it for an instant. Every day I hunt, and I never grow bored now, for I have a quarry with which I can match my wits."

Rainsford's bewilderment showed in his face.

"I wanted the ideal animal to hunt," explained the general. "So I said: 'What are the attributes of an ideal quarry?' And the answer was, of course: 'It must have courage, cunning, and, above all, it must be able to reason.'"

"But no animal can reason," objected Rainsford.

1 "My dear fellow," said the general, "there is one that can."

"But you can't mean—" gasped Rainsford.

"And why not?"

"I can't believe you are serious, General Zaroff. This is a grisly joke."

"Why should I not be serious? I am speaking of hunting."

"Hunting? Good God, General Zaroff, what you speak of is murder."

The general laughed with entire good nature. He regarded Rainsford quizzically. "I refuse to believe that so modern and civilized a young man as you seem to be harbors romantic ideas about the value of human life. Surely your experiences in the war—"

"Did not make me **condone** cold-blooded murder," finished Rainsford stiffly.

Laughter shook the general. "How extraordinarily droll you are!" he said. "One does not expect nowadays to find a young man of the educated class, even in America, with such a naive, and, if I may say so, mid-Victorian[14] point of view. It's like finding a snuff-box in a limousine. Ah, well, doubtless you had Puritan ancestors. So many Americans appear to have had. I'll wager you'll forget your notions when you go hunting with me. You've a genuine new thrill in store for you, Mr. Rainsford."

"Thank you, I'm a hunter, not a murderer."

"Dear me," said the general, quite unruffled, "again that unpleasant word. But I think I can show you that your scruples[15] are quite ill founded."

"Yes?"

"Life is for the strong, to be lived by the strong, and, if needs be, taken by the strong. The weak of the world were put here to give the strong pleasure. I am strong. Why should I not use my fist? If I wish to hunt, why should I not? I hunt the scum of the earth—sailors from tramp ships—lascars, blacks, Chinese, whites, mongrels[16]—a thoroughbred horse or hound is worth more than a score of them." ☆

"But they are men," said Rainsford hotly.

"Precisely," said the general. "That is why I use them. It gives me pleasure. They can reason, after a fashion. So they are dangerous." 2

"But where do you get them?"

The general's left eyelid fluttered down in a wink. "This island is called Ship-Trap," he answered. "Sometimes an angry god of the high seas sends them to me. Sometimes, when Providence is not so

1 Make and Verify Predictions About Plot *What animal do you think Zaroff will name?*

Vocabulary

condone (kən dōn′) *v.* to excuse or overlook an offense, usually a serious one, without criticism

14. Zaroff feels that Rainsford is quaint *(droll)*, innocent and unsophisticated *(naive)*, and old-fashioned *(mid-Victorian)*.
15. *Scruples* are beliefs about the morality or ethics of an act. To have scruples means you will not do something you believe is wrong.
16. *Lascars* are sailors from India. Zaroff uses the word *mongrel* to refer to people of mixed heritage.

Skills Practice

PARTNERS SPIRAL REVIEW

Punctuation and Dialogue When writing dialogue, authors sometimes tell which character is speaking before, after, or in the middle of a quotation, or not at all. Note that each time a character speaks, a writer often begins a new paragraph. This makes it easier to determine which character is speaking. Have students work with a partner to write an original conversation between Zaroff and Rainsford. Students should begin a new paragraph when a different character begins to speak. Remind students to use correct grammar and punctuation in their writing.

kind, I help Providence a bit. Come to the window with me."

Rainsford went to the window and looked out toward the sea.

"Watch! Out there!" exclaimed the general, pointing into the night. Rainsford's eyes saw only blackness, and then, as the general pressed a button, far out to sea Rainsford saw the flash of lights.

The general chuckled. "They indicate a channel," he said, "where there's none; giant rocks with razor edges crouch like a sea monster with wide-open jaws. They can crush a ship as easily as I crush this nut." He dropped a walnut on the hardwood floor and brought his heel grinding down on it. "Oh, yes," he said, casually, as if in answer to a question, "I have electricity. We try to be civilized here."

"Civilized? And you shoot down men?"

A trace of anger was in the general's black eyes, but it was there for but a second, and he said, in his most pleasant manner: "Dear me, what a righteous young man you are! I assure you I do not do the thing you suggest. That would be barbarous. I treat these visitors with every consideration. They get plenty of good food and exercise. They get into splendid physical condition. You shall see for yourself tomorrow."

"What do you mean?"

"We'll visit my training school," smiled the general. "It's in the cellar. I have about a dozen pupils down there now. They're from the Spanish bark *San Lucar* that had the bad luck to go on the rocks out there. A very inferior lot, I regret to say. Poor specimens and more accustomed to the deck than to the jungle."

Visual Vocabulary
A *bark* has from three to five masts, all but one of which are rigged with four-sided sails. The last mast has both three- and four-sided sails.

He raised his hand, and Ivan, who served as waiter, brought thick Turkish coffee. Rainsford, with an effort, held his tongue in check.

"It's a game, you see," pursued the general blandly. "I suggest to one of them that we go hunting. I give him a supply of food and an excellent hunting knife. I give him three hours' start. I am to follow, armed only with a pistol of the smallest caliber and range. If my quarry eludes me for three whole days, he wins the game. If I find him"—the general smiled—"he loses."

"Suppose he refuses to be hunted?"

"Oh," said the general, "I give him his option, of course. He need not play that game if he doesn't wish to. If he does not wish to hunt, I turn him over to Ivan. Ivan once had the honor of serving as official knouter[17] to the Great White Czar, and he has his own ideas of sport. Invariably, Mr. Rainsford, invariably they choose the hunt."

"And if they win?"

The smile on the general's face widened. "To date I have not lost," he said. Then he added, hastily: "I don't wish you to think me a braggart, Mr. Rainsford. Many of them afford only the most elementary sort of problem. Occasionally I strike a tartar.[18] One almost did win. I eventually had to use the dogs."

17. As the Czar's *knouter* (nou′ tər), Ivan was in charge of administering whippings and torture. A knout is a whip made of leather straps braided together with wires.
18. To *strike a tartar* is to take on someone who is stronger or abler.

3 Make and Verify Predictions About Plot *How do you think Zaroff will respond?*

Matters of Life and Death *What do you think happens to someone who "loses"?* **4**

Suspense *How does this statement increase the suspense?* **5**

Teach

Reading Strategy 3

Make and Verify Predictions About Plot
Answer: *Zaroff will become violent; he will hunt Rainsford.*

Big Idea 4

Matters of Life and Death
Answer: *The loser dies.*

Literary Element 5

Suspense **Answer:** *The statement shows how dangerous Zaroff is and suggests that the game is rigged; it is not a fair contest.*

English Learners

DIFFERENTIATED INSTRUCTION

Intermediate Point out the reference to the Spanish bark *San Lucar* and direct students to the Visual Vocabulary box on this page. Help students understand the story by providing them with the following meanings of words and phrases on pages 30 and 31:

- quarry—prey
- snuff-box—old-fashioned box used to hold tobacco
- Puritan ancestors—ancestors who were very moral
- after a fashion—after a while

Ask students to define these additional terms:

- Providence *(God or divine intervention)*
- held his tongue in check *(kept quiet)*
- eludes *(escapes)*
- grisly *(disgusting)*

Teach

Literary Element 1

Suspense **Answer:** *Like Rainsford, the reader knows that the general wants to show off his collection of human heads.*

View the Art ★

Answer: *Students should point out details that are similar, such as the heads of animals on the walls, as well as the general palatial feel of the room, which matches the descriptions of Zaroff's chateau.*

Kinloch Castle, on the Isle of Rhum in Scotland, is one of the best examples of an Edwardian country house. The castle was built between 1897 and 1901. *Kinloch* means "at the head of the loch"—in this case, referring to Loch Scresort.

View the Art In 1901, Sir George Bulloughs of Lancashire, England, bought the Isle of Rhum for use as a sporting estate. How does his trophy room, shown here, compare to Zaroff's home on Ship-Trap Island? ★

"The dogs?"

"This way, please. I'll show you."

The general steered Rainsford to a window. The lights from the windows sent a flickering illumination that made grotesque patterns on the courtyard below, and Rainsford could see moving about there a dozen or so huge black shapes; as they turned toward him, their eyes glittered greenly.

"A rather good lot, I think," observed the general. "They are let out at seven every night. If anyone should try to get into my house—or out of it—something extremely regrettable would occur to him." He hummed a snatch of song from the *Folies Bergère.*[19]

"And now," said the general, "I want to show you my new collection of heads. Will you come with me to the library?"

"I hope," said Rainsford, "that you will excuse me tonight, General Zaroff. I'm really not feeling well."

"Ah, indeed?" the general inquired solicitously.[20] "Well, I suppose that's only natural, after your long swim. You need a good, restful night's sleep. Tomorrow you'll feel like a new man, I'll wager. Then we'll hunt, eh? I've one rather promising prospect—" Rainsford was hurrying from the room.

19. The *Folies Bergère* (fô lē′ ber zher′) is a music hall in Paris, famed for its variety shows.

20. *Solicitously* means "in a caring or concerned manner."

Suspense *What is particularly foreboding about General Zaroff's statement at this point in the story?* 1

Reading Practice

SPIRAL REVIEW **Visualize Description** Point out the picture on the page. Ask students to name some elaborate features in the trophy room in the picture. Write their responses on the chalkboard. **Ask:** What might be different about Zaroff's trophy room? *(It might have different heads on the wall—even human heads.)*

Read aloud the description of the dogs on this page. **Ask:** What image is the author trying to convey in this description? *(He makes the dogs seem mysterious and scary.)* Have students write a description of Zaroff's house based on what they have read so far in the story.

"Sorry you can't go with me tonight," called the general. "I expect rather fair sport—a big, strong black. He looks resourceful—Well, good night, Mr. Rainsford; I hope you have a good night's rest."

The bed was good, and the pajamas of the softest silk and he was tired in every fiber of his being, but nevertheless Rainsford could not quiet his brain with the opiate of sleep. He lay, eyes wide open. Once he thought he heard stealthy steps in the corridor outside his room. He sought to throw open the door; it would not open. He went to the window and looked out. His room was high up in one of the towers. The lights of the chateau were out now, and it was dark and silent, but there was a fragment of sallow moon, and by its wan light he could see, dimly, the courtyard; there, weaving in and out in the pattern of shadow, were black, noiseless forms; the hounds heard him at the window and looked up, expectantly, with their green eyes. Rainsford went back to the bed and lay down. By many methods he tried to put himself to sleep. He had achieved a doze when, just as morning began to come, he heard, far off in the jungle, the faint report of a pistol.

General Zaroff did not appear until luncheon. He was dressed faultlessly in ☆ the tweeds of a country squire. He was solicitous about the state of Rainsford's health.

"As for me," sighed the general, "I do not feel so well. I am worried, Mr. Rainsford. Last night I detected traces of my old complaint."

To Rainsford's questioning glance the general said: "Ennui.[21] Boredom."

Then, taking a second helping of *Crêpes Suzette,* the general explained: "The hunting was not good last night. The fellow lost his head. He made a straight trail that offered no problems at all. That's the trouble with these sailors; they have dull brains to begin with, and they do not know how to get about in the woods. They do excessively stupid and obvious things. It's most annoying. Will you have another glass of *Chablis,*[22] Mr. Rainsford?"

Visual Vocabulary
Crêpes Suzette (kräps´ so͞o zet´) are thin pancakes rolled and heated in a sweet sauce flavored with orange or lemon juice and brandy.

"General," said Rainsford firmly, "I wish to leave this island at once."

The general raised his thickets of eyebrows; he seemed hurt. "But, my dear fellow," the general protested, "you've only just come. You've had no hunting—"

"I wish to go today," said Rainsford. He saw the dead black eyes of the general on him, studying him. General Zaroff's face suddenly brightened.

He filled Rainsford's glass with venerable *Chablis* from a dusty bottle.

"Tonight," said the general, "we will hunt—you and I."

Rainsford shook his head. "No, general," he said, "I will not hunt."

The general shrugged his shoulders and delicately ate a hothouse grape. "As you wish, my friend," he said. "The choice rests entirely with you. But may I not venture to suggest that you will find my idea of sport more diverting[23] than Ivan's?"

---

21. *Ennui* (än wē´)

22. *Chablis* (sha blē´) is a white wine.

23. *Diverting* means "entertaining" or "amusing."

Make and Verify Predictions About Plot *What effect will a poor hunt have on the general?* **2**

Teach

Reading Strategy 2

Make and Verify Predictions About Plot

Answer: *Poor hunting will probably leave the general bored and unsatisfied.*

APPROACHING Remind approaching-level students to make predictions and to verify those predictions as they continue reading.

Cultural History ☆

Clothing Style Zaroff wears "the tweeds of a country squire." English landowners, who were often addressed with the title *squire,* favored trousers and jackets made from tweed, a rough multicolored woolen fabric. **Ask:** What does this choice of clothing say about Zaroff? *(Since wool seems impractical for the tropics, it suggests he is obsessed with his image.)*

English Learners

DIFFERENTIATED INSTRUCTION

Early Advanced Explain to students that figurative language is used to evoke emotions and mental images and has meaning beyond its literal definition. For example, the phrase "dead black eyes" on page 33 does not mean that Zaroff's eyes are actually dead, but that they are as devoid of feeling as a dead person's eyes. Help students understand other examples of figurative language: "fragment of sallow moon"; "hogshead of a chest"; "worthy of my steel"; and "sharp rowels of something very like panic."

Teach

Reading Strategy 1

Make and Verify Predictions About Plot

Answer: *Rainsford will probably agree to the hunt rather than face certain death at Ivan's hands.*

Big Idea 2

Matters of Life and Death

Answer: *Zaroff will be determined to kill Rainsford rather than let him live to tell what Zaroff does on the island.*

Cultural History ☆

Moccasins Native Americans were some of the first people to wear moccasins: ankle-length or knee-length, heelless shoes made of deerskin. The upper parts of the shoes are often decorated with beads or embroidery.

He nodded toward the corner to where the giant stood, scowling, his thick arms crossed on his hogshead of a chest.

"You don't mean—" cried Rainsford.

"My dear fellow," said the general, "have I not told you I always mean what I say about hunting? This is really an inspiration. I drink to a foeman worthy of my steel—at last." The general raised his glass, but Rainsford sat staring at him.

"You'll find this game worth playing," the general said enthusiastically. "Your brain against mine. Your woodcraft against mine. Your strength and stamina against mine. Outdoor chess! And the stake is not without value, eh?"

"And if I win—" began Rainsford huskily.

"I'll cheerfully acknowledge myself defeated if I do not find you by midnight of the third day," said General Zaroff. "My sloop will place you on the mainland near a town." The general read what Rainsford was thinking.

"Oh, you can trust me," said the Cossack. "I will give you my word as a gentleman and a sportsman. Of course you, in turn, must agree to say nothing of your visit here."

"I'll agree to nothing of the kind," said Rainsford.

"Oh," said the general, "in that case— But why discuss that now? Three days hence we can discuss it over a bottle of *Veuve Cliquot*,[24] unless—"

The general sipped his wine. Then a businesslike air animated him. "Ivan," he said to Rainsford, "will supply you with hunting clothes, food, a knife. I suggest you wear moccasins; they leave a poorer trail. I ☆ suggest, too, that you avoid the big swamp in the southeast corner of the island. We call it Death Swamp. There's quicksand there. One foolish fellow tried it. The deplorable[25] part of it was that Lazarus followed him. You can imagine my feelings, Mr. Rainsford. I loved Lazarus; he was the finest hound in my pack. Well, I must beg you to excuse me now. I always take a siesta after lunch. You'll hardly have time for a nap, I fear. You'll want to start, no doubt. I shall not follow till dusk. Hunting at night is so much more exciting than by day, don't you think? Au revoir,[26] Mr. Rainsford, au revoir." General Zaroff, with a deep, courtly bow, strolled from the room.

Rainsford had fought his way through the bush for two hours. "I must keep my nerve. I must keep my nerve," he said through tight teeth.

He had not been entirely clear-headed when the chateau gates snapped shut behind him. His whole idea at first was to put distance between himself and General Zaroff, and, to this end, he had plunged along, spurred on by the sharp rowels[27] of something very like panic. Now he had got a grip on himself, had stopped, and was taking stock of himself and the situation. He saw that straight flight was futile; inevitably it would bring him face to face with the sea. He was in a picture with a frame of water, and his operations, clearly, must take place within that frame.

"I'll give him a trail to follow," muttered Rainsford, and he struck off from the rude path he had been following into the track-

24. *Veuve Cliquot* (vœv klē kō′) is a French champagne.

1 Make and Verify Predictions About Plot *What do you predict Rainsford will do?*

2 Matters of Life and Death *Why might Rainsford's statement put him in danger?*

25. *Deplorable* means "very bad" or "regrettable."

26. *Au revoir* (ō rə vwär′) is French for "good-bye" or "until we meet again."

27. *Rowel* is a wheel with sharp radiating points, as on the end of a rider's spur.

Writing Skills

Write Using Vivid Verbs Remind students that careful word choice brings their writing to life. Connell uses strong, specific, and vivid verbs to craft an engaging plot and draw interesting, believable characters. Ask students to locate examples of vivid verbs on pages 34 and 35. (nodded, sipped, snapped, plunged, muttered, climbed) Ask students to write several sentences about a physical activity, using specific, vivid verbs. Then have students exchange sentences with a partner to evaluate each other's verb choices.

Sea Piece by Moonlight. Caspar David Friedrich. Oil on canvas, 25 x 33 cm. Museum der bildenden Künste, Leipzig, Germany. ★

less wilderness. He executed a series of intricate loops; he doubled on his trail again and again, recalling all the lore of the fox hunt, and all the dodges of the fox. Night found him leg-weary, with hands and face lashed by the branches, on a thickly wooded ridge. He knew it would be insane to blunder on through the dark, even if he had the strength. His need for rest was **imperative** and he thought: "I have played the fox, now I must play the cat of the fable." A big tree with a thick trunk and outspread branches was near by, and, taking care to leave not the slightest mark, he climbed up into the crotch, and stretching out on one of the broad limbs, after a fashion, rested. Rest brought him new confidence and almost a feeling of security. Even so **zealous** a hunter as General Zaroff could not trace him there, he told himself; only the devil himself could follow that complicated trail through

Vocabulary

imperative (im per′ ə tiv) *adj.* absolutely necessary

Vocabulary

zealous (zel′ əs) *adj.* very eager; enthusiastic

Teach

View the Art ★

Scarred as a boy by the loss of his mother and a brother, Caspar David Friedrich (1774–1840) painted harsh, desolate landscapes. This painting suggests the isolation of the individual in the vastness of nature.

English Learners

DIFFERENTIATED INSTRUCTION

Intermediate Students may need the following background in order to understand the story. Clarify that on page 35 Rainsford refers to a fable by Aesop in which a fox challenges a cat to do tricks. The cat says that he does not know how to do tricks, but he knows how to do the most important things such as getting food and protecting himself. When some dogs come along, the fox continues acting "tricky" and is caught by the dogs. The cat simply climbs a tree, successfully avoiding capture.

Ask: How has Rainsford played the fox? *(He has given General Zaroff a trail to follow to trick him.)*

Ask: Why does he say he must now play the cat? *(He now needs to rest in a tree.)*

Teach

Literary Element 1

Figurative Language Point out the highlighted text and urge students to visualize this image of the night. Have them define *apprehensive. (worried and fearful)*

Ask: Does this word literally describe the night? *(No, the image reflects Rainsford's fear.)*

Literary Element 2

Suspense Answer: *Most students will say that "apprehensive," "like a wounded snake," and "a dead world" add to the suspense.*

Big Idea 3

Matters of Life and Death
Answer: *A cat will play with a mouse before killing it, just as Zaroff plays with Rainsford.*

the jungle after dark. But, perhaps the general was a devil—

An apprehensive night crawled slowly by like a wounded snake, and sleep did 1 not visit Rainsford, although the silence of a dead world was on the jungle. Toward morning when a dingy gray was varnishing the sky, the cry of some startled bird focused Rainsford's attention in that direction. Something was coming through the bush, coming slowly, carefully, coming by the same winding way Rainsford had come. He flattened himself down on the limb, and through a screen of leaves almost as thick as tapestry, he watched. . . . That which was approaching was a man.

He was General Zaroff. He made his way along with his eyes fixed in utmost concentration on the ground before him. He paused, almost beneath the tree, dropped to his knees and studied the ground. Rainsford's impulse was to hurl himself down like a panther, but he saw that the general's right hand held something metallic—a small automatic pistol.

The hunter shook his head several times, as if he were puzzled. Then he straightened up and took from his case one of his black cigarettes; its pungent incenselike smoke floated up to Rainsford's nostrils.

Rainsford held his breath. The general's eyes had left the ground and were traveling inch by inch up the tree. Rainsford froze there, every muscle tensed for a spring. But the sharp eyes of the hunter stopped before they reached the limb where Rainsford lay; a smile spread over his brown face. Very deliberately he blew a smoke ring into the air; then he turned his back on the tree and walked carelessly away, back along the trail he had come. The swish of the underbrush against his hunting boots grew fainter and fainter.

The pent-up air burst hotly from Rainsford's lungs. His first thought made him feel sick and numb. The general could follow a trail through the woods at night; he could follow an extremely difficult trail; he must have uncanny powers; only by the merest chance had the Cossack failed to see his quarry.

Rainsford's second thought was even more terrible. It sent a shudder of cold horror through his whole being. Why had the general smiled? Why had he turned back?

Rainsford did not want to believe what his reason told him was true, but the truth was as evident as the sun that had by now pushed through the morning mists. The general was playing with him! The general was saving him for another day's sport! The Cossack was the cat; he was the mouse. Then it was that Rainsford knew the full meaning of terror.

"I will not lose my nerve. I will not."

He slid down from the tree, and struck off again into the woods. His face was set and he forced the machinery of his mind to function. Three hundred yards from his hiding place he stopped where a huge dead tree leaned precariously on a smaller, living one. Throwing off his sack of food, Rainsford took his knife from its sheath and began to work with all his energy.

The job was finished at last, and he threw himself down behind a fallen log a hundred feet away. He did not have to wait long. The cat was coming again to play with the mouse.

Following the trail with the sureness of a bloodhound came General Zaroff. Nothing escaped those searching black

---

2 Suspense *What words and images does the author use in this passage to heighten the suspense?*

Matters of Life and Death *How are Zaroff and Rainsford like a cat and mouse?* 3

Skills Practice

SMALL GROUP

Figurative Language When Connell describes General Zaroff tracking Rainsford, he compares the behavior of both men to animals. He also describes their movements in words and phrases that are usually attributed to animals. Point out that on page 36, the author says that "Rainsford's impulse was to hurl himself down like a panther" and "The Cossack was the cat; he was the mouse."

Break students into small groups and have them reread pages 36 and 37 to find other instances where Connell makes the men sound as if they were animals. Have the groups share their findings with the class.

eyes, no crushed blade of grass, no bent twig, no mark, no matter how faint, in the moss. So intent was the Cossack on his stalking that he was upon the thing Rainsford had made before he saw it. His foot touched it, the general sensed his danger and leaped back with the agility of an ape. But he was not quick enough; the dead tree, delicately adjusted to rest on the cut living one, crashed down and struck the general a glancing blow on the shoulder as it fell; but for his alertness, he must have been smashed beneath it. He staggered, but he did not fall; nor did he drop his revolver. He stood there, rubbing his injured shoulder, and Rainsford, with fear again gripping his heart, heard the general's mocking laugh ring through the jungle.

"Rainsford," called the general, "if you are within sound of my voice, as I suppose you are, let me congratulate you. Not many men know how to make a Malay man-catcher. Luckily, for me, I, too, have hunted in Malacca.[28] You are proving interesting, Mr. Rainsford. I am going now to have my wound dressed; it's only a slight one. But I shall be back."

When the general, nursing his bruised shoulder, had gone, Rainsford took up his flight again. It was flight now, a desperate, hopeless flight, that carried him on for some hours. Dusk came, then darkness, and still he pressed on. The ground grew softer under his moccasins, the vegetation grew ranker, denser; insects bit him savagely. Then, as he stepped forward, his foot sank into the ooze. He tried to wrench it back, but the muck sucked viciously at his foot as if it were a giant leech. With a violent effort, he tore his feet loose. He knew where he was now. Death Swamp and its quicksand.

His hands were tight closed as if his nerve were something tangible that someone in the darkness was trying to tear from his grip. The softness of the earth had given him an idea. He stepped back from the quicksand a dozen feet or so and, like some huge prehistoric beaver, he began to dig.

Rainsford had dug himself in in France when a second's delay meant death. That had been a placid pastime compared to his digging now. The pit grew deeper; when it was above his shoulders, he climbed out and from some hard saplings cut stakes and sharpened them to a fine point. These stakes he planted in the bottom of the pit with the points sticking up. With flying fingers he wove a rough carpet of weeds and branches and with it he covered the mouth of the pit. Then, wet with sweat and aching with tiredness, he crouched behind the stump of a lightning-charred tree.

Visual Vocabulary
A *sapling* is a young tree.

He knew that his pursuer was coming; he heard the padding sound of feet on the soft earth, and the night breeze brought him the perfume of the general's cigarette. It seemed to Rainsford that the general was coming with unusual swiftness; he was not feeling his way along, foot by foot. Rainsford, crouching there, could not see the general, nor could he see the pit. He lived a year in a minute. Then he felt an impulse to cry aloud with joy, for he heard the sharp crackle of the breaking branches as the cover of the pit gave way; he heard the sharp scream of pain as the pointed stakes

28. The *Malay* are a people of southeast Asia, and *Malacca* (mə lak′ ə) is their home region.

4 Make and Verify Predictions About Plot *How do you think Zaroff will act after he returns? Why?*

Suspense *Why does this detail heighten the suspense?* **5**

Teach

Reading Strategy 4

Make and Verify Predictions About Plot

Answer: *He will be more determined and more careful.*

Literary Element 5

Suspense **Answer:** *The detail about Death Swamp and the quicksand raises the question of how Rainsford can avoid death there.*

Literary History ☆

Film Many movies, such as *The Fugitive,* and Alfred Hitchcock's *North by Northwest,* have depicted manhunts. Like this story, these films center on a battle of wits and endurance between the fugitive and the pursuer. A film version of Connell's story was released in 1932.

English Learners

DIFFERENTIATED INSTRUCTION

Early Advanced Remind students that a simile is a comparison of two things using *like* or *as.* Ask students to point out the similes in the story on pages 36 and 37.

- "An apprehensive night crawled slowly by like a wounded snake . . ." *(compares the passing of the night to an injured snake, which would move very slowly)*
- "He flattened himself down on the limb, and through a screen of leaves almost as thick as tapestry." *(compares the leaves to tapestry, a thick fabric)*
- "Rainsford's impulse was to hurl himself down like a panther . . ." *(compares Rainsford's first movement to a panther, which moves very quickly)*

Teach

Literary Element 1

Suspense **Answer:** *The short sentences speed up the pace and show how rapidly Rainsford must think. They add pressure and a feeling of panic to his decision.*

View the Art ★

Answer: *Students may say it would feel frightening, exciting, or awe-inspiring.*

William Trost Richards (1833–1905) began drawing as a boy in Philadelphia. Though he left school to support his family, he was able to study art at the Pennsylvania Academy of Fine Arts. Many of his paintings depict the rugged coast of Cornwall, in southwestern England. Land's End, the subject of this painting, is England's southwesternmost point.

found their mark. He leaped up from his place of concealment. Then he cowered back. Three feet from the pit a man was standing, with an electric torch in his hand.

"You've done well, Rainsford," the voice of the general called. "Your Burmese tiger pit has claimed one of my best dogs. Again you score. I think, Mr. Rainsford, I'll see what you can do against my whole pack. I'm going home for a rest now. Thank you for a most amusing evening."

At daybreak Rainsford, lying near the swamp, was awakened by a sound that made him know that he had new things to learn about fear. It was a distant sound, faint and wavering, but he knew it. It was the baying of a pack of hounds.

Rainsford knew he could do one of two things. He could stay where he was and wait. That was suicide. He could flee. That was postponing the inevitable. For a moment he stood there, thinking. An idea that held a wild chance came to him, and, tightening his belt, he headed away from the swamp.

Land's End—Cornwall, 1888. William Trost Richards. Oil on canvas, 62 x 50 in. The Butler Institute of American Art, Youngstown, OH.

View the Art What might it feel like to stand at the edge of cliffs like these? ★

The baying of the hounds drew nearer, then still nearer, nearer, ever nearer. On a ridge Rainsford climbed a tree. Down a watercourse, not a quarter of a mile away, he could see the bush moving. Straining his eyes, he saw the lean figure of General Zaroff; just ahead of him Rainsford made out another figure whose wide shoulders surged through the tall jungle weeds; it was the giant Ivan, and he seemed pulled forward by some unseen force; Rainsford knew that Ivan must be holding the pack in leash.

They would be on him any minute now. His mind worked frantically. He thought of a native trick he had learned in Uganda. He slid down the tree. He caught hold of a springy young sapling and to it he fastened his hunting knife, with the blade pointing down the trail; with a bit of wild grapevine he tied back the sapling. Then he ran for his life. The hounds raised their voices as

1 Suspense *How do the short sentences add to the feeling of suspense?*

Writing Practice

SPIRAL REVIEW **Write a New Ending**

Tell students that when authors flash forward, they interrupt the normal sequence of events in a story and skip ahead. A flash-forward is similar to a flashback except the action in the story moves into the future. Have students review the last two pages to identify the flash-forward at the very end of the story. Ask students to rewrite the ending of the story without the flash-forward. They can use their imaginations to describe the struggle between Zaroff and Rainsford that resulted in Zaroff's death.

they hit the fresh scent. Rainsford knew now how an animal at bay[29] feels.

He had to stop to get his breath. The baying of the hounds stopped abruptly, and Rainsford's heart stopped, too. They must have reached the knife.

He shinned excitedly up a tree and looked back. His pursuers had stopped. But the hope that was in Rainsford's brain when he climbed died, for he saw in the shallow valley that General Zaroff was still on his feet. But Ivan was not. The knife, driven by the recoil of the springing tree, had not wholly failed.

Rainsford had hardly tumbled to the ground when the pack took up the cry again.

"Nerve, nerve, nerve!" he panted, as he dashed along. A blue gap showed between the trees dead ahead. Ever nearer drew the hounds. Rainsford forced himself on toward that gap. He reached it. It was the shore of the sea. Across a cove he could see the gloomy gray stone of the chateau. Twenty feet below him the sea rumbled and hissed. Rainsford hesitated. He heard the hounds. Then he leaped far out into the sea. . . .

When the general and his pack reached the place by the sea, the Cossack stopped. For some minutes he stood regarding the blue-green expanse of water. He shrugged his shoulders. Then he sat down, took a drink of brandy from a silver flask, lit a cigarette, and hummed a bit from "Madame Butterfly."[30]

29. *At bay* refers to the position of a cornered animal that is forced to turn and confront its pursuers.

30. *Madame Butterfly* is an Italian opera by Giacomo Puccini.

2 Make and Verify Predictions About Plot *What do you think will happen to Rainsford as a result of this jump?*

General Zaroff had an exceedingly good dinner in his great paneled dining hall that evening. With it he had a bottle of *Pol Roger* and half a bottle of *Chambertin.* Two slight annoyances kept him from perfect enjoyment. One was the thought that it would be difficult to replace Ivan; the other was that his quarry had escaped him; of course the American hadn't played the game—so thought the general as he tasted his after-dinner liqueur. In his library he read. At ten he went up to his bedroom. He was deliciously tired, he said to himself, as he locked himself in. There was a little moonlight, so, before turning on his light, he went to the window and looked down at the courtyard. He could see the great hounds, and he called: "Better luck another time," to them. Then he switched on the light.

"Better luck another time."

A man, who had been hiding in the curtains of the bed, was standing there.

"Rainsford!" screamed the general. "How in God's name did you get here?"

"Swam," said Rainsford. "I found it quicker than walking through the jungle."

The general sucked in his breath and smiled. "I congratulate you," he said. "You have won the game."

Rainsford did not smile. "I am still a beast at bay," he said in a low, hoarse voice. "Get ready, General Zaroff."

The general made one of his deepest bows. "I see," he said. "Splendid! One of us is to furnish a repast[31] for the hounds. The other will sleep in this very excellent bed. On guard, Rainsford. . . ."

He had never slept in a better bed, ☆ Rainsford decided.

31. *Repast* means "meal" or "feast."

Matters of Life and Death *What does the phrase "a beast at bay" suggest about Rainsford?* **3**

Teach

Reading Strategy 2

Make and Verify Predictions About Plot

Answer: *Some students may predict his death, while others may predict that he will swim across the cove.*

Big Idea 3

Matters of Life and Death

Answer: *The phrase shows that Rainsford will not behave like a civilized man but rather as a beast in mortal peril; it suggests that he will show no mercy.*

Writer's Technique ☆

Flash-Forward In the last sentence, the story jumps forward in time. A flash-forward is often marked by a blank line, series of asterisks, or text ornament. Connell does not mark the jump, which makes it more startling. Students may need to reread to figure out what happened.

Progress Check

Can students explain suspense?

If No → See Unit 1 Teaching Resources Book, p. 41.

Approaching Level

DIFFERENTIATED INSTRUCTION

Emerging Help students understand that word choice helps authors craft engaging plots and characters as well as convey mood. Connell uses strong, specific, and vivid past-tense verbs throughout his story to advance these goals. Point out examples of these verbs on pages 38 and 39, such as *climbed, surged, tumbled, dashed,* and *rumbled.*

Remind students that the *-ly* ending often signals an adverb in English. Write examples on the chalkboard such as "We walked quickly" and "Our flight was especially smooth." Explain that adverbs modify verbs. Point out Connell's use of adverbs ending in *-ly* on these pages: *worked frantically, stopped abruptly, hardly tumbled,* and *deliciously tired.*

Assess

1. Ivan: his size and skill at torture; Zaroff: his contempt for the weak, coolness in killing, and hunting skill
2. (a) He accidentally falls off a boat while passing the island. (b) The island is far more dangerous than the sea.
3. (a) Zaroff had begun to hunt men. (b) Zaroff recognizes Rainsford's experience and skill and feels challenged by the idea of hunting him.
4. (a) Rainsford, the hunted, kills Zaroff, the hunter. (b) Zaroff may have thought that Rainsford would have committed suicide rather than continue playing.
5. Rainsford's knowledge helps because he uses tricks he had learned while hunting animals to elude and attack Zaroff.
6. Rainsford had no choice but to kill Zaroff, who would have killed him otherwise; Rainsford should have captured Zaroff and sought justice through legal means.
7. Answers will vary.
8. Zaroff only feels alive when causing death. Rainsford can only live if Zaroff dies.
9. Students should explain what characteristics and personality traits led to their choices.

For additional assessment, see Assessment Resources, pp. 43–44.

After You Read

Respond and Think Critically

Respond and Interpret

1. Who did you think was more frightening, Ivan or General Zaroff? Explain.
2. (a)How did Rainsford end up on Ship-Trap Island? (b)What is ironic about the comment, "All he knew was that he was safe from his enemy, the sea"?
3. (a)What solution had General Zaroff found to his problem of boredom with hunting? (b)Why is Zaroff excited to have Rainsford play his "game"?
4. (a)How did the game end? (b)What do you think Zaroff meant when he thought "the American hadn't played the game"?

Analyze and Evaluate

5. Did Rainsford's knowledge, experience, and training as a hunter help him stay alive? Explain.
6. Did Rainsford do the right thing at the end of the story? Defend or criticize his act and explain your reasons.
7. Would you recommend this story to a friend? Why or why not?

Connect

8. **Big Idea** **Matters of Life and Death** What is the relationship between Zaroff and Rainsford, or the hunter and the hunted? Explain.
9. **Connect to Today** If you were making a new movie based on this story, what actors would you cast to play Zaroff and Rainsford? Explain.

Visual Literacy

Plot Diagram

A typical plot diagram is shown here. Create a separate diagram that reflects the plot of "The Most Dangerous Game." Label your diagram so that a viewer can see which important events happen at each stage of the plot.

Group Activity Compare your diagram with a classmate's. Then discuss the following questions:

1. Which parts of the story contain suspense?
2. What makes the ending of this story different from many other stories?

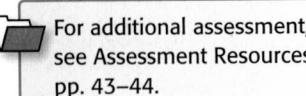

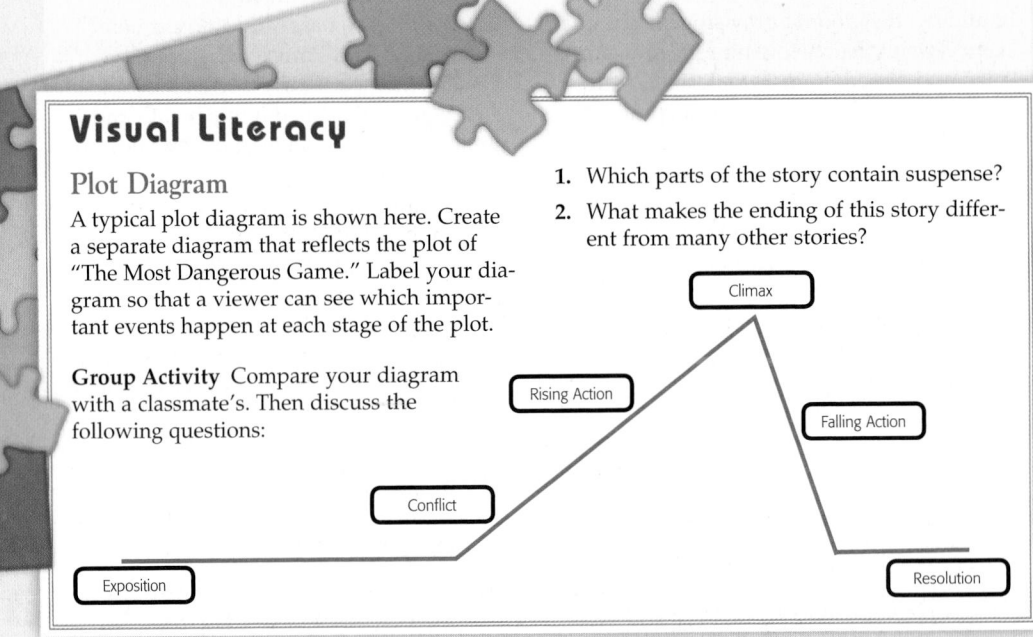

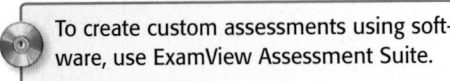

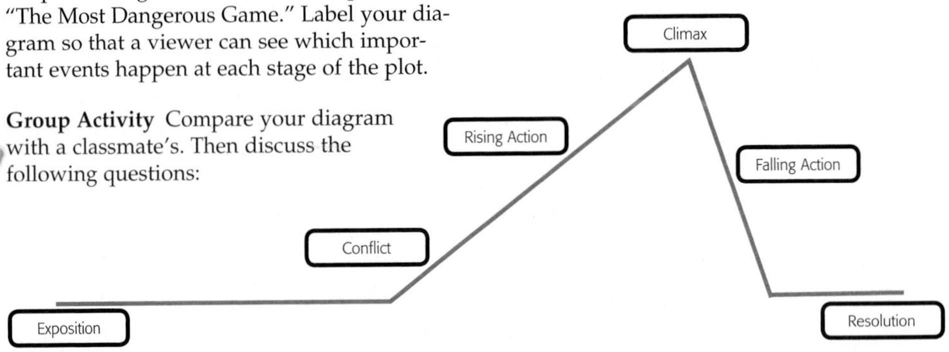

Visual Literacy

1. The long exposition builds suspense.
2. The entire story is filled with suspense.

To create custom assessments online, go to Progress Reporter Online Assessment.

To create custom assessments using software, use ExamView Assessment Suite.

Literary Element Suspense

Writers build **suspense** in several ways. For example, the writer may provide just enough information to keep the question "What will happen next?" burning in the reader's mind.

1. What information did the author include in the title and first three paragraphs to raise questions in readers' minds?
2. How does the setting add to the suspense? Consider not only where events take place but at what time of day.

Review: Conflict

As you learned on page 9, **conflict** is the struggle between opposing forces in a story. An external conflict exists when a character struggles against some outside force, such as another person, nature, society, or fate. An internal conflict is a struggle that takes place within a character's mind.

Partner Activity Meet with a classmate to discuss the conflicts in the story. Use a graphic like the one below to list internal and external conflicts. Create as many internal and external conflict boxes as you need. Discuss whether the story is driven primarily by internal conflicts, external conflicts, or a combination of both. Finally, identify the main conflict in the story and try to capture it in a phrase or short declarative sentence.

External Conflict: Rainsford must battle the sea to get to the island.

External Conflict:

Internal Conflict:

Main Conflict:

LOG ON **Literature** Online

Selection Resources For Selection Quizzes, eFlashcards, and Reading-Writing Connection activities, go to glencoe.com and enter QuickPass code GL49787u1.

Reading Strategy Make and Verify Predictions About Plot

Review the **prediction** chart you made while reading. Based on the story and your predictions, answer the following questions.

1. The story ends abruptly. What do you think is likely to happen next?
2. What story clues support this prediction?

Vocabulary Practice

Practice with Word Origins Studying the etymology, or origin and history, of a word can help you better understand and explore its meaning. Create a word map, like the one below, for each of these vocabulary words from the selection. Use a dictionary for help.

tangible discern condone
imperative zealous

Definition: marked by a constant effort; hard-working

Etymology: Latin *diligere* means "to love"

diligent

Sample Sentence: Sam's diligent studying resulted in high marks this semester.

Academic Vocabulary

Richard Connell **surveyed** the world from a variety of different perspectives.

Survey is an academic word that has different meanings in different contexts. Using context clues, try to figure out the meaning of *survey* in each sentence below and explain the difference between the two meanings.

1. He **surveyed** the forest, hoping to find prey.
2. The company's **survey** revealed customers' opinions about recent product changes.

For more on academic vocabulary, see pages 54–55 and R79–R81.

After You Read

Assess

Literary Element

1. The superlative in the title makes readers wonder, "What is the *most* dangerous game?" The questions of why sailors dread the place add suspense.
2. Because the game occurs on an island, there is no escape. The thick, dangerous jungle and the nighttime hunting create a sense of suspense.

Review: Conflict

External conflicts: the sea, the jungle, the quicksand, and Zaroff; Internal conflicts: Rainsford's battle to stay rational rather than succumb to fear; Main conflict: the life-and-death struggle between Rainsford and Zaroff; the story is driven by a combination of internal and external conflicts

Reading Strategy

1. Answers will vary.
2. Students should supoort their answer with clues from the story.

Academic Vocabulary

In the first sentence, *survey* means to examine by observing and in the second sentence it means to examine by questioning.

Vocabulary Practice

tangible: Etymology: Latin tangere means "to touch"; Definition: real; able to be touched; Sample Sentence: There is no tangible proof that the book was stolen.

discern: Etymology: Latin discernere means "to separate" or "to distinguish between"; Definition: to recognize; Sample Sentence: From a distance, the young child could discern the figure of her mother in the crowd.

condone: Etymology: Latin condonare means "forgive"; Definition: to voluntarily overlook something; Sample Sentence: We condone dishonesty by not punishing those who tell lies.

imperative: Etymology: Latin imperare means "to command"; Definition: necessary; Sample Sentence: It is imperative to stay calm in an emergency.

zealous: Etymology: Greek zelos means "ardor, jealousy"; Definition: having a strong interest in something; Sample Sentence: The zealous learner couldn't get her hands on enough books to satisfy her curiosity.

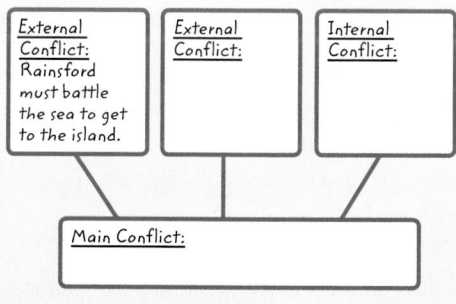

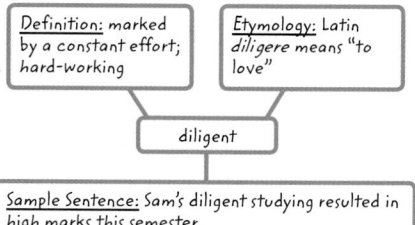

After You Read

Assess

Respond Through Writing

Students' summaries should

- be no more than 100 words
- include the main plot points
- be written in the present tense
  use correct grammar and punctuation

A student who meets all of these criteria should receive the equivalent of a 4-point response.

A student who fully meets two or partially meets three of these criteria should receive the equivalent of a 3-point response.

A student who fully meets one or partially meets two of these criteria should receive the equivalent of a 2-point response.

A student who partially meets one of these criteria should receive the equivalent of a 1-point response.

For grammar practice, see Unit 1 Teaching Resources Book, p. 45.

Respond Through Writing

Summary

Report Story Events When you write a summary of a story, you report the main events in sequence. A summary does not include personal opinions. In about 100 words, write a plot summary of "The Most Dangerous Game." Write your summary in the present tense.

Learning Objectives

In this assignment, you will focus on the following objectives:

Writing: Writing a summary.

Grammar: Understanding how to correct verb tense.

Understand the Task When you report events in **sequence,** you present them in the order as told in the original. In a **plot summary,** you report the main events and explain the main characters' problems and how they are resolved.

Prewrite Skim or reread the story, taking notes on what happens. You may want to create a timeline or plot outline (see page 40) as you take notes. Then answer questions about the main characters' problems and how they are resolved.

Draft Refer to the events you traced in your timeline as you write your summary. To show sequence, try using transitional words and phrases, such as *at first, next, when, then, before,* and *after.* Make sure you also include information about the characters' problems and resolutions. Be precise, and avoid including unnecessary details. Below is a sample summary of "The Lady, or the Tiger?" which appears on pages 12–18.

EXAMPLE:

In "The Lady, or the Tiger?" the king's daughter is in love with a young man, but the king doesn't like him. The king sentences the man to go to the arena where he must choose between two doors. Behind one is a man-eating tiger. Behind the other is a lady for him to marry. The princess is jealous of the lady behind the door, and finds out which door conceals her. When the young man enters the arena, the princess gives him a signal. He then opens the door she indicates. The reader is left to decide if the lady or the tiger emerges.

Revise Ask a classmate to check that your summary identifies the main characters, their problems, and how the problems are resolved, and that you have reported events in their original sequence. Revise your summary based on your classmate's comments.

Edit and Proofread Proofread your paper, correcting any errors in grammar, spelling, and punctuation. Use the Grammar Tip in the side column for help with correcting verb tense in your summary.

Grammar Tip

Present-Tense Verbs

When summarizing a story, use verbs in the present tense—even if events in the story are told in the past tense or if they happened in the past in the story. If you find yourself using the verbs *was* or *were* or using the verb form ending in *-ed,* such as *entered,* you are writing in the past tense. Go back and change the verbs to present tense.

EXAMPLE:

The princess ~~was~~ is jealous of the lady.

Assessment Practice

SPIRAL REVIEW SMALL GROUP

Revise Remind students that good writing is the result of good revision. Students should revise their papers to improve coherence and word choice. In small groups, have students discuss tips for improving their writing in the areas of organization, word choice, and coherence. Ask students to share their tips with the class to create a rubric for revising. Encourage students to use the list as they revise their summaries.

Before You Read

The Leap

Meet **Louise Erdrich**
(born 1954)

Storytelling is as natural as breathing for Louise Erdrich. Part Chippewa, she attributes her passion for writing to her Native American roots.

Growing Up The oldest of seven children, Erdrich was born in Minnesota and raised in North Dakota, where both of her parents worked for the Bureau of Indian Affairs. Her father, of German descent, and her mother, born on the Turtle Mountain Ojibwe (Chippewa) Reservation, both encouraged her early writing efforts. Her father rewarded her by paying her five cents for each story she wrote, and her mother affirmed her daughter's talent by creating book covers for the stories.

Erdrich was one of the first women admitted to Dartmouth University, where she continued to write and where she also met her future husband, Michael Dorris, a professor of Native American Studies. She and Dorris became successful literary collaborators, as well as parents to six children. They also became well-known and respected voices of Native American culture.

> *"All of our searches involve trying to discover where we are from."*
>
> —Louise Erdrich

Genres and Influences While some of Erdrich's earliest published work is poetry, her writing falls into a wide range of genres. Her novels, which include *Love Medicine* and *The Beet Queen*, were bestsellers as well as critical successes. Her short stories appear in numerous collections and her essays are also widely read and acclaimed. Among the many writers who influenced Erdrich's work are Flannery O'Connor and Gabriel García Márquez. Novelists Jane Austen, Toni Morrison, and William Faulkner also significantly shaped Erdrich's style and content.

Themes Erdrich often employs Native American themes, and many of her stories center on the notion of returning home. One of her most important themes is personal identity, both within the family and within the culture. She writes often, as she does in "The Leap," about women's personal power and the sacred struggle of mothers.

Erdrich is the recipient of several prizes for her writing, including the Pushcart Prize for poetry and the National Book Critics Circle Award for fiction. Erdrich continues to write, and she runs a small bookstore in Minnesota.

LOG ON **Literature** Online

Author Search For more about Louise Erdrich, go to glencoe.com and enter QuickPass code GL49787u1.

Before You Read

Focus

Bellringer Options

Selection Focus Transparency 3

Daily Language Practice Transparency 5

Or obtain a copy of the painting *The Circus* by Georges Seurat. Have students study it and then discuss circus acts and the courage they require.

Ask: What do you think motivates people to take great risks, physical or otherwise? *(Students may mention a desire for fame, to save a loved one, or to feel excitement.)* Have students consider as they read what compels the narrator's mother toward heroism and how her heroism affects the narrator.

Selection Skills

The Leap

Literary Elements
- Flashback (SE pp. 45–52)
- Setting (SE p. 52)

Listening/Speaking/Viewing Skills
- Interview (SE p. 53)
- Analyze Art (SE p. 48, 50; TE p. 45)

Reading Skills
- Sequence (SE pp. 45–53)

Vocabulary Skills
- Word Parts (SE pp. 44, 53)
- Academic Vocabulary (SE p. 53)

Writing Skills/Grammar
- Subordinate Clauses (TE p. 50)
- Compare and Contrast (TE p. 46)

Before You Read

Focus

Summary

The narrator is living in her childhood home with her blind, elderly mother. She states that she owes her life to her mother three times. She describes these three occasions in the story.

For summaries in languages other than English, see Unit 1 Teaching Resources Book, pp. 48–53.

Vocabulary

Grouping Words Have students come up with ways to categorize new vocabulary words. The categories can be as simple or as complex as students desire. Grouping the words in familiar categories can help the students remember the meaning of new vocabulary words. Then have students use each word in a sentence.

For additional vocabulary practice, see Unit 1 Teaching Resources Book, pp. 56–57.

For additional context, see Glencoe Visual Vocabulary CD-ROM.

Literature and Reading Preview

Connect to the Story

What personal qualities does it require to take a "leap" against great odds? Freewrite for a few minutes about a time when you or someone you know had to make such a leap. Describe the event and the results of the leap.

Build Background

Until the 1950s, most circus troupes performed in huge canvas tents that they carried around with them as they traveled from town to town. The canvas, however, like the sawdust that covered the dirt floors of the circus ring, was flammable, and circus tents sometimes became the scenes of terrible fires.

Set Purposes for Reading

Big Idea Matters of Life and Death

As you read "The Leap," ask yourself, How are death and life bound together in each part of the story?

Literary Element Flashback

A **flashback** is an interruption in the chronological order of a narrative to show an event that happened earlier. A flashback gives readers information that may help explain the main events of a story. As you read, ask yourself, How does the author use flashbacks to deepen the intensity of the story?

Reading Strategy Identify Sequence

Identifying sequence is finding the logical order of ideas or events. Understanding the sequence of ideas in a piece helps you follow a writer's train of thought. As you read, ask yourself, How does Erdrich use sequence to create greater suspense?

Tip: Make a Sequence Chain Create two sequence chains as you read the story: one showing the main events presented in flashbacks, and one showing the main events presented in present time.

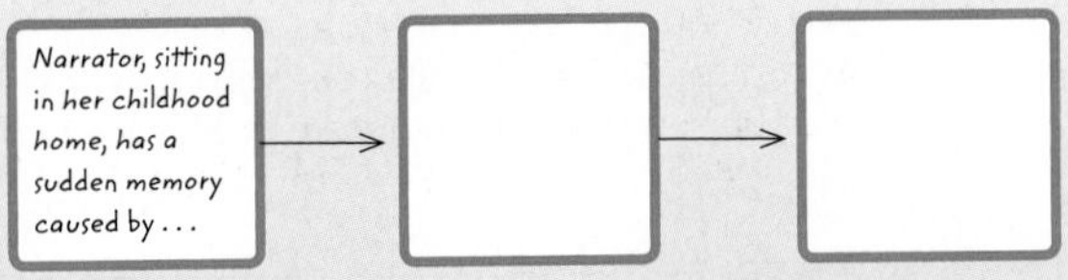

Narrator, sitting in her childhood home, has a sudden memory caused by . . .

Learning Objectives

For pages 43–53

In studying this text, you will focus on the following objectives:

Literary Study: Analyzing flashback.

Reading: Identifying sequence.

Speaking and Listening: Conducting an interview.

Vocabulary

commemorate (kə mem′ ə rāt′) *v.* to preserve the memory of; p. 46 *I chose to commemorate my grandfather's life by researching his past.*

extricate (eks′ trə kāt′) *v.* to release from entanglement or difficulty; to set free; p. 48 *John worked hard to extricate the animal from the trap.*

constricting (kən strikt′ ing) *adj.* restricting; limiting; p. 49 *The tiny space was constricting for the large man.*

perpetually (pər pech′ o͞o əl ē) *adv.* constantly; unceasingly; p. 49 *The busy waiters were perpetually moving from table to table.*

Tip: Word Parts When you encounter unfamiliar words, look for word parts such as prefixes and suffixes. Then look for familiar roots. For example, when you remove *com-* from *commemorate,* you can see the root *memor,* also used in *memory.*

Listening, Speaking, and Viewing Practice

SPIRAL REVIEW PARTNERS

Identify Sequence With a partner, have each student create a sequence chart to list the major activities he or she has completed so far during the day. For example, a student might say that she woke up, ate breakfast, dressed, took the bus to school, and so on. Ask a volunteer to present his or her chart to the class.

THE LEAP

Louise Erdrich

My mother is the surviving half of a blindfold trapeze act, not a fact I think about much even now that she is sightless, the result of encroaching and stubborn cataracts. She walks slowly through her house here in New Hampshire, lightly touching her way along walls and running her hands over knickknacks, books, the drift of a grown child's belongings and castoffs.

Au Cirque, 1976. Marc Chagall. Oil on canvas, 48 x 43¼ in. Private collection. ★

Teach

Big Idea 1

Matters of Life and Death

Say: Keep these questions in mind as you read: How is the narrator's approach to life and death different from her mother's? *(It is measured and logical, whereas her mother's is instinctive and emotional.)* **Ask:** How are the two approaches the same? *(Both people want to live.)*

View the Art ★

Marc Chagall (1887–1985) was born and grew up in Russia. He later lived in Paris and the United States. Chagall's work includes stage sets, a skill reflected in this painting's strong sense of place. The story's vividly described setting is suggested by the painting.

For an audio recording of this selection, use Listening Library Audio CD-ROM.

Readability Scores

Dale-Chall: 6.4

DRP: 64

Lexile: 1260

English Learners

DIFFERENTIATED INSTRUCTION

Beginning/Early Intermediate Explain that a trapeze artist does tricks or stunts high above the ground. Trapeze artists switch from one bar to another while sailing through the air. The author's mother did this blindfolded, which is extremely difficult. **Ask:** What physical abilities should a trapeze artist have? *(agility, speed, quickness)*

Intermediate Help students improve ***reading fluency*** by reading passages aloud. Have a student read aloud the opening paragraph. Then follow the reading by discussing unfamiliar words. Students may not be familiar with *knick-knacks* or *cataract*. Instruct students to use a dictionary to find the meaning of other unfamiliar words.

Teach

Reading Strategy 1

Identify Sequence
Answer: *The narrator is going to describe the three events in chronological order. The phrase "the first time" is a clue.*

For additional practice using the reading skill or strategy, see Unit 1 Teaching Resources Book, p. 55.

Literary Element 2

Flashback **Answer:** *She describes what she now thinks the day in the past was like. This gives a smooth link from present to past.*

Cultural History ☆

United States Climate People in the western United States can see storms coming because flat, open spaces make the sky visible. In the East, hills, trees, and buildings block views of the sky.

She has never upset an object or as much as brushed a magazine onto the floor. She has never lost her balance or bumped into a closet door left carelessly open.

It has occurred to me that the catlike precision of her movements in old age might be the result of her early training, but she shows so little of the drama or flair one might expect from a performer that I tend to forget the Flying Avalons. She has kept no sequined costume, no photographs, no fliers or posters from that part of her youth. I would, in fact, tend to think that all memory of double somersaults and heart-stopping catches had left her arms and legs were it not for the fact that sometimes, as I sit sewing in the room of the rebuilt house in which I slept as a child, I hear the crackle, catch a whiff of smoke from the stove downstairs, and suddenly the room goes dark, the stitches burn beneath my fingers, and I am sewing with a needle of hot silver, a thread of fire.

I owe her my existence three times. The first was when she saved herself. In the town square a replica tent pole, cracked and splintered, now stands cast in concrete. It **commemorates** the disaster that put our town smack on the front page of the Boston and New York tabloids.[1] It is from those old newspapers, now historical records, that I get my information. Not from my mother, Anna of the Flying Avalons, nor from any of her in-laws, nor certainly from the other half of her particular act, Harold Avalon, her first husband. In one news account it says, "The day was mildly overcast, but nothing in the air or temperature gave any hint of the sudden force with which the deadly gale would strike."

I have lived in the West, where you can see the weather coming for miles, and it is ☆ true that out here we are at something of a disadvantage. When extremes of temperature collide, a hot and cold front, winds generate instantaneously behind a hill and crash upon you without warning. That, I think, was the likely situation on that day in June. People probably commented on the pleasant air, grateful that no hot sun beat upon the striped tent that stretched over the entire center green. They bought their tickets and surrendered them in anticipation. They sat. They ate caramelized popcorn and roasted peanuts. There was time, before the storm, for three acts. The White Arabians of Ali-Khazar rose on their hind legs and waltzed. The Mysterious Bernie folded himself into a painted cracker tin, and the Lady of the Mists made herself appear and disappear in surprising places. As the clouds gathered outside, unnoticed, the ringmaster cracked his whip, shouted his introduction, and pointed to the ceiling of the tent, where the Flying Avalons were perched.

Visual Vocabulary
Here, *White Arabians* refers to performing Arabian horses.

They loved to drop gracefully from nowhere, like two sparkling birds, and blow kisses as they threw off their plumed helmets and high-collared capes. They laughed and flirted openly as they beat their way up again on the trapeze bars. In

1. Here, *tabloids* are newspapers with pages half the size of an ordinary newspaper page. They contain brief news articles and many pictures.

1 Identify Sequence *How is the narrator going to order the events of the story? How do you know?*

Vocabulary
commemorate (kə mem′ ə rāt′) *v.* to preserve the memory of

Flashback *How does this sentence serve as a transition from the narrator's present thoughts to her description of an event in the past?* **2**

Writing Practice

Write a Compare-and-Contrast Essay Remind students that the purpose of a comparison and contrast essay is to explain how two things are alike, how they differ, and then to draw one or more conclusions based on those similarities and differences. In "The Leap," Erdrich writes of Anna's transformation from someone with an exciting and unusual career to a life as a homemaker and an avid reader. Ask students to write about how Anna's two lives are similar and how they are different. Students should then draw a conclusion about Anna's character.

the final vignette[2] of their act, they actually would kiss in midair, pausing, almost hovering as they swooped past one another. On the ground, between bows, Harry Avalon would skip quickly to the front rows and point out the smear of my mother's lipstick, just off the edge of his mouth. They made a romantic pair all right, especially in the blindfold sequence.

That afternoon, as the anticipation increased, as Mr. and Mrs. Avalon tied sparkling strips of cloth onto each other's face and as they puckered their lips in mock kisses, lips destined "never again to meet," as one long breathless article put it, the wind rose, miles off, wrapped itself into a cone, and howled. There came a rumble of electrical energy, drowned out by the sudden roll of drums. One detail not mentioned by the press, perhaps unknown—Anna was pregnant at the time, seven months and hardly showing, her stomach muscles were that strong. It seems incredible that she would work high above the ground when any fall could be so dangerous, but the explanation—I know from ☆ watching her go blind—is that my mother lives comfortably in extreme elements. She is one with the constant dark now, just as the air was her home, familiar to her, safe, before the storm that afternoon.

From opposite ends of the tent they waved, blind and smiling, to the crowd below. The ringmaster removed his hat and called for silence, so that the two above could concentrate. They rubbed their hands in chalky powder, then Harry launched himself and swung, once, twice, in huge calibrated[3] beats across space. He hung from his knees and on the third swing stretched wide his arms, held his hands out to receive his pregnant wife as she dove from her shining bar.

It was while the two were in midair, their hands about to meet, that lightning struck the main pole and sizzled down the guy wires,[4] filling the air with a blue radiance that Harry Avalon must certainly have seen through the cloth of his blindfold as the tent buckled and the edifice[5] toppled him forward, the swing continuing and not returning in its sweep, and Harry going down, down into the crowd with his last thought, perhaps, just a prickle of surprise at his empty hands.

My mother once said that I'd be amazed at how many things a person can do within the act of falling. Perhaps, at the time, she was teaching me to dive off a board at the town pool, for I associate the idea with midair somersaults. But I also think she meant that even in that awful doomed second one could think, for she certainly did. When her hands did not meet her husband's, my mother tore her blindfold away. As he swept past her on the wrong side, she could have grasped his ankle, the toe-end of his tights, and gone down clutching him. Instead, she changed direction. Her body twisted toward a heavy wire and she managed to hang on to the braided metal, still hot from the lightning strike. Her palms were burned so terribly that once healed they bore no lines, only the blank scar tissue of a quieter future. She was lowered, gently, to the sawdust ring just underneath the dome of the

2. A *vignette* (vin yet′) is a short scene, sketch, or incident.
3. Here, *calibrated* means "precisely timed and measured."

4. A *guy* is a rope, cord, or cable used for steadying, guiding, or holding something. In this case, *guy wires* hold the main pole of the tent steady.
5. An *edifice* is a building or other structure (here, the tent), especially a large, impressive one.

3 Matters of Life and Death *What is the meaning of the quote from the newspaper article?*

Identify Sequence *Where would you place the conversation the narrator mentions here within the chronology of events described in the story so far?* **4**

Teach

Big Idea 3

Matters of Life and Death

Answer: *The two will never kiss again because they will be separated forever by death.*

Reading Strategy 4

Identify Sequence

Answer: *It was in the past ("once said") but after the narrator was born.*

APPROACHING Ask approaching-level students to think of words that identify sequence. Ask volunteers to share those words with the class. (first, next, last, finally)

Writer's Technique ☆

Motif A motif is a significant word, description, idea, or image that is repeated throughout a literary work and is related to its theme. In this story, Erdrich uses blindness as a motif.

Approaching Level

DIFFERENTIATED INSTRUCTION

Emerging Explain to students that the story takes place in the present, but the author tells about her mother's life in the past. On pages 46 and 47, the narrator describes a disaster her mother survived many years ago. Have students list the events on that day in the order that they occurred, starting at the paragraph which begins, "That afternoon . . ." on page 47.

Answer: *(tied sparkling strips of cloth onto each other's faces; kissed; waved to the crowd; rubbed their hands in powder; Harry launched; stretched his arms to catch his wife; tent buckles and he falls; Anna twists and grabs a heavy wire).*

Teach

Literary Element 1

Characterization Discuss techniques the author uses to characterize the narrator. Note the first-person point of view.

Ask: How does this affect characterization? *(The reader's idea of the main character is based on the narrator's own thoughts.)*

APPROACHING For approaching-level students, **ask:** How would you describe the narrator? *(She is introspective, sensitive, and analytical. She is loving and appreciates her mother's love.)*

Big Idea 2

Matters of Life and Death
Answer: *Students should infer that the unseen horizon is death.*

View the Art ★

Answer: *Students should point to elements of the stained glass such as the bright colors and the figures: an audience member and a performer.*

French artist Henri de Toulouse-Lautrec (1864–1901) is known for his paintings of residents of the Montmartre area of Paris at the end of the nineteenth century. This is one of his works done in stained glass by Louis Comfort Tiffany (1848–1933), an American artist known for his work in that medium.

canvas roof, which did not entirely settle but was held up on one end and jabbed through, torn, and still on fire in places from the giant spark, though rain and men's jackets soon put that out.

Three people died, but except for her hands my mother was not seriously harmed until an overeager rescuer broke her arm in **extricating** her and also, in the process, collapsed a portion of the tent bearing a huge buckle that knocked her unconscious. She was taken to the town hospital, and there she must have hemorrhaged,[6] for they kept her, confined to her bed, a month and a half before her baby was born without life.

Harry Avalon had wanted to be buried in the circus cemetery next to the original Avalon, his uncle, so she sent him back with his brothers. The child, however, is buried around the corner, beyond this house and just down the highway. 1 Sometimes I used to walk there just to sit. She was a girl, but I rarely thought of her as a sister or even as a separate person really. I suppose you could call it the egocentrism[7] of a child, of all young children, but I considered her a less finished version of myself.

When the snow falls, throwing shadows among the stones, I can easily pick hers out from the road, for it is bigger than the others and in the shape of a lamb at rest, its legs curled beneath. The carved lamb looms larger as the years pass, though it is probably only my eyes, the vision shifting, as what is close to me blurs and distances sharpen. In odd moments, I think it is the edge drawing near, the edge of everything, the unseen horizon we do not really speak of in the eastern woods. And it also seems to me, although this is probably an idle fantasy, that the statue is growing more sharply etched, as if, instead of weathering itself into a porous mass, it is hardening on the hillside with each snowfall, perfecting itself.

It was during her confinement in the hospital that my mother met my father. He was called in to look at the set of her arm,

Au Nouveau Cirque, Papa Chrysanthème. After Henri de Toulouse-Lautrec. 1894–95. Louis Comfort Tiffany. Musée d'Orsay, Paris.

View the Art Louis Comfort Tiffany created art in many media, but he is best known for his work in stained glass. How well does this stained glass window capture the mood of a circus? ★

6. To *hemorrhage* (hem′ ər ij) is to bleed heavily or excessively—in this case, probably because of internal injuries.
7. *Egocentrism* means "self-centeredness."

Vocabulary

extricate (eks′ trə kāt′) *v.* to release from entanglement or difficulty; to set free

Matters of Life and Death *What is the "unseen horizon" that the narrator mentions?* 2

Listening and Speaking Practice

SPIRAL REVIEW SMALL GROUP

Respond to Literature On page 48, the narrator discusses a sister who died before she was born. Break students into groups and have them reread page 48 to answer the following question: How does the narrator feel about her sister? Students should provide examples from the text to support their answers. Students should take notes during their discussion.

which was complicated. He stayed, sitting at her bedside, for he was something of an armchair traveler and had spent his war quietly, at an air force training grounds, where he became a specialist in arms and legs broken during parachute training exercises. Anna Avalon had been to many of the places he longed to visit—Venice, Rome, Mexico, all through France and Spain. She had no family of her own and was taken in by the Avalons, trained to perform from a very young age. They toured Europe before the war, then based themselves in New York. She was illiterate.

It was in the hospital that she finally learned to read and write, as a way of overcoming the boredom and depression of those weeks, and it was my father who insisted on teaching her. In return for stories of her adventures, he graded her first exercises. He bought her her first book, and over her bold letters, which the pale guides of the penmanship pads could not contain, they fell in love.

I wonder if my father calculated the exchange he offered: one form of flight for another. For after that, and for as long as I can remember, my mother has never been without a book. Until now, that is, and it remains the greatest difficulty of her blindness. Since my father's recent death, there is no one to read to her, which is why I returned, in fact, from my failed life where the land is flat. I came home to read to my mother, to read out loud, to read long into the dark if I must, to read all night.

3 Once my father and mother married, they moved onto the old farm he had inherited but didn't care much for. Though he'd been thinking of moving to a larger city, he settled down and broadened his practice in this valley. It still seems odd to me, when they could have gone anywhere else, that they chose to stay in the town where the disaster had occurred, and which my father in the first place had found so **constricting**. It was my mother who insisted upon it, after her child did not survive. And then, too, she loved the sagging farmhouse with its scrap of what was left of a vast acreage of woods and hidden hay fields that stretched to the game park. 3

I owe my existence, the second time then, to the two of them and the hospital that brought them together. That is the debt we take for granted since none of us asks for life. It is only once we have it that we hang on so dearly.

I was seven the year the house caught fire, probably from standing ash. It can rekindle, and my father, forgetful around the house and **perpetually** exhausted from night hours on call, often emptied what he thought were ashes from cold stoves into wooden or cardboard containers. The fire could have started from a flaming box, or perhaps a buildup of creosote inside the chimney was the culprit.[8] It started right around the stove, and the heart of the house was gutted. The babysitter, fallen asleep in my father's den on the first floor, woke to find the stairway to my upstairs room cut off by flames. She used the phone, then ran outside to stand beneath my window.

When my parents arrived, the town volunteers had drawn water from the fire pond and were spraying the outside of the house, preparing to go inside after me, not

---

8. *Creosote* (krē′ ə sōt′), an oily liquid that comes from the tar in wood and coal, would be a natural suspect as the *culprit,* or guilty party, in a chimney fire.

Identify Sequence *How do the words "second time" remind you of the sequence in the story, and to what do they refer?* 4

Vocabulary

constricting (kən strikt′ ing) *adj.* restricting; limiting

perpetually (pər pech′ o͞o əl ē) *adv.* constantly; unceasingly

Teach

Literary Element 3

Character Point out the narrator's descriptions of her father, beginning with "Once my father and mother . . ." and include the cause of the fire.

Ask: What is the father like? *(He is devoted to his wife—willing to ignore his own desires to live as she chooses—absent-minded, and hardworking.)*

Reading Strategy 4

Identify Sequence

Answer: *The narrator continues to present the past events in chronological order. The second time is the event she has just described: her parents' meeting at the hospital.*

English Learners

DIFFERENTIATED INSTRUCTION

Beginning/Early Intermediate Explain that *denotation* refers to the literal meaning of a word. It is the definition of the word you would find in a dictionary. *Connotation,* on the other hand, refers to the associations connected to a word and the emotions the word suggests. Have students read the sentences that include the words *perpetually* and *constricting.* Ask a volunteer to explain their connotation. *(Possible answers:* Constricting *does not sound comfortable; it makes you think of something negative, like being unable to breathe.* Perpetually *means lasting a long time. In the context of this story, it has a negative connotation; the father is always tired.)*

Teach

Literary Element 1

Flashback Answer: *This shows the importance of the circus episode in her life.*

View the Art ★

Answer: *The painting portrays the love, warmth, and security that the mother in the story provides for her daughter.*

Pablo Picasso (1881–1973), one of the foremost painters of the twentieth century, adopted many different artistic styles in his career. Here, his work mirrors the story: the mother and child are depicted realistically, but the background, like the story setting, is perhaps a bit fantastical.

La Maternité, 1901. Pablo Picasso. Oil on burlap. Private collection.

View the Art The title of this painting means "motherhood." How does this painting reflect the relationship of the mother and the daughter in the story? ★

As soon as I awakened, in the small room that I now use for sewing, I smelled the smoke. I followed things by the letter then, was good at memorizing instructions, and so I did exactly what was taught in the second-grade home fire drill. I got up, I touched the back of my door before opening it. Finding it hot, I left it closed and stuffed my rolled-up rug beneath the crack. I did not hide under my bed or crawl into my closet. I put on my flannel robe, and then I sat down to wait.

Outside, my mother stood below my dark window and saw clearly that there was no rescue. Flames had pierced one side wall, and the glare of the fire lighted the massive limbs and trunk of the vigorous old elm that had probably been planted the year the house was built, a hundred years ago at least. No leaf touched the wall, and just one thin branch scraped the roof. From below, it looked as though even a squirrel would have had trouble jumping from the tree onto the house, for the breadth of that small branch

knowing at the time that there was only one staircase and that it was lost. On the other side of the house, the superannuated[9] extension ladder broke in half. Perhaps the clatter of it falling against the walls woke me, for I'd been asleep up to that point.

9. Something that is *superannuated* has been set aside as too old and out-of-date to use.

Flashback *The author links this flashback to earlier details of the setting that launched her retelling of the circus episode. Why might she have done this?* 1

Grammar Practice

SPIRAL REVIEW PARTNERS

Subordinate Clauses Point out the first sentence which begins on page 49: "When my parents arrived, the town volunteers had drawn water from the fire pond and were spraying the outside of the house . . ."

Say: This sentence begins with a subordinate, or dependent clause. A subordinate clause begins with a subordinate conjunction and has a subject and a verb. It is not a complete thought, however, so it cannot stand alone as a sentence. It must be attached to a dependent clause.

Have students work with a partner to search for other examples of subordinate clauses at the beginning or end of sentences in the story. Ask students to identify the subordinate conjunction in each of these clauses.

Visual Vocabulary
An *extension ladder* has two or more sections joined together by a sliding mechanism that allows the ladder to be extended to its total length.

was no bigger than my mother's wrist.

Standing there, beside Father, who was preparing to rush back around to the front of the house, my mother asked him to unzip her dress. When he wouldn't be bothered, she made him understand. He couldn't make his hands work, so she finally tore it off and stood there in her pearls and stockings. She directed one of the men to lean the broken half of the extension ladder up against the trunk of the tree. In surprise, he complied. She ascended. She vanished. Then she could be seen among the leafless branches of late November as she made her way up and, along her stomach, inched the length of a bough that curved above the branch that brushed the roof.

Once there, swaying, she stood and balanced. There were plenty of people in the crowd and many who still remember, or think they do, my mother's leap through the ice-dark air toward that thinnest extension, and how she broke the branch falling so that it cracked in her hands, cracked louder than the flames as she vaulted with it toward the edge of the roof, and how it hurtled down end over end without her, and their eyes went up, again, to see where she had flown.

I didn't see her leap through air, only heard the sudden thump and looked out my window. She was hanging by the backs of her heels from the new gutter we had put in that year, and she was smiling. I was not surprised to see her, she was so matter-of-fact. She tapped on the window. I remember how she did it, too. It was the friendliest tap, a bit tentative, as if she was afraid she had arrived too early at a friend's house. Then she gestured at the latch, and when I opened the window she told me to raise it wider and prop it up with the stick so it wouldn't crush her fingers. She swung down, caught the ledge, and crawled through the opening. Once she was in my room, I realized she had on only underclothing, a bra of the heavy stitched cotton women used to wear and step-in, lace-trimmed drawers. I remember feeling light-headed, of course, terribly relieved, and then embarrassed for her to be seen by the crowd undressed.

I was still embarrassed as we flew out the window, toward earth, me in her lap, her toes pointed as we skimmed toward the painted target of the fire fighter's net.

I know that she's right. I knew it even then. As you fall there is time to think. Curled as I was, against her stomach, I was not startled by the cries of the crowd or the looming faces. The wind roared and beat its hot breath at our back, the flames whistled. I slowly wondered what would happen if we missed the circle or bounced out of it. Then I wrapped my hands around my mother's hands. I felt the brush of her lips and heard the beat of her heart in my ears, loud as thunder, long as the roll of drums.

2 Identify Sequence *Restate the sequence of events presented in this paragraph in your own words.*

Flashback *How do you know that the flashback is over?* **3**

Teach

Reading Strategy 2

Identify Sequence

Answer: *1. Her mother asks her father to unzip her dress. 2. Her mother tears off her dress. 3. Her mother asks a man to lean the ladder against the tree. 4. He does so. 5. She climbs the ladder and then the tree.*

Literary Element 3

Flashback Answer: *The change in verb tense indicates the end of the flashback as does the use of the word "then" in the second sentence to indicate the past.*

APPROACHING To aid approaching-level students in their comprehension of the Literary Element, ask a student to reread the explanation of flashback on page 44.

To check students' understanding of the selection, see Unit 1 Teaching Resources Book, p. 59.

Approaching Level

DIFFERENTIATED INSTRUCTION

Established Help students understand the Literary Element on page 50. Point out the words "the room that I now use for sewing." Explain that the author uses these words to link this part of the story with page 46 when she first mentions the sewing room. Tell students that both of the flashbacks in the story—the flashback of the accident at the circus and the flashback of the fire—are very long. When the author links the end of the story with the beginning, it makes the story more coherent.

To practice **reading fluency,** ask a volunteer to read aloud the second paragraph on page 46. Explain that the author's description ("I hear the crackle, catch a whiff . . .") refers to the fire they have just read about.

After You Read

Assess

1. The circus event (the risky trapeze act and fierce storm); the rescue (deadly fire, amazing leap)
2. (a) Lightning hit the pole, sending Harry to his death. Anna saved herself. (b) She wanted to forget the death of her husband and baby.
3. (a) She was trapped inside her burning house. (b) Their lives seemed miraculous and dramatic; both survived deadly events.
4. (a) The mother's first leap to save herself and the one to save her daughter (b) A leap of faith, such as the mother's courage in starting a new life and the daughter's faith that her mother would save her
5. Its unusual details stimulate the reader's interest.
6. (a) The sister seems unreal at first but later becomes a more definite presence. (b) As people age, they can visualize death more clearly.
7. Their calm attitude was realistic. The mother was trained to take great risks; a child might not appreciate the danger she faced or the finality of death.
8. Students may mention the mother's courage in times of danger, her ability to move on after tragedy, the daughter's ability to stay calm during the fire, and her faith in her mother.

Progress Check

Can students explain flashback?

If No → See Unit 1 Teaching Resources Book, p. 54.

After You Read

Respond and Think Critically

Respond and Interpret

1. What do you think is the most dramatic event in this story? Give details to explain your choice.
2. (a)What caused the disaster at the circus, and what happened to the Flying Avalons? (b)In your opinion, why didn't the mother save her costume or anything related to this period in her life?
3. (a)What happened to the narrator when she was seven? (b)What comparisons do you think the narrator would make between her life and her mother's? Provide evidence from the story to substantiate your claims.
4. (a)What specific event or events in this story does the title refer to? (b)What else might the title refer to?

Analyze and Evaluate

5. How effective is the author at capturing the reader's attention with the opening passage of this story? Explain.
6. (a)How does the narrator's attitude toward her dead half-sister change? (b)What does information about this sibling add to the story?

Connect

7. **Big Idea** **Matters of Life and Death** Both the narrator and her mother reacted to matters of life and death in this story. Did you find their reactions realistic? Explain.
8. **Connect to the Author** Louise Erdrich often writes about the personal power or strength of women. How do the narrator and her mother each show their personal strengths in this story?

Literary Element Flashback

A **flashback** can take the form of an earlier event, a prior conversation, or a complete episode. Flashbacks help the reader understand characters as well as events. Often presented as a memory of the narrator, a flashback may be sparked by one or more cues, such as a sound or odor associated with a prior experience or a visit to a related setting.

1. How do a sound, an odor, and a certain setting work together to spark the narrator's memory at the beginning of "The Leap"?
2. What other sensory details help to reveal the similarities between the two main flashbacks in the story?
3. Which of her mother's character traits were displayed throughout the narrator's flashbacks? How did the author's choice to use flashbacks help to better portray these traits? Give reasons for your opinion.

Review: Setting

As you learned on pages 8–9, **setting** is the time and place in which the events of a literary work occur. Setting includes not only the physical surroundings, but also the ideas, customs, values, and beliefs of a particular time and place.

Partner Activity Work with a classmate to record details of the setting. Create a chart like the one below and complete it with details from the story.

	Time	Place
Past	June, years ago	circus tent in a small New Hampshire town
Present		

Literary Element

1. They remind the narrator of her rescue from the fire.
2. The stitches that burn the narrator's fingers, the mother's burned hands; the mother's grace in the circus, her rescue of the narrator; the falls of the unborn child and the narrator, both held by the mother
3. Resilience, strength, grace, intuitiveness, balance, devotion; The reader sees the traits in action so they seem more real.

Review: Setting

Past: Time: Unnamed past—narrator's childhood and before; **Place:** Hospital; Cemetery; Burning house **Present: Time:** Unnamed present—narrator's adulthood; **Place:** New Hampshire farmhouse—sewing room

Reading Strategy Identify Sequence

ACT Skills Practice

1. Which event in the life of the narrator's mother occurs first?
   - **A.** She breaks her arm.
   - **B.** She loses her eyesight.
   - **C.** She leaps from the tree.
   - **D.** She marries a doctor.

Vocabulary Practice

Practice with Word Parts For each boldfaced vocabulary word in the left column, identify the related word with a shared root in the right column. Write both words and underline the part they have in common. Use a dictionary to look up the meaning of the related word. Then explain how it is related to the vocabulary word.

1. commemorate	restriction
2. extricate	intricately
3. constricting	petition
4. perpetually	memorial

Example:
innovation, renovate

Renovate means "to make new again."
An innovation is something that is new.

Academic Vocabulary

In "The Leap," the narrator ***sustains*** *suspense by revealing each life-saving incident slowly.*

If a business keeps growing from year to year, you could say that it has been successfully **sustaining** its growth. To study this word further, fill out the graphic organizer below.

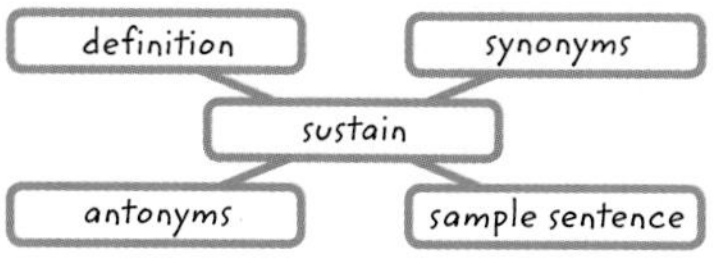

For more on academic vocabulary, see pages 54–55 and R79–R81.

Speaking and Listening

Interview

Assignment Imagine that you are a radio news reporter at the scene of the burning house. Interview witnesses (played by classmates) and create a news report to present the facts to your class. If you play the role of a witness, answer questions correctly and effectively.

Prepare Write a list of relevant questions phrased in mature and respectful language. Your questions should reflect your understanding of the situation. Leave space after each question to note answers.

Interview Speak to your interview subjects individually, taking notes on each subject's responses to your questions. In addition, make audio recordings of one or two statements from each "eyewitness."

During your interview, follow these tips:

- Allow your subject to respond completely; don't interrupt.
- Make frequent eye contact.
- If necessary, ask further questions to clarify information.
- Review your subject's statements as a final check.
- Thank your subject for his or her cooperation.

Report Organize your notes and compile the information to create a radio report. Write the news story in an engaging and objective style. Include audio clips that support or describe key details. Keep the clips brief and identify the speaker and his or her connection to the scene. Present your report to the class.

Evaluate Compare your final report to your original interview notes. Was your final report accurate? Did it include the most important details?

LOG ON **Literature** Online

Selection Resources For Selection Quizzes, eFlashcards, and Reading-Writing Connection activities, go to glencoe.com and enter QuickPass code GL49787u1.

After You Read

Assess

Reading Strategy

1. A is the correct answer. The mother breaks her arm as a result of her fall in the tent. The other events occur later in her life.

Vocabulary

1. commemorate, memorial
   A memorial helps people remember a person or event from the past. To commemorate something is to preserve its memory.
2. extricate, intricately
   Intricately means "in a complicated way." When you extricate something, you pull it out of entanglement, or complications.
3. constricting, restriction
   A restriction is something, such as a rule, that limits what you can do. Constricting refers to something that is tight and limiting.
4. perpetually, petition
   Perpetually means going or seeking constantly. To petition someone is to seek that person's approval on a request.

Academic Vocabulary

GO should include the following:
definition—to support or keep going
synonyms—maintain, preserve
antonyms—disrupt, terminate
sentence/image—(sample sentence) On the hike, I sustained my energy with water and snack bars.

Speaking and Listening

Students' reports should
- accurately reflect the details of the fire and the leap in Erdrich's short story
- be written in an engaging and objective style
- focus on information gathered from "eyewitnesses"
- analyze discrepancies between accounts
- include audio clips from "eyewitnesses"

Vocabulary Workshop

Academic Vocabulary

Focus

Ask students to identify their favorite subject. Then ask students to list words that are specific to their favorite subject. For instance, if a student likes history class, she may write the words *Rennaisance, imperialism,* and *rights*. After allowing students a few minutes to write, ask students to share words they listed. Follow with a discussion of why learning the vocabulary of a subject is beneficial.

Teach

Remind students that before beginning a new chapter in any subject, they should scan the material for key words. Point out that if their books do not always list vocabulary words, they can scan their textbooks for bold-faced words and research their meaning online or using a dictionary.

Learning Objectives

For pages 54–55

In this workshop, you will focus on the following objective:

Vocabulary: Understanding academic vocabulary.

For a complete list of academic vocabulary words, see pages R79–R81.

Tip

These key academic vocabulary words often appear on standardized tests.

Analyze: to systematically and critically examine all parts of an issue or event

Classify or categorize: to group items, based on common characteristics

Compare: to show how things are alike

Contrast: to show how things are different

Describe: to present a sketch or an impression

Discuss: to systematically write about all sides of an issue or event

Evaluate: to make a judgment and support it with evidence

Explain: to clarify or make plain

Vocabulary Workshop

Academic Vocabulary

What Is Academic Vocabulary? Words that are commonly used in academic texts such as textbooks, directions, and tests, are called **academic vocabulary.** Learning academic vocabulary will help you read, write, and research in many academic areas. These words will also help you succeed on standardized tests.

Different Kinds of Words Some words are specific to certain disciplines, or areas of study. For example, the words *onomatopoeia, free verse,* and *simile* pertain to literature. Other words, such as *analysis, definition,* and *estimate* are used in many areas of study. The charts below show more examples of both kinds of words.

Discipline-Specific Words

Discipline	Words
Math	integer, polynomial, ratio
Science	ecosystem, electron, polymer
Social Studies	commodity, expatriate, nomadic

General Academic Vocabulary

data	environment
factors	indicate
major	principle
process	theory

Academic Words in This Book You will learn about discipline-specific and general academic vocabulary words in this book. Words that are specific to literature and language arts will most often be introduced and explained in Literary Element and Reading Strategy features before and after you read literature selections. You will encounter more general academic vocabulary words in features called Academic Vocabulary that appear after literature selections.

Vocabulary Practice

Word Journal

Encourage students to keep a word journal in which they list new words as they learn them. Students should define these words and use each word in a sentence. They can divide the journal by subject if they want to include academic vocabulary, but encourage them to categorize the journal in a way that is meaningful and helpful for them.

A student might categorize the journal by words that are difficult to spell, words that have more than one meaning, or parts of speech. Ask students if they can come up with any other ways to divide their journals and to share their ideas with the class.

Multiple-Meaning Words Many academic vocabulary words, such as *uniform,* have more than one meaning. The first meaning is a literal, more common definition that you may already be familiar with (*uniform* means "the clothes worn by a specific group of people"). The second definition is more academic and may be unfamiliar to you (*uniform* also means "being consistently the same"). These two definitions are often related, however. In the case of *uniform,* the second, academic definition is connected to the common definition because "the clothes worn by a specific group of people" make those people consistently the same (at least in dress). The chart below lists additional examples of academic words with more than one meaning.

Words	Definitions	Relationship
conclusion	*n.* the outcome, such as of a story *n.* a generalization based on what a person has learned	Both definitions involve an outcome
select	*v.* to choose *adj.* of special importance or value	Both definitions involve choice: objects of special value would be chosen over similar objects of lesser value

As you encounter academic vocabulary words in this book, you will master the words through various activities. You'll have a chance to practice these activities in the exercise below.

Practice Using what you know about academic vocabulary, complete the following items.

1. *The princess in "The Lady, or the Tiger?" has* ***motivation*** *to direct the young man to the door with the tiger as well as to the door with the young woman.*

   Motivation is an academic word. In more casual conversation, someone might ask you where you find **motivation** to strive for excellence in a sport or school. Using context clues, try to figure out the meaning of the word in the sentence about "The Lady, or the Tiger?" above. Check your guess in a dictionary.

2. *Now that you know the basic elements of a short story, you could create your own* ***manual*** *on how to read and analyze them.*

   Manual is a word that has more than one meaning. Using context clues, try to figure out the meaning of *manual* in each sentence below and explain the difference between the two meanings.

   a. Before Eric started driving his parents' car, he read the owner's **manual.**

   b. Because the electric pencil sharpener was broken, Simone had to use the classroom's **manual** pencil sharpener.

Tip

These key academic vocabulary words often appear on standardized tests.

Illustrate: to provide examples or to show with a picture or another graphic

Infer: to read between the lines or to use knowledge or experience to draw conclusions, make generalizations, or form predictions

Justify: to prove or to support a position with specific facts and reasons

Predict: to tell what will happen in the future based on an understanding of prior events and behaviors

State: to briefly and concisely present information

Summarize: to give a brief overview of the main points of an event or issue

Trace: to present the steps or stages in a process or an event in sequential or chronological order

LOG ON **Literature** Online

Vocabulary For more vocabulary practice, go to glencoe.com and enter QuickPass code GL49787u1.

Assess

1. Students should determine that motivation means "something that gives a person reason to take a specific action."
2. **a.** a book explaining how to do something
   b. created, operated, or done by hand

For additional vocabulary practice, see Glencoe Interactive Vocabulary CD-ROM.

English Learners

DIFFERENTIATED INSTRUCTION

Advanced Less proficient readers may have a hard time understanding the definitions of complex academic terms. Tell students to search for more than one definition of troublesome words. If after comparing several definitions of the same word, they still do not understand the term, they should ask a teacher or fellow student to help them define the term.

Ask students if they have recently learned any new academic terms. Encourage them to share the new words and their definitions with the class. Also, in a discussion, ask students to share their tricks for learning new vocabulary.

Before You Read

Focus

Bellringer Options

Selection Focus Transparency 4

Daily Language Practice Transparency 6

Or **write on the board:** What scares you? Engage students in a discussion of what they find frightening. Encourage them to consider a broad range of topics, including places, sounds, animals, and insects. Broaden the discussion to entertainment, such as movies and books. Discuss the paradox of enjoying being frightened.

Before You Read

The Cask of Amontillado

Meet **Edgar Allan Poe**
(1809–1849)

Crumbling mansions, hearts that continue to beat after death, and insane killers are just a few of the ingredients in Edgar Allan Poe's fiction. His stories are not simple spine-tinglers, however. Poe travels deep into psychological territory, exploring guilt, rage, sorrow, madness, and fear.

A Loner Poe's life itself was a dark and often haunting tale. His parents were poverty-stricken actors. Poe's father left when Poe was two years old, and his mother died when he was three. Separated from his siblings, Poe was raised by John and Frances Allan. As Poe entered adolescence, he had a serious falling out with his foster father, who disapproved of his desire to write. Poe spent a few years in the army to try to regain his foster father's approval, but once it was clear that Allan was through with him, Poe moved to Baltimore and focused on writing.

> *"From childhood's hour I have not been*
> *As others were—I have not seen*
> *As others saw—"*
>
> —Edgar Allan Poe, "Alone"

Turmoil and Grief Poe began to write poetry as a teenager and published his first collection of poems in 1829. His short stories began appearing in magazines, and in 1833, one of his tales won a prize. This led to a job as a literary editor, a position that brought him great success, but which he lost due to his changeable nature and alcoholism. Most of the remainder of Poe's short life was spent in poverty and pain. He continued to work, but he did not achieve the public success he felt he deserved. Alcohol remained a problem, and he was often ill. He watched the love of his life, his wife Virginia Clemm, waste away and die from tuberculosis. Poe's loneliness, pain, and general inability to connect with others helped forge his uniquely dark vision.

A Literary Giant Poe's essays and reviews are still read today for their literary insights. His poetry, including such famous works as "The Raven" and "The Bells," lives on in countless collections of America's best writing. Perhaps most of all, his fictional works continue to frighten and delight readers worldwide.

Poe is classified as an American Romantic writer, a detective fiction writer, and a Gothic writer. Some critics refer to Poe as the first truly modern writer because he probed the individual and the mystery of the self.

LOG ON **Literature** Online

Author Search For more about Edgar Allan Poe, go to glencoe.com and enter QuickPass code GL49787u1.

Selection Skills

The Cask of Amontillado

Literary Elements
- Mood (SE pp. 57–66)
- Suspense (SE p. 66)

Listening/Speaking/Viewing Skills
- Analyze Art (TE p. 60)
- Visual Literacy (SE p. 65)

Reading Skills
- Paraphrase (SE pp. 57–66)
- Make a Chart (SE p. 57)

Vocabulary Skills
- Context Clues (SE p. 66)
- Academic Vocabulary (SE p. 66)

Writing Skills/Grammar
- Write a Research Report (SE p. 67)
- Colons (SE p. 67)

Literature and Reading Preview

Connect to the Story

What kinds of wrongs or injuries would make a person want to take revenge? Do you think getting revenge makes people feel better or worse? Discuss these questions with a partner.

Build Background

Much of this story is set in the catacombs of the Montresor family, which were also used as a wine cellar. Catacombs are underground cemeteries. The walls of the narrow passageways are lined with niches where bodies are placed. Carnival is an often uninhibited celebration involving costume parades, feasting, and other festivities. It takes place mainly in Roman Catholic regions during the weeks before Lent, a holy season of abstinence and prayer.

Set Purposes for Reading

Big Idea Matters of Life and Death

As you read "The Cask of Amontillado," ask yourself, How do details in the story evoke the idea of death?

Literary Element Mood

Mood is the emotional quality of a literary work. A writer's choice of language, subject matter, setting, and tone, as well as such sound devices as rhyme and rhythm, contribute to creating mood. As you read "The Cask of Amontillado," ask yourself, What emotions does the writing make me feel?

Reading Strategy Paraphrase

Paraphrasing is putting something into your own words. Unlike a summary, a paraphrase is usually about the same length as the original passage. As you read, ask yourself, How would I rephrase this passage in contemporary language?

Tip: Make a Chart Paraphrase difficult sentences, or parts of sentences, as you read.

Author's Words	My Paraphrase
p. 58 "The thousand injuries of Fortunato I had borne as I best could."	I had put up with the many wrongs Fortunato did to me as well as I could.

Learning Objectives

For pages 56–66

In studying this text, you will focus on the following objectives:

Literary Study: Analyzing mood.

Reading: Paraphrasing.

Vocabulary

preclude (pri klo͞od′) *v.* to prevent; to make impossible; p. 58 *Failing grades preclude the possibility of playing in Friday's basketball game.*

impunity (im pū′ nə tē) *n.* freedom from punishment, harm, or bad consequences; p. 58 *No one here knew him, so he thought he could lie with impunity.*

accost (ə kôst′) *v.* to approach and speak to, especially in an aggressive manner; p. 59 *The beggars accost and scare the shoppers.*

explicit (eks plis′ it) *adj.* definitely stated, clearly expressed; p. 60 *Ms. DePietro gave explicit instructions for each stage of the assignment.*

implore (im plôr′) *v.* to ask earnestly; to beg; p. 63 *Some parents implore their children to study.*

Before You Read

Focus

Summary

The narrator, Montresor, vows to exact revenge on Fortunato for an unspecified insult. He leads Fortunato into the catacombs beneath his palazzo. When they reach a niche in the cellar wall, Montresor chains Fortunato to the wall and fills in the niche with bricks and mortar. At the story's end, he states that the crime has gone undetected for fifty years.

For summaries in languages other than English, see Unit 1 Teaching Resources Book, pp. 61–66.

Interactive Read and Write

Other options for teaching this selection can be found in

- **Interactive Read and Write for EL Students, pp. 1–14**
- **Interactive Read and Write for Approaching-Level Students, pp. 1–14**
- **Interactive Read and Write for On-Level Students, pp. 1–14**

Vocabulary

Use New Words in New Ways Explain that many students have difficulty remembering the definitions of new words. Ask students to study the list of words on page 57. Instruct students to write a paragraph using the vocabulary words. Then ask students to use each word in a sentence. Volunteers may share their answers with the class.

For additional vocabulary practice, see Unit 1 Teaching Resources Book, p. 69.

English Learners

DIFFERENTIATED INSTRUCTION

Beginning/Early Intermediate Point out that on page 56 Poe is described as a "literary giant." Help students better understand this phrase. Brainstorm some literary giants and write their names on the board *(William Shakespeare, Emily Dickinson, Mark Twain, Eudora Welty)*.

Ask: What makes a writer a literary giant? *(Students may say that people have enjoyed their writing for many years and that they are famous and talented.)*

Teach

Reading Strategy 1

Paraphrase Discuss paraphrasing with students. **Say:** The first few paragraphs are the most demanding part of this story. The sentences are long and contain many difficult vocabulary words. Have students read closely and then paraphrase the first paragraph of the story. *(Possible Answer: I had always dealt with Fortunato's mistreatment as best I could, but this time he went too far. You know me well enough to know I would not threaten him. I will wait, and get my revenge without getting into trouble. True revenge does not harm the person taking it, but Fortunato must know that I am getting him back.)*

For additional practice using the reading skill or strategy, see Unit 1 Teaching Resources Book, p. 68.

For an audio recording of this selection, use Listening Library Audio CD-ROM.

Readability Scores

Dale-Chall: 9.8
DRP: 55
Lexile: 790

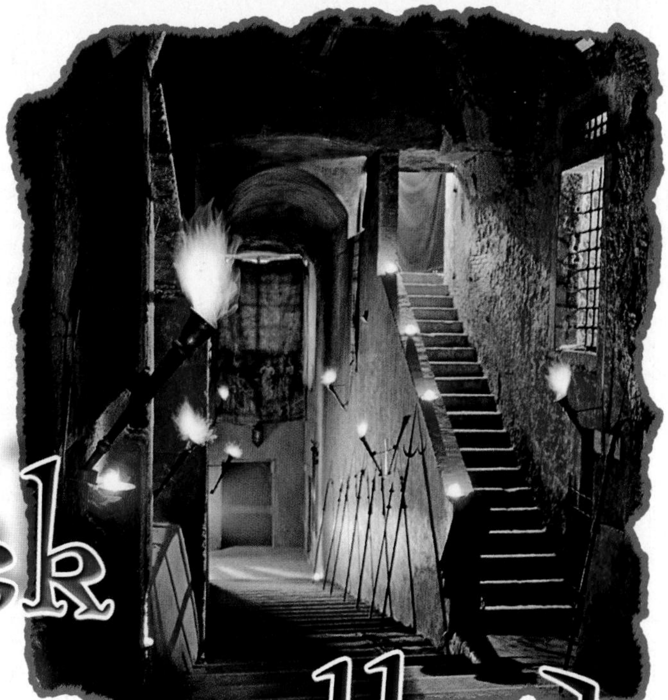

The Cask of Amontillado

Edgar Allan Poe

The thousand injuries of Fortunato[1] I had borne as I best could; but when he ventured upon insult, I vowed revenge. You, who so well know the nature
1 of my soul, will not suppose, however, that I gave utterance to a threat. *At length* I would be avenged; this was a point definitively settled—but the very definitiveness with which it was resolved, **precluded** the idea of risk. I must not only punish, but punish with **impunity.** A wrong is unredressed when retribution overtakes its redresser. It is equally unredressed when the avenger fails to make himself felt as such to him who has done the wrong.[2] 1

It must be understood, that neither by word nor deed had I given Fortunato cause

1. *Fortunato* (fôr′ to͞o nä′ tō)

2. *[A wrong is . . . done the wrong.]* These sentences might be rephrased this way: "A wrong is not avenged if the avenger either is punished for taking revenge or does not make the wrongdoer aware that he is taking revenge."

Vocabulary

preclude (pri klo͞od′) *v.* to prevent; to make impossible

Vocabulary

impunity (im pū′ nə tē) *n.* freedom from punishment, harm, or bad consequences

Vocabulary Practice

SMALL GROUP SPIRAL REVIEW **Use New Words** Explain that this story uses elaborate language, which may be difficult to understand at first. Break students into small groups. Have them read the definitions for the vocabulary words on these pages: *preclude, impunity, accosted,* and *explicit.* Have them write a sentence using each of the vocabulary words. Then ask them to use a dictionary to look up the following words on these pages. Have them write each word in a sentence:

- unredressed
- virtuoso
- imposture
- surmounted
- conical
- absconded
- sconces
- catacombs

to doubt my good-will. I continued, as was my wont, to smile in his face, and he did not perceive that my smile *now* was at the thought of his immolation.[3]

He had a weak point—this Fortunato—although in other regards he was a man to be respected and even feared. He prided himself on his connoisseurship[4] in wine. Few Italians have the true virtuoso spirit. For the most part their enthusiasm is adopted to suit the time and opportunity—to practice imposture upon the British and Austrian *millionnaires.* In painting and gemmary Fortunato, like his countrymen, was a quack—but in the matter of old wines he was sincere. In this respect I did not differ from him materially: I was skillful in the Italian vintages myself, and bought largely whenever I could.

"How remarkably well you are looking today!"

It was about dusk, one evening during the supreme madness of the carnival season, that I encountered my friend. He **accosted** me with excessive warmth, for he had been drinking much. The man wore motley.[5] He had on a tight-fitting parti-striped dress, and his head was surmounted by the conical cap and bells. I was so pleased to see him, that I thought I should never have done wringing his hand.

I said to him: "My dear Fortunato, you are luckily met. How remarkably well you are looking today! But I have received a pipe of what passes for Amontillado,[6] and I have my doubts." **3**

"How?" said he. "Amontillado? A pipe? Impossible! And in the middle of the carnival!"

"I have my doubts," I replied; "and I was silly enough to pay the full Amontillado price without consulting you in the matter. You were not to be found, and I was fearful of losing a bargain."

"Amontillado!"

"I have my doubts."

"Amontillado!"

"And I must satisfy them."

"Amontillado!"

"As you are engaged, I am on my way to Luchesi.[7] If anyone has a critical turn, it is he. He will tell me——"

"Luchesi cannot tell Amontillado from Sherry."

"And yet some fools will have it that his taste is a match for your own."

"Come, let us go."

"Whither?"

"To your vaults."

"My friend, no; I will not impose upon your good nature. I perceive you have an engagement. Luchesi—"

"I have no engagement;—come."

"My friend, no. It is not the engagement, but the severe cold with which I perceive

---

3. Here, *immolation* means "death or destruction."
4. *Connoisseurship* (kon ′ ə sur ′ ship) is expert knowledge that qualifies one to pass judgment in a particular area.
5. *Motley* is the multicolored costume of a court jester or clown.
6. A *pipe* is a wine barrel that holds 126 gallons. *Amontillado* (ə môn tē yä ′ dō) is a kind of pale, dry sherry from Spain.
7. *Luchesi* (lo͞o kā ′ sē)

2 Matters of Life and Death *What is the narrator's attitude toward the destruction of Fortunato?*

Vocabulary

accost (ə kôst ′) *v.* to approach and speak to, especially in an aggressive manner

Mood *How would you characterize this opening exchange between the two main characters?* **4**

Teach

Big Idea 2

Matters of Life and Death **Answer:** *He smiles at the thought of it; it gives Montresor pleasure.*

APPROACHING **Ask:** How do this comment and others on the first page affect your feelings about the narrator? Have students point out specific examples to support their opinions. *(Students may say they feel he is evil, based on details that highlight his obsession and delight with revenge.)*

Literary Element 3

Irony Irony is the contrast between appearance and reality.

Ask: Why is it ironic that Montresor says Fortunato is luckily met? *(Since Montresor plans to kill Fortunato, the meeting is hardly lucky for him.)*

Literary Element 4

Mood **Answer:** *It is friendly, cordial, and enthusiastic.*

English Learners

DIFFERENTIATED INSTRUCTION

Beginning/Early Intermediate English language learners may have particular difficulty with Poe's sentence structure. To improve ***reading fluency*** have students read a paragraph aloud and paraphrase what they have read at the end of each paragraph. Remind them that paraphrasing is restating the text in their own words. Model paraphrasing by reading aloud the first paragraph of the story. Then paraphrase the paragraph.

Say: The narrator has put up with Fortunato hurting him for a long time. Now he wants revenge. He wants to punish Fortunato without getting caught. He also wants Fortunato to know it is he who is punishing him.

Encourage students to discuss language they find unclear before continuing to the next section.

Teach

Reading Strategy 1

Paraphrase **Answer:** *Putting on my black mask and pulling my cape around me, I let him rush me home. Montresor is disguised so that no one will recognize him; he is making it seem as if Fortunato is in control of the situation.*

Carnival in Rome, 1839. Aleksandr Petrovich Myasoedov. Oil on canvas. State Russian Museum, St. Petersburg.

View the Art This painting depicts a street scene during Carnival. How would you describe the atmosphere in this painting? How does it compare with the opening scene from this story?

you are afflicted. The vaults are insufferably damp. They are encrusted with niter."[8]

"Let us go, nevertheless. The cold is merely nothing. Amontillado! You have been imposed upon. And as for Luchesi, he cannot distinguish Sherry from Amontillado."

Thus speaking, Fortunato possessed himself of my arm. Putting on a mask of black silk, and drawing a *roquelaure* closely about my person, I suffered him to hurry me to my palazzo.[9]

There were no attendants at home; they had absconded to make merry in honor of the time. I had told them that I should not return until the morning, and had given them **explicit** orders not to stir from the house. These orders were sufficient, I well knew, to insure their immediate disappearance, one and all, as soon as my back was turned.

I took from their sconces two flambeaux,[10] and giving one to Fortunato, bowed him through several suites of rooms to the archway that led into the vaults. I passed down a long and winding staircase, requesting him to be cautious as he followed. We came at length to the foot of the descent, and stood together on the damp ground of the catacombs of the Montresors.

The gait of my friend was unsteady, and the bells upon his cap jingled as he strode.

"The pipe?" said he.

"It is farther on," said I; "but observe the white web-work which gleams from these cavern walls."

8. *Niter* is a salt-like substance found in cool, damp places.
9. A *roquelaure* (rôk ə lor′) is a knee-length cloak that was popular in the 1700s. A *palazzo* (pə lät′sō) is a mansion or palace.
10. *Sconces* are wall brackets that hold candles or torches, and *flambeaux* (flam′ bō′) are lighted torches.

1 Paraphrase *Restate this sentence in your own words.*

Vocabulary

explicit (eks plis′ it) *adj.* definitely stated; clearly expressed

Writing Practice

SPIRAL REVIEW **Write Dialogue** Have students review the dialogue between Fortunato and Montresor on these pages. Point out the following techniques that Poe uses to make the dialogue seem realistic:

- The characters speak in incomplete sentences.
- Dashes are used at the end of a speech to indicate interruptions.
- Exclamation points are used occasionally to add strong emotion to the characters' comments.

Ask students to write a brief dialogue between Fortunato and Montresor, revealing the insult that causes Montresor to take revenge. Have them use Poe's techniques to make the dialogue realistic. Remind students to start a new paragraph each time a character speaks and to use quotation marks around spoken words. Point out that it is not always necessary to say "he said" or "she said."

He turned toward me, and looked into my eyes with two filmy orbs that distilled the rheum of intoxication.[11]

"Niter?" he asked, at length.

"Niter," I replied. "How long have you had that cough?"

"Ugh! ugh! ugh!—ugh! ugh! ugh!—ugh! ugh! ugh!—ugh! ugh! ugh!—ugh! ugh! ugh!"

My poor friend found it impossible to reply for many minutes.

"It is nothing," he said, at last.

"Come," I said, with decision, "we will go back; your health is precious. You are rich, respected, admired, beloved; you are happy, as once I was. You are a man to be missed. For me it is no matter. We will go back; you will be ill, and I cannot be responsible. Besides, there is Luchesi——"

"Enough," he said; "the cough is a mere nothing; it will not kill me. I shall not die of a cough."

"True—true," I replied; "and, indeed, I had no intention of alarming you unnecessarily; but you should use all proper caution. A draft of this Medoc[12] will defend us from the damps."

Here I knocked off the neck of a bottle which I drew from a long row of its fellows that lay upon the mold.

"Drink," I said, presenting him the wine.

He raised it to his lips with a leer. He paused and nodded to me familiarly, while his bells jingled.

"I drink," he said, "to the buried that repose[13] around us."

"And I to your long life."

He again took my arm, and we proceeded.

"These vaults," he said, "are extensive."

"The Montresors," I replied, "were a great and numerous family."

"I forget your arms."

"A huge human foot d'or, in a field azure; the foot crushes a serpent rampant[14] whose fangs are imbedded in the heel."

"And the motto?"

"*Nemo me impune lacessit.*"[15]

"Good!" he said.

The wine sparkled in his eyes and the bells jingled. My own fancy grew warm with the Medoc. We had passed through walls of piled bones, with casks and puncheons[16] intermingling, into the inmost recesses of the catacombs. I paused again, and this time I made bold to seize Fortunato by an arm above the elbow.

"The niter!" I said; "see, it increases. It hangs like moss upon the vaults. We are below the river's bed. The drops of moisture trickle among the bones. Come, we will go back ere it is too late. Your cough——"

"It is nothing," he said; "let us go on. But first, another draft of the Medoc."

I broke and reached him a flagon[17] of De Grâve. He emptied it at a breath. His eyes flashed with a fierce light. He laughed

Visual Vocabulary
Arms is short for "coat of arms," an arrangement of figures and symbols on or around a shield that, along with a motto, represents one's ancestry.

11. *[filmy orbs . . . intoxication]* This phrase describes Fortunato's eyes as clouded and watery from excessive drinking.
12. *Medoc* (mā dôk′) is a French red wine. A *draft* is the amount taken in one swig or swallow.
13. To *repose* is to lie at rest, either sleeping or in death.
14. The Montresor family's coat of arms includes a golden foot on a sky-blue background and a snake rising up.
15. The *motto* is Latin for "Nobody provokes me with impunity."
16. *Casks* and *puncheons* are large containers for storing liquids.
17. The *flagon* is a narrow-necked bottle with a handle.

2 Mood *What words in this passage suggest danger?*

Matters of Life and Death *How do these details add to the growing sense of entrapment in the story?* **3**

Teach

Literary Element 2

Mood Answer: *The word* alarming *suggests danger, and the request to "use all proper caution" also suggests that danger is lurking.*

APPROACHING Ask approaching-level students to think of other words that might suggest danger. *(warning, harm, risk, peril)*

Big Idea 3

Matters of Life and Death
Answer: *The mention of bones brings to mind death, while the references to catacombs suggest being trapped and cut off from the outside world.*

Advanced Learners

DIFFERENTIATED INSTRUCTION

Change the Point of View Challenge advanced students to rewrite the story from Fortunato's point of view. Remind them that the story is written from the third-person point of view. If they rewrite the story from Fortunato's point of view, he will tell the story and students will use the pronoun "I." Before they begin, brainstorm Fortunato's characteristics.

Ask: What can you tell about Fortunato from the story? Write their responses on the chalkboard. *(Fortunato knows a lot about wine, likes to drink, wears motley, coughs when he is cold, is a mason, can be rude [calls Luchesi an ignoramus])*

Teach

Literary Element 1

Mood **Answer:** *The characters are now surrounded by signs of death. Bones are piled to the ceiling. It is disturbing that the dead have not been left in peace; one wall of bones has been torn down. These details create a feeling of fear and horror.*

View the Art ★

The catacombs beneath Paris were originally limestone quarries. As churchyards began to fill, the quarries became catacombs, or underground cemeteries. They cover about 300 km under Paris and are estimated to hold from five to seven million graves.

★

and threw the bottle upward with a gesticulation I did not understand.

I looked at him in surprise. He repeated the movement—a grotesque one.

"You do not comprehend?" he said.

"Not I," I replied.

"Then you are not of the brotherhood."

"How?"

"You are not of the masons."[18]

"Yes, yes," I said; "yes, yes."

"You? Impossible! A mason?"

"A mason," I replied.

"A sign," he said.

"It is this," I answered, producing a trowel from beneath the folds of my *roquelaure.*

"You jest," he exclaimed, recoiling a few paces. "But let us proceed to the Amontillado."

"Be it so," I said, replacing the tool beneath the cloak, and again offering him my arm. He leaned upon it heavily. We continued our route in search of the Amontillado. We passed through a range of low arches, descended, passed on, and descending again, arrived at a deep crypt,[19] in which the foulness of the air caused our flambeaux rather to glow than flame.

At the most remote end of the crypt there appeared another less spacious. Its walls had been lined with human remains, piled to the vault overhead, in the fashion of the great catacombs of Paris. Three sides of this interior crypt were still ornamented in this manner. From the fourth the bones had been thrown down, and lay promiscuously upon the earth, forming at one point a mound of some size. Within the wall thus exposed by the displacing of the bones, we perceived a still interior recess, in depth about four feet, in width three, in height six or seven. It seemed to have been constructed for no especial use within itself, but formed merely

18. Here, *masons* is short for "Freemasons," an organization of stonecutters and bricklayers that was formed in the Middle Ages. By the time of this story, the masons had become a social group with secret rituals and signs.

19. A *crypt* is a burial chamber.

Mood *What emotion does the description in this paragraph create?* 1

Reading Practice

SMALL GROUP SPIRAL REVIEW **Compare and Contrast** In small groups, have students compare and contrast Montresor and Fortunato based on the details in the story. Ask students to create a graphic web showing each character's traits. **Ask:** What have you learned about Montresor's character? About Fortunato's? *(Students may say Montresor is obsessed and evil, and Fortunato is foolish and narcissistic.)*

Students should review the text to find page numbers indicating where each trait is displayed. When they finish, discuss the webs in class. Have students discuss the traits they listed on their webs. Encourage students to add traits from the discussion to their webs.

the interval between two of the colossal supports of the roof of the catacombs, and was backed by one of their circumscribing walls of solid granite.

It was in vain that Fortunato, uplifting his dull torch, endeavored to pry[20] into the depth of the recess. Its termination the feeble light did not enable us to see.

"Proceed," I said; "herein is the Amontillado. As for Luchesi——"

"He is an ignoramus," interrupted my friend, as he stepped unsteadily forward, while I followed immediately at his heels. In an instant he had reached the extremity of the niche,[21] and finding his progress arrested by the rock, stood stupidly bewildered. A moment more and I had fettered[22] him to the granite. In its surface were two iron staples, distant from each other about two feet, horizontally. From one of these depended a short chain, from the other a padlock. Throwing the links about his waist, it was but the work of a few seconds to secure it. He was too much astounded to resist. Withdrawing the key I stepped back from the recess.

3 "Pass your hand," I said, "over the wall; you cannot help feeling the niter. Indeed it is *very* damp. Once more let me **implore** you to return. No? Then I must positively leave you. But I must first render you all the little attentions in my power."

"The Amontillado!" ejaculated my friend, not yet recovered from his astonishment. 3

"True," I replied; "the Amontillado."

> "Indeed it is *very* damp."

As I said these words I busied myself among the pile of bones of which I have before spoken. Throwing them aside, I soon uncovered a quantity of building stone and mortar. With these materials and with the aid of my trowel, I began vigorously to wall up the entrance of the niche.

I had scarcely laid the first tier of the masonry when I discovered that the intoxication of Fortunato had in a great measure worn off. The earliest indication I had of this was a low moaning cry from the depth of the recess. It was *not* the cry of a drunken man. There was then a long and obstinate silence. I laid the second tier, and the third, and the fourth; and then I heard the furious vibrations of the chain. The noise lasted for several minutes, during which, that I might hearken to it with the more satisfaction, I ceased my labors and sat down upon the bones. When at last the clanking subsided, I resumed the trowel, and finished without interruption the fifth, the sixth, and the seventh tier. The wall was now nearly upon a level with my breast. I again paused, and holding the flambeaux over the mason-work, threw a few feeble rays upon the figure within.

A succession of loud and shrill screams, bursting suddenly from the throat of the chained form, seemed to thrust me violently

---

20. Here, *pry* means "to look closely; peer."
21. Here, the *extremity of the niche* (nich) is the farthest spot inside the recess.
22. *Fettered* means "bound with chains or shackles; restrained."

2 Paraphrase *Restate these sentences in your own words.*

Vocabulary

implore (im plôr′) *v.* to ask earnestly; to beg

Matters of Life and Death *What does Fortunato finally realize?* **4**

English Learners

DIFFERENTIATED INSTRUCTION

Intermediate Point out the visual vocabulary on page 61 and read it aloud. Explain that Poe uses many words that are uncommon in everyday speech. Instruct students to use a dictionary to look up unfamiliar words. Ask volunteers to look up the meaning of the following words: *remote, ornamented, recess, promiscuously, circumscribing, render, trowel, obstinate, hearken,* and *flambeaux.*

Teach

Reading Strategy 2

Paraphrase Answer: *Fortunato's torch did not give much light, so his staring into the dark recess did no good. He could not see to the end.*

Literary Element 3

Dialogue Ask: How has the dialogue changed? How does this contribute to the mood? *(Students may say that Montresor has gone from flattering Fortunato to mocking him. His delight in mocking Fortunato intensifies the horror.)*

Big Idea 4

Matters of Life and Death
Ask: What does Fortunado finally realize? *(Fortunato finally realizes that he will die in the crypt; he realizes Montresor's evil intent.)*

ADVANCED Point out to students that Fortunato never asks why Montresor is killing him. Ask students why they think this is. *(Students may say because he already knows or that he is too panicked to think that clearly.)*

Teach

Reading Strategy

Paraphrase Answer: *I echoed and added to the screams; I even screamed louder than Fortunato did. Then Fortunato stopped screaming. Montresor is mocking Fortunato.*

ENGLISH LEARNERS To help English learners comprehend the passage, have a student define *surpassed* and *clamorer,* using a dictionary.

To check students' understanding of the selection, see Unit 1 Teaching Resources Book, p. 72.

Visual Vocabulary
A *rapier* (rā′ pē ər) is a long, lightweight sword with a sharp point but no cutting edge.

back. For a brief moment I hesitated—I trembled. Unsheathing my rapier, I began to grope with it about the recess; but the thought of an instant reassured me. I placed my hand upon the solid fabric of the catacombs, and felt satisfied. I reapproached the wall. I replied to the yells of him who clamored. I re-echoed—I aided—I surpassed them in volume and in strength. I did this, and the clamorer grew still.

It was now midnight, and my task was drawing to a close. I had completed the eighth, the ninth, and the tenth tier. I had finished a portion of the last and the eleventh; there remained but a single stone to be fitted and plastered in. I struggled with its weight; I placed it partially in its destined[23] position. But now there came from out the niche a low laugh that erected the hairs upon my head. It was succeeded by a sad voice, which I had difficulty in recognizing as that of the noble Fortunato. The voice said——

"Ha! ha! ha!—he! he!—a very good joke indeed—an excellent jest. We will have many a rich laugh about it at the palazzo—he! he! he!—over our wine—he! he! he!"

"The Amontillado!" I said.

"He! he! he!—he! he! he!—yes, the Amontillado. But is it not getting late? Will not they be awaiting us at the palazzo, the Lady Fortunato and the rest? Let us be gone."

"Yes," I said, "let us be gone."

"For the love of God, Montresor!"

"Yes," I said, "for the love of God!"

But to these words I hearkened in vain for a reply. I grew impatient. I called aloud:

"Fortunato!"

No answer. I called again:

"Fortunato!"

No answer still. I thrust a torch through the remaining aperture and let it fall within. There came forth in return only a jingling of the bells. My heart grew sick—on account of the dampness of the catacombs. I hastened to make an end of my labor. I forced the last stone into its position; I plastered it up. Against the new masonry I re-erected the old rampart[24] of bones. For the half of a century no mortal has disturbed them. *In pace requiescat!*[25]

"For the love of God, Montresor!"

23. Here, *destined* means "intended for a particular purpose or use."

24. A *rampart* is a protective barrier or fortification.

25. *In pace requiescat* (in pä′chā rek′ wē es kät′) is Latin for "May he rest in peace."

1 Paraphrase *Restate these lines, and then explain why Montresor is doing what he is doing.*

Grammar Practice

SPIRAL REVIEW PARTNERS

Dashes A dash is used to show an interruption in thought. Have students work in pairs to find sentences on this page that contain a dash. Students should discuss other punctuation that could be used instead of the dash. For example, sometimes commas or ellipses could be used instead of the dash. Ask students to rewrite the sentences. Volunteers may share their revised sentences with the class.

After You Read

Respond and Think Critically

Respond and Interpret

1. What are one or two questions you would ask Montresor?

2. (a)How does Montresor get Fortunato to come with him to his vaults? (b)What is Montresor's motive for leading Fortunato there?

3. (a)Describe the conversation between Montresor and Fortunato as they walk in the catacombs. (b)What is ironic about Montresor's concern for Fortunato's health?

4. (a)What happens to Fortunato at the end of the story? (b)In what ways is this a "perfect" crime?

Analyze and Evaluate

5. What details does Poe include to show Montresor as a cold-blooded killer? Do you think his portrayal is effective? Why or why not?

6. Why might Poe have chosen to write this story from the first-person point of view, describing only Montresor's thoughts and not Fortunato's?

Connect

7. **Big Idea** Matters of Life and Death Do you believe that Montresor resolves his conflict with Fortunato? What else could Montresor have done to solve his problem?

8. **Connect to the Author** Poe is known as a master of the horror story. Based on this story, would you agree? Consider the following before making your decision. What is the moment of greatest horror in this story? How well does Poe build up to this moment?

Visual Literacy

Illustration

Famed British illustrator Arthur Rackham created this image in 1935 to illustrate "The Cask of Amontillado." Study the illustration, looking carefully at the subject matter and details.

Fortunado and Montresor, 1935. Arthur Rackham.

Group Activity Discuss the following questions with classmates. Use evidence from "The Cask of Amontillado" to support your answers.

1. How accurately does Rackham re-create the setting of "The Cask of Amontillado"? Consider the size of the niche, the number of levels of brick, the chains, and the niter.
2. How accurately does Rackham re-create the characters? Consider their clothing, the expressions on their faces, and their postures.
3. How well does Rackham capture the mood of this moment in the story? Explain.

After You Read

Assess

Respond and Interpret

1. "What was the insult that made you want to kill Fortunato?" or "Have you ever regretted your crime?"

2. (a) He tempts Fortunato to sample a fine wine. (b) To murder him

3. (a) Montresor fusses over Fortunato's health and suggests turning back. (b) His real intent is murder.

4. (a) He is entombed behind a wall. (b) The crime goes undetected.

5. The premeditated crime is coldly and methodically carried out despite his victim's screams; he drops a torch into the niche to make the death more brutal. Most students will say the portrayal was effective.

6. It lets readers into a killer's mind.

7. Answers will vary.

8. Answers will vary. The moment of greatest horror occurs when Montresor starts to fill the niche or when he throws in the torch. Poe builds up to this moment by first describing the descent into the catacombs, which then builds to the final horrible act.

Visual Literacy

1. Some may say the image looks too large; pictured niche might accommodate 14 rows of brick, rather than 11; niter and the chain near the waist look accurate; scene looks too bright, given that light was from a torch (not shown)

2. (a) Fortunato wears motley, cap, and bells as in story, but clothes should fit tighter; face and stance show his fear (b) Montresor's clothes look right, but inward-leaning posture suggests interest, not detachment; sword and trowel as in story

3. Some students may argue that adding light and color to such a darkly sinister moment detracts from the horror. Others may say that these features reflect Montresor's disturbing giddiness.

After You Read

Assess

Literary Element

1. The dark mood foreshadows a monstrous act of revenge.
2. Poe uses specific, vivid words: *damp, cold, remote, crypt,* and *foulness.*
3. The connotations of colorful gaiety contrast with the gloomy vault and emphasize Montresor's evil glee.

Progress Check

Can students analyze mood?

If No → See Unit 1 Teaching Resources Book, p. 67.

Review: Suspense

Details That Create Suspense	Why They Create Suspense
Niter everywhere	Niter suggests sense of suffocation, death
Reach far end of crypt	No place left to go—and no Amontillado
Montresor's "heart grew sick"	Does he realize the horror of his crime? Will he really leave Fortunato?

Reading Strategy

1. They help by replacing words such as *flambeaux, rheum,* and *orbs* with familiar terms.
2. "Thus speaking, Fortunato possessed himself of my arm" might become "As he spoke, Fortunato took my arm."

Literary Element Mood

Mood is the feeling that an author creates in a literary work. The mood can suggest an emotion, such as fear or joy; it can also suggest the quality of a setting, such as gloom or airiness. For example, if Poe had described the catacombs as "peaceful" or "still," he would have created a quiet, restful mood.

1. Describe the overall mood that Poe creates in this story. In what way does the mood contribute to the story's suspense?
2. How does Poe create the mood? Point to specific examples throughout the story to support your answer.
3. What impact does the Carnival setting have on the mood of this story?

Review: Suspense

As you learned on page 21, **suspense** is a feeling of curiosity, uncertainty, or dread about what will happen next in a story. Writers increase the level of suspense by creating a threat to the central character and raising questions in the reader's mind.

Partner Activity With a partner, create a chart that lists details in the story that create suspense. Then explain why they are suspenseful.

Details That Create Suspense	Why They Create Suspense
No one is home at Montresor's house.	No one can witness the crime.

LOG ON Literature Online

Selection Resources For Selection Quizzes, eFlashcards, and Reading-Writing Connection activities, go to glencoe.com and enter QuickPass code GL49787u1.

Reading Strategy Paraphrase

Review the chart you made while reading the story, and then answer the following questions.

1. Look at footnotes 10 and 11 on pages 60 and 61. Explain why footnotes and paraphrasing help you understand Poe's writing.
2. Compare your paraphrases from your chart with the original passages. How do Poe's vocabulary and sentence structures differ from contemporary English?

Vocabulary Practice

Practice with Context Clues Identify the context clues that help you determine the meaning of each boldfaced word.

1. Taking those classes will **preclude** the possibility of your working on the newspaper committee, which meets at the same time.
2. Would Joe be punished, or would he commit the crime with **impunity?**
3. Some people greet you in a timid way, while others **accost** you.
4. I have **explicit** instructions on how to get to the meet instead of a vague description.
5. "Please, please don't go to that party," Mrs. Weeks **implored.**

Academic Vocabulary

Poe's essays and reviews are still read today for their literary **insights.**
—Meet Edgar Allan Poe, page 56

Insights is an academic word. A sports reporter who thoroughly analyzes the strengths and weaknesses of a baseball team might be said to have **insights** into the game of baseball. Using context clues, try to figure out the meaning of the word in the sentence about Poe above. Check your guess in a dictionary.

For more on academic vocabulary, see pages 54–55 and R79–R81.

Vocabulary Practice

1. which meets at the same time
2. be punished, or
3. in a timid way, while others
4. instead of a vague description
5. Please, please

Academic Vocabulary

Students should figure out that *insights* means "understanding the complicated workings of something."

Respond Through Writing

Research Report

Investigate Setting In "The Cask of Amontillado," Poe's specific settings are fictional, but Carnival celebrations and catacombs do exist. Using primary and secondary sources, prepare a research report of 1,500 words or more on Carnival or catacombs.

Understand the Task **Primary sources** are firsthand accounts of an event, such as diaries or eyewitness news articles written at the time the event took place. **Secondary sources** are sources written by people who did not influence or experience the event.

Prewrite Write four or five questions to guide your research. Answer those questions by checking secondary sources and, if possible, primary sources. Prepare detailed notes, identifying your sources for each fact or idea. Create an outline like the one below to help structure your report, adding relevant information under each outline point.

The Catacombs of Europe

I. Purposes over the years
  a. Burial grounds
  b.
II. Construction
III.

Draft Develop a thesis statement that identifies your topic and explains what you plan to say about the topic. As you write, refer to your notes and outline to make sure you have included the correct information in a coherent order. Use your research to support your thesis and main points. You may also wish to include visual aids—photographs or period illustrations—to help readers visualize the setting of your report.

Revise As you incorporate the information in your notes, evaluate whether the information is relevant. Delete information unrelated to your thesis, and add any missing facts and ideas. If you have used any technical terms, make sure they are explained thoroughly and correctly to avoid any misunderstandings. Give credit where credit is due and cite your sources. See pages R33–R37 for information on avoiding plagiarism.

Edit and Proofread Proofread your paper, correcting any errors in spelling, grammar, and punctuation. Use the Grammar Tip in the side column to help you use colons correctly.

Learning Objectives

In this assignment, you will focus on the following objectives:

Writing: Writing a research report.

Grammar: Understanding how to use colons.

Grammar Tip

Colons

Colons can be used to introduce a list. Often, the words *the following, these,* or *as follows* can be a clue that you should use a colon. The words before a colon should form a complete sentence.

INCORRECT
In "The Cask of Amontillado," Montresor's catacombs contain: bones, niter, and wine.

CORRECT
In "The Cask of Amontillado," Montresor's catacombs contain the following: bones, niter, and wine.

After You Read

Assess

Respond Through Writing

Students' research reports should

- use information based on primary and secondary sources
- include a clear thesis and evidence to support it
- include source citations as necessary use correct grammar and punctuation

A student who meets all of these criteria should receive the equivalent of a 3-point response.

A student who fully meets one or partially meets two of these criteria should receive the equivalent of a 2-point response.

A student who partially meets one of these criteria should receive the equivalent of a 1-point response.

For grammar practice, see Unit 1 Teaching Resources Book, p. 71.

For additional selection assessment, see Assessment Resources, pp. 47–48.

Approaching Level

DIFFERENTIATED INSTRUCTION

Emerging Point out that there are several instances of foreshadowing in the story, and ask students if they remember any examples. After some discussion, have students scan the story looking for more examples of foreshadowing.

As students provide examples, **ask:** What event or action do you think Poe was foreshadowing? *(Answers will vary.)*

Vocabulary Workshop

Homonyms and Homophones

Focus

Assign individual student groups a homonym word pair to use in sentences that include context clues. Have the groups share their sentences and add context suggested by the class.

Teach

Write on the board: *its, it's, your, you're.* Have students differentiate by breaking down each contraction. **Say:** If the sentence calls for *it is,* use *it's.* If the sentence calls for *you are,* use *you're.*

ENGLISH LEARNERS Ask English learners to use these contractions in a sentence.

Assess

1. (a) wine, (b) cellar, (c) led
2. (a) arm: *n.* a body part, a limb; *n.* a weapon; *v.* to equip with weaponry; *v.* to prepare for warfare or conflict
   (b) ground: *n.* solid surface of the earth; *n.* soil or earth; *n.* an area of land designated for a particular purpose; *n.* a conductor that makes electrical connections with the earth; *v.* to place or cause to touch the ground; *v.* to connect to a ground
   (c) lie: *v.* to recline; *v.* to give false information; *n.* a falsehood
   (d) order: *n.* the arrangement of elements in a group; *n.* a command or direction; *v.* to command or instruct; *v.* to put in a methodical arrangement

Learning Objectives

In this workshop, you will focus on the following objective:

Vocabulary: Understanding homonyms and homophones.

Vocabulary Workshop

Homonyms and Homophones

Literature Connection In the sentence shown below, Edgar Allan Poe uses the homonym *respect.*

> *"In this respect, I did not differ from him materially."*
>
> —Edgar Allan Poe, from "The Cask of Amontillado"

Homonyms are words that sound alike and are spelled alike but have different meanings. Here, *respect* is a noun that means "particular detail." *Respect* is also a verb, however, that means "to consider worthy of esteem or regard."

Poe also uses the homophone *not* in this sentence. **Homophones** are words that sound alike but are spelled differently and have different meanings and histories. A word that sounds like *not* but is spelled differently and has a different meaning is *knot.*

Vocabulary Terms

Homonyms are words that sound alike and are spelled alike but have different meanings.

Homophones are words that sound alike but are spelled differently and have different meanings.

Tip

To determine the meaning of a homophone, use context clues. The part of speech can sometimes help you understand the intended meaning.

Examples

Homonym	Meaning
like	to care for
like	nearly the same
Homophone	**Meaning**
principal	person with authority; head of a school; most important
principle	basic truth, rule, policy, or law; moral conviction
sight	something seen; the ability to see
cite	to refer to; to acknowledge; to point out
site	a place; to locate

Practice

1. Choose the correct homophone to complete each sentence.
   a. Fortunato has expert knowledge about (whine, wine).
   b. Montresor takes Fortunato deeper into the (cellar, seller).
   c. Montresor has (lead, led) Fortunato to his death.
2. Use a dictionary to find more than one meaning for each homonym. Write at least two meanings.
   a. arm **b.** ground **c.** lie **d.** order

LOG ON Literature Online

Vocabulary For more vocabulary practice, go to glencoe.com and enter QuickPass code GL49787u1.

For additional vocabulary practice, see Glencoe Interactive Vocabulary CD-ROM.

Before You Read

Blues Ain't No Mockin Bird

Meet **Toni Cade Bambara**
(1939–1995)

Toni Cade Bambara once said that her mother never interrupted her if she was daydreaming. Bambara explained, "She recognized that as important work to do." Throughout her childhood, Bambara was encouraged to be creative, and she wrote on any slip of paper she could find.

A New Name As a young girl, Bambara asserted her independence by changing her first name, Miltona, to Toni. She adopted the last name "Bambara" after seeing the name in a sketchbook in her great-grandmother's attic. (The Bambara are an African people in Mali.)

> *"Words are to be taken seriously. . . . Words set things in motion."*
>
> —Toni Cade Bambara

Academia and Activism After receiving degrees in theater arts and American studies, Bambara taught at Rutgers University, Duke University, and Spelman College. Of her teaching, she said, "I'm a very seductive teacher, persuasive, infectious, overwhelming, irresistible. I worked hard in the classroom to teach students to critique me constantly, to protect themselves from my nonsense. . . . I would have to go into the classroom and beat them up for not taking me to the wall, for succumbing to mere charm and flash, when they should have been challenging me." During the turbulent years of the 1960s and 1970s, Bambara aligned herself with activists working to redress the injustices of American society. As part of that effort, she edited *The Black Woman,* an influential anthology.

Fiction and Film In 1972 Bambara published a collection of short stories entitled *Gorilla, My Love.* Of that collection, critic C. D. B. Bryan wrote, "Toni Cade Bambara tells me more about being black through her quiet, proud, silly, tender, hip, acute, loving stories than any amount of literary polemicizing could hope to do. She writes about love: a love for one's family, one's race, one's neighborhood, and it is the sort of love that comes with maturity and inner peace." Bambara published another short story collection, *The Sea Birds Are Still Alive,* in 1977 and a novel, *The Salt Eaters,* in 1980. In later years, she taught script writing at Scribe Video Center in Philadelphia. Bambara died from cancer at the age of 56.

LOG ON **Literature** Online

Author Search For more about Toni Cade Bambara, go to glencoe.com and enter QuickPass code GL49787u1.

Before You Read

Focus

Bellringer Options

Selection Focus Transparency 5

Daily Language Practice Transparency 7

Or prompt students to discuss the paparazzi. Note how famous people often object to being photographed by them. **Ask:** How would you feel if you were photographed without your consent? How do you think the photographer feels when taking such a picture? Discuss with students what they think is appropriate behavior for photographers.

Selection Skills

Blues Ain't No Mockin Bird

Literary Elements
- Description (SE pp. 70–78)
- Setting (SE p. 77)

Writing Skills/Grammar
- Write a Descriptive Essay (SE p. 78)
- Write Using Dialect (TE p. 70)

Reading Skills
- Concrete Details (SE pp. 70–78)

Vocabulary Skills
- Academic Vocabulary (SE p. 78)
- Analogies (SE p. 78)

Listening/Speaking/Viewing Skills
- Analyze Art (SE pp. 72, 74)

Before You Read

Focus

Summary

As the narrator plays with friends, Granny makes Christmas cakes on the back porch. Two men making a film for the county begin filming without her permission. Granny asks them to stop, but they don't. Eventually the men leave, but only after the narrator's grandfather uses a hammer to smash their camera.

For summaries in languages other than English, see Unit 1 Teaching Resources Book, pp. 74–79.

Vocabulary

Split Sheets Instruct students to draw a line down the center of a page. On one side of the line, they should write a vocabulary word. On the other side of the line, they should write the definition. Then have students fold the paper down the line. Students should study the vocabulary words by saying the definition of the word and then flipping the sheet to see if they are correct.

For additional vocabulary practice, see Unit 1 Teaching Resources Book, p. 82.

For additional context, see Glencoe Interactive Vocabulary CD-ROM.

Literature and Reading Preview

Connect to the Story

What would you say to someone who invaded your privacy? Freewrite for a few minutes about what you would say or do if someone were to invade your privacy and would not leave.

Build Background

The blues was born in the rural southern United States. There, African musical traditions were transformed to create a new music that spoke to the sadness and joy in African American life. The mockingbird is a songbird that mimics, or imitates, the songs of other birds.

Set Purposes for Reading

Big Idea Matters of Life and Death

As you read "Blues Ain't No Mockin Bird," ask yourself, What do the events reveal about the family's values?

Literary Element Description

Description is a detailed portrayal of a person, a place, an object, or an event. Descriptive writing helps readers imagine what characters see, hear, feel, taste, or touch. As you read, ask yourself, How does description help me visualize and further understand the characters?

Reading Strategy Analyze Concrete Details

Authors typically include specific, **concrete details** in descriptions of the people and events they portray. These details help readers to visualize setting, make inferences about characters, and understand plot. As you read, ask yourself, How do concrete details help give a precise image of the narrator, her family, and their home?

Tip: Record Details Use a diagram like the one below to list details from the story and explain what the details tell you about the character or setting. Add more boxes and circles as needed.

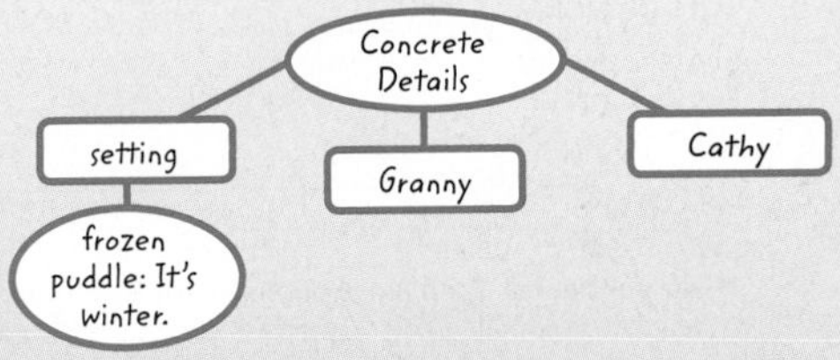

Learning Objectives

For pages 69–78

In studying this text, you will focus on the following objectives:

Literary Study: Analyzing description.

Reading: Analyzing concrete details.

Writing: Applying imagery in a descriptive essay.

Vocabulary

paperweight (pāp′ ər wāt′) *n.* a heavy, often decorative object traditionally used to hold down loose papers; p. 71 *After the wind blew papers off Terra's desk, she put to use the paperweight her father had given her.*

campaign (kam pān′) *n.* a series of related actions with the purpose of a specific goal, such as an election campaign; p. 72 *His campaign to become class president included a speech to the school.*

mortal (môrt′ əl) *adj.* deadly; p. 73 *During the joust, the knight received a mortal blow and died before sunset.*

molasses (mə las′ iz) *n.* a thick, dark brown syrup created by boiling down raw sugar; p. 76 *His father's cookie recipe uses both sugar and molasses.*

Tip: Analogies When completing an analogy, identifying the relationship between the first two words will allow you to apply that relationship to another pair of words. Some analogies are based on synonyms.

Writing Practice

SPIRAL REVIEW **Write Using Dialect** Explain to students that a dialect may suggest where a character comes from, what social group he or she belongs to, and what kind of education he or she has had. Talk about ways in which people in different regions of the country talk. Have students write a paragraph in a local dialect. Then ask them to rewrite the paragraph using Standard English.

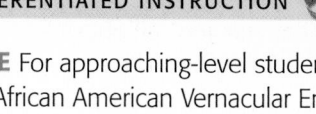

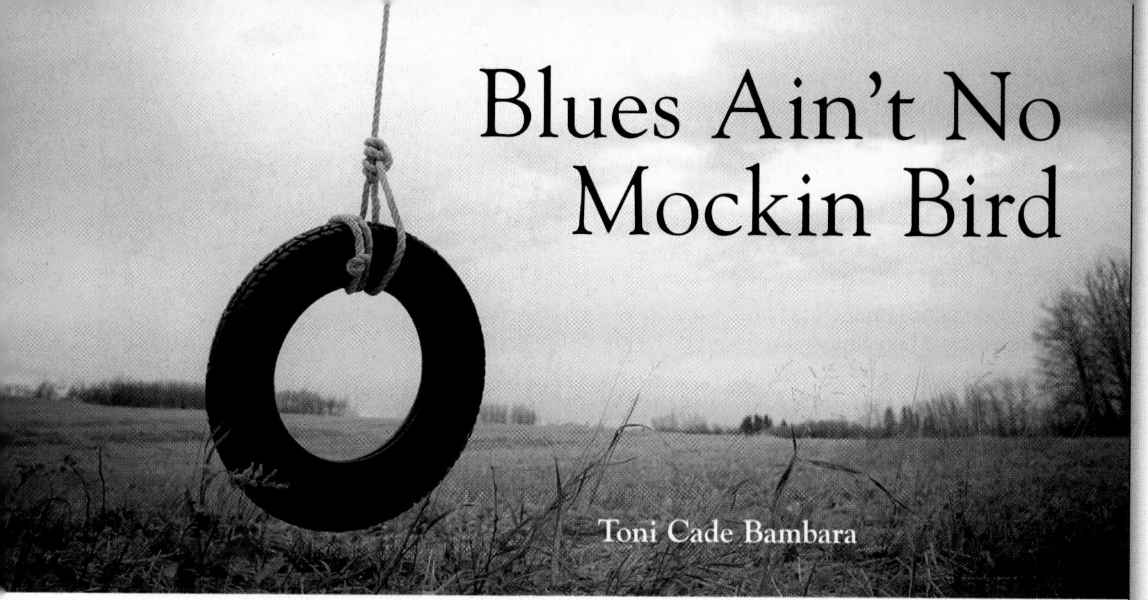

Blues Ain't No Mockin Bird

Toni Cade Bambara

The puddle had frozen over, and me and Cathy went stompin in it. The twins from next door, Tyrone and Terry, were swingin so high out of sight we forgot we were waitin our turn on the tire. Cathy jumped up and came down hard on her heels and started tap-dancin. And the frozen patch splinterin every which way underneath kinda spooky.

"Looks like a plastic spider web," she said. "A sort of weird spider, I guess, with many mental problems." But really it looked like the crystal **paperweight** Granny kept in the parlor. She was on the back porch, Granny was, making the cakes drunk. The old ladle dripping rum into the Christmas tins, like it used to drip maple syrup into the pails when we lived in the Judson's woods, like it poured cider into the vats when we were on the Cooper place, like it used to scoop buttermilk and soft cheese when we lived at the dairy.

"Go tell that man we ain't a bunch of trees."

"Ma'am?"

"I said to tell that man to get away from here with that camera." Me and Cathy look over toward the meadow where the men with the station wagon'd been roamin around all mornin. The tall man with a huge camera lassoed to his shoulder was buzzin our way.

"They're makin movie pictures," yelled Tyrone, stiffenin his legs and twistin so the tire'd come down slow so they could see.

"They're makin movie pictures," sang out Terry.

"That boy don't never have anything original to say," say Cathy grown-up.

By the time the man with the camera had cut across our neighbor's yard, the twins were out of the trees swingin low

---

Description *How is Cathy's description of the cracked ice more vivid than if she had said only that it looks like a spider web?*

Vocabulary

paperweight (pāpʹ ər wāt′) *n.* a heavy, often decorative object traditionally used to hold down loose papers

Teach

Literary Element

Description **Answer:** *Her description is much more specific. Saying it looks like the web of a weird spider with "many mental problems" gives the impression of chaotic, jagged cracks. It also gives the reader some insight into Cathy's personality.*

For additional literary element practice, see Unit 1 Teaching Resources Book, p. 80.

For an audio recording of this selection, use Listening Library Audio CD-ROM.

Readability Scores

Dale-Chall: 6.8

DRP: 53

Lexile: 960

English Learners

DIFFERENTIATED INSTRUCTION

Intermediate Help students understand the language in the story by explaining that dialect is a variation of language spoken by people in a particular region, certain area, or social class. Explain that the author often omits the letter g at the end of words ending in *-ing* (e.g., *stompin, swingin, mornin*) because she wants readers to omit this sound when they read the story.

Approaching Level

DIFFERENTIATED INSTRUCTION

AAVE For approaching-level students who use African American Vernacular English (AAVE), point out that the characters in this story often use double negatives: "That boy don't never have anything original to say." Explain that this, too, is part of the characters' dialect. Remind students that in Standard English, two negative words should not be used together in a sentence. Ask a student to revise the sentence, using Standard English. *(He never has anything original to say.)*

Teach

Reading Strategy 1

Analyze Concrete Details

Answer: *Bingo is a dog. This is clear from the context clue "bones on the kitchen floor."*

View the Art ★

Answer: *Students might infer that this is the face of a strong woman, who will speak with her facial expressions and stand her ground. Granny couldn't stand being taken advantage of, which was the reason for many of her actions.*

Elizabeth Catlett (1915–), an American printmaker and sculptor, has fought for equality for African American people and other people of color through her art.

and Granny was onto the steps, the screen door bammin soft and scratchy against her palms. "We thought we'd get a shot or two of the house and everything and then—"

"Good mornin," Granny cut him off. And smiled that smile.

"Good mornin," he said, head all down the way Bingo does when you yell at him about the bones on the kitchen floor. "Nice place you got here, aunty. We thought we'd take a—"

"Did you?" said Granny with her eyebrows. Cathy pulled up her socks and giggled.

"Nice things here," said the man, buzzin his camera over the yard. The pecan barrels, the sled, me and Cathy, the flowers, the printed stones along the driveway, the trees, the twins, the toolshed.

"I don't know about the thing, the it, and the stuff," said Granny, still talkin with her eyebrows. "Just people here is what I tend to consider."

Camera man stopped buzzin. Cathy giggled into her collar.

"Mornin, ladies," a new man said. He had come up behind us when we weren't lookin. "And gents," discoverin the twins givin him a nasty look. "We're filmin for the county," he said with a smile. "Mind if we shoot a bit around here?"

"I do indeed," said Granny with no smile. Smilin man was smiling up a storm. So was Cathy. But he didn't seem to have another word to say, so he and the camera man backed on out the yard, but you could hear the camera buzzin still. "Suppose you just shut that machine off," said Granny real low through her teeth, and took a step down off the porch and then another.

"Now, aunty," Camera said, pointin the thing straight at her.

1 Analyze Concrete Details *Who is Bingo? How do you know?*

Sharecropper, 1970. Elizabeth Catlett. Linoleum cut, 26 x 22 in. Hampton University Art Museum, VA. ©Elizabeth Catlett/ Licensed by VAGA, NY.

View the Art How would you describe the personality of this woman? How might she be similar to or different from Granny? ★

"Your mama and I are not related."

Smilin man got his notebook out and a chewed-up pencil. "Listen," he said movin back into our yard, "we'd like to have a statement from you . . . for the film. We're filmin for the county, see. Part of the food stamp **campaign.** You know about the food stamps?"[1]

Granny said nuthin.

"Maybe there's somethin you want to say for the film. I see you grow your own vegetables," he smiled real nice. "If more folks did that, see, there'd be no need—"

Granny wasn't sayin nuthin. So they backed on out, buzzin at our clothesline

1. *Food stamps* are coupons issued by the government to people with low incomes, who use the stamps, as if they were cash, to buy food at stores.

Vocabulary

campaign (kam pān′) *n.* a series of related actions with the purpose of a specific goal, such as an election campaign

Speaking and Viewing Practice

SPIRAL REVIEW **View the Art** Point out the art on this page. Ask students the View the Art question. Explain that the woman in the painting is a strong woman, like Granny, who can use facial expressions to show emotion. **Ask:** What are some facial expressions that can communicate feeling? *(raising eyebrows to show surprise, rolling eyes to show frustration, clenching teeth to show anger)*

Ask: What can you tell about the woman in the painting from her facial expression? *(She is stern and serious. She might be listening carefully to what someone is saying.)* As students read this page, have them jot down phrases that explain the ways in which Granny uses her facial expressions to communicate. *("And smiled that smile," "still talkin with her eyebrows," "with no smile," and "real low through her teeth.")*

and the twins' bicycles, then back on down to the meadow. The twins were danglin in the tire, lookin at Granny. Me and Cathy were waitin, too, cause Granny always got somethin to say. She teaches steady with no let-up. "I was on this bridge one time," she started off. "Was a crowd cause this man was goin to jump, you understand. And a minister was there and the police and some other folks. His woman was there, too."

"What was they doin?" asked Tyrone.

"Tryin to talk him out of it was what they was doin. The minister talkin about how it was a **mortal** sin,[2] suicide. His woman takin bites out of her own hand and not even knowin it, so nervous and cryin and talkin fast."

"So what happened?" asked Tyrone.

"So here comes . . . this person . . . with a camera, takin pictures of the man and the minister and the woman. Takin pictures of the man in his misery about to jump, cause life so bad and people been messin with him so bad. This person takin up the whole roll of film practically. But savin a few, of course."

"Of course," said Cathy, hatin the person. Me standin there wonderin how Cathy knew it was "of course" when I didn't and it was *my* grandmother.

After a while Tyrone say, "Did he jump?"

"Yeh, did he jump?" say Terry all eager.

And Granny just stared at the twins till their faces swallow up the eager and they don't even care any more about the man jumpin. Then she goes back onto the porch and lets the screen door go for itself. I'm lookin to Cathy to finish the story cause she knows Granny's whole story before me even. Like she knew how come we move so much and Cathy ain't but a third cousin we picked up on the way last Thanksgivin visitin. But she knew it was on account of people drivin Granny crazy till she'd get up in the night and start packin. Mumblin and packin and wakin everybody up sayin, "Let's get on away from here before I kill me somebody." Like people wouldn't pay her for things like they said they would. Or Mr. Judson bringin us boxes of old clothes and raggedy magazines. Or Mrs. Cooper comin in our kitchen and touchin everything and sayin how clean it all was. Granny goin crazy, and Granddaddy Cain pullin her off the people, sayin, "Now, now, Cora." But next day loadin up the truck, with rocks all in his jaw, madder than Granny in the first place.

"I read a story once," said Cathy soundin like Granny teacher. "About this lady Goldilocks who barged into a house that wasn't even hers. And not invited, you understand. Messed over the people's groceries and broke up the people's furniture. Had the nerve to sleep in the folks' bed."

"Then what happened?" asked Tyrone. "What they do, the folks, when they come in to all this mess?"

"Did they make her pay for it?" asked Terry, makin a fist. "I'd've made her pay me."

4 I didn't even ask. I could see Cathy actress was very likely to just walk away and leave us in mystery about this story which I heard was about some bears.

"Did they throw her out?" asked Tyrone, like his father sounds when he's bein extra nasty-plus to the washin-machine man.

"Woulda," said Terry. "I woulda gone upside her head with my fist and—"

2. In some Christian teachings, a *mortal sin* is one so terrible that it causes the death of the soul and results in eternal damnation.

2 Matters of Life and Death *What does Granny's story suggest about her values?*

Vocabulary

mortal (môrt′ əl) *adj.* deadly

3 Description *How do you picture Granddaddy Cain's face based on this description?*

Teach

Big Idea 2

Matters of Life and Death

Answer: *Students may say that Granny values her dignity and demands respect.*

ADVANCED Ask advanced learners to compare Granny to a character from another work who shows similar traits. *(Answers will vary.)*

Literary Element 3

Description Students might say they picture Granddaddy's face being red in anger and his jaw clenched.

Reading Strategy 4

Analyze Concrete Details

Ask: How does the narrator describe Cathy? *(Students may say that the narrator first says she sounds like "Granny teacher" and then calls her "Cathy actress.")*

APPROACHING **Ask:** Why do you think the narrator gives Cathy different titles? *(Students may say that the narrator is showing the different roles that Cathy takes on.)*

Approaching Level

DIFFERENTIATED INSTRUCTION

Emerging Explain that Granny's story about the photographers taking pictures of the man about to commit suicide shows that she thinks people have a right to privacy and should be treated respectfully. Ask students to identify other examples on this page that give insight into Granny's character. *(In the second column, the author says that the family moves often because people drive Granny crazy. She does not like it when people try to help her just because she is poor. She does not want boxes of old clothes or magazines and does not like it when people seem surprised that her house is clean.)*

Ask: What words would you use to describe her character? *(proud, independent, self-reliant)*

Teach

View the Art ★

Answer: *The settings are similar: a small, modest yet comfortable and cozy home in a peaceful rural setting.*

This painting is an example of folk art, artwork created by artists with little or no formal training. Folk artists often depict elements of everyday life.

"You woulda done whatcha always do—go cry to Mama, you big baby," said Tyrone. So naturally Terry starts hittin on Tyrone, and next thing you know they tumblin out the tire and rollin on the ground. But Granny didn't say a thing or send the twins home or step out on the steps to tell us about how we can't afford to be fightin amongst ourselves. She didn't say nuthin. So I get into the tire to take my turn. And I could see her leanin up against the pantry table, starin at the cakes she was puttin up for the Christmas sale, mumblin real low and grumpy and holdin her forehead like it wanted to fall off and mess up the rum cakes.

Behind me I hear before I can see Granddaddy Cain comin through the woods in his field boots. Then I twist around to see the shiny black oilskin[3] cuttin through what little left there was of yellows, reds, and oranges. His great white head not quite round cause of this bloody thing high on his shoulder, like he was wearin a cap on sideways. He takes the shortcut through the pecan grove, and the sound of twigs snapping overhead and underfoot travels clear and cold all the way up to us. And here comes Smilin and Camera up behind him like they was goin to do somethin. Folks like to go for him sometimes. Cathy say it's because he's so tall and quiet and like a

3. Here, *oilskin* is a coat made of cloth treated with oil to make it waterproof.

Our House, 1994. Jessie Coates. Acrylic on Masonite, 3½ x 5 in. Private collection.

View the Art This painting is an example of folk art. Folk art often shows elements of everyday life. How does this painting compare with the setting described in the story? ★

Research Practice

SPIRAL REVIEW **Research Information** Have students search the library or the Internet for articles written about privacy. Students should take notes on their findings and collect copies of articles, websites, etc.

Discuss the articles in class, addressing issues such as whether the public encourages invasion of privacy and how to remedy the situation. Students should support their answers with the information they have gathered.

Ask students to consider whether they think people have a right to take pictures on another person's property. Then ask students to discuss what the characters in the story could have done legally to make the men leave their property.

king. And people just can't stand it. But Smilin and Camera don't hit him in the head or nuthin. They just buzz on him as he stalks by with the chicken hawk slung over his shoulder, squawkin, drippin red down the back of the oilskin. He passes the porch and stops a second for Granny to see he's caught the hawk at last, but she's just starin and mumblin, and not at the hawk. So he nails the bird to the toolshed door, the hammerin crackin through the eardrums. And the bird flappin himself to death and droolin down the door to paint the gravel in the driveway red, then brown, then black. And the two men movin up on tiptoe like they was invisible or we were blind, one.

Visual Vocabulary
A *chicken hawk* is any hawk that preys on chickens.

1 "Get them persons out of my flower bed, Mister Cain," say Granny moanin real low like at a funeral.

"How come your grandmother calls her husband 'Mister Cain' all the time?" Tyrone whispers all loud and noisy and from the city and don't know no better. Like his mama, Miss Myrtle, tell us never mind the formality as if we had no better breeding than to call her Myrtle, plain. And then this awful thing—a giant hawk—come wailin up over the meadow, flyin low and tilted and screamin, zigzaggin through the pecan grove, breakin branches and hollerin, snappin past the clothesline, flyin every which way, flyin into things reckless with crazy.

"He's come to claim his mate," say Cathy fast, and ducks down. We all fall quick and flat into the gravel driveway, stones scrapin my face. I squinch my eyes open again at the hawk on the door, tryin to fly up out of her death like it was just a sack flown into by mistake. Her body holdin her there on that nail, though. The mate beatin the air overhead and clutchin for hair, for heads, for landin space.

The camera man duckin and bendin and runnin and fallin, jigglin the camera and scared. And Smilin jumpin up and down swipin at the huge bird, tryin to bring the hawk down with just his raggedy ole cap. 3 Granddaddy Cain straight up and silent, watchin the circles of the hawk, then aimin the hammer off his wrist. The giant bird fallin, silent and slow. Then here comes Camera and Smilin all big and bad now that the awful screechin thing is on its back and broken, here they come. And Granddaddy Cain looks up at them like it was the first time noticin, but not payin them too much mind cause he's listenin, we all listenin, to that low groanin music comin from the porch. And we figure any minute, somethin in my back tells me any minute now, Granny gonna bust through that screen with somethin in her hand and murder on her mind. So Granddaddy say above the buzzin, but quiet, "Good day, gentlemen." Just like that. Like he'd invited them in to play cards and they'd stayed too long and all the sandwiches were gone and Reverend Webb was droppin by and it was time to go.

They didn't know what to do. But like Cathy say, folks can't stand Granddaddy tall and silent and like a king. They can't neither. The smile the men smilin is pullin the mouth back and showin the teeth.

2 Analyze Concrete Details *How does the giant hawk behave as it approaches the family?*

Description *How does the description of Granddaddy Cain contrast with the descriptions of Camera and Smilin?*

Teach

Reading Strategy 1

Analyze Concrete Details
Ask: How does this description of Granny add to the mood of scene? *(Students may say the comment "moanin' real low like at a funeral" shows her grim view of the situation.)*

Reading Strategy 2

Analyze Concrete Details
Answer: *The hawk behaves unpredictably and violently.*

Literary Element 3

Description **Answer:** *Students should mention that while the camera man and his partner are jumping around scared and frantic, Granddaddy Cain is standing tall and calm.*

ENGLISH LEARNERS Ask English learners to think of words that describe the camera man in this passage. *(afraid, cowardly, fearful)*

Approaching Level

DIFFERENTIATED INSTRUCTION

Established Discuss the behavior of the hawk. **Ask:** In what ways are the hawk and the two men alike? Write students' responses on the chalkboard. *(Students may say they both intrude on the family and are uninvited; they both seem to want to do the family harm; and they both make unwanted noise.)*

Teach

Big Idea

Matters of Life and Death
Answer: *Students may say that Granddaddy values privacy and autonomy.*

To check students' understanding of the selection, see Unit 1 Teaching Resources Book, p. 85.

Progress Check

Can students analyze concrete details?

If No → See Unit 1 Teaching Resources Book, p. 81.

Lookin like the wolf man, both of them. Then Granddaddy holds his hand out—this huge hand I used to sit in when I was a baby and he'd carry me through the house to my mother like I was a gift on a tray. Like he used to on the trains. They called the other men just waiters. But they spoke of Granddaddy separate and said, The Waiter. And said he had engines in his feet and motors in his hands and couldn't no train throw him off and couldn't nobody turn him round. They were big enough for motors, his hands were. He held that one hand out all still and it gettin to be not at all a hand but a person in itself.

"He wants you to hand him the camera," Smilin whispers to Camera, tiltin his head to talk secret like they was in the jungle or somethin and come upon a native that don't speak the language. The men start untyin the straps, and they put the camera into that great hand speckled with the hawk's blood all black and crackly now. And the hand don't even drop with the weight, just the fingers move, curl up around the machine. But Granddaddy lookin straight at the men. They lookin at each other and everywhere but at Granddaddy's face.

"We filmin for the county, see," say Smilin. "We puttin together a movie for the food stamp program . . . filmin all around these parts. Uhh, filmin for the county."

"Can I have my camera back?" say the tall man with no machine on his shoulder, but still keepin it high like the camera was still there or needed to be. "Please, sir."

Then Granddaddy's other hand flies up like a sudden and gentle bird, slaps down fast on top of the camera and lifts off half like it was a calabash cut for sharing.

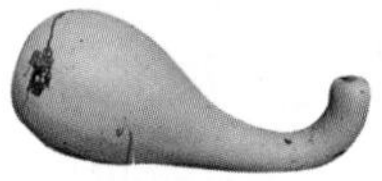

Visual Vocabulary
A *calabash* is the gourdlike fruit of a tropical American tree.

"Hey," Camera jumps forward. He gathers up the parts into his chest and everything unrollin and fallin all over. "Whatcha tryin to do? You'll ruin the film." He looks down into his chest of metal reels and things like he's protectin a kitten from the cold.

"You standin in the misses' flower bed," say Granddaddy. "This is our own place."

The two men look at him, then at each other, then back at the mess in the camera man's chest, and they just back off. One sayin over and over all the way down to the meadow, "Watch it, Bruno. Keep ya fingers off the film." Then Granddaddy picks up the hammer and jams it into the oilskin pocket, scrapes his boots, and goes into the house. And you can hear the squish of his boots headin through the house. And you can see the funny shadow he throws from the parlor window onto the ground by the string-bean patch. The hammer draggin the pocket of the oilskin out so Granddaddy looked even wider. Granny was hummin now—high, not low and grumbly. And she was doin the cakes again, you could smell the **molasses** from the rum.

"There's this story I'm goin to write one day," say Cathy dreamer. "About the proper use of the hammer."

"Can I be in it?" Tyrone say with his hand up like it was a matter of first come, first served.

"Perhaps," say Cathy, climbin onto the tire to pump us up. "If you there and ready." ∾

Matters of Life and Death *What does Granddaddy's explanation suggest about what he values?*

Vocabulary

molasses (mə las′ iz) *n.* a thick, dark brown syrup created by boiling down raw sugar

Literary Practice

Figurative Language Remind students that a simile is a comparison using *like* or *as*. The author uses several similes on this page. Read the following similes and have students explain the meaning of each.

- ". . . and he'd carry me through the house to my mother like I was a gift on a tray." *(He carried her very carefully.)*
- "Then Granddaddy's other hand flies up like a sudden and gentle bird . . ." *(His hand moves swiftly but gently.)*
- "He looks down into his chest of metal reels and things like he's protectin a kitten from the cold." *(The contents of the camera is fragile.)*

Ask students to select three things in the room and write a simile to describe them. For example, "This desk is as strong as steel." Have them share their similes with the class.

After You Read

Respond and Think Critically

Respond and Interpret

1. What images from the story linger in your mind?
2. (a)Who is the narrator, or person telling the story? (b)What details reveal the narrator's relationship to other characters in the story?
3. (a)What are the two men doing on the Cain family's property? (b)How would you describe the men's initial attitude toward Granny and the rest of the family? Include details from the story in your answer.
4. (a)Summarize Granny's experience on the bridge. (b)What does Granny's story about the man's suicide attempt reveal about her and her reactions to the men with the camera?

Analyze and Evaluate

5. The narrator says that Granny "always got somethin to say. She teaches steady with no let-up." (a)Does the narrator think Granny is a good teacher? (b)Do you think she is a good teacher? Support your opinion with evidence from the story.
6. Why do you think Toni Cade Bambara gave Granddaddy only fifteen words to say? Do you feel you got to know his character? Explain.
7. Do you think "Blues Ain't No Mockin Bird" is an appropriate title for this story? Explain.

Connect

8. **Big Idea** **Matters of Life and Death** How are the hawks like the men with the cameras? What kind of message might the hawks' death have sent to these men?
9. **Connect to the Author** One critic wrote that Toni Cade Bambara "writes about love." In what ways is this story about love?

Literary Element Description

By appealing to the senses, **description** helps readers visualize the characters and the action in a story. Good description can also help readers have a greater understanding for the reasons characters act as they do. Think about Toni Cade Bambara's use of description throughout this story, and then answer the following questions.

1. From the description of each, how does the chicken hawk's mate in the story remind you of Granddaddy?
2. What adjectives would you use to describe Camera and Smilin?

Review: Setting

As you learned on pages 8–9, **setting** is the time and place in which the events of a story occur. The history, customs, and beliefs of a place are also a part of setting. "Blues Ain't No Mockin Bird" is set in what is likely a poor rural county in the South during the late 1940s or 1950s. Bambara includes vivid details to help readers picture the Cain family home.

Partner Activity Imagine that you are in charge of finding a location to film a movie or television version of this story. With a partner, create a drawing and write a description of the setting. In the written description, include quotes and details from the story that support your choices.

Literary Element

1. Both are strong, dignified, loyal, and determined to defend their own against enemies.
2. Possible answers: *sneaky, condescending, arrogant, cowardly, offensive, intrusive.*

Review: Setting

Students' descriptions should include quotes and details from the story.

After You Read

Assess

1. Accept any reasonable answer that includes adequate support.
2. (a) The Cains' young granddaughter (b) Details such as the narrator's references to "Granny" and "Granddaddy"
3. (a) Making a film for the county's food stamp program (b) Presumptuous and rude
4. (a) Granny saw a man threatening to jump off a bridge. His minister and wife were trying to coax him down. A man took pictures of the incident, saving them in case the man jumped. (b) Granny thinks the two filmmakers are intrusive and exploitive.
5. (a) She respects but she does not entirely understand Granny. (b) Answers will vary.
6. His regal bearing and dramatic actions speak louder than words.
7. Students may say the title has something to do with realizing that it's wrong to exploit the serious troubles and hard times ("the blues") of other people.
8. Students may say they both intrude on the family and are uninvited; they both seem to want to do the family harm; and they both make unwanted noise.
9. Granny and Granddaddy Cain reveal their strong love for their family and the family's privacy. Granddaddy Cain kills the chicken hawks to protect the family's livelihood. He and Granny also protect their family from the intruders by taking a stand against them.

After You Read

Assess

Reading Strategy

1. D is the correct answer. The camera operator does not know Granny yet refers to her familiarly.

Vocabulary

1. a **2.** b **3.** a **4.** b

Academic Vocabulary

Answers may vary, sample response: I could use my experience taking care of my little brother to develop some income by baby-sitting for other families.

Write with Style

Students' essays should:

- accurately and engagingly describe a real location
- use imagery and sensory details in the descriptions
- organize the descriptions spatially
- use specific descriptive language

For grammar practice, see Unit 1 Teaching Resources Book, p. 84.

Reading Strategy Analyze Concrete Details

ACT Skills Practice

1. By calling Granny "aunty" the camera operator reveals that:

   A. He is related to her.
   B. He is on his best behavior.
   C. He finds her amusing.
   D. He has no respect for her.

Vocabulary Practice

Practice with Analogies To complete an analogy, first decide what relationship exists in a pair of words. Then choose the word that creates the same relationship in a second pair of words. For each item below, choose the word that best completes the analogy.

1. **wind : paperweight :: rain :**
   a. umbrella **b.** sunshine **c.** sweater
2. **drive : campaign :: competition :**
   a. amusement **b.** tournament **c.** sport
3. **injury : mortal :: mistake :**
   a. extreme **b.** benign **c.** failing
4. **syrup : molasses :: bird :**
   a. song **b.** hawk **c.** flight

Academic Vocabulary

In the story, the filmmakers are working on a piece about food stamps, which are meant to help people who have a low ***income.***

Income is an academic word. Some more familiar words that are similar in meaning are *salary, pay,* and *earnings.* What kinds of skills or experience could you use to increase your **income**?

For more on academic vocabulary, see pages 54–55 and R79–R81.

Write with Style

Apply Description

Assignment Consult maps and Internet searches to learn about the physical characteristics of a place you haven't been. Then, write a descriptive essay about the place.

Get Ideas While doing your Internet research, consult multiple Web sites. Find images and descriptions from a variety of online resources, such as encyclopedias, newspapers, and travel sites.

Give It Structure Organize the images and details into an outline. List each image and detail you want to describe, and group them spatially, focusing each section on a specific area within the place.

Look at Language Examine your language to make sure it accurately describes the details in an engaging way. Use synonym webs to vary or improve the language in your essay. In the center of the web, write a descriptive word; connect words with similar meanings. Extend the web with words that are synonyms for the first set of synonyms.

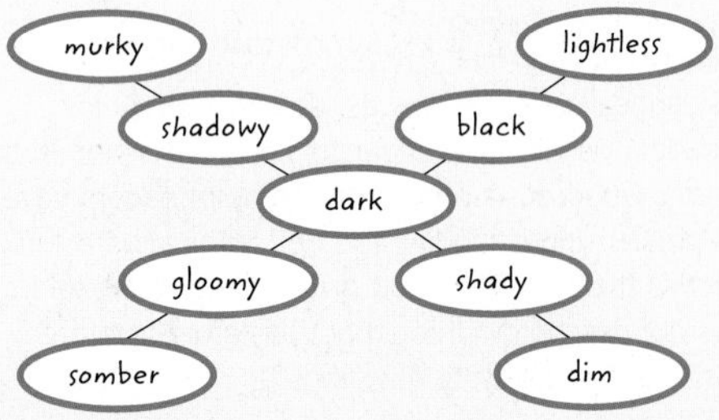

Select the most interesting word from the synonym web that describes your detail or image.

EXAMPLE:

Because the heavy jungle canopy blocks out most of the sun, the jungle floor is ~~dark~~ shadowy during the day.

LOG ON Literature Online

Selection Resources For Selection Quizzes, eFlashcards, and Reading-Writing Connection activities, go to glencoe.com and enter QuickPass code GL49787u1.

To create custom assessments online, go to Progress Reporter Online Assessment.

To create custom assessments using software, use ExamView Assessment Suite.

Before You Read

World Literature
England

The Interlopers

Meet **Saki**
(1870–1916)

Miserable old women eaten by ferrets, little girls who torment adults by making up strange tales, a cat who learns to talk so it can repeat the unkind comments it overhears—these are the plots and characters from the pen of the writer known as Saki. The stories are often a delightful mix of humor, horror, and plot-twisting irony that can be grim but unforgettable.

> *"A most improper story to tell the young children! You have undermined the effect of years of careful teaching."*
>
> —Saki, from "The Storyteller"

The Early Years Hector Hugh Munro was born in the former British colony of Burma, the third of three children. His mother died shortly after Hector's birth, so his father took the children to England. Leaving the children in the care of his two unmarried sisters, Hector's father returned to Burma. The aunts were extremely strict and rarely let the children play or go outside. Munro later related to his sister Ethel that he believed their unusual upbringing was responsible for their originality.

Saki Appears When Munro published *The Rise of the Russian Empire* in 1900, reviewers were quick to criticize his flippant style. However, the book contained elements that would survive in Saki's short stories: vivid descriptions of settings, scenes of pointless cruelty, and images of ferocious animals.

Munro then wrote a series of satiric pieces for a London newspaper. He began signing his work "Saki," a pseudonym he took from a twelfth-century Persian poem. He realized he had a talent for analyzing political intrigue, so he took a job as a foreign correspondent, traveling from one war-torn spot to the next.

In 1908 Munro returned to England. By 1909 he was able to earn a living as a freelance writer. Although he wrote two novels, Munro remains best known for his short stories. His biographer, Charles Gillen, believes that Munro's stories continue to be popular because readers see "something familiar and pertinent in Munro's cynicism and unflattering view of humanity."

When World War I began in 1914, Munro announced, "I have always looked forward to the romance of a European war." He enlisted and became one of the millions of soldiers who endured trench duty on the front lines. On a dark winter morning in 1916, he gave away his position when he ordered a soldier to put out a cigarette. Seconds later, Munro was killed by a shot through the head.

LOG ON **Literature** Online

Author Search For more about Saki, go to glencoe.com and enter QuickPass code GL49787u1.

Before You Read

Focus

Bellringer Options

Selection Focus Transparency 6

Daily Language Practice Transparency 8

Or **write on the board:** Do you think humanity is basically warlike or peaceful? Discuss whether most of humanity tends toward violence or peace.

Selection Skills

The Interlopers

Literary Elements
- Irony (SE pp. 80–88)
- Mood (SE p. 88)

Reading Skills
- Analyzing Cause-and-Effect Relationships (SE pp. 80–88)

Writing Skills/Grammar
- Write an Expository Essay (SE p. 89)
- Adverb Clauses (SE p. 89)

Vocabulary Skills
- Practice with Synonyms (SE p. 88)

Listening/Speaking/Viewing Skills
- Analyze Art (SE p. 82, 84)

Study Skills/Research/Assessment
- You're the Critic (SE p. 87)

Before You Read

Focus

Summary

The Gradwitz and Znaeym families have been fighting over a piece of forestland for generations. Ulrich von Gradwitz goes to the forest intent on catching Georg Znaeym poaching on his game and then killing him. When the two men meet, a tree falls on them. They reconcile as they lie pinned beneath the fallen tree, awaiting rescue. At the end of the story, they think they glimpse a rescue party but instead wolves appear.

For summaries in languages other than English, see Unit 1 Teaching Resources Book, pp. 87–92.

Vocabulary

Story Time Have students work in small groups to construct a story using all of the vocabulary words. When the students are finished, a representative of the group should read the story to the class.

For additional vocabulary practice, see Unit 1 Teaching Resources Book, p. 95.

For additional context, see Glencoe Interactive Vocabulary CD-ROM.

Literature and Reading Preview

Connect to the Story

Have you ever found that taking the time to talk to someone changed your opinion about that person? Write a journal entry about a time when you got to know someone better.

Build Background

Poachers are people who trespass on another person's land to hunt or fish, and they have long been a problem for landowners. Poaching has been a crime, sometimes punishable by death, for hundreds of years.

Set Purposes for Reading

Big Idea Matters of Life and Death

As you read "The Interlopers," ask yourself, How are the ideas of both death and new life always present in the woods?

Literary Element Irony

Irony is the contrast or discrepancy between appearance and reality. There are several forms of irony. **Situational irony** is a contrast between what is expected and what actually happens. As you read, ask yourself, How does Saki use situational irony to convey meaning about life and death?

Reading Strategy Analyze Cause-and-Effect Relationships

A cause is that which makes something happen. An effect is what happens as a result of the cause. When you **analyze a cause-and-effect relationship,** you explore the causes or reasons behind thoughts, actions, or events, and examine the results. You may find that an effect can in turn become the cause of the next effect. As you read, ask yourself, How does cause and effect control the plot and outcome of Saki's story?

Tip: List Causes and Effects Use a graphic organizer like the one below to record causes and effects in "The Interlopers."

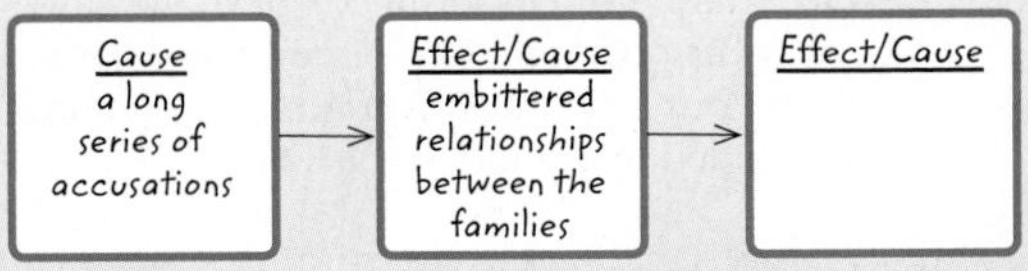

Learning Objectives

For pages 79–88

In studying this text, you will focus on the following objectives:

Literary Study: Analyzing irony.

Reading: Analyzing cause-and-effect relationships.

Vocabulary

acquiesce (ak′ wē es′) *v.* to consent or agree to without protest; p. 81 *He would not acquiesce to our plans for a surprise party.*

pious (pī′ əs) *adj.* having either genuine or pretended religious devotion; p. 83 *His pious acts included generosity to the poor and care for the sick.*

endeavor (en dev ər′) *n.* a serious or strenuous attempt to accomplish something; p. 84 *Despite their best endeavors, they could not rebuild the house in one day.*

languor (lang′ gər) *n.* weakness; fatigue; p. 85 *He could not explain the feeling of languor that made him want to sleep all day.*

reconciliation (rek′ ən sil′ ē ā′ shən) *n.* a settlement of a controversy or disagreement; p. 86 *Reconciliation between the two countries quickly brought an end to fighting.*

Literary Practice

Situational Irony Discuss the definition of situational irony on this page. Explain that writers often use this literary device to strengthen the plot. Tell students that in examples of situational irony, persons or events come together in unlikely situations. Give them the following examples:

- After two men rob a bank, they discover that their car has been stolen.
- A stunt woman trips over a curb and breaks her leg.
- A millionaire wins the lottery.
- You stay up all night finishing a research paper to learn that school is canceled because of snow.

Ask students to think of other examples of situational irony and share them with the class.

Poacher, 1894. Bruno Liljefors. Oil on canvas, 41 x 61 cm. Statens Konstmuseer, Stockholm. ©Estate of Bruno Liljefors. Licensed by VAGA, NY. ★

THE INTERLOPERS

Saki (H. H. Munro)

In a forest of mixed growth somewhere on the eastern spurs of the Carpathians,[1] a man stood one winter night watching and listening, as though he waited for some beast of the woods to come within the range of his vision, and, later, of his rifle. But the game for whose presence he kept so keen an outlook was none that figured in the sportsman's calendar as lawful and proper for the chase; Ulrich von Gradwitz[2] patrolled the dark forest in quest of a human enemy.

The forest lands of Gradwitz were of wide extent and well stocked with game; the narrow strip of precipitous[3] woodland that lay on its outskirt was not remarkable for the game it harbored or the shooting it afforded, but it was the most jealously guarded of all its owner's territorial possessions. A famous lawsuit, in the days of his grandfather, had wrested[4] it from the illegal possession of a neighboring family of petty landowners; the dispossessed party had never **acquiesced** in the judgment of the Courts, and a long series of poaching affrays[5] and similar scandals had embittered the relationships between the families for three generations. The neighbor feud had grown into a personal one since Ulrich had come to be head of his family; if there was a man in the world

---

1. The *Carpathians* are a mountain range in southeastern Europe, and *spurs* are ridges of mountains that extend from the main range.
2. *Ulrich von Gradwitz* (o͞ol′ rik fōn gräd′ vitz)
3. *Precipitous* means "very steep."
4. *Wrested* means "taken as if by force."
5. *Affrays* are disruptive, public quarrels or disagreements.

Irony *Explain how the description of the hunter and his game is an example of situational irony.* **1**

Analyze Cause-and-Effect Relationships *Why might it be significant that the feud became a "personal one"?* **2**

Vocabulary

acquiesce (ak′ wē es′) v. to consent or agree to without protest

Teach

Literary Element 1

Irony **Answer:** *Readers expect him to be hunting an animal; instead, he is hunting a human being.*

Reading Strategy 2

Analyze Cause-and-Effect Relationships **Answer:** *Because Ulrich takes it personally, he is less likely to let it go. Maintaining the feud is a matter of personal pride.*

For additional practice using the reading skill or strategy, see Unit 1 Teaching Resources Book, p. 94.

View the Art ★

Swedish artist Bruno Liljefors (1860–1939) is famous for his wildlife paintings. He painted outdoors in an effort to capture the true spirit of the natural world. His love of hunting is reflected in many of his paintings. Artistically, he was influenced by Impressionist and Japanese art.

For an audio recording of this selection, use Listening Library Audio CD-ROM.

Approaching Level

DIFFERENTIATED INSTRUCTION

Emerging Explain that the story takes place during the 1900s in the Carpathian Mountains, an area rich in vegetation and animals. **Ask:** Why would someone in the early 1900s consider land in this area valuable? *(They would be able to hunt and farm on the land.)*

Established Students may stumble over the unusual names in the story, which will slow down their reading. Instruct them to practice saying the names aloud until they are comfortable with them. Instruct students to look up unfamiliar words using a dictionary.

Readability Scores

Dale-Chall: 14.4
DRP: 65
Lexile: 1230

Teach

Big Idea 1

Matters of Life and Death
Answer: *There are hunters in the forest, so the animals may be running for their lives.*

Literary Element 2

Irony **Answer:** *Znaeym would know that Gradwitz was his enemy, and like the running deer, he should be trying to escape the hunter. Also, no hunter expects his prey to appear that suddenly.*

View the Art ★

Answer: *Some students may say that the deer running out of the woods accurately captures the setting of the story. Others may argue that the painting does not seem ominous enough.*

Gustave Courbet (1819–1877) is credited as an instigator and leader of the Realism art movement. Realism, as the term implies, relies on accurate depictions of subjects, with no embellishment. Courbet believed only in painting things that actually existed and that were of his time.

The Hunted Roe-Deer on the Alert, Spring, 1867. Gustave Courbet. Oil on canvas, 111 x 85 in. Musée d'Orsay, Paris.

View the Art Gustave Courbet was a leader of the Realist movement. He believed that the subjects of paintings should look as they do in real life. In your opinion, does this painting capture the setting of "The Interlopers"? Explain. ★

whom he detested and wished ill to it was Georg Znaeym,[6] the inheritor of the quarrel and the tireless game-snatcher and raider of the disputed border-forest. The feud might, perhaps, have died down or been compromised if the personal ill-will of the two men had not stood in the way; as boys they had thirsted for one another's blood, as men each prayed that misfortune might fall on the other, and this wind-scourged[7] winter night Ulrich had banded together his foresters to watch the dark forest, not in quest of four-footed quarry,[8] but to keep a look-out for the prowling thieves whom he suspected of being afoot from across the land boundary. The roebuck, which usually kept in the sheltered hollows during a storm-wind, were running like driven things tonight, and there was movement and unrest among the creatures that were wont[9] to sleep through the dark hours. Assuredly there was a disturbing element in the forest, and Ulrich could guess the quarter from whence it came.

He strayed away by himself from the watchers whom he had placed in ambush on the crest of the hill, and wandered far down the steep slopes amid the wild tangle of undergrowth, peering through the tree-trunks and listening through the whistling and skirling[10] of the wind and the restless beating of the branches for sight or sound of the marauders. If only on this wild night, in this dark, lone spot, he might come across Georg Znaeym, man to man, with none to witness—that was the wish that was uppermost in his thoughts. And as he stepped round the trunk of a huge beech he came face to face with the man he sought.

Visual Vocabulary
Beech trees have wide-spreading limbs and smooth, gray bark.

The two enemies stood glaring at one another for a long silent moment. Each had a rifle in his hand, each

6. *Georg Znaeym* (gaʹ ôrg znēʹ əm)
7. *Wind-scourged* means "wind-whipped."
8. *Quarry* (kwôrʹ ē) refers to an animal—or anything—that is being hunted or pursued.
9. *Wont* means "accustomed" or "used to."
10. *Skirling* is any long, shrill sound, but the word originally referred to the sound of a bagpipe.

Matters of Life and Death *How does the description of the behavior of the animals in the forest relate to the big idea?* **1**

Irony *Why is the appearance of Georg Znaeym unexpected?* **2**

Literary Practice

SPIRAL REVIEW **Imagery** Point out how Saki's word choice contributes to the mood of the story. Write on the chalkboard "restless beating of the branches." **Ask:** What mood does this create? *(Students may say that restless suggests tension and beating foreshadows violence.)* Have students skim page 82 for other examples of imagery. *(steep slopes amid the wild tangle of undergrowth; whistling and skirling; wild night)* Write these examples on the chalkboard. **Ask:** What mood do these images create? *(Answers will vary.)* Next have students write a paragraph describing the setting of the forest looks at night.

had hate in his heart and murder uppermost in his mind. The chance had come to give full play to the passions of a lifetime. But a man who has been brought up under the code of a restraining civilization cannot easily nerve himself to shoot down his neighbor in cold blood and without word spoken, except for an offense against his hearth[11] and honor. And before the moment of hesitation had given way to action a deed of Nature's own violence overwhelmed them both. A fierce shriek of the storm had been answered by a splitting crash over their heads, and ere[12] they could leap aside a mass of falling beech tree had thundered down on them. Ulrich von Gradwitz found himself stretched on the ground, one arm numb beneath him and the other held almost as helplessly in a tight tangle of forked branches, while both legs were pinned beneath the fallen mass. His heavy shooting-boots had saved his feet from being crushed to pieces, but if his fractures were not as serious as they might have been, at least it was evident that he could not move from his present position till some one came to release him. The descending twigs had slashed the skin of his face, and he had to wink away some drops of blood from his eyelashes before he could take in a general view of the disaster. At his side, so near that under ordinary circumstances he could almost have touched him, lay Georg Znaeym, alive and struggling, but obviously as helplessly pinioned[13] down as himself. All round them lay a thick-strewn wreckage of splintered branches and broken twigs.

Relief at being alive and exasperation at his captive plight brought a strange medley of **pious** thank-offerings and sharp curses to Ulrich's lips. Georg, who was nearly blinded with the blood which trickled across his eyes, stopped his struggling for a moment to listen, and then gave a short, snarling laugh.

"So you're not killed, as you ought to be, but you're caught, anyway," he cried; "caught fast. Ho, what a jest, Ulrich von Gradwitz snared in his stolen forest. There's real justice for you!"

And he laughed again, mockingly and savagely.

"I'm caught in my own forest-land," retorted Ulrich. "When my men come to release us you will wish, perhaps, that you were in a better plight than caught poaching on a neighbor's land, shame on you."

Georg was silent for a moment; then he answered quietly:

"Are you sure that your men will find much to release? I have men, too, in the forest tonight, close behind me, and *they* will be here first and do the releasing. When they drag me out from under these damned branches it won't need much clumsiness on their part to roll this mass of trunk right over on the top of you. Your men will find you dead under a fallen beech tree. For form's sake I shall send my condolences to your family."

"It is a useful hint," said Ulrich fiercely. "My men had orders to follow in ten minutes' time, seven of which must have gone by already, and when they get me out—I will remember the hint. Only as you

11. Here, *hearth* is used figuratively to mean "home and family."
12. *Ere* (ār) is an old word meaning "before."
13. To be pinioned is to be disabled by the binding of one's arms.

3 Analyze Cause-and-Effect Relationships *What causes the two men to hesitate instead of shooting immediately? What is the effect of their hesitation?*

4 Irony *What is ironic about the men's situation?*

Vocabulary

pious (pī′ əs) *adj.* having either genuine or pretended religious devotion

Teach

Reading Strategy 3

Analyze Cause-and-Effect Relationships Answer: *Despite their mutual hatred, they are civilized men who hesitate to kill a fellow human in cold blood. During that moment of hesitation, a tree falls on them.*

Literary Element 4

Irony Answer: *Each man thought that the other was the only enemy he had to worry about. Now both are trapped by a common "enemy," the tree.*

Advanced Learners

DIFFERENTIATED INSTRUCTION

Compare and Contrast Explain the conflict between the two families in the story: Both families believe they have a right to the land. Tell students about the famous McCoy-Hatfield family feud, which lasted over twenty years. This feud involved two families of the West Virginia-Kentucky area. Encourage students research this feud between the Hatfields and the McCoys and write an essay about it. Initiate a discussion in which students compare and contrast the feud between the families in the story with that of the Hatfields and the McCoys.

Teach

Big Idea 1

Matters of Life and Death
Answer: *They are trapped by a tree, not by one another. Their men might be long in coming. What else, besides the fallen tree, might occur in this dangerous forest?*

View the Art ★

Answer: *Students may say that the stark trees against a dark sky reflects the grim forest setting and the mood of menace and doom.*

William Fraser Garden (1856–1921) employed a technique known as photorealism. Although this is a painting, its precise attention to detail makes it look like a photograph.

The Wood at Dusk. William Fraser Garden. Watercolor. Private collection.

View the Art This painting is an example of photorealism—the details are so crisp that it looks like it could be a photograph. What elements of this painting are similar to elements in the story? ★

will have met your death poaching on my lands I don't think I can decently send any message of condolence to your family."

"Good," snarled Georg, "good. We fight this quarrel out to the death, you and I and our foresters, with no cursed interlopers[14] to come between us. Death and damnation to you, Ulrich von Gradwitz."

"The same to you, Georg Znaeym, forest-thief, game-snatcher."

Both men spoke with the bitterness of possible defeat before them, for each knew that it might be long before his men would seek him out or find him; it was a bare matter of chance which party would arrive first on the scene.

Both had now given up the useless struggle to free themselves from the mass of wood that held them down; Ulrich limited his **endeavors** to an effort to bring his one partially free arm near enough

Matters of Life and Death *Both men face death and threaten death at this moment. What about their situation suggests that life or death is not entirely in their own hands?* 1

Vocabulary

endeavor (en dev′ ər) *n.* a serious or strenuous attempt to accomplish something

14. *Interlopers* are people who violate or interfere with the rights of another, such as by trespassing.

Writing Practice

SPIRAL REVIEW

Respond to Literature

Point out the footnote for the word interloper on page 84. **Ask:** Why is "The Interlopers" a good title for this story? *(Both men think the other is trespassing on his property; Georg says that they are able to make peace because there are no interlopers from the outside to interfere.)*

Have students write a paragraph in which they answer the question. Suggest that they begin by rereading the beginning of the story and jotting down details about how each family feels about the other family and the land. Students should write a topic sentence for their paragraph that summarizes their reasons as to why the title is appropriate. Students should draft their paragraph and revise it so that it is well written and grammatically correct.

to his outer coat-pocket to draw out his wine-flask. Even when he had accomplished that operation it was long before he could manage the unscrewing of the stopper or get any of the liquid down his throat. But what a Heaven-sent draught[15] it seemed! It was an open winter, and little snow had fallen as yet, hence the captives suffered less from the cold than might have been the case at that season of the year; nevertheless, the wine was warming and reviving to the wounded man, and he looked across with something like a throb of pity to where his enemy lay, just keeping the groans of pain and weariness from crossing his lips.

"Could you reach this flask if I threw it over to you?" asked Ulrich suddenly; "there is good wine in it, and one may as well be as comfortable as one can. Let us drink, even if tonight one of us dies."

"No, I can scarcely see anything; there is so much blood caked round my eyes," said Georg, "and in any case I don't drink wine with an enemy."

Ulrich was silent for a few minutes, and lay listening to the weary screeching of the wind. An idea was slowly forming and growing in his brain, an idea that gained strength every time that he looked across at the man who was fighting so grimly against pain and exhaustion. In the pain and **languor** that Ulrich himself was feeling the old fierce hatred seemed to be dying down.

He looked across with something like a throb of pity to where his enemy lay . . .

"Neighbor," he said presently, "do as you please if your men come first. It was a fair compact.[16] But as for me, I've changed my mind. If my men are the first to come you shall be the first to be helped, as though you were my guest. We have quarreled like devils all our lives over this stupid strip of forest, where the trees can't even stand upright in a breath of wind. Lying here tonight, thinking, I've come to think we've been rather fools; there are better things in life than getting the better of a boundary dispute. Neighbor, if you will help me to bury the old quarrel I—I will ask you to be my friend."

Georg Znaeym was silent for so long that Ulrich thought, perhaps, he had fainted with the pain of his injuries. Then he spoke slowly and in jerks.

"How the whole region would stare and gabble[17] if we rode into the market-square together. No one living can remember seeing a Znaeym and a von Gradwitz talking to one another in friendship. And what peace there would be among the forester folk if we ended our feud tonight. And if we choose to make peace among our people there is none other to interfere, no interlopers from outside. . . . You would come and keep the Sylvester night beneath my roof, and I would

15. *Draught* is the amount taken in one drink. The word is pronounced the same as, and is often spelled, *draft.*

16. Here, *compact* means "agreement."

17. *Gabble* means "to talk rapidly and foolishly; jabber."

Vocabulary

languor (lang′ gər) *n.* weakness; fatigue

Irony *What is ironic about Ulrich's change of heart?* **2**

Analyze Cause-and-Effect Relationships *What effect do you think Ulrich's words will have on Georg?* **3**

Teach

Literary Element 2

Irony Answer: *It was Ulrich's becoming the head of his family that worsened the feud. No one would have imagined that his murderous hatred could fade.*

APPROACHING For approaching-level students, review the Literary Element on page 80. Ask a student to reread the explanation of irony.

Reading Strategy 3

Analyze Cause-and-Effect Relationships Answer: *Students may predict that Georg will gladly agree to end the feud. Others may predict that he will deny Ulrich a second time.*

English Learners

DIFFERENTIATED INSTRUCTION

Intermediate Remind students that many words in English have multiple meanings and can be used as different parts of speech. Ask students to think of two ways in which the word *party* can be used. *(one meaning is "a celebration"; another is "a group," which is used in the story)* Ask how Saki uses the word on the second column of page 84.

Have students work with a partner to read pages 84 and 85 carefully to identify words with more than one meaning *(bare, mass, open, fair, bury).* Instruct students to use dictionaries to find the meanings of those words and to choose a definition that fits the context of each word as it appears in the story.

Teach

Reading Strategy 1

Analyze Cause-and-Effect Relationships **Ask:** Given what you know about the feud, do you believe Georg is sincere in his promises of friendship to Ulrich? *(Students may say Georg was swept up in the moment and may not follow through. Others may feel he has truly changed.)*

Literary Element 2

Irony **Answer:** *Something will prevent their plan from being realized. Their men might attack before learning of their leaders' change of heart. Perhaps nature will again intervene.*

Big Idea 3

Matters of Life and Death **Answer:** *The two men will most likely die. They might have escaped this fate if they had made peace sooner.*

To check students' understanding of the selection, see Unit 1 Teaching Resources Book, p. 98.

come and feast on some high day[18] at your castle. . . . I would never fire a shot on your land, save when you invited me as a guest; and you should come and shoot with me down in the marshes where the wildfowl are. In all the countryside there are none that could hinder if we willed to make peace. I never thought to have wanted to do other than hate you all my life, but I think I have changed my mind about things too, this last half-hour. And you offered me your wine-flask. . . . Ulrich von Gradwitz, I will be your friend."

Visual Vocabulary *Wildfowl* refers to wild birds that are commonly hunted, such as ducks, geese, and swans.

1

For a space both men were silent, turning over in their minds the wonderful changes that this dramatic **reconciliation** would bring about. In the cold, gloomy forest, with the wind tearing in fitful gusts through the naked branches and whistling round the tree-trunks, they lay and waited for the help that would now bring release and succor[19] to both parties. And each prayed a private prayer that his men might be the first to arrive, so that he might be the first to show honorable attention to the enemy that had become a friend.

Presently, as the wind dropped for a moment, Ulrich broke silence.

"Let's shout for help," he said; "in this lull our voices may carry a little way."

"They won't carry far through the trees and undergrowth," said Georg, "but we can try. Together, then."

The two raised their voices in a prolonged hunting call.

"Together again," said Ulrich a few minutes later, after listening in vain for an answering halloo.

"I heard something that time, I think," said Ulrich.

"I heard nothing but the pestilential[20] wind," said Georg hoarsely.

There was silence again for some minutes, and then Ulrich gave a joyful cry.

"I can see figures coming through the wood. They are following in the way I came down the hillside."

Both men raised their voices in as loud a shout as they could muster.

"They hear us! They've stopped. Now they see us. They're running down the hill towards us," cried Ulrich.

"How many of them are there?" asked Georg.

"I can't see distinctly," said Ulrich; "nine or ten."

"Then they are yours," said Georg; "I had only seven out with me."

"They are making all the speed they can, brave lads," said Ulrich gladly.

"Are they your men?" asked Georg. "Are they your men?" he repeated impatiently as Ulrich did not answer.

"No," said Ulrich with a laugh, the idiotic chattering laugh of a man unstrung with hideous fear.

"Who are they?" asked Georg quickly, straining his eyes to see what the other would gladly not have seen.

"Wolves." ~

18. *Sylvester night* refers to New Year's Eve festivities honoring Saint Sylvester who, according to legend, converted Constantine the Great to Christianity after curing him of leprosy. A *high day* is any holy day (or holiday) in the church calendar.
19. To bring *succor* is to bring help, assistance, or relief.

20. Here, *pestilential* means "harmful" or "destructive."

2 **Irony** *What irony is suggested by this passage?*

Vocabulary

reconciliation (rek′ən sil′ē ā′shən) *n.* a settlement of a controversy or disagreement

Matters of Life and Death *What fate awaits the two men? What might have kept the men from this fate?* 3

Reading Practice

PARTNERS SPIRAL REVIEW

Dialogue The dialogue on page 86 conveys a great deal of emotion. The characters are hopeful and then fall into despair. Remind students that tone is a way of speaking or writing that conveys feeling. Ask students to practice reading the conversation between Ulrich and Georg. Students should indicate tone.

Have students read the dialogue with a partner, paying careful attention to tone.

Then **ask:** How does Ulrich probably feel when he suggests that they cry for help? *(The wind has stopped blowing and he is probably hopeful that someone will hear them and rescue them.)*

Ask: How do you think Ulrich feels when he sees what he believes are men running toward them? How does Georg feel when Ulrich tells him about this? *(Both men are very excited. They think they are about to be rescued.)*

After You Read

Respond and Think Critically

Respond and Interpret

1. (a)As you read the story, how did you think it would end? (b)What thoughts went through your mind at the end of the story?
2. (a)What started the feud between the von Gradwitz and Znaeym families? (b)In your opinion, why do Ulrich and Georg hate each other so much?
3. (a)How does the men's relationship gradually change while they are trapped under the tree? (b)What causes the change in the men's relationship? Explain.
4. (a)Who are the figures that Ulrich sees coming through the forest? (b)What is ironic about the way the story ends?

Analyze and Evaluate

5. To whom or what might the title of this story refer?
6. Do Ulrich and Georg seem to meet by chance or by design? Explain your answer.

Connect

7. **Big Idea** **Matters of Life and Death** What does Ulrich's statement that "there are better things in life than getting the better of a boundary dispute" suggest about how the two men have spent their lives?
8. **Connect to the Author** Saki is well known as a master of surprise endings, but he also drops hints to prepare a careful reader for the surprise. (a)What hints about the ending appear in "The Interlopers"? (b)How well has Saki prepared readers for the ending?

You're the Critic

Different Viewpoints

Read the two excerpts of literary criticism below. E. V. Knox notes how often Saki uses animals in his stories. Charles Gillen notes important features of Saki's surprise endings.

> *"The wild things run riot. They peep out in every plot. They peer from the corner of every conversation. . . . One creature or another, exotic or domesticated, is always playing a part in these tales, and sometimes a decisive part, terrible or whimsical. . . . Here is a world in which time after time in the author's eyes, human beings are a little lower than the animals."*
>
> —E. V. Knox

> *"It is difficult to give examples of [the surprise ending] aspect of Munro's writing without relating the entire plot of the story in point, so tightly knit was the preparation and skilled placing of false scents; the surprise ending of the story must be considered in relation to every little thing that has occurred before it."*
>
> —Charles Gillen

Group Activity Discuss the following questions with classmates. Refer to the excerpts and cite evidence from "The Interlopers."

1. How well do you think each critic's points are illustrated in "The Interlopers"? Give examples from the story.
2. Which element do you find more interesting—Saki's use of animals or his surprise endings? Explain.

After You Read

Assess

1. (a) Readers may have expected a "trick" ending. Others may have expected one man to be killed or that both would be saved. (b) Some may be startled or horrified by the end or hopeful that they may survive.
2. (a) Disputed ownership of the forestland (b) The feud was a family tradition.
3. (a) They decide to become friends. (b) Their life-or-death situation puts their pointless feud in perspective and creates a bond between them.
4. (a) Wolves (b) The men's conflict is about to destroy them just when they have finally resolved it.
5. Georg and his family trespassing on the Gradwitz land; Georg and Ulrich intruding in the wilderness; or the lurking wolves
6. By design; they are looking for each other.
7. They have wasted their lives in a petty dispute.
8. (a) "The roebuck . . . were running like driven things," suggests danger; "disturbing element in the forest . . ." suggests lurking menace. Several mentions of *interlopers* emphasize the idea of an intrusion. (b) Some may argue that these hints are too subtle.

You're the Critic

1. Many will agree Saki skillfully weaves together a series of ominous hints and "false scents." For example, because the men repeatedly insist their comrades are nearby, the reader expects the figures on the hill to be a search party. References to restless animals and repetition of the word *interloper* also foreshadow the men's fate. The plot twists keep the reader guessing.
2. Some will find the element of surprise suspenseful and fun. Others may prefer the use of animals as symbols and in imagery.

After You Read

Assess

Literary Element

1. Students may suggest that Saki wants readers to see the damage done by hatred and unresolved issues. He seems to warn readers to resolve conflicts before it is too late.
2. Students may say humans should recognize that they are part of a larger reality beyond their control. Both men felt in charge of the situation, but both soon learned they were at the mercy of chance and nature.

Progress Check

Can students identify irony?

If No → See Unit 1 Teaching Resources Book, p. 93.

Review: Mood

Details should include visual images of restless forest creatures, sounds of the wind blowing and the branches beating, and the fact that the story takes place on a winter night. Students may mention such words and phrases from the story as *prowling, unrest, disturbing,* and *wild tangle of undergrowth.*

Conclusion: The mood is scary and foreboding.

Literary Element Irony

Writers use **irony** to show meaning without giving readers a lecture or tacking on a moral to the story. For instance, a startling example of situational irony occurs in "The Interlopers" when the men, having agreed to end their feud and believing they are on the verge of being rescued by their comrades, discover to their horror that the "rescuers" are wolves. Saki leaves it up to readers to determine what the irony suggests about human beings and the way they live—or die. The situational irony of the story is that both men think only of their human enemy, but do not realize there are other elements that can determine their fates.

1. What do the numerous ironies in the story suggest about relationships between individuals?
2. What does the story's ironic ending suggest about human shortsightedness?

Review: Mood

As you learned on page 57, **mood** is the emotional quality of a literary work. A writer's choice of language, subject matter, setting, and tone contribute to creating mood.

Partner Activity Meet with another classmate and talk about what sort of mood Saki creates in "The Interlopers." Use a graphic like the one below to fill in descriptive details from the story and then form a conclusion about the mood based on those details.

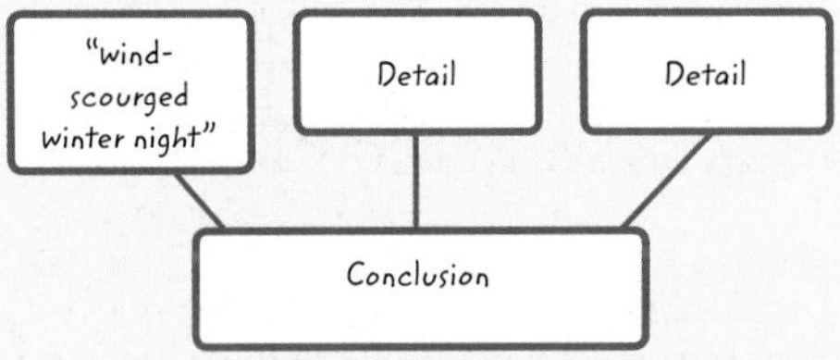

LOG ON **Literature** Online

Selection Resources For Selection Quizzes, eFlashcards, and Reading-Writing Connection activities, go to glencoe.com and enter QuickPass code GL49787u1.

Reading Strategy Analyze Cause-and-Effect Relationships

ACT Skills Practice

1. The tree that falls on Ulrich and Georg has which of the following effects?

   I. the reconciliation of both men
   II. the deaths of both men
   III. the renewed hatred of both men

   A. I and II only
   B. I, II, and III
   C. II and III only
   D. I only

Vocabulary Practice

Practice with Synonyms A synonym is a word that has a similar meaning as another word. With a partner, match each boldfaced vocabulary word with its synonym. You will not use all the answer choices. Use a thesaurus or dictionary to check your answers.

1. acquiesce	**a.** lethargy
2. pious	**b.** omission
3. endeavor	**c.** devout
4. languor	**d.** resolution
5. reconciliation	**e.** comply
	f. enthrall
	g. undertaking

Academic Vocabulary

In this story, Ulrich and Georg share a ***mutual*** *hatred.*

Mutual is an academic word. On its own, the word carries neither a negative nor a positive connotation. It can be used to indicate something negative (as in the sentence above) or something positive, such as, The new business partners felt **mutual** admiration for each other. Using context clues, try to figure out the meaning of the word in the sentences above.

For more on academic vocabulary, see pages 54–55 and R79–R81.

Reading Strategy

1. **A** is the correct answer. The fallen tree allows both men to settle their differences; it also renders them unable to defend themselves against the wolves.

Vocabulary

1. e **2.** c **3.** g **4.** a **5.** d

Academic Vocabulary

Answers may vary. Sample answer: Based on the use of "shared" and "for each other" in the context of both sentences, *mutual* means something in common or shared between people.

Respond Through Writing

Expository Essay

Analyze Cause and Effect The plot of "The Interlopers" is moved along by a series of cause-and-effect relationships. These relationships involve interactions between characters and between characters and nature. Write an essay in which you analyze a cause-and-effect chain in the story. Explain what the events suggest about the role of nature in the characters' lives. Use evidence from the text to support your thesis.

Understand the Task When you **analyze,** you identify the parts to find meaning in their relationships to the whole. A **thesis** is the main idea of a work of nonfiction, such as an essay. The thesis may be stated directly or implied.

Prewrite Review the graphic organizer you created for the Reading Strategy Tip on page 80. Take a few minutes to make any adjustments, adding information as needed. You can use these notes to help you organize your essay, following the chain of causes and effects chronologically in your essay.

Draft Use your chart to determine how each cause-and-effect relationship supports your thesis. You may want to use sentence frames as you draft your essay. Your body paragraphs should contain statements that support your thesis, such as the following:

The scene in which _____ *shows that* _____ *was the cause of* _____ *and* _____ .

Revise Ask a classmate to underline your thesis statement and highlight two statements that support your thesis. If this proves difficult, you may need to make your thesis and text support more clear. Get rid of superfluous or unrelated details. If you have used any technical terms, explain them thoroughly and correctly to avoid confusion. You may include all or part of your cause-and-effect chart in your essay as a visual aid.

Edit and Proofread Proofread your paper, correcting any errors in grammar, spelling, and punctuation. Use the Grammar Tip in the side column to help you with commas and adverb clauses.

Learning Objectives

In this assignment, you will focus on the following objectives:

Writing: Writing an expository essay.

Grammar: Understanding how to use commas with adverb clauses.

Grammar Tip

Commas and Adverb Clauses

Look at these two sentences. One has a comma and the other does not. Why?

After a tree falls on them, Ulrich and Georg find themselves trapped together and injured.

Ulrich and Georg find themselves trapped together and injured after a tree falls on them.

"After a tree falls on them" is an **adverb clause,** a dependent clause that modifies the verbs *trapped* and *injured* in the main clause.

When an adverb clause begins a sentence, it is set off by a comma. When an adverb clause follows the main clause, the comma is not needed.

After You Read

Assess

Respond Through Writing

Students' essays should

- have a clear thesis and supporting statements
- establish a logical organizational pattern
- establish and analyze cause-and-effect relationships
- be free of errors in grammar, spelling, and punctuation

A student who meets all of these criteria should receive the equivalent of a 4-point response.

A student who fully meets two or partially meets three of these criteria should receive the equivalent of a 3-point response.

A student who fully meets one or partially meets two of these criteria should receive the equivalent of a 2-point response.

A student who partially meets one of these criteria should receive the equivalent of a 1-point response.

For grammar practice, see Unit 1 Teaching Resources Book, p. 97.

For additional selection assessment, see Assessment Resources, pp. 51–52.

Approaching Level

DIFFERENTIATED INSTRUCTION

Emerging Guide students to see the irony in the story. Discuss the following:

- The two men planned to destroy each other, but nature destroyed them both.
- Ulrich tries to help the man he planned to kill.
- The two enemies reconcile, but no one will ever know.

To create custom assessments online, go to Progress Reporter Online Assessment.

To create custom assessments using software, use ExamView Assessment Suite.

TIME

Focus

Summary

John Beiler and his friends, Mike and Tom, go hunting on Alaska's Afognak Island. While alone, John breaks his leg. Stranded, he spends the night battling hypothermia, dehydration, and pain. At dawn, ravens overhead reveal his location. A helicopter flies John to a hospital. Although he spends Thanksgiving there, John is grateful to have survived his ordeal.

Teach

Preview the Article

Answers:

1. Excitement and a sense of danger
2. The final subhead is "Just in Time," which indicates that the outcome is probably positive.

Readability Scores

Dale-Chall: 7.1
DRP: 56
Lexile: 900

Learning Objectives

For pages 90–94

In studying this text, you will focus on the following objective:

Reading: Identifying problem and solution.

Set a Purpose for Reading

Read to learn about one man's struggle in a life-or-death situation.

Preview the Article

1. Read the *deck*, or the sentence that appears underneath the title. What emotions do you think the writer wants the reader to feel while reading this article?
2. Skim the boldfaced subheadings that appear in the article. Based on these, what do you think will be the outcome of the article?

Reading Strategy Identify Problem and Solution

Identifying problem and solution involves asking these questions:

- What is the main problem?
- What solutions are tried?
- What happens as a result?

As you read, ask yourself, What steps are taken to solve each problem? Use a chart like the one below.

Problem	Possible Solutions

TIME

Shattered

A terrible fall leaves a lone deer hunter with a shattered leg in the middle of brown-bear country. Now night is falling and nobody knows where he is.

By CHRISTOPHER BATIN

JOHN BEILER LIKED HUNTING SITKA BLACKTAIL DEER ON Alaska's Afognak Island. He loved the otter-filled bays, the scenic rock cliffs, the salmon streams, and just about all of the island's many natural wonders. Except one.

Afognak Island has a dark side. Typhoon winds can hammer the coastline without mercy for days at a time. Huge coastal brown bears roam the dark rain forests and salmon streams. Even hunters who are prepared for disasters often die or get seriously injured. For John Beiler, misfortune happened to others but not to him. Or so he thought.

At daybreak, Beiler and his hunting buddies Mike and Tom eyed the steep slopes of Mount Paramanof, rising 2,100 feet above their tidewater base camp. It was Thanksgiving week, and they were looking forward to blacktail steaks and mashed potatoes smothered in gravy. The hunters planned a several-hour climb to an alpine meadow where big bucks lived.

Beiler, who liked to hunt hillsides alone, left his buddies and crossed a marsh near the base of a steep cliff. He was a muscular, big-boned man, well suited to hunting the mountains. Although his rubber boots with tread soles didn't offer the best traction going uphill, they kept his feet dry as he crossed creeks and swamps.

By late afternoon, a light rain had filled the alpine landscape with the pungent-sweet smell of wet tundra. The approaching storm had caused the deer to hole up in thickets, and the dark outline of the beach below would take an hour to reach. Beiler walked faster so he could meet up with his friends before dark.

Reading Practice

Cause and Effect

SMALL GROUP SPIRAL REVIEW

Point out to students that the author builds the story through cause and effect. Remind students that what happens is the effect, and the reason it happens is the cause.

Ask: What is the main cause and effect of the story? *(Students may say that Beiler goes off on his own—cause—thereby causing him to break his leg and fight for his lfe—effect.)*

Break students into groups and have them find other causes and effects on page 90 and 91. *(Groups might note that his rubber boots, the approaching storm, and the slick grass and rotting plants may have caused him to fall.)* Ask students to design a cause-and-effect graphic organizer for the story. Have students continue to fill in their cause-and-effect organizer as they read.

The hillside's grass and rotting plants were as slick as greased ice. Leaning farther back for balance on the steep slope, he felt his right foot slide on an ice patch and shoot out from under him. He hit the ground with a jarring slam.

Beiler paused for a few moments to regain his breath. He tried to stand. Something wasn't right. 1

The sole of his left boot faced up, having slipped off in the fall. No big deal; he grabbed the boot top to pull it back on. His fingers slowed, then froze.

His foot was still inside the boot.

An Explosion of Pain

The horror of the moment paralyzed and confused him. He dug in his right heel and sat upright. There was no pain, yet the fall had snapped his leg in two places.

Beiler used his rifle barrel to straighten out his foot. The leg exploded in pain, taking away his breath and driving his head back in agony. He gritted his teeth and sucked air deep into his gut.

Long minutes passed before the pain lessened. The hill's steep angle made it impossible to move, so he took stock of the situation.

His survival gear consisted of a penlight, waterproof matches, three tea bags, a can of portable cooking fuel, aluminum foil, a candy bar, jerky, a knife, and 10 rounds of ammo. He was wearing a cap, gloves, a hoodless rubber-coated rain jacket, and the kind of waterproof pants used by fishers. Underneath he wore flannel-lined pants, cotton long johns, and a wool shirt. 2

Beiler decided to tough it out and let his friends find him. Being in the open, he would have a clear shot at any brown bears that viewed him as an easy meal.

The wool clothing soaked up drizzle like a dry sponge. Beiler sliced off his yellow rain pants, first down one leg, then the other. He pulled the fabric over his head and curled up against the storm.

Though he tried to hold his position, gravity kept biting away at his foothold, eroding the earthy stop under his right heel. He watched his injured leg twist grotesquely, then fold up like the edge of a pancake turned before its time. With teeth clenched tight, he eased uphill to straighten his leg. The pain swelled within him.

Using his fingers like claw hammers, he dug up clumps of mud and grass from the partly frozen ground. He slid into the dip and used the roots there to fashion a mud and grass splint around his leg. Then he braced 3

TIME

Teach

Big Idea 1

Matters of Life and Death
Ask: Why is it ironic that John Beiler is fighting for his survival in this story? *(Beiler is a hunter and went to the island to hunt deer. Instead, he is the one fighting for his life.)*

APPROACHING To assist approaching learners, **ask:** What problems might Beiler encounter now that he is injured? *(He is more likely to be attacked by a wild animal.)*

Reading Strategy 2

Visualizing **Ask:** What do the details about Beiler's survival gear tell you about him? *(Students may say the details tell them that he is an experienced hunter and is well prepared for his trip.)*

Cultural History ☆

Tundra Tundra comes from the Finnish word *tunturi,* meaning "arctic hill." Alpine tundra is one of two types of tundra in the world (the other is arctic) and is found at high altitudes on mountains. The tundra is characterized by cold temperatures, scarce vegetation, and permanently frozen ground called permafrost.

English Learners

DIFFERENTIATED INSTRUCTION

Early Advanced Remind English learners that compound words are formed by joining two words together to form a new word. Explain that by looking at the parts, students can figure out the meaning of many compounds. Point out the words *penlight* and *waterproof* on this page. Ask students to identify the component parts. *(pen* and *light; water* and *proof)* Penlight simply means a small pen-shaped light and something that is waterproof does not get wet. Ask students to find other compound words in the passage. Have them practice splitting the compounds into parts to decipher their meaning.

TIME

Teach

Literary Element 3

Mood Point out to students that through the use of descriptive details, authors can set the mood in nonfiction just as they do in fiction.

Ask: What is the mood of the article? *(Students may say suspenseful or scary.)*

ADVANCED **Ask:** How do the descriptive details enhance the mood? *Have students point out specific details in the story. (Students may say that using details like "twist grotesquely," "fingers like claw hammers," and "white-capped frenzy" creates tension.)*

3 himself and fired three shots. The recoil from the rifle set off more unbearable pain. Far down on the beach, a three-shot reply sailed past him and echoed off the rocks.

They heard him!

Back at Camp

Thinking Beiler had killed a deer, Mike and Tom returned to camp to start supper and await his return.

Beiler was realistic. The forested mountainside was now too dark and dangerous for his friends to begin looking for him. He knew he was on his own until morning.

Back at camp, Tom and Mike had made a bonfire. It roared and crackled, and served as a beacon for Beiler to follow. They shot their hunting rifles repeatedly.

Finally, they heard a single shot and knew he was alive.

From the mountain, Beiler watched the massive storm churn Shelik of Strait into a white capped frenzy. He saw a shrimp boat head for safety in the bay below. Soon after, a small runabout cut a wake to his hunting camp. No doubt his friends would ask the captain for help.

In the hours before midnight, steady rain and cold slowly numbed Beiler's legs and back. He was losing consciousness.

Beiler believed that if he fell asleep, he'd never wake up. He placed a tea bag in his mouth, steeping it in whatever saliva he could muster. The caffeine in the tea helped keep him awake. He sucked on the bags until the paper dissolved. Then he chewed on leaves and twigs. On the brushy alpine tundra, there was no wood.

Struggling to Survive

The cold rain trickled through his makeshift hood, inching through his underwear. He lit the cooking fuel and placed the hot metal can on his chest. Once warmed, he allowed the 50-knot gusts to put out the flame for a while.

He flashed his penlight to signal his location to anyone looking for him. The blackness failed to blink a reply. Around midnight, the last of the cooking fuel flickered out. His shivering became so intense that his gun barrel vibrated.

He twisted his mouth to catch rain. His clothes were soaked, yet he craved water. The wool gloves sopped up the puddles around him. With head back, he wrung every drop of the precious liquid into his mouth. A blast of rain pelted his face, and he prayed to survive the night.

The storm howled its opposition to the breaking

Writing Practice

SPIRAL REVIEW Mood

Remind students that the mood of an article or a story is the feeling that it evokes. **Ask:** What is the mood of this article? *(suspenseful)* Point out that many of the sentences are very short and that Beiler's situation is growing worse. This makes the reader want to keep reading to see what will happen.

Ask students to write a suspenseful nonfiction article. Students may choose to write about a real or an imagined event. They should choose their words carefully to ensure the correct mood. After they have drafted their articles, have students work in small groups to share their work with their peers, who should make suggestions on ways to make the mood more suspenseful.

dawn as the bay frothed in a tempest of whitecaps. The tops of hundred-year-old spruce trees whipped violently. Beiler had survived what seemed an eternity on this mountainside, and he was desperate for rescue.

Fifty yards away, a brush line snaked its way along the base of a shelf, taunting him with its promise of wood and fire. But the distance was just too great.

Survival became difficult. Hypothermia was a wrecking ball that continuously chipped away at his instinct for self-preservation, luring him into a world of neither pain nor cold. Beiler found an inner strength and calm thinking about his brothers, sisters, and family. He promised himself to give up his bad habits. And finally, he made his peace with his Maker, just in case.

Beiler snapped to full alert, fearful he had fallen asleep. Revitalized by the burst of adrenaline, he decided he was going to live. He wouldn't give up, no matter what.

The cold had left his leg and back muscles knotted up and useless. He pushed himself up with his arms, raising and balancing his torso on his numb, unbroken leg. Slowly he pushed himself upward and inched his broken leg forward. The world spun, and he hit the ground hard. He struggled to breathe as he slid and rolled headfirst for 20 feet before wedging into a clump of grass.

Beiler's left leg was as rigid as a wet towel and stuck out 90 degrees from his body. He gagged at the sight and would have vomited if he had had any food in his stomach.

A Long Crawl

Dragging his rifle, Beiler crawled to some brush 40 yards distant. His foot flopped and rotated as he did so. The pain stabbed him relentlessly, driving him crazy. But he kept crawling.

After reaching the brush, he reset his leg and took a breather. He cut pieces of wood and carefully arranged and tied them to his leg with strips of rain pant.

Meanwhile, at Mike and Tom's request, the shrimp boat captain radioed the Coast Guard that a hunter had spent a night on the mountain and was possibly in trouble. At the same time, the friends grabbed sleeping bags, food and water, and fired signal shots on the hillside below him.

Beiler knew they'd never see him in the brush. He tried to shout, but his throat was parched from thirst. Their rifle shots grew louder. He fired his last round, knowing that his rescue was now close at hand.

He tried to stand and again fell onto his back. Dazed, he looked up and witnessed a bizarre sight. Several ravens hovered over him on gusts of wind, performing an aerial circus of squawks and acrobatics. Mike and Tom saw the ravens and turned toward the commotion.

Beiler could hear shouts far off in the brush. He struggled to rise but couldn't. He was spent, exhausted. He gritted his teeth and slowly rose to his one good knee. If they passed him in the brush, it would be over.

With the gun as a crutch in his left hand, and the remnants of his yellow rain pants in his right, Beiler wobbled upright, teetered on one leg, and waved his pants and gun at the disappearing rescuers. His broken, cramped and tired limbs were unable to hold him, and he crumpled into a clump of broken flesh. He had given it everything he had.

Just in Time

It was enough. Mike and Tom saw him and busted through the brush to his side. Beiler's adrenaline surged at the sight of his rescuers, but he was in bad shape. Mike pulled out a candy bar, a fried-egg sandwich, and a cold soda. Beiler wolfed down the food. Ever so slowly, his limbs started to tingle with feeling.

Mike and Tom dressed him in a spare rain suit and roped both legs together from ankle to

> "Hypothermia was a wrecking ball that continuously chipped away at his instinct for self-preservation, luring him into a world of neither pain nor cold."

TIME

Teach

Cultural History ☆

Shelikof Strait The Strait lies between mainland Alaska and Afognak Island. Much of the island is devoted to a state park, one of the first conservation areas in the United States. In addition to the salmon, bears, and deer mentioned in the story, Afognak Island State Park is also home to the endangered marbled murrelet. In continuing conservation efforts, more land has been added to the park since its 1892 inception. Currently, the park is about 75,000 acres and covers most of the northern and eastern sides of the island.

Approaching Level

DIFFERENTIATED INSTRUCTION

Emerging Remind students that to paraphrase means to retell a story in their own words. To ensure that less proficient readers absorb the story, invite students to paraphrase the sections "A Long Crawl" and "Just in Time." Encourage them to jot down the events in sequential order as they read.

Established Explain that hypothermia is a condition where a person's body temperature is abnormally low. Windy and wet weather increases the chances of hypothermia. Explain that when the author says "Hypothermia was a wrecking ball that continuously chipped away at his instinct for self-preservation," he is using a metaphor. Hypothermia is not really a wrecking ball, but in this situation it is just as dangerous. Have students to provide other metaphors that reveal the danger of hypothermia.

TIME

Teach

Literary Element 1

Dialogue **Ask:** What effect does adding dialogue near the end have? *(Some may say that it reinforces the fictionlike feeling of the article; others will say that it lends realism.)*

Big Idea 2

Matters of Life and Death **Ask:** How does adding the detail about the dead man's clothes reinforce the life-and-death drama of the story? *(It reinforces how close Beiler came to dying and how easily he himself might have died.)*

Assess

1. Students' responses should summarize the article.
2. Some students will appreciate that many people enjoy risky pursuits. Others will think he was foolish.
3. (a) Beiler's leg broke in two places. (b) The description of the leg looking "like the edge of a pancake turned before its time"
4. (a) A storm comes. (b) Beiler's survival is threatened by the conditions.
5. The fear of losing his "instinct for self-preservation"
6. The detail is ironic. Beiler thinks that if he had not survived, his clothes would have been used in the same way. It also emphasizes the fragility of human life.
7. (a) Most will agree it was compelling because of the dramatic events and the vivid details, language, and imagery. (b) Some will say that such stories concern occurrences that do not happen to people every day. Others may say they remind people that life is precious.
8. Both men are hunters who find themselves in extreme conditions, where they become the hunted. Beiler's predator is nature, and Rainsford's predator is Zaroff.

thigh. Even his head was lashed forward to keep his neck from catching a log and snapping. They numbed him with pain medication and started their climb down to camp.

Once in the heavy timber and out of the wind, Mike stayed with Beiler and got a fire going. Tom descended to base camp for more supplies and to summon help.

The hot spruce fire pierced Beiler's stupor and drew him like a moth. The heat blistered the back of his rain jacket. Mike kept rolling Beiler away from the fire. Incoherent and suffering from hypothermia, Beiler didn't care if he was on fire. He needed heat desperately.

Mike piled more green sticks on the fire, and soon they could hear the rescue helicopter overhead. Mike dragged his friend into the open.

Gusts of wind howled across the mountaintop, as the copter dangled the rescue basket in front of Mike. He caught it single-handedly and strapped Beiler in before finally patting him on the chest.

"You're okay, John," Mike shouted over the noise of the chopper's blades.

"Tie me in tight, little buddy," Beiler replied, and gave him a thumbs up. 1

At Kodiak hospital, the doctor cut off the makeshift splint. Beiler's foot and leg flopped to the side. They cut off his wet, soiled clothes, set his leg, and treated him for hypothermia and dehydration.

Beiler spent Thanksgiving in the hospital, having cafeteria turkey instead of his blacktail venison. That weekend, with his leg in a full cast, he found himself with nothing to wear for his flight home to Fairbanks. A nurse brought him some clothes from a man who had recently died. 2

John thought about the many events that saved his life. A storm forced a fishing boat to seek shelter near their camp. The skipper had a radio that he used to call the Coast Guard for assistance. The ravens helped lead his buddies to his location. Had these things not happened, his clothes might have been the ones offered to someone else.

He hobbled upright on crutches out of the Kodiak hospital, a grateful man in borrowed clothes, having received a second chance at life.

—Updated 2005, from OUTDOOR LIFE, November 2004

Respond and Think Critically

Respond and Interpret

1. Write a brief summary of the main events in this article before you answer the following questions. For help on writing a summary, see page 42.
2. Beiler decides to hunt alone on Afognak Island, knowing that hunters "often die or get seriously injured" while doing so. How did you react to his story knowing that he willingly takes such a risk?
3. (a)What injury does Beiler suffer in the wilderness? (b)What details make Beiler's pain come alive for the reader?
4. (a)How does the weather change while Beiler is waiting for his friends to find him? (b)How do descriptions of the weather build suspense?

Analyze and Evaluate

5. Beiler faces an external conflict with nature. What internal conflict does he face? Support your answer with evidence from the text.
6. When Beiler was in the hospital, "a nurse brought him some clothes from a man who had recently died." Why does the writer include this detail?
7. (a)What makes Beiler's story compelling? (b)Why do you think people are interested in stories about matters of life and death?

Connect

8. How is Beiler's experience in Alaska similar to what happens to Ulrich and Georg in "The Interlopers"? What other stories from this unit are similar to the story described in this article?

PART 2

Rewards and Sacrifices

Stepping into the American Dream. Xavier Cortada. Acrylic on canvas, 96 x 97¾ in. Private collection.

View the Art Read the title of the painting above. What does "American dream" mean to you? What kinds of rewards and sacrifices might be involved in achieving "the American dream"? ★

BIG IDEA

Goals give purpose to life, and the struggles to attain them can bring both joy and heartache. The short stories in Part 2 deal with sacrifices people make as they strive to gain a reward or a goal. As you read the stories, ask yourself, Is the reward worth the characters' sacrifices?

95

UNIT ONE

PART 2

Analyze and Extend

Big Idea

Rewards and Sacrifices
Have students read the text under the Big Idea head. Urge them to discuss their long-term and short-term goals. Ask them to make a connection between their desire to reach their goals and the scene depicted in the art. Challenge students to consider the question, "Is the reward of attaining a goal worth the sacrifices?"

View the Art ★

Answer: *Students should give reasonable explanations of what "American dream" means to them. Students should explain why they name something as either a reward or a sacrifice.*

Cuban American artist Xavier Cortada (1964–) created *Stepping into the American Dream* in 2002 for the White House Conference on Minority Homeownership. Cortada specializes in large-scale public works, such as murals. For one mural in Miami, hundreds of people volunteered to paint.

English Learners

DIFFERENTIATED INSTRUCTION

Beginning/Early Intermediate Write the word *goal* on the board and make sure that students know its pronunciation and meaning. Allow students to generate a list of eight to ten words that describe a person who is able to reach his or her goals. Ask students to share their lists.

Approaching Level

DIFFERENTIATED INSTRUCTION

Emerging Ask students to think of a time during their lives when they reached a goal. Who originally set the goal for them? Did they have to make any sacrifices to reach that goal? Have students describe a time when they reached a goal.

For additional support for English Learners, see Unit 1 Teaching Resources Book, p. 111.

Focus

Bellringer Options

Daily Language Practice Transparency 9

Or display images of characters from popular culture. **Ask:** How would you describe these characters and their motivations? Have students consider what characters contribute to the stories as they read the selections.

Teach

Literary Element 1

Character Explain that many main characters in modern literature are flawed and morally ambiguous. Such protagonists are often referred to as antiheroes. Have students name heroes and antiheroes from stories or films.

View the Cartoon ★

Cartoonist Bill Watterson (1958–) drew the comic strip *Calvin and Hobbes* from 1985 to 1995.

Learning Objectives

For pages 95–97

In studying this text, you will focus on the following objective:

Literary Study: Analyzing character and theme.

LITERARY FOCUS

Character and Theme

How do the traits and actions of characters relate to theme?

Have you ever had to describe someone, perhaps when telling a story or recalling an event? Fiction writers describe a character's appearance, personality, and actions to give the reader a better understanding of the character's motivations, to reveal what makes the character tick. All of the information about the characters in a story, taken together with the plot and setting, can also reveal something about the overall meaning of the story.

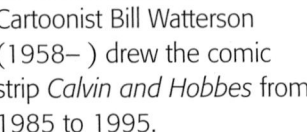

 ★

Character

Characters are the people, animals, and other individuals in a work of fiction. The most important characters in a story are called **main characters.** Among these main characters, there is a single **protagonist.** The protagonist is the central character around whom the central conflict revolves. **Minor characters** are those who help
1 or observe the protagonist solve the conflict.

Sheila was the middle daughter—at seventeen, all but out of reach. She would spend her days sunbathing on a float my Uncle Sierbert had moored in their cove, and before July was over I had learned all her moods.

—W. D. Wetherell, **from "The Bass, the River, and Sheila Mant"**

LOG ON Literature Online

Literature and Reading For more about literary elements, go to glencoe.com and enter QuickPass code GL49787u1.

Literary Element Practice

Character Words

Instruct students to create flashcards to help them remember literary terms associated with character. Have them write a literary term on the front of a card and its definition on the back. Students should use their flashcards to become familiar with the literary terms. Then ask students to think of a character that they like from a novel, story, television show, or movie. Ask students to decide what it is about this character that makes the character stand out in their mind. Ask students to apply each of the appropriate literary character terms to this character and write a brief explanation of why each term applies.

Round and Flat Characters Writers create two kinds of characters. A **round character** is complex, like people you know well. Like a real person, a round character has multiple and sometimes contradictory traits.

> There is within me (and with sadness I have watched it in others) a knot of cruelty borne by the stream of love, much as our blood sometimes bears the seed of our destruction, and at times I was mean to Doodle.
>
> —James Hurst, **from "The Scarlet Ibis"**

A **flat character,** on the other hand, shows only one or two personality traits. In "Rules of the Game," Lau Po is a flat character. His only role in the story is to teach the protagonist how to be a better chess player. A **stereotype,** such as a cruel headmaster or a jealous lover, is a flat character of a familiar type.

Dynamic and Static Characters Another way to describe characters is by watching to see how they change. A **dynamic character** develops or changes over the course of the story. Usually the development or change is spurred by the central conflict of the story. Very often, the change results in a character's newfound understanding of himself or herself or others.

> The truth was that after Liberty arrived, I never played with the others. It was as if I had found my double in another species.
>
> —Julia Alvarez, **from "Liberty"**

Static characters are characters that do not undergo a change. Most characters in a story are static so as not to distract the reader from the significant changes that occur in the protagonist.

Theme

The main idea, or message, of a literary work is called its **theme.** Keep in mind that a single work can have many themes, and that the theme of a story is different from its subject. The subject is what the story is about. The theme is the author's insight about life or human nature. "Rules of the Game" is about chess, but its theme addresses the generation gap that exists between mother and daughter.

> My mother had a habit of standing over me while I plotted out my games. I think she thought of herself as my protective ally. Her lips would be sealed tight, and after each move I made, a soft "Hmmmmph" would escape from her nose.
>
> "Ma, I can't practice when you stand there like that," I said one day. She retreated to the kitchen and made loud noises with the pots and pans.
>
> —Amy Tan, **from "Rules of the Game"**

Sometimes a story will have a **stated theme,** meaning the author expresses the theme directly. For example, fables have a stated theme. Most literary works, however, have implied themes. An **implied theme** is revealed gradually through a variety of literary elements, including plot, character, setting, figurative language, and point of view. **2**

Quickwrite

Chart Changes Think of a character from a story you know well. Using the graphic organizer below, describe how the character changes from the beginning of the story to the end.

Character Development

Beginning [ ] → Middle [ ] → End [ ]

UNIT ONE

PART 2

Teach

Reading Strategy 2

Make Inferences **Say:** Themes are rarely stated directly. You may have to "read between the lines" and review plot events to determine the story's message. When considering theme, try to complete the following sentences: "The message of the story is . . ." or "The point the writer wants to make is. . . ."

Assess

Quickwrite

Students should fill their graphic organizers with details about the character in the stories they choose. In most cases, the character will demonstrate some kind of development over the course of the story. Challenge students to make a generalization about the character's growth or lack of growth.

English Learners

DIFFERENTIATED INSTRUCTION

Beginning/Early Intermediate Remind students that a character trait is a distinguishing feature. Give them an example of a familiar character from a passage they have already read. Ask them to name some of the character's traits. Write these traits on the board.

Intermediate Ask a volunteer to read aloud the paragraphs about dynamic and static characters on page 97. Then ask students to provide examples of dynamic and static characters from a movie or book.

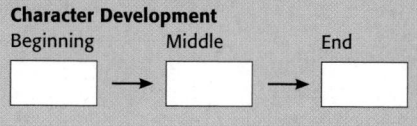

Before You Read

Focus

Bellringer Options

Selection Focus Transparency 7

Daily Language Practice Transparency 10

Or ask students to describe their neighborhoods. *(Crowded, public parks, businesses, vacant buildings, quiet, noisy, etc.)* Have students consider as they read how their neighborhoods affect their lives just as the narrator is affected by her life in San Francisco's Chinatown.

Cultural History ☆

Chinese Communism In 1921, Chinese politician Mao Zedong cofounded the Chinese Communist Party (CCP). This caused a political rift, and many Chinese fled. In 1949, the People's Republic of China was founded under a communist regime. Mao led the regime until his death in 1976.

Before You Read

Rules of the Game

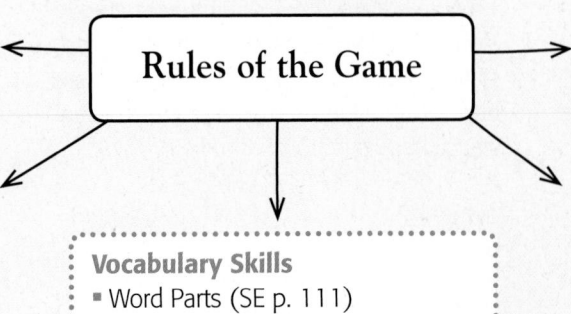

Meet **Amy Tan**

(born 1952)

Amy Tan's parents had very high expectations for her. "Of course, you will become a famous neurosurgeon," they said. In addition, they expected her to be a concert pianist in her spare time. Tan's parents were immigrants from China. Her father, John, came to the United States in 1947, and her mother, Daisy, fled here in ☆ 1949, just before the communist government came to power.

Tan remembers her father as playful, easygoing, and very loving. The pain and suffering of her mother's life in China, however, set the tone for the family. When Daisy became extremely unhappy, she had the urge to move to a new home. As a result, Tan attended eleven different schools before graduating from high school. The frequent moves made it hard for Tan to make close friends. To figure out how to fit in, she watched her classmates carefully. She would later draw on these observational skills when she began writing fiction.

> *"I enjoy the freedom to write whatever I feel like writing."*
>
> —Amy Tan

Tragedy Strikes When Tan was fifteen, a double tragedy transformed her life. Within several months, both her older brother and her father died of brain cancer. Tan's mother followed her pattern of moving the family to escape unhappiness. This time, she took Tan and her younger brother to Europe. First, they lived in the Netherlands. Later, they lived in Switzerland. Tan graduated from an international high school there and returned to the United States for college and graduate school.

On the Path to Writing Fiction Tan already had a successful career as a freelance technical writer when she began writing fiction as well. Eventually, she submitted her short story "Rules of the Game" to a publisher, along with an outline for a novel. Both were accepted, and Tan's first book, *The Joy Luck Club,* which incorporates "Rules of the Game," was published in 1989. *The Joy Luck Club* brought Tan overnight success. It was on the best-seller list for many months and has won many awards.

Tan has continued writing novels and has also written a memoir and two children's books. In addition, she is a vocalist in a rock band—Rock Bottom Remainders—that includes several other famous authors. This band tours the country and donates its profits to charity.

LOG ON **Literature** Online

Author Search For more about Amy Tan, go to glencoe.com and enter QuickPass code GL49787u1.

Selection Skills

Rules of the Game

Literary Elements
- Protagonist and Antagonist (SE pp. 99, 101, 106, 108–110)

Reading Skills
- Make Inferences About Characters (SE pp. 99, 101–104, 106, 109, 111)

Vocabulary Skills
- Word Parts (SE p. 111)

Listening/Speaking/Viewing Skills
- Analyze Art (SE pp. 102, 108)

Writing Skills/Grammar
- Research Report (SE p. 111)
- Semicolons (TE p. 104)

Literature and Reading Preview

Connect to the Story

Are clashes between generations inevitable? Discuss this question with a small group. Be sure each person explains his or her response.

Build Background

Like checkers, chess is a two-person game played on a board of sixty-four light and dark squares. The object of the game is to checkmate, or capture, the opponent's king. Chess players, like athletes, work their way up through the ranks by winning local, regional, national, and international tournaments. If they win enough tournaments at the international level, they reach grand master status.

Set Purposes for Reading

Big Idea Rewards and Sacrifices

As you read "Rules of the Game," ask yourself, What sacrifices are each of the characters willing to make for one another?

Literary Element Protagonist and Antagonist

The **protagonist** is the central character in a story. The **antagonist** is the character or force that opposes the protagonist. As you read "Rules of the Game," ask yourself, Who is the protagonist and who or what is the antagonist?

Reading Strategy Make Inferences About Characters

When you **make inferences about characters**, you pay attention to what the writer shows the characters doing and saying. Then you form ideas about their personality traits based on this evidence. As you read, ask yourself, What do each character's words and actions reveal about his or her personality?

Tip: Take Notes Make a web diagram like the one below for each character in this story. Use the diagrams to help you make inferences about characters.

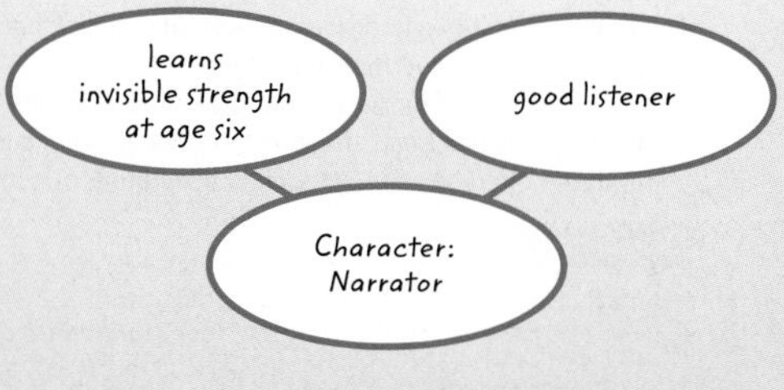

Learning Objectives

For pages 98–111

In studying this text, you will focus on the following objectives:

Literary Study: Analyzing protagonist and antagonist.

Reading: Making inferences about characters.

Research: Conducting Internet research.

Vocabulary

impart (im pärt′) *v.* to make known; to tell; p. 100 *Jan decided to keep her plan to herself and impart it to no one.*

relent (ri lent′) *v.* to become less harsh or strict; to yield; p. 104 *At first, they didn't want the younger athletes to play on their softball team, but later they decided to relent.*

adversary (ad′ vər ser′ ē) *n.* an opponent or enemy; p. 104 *Although he was friendly to me off the field, he was my adversary during the game.*

benevolently (bə nev′ ə lənt lē) *adv.* kindly; p. 105 *The conductor nodded benevolently to the young musicians after a great performance.*

malodorous (mal ō′ dər əs) *adj.* bad-smelling; stinky; p. 107 *The old sofa became malodorous after we left it out in the rain.*

Before You Read

Focus

Summary

Meimei is a Chinese-American girl growing up in San Francisco's Chinatown. She experiences a number of cultural clashes with her more traditional Chinese parents. These cultural differences worsen the generational gap between Meimei and her mother after Meimei becomes a chess champion.

For summaries in languages other than English, see Unit 1 Teaching Resources Book, pp. 112–117.

Vocabulary

Flash Cards Have students write each of the vocabulary words on a separate index card, with the definition on the other side. Pair up students and have them quiz each other using the cards. Then quiz students on the meaning of each vocabulary word.

For additional vocabulary practice, see Unit 1 Teaching Resources Book, p. 120.

For additional context, see Glencoe Interactive Vocabulary CD-ROM.

Approaching Level

DIFFERENTIATED INSTRUCTION

Established To help students better understand the game of chess, explain that it is a game for two players. At the start of the game, each player has sixteen pieces: one king and one queen, two rooks, two knights, two bishops, and eight pawns. Pieces can be moved in unique ways involving a great deal of strategy. A piece is captured when it can be moved onto a square occupied by the opponent's piece. Players take turns and attempt to make captures. A game between very skilled chess players can last for several hours. Ask students who are familiar with chess to share their opinions and/or experiences about players' skills and the strategies of the game.

Teach

Big Idea 1

Rewards and Sacrifices

Answer: *The narrator has learned exactly what her mother has tried to teach her—to apply self-control; her mother rewards her silence by buying what she knows the narrator wants.*

APPROACHING For approaching-level students **ask:** Which type of game is being referred to in the title? *(Most students will say the game is chess; some may say the game is the art of winning arguments.)*

Cultural History ☆

Ethnic Exclusion In 1882, the United States government passed an act called the "Chinese Exclusion Act." It placed restrictions on Chinese immigrants attempting to enter the United States. This act was finally lifted in 1943, about fifteen years before Amy Tan's story takes place.

For an audio recording of this selection, use Listening Library Audio CD-ROM.

Readability Scores

Dale-Chall: 7.3
DRP: 60
Lexile: 990

Rules of the Game

Amy Tan

I was six when my mother taught me the art of invisible strength. It was a strategy for winning arguments, respect from others, and eventually, though neither of us knew it at the time, chess games.

"Bite back your tongue," scolded my mother when I cried loudly, yanking her hand toward the store that sold bags of salted plums. At home, she said, "Wise guy, he not go against wind. In Chinese we say, Come from South, blow with wind—poom!—North will follow. Strongest wind cannot be seen."

The next week I bit back my tongue as we entered the store with the forbidden candies. When my mother finished her shopping, she quietly plucked a small bag of plums from the rack and put it on the counter with the rest of the items.

1 Rewards and Sacrifices *What has the narrator learned, and why does the mother respond the way she does?*

My mother **imparted** her daily truths so she could help my older brothers and me rise above our circumstances. We lived in San Francisco's Chinatown.[1] Like most of the other Chinese children who played in the back alleys of restaurants and curio shops, I didn't think we were poor. My bowl was always full, three five-course meals every day, beginning with a soup full of mysterious things I didn't want to know the names of.

We lived on Waverly Place, in a warm, clean, two-bedroom flat that sat above a small Chinese bakery specializing in steamed pastries and dim sum.[2] In the early morning, when the alley was still

1. *Chinatown* is a neighborhood or section of a city that is chiefly inhabited by Chinese people.
2. *Dim sum,* literally translated from the Chinese, means "dot-hearts," or "small treats that touch the heart." Dim sum foods are often bite-size dumplings, filled buns, or noodles.

Vocabulary

impart (im pärt′) *v.* to make known; to tell

Reading Practice

SPIRAL REVIEW Historical Approach

Explain to students that this story takes place in America during the 1950s, a time when many Chinese were immigrating to San Francisco and had been doing so for over 100 years. Ask students to answer these questions as they read:

- How does knowing about the wave of Chinese immigrating to California at this time help you to understand the beginning of the story?
- What do you understand about the characters after knowing more about Chinese immigration during that time?

As students read the story, have them note the ways in which Meimei's family is affected by the influx of Chinese immigrants in the 1950s in San Francisco.

quiet, I could smell fragrant red beans as they were cooked down to a pasty sweetness. By daybreak, our flat was heavy with the odor of fried sesame balls and sweet curried chicken crescents. From my bed, I would listen as my father got ready for work, then locked the door behind him, one-two-three clicks.

At the end of our two-block alley was a small sandlot playground with swings and slides well-shined down the middle with use. The play area was bordered by wood-slat benches where old-country people sat cracking roasted watermelon seeds with their golden teeth and scattering the husks to an impatient gathering of gurgling pigeons. The best playground, however, was the dark alley itself. It was crammed with daily mysteries and adventures. My brothers and I would peer into the medicinal herb shop, watching Old Li dole out onto a stiff sheet of white paper the right amount
3 of insect shells, saffron-colored[3] seeds, and pungent[4] leaves for his ailing customers. It was said that he once cured a woman dying of an ancestral curse that had eluded the best of American doctors. Next to the pharmacy was a printer who specialized in gold-embossed wedding invitations and festive red banners.

Farther down the street was Ping Yuen Fish Market. The front window displayed a tank crowded with doomed fish and turtles struggling to gain footing on the slimy green-tiled sides. A hand-written sign informed tourists, "Within this store, is all for food, not for pet." Inside, the butchers with their bloodstained white smocks deftly gutted the fish while customers cried out their orders and shouted, "Give me your freshest," to which the butchers always protested, "All are freshest." On less crowded market days, we would inspect the crates of live frogs and crabs which we were warned not to poke, boxes of dried cuttlefish, and row upon row of iced prawns, squid, and slippery fish. The sand dabs[5] made me shiver each time; their eyes lay on one flattened side and reminded me of my mother's story of a careless girl who ran into a crowded street and was crushed by a cab. "Was smash flat," reported my mother. 3

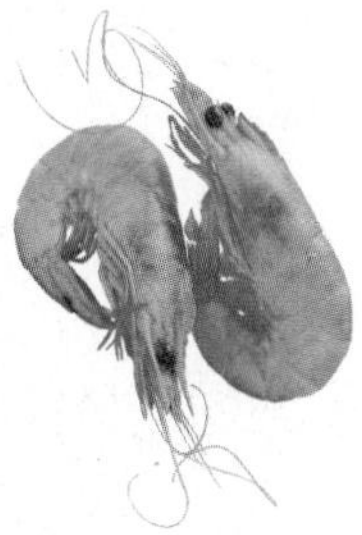

Visual Vocabulary
A *prawn* is a large shrimp.

At the corner of the alley was Hong Sing's, a four-table café with a recessed stairwell in front that led to a door marked "Tradesmen." My brothers and I believed the bad people emerged from this door at night. Tourists never went to Hong Sing's, since the menu was printed only in Chinese. A Caucasian[6] man with a big camera once posed me and my playmates in front of the restaurant. He had us move to the side of the picture window so the photo would capture the roasted duck with its head dangling from a juice-covered rope. After he took the picture, I told him he should go into Hong Sing's and eat dinner. When he smiled and asked me what they served, I shouted, "Guts and duck's feet and octopus gizzards!" Then I ran off with my friends, shrieking with laughter as we scampered across the alley and hid in the entryway grotto of the China

3. Anything *saffron-colored* is orange-yellow.
4. Anything that is *pungent* has a sharp smell or taste.

2 Protagonist and Antagonist *Who do you think will be the protagonist of this story? Why?*

4 Make Inferences About Characters *What can you infer about the narrator from this description?*

5. The *sand dab* is a small Pacific Coast flatfish related to the flounder.
6. *Caucasian* refers to the group of people who make up what is loosely known as the white race.

Teach

Literary Element 2

Protagonist and Antagonist **Answer:** *The little girl will be the protagonist because she tells the reader about herself.*

For additional literary element practice, see Unit 1 Teaching Resources Book, p. 118.

Literary Element 3

Setting Point out how the writer vividly creates the setting in which the story takes place. Explain that giving these details draws readers into the story by helping them create mental pictures of the place in which events will unfold. Ask students which detail is most vivid to them.

Reading Strategy 4

Make Inferences About Characters **Answer:** *She likes adventure and mystery; she appreciates small details of daily life.*

ADVANCED For advanced learners, **ask:** Based on the narrator's desire for adventure, what types of games would you expect her to play? *(Answers will vary.)*

English Learners

DIFFERENTIATED INSTRUCTION

Beginning/Early Intermediate Have students jot down unfamiliar words in their notebooks as they read. Help students use context clues to determine the meaning of these words. Guide them to use a dictionary to look up definitions. Explain that they will learn new words more easily if they use them in a sentence.

Approaching Level

DIFFERENTIATED INSTRUCTION

Established To practice *reading fluency,* have students read several paragraphs aloud. To demonstrate comprehension, ask students to make a judgment about the ideas presented in the text.

Teach

Reading Strategy 1

Make Inferences About Characters **Answer:** *She is daring and playful. She likes to have adventures and take risks.*

Reading Strategy 2

Make Inferences About Characters **Answer:** *She expects herself, her family, and other Chinese people to set high goals and to strive for excellence in everything they do.*

View the Art ★

Answer: *Students' responses will vary, but they should explain their answers.*

Russian born Alek Rapoport (1933–1997) immigrated to San Francisco when forced to leave the Soviet Union. Considered a dissident artist, Rapoport concentrated on inner life and spiritual objects in his work.

Dragon's Gate, Chinatown, San Francisco, 1986. Alek Rapoport. Tempera and masonite, 101.6 x 94 in. Private collection.

View the Art In the foreground, or front, of this painting are a child and an adult. Do they look the way you imagine Meimei and her mother to look? Explain. ★

Gem Company, my heart pounding with hope that he would chase us.

My mother named me after the street that we lived on: Waverly Place Jong, my official name for important American documents. But my family called me Meimei,[7] "Little Sister." I was the youngest, the only daughter. Each morning before school, my mother would twist and yank on my thick black hair until she had formed two tightly wound pigtails. One day, as she struggled to weave a hard-toothed comb through my disobedient hair, I had a sly thought.

I asked her, "Ma, what is Chinese torture?" My mother shook her head. A bobby pin was wedged between her lips. She wetted her palm and smoothed the hair above my ear, then pushed the pin in so that it nicked sharply against my scalp.

"Who say this word?" she asked without a trace of knowing how wicked I was being. I shrugged my shoulders and said, "Some boy in my class said Chinese people do Chinese torture."

"Chinese people do many things," she said simply. "Chinese people do business, do medicine, do painting. Not lazy like American people. We do torture. Best torture."

7. *Meimei* (mā′ mā)

1 Make Inferences About Characters *What can you infer about the narrator from this incident?*

Make Inferences About Characters *What goals and values can you infer the mother has, based on what she says here?* **2**

Writing Practice

SPIRAL REVIEW **Write Using Local Color** "Rules of the Game" is rich with local color, specific details that recreate the language, customs, and culture of a particular area. Explain to students that local color is an important element which helps to set the scene in Tan's short story. Ask students to review the story for passages in which the streets and alleyways of San Francisco's Chinatown are brought to life. Then have them write a brief essay in which they describe an event, giving special attention to the setting. Students might want to write about an experience that took place during a family vacation, a special event in their city or regional area, or a visit to a unique community. Students should use details that help to show the language, customs, and culture of the area.

My older brother Vincent was the one who actually got the chess set. We had gone to the annual Christmas party held at the First Chinese Baptist Church at the end of the alley. The missionary ladies had put together a Santa bag of gifts donated by members of another church. None of the gifts had names on them. There were separate sacks for boys and girls of different ages.

One of the Chinese parishioners had donned a Santa Claus costume and a stiff paper beard with cotton balls glued to it. I think the only children who thought he was the real thing were too young to know that Santa Claus was not Chinese. When my turn came up, the Santa man asked me how old I was. I thought it was a trick question; I was seven according to the American formula and eight by the Chinese calendar.[8] I said I was born on March 17, 1951. That seemed to satisfy him. He then solemnly asked if I had been a very, very good girl this year and did I believe in Jesus Christ and obey my parents. I knew the only answer to that. I nodded back with equal solemnity.

Having watched the other children opening their gifts, I already knew that the big gifts were not necessarily the nicest ones. One girl my age got a large coloring book of biblical characters, while a less greedy girl who selected a smaller box received a glass vial of lavender toilet water. The sound of the box was also important. A ten-year old boy had chosen a box that jangled when he shook it. It was a tin globe of the world with a slit for inserting money. He must have thought it was full of dimes and nickels, because when he saw that it had just ten pennies, his face fell with such undisguised disappointment that his mother slapped the side of his head and led him out of the church hall, apologizing to the crowd for her son who had such bad manners he couldn't appreciate such a fine gift.

As I peered into the sack, I quickly fingered the remaining presents, testing their weight, imagining what they contained. I chose a heavy, compact one that was wrapped in shiny silver foil and a red satin ribbon. It was a twelve-pack of Life Savers and I spent the rest of the party arranging and rearranging the candy tubes in the order of my favorites. My brother Winston chose wisely as well. His present turned out to be a box of intricate plastic parts; the instructions on the box proclaimed that when they were properly assembled he would have an authentic miniature replica of a World War II submarine.

Vincent got the chess set, which would have been a very decent present to get at a church Christmas party, except it was obviously used and, as we discovered later, it was missing a black pawn and a white knight. My mother graciously thanked the unknown benefactor,[9] saying, "Too good. Cost too much." At which point, an old lady with fine white, wispy hair nodded toward our family and said with a whistling whisper, "Merry, merry Christmas."

When we got home, my mother told Vincent to throw the chess set away. "She not want it. We not want it," she said, tossing her head stiffly to the side with a tight, proud smile. My brothers had deaf ears. They were already lining up the chess pieces and reading from the dog-eared instruction book.

8. By the *Chinese calendar,* the day on which a baby is born is counted as its first birthday. By this method, then, Meimei was one year old on the day she was born.

9. A *benefactor* is someone who gives financial aid; here, it refers to the gift giver.

Rewards and Sacrifices *What is Meimei's strategy for choosing the best present?* **3**

Make Inferences About Characters *How does what the mother says here contradict what she said earlier to the gift giver? What do her words reveal about her character?* **4**

Teach

Big Idea 3

Rewards and Sacrifices
Answer: *Meimei chooses the gift that weighs the most.*

Reading Strategy 4

Make Inferences About Characters **Answer:** *She is gracious and shows good manners to the gift giver, even though she is insulted by the gift; later on she is too proud and doesn't want to accept castoffs from others.*

ENGLISH LEARNERS For English learners, **ask:** Which of the mother's expressions and body language indicate that she is too proud to accept the gift? *(Students should note "tossing her head stiffly to the side" and "tight, proud smile.")*

Advanced Learners

DIFFERENTIATED INSTRUCTION

Understand Culture Tell students that each culture has features that make it unique. Ask students to point out references to Chinese culture on these pages. Encourage students to share aspects of their own ethnic culture. Prompt students by asking them what their families do on holidays. Point out that some of these traditions are part of their culture. Have students explain elements of their culture. Suggest that students provide examples reflecting language, traditions, dress, food, etc.

Teach

Big Idea 1

Rewards and Sacrifices
Answer: *She thinks the potential sacrifice of some of her candy will be well worth the reward of getting to play chess.*

Reading Strategy 2

Make Inferences About Characters **Answer:** *She is determined, disciplined, and systematic. She seems to learn things quickly.*

I watched Vincent and Winston play during Christmas week. The chess board seemed to hold elaborate secrets waiting to be untangled. The chessmen were more powerful than Old Li's magic herbs that cured ancestral curses. And my brothers wore such serious faces that I was sure something was at stake that was greater than avoiding the tradesmen's door to Hong Sing's.

"Let me! Let me!" I begged between games when one brother or the other would sit back with a deep sigh of relief and victory, the other annoyed, unable to let go of the outcome. Vincent at first refused to let me play, but when I offered my Life Savers as replacements for the buttons that filled in for the missing pieces, he **relented.** He chose the flavors: wild cherry for the black pawn and peppermint for the white knight. Winner could eat both.

As our mother sprinkled flour and rolled out small doughy circles for the steamed dumplings that would be our dinner that night, Vincent explained the rules, pointing to each piece. "You have sixteen pieces and so do I. One king and queen, two bishops, two knights, two castles, and eight pawns. The pawns can only move forward one step, except on the first move. Then they can move two. But they can only take men by moving crossways like this, except in the beginning, when you can move ahead and take another pawn."

"Why?" I asked as I moved my pawn. "Why can't they move more steps?"

"Because they're pawns," he said.

"But why do they go crossways to take other men. Why aren't there any women and children?"

"Why is the sky blue? Why must you always ask stupid questions?" asked Vincent. "This is a game. These are the rules. I didn't make them up. See. Here. In the book." He jabbed a page with a pawn in his hand. "Pawn. P-A-W-N. Pawn. Read it yourself."

My mother patted the flour off her hands. "Let me see book," she said quietly. She scanned the pages quickly, not reading the foreign English symbols, seeming to search deliberately for nothing in particular.

"This American rules," she concluded at last. "Every time people come out from foreign country, must know rules. You not know, judge say, Too bad, go back. They not telling you why so you can use their way go forward. They say, Don't know why, you find out yourself. But they knowing all the time. Better you take it, find out why yourself." She tossed her head back with a satisfied smile. ☆

I found out about all the whys later. I read the rules and looked up all the big words in a dictionary. I borrowed books from the Chinatown library. I studied each chess piece, trying to absorb the power each contained.

I learned about opening moves and why it's important to control the center early on; the shortest distance between two points is straight down the middle. I learned about the middle game and why tactics between two **adversaries** are like clashing ideas; the one who plays better has the clearest plans for both attacking and getting out of traps. I learned why it is essential in the

1 Rewards and Sacrifices *How do you think Meimei feels about the potential sacrifices and rewards in this situation?*

Vocabulary

relent (ri lent′) *v.* to become less harsh or strict; to yield

Make Inferences About Characters *What does the way in which Meimei learns to play chess tell you about her character?* **2**

Vocabulary

adversary (ad′ vər ser′ ē) *n.* an opponent or enemy

Grammar Practice

SPIRAL REVIEW SMALL GROUP **Use Semicolons** Remind students that a semicolon can be used to join two closely related independent clauses. Write this sentence on the board: "I said I couldn't finish my rice; my head didn't work right when my stomach was full." Tell students that Tan could have used a period instead of a semicolon or joined the sentences with a subordinate conjunction.

Write: "I said I couldn't finish my rice. My head didn't work right when my stomach was full."

Write: "I said I couldn't finish my rice because my head didn't work right when my stomach was full."

Break students into groups and have them reread pages 104 and 105 to look for places where Tan could have used a semicolon. Have them rewrite these sentences in their notebooks using the semicolon.

endgame[10] to have foresight, a mathematical understanding of all possible moves, and patience; all weaknesses and advantages become evident to a strong adversary and are obscured[11] to a tiring opponent. I discovered that for the whole game one must gather invisible strengths and see the endgame before the game begins.

I also found out why I should never reveal "why" to others. A little knowledge withheld is a great advantage one should store for future use. That is the power of chess. It is a game of secrets in which one must show and never tell.

I loved the secrets I found within the sixty-four black and white squares. I carefully drew a handmade chessboard and pinned it to the wall next to my bed, where at night I would stare for hours at imaginary battles. Soon I no longer lost any games or Life Savers, but I lost my adversaries. Winston and Vincent decided they were more interested in roaming the streets after school in their Hopalong Cassidy[12] cowboy hats.

On a cold spring afternoon, while walking home from school, I detoured through the playground at the end of our alley. I saw a group of old men, two seated across a folding table playing a game of chess, others smoking pipes, eating peanuts, and watching. I ran home and grabbed Vincent's chess set, which was bound in a cardboard box with rubber bands. I also carefully selected two prized rolls of Life Savers. I came back to the park and approached a man who was observing the game.

"Want to play?" I asked him. His face widened with surprise and he grinned as he looked at the box under my arm.

"Little sister, been a long time since I play with dolls," he said, smiling **benevolently.** I quickly put the box down next to him on the bench and displayed my retort.[13]

Lau Po, as he allowed me to call him, turned out to be a much better player than my brothers. I lost many games and many Life Savers. But over the weeks, with each diminishing roll of candies, I added new secrets. Lau Po gave me the names. The Double Attack from the East and West Shores. Throwing Stones on the Drowning Man. The Sudden Meeting of the Clan. The Surprise from the Sleeping Guard. The Humble Servant Who Kills the King. Sand in the Eyes of Advancing Forces. A Double Killing Without Blood.

There were also the fine points of chess etiquette.[14] Keep captured men in neat rows, as well-tended prisoners. Never announce "Check" with vanity, lest someone with an unseen sword slit your throat. Never hurl pieces into the sandbox after you have lost a game, because then you must find them again, by yourself, after apologizing to all around you. By the end of the summer, Lau Po had taught me all he knew, and I had become a better chess player.

A small weekend crowd of Chinese people and tourists would gather as I played and defeated my opponents one by one. My mother would join the crowds during these outdoor exhibition games. She sat proudly on the bench, telling my admirers with proper Chinese humility,[15] "Is luck."

10. When played at the expert level, a chess game has three parts—the *opening*, the *middle game*, and the *endgame*—each with its own tactics and strategies.
11. When something is *obscured*, it is difficult to see or understand.
12. *Hopalong Cassidy* is a fictional cowboy hero from early radio, movies, and television.

13. A *retort* (ri tôrt′) is a sharp, quick, witty reply.
14. *Chess etiquette* (et′ i kit) refers to the accepted practices or manners involved in playing chess.
15. *Humility* is the quality of being humble or modest.

3 Rewards and Sacrifices *When did Meimei first use the art of invisible strength to get a reward?*

Vocabulary

benevolently (bə nev′ ə lənt lē) *adv.* kindly

Teach

Big Idea 3

Rewards and Sacrifices

Answer: *At the beginning of the story, she gets her mother to buy salted plums.*

Cultural History ☆

U.S. Citizenship For an immigrant, becoming a U.S. citizen takes years. A person must first be a permanent resident for at least five years. Then, an applicant for citizenship must display knowledge of U.S. history and government, "the American rules" Meimei's mother mentions.

English Learners

DIFFERENTIATED INSTRUCTION

Early Advanced Explain to students that *syntax* is the grammatical arrangement of words in a sentence, and that the correct order of words in one language is often incorrect in another language. Point out these sentences on the page, which do not use correct syntax: "Little sister, been a long time since I play with dolls." "Is shame you fall down nobody push you," said my mother. Ask students to rewrite these sentences using correct syntax.

Teach

Literary Element 1

Protagonist and Antagonist **Answer:** *Meimei and her mother are in conflict over the best strategies for chess games. Some students may suggest that the mother is applying life lessons to the game.*

Reading Strategy 2

Make Inferences About Characters **Answer:** *The mother values her daughter's success greatly. She will release Meimei from family obligations to focus on chess.*

Writer's Technique ☆

Personification This is a figure of speech in which an animal, object, force of nature, or idea is given human qualities or characteristics. Amy Tan uses this technique in the fourth and fifth complete paragraphs on this page.

Ask: What is the author personifying? *(The wind)* What is the wind doing? *(It is giving Meimei advice about how to win the chess match.)*

A man who watched me play in the park suggested that my mother allow me to play in local chess tournaments. My mother smiled graciously, an answer that meant nothing. I desperately wanted to go, but I bit back my tongue. I knew she would not let me play among strangers. So as we walked home I said in a small voice that I didn't want to play in the local tournament. They would have American rules. If I lost, I would bring shame on my family.

"Is shame you fall down nobody push you," said my mother.

During my first tournament, my mother sat with me in the front row as I waited for my turn. I frequently bounced my legs to unstick them from the cold metal seat of the folding chair. When my name was called, I leapt up. My mother unwrapped something in her lap. It was her *chang*,[16] a small tablet of red jade which held the sun's fire. "Is luck," she whispered, and tucked it into my dress pocket. I turned to my opponent, a fifteen-year-old boy from Oakland. He looked at me, wrinkling his nose.

As I began to play, the boy disappeared, the color ran out of the room, and I saw only my white pieces and his black ones waiting on the other side. A light wind began blowing past my ears. It whispered secrets only I could hear.

"Blow from the South," it murmured. "The wind leaves no trail." I saw a clear path, the traps to avoid. The crowd rustled. "Shhh! Shhh!" said the corners of the room. The wind blew stronger. "Throw sand from the East to distract him." The knight came forward ready for the sacrifice. The wind hissed, louder and louder. "Blow, blow, blow. He cannot see. He is blind now. Make him lean away from the wind so he is easier to knock down." ☆

"Check," I said, as the wind roared with laughter. The wind died down to little puffs, my own breath.

My mother placed my first trophy next to a new plastic chess set that the neighborhood Tao[17] society had given to me. As she wiped each piece with a soft cloth, she said, "Next time win more, lose less."

"Ma, it's not how many pieces you lose," I said. "Sometimes you need to lose pieces to get ahead."

"Better to lose less, see if you really need."

At the next tournament, I won again, but it was my mother who wore the triumphant grin.

"Lost eight piece this time. Last time was eleven. What I tell you? Better off lose less!" I was annoyed, but I couldn't say anything.

I attended more tournaments, each one farther away from home. I won all games, in all divisions. The Chinese bakery downstairs from our flat displayed my growing collection of trophies in its window, amidst the dust-covered cakes that were never picked up. The day after I won an important regional tournament, the window encased a fresh sheet cake with whipped-cream frosting and red script saying, "Congratulations, Waverly Jong, Chinatown Chess Champion." Soon after that, a flower shop, headstone engraver, and funeral parlor offered to sponsor me in national tournaments. That's when my mother decided I no longer had to do the dishes. Winston and Vincent had to do my chores.

16. A *chang* is a good-luck charm.

17. *Tao* is short for *Taoism* (dou′ iz′ əm), one of the main religions of China. It is based on a belief in harmony with nature and one's fellow human beings.

1 Protagonist and Antagonist *What conflict has arisen between Meimei and her mother?*

2 Make Inferences About Characters *What does this decision indicate about the mother and her values?*

Reading Practice

Compare Characters
Remind students that character traits are distinguishing qualities that make up a character's personality. Meimei and her mother have some very strong character traits. Some of their traits are unique and some of their traits are shared. Ask students to complete a graphic organizer like the one that follows, in which they will list separate traits of Meimei and her mother, as well as those shared by both characters.

"Why does she get to play and we do all the work," complained Vincent.

"Is new American rules," said my mother. "Meimei play, squeeze all her brains out for win chess. You play, worth squeeze towel."

By my ninth birthday, I was a national chess champion. I was still some 429 points away from grand-master status, but I was touted as the Great American Hope, a child prodigy[18] and a girl to boot. They ran a photo of me in *Life* magazine next to a quote in which Bobby Fischer said, "There will never be a woman grand master." "Your move, Bobby," said the caption.

Visual Vocabulary
Considered to be one of the greatest players in the history of chess, American *Bobby Fischer* (1943–2008) became the youngest International Grandmaster at the age of fifteen.

The day they took the magazine picture I wore neatly plaited braids clipped with plastic barrettes trimmed with rhinestones. I was playing in a large high school auditorium that echoed with phlegmy coughs and the squeaky rubber knobs of chair legs sliding across freshly waxed wooden floors. Seated across from me was an American man, about the same age as Lau Po, maybe fifty. I remember that his sweaty brow seemed to weep at my every move. He wore a dark, **malodorous** suit. One of his pockets was stuffed with a great white kerchief on which he wiped his palm before sweeping his hand over the chosen chess piece with great flourish.

In my crisp pink-and-white dress with scratchy lace at the neck, one of two my mother had sewn for these special occasions, I would clasp my hands under my chin, the delicate points of my elbows poised lightly on the table in the manner my mother had shown me for posing for the press. I would swing my patent leather shoes back and forth like an impatient child riding on a school bus. Then I would pause, suck in my lips, twirl my chosen piece in midair as if undecided, and then firmly plant it in its new threatening place, with a triumphant smile thrown back at my opponent for good measure.

I no longer played in the alley of Waverly Place. I never visited the playground where the pigeons and old men gathered. I went to school, then directly home to learn new chess secrets, cleverly concealed advantages, more escape routes.

But I found it difficult to concentrate at home. My mother had a habit of standing over me while I plotted out my games. I think she thought of herself as my protective ally. Her lips would be sealed tight, and after each move I made, a soft "Hmmmmph" would escape from her nose.

"Ma, I can't practice when you stand there like that," I said one day. She retreated to the kitchen and made loud noises with the pots and pans. When the crashing stopped, I could see out of the corner of my eye that she was standing in the doorway. "Hmmmph!" Only this one came out of her tight throat.

My parents made many concessions to allow me to practice. One time I complained that the bedroom I shared was so noisy that I couldn't think. Thereafter, my brothers slept in a bed in the living room facing the street. I said I couldn't finish my rice; my head didn't work right when my stomach

18. A *prodigy* (prod ′ ə jē) is an extraordinarily gifted or talented person, especially a child.

Vocabulary

malodorous (mal ō ′ dər əs) *adv.* bad-smelling; stinky

Rewards and Sacrifices *What sacrifices does Meimei make to pursue chess? What rewards does she gain?* **3**

Teach

Big Idea 3

Rewards and Sacrifices

Answer: *She has given up exploring her neighborhood and her normal child's play. She has gained attention from her family as well as local and national fame.*

APPROACHING For approaching level students, **say:** In the beginning of the story, Meimei found adventure in playing in the alley, but now she prefers to play chess. **Ask:** Do you think Meimei finds chess adventurous? Explain. *(Students may say she thinks chess is adventurous because she describes learning "chess secrets" and "escape routes".)*

Approaching Level

DIFFERENTIATED INSTRUCTION

Established Expand on the Big Idea on this page. Point out the sacrifices Meimei's family makes so she can play chess. Ask students to discuss sacrifices they have made to help others or sacrifices that others have made to help them.

English Learners

DIFFERENTIATED INSTRUCTION

Intermediate Discuss the meaning of the phrase "to boot" as it is used by Meimei in the story. Also, ask students why they think that Meimei's gender became important when she started to excel in chess. Discuss how society has evolved away from such ideas, as well as ways in which it has held on to such thinking. Encourage students to use consistent standard English.

Teach

Literary Element 1

Protagonist and Antagonist **Answer:** *She is embarrassed by her mother's bragging; her mother thinks the narrator is embarrassed to be seen with her.*

View the Art ★

Answer: *Students should point out that the repeated squares obscure everything, including the players, around the table.*

The work of Portuguese-born artist Maria Helena Vieira da Silva (1908–1992) is often marked by a strong interest in perspective and its manipulation. *The Game of Chess* forcefully demonstrates this emphasis.

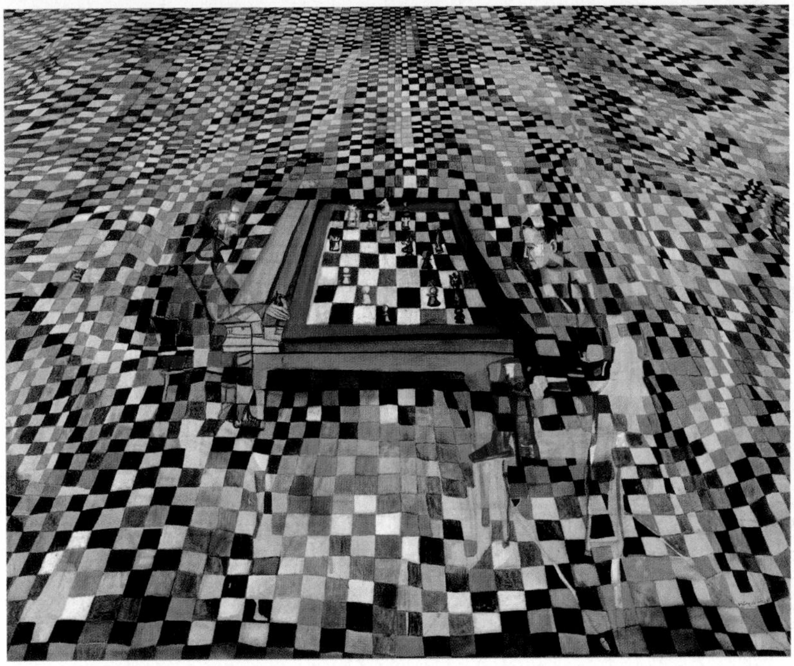

The Game of Chess, 1943. Maria Helena Vieira da Silva. Oil on canvas, 81 x 100 cm. Musée National d'Art Moderne, Centre Georges Pompidou, Paris.

View the Art Maria Helena Vieira da Silva often plays with perspective in her paintings. Do the repeated patterns of squares emphasize the chessboard table? Why or why not? ★

was too full. I left the table with half-finished bowls and nobody complained. But there was one duty I couldn't avoid. I had to accompany my mother on Saturday market days when I had no tournament to play. My mother would proudly walk with me, visiting many shops, buying very little. "This my daughter Wave-ly Jong," she said to whoever looked her way.

One day, after we left a shop I said under my breath, "I wish you wouldn't do that, telling everybody I'm your daughter." My mother stopped walking. Crowds of people with heavy bags pushed past us on the sidewalk, bumping into first one shoulder, then another.

"Aiii-ya. So shame be with mother?" She grasped my hand even tighter as she glared at me.

I looked down. "It's not that, it's just so obvious. It's just so embarrassing."

"Embarrass you be my daughter?" Her voice was cracking with anger.

"That's not what I meant. That's not what I said."

"What you say?"

I knew it was a mistake to say anything more, but I heard my voice speaking. "Why do you have to use me to show off? If you want to show off, then why don't you learn to play chess."

My mother's eyes turned into dangerous black slits. She had no words for me, just sharp silence.

Protagonist and Antagonist *Why is Meimei embarrassed? Why does her mother think she is embarrassed?* **1**

Listening and Speaking Practice

SPIRAL REVIEW SMALL GROUP

Group Discussion Point out that children often feel embarrassed by their parents or guardians as Meimei did. **Ask:** Can you remember a time when a parent or other adult accidentally embarrassed you?

In small groups, have students describe a situation in which an adult accidentally embarrassed them. After each student has shared his or her experience, ask the group to discuss the pros and cons of such an experience. Students should also discuss the lessons that can be learned from the experience. Encourage volunteers to share their responses with the class.

I felt the wind rushing around my hot ears. I jerked my hand out of my mother's tight grasp and spun around, knocking into an old woman. Her bag of groceries spilled to the ground.

"Aii-ya! Stupid girl!" my mother and the woman cried. Oranges and tin cans careened down the sidewalk. As my mother stooped to help the old woman pick up the escaping food, I took off.

I raced down the street, dashing between people, not looking back as my mother screamed shrilly, "Meimei! Meimei!" I fled down an alley, past dark curtained shops and merchants washing the grime off their windows. I sped into the sunlight, into a large street crowded with tourists examining trinkets and souvenirs. I ducked into another dark alley, down another street, up another alley. I ran until it hurt and I realized I had nowhere to go, that I was not running from anything. The alleys contained no escape routes.

My breath came out like angry smoke. It was cold. I sat down on an upturned plastic pail next to a stack of empty boxes, cupping my chin with my hands, thinking hard. I imagined my mother, first walking briskly down one street or another looking for me, then giving up and returning home to await my arrival. After two hours, I stood up on creaking legs and slowly walked home.

The alley was quiet and I could see the yellow lights shining from our flat like two tiger's eyes in the night. I climbed the sixteen steps to the door, advancing quietly up each so as not to make any warning sounds. I turned the knob; the door was locked. I heard a chair moving, quick steps, the locks turning—click! click! click!—and then the door opened.

"About time you got home," said Vincent. "Boy, are you in trouble."

He slid back to the dinner table. On a platter were the remains of a large fish, its fleshy head still connected to bones swimming upstream in vain escape. Standing there waiting for my punishment, I heard my mother speak in a dry voice.

"We not concerning this girl. This girl not have concerning for us."

Nobody looked at me. Bone chopsticks clinked against the insides of bowls being emptied into hungry mouths.

I walked into my room, closed the door, and lay down on my bed. The room was dark, the ceiling filled with shadows from the dinnertime lights of neighboring flats.

In my head, I saw a chessboard with sixty-four black and white squares. Opposite me was my opponent, two angry black slits. She wore a triumphant smile. "Strongest wind cannot be seen," she said.

Her black men advanced across the plane, slowly marching to each successive level as a single unit. My white pieces screamed as they scurried and fell off the board one by one. As her men drew closer to my edge, I felt myself growing light. I rose up into the air and flew out the window. Higher and higher, above the alley, over the tops of tiled roofs, where I was gathered up by the wind and pushed up toward the night sky until everything below me disappeared and I was alone.

I closed my eyes and pondered my next move. ~

---

2 Make Inferences About Characters *Why do you think Meimei runs away?*

Protagonist and Antagonist *Why do you think Meimei considers her mother the victor of their battle?* **3**

Teach

Reading Strategy 2

Make Inferences About Characters **Answer:** *Meimei might have been worried about what would happen because she blurted out her feelings to her mother, so she impulsively fled the situation.*

Literary Element 3

Protagonist and Antagonist **Answer:** *Meimei had to come home and her mother is treating her with anger and coldness.*

To check students' understanding of the selection, see Unit 1 Teaching Resources Book, p. 123.

Advanced Learners

DIFFERENTIATED INSTRUCTION

Understand Culture Ask students to consider the ways in which Meimei felt confined by her culture. Discuss why she felt this way and what she did to try to break out of this confinement. Talk about ways in which Meimei's culture helped her to reach her goals.

Finally, ask students to draw a conclusion as to whether Meimei's culture mostly helped or harmed her success. Have them write a paragraph explaining their thoughts about the subject.

After You Read

Assess

1. Some may like Meimei's determination to be independent of her mother. Others may say the mother is doing her best.
2. (a) Her mother taught her the art of invisible strength. She bit her tongue and got results. (b) She withholds knowledge.
3. (a) Her brother receives a set for Christmas. She reads, studies strategies, plays her brothers, and then challenges a man in the park. (b) It is a game of secrets.
4. (a) She acts uninterested in playing. (b) She says the right thing to get what she wants.
5. (a) Meimei tells her mother to stop showing off. Her mother thinks Meimei is embarrassed by her. (b) Students may say the issue is "Whose success is this?"
6. The mother is very proud. She brags to everyone.
7. Some may say the mother isn't justified; she is controlling. Others may say Meimei is not justified; she is ungrateful.
8. They have an adversarial relationship. Both try to anticipate each other's next move.
9. The parents sacrifice their traditional family values. Meimei and her mother sacrifice the good will between them.
10. Students might say that Amy Tan's observational skills enhance her writing by making her characters believable. The speech, mannerisms, and habits of her characters make them seem like real people and help readers feel close to them.

After You Read

Respond and Think Critically

Respond and Interpret

1. With whom do you sympathize most at the end of the story, Meimei or her mother? Explain why.
2. (a)What useful life lesson did Meimei's mother teach her when she was six years old? How did she learn it? (b)Explain how Meimei applies her mother's strategy to "winning arguments, respect for others, and . . . chess games."
3. (a)How and why does Meimei learn to play chess? (b)In your opinion, why does Meimei enjoy chess so much? Support your answer with evidence from the story.
4. (a)How does Meimei trick her mother into letting her play in her first chess tournament? (b)How does this scene reveal that Meimei can "see the endgame before the game begins"?
5. (a)What conflict arises when the mother and daughter go shopping? (b)What are Meimei and her mother really arguing about when they are shopping? Explain.

Analyze and Evaluate

6. How does the mother feel about her daughter's success? How can you tell?
7. Do you think the mother is justified in being angry? Is Meimei? Support your opinion with examples from your own experience or with details from the story.
8. How is Meimei's relationship with her mother like a game of chess?

Connect

9. **Big Idea** **Rewards and Sacrifices** What sacrifices do the main characters in this story make to pursue rewards?
10. **Connect to the Author** Amy Tan closely observed others when she was growing up. In your opinion, have her observational skills paid off? Does she portray each of the characters in a believable way? Explain.

Literary Element Protagonist and Antagonist

The **protagonist** and **antagonist** are important elements in this story. The action revolves around Meimei, the protagonist, who undergoes the main conflict. Readers are usually meant to identify with the protagonist and not with the antagonist.

1. Mrs. Jong is very supportive of Meimei's decision to play chess. What is the source of their conflict?
2. In what ways are Meimei and her mother victims of a "generation gap"?
3. Suppose the story had been told from the mother's point of view. Would Meimei still be the protagonist? Explain.

Review: Characters

As you learned on pages 96–97, **characters** are the people in the story. Meimei and her mother are the main characters in the story. Minor characters interact with the protagonist and antagonist to move the plot along.

Partner Activity Meet with a classmate to identify minor characters in this story. Discuss the roles they play in the plot. Make a chart like the one below to help you think about these characters.

Character	Role
Lau Po	teaches Meimei chess etiquette

Literary Element

1. Mrs. Jong brags about Meimei.
2. Meimei is comfortable with American customs; her mother is suspicious of them.
3. Meimei would probably be the antagonist. Mrs. Jong would be the protagonist because readers would see the story through her eyes.

Review: Characters

Students' charts should include minor characters such as the two brothers, Vincent and Winston, the father, and Lau Po, the man in the park. Have students devise questions about how they affect Meimei's motivation, ways of thinking, or character development.

Reading Strategy Make Inferences About Characters

SAT Skills Practice

1. At the end of the story, Meimei says, "I pondered my next move." This remark suggests that
   - (A) she acknowledges her mother's superiority
   - (B) she has learned the importance of obedience
   - (C) her days of attempting to please her mother are over
   - (D) she will remain in conflict with her mother
   - (E) her next attempt to escape will be successful

Vocabulary Practice

Practice with Word Parts Use a dictionary to find the meaning of each vocabulary word's root and to find the meanings of any prefixes or suffixes in the word. List the meanings in a diagram like the one shown. Then find three words that contain the same prefix, suffix, or root as the vocabulary word. Circle the word part that could help a person guess each word's meaning.

impart relent adversary benevolently malodorous

Example:

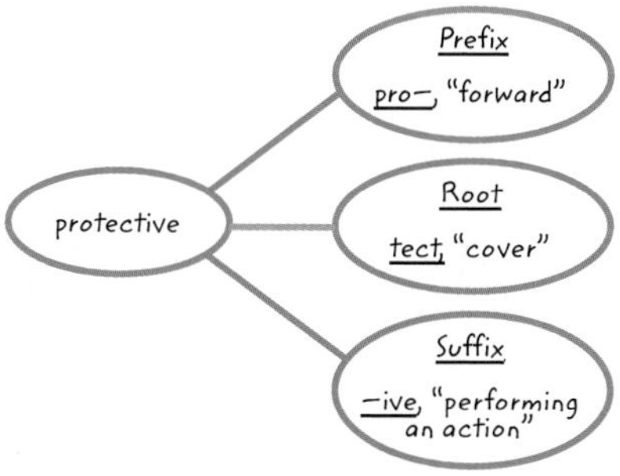

Related words: progress, detection, supportive

Research and Report

Internet Connection

Assignment Write a research report on the history of chess. Search several reliable online sources to answer questions such as: What cultures are known to have played chess? How does today's game differ from the game played hundreds of years ago? You may also want to search for information about rules and various strategies.

Get Ideas Make a list of key words to use in search engines and other Internet resources. During your research, add any related topics that you discover and want to investigate further.

Research Use your initial research as an overview of chess history and strategy. Choose two or three specific topics to focus on in your report, and research those areas. Make sure the information in the report is confirmed by multiple reliable sources.

Report To help organize the ideas for your report, create a web diagram for each of your main topics. Write the topic at the top of the diagram, and list the supporting details or ideas in the web below.

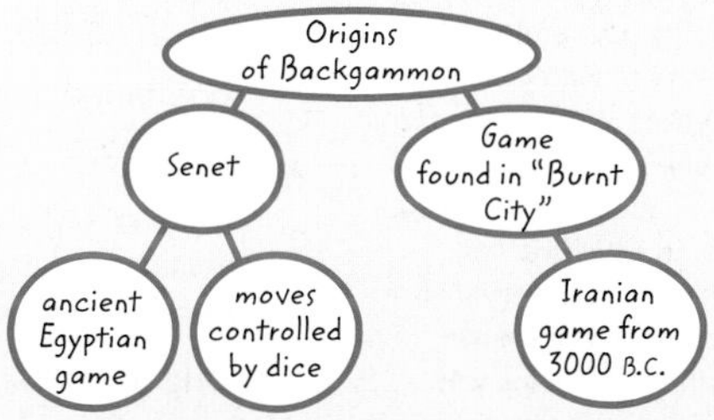

Use your diagrams to guide you as you write each section of the report. Make sure the transitions between sections convey how the topics are related. Include images in your report, such as photos of chess pieces or strategic diagrams, that support or help explain elements of your report.

LOG ON **Literature Online**

Selection Resources For Selection Quizzes, eFlashcards, and Reading-Writing Connection activities, go to glencoe.com and enter QuickPass code GL49787u1.

Research and Report

Students' reports should:

- provide accurate information about the history of chess and/or its rules and strategies
- focus on two or three specific topics discussed in-depth
- make use of graphic aids
- be engaging and well-organized

After You Read

Assess

Reading Strategy

1. D is the correct answer. Meimei has suffered a temporary setback, but she is already thinking of what next step to take in the conflict with her mother.

Progress Check

Can students make inferences about characters?

If No → See Unit 1 Teaching Resources Book, p. 119.

Vocabulary

impart:
Prefix im-, "not"
Root part, "divide"
Related words: imperfect, depart, partial

relent:
Prefix re-, "back"
Root lent, "to bend"
Related words: relenting, relentless, unrelenting,

adversary:
Root advers, "acting against"
Suffix -ary, "person engaged in"
Related words: adversity, revolutionary, visionary

benevolently:
Prefix bene-, "good"
Root volent, "wish"
Suffix -ly, "in a manner"
Related words: beneficial, malevolent, quickly

malodorous:
Prefix mal-, "bad"
Root odor, "smell"
Suffix -ous, "full of"
Related words: malnutrition, deodorant, poisonous

For grammar practice, see Unit 1 Teaching Resources Book, p. 122.

Focus

Activity

Write on the board: The coach supported the team. He wanted the players to do their best.

Ask students to identify possible ways to combine the two sentences. Rewrite the combined sentences on the board. (Possible answer: *The coach supported the team and wanted the players to do their best.*)

Teach

Combining Sentences

APPROACHING Point out to students that when two sentences are combined using the word *and,* students should remember to replace the capital letter in the second sentence with a lowercase letter.

Learning Objectives

For pages 112–113

In this workshop, you will focus on the following objective:

Grammar: Understanding how to combine sentences.

Grammar Workshop

Sentence Combining

Literature Connection In this quotation, Amy Tan combines several ideas into one sentence.

> *"As I peered into the sack, I quickly fingered the remaining presents, testing their weight, imagining what they contained."*
>
> —Amy Tan, "Rules of the Game"

If she had not combined the ideas, she might have written the passage something like this:

> "I peered into the sack. I quickly fingered the remaining presents. I tested their weight. I imagined what they contained."

To write effectively, you must make similar choices about sentence length and structure. Combining short sentences into longer ones helps you develop your own writing style.

Examples

Solution 1 Use a **prepositional phrase,** a group of words that begins with a preposition and ends with a noun or a pronoun.

Original: *Meimei's mother looked at her. Her face wore a scornful expression.*

Combined: *Meimei's mother looked at her <u>with a scornful expression</u>.*

Solution 2 Use an **appositive,** a noun or pronoun placed next to another noun or pronoun to give additional information about it. An **appositive phrase** is an appositive plus any words that modify it.

Original: *Meimei's mother was an opinionated woman. She wanted her daughter to be successful.*

Combined: *Meimei's mother<u>, an opinionated woman,</u> wanted her daughter to be successful.*

Solution 3 Use a participial phrase. A **participle** is a verb form, often ending in *-ing* or *-ed,* that functions as an adjective. A **participial phrase**—which includes a participle and other words that add to it—also functions as an adjective. In the sentence *Angered by her mother, Meimei ran away,* for example, *angered* is the participle and *angered by her mother* is the phrase. They both describe Meimei.

Drafting Tip

Vary the length and structure of your sentences. Work for a rhythmic, interesting balance of long and short sentences, remembering that brevity can have a dramatic force. By using different kinds of sentence openers—and by sometimes tucking information in the middle of a sentence—you can create stylistic interest.

Revising Tip

Read your draft aloud, stopping now and then to experiment with clusters of sentences. Whisper them to yourself in various combinations. As you read, listen to which version sounds most effective. This process is faster than rewriting and helps you decide on a "best sentence" to write down.

Writing Practice

SMALL GROUP **Sentence Combining** Have students work in small groups to create pairs of sentences. Students should then go back and rewrite a new sentence for each pair, using the sentence combining tips above. Allow volunteers to share their sentences with the rest of the class.

Original: Meimei took off through the dark streets. She ran frantically.

Combined: Running frantically, Meimei took off through the dark streets.

Solution 4 Use a **coordinating conjunction** to join words or groups of words with equal grammatical weight in a sentence. Coordinating conjunctions include words such as *and, but, or, so, nor, for,* and *yet.*

Original: Meimei worked hard at chess. She won many tournaments. She never satisfied her mother.

Combined: Meimei worked hard at chess and won many tournaments, but she never satisfied her mother.

Solution 5 Use a **subordinating conjunction** to join two clauses, or ideas, in such a way as to make one dependent upon the other. Subordinating conjunctions include words such as *after, although, as, because, if, since,* and *when.*

Original: Meimei finally returned home. She had nowhere else to go.

Combined: Meimei finally returned home because she had nowhere else to go.

Solution 6 Use an **adjective clause,** a group of words with a subject and a predicate that modify a noun or a pronoun. Adjective clauses often begin with *who, whom, whose, that,* and *which.*

Original: The chess set was missing two pieces. It belonged to Vincent.

Combined: The chess set, which belonged to Vincent, was missing two pieces.

Tip

Remember that there are many ways of combining sentences. When deciding which solution works best, ask yourself the following questions:

Is my solution free of excess words?

Does my solution emphasize the important idea of the sentence?

Does my solution flow naturally when I read it aloud?

Is my solution a complete sentence with a subject and predicate and not just a long fragment?

Revise

1. Use a participial phrase to combine the following sentences: *Meimei and her mother had an argument. They were standing on the sidewalk.*
2. Use the subordinating conjunctions *although* and *because* to combine these sentences: *The door was locked. She knew her parents were at home. She could hear them eating dinner.*
3. Combine the following sentences using an appositive phrase or an adjective clause: *Lau Po was Meimei's first teacher. He taught her everything he knew about chess.*

LOG ON **Literature** Online

Grammar For more grammar practice, go to glencoe.com and enter QuickPass code GL49787u1.

Assess

Revise

1. Standing on the sidewalk, Meimei and her mother had an argument.
2. Although the door was locked, she knew her parents were at home because she could hear them eating dinner.
3. appositive phrase: Lau Po, Meimei's first teacher, taught her everything he knew about chess. adjective clause: Lau Po, who was Meimei's first teacher, taught her everything he knew about chess.

For additional grammar practice, see Unit 1 Teaching Resources Book, p. 125.

Approaching Level

DIFFERENTIATED INSTRUCTION

Emerging Point out to students that semicolons can be valuable tools for combining sentences. A semicolon implies a stronger connection between sentences than a period does. On the board, **write:** "Her voice was hoarse; she had been to a football game the day before." Point out that this sentence has both two main clauses and internal punctuation, but they are closely related.

Have students review a recent writing assignment, looking for three sentences that could have been joined by semicolons instead of separated by periods or conjunctions. Ask students to rewrite these sentences using semicolons.

Before You Read

Focus

Bellringer Options

Selection Focus Transparency 8

Daily Language Practice Transparency 11

Or **say:** Describe a time when you made a sacrifice in order to solve a problem. *(Student answers will vary, but they should draw from experiences in their own life.)*

Ask: What personal items would you have a hard time giving up? *(Student answers will vary, but they should explain why they would have a hard time giving it up.)*

Have students consider as they read how the characters in the story are willing to sacrifice for each other.

Before You Read

The Gift of the Magi

Meet **O. Henry**

(1862–1910)

In the fall of 1903, O. Henry was living in a room at the small, rundown Hotel Marty in New York City. He had published a few stories in local magazines, but was still relatively unknown when editors at the *New York World* newspaper sent a young reporter to track down this mysterious writer. By the next day, O. Henry had an agreement with the newspaper to write one story a week for the magazine section of their Sunday edition. The *World* had the largest daily circulation in the world, and O. Henry's stories about New York life became immensely popular. By the time he left the newspaper after less than three years, O. Henry had established his reputation as a gifted storyteller and master of surprise endings.

> *"Life is made up of sobs, sniffles, and smiles, with sniffles predominating."*
>
> —O. Henry, from "The Gift of the Magi"

A Life of Twists O. Henry was the pen name used by William Sydney Porter, who was born in Greensboro, North Carolina. At the age of twenty, he moved to Austin, Texas, where he held a variety of jobs, eventually becoming a bank teller. He married and became a reporter and columnist for the *Houston Post*. After a few years, his wife was diagnosed with tuberculosis, and he was accused of embezzling from the bank where he worked. Some people have claimed that he was stealing money to help pay his wife's medical bills. O. Henry fled to Central America, but his wife was too ill to accompany him. Months later, when her condition worsened, he returned and turned himself in to the police. His wife soon died, and O. Henry spent three years in prison in Ohio. It was during his time in prison that he began writing the stories that would make him famous. W. S. Porter emerged from prison as O. Henry.

Success in the Big City In 1902 O. Henry moved to New York City and started trying to sell his stories. In a few years his luck changed for the better, and his position with the *New York World* helped make him a celebrated author. He published more than three hundred stories and gained worldwide acclaim. O. Henry's writing is admired for its colorful and realistic depictions of the everyday lives of New Yorkers. His stories are known for their plot twists and surprise endings. In fact, O. Henry's own life ended with a "twist"—his funeral was somehow scheduled in the same church at the same time as someone else's wedding! The O. Henry Award honors the authors of the best stories printed each year in American magazines.

LOG ON **Literature** Online

Author Search For more about O. Henry, go to glencoe.com and enter QuickPass code GL49787u1.

Selection Skills

The Gift of the Magi

Literary Elements
- Characterization (SE pp. 115–123)
- Plot (SE p. 123)
- Point of View (TE p. 119)

Reading Skills
- Analyze Description (SE pp. 115–123)
- Situational Irony (TE p. 118)

Vocabulary Skills
- Synonyms (SE pp. 115, 123)

Listening/Speaking/Viewing Skills
- Analyze Art (SE p. 118; TE p. 120)

Writing Skills/Grammar
- Reflective Essay (SE p. 123)
- Transitional Phrases (SE p. 123)

Literature and Reading Preview

Connect to the Story

What personal items would you have a hard time giving up and why? List the four items you would have the hardest time parting with.

Build Background

According to the New Testament of the Bible, the Magi were the three wise men who came from the East to give gifts to the newborn baby Jesus. Over time, the Magi have come to be associated with the practice of giving gifts.

Set Purposes for Reading

Big Idea Rewards and Sacrifices

As you read the story, ask yourself, What are the characters willing to sacrifice and what do they expect as rewards?

Literary Element Characterization

Characterization is the method a writer uses to reveal the personality traits of a character. A character's personality can be revealed through the narrator's commentary; through the character's words, thoughts, and actions; and through the thoughts and words of other characters. As you read, ask yourself, Based on their words and actions, what can I learn about the personality traits of the characters in this story?

Reading Strategy Analyze Description

When you **analyze description**, you examine the language the writer uses to portray a person, place, or experience. Good descriptive writing appeals to the senses through word choice, concrete details, and figurative language—language that uses expressions that are not literally true, such as comparing two seemingly unlike things. As you read, ask yourself, How does description help me visualize the people, places, and events?

Tip: List Details Use a diagram to list descriptive details about Della, Jim, their surroundings, and objects in the story.

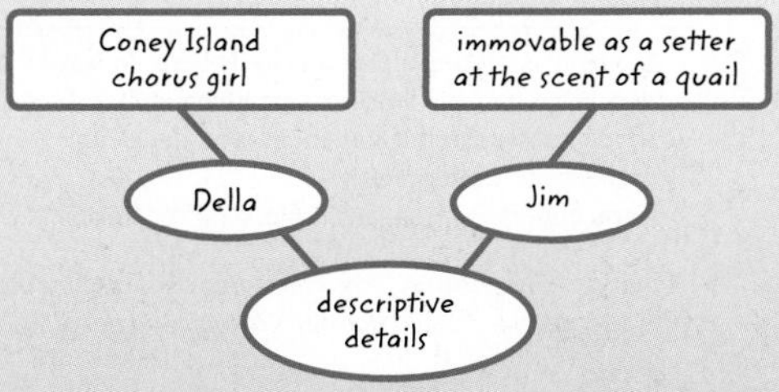

Learning Objectives

For pages 114–123

In studying this text, you will focus on the following objectives:

Literary Study: Analyzing characterization.

Reading: Analyzing description.

Vocabulary

imputation (im′ pyə tā′ shən) *n.* an accusation; p. 116 *He hadn't done anything wrong, so he didn't like the imputation.*

parsimony (pär′ sə mō′ nē) *n.* stinginess; p. 116 *Despite his great wealth, the man was known for his parsimony.*

depreciate (di prē′ shē āt′) *v.* to lessen the price or value of; p. 117 *The floodwater that soaked Anton's storage boxes depreciated his baseball card collection.*

prudence (pro͞od′ əns) *n.* caution; good judgment; p. 119 *It was a dangerous place, and therefore her prudence was wise.*

Tip: Synonyms Synonyms are words that have the same or similar meanings. Thinking of a familiar synonym for a vocabulary word can help you remember the meaning of the word. Example: You might think of *carefulness* as a synonym for *prudence.*

English Learners

DIFFERENTIATED INSTRUCTION

Beginning/Early Intermediate Point out the definition of *synonym* on this page. Have students list a synonym for each of these words:

- talk *(chat, speak, discuss, chatter)*
- flat *(even, level)*

Brainstorm with students some synonyms for the Vocabulary Preview words. Write their responses on the board.

- imputation *(allegation, charge, assertion, complaint)*
- parsimony *(thriftiness, cost-cutting, skimpiness)*
- depreciate *(decline, decrease, devalue, reduce)*
- prudence *(discretion, care, good sense)*

Before You Read

Focus

Summary

On Christmas Eve, Della Young has very little cash and no gift for her husband Jim. She decides to sell her hair, the only valuable thing she has, to buy Jim a chain for his watch. Meanwhile, Jim sells his watch to buy Della hair combs she had been admiring. Jim and Della soon discover that each has sold his or her prized possession to give the other a gift that would enhance the now gone possessions.

For summaries in languages other than English, see Unit 1 Teaching Resources Book, pp. 126–131.

Vocabulary

Extensions Have students discuss the meaning of each vocabulary word. Then ask students to write two sentences in their notebooks using each of these words. Ask for volunteers to read their sentences aloud. Discuss why the use of the vocabulary word is either correct or incorrect.

For additional vocabulary practice, see Unit 1 Teaching Resources Book, p. 134.

For additional context, see Glencoe Interactive Vocabulary CD-ROM.

Teach

Big Idea 1

Rewards and Sacrifices

Have students keep these questions in mind as they read.

Ask: What problem is faced by both characters? *(Neither has money to buy a gift for the other.)* How do they solve their problem? *(They each give up something they care about.)*

Reading Strategy 2

Analyze Description

Answer: *This detail, along with the shabby couch and the dysfunctional mailbox, shows that Della and Jim live in poverty.*

Writer's Technique ☆

Setting Writers often describe the time and location in which a story takes place to create an atmosphere or mood. **Ask:** Why might O. Henry describe the apartment house vestibule? *(To show that the couple cannot afford to live in a nicer apartment)*

For an audio recording of this selection, use Listening Library Audio CD-ROM.

Readability Scores

Dale-Chall: 8.0
DRP: 55
Lexile: 910

Picture Shop Window, 1907. John Sloan. Oil on canvas, 32 x 25⅛ in. Gift of Mrs. Felix Fuld, 1925. The Newark Museum, NJ.

The Gift of the Magi

O. Henry

One dollar and eighty-seven cents. That was all. And sixty cents of it was in pennies. Pennies saved one and two at a time by bulldozing the grocer and the vegetable man and the butcher until one's cheeks burned with the silent **imputation** of **parsimony** that such close dealing implied. Three times Della counted it. One dollar and eighty-seven cents. And
1 the next day would be Christmas.

There was clearly nothing to do but flop down on the shabby little couch and howl. So Della did it. Which instigates[1] the moral reflection that life is made up of sobs, sniffles, and smiles, with sniffles predominating.

While the mistress of the home is gradually subsiding from the first stage to the second, take a look at the home. A furnished flat at $8 per week. It did not exactly beggar description, but it certainly had that word on the lookout for the mendicancy squad.[2]

In the vestibule below was a letter-box ☆ into which no letter would go, and an electric button from which no mortal finger could coax a ring. Also appertaining[3]

1. To *instigate* is to stir up or cause something to happen.

Vocabulary

imputation (im′ pyə tā′ shən) *n.* an accusation
parsimony (pär′ sə mō′ nē) *n.* stinginess

2. O. Henry is making a play on words here. To *beggar* is to defy or go past the limits of something. A *mendicancy squad* consists of the authorities who deal with mendicants, or beggars.
3. Here, *appertaining* means "belonging" or "relating."

Analyze Description *What does this detail contribute to the description of Della and Jim's living conditions?* 2

Listening and Speaking Practice

SPIRAL REVIEW **Make Connections** After students read the first two pages of the story, ask them to consider how O. Henry's life may have influenced him to create certain elements in this story. Refer students back to the biographical information on page 114. **Ask:** What do you think O. Henry's life was like at the time he wrote this story? What parts of his life might be reflected in the story? *(Students may respond that O. Henry was in prison when he wrote this story, and that his environment was probably bleak. Many bleak elements appear in the story, such as poverty, the couple's shabby possessions, the drab colors of their clothes, Della's despair, the dreariness of winter, and ultimately, the ironic twist at the end of the story.)* Encourage students to respond to the answers provided by their classmates.

thereunto was a card bearing the name "Mr. James Dillingham Young."

The "Dillingham" had been flung to the breeze during a former period of prosperity when its possessor was being paid $30 per week. Now, when the income was shrunk to $20, the letters of "Dillingham" looked blurred, as though they were thinking seriously of contracting to a modest and unassuming[4] D. But whenever Mr. James Dillingham Young came home and reached his flat above he was called "Jim" and greatly hugged by Mrs. James Dillingham Young, already introduced to you as Della. Which is all very good.

Della finished her cry and attended to her cheeks with the powder rag. She stood by the window and looked out dully at a gray cat walking a gray fence in a gray backyard. Tomorrow would be Christmas Day, and she had only $1.87 with which to buy Jim a present. She had been saving every penny she could for months, with this result. Twenty dollars a week doesn't go far. Expenses had been greater than she had calculated. They always are. Only $1.87 to buy a present for Jim. Her Jim. Many a happy hour she had spent planning for something nice for him. Something fine and rare and sterling— something just a little bit near to being worthy of the honor of being owned by Jim.

There was a pier-glass[5] between the windows of the room. Perhaps you have seen a pier-glass in an $8 flat. A very thin and very agile person may, by observing his reflection in a rapid sequence of longitudinal strips, obtain a fairly accurate conception of his looks. Della, being slender, had mastered the art.

Suddenly she whirled from the window and stood before the glass. Her eyes were shining brilliantly, but her face had lost its color within twenty seconds. Rapidly she pulled down her hair and let it fall to its full length.

Now, there were two possessions of the James Dillingham Youngs in which they both took a mighty pride. One was Jim's gold watch that had been his father's and his grandfather's. The other was Della's ☆ hair. Had the Queen of Sheba lived in the flat across the airshaft, Della would have let her hair hang out the window some day to dry just to **depreciate** Her Majesty's jewels and gifts. Had King Solomon[6] been the janitor, with all his treasures piled up in the basement, Jim would have pulled out his watch every time he passed, just to see him pluck at his beard from envy.

So now Della's beautiful hair fell about her, rippling and shining like a cascade of brown waters. It reached below her knee and made itself almost a garment for her. And then she did it up again nervously and quickly. Once she faltered for a minute and stood still while a tear or two splashed on the worn red carpet.

On went her old brown jacket; on went her old brown hat. With a whirl of skirts and with the brilliant sparkle still in her eyes, she fluttered out the door and down the stairs to the street.

4. *Unassuming* means "not bold or boastful."
5. A *pier-glass* (pēr′ glas) is a tall, narrow mirror designed to be hung between two windows.

6. The Bible says that the *Queen of Sheba* visited *King Solomon,* bearing gifts that included great quantities of gold, spices, and jewels. Solomon is famous as the wisest and wealthiest man of his time.

3 Characterization *What can you tell about Della from the narrator's commentary?*

Analyze Description *What does the narrator compare Della's hair to?* **4**

Vocabulary

depreciate (di ′ prē ′shē āt) *v.* to lessen the price or value of

Teach

Literary Element 3

Characterization Answer: *She feels love and esteem for her husband. She wants to give Jim a Christmas present that is worthy of him.*

Reading Strategy 4

Analyze Description
Answer: *The narrator compares Della's hair to a waterfall.*

Cultural History ☆

History of Hair Hair has been a focus of most cultures since ancient times. While some practices, such as the use of human hair to make wigs, are still carried out today, others seem out of place in the modern world. For instance, in ancient Egypt, men and women often shaved their heads so that they could wear different wigs every day. The ancient Egyptians even had certain wigs for special ceremonies and celebrations. In seventeenth century France, men wore wigs to signify that they belonged to the aristocratic class; those without wigs were not considered refined.

Approaching Level

DIFFERENTIATED INSTRUCTION

Emerging Explain to students that stories are narrated in a first-, second-, or third-person point of view. Explain that in first-person narration, the narrator is a character in the story. First-person narration can be identified by the use of words such as "I" and "we." In second-person narration, the narrator speaks directly to the reader (identified by use of the word "you"). In third-person narration, the narrator is not actually in the story, but knows what is happening and what characters are thinking (identified by use of "he" and "she" without the use of "I"). To practice ***reading fluency,*** ask a student to read aloud the first few paragraphs of this passage. Point out that the narrator uses the pronouns "he" and "she," and therefore the story is written in the third person. Point out that stories written from the third-person point of view usually contain lots of description and dialogue. Note the description of Della's flat on page 116.

Teach

Big Idea 1

Rewards and Sacrifices

Answer: *Della has probably put aside her feelings of loss regarding her hair when she sees the perfect fob chain for Jim's watch.*

ENGLISH LEARNERS For English learners, explain that "must be" implies that Jim should own the watch chain not that Della saw something that already belonged to Jim.

View the Art ★

Answer: *Both Della and the woman in the painting have long, beautiful hair and seem to take pride in it.*

Edgar Degas (1834–1917) was one of the most famous of the French Impressionists. Best known for his paintings of dancers and for his portraits, Degas worked skillfully in a variety of media, including pastels. Explain to students that the word toilet in the title of the painting refers, in this context, to grooming.

Woman at Her Toilet. Edgar Degas. Oil pastel on paper. The Hermitage, St. Petersburg, Russia.

View the Art Many of Edgar Degas's paintings show people participating in everyday activities. How is the woman in the painting similar to Della? ★

Where she stopped the sign read: "Mme. Sofronie.[7] Hair Goods of All Kinds." One flight up Della ran, and collected herself, panting. Madame, large, too white, chilly, hardly looked the "Sofronie."

"Will you buy my hair?" asked Della.

"I buy hair," said Madame. "Take yer hat off and let's have a sight at the looks of it."

Down rippled the brown cascade.

"Twenty dollars," said Madame, lifting the mass with a practiced hand.

"Give it to me quick," said Della.

Oh, and the next two hours tripped by on rosy wings. Forget the hashed[8] metaphor. She was ransacking the stores for Jim's present.

She found it at last. It surely had been made for Jim and no one else. There was no other like it in any of the stores, and she had turned all of them inside out. It was a platinum fob chain simple and chaste[9] in design, properly proclaiming its value by substance alone and not by meretricious[10] ornamentation—as all good things should do. It was even worthy of The Watch. As soon as she saw it she knew that it must be Jim's.

Visual Vocabulary
A fob chain is attached to a pocket watch and worn hanging from a pocket.

7. *Mme. Sofronie* (mə dam′ sō frō′ nē)
8. O. Henry pokes fun at himself here. His metaphor is *hashed,* or mixed, because it combines parts of the familiar phrases "rose-colored glasses" and "on gossamer wings."
9. Here, *chaste* means "modest."
10. *Meretricious* means "cheap" or "showy."

Rewards and Sacrifices *How do you think Della feels about her sacrifice at this point?* 1

Reading Practice

SPIRAL REVIEW Situational Irony

The characters in "Gift of the Magi" make some important decisions on these pages that lead to the story's ironic conclusion. As students read the story, have them complete a chart like the one shown to ensure their understanding of the story's plot. When they have finished, tell them that situational irony is a contrast between what was expected and what actually happens. **Ask:** How do the character's actions contribute to the story's ironic ending?

Sequence Chart—Decision Making

Character	Objective	Obstacle	Solution
Della			
Jim			

It was like him. Quietness and value—the description applied to both. Twenty-one dollars they took from her for it, and she hurried home with the 87 cents. With that chain on his watch Jim might be properly anxious about the time in any company. Grand as the watch was, he sometimes looked at it on the sly on account of the old leather strap that he used in place of a chain.

2 When Della reached home her intoxication gave way a little to **prudence** and reason. She got out her curling irons and lighted the gas and went to work repairing the ravages[11] made by generosity added to love. Which is always a tremendous task, dear friends—a mammoth task.

Within forty minutes her head was covered with tiny, close-lying curls that made her look wonderfully like a truant schoolboy. She looked at her reflection in the mirror long, carefully, and critically.

"If Jim doesn't kill me," she said to herself, "before he takes a second look at me, he'll say I look like a Coney Island[12] chorus girl. But what could I do—oh! what could I do with a dollar and eighty-seven cents?"

At 7 o'clock the coffee was made and the frying pan was on the back of the stove hot and ready to cook the chops.

Jim was never late. Della doubled the fob chain in her hand and sat on the corner of the table near the door that he always entered. Then she heard his step on the stair away down on the first flight, and she turned white for just a moment. She had a habit of saying little silent prayers about the simplest everyday things, and now she whispered: "Please God, make him think I am still pretty."

The door opened and Jim stepped in and closed it. He looked thin and very serious. Poor fellow, he was only twenty-two—and to be burdened with a family! He needed a new overcoat and he was without gloves.

Jim stopped inside the door, as immovable as a setter at the scent of quail. His eyes were fixed upon Della, and there was an expression in them that she could not read, and it terrified her. It was not anger, nor surprise, nor disapproval, nor horror, nor any of the sentiments that she had been prepared for. He simply stared at her fixedly with that peculiar expression on his face.

Della wriggled off the table and went for him.

"Jim, darling," she cried, "don't look at me that way. I had my hair cut off and sold it because I couldn't have lived through Christmas without giving you a present. It'll grow out again—you won't mind, will you? I just had to do it. My hair grows awfully fast. Say 'Merry Christmas!' Jim, and let's be happy. You don't know what a nice—what a beautiful, nice gift I've got for you."

"You've cut off your hair?" asked Jim, laboriously, as if he had not arrived at that patent[13] fact yet even after the hardest mental labor.

"Cut it off and sold it," said Della. "Don't you like me just as well, anyhow? I'm me without my hair, ain't I?"

Jim looked about the room curiously.

"You say your hair is gone?" he said, with an air almost of idiocy.

11. *Ravages* means "destructive actions or their results." Here, it refers to the hasty cutting of Della's hair.
12. *Coney Island* is a famous beach and amusement park in Brooklyn, New York.

13. Here, Jim tries to grasp the obvious *(patent)* fact that Della has cut her hair.

3 Characterization *What does this detail reveal about Jim?*

Vocabulary

prudence (proo͞d′ əns) *n.* caution; good judgment

Analyze Description *What image of Jim does the word* idiocy *evoke?* 4

Teach

Literary Element 2

Point of View Explain to students that the story is being told in the third-person omniscient point of view. Discuss how the narrator uses the technique of addressing the reader directly. Have students find an example of this technique. *("Which is always a tremendous task, dear friends—a mammoth task.")*

ADVANCED Challenge advanced students to pick a portion of the text and rewrite the story, using the first-person point of view. Students may choose to write from either Della's or Jim's point of view.

Literary Element 3

Characterization **Answer:** *Although Jim tries to conceal his feelings, he is ashamed of his poverty.*

Reading Strategy 4

Analyze Description
Answer: *Jim is so stunned by the realization that Della won't be able to use the combs that he appears disoriented and out of his mind.*

English Learners

DIFFERENTIATED INSTRUCTION

Beginning/Early Intermediate
Explain to students that figurative language is often used for a descriptive effect. Figurative language is not literally true, but does have meaning. Define the term *simile* and provide an example. From the story, **read:** "Within forty minutes her head was covered with tiny, close-lying curls that made her look wonderfully like a truant schoolboy." Explain that Della doesn't really look like a boy. She just has short, curly hair. Ask students to explain the relationship between the description and how Della actually looks. Then instruct students to find examples of figurative language in the story.

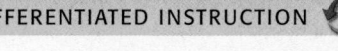

Teach

View the Art ★

Illustrator and painter Everett Shinn (1876–1953) was a member of the Ashcan School, a group of American artists working in the early twentieth century who realistically portrayed city life. **Ask:** Does the mood of the painting reflect the mood of the story? Explain.

Answer: *The tenement buildings crowded together on a city street, the snow, and the pedestrians reflect the hustle-bustle mood of the day before Christmas and the setting of the story.*

Fifth Avenue, 1910. Everett Shinn. Pastel on light tan laid paper, 12⅜ x 15¼ in. Brooklyn Museum, Brooklyn, NY. Gift of Samuel A. Lewisohn. ★

"You needn't look for it," said Della. "It's sold, I tell you—sold and gone, too. It's Christmas Eve, boy. Be good to me, for it went for you. Maybe the hairs of my head were numbered," she went on with a sudden serious sweetness, "but nobody could ever count my love for you. Shall I put the chops on, Jim?"

Out of his trance Jim seemed quickly to wake. He enfolded his Della. For ten seconds let us regard with discreet scrutiny some inconsequential object in the other direction.[14] Eight dollars a week or a million a year—what is the difference? A mathematician or a wit would give you the wrong answer. The Magi brought valuable gifts, but that was not among them. This dark assertion will be illuminated later on.[15]

Jim drew a package from his overcoat pocket and threw it upon the table.

"Don't make any mistake, Dell," he said, "about me. I don't think there's anything in the way of a haircut or a shave or a shampoo that could make me like my girl any less. But if you'll unwrap that package you may see why you had me going a while at first."

White fingers and nimble tore at the string and paper. And then an ecstatic

14. *[For ten seconds . . . other direction.]* O. Henry suggests that we give the couple privacy by examining some object on the other side of the room, as if we were physically in the couple's home.

15. *[This dark assertion . . . later on.]* O. Henry promises to explain, later, his statement in the preceding sentence.

Writing Practice

SPIRAL REVIEW **Demonstrate Author Style** After students have finished reading the story, ask them to reread the scenes in which Della decides to cut her hair and visits Madame Sofronie. Remind students to pay attention to O. Henry's writing style and the content of these scenes. Then ask students to write a scene in which Jim decides to sell his watch and then goes to a shop to sell it. Tell students that their writing should mimic O. Henry's style in writing this story. *(Students should set their scenes in a gloomy atmosphere. Jim should struggle with the decision before following through. The shopkeeper or other person purchasing the watch should be eccentric and should speak in dialect. Jim should feel remorse as the watch leaves his possession, but then joy at the thought of buying Della the combs for her beautiful hair.)*

scream of joy; and then, alas! a quick feminine change to hysterical tears and wails, necessitating the immediate employment of all the comforting powers of the lord of the flat.

Visual Vocabulary
This comb is designed both to fasten and adorn a woman's hair. Ordinary combs are used only to smooth and arrange it.

For there lay The Combs—the set of combs, side and back, that Della had worshipped for long in a Broadway window. Beautiful combs, pure tortoise shell, with jewelled rims—just the shade to wear in the beautiful vanished hair. They were expensive combs, she knew, and her heart had simply craved and yearned over them without the least hope of possession. And now, they were hers, but the tresses that should have adorned the coveted[16] adornments were gone.

But she hugged them to her bosom, and at length she was able to look up with dim eyes and a smile and say: "My hair grows so fast, Jim!"

And then Della leaped up like a little singed cat and cried, "Oh, oh!"

Jim had not yet seen his beautiful present. She held it out to him eagerly upon her open palm. The dull precious metal seemed to flash with a reflection of her bright and ardent spirit.

"Isn't it a dandy, Jim? I hunted all over town to find it. You'll have to look at the time a hundred times a day now. Give me your watch. I want to see how it looks on it."

Instead of obeying, Jim tumbled down on the couch and put his hands under the back of his head and smiled.

"Dell," said he, "let's put our Christmas presents away and keep 'em a while. They're too nice to use just at present. I sold the watch to get the money to buy your combs. And now suppose you put the chops on."

The Magi, as you know, were wise men—wonderfully wise men—who brought gifts to the Babe in the manger. They invented the art of giving Christmas presents. Being wise, their gifts were no doubt wise ones, possibly bearing the privilege of exchange in case of duplication. And here I have lamely related to you the uneventful chronicle of two foolish children in a flat who most unwisely sacrificed for each other the greatest treasures of their house. But in a last word to the wise of these days let it be said that of all who give gifts these two were the wisest. Of all who give and receive gifts, such as they are wisest. Everywhere they are wisest. They are the Magi. ~

16. Coveted means "strongly desired" or "wished for longingly."

Characterization *What do Jim's words reveal about his personality?* **1**

Rewards and Sacrifices *O. Henry is comparing the gifts that Jim and Della exchanged with the Magi's gifts. What does this comparison suggest about Jim's and Della's gifts?* **2**

Teach

Literary Element 1

Characterization **Answer:**

He reacts calmly and stoically to disappointment. He knows that the love and generosity he shares with Della are far more important than the acquisition of material objects.

Big Idea 2

Rewards and Sacrifices

Answer: *It suggests that Jim's and Della's gifts to each other were motivated by love. Jim and Della were poor, yet they found a way to give each other profound gifts. In the end, it was not the watch chain or the combs that mattered, but their willingness to make sacrifices for each other.*

APPROACHING Some approaching-level students may be confused by O.Henry's comparison. Point out that he uses words and phrases like "foolish children" and "unwisely" to initially describe Della's and Jim's sacrifice. However, in a last word, he then claims that they are the wisest like the Magi. **Ask:** By sacrificing for each other, what gift do Della and Jim really give each other? *(The gift of love)*

English Learners

DIFFERENTIATED INSTRUCTION

Early Advanced Explain to students that *dialect* is a variation of a language spoken by a group of people, often within a particular region. Tell students that dialects may differ from the standard form of a language in vocabulary, pronunciation, or grammatical forms. Point out that when Della says, "I'm me without my hair, ain't I?" the word "ain't" is an example of dialect. Then ask students to scan the story for other examples of dialect. (*"Take yer hat off." "Let's put our Christmas presents away and keep 'em awhile."*) **Ask:** Why do you think O. Henry included dialect in his characters' speech? *(Students may say because this is how these particular characters would have talked.)*

To check students' understanding of the selection, see Unit 1 Teaching Resources Book, p. 137.

After You Read

Assess

1. Answers will vary. Students should explain their answers.
2. (a) Della gives up her hair. Jim gives up his watch. Della buys Jim a watch chain. Jim buys Della hair combs. (b) They each bought something to go with the thing that the other person sold.
3. (a) Jim stares fixedly at her with a peculiar expression. (b) His reaction is ambiguous. He might be angry, or he might not have noticed that Della cut her hair. Both reactions would drastically change our view of Jim and change the outcome of the story.
4. When Jim sees Della, he quietly tries to comprehend the changes he sees in Della. When he does respond, he is calm and comforting. He states that the changes would never diminish his feelings for her.
5. (a) According to the narrator, Jim and Della are the Magi. (b) Their selfless gifts were the wisest of all.
6. Students' answers should include a brief explanation of their reasoning.
7. They each learn how much the other sacrificed and how much they love each other.
8. Students' answers should include a brief explanation of their opinions.

After You Read

Respond and Think Critically

Respond and Interpret

1. Were you surprised by the outcome of the story? Why or why not?
2. (a)What do Della and Jim give up for each other, and what gifts do they buy for each other? (b)Why do their choices turn out to be ironic, or different from what is expected?
3. (a)What is Jim's initial reaction to Della when he arrives home? (b)How does this reaction create suspense?

Analyze and Evaluate

4. Della compares the watch chain to Jim: "Quietness and value—the description applied to both." Does this description apply to Jim when he enters the flat? Explain.
5. (a)According to the narrator, who were the Magi? (b)Why do you think the narrator refers to Della and Jim as the Magi?
6. During O. Henry's time, his stories were praised for their surprise endings and plot twists, but later generations of readers criticized these same techniques. What is your opinion of the surprise ending in this story? Explain.

Connect

7. **Big Idea** **Rewards and Sacrifices** Even though neither Jim nor Della can use their gifts, how are they rewarded for their sacrifices?
8. **Connect to Today** Do you think the story's message is valuable to today's readers? Why or why not?

Primary Visual Artifact

Tortoiseshell Combs and a Platinum Fob Chain

The tortoiseshell combs and the platinum fob chain are objects that play a special role in "The Gift of the Magi." They have symbolic importance and add authenticity to the story's turn-of-the-century setting. Knowing what these objects look like and how they are used can add to your appreciation of the story.

1. How does the fob chain compare with the way that Jim has been carrying his watch?
2. How are the combs Della receives different from a regular comb?
3. If you were to write a modern-day version of this story, what gifts might you choose to replace these? Explain your choices.

Primary Visual Artifact

1. Jim had been using a leather strap. Unlike the leather strap, the chain matches the watch and is made from similar materials. It also attaches more securely than the leather strap.
2. These combs are designed to fasten and adorn a woman's hair. They are expensive and jeweled. Ordinary combs are used only to smooth and arrange hair.
3. Students' answers should provide a brief explanation of why they chose their gifts as replacements.

Literary Element Characterization

In **direct characterization,** a narrator who is not a character in the story makes statements about a character. In **indirect characterization,** the writer reveals information about a character through the character's words, thoughts, and actions and through the words and thoughts of other characters.

1. Is the characterization of Della and Jim direct, indirect, or both? Support your answer with examples from the story.
2. What method or methods of characterization are used to reveal Madame Sofronie's character? Provide examples from the text.

Review: Plot

As you learned on pages 8–9, **plot** is the sequence of events in a short story, novel, or drama. "The Gift of the Magi" is an example of a story that features a "plot twist," or surprise ending. Authors create plot twists by leading the reader to believe that something will happen and then having something unexpected happen instead.

Partner Activity With a partner, discuss other places in the story where you think a twist or surprise could have occurred. Together identify two places for a new plot twist and imagine how the twist would have changed the story. Using a chart like the one below, record your two new plot twists and briefly summarize how they would change the story.

Original Plot Event	New Plot Twist	How the Story Would Be Changed

Reading Strategy Analyze Description

Description is a detailed portrayal of a person, place, or thing. When you **analyze description,** you study the way the author uses concrete details and sensory language to describe tangible things, such as the appearance of a character or a material object, as well as intangible things, such as a character's thoughts or personality traits. Refer to the diagram of details you completed as you read to answer the following questions.

1. Identify details in the story that describe what Della and Jim look like. Cite examples from the text.
2. How do the details the narrator uses to describe the watch chain reflect Jim's character? Cite examples from the text.

Vocabulary Practice

Practice with Synonyms A **synonym** is a word that has the same or nearly the same meaning as another word. With a partner, match each boldfaced vocabulary word below with its synonym. You will not use all the answer choices. Use a thesaurus or dictionary to check your answers.

1. imputation	**a.** caution
2. parsimony	**b.** devalue
3. depreciate	**c.** minimal
4. prudence	**d.** accusation
	e. thriftiness
	f. supplement

LOG ON **Literature Online**

Selection Resources For Selection Quizzes, eFlashcards, and Reading-Writing Connection activities, go to glencoe.com and enter QuickPass code GL49787u1.

After You Read

Assess

Literary Element

1. Both direct and indirect characterization are used. Direct characterization is used when the narrator tells the reader that Della had saved money to buy a Christmas present for Jim. The narrator also reveals that Jim felt burdened by having a family. Indirect characterization is used when Della tells Jim that she couldn't live through Christmas without giving him a beautiful gift and when Jim tells Della that he sold his watch to get money to buy her combs.
2. Direct characterization is used when the narrator describes Madame Sofronie as "large, too white, chilly." Indirect characterization is used in Madame Sofronie's curt, business-like replies to Della. These details suggest that Madame Sofronie is insensitive and concerned only with making a profit.

Progress Check

Can students analyze characterization?

If No → See Unit 1 Teaching Resources Book, p. 132.

Review: Plot

Ask students to rewrite a part of the story using the new plot twist and share it with the class.

Reading Strategy

1. Della is described as slender, with shining eyes and long, luxurious hair. Jim is described as thin, serious, and shabbily dressed.
2. The narrator describes the watch chain as "simple and chaste in design, properly proclaiming its value by substance alone." Della reflects that the watch chain was like Jim in its "quietness and value." These comparisons suggest that Jim is unpretentious and a man of integrity.

Vocabulary

1. d **2.** e **3.** b **4.** a

For additional selection assessment, see Assessment Resources, pp. 57–58.

After You Read

Assess

Respond Through Writing

Students' essays should:

- share a personal gift-giving or receiving experience
- connect the experience to a broader theme in life
- relate the experience to the characters' experience in the story
- use imagery and sensory language to create an engaging description
- provide insight into the student's thoughts and feelings

A student who meets all of these criteria should receive the equivalent of a 5-point response.

A student who fully meets three or partially meets four of these criteria should receive the equivalent of a 4-point response.

A student who fully meets two or partially meets three of these criteria should receive the equivalent of a 3-point response.

A student who fully meets one or partially meets two of these criteria should receive the equivalent of a 2-point response.

A student who partially meets one of these criteria should receive the equivalent of a 1-point response.

For grammar practice, see Unit 1 Teaching Resources Book, p. 136.

To create custom assessments online, go to Progress Reporter Online Assessment.

To create custom assessments using software, use ExamView Assessment Suite.

Respond Through Writing

Reflective Essay

Apply Description Write a reflective essay about a special gift you have given or received, connecting the experience to a broader theme in your life. Use imagery to describe the gift and enhance your account.

Understand the Task In a **reflective essay,** you describe an experience to better understand what it means personally and what it might teach others. **Imagery** is descriptive language that appeals to one or more of the five senses. In your essay, you can use sensory details to help create an emotional response in the reader.

Prewrite Look through your belongings for any special gifts you have received, and look through old photos and diaries for reminders of special gifts in your past. Choose a gift that has unique meaning to you, and determine the broader theme or larger idea that the gift represents.

Draft Begin your essay by briefly comparing your experience giving or receiving the gift to Della or Jim's experience in "The Gift of the Magi." You can use this comparison to structure your essay's main idea. For example, your opening might include a sentence such as the following:

Like the character ______, I have had the experience of ______.

As you tell your experience, fully explain how it connects to a broader theme in your life. By revealing your inner thoughts and reasoning, you can help readers make the connections between your experience and the theme. Your descriptions should include descriptive details that support and reflect the theme.

Revise Make sure the essay effectively expresses why the experience was significant; it should be clear to readers why the gift is special. Revise your essay using the rubric on page 594.

Edit and Proofread Proofread your paper, correcting any errors in grammar, spelling, and punctuation. Use the Grammar Tip in the side column to help you with transitional phrases.

Learning Objectives

In this assignment, you will focus on the following objectives:

Writing: Applying description in a reflective essay.

Grammar: Understanding how and when to use transitional phrases.

Grammar Tip

Transitional Phrases

When recounting a sequence of events, you can use transitional phrases to connect events and indicate their order. These phrases are set apart by a comma.

First, I lifted the box to feel how heavy it was.

Transitional phrases can also be used to describe one event leading to another.

She shook her head yes, and as a result, I started to cry.

As shown in the examples above, transitional phrases can be used at the beginning of a sentence or in the middle of a compound sentence.

Vocabulary Workshop

Dictionary Use

Learning Objectives

In this workshop, you will focus on the following objective:

Vocabulary: Understanding how to use a dictionary.

Literature Connection In the following sentence, O. Henry uses one of those words that make English such an interesting language.

> *"And then Della leaped up like a little singed cat and cried, 'Oh, oh!'"*
>
> —O. Henry, from "The Gift of the Magi"

Singed looks as if it might be a form of the verb *sing,* but the past tense of *sing* is *sang.* Therefore, *singed* must have another meaning entirely. The dictionary will tell you.

Looking for a Word The main part of a dictionary consists of word entries and their definitions. Guide words at the top of each page tell you the first and last words listed on the page. They can help you locate entries quickly. Remember that the exact form of the word you are looking for may not be a main entry. Find an entry that is close in spelling to the word you want and see if it includes your word. *Singed* is not a main entry, but you will find it under *singe.*

The Main Entry A main entry tells you far more about a word than its definition. Here is what one dictionary says about *singe:*

The pronunciation is indicated in simplified spelling.

Other forms, such as past tense and present participle for a verb, are sometimes given.

singe (sinj) **singed, singeing.** *v.t.* **1.** to burn superficially or lightly; scorch; *The hot iron singed her dress.* **2.** to burn the ends or tips of (hair). *—n.* **1.** act of singeing. **2.** superficial burn. [Old English *sengan* to burn superficially.] —**Syn.** *v.t.* **1.** see **scorch.**

The part or parts of speech of the word are indicated.

Example sentences show how a word is used.

The etymology explains the history of a word.

Cross-references direct you to other related main entries.

Tip

If you do not know the spelling of a word, you can usually find it if you try to sound it out. Consider alternative spellings of vowels and consonants. For example, the *sh* sound can be found in *ocean* and *tissue.* The long *a* sound is in *paid, suede,* and *obey.*

Technology Tip

Using an online dictionary, you simply enter a search word to find its definition. Online dictionaries also offer features such as illustrations, word games, language tips, and fun facts.

Exercise Use the dictionary entry in this lesson to answer the following questions.

1. Why is the word *sengan* included in this entry?
2. What word is given as a synonym for *singe*?
3. *Singe* is often a verb. What other part of speech can it be?
4. When you add *-ing* to *singe,* do you drop the final *e* or leave it?
5. In the story, Della is compared to a *singed* cat. How is this a good description?

LOG ON **Literature** Online

Vocabulary For more vocabulary practice, go to glencoe.com and enter QuickPass code GL49787u1.

Vocabulary Workshop

Dictionary Use

Focus

This workshop explains how to use a dictionary to look up words. It includes a sample dictionary entry as a model for students.

Teach

Etymologies Explain that not all dictionaries include etymologies. If students are using a printed dictionary without etymologies, they might want to consult an online dictionary if they need to find a word's origin.

Assess

Exercise

1. *Sengan* means "to burn superficially" in Old English. It is included to show the origin of the word *singe.*
2. scorch
3. a noun
4. You leave the final *e.*
5. Possible answer: It is a good description because Della jumped up and screamed the way a cat would if it were burned.

For additional vocabulary practice, see Glencoe Interactive Vocabulary CD-ROM.

English Learners

DIFFERENTIATED INSTRUCTION

Beginning/Early Intermediate Point out the italicized sentence on this page. Show students where you would add the phrase "who is kindhearted and loving" to the sentence so that the phrase modifies Della. Point out the correct placement of commas since the phrase is nonrestrictive. (And then Della, who is kindhearted and loving, leaped up like a little singed cat and cried 'Oh, oh!')

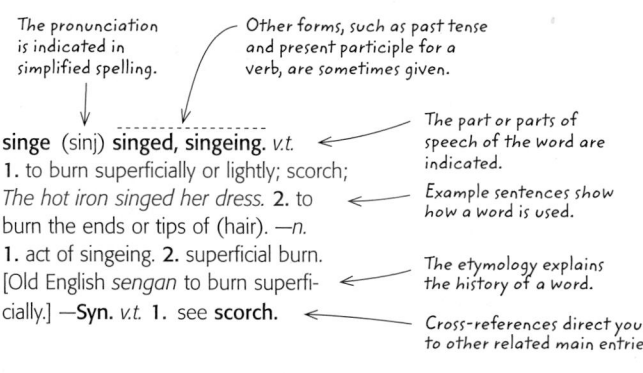

Comparing Literature

Across Genres

Focus

Bellringer Options

Literature Launchers: Pre-Reading Videos DVD, Selection Launcher

Daily Language Practice Transparency 12

Or display images of immigrants arriving in the United States at Ellis Island, San Francisco, and Florida. **Ask:** What emotions might these people be experiencing? Why might these people have come to the United States? What are some reasons they may have for leaving their homelands?

Connect to the Reading Selections

Have students share their responses to the opening questions. Then have them discuss what they already know about the history of immigrants to this country and the immigrants that continue to come to the United States today.

Comparing Literature

Across Genres

Learning Objectives

For pages 126–140

In studying these texts, you will focus on the following objectives:

Literary Study: Comparing themes. Analyzing motivation.

Reading: Responding to characters.

Writing: Writing an essay about theme.

Compare Literature About Immigration

The United States is sometimes referred to as a nation of immigrants. Many immigrants come seeking greater political freedom; others seek better opportunities to support themselves and their families. With their bravery, ingenuity, and hard work, immigrants make contributions that vastly enrich the nation as a whole. The three works compared here—by Julia Alvarez, Elizabeth Wong, and Pat Mora—explore the issues faced by people who leave behind their beloved homelands in order to build new lives and, in some cases, new identities.

COMPARE THE **Big Idea** Rewards and Sacrifices

Moving from one country to another can be exciting and rewarding. However, it can also be sad and painful. In these works, Julia Alvarez, Elizabeth Wong, and Pat Mora suggest that for immigrants, moving to the United States is a very big step. As you read, ask yourself, What sacrifices do these immigrants make to create new lives for themselves?

COMPARE Theme

The theme is the central message of a work of literature—an insight that readers can apply to their lives. As you read, ask yourself, What theme does each of these writers convey about the experience of immigration to the United States?

COMPARE Cultures

Though these authors write about immigrants from very different places, each author reflects on the importance of one's native culture. One cannot change culture like clothing or discard it like old newspapers. As you read, ask yourself, How would you describe the cultural conflicts explored in these selections?

LOG ON **Literature** Online

Author Search For more about Julia Alvarez, Elizabeth Wong, and Pat Mora, go to glencoe.com and enter QuickPass code GL49787u1.

126 COMPARING LITERATURE

Selection Skills

Comparing Literature

Literary Elements
- Motivation (SE pp. 128–135)
- Description (TE p. 132)
- Conflict (TE p. 137)

Vocabulary Skills
- Word Usage (SE pp. 128, 135)

Reading Skills
- Respond to Characters (SE pp. 128–135)
- Make Inferences (TE p. 129)
- Preview (TE p. 128)

Listening/Speaking/Viewing
- Analyze Art (SE pp. 129, 133)

Writing Skills/Grammar
- Essay (SE pp. 135, 140)
- Synthesize Information (TE p. 130)
- Dashes (TE p. 132)

Before You Read

Liberty

Meet **Julia Alvarez**
(born 1950)

At ten years old Julia Alvarez was a bewildered newcomer to the United States. Her family had recently escaped from the brutal regime of General Rafael Trujillo, military dictator of the Dominican Republic. In New York City, many miles away from the language and culture she grew up with, Alvarez felt out of place. "I looked around the schoolyard at unfriendly faces," she remembers.

A World of Words Unable to feel at home on the streets and playgrounds of New York City, Alvarez found a safe place in the world of words. "An English teacher asked us to write little stories about ourselves," she recalls. "I began to put into words some of what my life had been like in the Dominican Republic." Suddenly, Alvarez felt she had some control over her environment. "The boys in the schoolyard with ugly looks on their faces were not allowed into this world," she recalls.

> *"I found myself turning more and more to writing as the one place where I felt I belonged."*
>
> —Julia Alvarez

During high school and college, Alvarez dealt with problems by writing about them, and eventually she began to consider writing as a career. Her ambitions were startling for some people in her life. "I was raised in a very traditional, Old World family," she has explained, "so I never had thoughts about having a career. Moving to a new country, having to learn a new language, I got interested in words, and suddenly being in a world where there were books and encouragement of women to discover their talents contributed to my becoming a writer."

A Migrant Poet Alvarez graduated from Middlebury College in Vermont and received a graduate degree from Syracuse University. She then began her career as what she calls "a migrant poet." She began by teaching writing in prisons, retirement homes, and schools. "I would go anywhere," she told one interviewer. Finally she returned to Middlebury College, where she received tenure as a member of the English Department.

Writing from Experience Much of Alvarez's writing is about her homeland of the Dominican Republic and the lives of newcomers to the United States. Her first novel, *How the García Girls Lost Their Accents*, published in 1991, was an immediate success. It describes the struggles and successes of a family of Dominican immigrants.

LOG ON **Literature** Online

Author Search For more about Julia Alvarez, go to glencoe.com and enter QuickPass code GL49787u1.

Comparing Literature

Before You Read

Focus

Big Idea

Rewards and Sacrifices As students read, have them consider how the narrator feels when she finds out her family is moving to a new country. Then **ask:** What would you give up in moving to a new place? What might you gain? (Student answers will vary.)

ENGLISH LEARNERS Encourage English learners who have made such a move to share the sacrifices and rewards of their experiences.

Approaching Level

DIFFERENTIATED INSTRUCTION

Emerging Some students may be hampered by short attention spans. Suggest that students take notes while reading to monitor their comprehension. Suggest that students make a numbered list of events to help them understand the sequence of events. Remind them that if they take a break from reading, they can review the list each time before they resume reading the story. Also encourage students to write down any questions they might have about the text. They can search for answers to these questions as part of their review.

Before You Read

Focus

Summary

The narrator of this story, a young girl, has been hearing her parents talk about going to the United States. Her father, Papi, says he wants to go to school in the United States. Nothing seems to change until one day, with little warning, the children are told they will be leaving that very night for the United States. The narrator sees her world falling apart when she is told she must leave her pet dog, Liberty, behind.

For summaries in languages other than English, see Unit 1 Teaching Resources Book, pp. 140–145.

Vocabulary

Flash Cards Have students write each of the vocabulary words with the definition on the other side on separate index cards. Pair up students and have them use the cards to quiz each other, guessing the vocabulary word based on the definitions. Then quiz students on the meaning of each vocabulary word.

Comparing Literature

Literature and Reading Preview

Connect to the Story

Have you ever sacrificed something unwillingly, only to be thankful later that you did? Freewrite for a few minutes about a time when making a sacrifice led to a positive outcome.

Build Background

"Liberty" is set in an unnamed country that is likely meant to be the Dominican Republic, a Spanish-speaking country in the Caribbean. From 1930 to 1961, the country fell under the power of Rafael Trujillo, a dictator who eliminated political freedoms. Trujillo's secret police abducted and tortured many people thought to be guilty of disloyalty to the president. Trujillo was eventually overthrown by members of his own army.

Set Purposes for Reading

Big Idea Rewards and Sacrifices

As you read "Liberty," ask yourself, What sacrifices does the family have to make in order to leave their home country?

Literary Element Motivation

Motivation is the reason a character acts in a certain way. To understand a character's motivation, think about the character's attitude toward the events in the story. As you read, ask yourself, How would my reactions to each event be similar to and different from the characters' reactions?

Reading Strategy Respond to Characters

Some of the most interesting people you will ever meet are to be found in books. Ask them questions. Argue with them. In other words, **respond to characters** you meet when you read, just as you respond to people you meet in real life.

Tip: Record Your Responses Use a chart like the one below to record your responses to characters.

Character	Words, Thoughts, and Actions	My Response

Vocabulary

hyperactive (hī′ pər ak′ tiv) *adj.* overly energetic; very lively; p. 130 *Getting my hyperactive little brother to sit still for more than two minutes is next to impossible.*

distracted (dis trakt′ əd) *adj.* unable to pay attention; agitated; p. 130 *Distracted by thoughts of that evening's performance, Ara was unable to study.*

putrid (pū′ trid) *adj.* very nasty; disgusting; p. 131 *We threw out the rotten meat, but its putrid odor remained for days.*

admonition (ad′mə nish′ən) *n.* cautionary advice; warning; p. 132 *An admonition from a teacher is sometimes more effective than a scolding from a parent.*

inconsolable (in kən sō′ lə bəl) *adj.* heart-broken; impossible to comfort; p. 133 *The twins were inconsolable on hearing that the party had been canceled.*

Tip: Word Usage When you encounter new words, it might help you to answer a specific question about the word. For example, When do I most frequently feel *distracted* and how can I regain focus?

Reading Practice

SPIRAL REVIEW

Monitor Comprehension This story deals with the anguish and fears of a family on the brink of fleeing their homeland. It gives the reader a glimpse of the dangers the family faces if they stay and the risks they take by attempting to leave. Write these questions on the board for students to answer as they read:

- Why does Papi want to take his family to the United States?
- What is Mami's state of mind throughout the story?
- What sacrifices do family members make as they prepare to leave their homeland?

Interactive Read and Write

Other options for teaching this selection can be found in

- Interactive Read and Write for EL Students, pp. 15–32
- Interactive Read and Write for Approaching-Level Students, pp. 15–32
- Interactive Read and Write for On-Level Students, pp. 15–32

Comparing Literature

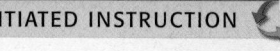

The Burning Passion. Tsing-Fang Chen.

View the Art This painting was created to commemmorate the Statue of Liberty's 100th birthday. What elements in the image make the Statue of Liberty recognizable? ★

Liberty

Julia Alvarez

Papi came home with a dog whose kind we had never seen before. A black-and-white-speckled electric current of energy. It was a special breed with papers, like a person with a birth certificate. Mami just kept staring at the puppy with a cross look on her face. "It looks like a mess!" she said. "Take it back."

"Mami, it is a gift!" Papi shook his head. It would be an insult to Mister Victor, who had given us the dog. The American consul[1] wanted to thank us for all we'd done for him since he'd been assigned to our country.

"If he wanted to thank us, he'd give us our visas,"[2] Mami grumbled. For a while now, my parents had been talking about going to the United States so Papi could return to school. I couldn't understand why a grown-up who could do whatever he wanted would elect to go back to a place I so much wanted to get out of.

On their faces when they talked of leaving there was a scared look I also couldn't understand. **1**

"Those visas will come soon," Papi promised. But Mami just kept shaking her head about the dog. She had enough with four girls to take on puppies, too. Papi explained

1. An *American consul* is an American government official in a foreign country, whose duties include helping people travel to the United States.
2. *Visas* are documents often necessary for traveling to other countries.

Teach

Reading Strategy 1

Make Inferences **Ask:** Why do you think Mami and Papi seem scared when they talk about going to the United States? *(Possible inferences: Mami and Papi are fearful of what life may be like in the United States; Mami and Papi are fearful of what might happen when they try to leave their homeland.)*

For additional practice using the reading skill or strategy, see Unit 1 Teaching Resources Book, p. 147.

View the Art ★

This painting by Taiwanese-born artist Tsing-Fang Chen (1936–) is one of a series of works that commemorate the centennial of the Statue of Liberty.

Answer: *Students' answers will vary. Students might point out details such as the shape of the crown and the extension of the figure's arm holding what appears to be a torch.*

English Learners

DIFFERENTIATED INSTRUCTION

Beginning/Early Intermediate The narrator states that she does not understand why her father would want to go back to school. It quickly becomes apparent that she does not understand why her parents want to move to the United States. Have students explain why the narrator does not understand these things, as well as why her parents might want these things.

Approaching Level

DIFFERENTIATED INSTRUCTION

Established Ask students what they know about immigration. Have them brainstorm reasons why people might want to leave other countries to live in the United States. Ask students why people might be afraid to make such a move, and discuss why some pursue this option despite their fear.

For an audio recording of this selection, use Listening Library Audio CD-ROM.

Readability Scores

Dale-Chall: 4.5
DRP: 50
Lexile: 840

Comparing Literature

Teach

Literary Element 1

Motivation Answer: *Students may say that Papi wishes to be polite to the American consul or that for Papi, the dog symbolizes the United States or freedom.*

APPROACHING For approaching-level students, **ask:** What qualities of an American might the dog possess? *(Students may say loyalty or obedience.)*

Reading Strategy 2

Respond to Characters Answer: *Answers will vary. Students may say that Mami is high-strung and Papi is kindhearted.*

that the dog would stay at the end of the yard in a pen. He would not be allowed in the house. He would not be pooping in Mami's orchid garden. He would not be barking until late at night. "A well-behaved dog," Papi concluded. "An American dog."

The little black-and-white puppy yanked at Papi's trouser cuff with his mouth. "What shall we call you?" Papi asked him.

"Trouble," Mami suggested, kicking the puppy away. He had left Papi's trousers to come slobber on her leg.

"We will call him Liberty. Life, liberty, and the pursuit of happiness." Papi quoted the U.S.A. Declaration of Independence. "Eh, Liberty, you are a lucky sign!"

Liberty barked his little toy barks and all us kids laughed. "Trouble." Mami kept shaking her head as she walked away. Liberty trotted behind her as if he agreed that that was the better name for him.

Mami was right, too—Liberty turned out to be trouble. He ate all of Mami's orchids, and that little **hyperactive** baton of a tail knocked things off the low coffee table whenever Liberty climbed on the couch to leave his footprints in among the flower prints. He tore up Mami's garden looking for buried treasure. Mami screamed at Liberty and stamped her foot. "Perro sin vergüenza!"[3] But Liberty just barked back at her.

"He doesn't understand Spanish," Papi said lamely. "Maybe if you correct him in English, he'll behave better!"

Mami turned on him, her slipper still in midair. Her face looked as if she'd light into him after she was done with Liberty. "Let him go be a pet in his own country if he wants instructions in English!" In recent weeks, Mami had changed her tune about going to the United States. She wanted to stay in her own country. She didn't want Mister Victor coming around our house and going off into the study with Papi to talk over important things in low, worried voices.

"All liberty involves sacrifice," Papi said in a careful voice. Liberty gave a few perky barks as if he agreed with that.

Mami glared at Papi. "I told you I don't want trouble—" She was going to say more, but her eye fell on me and she stopped herself. "Why aren't you with the others?" she scolded. It was as if I had been the one who had dug up her lily bulbs.

The truth was that after Liberty arrived, I never played with the others. It was as if I had found my double in another species. I had always been the tomboy, the live wire, the troublemaker, the one who was going to drive Mami to drink, the one she was going to give away to the Haitians. While the sisters dressed pretty and stayed clean in the playroom, I was out roaming the world looking for trouble. And now I had found someone to share my adventures.

"I'll take Liberty back to his pen," I offered. There was something I had figured out that Liberty had yet to learn: when to get out of Mami's way.

She didn't say yes and she didn't say no. She seemed **distracted**, as if something else was on her mind. As I led Liberty away by his collar, I could see her talking

3. *Perro sin vergüenza* means "shameless dog."

1 Motivation *Why does Papi want to keep the dog?*

2 Respond to Characters *What are your first impressions of Mami and Papi?*

Vocabulary

hyperactive (hī′ pər ak′ tiv) *adj.* overly energetic; very lively

Vocabulary

distracted (dis trakt′ əd) *adj.* unable to pay attention; agitated

Writing Practice

SPIRAL REVIEW **Synthesize Information** Explain to students that the characters in this story live in a country much like the Dominican Republic, which at the time, was ruled by a cruel and dangerous dictator. Ask students to use the Internet to research dictatorships and to find a country currently under the rule of a dictator. Have students prepare a short essay in which they explain this concept, present specific details about the country they have chosen, and explain why, in the story "Liberty," Papi and Mami live in fear. Students should use primary and secondary sources to support their ideas.

to Papi. Suddenly she started to cry, and Papi held her.

"It's okay," I consoled Liberty. "Mami doesn't mean it. She really does love you. She's just nervous." It was what my father always said when Mami scolded me harshly.

At the back of the property stood Liberty's pen—a chain-link fence around a dirt square at the center of which stood a doghouse. Papi had built it when Liberty first came, a cute little house, but then he painted it a **putrid** green that reminded me of all the vegetables I didn't like. It was always a job to get Liberty to go into that pen.

Sure enough, as soon as he saw where we were headed, he took off, barking, toward the house, then swerved to the front yard to our favorite spot. It was a grassy knoll[4] surrounded by a tall hibiscus hedge. At the center stood a tall, shady samán tree. From there, no one could see you up at the house. Whenever I did something wrong, this was where I hid out until the punishment winds blew over. That was where Liberty headed, and I was fast behind on his trail.

Inside the clearing I stopped short. Two strange men in dark glasses were crouched behind the hedge. The fat one had seized Liberty by the collar and was pulling so hard on it that poor Liberty was almost standing on his hind legs. When he saw me, Liberty began to bark, and the man holding him gave him a yank on the collar that made me sick to my stomach. I began to back away, but the other man grabbed my arm. "Not so fast," he said. Two little scared faces—my own—looked down at me from his glasses.

"I came for my dog," I said, on the verge of tears.

"Good thing you found him," the man said. "Give the young lady her dog," he ordered his friend, and then he turned to me. "You haven't seen us, you understand?"

I didn't understand. It was usually I who was the one lying and grown-ups telling me to tell the truth. But I nodded, relieved when the man released my arm and Liberty was back in my hands.

"It's okay, Liberty." I embraced him when I put him back in his pen. He was as sad as I was. We had both had a hard time with Mami, but this was the first time we'd come across mean and scary people. The fat man had almost broken Liberty's neck, and the other one had left his fingerprints on my arm. After I locked up the pen, I watched Liberty wander back slowly to his house and actually go inside, turn around, and stick his little head out the door. He'd always avoided that ugly doghouse before. I walked back to my own house, head down, to find my parents and tell them what I had seen.

Overnight, it seemed, Mister Victor moved in. He ate all his meals with us, stayed 'til late, and when he had to leave, someone from the embassy was left behind "to keep an eye on things." Now, when Papi and Mister Victor talked or when the *tíos*[5] came over, they all went down to the back of the property near Liberty's pen to talk. Mami had found some wires in the ☆ study, behind the portrait of Papi's great-grandmother fanning herself with a painted fan. The wires ran behind a screen and then out a window, where there was a

4. A *knoll* is a hill.

5. *Tíos* means "uncles" in Spanish.

Vocabulary

putrid (pū′ trid) *adj.* very nasty; disgusting

Motivation *Why would the stranger say this to the narrator?* **3**

Comparing Literature

Teach

Literary Element 3

Motivation **Answer:** *Students may say Papi does not wish to be too public about his plans or to let his children know exactly what is going on. Papi's plans are dangerous because the country where the family lives is ruled by a dictatorship.*

Writer's Technique ☆

Foreshadowing A writer often gives clues to prepare readers for events that will happen later in a story.

Ask: What clues in the selection prepare readers for future events? *(Possible answers: the strange men and their warning to the narrator, Mr. Victor's presence in the narrator's home, the hidden wires, the adults' reluctance to talk inside the house, and Mami's emotional state.)*

Approaching Level

DIFFERENTIATED INSTRUCTION

AAVE For approaching-level students who use African American Vernacular English (AAVE), explain the use of articles in Standard Academic English. Point out that in English grammar, the articles *a* and *an* are adjectives used to modify nouns. Remind students that *an* is used before vowel sounds and *a* is used before consonant sounds. **Write on the board:** an apple, an idea, an exam, an empty glass, a peach, a tree, a bank, a trumpet. Explain to students that an exception applies to words that begin with the letter "h" having a vowel sound. **Write:** an hour, an honor.

Teach

Reading Strategy 1

Respond to Characters
Answer: *Students may say the narrator's actions are humorous and understandable.*

Literary Element 2

Motivation **Answer:** *Students may say that Mami wishes to reassure the children.*

Literary Element 3

Description **Ask:** Which descriptive details about Mami express tension? *(Possible details: flashed a bright smile, as if someone were taking her picture; performance of happiness; looked like she wanted to cry; company smile, between clenched teeth)*

little box with lots of other wires coming from different parts of the house.

Mami explained that it was no longer safe to talk in the house about certain things. But the only way you knew what things those were was when Mami leveled her eyes on you as if she were pressing the off button on your mouth. She did this every time I asked her what was going on.

"Nothing," she said stiffly, and then she urged me to go outside and play. Forgotten were the **admonitions** to go study or I would flunk out of fifth grade. To go take a bath or the *microbios*[6] might kill me. To drink my milk or I would grow up stunted and with no teeth. Mami seemed absent and tense and always in tears. Papi was right—she was too nervous, poor thing.

1 I myself was enjoying a heyday of liberty. Several times I even got away with having one of Mister Victor's colas for breakfast instead of my boiled milk with a beaten egg, which Liberty was able to enjoy instead.

"You love that dog, don't you?" Mister Victor asked me one day. He was standing by the pen with Papi waiting for the uncles. He had a funny accent that sounded like someone making fun of Spanish when he spoke it.

I ran Liberty through some of the little tricks I had taught him, and Mister Victor laughed. His face was full of freckles—so that it looked as if he and Liberty were kin. I had the impression that God had spilled a lot of his colors when he was making American things.

Soon the uncles arrived and the men set to talking. I wandered into the pen and sat beside Liberty with my back to the house and listened. The men were speaking in English, and I had picked up enough of it at school and in my parents' conversations to make out most of what was being said. They were planning some hunting expedition for a goat with guns to be delivered by Mister Charlie. Papi was going to have to leave the goat to the others because his tennis shoes were missing. Though I understood the words—or thought I did—none of it made sense. I knew my father did not own a pair of tennis shoes, we didn't know a Mister Charlie, and who ever heard of hunting a goat?

As Liberty and I sat there with the sun baking the tops of our heads, I had this sense that the world as I knew it was about to end. The image of the two men in mirror glasses flashed through my head. So as not to think about them, I put my arm around Liberty and buried my face in his neck.

Late one morning Mami gave my sisters and me the news. Our visas had come. Mister Victor had arranged everything, and that very night we were going to the United States of America! Wasn't that wonderful! She flashed us a bright smile, as if someone were taking her picture. 3

We stood together watching her, alarmed at this performance of happiness when really she looked like she wanted to cry. All morning aunts had been stopping by and planting big kisses on our foreheads and holding our faces in their hands and asking us to promise we would be very good.

6. *Microbios* means "germs" in Spanish.

1 Respond to Characters *What is your reaction to the narrator and the way in which she enjoys her freedom from Mami's scrutiny?*

Vocabulary

admonition (ad′ mə nish′ ən) *n.* cautionary advice; warning

Motivation *Why does Mami try to seem happy?* 2

Grammar Practice

SPIRAL REVIEW **Use Dashes** Point out to students the places in the story where the writer has used a dash. Tell students that writers use a dash to signal a change in thought or to set off and emphasize supplemental information or parenthetical comments. Then write the following run-on and problematic sentences on the board:

- I love the library every time I go, I take out at least two books.
- Samir got a poster that looks just like or very close to the work of my favorite artist.
- Kendra knows best she is a lot older than we are.

Ask students to identify the proper placement of a dash or dashes in each sentence.

Until now, we hadn't a clue why they were so worked up.

Mami kept smiling her company smile. She had a little job for each of us to do. There would not be room in our bags for everything. We were to pick the one toy we wanted to take with us to the United States.

I didn't even have to think twice about my choice. It had suddenly dawned on me we were leaving, and that meant leaving *everything* behind. "I want to take Liberty."

Mami started shaking her head no. We could not take a dog into the United States of America. That was not allowed.

3 "Please," I begged with all my might. "Please, please, Mami, please." Repetition sometimes worked—each time you said the word, it was like giving a little push to the yes that was having a hard time rolling out of her mouth.

"I said no!" The bright smile on Mami's face had grown dimmer and dimmer. *"N–O."* She spelled it out for me in case I was confusing no with another word like yes. "I said a toy, and I mean a toy."

I burst into tears. I was not going to the United States unless I could take Liberty! Mami shook me by the shoulders and asked me between clenched teeth if I didn't understand we had to go to the United States or else. But all I could understand was that a world without Liberty would break my heart. I was **inconsolable.** Mami began to cry.

Tía Mimi took me aside. She had gone to school in the States and always had her nose in a book. In spite of her poor taste in how to spend her free time, I still loved her because she had smart things to say. Like telling Mami that punishment was not the

Portrait of Terrier. John Rabone Harvey. Private collection. John Noott Galleries, Broadway, Worcestershire, UK.

View the Art Compare and contrast the dog pictured here with the dog described in the story. ★

4 Respond to Characters *How does the narrator's reaction strike you? Could you see yourself behaving this way in a similar situation?*

Vocabulary

inconsolable (in kən sō′ lə bəl) *adj.* heart-broken; impossible to comfort

Comparing Literature

Teach

Reading Strategy 4

Respond to Characters

Answer: *Students may say the narrator's reaction is reasonable for a child. Others may say that they would not behave the same way, but would feel her deep sadness at having to leave a beloved pet behind.*

View the Art ★

Answer: *Liberty is "black-and-white-speckled" and very energetic. The breed is not given. The terrier is white with some brown on his ears and face. He sits quietly but alertly. Both seem to be intelligent and good companions.*

British artist John Rabone Harvey (1862–1933) painted *Portrait of Terrier.*

Approaching Level

DIFFERENTIATED INSTRUCTION

Emerging Direct students to the painting on this page. Ask students to discuss the effect of viewing the painting and reading the story together. Have students discuss how one enhances the other.

Advanced Learners

DIFFERENTIATED INSTRUCTION

Research Report Have students use the library or the Internet to find information about painter John Rabone Harvey. Students should write a one-page essay summarizing their findings. Remind students to cite their sources and use correct grammar, and punctuation.

Comparing Literature

Teach

Literary Element 1

Motivation Answer: *Students may say that Tía Mimi's words are motivated by her desire to encourage her niece and help her get to the United States.*

Literary Element 2

Motivation Ask: What motivates the narrator to free Liberty from his pen? *(Possible answer: She fears he will be harmed once her family leaves and the men in mirror glasses come to her home.)*

Big Idea 3

Rewards and Sacrifices
Answer: *Students may say that the narrator sacrifices the trusting friendship between her and her dog*

ENGLISH LEARNERS For English learners explain that "resort to Mami's techniques" means the narrator treats Liberty how Mami does in order to make Liberty stop following her. **Ask:** What does *tagging* mean in this paragraph? *(Following closely behind)*

way to make kids behave. "I'm going to tell you a little secret," she offered now. "You're going to find liberty when you get to the United States."

"Really?" I asked.

She hesitated a minute, and then she gave me a quick nod. "You'll see what I mean," she said. And then, giving me a pat on the butt, she added, "Come on, let's go pack. How about taking that wonderful book I got you on the Arabian Nights?" 1

Late in the night someone comes in and shakes us awake. "It's time!"

Half asleep, we put on our clothes, hands helping our arms to go into the right sleeves, buttoning us up, running a comb through our hair.

We were put to sleep hours earlier because the plane had not come in.

But now it's time.

"Go sit by the door," we are ordered, as the hands, the many hands that now seem to be in control, finish with us. We file out of the bedroom, one by one, and go sit on the bench where packages are set down when Mami comes in from shopping. There is much rushing around. Mister Victor comes by and pats us on the head like dogs. "We'll have to wait a few more minutes," he says.

In that wait, one sister has to go to the bathroom. Another wants a drink of water. I am left sitting with my baby sister, who is dozing with her head on my shoulder. I lay her head down on the bench and slip out.

Through the dark patio down the path to the back of the yard I go. Every now and then a strange figure flashes by. I have said good-bye to Liberty a dozen times already, but there is something else I have left to do.

Sitting on the bench, I had an image of those two men in mirror glasses. After we are gone, they come onto the property. They smash the picture of Papi's great-grandmother fanning herself. They knock over the things on the coffee table as if they don't know any better. They throw the flowered cushions on the floor. They smash the windows. And then they come to the back of the property and they find Liberty.

Quickly, because I hear calling from the big house, I slip open the door of the pen. Liberty is all over me, wagging his tail so it beats against my legs, jumping up and licking my face.

"Get away!" I order sharply, in a voice he is not used to hearing from me. I begin walking back to the house, not looking around so as not to encourage him. I want him to run away before the gangsters come. 2

He doesn't understand and keeps following me. Finally I have to resort to Mami's techniques. I kick him, softly at first, but then, when he keeps tagging behind me, I kick him hard. He whimpers and dashes away toward the front yard, disappearing in areas of darkness, then reappearing when he passes through lighted areas. At the front of the house, instead of turning toward our secret place, he keeps on going straight down the drive, through the big gates, to the world out there.

He will beat me to the United States is what I am thinking as I head back to the house. I will find Liberty there, like Tía Mimi says. But I already sense it is a different kind of liberty my aunt means. All I can do is hope that when we come back—as Mami has promised we will—my Liberty will be waiting for me here. 3

1 Motivation *What motivates Tía Mimi's words to the narrator?*

3 Rewards and Sacrifices *What sacrifice does the narrator make in order to keep Liberty safe?*

Reading Practice

SPIRAL REVIEW SMALL GROUP

Discover Wordplay

Explain to students that a *pun* is a play on words that is usually humorous, but can also be serious. In a pun, one word is assigned two separate meanings, both of which fit within the context of the text or idea. Have students form groups of three or four to examine the story and discover the pun in the first column. *(Though "Liberty" is the title of the story, and the pun on this word is apparent throughout the story, it is most apparent in the following sentence from page 134: "You're going to find liberty when you get to the United States.")*

To check students' understanding of the selection, see Unit 1 Teaching Resources Book, pp. 151–152.

After You Read

Respond and Think Critically

Respond and Interpret

1. What was your reaction at the end of this story? Explain.
2. (a)What gift does the American consul give the narrator's family at the beginning of the story? (b)What else does the family hope to obtain from the consul?
3. (a)Who narrates, or tells, the story? (b)How would you describe the narrator?
4. (a)How does Tía Mimi get the narrator to agree to go to the United States without her dog, Liberty? (b)What deeper meaning is there to her words? Explain.

Analyze and Evaluate

5. How believable was the story's portrait of the young narrator? Cite examples from the story to support your answer.
6. Do you think that over the course of the story, the narrator grows or changes in any way? Explain.

Connect

7. **Big Idea** **Rewards and Sacrifices** What sacrifices and rewards exist in this story? Are the rewards worth the cost? Why or why not?
8. **Connect to the Author** Much of Alvarez's writing focuses on the lives of immigrants. In what ways does "Liberty" explore this topic?

Literary Element Motivation

Characters usually have a reason for their behavior, but their motivation is not always directly stated.

1. What is Papi's reason for naming the dog "Liberty"?
2. What might be the larger meaning of the narrator's wish at the end of the story to find the dog Liberty safe when she returns? Explain.

Reading Strategy Respond to Characters

Review your character chart before answering the following questions. Explain each of your answers.

1. Which character did you find most interesting?
2. Which character did you find most irritating?
3. Which bit of dialogue, or words spoken by a character, did you find most memorable?
4. Which action seemed most important to you?

LOG ON Literature Online

Selection Resources For Selection Quizzes, eFlashcards, and Reading-Writing Connection activities, go to glencoe.com and enter QuickPass code GL49787u1.

Vocabulary Practice

Practice with Usage Respond to these statements to help you explore the meanings of the boldface vocabulary words from the selection.

1. Identify one way in which a **hyperactive** imagination might keep someone awake.
2. Describe how a **distracted** student might act during a lecture.
3. Give an example of something that has a **putrid** odor.
4. Tell about an **admonition** you've given to a friend or sibling.
5. Explain how a parent or other adult might react to an **inconsolable** child.

Writing

Write an Essay Write a brief essay in which you describe the story's theme—its central message or insight. How is the dog linked to the theme? Support your ideas with details from the story.

After You Read

Assess

1. Answers will vary.
2. (a) A puppy (b) Visas for travel to the United States
3. (a) A young girl (b) Students may say she is rebellious and a tomboy.
4. (a) She says liberty awaited the narrator in the United States. (b) She means that the girl and her family will find freedom and safety.
5. Students may say the portrayal of a young girl gripped by forces beyond her comprehension was believable.
6. She has learned to understand the need to let go of her home and her beloved pet.
7. They sacrifice their home; the girl sacrifices her dog. Students should support opinions with text examples.
8. Students should point out that the story mostly takes place in a country much like the Dominican Republic. In addition, they should recognize that while the family has not yet reached the U.S., they are preparing for and imagining their new lives there.

Vocabulary

Possible responses follow:

1. A hyperactive imagination might cause a person to be afraid of insignificant sounds.
2. The student might stare off into space or doodle in a notebook.
3. rotten fish
4. I warned my little brother not to cross the street without looking for cars first.
5. The adult would probably try to comfort the upset child by giving him a hug.

Literary Element

1. In honor of his goal of finding freedom in the United States
2. This might refer to her desire to find her country safe when she returns.

Reading Strategy

Answers will vary. Students should support answers with reasoning and story details.

Writing

Essays should explain the story's theme or message and give examples from the story that support their ideas.

Progress Check

Can students analyze motivation?

If No → See Unit 1 Teaching Resources Book, p. 146.

Before You Read

Focus

Summary

A girl and her brother of Chinese-American descent must attend Chinese school. The girl resists because she wants to be completely American. As an adult, she understands that her heritage is an important part of her.

Readability Scores

Dale-Chall: 4.5
DRP: 50
Lexile: 840

Build Background

In her essay, Elizabeth Wong describes the time she spent at Chinese school. Schools such as the one she describes grew out of immigrant parents' desire for their children to learn about their heritage. Often children attending these schools spend weekend afternoons at the school learning the language of their families' homeland as well as various cultural customs and history.

The Struggle to Be an All-American Girl

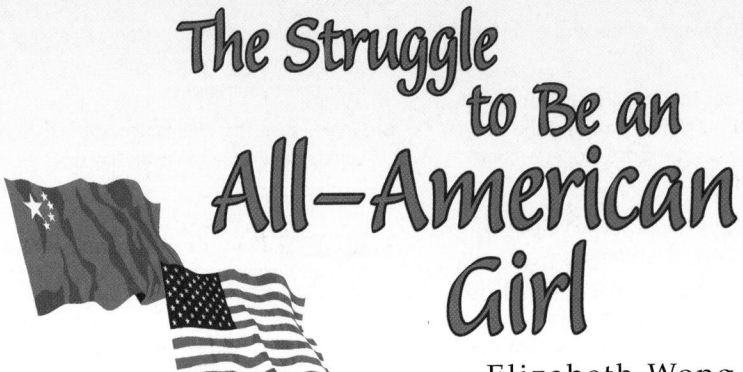

Elizabeth Wong

It's still there, the Chinese school on Yale Street where my brother and I used to go. Despite the new coat of paint and the high wire fence, the school I knew ten years ago remains remarkably, stoically[1] the same.

Every day at 5 PM, instead of playing with our fourth- and fifth-grade friends or sneaking out to the empty lot to hunt ghosts and animal bones, my brother and I had to go to Chinese school. No amount of kicking, screaming, or pleading could dissuade my mother, who was solidly determined to have us learn the language of our heritage.

Forcibly, she walked us the seven long, hilly blocks from our home to school, depositing our defiant tearful faces before the stern principal. My only memory of him is that he swayed on his heels like a palm tree, and he always clasped his impatient twitching hands behind his back. I recognized him as a repressed maniacal child killer,[2] and knew that if we ever saw his hands we'd be in big trouble.

We all sat in little chairs in an empty auditorium. The room smelled like Chinese medicine, an imported faraway mustiness. Like ancient mothballs or dirty closets. I hated that smell. I favored crisp new scents. Like the soft French perfume that my American teacher wore in public school.

There was a stage far to the right, flanked by an American flag and the flag of the Nationalist Republic of China,[3] which was also red, white and blue but not as pretty.

Although the emphasis at the school was mainly language—speaking, reading, writing—the lessons always began with an

1. *Stoically* here means "unaffected by outside influences."

2. The narrator uses the expression *repressed maniacal child killer* to humorously convey her childhood fear of her strict principal.

3. The *Nationalist Republic of China* is a country on the island of Taiwan. The People's Republic of China is on the mainland.

Reading Practice

SPIRAL REVIEW

Compare and Contrast

Have students fill in a Venn diagram comparing and contrasting the narrators of "Liberty" and "The Struggle to Be an All-American Girl." Then draw a large Venn diagram on the board and ask students to share the contents of their diagrams with the class. Encourage students to write their answers on the board. Have students incorporate additional details into their diagrams.

exercise in politeness. With the entrance of the teacher, the best student would tap a bell and everyone would get up, kowtow,[4] and chant, *"Sing san ho,"* the phonetic for "How are you, teacher?"

Being ten years old, I had better things to learn than ideographs[5] copied painstakingly in lines that ran right to left from the tip of a *moc but,* a real ink pen that had to be held in an awkward way if blotches were to be avoided. After all, I could do the multiplication tables, name the satellites of Mars, and write reports on Little Women and Black Beauty. Nancy Drew, my favorite book heroine, never spoke Chinese.

The language was a source of embarrassment. More times than not, I had tried to disassociate myself from the nagging loud voice that followed me wherever I wandered in the nearby American supermarket outside Chinatown. The voice belonged to my grandmother, a fragile woman in her seventies who could outshout the best of the street vendors. Her humor was raunchy, her Chinese rhythmless, patternless. It was quick, it was loud, it was unbeautiful. It was not like the quiet, lilting romance of French or the gentle refinement of the American South. Chinese sounded pedestrian.[6] Public.

In Chinatown, the comings and goings of hundreds of Chinese on their daily tasks sounded chaotic and frenzied. I did not want to be thought of as mad, as talking gibberish. When I spoke English, people nodded at me, smiled sweetly, said encouraging words. Even the people in my culture would cluck and say that I'd do well in life. "My, doesn't she move her lips fast," they would say, meaning that I'd be able to keep up with the world outside Chinatown.

My brother was even more fanatical than I about speaking English. He was especially hard on my mother, criticizing her, often cruelly, for her pidgin[7] speech—smatterings of Chinese scattered like chop suey in her conversation. "It's not 'What it is,' Mom," he'd say in exasperation. "It's 'What is it, what is it, what is it!'" Sometimes Mom might leave out an occasional "the" or "a," or perhaps a verb of being. He would stop her in mid-sentence: "Say it again, Mom. Say it right." When he tripped over his own tongue, he'd blame it on her: "See, Mom, it's all your fault. You set a bad example."

What infuriated my mother most was when my brother cornered her on her consonants, especially "r." My father had played a cruel joke on Mom by assigning her an American name that her tongue wouldn't allow her to say. No matter how hard she tried, "Ruth" always ended up "Luth" or "Roof."

After two years of writing with a *moc but* and reciting words with multiples of meanings, I finally was granted a cultural divorce. I was permitted to stop Chinese school.

I thought of myself as multicultural. I preferred tacos to egg rolls; I enjoyed Cinco de Mayo[8] more than Chinese New Year.

At last, I was one of you; I wasn't one of them.

Sadly, I still am.

Quickwrite

In two or three paragraphs, discuss the following questions: Who are the "you" and "them" that Wong refers to at the end of the essay? What is the meaning of the last sentence?

4. To *kowtow* means "to bow deeply and respectfully."
5. *Ideographs* are the symbols that make up traditional Chinese writing.
6. As used here, *pedestrian* means "ordinary."
7. *Pidgin* refers to a basic way of communicating, with a limited vocabulary and simplified grammar.
8. *Cinco de Mayo* means "fifth of May." It is a national holiday in Mexico.

Teach

Literary Element 1

Conflict Explain that conflict is the main struggle between two opposing forces in a story.

Ask: What is the conflict in this story? *(The narrator's desire to fit into American culture conflicts with her mother's determination that the children learn the language and customs of their Chinese heritage.)*

Quickwrite

Students' essays should explain that *you* refers to Americans. *Them* refers to people of Chinese heritage, such as her mother and grandmother. In the last line, the narrator, as an adult, seems to regret her resistance to Chinese culture.

Approaching Level

DIFFERENTIATED INSTRUCTION

Established Help students identify specific elements of Chinese culture on these pages. Write their responses on the board. Then ask them to contrast these elements with elements of American culture, both within and beyond the text.

Advanced Learners

DIFFERENTIATED INSTRUCTION

Autobiography The narrator in this story seems to regret her rejection of her culture as a child. **Ask:** As you grow older, do you regret something that you did or did not do in your past? Then have students write a short, autobiographical narrative describing such a situation in their own lives.

Before You Read

Focus

Summary

A poet writes about being an American who has emigrated from Mexico, and the loss of identity that comes with such a transition. She addresses the idea of being unaccepted by both Mexicans and Americans.

Legal Alien

Pat Mora

Ramon Gomez de la Serna, 1915. Diego Rivera. Oil on canvas, 109 x 90 cm. Private collection. ©Banco de Mexico Trust.

Writing Practice

SPIRAL REVIEW **Summarize** Explain to students that summarizing can help improve their comprehension of a poem. Have one student read the poem aloud to the class. Then have students write a summary of the poem. Ask students to share their summaries with the rest of the class. **Ask:** Do you think the effect of your prose writing is different from the effect of Mora's poem? How? *(Students should say that while their writing communicates the same meaning, it does not do so in an artistic, emotional way.)*

Build Background

The term *hyphenated identity* comes from the practice of using a hyphen to connect one's cultural heritage to one's country of birth: Mexican-American, for example. Because the hyphen implies that the person is neither Mexican nor American, this small punctuation mark has been the source of controversy. Pat Mora explores the issue of hyphenated identity in her poem "Legal Alien."

Bi-lingual, Bi-cultural,
able to slip from "How's life?"
to *"Me'stan volviendo loca,"*[1]
able to sit in a paneled office
drafting memos in smooth English,
able to order in fluent Spanish
at a Mexican restaurant,
American but hyphenated,
viewed by Anglos as perhaps exotic,
perhaps inferior, definitely different,
viewed by Mexicans as alien,
(their eyes say, "You may speak
Spanish but you're not like me")
an American to Mexicans
a Mexican to Americans
a handy token
sliding back and forth
between the fringes of both worlds
by smiling
by masking the discomfort
of being pre-judged
Bi-laterally.

---

1. *Me'stan volviendo loca* is Spanish for *They are driving me crazy.*

Discussion Starter

Meet with a small group to discuss the situation of the speaker of "Legal Alien." Consider what the title of the poem and phrases such as "the fringes of both worlds" suggest about her cultural conflict. Why does she feel like an outsider even though she is successful? Summarize your discussion for the rest of the class.

Teach

Reading Strategy 1

Draw Conclusions Ask students to draw conclusions about how the narrator of this poem feels about living in America. Have them use evidence from the poem to support their conclusions. *(Possible answer: Life in America is uncomfortable for the narrator because neither Mexicans nor Americans seem to accept her.)*

Discussion Starter

Students' discussions should touch on the speaker's dilemma of feeling rejected and judged by both cultures to which she belongs.

Approaching Level

DIFFERENTIATED INSTRUCTION

Established Have students conduct Internet research in order to find out more about Pat Mora's life and writings. Ask students to prepare a short essay in which they explain what they have discovered about the poet's life, accomplishments, and literary themes, as well as how this information ties into the theme of "Legal Alien."

Advanced Learners

DIFFERENTIATED INSTRUCTION

Analyze Poetry Have students read other poems by Mora and have them write an essay about some aspect of her poetry, such as her use of metaphors.

Wrap-Up: Comparing Literature

Across Genres

Assess

Compare the Big Idea

Evaluate student essays with these criteria:

- Do essays give reasons why immigrants make sacrifices to come to the United States?
- Do they tell what immigrants gain and sacrifice?
- Do essays conclude with students' ideas about the effects of immigrants on the United States?

Compare Theme

1. Possible answers: Alvarez says immigration is driven by a need for liberty and safety; people should appreciate the freedoms in the United States. Wong says immigrants and their children must decide what to retain of their old culture; they should not give up their heritage. Mora says it is difficult for Mexican Americans to fit in among Americans; at the same time, it is diffficult for them to fit in among Mexicans in Mexico.
2. Possible answers: Fiction was a good way for Alvarez to convey the feelings of a family beginning a journey to a new place. Memoir may have been the best way for Wong to reveal her personal feelings. Poetry may have been an appropriate way to convey Mora's delicate sentiments about loss of identity.
3. Answers will vary. Students should support their answers.

Wrap-Up: Comparing Literature

Across Genres

- ***Liberty*** by Julia Alvarez
- ***The Struggle to Be an All-American Girl*** by Elizabeth Wong
- ***Legal Alien*** by Pat Mora

COMPARE THE **Big Idea** Rewards and Sacrifices

Writing Activity The narrator of "Liberty," the author of "The Struggle to Be an All-American Girl," and the speaker in "Legal Alien" all make sacrifices in order to create a life in the United States. Why are they willing to make such sacrifices? What do they gain in return? What do they lose in the process? Think about the issues that seem to be common to immigrants from many places. Then write a brief essay discussing the different facets of the immigrant experience as revealed by these works. Conclude your essay with your thoughts about the impact the immigrant experience has had on U.S. society.

The Burning Passion. Tsing-Fang Chen.

COMPARE Theme

Group Activity A **genre** is a category, or type, of literature. Though the selections compared here come from different genres, each of the selections conveys a theme, or message, about immigration to the United States. With a small group, discuss the following questions:

1. What message about immigration does each writer share with the reader?
2. For each selection, in what way did the characteristics of the genre help convey the writer's message?
3. Which selection makes the most powerful statement about immigration? Support your answer with passages from the selections.

COMPARE Cultures

Speaking and Listening Julia Alvarez, Elizabeth Wong, and Pat Mora each emphasize different aspects of the immigrant experience. With a partner, discuss what each author suggests about the following issues:

- the importance of remembering one's origins
- the ways in which the United States is better or worse than other places
- the cultural conflicts that define the immigrant experience

Prepare a report to share your thoughts with your classmates.

LOG ON **Literature** Online

Selection Resources For Selection Quizzes, eFlashcards, and Reading-Writing Connection activities, go to glencoe.com and enter QuickPass code GL49787u1.

Compare Cultures

Evaluate students' discussions on these criteria:

- Do discussions include each author's beliefs?
- Do discussions touch on remembering one's origins, sacrifices, and gains made by the immigrant and how the immigrant combines love of his/her homeland and the United States?

For additional selection assessment, see Assessment Resources, pp. 59–60.

Before You Read

Sweet Potato Pie

Meet **Eugenia Collier**
(born 1928)

"Because racism is not over, writing still needs to define who we are." Eugenia Collier experienced racism firsthand as a young girl. The daughter of a doctor and an educator, she grew up in Baltimore, Maryland, where she attended segregated schools. After graduating with high honors from Howard University, earning her master's degree from Columbia University, and working as a public aid case worker for five years, Collier followed in her mother's footsteps by becoming a teacher.

The Educator Collier taught English at various colleges and universities in the metropolitan Baltimore-Washington, D.C., area. She was named one of the Outstanding Educators of America. Yet she herself continued to learn as well. "After a conventional Western-type education," Collier once stated, "I discovered the richness, the diversity, the beauty of my black heritage. This discovery has meant a coalescence of personal and professional goals. It has also meant a lifetime commitment."

> *"The fact of my blackness is the core and center of my creativity."*
>
> —Eugenia Collier

The Writer Collier merged her personal and professional lives by writing about the African American experience. In 1969 she won the Gwendolyn Brooks Award for Fiction for what is perhaps her most famous short story, "Marigolds." It tells the tale of a fourteen-year-old African American girl who comes of age in Maryland during the Great Depression. A one-act play based on her short story "Ricky" was staged in Chicago in 1976.

Collier has also written numerous critical essays about great African American authors such as Langston Hughes. In 1972, with collaborator Richard A. Long, she edited *Afro-American Writing: An Anthology of Prose and Poetry.* She has also contributed poems as well as stories and articles to both scholarly and popular publications, including *Black World, TV Guide,* and the *New York Times.*

"A Lifetime Commitment" In 1976 Collier obtained her doctorate from the University of Maryland. She continued to teach as well as write. Collier's career has shown the "lifetime commitment" to her African American heritage that she has previously expressed.

LOG ON **Literature** Online

Author Search For more about Eugenia Collier, go to glencoe.com and enter QuickPass code GL49787u1.

Before You Read

Focus

Bellringer Options

Selection Focus Transparency 9

Daily Language Practice Transparency 13

Or discuss the meaning of the phrase "comfort food and family traditions." Ask students if they have comfort foods or favorite family traditions. Have volunteers share the meaning of these special foods and traditions.

Ask: Why do people have comfort foods and favorite traditions? Have students consider as they read what makes the sweet potato pie a special food for the narrator.

For an audio recording of this selection, use Listening Library Audio CD-ROM.

Readability Scores

Dale-Chall: 6.7
DRP: 60
Lexile: 970

Selection Skills

Sweet Potato Pie

Literary Elements
- Theme (SE pp. 142–152)
- Character (SE p. 152)

Reading Skills
- Question (SE pp. 142–153)

Vocabulary Skills
- Word Parts (SE p. 153)
- Matching Game (TE p. 142)

Listening/Speaking/Viewing Skills
- Analyze Art (SE pp. 144, 149; TE p. 143)

Writing Skills/Grammar
- Research and Report (SE p. 153)
- Understand Dialect (TE p. 144)

Before You Read

Focus

Summary

Buddy was the youngest child of poor Southern sharecroppers. Now a college professor, Buddy drops in on his brother Charley's family in Harlem. He discovers that Charley, who sacrificed for Buddy all his life, will continue to do so forever.

For summaries in languages other than English, see Unit 1 Teaching Resources Book, pp. 153–158.

Vocabulary

Matching Game Group students in pairs. Distribute a list of vocabulary words to one partner in each pair. Distribute a list of definitions to the other partner. Tell students with the word lists to read aloud a word and have the partner read aloud the correct definition. That student should then read aloud another definition and have the partner read aloud the correct vocabulary word. Pairs should continue alternating in this manner until all words and definitions have been supplied. Then have them trade lists and repeat the process.

For additional vocabulary practice, see Unit 1 Teaching Resources Book, p. 161.

For additional context, see Glencoe Interactive Vocabulary CD-ROM.

Literature and Reading Preview

Connect to the Story

How do you define success? Write a journal entry about someone you consider to be successful. Why do you consider this person to be successful?

Build Background

Sharecropping was a farming system practiced in the South in the years between the Civil War and World War II. Landowners allowed people to live on and farm a portion of their land in exchange for half the crop. If the landowners provided supplies, the sharecropper could keep only about one-third of the crop. The sale of that amount barely covered basic necessities and kept sharecropping families in poverty.

Set Purposes for Reading

Big Idea Rewards and Sacrifices

As you read "Sweet Potato Pie," ask yourself, Which characters sacrifice the most, and which characters benefit most?

Literary Element Theme

The **theme** of a piece of literature is its central message about life or human nature. In some works, the theme is stated outright. In other works, the theme is implied and revealed gradually. As you read this story, ask yourself, What details reveal something about the central message or idea?

Reading Strategy Question

Asking **questions** as you read and looking for the answers, or even predicting them, can help you read more actively and intelligently. It can also help you better remember what you have read. As you read, ask yourself, Am I understanding the events and characters in the story?

Tip: Track Questions and Answers Use a chart to record your questions. Then, as you read, look for answers and record them as well.

Question	Clues/Answer
Why is Buddy's love "seasoned with gratitude"?	His brother Charley gave up his childhood.

Learning Objectives

For pages 141–153

In studying this text, you will focus on the following objectives:

Literary Study: Analyzing theme.

Reading: Questioning.

Research: Connecting literature to science.

Vocabulary

collective (kə lek′ tiv) *adj.* having to do with a group of persons or things; common; shared; p. 145 *The collective opinion of the jury was the man was guilty.*

antiquity (an tik′ wə tē) *n.* an ancient time or times; p. 145 *The pyramids of Egypt date back to antiquity.*

ubiquitous (ū bik′ wə təs) *adj.* seeming to be everywhere at once; p. 146 *Before the election, campaign posters were ubiquitous; in windows, on streets, on doors.*

futilely (fū′ til ē) *adv.* uselessly; vainly; hopelessly; p. 146 *The pedestrian futilely waved his arm at the taxicab as it sped by him.*

Tip: Word Parts Knowing what the parts of an unknown word mean can help determine the word's meaning. For example, if you know an *antique* is something old and that the suffix *–ity* means "state or condition," you might be able to get the idea that *antiquity* refers to the condition of being ancient or ancient times.

Literary Element Practice

SPIRAL REVIEW PARTNERS

Figurative Language Remind students that a simile is a comparison using the word *like* or *as.* Write these sentences on the board and point out the similes within them:

My cat Ninja is <u>as fast as lightning.</u>

Jamie's room looks <u>like a pigsty.</u>

Show students the simile in the first sentence of this story. Explain that the author compares Charley to an insect scurrying among other insects to show that Charley and those around him looked very small.

Pair up students and ask them to find two more similes on this page. *(". . . my thoughts hover over him like hummingbirds." ". . . as clearly as if I were looking at a split TV screen.")* Discuss their meaning.

Midtown Mayhem, 1999. Patti Mollica. Acrylic and pastel on paper. Collection of the artist. ★

Sweet Potato Pie

Eugenia Collier

1 From up here on the fourteenth floor, my brother Charley looks like an insect scurrying among other insects. A deep feeling of love surges through me. Despite the distance, he seems to feel it, for he turns and scans the upper windows, but failing to find me, continues on his way. I watch him moving quickly—gingerly,[1] it seems to me—down Fifth Avenue and around the corner to his shabby taxicab. In a moment he will be heading back uptown.

I turn from the window and flop down on the bed, shoes and all. Perhaps because of what happened this afternoon or maybe just because I see Charley so seldom, my thoughts hover over him like hummingbirds. The cheerful, impersonal tidiness of this room is a world away from Charley's walk-up flat in Harlem[2] and a hundred worlds from the bare, noisy shanty where he and the rest of us spent what there was of childhood. I close my eyes, and side by side I see the Charley of my boyhood and the Charley of this afternoon, as clearly as if I were looking at a split TV screen. Another surge of love, seasoned with gratitude, wells up in me.

As far as I know, Charley never had any childhood at all. The oldest children of sharecroppers never do. Mama and Pa were shadowy figures whose voices I heard vaguely in the morning when sleep was shallow and whom I glimpsed as they left for the field before I was fully awake or as they trudged wearily into the house at night when my lids were irresistibly heavy.

They came into sharp focus only on special occasions. One such occasion was the day when the crops were in and the sharecroppers were paid. In our cabin there was so much excitement in the air that even I, the "baby," responded to it. For weeks we had been running out of things that we could neither grow nor get on credit.

1. *Gingerly* means "with caution" or "carefully."
2. *Harlem* is a section of New York City mainly inhabited by African Americans and Hispanics.

2 Question *What question might this statement lead you to ask?*

Teach

Big Idea 1

Rewards and Sacrifices

Tell students to keep these questions in mind as they read.

Ask: What kind of relationship does the narrator have with Charley? *(He is Charley's younger brother.)* How does Charley's loving nature impact the life of the narrator? *(Charley cares for him as a father figure; he willingly makes sacrifices so the narrator can get an education.)*

Reading Strategy 2

Question **Answer:** *Students will likely ask, "What happened this afternoon between the two characters?"*

View the Art ★

Patti Mollica has created many urban street scenes, often set in New York City. Her work is characterized by bold colors. She sees the world as "a mosaic of shapes and color."

English Learners

DIFFERENTIATED INSTRUCTION

Beginning/Early Intermediate Write on the board *changed, toiled, looked,* and *hunted.* **Say:** These words refer to actions in the past. Not all past tense verbs end in *-ed.* Have students list the present tense of the past tense verbs *rode, sent,* and *sang.* Tell students to find verbs on this page and note their tense.

Approaching Level

DIFFERENTIATED INSTRUCTION

Established Explain that *flashback* is a literary device in which a narrator interrupts the chronological order of a narrative to describe an event that happened earlier. In this story, the narrator is remembering his childhood. This is a flashback. Flashbacks take you out of the current action of the story to tell you about the character's past. Why does the author do this? Flashbacks give you details about a character's past without interrupting the entire story. Ask students to think of other ways flashbacks might be used.

Teach

Literary Element 1

Theme Answer: *The description of the mother's face as beautiful and radiant despite her suffering is a clue to the theme of the story, which includes sacrifice.*

APPROACHING For approaching-level students, explain that the mother's face is not beautiful in a typical way; rather, the narrator expresses that Mama's face is beautiful because of her ability to persevere. **Ask:** What phrase indicates that Mama's beauty is not typical? *(Not with the hollow beauty of well-modeled features)*

View the Art ★

Answer: *The family in the painting might look like Buddy's family, although there were more children in Buddy's family.*

Ellis Wilson (1899–1977) grew up in Maysfield, Kentucky, a small town in tobacco country. He painted people going about everyday activities—cutting lumber in the swamps, harvesting and picking tobacco, going to church and market, and dancing.

Field Workers. Ellis Wilson. Oil on masonite, 29¾ x 34⅞ in. National Museum of American Art, Washington, DC.

View the Art Ellis Wilson often painted people, such as the family shown here, going about their daily activities. How is your impression of the narrator's family similar to or different from your impression of the family represented in this painting? ★

On the evening of that day we waited anxiously for our parents' return. Then we would cluster around the rough wooden table—I on Lil's lap or clinging to Charley's neck, little Alberta nervously tugging her plait,[3] Jamie crouched at Mama's elbow, like a panther about to spring, and all seven of us silent for once, waiting. Pa would place the money on the table—gently, for it was made from the sweat of their bodies and from their children's tears. Mama would count it out in little piles, her dark face stern and, I think now, beautiful. Not with the hollow beauty of well-modeled features but with the strong radiance of one who has suffered and never yielded.

Theme *So far, what possible clues to the story's theme do you notice?* 1

3. A *plait* (plāt) is a braid or pigtail.

Listening and Speaking Practice

SPIRAL REVIEW SMALL GROUP

Understand Dialect Break students into small groups and find places in the story where the characters speak in dialect. Assign each group a conversation from the story that contains dialect, and have group members orally translate the dialect into Standard Academic English. Have each group share its oral translation with the class. Initiate a discussion about the patterns students use in everyday speech. Write their responses on the board.

"This for store bill," she would mutter, making a little pile. "This for c'llection. This for piece o'gingham . . ."[4] and so on, stretching the money as tight over our **collective** needs as Jamie's outgrown pants were stretched over my bottom. "Well, that's the crop." She would look up at Pa at last. "It'll do." Pa's face would relax, and a general grin flitted from child to child. We would survive, at least for the present.

The other time when my parents were solid entities was at church. On Sundays we would don our threadbare Sunday-go-to-meeting clothes and tramp, along with neighbors similarly attired, to the Tabernacle Baptist Church, the frail edifice of bare boards held together by God knows what, which was all that my parents ever knew of security and future promise.

Being the youngest and therefore the most likely to err, I was plopped between my father and my mother on the long wooden bench. They sat huge and eternal like twin mountains at my sides. I remember my father's still, black profile silhouetted against the sunny window, looking back into dark recesses of time, into some dim **antiquity**, like an ancient ceremonial mask. My mother's face, usually sternly set, changed with the varying nuances[5] of her emotion, its planes shifting, shaped by the soft highlights of the sanctuary, as she progressed from a subdued "amen" to a loud "Help me, Jesus" wrung from the depths of her gaunt frame.

My early memories of my parents are associated with special occasions. The contours of my everyday were shaped by Lil and Charley, the oldest children, who rode herd on the rest of us while Pa and Mama toiled in fields not their own. Not until years later did I realize that Lil and Charley were little more than children themselves.

Lil had the loudest, screechiest voice in the county. When she yelled, "Boy, you better git yourself in here!" you *got* yourself in there. It was Lil who caught and bathed us, Lil who fed us and sent us to school, Lil who punished us when we needed punishing and comforted us when we needed comforting. If her voice was loud, so was her laughter. When she laughed, everybody laughed. And when Lil sang, everybody listened.

Charley was taller than anybody in the world, including, I was certain, God. From his shoulders, where I spent considerable time in the earliest years, the world had a different perspective: I looked down at tops of heads rather than at the undersides of chins. As I grew older, Charley became more father than brother. Those days return in fragments of splintered memory: Charley's slender dark hands whittling a toy from a chunk of wood, his face thin and intense, brown as the loaves Lil baked when there was flour. Charley's quick fingers guiding a stick of charred kindling over a bit of scrap paper, making a wondrous picture take shape—Jamie's face or Alberta's rag doll or the spare figure of our bony brown dog. Charley's voice low and terrible in the dark, telling ghost stories so delightfully dreadful that later in the night the moan of the wind through the chinks in the wall

---

4. *Gingham* (ging′ əm) is checked, striped, or plaid cotton fabric.
5. A *nuance* (no͞o′ äns) is a slight shade of tone, expression, or meaning.

2 Rewards and Sacrifices *What sacrifices have the parents in this family made?*

Vocabulary

collective (kə lek′ tiv) *adj.* having to do with a group of persons or things; common; shared

antiquity (an tik′ wə tē) *n.* an ancient time or times

Teach

Big Idea 2

Rewards and Sacrifices
Answer: *In order to support the children, the mother and father work long, hard hours and barely see their family.*

English Learners

DIFFERENTIATED INSTRUCTION

Intermediate Have students list words that they don't understand. Have them use a dictionary to look up the words on their list and use them in a new sentence. Encourage students to write the words, definitions, and new sentences in their vocabulary notebooks.

Early Advanced **Write** this hyperbole on the board: "Charley was taller than anyone else in the world, including, I was certain, God"; **Write** this example of personification: ". . . the moan of the wind through the chinks in the wall . . ." Have students identify other examples of figurative language. *("they sat huge and eternal like twin mountains at my sides," "her sister darted here and there like a merry little water bug.")*

Teach

Literary Element 1

Theme Answer: *Charley was a father figure for the narrator. He also was a brother to him and helped make the narrator's childhood happy.*

Reading Strategy 2

Question Answer: *Students may say the narrator received an education.*

ENGLISH LEARNERS For English learners, **ask:** Which words in the sentence serve as context clues to figure out the meaning of *futilely? (sought, feverishly, brute survival)*

Writer's Technique ☆

Using Dialect *Dialect* is a variation of a standard language spoken by a group of people, often within a particular region. Sentence structure, vocabulary, and pronunciation are affected by dialect. A writer uses dialect to enrich understanding of a character.

- Have a volunteer read aloud what Pa says to Buddy.
- Ask students to explain what Pa's language reveals about his character.

Visual Vocabulary
A *pallet* is a crude bed or mattress, usually filled with straw.

sent us scurrying to the security of Charley's pallet, Charley's sleeping form.

Some memories are more than fragmentary. I can still feel the *whap* of the wet dish rag across my mouth. Somehow I developed a stutter, which Charley was determined to cure. Someone had told him that an effective cure was to slap the stutterer across the mouth with a sopping wet dish rag. Thereafter whenever I began, "Let's g-g-g--," *whap!* from nowhere would come the **ubiquitous** rag. Charley would always insist, "I don't want hurt you none, Buddy—" and *whap* again. I don't know when or why I stopped stuttering. But I stopped.

Already laid waste by poverty, we were easy prey for ignorance and superstition, which hunted us like hawks. We sought education feverishly—and, for most of us, **futilely**, for the sum total of our combined energies was required for mere brute survival. Inevitably each child had to leave school and bear his share of the eternal burden.

Eventually the family's hopes for learning fastened on me, the youngest. I remember—I *think* I remember, for I could not have been more than five—one frigid day

1 Theme *During his childhood, what did the narrator receive from Charley?*

2 Question *"For most of us, futilely" implies that at least one child in the family did receive an education. Which one do you think received it?*

Vocabulary

ubiquitous (ū bik′ wə təs) *adj.* seeming to be everywhere at once

futilely (fū′ til ē) *adv.* uselessly; vainly; hopelessly

Pa, huddled on a rickety stool before the coal stove, took me on his knee and studied me gravely. I was a skinny little thing, they tell me, with large, solemn eyes.

"Well, boy," Pa said at last, "if you got to depend on your looks for what you get out'n this world, you just as well lay down right now." His hand was rough from the plow, but gentle as it touched my cheek. "Lucky for you, you got a *mind*. And that's something ain't everybody got. You go to school, boy, get yourself some learning. Make something out'n yourself. Ain't nothing you can't do if you got learning." ☆

Charley was determined that I would break the chain of poverty, that I would "be somebody." As we worked our small vegetable garden in the sun or pulled a bucket of brackish water[6] from the well, Charley would tell me, "You ain gon be no poor farmer, Buddy. You gon be a teacher or maybe a doctor or a lawyer. One thing, bad as you is you ain gon be no preacher."

I loved school with a desperate passion, which became more intense when I began to realize what a monumental struggle it was for my parents and brothers and sisters to keep me there. The cramped, dingy classroom became a battleground where I was victorious. I stayed on top of my class. With glee I out-read, out-figured, and outspelled the country boys who mocked my poverty, calling me "the boy with eyes in back of his head"—the "eyes" being the perpetual holes in my hand-me-down pants.

As the years passed, the economic strain was eased enough to make it possible for me to go on to high school. There were fewer mouths to feed, for one thing: Alberta went North to find work at sixteen; Jamie died at twelve.

6. *Brackish water* tastes bad.

Writing Practice

SPIRAL REVIEW

Understand Symbolism Tell students that this story contains many symbols. Explain that a symbol is a person, place, object, or event that exists on a literal level within a work but also represents something on a figurative level. **Ask:** What is the symbol for Buddy's achievement on these pages? *(Students should answer that Buddy's suit symbolizes his academic achievement and the support and love of his family.)* Have students write a paragraph in which they explain which object stands for the idea that Buddy, with the help of his family, has reached a goal.

I finished high school at the head of my class. For Mama and Pa and each of my brothers and sisters, my success was a personal triumph. One by one they came to me the week before commencement bringing crumpled dollar bills and coins long hoarded, muttering, "Here, Buddy, put this on your gradiation clothes." My graduation suit was the first suit that was all my own.

On graduation night our cabin (less crowded now) was a frantic collage of frayed nerves. I thought Charley would drive me mad.

"Buddy, you ain pressed out them pants right . . . Can't you git a better shine on them shoes? . . . Lord, you done messed up that tie!"

Overwhelmed by the combination of Charley's nerves and my own, I finally exploded. "Man, cut it out!" Abruptly he stopped tugging at my tie, and I was afraid I had hurt his feelings. "It's okay, Charley. Look, you're strangling me. The tie's okay."

Charley relaxed a little and gave a rather sheepish chuckle. "Sure, Buddy." He gave my shoulder a rough joggle. "But you gotta look good. You *somebody*."

My valedictory address[7] was the usual idealistic, sentimental nonsense. I have forgotten what I said that night, but the sight of Mama and Pa and the rest is like a lithograph[8] burned on my memory; Lil, her round face made beautiful by her proud smile; Pa, his head held high, eyes loving and fierce; Mama radiant. Years later when her shriveled hands were finally still, my mind kept coming back to her as she was now. I believe this moment was the apex of her entire life. All of them, even Alberta down from Baltimore—different now, but united with them in her pride. And Charley, on the end of the row, still somehow the protector of them all. Charley, looking as if he were in the presence of something sacred.

As I made my way through the carefully rehearsed speech it was as if part of me were standing outside watching the whole thing—their proud, work-weary faces, myself wearing the suit that was their combined strength and love and hope: Lil with her lovely, low-pitched voice, Charley with the hands of an artist, Pa and Mama with God knows what potential lost with their sweat in the fields. I realized in that moment that I wasn't necessarily the smartest—only the youngest.

And the luckiest. The war came along, and I exchanged three years of my life (including a fair amount of my blood and a great deal of pain) for the GI Bill[9] and a college education. Strange how time can slip by like water flowing through your fingers. One by one the changes came—the old house empty at last, the rest of us scattered; for me, marriage, graduate school, kids, a professorship, and by now a thickening waistline and thinning hair. My mind spins off the years, and I am back to this afternoon and today's Charley—still long and lean, still gentle-eyed, still my greatest fan, and still determined to keep me on the ball.

I didn't tell Charley I would be at a professional meeting in New York and would surely visit; he and Bea would have spent days in fixing up, and I would have had to be company. No, I would drop in on them,

7. A *valedictory address* is a graduation speech, traditionally given by the class's highest-ranked student—the valedictorian.

8. A *lithograph* is a picture printed by a process in which part of a flat surface is treated to retain ink, and part is treated to repel it.

9. The *G.I. Bill of Rights* provided educational and economic assistance to returning World War II soldiers.

3 Rewards and Sacrifices *How does this statement by the narrator relate to the theme of rewards and sacrifices?*

Theme *What did this insight help Buddy to understand about his family?* **4**

Teach

Big Idea 3

Rewards and Sacrifices **Answer:** *The family had worked in order for Buddy to succeed in school. His success was their reward.*

APPROACHING Explain to approaching-level students that because the rest of Buddy's family was unable to receive an education, they looked at his experience and achievements as their own. Ask students to describe orally an occasion when they felt connected to the success or achievements of a family member.

Literary Element 4

Theme **Answer:** *It helped Buddy realize that his family had consciously chosen to sacrifice their own dreams and potential to help him. He was not the most gifted member of the family, but he was the luckiest.*

English Learners

DIFFERENTIATED INSTRUCTION

Early Advanced Explain to students that some words are pronounced the same as others but have a different meaning. Tell them these words are called homophones. Help them find homophones on this page. *(*week *and* weak*;* rest *and* wrest*;* way *and* weigh*)*

Approaching Level

DIFFERENTIATED INSTRUCTION

AAVE One pattern of African American Vernacular English (AAVE) is the omission of the verb "to be". **Write on the board:** He happy. We sick. She funny. They nervous. Ask students to write the correct form of each sentence using Standard Academic English. *(He is happy. We are sick. She is funny. They are nervous.)* Have students identify an example of this pattern on this page and make the correction using Standard Academic English. *("You somebody." You are somebody.)*

Teach

Big Idea 1

Rewards and Sacrifices
Answer: *Charley had artistic talent but could never develop it nor get an education because he needed to work hard for the family and help raise his siblings. By doing so, he sacrificed any chance he had of living a better life when he got older.*

Literary Element 2

Theme **Answer:** *He does not begrudge or resent Buddy at all, even though he sacrificed greatly to help him.*

Writer's Technique ☆

Figurative Language Explain that writers often use figurative language to create powerful images in the reader's mind. To help students appreciate the simile "the subway which lurks like the dark, inscrutable *id* beneath the surface of the city," review the meaning of the word *id.*

Ask: How is the subway like the human id? *(Possible answer:* The subway is deep, dark, and somewhat primitive when compared with the surface streets of the city.)

take them by surprise before they had a chance to stiffen up. I was anxious to see them—it had been so long. Yesterday and this morning were taken up with meetings in the posh Fifth Avenue hotel—a place we could not have dreamed in our boyhood. Late this afternoon I shook loose and headed for Harlem, hoping that Charley still came home for a few hours before his evening run. Leaving the glare and glitter of downtown, I entered the subway which ☆ lurks like the dark, inscrutable *id*[10] beneath the surface of the city. When I emerged, I was in Harlem.

Whenever I come to Harlem I feel somehow as if I were coming home—to some mythic ancestral home. The problems are real, the people are real—yet there is some mysterious epic[11] quality about Harlem, as if all Black people began and ended there, as if each had left something of himself. As if in Harlem the very heart of Blackness pulsed its beautiful tortured rhythms. Joining the throngs of people that saunter Lenox Avenue late afternoons, I headed for Charley's apartment. Along the way I savored the panorama of Harlem—women with shopping bags trudging wearily home; little kids flitting saucily through the crowd; groups of adolescent boys striding boldly along—some boisterous, some ominously silent; tables of merchandise spread on the sidewalks with hawkers singing their siren songs[12] of irresistible bargains; a blaring microphone sending forth waves of words to draw passersby into a restless bunch around a slender young man whose eyes have seen Truth; defeated men standing around on street corners or sitting on steps, heads down, hands idle; posters announcing Garvey Day;[13] "Buy Black" stamped on pavements; store windows bright with things African; stores still boarded up, a livid[14] scar from last year's rioting. There was a terrible tension in the air; I thought of how quickly dry timber becomes a roaring fire from a single spark.

I mounted the steps of Charley's building—old and in need of paint, like all the rest—and pushed the button to his apartment. The graffiti on the dirty wall recorded the sexual fantasies of past visitors. Some of it was even a dialogue of sorts: Someone had scrawled, "Try Lola" and a telephone number, followed by a catalog of Lola's virtues. Someone else had written, "I tried Lola and she is a Dog." Charley's buzzer rang. I pushed open the door and mounted the urine-scented stairs.

"Well, do Jesus—it's Buddy!" roared Charley as I arrived on the third floor. "Bea! Bea! Come here, girl, it's Buddy!" And somehow I was simultaneously shaking Charley's hand, getting clapped on the back, and being buried in the fervor of Bea's gigantic hug. They swept me from the hall into their dim apartment.

"Lord, Buddy, what you doing here? Whyn't you tell me you was coming to New York?" His face was so lit up with pleasure that in spite of the inroads of time, he still looked like the Charley of years gone by, excited over a new litter of kittens.

10. In psychology, the *id* is the part of the personality that is associated with the most natural, primitive, and (to most people) mysterious drives for pleasure and satisfaction.
11. Here, *epic* means "majestic" or "heroic."
12. In mythology, *siren songs* were sung by sea nymphs, and sailors who heard these irresistible songs were drawn to their destruction.
13. *Garvey Day* is an unofficial holiday honoring Marcus Garvey (1887–1940), an African American leader during the 1920s.
14. *Livid* can mean both "angry" and "bruised."

Rewards and Sacrifices *How does the description of where Charley lives tie in with the idea of sacrifice?* **1**

Theme *What admirable quality does Charley display here?* **2**

Reading Practice

SPIRAL REVIEW **Repetition** Authors may repeat sounds, words, phrases, lines, or stanzas to emphasize and reinforce important ideas, to expand upon an idea, to create rhythm, and to increase the feeling of unity in a work. Have students point out the places in the story where Charley tells Buddy that he is "somebody."

Ask: Why does Charley repeat this idea so many times throughout the story? *(Students may say that the family was very poor and they wanted to make sure that Charley succeeded.)* Ask students to think of another way that Charley could have conveyed this idea to his brother.

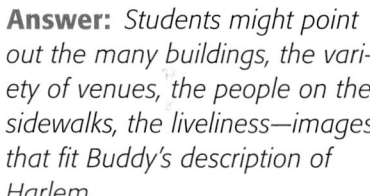

Rooftops (No. 1, This is Harlem), 1942–43. Jacob Lawrence. Gouache on paper, 14⅜ x 21⅞ in. Hirshhorn Museum and Sculpture Garden, Washington, DC.

View the Art Jacob Lawrence was more concerned about telling a story in his paintings than he was in artistic technique. What story of Harlem does this painting tell? Does it match Buddy's description of Harlem? Explain. ★

"The place look a mess! Whyn't you let us know?" put in Bea, suddenly distressed.

"Looks fine to me, girl. And so do you!"

And she did. Bea is a fine-looking woman, plump and firm still, with rich brown skin and thick black hair.

"Mary, Lucy, look, Uncle Buddy's here!"
3 Two neat little girls came shyly from the TV. Uncle Buddy was something of a celebrity in this house.

I hugged them heartily, much to their discomfort. "Charley, where you getting all these pretty women?"

We all sat in the warm kitchen, where Bea was preparing dinner. It felt good there. Beautiful odors mingled in the air. Charley sprawled in a chair near mine, his long arms and legs akimbo.[15] No longer shy, the tinier girl sat on my lap, while her sister darted here and there like a merry little water bug. Bea bustled about, managing to keep up with both the conversation and the cooking.

I told them about the conference I was attending and, knowing it would give them pleasure, I mentioned that I had addressed the group that morning. Charley's eyes glistened.

"You hear that, Bea?" he whispered. "Buddy done spoke in front of all them professors!"

---

15. *Akimbo* (ə kim′ bō) means "being in a bent, bowed, or arched position."

Teach

Reading Strategy 3

Connect Help students notice how Buddy's language becomes more like Charley's as they are speaking.

Ask: Why do you think Buddy starts using dialect when he is with Charley and Bea? *(Possible answer: Buddy is surrounded by his family, and he returns to speaking in a way that is more natural to him.)*

View the Art ★

Answer: *Students might point out the many buildings, the variety of venues, the people on the sidewalks, the liveliness—images that fit Buddy's description of Harlem.*

Jacob Lawrence (1917–2000) was one of the first painters to bring scenes of everyday African American life into mainstream consciousness. He painted images from his life experiences. His first concern was to convey a story; he was less interested in technique.

Approaching Level

DIFFERENTIATED INSTRUCTION

Established Ask students to think about the characters, setting, and themes in other stories previously covered in class. Briefly discuss these story elements. Then ask students to look for elements of "Sweet Potato Pie" that are similar. **Ask:** How are the characters' situations similar? What message can be found in both stories? *(Students should point out similarities and differences between the characters, settings, and themes of the stories.)*

Teach

Reading Strategy 1

Question **Answer:** *Some students may wonder what Buddy's speech was about and how good a speaker he is. Others may wonder if Buddy is being humble so as not to make himself seem better than his family.*

Literary Element 2

Theme **Answer:** *Buddy realizes how much his family sacrificed for him and how much gratitude he feels toward Charley.*

ENGLISH LEARNERS Point out the idiom "on the ball" to English learners. Guide students to interpret what this idiom means. Explain while Charley thinks of himself as just a cab driver, Buddy thinks of him as intelligent and responsible.

"Sure I hear," Bea answered briskly, stirring something that was making an aromatic steam. "I bet he weren't even scared. I bet them professors learnt something, too."

We all chuckled. "Well anyway," I said, "I hope they did."

We talked about a hundred different things after that—Bea's job in the school cafeteria, my Jess and the kids, our scattered family.

"Seem like we don't git together no more, not since Mama and Pa passed on," said Charley sadly. "I ain't even got a Christmas card from Alberta for three-four year now."

"Well, ain't no two a y'all in the same city. An' everybody scratchin to make ends meet," Bea replied. "Ain't nobody got time to git together."

"Yeah, that's the way it goes, I guess," I said.

"But it sure is good to see you, Buddy. Say, look, Lil told me bout the cash you sent the children last winter when Jake was out of work all that time. She sure preciated it."

"Lord, man, as close as you and Lil stuck to me when I was a kid, I owed her that and more. Say, Bea, did I ever tell you about the time—" and we swung into the usual reminiscences.

They insisted that I stay for dinner. Persuading me was no hard job: fish fried golden, ham hocks and collard greens, corn bread—if I'd *tried* to leave, my feet wouldn't have taken me. It was good to sit there in Charley's kitchen, my coat and tie flung over a chair, surrounded by soul food and love.

"Say, Buddy, a couple months back I picked up a kid from your school."

"No stuff."

"I axed him did he know you. He say he was in your class last year."

"Did you get his name?"

"No, I didn't ax him that. Man, he told me you were the best teacher he had. He said you were one smart cat!"

"He told you that cause you're my brother."

"Your *brother*—I didn't tell him I was your brother. I said you was a old friend of mine."

I put my fork down and leaned over. "What you tell him *that* for?"

Charley explained patiently as he had explained things when I was a child and had missed an obvious truth. "I didn't want your students to know your brother wasn't nothing but a cab driver. You *somebody*."

"You're a nut," I said gently. "You should've told that kid the truth." I wanted to say, I'm proud of you, you've got more on the ball than most people I know, I wouldn't have been anything at all except for you. But he would have been embarrassed.

Bea brought in the dessert—homemade sweet potato pie! "Buddy, I must of knew you were coming! I just had a mind I wanted to make some sweet potato pie."

There's nothing in this world I like better than Bea's sweet potato pie! "Lord, girl, how you expect me to eat all that?"

The slice she put before me was outrageously big—and moist and covered with a light, golden crust—I ate it all.

"Bea, I'm gonna have to eat and run," I said at last.

Charley guffawed. "Much as you et, I don't see how you gonna *walk*, let alone *run*." He went out to get his cab from the garage several blocks away.

Bea was washing the tiny girl's face. "Wait a minute, Buddy, I'm gon give you the rest of that pie to take with you."

1 Question *What questions do you have at this point?*

Theme *What does this passage suggest about the message of the story?* **2**

Writing Practice

SPIRAL REVIEW **Build Background** The neighborhood of Harlem plays a large symbolic role in this story. To help students fully understand the story and its characters, ask students to prepare a report on the history of Harlem. Have students prepare a report that explains:

- events that led to the development of the neighborhood *(housing boom, industry, immigration, etc.)*
- how African American culture developed with and because of the concentration of African American residents *(jazz, civil rights movement, Renaissance of the 1990s, etc.)*
- the economic ups and downs of the neighborhood and its residents
- how each of these ideas ties into and enhances students' understanding of "Sweet Potato Pie"

"Great!" I'd eaten all I could hold, but my spirit was still hungry for sweet potato pie.

Bea got out some waxed paper and wrapped up the rest of the pie. "That'll do you for a snack tonight." She slipped it into a brown paper bag.

I gave her a long good-bye hug. "Bea, I love you for a lot of things. Your cooking is one of them!" We had a last comfortable laugh together. I kissed the little girls and went outside to wait for Charley, holding the bag of pie reverently.

In a minute Charley's ancient cab limped to the curb. I plopped into the seat next to him, and we headed downtown. Soon we were assailed by the garish lights of New York on a sultry spring night. We chatted as Charley skillfully managed the heavy traffic. I looked at his long hands on the wheel and wondered what they could have done with artists' brushes.

We stopped a bit down the street from my hotel. I invited him in, but he said he had to get on with his evening run. But as I opened the door to get out, he commanded in the old familiar voice, "Buddy, you wait!"

For a moment I thought my fly was open or something. "What's wrong?"

"What's that you got there?"

I was bewildered. "That? You mean this bag? That's a piece of sweet potato pie Bea fixed for me."

"You ain't going through the lobby of no big hotel carrying no brown paper bag."

"Man, you *crazy!* Of course I'm going— Look, Bea fixed it for me—*That's my pie*—"

Charley's eyes were miserable. "Folks in that hotel don't go through the lobby carrying no brown paper bags. That's *country.* And you can't neither. You *somebody,* Buddy. You got to be *right.* Now, gimme that bag."

"I want that pie, Charley. I've got nothing to prove to anybody—"

I couldn't believe it. But there was no point in arguing. Foolish as it seemed to me, it was important to him.

"You got to look *right,* Buddy. Can't nobody look dignified carrying a brown paper bag."

So finally, thinking how tasty it would have been and how seldom I got a chance to eat anything that good, I handed over my bag of sweet potato pie. If it was that important to him.

I tried not to show my irritation. "Okay, man—take care now." I slammed the door harder than I had intended, walked rapidly to the hotel, and entered the brilliant, crowded lobby.

"That Charley!" I thought. Walking slower now, I crossed the carpeted lobby toward the elevator, still thinking of my lost snack. I had to admit that of all the herd of people who jostled each other in the lobby, not one was carrying a brown paper bag. Or anything but expensive attaché cases or slick packages from exclusive shops. I suppose we all operate according to the symbols that are meaningful to us, and to Charley a brown paper bag symbolizes the humble life he thought I had left. I was *somebody.*

Visual Vocabulary
An attaché (at´ ə shā´) case is a slim briefcase.

I don't know what made me glance back, but I did. And suddenly the tears and laughter, toil and love of a lifetime burst around me like fireworks in a night sky. **5**

For there, following a few steps behind, came Charley, proudly carrying a brown paper bag full of sweet potato pie. ∾

3 Question *Do you wonder why Charley is commanding Buddy to wait? What do you think he will say next?*

Rewards and Sacrifices *Why is Buddy willing to make this sacrifice for Charley?* **4**

Teach

Reading Strategy 3

Question Answer: *Students may or may not be able to predict that Charley will try to stop Buddy from carrying the bag with the pie into the hotel.*

Big Idea 4

Rewards and Sacrifices
Answer: *This is important to Charley, who has sacrificed much more for Buddy.*

Literary Element 5

Theme Ask: Why does Charley's action affect Buddy so strongly? *(It symbolizes a lifetime of familial love and sacrifice.)*

To check students' understanding of the selection, see Unit 1 Teaching Resources Book, p. 164.

Approaching Level

DIFFERENTIATED INSTRUCTION

Emerging One strategy for reading stories is to think of them as a series of problems and solutions. There is a problem. The characters attempt to solve it. By the end of the story, the problem is solved or unresolved.

- Have students work in small groups to find and write down the problems and solutions in the selection, indicating whether each solution worked or not.
- Compile a master list in which the problems and solutions follow the sequence of events in the story.

After You Read

Assess

1. Students may think Charley and the rest of the family are warm, appealing, and admirable because they make such sacrifices for Buddy.
2. (a) Lil and Charley (b) Buddy sees his siblings—especially Lil and Charley—as parental figures and appreciates their care. He says, "Lil . . . punished us when we needed punishing and comforted us when we needed comforting," and "Charley became more father than brother."
3. (a) He completes his education. (b) His older siblings, who had to work to support the family, had untapped potential.
4. (a) It symbolizes everything "country" and unsophisticated. (b) He is a "mere" cabdriver.
5. Students may say that Buddy and Charley have a special connection and try to protect each other.
6. The author shows that Buddy can move between his two lives and that he has not completely changed.
7. Students may say they learned from Charley that true and loving sacrifice has no time limit.
8. Students should support their answers. Some may respond that it is not an either-or situation—that what is most admired is achievement while staying true to oneself.

Literary Element

1. The implied central theme is familial love and sacrifice.
2. Answers will vary, but may include: Buddy's family sacrifices everything so he can break free of their life of poverty and hard work.

After You Read

Respond and Think Critically

Respond and Interpret

1. What are your feelings about Buddy's family and the sacrifices they make to help Buddy succeed? Explain.
2. (a)Who takes care of Buddy on a daily basis when he is a young boy? (b)How would you describe the relationship Buddy has with his siblings as he is growing up? Use details from the story to explain your response.
3. (a)What does Buddy accomplish that his parents and siblings do not? (b)What does Buddy mean when he says, "I wasn't necessarily the smartest—only the youngest."
4. (a)According to Buddy, what does the brown paper bag symbolize to Charley? (b)Why does Charley not mind carrying the paper bag?

Analyze and Evaluate

5. Charley withholds the truth about his identity from Buddy's former student. When Buddy hears this, he withholds the truth about his feelings for his brother. How are the brothers' decisions in keeping with their personalities?
6. **Dialect** is a variation of a language spoken by a group of people, often within a particular region. Why might Collier have chosen to have Buddy speak in dialect?

Connect

7. **Big Idea** **Rewards and Sacrifices** Explain what insights into the ideas of reward and sacrifice you gained from reading this story.
8. **Connect to Today** Is it more important in today's world to achieve the most one can or to stay true to one's inner self? Explain.

Literary Element Theme

Some works have a **stated theme,** which is expressed directly. Other works have an **implied theme,** which is revealed gradually through events, dialogue, or description. In addition, a literary work may have more than one theme.

1. In your opinion, what is the central theme in "Sweet Potato Pie"? Is this theme stated or implied? Explain.
2. What details and descriptions in the story support the theme? Explain.

Review: Character

As you learned on pages 96–97, a **character** is an individual in a literary work. You have probably read short stories that featured characters with heroic qualities—characters whose personalities or deeds inspired your admiration. In your opinion, which character or characters in "Sweet Potato Pie" are heroic?

Partner Activity With a partner, go back through "Sweet Potato Pie" and use webs like the one shown to record details that reveal the characters' admirable qualities and deeds. Then discuss which character you consider to be the real hero of the story. Share your thoughts with the class.

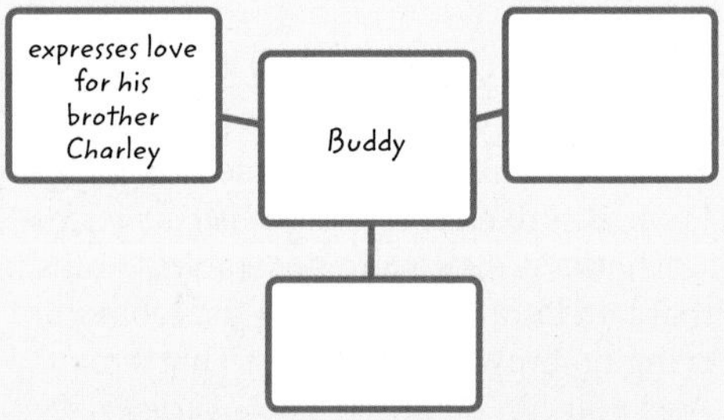

Review: Character

Students' character webs should include details and examples from the text that prove why the character is admirable. Encourage students to explain why they consider their choice the most heroic of all.

Progress Check

Can students identify theme?

If No → See Unit 1 Teaching Resources Book, p. 159.

Reading Strategy Question

Review your question-and-answer chart before answering the following questions.

1. Reread the second paragraph of "Sweet Potato Pie," beginning with "I turn from the window. . . ." Write three questions it might raise—one about plot, one about character, one about setting.
2. Work with a classmate to find clues and answers to your questions about the story.

Vocabulary Practice

Practice with Word Parts Use a dictionary to find the meaning of each vocabulary word's root and to find the meanings of any prefixes or suffixes in the word. List the meanings in a diagram like the one shown. Then find three words that contain the same prefix, suffix, or root as the vocabulary word. Circle the word part that could help a person guess each word's meaning.

collective antiquity ubiquitous futilely

Example:

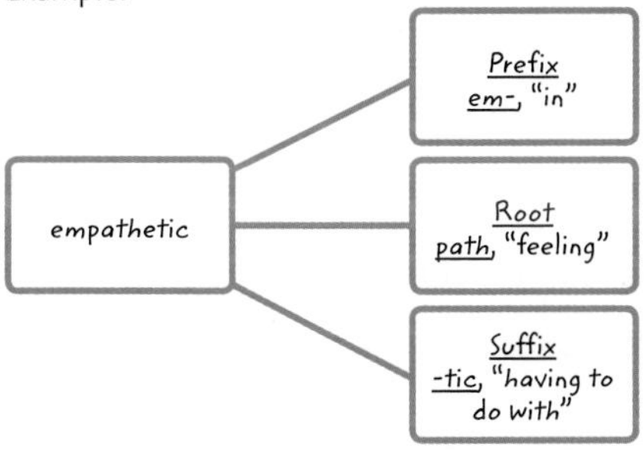

Related words: emphasis, sympathy, electronic

LOG ON Literature Online

Selection Resources For Selection Quizzes, eFlashcards, and Reading-Writing Connection activities, go to glencoe.com and enter QuickPass code GL49787u1.

Connect to *Science*

Research and Report

Assignment Research sweet potato pie or another common dish from the American South. Use your research to prepare an informative pamphlet about the way the body uses the nutrients in the dish. At the end of your pamphlet, provide a bibliography of reference materials, including a variety of consumer workplace and public documents, such as nutrition guides or publications from your state health department.

Investigate First make a list of possible sources of information, how to access them, and their likely reliability. Use a chart like the one below.

Source	Access	Reliability
Dr. Jenkins	ph: 555-1221	reliable (nutritionist)
food Web site	healthfuleating.com	questionable (business site)

Take notes on what you learn from each source. If there is contradictory information, use what you found in the most reliable source.

If you are unfamiliar with the scientific terms used in nutritional information, investigate further to clarify the meanings of those terms.

Create Your pamphlet should have an introduction, a section on each nutrient and how the body uses it, a conclusion, and a bibliography. You may want to include a graphic aid as well. See pages R34–R37 in the Writing Handbook for help in creating a bibliography.

Report If possible, use word processing software to make your pamphlet look professional. Create a three-panel pamphlet by setting the page layout to "landscape" and running the text in three columns.

After You Read

Assess

Reading Strategy

1. Sample questions: Plot: What happened this afternoon? Character: Why does the narrator visit Charley so seldom? Setting: Where is this impersonal, tidy room?
2. Students' responses will depend on the questions they have asked.

Progress Check

Can students develop questions about the text?

If No → See Unit 1 Teaching Resources Book, p. 160.

Vocabulary

collective:
Prefix: col-, "together"
Root: lect, "to gather"
Suffix: -ive, "performing an action"
Related words: collate, elect, definitive

antiquity:
Root: antique, "former, ancient"
Suffix: -ity, "state or condition"
Related words: antiquated, antiquarian, civility

ubiquitous:
Root: ubique, "everywhere"
Suffix: -ous, "full of"
Related words: ubiquity, adventurous, slanderous

futilely:
Root: futil, "useless"
Suffix: -ly, "in a manner"
Related words: futility, futilitarian, hungrily

Research and Report

Students' pamphlets should:

- provide accurate information about how the body uses the nutrients
- be well-organized, and include an introduction, sections on each nutrient, and a conclusion
- use a graphic aid
- include a bibliography

For grammar practice, see Unit 1 Teaching Resources Book, p. 163.

For additional selection assessment, see Assessment Resources, pp. 61–62.

Grammar Workshop

Misplaced Modifiers

Focus

Write this sentence on the board: A few steps behind came a brown paper bag full of sweet potato pie proudly carried by Charley.

Rewrite it to read: A few steps behind came Charley, proudly carrying a brown paper bag full of sweet potato pie. Discuss how misplacing modifiers in a sentence can change the meaning.

Teach

Avoid Misplaced Modifiers

When correcting misplaced modifiers, students should reread to be sure that they made the correct change. Have students read Problem 1 and Solution 1. **Say:** You could also revise this sentence to read, Charley, from the fourteenth floor, looks like an insect.

Assess

Possible Rewrites:

1. Correct
2. Della sells her hair, which reaches below her knees, to Madame Sofronie.
3. Meanwhile, Jim sells his watch for some hair combs for Della.

For additional grammar practice, see Unit 1 Teaching Resources Book, p. 166.

Learning Objectives

In this workshop, you will focus on the following objective:

Grammar: Understanding how to avoid misplaced modifiers.

Grammar Workshop

Misplaced Modifiers

Literature Connection Eugenia Collier places modifiers where they belong: near or next to the words they modify.

> *"Bea is a fine-looking woman, plump and firm still, with rich brown skin and thick black hair."*
>
> —Eugenia Collier, from "Sweet Potato Pie"

Look at the phrase "plump and firm still." It modifies, or tells more about, the word *woman.* Imagine, however, if the sentence had been written like this:

> "Bea is a fine-looking woman with rich brown skin and thick black hair, plump and firm still."

In this sentence, the modifying phrase *plump and firm still* is a **misplaced modifier.** The phrase modifies *hair*. A misplaced modifier is a word or phrase that makes a sentence confusing because the modifier is in the wrong place.

To correct misplaced modifiers, think about what you mean.

Problem 1 A misplaced phrase or group of words

Charley looks like an insect from the fourteenth floor.

Solution Move the word or phrase closer to the word it modifies.

From the fourteenth floor, Charley looks like an insect.

Problem 2 A misplaced word

Buddy only gives information about his family.

Solution Place modifiers such as *only* and *nearly* next to the word or words they modify.

Buddy gives information only about his family.

Misplaced Modifiers

A **misplaced modifier** is a word or phrase that makes a sentence confusing because the modifier is in the wrong place.

Tip

When you proofread your writing, examine the modifiers. Remember that modifiers can be just one word, such as *only* or *nearly*; prepositional phrases; or other phrases and clauses, such as groups of words that begin with *who* or *that*. Then check to see whether the modifiers are next to the words they are meant to modify.

Revise Rewrite the following sentences, correcting any misplaced modifiers. If the sentence is correct, write *Correct.*

1. At Christmas time, Della has only $1.87, which isn't enough money for the right gift for Jim.
2. Della sells her hair to Madame Sofronie, which reaches below her knees.
3. Meanwhile, Jim sells his watch for Della for some hair combs.

LOG ON **Literature Online**

Grammar For more grammar practice, go to glencoe.com and enter QuickPass code GL49787u1.

Grammar Practice

PARTNERS

Identify Misplaced Modifiers Have pairs of students revise the following sentences. Students should place modifiers close to the words they modify, in order to make the meaning of the sentence clear. Then have students explain the differences in meaning between the original sentence and their revised sentence.

1. *Meowing,* my brother rescued the cat.
2. *Bigger than most,* Alberto went to a new school.
3. The dog chased the cat *barking loudly.*
4. He easily spotted the eagle *with his high-powered binoculars.*

Before You Read

The Scarlet Ibis

Meet **James Hurst**
(born 1922)

Brown magnolia petals, honeysuckle, and purple phlox: these are just a few of the flowers that might have grown on James Hurst's childhood farm and home in North Carolina. At the very least, they grew in his memory and served as inspiration for the glories of nature that appear in "The Scarlet Ibis." As a child, Hurst gained first-hand knowledge not only of nature's beauty but also of its fury. In the coastal South, he likely experienced a hurricane similar to the storm that blows the scarlet ibis far to the north in this story.

> *"Authors seldom understand what they write. That is why we have critics."*
>
> —James Hurst

Not Only a Writer Hurst is a man of many experiences, talents, and careers. He holds a degree in chemical engineering from North Carolina State College and served in the army during World War II. To pursue his love of music, he studied at the Julliard School of Music in New York. He then went to Rome, where he lived for three years and continued to study music. When Hurst returned to the United States, he had a brief but unsuccessful career in opera. He then took a job at a large bank in New York City, where he worked for the next thirty-four years. While working at the bank, Hurst also wrote in his free time.

During the 1950s and early 1960s, he published several short stories and a play. The pinnacle of his writing career occurred when the *Atlantic Monthly* published "The Scarlet Ibis" in 1960.

A Great Story "The Scarlet Ibis" was immediately heralded as a great piece of literature and has been reprinted in nearly every major literature textbook and in many anthologies. There are numerous reasons for its success. The beauty of the language, lure of the setting, emotional power of the plot, and the power of its two central symbols, the scarlet ibis and the swamp, have made it a favorite with readers and critics alike. Hurst himself, however, is modest about the story. While he admits that the setting is as much a character as either the narrator or his brother Doodle, Hurst leaves further interpretation to his readers.

LOG ON **Literature** Online

Author Search For more about James Hurst, go to glencoe.com and enter QuickPass code GL49787u1.

Before You Read

Focus

Bellringer Options

Selection Focus Transparency 10

Daily Language Practice Transparency 14

Or invite volunteers to share challenging or satisfying experiences they have had growing up with younger siblings.

Ask: How have your feelings toward your siblings changed over time? Ask students to keep this discussion in mind as they read this story about a boy and his little brother.

Selection Skills

The Scarlet Ibis

Literary Elements
- Symbol (SE pp. 156–169)
- Setting (SE p. 169)
- Similes (TE p. 163)

Listening/Speaking/Viewing Skills
- Analyze Art (SE pp. 160, 163, 167; TE p. 157)

Reading Skills
- Compare and Contrast Characters (SE pp. 156–169)
- Character Analysis (TE p. 158)
- Identify Subtleties (TE p. 164)

Vocabulary Skills
- Word Origins (SE p. 169)

Writing Skills/Grammar
- Persuasive Essay (SE p. 170)
- Semicolons (SE p. 170)
- Personal Narrative (TE p. 160)
- Understand Symbolism (TE p. 162)

Before You Read

Focus

Summary

The narrator tells about his childhood on a cotton farm in the Deep South between 1912 and 1918. His younger brother Doodle was expected to die in infancy but survives. The narrator has to lug Doodle everywhere, which is a burden in many ways. Over time, the boys become inseparable. Together, they conquer the seemingly impossible and push toward even greater feats. In the process, they must face limitations and cope with shame.

For summaries in languages other than English, see Unit 1 Teaching Resources Book, pp. 167–172.

Vocabulary

Grouping Words Have students come up with ways to categorize new vocabulary words. The groups can be as simple or as complex as students desire. Grouping the words in familiar categories can help the students remember the meaning of new vocabulary words. Then have students use each word in a sentence.

For additional vocabulary practice, see Unit 1 Teaching Resources Book, p. 175.

For additional context, see Glencoe Interactive Vocabulary CD-ROM.

Literature and Reading Preview

Connect to the Story

What would it feel like to be embarrassed by or ashamed of someone you care about? Freewrite for a few minutes about a time when you felt embarrassed by someone close to you. How did it feel? How do you think it felt for the other person?

Build Background

A scarlet ibis is a tropical bird with bright red feathers. It is native to South America but can occasionally be spotted in Florida and on the Gulf coast of Texas and Louisiana.

Set Purposes for Reading

Big Idea Rewards and Sacrifices

As you read the story, ask yourself, What do the brothers gain from all that they sacrifice for each other?

Literary Element Symbol

A **symbol** is an object, person, place, or experience that exists on a literal level but also represents something else, often something abstract. For example, a wedding ring might symbolize marriage. As you read, ask yourself, What might this object, place, or character represent?

Reading Strategy Compare and Contrast Characters

When you **compare and contrast characters,** you look for the similarities and differences between two or more characters in a literary work. In "The Scarlet Ibis," exploring similarities between the narrator and his brother Doodle will help you better understand the characters' motivations, the plot's events, and the story's themes. As you read, ask yourself, In what ways are the brothers similar and in what ways are they different?

Tip: Diagram Similarities and Differences As you read, use a Venn diagram to organize your notes about the characters.

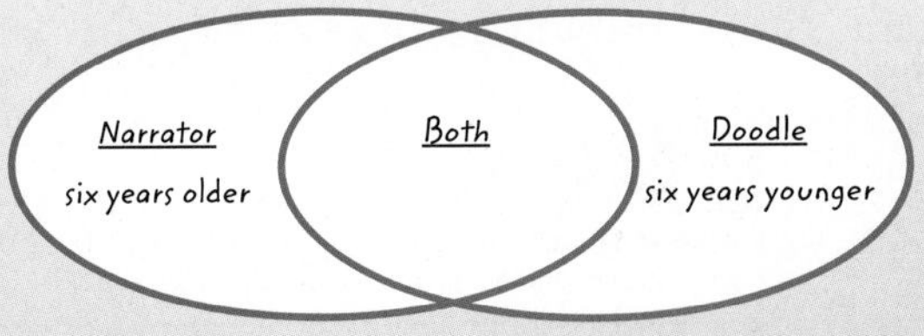

Learning Objectives

For pages 155–169

In studying this text, you will focus on the following objectives:

Literary Study: Analyzing symbol.

Reading: Comparing and contrasting characters.

Vocabulary

careen (kə rēn′) *v.* to tilt or sway while moving, as if out of control; p. 159 *The bicycle racers barely stay seated as they careen around the corner.*

serene (sə rēn′) *adj.* calm; peaceful; undisturbed; p. 162 *The water in the pond was still and serene.*

blighted (blīt′əd) *adj.* damaged or spoiled; p. 163 *The blighted crops could not be sold.*

reiterate (rē it′ ə rāt′) *v.* to say again or do again; repeat; p. 165 *For most patients, doctors reiterate the same advice for staying healthy.*

precariously (pri kār′ ē əs lē) *adv.* dangerously; insecurely; p. 165 *The bundle was perched precariously on the shelf and seemed about to fall.*

Tip: Word Origins Many words in English come from Latin, Greek, or French. Word origins can be found in a dictionary and are usually listed in brackets. For example, in a dictionary the word origin for *serene* would be listed as [Middle English, from Latin, *serenus* clear].

Reading Practice

SPIRAL REVIEW **Paraphrase** Remind students that when you paraphrase what you read, you restate it in your own words. Paraphrasing literature can help students better understand its content. Pair up students and ask them to read and orally paraphrase the information about James Hurst on page 155. Remind students to use correct grammar and complete sentences.

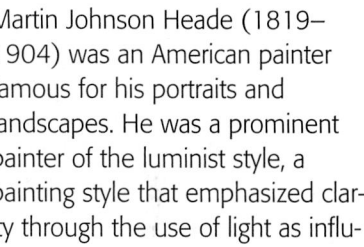

Sunset Over the Marshes. Martin Johnson Heade. ★

THE SCARLET IBIS

James Hurst

It was in the clove[1] of seasons, summer was dead but autumn had not yet been born, that the ibis lit in the bleeding tree. The flower garden was stained with rotting brown magnolia petals and ironweeds grew rank[2] amid the purple phlox. The five
1 o'clocks by the chimney still marked time, but the oriole nest in the elm was untenanted and rocked back and forth like an empty cradle. The last graveyard flowers were blooming, and their smell drifted across the cotton field and through every room of our house, speaking softly the names of our dead.

It's strange that all this is still so clear to me, now that that summer has long since fled and time has had its way. A grindstone stands where the bleeding tree stood, just outside the kitchen door, and now if an oriole sings in the elm, its song seems to die up in the leaves, a silvery dust. The flower garden is prim,[3] the house a gleaming white, and the pale fence across the yard stands straight and spruce. But sometimes (like right now), as I sit in the cool, green-draped parlor, the grindstone begins to turn, and time with all its changes is ground away—and I remember Doodle.

1. Here, a *clove* is a separation or split between two things.
2. Here, *rank* means "growing in vigorous, wild abundance."
3. Here, *prim* means "neat and trim."

Teach

Literary Element 1

Foreshadowing Point out the images of the rotting brown magnolia petals, the untenanted oriole nest that rocked like an empty cradle, and the graveyard flowers in the first paragraph. **Ask:** What do these images foreshadow? *(death)*

View the Art ★

Martin Johnson Heade (1819–1904) was an American painter famous for his portraits and landscapes. He was a prominent painter of the luminist style, a painting style that emphasized clarity through the use of light as influenced by the Hudson River school of painters of the late 1800s.

For an audio recording of this selection, use Listening Library Audio CD-ROM.

Readability Scores

Dale-Chall: 6.5
DRP: 57
Lexile: 1070

English Learners

DIFFERENTIATED INSTRUCTION

Early Advanced Read aloud the first two paragraphs of the story. Explain to students that authors often use figurative language. For example, this author compares the oriole nest to "an empty cradle" to show that it was sad and lifeless. He calls the oriole's song "a silvery dust" to show that it was weak and distant. Ask students to look for other examples of figurative language.

Approaching Level

DIFFERENTIATED INSTRUCTION

Emerging Have students read the first two paragraphs of the story, which contain several elements of figurative language. Students should think of how they would paraphrase what they have read. Then have students write a summary of the content of these paragraphs and share their summaries with the rest of the class.

Teach

Reading Strategy 1

Compare and Contrast Characters Answer: *The narrator is six years older.* **Ask:** How does the narrator explain that Miss Leedie is different from his brother? *(Doodle is a "nice crazy"; Miss Leedie is a "crazy crazy.")*

For additional practice using the reading skill or strategy, see Unit 1 Teaching Resources Book, p. 174.

Literary Element 2

Symbol Ask: How does the narrator feel about the name given to the baby? *(He does not think the name is appropriate for the baby; it is too "big" for such a little baby.)*

Reading Strategy 3

Compare and Contrast Characters Answer: *The narrator likes to run, jump, and climb; William Armstrong will never be able to do these things.*

ENGLISH LEARNERS For English learners **ask:** How does the narrator feel about having a brother who is "different"? *(He is disappointed and ashamed.)*

Doodle was just about the craziest brother a boy ever had. Of course, he wasn't a crazy crazy like old Miss Leedie, who was in love with President Wilson ☆ and wrote him a letter every day, but was a nice crazy, like someone you meet in your dreams. He was born when I was six and was, from the outset, a disappointment. He seemed all head, with a tiny body which was red and shriveled like an old man's. Everybody thought he was going to die—everybody except Aunt Nicey, who had delivered him. She said he would live because he was born in a caul[4] and cauls were made from Jesus' nightgown. Daddy had Mr. Heath, the carpenter, build a little mahogany coffin for him. But he didn't die, and when he was three months old Mama and Daddy decided they might as well name him. They named him William Armstrong, which was like
2 tying a big tail on a small kite. Such a name sounds good only on a tombstone.

I thought myself pretty smart at many things, like holding my breath, running, jumping, or climbing the vines in Old Woman Swamp, and I wanted more than anything else someone to race to Horsehead Landing, someone to box with, and someone to perch with in the top fork of the great pine behind the barn, where across the fields and swamps you could see the sea. I wanted a brother. But Mama, crying, told me that even if William Armstrong lived, he would never do these things with me. He might not, she sobbed, even be "all there." He might, as long as he lived, lie on the rubber sheet in the center of the bed in the front bedroom where the white marquisette curtains billowed out in the afternoon sea breeze, rustling like palmetto fronds.

Visual Vocabulary
Palmetto fronds are the large, divided leaves of the palmetto, a small, ornamental palm tree.

It was bad enough having an invalid brother, but having one who possibly was not all there was unbearable, so I began to make plans to kill him by smothering him with a pillow. However, one afternoon as I watched him, my head poked between the iron posts of the foot of the bed, he looked straight at me and grinned. I skipped through the rooms, down the echoing halls, shouting, "Mama, he smiled. He's all there! He's all there!" and he was.

When he was two, if you laid him on his stomach, he began to try to move himself, straining terribly. The doctor said that with his weak heart this strain would probably kill him, but it didn't. Trembling, he'd push himself up, turning first red, then a soft purple, and finally collapse back onto the bed like an old worn-out doll. I can still see Mama watching him, her hand pressed tight across her mouth, her eyes wide and unblinking. But he learned to crawl (it was his third winter), and we brought him out of the front bedroom, putting him on the rug before the fireplace. For the first time he became one of us.

As long as he lay all the time in bed, we called him William Armstrong, even though it was formal and sounded as if we were referring to one of our ancestors,

4. The *caul* is a membrane, or layer of tissue, that sometimes clings to a baby's head at birth. It is thought by some to bring good luck and protection.

1 Compare and Contrast Characters *What differences between the narrator and his brother does the narrator point out?*

3 Compare and Contrast Characters *What differences between the narrator and his brother can you infer from this paragraph?*

Political History ☆

President Woodrow Wilson
Woodrow Wilson, to whom Miss Leedie wrote daily, was the 28th president of the United States from 1913 to 1921. He led the country into World War I, and he also created and supported the League of Nations, forerunner of the United Nations, for which he received the Nobel Peace Prize.

Reading Practice

Character Analysis Discuss the following questions with students: How do the narrator's feelings about his brother fluctuate within the course of the story so far? What events in the story make the narrator constantly change his mind about Doodle? Have students draw a chart or diagram to illustrate this information. The chart can show a range of numbers from one to ten representing how much the narrator likes Doodle, with ten being the most and one being the least. Ask students to fill in each point on their charts or diagrams with a description from the story explaining what causes the narrator to feel this way.

but with his creeping around on the deer-skin rug and beginning to talk, something had to be done about his name. It was I who renamed him. When he crawled, he crawled backwards, as if he were in reverse and couldn't change gears. If you called him, he'd turn around as if he were going in the other direction, then he'd back right up to you to be picked up. Crawling backward made him look like a doodlebug,[5] so I began to call him Doodle, and in time even Mama and Daddy thought it was a better name than William Armstrong. Only Aunt Nicey disagreed. She said caul babies should be treated with special respect since they might turn out to be saints. Renaming my brother was perhaps the kindest thing I ever did for him, because nobody expects much from someone called Doodle.

Although Doodle learned to crawl, he showed no signs of walking, but he wasn't idle. He talked so much that we all quit listening to what he said. It was about this time that Daddy built him a go-cart and I had to pull him around. At first I just paraded him up and down the piazza,[6] but then he started crying to be taken out into the yard and it ended up by my having to lug him wherever I went. If I so much as picked up my cap, he'd start crying to go with me and Mama would call from wherever she was, "Take Doodle with you."

He was a burden in many ways. The doctor had said that he mustn't get too excited, too hot, too cold, or too tired and that he must always be treated gently. A long list of don'ts went with him, all of which I ignored once we got out of the house. To discourage his coming with me, I'd run with him across the ends of the cotton rows and **careen** him around corners on two wheels. Sometimes I accidentally turned him over, but he never told Mama. His skin was very sensitive, and he had to wear a big straw hat whenever he went out. When the going got rough and he had to cling to the sides of the go-cart, the hat slipped all the way down over his ears. He was a sight. Finally, I could see I was licked. Doodle was my brother and he was going to cling to me forever, no matter what I did, so I dragged him across the burning cotton field to share with him the only beauty I knew, Old Woman Swamp. I pulled the go-cart through the saw-tooth fern, down into the green dimness where the palmetto fronds whispered by the stream. I lifted him out and set him down in the soft rubber grass beside a tall pine. His eyes were round with wonder as he gazed about him, and his little hands began to stroke the rubber grass. Then he began to cry.

"For heaven's sake, what's the matter?" I asked, annoyed.

"It's so pretty," he said. "So pretty, pretty, pretty."

After that day Doodle and I often went down into Old Woman Swamp. I would gather wildflowers, wild violets, honeysuckle, yellow jasmine, snakeflowers, and water lilies, and with wire grass we'd weave them into necklaces and crowns. We'd bedeck ourselves with our handiwork

5. A *doodlebug* is the wormlike larva of the ant lion, which crawls backwards in order to dig a crater to trap ants and other insects.

6. A *piazza* (pē äz′ ə) is a large covered porch.

Rewards and Sacrifices *Why does the narrator consider it a sacrifice to have to play with his brother?* **4**

Symbol *Why might the narrator refer to the swamp as "Old Woman Swamp"?* **5**

Vocabulary

careen (kə rēn′) *v.* to tilt or sway while moving, as if out of control

Teach

Big Idea 4

Rewards and Sacrifices
Answer: *His brother cannot do the things the narrator can do. The narrator has to help his brother to do everything.*

Literary Element 5

Symbol **Answer:** *The narrator may refer to the swamp as a woman because of the beauty they find there. Some students may make a connection between "Old Woman" and a grandmother-like figure who offers comfort, familiarity, and security.*

Approaching Level

DIFFERENTIATED INSTRUCTION

Established Many kinds of plants and animals are mentioned in this story. Among these, the doodlebug is most important because it provides a name for Doodle. **Ask:** Why might Doodle be a good name for the boy? *(Doodle was like a doodlebug because he crawled backwards, and it was a good name because it made people not expect much from the sickly boy.)* Then, ask students to locate other kinds of plants and animals mentioned in the story. Help students understand that these living things create a background for the story. They help to show how the speaker and his family related to the world around them. *(Some of the plants mentioned in the story include magnolia, ironweeds, elm, palmetto, cotton, pine, wildflowers, wild violets, and sunflowers. Some of the animals in the story are orioles, screech owls, peacocks, hawks, frogs, locusts, and crabs. These living things help us picture the story as taking place in a countryside setting, probably in the South.)*

Teach

Reading Strategy 1

Compare and Contrast Characters **Answer:** *The narrator can be cruel, as he is in this scene when he forces Doodle to look at and touch his own coffin.*

APPROACHING For approaching level students **ask:** How does Doodle react to the way his brother treats him? *(Doodle does not get angry with his brother or return the cruelty. He tries to please his brother and stay close to him.)*

View the Art ★

Answer: *Students should point out that the painting shows a river, not a swamp, but should also recognize that the way the light filters through the trees is probably similar to the swamp setting.*

Peder Monsted (1859–1941), an acclaimed Danish impressionist artist, was born in Grend, Denmark. He often worked in oil, painting portraits and landscapes such as this one. His paintings show his control of light and paint. He is best known for his scenes of snow-covered mountains and forests.

The Lake in the Woods, 1891. Peder Monsted. Oil on canvas. Burlington Paintings, London.

View the Art Peder Monsted often painted portraits and landscapes, such as this one. Look at the way the light filters through the trees and is reflected in the river. In what ways is this scene similar to and different from the swamp setting in the story? ★

and loll about thus beautified, beyond the touch of the everyday world. Then when the slanted rays of the sun burned orange in the tops of the pines, we'd drop our jewels into the stream and watch them float away toward the sea.

There is within me (and with sadness I have watched it in others) a knot of cruelty borne by the stream of love, much as our blood sometimes bears the seed of our destruction, and at times I was mean to Doodle. One day I took him up to the barn loft and showed him his casket, telling him how we all had believed he would die. It was covered with a film of Paris green[7] sprinkled to kill the rats, and screech owls had built a nest inside it.

Doodle studied the mahogany box for a long time, then said, "It's not mine."

"It is," I said. "And before I'll help you down from the loft, you're going to have to touch it."

"I won't touch it," he said sullenly.

"Then I'll leave you here by yourself," I threatened, and made as if I were going down.

Doodle was frightened of being left. "Don't go leave me, Brother," he cried, and he leaned toward the coffin. His hand, trembling, reached out, and when he touched the casket he screamed. A screech owl flapped out of the box into our faces, scaring us and covering us with Paris green. Doodle was paralyzed, so I put him on my shoulder and carried him down the ladder, and even when we were outside in the bright sunshine, he clung to me, crying, "Don't leave me. Don't leave me."

When Doodle was five years old, I was embarrassed at having a brother of that age who couldn't walk, so I set out to teach him. We were down in Old Woman Swamp and it was spring and the sick-sweet smell of bay flowers hung everywhere like a mournful song. "I'm going to teach you to walk, Doodle," I said.

He was sitting comfortably on the soft grass, leaning back against the pine. "Why?" he asked.

I hadn't expected such an answer. "So I won't have to haul you around all the time."

7. *Paris green* is a poisonous green powder formerly used as a pesticide.

1 Compare and Contrast Characters *What qualities does the narrator have that are not evident in Doodle?*

Writing Practice

SPIRAL REVIEW **Personal Narrative** Direct students' attention to the point on page 161 where the narrator says, "I did not know then that pride is a wonderful, terrible thing." **Ask:** What does the narrator mean when he says this? Then ask students to think of a time in their own lives when they have experienced pride in a negative way. Have students write a short personal narrative in which they describe an event in their own lives involving some negative effect of pride. This assignment may involve personal stories that students are not willing to share with the class. Assure students that their essays will not be shared with other students. Essays should reflect an understanding of this concept of pride in the story.

"I can't walk, Brother," he said.

"Who says so?" I demanded.

"Mama, the doctor—everybody."

"Oh, you can walk," I said, and I took him by the arms and stood him up. He collapsed onto the grass like a half-empty flour sack. It was as if he had no bones in his little legs.

"Don't hurt me, Brother," he warned.

"Shut up. I'm not going to hurt you. I'm going to teach you to walk." I heaved him up again, and again he collapsed.

This time he did not lift his face up out of the rubber grass. "I just can't do it. Let's make honeysuckle wreaths."

"Oh yes you can, Doodle," I said. "All you got to do is try. Now come on," and I hauled him up once more.

It seemed so hopeless from the beginning that it's a miracle I didn't give up. But all of us must have something or someone to be proud of, and Doodle had become mine. I did not know then that pride is a wonderful, terrible thing, a seed that bears two vines, life and death. Every day that summer we went to the pine beside the stream of Old Woman Swamp, and I put him on his feet at least a hundred times each afternoon. Occasionally I too became discouraged because it didn't seem as if he was trying, and I would say, "Doodle, don't you *want* to learn to walk?"

He'd nod his head, and I'd say, "Well, if you don't keep trying, you'll never learn." Then I'd paint for him a picture of us as old men, white-haired, him with a long white beard and me still pulling him around in the go-cart. This never failed to make him try again.

Finally one day, after many weeks of practicing, he stood alone for a few seconds. When he fell, I grabbed him in my arms and hugged him, our laughter pealing through the swamp like a ringing bell. Now we knew it could be done. Hope no longer hid in the dark palmetto thicket but perched like a cardinal in the lacy toothbrush tree, brilliantly visible. "Yes, yes," I cried, and he cried it too, and the grass beneath us was soft and the smell of the swamp was sweet.

With success so imminent, we decided not to tell anyone until he could actually walk. Each day, barring rain, we sneaked into Old Woman Swamp, and by cotton-picking time Doodle was ready to show what he could do. He still wasn't able to walk far, but we could wait no longer. Keeping a nice secret is very hard to do, like holding your breath. We chose to reveal all on October eighth, Doodle's sixth birthday, and for weeks ahead we mooned around the house, promising everybody a most spectacular surprise. Aunt Nicey said that, after so much talk, if we produced anything less tremendous than the Resurrection,[8] she was going to be disappointed.

At breakfast on our chosen day, when Mama, Daddy, and Aunt Nicey were in the dining room, I brought Doodle to the door in the go-cart just as usual and had them turn their backs, making them cross their hearts and hope to die if they peeked. I helped Doodle up, and when he was standing alone I let them look. There wasn't a sound as Doodle walked slowly across the room and sat down at his place at the table. Then Mama began to cry and ran over to him, hugging him and kissing him. Daddy hugged him too, so I went to Aunt Nicey, who was thanks praying in the doorway, and began to waltz her around. We danced together quite well until she came down on my big toe with

8. Here, the *Resurrection* refers to the Christian belief that Jesus rose from the dead after his burial.

Symbol *What makes the Resurrection an appropriate symbol for Doodle's walking?* **2**

Teach

Literary Element 2

Symbol **Answer:** *Doodle's being able to walk would seem to be a miracle, just as Jesus' rising from the dead was miraculous.*

Approaching Level

DIFFERENTIATED INSTRUCTION

Emerging Ask students to discuss possible reasons for Doodle's initial acceptance that he is unable to walk and his initial unwillingness to learn. *(Students may say that he is afraid to try, that no one in his life has ever encouraged him to excel beyond his apparent means, or that he is comfortable relying on his older brother for support.)*

English Learners

DIFFERENTIATED INSTRUCTION

Beginning/Early Intermediate Create a handout defining and providing examples of the following elements of a sentence: noun, verb, article, adjective, adverb, pronoun, conjunction, preposition, and interjection. Then choose two or three shorter sentences from the story and have students write these sentences in their notebooks. Help students identify the grammatical elements of each sentence. For example, in the sentence "So I won't have to haul you around all the time," the word "haul" is a verb. Verbs are words that show action. The sentence "I heaved him up again, and again he collapsed," also contains verbs. "Heaved" and "collapsed" tell you what the characters did. Have students locate other action words in the text.

Teach

Big Idea 1

Rewards and Sacrifices

Answer: *The reward is no longer having to be ashamed of a crippled brother. The adults may think his reasons are less selfish—to help his brother.*

Ask: Do you think the narrator will be content with Doodle now that he has learned to walk? *(Now that the narrator has had a taste of success, he may continue to try to "improve" Doodle.)*

Reading Strategy 2

Compare and Contrast Characters

Answer: *Doodle has more need of a fictional world, as he faces disabilities in the real world. In his loneliness he has more time for an imaginative life.*

ADVANCED Challenge advanced level students and **ask:** All the people in Doodle's "lies" have wings and fly. What does this say about Doodle's internal fantasies? *(His lies are well-imagined and express his dream of a world where people don't need to walk.)*

Visual Vocabulary *Brogans* are sturdy, ankle-high shoes.

her brogans, hurting me so badly I thought I was crippled for life.

Doodle told them it was I who had taught him to walk, so everyone wanted to hug me, and I began to cry.

"What are you crying for?" asked Daddy, but I couldn't answer. They did not know that I did it for myself; that pride, whose slave I was, spoke to me louder than all their voices, and that Doodle walked only because I was ashamed of having a crippled brother.

Within a few months Doodle had learned to walk well and his go-cart was put up in the barn loft (it's still there) beside his little mahogany coffin. Now, when we roamed off together, resting often, we never turned back until our destination had been reached, and to help pass the time, we took up lying. From the beginning Doodle was a terrible liar and he got me in the habit. Had anyone stopped to listen to us, we would have been sent off to Dix Hill.[9]

My lies were scary, involved, and usually pointless, but Doodle's were twice as crazy. People in his stories all had wings and flew wherever they wanted to go. His favorite lie was about a boy named Peter who had a pet peacock with a ten-foot tail. Peter wore a golden robe that glittered so brightly that when he walked through the sunflowers they turned away from the sun to face him. When Peter was ready to go to sleep, the peacock spread his magnificent tail, enfolding the boy gently like a closing go-to-sleep flower, burying him in the gloriously iridescent,[10] rustling vortex.[11] Yes, I must admit it. Doodle could beat me lying.

Doodle and I spent lots of time thinking about our future. We decided that when we were grown we'd live in Old Woman Swamp and pick dog-tongue for a living. Beside the stream, he planned, we'd build us a house of whispering leaves and the swamp birds would be our chickens. All day long (when we weren't gathering dog-tongue) we'd swing through the cypresses on the rope vines, and if it rained we'd huddle beneath an umbrella tree and play stickfrog. Mama and Daddy could come and live with us if they wanted to. He even came up with the idea that he could marry Mama and I could marry Daddy. Of course, I was old enough to know this wouldn't work out, but the picture he painted was so beautiful and **serene** that all I could do was whisper Yes, yes.

Once I had succeeded in teaching Doodle to walk, I began to believe in my own infallibility and I prepared a terrific development program for him, unknown to Mama and Daddy, of course. I would teach him to run, to swim, to climb trees, and to fight. He, too, now believed in my infallibility, so we set the deadline for these accomplishments less than a year away, when, it had been decided, Doodle could start to school.

---

9. *Dix Hill* refers to the state mental hospital in Raleigh, North Carolina.

10. The feathers are iridescent, or shimmering with rainbow colors.

11. A *vortex* is a whirling mass, like a whirlwind or whirlpool. Here, it is the wide funnel-shaped curve of the peacock's tail feathers.

1 Rewards and Sacrifices *What does the narrator see as the reason, or reward, for teaching Doodle to walk? What do the adults probably think his reason is?*

Compare and Contrast Characters *Describe one possible reason for this difference between the two brothers.* 2

Vocabulary

serene (sə rēn′) *adj.* calm; peaceful; undisturbed

Writing Practice

SPIRAL REVIEW **Understand Symbolism** Tell students that this story contains many symbols. Remind students that in literature, a *symbol* is a person, place, object, or event that exists on a literal level within a work but also represents something on a figurative level. Ask students to read these pages of the story and consider what elements of the story may have a literal as well as figurative meaning. Then ask students to write a short essay in which they describe the symbols found on these pages of the story. *(Students may write that the placement of Doodle's coffin and go-cart in the barn's loft symbolize Doodle's achievement of things that no one thought he'd be able to do [e.g., live, walk]. Students may also write that elements of Doodle's "lies" represent his desire to continue to achieve the impossible [a boy who sleeps in the feathers of his pet peacock, a house of whispering leaves, a fantasy life of no responsibility, the boys' marriage to their parents]).*

Young Fishermen in a Rowboat, 1909. Adam Emory Albright. Oil on canvas, 24 x 36 in. Private collection.

View the Art How does the mood of this painting reflect the mood of the narrator and Doodle's summer? ★

That winter we didn't make much progress, for I was in school and Doodle suffered from one bad cold after another. But when spring came, rich and warm, we raised our sights again. Success lay at the end of summer like a pot of gold, and our campaign got off to a good start. On hot days, Doodle and I went down to Horsehead Landing and I gave him swimming lessons or
3 showed him how to row a boat. Sometimes we descended into the cool greenness of Old Woman Swamp and climbed the rope vines or boxed scientifically beneath the pine where he had learned to walk. Promise hung about us like the leaves, and wherever we looked, ferns unfurled and birds broke into song.

That summer, the summer of 1918, was **blighted.** In May and June there was no rain and the crops withered, curled up, then died under the thirsty sun. One morning in July a hurricane came out of the east, 3
tipping over the oaks in the yard and splitting the limbs of the elm trees. That afternoon it roared back out of the west, blew the fallen oaks around, snapping their roots

Vocabulary

blighted (blīt′ əd) *adj.* damaged or spoiled

Teach

Literary Element 3

Similes **Ask:** What similes are used on this page? *(like a pot of gold; like the leaves)* Discuss what two things are being compared in each simile and how they are alike.

View the Art ★

Answer: *The boys in the painting are shown enjoying a peaceful, idyllic time fishing in a boat. Like them, the boys in the story enjoyed a peaceful, idyllic summer, pursuing activities in a natural setting.*

Adam Albright was born in Monroe, Wisconsin. He was one of the first students of the prestigious Art Institute of Chicago, studying there from 1881 to 1883. Albright was noted for his landscapes, still lifes, and figures of country children, such as the boys shown in this image.

English Learners

DIFFERENTIATED INSTRUCTION

Intermediate Remind students that figurative language uses expressions that are not literally true. Remind students of the definitions of the terms *simile, metaphor, personification,* and other related terms. Help students understand the following examples of figurative language: *"collapsed back onto the bed like an old worn-out doll," "collapsed to the grass like a half-empty flour sack," "our laughter pealing through the swamp like a ringing bell,"; **metaphor:** "pride is . . . a seed that bears two vines, life and death"; "my fallen scarlet ibis"; **personification:** "palmetto fronds whispered by the stream," "a house of whispering leaves," "the thirsty sun.")*

Teach

Literary Element 1

Symbol **Answer:** *For the narrator, the beginning of fall represents the upcoming school year and the deadline to get Doodle to swim. Some students may recognize that fall symbolizes aging and nearing death.*

Prompt students by asking what images they associate with the word fall. *(changing leaves, the coming winter, and the death of plants)*

Reading Strategy 2

Compare and Contrast Characters **Answer:** *The narrator cares about Doodle's differences; Doodle does not.*

Big Idea 3

Rewards and Sacrifices **Answer:** *Doodle may be sacrificing his health.*

Language History ☆

Dog Days The Egyptians, Greeks, and Romans thought the "dog star," Sirius, lent its heat to the sun. The Romans called hot days in July and August *caniculares dies* ("days of the dog"). People began using the term *dog days* for any long period of hot days.

Visual Vocabulary
A *boll* is the rounded seed pod of the cotton plant.

and tearing them out of the earth like a hawk at the entrails of a chicken. Cotton bolls were wrenched from the stalks and lay like green walnuts in the valleys between the rows, while the cornfield leaned over uniformly so that the tassels touched the ground. Doodle and I followed Daddy out into the cotton field, where he stood, shoulders sagging, surveying the ruin. When his chin sank down onto his chest, we were frightened, and Doodle slipped his hand into mine. Suddenly Daddy straightened his shoulders, raised a giant knuckly fist, and with a voice that seemed to rumble out of the earth itself began cursing heaven, hell, the weather, and the Republican Party.[12] Doodle and I, prodding each other and giggling, went back to the house, knowing that everything would be all right.

And during that summer, strange names were heard through the house: Château Thierry, Amiens, Soissons, and in her blessing at the supper table, Mama once said, "And bless the Pearsons, whose boy Joe was lost at Belleau Wood."[13]

So we came to that clove of seasons. School was only a few weeks away, and Doodle was far behind schedule. He could barely clear the ground when climbing up the rope vines and his swimming was certainly not passable. We decided to double our efforts, to make that last drive and reach our pot of gold. I made him swim until he turned blue and row until he couldn't lift an oar. Wherever we went, I purposely walked fast, and although he kept up, his face turned red and his eyes became glazed. Once, he could go no further, so he collapsed on the ground and began to cry.

"Aw, come on, Doodle," I urged. "You can do it. Do you want to be different from everybody else when you start school?"

"Does it make any difference?"

"It certainly does," I said. "Now, come on," and I helped him up.

As we slipped through dog days,[14] ☆ Doodle began to look feverish, and Mama felt his forehead, asking him if he felt ill. At night he didn't sleep well, and sometimes he had nightmares, crying out until I touched him and said, "Wake up, Doodle. Wake up."

It was Saturday noon, just a few days before school was to start. I should have already admitted defeat, but my pride wouldn't let me. The excitement of our program had now been gone for weeks, but still we kept on with a tired doggedness. It was too late to turn back, for we had both wandered too far into a net of expectations and had left no crumbs behind.

Daddy, Mama, Doodle, and I were seated at the dining-room table having lunch. It was a hot day, with all the windows and doors open in case a breeze should come. In the kitchen Aunt Nicey

12. Daddy probably curses the *Republican Party* because he, like most Southerners at the time of the story, was a Democrat.

13. *Château Thierry* (shä tō tye rē′), *Amiens* (am ē ənz′), *Soissons* (swä sōn′), and *Belleau* (bel ō′) *Wood* were the sites of famous battles in France near the end of World War I.

14. *Dog days* are the hot, humid days of July and August.

1 **Symbol** *Here, "that clove of seasons" refers to the shift between summer and fall. What does this time of year represent for the narrator? What else might the beginning of fall represent?*

Compare and Contrast Characters *How does the dialogue between the brothers reveal differences between them?* 2

Rewards and Sacrifices *What is Doodle sacrificing for his brother's plans?* 3

Reading Practice

SMALL GROUP SPIRAL REVIEW

Identify Subtleties Explain to students that authors often infuse their stories with subtle elements that contribute to the story's overall meaning. Break students into small groups and ask them to identify places in this part of the story where the author gives readers subtle clues about what lies ahead. *(Students may say that the storm that ruins the family's crops begins the string of events that will hurt the family. Students may also recognize that Doodle's failing health and sleeping problems are a sign of bad things to come. Students may also say that the ibis' dramatic death is a portent of death, and that Doodle's compassion for the bird and role in burying the bird creates a direct tie between him and the impending doom that is building in the story.)*

was humming softly. After a long silence, Daddy spoke. "It's so calm, I wouldn't be surprised if we had a storm this afternoon."

"I haven't heard a rain frog," said Mama, who believed in signs, as she served the bread around the table.

"I did," declared Doodle. "Down in the swamp."

"He didn't," I said contrarily.

"You did, eh?" said Daddy, ignoring my denial.

"I certainly did," Doodle **reiterated,** scowling at me over the top of his iced-tea glass, and we were quiet again.

Suddenly, from out in the yard, came a strange croaking noise. Doodle stopped eating, with a piece of bread poised ready for his mouth, his eyes popped round like two blue buttons. "What's that?" he whispered.

I jumped up, knocking over my chair, and had reached the door when Mama called, "Pick up the chair, sit down again, and say excuse me."

By the time I had done this, Doodle had excused himself and had slipped out into the yard. He was looking up into the bleeding tree. "It's a great big red bird!" he called.

The bird croaked loudly again, and Mama and Daddy came out into the yard. We shaded our eyes with our hands against the hazy glare of the sun and peered up through the still leaves. On the topmost branch a bird the size of a chicken, with scarlet feathers and long legs, was perched **precariously.** Its wings hung down loosely, and as we watched, a feather dropped away and floated slowly down through the green leaves.

Vocabulary

reiterate (rē it′ə rāt′) *v.* to say again or do again; repeat

precariously (pri kār′ē əs lē) *adv.* dangerously; insecurely

"It's not even frightened of us," Mama said.

"It looks tired," Daddy added. "Or maybe sick."

Doodle's hands were clasped at his throat, and I had never seen him stand still so long. "What is it?" he asked.

Daddy shook his head. "I don't know, maybe it's—"

At that moment the bird began to flutter, but the wings were uncoordinated, and amid much flapping and a spray of flying feathers, it tumbled down, bumping through the limbs of the bleeding tree and landing at our feet with a thud. Its long, graceful neck jerked twice into an S, then straightened out, and the bird was still. A white veil came over the eyes and the long white beak unhinged. Its legs were crossed and its clawlike feet were delicately curved at rest. Even death did not mar its grace, for it lay on the earth like a broken vase of red flowers, and we stood around it, awed by its exotic beauty.

"It's dead," Mama said.

"What is it?" Doodle repeated.

"Go bring me the bird book," said Daddy.

I ran into the house and brought back the bird book. As we watched, Daddy ☆ thumbed through its pages. "It's a scarlet ibis," he said, pointing to a picture. "It lives in the tropics—South America to Florida. A storm must have brought it here."

Sadly, we all looked back at the bird. A scarlet ibis! How many miles it had traveled to die like this, in *our* yard, beneath the bleeding tree.

"Let's finish lunch," Mama said, nudging us back toward the dining room.

"I'm not hungry," said Doodle, and he knelt down beside the ibis.

Symbol *How is the bird like one of the characters in the story?* **4**

Teach

Literary Element 4

Symbol **Answer:** *The bird, like Doodle, seems awkward and ungainly, as it struggles to maintain its balance.*

Cultural History ☆

Bird Identification Bird identification, or bird-watching, is a popular hobby in the United States. It requires binoculars and a field guide. Tropical birds caught in storms can end up far from their usual habitats. Some birds, such as Doodle's scarlet ibis, do not survive.

English Learners

DIFFERENTIATED INSTRUCTION

Intermediate Ask students to make a list of words from these pages that are unfamiliar to them as they read. Have students call out words on the lists and write these words on the blackboard. Then go back to the story as a class and find the place where each word appears. Read the surrounding sentences and give students a chance to use the context clues to come up with a definition on their own before you provide students with the correct definition. Have students record the words and definitions in their vocabulary notebooks.

Teach

Reading Strategy 1

Compare and Contrast Characters **Answer:** *Doodle is moved by the death of the ibis and cannot eat, while the family is eating with great enthusiasm. Doodle seems more sensitive, or like a different species altogether.*

Visual Vocabulary
Cobbler is a deep-dish fruit pie with a thick top crust.

"We've got peach cobbler for dessert," Mama tempted from the doorway.

Doodle remained kneeling. "I'm going to bury him."

"Don't you dare touch him," Mama warned. "There's no telling what disease he might have had."

"All right," said Doodle. "I won't."

Daddy, Mama, and I went back to the dining-room table, but we watched Doodle through the open door. He took out a piece of string from his pocket and, without touching the ibis, looped one end around its neck. Slowly, while singing softly *Shall We Gather at the River,* he carried the bird around to the front yard and dug a hole in the flower garden, next to the petunia bed. Now we were watching him through the front window, but he didn't know it. His awkwardness at digging the hole with a shovel whose handle was twice as long as he was made us laugh, and we covered our mouths with our hands so he wouldn't hear.

When Doodle came into the dining room, he found us seriously eating our cobbler. He was pale and lingered just inside the screen door. "Did you get the scarlet ibis buried?" asked Daddy.

Doodle didn't speak but nodded his head.

"Go wash your hands, and then you can have some peach cobbler," said Mama.

"I'm not hungry," he said.

"Dead birds is bad luck," said Aunt Nicey, poking her head from the kitchen door. "Specially *red* dead birds!"

1 Compare and Contrast Characters *How does this scene underscore the differences between Doodle and his family?*

As soon as I had finished eating, Doodle and I hurried off to Horsehead Landing. Time was short, and Doodle still had a long way to go if he was going to keep up with the other boys when he started school. The sun, gilded with the yellow cast of autumn, still burned fiercely, but the dark green woods through which we passed were shady and cool. When we reached the landing, Doodle said he was too tired to swim, so we got into a skiff and floated down the creek with the tide. Far off in the marsh a rail[15] was scolding, and over on the beach locusts were singing in the myrtle trees. Doodle did not speak and kept his head turned away, letting one hand trail limply in the water.

After we had drifted a long way, I put the oars in place and made Doodle row back against the tide. Black clouds began to gather in the southwest, and he kept watching them, trying to pull the oars a little faster. When we reached Horsehead Landing, lightning was playing across half the sky and thunder roared out, hiding even the sound of the sea. The sun disappeared and darkness descended, almost like night. Flocks of marsh crows flew by, heading inland to their roosting trees, and two egrets, squawking, arose from the oyster-rock shallows and careened away.

Doodle was both tired and frightened, and when he stepped from the skiff he collapsed onto the mud, sending an armada of fiddler crabs rustling off into the marsh grass. I helped him up, and as he wiped the mud off his trousers, he smiled at me ashamedly. He had failed and we both knew it, so we started back home, racing the storm. We never spoke (What are the words that can solder[16] cracked pride?), but I knew he was watching me, watching for a sign of mercy. The lightning was near now, and

15. A *rail* is a small marsh bird.
16. *Solder* (sod′ er) means "to bond or repair."

Literary Element Practice

SPIRAL REVIEW **Understand Voice** Ask students to respond, in writing, to how Hurst's choice of narrator both shapes the story and affects readers. **Write** these questions on the board: How is the story shaped by its narrator? How does this make you feel about the narrator? What makes you feel this way? Do you feel the story's ending was fitting compared to the rest of the story? Also ask students how the story might have been different if it had been told from Doodle's point of view. *(Some students may feel that using the narrator's point of view makes readers strongly dislike the narrator because readers understand his selfish motivations and distasteful thoughts. Some may feel that the story's ending is fitting because Hurst signals throughout the story that the narrator's pride will eventually lead to Doodle's downfall. Students may indicate that if Doodle had told the story, readers would have known the narrator as he was seen by his brother and not as readers come to know him.)*

from fear he walked so close behind me he kept stepping on my heels. The faster I walked, the faster he walked, so I began to run. The rain was coming, roaring through the pines, and then, like a bursting Roman candle, a gum tree ahead of us was shattered by a bolt of lightning. When the deafening peal of thunder had died, and in the moment before the rain arrived, I heard Doodle, who had fallen behind, cry out, "Brother, Brother, don't leave me! Don't leave me!"

The knowledge that Doodle's and my plans had come to naught[17] was bitter, and that streak of cruelty within me awakened. I ran as fast as I could, leaving him far behind with a wall of rain dividing us. The drops stung my face like nettles, and the wind flared the wet glistening leaves of the bordering trees. Soon I could hear his voice no more.

I hadn't run too far before I became tired, and the flood of childish spite evanesced[18] as well. I stopped and waited for Doodle. The sound of rain was everywhere, but the wind had died and it fell straight down in parallel paths like ropes hanging from the sky. As I waited, I peered through the downpour, but no one came. Finally I went back and found him huddled beneath a red nightshade bush beside the road. He was sitting on the ground, his face buried in his arms, which were resting on his drawn-up knees. "Let's go, Doodle," I said.

He didn't answer, so I placed my hand on his forehead and lifted his head. Limply, he fell backwards onto the earth. He had been bleeding from the mouth, and his neck and the front of his shirt were stained a brilliant red.

"Doodle! Doodle!" I cried, shaking him, but there was no answer but the ropy rain. He lay very awkwardly, with his head thrown far back, making his vermilion[19] neck appear unusually long and slim. His little legs, bent sharply at the knees, had never before seemed so fragile, so thin.

I began to weep, and the tear-blurred vision in red before me looked very familiar. "Doodle!" I screamed above the pounding storm and threw my body to the earth above his. For a long long time, it seemed forever, I lay there crying, sheltering my fallen scarlet ibis from the heresy[20] of rain. ↜

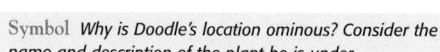

Boy with Green Cap. Robert Henri. Oil on canvas. ★

17. *Naught* (nôt) means "nothing."
18. *Evanesced* (ev′ ə nest′) means "faded away" or "vanished."
19. *Vermilion* is a bright red or scarlet color.
20. *Heresy* (her′ ə sē) is an action or opinion contrary to what is generally considered right, true, or proper.

2 Symbol *Why is Doodle's location ominous? Consider the name and description of the plant he is under.*

Teach

Literary Element 2

Symbol **Answer:** *Red is the color of blood and so is often associated with death.*

View the Art ★

Robert Henri (1865–1929) painted portraits as well as realistic city scenes. Henri was a member of the Ashcan School, a group of painters portraying the stark realities of urban life. An influential art teacher, Henri believed that art should embody the spirit of its time.

To check students' understanding of the selection, see Unit 1 Teaching Resources Book, p. 178.

Progress Check

Can students analyze symbol?

If No → See Unit 1 Teaching Resources Book, p. 173.

Approaching Level

DIFFERENTIATED INSTRUCTION

Emerging Have students study the painting on this page. Help students understand that it helps to view the painting while reading the story. **Ask:** What elements of Doodle's character are present in the painting? How does this add to the end of the story? *(Students may state that the boy in the painting appears to be frail and small, as Doodle is. They may also point out that his eyes appear kind, as Doodle is in the story, or that he looks a bit sad, as Doodle is after the ibis dies. Students may also say that seeing the boy's face and reading of the narrator's cruel treatment of his brother intensify the cruelty of the narrator's actions and evoke more sympathy for Doodle within the reader.)*

After You Read

Assess

1. Students may be upset, sad, or shocked at Doodle's death.
2. (a) He learns to crawl and to walk. (b) He has a strong will.
3. (a) He helps Doodle accomplish things but pushes him too hard. (b) He wants Doodle to be "normal" so he won't be embarrassed by him.
4. (a) He dies. (b) Some students may say the narrator pushes him too hard and possibly hastens Doodle's death.
5. Its death hints at Doodle's death in the same storm.
6. (a) Hurst may want to call attention to a bloody war and the idea that brothers kill brothers during war. (b) Answers will vary. Some students may say this adds another level of tragic loss to the story.
7. Doodle died; the narrator lost faith in himself. They gained companionship. Doodle walked; the narrator gained satisfaction.
8. Answers will vary. Students should use passages from the selection to support their responses.

After You Read

Respond and Think Critically

Respond and Interpret

1. What emotions did you feel as you read the story? Why?
2. (a)Name two things Doodle accomplishes despite the doctor's predictions. (b)What do his accomplishments reveal about his character?
3. (a)How is the narrator both kind and cruel to Doodle? (b)Why does he set high goals for his brother?
4. (a)What happens to Doodle at the end of the story? (b)Do you think what happens to Doodle is the narrator's fault? Explain.

Analyze and Evaluate

5. How does the death of the ibis serve as **foreshadowing**, or a clue that hints at later events in the plot?
6. (a)Why might Hurst have included references to World War I in the story? (b)Do these references enrich the story or move it away from its central focus? Explain.

Connect

7. **Big Idea** **Rewards and Sacrifices** What do the narrator and Doodle lose, or sacrifice, by being brothers, and what do they gain?
8. **Connect to the Author** James Hurst has said that "Old Woman Swamp" is as much a character in the story as the narrator and Doodle. Do you think the swamp functions as a character in the story? Explain.

Visual Literacy

Graphic Organizer

Story information travels clockwise around the chart shown below, ending at the bottom left with the story's resolution. Copy the map and fill in details from "The Scarlet Ibis."

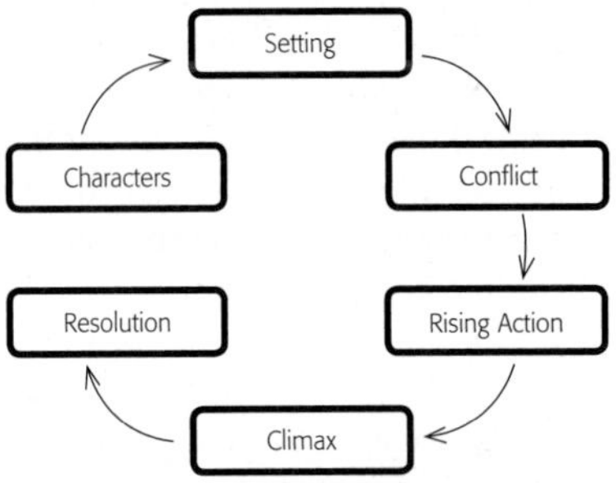

Group Activity Share your story map with several classmates. Then work together to complete the following items.

1. Develop a summary of the story.
2. Review your story map and summary as needed to discuss what each of the following adds to the story:
   - the setting—time and place
   - the fact that the ibis is not native to North Carolina
   - the narrator's point of view
   - the symbolism throughout

Visual Literacy

1. Summaries should name time and place, main characters, the conflict, and all major events of the plot as they appear in the story map.
2. Students' discussions should address the narrator's cruelty, the brothers' companionship, the sadness of changing seasons, superstitions and foreshadowing, and the ibis as a symbol of Doodle's fate.

Literary Element Symbol

After reading a story, you can identify its **symbols** by determining which objects or elements play an important role in the story. An object that an author focuses on or makes a significant part of the story may have a symbolic meaning.

1. Why is the presence of the scarlet ibis at the narrator's home in North Carolina unsettling?
2. Do you believe the ibis is a symbol for Doodle? Explain.
3. If the ibis is a symbol for Doodle, what does the bird's presence in North Carolina and ultimate death say about Doodle's existence and death?

Review: Setting

As you learned on pages 8–9, **setting** is the time and place in which the events of a literary work occur. Setting includes not only physical surroundings, but also the ideas and customs of a place and time. In "The Scarlet Ibis," the setting is so vivid that it takes on a life of its own.

Partner Activity Meet with a partner to discuss the setting of the swamp. Make a web diagram like the one below and complete it with details or interpretations from the story.

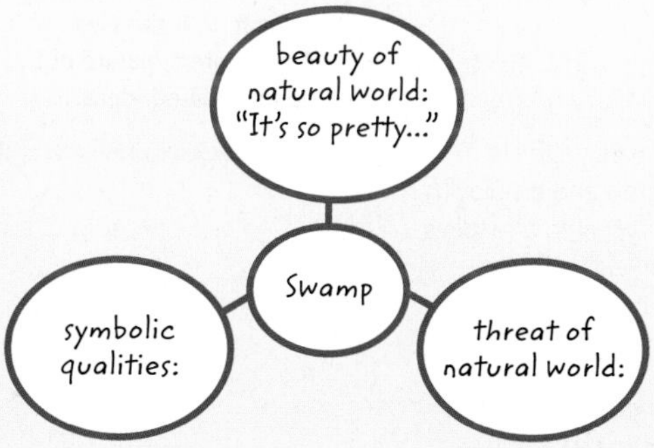

LOG ON **Literature** Online

Selection Resources For Selection Quizzes, eFlashcards, and Reading-Writing Connection activities, go to glencoe.com and enter QuickPass code GL49787u1

Reading Strategy Compare and Contrast Characters

ACT Skills Practice

1. Which of the following events underscores how Doodle differs from the rest of his family?

   A. He buries the scarlet ibis.

   B. He is delighted when he walks for the first time.

   C. When Brother takes him to the swamp, Doodle says it is "pretty."

   D. He makes up imaginative stories.

Vocabulary Practice

Practice with Word Origins Studying the etymology, or origin and history, of a word can help you better understand and explore its meaning. Some words can be traced far back into history, while others are of unknown origin. Create a word map, like the one below, for each of these vocabulary words from the selection. Use a dictionary for help.

careen serene blighted reiterate precariously

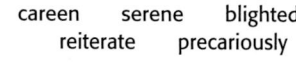

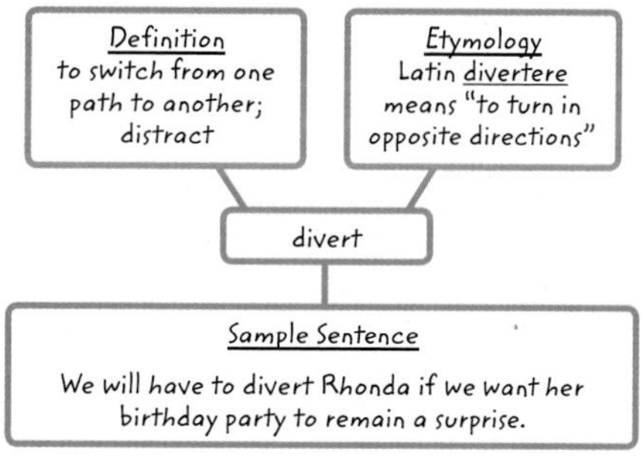

After You Read

Assess

Literary Element

1. The scarlet ibis is out of place so far north.
2. Students should use details from the story to support their responses.
3. Sample answer: It suggests that Doodle was doomed.

Review: Setting

- beauty of natural world—stream, palmetto fronds, "green dimness," saw-tooth fern, soft rubber grass, tall pine: "the only beauty I knew"
- threat of natural world—high winds, hurricane, lightning; disabled children; injured birds
- symbolic qualities—Memory is a swamp with lush growth, but not everything there is good. A swamp is a place to get stuck; in the story, it is a place of both death and beauty; it is a memory the narrator escapes, especially in a certain season

Reading Strategy

1. A is the correct answer. Other members of the family consider Doodle's desire to bury the ibis slightly comic.

Vocabulary

Sample responses follow:

careen: Etymology: Latin carina means "keel"
Definition: to lean over to one side
Sample Sentence: It's amazing how far the sailboats can careen without tipping over!

serene: Etymology: Latin serenus means "clear, unclouded"
Definition: calm, peaceful
Sample Sentence: I couldn't help but relax as my eyes wandered over the serene landscape.

blighted: Etymology: origin unknown
Definition: withered and deteriorated
Sample Sentence: The blighted houseplants will never again look strong and healthy.

reiterate: Etymology: Latin reiterare means "to repeat"
Definition: to say or do again
Sample Sentence: The microphone suddenly stopped working, so the speaker had to reiterate the last few points she had made.

precariously: Etymology: Latin precarius means "obtained by treaty"
Definition: in a way that is dependent on certain conditions
Sample Sentence: When the wind blew, the precariously balanced bag tumbled off the bench and onto the ground.

After You Read

Assess

Respond Through Writing

Students' essays should:

- begin with clear thesis about the use of red in Hurst's story
- support the thesis with evidence from the text
- use persuasive techniques to convince readers of the thesis
- present a thoughtful, well-organized argument

A student who meets all of these criteria should receive the equivalent of a 4-point response.

A student who fully meets two or partially meets three of these criteria should receive the equivalent of a 3-point response.

A student who fully meets one or partially meets two of these criteria should receive the equivalent of a 2-point response.

A student who partially meets one of these criteria should receive the equivalent of a 1-point response.

For additional grammar practice, see Unit 1 Teaching Resources Book, p. 177.

For additional selection assessment, see Assessment Resources, pp. 63–64.

Respond Through Writing

Persuasive Essay

Argue a Position Write a persuasive essay about the different uses of the color red (including scarlet, vermilion, and mahogany) in this story and its effectiveness as a symbol. Provide support for your conclusions.

Understand the Task To make a convincing argument, you will need to include **support**—material drawn directly from the text that provides evidence for your position.

Prewrite Prepare for your essay by tracking the instances of all shades of red throughout the story. Use a two-column chart to record each use of the color and note your ideas about its possible symbolism. Review your chart and determine your thesis. Highlight examples that best support your position.

Use of Red	What it Symbolizes
the mahogany coffin for William as a baby (p. 158)	Dark red symbolizes the dark future for William.

Draft The opening of your essay should provide a strong, clear explanation of your position. Before presenting any of your supporting evidence, you should briefly lay out your argument with a thesis statement, such as the following.

My own view is that _____, because _____ .

After summarizing your position, use the essay's body paragraphs to persuade the reader by presenting evidence from the text and employing other persuasive techniques. For example, you might appeal to a reader's emotions by discussing how the use of red evokes particular feelings. Make sure your conclusion ties your evidence together with your thesis.

Revise Using your chart for reference, review the examples you used and make sure that you included all of the best evidence from the text. Then exchange papers with a partner. Ask your partner to share any concerns about your position or your evidence. Then, address those concerns in your revisions.

Edit and Proofread Proofread your paper, correcting any errors in grammar, spelling, and punctuation. Use the Grammar Tip in the side column to help you with semicolons.

Learning Objectives

In this assignment, you will focus on the following objectives:

Writing: Writing a persuasive essay.

Grammar: Understanding how to use semicolons.

Grammar Tip

Semicolons

Semicolons separate main clauses that are not joined by a comma or coordinating conjunction (*and, but, or*). Semicolons can be used to help structure an argument/counterargument statement.

Some argue that Hurst's use of red is too subtle to be effective; I believe his subtlety helps to blend the symbolism into the story.

The semicolon helps to indicate that the two clauses are separate but closely related ideas.

To create custom assessments online, go to Progress Reporter Online Assessment.

To create custom assessments using software, use ExamView Assessment Suite.

Vocabulary Workshop

Multiple-Meaning Words

Literature Connection **Multiple-meaning words** are words that have several related definitions listed within a single dictionary entry. In the following sentence, W. D. Wetherell uses the multiple-meaning word *float.*

> *"She would spend her days sunbathing on a float my Uncle Sierbert had moored in their cove, and before July was over I had learned all her moods."*
>
> —W. D. Wetherell, "The Bass, the River, and Sheila Mant"

Float can refer to a raft, the action of floating, or a drink made with ice cream and soda.

Examples

Word	Meanings	Examples
crawl	a crawling movement	Would the narrator *crawl* on hands and knees to get Sheila's attention?
	a particular swim stroke	The narrator swims the *crawl* in the cove.
figure	shape, outline, or form	Sheila's *figure* attracts the narrator.
	person or personality	Sheila is an important *figure* in the narrator's summer.
line	a strong cord with a hook used for fishing	During the boat ride, a large bass gets hooked on the narrator's *line*.
	a short letter or note	If Sheila sent the narrator a *line*, what would it say?
	a boundary	The narrator fails to draw a *line* between fishing and dating.

Practice Use context clues to help you determine the meaning of each underlined word. Write down this meaning. Then write down at least one additional dictionary meaning for the word.

1. The scarlet ibis is a <u>symbol</u>.
2. The bird has been blown off <u>course</u> and is far from its natural surroundings.
3. Doodle buries the ibis in the front <u>yard</u>.

Learning Objectives

In this workshop, you will focus on the following objective:

Vocabulary: Understanding multiple-meaning words.

Vocabulary Terms

A **multiple-meaning word** is a word that has several related definitions listed within a single dictionary entry.

Tip

To determine the intended use of a multiple-meaning word, look for context clues such as synonyms, antonyms, and examples.

LOG ON **Literature Online**

Vocabulary For more vocabulary practice, go to glencoe.com and enter QuickPass code GL49787u1.

Vocabulary Workshop

Multiple-Meaning Words

Focus

A multiple-meaning word may be used as more than one part of speech. For example, *float* can be a noun—a raft. It can be a verb—to go down a river.

Teach

Multiple-Meaning Words

Tell students to determine what part of speech the word is as it is used in the sentence. Then they should find context clues to help determine the word's meaning.

Assess

1. Something used to represent something else; a written or printed sign used to represent an action or a relationship
2. The direction of movement; an area where a race is held
3. Ground around a building; an area where trains are switched or stored

For additional vocabulary practice, see Glencoe Interactive Vocabulary CD-ROM.

English Learners

DIFFERENTIATED INSTRUCTION

Intermediate English Learners may have difficulty using a dictionary, particularly when checking multiple meaning words. Help students review the entry for the word *yard.* Explain that it has two entries in the dictionary, with a different word origin for each. The first entry comes from a Middle English word meaning "rod or staff." The second come from a Middle English word meaning "enclosure." Review the definitions for each entry, noting the relation of the definition to the word's origin.

Before You Read

Focus

Bellringer Options

Selection Focus Transparency 12

Daily Language Practice Transparency 15

Or **ask:** Have you ever observed someone pretending to be something that he or she was not in order to impress another person? What did you think of that person's behavior?

As they read, students should observe how the main character behaves and the outcome of that behavior.

Before You Read

The Bass, the River, and Sheila Mant

Meet **W. D. Wetherell**

(born 1948)

Author and fishing enthusiast W. D. Wetherell has been hooking readers since he first began publishing in the early 1980s. Born in a small town in New York, Wetherell was a shy child. By the time he was ten or eleven years old, he was interested in becoming a writer. Around the same time, Wetherell developed a passion for the outdoors of New England, and in particular for fishing.

> *"Living modestly, with a certain leanness, brings joy unknown to those for whom money is no object."*
>
> —W. D. Wetherell

Early Career Wetherell wrote his first short story on the ping-pong table in his parents' basement at the age of nineteen. His early career was typical of that of many writers. He experienced eight long years of rejections before getting a piece accepted for publication. While attempting to make a living as a writer, Wetherell tried many jobs, from movie extra to tour guide. He refused to be deterred by early difficulties and eventually built a successful life as a writer. Wetherell has said that his work is "a testament of faith—in the power of art in general, and in the importance of fiction in particular."

The Country Life For many years, Wetherell has lived with his family in western New Hampshire, close enough to water to cast a fishing line. Without a computer or television, he lives a quiet life, enjoying the simple pleasures of fishing, watching the stars, reading poetry, and collecting local history.

In his work, Wetherell promotes a way of life that he believes is fast disappearing: a simple life spent in tune with nature. He calls himself "a walker in a sedentary age; a lover of quiet in a century that has the volume turned up full blast; a reader in a visual age; a writer in one that is increasingly aliterate."

Wetherell has published several novels as well as collections of short stories and essays. His work has earned him many prestigious awards; he has received the O. Henry Award for fiction twice.

LOG ON Literature Online

Author Search For more about W. D. Wetherell, go to glencoe.com and enter QuickPass code GL49787u1.

Selection Skills

The Bass, the River, and Sheila Mant

Literary Elements
- Dialogue (SE pp. 173–181)
- Plot (SE p. 185)

Reading Skills
- Connect to Personal Experience (SE pp. 173–182)
- Make Predictions (TE p. 176)

Vocabulary Skills
- Analogies (SE pp. 173, 182; TE p. 176)

Listening/Speaking/Viewing Skills
- Analyze Art (SE pp. 176, 179)

Writing Skills/Grammar
- Apply Dialogue (SE p. 182)

Literature and Reading Preview

Connect to the Story

When faced with a choice between two things you want, how do you make the decision? Freewrite for a few minutes about how you make difficult choices.

Build Background

The average largemouth bass lives about eight years, measures just over fourteen inches, and weighs one and one half pounds, but some bass weigh as much as eleven pounds. The river in the title of this story is the Connecticut River, which runs between New Hampshire and Vermont.

Set Purposes for Reading

Big Idea Rewards and Sacrifices

As you read, ask yourself, What does the narrator in the story hope to gain—and what is he willing to sacrifice to get it?

Literary Element Dialogue

Conversation between characters in a literary work is called **dialogue.** Dialogue brings characters to life by revealing their personality traits and by showing what they are thinking and feeling as they react to other characters. As you read, ask yourself, What does Wetherell reveal about his characters through dialogue?

Reading Strategy Connect to Personal Experience

When you **connect a story to your personal experience,** you link it to events in your own life. Connecting can help you to better appreciate and understand the story. As you read, ask yourself, What does it feel like to have an intense crush on someone?

Tip: Make a Chart As you read, make a chart to show the connections you share with characters and events in the story.

Detail	My Connection
p. 174 "... before July was over I had learned all her moods."	I know when my best friend is feeling sad or angry or happy.

Learning Objectives

For pages 172–182

In studying this text, you will focus on the following objectives:

Literary Study: Analyzing dialogue.

Reading: Connecting to personal experience.

Writing: Applying dialogue.

Vocabulary

pensive (pen′ siv) *adj.* thinking deeply, often sadly; p. 174 *Rowena was pensive as she studied the photograph of the forest fire.*

dubious (do͞o′ bē əs) *adj.* skeptical; feeling doubt; p. 177 *I was dubious when Lee claimed that she had jumped ten feet.*

surreptitiously (sur′ əp tish′ əs lē) *adv.* secretly or slyly; p. 178 *Sara neared the cookie jar surreptitiously.*

inhibition (in′ i bish′ ən) *n.* a restraint on one's natural impulses; p. 178 *An inhibition prevented Jody from laughing in the presence of elders.*

lithe (līth) *adj.* limber; bending easily; p. 180 *The lithe gymnast easily bent to touch her toes.*

Tip: Analogies To complete an analogy, decide what relationship exists in a pair of words. Then choose the word that creates the same relationship in a second pair. Example: considerate : thoughtfulness :: dubious : _____ A *considerate* person shows *thoughtfulness;* a *dubious* person shows *doubt.*

English Learners

DIFFERENTIATED INSTRUCTION

Intermediate Help students understand the meaning of uncommon words and phrases and words with multiple meanings on page 172. Point out and discuss the meanings of the following examples:

- hooking readers (*making readers want to keep on reading*)
- solitary (*alone*)
- deterred (*let down or stopped*)
- promotes (*thriftiness, cost-cutting, skimpiness*)
- in tune with nature (*enjoying nature*)
- prestigious (*important or impressive*)

Have students jot down new words as they read. Ask them to use a dictionary to determine their meaning.

Before You Read

Focus

Summary

A 14-year-old boy who is an avid fisherman develops a crush on Sheila Mant, the 17-year-old girl next door. As he paddles her in his canoe, Sheila announces that fishing is dumb, just as a fish attacks his lure. During the journey, the boy is torn between the girl of his dreams and the biggest bass he ever hooked. In the end, he makes a choice between the two and learns a valuable lesson about life and love.

For summaries in languages other than English, see Unit 1 Teaching Resources Book, pp. 180–185.

Vocabulary

Use Context Clues On the board, write three sentences that each contain one of the vocabulary words and appropriate context clues. Ask volunteers to come to the board and underline the context clues in the sentence that help reveal the meaning of each vocabulary word.

For additional vocabulary practice, see Unit 1 Teaching Resources Book, p. 188.

For additional context, see Glencoe Interactive Vocabulary CD-ROM.

Teach

Vocabulary 1

Multiple-Meaning Words
Point out the multiple-meaning word *observant* on this page. One meaning is "conscientious about observing a custom or a rule."
Ask: What is another meaning of this word? Which definition applies to the word in this case? *(Another meaning is "alert, or quick to notice"; this definition fits the use on this page.)*

For an audio recording of this selection, use Listening Library Audio CD-ROM.

Readability Scores
Dale-Chall: 9.4
DRP: 62
Lexile: 1110

The Bass, the River, and Sheila Mant

W. D. Wetherell

There was a summer in my life when the only creatur e that seemed lovelier to me than a largemouth bass was Sheila Mant. I was fourteen. The Mants had rented the cottage next to ours on the river; with their parties, their frantic games of softball, their constant comings and goings, they appeared to me denizens[1] of a brilliant existence.

"Too noisy by half," my mother quickly decided, but I would have given anything to be invited to one of their parties, and when my parents went to bed I would sneak through the woods to their hedge and stare enchanted at the candlelit swirl of white dresses and bright, paisley skirts.

Sheila was the middle daughter—at seventeen, all but out of reach. She would spend her days sunbathing on a float my Uncle Sierbert had moored in their cove, and before July was over I had learned all her moods. If she lay flat on the diving board with her hand trailing idly in the water, she was **pensive**, not to be disturbed. On her side, her head propped up
by her arm, she was observant, considering 1
those around her with a look that seemed queenly and severe. Sitting up, arms tucked around her long, suntanned legs, she was approachable, but barely, and it was only in those glorious moments when she stretched herself prior to entering the water that her various suitors found the courage to come near.

These were many. The Dartmouth heavyweight crew[2] would scull[3] by her

1. A *denizen* (den′ ə zən) is an inhabitant or occupant.

2. *Dartmouth heavyweight crew* refers to one of the rowing teams from Dartmouth College in Hanover, New Hampshire.

3. Here, *scull* means "propel by rowing."

Vocabulary

pensive (pen′ siv) *adj.* thinking deeply, often sadly

Research Practice

SPIRAL REVIEW **Build Background** This story takes place in a town on the Connecticut River, which separates the states of Vermont and New Hampshire. Ask students to find this river on a map. Explain that many people travel to this area to go fishing and that fishing will be a big part of the story. Then ask students to research fishing in this area. Have them find out more about the kinds of fish that live in the river, as well as what they eat, how big they get, why people enjoy fishing in this area, and other details that may enhance readers' understanding of the narrator's love of fishing. Ask students to write about what they have learned. Also ask students to find definitions for the following fishing terms from the story: *rod, reel, line, drag, cast, plug, lure, spinning rod,* and *spool.*

house on their way upriver, and I think all eight of them must have been in love with her at various times during the summer; the coxswain[4] would curse at them through his megaphone, but without effect—there was always a pause in their pace when they passed Sheila's float. I suppose to these jaded twenty-year-olds she seemed the incarnation of innocence and youth,[5] while to me she appeared unutterably suave, the epitome of sophistication.[6] I was on the swim team at school, and to win her attention would do endless laps between my house and the Vermont shore, hoping she would notice the beauty of my flutter kick, the power of my crawl. Finishing, I would boost myself up onto our dock and glance casually over toward her, but she was never watching, and the miraculous day she was, I immediately climbed the diving board and did my best tuck and a half for her, and continued diving until she had left and the sun went down and my longing was like a madness and I couldn't stop.

It was late August by the time I got up the nerve to ask her out. The tortured will-I's, won't-I's, the agonized indecision over what to say, the false starts toward her house and embarrassed retreats—the details of these have been seared from my memory, and the only part I remember clearly is emerging from the woods toward dusk while they were playing softball on their lawn, as bashful and frightened as a unicorn. Sheila was stationed halfway between first and second, well outside the infield. She didn't seem surprised to see me—as a matter of fact, she didn't seem to see me at all.

"If you're playing second base, you should move closer," I said.

She turned—I took the full brunt of her long red hair and well-spaced freckles.

"I'm playing outfield," she said, "I don't like the responsibility of having a base."

"Yeah, I can understand that," I said, though I couldn't. "There's a band in Dixford tomorrow night at nine. Want to go?"

One of her brothers sent the ball sailing over the leftfielder's head; she stood and watched it disappear toward the river.

"You have a car?" she said, without looking up.

I played my master stroke. "We'll go by canoe."

I spent all of the following day polishing it. I turned it upside down on our lawn and rubbed every inch with Brillo, hosing off the dirt, wiping it with chamois until it gleamed as bright as aluminum ever gleamed.[7] About five, I slid it into the water, arranging cushions near the bow so Sheila could lean on them if she was in one of her pensive moods, propping up my father's transistor radio by the middle thwart[8] so we could have music when we came back. Automatically, without thinking about it, I mounted my Mitchell reel on my Pfleuger spinning rod and stuck it in the stern.

4. On a crew team, the *coxswain* (kok′ sən) steers the boat and directs the timing of the team's oar strokes.
5. The narrator imagines that the college men, being dulled by long experience *(jaded)* with women, see Sheila as the personification or purest form *(incarnation)* of adolescent innocence.
6. The narrator believes Sheila is polished and gracious *(suave)* beyond words *(unutterably)* and the *epitome* (i pit′ ə mē), or perfect example, of mature, worldly experience.

7. *Brillo* is the brand name of a steel-wool pad used to scrub and clean, and *chamois* (sham′ ē) is a very soft, absorbent leather used to dry and polish.
8. In a canoe, a *thwart* is a brace running from side to side.

2 Connect to Personal Experience *How do you act when you want to impress someone?*

Rewards and Sacrifices *Why is the narrator willing to sacrifice truthfulness?* **3**

Dialogue *What does this dialogue reveal about the two characters?* **4**

Teach

Reading Strategy 2

Connect to Personal Experience **Answer:** *Answers will vary. Students may say they relate to the narrator's attempts to impress Sheila.*

Big Idea 3

Rewards and Sacrifices
Answer: *Perhaps the narrator's crush on Sheila is "like a madness," and he has lost all perspective.*

Literary Element 4

Dialogue **Answer:** *Each character is trying to impress the other. Sheila Mant insinuates that she only goes out with boys who have cars. The narrator thinks that Sheila will be impressed by a canoe ride.*

ENGLISH LEARNERS English learners may be confused by the line "I played my master stroke." Help them to understand this idiom by explaining that the narrator's best opportunity to take Sheila to the dance is to provide her with transportation.

English Learners

DIFFERENTIATED INSTRUCTION

Beginning/Early Intermediate

Explain that writers often use contractions to improve the flow of writing, or the flow of a character's speech in a story. Explain that contractions are shortened forms of two words that use apostrophes in place of omitted letters. Explain the difference between a contraction and a possessive pronoun (*it's* and *its, they're* and *their, you're* and *your*). Then ask students to find three instances on this page in which the author has used contractions as the shortened form of two words. (*You're, don't, couldn't, we'll, wasn't.*) Have students record the contractions on paper and write out the two words they represent.

Teach

Vocabulary

Analogies Refer students to the vocabulary word *dubious* and its definition on page 177. Then have students complete the following analogy:

dubious : certain :: solitude :

______

(Students may suggest words such as companionship *or* company.*)*

Ask: What is the relationship between the words in this analogy? *(These words are antonyms.)*

View the Art ★

Answer: *Students may say that the quiet, sheltered scene showing a waterfront house, pier, and canoe are similar to the story setting they imagine.*

Award-winning artist Ed Labadie paints in watercolor and oil. He uses vivid colors and geometric shapes to create compelling compositions. His works include abstracts, outdoor scenes, and images of wildlife.

Country House with Canoe, 1996. Ed Labadie. Watercolor on paper, 17½ x 10½ in. Collection of the artist.

View the Art How well does the scene in this painting match how you imagine the story's setting? ★

Reading Practice

SPIRAL REVIEW **Make Predictions** A prediction is an informed guess about what will happen in a story based both on textual evidence and on personal experience. Ask students to predict whether the narrator's evening with Sheila will be a pleasant experience. Have them consider the following questions:

- How has Sheila treated the narrator up to this point in the story?
- Sheila sits with her back to the narrator. What does this detail tell you about Sheila and about the evening?
- What is the significance of Sheila's comment that Eric Caswell will be at the dance?

1 I say automatically, because I never went anywhere that summer without a fishing rod. When I wasn't swimming laps to impress Sheila, I was back in our driveway practicing casts, and when I wasn't practicing casts, I was tying the line to Tosca, our springer spaniel, to test the reel's drag, and when I wasn't doing any of those things, I was fishing the river for bass.

Too nervous to sit at home, I got in the canoe early and started paddling in a huge circle that would get me to Sheila's dock around eight. As automatically as I brought along my rod, I tied on a big Rapala plug, let it down into the water, let out some line and immediately forgot all about it.

It was already dark by the time I glided up to the Mants' dock. Even by day the river was quiet, most of the summer people preferring Sunapee or one of the other nearby lakes, and at night it was a solitude difficult to believe, a corridor of hidden life that ran between banks like a tunnel. Even the stars were part of it. They weren't as sharp anywhere else; they seemed to have chosen the river as a guide on their slow wheel toward morning, and in the course of the summer's fishing, I had learned all their names.

I was there ten minutes before Sheila appeared. I heard the slam of their screen door first, then saw her in the spotlight as she came slowly down the path. As beautiful as she was on the float, she was even lovelier now—her white dress went perfectly with her hair, and complimented her figure even more than her swimsuit.

It was her face that bothered me. It had on its delightful fullness a very **dubious** expression.

"Look," she said. "I can get Dad's car."

"It's faster this way," I lied. "Parking's tense up there. Hey, it's safe. I won't tip it or anything."

She let herself down reluctantly into the bow. I was glad she wasn't facing me. When her eyes were on me, I felt like diving in the river again from agony and joy.

I pried the canoe away from the dock and started paddling upstream. There was an extra paddle in the bow, but Sheila made no move to pick it up. She took her shoes off, and dangled her feet over the side.

Ten minutes went by.

"What kind of band?" she said.

"It's sort of like folk music. You'll like it."

"Eric Caswell's going to be there. He strokes number four."[9]

"No kidding?" I said. I had no idea who she meant.

"What's that sound?" she said, pointing toward shore.

"Bass. That splashing sound?"

"Over there."

"Yeah, bass. They come into the shallows at night to chase frogs and moths and things. Big largemouths. *Micropetrus salmonides*,"[10] I added, showing off.

"I think fishing's dumb," she said, making a face. "I mean, it's boring and all. Definitely dumb."

Now I have spent a great deal of time in the years since wondering why Sheila Mant should come down so hard on fishing. Was her father a fisherman? Her

9. Eric *strokes*, or rows, in the *number four* position in the racing scull.

10. The narrator probably means to say *Micropterus salmoides* (mī crop ′ tə rəs sal moi ′ dēz), the scientific name for the largemouth bass.

Vocabulary

dubious (do͞o ′ bē əs) *adj*. skeptical; feeling doubt

Connect to Personal Experience *Can you imagine feeling the way the narrator is feeling? Explain.* **2**

Dialogue *What differences between the two characters does this conversation reveal?* **3**

English Learners

DIFFERENTIATED INSTRUCTION

Intermediate Ask the class for two volunteers: one to read the story aloud and one to look up words in the dictionary. Tell the students to raise their hands when the reader gets to a word that they do not know. Ask the reader to stop reading while you write the word on the board.

The other volunteer should look up the word in the dictionary. This student should then read the definition of the word to the class, allowing the other students time to copy the word and definition into their vocabulary notebooks. Then allow the reader to continue reading the story. After two or three pages, ask for two more volunteers to fill these jobs.

Teach

Big Idea 1

Rewards and Sacrifices

Have students read the bracketed passage.

Ask: Based on this passage, and what you have read so far about the narrator's feelings, do you think it would be a great sacrifice for him to give up fishing to impress Sheila? Why or why not? *(Some students may say it would not be a great sacrifice, since he has such a crush on Sheila; others may say fishing is very important to him; giving it up would be a great sacrifice.)*

Reading Strategy 2

Connect to Personal Experience

Answer: *Students may say they have felt this way before.* **Ask:** Why do you think Sheila does not face the narrator in the boat? *(Students may suggest that Sheila is not really interested in the narrator. She just wants a ride to the dance.)*

Literary Element 3

Dialogue

Answer: *It reveals a difference in their interests, which may reflect their relative ages. At fourteen, although the narrator is interested in Sheila, he is also interested in fishing. At seventeen, Sheila is primarily interested in flirting with boys.*

Teach

Reading Strategy 1

Connect to Personal Experience **Ask:** How does Sheila respond to the explanation that the buzzing sound is bats? *(She shudders and takes her feet out of the water.)*

Ask: How would you respond? Why? *(Most students would respond the same way, because most people find bats distasteful.)*

APPROACHING For approaching level students, **ask:** What does Sheila's easy acceptance of the explanation tell you about her? *(She has never heard a bat or been around people fishing, or she would have recognized the sound of the reel.)*

Literary Element 2

Dialogue **Answer:** *While the narrator is preoccupied with the hooked bass, Sheila is preoccupied with herself. She chatters away about herself and has no idea what is happening in the boat. Sheila seems to be shallow.*

antipathy[11] toward fishing nothing more than normal filial rebellion? Had she tried it once? A messy encounter with worms? It doesn't matter. What does, is that at that fragile moment in time I would have given anything not to appear dumb in Sheila's severe and unforgiving eyes.

She hadn't seen my equipment yet. What I *should* have done, of course, was push the canoe in closer to shore and carefully slide the rod into some branches where I could pick it up again in the morning. Failing that, I could have **surreptitiously** dumped the whole outfit overboard, written off the forty or so dollars as love's tribute.[12] What I actually *did* do was gently lean forward, and slowly, ever so slowly, push the rod back through my legs toward the stern where it would be less conspicuous.

It must have been just exactly what the bass was waiting for. Fish will trail a lure sometimes, trying to make up their mind whether or not to attack, and the slight pause in the plug's speed caused by my adjustment was tantalizing enough to overcome the bass's **inhibitions**. My rod, safely out of sight at last, bent double. The line, tightly coiled, peeled off the spool with the shrill, tearing zip of a high-speed drill.

Four things occurred to me at once. One, that it was a bass. Two, that it was a big bass. Three, that it was the biggest bass I had ever hooked. Four, that Sheila Mant must not know.

"What was that?" she said, turning half around.

11. *Antipathy* (an tip′ ə thē) means "intense dislike."
12. Here, a *tribute* is a payment showing devotion, respect, or gratitude.

Vocabulary

surreptitiously (sur′ əp tish′ əs lē) *adv.* secretly or slyly

inhibition (in′ i bish′ ən) *n.* a restraint on one's natural impulses

"Uh, what was what?"

"That buzzing noise."

"Bats." 1

She shuddered, quickly drew her feet back into the canoe. Every instinct I had told me to pick up the rod and strike back at the bass, but there was no need to—it was already solidly hooked. Downstream, an awesome distance downstream, it jumped clear of the water, landing with a concussion heavy enough to ripple the entire river. For a moment, I thought it was gone, but then the rod was bending again, the tip dancing into the water. Slowly, not making any motion that might alert Sheila, I reached down to tighten the drag.

While all this was going on, Sheila had begun talking and it was a few minutes before I was able to catch up with her train of thought.

"I went to a party there. These fraternity men. Katherine says I could get in there if I wanted. I'm thinking more of UVM or Bennington.[13] Somewhere I can ski."

The bass was slanting toward the rocks on the New Hampshire side by the ruins of Donaldson's boathouse. It had to be an old bass—a young one probably wouldn't have known the rocks were there. I brought the canoe back out into the middle of the river, hoping to head it off.

"That's neat," I mumbled. "Skiing. Yeah, I can see that."

"Eric said I have the figure to model, but I thought I should get an education first. I mean, it might be a while before I get started and all. I was thinking of getting my hair styled, more swept back? I mean, Ann-Margret?[14] Like hers, only shorter."

13. *UVM* refers to the University of Vermont at Burlington; *Bennington* is a small, private college, also in Vermont.
14. *Ann-Margret* is an actress and singer who was a young, glamorous movie star at the time of the story.

Dialogue *What do Sheila's words reveal about her?* 2

Reading Practice

Character Dialogue As the narrator's mind is consumed with the bass he has unintentionally hooked and how he is going to hide the fish, Sheila keeps up a constant stream of chatter, though she does not realize that her conversation is, for the most part, one-sided. **Ask:** What does Sheila talk about? Why doesn't she realize that the narrator is not listening to her? How does what she says make you, as a reader, feel about her? *(Students may respond that Sheila talks about herself almost the entire time they are in the boat. Students may say that she doesn't realize that the narrator isn't listening because she is focused on herself and not on the narrator. Students may express that this makes readers dislike Sheila because she is self-centered and arrogant, and because it is obvious that she doesn't care about the narrator.)*

Trout Fishing, Lake St. John, 1895. Winslow Homer. William Wilkens Warren Fund.

View the Art The artist, Winslow Homer, chose to paint this image in shades of brown. In your opinion, what mood does the color of the painting evoke? ★

She hesitated. "Are we going backwards?"

We were. I had managed to keep the bass in the middle of the river away from the rocks, but it had plenty of room there, and for the first time a chance to exert its full strength. I quickly computed the weight necessary to draw a fully loaded canoe backwards—the thought of it made me feel faint.

"It's just the current," I said hoarsely. "No sweat or anything."

I dug in deeper with my paddle. Reassured, Sheila began talking about something else, but all my attention was taken up now with the fish. I could feel its desperation as the water grew shallower. I could sense the extra strain on the line, the frantic way it cut back and forth in the water. I could visualize what it looked like—the gape of its mouth, the flared gills and thick, vertical tail. The bass couldn't have encountered many forces in its long life that it wasn't capable of handling, and the unrelenting tug at its mouth must have been a source of great puzzlement and mounting panic.

Me, I had problems of my own. To get to Dixford, I had to paddle up a sluggish stream that came into the river beneath a covered bridge. There was a shallow sandbar at the mouth of this stream—weeds on one side, rocks on the other. Without doubt, this is where I would lose the fish.

"I have to be careful with my complexion. I tan, but in segments. I can't figure out if it's even worth it. I wouldn't even do it probably. I saw Jackie Kennedy[15] in Boston and she wasn't tan at all."

3 Rewards and Sacrifices *What choice is the narrator struggling with?*

15. *Jackie Kennedy* (1929–1994), President John F. Kennedy's wife, was admired by many as a role model and style setter.

Teach

Big Idea 3

Rewards and Sacrifices

Answer: *He struggles to choose between impressing Sheila and catching the large bass, thus revealing himself as a fisherman.*

Ask: How does each choice represent both a reward and a sacrifice? *(Impressing Sheila is a reward, but he must make the sacrifice of giving up the bass. Catching the bass is a reward, but he must sacrifice Sheila's good impression of him.)*

View the Art ★

Answer: *Students may say that the brown colors give the image a sense of simplicity and nostalgia.*

American artist Winslow Homer (1836–1910) painted scenes of people interacting with nature and of everyday rural life in America.

Approaching Level

DIFFERENTIATED INSTRUCTION

Established Have students discuss the events leading to the story's climax. **Ask:** Why does the narrator try to paddle the canoe into the middle of the lake? Why does he hesitate when he reaches for his fishing rod? *(Students may say that the narrator is trying not to lose the fish, even though he doesn't know what he would do with it if he caught it. Students may also say that he hesitates when he reaches for the fishing rod because he wants to catch the bass, but doesn't want Sheila to think that he is stupid, which is what she thinks of fishing.)*

Advanced Learners

DIFFERENTIATED INSTRUCTION

Story Development Ask students what might have been different if the narrator had reeled in the bass. **Ask:** What might have changed? *(Students may answer that Sheila might have changed her mind about fishing being "boring" if she had seen the narrator reel in the biggest bass of his life.)*

Teach

Reading Strategy 1

Connect to Personal Experience **Answer:** *Answers will vary. Students may relate to the narrator's decision to prioritize his crush over his hobby.*

Literary Element 2

Dialogue **Answer:** *The narrator is probably realizing that Sheila is more interested in Eric Caswell because he is a college student and owns a Corvette. He also realizes that his choice to cut the bass loose was a mistake due to his immature infatuation with Sheila, who is not worth his attention.*

To check students' understanding of the selection, see Unit 1 Teaching Resources Book, p. 191.

Progress Check

Can students analyze dialogue?

If No → See Unit 1 Teaching Resources Book, p. 186.

Taking a deep breath, I paddled as hard as I could for the middle, deepest part of the bar. I could have threaded the eye of a needle with the canoe, but the pull on the stern threw me off and I overcompensated—the canoe veered left and scraped bottom. I pushed the paddle down and shoved. A moment of hesitation . . . a moment more. . . . The canoe shot clear into the deeper water of the stream. I immediately looked down at the rod. It was bent in the same, tight arc—miraculously, the bass was still on.

The moon was out now. It was low and full enough that its beam shone directly on Sheila there ahead of me in the canoe, washing her in a creamy, luminous glow. I could see the **lithe**, easy shape of her figure. I could see the way her hair curled down off her shoulders, the proud, alert tilt of her head, and all these things were as a tug on my heart. Not just Sheila, but the aura[16] she carried about her of parties and casual touchings and grace. Behind me, I could feel the strain of the bass, steadier now, growing weaker, and this was another tug on my heart, not just the bass but the beat of the river and the slant of the stars and the smell of the night, until finally it seemed I would be torn apart between longings, split in half. Twenty yards ahead of us was the road, and once I pulled the canoe up on shore, the bass would be gone, irretrievably gone. If instead I stood up, grabbed the rod and started pumping, I would have it—as tired as the bass was, there was no chance it could get away. I reached down for the rod, hesitated, looked up to where Sheila was stretching herself lazily toward the sky, her small breasts rising beneath the soft fabric of her dress, and the tug was too much for me, and quicker than it takes to write down, I pulled the penknife from my pocket and cut the line in half.

With a sick, nauseous feeling in my stomach, I saw the rod unbend.

"My legs are sore," Sheila whined. "Are we there yet?"

Through a superhuman effort of self-control, I was able to beach the canoe and help Sheila off. The rest of the night is much foggier. We walked to the fair—there was the smell of popcorn, the sound of guitars. I may have danced once or twice with her, but all I really remember is her coming over to me once the music was done to explain that she would be going home in Eric Caswell's Corvette.

"Okay," I mumbled.

For the first time that night she looked at me, really looked at me.

"You're a funny kid, you know that?"

Funny. Different. Dreamy. Odd. How many times was I to hear that in the years to come, all spoken with the same quizzical, half-accusatory tone Sheila used then. Poor Sheila! Before the month was over, the spell she cast over me was gone, but the memory of that lost bass haunted me all summer and haunts me still. There would be other Sheila Mants in my life, other fish, and though I came close once or twice, it was these secret, hidden tuggings in the night that claimed me, and I never made the same mistake again. ∾

16. Here, Sheila's *aura* is a sort of atmosphere or quality that the narrator senses around her.

Vocabulary

lithe (līth) *adj.* limber; bending easily

Connect to Personal Experience *If you had been in this situation, how would you have responded?* **1**

Dialogue *What do you think the narrator is thinking as he says this one simple word?* **2**

Writing Practice

SPIRAL REVIEW **Personal Narrative** Ask students if they have ever sacrificed something that they loved only to discover that the sacrifice was not worth the result. Ask readers how they felt after it happened, and if they thought that any good came out of it at all. Then ask readers how their own experience contributed to their reactions to the story. Have students explain their situations and answer these questions in a short written narrative.

(Students may write that they were disappointed when the situation did not turn out the way that they hoped it would. Some students may realize that a positive result of the situation may have been that students learned a lesson that they would carry with them, as did the narrator in the story.)

After You Read

Respond and Think Critically

Respond and Interpret

1. Did you find this story to be humorous, serious, or both? Explain.
2. (a)How old is the narrator, and how old is Sheila Mant? (b)What makes Sheila so attractive to the narrator, and why is she "all but out of reach"?
3. (a)Which of the narrator's special hobbies or skills does he openly reveal to Sheila, and which does he keep secret? (b)How important is fishing to the narrator? Support your answer.
4. (a)How does the narrator's date with Sheila end? (b)The narrator says that there would be "other Sheila Mants" in his life. What does Sheila Mant come to represent for the narrator?

Analyze and Evaluate

5. How well does the story demonstrate the differences between the narrator and Sheila? Cite examples from the story.
6. Choose a passage that helps you feel sympathy for the narrator's actions and explain why it is effective.

Connect

7. **Big Idea** Rewards and Sacrifices Do you think the narrator made the right choice in putting aside his interests for Sheila? Explain.
8. **Connect to the Author** W. D. Wetherell often writes about fishing. Does this story help you understand the passion many fishing enthusiasts feel for the sport? Explain.

Literary Element Dialogue

In addition to revealing personality and character, writers use **dialogue** to create mood, advance the plot, and develop theme.

1. Reread the dialogue between the narrator and Sheila on page 177 that takes place toward the beginning of their canoe ride. How does this conversation advance the plot of the story?
2. Reread the brief dialogue on page 178 in which the narrator tells Sheila that the buzzing noise she hears comes from bats. How does this dialogue contribute to the comic mood of the story?
3. How does the final dialogue between the narrator and Sheila on page 180 develop the theme of growing up in the story?

Review: Plot

As you learned on pages 8–9, in a story's **plot,** the **falling action** shows what happens to the characters after the climax. The **resolution** of the plot explains the final outcome of the story and ties up any loose ends.

1. What events make up this story's falling action?
2. In your opinion, is Sheila's comment that the narrator is a "funny kid" part of the falling action or part of the resolution? Why?
3. Did you find the resolution surprising, or was it predictable? Explain your answer.

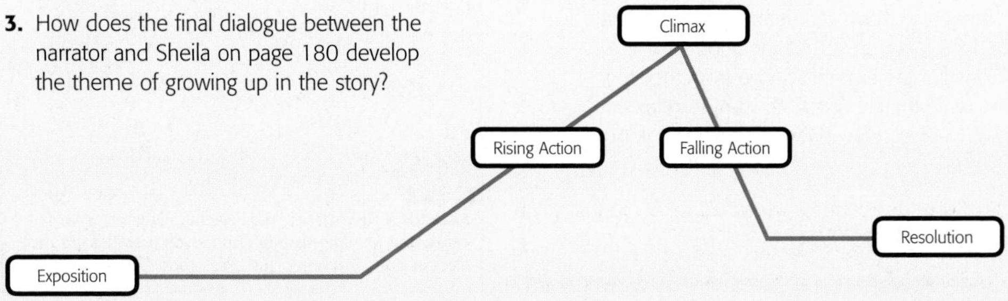

After You Read

Assess

1. Students may find the subject serious but the treatment humorous.
2. (a) He is 14. She is 17.
   (b) She is lovely and three years older than the narrator.
3. (a) Reveals swimming; hides fishing (b) Very important; he spends most of his time at it.
4. (a) She goes home with Eric.
   (b) The temptation to gain others' approval at any cost
5. She is older and cares about her tan, college, and hair; she is a poor baseball player and a bad date. He is quiet and obsessed with her and fishing.
6. Students may say the author shows what it is like to be a sensitive, awkward adolescent with a crush.
7. Possible answers: He was wrong because she was not a "better catch"; he was right because it would be rude to value fishing above another person.
8. Students should point to passages in the story and explain why they think the story was either successful or unsuccessful at helping them to understand the passion fishing enthusiasts feel for the sport.

Literary Element

1. The narrator has been trying to impress Sheila with his skill at canoeing and knowledge of fishing until she says, "I think fishing is dumb." Afterwards, he attempts to hide his interest in fishing, including his encounter with the bass.
2. The narrator's need to tell the lie that the noise comes from bats and Sheila's reaction are comic.
3. The narrator realizes that his futile attempt to please Sheila was not worth giving up the bass. He becomes aware that adolescent flirtations with girls are fleeting, while fishing is an important and enduring avocation. He learns to respect and follow his true inclinations.

Review: Plot

1. Sheila says she is leaving with Eric.
2. It is part of the falling action because after that his crush continues for a while longer.
3. Answers will vary. Students should provide support for their answers.

After You Read

Assess

Reading Strategy

1. Students should support their answers.
2. Students may say that unique abilities may make a person feel isolated but are rewarding.

Progress Check

Can students connect to personal experience?

If No → See Unit 1 Teaching Resources Book, p. 187.

Vocabulary

1. b **2.** a **3.** b **4.** a **5.** a

Academic Vocabulary

He wanted to be able to enjoy Sheila's company, but he also wanted to focus on catching the big bass.

Write with Style

Students' dialogues should:

- feature two distinct, realistically-portrayed characters
- include dialogue that uses language that is appropriate for each character and reflects each character's personality
- include characters' thoughts and actions in addition to the dialogue
- clearly attribute dialogue and actions to specific characters

For grammar practice, see Unit 1 Teaching Resources Book, p. 190.

Reading Strategy Connect to Personal Experience

Review the connections chart you created as you read. Then answer the following questions.

1. What about the narrator's feelings or experiences did you relate to most? Explain.
2. The narrator says that over the years, people have called him *funny*, *different*, *dreamy*, and *odd*. Have you ever felt that you were different from the people around you? Explain the advantages and disadvantages of having unique abilities or characteristics that others do not appreciate.

Vocabulary Practice

Practice with Analogies Choose the word that best completes each analogy.

1. **muscular : strength :: lithe :**
   a. cleverness **b.** flexibility
2. **restraint : inhibition :: acknowledgment :**
   a. recognition **b.** termination
3. **thinking : pensive :: thanking :**
   a. tentative **b.** appreciative
4. **skeptic : dubious :: fan :**
   a. enthusiastic **b.** imitative
5. **openly : surreptitiously :: abundantly :**
   a. scarcely **b.** regretfully

Academic Vocabulary

*After hooking the fish, the narrator was unable to **relax** and enjoy his boat ride with Sheila.*

Relax is an academic word that means "to become less tense." It is important to **relax** sometimes; however, **relaxing** can cause you to lose focus on something important. Consider the example above from the story. Why did the narrator both want to **relax** and not want to **relax** during his boat ride with Sheila?

For more on academic vocabulary, see pages 54–55 and R79–R81.

Write with Style

Apply Dialogue

Assignment Use the narrator and Sheila's conversation in the canoe as a model for a dialogue in which one character is distracted and the other character doesn't realize it.

Get Ideas Use a Venn diagram to list what the distracted person is focused on and what the main speaker is talking about. Organize your ideas within the circles; the overlapping area contains the part of the dialogue to which both characters are attentive.

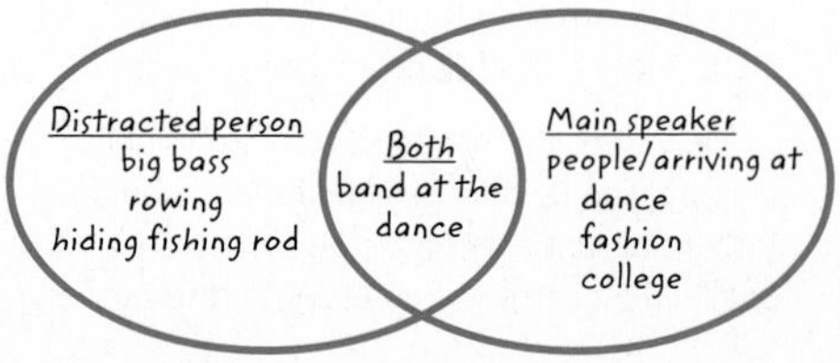

Give It Structure To build the full scene, include descriptions of the characters' thoughts or actions between the passages of dialogue. Each paragraph of dialogue and description should focus on one character. Make sure that it is clear who is speaking, or whose thoughts or actions are being described.

EXAMPLE:

With a sick, nauseous feeling in my stomach, I saw the rod unbend.

"My legs are sore," Sheila whined. "Are we there yet?"

Look at Language Review the dialogue to make sure it reflects two distinct characters and the specific language that each character would use.

LOG ON Literature Online

Selection Resources For Selection Quizzes, eFlashcards, and Reading-Writing Connection activities, go to glencoe.com and enter QuickPass code GL49787u1.

For additional selection assessment, see Assessment Resources, pp. 65–66.

To create custom assessments online, go to Progress Reporter Online Assessment.

To create custom assessments using software, use ExamView Assessment Suite.

PART 3

Dreams and Reality

The Sleeping Gypsy, 1897. Henri Rousseau. Oil on canvas, 51 x 79 in. The Museum of Modern Art, New York.

View the Art When Henri Rousseau's paintings were first displayed, the public ridiculed them. Later, however, his work influenced many younger artists including the famous Pablo Picasso. How does this painting evoke a dream-like state? ★

BIG IDEA

When reality intrudes on a person's dreams and daydreams, he or she must face choices. The actions taken then reveal much about his or her personality. In the short stories in Part 3, you will read about clashes between dreams and reality. As you read, ask yourself, How well do these dreams mesh with reality?

183

UNIT ONE

PART 3

Analyze and Extend

Big Idea

Dreams and Reality After students have read the text under the Big Idea head, discuss the distinction between dreams and reality. Challenge students to consider the question, "How well do dreams connect to reality?" Return to this question after students have read the selections and have them reconsider their answers.

View the Art ★

The Sleeping Gypsy is the painting that secured the reputation of self-taught French painter Henri Rousseau (1844–1910). Rousseau was a public servant who took up painting at the age of 40.

Answer: *Students might mention the soft colors and gentle sloping lines of the painting. They might also point out the surreal scene of a woman sleeping while a lion calmly walks around her.*

English Learners

DIFFERENTIATED INSTRUCTION

Early Advanced The relationship between dreams and reality is not viewed the same way in every culture. Invite English learners to talk about the role of dreams in their culture. As a class, make comparisons with modern American culture and provide examples as support.

Advanced Learners

DIFFERENTIATED INSTRUCTION

Analyze Dreams in Stories Invite advanced readers to think about literature in which dreams play an important part. Encourage them to offer examples and explain the role of the dream in the story. Discuss how dreams contribute to the work's meaning and how dreams often provide insight into a character's mind.

Focus

Bellringer Options

Daily Language Practice Transparency 16

Or display photos or artwork that show different points of view—for example, views from great heights or ground level, close-ups, and wide-angle shots.

Ask: How does the point of view affect what we can see in these photographs? Why is point of view important? Have students consider as they read why an author chose to write from a particular point of view.

Teach

Literary Element 1

Narrator's Point of View

Say: Point of view refers to the relationship of the narrator to the story. It determines the information that the reader gets. The first-person point of view, for example, gives readers access to the narrator's thoughts and feelings. Have students recall a story they have read recently and ask them to identify the point of view.

For additional support for English Learners, see Unit 1 Teaching Resources Book, p. 195.

Learning Objectives

For pages 183–185

In studying this text, you will focus on the following objective:

Literary Study: Analyzing narrator, point of view, and voice.

LITERARY FOCUS

Narrator and Voice

How do narrator and voice affect a story?

Think of a narrator as a guide—someone who takes the reader from place to place, scene to scene, pointing out objects of interest along the way. The narrator may be a character in the story whose point of view and misunderstandings add suspense or interest to a story. Or, the narrator can be a trustworthy, reliable guide.

from *The Son from America*

by Isaac Bashevis Singer

The couple had a son, Samuel, who had gone to America forty years ago. It was said in Lentshin that he became a millionaire there. Every month, the Lentshin letter carrier brought old Berl a money order and a letter that no one could read because it was in English. How much money Samuel sent his parents remained a secret. Three times a year, Berl and his wife went on foot to Zakroczym and cashed the money orders there. But they never seemed to use the money. What for? The garden, the cow, and the goat provided most of their needs. Besides, Berlcha sold chickens and eggs, and from these there was enough to buy flour for bread.

The Smith at Szeliwy, Poland, 1904.
Robert Polhill Bevan. Oil on board, 26 x 37 cm.
Private collection.

Narrator

1 The **narrator** is the person who tells a story. The narrator can be a character in the story or an outside observer. The choice of a narrator influences how the story is revealed to the reader. Sometimes a narrator is unreliable. An **unreliable narrator** does not tell the story accurately either deliberately or because he or she does not know any better.

> She dressed plainly because she could not afford fine clothes, but was as unhappy as a woman who has come down in the world; for women have no family rank or social class.
>
> —Guy de Maupassant, **from "The Necklace"**

Writing Practice

Point of View Tell students to think of a scene from a familiar story, such as a fairy tale or one of the passages from a previous selection. **Ask:** From whose point of view is the story told? Why was it important that the story be told from that point of view? Allow students to write for a few minutes in their notebooks. Then have them share their findings with the class.

Choose one familiar story and randomly assign different points of view to students. Have them rewrite the scene using the assigned perspective. Then have students read their work aloud. Students should explain how the point of view used by the author compares to their version. Discuss how point of view can affect the text.

Point of View

Point of view refers to the relationship of the narrator to the story.

First Person In a story with **first-person point of view,** the narrator is a character in the story, referred to as *I.* The reader is restricted to the thoughts and feelings of that character.

I had a view of their kitchen and their backyard, and though I could not hear what they said, I knew when they were arguing, when one of them was sick, and many other things. I knew all this by watching them at mealtimes.

—Judith Ortiz Cofer, **from "American History"**

A first-person narrator can be the protagonist, one of the minor characters, an outside observer, or a person who has heard the story second-hand.

Third-Person Omniscient In a story with **third-person omniscient point of view,** the narrator is not a character in the story and uses the words *he* and *she* to describe the events of the story. This type of narrator can move from one place to another and back and forth through time. In addition, the omniscient narrator knows the characters' thoughts and feelings and may reveal details the characters themselves could not reveal.

He stopped talking, dazed and distracted to see his wife burst out weeping. Two large tears slowly rolled from the corners of her eyes to the corners of her mouth; he gasped, "Why, what's the matter? What's the trouble?"

By sheer will power she overcame her outburst and answered in a calm voice while wiping the tears from her wet cheeks.

—Guy de Maupassant, **from "The Necklace"**

Third-Person Limited In a story with **third-person limited point of view,** the narrator knows the thoughts and feelings of only one character, usually the protagonist. The way people, places, and events appear to that character is the way they appear to the reader.

Walter Mitty began to wonder what the other thing was his wife had told him to get. She had told him, twice, before they set out from their house for Waterbury. In a way he hated these weekly trips to town—he was always getting something wrong.

—James Thurber, **from "The Secret Life of Walter Mitty"**

Voice

The distinctive use of language that conveys the author's or narrator's personality is called **voice.** Voice is determined by word choice or by the author's attitude toward the subject or audience (tone) and by the overall emotional quality of the work (mood). 2

Well Marge, you haven't heard anything! You should hear the woman I work for . . . she's really something. Calls herself "Mrs. James!" All the time she says "Mrs. James."

—Alice Childress, **from "Mrs. James"**

Quickwrite

Describe Author's Voice Think of a writer with a strong, distinctive voice. Describe this author's voice and the qualities that make it memorable.

LOG ON **Literature** Online

Literature and Reading For more about literary elements, go to glencoe.com and enter QuickPass code GL49787u1.

UNIT ONE

PART 3

Focus

Reading Strategy 2

Make Generalizations

Ask: How do narrator, point of view, and voice affect a story? *(Students should note that the point of view affects how much information is shared with the reader. It also affects voice. The narrator's voice is shaped by what he or she knows.)*

Assess

Quickwrite

Students' answers should include adjectives that describe the author's voice. If students have trouble thinking of an author, remind them to review the stories they have read so far. Remind them to look at the author's choice of words, sentence length, and use of imagery to analyze the voice.

Approaching Level

DIFFERENTIATED INSTRUCTION

Established Ask: What is the literary term used to identify the person telling the story? *(narrator)* According to the Literary Focus, what conveys the attitude and personality of the narrator? *(voice)*

Advanced Learners

DIFFERENTIATED INSTRUCTION

Match Voice and Music Students who are musical will grasp how a writer's voice conveys a particular mood. Have them select music that expresses the same personality, mood, or tone as the voice in a story of their choosing. Students should play the music for the class and explain their choice.

Before You Read

Focus

Bellringer Options

Selection Focus Transparency 12

Daily Language Practice Transparency 17

Or have students brainstorm a list of things that they daydream about.

Ask: Do you daydream about things that could never come true, or things that could actually happen? Have students arrange their lists in two columns: things that could never come true and things that they could accomplish. Ask volunteers to share one of their daydreams with the class.

Before You Read

The Secret Life of Walter Mitty

Meet **James Thurber**

(1894–1961)

When he was six years old, James Thurber stood with an apple on his head while his older brother aimed a homemade arrow at the fruit. The arrow pierced Thurber's left eye, blinding him in that eye. Aside from that ill-advised decision to assist in his brother's re-creation of William Tell's famous act, Thurber had a relatively normal childhood in Columbus, Ohio.

A Working Writer Thurber's professional writing career began in 1920 when he took a job as a reporter for the *Columbus Dispatch.* In 1927, E. B. White, author of the children's classics *Stuart Little* and *Charlotte's Web,* helped Thurber get a job with *The New Yorker* magazine. For more than thirty years, he delighted its readers with humorous stories, essays, fables, and cartoons.

> *"I write basically because it's so much fun."*
>
> —James Thurber

As Thurber aged, the vision in his right eye declined. As a result, he sometimes wrote with a black crayon on yellow paper, filling the page with just twenty words. His usual method of writing, however, was a mental process. Once he had worked out an idea in his mind, he would dictate his thoughts to a secretary, usually about two thousand words in an afternoon.

The Humorist James Thurber has been called the "funniest American writer of his day" and "one of the world's greatest humorists." However, some critics see Thurber's humor as far from lighthearted. In *Thurber: A Collection of Critical Essays,* John Updike wrote that "Thurber's genius was to make of our despair a humorous fable."

Thurber did not consider his humor gentle either. Instead, his stories are edgy and tense, typically reflecting the unsettling problems and disasters that befall humans. Much of his work was satire, a form of writing that ridicules people, practices, or institutions in order to point out their failings. Thurber's satire was social, not political. The institution of marriage was one of his chief targets. But many of his pieces are just plain fun. Thurber once said, "Humor is a serious thing. I like to think of it as one of our greatest earliest natural resources, which must be preserved at all cost."

LOG ON **Literature** Online

Author Search For more about James Thurber, go to glencoe.com and enter QuickPass code GL49787u1.

Selection Skills

The Secret Life of Walter Mitty

Literary Elements
- Diction (SE pp. 187–193)
- Narrator (SE p. 193)

Listening/Speaking/Viewing Skills
- Analyze Art (SE p. 188, 191)
- Oral Interpretation (SE p. 194)

Reading Skills
- Visualize (SE pp. 187–193)

Vocabulary Skills
- Synonyms (SE pp. 187, 194)
- Academic Vocabulary (SE p. 194)

Writing Skills/Grammar
- Essay Question (SE p. 192)

Literature and Reading Preview

Connect to the Story

Do you ever daydream? Write a journal entry about when you find yourself daydreaming and what you daydream about.

Build Background

This story depicts a person's daydreams about heroic real-life situations, but many of the details of these situations are invented. For example, one daydream includes an eight-engine Navy hydroplane, but there is no such thing. There is also a reference to a 50.80 caliber pistol, which in reality would be bigger than a cannon.

Set Purposes for Reading

Big Idea Dreams and Reality

As you read, ask yourself, What separates Walter Mitty's real world from the world of his daydreams?

Literary Element Diction

Diction is a writer's choice of words and the arrangement of those words in phrases, sentences, or lines of a poem. As you read, ask yourself, How does Thurber's word choice differ in each scene of the story?

Reading Strategy Visualize

Visualizing is picturing a writer's ideas or descriptions in the mind's eye. As you read, ask yourself, What descriptive details in the story help the reader visualize settings, characters, and events in Mitty's daydreams and in his real life?

Tip: Gather Details Use a chart like the one below to record details that will help you visualize details in the story.

First Daydream

What do I see?	What do I hear?	How do I feel?
commander in full-dress uniform	voice like thin ice breaking	confident, in control

Learning Objectives

For pages 186–194

In studying this text, you will focus on the following objectives:

Literary Study: Analyzing diction.

Reading: Visualizing.

Speaking and Listening: Presenting an oral interpretation.

Vocabulary

distraught (dis trôt′) *adj.* very upset; confused; p. 189 *She was distraught after the car accident.*

haggard (hag′ ərd) *adj.* having a worn and tired look; p. 189 *Anyone would look haggard after two days without sleep.*

craven (krā′ vən) *adj.* extremely cowardly; p. 190 *To let someone else take the punishment for his misdeeds was a truly craven act.*

pandemonium (pan′ də mō′ nē əm) *n.* wild uproar; p. 191 *When the mob began shouting and shoving, pandemonium ensued.*

disdainful (dis dān′ fəl) *adj.* showing scorn for something or someone regarded as unworthy; p. 192 *She gave her boss a disdainful look that showed no respect for his feelings.*

Tip: Synonyms Synonyms are words that have the same or similar meanings. Thinking of a familiar word that is a synonym for a vocabulary word can help you remember the meaning of the new word.

English Learners

DIFFERENTIATED INSTRUCTION

Beginning/Early Intermediate Ask students to make a list of synonyms for each of the vocabulary words on this page. Students may use a dictionary to develop their lists.

Intermediate Help students understand John Updike's quote about Thurber on page 186—"Thurber's genius was to make of our despair a humorous fable." **Ask:** What do you think Updike meant by this statement? *(Possible answer: Thurber was able to make the reality of sadness something to laugh at.)*

Before You Read

Focus

Summary

Meek, ineffectual Walter Mitty has the world at his feet in his daydreams. He repeatedly drifts into this fantasyland during a shopping outing with his overbearing wife. However, the real world keeps intruding, as his wife, a police officer, a parking attendant, and even passersby interrupt his daydreams with duties he'd rather forget and remind him of mistakes caused by his inattention.

For summaries in languages other than English, see Unit 1 Teaching Resources Book, pp. 196–201.

Vocabulary

Use New Vocabulary

To test vocabulary comprehension, have students write a paragraph using each of the vocabulary words at least once. Ask students who have used the words in the best and most creative ways to share their stories with the rest of the class.

For additional vocabulary practice, see Unit 1 Teaching Resources Book, p. 204.

For additional context, see Glencoe Interactive Vocabulary CD-ROM.

Teach

Big Idea 1

Dreams and Reality **Ask:** Why might it be easier to live in a daydream than in reality? *(In daydreams one can ignore one's problems and shortcomings.)*

APPROACHING To guide approaching learners, **ask:** What effect can constant daydreaming have on one's life? *(It can result in blunders and keep a person from participating in real life.)*

Literary Element 2

Diction **Answer:** *He is decisive and authoritative.*

View the Art ★

British landscape artist George Horace Davis (1881–1963) painted aerial diagrams that were used to train pilots in the royal Air Force (RAF). **Answer:** *Students should compare their visualizations with the painting.*

For an audio recording of this selection, use Listening Library Audio CD-ROM.

Readability Scores

Dale-Chall: 3.3
DRP: 52
Lexile: 700

The Secret Life of Walter Mitty

James Thurber

1 "We're going through!" The Commander's voice was like thin ice breaking. He wore his full-dress uniform, with the heavily braided white cap pulled down rakishly[1] over one cold gray eye. "We can't make it, sir. It's spoiling for a hurricane, if you ask me."

2 "I'm not asking you, Lieutenant Berg," said the Commander. "Throw on the power lights! Rev her up to 8,500! We're going through!" The pounding of the cylinders increased: ta-pocketa-pocketa-pocketa-*pocketa-pocketa*. The Commander stared at the ice forming on the pilot window. He walked over and twisted a row of complicated dials. "Switch on No. 8 auxiliary!" he shouted. "Switch on No. 8 auxiliary!" repeated Lieutenant Berg. "Full strength in No. 3 turret!" shouted the Commander. "Full strength in No. 3 turret!" The crew, bending to their various tasks in the huge, hurtling eight-engined Navy hydroplane,[2] looked at each other and grinned. "The Old Man'll get us

Putting Out His Eyes, 1919. George Horace Davis. Imperial War Museum, London.

View the Art Is this how you picture the first scene of the story? Why or why not? ★

1. *Rakishly* means "in a dashing or jaunty manner."
2. A *hydroplane* is an airplane equipped with floats that allow it to take off from and land on water.

2 Diction *What does the Commander's style of speaking tell you about him?*

Reading Practice

SPIRAL REVIEW **Understand Contradictions** Have students define *contradiction* using a dictionary. Explain that Thurber shifts between Walter Mitty's real life and his fantasy world to emphasize the contradictions between two. Have students find the first interruption between Walter's real world and his fantasy world. *(See top of page 189 where Mrs. Mitty tells Walter he's driving too fast.)* Tell students that as they read, think about how the two worlds in the story contradict each other.

Write "Real World" and "Dream World" on the board. Have students suggest ways in which the two worlds are different. Once several differences are written on the board, ask students why they think Mitty's fantasies are so extreme. *(Students may indicate that in his dreams Mitty can do whatever he wants.)* Point out that the exciting dream world makes the real world seem especially dull.

through," they said to one another. "The Old Man ain't afraid of Hell!" . . .

"Not so fast! You're driving too fast!" said Mrs. Mitty. "What are you driving so fast for?"

"Hmm?" said Walter Mitty. He looked at his wife, in the seat beside him, with shocked astonishment. She seemed grossly unfamiliar, like a strange woman who had yelled at him in a crowd. "You were up to fifty-five," she said. "You know I don't like to go more than forty. You were up to fifty-five." Walter Mitty drove on toward Waterbury in silence, the roaring of the SN202 through the worst storm in twenty years of Navy flying fading in the remote, intimate airways of his mind. "You're tensed up again," said Mrs. Mitty. "It's one of your days. I wish you'd let Dr. Renshaw look you over."

Walter Mitty stopped the car in front of the building where his wife went to have her hair done. "Remember to get those overshoes while I'm having my hair done," she said. "I don't need overshoes," said Mitty. She put her mirror back into her bag. "We've been all through that," she said, getting out of the car. "You're not a young man any longer." He raced the engine a little. "Why don't you wear your gloves? Have you lost your gloves?" Walter Mitty reached in a pocket and brought out the gloves. He put them on, but after she had turned and gone into the building and he had driven on to a red light, he took them off again. "Pick it up, brother!" snapped a cop as the light changed, and Mitty hastily pulled on his gloves and lurched ahead. He drove around the streets aimlessly for a time, and then he drove past the hospital on his way to the parking lot.

. . . "It's the millionaire banker, Wellington McMillan," said the pretty nurse. "Yes?" said Walter Mitty, removing his gloves slowly. "Who has the case?" "Dr. Renshaw and Dr. Benbow, but there are two specialists here, Dr. Remington from New York and Mr. Pritchard-Mitford from London. He flew over." A door opened down a long, cool corridor and Dr. Renshaw came out. He looked **distraught** and **haggard.** "Hello, Mitty," he said. "We're having the devil's own time with McMillan, the millionaire banker and close personal friend of Roosevelt. Obstreosis of the ductal tract. Tertiary. Wish you'd take a look at him." "Glad to," said Mitty.

In the operating room there were whispered introductions: "Dr. Remington, Dr. Mitty. Mr. Pritchard-Mitford, Dr. Mitty." "I've read your book on streptothricosis," said Pritchard-Mitford, shaking hands. "A brilliant performance, sir." "Thank you," said Walter Mitty. "Didn't know you were in the States, Mitty," grumbled Remington. "Coals to Newcastle,[3] bringing Mitford and me up here for a tertiary." "You are very kind," said Mitty. A huge, complicated machine, connected to the operating table, with many tubes and wires, began at this moment to go pocketa-pocketa-pocketa. "The new anesthetizer is giving way!" shouted an intern. "There is no one in the East who knows how to fix it!" "Quiet, man!" said Mitty, in a low, cool voice. He sprang to the machine, which was now going pocketa-pocketa-queep-

3. Carrying *coals to Newcastle* would be a waste of time and energy, since Newcastle, England, is a coal-mining town.

3 Diction *How does Thurber's word choice here help convey Mitty's character?*

Dreams and Reality *How does Thurber tie this daydream to what Mitty is experiencing in real life?* **4**

Vocabulary

distraught (dis trôt′) *adj.* very upset; confused

haggard (hag′ ərd) *adj.* having a worn and tired look

Teach

Literary Element 3

Diction Answer: *"Hastily pulled on his gloves" suggests meek obedience. "Lurched ahead" suggests he is an incompetent driver.*

ENGLISH LEARNERS To aid English learners, have a student define *hastily* and *lurched.* Ask students to use these words in a sentence.

Big Idea 4

Dreams and Reality

Answer: *This daydream is taking place in a hospital and Mitty is a doctor. In real life, Mitty has just driven past a hospital, and earlier his wife said he should see a doctor. In the daydream, Mitty removes his gloves slowly. In real life, he pulls on his gloves hastily.*

English Learners

DIFFERENTIATED INSTRUCTION

Beginning/Early Intermediate
To practice **reading fluency** ask a volunteer to read the passages where ellipses occur on these two pages. Explain that ellipses often indicate an unfinished thought or speech that trails off. **Ask:** What is the purpose of the ellipses in this part of the story? *(The ellipses introduce a transition between Witty's fantasy world and his reality.)*

Approaching Level

DIFFERENTIATED INSTRUCTION

Emerging Point out that students should pay attention to how characters treat one another. Readers can learn about a character by observing how he or she is treated by other characters. Write "Wife" on one side of the board and "Doctors" on the other. Have students list words that describe how the wife and doctors treat Mitty.

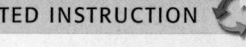

Teach

Reading Strategy 1

Visualize Answer: *The details "vaulted into the car" and "insolent skill" help create an image of a cocky young man whose skillful driving is intuitive. In contrast, Mitty drives in the wrong lane and is extremely cautious.*

For additional practice using the reading skill or strategy, see Unit 1 Teaching Resources Book, p. 203.

Writer's Technique ☆

Characterization Thurber gives readers a glimpse into Mitty's thought process about a real event and gives them a chance to draw a conclusion about what Mitty thinks of his true abilities.

pocketa-queep. He began fingering delicately a row of glistening dials. "Give me a fountain pen!"[4] he snapped. Someone handed him a fountain pen. He pulled a faulty piston out of the machine and inserted the pen in its place. "That will hold for ten minutes," he said. "Get on with the operation." A nurse hurried over and whispered to Renshaw, and Mitty saw the man turn pale. "Coreopsis[5] has set in," said Renshaw nervously. "If you would take over, Mitty?" Mitty looked at him and at the **craven** figure of Benbow, who drank, and at the grave, uncertain faces of the two great specialists. "If you wish," he said. They slipped a white gown on him; he adjusted a mask and drew on thin gloves; nurses handed him shining . . . .

"Back it up, Mac! Look out for that Buick!" Walter Mitty jammed on the brakes. "Wrong lane, Mac," said the parking-lot attendant, looking at Mitty closely. "Gee. Yeh," muttered Mitty. He began cautiously to back out of the lane marked "Exit Only." "Leave her sit there," said the attendant. "I'll put her away." Mitty got out of the car. "Hey, better leave the key." "Oh," said Mitty, handing the man the ignition key. The attendant vaulted into the car, backed it up with insolent[6] skill, and put it where it belonged.

They're so damn cocky, thought Walter Mitty, walking along Main Street; they think they know everything. Once he had tried to take his chains[7] off, outside New Milford, and he had got them wound around the axles. A man had had to come out in a wrecking car and unwind them, a young, grinning garageman. Since then Mrs. Mitty always made him drive to a garage to have the chains taken off. The next time, he thought, I'll wear my right arm in a sling; they won't grin at me then. ☆ I'll have my right arm in a sling and they'll see I couldn't possibly take the chains off myself. He kicked at the slush on the sidewalk. "Overshoes," he said to himself, and he began looking for a shoe store.

When he came out into the street again, with the overshoes in a box under his arm, Walter Mitty began to wonder what the other thing was his wife had told him to get. She had told him, twice, before they set out from their house for Waterbury. In a way he hated these weekly trips to town—he was always getting something wrong. Kleenex, he thought, Squibb's, razor blades? No. Toothpaste, toothbrush, bicarbonate, carborundum, initiative and referendum?[8] He gave it up. But she would remember it. "Where's the what's-its-name?" she would ask. "Don't tell me you forgot the what's-its-name." A newsboy went by shouting something about the Waterbury trial.

. . . "Perhaps this will refresh your memory." The District Attorney suddenly thrust a heavy automatic at the quiet figure on the witness stand. "Have you ever seen this before?" Walter Mitty took the gun

4. A *fountain pen* has a reservoir or replaceable cartridge that automatically feeds a steady supply of ink to the nib, or pen point.
5. If *coreopsis* really has set in, the patient may need a gardener. This is the name of a daisy-like flowering plant.
6. *Insolent* means "so rude or proud as to be offensive."

1 Visualize *What details help you visualize the attendant? How does this image contrast with the image you formed of Mitty trying to park?*

Vocabulary

craven (krā′ vən) *adj.* extremely cowardly

7. In some areas, people put *chains* on tires to provide better traction on ice and snow.
8. Mitty's shopping list is partially nonsense: *Carborundum* is the brand name of an industrial compound used to grind and polish, an *initiative* is a procedure enabling voters to propose new laws, and a *referendum* is a direct popular vote on a public issue.

Writing Practice

SPIRAL REVIEW **Essay Question** Ask students what they have learned about Walter Mitty by reading the story. Write their answers on the board. Once a sufficient description of Walter is on the board, have students write an answer to the following essay question: Why does Walter Mitty daydream? Before they begin to write, explain that they should support their ideas with at least three specific details from the story. After allowing students fifteen minutes to write, ask them to share their writings with the class.

and examined it expertly. "This is my Webley-Vickers 50.80," he said calmly.

An excited buzz ran around the courtroom. The Judge rapped for order. "You are a crack shot with any sort of firearms, I believe?" said the District Attorney, insinuatingly.[9] "Objection!" shouted Mitty's attorney. "We have shown that the defendant could not have fired the shot. We have shown that he wore his right arm in a sling on the night of the fourteenth of July." Walter Mitty raised his hand briefly and the bickering attorneys were stilled. "With any known make of gun," he said evenly, "I could have killed Gregory Fitzhurst at three hundred feet *with my left hand*." **Pandemonium** broke loose in the courtroom. A woman's scream rose above the bedlam and suddenly a lovely, dark-haired girl was in Walter Mitty's arms. The District Attorney struck at her savagely. Without rising from his chair, Mitty let the man have it on the point of the chin. "You miserable cur!" . . .[10]

"Puppy biscuit," said Walter Mitty. He stopped walking and the buildings of Waterbury rose up out of the misty courtroom and surrounded him again. A woman who was passing laughed. "He said 'Puppy biscuit,'" she said to her companion. "That man said 'Puppy biscuit' to himself." Walter Mitty hurried on. He went into an A. & P.,[11]

Hotel Lobby, 1943. Edward Hopper. Oil on canvas, 82 x 103.5 cm. Indianapolis Museum of Art, IN.

View the Art Edward Hopper's works often suggest that the figures depicted are alone, even if they are surrounded by others. Do the figures in this painting seem to be alone? Is this painting appropriate for the story? Explain. ★

not the first one he came to but a smaller one farther up the street. "I want some biscuit for small, young dogs," he said to the clerk. "Any special brand, sir?" The greatest pistol shot in the world thought a moment. "It says 'Puppies Bark for It' on the box," said Walter Mitty.

His wife would be through at the hairdresser's in fifteen minutes, Mitty saw in looking at his watch, unless they had trouble drying it; sometimes they had trouble drying it. She didn't like to get to the hotel first; she would want him to be there waiting for her as usual. He found a big leather chair in the lobby, facing a window, and he put the overshoes and the puppy biscuit on the floor beside it. He picked up an old copy of *Liberty* and sank down into the chair. "Can Germany Conquer the World Through the Air?" Walter Mitty looked at the pictures of bombing planes and of ruined streets.

. . . "The cannonading has got the wind up in young Raleigh, sir," said the ser-

9. Here *insinuatingly* (in sin′ ū āt′ ing lē) means "in a way to suggest guilt."
10. A *cur* can be either a mean, rude person or a mixed-breed dog.
11. *A. & P.*, short for Atlantic & Pacific Tea Company, is a chain of grocery stores.

2 Diction *Why does Thurber include this reference to something that does not really exist?*

3 Visualize *What details help you visualize this scene?*

Vocabulary

pandemonium (pan′ də mō′ nē əm) *n.* wild uproar

Dreams and Reality *What triggers this daydream for Mitty?* **4**

Teach

Literary Element 2

Diction **Answer:** *It creates a false sense of authenticity in Mitty's daydream.*

Reading Strategy 3

Visualize **Answer:** *Details include repetition of the phrase "Puppy biscuit," the references to Waterbury and the A & P, and the mocking woman.*

ADVANCED For advanced learners, **say:** Thurber contrasts the melodramatic courtroom scene with the quietly mundane "puppy biscuit" episode to hilarious effect. What are some contrasting details that emphasize the difference between Mitty's two lives? *(Authority, action, passion, "raised his hand briefly," "crack shot," "pandemonium," and girl in his arms versus the mildness of puppies, his absent-minded dealings with the A & P clerk, and the mocking woman.)*

Big Idea 4

Dreams and Reality
Answer: *Mitty was looking at pictures of bombing planes and ruined streets in the magazine* Liberty.

Approaching Level

DIFFERENTIATED INSTRUCTION

Established Have students read the final paragraph on page 191. Ask students what Walter Mitty's actions and thoughts say about him. **Ask:** Does Walter bring the way others treat him on himself? How could he change his own behavior to make people treat him more like they do in his daydreams? *(Answers will vary.)*

Emerging Have one student read the interaction between the women walking down the street and Walter. **Ask:** What can you infer about Walter from this exchange? *(Walter's lack of response shows his inability to confront people in the real world.)*

View the Art ★

Answer: *Students should explain their responses using details from the story and the painting.* American realist painter Edward Hopper (1882–1967) is known for his often stark scenes of everyday twentieth-century American life.

Teach

Reading Strategy 1

Visualize **Ask:** *What sounds help you create a vivid picture of this scene in your mind? (Sounds include the cannon's pounding, machine guns' rat-tat-tatting, flame-throwers' pocketa-pocketa-pocketa, and Mitty's humming.)*

Literary Element 2

Diction **Answer:** *Even the revolving door appears to be ridiculing Mitty.*

To check students' understanding of the selection, see Unit 1 Teaching Resources Book, p. 207.

geant. Captain Mitty looked up at him through tousled hair. "Get him to bed," he said wearily. "With the others. I'll fly alone." "But you can't, sir," said the sergeant anxiously. "It takes two men to handle that bomber and the Archies are pounding hell out of the air. Von Richtman's circus is between here and Saulier."[12] "Somebody's got to get that ammunition dump," said Mitty. "I'm going over. Spot of brandy?" He poured a drink for the sergeant and one for himself. War thundered and whined around the dugout and battered at the door. There was a rending of wood and splinters flew through the room. "A bit of a near thing," said Captain Mitty carelessly. "The box barrage[13] is closing in," said the sergeant. "We only live once, Sergeant," said Mitty, with his faint, fleeting smile. "Or do we?" He poured another brandy and tossed it off. "I never see a man could hold his brandy like you, sir," said the sergeant. "Begging your pardon, sir." Captain Mitty stood up and strapped on his huge Webley-Vickers automatic. "It's forty kilometers through hell, sir," said the sergeant. Mitty finished one last brandy. "After all," he said softly, "what isn't?" **1** The pounding of the cannon increased; there was the rat-tat-tatting of machine guns, and from somewhere came the menacing pocketa-pocketa-pocketa of the new flame-throwers. Walter Mitty walked to the door of the dugout humming "Auprès de Ma Blonde."[14] He turned and waved to the sergeant. "Cheerio!" he said . . .

Something struck his shoulder. "I've been looking all over this hotel for you," said Mrs. Mitty. "Why do you have to hide in this old chair? How did you expect me to find you?" "Things close in," said Walter Mitty vaguely. "What?" Mrs. Mitty said. "Did you get the what's-its-name? The puppy biscuit? What's in that box?" "Overshoes," said Mitty. "Couldn't you have put them on in the store?" "I was thinking," said Walter Mitty. "Does it ever occur to you that I am sometimes thinking?" She looked at him. "I'm going to take your temperature when I get you home," she said.

They went out through the revolving doors that made a faintly derisive[15] whistling sound when you pushed them. It was two blocks to the parking lot. At the drugstore on the corner she said, "Wait here for me. I forgot something. I won't be a minute." She was more than a minute. Walter Mitty lighted a cigarette. It began to rain, rain with sleet in it. He stood up against the wall of the drugstore, smoking. . . . He put his shoulders back and his heels together. "To hell with the handkerchief," said Walter Mitty scornfully. He took one last drag on his cigarette and snapped it away. Then, with that faint, fleeting smile playing about his lips, he faced the firing squad; erect and motionless, proud and **disdainful**, Walter Mitty the Undefeated, inscrutable[16] to the last.

12. Mitty blends fantasy with the realities of World War I. *Archies* was the British name for anti-aircraft guns and their shells. *Von Richtman* suggests Manfred von Richthofen, the German flying ace known as the Red Baron. *Saulier* appears to be a made-up name for a town in France.
13. *Box barrage* refers to artillery fire used to hold back the enemy or to protect one's own soldiers.
14. *"Auprès de Ma Blonde"* (ō prā də mä blōnd) is a French song ("Near My Blonde") that was popular during World War I.
15. *Derisive* (di rī′ siv) means mocking, jeering, or ridiculing.
16. *Inscrutable* (in skro͞o′ tə bəl) means "mysterious."

Diction *Why do you think Thurber describes the sound of the door as "derisive"?* **2**

Vocabulary

disdainful (dis dān′ fəl) *adj.* showing scorn for something or someone regarded as unworthy

Reading Practice

SPIRAL REVIEW **Understand Voice** Remind students that stories are told in first-, second-, and third-person point of view. Authors must decide the best way to tell a story. **Ask:** Why did Thurber most likely choose to tell this story in the third person? *(Students may answer that third person narration can easily move back and forth through time and can reveal details about Mitty that the he may not be able to reveal about himself.)*

Have students retell the scene in the parking lot using the first person point of view. Have students explain whether they think the first-person narrator is most effective. *(Students should support their answers with examples.)*

After You Read

Respond and Think Critically

Respond and Interpret

1. Did you identify with Walter Mitty as you read this story? Explain.
2. (a)What roles does Mitty play in his different daydreams? (b)What is ironic, or contradictory, about the way in which Mitty sees himself in his daydreams?
3. (a)Which of Mitty's traits causes his wife, the police officer, and the parking attendant to scold him? (b)Why do they treat him this way?
4. (a)How does Mitty's wife greet him at the hotel? (b)What does Mitty's conversation with his wife at the hotel tell you about their relationship?

Analyze and Evaluate

5. (a)What is the main conflict in the story? (b)Is the conflict resolved in a way that is satisfying to you? Why or why not?
6. (a)How does Thurber tie the beginning of the story to the ending? (b)Why do you think he does this?

Connect

7. **Big Idea** **Dreams and Reality** What is missing in Walter Mitty's real life that he tries to fulfill in his daydreams?
8. **Connect to Today** This story was first published in 1939. Is it still relevant in today's world? Is it still funny? Explain.

Literary Element Diction

Diction allows writers to establish setting, convey meaning, and create different tones, moods, and images. For example, in "The Secret Life of Walter Mitty," Thurber deliberately misuses real words. This helps establish a humorous tone and, at the same time, reveals Mitty's daydreams as preposterous.

1. Reread the last line of the story. How do the adjectives used to describe Mitty compare with the way he really is?
2. Give examples of language Mitty uses to speak to others in his daydreams and language he uses to speak to his wife. What do these examples reveal about his character?
3. Besides the deliberate misuse of words, how does Thurber's diction contribute to the humorous tone of the story and help characterize Mitty as absurd and inept?

Review: Narrator

As you learned on pages 184–185, the **narrator** is the person who tells a story. An unreliable narrator presents an untrustworthy account of people and events. The narrator of "The Secret Life of Walter Mitty" shifts between the real world and Mitty's dream world. Does this shifting make the narrator unreliable?

Partner Activity Meet with a classmate and discuss how the story's narrator could be perceived as unreliable. Working with your partner, create a web diagram like the one below. Then fill it in with evidence that proves (or disproves) that the narrator is unreliable.

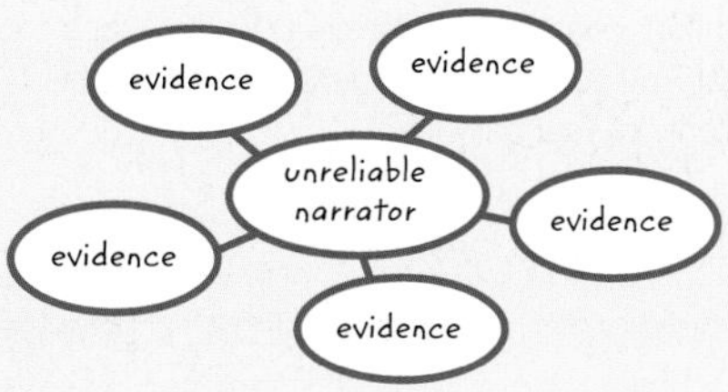

Literary Element

1. The real Mitty is a chronically defeated sad sack.
2. Daydreams: "I'm not asking you," and "Quiet, man!" Wife: "Hmm?" and "Things close in." They show his divided character—the gap between his true self and what he would like to be.
3. Students may point to the Puppy biscuit incident and to Mitty's invention of a disease.

Progress Check

Can students analyze diction?

If No → See Unit 1 Teaching Resources Book, p. 202.

After You Read

Assess

1. Answers will vary.
2. (a) A Navy flight commander, a surgeon, a wrongly accused defendant and crack shot, a World War I captain, and a man facing a firing squad (b) He is fearless and admired, the exact opposite of how he is viewed in real life.
3. (a) Inattentiveness (b) He never stands up for himself.
4. (a) She accuses him of being hard to find. (b) There is no real closeness or communication in their marriage.
5. (a) The conflict between his real life and his fantasy life (b) Accept any reasonable answer.
6. (a) It begins and ends in fantasy. (b) To show that Walter will cling to his fantasies to the end
7. Respect, excitement, power, admiration, and self-worth
8. Students should point to specific details in the selection as well as specific details in today's world to support their answers.

Review: Narrator

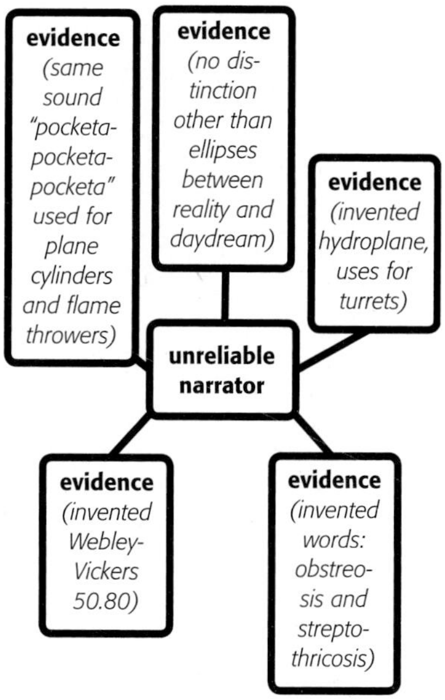

After You Read

Assess

Reading Strategy

1. Images of Mitty as authoritative and admired (he silences the lawyers, "crack shot" girl's embrace) and wildly dramatic events (pandemonium, bedlam) are offset by opposing images of mildness, dullness, and mockery (puppies, A & P, laughing woman).
2. Accept answers that are well supported by sensory details.

Vocabulary

1. c **2.** e **3.** a **4.** g **5.** f

Speaking and Listening

Student's oral presentations should

- present a dramatic oral version of two scenes from the story
- provide an engaging, well-paced, and easily understood reading of the scenes
- clearly and creatively indicate the transition between reality and daydreams
- conclude with a discussion of the story and presentation

Reading Strategy Visualize

By **visualizing** as you read, you can better understand what is happening and why. Review the sensory chart you created for visualizing important characters and events in the story.

1. Point out details that allow you to visualize the courtroom scene and the "puppy biscuit" scene. How does Thurber use these details to create parallels between the two scenes?
2. What scene in the story is most memorable to you? What specific details help you visualize this scene?

Vocabulary Practice

Practice with Synonyms A **synonym** is a word that has the same or nearly the same meaning as another word. Match each boldfaced vocabulary word below with its synonym. Use a thesaurus or dictionary to check your answers. You will not use all the answer choices.

1. distraught	**a.** spineless
2. haggard	**b.** boredom
3. craven	**c.** agitated
4. pandemonium	**d.** terrified
5. disdainful	**e.** exhausted
	f. haughty
	g. mayhem

Academic Vocabulary

Fantasies and daydreams **constitute** *much of Walter Mitty's daily experience.*

Constitute is an academic word that refers to the make-up of something. For example, if a recipe is mostly eggs and flour, you could say that eggs and flour **constitute** the majority of the recipe. What "ingredients" or elements **constitute** the majority of your daily life?

For more on academic vocabulary, see pages 54–55 and R79–R81.

Speaking and Listening

Oral Interpretation

Assignment With a small group, organize and present an oral interpretation of two scenes from "The Secret Life of Walter Mitty" to illustrate the transitions between Mitty's real and secret lives.

Prepare Choose two scenes from the story and review them, discussing any confusing areas. Select a director and a person to create sound effects. Assign actors to be the characters. Some actors may need to play more than one character.

Discuss the transitions between Mitty's two lives. On a timeline, plot the real-life action of the story on top, and note the small dramas that occur in the daydreams on the bottom.

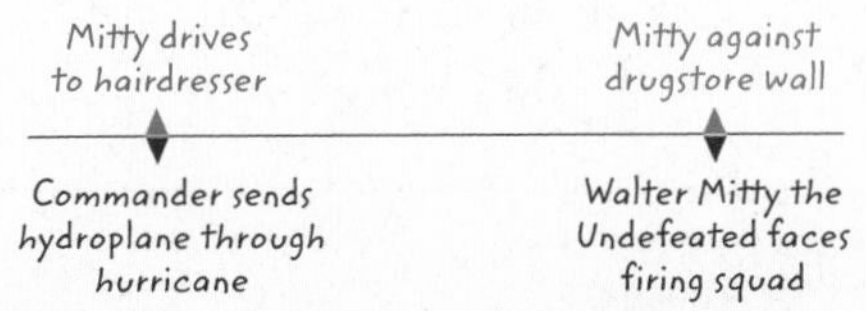
Mitty drives to hairdresser
Mitty against drugstore wall
Commander sends hydroplane through hurricane
Walter Mitty the Undefeated faces firing squad

Discuss the way the action rises and falls around transitions in your scenes. Discuss what story elements are implied in the dialogue and how you can make the events clear in your dramatization. Jot down notes to explain the transitions to the audience after the performance. Rehearse the story until you can all perform it smoothly, focusing on volume, pacing, eye contact, and gestures.

Perform Present your dramatic reading to the class. Pause for audience laughter and read slowly and clearly. After the reading, talk about how the story moves between the daydreams and Mitty's real life. Explain how your group clarified the transitions.

Evaluate Discuss your performance with group members. Write a few paragraphs about the experience, noting areas that could be improved.

LOG ON **Literature** Online

Selection Resources For Selection Quizzes, eFlashcards, and Reading-Writing Connection activities, go to glencoe.com **and enter QuickPass code GL49787u1.**

For additional selection assessment, see Assessment Resources, pp. 67–68.

To create custom assessments online, go to Progress Reporter Online Assessment.

To create custom assessments using software, use ExamView Assessment Suite.

Grammar Workshop

Run-on Sentences

Learning Objectives

In this workshop, you will focus on the following objective:

Grammar: Understanding how to avoid run-on sentences.

Connecting to Literature James Thurber presents connected ideas in a **compound sentence**—a sentence with two or more main clauses.

> *"He drove around the streets aimlessly for a time, and then he drove past the hospital on his way to the parking lot."*
>
> —James Thurber, from "The Secret Life of Walter Mitty"

Sometimes, however, writers fail to punctuate two or more main clauses correctly. This creates a **run-on sentence,** two or more complete sentences written incorrectly as a single sentence.

Note the following run-on sentence problems and their solutions.

Problem 1 Two main clauses are separated with only a comma.

The doctor introduced himself, Mitty shook hands with him.

Problem 2 Two main clauses appear with no punctuation between them.

The machine doesn't operate correctly Mitty repairs it.

Solution A Rewrite the sentence as two short sentences.

The doctor introduced himself. Mitty shook hands with him.
The machine doesn't operate correctly. Mitty repairs it.

Solution B Insert a coordinating conjunction preceded by a comma.

The doctor introduced himself, and Mitty shook hands with him.
The machine doesn't operate correctly, so Mitty repairs it.

Solution C Insert a semicolon between principal clauses.

The doctor introduced himself; Mitty shook hands with him.
The machine doesn't operate correctly; Mitty repairs it.

Run-on Sentences

A **run-on sentence** is two or more complete sentences written incorrectly as a single sentence.

Tip

Sometimes you will see a compound sentence that has a coordinating conjunction, but no punctuation, between independent clauses. To correct this error, simply insert a comma after the first clause. If the clauses are closely connected, you may insert a semicolon and delete the conjunction instead.

Language Handbook

For more about run-on sentences, see Language Handbook, pp. R47–R48.

Revise Rewrite these sentences, applying one of the solutions shown above.

1. Mitty is ordinary, he imagines himself as extraordinary.
2. Mitty is running errands he is daydreaming at the same time.
3. Mitty's wife tells him what to do but she doesn't control his inner life.

LOG ON **Literature Online**

Grammar For more grammar practice, go to glencoe.com and enter QuickPass code GL49787u1.

Writing Practice

Avoid Run-On Sentences Have students read paragraphs from the selection, noting compound and complex sentences. Copy three examples onto the board and discuss the logic used in joining these clauses. Have students write a narrative paragraph in which Mitty daydreams. Students should use the solutions suggested above to avoid run-on sentences. Finally, have students read their own paragraphs aloud, using punctuation to cue appropriate pauses.

Grammar Workshop

Run-on Sentences

Focus

Write this sentence on the board: "Pick it up, brother!" snapped a cop as the light changed, and Mitty hastily pulled on his gloves and lurched ahead.

Discuss what makes this sentence compound and not a run-on.

Teach

Compound Subjects and Verbs Explain the difference between a compound sentence and compound subjects or verbs. Emphasize that a compound sentence is made up of two simple sentences, each of which has a subject and a verb. Note that compound subjects or verbs are not separated by a comma.

Assess

1. Mitty is ordinary, but he imagines himself as extraordinary.
2. Mitty is running errands; he is daydreaming at the same time.
3. Mitty's wife tells him what to do, but she doesn't control his inner life.

For additional grammar practice, see Unit 1 Teaching Resources Book, p. 209.

Before You Read

Focus

Bellringer Options

Selection Focus Transparency 13

Daily Language Practice Transparency 18

Or **ask:** What are some items that people will go into debt to buy? *(Cars, houses, furniture, entertainment systems)* **Ask:** Why do people buy things that will cause them to go into debt? *(Financing a basic need such as a home or car is easier than buying outright. People who charge costly luxury items usually want instant gratification.)* Ask students to think about the emotional, as well as the economic, costs of debts as they read.

Before You Read

World Literature
France

The Necklace

Meet **Guy de Maupassant**
(1850–1893)

Guy de Maupassant ranks with the world's greatest short story writers. Though he was the child of wealthy parents, he grew up among the children of peasants and sailors who lived near his mother's estates in northwestern France. Their hard-working lives and colorful customs captured the young Maupassant's imagination. When he went away to school, Maupassant spent occasional Sundays with the great French novelist Gustave Flaubert, his mother's childhood friend. Flaubert encouraged the young Maupassant's literary efforts and suggested that he experiment with poetry in order to practice clarity and concision.

> *"She had been born for all the little niceties and luxuries of living."*
>
> —Guy de Maupassant, from "The Necklace"

From War to Writing The young Maupassant served in the Franco-Prussian War from late 1869 to July of 1871, an experience which gave him a strong distaste for war. Upon returning home, he became a government clerk, devoting his free time to writing. Flaubert helped Maupassant to join the flourishing Parisian literary scene, introducing Maupassant to such important writers as Émile Zola, Ivan Turgenev, and Henry James. At the age of thirty, Maupassant published his own work in a volume of stories by up-and-coming authors. Flaubert declared the story a masterpiece. Maupassant became famous and successful.

Putting the working world behind him, Maupassant began to live extravagantly. He built himself a villa, purchased a boat, and traveled around Europe. Eventually his extravagances forced him into debt. To keep up with expenses, he began writing at a frenetic pace. Between 1880 and 1890, he authored three hundred short stories, six novels, three travel books, and his only volume of verse.

Life's Catastrophes Maupassant's own life experiences were reflected in his work. He wrote of peasants, soldiers, and ordinary people caught in disastrous or demeaning situations. Maupassant described his subject as life's "inexplicable, illogical, and contradictory catastrophes" and said writing should aim not at "telling a story or entertaining us or touching our hearts but at forcing us to think and understand the deeper, hidden meaning of events."

LOG ON **Literature** Online

Author Search For more about Guy de Maupassant, go to glencoe.com and enter QuickPass code GL49787u1.

Selection Skills

The Necklace

Literary Elements
- Point of View (SE pp. 197–206)

Reading Skills
- Analyze Cause-and-Effect Relationships (SE pp. 197–206)

Vocabulary Skills
- Word Usage (SE p. 197)

Listening/Speaking/Viewing Skills
- Analyze Art (SE pp. 201, 203)

Writing Skills/Grammar
- Write a Short Story (SE p. 207)
- Write a Monologue (TE p. 202)

Literature and Reading Preview

Connect to the Story

How important is it to be proper and respectable? Discuss this question with a partner and consider what it means.

Build Background

In Paris in the 1800s, a class structure defined society. At the top of the social ladder were the wealthy aristocrats. Next was a middle class, who lived in modest homes and could afford a few servants. Even if money was tight, custom forbade middle-class women from working. Below this class was a huge number of farmers and servants, who worked for the rich.

Set Purposes for Reading

Big Idea Dreams and Reality

As you read, ask yourself, How can the reality of a character's situation be hidden behind a different outer appearance?

Literary Element Point of View

Point of view refers to the relationship of the narrator to the story. In a story with *third-person limited* point of view, the narrator reveals the thoughts and observations of only one character, referring to that character as "he" or "she." The narrator in *third-person omniscient* point of view also refers to characters as "he" or "she." However, the omniscient, or all-knowing, narrator knows everything about the characters and may reveal details that they could not reveal themselves. As you read, ask yourself, What does the narrator reveal about each character?

Reading Strategy Analyze Cause-and-Effect Relationships

A **cause-and-effect relationship** is made up of an event, or cause, and the result of the event, or the effect. When you analyze cause and effect, you look closely at the reasons events happen. As you read, ask yourself, What caused this event? What other effects and causes did the event lead to?

Tip: Make a Cause-and-Effect Chain As you read, keep track of relationships between events by making a chain.

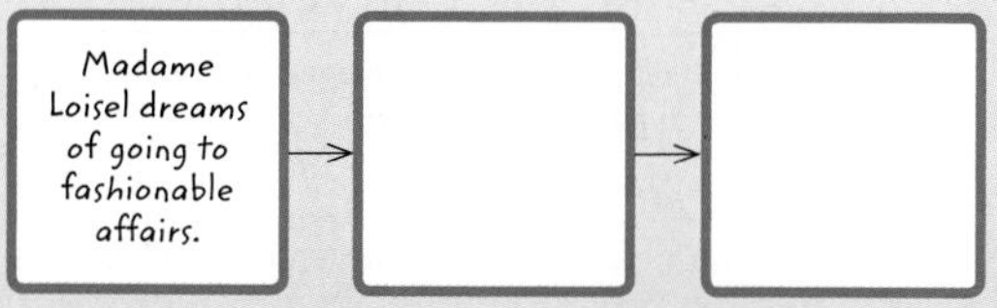

Madame Loisel dreams of going to fashionable affairs.

Learning Objectives

For pages 196–206

In studying this text, you will focus on the following objectives:

Literary Study: Analyzing third-person point of view.

Reading: Analyzing cause-and-effect relationships.

Vocabulary

incessantly (in ses′ ənt lē) *adv.* endlessly; constantly; p. 198 *The crickets would not stop chirping; they called out incessantly.*

disconsolate (dis kon′ sə lit) *adj.* so unhappy that nothing can comfort; hopeless and depressed; p. 199 *The fans were disconsolate when their team lost the game.*

aghast (ə gast′) *adj.* filled with fear, horror, or amazement; p. 202 *She was aghast at the possibility of failing the class.*

gamut (gam′ ət) *n.* the entire range or series of something; p. 203 *You can buy food dye in a gamut of colors, from black to red to white.*

privation (prī vā′ shən) *n.* the lack of comforts or basic necessities; p. 203 *Their growing debts led to a life of privation.*

Tip: Word Usage When you encounter new words, it might help you to answer a specific question about a word. For example, When would I feel **aghast** about something?

Before You Read

Focus

Summary

When Mathilde Loisel, a clerk's wife who dreams of wealth and glamour, is invited to a ball, she borrows a diamond necklace from a rich friend. Her social triumph turns into a disaster when she loses the necklace. The Loisels keep the loss a secret and borrow heavily to buy an identical piece. After ten years of toil and misery, they learn the borrowed jewels were fake.

For summaries in languages other than English, see Unit 1 Teaching Resources Book, pp. 210–215.

Vocabulary

Picture Words Explain that one way to remember the meaning of words is to associate a picture with the word. Have each student choose a vocabulary word, use the word in a sentence, and then draw a picture of what is happening in the sentence. Ask for volunteers to show their pictures to the class.

For additional vocabulary practice, see Unit 1 Teaching Resources Book, p. 218.

For additional context, see Glencoe Interactive Vocabulary CD-ROM.

Approaching Level

DIFFERENTIATED INSTRUCTION

Emerging Help students better understand the Reading Strategy on this page by pointing out the cause and the effect in each of these examples.

- The grass in our yard is very green *(effect)* because it rained often this summer *(cause).*
- Emily spent many hours studying for her history test *(cause)* and answered most of the questions correctly *(effect)*.
- My alarm clock did not go off this morning *(cause),* and I missed my bus *(effect).*

Have students write three sentences of their own that show cause-and-effect relationships. Students should use correct grammar and sentence structure.

Teach

Big Idea 1

Dreams and Reality **Ask:** Why do some people pretend to be richer or more important than they really are? *(They are ashamed of or disappointed in their status in life.)*

APPROACHING For approaching-level students **ask:** Why is accepting the reality of their lives so hard for such people? *(They are obsessed with appearances, desire admiration or attention, or lack self-worth.)*

Cultural History ☆

Brittany Brittany is located on the northwestern coast of France. Originally settled by the Celts, Brittany became part of France in 1532. Many of its natives can still speak the Celtic language Breton. Brittany is famous for its many historic sites and Neolithic monuments.

For an audio recording of this selection, use Listening Library Audio CD-ROM.

Readability Scores

Dale-Chall: 6.9
DRP: 61
Lexile: 950

The Toilette. Charles Robert Leslie. Oil on panel, 12 x 10 in. Victoria and Albert Museum, London.

The Necklace

Guy de Maupassant

She was one of those pretty and charming girls, born, as if by an accident of fate, into a family of clerks. With no dowry,[1] no prospects, no way of any kind of being met, understood, loved, and married by a man both prosperous and famous, she was finally married to a minor clerk in the Ministry of Education.

She dressed plainly because she could not afford fine clothes, but was as unhappy as a woman who has come down in the
1 world; for women have no family rank or social class. With them, beauty, grace, and charm take the place of birth and breeding. Their natural poise, their instinctive good taste, and their mental cleverness are the sole guiding principles which make daughters of the common people the equals of 1
ladies in high society.

She grieved **incessantly**, feeling that she had been born for all the little niceties and luxuries of living. She grieved over the shabbiness of her apartment, the dinginess of the walls, the worn-out appearance of the chairs, the ugliness of the draperies. All these things, which another woman of her class would not even have noticed, gnawed at her and made her furious. The sight of the little Breton[2] girl who did her humble ☆

1. A *dowry* is money or property that a woman brings to her husband at the start of a marriage.

2. *Breton* (bret′ ən) refers to someone or something from the French province of Brittany.

Vocabulary

incessantly (in ses′ ənt lē) *adv.* endlessly; constantly

Reading Practice

SMALL GROUP SPIRAL REVIEW **Understand Character Traits** In small groups, have students read the first three paragraphs of the story. Then ask the groups to discuss the woman described in these paragraphs. Students should address the following questions: What kind of person does the woman seem to be? How would you describe her? *(Students might say that she seems ungrateful, spoiled, greedy, or sad.)* Students should then identify areas of the text that characterize the woman. For example, if students say she seems greedy, they should find places in the text that support this idea. During this activity, students should take notes to share highlights of their discussion with the rest of the class.

housework roused in her **disconsolate** regrets and wild daydreams. She would dream of silent chambers, draped with Oriental tapestries and lighted by tall bronze floor lamps, and of two handsome butlers in knee breeches, who, drowsy from the heavy warmth cast by the central stove, dozed in large overstuffed armchairs.

She would dream of great reception halls hung with old silks, of fine furniture filled with priceless curios,[3] and of small, stylish, scented sitting rooms just right for the four o'clock chat with intimate friends, with distinguished and sought-after men whose attention every woman envies and longs to attract.

Visual Vocabulary
A *tureen* is a deep dish used for serving soup or other food at the table.

When dining at the round table covered for the third day with the same cloth, opposite her husband, who would raise the cover of the soup tureen, declaring delightedly, "Ah! a good stew! There's nothing I like better . . ." she would dream of fashionable dinner parties, of gleaming silverware, of tapestries making the walls alive with characters out of history and strange birds in a fairyland forest; she would dream of delicious dishes served on wonderful china, of gallant compliments whispered and listened to with a sphinxlike[4] smile as one eats the rosy flesh of a trout or nibbles at the wings of a grouse.

She had no evening clothes, no jewels, nothing. But those were the things she wanted; she felt that was the kind of life for her. She so much longed to please, be envied, be fascinating and sought after.

She had a well-to-do friend, a classmate of convent-school days whom she would no longer go to see, simply because she would feel so distressed on returning home. And she would weep for days on end from vexation,[5] regret, despair, and anguish.

Then one evening, her husband came home proudly holding out a large envelope.

"Look," he said, "I've got something for you."

She excitedly tore open the envelope and pulled out a printed card bearing these words:

"The Minister of Education and Mme. Georges Ramponneau beg M. and Mme. Loisel[6] to do them the honor of attending an evening reception at the Ministerial Mansion on Friday, January 18."

Instead of being delighted, as her husband had hoped, she scornfully tossed the invitation on the table, murmuring, "What good is that to me?"

"But, my dear, I thought you'd be thrilled to death. You never get a chance to go out, and this is a real affair, a wonderful one! I had an awful time getting a card. Everybody wants one: it's much sought after, and not many clerks have a chance at one. You'll see all the most important people there."

3. *Priceless curios* are rare or unusual ornamental objects that are very valuable.
4. *Sphinxlike* means "mysterious," referring to a creature in Greek mythology that killed anyone who could not answer its riddle.
5. Here, *vexation* means "distress."
6. *Georges Ramponneau* (ram pə nō´); *Loisel* (lwä zel´). The abbreviations *M.* and *Mme.* are the French versions of *Mr.* and *Mrs.* and stand for *Monsieur* (mə syœ´) and *Madame* (mə dam´).

2 Dreams and Reality *How does the husband's attitude toward the reality of his family's life differ from his wife's?*

Vocabulary

disconsolate (dis kon´ sə lit) *adj.* so unhappy that nothing can comfort; hopeless and depressed

Analyze Cause-and-Effect Relationships *Why does the husband go to great lengths to obtain the invitation? How does he expect his wife to react?* **3**

Teach

Big Idea 2

Dreams and Reality

Answer: *He is content with their circumstances; she despises them.*

Reading Strategy 3

Analyze Cause-and-Effect Relationships

Answer: *He knows she craves a glamorous lifestyle and wants to please her. He thought she would be thrilled.*

Ask: Why does Mathilde react to her husband's surprise with scorn and irritation? *(The invitation is not enough; she wants the lifestyle that the other guests have. Her plain dress will reveal her true station.)*

For additional practice using the reading skill or strategy, see Unit 1 Teaching Resources Book, p. 217.

Cultural History ☆

Sphinx According to myth, a Sphinx has the head of a woman and the body of a lion. Besides the Greek mythological Sphinx, there are famous statues of sphinxes in Egypt. The Great Sphinx of Giza, with the head of a pharaoh and the body of a lion, has become a national symbol of Egypt.

English Learners

DIFFERENTIATED INSTRUCTION

Intermediate Remind students that a pronoun is a word that takes the place of a specific noun often referred to as an antecedent. **Write:** David made a pie. He used fresh apples to make it. Point out that *He* is the pronoun for the antecedent *David* and *it* is the pronoun for the antecedent *pie.* Explain that in "The Necklace," the author's reliance on pronouns to identify the characters and other nouns may be confusing. Students can find the antecedent by asking simple questions, such as "Who or what is being talked about?"

Write: "I had an awful time getting a card. Everybody wants one . . ." Ask students to identify the antecedent and pronoun. *(Card is the antecedent. One is the pronoun.)*

Teach

Literary Element 1

Point of View **Answer:** *By revealing the husband's unspoken thoughts, the narrator enables readers to see how willing the husband is to sacrifice his own desires to please his wife.*

Big Idea 2

Dreams and Reality

Answer: *She must look as rich as the other guests.*

ENGLISH LEARNERS Ask English learners to think of synonyms for *humiliating.* Have volunteers share their answers with the class. *(embarrassing, shameful, degrading)*

She gave him an irritated glance and burst out impatiently, "What do you think I have to go in?"

He hadn't given that a thought. He stammered, "Why, the dress you wear when we go to the theater. That looks quite nice, I think."

He stopped talking, dazed and distracted to see his wife burst out weeping. Two large tears slowly rolled from the corners of her eyes to the corners of her mouth; he gasped, "Why, what's the matter? What's the trouble?"

By sheer will power she overcame her outburst and answered in a calm voice while wiping the tears from her wet cheeks:

"Oh, nothing. Only I don't have an evening dress and therefore I can't go to that affair. Give the card to some friend at the office whose wife can dress better than I can."

He was stunned. He resumed, "Let's see, Mathilde.[7] How much would a suitable outfit cost—one you could wear for other affairs too—something very simple?"

She thought it over for several seconds, going over her allowance and thinking also of the amount she could ask for without bringing an immediate refusal and an exclamation of dismay from the thrifty clerk.

Finally, she answered hesitatingly, "I'm not sure exactly, but I think with four hundred francs I could manage it."

He turned a bit pale, for he had set aside just that amount to buy a rifle so that, the following summer, he could join some friends who were getting up a group to shoot larks on the plain near Nanterre.

However, he said, "All right. I'll give you four hundred francs. But try to get a nice dress."

As the day of the party approached, Mme. Loisel seemed sad, moody, and ill at ease. Her outfit was ready, however. Her husband said to her one evening, "What's the matter? You've been all out of sorts for three days."

And she answered, "It's embarrassing not to have a jewel or a gem—nothing to wear on my dress. I'll look like a pauper:[8] I'd almost rather not go to that party."

"I'll look like a pauper: I'd almost rather not go to that party."

He answered, "Why not wear some flowers? They're very fashionable this season. For ten francs you can get two or three gorgeous roses."

She wasn't at all convinced. "No . . . There's nothing more humiliating than to look poor among a lot of rich women."

But her husband exclaimed, "My, but you're silly! Go see your friend Mme. Forestier[9] and ask her to lend you some jewelry. You and she know each other well enough for you to do that."

She gave a cry of joy, "Why, that's so! I hadn't thought of it."

The next day she paid her friend a visit and told her of her predicament.

Mme. Forestier went toward a large closet with mirrored doors, took out a large

7. *Mathilde* (mä tēld′)

8. A *pauper* is a very poor person.

9. *Forestier* (fô res tyā′)

Point of View *What does the narrator help the reader to fully appreciate about the husband's feelings for his wife?* **1**

Dreams and Reality *What does Madame Loisel require in order to enjoy the party?* **2**

Literary Practice

SPIRAL REVIEW **Symbolism** Explain that symbolism is when a person, animal, place, object, or event is used to represent something else. Guide students to think about why Mme. Loisel wants the necklace. **Ask:** What do you think the necklace represents? *(The necklace represents a lavish, opulent life. It represents wealth and status.)* Remind students that symbols help writers explain abstract concepts. Since the necklace represents wealth, readers should pay close attention to it. What happens to the necklace will reveal how the author feels about appearances. Ask students to think of a story they have heard or read that uses symbolism to represent an idea. Ask students to share these stories with the class and explain the use of symbolism in the story.

jewel box, brought it over, opened it, and said to Mme. Loisel: "Pick something out, my dear."

At first her eyes noted some bracelets, then a pearl necklace, then a Venetian cross, gold and gems, of marvelous workmanship. She tried on these adornments in front of the mirror, but hesitated, unable to decide which to part with and put back. She kept on asking, "Haven't you something else?"

"Oh, yes, keep on looking. I don't know just what you'd like."

The Hunt Ball, 1885. Julius L. Stewart. Phototype, colored after a painting. Private collection.

View the Art Julius L. Stewart often painted scenes of the European elite. What might Mme. Loisel find particularly exciting about this party? ★

All at once she found, in a black satin box, a superb diamond necklace; and her pulse beat faster with longing. Her hands trembled as she took it up. Clasping it around her throat, outside her high-necked dress, she stood in ecstasy looking at her reflection.

Then she asked, hesitatingly, pleading, "Could I borrow that, just that and nothing else?"

"Why, of course."

She threw her arms around her friend, kissed her warmly, and fled with her treasure.

The day of the party arrived. Mme. Loisel was a sensation. She was the prettiest one there, fashionable, gracious, smiling, and wild with joy. All the men turned to look at her, asked who she was, begged to be introduced. All the Cabinet officials wanted to waltz with her. The minister took notice of her.

She danced madly, wildly, drunk with pleasure, giving no thought to anything in the triumph of her beauty, the pride of her success, in a kind of happy cloud composed of all the adulation,[10] of all the admiring glances, of all the awakened longings, of a sense of complete victory that is so sweet to a woman's heart.

She left around four o'clock in the morning. Her husband, since midnight, had been dozing in a small empty sitting room with three other gentlemen whose wives were having too good a time.

He threw over her shoulders the wraps he had brought for going home, modest garments of everyday life whose shabbiness clashed with the stylishness of her evening clothes. She felt this and longed to escape, unseen by the other women who were draped in expensive furs.

Loisel held her back.

"Hold on! You'll catch cold outside. I'll call a cab."

But she wouldn't listen to him and went rapidly down the stairs. When they were on the street, they didn't find a carriage; and

3 Dreams and Reality *What reasons might there be for Madame Loisel's success at the party?*

10. Here, *adulation* means "plentiful praise" or "flattery."

Teach

Big Idea 3

Dreams and Reality

Answer: *She looked lovely and was confident, vivacious, and charming.*

View the Art ★

Answer: *(The luxurious setting, chandeliers, gilt trimmings, draperies, and splendid formal attire would excite her.)* Students should use details from the painting and the story to support their opinions.

Julius L. Stewart (1855–1919) was the son of a wealthy American who lived in Europe. The social gatherings of the European elite inspired many of his paintings. His painting, *The Hunt Ball,* emerged around the same time as Maupassant's story, "The Necklace."

Approaching Level

DIFFERENTIATED INSTRUCTION

Emerging Remind students that literature offers them a chance to live someone else's life for a while. If they do not understand a character, they should imagine what the character is going through.

Say: Imagine what it would be like to be Mme. Loisel think of something that you have wanted for your entire life. Now imagine being told that you can have it, but just for one night. What sort of conflicting emotions would you feel? Why might this decision be so important to Mme. Loisel? *(Answers will vary.)* Answering these questions might help students empathize with the main character.

Teach

Literary Element 1

Point of View **Answer:** *The husband patiently waits with other husbands while Madame Loisel circulates at the party. He is not dazzled by glamorous affairs. His thoughts at the end of the night are on another day of labor.*

Reading Strategy 2

Analyze Cause-and-Effect Relationships **Answer:** *They must decide whether to tell Madame Forestier the truth about losing the necklace or to find some alternative.*

Cultural History ☆

Palais Royal The Palais Royal was orginally a theater that was part of Cardinal Richelieu's residence. After Richelieu's death, the Palais was inherited by Louis the XIII and became a royal property. Since then, the Palais has housed several theaters and has been used for entertainment purposes.

they set out to hunt for one, hailing drivers whom they saw going by at a distance.

They walked toward the Seine,[11] disconsolate and shivering. Finally on the docks they found one of those carriages that one sees in Paris only after nightfall, as if they were ashamed to show their drabness during daylight hours.

It dropped them at their door in the Rue des Martyrs,[12] and they climbed wearily up to their apartment. For her, it was all over. For him, there was the thought that he would have to be at the Ministry at ten o'clock.

Before the mirror, she let the wraps fall from her shoulders to see herself once again in all her glory. Suddenly she gave a cry. The necklace was gone.

Her husband, already half undressed, said, "What's the trouble?"

She turned toward him despairingly, "I . . . I . . . I don't have Mme. Forestier's necklace."

"What! You can't mean it! It's impossible!"

They hunted everywhere, through the folds of the dress, through the folds of the coat, in the pockets. They found nothing.

He asked, "Are you sure you had it when leaving the dance?"

"Yes, I felt it when I was in the hall of the Ministry."

"But if you had lost it on the street we'd have heard it drop. It must be in the cab."

"Yes, quite likely. Did you get its number?"

"No. Didn't you notice it either?"

"No."

They looked at each other **aghast**. Finally Loisel got dressed again.

"I'll retrace our steps on foot," he said, "to see if I can find it."

And he went out. She remained in her evening clothes, without the strength to go to bed, slumped in a chair in the unheated room, her mind a blank.

Her husband came in about seven o'clock. He had had no luck.

He went to the police station, to the newspapers to post a reward, to the cab companies, everywhere the slightest hope drove him.

That evening Loisel returned, pale, his face lined; still he had learned nothing.

"We'll have to write your friend," he said, "to tell her you have broken the catch and are having it repaired. That will give us a little time to turn around."

She wrote to his dictation.

At the end of a week, they had given up all hope.

And Loisel, looking five years older, declared, "We must take steps to replace that piece of jewelry."

The next day they took the case to the jeweler whose name they found inside. He consulted his records. "I didn't sell that necklace, madame," he said. "I only supplied the case."

Then they went from one jeweler to another hunting for a similar necklace, going over their recollections, both sick with despair and anxiety.

They found, in a shop in Palais Royal, a ☆ string of diamonds which seemed exactly

---

11. The *Seine* (sen) is a river that flows through Paris.
12. A Paris street, *Rue des Martyrs* (ro͞o dā mär tēr′) translates as "Street of Martyrs." A *martyr* is a person who suffers greatly or sacrifices all for a belief, principle, or cause.

1 Point of View *What details suggest the husband's down-to-earth simplicity?*

Analyze Cause-and-Effect Relationships *What dilemma does the couple face because they cannot find the necklace?* 2

Vocabulary

aghast (ə gast′) *adj.* filled with fear, horror, or amazement

Writing Practice

SPIRAL REVIEW **Write a Monologue** In third-person stories, the reader must infer a character's thoughts by observing his or her actions and dialogue as communicated by the narrator. Explain that stories told in the third person may not always reveal a character's thoughts as the story takes place. Have students write a monologue for Mme. Loisel revealing her own personal thoughts after she lost the necklace.

The monologue should be written in the first-person and should include the words *I* and *we.* Ask students to share their their work with the class. *(Students' writing should reflect the characters and events in the story.)* Students should use precise language, sensory details, and active verbs to enhance their writing.

like the one they were seeking. It was priced at forty thousand francs. They could get it for thirty-six.

They asked the jeweler to hold it for them for three days. And they reached an agreement that he would take it back for thirty-four thousand if the lost one was found before the end of February.

Loisel had eighteen thousand francs he had inherited from his father. He would borrow the rest.

He went about raising the money, asking a thousand francs from one, four hundred from another, a hundred here, sixty there. He signed notes, made ruinous deals, did business with loan sharks, ran the whole **gamut** of moneylenders. He compromised the rest of his life, risked his signature without knowing if he'd be able to honor it, and then, terrified by the outlook for the future, by the blackness of despair about to close around him, by the prospect of all the **privations** of the body and tortures of the spirit, he went to claim the new necklace with the thirty-six thousand francs which he placed on the counter of the shopkeeper.

When Mme. Loisel took the necklace back, Mme. Forestier said to her frostily, "You should have brought it back sooner; I might have needed it."

She didn't open the case, an action her friend was afraid of. If she had noticed the substitution, what would she have thought? What would she have said? Would she have thought her a thief?

The Champs Élysées, Paris. Georges Stein. Gavin Graham Gallery, London. Private collection.

View the Art French painter Georges Stein focused on scenes of Paris in the late 1800s and early 1900s. Does this painting change your impression of late nineteenth-century Paris as it is described in the story? Explain. ★

Mme. Loisel experienced the horrible life the needy live. She played her part, however, with sudden heroism. That frightful debt had to be paid. She would pay it. She dismissed her maid; they rented a garret under the eaves.[13]

She learned to do the heavy housework, to perform the hateful duties of cooking. She washed dishes, wearing down her shell-pink nails scouring the grease from pots and pans; she scrubbed dirty linen, shirts, and cleaning rags which she hung on a line to dry; she took the garbage down to the street each morning and brought up water, stopping on each landing to get her breath. And, clad like a peasant woman, basket on arm, guarding sou[14] by sou her

3 Dreams and Reality *How has Madame Loisel's dream turned into a difficult reality for her husband?*

Vocabulary

gamut (gam′ ət) n. the entire range or series of something

privation (prī vā′ shən) n. the lack of comforts or basic necessities

13. A *garret under the eaves* would be a small attic apartment.

14. The *sou* (so͞o) is a French coin worth about one-twentieth of a franc.

Teach

Big Idea 3

Dreams and Reality

Answer: *He sacrifices his security and risks his reputation to replace the necklace.*

View the Art ★

Answer: *Answers will vary. Students should support their answers.* The Champs Élysées, one of the great Parisian boulevards, has traditionally been lined with luxury apartments, high-end boutiques, and a bustling swath of restaurants, cafés, theaters, museums, and parks.

English Learners

DIFFERENTIATED INSTRUCTION

Intermediate Tell students that summarizing can help them keep track of characters, events, and other details as they read. If a passage seems unclear, students should first identify the key characters and actions in a passage. Then write down a brief summary of what was read. Have students practice with the following passage on this page. **Read:** "Mme. Loisel experienced the horrible life the needy live. She played her part, however, with sudden heroism. That frightful debt had to be paid. She would pay it. She dismissed her maid; they rented a garret under the eaves." Ask students to summarize the passage. *(Mme. Loisel bravely resigned herself to a life of poverty to repay her debt.)*

Teach

Big Idea 1

Dreams and Reality

Answer: *She becomes the "pauper" she feared she would resemble at the ball.*

Reading Strategy 2

Analyze Cause-and-Effect Relationships

Answer: *They descend into a life of poverty and unceasing drudgery.*

Writer's Technique ☆

Irony Irony is a figurative use of expression that occurs when an outcome is the opposite of what is expected. Maupassant creates irony in Mathilde's circumstances, her appearance, and her thinking.

To check students' understanding of the selection, see Unit 1 Teaching Resources Book, p. 221.

scanty allowance, she bargained with the fruit dealers, the grocer, the butcher, and was insulted by them.

Each month notes had to be paid, and others renewed to give more time.

Her husband labored evenings to balance a tradesman's accounts, and at night, often, he copied documents at five sous a page.

And this went on for ten years.

Finally, all was paid back, everything including the exorbitant[15] rates of the loan sharks and accumulated compound interest.

Mme. Loisel appeared an old woman, now. She became heavy, rough, harsh, like one of the poor. Her hair untended, her skirts askew,[16] her hands red, her voice shrill, she even slopped water on her floors and scrubbed them herself. But, sometimes, while her husband was at work, she would sit near the window and think of that long-ago evening when, at the dance, she had been so beautiful and admired.

What would have happened if she had not lost that necklace? Who knows? Who can say? How strange and unpredictable life is! How little there is between happiness and misery!

Then one Sunday when she had gone for a walk on the Champs Élysées[17] to relax a bit from the week's labors, she suddenly noticed a woman strolling with a child. It was Mme. Forestier, still young-looking, still beautiful, still charming.

Mme. Loisel felt a rush of emotion. Should she speak to her? Of course. And now that everything was paid off, she would tell her the whole story. Why not?

She went toward her. "Hello, Jeanne."

The other, not recognizing her, showed astonishment at being spoken to so familiarly by this common person. She stammered, "But . . . madame . . . I don't recognize . . . You must be mistaken."

"No, I'm Mathilde Loisel."

Her friend gave a cry, "Oh, my poor Mathilde, how you've changed!"

"Yes, I've had a hard time since last seeing you. And plenty of misfortunes—and all on account of you!"

"Of me . . . How do you mean?"

"Do you remember that diamond necklace you loaned me to wear to the dance at the Ministry?"

"Yes, but what about it?"

"Well, I lost it."

"You lost it! But you returned it."

"I brought you another just like it. And we've been paying for it for ten years now. You can imagine that wasn't easy for us who had nothing. Well, it's over now, and I am glad of it."

Mme. Forestier stopped short. "You mean to say you bought a diamond necklace to replace mine?"

"Yes. You never noticed, then? They were quite alike."

And she smiled with proud and simple joy.

Mme. Forestier, quite overcome, clasped her by the hands. "Oh, my poor Mathilde. ☆ But mine was only paste.[18] Why, at most it was worth only five hundred francs!"

15. *Exorbitant* means "beyond what is reasonable or fair" or "excessive."
16. *Askew* (ə skyo͞o′) means "crooked" or "to one side."
17. *Champs Élysées* (shän′ zā lē zā′) is a fashionable, tree-lined avenue in Paris.
18. Here, *paste* is a hard, brilliant glass used to make artificial jewels.

1 Dreams and Reality *In what sense are Madame Loisel's worst fears coming true?*

2 Analyze Cause-and-Effect Relationships *What happens to the couple because of Madame Loisel's losing the necklace?*

Listening and Speaking Practice

SMALL GROUP SPIRAL REVIEW **Notetaking** Maupassant describes the Loisels' actions as heroic because the couple does what has to be done to pay their debt, no matter how hard or unpleasant. In small groups, have students discuss recent stories from newspapers, magazines, and other sources and identify a person whom they consider a hero. Students should take notes during their discussion. Remind them that Maupassant found heroic qualities in an unlikely couple. Encourage them to name unlikely heroes. Have students work together to create a list of actions and qualities that make a person heroic. Have groups present their findings to the class. A chosen speaker should summarize the group's discussion and share the group's list with the class.

After You Read

Respond and Think Critically

Respond and Interpret

1. Could you imagine feeling and acting as Madame Loisel does in the story? Why or why not?
2. (a)At the beginning of the story, why is Madame Loisel unhappy with her life? (b)How would you characterize her ideas about what gives happiness in life?
3. (a)How does Madame Loisel react to the party invitation? (b)What do Monsieur Loisel's reactions to her suggest about him?
4. (a)How do the Loisels pay for the replacement necklace? (b)In your opinion, why do the Loisels decide not to tell Madame Forestier that they lost the necklace?

Analyze and Evaluate

5. Do you think the Loisels' efforts to replace the necklace are admirable or foolish? Give reasons for your opinion.
6. When she finds herself in debt, Madame Loisel "plays her part . . . with sudden heroism." (a)What does she do that might be called heroic? (b)Why might those actions seem surprising?

Connect

7. **Big Idea** **Dreams and Reality** In your opinion, when are dreams for a better life beneficial, and when are they harmful? Explain.
8. **Connect to Today** How is Madame Loisel's situation in the story similar to and different from what it might be today?

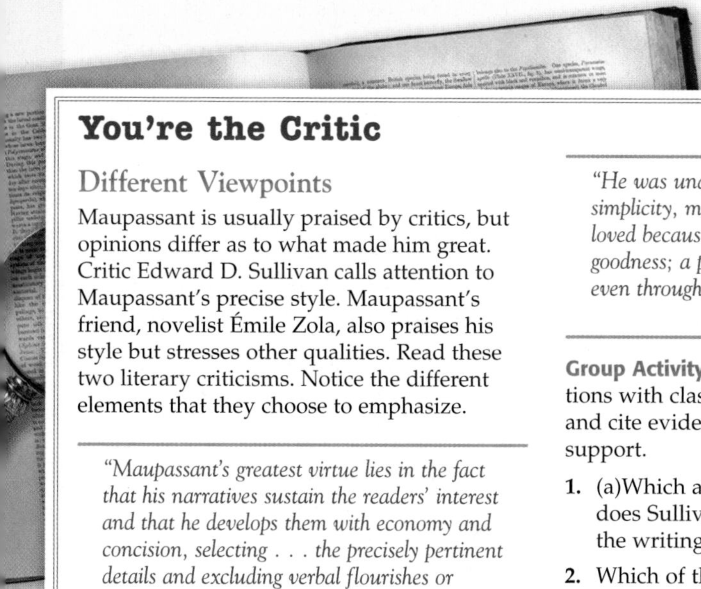

You're the Critic

Different Viewpoints

Maupassant is usually praised by critics, but opinions differ as to what made him great. Critic Edward D. Sullivan calls attention to Maupassant's precise style. Maupassant's friend, novelist Émile Zola, also praises his style but stresses other qualities. Read these two literary criticisms. Notice the different elements that they choose to emphasize.

"Maupassant's greatest virtue lies in the fact that his narratives sustain the readers' interest and that he develops them with economy and concision, selecting . . . the precisely pertinent details and excluding verbal flourishes or elaborate enumeration."

—Edward D. Sullivan

"He was understood because he had clarity, simplicity, moderation, and strength. He was loved because he possessed a laughing goodness; a profound satire which persists even through tears."

—Émile Zola

Group Activity Discuss the following questions with classmates. Refer to the excerpts and cite evidence from "The Necklace" for support.

1. (a)Which aspects of Maupassant's writing does Sullivan praise? (b)What aspects of the writing does Zola emphasize?
2. Which of the critical assessments most closely captures your own opinion? Cite evidence from the story.

After You Read

Assess

1. Students should support their answers.
2. (a) She longs for a life of luxury and attention. (b) She believes happiness comes from wealth, status, and admiration.
3. (a) Madame Loisel is depressed and refuses to go without the proper clothes. (b) His patient concern for his wife suggests he is loving, kind, and self-sacrificing.
4. (a) They acquire steep debts, which they labor for ten hard years to pay off. (b) Possible answers: fear that she will accuse them of theft; embarrassment
5. Answers will vary.
6. (a) She works hard and uncomplainingly. (b) She seemed idle and given to daydreaming and self-pity.
7. Students should support their answers.
8. Students might say that in today's world, Madame Loisel might have a career. Others might argue that she might still be in a social class that would expect her not to work.

For additional selection assessment, see Assessment Resources, pp. 69–70.

You're the Critic

1. (a) Sullivan praises his economy, precision, and ability to entertain. (b) Zola praises not only his concise style but also his ironic yet moving portrayal of human weakness.
2. Students should support their answers with evidence from the text.

After You Read

Assess

Literary Element

1. The narrator gives no hints that the necklace is a fake.
2. Possible answer: Without the comments, the reader would have too limited a view of the motivations and feelings of the characters. Students should support their answers.

Progress Check

Can students identify point of view?

If No → See Unit 1 Teaching Resources Book, p. 216.

Review: Symbol

1. It represents the life Madame Loisel desired.
2. Possible answers: A symbol of their ruin or of the life they will never have because of their debt
3. Possible answers: It then becomes a symbol of the emptiness of Mathilde's vanity and her illusions about happiness.

Reading Strategy

1. C is the correct answer. Madame Loisel's desire for a life of grandeur is the starting point for all of the couple's misfortunes.

Literary Element Point of View

Stories told from a **third-person point of view** are told by a narrator who is not a character in the story, but someone who stands outside the story and comments on the action.

1. Think about how Maupassant makes use of the third-person point of view in this story. Why is the information revealed at the end so surprising? Explain.
2. The narrator comments in detail about both Madame and Monsieur Loisel. If these comments were removed from the story altogether, how might your perception of the story be different? Would you have greater, less, or the same amount of sympathy for the characters? Explain.

Review: Symbol

As you learned on page 156, a **symbol** is an object, person, place, or experience that represents something else, usually something abstract. In this story, a fancy evening dress is a symbol of class and distinction. A symbol may have more than one meaning, or its meaning may change from the beginning to the end of a literary work.

Partner Activity Meet with a partner to consider the importance of the diamond necklace as a symbol in the story. Then work together to answer the following questions. When you are finished, share your thoughts with the class.

1. What does the necklace represent when Madame Loisel first sees it in its black satin box?
2. What does the necklace symbolize after Madame Loisel discovers that it is lost?
3. How does the meaning of the symbol change when it is revealed that the diamonds in the necklace were fake?

LOG ON **Literature** Online

Selection Resources For Selection Quizzes, eFlashcards, and Reading-Writing Connection activities, go to glencoe.com and enter QuickPass code GL49787u1.

Reading Strategy Analyze Cause-and-Effect Relationships

ACT Skills Practice

1. The Loisels endure years of poverty and suffering because:

   A. Monsieur Loisel is a minor clerk in the Ministry of Education.

   B. the borrowed diamonds are artificial.

   C. Madame Loisel has a deep desire for luxury and entertainment.

   D. Monsieur Loisel borrows money from loan sharks.

Vocabulary Practice

Practice with Usage Respond to these statements to help you explore the meanings of vocabulary words from the selection.

1. Give an example of something a child might ask for **incessantly.**
2. Describe how a **disconsolate** person acts.
3. Identify a situation where someone might be **aghast.**
4. Name something that would have a **gamut.**
5. Explain the living conditions of someone experiencing **privation.**

Academic Vocabulary

French writer Gustave Flaubert believed that Maupassant was ***capable*** *of great things.*

Capable is an academic word. In more casual conversation someone might say that a favorite team is **capable** of winning an upcoming game. Think of something difficult or challenging that you want to do in your future. Why do you think you will be **capable** of doing it?

For more on academic vocabulary, see pages 54–55 and R79–R81.

Vocabulary

Answers will vary. Sample responses:

1. A child who likes action figures might ask for one incessantly.
2. A disconsolate person acts gloomy, hopeless, and depressed.
3. If their favorite team loses a big game, a person would be aghast.
4. emotions, books, and colors would have a gamut
5. A person experiencing privation would live a very simple life perhaps without running water or electricity.

Academic Vocabulary

Answers may vary, but students' explanations should use the word capable correctly.

Respond Through Writing

Short Story

Apply Point of View Write a story of at least 1,500 words about a character who gets into trouble as a result of miscommunication or misunderstanding in a serious situation. Describe what happens and explain what the character learns from the experience. Clearly show the cause of the misunderstanding and its undesired effects. Write your story from the third-person omniscient point of view.

Understand the Task In **third-person omniscient point of view,** the all-knowing narrator is not a character in the story. Unlike third-person limited—in which an outside narrator focuses on just one character's experience—an omniscient narrator can share the thoughts and experiences of any character in the story.

Prewrite Freewrite about some misunderstandings that have gotten you into trouble; search newspapers or magazines for problems caused by miscommunications. Then brainstorm a plot that is built around a misunderstanding. Create a plot diagram such as the one on page 40 to help guide your writing.

Draft As you write a first draft, use your plot diagram to help you pace the action; always keep in mind where you are in the overall story. Focus on clearly presenting the significance of events and how they contribute to or are affected by the misunderstanding. Ground the story's events by setting them in distinct, vividly described locations.

Revise Use your revisions as a chance to expand the scope of the situation. Keep in mind that your narrator can share any detail about settings. Give each scene in your story a strong sense of place. As you revise, add more sensory details about the settings and characters. Provide details about the main character's thoughts and feelings about the misunderstanding.

After finishing your first revision, exchange stories with a classmate. Share your responses to each other's stories, and provide constructive comments. Use the comments and suggestions you received to make one more round of revisions.

Edit and Proofread Proofread your paper, correcting any errors in grammar, spelling, and punctuation. Use the Grammar Tip in the side column to help you with comparative and superlative adjectives.

Learning Objectives

In this assignment, you will focus on the following objectives:

Writing: Applying point of view in a short story.

Grammar: Understanding how to use comparative and superlative adjectives.

Grammar Tip

Comparative and Superlative Adjectives

A comparative adjective compares two things:

Steve is taller *than Jeremy.*

A superlative adjective compares three or more things:

Steve is the tallest *man in their club.*

The -*er* and -*est* versions are regular forms of comparative and superlative adjectives. Some comparative and superlative adjectives use *more* and *most* instead, and are referred to as irregular. For example:

Steve is more serious *than Jeremy.*

Steve is the most serious *man in their club.*

After You Read

Assess

Respond Through Writing

Students' short stories should:

- explain what the character learns
- show the cause of a misunderstanding
- show the effect of a misunderstanding
- be written from the third-person point of view

A student who meets all of these criteria should receive the equivalent of a 4-point response.

A student who fully meets two or partially meets three of these criteria should receive the equivalent of a 3-point response.

A student who fully meets one or partially meets two of these criteria should receive the equivalent of a 2-point response.

A student who partially meets one of these criteria should receive the equivalent of a 1-point response.

For grammar practice, see Unit 1 Teaching Resources Book, p. 220.

To create custom assessments online, go to Progress Reporter Online Assessment.

To create custom assessments using software, use ExamView Assessment Suite.

Before You Read

Focus

Bellringer Options

Literature Launchers:
Pre-Reading Videos DVD, Selection Launcher

Selection Focus
Transparency 14

Daily Language Practice
Transparency 19

Or **write the following phrases on the board:** Kennedy Assassinated, Civil Rights Movement, Vietnam War, Martin Luther King, Jr. Assassinated.

Ask: What do these events have in common? *(All of these events happened in the 1960s.)* Tell students that the story "American History" is set during the early 1960s.

Before You Read

American History

Meet **Judith Ortiz Cofer**
(born 1952)

Judith Ortiz Cofer brings her readers on a journey. It is not a journey to a distant past or an exotic place, or even an imaginary world; it is, according to one critic, "a quest to discover what it means to be a person in a specific place and culture." Ortiz Cofer can describe this quest with great depth and precision because she has been engaged in it her entire life.

Born in a small town in Puerto Rico, Ortiz Cofer moved with her parents to the United States when she was very young. Her father joined the U.S. Navy, and the family lived in Paterson, New Jersey. About every six months, the Navy sent her father to Europe. While he was away, her mother would take the family back to Puerto Rico. As a result, Ortiz Cofer's childhood was split between an industrialized East Coast city and a rural town on the island of Puerto Rico.

> *"I absorbed literature, both spoken* cuentos *and books, as a creature who breathed ink."*
>
> —Judith Ortiz Cofer

Two Distinct Worlds Always the new girl, Ortiz Cofer often felt out of place in both New Jersey and Puerto Rico. When she was in New Jersey, she spent a lot of time reading books from the library and the romance novels (in Spanish) that her mother brought from Puerto Rico. While in Puerto Rico, Ortiz Cofer became absorbed in family stories called *cuentos*. Her grandmother was an especially gifted storyteller. Her grandfather was a carpenter and a poet, and he often read his poems to his granddaughter. A love of language fed Ortiz Cofer's dreams of going to college and becoming a teacher.

A Literary Life In 1970 Ortiz Cofer realized her dream of attending college and went on to become a bilingual teacher. While in graduate school, she began writing poetry. She published her first book of poetry in 1980. Since then she has won awards not only for her poems, but also for her short stories, essays, and novels.

Ortiz Cofer continues to write and teach. She is a professor of English and creative writing at the University of Georgia.

LOG ON **Literature** Online

Author Search For more about Judith Ortiz Cofer, go to glencoe.com and enter QuickPass code GL49787u1.

Selection Skills

American History

Literary Elements
- Point of View (SE pp. 209–218)

Reading Skills
- Make Inferences About Character (SE pp. 209–218)

Vocabulary Skills
- Analogies (SE p. 219)
- Academic Vocabulary (SE p. 219)

Listening/Speaking/Viewing Skills
- Analyze Art (SE p. 213, 217)
- Literature Groups (SE p. 219)

Writing Skills/Grammar
- Write a Report (TE p. 210)

Literature and Reading Preview

Connect to the Story

Have you ever met a person whom you liked right away, but something prevented the friendship from growing? Write a journal entry about someone you would like to get to know better and what is standing in the way.

Build Background

John F. Kennedy—the youngest man to be elected President of the United States—was a dynamic, popular leader who energized the American people and instilled in them a sense of hope for the future. During his brief term, Kennedy urged Congress to pass sweeping civil rights legislation, saying, "race has no place in American life or law."

Set Purposes for Reading

Big Idea Dreams and Reality

As you read "American History," ask yourself, How do dreams and reality clash for the characters in this story?

Literary Element Point of View

Point of view is the relationship of the narrator to the story. In a story with **first-person point of view,** the narrator is a character in the story and uses the words *I, me,* and *we*. As you read, ask yourself, How does the narrator's perspective shape the story?

Reading Strategy Make Inferences About Characters

When you **make inferences about characters,** you draw generalizations about the characters based on their actions and on what they say about themselves or other characters. As you read, ask yourself, What can I infer about the characters in the story based on what the narrator says?

Tip: Chart Inferences In a three-column chart, record your inferences about the characters in the story.

Character	Example	Inference
Narrator	"to read my library books in the summer"	She is studious rather than athletic.

Learning Objectives

For pages 208–219

In studying this text, you will focus on the following objectives:

Literary Study: Analyzing first-person point of view.

Reading: Making inferences about characters.

Speaking and Listening: Participating in a literature group.

Vocabulary

discreet (dis krēt′) *adj.* showing good judgment; cautious; p. 212 *Although neither the food nor the service Jon received at the restaurant was good, his comments to the manager were discreet.*

vigilant (vij′əl ənt) *adj.* alert and watchful for danger or trouble; p. 213 *The monitors were vigilant for any signs of cheating or other misconduct during the standardized test.*

enthrall (en thrôl′) *v.* to hold spellbound; fascinate; p. 214 *We were enthralled by the flute solo and its high, clear, sweet melody.*

elation (i lā′shən) *n.* a feeling of great joy; ecstasy; p. 215 *When the blizzard made it impossible for them to get to school, their elation at the unexpected snow day was obvious.*

Approaching Level

DIFFERENTIATED INSTRUCTION

Emerging Have students think of people, places, or activities that are associated with or can be described using one of the vocabulary words. For example, "a security guard" might be described as "vigilant." "A lottery winner" would show "elation."

Before You Read

Focus

Summary

Elena wants desperately to be friends with Eugene, who lives in the house next to her tenement building. Both teens are studious and outcasts in their bleak public school. Although Eugene is friendly to Elena, his mother prevents them from studying together; she makes it clear that race is the problem.

For summaries in languages other than English, see Unit 1 Teaching Resources Book, pp. 223–228.

Interactive Read and Write

Other options for teaching this selection can be found in

- Interactive Read and Write for EL Students, pp. 33–48
- Interactive Read and Write for Approaching-Level Students, pp. 33–48
- Interactive Read and Write for On-Level Students, pp. 33–48

Vocabulary

Word Games Write each word and its definition on an index card. Invite two volunteers to the front of the class, and give one student a cards listing a vocabulary word and its definition. The student with the cards must provide clues to help the other student guess the word on the cards. Students should provide a definition, synonyms, antonyms, or other word clues.

For additional vocabulary practice, see Unit 1 Teaching Resources Book, p. 231.

Teach

Big Idea 1

Dreams and Reality **Say:** Keep these questions in mind as you read: What dreams and realities have you shared with new friends?

APPROACHING To further assist approaching-level students **ask:** how would you react if authority figures, such as parents and teachers, tried to interfere with your dreams?

Literary Element 2

Point of View **Answer:** *The writer establishes a first-person point of view by starting with the word I.*

For additional literary element practice, see Unit 1 Teaching Resources Book, p. 229.

View the Art ★

Many of O. Louis Guglielmi's (1906–1956) paintings were created while he worked with the Works Progress Administration. The WPA was set up by the federal government during the Great Depression to help Americans make ends meet. Guglielmi's paintings are noted for their strong colors and unusual perspective.

View in Chambers Street, 1936. O. Louis Guglielmi. Oil on canvas, 30¼ x 24¼ in. The Newark Museum, NJ. ★

AMERICAN HISTORY

Judith Ortiz Cofer

I once read in a *Ripley's Believe It or Not* column that Paterson, New Jersey, is the place where the Straight and Narrow (streets) intersect. **1** The Puerto Rican tenement[1] known as El Building was one block up from Straight. It was, in fact, the corner of Straight and Market; not "at" the corner, but *the* corner.

1. A *tenement* is a run-down apartment building, generally with low rent.

Point of View *What point of view does the writer use for this story? How do you know?* **2**

Writing Practice

SPIRAL REVIEW **Write a Report** Have students use the library or the Internet to find information about painter O. Louis Guglielmi. Students should write a one-page report on their findings. Students should integrate quotations within their essay to support ideas. Remind them to cite their sources and use correct grammar and punctuation.

For an audio recording of this selection, use Listening Library Audio CD-ROM.

Readability Scores

Dale-Chall: 5.6
DRP: 55
Lexile: 990

At almost any hour of the day, El Building was like a monstrous jukebox, blasting out *salsas*[2] from open windows as the residents, mostly new immigrants just up from the island,[3] tried to drown out whatever they were currently enduring with loud music. But the day President Kennedy was shot, there was a profound silence in El Building; even the abusive tongues of viragoes,[4] the cursing of the unemployed, and the screeching of small children had been somehow muted. President Kennedy was a saint to these people. In fact, soon his photograph would be hung alongside the Sacred Heart[5] and over the spiritist altars that many women kept in their apartments. He would become part of the hierarchy of martyrs[6] they prayed to for favors that only one who had died for a cause would understand.

On the day that President Kennedy was shot, my ninth grade class had been out in the fenced playground of the Public School Number 13. We had been given "free" exercise time and had been ordered by our P.E.[7] teacher, Mr. DePalma, to "keep moving." That meant that the girls should jump rope and the boys toss basketballs through a hoop at the far end of the yard. He in the meantime would "keep an eye" on us from just inside the building.

It was a cold gray day in Paterson. The kind that warns of early snow. I was miserable, since I had forgotten my gloves and my knuckles were turning red and raw from the jump rope. I was also taking a lot of abuse from the black girls for not turning the rope hard and fast enough for them.

"Hey, Skinny Bones, pump it, girl. Ain't you got no energy today?" Gail, the biggest of the black girls who had the other end of the rope yelled, "Didn't you eat your rice and beans and pork chops for breakfast today?"

The other girls picked up the "pork chop" and made it into a refrain: "pork chop, pork chop, did you eat your pork chop?" They entered the double ropes in pairs and exited without tripping or missing a beat. I felt a burning on my cheeks, and then my glasses fogged up so that I could not manage to coordinate the jump rope with Gail. The chill was doing to me what it always did, entering my bones, making me cry, humiliating me. I hated the city, especially in winter. I hated Public School Number 13. I hated my skinny flat-chested body, and I envied the black girls who could jump rope so fast that their legs became a blur. They always seemed to be warm while I froze.

There was only one source of beauty and light for me that school year. The only thing I had anticipated at the start of the semester. That was seeing Eugene. In August, Eugene and his family had moved into the only house on the block that had a yard and trees. I could see his place from my window in El Building. In fact, if I sat on the fire escape I was literally suspended above Eugene's backyard. It was my favorite spot to read my library books in the summer. Until that August the house had

2. *Salsas* are Latin American dance tunes.
3. When the writer refers to "the island" in this story, she is referring to Puerto Rico, an island in the Caribbean Sea, which is a self-governing commonwealth of the United States.
4. *Viragoes* (vi rä′ gōz) are bad-tempered, scolding women who, here, use coarse or insulting (*abusive*) language.
5. The *Sacred Heart* is a picture of the wounded heart of Jesus, sometimes encircled in a crown of thorns and giving off rays of golden light.
6. The *hierarchy* (hī ə rär′ kē) *of martyrs* (mär′ tərz) is the ranking of those who have suffered or died for their religion.
7. Here, *P.E.* stands for "physical education."

Make Inferences About Characters *Based on this physical description, what can you infer about how the narrator is feeling?* **3**

Teach

Reading Strategy 3

Make Inferences About Characters **Answer:** *Her cheeks blush with shame because she is hurt by the racial slurs of the other girls jumping rope.*

Advanced Learners

DIFFERENTIATED INSTRUCTION

Literary Criticism To practice **reading fluency,** have a student read aloud the passage on page 211 starting at, "There was only one source . . ." **Ask:** What word describes the tone of the passage? *(innocent, idealistic, romantic)* Remind students that the author's tone and choice of words often help the reader visualize and understand the character as well as the story. Explain that the author's stylistic choices and how these choices affect the reader are often debated among literary critics.

Say: As you read, pay attention to how word choice and tone affect your emotions. Have students to note where these stylistic choices stir their emotions. Ask students to point out these passages and explain how the author uses language and tone to impact mood.

Teach

Literary Element 1

Point of View **Answer:** *She reveals that she is a close observer of people and strongly empathizes with their feelings. Some students may also mention that the narrator seems to have a strong desire to be a part of a different family.*

Big Idea 2

Dreams and Reality
Answer: *Some might think that she does because they both seem to be quiet and like to read; others may argue that she has only watched him and their backgrounds are different.*

Reading Strategy 3

Make Inferences About Characters **Answer:** *She might assume that Eugene would reject her because of their racial differences or because he was not interested in her.*

been occupied by an old Jewish couple. Over the years I had become part of their family, without their knowing it, of course. I had a view of their kitchen and their backyard, and though I could not hear what they said, I knew when they were arguing, when one of them was sick, and many other things. I knew all this by watching them at mealtimes. I could see their kitchen table, the sink and the stove. During good times, he sat at the table and read his newspapers while she fixed the meals. If they argued, he would leave and the old woman would sit and stare at nothing for a long time. When one of them was sick, the other would come and get things from the kitchen and carry them out on a tray. The old man had died in June. The last week of school I had not seen him at the table at all. Then one day I saw that there was a crowd in the kitchen. The old woman had finally emerged from the house on the arm of a stocky middle-aged woman whom I had seen there a few times before, maybe her daughter. Then a man had carried out suitcases. The house had stood empty for weeks. I had had to resist the temptation to climb down into the yard and water the flowers the old lady had taken such good care of.

By the time Eugene's family moved in, the yard was a tangled mass of weeds. The father had spent several days mowing, and when he finished, I didn't see the red, yellow, and purple clusters that meant flowers to me from where I sat. I didn't see this family sit down at the kitchen table together. It was just the mother, a red-headed tall woman who wore a white uniform—a nurse's, I guessed it was; the father was gone before I got up in the morning and was never there at dinner time. I only saw him on weekends when they sometimes sat on lawn chairs under the oak tree, each hidden behind a section of the newspaper; and there was Eugene. He was tall and blond, and he wore glasses. I liked him right away because he sat at the kitchen table and read books for hours. That summer, before we had even spoken one word to each other, I kept him company on my fire escape.

Once school started I looked for him in all my classes, but P.S. 13[8] was a huge, overpopulated place and it took me days and many **discreet** questions to discover that Eugene was in honors classes for all his subjects; classes that were not open to me because English was not my first language, though I was a straight A student. After much maneuvering I managed "to run into him" in the hallway where his locker was—on the other side of the building from mine—and in study hall at the library, where he first seemed to notice me but did not speak; and finally, on the way home after school one day when I decided to approach him directly, though my stomach was doing somersaults.

I was ready for rejection, snobbery, the worst. But when I came up to him, practically panting in my nervousness, and blurted out: "You're Eugene. Right?" He smiled, pushed his glasses up on his nose, and nodded. I saw then that he was blush-

8. Here, *P.S.* stands for "public school."

1 Point of View *What does the narrator reveal about herself through her description of the neighbors' house and family?*

Dreams and Reality *Do you think that the narrator has a basis for forming such a positive impression of Eugene? Why or why not?* 2

Make Inferences About Characters *Why do you think the narrator assumes that Eugene will reject her?* 3

Vocabulary

discreet (dis krēt′) *adj.* showing good judgment; cautious

Research Practice

SPIRAL REVIEW **Puerto Rican Culture** Have students use a variety of sources to learn about Puerto Rican culture. Students should also learn about ways in which Puerto Ricans have contributed to major fields such as science, art, politics, music, medicine, literature, etc. Have students develop a list of questions to guide their research. Some questions to guide their reading might include: Who are some well-known Puerto Rican men and women? What contributions have they made to society? Students can share their findings in small groups or present their research to the class.

Soho Fire Escapes, 2001. Patti Mollica.

View the Art The energy of New York is a frequent subject for Patti Mollica. Although this painting shows a building in New York City's Soho neighborhood, does it look the way you imagine the fire escape that the narrator describes in the story? Why or why not? ★

ing deeply. Eugene liked me, but he was shy. I did most of the talking that day. He nodded and smiled a lot. In the weeks that followed, we walked home together. He would linger at the corner of El Building for a few minutes then walk down to his two-story house. It was not until Eugene moved into that house that I noticed that El Building blocked most of the sun and that the only spot that got a little sunlight during the day was the tiny square of earth the old woman had planted with flowers.

I did not tell Eugene that I could see inside his kitchen from my bedroom. I felt dishonest, but I liked my secret sharing of his evenings, especially now that I knew what he was reading, since we chose our books together at the school library.

One day my mother came into my room as I was sitting on the windowsill staring out. In her abrupt way she said: "Elena, you are acting 'moony.' " *Enamorada*[9] was what she really said—that is, like a girl stupidly infatuated. Since I had turned fourteen and started menstruating my mother had been more **vigilant** than ever. She acted as if I was going to go crazy or explode or something if she didn't watch me and nag me all the time about being a señorita[10] now. She kept talking about virtue, morality, and other subjects that did not interest me in the least. My mother was unhappy in Paterson, but

9. *Enamorada* (en ăm′ ər ä′ dä)
10. *Señorita* (sen′ yə rē′ tə) is Spanish for *young lady.*

4 Dreams and Reality *Do you think that the narrator's beliefs about Eugene are rooted in reality, or not? Explain.*

Point of View *How does the author reveal the narrator's name? Why might the author have revealed it in this way?* **5**

Vocabulary

vigilant (vij′ əl ənt) *adj.* alert and watchful for danger or trouble

Teach

Big Idea 4

Dreams and Reality

Answer: *They seem to be realistic, given that Eugene seems to be happy to talk with her.*

Literary Element 5

Point of View **Answer:** *The mother calls her by name. Since Elena is the narrator, revealing her name this way is more realistic than having her tell her name.*

View the Art ★

American contemporary illustrator and graphic designer Patti Mollica combines bold and vigorous use of color with composition influenced by strong graphic design.

Answer: *Students should point to details in the selection and the artwork to support their opinions.*

English Learners

DIFFERENTIATED INSTRUCTION

Beginning/Early Intermediate Have students read the definition of *viligant* at the bottom of page 213. Then ask a student to reread the paragraph on page 213 that features the word. Have students use the word in a sentence and provide an example of why someone would be vigilant.

Approaching Level

DIFFERENTIATED INSTRUCTION

Established Have students view the painting above. Discuss elements of the painting such as color and details. Ask students to explain whether this painting reflects the neighborhood in which they live. Have students support their answers with reasons and examples. Ask students to present ideas for a painting that would reflect their neighborhood.

Teach

Big Idea 1

Dreams and Reality

Answer: *The narrator has unpleasant memories of Puerto Rico and does not consider it her home; her parents remember it as paradise and dream about returning there.*

Reading Strategy 2

Make Inferences About Characters

Answer: *Like Eugene, Elena is studious. She wants to become educated and enter a profession where she can use her intellect. Also, she is glad to return to Paterson after her vacation in Puerto Rico, unlike her parents, who dream of retiring to a beach there.*

my father had a good job at the blue jeans factory in Passaic, and soon, he kept assuring us, we would be moving to our own house there. Every Sunday we drove out to the suburbs of Paterson, Clifton, and Passaic, out to where people mowed grass on Sundays in the summer and where children made snowmen in the winter from pure white snow, not like the gray slush of Paterson, which seemed to fall from the sky in that hue. I had learned to listen to my parents' dreams, which were spoken in Spanish, as fairy tales, like the stories about life in the island paradise of Puerto Rico before I was born. I had been to the Island once as a little girl, to grandmother's funeral, and all I remembered was wailing women in black, my mother becoming hysterical and being given a pill that made her sleep two days, and me feeling lost in a crowd of strangers all claiming to be my aunts, uncles, and cousins. I had actually been glad to return to the city. We had not been back there since then, though my parents talked constantly about buying a house on the beach someday, retiring on the island—that was a common topic among the residents of El Building. As for me, I was going to go to college and become a teacher.

But after meeting Eugene I began to think of the present more than of the future. What I wanted now was to enter that house I had watched for so many years. I wanted to see the other rooms where the old people had lived and where the boy I liked spent his time. Most of all, I wanted to sit at the kitchen table with Eugene like two adults, like the old man and his wife had done, maybe drink some coffee and talk about books. I had started reading *Gone with the Wind*.[11] I was **enthralled** by it, with the daring and the passion of the beautiful girl living in a mansion, and with her devoted parents and the slaves who did everything for them. I didn't believe such a world had ever really existed, and I wanted to ask Eugene some questions, since he and his parents, he had told me, had come up from Georgia, the same place where the novel was set. His father worked for a company that had transferred him to Paterson. His mother was very unhappy, Eugene said, in his beautiful voice that rose and fell over words in a strange, lilting way. The kids at school called him the Hick and made fun of the way he talked. I knew I was his only friend so far, and I liked that, though I felt sad for him sometimes. Skinny Bones and the Hick was what they called us at school when we were seen together.

The day Mr. DePalma came out into the cold and asked us to line up in front of him was the day that President Kennedy was shot. Mr. DePalma, a short, muscular man with slicked-down black hair, was the science teacher, P.E. coach, and disciplinarian at P.S. 13. He was the teacher to whose homeroom you got assigned if you were a troublemaker, and the man called out to break up playground fights, and to escort violently angry teenagers to the office. And Mr. DePalma was the man who called your parents in for "a conference."

That day, he stood in front of two rows of mostly black and Puerto Rican kids,

1 Dreams and Reality *How do Elena's ideas and feelings about Puerto Rico contrast with those of her parents?*

2 Make Inferences About Characters *How is Elena more like Eugene than she is like her parents?*

11. *Gone with the Wind* is a romantic novel about the South during and after the Civil War.

Vocabulary

enthrall (en thrôl′) *v.* to hold spellbound; fascinate

Speaking Practice

SMALL GROUP SPIRAL REVIEW

Compare Media Genres Assign students to small groups. Ask groups to research the public response to the assassination of President Kennedy. Have them check accounts in newspapers, news magazines, documentaries, and reports stored online. Tell students to focus on quotations and reactions from ordinary citizens. Ask groups to present their findings by discussing differences and similarities between the various types of media accounts. Conclude by having students evaluate if the reactions of the characters in the story are realistic.

brittle from their efforts to "keep moving" on a November day that was turning bitter cold. Mr. DePalma, to our complete shock, was crying. Not just silent adult tears, but really sobbing. There were a few titters from the back of the line where I stood, shivering.

"Listen," Mr. DePalma raised his arms over his head as if he were about to conduct an orchestra. His voice broke, and he covered his face with his hands. His barrel chest was heaving. Someone giggled behind me.

"Listen," he repeated, "something awful has happened." A strange gurgling came from his throat, and he turned around and spit on the cement behind him.

"Gross," someone said, and there was a lot of laughter.

"The president is dead, you idiots. I should have known that wouldn't mean anything to a bunch of losers like you kids. Go home." He was shrieking now. No one moved for a minute or two, but then a big girl let out a "yeah!" and ran to get her books piled up with the others against the brick wall of the school building. The others followed in a mad scramble to get to their things before somebody caught on. It was still an hour to the dismissal bell.

A little scared, I headed for El Building. There was an eerie feeling on the streets. I looked into Mario's drugstore, a favorite hangout for the high school crowd, but there were only a couple of old Jewish men at the soda bar, talking with the short order cook in tones that sounded almost angry, but they were keeping their voices low. Even the traffic on one of the busiest intersections in Paterson—Straight Street and Park Avenue—seemed to be moving slower. There were no horns blasting that day. At El Building, the usual little group of unemployed men were not hanging out on the front stoop, making it difficult for women to enter the front door. No music spilled out from open doors in the hallway. When I walked into our apartment, I found my mother sitting in front of the grainy picture of the television set.

She looked up at me with a tear-streaked face and just said: *"Dios mío,"*[12] turning back to the set as if it were pulling at her eyes. I went into my room.

Though I wanted to feel the right thing about President Kennedy's death, I could not fight the feeling of **elation** that stirred in my chest. Today was the day I was to visit Eugene in his house. He had asked me to come over after school to study for an American history test with him. We had also planned to walk to the public library together. I looked down into his yard. The oak tree was bare of leaves, and the ground looked gray with ice. The light through the large kitchen window of his house told me that El Building blocked the sun to such an extent that they had to turn lights on in the middle of the day. I felt ashamed about it. But the white kitchen table with the lamp hanging just above it looked cozy and inviting. I would soon sit there, across from Eugene, and I would tell him about my perch just above his house. Maybe I would.

In the next thirty minutes I changed clothes, put on a little pink lipstick, and got my books together. Then I went in

12. *Dios mío* (dē′ os mē′ ō) is Spanish for *My God.*

Dreams and Reality *What is the narrator's mother watching? Based on what you already know, why is she so sad?* **3**

Point of View *How does the writer's use of point of view influence how you react to the information given here?* **4**

Make Inferences About Characters *What can you infer about Elena's feelings toward Eugene?* **5**

Vocabulary

elation (i lā′ shən) *n.* a feeling of great joy; ecstasy

Teach

Big Idea 3

Dreams and Reality

Answer: *She is watching news coverage related to President Kennedy's assassination; she is very upset; the narrator noted earlier that Puerto Ricans in her building admired the President.*

Literary Element 4

Point of View

Answer: *Experiencing the story through the narrator's eyes will prompt most students to empathize with her elation at realizing her dream of visiting Eugene's house rather than condemning her lack of involvement in the nation's mourning.*

Reading Strategy 5

Make Inferences About Characters

Answer: *The fact that Elena considers confiding her secret to Eugene suggests that she feels a bond with him and trusts him, even though they do not know each other well yet.*

Approaching Level

DIFFERENTIATED INSTRUCTION

Established This story contains many words about feelings and emotions. Less proficient readers can relate to the climax of the story if they understand the emotional words in a familiar context. List the following words on the board and have students define each using a dictionary: *elation, distraught, disbelief, hope,* and *humiliation.* Have students explain the connotation of each word. Then ask students to recall specific incidents when they felt these emotions. In their notebooks, students should write the word at the top of the page and then describe the situation in which they felt that way.

Teach

Big Idea 1

Dreams and Reality
Answer: *Students should mention the mother's ominous warning that Elena is heading for "humiliation and pain." The narrator is hoping that instead she and Eugene will enjoy their time together.*

Literary Element 2

Point of View **Answer:** *Because this description of El Building comes from the narrator's point of view, the reader recognizes that it reflects her feelings of awkwardness and shame.*

to tell my mother that I was going to a friend's house to study. I did not expect her reaction.

"You are going out *today*?" The way she said "today" sounded as if a storm warning had been issued. It was said in utter disbelief. Before I could answer, she came toward me and held my elbows as I clutched my books.

"*Hija*,[13] the president has been killed. We must show respect. He was a great man. Come to church with me tonight."

She tried to embrace me, but my books were in the way. My first impulse was to comfort her, she seemed so distraught, but I had to meet Eugene in fifteen minutes.

"I have a test to study for, Mama. I will be home by eight."

"You are forgetting who you are, *Niña*.[14] I have seen you staring down at that boy's house. You are heading for humiliation and pain." My mother said this in Spanish and in a resigned tone that surprised me, as if she had no intention of stopping me from "heading for humiliation and pain." I started for the door. She sat in front of the TV, holding a white handkerchief to her face.

I walked out to the street and around the chain-link fence that separated El Building from Eugene's house. The yard was neatly edged around the little walk that led to the door. It always amazed me how Paterson, the inner core of the city, had no apparent logic to its architecture. Small, neat, single residences like this one could be found right next to huge, dilapidated apartment buildings like El Building. My guess was that the little houses had been there first, then the immigrants had come in droves, and the monstrosities had been raised for them—the Italians, the Irish, the Jews, and now us, the Puerto Ricans, and the blacks.

13. *Hija* (ē′ hä) is Spanish for *daughter*.
14. *Niña* (nēn yä) is Spanish for *girl*.

The door was painted a deep green: *verde*, the color of hope. I had heard my mother say it: *Verde-Esperanza*.[15]

I knocked softly. A few suspenseful moments later the door opened just a crack. The red, swollen face of a woman appeared. She had a halo of red hair floating over a delicate ivory face—the face of a doll—with freckles on the nose. Her smudged eye makeup made her look unreal to me, like a mannequin seen through a warped store window.

"What do you want?" Her voice was tiny and sweet-sounding, like a little girl's, but her tone was not friendly.

"I'm Eugene's friend. He asked me over. To study." I thrust out my books, a silly gesture that embarrassed me almost immediately.

"You live there?" She pointed up to El Building, which looked particularly ugly, like a gray prison with its many dirty windows and rusty fire escapes. The woman had stepped halfway out, and I could see that she wore a white nurse's uniform with "St. Joseph's Hospital" on the name tag.

"Yes. I do."

She looked intently at me for a couple of heartbeats, then said as if to herself, "I don't know how you people do it." Then directly to me: "Listen. Honey. Eugene doesn't want to study with you. He is a smart boy. Doesn't need help. You understand me. I am truly sorry if he told you you could come over. He cannot study with you. It's nothing personal. You understand? We won't be in this place much longer, no need for him to get close to

15. Translated directly, *Verde-Esperanza* (vār′ dā es pe rän′ zə) is Green-Hope.

Dreams and Reality *Why might seeing a sign of hope be especially important to the narrator at this moment?* **1**

Point of View *How does the narrator's description of the building reflect her own mood at the moment?* **2**

Grammar Practice

SPIRAL REVIEW **Understand Adverbs** Explain to students that adverbs modify verbs, adjectives, or other adverbs by telling *when, where, how,* and *to what degree.* Write the following sentences on the board: "I turned away from the green door and heard her close it gently."

Discuss how adverbs add to the meaning of the sentence. Show how the adverb answers a question: How did Eugene's mother close the door? *(gently)* Have students to find other adverbs in the selection and write them in your notebook, along with the word they modify. Ask students to use the adverb in a sentence of their own.

Flash—November 22, 1963, 1968. Andy Warhol. Silkscreen on paper, from a portfolio of 11 screenprints, colophon and text, 21 x 21 in. The Andy Warhol Foundation, Inc.

View the Art Why might Elena think of Kennedy this way—in harsh colors and abstract shapes? ★

people—it'll just make it harder for him later. Run back home now."

I couldn't move. I just stood there in shock at hearing these things said to me in such a honey-drenched voice. I had never heard an accent like hers except for Eugene's softer version. It was as if she were singing me a little song.

"What's wrong? Didn't you hear what I said?" She seemed very angry, and I finally snapped out of my trance. I turned away from the green door and heard her close it gently.

Our apartment was empty when I got home. My mother was in someone else's kitchen, seeking the solace[16] she needed. Father would come in from his late shift at midnight. I would hear them talking softly in the kitchen for hours that night. They would not discuss their dreams for the future, or life in Puerto Rico, as they often did; that night they would talk sadly about the young widow and her two children, as if they were family. For the next few days, we would observe *luto*[17] in our apartment; that is, we would practice restraint and silence—no loud music or laughter. Some of the women of El Building would wear black for weeks.

That night, I lay in my bed, trying to feel the right thing for our dead president. But the tears that came up from a deep source inside me were strictly for me. When my mother came to the door, I pretended to be sleeping. Sometime during the night, I saw from my bed the streetlight come on. It had a pink halo around it. I went to my window and pressed my face to the cool glass. Looking up at the light I could see the white snow falling like a lace veil over its face. I did not look down to see it turning gray as it touched the ground below. ∾

16. *Solace* is "relief from sorrow or disappointment;" it also means "comfort."

17. *Luto* (lo͞o′ tō) is Spanish for *mourning.*

Dreams and Reality *How does this passage reflect both dreams and realities?* **3**

Teach

Big Idea 3

Dreams and Reality

Answer: *When the narrator describes the suburbs, she mentions that the children play in white snow, unlike the gray slush she is used to in Paterson. The white snow represents dreams of a better life; the grey slush is the reality of her life now.*

View the Art ★

Answer: *Harshness of color balances the starkness of the announcement and Elena's surroundings; like the shapes, Kennedy is an abstraction, or idea, to Elena. She does not feel a personal, emotional connection to Kennedy but realizes he is important to her community.*

Andy Warhol was the most innovative producer of Pop art, a form that features commonplace and commercial elements of technological society. According to Warhol, its intent is to bore the audience and show how dehumanizing life has become.

To check students' understanding of the selection, see Unit 1 Teaching Resources Book, p. 234.

Approaching Level

DIFFERENTIATED INSTRUCTION

Established Discuss the title of the story. **Ask:** Why do you think the author chose the title American History? Point out that the story blends an event from national history (the death of President Kennedy) with an event from the character's personal history (the situation with Eugene). Let students share their ideas in a class discussion. Encourage them to back up their assertions with examples from the story.

After You Read

Assess

1. Accept reasonable answers.
2. (a) The house next door (b) She finds normalcy and comfort in their daily routines.
3. (a) She is invited to Eugene's house. His mother sends her home. (b) She may have been racially prejudiced.
4. To contrast with her message and underline her cruelty
5. Accept answers supported by details.
6. The title refers to the assassination, the subject Elena and Eugene plan to study, and the country's history of racial division.
7. Assassination shattered the dreams of those who believed in Kennedy; life in the tenement eclipsed the parents' dream of a beach house; Elena's dreams of Eugene's friendship are shattered by his mother's prejudice.
8. Most students will agree because the setting and characters' cultures play such a large role in the story. Students should point to details in the story to support their answers.

For additional selection assessment, see Assessment Resources, pp. 71–72.

After You Read

Respond and Think Critically

Respond and Interpret

1. How do you feel about what happens to the narrator at Eugene's house?
2. (a)What does Elena enjoy looking at from her window? (b)In your opinion, why is Elena interested in the daily habits of the old Jewish couple and later of Eugene's family?
3. (a)Why does Elena feel particularly happy on the day the story takes place and sorrowful that night? (b)What factors might have led Eugene's mother to react as she did to Elena? Use details from the story to support your opinion.

Analyze and Evaluate

4. A character trait is a habit, a physical attribute, or an attitude that helps define a character. Why might Ortiz Cofer have given Eugene's mother the character traits of a face like a doll and a tiny, sweet-sounding voice?
5. Do you think the author expressed the feelings of a ninth-grade girl realistically? Support your response with details from the story as well as from your own experience.
6. In your opinion, why might the writer have titled this story "American History"?

Connect

7. **Big Idea** **Dreams and Reality** Describe three ways in which dreams are overshadowed by reality in this story.
8. **Connect to the Author** One critic has said that Judith Ortiz Cofer takes reading on "a quest to discover what it means to be a person in a specific place and culture." Do you think that is a good way to describe this story? Why or why not?

Literary Element Point of View

The choice of **point of view** can greatly influence how a story unfolds. A writer will usually choose a narrator whose point of view effectively communicates the main ideas and themes.

1. How does the first-person point of view in "American History" shape how readers feel about the interactions between people of different cultures or ethnic groups?
2. If Ortiz Cofer had chosen to tell this story from the point of view of one of the adults, how might that choice have changed the focus of the story?

Review: Setting

As you learned on pages 8–9, **setting** is the time and place in which the events of a literary work occur. Setting also includes the ideas, customs, beliefs, and values of the time and place.

Group Activity Work with a small group to create a web diagram listing details the writer gives in "American History" to evoke the setting of El Building in 1963, home to many Puerto Ricans who have moved to Paterson, New Jersey. Try to include at least one example for each category in the web below.

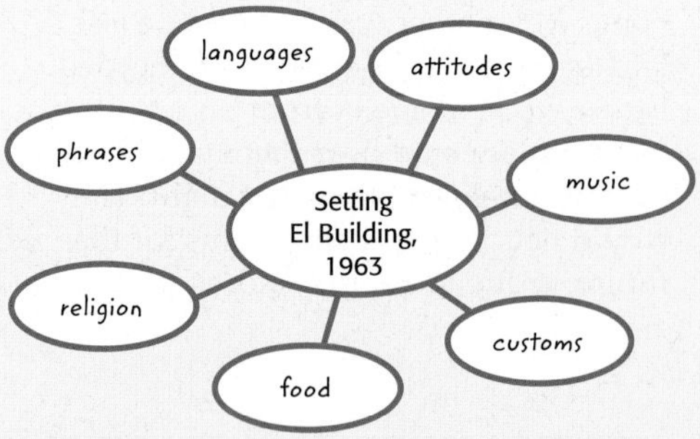

Literary Element

1. The first-person point of view helps readers empathize with ethnic groups facing prejudice.
2. The focus might be the assassination.

Review: Setting

Attitudes: Stick with your own ethnic group

Customs: *luto* (silent mourning)

Phrases: moony or *enamorada*

Languages: Spanish

Music: *salsas*

Food: rice, beans, pork chops

Religion: Spiritist altars

Reading Strategy Make Inferences About Characters

Refer to your inferences chart to help you answer the following questions. In your answers, cite examples from the story.

1. What can you infer about Elena when she says that Eugene was the "only . . . source of beauty and light" for her during the school year?
2. What can you infer about Elena's mother when she warns Elena that she is "heading for humiliation and pain"?

Vocabulary Practice

Practice with Analogies Choose the word that best completes the analogy.

1. elation : pleasure :: terror :
   a. happiness **c.** silliness
   b. fear **d.** anger
2. interest : enthrall :: moisten :
   a. dry **c.** select
   b. measure **d.** soak
3. discreet : careless :: cautious :
   a. careful **c.** reckless
   b. safe **d.** distant
4. alert : vigilant :: happy :
   a. overjoyed **c.** sad
   b. penitent **d.** joyless

Academic Vocabulary

*Eugene's mother tells Elena that her friendship with Eugene is not **appropriate.***

Appropriate is an academic word. In casual conversation, Elena's mother might tell Elena that shorts and a t-shirt are not **appropriate** clothes on a cold, rainy day. Using the context clues in both examples, try to figure out the meaning of the word.

For more on academic vocabulary, see pages 54–55 and R79–R81.

Speaking and Listening

Literature Groups

Assignment Some literary works have universal appeal: any reader can personally connect to the text because he or she can relate to the events described. Reviewer Nancy Vasilakis writes that Ortiz Cofer's narratives "have a universal resonance in the vitality, the brashness, the self-centered hopefulness, and the angst [anxiety] expressed by the teens." In a small group, discuss whether you agree with Vasilakis's statement.

Prepare As a group, review the story and identify examples of youthful vitality, brashness, self-centered hopefulness, and angst. Use a four-column chart to list and organize your examples according to each of the four categories.

Discuss During your group's discussion of Cofer's appeal to teens, follow these guidelines:

- Listen to each other's opinions with an open mind. Even if you don't agree, carefully consider the reasoning and evidence presented by other group members.
- Listen actively; make mental or written notes about ideas you share or questions you have.
- When presenting your viewpoint, support it with specific examples from the story. Clearly explain how the examples support your opinion.

Report Have two group members present the class with summaries of the two viewpoints: those who agree with Vasilakis and those who disagree. Each presenter should speak with confidence. Group members should be prepared to respond to follow-up questions from the audience.

Evaluate Write a paragraph in which you assess the effectiveness of your discussion. Use the checklist on page 249 to help in your evaluation.

LOG ON **Literature** Online

Selection Resources For Selection Quizzes, eFlashcards, and Reading-Writing Connection activities, go to glencoe.com and enter QuickPass code GL49787u1.

To create custom assessments online, go to Progress Reporter Online Assessment.

To create custom assessments using software, use ExamView Assessment Suite.

After You Read

Assess

Reading Strategy

1. **Answer:** Elena is lonely because she does not fit in with the other students. Eugene is a "source of beauty and light" because he admires Elena for her intrinsic qualities.
2. **Answer:** Elena's mother has suffered from prejudice and is trying to protect Elena from similar humiliation and pain.

Progress Check

Can students make inferences about characters?

If No → See Unit 1 Teaching Resources Book, p. 230.

Vocabulary

1. b **2.** d **3.** c **4.** a

Academic Vocabulary

Answers may vary, but students' definitions should reflect a meaning similar to "especially suitable."

Speaking and Listening

Students should

- identify examples of "youthful vitality, brashness, self-centered hopefulness, and angst" in the story
- listen to each other's opinions attentively and actively
- support their own opinions with evidence from the story
- develop succinct summaries of the group's conclusions
- present the summaries in a well-organized and engaging fashion
- answer follow-up questions thoughtfully

Focus

Summary

This passage from *A Thousand Days* begins with the author hearing the news that President Kennedy was shot. The author then lists the responses of many people in America and around the world to the death of an American President.

Teach

Big Idea 1

Dreams and Reality Many people saw the young, energetic President as a source of hope. His assassination left some feeling that the American dream had been damaged if not altogether destroyed.

Ask: Why would Kennedy's assassination demoralize so many people across the country? *(People hoped Kennedy would improve their lives. Also, the reality of violence is shocking to many.)*

ENGLISH LEARNERS To help English learners identify with President Kennedy ask them to name a well-known and admired leader from their native country who has influenced the lives of others. Have students explain why he or she is admired by others.

For an audio recording of this selection, use Listening Library Audio CD-ROM.

Readability Scores

Dale-Chall: 8.4
DRP: 61
Lexile: 1020

Historical Perspective
on *American History*

Learning Objectives

For pages 220–224

In studying this text, you will focus on the following objective:

Reading: Recognizing bias. Analyzing historical context. Making connections across literature.

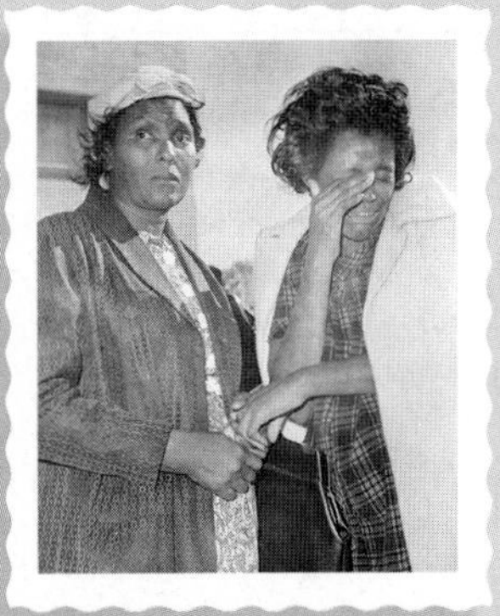

The Drums of Washington

Arthur M. Schlesinger Jr.

Pulitzer Prize Winner

Set a Purpose for Reading

Read to discover the reactions of people around the world to the assassination of President Kennedy.

Build Background

John F. Kennedy, who in 1960 was the youngest person ever elected president of the United States, is revered for his charisma and vision. Despite crises abroad, the Kennedy administration managed to make progress in foreign and domestic policy. During Kennedy's presidency, Arthur M. Schlesinger Jr. served as his adviser and later as a special assistant for Latin American affairs. In this excerpt, Schlesinger explores the grief that overwhelmed the world upon the assassination of President Kennedy on November 22, 1963.

Reading Strategy

Recognize Bias

When you read to determine if the author has an inclination toward a certain opinion or position, you are **recognizing bias.** As you read "The Drums of Washington," ask yourself, Do any statements made by Schlesinger suggest bias?

On Friday morning I had flown to New York with Katharine Graham,[1] whose husband Philip had died three months before, for a luncheon with the editors of her magazine *Newsweek.* Kenneth Galbraith[2] had come down from Cambridge for the occasion. We were still sipping drinks before luncheon in an amiable mood of Friday-before-the-Harvard-Yale game relaxation when a young man in shirtsleeves entered the room and said, a little tentatively, "I am sorry to break in, but I think you should know that the President has been shot in the head in Texas." For a flash one thought this was some sort of ghastly office joke. Then we knew it could not be and huddled desperately around the nearest television. Everything was confused and appalling. The minutes dragged along. Incomprehensible bulletins came from the hospital.

1 2

1. *Katharine Graham* (1917–2001) was an owner and publisher of news media, including the *Washington Post.*
2. *Kenneth Galbraith* (1908–2006) was an economist who served as an ambassador to India and an adviser during the Kennedy administration.

Viewing Practice

SMALL GROUP SPIRAL REVIEW **Analyze the Photographs** Have students view the photographs that appear with this selection. In small groups, students should take notes while answering the following questions:

- What ideas come to mind when you view each photograph?
- Why do you think the photographer felt it necessary to capture this image?

Students should also discuss the importance of having visual images accompany literature and informational text. Ask students to share points of their discussion with the rest of the class. They can use their notes to present information to the class.

2 Suddenly an insane surge of conviction flowed through me: I felt that the man who had survived the Solomon Islands[3] and so much illness[4] and agony, who so loved life, embodied it, enhanced it, could not possibly die now. He would escape the shadow as he had before. Almost immediately we received the irrevocable word.

Commuters in New York read about Kennedy's assassination.

In a few moments Galbraith and I were on Katharine Graham's plane bound for Washington. It was the saddest journey of one's life. Bitterness, shame, anguish, disbelief, emptiness mingled inextricably in one's mind. When I stumbled, almost blindly, into the East Wing, the first person I encountered was Franklin D. Roosevelt Jr. In a short time I went with my White House colleagues to Andrews Field to await the return of Air Force One from Texas. A small crowd was waiting in the dusk, McNamara,[5] stunned and silent, Harriman,[6] haggard and suddenly looking very old, desolation everywhere. We watched incredulously as the casket was carefully lifted out of the plane and taken to the Naval Hospital at Bethesda. Later I went to my house in Georgetown. My weeping daughter Christina said, "Daddy, what has happened to our country? If this is the kind of country we have, I don't want to live here any more." The older children were already on their way back from college to Washington.

Still later I went back to the White House to await the last return. Around four in the morning the casket, wrapped in a flag, was brought from the Naval Hospital and placed on a stand in the East Room. Tapers were lit around the bier,[7] and a priest said a few words. Then Jacqueline approached the bier, knelt for a moment and buried her head in the flag. Soon she walked away. The rest of us waited for a little while in the great hall. We were beyond consolation, but we clung ☆ to the comradeship he had given us. Finally, just before daybreak, we bleakly dispersed into the mild night.

We did not grieve alone. Sorrow engulfed America and the world. At Harvard Yard the bells tolled in Memorial Church, a girl wept hysterically in Widener Library,[8] a student slammed a tree, again and again, with his fist. Negroes mourned, and A. Philip Randolph[9] said that his "place in history will be next to Abraham Lincoln." Pablo

3. Schlesinger is referring to Kennedy's service in the U.S. Navy. In 1943 Kennedy was seriously injured while commanding a patrol torpedo boat that was sunk by a Japanese destroyer in the Solomon Islands in the South Pacific.
4. The *illness* to which Schlesinger is referring is Addison's disease.
5. *Robert S. McNamara* (1916–) served as the U.S. Secretary of Defense from 1961 to 1968.
6. *W. Averell Harriman* (1891–1986) served as the assistant secretary for Far Eastern affairs from 1961 to 1963.
7. *Tapers* are candles. A *bier* is "the stand on which a coffin is placed before burial."
8. *Widener Library* is the main library at Harvard University.
9. *A. Philip Randolph* (1889–1979) was a trade unionist and civil rights leader who served as the first president of the Negro American Labor Council (1960–1966).

Teach

Reading Strategy 2

Recognize Bias

Ask: What is the mood in the first paragraph? *(Schlesinger and his friends are relaxed and happy.)* What causes the mood to change? *(A young man informs them that the President has been shot.)*

ADVANCED Does Schlesinger's reaction to the news suggest bias? *(Schlesinger reacts by watching television, but the words he uses to describe how he felt are emotionally charged and suggest bias.)*

Political History ☆

The Assassin Lee Harvey Oswald was the man who assassinated President Kennedy. Oswald, who was born in 1939 in New Orleans, served in the Marine Corps. On the same day as the assassination, Oswald also shot and killed a police officer who stopped to question him.

Approaching Level

DIFFERENTIATED INSTRUCTION

Emerging Point out that this story deals with some of the same topics discussed in the previous story, "American History." **Ask:** How is this story similar to "American History"? *(the death of President Kennedy)* **Ask:** How does the narrator in this passage view President Kennedy's death differently from the narrator in "American History"? *(Elena did not know how to feel about the incident. For her, the event seemed far away. For Schlesinger, the event hits very close to home.)*

Teach

Reading Strategy 1

Recognize Bias **Ask:** How does the writer suggest bias? *(Students may say he lists many people who shared his opinion of Kennedy.)*

APPROACHING Why do you think the writer included comments by other political leaders? *(To add validity to his view of Kennedy)*

ADVANCED How does describing Kennedy as a "young hero of far away, the slayer of the dragons of discrimination, poverty, ignorance, and war" show bias? *(It exaggerates Kennedy as a heroic figure.)*

For activities related to this selection, see Unit 1 Teaching Resources Book, pp. 236–244.

For additional selection assessment, see Assessment Resources, pp. 73–74.

Casals[10] mused that he had seen many great and terrible events in his lifetime—the Dreyfus case,[11] the assassination of Gandhi[12]—"but in recent history—and I am thinking of my own lifetime—there has never been a tragedy that has brought so much sadness and grief to as many people as this." "For a time we felt the country was ours," said Norman Mailer.[13] "Now it's theirs again." Many were surprised by the intensity of the loss. Alistair Cooke[14] spoke of "this sudden discovery that he was more familiar than we knew." "Is there some principle of nature," asked Richard Hofstadter,[15] "which requires that we never know the quality of what we have had until it is gone?" Around the land people sat desperately in front of television sets watching the bitter drama of the next four days. In Washington Daniel Patrick Moynihan, the Assistant Secretary of Labor, said, "I don't think there's any point in being Irish if you don't know that the world is going to break your heart eventually. I guess that we thought we had a little more time. . . . Mary McGrory[16] said to me that we'll never laugh again. And I said, 'Heavens, Mary. We'll laugh again. It's just that we'll never be young again.' "

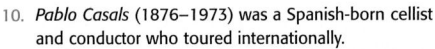

Women in Germany place flowers next to a picture of John F. Kennedy to honor him after his death.

In Ireland, "Ah, they cried the rain down that night," said a Fitzgerald of Limerick; he would not come back in the springtime. David Bruce reported from London, "Great Britain has never before mourned a foreigner as it has President Kennedy." As the news spread around London, over a thousand people assembled before the embassy in Grosvenor Square; they came in endless thousands in the next days to sign the condolence book. . . . In West Berlin people lighted candles in darkened windows. In Poland there was a spontaneous mass mourning by university students; church bells tolled for fifteen minutes on the night of the funeral. In Yugoslavia Tito,[17] so overcome that he could hardly speak, phoned the American chief of mission; later he read a statement over the state radio and went in person to the embassy to sign the book. The

10. *Pablo Casals* (1876–1973) was a Spanish-born cellist and conductor who toured internationally.
11. The *Dreyfus case* occurred in 1894 in France, when an army officer, Captain Alfred Dreyfus, was sentenced to life imprisonment for selling military secrets to Germany. It was later discovered that another officer committed the crime, yet officials refused to reopen the case.
12. *Mohandas Gandhi* (1869–1948) led the Indian national movement by means of nonviolent protest to eliminate British rule in India.
13. *Norman Mailer* (1923–2007) was an American novelist who often criticized totalitarianism.
14. *Alistair Cooke* (1908–2004) was a journalist who commented on history and culture.
15. *Richard Hofstadter* (1916–1970) was an American historian and recipient of two Pulitzer Prizes.
16. *Mary McGrory* (1918–2004) was a newspaper columnist who frequently wrote for the *Washington Post*. She was also a recipient of the Pulitzer Prize.
17. *Josip Broz Tito* (1892–1980) was the president of the Communist Party of Yugoslavia from 1939 to 1980.

Vocabulary Practice

PARTNERS SPIRAL REVIEW **Negative Prefixes** The writer uses several words that begin with a negative prefix. Examples of negative prefixes include *in-*, *im-*, *il-*, and *ir-*. Explain that usually these prefixes mean "not," "without," or "the opposite of." They often imply the opposite meaning of the words to which they are attached. **Say:** When the news bulletins about President Kennedy were incomprehensible, it means the writer could not understand what he was hearing. Have partners scan the story with a partner to find other examples of words with negative prefixes. Students should make a list of the words they find, and then write two sentences using each word. Have students share their sentences with the class.

national flag was flown at half-mast, and schools were instructed to devote one full hour to a discussion of the President's policies and significance. In Moscow Khrushchev[18] was the first to sign the book, and the Soviet television carried the funeral, including the service in the church.

Latin America was devastated. Streets, schools, housing projects were named after him, shrines set up in his memory; his picture, torn from the newspaper, hung on the walls of workers' shacks and in the hovels of the *campesinos.*[19] "For Latin America," said Lleras Camargo,[20] "Kennedy's passing is a blackening, a tunnel, a gust of cloud and smoke." Castro[21] was with Jean Daniel when the report came; he said, *"Es una mala noticia"* ("This is bad news"). In a few moments, with the final word, he stood and said, "Everything is changed. . . . I'll tell you one thing: at least Kennedy was an enemy to whom we had become accustomed." In Cambodia Prince Sihanouk ordered court mourning: "a light was put out," he later said, "which may not be re-lit for many years to come." In Indonesia flags flew at half-mast. In New Delhi people cried in the streets. In Algiers Ben Bella[22] phoned Ambassador Porter in tears and said, "I can't believe it. Believe me, I'd rather it happen to me than to him." In Guinea Sékou Touré[23] said, "I have lost my only true friend in the outside world." The embassy reported, "People expressed their grief without restraint, and just about everybody in Guinea seemed to have fallen under the spell of the courageous young hero of far away, the slayer of the dragons of discrimination, poverty, ignorance, and war." **1** In N'zérékoré[24] in the back country, where one would hardly think they had heard of the United States let alone the American President, a group of natives presented a sum of money to their American pastor to buy, according to the custom of the Guerze people, a rush mat in which to bury President Kennedy. In Kampala Ugandans crowded the residence of the American Ambassador; others sat silently for hours on the lawns and hillsides waiting. In Mali, the most left-wing of African states, President Keita came to the embassy with an honor guard and delivered a eulogy. In the Sudan a grizzled old Bisharine tribesman told an American lawyer that it was terrible Kennedy's son was so young; "it will be a long time before he can be the true leader." *Transition,* the magazine of African intellectuals, said, "In this way was murdered the first real chance in this century for an intelligent and new leadership to the world. . . . More than any other person, he achieved the intellectual's ideal of a man in action. His death leaves us unprepared and in darkness."

In Washington grief was an agony. **2** Somehow the long hours passed, as the new President took over with firmness ☆ and strength, but the roll of the drums, when we walked to St. Matthew's Cathedral on the frosty Monday, will sound forever in my ears, and the wildly twittering birds during the interment at Arlington[25] while the statesmen of the

18. *Nikita Sergeyevich Khrushchev* was the premier of the Soviet Union from 1958 to 1964.
19. *Campesinos* is Spanish for "farmers."
20. *Alberto Lleras Camargo* (1906–1990) was the president of Colombia from 1945 to 1946 and 1958 to 1962.
21. *Fidel Castro* (c. 1926–) is the Cuban premier.
22. *Ahmed Ben Bella* (1918–) served as the first prime minister (1962–1963) and first president (1963–1965) of the Algerian republic.
23. *Sékou Touré* (1922–1984) served as the first president of the Republic of Guinea from 1958 to 1984.
24. *N'zérékoré* is a town in southeastern Guinea.
25. *Interment* means "the act of placing in a grave." Arlington refers to Arlington National Cemetery, in Virginia.

Historical Perspective
on *American History*

Teach

Reading Strategy 2

Recognize Bias Say: A writer shows bias when he or she demonstrates a strong, personal, and sometimes unreasonable opinion. Readers should analyze how a writer's bias influences his or her writing. What bias is clear in this selection? *(Students may say that Schlesinger has a strong positive bias toward Kennedy because he worked with him and admired him.)*

Tell students to choose examples from the selection that reveal the author's bias and share them with the class.

Political History ☆

The New President When the President of the United States dies, resigns, or is removed from office, the Vice President becomes President. Lyndon B. Johnson became President upon Kennedy's death and was later elected to a full term.

Approaching Level

DIFFERENTIATED INSTRUCTION

Emerging Reading this selection aloud will convey the depth of Schlesinger's emotions and help students practice **reading fluency.** Assign students a paragraph from the selection. Have them take turns reading in a tone that communicates the writer's feelings. Students should use verbal techniques for emphasis.

Established Have students identify areas of the text that greatly affect their emotions. **Ask:** Why does this passage stir your emotions? Students should analyze such effective techniques so they can use them in their own writing. Ask students to review the article and find places where the author uses language, tone, and mood to stir the emotions of the reader. Students should make a judgment of how well the author uses these literary elements.

Assess

1. Students' summaries should reflect the the main ideas in this selection.
2. Students should be able to support their answer by explaining how the quotation established the mood of the time period described.
3. (a) His daughter had an intense reaction. She said, "If this is the kind of country we have, I don't want to live here anymore." (b) Accept any well-reasoned answer.
4. (a) Khrushchev was the first person in Moscow to sign the condolences book, and Castro said "This is bad news. Everything is changed. . . . I'll tell you one thing: at least Kennedy was an enemy to whom we had become accustomed." (b) Students should realize that in foreign relations, even with nations with whom the United States experienced tensions, President Kennedy commanded respect, and many foreign leaders liked him personally.
5. Students may feel he quotes too many people without providing enough background. Others may feel this approach conveys his sense that the whole world was affected by President Kennedy's assassination.
6. Possible answers: He was using language to set a somber mood to influence the reaction of the reader; he was making a broader statement about Kennedy's presidency being a time when there was a different sort of energy and spirit leading the nation.

world looked on. It was all so grotesque and so incredible. One remembered Stephen Spender's poem:

I think continually of those who were truly great. . . .
The names of those who in their lives fought for life,
Who wore at their hearts the fire's center.
Born of the sun they traveled a short while towards the sun,
And left the vivid air signed with their honor.

It was all gone now—the life-affirming, life-enhancing zest, the brilliance, the wit, the cool commitment, the steady purpose. . . .

Kennedy transformed the American spirit—and the response of his people to his murder, the absence of intolerance and hatred, was a monument to his memory. The energies he released, the standards he set, the purposes he inspired, the goals he established would guide the land he loved for years to come. Above all he gave the world for an imperishable moment the vision of a leader who greatly understood the terror and the hope, the diversity and the possibility, of life on this planet and who made people look beyond nation and race to the future of humanity. So the people of the world grieved as if they had terribly lost their own leader, friend, brother.

On December 22, a month after his death, fire from the flame burning at his grave in Arlington was carried at dusk to the Lincoln Memorial. It was fiercely cold. Thousands stood, candles in their hands; then, as the flame spread among us, one candle lighting the next, the crowd gently moved away, the torches flaring and flickering, into the darkness. The next day it snowed—almost as deep a snow as the inaugural blizzard. I went to the White House. It was lovely, ghostly, and strange.

It all ended, as it began, in the cold.

Respond and Think Critically

Respond and Interpret

1. Write a brief summary of the main ideas in this excerpt before you answer the following questions. For help on writing a summary, see page 421.
2. Schlesinger uses quotations from many people around the world. Which quotation do you think especially captured how people reacted to President Kennedy's assassination? Why?
3. (a)How did Schlesinger's daughter react to the assassination of President Kennedy? (b)Do you think an American child living today would have a similar reaction to a U.S. president's assassination? Why or why not?
4. (a)How did the Soviet premier, Nikita Khrushchev, and Cuba's leader, Fidel Castro, react to President Kennedy's assassination? (b)During Kennedy's presidency, there was much tension between the United States and both Cuba and the Soviet Union. What do the reactions of Khrushchev and Castro say about how President Kennedy served in U.S. foreign relations?

Analyze and Evaluate

5. The author supports his opinion of President Kennedy by using quotations. Do you think this is effective? Why or why not?
6. This excerpt closes with the statement, "It all ended, as it began, in the cold." Literally, Schlesinger is referring to the day of President Kennedy's inauguration and the day of his assassination. What effect may he be trying to create?

Connect

7. Schlesinger in *Drums of Washington* and Judith Ortiz Cofer in "American History" both attempt to capture the mood of November 22, 1963, the day of President Kennedy's assassination. Which do you think is more effective and why?

7. Possible answers: The perspective of someone their own age may be more accessible for some students; others may find the voice of a witness to that moment in history more compelling.

Before You Read

Mrs. James

Meet **Alice Childress**
(1920–1994)

When Alice Childress was a girl, she lived with her grandmother in the Harlem section of New York City. Her grandmother encouraged Childress to believe that her ideas were valuable, and she urged her granddaughter to write them down. The young girl embraced this concept and dedicated herself to becoming a writer. She also became an accomplished actress and playwright, and was the first African American woman to have a play produced on Broadway.

Young Ambitions Although she was born in Charleston, South Carolina, in 1920, Childress spent most of her childhood in Harlem. At the age of twenty, Childress began her theater career by joining Harlem's American Negro Theater (ANT). She began as an actress and a technical staffer, but within a year Childress became the director of the ANT, a position she held until 1952. Not content to only act and direct, she began writing her own plays, and in 1949, the ANT presented Childress's first play, *Florence*. Despite her success during her time at the ANT, Childress supported herself financially through a series of other jobs. Some of the jobs she held included working as a machinist, a governess, a salesperson, and an insurance agent. The influence of these work experiences can be found throughout her writing.

Flourishing on the Big Stage By her mid-thirties, Childress's career was beginning to bloom. In 1956 her play *Trouble in Mind*—her first to be produced outside of Harlem—won the 1956 Obie award for best original off-Broadway play. That same year she published her first short story collection, *Like One of the Family: Conversations from a Domestic's Life*.

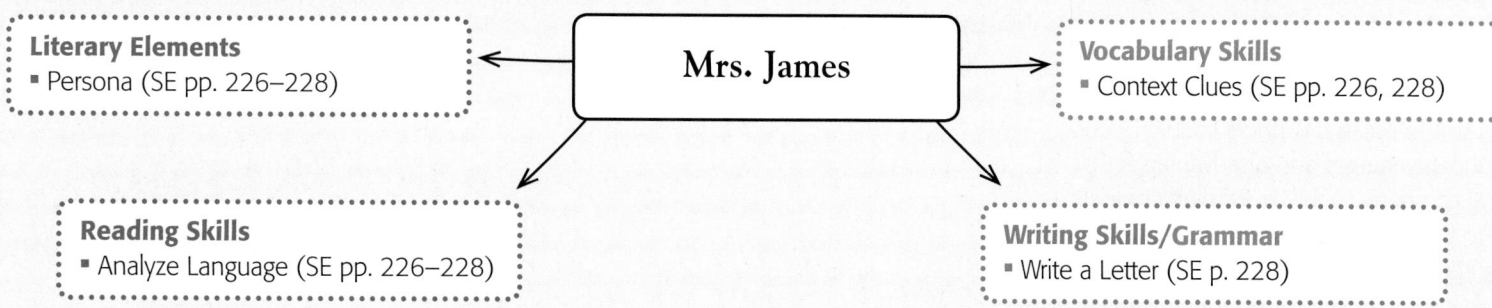

"All of us have heard, felt, and seen racism, but many do not wish to see it. It's too painful."

—Alice Childress

Childress continued to live in Manhattan, writing acclaimed plays and novels, as well as award-winning children's and young-adult books. In addition to writing, she lectured at Fisk University and Radcliffe College. She remained involved in theater until her death in 1994.

LOG ON **Literature** Online

Author Search For more about Alice Childress, go to glencoe.com and enter QuickPass code GL49787u1.

Before You Read

Focus

Bellringer Options

Daily Language Practice Transparency 20

Or ask students to talk about a job they once had. **Ask:** What did you like about the job and what did you dislike? After some discussion, instruct students to list the qualities of a good job. Then ask students to explain why these qualities are important to them. Explain that aside from the most obvious choices, such as high pay and time off, they should think about other benefits, such as being appreciated or having a good relationship with coworkers.

Selection Skills

Mrs. James

Literary Elements
- Persona (SE pp. 226–228)

Vocabulary Skills
- Context Clues (SE pp. 226, 228)

Reading Skills
- Analyze Language (SE pp. 226–228)

Writing Skills/Grammar
- Write a Letter (SE p. 228)

Before You Read

Focus

Summary

The narrator, Mildred, tells her friend about her wealthy boss, Mrs. James. Mrs. James can be irritating, but Mildred explains how she puts her boss in her place.

For summaries in languages other than English, see Unit 1 Teaching Resources Book, pp. 245–250.

Vocabulary

Use New Vocabulary To test vocabulary comprehension, have students write a paragraph using each of the vocabulary words at least once. Ask students who have used the words in the best and most creative ways to share their stories with the rest of the class.

For additional vocabulary practice, see Unit 1 Teaching Resources Book, p. 253.

For additional context, see Glencoe Interactive Vocabulary CD-ROM.

Literature and Reading Preview

Connect to the Story

Have you ever done work or chores? Write a journal entry about what it felt like to work for someone else.

Build Background

This story takes place in New York City, probably sometime in the late 1940s or early 1950s. At this time, the Great Depression, a period of great economic hardship for most Americans, was still a vivid memory. Although the economy had recovered and work was abundant, the difficulties of Depression-era life still haunted many people.

Set Purposes for Reading

Big Idea Dreams and Reality

As you read, ask yourself, How do you think Mildred's actual life compares to what she wishes her life were like?

Literary Element Persona

A **persona** is a narrator or person created by an author to tell a story. The attitudes and beliefs of the persona may differ from the author's. As you read, ask yourself, What characteristics define the personality of the narrator in "Mrs. James"?

Reading Strategy Analyze Language

When you **analyze language,** you determine how the author's use of language helps to create an authentic **tone.** For example, an author might have characters speak in a **dialect,** a specific variation of a language spoken by a group of people, often within a particular region. As you read, ask yourself, How does the narrator's language affect the tone of the story?

Tip: Take Notes As you read, use a simple three-column chart to take notes on the language.

Example of Dialect	What Character is Expressing	How Language Affects Tone
"she come into the kitchen and says,"	Mrs. James walked in and said...	

Learning Objectives

For pages 225–228

In studying this text, you will focus on the following objectives:

Literary Study: Analyzing persona.

Reading: Analyzing language.

Writing: Writing a letter.

Vocabulary

pantry (pan′ trē) *n.* room or closet in which food and articles for preparing and serving food are kept; p. 227 *The pantry was fully stocked once I made a quick trip to the grocery store.*

sashay (sa shā′) *v.* to walk or move in a way that shows indifference or a lack of interest; p. 227 *She sashayed by without even looking at her ex-boyfriend.*

Tip: Context Clues To decipher the meaning of an unfamiliar word, determine what the rest of the sentence is describing. Try to figure out how the unfamiliar word relates to what is being described. Example: *The pantry was fully stocked once I made a quick trip to the grocery store.* Based on the rest of the sentence, the *pantry* must be something that is filled with things from a grocery store, or food.

Listening and Speaking Practice

Pros and Cons Have students work with a partner to discuss their future career plans. Each student should develop a list of three job positions that he or she might want to pursue. Partners should discuss the advantages and disadvantages that accompany each job. Remind students to take notes during their discussion and use their notes to chart the pros and cons. Ask volunteers to present their information to the class. After each presentation, **ask:** If you had to choose one of these jobs today, which one would you choose and why? Students should support their answers.

Mrs. James

Alice Childress

Well Marge, you haven't heard anything! You should hear the woman I work for . . . she's really something. Calls herself "Mrs. James!" All the time she says "Mrs. James."

The first day I was there she come into the kitchen and says, "Mildred, Mrs. James would like you to clean the **pantry**." Well I looked 'round to see if she meant her mother-in-law or somebody and then she adds, "If anyone calls, Mrs. James is out shopping." And with that she **sashays** out the door.

Now she keeps on talking that way all the time, the whole time I'm there. That woman wouldn't say "I" or "me" for nothing in the world. The way I look at it . . . I guess she thought it would be too personal.

Now Marge, you know I don't work Saturdays for nobody! Well sir! Last Friday she breezed in the kitchen and fussed around a little . . . movin' first the salt and then the pepper, I could feel something brewin' in the air. Next thing you know she speaks up. "Mildred," she says, "Mrs. James will need you this Saturday." I was polishin' silver at the time but I turned around and looked her dead in the eye

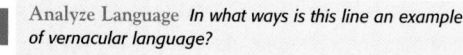

and said, "Mildred does not work on Saturdays."

Well, for the rest of the day things went along kind of quiet-like but just before time for me to go home she drifted by the linen closet to check the ruffle on a guest towel and threw in her two cents more. "Mildred," she says, "a depression might do this country some good, then some people might work eight days a week and be glad for the chance to do it."

I didn't bat an eyelash, but about 15 minutes later when I was headin' for home, I stopped off at the living room and called to her, "That's very true, but on the other hand some folks might be doin' their own housework . . . don'tcha know." With that and a cool "goodnight" I gently went out the front door. . . .

Oh, but we get along fine now. . . . Just fine!

1 Analyze Language *In what ways is this line an example of vernacular language?*

Vocabulary

pantry (pan′ trē) *n.* room or closet in which food and articles for preparing and serving food are kept

sashay (sa shā′) *v.* to walk or move in a way that shows indifference or a lack of interest

Dreams and Reality *Why do you think it is important to Mildred that she not work on Saturdays?* 2

Teach

Reading Strategy 1

Analyze Language

Answer: *The line uses technically incorrect grammar—a double negative—in order to create a realistic voice for the character. Although the language is ungrammatical, it reflects the everyday language used by the characters.*

Big Idea 2

Dreams and Reality

Answer: *It is important because she has very little time for herself, and it is also one of the only parts of her job that she can control and make her own decisions about.*

To check students' understanding of the selection, see Unit 1 Teaching Resources Book, p. 255.

Progress Check

Can students identify persona?

If No → See Unit 1 Teaching Resources Book, p. 251.

For an audio recording of this selection, use Listening Library Audio CD-ROM.

Readability Scores

Dale-Chall: 4.2
DRP: 56
Lexile: 880

Approaching Level

DIFFERENTIATED INSTRUCTION

AAVE One pattern of African American Vernacular English (AAVE) is dropping the /g/ sound at the end of words ending in *-ing*. **Say:** Some speakers may say *lookin'* instead of *looking* or *helpin'* instead of *helping.* Ask students to find examples of this pattern within the story. *(movin', brewin', polishin', headin', doin')* To practice **reading fluency,** have students read these sentences aloud. Thank ask them to replace the vernacular with the standard English form of the word. Explain that some stories are written using AAVE to help characterize the speaker. Remind students that AAVE is not always appropriate in writing. Point out that it would not be acceptable in a research paper or business letter.

After You Read

Assess

1. Answers will vary.
2. (a)Mrs. James asks Mildred to work on Saturday. (b)Mrs. James fusses with the shakers because she is afraid to ask Mildred.
3. (a)She says a depression might make some people work more. (b)Her remark shows that she thinks Mildred should simply be grateful that she has a job.
4. Possible answer: By leaving quietly instead of angrily, Mildred's departure shows dignity and self-control.
5. Answers will vary.
6. Mrs. James has probably never been poor or had to work very hard, so her reality is one of comfort and luxury. This contrasts strongly with the reality in Mildred's life, which is filled with hard work and a background of struggling.
7. Possible answers: The details of her work, such as cleaning the pantry, and the ruffles on the linen towels; the routine of Mildred's day.

Literary Element

1. Mildred's persona could be seen to represent the "working class" in general, the people who are often at the mercy of employers who don't respect them as people.
2. By using the word "you" frequently, the persona draws the reader in and makes the reader feel like a part of the story.

After You Read

Respond and Think Critically

Respond and Interpret

1. Would you want to meet either Mildred or Mrs. James? Explain.
2. (a)What does Mrs. James ask Mildred to do that Mildred finds very upsetting? (b)During this scene, how do the two characters seem to feel?
3. (a)What does Mrs. James say to Mildred after their confrontation about Saturdays? (b)What does Mrs. James mean by her comment?

Analyze and Evaluate

4. Why do you think Childress has Mildred leave "gently" instead of doing something like slamming the door?
5. Do you think this very short text is a complete and effective story? Why or why not?

Connect

6. **Big Idea** **Dreams and Reality** What differences between Mrs. James's and Mildred's realities make it difficult for them to understand each other?
7. **Connect to the Author** Early in her career, Alice Childress worked as a domestic, or a household servant such as a maid. What specific details in the story reveal this firsthand experience?

Literary Element Persona

Authors often intend for a **persona** to reflect one or more parts of society, giving the story a larger meaning. For example, an author might use a child persona as a representative of all children in order to say something about childhood.

1. In this story, what group of people does the persona represent?
2. What is the effect of the persona's method of telling the story?

Reading Strategy Analyze Language

Review the note-taking chart that you kept while reading and then answer the following questions.

1. How does the dialogue reflect the differences between the two women's personalities?
2. How does Childress's use of dialect and vernacular affect the tone of the story?

LOG ON Literature Online

Selection Resources For Selection Quizzes, eFlashcards, and Reading-Writing Connection activities, go to glencoe.com and enter QuickPass code GL49787u1.

Vocabulary Practice

Practice with Context Clues Identify the context clues in the following sentences that help you determine the meaning of each boldfaced vocabulary word.

1. The children kept sneaking into the **pantry** and stealing cookies, chips, and other snacks.
2. The woman was clearly uninterested in anything in the store as she **sashayed** through the cosmetics department.

Writing

Write a Letter Write a letter to Mrs. James, giving her advice about how to treat household employees. Write the letter using the persona of someone who has spent many years as a domestic worker or as someone who has his or her own household employees. Make sure the persona strongly reflects the character's personality.

Reading Strategy

1. Mrs. James' dialogue reflects her stiff, cold personality, and Mildred's dialogue expresses her warmth and expressiveness.
2. The use of the vernacular creates an engaging tone that gives the reader the feeling of being in the story's setting.

Vocabulary Practice

1. *cookie, chips, and other snacks*
2. *uninterested*

Writing

Students' letters should

- follow the standard conventions of letter-writing form
- directly address Mrs. James and convey to her advice on household employees
- be written in a distinct persona

Before You Read

World Literature
Poland

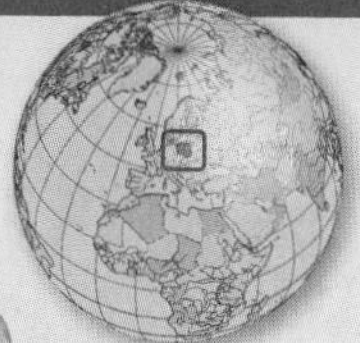

The Son from America

Meet **Isaac Bashevis Singer** (1904–1991)

"Of course, I believe in free will," Isaac Bashevis Singer once said. "I have no choice." This is the kind of sweetly humorous and delightfully human contradiction that marked his fiction, and, to some extent, his life.

Childhood in Poland Singer was born in a shtetl—a small, Jewish village—near Warsaw, Poland. When he was four, his family moved to Warsaw, where he spent most of his childhood. His father and both of his grandfathers were rabbis, and Singer passed his boyhood immersed in religious studies. The expectation was that he would be a rabbi, too, but at a very young age he began to have doubts about religion.

> *"The greatness of art is not to find what is common but what is unique."*
>
> —Isaac Bashevis Singer

Besides his constant reading, two experiences proved very important for the future writer. One was listening to the people who came to his father for advice. The young Singer overheard their stories, their conflicts, and their individual and collective voices. Another important experience was living in his grandfather's village, Bilgoray, for three or four years when he was an adolescent. There, according to Singer, "the traditions of hundreds of years ago still lived," and he "learned a lot about Jewishness."

A Son from America In some ways, Singer himself became a "son from America." First, he did not follow the path his parents wanted him to pursue: instead of becoming a rabbi, he became a writer. He also left home for the United States—although with Hitler in power in Germany and conflict on the rise, leaving Europe was as much necessity as choice. In 1935, Singer joined his older brother who already worked in the United States as a writer.

Once in the United States, Singer wrote extensively. Working for the *Jewish Daily Forward*, he published one or two stories or chapters a week for more than forty years. All together, he wrote forty-five volumes of short stories, as well as novels, plays, autobiographies, and children's stories.

A Lifetime of Achievement Singer received numerous awards, including the Nobel Prize in Literature in 1978. His short story collection *A Crown of Feathers*, which includes "The Son from America," won a National Book Award in 1974.

LOG ON **Literature** Online

Author Search For more about Isaac Bashevis Singer, go to glencoe.com and enter QuickPass code GL49787u1.

Before You Read

Focus

Bellringer Options

Selection Focus Transparency 15

Daily Language Practice Transparency 21

Or have students discuss the following question: Are your memories of the past usually accurate, or do you tend to forget significant details? Ask volunteers to share their earliest memories. Then ask students to explain why memories are so important. As students read, they should consider the difference between Samuel's memory of his home village and the reality.

Selection Skills

The Son from America

Literary Elements
- Style (SE pp. 230–238)
- Voice (SE p. 238)

Reading Skills
- Make Inferences About Theme (SE pp. 230–239)

Vocabulary Skills
- Word Origins (SE p. 230)
- Academic Vocabulary (SE p. 239)

Listening/Speaking/Viewing Skills
- Analyze Art (TE pp. 234, 237)

Writing Skills
- Apply Tone (SE p. 239)

Before You Read

Focus

Summary

Life in the tiny Polish village of Lentshin continues uneventfully, as it always has for Berl and his wife Berlcha. Then one day, their son returns from the United States after 40 years, bearing gifts and modern ideas about wealth and happiness.

For summaries in languages other than English, see Unit 1 Teaching Resources Book, pp. 257-262.

Vocabulary

Synonym Chains Have one student read the first vocabulary word and definition. Then, ask the student to finish this sentence: "A synonym of the word is . . ." The next student should repeat the new word, define it, and finish the sentence: "A synonym of the word is . . ." Keep the chain going until a student cannot come up with an additional synonym. Then move on to the next vocabulary word.

Literature and Reading Preview

Connect to the Story

Do you think the simpler life of earlier generations is superior to modern life? Discuss this question with a small group.

Build Background

This story takes place sometime between 1896 and 1917. The setting is the fictional town of Lentshin, Poland, a Jewish community in which the Sabbath (the holy day), the synagogue (the place of worship), and Jewish rites and rituals create the daily round of life. Thus, one of the main characters, Berlcha, lights candles on the Sabbath and keeps separate shelves for meat and for dairy.

Set Purposes for Reading

Big Idea Dreams and Reality

As you read "The Son from America," ask yourself, What is dreamlike about the setting, and how does it contrast with ideas of "real" or modern life?

Literary Element Style

Style is the expressive qualities that distinguish an author's work, including word choice, the length and arrangement of sentences, and the use of figurative language and imagery. As you read, ask yourself, What are the effects of Singer's choices of words and sentence and paragraph structures?

Reading Strategy Make Inferences About Theme

A **theme** is a work's main idea or message. Sometimes, the reader has to **infer** the author's theme, or use his or her reason and experience to deduce what an author is saying indirectly. As you read, ask yourself, Based on the details, what can I infer about the overall meaning of the story?

Tip: Take Notes Use a chart to help you track your inferences about the theme.

Example	Inference
"But they never seemed to use the money. What for?"	Although the couple have little material wealth, they feel they have all that they need.

Learning Objectives

For pages 229–239

In studying this text, you will focus on the following objectives:

Literary Study: Analyzing style.

Reading: Making inferences about theme.

Writing: Applying tone in retellings of a folktale.

Vocabulary

mock (mok) *v.* to make fun of or ridicule; p. 231 *The mean boys mock the strange behaviors of the newcomer.*

contour (kon′ toor) *n.* outline or general shape; p. 235 *When deciding where to place the house, the architect considered the contour of the land.*

benediction (ben′ ə dik′ shən) *n.* short prayer used as a blessing; p. 235 *The priest gave the benediction before the meal.*

bestow (bi stō′) *v.* to give as a gift; p. 237 *The parents bestowed their treasures on their children.*

tread (tred) *n.* step or footstep; p. 237 *We barely heard the soft tread of the child's feet on the stairs.*

Tip: Word Origins Knowing the origin of a word can help you remember its meaning. For example, the word *benediction* was formed from the words *bene* (meaning "well") and *dicere* (meaning "speak").

Grammar Practice

Verb Tense Point out that the vocabulary words *mock* and *bestow* are verbs. Remind students that verb tense should be consistent, or parallel, within a sentence. Put the following sentences on the board. Ask students to find the error and rewrite each sentence.

- We watched a movie and talk about it afterward. *(talked)*
- Shelby knows that she will do well on the math test and thought she will do well on the English test, too. *(thinks)*
- The wind blew fiercely and the waves crashing into the rocks near the shore. *(crashed)*

Mount Kosciusko, 1955. Konrad Winkler. Oil on canvas, 51 x 66 in. National Museum, Krakow, Poland.

The Son from America

Isaac Bashevis Singer

The village of Lentshin was tiny—a sandy marketplace where the peasants of the area met once a week. It was surrounded by little huts with thatched roofs or shingles green with moss. The chimneys looked like pots. Between the huts there were fields, where the owners planted vegetables or pastured their goats.

In the smallest of these huts lived old Berl, a man in his eighties, and his wife, who was called Berlcha (wife of Berl). Old Berl was one of the Jews who had been driven from their villages in Russia and had settled in Poland. In Lentshin, they **mocked** the mistakes he made while praying aloud. He spoke with a sharp "r." He

Style *What images and figurative language do you find in this passage?*

Vocabulary

mock (mok) *v.* to make fun of or ridicule

Teach

Literary Element

Style **Answer:** *Images include little huts with thatched roofs and mossy shingles. The simile compares chimneys to pots.*

Ask: What do the author's choice of image and words suggest about his writing style? *(Students may say that the writer's style is down-to-earth and honest.)*

ENGLISH LEARNERS Inform English learners that this story is set in a small country village. Students should look for unfamiliar words that help to describe the village and the lives of those who live there. Remind students to use a dictionary to define unfamiliar words.

For an audio recording of this selection, use Listening Library Audio CD-ROM.

Readability Scores

Dale-Chall: 3.8
DRP: 54
Lexile: 760

Approaching Level

DIFFERENTIATED INSTRUCTION

Established Writers often give hints about a character by using vivid details to describe the character's actions, words, and physical appearance. Readers may then draw conclusions about the character's personality or values on the basis of these details. Read the following passage aloud: "Old Berl was one of the Jews who had been driven from their villages in Russia and had settled in Poland. In Lentshin, they mocked the mistakes he made while praying aloud. He spoke with a sharp 'r.'"

Ask: What do these details reveal about Berl? What kind of person do you think he is, based on this description? *(Possible answer: The details reveal that Berl is a survivor, even though others may see him as laughable.)*

Teach

Literary Element 1

Style **Answer:** *It is short and informal. Although it is not dialogue, it reflects the way some people speak.*

APPROACHING To aid approaching-level students, **ask:** Whose voice is reflected here? *(Students should realize that the voice could be that of Berl or of any person living in the village.)*

Reading Strategy 2

Make Inferences About Theme **Answer:** *The reader can infer from the couple's modest lifestyle that the theme will concern the relative value of material possessions and the question of what is required to lead a good and happy life.*

For additional practice using the reading skill or strategy, see Unit 1 Teaching Resources Book, p. 264.

was short, broad-shouldered, and had a small white beard, and summer and winter he wore a sheepskin hat, a padded cotton jacket, and stout boots. He walked slowly, shuffling his feet. He had a half acre of field, a cow, a goat, and chickens.

The couple had a son, Samuel, who had gone to America forty years ago. It was said in Lentshin that he became a millionaire there. Every month, the Lentshin letter carrier brought old Berl a money order and a letter that no one could read because many of the words were English. How much money Samuel sent his parents remained a secret. Three times a year, Berl and his wife went on foot to Zakroczym and cashed the money orders there. But they never seemed to use the money. What for? The garden, the cow, and the goat provided most of their needs. Besides, Berlcha sold chickens and eggs, and from these there was enough to buy flour for bread.

Her face was yellowish and wrinkled like a cabbage leaf.

No one cared to know where Berl kept the money that his son sent him. There were no thieves in Lentshin. The hut consisted of one room, which contained all their belongings: the table, the shelf for meat, the shelf for milk foods, the two beds, and the clay oven. Sometimes the chickens roosted in the woodshed and sometimes, when it was cold, in a coop near the oven. The goat, too, found shelter inside when the weather was bad. The more prosperous villagers had kerosene lamps, but Berl and his wife did not believe in newfangled gadgets. What was wrong with a wick in a dish of oil? Only for the Sabbath would Berlcha buy three tallow candles at the store. In summer, the couple got up at sunrise and retired with the chickens. In the long winter evenings, Berlcha spun flax[1] at her spinning wheel and Berl sat beside her in the silence of those who enjoy their rest.

Once in a while when Berl came home from the synagogue[2] after evening prayers, he brought news to his wife. In Warsaw there were strikers who demanded that the czar abdicate.[3] A heretic by the name of Dr. Herzl had come up with the idea that Jews should settle again in Palestine.[4] Berlcha listened and shook her bonneted head. Her face was yellowish and wrinkled like a cabbage leaf. There were bluish sacks under her eyes. She was half deaf. Berl had to repeat each word he said to her. She would say, "The things that happen in the big cities!"

Here in Lentshin nothing happened except usual events: a cow gave birth to a calf, a young couple has a bris,[5] or a girl was born and there was no party. Occasionally, someone died. Lentshin had no cemetery, and the corpse had to be taken to Zakroczym. Actually, Lentshin had become a village with few young people. The young men left for Zakroczym, for Nowy Dwor, for Warsaw, and sometimes

1 Style *How does this sentence contribute to style?*

2 Make Inferences About Theme *What details in these first paragraphs could you use to make inferences about the theme?*

1. *Flax* is a fiber made from the stem of a plant.
2. A *synagogue* (sin′ ə gog′) is a place for worship and religious instruction.
3. *Czar* is the title for Russian rulers until 1917. Russia ruled Poland at the time of the story. Abdicate means "to give up rule."
4. *Herzl* (1860–1904) refers to Dr. Theodor Herzl, the founder of Zionism, the movement to establish a Jewish state in Palestine, the biblical homeland of the Jews.
5. A *bris* is a Jewish ritual and celebration accompanying the birth of a male child.

Reading Practice

SPIRAL REVIEW **Predict**

Remind students that to predict means to make guesses about what will happen next in a story. **Say:** To make good predictions, pay attention to details in the story and use what you know about the subject of the story. After reading page 232, ask students to make predictions about what they think will happen next. Then ask them to make a note of these predictions. As students read, they should check to see if their predictions were correct.

for the United States. Like Samuel's, their letters were illegible, the Yiddish mixed with the languages of the countries where they were now living. They sent photographs in which the men wore top hats and the women fancy dresses like squiresses.

Berl and Berlcha also received such photographs. But their eyes were failing and neither he nor she had glasses. They could barely make out the pictures. Samuel had sons and daughters with Gentile[6] names—and grandchildren who had married and had their own offspring. Their names were so strange that Berl and Berlcha could never remember them. But what difference do names make? America was far, far away on the other side of the ocean, at the edge of the world. A Talmud[7] teacher who came to Lentshin had said that Americans walked with their heads down and their feet up. Berl and Berlcha could not grasp this. How was it possible? But since the teacher said so it must be true. Berlcha pondered for some time and then she said, "One can get accustomed to everything."

From too much thinking—God forbid—one may lose one's wits.

And so it remained. From too much thinking—God forbid—one may lose one's wits.

One Friday morning, when Berlcha was kneading the dough for the Sabbath loaves, the door opened and a nobleman entered. He was so tall that he had to bend down to get through the door. He wore a beaver hat and a cloak bordered with fur. He was followed by Chazkel, the coachman from Zakroczym, who carried two leather valises with brass locks. In astonishment Berlcha raised her eyes.

The nobleman looked around and said to the coachman in Yiddish, "Here it is." He took out a silver ruble[8] and paid him. The coachman tried to hand him change but he said, "You can go now."

When the coachman closed the door, the nobleman said, "Mother, it's me, your son Samuel—Sam."

Berlcha heard the words and her legs grew numb. Her hands, to which pieces of dough were sticking, lost their power. The nobleman hugged her, kissed her forehead, both her cheeks. Berlcha began to cackle like a hen, "My son!" At that moment Berl came in from the woodshed, his arms piled with logs. The goat followed him. When he saw a nobleman kissing his wife, Berl dropped the wood and exclaimed, "What is this?"

The nobleman let go of Berlcha and embraced Berl. "Father!"

For a long time Berl was unable to utter a sound. He wanted to recite holy words that he had read in the Yiddish Bible, but he could remember nothing. Then he asked, "Are you Samuel?"

"Yes, Father, I am Samuel."

"Well, peace be with you." Berl grasped his son's hand. He was still not sure that he was not being fooled. Samuel wasn't as tall and heavy as this man, but then Berl

---

6. A *Gentile* is a person who is not Jewish, usually someone who is Christian.
7. *Talmud* (täl′ mood) is a collection of Jewish civil and religious laws. A Talmud teacher explains the complications of the law to the people.
8. A *ruble* (ro͞o′ bəl) is a monetary unit in Russia and, in this case, Russian-occupied Poland.

3 Dreams and Reality *What makes these foreign places dreamlike to the parents who stay in Poland?*

Style *What is unusual about this sentence? What effect does it have?* **4**

Teach

Big Idea 3

Dreams and Reality
Answer: *Everything about them is beyond the realm of the parents' experience or understanding.*

Literary Element 4

Style **Answer:** *This sentence has an unexpected or inverted word order. The reversed word order puts more emphasis on Berlcha's astonishment.*

English Learners

DIFFERENTIATED INSTRUCTION

Early Advanced Students may be unfamilar with words related to Jewish customs and traditions. Write these words on the board: *synagogue, czar, bris, gentile, Talmud, ruble, Kaddish, Gefilte,* and *Torah.* Have students find the definitions of these words in the footnotes. Then, have volunteers read the definitions aloud.ELD R B 4

Approaching Level

DIFFERENTIATED INSTRUCTION

Established Some students may have difficulty visualizing the world of Lentshin, but it is important for their understanding of the story. Tell students to note details about the location as they read the story. When finished, have students describe Lentshin in a class discussion.

Teach

Reading Strategy 1

Make Inferences About Theme **Answer:** *It emphasizes the different life styles of the old couple and their son.*

Cultural History ☆

The Jewish Sabbath The Sabbath, or day of rest, is an important Jewish tradition. The Jewish Sabbath is observed from sunset on each Friday to sunset on Saturday. On the Sabbath, Jews do not work but attend religious services and gather for a festive meal. Sabbath customs prohibit the handling of money or traveling.

View the Art ★

Answer: *Students should point to passages in the text and details in the art to support their opinions.*

Peasants, 1914. Zinaida Serebryakova. The State Russian Museum, Moscow.

View the Art In what ways does this painting reflect life in the village of Lentshin? ★

reminded himself that Samuel was only fifteen years old when he had left home. He must have grown in that faraway country. Berl asked, "Why didn't you let us know that you were coming?"

"Didn't you receive my cable?" Samuel asked.

Berl did not know what a cable was.

Berlcha had scraped the dough from her hands and enfolded her son. He kissed her again and asked, "Mother, didn't you receive a cable?"

"What? If I lived to see this, I am happy to die," Berlcha said, amazed by her own words. Berl, too, was amazed. These were just the words he would have said earlier if he had been able to remember. After a while Berl came to himself and said, "Pescha, you will have to make a double Sabbath pudding in addition to the stew." ☆

It was years since Berl had called Berlcha by her given name. When he wanted to address her, he would say, "Listen," or "Say." It is the young or those from the big cities who call a wife by her name. Only now did Berlcha begin to cry. Yellow tears ran from her eyes, and everything became dim. Then she called out, "It's Friday— I have to prepare for the Sabbath." Yes, she had to knead the dough and braid the

Make Inferences About Theme *How does this passage change or reinforce your ideas about the theme?* 1

Reading Practice

SPIRAL REVIEW **Infer and Conclude** Although a U.S. resident at the time, Isaac Bashevis Singer wrote this story in his native Yiddish. **Ask:** Is Singer sentimental about the old country and its ways? How does he feel about American ways? Does he prefer one way of life to the other? Have students take notes as they read. Invite volunteers to share their conclusions and the details supporting them.

Ask students if "a longing for the past" is a common theme in literature. Have students suggest other stories in which this theme is present.

loaves. With such a guest, she had to make a larger Sabbath stew. The winter day is short and she must hurry.

Her son understood what was worrying her, because he said, "Mother, I will help you."

Berlcha wanted to laugh, but a choked sob came out. "What are you saying? God forbid."

The nobleman took off his cloak and jacket and remained in his vest, on which hung a solid-gold watch chain. He rolled up his sleeves and came to the trough. "Mother, I was a baker for many years in New York," he said, and he began to knead the dough.

"What! You are my darling son who will say Kaddish[9] for me." She wept raspingly. Her strength left her, and she slumped onto the bed.

Berl said, "Women will always be women." And he went to the shed to get more wood. The goat sat down near the oven; she gazed with surprise at this strange man—his height and his bizarre clothes.

The neighbors had heard the good news that Berl's son had arrived from America and they came to greet him. The women began to help Berlcha prepare for the Sabbath. Some laughed, some cried. The room was full of people, as at a wedding. They asked Berl's son, "What is new in America?" And Berl's son answered, "America is all right."

"Do Jews make a living?"

"One eats white bread there on weekdays."

"Do they remain Jews?"

☆ "I am not a Gentile."

After Berlcha blessed the candles, father and son went to the little synagogue across the street. A new snow had fallen. The son took large steps, but Berl warned him, "Slow down."

In the synagogue the Jews recited "Let Us Exult" and "Come, My Groom." All the time, the snow outside kept falling. After prayers, when Berl and Samuel left the Holy Place, the village was unrecognizable. Everything was covered in snow. One could see only the **contours** of the roofs and the candles in the windows. Samuel said, "Nothing has changed here."

Berlcha had prepared gefilte fish,[10] chicken soup with rice, meat, carrot stew. Berl recited the **benediction** over a glass of ritual wine. The family ate and drank, and when it grew quiet for a while one could hear the chirping of the house cricket. The son talked a lot, but Berl and Berlcha understood little. His Yiddish was different and contained foreign words.

After the final blessing Samuel asked, "Father, what did you do with all the money I sent you?"

Berl raised his white brows. "It's here."

"Didn't you put it in a bank?"

"There is no bank in Lentshin."

"Where do you keep it?"

Berl hesitated. "One is not allowed to touch money on the Sabbath, but I will show you." He crouched beside the bed and began to shove something heavy. A boot appeared. Its top was stuffed with straw. Berl removed the straw and the son saw that the boot was full of gold coins. He lifted it.

9. *Kaddish* (kä′ dish) is a prayer, generally recited by mourners.

10. *Gefilte* (gə fil′ tə) *fish* is a preparation of minced fish and other ingredients shaped into balls or cakes.

2 Style *In your opinion, why might Singer have chosen to give the goat human-like qualities here?*

Dreams and Reality *What details make the village seem like a dream world?* **3**

Vocabulary

contour (kon′ toor) *n.* outline or general shape

benediction (ben′ ə dik′ shən) *n.* short prayer used as a blessing

Teach

Literary Element 2

Style Answer: *Students may say that the goat represents the parents' rural culture. Others may say that it adds humor to an emotional moment.*

Big Idea 3

Dreams and Reality

Answer: *The snow covers everything, making it unrecognizable. The village seems wrapped in a white shroud, a world that time forgot.*

Language History ☆

Gentile Pronounced jen′ tīl, the word literally means "nation" and comes from the Latin root gens for "race or people." Centuries ago, Jews applied the word to "heathens"—people who practiced polytheism. Later, it came to be used as a term for Christians.

English Learners

DIFFERENTIATED INSTRUCTION

Beginning/Early Intermediate Explain that time-order words and phrases, such as *when, a moment later,* and *for a long time,* help readers link events in the story. Have English language learners reread the page to identify time-order words and phrases. Ask them to write down these words and phrases, along with the events that happen after each one.

Intermediate Have students practice their understanding of chronological order by writing a list of what happens once Samuel arrives in Lentshin. When everyone is finished, have students compare their lists in a class discussion.

Teach

Literary Element 1

Style Answer: *It seems to suggest he does not know what to say or do with so much money, while at the same time implying that for them this wealth is not really a treasure.*

ADVANCED To challenge advanced learners, **ask:** What is ironic about Samuel's comment that "Nothing has changed here"? *(The village was just described as unrecognizable under the snow, but Samuel sees it as exactly the same.)*

Reading Strategy 2

Make Inferences About Theme Answer: *They were completely content with what they had.*

Big Idea 3

Dreams and Reality
Answer: *Some students will say he is more in touch with the practical realities of today's world than his parents; others will argue that the parents' simpler existence is more authentic and meaningful.*

"Father, this is a treasure!" he called out.

"Well."

"Why didn't you spend it?"

"On what? Thank God, we have everything."

"Why didn't you travel somewhere?"

"Where to? This is our home."

The son asked one question after the other, but Berl's answer was always the same: they wanted for nothing. The garden, the cow, the goat, the chickens provided them with all they needed. The son said, "If thieves knew about this, your lives wouldn't be safe."

"There are no thieves here."

"What will happen to the money?"

"You take it."

Slowly, Berl and Berlcha grew accustomed to their son and his American Yiddish. Berlcha could hear him better now. She even recognized his voice. He was saying, "Perhaps we should build a larger synagogue."

"The synagogue is big enough," Berl replied.

"Perhaps a home for old people."

"No one sleeps in the street."

The next day after the Sabbath meal was eaten, a Gentile from Zakroczym brought a paper—it was the cable. Berl and Berlcha lay down for a nap. They soon began to snore. The goat, too, dozed off. The son put on his cloak and his hat and went for a walk. He strode with his long legs across the marketplace. He stretched out a hand and touched a roof. He wanted to smoke a cigar, but he remembered it was forbidden on the Sabbath. He had a desire to talk to someone, but it seemed that the whole of Lentshin was asleep. He entered the synagogue. An old man was sitting there, reciting psalms. Samuel asked, "Are you praying?"

"What else is there to do when one gets old?"

"Do you make a living?"

The old man did not understand the meaning of these words. He smiled, showing his empty gums, and then he said, "If God gives health, one keeps on living."

Samuel returned home. Dusk had fallen. Berl went to the synagogue for the evening prayers and the son remained with his mother. The room was filled with shadows.

"If God gives health, one keeps on living."

Berlcha began to recite in a solemn singsong, "God of Abraham, Isaac, and Jacob,[11] defend the poor people of Israel and Thy name. The Holy Sabbath is departing; the welcome week is coming to us. Let it be one of health, wealth, and good deeds."

"Mother, you don't need to pray for wealth," Samuel said. "You are wealthy already."

Berlcha did not hear—or pretended not to. Her face had turned into a cluster of shadows.

In the twilight Samuel put his hand into his jacket pocket and touched his passport, his checkbook, his letters of credit. He had

11. *Abraham, Isaac, and Jacob* are the original ancestors of the Jewish people. Abraham was the father of Isaac, who was the father of Jacob. They appear in the Torah and the Old Testament of the Bible.

1 Style *How does this single word convey a great deal of meaning?*

Make Inferences About Theme *In what ways are Berl and Berlcha wealthy?* 2

Dreams and Reality *Do you think Samuel represents the real world? Explain.* 3

Listening Practice

SMALL GROUP SPIRAL REVIEW **Group Discussion** Discuss the emotional state of Samuel and his parents during their reunion. *(The parents are overwhelmed, surprised, and a little disbelieving; Samuel is expectant and joyful.)* Invite volunteers to demonstrate how each character would speak, move, and gesture to convey these feelings.

Have groups of three act out the scene for the class. Remind students to base their performances on details from the text. When the students are finished performing, ask questions about the speech, movements, and gestures they made. Have them describe the emotions of the characters, how they chose to express these emotions, and why.

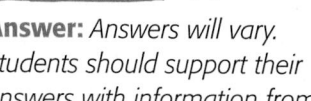

Shiviti, 19th century Jewish folk art from Poland. Collection of Isaac Einhorn. Tel Aviv, Israel.

View the Art A *shiviti* is a decorative plaque or artistic work based on the Biblical verse, "I have set the Lord always before me." Is this an appropriate piece of art to go with the story? Why or why not? ★

come here with big plans. He had a valise filled with presents for his parents. He wanted to **bestow** gifts on the village. He brought not only his own money but funds from the Lentshin Society in New York, which had organized a ball for the benefit of the village. But this village in the hinterland needed nothing. From the synagogue one could hear hoarse chanting. The cricket, silent all day, started again its chirping. Berlcha began to sway and utter holy rhymes inherited from mothers and grandmothers:

Thy holy sheep
In mercy keep,
In Torah[12] *and good deeds;*
Provide for all their needs,
Shoes, clothes, and bread
And the Messiah's ***tread.*** ∾

12. *Torah* (tôr′ə) can be narrowly defined as the five books of Moses or broadly defined as a collection of Jewish texts including scripture and law.

Vocabulary

bestow (bi stō′) *v.* to give as a gift

Vocabulary

tread (tred) *n.* step or footstep

Teach

View the Art ★

Answer: *Answers will vary. Students should support their answers with information from the text.*

In the 18th and 19th centuries, these elaborate works of art often hung in synagogues and Jewish homes.

To check students' understanding of the selection, see Unit 1 Teaching Resources Book, p. 268.

Progress Check

Can students analyze style?

If No → See Unit 1 Teaching Resources Book, p. 263.

English Learners

DIFFERENTIATED INSTRUCTION

Intermediate Readers may have trouble identifying the speakers when the dialogue does not contain tags. To practice **reading fluency,** suggest that students work in groups to read page 236 aloud. Before students begin, they should decide who will read the narrator's words, Samuel's words, Berl's words, and the words of the old man outside of the synagogue. Have students read the scene aloud. After reading, ask students to describe each character based on the dialogue from page 236.

After You Read

Assess

1. Students may sympathize with Samuel's desire to share his wealth with the villagers.
2. (a) A half-acre, a cow, a goat, chickens, a table, two shelves, two beds, and an oven (b)There is nothing to steal; also the people do not consider themselves poor.
3. (a) Forty years ago; He went to the United States, became a baker, and had children and grandchildren. (b) To visit his parents and to provide for the community
4. (a) They never spent it. (b) He cannot understand why they would not want to "improve" their lives.
5. (a) The idea that "from too much thinking . . . one may lose one's wits"; the arrival of the cable one day after Samuel; the goat's "surprise" at Samuel; and Berl's suggestion that Samuel take the money (b) It entertains and provides insight into human nature.
6. Yes, it reinforces the importance and changelessness of tradition.
7. The story mixes these elements. Berlcha and Berl are predictable, and the ending of the story for them is clear. But the story is full of ambiguity. Both parents and child are sympathetic characters.
8. (a) It is a faraway land with strange ways and untold wealth. (b) It is stuck in time, untouched by the modern world
9. Answers may vary. Students may mention such technologies as text messaging and Internet activities.

After You Read

Respond and Think Critically

Respond and Interpret

1. If you were Samuel, how would you feel about your visit to Lentshin?
2. (a)Name five things that Berl and his wife own. (b)Why are there no thieves in Lentshin?
3. (a)When did Samuel leave home, and what happened to him since Berl and Berlcha last saw him? (b)Why does Samuel return?
4. (a)What does Samuel learn about the money that he has sent his parents? (b)Why is he amazed at what he learns?

Analyze and Evaluate

5. (a)There is some gentle humor in this story. Identify two examples. (b)What does the humor add to the story?
6. Do you think that the "holy rhymes" make a good conclusion for the story?
7. In modern fiction, characters, motives, outcomes, and themes can be highly complex and ambiguous. Alternatively, in a folk story, the characters are often predictable and the outcome is clear. Do you think "The Son from America" is more like a folktale or modern fiction? Explain using examples from the story.

Connect

8. **Big Idea** Dreams and Reality (a)In what ways does America seem like a dream to Berl and Berlcha? (b)In what ways does Lentshin seem to be a dreamlike or fantastic place to their son?
9. **Connect to Today** Samuel and his parents have a difficult time understanding one another. What new technologies, or ways of doing things, might cause parents and children of today to disagree?

Literary Element Style

SAT Skills Practice

1. In describing what Berl had done with his money (pages 235–236), the author's tone is
   (A) amused and affectionate
   (B) mocking and ironic
   (C) sad and regretful
   (D) critical and superior
   (E) angry and passionate
2. The description of the village and of old Berl in the first two paragraphs (page 231) give this story the flavor of a
   (A) tall tale
   (B) folktale
   (C) myth
   (D) science fiction story
   (E) drama

Review: Voice

As you learned on pages 184–185, **voice** is the distinctive use of language that conveys the author's or narrator's personality to the reader. In "The Son from America," the narrator's voice is that of a Yiddish storyteller.

Partner Activity Work with a partner to find examples of things that are said in the story in a voice that sounds different to you from that of a typical American English speaker. From that list, draw a conclusion about Yiddish vocabulary, word order, or sentences.

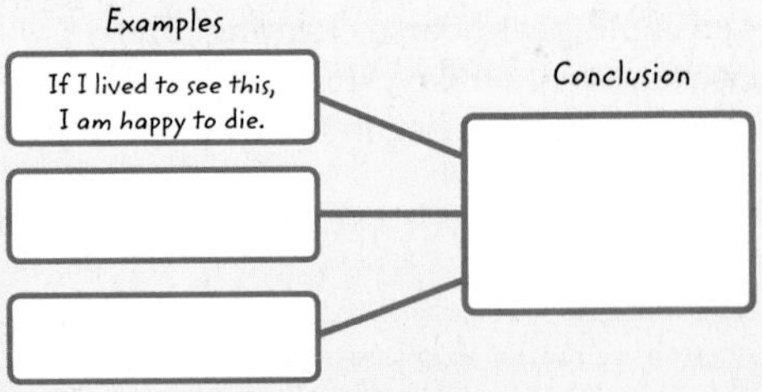

Literary Element

1. A is the correct answer. The narrator uses humor throughout the story and is clearly fond of his characters.
2. B is the correct answer. The distant setting, simple style, and fond description of old Berl are reminiscent of a folktale.

Review: Voice

Students may point to additional examples, such as "The cricket, silent all day, started again its chirping" and "With such a guest, she had to make a larger Sabbath stew." Students should conclude that, in Yiddish, word order is often inverted.

Reading Strategy Make Inferences About Theme

Most literary works have an **implied theme,** which is revealed gradually through events, dialogue, or description. Learning to accurately **make inferences** will allow you to find deeper meaning in any work of literature. Review your inferences chart, and then answer the following questions.

1. What do you think is the primary theme in "The Son from America"?
2. What is one secondary, or minor, theme in the story? Point to specific passages in the story as evidence.

Vocabulary Practice

Practice with Word Origins Studying the etymology, or origin and history, of a word can help you better understand and explore its meaning. Create a word map for each of these boldface vocabulary words from the selection. Use a dictionary for help.

mock **contour** **benediction** **bestow** **tread**

Etymology: Latin solari means "to console"

Definition: relief from sorrow or disappointment

solace

Sample Sentence: The grieving woman found solace in the star-filled sky.

Academic Vocabulary

In the story, it takes a while for Berl to ***register*** *the identity of the "nobleman."*

When someone comprehends or becomes aware of something, you might say that the person *registered* it. Why doesn't Berl **register** the identity of the "nobleman" right away?

For more on academic vocabulary, see pages 54–55 and R79–R81.

Write with Style

Apply Tone

Assignment Choose a folktale and write two brief versions of it, changing the tone, but not the action, for each draft. Tone is the author's attitude, such as serious or humorous, toward the subject matter.

Get Ideas Find and review two versions of a folktale. Note how each one has its own distinct tone. Think about what tone you want to use for each version of the folktale you have chosen to retell.

Give It Structure Although the language will be different in each of your versions, the structure of the action should be the same. Use a chart to lay out the action in the folktale in chronological order.

Paul Bunyan raises a blue ox.
↓
Babe grows into giant.
↓
Babe straightens logging roads.
↓
Babe pulls wagon that leaks and creates Mississippi.

Use these events to structure your versions, but make sure your descriptions of the events reflect the tone that you have chosen for each version.

Look at Language Pay close attention to word choice; it is key to creating a distinct tone. Choose language that strongly evokes the appropriate tone.

EXAMPLE:

Admiring tone: *Babe quickly grew into a beautiful giant—a grand, towering animal.*

Intimidated tone: *Babe grew fast and soon became a heavy, thundering, oversized creature.*

LOG ON **Literature Online**

Selection Resources For Selection Quizzes, eFlashcards, and Reading-Writing Connection activities, go to glencoe.com and enter QuickPass code GL49787u1.

After You Read

Assess

Reading Strategy

1. That wealth and poverty are not absolute terms but are relative to the society in which one lives
2. Samuel's desire to improve the lives of the villagers by giving them money illustrates the theme that good intentions are often out of touch with reality.

Vocabulary Practice

mock: Etymology: Middle French mocquer means "to ridicule"
Definition: to make fun of or ridicule
Sample Sentence: The children continued to mock the little boy's hat, even after he started crying.

contour: Etymology: Latin contornare means "to go around"
Definition: the outline of a figure or shape
Sample Sentence: The contour of the chair fits perfectly into the curve of my back.

benediction: Etymology: Latin benedicere means "to speak well of"
Definition: a blessing
Sample Sentence: The minister gave a benediction at the end of the marriage ceremony.

bestow: Etymology: Middle English bestowen means "to place"
Definition: to give as a gift
Sample Sentence: We visited my aunt to bestow gifts on her and her new baby.

tread: Etymology: Old English tredan means "tread"
Definition: a step
Sample Sentence: As the hiker's legs grew tired, her tread became heavier and heavier.

Academic Vocabulary

He doesn't register his identity right away because he has not seen his son since he was a teenager and still imagined him as a boy, not as a full grown man.

Write with Style

Students' folktales should:

- include the main events and characters from the source folktale
- share a similar plot structure in both versions
- present the events clearly and in proper chronological order
- use word choice to create a distinctly different tone in each version
- maintain a consistent tone throughout each version

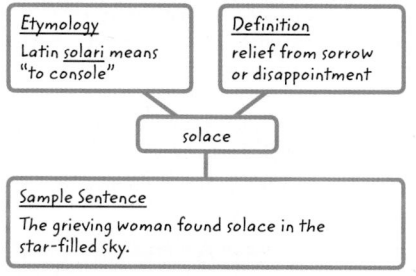

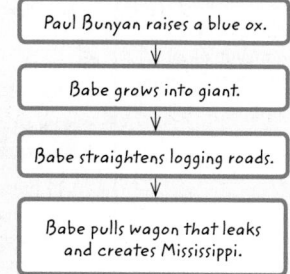

Writing Workshop

Response to Literature

Focus

Bellringer

Have students recall a favorite story. **Ask:** Why did the story become a favorite? Can you remember what you thought or felt the first time you read it? Ask students to reflect on their original response to their favorite story as they learn to write a response to literature.

Summary

In this workshop, students will write and present a response to literature. They will follow the stages of the writing process, including prewriting, drafting, revising, and editing. In addition, the workshop provides two mini-lessons, on including clear examples and correcting sentence fragments.

Learning Objectives

For pages 240–247

In this workshop, you will focus on the following objectives:

Writing:
Writing a response to literature using the writing process.
Using clear examples to support a thesis.

Grammar: Understanding how to correct sentence fragments.

Writing Process

At any stage of a writing process, you may think of new ideas. Feel free to return to earlier stages as you write.

- Prewrite
- Draft
- Revise
- Focus Lesson: Clear Examples
- Edit and Proofread
- Focus Lesson: Sentence Fragments
- Present/Publish

LOG ON **Literature Online**

Writing and Research For prewriting, drafting, and revising tools, go to glencoe.com and enter QuickPass code GL49787u1.

Writing Workshop

Response to Literature

Literature Connection What reader could fail to respond to this grim foreshadowing of death in Edgar Allan Poe's "The Cask of Amontillado"?

> *"At the most remote end of the crypt there appeared another less spacious. Its walls had been lined with human remains, piled to the vault overhead."*

Perhaps Poe caused you to recoil a bit as you read these details about human remains piled several feet high. Perhaps he scared you as he led you deeper and deeper into the crypt, or burial vault. Those personal reactions are fodder for a response to literature: a personal reaction to some aspect of a work. Read these goals and strategies for writing an effective response to literature.

Checklist

Goals	Strategies
To present your personal response to and thorough understanding of a story	☑ Focus on your feelings and thoughts as you demonstrate awareness of and appreciation for the author's style
To organize and focus your response with an introduction, body, and conclusion	☑ Introduce the work ☑ Present a thesis clearly stating your personal perspective ☑ Maintain your focus in the body paragraphs ☑ Summarize your response
To use examples to support your response	☑ Provide accurate and detailed references to the text to support your thesis ☑ Connect your examples to your response
To engage your audience	☑ Use first-person point of view and an active voice ☑ Use precise language and sensory details ☑ Match your tone to your response and keep it consistent

Workshop Resources

Print Materials

- Unit 1 Teaching Resources pp. 271–273
- Writing Kit
- Success in Writing: Research and Reports

Technology

- Literature Online: Writing Resources and Grammar Resources, www.glencoe.com
- Online Essay Grader, www.glencoe.com
- Student Presentation Builder on StudentWorks Plus CD-ROM
- Media Workshop DVD
- Online Student Edition

Assignment: Respond to a Short Story

Write a response of at least 1,000 words to a short story. Include specific details and quotations to support a viewpoint about one aspect of the work, such as characters, events, or setting.

Audience: peers, classmates, and teacher

Purpose: to express a clear, focused response to a short story

Analyzing a Professional Model

In this selection, Oscar Hijuelos describes his first reading of a short story that inspired him to become a writer. Note how Hijuelos creates a controlling perspective through his unified focus, word choice, and tone. The comments in the margin point out features to include in your response.

Real-World Connection

In the workplace, you may be asked to respond to a draft proposal, memo, or other document. This task will require many of the same skills you use in responding to literature: writing in the first person, presenting a controlling perspective, organizing your response logically and coherently, maintaining your focus, and using an appropriate tone for your audience and purpose.

"On 'The Aleph'" by Oscar Hijuelos ☆

I first encountered "The Aleph" by the great Argentine writer Jorge Luis Borges one afternoon over twenty years ago, in 1973—I believe—when I was down on the Lower East Side visiting a friend, a young Armenian intellectual, such as one might meet at City College in those days. While he fiddled about in his kitchen (or walked his dog, or pleaded/conversed with his girlfriend on the telephone), I sat on his itchy, cat-haired, roach-egged couch, idly riffling through a pile of books that I had pulled from his shelves, among them a mildewed, jaundiced-looking, much-read-over pocketbook edition of *The Aleph and Other Stories* by Borges. Now, just a few days earlier I had been informed about the results of an aptitude test I had taken, the upshot being that I was apparently most suited for the profession of accounting. That well may have been my destiny, but I am happy (unhappy?) to report that the experience of reading "The Aleph" for the first of many times had a great effect upon me and my future; I have loved and will always love that story—and I will always be indebted to Borges for

Audience Engagement

Use first-person point of view, active voice, precise language, and sensory details.

Writing Workshop

Response to Literature

Teach

Big Idea

Dreams and Reality **Ask:** Have you ever become so involved in the fantasy world of a book or a movie that it seemed real to you? *Discuss students' favorite works of fantasy, guiding them to recognize the role of concrete, realistic detail in creating a believable fantasy world.*

Say: Think back on the selections you have read in this unit. Can you think of any examples of realistic, concrete details that helped to create a convincing fantasy world?

Literary History ☆

Oscar Hijuelos In 1990, Hijuelos (1951–) became the first Hispanic to win the Pulitzer Prize in fiction. He received the award for his novel *The Mambo Kings Play Songs of Love,* which concerns two Cuban brothers who immigrate to New York in 1949 and become professional musicians. The novel was adapted into both a movie and a Broadway musical. Hijuelos was born and raised in New York City. He has written several other critically acclaimed novels.

Approaching Level

DIFFERENTIATED INSTRUCTION

Emerging Tell students they are about to write a response to a story. Remind students that when they write, they must follow the steps of the writing process *(prewriting, drafting, revising, editing and proofreading, and presenting).* As a prewriting activity, ask students to think of a story they would like to write about and then answer the following activities. Why would you want to write about this story? What did you like or dislike about the story? What did you learn from the story? What did you notice about the writer's style, use of description, and use of language?

Writing Workshop

Response to Literature

Teach

Writing Skills

Main Idea Remind students that every piece of writing should have a main idea.

Ask: What is the main idea of the professional model? *(Writers need to be aware of the contract they have with readers to tell* the truth.)

Writing Skills

Model Point out that Hijuelos was fascinated by the complexity of Borges's story: it has the characteristics of a love story, a horror tale, and a screenplay. Ask students to think of other stories that have the characteristics of more than one genre. *(Students may mention "The Scarlet Ibis," which combines poetic description with an emotional narrative.)*

Literary History ☆

Jorge Luis Borges (1899–1986) was born in Argentina and became one of the greatest writers of the 1900s. He gained fame for his poems, essays, and short fiction.

Thesis

Convey a clear and personal perspective.

Support

Demonstrate your appreciation for the author's style and support your thesis by making accurate and detailed references to the text.

Tone and Focus

Maintain a consistent tone and focus.

having written it—because, aside from its many wonderful qualities, it will always hold a special meaning for me: quite simply, "The Aleph" is the story that first inspired in me the desire to one day write.

The Result, 1924. William McCance. Oil on canvas, 69.8 x 90.1 cm. The Fleming-Wyfold Art Foundation, London.

As for the story itself, "The Aleph" is part love tale, told in a voice that is both obsessively introspective and delicately urbane; it has an undertone of near horror, like a ghost story—as in an Edgar Allan Poe tale, the object of the narrator's love, Beatriz Viterbo, exerts a great power long after she has been dead; it has a quite visual, nearly cinematic, narrative that is a pleasure to read. Ironically, Borges, who suffered from a hereditary progressive blindness, had often spoken about the influence of film upon his writing. In the economy and vividness of its details, it is instructive to young writers—note how effortlessly Borges suggests the shifting universe by opening with a most introspective and bemused narrator noticing yet another new brand of American cigarette being advertised on the billboards of Constitution Plaza in Buenos Aires. And it is quite funny—especially to writers—when, for example, the narrator, Borges himself, muses over the critical success of a decidedly second-rate talent, Carlos Argentino Daneri, who to the narrator's chagrin has risen to the top of the poet's profession while the narrator has not.

For a final note; without betraying the essence of the story, which is the "Aleph" itself, nor this story's spectacular climax, I will leave the reader with my sense that in this work, as in certain others—"Funes, the Memorious," for example—Borges is really writing about and paying tribute to the writer's

Reading Practice

SPIRAL REVIEW **Take Notes** Remind students it is important to review a story and think about what you want to say in your written response before you actually begin writing. Have students review the story they will write about. Students should evaluate the aesthetic qualities of style, figurative language, mood, and theme, using the terminology of literary criticism. Ask students to take notes on the following as they review:

- main idea
- supporting details
- author's purpose and tone
- rhetorical and literary devices
- word choice

consciousness, which, through its command of and access to the imagination and language, can contain and replicate everything that has existed or will ever exist in this universe.

Reading–Writing Connection Think about the writing techniques you just encountered and try them out in your response to a short story.

Prewrite

Gather Ideas Begin with your overall response to the story, such as fear, astonishment, or inspiration. Use one or more of the following methods to develop that response.

- Relate the story to your own experience. Is the character in some way like you or someone you know? Has anything like this ever happened to you? Have you read other stories like this?
- Make a habit of keeping a response journal. Jot down notes in it while you are reading a story or book. You can go back and review these notes to write a response to the story.
- Consider the different elements in the story. You might react to a character, the plot, the setting, or the theme. Look for specific details in the story to use as support for your response. Use a chart to organize your thoughts about the story. Write an example or quote from the story in the left column and your response in the right column.

Example from story	My response to the example

Narrow Your Focus Write a working thesis—a statement you can revise for accuracy or clarity later. Then decide on your tone.

Talk About Your Ideas Make a writing plan. Meet with a partner to discuss ways to

- create an engaging introduction;
- frame topic sentences that relate clearly to your thesis and help to organize your essay; and
- conclude memorably.

Exposition

Demonstrate a Solid Reading

Remember that an effective personal response goes well beyond "I thought" and "I felt." It must also show your understanding of the work. Be sure you can cite ample evidence from the text to support your thesis—in the form of both paraphrases and direct quotations—before you begin to write.

Avoid Plagiarism

The best way to avoid plagiarism when writing a response to literature is to refrain from consulting any outside sources. Trust your own response.

English Learners

DIFFERENTIATED INSTRUCTION

Intermediate Remind students that authors must often choose the words that best express what they want to convey to readers. Ask students to think about what makes a piece of writing interesting to readers. **Ask:** How does an author's word choice influence your opinion of his or her writing? *(Answers will vary.)* Remind students that they can use a thesaurus to help them think of interesting and engaging language to include in their writing. Students' responses should include detailed sentences and transitions.

Teach

Writing Process

Prewrite Explain that the purpose of most literary criticism is to inform or to persuade. Students should understand that they may do both in their own responses. They will inform readers of their responses and also try to convince readers to see the story through their eyes.

Writing Skills

Generate Examples
Encourage students to create a graphic organizer like the one on page 243 and to fill it in with as many examples as possible. Later they can choose the examples that are most interesting. They should look at their examples and identify common ideas. For example, all of the examples might involve one character. Seeing a commonality among the examples will help students formulate their main ideas.

Teach

Writing Process

Draft Encourage students to devote one paragraph to each response from their prewriting graphic. They can rearrange the ideas in each paragraph as they revise; in the drafting stage they need not worry about organization.

Writing Skills

Thesis **Answer:** *It presents the reader's perspective and clearly explains how the reader was affected by the text.*

Writing Skills

Audience Engagement
Answer: *The author uses details and engaging language that captures the attention of the reader.*

Draft

Put Your Thoughts Down on Paper Begin drafting your response using your plan as a guide. Occasionally look back at your unfinished draft and check that the details you include contribute to the main point you want to make about the story. If your writing is leading you in a new direction, you may want to follow it. Keep in mind that you can polish your response later.

Writing Frames

As you read the workshop model, think about the writer's use of the following frames:

Reading this story left me feeling ____.

It convinced/showed/taught me that ____.

As the story continued, I became ____.

Consider using frames like these in your own response.

Analyze a Workshop Model

Here is a final draft of a response to a story. Read the response and answer the questions in the margin. Use the answers to these questions to guide you as you write.

Thesis

What makes this thesis personal, clear, and focused?

Audience Engagement

How does the writer use the active voice, precise language, and quoted evidence to show appreciation and engage the audience?

My Response to "The Leap"

"The Leap," by Louise Erdrich, is about a remarkable woman who risks her life to save her daughter. The mother has lost her eyesight as a result of cataracts, but even without sight, her life is a reflection of precise vision and courage. Her dexterity and skill achieved as a young trapeze artist saved a life not once, but twice. Reading this story left me feeling stunned by her courage and physical skill, and it convinced me that even when you are terrified, you can and do make life-and-death decisions.

I can only imagine how the narrator's mother must have felt to lose the man she loved and the father of her unborn baby girl. I could feel the love and trust these two people shared. They were "like two sparkling birds" passing each other so high in the air, pausing and kissing "as they swooped past one another" during their trapeze act. When the storm struck and lightning destroyed the main pole of the circus tent, the couple began to fall to their death. This woman made a split-second decision not to cling to the man she loved, but to save herself and the child growing within her. She "changed direction" in midair, and her husband fell

Grammar Practice

SPIRAL REVIEW **Active Voice** Explain the difference between active and passive voice. Tell students that in active voice, the subject acts, or performs an action. **Say:** Using active voice in your writing makes your message clear and direct. Then tell students that in passive voice, the subject receives the action of the verb. Provide students with examples of both types of writing. Write the following sentences on the board and have students identify whether each sentence is written in the active or passive voice.

- Her mother scolded her for staying out too late. *(active voice)*
- She was scolded by her mother for staying out too late. *(passive voice.)*
- My German shepherd scared a big, gray cat today. *(active voice)*
- Today the big, gray cat was scared away by my German shepherd. *(passive voice)*

to his death. The baby did not survive. As the story continued, I became even more amazed by this courageous woman. Although talented and capable on the trapeze, she was illiterate. She was taught to read by her future husband during her recovery in the hospital. Books became a constant part of her life, and I found it tragic that life could be so unkind as to leave her without sight in the end. Yet I somehow think she always had enough inner strength to handle whatever she encountered.

The mother remarried and had a daughter. Reading about how she saved her daughter from the fire in their home, when rescue seemed hopeless, left me with a feeling of awe. I couldn't believe it was possible to do something this brave. I was struck by how she took control of the situation. With no time to think about the consequences, this woman acted because it was necessary to save the life of her child. She climbed out on a tree branch near her daughter's window and jumped—flew—into the child's room. I could almost hear the tree branch as it broke, "so that it cracked in her hands, cracked louder than the flames as she vaulted with it toward the edge. . . ."

The story ends with a sentence that I needed to think about: "As you fall there is time to think." I guess there will be times in my life when I will have to make such quick, critical decisions. I just hope I will have as much strength and courage as the woman in this story when I need it most.

Exposition

Support
How do detailed references to the text support the thesis?

Tone and Focus
How do the tone and focus here match the tone and focus in other parts of the response?

Writing Workshop

Response to Literature

Teach

Writing Skills

Support **Answer:** *Information here points back to the thesis statement.*

Writing Skills

Tone and Focus **Answer:** *The writer uses a very personal tone. The writer uses "I" to express ideas. This is found throughout the writing.*

Writing Skills

Punctuation Remind students of the importance of using correct punctuation in their writing. Note that the titles of short stories and poems should be set inside quotation marks and that titles of novels and films should be underlined or set in italics. Remind students that direct quotations from the original work of literature should appear in quotation marks too. Point out the quotations that appear in the second paragraph of the model.

Approaching Level

DIFFERENTIATED INSTRUCTION

Emerging Remind students they can use graphic organizers to help them prepare to write. On the board, show students some examples of graphic organizers that they might find helpful. Have them copy these examples into their notebooks. Examples might include a web diagram, a Venn diagram, a two-column chart, or an outline.

Writing Workshop

Response to Literature

Teach

Writing Process

Revise Students may wish to read their drafts to a partner or into a tape recorder. They should read only what is written. If students find themselves rewriting as they read aloud, they should make a note of the revisions in the margins of their paper.

Writing Skill

Reconsider Examples

As they revise, students should make sure the examples they provide actually support their points. Have students ask themselves these questions:

- What is my point here?
- What example do I provide to support my point?
- Why did I choose this example?
- Can I clearly explain how this example supports my point?
- Will readers understand the connection between my example and my point?

Students should also use the revising stage to consider the strength and the arrangement of their ideas.

Traits of Strong Writing

Include these traits of strong writing to express your ideas effectively.

Ideas message or theme and the details that develop it

Organization arrangement of main ideas and supporting details

Voice writer's unique way of using tone and style

Word Choice vocabulary a writer uses to convey meaning

Sentence Fluency rhythm and flow of sentences

Conventions correct spelling, grammar, usage, and mechanics

Presentation the way words and design elements look on a page

See also pages R28–R30.

Word Choice

This academic vocabulary word appears in the student model:

capable (kā′ pə bəl) *adj.* 1. having the qualities needed to accomplish something; 2. having the traits that could permit a future act; *Although talented and capable on the trapeze, she was illiterate.* Try to use academic vocabulary when it will strengthen your writing. (See pages R79–R81.)

Revise

Peer Review Exchange drafts with a classmate. Identify and discuss the thesis, organization, supporting details, and conclusion in each paper. Have your partner note any areas that could be improved. Use the checklist below to evaluate and strengthen each other's essays.

Checklist

- ☑ Do you focus on your own response while demonstrating a thorough understanding of the story?
- ☑ Do you state a clear thesis and support it with examples?
- ☑ Do you include accurate and detailed references to the text?
- ☑ Do you keep your tone and focus consistent?
- ☑ Do you use the first person, the active voice, and sensory language?

Focus Lesson

Clear Examples

Your response should include examples—facts, explanations, vivid details, or descriptions—that support your main point. The revision of this sentence from the Workshop Model includes clear examples.

Draft:

I couldn't believe it was possible to do something this brave.

Revision:

I couldn't believe it was possible to do something this brave. With no time to think about the consequences, this woman acted because it was necessary to save the life of her child.[1] She climbed out on a tree branch near her daughter's window and jumped—flew—into the child's room.[2] I could almost hear the tree branch as it broke, "so that it cracked in her hands, cracked louder than the flames as she vaulted with it toward the edge. . . ."[3]

1: Explanation of the situation
2: Vivid description of the action
3: Sensory imagery through descriptive details

Writing Practice

SPIRAL REVIEW **Sentence Structure** Explain to students that a run-on sentence occurs when two sentences are joined without the correct punctuation or adjoining word. Tell students that a fragment is a group of words that do not form a complete sentence because of essential missing elements (e.g., a verb, a subject, etc.). A run-on sentence is two or more sentences incorrectly written as one sentence.

Provide students with the examples below and ask them to identify the error for each sentence and explain how the error can be corrected.

- When I got home from soccer practice I was tired I took a nap. *(Run-on)*
- When I got home from soccer practice. *(Fragment)*

Then ask students to reread their drafts and revise run-ons, fragments.

Edit and Proofread

Get It Right When you have completed the final draft of your essay, proofread for errors in grammar, usage, mechanics, and spelling. Refer to the Language Handbook, pages R40–R59, as a guide.

Focus Lesson

Sentence Fragments

A sentence fragment is a group of words that lacks a subject, a verb, or both. To correct the fragment, add the missing part or parts. Sometimes a fragment is a subordinate clause. It needs to be rewritten as a complete sentence or added to a sentence.

Sentence Fragment:

When the storm struck and lightning destroyed the main pole of the circus tent.

Solution A: To avoid the fragment, rewrite it as a complete sentence.

The storm struck and lightning destroyed the main pole of the circus tent.

Solution B: Connect the fragment to a sentence and set it off with a comma.

When the storm struck and lightning destroyed the main pole of the circus tent, the couple began to fall to their death.

Peer Review Tips

A classmate may ask you to read his or her response. Take your time and jot down notes as you read so you can give constructive feedback. Use the following questions to get started:

Does the introduction name the short story and author, and does it clearly state a thesis?

Do the body paragraphs clearly support the thesis by providing clear topic sentences, support, and explanation?

Word-Processing Tip

Use white, 8½ x 11-inch paper. Leave one-inch margins at the top, bottom, and both sides of the page. The left-hand margin should be perfectly straight except for paragraph indents, bullets, or a centered title.

Present/Publish

The Final Touch Reread the assignment and any guidelines your teacher established for the number of words, the spacing, and the margins. Check to see if you have followed these exactly. Remember that a neat paper free of errors in spelling, grammar, usage, and mechanics makes a good impression.

Writer's Portfolio

Place a clean copy of your response to a short story in your portfolio to review later.

Writing Workshop

Response to Literature

Teach

Writing Process

Edit Remind students that although sentence fragments are often used in daily speech, they are not acceptable in formal writing situations, such as a response to literature. Tell students that every sentence in their essay should contain a subject and a verb—unless the sentence fragment is a direct quotation from the literature.

Writing Process

Present Showing pride in your work is one way of convincing others that you have something valuable to say. Attention to detail is the hallmark of an effective presentation. Have a partner look over your work to ensure that it looks neat and precise.

Approaching Level

DIFFERENTIATED INSTRUCTION

Emerging Remind students to think about their audience as they write.
Say: Who will read your writing? How might this affect your writing? What is the purpose of your writing? Discuss how an author's choice of tone is largely based on the author's audience.

Point out that students should reread their drafts, keeping in mind their audience, the tone of the writing, and the purpose of the writing. Students may make revisions, if necessary, before the draft is considered final.

Speaking, Listening, and Viewing Workshop

Discuss Ideas About Literature

Focus

Summary

In this workshop, students will learn how to plan and participate in an oral discussion about literature.

Teach

Speaking Skills

Establish Discussion Rules
Students may feel more comfortable about participating in group discussions if some ground rules are provided. Share the following guidelines:

- Every group member must participate at least once.
- Ideas and comments such as "I liked it" or "I agree" must be supported with reasons.
- Participants who disagree with others' comments must not insult or dismiss them, but provide factual and/or textual support for their differing opinions.
- Students may not speak for more than two minutes at a time.

Learning Objectives

For pages 248–249

In this workshop, you will focus on the following objective:

Speaking and Listening: Participating in a literature discussion.

Speaking, Listening, and Viewing Workshop

Discuss Ideas About Literature

Literature Connection Following a reading of "American History" in the town where it is set, author Judith Ortiz Cofer responded to a comment about the accuracy of a detail. Many contemporary authors read passages from their work and then respond to comments and questions from the audience. You respond to literature and to others' ideas when you participate in a group discussion.

Assignment **Work in a small group to read and discuss "The Necklace" or another short story. Explain your feelings and thoughts about the main characters.**

Plan for the Discussion

Plan for a discussion to make sure you are ready to comment and respond to others in your group.

- Review the story.
- Make notes about your reactions to the characters and events in the story.
- Find examples, including details and quotations, to support your feelings and thoughts about the characters or events.
- Assess how irony or other aspects of the text affect your response to the characters.

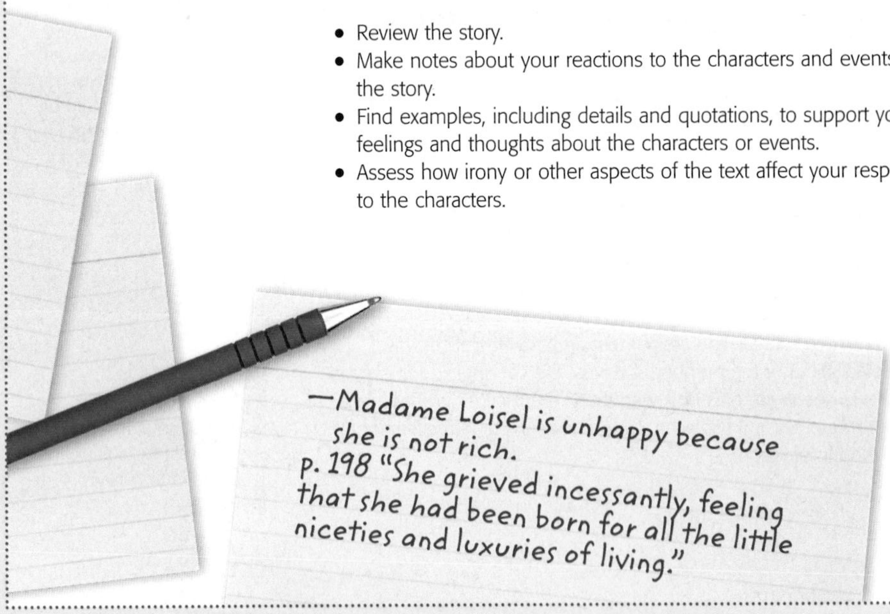

—Madame Loisel is unhappy because
she is not rich.
p. 198 "She grieved incessantly, feeling
that she had been born for all the little
niceties and luxuries of living."

Listening Practice

Summarize and Review Tell students that a good way to remember ideas shared during a discussion is to stop periodically and summarize what has been discussed. Tell students to take notes of the main points in the discussion, along with who made the points. At the end of the discussion, or at a logical stopping point, give students time to look over their notes and develop a review of the discussion. **Say:** In your review, you should sum up the main ideas of the discussion, point out who made the most interesting points and why, and explain your own ideas about what was discussed. Have volunteers share their reviews with the class.

Create a Graphic Organizer

Make a visual to show a main idea about a character from the story and textual evidence that supports your main idea. Refer to your graphic organizer to recall ideas as you speak; display your graphic organizer to help listeners follow your ideas as you speak.

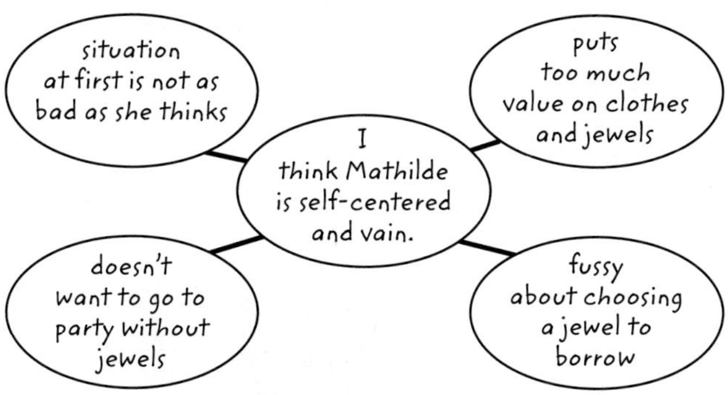

Make and Support Judgments

As you listen, make judgments about the comments others make. Remember that a discussion is a give and take, and you should respond to others' comments—by agreeing, disagreeing, asking questions, or speculating. Explain and support your responses to others by referring to the text. You might cite a character's thoughts, actions, and words, as well as what other characters think and say about the character.

Techniques for Responding in a Discussion

Verbal Techniques	Nonverbal Techniques
☑ **Speak** Enunciate your words clearly and speak loudly enough to be heard easily.	☑ **Make Eye Contact** Look at others both as you speak and as you listen.
☑ **Participate, Don't Monopolize** Offer your comments but give others a chance to speak.	☑ **Be Courteous** Do not act rudely or become angry when disagreeing with others.
☑ **Encourage Others to Speak** Ask an open-ended question to spark a response from the shy members of your group.	☑ **Listen** Focus your attention on others when they are speaking.

Speaking Frames

Consider using the following frames as you respond to others:

I like the point ____ made about ____ because ____.

I take your point that ____, but I still think ____ because of the part of the story that says ____.

Discussion Tips

Use the following checklist to evaluate your group discussion.

☑ Did all group members participate, both by presenting their own ideas and by responding to the ideas of others?

☑ Did group members support their own points and their responses to others' points with accurate references to the story?

LOG ON Literature Online

Speaking, Listening, and Viewing For project ideas, templates, and presentation tips, go to glencoe.com and enter QuickPass code GL49787u1.

Speaking, Listening, and Viewing Workshop

Discuss Ideas About Literature

Teach

Listening Skills

Group Discussion Students need to be good listeners as well as informed speakers. They should listen carefully to other ideas before speaking and should make sure they do not repeat ideas that have been covered. Students should make sure others have exhausted their ideas about the current subject before introducing a new idea.

Listening Skills

Discussion Assessment

Ask students to write a two-paragraph assessment of their discussion. Their assessment should answer the following questions:

- Did I correctly summarize the discussion's main ideas?
- Did I understand what my peers were saying?
- Did I ask questions to clarify misunderstandings?
- Were other students attentive listeners? Why or why not?

Ask volunteers to submit their assessments.

English Learners

DIFFERENTIATED INSTRUCTION

Intermediate Challenge students to elaborate on their ideas by asking them questions that require a longer and more thought-out answer. Monitor students' responses and during their discussion, ask one or two of the following questions:

- Which character did you relate to most and why?
- Did any of the events in the story surprise you? Why? What were you expecting?
- Do you feel you learned any lessons from reading the story? What are they? How did the story teach you that?

Independent
Reading

Focus

Summary

In this lesson, students will read summaries of short story collections and novels that deal with a range of themes, including the challenges young people face as they grow up. Encourage students to read these selections and to think about how they portray the dreams and reality of young people.

Literary History ☆

Lori Carlson Writer, editor, and translator Lori Carlson (1957–) is best known for works that celebrate Hispanic culture. She has produced an anthology of plays for young adults, written in English and Spanish, and a collection of poems, essays, and artworks by three generations of Hispanic artists. She has expressed interest in Asian and Native American cultures, and her goal is to help readers appreciate the variety of cultures that coexist in the United States.

Independent Reading

Short Stories and Novels

LIKE ANY GOOD NOVEL, a short story can take you to new places or on new adventures. Along the way, it might give you new insights into human motivation and behavior. It might also make you laugh, ponder, praise, or cry out in horror. For more short stories on a range of themes, try the suggestions on these pages. For novels that treat the Big Ideas of *Matters of Life and Death, Rewards and Sacrifices,* and *Dreams and Reality,* try the titles from the Glencoe Literature Library on the next page.

American Eyes: New Asian-American Short Stories

edited by Lori Carlson ☆

These ten short stories present the conflicts faced by Asian Americans whose families have immigrated from Taiwan, China, Japan, Korea, Vietnam, and other Asian nations. They explore issues of finding one's own identity in a new culture, as well as common universal themes such as the generation gap. They also look at American pop culture through the eyes of people who are seeing some of it for the first time. Conflicts range from the difficulties of growing up to the struggles of getting by financially.

An Island Like You: Stories from the Barrio

Judith Ortiz Cofer

Here are more stories about young people caught between two worlds: the one their parents left behind in Puerto Rico, and the one they now inhabit in Paterson, New Jersey. A different voice tells each story, though some characters reappear in different roles in other stories. The pages are packed with emotion: love and tenderness between generations; disappointment and rage; humor, hope, and friendship between teens; and dashed hopes and resentments. Everything is here from celebration to sorrow, but there are no neat and tidy endings.

Listening, Speaking, and Viewing Practice

Adaptation Choose a scene from John Knowles's novel *A Separate Peace.* Hand out copies of the passage to the class and read the scene aloud. Then, break students into groups and have them write a short drama script of the scene. Instruct them to describe the characters' appearances and actions, and to include dialogue. Then encourage the groups to perform or read aloud their scene for the class. Students should use effective verbal and nonverbal techniques in their presentation. If time allows, show students the same scene as it appears in the film version of the novel. Ask them to compare and contrast the different versions of the scene. Encourage students to comment on the director's choices and what they would have done differently.

GLENCOE LITERATURE LIBRARY

A Separate Peace

John Knowles

Two boys at a boarding school struggle with matters of life and death.

Winter Thunder

Mari Sandoz

Based on a real-life event, this gripping story of survival describes rewards and sacrifices.

The Metamorphosis

Franz Kafka

One man straddles dreams and reality in a bizarre world.

CRITICS' CORNER

"Toni Cade Bambara's stories do more than paint a picture of black life in contemporary black settings. . . . Her characters achieve a personal identity as a result of their participation in the human quest for knowledge, which brings power. Bambara's skill as a writer saves her characters from being stereotypic cutouts."

—Martha M. Vertreace, from *American Women Writing Fiction: Memory, Identity, Family, Space*

Gorilla, My Love

Toni Cade Bambara ☆

This collection of fifteen short stories includes the well-known "Raymond's Run," the story of a young female track star who takes care of her older brother Raymond. Most of the narrators are spirited young women.

Write a Review

Read one of the books listed on these pages and write a review of it for your classmates. Be sure to explain why other students might enjoy the book, or offer suggestions on how they might overcome difficulties in reading the book. Present your review to the class.

Approaching Level

DIFFERENTIATED INSTRUCTION

Established After students have written and presented their reviews, **Ask:** Did you notice any similarities between the book you read and other selections previously read in class? Guide students by writing these words on the board:

- Characters
- Themes
- Plot

Ask students to freewrite about similarities in these three areas. After a few minutes of writing, ask students to share the similarities they found. Explain that the physical act of writing ideas helps our minds make connections.

Teach

Literary History ☆

Toni Cade Bambara Toni Cade was born in New York City in 1939. Cade became a writer before she finished college, adding Bambara to her pen name in honor of her great-grandmother. Most of her writings feature realistic portrayals of African American characters who are trying to figure out who they are and what their place is in the world.

Glencoe Literature Library

Glencoe Literature Library offers an extensive collection of hardcover books that help you encourage your students to read independently. Choose among the more than 120 full-length literary works—novels, novellas, plays, and nonfiction. Each book includes related readings from a broad range of genres. Go to glencoe.com for more information.

Write a Review

Students' reviews should address one book mentioned in the Independent Reading feature and should include reasons why others might like the book as well as tips on how to overcome difficulties reading it.

For access to all study guides for the Glencoe Literature Library, see the Literature Library Teacher Resources CD-ROM.

To create customized reading lists use BookLink K–12 CD-ROM.

Focus

Bellringer Options

Explain that on some tests, students will be asked to read a piece of fiction and answer questions about the selection.

Ask: How would your approach to reading fiction change in a test situation? Have students list the elements they would pay attention to when reading fiction for a test. Review these lists and discuss any missing elements.

Teach

Assessment Inform students that in this section, they will first be asked to read a fiction selection and answer comprehension, context-clue, and inference questions. Then they will be asked to answer paragraph-improvement questions and respond to a short reflective essay question.

Assessment

English Language Arts

Reading: Fiction

Read the following passage. Then, on a separate sheet of paper, answer the questions on pages 253 and 254.

from *"The Lumber Room"* by Saki (H. H. Munro)

Presently the angry repetitions of Nicholas' name gave way to a shriek, and a cry for somebody to come quickly. Nicholas shut the book, restored it carefully to its place in a corner, and shook some dust from a neighboring pile of newspapers over it. Then he crept from the room, locked the door, and replaced the key exactly where he had found it. His aunt was still calling his name when he sauntered into the front garden.

"Who's calling?" he asked.

"Me," came the answer from the other side of the wall; "didn't you hear me? I've been looking for you in the gooseberry garden and I've slipped into the rain-water tank. Luckily there's no water in it, but the sides are slippery and I can't get out. Fetch the little ladder from under the cherry tree—"

"I was told I wasn't to go into the gooseberry garden," said Nicholas promptly.

"I told you not to, and now I tell you that you may," came the voice from the rain-water tank, rather impatiently.

"Your voice doesn't sound like Aunt's," objected Nicholas; "you may be the Evil One tempting me to be disobedient. Aunt often tells me that the Evil One tempts me and that I always yield. This time I'm not going to yield."

"Don't talk nonsense" said the prisoner in the tank; "go and fetch the ladder."

"Will there be strawberry jam for tea?" asked Nicholas innocently.

"Certainly there will be," said the aunt, privately resolving that Nicholas should have none of it.

"Now I know that you are the Evil One and not aunt," shouted Nicholas gleefully; "when we asked aunt for strawberry jam yesterday she said there wasn't any. I know there are four jars of it in the store cupboard, because I looked, and of course you know it's there, but she doesn't, because *she* said there wasn't any. Oh, Devil, you *have* sold yourself!"

There was an unusual sense of luxury in being able to talk to an aunt as though one was talking to the Evil One, but Nicholas knew, with childish discernment, that such luxuries were not to be overindulged in. He walked noisily away and it was a kitchenmaid, in search of parsley, who eventually rescued aunt from the rain-water tank.

Writing Practice

Test-Taking Strategies Tell students that most standardized tests are open-book tests; after reading a passage, they will be able to look back at the passage to find evidence or clues to answer questions. Have students develop a checklist for taking a test that includes a reading passage followed by multiple-choice questions. Check to see that students' lists include the following steps.

- Read the passage, stopping to paraphrase the information in your head.
- Read the question to be sure you understand what answer is needed.
- Eliminate answers that are incorrect.
- Look back at the passage for confirmation before marking your final choice.
- Mark your final answer.

1. What was the aunt doing in the garden?
   A. drinking tea
   B. eating jam
   C. looking for a ladder
   D. looking for Nicholas

2. From the context, what do you conclude that the word *sauntered,* in line 5, means?
   A. departed
   B. returned
   C. strolled
   D. yelled

3. Why does Nicholas say that he is certain that he is not really speaking with his aunt?
   A. She grew very angry with him.
   B. She agreed to give him jam.
   C. She said she fell inside the tank.
   D. She told him to come to the front garden.

4. What does the passage suggest that Nicholas was doing when his aunt called to him?
   A. cleaning
   B. playing
   C. reading
   D. sleeping

5. How does this passage reveal Nicholas's personality?
   A. through irony
   B. through direct characterization
   C. through indirect characterization
   D. through dialect

6. What is the overall tone of this passage?
   A. angry
   B. disapproving
   C. objective
   D. playful

7. What can the reader infer from Nicholas's actions in the first paragraph?
   A. He is in a place where he does not belong.
   B. He is about to displease his aunt.
   C. He is responsible for his aunt's emergency.
   D. He is happy that he is not alone in the house.

8. What literary device makes the reader wonder what will happen to the aunt?
   A. dialect
   B. motivation
   C. suspense
   D. motif

9. From the context, what do you conclude that the word *resolving,* in line 19, means?
   A. answering
   B. deciding
   C. fixing
   D. settling

10. Which of the following best describes Nicholas's tone when talking to his aunt?
   A. concerned
   B. despairing
   C. ironic
   D. sad

11. Which of the following best describes the author's purpose in this passage?
   A. to entertain
   B. to persuade
   C. to describe
   D. to explain

LOG ON **Literature** Online

Assessment For additional test practice, go to glencoe.com and enter QuickPass code GL49787u1.

English Learners

DIFFERENTIATED INSTRUCTION

Intermediate Model the correct way to approach a multiple-choice question by helping students answer the first item. Explain that a multiple-choice question offers a question and four possible answers. Instruct the students to choose only one answer. Explain to students the importance of reading the question and all answer choices before choosing an answer. Remind them they have a 25 percent chance of answering the question correctly, so even if they are unsure of the answer, they should make an educated guess. Guide students to cross out answers they know are incorrect and choose from the answers that remain.

Assess

Reading

1. D is the correct answer because the aunt says, "I've been looking for you in the gooseberry garden. . . ." DOK 1

2. C is the correct answer. *Saunter* means "to walk" or "to stroll." DOK 1

3. B is the correct answer because he says that only the Evil One could have known there was jam in the cupboard. DOK 1

4. C is the correct answer because Nicholas puts away a book. DOK 2

5. C is the correct answer because the dialogue and the descriptions of Nicholas's actions give an impression of his personality. DOK 2

6. D is the correct answer because Nicholas is amused at his aunt's expense. DOK 3

7. A is the correct answer because he conceals the fact that he was in the room. DOK 2

8. C is the correct answer because the reader wonders if Nicholas will rescue his aunt. DOK 2

9. B is the correct answer because the aunt has made a decision not to give jam to Nicholas, despite what she says. DOK 1

10. C is the correct answer because Nicholas says things he doesn't mean. DOK 2

11. A is the correct answer because the passage is meant to entertain. DOK 3

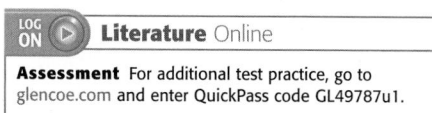

Assessment

English Language Arts

Assess

12. B is the correct answer because Nicholas sees through the Devil's ruse and uses language referring to the idea of selling one's soul to the Devil. DOK 2

13. C is the correct answer because childish discernment refers to Nicholas's perception. DOK 1

14. D is the correct answer because the narration describes the thoughts of both main characters from the perspective of someone outside the story. DOK 4

15. D is the correct answer because Nicholas reasons that the voice coming from the tank is the Evil One's so he won't have to help his aunt. DOK 2

12. The exclamation "Oh, Devil, you *have* sold yourself!" in line 23 means what?
    A. The Evil One has struck a bargain with the aunt.
    B. The Evil One has revealed himself through his words.
    C. Nicholas has purchased the Evil One's services.
    D. Aunt has brought home the Evil One as a gift for Nicholas.

13. From the context, what do you conclude that the word *discernment,* in line 25, means?
    A. cruelty
    B. deception
    C. comprehension
    D. sympathy

14. From what point of view is this passage written?
    A. first person
    B. second person
    C. third-person limited
    D. third-person omniscient

15. Which of the following best describes the main idea of this excerpt from "The Lumber Room"?
    A. Adults often keep the truth from children for their own good.
    B. Adults can usually get their way through bargaining.
    C. Children are usually more superstitious than adults.
    D. The lies of adults can be used against them by clever children.

Reading Practice

Reading for Purpose While reading a passage on a test, students should look for clues to the author's purpose: is the author making an argument, describing a historical event, or telling a story? Students should also look for clues to the author's tone: is the tone objective or subjective, argumentative or impassioned? Encourage them to get in the habit of jotting down brief notes in the margins, such as *genre: fiction; purpose: to entertain; tone: ironic.*

For practice have students jot down notes about the passage on page 252, and then discuss their responses.

Vocabulary Skills: Sentence Completion

For each question in the Vocabulary Skills section, choose the word that best completes the sentence.

1. The father was _______ after hearing about his daughter's death.
   A. blighted
   B. inconsolable
   C. disdainful
   D. disconsolate

2. It took hours for everything to settle down following the _______ created by the emergency.
   A. conspiracy
   B. impunity
   C. pandemonium
   D. adversary

3. After she _______ struggled to escape on her own, the woman was rescued from the well.
   A. futilely
   B. indiscernibly
   C. perpetually
   D. fervently

4. Plagued in childhood with shyness and _______, Lincoln nevertheless became an eloquent speaker.
   A. languor
   B. reconciliation
   C. admonition
   D. inhibition

5. Since the boy was _______ of his aunt's promises, he did not answer her call for help.
   A. dubious
   B. impartial
   C. pensive
   D. zealous

6. Eager to avoid the influence of evil, he became extremely _______ and particular.
   A. explicit
   B. discreet
   C. hesitant
   D. vigilant

7. The lack of nutritious food is just one of the _______ of long-term captivity.
   A. absurdities
   B. elations
   C. imputations
   D. privations

8. Their _______ day by the lake was interrupted by the unexpected arrival of rowdy guests.
   A. serene
   B. craven
   C. distraught
   D. commonplace

9. Although she called for help _______, no one responded for hours.
   A. benevolently
   B. incessantly
   C. precariously
   D. surreptitiously

10. Even though he was exhausted for two days after the marathon, Daniel was proud that his _______ ended in success.
    A. endeavor
    B. gratification
    C. parsimony
    D. principle

Assess

Vocabulary Skills

1. **B** is the correct answer. *Inconsolable* means unable to be comforted. **DOK 1**
2. **C** is the correct answer. *Pandemonium* means extreme chaos or disorder. **DOK 1**
3. **A** is the correct answer. Futile, or fruitless, escape attempts would leave her stranded. **DOK 1**
4. **D** is the correct answer. *Inhibition* means restraint in behavior. **DOK 1**
5. **A** is the correct answer. *Dubious* means doubtful. **DOK 1**
6. **D** is the correct answer. No other option makes sense in this context. **DOK 1**
7. **D** is the correct answer. Privations are the lack of something necessary or desirable. **DOK 1**
8. **A** is the correct answer. *Serene* is the opposite of *rowdy.* **DOK 1**
9. **B** is the correct answer. No other option makes sense in this context. **DOK 1**
10. **A** is the correct answer. *Endeavor* means determined effort. **DOK 1**

English Learners

DIFFERENTIATED INSTRUCTION

Intermediate Write: Alex, who loves to ride horses, work at a stable. Ask students to identify the subject and the verb of the sentence. Then ask students if they can find any errors in the sentence. (work needs an s to agree with the singular subject) Explain to students that identifying the subject and the verb of a sentence is a good way to find errors in agreement as well as several other types of mistakes.

Assess

Grammar and Writing Skills

1. C is the correct answer because the sentence contains a comma splice, and people are born in, not at, countries. DOK 1
2. D is the correct answer because a past-tense verb is needed to maintain verb-tense consistency. DOK 2

Grammar and Writing Skills: Paragraph Improvement

The following passage is the first draft of a student's research essay on Saki. It may contain errors in grammar and punctuation. As you read, pay close attention to the writer's sentence structure, subject and verb agreement, and flow of ideas. Some questions may refer to numbered sentences. Read the essay and then, on a separate sheet of paper, answer the questions on pages 256–257.

Saki

(1) Saki was the pen name of Hector Hugh Munro, he was born in 1870 at Burma. (2) His father was a member of the police force at the time that the country, called Myanmar now, is still part of the British Empire. (3) He was raised in England by his grandmother and aunts. (4) The strictness of households like his became the subject of many of his stories. (5) His short stories made fun of Edwardian society. (6) He wrote several novels and wrote plays also.

(7) In 1893 Munro returned to Burma and joined the police force. (8) Three years later, because of illness, quit and he returned to England. (9) Munro's first book, The Rise of the Russian Empire, a historical study, was published in 1900. (10) It was followed in 1902 by a collection of short stories. (11) Many more short stories appeared in subsequent years, which were widely read.

(12) Munro was also a correspondent for The Morning Post from 1902 to 1908, reporting throughout Europe. (13) He had started his career of journalism even earlier he started right after moving back to England. (14) After roving through Europe as a correspondent, he permanently settled in London. (15) Many of the stories from this period feature characters taking pleasure in the misfortune of their elders.

(16) After World War I began, Munro enlisted the Army as an ordinary soldier even though his age exceeded the official limit. (17) He was killed during the war in France in 1916, he was in a shell crater at the time. (18) Much of his work was published after he died.

1. Which of the following is the best revision of sentence 1?
   - **A.** Saki was the pen name of Hector Hugh Munro, born in 1870 Burma.
   - **B.** Saki was the pen name for Hector Hugh Munro, born in 1870 in Burma.
   - **C.** Saki was the pen name of Hector Hugh Munro, who was born in 1870 in Burma.
   - **D.** Saki is the pen name for Hector Hugh Munro, who was born in 1870 Burma.

2. Which of the following errors appears in sentence 2?
   - **A.** lack of subject-verb agreement
   - **B.** misplaced modifier
   - **C.** run-on sentence
   - **D.** lack of verb-tense consistency

Grammar Practice

Evaluating Sentence Errors

As experienced readers, students can evaluate whether a sentence contains a grammatical error without even knowing exactly what the error is. Demonstrate by reading aloud a sentence in the exercise as students follow along. Have students raise their hands if they think that something is wrong with the sentence. Ask students why they think the sentence is wrong. Tell students as they complete the paragraph-improvement section to read the sentences aloud in a quiet voice and to put a mark next to the sentences they think contain errors.

3. Which of the following is the best revision of sentence 8?
   A. Three years later, illness forced Munro to quit, he returned to England.
   B. Three years later, illness forced Munro to quit, but he returned to England.
   C. Three years later, illness forced Munro to quit, return to England.
   D. Three years later, illness forced Munro to quit, and he returned to England.

4. Which of the following errors appears in sentence 11?
   A. run-on sentence
   B. misplaced modifier
   C. lack of parallelism
   D. split infinitive

5. Which sentence is not related to the main idea of the third paragraph?
   A. 12
   B. 13
   C. 14
   D. 15

6. Which of the following errors appears in sentence 13?
   A. run-on sentence
   B. lack of subject-verb agreement
   C. sentence fragment
   D. misplaced modifier

7. Which of the following errors appears in sentence 16?
   A. a missing word and a missing comma
   B. a missing comma and a missing semicolon
   C. an extra word and an unnecesssary comma
   D. a missing subject or a missing predicate

8. Which of the following errors appears in sentence 17?
   A. comma splice
   B. sentence fragment
   C. dangling modifier
   D. lack of subject-verb agreement

9. What is most notably missing from this essay?
   A. supporting arguments
   B. historical quotations
   C. a concluding paragraph
   D. a personal photograph

10. Which of the following titles would best suit this essay?
   A. "England's Greatest Journalist"
   B. "The Life and Career of Saki"
   C. "Munro's Family Fortunes"
   D. "History of the Short Story"

Essay

In the excerpt from "The Lumber Room," why does Nicholas say that his aunt is the "Evil One"? Write a short essay in which you explain Nicholas's behavior. Be sure to include quotations from the text to support your position. As you write, keep in mind that your essay will be evaluated for **ideas, organization, voice, word choice, sentence fluency, conventions,** and **presentation.**

Checklist for Your Writing
The following checklist will help you write your essay. Make sure to
☐ brainstorm for ideas.
☐ organize your writing with an introduction, a body, and a conclusion.
☐ pay attention to your word choice and voice.
☐ edit for sentence fluency and conventions.
☐ have a neat and organized presentation.

English Learners

DIFFERENTIATED INSTRUCTION

Early Advanced Remind students that in a timed writing, what is most important is to stay calm and to write clearly and simply. Tell students that a good way to achieve this calm is to create a plan for their writing. Remind students to read the writing prompt carefully and explain Nicholas's behavior, providing examples from the story. Tell students that they can use a graphic organizer in their notes. They should focus on their main idea and the ideas that support it. Also, remind students to review their writing for errors.

Assess

Grammar and Writing Skills

3. D is the correct answer. Sentence 7 is a fragment because the first verb lacks a noun. DOK 1

4. B is the correct answer. The clause "which were widely read" should modify "short stories," not "following years." DOK 1

5. C is the correct answer. Sentence 14 is the only sentence discussing Saki's stories. DOK 3

6. A is the correct answer. Sentence 12 is a run-on sentence. DOK 1

7. A is the correct answer. Sentence 15 is missing a comma and the word *in.* DOK 1

8. A is the correct answer. DOK 1

9. C is the correct answer. This biographical passage has no concluding passage. DOK 3

10. B is the correct answer. DOK 4

Essay

Evaluate essays for the following:
- a clearly stated analysis of Nicholas's behavior supported by quotations, examples, and details from the passage
- effective voice, word choice, and sentence variety
- effective presentation, with attention to grammar and spelling conventions DOK 3

Skills Scope and Sequence

Readability Scores Key: Dale-Chall/DRP/Lexile

PART 1: Looking Into Lives

Selections and Features	Literary Elements
Unit Introduction pp. 258–264	Nonfiction **SE** pp. 260–261 Autobiography and Biography **SE** p. 260 Personal and Expository Essay **SE** p. 261 Persuasive Essay and Speech **SE** p. 261
Literary Focus pp. 266–267	Autobiography **SE** p. 266 Biography **SE** p. 267
Biographical Essay Of Dry Goods and Black Bow Ties, by Yoshiko Uchida **6.7/62/1230** pp. 268–275	Author's Purpose **SE** p. 269
Memoir Only Daughter, by Sandra Cisneros **5.7/57/900** pp. 276–281	Memoir **SE** p. 277
Historical Narrative A Brother's Crime *from* **Good Brother Bad Brother,** by James Cross Giblin **7.7/60/1110** pp. 282–291	Historical Narrative **SE** p. 283 Characterization **TE** p. 287 Narrator (review) **SE** p. 290
Visual Perspective *from* **The Murder of Abraham Lincoln,** by Rick Geary pp. 292–296	
Autobiography *from* **Black Boy,** by Richard Wright **7.8/50/740** pp. 297–305	Anecdote **SE** p. 298 Author's Purpose (review) **SE** p. 304
Grammar Workshop p. 306	
Autobiography Escape from Afghanistan *from* **The Story of My Life,** by Farah Ahmedi **5.8/54/820** pp. 307–317	Tone **SE** p. 308 Historical Narrative (review) **SE** p. 316

Reading Skills and Strategies	Vocabulary	Writing Grammar	Speaking, Listening, and Viewing
Recognize Facts and Opinions **TE** p. 261 Identify the Main Idea **TE** p. 262 Identify Bias **TE** p. 262 Analyze **SE** p. 263 Evaluate **TE** p. 263		Write an Autobiography **TE** p. 260	
Identify Bias **TE** p. 267		Choose an Angle **TE** p. 266 Evaluate **SE** p. 267	
Analyze Cause-and-Effect Relationships **SE** p. 269 Understand Character **TE** p. 272	Synonyms **SE** p. 275	Write a Biography **TE** p. 270 Conduct Research **TE** p. 274 Write a News Story **SE** p. 275	
Draw Conclusions About Author's Beliefs **SE** p. 277 Evaluate Style **TE** p. 280	Analogies **SE** p. 281	Write an Essay **TE** p. 278 Write a Summary **SE** p. 281	
Activate Prior Knowledge **SE** p. 283 Evaluate **TE** p. 286 Analyze a Speech **TE** p. 286	Word Origins **SE** p. 290 Academic Vocabulary **SE** p. 290	Write a Summary **TE** p. 284 Sentence Fragments **TE** p. 288 Write a Biographical Narrative **SE** p. 291 Absolute Phrases **SE** p. 291	
Identify Genre **SE** p. 292 Connect **TE** p. 294 Check Comprehension **TE** p. 295	Decoding Vocabulary **TE** p. 292		Present a Speech **TE** p. 296
Connect to Personal Experience **SE** p. 298	Word Usage **SE** p. 305 Academic Vocabulary **SE** p. 305	Write an Autobiographical Essay **TE** p. 298 Respond to Literature **TE** p. 302	Practice Dialogue **TE** p. 300 Interview **SE** p. 305
		Dialogue and Speaker Tags **SE** p. 306	
Analyze Cultural Context **SE** p. 308 Make Inferences **TE** p. 315	Context Clues **SE** p. 317 Academic Vocabulary **SE** p. 317	Understand Adverbs **TE** p. 308 Write a Summary **TE** p. 310 Prepositional Phrases **TE** p. 314	Research and Report **SE** p. 317

Readability Scores Key: Dale-Chall/DRP/Lexile

PART 1: Looking Into Lives *(continued)*

Selections and Features	Literary Elements
Media Workshop pp. 318–324	

PART 2: On the Move

Literary Focus pp. 326–327	Essay **SE** p. 326 Personal, Expository, and Persuasive Essays **SE** pp. 327 Audience **TE** p. 326
Narrative Essay *from* **All God's Children Need Traveling Shoes,** by Maya Angelou **7.4/61/960** pp. 328–339	Narrative Essay **SE** p. 329 Author's Purpose (review) **SE** p. 338
Descriptive Essay Walking, by Linda Hogan **6.4/56/1060** pp. 340–346	Descriptive Essay **SE** p. 341 Setting (review) **SE** p. 345
Grammar Workshop p. 347	
Essay Sayonara, by Anne Morrow Lindbergh **9.1/59/1060** pp. 348–354	Thesis **SE** p. 349 Descriptive Essay (review) **SE** p. 353
Memoir *from* **Into Thin Air,** by Jon Krakauer **9.4/64/1160** pp. 355–368	Structure **SE** p. 356 Dialogue (review) **SE** p. 367
Informational Text TIME: Adventure to Antarctica, by Rob Johnson **7.6/61/1020** pp. 369–373	
Vocabulary Workshop p. 374	

Reading Skills and Strategies	Vocabulary	Writing Grammar	Speaking, Listening, and Viewing
Compare Media Genres **SE** pp. 318–324 Analyze Author's Purpose **TE** p. 322	Loaded Words **TE** p. 318	Create a Comparison Chart **SE** p. 319 Research and Summarize **TE** p. 320 Form an Argument **TE** p. 324	Discussion Groups **SE** p. 324
Evaluate Credibility **TE** p. 326 Identify Facts **TE** p. 327		Describe a Journey **SE** p. 327	
Identify Problem and Solution **SE** p. 329 Identify Imagery **TE** p. 330 Analyze Character **TE** p. 332 Make Inferences **TE** p. 332	Synonyms **SE** p. 338 Academic Vocabulary **SE** p. 338	Commas in a Series **TE** p. 334 Modifiers **TE** p. 336 Write an Autobiographical Narrative **SE** p. 339 Possessive Pronouns **SE** p. 339	
Visualize **SE** p. 341 Identify Personification **TE** p. 342	Word Usage **SE** p. 346 Academic Vocabulary **SE** p. 346	Write a Poem **TE** p. 344 Apply Imagery and Sensory Details **SE** p. 346	
		Clauses and Phrases **SE** p. 347	
Analyze Rhetorical Devices **SE** p. 349 Synthesize **TE** p. 350	Analogies **SE** p. 354 Academic Vocabulary **SE** p. 354	Write a Poem **TE** p. 352 Apply Repetition **SE** p. 354	
Monitor Comprehension **SE** p. 356 Identify Cause and Effect **TE** p. 358 Identify Problems and Solutions **TE** p. 364	Word Usage **SE** p. 368 Academic Vocabulary **SE** p. 368	Semicolons and Colons **TE** p. 366 Research and Report **SE** p. 368	Research and Present **TE** p. 356 Analyze Media **TE** p. 360
Analyze Text Structure **SE** p. 369 Prepare a Bibliography **TE** p. 370		Identify Sensory Details **TE** p. 372	
	Jargon **SE** p. 374	Collect and Use Jargon **TE** p. 374	

Readability Scores Key: Dale-Chall/DRP/Lexile

PART 3: Finding Common Ground

Selections and Features	Literary Elements
Literary Focus pp. 376–377	Persuasive Essay and Speech **SE** pp. 376–377 Diction **TE** p. 376
Speech **A New Generation of Americans: Inaugural Address,** by John F. Kennedy **10.1/65/1360** pp. 378–385	Historical Devices **SE** p. 379 Tone **TE** p. 381 Rhetorical Devices **TE** p. 381
Essay **That One Man's Profit Is Another's Loss,** by Michel de Montaigne **9.9/64/1140** pp. 386–389	Antithesis **SE** p. 387
Essay **Daylight Saving,** by Benjamin Franklin **10.3/62/1240** pp. 390–397	Humor **SE** p. 391 Rhetorical Devices (review) **SE** p. 396
Comparing Literature **Thoughts on Fenway Park**, by various authors **7.4/59/930** **Taxpayers Will Get a Return on Investment** (editorial), by John L. Harrington **10.0/66/1260** **Other Revenue Sources Should Be Pursued** (editorial), by William M. Straus **8.6/67/1360** pp. 398–411	Persuasion **SE** p. 398 Author's Viewpoint **SE** p. 398 Rhetorical Devices **SE** p. 400
Speech **Put Down the Backpack: Commencement Speech at Holyoke College,** by Anna Quindlen **7.4/57/1020** pp. 412–421	Author's Purpose **SE** p. 413 Argument (review) **SE** p. 420
Writing Workshop pp. 422–429	
Speaking, Listening, and Viewing Workshop pp. 430–431	Sound Devices **TE** p. 430
Independent Reading pp. 432–433	
Assessment pp. 434–439	

Reading Skills and Strategies	Vocabulary	Writing Grammar	Speaking, Listening, and Viewing
Evaluate Assertions **TE** p. 377		List Persuasive Techniques **TE** p. 376 Convince Others **SE** p. 377	
Recognize Bias **SE** p. 379			Analyze Oral Communications **TE** p. 380 Analyze Media Coverage **TE** p. 382
Analyze Argument **SE** p. 387 Reread **TE** p. 388	Word Usage **TE** p. 387 Word Usage **SE** p. 389	Write a Summary **SE** p. 389	
Analyze Humor **SE** p. 391 Analyze Evidence **TE** p. 393 Paraphrase **TE** p. 394	Context Clues **SE** p. 397	Write a Humorous Essay **SE** p. 397	
Identify Author's Purpose **TE** p. 399 Evaluate Credibility **SE** p. 400 Scan for Information **TE** p. 408 Evaluate an Argument **TE** p. 408	Synonyms **SE** p. 410	Correct Sentence Fragments **TE** p. 400 Write a Persuasive Essay **TE** p. 402 Write an Editorial **TE** p. 406 Write a Business Letter **SE** p. 410	Oral Presentation **SE** p. 411
Evaluate Evidence **SE** p. 413 Synthesize **TE** p. 416 Interpret **TE** p. 418 Paraphrase **TE** p. 418	Analogies **SE** p. 420 Academic Vocabulary **SE** p. 420	Write a Summary **SE** p. 421 Specific Nouns **SE** p. 421	
		Prewrite **SE** p. 425 Draft **SE** p. 426 Revise **SE** p. 428 Write an Autobiographical Narrative **SE** p. 429 Pronoun-Antecedent Agreement **SE** p. 429	
			Narrative Presentation **SE** p. 430
		Write a Review **SE** p. 433	
Review Literary Devices **TE** p. 438		Write an Essay **SE** p. 439	

UNIT TWO

Focus

Bellringer Options

Literature Launchers Pre-Reading Videos: Unit 2

Daily Language Practice Transparency 24

Or write on the board: Why do people tell stories about real-life events?

Say: Identify some reasons why people write about their lives, the lives of others, and the world around them. *(Guide students to recognize that telling true stories helps people make sense of the world and preserve memories.)*

For school-to-home activities, see Unit 2 Teaching Resources Book, pp. 5–11.

For students who would profit from independent novel study, see Novel Companion pp. 75–118.

The Three Graces. Freeman. Oil on canvas, 91.4 x 121.9 cm. Private collection.

View the Art Many of Kathryn Freeman's paintings show ordinary people and places, but others have a magical quality. How would you describe this painting? Does this painting suggest the idea of nonfiction? Why or why not? ★

Unit Introduction Skills

Nonfiction

Literary Elements
- Autobiography and Biography (SE p. 260)
- Personal and Expository Essay (SE p. 261)
- Persuasive Essay and Speech (SE p. 261)

Listening/Speaking/Viewing Skills
- Discuss (SE p. 264)
- Visual Literacy (SE p. 264)
- Analyze Art (TE pp. 258)

Reading Skills
- Reading Nonfiction (SE p. 264)
- Identifying Bias (TE p. 262)

Writing Skills/Grammar
- Autobiography (TE p. 260)
- Take Notes (SE p. 264)

UNIT TWO

NONFICTION

Looking Ahead

Nonfiction is the broadest category of literature and includes autobiographies, memoirs, biographies, letters, essays, speeches, and news articles, to name a few. All types of nonfiction concern real, rather than imaginary, subjects and are written, in part, to convey information to readers.

Each part in Unit Two focuses on a Big Idea that can help you connect to the selections.

PREVIEW	Big Ideas	Literary Focus
PART 1	Looking into Lives	Autobiography and Biography
PART 2	On the Move	Personal and Expository Essay
PART 3	Finding Common Ground	Persuasive Essay and Speech

259

UNIT TWO

Focus

Summary

This unit identifies several kinds of nonfiction. An excerpt by Julia Alvarez is provided for students to read and analyze. Insights from professional writers of nonfiction are included. Activities to help students review the elements of nonfiction conclude the section.

View the Art ★

Answer: *Students should support their answers with a reasonable explanation.*

American artist Kathryn Freeman specializes in painting figures in motion. Many of Freeman's paintings show ordinary places and people, but others have a magical or fairy-tale quality. Her use of color and shading give her works a hazy, dreamlike atmosphere.

For diagnostic and end-of-unit assessment, see Assessment Resources, pp. 7–12, 227–228.

Unit Resources

Print Materials

- Unit 2 Teaching Resources, pp. 1–268
- Interactive Read and Write (On Level/ Approaching, EL), pp. 49–98
- Novel Companion, pp. 75–118
- Bellringer Option Transparencies: Selection Focus 16–18; Daily Language Practice 24–42
- Literary Element Transparencies 12, 16, 37, 38
- Assessment Resources, Unit Assessment, pp. 7–12
- Assessment Resources, Selection Assessment, pp. 79–110

Technology

- TeacherWorks Plus CD
- StudentWorks Plus CD
- Literature Launchers: Pre-Reading Videos DVD, Unit 2
- Literature Online
- Interactive Vocabulary CD-ROM
- Listening Library CD-ROM
- ExamView CD-ROM
- Skill Level Up! CD-ROM

UNIT TWO

Teach

- Note that each of the selections that students will read illustrates one form of nonfiction.
- Invite volunteers to read each explanation and then the exerpt example beside it aloud. Point out how the excerpt illustrates the form.

Learning Objectives

For pages 258–264

In studying this text, you will focus on the following objective:

Literary Study: Analyzing literary genres.

Genre Focus: Nonfiction

What are the different types of nonfiction?

Nonfiction is the broadest category of literature. Autobiographies, biographies, memoirs, letters, essays, speeches, and news articles are just a few of the many types of nonfiction writing. All of these forms of prose concern real, rather than imaginary, subjects.

Nonfiction writers in particular know the importance of being clear. In addition, they understand that what they write must be of interest, or no one will want to read what they have to say. Even though nonfiction is about real people and real events, nonfiction writing can also be creative.

Autobiography and Biography

Writing About Oneself

An **autobiography** is the story of a person's life written by that person. Autobiographies are presented from the first-person point of view and may be based entirely on the writer's memory. A **memoir** is also about the person who has written it, but a memoir usually focuses on one experience or period in the person's life.

Once, several years ago, when I was just starting out my writing career, I was asked to write my own contributor's note for an anthology I was part of. I wrote: "I am the only daughter in a family of six sons. *That* explains everything."

—Sandra Cisneros, **from "Only Daughter"**

Writing About Another

A **biography** is the story of a person's life written by someone other than that person. In addition to recounting the events of the subject's life, most biographers explore the person's reactions to those events and the effects they had on his or her personality.

My father came to America in 1906 when he was not yet twenty-one. Sailing from Japan on a small six-thousand-ton ship which was buffeted all the way by rough seas, he landed in Seattle on a bleak January day.

—Yoshiko Uchida, **from "Of Dry Goods and Black Bow Ties"**

Writing Practice

SPIRAL REVIEW **Autobiography** Have students write a one-page autobiographical story connected to a childhood experience. Remind them to address the basic questions—*Who? What? Where? When? Why? How?* Ask volunteers to read their essays aloud. Then discuss the different approaches writers took. Did they start with their birth and list events sequentially, or did they focus on one portion of their life? After students read selections in the unit, have them reevaluate their methods.

Personal and Expository Essay

Formal and Informal Essays

An **essay** is a relatively short piece of nonfiction in which the writer explores a single topic from his or her own perspective. Essays can be formal or informal. The most common type of informal essay is the **personal essay,** in which the writer's purpose is to entertain or share personal experiences with the reader. Formal essays are more serious in tone. They include the **expository** (or explanatory) essay and the **persuasive** essay.

For *Sayonara,* literally translated, "Since it must be so," of all the good-byes I have heard is the most beautiful. Unlike *Auf Wiedersehens* and *Au revoirs,* it does not try to cheat itself by any bravado "Till we meet again," any sedative to postpone the pain of separation.

—Anne Morrow Lindbergh, **from "Sayonara"**

Persuasive Essay and Speech

Writing to Persuade

One type of formal essay is the **persuasive essay** or speech. In persuasive writing, the writer tries to influence the reader's or listener's ideas or actions. A persuasive essay or speech may contain emotional appeals. However, a specific type of persuasive writing, known as **argument,** relies on logic, reason, and evidence to convince the reader.

"So let us begin anew—remembering on both sides that civility is not a sign of weakness, and sincerity is always subject to proof. Let us never negotiate out of fear. But let us never fear to negotiate."

—John F. Kennedy, **from *"A New Generation of Americans"***

Paddywagon Party, 2001. Colin Bootman. Oil on canvas. Private collection. ★

LOG ON **Literature** Online

Literature and Reading For more selections, go to glencoe.com and enter QuickPass code GL49787u2.

UNIT TWO

Teach

Reading Strategy

Recognize Facts and Opinions **Say:** Expository essays usually contain facts. Facts are provable statements. **Ask:** What facts appear in the excerpt from "Sayonara"? (Sayonara means "since it must be so.")

ENGLISH LEARNERS To assist English learners, **say:** Essays may also contain opinions. Opinions are ideas or beliefs that cannot be proven, only argued. Ask students to state a fact and then to state an opinion.

APPROACHING To assist approaching-level students, **ask:** What opinion is expressed in "Sayonara"? *(That the word sayonara is more beautiful than other words for "good-bye")*

View the Art ★

Colin Bootman was born in Trinidad and came to the United States at an early age. Primarily an illustrator of children's books, he was inspired to draw by his first American comic book.

English Learners

DIFFERENTIATED INSTRUCTION

Intermediate Encourage students to keep a list of the different types of nonfiction and their characteristics in their notebooks. **Say:** On these pages, you read about autobiographies. **Ask:** What characteristics would you list in your journal under autobiography? *(possible answer: informs readers about the author's life, story is told by the author in the first person)*

Encourage students to refer to the list to categorize the nonfiction selections they read. As students progress through Unit 2, encourage them to scan a selection before they read and make predictions what type of nonfiction it may be.

Teach

Reading Strategy 1

Identify the Main Idea

Say: In personal essays, the main idea may be stated directly or implied. If it is implied, you must pay attention to the details and consider what idea they support. **Ask:** What is the main idea of the first paragraph of Alvarez's essay? *(Alvarez discovered something about herself by reading an author from another culture.)*

APPROACHING To aid approaching-level students, **ask:** Was the main idea stated or implied? *(It was stated in the first sentence.)*

Writer's Technique ☆

Sentence Variety Note that one strategy Alvarez uses to keep readers' interest is to vary the lengths of her sentences. Most sentences are long. Occasionally she interrupts them with short sentences, such as, "Wow! The silence within me broke." The contrast makes readers pay attention.

LITERARY ANALYSIS MODEL

How do literary elements create meaning in nonfiction?

In the essay that follows, Alvarez explains her roots as a writer and the joy she feels at being part of a *comunidad*—community—of authors. Notice how she uses elements of the various types of nonfiction discussed on pages 260–261.

from *On Finding a Latino Voice*

by Julia Alvarez

APPLYING Literary Elements

Autobiography
Alvarez's use of the first-person point of view is a clue that the selection may be an autobiography or a personal essay.

Personal Essay
Alvarez focuses on the lack of women authors represented in Latino writing. This focus is a clue that the selection is a personal essay, describing her thoughts about Latina writers.

1 How I discovered a way into my bicultural, bilingual experience was paradoxically not through a Hispanic-American writer, but an Asian-American one. Soon after it came out, I remember picking up *The Woman Warrior* by Maxine Hong Kingston. I gobbled up the book and then I went back to the first page and read it through again. She addressed the duality of her experience, the Babel of voices in her head, the confusions and pressures of being a Chinese-American female. Wow! ☆ The silence within me broke.

With her as my model, I set out to write about my own experience as a Dominican American. And now that I had a name for what I had been experiencing, I could begin to understand it as not just my personal problem. I combed the bookstores and libraries. I discovered Latino writers I had never heard of: Piri Thomas, Ernesto Galarza, Rudolfo Anaya, Jose Antonio Villareal, Gary Soto. But I could not find any women among these early Latino writers.

The '80s changed all that. In 1983, Alma Gomez, Cherrie Moraga, and Mariana Romo-Carmona came out with *Cuentos: Stories by Latinas*. It was an uneven collection, but the introduction, titled "Testimonio," was like a clarion call: "We need *una literatura* that testifies to our lives, provides acknowledgement of who we are: an exiled people, a migrant people, *mujeres en la lucha*[1] . . . What hurts is the discovery of the measure of our

1. *Mujeres en la lucha* is Spanish for "Women in the struggle."

Reading Practice

SPIRAL REVIEW **Identify Bias** Explain that an author may express bias, or strong feelings for or against something. Have students practice identifying bias by answering the following questions:

- What does Alvarez think about the writers she mentions in the second paragraph? *(She is disappointed that they are all men.)*
- Is Alvarez in favor of identifying with one's culture? *(She thinks it is good to find a community and form a tradition.)* Ask students to explain how bias can affect a reader's opinion of a text. (Possible answer: If a reader senses that an author is biased, he or she may begin to question the credibility of the author's information.

silence. How deep it runs. How many of us are indeed caught, unreconciled between two languages, two political poles, and suffer the insecurities of that straddling."

The very next year Sandra Cisneros published her collection of linked stories, *The House on Mango Street;* Ana Castillo published her book of poems, *Women Are Not Roses;* I published *Homecoming.* Up at Bread Loaf, I met Judith Ortiz Cofer and heard her read poems and stories that would soon find their way into her books of poems, stories, and essays and her novel *The Line of the Sun.* Cherrie Moraga, Helena Maria Viramontes, Denise Chavez. Suddenly there was a whole group of us, a tradition forming, a dialogue going on. And why not? If Hemingway and his buddies could have their Paris group and beat poets their Black Mountain School,[2] why couldn't we Latinos and Latinas have our own made-in-the-U.S.A. boom? ☆ 2

Personal and Expository Essay
Phrases like "the very next year" help the reader track the sequence of events Alvarez describes in her essay.

Still, I get nervous when people ask me to define myself as a writer. I hear the cage of a definition close around me with its "subject matter," "style," "concerns." I find that the best way to define myself is through the stories and poems that do not limit me to a simple label, a choice. Maybe it is part of my immigrant uneasiness at the question, in whatever form, "Do you have something to declare?"[3] Maybe, too, after years of feeling caught between being a "real Dominican" and being American, I shy away from simplistic choices that will leave out an important part of who I am or what my work is about.

Certainly none of us serious writers of Latino origin wants to be a mere flash in the literary pan. We want to write good books that touch and move all our readers, not just those of our own particular ethnic background. And speaking for myself, I very much agree with the advice given to writers by Jean Rhys, "Feed the sea, feed the sea." The little rivers dry up in the long run, but the sea grows. What matters is the great body of all that has been thought and felt and written by writers of different cultures, languages, experiences, classes, races.

At last, I have found a *comunidad* in the word that I had never found in a neighborhood in this country. By writing powerfully about our Latino culture, we are forging a tradition and creating a literature that will widen and enrich the existing canon. So much depends upon our feeling that we have a right and responsibility to do this.

Argument
Alvarez's thesis—that she and writers like her are forging a new tradition—appears at the end. Details in the preceding paragraphs support the thesis.

2. The *Black Mountain School* was a group of experimental poets in the 1950s.
3. People entering the United States are required to "declare" to a customs agent any valuable property they are carrying and possibly to pay taxes on it.

Reading Check
Analyze What *comunidad* does Alvarez describe?

Teach

Reading Check

Answer: *A community where she can take pride in her heritage and can explore it in her writing*

Reading Strategy 2

Evaluate **Say:** As you read nonfiction, you should evaluate whether the details support the writer's main idea.

Ask: What details support the author's idea that she "gets nervous when people ask *(her)* to define *(herself)*"? *(Her memory of having to declare each time she came back to the United States)*

Cultural History ☆

Latinos in the United States
The word *Latino* came into use after World War II to identify Latin-American people living in the United States. The word is generally interchangeable with *Hispanic.* Latinos come from a wide range of countries, including Mexico, the Caribbean, and Central and South America. Today, one eighth of the population of the United States identifies itself as Hispanic/Latino.

Approaching Level

DIFFERENTIATED INSTRUCTION

Emerging Alvarez's sentences vary in length. Reading passages aloud will help students appreciate the rhythm of her prose. To practice **reading fluency,** have students take turns reading aloud with a partner. After each student reads, his or her partner should ask questions and clarify meanings.

Established Point out that in her essay, Alvarez includes sentences that vary in length. Encourage students to scan their writing when they revise. If they tend to write long sentences, try to shorten a few, and vice versa. Explain that varying sentence length makes for interesting writing and reading.

UNIT TWO

Assess

Guide to Reading Nonfiction

Remind students to ask questions, make connections, and evaluate the writers' truthfulness as they read the selections.

Types of Nonfiction

Explain that recognizing the types of nonfiction in the unit will help students set a purpose for reading.

FOLDABLES Study Organizer

Have students make and label the Layered-Look Book. As they read each selection in this unit, they can record notes under the question headings.

Wrap-Up:

Guide to Reading Nonfiction

- When reading nonfiction, first determine what type of work you are reading.
- Try to identify the author's purpose. Is he or she writing to inform, to entertain, or to persuade?
- If the author's purpose is to inform, look for a thesis statement and support for the thesis.
- If the author's purpose is to entertain, look for literary elements, such as figurative language, dialogue, or suspense.
- If the author's purpose is to persuade, determine whether the author is presenting an argument, emotional appeals, or a combination of both.

Types of Nonfiction

- **Nonfiction** is writing about real people and real events.
- An **autobiography** tells the story of the writer's own life.
- A **biography** tells the story of another person's life.
- An **essay** is a short work of nonfiction on a single topic. An essay can be **formal** or **informal.**
- Informal, or **personal,** essays are meant primarily to entertain. Formal essays are intended to explain, inform, or persuade.
- **Persuasive** essays and speeches are intended to change the way people act and think. Some persuasive essays and speeches contain arguments that persuade through logic, reason, and evidence.

LOG ON Literature Online

Unit Resources For additional skills practice, go to glencoe.com and enter QuickPass code GL49787u2.

Activities

Use what you have learned about reading and analyzing nonfiction to complete one of the following activities.

1. **Discuss** In small groups, discuss the excerpt from Julia Alvarez's essay "On Finding a Latino Voice." In your discussion, identify three events that helped the author find her voice.
2. **Visual Literacy** Create a Venn diagram to show the similarities and differences between autobiography and biography.
3. **Take Notes** Try using the study organizer at right to jot down questions you have about the readings in this unit. See pages R20–R21 for folding instructions.

FOLDABLES Study Organizer **LAYERED-LOOK BOOK**

Activities

1. **Discuss** Students should include quotations and specific details from the text to support their ideas.
2. **Visual Literacy** Draw a Venn diagram on the board. Explain that shared characteristics should appear in the area where the circles overlap.
3. **Take Notes** Students should question the text and express a clear opinion or judgment.

PART 1

LOOKING INTO LIVES

The Quest. Tomar Levine. Watercolor on paper. Private collection.

View the Art There is a painting within this painting. How might the objects at the bottom of the painting be relevant to the picture shown? What is the connection between the art and the Big Idea? ★

BIG IDEA

Writers create portraits that allow readers to look into the lives of people both familiar and exotic. The selections in this part look into the lives of people from all walks of life. As you read, ask yourself, In what ways are these people different from people I know, and in what ways are they similar?

UNIT TWO

PART 1

Analyze and Extend

Big Idea

Looking into Lives Have students read the text under the "Big Idea" head and study the artwork. Discuss why artists are interested in writing or painting other people's portraits. As students look at the artwork, have them answer the question at the bottom of the page.

View the Art ★

Answer: *Answers will vary. Students should support their answers.*

Tomar Levine is known for his still-life paintings that feature shells, rocks, and bottles. The placement of these objects in each work is highly symbolic. He spends months on each painting.

For additional support for English Learners, see Unit 2 Teaching Resources Book, p. 21.

English Learners

DIFFERENTIATED INSTRUCTION

Beginning/Early Intermediate

Review the term *portrait.* If possible, show students a variety of portraits from fine art and photography. Explain that a portrait captures a person at one point in time in his or her life, either formally posed or engaged in an activity. **Ask:** If someone were painting or writing a portrait of you, what would you want them to show? Why? Ask students to share their answers in a class discussion. To promote discussion, encourage students to ask classmates questions for clarification and elaboration.

Focus

Bellringer Options

Daily Language Practice Transparency 25

Or display an image of a famous public figure such as Abraham Lincoln.

Ask: What do you know about this person? How did you learn about him or her? What opinions have you developed about him or her based on what you have learned? *(Students may mention textbooks or biographies.)*

Teach

Literary Element | 1

Autobiography Remind students to be skeptical when they read autobiographies. Note that the writers are telling about their own lives and may try to present themselves in the best possible light.

Writing Practice

SPIRAL REVIEW **Choose an Angle** Explain that nonfiction authors have to sort through all of the facts and reorganize them to create a story—something with a beginning, a middle, and an end—and a message or theme. Sometimes, choosing an angle means cutting out interesting facts that don't fit into the story, even though they may be interesting or funny. Ask students to think of ideas to write their own autobiographical narrative.

Have students create an outline to help them organize their ideas. Students should use the outline to draft a short autobiographical story. During the revision process, students should eliminate insignificant details.

Learning Objectives

For pages 265–267

In studying this text, you will focus on the following objective:

Literary Study: Analyzing autobiography and biography.

LITERARY FOCUS

AUTOBIOGRAPHY AND BIOGRAPHY

How do nonfiction writers choose which details to include?

Foxtrot ©2006 Bill Amend. Reprinted with permission of Universal Press Syndicate. All rights reserved.

Autobiography 1

An **autobiography** is the story of a person's life written by that person. Usually it is written in the first-person point of view. For example, in the excerpt shown at right, Farah Ahmedi describes the plan she and her mother develop to leave Afghanistan.

Most autobiographies are organized chronologically and reveal the events and ideas that shaped the writer's life.

> We made inquiries and learned that we could pay a man to serve as our escort on the bus to Jalalabad. That would get us out of Taliban-dominated Kabul. From Jalalabad to the border, we would be on our own. As for getting across the border, no one knew what that entailed.
>
> —Farah Ahmedi, **from "Escape from Afghanistan"**

Memoir Like an autobiography, a **memoir** is a first-person account of a person's life written by that person. The chief difference between the two is that an autobiography is a more complete summation of a person's life. A memoir focuses on one period or significant episode in a person's life. For example, Sandra Cisneros writes about her life as the only daughter in a family of boys.

> Being an only daughter in a family of six sons forced me by circumstance to spend a lot of time by myself because my brothers felt it beneath them to play with a *girl* in public. But that aloneness, that loneliness, was good for a would-be writer—it allowed me time to think and think, to imagine, to read and prepare myself.
>
> —Sandra Cisneros, **from "Only Daughter"**

The Seaside, 1895–1905. Francois Flameng. ★

Biography

A **biography** is the account of a person's life written by someone other than that person. Unlike an autobiographer—who can write mostly from memory—biographers consult a variety of sources when gathering information about the subject. Most biographies are organized chronologically, and many reflect the attitude the author has toward his or her subject. Biographies can vary in length, from brief encyclopedia entries to works that span several volumes.

In his book *Good Brother, Bad Brother,* James Cross Giblin presents a biography about Edwin Booth, the brother of the man who assassinated Abraham Lincoln. In order to gather information for the biography, Giblin read documents such as newspaper articles and personal letters to and from Edwin Booth.

> That night Edwin, who was staying at a friend's house in Boston, had trouble getting to sleep. But he still had no intimation of the shock that was in store for him the next morning. Without knocking first, his valet burst into his bedroom shortly after seven. Thrusting a newspaper in front of a dazed Edwin, the man exclaimed, "Mr. Booth, President Lincoln has been shot!" Before Edwin could absorb that terrible fact, the valet went on: "And—oh, Mr. Booth—they say your brother John has done it!"
>
> —James Cross Giblin, **from "A Brother's Crime"** 2

LOG ON **Literature** Online

Literature and Reading For more about literary elements, go to glencoe.com and enter QuickPass code GL49787u2.

Quickwrite

Evaluate Reread the excerpts on these pages and consider each author's style. In a paragraph, explain which style you prefer and why.

UNIT TWO

PART 1

Teach

Reading Strategy 2

Identify Bias **Ask:** In the excerpt from "A Brother's Crime," what does the author feel about his subject? *(The author makes the subject appear innocent; his shock at the news suggests his innocence.)*

View the Art ★

Francois Flameng (1856–1923) was a French artist known for his portraits, historical paintings, and decorative work. He painted many ceilings and panels in buildings around the world.

Assess

Quickwrite

The title should reflect understanding of the person's accomplishments and reputation.

English Learners

DIFFERENTIATED INSTRUCTION

Early Advanced Students may better understand the emotions of a text if they hear the passage read aloud. After all students independently read page 267, ask proficient readers to read the excerpts on this page. Allow them time to accurately practice reading and using their voices to express the excerpts' emotions.

After the readings, have students discuss what they learned from hearing the story that they did not learn from reading the story. **Say:** Hearing text read aloud works even when you're reading independently, so if you are not sure of a text's meaning, try reading it aloud.

Before You Read

Focus

Bellringer Options

Literature Launchers: Pre-Reading Videos DVD, Selection Launcher

Selection Focus Transparency 16

Daily Language Practice Transparency 26

Or discuss students' concept of success. Invite small groups of students to compile a list of five different types of rewards that might stem from success. Start them off with some examples, such as personal fulfillment, financial security, and professional reputation.

Ask: What types of success do you think are most important to immigrants to the United States? *(Students may mention financial success or political freedom.)*

Before You Read

Of Dry Goods and Black Bow Ties

Meet **Yoshiko Uchida**

(1921–1992)

The stories of millions of people who left their homes to seek better lives in the United States make up one of the most interesting chapters in American history. The parents of Yoshiko Uchida, Dwight and Iku, were a part of this chapter. They immigrated to the United States from Japan.

Treated Like an Enemy Yoshiko Uchida was born in Alameda, California. Raised in the nearby community of Berkeley, Uchida finished high school early. She enrolled in college when she was only sixteen years old. In 1941 she was studying for final exams at the University of California in Berkeley when she learned that Japanese warplanes had bombed Pearl Harbor. Then the United States declared war on Japan.

> *"I write to celebrate our common humanity, for the basic elements of humanity are present in all our strivings."*
>
> —Yoshiko Uchida

Not long after, the United States government decided to imprison thousands of Japanese Americans. Citizens or not, those of Japanese heritage remained in "relocation centers" or internment camps for months or even years. Uchida and her family were among them. They had to leave everything behind and go to an internment camp. Until 1943 they lived in a remote, guarded camp in the Utah desert. Uchida later recalled this experience in *Journey to Topaz* and its sequel, *Journey Home*.

After Uchida was released in 1943, she earned a master's degree in education from Smith College in Massachusetts. She did not teach, however. Instead, she worked as a secretary during the day and wrote in the evenings. Uchida published her first book, *The Dancing Kettle and Other Japanese Folk Tales*, in 1949.

Visit to Japan In 1952 Uchida won a Ford Foundation research grant to study in Japan. Over a period of two years, she traveled around the country collecting folktales. She also learned about Japanese arts and crafts. As a result of her experiences in Japan, Uchida gained a deeper awareness of herself as a Japanese American. She also developed an increased "respect and admiration for the culture that had made my parents what they were."

Uchida eventually became an award-winning author of more than twenty children's books. They include *A Jar of Dreams*, *The Bracelet*, and *The Magic Purse*. Influenced by her heritage, she focused on Japanese American themes in her work.

LOG ON **Literature** Online

Author Search For more about Yoshiko Uchida, go to glencoe.com and enter QuickPass code GL49787u2.

Selection Skills

Of Dry Goods and Black Bow Ties

Literary Elements
- Author's Purpose (SE pp. 269–275)

Vocabulary Skills
- Synonyms (SE p. 269)

Reading Skills
- Analyzing Cause-and-Effect Relationships (SE pp. 269–275)

Writing Skills
- Write a News Story (SE p. 275)

Listening/Speaking/Viewing Skills
- Analyze Art (SE p. 273)

Literature and Reading Preview

Connect to the Biography

What does it mean to be successful? Write a journal entry about your idea of what it means to be successful in life.

Build Background

In this biographical essay, Yoshiko Uchida describes events that happened between 1880 and 1929 in Seattle, Portland, and San Francisco. One event that is not directly discussed but that affected a central figure in this selection was a financial panic that triggered widespread selling of stocks on the New York Stock Exchange. This panic helped begin the Depression era in the United States. Many businesses failed at this time, including a store in which Uchida's father had worked.

Set Purposes for Reading

Big Idea Looking into Lives

As you read, ask yourself, What facts and details in the selection help bring to life the relationship between Uchida's father and Shozo Shimada, a Japanese American businessman?

Literary Element Author's Purpose

An **author's purpose,** or reason for writing, may be to entertain, to persuade, to express opinions, to describe, or to inform. Paying attention to words, phrases, and details in a selection can help you determine the author's purpose. As you read, ask yourself, What clues reveal Uchida's purpose for writing?

Reading Strategy Analyze Cause-and-Effect Relationships

A **cause** is any event that leads to an **effect,** or result. For example, because Mr. Shimada can sew and speak Japanese, Japanese women come to his shop. As you read, ask yourself, What other cause-and-effect relationships are in the story?

Tip: Create Organizers Use cause-and-effect diagrams like the one shown below to record other examples of cause-and-effect relationships that you find in this selection. You may have to add *Effect* boxes if a cause has more than one effect.

Cause
Mr. Shimada can sew and speak Japanese.

→

Effect
Japanese women come to his dress-making shop.

Learning Objectives

For pages 268–275

In studying this text, you will focus on the following objectives:

Literary Study: Analyzing author's purpose.

Reading: Analyzing cause-and-effect relationships.

Writing: Writing a newspaper article.

Vocabulary

confidant (kon′ fə dant′) *n.* a person to whom secrets are entrusted; p. 271 *My best friend is a true confidant; I can tell her anything.*

imposing (im pō′ zing) *adj.* impressive in appearance or manner; p. 272 *The pyramids in Egypt are imposing monuments.*

exhilarated (ig zil′ ə rāt′ əd) *adj.* cheerful, lively, or excited; p. 272 *The exhilarated cast took its final bow after a terrific performance.*

irreverent (i rev′ ər ənt) *adj.* showing a lack of proper respect; p. 273 *Jim felt that the unflattering jokes about our country's leaders were irreverent.*

Tip: Synonyms Synonyms are words that have the same or nearly the same meaning. Remember that synonyms are always the same part of speech. For example, the word *disrespectful* is a synonym for the vocabulary word *irreverent.* Both words are adjectives.

English Learners

DIFFERENTIATED INSTRUCTION

Intermediate Tell students that the selection they are about to read is about a man who moves from Japan to the United States. **Say:** This selection looks at some of the hardships of not knowing the language of the country in which you live. English language learners may sympathize with the desire of Mr. Shimada's customers to do business with a native Japanese speaker.

Struggling to communicate in an unfamiliar language can be a difficult and an isolating experience. Encourage students to discuss whether they enjoy speaking in their native tongue and how they feel when they meet someone who can speak their first language.

Before You Read

Focus

Summary

Yoshiko Uchida explores her father's relationship with his first employer, Mr. Shimada, a successful Japanese American businessman. Mr. Shimada says, "One never knows when one might be indebted to even the lowliest of beggars." Uchida's father never forgets Mr. Shimada's wisdom.

For summaries in languages other than English, see Unit 2 Teaching Resources Book, pp. 22–27.

Interactive Read and Write

Other options for teaching this selection can be found in

- Interactive Read and Write for EL Students, pp. 49–60
- Interactive Read and Write for Approaching-Level Students, pp. 49–60
- Interactive Read and Write for On-Level Students, pp. 49–60

Vocabulary

Use Memory Tricks Have students develop mnemonic devices to help them remember the meaning of a word. For example, the word *confidant* means "a person to whom secrets can be entrusted." A student might write, "I'm confident I can trust my confidant." Have students think of as many mnemonic devices for remembering vocabulary words as possible. Encourage them to share these with the class.

For additional vocabulary practice, see Unit 2 Teaching Resources Book, pp. 30–31.

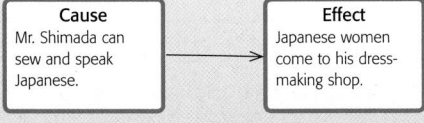

Teach

Literary Element 1

Author's Purpose Answer: *The author includes factual information about her father. Students should infer that the author's purpose is to inform.*

Big Idea 2

Looking into Lives
Answer: *It suggests he felt discouraged and isolated.*

For an audio recording of this selection, use Listening Library Audio CD-ROM.

Readability Scores

Dale-Chall: 6.7
DRP: 62
Lexile: 1230

Of Dry Goods and Black Bow Ties

Yoshiko Uchida

Long after reaching the age of sixty, when my father was persuaded at last to wear a conservative four-in-hand tie,[1] it was not because of his family's urging, but because Mr. Shimada[2] (I shall call him that) had died. Until then, for some forty years, my father had always worn a plain black bow tie, a formality which was required on his first job in America and which he had continued to observe as faithfully as his father before him had worn his samurai[3] sword.

My father came to America in 1906 when he was not yet twenty-one. Sailing from Japan on a small six-thousand-ton ship which was buffeted all the way by rough seas, he landed in Seattle on a bleak January day. He revived himself with the first solid meal he had enjoyed in many days, and then allowed himself one day of rest to restore his sagging spirits. Early on the second morning, wearing a stiff new bowler,[4] he went to see Mr. Shozo Shimada to whom he carried a letter of introduction.

At that time, Shozo Shimada was Seattle's most successful Japanese businessman. He owned a chain of dry goods stores which extended not only from Vancouver to Portland, but to cities in Japan as well. He had come to America in 1880, penniless but enterprising, and sought work as a laborer. It wasn't long, however, before he saw the futility of trying to compete with American laborers whose bodies were twice his in muscle and bulk. He knew he would never go far as a laborer, but he did

1. A *four-in-hand tie* is a man's necktie that is tied in a slip knot with the ends hanging down vertically.
2. *Shimada* (shē mä′ dä)
3. In feudal Japan, the sword-carrying *samurai* (sam′ oo rī′) were an aristocratic class of warriors who valued honor above life itself.
4. A *bowler* is a hard, round hat with a narrow, curled brim.

1 Author's Purpose *What can you infer about the author's purpose based on the text so far?*

Looking into Lives *How might this description reflect his mood, or how he feels when he arrives?* **2**

Writing Practice

SPIRAL REVIEW **Biography** Point out that this selection is a biography—the author is telling about her father's life beginning with his arrival in the United States. After students have read these pages, have them write a short biography of a relative. Encourage them to weave accounts of their family members and friends into their writing. Ask these questions to help students get started:

- Where was the family member born?
- Where did he or she grow up?
- What is unique about this person's life?

When they finish, have volunteers read aloud their biographies for the class.

possess another skill that could give him a start toward better things. He knew how to sew. It was a matter of expediency[5] over masculine pride. He set aside his shovel, bought a second-hand sewing machine, and hung a dressmaker's sign in his window. He was in business.

In those days, there were some Japanese women in Seattle who had neither homes nor families nor sewing machines, and were delighted to find a friendly Japanese person to do some sewing for them. They flocked to Mr. Shimada with bolts of cloth, elated to discover a dressmaker who could speak their native tongue and, although a male, sew western-styled dresses for them.

Mr. Shimada acquainted himself with the fine points of turning a seam, fitting sleeves, and coping with the slippery folds of satin, and soon the women ordered enough dresses to keep him thriving and able to establish a healthy bank account. He became a trusted friend and **confidant** to many of them and soon they began to bring him what money they earned for safekeeping.

"Keep our money for us, Shimada-san,"[6] they urged, refusing to go to American banks whose tellers spoke in a language they could not understand.

At first the money accumulated slowly and Mr. Shimada used a pair of old socks as a repository,[7] stuffing them into a far corner of his drawer beneath his union suits.[8] But after a time, Mr. Shimada's private bank began to overflow and he soon found it necessary to replenish his supply of socks. ☆

He went to a small dry goods store downtown, and as he glanced about at the buttons, threads, needles, and laces, it occurred to him that he owed it to the women to invest their savings in a business venture with more future than the dark recesses of his bureau drawer. That night he called a group of them together.

"Think, ladies," he began. "What are the two basic needs of the Japanese living in Seattle? Clothes to wear and food to eat," he answered himself. "Is that not right? Every man must buy a shirt to put on his back and pickles and rice for his stomach."

The women marveled at Mr. Shimada's cleverness as he spread before them his fine plans for a Japanese dry goods store that would not only carry everything available in an American dry goods store, but Japanese foodstuff as well. That was the beginning of the first Shimada Dry Goods Store on State Street.

By the time my father appeared, Mr. Shimada had long since abandoned his sewing machine and was well on his way to becoming a business tycoon.[9] Although he had opened cautiously with such stock items as ginghams, flannel, handkerchiefs, socks, shirts, overalls, umbrellas, and ladies' silk and cotton stockings, he now carried tins of salt, rice crackers, bottles of soy sauce, vinegar, ginger root, fish-paste cakes, bean paste, Japanese pickles, dried mushrooms, salt fish, red beans, and just about every item of canned food that could be shipped from Japan. In addition, his was the first Japanese store to install a U.S. Post Office Station, and he therefore flew

5. *Expediency* is a means of achieving a particular goal, or the quality of being appropriate to the end in view.
6. According to Japanese custom, the suffix *-san* (sän) is added after a person's name to express respect.
7. A *repository* is a place or object in which something may be stored for safekeeping.
8. *Union suits* are one-piece undergarments that combine a shirt with long pants.

9. A *tycoon* is a wealthy, powerful businessman.

Vocabulary

confidant (kon′ fə dant′) *n.* a person to whom secrets are entrusted

Analyze Cause-and-Effect Relationships *What causes Mr. Shimada to establish a dry goods store?* **3**

Teach

Reading Strategy 3

Analyze Cause-and-Effect Relationships **Answer:** *He wanted to help the women profit from their investment and saw this as a good opportunity to fill a need in the Japanese emigrant community.*

ENGLISH LEARNERS To assist English learners, ask a volunteer to point out the words in this passage that identify sequence. *(beginning, first)* Remind students that sequence means an arrangement of order or time.

Writer's Technique ☆

Humor Note that authors sometimes use humorous anecdotes as an engaging way to advance a narrative.

Ask: Why does the author tell the story about Mr. Shimada and his sock bank? *(The anecdote leads into an explanation of how he decided to open a dry goods store.)*

Approaching Level

DIFFERENTIATED INSTRUCTION

Emerging Help students better understand the progression of events in Mr. Shimada's life on these pages. Explain that he worked as a laborer when he first arrived in America but realized he could earn a better living sewing clothes for Japanese immigrants. In time, he opened his own store. Tell students that a dry goods store sold cloth, clothing, and goods that did not require refrigeration (rice, pasta, canned foods). Mr. Shimada turned his dry goods store into a one-stop shop for Japanese immigrants who could purchase anything they needed.

Teach

Big Idea 1

Looking into Lives
Answer: *The details show how successful he is.*

Literary Element 2

Author's Purpose Answer: *The explanation is given to reveal the motivation of Uchida's father to attain success without sacrificing honor and dignity.*

APPROACHING To aid approaching-level students, remind students to ask questions to help them understand the writer's purpose, such as: Why does the writer include this information?

For additional literary element practice, see Unit 2 Teaching Resources Book, p. 28.

an American flag in front of the large sign that bore the name of his shop.

When my father first saw the big American flag fluttering in front of Mr. Shimada's shop, he was overcome with admiration and awe. He expected that Mr. Shozo Shimada would be the finest of Americanized Japanese gentlemen, and when he met him, he was not disappointed.

Although Mr. Shimada was not very tall, he gave the illusion of height because of his erect carriage. He wore a spotless black alpaca[10] suit, an immaculate[11] white shirt, and a white collar so stiff it might have overcome a lesser man. He also wore a black bow tie, black shoes that buttoned up the side and a gold watch whose thick chain looped grandly on his vest. He was probably in his fifties then, a ruddy-faced man whose hair, already turning white, was parted carefully in the center. He was an **imposing** figure to confront a young man fresh from Japan with scarcely a future to look forward to. My father bowed, summoned as much dignity as he could muster, and presented the letter of introduction he carried to him.

Mr. Shimada was quick to sense his need. "Do you know anything about bookkeeping?" he inquired.

"I intend to go to night school to learn this very skill," my father answered.

Mr. Shimada could assess a man's qualities in a very few minutes. He looked my father straight in the eye and said, "Consider yourself hired." Then he added, "I have a few basic rules. My employees must at all times wear a clean white shirt and a black bow tie. They must answer the telephone promptly with the words, 'Good morning or good afternoon, Shimada's Dry Goods,' and they must always treat each customer with respect. It never hurts to be polite," he said thoughtfully. "One never knows when one might be indebted to even the lowliest of beggars."

My father was impressed with these modest words from a man of such success. He accepted them with a sense of mission and from that day was committed to white shirts and black bow ties, and treated every customer, no matter how humble, with respect and courtesy. When, in later years, he had his own home, he never failed to answer the phone before it could ring twice if at all possible.

My father worked with Mr. Shimada for ten years, becoming first the buyer for his Seattle store and later, manager of the Portland branch. During this time Mr. Shimada continued on a course of **exhilarated** expansion. He established two Japanese banks in Seattle, bought a fifteen-room house outside the dreary confines of the Japanese community and dressed his wife and daughter in velvets and ostrich feathers. When his daughter became eighteen, he sent her to study in Paris, and the party he gave on the eve of her departure, with musicians, as well as caterers to serve roast turkey, venison, baked ham, and champagne, seemed to verify rumors that

10. *Alpaca* (al pak′ ə) is the fleece of the alpaca, a South American mammal related to the llama.

11. *Immaculate* (i mak′ yə lit) means "perfectly clean" or "spotless."

1 Looking into Lives *What do these details reveal about Mr. Shimada?*

Vocabulary

imposing (im pō′ zing) *adj.* impressive in appearance or manner

2 Author's Purpose *Why do you think Uchida explains her father's feelings here?*

Vocabulary

exhilarated (ig zil′ ə rāt′ əd) *adj.* cheerful, lively, or excited

Reading Practice

SMALL GROUP SPIRAL REVIEW

Understand Character Point out that pages 272 and 273 are mainly about Mr. Shimada's life and character. Break students into groups and have them create a word web. Tell them to write Mr. Shimada's name in the center circle of the web diagram. Then have them review the pages. Students should use the author's description to draw conclusions about the character traits of Mr. Shimada. Instruct students to add these traits to their graphic organizer.

Ask: Do you know of any people with similar traits? Do you think these traits are more or less common today? *(Students may say that they know of a grandparent or older person with these traits. They will likely say that these traits are not as common today, that people are not as loyal and trusting.)*

View the Photograph This photograph was taken in 1903 in Sacramento, California. How might the dry goods store shown compare with Mr. Shimada's store? ★

he had become one of the first Japanese millionaires of America.

In spite of his phenomenal success, however, Mr. Shimada never forgot his early friends nor lost any of his generosity, and this, ironically enough, was his undoing. Many of the women for whom he had once sewn dresses were now well established, and they came to him requesting loans with which they and their husbands might open grocery stores and laundries and shoe repair shops. Mr. Shimada helped them all and never demanded any collateral.[12] He operated his banks on faith and trust and gave no thought to such common prudence as maintaining a reserve.[13]

When my father was called to a new position with a large Japanese firm in San Francisco, Mr. Shimada came down to Portland to extend personally his good wishes. He took Father to a Chinese dinner

12. A moneylender sometimes requires a borrower to provide collateral: something of equivalent value offered or promised as proof that a loan will be repaid.
13. A bank maintains a reserve of uninvested funds to meet possible demands or emergencies (such as a drop in the value of its invested funds).

3 Looking into Lives *What positive characteristics and traits does Mr. Shimada have?*

and told him over the peanut duck and chow mein that he would like always to be considered a friend.

"If I can ever be of assistance to you," he said, "don't ever hesitate to call." And with a firm shake of the hand, he wished my father well.

That was in 1916. My father wrote regularly to Mr. Shimada telling him of his new job, of his bride, and later, of his two children. Mr. Shimada did not write often, but each Christmas he sent a box of Oregon apples and pears, and at New Year's a slab of heavy white rice paste from his Seattle shop.

In 1929 the letters and gifts stopped coming and Father learned from friends in Seattle that both of Mr. Shimada's banks had failed. He immediately dispatched a letter to Mr. Shimada, but it was returned unopened. The next news he had was that Mr. Shimada had had to sell all of his shops. My father was now manager of the San Francisco branch of his firm. He wrote once more asking Mr. Shimada if there was anything he could do to help. The letter did not come back, but there was no reply, and my father did not write again. After all, how do you offer help to the head of a fallen empire? It seemed almost **irreverent.**

Vocabulary

irreverent (i rev′ ər ənt) *adj.* showing a lack of proper respect

YOSHIKO UCHIDA **273**

Teach

Big Idea | **3**

Looking into Lives
Answer: *He is intelligent, trusting, polite, hardworking, kind, generous, and loyal.*

View the Photograph ★
Answer: *Students should note that the stores are of the same time period, the same general geographic area (the West coast), and both appear to sell Japanese goods.*

Photos taken between 1889 and the 1920s used nitrate-based film. Although black and white photos last longer, nitrate film degrades over time, becoming highly flammable and explosive. This film requires special care and storage.

English Learners

DIFFERENTIATED INSTRUCTION

Beginning/Early Intermediate Help English learners understand the author's description of Mr. Shimada and her father on page 272. Read aloud the paragraph which begins, "Although Mr. Shimada . . ." Then ask students to explain the meaning of "erect carriage" (*stands very straight*), "ruddy-faced" (*darker-colored skin*), and "summoned" (*pulled together*).

Advanced Learners

DIFFERENTIATED INSTRUCTION

Explain and Support Help students understand Mr. Shimada's philosophy on page 272: "One never knows when one might be indebted to even the lowliest of beggars." Have a student explain the meaning of indebted. (*to owe someone something*) Then ask students to explain the meaning of this statement. (*Students might say that you never know who you may need to go to for a favor.*) Have stu-

dents to provide an example that supports the quotation.

Teach

Big Idea 1

Looking into Lives
Answer: *He is still loyal and respectful toward Shimada.*

Reading Strategy 2

Analyze Cause-and-Effect Relationships
Answer: *He ends up a poor door-to-door salesman.*

To check students' understanding of the selection, see Unit 2 Teaching Resources Book, p. 33.

It was many years later that Mr. Shimada appeared one night at our home in Berkeley. In the dim light of the front porch my mother was startled to see an elderly gentleman wearing striped pants, a morning coat, and a shabby black hat. In his hand he carried a small black satchel. When she invited him inside, she saw that the morning coat was faded, and his shoes badly in need of a shine.

Visual Vocabulary
A *morning coat* is a man's jacket for formal daytime wear, traditionally worn with striped trousers and a top hat.

"I am Shimada," he announced with a courtly bow, and it was my mother who felt inadequate to the occasion. She hurriedly pulled off her apron and went to call my father. When he heard who was in the living room, he put on his coat and tie before going out to greet his old friend. **1**

Mr. Shimada spoke to them about Father's friends in Seattle and about his daughter who was now married and living in Denver. He spoke of a typhoon that had recently swept over Japan, and he drank the tea my mother served and ate a piece of her chocolate cake. Only then did he open his black satchel.

"I thought your girls might enjoy these books," he said, as he drew out a brochure describing *The Book of Knowledge.*

"Fourteen volumes that will tell them of the wonders of this world." He spread his arms in a magnificent gesture that recalled his eloquence of the past. "I wish I could give them to your children as a personal gift," he added softly. **2**

Without asking the price of the set, my father wrote a check for one hundred dollars and gave it Mr. Shimada.

Mr. Shimada glanced at the check and said, "You have given me fifty dollars too much." He seemed troubled for only a moment, however, and quickly added, "Ah, the balance is for a deposit, is it? Very well, yours will be the first deposit in my next bank."

"Is your home still in Seattle then?" Father asked cautiously.

"I am living there, yes," Mr. Shimada answered.

And then, suddenly overcome with memories of the past, he spoke in a voice so low he could scarcely be heard.

"I paid back every cent," he murmured. "It took ten years, but I paid it back. All of it. I owe nothing."

"You are a true gentleman, Shimada-san," Father said. "You always will be." Then he pointed to the black tie he wore, saying, "You see, I am still one of the Shimada men."

That was the last time my father saw Shozo Shimada. Some time later he heard that he had returned to Japan as penniless as the day he set out for America.

It wasn't until the Christmas after we heard of Mr. Shimada's death that I ventured to give my father a silk four-in-hand tie. It was charcoal gray and flecked with threads of silver. My father looked at it for a long time before he tried it on, and then fingering it gently, he said, "Well, perhaps it is time now that I put away my black bow ties." ~

1 Looking into Lives *What does this action tell you about Uchida's father?*

2 Analyze Cause-and-Effect Relationships *How does Mr. Shimada's life change after the Great Depression?*

Writing Practice

PARTNERS SPIRAL REVIEW **Conduct Research** Explain to students that Mr. Shimada's banks failed during the Great Depression, a time when many Americans suffered economic hardship. Pair up students and have them research bank failures during the Great Depression. Have students find at least one reputable Internet source and two print resources. Have students write a few paragraphs on what happened to the banks during the Great Depression. Then initiate a discussion about what happened to Mr. Shimada and others during the Great Depression. Discuss how their lives changed using details from their research.

After You Read

Respond and Think Critically

Respond and Interpret

1. Describe your reaction to what happens to Mr. Shimada.
2. (a)What happens after people entrust Mr. Shimada with their savings? (b)What traits do you think help him become a business success?
3. (a)Summarize what happens to Mr. Shimada and his businesses after 1929. (b)Why is Mr. Shimada's generosity his "undoing"?

Analyze and Evaluate

4. What are the most important lessons that the author's father learned from Mr. Shimada?
5. What conclusions can you draw about the impact of the stock market crash of 1929 and the Great Depression on the lives of Americans?

Connect

6. **Big Idea** Looking into Lives Would you work for a boss like Mr. Shimada? Explain.
7. **Connect to Today** Many of the events in this essay take place between 1880 and 1929. How is Uchida's story about Mr. Shimada and her father relevant in today's society? Support your answer with facts and details from the story.

Literary Element Author's Purpose

An author may have more than one purpose for writing. For example, you may find Uchida's essay entertaining. However, Uchida also has something important to say about true gentlemen in society.

1. In your opinion, what was Uchida's primary purpose in writing this biographical essay?
2. How does the fact the author was born in this country help to explain her purpose for writing?

Reading Strategy Analyze Cause-and-Effect Relationships

Sometimes, authors use **cause-and-effect relationships** clue words such as *because, as a result, since,* or *when.* Review the diagrams you created as you read and answer these questions.

1. Identify two clue words that Uchida uses to signal cause-and-effect relationships in this essay.
2. Identify a cause that has multiple effects.

Vocabulary Practice

Practice with Synonyms A synonym is a word that has the same or nearly the same meaning as another word. With a partner, match each boldfaced vocabulary word below with its synonym. Use a thesaurus or dictionary to check your answers. You will not use all the answer choices.

1. **confidant**	a. unimportant
2. **imposing**	b. elated
3. **exhilarated**	c. friend
4. **irreverent**	d. magnificent
	e. facetious
	f. certain

Writing

Write a News Story How does the author's purpose affect your understanding of the story? Write Mr. Shimada's story from the objective point of view of a newspaper reporter. Consider the purpose of a news report, and how that purpose might affect how the story is told.

LOG ON **Literature** Online

Selection Resources For Selection Quizzes, eFlashcards, and Reading-Writing Connection activities, go to glencoe.com and enter QuickPass code GL49787u2.

After You Read

Assess

1. Students' answers should reflect an understanding of the tragedy of his fate.
2. (a) He invested their money in a dry goods store. (b) Hard-working, trustworthy, and perceptive about the needs of his community
3. (a) His banks failed, and he had to sell all his stores. (b) He loaned money without any guarantees of repayment.
4. Generosity, loyalty, respect for others
5. Answers should reflect understanding of its devastating impact on individuals and communities.
6. Students should identify his various qualities to support their answers.
7. Students may say that stories about mentors are always relevant because people naturally look to those who are successful to learn how to become successful themselves.

Vocabulary Practice

1. c **2.** d **3.** b **4.** e

Writing

Students' reports should maintain an objective point of view.

Literary Element

1. Possible answers: to show that honor, respect, and dignity can be aspired to in any society; to show that success is determined in large part by a willingness to work hard while living according to high principles.
2. Possible answers: The author may wish to show that her attitudes have been formed in part by her exposure to two cultures. She may seek to show that principles can be applied equally in any culture.

Reading Strategy

1. Therefore; when
2. Cause: Shimada was generous and helpful. Effects: People trusted and relied on him. His bank failed because of unsecured loans.

Progress Check

Can students analyze cause-and-effect relationships?

If No → See Unit 2 Teaching Resources Book, p. 29.

Before You Read

Focus

Bellringer Options

Selection Focus Transparency 17

Daily Language Practice Transparency 27

Or tell students that this selection focuses on family in an especially personal, vivid way.

Ask: Does being a family's only daughter or son—or being an eldest, middle, or youngest child—affect a person's sense of who he or she is? Have small groups of students discuss the effect of family structure on their feelings about themselves or on someone they know.

Before You Read

Only Daughter

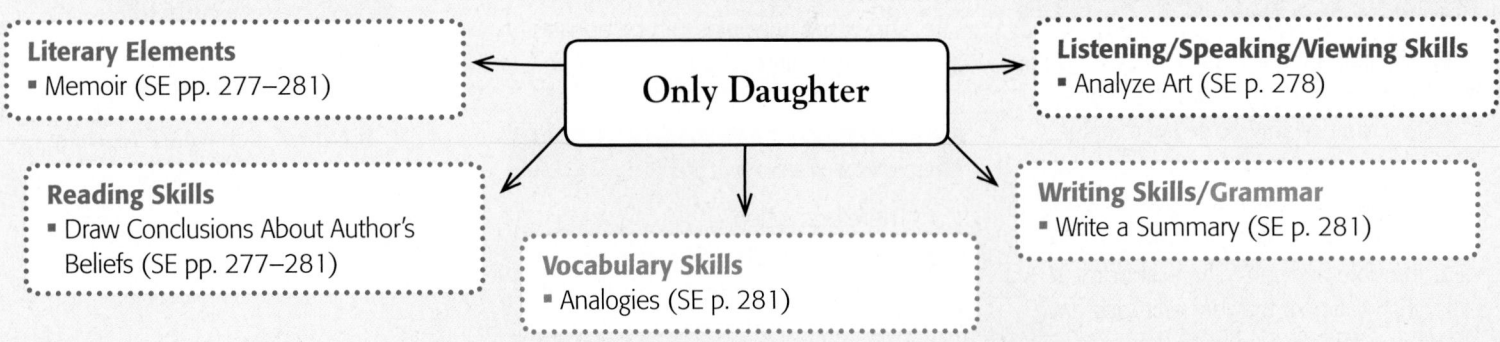

Meet **Sandra Cisneros**

(born 1954)

Sandra Cisneros says that coming from a Mexican American family gives her "two ways of looking at the world" and "twice as many words to pick from." Although Cisneros weaves Spanish words and phrases into her writing, she writes poetry and fiction primarily in English.

Poverty and Alienation Cisneros grew up in Chicago, Illinois, in a working-class Mexican American family. As she explains in her essay "Only Daughter," she was the only girl in a family of seven children. As a child, she experienced poverty firsthand. She also felt alienated because her family moved frequently between the United States and Mexico. As a result of moving and changing schools frequently, Cisneros had difficulty making friends and spent a lot of time alone.

Finding Her Voice After graduating from high school, Cisneros studied English at Loyola University in Chicago. Later, she attended graduate school at the University of Iowa where she earned a master's degree in poetry from the famed Iowa Writers' Workshop. While she was in graduate school, she realized that she wanted to write about her unique experiences as a Mexican American.

At this point in her life, Cisneros also began to write the vignettes that were later published in her acclaimed work of fiction *The House on Mango Street* (1984). In that collection of connected stories, as well as in her other writing, she focused on poor families—the people she "knew and loved but never saw in the pages of the books" that she borrowed from the library.

"I am a woman and a Latina. Those are the things that make my writing distinctive. Those are the things that give my writing power."

—Sandra Cisneros

A Writer's Life Despite the success of *The House on Mango Street,* which won the American Book Award, Cisneros struggled to earn a living after she finished graduate school. She worked as a high school teacher, a college recruiter, and a college professor while writing at night at her kitchen table. After she received a National Endowment for the Arts grant in 1988, Cisneros was able to work on *Woman Hollering Creek and Other Stories,* which was published in 1991. Since then, she has published a fourth book of poems, a children's book, and her first novel, *Caramelo.*

LOG ON **Literature** Online

Author Search For more about Sandra Cisneros, go to glencoe.com and enter QuickPass code GL49787u2.

Selection Skills

Only Daughter

Literary Elements
- Memoir (SE pp. 277–281)

Listening/Speaking/Viewing Skills
- Analyze Art (SE p. 278)

Reading Skills
- Draw Conclusions About Author's Beliefs (SE pp. 277–281)

Vocabulary Skills
- Analogies (SE p. 281)

Writing Skills/Grammar
- Write a Summary (SE p. 281)

Literature and Reading Preview

Connect to the Memoir

How does being the eldest, middle, youngest, or only child in a family affect a person? Freewrite for a few minutes about your position in your family and how it affects who you are.

Build Background

In "Only Daughter," Cisneros remembers her father referring to his children as *"hijos"* (ē′ hōs). In Spanish, *hijos* means "sons," but it also means "children." When Cisneros's father speaks directly to his daughter, he uses the feminine equivalent of the word *hijo,* which is *hija* (ē′ hä). He says *"mi'ja"* (mē′ hä), which is a shortening of *mi* and *hija*, meaning "my daughter."

Set Purposes for Reading

Big Idea Looking into Lives

As you read, ask yourself, What details about growing up as the family's only daughter do I find most powerful and descriptive?

Literary Element Memoir

A **memoir** is a type of narrative nonfiction that presents an account of an event or period in the author's life. It is told from the first-person point of view and emphasizes the author's personal experience. As you read, ask yourself, What can I learn about Sandra Cisneros from reading this memoir?

Reading Strategy Draw Conclusions About Author's Beliefs

When you draw a conclusion, you use a number of pieces of information to make a general statement about people, places, events, or ideas. By **drawing conclusions about an author's beliefs,** you can better understand how an author's ideas and opinions are related to what you are reading. As you read, ask yourself, What conclusions can I draw about Cisneros's beliefs?

Tip: Note Details Use a graphic organizer to note details that will help you draw conclusions about Cisneros's beliefs regarding women, education, and becoming a writer.

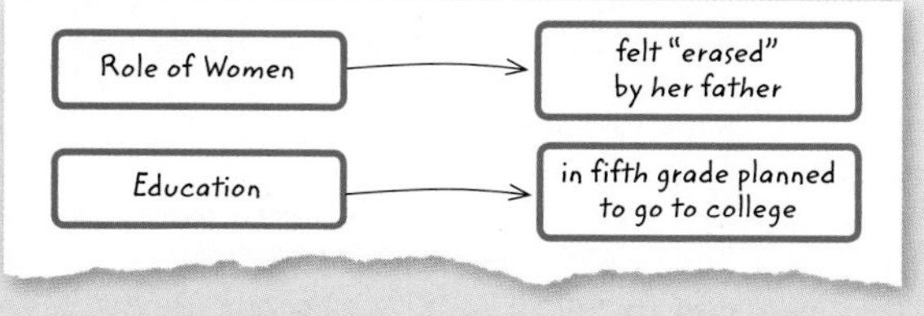

Learning Objectives

For pages 276–281

In studying this text, you will focus on the following objectives:

Literary Study: Analyzing memoir.

Reading: Drawing conclusions about author's beliefs.

Writing: Writing a summary.

Vocabulary

anthology (an thol′ ə jē) *n.* a collection of written works, such as poems, stories, or essays, in a single book or set; p. 278 *My favorite story and Sam's favorite story are both in an anthology,* Best Short Stories About New England.

retrospect (ret′ rə spekt′) *n.* the act of looking back or thinking about the past; p. 279 *In retrospect the detective realized that he had missed an important clue.*

embroider (em broi′ dər) *v.* to make a story more interesting with imaginary details or exaggerations; p. 279 *Cal did not embroider his account of being lost at sea; the true story was thrilling enough.*

fulfill (fool fil′) *v.* to measure up to, or satisfy; to bring to pass; p. 279 *Dawn is determined to fulfill her dream of competing in the Olympics.*

Before You Read

Focus

Summary

Sandra Cisneros is a young Mexican American woman who aspires to become a writer. She graduates from college, but, to her father's dismay, does not find a husband. After achieving professional recognition, she returns home with a published story. After reading the story, her father asks for copies for their relatives.

For summaries in languages other than English, see Unit 2 Teaching Resources Book, pp. 35–40.

Vocabulary

The Prefix Strategy Remind students that if they don't know the meaning of a word, they can use common prefixes and suffixes to help them. If a student knows the prefix *retro-* means "back," they can decode the word *retrospect.* The same goes for suffixes. Encourage students to try to find the meaning of unfamiliar words by identifying the meanings of prefixes, roots, and suffixes.

For additional vocabulary practice, see Unit 2 Teaching Resources Book, pp. 43–44.

For additional context, see Glencoe Interactive Vocabulary CD-ROM.

English Learners

DIFFERENTIATED INSTRUCTION

Intermediate While reading "Only Daughter," English language learners may have trouble understanding words with multiple meanings. Write the following phrases on the board.

- "The house was throbbing . . ." *(filled with activity)*
- ". . . hot tamales and sweet tamales hissing in my mother's pressure cooker." *(sizzling)*
- " . . . my father likes to spend his leisure hours horizontally." *(lying down)*
- " . . . punched the mute button" *(pressed the mute button)*

Ask students to explain the meaning of the underlined word as it is used in each phrase.

Teach

Reading Strategy 1

Draw Conclusions About Author's Beliefs
Answer: *Students may conclude she thinks becoming a writer is a long, complex process.*

For additional practice using the reading skill or strategy, see Unit 2 Teaching Resources Book, p. 42.

Literary Element 2

Memoir **Answer:** *The father sends his daughter to college to find a good husband. By wishing to attain a college education as a springboard to a writing career, Cisneros is part of the emerging generation that values education for both sexes.*

View the Art ★

Answer: *The artist's use of color and definitive lines makes the woman in the painting stand out from her background—just as the author wants to "stand out."*

For an audio recording of this selection, use Listening Library Audio CD-ROM.

Readability Scores

Dale-Chall: 5.7
DRP: 57
Lexile: 900

Only Daughter

Sandra Cisneros

Woman in Cordilleran Night, 1996. Maria Eugenia Terrazas. Watercolor, 70 x 70 cm. Kactus Foto, Santiago, Chile.

View the Art How does the artist's use of color and lines affect the mood of this painting? Compare and contrast this woman with the narrator in this selection. ★

Once, several years ago, when I was just starting out my writing career, I was asked to write my own contributor's note for an **anthology** I was part of. I wrote: "I am the only daughter in a family of six sons. *That* explains everything."

Well, I've thought about that ever since, and yes, it explains a lot to me, but for the reader's sake I should have written: "I am the only daughter in a *Mexican* family of six sons." Or even: "I am the only daughter of a Mexican father and a Mexican-American mother." Or: "I am the only daughter of a working-class family of nine." All of these had everything to do with who I am today.

I was/am the only daughter and *only* a daughter. Being an only daughter in a family of six sons forced me by circumstance to spend a lot of time by myself because my brothers felt it beneath them to play with a *girl* in public. But that aloneness, that loneliness, was good for a would-be writer—it allowed me time to think and think, to imagine, to read and prepare myself.

Being only a daughter for my father meant my destiny would lead me to become someone's wife. That's what he believed. But when I was in the fifth grade and shared my plans for college with him, I was sure he understood. I remember my father saying, "*Qué bueno, mi'ja,*[1] that's good." That meant a lot to me, especially since my brothers thought the idea hilarious. What I didn't realize was that my father thought college was good for girls—good for finding a husband. After four years in college and two more in graduate school, and still no

Vocabulary

anthology (an thol′ ə jē) *n.* a collection of written works, such as poems, stories, or essays, in a single book or set

1. *Qué bueno, mi'ja* (kā bwā′ nō mē′ hä)

Draw Conclusions About Author's Beliefs *What conclusion can you draw about Cisneros's beliefs on what it takes to become a writer?* **1**

Memoir *How does Cisneros's experience reflect a generation gap in the Mexican American community?* **2**

Writing Practice

SMALL GROUP SPIRAL REVIEW

Narrative Cisneros feels that being the only daughter in a family of six sons contributed to her becoming a writer. Break students into small groups and have them discuss how a person's role in a family can affect his or her life. Ask them to consider the following:

- What is life like for the oldest child in a family? The youngest child? Children in the middle?
- What is life like for an only child?

Then have students individually write an essay in which they discuss how their place in their family has affected their life so far and how it will affect their lives in the future.

husband, my father shakes his head even now and says I wasted all that education.

In **retrospect,** I'm lucky my father believed daughters were meant for husbands. It meant it didn't matter if I majored in something silly like English. After all, I'd find a nice professional eventually, right? This allowed me the liberty to putter about **embroidering** my little poems and stories without my father interrupting with so much as a "What's that you're writing?"

But the truth is, I wanted him to interrupt. I wanted my father to understand what it was I was scribbling, to introduce me as "My only daughter, the writer." Not as "This is only my daughter. She teaches." *Es maestra*—teacher. Not even *profesora.*[2]

In a sense, everything I have ever written has been for him, to win his approval even though I know my father can't read English words, even though my father's only reading includes the brown-ink *Esto*[3] sports magazines from Mexico City and the bloody *¡Alarma!* magazines[4] that feature yet another sighting of *La Virgen de Guadalupe*[5] on a tortilla or a wife's revenge on her philandering husband[6] by bashing his skull in with a *molcajete* (a kitchen mortar[7] made of volcanic rock). Or the *fotonovelas,*[8] the little picture paperbacks with tragedy and trauma erupting from the characters' mouths in bubbles.

My father represents, then, the public majority. A public who is disinterested in reading, and yet one whom I am writing about and for, and privately trying to woo. **5**

When we were growing up in Chicago, we moved a lot because of my father. He suffered bouts of nostalgia.[9] Then we'd have to let go our flat, store the furniture with mother's relatives, load the station wagon with baggage and bologna sandwiches and head south. To Mexico City.

We came back, of course. To yet another Chicago flat, another Chicago neighborhood, another Catholic school. Each time, my father would seek out the parish priest in order to get a tuition break, and complain or boast: "I have seven sons."

He meant *siete hijos,*[10] seven children, but he translated it as "sons." "I have seven sons." To anyone who would listen. The Sears Roebuck employee who sold us the washing machine. The short-order cook where my father ate his ham-and-eggs breakfasts. "I have seven sons." As if he deserved a medal from the state.

My papa. He didn't mean anything by that mistranslation, I'm sure. But somehow I could feel myself being erased. I'd tug my father's sleeve and whisper: "Not seven sons. Six! and *one daughter.*"

When my oldest brother graduated from medical school, he **fulfilled** my

2. *Es maestra* (es mī äs′ trə); *profesora* (prō fes ō rə) means "professor."
3. *Esto* (äs′ tō)
4. *¡Alarma! magazines* feature exciting stories about famous people, strange events, and shocking crimes.
5. *La Virgen de Guadalupe* (lä vēr′ hin dä gwä də loo′ pā), meaning "the Virgin of Guadalupe," is a name for Jesus's mother, Mary, the patron saint of Mexico.
6. A *philandering husband* is one who cheats on his wife.
7. A *molcajete* (mōl′ kə hä′ tā), or *kitchen mortar,* is a thick bowl used to crush substances, such as dried spices, into a powder or paste.
8. *fotonovelas* (fō′ tō nō vä′ läs)
9. *Nostalgia* is a sentimental longing for the past.
10. *Siete hijos* (sye′ tā ē′ hōs)

Vocabulary

retrospect (ret′ rə spekt′) *n.* the act of looking back or thinking about the past

embroider (em broi′ dər) *v.* to make a story more interesting with imaginary details or exaggerations

Memoir *How does this passage reveal Cisneros's main goal as a writer?* **3**

Looking into Lives *Why does the author's father boast about having seven sons rather than seven children?* **4**

Vocabulary

fulfill (fool fil′) *v.* to measure up to, or satisfy; to bring to pass

Teach

Literary Element 3

Memoir **Answer:** *Cisneros reveals that her main goal is to educate. She also hopes to gain the respect of Mexican immigrants like her father.*

APPROACHING Remind approaching-level students that "Only Daughter" is a memoir. For review, ask students to explain what a memoir is and its characteristics. *(Students' answers should reflect the explanation provided on page 277.)*

Big Idea 4

Looking into Lives
Answer: *In some cultures, sons are more valued than daughters. Mr. Cisneros feels that people will be more impressed with him if he says all his children are sons.*

Reading Strategy 5

Draw Conclusions About Author's Beliefs **Ask:** What does this passage suggest about the writer's feelings about the reading public? *(She regrets that most people are not interested in serious literature, but wants to write literature they will read.)*

Approaching Level

DIFFERENTIATED INSTRUCTION

Emerging Write these sentences on the board: "I am the *only* daughter" and "I am *only* a daughter." Have a student point out the difference in meaning.

Established Read aloud the paragraph on page 279 that begins "When we were growing up in Chicago . . ." Ask a student to explain what Cisneros means when she says her father suffers from "bouts of nostalgia." (At times he remembers his past experiences in Mexico and he misses his country badly.)

Teach

Literary Element 1

Memoir **Answer:** *She has succeeded in writing a story that her father enjoys and can identify with his own experiences; consequently, she has piqued his interest in reading and has gained his respect.*

ENGLISH LEARNERS Ask English learners to think of someone from their culture whose life story would make an interesting memoir. Have students share their answers with the class and explain. They should support their answers with a reasonable explanation.

Reading Strategy 2

Draw Conclusions About Author's Beliefs **Ask:** Why is this experience important to Cisneros as a daughter, as a Mexican American woman, and as a writer? *Cisneros finally gets the recognition she deserves from her father and feels proud that she is able to win over someone who ordinarily does not enjoy reading serious fiction. She has finally connected with her father in a way they can both understand.*

Progress Check

Can students analyze memoir?

If No → See Unit 2 Teaching Resources Book, p. 41.

To check students' understanding of the selection, see Unit 2 Teaching Resources Book, pp. 46–47.

father's dream that we study hard and use this—our heads, instead of this—our hands. Even now my father's hands are thick and yellow, stubbed by a history of hammer and nails and twine and coils and springs. "Use this," my father said, tapping his head, "and not this," showing us those hands. He always looked tired when he said it.

Wasn't college an investment? And hadn't I spent all those years in college? And if I didn't marry, what was it all for? Why would anyone go to college and then choose to be poor? Especially someone who had always been poor.

Last year, after ten years of writing professionally, the financial rewards started to trickle in. My second National Endowment for the Arts[11] Fellowship. A guest professorship at the University of California, Berkeley. My book, which sold to a major New York publishing house.

At Christmas, I flew home to Chicago. The house was throbbing, same as always: hot *tamales*[12] and sweet *tamales* hissing in my mother's pressure cooker, and everybody—my mother, six brothers, wives, babies, aunts, cousins—talking too loud and at the same time, like in a Fellini[13] film, because that's just how we are.

I went upstairs to my father's room. One of my stories had just been translated into Spanish and published in an anthology of Chicano[14] writing, and I wanted to show it to him. Ever since he recovered from a stroke two years ago, my father likes to spend his leisure hours horizontally. And that's how I found him, watching a Pedro Infante movie on Galavision[15] and eating rice pudding.

There was a glass filmed with milk on the bedside table. There were several vials of pills and balled Kleenex. And on the floor, one black sock and a plastic urinal that I didn't want to look at but looked at anyway. Pedro Infante was about to burst into song, and my father was laughing.

I'm not sure if it was because my story was translated into Spanish, or because it was published in Mexico, or perhaps because the story dealt with Tepeyac, the *colonia*[16] my father was raised in and the house he grew up in, but at any rate, my father punched the mute button on his remote control and read my story.

I sat on the bed next to my father and waited. He read it very slowly. As if he were reading each line over and over. He laughed at all the right places and read lines he liked out loud. He pointed and asked questions: "Is this So-and-so?" "Yes," I said. He kept reading.

When he was finally finished, after what seemed like hours, my father looked up and asked: "Where can we get more copies of this for the relatives?"

Of all the wonderful things that happened to me last year, that was the most wonderful. 2

11. The *National Endowment for the Arts* is a U.S. government agency that awards money in the form of grants and fellowships to writers and other artists.
12. A *tamale* (tə mä′ lā) is a Mexican dish made of highly seasoned ground meat that is rolled in cornmeal dough, wrapped in corn husks, and steamed.
13. The movies of Italian director Federico Fellini (1920–1993) are often filled with strange characters and noisy, chaotic events.
14. *Chicano* (chi kä′ nō) means "Mexican American."
15. *Pedro Infante* (in fän′ tā) is a popular Mexican movie star who can occasionally be seen on *Galavision*, a Spanish-language, cable-television channel.
16. *Tepeyac* (tā pā yäk) is a district *(colonia)* of Mexico City.

Memoir *How has Cisneros fulfilled her ambitions as a writer?* 1

Reading Practice

SMALL GROUP SPIRAL REVIEW **Evaluate Style** Ask a volunteer to read the first two paragraphs on page 280. In the second paragraph, the author asks a series of questions. **Ask:** Who do you think is asking these questions? And why aren't they in quotation marks? *(Students may say that Cisneros is repeating questions her father has repeatedly asked. She doesn't use quotation marks because she isn't quoting his exact words but is instead summarizing how he feels.)*

In small groups, have students rewrite the paragraph without the questions. Remind them to demonstrate a control of grammar, diction, and paragraph structure. Then have them discuss whether the paragraph they have written is more or less effective than Cisneros's paragraph.

After You Read

Respond and Think Critically

Respond and Interpret

1. How did you react to the author's experience as an only daughter?
2. (a)Describe Cisneros's family. (b)Why do you think Cisneros writes more about her father in the essay than about other family members?
3. (a)How did her father's attitude about Cisneros's education differ from his attitude toward his sons' educations? (b)Do you think that Cisneros was affected by his attitude? Why or why not?

Analyze and Evaluate

4. "I am the only daughter in a family of six sons. *That* explains everything." In what ways does the essay confirm or contradict this statement?
5. Explain how being the only daughter, and "only" a daughter, has proven to be both a positive and a negative experience for Cisneros.

Connect

6. **Big Idea** Looking into Lives How does the use of Spanish words, as well as the references to Mexican television, food, and magazines, help you look into Cisneros's life?
7. **Connect to the Author** Cisneros seeks approval from her father. In your experience, is this a goal that is specific to certain cultures or a common goal of all children? Explain.

Literary Element Memoir

A memoir usually presents the author's thoughts and feelings, their relationships with other people, or the impact of significant events in his or her life.

1. How does Cisneros feel about being the only daughter among her father's seven children?
2. What is the significance to Cisneros that one of her stories was translated into Spanish and published in an anthology of Chicano writing?

Reading Strategy Draw Conclusions About Author's Beliefs

Refer to your graphic organizer to answer the following questions.

1. What conclusion can you draw about Cisneros's beliefs about the role of women?
2. What conclusion can you draw about Cisneros's beliefs about getting an education?

LOG ON **Literature** Online

Selection Resources For Selection Quizzes, eFlashcards, and Reading-Writing Connection activities, go to glencoe.com and enter QuickPass code GL49787u2.

Vocabulary Practice

Practice with Analogies Complete each analogy below by identifying the relationship between the first pair of words and applying that relationship to the second pair of words.

1. **poem : anthology :: episode :**
   a. story **b.** series **c.** play
2. **embroider : exaggerate :: lie :**
   a. lesson **b.** deceive **c.** disagree
3. **retrospect : remember :: opinion :**
   a. believe **b.** fact **c.** debate
4. **fulfill : abandon :: succeed :**
   a. ascertain **b.** overcome **c.** fail

Writing

Write a Summary Summarizing an essay can help you better understand the main ideas and details an author uses to support her purpose. Write a summary of "Only Daughter." Remember that a summary should be shorter than the original because the idea is to highlight key points. For more help writing a summary, see page 421.

After You Read

Assess

1. Students' responses should give reasons for their reactions.
2. (a) Large, working-class Mexican American family (b) Her desire to win her father's approval had the most impact on her development as a writer.
3. (a) He expected his sons to become well-paid professionals and his daughter to marry well. (b) Students should support their answers with information from the text.
4. Confirms: Her family and her role in it shaped her development as a writer. Contradicts: She became a writer in spite of these facts.
5. It resulted in having solitude and time to think but also distanced her from father.
6. They bring to life the culture that helped shape her father's experience and her own.
7. Possible answers: All children want this approval; culture, personality, gender, may affect how some feel.

For additional assessment, see Assessment Resources, pp. 81–82.

Literary Element

1. Cisneros loves her father and, although she mildly satirizes his attitude toward women, she does not appear to hold his chauvinism against him. She says that everything she has ever written has been to win his approval.
2. Her father would be able to read her work and gain respect for her as a writer.

Reading Strategy

1. She believes that women should be able to have a career and do not necessarily have to be wives and mothers.
2. Cisneros believes education is valuable for its own sake.

Vocabulary

1. b **2.** b **3.** a **4.** c

Writing

Students' summaries should

- be no more than 100 words
- include the main ideas
- be written in the present tense

Before You Read

Focus

Bellringer Options

Daily Language Practice Transparency 28

Or discuss with students the idea of family loyalties. Could there be a situation in which loyalty to a family member is severely tested?

Ask: What kind of situation might make you reconsider your loyalty to a member of your own family?

Before You Read

A Brother's Crime

Meet **James Cross Giblin** (born 1933)

Who wants to write about the "bad guys" in history? James Cross Giblin does. He has already written about Adolf Hitler and John Wilkes Booth, Abraham Lincoln's assassin. He is currently working on the biography of Senator Joseph McCarthy, the man whose investigations of suspected Communists ruined so many lives in the 1950s. For Giblin, "bad guys"—who often see themselves as heroes—make terrific stories.

Theater Background Giblin, who wrote his own comic strips as a child, was more interested in acting than writing when he was in high school. After seeing a notice in a local newspaper, he auditioned for a role in a community play and got the part. After the play was over, he said, "I was hooked on the theater." In college, he studied drama and performed in many plays.

> *"I approach my nonfiction topics as if I were playing detective."*
>
> —James Cross Giblin

Giblin feels that his acting work actually helps him develop narrative interest and pacing in his nonfiction writing. "My training in the theater has given me a sense of drama that comes in handy when I'm trying to shape [my writing] in a way that will catch and hold the reader's attention," he says. He explains that actors ask themselves, "What is my character's chief goal, and how does he or she go about trying to achieve it?" This is similar, Giblin points out, to the biographer's job of determining his or her subject's motivations and inner life.

The Writing Life Because acting was an unpredictable career, Giblin started working as an editor. He enjoyed this career tremendously and discovered that he particularly liked working on books for young audiences. From editing, the transition to writing was natural, and in 1980, working with collaborator Dale Ferguson, Giblin published *The Scarecrow Book.* It was the beginning of a long list of nonfiction titles on topics ranging from skyscrapers and defensive walls to windows, pasteurized milk, and famous people.

Finding the Facts Giblin enjoys the research required to write a nonfiction book. Tracking down information seems to come naturally to him, and many critics have noted his thoroughness in this area. Giblin does not do his research exclusively in libraries. For his biography of Hitler, for example, he traveled across Europe twice.

LOG ON **Literature** Online

Author Search For more about James Cross Giblin, go to glencoe.com and enter QuickPass code GL49787u2.

Selection Skills

A Brother's Crime

Literary Elements
- Historical Narrative (SE pp. 283–290)
- Narrator (SE p. 290)

Writing Skills/Grammar
- Autobiographical Narrative (SE p. 291)
- Sentence Fragments (TE p. 288)

Reading Skills
- Activate Prior Knowledge (SE pp. 283–290)
- Evaluate (TE p. 286)

Vocabulary Skills
- Word Origins (SE p. 283, 290)
- Academic Vocabulary (SE p. 290)

Literature and Reading Preview

Connect to the Biography

What makes a news story particularly shocking? List some recent events that you found especially shocking.

Build Background

Stage actors were the celebrities of the nineteenth century. Perhaps the greatest actor of his day was Edwin Booth, of whom one admiring critic wrote, "Edwin Booth has done more for the stage in America than any other man." Abraham Lincoln, who was an enthusiastic and regular theatergoer, saw Edwin Booth perform many times. Edwin's brother, John Wilkes Booth, was also an accomplished actor. John Wilkes Booth shot Lincoln, jumped onto the stage, and cried out *"Sic semper tyrannis,"* which means "death always to tyrants."

Set Purposes for Reading

Big Idea Looking into Lives

As you read "A Brother's Crime," ask yourself, How does Giblin reveal Edwin Booth's thoughts, feelings, and attitudes at this key moment in his life?

Literary Element Historical Narrative

A **historical narrative** is a work of nonfiction that tells the story of important historical events or developments. As you read, ask yourself, How does this narrative help me learn facts and gain insights into the lives of real people, as well as into the time period?

Reading Strategy Activate Prior Knowledge

Activating prior knowledge is considering what you already know about a person, place, idea, or event in a literary work and using that knowledge to deepen your understanding of what you are reading. As you read, ask yourself, How can I use my prior knowledge of Lincoln, the Civil War, and human nature to further understand this biography?

Tip: Record What You Know Record details about which you have prior knowledge.

Detail	Prior Knowledge
p. 284 "April 14, 1865"	This is near the end of the Civil War.

Learning Objectives

For pages 282–290

In studying this text, you will focus on the following objectives:

Literary Study: Analyzing a historical narrative.

Reading: Activating prior knowledge.

Vocabulary

premonition (prē′ mə nish′ ən) *n.* anticipation of an event without outside warning or reason; p. 284 *Dad had a premonition about the storm, so we took cover.*

intimation (in′ tə mā′ shən) *n.* a suggestion or hint; p. 285 *The tic in the applicant's eye was the only intimation of his nervousness.*

calamity (kə lam′ ə tē) *n.* a disastrous event; p. 286 *The hurricane was a calamity for which few people were fully prepared.*

perpetrator (pur′ pə trā′ tər) *n.* one who commits a crime or other similar act; p. 286 *Police quickly captured the perpetrator.*

incriminating (in krim′ ə nāt′ ing) *adj.* showing involvement in a crime; p. 287 *Police found stolen goods and other incriminating items.*

Tip: Word Origins To find a word's origins refer to a dictionary. For example, the word *perpetrator* comes from the Latin word *patrare,* meaning "to bring about." Knowing this makes it easier to recall the meaning of *perpetrator*—one who brings about or carries out a crime.

Approaching Level

DIFFERENTIATED INSTRUCTION

Emerging Prepare students for "A Brother's Crime" by explaining that the excerpt focuses on a true historical event, but is told in narrative form. **Say:** The writer tells the story of Edwin Booth, whose brother committed a serious crime that changed the history of the United States.

Tell students that the crime took place during the Civil War era. Ask students to share what they know about the Civil War. The background information will help students understand the significance of the passage.

Before You Read

Focus

Summary

In this historical narrative, the author describes the feelings and actions of Edwin Booth, brother of John Wilkes Booth. The narrative is set when Edwin learns that his younger brother, a fellow actor, has assassinated President Abraham Lincoln. Unlike his brother, Edwin is an admirer of Lincoln, and he knows that his life will never be the same again.

For summaries in languages other than English, see Unit 2 Teaching Resources Book, pp. 48–53.

Vocabulary

Word Scramble Rewrite each vocabulary word on the board, rearranging the order of the letters in each word. Have students guess the vocabulary word for each group of letters. Then have students define the term in their own words and then use the term in a sentence.

For additional vocabulary practice, see Unit 2 Teaching Resources Book, p. 56.

For additional context, see Glencoe Interactive Vocabulary CD-ROM.

Teach

Literary Element 1

Historical Narrative
Answer: *The date is April 14, 1865 (Good Friday), and the place is the Boston Theatre. Edwin Booth is the subject of the narrative.*

Literary Element 2

Historical Narrative Ask: How does the author of this narrative set the scene in historical context? *(He describes Booth as one of the finest actors of the day, and he refers specifically to the end of the Civil War in 1865.)*

Reading Strategy 3

Activate Prior Knowledge
Answer: *Students may name emotions ranging from grief to violent resentment.*

For additional practice using the reading skill or strategy, see Unit 2 Teaching Resources Book, p. 55.

Readability Scores

Dale-Chall: 7.7
DRP: 60
Lexile: 1110

A BROTHER'S CRIME

James Cross Giblin

Edwin Booth often had **premonitions** that something bad was going to happen. But there is no evidence that he had any advance warning on April 14, 1865, of the terrible event
2 that was about to befall him and the nation. On that Friday—Good Friday[1]—Booth sat in his dressing room at the Boston Theatre, applying his makeup for the evening performance. The theater's manager had told him the house was sold out, and Booth wanted to give the crowd his best.

An air of eager expectation filled the auditorium as the audience members took their seats in the orchestra[2] or climbed the steep stairs to the balcony. Many had come just to see Booth, who, at thirty-one, was considered one of America's finest actors, if not the finest. But many others had come to celebrate the end of the Civil War.

The Sunday before, on April 9, the Confederate general, Robert E. Lee, had surrendered to the Union commander, Ulysses S. Grant, at the little town of Appomattox Courthouse in Virginia. Four years of increasingly bloody warfare had ended in victory for the North. Now, while the South mourned its loss, people all

1. *Good Friday* is the day that Christians observe as the anniversary of Christ's crucifixion.

2. Here, *orchestra* refers to a seating area on the first floor of a theater.

1 Historical Narrative *Identify the time, the place, and the person who is the subject of this historical narrative.*

Vocabulary

premonition (prē′ mə nish′ ən) *n.* anticipation of an event without outside warning or reason

Activate Prior Knowledge *How did many Southerners feel at this time?* 3

Research Practice

SPIRAL REVIEW

Synthesizing Information

Explain to students that the Civil War was a tumultuous time for Americans in both the North and the South. Tell them that at the end of the war, the South was ravaged, and Southerners experienced bitter defeat, while Northerners savored their victory. Newspapers across the country published accounts of the war, as well as opinions on the outcome.

Ask students to research the effects of the Civil War how it impacted the Northern and Southern residents. Students should develop a list of questions to guide them in their research. Then have students write a short summary of their findings in which they examine how this information relates to the social issues mentioned in "A Brother's Crime."

across the North rejoiced that the fighting was over. The Union flag—the American flag—flew everywhere, and red-white-and-blue bunting[3] decorated lampposts and storefronts in towns large and small.

On Good Friday, thousands of Northerners gave thanks for the victory by attending church services in the morning. That evening, theaters were packed in cities throughout the North—and Boston was no exception. For the occasion, Edwin Booth, who was famed for his performances in Shakespeare's plays, chose something in a less classical vein. He decided to appear as the villain, Sir Edward Mortimer, in a melodrama[4] that never failed to please the ☆ crowd: *The Iron Chest.*

When Edwin made his entrance, clad[5] in black velvet, the audience greeted him with loud applause. Unlike most actors of his day, Booth never indulged in grand gestures or studied[6] poses. Instead, he acted in a more realistic style, relying on his low, intense voice and piercing dark eyes to compel the spectators' attention. Not a sound could be heard in the vast theater during the climactic death scene, when Booth, as Sir Edward, finally admitted his guilt. And at the end, he was brought back for curtain call after curtain call.

That night Edwin, who was staying at a friend's house in Boston, had trouble getting to sleep. But he still had no **intimation** of the shock that was in store for him the next morning. Without knocking first, his valet[7] burst into his bedroom shortly after seven. Thrusting a newspaper in front of a dazed Edwin, the man exclaimed, "Mr. Booth, President Lincoln has been shot!" Before Edwin could absorb that terrible fact, the valet went on: "And—oh, Mr. Booth—they say your brother John has done it!"

His brother John . . . how could that be? Edwin knew that John strongly supported the South and hated Abraham Lincoln. He'd often heard John state, without any evidence, that Lincoln would make himself king of the United States if the North won the war. The last time they'd been together, John had stormed out of the room when Edwin, whose sympathies were with the North, told him that he'd voted for Lincoln's re-election. Oh, John could be headstrong.[8] But to shoot the president—to try to kill him? That wasn't the brother he knew and loved.

Edwin grabbed the newspaper from the valet and quickly scanned the story of the shooting, which occupied the entire front page. It said that President Lincoln had been shot and gravely wounded in his box at Ford's Theatre in Washington, where he and his wife had gone to see a play. And there it was, the name of the attacker, who had been recognized at once by many in the audience. He was the dashing, dark-haired young actor who stirred many feminine hearts when he played Romeo in Shakespeare's *Romeo and Juliet* and other romantic roles: John Wilkes Booth.

Later, Edwin would write to a friend that when he saw his brother's name in

3. *Bunting* is loosely woven fabric or coarse muslin used for flags and other decorations.
4. A *melodrama* is a type of play that emphasizes action and dramatic effects over characterization and theme.
5. Here, *clad* means "dressed."
6. Here, *studied* means "carefully prepared."
7. A *valet* is a personal servant.
8. *Headstrong* means "impatient" or "unwilling to accept advice or control."

4 Looking into Lives *What do these details suggest about Booth's personality?*

Vocabulary

intimation (in′ tə mā′ shən) *n.* a suggestion or hint

Activate Prior Knowledge *What types of stories typically appear on the front pages of newspapers?* **5**

Teach

Big Idea 4

Looking into Lives

Answer: *The details suggest that Booth was not overly dramatic or a person who wanted attention, but rather a restrained professional.*

ENGLISH LEARNERS To assist English learners, be sure that students understand the meaning of *intense, piercing,* and *compel.* Have students define these words using a dictionary and use each word in a sentence.

Reading Strategy 5

Activate Prior Knowledge

Answer: *Most students will know that the more important stories are placed on the front page.*

Cultural Note ☆

The Iron Chest George Colman the Younger wrote *The Iron Chest* in 1796, based on William Godwin's popular 1794 novel, *Caleb Williams*. The play is a drama involving murder and deceit, with the lowly but good steward Willard (Caleb Williams) facing off with his villainous master, Sir Edward Mortimer.

Approaching Level

DIFFERENTIATED INSTRUCTION

Emerging Remind students that foreshadowing is an author's use of clues to prepare readers for events that will happen later in the story. Tell students that the author includes two instances of foreshadowing on these pages of the text. Ask students to find these instances of foreshadowing on these two pages.

(Page 284: ". . . there is no evidence that he had any advance warning of the terrible event that was about to befall him and the nation"; page 285: "But he still had no intimation of the shock that was in store for him the next morning.")

Teach

Reading Strategy 1

Evaluate **Ask:** Do you think the theater manager made the correct decision? Why or why not? *(Students may say that his fear of possible violence was well founded but that he could have written more tactfully to Edwin.)*

print, he felt "as if I had been struck on the head by a hammer." As he struggled to comprehend the dreadful news, his mind was a jumble of worries and fears. He thought of his mother, at home in New York with his older sister, Rosalie. John had always been his mother's favorite; how would she deal with the news? Would she have the strength to go on? And where was John now? The newspaper said he had escaped—where had he gone?

While Edwin was still sorting out his reactions and trying to decide what to do, word came that Lincoln had lost his night-long battle for life. The president had died early that morning without ever regaining consciousness. Shortly after that, a messenger arrived with a letter from the manager of the Boston Theatre. "My dear sir," the letter began. "A fearful **calamity** is upon us. The President of the United States has fallen by the hand of an assassin, and I am shocked to say suspicion points to one nearly related to you as the **perpetrator** of this horrid deed. God grant it may not prove so!"

1 But the manager was taking no chances. He went on: "With this knowledge, and out of respect for the anguish which will fill the public mind as soon as the

SURRAT.
BOOTH.
HAROLD.
War Department, Washington, April 20, 1865,
$100,000 REWARD!
THE MURDERER
Of our late beloved President, Abraham Lincoln,
IS STILL AT LARGE.
$50,000 REWARD
Will be paid by this Department for his apprehension, in addition to any reward offered by Municipal Authorities or State Executives.
$25,000 REWARD
Will be paid for the apprehension of JOHN H. SURRATT, one of Booth's Accomplices.
$25,000 REWARD
Will be paid for the apprehension of David C. Harold, another of Booth's accomplices.
LIBERAL REWARDS will be paid for any information that shall conduce to the arrest of either of the above-named criminals, or their accomplices.
All persons harboring or secreting the said persons, or either of them, or aiding or assisting their concealment or escape, will be treated as accomplices in the murder of the President and the attempted assassination of the Secretary of State, and shall be subject to trial before a Military Commission and the punishment of DEATH.
Let the stain of innocent blood be removed from the land by the arrest and punishment of the murderers.
All good citizens are exhorted to aid public justice on this occasion. Every man should consider his own conscience charged with this solemn duty, and rest neither night nor day until it be accomplished.
EDWIN M. STANTON, Secretary of War.
DESCRIPTIONS.—BOOTH is Five Feet 7 or 8 inches high, slender build, high forehead, black hair, black eyes, and wears a heavy black moustache.
JOHN H. SURRAT is about 5 feet, 9 inches. Hair rather thin and dark; eyes rather light; no beard. Would weigh 145 or 150 pounds. Complexion rather pale and clear, with color in his cheeks. Wore light clothes of fine quality. Shoulders square; cheek bones rather prominent; chin narrow; ears projecting at the top; forehead rather low and square, but broad. Parts his hair on the right side; neck rather long. His lips are firmly set. A slim man.
DAVID C. HAROLD is five feet six inches high, hair dark, eyes dark, eyebrows rather heavy, full face, nose short, hand short and fleshy, feet small, instep high, round bodied, naturally quick and active, slightly closes his eyes when looking at a person.
NOTICE.—In addition to the above, State and other authorities have offered rewards amounting to almost one hundred thousand dollars, making an aggregate of about TWO HUNDRED THOUSAND DOLLARS.

Vocabulary

calamity (kə lam′ ə tē) *n.* a disastrous event

perpetrator (pur′ pə trā tər) *n.* one who commits a crime or other similar act

Reading Practice

SPIRAL REVIEW **Analyze a Speech** Obtain a copy of Lincoln's second inaugural address, which he delivered just a few weeks before his assassination. Distribute copies to the class, pointing out that the last paragraph is one of Lincoln's most-quoted statements. Ask students to analyze the speech for rhetorical devices and memorable features. Remind them that rhetorical devices include such elements as repetition, parallelism, and appeals to authority. Ask them to provide examples of each of these three devices. (Students may identify the repetition and parallelism in the last paragraph and the frequent mentions of God in the second half of the speech.)

1 appalling[9] fact shall be fully revealed, I have concluded to close the Boston Theatre until further notice." The manager ended on a cool, impersonal note. "Please signify to me[10] your cooperation in this matter."

Edwin drafted a quick response to the manager's letter. It was written in the formal style of the time, but Edwin's feelings can be sensed between the lines. "With deepest sorrow and great agitation, I thank you for relieving me from my engagement[11] with yourself and the public," he wrote. "The news of the morning has made me wretched indeed, not only because I received the unhappy tidings of the suspicion of a brother's crime, but because a good man, and a most justly honored and patriotic ruler, has fallen by the hand of an assassin."

Edwin concluded the letter with a strong statement of his own loyalty and patriotism. "While mourning, in common with all other loyal hearts, the death of the President, I am oppressed by a private woe[12] not to be expressed in words. But whatever calamity may befall me or mine, my country, one and indivisible, has my warmest devotion."

Now that the Boston Theatre was closed, Edwin had no reason to stay on in Boston. He decided to return to New York as soon as possible and sent a telegram to his mother saying he would take the midnight train and be home on Sunday morning. But he had to delay his departure. Federal marshals[13] wanted to question him about his relations with his brother and what, if anything, he knew about the assassination of the president. They also wanted to conduct a thorough search of his luggage.

Edwin did not keep a diary or journal, so there's no way of knowing what questions the authorities asked him or how he answered them. But an indication of his mood at this time can be glimpsed in a letter he wrote his friend Adam Badeau while waiting for permission to leave Boston.

"You know, Ad, how I have labored to establish a name that all my friends would be proud of; how I have always toiled for the comfort and welfare of my family—and how loyal I have been from the first of this rebellion [the Civil War]. And you must feel deeply the agony I bear in thus being blasted in all my hopes by a villain [John] who seemed so lovable and in whom all 2 his family found a source of joy in his boyish and confiding nature." Booth ended on a slightly more positive note: "I have a great deal to tell you of myself & the beautiful plans I had for the future—but must wait until my mind is more settled. I am half crazy now—"

The federal marshals found nothing **incriminating** in Edwin's trunks, or in his correspondence. He was not given clearance[14] to travel, though, until several prominent friends, including the governor of Massachusetts, spoke to the authorities on his behalf. At last, on Easter Sunday afternoon, he received official permission to leave Boston. His friend Orlando Tompkins volunteered to accompany him, and they reserved seats on the midnight

9. *Appalling* means "horrifying."
10. *Signify to me* is an old-fashioned way of saying "Let me know of."
11. Here, *engagement* means "period of time working."
12. *Woe* is sorrow.
13. *Federal marshals* are law enforcement officers concerned with national issues.

14. Here, *clearance* means "permission from an authority."

Historical Narrative *How does this account differ from anything else you have read or heard about the events following Lincoln's assassination?* 3

Vocabulary

incriminating (in krim′ ə nāt′ ing) *adj.* showing involvement in a crime

Teach

Literary Element 2

Characterization Ask: What does this passage reveal about Edwin's personality? *(He worked hard to gain a reputation for integrity, is sensitive to family ties, and is basically optimistic, even at a time of crisis.)*

Literary Element 3

Historical Narrative
Answer: *This account gives a personal account of the assassin's brother, rather than an account of either Lincoln or John Wilkes Booth.*

English Learners

DIFFERENTIATED INSTRUCTION

Beginning/Early Intermediate Remind students that some words have more than one meaning, and that these words are called homographs. Provide them with examples from the story. *(agitation, engagement, players, etc.)* Have students use these words in sentences to demonstrate an understanding of their different meanings.

Advanced Learners

DIFFERENTIATED INSTRUCTION

Compare and Contrast Point out to students the poster on page 286, which offers a $100,000 reward for the capture of John Wilkes Booth and his accomplices. Tell students that this amount in 1865 was equivalent to approximately $1,200,000 today. Ask students to explain what this might suggest about how the American people valued their president.

Then have students consider the assassinations of Abraham Lincoln and John F. Kennedy. Ask students to compare and contrast the two events. *(Answers will vary. Students may refer to "The Drums of Washington" on page 220.)*

Teach

Big Idea 1

Looking into Lives

Answer: *Taking a midnight train and pulling his hat low suggest that he was worried about being recognized and injured.*

Literary Element 2

Historical Narrative

Say: Although no one really knows what was on Edwin's mind, the writer offers his guesses, or conjectures, about Edwin's thoughts.

ADVANCED **Ask:** Do you think these guesses are reasonable? Why or why not? *(Students may say yes because Edwin is known to have admired Lincoln, and he would naturally be concerned about his career.)*

Progress Check

Can students analyze historical narrative?

If No → See Unit 2 Teaching Resources Book, p. 54.

To check students' understanding of the selection, see Unit 2 Teaching Resources Book, p. 59.

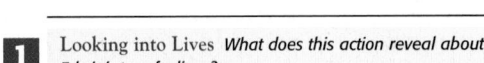

Edwin Thomas Booth, 1860. Matthew Brady. Wet collodion photograph.

train for New York. At that late hour, fewer people would be on the streets and there'd be less chance of Edwin being recognized. 1

The assassination had aroused strong feelings of outrage throughout the nation. Everyone who had any connection with John came under suspicion, and Edwin's friends feared that the hatred of his brother would rub off on him. Edwin shrugged off their worries. But before leaving for the railroad station, he pulled his wide-brimmed hat down low over his forehead so as to conceal as much of his face as possible.

He and Tompkins boarded the New York train without incident and found their seats in the nearly empty parlor car.[15] Exactly at midnight, the train pulled out of Boston's South Street Station and began the five-and-a-half-hour trip to New York. There's no way of knowing what was on Edwin's mind as he sat back in his seat and stared out into the darkness. No doubt his thoughts centered largely on his brother and the horrible thing he had done. But he must have wondered about his own future, too. Would he ever act again, or would audiences reject him because he was a Booth—the brother of the man who had killed President Lincoln?

A Booth. Earlier he had reminded Adam Badeau how hard he had labored to establish a name that he and all his friends would be proud of. He wasn't the first Booth to do so. Or the first Booth to make his reputation in the theater. His father, the actor Junius Brutus Booth, had emigrated from England in 1821 and, within a short time, had been recognized as one of the finest players American audiences had ever seen. 2

Edwin always spoke kindly of Junius—his gifted, eccentric,[16] lovable, and often maddening father. Junius had introduced him to the world of the theater and taught him much of what he knew about acting. Now, as he rode southward toward New York and an uncertain future, Edwin may have been wishing his father were still alive to offer advice and support.

1 Looking into Lives *What does this action reveal about Edwin's true feelings?*

15. A *parlor car* was a railroad car for which passengers paid extra fare in order to sit in individual chairs.
16. *Eccentric* means "odd."

Grammar Practice

SPIRAL REVIEW **Sentence Fragments** Explain that writers sometimes use sentence fragments for effect. Have students identify the two fragments on page 288. *("A Booth" and "Or the first Booth to make his reputation in the theatre.")* Have students correct the fragments by forming complete sentences. Encourage students to also consider how they might be able to combine the fragment with other sentences in the paragraph. Ask volunteers to write their sentences on the board.

After You Read

Respond and Think Critically

Respond and Interpret

1. What was the most surprising or interesting thing you learned from this selection?
2. (a)How did the audience respond to Edwin Booth during his last performance? (b)How did attitudes toward him change the next day?
3. (a)What did Edwin learn from his valet? (b)Why did this information shock him?
4. (a)What did the theater manager tell Edwin Booth? (b)What qualities did Edwin exhibit in his response to the manager?

Analyze and Evaluate

5. What is the author's attitude toward Edwin Booth? Cite details from the selection that support your opinion.
6. How well does Giblin show the effect of John's action on Edwin?
7. How credible do you think Giblin is as a source of information about the Booths? Do you think that he has any biases? Explain.

Connect

8. **Big Idea** **Looking into Lives** After reading this biography, do you feel like you have learned something new about the days around President Lincoln's assassination? Explain.
9. **Connect to the Author** Review the short biography of James Cross Giblin on page 282. Why do you think Giblin chose to look into the life of Edwin Booth?

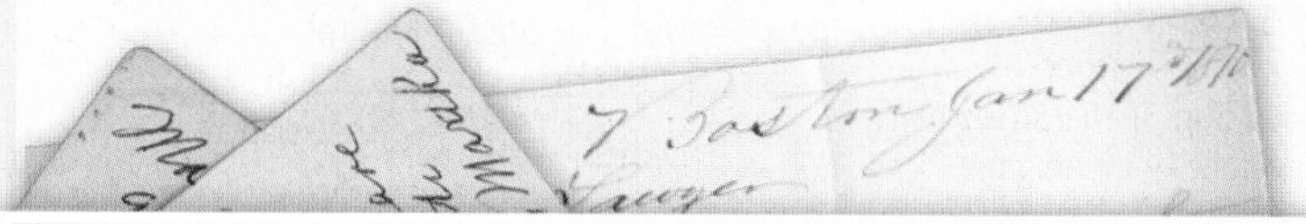

Primary Source Quotation

Booth Rescues Lincoln

A few years before John Wilkes Booth assassinated President Lincoln, an ironic event occurred. The president's son Robert was rescued from a potentially fatal accident in a railway station by Edwin Booth, the assassin's brother. In 1909 Robert recalled the incident.

"There was some crowding, and I happened to be pressed by it against the car body while waiting my turn. In this situation the train began to move, and by the motion I was twisted off my feet, and had dropped somewhat, with feet downward, into the open space, . . . when my coat collar was vigorously seized and I was quickly pulled up and out to a secure footing on the platform. Upon turning to thank my rescuer I saw it was Edwin Booth, whose face was of course well known to me, and I expressed my gratitude to him, and in doing so, called him by name."

Group Activity Discuss these questions with a group of classmates. Refer to the quotation and to the selection to support your answers.

1. Why do you think it was important for Robert Lincoln to recount this event forty-five years after it occurred?
2. Edwin Booth died before Robert Lincoln gave his account of the rescue. How do you think Booth would have felt had he been able to read Robert's account?
3. How does this quotation add to Giblin's portrayal of Edwin Booth in the selection?

After You Read

Assess

1. Answers will vary.
2. (a) Entrance was applauded; received curtain calls (b) Lost his job and fell under suspicion
3. (a) His brother was accused of shooting Lincoln. (b) He had thought his brother incapable of such a crime.
4. (a) Tells Edwin the theater will close (b) Acts graciously, thanks manager, and expresses regret over Lincoln's death
5. Possible answer: Sympathetic: interior monologue shows his decency and compassion.
6. Possible answer: Details about Edwin's loss of his job, his questioning by authorities, and his abrupt nighttime departure clearly show the effect.
7. Possible answer: Seems credible: uses primary sources, makes reasonable inferences, notes that some facts remain unknown; Unbiased: humanizes killer by showing him through brother's eyes
8. Answers will vary. Students should explain their responses by pointing to specific examples.
9. Students may mention that Giblin was an actor, and so he may feel a connection to Edwin Booth as an actor.

Primary Source Quotation

1. Students may say that Lincoln's gratitude to Booth prompted him to help restore Booth's reputation, which was temporarily tainted by his brother's crime.
2. Students may say that Booth would have been grateful to Robert Lincoln and would have possibly derived some comfort from the memory of saving the life of President Lincoln's son.
3. Students may say that this quotation enhances the positive portrayal of Edwin Booth in the excerpt from Giblin's biography. It adds bravery and heroism to his other admirable qualities.

After You Read

Assess

Literary Element

1. The events occur in April of 1865 in Boston and on a train to New York.
2. He describes their appearance, actions, and effect on audiences and portrays Edwin's thoughts in interior monologues and with quotations.
3. Edwin's internal conflict over whether to believe the accusation about his brother, and his external conflicts with those who associate him with his brother's crime.

Review: Narrator

Other examples of interior monologue appear on page 330 ("His brother John . . . How could that be?"; "how would she deal with the news?"). The monologue shows John's hatred of Lincoln, his tendency to be headstrong, and Edwin's concern for his mother.

Reading Strategy

1. Most students can probably recall hearing shocking news about someone they thought they knew well.
2. Students will probably recall similar worries of their own or of people they know.

Vocabulary

premonition: Etymology: Latin praemonēre means "to name in advance" Definition: anticipation of a future event Sample Sentence: Tom had a premonition about the boat, so we did not sail.

intimation: Etymology: Latin intimus means "innermost" Definition: a hint Sample Sentence: Michelle didn't tell us that she made the team, but her smile was a strong intimation.

calamity: Etymology: Latin calamitatem means "damage, disaster" Definition: a disastrous event Sample Sentence: Failing my exams and spending the summer in school would be a calamity.

perpetrator: Etymology: Latin per- means "through" and patrare means "to bring about" Definition: one who brings about or carries out a crime Sample Sentence: The perpetrator was gone by the time the police arrived at the house.

incriminating: Etymology: Latin in- means "in" and crimen means "crime" Definition: showing evidence of involvement in a crime Sample Sentence: The villain's expression was as incriminating as the stolen goods themselves.

Academic Vocabulary

Answers will vary.

Literary Element Historical Narrative

A **historical narrative** contains many elements found in fictional narratives. For example, the people described in a historical narrative are real people, but they are also like characters in fiction: they have motives, and authors can reveal them through their words, actions, appearance, and other details.

1. What is the setting of Giblin's narrative?
2. What techniques does Giblin use to characterize the Booth brothers? Give examples.
3. What conflict(s) does Giblin present?

Review: Narrator

As you learned on pages 184–185, a **narrator** is the person or voice that tells a story. In "A Brother's Crime," the narrator uses a technique called **interior monologue.** This technique presents one character's thoughts as they occur to him or her. It is a monologue in the character's mind. Interior monologue allows the reader to get a more complete picture of a character by revealing thoughts and feelings that may not be obvious from a character's spoken dialogue or actions. Carefully examining the thoughts expressed in an interior monologue can help you to more fully understand a character.

Partner Activity With a partner, identify examples of interior monologue in the selection. Use a chart to record what each reveals about Edwin and/or John.

Interior Monologue	What It Shows About Edwin	What It Shows About John
"Would he ever act again . . . ?"	He is worried about his future.	

LOG ON Literature Online

Selection Resources For Selection Quizzes, eFlashcards, and Reading-Writing Connection activities, go to glencoe.com and enter QuickPass code GL49787u2.

Reading Strategy Activate Prior Knowledge

In "A Brother's Crime," Giblin assumes that you have **prior knowledge** of President Lincoln and the Civil War, but not of Edwin Booth. Review your chart, and then answer the following questions.

1. How does prior knowledge help you understand what Edwin Booth must have felt when he got the news of his brother's crime?
2. How does your understanding of people in general help you understand Edwin's concern for his family and fears for his future?

Vocabulary Practice

Practice with Word Origins Studying the origin of a word can help you understand its meaning. Create a word map, like the one below, for each of these vocabulary words from the selection. Use a dictionary for help.

premonition **intimation** **calamity** **perpetrator** **incriminating**

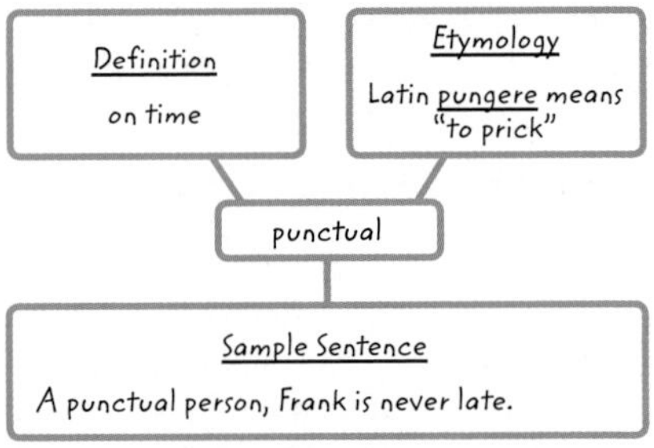

Academic Vocabulary

Although Giblin's biography of Edwin Booth is a narrative, his telling ***retains*** *the facts of the real-life events.*

Retain is an academic word. By **retaining** the facts in his narrative, Giblin makes it historically accurate. What fact from the biography are you most likely to **retain?** Why will you **retain** it?

For more on academic vocabulary, see pages 54–55 and R79–R81.

Respond Through Writing

Biographical Narrative

Apply Characterization Think about a famous person you have learned about. Research his or her family life, evaluating your sources for reliability and consistency. Write a biographical narrative about a critical moment of the person's life. Incorporate historical context.

Understand the Task A **biographical narrative** tells a true story about the life of a real person in a format that uses plot, setting, and character in the same way as a fictional story. **Historical context** refers to the historical elements of the specific time and place in which the events described occurred.

Prewrite Seek out a variety of sources for researching your subject's family life. You can use biographical texts, newspaper and magazine articles, interviews of your subject, or interviews of family members or other people who knew your subject's family.

Once you have determined the critical moment that you plan to write about, do additional research on the historical context. As you research, identify how the historical context relates to or provides a setting for your biographical narrative.

Draft Although it is based on factual research, write your draft in a narrative form and not as a report. Use the historical context as part of your setting, and build up to the critical moment using the pacing and plotting of a short story. In addition, make sure the narrative conveys the significance of the moment in your subject's life.

Revise When revising your draft, help bring your characters and setting to life by adding specific sensory details that enhance your descriptions. After finishing your first revision, exchange narratives with a classmate and provide constructive comments about any elements that could be improved in each other's narratives.

Edit and Proofread Proofread your paper, correcting any errors in grammar, spelling, and punctuation. Use the Grammar Tip in the side column to help you with absolute phrases.

Learning Objectives

In this assignment, you will focus on the following objectives:

Writing: Writing a biographical narrative.

Grammar: Understanding how to use absolute phrases.

Grammar Tip

Absolute Phrases

An absolute phrase consists of a noun or pronoun that is modified by a participle or participial phrase, but has no grammatical relation to the complete subject or predicate. For example:

The sun having set, *they began lighting the candles.*

Absolute phrases can be used to provide enhanced description and as a way to vary your sentence structure. For example, the sample sentence above might be used to replace these two sentences with the similar structure:

The sun had set. They began lighting the candles.

After You Read

Assess

Respond Through Writing

Students' narratives should

- accurately depict a critical moment in their famous subject's life
- present factual biographical information in a narrative format
- use plot, setting, and character to build a compelling narrative
- incorporate the setting's historical context into the narrative

A student who meets all of these criteria should receive the equivalent of a 4-point response.

A student who fully meets two or partially meets three of these criteria should receive the equivalent of a 3-point response.

A student who fully meets one or partially meets two of these criteria should receive the equivalent of a 2-point response.

A student who partially meets one of these criteria should receive the equivalent of a 1-point response.

For grammar practice, see Unit 2 Teaching Resources Book, p. 58.

To create custom assessments online, go to Progress Reporter Online Assessment.

To create custom assessments using software, use ExamView Assessment Suite.

Visual Perspective on *Abraham Lincoln*

Focus

Summary

The graphic novel tells the story of Lincoln's second inauguration, juxtaposing parts of Lincoln's speech with scenes depicting the reactions of his listeners.

Teach

Reading Strategy

Identify Genre Guide a discussion on the essential features of comics: panels of graphics that tell a story through both images and words. The words in comics, and in graphic novels, are set apart in bubbles called speech balloons. Have students examine and discuss some sample comics clipped from a daily newspaper.

For activities related to this selection, see Unit 2 Teaching Resources Book, pp. 61–69.

For an audio recording of this selection, use Listening Library Audio CD-ROM.

Visual Perspective on *Abraham Lincoln*

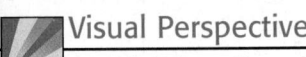

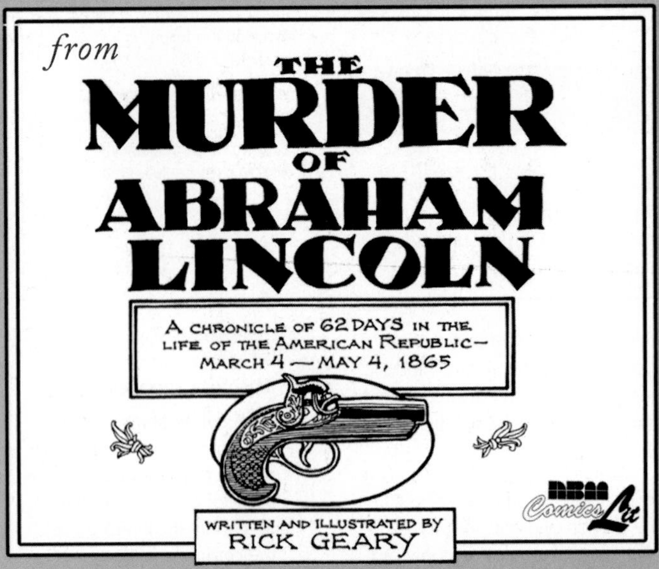

from
THE MURDER OF ABRAHAM LINCOLN
A CHRONICLE OF 62 DAYS IN THE LIFE OF THE AMERICAN REPUBLIC— MARCH 4 — MAY 4, 1865
WRITTEN AND ILLUSTRATED BY RICK GEARY
NBM ComicsLit

Learning Objectives

For pages 292–296

In studying this text, you will focus on the following objective:

Reading: Identifying genre.

Set a Purpose for Reading

Read to experience a graphic novel interpretation of an important episode in Lincoln's life.

Build Background

Comic books have been an important part of U.S. popular culture since superheroes such as Superman and Batman first appeared in the late 1930s. In the 1970s, comic books took a new direction, which was soon referred to as the "graphic novel." Graphic novels have the same basic panel format as comic books and use the same visual techniques, such as speech balloons and inset panels. But the two forms differ in important ways. Graphic novels are longer than the standard comic book; they usually present only a single story; and they often deal with more realistic subject matter.

Rick Geary's graphic novel, *The Murder of Abraham Lincoln*, deals with the events immediately before and after the assassination of President Abraham Lincoln on April 14, 1865. This excerpt, which opens the novel, presents Lincoln's delivery of his Second Inaugural Address on March 4, 1865.

Reading Strategy Identify Genre

Like literature, visual art has different genres, or types, such as the portrait and the landscape. The comic is another visual genre. **Identifying genre** means recognizing the characteristic elements of a particular type of art. As you read Rick Geary's graphic novel, ask yourself, How does he use elements of the comic book genre to tell a true story? Use a two-column chart like the one below to record your notes.

Example	Genre Element
p. 293 The setting is established	boxed text over illustration

Vocabulary Practice

SMALL GROUP SPIRAL REVIEW

Decoding Vocabulary This selection contains several words that may be unfamiliar to most students. As they read the selection, ask students to write down words that are unfamiliar to them, along with the page number where the word appears. When they have finished reading the selection, have students share their word lists in a small group. Encourage students to use context clues to guess the meaning of each word. Students should then look up the definitions in a dictionary to confirm and/or adjust their comprehension of the words. *Unfamiliar words may include the following: brevity, deprecated, perish, refuge, pinnacle, fervently, scourge, and reconciliation.*

Visual Perspective

on *Abraham Lincoln*

Teach

Historical Note ☆

Salmon P. Chase Salmon Chase (1808–1873) helped form and lead the antislavery Liberty party. At various times a lawyer, governor of and senator from Ohio, and U.S. Secretary of the Treasury, Chase was nominated to the Supreme Court by President Lincoln. He eventually became Chief Justice.

English Learners

DIFFERENTIATED INSTRUCTION

Intermediate Discuss the idea that speechwriters and public speakers often use a style of language different from the language people use in everyday life. **Read:** "At this second appearing to take the oath of presidential office, there is less occasion for an extended address than there was at the first." Ask students to restate this sentence using words that are easier to comprehend. *(Sample response: As I am about to take the oath as president for a second time, there is really no need for a long, detailed speech like the one I gave before.)*

Teach

Reading Strategy 1

Connect **Ask:** How do the descriptions of the crowd's feelings enhance your reading of Lincoln's speech? *(Answers will vary. Students may say that understanding the responses of the crowd makes the speech more vibrant and real to them and helps them to empathize with the crowd and connect with the speech.)*

Reading Strategy 2

Connect **Ask:** How does the artwork relate to the written words? *(Students should note that the images illustrate Lincoln's speech.)*

ENGLISH LEARNERS To assist English learners, **ask:** How does this affect your understanding of the speech? *(Students may say that seeing the images clarifies what they are reading.)*

1

2

Viewing Practice

SPIRAL REVIEW **Visual Characterization** Ask students to study the pictures of Abraham Lincoln in the graphic novel excerpt. Point out to students the details of facial expressions, body language, and other visual elements. **Ask:** What do these pictures tell you about what kind of man Lincoln was? *(Possible answer: He was serious and held people's attention when he spoke.)* Then ask students to research Lincoln's life to find out more about the details of his character. **Ask:** Do you think the artist has done a good job at portraying Lincoln the way he really was? Explain what leads you to draw this conclusion.

3

4

Visual Perspective
on *Abraham Lincoln*

Teach

Reading Strategy 3

Read Aloud Invite volunteers to read the parts of President Lincoln and the narrator.

Ask: How does hearing the text aloud, while looking at the images, enhance your understanding?

APPROACHING Ask approaching-level students to explain the advantages of hearing the text while viewing the images.

Reading Strategy 4

Comprehension **Ask:** Why do you think some people found Lincoln to be "an object of scorn and deep loathing" (Students may cite the Civil War and Lincoln's emancipation of the slaves as reasons.)

Approaching Level

DIFFERENTIATED INSTRUCTION

Early Advanced Remind students of the importance of using word roots to help them decipher vocabulary. Explain that several words are similar in many languages because they are based on Greek or Latin root words. Write the word *tyrant* on the board, and have students use a dictionary to search for the definition of the word. While they search, write the word *tyrannos* on the board. Explain that *tyrannos* is the Greek word for a tyrant. Explain that knowing some Greek or Latin words can help them figure out the meaning of unfamiliar English words without always needing a dictionary.

Assess

1. Students' summaries should highlight the main idea and key details from the excerpt.
2. Students should use such words as *heroic, noble, thoughtful, earnest, eloquent,* and *brave.*
3. (a) Lincoln's second inauguration outside the Capitol in Washington, D.C. (b) The vertical composition elevates the central figure of Lincoln, who stands above the spectators, by leading the eye up the Capitol's portico to the top of its dome.
4. (a) It shows Lincoln's hand on the Bible as he takes the oath of office. (b) The inset panel dramatizes the narrative.
5. (a) On page 294, the speech balloons connect Lincoln's words to panels illustrating the events he refers to. On page 296, the speech balloons divide the final part of Lincoln's speech into three parts that comprise his presidency's goals: finish the war, heal the country, and establish peace. (b) The arrangements show the context of Lincoln's words.
6. (a) Several panels show the hatred and violence directed at Lincoln throughout the war. (b) This foreshadows the President's assassination.
7. Both present Lincoln as heroic. Giblin concentrates on the assassin's single historically significant deed and its tragic effect on his brother. Geary focuses on Lincoln's last days and the national tragedies of the Civil War and the assassination.

Respond and Think Critically

Respond and Interpret

1. Write a brief summary of the main ideas in this graphic story before you answer the following questions. For help on writing a summary, see page 421.
2. What words would you use to describe the way that Abraham Lincoln is presented in this excerpt?
3. (a)What is the setting of page 293? (b)What is the effect of the visual composition of this panel?
4. (a)What appears in the inset panel on page 293? (b)What storytelling purpose does the inset serve?

Analyze and Evaluate

5. (a)How does Geary arrange the speech balloons on pages 294 and 296? (b)What is the purpose of the arrangement in each case?
6. (a)How does Geary visually interrupt the presentation of Lincoln's Second Inaugural Address on page 294? (b)What effect does this interruption have?

Connect

7. How is the overall effect of this excerpt similar to and different from that of "A Brother's Crime"?

Speaking Practice

SPIRAL REVIEW **Present a Speech** Ask students to use the library and the Internet to find another historically significant speech. Students should understand the purpose and influence of the speech during the time it was written. Have students read an excerpt from the speech. Encourage them to use body language and a voice appropriate for the speech they have chosen. Students should explain the significance of the speech and their reason for selecting it. Have students discuss rhetorical devices and features that may have contributed to the popularity of the speech over the years.

Before You Read

from *Black Boy*

Meet **Richard Wright**

(1908–1960)

After struggling through a youth of extreme poverty and racial inequality, Richard Wright emerged as one of America's first prominent African American writers. Wright tells of his childhood in the acclaimed autobiography, *Black Boy* (1945), a firsthand account of hardship and discrimination in the early twentieth century.

Carving a Path Out of Poverty Wright was born on a plantation near Natchez, Mississippi. After struggling for several years in Mississippi, Wright's family moved to Memphis, Tennessee. Their fortunes did not improve in Memphis, and soon Wright's parents broke up. By the time he was twelve, Wright had returned to Mississippi and was living in Jackson with his mother.

> *"My deepest thoughts are communicated to no one. No one around me. I just think them and try to write them."*
>
> —Richard Wright

In Jackson, Wright attended public school for a few years, and then spent some time working menial jobs, but his real interest was writing. At the age of sixteen, he published his first story in the local black newspaper, *Southern Register* (an event he recounts in the following excerpt from *Black Boy*). By the time he left the South at the age of nineteen, the self-educating Wright was already poring through the works of literary legends like H. L. Menken, Theodore Dreiser, and Sinclair Lewis.

Creating a Legacy In 1927 Wright moved to Chicago, finally escaping some of the restraints imposed by the open discrimination in the South. Early on, the Great Depression of the 1930s made Wright's life in the North a struggle, but he continued to write. His 1938 collection of stories, *Uncle Tom's Children,* received a prize from *Story* magazine. Just two years later, after publishing his first novel, *Native Son,* Wright was considered the nation's leading African American author.

Seeking Tolerance Through his writing career, Wright was able to escape the hardship of his younger years but not the discrimination. Despite achieving fame, fortune, awards, and critical praise as a writer, Wright continued to suffer greatly from racism. In an effort to find a more tolerant society, Wright eventually left America and moved to Paris, France, where he lived from 1947 until his death.

LOG ON **Literature** Online

Author Search For more about Richard Wright, go to glencoe.com and enter QuickPass code GL49787u2.

Before You Read

Focus

Bellringer Option

Literature Launchers: Pre-Reading Videos DVD, Selection Launcher

Daily Language Practice Transparency 29

Or tell students about something you've done that you are proud of today. Remind students that they can aways build their confidence by remembering a past accomplishment. **Ask:** What accomplishment are you proud of the most and why? Encourage students to share their answers with the class.

Selection Skills

from Black Boy

Literary Elements
- Anecdote (SE pp. 298–304)
- Author's Purpose (SE p. 304)

Listening/Speaking/Viewing Skills
- Interview (SE p. 305)
- Practice Dialogue (TE p. 305)

Reading Skills
- Connect to Personal Experience (SE pp. 298–304)

Vocabulary Skills
- Word Usage (SE p. 298)
- Academic Vocabulary (SE p. 305)

Writing Skills/Grammar
- Write a Report (SE p. 305)
- Respond to Literature (TE p. 302)

Before You Read

Focus

Summary

When he was in eighth grade, Richard Wright wrote a story because he was bored. He took his story to a newspaper editor and insisted the editor consider it for publication. Wright gets his story published, and wins a new job, but his friends and family aren't quite as impressed as he thinks they should be.

For summaries in languages other than English, see Unit 2 Teaching Resources Book, pp. 70–75.

Vocabulary

Act Out to Remember Give students five minutes to review the vocabulary list above. Then have volunteers pick a word from the vocabulary list and act out the word before the class. Have the other students in the class guess which word the volunteer is presenting. The student who guesses the word should read the definition of the word and try using the word in a sentence.

Literature and Reading Preview

Connect to the Autobiography

What are you most passionate about in your life? Freewrite for a few minutes about what first inspired this passion and about how you might pursue your interest in the future.

Build Background

In this excerpt from the autobiography *Black Boy,* Wright recalls events that occurred in Jackson, Mississippi, in 1923. In the post-Civil War South, many states passed unfair local laws to deny civil rights to African Americans. These laws were called "Jim Crow," named after a character in a song. Most Jim Crow laws required that blacks and whites use separate public facilities, including schools.

Set Purposes for Reading

Big Idea Looking into Lives

As you read this excerpt from *Black Boy,* ask yourself, How did Wright's high school experience differ from the experience of most white high school students at the time?

Literary Element Anecdote

An **anecdote** is a brief account of an interesting or significant occurrence. Writers often use anecdotes to illustrate their points, to get a reader's attention, to clarify their ideas, or to convey a story element, such as setting or rising action. As you read, ask yourself, Why does Wright describe in detail his first exchange with the newspaper editor?

Reading Strategy Connect to Personal Experience

To **connect to personal experience** is to use experiences in your own life in order to understand characters and events in literature. For example, by freewriting earlier about your own passion, you might better understand the passion that Wright expresses in the excerpt. As you read, ask yourself, What are the similarities between Wright's life and my own?

Tip: Take Notes Use a simple chart to note connections that you find between Wright's life and your own life.

Detail	My Personal Experience
Wright brought his story to the newspaper editor.	I write for the school paper and turn my stories in to an editor.

Learning Objectives

For pages 297–305

In studying this text, you will focus on the following objectives:

Literary Study: Analyzing anecdote.

Reading: Connecting to personal experience.

Speaking and Listening: Conducting an interview.

Vocabulary

intuitive (in too͞o′ ə tiv) *adj.* rising from an impulse or natural tendency; instinctive; not learned; p. 299 *Although he'd only played a little baseball, he seemed to have an intuitive understanding of the game.*

conviction (kôn vik′ shən) *n.* a firmly established opinion or belief; p. 300 *She believed in freedom for all people, and her conviction was unshakeable.*

naive (nä′ ēv) *adj.* innocent; unsophisticated; p. 303 *He was bright but inexperienced, so he still sounded naive when he talked about the world.*

articulate (är tik′ yə lit) *adj.* able to express oneself well or effectively; p. 303 *After giving speeches for years, he was comfortable and articulate in front of a microphone.*

Tip: Word Usage Adjectives can be used in their adverb form to describe an action directly. Using the adverb form of an adjective is one way to make your sentences more active. For example: *She learned new languages* intuitively.

Writing Practice

SMALL GROUP SPIRAL REVIEW **Autobiography** Remind students that an autobiography is a first-person account of an experience. Have students complete the Connect to the Autobiography activity on this page, in which they freewrite for a few minutes about what first inspired them to become passionate about something. To help students get started, **Ask:** What do you like to do? Do you like to play an instrument? A sport? Do you like to write?

When students have finished freewriting, break them into small groups. Have them share their freewriting with their group members. Tell students to help each other use their freewriting, develop ideas for a short essay about what first inspired their passion. Have students draft and revise their essays on their own.

from Black Boy

Richard Wright

The eighth grade days flowed in their hungry path and I grew more conscious of myself; I sat in classes, bored, wondering, dreaming. One long dry afternoon I took out my composition book and told myself that I would write a story; it was sheer idleness that led me to it.

What would the story be about? It resolved itself into a plot about a villain who wanted a widow's home and I called it *The Voodoo of Hell's Half-Acre.* It was crudely atmospheric, emotional, **intuitively** psychological, and stemmed from pure feeling. I finished it in three days and then wondered what to do with it.

The local Negro newspaper! That's it . . . I sailed into the office and shoved my ragged composition book under the nose of the man who called himself the editor.

"What is that?" he asked.

"A story," I said.

"A news story?"

"No, fiction."

"All right. I'll read it," he said.

He pushed my composition book back on his desk and looked at me curiously, sucking at his pipe.

"But I want you to read it *now,*" I said.

He blinked. I had no idea how newspapers were run. I thought that one took a story to an editor and he sat down then and there and read it and said yes or no.

"I'll read this and let you know about it tomorrow," he said.

I was disappointed; I had taken time to write it and he seemed distant and uninterested.

"Give me the story," I said, reaching for it.

He turned from me, took up the book and read ten pages or more.

"Won't you come in tomorrow?" he asked. "I'll have it finished then."

Connect to Personal Experience *What kinds of things have you tried creating just because you were bored?*

Vocabulary

intuitive (in too͞′ ə tiv) *adj.* rising from an impulse or natural tendency; instinctive; not learned

Teach

Reading Strategies

Connect to Personal Experience **Answer:** *Sample answer: I have written poems and stories before simply because I was bored and wanted to create something to pass the time.*

Interactive Read and Write

Other options for teaching this selection can be found in

- Interactive Read and Write for EL Students, pp. 61–72
- Interactive Read and Write for Approaching-Level Students, pp. 61–72
- Interactive Read and Write for On-Level Students, pp. 61–72

For an audio recording of this selection, use Listening Library Audio CD-ROM.

Readability Scores

Dale-Chall: 7.8
DRP: 50
Lexile: 740

English Learners

DIFFERENTIATED INSTRUCTION

Beginning/Early Intermediate Help students understand the author's use of description on this page. Ask English learners to explain the meaning of these phrases:

- "flowed in their hungry path" *(passed by quickly)*
- "sheer idleness" *(complete boredom)*
- "crudely atmospheric, emotional" *(lacked sophistication; not polished or professional)*
- "sailed into the office" *(walked quickly and confidently)*

Teach

Big Idea

Looking into Lives

Answer: *Sample answer: It shows that he is tough-nosed, smart, and confident in himself.*

APPROACHING Ask students to point out dialogue on the page that reveals Wright's personality and attitude about his work.

I honestly relented.

"All right," I said. "I'll stop in tomorrow."

I left with the **conviction** that he would not read it. Now, where else could I take it after he had turned it down? The next afternoon, en route to my job, I stepped into the newspaper office.

"Where's my story?" I asked.

"It's in galleys," he said.

"What's that?" I asked; I did not know what galleys were.

"It's set up in type," he said. "We're publishing it."

"How much money will I get?" I asked, excited.

"We can't pay for manuscript," he said.

"But you sell your papers for money," I said with logic.

"Yes, but we're young in business," he explained.

"But you're asking me to *give* you my story, but you don't *give* your papers away," I said.

He laughed.

"Look, you're just starting. This story will put your name before our readers. Now, that's something," he said.

"But if the story is good enough to sell to your readers, then you ought to give me some of the money you get from it," I insisted.

He laughed again and I sensed that I was amusing him. "I'm going to offer you something more valuable than money," he said. "I'll give you a chance to learn to write."

I was pleased, but I still thought he was taking advantage of me.

"When will you publish my story?"

"I'm dividing it into three installments," he said. "The first installment appears this week. But the main thing is this: Will you get news for me on a space rate basis?"[1]

"I work mornings and evenings for three dollars a week," I said.

"Oh," he said. "Then you better keep that. But what are you doing this summer?"

"Nothing."

"Then come to see me before you take another job," he said. "And write some more stories."

A few days later my classmates came to me with baffled eyes, holding copies of the *Southern Register* in their hands.

"Did you really write that story?" they asked me.

"Yes."

"Why?"

"Because I wanted to."

"Where did you get it from?"

"I made it up."

"You didn't. You copied it out of a book."

"If I had, no one would publish it."

"But what are they publishing it for?"

"So people can read it."

"Who told you to do that?"

"Nobody."

"Then why did you do it?"

"Because I wanted to," I said again.

They were convinced that I had not told them the truth. We had never had any instruction in literary matters at school; the literature of the nation or the Negro had never been mentioned. My schoolmates could not understand why anyone would want to write a story; and, above all, they could not understand why I had called it *The Voodoo of Hell's Half-Acre.* The mood out of which a story was written

Looking Into Lives *What does Wright's behavior here reveal about his personality as a teenager?*

Vocabulary

conviction (kôn vik′ shən) *n.* a firmly established opinion or belief

1. On a *space rate basis* means that payment would vary according to the length of each news article.

Speaking Practice

PARTNERS SPIRAL REVIEW **Practice Dialogue** Remind students that when authors include dialogue, they use punctuation to let readers know who is speaking and how. **Write:** Charlie exclaimed, "Stop the car!" Explain that in this example, the punctuation lets you know that Charlie is shouting. Pair up students and have them read the dialogue between the author and the editor on this page. Students should use punctuation to indicate how the author and the editor might sound. Ask students to explain the attitude of both speakers based on the dialogue. *(The author is overconfident and the editor probably finds this amusing.)*

My Brother, 1942. John Wilson. Oil on panel, 12 x 10⅝ in. Smith College Museum of Art, Northampton, MA. Licensed by VAGA, NY.

Teach

Cultural History ☆

The Richmond Planet

America's first African American newspaper, *The Richmond Planet,* was founded by a group of thirteen former slaves in 1883. The most famous figure associated with this paper, John Mitchell Jr., became editor when he was only 21 years old. Through the newspaper, Mitchell fought for equal rights for African Americans, and he used the paper to protest the Jim Crow laws, which prohibited African Americans from attending public schools and occupying restaurants, theaters, and other public places. *The Richmond Planet,* which became *The Richmond Afro-American Planet* in 1938, was published until 1996.

English Learners

DIFFERENTIATED INSTRUCTION

Intermediate Students may be confused by the dialogue between the author and his classmates in the second column on page 300. The author does not use tags to give the reader the names of his classmates or to indicate who is speaking. **Ask:** Why do you think the author does this? *(Students may say that it is not important which classmates are speaking because the individuals here have a very minor role in the story.)*

Ask: How would you describe the classmates here in the story? *The classmates don't believe Wright and can't understand that he enjoys writing.)*

Teach

Literary Elements 1

Anecdote Answer: *He uses previous anecdotes to show how people around him were not supportive of his dream.*

For additional literary element practice, see Unit 2 Teaching Resources Book, p. 76.

Big Idea 2

Looking into Lives
Answer: *This whole episode was one of the first events that inspired him to follow his dreams and pursue a career as a writer.*

was the most alien thing conceivable[2] to them. They looked at me with new eyes, and a distance, a suspiciousness came between us. If I had thought anything in writing the story, I had thought that perhaps it would make me more acceptable to them, and now it was cutting me off from them more completely than ever.

At home the effects were no less disturbing. Granny came into my room early one morning and sat on the edge of my bed.

"Richard, what is this you're putting in the papers?" she asked.

"A story," I said.

"About what?"

"It's just a story, granny."

"But they tell me it's been in three times."

"It's the same story. It's in three parts."

"But what is it about?" she insisted.

I hedged,[3] fearful of getting into a religious argument.

"It's just a story I made up," I said.

"Then it's a lie," she said.

"Oh, Christ," I said.

"You must get out of this house if you take the name of the Lord in vain," she said.

"Granny, please . . . I'm sorry," I pleaded. "But it's hard to tell you about the story. You see, granny, everybody knows that the story isn't true, but . . ."

"Then why write it?" she asked.

"Because people might want to read it."

"That's the Devil's work," she said and left.

My mother also was worried.

"Son, you ought to be more serious," she said. "You're growing up now and you won't be able to get jobs if you let people think that you're weak-minded. Suppose the superintendent of schools would ask you to teach here in Jackson, and he found out that you had been writing stories?"

I could not answer her.

"I'll be all right, mama," I said.

Uncle Tom, though surprised, was highly critical and contemptuous.[4] The story had no point, he said. And whoever heard of a story by the title of *The Voodoo of Hell's Half-Acre*? Aunt Addie said that it was a sin for anyone to use the word "hell" and that what was wrong with me was that I had nobody to guide me. She blamed the whole thing upon my upbringing.

In the end I was so angry that I refused to talk about the story. From no quarter,[5] with the exception of the Negro newspaper editor, had there come a single encouraging word. It was rumored that the principal wanted to know why I had used the word "hell." I felt that I had committed a crime. Had I been conscious of the full extent to which I was pushing against the current of my environment, I would have been frightened altogether out of my attempts at writing. But my reactions were limited to the attitude of the people about me, and I did not speculate or generalize.[6]

I dreamed of going north and writing books, novels. The North symbolized to me all that I had not felt and seen; it had no relation whatever to what actually existed. Yet, by imagining a place where everything was possible, I kept hope alive in me. But

2. It was the strangest *(most alien)* idea imaginable *(conceivable)*.
3. Wright *hedged* when he avoided giving a direct answer or committing himself.

4. *Contemptuous* means "scornful, lacking respect for something."
5. Here, *quarter* means "person, place, or group."
6. Here, to *speculate* is to guess, and to *generalize* is to form a general opinion based on particular facts or instances.

1 Anecdote *How does Wright use the previous anecdotes to illustrate this statement?*

2 Looking into Lives *How does this sentence reveal the significance of the period in Wright's life described in the excerpt?*

Writing Practice

SPIRAL REVIEW **Respond to Literature** Point out that with the exception of the newspaper editor, no one reacted positively to the narrator's story. Have students reread parts of the selection and note how the narrator's friends and family felt about his story. Have students write responses to the following questions: Why did people react so negatively to the narrator's story being published in the paper? Why do you think the newspaper editor was more supportive? *(Students may write that the narrator's friends and family did not understand his desire to succeed, and perhaps on some level, thought it might get him into trouble; whereas the newspaper editor was likely educated and accustomed to African Americans in white-collar jobs.)*

where had I got this notion of doing something in the future, of going away from home and accomplishing something that would be recognized by others? I had, of course, read my Horatio Alger stories, my pulp stories, and I knew my Get-Rich-Quick Wallingford series[7] from cover to cover, though I had sense enough not to hope to get rich; even to my **naive** imagination that possibility was too remote. I knew that I lived in a country in which the aspirations of black people were limited, marked-off. Yet I felt that I had to go somewhere and do something to redeem[8] my being alive.

I was building up in me a dream which the entire educational system of the South had been rigged to stifle.[9] I was feeling the very thing that the state of Mississippi had spent millions of dollars to make sure that I would never feel; I was becoming aware of the thing that the Jim Crow laws had been drafted and passed to keep out of my consciousness; I was acting on impulses that southern senators in the nation's capital had striven[10] to keep out of Negro life; I was beginning to dream the dreams that the state had said were wrong, that the schools had said were taboo.[11]

7. *Horatio Alger stories, pulp stories,* and the *Wallingford series* are all works—some fictional and some claiming to be true—about people who achieved financial success through hard work or cleverness.
8. In this context, *redeem* means "to justify."
9. To *stifle* means "to smother."
10. *Striven* means "to have made an intense effort."
11. *Taboo* means "prohibited or forbidden."

Vocabulary

naive (nä ′ ēv) *adj.* innocent; unsophisticated

Had I been **articulate** about my ultimate aspirations, no doubt someone would have told me what I was bargaining for; but nobody seemed to know, and least of all did I. My classmates felt that I was doing something that was vaguely wrong, but they did not know how to express it. As the outside world grew more meaningful, I became more concerned, tense; and my classmates and my teachers would say: "Why do you ask so many questions?" Or: "Keep quiet."

I was in my fifteenth year; in terms of schooling I was far behind the average youth of the nation, but I did not know that. In me was shaping a yearning for a kind of consciousness, a mode[12] of being that the way of life about me had said could not be, must not be, and upon which the penalty of death had been placed. Somewhere in the dead of the southern night my life had switched onto the wrong track and, without my knowing it, the locomotive of my heart was rushing down a dangerously steep slope, heading for a collision, heedless of the warning red lights that blinked all about me, the sirens and the bells and the screams that filled the air. ∾

12. A *mode* is a manner or way.

Connecting to Personal Experience *How do you think your educational opportunities compare to Wright's educational opportunities?* **3**

Vocabulary

articulate (är tik ′ yə lit) *adj.* able to express oneself well or effectively

Teach

Reading Strategies 3

Connect to Personal Experience **Answer:** *Answers may vary. Students should support their answers with personal experiences and information from the text.*

ENGLISH LEARNERS Encourage English learners to speak clearly and use consistent Standard English.

Progress Check

Can students connect to personal experience?

If No → See Unit 2 Teaching Resources Book, p. 77.

To check students' understanding of the selection, see Unit 2 Teaching Resources Book, p. 81.

Approaching Level

DIFFERENTIATED INSTRUCTION

Established Explain that Jim Crow laws were state and local laws in the South that separated blacks and whites in public places such as schools and restaurants. The author says these laws were passed to keep blacks from succeeding. **Ask:** How does this selection reflect the historical period? *(Possible response: It shows how racism tried to limit African Americans and their ability to succeed.)*

After You Read

Assess

1. Answers will vary.
2. (a) At first the editor says he will read it later, then eventually reads part of it after Wright threatens to take it back. (b) He views Wright as naive and inexperienced, but also sees a passion and intelligence in him.
3. (a) Granny is worried that the story is offensive to God, and his mother is worried that it is offensive to the school and colleges. (b) It shows that Granny's concerns are more spiritual and Wright's mother's worries are more practical.
4. (a) It inspired him to leave the South and become a writer. (b) This was a victory over racism because the racist system was designed to keep Wright from achieving success.
5. Almost all of the dialogue shows Wright in conflict with people. It makes it feel as if most of his interactions at that time were a struggle.
6. Answers will vary. Students should support their answers with information from the text.
7. Answers may vary. Sample answer: His responses reflect that he believes in his writing and his reasons for writing. Instead of doubting himself when challenged, he defends his work and stands strong.
8. Answers will vary. Students should support their answers with information from the text.

After You Read

Respond and Think Critically

Respond and Interpret

1. How did you feel about the way Wright's family, teachers, and classmates reacted to his story?
2. (a)How does the newspaper editor respond when Wright shows him the story? (b)What impression do you think the editor has of Wright during this encounter?
3. (a)How does Granny's response to the story differ from Wright's mother's? (b)What differences does this reflect in their personalities?
4. (a)What dream did Wright's newspaper experience inspire in him? (b)In what ways did this dream represent a victory over racism?

Analyze and Evaluate

5. How does Wright use dialogue in this excerpt to reflect the struggle of his first writing experience?
6. Do you think Wright's depiction of his family and classmates is biased because they did not like his story? Or do you think he presents a fair portrayal of them? Explain your answer.

Connect

7. **Big Idea** Looking into Lives What do Wright's responses to the criticism of his story reflect about his personality?
8. **Connect to the Author** Based on this excerpt, why do you think Wright might have chosen *Black Boy* as the title of his autobiography?

Literary Element Anecdote

An **anecdote** is a brief account of an interesting or amusing incident. An anecdote is often used to explain or support an idea, to entertain readers, or to reveal the personality of an author or another person.

1. Which anecdote do you think best reflects Wright's passion for writing? Explain.
2. Which anecdote did you find most amusing? What does it reveal about the characters involved?
3. Which anecdote do you think most powerfully illustrates the challenges Wright faced because of racism? Explain.

Review: Author's Purpose

As you learned on page 269, **author's purpose** is the author's reason for writing. For example, the purpose may be to entertain, to persuade, to inform, or to express an opinion. Sometimes an author may have more than one purpose for writing.

Partner Activity With a classmate, create a chart like the one below to find clues that suggest what Wright's primary purpose is in this excerpt.

Evidence	Purpose
p. 299 opens by telling about writing the story	Wright intends to show us why writing this short story was an important event in his life.

LOG ON **Literature** Online

Selection Resources For Selection Quizzes, eFlashcards, and Reading-Writing Connection activities, go to glencoe.com and enter QuickPass code GL49787u2.

Literary Element

1. Answers will vary. Students should summarize an anecdote and support their answers.
2. Answers will vary. Students should summarize an anecdote and support their answers.
3. Answers will vary. Students should summarize an anecdote and support their answers.

Review: Author's Purpose

Students' charts should include evidence from the story and an explanation of its purpose.

For additional selection assessment, see Assessment Resources, pp. 87–88.

Reading Strategy Connect to Personal Experience

Review your note-taking chart and think about which of Wright's experiences you connected to your own experiences.

1. Among the experiences you noted, which one(s) changed you or altered your life in some way? Explain.
2. How might you apply the lessons from Wright's experience to your own life?
3. Which of Wright's personal experiences did you feel the strongest connection to? Explain.

Vocabulary Practice

Practice with Word Usage Respond to these statements to help you explore the meanings of vocabulary words from the selection.

1. Why might it be difficult for an **intuitive** athlete to explain his or her techniques?
2. How might strong **convictions** cloud your judgment during a disagreement?
3. In what ways would traveling the world help to make someone less **naive**?
4. Why might being **articulate** make someone more persuasive?

Academic Vocabulary

Wright did not believe that his education was ***equivalent*** *to the education that white students were receiving.*

Equivalent is an academic word. Other words that are similar in meaning are *equal* and *comparable.* To study this word further, fill out the graphic organizer below.

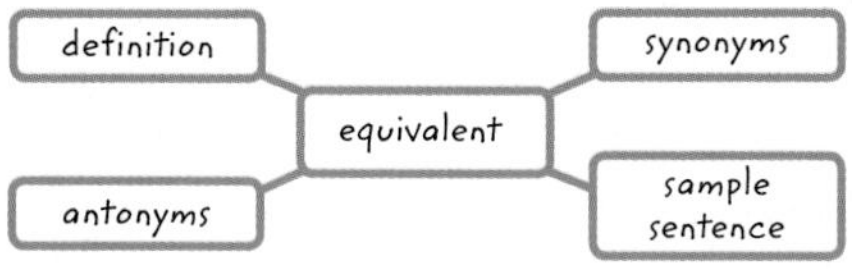

For more on academic vocabulary, see pages 54–54 and R79–R81.

Speaking and Listening

Interview

Assignment Conduct an interview with a friend or family member about a key moment in his or her life. Build the interview around that moment, or anecdote, and compile the story in a written report.

Prepare Write a list of relevant questions phrased in mature, sensitive, respectful language. Your questions should reflect your understanding of the key moment's significance. Leave space after each question to note answers. Before conducting the interview, practice reading some of the questions aloud.

Interview During the interview, maintain appropriate body language, tone, and eye contact. Listen with care and take notes. As you ask questions and take notes, follow these tips:

- Allow your subject to respond completely; don't interrupt. If you are the interview subject, respond correctly and effectively.
- Adjust your tone of voice in response to what your subject tells you.
- If necessary, ask further questions to clarify information.
- Review your subject's statements as a final check.
- Thank your subject for his or her cooperation.

Report Review the notes from your interview and determine what to include in your report. Compile and organize this information in an outline. Arrange the outline so that it reflects the sequence of events and make sure it includes all of the key details.

Using your outline as a guide, write a report about your subject's key moment. Create a report that accurately conveys the facts while telling the story in a compelling fashion. Add authenticity by including direct quotes from your subject throughout the report. Use the quotes to highlight important details and make sure to properly attribute them.

Evaluate Compare your final report to your original interview notes. Did you effectively convey the significance of the moment? Does your report accurately represent the details as reflected in your notes?

After You Read

Assess

Reading Strategy

1. Sample answer: Like Wright getting his first story published, getting my school to start a recycling program has given me the confidence to move forward with things that are important to me.
2. Sample answer: I can learn perseverance from Wright's experience. He continued to push forward even when he was on his own.
3. Sample answer: I related to him feeling misunderstood by his family. I often feel like they do not understand why I do what I do.

Vocabulary

1. Because it comes naturally, he or she may not have ever given the technique much thought.
2. Because your beliefs are already strong, they could make you less likely to change your mind, even if you are wrong.
3. A person would learn about other places and cultures and become less innocent and sheltered.
4. Someone who is more articulate would likely be more persuasive because they would be able to make use of the language better.

Academic Vocabulary

Definition: equal; Synonyms: equal, same; Antonyms: unequal; inequitable; Sample Sentence: We should receive equivalent pay since we both do the same job.

To create custom assessments online, go to Progress Reporter Online Assessment.

To create custom assessments using software, use ExamView Assessment Suite.

Speaking and Listening

Students' reports should

- focus on a key moment in the subject's life
- convey the moment in an engaging story-like fashion
- report the facts about the events accurately
- include direct quotes from the subject

Focus

Explain that dialogue, or direct discourse, quotes a speaker's exact words. Note that dialogue is enclosed in quotation marks and is often accompanied by speaker tags that identify who is talking. **Write:** "What do you mean?" Rosalie asked.

Explain that unlike dialogue, indirect discourse reports or describes rather than quotes what a person has said. **Write:** Rosalie asked what he meant.

Teach

Placement of End Punctuation

Emphasize that the placement of end punctuation with quotation marks depends on whether a question or an exclamation is, or is not, part of the quotation.

Assess

1. "Are you an only daughter?" Neil asked.
   "Yes, I am," Marisa said.
2. "Well, you might like this essay," Neil said. "It's by Sandra Cisneros."
3. "Oh, I think I have already read that!" Marisa exclaimed.
4. "You're kidding!" Neil said. Marisa explained, "We had to read it in class."
5. "Did you enjoy it?" Neil asked. "I thought it was terrific," Marisa replied.

Learning Objectives

In this workshop, you will focus on the following objective:

Grammar: Understanding how to use dialogue and speaker tags.

Writing Dialogue

Dialogue is the exact words that characters exchange. Writers use **speaker tags** or tag lines to identify who is speaking in a dialogue.

Tip

When you are writing or proofreading dialogue, always check for the end quotation mark. Writers often accidentally omit it.

Language Handbook

For more about puncutation, see Language Handbook, pp. R53–R56.

LOG ON Literature Online

Grammar For more grammar practice, go to glencoe.com and enter QuickPass code GL49787u2.

Grammar Workshop

Dialogue and Speaker Tags

Literature Connection Richard Wright uses dialogue to break up paragraphs and to show speakers' exact words. He encloses speakers' words in quotation marks, begins their statements with a capital letter, and usually identifies speakers with speaker tags or tag lines.

> *"I'm going to offer you something more valuable than money," he said.*
>
> —Richard Wright, from *Black Boy*

Speaker tags, phrases such as *he said* and *I replied,* identify speakers and often convey additional information, such as tone of voice.

Remember these additional rules for quoting dialogue.

- If the speaker tag comes before the speaker's words, follow the tag with a comma, but before the opening quotation mark. Place the end punctuation inside the closing quotation mark.

  I said with logic, "But you sell your papers for money."

- If the speaker tag comes after the speaker's words in a declarative sentence, place a comma inside the closing quotation mark.

  "We can't pay for manuscript," he said.

- If the speaker tag comes after the speaker's words in an interrogative or exclamatory sentence, keep the question mark or exclamation point inside the closing quotation mark and do not add a comma.

  "How much money will I get?" I asked, excited.

Begin a new paragraph each time the speaker changes.

Revise Rewrite the dialogue below. Add punctuation, capitalization, indentation, and speaker tags as needed.

1. Are you an only daughter? Neil asked. Yes, I am.
2. Well, you might like this essay. It's by Sandra Cisneros.
3. Oh, I think I have already read that!
4. You're kidding! Neil said. Marisa explained we had to read it in class.
5. Did you enjoy it? I thought it was terrific!

For additional grammar practice, see Unit 2 Teaching Resources Book, p. 83.

Before You Read

World Literature
Afghanistan

Escape from Afghanistan

Meet **Farah Ahmedi**
(born 1988)

One day when Farah Ahmedi was in second grade and walking to school in her home city of Kabul, Afghanistan, she stepped on a landmine. At first, her parents thought she would die. Luckily, however, a humanitarian organization flew her to Germany for medical care. She spent two years there, all the time believing she would never walk again or see her family again. Ahmedi did lose one leg, and the other remained permanently rigid. Nevertheless, she was able to walk because of a prosthesis, or artificial replacement device.

Not long after Ahmedi returned to Afghanistan, a rocket hit her home in Kabul. Her father and two sisters were killed in the explosion. Her brothers left the country in order to avoid the Taliban, a militant Islamic group. Ahmedi never heard from them again. She and her mother were left full of grief and alone.

> *"I was so scared. A lot of times I wonder why I didn't die. Those were hard times."*
>
> —Farah Ahmedi

Arrival in America During the time Ahmedi and her mother lived alone in Afghanistan, the Taliban gained control of the country. The Taliban government persecuted Ahmedi's ethnic group, the Hazara. Because Ahmedi's mother had a cousin in Pakistan who was willing to help them, they decided to flee their country. Ahmedi was only ten years old. After spending several years in a refugee camp in Pakistan, they were finally allowed to come to the United States in 2002, where Ahmedi entered high school at the age of fourteen.

A Contest Changes Her Life Only a couple years after Ahmedi's arrival, *Good Morning America* and the publisher Simon & Schuster offered a writing contest. It invited viewers to write their life stories. Ahmedi submitted an essay and was selected as one of three finalists. Then the publisher assigned a professional writer, Tamim Ansary, to write Ahmedi's story. Comfortable with Ansary, who was also from Afghanistan and spoke her native language of Farsi, Ahmedi spent five days recounting her story to him. The result was a full-length book. When viewers chose her book as the best, it was published as *The Story of My Life: An Afghan Girl on the Other Side of the Sky*.

A Bright Future Ahmedi has been named a youth ambassador for the Adopt-a-Minefield Program. That organization works to clear landmines and help landmine survivors in the six most heavily mined countries in the world, one of which is Afghanistan. She is proud and happy to live in the United States, where she knows she has excellent opportunities for independence and education.

LOG ON **Literature** Online

Author Search For more about Farah Ahmedi, go to glencoe.com and enter QuickPass code GL49787u2.

Before You Read

Focus

Bellringer Options

Daily Language Practice Transparency 30

Or invite volunteers to give examples of regions where war, famine, or persecution has prompted people to flee to other countries either recently or in the past. *(Africa, Ireland, Germany)*

Ask: How would you feel if you suddenly had to leave your native country and live in exile? What hopes and fears might preoccupy your mind?

Selection Skills

Escape from Afghanistan

Literary Elements
- Tone (SE pp. 308–316)
- Historical Narrative (SE p. 316)

Listening/Speaking/Viewing Skills
- Analyze Art (SE p. 313, 314)
- Oral Report (SE p. 317)

Reading Skills
- Analyze Cultural Context (SE pp. 308–316)
- Make Inferences (TE p. 315)

Vocabulary Skills
- Context Clues (SE pp. 308, 317)
- Academic Vocabulary (SE p. 317)

Writing Skills/Grammar
- Adverbs (TE p. 308)
- Write a Summary (TE p. 310)

Before You Read

Focus

Summary

In this suspenseful excerpt from her autobiography, Farah Ahmedi recounts how she and her mother made a harrowing journey across the border into Pakistan to escape persecution by the Taliban regime in Afghanistan and begin a new life.

For summaries in languages other than English, see Unit 2 Teaching Resources Book, pp. 84–89.

Vocabulary

Fill in the Blanks Have students create a fill-in-the-blank exercise using the vocabulary words. When students finish, collect the exercises and randomly hand them out to the class. Creating the exercise will help teach the vocabulary. Completing the exercise will measure how much they have learned.

For additional vocabulary practice, see Unit 2 Teaching Resources Book, p. 92.

For additional context, see Glencoe Interactive Vocabulary CD-ROM.

Literature and Reading Preview

Connect to the Autobiography

What might make you leave your country with only a bundle of belongings? Discuss this question with a small group.

Build Background

Throughout history, Afghanistan has lacked unity because of its mix of religions and cultures. About 85% of Afghans are Sunni Muslims. Shi'ite Muslims make up most of the remaining 15%. Afghans also are divided by language and ethnicity. The major ethnic group is the Pashtun. When the Taliban took over in the 1990s, conflict between the Pashtun and other groups intensified and led to the massacres of Shi'ite Muslims and others.

Set Purposes for Reading

Big Idea Looking into Lives

As you read, ask yourself, In what ways is Ahmedi's autobiography a tale of survival against all odds?

Literary Element Tone

Tone is an author's attitude toward a subject matter. Tone is conveyed through elements such as word choice, sentence structure, and figures of speech. As you read, ask yourself, How does word choice reveal the author's feelings and attitudes?

Reading Strategy Analyze Cultural Context

Analyzing cultural context is thinking about the time and place of a story and the values of the people in that time and place, and determining how those factors affect the work. As you read, ask yourself, How is the culture described in this story similar to and different from the culture in which I live?

Tip: Track Details As you read, track details that show the time, place, values, or attitudes in an organizer like the one shown.

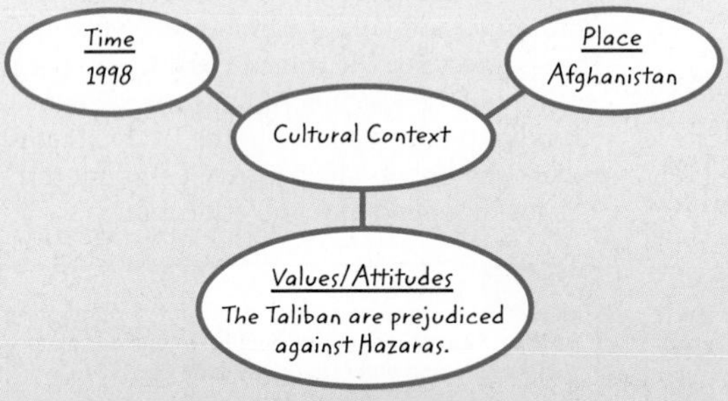

Learning Objectives

For pages 307–317

In studying this text, you will focus on the following objectives:

Literary Study: Analyzing tone.

Reading: Analyzing cultural context.

Research: Using the Internet to conduct research.

Vocabulary

quandary (kwon′ drē) *n.* state of indecision or doubt; p. 309 *Lisa was in a quandary over which class to take.*

surge (surj) *v.* to move suddenly in a wave; p. 311 *The fans surge forward when the rock star comes on stage.*

pervade (pər vād′) *v.* to go through or fill every part of; p. 311 *After each win, joy pervades the locker room.*

stoke (stōk) *v.* to stir up; to cause to increase; p. 312 *Robert's part in the prank stoked bad feelings in many of the faculty members.*

chide (chīd) *v.* to express disapproval; p. 315 *My parents chide me for putting off my homework until the last minute.*

Tip: Context Clues To figure out the meanings of unfamiliar words, look for context clues, or words about meaning, in the words and phrases around the unfamiliar word.

Grammar Practice

SPIRAL REVIEW **Understand Adverbs** Explain to students that adverbs modify verbs, adjectives, or other adverbs by telling *when, where, how,* and *to what degree.* Write the following lines on the board: I watched closely and saw that it was true.

Show how the adverb answers a question: How did the narrator watch? *(closely)*

Ask: How else could someone describe how they watched someone? *(possible answers: secretly, quietly)* Have students find other adverbs in the selection and write them in their notebook, along with the words they modify.

ESCAPE from Afghanistan

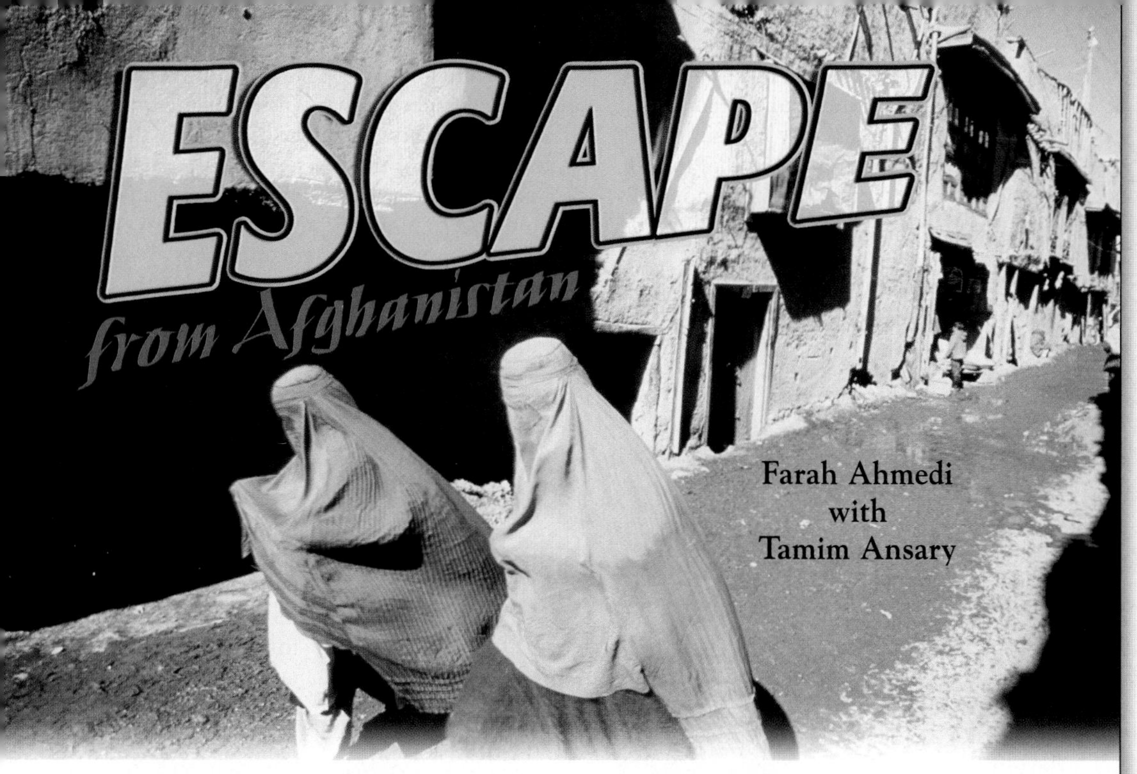

Farah Ahmedi
with
Tamim Ansary

One day we got a letter, hand-carried to us by some traveler. Alas, it was not from my brothers. It came from my mother's cousin in Quetta, a city on the Pakistan side of the Afghan border. We had lost track of her and did not even know she was there, but somehow, six months after my father's death, she had heard about the event and about our **quandary.**

Come to Quetta, she wrote. *Get across the border somehow, and then come directly to Quetta. Do not tarry*[1] *in Peshawar.*[2] *That is a Taliban stronghold, a Pashtun city. You won't be welcome there. In fact, you will be in danger, for the Taliban come from that region, and they are prejudiced against Hazaras. Peshawar is a dangerous place for two Hazara women on their own. Do not even go into the city, if you can avoid it. Just come to Quetta.* And she gave directions for finding her house once we got to her city.

3 This cousin of my mother's had moved to Quetta some time ago. She had a settled life there. She had lost her husband, but she had a brother and two sons living in Turkmenistan.[3] Those men had gotten out of Afghanistan during the Communist era.[4]

1. Here, to *tarry* means "to delay" or "to stay longer than the minimum necessary."
2. *Peshawar* is the first major city in Pakistan below the Khyber Pass from Afghanistan.
3. *Turkmenistan* borders Afghanistan on the north.
4. The *Communist era* began in 1979 when the Soviets took control of Afghanistan. That occupation began the Afghanistan War, which lasted until 1989, devastating the country.

1 Tone *What tone or attitude do you hear in this sentence?*

2 Analyze Cultural Context *What appears to be part of the culture of Peshawar, Pakistan?*

Vocabulary

quandary (kwon′ drē) n. state of indecision or doubt

Teach

Literary Element 1

Tone **Answer:** *The terse imperative sentence creates an urgent tone.*

For additional literary element practice, see Unit 2 Teaching Resources Book, p. 90.

Reading Strategy 2

Analyze Cultural Context **Answer:** *There is prejudice against the Hazara and especially against Hazara women. There may be a threat of violence there.*

Literary Element 3

Tone **Ask:** How would you describe the tone of this paragraph? *(The tone is factual and objective. There are many details but little personal commentary or emotional reaction.)*

For an audio recording of this selection, use Listening Library Audio CD-ROM.

Readability Scores

Dale-Chall: 5.8
DRP: 54
Lexile: 820

English Learners

DIFFERENTIATED INSTRUCTION

Intermediate Many words in the selection may be unfamiliar to English language learners. Direct students' attention to the second paragraph on page 309. Note the words *border, directly, tarry, stronghold, welcome, region, prejudiced,* and *avoid.* Explain that context clues can often help readers figure out a word's meaning. As they read, have students create a list of unfamiliar words from the text. Students should define each word using a dictionary. Students can then use their lists to quiz each other on the words they selected.

Teach

Big Idea 1

Looking into Lives

Ask: If you were in these travelers' position and had to choose just a few possessions to carry by hand, what would they be? *(Encourage students to offer support for their choices.)*

APPROACHING Ask an approaching-level student to summarize the information presented in this passage.

Reading Strategy 2

Analyze Cultural Context

Answer: *It suggests that women cannot safely travel alone on buses there.*

Big Idea 3

Looking into Lives

Answer: *Their situation must be dire.*

3 They had gone to Turkmenistan to study, and then, because the country had dissolved into civil war, they had simply stayed. They now worked in that former Soviet republic and sent bits of money from time to time; that's what my mother's cousin lived on.

Well, we talked it over with our neighbors and decided that we had to do it. We made inquiries and learned that we could pay a man to serve as our escort on the bus to Jalalabad.[5] That would get us out of Taliban-dominated Kabul.[6] From Jalalabad to the border, we would be on our own. As for getting across the border, no one knew what that entailed. And as for making the journey from the border to Quetta, that was like asking how to get from one part of the moon to another part. No one could give us any advice on that subject. We would just have to figure things out when we got there.

This map shows the location of the cities and countries mentioned in the selection.

1 By the time we left Afghanistan, the warm days had come. We wrapped the few possessions we would take along in little cloth bundles. We could not take much, for we would have to carry whatever we took, and while I could not handle much of a load, my poor mother was in even worse shape. The day my father died, her asthma took a turn for the worse. Now she was rasping with every breath, and exertion of any kind tightened up her air passages. We had no medicine for her condition. When it got bad, all she could do was rest, so the last thing we needed was extra baggage. 1

We made it to Jalalabad by bus. We could not have gotten there any other way. The stretch of road between Kabul and Jalalabad goes over some of the country's steepest mountains, cutting through two rugged gorges. The Kabul River pours through those gorges in a series of thundering cataracts,[7] and the highway has been cut into nearly solid rock, folding back and forth, back and forth like a ribbon along the riverbank.

Once the road descended out of those gorges, the weather changed. The temperature rose. Now we were in the Jalalabad valley, which was dotted with groves of orange trees and lemon trees. The bus let us off in a crowded bazaar. We were frightened to be there alone and frightened to

5. *Jalalabad* is the last major city in Afghanistan before the Khyber Pass. It is southeast of Kabul.
6. *Kabul* is the capital city of Afghanistan, located in the eastern part of the country.
7. *Gorges* are canyons or narrow passages through the land; *cataracts* are steep rapids.

2 Analyze Cultural Context *What does this tell you about the culture of Afghanistan?*

Looking into Lives *The author and her mother face incredible challenges. What does their willingness to forge ahead tell you about their situation?* 3

Writing Practice

SPIRAL REVIEW SPIRAL REVIEW **Write a Summary** Remind students that following the sequence, or order in which events occur is important to understanding the text. Point out that the author may or may not use clue words such as *first, next, last,* and *then.* Have students construct a timeline showing the events in the selection. Then ask students to write a brief summary of the story.

have to ask for advice and directions, but we addressed our questions to women as much as possible or to family groups that included women. In this way we found out how to get to the "other" bus station.

This other bus station wasn't really a station. There was no building, no ticket booth, and no station agent—nothing like that. The so-called bus station looked like any other part of the bazaar: It was just a road lined
4 on both sides with merchants' stalls. Along this strip of bazaar, however, men cruised back and forth in vans they owned, looking for people who wanted to go to the border. If you just stood at the curb, they pulled over and offered you a ride.

Before we got on, though, other people waiting there for rides advised us to get some plastic bags. We didn't know why, but we figured we had better do whatever other travelers were doing. They no doubt knew more than we did. Curiously enough, some of the stalls in that vicinity sold plastic bags as if this were a normal travel need.

Shortly after we took up our post by the side of the road, a van pulled over. Instantly, a crowd **surged** toward its door. People fought and threw elbows to get to the front so they could board. That's how it was at the "bus station." Only the most aggressive travelers got rides. Each van could carry ten or twelve people, if they squeezed; and they always squeezed. The drivers wanted to make as much money as they could. We were unable to get onto the first van. We could not get on the next one, either. By the third one, however, I saw what we needed to do, and taking my mother by the arm, I shoved and pushed with the others until we made it to the door of the van.

It wasn't all that far from Jalalabad to the border, but we were traveling in the heat of mid-afternoon. Dust boiled up around the car and got in through the windows. My mother began to wheeze and gasp. I worried that she might stop breathing right then and there, so I tried to shield her with my body, tried to keep the other passengers from pressing in on her so that she would have her own space to breathe out of. Meanwhile, the dust mingled with the sweat running down my face, turning to mud by the time it reached my chin.

At that moment I discovered what the plastic bags were for: One of the men in the backseat vomited loudly, barely getting his awful stew into his bag. The nasty odor immediately **pervaded** the entire van. My nostrils puckered, and I felt my own vomit rising. I grabbed for my bag. Within minutes, all of us passengers were filling up our plastic bags. No, it wasn't far from Jalalabad to the border, just a couple of hours, but that ride felt like it would never end.

About half a mile from the border the van pulled over to the side of the road. "This is as far as we go," the driver said. "That's the border up ahead. You see those two buildings and the gate between them? That's it. If you can get through that gate, you're in Pakistan. About half a mile up the road on the other side, if you can get to the other side, you'll find other cars like this one offering rides to Peshawar."

Well, we got out and started trudging toward the border station. We were not alone. The whole stretch of road was filled

5 Looking into Lives *What does the description of this bus station tell you about the trip Ahmedi and her mother are taking?*

Vocabulary

surge (surj) *v.* to move suddenly in a wave

Vocabulary

pervade (pər vād′) *v.* to go through or fill every part of

Teach

Reading Strategy 4

Analyze Cultural Context

Ask students to visualize the "other bus station."

Ask: Why do you think the men in the vans acted this way? *(Possible answer: The rides they offered to the border were* a violation of the law.)

Big Idea 5

Looking into Lives

Answer: *Their trip is obviously dangerous because they are relying on other people to help them. They are unsure where they are going and how exactly to get there.*

English Learners

DIFFERENTIATED INSTRUCTION

Intermediate Visual learners respond well to descriptive passages such as the paragraph on page 310 which begins, "We made it to Jalalabad by bus." Encourage students to use that paragraph as the basis for a drawing, painting, or collage. They may choose to illustrate the entire scene described, or they may select a portion of the scene. Ask students to present their artwork. As a class, look at specific pieces and invite the artists to speak about what they depicted. Invite others to comment on the work.

Teach

Literary Element 1

Tone **Answer:** *Worry, anxiety, and desperation*

Literary Element 2

Tone **Answer:** *Although she is in an extremely difficult situation, she feels "blessed" in some ways, such as not being alone or too cold. She is emotional about the few positive things she experienced.*

with people hoping to get across the border that day—hundreds of families. I don't know how many. I wasn't counting. I didn't count. I was distracted by the scene I saw up ahead.

The gate to Pakistan was closed, and I could see that the Pakistani border guards were letting no one through. People were pushing and shoving and jostling up against that gate, and the guards were driving them back. As we got closer, the crowd thickened, and I could hear the roar and clamor at the gate. The Afghans were yelling something, and the Pakistanis were yelling back. My mother was clutching her side and gasping for breath, trying to keep up. I felt desperate to get through, because the sun was setting, and if we got stuck here, what were we going to do? Where would we stay? There was nothing here, no town, no hotel, no buildings, just the desert.

Yet we had no real chance of getting through. Big strong men were running up to the gate in vain. The guards had clubs, and they had carbines,[8] too, which they turned around and used as weapons. Again and again, the crowd surged toward the gate and the guards drove them back with their sticks and clubs, swinging and beating until the crowd receded. And after that, for the next few minutes, on our side of the border, people milled about and muttered and **stoked** their own impatience and worked up their rage, until gradually the crowd gathered strength and surged against that gate again, only to be swept back.

We never even got close to the front. We got caught up in the thinning rear end of the crowd, and even so, we were part of each wave, pulled forward, driven back. It was hard for me to keep my footing, and my mother was clutching my arm now, just hanging on, just trying to stay close to me, because the worst thing would have been if we had gotten separated. Finally, I saw that it was no use. We were only risking injury. We drifted back, out of the crowd. In the thickening dusk we could hear the dull roar of people still trying to get past the border guards, but we receded into the desert, farther and farther back from the border gate.

Night was falling, and we were stranded out there in the open.

But at least it wasn't cold; that was a blessing. And at least we were not alone. For that, too, I felt grateful. Hundreds of us were hunkering out there on the desert floor, in the shadows of the high hills that marked the border. We were clotted into family groups. Some groups managed to get fires going, which added a feeling of cheer. They chatted quietly around their fires, and we could hear their voices. There was something companionable about it, really. We were all just ordinary folks caught in a bad situation, sharing the same fate. No one there meant anybody harm.

Had I been alone, I would have felt frightened, but with that sea of families surrounding me, I felt safe, even if they were strangers. My mother and I had our little cloth bundles, in which we were each carrying some extra clothes, and we had our head scarves. We put those under our heads as pillows and slept under the stars. It wasn't bad. We did manage to catch some sleep.

Then dawn came, and we again had to make our way to the road and try to get

8. *Carbines* are a type of firearm.

1 Tone *What emotions do you hear in the author's voice?*

Vocabulary

stoke (stōk) *v.* to stir up; to cause to increase

Tone *What is the author's attitude toward her situation?* **2**

Research Practice

SMALL GROUP SPIRAL REVIEW **Citizenship** Have students search newspapers, magazines, documentaries, and the Internet for articles that describe the current lifestyle in Afghanistan. Assign students to small groups and ask them to compare and contrast information from two different media sources. Have the groups answer questions such as these:

- How has life in Afghanistan changed since the author left?
- What has your research helped you to understand about the selection? Explain.
- After researching Afghanistan, what insight do you have concerning the author's decision to leave?

Mountains near Badakhshan, Afghanistan.

View the Photograph The impressive mountain range shown here characterizes the geography of Afghanistan. Does seeing the terrain make Ahmedi's journey seem more difficult? Explain. ★

across that border. What else could we do? We could not go back, nor could we stay in that wasteland indefinitely. We *had* to get through. But once again, the guards were keeping the gate closed, beating and hitting anyone who got close enough each time the crowd rushed.

On that second day, however, I learned that it was all a question of money. Someone told me about this, and then I watched closely and saw that it was true. Throughout the day, while some of the guards confronted the crowds, a few others lounged over to the side. People approached them quietly. Money changed hands, and the guards then let those people quietly through a small door to the side.

3 Analyze Cultural Context *What do these details tell you about the guards at this border station?*

Hundreds could have flowed through the main gate had it been opened, but only one or two could get through the side door at a time. The fact that the guards were taking bribes did us no good whatsoever. We did not have the money to pay them. What little we had we would need to get from Peshawar to Quetta. And so the second day passed.

At the end of that day we found ourselves camping near a friendly family. We struck up a conversation with them. The woman told us that her husband, Ghulam Ali, had gone to look for another way across the border. He was checking out a goat path that supposedly went over the mountains several miles northeast of the border station. If one could get to Pakistan safely by that route, he would come back for his family. "You can go with us," the woman said.

Teach

Reading Strategy 3

Analyze Cultural Context

Answer: *Smuggling is commonplace and accepted. Students may mention that it is not only at the official border that bribes are commonplace, but that most of the border guards are likely corrupt.*

ENGLISH LEARNERS To assist English learners, ask students to think of words that describe the guards mentioned in this paragraph. (corrupt, dishonest)

View the Photograph ★

Answer: *Answers will vary. Students should support their answers.*

The Hindu Kush spans 500 miles and spreads southwest into Afghanistan from Pakistan. Around 1500 B.C., people from Central Asia crossed through the range and brought with them the beginnings of Indo-Iranian languages.

Approaching Level

DIFFERENTIATED INSTRUCTION

Emerging To practice ***reading fluency,*** have students read the paragraph on page 313 which begins, "On that second day. . . " Ask students if this passage reminds them of anything that happened earlier in the story. *(Students might compare this scene to the learning experience the narrator had at the "bus station.")*

Established Say: The narrator admits that she does not know how to cross the border and that she watches others to learn. **Ask:** What does this admission show about the narrator? *(Students may point out that the narrator is very brave to forge ahead when she does not know what to expect. They might also say that she is a good observer and a fast learner.)*

Teach

Reading Strategy 1

Analyze Cultural Context
Answer: *The Islamic faith is a vital part of the culture. Even at the border crossing, there is a mosque. Despite the need for haste, prayers are observed.*

View the Photograph ★

Answer: *Students might say that the image of the massed crowds behind the wire fence corresponds to Ahmedi's description.*

The terrain along the border between Afghanistan and Pakistan is rugged and mountainous; much of the border runs along the Hindu Kush mountain range.

View the Photograph In this photo, taken November 15, 2000, at Torkham border post, 55 kilometers (34 miles) northwest of Peshawar, Pakistani border security guards stand in front of the Pakistan-Afghanistan border to stop Afghan refugees. Based on Ahmedi's description, how well does this photo capture the scene at the border? ★

Later that night her husband showed up. "It works," he said. "Smugglers use that path, and they bribe the guards to leave it unguarded. Of course, we don't want to run into any smugglers, either, but if we go late at night, we should be fine."

His wife then told him our story, and Ghulam Ali took pity on us. "Yes, of course you can come with us," he said. "But you have had two hard days. You will need some rest before you attempt this mountain crossing. Spend tonight here and sleep well, knowing that you will have nothing to do tomorrow except lounge around, rest, and catch your breath. Tomorrow, do not throw yourself against those border guards again. Let your only work be the gathering of your strength. Then tomorrow night we will all go over the mountain together, with God's grace. I will show you the way. If God wills it,[9] we will follow that smugglers' path to safety. You and your mother are in my care now."

So we spent the whole next day there. It was terribly warm and we had no water, but we walked a little way and found a mosque that refugees like us had built over the years, so that people waiting to get across the border would have a place to say their prayers. We got some water to drink at the mosque, and we said *namaz*[10] there too. Somehow we obtained a bit of bread as well. I can't remember how that turned up, but there it was, and we ate it. We sustained our strength. After sunset we lay down just as if we were going to spend another night. In fact, I did fall asleep for a while. Long after dark—or early the next morning, to be exact, before the sun came up—that man shook us awake. "It's time," he said.

We got up and performed our ablutions[11] quickly in the darkness, with just sand because that's allowed when you have no access to water. We said our prayers. Then Ghulam Ali began to march into the darkness with his family, and we trudged along silently behind them. After several miles the path began to climb, and my mother

9. Throughout the Muslim world, expressions that show an awareness of God are common. Here, typical phrases are used to show that people's fortunes are dependent on God's will or grace.
10. *Namaz* is prayer.
11. *Ablutions* refers to ritual washing before prayer.

Analyze Cultural Context *What does this tell you about the author's culture?* **1**

Grammar Practice

SPIRAL REVIEW **Prepositional Phrases** Write the phrase *"over the mountains"* on the board. Explain that prepositional phrases consist of a preposition *(over)* and an object of the preposition *(mountains)*. Note that prepositional phrases often clarify spatial relationships. For example, Ahmedi uses the phrases *"through the main gate," "from Peshawar to Quetta," "near a friendly family,"* and *"across the border."*

Have students write at least two prepositional phrases in sentences to clarify a spatial relationship.

began to wheeze. Her asthma was pretty bad at this point, poor thing. No doubt, her anxiety made it worse, but in such circumstances how could she rid herself of anxiety? It was no use knowing that her difficulty was rooted in anxiety, just as it was no use knowing that we could have moved more quickly if we had possessed
2 wings. Life is what it is. The path over that mountain was not actually very long, only a couple of miles. Steep as it was, we could have gotten over in little more than an hour if not for my mother. Because of her, we had to pause every few minutes, so our journey took many hours.

I myself hardly felt the exertion. I was walking quite well that day, quite athletically. I had that good prosthetic leg from Germany. The foot was a little worn by then, but not enough to slow me down. Thinking back, I'm puzzled, actually. How did I scale that mountain so easily? How did I climb down the other side? These days I find it hard to clamber up two or three flights of stairs, even. I don't know what made me so supple[12] and strong that day, but I felt no hardship, no anxiety or fear, just concentration and intensity. Perhaps my mother's problems distracted me from my own. That might account for it. Perhaps desperation gave me energy and made me forget the rigor of the climb. Well, whatever the reason, I scrambled up like a goat. The family we were following had a girl only a bit younger than me, and she was moving slowly. Her family used my example to **chide** her. They kept saying, "Look at that girl. She's missing a leg, and yet she's going faster than you. Why can't you keep up? Hurry now!"

That Ghulam Ali was certainly a good man, so patient with us and so compassionate. He had never seen us before, and yet when he met us, he said, "I will help you." That's the thing about life. You never know when and where you will encounter a spot of human decency. I have felt alone in this world at times; I have known long periods of being no one. But then, without warning, a person like Ghulam Ali just turns up and says, "I see you. I am on your side." Strangers have been kind to me when it mattered most. That sustains a person's hope and faith.

Anyway, climbing up that mountain on the Afghanistan side took some effort, but after we topped the crest, even my mother found the going down part fairly easy. We hardly stopped at all on the downward side. Going up took hours; coming down took minutes, or so it seemed.

As soon as we reached the bottom of the slope, Ghulam Ali told us we were now officially in Pakistan. We peered around. The landscape looked just the same here as it did back where we came from. And yet we were in Pakistan. We had escaped from Afghanistan. We started laughing. We couldn't stop. We tried to stop our mouths with our palms, and we could not do it. The laughter just insisted on bursting forth from us. Happiness filled our hearts. My mother's asthma disappeared without a trace for one whole hour. Yes, for one whole hour there, my mother could breathe. You might as well say we had been in prison for thirty years and had suddenly been released—that was the kind of joy we felt.

12. Here, *supple* means "able to adapt or respond to a new situation."

3 Tone *What tone or attitude do you hear in this statement?*

Vocabulary

chide (chīd) *v.* to express disapproval

Looking into Lives *How does the author draw the reader into the giddy happiness she felt on the other side of the mountain?* **4**

Teach

Reading Strategy 2

Make Inferences **Ask:** What can you infer about the narrator's attitude toward challenges in life? *(She believes confronting challenges may give a person energy and spirit.)*

Literary Element 3

Tone **Answer:** *Students may hear resignation, acceptance, or endurance.*

Big Idea 4

Looking into Lives
Answer: *Her word choice and repeated mentions of the laughing draw the reader in, as does the repetition of her mother being able to breathe, along with the informal "Yes."*

To check students' understanding of the selection, see Unit 2 Teaching Resources Book, p. 95.

Advanced Learners

DIFFERENTIATED INSTRUCTION

Analyze Tone Have a student read aloud the paragraph that begins "That Ghulam Ali was certainly a good man. . . " **Ask:** How does the tone of this paragraph contradict with the tone of the rest of the story? *(Students may say that this paragraph is filled with hope and gratitude, while the rest of the passage has a tone of desperation and suspense.)*

Ask: How does word choice and the narrator's voice affect the tone of the paragraph? *(The narrator uses words such as "so compassionate," "human decency," "kind tone," "hope and faith." These words reflect a positive attitude and set a positive tone here in this paragraph.)*

After You Read

Assess

1. Answers will vary.
2. (a) From Kabul, Afghanistan, to Quetta, Pakistan; (b) They are in danger from the Taliban.
3. (a) They take a bus to Jalalabad and then continue in a van. (b) Possible answers: Need for male escort, armed border guards, unruly crowd at the border
4. (a) Ghulam Ali guides them along a smugglers' path through the mountains. (b) People have to bribe guards to get across. It was lucky to find someone who could help them across the border.
5. Mention of Taliban in both Afghanistan and Peshawar, Pakistan, and that they are hostile toward her people
6. Vivid sensory details: van's stench, clamor and pressure of the frenzied throng, heat and dust of the desert
7. Answers will vary. Students should support their answers with reasonable explanations.
8. Students should use specific examples from the text to show how different Ahmedi's life in the United States might be.

For additional selection assessment, see Assessment Resources, pp. 89–90.

After You Read

Respond and Think Critically

Respond and Interpret

1. What part of this autobiography do you think you will remember longest? Why?
2. (a)Where do the author and her mother start out, and where are they going? (b)What can you infer about why they are going?
3. (a)How do the author and her mother reach the border? (b)What details of the journey hint at danger?
4. (a)How do the author and her mother cross the border? (b)Why could they be considered lucky to have gotten across the border?

Analyze and Evaluate

5. How does the author make it clear that she and her mother faced problems in both Afghanistan and Pakistan?
6. How well does the author give you a "you-are-there" sense of the journey? Cite passages from the text that provide sensory details.

Connect

7. **Big Idea** Looking into Lives Do you agree that Ahmedi's story is a tale of survival against all odds? Why or why not?
8. **Connect to the Author** Look back at the graphic organizer you made while reading. In what ways is Ahmedi's life in the United States probably different from her life in Afghanistan?

Literary Element Tone

SAT Skills Practice

1. The paragraph beginning "Then dawn came . . ." (page 312) is written in a tone of
   (A) casual humor
   (B) great urgency
   (C) angry mockery
   (D) deep pessimism
   (E) impartial neutrality
2. With the arrival of Ghulam Ali (page 314), the tone of the narrative changes from
   (A) ironic to sincere
   (B) playful to emotional
   (C) balanced to biased
   (D) serious to optimistic
   (E) grim to light-hearted

Review: Historical Narrative

As you learned on page 283, a **historical narrative** is a work of nonfiction that tells the story of important historical events or developments.

Partner Activity Work with a classmate to record information you learned in this autobiography about Afghanistan during the Taliban regime. Use a cluster chart like this one.

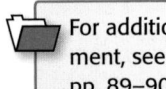

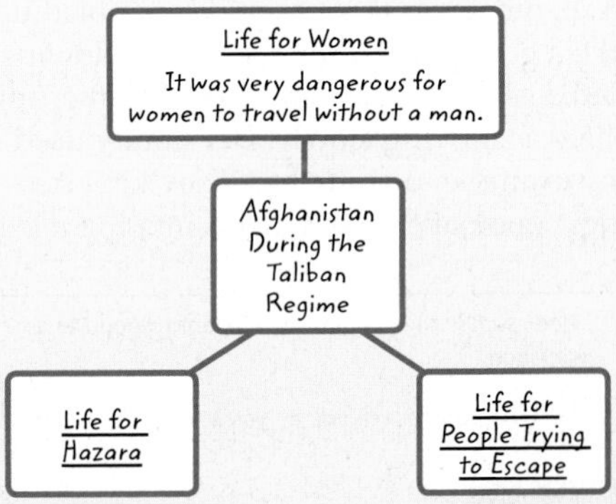

Literary Element

1. B is the correct answer. The narrator and her mother have no choice but to get across the border.
2. D is the correct answer. The arrival of this generous man allows the narrator a ray of hope.

Review: Historical Narrative

Sample answers for chart:

Life for Women: Need escort to travel
Life for Hazara: Hostility from the Taliban
Life for People Trying to Escape: No safe way across the border; must pay bribes or sneak across

Reading Strategy Analyze Cultural Context

Much of what makes "Escape from Afghanistan" so interesting is that it is set in such a different world than the one most readers inhabit. Review the cultural details you noted as you read.

1. In what ways does this autobiography take you to a different world than the one you live in?
2. How do the details about life in Afghanistan and the crossing to Pakistan interest you?

Vocabulary Practice

Practice with Context Clues Look back at pages 309–315 to find context clues for the boldface vocabulary words below. Record your findings in a chart like the one here.

quandary surge pervade stoke chide

Example:

Word: jostle
↓
Clues: Pushing and shoving led to jostling "up against that gate" so they were pushed into it.
↓
Meaning: to bump or be pushed against

Academic Vocabulary

Because of the help of a humanitarian ***network,*** *Ahmedi was able to survive and recover from stepping on a landmine.*

Network is an academic word. In order to escape from Afghanistan, Ahmedi relied on a **network** of many people who were committed to helping refugees from her country. What are some of the key **networks** that you rely on?

For more on academic vocabulary, see pages 54–55 and R79–R81.

Connect to *Social Studies*

Research and Report

Assignment How have the many years of civil war, as well as the recent U.S. war against the Taliban, affected Afghan teenagers? Use the Internet to find information. You might look for information about interrupted education, landmines, orphans, and refugees. Present your findings in an engaging and well-organized poster.

Investigate Begin by searching the Internet for sources that discuss life in Afghanistan in recent years. Research a variety of resources, such as newspaper and magazine articles, first-hand accounts, and academic reports. Read carefully and follow any technical directions you encounter in access guides to Internet sites. When deciding which sources to use, determine the credibility of the authors and publications, and use the most informed and reliable sources.

Use cause-and-effects charts to collect and combine information gathered from multiple sources. In the left box, write one of the major factors affecting Afghan teenagers. In the right boxes, list the various effects you encounter in your research.

Cause: a lack of schools and teachers after years of war → Effect: most school-age children do not attend school

Create Choose images and text that clearly depict some of the most significant effects of the wars on Afghan teens. Organize these elements together in a large poster that both engages and informs.

Report Prepare a brief oral report that explains the causes of the effects depicted in the poster. Present the poster first, then follow up with your oral report.

LOG ON Literature Online

Selection Resources For Selection Quizzes, eFlashcards, and Reading-Writing Connection activities, go to glencoe.com and enter QuickPass code GL49787u2.

After You Read

Assess

Reading Strategy

1. Students may be unfamiliar with bazaars, ritual washing before prayer, and restrictions on women's freedom.
2. Accept any reasonable answer.

Progress Check

Can students analyze cultural context?

If No → See Unit 2 Teaching Resources Book, p. 91.

Vocabulary

Word: quandary Textual Clues: One city is a "dangerous place for two Hazara women on their own," so they probably don't know what to do now that the girl's father has died. Meaning: a state of uncertainty

Word: surge Textual Clues: "Instantly," the crowd moved toward the van door, so all of the people moved as one. Meaning: a strong, wavelike movement

Word: pervade Textual Clues: The "entire van" smelled like vomit, so the smell must have spread. Meaning: to spread throughout

Word: stoke Textual Clues: The people "worked up their rage," so they became more impatient. Meaning: to build up; to cause to increase

Word: chide Textual Clues: The family was unhappy with the girl and said, "She's missing a leg, and yet she's going faster than you." Meaning: to express disapproval

To create custom assessments online, go to Progress Reporter Online Assessment.

Academic Vocabulary

Answers may vary. Sample response: I rely on a network of teachers and administrators for my education, and a network of doctors and nurses for my health.

To create custom assessments using software, use ExamView Assessment Suite.

Connect to *Social Studies*

Research and Report

Students' brief oral reports should

- explain the causes of the effects shown in the poster's images and text
- provide accurate background information on the situation in Afghanistan

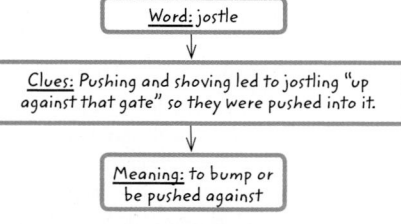

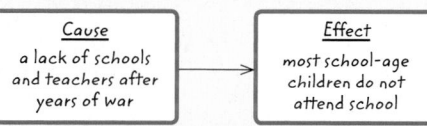

Focus

Bellringer Options

Show students a newspaper article about an important current event. **Ask:** Where else have you seen stories or reports about this subject? *(tv, radio, Internet)* Have students list as many mediums as they can as you write them on the board. Then ask students which medium they prefer most and why. Ask students to compare and contrast the ways in which these sources present information.

Summary

In this workshop, students will learn about the characteristics of different types of media. Students will learn various strategies for comparing media genres.

Learning Objectives

For pages 318–324

In this workshop, you will focus on the following objectives:

Media Literacy:
Comparing forms of media.
Distinguishing between propaganda and ethical reasoning strategies.
Explaining how text features, such as subheads, captions, and illustrations, aid the reader's understanding.

Media Workshop

Compare Media Genres

Literature Connection In 1995 Farah Ahmedi, author of "Escape from Afghanistan," stepped on a landmine and lost the use of her leg. After enduring great hardship, Ahmedi and her mother eventually made their way to the United States in 2002. Three years later, Ahmedi was named a youth ambassador for the United Nations Adopt-a-Minefield Program, which works to clear landmines in the most heavily mined countries worldwide. Such organizations often use the power of the media to gain support for their causes from viewers and readers.

Forms of Media

Every day you are bombarded by media messages in a variety of **genres,** or forms. **Print media** communicate through images and texts, and include newspapers, magazines, books, and billboards. **Electronic media** rely on sound and moving images to reach its audience. Radio, television, CDs, DVDs, movies, videotapes, documentary films, and the Internet are all electronic media.

The message and its impact on you are largely determined by the media genre. Each genre has distinct characteristics and limitations. For example, suppose you were researching a news event about the crisis of landmines. You would discover notably different presentations on the topic in a television documentary and a newspaper article. All media genres have strengths and weaknesses, and all are intended to affect their audiences in different ways.

Strategies for Comparing Media Genres

The information presented in a media message reflects the viewpoints, beliefs, and sometimes biases of those who create it. In crafting their messages, the creators determine which genre will be most effective in reaching their intended audience and which genre techniques can be used to make the message as powerful and effective as possible. When comparing how different media genres cover or present information on the same subject, it is helpful to look at the elements the genres have in common. Sources, language, images—these are basic media elements you'll find in most print and electronic media. Also consider the genres' strengths: TV is a visual medium, radio is all about sounds, and newspapers are primarily text-based. Refer to the chart to help analyze, or deconstruct, and compare media strategies and genres.

LOG ON Literature Online

Media Literacy For project ideas, templates, and media analysis guides, go to glencoe.com and enter QuickPass code GL49787u2.

Vocabulary Practice

SPIRAL REVIEW **Adopted Words** Point out that *ad hominem* in the Focus Lesson on page 319 is a Latin word, but it is commonly used in English to mean an attack against a person instead of a response to the person's ideas. Encourage students to think of other words English has adopted from other languages. **Ask:** What term do you use to show that more items can be added to a list? *(etc. or et al.)* Have students check a dictionary to see what language those terms come from. *(Latin)* Brainstorm a list of other words from other languages. Suggest thinking about foods (espresso, croissant, burrito, sushi, borscht, hors d'oeuvres), terms related to war or government (corps, coup d'etat, blitzkrieg, ad hoc, caveat), or current events (jihad, hijab) and have groups use dictionaries to find what language each comes from.

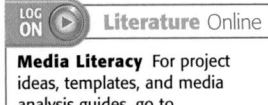

Media Strategies to Compare	
Strategy	**Questions to Ask Yourself**
source	☑ Who created the media message? How believable is the evidence that the source uses to support the message? Do the creators' viewpoints or biases interfere in any way with the message?
purpose	☑ Why was this message created? To entertain? To persuade? To inform? Is the media genre well suited to the purpose of the message?
language	☑ How do the creators use language in the message? Is the language formal? Informal? Technical? Does the language convey cultural or political ideas, trends, or beliefs?
target audience	☑ Who is this message intended to affect? Do the creators use stereotypes of people—such as children or teenagers—to try to sway the viewer? Does the genre being used exclude certain audiences?
design elements and/or film techniques	☑ How do the creators visually compose the message? Are visual symbols used to represent popular ideas or values? What do you notice about the colors, lines, shapes, or texture? Are film techniques or special effects used to influence the audience?

Focus Lesson

Persuasive Techniques: Logical Fallacies

Many media messages want you to agree with a point of view or to take a specific action. Creators of media messages sometimes use the persuasive technique of logical fallacy, or purposeful error in reasoning, to try to sway the audience. Sometimes logical fallacies are used for humor (as in a funny product ad), but they are too often used for more serious purposes, including propaganda—the use of ideas, information, or rumors to spread information or beliefs. Try to spot the following types of logical fallacies in all media genres you encounter:

- **bandwagon** urging people to do something because everyone else is doing it
- ***ad hominem*** personally attacking someone to shift attention away from the person's views or ideas
- **overgeneralization** using broad, sweeping statements with no reasonable supporting evidence as proof
- **either-or fallacy** presenting only two possible sides or solutions to an issue when there are more options
- **red herring** changing the subject on purpose in order to avoid the issue at hand
- **false cause** drawing a cause-and-effect relationship between two unrelated events that happen to follow one after another

Activity

Create a Comparison Chart

Use the Media Strategies chart on this page as a guide to compare a news event from two different media genres—for example, a TV report and a newspaper article. Create a chart in which you add a third and fourth column, one for each media genre you examine. Use the new columns to answer the questions in the second column. Remember to choose an event that is appropriate to discuss in your classroom.

Teach

Big Idea

Looking Into Lives **Ask:** In your opinion, which medium offers the most insight into the lives of others? Students should support their answers. *(Possible answer: Television because it provides information through sound and images.)*

Activity

Create a Comparison Chart Students' charts should compare different media genres and address a variety of questions from the Media Strategies chart on this page.

For video presentations related to this workshop, see Media Workshop DVD.

English Learners

DIFFERENTIATED INSTRUCTION

Early Intermediate Explain to students that the media forms they commonly encounter might include television, radio, newspapers, and magazines. Media messages often use persuasive techniques to convince their audience. Ask students to provide an example of how media messages are used to persuade an audience. *(Possible answers: Politicians use radio and television commercials to persuade people to vote for them. Advertisers try to persuade consumers to buy products using print ads and commercials.)* Have a student read aloud the questions provided at the top of the page which relate to the source strategy. **Say:** You probably ask similar questions when someone tries to convince you something is true. **Ask:** What additional questions might you ask? *(Possible answers: Can I believe this person? Is this information based on fact or an opinion? Does this person's position in life affect how he or she feels?)*

Compare Media Genres

Teach

Media Skills

Design Element Ask: How is a photograph like a summary of an event? (Possible answer: In one picture, photographers try to tell a story or capture a main idea.)

ADVANCED To challenge advanced students, ask them to think of a historical photograph they have seen that tells a story. Ask students to explain the ideas these photographs capture. *(Answers will vary.)*

Media Genre: **Online Slide Show**

Build Background Schools Demining Schools (SDS) is a United Nations organization working to educate young people like you about the dangers of landmines. SDS urges young people to get involved in the worldwide effort to remove existing mines and to ban the use of landmines in the future. These examples from the SDS online slide show, shown on its Web site, combine images and text to introduce the problem of landmines.

Design Elements

The photographer links the image of the burned-out bus—perhaps from an explosion—with the red triangle warning sign suggesting that landmines are in the area. The photographer effectively creates the association between the sign in the background and the remains of the bus.

Landmines are silent, secret weapons. People can't see them and step on them, causing death and injury. Millions of landmines are lying in the ground in over 60 countries. Landmines claim thousands of victims each year, and many live in the poorest parts of the world.

Factual Illustration

This close-up image is intended to let viewers know exactly what a common landmine looks like and how it is placed in the ground.

Landmines and unexploded ordnances (also known as UXO) were originally developed for military use during times of war and conflict. However, long after these wars and conflicts have ended, landmines and UXO continue to kill and maim the individuals who live in the areas where they have been placed.

Research Practice

PARTNERS SPIRAL REVIEW **Fact and Opinion**

Say: An example of a fact about landmines is "Landmines are found in over 60 countries." An example of an opinion about landmines is "Landmines are one of the biggest problems plaguing these countries." Explain that one of the challenges of understanding media messages is deciphering fact from opinion. Ask students to research information on landmines with a partner by visiting the library and/or searching the Internet. Ask students to locate a source about landmines and make a list of facts and a list of opinions presented by the source. Students should evaluate its credibility by answering questions presented in the chart on page 319. Have students briefly summarize their findings and their evaluation of the articles.

In this Web site, Schools Demining Schools, you will find out about the use of landmines around the world, the destruction they cause, and what you can do about it. Kids like you are taking action to heal the world from these weapons. You can start by:

- Learning everything you can about landmines and mine action.
- Questioning why they continue to be used.
- Imagining ways you might be able to help.
- Taking action by joining other children and activists around the world, who are taking mine action. You can begin by joining this project and working with the United Nations and kids like you to prevent landmines from further destroying the lives and communities of children around the world.

Getting involved makes a difference in the lives of those affected by landmines, and in your life as well. YOU CAN HELP!

Language

The photo shows children involved in a landmine awareness activity. The caption lists some steps that young people can take to solve the problem. Notice that every bulleted point begins with an action verb.

Activity

Listening and Speaking

Meet in small groups to discuss the following questions:

1. Which image from the slide show made the biggest impact on you? Why?
2. How would you describe the slide show creators' point of view? What words (or language) are used in the captions that reveal any bias?

Persuasive Technique

The text that accompanies this photo concludes the slide show with a call to action, urging young people to make a difference and get involved. The phrase "YOU CAN HELP!" in capital letters resembles an advertising slogan.

Teach

Activity

Listening and Speaking

1. Answers will vary. Students should support their answers.
2. Answers will vary. Some students may say that the slide show creator is passionate about the dangers of landmines and the terrible damage they do. Words like *death, victims, kill,* and *maim* convey the destructive power of the mines. Words and phrases like *heal, learning, taking action, activists,* and *getting involved* convey passion for the group's mission to prevent landmine disasters.

Approaching Level

DIFFERENTIATED INSTRUCTION

Established Have a student read the bulleted list on page 321. Ask them to explain why a writer might use a bulleted list. *(to organize information in an easy-to-read format)* Point out how the first three bullets are very concise and the final bullet is more detailed. **Ask:** Why might the author have done this? *(Perhaps the writer does this to make it seem as if the first steps toward action are easy to do.)*

Compare Media Genres

Teach

Media Skills

Caption Inform students that the purpose of a caption is to provide the reader with information about an image or photograph that accompanies the text.

APPROACHING After reading the first few paragraphs of the article, ask students to think of a new caption for the image on page 322 and to share their caption with the class.

Media Skills

Title Point out the title of the article that begins on page 322 and explain that the purpose of a title is to identify a piece of writing and attract readers' attention. Have students name their favorite titles and explain how the title reflects the main idea of a story or film.

Media Genre: **Web Site Report**

Build Background UNICEF—the United Nations International Children's Emergency Fund—was founded in 1946. After World War II ended, UNICEF's first assignment was helping European children who were suffering from starvation and disease. Since then, UNICEF has come to symbolize peaceful humanitarian care for children all around the globe. Beginning in the mid-1990s, one of UNICEF's ongoing projects is tackling the problem of landmines—a dangerous outcome of modern warfare. The UNICEF report below summarizes a United Nations (UN) report on this issue.

Afghan boys and girls stage a march for landmine safety.

Title

The title grabs the readers' attention and points to the main idea. The words *Deadly Inheritance* suggests that the report will be about something fatal that is left to children.

Source

A UN report—the source of information for this UNICEF report—explains the effects of warfare on children. Graça Machel is an expert on the subject.

Information—Impact of Armed Conflict on Children

LANDMINES: A DEADLY INHERITANCE

Landmines represent "an insidious and persistent danger" to children affected by war, says a new United Nations report on the impact of armed conflict on children, by Graça Machel, the UN Secretary-General's Expert on the Impact of Armed Conflict on Children.

Children are particularly vulnerable to landmines in a number of ways. If they are too young to read or are illiterate, signs posted to warn them of the presence of mines are useless. Also, children are far more likely to die from their mine injuries than are adults. Of those maimed children who survive, few will receive prostheses that keep up with the continued growth of their stunted limbs.

Reading Practice

Author's Purpose Explain that writers can make different types of arguments. Writers will sometimes try to persuade people using emotional appeal, facts, or comparisons. Have students find a persuasive article and bring it to class. With a partner, students should discuss the articles and the persuasive techniques used by the author. Have each group share highlights of their discussion with the class.

Compare Media Genres

Teach

Media Skills

Question Encourage students to jot down questions as they read the article. **Say:** Questioning what you have read will help you understand the information you are reading. As you answer your own questions, you are making sure you understand the information in the text.

The report calls on governments and the international community to design mine awareness programs and physical rehabilitation programs with children's needs in mind. The report urges that humanitarian mine clearance be made a standard part of peace agreements. Above all, it calls on governments to enact immediate legislation banning the production, use, trade, and stockpiling of landmines and to support the campaign for a worldwide ban. Some 41 nations are now on record as being in favor of the permanent elimination of landmines.

Purpose

The goal of the UN report is to persuade governments to solve the problem of landmines.

"Landmines are uniquely savage in the history of modern conventional warfare not only because of their appalling individual impact, but also their long-term social and economic destruction," says Ms. Machel.

Children in at least 68 countries are today threatened by what may be the most toxic pollution facing mankind—the contamination by mines of the land they live on. Over 110 million landmines of various types—plus millions more unexploded bombs, shells, and grenades—remain hidden around the world, waiting to be triggered by the innocent and unsuspecting, the report says. So common are mines in Cambodia that they are now used for fishing, to protect private property, and even to settle private disputes.

Evidence: Statistics

Reporters use statistics to provide concrete factual support. Here the reporter includes many statistics about landmines and their devastation.

Afghanistan, Angola, and Cambodia have suffered 85% of the world's landmine casualties. Overall, African children live on the most mine-plagued continent, with an estimated 37 million mines embedded in the soil of at least 19 countries. Angola alone has an estimated 10 million landmines and an amputee population of 70,000, of whom 8,000 are children. Since May 1995 children have made up about half the victims of the 50,000–100,000 anti-personnel mines laid in Rwanda.

Once laid, a mine may remain active for up to 50 years. Unless vigorous action is taken, mines placed today will still be killing and maiming people well into the middle of the next century. In just one district of Viet Nam, 300 children have died, 42 have lost one or more limbs, and 16 have been blinded as a result of landmines laid during the Viet Nam war. As one Khmer Rouge general put it, a landmine is the most excellent of soldiers, for it is "ever courageous, never sleeps, never misses."

Language

The Khmer Rouge general, quoted here, uses figurative language to personify a landmine as the "most excellent of soldiers." This description underscores the fierce power of landmines. *(Note:* In 1975, Cambodia fell under the brutal rule of the Khmer Rouge, a Communist group.)

Landmines pose particular dangers for children. Naturally curious, children are likely to pick up strange objects, such

English Learners

DIFFERENTIATED INSTRUCTION

Intermediate Explain that some of the information in this report is statistical information. **Say:** A statistic is a fact that can be calculated or numbered. Statistics provide measurable facts and dates. Ask students to identify statistics represented on page 323. *(Possible answer: "Since May 1995 children have made up about half the victims of the 50,000–100,000 anti-personnel mines laid in Rwanda.")*

Compare Media Genres

Teach

Activity

Listening and Speaking

1. Answers will vary. Some students may say that the article focuses on the damage done to children because that has the biggest effect on readers' emotions.
2. Answers will vary. Students should support their answers with information from the article.
3. Answers will vary. Students should support their answers with examples. Photos and images help people to see what the writer is trying to convey with written words.
4. Answers will vary. Some students may choose to use an online slide show because the combination of powerful images and informative text would have a strong impact on viewers.

Activity

Listening and Speaking

Meet in small groups to discuss the following questions:

1. Does the language in the report reveal any bias? Give examples to support your answer.
2. From which of these genres—slide show or Web site report—did you learn more about the issue of landmines?
3. What advantages do photos and images have over text in conveying information about an issue? What are the disadvantages?
4. Imagine you are planning a campaign to raise awareness of an issue in your town. Which genre would you use—a Web site report or an online slide show? Why?

Source

Quoting expert sources adds credibility to reporting. Ms. Machel's comments also logically support her ethical, or moral, views about clearing fields of landmines.

Persuasive Technique

This paragraph directly quotes the UN report's call to action. The UN is putting political and financial pressure on countries and companies responsible for the use of landmines.

as the infamous toy-like "butterfly" mines that Soviet forces spread by the millions in Afghanistan. In northern Iraq, Kurdish children have used round mines as wheels for toy trucks, while in Cambodia, children use B40 anti-personnel mines to play "boules," notes the report.

Landmines also have more catastrophic effects on children, whose small bodies succumb more readily to the horrific injuries mines inflict. In Cambodia, an average of 20% of children injured by mines and unexploded ordnance die from their injuries. Children who manage to survive explosions are likely to be more seriously injured than adults, and often permanently disabled. Because a child's bones grow faster than the surrounding tissue, a wound may require repeated amputation and a new artificial limb as often as every six months—although the prosthesis is not likely to be available. Moreover, competing demands for scarce medical services also mean that children injured by mines seldom receive the care they deserve. Only 10–20% of children disabled by mines in El Salvador receive any rehabilitative therapy.

Landmines also strike insidiously at a war-torn country's reconstruction and development. The widespread practice of mining agricultural land has led to malnutrition, even to famine and starvation. Mines laid along roads and tracks prevent the safe repatriation of refugees and impede the delivery of aid. Cambodian farmland has been so severely contaminated by mines, for example, that only 2,435 families were able to take up allocations of land out of the 85,000 originally scheduled.

"Clearing a field of mines gives life back to a local community," says Ms. Machel. "It gives people the chance to grow their own crops rather than rely on international assistance. In short, it restores human dignity and promotes human security."

Protecting children from landmines calls for a major international commitment to large-scale mine clearance and the development of child-oriented programs for mine awareness and physical rehabilitation, the report states. It is essential for children in high-risk areas to receive more innovative education in mine awareness by utilizing, for example, child-to-child approaches, role-playing, and the use of survivors as educators.

324 UNIT 2 NONFICTION

Writing Practice

SPIRAL REVIEW **Forming an Argument** Explain that one of the major points of this report is to inform people about a problem and to persuade them to take action. This report uses phrases such as "calls for a major international commitment" to make an argument, and it uses loaded words like "catastrophic" and "famine." Ask students to think of a topic that is important to them and then find facts and opinions about their topic. Have students write a three-paragraph argument that informs and persuades readers to take action. Students should use persuasive techniques such as emotional appeal, factual support, and loaded words to help support their essays. Have students present their essays to the class.

PART 2

On the Move

Harbor, Lofoten, Norway, 1937. William Johnson. Smithsonian American Art Museum, Washington, DC.

View the Art Bold colors and strong swirly lines dominate this painting of a harbor in Norway. How do the colors and lines create a sense of movement? Is it effective or distracting? ★

BIG IDEA

The world and its richness is a favorite subject of essayists. Travel and adventure writers describe their travels in vivid detail and draw lessons from exploring the world or experiencing the wonders of nature. In the essays in Part 2, the writers not only tell of their experiences, they often offer personal messages—as if they were thinking aloud and talking only to you. As you read these essays, ask yourself, What message is the author trying to convey?

UNIT TWO

PART 2

Analyze and Extend

Big Idea

On the Move After students have read the text under the "Big Idea" heading, have them study the artwork. Note how the artist uses details to convey the place's appearance and mood. Lead a discussion in which students answer the question, "What is the artist trying to convey?"

View the Art ★

Answer: *The swirling lines create a sense of ocean waves even on the land. Students should support their opinions by pointing out the details in the painting.*

African American artist William Johnson (1901–1970) studied at the National Academy of Art in Harlem, New York. After graduating, he moved to Paris and traveled around Europe, living in Denmark and Norway. In 1938, Johnson returned to the United States and devoted himself to depicting the lives of African Americans during the Depression.

English Learners

DIFFERENTIATED INSTRUCTION

Beginning/Early Intermediate Review the term *adventurous*. Explain that an adventurous person is generally someone who is daring and enjoys taking risks. **Ask:** What might an adventurous person like to do? Encourage students to share their ideas about activities an adventurous person would do in a class discussion. Write their ideas on the board. Point out that people might have different ideas about what it means to be adventurous.

Then ask students to write a few sentences about an adventurous person. When they finish, have them read their work aloud. **Ask:** How does your idea of an adventurous person compare with those of your classmates? Encourage students to share their thoughts with the class.

For additional support for English Learners, see Unit 2 Teaching Resources Book, p. 100.

UNIT TWO

PART 2

Focus

Bellringer Options

Daily Language Practice Transparency 31

Or present an example of an informative or persuasive essay from a newspaper.

Ask: Why do people read informative or persuasive essays? Why do newspapers print such essays? *Have students consider their purpose for reading as they read the essays.*

Teach

Literary Element 1

Audience Explain that essay writers consider their audiences before they write. They think about what the readers will need or want to know. As students read these excerpts, have them identify the essays' likely audiences.

View the Art ★

Elizabeth Barakah Hodges is an artist and educator who lives in Florida. She describes her work as "magic realism" and says she focuses on "the beauty of the spirit."

Learning Objectives

For pages 325–327

In studying this text, you will focus on the following objective:

Literary Study: Analyzing essays.

LITERARY FOCUS

Personal and Expository Essay

What is an essay?

An **essay** is a short piece of nonfiction writing that usually deals with a single subject. But an essay can deal with virtually any subject in a variety of ways. Many essays, regardless of their type, share the author's thoughts about a subject or an experience. In the excerpt in Part 2 from *All God's Children Need Traveling Shoes*, Maya Angelou tells of a weekend drive out of Accra to see the countryside of Ghana. 1

from *All God's Children Need Traveling Shoes*

by Maya Angelou

The too sweet aromas of flowers, the odors of freshly fried fish and stench from open sewers hung in my clothes and lay on my skin. Car horns blew, drums thumped. Loud radio music and the muddle of many languages shouted or murmured. I needed country quiet.

The Fiat was dependable, and I had a long weekend, money in my purse, and a working command of Fanti, so I decided to travel into the bush.

The essays in this part were written to inform or to share experiences with the reader. For example, in the above excerpt, Maya Angelou shares her impressions of the sights, sounds, and smells of Accra. Essays are generally categorized as **personal, expository,** or **persuasive.**

Africa, 1995. Elizabeth Barakah Hodges. Acrylic on canvas, 25 x 18 in. Private collection. ★

Reading Practice

SPIRAL REVIEW **Evaluate Credibility Say:** It is important to evaluate the author's credibility when reading nonfiction. Questioning the author's intent and qualifications on the topic, helps students to better recognize propaganda and bias.

Remind students that the easiest way to examine an author's credibility is to ask questions relating to the author's purpose for writing. **Ask:** What questions would help you assess the author's credibility? Encourage students to brainstorm questions and write them on the board. Tell students to record their questions in their journals so that they can refer back to them while reading.

The Personal Essay

Personal essays are usually informal in their language and tone. A personal essay often reflects on an incident in the writer's life. The writer may share a life lesson with the reader or perhaps reminisce about a past experience.

2 The voices outside rose in a flurry of noise, like a flock of frightened birds. But above the conglomerate sound there was always one voice, clean and sharp and individual and yet representative of the mass like that one face in the front line that holds the meaning of the whole crowd—one cry "Sayonara." The impression was intensified perhaps because it was the one word of Japanese I understood—"Sayonara" ("Good-bye").

—Anne Morrow Lindbergh, **"Sayonara"**

The Expository Essay

The word *expository* is a derivative of the word *expose*, which means "to make known or explain." Whenever you write to inform, give directions, explain an idea, or make something clear, you are writing an **expository essay.**

In this one plant, in one summer season, a drama of need and survival took place. Hungers were filled. Insects coupled. There was escape, exhaustion, and death. Lives touched down a moment and were gone.

—Linda Hogan, **"Walking"**

Chefs in Paris, 2003. Pam Ingalls. ★

The Persuasive Essay

In a **persuasive essay,** the writer attempts to influence the reader to accept an idea, adopt a point of view, or perform an action. Persuasive writing may appeal to the reader's emotions. However, a type of persuasive writing called **argument** relies on reason, logic, and evidence to convince the reader. Most persuasive essays and speeches use a combination of argument and emotional appeal. You will encounter persuasive writing and speaking in Part 3 of this unit.

LOG ON **Literature** Online

Literature and Reading For more about literary elements, go to glencoe.com and enter QuickPass code GL49787u2.

Quickwrite

Describe a Journey Describe your journey to school on a particular day. What main point will you make? What are your thoughts about your experience? Include details about what you see, hear, smell, taste, and touch that support your main point.

Approaching Level

DIFFERENTIATED INSTRUCTION

Emerging Explain that certain topics are better suited to certain types of essays. Ask students to come up with ideas for essay topics. Encourage them to write their ideas on the board. Then lead a class discussion on the differences among personal, expository and persuasive essays, referring to the information on this page. On the board draw three columns: personal essays, expository essays, and persuasive essays. Ask volunteers to choose a topic from the list and put it in the correct column. Then ask students to pick one of these topics and write a brief essay about it. Remind them to choose details carefully so that their essays are clear and factual.

Teach

Reading Strategy 2

Identify Facts **Say:** In nonfiction, writers provide details that help the reader picture the setting and the people, but those details must be factual. **Ask:** What details would you use to describe the setting of your classroom today? Remind students to use facts and details that would help a reader picture the setting.

View the Art ★

Pam Ingalls began studying art with her father, the founder of the art department at Gonzaga University in Washington. She favors bold colors and simple subjects. Ingalls has won over 60 prizes for her work.

Assess

Quickwrite

Descriptions should include sensory details that bring the scene or events to life. Students should use the details to support a larger point about life and describe their thoughts and feelings.

Before You Read

Focus

Bellringer Options

Daily Language Practice Transparency 32

Or discuss journeys students have taken to other states or countries, either physically or by reading a book or magazine.

Ask: Why do you think people like to travel? *(Students may mention curiosity, relaxation, or family bonds)* How are people different when traveling than when at home? *(Possible answer: They may be more adventurous; they may reinvent themselves a bit.)*

Before You Read

from *All God's Children Need Traveling Shoes*

Meet **Maya Angelou**

(born 1928)

How many careers can one person have? Maya Angelou has been a cook, waitress, singer, actor, and dancer. She was the first female African American streetcar conductor in San Francisco. During the 1960s, she was a coordinator for the Southern Christian Leadership Conference and a voice of the Civil Rights Movement. She was a television and movie star, as well as a political activist for women's rights. On top of all that, she is an award-winning author.

Six Autobiographies Born in St. Louis, Missouri, Angelou spent much of her childhood in rural, racially segregated Stamps, Arkansas. She wrote eloquently about this and other periods of her life in a series of six autobiographical books. *All God's Children Need Traveling Shoes* is the fifth in the series. It recounts Angelou's years in Ghana, where she enrolled her son in college.

> *"[Travel] can introduce the idea that if we try to understand each other, we may even become friends."*
>
> —Maya Angelou

Angelou began writing autobiographies when she returned home from Ghana. Although she never planned to write more than one volume, she published more and more books over the years. In addition to autobiographies, Angelou has published children's books, poetry, essays, plays, and film and television scripts.

On the Move Angelou has crossed the United States as well as other countries and continents to write, perform, appear on talk shows, receive honorary degrees, and fight for the rights of women and the underprivileged. A savvy traveler, Angelou speaks five languages in addition to English: Spanish, French, Italian, Arabic, and Fanti, a language spoken in Ghana. She knows that travel is not a cure for the world's problems, but she does think it has great potential for bringing people together.

Awards and Accomplishments Angelou has been honored in many ways. President Bill Clinton chose her to write and read a poem at his first inaugural ceremony in January 1993. Angelou was also chosen to write and read a poem for the fiftieth anniversary of the United Nations in 1995. She received the NAACP's Spingarn Medal in 1993.

LOG ON **Literature** Online

Author Search For more about Maya Angelou, go to glencoe.com and enter QuickPass code GL49787u2.

Selection Skills

from All God's Children Need Traveling Shoes

Literary Elements
- Narrative Essay (SE pp. 329–338)
- Author's Purpose (SE p. 338)

Listening/Speaking/Viewing Skills
- Analyze Art (SE p. 332; TE p. 334)
- Group Activity (SE p. 337)

Reading Skills
- Identify Problem and Solution (SE pp. 329–338)

Vocabulary Skills
- Synonyms (SE pp. 329, 338)

Writing Skills/Grammar
- Autobiographical Narrative (SE p. 339)
- Possessive Pronouns (SE p. 339)

Literature and Reading Preview

Connect to the Narrative Essay

How would you act if you were not sure you would be accepted among strangers? Freewrite for a few minutes about a time when you found yourself among strangers.

Build Background

This selection takes place in the 1960s in Ghana, a nation that lies on the coast of West Africa. When fifteenth-century explorers arrived in the region now known as Ghana, they found so much gold that they named it the Gold Coast. In 1957 the nation attained its independence and renamed itself Ghana.

Big Idea On the Move

As you read, ask yourself, What does Angelou learn and feel during her journey?

Literary Element Narrative Essay

A **narrative essay** is a nonfiction story. In this short form, authors present a real time and place, real people as characters, and events that actually happened. Often a narrative essay includes a central conflict or problem, as well as a climax and resolution. As you read, ask yourself, How do the elements of a narrative essay work together to tell a story?

Reading Strategy Identify Problem and Solution

When you **identify problem and solution,** you look for conflicts and problems and identify how they are or can be solved. This process can give you insight into a literary work and its characters. As you read, ask yourself, What problems arise as the narrator travels in Ghana and what solutions does she find?

Tip: Chart Problems and Solutions As you read, use a graphic organizer to chart problems and solutions.

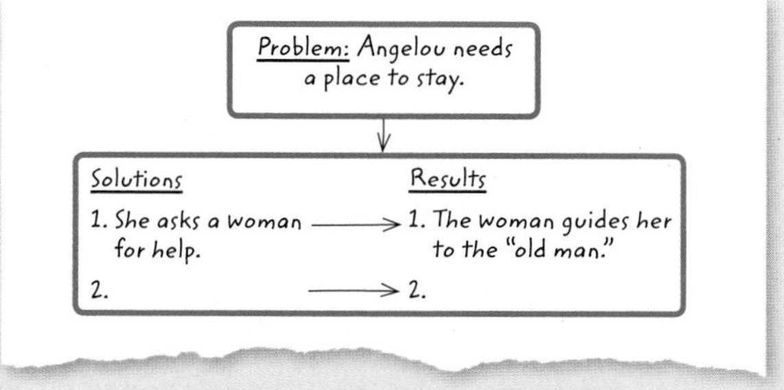

Problem: Angelou needs a place to stay.
Solutions
Results
1. She asks a woman for help.
1. The woman guides her to the "old man."
2.
2.

Learning Objectives

For pages 328–338

In studying this text, you will focus on the following objectives:

Literary Study: Analyzing narrative essay.

Reading: Identifying problem and solution.

Vocabulary

throng (thrông) *n.* a large number of people or things crowded together; p. 330 *Cars could not pass through the throng of tourists.*

pang (pang) *n.* a sudden sharp feeling of pain or distress; p. 331 *The woman felt a pang as she recalled the scene of the accident.*

suffuse (sə fūz′) *v.* to spread through or over; p. 331 *The smell of baking bread suffused the house.*

impervious (im pur′ vē əs) *adj.* incapable of being passed through, affected, or disturbed; p. 333 *The manager was impervious to the customer's complaints and refused to issue a refund.*

reverberate (ri vur′ bə rāt′) *v.* to echo; resound; p. 336 *The noise of the cars passing through the tunnel reverberated off its walls.*

Tip: Synonyms Paying attention to the differences between synonyms will help you communicate more clearly. For example, both *crowd* and *throng* refer to a large group of people. However, *crowd* suggests the people are close and pressed together while *throng* implies movement and pushing.

Before You Read

Focus

Summary

During her stay in Ghana, Maya Angelou is overcome with emotion at her thoughts about the slave dungeons. She stops overnight in the town of Dunkwa. A woman there brings her to a private home. She allows herself to be mistakenly identified as a Bambara from Liberia instead of an American and spends the night as an honored guest.

For summaries in languages other than English, see Unit 2 Teaching Resources Book, pp. 101–106.

Vocabulary

Use Context Clues Have students write sentences with context clues for each vocabulary word. Have them leave a blank for the vocabulary word and ask a partner to use the context clues to guess the correct vocabulary word to complete each sentence. Encourage students to use a variety of context clues, such as cause-effect, synonym, contrast, definition, and example. When partners are finished, have students identify their best sentences to share with the class.

Approaching Level

DIFFERENTIATED INSTRUCTION

Established Maya Angelou was raised in the southern United States at a time when the country was racially segregated. At that time, African Americans were not allowed to occupy the same public spaces—such as schools, restaurants, and public restrooms—as white Americans were.

Ask: How do you think it felt to be treated this way? Think of a single word to describe your feelings and explain why you chose that word.

For additional vocabulary practice, see Unit 2 Teaching Resources Book, p. 109.

For additional context, see Glencoe Visual Vocabulary CD-ROM.

Teach

Big Idea 1

On the Move **Ask:** What makes the narrator feel able to travel in the bush? *(She has plenty of money, she knows Fanti, the language of the bush, and she has a dependable car.)*

Literary Element 2

Narrative Essay **Possible answer:** *Ghana has a colorful, diverse culture.*

Cultural History ☆

Cape Coast, Ghana Historic Cape Coast has some of Ghana's best schools and museums. Cape Coast was the capital of the Gold Coast from 1700 to 1877.

For an audio recording of this selection, use Listening Library Audio CD-ROM.

Readability Scores

Dale-Chall: 7.4
DRP: 61
Lexile: 960

from All God's Children Need Traveling Shoes

Maya Angelou

Each morning Ghana's seven-and-one-half million people seemed to crowd at once into the capital city where the broad avenues as well as the unpaved rutted lanes became gorgeous with moving pageantry: bicycles, battered lorries, hand carts, American and European cars, chauffeur-driven limousines. People on foot struggled for right-of-way, white-collar workers wearing white knee-high socks brushed against market women balancing large baskets on their heads as they proudly swung their wide hips. Children, bright faces shining with palm oil, picked openings in the **throng**, and pretty young women in western clothes affected not to notice the attention they caused as they laughed together talking in the musical Twi language. Old men sat or stooped beside the road smoking homemade pipes and looking wise as old men have done eternally.

The too sweet aromas of flowers, the odors of freshly fried fish and stench from open sewers hung in my clothes and lay on my skin. Car horns blew, drums thumped. Loud radio music and the muddle of many languages shouted or murmured. I needed country quiet.

The Fiat was dependable, and I had a long weekend, money in my purse, and a working command of Fanti,[1] so I decided to travel into the bush. I bought roasted plantain stuffed with boiled peanuts, a quart of Club beer and headed my little car west. The stretch was a highway from Accra to Cape Coast,[2] filled with trucks and private cars passing from lane to lane with abandon. People hung out of windows of the crowded mammie lorries,[3] and I could hear singing and shouting when the drivers careened those antique vehicles up and down hills as if each was a little train out to prove it could.

Vocabulary

throng (thrông) *n.* a large number of people or things crowded together

1. *Fanti* (fan′ tē) is a dialect of Akan spoken by one of Ghana's many ethnic groups.
2. *Accra* is Ghana's capital and largest city; the town of *Cape Coast* is about 75 miles southwest of Accra.
3. *Mammie lorries* are small trucks or open-sided buses used for public transportation.

Narrative Essay *What do these details reveal about Ghana?*

Reading Practice

SPIRAL REVIEW **Imagery** Tell students that Angelou uses vivid details to create an image of Ghana on this page. Read the first paragraph aloud.
Ask: What are some vivid details in this paragraph? *(Students may note the following details: "unpaved rutted lane," "white-collar workers wearing white knee-high socks," "market women balancing large baskets on their heads as they proudly swung their wide hips," "bright faces shining with palm oil")* Have students jot down details as they read pages 330 and 331. Then ask for some examples of vivid imagery and write these responses on the board.

I stopped in Cape Coast only for gas. Although many black Americans had headed for the town as soon as they touched ground in Ghana, I successfully avoided it for a year. Cape Coast Castle and the nearby Elmina Castle[4] had been holding forts for captured slaves. The captives had been imprisoned in dungeons beneath the massive buildings, and friends of mine who had felt called upon to make the trek reported that they felt the thick stone walls still echoed with old cries.

The palm tree-lined streets and fine white stone buildings did not tempt me to remain any longer than necessary. Once out of the town and again onto the tarred roads, I knew I had not made a clean escape. Despite my hurry, history had invaded my little car. **Pangs** of self-pity and a sorrow for my unknown relatives **suffused** me. Tears made the highway waver and were salty on my tongue.

What did they think and feel, my grandfathers, caught on those green savannas, under the baobab trees? How long did their families search for them? Did the dungeon wall feel chilly and its slickness strange to my grandmothers, who were used to the rush of air against bamboo huts and the sound of birds rattling their grass roofs?

I had to pull off the road. Just passing near Cape Coast Castle had plunged me back into the eternal melodrama.[5]

There would be no purging,[6] I knew, unless I asked all the questions. Only then would the spirits understand that I was feeding them. It was a crumb, but it was all I had.

I allowed the shapes to come to my imagination: children passed tied together by ropes and chains, tears abashed, stumbling in dull exhaustion, then women, hair uncombed, bodies gritted with sand, and sagging in defeat. Men, muscles without memory, minds dimmed, plodding, leaving bloodied footprints in the dirt. The quiet was awful. None of them cried, or yelled, or bellowed. No moans came from them. They lived in a mute territory, dead to feeling and protest. These were the legions, sold by sisters, stolen by brothers, bought by strangers, enslaved by the greedy, and betrayed by history.

For a long time, I sat as in an open-air auditorium watching a troop of tragic players enter and exit the stage.

The visions faded as my tears ceased. Light returned and I started the car, turned off the main road, and headed for the interior. Using rutted track roads, and lanes a

Visual Vocabulary
Found mostly in tropical Africa, *baobab* (bā′ ō bab′) *trees* have very broad trunks, thick branches, and large white flowers. They grow well on *savannahs,* which are open grasslands with scattered trees and shrubs.

4. *Cape Coast Castle* and *Elmina Castle* are two slave-trade era fortifications. The castles' dungeons held thousands of captured men, women, and children in chains as they awaited export to North America as slaves. The United Nations has designated the buildings as World Heritage Monuments.

5. *[eternal melodrama]* Angelou compares the experience of slavery to a play that never fails to stir the emotions deeply.

6. A *purging* is a removal of something that is unclean or undesirable.

Vocabulary

pang (pang) *n.* a sudden sharp feeling of pain or distress

suffuse (se fūz′) *v.* to spread through or over

On the Move *What important connection came about because of this interruption in the narrator's journey?* **3**

Narrative Essay *What happens in the narrative at this point and how do you know that something has changed?* **4**

Teach

Big Idea 3

On the Move Answer: *The interruption helps the narrator connect with the experiences of the slaves and with her feelings about Cape Coast Castle's sad history.*

Literary Element 4

Narrative Essay Answer: *The narrator resumes her trip to the "bush" by starting her car decisively and turning off the main road. In addition, restarting her journey may be a metaphor for resolving the emotions that Cape Coast evoked in her.*

Approaching Level

DIFFERENTIATED INSTRUCTION

Emerging As they read page 331, help students better understand the sequence of events by having them note the following:

- The narrator stops for gas in Cape Coast.
- She pulls back onto the road.
- She wonders what her ancestors thought and felt.
- She pulls off the road.
- She imagines what her ancestors must have gone through.

Established Help students understand Angelou's language in the second-to-last paragraph on page 331. Explain that the "auditorium" is her imagination and "the troop of tragic players" are her ancestors as she sees them in her mind.

Teach

Reading Strategy 1

Analyze Character Have a volunteer read the last paragraph on this page. **Ask:** What does this paragraph tell you about the narrator *(She hopes to pass herself off as a native Ghanaian.)*

ENGLISH LEARNERS Ask English learners if they have ever felt the need to try to blend in with a different culture. Students should explain why or why not? *(Answers will vary.)*

View the Art ★

Possible answer: *The colors in* Small Town in Africa *make it seem as if the town is in an area where the weather is hot and breezy.*

Irish-born Rosemary Woods reflects her heritage in much of her artwork. She likes using rich colors.

Small Town in Africa. Rosemary Woods

View the Art Rosemary Woods used bold reds and oranges to depict this town in Africa. How do the colors affect your sense of place? ★

little larger than foot paths, I found the River Pra. The black water moving quietly, ringed with the tall trees, seemed enchanted. A fear of snakes kept me in the car, but I parked and watched the bright sun turn the water surface into a rippling cloth of lamé.[7] I passed through villages which were little more than collections of thatch huts, with goats and small children wandering in the lanes. The noise of my car brought smiling adults out to wave at me.

In the late afternoon, I reached the thriving town that was my destination. A student whom I had met at Legon had spoken to me often of the gold-mining area, of Dunkwa, his birthplace. His reports had so glowed with the town's virtues, and I had chosen that spot for my first journey.

My skin color, features, and the Ghana cloth I wore made me look like any young Ghanaian[8] woman. I could pass if I didn't talk too much. 1

7. *Lamé* (la mā′) is a fabric woven with metallic threads that give it a glittering appearance.

8. *Ghanaian* (gä′ nə yən)

Reading Practice

SPIRAL REVIEW **Making Inferences** Making inferences means figuring out what an author means but does not directly state. Authors often provide clues for readers to piece together. For example, the villagers find the idea of one person from Accra (one Nkran) amusing. Point out clues that explain their reaction, such as the meaning of the word *Nkran,* which suggests millions of occupants living and building dwellings together.

Ask: Explain the villagers' reaction? (If she is an "ant" from Nkran, it is funny to think she would be alone and without a dwelling.)

As usual, in the towns of Ghana, the streets were filled with vendors selling their wares of tinned pat milk, hot spicy Killi Willis (fried, ripe plantain chips), Pond's cold cream, and antimosquito incense rings. Farmers were returning home, children returning from school. Young boys grinned at mincing[9] girls and always there were the market women, huge and **impervious.** I searched for a hotel sign in vain and as the day lengthened, I started to worry. I didn't have enough gas to get to Koforidua, a large town northeast of Dunkwa, where there would certainly be hotels, and I didn't have the address of my student's family. I parked the car a little out of the town center and stopped a woman carrying a bucket of water on her head and a baby on her back.

"Good day." I spoke in Fanti, and she responded. I continued, "I beg you, I am a stranger looking for a place to stay."

She repeated, "Stranger?" and laughed. "You are a stranger? No. No."

To many Africans only whites could be strangers. All Africans belonged somewhere, to some clan. All Akan-speaking[10] people belong to one of eight blood lines (Abosua) and one of eight spirit lines (Ntoro).

I said, "I am not from here."

For a second fear darted in her eyes. There was the possibility that I was a witch or some unhappy ghost from the country of the dead. I quickly said, "I am from Accra." She gave me a good smile. "Oh, one Accra. Without a home." She laughed. The Fanti word *Nkran,* for which the capitol was named, means the large ant that builds ten-foot-high domes of red clay and lives with millions of other ants.

"Come with me." She turned quickly, steadying the bucket on her head, and led me between two corrugated tin shacks. The baby bounced and slept on her back, secured by the large piece of cloth wrapped around her body. We passed a compound where women were pounding the dinner foo foo[11] in wooden bowls.

The woman shouted, "Look what I have found. One Nkran has no place to sleep tonight." The women laughed and asked, "One Nkran? I don't believe it."

"Are you taking it to the old man?"

"Of course."

"Sleep well, alone, Nkran, if you can." My guide stopped before a small house. She put the water on the ground and told me to wait while she entered the house. She returned immediately followed by a man who rubbed his eyes as if he had just been awakened.

He walked close and peered hard at my face. "This is the Nkran?" The woman was adjusting the bucket on her head.

"Yes, Uncle. I have brought her." She looked at me, "Good-bye, Nkran. Sleep in peace. Uncle, I am going." The man said, "Go and come, child," and resumed studying my face. "You are not Ga." He was reading my features.

A few small children had collected around his knees. They could barely hold back their giggles as he interrogated me.

"Aflao?"[12]

9. The *mincing* girls are trying to appear dainty and refined.
10. *Akan* (ä′ kän′) is the language spoken in southern Ghana; Fanti is a dialect of Akan.
11. *Foo foo* is a dough made from mashed yams, plantains, or other starchy fruits.
12. Here and in the next few paragraphs, the man guesses at Angelou's ethnic group in the mistaken belief that she is a native West African.

2 Identify Problem and Solution *When do you first realize that the narrator is in trouble and how does she convey the significance of her predicament?*

Vocabulary

impervious (im pur′ vē əs) *adj.* incapable of being passed through, affected, or disturbed

Narrative Essay *What does the woman's response to the narrator suggest about her role in the narrative and the ensuing events?* **3**

Teach

Reading Strategy 2

Identify Problem and Solution **Answer:** *The first sign of trouble is that the narrator cannot find a hotel and begins "to worry." She explains that she is short on gas and does not know the address of her student's family. Listing these unavailable solutions heightens the narrator's problem.*

For additional practice using the reading skill or strategy, see Unit 2 Teaching Resources Book, p. 108.

Literary Element 3

Narrative Essay **Answer:** *The woman's command to come with her implies that she has a solution to the narrator's problem. The unclear nature of the woman's solution may deepen the narrator's unease even as it develops the narrative.*

Cultural History ☆

Agriculture The rich soil and favorable climate in Ghana allows farmers to grow several crops, including coffee beans, fruits, and vegetables for both domestic consumption and export. However, the most profitable export is the cocoa bean.

Approaching Level

DIFFERENTIATED INSTRUCTION

Established Help students understand figurative language on this page. Point out the phrase "fear darted in her eyes" on page 333 and explain that this is an example of personification.

Teach

Reading Strategy 1

Identify Problem and Solution **Answer:** *The narrator finds it difficult to explain her identity as an African American in a country where only white people are considered strangers. This difficulty is heightened by the man's unwillingness to let her speak and assumption that he can figure out her identity.*

APPROACHING For approaching level students, **ask:** Is it possible to tell what region a person is from by the way he or she speaks? Explain. *(Students may say that an accent, certain colloquialisms, or dialect might help to identify where a person is from.)*

View the Art ★

Tilly Willis paints landscapes, still lifes, and portraits. Her work has been published in various media, including cards, books, and prints. Much of Willis's art is influenced by her travels to Africa, Russia, and the Middle East.

Calabash Girls, 1991. Tilly Willis. Oil on canvas. Private collection. ★

I said, "No."

"Brong-ahafo?"

I said, "No. I am—." I meant to tell him the truth, but he said, "Don't tell me. I will soon know." He continued staring at me. "Speak more. I will know from your Fanti."

"Well, I have come from Accra and I need to rent a room for the night. I told that woman that I was a stranger . . ."

He laughed. "And you are. Now, I know. You are Bambara from Liberia. It is clear you are Bambara." He laughed again. "I always can tell. I am not easily fooled." He shook my hand. "Yes, we will find you a place for the night. Come." He touched a boy at his right. "Find Patience Aduah, and bring her to me."

The children laughed and all ran away as the man led me into the house. He pointed me to a seat in the neat little parlor and shouted, "Foriwa, we have a guest. Bring beer." A small black woman with an imperial air entered the room. Her knowing face told me that she had witnessed the scene in her front yard.

She spoke to her husband. "And, Kobina, did you find who the stranger was?" She walked to me. I stood and shook

1 Identify Problem and Solution *What are the complexities of the problem that the narrator has at this moment?*

Grammar Practice

SPIRAL REVIEW **Commas in a Series** Point out the following phrases from the selection: *My skin color, features, and the Ghana cloth . . .; . . . fried plantain, dukuno, shrimp, fish cakes, and more.* Explain that in a series of three or more items, a comma is used after each item except the last. Ask students to write five sentences demonstrating the correct use of commas in a series. Have volunteers write one of their sentences on the board.

her hand. "Welcome, stranger." We both laughed. "Now don't tell me, Kobina, I have ears, also. Sit down, Sister, beer is coming. Let me hear you speak."

We sat facing each other while her husband stood over us smiling. "You, Foriwa, you will never get it."

I told her my story, adding a few more words I had recently learned. She laughed grandly. "She is Bambara. I could have told you when Abaa first brought her. See how tall she is? See her head? See her color? Men, huh. They only look at a woman's shape."

Two children brought beer and glasses to the man who poured and handed the glasses around. "Sister, I am Kobina Artey; this is my wife Foriwa and some of my children."

I introduced myself, but because they had taken such relish in detecting my tribal origin I couldn't tell them that they were wrong. Or, less admirably, at that moment I didn't want to remember that I was an American. For the first time since my arrival, I was very nearly home. Not a Ghanaian, but at least accepted as an African. The sensation was worth a lie.

Voices came to the house from the yard. "Brother Kobina," "Uncle," "Auntie."

Foriwa opened the door to a group of people who entered speaking fast and looking at me.

"So this is the Bambara woman? The stranger?" They looked me over and talked with my hosts. I understood some of their conversation. They said that I was nice looking and old enough to have a little wisdom. They announced that my car was parked a few blocks away. Kobina told them that I would spend the night with the newlyweds, Patience and Kwame Duodu. Yes, they could see clearly that I was a Bambara.

"Give us the keys to your car, Sister; someone will bring your bag."

I gave up the keys and all resistance. I was either at home with friends, or I would die wishing that to be so.

Later, Patience, her husband, Kwame, and I sat out in the yard around a cooking fire near to their thatched house which was much smaller than the Artey bungalow. They explained that Kobina Artey was not a chief, but a member of the village council, and all small matters in that area of Dunkwa were taken to him. As Patience stirred the stew in the pot, which was balanced over the fire, children and women appeared sporadically out of the darkness carrying covered plates. Each time Patience thanked the bearers and directed them to the house, I felt the distance narrow between my past and present.

In the United States, during segregation, black American travelers, unable to stay in hotels restricted to white patrons, stopped at churches and told the black ministers or deacons of their predicaments. Church officials would select a home and then inform the unexpecting hosts of the decision. There was never a protest, but the new hosts relied on the generosity of their neighbors to help feed and even entertain their guests. After the travelers were settled, surreptitious knocks would sound on the back door.

In Stamps, Arkansas, I heard so often, "Sister Henderson, I know you've got guests. Here's a pan of biscuits."

"Sister Henderson, Mama sent a half a cake for your visitors."

---

2 Identify Problem and Solution *What problem is solved in this exchange with the Ghanaians, and what does this solution suggest about the narrator's sense of who she is?*

Identify Problem and Solution *In what ways is this statement a solution to the narrator's earlier problems?* **3**

Teach

Reading Strategy 2

Identify Problem and Solution Answer: *The narrator is accepted as an African. Her happiness at this suggests that she does not feel "at home" in her American identity.*

Reading Strategy 3

Identify Problem and Solution Answer: *She has solved her problems of needing a place to stay and of finding an African identity for herself.*

ENGLISH LEARNERS To assist English learners, review the explanation of the Reading Strategy on page 329.

English Learners

DIFFERENTIATED INSTRUCTION

Beginning/Early Intermediate Explain the use of the term "Sister" throughout the selection. Tell students that this is an example of dialect, or regional variety of a language with differences in vocabulary, grammar, and punctuation. Explain that Patience and her family consider the narrator to be one of their group—the group of Africans—and so they call her Sister. It does not mean that she is literally their sister. Point out the use of the word Sister in the first column of page 335 when the narrator tells about her time in Arkansas. Ask students to find another similar label used in the selection. *(Auntie)*

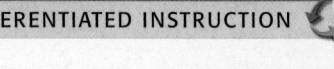

Teach

Big Idea 1

On the Move Answer: *She recognizes the generosity of the Ghanaians and relates it to hospitality in her Arkansas hometown, specifically, when families took in African Americans banned from hotels by segregation. Travel illuminates her past and connects the two cultures.*

Literary Element 2

Narrative Essay Answer: *She learned in her childhood the appropriate way to act in similar situations.*

Cultural History ☆

Food Corn, cassava, yams, and bananas are staples in most African regions. Groundnuts are the same as peanuts in the United States. Groundnut stew is made with okra, squash, groundnuts, and meat.

To check students' understanding of the selection, see Unit 2 Teaching Resources Book, p. 112.

"Sister Henderson, I made a lot of macaroni and cheese. Maybe this will help with your visitors."

My grandmother would whisper her thanks and finally when the family and guests sat down at the table, the offerings were so different and plentiful, it appeared that days had been spent preparing the meal.

Patience invited me inside, and when I saw the table I was confirmed in my earlier impression. Groundnut stew, garden egg stew, hot pepper soup, *kenke, kotomre,* fried plantain, *dukuno,* shrimp, fish cakes, and more, all crowded together on variously patterned plates.

In Arkansas, the guests would never suggest, although they knew better, that the host had not prepared every scrap of food, especially for them.

I said to Patience, "Oh, Sister, you went to such trouble."

She laughed, "It is nothing, Sister. We don't want our Bambara relative to think herself a stranger anymore. Come, let us wash and eat."

After dinner I followed Patience to the outdoor toilet, then they gave me a cot in a very small room.

In the morning I wrapped my cloth under my arms, sarong fashion, and walked with Patience to the bathhouse. We joined about twenty women in a walled enclosure that had no ceiling. The greetings were loud and cheerful as we soaped ourselves and poured buckets of water over our shoulders.

1 On the Move *How does the narrator's description of her meal at Dunkwa reveal the importance of travel to her?*

Patience introduced me. "This is our Bambara sister."

"She's a tall one all right. Welcome, Sister."

"I like her color."

"How many children, Sister?"

I apologized, "I only have one."

"One?"

"One?"

"One!" Shouts **reverberated** over the splashing water. I said, "One, but I'm trying."

They laughed. "Try hard, sister. Keep trying."

We ate leftovers from the last night feast and I said a sad good-bye to my hosts. The children walked me back to my car with the oldest boy carrying my bag. I couldn't offer money to my hosts, Arkansas had taught me that, but I gave change to the children. They bobbed and jumped and grinned.

"Good-bye, Bambara Auntie."

"Go and come, Auntie."

"Go and come."

I drove into Cape Coast before I thought of the gruesome castle and out of its environs before the ghosts of slavery caught me. Perhaps their attempts had been halfhearted. After all, in Dunkwa, although I let a lie speak for me, I had proved that one of their descendants, at least one, could just briefly return to Africa, and that despite cruel betrayals, bitter ocean voyages, and hurtful centuries, we were still recognizable. ᔓ

Narrative Essay *How has the narrator's past helped her act appropriately in the present?* **2**

Vocabulary

reverberate (ri vur′ bə rāt′) *v.* to echo; resound

Grammar Practice

SPIRAL REVIEW **Modifiers** Remind students that modifiers are descriptive words—adjectives and adverbs—that make the picture more clear in the reader's mind. **Write:** The cat slept in the sun. **Ask:** What do you picture when you read that sentence? **Write:** The large gray cat slept peacefully in the sun. **Ask:** Now what do you see?

Point out that *large* and *gray* are adjectives that modify *cat* and *peacefully* is an adverb that modifies *slept.* Have students write sentences using modifiers and share their sentences with the class.

After You Read

Respond and Think Critically

Respond and Interpret

1. Which emotion described in this selection could you relate to most? What specifically about the writing evokes this emotion?
2. (a)Describe what happened when Angelou pulled her car off the road after passing Cape Coast Castle. (b)What issues and emotions might Cape Coast Castle raise for her?
3. (a)What nationality do Kobina and Foriwa think Angelou is? What reason does she offer for not correcting them? (b)What unspoken reasons might Angelou have for not correcting her hosts when they misidentify her?
4. (a)What does Angelou feel that she proved in Dunkwa? (b)How do you think this resolution relates to her experience at Cape Coast Castle at the beginning of her journey?

Analyze and Evaluate

5. (a)How does the discussion of Cape Coast Castle introduce a new mood in this selection? (b)How well does Angelou succeed in creating this mood here and elsewhere in the selection?
6. How is the information about Stamps, Arkansas, important in the story of Angelou's travels?

Connect

7. **Big Idea** On the Move Do you think traveling to Dunkwa was the only way Angelou could have quieted the "ghosts of slavery"? Explain.
8. **Connect to the Author** Based on what you know from the biography on page 328 and the essay, why do you think it was important to Angelou to be seen as a Ghanaian woman?

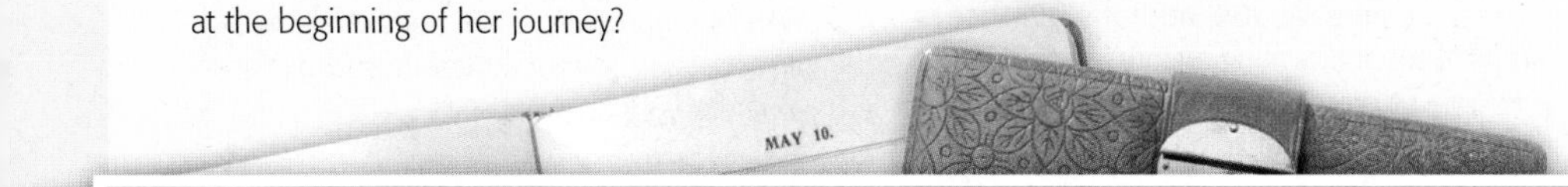

Daily Life & Culture

Life in Rural Ghana

In Ghana in the 1960s, most people lived in towns and villages that did not yet have electricity. Dirt roads and waterways connected them. In the greener, wealthier south, picturesque villages sat beneath trees and were surrounded by banana groves and coconut palms. In the dryer, poorer north, mud huts baked in the hot sun. In the villages and towns, women and girls carried water in buckets or pots, sometimes on their heads, from nearby streams or pipes; did washing by hand; pounded maize, cassava, and other starchy fruits and vegetables using a heavy mortar and pestle; and cooked over an open fire in the courtyard.

Group Activity Work with classmates to discuss and answer the following questions.

1. How full or complete a picture do you get of life and culture in Ghana in the early 1960s from Angelou's essay?
2. What do you learn from this feature about daily life and culture that is not stated in Angelou's essay?

After You Read

Assess

1. Possible answers: Her pain and anger about slavery or her feelings of warmth and closeness toward the villagers; she evokes emotion by showing that travel illuminates critical aspects of identity and home.
2. (a) She has a vision of the slaves at the castle. (b) Feelings of fear, anger, and sadness
3. (a) Bambara from Liberia; they were proud of figuring it out (b) she wanted to be seen as an African; she did not wish to be seen as American.
4. (a) The descendant of an African slave could return to Africa as an African. (b) The villagers give her a positive image to balance the negative one of African slaves.
5. (a) Her tears create a mood of pain and sadness. (b) She succeeds well. She creates a somber mood, shifts to buoyancy in Dunkwa, and then recalls the somber mood in the last lines.
6. It shows that hospitality in the two places is alike. The references connect the past and present, and Angelou's ancestors and present-day hosts.
7. Possible answer: Balancing the castle with a good experience helps her quiet the ghosts. She might have resolved her feelings by studying slavery at home.
8. She wants to be African and reclaim some of her stolen heritage.

Daily Life & Culture

1. The selection of details is not a complete picture, but readers can learn a lot about the city and country people.
2. Students should note they learn about the simple living conditions, including details about housing, cooking, and washing clothes.

After You Read

Assess

Literary Element

1. A is the correct answer. The author describes the bustling city life of Ghana before setting out on her journey.
2. H is the correct answer. As a result of the warm welcome she receives from perfect strangers, Angelou understands that she is one of their descendants.

Progress Check

Can students define narrative essay?

If No → See Unit 2 Teaching Resources Book, p. 107.

Review: Author's Purpose

One main idea is centered on the busy city streets. Another main idea addresses what happened at the castle. A third main idea is concerned with the author and how she is like and unlike Ghanaian women. The author's purpose is to inform.

Vocabulary Practice

1. d **2.** b **3.** e **4.** c **5.** a

Academic Vocabulary

Sample answer: Hotels, motels, campgrounds, and hostels are some of the places that are often available for travelers to stay at.

Literary Element Narrative Essay

ACT Skills Practice

1. The description of Accra fills what role in this narrative?

   A. exposition
   B. rising action
   C. climax
   D. resolution

2. The resolution of this essay might BEST be identified as the author's:

   F. inability to tell the truth about her origins.
   G. memory of her days as a girl in Stamps, Arkansas.
   H. feeling of kinship with the people of Ghana.
   J. happy dinner party with her hosts.

Review: Author's Purpose

As you learned on page 269, **author's purpose** is the author's intent in writing a story. Authors often write for one or more of these purposes: to inform, to explain, to entertain, or to describe.

Partner Activity With a partner, discuss Angelou's purpose in writing this selection. Make a diagram like the one below. List three important points or ideas of the essay. Draw a conclusion about her purpose based on the details.

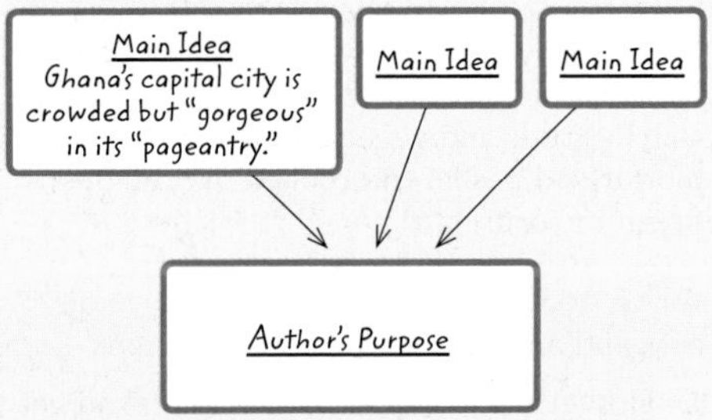

LOG ON Literature Online

Selection Resources For Selection Quizzes, eFlashcards, and Reading-Writing Connection activities, go to glencoe.com and enter QuickPass code GL49787u2.

Reading Strategy Identify Problem and Solution

In Angelou's narrative essay, some of the **problems and solutions** lead to new problems and solutions, creating a chain of events. Review the list of problems and solutions you created while reading this essay and note which solutions led to new problems.

1. Which problems and solutions in this essay appear to lead to new problems?
2. In what way is the problem-solution structure of this essay related to the Big Idea of being "On the Move"? Use events from the narrative to support your answer.

Vocabulary Practice

Practice with Synonyms A **synonym** is a word that has the same or nearly the same meaning as another word. With a partner, match each boldfaced vocabulary word below with its synonym. You will not use all the answer choices. Use a thesaurus or dictionary to check your answers.

1. throng
2. pang
3. suffuse
4. impervious
5. reverberate

a. echo
b. twinge
c. resistant
d. multitude
e. permeate
f. wither
g. commanding

Academic Vocabulary

*When Angelou first arrives in Dunkwa, there is no place **available** for her to stay.*

If a place or a thing is *available,* you could say that it is "present and ready." So when the villager prepared and offered her home to Angelou, there was finally some place **available** for Angelou to stay. What kinds of places are often **available** for travelers to stay?

For more on academic vocabulary, see pages 54–55 and R79–R81.

Reading Strategy

1. Seeking a hotel: new problem of having to explain her identity; identified as a Bambara: new problem of not wanting to correct the proud host; giving up car keys: new problem of being at host's mercy; driving past Castle: new problem of emotions.
2. Being "on the move" entails difficulties, such as running out of gas, needing a place to stay, or searching for identity. It also brings solutions: getting past the castle literally and metaphorically, and feeling at home in Ghana.

Respond Through Writing

Autobiographical Narrative

Learning Objectives

In this assignment, you will focus on the following objectives:

Writing: Writing an autobiographical narrative.

Grammar: Understanding how to use possessive pronouns.

Apply Flashback Angelou expects to have no problem finding a place to stay in Dunkwa, but it proves to be difficult. Write an autobiographical narrative of at least 1,500 words about a time you encountered an unexpected problem and needed help from someone else to find a solution. Use flashback to structure your narrative.

Understand the Task In an **autobiographical narrative,** the author tells a true story about his or her own life. This nonfiction format uses real life events, places, and people for the story's plot, setting, and character. A **flashback** interrupts the chronological order of a narrative to describe an event that happened earlier.

Prewrite Think of an experience involving an unexpected problem. Choose something that would make a good narrative. Use a graphic organizer similar to the one on page 329 to lay out the main problem and attempted solutions that you will build your narrative around.

Draft Using your organizer as a guide, write a draft of your narrative. Begin your draft in the present and set up the story from your current point of view. Then, use a flashback to jump back to the time in which the problem occurred. Structure your narrative around flashbacks—telling most of the story in the past, and occasionally returning to the present to comment on the events from your perspective now.

Revise As you revise your draft, make sure it is clear where and when the action in the flashbacks takes place. Add details to the setting to make your flashbacks more concrete. In addition, enhance your character descriptions in the flashbacks with sensory details that describe appearance, actions, gestures, and other concrete elements. Add more depth by using interior monologue. Although it is part of the flashback, the interior monolgue shows what you were thinking in the actual moment, so it should be written in present tense.

After finishing your revision, check your essay against your organizer and make sure all of the ideas and events have been fleshed out in the narrative.

Edit and Proofread Proofread your paper, correcting any errors in grammar, spelling, and punctuation. Use the Grammar Tip in the side column to help you with possessive pronouns.

Grammar Tip

Possessive Pronouns

Possessive pronouns show ownership. They take the place of possessive nouns and can be singular (such as *my, his, hers*) or plural (such as *our, ours, their*).

We sat facing each other while her *husband stood over us smiling.*

In this sentence from Angelou's essay, the possessive pronoun *her* replaces the possessive noun "the woman's." Possessive pronouns are frequently misused. Check the usage in your essay, identifying possessive pronouns and the nouns they replace.

English Learners

DIFFERENTIATED INSTRUCTION

Intermediate Expand on the discussion of pronouns on this page. Tell students that a pronoun and its subject must agree in number—a singular subject needs a singular pronoun and a plural subject needs a plural pronoun. **Write:** Each of the students know their locker combination.

Explain the error in this sentence: The subject of the sentence *(each)* is singular and the pronoun in the sentence *(their)* is plural. Have the students revise the sentence. *(Each of the students knows his or her locker combination.)* Point out that the following revision is also correct: *All of the students know their locker combinations.*

After You Read

Assess

Respond Through Writing

Students' narratives should:

- recount an unexpected problem and a solution involving someone else's help
- present the story in a narrative form using elements such as plot, setting, and character
- use flashback to structure the narrative
- use interior dialogue to reveal their thoughts during the events

A student who meets all of these criteria should receive the equivalent of a 4-point response.

A student who fully meets two or partially meets three of these criteria should receive the equivalent of a 3-point response.

A student who fully meets one or partially meets two of these criteria should receive the equivalent of a 2-point response.

A student who partially meets one of these criteria should receive the equivalent of a 1-point response.

For grammar practice, see Unit 2 Teaching Resources Book, p. 111.

To create custom assessments online, go to Progress Reporter Online Assessment.

Before You Read

Focus

Bellringer Option

Daily Language Practice Transparency 33

Or show students a picture of a field of flowers, and ask them to write a short descriptive paragraph about it. Then, show a close-up picture of one flower, and have them write a short descriptive paragraph. Finally, show the first picture again.

Say: Just imagine that every flower in the field has just as much detail as the close-up picture. In "Walking," Hogan asks readers to stop and closely study our natural world.

Before You Read

Walking

Meet **Linda Hogan**

(born 1947)

"We want to live as if there is no other place, as if we will always be here."

—Linda Hogan

Inspired by her Chickasaw heritage, Linda Hogan holds a deep belief in the sacredness of all living things. An award-winning poet, novelist, playwright, and essayist, Hogan writes eloquently about the beauty of the natural world and the need to respect and preserve the environment.

Sharing a Culture and Heritage Linda Hogan was born in Denver, Colorado, in 1947. She received her degree in English and creative writing in 1978 from the University of Boulder. She soon went on to become poet-in-the-schools for the states of Colorado and Oklahoma. In her mid-thirties, Hogan began teaching Native American Studies, and she is currently a professor at the University of Colorado at Boulder. As evidence of her devotion to nature, Hogan also spends time volunteering at a Wildlife Rehabilitation Clinic.

Writing in the Voice of Ancestors Over the course of her career Hogan has become one of the most accomplished Native American writers of her generation. She began her literary career while serving as a poet-in-the-schools, publishing the chapbook *Calling Myself Home*. Like much of her writing, these first poems evoked her Indian heritage. She has since published four other collections of poems *Eclipse* (1983), *Seeing Through the Sun* (1985), *Savings* (1988), and *The Book of Medicines* (1993).

In addition to writing poetry, Hogan is an acclaimed novelist. Her first novel *Mean Spirit* (1990)—about American Indian communities in Oklahoma in the 1920s—was nominated for a Pulitzer Prize. She followed it up with her novel *Solar Storms* (1995), which explores another ancestral journey.

The following essay is from Hogan's first nonfiction collection, *Dwellings: A Spiritual History of the Living World* (1995). The collection explores the idea that people "dwell" on earth and how our relationship with the planet's other creatures and elements is an important part of our daily lives.

LOG ON **Literature** Online

Author Search For more about Linda Hogan, go to glencoe.com and enter QuickPass code GL49787u2.

Selection Skills

Walking

Literary Elements
- Descriptive Essay (SE pp. 341, 342, 345)
- Setting (SE p. 345)

Listening/Speaking/Viewing Skills
- Analyze Art (SE p. 344)

Reading Skills
- Visualize (SE pp. 341, 344, 346)
- Personification (TE p. 342)

Vocabulary Skills
- Word Usage (SE pp. 341, 346)
- Synonyms and Antonyms (TE p. 341)

Writing Skills/Grammar
- Write a Descriptive Essay (SE p. 346)

Literature and Reading Preview

Connect to the Descriptive Essay

What about nature do you find most interesting or inspiring? List several elements of nature that inspire or intrigue you and explain why you are interested in them.

Build Background

Sunflowers have showy yellow blossoms and may grow up to fifteen feet tall. A sunflower's head may reach a diameter of more than one foot and produce thousands of seeds. Wild sunflowers grow in meadows, on hillsides, and in gullies along roads and highways throughout the United States.

Set Purposes for Reading

Big Idea On the Move

As you read the essay "Walking," ask yourself, Why did Hogan's walks through natural landscapes cause her to reflect on larger things?

Literary Element Descriptive Essay

Descriptive essays use carefully selected details to help readers picture an object or place. In this essay, Hogan uses vivid details to describe her observations of nature. Many of these details are sensory details, words that convey experiences of the sense, such as seeing, hearing, touching, tasting, and smelling. As you read this essay, ask yourself, Which sensory details have the most impact or leave the deepest impression?

Reading Strategy Visualize

Visualizing is picturing a writer's ideas or descriptions in your mind's eye. Visualizing can help you better understand what an author is trying to show you or tell you. It also can help you to remember what you read. As you read this excerpt, ask yourself, Which images and descriptions are the easiest to visualize?

Tip: Sketch As you read, pause to visualize the descriptions presented by Hogan. Jot down quick sketches of what you see in your mind's eye.

Learning Objectives

For pages 340–346

In studying this text, you will focus on the following objectives:

Literary Study: Analyzing a descriptive essay.

Reading: Visualizing.

Writing: Applying imagery and sensory details in a descriptive essay.

Vocabulary

elemental (el′ ə ment′ əl) *adj.* of or like the forces of nature; ancient and powerful; p. 342 *The giant full moon looming above us was an elemental presence.*

diverse (di vurs′) *adj.* markedly different; varied; p. 342 *Dining options in our neighborhood are diverse; we can have food from a different culture every night.*

evade (i vād′) *v.* to escape or avoid, often by cleverness; p. 343 *The cat evaded the dog by sneaking into a small pipe.*

communal (kə mūn′əl) *adj.* belonging to a community, society, or group; common; shared; p. 343 *The communal pool is open to all residents of the town.*

audible (ô′ də bəl) *adj.* loud enough to be heard; p. 343 *Her voice was barely audible over the sounds of the busy traffic.*

Tip: Word Usage The vocabulary words *elemental* and *communal* both have *-al* endings. This helps indicate they are adjective forms of nouns (*element* and *community*).

Before You Read

Focus

Summary

In her essay "Walking," Linda Hogan describes her nature walks and explains a life lesson she learned from closely watching the growth of a sunflower over a summer. Hogan comes to the conclusion that nature has a language of its own that human beings can hear if they take the time to listen to the natural world around them.

For summaries in languages other than English, see Unit 2 Teaching Resources Book, pp. 114–119.

Vocabulary

Synonyms and Antonyms Organize students into pairs, and have them look up synonyms and antonyms for each new vocabulary word. Then have the students test one another to guess the vocabulary word by its synonym or antonym.

For additional vocabulary practice, see Unit 2 Teaching Resources Book, p. 122.

For additional context, see Glencoe Visual Vocabulary CD-ROM.

Approaching Level

DIFFERENTIATED INSTRUCTION

Emerging In the essay "Walking," Hogan allows readers to share the experiences of her ritual nature walks and explains why they are important. **Ask:** What rituals do you have that are important to you? What experiences have you had that might be interesting to others? Have students write a paragraph in which they explain an important ritual or interesting experience. Remind students to use descriptive language in their essays. Then invite volunteers to share their essays with the class.

Teach

Literary Element 1

Descriptive Essay Answer: *Just as the plant is getting started growing, so is the author's essay.*

ADVANCED For advanced students, point out the opening line "It began in dark and underground weather." **Ask:** How does the narrator know this information? *(The growth process can be inferred; the narrator is omniscient)*

For additional literary element practice, see Unit 2 Teaching Resources Book, p. 120.

For an audio recording of this selection, use Listening Library Audio CD-ROM.

Readability Scores

Dale-Chall: 6.4
DRP: 56
Lexile: 1060

Walking

Linda Hogan

It began in dark and underground weather, a slow hunger moving toward light. It grew in a dry gulley beside the road where I live, a place where entire hillsides are sometimes yellow, windblown tides of sunflower plants. But this plant was different. It was alone and larger than the countless others that had established their lives farther up the hill. This one was a traveler, a settler, and like a dream beginning in conflict, it grew where the land had been disturbed.

I saw it first in early summer. It was a green and sleeping bud, raising itself toward the sun. Ants worked around the unopened bloom, gathering aphids and sap. A few days later, it was a tender young flower, soft and new, with a pale green center and a troop of silver-gray insects climbing up and down the stalk.

Over the summer this sunflower grew into a plant of incredible beauty, turning its face daily toward the sun in the most subtle of ways, the black center of it dark and alive with a deep blue light, as if flint had sparked an **elemental** fire there, in community with rain, mineral, mountain air, and sand.

As summer changed from green to yellow there were new visitors daily, the lace-winged insects, the bees whose legs were fat with pollen, and grasshoppers with their clattering wings and desperate hunger. There were other lives I missed, those too small or hidden to see. It was as if this plant with its host of lives was a society, one in which moment by moment, depending on light and moisture, there was great and **diverse** change.

1 Descriptive Essay *Why is this description appropriate at the beginning of an essay?*

Vocabulary

elemental (el′ ə ment′ əl) *adj.* of or like the forces of nature; ancient and powerful

diverse (di vurs′) *adj.* markedly different; varied

Literary Practice

SMALL GROUP SPIRAL REVIEW **Personification** Writers use many tools to draw readers into a story. One of these tools is personification, or giving human traits to nonhuman objects. Explain this literary device to students and give some examples, such as "the grass danced in the breeze." Then group students and challenge them to find examples of personification in the story.

Say: This story is mostly about a sunflower and the things that happen to it. The sunflower is not a person, but the author views it, and other plants, as humanlike. Then review some of the examples of personification found by the students. These examples may include the suggestion that bamboo has an "inner language" or that the redwood forest has a kind of heartbeat.

There were changes in the next larger world around the plant as well. One day I rounded a bend in the road to find the disturbing sight of a dead horse, black and still against a hillside, eyes rolled back. Another day I was nearly lifted by a wind and sandstorm so fierce and hot that I had to wait for it to pass before I could return home. On this day the faded dry petals of the sunflower were swept across the land. That was when the birds arrived to carry the new seeds to another future.

In this one plant, in one summer season, a drama of need and survival took place. Hungers were filled. Insects coupled. There was escape, exhaustion, and death. Lives touched down a moment and were gone.

I was an outsider. I only watched. I never learned the sunflower's golden language or the tongues[1] of its citizens. I had a small understanding, nothing more than a shallow observation of the flower, insects, and birds. But they knew what to do, how to live. An old voice from somewhere, gene or cell, told the plant how to **evade** the pull of gravity and find its way upward, how to open. It was instinct, intuition, necessity. A certain knowing directed the seed-bearing birds on paths to ancestral homelands they had never seen. They believed it. They followed.

There are other summons and calls, some even more mysterious than those commandments to birds or those survival journeys of insects. In bamboo plants, for instance, with their thin green canopy of light and golden stalks that creak in the wind. Once a century, all of a certain kind of bamboo flower on the same day. Neither the plants' location, in Malaysia or in a greenhouse in Minnesota, nor their age or size make a difference. They flower. Some current of an inner language passes among them, through space and separation, in ways we cannot explain in our language. They are all, somehow, one plant, each with a share of **communal** knowledge.

John Hay, in *The Immortal Wilderness,* has written: "There are occasions when you can hear the mysterious language of the Earth, in water, or coming through the trees, emanating[2] from the mosses, seeping through the undercurrents of the soil, but you have to be willing to wait and receive."

Sometimes I hear it talking. The light of the sunflower was one language, but there are others more **audible**. Once, in the redwood forest, I heard a beat, something like a drum or heart coming from the ground and trees and wind. That underground current stirred a kind of knowing inside me, a kinship and longing, a dream barely remembered that disappeared back to the body. Another time, there was the booming voice of an ocean storm thundering from far out at sea, telling about what lived in the distance, about the rough water that would arrive, wave after wave revealing the disturbance at center.

Tonight I walk. I am watching the sky. I think of the people who came before me and how they knew the placement of stars in the sky, watched the moving sun long and hard enough to witness how a certain angle of light touched a stone only once a year. Without written records, they knew

---

1. Here, *tongues* means "languages."

2 **On the Move** *How does Hogan's description evoke a sense of movement?*

Vocabulary

evade (i vād′) *v.* to escape or avoid, often by cleverness

2. *Emanating* means "coming, issuing, or flowing from."

Vocabulary

communal (kə mūn′əl) *adj.* belonging to a community, society, or group; common; shared

audible (ô′də bəl) *adj.* loud enough to be heard

Teach

Big Idea 2

On the Move **Answer:** *The surroundings change and become like different places, as if you are physically traveling to different locations.*

Advanced Learners

DIFFERENTIATED INSTRUCTION

Analyze Title **Ask:** How does this title fit with the events in the story? How is the idea of "walking" related to the growing plants? Allow students to develop some theories about the title. Students may reply that the title comes from the writer's walking around the hills and forests, watching the plants.

Ask students if they feel the title works well with the content of the story. If they think so, have them explain why. If not, ask for suggestions for alternate titles. *(Students may say a title like "Sunflower's Soul" better shows the life and spirit of the plant, or "Thoughts on a Flower" might better reflect the writer's part in the story.)*

Teach

Reading Strategy 1

Visualize Answer: *It is almost as if you are flying from location to location, traveling in mind and through the air between the different places that Hogan has described earlier.*

Big Idea 2

On the Move Answer: *They might have wanted her to take some time to observe the wonders in the world around her and see how she is a part of the wonder.*

APPROACHING For approaching-level students, **ask:** Who do you think appreciates nature more, you or your ancestors? *(Answers will vary. Students should support their answers.)*

View the Art ★

Answer: *The painting captures what Hogan typically sees, "tides of sunflower plants." However, she describes one specific, isolated sunflower that she encounters.*

To check students' understanding of the selection, see Unit 2 Teaching Resources Book, p. 125.

Sunflowers. Frederick John Pym Gore. Christie's, London.

View the Art How well does this painting capture the sight Linda Hogan encountered? ★

the gods of every night, the small, fine details of the world around them and of immensity above them.

Walking, I can almost hear the redwoods beating. And the oceans are above me here, rolling clouds, heavy and dark, considering snow. On the dry, red road, I pass the place of the sunflower, that dark and secret location where creation took place. I wonder if it will return this summer, if it will multiply and move up to the other stand of flowers in a territorial struggle.

It's winter and there is smoke from the fires. The square, lighted windows of houses are fogging over. It is a world of elemental attention, of all things working together, listening to what speaks in the blood. Whichever road I follow, I walk in the land of many gods, and they love and eat one another. Walking, I am listening to a deeper way. Suddenly all my ancestors are behind me. Be still, they say. Watch and listen. You are the result of the love of thousands.

1 Visualize *How does Hogan's language help you visualize her walk?*

On the Move *Why might Hogan imagine her ancestors would tell her to be still?* 2

Writing Practice

Poetry Ask students to think about a time when they enjoyed an experience with nature. Encourage students to think of times they have gone on vacation or on an outing with a family member or friend. Memories might lead them to also think about a time at the beach, fishing on a lake, or hiking with a friend. Let them know that their experience could also be linked to a place closer to home such as a local park or even their very own back yard. Have students write a poem about a time they experienced a connection with nature.

After You Read

Respond and Think Critically

Respond and Interpret

1. What image or description in this essay did you find most powerful? Explain.
2. (a)Name two things that impress Hogan about the sunflower she sees along her walk. (b)What do these things suggest about Hogan herself?
3. (a)What disturbing sight does Hogan find one day after rounding the bend in the road? (b)How does this image contrast with the image of sunflowers?
4. (a)What season does Hogan describe at the end of the essay? (b)In your own words, explain what Hogan is saying in the last paragraph of this essay.

Analyze and Evaluate

5. Why do you think Hogan chooses to talk about bamboo even though she did not encounter it in her walks?
6. Do you think the sunflower is the image that best reflects Hogan's message? Or do you think one of the other images, such as the bamboo, redwoods, or ocean should have been the main image? Explain.

Connect

7. **Big Idea** On the Move Based on Hogan's essay, why do you think it would be good to experience a variety of natural environments?
8. **Connect to the Author** In your opinion, why does Hogan think of her ancestors as she walks?

Literary Element Descriptive Essay

A **descriptive essay** gives a carefully detailed portrayal of a place or a thing. Writers often use sensory details in their description to help readers understand what something looks like, sounds like, and feels like.

1. List four descriptive details that help you picture the sunflower. What do you find interesting or evocative about the details?
2. What details does Hogan use to describe the bamboo?
3. What details does she use to convey winter?

Review: Setting

As you learned on pages 8–9, **setting** is the time and place in which the events of a work occur. In addition to a place's physical characteristics, setting also includes the history, customs, and values of the people who live there.

Partner Activity With a classmate, discuss this essay's natural setting and the Native Americans who once lived there. What inferences can you make about what that lifestyle would have been like? With your partner, create a chart like the one shown. List details about the setting in the first column. Then record your inferences in the second column.

Details	Inferences
They could read the stars in the sky.	The nights must have been dark and peaceful.

LOG ON **Literature** Online

Selection Resources For Selection Quizzes, eFlashcards, and Reading-Writing Connection activities, go to glencoe.com and enter QuickPass code GL49787u2.

After You Read

Assess

Respond and Think Critically

1. Answers may vary. Students should support their answers with information from the text.
2. (a) It rose towards the sun on its own, and it supported an entire community of creatures. (b) This shows that she admires the power of nature to thrive on its own, or that she appreciates the interaction between different elements of nature.
3. (a) She finds a dead horse along the hillside. (b) This image contrasts the life shown by the sunflower and reminds us that the natural world includes both life and death.
4. (a) Winter (b) She is talking about links connecting all forms of life.
5. It is an example of how mysterious nature is, and how other living things communicate in ways we cannot understand.
6. Answers may vary. Students should support their answers with information from the text.
7. Sample answer: Experiencing different environments can help you understand nature's power and diversity. It can broaden your perspective of the universe by spurring new thoughts.
8. Sample answer: She thinks of her ancestors because these are the same kinds of walks, paths, and views that they might have had themselves centuries ago; and she becomes aware of the roles of those who came before her.

Literary Element

1. Sample answer: It grew in a dry gully; it began as a "green and sleeping bud"; it grew into a plant of incredible beauty; it was "alive with a deep blue light." The black center actually seeming to glow a deep blue is the most interesting detail about the sunflower.
2. She says the bamboo is a "thin green canopy of light and stalks that creak in the wind." And she details how they all flower together, at all ages and places, on the same day every 100 years.
3. She conveys winter by detailing smoke from fires and square lighted windows fogging over.

Review: Setting

Students' chart should list details from the story and inferences made from those details.

After You Read

Assess

Reading Strategy

1. Students might identify images of sunflowers, insects on flowers or flying, bamboo trees, the stars in the night sky, redwood trees, an ocean storms, waves, a dirt road, and a small town in winter.
2. Answers may vary.

Progress Check

Can students explain the Reading Strategy?

If No → See Unit 2 Teaching Resources Book, p. 121.

Vocabulary

1. Because it is one of the most basic substances and is essential for life.
2. It would contain a wide variety of flowers and vegetables.
3. Sample answer: I would sneak down an alley if I were trying to evade someone.
4. People need to share with each other and live among each other.
5. Sample answer: A whisper is barely audible.

Write with Style

Students' essays should

- open by clearly describing the place that they will be writing about
- use sensory details
- present creative, engaging descriptions
- reflect their personality in the writing

For grammar practice, see Unit 2 Teaching Resources Book, p. 124.

Reading Strategy Visualize

Visualizing is one of the best ways to understand and remember information in an essay. Review the sketches that you visualized, then answer these questions.

1. What pictures or images would you include in a video depicting Hogan's walks?
2. As you recall the essay, which images are most memorable? Why?

Vocabulary Practice

Practice with Word Usage Respond to these statements to help you explore the meanings of vocabulary words from the selection.

1. Why would water be considered **elemental?**
2. What would a **diverse** garden contain?
3. Where might you go if you were trying to **evade** someone?
4. What do people need to do to take part in **communal** living?
5. Describe a sound that is barely **audible.**

Academic Vocabulary

*The **scope** of this essay ranges across time and generations.*

Scope is an academic word that refers to the extent of one's perceptions, thoughts, or actions. To study this word further, fill out the graphic organizer below.

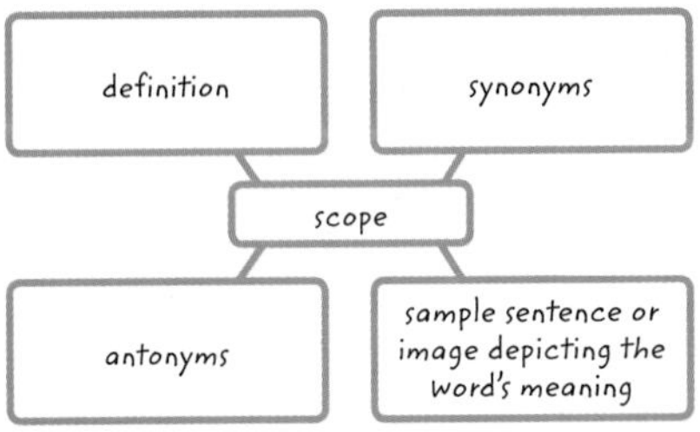

For more on academic vocabulary, see pages 54–55 and R79–R81.

Write with Style

Apply Imagery and Sensory Details

Assignment Think of a place that you know well and can picture easily in your mind. Write a descriptive essay about the place using strong imagery and sensory details.

Get Ideas Once you've chosen a place, spend some time visualizing it in detail. Explore the place in your mind, part by part, and try to recall as many sensory details as possible. Think beyond just sight. What are the smells? The sounds? The feel? As you recall the details, use an organizer like the one below to help you keep track of your recollections. Write a general description of the place in the left box and sensory details in the right boxes.

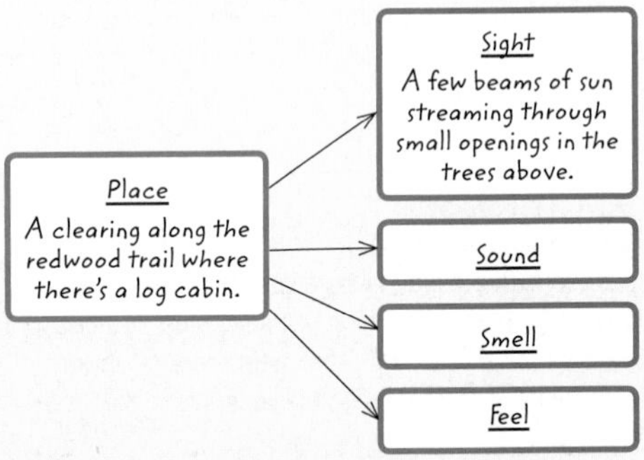

Give It Structure Use the details in your chart as a source for the descriptions in your essay. Weave the details together so it is easy for your readers to visualize the place.

Look at Language Make sure the style of your writing reflects your personality. Check for sentence variation—if you have written a lot of short, declarative sentences, try combining some of them into longer sentences. Rewrite dull descriptions using more engaging language.

EXAMPLE:

was covered with a carpet of soft pine needles.
The forest floor ~~had pine needles on it~~.

To create custom assessments online, go to Progress Reporter Online Assessment.

To create custom assessments using software, use ExamView Assessment Suite.

Grammar Workshop

Clauses and Phrases

Learning Objectives

In this workshop, you will focus on the following objective:

Grammar: Understanding how to use clauses and phrases.

Literature Connection The following sentence is made up of an independent, or main, clause: *I pass the place of the sunflower* and a subordinate, or dependent, clause: *that dark and secret location where creation took place.*

> *"On the dry, red road, I pass the place of the sunflower, that dark and secret location where creation took place."*
>
> —Linda Hogan, from "Walking"

Both clauses contain a subject and a verb, but the dependent clause cannot stand alone as a sentence. It depends on the independent clause to complete its meaning.

A **phrase** is a group of related words, lacking a subject or a predicate, that acts as a single part of speech in a sentence. A phrase can be used as a noun, a verb, or a modifier. A prepositional phrase is one type of phrase. It consists of a preposition, its object, and any modifiers of the object: *on the dry, red road.*

Examples

Because the sunflower grew in a gulley, it was a settler.

The underlined clause tells why and modifies the word *settler.*

The sunflowers on the hillside were very colorful.

The underlined phrase tells where and modifies the noun *sunflowers.*

Clauses and Phrases

Clauses are groups of words that have a subject and a verb and that are used as part of a sentence. **Phrases** are groups of words that act in a sentence as a singular part of speech.

Tip

When a dependent clause or phrase appears at the beginning of a sentence, separate it from the main clause with a comma. Very short introductory prepositional phrase, such as *In the summer* or *After dark,* do not require a comma. However, it is not wrong to use a comma after them.

Language Handbook

For more on subordinate clauses, see Language Handbook, pp. R40–R41.

Revise Write a sentence that contains each group of elements. Underline each clause or phrase you create, and circle the word the clause or phrase modifies.

1. **Clause:** Maya Angelou decided to travel
   Clause: she had a long weekend
   Conjunction: because
2. **Clause:** she let a lie speak for her
   Clause: she had proved that one could return to Africa
   Conjunction: although
3. **Clause:** she reached the thriving town
   Phrase: the late afternoon
   Preposition: in

LOG ON **Literature** Online

Grammar For more grammar practice, go to glencoe.com and enter QuickPass code GL49787u2.

Grammar Workshop

Clauses and Phrases

Focus

Write: Using rutted track roads, and lanes a little larger than foot paths, I found the River Pra. Explain that this sentence contains two parts. The first clause provides detail about the second clause but is not necessary to make a complete sentence.

Teach

Adverb Clauses

Point out the second example. Clarify that adverb clauses can appear at the beginning, middle, or end of a sentence.

Assess

1. Because she had a long weekend, Maya Angelou decided to (travel.)
2. Although she let a lie speak for me, she had (proved) that one could return to Africa.
3. In the late (afternoon,) she reached the thriving town.

For additional grammar practice, see Unit 2 Teaching Resources Book, p. 127.

Approaching Level

DIFFERENTIATED INSTRUCTION

Established Explain that there are three basic types of sentences: simple, complex, and compound. Each contains an independent clause. Write these examples on the board and explain that the independent clause is underlined:

- simple—one independent clause (e.g., The quiet was awful.)
- compound—two or more independent clauses joined (e.g., We ate leftovers from the last night feast, and I said a sad good-bye to my hosts.)
- complex—one independent clause and at least one dependent clause joined (e.g., I could pass if I didn't talk too much.) Explain that using different types of sentences makes writing sound more interesting.

Have students write one of each type of sentence, underline the independent clauses, and share their work with the class.

Before You Read

Focus

Bellringer Options

Daily Language Practice Transparency 34

Or have students recall their parting words to a family member, friend, or teacher from the past few days.

Ask: How do your parting words differ from one situation to another? *(Students should recognize that they say goodbye in different ways.)*

As they read, have students consider why the author likes the good-bye "Sayonara."

Before You Read

Sayonara

Meet **Anne Morrow Lindbergh**
(1906–2001)

Imagine soaring above the earth in a tiny single-engine plane—nothing but blue sky and ocean water as far as the eye can see. That is how Anne Morrow Lindbergh spent much of the early years of her marriage to aviation pioneer Charles Lindbergh. In 1927 Charles became the first person to fly solo over the Atlantic Ocean, and he was greeted with worldwide adoration. Later that year, he was invited to visit Mexico by Dwight Morrow, the U.S. ambassador to that country. There he met Morrow's daughter, Anne.

The Daring Pilot Born in Englewood, New Jersey, Anne Morrow was a quiet girl who wrote poetry. During their courtship, Charles taught her how to fly. The two married in 1929 after Anne graduated from college.

> *"Writing is thinking. It is more than living, for it is being conscious of living."*
>
> —Anne Morrow Lindbergh

Anne became an accomplished pilot, navigator, and radio operator. Together with Charles, she made historic flights all over the world, charting routes for the fledgling airline industry. The couple crisscrossed continents in their single-engine plane. In 1931 they flew an uncharted route over Canada, Alaska, and the northern Pacific Ocean to China.

A Gifted Writer Anne's interest in aviation was matched by a devotion to writing. In fact, her flying was the source of inspiration for some of her work. In all, Anne wrote more than a dozen books and published five volumes of her diaries and letters. Her most popular and enduring work, however, was not about flying at all. In *Gift from the Sea,* Anne's contemplative nature was revealed in essays about a woman's role in modern life.

Home Life/Public Life Anne gave birth to the first of her six children, Charles A. Lindbergh III, in 1930. In 1932 the young boy was kidnapped and murdered. The press sensationalized the crime and, later, the trial of the accused kidnapper. For the sake of their privacy and security, the Lindberghs left the United States to live in Europe.

Later in life, they journeyed through Asia and Africa, working for conservation and the protection of endangered animals. After Charles's death, Anne moved back to the East Coast, where she lived the rest of her life.

LOG ON **Literature** Online

Author Search For more about Anne Morrow Lindbergh, go to glencoe.com and enter QuickPass code GL49787u2.

Selection Skills

Sayonara

Literary Elements
- Thesis (SE pp. 349–353)
- Descriptive Essay (SE p. 353)

Listening/Speaking/Viewing Skills
- Analyze Art (SE p. 351)

Reading Skills
- Analyze Rhetorical Devices (SE pp. 349–354)

Vocabulary Skills
- Analogies (SE pp. 349, 354)
- Academic Vocabulary (SE p. 354)

Writing Skills/Grammar
- Apply Repitition (SE p. 354)
- Write a Poem (TE p. 352)

Literature and Reading Preview

Connect to the Essay

How does it feel to have to say good-bye to someone or something you love? Freewrite about a time you had to say good-bye to someone and describe how you said good-bye.

Build Background

In 1931 the Lindberghs flew their small plane to Asia. When the plane was damaged in China, they traveled by boat to Japan. They then had to travel by train across Japan to the ship that would carry them to the United States.

Set Purposes for Reading

Big Idea On the Move

As you read, ask yourself, What are the various ways of saying good-bye and what are the differences in their meanings?

Literary Element Thesis

A **thesis** is the main idea of an essay or other nonfiction work. It is generally stated in one or two sentences. This brief summary is called the **thesis statement.** Identifying the thesis can help you better understand a work as a whole. As you read, ask yourself, What clues are there to help me determine the thesis?

Reading Strategy Analyze Rhetorical Devices

Rhetorical devices are techniques an author uses to express ideas, persuade, or evoke an emotional response. Rhetorical devices include repetition; analogy—explaining an unfamiliar idea by comparing it with a familiar one; juxtaposition—placing two or more distinct things side by side in order to compare or contrast them; and parallelism—using a series of similar grammatical structures. As you read, ask yourself, How does Lindbergh use rhetorical devices in this essay?

Tip: Listen Use a chart like the one below to record the repetition of the word *Sayonara.* List who says the word and why.

Sayonara Used	Who Says It	Circumstance
p. 350, paragraph 4	Japanese family	on a train saying good-bye to their family

Learning Objectives

For pages 348–354

In studying this text, you will focus on the following objectives:

Literary Study: Analyzing thesis.

Reading: Analyzing rhetorical devices.

Writing: Applying repetition in an essay.

Vocabulary

conglomerate (kən glom′ ər it) *adj.* made up of separate parts collected together as one; p. 350 *The salad was a conglomerate of lettuce, carrots, and tomatoes.*

unintelligible (un′ in tel′ ə jə bəl) *adj.* not able to be understood; p. 352 *Her voice was low and unintelligible on the cell phone.*

bravado (brə vä′dō) *n.* pretended courage or confidence; p. 352 *Although the boxer entered the ring with bravado, he had sweaty palms.*

Tip: Analogies Some analogies feature words that have opposite meanings but aren't true antonyms.

comprehend : unintelligible :: smell : odorless

A person cannot *comprehend* something that is *unintelligible;* a person cannot *smell* something that is *odorless.* The paired words have opposite meanings, but they are not antonyms because they are not the same part of speech.

Before You Read

Focus

Summary

In this essay, the author describes her journey across Japan by train. She offers details about the Japanese countryside and culture, and pays particular attention to the way people conduct their farewells. When she departs a Japanese port by boat, the author considers how the Japanese good-bye—Sayonara—differs from and improves upon other good-byes.

For summaries in languages other than English, see Unit 2 Teaching Resources Book, pp. 128–133.

Vocabulary

Memory Challenge Write the list of vocabulary words and the words' definitions on the chalkboard. Tell students to study the list and review any words the students do not understand. Erase the words while leaving the definitions on the board. Have students recreate the list with the words and the words' definitions on a sheet of paper.

For additional vocabulary practice, see Unit 2 Teaching Resources Book, p. 136.

For additional context, see Glencoe Interactive Vocabulary CD-ROM.

Approaching Level

DIFFERENTIATED INSTRUCTION

Established Encourage students to pay attention to the speaker's tone and observations as they read. This will help the students develop a picture of the speaker and a sense of her personality and beliefs. Ask the students to think about what kind of person she may be.

Ask: What kinds of things does the speaker notice? How does she react to them? *(Students may answer that the speaker is very observant. When she hears people talking, she thinks about the meaning and importance of their words.)*

Teach

Big Idea 1

On the Move **Say:** Keep these questions in mind as you read: How does the author feel about traveling? *(Possible answer: She is fascinated by it.)*

APPROACHING What aspects of traveling are most engaging to the author? *(She is engaged by the many sights and sounds of the culture and land around her.)*

Literary Element 2

Thesis **Possible answer:** *The essay's thesis is that saying good-bye is difficult.*

Cultural History ☆

Clothing Today, most Japanese dress in "Western style" clothes. At the time of Lindbergh's visit, however, more Japanese—especially women—may have worn traditional kimonos.

For an audio recording of this selection, use Listening Library Audio CD-ROM.

Readability Scores

Dale-Chall: 9.1
DRP: 59
Lexile: 1060

SAYONARA

Anne Morrow Lindbergh

1 "Sayonara, Sayonara!" I was in my stateroom[1] but I could hear them, outside on the deck of the Japanese boat, calling to friends and relatives on the dock at Shanghai. "Sayonara"—up and down the gangplank and over the rails. A boatload of Japanese were leaving China for home, as we were. "Sayonara," the chains clanked and the warning whistle shook the boat. The voices outside rose in a flurry of noise, like a flock of frightened birds. But above the **conglomerate** sound there was always one voice, clean and sharp and individual and yet representative of the mass like that one face in the front line that holds the meaning of the whole crowd—one cry, "Sayonara." The impression was intensified perhaps because it was the one word of Japanese I understood—"Sayonara" ("Good-bye").

I was to hear it again, all along our trip home. For we crossed Japan by train from the southern tip to Yokohama, where we boarded the boat for America.

"Sayonara": the clatter of wooden clogs[2] along the station platform; the flutter of kimonos;[3] babies jogging on their mothers' ☆ backs; men carrying four or five small bundles tied up in different-colored furoshiki (squares of parti-colored silk or cotton); old women knocking along with their sticks, their brown faces hidden under enormous rooflike hats of straw; a man shouting his wares. We leaned out of the window at one of these stations and motioned to a vender for some tea. He poured out of his big tin into a little brown clay teapot like a child's toy, with a saucer for a lid and an inverted cup on top. "Two! Two!" we shouted and signaled as the train jerked forward, starting to pull out. The vender ran after us with another teapot swinging from its wire handle and pushed it in our window.

"Sayonara—Sayonara!" cried the passengers who had just stepped on board. A Japanese family across the aisle from us leaned out of the window to say a few last words. They occupied two long seats raised on a slight platform, separated from the next family by a partition. The mother and nurse (or older sister) were dressed in

1. A *stateroom* is a private room aboard a ship.

2 Thesis *Based on your reading so far, what do you think the thesis of this essay is?*

Vocabulary

conglomerate (kən glom′ ər it) *adj.* made up of separate parts collected together as one

2. Here, *clogs* refers to a type of sandal.
3. *Kimonos* (ki mō′ nōz) are loose gowns tied with a sash, part of the traditional clothing worn by Japanese men and women.

Reading Practice

SPIRAL REVIEW **Synthesize** Have students read other examples of travel writing by Lindbergh. Possible sources include her early works North to the Orient and Listen! The Wind as well as the diaries that she published later in life. Ask students to paraphrase the main ideas of these works. Have them write several paragraphs, comparing these ideas with ideas from other travel writing they have read or from television programs dealing with travel.

Postcard for the Nippon Yusen Kaisha line, c. 1929. Private collection.

View the Art How well does this postcard from 1929 illustrate the scene on the ship that Anne Morrow Lindbergh describes? ★

Japanese kimonos, the father in Western business suit, the two little girls in green challis[4] suits with Irish-lace collars, and the baby in woolens. They had already kicked off their shoes, in Japanese fashion, and were squatting on their feet on the blue plush seats. They held the baby up to the window for the last good-bye—"Sayonara"; and then the monotonous doggerel rhythm of the train, quickening to a roar, drowned all noise. We were off.

4. *Challis* (shal′ ē) is a lightweight cloth made of cotton or wool.

Teach

View the Art ★

Answer: *The postcard is a good depiction of the author's description; similarly, the author describes people throwing colored paper and saying their good-byes from the ship.*

Today, Nippon Yusen Kaisha is one of the largest shipping companies in the world. Aside from shipping, the company also provides luxury cruise ship services in the United States and Japan.

English Learners

DIFFERENTIATED INSTRUCTION

Intermediate In this story, the writer lists several ways people around the world say "good-bye." Pair up students and instruct them to list these terms, as well as the writer's attitude toward each. *(For example, the author thinks that the French term* au revoir *("Till we meet again") ignores the unpleasant feelings of separation.)*

Ask: Which way of saying good-bye do you prefer? Do you have your own way of saying this? Invite students to share terms for "good-bye" in their native language. Then make a list and discuss what each term means, and which ones the students prefer.

Teach

Reading Strategy 1

Analyze Rhetorical Devices **Answer:** *She uses parallelism to convey her fondness for Japan.*

APPROACHING For approaching-level students, **ask:** What other literary device does the author use in this paragraph? *(simile)*

For additional practice using the reading skill or strategy, see Unit 2 Teaching Resources Book, p. 135.

Literary Element 2

Thesis **Answer:** *"Farewell" says too little; it hides the emotion of departure. Other terms say too much, but deny that people will be apart. She prefers Sayonara because it is an acceptance.*

To check students' understanding of the selection, see Unit 2 Teaching Resources Book, p. 138.

It was good-bye for us too, as we rushed through Japan on our way to the boat. Good-bye to the rice fields terraced up a narrow gully in the hills; to thatched roofs and paper walls; to heavy-headed grain bent to a curve; to a field of awkward lotus leaves, like big elephant ears flapping on their tall stalks; to a white road leading up a hill to a pine grove and the flicker of red of a shrine gate. Good-bye to the little towns we rattled through, with their narrow cobbled streets lined with shops, open to the passerby except for fluttering blue-toweling curtains or bright paper and cloth flag-signs. Good-bye to blue paper umbrellas in the rain and little boys chasing dragon flies.

Our real good-bye was not until the boat pulled out of the dock at Yokohama, when the crowd of Japanese leaning over the rails of the decks shot twirling strands of serpentine[5] across to those they had left behind on shore—a rain of bright fireworks. One end of these colored paper ribbons was held in the hands of those on deck; the other, by those on shore, until a brilliant multicolored web was spun between ship and shore. This and the shouts of conversation **unintelligible** to me, interlacing back and forth across the gap, made up a finely woven band—a tissue, intricately patterned and rich in texture which held together for a few more seconds those remaining and those departing. Then the gap of water slowly widening between dock and ship, the ribbons tautened and snapped, the broken and raveled ends twirling off idly into the water, floating away with the unfinished ends of sentences. And nothing could bridge the gap but "Sayonara!"

For *Sayonara,* literally translated, "Since it must be so," of all the good-byes I have heard is the most beautiful. Unlike the *Auf Wiedersehens* and *Au revoirs,* it does not try to cheat itself by any **bravado** "Till we meet again," any sedative to postpone the pain of separation. It does not evade the issue like the sturdy blinking *Farewell. Farewell* is a father's *good-bye.* It is—"Go out in the world and do well, my son." It is encouragement and admonition. It is hope and faith. But it passes over the significance of the moment; of parting it says nothing. It hides its emotion. It says too little. While *Good-bye* ("God be with you") and *Adios* say too much. They try to bridge the distance, almost to deny it. *Good-bye* is a prayer, a ringing cry. "You must not go—I cannot bear to have you go! But you shall not go alone, unwatched. God will be with you. God's hand will be over you" and even—underneath, hidden, but it is there, incorrigible—"I will be with you; I will watch you—always." It is a mother's *good-bye.* But Sayonara says neither too much nor too little. It is a simple acceptance of fact. All understanding of life lies in its limits. All emotion, smoldering, is banked up behind it. But it says nothing. It is really the unspoken good-bye, the pressure of a hand, "Sayonara."

5. *Serpentine* are streamers of rolled colored paper that unwind when thrown.

1 Analyze Rhetorical Devices *What is the effect of Morrow's use of parallelism in this sentence?*

Vocabulary

unintelligible (un´ in tel´ ə jə bəl) *adj.* not able to be understood

2 Thesis *What does the author mean by "too much" and "too little," and why does she prefer the term* Sayonara?

Vocabulary

bravado (brə vä´ dō) *n.* pretended courage or confidence

Writing Practice

SPIRAL REVIEW **Write a Poem** Have students write a poem about a time they had to tell someone good-bye. **Ask:** How did you say good-bye? Did you talk, write, or use another form of communication? How did you feel? Was it difficult to say good-bye? Why or why not? Tell students that their poems should reflect these questions. Remind them to use descriptive language and sensory details to enhance their writing.

After You Read

Respond and Think Critically

Respond and Interpret

1. Do you agree with Lindbergh that *Sayonara* is the best parting expression? Explain.
2. (a)Why does Lindbergh hear the word *Sayonara* again and again? (b)Why do you think she uses the experience to make a generalization about life?
3. (a)What do the people on the boat do as it is leaving? (b)What does their action symbolize?
4. (a)What does *Sayonara* literally mean? (b)What does this meaning suggest about the Japanese view of life?

Analyze and Evaluate

5. In the passage beginning, " . . . the clatter of wooden clogs," the author uses parallel phrases: "babies jogging . . . men carrying . . . old women knocking . . ." How does the first half of this paragraph differ from the second half? Which style is more effective in describing the scene?
6. Why does Lindbergh contrast the words *farewell* and *good-bye*?
7. When the author says, "But it says nothing," does she really mean that *Sayonara* has no meaning? Explain.

Connect

8. **Big Idea** **On the Move** Although the idea of saying good-bye seems sad, the ending of the essay is neither sad nor happy. Why might this be important to Lindbergh?
9. **Connect to Today** How is saying good-bye to family today similar to or different from saying good-bye when the essay was written?

Literary Element Thesis

ACT Skills Practice

1. Which of the following statements best identifies the thesis of "Sayonara"?

   A. We say good-bye many times throughout our lives.

   B. Parting with loved ones is a sad experience.

   C. The Japanese language is more expressive than most European languages.

   D. In saying good-bye, we must accept an inevitable human experience.

2. The thesis of the essay is best supported by the image of:

   F. paper streamers breaking as an ocean liner pulls away from a dock.

   G. hundreds of voices calling out "Sayonara."

   H. little boys chasing dragon flies.

   J. the bustle of people along a station platform.

Review: Descriptive Essay

As you learned on page 341, a **descriptive essay** creates a picture in the reader's mind of an actual person, object, or place. The essayist uses descriptive details and concrete language, which appeal to one or more of the senses, to create this picture.

Partner Activity With a partner, reread the scene at the train station. Note the details described, and classify each as a detail of sight or sound. Write a description of the impression the images give you.

Sights	Sounds

After You Read

Assess

1. Answers will vary.
2. (a) Because she is crossing Japan by train (b) She wants to express the pain and difficulty of separating from loved ones.
3. (a) Throw paper streamers to people on the dock (b) Separation as the streamers break
4. (a) "Since it must be so" (b) An acceptance of life as it is
5. Possible answer: The first half is purely descriptive and contains parallelism. The second half uses phrases and no parallelism. Students may say the first half is more effective because it provides more details.
6. Possible answers: She underscores the nuances of various departing sentiments.
7. She means that it is neutral, an acknowledgement of fact.
8. For her, good-bye was a "simple acceptance of fact."
9. Students' answers will vary. Students should draw parallels or demonstrate differences between good-byes today and in the 1930s.

Review: Descriptive Essay

Possible answers: Sights: *babies jogging on mother's backs, men carrying different-colored bundles, brown faces under roof-like straw hats;* **Sounds:** *clatter of wooden clogs, sticks of old women knocking, man shouting;* The overall impression is one of noisy, colorful confusion.

Literary Element

1. D is the correct answer. The author states that sayonara, meaning "since it must be so," is the most realistic expression to use when parting.
2. F is the correct answer. This image captures Lindbergh's argument that parting is inevitable.

Progress Check

Can students explain thesis?

If No → See Unit 2 Teaching Resources Book, p. 134.

After You Read

Assess

Reading Strategy

1. Possible answer: The voices outside the boat in China rising like a flock of birds (similarity: sound)
2. Possible answer: The tangible web of streamers and the intangible web of back-and-forth shouts

Vocabulary

1. a
2. a
3. b

Academic Vocabulary

definition: to call upon

synonyms: summon, cite, evoke

sentence: For strength, the gymnast **invoked** the name of her coach before attempting the difficult trick.

Write with Style

Students' essays should

- explore everyday language by using the repetition of a word or phrase
- present a clear thesis and repeat it in the supporting ideas throughout
- use varied language and sentence structure in the repetition of the main idea
- be organized logically and build toward the conclusion

Reading Strategy Analyze Rhetorical Devices

The **rhetorical devices** of analogy and juxtaposition are methods of comparison. Analogy compares two dissimilar things by showing how they are similar. Juxtaposition compares or contrasts two distinct things placed side by side.

1. Find an example of analogy in "Sayonara." What is being compared? How are they similar?
2. Find an example of juxtaposition. What is juxtaposed? How are they similar or dissimilar?

Vocabulary Practice

Practice with Analogies Choose the word pair that best completes the analogy.

1. conglomerate : individuals ::
   a. team : players **b.** teacher : students
2. unintelligible : understand ::
   a. hidden : see **b.** broken : mend
3. bravado : nervousness ::
   a. joy : emotion **b.** calmness : anxiety

Academic Vocabulary

In this essay, Lindbergh **invokes** the word *Sayonara* almost like a blessing or a wish.

Invoke is an academic word that means to "call on" or "appeal to" something. To study the word further, complete a graphic organizer like the one shown.

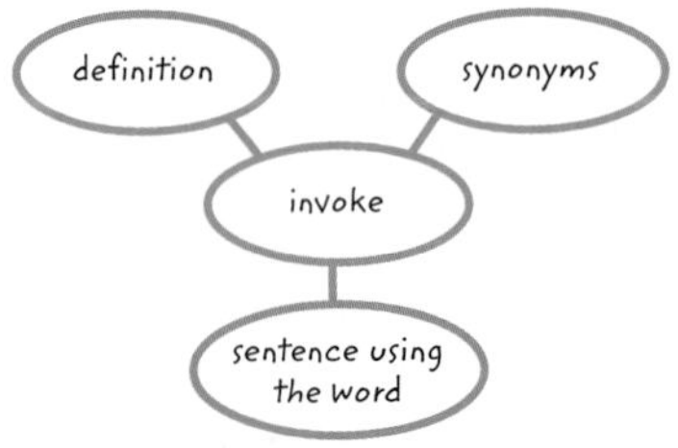

For more on academic vocabulary, see pages 54–55 and R79–R81.

Write with Style

Apply Repetition

Assignment Write an essay modeled after "Sayonara," in which you discuss a common word or phrase. Use repetition to explain the word or phrase's usage and its potential for multiple meanings.

Get Ideas Start with a dictionary to review your word's meaning and origin. Then search the library or Internet for articles about the word's etymology, or history. Create a word web with your word or phrase in the center and its different uses and meanings branching off. Determine your thesis, and use ideas on the outer branches of the word web as supporting ideas.

Give It Structure Organize your thesis and supporting details into an outline that includes an introduction, a body, and a conclusion. The outline should map out a logical development of your thesis. Group details that support the same idea, and build toward the conclusion. Refer to the repetition chart you made to review how Lindbergh uses repetition to strengthen her ideas. The supporting material should reiterate the essay's main idea.

Look at Language Although you are repeating a word or phrase throughout your essay, you should still vary the ways in which the word or phrase is used. Evaluate your use of repetition, making sure each occurrence adds some variation.

EXAMPLE:

will holler it—"Timeout!"—

Adults ~~say it to each other, usually~~ when an argument gets too intense ~~, "Timeout!"~~ .

Even toddlers hear it, usually when they're being bad: "Timeout!"

LOG ON Literature Online

Selection Resources For Selection Quizzes, eFlashcards, and Reading-Writing Connection activities, go to glencoe.com and enter QuickPass code GL49787u2.

For grammar practice, see Unit 2 Teaching Resources Book, p. 137.

To create custom assessments online, go to Progress Reporter Online Assessment.

To create custom assessments using software, use ExamView Assessment Suite.

Before You Read

from *Into Thin Air*

Meet **Jon Krakauer**
(born 1954)

Jon Krakauer got started as a writer when a mountain climbing club asked him to write an article about his ascent of three previously unclimbed Alaskan peaks. Three years later, a British magazine paid him to write another article, this time about climbing Devil's Thumb near Petersburg, Alaska. After that, Krakauer quit his carpentry job to become a freelance writer. His experience as a carpenter and commercial fisherman enabled him to write articles for *Architectural Digest* and *Smithsonian,* but he soon realized that only writing about the outdoors truly satisfied him.

Climbing and Writing Krakauer spent most of his childhood in Oregon, where he began climbing at age eight with his father. Krakauer never lost his love of climbing. After graduating from college, he spent part of each year working and the rest in the mountains. After publishing his first few articles, Krakauer turned to full-length books. His story of a young man who travels alone into the Alaskan wilderness, *Into the Wild,* became a bestseller.

Mount Everest In 1996 Krakauer was hired to write about how climbing Mount Everest was turning into a big business. Everyday adventurers would pay large sums for the thrill of saying they had climbed the world's tallest mountain. Krakauer admits that there were many reasons for not going but he could not resist the opportunity. He joined a climbing team led by the legendary Rob Hall. Hall, who had reached the top of Mount Everest seven times, would be one of several people to die on the May 1996 expedition.

Nevertheless, within a few years of the disaster, Krakauer chronicles his experience in *Into Thin Air,* and he returned to climbing. He explains, "I'd give up writing before I gave up climbing."

> *"The plain truth is that I knew better but I went to Everest anyway."*
>
> —Jon Krakauer

Fact That Reads Like Fiction One reason for Krakauer's success as a writer is his ability to tell a story. His nonfiction has the drama, the pacing, and the qualities of rising action—including suspense—that are found in fiction. His people are well-developed characters full of complex motives and emotions. Krakauer admits that he works very hard to achieve these effects, sometimes taking days to hammer out a single sentence.

LOG ON **Literature** Online

Author Search For more about Jon Krakauer, go to glencoe.com and enter QuickPass code GL49787u2.

Before You Read

Focus

Bellringer Option

Daily Language Practice Transparency 35

Or show students photographs of remote natural locations, such as Mount Everest, Antarctica, and the Brazilian rainforest.

Ask: How would travel to all these places be similar? *(All are remote and hard to reach. All have potential dangers and amazing natural beauty.)*

As they read, have students consider how the author's journey to the summit of Mount Everest is like and unlike other journeys to remote natural locations.

Selection Skills

***from* Into Thin Air**

Literary Elements
- Structure (SE pp. 356–367)
- Dialogue (SE p. 367)

Reading Skills
- Monitor Comprehension (SE pp. 356–368)
- Cause and Effect (TE p. 358)

Vocabulary Skills
- Word Usage (SE p. 356, 368)
- Academic Vocabulary (SE p. 368)

Listening/Speaking/Viewing Skills
- View the Photograph (SE p. 359; TE 366)

Writing Skills/Grammar
- Semicolons and Colons (TE p. 366)

Study Skills/Research/Assessment
- Internet Connection (SE p. 368)

Before You Read

Focus

Summary

In this excerpt from his memoir, the author describes his ascent to the summit of Mount Everest. On the journey up to the summit and back to the base camp, Krakauer records the many decisions that led to problems for him and his climbing mates.

For summaries in languages other than English, see Unit 2 Teaching Resources Book, pp. 140–145.

Vocabulary

Practicing With Poetry
Provide students with two lines of a popular poem. Have students complete the poem in their own words, using at least two new vocabulary words in their versions of the poem.

For additional vocabulary practice, see Unit 2 Teaching Resources Book, p. 148.

Literature and Reading Preview

Connect to the Essay

If you had the chance, would you accept the challenge to climb the world's highest mountain? Freewrite for a few minutes and explain why you would or would not make the climb.

Build Background

At 29,028 feet, Mount Everest claimed the lives of dozens of climbers before it was first successfully conquered in 1953. Besides ice, snow, and changing weather conditions, a central problem for climbers is the "thin air," or lack of oxygen, at higher elevations. Most climbers carry bottled oxygen. Climbers who do not get enough oxygen enter a state of hypoxia, which includes disorientation, dizziness, and hallucinations.

Set Purposes for Reading

Big Idea On the Move

As you read, ask yourself, What is it like to be on the move in one of the most dangerous places on earth?

Literary Element Structure

Structure is the particular order a writer uses to present ideas. Narratives commonly follow a chronological order. As you read, ask yourself, What words or phrases does Krakauer use to show chronological order?

Reading Strategy Monitor Comprehension

Monitoring comprehension is thinking about whether you understand what you are reading. You can improve your comprehension by rereading or asking yourself questions about central ideas, characters, and events. As you read, ask yourself, Where do I need to review and read at a slower pace?

Tip: Record Rereading Keep a record of where you stop to reread. For each instance, jot down basic facts about who, what, where, when, why, and how.

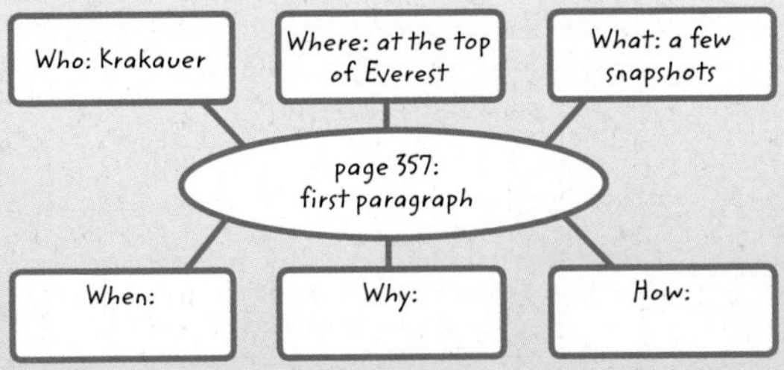

Learning Objectives

For pages 355–368

In studying this text, you will focus on the following objectives:

Literary Study: Analyzing structure.

Reading: Monitoring comprehension.

Research: Conducting Internet research.

Vocabulary

tenuously (ten′ ū əs lē) *adv.* uncertainly; shakily; p. 360 *The climber was perched tenuously on a crag above the cliff face.*

exacerbate (ig zas′ ər bāt′) *v.* to make worse, more violent, or more bitter; p. 361 *The foul weather exacerbated her headache.*

invincible (in vin′ sə bəl) *adj.* not able to be beaten or overcome; p. 361 *Ann was invincible at chess; no one could beat her.*

terrain (tə rān′) *n.* the physical features of the land; p. 363 *The team made slow progress over the rocky terrain.*

detachment (di tach′ mənt) *n.* indifference; a state of being apart from; p. 365 *His detachment was normal; he liked being alone.*

Tip: Word Usage Knowing the root of an unfamilar word can help figure out its meaning. For example, knowing that the root *terr* means "earth" can help you figure out that *terrain* means "a piece of land."

Research Practice

SPIRAL REVIEW **Compare and Contrast** Read aloud the Build Background on this page. **Ask:** What do you think would be the greatest challenges of mountain climbing? *(Students may say that dangers such as falling or being injured in an avalanche would be great challenges.)*

Ask: Why do you think people want to climb Mount Everest? *(Students may say to challenge themselves and accomplish something great.) Break students into groups. Have groups go to the library to conduct research to compare and contrast the clothing and gear used by past climbers of Mount Everest with that used today. Students should write a brief summary of their findings. Have groups present their findings to the class.*

Near the top of Khumbu Icefall, Scott Fischer ascends the large overhanging serac known as the mouse trap, during the May 1996 ascent on Mount Everest.

from Into Thin Air

Jon Krakauer

In my backpack was a banner from *Outside* magazine, a small pennant emblazoned with a whimsical lizard that Linda, my wife, had sewn, and some other mementos[1] with which I'd intended to pose for a series of triumphant photos. Cognizant[2] of my dwindling oxygen reserves, however, I left everything in my pack and stayed on top of the world just long enough to fire off four quick shots of Andy Harris and Anatoli Boukreev posing
1 in front of the summit survey marker.

Then I turned to descend. About twenty yards below the summit I passed Neal Beidleman and a client of Fischer's named Martin Adams[3] on their way up. After exchanging a high five with Neal, I grabbed a handful of small stones from a wind-scoured patch of exposed shale, zipped the souvenirs into the pocket of my down suit, and hastened down the ridge.

1. *Mementos* are souvenirs.
2. Here, *cognizant* means "aware."
3. Throughout this essay, Krakauer mentions the names of many other climbers, including guides Andy Harris, Anatoli Boukreev, Andy Fischer, and Neal Beidleman. He also mentions climbers who were led by these guides, including Martin Adams.

Structure *What is the first thing Krakauer tells his readers?* **2**

Teach

Big Idea 1

On the Move **Say:** Keep these questions in mind as you read: How do our surroundings contribute to our ability to be on the move? *(They affect how easy or difficult it is to move, and they can make it impossible to move.)*

APPROACHING How do Krakauer's surroundings make it life-threatening to be on the move? *(They make him short of oxygen, subject to freezing temperatures, and at risk of falling.)*

Literary Element 2

Structure **Possible answer:** *Krakauer first describes being on the top of Mount Everest.*

ENGLISH LEARNERS To guide English learners, ask a student to look up the word *summit* in the dictionary. Have another student use the word in a sentence.

For an audio recording of this selection, use Listening Library Audio CD-ROM.

Readability Scores

Dale-Chall: 9.4
DRP: 64
Lexile: 1160

Approaching Level

DIFFERENTIATED INSTRUCTION

Emerging Help students understand the different people in the essay by making a chart. Include names and descriptions or words from the essay that will help students identify the various people, locations, events, etc. Students should add information to the chart as they continue their reading. Encourage students to analyze how the actions of one person affect others mentioned in the story.

Teach

Big Idea

On the Move Answer: *Adams's experience as a pilot makes him recognize the approaching danger of the storm, while Krakauer remains focused on the danger of running out of oxygen.*

A moment earlier I'd noticed that wispy clouds now filled the valleys to the south, obscuring all but the highest peaks. Adams—a small, pugnacious[4] Texan who'd gotten rich selling bonds during the booming 1980s—is an experienced airplane pilot who'd spent many hours gazing down on the tops of clouds; later he told me that he recognized these innocent-looking puffs of water vapor to be the crowns of robust thunderheads immediately after reaching the top. "When you see a thunderhead in an airplane," he explained, "your first reaction is to get out of there. So that's what I did."

But unlike Adams, I was unaccustomed to peering down at cumulonimbus cells from 29,000 feet, and I therefore remained ignorant of the storm that was even then bearing down. My concerns revolved instead around the diminishing supply of oxygen in my tank.

Fifteen minutes after leaving the summit I reached the top of the Hillary Step,[5] where I encountered a clot of climbers chuffing up the single strand of rope, and my descent came to an enforced halt.[6] As I waited for the crowd to pass, Andy arrived on his way down. "Jon," he asked, "I don't seem to be getting enough air. Can you tell if the intake valve to my mask is iced up?"

A quick check revealed a fist-sized chunk of frozen drool blocking the rubber valve that admitted ambient air into the mask from the atmosphere. I chipped it off with the pick of my ice ax, then asked Andy to return the favor by turning off my regulator in order to conserve my gas until the Step cleared. He mistakenly opened the valve instead of closing it, however, and ten minutes later all my oxygen was gone. My cognitive functions, which had been marginal before, instantly went into a nosedive. I felt like I'd been slipped an overdose of a powerful sedative.

I fuzzily remember Sandy Pittman climbing past as I waited, bound for the summit, followed an indeterminate time later by Charlotte Fox and then Lopsang Jangbu. Yasuko materialized next, just below my precarious stance, but was flummoxed[7] by the last and steepest portion of the Step. I watched helplessly for fifteen minutes as she struggled to haul herself up the uppermost brow of rock, too exhausted to manage it. Finally Tim Madsen, who was waiting impatiently directly below her, put his hands beneath her buttocks and pushed her to the top.

Rob Hall appeared not long after that. Disguising my rising panic, I thanked him for getting me to the top of Everest. "Yeah, it's turned out to be a pretty good expedition," he replied, then mentioned that Frank Fischbeck, Beck Weathers, Lou Kasischke, Stuart Hutchison, and John Taske had all turned back. Even in my state of hypoxic imbecility, it was obvious Hall was profoundly disappointed that five of his eight clients had packed it in—a sentiment that I suspected was heightened by the fact that Fischer's entire crew appeared to be plugging toward the summit. "I only wish we could have gotten more clients to the top," Rob lamented before continuing on his way.

Soon thereafter, Adams and Boukreev arrived on their way down, stopping immediately above me to wait for the traffic to clear. A minute later the overcrowding atop

4. Here, *pugnacious* suggests someone who is not easy to get along with.
5. Named for Sir Edmund Hillary, *Hillary Step* is the last difficult ascent before the summit.
6. One of Krakauer's points is that there were so many climbers on the mountain that it was like a traffic jam.
7. *Flummoxed* means "confused."

On the Move *How do Krakauer's and Adams's different travel experiences affect their assessment of the situation on Mount Everest?*

Reading Practice

SPIRAL REVIEW **Cause and Effect** Remind students that causes are the reasons events happen, and effects are the results of causes. Krakauer repeatedly looks at causes and effects. For example, running out of oxygen caused Krakauer to panic. Ask students to read page 358 and look for other cause-and-effect relationships. Have them identify these in single sentences:

- _____ caused _____.
- _____ happened because of _____.

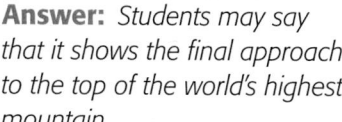

The summit ridge viewed from the South Summit in the early afternoon of May 10, 1996, as the climbers moved to the top.

View the Art What do you find most striking about this photograph? Explain. ★

Teach

View the Photograph ★

Answer: *Students may say that it shows the final approach to the top of the world's highest mountain.*

The South Summit of Everest is located at 28,700 feet. Traditionally, this is the place where climbers decide to tackle the remaining challenges on the way to the summit, or turn around.

English Learners

DIFFERENTIATED INSTRUCTION

Intermediate English learners might have trouble understanding some of the difficult vocabulary in the essay. **Say:** Find the word *descent* in the third paragraph on page 358. **Ask:** What do you think *descent* means? *(possible answer: the act of moving downward)*

Encourage students to look up the meaning of the word *descent* in the dictionary. Do the same for the following words: *cognitive, marginal, indeterminate, materialized, precarious, lamented, supplemental,* and *cerebral cortex.*

Teach

Literary Element 1

Structure Answer: *Krakauer is still at the Hillary Step, 28,900 feet above sea level. He is describing the altitude's effects on him and the movement of the climbers around him.*

Big Idea 2

On the Move Possible answer: *The presence of other people has both hindered and helped Krakauer's movement. Without the traffic jam, he would not have run out of oxygen so soon. Without Mike Groom, he would have been stuck on Hillary Step.*

View the Photograph ★

As a result of Everest's growing popularity with climbers, the mountain has become polluted. For example, the South Col at 26,000 feet is cluttered with items, such as bottles and climbing poles. *Col* is Welsh for "pass," and the South Col is the pass between Everest and Lhotse.

Doug Hansen approaching the summit, with Mike Groom descending behind. ★

the Step intensified further as Makalu Gau, Ang Dorje, and several other Sherpas[8] came up the rope, followed by Doug Hansen and Scott Fischer. Then, finally, the Hillary Step was clear—but only after I'd spent more than an hour at 28,900 feet without supplemental oxygen.

By that point, entire sectors of my cerebral cortex seemed to have shut down altogether. Dizzy, fearing that I would black out, I was frantic to reach the South Summit, where my third bottle was waiting. I started **tenuously** down the fixed lines,[9] stiff with dread. Just below the step, Anatoli and Martin scooted around me and hurried down. Exercising extreme caution, I continued descending the tightrope of the ridge, but fifty feet above the oxygen cache the rope ended, and I balked at going farther without gas.

Over at the South Summit, I could see Andy Harris sorting through a pile of orange oxygen bottles. "Yo, Harold!"[10] I yelled, "Could you bring me a fresh bottle?"

"There's no oxygen here!" the guide shouted back. "These bottles are all empty!" This was disturbing news. My brain screamed for oxygen. I didn't know what to do. Just then, Mike Groom caught up to me on his way down from the summit. Mike had climbed Everest in 1993 without gas, and he wasn't overly concerned about going without. He gave me his oxygen bottle, and we quickly scrambled over to the South Summit.[11]

When we got there, an examination of the oxygen cache immediately revealed that there were at least six full bottles. Andy, however, refused to believe it. He kept insisting that they were all empty, and nothing Mike or I said could convince him otherwise.

The only way to know how much gas is in a canister is to attach it to your regulator and read the gauge; presumably this is how Andy had checked the bottles at the South Summit. After the expedition, Neal

8. *Sherpas* are people who live in the Himalayas and are hired to carry supplies and otherwise assist mountain climbers in their ascents.
9. *Fixed lines,* also referred to later as *fixed ropes,* are ropes that have been put in place by others in the most challenging parts of the mountain. Climbers are supposed to clip a short safety tether to these ropes as they ascend or descend.

10. *Harold* was Andy Harris's nickname.
11. The *South Summit* is a short distance below Hillary Step.

1 Structure *Where is Krakauer? How is he using his location to tell his story?*

Vocabulary

tenuously (ten′ ū əs lē) *adv.* uncertainly; shakily

On the Move *How important is the presence of other people on Mount Everest to Krakauer's ability to move safely?* **2**

Listening and Speaking Practice

Analyze Media Obtain a copy of *Into Thin Air: Death on Everest,* the 1997 TV movie adapted from Krakauer's book. Show students the scenes that correspond with the book excerpt reproduced here. Then have the class discuss the aesthetic effects of the movie by asking questions such as the following:

- In what ways does the movie differ from the book? Why do you think the screenwriter chose to make these changes?
- How does the director use camera angles, movements, and close-ups to heighten the dramatic action?
- Do you think the movie scenes are effective? Why or why not?

Beidleman pointed out that if Andy's regulator had become fouled with ice, the gauge might have registered empty even though the canisters were full, which would explain his bizarre obstinacy. And if his regulator was perhaps on the fritz and not delivering oxygen to his mask, that would also explain Andy's apparent lack of lucidity.[12]

This possibility—which now seems so self-evident—didn't occur to either Mike or me at the time, however. In hindsight,[13] Andy was acting irrationally and had plainly slipped well beyond routine hypoxia, but I was so mentally impeded myself that it simply didn't register.

My inability to discern the obvious was **exacerbated** to some degree by the guide-client protocol. Andy and I were very similar in terms of physical ability and technical expertise; had we been climbing together in a nonguided situation as equal partners, it's inconceivable to me that I would have neglected to recognize his plight.[14] But on this expedition he had been cast in the role of **invincible** guide, there to look after me and the other clients; we had been specifically indoctrinated not to question our guides' judgment. The thought never entered my crippled mind that Andy might in fact be in terrible straits—that a guide might urgently need help from me.

12. *Lucidity* means "mental clarity."
13. *Hindsight* is the ability to see past events clearly and with wisdom, often in a way that was not possible at the time the events occurred.
14. Here, *plight* means "a dangerous condition or state."

3 Monitor Comprehension *Monitor your comprehension by explaining Andy Harris's behavior. If necessary, reread.*

Vocabulary

exacerbate (ig zas′ ər bāt′) *v.* to make worse, more violent, or more bitter

invincible (in vin′ sə bəl) *adj.* not able to be beaten or overcome

As Andy continued to assert that there were no full bottles at the South Summit, Mike looked at me quizzically. I looked back and shrugged. Turning to Andy, I said, "No big deal, Harold. Much ado about nothing." Then I grabbed a new oxygen canister, screwed it onto my regulator, and headed down the mountain. Given what unfolded over the hours that followed, the ease with which I abdicated responsibility—my utter failure to consider that Andy might have been in serious trouble—was a lapse that's likely to haunt me for the rest of my life.

Around 3:30 PM I left the South Summit ahead of Mike, Yasuko, and Andy, and almost immediately descended into a dense layer of clouds. Light snow started to fall. I could scarcely tell where the mountain ended and where the sky began in the flat, diminishing light; it would have been very easy to blunder off the edge of the ridge and never be heard from again. And the conditions only worsened as I moved down the peak.

At the bottom of the rock steps on the Southeast Ridge I stopped with Mike to wait for Yasuko, who was having difficulty negotiating the fixed ropes. He attempted to call Rob on the radio, but Mike's transmitter was working only intermittently and he couldn't raise anybody. With Mike looking after Yasuko, and both Rob and Andy accompanying Doug Hansen—the only other client still above us—I assumed the situation was under control. So as Yasuko caught up to us, I asked Mike's permission to continue down alone. "Fine," he replied. "Just don't walk off any cornices."[15]

15. *Cornices* are snowy, unsupported overhangs.

4 Monitor Comprehension *What does Krakauer mean by "a lapse"? Why will the lapse haunt him? If you are not sure of the answers, reread.*

Teach

Reading Strategy 3

Monitor Comprehension

Answer: *Andy thought all the oxygen bottles were empty at the time, but they were not. Reflecting on this later, Krakauer realizes that Harris was probably not getting enough oxygen.*

For additional practice using the reading skill or strategy, see Unit 2 Teaching Resources Book, p. 147.

Reading Strategy 4

Monitor Comprehension

Answer: *The lapse was not realizing that Andy might have been in serious trouble. This will haunt him "given what unfolded over the hours that followed": a foreshadowing of disaster for Andy.*

Approaching Level

DIFFERENTIATED INSTRUCTION

Emerging Krakauer includes a lot of dialogue, thus creating a storylike narrative in his essay. To practice reading fluency, have several students read passages aloud. Ask them to clarify who is speaking to monitor their comprehension. Stop periodically to clarify what is happening..

English Learners

DIFFERENTIATED INSTRUCTION

Intermediate Pair up students and have them identify unfamiliar vocabulary on these pages before reading aloud. Unfamiliar vocabulary might include words such as *protocol* and *abdicated,* figurative language such as *My brain screamed,* and idioms such as *fouled with ice* and *on the fritz*

Teach

Literary Element 1

Structure Answer: *The time and location are both given. It is later in the day (the last mention of time was 3:30 PM) and lower on the mountain.*

Big Idea 2

On the Move Answer: *Beck is determined and perhaps irrational; he has climbed part of the mountain in an almost blind condition. This mountain is challenging even for sighted climbers.*

Medical History ☆

Eye Surgery Nearsightedness, also called myopia, is the inability to see things in the distance. During radial keratotomy surgery, incisions are made in the cornea. This allows the cornea to flatten, bringing the focal point closer to the retina, and improving distance vision.

About 4:45 PM, when I reached the Balcony[16]—the promontory at 27,600 feet on the Southeast Ridge where I'd sat watching the sunrise with Ang Dorje—I was shocked to encounter Beck Weathers, standing alone in the snow, shivering violently. I'd assumed that he'd descended to Camp Four[17] hours earlier. "Beck!" I exclaimed, "what are you still doing up here?"

Years earlier, Beck had undergone a ☆ radial keratotomy[18] to correct his vision. A side effect of the surgery, he discovered early in the Everest climb, was that the low barometric pressure that exists at high altitude caused his eyesight to fail. The higher he climbed, the lower the barometric pressure fell, and the worse his vision became.

The previous afternoon as he was ascending from Camp Three to Camp Four, Beck later confessed to me, "my vision had gotten so bad that I couldn't see more than a few feet. So I just tucked right behind John Taske and when he'd lift a foot I'd place my foot right in his bootprint."

Beck had spoken openly of his vision problem earlier, but with the summit in reach he neglected to mention its increasing severity to Rob or anyone else. His bad eyes notwithstanding, he was climbing well and feeling stronger than he had since the beginning of the expedition, and, he explained, "I didn't want to bail out prematurely."

Climbing above the South Col through the night, Beck managed to keep up with the group by employing the same strategy he'd used the previous afternoon—stepping in the footsteps of the person directly in front of him. But by the time he reached the Balcony and the sun came up, he realized his vision was worse than ever. In addition, he'd inadvertently rubbed some ice crystals into his eyes, lacerating both corneas.[19]

"At that point," Beck revealed, "one eye was completely blurred over, I could barely see out of the other, and I'd lost all depth perception. I felt that I couldn't see well enough to climb higher without being a danger to myself or a burden to someone else, so I told Rob what was going on."

"Sorry pal," Rob immediately announced, "you're going down. I'll send one of the Sherpas down with you." But Beck wasn't quite ready to give up his summit hopes: "I explained to Rob that I thought there was a pretty good chance my vision would improve once the sun got higher and my pupils contracted. I said I wanted to wait a little while, and then boogie on up after everybody else if I started seeing more clearly."

Rob considered Beck's proposal, then decreed, "O.K., fair enough. I'll give you half an hour to find out. But I can't have you going down to Camp Four on your own. If your vision isn't better in thirty minutes I want you to stay here so I know exactly where you are until I come back from the summit, then we can go down together. I'm very serious about this: either you go down right now, or you promise me you'll sit right here until I return."

"So I crossed my heart and hoped to die," Beck told me good-naturedly as we stood in the blowing snow and waning light. "And I've kept my word. Which is why I'm still standing here."

16. The *Balcony* is a projecting mass of land on the Southeast Ridge, the place where two of the faces or slopes of Mount Everest meet.
17. *Camp Four* is the highest camp.
18. A *radial keratotomy* is surgery for nearsightedness.
19. The ice crystals cut the *cornea,* a clear layer that covers the iris and pupil, of each of Beck's eyes.

1 Structure *What clues are given here to chronological and spatial order?*

On the Move *How would you describe Beck's desire to continue the climb?* **2**

Reading Practice

SMALL GROUP SPIRAL REVIEW

Time and Sequence Krakauer jumps back and forth in time to provide background about his fellow climbers. He uses literary devices such as flashbacks and foreshadowing. He also uses chronological words and phrases to orient readers. For example, he says *Years earlier* before explaining Beck Weathers' eye surgery and its impact on Beck's eyesight while on the climb. Break students into groups and have them find other examples of signal words that Krakauer uses to orient readers in time and space. Invite groups to share their findings with the class.

Shortly after noon, Stuart Hutchison, John Taske, and Lou Kasischke had gone past on their way down with Lhakpa and Kami, but Weathers elected not to accompany them. "The weather was still good," he explains, "and I saw no reason to break my promise to Rob at that point."

Late in the afternoon during the descent from the summit of Mount Everest.

Now, however, it was getting dark and conditions were turning grim. "Come down with me," I implored. "It will be at least another two or three hours before Rob shows up. I'll be your eyes. I'll get you down, no problem." Beck was nearly persuaded to descend with me when I made the mistake of mentioning that Mike Groom was on his way down with Yasuko, a few minutes behind me. In a day of many mistakes, this would turn out to be one of the larger ones.

"Thanks anyway," Beck said. "I think I'll just wait for Mike. He's got a rope; he'll be able to short-rope[20] me down."

"O.K., Beck," I replied. "It's your call. I guess I'll see you in camp, then." Secretly, I was relieved that I wouldn't have to deal with getting Beck down the problematic slopes to come, most of which were not protected by fixed lines. Daylight was waning, the weather was worsening, my reserves of strength were nearly gone. Yet I still didn't have any sense that calamity[21] was around the corner. Indeed, after talking with Beck I even took the time to find a spent oxygen canister that I'd stashed in the snow on the way up some ten hours earlier. Wanting to remove all my trash from the mountain, I stuffed it into my pack with my other two bottles (one empty, one partially full) and then hurried toward the South Col, 1,600 feet below.

From the Balcony I descended a few hundred feet down a broad, gentle snow gully without incident, but then things began to get sketchy. The route meandered through outcroppings of broken shale blanketed with six inches of fresh snow. Negotiating the puzzling, infirm[22] **terrain** demanded unceasing concentration, an all-but-impossible feat in my punch-drunk state.

Because the wind had erased the tracks of the climbers who'd gone down before me, I had difficulty determining the correct route. In 1993, Mike Groom's partner—

20. To *short-rope* is to pull a second climber along using a rope attached to a leading climber.
21. A *calamity* is a great loss.

22. Here, *infirm* means "not solid."

3 Structure *How does Krakauer remind the reader of the chronological structure?*

Monitor Comprehension *Describe the encounter between Krakauer and Beck. If necessary, reread.* **4**

Vocabulary

terrain (tə rān′) *n.* the physical features of the land

Teach

Literary Element 3

Structure Answer: *He notes the coming darkness, the approach of night.*

ADVANCED **Ask:** How does the reference to night link readers to Beck's earlier discussion of his vision problem? *(Beck said earlier that he hoped his vision would clear in greater daylight. This implies the problem will get worse in fading light.)*

Reading Strategy 4

Monitor Comprehension
Answer: *Krakauer urges Beck to descend with him but is relieved when Beck refuses. Krakauer does not feel the sense of urgency at this moment that he should have felt.*

Advanced Learners

DIFFERENTIATED INSTRUCTION

Roots and Affixes Explain that the prefixes *in-* and *im-* are examples of negating prefixes. Usually, they mean "not," "without," or "the opposite of," and reverse the meaning of the attached root word. When the terrain is "infirm," it is "not firm." Sometimes the letters *in* appear at the beginning of words, such as *incident,* and are not negating prefixes but are part of the root word. Have students find three words in the essay that begin with *in-*, *im-*, or the other variations *il-* or *ir-*. They should define those that begin with negating prefixes.

Teach

Literary Element 1

Structure Point out the words "In the morning. . . ."

Ask: What do these words suggest about the order of events in this paragraph? *(They suggest a brief flashback to the morning's events.)*

Reading Strategy 2

Monitor Comprehension

Answer: *Students may say that they knew what was coming (an earlier conversation between Adams and Krakauer on page 358 alludes to the storm), and so they could read at a fairly rapid pace.*

Cultural History ☆

Tenzing Norgay For more than 20 years, Tenzing Norgay climbed with expeditions trying to reach the summit of Mt. Everest. After reaching his goal in 1953, Norgay became a representative of the high altitude Sherpas.

Lopsang Tshering Bhutia, a skilled Himalayan climber who was a nephew of ☆ Tenzing Norgay's[23]—had taken a wrong turn in this area and fallen to his death. Fighting to maintain a grip on reality, I started talking to myself out loud. "Keep it together, keep it together, keep it together," I chanted over and over, mantra-like.[24] "This is way serious. Keep it together."

I sat down to rest on a broad, sloping ledge, but after a few minutes a deafening boom! frightened me back to my feet. Enough new snow had accumulated that I feared a massive slab avalanche had released on the slopes above, but when I spun around to look I saw nothing. Then there was another boom!, accompanied by a flash that momentarily lit up the sky, and I realized I was hearing the crash of thunder.

1 In the morning, on the way up, I'd made a point of continually studying the route on this part of the mountain, frequently looking down to pick out landmarks that would be helpful on the descent, compulsively memorizing the terrain: "Remember to turn left at the buttress that looks like a ship's prow.[25] Then follow that skinny line of snow until it curves sharply to the right." This was something I'd trained myself to do many years earlier, a drill I forced myself to go through every time I climbed, and on Everest it may have saved my life. By 6:00 PM, as the storm escalated into a full-scale blizzard with driving snow and winds gusting in excess of 60 knots,[26] I came upon the rope that had been fixed by the Montenegrins on the snow slope 600 feet above the Col. Sobered by the force of the rising tempest, I realized that I'd gotten down the trickiest ground just in the nick of time.

Wrapping the fixed line around my arms to rappel,[27] I continued down through the blizzard. Some minutes later I was overwhelmed by a disturbingly familiar feeling of suffocation, and I realized that my oxygen had once again run out. Three hours earlier when I'd attached my regulator to my third and last oxygen canister, I'd noticed that the gauge indicated that the bottle was only half full. I'd figured that would be enough to get me most of the way down, though, so I hadn't bothered exchanging it for a full one. And now the gas was gone.

I pulled the mask from my face, left it hanging around my neck, and pressed onward, surprisingly unconcerned. However, without supplemental oxygen, I moved more slowly, and I had to stop and rest more often.

The literature of Everest is rife[28] with accounts of hallucinatory experiences attributable to hypoxia and fatigue. In 1933, the noted English climber Frank Smythe observed "two curious looking objects floating in the sky" directly above him at 27,000 feet: "[One] possessed what appeared to be squat underdeveloped wings, and the other a protuberance[29] suggestive of a beak. They hovered motionless but seemed slowly to pulsate." In 1980, during his solo ascent, Reinhold Messner imagined that an invisible companion was

23. Tenzing Norgay and Edmund Hillary were the first climbers ever to reach the top of Mount Everest.
24. A *mantra* is a prayerlike repetition of syllables, words, or phrases for mystical purposes.
25. Krakauer describes a *buttress,* or a large, projecting rock, that looks like a *prow,* or the front part of a ship or boat.
26. *60 knots* is about 69 mph.
27. To *rappel* is to descend from a height by sliding down a rope.
28. Here, *rife* means "full of" or "overflowing with."
29. A *protuberance* is something that sticks out.

2 Monitor Comprehension *Did you slow down, speed up, or maintain the same reading rate as you read this paragraph? Explain.*

Reading Practice

PARTNERS SPIRAL REVIEW **Problem and Solution** Identifying problems and solutions can help students understand narrative nonfiction.

Ask: What is the main problem on this page? *(The narrator has to find his way down the summit in a terrible storm without enough oxygen.)* Who has the problem? *(Kraukaer)* What solutions are tried? *(He tries to remember what he saw on the way up the summit.)* What happens as a result? *(He makes it down the trickiest part just in time.)* Explain that Krakauer discusses many problems—his own and others'—as he recounts his attempt to solve his problem of getting off the summit alive.

Pair up students and have them find at least three other problems and solutions on these pages. Have volunteers share their findings with the class. Write their responses on the board.

climbing beside him. Gradually, I became aware that my mind had gone haywire in a similar fashion, and I observed my own slide from reality with a blend of fascination and horror.

I was so far beyond ordinary exhaustion that I experienced a queer **detachment** from my body, as if I were observing my descent from a few feet overhead. I imagined that I was dressed in a green cardigan and wingtips. And although the gale was generating a windchill in excess of seventy below zero Fahrenheit, I felt strangely, disturbingly warm.

At 6:30, as the last of the daylight seeped from the sky, I'd descended to within 200 vertical feet of Camp Four. Only one obstacle now stood between me and safety: a bulging incline of hard, glassy ice that I would have to descend without a rope. Snow pellets borne by 70-knot gusts stung my face; any exposed flesh was instantly frozen. The tents, no more than 650 horizontal feet away, were only intermittently visible through the whiteout. There was no margin for error. Worried about making a critical blunder, I sat down to marshal[30] my energy before descending further.

Once I was off my feet, inertia[31] took hold. It was so much easier to remain at rest than to summon the initiative to tackle the dangerous ice slope; so I just sat there as the storm roared around me, letting my mind drift, doing nothing for perhaps forty-five minutes.

30. To *marshal* is to bring together in an effective way.
31. Here, *inertia* means "the tendency of a body at rest to remain at rest."

3 Structure *Summarize how time and place have changed since the beginning of the essay.*

Vocabulary

detachment (di tach′ mənt) *n.* indifference; a state of being apart from

I'd tightened the drawstrings on my hood until only a tiny opening remained around my eyes, and I was removing the useless, frozen oxygen mask from beneath my chin when Andy Harris suddenly appeared out of the gloom beside me. Shining my headlamp in his direction, I reflexively recoiled when I saw the appalling condition of his face. His cheeks were coated with an armor of frost, one eye was frozen shut, and he was slurring his words badly. He looked in serious trouble. "Which way to the tents?" Andy blurted, frantic to reach shelter.

I pointed in the direction of Camp Four, then warned him about the ice just below us. "It's steeper than it looks!" I yelled, straining to make myself heard over the tempest. "Maybe I should go down first and get a rope from camp—" As I was in midsentence, Andy abruptly turned away and moved over the lip of the ice slope, leaving me sitting there dumbfounded.[32]

Scooting on his butt, he started down the steepest part of the incline. "Andy," I shouted after him, "it's crazy to try it like that! You're going to blow it for sure!" He yelled something back, but his words were carried off by the screaming wind. A second later he lost his purchase, flipped ass over teakettle, and was suddenly rocketing headfirst down the ice.

Two hundred feet below, I could just make out Andy's motionless form slumped at the foot of the incline. I was sure he'd broken at least a leg, maybe his neck. But then, incredibly, he stood up, waved that he was O.K., and started lurching[33] toward

32. *Dumbfounded* means "so surprised that one cannot speak."
33. To *lurch* is to move in a sudden, irregular way.

On the Move *What is Andy's attitude toward the climb at this point?* **4**

Teach

Literary Element 3

Structure Answer: *More than four hours have passed. He is within 200 vertical feet of his destination instead of at the top of the mountain.*

APPROACHING **Ask:** How do you know it is 6:00 PM and not 6:00 AM? *(He says "the last of the daylight seeped from the sky.")*

Big Idea 4

On the Move Answer: *Andy is near panic and wants the climb to be over.*

APPROACHING For approaching-level students, **ask:** How does Andy's emotional state affect his judgment? *(He rushes down the slope without evaluating its steepness, and ends up falling.)*

Approaching Level

DIFFERENTIATED INSTRUCTION

Emerging In the first column on page 364, Krakauer says that snow pellets traveling in wind gusts of 70 knots hit his face. Tell students that a knot is a unit of measurement that is a little more than mile. This is as strong as wind during a hurricane.

Teach

Reading Strategy 1

Monitor Comprehension
Answer: *They are about Andy's almost miraculously safe descent, his making it almost (and presumably) to safety, and Krakauer's momentary jealousy of that fact.*

Literary Element 2

Structure Answer: *He uses both orders throughout the essay. He only deviates to give background information about past climbers.*

ENGLISH LEARNERS Ask English learners to explain how Krakauer's use of sequence can help the reader. *(Possible answer: The use of sequence helps to organize information and helps the reader follow the events in an organized way.)*

To check students' understanding of the selection, see Unit 2 Teaching Resources Book, p. 151.

View the Photograph ★

This photograph was taken by Caroline Mackenzie, the Base Camp doctor for the expedition. Lack of oxygen (hypoxia), frostbite, and brain swelling are just some of the problems that face doctors on Everest.

Members of the ill-fated Mount Everest expedition led by Rob Hall (center right) and guide Scott Fischer (center left). John Krakauer is third from left. ★

Camp Four, which, at the moment was in plain sight, 500 feet beyond.

I could see the shadowy forms of three or four people standing outside the tents; their headlamps flickered through curtains of blowing snow. I watched Harris walk toward them across the flats, a distance he covered in less than ten minutes. When the clouds closed in a moment later, cutting off my view, he was within sixty feet of the tents, maybe closer. I didn't see him again after that, but I was certain that he'd reached the security of camp, where Chuldum and Arita would doubtless be waiting with hot tea. Sitting out in the storm, with the ice bulge still standing between me and the tents, I felt a pang of envy. I was angry that my guide hadn't waited for me.

My backpack held little more than three empty oxygen canisters and a pint of frozen lemonade; it probably weighed no more than sixteen or eighteen pounds. But I was tired, and worried about getting down the incline without breaking a leg, so I tossed the pack over the edge and hoped it would come to rest where I could retrieve it. Then I stood up and started down the ice, which was as smooth and hard as the surface of a bowling ball.

Fifteen minutes of dicey, fatiguing crampon[34] work brought me safely to the bottom of the incline, where I easily located my pack, and another ten minutes after that I was in camp myself. I lunged into my tent with my crampons still on, zipped the door tight, and sprawled across the frost-covered floor too tired to even sit upright. For the first time I had a sense of how wasted I really was: I was more exhausted than I'd ever been in my life. But I was safe. Andy was safe.[35] The others would be coming into camp soon. We'd done it. We'd climbed Everest. It had been a little sketchy there for a while, but in the end everything had turned out great.

It would be many hours before I learned that everything had not in fact turned out great—that nineteen men and women were stranded up on the mountain by the storm, caught in a desperate struggle for their lives. ∾

34. *Crampons* are steel spikes attached to mountaineering boots to prevent sliding on ice and snow.

35. As Krakauer would realize later, he had mistaken Martin Adams for Andy Harris. In fact, Harris died on the climb while trying to help others reach safety.

1 Monitor Comprehension *Monitor your comprehension by telling who and what the preceding two paragraphs are about. If necessary, reread.*

Structure *How consistently does Krakauer use time and spatial order in this essay?* 2

Grammar Practice

Semicolons and Colons

Tell students that Krakauer frequently uses the semicolon to join closely related independent clauses. Read aloud the first sentence of the second paragraph on this page. Point out that the idea in the first independent clause *(that his backpack had little in it)* is closely related to the idea in the second independent clause *(that it weighed no more than sixteen or eighteen pounds).*

Show students Krakauer's use of the colon in the second column on this page. In this instance, he uses the colon to separate a statement from an example. Have students write three sentences using a semicolon and three sentences using a colon the way that Krakauer does. Have students write examples of sentences on the board.

After You Read

Respond and Think Critically

Respond and Interpret

1. What part of this essay interested or startled you the most? Explain.
2. (a)Where is Krakauer at the beginning of this selection? (b)How would you describe his mood or state of mind?
3. (a)What problems does Krakauer have with the climate on the mountain? (b)How do these problems lead to a crucial error on Krakauer's part?

Analyze and Evaluate

4. (a)What storytelling elements appear in this nonfiction selection? (b)How well does Krakauer tell the story of the climb? Use examples from the selection to support your opinion.
5. How well does the author convey the dangers the climbers faced?
6. How does Krakauer let the reader know that there are too many people on the mountain and, perhaps, that there are people who should not have been there?

Connect

7. **Big Idea** **On the Move** How does this selection make you feel about the risks and rewards of climbing Mount Everest?
8. **Connect to the Author** What facts about Krakauer might lead someone to have expected that he would be capable of successfully climbing Mount Everest?

Literary Element Structure

In this excerpt from *Into Thin Air,* Krakauer arranges the facts of his narrative in both spatial and chronological order. Spatial order shows the descent from the summit, while chronological order shows the passage of time.

1. Where is Krakauer at the beginning of the selection, and where is he at the end? State, in order, at least two places he stops along the way.
2. Explain how elevations, or heights measured in feet, provide a guide to the structure of this selection.
3. How much time would you guess elapses from the beginning of the action to the end? Cite evidence from the selection to support your answer.

Review: Dialogue

As you learned on page 173, **dialogue** is conversation between characters in a literary work. Dialogue is usually set off with quotation marks and dialogue tags, or markers that tell the reader who said what.

Partner Activity Work with a partner to record at least five examples of dialogue from the essay. For each one, identify the speakers, and reflect on the purpose of the dialogue. That is, tell whether the dialogue contributes to characterization, establishes mood, advances the action, helps develop a thesis or theme, or serves some other purpose.

Dialogue	Speakers	Purpose

After You Read

Assess

1. Possible answers: difficulties with oxygen; the bravery/recklessness of a near-blind climber wanting to continue
2. (a) At the top of Mount Everest (b) Eager to descend; his oxygen is running low
3. (a) The thin air deprives his brain of oxygen, and he gets dizzy and confused. (b) He fails to notice Andy Harris's advanced hypoxia.
4. (a) Characters, setting, events, rising action, suspense, and some foreshadowing (b) Students should support their answers with examples from the text.
5. He conveys the danger very well through descriptive language.
6. Krakauer details his long wait at the Hillary Step because of "overcrowding," Beck's will despite near blindness, Yasuko's need to be boosted to the top, and his reaction to Andy's reckless final descent.
7. Possible answer: This essay clearly shows the extraordinary danger of such an adventure.
8. He's an experienced climber. He began climbing at eight years old. He made the ascent of three previously unclimbed Alaskan peaks.

Review: Dialogue

Sample answers:

Andy Harris says, "I don't seem to be getting enough air." The purpose is to create a mood of danger, to show something about his character, and to advance the action.

Krakauer says, "Yo, Harold." The purpose is to show his goodwill toward Andy.

Literary Element

1. beginning: the summit; end: at Camp Four; on the way down: the Hillary Step and the Balcony
2. Elevations are presented in descending order.
3. More than 5 and a half hours pass; students should calculate times based on the hours in the essay.

Progress Check

Can students explain structure?

If No → See Unit 2 Teaching Resources Book, p. 146.

After You Read

Assess

Reading Strategy

1. Possible answer: The footnote about short-roping
2. Possible answer: Footnotes helped clarify location and unfamiliar hiking terms

Vocabulary

Answers will vary. Sample responses:

1. A person acting tenuously will look uncertain and shaky.
2. Seeing someone else fail might exacerbate a person's nervousness.
3. I felt invincible when my team won a close game.
4. Mountains, plains, and pastures are all types of terrain.
5. A doctor has to act with detachment so he or she can help his or her patient.

Academic Vocabulary

1. *Recover* means "to find or regain."
2. *Recover* means "to return to normal."

Research and Report

Students' reports should

- present information on multiple climbers
- present information about different aspects of their expeditions (i.e., routes, conditions, accomplishments, challenges).
- present the information in a web or multimedia format
- combine both visual and text in the presentation

Reading Strategy Monitor Comprehension

Krakauer assumes that his readers have some knowledge about mountaineering, Mount Everest, and the problems of thin air. Review the graphic organizer you created while reading, and then answer the following questions.

1. Name at least one place where you slowed down to refer to a footnote.
2. Explain how the footnotes helped you understand the features of Mount Everest.

Vocabulary Practice

Practice with Usage Respond to these statements to help you explore the meanings of boldface vocabulary words from the selection.

1. Describe the behavior of someone acting **tenuously.**
2. Give an example of a situation that might **exacerbate** someone's nervousness.
3. Identify a time when you felt **invincible.**
4. Describe the **terrain** of your neighborhood.
5. Give an example of a time you saw someone acting with **detachment.**

Academic Vocabulary

*The conditions during the climb made it difficult for Krakauer to **recover** from his state of dizziness and mental confusion.*

Recover is an academic word that has different meanings. Using context clues, figure out the meaning of *recover* in each sentence and explain the difference between the meanings.

1. She **recovered** the paddle from the river.
2. After a few days of rest, he **recovered** from the sickness.

For more on academic vocabulary, see pages 54–55 and R79–R81.

Research and Report

Internet Connection

Assignment Use the Internet to learn about other Mount Everest expeditions and climbers such as George Leigh Mallory, Tom Hornbein, Willi Unsoeld, David Breashears, and Ed Viesturs. Create a web page or a multimedia report about their challenges and triumphs, including facts about their routes, the conditions of their ascents, and first-time feats.

Get Ideas Keep in mind that you will be reporting on the climbers and their Everest expeditions. Use web diagrams to help you brainstorm research questions. When you decide on a topic for your research, write it in the middle oval of a web diagram. Then list questions about the topic in the surrounding ovals.

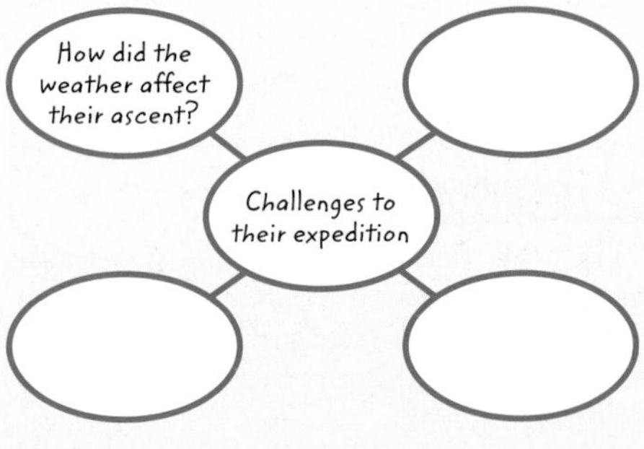

Research Choose a few climbers to focus on in your research. Then use the questions you developed in your web diagrams to gather information on each climber and their expedition. Organize your final research in an outline.

Report Using your outline as a guide, create a web page or multimedia report that combines text and visuals that convey the information gathered in your research. Provide a bibliography of the materials you used. See pages R34–R37 in the Writing Handbook for help in creating a bibliography.

LOG ON **Literature** Online

Selection Resources For Selection Quizzes, eFlashcards, and Reading-Writing Connection activities, go to glencoe.com and enter QuickPass code GL49787u2.

For additional assessment, see Assessment Resources, pp. 97–98.

To create custom assessments online, go to Progress Reporter Online Assessment.

For grammar practice, see Unit 2 Teaching Resources Book, p. 150.

To create custom assessments using software, use ExamView Assessment Suite.

Learning Objectives

For pages 369–373

In studying this text, you will focus on the following objectives:

Reading:
Previewing the article.
Analyzing text structure.

Set a Purpose for Reading

Read to learn about an explorer's journey to the shores of Antarctica.

Preview the Article

1. What do you already know about Antarctica?
2. Read the *deck,* or the text in large type that appears underneath the title. What type of emotion do you think the author wants you to feel about the trip he is about to describe?

Reading Strategy Analyze Text Structure

Analyzing text structure involves recognizing the pattern of organization the author uses. The following selection's main pattern of organization is problem and solution. As you read the selection, identify the problem the author illustrates. Then ask yourself, What possible solution or solutions does he provide? Use a graphic organizer like the one below.

Problem	Possible Solutions

TIME

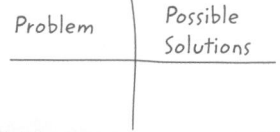

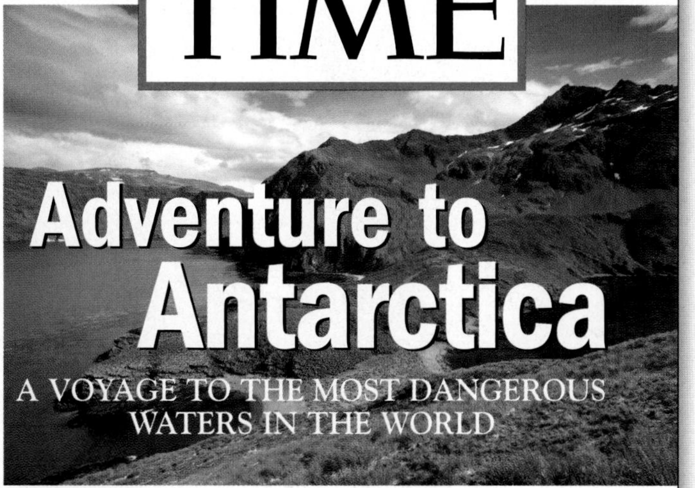

Adventure to Antarctica

A VOYAGE TO THE MOST DANGEROUS WATERS IN THE WORLD

By ROB JOHNSON

SOUTH GEORGIA ISLAND, LOCATED IN THE SOUTH Atlantic Ocean, is the breeding ground of Antarctica. Birds and seals live and reproduce there. The island is also the site of the whaling industry in the Southern Ocean for much of the 20th century. This cold and windswept, rocky land is the final resting place and center of drama for the life of British explorer Sir Ernest Shackleton, who wanted to be the first person to cross the frozen continent.

Surrounded by ice and the most famous and dangerous waters in the world, South Georgia Island (SGI) represents the ultimate destination on Earth. With this in mind, I set my sights on sailing to her shores. But nearly 10 years of reading, planning, dreaming, and voyaging would pass before we cast off.

The first thing I had to do was to build *Shaman,* the ship that would take us on our adventure. Her design and construction became the cornerstone of the adventure. My vision of sailing to South Georgia Island became the tool I used to inspire the designer, project manager, boatbuilder, and sail maker as each joined me in creating this 88-foot sailing yacht. Everything about *Shaman* was created with the South Georgia mission in mind. We launched her in 1997, and every voyage aboard her—past many glaciers, through many storms—built my confidence for the passage to South Georgia.

The Management of Fear

To dream and consider is not the same as to act. Setting out on an expedition to SGI is challenging—the water tempera-

TIME

Focus

Summary

Author Rob Johnson recounts his journey to Antarctica, inspired by his wish to see the final resting place of explorer Sir Ernest Shackleton. Johnson builds a boat, assembles a crew, and sets sail for Antarctica. Once there, the crew visits South Georgia Island, where Shackleton died, and Albatross Island. Johnson is deeply affected by his journey.

Teach

Preview the Article

1. Possible answer: Antarctica is a large, mostly uninhabited continent in the Southern Ocean at the South Pole.
2. Possible answer: The author creates an exciting mood by commenting on the perils of the story to come.

Reading Strategy

Analyze Text Structure

Problems may require many solutions and solutions can be multifaceted. Some problems are abstract, as in emotions such as fear. Others are concrete, as in staying aboard a ship in high seas.

Readability Scores

Dale-Chall: 7.6
DRP: 61
Lexile: 1020

English Learners

DIFFERENTIATED INSTRUCTION

Beginning/Early Intermediate Have students to read the first paragraph independently. Help students understand the location of South Georgia Island (SGI) by showing them the island on a globe. Tell them that SGI is one of a group of islands. Explain that no one lives permanently on the island because of its harsh climate. The temperature on the island drops below zero in the winter and remains cool even during the summer. With its snow-covered mountain peaks and blue glacier ice, SGI is a beautiful place, however, and is one of the most important penguin nesting sites in the world. The wind and rough waters surrounding the island make it difficult to approach by ship.

TIME

Teach

Big Idea 1

On the Move Point out that in the article, Rob Johnson acknowledges that fear is a component of every journey. His goal was to use that fear in the service of the journey, rather than allowing it to detour the journey.

Reading Strategy 2

Analyze Text Structure
Say: As you read the subhead The Team, ask yourself how each crew member solves a particular problem.

Cultural History ☆

Shaman Rob names his boat *Shaman,* a term that refers to a spiritual leader in many cultures. In some Asian and American Indian cultures, a shaman possesses healing powers. The term may also be used to suggest the power to control events, as perhaps Rob hoped for with his choice of name.

ture is 30 degrees Fahrenheit, winds are often stronger than 50 knots, and waves frequently reach a height of 50 feet.

We expected to hike on land **1** that features elevation changes of 2,000 to 3,000 feet in a day's trek, and as much as 10,000 feet just a few miles from shore. Besides the weather and the land, there were other dangers to face. Animals, in this case fur seals, can bite, leaving a deadly infection, and South Georgia does not have a hospital.

Fear will always be present when risk and danger are real, yet too much fear can limit an adventure. Much pleasure, excitement, and achievement are lost if you give in to it. Yet you can't ignore fear. It is more dangerous to say it doesn't exist.

I believe that the central focus of expedition sailing is fear management. Are the boat, the equipment, the team, and the preparation thorough enough to manage the risk of a dangerous expedition? Does the crew get along and do they trust and support one another? How does the team work together to roll back the envelope of the fear that limits action—roll back, but not eliminate, fear to get the most from the experience?

The Team 2

I selected a team of nine people, including myself. Raymond Wroe Street and Kim Broas had been aboard *Shaman* for four ☆ years. They knew her inside out and were in charge of the mechanical and logistics preparations. Raymond's brother, Grant, and Simon Laight were the athletes. Grant was an experienced outdoorsman, hiker, and climber. We would need Simon's and Grant's help once we landed on the island.

Since the Southern Ocean is so dangerous, I needed experienced sailors, some of whom knew how to steer in heavy seas. An 88-foot sloop, such as *Shaman*, can reach speeds of 20 knots or more in the conditions that sailors find in the rough Southern Ocean. A mistake aboard a 100,000 pound yacht hurtling through confused seas at that speed can be costly.

Erik Soper had a strong spirit. He came to be known as Crean after the member of Shackleton's crew Tom Crean, who was at Shackleton's side throughout his voyage. Every job was his job in his mind. Erik proved to us all that we could do more.

Reading Practice

SPIRAL REVIEW **Prepare a Bibliography** Ask students to imagine that they have written a report on how people can take a trip to Antarctica. Have them prepare a bibliography for the report in which they include a variety of consumer and public documents. They might consult government websites that show wildlife preserves and other restricted areas. They might also consult travel agencies for information about boat travel to the area and the best times to avoid severe weather. Emphasize that students should present their bibliographies in a standard format that meets manuscript requirements.

THIS IS THE MOST AMAZING PLACE I HAVE EVER BEEN. IT WILL PROBABLY BE THE MOST AMAZING PLACE I WILL EVER GO.

The crew socialized with the residents of Albatross Island.

Onne van der Wal was our photographer. He is a fine sailor and had sailed the Southern Ocean before. His skill as a seaman added to our confidence, and his pictures preserved our memories so we could share them forever.

Peter Wilson was the project manager in the building of *Shaman*, and an experienced seaman. He was formerly a captain and ocean racer. I was delighted that he had the chance to experience firsthand the ship which he had helped create.

We also needed knowledge of the island, its harbors, and its dangers. We were very fortunate to find a guide in Eef Willems. Eef had been to SGI several times, taking part in studies of the island's animal population. He also knew SGI's geology, animal life, wind conditions, and places to go for shelter. Eef had a very loving, enthusiastic, and encouraging way about her that was so important to her leadership. We could feel that she wanted us to stretch to see what she knew was waiting for us, and that she cared about our safety.

Departure 3

We left Ushuaia, Argentina, on February 7, 2003, and stopped briefly in Chile. Then we sailed out into the ocean, where light winds greeted us, eventually growing to 25 knots. We clipped along at 10–12 knots, at last on our way. Eef told us what we could expect during the 1,300-mile trip to SGI. Temperatures were cool and we spent time reviewing safety procedures. Everyone on deck had to wear a safety harness and be clipped to a tether so we wouldn't fall overboard. In addition, everyone on deck wore a life jacket and an emergency radio locator in case we *did* fall overboard!

Our trip was largely uneventful for 800 miles. Eef continued to tell stories about the island, which made us excited to see it. As we got closer, icebergs, 200 to 400 feet high, began to appear on the horizon. We were able to see the ice on radar, and during the daylight hours (about 19 hours of the day in the Antarctic summer), we could spot them in the distance. As the ice masses grew in number, Eef requested that we slow the boat to 5 knots or less during darkness. She also suggested that we put a crew member on the ship's bow during daylight as a lookout for ice. As excited as we were to reach the island, we were all in favor of Eef's safer—if slower—approach.

Approach and First Landing

On a slightly hazy and overcast day, we sailed up to the northwest corner of the island toward Right Whale Bay. As we approached the anchorage, two things were clear. First, the symphony of animal cries was worthy of a Steven Spielberg

TIME

Teach

Reading Strategy 3

Analyze Text Structure

Say: Each subhead identifies new problems. What are the problems in the section under the subhead Departure? *(Possible answers: not falling overboard; avoiding icebergs)*

For activities related to this selection, see Unit 2 Teaching Resources Book, pp. 153–161.

For an audio recording of this selection, use Listening Library Audio CD-ROM.

For additional assessment, see Assessment Resources, pp. 99–100.

Approaching Level

DIFFERENTIATED INSTRUCTION

Emerging Johnson tells about each of the members of his team and why they were chosen. As they read, have students jot down the name of each person and the reason he or she was chosen. Help students pronounce unfamiliar names. After reading page 371, ask students to explain why Johnson chose each member of his team.

Established Point out that on page 370, Johnson says that Raymond Wroe Street and Kim Broas had been aboard *Shaman* for four years—a long time. Their length of time on the ship shows how long Johnson prepared for this journey and how important it was to him. Have students share a time when they strategically planned for something. Ask them to explain why they gave so much attention to planning.

TIME

Teach

Reading Strategy 1

Analyze Text Structure
Ask: What personal characteristics does Shackleton use to solve his problems? *(Possible answer: courage, endurance, persistence, physical stamina)*

Cultural History ☆

Heroic Era Ernest Shackleton went to Antarctica several times. On one journey in 1907, he and his crew traveled to within 100 nautical miles of the South Pole. They confirmed that the site was on actual land, not ice. These explorations occurred during an era of great exploration at the poles. Known as the Heroic Era, it features the race between Captain Scott and Roald Amundsen to reach the South Pole. Amundsen won the race. Scott made it but perished on the return trip.

movie. Fur seals, elephant seals, and penguins provided a continuous soundtrack. As dusk approached, we could make out the outlines of the many animals playing on the beach.

Second, our sense of smell told us that this place was different from any most of us had ever visited. Not even the monkey house at the San Diego Zoo could compare with this notification that animal life was abundant. In my journal of the day I wrote:

Animal cries were everywhere. Awe was in every pair of eyes I explored. The excitement of the romantic quest to the land of Shackleton had given way to that which was before our eyes and in our ears.

1 Ernest Henry Shackleton

Many times, close examination deflates the reputation of a heroic figure. In this case, though, the more we explored the experience of Shackleton, the more powerful his heroism became. Shackleton, who had hoped to be the first person to travel across Antarctica, had the sense to place the value of human life above his personal record of achievement. In the end he is all the more heroic for the choices he made.

In 1915, Shackleton's ship was crushed in the ice near Elephant Island, about 800 miles from a whaling center on SGI. To save his crew, the explorer and five of his strongest men sailed and rowed 800 miles in a 22-foot boat to get help from the whalers. As we visited the beach where Shackleton landed after his trip, and as we traced parts of his dangerous three-day hike across the island, we could see and feel how dismaying the task must have been to the men seeking help for their stranded crew.

Perhaps even more remarkable was that Shackleton returned to Elephant Island and rescued all of his team. Every one of them was alive after months of living on the ice, eating penguins, and burning seal blubber for warmth.

Shackleton died in 1922, aboard ship while docked at a harbor along SGI. On February 15, 2003, the 129th anniversary of Shackleton's birth, we visited his grave on South Georgia and had cake inscribed with the Shackleton family motto, "By Endurance We Conquer." Written on the back of the gravestone is the following: "I held that a man should strive to the uttermost for his life's set prize. —Robert Browning." ☆

Albatross Island

We spent two days on Albatross Island playing with the wandering albatross, the largest existing bird species that can fly. This last stop was the most moving of experiences for me. I stood in the grass with my still and video cameras, and watched birds perform their mating dance. As they flew overhead, their 11-foot wingspan ripped the winds. At one point, two birds came up next to me. One of them nibbled on my glove. It then turned and sat down not 18 inches from my right thigh. I took off my glove and sat there petting its beautiful white-feathered back. Tears flowed down my cheeks. Tenderness and wonder filled my spirit.

After returning to *Shaman* I wrote in my journal: *I touched a bird and something in me was touched. At that moment, standing with Simon, Eef, Peter, and Onne, I could feel that I have completed what I came here to do. I cannot tell you what it is that I came here to do. But I know I have completed it. I am ready to come home. I do not entirely know why I built this boat. I do not know why South Georgia Island was my ultimate destination from the beginning. When we took off, I expected it to*

Writing Practice

SPIRAL REVIEW **Sensory Details** Johnson describes his surroundings and the trip with sensory details—sound, sights, smell, and touch. Point out his use of sensory details in this sentence: "A beautiful sunrise and Van Morrison on the stereo brought relief to everyone." **Say:** In this sentence, Johnson tells you what he sees—the beautiful sunrise—and what he hears—Van Morrison playing on the stereo. Have students create a chart with these headings: Sounds, Sights, Smells, Touch. Tell students to read these pages and fill in their charts with sensory details.

be stimulating and, at times, stunning. But I did not know all of what I wanted to accomplish. I did not know either, early on, what would free my mind to set sail away from here feeling. . . . satisfied . . . . We have seen a lot, and the experience of this island has been significantly more powerful than I had expected. Even with high expectations, I do not know now why this moment with the wandering albatross completed my satisfaction, and I do not even know what it is that constitutes completeness. I just feel it. I can come home now.

2 Heading Home

The magnetic pull of family, business, and friendships grew increasingly strong. Snow was falling on the mountains as we left, and winds were moderate. Dolphins and albatross took turns as escorts, leading our parade toward home. Winds and seas continued to build as we crossed the rough waters.

This was our final test. Four times, waves crashing into the steering cockpit knocked the helmsman off of his feet. The power of the Southern Ocean lived up to the tales, and I knew we did not see the worst of its anger. *Shaman* was strong and the crew was capable, but we were aware that the sea could take us if it wanted to.

As we sailed north, the conditions eased and the temperatures warmed enough to let us step out of our woolies and wet gear. A beautiful sunrise and Van Morrison on the stereo brought relief to everyone.

That evening, we landed in Montevideo, Uruguay, and tied the ship to the dock. *Shaman* had safely completed that which she had been designed to do. It was the trip of a lifetime. I am so grateful.

—Updated 2005, from *Yachting*, October 2004

Respond and Think Critically

Respond and Interpret

1. Write a brief summary of the main events in this article before you answer the following questions. For help on writing a summary, see page 42.
2. After reading about Johnson's travels, how would you describe his personality?
3. (a)How long did Johnson prepare for the voyage? (b)How do you think the time he spent preparing affected his coping skills while on the voyage?
4. (a)What does Johnson think about fear? (b)Do you agree with his philosophy? Why or why not?
5. (a)What did Ernest Shackleton do to save his crew? (b)How do you think Shackleton's rescue efforts inspired Johnson's idea of a team?

Analyze and Evaluate

6. Why does Johnson describe each member of his team?
7. Why do you think Johnson points out the Shackleton family motto, "By Endurance We Conquer"? What does this say about Johnson's values?
8. Johnson wrote in his journal, "I could feel that I completed what I came here to do. I cannot tell you what it is that I came here to do. But I know I have completed it." Why may he have felt this?

Connect

9. Consider the article, "Adventure to Antarctica," and the excerpt from *Into Thin Air*. How does the team mentality differ in each selection?

TIME

Teach

Reading Strategy 2

Analyze Text Structure
Direct students to the subhead Heading Home.

Ask: How does the subhead foreshadow the problem and solution of this subsection? (The problem will be getting home, and it will probably be solved.)

Assess

1. Students' summaries should reflect the main ideas of the article.
2. Possible answer: Johnson is an optimist because he set out to accomplish a difficult goal and led a team to achieve it.
3. (a) Close to ten years (b) The preparation helped prepare Johnson for any unexpected events.
4. (a) Fear should be managed, through preparation and by respecting danger. (b) Students should support their answers.
5. (a) Shackleton took his strongest men on a dangerous trip to get help for his stranded crew. (b) Johnson respected Shackleton's priority to protect his crew and the way the crew carried equal weight.
6. He wants to show that each individual on a team is important.
7. The motto inspires Johnson to adventure. He feels that endurance tests a person's will.
8. Johnson feels he has completed a quest he's had for many years. The sense of completion comes also from pleasure in Antarctica.
9. In "Adventure to Antarctica," each team member is assigned a specific task that benefits the team. In *Into Thin Air,* the hikers' tasks are more individual in nature. Also, the team has leaders with specific jobs.

Vocabulary Workshop

Jargon

Focus

Work with students to identify technical words or jargon and discuss their meanings.

Teach

Technical Words Recall that technical words can be specialized vocabulary, such as *spam,* or ordinary words used in specialized ways, such as *bug.*

Assess

Exercise

1. A *composition book* is a notebook to write stories and essays in.
2. *Galleys* are newspaper pages that are ready to be printed.
3. *Installments* are parts of a story that are printed at different times.
5. *Pulp stories* are books printed on inexpensive paper that are often about action and adventure.

For additional vocabulary practice, see Glencoe Visual Vocabulary CD-ROM.

Learning Objectives

In this workshop, you will focus on the following objective:

Grammar: Understanding jargon.

Vocabulary Workshop

Jargon

Literature Connection When Krakauer writes about mountain climbing, his language is full of words that climbers understand, such as references to fixed ropes and knots, or wind speeds. This specialized vocabulary is jargon.

> *"By 6:00* PM*, as the storm escalated into a full-scale blizzard with driving snow and winds gusting in excess of 60 knots, I came upon the rope that had been fixed by the Montenegrins on the snow slope 600 feet above the Col."*
>
> —Jon Krakauer, from *Into Thin Air*

Jargon is any technical or specialized language specific to a particular sport, trade, hobby, or field. For example, the jargon of computer users includes terms such as *bug, boot up, spam, Usenet,* and *blog.* The jargon of bodybuilders includes terms such as *rep, lats, mass,* and *set.*

Examples

Word	Meaning	Why the Word Is Used
intake valve	device used to control the flow of oxygen into an oxygen mask	Krakauer wore an oxygen mask, which he depended on to survive his climb.
cornice	a snowy, unsupported overhang on a mountain	Climbers who walked onto cornices could fall, possibly to their deaths.
crampons	steel spikes attached to boots to prevent sliding on ice or snow	Krakauer used crampons to descend icy, steep slopes.

Practice Identify jargon, or specialized vocabulary, in each sentence below. Use a dictionary or context clues to help you find each meaning. Then give a reason why the author may have used the term.

1. Richard Wright wrote one of his first stories in a composition book.
2. The editor set up Wright's story in galleys.
3. Wright's story was published in three installments.
4. The newspaper editor offered to pay Wright on a space rate basis.
5. As a boy, Wright enjoyed reading pulp stories.

Jargon

Jargon is any technical or specialized language specific to an occupation, activity, or group.

Technology Tip

If you come across a word that you believe is jargon, you can follow several approaches to determine its meaning.

Use context clues. Read the surrounding sentences carefully, looking for clues to the meaning.

Analyze word parts to see if you recognize the root or any affixes.

Use a search engine to look up the term online. Type *define:* and the term you want defined. For example, type *define: knot,* and several sites and definitions will appear. Different search engines will yield different results, so if you do not find what you need immediately, try another engine.

LOG ON **Literature** Online

Vocabulary For more vocabulary practice, go to glencoe.com and enter QuickPass code GL49787u2.

Writing Practice

SMALL GROUP **Jargon** Expand on the discussion of jargon on this page. Break students into small groups. Have them go to the library or conduct research online to find examples of jargon in another field, such as sports, medicine, or publishing. Suggest that they look through articles related to the field they choose. Encourage group members to think of other fields in which jargon might be used.

Once each group has compiled a list of terms, have members collectively use their new words in several sentences.

PART 3

FINDING COMMON GROUND

United Front (Un solo frente), ca. 1928. Diego Rivera. Mural 6.69 x 5.28 ft. Court of Fiestas, Level 3, South Wall. Secretaria de Educacion Publica, Mexico City.

View the Art Mexican artist Diego Rivera created this huge mural celebrating his heritage. How does this mural illustrate the Big Idea? ★

BIG IDEA

One of the most powerful forces in the world is that which comes about when people join with others who share their point of view. A major concern for citizens is how to get people to agree with one another and to join a common effort. The writers in Part 3 demonstrate their powers of persuasion. As you read these speeches, essays, and articles, ask yourself, How do you convince others to share your opinions? What do you do when someone does not agree with you?

375

UNIT TWO

PART 3

Analyze and Extend

Big Idea

Find Common Ground

Have students read the text under the "Big Idea" heading. Ask them to connect the idea of finding common ground to the artwork. Invite students to discuss how they deal with conflict. Return to this discussion later, after students have read selections from Part 3. Ask students to update their responses based on their reading.

View the Art ★

Answer: *Students should recognize that the two men shaking hands illustrate the Big Idea. Encourage them to point out details that reveal what differences they may have had.*

Mexican artist Diego Rivera (1886–1957) painted the great mural, *United Front*. Rivera revived the art of mural painting in his native country. Spurred by his interest in world politics, Rivera created huge murals that celebrated his heritage and depicted vibrant Mexican communities at work, at play, and at war.

Approaching Level

DIFFERENTIATED INSTRUCTION

Emerging Discuss with students different ways that people from different groups or cultures often come together. *(For example, immigrants moving to a new country, families joined through marriage, an employee joining a new company.)* Point out that in many of these situations, one person must join a larger group of individuals who share common interests, beliefs, or customs.

Ask: Has there ever been a time when you found it difficult to fit in with another group of people? Were you able to find common ground? What does the phrase "common ground" mean to you? Have students write a short reflective paragraph in which they address these questions.

For additional support for English Learners, see Unit 2 Teaching Resources Book, p. 164.

UNIT TWO

PART 3

Focus

Bellringer Options

Daily Language Practice Transparency 37

Or provide students with copies of an advertisement or a political flier.

Ask: How does the ad or flier make you feel? What does it make you think about? How does it try to influence you?

Teach

Literary Element

Diction **Ask:** What words in Lincoln's address might make the audience believe that the war is a worthy cause? *(Students may mention words and phrases such as "great civil war," "great battle-field," "brave men.")*

View the Art ★

President Lincoln (1809–1865) was the subject of many paintings such as this one by William Willard. Lincoln was also the first American president to be regularly photographed.

Ask: What character traits does the portrait of Lincoln suggest? *(Poise, thoughtfulness, intelligence)*

Learning Objectives

For pages 375–377

In studying this text, you will focus on the following objective:

Literary Study: Analyzing argument and persuasion.

LITERARY FOCUS

Persuasive Essay and Speech

What techniques make persuasive writing compelling?

On November 19, 1863, President Abraham Lincoln went to Gettysburg, Pennsylvania, to speak at the dedication of a cemetery that was to honor the Union war dead. One of Lincoln's goals in his speech was to persuade his audience to continue their support of the Civil War, no matter how terrible the losses.

The Gettysburg Address

by Abraham Lincoln

Four score and seven years ago our fathers brought forth on this continent, a new nation, conceived in liberty, and dedicated to the proposition that all men are created equal. Now we are engaged in a great civil war, testing whether that nation or any nation so conceived and so dedicated, can long endure. We are met on a great battle-field of that war. We have come to dedicate a portion of that field, as a final resting place for those who here gave their lives that that nation might live. It is altogether fitting and proper that we should do this.

But, in a larger sense, we cannot dedicate—we cannot consecrate—we cannot hallow—this ground. The brave men, living and dead, who struggled here, have consecrated it, far above our poor power to add or detract. The world will little note, nor long remember what we say here, but it can never forget what they did here. It is for us the living, rather, to be here dedicated to the great task remaining before us—that from these honored dead we take increased devotion to that cause for which they here gave the last full measure of devotion—that we here highly resolve that these dead shall not have died in vain—that this nation, under God, shall have a new birth of freedom—and that government of the people, by the people, for the people shall not perish from the earth.

Abraham Lincoln, 1864. William Willard. Oil on canvas, 61 x 45.5 cm. National Portrait Gallery, Smithsonian Institution, Washington, D.C. ★

Writing Practice

List Persuasive Techniques

Discuss the concept of persuasive speaking and writing. Then ask students to brainstorm different ways that people try to persuade them. *(Students might say that television commercials are persuasive, or that their siblings have certain ways of persuading them to do favors.)* Have students develop a list of techniques people often use to persuade others. Then ask students to write two paragraphs explaining how they were convinced at one time by an advertisement, article, or speech. Students should explain which persuasive techniques were used and why they felt convinced by the source.

By speaking of the sacrifice of the fallen soldiers and emphasizing the importance of the cause—liberty not just for the United States but for the whole world—Lincoln made a strong persuasive speech in favor of continuing the war.

Persuasion Persuasion is writing that attempts to convince readers to think or act in a particular way. Writers of persuasive essays and speeches appeal to logic and reason, but they also appeal to emotion. Notice how Lincoln uses patriotic appeals in referring to the "honored dead" and "this nation, under God."

Argument Argument is a specific type of persuasive writing or speaking in which logic and evidence are used to appeal to the reader's or listener's reason. Notice for example how Lincoln employs logic in saying that the hallowed ground cannot be consecrated because it has already been consecrated by the dead soldiers.

An effective argument has four primary parts: (1) the assertion or opinion statement, (2) support for the assertion, (3) acknowledgement of opposing arguments, and (4) a recommendation. The four parts of an argument can come in any order, or they can be mixed together.

Assertion An assertion is a statement of belief. A good assertion is short, precise, and direct. The writer or speaker names the topic and then states his or her position.

> Let the word go forth from this time and place, to friend and foe alike, that the torch has been passed to a new generation of Americans—born in this century, tempered by war, disciplined by a hard and bitter peace, proud of our ancient heritage—and unwilling to witness or permit the slow undoing of those human rights to which this nation has always been committed, and to which we are committed today at home and around the world.
>
> —John F. Kennedy, **from "A New Generation of Americans"**

LOG ON Literature Online

Literature and Reading For more about literary elements, go to glencoe.com and enter QuickPass code GL49787u2.

Evidence in support of an argument's assertion should be fact-based. It can come from a variety of sources, including research, expert opinion, and personal experience.

> When I quit the *New York Times* to be a full-time mother, the voices of the world said that I was nuts. When I quit it again to be a full-time novelist, they said I was nuts again. But I am not nuts. I am happy. I am successful on my own terms.
>
> —Anna Quindlen, **from "Put Down the Backpack"**

Refuting the opposing argument means anticipating what the opposition will say, and then explaining why these arguments are illogical, impractical, or unsound.

A good persuasive piece also includes a solution to the problem or a recommendation of what the reader or audience should do, think, or say as a result of the argument.

> Begin to say no to the Greek chorus that thinks it knows the parameters of a happy life when all it knows is the homogenization of human experience. Listen to that small voice from inside you, that tells you to go another way.
>
> —Anna Quindlen, **from "Put Down the Backpack"**

Quickwrite

Convince Others Write an e-mail to a family member persuading him or her to allow you to go to an amusement park with friends. Then read what you wrote. Label the sentences in which you make the assertion, provide support, acknowledge opposing arguments, and make your recommendation.

Teach

Reading Strategy

Evaluate Assertions Make sure that students understand the concept of assertion.

Ask: What is the assertion in John F. Kennedy's inaugural speech? *(He is claiming that Americans are committed to supporting human rights all around the world.)*

Assess

Quickwrite

Students' e-mails should contain an assertion, supporting facts, an opposing view, and a recommendation, all of which should be labeled. If students have trouble thinking of ideas, allow them to meet in groups to share their thoughts.

English Learners

DIFFERENTIATED INSTRUCTION

Beginning/Early Intermediate

Provide English learners with a list of vocabulary words associated with persuasion *(argument, assertion, position statement, opinion,* and *support).* Explain the meanings of these words to students and provide them with examples of each. Have students record words and examples in their vocabulary notebooks. Test their comprehension of these words by presenting them with more examples and asking them to identify each example.

Before You Read

Focus

Bellringer Options

Daily Language Practice Transparency 38

Or display images of important people and events from the 1960s era, such as President Kennedy, the Cuban missile crisis, Martin Luther King Jr., the Civil Rights Movement, American and Russian space satellites, and astronaut Alan Shepard.

Before You Read

A New Generation of Americans

Meet **John F. Kennedy**
(1917–1963)

John F. Kennedy was the youngest person ever elected president of the United States. He was a positive leader who had many ideas about how to change the country for the better. Although his time in office ended tragically when he was assassinated, he accomplished much in his short presidency.

Early Years Kennedy was born in Brookline, Massachusetts. His father was a successful businessman who encouraged all nine of his children to try to win in whatever they might do. One of his father's favorite sayings was "Second place is a loser." Kennedy graduated from Harvard in 1940, shortly before the United States entered World War II.

> *"Change is the law of life. And those who look only to the past or present are certain to miss the future."*
>
> —John F. Kennedy

Soldier and Statesman Kennedy joined the Navy and served as a lieutenant during the war. In 1943, when he was a commander in the South Pacific, a Japanese destroyer sank his PT (patrol torpedo) boat. Kennedy led the ten other survivors to safety, despite his own serious injuries. For his bravery, Kennedy received recognition as a hero.

After the war ended, Kennedy became a Democratic Congressman, and he advanced to the Senate in 1953. Two years later, he wrote a book, *Profiles in Courage*, about politicians who stay true to their principles despite difficult circumstances. This book was awarded the Pulitzer Prize for history.

Challenges as President Kennedy's popularity increased, and he won the presidential election in 1960. He called for new civil rights laws as well as additional government funding for education and better medical care. He also emphasized the need to help developing countries and started the Peace Corps, an organization that sends U.S. volunteers overseas.

Kennedy had to deal with threats from the Communist countries of Cuba and the Soviet Union. One significant event of his presidency was the Cuban missile crisis. In October 1962, a terrifying situation developed when the Soviets tried to bring nuclear missiles to Cuba. The United States feared that Cuba might use them to attack the United States and start a nuclear war. Kennedy was able to resolve the situation peacefully, and the Russians removed the missiles. In return, the United States promised not to invade Cuba.

Kennedy was assassinated on November 22, 1963. He was shot while riding in a presidential motorcade during a campaign trip to Dallas, Texas.

LOG ON **Literature** Online

Author Search For more about John F. Kennedy, go to glencoe.com and enter QuickPass code GL49787u2.

Selection Skills

A New Generation of Americans

Literary Elements
- Rhetorical Devices (SE pp. 379–384)
- Structure (SE p. 384)

Writing Skills/Grammar
- Persuasive Essay (SE p. 385)
- Infinitives (SE p. 385)

Reading Skills
- Recognize Bias (SE pp. 379–384)

Vocabulary Skills
- Word Origins (SE p. 384)

Listening/Speaking/Viewing Skills
- Analyze Oral Communications (TE p. 380)
- Analyze Media Coverage (TE p. 382)

Literature and Reading Preview

Connect to the Speech

What ideals are so important to you that you would make sacrifices to protect them? Discuss this question with a partner. Consider how much you would sacrifice to maintain the ideals.

Build Background

When Kennedy gave his inaugural address in January 1961, the hardships of World War II were still fresh in the nation's memory. The atomic bomb used to end the war had caused destruction unlike anything seen before. Americans feared nuclear war as tensions between the United States and the Soviet Union escalated.

Set Purposes for Reading

Big Idea Finding Common Ground

As you read "A New Generation of Americans," ask yourself, How does Kennedy encourage Americans to focus on the common experiences that draw them together?

Literary Element Rhetorical Devices

Rhetorical devices are techniques an author uses to create particular effects or to engage the reader. These devices use language in artistic ways that make passages more memorable and more persuasive. As you read, ask yourself, What effect does Kennedy's use of rhetorical devices have on me?

Reading Strategy Recognize Bias

Bias is an opinion or position on a topic that may stem from prejudice. An author who shows bias is inclined to think in a particular way and may have something to gain from the viewpoint he or she supports. As you read, ask yourself, How does the speech reveal Kennedy's opinions and goals?

Tip: Make a Chart Use a chart to record instances of bias in Kennedy's address.

Passage	Bias
"human rights to which this nation has always been committed"	human rights have not always been protected in the United States

Learning Objectives

For pages 378–384

In studying this text, you will focus on the following objectives:

Literary Study: Analyzing rhetorical devices.

Reading: Recognizing bias.

Vocabulary

venture (ven′ chər) *n.* an undertaking involving chance, risk, or danger; p. 381 *Though they were unsure of its chances for success, Mick's friends supported his business venture.*

negotiate (ni gō′ shē āt′) *v.* to discuss or compromise; p. 381 *The two countries were able to negotiate a peace treaty.*

eradicate (i rad′ ə kāt′) *v.* to get rid of completely; p. 382 *Some household pests can be difficult to eradicate.*

testimony (tes′ tə mō′ nē) *n.* a solemn declaration; p. 382 *The witness gave testimony in court that showed that the defendant had been innocent all along.*

Tip: Word Origins The etymology, or history, of some words is relatively obvious. For example, a dictionary will tell you that the word *venture* is a variation of *adventure.* You probably know that an adventure is an exciting or unusual experience, so you might have guessed that the two words are related.

Before You Read

Focus

Summary

In his inaugural address, John F. Kennedy speaks about renewal and change. He pledges his allegiance to the beliefs of our American forefathers but serves notice that the world has changed, and there is a new generation of Americans. He proclaims that this new generation is ready and willing to take responsibility for preserving the ideals of equality and liberty. In his speech, Kennedy reaches out to all people and nations and implores them to join together to make a better world.

For summaries in languages other than English, see Unit 2 Teaching Resources Book, pp. 165–170.

Vocabulary

The Power of Metaphor and Simile Compile a list of metaphors and similes that use words from the vocabulary list. Put students into groups of three or four to discuss the meaning of one or two of the phrases. Tell students to discuss what the phrases mean and why an author might choose to use metaphors and similes in his or her writing.

Approaching Level

DIFFERENTIATED INSTRUCTION

Emerging One of the most famous aspects of Kennedy's speech is the symbolism he uses. Explain to students that authors often use symbols (objects or images that stand for important ideas) in their writing. Encourage students to keep this in mind as they read the speech and to look for symbolism in Kennedy's words. Perhaps the most prominent symbol in this speech is that of a torch. Kennedy declares that "the torch has been passed to a new generation of Americans." To him, the torch is a symbol of the hopes and dreams of the people who founded America. He believes every generation has the responsibility to help carry that torch.

For additional vocabulary practice, see Unit 2 Teaching Resources Book, p. 173.

For additional context, see Glencoe Interactive Vocabulary CD-ROM.

Teach

Big Idea 1

Finding Common Ground
Answer: *The difficulties of war and of maintaining peace have brought Americans together and renewed their pride in their shared history.*

Literary Element 2

Rhetorical Devices
Answer: *The repetitions make the passage more powerful or create a sense of urgency by adding emphasis.*

ENGLISH LEARNERS Ask an English learner to look up *repetition* in a dictionary and to read the definition aloud.

For an audio recording of this selection, use Listening Library Audio CD-ROM.

Readability Scores
Dale-Chall: 10.1
DRP: 65
Lexile: 1360

John F. Kennedy

We observe today not a victory of a party but a celebration of freedom—symbolizing an end as well as a beginning—signifying renewal as well as change. For I have sworn before you and Almighty God the same solemn oath our forebears[1] prescribed nearly a century and three quarters ago.

The world is very different now. For man holds in his mortal hands the power to abolish[2] all forms of human poverty and all forms of human life. And yet the same revolutionary beliefs for which our forebears fought are still at issue around the globe—the belief that the rights of man come not from the generosity of the state but from the hand of God.

We dare not forget today that we are the heirs of that first revolution. Let the word go forth from this time and place, to friend and foe alike, that the torch has been passed to a new generation of Americans—born in this century, tempered[3] by war, disciplined by a hard and bitter peace, proud of our ancient heritage—and unwilling to witness or permit the slow undoing of those human rights to which this nation has always been committed, and to which we are committed today at home and around the world.

Let every nation know, whether it wishes us well or ill, that we shall pay any price, bear any burden, meet any hardship, support any friend, oppose any foe to assure the survival and success of liberty.

This much we pledge—and more.

To those old allies whose cultural and spiritual origins we share, we pledge the loyalty of faithful friends. United, there is

1. *Forebears* are ancestors; Kennedy is referring here to the founders of the United States.
2. *Abolish* means "to end or destroy."
3. Here, *tempered* means "made stronger through hardship."

Finding Common Ground *According to Kennedy, what was one of the effects of war on the people of the United States?* 1

Rhetorical Devices *What is the effect of the repetitions in this passage?* 2

Listening Practice

SPIRAL REVIEW **Analyze Oral Communications** Play an audio or video recording of the speech for the class. Review the rhetorical devices identified by the questions and other material in the student edition. Have students take notes on the way Kennedy delivers the speech. Tell them to watch for gestures, tone, and changes in pace and volume. Conclude by discussing which aspects of the speech make it memorable.

little we cannot do in a host of cooperative **ventures**. Divided, there is little we can do—for we dare not meet a powerful challenge at odds and split asunder.

To those new states whom we welcome to the ranks of the free, we pledge our word that one form of colonial control shall not have passed away merely to be replaced by a far more iron tyranny.[4] We shall not always expect to find them supporting our view. But we shall always hope to find them strongly supporting their own freedom—and to remember that, in the past, those who foolishly sought power by riding the back of the tiger ended up inside.

To those peoples in the huts and villages of half the globe struggling to break the bonds of mass misery, we pledge our best efforts to help them help themselves, for whatever period is required—not because the Communists may be doing it, not because we seek their votes, but because it is right. If a free society cannot help the many who are poor, it cannot save the few who are rich.

To our sister republics south of our border, we offer a special pledge—to convert our good words into good deeds—in a new alliance for progress—to assist free men and free governments in casting off the chains of poverty. But this peaceful revolution of hope cannot become the prey of hostile powers. Let all our neighbors know that we shall join with them to oppose aggression or subversion[5] anywhere in the Americas. And let every other power know that this hemisphere intends to remain the master of its own house.

To that world assembly of sovereign[6] states, the United Nations, our last best hope in an age where the instruments of war have far outpaced the instruments of peace, we renew our pledge of support—to prevent it from becoming merely a forum for invective[7]—to strengthen its shield of the new and the weak—and to enlarge the area in which its writ[8] may run.

Finally, to those nations who would make themselves our adversary, we offer not a pledge but a request: that both sides begin anew the quest for peace, before the dark powers of destruction unleashed by science engulf all humanity in planned or accidental self-destruction. **4**

We dare not tempt them with weakness. For only when our arms are sufficient beyond doubt can we be certain beyond doubt that they will never be employed.

But neither can two great and powerful groups of nations take comfort from our present course—both sides overburdened by the cost of modern weapons, both rightly alarmed by the steady spread of the deadly atom, yet both racing to alter that uncertain balance of terror that stays the hand of mankind's final war.

So let us begin anew—remembering on both sides that civility is not a sign of weakness, and sincerity is always subject to proof. Let us never **negotiate** out of fear. But let us never fear to negotiate.

4. *Tyranny* means "oppressive power."
5. *Subversion* is a systematic attempt to overthrow a government.

6. Here, *sovereign* means "independent."
7. *Invective* means "insulting or abusive language."
8. A *writ* is a law or a formal written command or order. Kennedy is promising to help the United Nations extend its power.

3 Recognize Bias *Who here defines what deeds are good and what constitutes progress?*

Vocabulary

venture (ven′ chər) *n.* an undertaking involving chance, risk, or danger

Rhetorical Devices *What technique does Kennedy use to make this passage memorable?* **5**

Vocabulary

negotiate (ni gō′ shē āt′) *v.* to discuss or compromise

Teach

Reading Strategy 3

Recognize Bias Answer: *Kennedy and the United States define what progress would benefit these developing countries.*

APPROACHING For approaching-level students, review the Reading Strategy on page 379, and ask a student to reread the explanation of recognize bias.

Literary Element 4

Tone Ask: What tone does Kennedy use to address "nations who would make themselves our adversary"? *(Possible answer: The tone is firm but not threatening; he asks nations to work together.)*

Literary Element 5

Rhetorical Devices
Answer: *His use of the same words in two consecutive sentences with opposite meanings emphasizes the importance of negotiation.*

English Learners

DIFFERENTIATED INSTRUCTION

SMALL GROUP

Intermediate Point out to students Kennedy's repetition of the word "to" on this page ("To those," "To our," "To that"). **Ask:** Why does President Kennedy start each paragraph with these words? What is he trying to tell his listeners? Explain to students that repetition in a speech or story can help make the writer's points stronger and more memorable.

Break students into small groups. Give each group a short story, speech, or poem. Then, challenge the students to rearrange the writing so that part of it repeats. Read some examples to the class and discuss how the repetition changes the flow of the writing and emphasizes certain ideas and images.

Teach

Literary Element 1

Rhetorical Devices
Answer: *It emphasizes the difficulty of his goals.*

ENGLISH LEARNERS To help English learners comprehend the usage of *nor,* have a student define *nor* using a dictionary and then use the word in a sentence.

Reading Strategy 2

Synthesize **Say:** Near the end of the address, Kennedy speaks of "defending our freedom in its maximum hour of danger." Explain that he is referring to the nuclear arms race between the United States and the Soviet Union. Have students research other speeches by Kennedy dealing with U.S.-Soviet relations, such as those made during the Cuban Missile Crisis of October 1962. Then discuss the ways in which recent presidents have chosen to have the United States defend freedom.

To check students' understanding of the selection, see Unit 2 Teaching Resources Book, p. 176.

Let both sides explore what problems unite us instead of belaboring those problems which divide us. Let both sides, for the first time, formulate serious and precise proposals for the inspection and control of arms—and bring the absolute power to destroy other nations under the absolute control of all nations.

Let both sides seek to invoke[9] the wonders of science instead of its terrors. Together let us explore the stars, conquer the deserts, **eradicate** disease, tap the ocean depths, and encourage the arts and commerce.

Let both sides unite to heed in all corners of the earth the command of Isaiah[10]—to "undo the heavy burdens and to let the oppressed go free."

And if a beachhead[11] of cooperation may push back the jungle of suspicion, let both sides join in a new endeavor—not a new balance of power, but a new world of law, where the strong are just and the weak secure and the peace preserved.

All this will not be finished in the first one hundred days. Nor will it be finished in the first one thousand days, nor in the life of this administration, nor even perhaps in our lifetime on this planet. But let us begin.

In your hands, my fellow citizens, more than mine, will rest the final success or failure of our course. Since this country was founded, each generation of Americans has been summoned to give **testimony** to its national loyalty. The graves of young Americans who answered the call to service surround the globe.

Now the trumpet summons us again—not as a call to bear arms, though arms we need—not as a call to battle, though embattled[12] we are—but a call to bear the burden of a long twilight struggle, year in and year out, "rejoicing in hope, patient in tribulation"[13]—a struggle against the common enemies of man: tyranny, poverty, disease, and war itself.

Can we forge against these enemies a grand and global alliance, North and South, East and West, that can assure a more fruitful life for all mankind? Will you join in that historic effort?

In the long history of the world, only a few generations have been granted the role of defending freedom in its hour of maximum danger. I do not shrink from this responsibility—I welcome it. I do not believe that any of us would exchange places with any other people or any other generation. The energy, the faith, the devotion which we bring to this endeavor will light our country and all who serve it—and the glow from that fire can truly light the world. 2

And so, my fellow Americans, ask not what your country can do for you—ask what you can do for your country.

My fellow citizens of the world, ask not what America will do for you, but what together we can do for the freedom of man.

Finally, whether you are citizens of America or citizens of the world, ask of us here the same high standards of strength and sacrifice which we ask of you. With a good conscience our only sure reward, with history the final judge of our deeds, let us go forth to lead the land we love, asking his blessing and his help, but knowing that here on earth God's work must truly be our own.

9. To *invoke* means "to put into effect or operation."
10. *Isaiah* is a prophet in the Old Testament of the Bible.
11. A *beachhead* is an occupied area in an enemy country where troops and supplies can land.

1 Rhetorical Devices *What is the effect of the repetition of the word* nor?

Vocabulary

eradicate (i rad′ ə kāt′) *v.* to get rid of completely
testimony (tes′ tə mō′ nē) *n.* a solemn declaration

12. *Embattled* means "prepared for battle."
13. A *tribulation* is a difficult experience.

Speaking Practice

SMALL GROUP **Analyze Media Coverage** Remind students that this inaugural address by President Kennedy was delivered in January 1961. Have small groups research coverage of that event in newspaper and news magazine articles, DVDs of television news reports, documentaries, and reports stored on the Internet. Groups can present their findings in the form of a panel discussion in which they compare and contrast the way different media covered the event.

After You Read

Respond and Think Critically

Respond and Interpret

1. How does Kennedy's speech make you feel about the United States?
2. (a)According to Kennedy, in which ways has the world changed? (b)What does he expect of this new generation of Americans?
3. (a)What does Kennedy promise to the people of less developed countries? (b)How do you think his promises to these countries relate to his goals for the United States?

Analyze and Evaluate

4. (a)What are the main arguments Kennedy uses to try to inspire the American people? (b)How persuasive is he? Explain.
5. Kennedy says that "sincerity is always subject to proof." Does his speech strike you as sincere?

Connect

6. **Big Idea** Finding Common Ground (a) What groups of people does Kennedy encourage to find common ground? (b)What are some specific ways he mentions for this to be achieved?
7. **Connect to the Author** When Kennedy served in the Navy during World War II, a Japanese destroyer sank his patrol boat. How does Kennedy present his attitude toward war in this speech? How might his experiences in World War II have affected his opinion about war?

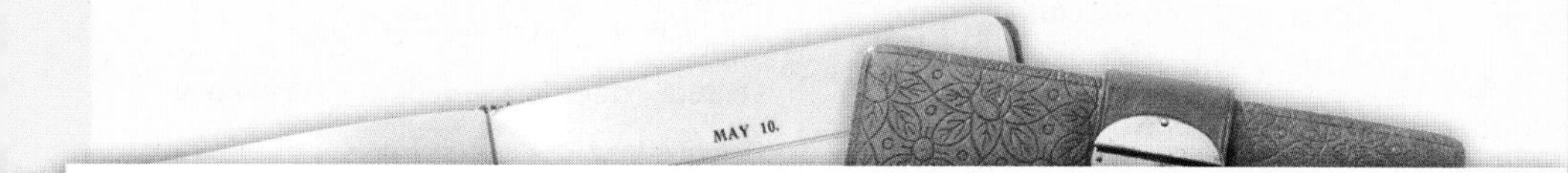

Daily Life & Culture

Inaugurating a New Decade

President Kennedy inherited a sharply divided country. For the white American middle class, the 1950s were a time of stability and increased consumerism. For many African Americans, however, it was a time of racism and oppression. Happy nuclear families ate TV dinners while watching "Lassie" or "I Love Lucy," but there were fallout shelters in the yard, bomb drills in the classroom, young U.S. soldiers dying in Korea, and the creeping fear of Communism. In his inauguration speech, Kennedy expressed the hope that people would unite in order to dispel the increasing polarization of both the country and the world.

Group Activity Discuss the questions on the right with your classmates.

1. What do you know about the 1950s from popular culture, such as movies and television shows? What have your parents, grandparents, or other family members told you about life in the 1950s?
2. Compare and contrast life in the 1950s with life in the United States today.

A family gathers around the television in 1956.

Daily Life & Culture

1. Answers will vary.
2. Answers will vary.

After You Read

Assess

1. Students may say they feel proud or optimistic about the United States.
2. (a) The world is different because people have the power to achieve more things, both good and bad, than they have before. (b) Americans will join together to use this power for the good of their country and the world.
3. (a) He promises to "help them help themselves, for whatever period is required." He pledges the United States will work with them to achieve freedom from tyranny and disease. (b) Students may say these are part of his vision of using American strength to create a better world.
4. (a) He says Americans share experiences with people across the world who struggle for freedom because Americans fought for these same rights. Therefore, Americans must help developing countries and make sacrifices to preserve liberty around the world. (b) Answers will vary. Students should support opinions with examples from the text.
5. Some students may say he sounds sincere and uses sound reasoning. Others may distrust his patriotic and idealistic tone.
6. (a) Americans and people from other countries, specifically developing nations and the Soviet Union. (b) He proposes working together against common problems or in the areas of science and art.
7. He thinks war is necessary, but only as a last resort; increasing the nation's power and readiness for war may deter other countries.

After You Read

Assess

Literary Element

1. "both sides overburdened . . ."; "And so, my fellow Americans . . ."
2. The devices are emphatic, persuasive, or inspiring.

Progress Check

Can students identify rhetorical devices?

If No → See Unit 2 Teaching Resources Book, p. 171.

Review: Structure

Invite students to compare their charts and read aloud each section of the speech.

Reading Strategy

1. D is the correct answer. Kennedy has no plans for territorial expansion. He is not so interested in the freedom of South American countries as in the security of the United States.

Progress Check

Can students recognize bias?

If No → See Unit 2 Teaching Resources Book, p. 172.

Vocabulary Practice

venture Etymology: Latin aventure means "adventure" Definition: an undertaking involving chance and risk Sample Sentence: The rock-climbing venture ended early when my friend slipped and twisted his ankle.

negotiate Etymology: Latin neg- means "not" and otium means "leisure" Definition: to reach an agreement Sample Sentence: My sister and I often have to negotiate the use of the bike we share.

eradicate Etymology: Latin e- (ex-) means "out" and radix means "root" Definition: to totally remove or destroy Sample Sentence: No matter how hard Gene tries, he cannot eradicate the weeds from his lawn.

testimony Etymology: Latin testimonium means "evidence, witness" Definition: a solemn declaration often made by a witness Sample Sentence: Sandra's testimony confirmed that Tia wasn't home Tuesday night.

Literary Element Rhetorical Devices

A writer can draw from a variety of **rhetorical devices** to create a particular effect. Rhetorical devices are often used to persuade or move an audience. Parallelism and repetition are examples of rhetorical devices that appear in Kennedy's address. Parallelism is the use of a series of words, phrases, or sentences that have a similar grammatical form. This sentence structure emphasizes the items that are arranged in a similar way. Repetition emphasizes words or phrases that appear more than once.

1. Examine Kennedy's speech to find one example of parallelism and one example of repetition.
2. For both passages you have chosen, describe how the rhetorical device is effective and what kind of reaction it is meant to evoke in the reader or listener.

Review: Structure

As you learned on page 356, **structure** is the particular order or pattern a writer uses to present ideas.

Partner Activity With a classmate, discuss the structure of Kennedy's speech. Create a chart like the one below. Fill in the first column with names for each section of the speech, such as *introduction* or *first main idea.* In the second column, note how long the section is. In the third column, summarize the main points presented in the section.

Section	Length	Main Points
Introduction	First 2 paragraphs	The world is changing, and people have more power.

LOG ON Literature Online

Selection Resources For Selection Quizzes, eFlashcards, and Reading-Writing Connection activities, go to glencoe.com and enter QuickPass code GL49787u2.

Reading Strategy Recognize Bias

SAT Skills Practice

1. What message underlies the paragraph beginning "To our sister republics south of our border . . ." (page 381)?
   (A) Latin American countries must be prepared to defend themselves.
   (B) The United States has the intention of creating one federal American state.
   (C) Latin American countries are democratic and must remain so.
   (D) The United States will not tolerate any foreign meddling in Latin America.
   (E) Poverty must end in Latin America.

Vocabulary Practice

Practice with Word Origins Studying the etymology of a word can help you understand and explore its meaning. Create a word map for each of these vocabulary words from the selection. Use a dictionary for help.

venture **negotiate** **eradicate** **testimony**

Example:

Definition: ordinary, commonplace, earthly

Etymology: Latin, mundus means "world"

mundane

Sample Sentence: Levi grew tired of his mundane life and took off on a trip around the world.

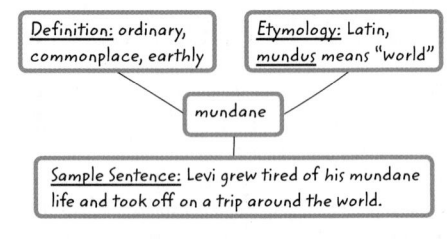

Respond Through Writing

Persuasive Essay

Argue a Position Perhaps the most famous line from Kennedy's speech is "Ask not what your country can do for you—ask what you can do for your country." Write an essay in which you argue whether it would be appropriate for a president today to make this same request. Provide support for your opinion, and use a rhetorical device such as parallelism or repetition to underscore your point.

Understand the Task **Parallelism** is the use of a series of words or phrases that have similar grammatical form. Use parallelism in your essay to show the relationship between ideas and to emphasize thoughts. You can also connect and emphasize ideas by using **repetition,** which is the recurrence of sounds, phrases, or lines.

Prewrite Once you have determined your position, brainstorm and create a list of arguments in favor of your stance. Discuss the issue with classmates and note the responses (supporting and opposing) to your arguments on another list. Review both of your lists and develop a thesis statement (a statement of the main idea) for your essay.

Draft Using your thesis statement as a starting point, begin writing a draft of your essay. Based on the lists you created, select the three strongest arguments supporting your position and build your draft around them.

After your introductory paragraph, introduce your supporting arguments one paragraph at a time. After stating your position at the beginning of each paragraph, address the opposing position. Use the lists from your discussions to state opposing arguments. Conclude each paragraph by refuting the opposing argument with evidence supporting your position.

Reinforce this parallel structure with the use of parallel language and repetition from paragraph to paragraph. This will help you to connect the essay and emphasize your main ideas.

Revise When revising your draft, make sure that the opening and closing paragraphs make a strong emotional, ethical, or logical appeal. Share your essay with one of the classmates whom you originally discussed the issue with. Use the feedback to guide your final revisions.

Edit and Proofread Proofread your paper, correcting any errors in grammar, spelling, and punctuation. Use the Grammar Tip in the side column to help you with infinitives and infinitive phrases.

Learning Objectives

In this assignment, you will focus on the following objectives:

Writing: Writing a persuasive essay.

Grammar: Understanding how to use infinitives and infinitive phrases.

Grammar Tip

Infinitives and Infinitive Phrases

A finite verb changes according to the number and person it is being used with (i.e., *run, ran, running*). An infinitive does not change and usually begins with *to* (i.e., *to run*).

You can use infinitive phrases to create effective parallelism in an essay or speech. For example:

The people need to create their own opportunities, to believe in themselves again, and to work together for the community.

For additional selection assessment, see Assessment Resources, pp. 101–102.

To create custom assessments online, go to Progress Reporter Online Assessment.

To create custom assessments using software, use ExamView Assessment Suite.

After You Read

Assess

Respond Through Writing

Students' essays should:

- clearly state a position supporting or opposing Kennedy's statement
- support their position with evidence or examples
- provide strong arguments supporting their position
- respond to opposing arguments
- use parallelism and/or repetition for structure and emphasis
- make an emotional, ethical or logical appeal in the introduction and conclusion

A student who meets all of these criteria should receive the equivalent of a 6-point response.

A student who fully meets four or partially meets five of these criteria should receive the equivalent of a 5-point response.

A student who fully meets three or partially meets four of these criteria should receive the equivalent of a 4-point response.

A student who fully meets two or partially meets three of these criteria should receive the equivalent of a 3-point response.

A student who fully meets one or partially meets two of these criteria should receive the equivalent of a 2-point response.

A student who partially meets one of these criteria should receive the equivalent of a 1-point response.

For grammar practice, see Unit 2 Teaching Resources Book, p. 175.

Before You Read

Focus

Bellringer Options

Daily Language Practice Transparency 39

Or **ask** students if they agree with the statement: No gain can be made except at someone else's loss. *(Students' answers will vary, but students should be able to support their opinions.)* Have students consider as they read how the author presents and supports his argument.

Before You Read

World Literature
France

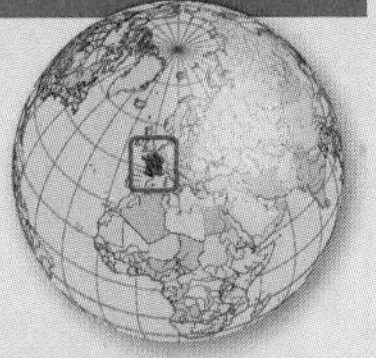

That One Man's Profit Is Another's Loss

Meet **Michel de Montaigne** (1533–1592)

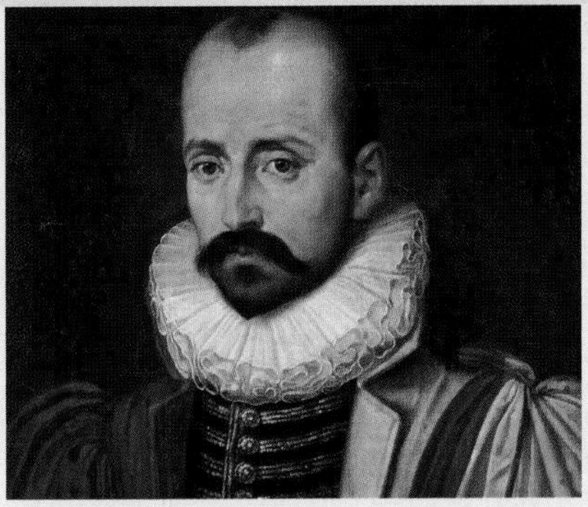

An influential Renaissance thinker, humanist, and one of the world's greatest essayists, Michel de Montaigne (män tān′) had an unusual childhood. He was born near Bordeaux, France, to a wealthy merchant family and was educated according to his father's personal views, in an environment of gentle encouragement. He was taught Latin, the language of the educated in Europe at the time, and did not learn French until he was six years old. As a child, he was curious about everything, especially people and their motives. As an adult, he called into question many of the beliefs of his time.

Father of the Essay When Montaigne was six years old, he was sent to the famous humanist school, Collège de Guyenne. He went on to study law, and became a councilor in the Bordeaux parliament in 1554.

> *"I write to keep from going mad from the contradictions I find among mankind—and to work some of those contradictions out for myself."*
>
> —Michel de Montaigne

In 1568 his father died, and he inherited the family estate. He left his government position to settle at the family château where he began to write. Montaigne is called the "father of the familiar essay" because he revived the ancient literary form, named it (the French *essais* means "attempts"), and made it popular. Montaigne wrote about humankind by observing and analyzing his own behavior and opinions and comparing them with those of others. His essays cover a wide range of topics, such as how to read well, how to endure pain, and how to raise children. Montaigne traveled to Paris to present a copy of his famous *Essays* to the king, Henry III, in 1580.

A Progressive Thinker When drawing conclusions, Montaigne tried to use what he called his "natural judgment" rather than things he learned from books. He wrote in a clear, nontechnical style, and tried to humble his readers by calling attention to excessive pride. Montaigne wanted to challenge what other people accepted as truth. He pointed out the danger of believing in anything without thoroughly examining it. Living in an age when religious intolerance ran high, Montaigne thought that the beliefs and customs of different cultures should be respected.

Unlike other writers of his time, he structured his essays through free association. This distinctive style influenced later essayists, such as Francis Bacon and Ralph Waldo Emerson.

LOG ON **Literature** Online

Author Search For more about Michel de Montaigne, go to glencoe.com and enter QuickPass code GL49787u2.

Selection Skills

That One Man's Profit Is Another's Loss

Literary Elements
- Antithesis (SE pp. 387–389)

Listening/Speaking/Viewing Skills
- Analyze Art (TE p. 388)

Reading Skills
- Analyze Argument (SE pp. 387, 389)
- Reread (TE p. 388)

Vocabulary Skills
- Word Origins (SE pp. 387, 389)

Writing Skills/Grammar
- Write a Summary (SE p. 389)

Literature and Reading Preview

Connect to the Essay

Is it possible to be successful without taking advantage of others? Discuss this question with a partner. Consider how one person's gain might have a negative effect on someone else.

Build Background

Michel de Montaigne was highly influenced by the works of Seneca, an ancient Roman writer and philosopher. "That One Man's Profit Is Another's Loss" opens with a reference to a character, Demades the Athenian, from Seneca's essay "De Beneficiis," or "On Benefits." Seneca's works influenced many writers from the sixteenth century to the eighteenth century.

Set Purposes for Reading

Big Idea Finding Common Ground

As you read this essay, ask yourself, What assumption does Montaigne make about people in general?

Literary Element Antithesis

Antithesis is a contrasting relationship between two ideas. An author uses antithesis by placing two contrasting ideas together, often in parallel structure. Mentioning the two ideas next to each other highlights their differences. As you read, ask yourself, Where in the essay does Montaigne make use of antithesis?

Reading Strategy Analyze Argument

An **argument** is a technique an author uses to present an idea in a convincing way. Arguments use reasons and facts to support an idea or opinion. As you read, ask yourself, What kinds of arguments does Montaigne use to persuade the reader?

Tip: Take Notes As you read the essay, note Montaigne's arguments and identify the supporting details. Create web diagrams like the one below. Write one of Montaigne's arguments in the center circle and fill the surrounding circles with supporting details.

Learning Objectives

For pages 386–389

In studying this text, you will focus on the following objectives:

Literary Study: Analyzing antithesis.

Reading: Analyzing argument.

Writing: Writing a summary.

Vocabulary

condemn (kən dem′) *v.* to declare to be wrong; to pronounce guilty; p. 388 *She condemned his cruelty to animals.*

contention (kən ten′shən) *n.* a point advanced in a debate or argument; p. 388 *The speaker's contention was well supported and won the approval of the audience.*

vice (vīs) *n.* a moral fault or failing; p. 388 *She considered eating junk food a vice and decided to break her habit.*

Tip: Word Usage When you encounter new words, it might help you to answer a specific question about the word. For example, you might ask yourself, When have I experienced a point of *contention* with someone and how did we solve the issue?

Before You Read

Focus

Summary

The speaker begins his speech with an anecdote about a man in ancient Greece who is condemned by another because he earns a living by selling funeral materials. The accuser claimed the man charged too much for his goods and made his profits from the deaths of many people. The speaker then ponders the question: Aren't all gains acquired at the expense of something or someone else?

For summaries in languages other than English, see Unit 2 Teaching Resources Book, pp. 178–183.

Vocabulary

Talking Points Review the vocabulary list with the students and give them examples of the words being used in sentences. Have a contest to see which student can use the most vocabulary words during the rest of the class period. Tell students to use the words in regular conversation and give a student a point each time he or she uses one of the new words correctly. The student with the most points wins.

For additional vocabulary practice, see Unit 2 Teaching Resources Book, p. 186.

Approaching Level

DIFFERENTIATED INSTRUCTION

Emerging Read aloud the Literary Element on this page. Explain that the word *antithesis* comes from the Greek word *opposition.* Give students the following examples to illustrate the concept. Point out the contrasting elements in each.

- "It was the best of times, it was the worst of times;" (Charles Dickens, *A Tale of Two Cities*)
- "We must learn to live together as brothers or perish together as fools." (Martin Luther King Jr.)
- ". . . one small step for a man, one giant leap for mankind." (Neil Armstrong)

Teach

Literary Element 1

Antithesis **Answer:** *Yes; it contrasts gain and loss. Montaigne presents Demades's "ill-reasoned" idea and then argues that no profit can be made except at another's expense.*

For additional literary element practice, see Unit 2 Teaching Resources Book, p. 184.

View the Art ★

Albert Hahn (1877–1918) was a Dutch artist known for his political cartoons, which were often critical of the militarism that he felt led to World War I.

To check students' understanding of the selection, see Unit 2 Teaching Resources Book, p. 188.

Interactive Read and Write
Other options for teaching this selection can be found in

- Interactive Read and Write for EL Students, pp. 91–98
- Interactive Read and Write for Approaching-Level Students, pp. 91–98
- Interactive Read and Write for On-Level Students, pp. 91–98

Readability Scores

Dale-Chall: 9.9
DRP: 64
Lexile: 1140

That One Man's Profit Is Another's Loss

Michel de Montaigne

"The Man of the Century" (Caricature of entrepreneur), c.1890. Albert Hahn. Graphic art. ★

Demades the Athenian **condemned** a man of his city whose trade was to sell what is needed for funerals, on the ground that he asked too high a profit, and that he could only make this profit by the death of a great many people. This seems an ill-reasoned judgment, since no profit can be made except at another's expense, and so by this rule we should have to condemn every sort of gain.

The merchant only thrives on the extravagance of youth; the farmer on the high price of grain; the architect on the collapse of houses; the officers of the law on men's suits[1] and **contentions;** even the honor and practice of ministers of religion depend on our deaths and our **vices.** No physician takes pleasure in the health even of his friends, says the ancient Greek comedy-writer,[2] no soldier in the peace of his city, and so on. And what is worse, let anyone search his heart and he will find that our inward wishes are for the most part born and nourished at the expense of others.

As I was reflecting on this, the fancy came upon me that here nature is merely following her habitual policy. For natural scientists hold that the birth, nourishment, and growth of each thing means the change and decay of something else:

Nam quodcumqus suis mutatum
finibus exit,
continuo hoc mors est illius,
quod fuit ante.[3] ∾

1. Here, *suits* refers to processes in a court for the recovery of a right or claim.

1 Antithesis *Is this statement an antithesis? Explain.*

Vocabulary

condemn (kən dem′) *v.* to declare to be wrong; to pronounce guilty
contention (kən ten′ shən) *n.* a point advanced in a debate or argument
vice (vīs) *n.* a moral fault or failing

2. Montaigne is referring to Philemon, an ancient Greek writer of comedies.
3. "Whenever a thing changes and alters its nature, at that moment comes the death of what it was before." This sentence is a quotation from the Roman philosopher Lucretius (c. 96 to c. 55 B.C.).

Reading Practice

SPIRAL REVIEW **Reread** Students may have to reread the selection several times to understand it. Help them understand the selection by asking these questions:

- What is the main idea? *(Students may say that people get what they want at the expense of others.)*
- What is the author's purpose? *(to persuade; to make readers think)*
- What is his tone? *(Students may say assertive or reflective)*

Read aloud the second paragraph. **Ask:** Are Montaigne's assertions true? *(Students may say they are true but that people do not mean to hurt others.)* Read aloud the translation of the last two lines of the essay. Pair students. Have them think of examples to support this assertion.

After You Read

Respond and Think Critically

Respond and Interpret

1. Do you agree with Montaigne's ideas about profit and loss? Explain your answer.
2. (a)Why does Demades the Athenian criticize the funeral director? (b)How does Demades' complaint set the stage for Montaigne's declaration?
3. (a)What does Montaigne say anyone will find if he searches his own heart? (b)What does Montaigne's statement tell you about his view of human nature?

Analyze and Evaluate

4. (a)What does Montaigne mean when he says that "No physician takes pleasure in the health even of his friends"? (b)How would you describe Montaigne's tone in this sentence?
5. In the last paragraph of the essay, Montaigne writes, "As I was reflecting on this, the fancy came upon me. . . ." What effect do the content, tone, and language of this sentence have on the reader?
6. Are you convinced by Montaigne's arguments in this essay? Explain using examples from the text.

Connect

7. **Big Idea** Finding Common Ground How does Montaigne employ the idea of nature as a way to establish common ground?
8. **Connect to the Author** Review the biographical sketch of Michel de Montaigne on page 386. Identify events in Montaigne's life that support his ideas about profit and loss.

Literary Element Antithesis

Authors use **antithesis** to make comparisons more powerful and to more clearly define the contrasting relationship between two things.

1. Where does Montaigne use antithesis to try to lead the reader to a certain conclusion? Explain.
2. In what ways is Montaigne's whole essay based on antithesis?

Reading Strategy Analyze Argument

In order to persuade, an author must support his or her argument with statements, facts, and reasons that are certain to have a great impact on the reader.

1. What kinds of reasons or facts does Montaigne use to support his main argument?
2. What kind of support in this essay do you find most persuasive? Explain.

LOG ON **Literature** Online

Selection Resources For Selection Quizzes, eFlashcards, and Reading-Writing Connection activities, go to glencoe.com and enter QuickPass code GL49787u2.

Vocabulary Practice

Practice with Usage Respond to these statements to help you explore the meanings of the boldface vocabulary words from the selection.

1. Explain a situation where a judge might **condemn** a person.
2. Identify a point of **contention** you have recently seen between two people.
3. Give an example of a **vice** you would like to stop or give up.

Writing

Write a Summary Summarizing an essay can help you to understand its main ideas and organizational structure. Write a one-paragraph summary of "That One Man's Profit Is Another's Loss." Remember to highlight the main idea and key points of the essay. For help writing a summary, see page 421.

After You Read

Assess

1. Answers will vary.
2. (a) The funeral director profits from people's deaths. (b) By highlighting this "ill-reasoned judgment," Montaigne makes his position sound reasonable.
3. (a) Our deepest wishes are "born and nourished at the expense of others." (b) He is pessimistic; he thinks people care only about themselves.
4. (a) A physician who cares about profit loses if anyone is healthy. (b) humorous; he exaggerates to make a point
5. This line strikes a casual and conversational tone, as if his conclusion occurred to him spontaneously.
6. Answers will vary.
7. He appeals to the "habitual policy" of nature. Laws of nature include growth and decay; the laws also apply to profit and loss.
8. He inherited the family estate due to the death of his father. He moved into the family château and his career as a writer began, but only after he gave up his government position.

Literary Element

1. He shows the reader how most professions profit. He focuses on negative aspects of jobs so readers will find them ruthless.
2. The title has an antithesis. The theme, that one person's profit is another's loss, is an antithesis.

For additional selection assessment, see Assessment Resources, pp. 103–104.

Reading Strategy

1. He examines jobs that most people would not find distasteful and shows how each profession gains from loss. He states that this theory agrees with the laws of nature.
2. Answers will vary.

Vocabulary Practice

Answers will vary. Sample responses:

1. A murder trial
2. What to eat for dinner is a point of contention in my family.
3. I would like to stop drinking soda.

Writing

Students' summaries should: state the essay's main idea and highlight key points.

Before You Read

Focus

Bellringer Options

Daily Language Practice Transparency 40

Or invite students to name their favorite comedian or comedy show on television.

Ask: Why does the comedian or television show appeal to you? As they read, have students consider the characteristics of humor and why people respond to humor.

Before You Read

Daylight Saving

Meet **Benjamin Franklin**
(1706–1790)

"If you would not be forgotten, as soon as you are dead, either write things worth reading, or do things worth the writing."

—Benjamin Franklin

Born in Boston, Massachusetts, Benjamin Franklin attended school for only two years before beginning work in his father's shop. When his brother James returned from England in 1718 and set up a printing shop, Franklin became James's apprentice. Franklin developed a great love of books. In fact, he would eventually establish America's first public library.

Literary Career When Franklin was sixteen, he began to write anonymously for the *New England Courant,* a newspaper that James had started. Franklin wrote under the pen name "Silence Dogood," thinking that his brother would not take his work seriously. In 1723 Franklin moved to Philadelphia, where he established a printing shop in 1728. One year later, he purchased a local newspaper, the *Pennsylvania Gazette.*

Franklin married Deborah Read Rogers in 1730, and they raised three children. Two years later, Franklin started writing and publishing what became known as *Poor Richard's Almanack,* which was extremely popular for its engaging prose and useful information.

Scientist and Revolutionary Franklin busied himself conducting scientific experiments. During his lifetime, he was better known for his scientific achievements than for his writing accomplishments. For example, he devised a new way of printing paper money to make counterfeiting more difficult. He also made many important discoveries concerning electricity and invented the grounding rod, which protected buildings from lightning strikes.

Franklin also was an important figure in the struggle to achieve American independence from England. He was elected Speaker of the Pennsylvania House in 1764 and became one of the chief spokespersons for the colonies. In 1776 he served on the committee to draft the Declaration of Independence and then went to France as an ambassador. While there he negotiated the Treaty of Paris, which formally ended the American Revolutionary War. He is considered by many historians to be the most celebrated early American after George Washington.

LOG ON **Literature** Online

Author Search For more about Benjamin Franklin, go to glencoe.com and enter QuickPass code GL49787u2.

Selection Skills

Daylight Saving

Literary Elements
- Humor (SE pp. 391, 394, 396)
- Rhetorical Devices (SE p. 396)

Listening/Speaking/Viewing Skills
- Analyze Art (SE p. 395)

Reading Skills
- Analyze Humor (SE pp. 391, 393, 394, 397)
- Evaluate Evidence (TE p. 392)

Vocabulary Skills
- Context Clues (SE pp. 391, 397)

Writing Skills/Grammar
- Apply Irony and Hyperbole (SE p. 397)
- Research Daylight Savings (TE p. 392)

Literature and Reading Preview

Connect to the Letter

When have you shared a humorous incident with your friends or family members to convince them of something? Discuss this question with a partner. Consider why it can be helpful to use humor when trying to convince people of something.

Build Background

Daylight saving time comes from an idea of Benjamin Franklin's. The system was not seriously suggested, however, until 1907, when German William Willett proposed moving clocks forward in April and moving clocks back in September. His proposal met with a great deal of criticism. Today, most areas of the United States follow daylight saving time laws.

Set Purposes for Reading

Big Idea Finding Common Ground

As you read, ask yourself, How does Franklin find common ground with readers as he argues taking advantage of sunlight?

Literary Element Humor

Humor is the quality of a literary work that makes the characters, situations, or events appear funny or ridiculous. Humor can appear in many forms and can be used in a serious work to provide comic relief or make a point. As you read, ask yourself, What types of humor does Franklin use in his letter?

Reading Strategy Analyze Humor

When you **analyze humor,** you determine the function of humor in a literary selection. As you read, ask yourself, What is Franklin's primary purpose in using humor in this letter?

Tip: Make a Chart In a two-column chart similar to the one below, track Franklin's use of persuasive humor.

Examples of Humor	Persuasive Intent
p. 393 "he used many ingenious arguments"	ridicules a "learned natural philosopher" who has knowledge from books, not observation

Learning Objectives

For pages 390–397

In studying this text, you will focus on the following objectives:

Literary Study: Identifying humor.

Reading: Analyzing humor.

Writing: Applying irony and hyperbole in a humorous essay.

Vocabulary

negligently (neg′ li jənt lē) *adv.* in a carelessly inattentive manner; p. 392 *She negligently allowed the children to go swimming alone.*

subsequent (sub′ sə kwənt) *adj.* following in time, order, or place; p. 393 *After their first research paper, the students hoped that subsequent papers would be easier.*

obstinately (ob′ stə nit lē) *adv.* stubbornly; in spite of reason or persuasion; p. 394 *He obstinately refused to change his plans.*

prudent (pro͞od′ ənt) *adj.* showing wisdom and good judgment; p. 395 *She asked the advice of a prudent friend before making a big decision.*

Tip: Context Clues You can figure out the meaning of an unfamiliar word by its context, or the words around it. For example, in the sentence *I was nervous before the first show, but I felt more at ease at subsequent shows,* the word *first* lets you know that *subsequent* refers to later shows.

English Learners

DIFFERENTIATED INSTRUCTION

Early Intermediate Point out the vocabulary words on this page. Read aloud each word and its definition. Point out that the words *negligently* and *obstinately* are adverbs. Remind students that adverbs modify verbs. **Write:** The tall man ducked quickly. **Say:** The word *quickly* is an adverb that modifies the verb *ducked.* It tells how the man ducked.

Tell students that while adverbs often end in *-ly,* some adverbs do not. **Write:** We will go to the movies soon. **Say:** In this sentence, the word *soon* is an adverb because it modifies the verb *go*—it tells when we will go to the movies.

Before You Read

Focus

Summary

While visiting France, Benjamin Franklin witnesses the unveiling of a new type of lamp. A discussion follows about how economical using the lamp will be. A satisfactory conclusion is not reached. Franklin writes a humorous letter to the *Journal of Paris* describing the problem and a wonderful discovery he has made about the sun that will be the solution to the problem of saving daylight.

For summaries in languages other than English, see Unit 2 Teaching Resources Book, pp. 190–195.

Vocabulary

Word Origins Ask students to find the etymology of the vocabulary words. Have them focus on and copy all the abbreviations in the etymology, or the portion of the entry that details the word's origins.

For additional vocabulary practice, see Unit 2 Teaching Resources Book, p. 198.

For additional context, see Glencoe Visual Vocabulary CD-ROM.

Teach

Big Idea 1

Finding Common Ground

Say: Keep these questions in mind as you read: What is the purpose of Franklin's letter? *(To provide information in a humorous way about saving money on lighting.)*

APPROACHING For approaching-level students, **ask:** How does Franklin use humor to make his point? *(He uses humor to poke fun at the people discussing the issue because they are oblivious to a simple solution.)*

Big Idea 2

Finding Common Ground

Answer: *He mentions people's desire to save money. The title connects saving money and "saving" daylight.*

Reading Strategy 3

Evaluate Evidence

Ask: How does Franklin support his claim that the sun was supposed to rise at six o'clock? *(He looked at his watch and in an almanac.)*

For an audio recording of this selection, use Listening Library Audio CD-ROM.

Readability Scores

Dale-Chall: 10.3
DRP: 62
Lexile: 1240

Shakespeare's Bed, 2003. Pam Ingalls.

Daylight Saving

Benjamin Franklin

MESSIEURS,[1]

1 You often entertain us with accounts of new discoveries. Permit me to communicate to the public, through your paper, one that has lately been made by myself, and which I conceive may be of great utility.

I was the other evening in a grand company, where the new lamp of Messrs. Quinquet and Lange was introduced, and much admired for its splendor; but a general inquiry was made, whether the oil it consumed was not in proportion to the light it afforded, in which case there would be no saving in the use of it. No one present could satisfy us in that point, which all agreed ought to be known, it being a very desirable thing to lessen, if possible, the expense of lighting our apartments, when every other article of family expense was so much augmented.

I was pleased to see this general concern for economy, for I love economy exceedingly.

I went home, and to bed, three or four hours after midnight, with my head full of the subject. An accidental sudden noise waked me about six in the morning, when I was surprised to find my room filled with light; and I imagined at first, that a number of those lamps had been brought into it; but, rubbing my eyes, I perceived the light came in at the windows. I got up and looked out to see what might be the occasion of it, when I saw the sun just rising above the horizon, from whence he poured his rays plentifully into my chamber, my domestic[2] having **negligently** omitted, the preceding evening, to close the shutters.

I looked at my watch, which goes very well, and found that it was but six o'clock; 3 and still thinking it something extraordinary that the sun should rise so early, I

1. *Messieurs* (mes′ ərz), abbreviated as *Messrs.*, is the plural of *Monsieur* (mə syœ′), the French equivalent of the English title "Mister."

2 Finding Common Ground *What common concern does Franklin mention here, and how is it related to the title of the essay?*

2. A *domestic* is a household servant.

Vocabulary

negligently (neg′ li jənt lē) *adv.* in a carelessly inattentive manner

Writing Practice

SPIRAL REVIEW

Research Daylight Savings

Students may know that hours of daylight and darkness vary during the year with the changing seasons. Explain that daylight savings time is a way to save energy by changing time so that it is light outdoors when people are awake. Tell students that daylight savings time essentially moves an hour of daylight from the morning to the evening. Have students research the history of daylight savings time in the United States and write a summary of their findings.

3 looked into the almanac,[3] where I found it to be the hour given for his rising on that day. I looked forward, too, and found he was to rise still earlier every day till towards the end of June; and that at no time in the year he retarded his rising so long as till eight o'clock. Your readers, who with me have never seen any signs of sunshine before noon, and seldom regard the astronomical[4] part of the almanac, will be as much astonished as I was, when they hear of his rising so early; and especially when I assure them, *that he gives light as soon as he rises.* I am convinced of this. I am certain of my fact. One cannot be more certain of any fact. I saw it with my own eyes. And, having repeated this observation the three following mornings, I found always precisely the same result.

Yet it so happens, that when I speak of this discovery to others, I can easily perceive by their countenances,[5] though they forbear expressing it in words, that they do not quite believe me. One, indeed, who is a learned natural philosopher, has assured me that I must certainly be mistaken as to the circumstance of the light coming into my room; for it being well known, as he says, that there could be no light abroad at that hour, it follows that none could enter from without; and that of consequence, my windows being accidentally left open, instead of letting in the light, had only served to let out the darkness; and he used many ingenious arguments to show me how I might, by that means, have been deceived. I owned[6] that he puzzled me a little, but he did not satisfy me; and the **subsequent** observations I made, as above mentioned, confirmed me in my first opinion.

This event has given rise in my mind to several serious and important reflections. I considered that, if I had not been awakened so early in the morning, I should have slept six hours longer by the light of the sun, and in exchange have lived six hours the following night by candlelight; and, the latter being a much more expensive light than the former, my love of economy induced me to muster up what little arithmetic I was master of, and to make some calculations, which I shall give you, after observing that utility is, in my opinion the test of value in matters of invention, and that a discovery which can be applied to no use, or is not good for something, is good for nothing.

I took for the basis of my calculation the supposition that there are one hundred thousand families in Paris, and that these families consume in the night half a pound of bougies, or candles, per hour. I think this is a moderate allowance, taking one family with another; for though I believe some consume less, I know that many consume a great deal more. Then estimating seven hours per day as the medium quantity between the time of the sun's rising and ours, he rising during the six following months from six to eight hours before noon, and there being seven hours of course per night in which we burn candles, the account will stand thus;—

3. An *almanac* is a publication that gives the times of sunrise and sunset, the cycles of the moon, and the weather, among other things.
4. The *astronomical* part of the almanac refers to information about the sun, moon, and stars.
5. Here, *countenance* means "face."
6. Here, *own* means "admit."

4 Finding Common Ground *Why do you think that Franklin includes himself with the readers here?*

Analyze Humor *How does Franklin try to win over his readers with this humorous remark?* 5

Vocabulary

subsequent (sub′ sə kwənt) *adj.* following in time, order, or place

Teach

Big Idea 4

Finding Common Ground

Answer: *He may not wish to appear smarter than others; saying that his readers will be as astonished as he was is humorous.*

Reading Strategy 5

Analyze Humor

Answer: *By using exaggerated modesty, Franklin pokes fun at himself. In so doing, he comes across as an "everyman."*

APPROACHING To assist approaching-level students, ask for other example sentences where Franklin pokes fun at himself. *(Sample answer: muster up what little arithmetic I was master of)*

Approaching Level

DIFFERENTIATED INSTRUCTION

Emerging Point out Franklin's use of personification on this page. Read aloud the paragraph that begins "I looked at my watch. . . ." Use expression to show students that Franklin uses personification to make his readers laugh. Franklin makes the sun seem uncooperative and unreasonable.

Established Students may have trouble understanding Franklin's ideas about daylight savings time. Tell students that Franklin's point is that he is wasting candles at night when he could be making use of the free sunlight during the day if he changed his schedule.

Teach

Reading Strategy 1

Analyze Humor Answer: *The humor derives from Franklin's preposterous assertion that his readers must learn an obvious fact from his letter—that daylight occurs when the sun rises. It persuades his audience by insinuating that anyone who refuses to rise with the sun lacks common sense. Franklin's personification of the sun creates the illusion of a joint effort between people and the sun in their endeavor to rise early.*

ADVANCED For advanced students, **ask:** How does the use of humor enhance the mood of the selection? *(Answers will vary.)*

Literary Element 2

Humor Answer: *Franklin employs hyperbole in a series of exaggerations and he also puns on the phrase "open their eyes," which is meant to be taken literally, as in waking, and figuratively, as in a revelation.*

In the six months between the 20th of March and the 20th of September, there are

Nights	183
Hours of each night in which we burn candles	7
Multiplication gives for the total number of hours	1,281
These 1,281 hours multiplied by 100,000, the number of inhabitants, give	128,100,000
One hundred twenty-eight millions and one hundred thousand hours, spent at Paris by candlelight, which, at half a pound of wax and tallow[7] per hour, gives the weight of	64,050,000
Sixty-four millions and fifty thousand of pounds, which, estimating the whole at the medium price of thirty sols[8] the pound, makes the sum of ninety-six millions and seventy-five thousand livres tournois[9]	96,075,000

An immense sum! that the city of Paris might save every year, by the economy of using sunshine instead of candles. If it should be said, that people are apt to be **obstinately** attached to old customs, and that it will be difficult to induce them to rise before noon, consequently my discovery can be of little use; I answer, *Nil desperandum.*[10] I believe all who have common sense, as soon as they have learnt from this paper that it is daylight when the sun rises, will contrive to rise with him; and, to compel the rest, I would propose the following regulations; First. Let a tax be laid of a louis[11] per window, on every window that is provided with shutters to keep out the light of the sun.

Second. Let the same salutary[12] operation of police be made use of, to prevent our burning candles, that inclined us last winter to be more economical in burning wood; that is, let guards be placed in the shops of the wax and tallow chandlers,[13] and no family be permitted to be supplied with more than one pound of candles per week.

Third. Let guards also be posted to stop all the coaches, &c. that would pass the streets after sunset, except those of physicians, surgeons, and midwives.

Fourth. Every morning, as soon as the sun rises, let all the bells in every church be set ringing; and if that is not sufficient?, let cannon be fired in every street, to wake the sluggards[14] effectually, and make them open their eyes to see their true interest.

All the difficulty will be in the first two or three days; after which the reformation will be as natural and easy as the present irregularity; for, *ce n'est que le premier pas qui coûte.*[15] Oblige a man to rise at four in the

7. *Tallow* is a white, nearly solid fat from cattle and sheep that is used to make soap and candles.
8. A *sol* was a French unit of currency.
9. *Livres tournois* refers to currency coined in Tours, a provincial French city in west-central France along the Loire River. This currency was worth one-fifth less than the money made in Paris.

Vocabulary

obstinately (ob′ stə nit lē) *adv.* stubbornly; in spite of reason or persuasion

10. *Nil desperandum* means "Never despair" in Latin.
11. A *louis* was a French unit of currency.
12. *Salutary* means "beneficial."
13. A *chandler* is a maker or seller of tallow, wax candles, or soap.
14. A *sluggard* is a habitually lazy person.
15. *Ce n'est que le premier pas qui coûte* means "It is only the first step that counts" in French.

Analyze Humor *What is humorous about this statement, and how is it intended to persuade the reader?* **1**

Humor *What type of humor does Franklin develop in this passage?* **2**

Reading Practice

SMALL GROUP SPIRAL REVIEW

Paraphrase Franklin uses many words and phrases that are no longer used in everyday conversation. Remind students that when you paraphrase writing, you put it into your own words. Tell them that paraphrasing writing can help them better understand what they have read. Break students into small groups and have them paraphrase this page of the essay. Help students get started by reading aloud the portion of the paragraph beginning with "In the six months between the 20th" and ending with "Multiplication gives for the total number of hours." **Ask:** What does this mean? *(Students may say that there are 183 nights in the six months between March 20 and September 20 and people burn candles for 7 hours each night. If you multiply the number of nights by the number of candles burned, you get a total of 1,281 hours.)*

morning, and it is more than probable he will go willingly to bed at eight in the evening; and, having had eight hours sleep, he will rise more willingly at four in the morning following. But this sum of ninety-six millions and seventy-five thousand livres is not the whole of what may be saved by my economical project. You may observe, that I have calculated upon only one half of the year, and much may be saved in the other, though the days are shorter. Besides, the immense stock of wax and tallow left unconsumed during the summer, will probably make candles much cheaper for the ensuing winter, and continue them cheaper as long as the proposed reformation shall be supported.

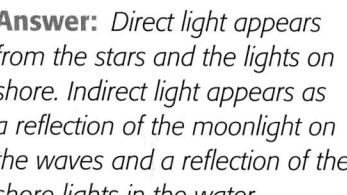

Starry Night, Arles, 1888. Vincent Van Gogh. Musee d'Orsay, Paris.

View the Art Vincent Van Gogh created many paintings in which light and dark are prominent subject areas. What forms of light appear in this painting? Does the painting support Franklin's ideas in this letter? Explain why or why not. ★

For the great benefit of this discovery, thus freely communicated and bestowed by me on the public, I demand neither place, pension, exclusive privilege, nor any other reward whatever. I expect only to have the honor of it. And yet I know there are little, envious minds, who will, as usual, deny me this and say, that my invention was known to the ancients, and perhaps they may bring passages out of the old books in proof of it. I will not dispute with these people, that the ancients knew not the sun would rise at certain hours; they possibly had, as we have, almanacs that predicted it; but it does not follow thence, that they knew *he gave light as soon as he rose.* This is what I claim as my discovery. If the ancients knew it, it might have been long since forgotten; for it certainly was unknown to the moderns, at least to the Parisians, which to prove, I need use but one plain simple argument. They are as well instructed, judicious,[16] and **prudent** a people as exist anywhere in the world, all professing, like myself, to be lovers of economy; and, from the many heavy taxes required from them by the necessities of the state, have surely an abundant reason to be economical. I say it is impossible that so sensible a people, under such circumstances, should have lived so long by the smoky, unwholesome, and enormously expensive light of candles, if they had really known, that they might have had as much pure light of the sun for nothing. I am, &c.

A SUBSCRIBER

16. *Judicious* means "using good judgment."

Analyze Humor *How is Franklin using humor in this passage to persuade his audience?* **3**

Vocabulary

prudent (prōōd′ ənt) *adj.* showing wisdom and good judgment

Teach

Reading Strategy 3

Analyze Humor Answer: *Franklin uses mock flattery in saying that the French are too intelligent to have ignored the obvious fact that the sun gives light as it rises. He concludes that they must not have known about it until he made his great "discovery."*

View the Art ★

Answer: *Direct light appears from the stars and the lights on shore. Indirect light appears as a reflection of the moonlight on the waves and a reflection of the shore lights in the water.*

Although 1888 saw the maturation of Van Gogh's technique, it was also a year of great mental turmoil for him. In December, he suffered a psychotic episode resulting in the infamous incident where he cut off part of his own ear.

To check students' understanding of the selection, see Unit 2 Teaching Resources Book, p. 201.

English Learners

DIFFERENTIATED INSTRUCTION

PARTNERS

Intermediate Point out the words *ce n'est que le premier pas qui coûte* on page 394 and explain that the words are italicized because they are French words. When foreign words are accepted into English, they are not italicized. Pair English learners with English-speaking classmates. Have partners compile lists of borrowed words. Challenge students to identify words that took on English spellings and pronunciations and words that kept their original spellings. Students may use the Internet or a dictionary for assistance.

After You Read

Assess

1. Students should distinguish between our daylight saving time and Franklin's parody.
2. (a) They do not believe him. (b) He teases others, but also mocks himself.
3. (a) As wise people, they would have risen early and passed on such knowledge. (b) The ancients knew economics and most of Franklin's reasons save money.
4. His tone and use of detail add to the humor. Examples: He describes his gradual realization of the light source; he did not realize at once it was the sun.
5. His arguments state the obvious, but include facts as well.
6. (a) His essay is humorous, yet his letter explains that people waste daytime light and nighttime candles. He pokes fun at those who dispute his discovery's usefulness, and exaggerates ways to implement his plan. His discovery's economic benefits are real. (b) Answers will vary.
7. He makes fun of himself as well as them.
8. Student responses will vary. Students should point to specific suggestions from Franklin's letter to support their answers.

Literary Element

1. Possible answer: His surprise upon waking at six in the morning and finding his room full of light.
2. He insists that his realization about the sun is an ingenious discovery.

After You Read

Respond and Think Critically

Respond and Interpret

1. How does Franklin's essay affect your thoughts on our current daylight saving time program?
2. (a)Franklin describes sharing his discovery with several people. How do they react? (b)How does the way he talks about these people relate to his purpose in writing the essay?
3. (a)How does Franklin show that he "knows" the ancients did not perceive that the sun "gave light as soon as he rose"? (b)How do these reasons relate to what he considers the most important motive for proposing daylight saving?

Analyze and Evaluate

4. How does Franklin's description of his discovery of early morning sunlight add to the humor of the essay?
5. Franklin says that a discovery that is not useful is good for nothing. How convincing is he in portraying daylight saving as useful?
6. (a)How does Franklin balance serious and humorous elements in his essay? (b)Do you take him seriously in spite of his humorous style? Explain.

Connect

7. **Big Idea** **Finding Common Ground** How does Franklin establish common ground with his audience?
8. **Connect to Today** How do you think people of today would react to a similar letter with the same suggestions?

Literary Element Humor

Humor is often used to point out human failings and the ironies of everyday life. Humorous devices include sarcasm, exaggeration, puns, and verbal irony. Humor that is ironic presents a statement that is the opposite of what is true, or the opposite of what the author really means.

1. What is an example of exaggeration in Franklin's letter?
2. Where does Franklin use verbal irony?

Review: Rhetorical Devices

As you learned on page 379, **rhetorical devices** are techniques that an author uses in order to heighten a particular effect or engage the attention of the reader. One of these techniques is the deliberate repetition of sentence structures, which is called parallelism.

Partner Activity With a classmate, look through Franklin's letter to find examples of parallelism. Use a chart like the one below to record the examples and their effects.

Example of Parallelism	Effect
"I looked at my watch" "I looked into the almanac" "I looked forward, too"	Humorous—he seems to need a lot of evidence that the sun comes up in the morning, something we all know.

Progress Check

Can students identify humor?

If No → See Unit 2 Teaching Resources Book, p. 196.

Review: Rhetorical Devices

Students' answers will vary. They should include the effects of each example of parallelism.

Reading Strategy Analyze Humor

SAT Skills Practice

1. Franklin achieves a humorous effect in the paragraph beginning "I looked at my watch . . ." (page 392) by
   (A) pretending to be superior to the average Parisian
   (B) using highly sarcastic language
   (C) contrasting his habits favorably with those of other people
   (D) mocking the human failings of both Parisians and Americans
   (E) stating an obvious truth as if it were a new discovery

Vocabulary Practice

Practice with Context Clues In the following sentences, identify the context clues that help you determine the meaning of each boldfaced vocabulary word.

1. He **negligently** forgot to check the safety of the machinery, which led to an accident.
2. The introduction to his speech was very interesting, but his **subsequent** points were less than inspiring.
3. Merle refused to learn to type correctly and **obstinately** kept typing in her own, much slower, way.
4. She wanted to start skiing down steep slopes immediately, but she made the more **prudent** decision to practice on gentler slopes first.

LOG ON **Literature** Online

Selection Resources For Selection Quizzes, eFlashcards, and Reading-Writing Connection activities, go to glencoe.com and enter QuickPass code GL49787u2.

Write with Style

Apply Irony and Hyperbole

Assignment Write a humorous essay about an ordinary part of life that you find ironic. Use **irony,** or a contrast between what is expected and what actually happens, and **hyperbole,** or exaggeration that expresses strong emotion, makes a point, or evokes humor.

Get Ideas Use personal sources, such as a journal, datebook, or e-mail, to create a list of ironic situations you have encountered in your daily life. Then choose a topic from the list and brainstorm some hyperboles that describe or elaborate on it.

Give It Structure Begin with a thesis statement that briefly describes the topic and your humorous perspective on it. In each paragraph, include a hyperbole that expresses or supports the paragraph's main idea.

Look at Language Irony can be challenging to convey; make sure your opening paragraph uses precise language that clearly describes the irony in your situation. The language should accurately convey how the situation's outcome or reality differs from what is expected.

EXAMPLE:

~~*Despite all my best efforts, and no matter how hard I try, I can never get to school early.*~~

Every morning when I wake up, my first thought is, "I'm going to get to school early today!" And yet, every morning, I'm running through the doors just before the first bell.

Avoid trite language and clichés in your hyperboles; replace overly familiar phrases with more original descriptions. Get creative—use the hyperboles to express your style and create your own unique, humorous voice.

EXAMPLE:

~~*Picking out my clothes takes forever and a day.*~~

Most people could dress an entire army in the time I take to choose a shirt.

After You Read

Assess

Reading Strategy

1. E is the correct answer. Everyone is aware that the sun often rises before people are awake, but Franklin pretends that this is not general knowledge.

Progress Check

Can students analyze humor?

If No → See Unit 2 Teaching Resources Book, p. 197.

Vocabulary Practice

1. "forgot"
2. "introduction"
3. "refused"
4. "gentler slopes first"

Write with Style

Students' essays should:

- use humor to discuss an ironic situation in everyday life
- include a thesis statement that reflects a humorous perspective
- employ a hyperbole in each paragraph to support the main idea
- use creative language in its descriptions

For grammar practice, see Unit 2 Teaching Resources Book, p. 200.

To create custom assessments online, go to Progress Reporter Online Assessment.

For additional selection assessment, see Assessment Resources, pp. 105–106.

To create custom assessments using software, use ExamView Assessment Suite.

Comparing Literature

Different Viewpoints

Focus

Bellringer Options

Daily Language Practice Transparency 41

Or display images of Fenway Park from the past and present. Discuss students' experiences in a sports stadium or at a match or a game.

Ask: Why are sports fans so dedicated to their favorite teams? Why do some people have an emotional attachment to Fenway Park?

Connect to the Reading Selections

Allow students to share their responses to the opening question. Then have students discuss what they know about the social, communal, and economic value of living near a sports stadium.

Comparing Literature

Different Viewpoints

Learning Objectives

For pages 398–411

In studying these texts, you will focus on the following objectives:

Literary Study:
Comparing persuasion.
Comparing author's viewpoint.
Analyzing rhetorical devices.

Reading: Evaluating credibility.

Compare Literature About a Controversial Issue

Many cities throughout the United States have faced this dilemma: What should be done about aging sports stadiums that lack the features team owners claim are essential to modern sports franchises? Many fans argue passionately for the preservation of their beloved stadiums. Others urge that new facilities are needed for teams to survive. In the works compared here, writers argue for and against the demolition of historic Fenway Park, home of the Boston Red Sox.

COMPARE THE Big Idea Finding Common Ground

Even though these writers take different sides on the issue of whether to preserve or demolish Fenway Park, they all try to build rapport with their audience. As you read, ask yourself, How does each writer establish common ground with the reader?

COMPARE Persuasion

The art of persuasion is the art of convincing someone to adopt a certain belief or to take a certain action. For instance, you might try to persuade your friends that one candidate for class president is better than another, or you might try to persuade your parents to watch a particular movie. In these selections, the authors make different appeals to persuade readers to adopt their ideas. As you read, ask yourself, What persuasive appeals does each writer use?

COMPARE Author's Viewpoint

The author's viewpoint is the author's opinion about, or approach to, an issue. In persuasive writing, the author's viewpoint helps shape both form and content, both what the author says and how he or she says it. As you read, ask yourself, What is each author's viewpoint?

LOG ON **Literature Online**

Author Search For information about the authors, go to glencoe.com and enter QuickPass code GL49787u2.

Selection Skills

Comparing Literature

Literary Elements
- Rhetorical Devices (SE pp. 402–408)

Listening/Speaking/Viewing Skills
- Analyze Art (TE pp. 401, 405)
- Discussion Starter (SE p. 406)

Reading Skills
- Evaluate Credibility (SE pp. 401–408)
- Identify Author's Purpose (TE p. 399)
- Evaluate an Argument (TE p. 408)

Vocabulary Skills
- Synonyms (SE p. 410)
- Etymology (TE p. 400)

Writing Skills/Grammar
- Quickwrite (SE p. 403)
- Write a Business Letter (SE p. 410)
- Compare/Contrast Essay (SE p. 411)

Before You Read

Persuasive Text

Reading and Analyzing Persuasive Text

An argument is a type of persuasive writing in which logic or reason is used to try to influence the reader's ideas or actions. When reading an argument, it is important to be cautious about its claims. First, determine the author's position. Then identify the structure of the argument. Is the structure logical? Does the author provide strong evidence to support his or her opinions?

The Structure of an Argument At its most basic, an argument consists of a specific position plus evidence supporting that position. The strongest argument is a logical one, which means that the argument is structured in such a way that it makes sense. An argument can be structured logically by the use of either inductive or deductive reasoning.

Inductive reasoning involves drawing a general conclusion from a series of specific facts. When scientists draw conclusions based on data from experiments and observations, they are using inductive reasoning. The chart below shows how inductive reasoning led some scientists to conclude that Earth had been hit by a meteorite.

Fact: Iridium, a chemical element, is found in layers of rock in Italy, Denmark, and New Zealand.

Fact: Iridium is rarely found on Earth but is found in meteorites.

Fact: The rock containing the iridium is about 66 million years old.

→ **Generalization:** A meteorite hit Earth about 66 million years ago.

Deductive reasoning applies a generalization to a specific example, or set of examples, to arrive at a conclusion. The chart below outlines the deductive reasoning used by the people who left Love Canal, a community in upstate New York, when they discovered that it had been built on a toxic waste dump.

Generalization: Toxic chemical waste is dangerous to humans.

↓

Fact: Love Canal is located on top of a layer of toxic waste.

↓

Conclusion: Love Canal is a dangerous place to live.

Common Pitfalls When analyzing arguments, be aware of faulty reasoning in the form of hasty generalizations and invalid assumptions. **Hasty generalizations** occur when a conclusion goes further than the evidence permits. For example, if you saw a group of drummers who were boys, you might reason inductively that only boys play drums, but your reasoning would be incorrect because it is based on too small a sample of drummers.

In deductive reasoning, the chain of reasoning can be invalidated by an incorrect statement. For example, consider this line of reasoning: *To attract top-notch students, a school needs a good science program; our school wants to attract top-notch students; therefore, we need to improve our science program.* Not everyone may agree with the first assumption. In this case, the reasoning is well-constructed but the conclusion is not necessarily true.

As you review an argument, also be sure to examine the evidence the author provides. Is the evidence credible? Does the evidence, in fact, support the author's opinions?

Comparing Literature

Before You Read

Focus

Reading Strategy

Identify Author's Purpose
Have students attempt to identify the author's opinion about the issue at hand. Remind students that in persuasive writing, the author wants to convince the reader that his or her viewpoint is correct.

Ask: What clues do you find in the selection to tell you about the author's purpose? *(The writers have specific opinions and present arguments to support these viewpoints.)*

APPROACHING For approaching-level students, **Say:** Keep this question in mind as you read: What argument is the author using to convince the reader of his or her viewpoint?

Approaching Level

DIFFERENTIATED INSTRUCTION

Established Help students understand persuasive writing by explaining the difference between a fact and an opinion. **Say:** A fact is a statement that can be proven. An opinion is what someone thinks. Ask students whether each of these sentences is a fact or an opinion.

- Krista has the best shot on the basketball team. *(opinion)*
- Krista has scored the most points on the basketball team. *(fact)*
- Mr. Richards is a great teacher. *(opinion)*
- Mr. Richards is the most experienced teacher in our school. *(fact)*

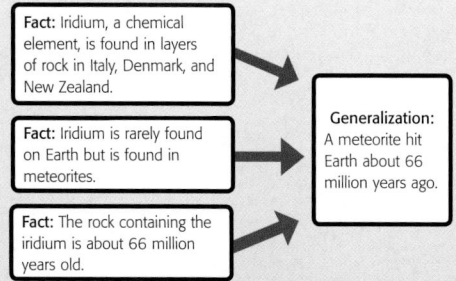

Before You Read

Focus

Summary

Sportswriters, the CEO of the Boston Red Sox, and a member of the Massachusetts House of Representatives speak out about the fate of Fenway Park, a landmark sports stadium in Massachusetts. Conflicting perspectives are presented: Save Fenway because of its historic and nostalgic value or build a new stadium, which would help provide funds and field a top team; let the state help with the funding or let private funds carry most of the cost. The selections introduce the reader to a variety of rhetorical devices.

For summaries in languages other than English, see Unit 2 Teaching Resources Book, pp. 204–209.

Vocabulary

Etymology Put the students into small groups and assign each group a word from the vocabulary list. Have the groups trace the etymology of their words with dictionaries and the Internet. Have each group give a short history of the word and how the word became part of the English language.

For additional vocabulary practice, see Unit 2 Teaching Resources Book, p. 212.

For additional context, see Glencoe Visual Vocabulary CD-ROM.

Literature and Reading Preview

Connect to the Arguments

What public building or other public space has special meaning for you, and why? Write a journal entry describing how you would feel if that place were destroyed or replaced.

Build Background

In 1999 the Yawkey Trust, then-owner of the Boston Red Sox, proposed that a new stadium be built to replace Fenway Park. Many fans were shocked and dismayed at the thought of their team playing home games anywhere other than Fenway Park, which has been home to the Red Sox since April 20, 1912.

Set Purposes for Reading

Big Idea Finding Common Ground

As you read the arguments about Fenway Park, ask yourself, What points do these writers with differing opinions agree on?

Literary Element Rhetorical Devices

Rhetorical devices are ways in which authors support their arguments and persuade their audiences. Such devices include appeals to logic, emotion, ethics, and authority. As you read, ask yourself, Why do I agree or disagree with this writer?

Reading Strategy Evaluate Credibility

To analyze an argument in a persuasive essay, you must **evaluate the credibility** of the author. You must read carefully to separate facts from opinions and detect bias, or a prejudice toward a favored viewpoint. It is also helpful to examine the author's credentials, or qualifications, that determine the reliability of his or her opinions. As you read, ask yourself, Why should I believe the arguments or opinions presented by this writer?

Tip: Examine Credentials Use a chart to list each writer, his or her credentials, and any bias the person may have.

Writer	Credentials	Bias
Stark	Sportscaster	personal nostalgia for old-time ballparks

Vocabulary

cathedral (kə thē′ drəl) *n.* a large, important church; sometimes used to describe something of great importance; p. 401 *The redwood forests of California are nature's cathedrals.*

nostalgia (nos tal′ jə) *n.* a feeling of longing experienced when remembering the past; an overly sentimental feeling; p. 402 *As they listened to music from the 1980s, a wave of nostalgia washed over them.*

staggering (stag′ ər ing) *adj.* shocking; overwhelming; p. 404 *When I returned from vacation, I found a staggering tower of bills.*

magnitude (mag′ nə to͞od) *n.* great size, volume, or extent; importance; significance; p. 409 *The bride had never in her life seen a cake of such magnitude.*

Tip: Synonyms Synonyms are always the same part of speech. For example, the words *magnitude* and *immense* have similar meanings but are not synonyms. *Magnitude* is a noun; *immense* is an adjective. However, *magnitude* and *immensity* are synonyms; they have similar meaning and they are both nouns.

Grammar Practice

Sentence Fragments Explain that writers sometimes use sentence fragments for effect, but in general, students should make sure the sentences they write are complete sentences that have subjects and verbs.

Have students correct the following sentence fragments:

1. I swim every day. Get exercise. *(I swim every day to get exercise.)*
2. Jeff learned to type. Works faster. *(Jeff learned to type, so he could work faster.)*
3. Each afternoon. My brother takes our dog Rusty for a walk.

(Each afternoon, my brother takes our dog Rusty for a walk.)

Thoughts on Fenway Park

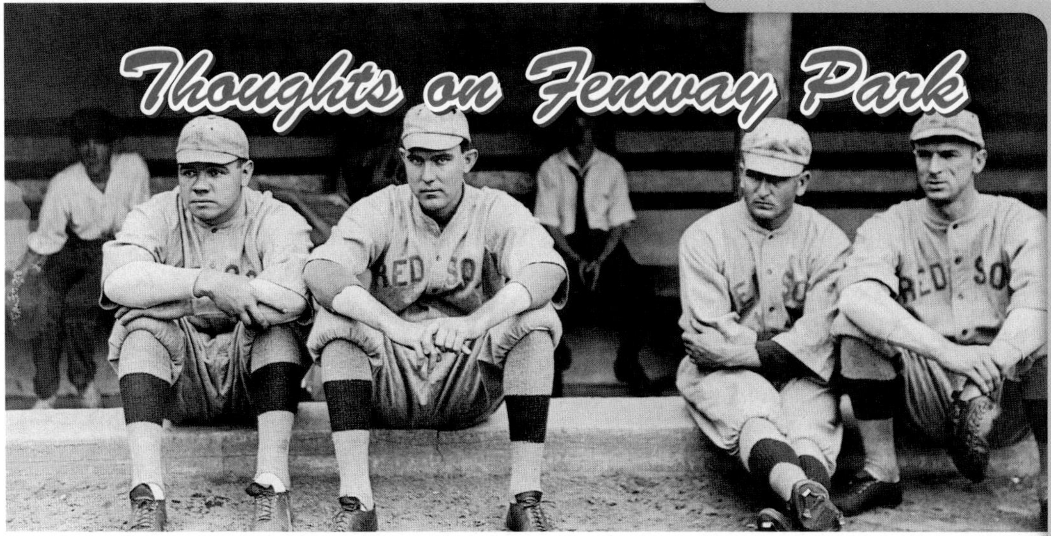

Babe Ruth, Ernie Shore, Rube (George) Foster, and Del Gainer rest on the edge of their dugout during a game at Fenway Park, ca. 1915. ★

In 2000 sportscasters were invited to respond to the question, "Should Fenway Park be replaced?" Following are some of their responses.

Jayson Stark

No. Please. I may not be Paul Volcker,[1] but I understand modern baseball economics. And I'm tired of baseball's inclination to bulldoze its history in the name of economics. To me, places like Fenway and Wrigley and Yankee Stadium[2] aren't mere ballparks. They're national historic monuments. So we should no more consider blowing up Fenway than we would Independence Hall.[3]

I've seen the way players react after entering Fenway for the first time. They go knock on the Monster, climb inside the scoreboard, wander up to sit in The Ted Williams Seat[4] in the bleachers, think about Babe Ruth and Ty Cobb[5] dressing in the same clubhouse they now occupy. It's awesome. Believe me, nobody reacts this way when they enter Stade Olympique[6] for the first time.

So rather than tear down these **cathedrals**, the people who run the sport need to work with these teams to figure out ways

1. *Paul Volcker* is a financial expert who has served as undersecretary of the U.S. Treasury and president of New York's Federal Reserve Bank.
2. *Wrigley Field* and *Yankee Stadium* are located respectively in Chicago and New York City.
3. *Independence Hall* is the building in Philadelphia, Pennsylvania, in which the Declaration of Independence and the Constitution were signed.
4. *The Ted Williams Seat* is the seat in the stands at Fenway where Ted Williams's longest home run (also the longest ever hit in Fenway) landed. The seat back is red, which sets it apart from the other green seats.
5. *Ty Cobb* played baseball for the Detroit Tigers between 1905 and 1926. He is still considered one of baseball's greatest players.
6. The *Stade Olympique* is the large, modern stadium that housed the Montreal Expos baseball team until 2005.

1 Evaluate Credibility *Is the writer's argument based on fact or opinion? How can you tell?*

Vocabulary

cathedral (kə thē′ drəl) *n.* a large, important church; sometimes used to describe something of great importance

English Learners

DIFFERENTIATED INSTRUCTION

Intermediate Newcomers to the United States may be unfamiliar with baseball, but they may understand the concept of a national sport. In most countries, soccer is the most popular sport. In some countries, such as India, cricket (a game similar to baseball) is popular. Ask students to describe a popular sport in their homeland. Prompt students to talk about how sports can help bring people from various backgrounds and cultures together. Have them share information about their favorite teams and players.

Comparing Literature

Teach

Reading Strategy 1

Evaluate Credibility

Answer: *Opinion. The statements begins "to me," which expresses a personal opinion.*

ENGLISH LEARNERS Check to make sure English learners understand the difference between fact and opinion. Have a student define the two terms using a dictionary.

View the Photograph ★

This photograph, taken in about 1915, shows how long baseball has been a part of U.S. culture. Baseball evolved from much earlier ball games but was systematized in the early nineteenth century. Its present form is generally attributed to Alexander Cartwright, but there has been some controversy regarding this identification over the years. **Ask:** How do these players look different from baseball players today? *(Students may point out that the uniforms are an older style.)*

For an audio recording of this selection, use Listening Library Audio CD-ROM.

Readability Scores

Dale-Chall: 7.4

DRP: 59

Lexile: 930

Comparing Literature

Teach

Big Idea 1

Finding Common Ground

Ask: What device does Campbell use to connect with readers? *(He uses a personal anecdote about his favorite ballpark to prove he understands how fans feel about Fenway.)*

Big Idea 2

Finding Common Ground

Answer: *Campbell tries to appeal to both sides through a compromise.*

Literary Element 3

Rhetorical Devices

Answer: *It appeals to emotion. He says Fenway's replacement is "inevitable." He implies "Save Fenway" groups are not moving into "the 21st century." These statements cannot be proven.*

to preserve their great ballparks and still keep them economically viable.[7] There is no equivalent to Fenway in *any* other sport. And it ought to dawn on our leaders one of these days that baseball needs to capitalize on[8] places like Fenway, not abandon them. The NFL has a new-stadium fund. Shouldn't baseball have an *old*-stadium fund?

Dave Campbell

1 Yes, Fenway should be replaced. I know it's tough for the fans in New England. I grew up in Michigan and Tiger Stadium[9] was the ultimate institution for me; it was my Fenway. It was the stadium I grew up in, with all the memories and **nostalgia** involved. Tiger Stadium was a wonderful sea of green and had a magical charm about it. In fact, Fenway and Tiger opened the exact same day—April 20, 1912.

Unfortunately, the bottom line in today's economy is that you have to create a stadium that can generate a lot of revenue from places other than ticket sales. Right now, the Red Sox have the most expensive ticket prices in baseball and that is because they only have 33,000 seats. They need to have a stadium with corporate luxury suites; and I mean real, top-notch suites, not those things they threw up like a glorified backstop in recent years.

In Detroit they revamped[10] everything. There is nothing in the new stadium that reminds you of Tiger Stadium. But it doesn't have to be that way. Build a new stadium for the Red Sox and find a way to keep the Green Monster.

There was a tremendous amount of opposition to tearing down Tiger Stadium. They had all kinds of "Save Tiger" groups, just like they do in Boston now. The bottom line is Fenway Park is, like Tiger Stadium was, antiquated,[11] old, and probably getting to the point of unsafe. "Save Fenway" groups only put off the inevitable. It's time to move into the 21st century.

Tim Kurkjian

Absolutely not. There is so much history and tradition at Fenway, I would hate to see it go. I know it's getting a little old, and I know I sit in the press box and not behind some pole obstructing my view in the stands, but every time I walk in that place, I think about Ted Williams and Babe Ruth, and that stuff is really important. Even if they build a park to look just like it, it won't be the same.

Financially, I understand why new parks are necessities. Today's game is built around luxury suites, big-time corporate backing, and over 40,000 seats; and Fenway doesn't have any of those. The only way to make Fenway a financially viable park is to tear it down and build a new one. I know Fenway will be replaced eventually, and I'll be sad when it is.

7. *Viable* means "able to be done."
8. Here, *capitalize on* means "treat as an asset rather than as an expense."
9. *Tiger Stadium* was the stadium for the Detroit Tigers baseball team until 1999.
10. Revamped means "altered" or "renovated."

11. *Antiquated* means "out of date."

Vocabulary

nostalgia (nos tal′ jə) *n.* a feeling of longing experienced when remembering the past; an overly sentimental feeling

Finding Common Ground *In this passage, to whom is the author trying to appeal?* 2

Rhetorical Devices *Does this part of the writer's argument appeal to logic, emotion, ethics, or authority? How can you tell?* 3

Writing Practice

Persuasive Essay Explain that persuasive writing tries to convince someone to adopt a certain belief or action. Discuss the Big Idea of Finding Common Ground. Explain that this is important when writing persuasive essays. Ask students to write a persuasive essay about an issue relevant to them. Have students present their essays to the class for critiquing.

Have students use the following questions to critique their essays:

- Is the author's purpose clearly stated?
- Does the author find common ground with the audience?

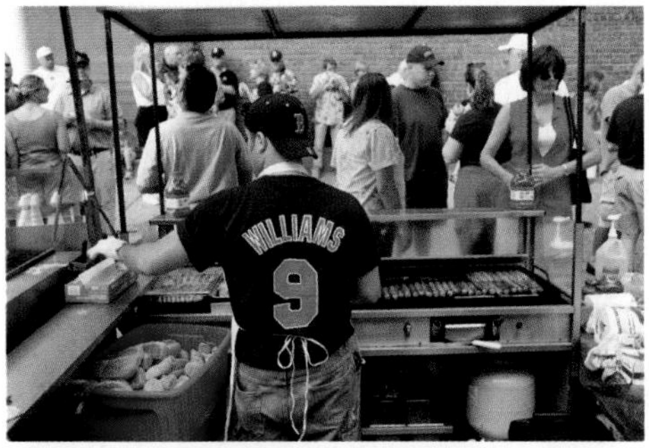

A Fenway Park vendor wears a shirt honoring former Red Sox player Ted Williams, who died in 2002.

Brian McRae

From a nostalgic standpoint, you can't tear down Fenway. But from an economic standpoint, the Red Sox are losing so much money, they need to get a new ballpark. The amount of money it costs just to maintain Fenway is amazing. The way the economics of baseball are today, if the Red Sox don't get a new stadium, 10 years from now it will be hard for them to compete and put a championship-caliber[12] team on the field. I think the fans would rather see a championship-caliber team in a new park than a last-place team in an old, broken-down Fenway Park. It's inevitable.

Rob Dibble

No. There are very few old-time structures left in the league. In the NL, it's Wrigley; in the AL,[13] it's Yankee Stadium and Fenway. Those parks are monuments and are like museums. Babe Ruth, Yaz,[14] Ted Williams . . . great players have walked across that field. I love the historical aspect of baseball and the history of Fenway makes saving it worth more than any economic downside.

There is enough technology to refurbish[15] the stadium without having to tear it down. You should be able to rebuild it from within. I understand that, economically, something has to be done. And the facilities aren't the greatest; the locker rooms are way too small. It needs to be upgraded in the worst way, but it's difficult to imagine Fenway not existing.

Buck Martinez

Yes. Fenway Park should be replaced because the locker-room facilities, the fan-comfort facilities and the concession stands are all antiquated. But when they replace it, they have to pay particular attention to keeping the new park as close to what it is now as possible. Fenway Park is baseball history and a remarkable baseball setting. They would make a terrible mistake if they don't include the Green Monster in whatever new ballpark is built. But the economics of the game today dictate that they need more luxury boxes and more fan amenities[16] because that is the way the game is headed.

12. *Caliber* means "degree of excellence or importance."
13. *NL* stands for National League, and *AL* stands for American League. These are the two leagues that make up Major League Baseball (MLB).
14. *Yaz* refers to Carl Yastrzemski, the Red Sox player who replaced Ted Williams as left fielder in 1961.
15. *Refurbish* means "to restore to the original state"; or "to renovate."
16. *Amenities* are benefits that make places more attractive to customers.

4 Evaluate Credibility *Is this either-or argument valid? Explain.*

Quickwrite

The sportswriters who responded to the question "Should Fenway Park be replaced?" gave a variety of opinions. Choose the response you think is the strongest and write a paragraph explaining why you chose it.

Teach

Reading Strategy 4

Evaluate Credibility

Answer: *The writer suggests that the additional revenue created by having a newer and larger stadium would guarantee a "championship-caliber team." Students should recognize the faulty logic in this argument.*

Assess

Quickwrite

Students' paragraphs should express their choice of the strongest opinion and refer to specific points in the text to support their choice.

To check students' understanding of the selection, see Unit 2 Teaching Resources Book, p. 215.

English Learners

DIFFERENTIATED INSTRUCTION

Beginning/Early Intermediate Explain to English learners that a footnote in a prose selection is numbered in both the text and at the bottom of the page. Remind students that footnotes are used because a book cannot explain every reference or definition within a text. Have English learners work with English-proficient students to suggest additional words and phrases they think should be footnoted. Guide students to use a dictionary and write footnotes for their additions.

Before You Read

Teach

Reading Strategy 1

Evaluate Credibility

Ask: What concrete evidence is given about the team's commitment to build a new stadium? *(The team is committing over $350 million to the project.)*

APPROACHING For approaching-level students, ask for another example of evidence of the team's commitment to building a new stadium. *(a plan to be responsible for cost overruns)*

Cultural History ☆

In 2004 fans were overjoyed when the Red Sox finally won the World Series. The team hadn't won since they traded Babe "the Bambino" Ruth 86 years earlier. The dry spell was referred to as "The Curse of the Bambino."

For an audio recording of this selection, use Listening Library Audio CD-ROM.

Readability Scores

Dale-Chall: 10.0

DRP: 66

Lexile: 1260

Build Background

John L. Harrington served as Chief Executive Officer of the Boston Red Sox from 1992 to 2001. During that time, Fenway Park was expanded and refurbished, and the spring training site was moved to a state-of-the-art facility in Fort Myers, Florida. In an interview, Harrington said, "People refer to the Red Sox as an institution and look on me as a caretaker. And that's fine with me." The following article, which originally appeared in 2000, was excerpted from the official Web site of the Boston Red Sox.

Taxpayer$ Will Get A Return On Inve$tment

John L. Harrington

With all of the talk and discussions today surrounding our new ballpark project, I wanted to communicate directly with you to update you on recent developments in our effort to build a new ballpark—the step we believe is essential to the future of the Boston Red Sox.

The Red Sox have committed to privately finance the entire new ballpark. We will put more private dollars into the new ballpark than any sports team in history has put into its facility. In absolute dollar
1 terms, at the costs we face today, we are committing to over $350 million for the new ballpark. Furthermore, we will take responsibility for any cost overruns involved in the park's construction.

This is not easy for us. To raise this **staggering** amount will require us to use a combination of ticket revenues, in-park marketing and advertising revenues, up-front payments for club seats and suites, deposits from season-ticket holders, naming rights,[1] and revenue from major league baseball and our limited partners.

1. Sponsors who make very large contributions to an organization are sometimes given *naming rights,* or the opportunity to name a piece of property, such as a ball park, theater, or stadium.

Vocabulary

staggering (stag′ ər ing) *adj.* shocking; overwhelming

Skills Practice

SPIRAL REVIEW Identify Author's Purpose

Ask: Why do writers write? Encourage students to share their answers in a class discussion and list their responses on the board. Explain that an author's motivation for writing can affect his or her work. Tell students to keep this in mind as they read the selections in this unit.

As students read, have them point out specific lines of a passage where the author's purpose for writing becomes clear. After they have finished reading, ask students if the author's purpose had an effect on the credibility of the author's argument.

By taking this approach, we will be required to consider certain steps that I have been very reluctant to think about, such as naming rights and season ticket deposits. Our reluctance has stemmed from our desire to protect you, our fans. I recognize that many fans care deeply about their season tickets and about the name of the ballpark. But we do not think we can ask for the first public dollar until we have shown our willingness to consider every possible private dollar.

As you know, the Red Sox do not have the limitless pockets that some suggest we have. Our financial objective, carried forward from the Yawkey years,[2] is to break even—not to turn a profit. Because I run a trust[3] and not a traditional profit-making enterprise, and because the mandate[4] of that trust was to serve the best interests of the baseball team, we plow all our revenues back into the Red Sox organization.

The twin goals of the organization that we must balance are the fielding of a strong, competitive team and the preservation of Red Sox baseball as affordable family entertainment. These goals are increasingly difficult in Fenway Park, the oldest and smallest park in the major leagues. We have stayed competitive, but we have maxed out ticket prices. Frankly, ticket prices are much higher than we'd like them to be, but we have no other way to raise revenue to field a team. In the economics of today's baseball, in a tiny ballpark, these twin goals are in conflict.

To meet our goal of fielding a competitive team, we must bear in mind that much of our competition plays in ballparks substantially built by their host municipalities.[5] This means that they enjoy a competitive advantage over us.

So be it. We want to play baseball here in Massachusetts, in Boston, in the Fenway, and we accept the political realities that go along with that.

But to play here for another hundred years we do need the kinds of public investments that have been made here in Massachusetts in the past. We believe that those public investments are justified by the return to the state and the city—in hard economic benefits, in increased income, sales, hotel and property taxes, and in the quality of life that a major league baseball team helps bring to a city.

The Red Sox also bring a special return through the ownership arrangement: the Yawkey Foundation[6] will be the biggest beneficiary of any future sale of the team, and Yawkey Foundation charities—educational, health care, and youth programs—will receive millions of dollars. That ownership arrangement, and that public benefit, is uniquely different from every other sports team in Massachusetts, and probably unique in American sports. . . .

We need assistance from the city we have called home for a hundred years, consistent with the steps the city has taken

2. *The Yawkey years* refers to the time period during which the Red Sox were owned by Tom Yawkey (1933–1976).
3. Here, *trust* means "a corporation legally responsible for managing the money or property of another person."
4. A *mandate* is an official duty or order.
5. Here, *host municipalities* are the towns or cities in which the teams play.
6. *The Yawkey Foundation* is a charitable organization that comprises Tom Yawkey's Foundation I and Jean Yawkey's Foundation II.

2 Rhetorical Devices *For what rhetorical purpose does the author bring up the subject of naming rights?*

3 Evaluate Credibility *How does Harrington attempt to establish his credentials?*

4 Rhetorical Devices *Which of these examples appeal to logic? Explain.*

Comparing Literature

Teach

Literary Element 2

Rhetorical Devices
Answer: *To remind readers that if they do not push for public funding, naming rights will have to be sold. He might seem to be appealing to logic, but he is actually making a veiled appeal to fans' emotions.*

Reading Strategy 3

Evaluate Credibility
Answer: *He uses the authority of his position as CEO of the Boston Red Sox to persuade the fans that his intentions are honorable. He claims that he is not motivated by profits.*

Literary Element 4

Rhetorical Devices
Answer: *Increased income, sales, and hotel and property taxes are examples that appeal to logic because they are measurable. Quality of life is not as easily measured; it is subjective.*

English Learners

DIFFERENTIATED INSTRUCTION

Intermediate English language learners may struggle with some words and phrases on this page. **Write** the following words and phrases on the board and discuss their meaning:

- limitless pockets *(an unlimited supply of money)*
- financial objective *(goal for money)*
- plow *(put strongly)*
- fielding *(putting together)*
- maxed out *(used up)*
- bear in mind *(keep in mind)*

Have students jot down unfamiliar words as they read. When they finish, guide them to look up the definitions of each word and use it in a sentence.

Teach

Reading Strategy 1

Evaluate Credibility

Answer: *His only support for the opinion is that most of the other major league teams have decided to build new ballparks. This does not prove the necessity for a new park in Boston because he has ignored the possibility that continued remodeling of the park will be successful.*

Literary Element 2

Rhetorical Devices

Ask: How does the writer attempt to manipulate the reader? *(Possible answer: He tries to create urgency by saying this "may be the last chance.")*

APPROACHING For approaching-level students, **ask:** Does the writer succeed in influencing the reader? *(Answers will vary.)*

Big Idea 3

Finding Common Ground

Answer: *He first says the owners are open to other options and stresses the need for consensus. Then he presses for the decision he wants; consensus is less important than adopting the plan.*

Assess

Discussion Starter

Groups should come to a consensus and come up with clear, logical arguments to counter the proposal.

on other projects like the Convention Center. As Boston did with the Convention Center, the Red Sox need for the city to acquire the land and prepare the site. We believe this investment is more than justified by the economic benefits the Red Sox will generate in a new park, but we understand the city needs some revenue streams to support their investment.

This legislative session has about eight weeks left. Last year's legislation for the new Patriots[7] stadium was passed in three weeks. But this year's window of opportunity closes on July 31, and if action is not taken by then, the opening date will be pushed back another year, or several years. That in turn means higher interest rates, construction costs, and possibly years without the benefits the new ballpark will bring to the fans, the team, the city, and the state.

Time is not on our side, and doing nothing is not an option. Fenway was built in 1912. We started trying to build a new ballpark in 1965, and have invested close to $100 million in Fenway maintenance and upkeep since then. In competitiveness—baseball survival—terms, we are one of the last teams in baseball still trying to build a new ballpark. New ballparks put teams like the Orioles and Indians back into contention,[8] and other cities followed: twenty-six of the other twenty-nine major league teams have either built new ballparks or are in the planning stages. If we do nothing, we will be left behind.

7. The *Patriots* are the New England Patriots football team, who play their home games at Gillette Stadium in Foxborough, Massachusetts.
8. Here, *contention* means "competition."

1 Evaluate Credibility *Evaluate the evidence Harrington uses to support this opinion.*

This legislative session may be the last chance to build this in the way we want it built. Since Tom Yawkey bought this team more than sixty-five years ago, there has been an extraordinary relationship with this community, which has made this team one of the most beloved sports franchises[9] in the world. We know how people feel about the Red Sox, and we feel the same way about Boston. The Boston Red Sox have never contemplated any other way to run this team or this franchise. 2

There's more than one way to finance a ballpark project, but the best overall financing plan is the one that is acceptable to all the essential parties—the team, the city, and the state. We are open to any reasonable plan that can achieve a consensus[10] agreement in time for action in this legislative session.

The Boston Red Sox are prepared to do what we must to make this new park a reality. We ask you and our other fans and friends to speak out on this issue, let your public officials know how you feel, and encourage them to show the same kind of leadership they've shown in the past on similar projects.

9. *Sports franchises* are professional teams that compete in a league.
10. Here, *consensus* means "among all members of a group."

Finding Common Ground *What attitude is the author expressing here? Why?* 3

Discussion Starter

Harrington presents several reasons for both building a new ballpark and using tax money to pay for it. With a group of classmates discuss Harrington's main points. Does your group agree with him? What arguments can you make to counter his proposal?

Writing Practice

Editorial Explain that this passage is an example of an editorial. An editorial is a kind of writing, usually meant to inform or persuade, that is printed in a newspaper. Editorials may be about happenings in a neighborhood, differences between political candidates, or (in this case) options in dealing with public financial concerns.

Group students and help each group brainstorm for suitable topics for editorials. Then, instruct students to write editorials that are meant to persuade readers to agree with the writer's opinion. This may be challenging, so be sure to make yourself available to answer questions and offer guidance.

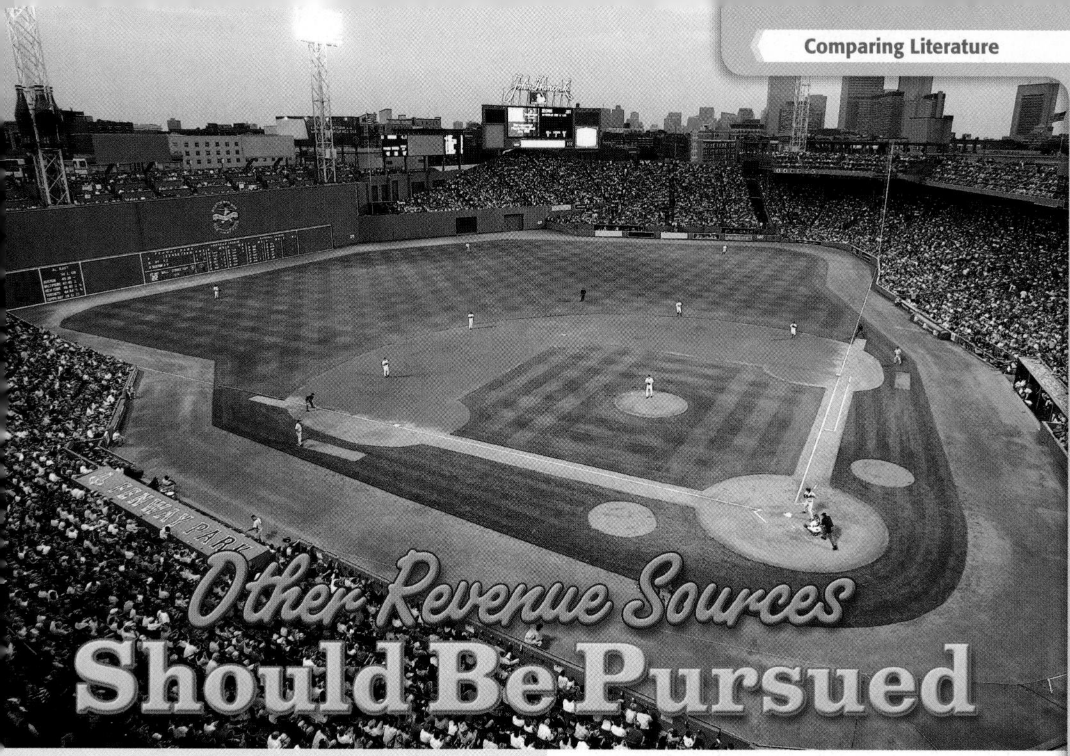

Other Revenue Sources Should Be Pursued

William M. Straus

Build Background

After earning a law degree from Georgetown University, William M. Straus served as an Assistant District Attorney in Bristol County, Massachusetts, for six years. He has represented the 10th Bristol District in the Massachusetts state House of Representatives since 1992. Straus grew up in South Orange, New Jersey, and remains a loyal Yankees fan. Nevertheless, he says he loves to see a game at Fenway Park. The following article was excerpted from the Web site of the New Bedford, Massachusetts, *Standard-Times* newspaper and originally appeared in 2000.

There's something different in the air in Massachusetts whenever the discussion involves major league sports and stadiums. In 1993 we saw this play out with the financing of the FleetCenter[1] and last year with the Patriots and their whirlwind trip to Connecticut and back.[2]

And now it is the Red Sox's turn at bat. To its credit, the team has stated clearly its

1. The *FleetCenter* was the former name of a Boston sports arena that hosts hockey and basketball games as well as concerts and other events. The arena is now called the TD Banknorth Garden.
2. *Their whirlwind trip to Connecticut and back* refers to the time in which the Patriots football team left Boston briefly because the state legislature would not finance improvements to the Patriots' old stadium.

Finding Common Ground *What does the author hope to do by using the word we?* **4**

Teach

Big Idea

Finding Common Ground
Say: As you read, answer this question: What is Straus's position on building a new stadium? *(He wants more financial research analyzed before a decision is made.)*

ENGLISH LEARNERS To assist English learners, explain that *position* has several different meanings. Guide a student to find the correct definition of this usage in a dictionary.

Big Idea 4

Finding Common Ground
Answer: *To convince readers that this decision affects him, too.*

For an audio recording of this selection, use Listening Library Audio CD-ROM.

Readability Scores

Dale-Chall: 8.6
DRP: 67
Lexile: 1330

Approaching Level

DIFFERENTIATED INSTRUCTION

Emerging Point out that this passage begins with a description of the author. Tell students that learning about the author can help them better understand a selection. Read aloud the background information about William M. Straus. With the class, make a list of facts about him. **Ask:** What kind of person does the author seem to be? How might his personality affect his writing? *(Students may think that the author seems like a busy person who is concerned with the people around him, as well as a dedicated baseball fan.)*

Comparing Literature

Teach

Reading Strategy 1

Evaluate Credibility
Answer: *By complimenting his opponent, he tries to gain the reader's trust by showing that he is fair minded. Also, as an elected official of Massachusetts, he wants to establish at the outset that he is primarily concerned with protecting the rights of taxpaying citizens.*

Reading Strategy 2

Scan for Information
Ask: What is the first area that Straus wants the Red Sox to rethink? *(Private sources of money)*

Literary Element 3

Rhetorical Devices
Answer: *People should not let love of the team cloud their judgment in money matters. The phrase "natural tendency" softens his criticism. The words emotional and nostalgic appeal to readers' logic.*

intention to remain in Boston with no threat to go elsewhere. In addition, the Red Sox contribution to the welfare of Massachusetts and its citizens has been exemplary,[3] whether in the field of charity or as a business neighbor.

Although the need for a new ballpark has been discussed for nearly twenty years, it was only in May that the team first went public with hard numbers on a request for taxpayer help. In a familiar negotiation approach, the Sox also stated that the deal had to be done by July 31, before the end of this year's legislative session. The imposition[4] of artificial deadlines usually doesn't help resolve negotiations, particularly when the deadline is set by someone who is asking for more than $200 million.

Unfortunately, the Red Sox request fell short in a number of respects. As of now, they are, in the phrase of the moment, "sharpening their pencils" to reduce the taxpayer's exposure in the costs of developing a new stadium. A quick review of the numbers helps explain the problem with the Red Sox's initial request.

The Sox priced the project at $627 million. The team was to provide $352 million to build the stadium, the city of Boston was being asked for $140 million for site acquisition and related costs, and the state of Massachusetts would put up $135 million for building two parking garages, utilities,[5] and road and subway improvements near the park.

The real cost of the subway and road projects, projected at around $50 million by the Red Sox, is more likely to come in at about $100 million. Even more disturbing is that the Sox did not identify the borrowing costs to the state or city for coming up with this amount of money. Given the current bond capacity[6] of the state, and the fact that this fall's ballot contains tax-cut proposals reducing annual state revenues by at least $1.5 billion, the carrying costs of the Sox proposal are a serious concern.

I believe there are two broad areas that caused this plan to fail and unless they are confronted in the next proposal by the Red Sox, will continue to plague the completion of the project.

First, have all private revenue sources been pursued? We are dealing with a private for-profit business enterprise. While public help for businesses in Massachusetts has occurred before, the private contribution is to be maximized. The natural tendency to view sports teams in emotional or nostalgic terms cannot overwhelm other considerations. When tax increment financing[7] is used in our region or other parts of the state, some balance of local return is analyzed and weighed. 2

In this case, the Sox plan has not considered a number of other private sources of money that have been employed around the country for financing stadium projects. Naming rights to the stadium is the most obvious example which so far has been missing; published reports indicate that in

3. *Exemplary* means "so good that others should use it as an example."
4. *Imposition* means "an unreasonable request."
5. *Utilities* refer to services, such as water and electricity, that a city provides to homes and businesses.
6. *Bond capacity* refers to a way in which city, state, and federal governments borrow money for public projects. They sell bonds to citizens to raise funds and pay back the money, with interest, at a later date.
7. *Tax increment financing* refers to the use of tax increases to finance local projects.

1 Evaluate Credibility *How does Straus attempt to demonstrate his reliability in this paragraph?*

Rhetorical Devices *What does the author mean here? How does his word choice affect his message?* 3

Reading Practice

Evaluate an Argument The author of this passage is trying to persuade readers to feel a certain way about the Red Sox construction project. **Ask:** How does the author feel about the project? How does he want readers to feel? Poll students on their reaction to the author's arguments and then discuss whether the author made a successful case.

Ask students to consider the ways the author presented his information and suggestions. *(Students may note that he used facts and figures to deal with the prices of certain renovations.)*

some cases, companies have paid nearly $100 million for multiyear agreements for the right to name a facility. Another potential source of revenue is the inclusion of new private partners in the project. It has also been reported that other businesses might agree to help finance the $81 million in parking garages in return for their use outside of the eighty or so game dates needed by the Sox.

☆ Another private source of funds may be the private land owners whose land the Sox are asking be taken by the city of Boston in eminent domain[8] proceedings. And finally, many teams have raised money by selling private licenses for long-term seat ownership by the fans who attend the games. Until these avenues are exhausted, the Sox will have a hard time coming to the taxpayers for help.

The second broad area for the Sox to consider is the question of repayment to the taxpayers for the money put up by the state. The Sox proposed that they retain most of the revenue stream from the parking garage, which was to be built entirely by the state. This simply will not work. Assuming that it is even appropriate for the state to build a facility that private parties might be just as willing to construct, there seems to be no logic in simply handing over future income to the team from parking revenues. . . .

Some public assistance for a project of this **magnitude** can be justified by the overall improvement to tax revenues for both the state and the city. But such numbers cannot be glossed over and should be based upon serious calculations and benefits to the public. What the final mix should be on the contributions for infrastructure[9] improvements remains open and will take shape in the unusual process of negotiation which occurs on sports facilities.

No one can say for sure when this project will get its approvals. The process is both public and private. As we've seen in the few weeks since the Red Sox came forward with a real spending plan, much give and take has occurred and will occur in the coming weeks. The Legislature has a responsibility to act prudently so that the Red Sox are treated no better or worse than others who seek public help for their projects.

8. *Eminent domain* is the right of the government to take private land if it can prove that its use of the land will benefit the public.

9. *Infrastructure* is the network of public systems that includes roads, telephone wires, water pipes, and other means of public communication, transportation, and operation.

Vocabulary

magnitude (mag′ nə tōōd′) *n.* great size, volume, or extent; importance; significance

Finding Common Ground *Who does the author see as part of the "give and take"?* **4**

Quickwrite

If you were a taxpayer in Boston, would you approve of paying more taxes in order to fund a new baseball park? Write a paragraph explaining why or why not.

Comparing Literature

Teach

Big Idea 4

Finding Common Ground
Answer: *The author sees the Red Sox owners, the city of Boston, the fans, and the state of Massachusetts as part of this give and take.*

ENGLISH LEARNERS To aid English learners, explain that *give* and *take* means "compromise" or "a friendly exchange." Ask English learners to share similar words or phrases in their language.

Assess

Quickwrite

Encourage students to consider writing two paragraphs; one for each side of the question. Divide the class in half and assign one viewpoint to each group. Invite one student from each group to face off and debate the two positions.

Cultural History ☆

Building Fenway John Taylor, former owner of the Boston Red Sox, built Fenway Park on land he owned. The stadium was built for the team and opened in 1912.

English Learners

DIFFERENTIATED INSTRUCTION

SMALL GROUP

Intermediate This passage contains many words that may be difficult to English learners. Ask students to write down all unfamiliar words as they read this passage. Then, group the students and instruct them to use a dictionary to define each word.

When the students are finished, compare their lists and make a combined list of new vocabulary. This list will likely contain such difficult words and terms as *financing, credit, negotiation, maximizing,* and *revenue stream.*

After You Read

Assess

1. Answers will vary.
2. (a) A new ballpark (b) Red Sox might become a bad team.
3. (a) Naming rights (b) Fans may want a new stadium to be called Fenway Park.
4. Answers will vary. Harrington is sincere and promises to keep the Red Sox in Boston. Straus uses real numbers.
5. Harrington's calculations were not accurate and the benefits were not clear.
6. Students should support their responses.
7. Students should explain their reasons logically.

Literary Element

1. Answers should describe appeals to logic, emotion, ethics, or authority. Effects might be urgency, trust, desperation, or anger.
2. Answers will vary.

Progress Check

Can students identify rhetorical devices?

If No → See Unit 2 Teaching Resources Book, p. 210.

Comparing Literature

After You Read

Respond and Think Critically

Respond and Interpret

1. Who do you think presented the most persuasive argument about Fenway Park? Explain.
2. (a)According to John L. Harrington, what is essential to the future of the Red Sox? (b)What does he think would be the most negative repercussion if this project is stalled?
3. (a)According to William M. Straus, what is the most obvious source of private funding for a new Red Sox stadium? (b)What might Red Sox fans dislike about this kind of funding?

Analyze and Evaluate

4. Harrington argues that the Yawkey Trust is "not a traditional profit-making enterprise." But Straus refers to the Yawkey Trust as "a private for-profit business enterprise." Whom do you believe, and why?
5. What does Straus suggest about the financial numbers Harrington cites?

Connect

6. **Big Idea** **Finding Common Ground** After reading these opinions and arguments, what ideas do you have about how opposing sides might find common ground?
7. **Connect to Today** What building or place do you know of that might be knocked down or replaced? On which side of the issue would you argue? Why?

Literary Element Rhetorical Devices

Review the various types of appeals—to logic, emotion, ethics, and authority—listed on page 400. Consider how each type of appeal works as a rhetorical device. Then answer the following questions.

1. Describe a rhetorical device used in one of the selections. What is the effect of the device?
2. Which of the authors did you find most trustworthy? Explain your answer in terms of the rhetorical devices the author uses.

Reading Strategy Evaluate Credibility

Refer to the chart you made as you read, and then answer the following questions.

1. Who is Harrington's primary audience? How does his audience and purpose affect his tone?
2. Who is Straus's primary audience? What bias may he have regarding Fenway Park?

Vocabulary Practice

Practice with Synonyms With a partner, match each boldfaced vocabulary word below with its synonym. You will not use all the answer choices.

1. cathedral	a. church
2. nostalgia	b. remember
3. staggering	c. attractive
4. magnitude	d. enormity
	e. awesome
	f. wistfulness

Writing

Write a Business Letter Write a letter to one of the writers featured here evaluating the credibility of his argument. Critique the relationship between generalizations and evidence, the comprehensiveness of evidence, and the way in which his intent affects the structure and tone of his writing. For help on writing a letter, see pages 1112 and R22.

Reading Strategy

1. Harrington addresses fans. His tone is friendly and inclusive.
2. Straus's audience may be taxpayers or the Legislature. Straus is a state legislator and likely wants to continue to be involved in politics. Students may say that his bias comes from a desire to be re-elected.

Progress Check

Can students evaluate credibility?

If No → See Unit 2 Teaching Resources Book, p. 211.

Vocabulary Practice

1. a **2.** f **3.** e **4.** d

Write

Students' letters should critique the relationship between generalizations and evidence and should address the way the author's intent affects his writing.

For additional selection assessment, see Assessment Resources, pp. 107–108.

Wrap-Up: Comparing Literature

Different Viewpoints

- *Thoughts on Fenway Park* by various authors
- *Taxpayers Will Get a Return on Investment* by John L. Harrington
- *Other Revenue Sources Should Be Pursued* by William M. Straus

COMPARE THE Big Idea Finding Common Ground

Writing Each of the writers in this feature attempts to find common ground with the audience. For example, they may mention ideas or facts that they know will resonate with their audience. Write a brief essay in which you compare the ways that three of the writers seek to establish common ground with the reader. Cite evidence from the selections to support your ideas.

COMPARE Persuasion

Group Activity As an attempt to influence, a persuasive appeal can be a very powerful thing. It is important to identify these appeals so you can draw informed conclusions. With a small group, discuss the following questions:

1. What is each writer trying to communicate about Fenway Park?
2. What persuasive appeals does each writer use to influence the reader?
3. Which of the selections presents the strongest argument? Support your answer with passages from the selections.

COMPARE Author's Viewpoint

Speaking and Listening With a partner, research one of the following questions using the resources at the library and on the Internet. Present your findings in an oral presentation to your class.

1. Why did John L. Harrington sell the Boston Red Sox in 2002?
2. What recent renovations have been made to Fenway Park? Who is paying for these improvements?
3. How has the neighborhood around Fenway Park changed in the past ten years?
4. What issues are Red Sox fans currently debating?

LOG ON **Literature Online**

Selection Resources For Selection Quizzes, eFlashcards, and Reading-Writing Connection activities, go to glencoe.com and enter QuickPass code GL49787u2.

Wrap-Up: Comparing Literature

Different Viewpoints

Assess

Compare the Big Idea

Critique student essays on these criteria:

- Do students discuss how the authors establish common ground with their readers?
- Do students support their ideas with evidence from the selections?

Compare Persuasion

Students should support their answers with details from the text. They should note where authors employed similar persuasive appeals to different ends.

Compare Author's Viewpoint

Students' presentations should be well-researched and provide facts to answer the question they choose.

English Learners

DIFFERENTIATED INSTRUCTION

SMALL GROUP

Beginning/Early Intermediate This passage provides many ideas and details. It may be challenging for English learners to decide which are the most important concepts in the passage. Group students and have them help one another in evaluating the information given by the writer. Ask them to list five details as well as the main idea of the passage. Encourage students to share the results of their reading.

They may offer a wide variety of details from the passage, such as the cost of the stadium, the money that would be paid by Boston, or the importance of the stadium's name. The main idea is that the Red Sox should consider other options in terms of finding financial support for their projects.

Before You Read

Focus

Bellringer Options

Selection Focus Transparency 18

Daily Language Practice Transparency 42

Or display images of students from the 1940s and 1950s. Show students standing in lines, seated at a school assembly—situations that required students to behave themselves in an orderly and quiet fashion.

Ask: How might student life today be similar to or different from student life in the 1940s or 1950s? Have students consider as they read what they might have in common with the author.

Before You Read

Put Down the Backpack

Meet **Anna Quindlen**
(born 1952)

Anna Quindlen knows the power of language. She once said that reading "has made me more human by exposing me to worlds I might never have entered and people I might never meet." Her love of reading and writing led to a successful career as a journalist and fiction writer.

Quindlen was born in Philadelphia. From an early age, she knew that she wanted to be a writer. At the age of eighteen, Quindlen worked part-time as a reporter for the *New York Post* while attending Barnard College, where she earned a bachelor's degree in English literature. In 1977 she left the *Post* for the *New York Times*.

> *"There's no greater happiness than doing something every day that you love."*
>
> —Anna Quindlen

Trailblazer By 1983 Quindlen was writing editorial columns for the *New York Times*. In 1985 she began writing "Life in the 30s." In the column, Quindlen openly discussed her own childhood, the struggles of parenting, and a variety of political issues. Readers were drawn to the honest nature of her writing.

With her next column, "Public and Private," Quindlen became the third woman in the *New York Times'* history to write a regular column on the prestigious op-ed page. She was awarded a Pulitzer Prize for "Public and Private" in 1992. A collection of Quindlen's essays, *Thinking Out Loud,* was published in 1993.

A Novelist, Too Quindlen's first novel, *Object Lessons,* was published in 1991. It was followed by *One True Thing* and the bestselling *Black and Blue.* In her fiction, she explores themes of tragedy, loss, violence, and power. Despite these grave themes, Quindlen's message often is about finding happiness and meaning in life.

Quindlen's successful career as a novelist, social critic, and prize-winning journalist continues today. Currently, she writes for the popular column "The Last Word" in *Newsweek* magazine. She lives in New York with her husband and three children.

LOG ON **Literature** Online

Author Search For more about Anna Quindlen, go to glencoe.com and enter QuickPass code GL49787u2.

Selection Skills

Put Down the Backpack

Literary Elements
- Author's Purpose (SE pp. 415–420)

Reading Skills
- Evaluate Evidence (SE pp. 415–420)

Vocabulary Skills
- Analogy (SE pp. 413, 420)

Listening/Speaking/Viewing Skills
- Analyze Art (SE pp. 417, 418)

Writing Skills/Grammar
- Summary (SE p. 421)
- Freewrite (TE p. 414)

Literature and Reading Preview

Connect to the Speech

How do you see yourself as unique from other people? List several qualities that make you unique and explain each one.

Build Background

Quindlen delivered this speech at Mount Holyoke College in South Hadley, Massachusetts. Mount Holyoke is a women's college, similar to Barnard College, which Quindlen attended. Both colleges were founded in the 1800s, at times when many universities did not admit women.

Set Purposes for Reading

Big Idea Finding Common Ground

As you read "Put Down the Backpack," ask yourself, How does Quindlen establish common ground with her audience?

Literary Element Author's Purpose

An **author's purpose** might be one or more of the following: to inform, to explain, to entertain, or to persuade. Being aware of author's purpose gives the reader a clearer understanding of the meaning and intent of a writer. As you read, ask yourself, What is Quindlen's purpose in writing for this audience?

Reading Strategy Evaluate Evidence

In a persuasive essay, a writer attempts to convince the reader to adopt an idea or to take action on an issue. A persuasive technique is to give reasons in the form of generalizations supported by evidence. When you **evaluate evidence,** you judge the adequacy of the evidence used to support each generalization. As you read, ask yourself, How well does Quindlen support her generalizations with convincing evidence?

Tip: **Make a Web** As you read, track Quindlen's generalizations and how she supports them. Make a web diagram like the one below for each generalization to help you evaluate her evidence.

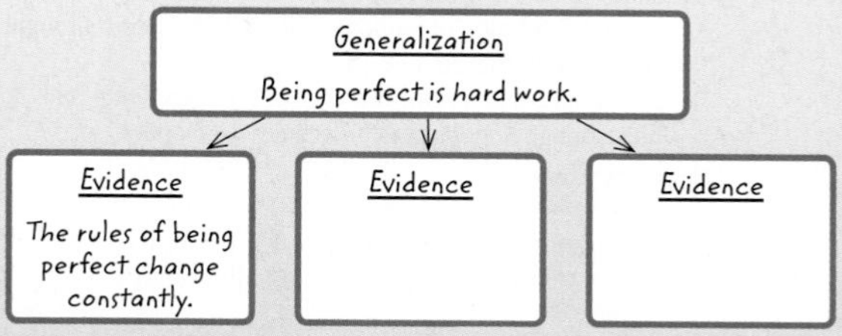

Learning Objectives

For pages 412–420

In studying this text, you will focus on the following objectives:

Literary Study: Analyzing author's purpose.

Reading: Evaluating evidence.

Vocabulary

monogrammed (mon′ə gramd) *adj.* decorated with a design of one or more letters, usually the initials of a name; p. 414 *They got monogrammed towels as a gift.*

template (tem′ plāt) *n.* a pattern that serves as a guide to making something accurately; p. 415 *The students used a template when drawing their graphic organizers.*

redundant (ri dun′dənt) *adj.* unnecessarily repetitive; without a purpose; p. 416 *Carla thought repeating the story was redundant.*

denigrate (den′ə grāt′) *v.* to criticize or belittle; p. 418 *The coach did not denigrate the kicker for the missed field goal.*

Tip: **Analogies** To complete an analogy, make up a sentence that shows a relationship between two words. Then look for another pair of words that, when put into the same sentence, also results in a true statement. For example:

redundant : boring :: novel : exciting

Something *redundant* can be *boring;* something *novel* can be *exciting*.

Approaching Level

DIFFERENTIATED INSTRUCTION

Emerging Explain to students that the selection they are going to read is a speech once presented to college students on graduation day. **Ask:** In your opinion, what makes a good speech? *(Possible answers: personal experiences, funny jokes, everyday language, familiar quotes, events the audience will recognize, and stories that have common themes.)*

Tell students that the author, in her speech, uses her own experiences to relate to students. She also uses humor, figurative language, and quotes from other authors.

Before You Read

Focus

Summary

An author uses her youthful quest for perfection as the topic of a graduation speech. She explains that being perfect in the eyes of the world is hard work, but it is an attainable goal. However, the more difficult task is finding out who you are as an individual. It is also by far the most rewarding task a person can undertake.

For summaries in languages other than English, see Unit 2 Teaching Resources Book, pp. 217–222.

Vocabulary

Definition Game Split the class into two teams. Give each team flash cards with a vocabulary word printed on each. Read the definitions of the vocabulary words aloud. Have a student from each team bring up the card with the word that you defined. The team that gets the correct card to the front of the room first gets one point. The team with the most points at the end of the game wins.

For additional vocabulary practice, see Unit 2 Teaching Resources Book, p. 225.

For additional context, see Glencoe Interactive Vocabulary CD-ROM.

Teach

Big Idea 1

Finding Common Ground

Answer: *She creates a bond with her audience by showing she was once where they are. This common ground makes it more likely they will listen to what she says and consider her advice.*

APPROACHING For approaching-level students, **ask:** How would you describe the writer? *(Answers will vary.)*

Writer's Technique ☆

Repetition Writers often repeat sounds, words, or phrases to emphasize an idea. **Ask:** Why does the writer repeat the phrase "to be perfect in every possible way" in the second paragraph? *(To emphasize her goal; it is a mantra in her quest for perfection.)*

For an audio recording of this selection, use Listening Library Audio CD-ROM.

Readability Scores

Dale-Chall: 7.4
DRP: 57
Lexile: 1020

Put Down the Backpack

Anna Quindlen

I look at all of you today and I cannot help but see myself twenty-five years ago, at my own Barnard commencement. I sometimes seem, in my mind, to have as much in common with that girl as I do with any stranger I might pass in the doorway of a coffee shop or in the aisle of an airplane. I cannot remember what she wore or how she felt that day. But I can tell you this about her without question: she was perfect.

Let me be very clear what I mean by that. I mean that I got up every day and tried to ☆ be perfect in every possible way. If there was a test to be had, I had studied for it; if there was a paper to be written, it was done. I smiled at everyone in the dorm hallways, because it was important to be friendly, and I made fun of them behind their backs because it was important to be witty. And I worked as a residence counselor[1] and sat on housing council. If anyone had ever stopped and asked me why I did those things—well, I'm not sure what I would have said. But I can tell you, today, that I did them to be perfect, in every possible way.

1. A *residence counselor* is an older student who lives with and supervises other students in a college dormitory.

1 Finding Common Ground *Why do you think the author opens her speech with this reference to Barnard?*

Being perfect was hard work, and the hell of it was, the rules of it changed. So that while I arrived at college in 1970 with a trunk full of perfect pleated kilts and perfect **monogrammed** sweaters, by Christmas vacation I had another perfect uniform: overalls, turtlenecks, and the perfect New York City Barnard College affect[2]—part hyper-intellectual, part ennui.[3] This was very hard work indeed. I had read neither Sartre nor Sappho,[4] and the closest I ever came to being bored and above it all was falling asleep. Finally, it was harder to become perfect because I realized, at Barnard, that I was not the smartest girl in the world. Eventually being perfect day after day, year after year, became like always carrying a backpack filled with bricks on my back. And oh, how I secretly longed to lay my burden down.

2. Here, *affect* (af′ ekt) is a noun meaning "a quality pretended to impress others."
3. *Ennui* (än wē′) is the French word for *boredom*. The word has a connotation of world weariness or boredom brought on by intellectual superiority.
4. *Jean-Paul Sartre* (1905–1980) was a French writer and philosopher. *Sappho* was an ancient Greek poet.

Vocabulary

monogrammed (mon′ ə gramd) *adj.* decorated with a design of one or more letters, usually the initials of a name

Writing Practice

Relate to the Selection Read aloud the second paragraph to demonstrate how the speaker tried to be perfect. Explain that the speaker tried to wear the right clothes, get the right grades, and say the right things. Attempting to be perfect is a common theme. Ask students whether they can relate to the selection's point about trying to be perfect. Mention that people try to be perfect in different ways for different aspects of their lives. For example perfect for a teacher is different than being perfect for friends. **Ask:** How have you tried to be perfect for your friends, family, or school? Have students freewrite about ways that they try to be perfect. Students may use the freewrite as prewriting material to begin a one-page essay

2 So what I want to say to you today is this: if this sounds, in any way, familiar to you, if you have been trying to be perfect in one way or another, too, then make today, when for a moment there are no more grades to be gotten, classmates to be met, terrain to be scouted, positioning to be arranged—make today the day to put down the backpack. Trying to be perfect may be sort of inevitable for people like us, who are smart and ambitious and interested in the world and in its good opinion. But at one level it's too hard, and at another, it's too cheap and easy. Because it really requires you mainly to read the zeitgeist[5] of wherever and whenever you happen to be, and to assume the masks necessary to be the best of whatever the zeitgeist dictates or requires. Those requirements shapeshift, sure, but when you're clever you can read them and do the imitation required.

3 But nothing important, or meaningful, or beautiful, or interesting, or great ever came out of imitations. The thing that is really hard, and really amazing, is giving up on being perfect and beginning the work of becoming yourself.

This is more difficult, because there is no zeitgeist to read, no **template** to follow, no mask to wear. Set aside what your friends expect, what your parents demand, what your acquaintances require. Set aside the messages this culture sends, through its advertising, its entertainment, its disdain and its disapproval, about how you should behave.

5. *Zeitgeist* means "the culture of a particular place and time."

3 Finding Common Ground *What effect might this phrase have on the audience at this point in the speech?*

4 Evaluate Evidence *What evidence does Quindlen cite to support this generalization?*

Vocabulary

template (tem′ plāt) *n.* a pattern that serves as a guide to making something accurately

Set aside the old traditional notion of female as nurturer[6] and male as leader; set aside, too, the new traditional notions of female as superwoman and male as oppressor.[7] Begin with that most terrifying of all things, a clean slate. Then look, every day, at the choices you are making, and when you ask yourself why you are making them, find this answer: for me, for me. Because they are who and what I am, and mean to be.

This is the hard work of your life in the world, to make it all up as you go along, to acknowledge the introvert, the clown, the artist, the reserved, the distraught, the goofball, the thinker. You will have to bend all your will not to march to the music that all of those great "theys" out there pipe on their flutes. They want you to go to professional school, to wear khakis, to pierce your navel, to bare your soul. These are the fashionable ways. The music is tinny, if you listen close enough. Look inside. That way lies dancing to the melodies spun out by your own heart. This is a symphony. All the rest are jingles.[8]

4 This will always be your struggle whether you are twenty-one or fifty-one. I know this from experience. When I quit the *New York Times* to be a full-time mother, the voices of the world said that I was nuts. When I quit it again to be a full-time novelist, they said I was nuts again. But I am not nuts. I am happy. I am successful on my own terms. Because if your success is not on your own terms, if it looks good to the world but does not feel good in your heart, it is not success at

6. A *nurturer* is someone who takes care of others.
7. An *oppressor* is someone who dominates others through an unjust use of force or authority.
8. Here, *jingles* refers to the short, catchy songs used in advertising.

Author's Purpose *What is the author's purpose in this paragraph? How can you tell?* **5**

Teach

Big Idea 2

Finding Common Ground

Ask: What metaphor does Quindlen use to represent the burden of trying to be perfect? *(A heavy backpack)* What suggestion does she make to her audience? *(Stop trying to be perfect; put the backpack down.)*

Big Idea 3

Finding Common Ground

Answer: *By allying herself with her listeners, the speaker increases her chances of convincing them that her message is valid.*

Reading Strategy 4

Evaluate Evidence

Answer: *She uses an example from literature to show that an author must use her own personality, voice, and character to prevent her work from being redundant.*

Literary Element 5

Author's Purpose

Answer: *She wants people to develop themselves as individuals.*

English Learners

DIFFERENTIATED INSTRUCTION

Intermediate This selection uses figurative language to add humor. Encourage students to make a list of figurative language that they do not understand. *(Possible language that students might not understand includes "Those requirements shapeshift," "a clean slate," "dancing to the melodies spun out by your own heart," and "crowned by an abstract design that is completely different than those of anyone in this crowd.")* Instruct students to closely look at context clues surrounding figurative language. These clues may help students decipher the language.

Teach

Literary Element 1

Author's Purpose

Ask: Why does the author end the paragraph with a rhetorical question? *(Possible answer: The question helps her transition between two ideas.)*

ENGLISH LEARNERS Ask an English learner to look up *rhetorical* in a dictionary and read the definition aloud.

Literary Element 2

Author's Purpose

Answer: *She uses imperative sentences to persuade her audience to do something. The repetition strengthens the persuasion. She wants the graduates to be as a child is, unaware of others' expectations.*

all. Remember the words of Lily Tomlin:[9] If you win the rat race, you're still a rat.

Look at your fingers. Hold them in front of your face. Each one is crowned by an abstract design that is completely different than those of anyone in this crowd, in this
1 country, in this world. They are a metaphor for you. Each of you is as different as your fingerprints. Why in the world should you march to any lockstep?[10]

The lockstep is easier, but here is why you cannot march to it. Because nothing great or even good ever came of it. When young writers write to me about following in the footsteps of those of us who string together nouns and verbs for a living, I tell them this: every story has already been told. Once you've read *Anna Karenina, Bleak House, The Sound and the Fury, To Kill a Mockingbird,* and *A Wrinkle in Time,* you understand that there is really no reason to ever write another novel. Except that each writer brings to the table, if she will let herself, something that no one else in the history of time has ever had. And that is herself, her own personality, her own voice. If she is doing Faulkner[11] imitations, she can stay home. If she is giving readers what she thinks they want instead of what she is, she should stop trying.

But if her books reflect her character, who she really is, then she is giving them a new and wonderful gift. Giving it to herself, too.

And that is true of music and art and teaching and medicine. Someone sent me a T-shirt not long ago that read "Well-Behaved Women Don't Make History." They don't make good lawyers, either, or doctors or businesswomen. Imitations are **redundant**. Yourself is what is wanted.

You already know this. I just need to remind you. Think back. Think back to first or second grade, when you could still hear the sound of your own voice in your head, when you were too young, too unformed, too fantastic[12] to understand that you were supposed to take on the protective coloration of the expectations of those around you. Think of what the writer Catherine Drinker Bowen[13] once wrote, more than half a century ago: "Many a man who has known himself at ten forgets himself utterly between ten and thirty." Many a woman, too.

You are not alone in this. We parents have forgotten our way sometimes, too. I say this as the deeply committed, often flawed mother of three. When you were first born, each of you, our great glory was in thinking you absolutely distinct from every baby who had ever been born before. You were a miracle of singularity, and we knew it in every fiber of our being.

But we are only human, and being a parent is a very difficult job, more difficult than any other, because it requires the shaping of other people, which is an act of extraordinary hubris.[14] Over the years we learned to want for you things that you did not want for yourself. We learned to want the lead in the play, the acceptance to our own college, the straight and narrow path

---

9. *Lily Tomlin* (1939–) is a U.S. comedian and actress.
10. A *lockstep* is any process or method of doing something that is adhered to strictly and without question or thought. The word comes from a style of marching in which a group march as one, precisely in step and very close together.
11. *William Faulkner* (1897–1962) was a renowned American writer.
12. Here, *fantastic* means "reliant on imagination."
13. *Catherine Drinker Bowen* (1897–1973) was an American writer of what she called "semifictional biographies."
14. *Hubris* means "arrogance or excessive pride."

Author's Purpose *What do the writing techniques in this paragraph reveal about the author's purpose? What is unusual about her purpose in this passage?* 2

Vocabulary

redundant (ri dun′dənt) *adj.* unnecessarily repetitive; without a purpose

Reading Practice

SPIRAL REVIEW **Synthesize** Explain to students that Quindlen is one of most well-respected essayists in the United States in the area of social commentary. Have them read additional works from her collected essays, which include the books Thinking Out Loud and Loud and Clear. Tell them to take notes on the main ideas of the essays and to summarize them in a list. Then ask them to compare these ideas with their own ideas about life in American society. Have a class discussion in which students indicate which of Quindlen's ideas they agree with and which they disagree with.

Ciurana, the path, 1917. Joan Miró. Coll. Tappenbeck, Mouzay, France

View the Art Joan Miró's early work was influenced by Catalan folk art. This style of art is known for its flat appearance—it lacks a sense of being three-dimensional. Would you describe this painting as flat? Why or why not? ★

that often leads absolutely nowhere. Sometimes we wanted those things because we were convinced it would make life better, or at least easier for you. Sometimes we had a hard time distinguishing between where you ended and we began.

So that another reason that you must give up on being perfect and take hold of being yourself is because sometime, in the distant future, you may want to be parents, too. If you can bring to your children the self that you truly are, as opposed to some amalgam[15] of manners and mannerisms, expectations and fears that you have acquired as a carapace[16] along the way, you will give them, too, a great gift. You will teach them by example not to be terrorized by the narrow and parsimonious[17] expectations of the world, a world that often likes to color within the lines when a spray of paint, a scrawl of crayon, is what is truly wanted.

Remember yourself, from the days when you were younger and rougher and wilder, more scrawl than straight line. Remember all of yourself, the flaws and faults as well as the many strengths. Carl Jung[18] once said, "If people can be educated to see the lowly side of their own natures, it may be hoped that they will also learn to understand and to love their fellow men better. A little less hypocrisy[19] and a little more tolerance toward oneself can only have good results in respect for our neighbors, for we are all too prone to transfer to our fellows the injustice and violence we inflict upon our own natures."

Most commencement speeches suggest you take up something or other: the challenge of the future, a vision of the twenty-first century. Instead I'd like you to give up. Give up the backpack. Give up the nonsensical and punishing quest for perfection that

15. An *amalgam* is a mixture of different elements.
16. A *carapace* is a figurative shell that protects a person, just as the literal shell of a turtle protects it.
17. *Parsimonious* means "stingy or ungenerous."

18. *Carl Jung* (1875–1961) was a Swiss psychiatrist who wrote about the human unconscious.
19. *Hypocrisy* is the act of pretending to have certain values, beliefs, or feelings in order to appear moral or superior to others.

Evaluate Evidence *Why do you think Quindlen includes this quote from Carl Jung?* **3**

Author's Purpose *How is Quindlen's repetition of the phrase "give up" in this passage related to her purpose?* **4**

Teach

Reading Strategy 3

Evaluate Evidence

Answer: *Because Jung, a famous psychologist, was an authority on the human mind and behavior, Quindlen uses his words as evidence that self-knowledge and self-respect can enable parents to raise children who are resistant to the conformist expectations of the world.*

Literary Element 4

Author's Purpose

Answer: *Her purpose is to persuade the audience to give up the quest for perfection based on external expectations. Her repetition emphasizes the importance of this message.*

View the Art ★

Answer: *Most students will probably say the painting does not appear all that flat since it does utilize perspective.*

Advanced Learners

DIFFERENTIATED INSTRUCTION

Literary Allusions An allusion is a reference to another author or work in literature. Quindlen makes many allusions to authors and their works in her selection. Have a student read the paragraph that begins "The lockstep is easier . . ." on page 416. **Ask:** Why does Quindlen mention so many books by other authors? Why does she mention William Faulkner? *(To relate her point to books college students may have read)*

Explain to students that by using literary allusions to authors and their works, Quindlen relates to her audience—college graduates who have probably read all of the works she mentioned. Quindlen also displays her writing knowledge to the audience to make herself seem more credible. **Ask:** After reading this list of books, do you find Quindlen more credible? *(Answers will vary.)*

Teach

Big Idea 1

Finding Common Ground
Answer: *She may use us and our to indicate solidarity with the members of her audience and all people.*

Reading Strategy 2

Evaluate Evidence
Answer: *Quindlen has cited her personal experience to show that a person is happier when she frees herself from the expectations of others. She now extends the generalization to include the related point that a person will be unable to cope with disappointment or failure without a strong sense of selfhood.*

Reading Strategy 3

Interpret **Ask:** How does Eliot's quote apply to you? *(There is no time limit on when a person can take up the task of finding his or her inner self.)*

APPROACHING Ask approaching-level students to think of other famous quotes that they think applies to them.

View the Art ★

Answer: *In this painting, two women look into a mirror and see one reflection. Quindlen argues that the pursuit of perfection is driven by societal pressure, which cripples creativity. It is our imperfections, she believes, that mark us as individuals.*

To check students' understanding of the selection, see Unit 2 Teaching Resources Book, p. 228.

Two Women and Mirror. Ludvik Glazer-Naudé.

View the Art Ludvik Glazer-Naudé's unusual illustrations are influenced by a variety of art forms, including graphic design and painting. In what ways does this picture reflect Quindlen's call to "put down the backpack"? ★

dogs too many of us through too much of our lives. It is a quest that causes us to doubt and **denigrate** ourselves, our true selves, our quirks and foibles[20] and great leaps into the unknown, and that is bad enough.

But this is worse: that someday, sometime, you will be somewhere, maybe on a day like today—a berm[21] overlooking a pond in Vermont, the lip of the Grand Canyon at sunset. Maybe something bad will have happened: you will have lost someone you loved, or failed at something you wanted to succeed at very much.

And sitting there, you will fall into the center of yourself. You will look for that core to sustain you. If you have been perfect all your life, and have managed to meet all the expectations of your family, your friends, your community, your society, chances are excellent that there will be a black hole where your core ought to be.

Don't take that chance. Begin to say no to the Greek chorus[22] that thinks it knows the parameters of a happy life when all it knows is the homogenization[23] of human experience. Listen to that small voice from inside you, that tells you to go another way. George Eliot[24] wrote, "It is never too late to be what you might have been." It is never too early, either. And it will make all the difference in the world. Take it from someone who has left the backpack full of bricks far behind. Every day feels light as a feather. 3

20. *Quirks and foibles* are odd qualities and small weaknesses in a person's character.
21. A *berm* is a narrow path along the top or bottom of a hill.
22. A *Greek chorus* is a group of actors in an ancient Greek play who comment in unison on what is happening.
23. *Homogenization* means "making the same."
24. *George Eliot* was the pen name of British novelist Mary Ann Evans (1819–1880).

1 **Finding Common Ground** *Quindlen has established that she has given up the quest for perfection. Why then do you think she uses the pronouns* us *and* our *in this sentence?*

Evaluate Evidence *What evidence has Quindlen cited in the speech to support this generalization?* 2

Vocabulary
denigrate (den′ ə grāt′) *v.* to criticize or belittle

Reading Practice

SPIRAL REVIEW **Paraphrase** Explain that paraphrasing—rewriting a selection in your own words—can help improve comprehension of the selection. **Model** this activity by paraphrasing the last paragraph on the board. **Write:** Don't risk your life by letting others narrate what is best for you. Listen to yourself, and take the path you want to take. Make your life easier; don't try to be perfect.

Break students into groups. Have them paraphrase the paragraph on page 418 that begins "But this is worse." *(Possible answer: Someday, you will be in a very different place and time. Something terrible may happen such as the death of a loved one or the loss of a goal.)*

After You Read

Respond and Think Critically

Respond and Interpret

1. Did Quindlen's speech persuade you to change the way in which you think about success? Explain your answer using examples from the speech.
2. (a)In Quindlen's view, what is the problem with imitation? (b)How does her opinion of imitation relate to her message of "becoming yourself"?
3. (a)Why does Quindlen urge the members of her audience to remember being children? (b)When might "coloring outside the lines" be beneficial?

Analyze and Evaluate

4. Why might "marching in lockstep" with the rest of the world be preferable for some people?
5. Explain whether you think Quindlen was a good choice of speaker at this college's graduation.

Connect

6. **Big Idea** Finding Common Ground Does Quindlen's speech reach out to all types of students? Use examples from the text to explain your answer.
7. **Connect to Today** Explain how Quindlen's standards compare to messages often sent through today's advertising and entertainment.

Visual Literacy

Topics and Transitions

In her speech, Quindlen establishes clear topics and then links those topics together with transition sentences. Make a flowchart like the one shown to identify the topics and transitions in Quindlen's speech. Fill in the chart with topics by summarizing Quindlen's main ideas in your own words. Then identify the sentences from the speech that connect Quindlen's ideas to one another. Note words or phrases that connect the transition sentence to the previous topic and the following topic.

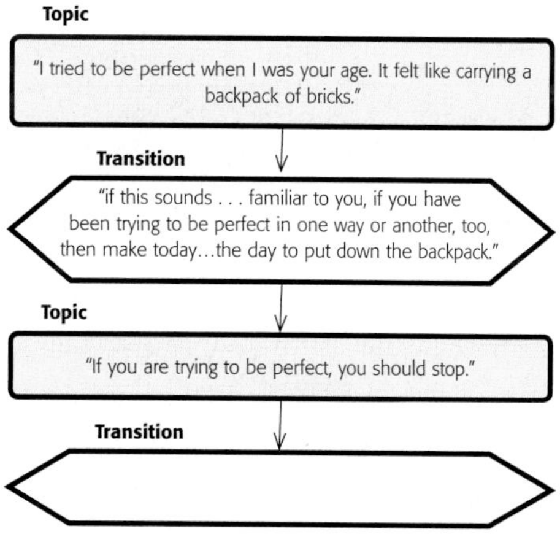

Topic
"I tried to be perfect when I was your age. It felt like carrying a backpack of bricks."
Transition
"if this sounds . . . familiar to you, if you have been trying to be perfect in one way or another, too, then make today...the day to put down the backpack."
Topic
"If you are trying to be perfect, you should stop."
Transition

1. How does Quindlen help her audience follow the flow of her ideas? Use examples from your chart to illustrate your answer.
2. Why does the author of a speech need to make sure that all topics and transitions are clear and easy to follow?

After You Read

Assess

1. Students may be persuaded that success should be measured by internal factors rather than outside forces. Others may say she is unrealistic and success is dictated by factors such as wealth and status.
2. (a) She says "nothing important, or meaningful, or beautiful, or interesting, or great ever came out of imitations." (b) She urges listeners to pursue their own paths.
3. (a) Children are free and do not face expectations from the outside world. (b) When facing a problem or situation that requires original and creative thinking.
4. They would not have to think about what to do.
5. Possible answer: Excellent choice—she attended a women's college, became a successful writer, and is a role model for the graduates.
6. Yes, especially those who strive to be perfect. Her speech validates those who have established their own paths.
7. Her standards are not the messages transmitted through our culture. One should define success using his or her own parameters.

For additional selection assessment, see Assessment Resources, pp. 109–110.

Visual Literacy

1. She uses transition words such as *this, that,* and *but* to signal a connection or a contrast between ideas. She repeats key words and phrases such as *perfect, imitation,* and *give up* to help the audience follow her ideas.
2. The audience for a speech, unlike readers, cannot follow along on the page or go back to clarify a word or concept.

After You Read

Assess

Literary Element

1. She wants graduates to lead fulfilled lives by determining their own success rather than following cultural norms.
2. Students should support their analysis with evidence. Her purpose is persuasion.

Progress Check

Can students identify author's purpose?

If No → See Unit 2 Teaching Resources Book, p. 223.

Review: Argument

Invite students to share their completed charts with the class. Discuss how the quotations appeal to reason or emotion.

Reading Strategy

1. B is the correct answer. Quindlen's key evidence here is that she has taken her own advice (put down her backpack) and is feeling "light as a feather."

Progress Check

Can students evaluate evidence?

If No → See Unit 2 Teaching Resources Book, p. 224.

Literary Element Author's Purpose

An author can have several **purposes** in writing. A columnist, for example, may seek to inform, explain, and entertain all at once. A speech writer, on the other hand, most likely wants to persuade.

1. Describe Quindlen's possible intent in speaking on this particular topic to this particular audience.
2. Choose one or two paragraphs from the speech and analyze Quindlen's purpose(s). Support your analysis with examples from the text.

Review: Argument

As you learned on page 377, an **argument** is a type of persuasive writing where logic and reason are used to influence a reader's ideas.

Partner Activity Look for places in the speech when Quindlen appeals to either logic or emotion. Working with a partner, create a chart similar to the one below. Fill in the left-hand column with examples you have chosen. Next explain how each example appeals to logic or to emotion. Then rewrite the text so that it appeals to emotion, and rewrite the emotion-driven text to appeal to logic.

Text	Appeals to Logic/ Emotion	Rewrite
"I cannot help but see myself . . . at my own Barnard commencement."	Logic: The speaker was a student at Barnard, so she can relate to her audience.	"I can imagine your excitement and anticipation at finishing college."

LOG ON **Literature** Online

Selection Resources For Selection Quizzes, eFlashcards, and Reading-Writing Connection activities, go to glencoe.com and enter QuickPass code GL49787u2.

Reading Strategy Evaluate Evidence

SAT Skills Practice

1. In the concluding paragraph of her speech (page 418), Quindlen suggests that
   (A) her listeners can become high achievers by exploring their identities
   (B) her own happiness is proof that she is offering good advice
   (C) most people make unwise decisions
   (D) educated people should be familiar with the work of George Eliot
   (E) her listeners should never take advice from others

Vocabulary Practice

Practice with Analogies Complete each analogy below. Use a dictionary if you need help.

1. **monogrammed : undecorated :: creation :**
   a. destruction **b.** evolution **c.** war
2. **templates : identical :: paupers :**
   a. hungry **b.** poor **c.** unclean
3. **imitation : redundant :: singularity :**
   a. unique **b.** identical **c.** parallel
4. **denigrate : elevate :: move :**
   a. wander **b.** settle **c.** travel

Academic Vocabulary

*Quindlen does not believe people should **submit** to the cultural standards of success.*

In the context above, *submit* is an academic word that means "to subject oneself to." *Submit* also has another meaning—"to give." For example, *I **submitted** my assignment to the teacher yesterday.* Write two sentences that use the word *submit* and demonstrate these two different meanings through context clues.

For more on academic vocabulary, see pages 54–55 and R79–R81.

Vocabulary Practice

1. a **2.** b **3.** a **4.** b

Academic Vocabulary

He submitted to his parents' demands and stayed home for the night.

She didn't submit her application in time and couldn't go.

Respond Through Writing

Summary

Report Main Ideas and Events When you write a summary of nonfiction, you restate the main ideas or events in a short version of the original. A summary does not include personal opinions. In about 100 words, summarize "Put Down the Backpack."

Understand the Task When you **restate,** you retell written or spoken text in your own words and do not copy exact words from the original material.

Prewrite To write a strong summary, you need to cover the main ideas of the selection. Before you begin your draft, review the speech. Then use a chart like the one below to help you determine which ideas you will feature in your summary.

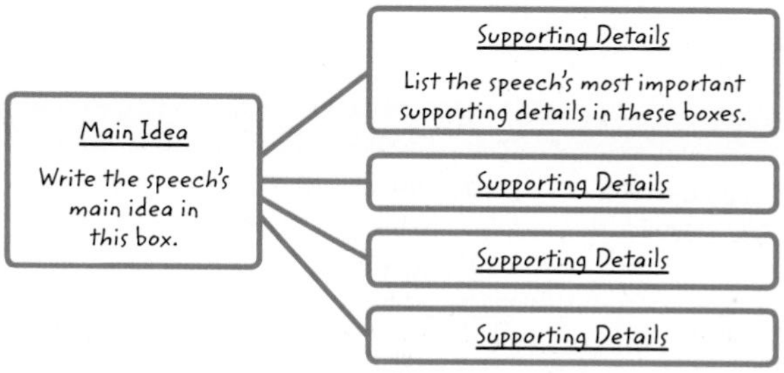

Draft Build your draft around the main idea and supporting details noted on your chart. Because the summary needs to explain all of these ideas in a limited space, the language must be concise—brief, but comprehensive.

Your summary should present Quindlen's ideas in a structure that is similar to the structure of her speech. Refer to her speech as you create your draft and use it to guide the structure of your summary.

Revise Read your draft to a classmate. Discuss whether your summary misses any important ideas. In your revision, add any key ideas that you missed. If you are tight on space, remove the least important details from your summary.

Edit and Proofread Proofread your paper, correcting any errors in grammar, spelling, and punctuation. Use the Grammar Tip in the side column to help you with parts of speech.

Learning Objectives

In this assignment, you will focus on the following objectives:

Writing: Writing a summary.

Grammar: Understanding how to choose precise words.

Grammar Tip

Specific Nouns

Using *specific nouns* can help you to be more concise. Instead of using two-word *adjective/noun constructions,* use a single specific noun to tighten up the language. For example, instead of writing:

She spoke in front of a large group.

you could write:

She spoke in front of a crowd.

This technique is especially useful when you are trying to write something short, like a summary.

After You Read

Assess

Respond Through Writing

Students' summaries should:

- not exceed 100 words
- accurately and comprehensively restate the speech's main and supporting ideas
- use concise, creative language
- present an emotional appeal

A student who meets all of these criteria should receive the equivalent of a 4-point response.

A student who fully meets two or partially meets three of these criteria should receive the equivalent of a 3-point response.

A student who fully meets one or partially meets two of these criteria should receive the equivalent of a 2-point response.

A student who partially meets one of these criteria should receive the equivalent of a 1-point response.

For grammar practice, see Unit 2 Teaching Resources Book, p. 227.

To create custom assessments online, go to Progress Reporter Online Assessment.

To create custom assessments using software, use ExamView Assessment Suite.

Approaching Level

DIFFERENTIATED INSTRUCTION

Emerging Stress that while approaching-level students are drafting, it is most important to concentrate on only the central ideas of the speech. Remind students that they can focus on improving and correcting other issues during the revision and editing stages. **Say:** During the revision process, improve upon word choice, tone, and coherence. In the final stages of editing and proofreading, check for errors in spelling, grammar, and punctuation. Explain that their skills will improve with practice.

Writing Workshop

Autobiographical Narrative

Focus

Display images of events you would be likely to find in a photo album, such as a birthday party, a wedding, a graduation, and a vacation trip. **Ask:** What kinds of events do you include in a photo album? Brainstorm with students to develop a list of events, people, and places they would capture in photographs.

Summary

In this workshop, students will write and present an autobiographical narrative. Students will follow the stages of the writing process, including prewriting, drafting, revising, and editing. In addition, the workshop provides two focus lessons, on developing voice and on pronoun-antecedent agreement.

Learning Objectives

For pages 422–429

In this workshop, you will focus on the following objectives:

Writing: Writing an autobiographical narrative using a writing process. Developing your voice.

Grammar: Understanding pronoun-antecedent agreement.

Writing Process

At any stage of a writing process, you may think of new ideas. Feel free to return to earlier stages as you write.

- Prewrite
- Draft
- Revise
- Focus Lesson: Voice
- Edit and Proofread
- Focus Lesson: Pronoun-Antecedent Agreement
- Present/Publish

LOG ON Literature Online

Writing and Research For prewriting, drafting, and revising tools, go to glencoe.com and enter QuickPass code GL49787u2.

Writing Workshop

Autobiographical Narrative

Literature Connection In "Only Daughter," Sandra Cisneros reflects on how growing up in Chicago with her parents and six brothers helped make her a writer.

> *"Being an only daughter in a family of six sons forced me by circumstance to spend a lot of time by myself because my brothers felt it beneath them to play with a girl in public. But that aloneness, that loneliness, was good for a would-be writer—it allowed me time to think and think, to imagine, to read and prepare myself."*

Autobiographical narratives generally focus on memories and their significance to the writer. Specific goals and strategies of autobiographical narratives follow.

Checklist

Goals	Strategies
To relate a personally meaningful experience	☑ Present a clear, focused, and unified sequence of events ☑ Use first-person point of view
To locate scenes and incidents in specific places	☑ Use concrete and sensory details, the active voice, precise word choice, and imagery
To entertain by presenting an engaging plot and using effective narrative techniques	☑ Use dialogue, gestures, and interior monologue to reveal characters ☑ Pace the action effectively
To communicate the significance of the events	☑ Point out how your experiences helped you understand people, yourself, or a situation

Workshop Resources

Print Materials

- Unit 2 Teaching Resources, pp. 231–235
- Writing Kit
- Success in Writing: Research and Reports

Transparencies

- Grammar and Language Transparency 39
- Writing Workshop Transparencies 11, 12, 13, 14, 15

Technology

- Literature Online: Writing Resources and Grammar Resources, www.glencoe.com
- Online Essay Grader, www.glencoe.com
- Student Presentation Builder on StudentWorks Plus CD-ROM
- Media Workshop DVD
- Online Student Edition

Writing Workshop

Autobiographical Narrative

Assignment: Write About a Personal Experience

Write an autobiographical narrative of about 1,500 words in which you explain how a personal experience was meaningful in your life.

Audience: peers, classmates, and teacher

Purpose: to relate a personal experience and explain why it was meaningful

Analyze a Professional Model

In the following selection, Isaac Bashevis Singer describes a memorable experience from his childhood. Notice Singer's use of the first-person point of view, concrete words, and dialogue. The comments in the margin point out features to include in your own autobiographical narrative.

Real-World Connection

From ex-presidents to professional baseball players, people often write autobiographical narratives about their experiences. You may be required to write your life story, or part of it, for a college or job application.

"*A Day of Pleasures*" from *In My Father's Court* by Isaac Bashevis Singer ☆

When times were good, I would get a two-groschen piece from Father or Mother every day. For me this piece—or kopeck—represented all worldly pleasures. Across the street was Esther's sweetshop, where one could buy chocolates, jelly beans, candy squares, ice cream, caramels, and all sorts of cookies. Since I had begun at an early age to write copy exercises, and had a weakness for drawing and coloring with crayons, which cost money, a kopeck proved not nearly so large a coin as Father and Mother made it out to be. There were times when I was forced to borrow money from a heder classmate, a young usurer who demanded interest—for every four groschen, I paid a groschen a week.

Now imagine the indescribable joy that I felt when I once earned a whole ruble—that is, one hundred kopecks!

I no longer remember exactly how I came to earn that ruble. I think it happened like this: Someone had ordered a pair of kidskin boots from a shoemaker, but upon delivery

Locate Scenes and Incidents

Use concrete and sensory details to establish time and place and to interest the reader.

First-Person Point of View

Engage your reader by using the first-person point of view, the active voice, and precise word choice.

Teach

Big Idea

Finding Common Ground

Ask: How might an autobiographical narrative aid people in finding common ground? *(Students may say that in an autobiography an author shares his or her experiences, ideas, and feelings. This gives the reader the chance to experience what the author has experienced and to find common ground.)* Point out to students that one advantage of an autobiography is that the author, by speaking from a first-person point of view, speaks directly to readers in sharing an experience.

Literary History ☆

Isaac Bashevis Singer

Although he immigrated to the United States in 1935, writer Isaac Bashevis Singer (1904–1991) conjured up the Poland of his childhood in his writings. Poland's Jewish community was destroyed in World War II, so Singer's writings serve as a window to a time, a place, and a culture that have been lost. Singer won the Nobel Prize in Literature in 1978.

Approaching Level

DIFFERENTIATED INSTRUCTION

Emerging Have a student read the Real-World Connection near the top right corner of this page. Explain that an autobiography is a story of a person's life told by that person. Autobiographies are written using the first-person point of view. **Say:** **People speak using the first-person point of view when they use the pronouns "I" and "me."** Tell students that any time they speak to others about themselves, it is very much like an autobiography.

Have students speak about their own childhood, using the first-person point of view. Then have them speak about someone else's childhood, using the third-person point of view to point out how different it sounds. *(Correct examples of the third-person point of view will include the use of* he *or* she*, and the name of the person they are describing.)*

Writing Workshop

Autobiographical Narrative

Teach

Writing Skills

Dialogue Invite students to explain who is speaking in this conversation. **Ask:** What effect does adding dialogue at the end have for the reader? *(Students may say that the dialogue breaks up the narration, that it engages the reader, or that it adds humor.)*

Visualization Have students reread the dialogue at the end of Singer's story. **Ask:** Can you describe Singer's expression when he shows the ruble to the driver? *(Students should be able to visualize a look of triumph, satisfaction, or glee on Singer's face from the details given.)*

APPROACHING Point out to approaching-level students that having a detailed image in mind when they write will help them create something that the reader can visualize clearly.

The Village Sweet Shop, 1897. Ralph Hedley. Oil on canvas.

the boots proved to be either too tight or too loose. The man who had ordered them refused to accept them, and the shoemaker summoned him to a Din Torah. Father sent me to another shoemaker to ask him to appraise the value of the boots or perhaps even to buy them, since he also dealt in ready-made footwear. It so happened that the second shoemaker had a customer who wanted the boots and was prepared to pay a good price for them. I do not recall all the details, but I remember that I carried a pair of brand-new boots around, and that one of the litigants rewarded me with a ruble.

Engaging Plot
Note conflicts, reveal feelings, and pick up or slow down the pace as the mood and time change.

I knew that if I stayed home my parents would ruin that ruble. They would buy me something to wear which I would have got in any case, or they would borrow the ruble from me and, though they would never deny the debt, I would never see it again. I therefore took the ruble and decided for once to indulge myself in the pleasures of this world, to enjoy all those good things for which my heart yearned.

Order of Events
Use a logical order or sequence to show the events in the narrative.

I quickly passed through Krochmalna Street. Here everyone knew me too well. Here I could not afford to act the profligate. But on Gnoyna Street I was unknown. I signaled to the driver of a droshky, and he stopped.

Dialogue
Use dialogue, gestures, or interior monologue to move your story along and to bring your characters and the scene to life.

"What do you want?"

"To ride."

"Ride where?"

"To the other streets."

"What other streets?"

"To Nalewki Street."

"That costs forty groschen. Have you got the money to pay?"

Tone/Focus/Perspective
Maintain a consistent tone, focus, and controlling perspective from start to finish.

I showed him the ruble.

Reading–Writing Connection Try applying the writing techniques you have just encountered in the autobiographical narrative you write.

Writing Practice

SMALL GROUP

Dialogue Remind students that dialogue is a conversation in a fiction or nonfiction selection. It can be difficult for authors to write dialogue as people would actually speak. Break students into groups of three. In each group, designate one student as an author and two students as speakers. Direct the speakers to have a conversation while the group author writes down the conversation.

Tell the authors that they can change the speakers' words if they want to, but they must keep the same idea. When they finish, have groups evaluate the dialogue. **Ask:** Were any changes made to the dialogue? Does the dialogue still sound like a real conversation between students? What does or does not sound like actual speech?

Prewrite

Choose an Experience As you consider subjects to write about, think of experiences that have been meaningful in your life. Also consider what experiences will be interesting to others. Choose an experience you want to share with readers, and one that you remember in detail.

Gather Your Thoughts Use the following criteria to help you choose a meaningful experience to describe.

- ▶ Think About the Experience Recall the details by asking yourself what happened and when. Try replaying the experience in your mind and talking about it with others who were there. You might have a photo or diary entry that will provide details you have forgotten.
- ▶ Connect to Your Audience Consider what details will be interesting to your readers. Your readers will feel like participants in the experience if you include specific details and concrete words. Sensory images, dialogue, gestures, interior monologue, and your own thoughts about the experience will make it come alive for your readers.

Make a Plan To write an autobiographical narrative, you may want to tell what happened in chronological order. A flow chart or timeline can help you get organized during the prewriting step. Put the events in the sequence in which they happened. Draw arrows to show how one idea flows into the next.

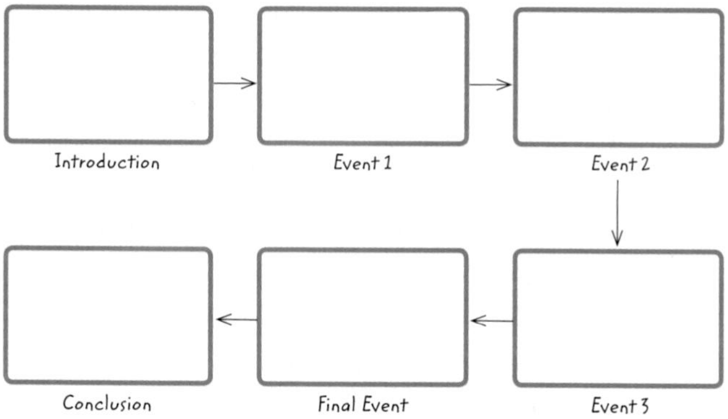

Discuss Your Ideas Before you begin drafting, meet with a partner to talk about the details of your autobiographical narrative. Talking through the experience will help you recall events and specific details that you may not have thought about for a long time. Jot down notes to refer to as you write.

Tell a Story

Remember that a narrative tells a story. Be sure to include the elements of a good narrative. Begin with an exposition, or introduction. Identify the setting, characters, and conflict. Tell what happens as the suspense builds to a high point and then comes to a conclusion.

Avoid Plagiarism

Did you "happen upon" a paper that answers this assignment—perhaps from an older student or on the Internet? One reason not to use it is consequences: your school may have a policy that responds to plagiarism with suspension or other serious punishment.

Teach

Writing Skills

Connect to the Audience
Suggest that students ask their peers for feedback if they have trouble settling on an idea. Have students work in pairs to discuss possible subjects. Instruct students to list the ideas that elicit the strongest responses and to choose an idea from this list.

Writing Process

Prewrite For many students, choosing a topic to write about is the most challenging part of the writing process. Many students become tense when they are faced with essay choices on a test. Encourage students to approach the brainstorming process as an opportunity to be creative rather than as something stressful. Point out that this is one of the few times when they are encouraged to daydream!

Approaching Level

DIFFERENTIATED INSTRUCTION

Established The most difficult part of writing is getting started. Explain to students that prewriting can help them decide what to write about. Tell students that prewriting can be very informal. Students often feel that they must follow a certain format for prewriting, but prewriting should be something each student does differently.

Ask: If a friend were to ask what you did last weekend, what would you say? Have students write down their answers. If students answer "nothing," explain that even if they were bored, they were probably doing something.

Writing Workshop

Autobiographical Narrative

Teach

Writing Process

Draft At this stage, students should work on obvious errors or solve structural problems. Students must be flexible during the drafting process. They may use ideas from prewriting but can also extend those ideas or explore new ones.

Writing Skills

Dialogue/First-Person Point of View

Answer: *The writer tells about his own life experiences.*

Locate Scenes and Incidents

Answer: *They help readers feel that they are living through the experience.*

Order of Events

Answer: *It is organized in chronological order.*

Draft

Put Your Words Down on Paper Using your plan as a guide, draft your autobiographical narrative. Because you are writing a narrative, you should incorporate conflict and suspense into it. You may find that writing about a personal experience gives you a fresh understanding of it.

Analyze a Workshop Model

Here is a final draft of an autobiographical narrative. Read the narrative and answer the questions in the margin. Use the answers to these questions to guide you as you write.

Writing Frames

As you read the workshop model, think about the writer's use of the following frames:

When I/As I ____ . . .

The ____ continued . . .

I had learned something new about . . . ____.

Consider using frames like these in your own narrative.

Surprise! Surprise!

I should have been more suspicious from the start. A few weeks before my birthday, my mother said casually, "Now that you are in high school, it's time to give up those big parties. Why don't you go out for pizza and a movie? You can treat yourself and three friends."

Dialogue/First-Person Point of View
How does the writer create interest in the opening paragraph(s)?

"That sounds like a great idea," I replied. What I didn't know was that she was setting me up. My friends were integral to her scheme. I found out later that she had called Jason, Darryl, and Will and sworn them to secrecy.

My dad was sworn to secrecy, too. He gave me a ten-dollar bill and two twenties before we got in the car. Then he picked up my three friends and dropped us off at the movie theater. Dad said, "I'll pick you up in front of Pat's Pizza Place at 7:30."

Meanwhile, my mom was decorating the backyard with blue and orange streamers and balloons in honor of my favorite football team. My sister hung a banner between two trees.

Locate Scenes and Incidents
How do sensory details, precise word choice, and imagery convey time and place?

Dad picked us up at exactly 7:30. During the drive home, he made comments like, "I bet this was your best birthday celebration ever." His words signaled that the party was over. As we pulled up to the house at quarter to eight, he said, "Why don't you guys come in for an hour. I want to watch a television

Order of Events
How is this essay organized?

Writing Practice

SPIRAL REVIEW **Point of View** Explain to students that first-person point of view is not objective. The author can convey his or her thoughts and emotions instead of just facts. This is good in some writing, but other writing should be written without bias. Have students write a paragraph from a first-person point of view.

Then, have students write a similar paragraph about the same topic from a third-person point of view. **Ask:** What is different about the two paragraphs? What types of details are there in the first-person and third-person paragraphs? *(Students may answer that the first-person draft expresses more details about feelings, while the third-person draft expresses more details about the topic.)*

show at 8:00. Then I'll drive all of you home." My father had successfully set the trap.

As I walked with the guys into the house, my mom said, "Why don't you go out to the backyard so your dad can watch his show uninterrupted?"

When I walked out the patio door, I heard faceless voices yelling, "Surprise! Surprise!" Then suddenly people started popping up from behind the trees and bushes all over the backyard. "Happy Birthday, Andy." I was stunned! At least twenty of my friends from school were in the yard.

I congratulated my parents on their plan to surprise me. Few people are clever enough to throw a surprise party that really is a surprise. I felt like I was getting a double party—the one with a movie and pizza and now this one.

The party continued, and the surprises kept coming. As everyone was singing "Happy Birthday," three strangers dressed in black and wearing sunglasses appeared in the backyard. They carried large wire cages draped with black scarves.

My mom introduced the mysterious guests. She said, "May I have your attention. I would like to introduce Craig, Tim, and Wanda, animal trainers from Creepy Crawling Creatures."

Wanda, the head animal trainer, slipped off the black scarves covering the cages. Everyone gasped!

"Wow!"

"What kind of snakes are they?"

Craig said, "Each cage holds a huge boa constrictor."

"These snakes are more than seven feet long. They are all tame. Don't be afraid," Tim continued.

Darryl was brave enough to let Wanda wrap one of the boa constrictors around his neck like a scarf.

My friend Martha said, on her way out the door at the end of the party, "We surprised you, but those snakes surprised us."

I just smiled. I had learned something new about my parents: Expect the unexpected.

Narration

Narrative Techniques
How do emotions, gestures, and dialogue help tell the story?

Focus/Tone
How does the writer maintain a consistent tone and focus?

Engaging Plot
How can you create conflict or tension in a narrative? How can you pace your story to help create its mood?

Dialogue
How does dialogue add interest to a narrative?

Controlling Perspective/Tone/Focus
How does the writer maintain a consistent tone, focus, and controlling perspective from beginning to end?

Teach

Writing Skills

Narrative Techniques
Answer: *They help make the events seem real to the reader.*

Tone/Focus
Answer: *The writer continues with chronological order and first-person narration.*

Engaging Plot
Answer: *Including the unexpected or disagreement among characters can create tension. Students can pace their stories by providing careful details leading up to an event or action.*

Dialogue
Answer: *It provides detail and makes the reader feel part of the events.*

Controlling Perspective/Tone/Focus
Answer: *Through the use of dialogue and repetition*

Approaching Level

DIFFERENTIATED INSTRUCTION

Emerging Encourage approaching-level students to practice autobiographical writing by having them write short journal entries each night. Instruct students to discuss events of the day, the things they have seen, the emotions that they felt, and other detailed descriptions of their lives.

Collect journal entries and include comments to guide students who struggle with writing journal entries.

After collecting students' journal entries, pick two or three of the best written entries and ask students privately if they would like to share their entries with the class. Ask the class to discuss what makes the journal entry a good piece of writing.

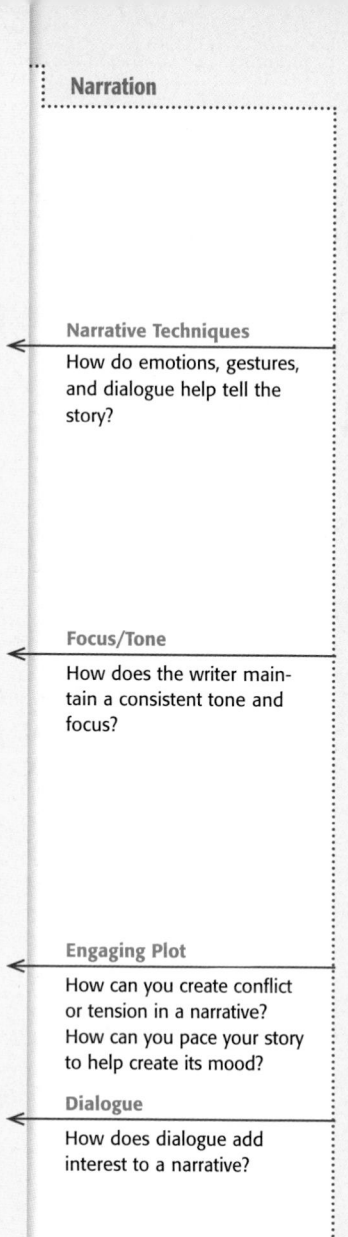

Teach

Writing Process

Revise Ask: Why is it helpful to separate the drafting and revising processes? *(Students may say that if they try to revise while they are drafting, they interrupt their writing flow.)* Suggest that if students revise while they write, they may take longer to finish the story. Suggest that they take a break before they revise their work so that they may look at their writing with a fresh perspective.

Writing Skills

Voice Have students talk with their peer reviewer about voice and see what elements of individual style the reviewer notices. **Ask:** How would you describe your voice? *(Students might note their use of vocabulary or detail.)* Instruct students to note their strengths and also where they could use improvement.

Traits of Strong Writing

Include these traits of strong writing to effectively express your ideas.

Ideas

Organization

Voice

Word Choice

Sentence Fluency

Conventions

Presentation

For more information on using the Traits of Strong Writing, see pages R28–R30.

Revise

Peer Review Exchange completed drafts with a partner. Review the drafts for conflict development and use of effective details. Use the checklist below to evaluate and strengthen each other's essays.

Checklist

- [x] Does your narrative present a focused and unified sequence of events?
- [x] Do you use the first-person point of view?
- [x] Do you entertain your audience with effective dialogue, monologue, or gestures?
- [x] Do you pace the narrative effectively?
- [x] Do you use concrete and sensory details, precise words, and imagery?
- [x] Do you effectively communicate the significance of the events?

Word Choice

This academic vocabulary word appears in the student model:

integral (in′ ti grəl) *adj.* 1. essential to; 2. required to make complete; 3. *Mathematics:* relating to an integer. *My friends were integral to her scheme.* Using academic vocabulary may help strengthen your writing. Try to use one or two academic vocabulary words in your narrative. See the complete list on pages R79–R81.

Focus Lesson

Voice

Your voice is what gives your writing its own style. Voice is determined by your use of language, your choice of words, and your tone, or attitude toward your subject. As you revise your narrative, use vivid words and expressive details to create your own voice.

Draft:

"That sounds fine," I replied. What I didn't know was her plan. My friends were involved.

Revision:

"That sounds like a great idea,"[1] I replied. What I didn't know was that she was setting me up.[2] My friends were integral to her scheme.[3]

1: tone **2:** language (idiom) **3:** word choice

Writing Practice

PARTNERS

Diction Explain that word choice is one of the most important elements of good writing. Have peer review partners identify places where word choice can be improved. **Say:** Keep in mind your audience and purpose as you consider word choice in your drafts. Provide students with a thesaurus to help them choose stronger words that they might include in their drafts. Caution students to look up definitions of new words in a dictionary to ensure that they are using the correct connotation of the word.

Edit and Proofread

Get It Right When you have completed your final draft, proofread it to correct errors in grammar, usage, mechanics, and spelling. Refer to the Language Handbook, pages R40–R59, as a guide.

Focus Lesson

Pronoun-Antecedent Agreement

A pronoun is a word that takes the place of or refers back to a noun, a noun phrase, or another pronoun. The antecedent is the word or words the pronoun replaces. The pronoun must agree with its antecedent in number, gender, and person.

Problem: It is unclear which antecedent the pronoun refers to.

My sister made a banner and a sign. She hung it between two trees.

Solution: To avoid an unclear pronoun reference, revise by using the noun or otherwise making the meaning clear.

My sister made a banner and a sign. She hung the banner between two trees.

Problem: A pronoun does not agree with its antecedent in number.

I found out later that she had called Jason, Darryl, and Will and sworn him to secrecy.

Solution: Use a singular pronoun if the antecedent is singular; use a plural pronoun if the antecedent is plural.

I found out later that she had called Jason, Darryl, and Will and sworn them to secrecy.

Present/Publish

The Right Look Before you turn in your autobiographical narrative, make sure it is neat and presentable. Your narrative should be typed with appropriate margins or neatly handwritten. Check with your teacher for additional presentation guidelines.

Peer Review Tips

A classmate may ask you to read his or her narrative. Take your time and jot down notes as you read so you can give constructive feedback. Use the following questions to get started:

Is the narrative clear and easy to read?

Do you understand the significance of the experience?

Does the writer's tone match the content and purpose of the essay?

Word-Processing Tip

Your teacher may require a title sheet or cover page. If your teacher does not specify different requirements for a cover sheet, include your name, your teacher's name, the course name, and the date in the upper right-hand corner. Center your title in the middle of the page. Do not include a page number.

Writer's Portfolio

Place a clean copy of your autobiographical narrative in your portfolio to review later.

LOG ON Literature Online

Writing and Research
For editing and publishing tools, go to glencoe.com and enter QuickPass code GL49787u2.

Teach

Writing Process

Proofread Remind students that relying on a computer's spell-check program to catch all their errors will not work. Point out that the computer will not find a common typing error such as typing *form* instead of *from* because the word is not spelled incorrectly.

Say: Make sure you examine spelling, grammar, and overall flow in your final draft before turning in your work.

Writing Skills

Test-Taking Tip Point out to students that it is common on standardized tests to have grammar questions about catching and correcting pronoun errors. Suggest that when taking a grammar test, students check to be sure that pronouns match their antecedents in number, gender, and case and that the antecedents are clear.

Approaching Level

DIFFERENTIATED INSTRUCTION

AAVE Review subject/verb agreement with approaching-level students who use African American Vernacular English (AAVE). Tell students that the subject of a sentence must agree with the verb in number (singular, plural) and in tense (past, present, future). **Write:** Her brother and sister _____ both very nice. *(are)*

Ask students which form of the verb "to be" belongs in the blank. **Write:** When she was in high school, Trish _____ the best player on her softball team. Ask students to fill in the blank with the correct form of the verb "to be." *(was)*

Speaking, Listening, and Viewing Workshop

Narrative Presentation

Focus

Summary

In this workshop, students will learn techniques for planning, preparing, and gathering props for an autobiographical narrative presentation.

For help with creating presentations, see Student Presentation Builder on StudentWorks Plus.

Teach

Speaking Skills

Memorization To some students, the idea of "learning lines" seems daunting. Share the following tips to help them feel more comfortable:

- Memorize the order. Make a list of the events in order and become familiar with it.
- Break the list into sections, such as beginning, middle, and end. Think about the effect each section should have.
- Memorize one section at time.
- Practice reading through the entire story every day, working on the flow between sections.

Learning Objectives

For pages 430–431

In this workshop, you will focus on the following objective:

Speaking and Listening: Delivering a narrative presentation.

Speaking, Listening, and Viewing Workshop

Narrative Presentation

Literature Connection Sandra Cisneros is a master storyteller whose work, which often deals with themes of identity and heritage, is emotional and gripping. When you present your autobiographical narrative, it is important to understand the themes and emotions you want to convey to your audience. To present a narrative effectively, use eye contact, facial expressions, and gestures to communicate your message.

Assignment **Create an oral presentation of your autobiographical narrative and present it to an audience.**

Plan Your Presentation

Reread your narrative, keeping in mind that your audience has changed from readers to listeners and viewers. Look for places to engage their eyes and ears. Make notations for places to add the following:

- actions or movements, such as those that show feelings of surprise, confusion, or irritation
- gestures and facial expressions, such as those that show feelings, as well as those that might signal a change of scene or focus
- changes in loudness and tone, especially for emphasis

In addition, mark your narrative for places to speed up or slow down. Pick up the pace where needed to keep your audience involved. Slow it down to build suspense or to complement a shift to a sad or serious mood.

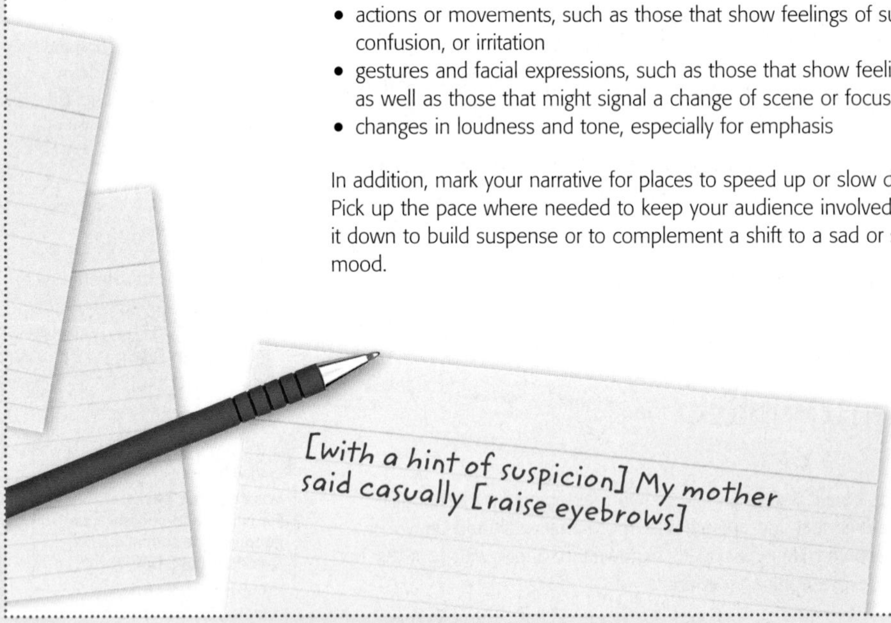

[with a hint of suspicion] My mother
said casually [raise eyebrows]

Listening Practice

Sound Devices Point out that sound devices can create atmosphere and rhythm, and can engage the listener. **Ask:** What sound devices might you use? *(Students may suggest rhythm, repetition, or alliteration.)* How might word repetition affect a story presentation? *(Repetition can link ideas and build tension.)*

Be sure students know what alliteration and onomatopoeia are. Discuss the effect of alliteration and onomatopoeia on the listener. Have students volunteer examples of each and note the reactions of their classmates.

Gather Your Props

Storytellers often use objects to help show time, place, and character. For example, the writer of "Surprise! Surprise!" might use a movie ticket stub, balloons, a banner, and a black scarf. Decide what props you will use and how you will use them to locate scenes, show character, and create interest. Brainstorm ideas in a chart like the one below.

What objects show time, place, or character in my narrative?	Which of these are easy to find and carry around?	How can I display the objects during my presentation?

Rehearse

You will need a lot of practice to remember all of the details when you present your narrative in front of an audience. Begin by reviewing the story several times to fix the order of events in your mind. Then invite members of your family to a dress rehearsal. They may be able to suggest additional details to enhance the story. Ask them to comment on how clearly you are speaking and on the effectiveness of your props.

Use the verbal and nonverbal techniques mentioned below.

Techniques for Delivering an Effective Presentation

Verbal Techniques	Nonverbal Techniques
☑ **Emphasis** Speak expressively. Stress important words that help communicate the meaning of the experience.	☑ **Posture** Stand with confidence to show you believe you have a good story to tell.
☑ **Pace** Vary your rate to show that the time or the mood is changing. Use dramatic pauses.	☑ **Eye Contact** Look at your audience. Relate to them. Make eye contact.
☑ **Tone** Make sure your tone of voice reflects the subject matter.	☑ **Gestures** Use gestures and facial expressions to communicate with your audience.

Make a Videotape

Have someone videotape your presentation. View it to evaluate your delivery. Make adjustments based on your evaluation.

Speaking Frames

Consider using the following frames in your narrative presentation.

When I/As I ____.

I realized that ____.

I learned something new about ____.

Presentation Tips

Use the following checklist to evaluate your narrative presentation.

☑ Did you engage your listeners and viewers from beginning to end?

☑ Which props were most or least effective? Why?

☑ Which verbal and nonverbal techniques served you best? Why?

LOG ON **Literature Online**

Speaking, Listening, and Viewing For project ideas, templates, and presentation tips, go to glencoe.com and enter QuickPass code GL49787u2.

Teach

Speaking Skills

Use Props Point out that working with props takes practice. If used awkwardly, props can detract from, rather than add to, the story. To avoid prop difficulties, ask students to bring props to class. Have students work in pairs to practice incorporating their props into their presentations. Instruct students to point out to their partners any areas of awkwardness or difficulty in prop use.

Viewing Skills

Analyze the Presentation Have students present their stories to partners. Advise the partners to write an evaluation based on these physical aspects of the presentation:

- Is the speaker wiggling or rocking back and forth?
- Does the speaker use hand movements or arm waving that distracts the audience?
- Is the speaker's gaze on the audience or elsewhere?

Approaching Level

DIFFERENTIATED INSTRUCTION

Established Explain that some speakers may feel self-conscious when giving their speech. Remind students that nervousness often makes people speak too quickly and too softly. Tell students to be aware of their pacing and whether they can be heard by the audience. Explain that students should also be aware of other verbal and nonverbal techniques such as using eye contact, hand gestures, and tone of voice for effect when necessary. Advise them to practice their speech in front of others or while looking in a mirror.

Focus

Summary

This Independent Reading feature encourages students to read nonfiction by introducing them to the wide variety of subjects and styles that are available.

Teach

Literary History ☆

Douglas Adams British author Douglas Adams (1952–2001) worked in many genres besides nonfiction. For his *Hitchhiker's Guide to the Galaxy* series, he adapted the story for radio, television, novels, a computer game, stage, and most recently film. Adams is known for the unique sense of humor with which he imbues his writing, regardless of genre.

Independent Reading

Nonfiction and Novels

NONFICTION WRITING RANGES FROM DIARY ENTRIES TO COOKBOOKS. It can tell us how, why, what, and when. Some nonfiction selections look back and reflect on entire lives, while others describe just one experience in a life. For more nonfiction on a range of themes, try the suggestions on these pages. For novels that incorporate the Big Ideas of *Looking into Lives, On the Move,* and *Finding Common Ground,* try the titles from the Glencoe Literature Library on the next page.

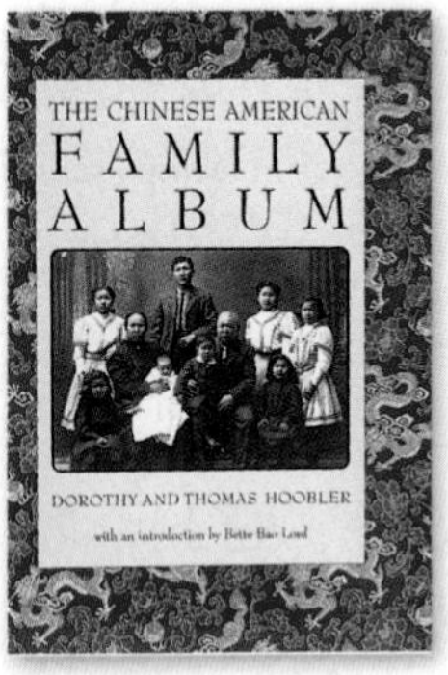

The Chinese American Family Album

Dorothy and Thomas Hoobler

In order to tell the story of Chinese immigration to the United States, the Hooblers gathered photographs, letters, journals, and other firsthand accounts from the people who made the trip from one country to the other. Challenges in the new country, including clashes of culture, are presented in personal, intimate detail. Other topics include the Gold Rush, the construction of the transcontinental railroad, and the establishment of Chinese businesses.

Last Chance to See

Douglas Adams and Mark Carwardine ☆

A best-selling author and a well-known zoologist team up to travel the world looking for endangered species. They meet up with exotic species such as the Komodo dragon, the northern white rhinoceros, and the mountain gorilla. Adams and Carwardine retell some of their adventures with sidesplitting humor and flair. At the same time, they describe the heartbreaking plight of the animals they encounter and make a convincing case for greater awareness and conservation efforts.

Reading Practice

SPIRAL REVIEW **Research Nonfiction** When approaching the nonfiction genre, students imagine dry, boring, informational texts. Point out that nonfiction includes a wide range of topics and styles, such as humorous opinion pieces, magazine articles, and topical essays.

Invite students to research the nonfiction genre in the library or on the Internet and create a list of subjects, authors, and styles that interest them. Have them read further on those topics.

GLENCOE LITERATURE LIBRARY

Great Expectations

Charles Dickens

This coming-of-age novel looks into the life of a boy as he becomes a man in Victorian England.

. . . And the Earth Did Not Devour Him

Tomás Rivera

This collection of related stories recounts the struggles, hopes, and dreams of migrant workers on the move.

To Kill a Mockingbird

Harper Lee

Set in the rural south of the 1930s, this is a tale of justice and injustice, family, community, and the courage needed to find common ground.

CRITICS' CORNER

"Sarah and Annie Elizabeth Delany . . . were taught to participate in history, not just witness it, and they have had the wit to shape their histories with style. . . . And no, I am not saying their memoirs, deftly arranged in alternating chapters by the journalist Amy Hill Hearth, are literature: I am saying that they are literature's living kin."

—Margo Jefferson, the *New York Times*

Having Our Say

Sarah L. and A. Elizabeth Delany with Amy Hill Hearth

This is the remarkable story of two sisters, who were 101 and 103 when they told their stories. Born to a former slave, the Delany sisters lived through most of the twentieth century and all of its changes. They were pioneers in the era that ended segregation and began civil rights. Their insights into history and life reflect the wisdom gained over a century.

Write a Review

Read one of the books listed on these pages and write a review of it for your classmates. Be sure to explain why other students might enjoy the book, or offer suggestions on how they might overcome difficulties in reading the book. Present your review to the class.

Approaching Level

DIFFERENTIATED INSTRUCTION

Emerging Encourage approaching-level students to try writing nonfiction. Students may attempt to write a variety of nonfiction pieces. Instruct students to incorporate one of the Big Ideas from Unit 2 into their writing. Encourage students to experiment with tone in their nonfiction writing.

Established Point out to students that reading nonfiction is a good way to hone their language skills while learning more about subjects that interest them. Encourage students to bring nonfiction magazine articles to class for discussion.

Teach

Glencoe Literature Library

Glencoe Literature Library offers an extensive collection of hardcover books that help you encourage your students to read independently. Choose among the more than 120 full-length literary works—novels, novellas, plays, and nonfiction. Each book includes related readings from a broad range of genres. Go to glencoe.com for more information.

For access to all study guides for the Glencoe Literature Library, see the Literature Library Teacher Resources CD-ROM.

To create customized reading lists from a database of more than 30,000 titles, use BookLink K–12 CD-ROM.

Assess

Write a Review

Students' reviews should address one book mentioned in the Independent Reading feature and should include reasons why others might like the book as well as tips on how to overcome difficulties reading it.

Assessment

English Language Arts

Focus

Bellringer Options

Ask: What is the most challenging part of a test for you? *(Students may say that reading a passage or answering multiple-choice questions is most difficult.)* Discuss students' test-taking fears and challenges; list them on the board. Each time they address one of these challenges in class, cross it off the board.

Teach

Assessment Explain to students that the Assessment is intended to reinforce general test-taking strategies.

Assessment

English Language Arts

Reading: Nonfiction

Carefully read the following passage. Use context clues to help define any words with which you are unfamiliar. Pay close attention to the author's main idea and her use of rhetorical devices. Then, on a separate sheet of paper, answer the questions on pages 435–436.

from *To Be Young, Gifted, and Black* by Lorraine Hansberry

R—O—S—S
This spells Ross
We'll get along at any old cost
With one good Principal
& teachers all so fine
You may search the wide world over
No school like Ross you'll find.

The heartbreaking part was this: It was *not* an old building but, on the contrary, a relatively new and modern one. Its substandard quality had been planned from the drawing board. For from its inception Betsy Ross had been earmarked as a ghetto school, a school for black children and, therefore, one in which as many things as possible might be safely thought of as "expendable." That, after all, was why it existed: *not* to give education but to withhold as much as possible, just as the ghetto itself exists not to give people homes but to cheat them out of as much decent housing as possible.

I was given, during the grade school years, one-half the amount of education prescribed by the Board of Education of my city. This was because the children of the Chicago ghetto were jammed into a segregated school system. I am a product of that system and one result is that—to this day—I cannot count properly. I do not add, subtract, or multiply with ease. Our teachers, devoted and indifferent alike, had to sacrifice something to make the system work at all—and in my case it was arithmetic that got put aside most often. Thus, the mind which was able to grasp university level reading materials in the sixth and seventh grades had not been sufficiently exposed to elementary arithmetic to make even simple change in the grocery store.

This is what is meant when we speak of the scars, the marks that the ghettoized child carries through life. To be imprisoned in the ghetto is to be forgotten—or deliberately cheated of one's birthright—at best.

. . .

Reading Practice

Be an Active Reader Explain to students that there are different ways to read. Sometimes people read for enjoyment. Other times, such as during a test, people read for understanding. Tell students that a good way to read for understanding is to pick out the main idea or topic sentence. Have students carefully reread the first paragraph of the story above.

Ask: Which sentence in this paragraph tells you the main idea of the story? Tell students that the main idea sentence in the first paragraph is the sentence that beigns "For from its inception Betsy Ross . . ." Explain that this sentence tells the reader that the story is going to be about the speaker's problems at Betsy Ross school.

I recall being the only child in my classes who did not come from the Rooseveltian atmosphere of the homes of the Thirties. Father ran for Congress as a Republican. He believed in American private enterprise and, among other things which he had done by the time I was old enough to be aware of him, amassed—in the terms of his community—a "fortune" (though actually he had done absolutely nothing of the kind: relative to American society of the Nineteen Thirties and Forties Carl A. Hansberry had simply become a reasonably successful businessman of the middle class). But we are all shaped, are we not, by that particular rim of the soup-bowl where we swim, and I have remained throughout the balance of my life a creature formed in a community atmosphere where I was known as—a "rich" girl.

In any case, my mother sent me to kindergarten in white fur in the middle of the depression; the kids beat me up; and I think it was from that moment I became—a rebel. . . .

1. According to Hansberry, what factor led to her attending the kind of school she did?
   A. family
   B. politics
   C. race
   D. talent

2. From the context, what do you conclude that the word *substandard,* in line 9, means?
   A. average
   B. high
   C. inferior
   D. unusual

3. What does Hansberry suggest was the most serious issue in her school?
   A. busing
   B. money
   C. students
   D. teachers

4. What literary element is most evident in the sentence beginning on line 30?
   A. allusion
   B. metaphor
   C. simile
   D. symbol

5. What does Hansberry refer to when she writes, in the third paragraph, of "scars"?
   A. lasting effects of prejudice
   B. shame of feeling left out
   C. suffering caused by poverty
   D. corruption in public schools

6. What factor led Hansberry to be thought of in a specific way by others in her school?
   A. Her father had become wealthy as a business leader.
   B. Her father was more successful than most others in the community.
   C. She attended a segregated school even though she did not have to.
   D. She was far ahead of her classmates in reading and writing.

LOG ON **Literature** Online

Assessment For additional test practice, go to glencoe.com and enter QuickPass code GL49787u2.

Assess

Reading

1. C is the correct answer. The school was racially segregated. DOK 1

2. C is the correct answer. It means "of low quality." DOK 1

3. B is the correct answer. She suggests that her school was deliberately poorly funded. DOK 1

4. B is the correct answer. The "soup bowl" is metaphorical. DOK 2

5. A is the correct answer. The scars are the long-term effects of prejudice, such as the effects of being poorly educated. DOK 2

6. B is the correct answer because Hansberry's father was thought to be wealthy, but in fact he was a middle-class businessman. DOK 1

Approaching Level

DIFFERENTIATED INSTRUCTION

Established Remind students of the importance of reading, the title, the name of the author, and the information in the introduction, if one is provided. **Ask: What can you learn from the title of the passage on page 434?** (The title suggests that the author is African American and talented. The title also suggests that she will discuss her childhood.)

Assess

Reading

7. A is the correct answer because Hansberry relates the story of her own life. DOK 4

8. D is the correct answer. Hansberry notes that the teachers purposely did not focus on teaching her math skills. DOK 1

9. B is the correct answer. She sees a good education as every child's birthright. DOK 1

10. C is the correct answer because Hansberry describes her father's personal beliefs directly. DOK 1

11. A is the correct answer. "Rooseveltian atmosphere" alludes to the mood during the presidency of Franklin D. Roosevelt. DOK 2

12. A is the correct answer because she says the students "had not been sufficiently exposed to elementary arithmetic." DOK 1

13. D is the correct answer because the author is explaining how segregation affected her life. DOK 4

14. A is the correct answer. The author is angry about the lasting effects of segregation on her life. DOK 4

15. Answers will vary. Students should recognize that Hansberry is explaining how segregation affected her social and learning experiences. DOK 3

7. From what point of view is this passage written?
   A. first person
   B. second person
   C. third-person limited
   D. third-person omniscient

8. From the context, what do you conclude that the word *indifferent*, in line 17, means?
   A. apart
   B. dislocated
   C. similar
   D. uncaring

9. What does Hansberry mean when she writes about being "cheated of one's birthright"?
   A. Her parents were not respected enough in the community.
   B. Many children were not receiving the education they deserved.
   C. Some children suffered terribly during the Thirties.
   D. Her upbringing was unusual for the time.

10. In this passage, how does Hansberry convey the personality of her father?
   A. through allegory
   B. through personification
   C. through direct characterization
   D. through indirect characterization

11. What literary element is used in the sentence beginning on line 25?
   A. allusion
   B. hyperbole
   C. metaphor
   D. personification

12. What subject does Hansberry say was not taught properly to her in school?
   A. math
   B. history
   C. reading
   D. science

13. Which of the following best describes the author's purpose in this passage?
   A. to entertain
   B. to persuade
   C. to describe
   D. to explain

14. What is the overall tone of this passage?
   A. angry
   B. mysterious
   C. relaxed
   D. sarcastic

15. **Short Response** In a short paragraph, describe the theme of this essay. Support your answer with details from the essay.

Reading Practice

Reading Practice and Summary Students may feel pressured by the time constraints of a test. They may feel they do not have enough time to read and comprehend a passage well enough to answer questions correctly. Students should practice reading nonfiction passages to improve reading fluency and comprehension. Have students work in pairs to read the excerpt. Partners should first read the passage silently. Then each partner should read paragraphs aloud and practice summarizing the content of each.

Vocabulary Skills: Sentence Completion

For each question in the Vocabulary Skills section, choose the word that best completes the sentence. Write your answers on a separate sheet of paper.

1. Although the offense did their best to break through, the defensive line was ______.
   A. ponderous
   B. pernicious
   C. mortal
   D. impervious

2. As darkness fell, a feeling of relaxation would ______ the entire neighborhood.
   A. incriminate
   B. replenish
   C. implore
   D. suffuse

3. As soon as the gates to the amusement park opened, the waiting crowd ______ forward.
   A. surged
   B. detached
   C. embroidered
   D. evaded

4. Many voters enjoyed listening to the young candidate speak because he was so ______.
   A. incriminating
   B. elemental
   C. articulate
   D. audible

5. In revealing personal details about her childhood, the author addresses the reader as a ______.
   A. fugitive
   B. confidant
   C. throng
   D. perpetrator

6. Unlike her ______ classmates, Hansberry was always respectful toward her teachers.
   A. irreverent
   B. adamant
   C. inherent
   D. prudent

7. Hansberry never ______ the scars of growing up under segregation.
   A. eradicated
   B. consoled
   C. fulfilled
   D. denigrated

8. Hansberry saw in ______ that many of her childhood teachers had worked very hard.
   A. severance
   B. expediency
   C. retrospect
   D. languor

9. The young girl displayed great ______ by not crying after skinning her knee.
   A. detachment
   B. bravado
   C. intimation
   D. magnitude

10. The new teacher was so ______ that the students always quietly obeyed his instructions.
   A. haphazard
   B. imposing
   C. symmetrical
   D. distraught

English Learners

DIFFERENTIATED INSTRUCTION

Intermediate Ask students to look at their paragraph improvement exercises to discover which grammatical concepts might be giving them the most trouble. Encourage students to keep a list of these grammatical concepts, along with tips on how to correct possible errors. Provide clarification of these concepts for students.

Assess

Vocabulary Skills

1. **D** is the correct answer. The offense tried to break through but could not. DOK 1
2. **D** is the correct answer. The word *entire* suggests that the feeling blankets the neighborhood. DOK 1
3. **A** is the correct answer. The opening gates imply that the waiting crowd would rush in. DOK 1
4. **C** is the correct answer. An articulate speaker would likely hold an audience's attention. DOK 1
5. **B** is the correct answer. The author reveals personal details, which suggests a level of familiarity. DOK 1
6. **A** is the correct answer. Prudent students would be respectful, so option **D** is incorrect. Options **B** and **C** make no sense here. DOK 1
7. **A** is the correct answer. The fact that she has scars suggests that the effects of segregation never faded. DOK 1
8. **C** is the correct answer. Hansberry is remembering her childhood, which was in the past. DOK 1
9. **B** is the correct answer. By not crying about something painful, the girl exhibits courage. DOK 1
10. **B** is the correct answer. Haphazardly taught students would have difficulty obeying instructions, so option **A** is incorrect. A distraught teacher would have difficulty giving instructions so option **D** is incorrect. Option **C** makes no sense. DOK 1

Assessment

English Language Arts

Assess

Grammar and Writing

1. A is the correct answer. There is a wrong verb form in the original. No other option corrects this error without introducing further errors. DOK 1
2. C is the correct answer. No comma appears after the introductory clause. No other option corrects this error without introducing further errors. DOK 1
3. C is the correct answer. Two main clauses are joined with a comma here. DOK 1

Grammar and Writing Skills: Paragraph Improvement

Carefully read the following excerpt from the first draft of a student's essay. Pay close attention to verb tense, punctuation, and parallel construction. Then, on a separate sheet of paper, answer the questions on pages 438–439.

(1) *There is a long history of segregation in American public schools.* (2) *Prejudice and racism had keeping minorities out of white schools.* (3) *Even though much progress had been made in Civil Rights during the nineteenth century segregation practices continued.* (4) *In a famous 1896 case, the Supreme Court ruled that "separate but equal" facilities for Whites and African Americans were acceptable.* (5) *That ruling allowed public school systems to continue segregating students.*

(6) *It was many decades before the Supreme Court finally changed its position, it held that "separate but equal" was no longer acceptable.* (7) *Many schools were forced to admit African American students for the first time.* (8) *While many people applauded this change, others were outraged.* (9) *Schools throughout the country were segregated in the nineteenth century.*

(10) *Even the Supreme Court could not fully integrate schools, however.* (11) *The fact is that most children attend schools in their own communities.* (12) *Many communities not integrated.* (13) *In order to address this problem, many cities would have students travel to other communities to desegregate its schools.* (14) *This policy was known as "busing."*

(15) *Today many people see segregation in public schools as resulting from other factors that are not racially diverse.* (16) *Fewer whites live in central cities than in previous eras.* (17) *This "white flight" has left many school districts populated mostly by minority groups.* (18) *Since busing is not so common today as it once was, many public schools are not integrated.* (19) *Although the causes of racial separation have changed, however, many believe that the effects are similar.*

1. Which of the following is the best revision of sentence 2?
   - **A.** Prejudice and racism kept minorities out of white schools.
   - **B.** Prejudice and racism keeps minorities out of white schools.
   - **C.** Prejudice and racism had kept minorities, out of white schools.
   - **D.** Prejudice and racism was keeping minorities, out of white schools.

2. Which is the best way to revise sentence 3?
   - **A.** Make no change.
   - **B.** Insert commas after *Rights* and after *practices.*
   - **C.** Insert a comma after *century.*
   - **D.** Insert a comma after *Rights.*

3. Which error appears in sentence 6?
   - **A.** incorrect verb tense
   - **B.** misplaced modifier
   - **C.** run-on sentence
   - **D.** sentence fragment

Skills Practice

Review Literary Devices Tell students to read the writing task assignment on page 439. The task asks students to identify literary devices, specifically metaphor and hyperbole, that Hansberry uses to help express her point of view. Review the different types of literary devices that an author might use: *metaphor, simile, hyperbole, allusion, imagery, allegory, symbolism, etc.* As a class brainstorm definitions of each of the literary devices then have volunteers provide an example for each found in Hansberry's writing. Remind students to flesh out these ideas and examples in their essays and to use the provided hints as a guideline.

4. Which sentence is not related to the main idea of the second paragraph?
   A. 6
   B. 7
   C. 8
   D. 9

5. Which error appears in sentence 12?
   A. incorrect parallelism
   B. misplaced modifier
   C. run-on sentence
   D. sentence fragment

6. Which is the best revision of sentence 13?
   A. To address this problem many cities would have students travel, to other communities, to desegregate its schools.
   B. To address this problem many cities would have students travel to other communities, to desegregate its schools.
   C. In order to address this problem, many cities would have students travel to another community to desegregate their schools.
   D. In order to address this problem, many cities would have students travel to other communities to desegregate their schools.

7. Which error appears in sentence 15?
   A. incorrect parallelism
   B. misplaced modifier
   C. run-on sentence
   D. sentence fragment

8. What material would best fit in a paragraph inserted between the last two paragraphs?
   A. a discussion of the origins of segregation
   B. a discussion of busing-program results
   C. an explanation of the Supreme Court's decisions
   D. an explanation of nineteenth-century Civil Rights laws

9. What is most needed in this essay?
   A. footnotes
   B. a conclusion
   C. quotations
   D. visual aids

Essay

WRITING SITUATION: Imagine discussing with the author the use of literary elements to connect her personal experience to ideas about society.

DIRECTIONS FOR WRITING: Think about how literary elements, such as metaphor and hyperbole, help express the author's point of view. Now write an essay in which you argue for or against the use of these literary elements in writing about history.

REMEMBER—YOU SHOULD:
- write about the assigned topic
- make your writing thoughtful and interesting
- make each sentence you write contribute to your composition as a whole
- make sure that your ideas are clear and well organized
- write about your ideas so that the reader can understand your argument
- proofread and edit your writing to correct errors in spelling, punctuation, grammar, and sentence structure

Approaching Level

DIFFERENTIATED INSTRUCTION

Emerging Tell students that they will have enough time to read a passage, analyze its information, and answer questions about the passage if they focus on the content. Explain that text features (headings, capitalized words, boldface and italicized words, dates, words in quotation marks, graphics, and so forth) can help them focus on important information in a text. Ask students to find a text that contains two or more of these features. Discuss with students how these features can help them quickly find important information in a passage.

Assess

Grammar and Writing Skills

4. D is the correct answer. Segregation in the nineteenth century does not directly relate to the changes that occurred later. DOK 2

5. D is the correct answer. The sentence lacks a verb. DOK 1

6. D is the correct answer. The pronoun *its* does not agree with its antecedent, *communities.* DOK 1

7. B is the correct answer. The phrase at the end of the sentence appears to modify *other factors* when it should modify *public schools.* DOK 1

8. B is the correct answer. The third paragraph ends with a statement about busing, and the fourth paragraph says that busing is no longer widespread. DOK 3

9. B is the correct answer. An introductory paragraph is missing from this essay, which has a concluding paragraph and does not need quotations or visual aids. DOK 3

Essay

Remind students to present their position clearly, support it with examples, and provide a summary conclusion. DOK 4

Skills Scope and Sequence

Readability Scores Key: **Dale-Chall/DRP/Lexile**

PART 1: Nature Inspires

Selections and Features	Literary Elements
Unit Introduction pp. 440–446	Poetry **SE** p. 442
Literary Focus pp. 448–449	Poetry **SE** p. 448 Form and Structure **SE** p. 448 Rhythm **SE** p. 449 Rhyme **SE** p. 449
Poem I Wandered Lonely as a Cloud, by William Wordsworth pp. 450–454	Rhyme and Rhyme Scheme **SE** p. 451
Poems who are you, little i and **l(a,** by e. e. cummings pp. 455–460	Form **SE** p. 456
Poem A Red, Red Rose, by Robert Burns pp. 461–464	Meter and Rhythm **SE** p. 462
Poem A Noiseless Patient Spider, by Walt Whitman pp. 465–469	Free Verse **SE** p. 466 Tone (review) **SE** p. 468
Informational Text TIME: The Island Within, by Leslie Marshall **7.0/60/1130** pp. 470–473	
Comparing Literature **An Indian Summer Day on the Prairie** (poem), by Vachel Lindsay **On Summer** (memoir), by Lorraine Hansberry **6.2/89/1140** **Monument** (poem), by Natasha Tretheway pp. 474–485	Line and Stanza **SE** p. 476
Poem The Black Snake, by Mary Oliver pp. 486–490	Parallelism **SE** p. 487, **TE** p. 488 Free Verse (review) **SE** p. 489
Poem The Peace of Wild Things, by Wendell Berry pp. 491–494	Enjambment **SE** p. 492
Grammar Workshop p. 495	

Reading Skills and Strategies	Vocabulary	Writing Grammar	Speaking, Listening, and Viewing
Analyze Imagery **TE** p. 442		Note Taking **TE** p. 444 Write an Expository Essay **SE** p. 446 Write a Poem **TE** p. 446	Oral Interpretation **SE** p. 446
		Write a Poem **TE** p. 448	
Preview **SE** p. 451	Word Origins **SE** p. 454 Academic Vocabulary **SE** p. 454	Write a Poem **SE** p. 454	
Analyze Style **SE** p. 456		Write a Poem **TE** p. 456 Write About Style **TE** p. 458	
Make Inferences About Speaker **SE** p. 462 Understand Standard Verse Forms **TE** p. 462	Academic Vocabulary **SE** p. 464	Write a Poem **SE** p. 464	
Monitor Comprehension **SE** p. 466	Synonyms **TE** p. 466 Word Usage **SE** p. 469 Academic Vocabulary **SE** p. 469	Write a Poem **TE** p. 466 Apply Rhythm **SE** p. 469	
Preview SE p. 470 Determine Main Idea and Supporting Details **SE** p. 470		Write a Description **TE** p. 470	Research Careers **TE** p. 472
Compare and Contrast **SE** p. 474 Compare and Contrast Imagery **SE** p. 476 Analyze Tone and Mood **TE** p. 480	Academic Vocabulary **SE** p. 478	Use Metaphors **TE** p. 476 Write a Timeline **SE** p. 478 Write an Explanation **TE** p. 482 Analyze Active and Passive Voice **TE** p. 484	Discussion **SE** p. 485
Analyze Mood **SE** p. 487	Academic Vocabulary **SE** p. 490	Write a Literary Analysis **SE** p. 490	
Analyze Cause-and-Effect Relationships **SE** p. 492	Synonyms **SE** p. 494	Write a Flyer **SE** p. 494	
		Subject-Verb Agreement **SE** p. 495	

Readability Scores Key: **Dale-Chall/DRP/Lexile**

PART 1: Nature Inspires *(continued)*

Selections and Features	Literary Elements
Poems Haiku by Matsuo Bashō, Katy Peake, Chiyu, and Paula Yup pp. 496–501	Haiku **SE** p. 497 Diction (review) **SE** p. 500
Vocabulary Workshop p. 502	

PART 2: Life Lessons

Literary Focus pp. 504–505	Language of Poetry **SE** p. 504
Poem How Things Work, by Gary Soto pp. 506–509	Imagery **SE** p. 507
Poem I Was a Skinny Tomboy Kid, by Alma Luz Villanueva pp. 510–514	Free Verse **SE** p. 511
Poem Choices, by Nikki Giovanni pp. 515–518	Speaker **SE** p. 516
Poems "Hope" is the thing with feathers— and **I'm nobody! Who are you?,** by Emily Dickinson pp. 519–525	Metaphor **SE** p. 520 Meter (review) **SE** p. 524
Poem Defining the Grateful Gesture, by Yvonne Sapia pp. 526–530	Metaphor and Simile **SE** p. 527
Poem Sympathy, by Paul Laurence Dunbar pp. 531–535	Symbol **SE** p. 532 Metaphor (review) **SE** p. 534
Poem Remember, by Joy Harjo pp. 536–539	Repetition **SE** p. 537
Poem The Road Not Taken, by Robert Frost pp. 540–545	Lyric Poetry **SE** p. 541 Rhythm (review) **SE** p. 544
Poem Time, by Joseph Bruchac pp. 546–549	Personification **SE** p. 547
Poem Theme for English B, by Langston Hughes pp. 550–555	Voice **SE** p. 551 Lyric Poetry **SE** p. 554
Poem The Secret, by Denise Levertov pp. 556–560	Paradox **SE** p. 557 Free Verse **SE** p. 559

Reading Skills and Strategies	Vocabulary	Writing Grammar	Speaking, Listening, and Viewing
Interpret Imagery **SE** p. 497	Analogies **SE** p. 500 Academic Vocabulary **SE** p. 500	Write About Style **TE** p. 498 Write a Research Report **SE** p. 501 Italics **SE** p. 501	Discussion **SE** p. 499
	Thesaurus Use **SE** p. 502		

		Write a Description **SE** p. 505	
Analyze Structure **SE** p. 507	Context Clues **SE** p. 509	Write a Paragraph **TE** p. 508 Write a Graphic Story **SE** p. 509	
Analyze Sensory Details **SE** p. 511 Analyze Character **TE** p. 512	Academic Vocabulary **SE** p. 514	Write a Poem **SE** p. 514	
Analyze Language **SE** p. 516	Academic Vocabulary **SE** p. 518	Write a List **SE** p. 518	Discussion **TE** p. 516
Compare and Contrast Imagery **SE** p. 520	Analogies **SE** p. 524	Write a Short Story **SE** p. 525 Hyphens **SE** p. 525	
Connect to Personal Experience **SE** p. 527	Denotation and Connotation **SE** p. 530	Write a Poem **SE** p. 530	
Apply Background Knowledge **SE** p. 532	Analogies **SE** p. 535 Academic Vocabulary **SE** p. 535	Apply Symbolism **SE** p. 535	
Draw Conclusions About Author's Beliefs **SE** p. 537	Academic Vocabulary **SE** p. 539	Write a Personal Essay **SE** p. 539	Oral Response to Literature **TE** p. 538
Make Inferences About Theme **SE** p. 541	Context Clues **SE** p. 544	Write a Response to Literature **TE** p. 542 Write an Expository Essay **SE** p. 545 In-text Quotations **SE** p. 545	Discussion **SE** p. 543
Identify Irony **SE** p. 547	Academic Vocabulary **SE** p. 549	Write a Memo **SE** p. 549	Discussion **TE** p. 548
Analyze Style **SE** p. 551	Academic Vocabulary **SE** p. 555	Apply Tone **SE** p. 555	Partner Reading **SE** p. 554
Analyze Parallelism with Juxtaposition **SE** p. 557	Academic Vocabulary **SE** p. 560	Write Paradoxes **TE** p. 558	Partner Reading **SE** p. 559 Literature Group **SE** p. 560

Readability Scores Key: Dale-Chall/DRP/Lexile

PART 3: The Strength of Family

Selections and Features	Literary Elements
Literary Focus pp. 562–563	Sound Devices **SE** p. 563
Poem Grape Sherbet, by Rita Dove pp. 564–568	Assonance and Consonance **SE** p. 565 Exact Rhyme and Slant Rhyme **TE** p. 566 Metaphor **SE** p. 567
Poem "Good Night, Willie Lee, I'll See You in the Morning," by Alice Walker pp. 569–572	Epiphany **SE** p. 570
Poem Where Are Those Songs?, by Micere Githae Mugo pp. 573–579	Rhythm **SE** p. 574 Assonance **SE** p. 578
Poem My Mother Combs My Hair, by Chitra Banerjee Divakaruni pp. 580–586	Simile **SE** p. 581 Character Traits **TE** p. 582 Form **SE** p. 585
Visual Perspective *from* **Bone: Out from Boneville,** by Jeff Smith pp. 587–589	
Poem Lineage, by Margaret Walker pp. 590–593	Alliteration **SE** p. 591
Writing Workshop pp. 594–601	
Speaking, Listening, and Viewing Workshop pp. 602–603	
Independent Reading pp. 604–605	
Assessment pp. 606–611	Humor **TE** p. 607

Reading Skills and Strategies	Vocabulary	Writing Grammar	Speaking, Listening, and Viewing
Analyze Literary Devices **SE** p. 562		Write a Paragraph **SE** p. 563	
Make Inferences About Setting **SE** p. 565	Analogies **SE** pp. 565, 568 Academic Vocabulary **SE** p. 568	Apply Diction **SE** p. 568	
Make Generalizations **SE** p. 570	Word Roots **TE** p. 570 Academic Vocabulary **SE** p. 572	Write a Journal Entry **SE** p. 572	
Analyze Structure **SE** p. 574 Paraphrase to Understand **TE** p. 576	Academic Vocabulary **SE** p. 579	Write a Poem **SE** p. 578 Write a Speech **SE** p. 579	Speech **SE** p. 579
Visualize **SE** p. 581	Analogies **SE** pp. 581, 585 Academic Vocabulary **SE** p. 585	Rewrite a Poem **SE** p. 585 Write an Essay **SE** p. 586 Paragraphing **SE** p. 586	Discussion **SE** p. 585
Interpret Graphic Forms of Literature **SE** p. 587		Write a Summary **SE** p. 589	Discussion **TE** p. 588
Analyze Rhythm **SE** p. 591	Synonyms **SE** pp. 591, 593	Write a Dialogue **SE** p. 593	Discussion **TE** p. 592
Peer Review **SE** p. 601		Write a Descriptive Essay **SE** pp. 594–601 Write Descriptive Statements **TE** p. 596 Precise Adjectives **SE** p. 600 Misplaced Modifiers **SE** p. 601	
		Develop a Presentation **SE** p. 603 Assess a Presentation **TE** p. 603	Presentation **SE** p. 603
		Write a Review **SE** p. 605	Present a Poem **TE** p. 604 Review **SE** p. 605
Visualize **TE** p. 606		Create a Comparison Chart **TE** p. 610 Write an Essay **SE** p. 611	

UNIT THREE

Focus

Bellringer Options

Literature Launcher
Pre-Reading Video Unit 3
Daily Language Practice Transparency 43

Or tell students that they have been studying poetry, in many forms, since early childhood. Point out to students that nursery rhymes are a form of poetry.

Ask: What other types of poetry do you recall? Have students volunteer poems that they remember and explain why the poems made an impression on them.

For school-to-home activities, see Unit 3 Teaching Resources Book, pp. 5–11.

For students who would profit from independent novel study, see Novel Companion, pp. 119–162.

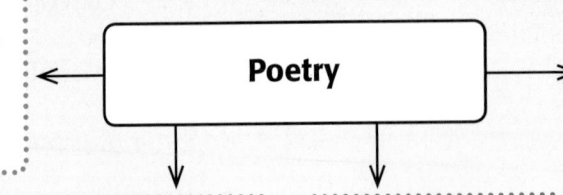

Pollard Willows and Setting Sun, 1888. Vincent van Gogh. Rijksmuseum Kroeller-Mueller, Otterio, The Netherlands.

View the Art Vincent van Gogh moved to the south of France in 1888. The landscapes there inspired him to create paintings such as this one. What types of poetry does this painting remind you of?

440

Unit Introduction Skills

Poetry

Writing Skills/Grammar
- Metaphor and Simile Essay (SE p. 446)
- Concrete and Abstract Nouns (TE p. 510)
- Take Notes (TE p. 444)

Literary Elements
- Form and Structure (SE p. 442)
- Language of Poetry (SE p. 443)
- Sound of Poetry (SE p. 443)
- Literary Analysis (SE pp. 444–445)

Listening/Speaking/Viewing Skills
- Memorize a Stanza (SE p. 446)
- Analyze Art (TE pp. 441, 445)

Reading Skills
- Read Poetry (SE pp. 442–443)

UNIT THREE

Poetry

Looking Ahead

According to Nicaraguan poet Daisy Zamora, poetry is "a way of feeling life." How does poetry help us "feel" life? Poetry captures intense experiences or creative perceptions of the world in a musical language. If prose is like talking, poetry is like singing.

Each part in Unit Three focuses on a Big Idea that can help you connect the selection to your life.

PREVIEW	Big Ideas	Literary Focus
PART 1	Nature Inspires	Form and Structure
PART 2	Life Lessons	Language
PART 3	The Strength of Family	Sound Devices

UNIT THREE

Focus

Summary

The unit begins with an introduction to form, structure, language, and sound in poetry. It includes quotes from writers on reading poetry as well as an analysis of "The Charge of the Light Brigade."

View the Art ★

Answer: *(Prompt students to include rhymes, song lyrics, and plays written in verse.)*

Pollard Willows and Setting Sun was painted by Vincent van Gogh (1853–1890) in 1888, the year he moved from Paris to Arles in Provence, in the south of France. The light, colors, and landscapes of Provence inspired Van Gogh. During this prolific period, his technique matured, and many of his works were saturated with color, such as his famous *Sunflowers*.

Unit Resources

Print Materials

- Unit 3 Teaching Resources, pp. 1–368
- Interactive Read and Write (On Level/Approaching, EL), pp. 99–166
- Novel Companion, pp. 119–162
- Bellringer Option Transparencies: Selection Focus 19–29; Daily Language Practice 43–70
- Literary Element Transparencies 52, 88, 107
- Assessment Resources, Unit Assessment, pp. 229–230
- Assessment Resources, Selection Assessment, pp. 111–162

Technology

- TeacherWorks Plus CD
- StudentWorks Plus CD
- Literature Launchers: Pre-Reading Videos DVD, Unit 3
- Literature Online
- Interactive Vocabulary CD-ROM
- Listening Library CD-ROM
- ExamView CD-ROM
- Skill Level Up! CD-ROM

UNIT THREE

Teach

Write on the board:

- Imagery
- Figures of Speech
- Simile
- Metaphor
- Personification
- Rhythm and Meter
- Rhyme

Leave space under each heading. As you go through the section, pause at each topic and ask students for examples. List examples under the appropriate headings and have students copy the lists into their notebooks.

Writer's Technique ☆

Sound Elements The use of sound elements such as rhythm, meter, and rhyme is an integral part of a poet's technique. Shakespeare, for example, is known for his use of iambic pentameter. Edna St. Vincent Millay is noted for her sonnets.

Learning Objectives

For pages 440–446

In studying this text, you will focus on the following objectives:

Literary Study:
Analyzing poetry.
Connecting to literature.

Genre Focus: Poetry

What distinguishes poetry from prose?

Mexican poet Octavio Paz believed that "the poem is an original and unique creation, but it is also reading and recitation: participation." Paz's point was that poetry is meant to be read, understood, and *enjoyed.* Literary elements such as figurative language, rhyme, and rhythm help us to enjoy a poem.

The Form and Structure of Poetry ☆

Organization

In literature, **structure** is the organization of images, ideas, and words. Poets often organize the ideas in their poems into **stanzas**—the "paragraphs" of poetry. Each stanza is made up of **lines,** or rows of words that may or may not form sentences. **Form,** or the external pattern of a poem, often dictates such elements as rhythm, meter, and rhyme.

O, my love is like a red, red rose,
That's newly sprung in June.
O, my love is like the melody,
That's sweetly play'd in tune.

—Robert Burns, **from "A Red, Red Rose"**

Rhythm and Meter

Rhythm is the pattern of stressed and unstressed syllables in a line of poetry. A poem's rhythm can be regular or irregular. **Meter** is the regular pattern of stressed and unstressed syllables that can establish the rhythm of a poem.

I've heard it in the chillest land—
And on the strangest Sea—
Yet, never, in Extremity,
It asked a crumb—of Me.

—Emily Dickinson, **from "'Hope' is the thing with feathers—"**

Rhyme

Rhyme is the repetition of the same stressed vowel sounds and any succeeding sounds in two or more words. For example, *stop* rhymes with *drop.* **Internal rhyme** occurs when two words in the same line rhyme. **End rhyme** occurs at the end of lines. In this passage, the end rhymes are underlined.

I know what the caged bird feels, <u>alas</u>!
When the sun is bright on the upland slopes;
When the wind stirs soft through the springing <u>grass</u>,
And the river flows like a stream of <u>glass</u>;

—Paul Laurence Dunbar, **from "Sympathy"**

Reading Practice

Imagery Say: Many of the words used in poems are meant to excite the senses. A poem about a storm may describe how cold wind and rain feels on a person's skin. A poem about flowers would likely tell how good the plants smell. Ask students to think about different imagery words, or words that can stir up the senses.

Make a list of the words the students volunteer. Then, with the class, discuss how each word works with a particular sense. For example, the word "delicious" appeals to our sense of taste. Perhaps a student will suggest a term like "fresh-baked bread." That term might appeal to the senses of smell, taste, or sight.

The Language of Poetry

Imagery

Imagery is descriptive language that appeals to one or more of the five senses: sight, sound, touch, taste, and smell. Some images appeal to more than one sense.

The room is full
of the scent of crushed hibiscus,
my mother's breath.

—Chitra Banerjee Divakaruni, **from "My Mother Combs My Hair"**

Figures of Speech

A **figure of speech** is a word or expression that is not meant to be taken literally. Similes, metaphors, and personification are all figures of speech.

A **simile** uses the word *like* or *as* to compare two seemingly unlike things.

A **metaphor** compares two or more different things by stating or implying that one thing *is* another.

Personification attributes human characteristics to an animal, object, or idea.

How dreary—to be—Somebody!
How public—like a Frog—

—Emily Dickinson, **from "I'm Nobody! Who are you?"**

The sun is a smoldering fire,
That creeps through the high gray plain, **1**

—Vachel Lindsay, **from "An Indian Summer Day on the Prairie"**

The Sound of Poetry

Sound Devices

Writers use **sound devices** to underscore the meaning of certain words, to enhance rhythm, and to add to the musical quality of the work. For example, a poet might use **alliteration**—repetition of consonant sounds at the beginnings of words—to draw the reader's attention to the words and ideas behind them.

The **repetition** of a sound, word, phrase, line, or even an entire stanza is another frequently used sound device.

They were full of sturdiness and singing. **2**
My grandmothers were strong.

—Margaret Walker, **from "Lineage"**

LOG ON **Literature** Online

Literature and Reading For more selections, go to glencoe.com and enter QuickPass code GL49787u3.

UNIT THREE

Teach

Literary Element 1

Metaphor Have a volunteer read the lines from Vachel Lindsay aloud. **Ask:** In what ways is the sun similar to a smoldering fire? *(The sun slowly lightens the land as it rises.)* What effect do you think the author wanted the metaphor to have? *(Possible answers: for the reader to feel the moment of the sunrise; to create a visual effect of the light moving across the plain.)*

Literary Element 2

Sound Devices **Ask:** How does the repetition of the *s* sound affect these lines of the poem? *(The grandmothers are closely connected to the words* sturdiness, singing, *and* strong.*)*

Approaching Level

DIFFERENTIATED INSTRUCTION

Emerging Some students may have difficulty understanding literary devices such as simile and metaphor. Show students that there is an easy way to tell the difference between the two. **Say:** *Simile* is related to *similar*. Similar things are *as* or *like* each other, but not exactly the same. A metaphor suggests something in common but does not use *like* or *as*.

Reinforce this lesson with an activity. Pair students and ask each group to make two lists: one for similes and one for metaphors. Then, ask the groups to think of at least five examples for each list. *(An example simile is "quiet as a mouse," and an example metaphor is "the car is lightning-fast.")*

UNIT THREE

Teach

Reading Strategy 1

Reading Poetry **Ask:** How does the poem's rhythm and rhyme affect you? *(Urge students to characterize these elements and explain their personal reactions.)* Suggest that when they read a poem, they should ask themselves the following questions:

- What is the rhythm like—fast, slow, regular, or irregular?
- What sound devices are used?
- What effect do these elements have on the mood and on me?

Writer's Technique ☆

Repetition Note Tennyson's use of repetition. The pounding rhythm of the poem echoes the sound of marching, drumming, hoof beats, and gunfire, bringing the battle to life and drawing the reader into the center of the drama.

Literary Analysis Model

How do literary elements create meaning in a poem?

In his poem "The Charge of the Light Brigade," Alfred, Lord Tennyson pays tribute to the 673 soldiers who made an ill-advised charge against Russian artillery positions near Sebastopol, Russia, during the Crimean War (1853–1856). Fought largely on the Crimean Peninsula in what is now Ukraine, the war began after Russia tried to expand into the Black Sea region by invading Turkish territory.

APPLYING Literary Elements

Repetition ☆

The repeated phrases of the first stanza suggest galloping horses. Tennyson maintains this rhythm throughout.

Rhyme

Notice that the last word in line 12 rhymes with the last word of the fourth line of stanzas 3 and 5 as well as the words *wondered* and *sundered* in stanzas 4 and 6. It also forms a slant rhyme with *hundred* throughout the poem.

The Charge of the Light Brigade

by Alfred, Lord Tennyson

Half a league, half a league,
Half a league, onward
All in the valley of Death
   Rode the six hundred.
"Forward, the Light Brigade!
Charge for the guns!" he said.
Into the valley of Death
   Rode the six hundred.

"Forward, the Light Brigade!"
Was there a man dismayed?
Not though the soldier knew
   Someone had blundered.
Theirs not to make reply,
Theirs not to reason why,
Theirs but to do and die.
Into the valley of Death
   Rode the six hundred.

Cannon to right of them,
Cannon to left of them,
Cannon in front of them,
   Volleyed and thundered;
Stormed at with shot and
   shell,
Boldly they rode and well,

John Charlton 1889 reproduced in "The Nation's Pictures."

Writing Practice

Take Notes This poem tells a story about people, but it does not give any of these characters' names. Explain to students that they need to read the poem carefully to decide who the characters are and what kind of people they might be. Ask students to keep a list of character information as they read the poem.

Students may write down many kinds of information. For example, the people in the poem are known as the "Light Brigade." They seem to be soldiers riding into a battle. Some students may point out that the soldiers are brave and committed to their duty—"to do and die" without hesitating.

Into the jaws of Death,
Into the mouth of hell
Rode the six hundred.
Flashed all their sabers bare,
Flashed as they turned in air
Sabering the gunners there,
Charging an army, while
All the world wondered.
Plunged in the battery smoke
Right through the line they broke;
Cossack and Russian
Reeled from the saber stroke
Shattered and sundered.
Then they rode back, but not,
Not the six hundred.

Cannon to right of them,
Cannon to left of them,
Cannon behind them
Volleyed and thundered;
Stormed at with shot and shell,
While horse and hero fell,
They that had fought so well
Came through the jaws of Death,
Back from the mouth of hell,
All that was left of them,
Left of six hundred.

When can their glory fade?
O the wild charge they made!
All the world wondered.
Honor the charge they made!
Honor the Light Brigade,
Noble six hundred!

Metaphor

Tennyson uses fiercely dramatic metaphors (24 "jaws of death", 25 "mouth of hell") to describe the challenge the soldiers face in the charge.

Imagery

Words like *volleyed* and *thundered* help the reader "hear" the action on the battlefield.

Form

Tennyson shortened the final stanza in order to emphasize his themes of courage and honor.

Alfred, Lord Tennyson, ca. 1860. Mathew Brady. Photograph. ★

Reading Check

Interpret What effect does the repetition of words and lines have on the depiction of the battle?

Teach

Reading Check

Answer: *The repetition re-creates the sounds of battle and evokes a feeling of inevitability and omnipresent danger. The soldiers must do their duty and ride into the fray even though they are surrounded. The relentless rhythm gradually builds a sense of impending doom.*

Literary Element 2

Imagery **Ask:** In addition to *volleyed* and *thundered*, what other words from this stanza evoke strong images? *(Possible answers: "jaws of Death" or "mouth of hell.")*

English Learners

DIFFERENTIATED INSTRUCTION

Early Advanced This poem tells a simple story, but it does so with poetic language. Some of the words are unusual, and many of the sentences are structured in nonstandard ways. Although this may help the flow and emotion of the poem, it may confuse English learners. Take time to help students rearrange these sentences to discover their meaning.

Some problematic sentences have inverted subject-verb order, such as, *Into the mouth of hell rode the six hundred.* Write these lines on the board and show students how they would be said in everyday language: *The six hundred rode into the mouth of hell.* Help students with any other confusing word arrangements in the poem.

View the Photograph ★

Mathew Brady (1823–1896) is probably best known for his striking Civil War photographs, but he started out as a portrait photographer. He photographed many famous people of his time including politicians and authors. When the Civil War began in 1861, Brady hired a team of photographers to document the war. Although Brady rarely photographed the war himself, the photos are attributed to him because he would not credit them to his staff members.

UNIT THREE

Assess

Guide to Reading Poetry

Suggest to students that they consider the following when reading a poem three times:

- On the first reading, consider your overall response to the poem.
- On the second, ask what ideas, emotions, and images the poet is trying to convey.
- On the third, read for structure and language and make notes about the different elements.

Elements of Poetry

Suggest that students make a checklist of all the elements of poetry to reference.

Activities

1. **Speaking/Listening** Suggest that while practicing in front of a mirror, students experiment with tone of voice and hand gestures.
2. **Writing** Remind students that they can use everyday objects in their metaphors.
3. **Note Taking** Remind students to take brief notes on each Big Idea.

FOLDABLES® Study Organizer

Have students make and label the Three-Pocket Book. They can insert their notes on each Big Idea in the pockets.

Wrap-Up:

Guide to Reading Poetry

- Pay attention to the ways a poem may "refresh language" and make it seem new.
- Use your emotions, experiences, and imagination to help you create meaning in a poem.
- Read a poem at least three times: once for enjoyment, once for meaning, and once for structure and language.
- Respond to a poem as a whole before analyzing its details.

LOG ON Literature Online

Unit Resources For additional skills practice, go to glencoe.com and enter QuickPass code GL49787u3.

Elements of Poetry

- Poems are organized into stanzas. Each **stanza** contains one or more **lines.**
- **Imagery** is descriptive language that appeals to the five senses: sight, sound, smell, touch, taste.
- **Figurative language** is language used for descriptive effect, often to imply ideas indirectly.
- A **figure of speech** is a word or expression that is not meant to be taken literally.
- **Rhythm** is the pattern of stressed and unstressed syllables in a line of poetry.
- **Rhyme** and other sound devices repeat certain sounds to create musical effects.

Activities

Use what you have learned about reading and analyzing poetry to complete one of the following activities.

1. **Speaking/Listening** Memorize a stanza of Tennyson's "Charge of the Light Brigade." Practice your delivery in front of a mirror, and then recite your stanza for the class.
2. **Writing** Write a brief essay explaining the difference between the terms *metaphor* and *simile.* Write your own examples of each type of figurative language to include.
3. **Note Taking** Try using this study organizer to keep track of the Big Ideas in this unit. See pages R20–R21 for folding instructions.

FOLDABLES Study Organizer **THREE-POCKET BOOK**

Writing Practice

Write a Poem In this introduction, students received an overview of several imporant aspects of poetry. These concepts include structure; imagery; and figurative language such as similes, metaphors, and personification. Review each term with students and then define the terms on the board, along with an example of each.

Place students into small groups. Instruct each group to write a short poem using a definite structure, imagery, and at least one example of figurative language. Poems can be silly or serious, as long as they illustrate the concepts in this introduction.

PART 1

Nature Inspires

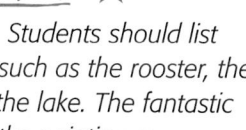

The Rooster, 1928. Marc Chagall. Fundacion Coleccion Tthyssen-Bornemisza, Madrid, Spain.

View the Art This painting by Marc Chagall has a dreamlike quality. What elements of nature are depicted? How does the dreamlike quality suggest inspiration? ★

BIG IDEA

Many poets take their subjects from nature. A flower, a bug, a morning, or an entire day—from these natural elements poets draw lessons about the human condition. The poems in Part 1 react to nature in various ways. As you read them, ask yourself, How much of the world around me do I really see?

447

UNIT THREE

PART 1

Analyze and Extend

Big Idea

Nature Inspires **Ask:** When is the last time you saw a sunset? *Engage students in a discussion of subjects from the natural world that could inspire them to create art. Suggest students list elements of nature that they see on the way to and from school. Have students share their observations with the class.*

View the Art ★

Answer: *Students should list elements such as the rooster, the tree, and the lake. The fantastic nature of the painting may suggest inspiration.*

For additional support for English Learners, see Unit 3 Teaching Resources Book, p. 21.

Approaching Level

DIFFERENTIATED INSTRUCTION

Emerging Sometimes writing and visual arts can be very closely connected. Many visual artists are inspired by writers, and vice versa. Ask students to look carefully at the painting on this page. **Ask:** What do you see when you look at this picture? How do you think the artist feels about the natural things he is painting? *(Students' interpretations will vary.)*

Encourage students to brainstorm further by posing more questions. **Ask:** What are the figures doing in the painting? *(A person is riding a giant rooster; people are riding in a rowboat)* **Ask:** Where is this action taking place? *(outside, next to a lake)* Instruct students to write out their ideas and develop a short story about the painting.

Focus

Bellringer Options

Daily Language Practice Transparency 44

Or build a house of cards. Pull a card out from the foundation. When the house collapses, have students explain the importance of form and structure in architecture. *(The need for a firm foundation and the visual effect of the building)* Note that form and structure are just as crucial in poetry. Discuss how these elements relate to poetry.

Learning Objectives

For pages 447–449

In studying this text, you will focus on the following objective:

Literary Study: Analyzing the form and structure of poetry.

LITERARY FOCUS

Form and Structure

How do form and structure affect meaning in a poem?

Poets pack a lot into a small space. When you read a poem, you can be sure that each word and phrase was chosen carefully by the poet. **1** Even the organization and appearance of a poem can be important aspects of fully understanding the meaning. Form and structure both address organization in poetry—the order of the ideas presented and the sound and visual patterns created by the poet's choices.

Form and Structure

The **form** of a poem is its prescribed pattern, usually involving meter, rhyme, rhyme scheme, and structure. The **structure** of a poem is created through the organization of its images, ideas, and words. A poet may use rhythm and rhyme to connect ideas, or he or she may use stanzas to separate the poem into distinct parts, in much the same way paragraphs separate the ideas in an essay. Each stanza within a poem may serve a different purpose. For example, one stanza could describe a problem, one stanza could explore its solutions, and one stanza could re-create a time before the problem existed.

Stanza The basic unit of form is the **stanza**—a group of lines that create a unit. A **line** of poetry is a word or row of words that may or may not form a complete sentence. Calvin's poem about Hobbes is written in couplets, or sets of two rhyming lines. The chart on the next page shows several options for stanza length. Poets are not limited by these options, however. Some poems have stanzas of varying lengths, and other poems have no stanza divisions at all.

Teach

Literary Element 1

Form and Structure Ask: Do you have a preference for a particular structure or form in poetry? Why? *Discuss why certain elements in poetry appeal to them.*

Writing Practice

Use a Poetic Form This unit will introduce students to several kinds of poetic forms, including ballads, sonnets, quatrains, and couplets. Divide the class into four groups and assign each group to study one of these structures. Ask the students to find a clear definition of their assigned structure as well as some examples. Have each student write a poem using the poetic form studied within his or her group. Students may present their poems to the class. Students' poetry should use precise language, active verbs, and sensory details.

Some Common Stanza Types

Type	Lines per stanza
couplet	two
quatrain	four
cinquain	five
sestet	six
octave	eight

Rhythm

Rhythm is the pattern of sound created by the arrangement of stressed and unstressed syllables in a line. Rhythm can be regular or irregular. **Meter** is a regular pattern of stressed and unstressed syllables, which sets the overall rhythm of certain poems. The basic unit of meter is the foot. A foot usually contains two or three syllables with varying patterns of stress.

Scansion The analysis of the meter in a line of poetry is called scansion. To scan a line of poetry means to note the stressed (ˊ) and unstressed (˘) syllables and to divide the line into its feet, or rhythmic units.

˘ And fáre | thĕe wéel, | mў ón | lў lóve,
˘ And fáre | thĕe wéel | ă while!

—Robert Burns, **from "A Red, Red Rose"**

LOG ON ▶ **Literature** Online

Literature and Reading For more about literary elements, go to glencoe.com and enter QuickPass code GL49787u3.

Rhyme

Rhyme is the repetition of the same stressed vowel sounds and any succeeding sounds in two or more words. **End rhyme** is the rhyming of words at the end of a line, while internal rhyme is the rhyming of words within a single line. **Slant rhyme** occurs when the sounds of words are similar but not identical. For example, *soul* and *all* are slant rhymes in this poem by Emily Dickinson.

"Hope" is the thing with feathers—
That perches in the <u>soul</u>—
And sings the tune without the words—
And never stops—at <u>all</u>—

—Emily Dickinson, **from "'Hope' is the Thing with Feathers—"**

Rhyme Scheme The **rhyme scheme** is the pattern of end rhyme in a poem. You can mark the rhyme scheme of a poem by using a different letter of the alphabet for each new rhyme. Using *a* to denote the first rhyme, *b* the second, and so on, you can see that the poem below follows an *abab* rhyme scheme.

who are you,little <u>i</u> a
(five or six years <u>old</u>) b
peering from some <u>high</u> a
window;at the <u>gold</u> b

—E. E. Cummings, **from "who are you,little i"**

Quickwrite

Write Recall the nursery rhymes you heard as a child, such as "Humpty Dumpty" and "Hickory Dickory Dock." What can you remember about their form and structure? What did their rhythm sound like? What were their rhyme schemes? Write your recollections.

LITERARY FOCUS **449**

English Learners

DIFFERENTIATED INSTRUCTION

Early Advanced Review with students the types of rhyme explained on this page. Some English learners may find certain varieties difficult, especially slant rhymes. Read the example poem from Emily Dickinson and note its use of slant rhyme ("soul" and "all"). Demonstrate to the class how these words do not truly rhyme, but sound like it when read aloud.

Rhyming can be a fun way to enhance vocabulary lessons. When you introduce vocabulary to the class, consider adding the new words into rhymes, or assigning students to do so. Challenge students to use newly learned words in various rhyme schemes including end rhyme and slant rhyme.

UNIT THREE

PART 1

Teach

Reading Strategy	2

Reading Poetry Suggest that when analyzing a poem for rhyme, students first look at the way each line ends to note all the end rhyme patterns before searching for internal rhymes within each line.

View the Cartoon ★

Bill Watterson's *Calvin and Hobbes* has run in more than 2,400 papers and is one of the most popular cartoons of all time. The hallmarks of Watterson's style include fine drawing and character-driven humor.

Ask: How do the form and structure of Calvin's poem affect your understanding of it? *(Students may say that the structure makes the poem easy to understand and adds to the humor.)*

Assess

Quickwrite

Students' memories will vary. Make sure their written recollections are specific and address various aspects of form and structure.

Before You Read

Focus

Bellringer Options

Selection Focus Transparency 28

Daily Language Practice Transparency 45

Or display images of nature (flowers, trees, animals in their natural habitats).

Ask: What do you feel when you look at these images? How does nature affect your life? Have students consider as they read how nature affects the poem's speaker.

Before You Read

World Literature
England

I Wandered Lonely as a Cloud

Meet **William Wordsworth** (1770–1850)

English literature in the 1700s was dominated by values of intellect, order, and restraint—values some people found stifling. Then a rebellious young genius came along and revitalized poetry. His name was William Wordsworth.

Exciting Education Wordsworth was born and raised in England's Lake District, an area of breathtaking scenery. His mother died when he was eight, and he and his three brothers were sent to live at a boarding school. There, Wordsworth was free to hike, skate, and explore the countryside. As an adult, he often wrote about these happy times.

> *"One impulse from a vernal wood*
> *May teach you more of man,*
> *Of moral evil and of good,*
> *Than all the sages can."*
>
> —William Wordsworth
> from "The Tables Turned"

After completing his studies at Cambridge University, Wordsworth visited France, where he became an ardent supporter of the French Revolution. He wished to stay in France, but a lack of money forced him to return to England. There, unhappiness at not finding suitable employment, and the growing conviction that the revolution had compromised its democratic ideals, brought Wordsworth to the brink of mental collapse.

Pioneer of Poetry In 1795 Wordsworth began to enjoy happier times. He came into enough money to move into a small cottage with his sister Dorothy, who was his close friend and confidante, and soon afterward, he met the poet and critic Samuel Taylor Coleridge. The meeting resulted in what has been called the most significant friendship in English literature. Coleridge inspired new ideas in Wordsworth and encouraged Wordsworth to follow his own path as a writer.

Wordsworth and Coleridge placed a high value on nature and intuition and advocated a poetry that spoke simply and to the heart. Together, the poets championed many ideas that continue to influence literature.

LOG ON **Literature** Online

Author Search For more about William Wordsworth, go to glencoe.com and enter QuickPass code GL49787u3.

Selection Skills

I Wandered Lonely as a Cloud

Literary Elements
- Rhyme and Rhyme Scheme (SE pp. 451, 453)

Writing Skills/Grammar
- Apply Imagery (SE p. 454)

Reading Skills
- Preview (SE pp. 451, 452, 454)
- Paraphrase (TE p. 452)

Vocabulary Skills
- Word Origins (SE pp. 451, 454)
- Academic Vocabulary (SE p. 454)

Literature and Reading Preview

Connect to the Poem

What are the rewards of solitude? Write a journal entry about the benefits of spending time alone.

Build Background

The Lake District in England is famous for its scenic mountains, hills, and lakes. The experience that inspired "I Wandered Lonely as a Cloud" occurred on a walk that Wordsworth took in the Lake District countryside on April 15, 1802.

Set Purposes for Reading

Big Idea Nature Inspires

As you read the poem, ask yourself, How can nature's beauty provide encouragement and joy in times of trouble?

Literary Element Rhyme and Rhyme Scheme

Rhyme is the repetition of the same stressed vowel sounds and any succeeding sounds in two or more words. **End rhyme** occurs at the ends of lines of poetry. **Rhyme scheme** is the pattern of end rhymes in a poem. As you read, ask yourself, What mood does the rhyme in this poem evoke?

Reading Strategy Preview

To **preview** a text, first think about what the title may mean. Look at images and at how the text is organized. Skim the text to get a sense of what it is about. Then predict what the author's purpose for writing might be. Finally, before you read, ask yourself, What is my purpose for reading this work?

Tip: Take Notes Use a chart to record your thoughts as you preview the poem. Jot down your predictions about the poem.

My thoughts after . . .	
reading title	
looking at art	
skimming poem	

My prediction(s) about poem:

Learning Objectives

For pages 450–454

In studying this text, you will focus on the following objectives:

Literary Study: Analyzing rhyme and rhyme scheme.

Reading: Previewing.

Writing: Applying imagery in a poem.

Vocabulary

host (hōst) *n.* a great number; a multitude; p. 452 *We saw a host of animals at the zoo.*

solitude (sol′ ə tōōd′) *n.* isolation; the state of being alone; p. 452 *After a hectic day of working with others, Maria retreated to the solitude of her apartment.*

Tip: Word Origins The origin and history of a word is called its etymology. Use a dictionary to find information on the history and origin of a word. Word origins are usually listed in brackets. For example, a sample word origin for *solitude* is [ME, fr. MF, fr. L *solitudin-, solitudo,* fr. *solus*]. The abbreviations are explained in the front of the dictionary.

Before You Read

Focus

Summary

The poem's speaker recalls taking a walk and seeing a field of yellow daffodils. He does not understand the flowers' impact on him until the memory provides him with pleasure at a later time.

For summaries in languages other than English, see Unit 3 Teaching Resources Book, pp. 22–27.

Interactive Read and Write

Other options for teaching this selection can be found in

- Interactive Read and Write for EL Students, pp. 99–106
- Interactive Read and Write for Approaching-Level Students, pp. 99–106
- Interactive Read and Write for On-Level Students, pp. 99–106

Vocabulary

Vocabulary Adventure

Have the class brainstorm outdoor activities they enjoy. Tell students to pick one of the activities from the list and write a paragraph using the new vocabulary words.

For additional vocabulary practice, see Unit 3 Teaching Resources Book, p. 30.

For additional context, see Glencoe Visual Vocabulary CD-ROM.

English Learners

DIFFERENTIATED INSTRUCTION

Early Advanced Review figurative language including personification, simile, and metaphor. Remind students that figurative language has meaning beyond what it says on the page. Group students and have them develop one example each of personification, simile, and metaphor. Have groups read aloud their examples. Tell students to look for examples of figurative language as they read Wordsworth's poem.

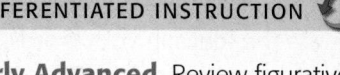

Teach

Big Idea 1

Nature Inspires

Ask: How is the speaker affected by the flowers? *(He feels great pleasure when he remembers them.)*

APPROACHING To assist approaching level learners, **say:** Seeing the daffodils was a valuable experience for the poet because thinking of the daffodils and their beauty brings him great pleasure when he is alone.

Reading Strategy 2

Preview **Answer:** *Students may say the poem will be about loneliness or isolation. They may find the comparison with a cloud intriguing and suggest that the poem will talk about the spirit.*

Say: Look for clues in the text and use your own experiences to make a prediction. As you read, confirm or correct your predictions.

Literary History ☆

The Romantic Movement

In the preface to *Lyrical Ballads,* Wordsworth signaled a momentous cultural change. He called poetry the expression of a "spontaneous overflow of feeling." In stressing feeling over intellect and individuals over society, he helped define Romanticism. This movement embraced folk tradition, explored spirituality, and glorified human struggles.

To check students' understanding of the selection, see Unit 3 Teaching Resources Book, p. 32.

I Wandered Lonely as a Cloud

William Wordsworth

Big Daffodils, 1990. John Newcomb. Casein on canvas. Private collection.

☆ 1
I wandered lonely as a cloud
That floats on high o'er vales and hills,
When all at once I saw a crowd,
A **host**, of golden daffodils;
Beside the lake, beneath the trees,
Fluttering and dancing in the breeze.

Continuous as the stars that shine
And twinkle on the milky way,
They stretched in never-ending line
Along the margin of a bay:
Ten thousand saw I at a glance,
Tossing their heads in sprightly[1] dance.

The waves beside them danced; but they
Outdid the sparkling waves in glee:
A poet could not but be gay,
In such a jocund[2] company:
I gazed—and gazed—but little thought
What wealth the show to me had brought:

For oft,[3] when on my couch I lie
In vacant or in pensive mood,
They flash upon that inward eye
Which is the bliss of **solitude**;
And then my heart with pleasure fills,
And dances with the daffodils.

1. *Sprightly* (sprīt′ lē) means "lighthearted" or "merry."
2. *Jocund* (jok′ ənd) means "cheerful" or "carefree."
3. *Oft* is an old, poetic form of "often."

2 Preview *After reading the title and first line, what do you think the poem might be about?*

Vocabulary

host (hōst) *n.* a great number; a multitude

Vocabulary

solitude (sol′ ə to͞od′) *n.* isolation; the state of being alone

Writing Practice

SPIRAL REVIEW **Paraphrase Poetry** Explain that a good way to respond to and understand poetry is to paraphrase it. To paraphrase means to restate what you have read or heard, using your own words. Have students paraphrase Wordsworth's poem in a paragraph. Ask volunteers to read their paraphrased versions. Lead a class discussion to ensure that students fully comprehend the meaning of the poem. **Say:** When you read a difficult text, break it into smaller parts, and restate the ideas in your words. This will help you gain a better understanding of it.

After You Read

Respond and Think Critically

Respond and Interpret

1. Which lines from the poem did you find most memorable, powerful, or surprising? Explain.
2. (a)In your own words, describe the scene that the speaker sees. (b)Why does the speaker find the sight so special?
3. (a)What is the "wealth" that the sight brings to the speaker? (b)Why do you think the speaker experiences that "wealth" after the fact, rather than at the moment of his vision?

Analyze and Evaluate

4. "I Wandered Lonely as a Cloud" is considered to be one of Wordsworth's most memorable poems. What makes it memorable?
5. Wordsworth uses **personification** in this poem, that is, he gives human qualities or characteristics to elements in nature. What does his use of this technique suggest about his response to the scene?

Connect

6. **Big Idea** **Nature Inspires** The **theme** of a poem is its overall message about life or human nature. What, in your opinion, is the theme of this poem?
7. **Connect to Today** Wordsworth's poetry reflects the value he placed on nature. In what ways have you seen people express their appreciation and respect for nature today?

Literary Element Rhyme and Rhyme Scheme

Wordsworth uses **end rhyme** and a particular **rhyme scheme** in "I Wandered Lonely as a Cloud" to create various effects. For example, the emphasis of certain sounds helps create a **mood,** or feeling. Rhyme scheme is designated by the assignment of a different letter of the alphabet to each new rhyme. The first four lines of Wordsworth's poem have an *abab* rhyme scheme.

1. What is the rhyme scheme of the entire poem?
2. What is the mood of the poem? Explain how rhyme and rhyme scheme contribute to the mood.

LOG ON **Literature** Online

Selection Resources For Selection Quizzes, eFlashcards, and Reading-Writing Connection activities, go to glencoe.com and enter QuickPass code GL49787u3.

Review: Form and Structure

As you learned on pages 448–449, **form** is the external pattern of a poem—its rhythm, rhyme scheme, and organization by line and stanza. **Structure** is the organization of images, ideas, and words. Without an organized form and structure, a poem would not be a coherent whole.

Partner Activity Work with a partner to create a web diagram like the one below. Fill in the diagram with examples of elements that help unify "I Wandered Lonely as a Cloud."

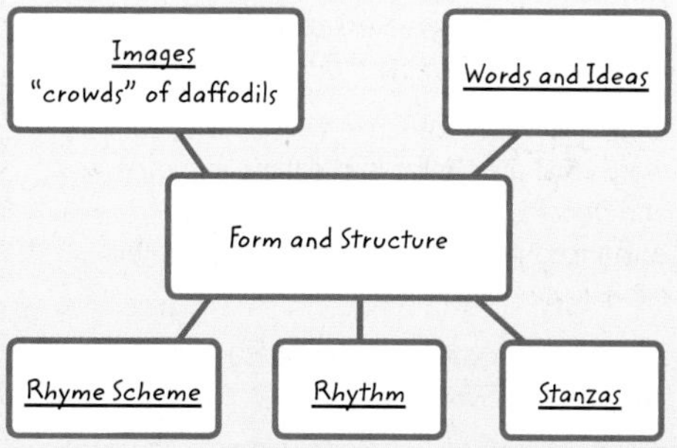

After You Read

Assess

1. Answers will vary.
2. (a) The speaker sees a field of daffodils beside a lake; the flowers and water ripple in the wind. (b) The color, movement, and sudden appearance of the view surprise and delight him.
3. (a) The "wealth" is a recurring image of the daffodils, which brings pleasure and lightens his mood. (b) The speaker enjoys many returns; he experiences the vision of the flowers again and again in his memory.
4. Students may say that the poem is memorable because its elements reinforce the happy mood and theme of "bliss of solitude." A harmony of sounds, clear and appealing images, and positive language create a pleasing whole.
5. By making the daffodils dance, the speaker conveys not only the movement of the flowers but his delight in them.
6. Students may mention the restorative power of nature.
7. Students should support their answers with examples.

Literary Element

1. The rhyme scheme may be described as *ababcc.*
2. The rhyme helps create a mood of cheerful harmony, with each stanza's musical rhyme unifying the whole effect.

Progress Check

Can students identify rhyme and rhyme scheme?

If No → See Unit 3 Teaching Resources Book, p. 28.

Review: Form and Structure

Students' web diagrams should indicate how the parts of the poem interact. Students should see how the stanzas (with regular rhyme scheme and rhythm, and uniform length) and the poet's choice of words help express the idea that nature can be a source of delight and inspiration.

After You Read

Assess

Reading Strategy

1. Students may say that they thought the poem would be sadder than it turned out to be.
2. Students may say that they predicted the author's purpose would be to make connections with nature, and the subject would be clouds, flowers, or other natural objects.
3. Answers will vary. Students should support their answers. They may say that by previewing the poem, they were prepared to learn about or enjoy one writer's views on nature.

Progress Check

Can students preview?

If No → See Unit 3 Teaching Resources Book, p. 29.

Vocabulary

Word: host; Definition: a great number; a multitude; Etymology: from LL *hostis,* from L "stranger," "enemy"; Sample Sentence: A host of people attended the concert. Word: solitude; Definition: isolation; the state of being alone; Etymology: from L *solus;* Sample Sentence: Mary enjoyed her solitude in the forest.

Academic Vocabulary

His life is **enhanced** by the memories of the experience and his ability to recall the moment whenever he wants.

Reading Strategy Preview

Review the chart you created when you previewed the poem. Then answer the following questions.

1. How did your initial thoughts about the meaning of the title change as you read the poem?
2. What did you predict the author's purpose would be? What did you predict the subject of the poem would be?
3. How did previewing help prepare you for reading?

Vocabulary Practice

Practice with Word Origins Studying the etymology of a word can help you better understand and explore its meaning. Create a word map, like the one below, for each of the boldface vocabulary words from the poem. Use a dictionary for help.

host solitude

Example:

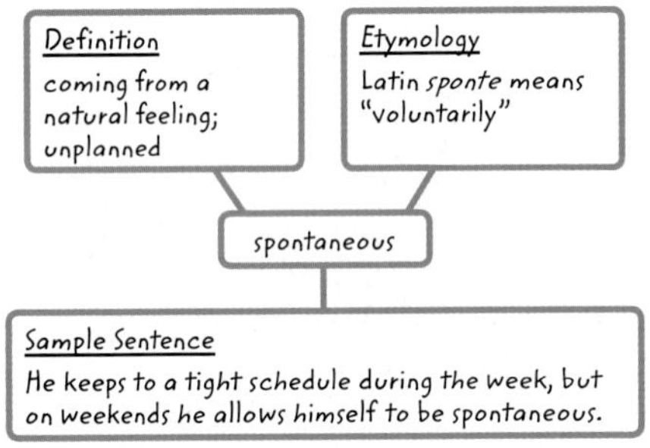

Definition
coming from a natural feeling; unplanned
Etymology
Latin *sponte* means "voluntarily"
spontaneous
Sample Sentence
He keeps to a tight schedule during the week, but on weekends he allows himself to be spontaneous.

Academic Vocabulary

In this poem, the speaker's experience is ***enhanced*** *by the natural beauty he encounters.*

Enhanced is an academic word. More familiar words that are similar in meaning are *improved* and *boosted.* How is the speaker's life **enhanced** by his experience even after the experience is over?

For more on academic vocabulary, see pages 54–55 and R79–R81.

Write with Style

Apply Imagery

Assignment Write a poem that has the same rhyme scheme as Wordsworth's poem and includes examples of imagery.

Get Ideas Choose a subject for your poem—something that can be described in a visual way. Write your subject in the center of a spider map like the one below. Think of imagery for your poem and list four main images on the chart's diagonal lines. On the horizontal lines, write two specific details that describe each image. Choose images and details to help the reader visualize the subject.

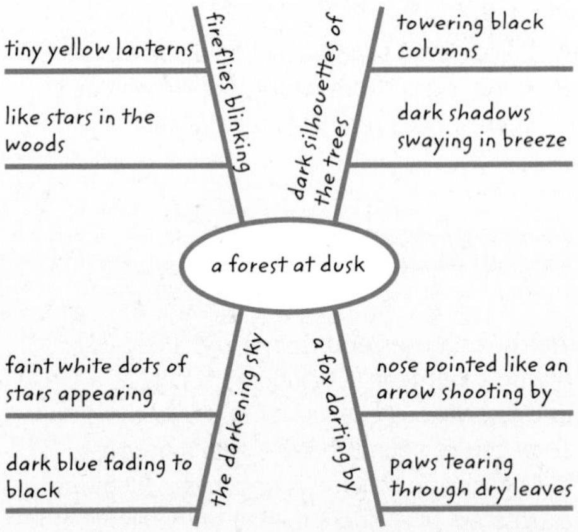

a forest at dusk
fireflies blinking

like stars in the woods
dark silhouettes of the trees
towering black columns
dark shadows swaying in breeze
the darkening sky
faint white dots of stars appearing
dark blue fading to black
a fox darting by
nose pointed like an arrow shooting by
paws tearing through dry leaves

Give It Structure Write your poem in six-line stanzas that follow Wordsworth's rhyme scheme. Focus on describing one or two images in each stanza.

Look at Language Exploring different word choices can help you create more interesting rhymes. Try out different words and combinations; rewrite any forced, imprecise, or nonsense rhymes.

EXAMPLE:

Tiny yellow lanterns ~~flutter~~ *hovered*

In the darkness ~~like no other.~~ *now uncovered.*

For additional selection assessment, see Assessment Resources, pp. 111–112.

To create custom assessments online, go to Progress Reporter Online Assessment.

To create custom assessments using software, use ExamView Assessment Suite.

Write with Style

Students' poems should

- be written in six-line stanzas
- follow Wordsworth's rhyme scheme (ababcc)
- not include forced or nonsense rhymes
- make heavy use of imagery
- use detail in describing images

For grammar practice, see Unit 3 Teaching Resources Book, p. 31.

Before You Read

who are you,little i
l(a

Meet **E. E. Cummings**
(1894–1962)

In a presentation that was later published as part of a collection titled *i: Six Nonlectures,* E. E. Cummings stated, "Poetry and every other art was and is and forever will be strictly and distinctly a question of individuality. . . ." That "i" was an important theme for this ardent individualist.

A painter, playwright, and novelist, Edward Estlin Cummings was born in Cambridge, Massachusetts, in 1894. He determined very early to become a poet, and his mother made up word games and other activities to nurture her son's creativity. After high school, Cummings went to Harvard. He studied Latin, Greek, and literature, exploring poetry and its traditional forms. He also published poetry in Harvard magazines, which led to his meeting people who would encourage him throughout most of his career.

From War to Writer After receiving his master's degree, Cummings went to New York City to work as a painter and poet. But when World War I began, Cummings volunteered as an ambulance driver in France. There he and a friend were arrested by the French on suspicion of spying. The two were kept with other prisoners in a large room in a detention camp. Cummings's father wrote to President Woodrow Wilson asking for help, and the poet and his friend were soon free. Out of this experience, however, came Cummings's first book, *The Enormous Room,* a witty attack on bureaucracy published in 1922.

"Poetry is being, not doing."

—E. E. Cummings

The "lowercase poet" When Cummings moved back to New York City in 1924, he was already a celebrated writer. John Dos Passos, a friend from Harvard and a successful author himself, had helped Cummings get his first collection of poems, *Tulips and Chimneys,* published in 1923. While living in Greenwich Village, Cummings developed the style of poetry writing for which he became renowned, with its unconventional use of capitalization, punctuation, spacing, and structure.

As both a person and a poet, Cummings was a champion of freedom and of the individual. His fight for individualism and nonconformity was balanced by his sense of wonder about nature and his love of family.

LOG ON **Literature** Online

Author Search For more about E. E. Cummings, go to glencoe.com and enter QuickPass code GL49787u3.

Before You Read

Focus

Bellringer Options

Selection Focus Transparency 20

Daily Language Practice Transparency 46

Or display an image of a sunset.

Ask: Have you ever stopped to watch a sunset? What did it make you feel or think? Have students consider as they read the poem how nature affects the speaker.

Selection Skills

who are you,little i
l(a

Reading Skills
- Analyze Style (SE pp. 456, 457, 460)

Writing Skills/Grammar
- Connect to Art (SE p. 460)

Literary Elements
- Form (SE pp. 456, 457, 458, 459)

Before You Read

Focus

Summary

The speaker recalls a moment from childhood when he thoughtfully watched a sunset.

For summaries in languages other than English, see Unit 3 Teaching Resources Book, pp. 34–39.

Literature and Reading Preview

Connect to the Poem

What setting, object, or image makes you think of solitude or loneliness? Freewrite for a few minutes about why you associate it with solitude or loneliness.

Build Background

Unconventional capitalization, punctuation, and spacing are the hallmarks of E. E. Cummings's poetry. The poet also has been known to weave slang, jazzy rhythms, and invented words into his poems. Despite their nontraditional form, Cummings's poems often utilize rhyme and sound patterns.

Set Purposes for Reading

Big Idea Nature Inspires

As you read these poems, ask yourself, How does Cummings use nature to convey emotion?

Literary Element Form

Form refers to the external pattern of a poem, including the way lines and stanzas are organized. Form also dictates such elements as rhythm, meter, and rhyme. As you read, ask yourself, How does the form of the poem relate to what it is about?

Reading Strategy Analyze Style

Style is the expressive qualities that distinguish an author's work, including word choice, sentence length and arrangement, and the use of descriptive language and imagery. To **analyze** Cummings's unconventional style, closely examine his use of punctuation and how he breaks lines and words. As you read these poems, ask yourself, How do breaks in the lines and words impact the theme of each of the poems?

Tip: Read First It is easier to analyze a poem after reading through it first. After you have read it, examine the style more closely. Use a web diagram like the one below to list examples of rhythm, repetition, and images from each poem.

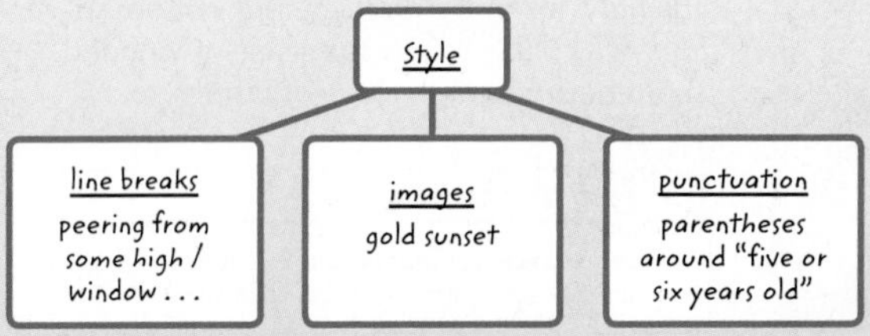

Learning Objectives

For pages 455–460

In studying this text, you will focus on the following objectives:

Literary Study: Analyzing form.

Reading:
Analyzing style.
Connecting literature to art.

Writing Practice

SMALL GROUP

Write to Model Style Expand on the Connect to the Poem feature on this page. When students finish freewriting about a setting, an object, or an image that makes them think of solitude, have them use their freewriting to write a poem. Tell students to write their poems in a style similar to Cummings's with little or no punctuation or capitalization. Break students into small groups and have them review each other's poems. Have them offer suggestions to make their poems more descriptive or appealing to readers.

Songs of Sunset Series 1. Ashton Hinrichs.

who are you, little i

E. E. Cummings

who are you,little i

(five or six years old)
peering from some high

window;at the gold

of november sunset

(and feeling:that if day
has to become night

this is a beautiful way) ☆

1 Analyze Style *What is unusual about the punctuation in this line?*

2 Form *How would you describe the stanzas in this poem?*

Teach

Reading Strategy 1

Analyze Style **Answer:** *The comma does not have a space following it, and although it is a question, there is no question mark at the end.*

ENGLISH LEARNERS To assist English learners, **say:** E. E. Cummings uses unconventional capitalization, punctuation, and spelling to create his unique style. However, this style can make his poetry difficult to read. Have English learners edit the poem for correct capitalization, punctuation, and spelling to help them read the poem more fluently.

Literary Element 2

Form **Answer:** *There are a total of six stanzas with varied length. Four stanzas are only one line long while the other two are two lines long.*

Writer's Technique ☆

Parentheses Parentheses usually set off supplemental information in a text. In Cummings's poem, however, some key details are enclosed in parentheses—the age of the young person and the young person's realization. Cummings's technique challenges a reader's expectation of how punctuation is used.

Approaching Level

DIFFERENTIATED INSTRUCTION

Established Remind students that all poems are meant to be read aloud. Read the poem aloud for students, taking care to pause appropriately. **Ask:** What does the speaker's voice sound like in your mind? *(Students may say that he speaks softly and calmly.)* **Ask:** Who is the speaker and what is he like? *(Students may say that he is a grown man thinking back on this childhood; they may say he is thoughtful and sentimental.)*

Teach

Big Idea 1

Nature Inspires
Answer: *The speaker is describing a leaf.*

Literary Element 2

Form **Answer:** *It makes the letter l look like the number one.*

To check students' understanding of the selection, see Unit 3 Teaching Resources Book, p. 43.

l(a

E. E. Cummings

l(a

le
af
fa

ll

s)
one
l

iness

In Front of the Gas Lamp, 1915. Paul Klee. Galleria Nazionale d'Arte Moderna, Rome, Italy. ©ARS, NY

1 Nature Inspires *What element of nature is the speaker describing?*

2 Form *What is the effect of leaving this letter by itself on this line?*

Writing Practice

SMALL GROUP

Write About Style Have students go to a library to find other poems by E. E. Cummings to bring to class. Encourage students to choose poems that they enjoy reading. Break students into groups to discuss the style of the two poems on these pages and the other poems. Students should consider Cummings's use of space, punctuation, capitalization (or lack thereof), and line length. Point out that Cummings does not capitalize the pronoun *I*, which shows humility and reminds readers that one person is just a "little i." Have students individually write an essay about the style of Cummings's poems.

After You Read

Respond and Think Critically

Respond and Interpret

1. What was your initial reaction to Cummings's unusual style?
2. (a)In "who are you,little i," what is "little i" doing? (b)What is the relationship between "little i" and the speaker of the poem?
3. (a)What does "little i" think is beautiful? (b)What does this beauty help to make up for?
4. (a)In "l(a" what is falling? (b)How does this image relate to the rest of the poem?

Analyze and Evaluate

5. In "who are you,little i," what do the time of day and time of year suggest about the speaker?
6. Explain the **pun**, or play on words, in the name "little i" that is related to what "little i" is doing.

Connect

7. **Big Idea** **Nature Inspires** These poems use natural images to evoke, or stir up, emotions in the reader. Do you think the images are effective in evoking emotion? Explain your response.
8. **Connect to Today** During Cummings's era, his poems were considered rebellious. Do you think they still seem rebellious today? Explain your response.

Literary Element Form

Poets have used **form** in a wide variety of ways—from traditional forms, such as sonnets and haiku, to the experimental forms of poets like Cummings.

1. Cummings uses form to help divide "who are you,little i" in half. How does he use a pattern in the poem's stanzas to divide the poem into two parts?
2. In "l(a" how does the shape of the poem reflect its content?
3. In the second stanza of "l(a," each line alternates in a pattern of one short letter and one tall letter. What natural motion (illustrated in the poem) might Cummings be mimicking with this visual effect?

Review: Structure

As you learned on pages 448–449, **structure** refers to the organization of words, images, and ideas in a poem. Think about how form and structure work together in Cummings's poems.

Partner Activity With a classmate, examine how Cummings organizes the ideas in each of these poems. Create a graphic organizer like the one shown below for each poem. List the **theme,** or main idea, of the poem in the first box and then list the images and ideas from the poem that are related to the theme.

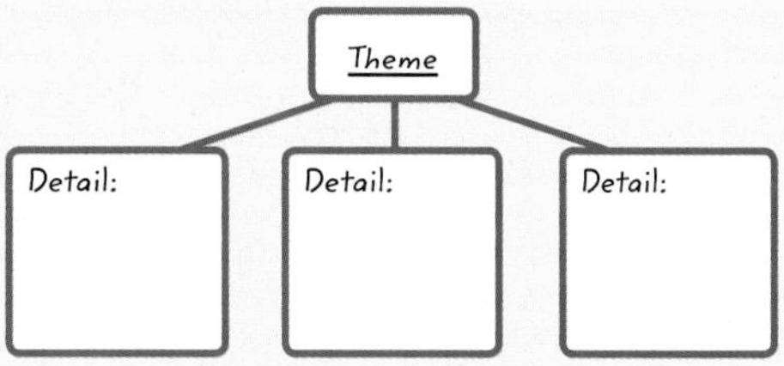

After You Read

Assess

1. Sample answer: It seemed playful and made me more interested in the poems.
2. (a) "little i" is looking out of a window at the sunset. (b) They are the same person at different times in life.
3. (a) "little i" thinks the sunset is beautiful. (b) It makes up for the sadness of the day ending.
4. (a) A leaf is falling. (b) The rest of the poem—the word "loneliness"—describes the feeling that the image of a solitary leaf evokes.
5. They suggest that the speaker himself might be nearing the "sunset" or "autumn" of his own life now.
6. The pun refers to the speaker's younger self and to the "little eye" looking out the window.
7. Students should support their answers.
8. Students should support their answers.

Literary Element

1. Cummings repeats the same stanza pattern one-line, two-line, one-line in the top half and the bottom half of the poem, and adds extra space between these two halves.
2. The tall thin shape is like the path of the falling leaf described in the poem. Or, The poem is shaped like the number one, which appears several times in the poem and also reflects the idea of being alone.
3. He is likely mimicking the twisting or swaying of a leaf floating to the ground.

Progress Check

Can students identify form?

If No → See Unit 3 Teaching Resources Book, p. 40.

Review: Structure

Responses will vary. Students should support their themes with evidence from the text.

After You Read

Assess

Reading Strategy

1. C is the correct answer. By breaking the word *loneliness* into smaller parts Cummings is able to create multiple ideas.

Progress Check

Can students analyze style?

If No → See Unit 3 Teaching Resources Book, p. 41.

For additional selection assessment, see Assessment Resources, pp. 113–114.

To create custom assessments online, go to Progress Reporter Online Assessment.

To create custom assessments using software, use ExamView Assessment Suite.

Academic Vocabulary

definition: feeling or showing nervous tension
synonyms: stressed, nervous
antonyms: relaxed, carefree
sample sentence: I always feel tense the night before a test.

Reading Strategy Analyze Style

SAT Skills Practice

1. Cummings probably placed the letters *one* in line 7 of "l(a" in order to
   (A) create a stanza with lines of one, two, and three characters
   (B) make the poem easier to read
   (C) reinforce the sense of loneliness with the word *one*
   (D) represent a pile of fallen leaves
   (E) emphasize that the whole poem resembles the numeral 1

Academic Vocabulary

*In "who are you,little i," the beauty of the sunset relaxes the speaker and keeps him from feeling **tense** about the day ending.*

Tense is an academic word. More familiar words that are similar in meaning are *nervous, worried,* and *edgy.* To study this word further, fill out the graphic organizer below.

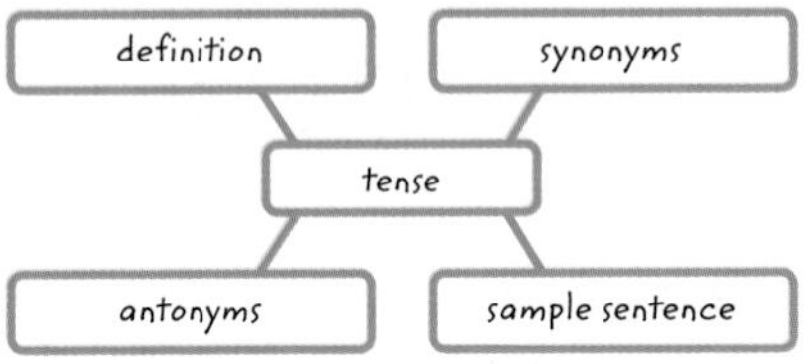

For more on academic vocabulary, see pages 54–55 and R79–R81.

Connect to *Art*

Create a Collage

Assignment Using words and images, make a collage about a particular place in nature.

Investigate Choose a specific place in nature that inspires you, and freewrite for several minutes to develop ideas about the place. Then review your writing to create a list of the ideas that you feel best reflect the place.

Create Using your idea list, begin searching through old magazines, newspapers, and other print media products. Cut out words and images that match or are similar to the ideas you listed. You also can search for images online and print them out.

Once you have your words and images printed or cut, organize them into a collage. Plan to keep words and images that are related near each other. For example, if you have an image of something that is meant to be beautiful, you might consider putting the word *beautiful* across or near the image.

Once you have your collage organized, begin to glue or paste everything down. Be sure to start with the bottom layers. If you have access to creative software, you can follow these steps and create a collage on a computer using only digital images.

Report Write a descriptive paragraph about your chosen place. The paragraph should be written as a companion piece to the collage. In other words, it should elaborate on the words and images in the collage, explaining how everything ties together to suggest the place you chose.

LOG ON Literature Online

Selection Resources For Selection Quizzes, eFlashcards, and Reading-Writing Connection activities, go to glencoe.com and enter QuickPass code GL49787u3.

Connect to *Art*

Students' collages should
- depict or reflect a specific place in nature
- combine a variety of words and images
- use the words and images to support each other
- be accompanied by a descriptive paragraph that elaborates on the collage

For grammar practice, see Unit 3 Teaching Resources Book, p. 42.

Before You Read

World Literature
Scotland

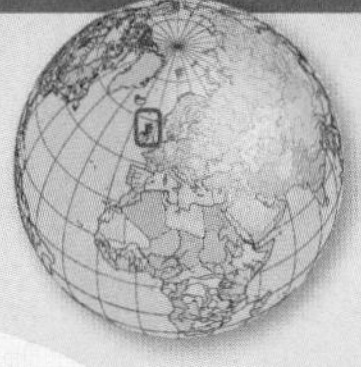

A Red, Red Rose

Meet **Robert Burns**
(1759–1796)

Robert Burns wrote more than six hundred poems. If you have ever sung "Auld Lang Syne" on New Year's Eve, then you are familiar with one of his most famous works. He is considered the national poet of Scotland, and the critic Raymond Bentman says, "Robert Burns is the first truly modern poet in British literature."

> *"For my own part I never had the least thought or inclination of turning poet till I got once heartily in Love. . . ."*
>
> —Robert Burns

Early Years Burns was born in Alloway, Scotland. His father was a tenant farmer, and Burns worked as a plowboy. However, because his family valued reading and writing, his father tutored Burns and his brothers at home. Burns grew up poor but well read. He even taught himself to read French. He also began writing poetry in Scottish dialect. As an adult, he was unsuccessful in making a living at farming and even less so as a flax weaver.

Unexpected Success In addition to his financial woes, Burns had other problems. He wanted to marry his girlfriend Jean Armour. When her family refused to let them marry, Burns decided to leave Scotland for the West Indies (Jamaica). To raise money for the voyage, he planned to sell a volume of the poems he had written. This book, *Poems, Chiefly in the Scottish Dialect,* was an immediate success and Burns suddenly found himself famous. Armour's parents now considered Burns to be more worthy of their daughter and allowed them to marry.

Style and Form Burns wrote in the standard verse forms for eighteenth-century poets, namely epistles (verse letters), satires, epigrams, and elegies. But perhaps he realized that lyric poems would appeal to a wider audience, because in his later years he mainly wrote songs in Scottish dialect. These poems express a wide range of emotions, from rapture to despair. Some of the lyrics, such as those in "A Red, Red Rose," are deceptively simple. Burns was also sensitive enough to write many of these poems from a female point of view, often reflecting the perspective of women suffering from betrayal or loss of love. Burns's works have been translated into nearly fifty languages and have remained in print since 1786.

LOG ON **Literature** Online

Author Search For more about Robert Burns, go to glencoe.com and enter QuickPass code GL49787u3.

Before You Read

Focus

Bellringer Options

Daily Language Practice Transparency 47

Or display images associated with love, such as roses, hearts, and cupids.

Ask: What do these images suggest about the nature of romantic love? Have students consider as they read the poem how the speaker's love is or is not like a flower.

Selection Skills

A Red, Red Rose

Literary Elements
- Meter and Rhythm (SE pp. 462, 464)

Reading Skills
- Making Inferences About the Speaker (SE pp. 462, 463, 464)

Writing Skills/Grammar
- Write a Poem (SE p. 464)

Before You Read

Focus

Summary

The speaker describes his deep love by comparing it to a red rose and a melody. He says his love will last across years and miles.

For summaries in languages other than English, see Unit 3 Teaching Resources Book, pp. 45–50.

Literature and Reading Preview

Learning Objectives

For pages 461–464

In studying this text, you will focus on the following objectives:

Literary Study: Analyzing meter and rhythm.

Reading: Making inferences about the speaker.

Writing: Writing a poem.

Connect to the Poem

What images in nature would you use to express love? Write a journal entry about vivid images from nature you can use to express the emotion love.

Build Background

"A Red, Red Rose" is a love song that Robert Burns modeled after bits and pieces from various Scottish folk songs. He composed it to the tune of "Major Graham," a song from *Oswald's Companion Book,* published in the mid-1700s.

Set Purposes for Reading

Big Idea Nature Inspires

As you read "A Red, Red Rose," ask yourself, How does the author use aspects of nature in this poem?

Literary Element Meter and Rhythm

Rhythm is the pattern of beats created by the arrangement of stressed and unstressed syllables. Rhythm can be regular, with a predictable pattern, or irregular. When a poem has regular rhythm, the predictable pattern of syllables is called **meter.** Being aware of meter and rhythm can help you appreciate the beauty of a poem and help you grasp its purpose and meaning. As you read, ask yourself, How do the poem's meter and rhythm emphasize words and help convey meaning?

Reading Strategy Make Inferences About the Speaker

When you infer, you use reason and your experience to decipher the author's implied meaning. **Making inferences about the speaker** helps you determine and understand the author's purpose for writing a work of literature. As you read, ask yourself, What do the poem's details suggest about the speaker's tone and attitude, as well as about whom the speaker is addressing?

Tip: Chart Inferences Use a chart to record inferences that you draw about the speaker based on the details presented.

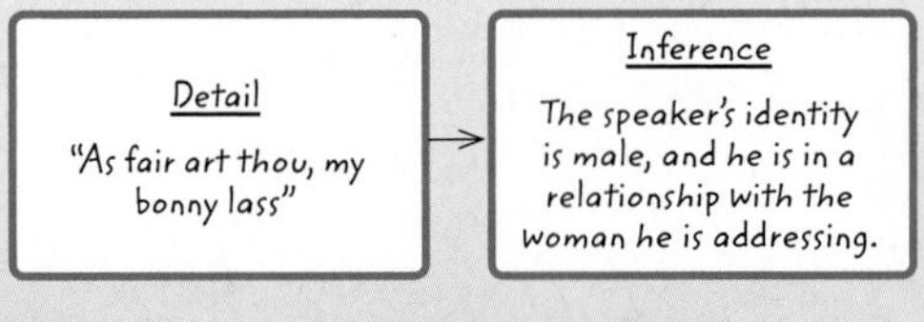
Detail
"As fair art thou, my bonny lass"
Inference
The speaker's identity is male, and he is in a relationship with the woman he is addressing.

FOX TROT by Bill Amend

Reading Practice

SMALL GROUP

Understand Standard Verse Forms Point out the standard verse forms used by Burns and other eighteenth-century poets. **Say:** An *epistle* is a letter. *Satire* uses wit to criticize people or societies. An *epigram* is a short poem that expresses a single thought. An *elegy* is a poem written to honor someone who has died. Ask students to provide examples of each. *(Students may name a television show that is satirical; say that a greeting card might be similar to an epigram. Students may also point out that a eulogy or obituary is similar to an elegy.)* Put students' responses on the board. Break students into groups and have them think of modern forms of communication that are similar to these verse forms. **Ask:** You probably don't write a lot of letters, but how do you communicate in writing with friends? *(Students may say that they send e-mail or text messages.)*

A Red, Red Rose

Robert Burns ☆

I

O, my love is like a red, red rose,
That's newly sprung in June.
O, my love is like the melody,
That's sweetly play'd in tune.

II

As fair art thou, my bonny lass,[1]
So deep in love am I,
And I will love thee still, my dear,
Till a' the seas gang dry.[2]

III

Till a' the seas gang dry, my dear,
And the rocks melt wi' the sun!
And I will love thee still, my dear,
While the sands o' life shall run.

IV

And fare thee weel,[3] my only love,
And fare thee weel a while!
And I will come again, my love,
Tho' it were ten thousand mile!

Rosa indica cruenta (blood-red Bengal rose). Pierre Joseph Redoute. Coloured Aquatint, 36.8 x 26.7 cm. Private collection.

1. *Bonny lass* means "pretty young woman" or "sweetheart."
2. *[Till a' the seas gang dry]* This line, in Standard English, is "Until all the seas go dry."
3. *Weel* means "well."

1 Nature Inspires *How does nature compare with the speaker's love?*

2 Make Inferences About the Speaker *What can you infer about the speaker's devotion to his love from these lines?*

Teach

Big Idea 1

Nature Inspires Answer: *Like the rose, the speaker's love is beautiful, fresh, and vibrant.*

Reading Strategy 2

Make Inferences About the Speaker Answer: *The speaker is committed to returning to his love, regardless of the obstacles that stand between them.*

ADVANCED **Ask advanced learners:** What can you infer about the speaker from the line "Till a' the seas gang dry, my dear," and "And fare thee weel, my only love,"? **Answer:** *The poet probably speaks in a dialect that he is trying to capture with his poetic style.*

Literary History ☆

From Rebel to Traditionalist

As a young man, Robert Burns considered himself a rebel. However, after the publication of his *Poems,* he wished to serve his Scottish people and preserve their songs. He spent the last years of his life collecting, editing, updating, and writing songs and poems in the Scottish tradition.

To check students' understanding of the selection, see Unit 3 Teaching Resources Book, p. 54.

Approaching Level

DIFFERENTIATED INSTRUCTION

Emerging Students may have trouble understanding the language in the poem. Read aloud the footnotes at the bottom of the page. Explain that Burns frequently uses the apostrophe in the poem to show that letters from words have been omitted. **Ask:** Why do you think he does this? Why doesn't he just spell out the entire word in the poem? *(Students may say that he does this to maintain the rhythm of the poem and to show how he wants the words to be spoken.)*

After You Read

Assess

1. Answers will vary.
2. (a) A newly bloomed rose and a pleasing melody (b) He may refer to both the woman's beauty and the depth of his love.
3. (a) He is leaving. (b) He will return no matter what.
4. Examples: "Till a' the seas gang dry" and "rocks melt wi' the sun." These show that his love is deep, long-lasting, and sincere.
5. Students should understand Keith's point that Burns knew that saturating a poem with love made for good poetry.
6. He uses vivid natural images of a red rose, seas drying, and rocks melting.
7. Answers will vary. Students should support their answer.

Literary Element

1.
Ó, mў lóve ĭs líke ă réd, réd róse,
Thăt's néwlў sprúng ĭn Júne.
Ó, mў lóve ĭs líke thĕ mélŏdў,
Thăt's swéetlў pláy'd ĭn túne.

2. The meter and rhythm stress key words and ideas.

Progress Check

Can students identify meter and rhythm?

If No → See Unit 3 Teaching Resources Book, p. 51.

For additional selection assessment, see Assessment Resources, pp. 115–116.

After You Read

Respond and Think Critically

Respond and Interpret

1. What image in the poem was most memorable or surprising to you? Explain.
2. (a)To what two things does the speaker compare his love in the first stanza? (b)When the speaker says "my love," do you think he refers to the person he loves or to the love that he feels for her? Explain.
3. (a)In the last stanza, what event is about to happen? (b)What do you think the speaker is trying to convey by mentioning the number of miles?

Analyze and Evaluate

4. How does the speaker use **hyperbole,** or exaggeration, in the poem? What is its purpose?
5. Literary critic Christina Keith wrote: "Each of Burns's four verses leads on to the next, with love, like a thread of gold, linking them all together. Love is the recurrent motif. Burns has at last realized you cannot have too much of it in a love-song. Or bring it in too soon. Or pitch it too high." What do you think she meant?

Connect

6. **Big Idea** **Nature Inspires** What descriptions from nature does Burns use to describe the power of his love?
7. **Connect to Today** Burns wrote this poem in traditional Scottish dialect. Do you think the poem would be as effective if it were written in modern-day English? Explain.

Literary Element Meter and Rhythm

Readers can analyze a poet's use of **meter** and **rhythm** by mapping the rhythm. This type of mapping is called **scansion**. To write out scansion, you write each line of the poem and use symbols above each syllable to show the rhythm. A ˘ indicates an unstressed syllable and a ´ shows stressed syllables.

1. Write out the scansion for the first four lines of the poem.
2. How effective did you find Burns's use of meter and rhythm in the poem? Explain.

Reading Strategy Make Inferences About the Speaker

Use the **inferences** you have made about the speaker to help you answer the following questions.

1. Who is the speaker and to whom is he speaking?
2. What did you infer about the speaker's feelings?

LOG ON **Literature** Online

Selection Resources For Selection Quizzes, eFlashcards, and Reading-Writing Connection activities, go to glencoe.com and enter QuickPass code GL49787u3.

Academic Vocabulary

Burns's first book of poetry helped him to ***attain*** *sudden, unexpected fame.*

Attain is an academic word. Like its more familiar synonym *achieve,* the word *attain* is typically used to describe an impressive accomplishment. Would you rather **attain** fame or wealth? Explain.

For more on academic vocabulary, see pages 54–55 and R79–R81.

Writing

Write a Poem in Verse Write a two- or three-stanza poem following the scansion you mapped out for "A Red, Red Rose." The poem can be about any subject, but it should employ a simple rhyme scheme. When you are done, check the meter by tapping the syllables.

Reading Strategy

1. A lover; the woman he loves
2. His love is sincere but his expression is exaggerated.

Academic Vocabulary

Answers will vary. Students' answers should demonstrate an understanding of *attain.*

Writing

Students' poems should

- have two or three stanzas
- employ simple rhyme

Before You Read

A Noiseless Patient Spider

Meet **Walt Whitman**
(1819–1892)

When Walt Whitman first published *Leaves of Grass,* a collection of poetry that broke with tradition both in form and content, it caused an uproar. A critic for the *Boston Intelligencer* wrote, "The author should be kicked from all decent society as below the level of brute . . . it seems to us that he must be some escaped lunatic, raving in pitiable delirium."

Whitman, however, refused to give up. After all, not everyone disliked *Leaves of Grass.* Ralph Waldo Emerson, a major figure in American literature, praised the collection of poems as "the most extraordinary piece of wit and wisdom" the United States had yet produced. Today, *Leaves of Grass* is considered one of the most important works in American literature, and Whitman is regarded as one of the first uniquely American poets.

> *"I am as bad as the worst, but thank God I am as good as the best."*
>
> —Walt Whitman

Early Years Walt Whitman was born in Long Island, New York. His family moved to Brooklyn when he was four years old. Unfortunately, the move proved to be financially unsuccessful, and young Walt was forced to leave school to help support the growing family. Whitman's early departure from school did not prevent him from obtaining an education. While working for a printer, he discovered a love of books and literature, and read everything he could find. When he was seventeen, Whitman became a schoolteacher. He left teaching to pursue his interest in journalism, working as an editor for several New York and Brooklyn newspapers. On his own time, he began to experiment with writing poetry.

Civil War Years During the Civil War, Whitman went to Virginia to care for his injured brother George. While in Virginia, he published two more collections of poetry, *Drum-Taps* and *Sequel to Drum-Taps.* Two of Whitman's most famous poems, "When Lilacs Last in the Dooryard Bloom'd" and "O Captain! My Captain!" are found in these volumes. Both poems are elegies written for Abraham Lincoln, whom Whitman greatly admired.

Final Years Whitman spent his final years in his modest home in Camden, New Jersey. One year before he died, Whitman wrote an essay in which he looked back upon his life. He ended the essay on a hopeful note, saying, "The strongest and sweetest songs remain yet to be sung."

LOG ON **Literature** Online

Author Search For more about Walt Whitman, go to glencoe.com and enter QuickPass code GL49787u3.

Before You Read

Focus

Bellringer Options

Selection Focus Transparency 21

Daily Language Practice Transparency 48

Or display images of spiders.

Ask: What associations might people have with spiders? Have students consider as they read what the spider and its web stand for in the poem.

Selection Skills

A Noiseless Patient Spider

Literary Elements
- Free Verse (SE pp. 466, 467, 468)
- Tone (SE p. 468)

Vocabulary Skills
- Word Usage (SE p. 469)
- Academic Vocabulary (SE p. 469)

Reading Skills
- Monitor Comprehension (SE pp. 466, 469)

Writing Skills/Grammar
- Apply Rhythm (SE p. 469)

Before You Read

Focus

Summary

The poem's speaker contemplates a spider as it casts its web into a vast open space and suggests that he and the spider share the same destiny.

For summaries in languages other than English, see Unit 3 Teaching Resources Book, pp. 56–61.

Vocabulary

Synonym Scramble Write the three new vocabulary words on the chalkboard. In the middle of the board, tape synonyms of each vocabulary word. Have volunteers come up to the board and move the synonyms into the correct column.

For additional vocabulary practice, see Unit 3 Teaching Resources Book, p. 64.

Literature and Reading Preview

Connect to the Poem

What unique qualities come to mind when you think about a spider? List these qualities and provide an example of or explanation for each quality.

Build Background

Spiders can spin a long thread called a dragline, which they use to cross through the air from one point to another. The spider spins a ball of thread to form a sticky anchor. Then it swings on the dragline to a new place. Upon landing, it spins a new anchor, creating a bridge to move back and forth on.

Set Purposes for Reading

Big Idea Nature Inspires

As you read the poem, ask yourself, How does the speaker compare the spider's actions to aspects of human behavior?

Literary Element Free Verse

Free verse is poetry that has no fixed pattern of meter, rhyme, line length, or stanza arrangement. As you read, ask yourself, What effects does Whitman achieve by not following meter, rhyme, and traditional poetic structures?

Reading Strategy Monitor Comprehension

When you **monitor your comprehension,** you think about how well you understand what you are reading. A poem can pack a lot into a few lines. So it is important to often pause to ask questions. As you read, ask yourself, How could I restate these lines? Is there another meaning beneath the literal one? and How can I use my own knowledge and experiences to understand the poet's meaning?

Tip: Paraphrase As you ask questions to monitor your comprehension, use a chart to restate the poet's thoughts in your own words.

Lines of Poem	Restated
1 and 2	I saw a quiet, patient spider standing alone on the edge of a rock.

Learning Objectives

For pages 465–469

In studying this text, you will focus on the following objectives:

Literary Study: Analyzing free verse.

Reading: Monitoring comprehension by paraphrasing and questioning.

Writing: Applying rhythm in a poem.

Vocabulary

isolated (ī′ sə lāt′ əd) *adj.* alone, cut off from others; p. 467 *The cabin stood in an isolated clearing, far away from any other structures.*

detached (di tacht′) *adj.* separated, apart; p. 467 *After moving to a new town, I felt detached from my old friends and surroundings.*

ceaselessly (sēs′ lis lē) *adv.* without stopping; continually; p. 467 *The speaker went on and on, ceaselessly stressing his point of view.*

Tip: Word Usage When you encounter a new word, it might help you to answer a specific question about it. For example, upon encountering the word *isolated,* you might ask yourself, When have I felt isolated from something and how did I correct the situation to make that feeling go away?

Writing Practice

Write a Poem in Free Verse Tell students that free verse has no boundaries, patterns, or rules. Poets can write any way they choose. Point out while poets writing in free verse do not worry about meter, rhythm, and rhyme, they do weave other literary devices into their poems such as symbolism and figurative language.

Have students write a poem in free verse about an inspiring creature of nature. Have students read the poem to the class. Then ask students to explain why they chose the creature of their choice.

A Noiseless Patient Spider

Walt Whitman

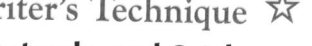

Crossing the Spider Web (detail). Victor Hugo. Musee de la Ville de Paris, France.

A noiseless patient spider,
I mark'd where on a little promontory[1] it stood **isolated**,
Mark'd how to explore the vacant vast surrounding,
It launch'd forth filament,[2] filament, filament, out of itself,
Ever unreeling them, ever tirelessly speeding them.

☆ And you O my soul where you stand,
Surrounded, **detached**, in measureless oceans of space,
Ceaselessly musing, venturing, throwing, seeking the spheres[3]
to connect them,
1 Till the bridge you will need be form'd, till the ductile[4]
anchor hold,
2 Till the gossamer[5] thread you fling catch somewhere, O my soul.

1. A *promontory* is a high ridge of rock or land, jutting out into a body of water.
2. Here, *filament* refers to the spider's thin thread of silk.
3. The phrase *seeking the spheres* means "seeking the truth about the heavens."
4. Something that is *ductile* (dukt′ əl) is easily molded or shaped.
5. Here, *gossamer* means "light, delicate, filmy."

3 Free Verse *In what ways are lines 3–4 good examples of free verse?*

Vocabulary

isolated (ī′ sə lāt′ əd) *adj.* alone, cut off from others
detached (di tacht′) *adj.* separated, apart
ceaselessly (sēs′ lis lē) *adv.* without stopping; continually

Teach

Big Idea 1

Nature Inspires **Ask:** What is the connection between the spider and the speaker's soul? *(The spider's weaving its clinging threads reminds the speaker of his soul's search for meaning.)*

Reading Strategy 2

Monitor Comprehension

ENGLISH LEARNERS Help English learners to understand the poem by having them paraphrase each stanza to monitor comprehension.

Literary Element 3

Free Verse **Answer:** *The lines are of different lengths; there is no regular meter; there is no rhyme.*

Writer's Technique ☆

Apostrophe and Catalog

Whitman uses two traditional poetic devices in this poem—apostrophe and catalog. Apostrophe is the addressing of a person or object. It often begins with an exclamation, such as *O* or *Oh*. A catalog is a list of people, things, or attributes. In this poem, Whitman addresses his soul ("O my soul") and catalogs its ceaseless activity (musing, venturing, throwing, and seeking).

Approaching Level

DIFFERENTIATED INSTRUCTION

Emerging Students may need guidance to understand the meaning of the poem. Read the poem aloud and have students use the footnotes to determine the meaning of unfamiliar words. Explain that in the first stanza, the speaker is watching a spider spin its web. The spider throws out filaments many times into its vast surroundings. It is trying to find a place to anchor the filaments so it can spin a web.

In the second stanza, Whitman speaks directly to his own soul. He feels like the spider—alone in a vast world—and is searching for a connection.

To check students' understanding of the selection, see Unit 3 Teaching Resources Book, p. 66.

After You Read

Assess

1. Students' answers will vary.
2. (a) It stands on a rocky overlook casting out silk strands. (b) It may use the strands to travel to a new location.
3. (a) *Patient, noiseless, isolated, tireless in its efforts* (b) He admires and respects it for its hard work and courage.
4. (a) Both are isolated in empty space and try to find an anchor. (b) The speaker might be seeking answers about life.
5. (a) Unlike the quiet, hard-working spider, the speaker is restless and unsure. (b) Students should support their answers with reasons.
6. (a) The filament is the spider's silky thread. The speaker's gossamer thread is a metaphor for the speaker's searching soul. (b) It is effective because it is visual, tactile, and easy to imagine.
7. (a) He admires the spider's courage and tenacity; he identifies with the difficulty of its task. (b) Some students may have new respect for what spiders do.
8. The speaker is inspired by the spider's actions; the spider has caused him to examine his own feelings, needs, and emotions.
9. When critics did not accept his work, Whitman may have felt lonely and isolated, like the spider. As the spider tirelessly produced the silky thread, Whitman continued to write, despite the critics. Answers may vary.

After You Read

Respond and Think Critically

Respond and Interpret

1. What did you like best about this poem? What did you like least? Explain.
2. (a)Where is the spider and what is it doing? (b)What might be the purpose of the spider's actions?
3. (a)What adjectives does the speaker use to describe the spider and its actions? (b)What do those adjectives suggest about his feelings toward the spider?
4. (a)How is the predicament of the speaker's soul like that of the spider? (b)What might the speaker be looking or hoping for?

Analyze and Evaluate

5. (a)How might the speaker be using the words *noiseless* and *patient* to contrast the spider with himself? (b)Do you feel sympathy for the speaker? Explain why or why not.
6. (a)The speaker compares the spider's "filament" with his soul's "gossamer thread." What is the meaning of each term? (b)Do you think the image of a person's "gossamer thread" is effective? Explain.
7. (a)In your own words, summarize the speaker's feelings for the spider. (b)Does this poem make you think about spiders in a different way? Explain why or why not.

Connect

8. **Big Idea** **Nature Inspires** In your opinion, why does this poem fit into the Big Idea of "Nature Inspires"?
9. **Connect to the Author** Reviews of Walt Whitman's early poetry were very negative, but he kept writing. In what ways might the first stanza of the poem be a reflection of Whitman and his career?

Literary Element Free Verse

When writing **free verse,** a poet varies meter, rhyme, line length, and stanza arrangement to emphasize an idea or create a tone. Whitman's use of free verse initially shocked critics and readers who thought that he had broken the rules of poetry.

1. When free verse was first used, it forced people to redefine poetry. What do you think is poetic about Whitman's work? Provide examples from the text.
2. In "A Noiseless Patient Spider," how is free verse like ordinary speech? How is it different?

Review: Tone

As you learned on page 308, **tone** is the author's attitude toward his or her subject matter. Tone is conveyed through elements such as word choice, sentence structure, and figures of speech or comparisons. A writer's tone might convey a variety of attitudes, such as sympathy, objectivity, or humor.

Partner Activity Meet with a classmate to identify the overall tone of "A Noiseless Patient Spider." Use a diagram like the one shown.

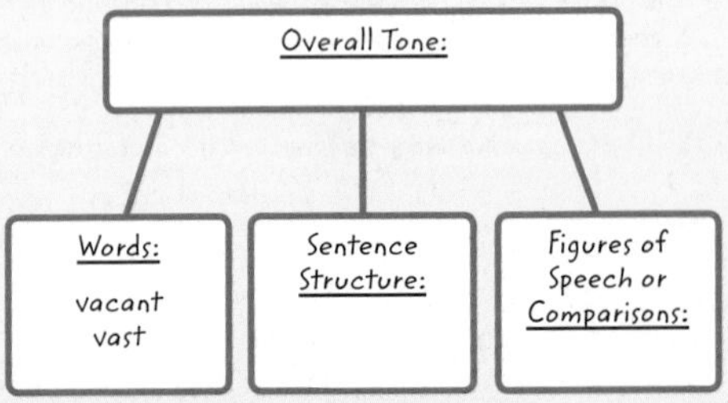

Literary Element

1. Students should support answers with references to the poem.
2. It expresses thoughts in sentences. Some of the language is poetic with a distinct and regular meter or vivid vocabulary—*promontory, filament,* and *gossamer.* The speaker addresses his soul in a poetic manner.

Progress Check

Can students identify free verse?

If No → See Unit 3 Teaching Resources Book, p. 62.

Review: Tone

Students may find that the tone is reverent, awed, or searching. Challenge students to explain how their evidence supports their ideas.

Reading Strategy Monitor Comprehension

A reader can find deeper meanings by pausing from time to time to ask questions and to rephrase certain lines in his or her own words. Review the chart you created while reading the poem.

1. Reread lines 6–7. What does the speaker mean by "detached, in measureless oceans of space"?
2. Reread lines 9–10. What does the image of building a bridge suggest?
3. In the final line, why might the speaker have chosen to use the vague word "somewhere"?

Vocabulary Practice

Practice with Usage Respond to these statements to help you explore the meanings of the boldface vocabulary words from the selection.

1. Explain a situation where someone might feel **isolated.**
2. Describe the behavior of a person who is **detached.**
3. Give an example of a cause or idea you would work **ceaselessly** for.

Academic Vocabulary

Like other poets, Whitman explored ***abstract*** *concepts, such as eternity and beauty.*

Abstract is a word that has different meanings. Using context clues, try to figure out the meaning of *abstract* in each sentence and explain the difference between the two meanings.

1. The teacher called Frankie's painting of swirled colors **abstract,** because there weren't any concrete objects or people in it.
2. The paragraph-long **abstract** beginning the article help me to quickly learn if the article had the information I needed for my report.

For more on academic vocabulary, see pages 54–55 and R79–R81.

Write with Style

Apply Rhythm

Assignment Spend time listening to how people talk. Listen specifically for the rhythm of conversational speech. Write a poem that uses the rhythms of natural speech, and read it aloud to the class.

Get Ideas Whitman used an observation from nature to express his ideas in "A Noiseless, Patient Spider." Before choosing a topic for your poem, spend time observing the world around you. Flip through magazines and newspapers. What is interesting to you? What reminds you of your own life?

Use a web diagram to brainstorm ideas about one of your observations. Then make a statement about what you observed and how it relates to life.

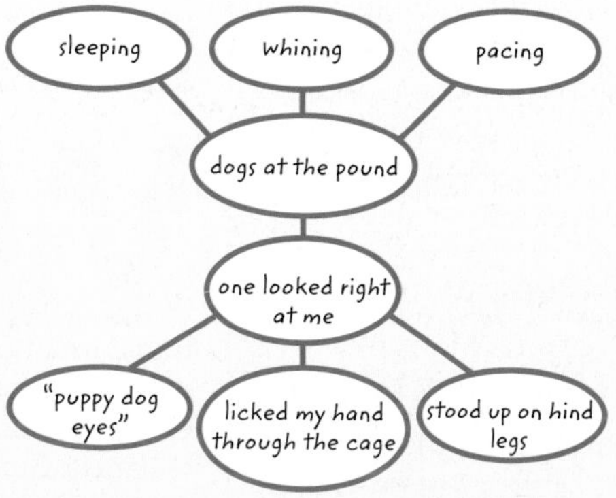

A good dog is like a good friend—it understands you right from the start.

Give It Structure Use your diagram as a springboard to elaborate on your subject. Speak or write about it in a conversational way—as if you were passionately sharing your thoughts with a friend.

Look at Language Choose language that directly engages listeners. Make sure the poem's language and rhythms reflect your own style of speech.

LOG ON **Literature Online**

Selection Resources For Selection Quizzes, eFlashcards, and Reading-Writing Connection activities, go to glencoe.com and enter QuickPass code GL49787u3.

For grammar practice, see Unit 3 Teaching Resources Book, p. 65.

For additional selection assessment, see Assessment Resources, pp. 117–118.

To create custom assessments online, go to Progress Reporter Online Assessment.

To create custom assessments using software, use ExamView Assessment Suite.

After You Read

Assess

Reading Strategy

1. The speaker feels isolated, small, and insignificant in the vast universe.
2. The narrator yearns to be able to cross into a new and meaningful part of his life.
3. The speaker does not know where he will find answers, but yearns to make a connection somewhere.

Progress Check

Can students monitor comprehension?

If No → See Unit 3 Teaching Resources Book, p. 63.

Vocabulary

Answers will vary. Sample responses:

1. A student new to a school might feel isolated.
2. A person who is detached acts remote and uninterested.
3. I would work ceaselessly for helping homeless people in my neighborhood.

Academic Vocabulary

1. *Abstract* means "not concrete."
2. An abstract is a summary.

Write with Style

Students' poems should

- be written in the rhythms of natural speech
- be conversational and expressive
- focus on a specific subject—personal, social, or political
- use strong, engaging language

TIME

Focus

Summary

After describing how her visits to Cumberland Island refresh her spirit, the writer tells of a recent visit there with a naturalist. Later, as she walks alone, she thinks about life cycles and how life is a gift and a miracle.

For summaries in languages other than English, see Unit 3 Teaching Resources Book, pp. 68–73.

Teach

Preview the Article

1. The writer's feelings and thoughts
2. The writer's feelings about the island

For an audio recording of this selection, use Listening Library Audio CD-ROM.

Readability Scores

Dale-Chall: 7.0
DRP: 60
Lexile: 1130

Learning Objectives

For pages 470–473

In studying this text, you will focus on the following objectives:

Reading:
Previewing the article.
Determining main idea and supporting details.

Set a Purpose for Reading

Read to understand how nature influences one writer's perspective on life.

Preview the Article

1. Based on the title, what do you think this article will be about?
2. Scan the article's subheadings. What do you think the writer will describe?

Reading Strategy

Determine Main Idea and Supporting Details

The **main idea** of a text is the most important thing the writer wants to convey about their subject. The main idea is not always obvious; you may have to identify it from the details in the text.

As you read, use a graphic organizer to organize your thoughts.

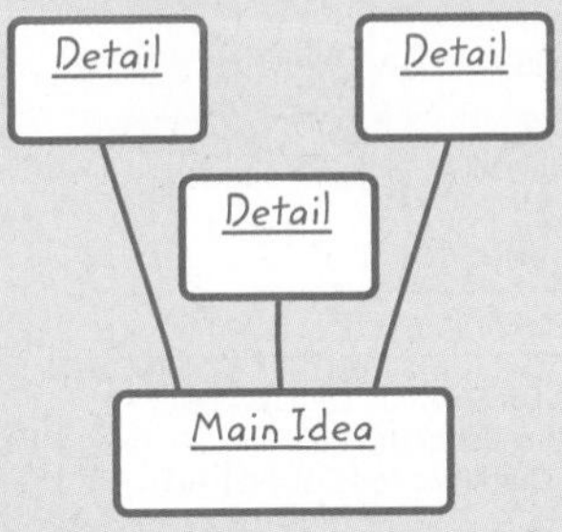

TIME

The Island Within

On a walk on Cumberland Island, a writer dusts off her sense of wonder—and discovers the healing power of nature.

By LESLIE MARSHALL

WHENEVER I FEEL WEARY, WORN OUT, AND bogged down by the complications of my modern life, all I have to do is walk into nature. The moment I step off the path of my daily routine and let myself wander, a transformation begins. For me, a walk just about anywhere will do. But a walk on Cumberland Island, off the coast of Georgia, is as good as it gets.

Part of Cumberland's appeal is classic island magic—that mix of adventure and simplicity that comes with geographic isolation. During a visit to this 36,415-acre wilderness, there will be no shopping, no catching a movie or a play, no working out at the gym. There will be only that rare luxury: free time.

Every time I set foot on Cumberland, I experience the fresh sense of arriving on a new stage. It is as if I am shedding my skin. Upon arriving, I am certain that my spirit will be restored by the time I leave. The island will do its work, and so will I.

Stepping Stones to Growth

I have been coming to Cumberland for years; it is a place layered with personal memories. The trips I have made here over time—some alone, some with large groups of friends, some with my husband and three children—form a series of stepping stones that chart a path of self-knowledge and growth. I have experienced some of my most peaceful moments here—and

Writing Practice

Write a Description Point out that on this page the author introduces readers to Cumberland Island, a place that is special to her because it allows her to step off the path of her daily routine and relax. Read aloud this sentence to students: "Upon arriving, I am certain that my spirit will be restored by the time I leave." Initiate a discussion in which students brainstorm places where they go to rest and feel restored. Write some of their responses on the board. Have students write a descriptive essay about their special place. Students may choose to model their description after the author's description in this essay. Their writing should demonstrate an understanding of correct use of grammar, punctuation, and sentence structure.

MAGNOLIA PETALS ARE LANDING STRIPS FOR POLLINATING INSECTS.

SALT MARSHES AND BOGS ARE HOMES FOR A DIVERSITY OF WILDLIFE.

some of the most harrowing. And I have had a few lessons in the art of holding on and letting go.

On this particular trip, I have come alone, leaving my children safe at home on another island, Manhattan. After a long, gray winter in the city, I have come to dust off my sense of wonder. I have no doubt that Cumberland will jump-start my heart, mind, and imagination.

1 Walking in Wonder

Stacia Hendricks, a naturalist who has lived on Cumberland for 14 years, is sitting beside me at sunrise, softly sharing her understanding of nature. "We are sitting on top of the forest right now," she tells me. "Those are the tops of live oak trees and wax myrtle bushes sticking out of the sand. They are the reason the dunes are here. They anchor the dunes." Her hushed enthusiasm is contagious. "Look at this guy," she exclaims, holding up a sea-oat seed that has sprouted a shoot of green. "Isn't he beautiful?" Stacia explains how over the years the dunes shift in response to wet and dry cycles, in a slow-motion imitation of the sea.

To walk six square feet of forest, dune field, or marsh with Stacia is to invite a lifetime of insights into the complex play of nature, science, history, commerce, and human emotion. After one early-morning inland walk, I rush home and fill several pages of a journal with a quick summary of what I've just learned. I write about allelopathic trees, like the magnolia, whose leaves contain a toxic substance that is drawn out by rain. When they fall and cover the ground, these leaves prevent other plants from growing. I write about epiphytic plants, like the Spanish moss that hangs from the live oaks all over the island. These plants have no roots, but they absorb enough moisture through their fuzzy bodies to get nourishment and thrive.

Reading the Landscape

Walking through the forest, Stacia has shown me the Lyonia plant, which is the first plant to burst into flames as fire approaches. Remarkably enough, it is also the first plant to begin growing after a fire (thanks to its nutrient-rich ashes). Stacia also shows me the sensitive (or "shy") plant, a delicate fern-like creation with a bright fuchsia blossom, which folds up its leaves when touched. Then she points out the woolly mullein plant (also known as Hunter's Friend

TIME

Teach

Reading Strategy 1

Determine Main Idea and Supporting Details Ask students to read the subheads to predict the writer's thoughts and ideas.

Ask: What do you think Marshall will talk about in the section called "Walking in Wonder"? *(She may recall amazing things she saw on a walk.)*

ENGLISH LEARNERS Point out to English learners that *wonder* is a multiple-meaning word. Have students look up *wonder* in a dictionary to help them make predictions about what the section entitled "Walking in Wonder" will contain.

English Learners

DIFFERENTIATED INSTRUCTION

Intermediate Students may have trouble with the scientific plant names in the essay. Have them list difficult or unfamiliar words such as live oak, wax myrtle bushes, sea-oat, allelopathic trees, and epiphytic trees. Have students work together using library resources or the Internet to find information about the plants. Encourage them to print a picture of each. Students who are interested in botany may wish to create a visual multimedia presentation to illustrate and discuss plants on Cumberland Island.

TIME

Teach

Reading Strategy 1

Determine Main Idea and Supporting Details

Ask: What is the main idea of the paragraph that begins "There is so much I haven't yet touched on." *(The writer realizes there is much more to learn from the land.)* **Ask:** What details support this idea? *(She points to all the things she wants to learn about and what her friend has taught her.)*

Writer's Technique ☆

Parenthetical Information

Parentheses provide nonessential but related information in a sentence or paragraph. This parenthetical information adds color and detail to the selection and creates an informal tone.

To check students' understanding of the selection, see Unit 3 Teaching Resources Book, p. 75.

SOUTHERN RED CEDAR BERRIES IN SPRING

WILD POINSETTIA SEEDS STUDIED UP CLOSE

because its leaves make good emergency toilet paper); Lion's Paw (often considered a weed, ☆ it actually produces a beautiful orange flower); and the prickly ash, called the toothache tree by Native Americans because chewing its bark numbs the mouth. (I tried it—it works!)

Stacia tells me that Native Americans, Cumberland's first residents, began living here around 2000 B.C. Next came the Spanish, who brought horses to the island. The wild horses that roam everywhere now are descendants of their horses, the work horses kept by plantation owners who came later, and the fancy riding horses imported in the 20th century. Today, most of the island is owned by the National Park Service.

1 There is so much I haven't yet touched on—the details of animal, fish, and bird life, the sweet symphony of sounds that has begun to sift into recognizable voices. ("Sweet, sweet, I'm so sweet!" calls the yellow-throated warbler.) It is not that I need to know all these things, or care if I get them exactly right. But a nature-walk tutorial from Stacia reminds me of how much is to be read in the activity in the landscape. After spending time with Stacia, I am ready to explore this island alone, and to explore my own inner island.

A Solitary Stroll

I am walking in the heat of midmorning around the ruins of Dungeness, a huge mansion that was rebuilt by Thomas and Lucy Carnegie in 1881 and burned down in 1959. (Thomas Carnegie, a steel baron, bought a large part of the island in 1881.) Along the way, I have stopped to tease a few doodlebugs—small insects that hide in the sand and wait to catch unlucky ants. I have picked up a beautiful owl feather and, after admiring the way it tapers off to make owls the quietest fliers, I've tucked it behind my ear. (Airplane designers studied owl feathers, Stacia says.) Even in the morning light, the ivy-covered remains of Dungeness are grand and exotic. "It makes a much more beautiful ruin than it ever did a mansion," the late Lucy Ferguson, granddaughter of Lucy and Thomas Carnegie, is said to have commented. It's impossible to stroll across the former lawns and gardens, now the home of wild horses and pigs, without feeling a rush of nostalgia. Everything passes, everything rots, everything gets recycled, this once grand home seems to say.

On the front lawn, a dead magnolia tree lost to lightning stands against a backdrop of

Research Practice

SPIRAL REVIEW **Research Careers** Tell students that a *naturalist* is a biologist who studies natural history, including botany, which is the study of plants, and zoology, which is the study of animals. Invite interested students to learn about becoming a naturalist. Have them use library and Internet resources to read about how they would prepare for this career and what kind of activities they would perform on the job. Students should create a list of questions to help guide their research. Allow students to share their findings.

THE WRITER SITTING UNDER AN ANCIENT OAK

lush, green marsh. The magnolia must no longer be emitting its allelopathic poisons, for underneath it, all kinds of ragged plants have sprung up. Lightning is so random and so fierce.

Deeper in the forest now, on a road that leads to a pair of abandoned silos near where Stacia keeps her beehives, I pass a rotting log and a patch of mushrooms.

I remember what Stacia has explained about the wonders of bacteria—what a crucial role it plays in the cycles of decay and life. Death as a process is visible everywhere on this island. Cemeteries abound. A big Indian burial mound rises from the flat of the landing field; a plantation-era group of graves lies near the marsh. I pause and listen to the multitoned whisper of the forest. It is then that I come to a realization: The miracle is not that we die, but that we are given a chance to live. Cumberland jams the circuits with evidence of this simple, radical truth; but I remind myself that a walk anywhere, properly conducted, can do the same.

—Updated 2005, from REAL SIMPLE, August 2000

Respond and Think Critically

Respond and Interpret

1. Write a brief summary of the main ideas in this article before you answer the following questions. For help on writing a summary, see page 421.
2. In what ways do you think people can find solace in nature?
3. (a)With whom has Marshall made trips to Cumberland Island? (b)Why does she travel there so often?
4. (a)What kinds of information does Stacia Hendricks, the naturalist, share with the writer? (b)How does this knowledge affect Marshall?

Analyze and Evaluate

5. What adjectives would you use to describe Marshall's personality?
6. (a)Give examples from the text of figurative language. (b)Do they work well in this context? Why or why not?
7. Of all the trips Marshall has made to Cumberland Island, why do you think she chose to write about this one?

Connect

8. Compare the literary function and purpose of the spider in Walt Whitman's "A Noiseless Patient Spider" with that of the island in Leslie Marshall's "The Island Within."

TIME

Assess

1. Summaries should reflect the main ideas of the article.
2. Nature may comfort or awe with its silence and beauty.
3. (a) Her friends and her family (b) For peace of mind and inspiration
4. (a) Information about the island's plants and settlers (b) She contemplates the source of living things and their end.
5. *Optimistic, open, observant, introspective, and imaginative*
6. (a) "Arriving on a new stage," "as if I'm shedding my skin," "dust off my sense of wonder," and "read in the activity of the landscape" (b) They enhance the writer's style and give her narrative a lyrical tone.
7. Because of the new insights into nature she learned from Stacia Hendricks
8. Both the spider and the island are symbols of isolation and forms of inspiration.

For additional selection assessment, see Assessment Resources, pp. 121–122.

Approaching Level

DIFFERENTIATED INSTRUCTION

Emerging Help students see the connection between Marshall's experience at Cumberland Island and Whitman's observations in "A Noiseless Patient Spider." **Ask:** How do Marshall and Whitman feel when they observe nature? How do they connect with nature? *(Students may say that they feel calm and inspired when they observe nature. They may say that they connect with nature by noting how similar they are to nature—Whitman feels he is reaching out in the vastness around him like the spider, and Marshall contemplates that like everything else on Cumberland Island, she lives and will one day die.)*

Focus

Bellringer Options

Daily Language Practice Transparency 49

Or display images of the sky during different seasons or kinds of weather.

Ask: What do you notice about the sun and the sky during your day? How does the sky affect the way you feel?

As students read the selections, ask them to think about how the sun and sky affect the writers.

Connecting to the Reading Selections

Allow students to share their responses to the opening statement. Then have students discuss their experiences of reading the nature writing they have encountered in this unit. Challenge them to list characteristics of nature writing based on their experiences as readers.

Comparing Literature

Across Genres

Learning Objectives

For pages 474–485

In studying these texts, you will focus on the following objectives:

Literary Study: Comparing structure. Analyzing line and stanza.

Reading: Comparing author's ideas. Comparing and contrasting imagery.

Writing: Creating a timeline.

Compare Literature About Nature

You may have heard or read the phrase "communing with nature." When we commune with nature, we observe it closely, ponder it, and even lose ourselves in it. The three literary works compared here—two poems and a memoir—celebrate nature and demonstrate how deeply it rewards our close attention.

COMPARE THE Big Idea Nature Inspires

Nature inspires different thoughts in different people. One person may perceive nature as a safe, open place for people to play in. Others may perceive it as a deep mystery. Still others view nature as a school for sharpening the senses. As you read, ask yourself, What images does each writer use to suggest his or her view of nature?

COMPARE Structure

Literary works can be patterned in different ways. In poems, **structure** is sometimes created with rhythm, rhyme, repetition, or stanzas. In works of prose, there may be a variety of structures at work. For instance, works of prose may be structured by the order of the events they describe or by the elaboration of a simple idea during the course of the work. As you read, ask yourself, What pattern helps give coherence to each work?

COMPARE Ideas

The authors featured here have both similar and different ideas about nature's meaning and value. These ideas are sometimes stated outright; at other times, they are implied through the details of the works. As you read, ask yourself, What ideas about nature does each writer convey?

LOG ON Literature Online

Author Search For more about Vachel Lindsay, Lorraine Hansberry, and Natasha Trethewey, go to glencoe.com and enter QuickPass code GL49787u3.

Selection Skills

Comparing Literature

Literary Elements
- Structure (SE pp. 474, 485)
- Line and Stanza (SE pp. 476, 477, 478)

Reading Skills
- Compare and Contrast Imagery (SE pp. 476, 477, 478)

Vocabulary Skills
- Academic Vocabulary (SE, p. 478)

Listening/Speaking/Viewing Skills
- Visual Display (SE p. 485)

Writing Skills/Grammar
- Write a Timeline (SE, p. 478)

Before You Read

An Indian Summer Day on the Prairie

Meet **Vachel Lindsay**
(1879–1931)

Born in Springfield, Illinois, in a house associated with Abraham Lincoln's family, Lindsay considered himself to be a Midwesterner through and through. In his work, he attempted to embody the region's love of democracy, faith, and nature. Lindsay's parents hoped their son would become a doctor. To that end, Lindsay studied science at Hiram College. He also studied oratory, or the art of effective public speaking.

☆ **The Troubadour** After giving up his scientific studies, Lindsay spent time studying art in both Chicago and New York City. In New York, he lectured on art at a local YMCA. Through the experience, art and public speaking became intertwined in his life. At this time, Lindsay was also writing poems but having little success getting them published.

> *"No one cared for my pictures, no one cared for my verse, and I turned beggar in sheer desperation."*
>
> —Vachel Lindsay

At the age of twenty-seven, Lindsay began what was to become a famous walking trip from Florida to Illinois by way of Georgia, the Carolinas, and Kentucky. To support himself, Lindsay traded lectures and poetry recitals for food and shelter. He became a troubadour, or a wandering artist. It was a role that he would repeat many times in his life.

A Democratic Poet At thirty-four, Lindsay published his first book of poetry, *General William Booth Enters into Heaven and Other Poems.* Although this book did not receive high praise, Lindsay's next book, *The Congo and Other Poems,* thrust the poet into the public eye. In 1914 Lindsay recited his poem "The Congo" at a banquet sponsored by a poetry magazine. Many famous poets, including Carl Sandburg, were in attendance. When Lindsay read his poetry, he swayed, chanted, and shouted out words. Viewers said "he rocked on the balls of his feet—his eyes blazing, his arms pumping like pistons" and "his tone [changed] color in response to the noise and savage imagery of the lines."

Lindsay believed that poetry was an oral art form that all people could appreciate. In order to appeal to a broad audience, Lindsay consciously echoed vaudeville—popular variety shows that were performed before live audiences—in his rhythms and performance style. To this day, his poems are admired for their vivid imagery and persistent, thumping rhythms.

Before You Read

Focus

Big Idea

Nature Inspires **Ask:** What images and words come to mind when you recall a beautiful sunrise or sunset? Have students consider as they read how the poet uses words and imagery to describe the sun as it appears to move across the sky.

Cultural History ☆

Traveling Troubadours The tradition of the troubadour, or wandering minstrel, began during the Middle Ages throughout parts of western Europe. These poets and musicians often supported themselves by telling stories to large crowds at town events such as weddings and fairs. Thirsty for entertainment, the people of the era were captivated by the troubadours' lyrical stories of love and bravery.

Approaching Level

DIFFERENTIATED INSTRUCTION

Established Read the paragraph at the top of page 474. Have students connect to the selection by recalling a time when they communed with nature. Suggest that they write a paragraph about this experience. Remind students to produce legible work that shows accurate spelling and correct use of grammar, punctuation, and capitalization.

Before You Read

Focus

Summary

The speaker describes the sun at four times of the day. He compares it to a huntress, a fire, a wounded deer, and an aging eagle.

For summaries in languages other than English, see Unit 3 Teaching Resources Book, pp. 78–83.

Vocabulary

Words from Around the World Most students already know that many words in the English language have Greek and Latin roots. However, some foreign words have become such a part of the English language that we don't even realize that they aren't English words. You might point out that the word *troubadour* is French. Ask students to think of other foreign words that are commonly used in English. Some examples might be *petite* (French), *blitz* (German), and *plaza* (Spanish).

Literature and Reading Preview

Connect to the Poem

How would you describe a beautiful summer day? Write a journal entry describing a summer day from morning to evening.

Wigeon at Sunrise, 1994. Julian Novorol. Oil on canvas. Private collection.

Build Background

Dating back to as early as the late 1700s, the term *Indian summer* refers to the warm, dry, hazy days that occur during the autumn months after a killing frost.

Set Purposes for Reading

Big Idea Nature Inspires

As you read the poem, ask yourself, What parts of nature seem to have most inspired Vachel Lindsay?

Literary Element Line and Stanza

A **line** is a row of words in a poem. A **stanza** is a group of lines that forms a unit in a poem, much like a paragraph forms a unit in a prose selection. Usually stanzas are indicated by lines of space. As you read, ask yourself, How do the line and stanza breaks support the series of ideas in the poem?

Reading Strategy Compare and Contrast Imagery

Images are the "word pictures" that writers use to evoke emotional responses in readers. Most images appeal to one or more of the five senses. As you read, ask yourself, What ideas or feelings do the images convey?

Tip: Note Imagery Use a chart to note details that appeal to the five senses.

Image	Sense	Idea or Feeling Suggested by Image
huntress	sight	beauty

Reading Practice

SMALL GROUP

Metaphor Tell students that in the poem "An Indian Summer Day on the Prairie" Lindsay uses metaphors, a type of figurative language, to describe the sun. Pair up students and have them work together to revise their journal entries describing a summer day. Have students include metaphors in their journal entries. Encourage them to create metaphors for the sun. When they finish, ask volunteers to give examples. Write them on the board.

Ask: Do metaphors make your writing more descriptive? Why or why not? *(Some students may feel that metaphors help them create a more vivid picture in the reader's mind; others may feel that they make their writing difficult to understand.)*

An Indian Summer Day on the Prairie

Vachel Lindsay

Sunset, Hans Agersnap. Private collection.

In the Beginning
The sun is a huntress young,
The sun is red, red joy,
The sun is an Indian girl,
Of the tribe of the Illinois.[1]

Mid-morning
The sun is a smoldering fire,
That creeps through the high gray plain,
And leaves not a bush of cloud
To blossom with flowers of rain.

Noon
The sun is a wounded deer,
That treads pale grass in the skies,
Shaking his golden horns,
Flashing his baleful[2] eyes.

Sunset
The sun is an eagle old;
There in the windless west,
Atop of the spirit-cliffs
He builds him a crimson nest. ☆

1. The *Illinois,* or Illini, are a tribe of Native Americans who once lived in what is now the state of Illinois. Their descendants maintain headquarters in Miami, Oklahoma.

2. *Baleful* means "threatening" or "deadly."

1 Line and Stanza *What does each stanza describe?*

Compare and Contrast Imagery *In what way is this image like the one that begins the poem? How is it different?* **2**

Comparing Literature

Teach

Literary Element 1

Line and Stanza **Answer:** *Each stanza describes a particular time of day.*

Reading Strategy 2

Compare and Contrast Imagery **Answer:** *Both are metaphors that compare the sun to youth and age.*

APPROACHING Explain to approaching level learners that the poet uses a metaphor to compare the sun to living things. **Say:** Lindsay compares the sun to living things in order to make the sun more relatable to human experience.

For additional practice using the reading skill or strategy, see Unit 3 Teaching Resources Book, p. 85.

Writer's Technique ☆

Rhyme and Rhythm

Lindsay's poem uses a rhyme scheme and meter found in many traditional ballads and songs. In each stanza, the second and fourth lines rhyme, and each line contains three beats.

English Learners

DIFFERENTIATED INSTRUCTION

Early Advanced Students may need help understanding the many metaphors in Lindsay's poem. Remind them that a metaphor compares two things without using the words *like* or *as.* Point out that each stanza contains a metaphor and has a heading above it. Have them consider what the poet is saying about the sun through these metaphors. **Ask:** Why do you think the poet compared the early morning sun to an Indian girl? *(Students may say because the sun is young in the beginning of the day but grows older as it sets.)*

Interactive Read and Write

Other options for teaching this selection can be found in

- Interactive Read and Write for EL Students, pp. 107–111
- Interactive Read and Write for Approaching-Level Students, pp. 107–111
- Interactive Read and Write for On-Level Students, pp. 107–111

After You Read

Assess

1. Answers will vary.
2. (a) An Indian girl, a smoldering fire, a wounded deer, an old eagle (b) Each describes the sun at a different time of day.
3. (a) It is rising higher. (b) The sun destroys the clouds and, therefore, the chance of rain.
4. It shows the setting. The Indian, the huntress, the deer, and the eagle might have appeared on prairies.
5. (a) Possible answers: regular, persistent, driving (b) Possible answer: The rhythm helped make the poem clear.
6. He is captivated or enthralled.
7. Answers may vary. Students should support their answers.

Literary Element

1. Students should cite specific lines and give clear reasons.
2. First: red morning sun; second: hot mid-morning sun; third: noon sun shimmering high in the sky; fourth: red sun losing strength in the west. Together they create a picture of a dazzling, powerful phenomenon of nature.

Progress Check

Can students identify line and stanza?

If No → See Unit 3 Teaching Resources Book, p. 84.

For additional selection assessment, see Assessment Resources, pp. 121–122.

After You Read

Respond and Think Critically

Respond and Interpret

1. In your opinion, which image from the poem most vividly portrays the sun? Explain.
2. (a)What does the speaker compare the sun to at the beginning of each stanza? (b)Why do the comparisons differ?
3. (a)Where is the sun at sunset? (b)Why is its nest crimson?

Analyze and Evaluate

4. What details in the poem justify the inclusion of "on the prairie" in the title?
5. (a)How would you describe the poem's **rhythm,** or pattern of beats? (b)How did it contribute to your enjoyment of the poem? Explain.

Connect

6. **Big Idea** Nature Inspires What feelings does nature seem to inspire in the speaker of this poem? Explain.
7. **Connect to Today** This poem was originally published in 1914. In your opinion, are the descriptions still valid and accurate? Why or not?

Literary Element Line and Stanza

Each **line and stanza** in a poem contains distinct ideas that contribute to the poem's overall message.

1. Which lines in the poem did you consider especially vivid or memorable?
2. What key ideas are expressed by each of the stanzas? What impression of the sun do the four stanzas create?

Reading Strategy Compare and Contrast Imagery

Review the imagery chart you created while you read the poem.

1. Which images convey joy, and which images convey power or might? Explain.
2. In your opinion, what do the images in stanzas two and three have in common with one another? How are they different? Explain.

LOG ON **Literature** Online

Selection Resources For Selection Quizzes, eFlashcards, and Reading-Writing Connection activities, go to glencoe.com and enter QuickPass code GL49787u3.

Academic Vocabulary

Lindsay's poem follows the sun's ***transit*** *across the sky.*

Transit is an academic word. More familiar words that are similar in meaning are *journey* and *passage.* Using context clues, try to figure out the meaning of the word in the sentence about Lindsay's poem above. Check your guess in a dictionary.

For more on academic vocabulary, see pages 54–55 and R79–R81.

Writing

Write a Timeline Create a timeline labeled with the stanza headings from the poem. Then choose a place and an element of nature specific to that place (a birch tree in a park, for example). Note changes that take place over the course of a day, and plot the events on your timeline. Describe how the element of nature changes as the day passes.

Reading Strategy

1. Students may say the images in the first two stanzas, when the sun is young and beautiful.
2. Students may say the deer and the fire both creep slowly and are beautiful.

Academic Vocabulary

Transit is used as a noun meaning "a trip."

Writing

Students' timelines should

- feature a place and a natural element specific to the poem
- note the changes that take place in a day

Build Background

Best known for *A Raisin in the Sun,* the first play written by an African American woman to appear on Broadway, Lorraine Hansberry (1930–1965) grew up in the city of Chicago. In this memoir, she describes her impressions of summer and her changing attitude toward the season.

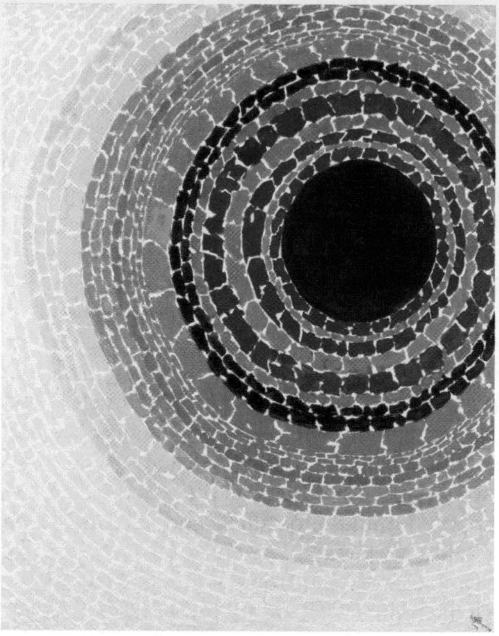

The Eclipse, 1970. Alma Woodsey Thomas. Acrylic on canvas, 62 x 49¾ in. Smithsonian American Art Museum, Washington, DC.

On Summer

Lorraine Hansberry

1 It has taken me a good number of years to come to any measure of respect for summer. I was, being May-born, literally an "infant of the spring" and, during the later childhood years, tended, for some reason or other, to rather worship the cold aloofness of winter. The adolescence, admittedly lingering still, brought the traditional passionate commitment to melancholy[1] autumn—and all that. For the longest kind of time I simply thought that summer was a mistake.

In fact, my earliest memory of anything at all is of waking up in a darkened room where I had been put to bed for a nap on a summer's afternoon, and feeling very, very hot. I acutely disliked the feeling then and retained the bias for years. It had originally been a matter of the heat but, over the years, I came actively to associate displeasure with most of the usually celebrated natural features and social by-products of the season: the too-grainy texture of sand; the too-cold coldness of the various waters we constantly try to escape into; and the icky-perspiry feeling of bathing caps. 2

1. *Melancholy* means "sad" or "dismal."

Comparing Literature

Focus

Summary

The author recalls her initial impressions of summer—the sticky heat, the overwhelming brightness, and the length of the never-ending days. She then explains that she gained a new appreciation for the season after meeting a woman with cancer who wished to see just one more summer in her life.

Big Idea 1

Nature Inspires **Ask:** Which season do you feel is most inspiring? As students read, have them consider what factors make a particular season their favorite. They should pay attention to how the narrator gives each season a feeling and tone.

Reading Strategy 2

Compare and Contrast Imagery **Ask:** How does Hansberry's imagery of summer compare to Lindsay's? **Answer:** *Lindsay's imagery makes a summer day seem beautiful and exciting, while Hansberry's imagery makes summer seem uncomfortable and unpleasant.*

Interactive Read and Write

Other options for teaching this selection can be found in

- Interactive Read and Write for EL Students, pp. 107–118
- Interactive Read and Write for Approaching-Level Students, pp. 107–118
- Interactive Read and Write for On-Level Students, pp. 107–118

English Learners

DIFFERENTIATED INSTRUCTION

Intermediate Have students scan the text and create a list of descriptive words and phrases that the author uses to describe summer, such as "a mistake," "maddeningly excessive," "icky-perspiry," and "light too blinding." **Say:** An author's choice of words can tell you how he or she thinks or feels. **Ask:** What do the author's words suggest about her feelings toward summer? *(Sample answer: She seems to dislike everything about summer—the way its looks, sounds, and feels.)*

Teach

Literary Element 1

Imagery **Ask:** How does the author use imagery in these lines to help readers visualize her summers as a child? *(The author calls readers to imagine "ordinary" or typical city summers. The author uses an image common to many readers.)*

Reading Strategy 2

Draw Conclusions **Ask:** Who is most likely the master to which the narrator refers? *(The narrator is alluding to the fact that her grandfather was a slave. His master is the person who enslaved him.)*

APPROACHING Help approaching level learners understand the identity of the master that the author refers to. **Say:** Since Lorraine Hansberry was born in 1930, her grandfather is probably old enough to have lived before slavery was abolished in the United States. The master she refers to is probably the slave holder who had enslaved her grandfather.

It also seemed to me, esthetically[2] speaking, that nature had got inexcusably carried away on the summer question and let the whole thing get to be rather much. By duration alone, for instance, a summer's day seemed maddeningly excessive; an utter overstatement. Except for those few hours at either end of it, objects always appeared in too sharp a relief against backgrounds; shadows too pronounced and light too blinding. It always gave me the feeling of walking around in a motion picture which had been too artsily-craftsily exposed. Sound also had a way of coming to the ear without that muting influence, marvelously common to winter, across patios or beaches or through the woods. I suppose I found it too stark[3] and yet too intimate a season.

1 My childhood Southside[4] summers were the ordinary city kind, full of the street games which the other rememberers have turned into fine ballets these days and rhymes that anticipated what some people insist on calling modern poetry:

Oh, Mary Mack, Mack, Mack
With the silver buttons, buttons, buttons
All down her back, back, back
She asked her mother, mother, mother
For fifteen cents, cents, cents
To see the elephant, elephant, elephant
Jump the fence, fence, fence
Well, he jumped so high, high, high
'Til he touched the sky, sky, sky
And he didn't come back, back, back
'Til the Fourth of Ju-ly, ly, ly!

Evenings were spent mainly on the back porches where screen doors slammed in the darkness with those really very special summertime sounds. And, sometimes, when Chicago nights got too steamy, the whole family got into the car and went to the park and slept out in the open on blankets. Those were, of course, the best times of all because the grownups were invariably reminded of having been children in rural parts of the country and told the best stories then. And it was also cool and sweet to be on the grass and there was usually the scent of freshly cut lemons or melons in the air. And Daddy would lie on his back, as fathers must, and explain about how men thought the stars above us came to be and how far away they were. I never did learn to believe that anything could be as far away as *that*. Especially the stars.

My mother first took us south to visit her Tennessee birthplace one summer when I was seven or eight, I think. I woke up on the back seat of the car while we were still driving through some place called Kentucky and my mother was pointing out to the beautiful hills on both sides of the highway and telling my brothers and my sister about how her father had run away and hidden from his master in those very hills when he was a little boy. 2 She said that his mother had wandered among the wooded slopes in the moonlight and left food for him in secret places. They were very beautiful hills and I looked out at them for miles and miles after that wondering who and what a *master* might be.

I remember being startled when I first saw my grandmother rocking away on her porch. All my life I had heard that she was a great beauty and no one had ever remarked that they meant a half century before. The woman that I met was as wrin-

2. *Esthetically* means "in a way that pertains to beauty."
3. *Stark* means "blunt."
4. *Southside* refers to the part of Chicago south of the Loop, the central, downtown area.

Reading Practice

SPIRAL REVIEW **Analyze Tone and Mood** Explain the difference between *tone* (the author's attitude toward his or her subject) and *mood* (the feeling that an author's work creates in a reader). Have students read the paragraph beginning "I remember being startled . . ." **Say:** The author's tone in this paragraph is amused. She is amused by her grandmother's prune-like appearance, wonderful cupcakes, and fascination with cars. Encourage students to suggest other words to describe the author's tone. **Ask:** What is the mood of the paragraph? How does it make you feel when you read it? *(Students may say that the paragraph makes them feel nostalgic, calm, lighthearted, etc.)*

House at Provincetown, 1930. Edward Hopper. Watercolor on paper. Fred Jones Jr. Museum of Art, University of Oklahoma.

kled as a prune and could hardly hear and barely see and always seemed to be thinking of other times. But she could still rock and talk and even make wonderful cupcakes which were like cornbread, only sweet. She was captivated by automobiles and, even though it was well into the Thirties, I don't think she had ever been in one before we came down and took her driving. She was a little afraid of them and could not seem to negotiate the windows, but she loved driving. She died the next summer and that is all that I remember about her, except that she was born in slavery and had memories of it and they didn't sound anything like *Gone with the Wind.*[5]

Like everyone else, I have spent whole or bits of summers in many different kinds of places since then: camps and resorts in the Middle West and New York State; on an island; in a tiny Mexican village; Cape Cod, perched atop the Truro bluffs at Longnook Beach that Millay[6] wrote about; or simply strolling the streets of Provincetown before the hours when the parties begin.

And, lastly, I do not think that I will forget days spent, a few summers ago, at a beautiful lodge built right into the rocky cliffs of a bay on the Maine coast. We met a woman there who had lived a purposeful and courageous life and who was then dying of cancer. She had, characteristically, just written a book and taken up painting.

5. *Gone with the Wind* refers to Margaret Mitchell's novel set in the South during the Civil War era or to the film adaptation of it.

6. *Millay* refers to the American poet Edna St. Vincent Millay (1892–1950).

Comparing Literature

Teach

Literary Element 3

Imagery Have a volunteer read aloud the section about taking the grandmother driving. **Ask:** What details does the narrator give about the grandmother driving? *(She liked cars; She'd never been in a car; She could not work the windows)*

Approaching Level

DIFFERENTIATED INSTRUCTION

Emerging Tell students to scan the text and make a list of unfamiliar words (e.g., *radical, devastating, palpable, despondency,* etc.). Choose students to look up the meanings of these words in a dictionary and read them aloud to the class.

Established After reviewing difficult vocabulary words, tell students to read the paragraphs about the woman with cancer that Hansberry met one summer. Have students choose a partner with whom to discuss the text and instruct students to explain to their partner what they think the text means. Lead a discussion to help students fully understand this portion of the text.

Teach

Reading Strategy 1

Compare and Contrast Imagery **Ask:** What belief is the author introducing through the repetition of the image of reaching for the stars? *(The author introduces the belief that through science anything can be accomplished—even a cure for cancer.)*

Literary Element 2

Structure **Ask:** Why do you think the author gives so much space in the story to this woman? *(The woman changed the narrator's lifelong outlook on summer, so she is a very important part of the story.)*

Discussion Starter

Her attitude toward summer changes because of her experience with the woman who has cancer. She concludes that summer is the noblest season because it represents life at its "apex." Students should support their responses.

She had also been of radical viewpoint all her life; one of those people who energetically believe that the world *can* be changed for the better and spend their lives trying to do just that. And that was the way she thought of cancer; she absolutely refused to award it the stature of tragedy, a devastating instance of the brooding doom and inexplicability[7] of the absurdity of human destiny, etc., etc. The kind of characterization given, lately, as we all know, to far less formidable[8] foes in life than cancer.

But for this remarkable woman it was a matter of nature in imperfection, implying, as always, work for man to do. It was an *enemy,* but a palpable one with shape and effect and source; and if it existed, it could be destroyed. She saluted it accordingly, without despondency, but with a lively, beautiful and delightfully ribald[9] anger. There was one thing, she felt, which would prove equal to its relentless ravages and that was the genius of man. 1 Not his mysticism,[10] but man with tubes and slides and the stubborn human notion that the stars are very much within our reach.

The last time I saw her she was sitting surrounded by her paintings with her manuscript laid out for me to read, because, she said, she wanted to know what a *young person* would think of her thinking; one must always keep up with what *young people* thought about things because, after all, they were *change.*

Every now and then her jaw set in anger as we spoke of things people should be angry about. And then, for relief, she would look out at the lovely bay at a mellow sunset settling on the water. Her face softened with love of all that beauty and, watching her, I wished with all my power what I knew that she was wishing: that she might live to see at least one more *summer.* Through her eyes I finally gained the sense of what it might mean; more than the coming autumn with its pretentious[11] melancholy; more than an austere and silent winter which must shut dying people in for precious months; more even than the frivolous[12] spring, too full of too many false promises, would be the gift of another summer with its stark and intimate assertion of neither birth nor death but life at the apex; with the gentlest nights and, above all, the longest days.

I heard later that she did live to see another summer. And I have retained my respect for the noblest of the seasons. 2

7. *Inexplicability* means "the quality of being impossible to explain."
8. *Formidable* means "causing fear."
9. *Ribald* means "crude" or "offensive."
10. *Mysticism* is the belief that direct knowledge of reality can be obtained through visions or trances.

11. *Pretentious* means "assuming a false sense of importance."
12. *Frivolous* means "lacking in seriousness."

Discussion Starter

Why does Hansberry's attitude toward summer change? Why does she finally conclude that summer is the "noblest of the seasons"? Use details from the selection to support your responses.

Writing Practice

Write an Explanation Tell students that to extend their understanding of a text, they must analyze the text and think beyond what the author has written. **Say:** Choose the event in Hansberry's essay that you think is most important and write an explanation of why you chose that event. Give students a few minutes to compose their responses. Encourage students to share their responses and discuss them with the rest of the class.

Build Background

Natasha Trethewey, an African American poet, was born in Gulfport, Mississippi, in 1966. "Monument" is from her collection *Native Ground,* which received the 2007 Pulitzer Prize for Poetry. In this poem, Trethewey commemorates her mother, who passed away in 1985. **3**

MONUMENT

Natasha Trethewey

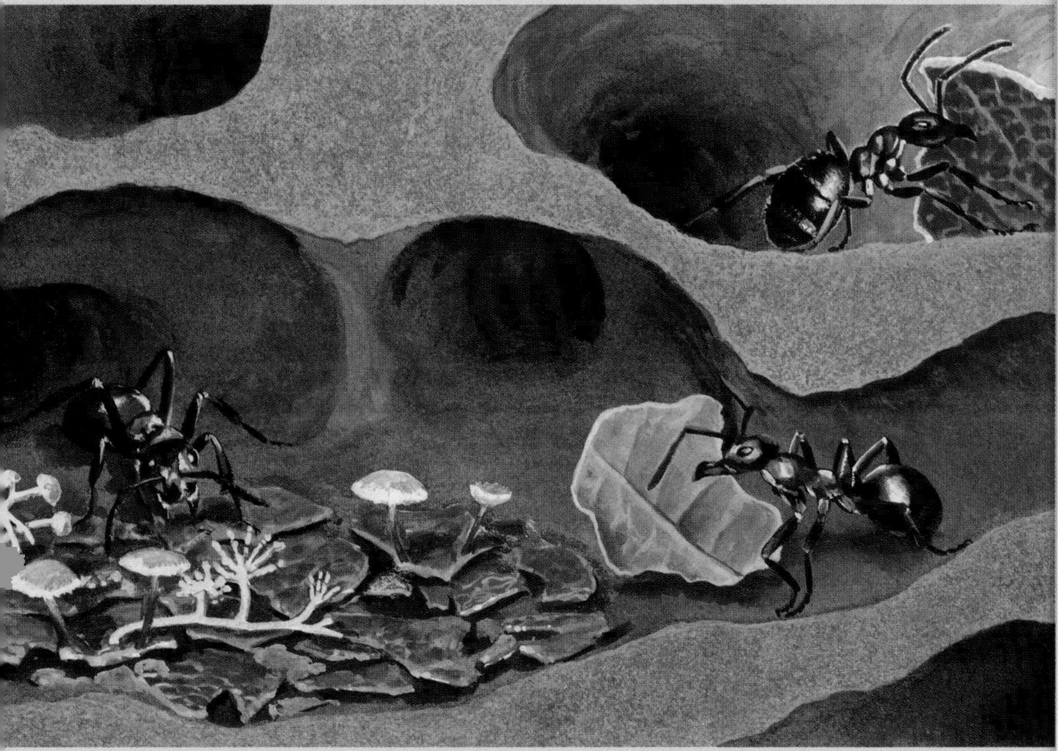

Three ants in an anthill. De Agostini Picture Library.

Focus

Summary

When the speaker sees ants near her front step, she is reminded of an anthill on her mother's grave.

Big Idea 3

Nature Inspires **Say:** People often compare the events of life to events in nature—for example, the cycles of birth, youth, old age, and death are mirrored through spring, summer, fall, and winter. **Ask:** What life lessons have you learned from nature? *(Answers will vary.)*

Interactive Read and Write

Other options for teaching this selection can be found in

- Interactive Read and Write for EL Students, p. 117
- Interactive Read and Write for Approaching-Level Students, p. 117
- Interactive Read and Write for On-Level Students, p. 117

Approaching Level

DIFFERENTIATED INSTRUCTION

Emerging Help students understand the poem by pointing out the simile "in and out like arteries" and the metaphor "the mound is a blister on my heart." Explain that the author uses the simile to compare the ants going in and out of the anthills to arteries to show that there are many lines of ants in constant motion. Explain the meaning of the metaphor: She feels guilty about the ant mound on her mother's grave—it breaks her heart—because she has not tended to it.

Established Point out that while the poem begins in the present, throughout most of the poem the author is remembering an event from the past. Show students the transitional words "In the cemetery last June."

Teach

Literary Element 1

Line and Stanza **Say:** One stanza is used to carry out the poem's ideas. Notice how the poet uses dashes throughout the lines of the poem to introduce additional thoughts in the middle of a sentence.

ADVANCED **Ask:** Why do you think the poet did not include any breaks between lines or stanzas? **Answer:** *Students may say that the poem continues on without pause just as the ants it describes.*

Quickwrite

Students' paragraphs should

- explore the use of figurative language in conveying theme
- cite specific phrases and lines from the poem
- address the question of why the ants' work disturbs the speaker

Today the ants are busy
beside my front steps, weaving
in and out of the hill they're building.
I watch them emerge and—
like everything I've forgotten—disappear
into the subterranean[1], a world
made by displacement. In the cemetery
last June, I circled, lost—
weeds and grass grown up all around— **1**
the landscape blurred and waving.
At my mother's grave, ants streamed in
and out like arteries, a tiny hill rising
above her untended plot. Bit by bit,
red dirt piled up, spread
like a rash on the grass; I watched a long time
the ants' determined work,
how they brought up soil
of which she will be part,
and piled it before me. Believe me when I say
I've tried not to begrudge[2] them
their industry, this reminder of what
I haven't done. Even now,
the mound is a blister on my heart,
a red and humming swarm.

1. *Subterranean* means "underground."
2. *Begrudge* means "look upon with disapproval."

Quickwrite

In this poem, the speaker describes ants busily at work. Why does their work disturb the speaker? Write a paragraph to explore this question. In your paragraph, comment on the use of **figurative language**—language that expresses some truth beyond the literal level—to suggest the theme. Cite lines from the poem to support your ideas.

Reading Practice

SMALL GROUP

Active vs. Passive Voice Point out that Trethewey uses the active voice in this poem. In sentences written in the active voice, the subject *performs* the action. In sentences written in the passive voice, the subject *receives* the action. **Write on the board:** The boys won the game. **Ask:** Does this sentence use active or passive voice. Explain your answer. *(active voice; the subject, the boys, performs the action)*

Write on the board: The game was won by the boys. **Ask:** Does this sentence use active or passive voice? Explain your answer. *(passive voice; the subject, the game, receives the action)* Break students into groups and have them write three sentences in both the active and passive voice.

Wrap-Up: Comparing Literature

Across Genres

- ***An Indian Summer Day on the Prairie*** by Vachel Lindsay
- ***On Summer*** by Lorraine Hansberry
- ***Monument*** by Natasha Trethewey

COMPARE THE Big Idea Nature Inspires

Sunset at Sea. Odilon Redon. Private collection.

Visual Display Each one of these writers—Vachel Lindsay, Lorraine Hansberry, and Natasha Trethewey—was inspired by nature to create a work of literature. Their works include vivid images that help readers see and feel details of nature. Create a collage of the images in each work that you find most inspirational or thought-provoking. Begin by reviewing the selections to determine which images you want to capture. Then find visual aids, such as copies of photographs or works of fine art, that contain images similar to the ones described by the writers. Assemble the images into three collages and present your collages to the class. Quote lines from the poems and the memoir that helped you select your images, and explain what makes these nature images memorable to you.

COMPARE Structure

Writing The **structure** of a literary work gives it coherence and order. Structure allows the reader to perceive relationships and to carefully build an understanding of the work's theme, or central insight. Look at Hansberry's memoir and either Lindsay's or Trethewey's poem. Write a brief essay describing each work's structure. How are the structures similar? How are they different? Are the authors' messages especially suited to the structures they selected? Why or why not? Cite evidence from the selections to support your ideas.

COMPARE Ideas

Group Activity To draw conclusions about an author's ideas, closely examine the details of his or her work. In a small group, discuss the ideas that Lindsay, Hansberry, and Trethewey express. As you answer the following questions, cite evidence from the selections to support your points.

1. What is the topic or subject of each work? What attitudes or ideas does each author seem to be expressing toward his or her topic?
2. What is each author's opinion of the relationship between humans and the natural world?

LOG ON Literature Online

Selection Resources For Selection Quizzes, eFlashcards, and Reading-Writing Connection activities, go to glencoe.com and enter QuickPass code GL49787u3.

Wrap-Up: Comparing Literature

Across Genres

Assess

Compare the Big Idea

Students' collages and presentations should

- show images from each work
- depict key images
- identify the source of each image

Compare Structure

Students' essays should

- compare and contrast the structure of one memoir and one of the two other works
- identify structural patterns in both works
- explain the relationship between an author's theme and choice of structure
- include specific details as supporting evidence

Compare Ideas

Students should support their answers with evidence from the texts.

English Learners

DIFFERENTIATED INSTRUCTION

Beginning/Early Intermediate Tell students that there are guidelines for reading a poem that will help them read more fluidly. Tell students to pause after reading punctuation marks instead of at the end of each line. Suggest that students pause briefly after a comma and slightly longer after a period. Encourage students to read other poems aloud softly to themselves several times until they feel they can read them without hesitating.

Approaching Level

DIFFERENTIATED INSTRUCTION

African American Vernacular English Approaching-level students who are users of African American vernacular English should be careful to pronounce the *-ed* sound at the end of past tense verbs. For example, students should say, "He walked outside," instead of "He walk outside."

Before You Read

Focus

Bellringer Options

Daily Language Practice Transparency 50

Or display images of snakes—real snakes and snakes that appear in art, logos, and symbols or seals.

Ask: What is your reaction to seeing a snake? What do they often represent in art and in literature? Have students consider as they read how the poem's speaker feels about the snake she encounters.

Before You Read

The Black Snake

Meet **Mary Oliver**
(born 1935)

Mary Oliver once told an interviewer, "I don't think I have ever been bored one day in my life." Yet Oliver leads and always has led a relatively quiet life. She was born in Maple Heights, Ohio, in 1935. As a child, she developed the strong bond with the natural world that informs and enlivens her work and serves as a guiding principle in her life.

Learning the Craft Oliver attended college, but never graduated. Nevertheless, she began to hone her craft. As she says, "To keep writing was always a first priority."

> *"I have never felt yet that I've done it right. This is the marvelous thing about language. It can always be done better."*
>
> —Mary Oliver

Oliver's first collection of poems, *No Voyage,* was published in 1963. She acknowledges that her early work is derivative, that is, clearly influenced by the poets she was reading at the time—Robert Frost, William Carlos Williams, Edna St. Vincent Millay, and James Wright, among others. "Every poet learns by imitating other poets," she says, "but there is finally a time when you begin to hear something new and different—something of your own—and that's the part of your work you want then to cherish, to make strong."

Oliver continued to read and write every day, often waking at 4:30 or 5:00 in the morning and writing for several hours before work.

Over the years, she developed her distinctive voice. In 1983 she published *American Primitive,* a collection of poetry with one voice throughout—a voice that she says "can, imaginatively, become the reader's inner voice." This book was well received and won the Pulitzer Prize in 1984.

Meticulous Technique Writing is not an effortless act of creation for Oliver. She revises extensively, often producing up to sixty drafts. She prefers to use an electric typewriter, pens, and pencils—or, as she calls them, "the old-fashioned stuff."

As her meticulous technique suggests, Oliver examines her subjects in great detail. But it is her ability to translate these details into universal experience that makes her work great poetry.

Today, Mary Oliver lives in Provincetown, Massachusetts, where she teaches, writes, and revels in the natural world. Oliver keeps a notebook with her at all times, so that she can write down immediate impressions. She has a keen appreciation for the natural world, and she has always tried to share that with her readers.

LOG ON **Literature** Online

Author Search For more about Mary Oliver, go to glencoe.com and enter QuickPass code GL49787u3.

Selection Skills

The Black Snake

Literary Elements
- Parallelism (SE pp. 487, 488, 489)

Writing Skills/Grammar
- Literary Criticism(SE p. 490)
- Use Parallelism (TE p. 488)

Reading Skills
- Analyze Mood (SE pp. 487, 488, 490)

Vocabulary Skills
- Academic Vocabulary (SE p. 490)

Literature and Reading Preview

Connect to the Poem

What animal makes you think about an important idea or issue in life? With a partner, discuss the question above. Be sure to support your answer with an explanation and specific examples.

Build Background

Snakes have much more reason to fear people, their worst enemies, than people have to fear snakes. In fact, many ancient and modern cultures have considered snakes to be valuable or even sacred. For example, the Aztecs worshipped the feathered serpent god Quetzalcoatl. In Arizona, Hopi people still perform the snake-antelope dance, a ceremony using live snakes, to plea for rain from the gods.

Set Purposes for Reading

Big Idea Nature Inspires

As you read "The Black Snake," ask yourself, How does the snake inspire the speaker to contemplate life and death?

Literary Element Parallelism

Parallelism is the use of a series of words, phrases, or sentences that have similar grammatical form. It is a form of repetition that emphasizes the items that are arranged in similar structures. Understanding parallelism will help you to identify ideas the author considers important. As you read, ask yourself, What examples of parallelism can I find in this poem?

Reading Strategy Analyze Mood

Mood is the feeling or emotional quality of a literary work. Mood can suggest a specific emotion, such as excitement or fear. In a poem, word choice, line length, rhythm, and other elements contribute to mood. Descriptive language and figures of speech also help establish the mood. As you read, ask yourself, What emotion does the language and imagery of this poem evoke?

Tip: Note Mood Words As you read the poem, use a chart to record the words that suggest a particular mood.

Word	Mood Suggested
flashed	excitement

Learning Objectives

For pages 486–490

In studying this text, you will focus on the following objectives:

Literary Study: Analyzing parallelism.

Reading: Analyzing mood.

Writing: Reporting on literary criticism.

A sculpture of the god Quetzalcoatl, depicted as a plumed serpent, adorns the outside of a temple in his honor in Teotihuacan, Mexico.

Before You Read

Focus

Summary

A snake crawls onto a road and is killed by an oncoming truck. The speaker stops her car and moves the snake's body to the side of the road. As she drives off, she thinks about death and how our deepest impulse is to think that we will never die.

For summaries in languages other than English, see Unit 3 Teaching Resources Book, pp. 89–94.

Approaching Level

DIFFERENTIATED INSTRUCTION

Emerging Read aloud the Reading Strategy on this page. Help students grasp the concept of mood.

Write: foggy, damp, icy, dark **Ask:** What kind of mood do these words create? *(gloomy, sad)* **Write:** cool, soft, quiet, gentle **Ask:** What kind of mood do these words create? *(peaceful, restful)* Tell students to look for words that create mood as they read Oliver's poem.

Teach

Reading Strategy 1

Analyze Mood Answer: *Students may say that the mood is melancholy or pensive. The once vital snake is now something to be thrown away.* Explain that mood is a feeling that is evoked by images, sounds, and words.

ADVANCED **Ask:** Why does the image of the tire evoke such feelings? *(Possible answer: The image of something useless and limp makes readers feel something has been lost or wasted.)*

Literary Element 2

Parallelism Answer: *The phrase "he is" is followed twice by a pair of adjectives and a simile—"he is as cool and gleaming as a braided whip . . . beautiful and quiet as a dead brother" (ll. 9–11). The snake is compared to both a whip and a dead brother.*

To check students' understanding of the selection, see Unit 3 Teaching Resources Book, p. 98.

The Black Snake

Mary Oliver

Snake and Plant, ca. 1731–1743. Mark Catesby. Academy of Natural Sciences of Philadelphia.

When the black snake
flashed onto the morning road,
and the truck could not swerve—
death, that is how it happens.

Now he lies looped and useless
as an old bicycle tire.
I stop the car
and carry him into the bushes.

He is as cool and gleaming
as a braided whip, he is as beautiful and quiet
as a dead brother.
I leave him under the leaves

and drive on, thinking
about *death:* its suddenness,
its terrible weight,
its certain coming. Yet under

reason burns a brighter fire, which the bones
have always preferred.
It is the story of endless good fortune.
It says to oblivion:[1] not me!

It is the light at the center of every cell.
It is what sent the snake coiling and flowing forward
happily all spring through the green leaves before
he came to the road.

---

1. *Oblivion* is the state of being entirely forgotten.

1 Analyze Mood *What mood does this comparison convey?*

2 Parallelism *Identify the parallelism in this sentence. To what unlikely things is the snake being compared?*

Writing Practice

Use Parallelism

Tell students that good writers use parallel structure within their sentences. Explain that sentences with correlative expressions (both/and, not/but; not only/but also, either/or; first, second, third) should be parallel. **Write:** It is a day not for fun but work. *(not parallel)* **Write:** It is a day not for fun but for work. *(parallel)*

Have students work with a partner to revise each of the following sentences to make it parallel.

- It was both a hot day and very humid. *(The day was both hot and humid.)*
- Either you must listen to your mother or suffer the consequences. *(You must either listen to your mother or suffer the consequences.)*

After You Read

Respond and Think Critically

Respond and Interpret

1. What was your reaction to the speaker's description of the snake?
2. (a)What does the speaker do with the snake? (b)What does this tell you about the speaker?
3. (a)What image begins and ends the poem? (b)What does the repetition of this image suggest?
4. (a)What is the "brighter fire, which the bones / have always preferred"? (b)Why is the fire brighter?

Analyze and Evaluate

5. (a)Identify words and phrases that describe circles. (b)Why does the author repeat the image of a circle?
6. How does the idea of a "light at the center of every cell" tie in with the speaker's thoughts?
7. The **speaker** in a poem is the voice that communicates with the reader. Why do you suppose Oliver wrote so little about the speaker and so much about the snake?

Connect

8. **Big Idea** Nature Inspires What does this poem suggest about the ability of nature to provide inspiration?
9. **Connect to the Author** Mary Oliver often examines her subjects in great detail. Do you think this poem is a good example of that quality of her writing? Why or why not?

Literary Element Parallelism

SAT Skills Practice

1. The use of parallelism in stanza 4 serves primarily to
   (A) reveal the speaker's fear of death
   (B) suggest that life is an illusion
   (C) foreshadow a new, optimistic mood
   (D) point out the dangers involved in any journey
   (E) underscore the reality and seriousness of death

Review: Free Verse

As you learned on page 466, **free verse** is poetry that has no fixed pattern of meter, rhyme, line length, or stanza arrangement. Free verse is very popular in modern poetry because it allows the speaker to address the reader in an informal, conversational style.

Partner Activity Despite their lack of form, free verse poems do contain poetic techniques. With a partner, identify the following literary elements that Mary Oliver uses in "The Black Snake":

- **simile,** an explicit comparison between two seemingly unlike things
- **repetition** of key words
- **alliteration,** the repetition of consonant sounds at the beginning of words.

Use a web similar to the one below.

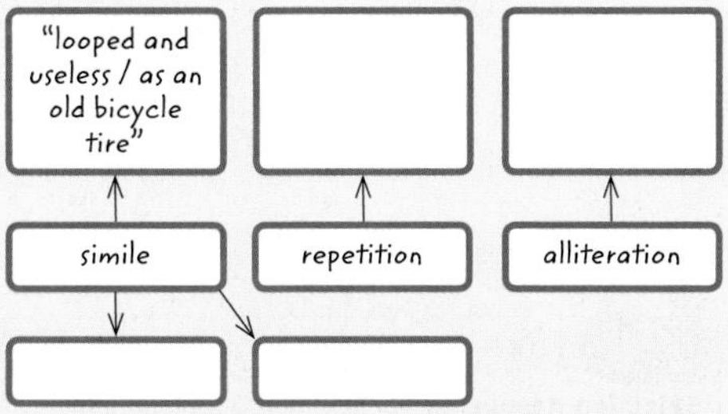

Progress Check

Can students identify parallelism?

If No → See Unit 3 Teaching Resources Book, p. 95.

For additional selection assessment, see Assessment Resources, pp. 125–126.

After You Read

Assess

1. Answers will vary.
2. (a) Places it under the leaves (b) She has respect and sympathy for the snake.
3. (a) The living snake on the road (b) The cycle of life
4. (a) The life force (b) The life force gives the illusion of immortality.
5. (a) *looped, tire, coiling,* (b) It symbolizes the cycle of life and death.
6. It may refer to the will to survive.
7. The snake symbolizes natural forces; the speaker is merely a witness.
8. Despite our knowledge of certain death, humans want to live forever.
9. Students should support their opinions with examples from the poem.

Literary Element

1. E is the correct answer. The speaker mentions death's suddenness, terrible weight and certain coming.

Review: Free Verse

simile: "as cool and gleaming / as a braided whip," ll. 9–10; "as beautiful and quiet / as a dead brother," ll. 10–11

repetition: *"death,"* ll. 4 and 14

alliteration: "flowing forward," l. 22

After You Read

Assess

Reading Strategy

1. sober and reflective; death, useless, beautiful, quiet, dead brother
2. (a) The mood moves from mournful to life-affirming. (b) No. It is consistent with the life-affirming mood.

Academic Vocabulary

Sample answers: Definition: cause; Synonyms: convince, persuade; Antonyms: dissuade, detract; Sample Sentence: The sight of a nearby predator or food might induce a snake to move through the grass.

Research and Report

Students' essays should

- present a clear, concise thesis statement in the opening paragraph
- respond to the quote's analysis of Oliver
- use a comparison from the poem to illustrate their position
- analyze the language used in the comparison
- cite examples from the text to support their analysis

For grammar practice, see Unit 3 Teaching Resources Book, p. 97.

To create custom assessments online, go to Progress Reporter Online Assessment.

To create custom assessments using software, use ExamView Assessment Suite.

Reading Strategy Analyze Mood

Often, the **mood** of a work of literature changes as the work progresses. Review the mood chart you created as you read and note if and where the mood of the poem changes.

1. What is the mood at the beginning of the poem? What words or images help evoke this mood?
2. (a)How does the poem's structure reflect a change in mood? (b)Does the final line of the poem affect the mood? Explain.

Academic Vocabulary

According to the poem, it was "the light at the center of every cell" that ***induced*** *the snake to spring through the green leaves.*

Induce is an academic word. More familiar words that are similar in meaning are *cause, encourage,* and *persuade.* To study this word further, fill out the graphic organizer below.

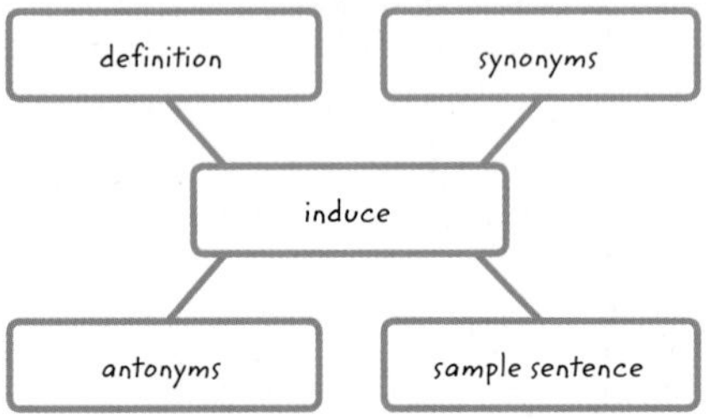

For more on academic vocabulary, see pages 54–55 and R79–R81.

LOG ON Literature Online

Selection Resources For Selection Quizzes, eFlashcards, and Reading-Writing Connection activities, go to glencoe.com and enter QuickPass code GL49787u3.

Research and Report

Literary Criticism

Assignment Consider the following quotation by author Joyce Carol Oates:

> "[Mary Oliver] sees the true 'terror' of the country as nature's pitiless regard for the individual, whether prey or predator; she cannot divide the world into victim and oppressor."

Do you agree with Oates's analysis? Review "The Black Snake" to analyze Oliver's use of comparisons in the poem (life and death, reason and emotion, the speaker and the snake). Write a brief essay in which you describe one of these comparisons, and evaluate how it contributes to the poem's sense of "nature's pitiless regard for the individual." Explain whether you think the roles of "victim and oppressor" are present. Provide examples from the poem to support your main points.

Prepare First, determine whether you agree with the quote's analysis. As you determine your position, consider these questions: *What is Oliver's intended effect? Do you think she has succeeded?* Then, choose a comparison in the poem that illustrates or supports your position.

Draft a thesis statement that briefly expresses how the comparison supports your position. Your thesis could be structured like this:

The poet uses the comparison between _____ and _____ to show _____ .

Review the text of the poem for specific examples that support your thesis. Your examples should highlight language that the poet uses in her comparison.

Report As you write your essay, support your thesis with logical arguments. Make sure that you clearly explain how your examples support your position.

Evaluate Create a short checklist to use in evaluating your essay. Your list should include items such as presenting a thesis statement and providing supporting examples.

Research Practice

SMALL GROUP

Research to Understand Voice Read aloud the quotation by Joyce Carol Oates on this page. Break students into groups and have them research Oates's life and work. Have them answer this question based on their research: Do you think Oates views nature in the same way Oliver does? *(Students will likely say no; since Oates often writes in the horror genre, her views of nature will not be as compassionate.)*

Before You Read

The Peace of Wild Things

Meet **Wendell Berry**
(born 1934)

Wendell Berry is a farmer without a tractor and a writer without a computer. Berry does not believe in modern technology, but he does believe in the importance of sustaining local community life, small farms, and family heritage. Nature and the environment are central to his writing and his work.

Love of the Land Berry was born in New Castle, Kentucky, and grew up on his family's farm. After earning a bachelor's degree and a master's degree in English at the University of Kentucky, Berry taught at Georgetown College from 1957 to 1959. Later, he taught at the creative writing center at Stanford University and then at New York University. While at Stanford, Berry wrote his first novel, entitled *Nathan Coulter*. Published in 1960, it was the first in his series of "Port William" novels. The series deals with the themes of family, community, and love of the land.

> *"My work has been motivated by a desire to make myself responsible at home in this world and in my native and chosen place."*
>
> —Wendell Berry

In addition to being a novelist, Berry is also a poet, an essayist, and the author of more than thirty books. His nature writing is often compared with that of William Wordsworth and Henry David Thoreau. Farming and community continue to be the focus of his writing.

Organics, Pencils, and Paper Today, Berry lives in the county where he was born, on a 125-acre farm where members of the Berry family have lived since the early 1800s. He and his wife came to the farm for a vacation in 1965 but decided to stay. "It is a real farm," Berry has said, "not a writer-professor's country estate." He farms organically—using no chemical pesticides or herbicides. Berry does not use modern farm equipment, preferring to use draft horses to plow his fields instead of "exhaust-stinking, engine-roaring, gasoline-guzzling tractors."

Berry also refuses to use a computer to write, explaining his reasons in an essay entitled "Why I Am Not Going to Buy a Computer." He does not want to use electricity generated by the burning of strip-mined coal.

In all of his writing, Berry promotes the message that respect and appreciation for nature are essential to human life.

LOG ON **Literature** Online

Author Search For more about Wendell Berry, go to glencoe.com and enter QuickPass code GL49787u3.

Before You Read

Focus

Bellringer Options

Daily Language Practice Transparency 51

Or display images of water scenes—ponds, seascapes, and river views.

Ask: How do these scenes make you feel? Why do you think people enjoy spending time near the water? *Have students consider as they read the poem how nature soothes the speaker's worries.*

Selection Skills

The Peace of Wild Things

Literary Elements
- Enjambment (SE pp. 492, 493, 494)

Writing Skills/Grammar
- Write a Flyer (SE p. 494)

Reading Skills
- Analyze Cause-and-Effect Relationships (SE pp. 492, 494)

Vocabulary Skills
- Synonyms (SE p. 494)

Before You Read

Focus

Summary

The speaker tells how, when his worries wake him at night, he goes down to the water to watch the birds and stars and feels comforted.

For summaries in languages other than English, see Unit 3 Teaching Resources Book, pp. 100–105.

Vocabulary

Write with Vocabulary
Have students read the vocabulary words and their definitions. Then have them write a paragraph about a recent event in their lives. Students must use both of the vocabulary words from the list.

For additional vocabulary practice, see Unit 3 Teaching Resources Book, p. 108.

Literature and Reading Preview

Connect to the Poem

Why might someone feel despair for the world? Discuss this question with a partner. Consider ways in which nature could help overcome feelings of despair.

Build Background

The setting of the poem is "still water," that is, a lake or pond where waterfowl, such as wood ducks and herons, stop to feed or nest. The wood drake, or male wood duck, is marked by bright green and blue. The heron wades in water to fish.

Set Purposes for Reading

Big Idea Nature Inspires

As you read "The Peace of Wild Things," ask yourself, What role does nature play in the speaker's life?

Literary Element Enjambment

Enjambment is the continuation of a sentence from one line of a poem into the next. Also called a run-on line, enjambment draws the reader to the next line and makes the poem's meter and rhythm flow naturally. If a line of poetry has no end punctuation, see if the poet is using enjambment. As you read, ask yourself, How does enjambment help the flow of this poem?

Reading Strategy Analyze Cause-and-Effect Relationships

When a writer presents a **cause-and-effect relationship,** he or she explains why something happens or shows both an action and its result. A single cause may have many effects. As you read, ask yourself, What cause-and-effect relationships exist in this poem?

Tip: Note Cause and Effect Read the poem at least twice. Then identify the cause-and-effect relationships in the poem, and record them in a chart like the one below.

Cause	Effect
despair and fear	waking in the night

Learning Objectives

For pages 491–494

In studying this text, you will focus on the following objectives:

Literary Study: Analyzing enjambment.

Reading: Analyzing cause-and-effect relationships.

Writing: Writing a flyer.

Vocabulary

tax (taks) *v.* to place a heavy burden on; to strain; p. 493 *Studying for long hours without a break can tax your brain.*

forethought (for′ thôt′) *n.* thinking or planning beforehand; p. 493 *We had the forethought to make alternate plans in case of rain.*

Tip: Synonyms Synonyms are words that have the same or similar meanings. Paying attention to the differences that exist between synonyms will help you more clearly communicate and better understand what you read. For example, *tax* and *strain* are synonyms, but they do not mean exactly the same thing. The verb *tax* implies "making challenging demands on," while *strain* implies maximum exertion, perhaps even too much exertion.

Writing Practice

Write Poetry Expand on the Big Idea on this page and have students consider the role that nature plays in their lives. **Ask:** Is there a favorite place outdoors that you go to escape daily life? What do you like about this place? *(Students may say that they like to go hiking on a mountain or travel to a beach because these places are very different from school and home.)*

Have students write a short poem about their favorite outdoor place. Tell them that *enjambment* is the continuation of a sentence from one line in a poem to the next. Show them examples of enjambment in Berry's poem. Encourage them to use enjambment in their poems about nature.

The Peace of Wild Things

Wendell Berry

Tranquility. Nilaus Fristrup. Bourne Gallery, Reigate, Great Britain.

When despair for the world grows in me
and I wake in the night at the least sound
in fear of what my life and my children's lives may be,
☆ I go and lie down where the wood drake
rests in his beauty on the water, and the great heron feeds.
I come into the peace of wild things
who do not **tax** their lives with **forethought**
1 of grief. I come into the presence of still water.
And I feel above me the day-blind stars
waiting with their light. For a time
I rest in the grace of the world, and am free.

2 Enjambment *Why would it sound unnatural to pause at the end of this line? Where is a more natural place to pause?*

Vocabulary

tax (taks) *v.* to place a heavy burden on; to strain
forethought (for′ thôt′) *n.* thinking or planning beforehand

Approaching Level

DIFFERENTIATED INSTRUCTION

Emerging Remind students that poetry is meant to be read aloud. Tell them to note the punctuation in Berry's poem. Remind them not to stop reading at the end of a line. Tell them to keep reading until they come to a period.

Have them think about the tone of Berry's poem as they read. Explain that they may have to read the poem aloud several times to get a sense of the rhyme scheme and rhythm.

Teach

Reading Strategy 1

Analyze Cause-and-Effect Relationships **Ask:** What causes the speaker to go down to the water? **Answer:** *He is worried about his and his children's future.*

APPROACHING Help approaching level learners understand the cause-and-effect relationship in this poem. **Say:** The speaker is so worried about his and his children's futures that he cannot sleep. He goes down to the water because it is a very calm place that helps him relax. The tranquility of that place causes him to forget about his troubles for a time.

Literary Element 2

Enjambment Enjambment is often used in free verse. Without the structure of meter and rhyme scheme, poets can break lines where they wish to focus on the visual aspect of the poem or to build suspense.

Answer: *The thought sounds incomplete; a verb is missing. Students would normally pause after "on the water."*

Language History ☆

Drake The word *drake* dates back to the thirteenth century. It is derived from a Germanic word *draak, drake,* or *drache.* For medieval Germans, *drake* was part of a compound word *anddrake,* which meant "duck drake." English speakers borrowed the second part, *drake,* to refer to a male duck.

To check students' understanding of the selection, see Unit 3 Teaching Resources Book, p. 110.

After You Read

Assess

1. Answers will vary.
2. (a) Worry about the future (b) To live in the present
3. (a) Only "for a time" (b) He is free from worry and fear.
4. (a) That wild things provide peace (b) Wild things live without "forethought of grief."
5. Answers will vary.
6. (a) It warns the reader that peace is temporary. (b) It is effective because it is true.
7. Answers will vary.
8. By turning to nature to find peace, the speaker of the poem reveals a deep level of respect and care for the natural world.

Literary Element

1. The phrase is emphasized by being suspended.
2. The break after *stars* in line 9 builds suspense.

Progress Check

Can students identify enjambment?

If No → See Unit 3 Teaching Resources Book, p. 106.

Reading Strategy

1. Despair and fear for his and his children's future
2. He lies down near water. He gains peace of mind from nature.

Vocabulary

1. d **2.** a

After You Read

Respond and Think Critically

Respond and Interpret

1. Which lines from this poem did you find most memorable, powerful, or surprising? Explain.
2. (a)What is it that people do that "wild things" do not? (b)What do wild things teach the speaker and reader about living?
3. (a)For how long does the experience with nature allow the speaker to be free? (b)What is the nature of this freedom?

Analyze and Evaluate

4. (a)What ironic contrast is presented in the title of the poem? (b)How does the title reflect the poem's content?
5. How well do you think the poem evokes the feeling of peace in nature? Support your answer with details from the poem.
6. (a)What does the phrase "For a time" in line 10 contribute to the mood, or emotional quality, of the poem? (b)Is this choice of words effective?

Connect

7. **Big Idea** **Nature Inspires** How does your experience with nature compare with the experience described in the poem?
8. **Connect to the Author** Berry's concern about the environment and nature is well-known. How does the poem reflect this attitude?

Literary Element Enjambment

Poetry that has punctuation at the ends of its lines gives a sense of structure and order. **Enjambment,** on the other hand, can create a sense of disorder.

1. What effect does breaking line 10 after "For a time" have on the flow of the poem? Explain your answer.
2. Identify one other example of enjambment in the poem. What effect does it have?

Reading Strategy Analyze Cause-and-Effect Relationships

Review the cause-and-effect chart you made while reading. Then answer the following questions.

1. What are the initial feelings that cause the speaker to take action?
2. What action does the speaker take as a result of these feelings? What is the effect of his action?

LOG ON **Literature** Online

Selection Resources For Selection Quizzes, eFlashcards, and Reading-Writing Connection activities, go to glencoe.com and enter QuickPass code GL49787u3.

Vocabulary Practice

Practice with Synonyms With a partner, match each boldface vocabulary word below with its synonym. You will not use all the answer choices. Use a thesaurus or dictionary to check your answers.

1. tax	a. premonition
2. forethought	b. preparation
	c. money
	d. challenge

Writing

Write a Flyer The speaker goes to nature to escape the anxieties of the world. Think about a place you visit to relax. Is it a natural setting? Is it indoors? Do you go there alone or with other people? Write a one-page flyer about a place that gives you peace. Include details about its location, and highlight its unique qualities. Add an illustration if you have space.

Writing

Students' fliers should show and explain a place where they go to escape.

For additional selection assessment, see Assessment Resources, pp. 125–126.

Grammar Workshop

Subject-Verb Agreement

Literature Connection When the speaker in Berry's poem says "I rest" and "am free," both verb forms agree with the subject *I*.

> *"For a time I rest in the grace of the world, and am free."*
>
> —Wendell Berry, from "The Peace of Wild Things"

The **subject,** or person or thing performing the action, and the **verb,** or action or state of being, must agree in number. If the subject of a sentence is singular (*he, it*), the verb must be singular (*eats, describes*).

Learn to identify agreement problems and correct them.

Problem 1 A prepositional phrase or other words come between the subject and the verb.

The speaker of these lines celebrate the peace of wild things.

Solution Make the verb agree with the subject, not with the object of the preposition.

The speaker of these lines celebrates the peace of wild things.

Problem 2 The subject is a compound joined by *and.*

The great heron and the wood drake feeds at the pond.

Solution Be sure to use the plural form of the verb.

The great heron and the wood drake feed at the pond.

Problem 3 A compound subject is joined by *or* or *nor.*

Fear or worries fades away.
Neither the stars nor water destroy the speaker's peace.

Solution Make the verb agree with the subject that is closer to it.

Fear or worries fade away.
Neither the stars nor water destroys the speaker's peace.

Revise Rewrite these sentences, correcting any agreement problems. If the sentence is correct, write *Correct.*

1. A crowd of golden daffodils catch the speaker's eye.
2. The trees and the lake frames the field of flowers.
3. Along the bay are ten thousand daffodils.
4. Neither the daffodils nor the landscape call out to me.

Learning Objectives

In this workshop, you will focus on the following objective:

Grammar: Understanding how to correct subject-verb agreement problems.

Subject and Verb
The **subject** of a sentence is the person or thing that performs the action or exists; the **verb** is the action or state of being.

Tip
Check for subject-verb agreement as a separate step in the proofreading process. Look twice at sentences with unexpected word order, compound subjects, and words or phrases between the subject and verb.

Language Handbook
For more about subject-verb agreement, see Language Handbook, pp. R48–R49.

LOG ON Literature Online

Grammar For more Grammar practice, go to glencoe.com and enter QuickPass code GL49787u3.

Grammar Workshop

Subject-Verb Agreement

Focus

Write this sentence on the board:

Many works by this author is nonfiction. Discuss why this sentence is incorrect. Remind students that verbs should agree with the subject of the sentence in person and number and that the subject does not always immediately precede the verb.

Teach

Subject-Verb Agreement

Point out that the verb must agree with its subject in number and person. To help eliminate errors in subject-verb agreement, students may identify and mentally place the subject next to the verb.

Assess

1. A crowd of golden daffodils catches the speaker's eye.
2. The trees and the lake frame the field of flowers.
3. Correct
4. Neither the daffodils nor the landscape calls out to me.

Approaching Level

DIFFERENTIATED INSTRUCTION

African American Vernacular English For approaching-level students who are users of African American vernacular English, help them understand the present, past, and future tenses of the verbs *do, have,* and *was*. **Write:** does *(singular)* do *(plural)*; has *(singular)* have *(plural)*; was *(singular)* were *(plural)* Point out the subject-verb agreement in each of these sentences:

- Tommy does like to eat broccoli. *(singular subject-singular verb)*
- She has basketball practice after school. *(singular subject-singular verb)*
- Sandy and Joe were our neighbors for ten years. *(plural subject-plural verb)*

Before You Read

Focus

Bellringer Options

Selection Focus Transparency 22

Daily Language Practice Transparency 52

Or display images associated with traditional Japanese culture—cherry trees in blossom, Mount Fuji, kimonos, or Buddhist temples.

Ask: What do these images tell you about the relationship between traditional Japanese culture and nature?

Have students consider as they read how important nature has been to haiku writers.

Before You Read

Haiku

Meet the **Poets**

How much can seventeen syllables say? In the form of a haiku, they can express simple yet profound ideas and observations. Here are four haiku writers—two traditional masters from Japan and two modern voices.

Matsuo Bashō (1644–1694) Bashō is revered as one of Japan's greatest masters of haiku. Born into the samurai class of society, he received an education in Japanese and Chinese classics and began writing at an early age. When he was twelve, he entered the service of a local feudal lord. After his lord's death, Bashō traveled to the capital, Edo (now Tokyo), where he worked for four years as a clerk in the waterworks. However, the life of a civil servant was not for Bashō. He started a school of haiku and soon attracted a group of patrons and students whose support made it possible for him to spend his life traveling, writing, and meditating.

Widely respected in his own lifetime, Bashō's influence continued to grow in the twentieth century.

Chiyo (1703–1775) Kihaku, a well-known disciple of Bashō, discovered Chiyo's poetry when Chiyo was eighteen years old. Kihaku sought her out and helped to make her famous throughout Japan. Chiyo's poetry was greatly influenced by Bashō's work and shared its emphasis on a "oneness with nature." Nevertheless, Chiyo developed her own voice as an honest observer of nature. For Chiyo, writing poetry was a source of awakening that allowed her to live with simplicity and clarity.

Matsuo Bashō

Katy Peake (1917–1995) Catherine Anne (Katy) Peake was a poet, artist, author of children's stories, and social activist from Santa Barbara, California. Her work includes *The Indian Heart of Carrie Hodges* (1972), *A Four Gathering* (1981), and *Dancing Among Foxes* (1993). She was also a photographer.

Paula Yup (born 1957) Born in Phoenix, Arizona, Chinese American poet Paula Yup spent two years in Japan studying Japanese language and literature. She has published more than seventy poems. In addition to writing poetry, she translates Japanese poems into English.

LOG ON **Literature** Online

Author Search For more about the authors, go to glencoe.com and enter QuickPass code GL49787u3.

Selection Skills

Haiku

Literary Elements
- Haiku (SE pp. 497, 498, 500)
- Diction (SE p. 500)

Writing Skills/Grammar
- Research Report (SE p. 501)
- Italics (SE p. 501)
- Write About Style (TE p. 498)

Reading Skills
- Interpret Imagery (SE pp. 497, 498, 500)

Vocabulary Skills
- Analogies (SE pp. 497, 500)
- Academic Vocabulary (SE p. 500)

Literature and Reading Preview

Connect to the Poems

Have you ever struggled to find the right words to describe something? Write a description of a memorable moment in your life, using fifteen words or less.

Build Background

The purpose of a haiku, traditionally an untitled, unrhymed, seventeen-syllable poem, is to capture a flash of insight based on a solitary observation of nature. Since nature may change suddenly, the poet's challenge in writing a haiku is to record a fleeting moment in precise language.

Set Purposes for Reading

Big Idea Nature Inspires

As you read, think about the image from nature that gave rise to each haiku. Ask yourself, Why did that image inspire the poet?

Literary Element Haiku

Haiku is a traditional Japanese form of poetry that has three lines and seventeen syllables. The first and third lines have five syllables each; the middle line has seven syllables. As you read these haiku, ask yourself, How well does each poem capture a single moment in nature?

Reading Strategy Interpret Imagery

Imagery is the "word pictures" that writers create to evoke an emotional response in readers. In creating effective images, writers use sensory details or descriptions that appeal to one or more of the five senses: sight, hearing, touch, taste, and smell. **Interpreting imagery** means deciding how these descriptions create or affect a text's meaning.

Tip: **Take Notes** Use a chart to record images and your interpretations.

Image	Interpretation
old pond	represents stillness, maybe old age

Learning Objectives

For pages 496–500

In studying these texts, you will focus on the following objectives:

Literary Study: Analyzing haiku.

Reading: Interpreting imagery.

Vocabulary

calligraphy (kə lig′ re fē) *n.* artistic, decorative, or stylized writing or lettering; p. 498 *Written in calligraphy, the message was beautiful but difficult to read.*

twine (twīn) *v.* to coil around; p. 498 *The ivy twined around the chimney, covering it on all sides.*

Tip: **Analogies** Comparisons that reveal the relationship between two things or ideas are called analogies. One way to approach an analogy is to make up a sentence describing the relationship between the first pair of words. Then look for another pair of words that, when put into the same sentence, also results in a true statement.

calligraphy : writing :: jumping : movement

You might think, "*Calligraphy* is a type of *writing; jumping* is a type of *movement.*"

Before You Read

Focus

Summary

Each haiku conveys an ordinary but beautiful natural event—a frog jumping, a sky clearing, a flower growing, and a butterfly resting.

For summaries in languages other than English, see Unit 3 Teaching Resources Book, pp. 113–118.

Vocabulary

Draw Definitions Have students write a short story using the new vocabulary words. Tell students to illustrate their stories by creating a collage, using pictures from magazines or newspapers.

For additional vocabulary practice, see Unit 3 Teaching Resources Book, p. 121.

English Learners

DIFFERENTIATED INSTRUCTION

Beginning/Early Intermediate Give English learners extra help in understanding analogies. Tell them that they need to think about the relationship between the literal meaning of each word in an analogy. Explain that analogies can represent different relationships, such as part/whole and classification/type. **Write:** finger : hand :: petal : flower. Explain that a finger is part of a hand and a petal is part of a flower. **Write:** poodle : dog :: oak : tree. Ask students to verbalize this analogy. *(Poodle is a kind of dog just as oak is a kind of tree.)* Encourage students to think of other analogies to represent these relationships.

Teach

Reading Strategy 1

Interpret Imagery
Answer: *Students may say that the morning glory is receiving water from the bucket or has set roots down in it.*

Literary Element 2

Haiku **Answer:** *Students may say that the image of the butterfly captures a few seconds in time—butterflies rarely linger and they do not live long.*

View the Art ★

Although the kimono has long been associated with traditional Japanese culture, it originally came from China. The Chinese wore kimonos until the overthrow of the Ming dynasty. The Japanese adopted the kimono in the eighth century. The long, wide-sleeved robe is secured only with a wide sash called an obi and is traditionally worn by both men and women.

To check students' understanding of the selection, see Unit 3 Teaching Resources Book, p. 123.

Haiku

The old pond;
A frog jumps in:
Sound of water.

Matsuo Bashō
Translated by Robert Hass

a clear sheet of sky
calligraphy of blackbirds
written and erased

Katy Peake

The bottom of the bucket which Lady Chiyo filled has fallen out; the moon has no home in the water, November, 1889. Yoshitoshi. ★

A morning glory
Twined round the bucket:
I will ask my neighbor for water.

Chiyo
Translated by Yasuko Horioka

Peace

I spy butterfly
In quietly still waters
living for today.

Paula Yup

1 Interpret Imagery *What is the relationship between the morning glory and the bucket?*

Vocabulary

calligraphy (kə lig′ rə fē) *n.* artistic, decorative, or stylized writing or lettering

twine (twīn) *v.* to coil around

Haiku *How well does this haiku capture a single moment?* **2**

Writing Practice

SPIRAL REVIEW **Write About Style** Have students recall poems that they have read in this unit and compare their different styles. Students should note the techniques within each poem—rhyme, rhythm, meter, free verse, enjambment, and haiku. Students may also consider the use of figurative language in a poem.

Have them write responses to the following questions:

- What style appeals to you most? *(Answers will vary.)*
- What style do you think is the easiest to write? The most difficult? *(Students may say that free verse is the easiest to write and that poems with very specific patterns of rhyme and rhythm are the most difficult to write.)*

Then have students write a paragraph that summarizes their answers.

After You Read

Respond and Think Critically

Respond and Interpret

1. Which of the haiku gives you the clearest image of a specific moment in time in a natural setting? Explain.

2. (a)What does the speaker in Bashō's haiku see and hear? (b)What makes this a fleeting moment?

3. (a)What event in nature does Katy Peake's haiku describe? (b)What human activity does she compare it with?

Analyze and Evaluate

4. Reread Bashō's haiku. In which season do you think this moment took place? Explain your opinion.

5. The speaker in most traditional haiku does not often appear in the poem as "I." Do you think Chiyo's break with tradition makes her haiku more or less effective? Explain.

6. Explain how Paula Yup's poem is both similar to and different from traditional Japanese haiku.

Connect

7. **Big Idea** Nature Inspires What image or natural scene would you use in a haiku? Explain.

8. **Compare to Today** As an art form, the haiku has sometimes been compared to the photograph, which can capture a fleeting moment. Do you think this is an appropriate comparison? Explain.

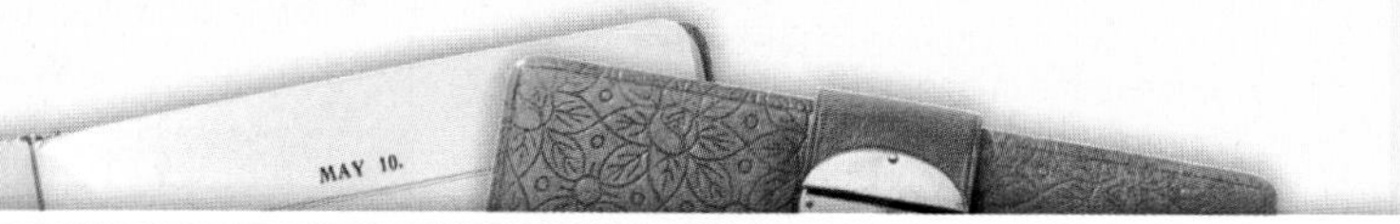

Daily Life & Culture

Early Japanese Women Writers

During the Heian Period (794–1192), the development of *kana*—a Japanese phonetic syllabary—made writing the native Japanese language much easier. As scholars and government officials, men remained under pressure to use the Chinese language, which was in political favor at the time. Women, however, did not hold such positions at court, and they were able to write privately in *kana*.

In fact, during this time period, many women published prose anthologies or collections that often combined stories, catalogues, and other "bits" of personal nonfiction from diaries.

Matsushima no Tsubone, 1875. Yoshitoshi Taiso. Woodblock print, 14¼ x 9½ in. Private collection.

Group Activity Work with classmates to discuss and answer the following questions.

1. Why were women uniquely positioned to play an important role in the development of native Japanese culture?
2. (a)What form did the earliest writing by Japanese women take? (b)Why do you think it took this form?
3. What might a diary entry and a haiku have in common?

After You Read

Assess

1. Students may suggest the image of blackbirds scrawled against the sky or the flower growing around the bucket.

2. (a) The speaker sees a pond and a frog; he hears a splash of water. (b) The movement of the frog is quick. The reader knows that the sound and ripples in the water will fade quickly.

3. (a) A flock of blackbirds flying through the sky (b) Handwriting that is quickly erased

4. The season is probably spring or summer because the pond is not frozen.

5. Students may say the "I" makes the poem more effective because it shows the relationship between the speaker and nature.

6. Similar: It focuses sharply on one natural image at a particular moment and has the traditional line and syllable requirements. Different: It has a title and there is no punctuation separating the final line from the rest of poem.

7. Answers will vary.

8. Some students may say that the comparison to a photograph is apt because both capture a fleeting image in the moment.

For additional selection assessment, see Assessment Resources, pp. 127–128.

Daily Life & Culture

1. Women did not have roles at court that required them to use Chinese.

2. (a) diaries and lists (b) Women did not participate in public life. Their work was not meant for publication.

3. Both often include observations about the human experience.

After You Read

Assess

Literary Element

1. It shows how patterns are written and erased in the sky. The poem illustrates that nothing is constant.
2. It shows how a morning glory becomes part of a bucket and how a human is affected by this natural occurrence. It illustrates the connection between the human and the natural worlds.
3. The poem suggests silence before the frog jumps and after the sound of the water fades away.

Progress Check

Can students identify haiku?

If No → See Unit 3 Teaching Resources Book, p. 119.

Review: Diction

Students might brainstorm synonyms for these words and use them to write a new version of the haiku with the traditional syllable pattern: *twined, round, bucket, ask, neighbor, water, old, pond, jumps, sound*

Reading Strategy

1. The water is still, clear, and mirror-like; the butterfly is fluttering and colorful. The butterfly's life is short; the water will last. The butterfly is not conscious of or worried about the passage of time; it simply exists in the moment.
2. A morning glory is a vine-like flower that grows rapidly. The flowers might literally appear in the bucket overnight. Most other flowers, such as tulips or daisies, cannot grow around an object. Also, morning glories are seasonal. The flower may be a *kigo* signifying summer.

Progress Check

Can students interpret imagery?

If No → See Unit 3 Teaching Resources Book, p. 120.

Vocabulary

1. a **2.** c

Academic Vocabulary

definition—to improve or perfect
synonyms—hone, polish
sample sentence—The pitcher refined his delivery until it was perfect.

Literary Element Haiku

Most **haiku** use vivid but fleeting images to sketch a scene that usually involves the world of nature and says something about the human experience. This tradition revolves around some key Buddhist principles about the natural world: that all things change; that all things are interrelated; and that all things suffer. Another Buddhist principle that underlies haiku is a respect or concern for silence.

1. How does Peake's haiku demonstrate that all things change?
2. How does Chiyo's poem show that all things are related to each other?
3. Explain how Bashō's poem is concerned with silence.

Review: Diction

As you learned on page 187, **diction** is a writer's choice of words. Translators are keenly aware of diction. A single word in one language may have many counterparts in another language, and the translator must choose the word that best conveys the meaning of the original text.

Partner Activity Meet with a partner to discuss the translated poems. Count the syllables in each line to find places where the poem veers from the traditional syllable pattern. Brainstorm a list of words and phrases that have the same or similar meaning as those in the poem. Using your list of words, write a new version of the haiku that follows the traditional 5-7-5 syllable pattern. Share your haiku with the rest of the class.

LOG ON Literature Online

Selection Resources For Selection Quizzes, eFlashcards, and Reading-Writing Connection activities, go to glencoe.com and enter QuickPass code GL49787u3.

Reading Strategy Interpret Imagery

An **image** brings a picture, sound, or other sensory experience to mind, but it may also have some sort of symbolic value. Look back at the chart you created, and think about the deeper meanings of the images in the poems.

1. In Yup's haiku, how do you suppose the appearance of the water compares with that of the butterfly? Why might Yup think that the butterfly is "living for today"?
2. One image in Chiyo's poem is the morning glory. Why do you think she chose this vinelike plant, which grows very fast?

Vocabulary Practice

Practice with Analogies Choose the word that best completes each analogy.

1. **photography : camera :: calligraphy :**
   a. brush **b.** appliance **c.** hoe
2. **broken : split :: twined :**
   a. open **b.** doubled **c.** twisted

Academic Vocabulary

*In order to achieve precise effects, haiku writers must carefully **refine** their language.*

Refine is an academic word. In more casual conversation, someone might say that the valedictorian of the class had **refined** his or her study skills. To study this word further, fill out the graphic organizer below.

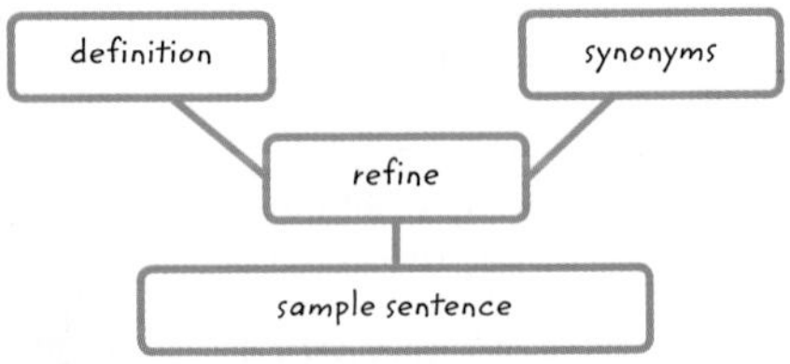

For more on academic vocabulary, see pages 54–55 and R79–R81.

Respond Through Writing

Research Report

Investigate the History of Haiku Write a research report of at least 1,500 words explaining why haiku is a distinctively Japanese art form.

Prewrite To create a foundation for your research, begin by investigating the basic information about haiku's origins. Use an organizer like the one below to guide and record your initial research. In the center box, write the general topic of your investigation. In the outer boxes, record the answers to the basic questions: *Who? What? Where? How? Why? When?*

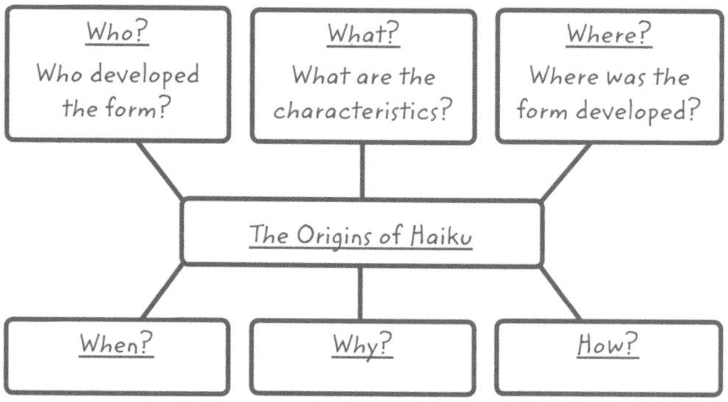

Do further research on the important names, places, and ideas discovered in your initial investigation. In your research, use a variety of sources—Web sites, encyclopedias, magazines, and books.

Draft Choose a central idea for your report—one that is strongly supported by your research. Express this idea clearly in a thesis statement in your report's opening. In your draft, include information that best supports your thesis and addresses the reader's most likely questions. As you write, accurately convey the results of your research.

Revise As you revise your draft, identify places in the report that could be enhanced by visual aids, such as Japanese images, art, or photos. Make sure that you use all haiku or Japanese terminology correctly. Review your report using the rubric on page 962 and revise as necessary.

Edit and Proofread Proofread your paper, correcting any errors in spelling, grammar, and punctuation. Use the Grammar Tip in the side column to help you use italics correctly.

Learning Objectives

In this workshop, you will focus on the following objectives:

Writing: Writing a research report.

Grammar: Understanding when to use italics for titles of works.

Grammar Tip

Italics

With each quotation, summary, or paraphrased text in your final report, you must include a reference to your source. Titles of complete works, such as books, magazines, Web sites, and newspapers, should appear in italics.

The Encyclopedia of Japanese Art

Titles of shorter pieces that appear in a larger work, such as articles that appear in a magazine or on a Web site, should be surrounded by quotation marks.

"Haiku in Modern Japan" from *The Encyclopedia of Japanese Art*

See pages R34–R37 for more information on citing sources in a research paper.

After You Read

Assess

Respond Through Writing

Students' reports should:

- explore the history of haiku as a distinctly Japanese art form
- include a clear, concise thesis statement with supporting evidence
- focus on the form's origins and provide all of the essential information about these origins
- explore specific areas of the form's history in more depth
- include relevant visual aids

A student who meets all of these criteria should receive the equivalent of a 4-point response.

A student who fully meets four or partially meets five of these criteria should receive the equivalent of a 3-point response.

A student who fully meets two or three or partially meets four of these criteria should receive the equivalent of a 2-point response.

A student who partially meets two or fully meets one of these criteria should receive the equivalent of a 1-point response.

Approaching Level

DIFFERENTIATED INSTRUCTION

Emerging Tell students that a thesis statement is a sentence in the introduction of an essay that states what will be proven in the essay.

Remind students to make their thesis as specific as possible. **Write:** George Washington Carver was a famous inventor who helped people in many ways. Explain that this thesis is too broad. The phrase "in many ways" is not specific.

Write: George Washington Carver was a scholar and inventor who is best known for creating innovative ways of helping people. Discuss the ways in which this statement is more specific.

Focus

The words in the Practice are all verbs or adjectives. Students should find synonyms that are the same part of speech and can be used correctly in the sentences.

Assess

Practice

1. Possible synonyms:
   - **a.** swerve—veer, turn
   - **b.** reconcile—reunite, settle
   - **c.** isolated—separated, secluded
   - **d.** vast—huge, giant
   - **e.** vacant—empty, absent
2. Possible sentences:
   - **a.** You have to swerve to avoid the pothole.
     Turn to the right at the stop sign.
     Veer away from the shoulder, or you will skid.
   - **b.** The sisters will reconcile their differences.
     Bob hopes to reunite the arguing brothers.
     Can you settle the differences between those two teams?
   - **c.** The isolated village was far from the highway.
     The secluded house could not be seen from the street.
     The separated children ate lunch at different desks.
   - **d.** The universe is vast.
     The auditorium is huge.
     The servings are enormous.
   - **e.** The apartment is vacant.
     The pot is empty.
     The student was absent from class.

For additional vocabulary practice, see Glencoe Interactive Vocabulary CD-ROM.

Learning Objectives

In this workshop, you will focus on the following objective:

Vocabulary: Understanding how to use a thesaurus.

Vocabulary Workshop

Thesaurus Use

Literature Connection Some synonyms, such as *twined* and *wound,* are practically interchangeable; others can have subtly different meanings. For instance, *still* means "motionless," as well as "quiet."

> "*I spy butterfly / In quietly still waters / living for today.*"
>
> —Paula Yup, "Peace"

Learning the differences between similar words can help you read better, write more expressively and precisely, and speak and listen more effectively.

Dictionaries sometimes provide a list of **synonyms** at the end of an entry and explain their shades of meaning. A **thesaurus** is a more specialized reference work for finding synonyms and **antonyms,** or words with opposite meanings. Thesauruses are available in different formats: online, on CD-ROMs, in word-processing software, and in print. Thesauruses may be organized traditionally or in dictionary order.

Traditional Organization The traditional organization for a thesaurus is based on concepts. To use such a thesaurus, look up the target word, such as *remove,* in the index. Then choose the subentry closest to the meaning you want, such as *subtract.* That subentry will direct you to a list of synonyms under the heading *subtraction.*

Dictionary Organization Some thesauruses are organized like dictionaries. You simply look up the word you know. The sample entry below is from a thesuarus organized like a dictionary.

The part of speech is indicated. *A sample sentence is provided.*

quiet *adj. The night was quiet:* silent, calm, soundless, noiseless, hushed, still, making no sound, not busy ← *The most common synonyms are listed first.*

Ant. loud, noisy, active, busy ← *A list of antonyms is also provided.*

Practice Using a thesaurus, find two synonyms for each word below. Find the definitions of those synonyms in a dictionary to identify the precise meaning of each one. Write a sentence for each word below. Each sentence should include one of the words as well as two synonyms for each word. Be sure that your sentences reflect the slight differences in meaning among each group of synonyms.

a. swerve **b.** reconcile **c.** isolated **d.** vast **e.** vacant

Thesauruses, Synonyms, and Antonyms

A **thesaurus** is a reference source containing synonyms and antonyms, in which terms are arranged either alphabetically or by subject area. **Synonyms** are words with the same or nearly the same meanings. **Antonyms** are words with opposite meanings.

Tip

To decide whether two words are synonyms, first determine what part of speech each word is. Synonyms are always the same part of speech.

LOG ON **Literature Online**

Vocabulary For more vocabulary practice, go to glencoe.com and enter QuickPass code GL49787u3.

Vocabulary Practice

SMALL GROUP SPIRAL REVIEW **Denotation and Connotation** Inform students that synonyms often have similar meanings but do not necessarily have the same denotation, or dictionary definition. Have students work in small groups and share the synonyms that they came up with for each word in the Practice exercise. Have students discuss the denotations of each of the synonyms. Then, have students identify which of the three words have the strongest connotation, or the undertone or implied meaning of a word. For example, two synonyms for the word *swerve* are *veer* and *turn*. Since *swerve* means an abrupt turn and *veer* implies a more gradual shift in turning, *swerve* has the stronger connotation of all the words.

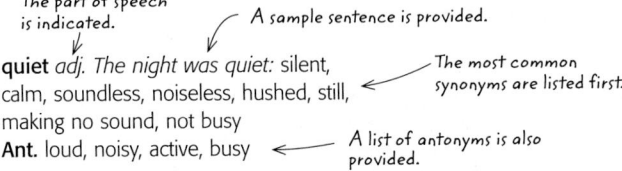

PART 2

Life Lessons

Spectators, 20th century. Andrew Gadd. Oil on canvas, 47 x 71 in.

View the Art Many of Andrew Gadd's artworks are allegorical—they have meaning beyond the literal. What does this painting literally show? What might this painting represent figuratively? ★

BIG IDEA

Perhaps the most important thing life teaches us is that there is always more to learn. Every experience brings a new lesson. The selections in this part explore the wisdom gained from some of life's greatest teachers—love, family, and nature. As you read these poems, ask yourself, What lesson has each speaker learned?

503

UNIT THREE

PART 2

Analyze and Extend

Big Idea

Life Lessons Encourage students to look at the art and discuss who, if anyone, is learning a lesson.

Ask: What is one of the most important life lessons you have learned? *(Answers will vary.)*

View the Art ★

Answer: *(The painting literally shows some kids watching something. Answers will vary as to the figurative meaning.)*

While English artist Andrew Gadd's (1968–) technique shows classic influences, his subjects are contemporary. Gadd is a figurative painter—he paints real subjects that may not strictly represent what they are—and his work is often allegorical.

English Learners

DIFFERENTIATED INSTRUCTION

Intermediate Have a student read the Big Idea note above. Engage students in a discussion of what this Big Idea means. **Ask:** How are love, family, and nature life's greatest teachers? *(Students may answer that people learn, gain their personalities, and develop humor from watching their families and those who they love. People also learn lessons from watching things that happen in nature.)*

Ask students to discuss some of their "greatest teachers." Encourage students to write down something they have learned from love, family, or nature. After they read, they can compare what they have learned to what other students may have learned.

UNIT THREE

PART 2

Focus

Bellringer Options

Daily Language Practice Transparency 53

Or **write** on the board: It was so hot I could have fried an egg on the sidewalk. Point out to students that imagery can be fun and funny. Have students complete the following: It was so cold . . . ; It rained so hard . . . ; The fog was so dense . . . .

For additional support for English Learners, see Unit 3 Teaching Resources Book, p. 127.

View the Cartoon ★

Cartoonist Wiley Miller has received four National Cartoonist Society Reuben Awards for "Non Sequitur." The cartoon is not confined to any specific subject, but ranges from political satire to pure comedy.

Learning Objectives

For pages 503–505

In studying this text, you will focus on the following objective:

Literary Study: Analyzing figurative language and imagery.

LITERARY FOCUS

The Language of Poetry

In what distinctive ways does poetry use language?

 ★

Imagery

Imagery refers to the word pictures that can remind readers of something they have seen, heard, tasted, smelled, or touched. To create an image, the poet uses sensory details: words that appeal to one or more of the five senses.

Figurative Language

Figurative language is language used for descriptive effect, often to imply meanings indirectly. The words in figurative language suggest more than their ordinary, literal meanings. All writers use figurative language, although it is particularly important to poets, who rely on it to bring power, vitality, and freshness to their writing. Notice the way Yvonne Sapia uses the word *passenger* in this excerpt from "Defining the Grateful Gesture."

but she would eat it
to gain back the strength
taken from her by long hot days
of working in her mother's house
and helping her father make
candy in the family kitchen.
No idle passenger
Traveling through life was she.

—Yvonne Sapia, **from "Defining the Grateful Gesture"**

Writing Practice

Write Using Figurative Language Explain that authors use figurative language to describe a setting, object, or person to readers. Figurative language such as imagery, personification, and metaphors help readers to understand something better. Tell students to think of a place that they like to visit, such as a family member's house, a park, or a museum. **Ask:** To which of your senses does the place appeal? *(Students will answer with different sights, sounds, smells, tastes, or feels. They may like music, food, or pictures.)* Tell students to write a paragraph describing the place and to use figurative language. Instruct them to attempt at least one simile or metaphor and to use imagery by describing how the place appeals to at least two of their five senses.

Figurative language is based on figures of speech. A **figure of speech** is an expression in which words are used in unusual ways to create vivid or dramatic effects. Simile, metaphor, personification, and hyperbole are all figures of speech.

Simile A **simile** is a comparison of two unlike things that uses the word *like* or *as*. Poets employ similes to help the reader understand an abstraction—to make it easier for the reader to grasp what is being described.

He is as cool and gleaming as a braided whip

—Mary Oliver, **from "The Black Snake"**

The simile comparing a snake to a braided whip helps the reader see the snake in a new way. A simile can also startle the reader and inject fresh life into a familiar idea, as does William Shakespeare's simile, "Death lies on her, like an untimely frost."

Metaphor Like a simile, a **metaphor** is a direct comparison between two unlike things. However, in a metaphor, the comparison is implied rather than stated; there is no use of connective words such as *like* or *as*.

a clear sheet of sky
calligraphy of blackbirds

—Katy Peake, **from "Haiku"**

In her haiku, Katy Peake compares the sky to a clean sheet of paper and the appearance of birds as handwriting on the paper. In most metaphors, the first object is seen as having similar qualities to the second object. Poets use metaphors to enliven language and to help readers see a familiar subject in a new way.

Personification When a writer gives human qualities to nonhuman things, he or she is using **personification**. Poets use personification for the same reasons they use a metaphor: to help the reader see something familiar in a slightly different way.

And then my heart with pleasure fills,
And dances with the daffodils.

—William Wordsworth, **from "I Wandered Lonely as a Cloud"**

Hyperbole This figure of speech uses overstatement or exaggeration for dramatic effect. Poets use hyperbole to add flavor to their writing and bring emphasis to their images:

And you O my Soul where you stand,
Surrounded, detached, in measureless oceans
of space

—Walt Whitman, **from "A Noiseless Patient Spider"**

Quickwrite

Describe Winter What sights, smells, or tastes come to mind when you think of winter? Can you smell chestnuts roasting? Can you taste a snowflake on your tongue? Or do you feel the warmth of the sun on your face? Jot down images that would help a reader who lives in a different part of the country see, hear, smell, taste, and touch a typical winter day where you live.

LOG ON **Literature** Online

Literature and Reading For more about literary elements, go to glencoe.com and enter QuickPass code GL49787u3.

UNIT THREE

PART 2

Teach

Reading Strategy

Understand Imagery

Have students read each of the poem excerpts aloud. After each excerpt is read, pause and **ask:** What images do you see when you read the poem? Encourage students to be specific. Point out any figurative language the students use as they talk.

Assess

Quickwrite

Answers will vary. Make sure students are specific and that their images address all five senses.

English Learners

DIFFERENTIATED INSTRUCTION

Intermediate Have students look at the cartoon on page 504. **Ask:** What does the saying "the pen is mightier than the sword" mean? *(Students may answer that the saying means that words solve more problems than violence does.)* Have students look carefully at the boxes, which are marked "pens." Explain that the caption "Learning the Proper Use of Metaphor" hints that metaphors are not to be taken literally. **Say:** If you call someone a cheetah, you probably mean that they are very fast. You do not mean that the person is actually a cheetah.

Before You Read

Focus

Bellringer Options

Daily Language Practice Transparency 54

Or **say:** Buying, selling, and trading are basic to modern life. **Ask:** What do you buy or trade? How might surfing the Web or downloading information be considered a form of commerce? *(Possible answers: Companies provide information in return for your exposure to their ads; information might be seen as a type of currency.)* Encourage students to discuss how these forms of commerce affect their personal economics.

Before You Read

How Things Work

Meet **Gary Soto**

(born 1952)

Gary Soto first became interested in poetry while procrastinating on a college research paper. Instead of writing, he picked up an anthology of poetry and began leafing through it. Excited by what he found there, Soto decided to write poetry himself.

Handle with Care Soto was born and raised in Fresno, California, in the *barrio,* a working-class Mexican American neighborhood. There were no books in his home, and he was not encouraged to read. Still, he developed an interest in geography and eventually went to college at Fresno State University. There, he enrolled in a writing class where he learned "to handle language with care." Soto memorized the poems of English and Chinese authors, because this practice was supposed to help his writing. However, he was more interested in Spanish and Latin American poets.

> *"I woke up to poetry and went to bed with poetry."*
>
> —Gary Soto

Soto received his Master of Fine Arts degree in creative writing from the University of California, Irvine. A year later, his first collection of poetry, *The Elements of San Joaquin* (1977), was published. A reviewer for *Western American Literature* called Soto "considerably more than just a good ethnic writer, he is a good poet."

A Writer and a Teacher Since his first book of poems, Soto has written memoirs, novels, plays, films, and an opera libretto. His writing appeals to all age groups and his work has won many awards, including the Academy of American Poets Prize and the Andrew Carnegie Medal. He encourages young poets and writers by telling them to look within themselves for inspiration.

Examining Life Unlike some authors, Soto does not begin writing with a particular audience in mind. As a result, his work often appeals to adults and young adults alike. His writing encourages readers to recall the details of their own childhoods. Most of Soto's work describes the pain and promise of growing up. His memoir *Living Up the Street* is a collection of 21 anecdotes about his life growing up in the *barrio.* In one chapter, he writes about struggling to make his world like the one he sees on 1950s television by trying to get his rowdy siblings to dress for dinner as they do in "Leave It to Beaver."

LOG ON **Literature** Online

Author Search For more about Gary Soto, go to glencoe.com and enter QuickPass code GL49787u3.

Selection Skills

How Things Work

Reading Skills
- Analyzing Structure (SE pp. 507, 509)
- Use a Chart (SE p. 507)

Writing Skills/Grammar
- Write a Graphic Story (SE p. 509)
- Write a Paragraph (TE p. 508)

Literary Elements
- Imagery (SE pp. 507, 509)

Vocabulary Skills
- Context Clues (SE pp. 507, 509)

Literature and Reading Preview

Connect to the Poem

Would anyone's life change if you stopped spending money on everyday things? List several items you buy regularly and explain how not buying them could affect other people.

Build Background

In 1982 the United States suffered a recession that was the worst economic downturn since the Great Depression of the 1930s. Businesses failed, farms went bankrupt, and many were jobless. By 1985, when Gary Soto published the poem "How Things Work," the U.S. economy was beginning to turn around and the country's mood was more hopeful.

Set Purposes for Reading

Big Idea Life Lessons

As you read "How Things Work," ask yourself, What lesson might the speaker be encouraging his daughter to learn?

Literary Element Imagery

Imagery refers to "word pictures" writers create to evoke an emotional response in the reader. In creating effective images, writers use sensory details—descriptions that appeal to one or more of your senses. As you read, ask yourself, Which of Soto's words and phrases create imagery and an emotional response?

Reading Strategy Analyze Structure

The **structure** of a poem is created through the organization of images, ideas, and words. Without organized structure, a poem, or any other piece of writing, would not be a coherent whole. As you read, ask yourself, What structure does Soto use?

Tip: Reread Read the poem, thinking about what the words mean. Then read it again, concentrating on structure. Use a chart to record the ways the structure adds meaning.

Structure	Purpose
short sentences	emphasize a point

Learning Objectives

For pages 506–509

In studying this text, you will focus on the following objectives:

Literary Study: Analyzing imagery.

Reading: Analyzing structure.

Writing: Writing a graphic story.

Vocabulary

rosin (roz′ in) *n.* a resin made from the sap of various pine trees used to increase sliding friction on the bows of certain stringed instruments; p. 508 *New violin students have to learn when and where to use rosin on the bow.*

belligerent (bə lij′ ər ənt) *adj.* inclined or eager to fight; p. 508 *The opposing team's belligerent coach screamed and kicked dirt when the umpire made a questionable call.*

Tip: Context Clues When you encounter an unfamiliar word, you often can figure out its meaning by looking at the words and sentences that surround it. For example, in the sentence *The belligerent woman was hostile and angry toward the salesperson for making a mistake,* the words "angry," "hostile," and "for making a mistake" tell you that *belligerent* means "aggressive" and "inclined to fight."

Before You Read

Focus

Summary

The speaker first describes how he spends his 20 dollars. Then he theorizes how the people who received the money will use it. He explains to his daughter that by purchasing something, he indirectly helps others buy things of their own. But he admits some uncertainty about whether this is true or not.

For summaries in languages other than English, see Unit 3 Teaching Resources Book, pp. 128–133.

Vocabulary

Prompting Learning Give students sheets of paper with the line, "This morning on my way to school I saw . . ." at the top of the page. Have students finish the story in one or two paragraphs. Tell students to try to include the words *rosin* and *belligerent* in their paragraphs. Have volunteers read their paragraphs aloud.

For additional vocabulary practice, see Unit 3 Teaching Resources Book, p. 136.

For additional context, see Glencoe Visual Vocabulary CD-ROM.

Approaching Level

DIFFERENTIATED INSTRUCTION

Emerging Explain to students that many readers think poems must rhyme. Tell students that poems do not have to rhyme, but should have a rhythm. Encourage students to read the poem twice. The first time they read, they should try to understand the meaning. The second time they read, they should notice the rhythm of the poem. Ask students to comment on the author's use of style and language.

Teach

Big Idea 1

Life Lessons Answer: *To admit his uncertainty*

ADVANCED For advanced-level students, **ask:** How does this admission affect the reader? *(Students may say that it makes him seem honest and human; rather than claiming to be all knowing, he questions his own wisdom. By establishing the persona of a "regular guy," he encourages readers to identify with him.)*

View the Art ★

The influence of Impressionism and Cubism can clearly be seen in French artist Robert Delaunay's (1885–1941) unique painting style. Delaunay often collaborated with his wife, artist Sonia Terk.

To check students' understanding of the selection, see Unit 3 Teaching Resources Book, p. 138.

How Things Work

Gary Soto

Menage de Cochon or Menage Electrique. Robert Delaunay. Musee National d'Art Moderne, Centre Georges Pompidou, Paris. ★

Today it's going to cost us thirty-five dollars
To live. Six for a softball. Eight for a book,
A handful of ones for coffee and two sweet rolls,
Bus fare, **rosin** for your mother's violin.
We're completing our task. The tip I left
For the waitress filters down
Like rain, wetting the new roots of a child
Perhaps, a **belligerent** cat that won't let go
Of a balled sock until there's chicken to eat.
As far as I can tell, daughter, it works like this:
You buy crayons from a stationer, a bag of apples
From the farmer's market, and what dollars
Are passed on help others buy pencils, a guitar,
Tickets to a matinee movie.
If we buy a goldfish, someone tries on a hat.
If we buy crayons, someone walks home with a broom.
A tip, a small purchase here and there,
And things just keep going. I guess.

1 Life Lessons *Why might the speaker start his lesson with this phrase? Explain.*

Vocabulary

rosin (roz′ in) *n.* a resin made from the sap of various pine trees used to increase sliding friction on the bows of certain stringed instruments

belligerent (be lij′ ər ənt) *adj.* inclined or eager to fight

Writing Practice

SPIRAL REVIEW **Write a Paragraph** In "How Things Work," Gary Soto writes about the cause-and-effect relationship of money and the economy. Ask students if they have ever thought about what happens to their money after they spend it. **Ask:** Where do you spend your money? Where does the money go after you spend it? Then have students write a paragraph from the point of view of a one dollar bill. In the paragraph, students should consider where a one dollar bill might travel throughout a day. Ask volunteers to present their paragraphs to the class.

After You Read

Respond and Think Critically

Respond and Interpret

1. Do you agree with the speaker's interpretation of how things work? Explain.
2. (a)What does the speaker say it will cost today to live? (b)What do you think "to live" means in the context of the poem?
3. (a)What happens if the characters "buy a goldfish"? (b)What does the speaker mean by this?

Analyze and Evaluate

4. What might the speaker mean by "We're completing our task"? Explain.
5. What emotion does the image in line 7 evoke in the reader?
6. How appropriate or effective do you think the poem's title is?

Connect

7. **Big Idea** Life Lessons What does the speaker of the poem seem to be teaching his daughter about money and life?
8. **Connect to the Author** Soto's writings often appeal to adults and young adults. Do you think readers of all age groups can learn from this poem? Explain.

Literary Element Imagery

Poets and other writers use **imagery** to communicate what they see, hear, feel, taste, and smell. Appealing to the senses draws readers into the writing and encourages them to develop a personal relationship with the text. Soto relies on imagery throughout his poem to help readers understand his ideas.

1. Identify two examples of imagery in this poem.
2. Why do you think Soto chose not to create images of the father or the daughter in the poem?

Reading Strategy Analyze Structure

The **structure** of a poem includes the organization of images, ideas, words, and lines and is sometimes created through the use of rhythm, rhyme, repetition, or stanzas. Review the structure chart you made while reading. Then answer the following questions.

1. Find two lines in the poem that end in **enjambment,** or the breaking of a sentence where there is not a natural pause.
2. What is the effect of these enjambments?

Vocabulary Practice

Practice with Context Clues Identify the context clues in the following sentences that help you determine the meaning of each boldface vocabulary word.

1. The musician used **rosin** on her cello bow to keep it from getting too slippery.
2. As usual, the **belligerent** coach became aggressive when arguing with the referee and was thrown out of the game.

Writing

Write a Graphic Story The poem's imagery follows the journey of a few dollars. Write and illustrate a brief (six-panel) graphic story that follows a dollar as it is traded for things like food, entertainment, and transportation in the everyday cycle of work, wages, and goods.

LOG ON **Literature** Online

Selection Resources For Selection Quizzes, eFlashcards, and Reading-Writing Connection activities, go to glencoe.com and enter QuickPass code GL49787u3.

After You Read

Assess

1. Students should support their answers.
2. (a) Thirty-five dollars (b) "To live" means to buy what is needed to sustain their daily routines. Some may argue that the literal cost of living is much higher; explain that the small dollar amount points to Soto's meaning.
3. (a) Someone may try on a hat. (b) This sale paid for the hat.
4. They are doing their duty by contributing to the economy.
5. Tender or caring; the flow of money may be seen as contributing to child raising.
6. Students should support their answers.
7. He suggests that because this cycle sustains daily life, we have a duty to participate; yet he also questions the truth of this idea.
8. Most students will agree that the poem can be a lesson for all age groups. Students should support their responses with examples from the poem, such as Soto including items that many people can relate to including tipping, crayons, and guitars.

For additional selection assessment, see Assessment Resources, pp. 129–130.

Reading Strategy

1. 1, 5, 8, 12
2. The line breaks add emphasis to the words that follow the break.

Vocabulary Practice

1. "keep it from getting too slippery"
2. "became aggressive;" "when arguing"

Literary Element

1. "Filters down like rain"; "someone walks home with a broom"
2. His focus is on a political and philosophical statement about consumer society, not characters.

Writing

Students may adapt their paragraphs from the Writing Practice activity on TE p. 508. Students' graphic stories should:

- illustrate the story of a dollar as it travels through everyday life

For grammar practice, see Unit 3 Teaching Resources Book, p. 137.

Before You Read

Focus

Bellringer Options

Selection Focus Transparency 23

Daily Language Practice Transparency 55

Or **write** on the board: Are you a rebel? Discuss which societal and cultural rules students conform to. Then ask which restrictions they rebel against. Point out that the word *rebellious* can have negative connotations.

Ask: Do you think being rebellious is a bad thing? Explain.

Before You Read

I Was a Skinny Tomboy Kid

Meet **Alma Luz Villanueva**

(born 1944)

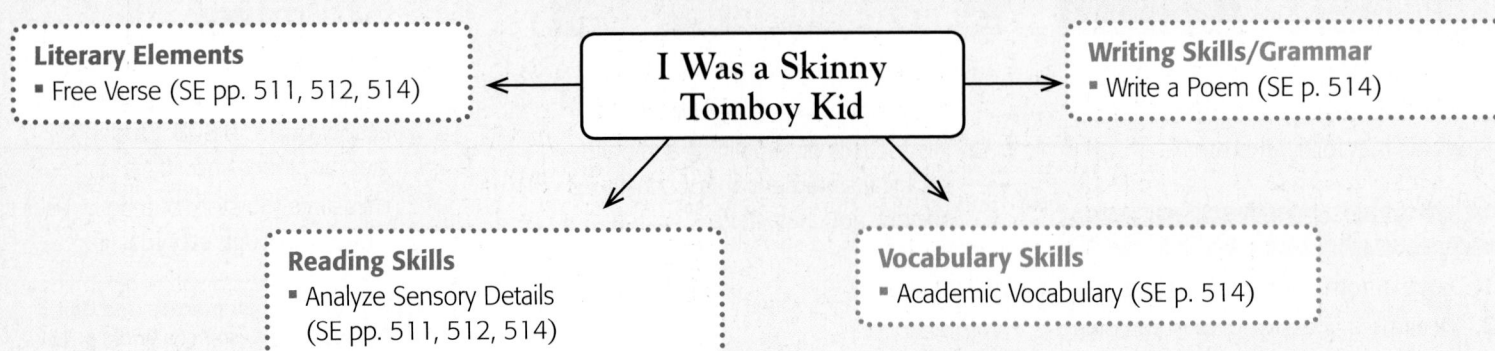

Alma Luz Villanueva writes about the struggles and joys of life in a personal voice that suggests universal feelings and experiences. Her writing explores the roles of women and her Mexican American, or Chicana, culture. Her works incorporate the themes of identity, love, and nature.

One with Nature Born in Lompoc, California, and raised in San Francisco, Villanueva never knew her German father. Her grandmother, a native of Mexico's Yaqui tribe, taught Villanueva about Mexican culture as well as her German heritage. Her grandmother also told her stories of the Yaqui people. When Villanueva was eleven years old, her grandmother died. Later, Villanueva would heal the pain of her loss through writing.

Villanueva left high school in tenth grade. She married young, and while her husband was overseas with the U.S. Marines, Villanueva worked two jobs to support herself and the first of their three children. Her marriage ended, and Villanueva left San Francisco to live in the Sierra Nevadas. She enjoyed the peace and the gentle sounds of nature.

Villanueva returned to school to receive her high school diploma and then went on to earn a degree in creative writing. She married a Chicano artist, Wilfredo Castaño. Not until she was thirty years old was she able to write on a regular basis. Through her writing, she began to explore themes of nature and her own difficult childhood. In 1977 her first book, *Bloodroot,* was published. In *Bloodroot,* Villanueva develops the connection between humans and nature, a theme she had heard in her grandmother's stories.

Illuminated Self In 1978 Villanueva's second book, *Mother, May I?,* was published. It is a long autobiographical poem in which she reflects upon the death of her grandmother, the struggles of growing up poor, and the alienation she felt as a tomboy in a culture that values femininity.

> *"Almost daily I will sit down to my poetry first and see what it has to tell me."*
>
> —Alma Luz Villanueva

Life Span, a book of poems written in the isolation of the mountains, was published in 1985. In these poems, Villanueva relied on her Chicana background and the wisdom she learned from her grandmother. Villanueva has gone on to publish a novel and short stories that, like her poetry, explore the unique experiences of her life.

LOG ON **Literature** Online

Author Search For more about Alma Luz Villanueva, go to glencoe.com and enter QuickPass code GL49787u3.

Selection Skills

I Was a Skinny Tomboy Kid

Literary Elements
- Free Verse (SE pp. 511, 512, 514)

Writing Skills/Grammar
- Write a Poem (SE p. 514)

Reading Skills
- Analyze Sensory Details (SE pp. 511, 512, 514)

Vocabulary Skills
- Academic Vocabulary (SE p. 514)

Literature and Reading Preview

Connect to the Poem

What expectations keep you from expressing who you really are? Quickwrite for a few minutes about how you might express yourself if you were not bound by these expectations.

Build Background

In the 1400s, the word *tomboy* meant "a rude, forward boy"; by the late 1500s, it meant "a bold or immodest woman." Modern definitions of *tomboy*—"a wild romping girl who behaves like a boy" and "a girl who enjoys activities and interests usually considered to be preferred by boys"—continue to imply that girls' interests should be different from those of boys.

Set Purposes for Reading

Big Idea Life Lessons

As you read, ask yourself, What life lessons has the speaker of the poem learned since she was a child?

Literary Element Free Verse

Free verse poetry has no fixed pattern of meter, rhyme, line length, or stanza arrangement. Although poets who write free verse do not follow traditional rules of form, meter, and rhyme, they use other techniques to create patterns. As you read, ask yourself, How does Villanueva create patterns in this poem?

Reading Strategy Analyze Sensory Details

Sensory details are the words or phrases in a work of literature that appeal to one or more of the five senses. As you read, ask yourself, How do the sensory images affect me?

Tip: Make a Chart As you read, use a chart like the one below to categorize the sensory details Villanueva uses.

Detail	Sense	Effect
"my fists clenched into / tight balls"	Touch Sight	Helps the reader identify physically with the speaker of the poem

Learning Objectives

For pages 510–514

In studying this text, you will focus on the following objectives:

Literary Study: Analyzing free verse.

Reading: Analyzing sensory details.

Writing: Writing a poem in free verse.

Before You Read

Focus

Summary

Poet Alma Luz Villanueva describes growing up as a tomboy. Activities such as walking along rooftops and fishing made her feel victorious and independent. Fearful of becoming like her mother, whom she saw as helpless, she invented a heroic self-image. Only as an adult did she realize how strong her mother was. Sometimes, she reexperiences the old fear and anger and has to comfort the child inside of her.

For summaries in languages other than English, see Unit 3 Teaching Resources Book, pp. 140–145.

Interactive Read and Write

Other options for teaching this selection can be found in

- Interactive Read and Write for EL Students, pp. 119–126
- Interactive Read and Write for Approaching-Level Students, pp. 119–126
- Interactive Read and Write for On-Level Students, pp. 119–126

Approaching Level

DIFFERENTIATED INSTRUCTION

Emerging In every culture, males and females are viewed differently. Often men are expected to be strong and decisive and women are expected to be caring and supportive. Discuss this idea with students. **Ask:** How do these expectations affect the way men and women are often treated or expected to behave? Encourage them to think about whether they think women and men should be treated differently or alike.

Ask: Have you ever been treated differently because of your gender? *(Answers will vary. Students should explain their answers.)* Encourage students to describe how they believe people should be treated.

Teach

Literary Element 1

Free Verse **Answer:** *She probably isolated the words "tight balls" at the far right to emphasize them. This line breaks the rhythm, jolting the reader in a way that echoes the sudden tensing of her clenched fists.*

APPROACHING To help approaching level students, **say:** A poet using free verse can alter the structure of a poem to emphasize the imagery. The break in the line before "tight balls" echoes the sudden tensing of the speaker's fists.

Reading Strategy 2

Analyze Sensory Details
Answer: *It appeals to the sense of touch.*

For additional practice using the reading skill or strategy, see Unit 3 Teaching Resources Book, p. 147.

Big Idea 3

Life Lessons **Ask:** What does the speaker learn about herself from the feeling inspired by walking on the rooftops? *(The line "I liked the edge of almost not making it" suggests she enjoys danger.)*

I Was a Skinny TOMBOY Kid

Alma Luz Villanueva

I was a skinny tomboy kid
who walked down the streets
with my fists clenched into
tight balls.
I knew all the roofs
and back yard fences,
I liked traveling that way
sometimes
not touching
the sidewalks
for blocks and blocks
it made
me feel

victorious
somehow
over the streets.
I liked to fly
from roof
to roof
the gravel
falling
away
beneath my feet,
I liked
the edge
of almost
not making it.
And the freedom
of riding
my bike
to the ocean
and smelling it
long before
I could see it,

1 Free Verse *Why do you think Villanueva chose to make this line look this way?*

2 Analyze Sensory Details *To which of the five senses does this detail appeal?*

Reading Practice

PARTNERS SPIRAL REVIEW **Analyze Character** In this poem, the speaker gives personal information about herself, including what she does and how she feels. Readers can use this information to make judgments about the character of the speaker. Have students read the poem with a partner. Then ask them to list interesting things about the speaker.

After students have finished reading, discuss the points that they have listed. In a class discussion, try to determine what kind of person the narrator is. **Ask:** What does the narrator like to do? How does that make her feel? *(Students may reply that the speaker likes to jump across rooftops because it makes her feel excited and victorious.)*

and I traveled disguised
as a boy
(I thought)
in an old army jacket
carrying my
fishing tackle
to the piers, and
bumming bait
and a couple of cokes
and catching crabs
sometimes and
selling them
to some Chinese guys
and I'd give
the fish away,
I didn't like fish
I just liked to fish—
and I vowed
to never
grow up
to be a woman
and be helpless
like my mother,
but then I didn't realize
the kind of guts
it often took
for her to just keep
standing
where she was.
I grew like a thin, stubborn weed
watering myself whatever way I could
believing in my own myth
transforming my reality
and creating a
legendary/self
every once in a while
late at night

Bicycle in Front of Nine Yellow Houses. Montse Roldos. Watercolor on paper. Private collection.

in the deep
darkness of my sleep
I wake
with a tenseness
in my arms
and I follow
it from my elbow to
my wrist
and realize
my fists are tightly clenched
and the streets come grinning
and I forget who I'm protecting
and I coil up
in a self/mothering fashion **5**
and tell myself
it's o.k.

4 Life Lessons *What has the speaker of the poem learned about her childhood view of her mother as helpless?*

Teach

Big Idea 4

Life Lessons Answer: *Villanueva saw her mother as weak for not rebelling against her role, but then realized she actually showed strength and courage by fulfilling it.*

Reading Strategy 5

Clarify Have students paraphrase what happens at the end of the poem.

APPROACHING To aid approaching-level students, ask what the speaker's action reveals about herself? *(She still feels at odds with the world and alone; she needs solace and mothering.)*

To check students' understanding of the selection, see Unit 3 Teaching Resources Book, p. 149.

English Learners

DIFFERENTIATED INSTRUCTION

Beginning/Early Intermediate This poem is written in an informal tone. The speaker uses conversational language and some slang terms which may be difficult for English learners. Ask the students to scan the poem and pick out any words that are unfamiliar to them. Then encourage students to look up the words in a dictionary.

For example, English learners may have trouble understanding slang terms like "bumming bait" and "the kind of guts it often took." **Ask:** Using the information in the poem, what do you think these unusual terms mean? *(In these cases, "bumming" means asking for; "guts" means bravery.)*

After You Read

Assess

1. Accept reasonable answers.
2. (a) Flying from roof to roof, almost not making it; riding her bike to the ocean; fishing (b) She craved thrills, challenges, and freedom.
3. (a) Line 74 (b) She is now an adult looking back.
4. A woman remembering her tomboy phase; tense shift in line 74 and *was* in the title
5. (a) To rebel against the image of girls as helpless (b) By inventing a heroic self-image
6. Possible answer: It conveys a long, convoluted life journey; its rhythm is tedious; the syntax, confusing.
7. She can be herself without rejecting her femininity.
8. Students may point to the speaker's comment that she doesn't want to be helpless like her mother.

Literary Element

1. In line 7, the indentation implies traveling; lines 14 and 15 are isolated, "being above it all"; lines 17–23 mimic the speaker's action.
2. The sense of free exploration might be lost.

Progress Check

Can students identify free verse?

If No → See Unit 3 Teaching Resources Book, p. 146.

Reading Strategy

1. Sight, touch, smell, and taste
2. Accept reasonable answers.

After You Read

Respond and Think Critically

Respond and Interpret

1. In what ways can you relate to the speaker of this poem?
2. (a)What does the speaker of the poem say she liked as a girl? (b)What can you tell about her from these details?
3. (a)Identify the point in the poem where the verb tense changes. (b)What does this change indicate?

Analyze and Evaluate

4. Who is the speaker of this poem? Use clues from the text to support your answer.
5. (a)Why does the speaker of the poem want to disguise herself as a boy? (b)In what other ways does the speaker disguise herself?
6. One sentence in this poem runs from line 28 to line 63. What might have been the author's purpose in making this sentence so long?

Connect

7. **Big Idea** Life Lessons What lessons has the speaker of the poem learned about being female?
8. **Connect to the Author** As a girl, Villanueva felt alienated because of her tomboy attitude. Where in the poem does this alienation appear?

Literary Element Free Verse

Before the twentieth century, most poets used regular meter and rhyme. Modern poets, rebelling against tradition, began writing in **free verse,** creating patterns with irregular meter and form.

1. Identify two places in "I Was a Skinny Tomboy Kid" where Villanueva uses the poem's form to emphasize the content of the poem.
2. How would "I Was a Skinny Tomboy Kid" differ if Villanueva had written it using regular meter and rhyme rather than free verse?

Reading Strategy Analyze Sensory Details

Many authors use **sensory details** to help readers imagine the characters, setting, and action in a piece of writing. Review the chart you created, and then answer the following questions.

1. What types of sensory details does Villanueva use most often in her poem? Support your answer with examples from the text.
2. Which of the sensory details in the poem do you find most striking or effective? Explain.

Academic Vocabulary

At the end of the poem, the speaker ***assures*** *herself that everything is okay.*

Assure is an academic word. More familiar words that are similar in meaning are *convince, guarantee,* and *promise.* In your life, what do you sometimes have to **assure** yourself about?

For more on academic vocabulary, see pages 54–55 and R79–R81.

Writing

Write a Poem in Free Verse Think about how free verse is suited for a poem about childhood. Write a poem in free verse about yourself as a child. Remember that free verse can take whatever form best supports your poem's imagery, rhythm, and subject matter.

LOG ON **Literature** Online

Selection Resources For Selection Quizzes, eFlashcards, and Reading-Writing Connection activities, go to glencoe.com and enter QuickPass code GL49787u3.

Academic Vocabulary

Answers will vary.

For additional assessment, see Assessment Resources, pp. 131–132.

Writing

Students' poems should

- include a childhood image
- use free verse effectively

For grammar practice, see Unit 3 Teaching Resources Book, p. 148.

Before You Read

Choices

Meet **Nikki Giovanni**

(born 1943)

In the early 1960s, Nikki Giovanni's sister was one of the first African American students to attend a previously all-white high school in Cincinnati, Ohio. Giovanni herself, however, chose to continue her education in the all-black schools she had always attended.

Giovanni was born Yolande Cornelia Giovanni Jr. in Knoxville, Tennessee. When she was still an infant, the family moved to Cincinnati, where her parents were employed as teachers. At that time, many neighborhoods had restricted policies that prevented non-whites from buying property in them, so Giovanni's parents bought a house in Lincoln Heights, an all-black suburb. Sometime before Yolande turned three, she acquired the nickname Nikki.

Early Protests During high school, Giovanni returned to Knoxville to live with her grandparents and attend the school where her grandfather taught Latin. It was in Knoxville that she began accompanying her grandmother to rallies protesting racial inequality.

> *"Life, I believe is not only a journey, it is an adventure. Every day there is something new and wonderful about life."*
>
> —Nikki Giovanni

As the end of high school neared, Giovanni applied and was accepted to Fisk University, an all-black college. But when she openly voiced her contempt for the school's rules during her first semester, Giovanni was expelled. Three years later, a new dean of students invited her to return to Fisk, where she eventually graduated with honors in history.

A Passion for Poetry Giovanni began writing poetry when she was a teen. After the death of her grandmother, she used her writing more and more as a refuge from emotional pain. In 1968, using borrowed money, Giovanni self-published her first book, *Black Feeling, Black Talk*. Most of the poems were the ones she had written while in mourning for her grandmother. That same year, with the profits from her first book and an arts grant, Giovanni published her second book, *Black Judgement*. By that time, Giovanni was being invited to speak and read her poetry regularly.

Woman of the Year In 1970, *Ebony* magazine named Giovanni "Woman of the Year." Although her writing continued to reflect a radical point of view, the mainstream magazine *Mademoiselle* named her "Woman of the Year" in 1971. Her activism led to national and international honors and awards.

LOG ON **Literature** Online

Author Search For more about Nikki Giovanni, go to glencoe.com and enter QuickPass code GL49787u3.

Before You Read

Focus

Bellringer Options

Daily Language Practice Transparency 56

Or **ask:** What do you do when you have to make a difficult choice? Discuss the importance of making choices and having the right to make personal decisions.

Selection Skills

Choices

Literary Elements
- Speaker (SE pp. 516–518)

Writing Skills/Grammar
- Write a List (SE p. 518)
- Write a Summary (TE p. 516)

Reading Skills
- Analyze Language (SE pp. 516–518)

Before You Read

Focus

Summary

The poem describes and communicates the deep pain of loneliness. The speaker's overwhelming need to connect is reflected in humanized images of the natural world.

For summaries in languages other than English, see Unit 3 Teaching Resources Book, pp. 151–156.

Literature and Reading Preview

Connect to the Poem

How can you turn a disappointment into something positive? Freewrite for a few minutes about an experience in which you turned a disappointment into something positive.

Build Background

Giovanni's style shows the influence of modern poets who experimented with form and style. In this poem, instead of punctuation, Giovanni uses line breaks and extra spaces to indicate pauses or to separate certain thoughts or ideas.

Set Purposes for Reading

Big Idea Life Lessons

As you read "Choices," ask yourself, How does the speaker respond to disappointment?

Literary Element Speaker

The **speaker** is the person (or animal or thing) that is speaking in a poem. Sometimes the speaker's voice is that of the poet. However, one should never assume that the speaker and the poet are the same. As you read "Choices," ask yourself, How would I describe the speaker's personality?

Reading Strategy Analyze Language

Although the language in this poem is simple, Giovanni uses it to create rhythmic and melodic lines. By **analyzing language** you can explore the ways Giovanni uses elements like repetition and wordplay to make the poem more musical. As you read, ask yourself, How does the language create rhythm in this poem?

Tip: Read First, Then Analyze Before analyzing a poem, it is best to read it at least one time straight through. When returning to the poem to analyze it, your familiarity will make it easier to understand how the language is working. After reading the poem once, use a chart like the one below to identify and track important words or phrases that are repeated in the poem.

Word/Phrase	Where It Occurs
"what i"	lines 2, 4, 10, 25, 27

Learning Objectives

For pages 515–518

In studying this text, you will focus on the following objectives:

Literary Study: Analyzing speaker.

Reading: Analyzing language.

Writing: Writing a list.

Writing Practice

PARTNERS SPIRAL REVIEW **Write a Summary**

Say: When you summarize, you want to restate the main ideas. Look for the most important ideas and then put them into your own words. With a partner, ask students to summarize the poem aloud, and then write a brief summary of the poem in a paragraph. Then have the partners evaluate the poem and discuss how the poem connects to their own lives. Ask students to share interesting points of their discussion with the class.

Petit Alleluia (For a Wedding), 1970. Alfred Manessier. Lithograph, 42 x 33.5 cm. Private collection.© ARS, NY.

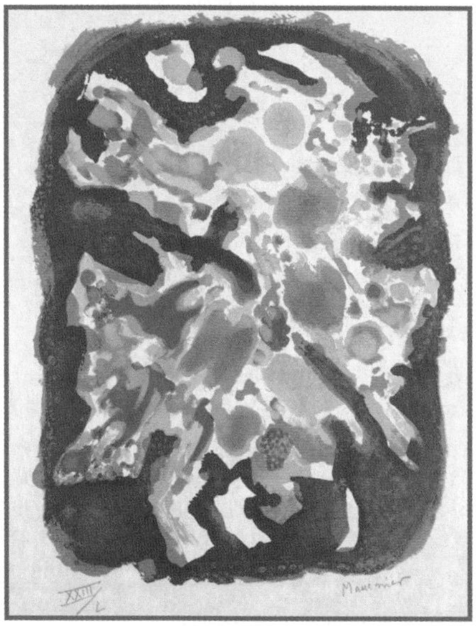

Choices

Nikki Giovanni

if i can't do
what i want to do
then my job is to not
do what i don't want
to do

it's not the same thing
but it's the best i can
do

if i can't have
what i want then
my job is to want
what i've got
and be satisfied
that at least there
is something more
to want

since i can't go
where i need
to go then i must go
where the signs point
though always understanding
parallel movement
isn't lateral

when i can't express
what i really feel
i practice feeling
what i can express
and none of it is equal
i know
but that's why mankind
alone among the mammals
learns to cry

1 Speaker *What is the speaker's attitude?*

2 Life Lessons *What is the message about life that is conveyed in these lines?*

3 Analyze Language *What phrase from earlier in the poem expresses an idea very similar to this?*

Teach

Literary Element 1

Speaker Answer: *The speaker seems defiant here, as if she will not be defeated.*

For additional literary element practice, see Unit 3 Teaching Resources Book, p. 157.

Big Idea 2

Life Lessons Answer: *The message of these lines is that sometimes having desire or motivation for things in life can be a positive thing.*

Reading Strategy 3

Analyze Language
Answer: *The phrase from the second stanza, "it's not the same thing."*

ADVANCED To challenge advanced learners, **ask:** What effect does repeating this idea throughout the poem have? *(The repetition helps create rhythm and gives the poem a musical quality, like the chorus of a song.)*

For additional practice using the reading skill or strategy, see Unit 0 Teaching Resources Book, p. 158.

To check students' understanding of the selection, see Unit 3 Teaching Resources Book, p. 160.

Approaching Level

DIFFERENTIATED INSTRUCTION

Established Lead approaching-level students in a discussion about the poem's title. **Ask:** Is the title of the poem appropriate for the poem's message? *(Some students may say the title is appropriate because the poem reflects different choices. Others may disagree because the poet performs an action based on lack of choice.)* Explore the idea of choice within the poem. Direct students' attention to the phrase "i can't" within each stanza. **Say:** The speaker is saying that if she is unable to do one thing than she will do the other. **Ask:** If the speaker is not allowed the first option, for example, with "if i can't have what i want", then does the speaker really have a choice? *(Answers will vary. Students should support their answers.)*

After You Read

Assess

1. Answers will vary.
2. (a) Because it's the best she can do (b) It tells you that she is willing to make the best out of a bad situation.
3. (a) Because she can't go where she needs to go (b) She means that she will go wherever it seems obvious to go or wherever is available to go.
4. (a) They learn to cry in response to, or in order to, express the frustrations of life. (b) In the rest of the poem the speaker seems to be accepting of the disappointments, but here she suggests being sad or upset over the disappointments.
5. Most of the poem only seems restricted to the speaker's personal experience. The ending makes the poem more about people in general.
6. Answers will vary.
7. Students should support their answers.
8. Possibly discrimination as a woman and as an African American

Literary Element

1. Answers will vary.
2. Answers will vary.

For additional assessment, see Assessment Resources, pp. 133–134.

After You Read

Respond and Think Critically

Respond and Interpret

1. How did the poem make you feel? Why?
2. (a)In the beginning of the poem, why does the speaker do something even though "it's not the same thing" as what she wants to do? (b)What does this tell you about the speaker's attitude?
3. (a)Why does the speaker "go where the signs point"? (b)What does the speaker mean when she says this?
4. (a)According to the poem, why do humans learn to cry? (b)In what ways does this ending reflect a change from the speaker's attitude in the rest of the poem?

Analyze and Evaluate

5. How does the ending of the poem broaden the message?
6. How well do you think the content and message in the poem reflect the title? Explain.

Connect

7. **Big Idea** Life Lessons What do you think the poet wanted to teach her readers about life?
8. **Connect to the Author** Considering the attitudes of society during Giovanni's youth, what kinds of frustrations do you think she likely faced?

Literary Element Speaker

The **speaker** of a poem is the voice that communicates with the reader. The speaker's words communicate a particular tone, or attitude, toward the subject of the poem.

1. Does the speaker seem old and wise, young and naïve, or somewhere in between? Explain.
2. How much courage do you think the speaker shows in her approach to life? Explain.

Reading Strategy Analyzing Language

Review the important words and phrases that you noted in your chart. Then answer these questions.

1. What is the effect of the repeated words and phrases throughout the poem?
2. The language in this poem is simple, even though the form is complicated. Do you think the poem's message would be more effective if the language were more complicated? Explain.

LOG ON **Literature** Online

Selection Resources For Selection Quizzes, eFlashcards, and Reading-Writing Connection activities, go to glencoe.com and enter QuickPass code GL49787u3.

Academic Vocabulary

*Because she is a **dynamic** speaker, Nikki Giovanni is often asked to give public readings of her poetry.*

Dynamic is an academic word. In more casual conversation, someone might say the lead scorer on the basketball team was a **dynamic** player. Using context clues, try to figure out the meaning of the word in the sentence about Giovanni above. Check your guess in a dictionary.

For more on academic vocabulary, see pages 54–55 and R79–R81.

Writing

Write a List Giovanni's poem presents a series of choices that are all related or linked together. Think about how one decision can lead to a series of choices like those in the poem. Create your own list of a series of choices that stem from one decision. Make sure that it is clear how the choices in the list are related.

Reading Strategy

1. It helps to connect the different parts of the poem and emphasizes which ideas are most important to the poem's message.
2. Answers will vary. Students should support their answers.

Writing

Students' lists should

- begin with a decision that leads to a series of choices
- present a series of choices that stem from the decision
- present the choices in order of sequence
- clearly demonstrate how the choices are related

Before You Read

"Hope" is the thing with feathers— I'm Nobody! Who are you?

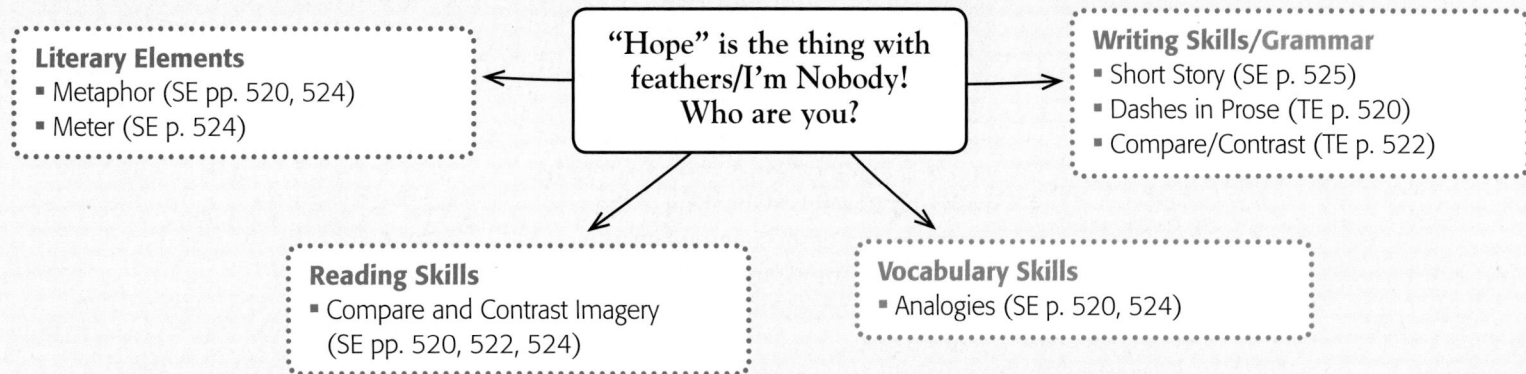

Meet **Emily Dickinson**
(1830–1886)

Few people who lived in Amherst, Massachusetts, in the mid-1800s probably suspected that their neighbor Emily Dickinson would come to be known as one of the greatest poets in American literature. Dickinson appeared proper and shy to her neighbors, but as a writer she was bold, daringly experimental, and spontaneous. Her poems broke conventions and spoke in a fresh, unique voice.

> *"I find ecstasy in living."*
>
> —Emily Dickinson

Experiences Common and Unique Dickinson came from a family that encouraged learning. Her grandfather founded Amherst College, and her father was a lawyer and treasurer of the college. Her home was filled with books. Among Emily's favorite authors were William Shakespeare, Ralph Waldo Emerson, and Emily Brontë.

Dickinson attended Mount Holyoke Female Seminary from 1847 to 1848. There, religious education and growth were just as important as intellectual development. Unlike most of her classmates, Dickinson remained a skeptic. Nevertheless, her poems often touch on religious themes.

Several of her letters express longing for a character named "Master," but it is unclear who he was. It seems, though, that Dickinson was disappointed in love. As time went by, she became a recluse. She walked often—but only on her father's property. Even though nature is a strong theme in her poetry, her own yard seemed to provide all the inspiration she needed.

A Prolific Poet Dickinson wrote about 1,775 poems and just as many letters. She wrote most of her poems on scraps of paper. She saved the poems in bureau drawers. Only seven of her poems were published during her lifetime. Her sister discovered the rest after Dickinson's death.

The first volume of Dickinson's poetry was published in 1890, four years after her death. The book was organized into five sections—Life, Love, Nature, Time, and Eternity. The volume was an immediate success. However, it was not until the 1950s that her poems were published exactly as she had written them, complete with all her dashes and capitalizations. It was then that people began to appreciate her work anew.

LOG ON **Literature** Online

Author Search For more about Emily Dickinson, go to glencoe.com and enter QuickPass code GL49787u3.

Before You Read

Focus

Bellringer Options

Daily Language Practice Transparency 57

Or **write** on the board: How do you know when your work is ready for public scrutiny? Note that many celebrated artists, such as Dickinson and Van Gogh, received recognition only after their death. Brainstorm innovative methods of presenting work to the public, such as blogging and posting photos and art on Web sites.

Selection Skills

"Hope" is the thing with feathers/I'm Nobody! Who are you?

Literary Elements
- Metaphor (SE pp. 520, 524)
- Meter (SE p. 524)

Writing Skills/Grammar
- Short Story (SE p. 525)
- Dashes in Prose (TE p. 520)
- Compare/Contrast (TE p. 522)

Reading Skills
- Compare and Contrast Imagery (SE pp. 520, 522, 524)

Vocabulary Skills
- Analogies (SE p. 520, 524)

Before You Read

Focus

Summary

In "'Hope' is the thing with feathers—," Emily Dickinson uses bird imagery to describe the nature of hope. In "I'm Nobody! Who are you?" Dickinson invites another "nobody" to join forces with her. She compares being "somebody" to a frog constantly singing its own praises to its admirers.

For summaries in languages other than English, see Unit 3 Teaching Resources Book, pp. 162–167.

Vocabulary

Flash Cards Have students write each of the vocabulary words on a separate index card, with the definition on the other side. Pair up students and have them quiz each other using the cards. Then quiz students on the meaning of each vocabulary word.

For additional vocabulary practice, see Unit 3 Teaching Resources Book, p. 170.

For additional context, see Glencoe Visual Vocabulary CD-ROM.

Literature and Reading Preview

Connect to the Poems

How can observing nature suggest new ways to look at important issues? Freewrite for a few minutes about how nature could inspire you when trying to resolve a personal problem.

Build Background

Emily Dickinson's poetry is full of unusual capitalization and dashes. The capitalization puts extra emphasis on certain words. The dashes serve as interrupters, breaking up text, slowing the reader down, and usually adding emphasis.

Set Purposes for Reading

Big Idea Life Lessons

As you read Dickinson's poems, ask yourself, How can everyday sights illustrate abstract concepts?

Literary Element Metaphor

A **metaphor** is a figure of speech that compares or equates two seemingly unlike things. Unlike a simile, a metaphor does not use the words *like* or *as;* instead, the comparison is implied. An **extended metaphor** compares two unlike things in various ways throughout a stanza or an entire selection. As you read, ask yourself, Where does Dickinson use metaphors?

Reading Strategy Compare and Contrast Imagery

Imagery is the "word pictures" that authors create to evoke an emotional response in readers. These images can involve any of the five senses. As you read, ask yourself, How is the imagery in these two poems alike and different? Note the natural associations and meanings that you draw from the imagery.

Tip: Take Notes Use a chart similar to the one below to help organize your ideas.

"Hope" is the thing with feathers—

Image	Associations	Possible meaning
a bird singing an endless song	bird: freedom, flight; endless song: eternity	

Learning Objectives

For pages 519–524

In studying this text, you will focus on the following objectives:

Literary Study: Analyzing metaphor.

Reading: Comparing and contrasting imagery.

Vocabulary

gale (gāl) *n.* a very strong wind; p. 521 *The gale blew the lawn chairs down the street.*

abash (ə bash′) *v.* to make ashamed or uneasy; to embarrass; p. 521 *Jean was abashed when she was insulted in front of her friends.*

dreary (drēr′ē) *adj.* depressing; sad; dull; uninteresting; p. 522 *The rain and dark clouds made the day seem dreary.*

livelong (liv′lông′) *adj.* complete; whole; used to emphasize the length of a period of time; p. 522 *It seemed to snow throughout the livelong winter.*

bog (bog) *n.* a wetland ecosystem where shrubs and peat moss grow and various animals live; p. 522 *They pulled on tall rubber boots before heading into the bog.*

Tip: Analogies To complete an analogy, decide what relationship exists between the meanings of the first two words. Then apply that relationship to another pair of words.

Grammar Practice

SPIRAL REVIEW **Dashes in Prose** **Ask:** When are dashes used in prose? *(in dialogue; to replace commas or parentheses; when providing additional information)* Mention that if the information between the dashes can be deleted without changing the meaning of the sentence, the dashes are probably correct. **Write:** The Grand Canyon, one of the wonders of the American West, is in Arizona.

Ask: Where might dashes be used? *(In place of the commas)* Note that dashes can indicate a change in thought. Have students write 10 sentences using dashes.

"Hope" is the thing with feathers—

Emily Dickinson

"Hope" is the thing with feathers—
That perches in the soul—
And sings the tune without the words—
1 And never stops—at all—

And sweetest—in the **Gale**—is heard—
And sore[1] must be the storm—
That could **abash** the little Bird
That kept so many warm—

I've heard it in the chillest land—
And on the strangest Sea—
Yet, never, in Extremity,[2]
It asked a crumb—of Me.

1. Here, *sore* means "dreadful" or "terrible."
2. Here, *extremity* means "great danger" or "distress."

2 Life Lessons *What does the bird teach us about the nature of hope?*

Vocabulary

gale (gāl) *n.* a very strong wind
abash (ə bash′) *v.* to make ashamed or uneasy; to embarrass

Teach

Literary Element 1

Dash **Ask:** What is the effect of the final dashes in the first stanza? *(It may suggest an unfinished thought or introduce the next element.)*

APPROACHING For approaching-level students, **ask:** What other punctuation might substitute for the dash? *(An ellipsis for an unfinished thought; a period to suggest a complete thought; an exclamation point to emphasize the thought)*

Big Idea 2

Life Lessons **Answer:** *Hope is a gift available to everyone and costs nothing. It resides in the soul and can endure all but the most brutal trials.*

For an audio recording of this selection, use Listening Library Audio CD-ROM.

Approaching Level

DIFFERENTIATED INSTRUCTION

AAVE Point out that approaching-level speakers of African American Vernacular English (AAVE) sometimes show a tendency to drop the second consonant sound in words that end with two consonants. On the board, **write:** *mist, list, told, task, test.* **Say:** Speakers might say *mis-* instead of *mist, lis-* instead of *list, tol-* instead of *told, tas-* instead of *task,* or *tes-* instead of *test.* Have students write sentences using the following words: *desk, fold, mild, find, best, least, cost.* Then have students read their sentences aloud. Correct their pronunciation if needed.

Teach

Big Idea 1

Life Lessons Ask: What does the "Nobody" teach us about being a "Somebody"? *(Being a somebody is overrated. Somebodies are loud, self-aggrandizing, and trite.)*

Reading Strategy 2

Compare and Contrast Imagery Answer: *Most students will say the frog is very different from the bird. They may associate frogs with ugliness and birds with beauty.*

Literary Element 3

Metaphor Ask: What is the bog a metaphor for? *(The general public or any undiscerning audience)*

ENGLISH LEARNERS English learners may be unfamiliar with the word *bog.* Have them look *bog* up in a dictionary and use the word in a sentence.

For additional literary element practice, see Unit 3 Teaching Resources Book, p. 168.

To check students' understanding of the selection, see Unit 3 Teaching Resources Book, p. 173.

I'm Nobody! Who are you?

Emily Dickinson

Sun Shower, 1995. Diana Ong. Computer graphics, 5 x 4 in. Chrome.

I'm Nobody! Who are you?
Are you—Nobody—Too?
Then there's a pair of us!
Don't tell! they'd advertise—you know!

How **dreary**—to be—Somebody!
1 How public—like a Frog—
To tell one's name—the **livelong** June—
3 To an admiring **Bog**!

Vocabulary

dreary (drēr′ē) *adj.* sad; depressing; dull; uninteresting

livelong (liv′ lông′) *adj.* complete; whole; used to emphasize the length of a period of time

bog (bog) *n.* a wetland ecosystem where shrubs and peat moss grow and various animals live

2 Compare and Contrast Imagery *How is the frog similar to or different from the bird in "'Hope' is the thing with feathers—"? What meanings do these associations convey?*

Writing Practice

SMALL GROUP **Compare and Contrast** Break students into groups and have them compare and contrast Dickinson's style in this poem with the poem on the previous page. Have them take notes about Dickinson's use of punctuation, capitalization, and rhyme and rhythm. Then ask groups to discuss the tone in each of the poems and her subject matter. **Ask:** What is her tone in the first poem? In the second? *(Students may say that her tone in the first poem is friendly and cheerful while her tone in the second poem is more critical or serious.)* Then have students work independently to write a compare-and-contrast essay based on the discussion.

After You Read

Respond and Think Critically

Respond and Interpret

1. Which of the Dickinson poems did you prefer? Explain.
2. (a)In "'Hope' is the thing with feathers—," where does hope perch? (b)Why do you think Dickinson uses the verb *perches*?
3. (a)In "I'm Nobody! Who are you?" what does the speaker say will happen if people discover a pair of nobodies? (b)What is the speaker's tone, or attitude?
4. (a)In the second poem, what adjective does Dickinson use to describe the bog? (b)What does the bog represent? Explain.

Analyze and Evaluate

5. Why might Dickinson have chosen to capitalize words in the middle or at the end of a sentence? Use specific examples from the two poems to support your answer.
6. (a)In "I'm Nobody! Who are you?," how does the speaker feel about being "Nobody"? Explain. (b)Why do you suppose she feels this way?

Connect

7. **Big Idea** **Life Lessons** What do these poems reveal about the speakers' values? Explain.
8. **Connect to the Author** Dickinson was a quiet and reclusive person, yet her poems reveal a writer who was bold and spontaneous. Which persona does her poem "I'm Nobody! Who are you?" reflect? Explain.

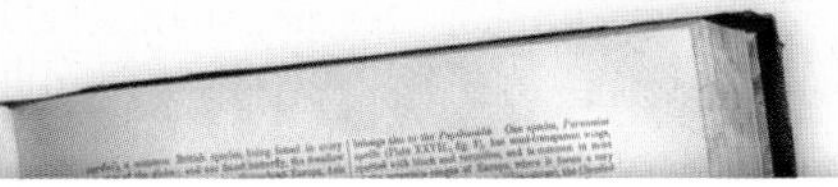

You're the Critic

Her Own Style

When Dickinson's first volume of poetry appeared in 1890, it received mixed critical reviews. Arlo Bates, a Boston critic, and William Dean Howells, a novelist and editor of the *Atlantic Monthly* magazine, agreed that Dickinson's poetry was like nothing they had ever seen before. As you read these two excerpts, note how each writer interprets Dickinson's nontraditional techniques somewhat differently.

> *"[Her poetry is] so wholly without the pale of conventional criticism, that it is necessary at the start to declare the grounds upon which it is to be judged as if it were a new species of art."*
>
> —Arlo Bates

> *"[I]f nothing else had come out of our life but this strange poetry we should feel that in the work of Emily Dickinson America, or New England rather, had made a distinctive addition to the literature of the world."*
>
> —William Dean Howells

Group Activity With one or two other students, gather evidence from Dickinson's poems to demonstrate how her writing style was innovative. Then consider the following questions.

1. What aspects of Dickinson's poetry may have surprised Arlo Bates and William Dean Howells?
2. What aspects of Dickinson's poems are nontraditional? What are the effects of these techniques?

After You Read

Assess

1. Students should support their answers with specific reasons.
2. (a) In the soul (b) She strengthens the bird metaphor; *perches* suggest that hope, like a bird, can easily come and go.
3. (a) "They'd advertise." (b) Intimate
4. (a) Admiring (b) The public; she imagines the admiring public as a gross, undifferentiated mass.
5. Possible answers: "'Hope' . . ." capitalizes *Gale, Bird, Sea, Extremity,* and *Me* to emphasize those words; "I'm Nobody!" *Nobody, Too, Somebody, Frog, Bog*
6. (a) The exclamation point suggests that the speaker is happy or proud to be Nobody and content to be ignored. (b) The speaker enjoys privacy and disdains public opinion.
7. The speaker is thoughtful, positive, and ironically humorous and values humility and privacy.
8. Most students will state that Dickinson's quiet persona is reflected in the poem. Students should point to phrases in the poem to support their answers.

You're the Critic

1. Broken meter created by dashes, capitalization, unconventional metaphors
2. Her use of capitalization and punctuation and the meter of her poems seem nontraditional. For example, in "I'm Nobody! Who are you?" the rhyme scheme is *aabc defe.* The effect of such irregularity is that the subject matter is made new and surprising.

After You Read

Assess

Literary Element

1. **C** is the correct answer. The bird is an extended metaphor for hope throughout the poem.
2. **D** is the correct answer. The "Bog" is Dickinson's dismissive metaphor for people who listen willingly to self-important speakers.

Review

"Hope" is the thing with feathers—

"Hope" is the thing with feathers—
That perches in the soul—
And sings the tune without the
words—
And never stops—at all—

"I'm Nobody! Who are you?"

I'm Nobody! Who are you?
Are you—Nobody—Too?
Then there's a pair of us!
Don't tell! They'd advertise—you
know!

Most students will say that Dickinson uses meter effectively to stress key words, such as *hope, soul, sings, tune, words,* and *stops* in the first poem and the *No-* in *Nobody, Who, too, pair,* and *know* in the second poem.

Literary Element Metaphor

SAT Skills Practice

1. In "'Hope' is the thing with feathers—," what is the "little Bird" referred to in line 7?
   (A) The human soul
   (B) Happiness
   (C) Hope
   (D) The need for comfort in times of hardship
   (E) God
2. In "I'm Nobody! Who are you?" what does the speaker mean by the "Bog" (line 8)?
   (A) Frogs and other swamp creatures
   (B) A place unfit for human beings to inhabit
   (C) An audience that doesn't value one's opinion
   (D) A general public thirsty for celebrity
   (E) A depressed state of mind

Review: Meter

As you learned on page 462, **meter** is the regular pattern of stressed and unstressed syllables that gives a line of poetry a predictable rhythm. The unit of meter within a line is called the **foot.** Each foot has a distinctive pattern of stressed (ʹ) and unstressed (˘) syllables. Mapping the meter is called **scansion.** Meter gives poetry its musical quality and can be used by the poet to stress key words and ideas in the poem.

Partner Activity With a partner, take turns reading each of the Dickinson poems aloud. As your partner reads the poem, listen closely to get a sense of the meter. Then scan the first stanza of each poem. Reread the poems to each other, using your scansion marks to accentuate the meter. How successful is Dickinson in using meter to stress key words or ideas in each poem? Discuss this question with your partner.

Reading Strategy Compare and Contrast Imagery

Imagery is an important component of both "'Hope' is the thing with feathers—" and "I'm Nobody! Who are you?" Dickinson often used sensory details from the natural world in her poems.

1. List three sensory details from "'Hope' is the thing with feathers—" and "I'm Nobody! Who are you?" that have to do with nature.
2. Explain how the images are alike and different. What purpose does each image serve?

Vocabulary Practice

Practice with Analogies An analogy shows the relationships between words. The symbol : means "is to," and the symbol :: means "as." Find the word that completes each of the analogies below.

1. **abash : humiliate :: understand :**
   a. comprehend **b.** confuse **c.** tolerate
2. **gale : storm :: field :**
   a. tractor **b.** corn **c.** farm
3. **dreary : exciting :: perfect :**
   a. interesting **b.** lifeless **c.** flawed
4. **livelong : whole :: chilly :**
   a. cold **b.** shivering **c.** icy
5. **peat moss : bog :: seaweed :**
   a. mountain **b.** ocean **c.** valley

LOG ON **Literature** Online

Selection Resources For Selection Quizzes, eFlashcards, and Reading-Writing Connection activities, go to glencoe.com and enter QuickPass code GL49787u3.

Reading Strategy

1. Possible answers: feathers, bird, birdsong, gale, storm, cold, sea, frog, June, bog
2. Responses should include analysis of how images are alike and different and how the poet uses the images.

Vocabulary Practice

1. a **2.** c **3.** c **4.** a **5.** b

Progress Check

Can students compare and contrast imagery?

If No → See Unit 3 Teaching Resources Book, p. 169.

Respond Through Writing

Short Story

Apply Imagery Write a short story of at least 1,500 words using the theme of one or both of Dickinson's poems. Use imagery to bring your story to life.

Understand the Task A **theme** is the main idea or message of a literary work. It often is expressed as a general statement about life. The theme of a work can be stated directly or implied through elements such as plot, character, setting, point of view, and symbol.

Prewrite Choose a theme and develop a storyline based on it. Before you begin writing, look at the imagery charts you created as you read the poems to review the ways imagery functions in them. Then create an outline to organize the elements of your story. Your outline should include details about characters, setting (time and place), and plot (conflict, climax, and resolution). You might also include any ideas you have regarding the use of imagery in your story.

Draft Using your outline as a guide, write a draft of your story. As you describe the unfolding events, make sure that the pace of the story gains momentum as it builds toward the climax. You can create momentum by increasing the tension or action as the plot moves forward. In addition to showing how the events occurred, your story should express or reflect how the events support your theme.

As you write your draft, use imagery to fill out the setting and to give each scene a strong sense of place. The imagery should provide concrete details that allow readers to clearly picture the story's locations. To develop details for your story, imagine yourself in each scene's setting and visualize the place in your mind. Use these visualizations to create the concrete details for your descriptions.

Revise When you revise your draft, closely review your descriptions of the setting and characters. Make sure your descriptions appeal to a variety of senses—including details about sound, smell, and texture, in addition to visual elements.

Edit and Proofread Proofread your paper, correcting any errors in grammar, spelling, and punctuation. Review the Grammar Tip in the side column to help you with hyphens.

Learning Objectives

In this assignment, you will focus on the following objectives:

Writing: Writing a short story.

Grammar: Using hyphens correctly.

Grammar Tip

Hyphens

When two words are used together as a single adjective before a noun, they are connected by a hyphen:

Trapeze artists are high-flying daredevils.

You can use this hyphenation of adjectives to add variety to your descriptions. Keep in mind that this rule does not apply when the words are used in a list as two separate adjectives.

Trapeze artists are brave, graceful daredevils.

Assess

Respond Through Writing

Students' short stories should

- be at least 1,500 words
- relate to a theme from one of Dickinson's poems
- present well-developed plot and characters
- build momentum toward a climax
- use imagery to create a strong setting
- use concrete sensory details to describe the imagery

For grammar practice, see Unit 3 Teaching Resources Book, p. 172.

For additional assessment, see Assessment Resources, pp. 135–136.

To create custom assessments using software, use ExamView Assessment Suite.

To create custom assessments online, go to Progress Reporter Online Assessment.

Before You Read

Focus

Bellringer Options

Daily Language Practice Transparency 58

Or **write** on the board: Family Dinner. Invite volunteers to share their descriptions of a typical family meal. **Ask:** Is it a boisterous gathering or a more solemn affair? What happens when the meal includes extended family? Are certain traditions or foods included? Invite students to compare and contrast their family mealtime traditions.

Before You Read

Defining the Grateful Gesture

Meet **Yvonne Sapia**

(born 1946)

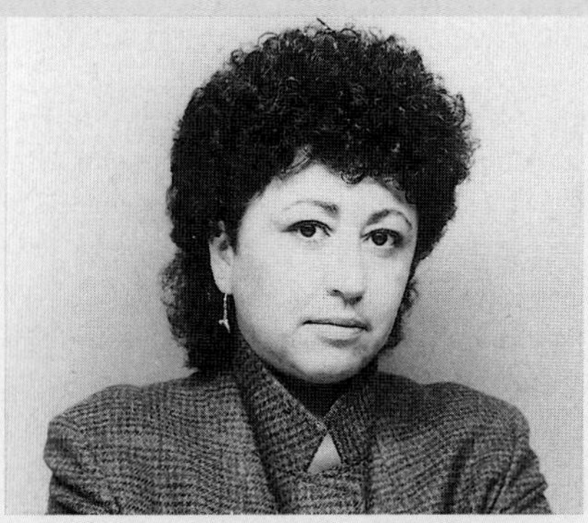

Poet Yvonne Sapia counts among her influences Robert Frost and Mother Goose, whose rhymes she describes as "funny, sad, and inspiring." Sapia was born in 1946 in New York City to parents who had emigrated from Puerto Rico during the 1920s. Her father was a barber, and her mother was a homemaker. Her father was known in his Bronx neighborhood for having cut the hair of silent film star Rudolph Valentino. Sapia swept the floor of her father's shop when she was a girl.

> *"Reading poetry is cool stuff. It always provides a solution and then years later it provides a new solution because we change."*
>
> —Yvonne Sapia

Mourning and Imagination As a young woman, Sapia left New York and went to Florida to attend college. She graduated from Florida Atlantic University in Boca Raton. Sapia then entered the working world as a newspaper reporter and a writer of technical books on horticulture, the science of cultivating plants. Sapia wanted to write poetry and novels, so she returned to college to earn a Master of Fine Arts degree in creative writing from the University of Florida in Gainesville. In 1976 she became a poet-in-residence and English professor at Lake City Community College in Lake City, Florida, where she still writes and teaches today.

In 1983 Sapia published her first collection of poetry, *Fertile Crescent,* which won the Florida Chapbook Award. She titled her second book after her poem "Valentino's Hair," which tells the story of a Puerto Rican barber in New York City during the 1920s. The poem is a tribute to Sapia's father, who died when she was nineteen. The book *Valentino's Hair* won the Samuel French Morse Prize for poetry in 1987, and the title poem was included in the *Best American Poetry* anthology.

Moment of Discovery Sapia has been writing and teaching for many years at Lake City Community College. She loves the moment when students discover that they, too, can draw on their own thoughts and experiences in order to write poetry. Sapia hopes that her poetry will serve as a legacy and inspiration for her students. She describes her poems as a reflection of "being a Puerto Rican American woman in the late 20th century. . . . They convey what this Latina thought at this point in time. I see students as books, a story waiting to be shared, written. Everyone has a human experience to share."

LOG ON **Literature** Online

Author Search For more about Yvonne Sapia, go to glencoe.com and enter QuickPass code GL49787u3.

Selection Skills

Defining the Grateful Gesture

Literary Elements
- Metaphor and Simile (SE pp. 527, 528, 530)

Writing Skills/Grammar
- Write a Poem (SE p. 530)

Reading Skills
- Connect to Personal Experience (SE pp. 527, 530)

Vocabulary Skills
- Denotation and Connotation (SE pp. 527, 530)

Literature and Reading Preview

Connect to the Poem

What do you feel especially grateful for in your own life? Write a journal entry about one thing that you feel grateful for and why you feel grateful for it.

Build Background

The childhood home of the mother in "Defining the Grateful Gesture" is Puerto Rico, a small, resource-poor island that has long suffered the effects of overpopulation. By U.S. standards, Puerto Rico has a high rate of unemployment and poverty. The situation today, however, is much better than it was in the past.

Set Purposes for Reading

Big Idea Life Lessons

As you read "Defining the Grateful Gesture," ask yourself, How does Sapia portray gratitude as an important life lesson?

Literary Element Metaphor and Simile

A **simile** is a figure of speech that uses *like* or *as* to compare seemingly unlike things. A **metaphor** compares two seemingly unlike things, but implies the comparison instead of stating it directly. Identifying metaphors and similes will help you understand the poet's meaning. As you read, ask yourself, How does Sapia use metaphors and similes to stress the mother's lesson?

Reading Strategy Connect to Personal Experience

Connecting to personal experience can make a literary work more real to you and help you understand its meaning. As you read this poem, ask yourself, What connections can I make between the lives of the children and their mother's childhood and my own experiences?

Tip: Chart Connections As you read, use a chart to record your personal connections to the poem.

Line from Poem	Personal Experience
and helping her father make candy in the family kitchen.	I help my father in his carpentry shop.

Learning Objectives

For pages 526–530

In studying this text, you will focus on the following objectives:

Literary Study: Analyzing metaphor and simile.

Reading: Connecting to personal experience.

Writing: Writing a poem using metaphors and similes.

Vocabulary

reverent (rev′ ər ənt) *adj.* feeling or expressing respect or courtesy; p. 528 *Faye was always reverent in the presence of her teachers.*

archetypal (är′ kə tī′ pəl) *adj.* serving as an ideal model or perfect example; p. 528 *Achilles is the archetypal hero with only one weakness—his heel.*

supplicant (sup′ lə kənt) *n.* one who asks humbly and earnestly; p. 529 *The supplicants begged the king to grant their requests.*

Tip: Denotation and Connotation **Denotation** is the literal meaning of a word. **Connotation** is the suggested or implied meaning associated with a word. For example, the denotation of the word *reverent* is "deeply respectful." The connotations of *reverent* include "serious" and "in awe." Knowing both meanings of words will help you better understand what you read and communicate more clearly.

Before You Read

Focus

Summary

Yvonne Sapia recalls a typical family dinner. Her mother would lecture Sapia and her brother about appreciating their food and contrast her children's lives with her own poor, hardworking childhood. The children tried to seem sufficiently grateful to please their mother, but always fell short.

For summaries in languages other than English, see Unit 3 Teaching Resources Book, pp. 175–180.

Vocabulary

Interview Exercise Have students brainstorm a list of famous people they would like to interview. Tell students to pick a famous person from the list and compose questions they would like to ask that person. Tell students to use the vocabulary words to develop their questions.

For additional vocabulary practice, see Unit 3 Teaching Resources Book, p. 183.

For additional context, see Glencoe Visual Vocabulary CD-ROM.

English Learners

DIFFERENTIATED INSTRUCTION

Beginning/Early Intermediate Explain to students that poets typically organize their poems around a certain theme. The theme is the main message that the poet wants to convey. The theme may express the author's opinion or make a general statement about life. For example, in a poem about friendship, the theme might be "Friends are like air: You need them to survive." **Say:** As you read the poem by Yvonne Sapia, identify the theme and think about how it relates to your own life.

Teach

Literary Element 1

Metaphor and Simile
Answer: *Metaphor; students should recognize that the mother was not a lazy or passive person.*

ENGLISH LEARNERS Have English learners look up the words *idle* and *passenger* to help them understand the metaphor in this line. Then **ask:** What does it mean to say that the speaker's mother was not an "idle passenger through life"? *(The mother was not a lazy person.)*

For additional literary element practice, see Unit 3 Teaching Resources Book, p. 181.

For an audio recording of this selection, see Listening Library Audio CD-ROM.

Defining the Grateful Gesture

Yvonne Sapia

According to our mother,
when she was a child
what was placed before her
for dinner was not a feast,
but she would eat it
to gain back the strength
taken from her by long hot days
of working in her mother's house
and helping her father make
candy in the family kitchen.
No idle passenger
Traveling through life was she.

And that's why she resolved
to tell stories about
the appreciation for satisfied hunger.
When we would sit down
for our evening meal
of arroz con pollo[1]
or frijoles negros con plátanos[2]
she would expect us
to be **reverent** to the sources
of our undeserved nourishment
and to strike a thankful pose
before each lift of the fork
or swirl of the spoon.
For the dishes she prepared,
we were ungrateful,
she would say, and repeat
her **archetypal** tale about the Pérez
brothers who stumbled over
themselves
with health in her girlhood town
of Ponce,[3] looking like ripe mangoes,
their cheeks rosed despite poverty.

1. *Arroz con pollo* (ä rōs′ kōn pō′ yō) is Spanish for "rice with chicken."

1 Metaphor and Simile *What figure of speech is this and what does it mean?*

2. *Frijoles negros con plátanos* (frē hō′ les neg′ rōs′ kōn plä′ tä nōs) are black beans with plantains (plant′ ənz). Plantain is a banana-like fruit that is starchy and eaten cooked.
3. *Ponce* (pōn′ sā) is a city in Puerto Rico.

Vocabulary

reverent (rev′ ər ənt) *adj.* feeling or expressing respect or courtesy

archetypal (är′ kə tī′ pəl) *adj.* serving as an ideal model or perfect example

Vocabulary Practice

SPIRAL REVIEW **Denotations and Connotations**
Explain the difference between denotations (literal meanings) and connotations (unspoken meanings and associations) of words. **Say:** Understanding the connotations of words can help you appreciate the various layers of meaning in poetry. Play a game of word association using words from the poem. Have students choose a word, consider its context, and discuss its associations. For example, notice how the connotations of virtue and purity associated with *white* deepen the poem's religious overtones.

The Meal (The Bananas), 1891. Paul Gauguin. Oil on canvas. Musee d'Orsay, Paris.

My mother would then tell us about
the day
she saw Mrs. Pérez searching
the neighborhood garbage,
picking out with a missionary's care
the edible potato peels, the plantain
skins,
the shafts of old celery to take
home to her muchachos[4]
who required more food
than she could afford.

Although my brothers and I
never quite mastered the ritual
of obedience our mother craved,
and as **supplicants** failed
to feed her with our worthiness,
we'd sit like solemn loaves of bread,
sighing over the white plates
with a sense of realization, or relief,
guilty about possessing appetite.

4. *Muchachos* (mo͞o chä′ chōs) means "boys" in Spanish.

2 Life Lessons *What does the mother hope to accomplish by sharing this tale with her children?*

Vocabulary

supplicant (sup′ lə kənt) *n.* one who asks humbly and earnestly

Teach

Big Idea 2

Life Lessons Answer: *To teach gratitude for their food and the hard work that brought it to them*

ADVANCED For advanced students, **ask:** What can you infer about the mother's attitude toward her children from the lesson she is teaching? *(By taking the time to reinforce this lesson, the mother shows she cares about her children and does not want them to be spoiled.)*

To check students' understanding of the selection, see Unit 3 Teaching Resources Book, p. 185.

Approaching Level

DIFFERENTIATED INSTRUCTION

Emerging To practice **reading fluency,** have approaching-level students read parts of the poem aloud. Then have students identify the similes and metaphors in the text. Lead a discussion to help students understand the meaning of each one.

Established Explain that poets use figurative language and imagery to paint pictures with words. Point out examples from the poem such as the Pérez boys "looking like ripe mangoes" and "Mrs. Pérez searching the neighborhood garbage." Encourage students to discuss how these images enhace the poem and stir their emotions.

After You Read

Assess

1. Students should support their answers.
2. (a) She helped her mother with housework and helped her father make candy. (b) The candy connects with the food motif.
3. (a) They don't work for their food. (b) They take food for granted; she earned hers and ate whatever was served.
4. The poverty of the Pérez boys; It suggests that the children's health depended on their mother's labor and sacrifice.
5. It enables the mother to show her children the difficulty of feeding one's family and how lucky they are.
6. They do not express the degree of gratitude their mother desires.
7. Students should support their responses. Possible answer: the speaker eats traditional Puerto Rican food for dinner.

Literary Element

1. They are supposed to "feed" their mother. It fits the food motif.
2. Answers will vary.

Reading Strategy

1. Answers will vary.
2. Accept reasonable answers.

Progress Check

Can students connect to personal experience?

If No → See Unit 3 Teaching Resources Book, p. 182.

After You Read

Respond and Think Critically

Respond and Interpret

1. How do the mother's stories make you feel about showing thanks? Explain.
2. (a)How did the mother help her family when she was young? (b)What is significant about this detail?
3. (a)What does the speaker mean by the children's "undeserved nourishment"? (b)How does their situation compare with their mother's childhood experiences?

Analyze and Evaluate

4. What do the mangoes in the poem contrast with? How is this contrast related to the theme?
5. Why does the author include the story about the Pérez family in her poem?

Connect

6. **Big Idea** Life Lessons Have the children learned the lesson their mother was trying to teach them? Explain.
7. **Connect to the Author** Where in this poem are Sapia's experiences as a Puerto Rican American portrayed?

Literary Element Metaphor and Simile

Poets use metaphors and similes to create powerful images and to imply meaning, rather than state it directly.

1. How are the speaker and her brothers "like solemn loaves of bread"? Is this a suitable simile for this poem? Explain.
2. The speaker says that she and her brothers "failed to feed" their mother with their worthiness. Is this an appropriate metaphor? Explain.

Reading Strategy Connect to Personal Experience

Review the chart you made while reading the poem and answer the following questions.

1. What elements of the poem are unfamiliar to you?
2. What elements of the poem can you connect to your own life?

LOG ON Literature Online

Selection Resources For Selection Quizzes, eFlashcards, and Reading-Writing Connection activities, go to glencoe.com and enter QuickPass code GL49787u3.

Vocabulary Practice

Practice with Denotation and Connotation
Denotation is the literal meaning of a word. **Connotation** is the implied meaning of a word. For example, the words *upset* and *devastated* have a similar denotation, "disturbed," but they have different connotations:

Weaker	**Stronger**
upset	devastated

Each boldface vocabulary word is listed with a word that has a similar denotation. Choose the word that has a stronger connotation.

1. reverent	considerate
2. archetypal	typical
3. supplicant	asker

Writing

Write a Poem Sapia encloses meaning in the metaphors and similes of "Defining the Grateful Gesture." Write a poem to describe a person, thing, or event using similes and metaphors. Use at least one metaphor and at least one simile in the poem.

Vocabulary Practice

Possible answers:

1. *Reverent* has the stronger connotation. *Considerate* implies general kindness, while *reverent* implies feelings of profound respect and awe.
2. *Archetypal* has the stronger connotation. It implies a sense of perfection, while *typical* simply implies "normal."
3. *Supplicant* has the stronger connotation. *Asker* implies a general inquiry, while *supplicant* implies a serious plea.

Writing

Students' poems should

- describe a person, thing, or event
- include both similes and metaphors

Before You Read

Sympathy

Meet **Paul Laurence Dunbar**
(1872–1906)

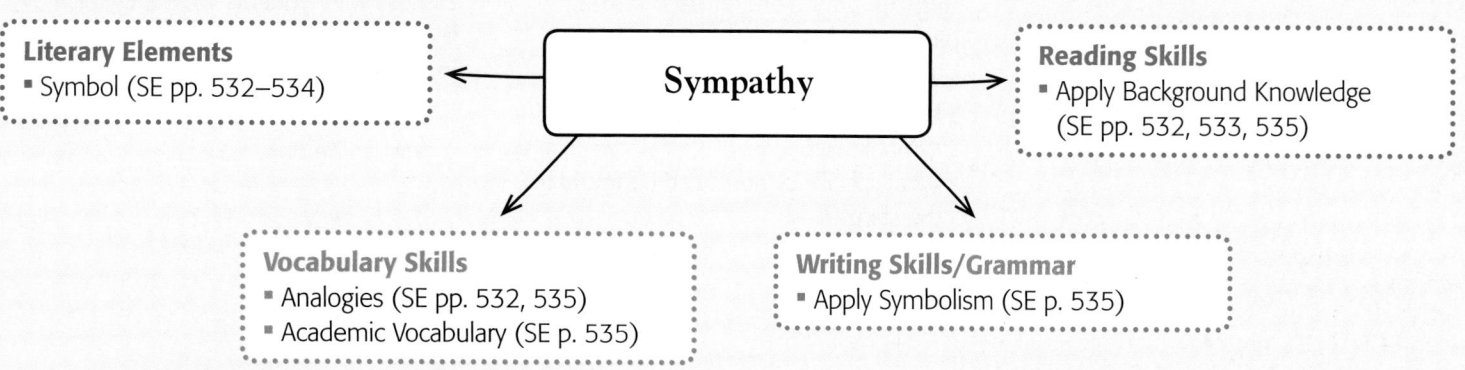

The only African American in his high school class in Dayton, Ohio, Paul Laurence Dunbar was class president, editor of the school newspaper, and president of the literary society. While still in school, he also edited an African American newspaper funded by the Wright brothers, the *Dayton Tattler,* and published poems in the *Dayton Herald.* As a young man, Dunbar wrote that his ambition was to "be able to interpret my own people through song and story, and to prove to the many that after all we are more human than African."

Although Dunbar grew up in the post–Civil War North, both of his parents had been enslaved. When he graduated from high school in 1891, despite the excellence he had achieved, racism in society limited his prospects. Dunbar was only able to obtain work as an elevator operator in Dayton's Callahan Building. During downtime on the job, the young Dunbar wrote poetry, including a first draft of the poem that would become his most well known: "Sympathy."

> *"With our short sight we affect to take a comprehensive view of eternity. Our horizon is the universe."*
>
> —Paul Laurence Dunbar

Early Acclaim and Continued Success Dunbar found a publisher for his first book of poems, *Oak and Ivy,* and published it in 1892. He sold copies of his book to people who rode the elevator that he operated. As word of the young "elevator boy poet" got around, several respected writers and critics began applauding his work.

Dunbar also branched out into other forms of writing. At the height of his career, he contributed songs to the first full-length African American musical on Broadway, *In Dahomey* (1902). He also published several novels and a well-received collection of short stories, *The Strength of Gideon and Other Stories* (1900).

Diverse Styles Like other popular poets of the time, Dunbar wrote in Standard English and imitated classical verse. He also found inspiration in John Whitcomb Riley's nostalgic poems, which were largely written in dialect and described ordinary people. Some of Dunbar's most highly praised poems were written in an authentic dialect form that imitated the conventions of plantation life.

LOG ON **Literature** Online

Author Search For more about Paul Laurence Dunbar, go to glencoe.com and enter QuickPass code GL49787u3.

Before You Read

Focus

Bellringer Options

Selection Focus Transparency 24

Daily Language Practice Transparency 59

Or **ask:** Can an individual be free while imprisoned? Are there other kinds of prisons besides jail? Discuss how a person might be free in mind and spirit while physically incarcerated. Then ask students to consider how a person who is literally free might feel psychologically or spiritually imprisoned by society's rules and prejudices.

Selection Skills

Sympathy

Literary Elements
- Symbol (SE pp. 532–534)

Reading Skills
- Apply Background Knowledge (SE pp. 532, 533, 535)

Vocabulary Skills
- Analogies (SE pp. 532, 535)
- Academic Vocabulary (SE p. 535)

Writing Skills/Grammar
- Apply Symbolism (SE p. 535)

Before You Read

Focus

Summary

Paul Laurence Dunbar uses the suffering of a caged bird as a metaphor for his own feelings of imprisonment. In the first stanza, he relates to how the bird feels looking out from its cage. In the second, he relates to its struggle against confinement. In the final stanza, he compares the bird's singing to a prayer.

For summaries in languages other than English, see Unit 3 Teaching Resources Book, pp. 187–192.

Vocabulary

Write Sentences Have students discuss the meaning of each vocabulary word. Then ask students to write two sentences in their notebooks using each of these words. Ask for volunteers to read their sentences aloud. Discuss why the use of the vocabulary word is either correct or incorrect.

For additional vocabulary practice, see Unit 3 Teaching Resources Book, p. 195.

For additional context, see Glencoe Visual Vocabulary CD-ROM.

Literature and Reading Preview

Connect to the Poem

How would your life change if you no longer had the freedom to do the things you wanted to do? Discuss this question with a partner. Explain how you would feel if your freedoms were taken away.

Build Background

In 1863, during the Civil War, President Abraham Lincoln banned slavery in the states that had seceded from the Union. Many enslaved people rejoiced, but their fight against discrimination and persecution was far from over. Shortly after 1877, southern states enacted Jim Crow laws to restrict the rights of African Americans.

Set Purposes for Reading

Big Idea Life Lessons

As you read "Sympathy," ask yourself, How might Dunbar have wanted his poem to affect those who were not confronted with discrimination?

Literary Element Symbol

A **symbol** is any object, person, or place that has meaning in itself but also stands for something else, usually on an abstract level. As you read, ask yourself, How does Dunbar use the image of the bird to symbolize something deeper?

Reading Strategy Apply Background Knowledge

A reader can **apply background knowledge** to understand an author's point of view. Knowing the perspective from which an author writes can help you evaluate and more deeply understand a literary work. As you read, ask yourself, How might events in Dunbar's life be reflected in the theme of the poem?

Tip: Create a Web Use a graphic organizer like the one below to record experiences in Dunbar's life that would lead him to sympathize with a caged bird.

Learning Objectives

For pages 531–535

In studying this text, you will focus on the following objectives:

Literary Study: Analyzing symbol.

Reading: Applying background knowledge.

Writing: Applying symbolism in a poem.

Vocabulary

chalice (chal′ is) *n.* drinking cup; a cup-shaped interior of a flower; p. 533 *The bee nestled in the chalice of the flower.*

keen (kēn) *adj.* sharp; intense; p. 533 *She hurt her friend's feelings with her keen sarcasm.*

Tip: Analogies An analogy conveys a relationship between things or ideas. To finish an analogy, decide what relationship exists between the first pair of words and then apply that relationship to the second pair of words. Some analogies feature words that are antonyms, or opposites.

Example:
keen : blunt :: mysterious : obvious

Literary Element Practice

Symbol At the end of each stanza, pause and discuss the following:

- What is the literal meaning of this stanza?
- How might the stanza be interpreted symbolically?
- What specific symbols can be found in the stanza?

Discuss with students what they think the author's overall intention is and what impression he wants to leave with the reader.

Sympathy

Paul Laurence Dunbar

Parrot outside his cage. Cornelis Biltius. Private collection.

I know what the caged bird feels, alas!
When the sun is bright on the upland slopes;
When the wind stirs soft through the springing grass,
And the river flows like a stream of glass;
When the first bird sings and the first bud opes,[1]
And the faint perfume from its **chalice** steals—
I know what the caged bird feels!

I know why the caged bird beats his wing
Till its blood is red on the cruel bars;
For he must fly back to his perch and cling
When he fain[2] would be on the bough a-swing;[3]
And a pain still throbs in the old, old scars
And they pulse again with a **keener** sting—
I know why he beats his wing!

I know why the caged bird sings, ah me,
When his wing is bruised and his bosom sore,—
When he beats his bars and he would be free;
It is not a carol of joy or glee,
But a prayer that he sends from his heart's deep core,
But a plea, that upward to Heaven he flings—
I know why the caged bird sings!

1. *Opes* means "opens."
2. *Fain* means "gladly" or "preferably."
3. *A-swing* means "swinging."

Apply Background Knowledge *Why might Dunbar identify with the caged bird's throbbing pain and old scars?*

Symbol *What kind of "bars" did Dunbar run up against?*

Vocabulary

chalice (chal′ is) *n.* drinking cup; a cup-shaped interior of a flower
keen (kēn) *adj.* sharp; intense

Teach

Reading Strategy 1

Apply Background Knowledge Answer: *Dunbar's identification with the bird may be rooted in the pain that resulted from knowing the terrible hardships his parents faced as enslaved people and from the racial prejudice that he experienced.*

Literary Element 2

Symbol Answer: *Obstacles such as racism and lack of economic opportunity*

APPROACHING To assist approaching-level students, **ask:** Who does the bird represent? What does the cage represent? *(The bird represents either the poet or African Americans in general, and the cage represents the racism that prevents them from enjoying all of their rights.)*

To check students' understanding of the selection, see Unit 3 Teaching Resources Book, p. 197.

Approaching Level

DIFFERENTIATED INSTRUCTION

Established To practice ***reading fluency,*** have a student read the first and last line of the first stanza. Point out that these two lines are the same. Explain that the author used repetition to create a rythmic sound similar to what you might hear in a song. Ask students to consider why the author wrote the poem this way. Ask students to share their opinions about how repetition affects the poem.

After You Read

Assess

1. Accept reasonable answers.
2. (a) Shining sun, wind softly blowing, springing grass, river flowing, flowers opening
(b) The vowel sounds and the one-syllable words lend a sense of serenity, ease, and freedom.
3. (a) Repeatedly running into the same barriers brings back the pain of imprisonment and intensifies it (b) to emphasize the pain caused by these constraints
4. (a) The hope for freedom is renewed despite the pain.
(b) To contradict comforting assumptions and alert people to suffering
5. (a) "Till its blood is red on the cruel bars"; "he fain would be on the bough a-swing"; "When his wing is bruised" (b) Students should support their answers.
6. Possible answers: To achieve a songlike effect; for emphasis
7. Answers will vary.
8. Members of minorities, political prisoners, or the physically disabled might write on this theme.

Literary Element

1. The caged bird symbolizes the oppression of African Americans. The symbol is traditional because the caged bird has been used as a symbol for cruel and unnatural bondage, or lack of freedom.
2. Traditional symbols; accept reasonable answers.

Progress Check

Can students explain symbol?

If No → See Unit 3 Teaching Resources Book, p. 193.

After You Read

Respond and Think Critically

Respond and Interpret

1. How does the bird's life help you understand the lives of the oppressed?
2. (a)What images from nature does Dunbar use in the first stanza? (b)In what ways does Dunbar create a sense of freedom with his words?
3. (a)What causes the bird in the poem to bleed? (b)What conclusion do you think Dunbar wanted the reader to draw from this image?
4. (a)According to Dunbar, why do the caged bird's scars "pulse again with a keener sting"? (b)Why do you think Dunbar emphasizes that the bird's singing is not a joyful or gleeful carol?

Analyze and Evaluate

5. (a)What passages most focus your attention on the idea of sympathy? (b)Is Dunbar's use of the bird as a symbol of this idea effective? Explain.
6. Why do you think Dunbar uses the same rhyming sound for the final couplets in the second and third stanzas?

Connect

7. **Big Idea** **Life Lessons** What life lesson might Dunbar have wanted the reader to learn from reading "Sympathy"?
8. **Connect to Today** Dunbar struggled against discrimination to become a writer and poet. What circumstances might lead a person today to write a poem like "Sympathy"?

Literary Element Symbol

A traditional **symbol** may be recognized by most people and usually is met with a predictable response. For example, a thorn on a rose might symbolize both good and bad existing together. Sometimes an author will use an original symbol, for which the meaning is not as easily recognized and requires analysis.

1. What does the caged bird symbolize in this poem? Is it a traditional or an original symbol? Explain.
2. How effectively do you think Dunbar uses symbols to represent abstract concepts?

Review: Metaphor

As you learned on page 520, a **metaphor** is a type of figurative language in which two seemingly unlike things are compared to reveal their underlying similarities. Unlike a simile, which states the comparison directly with the words *like* or *as,* the comparison in a metaphor is implied. Identifying and understanding the poet's metaphors is often vital to understanding a poem's meaning.

Partner Activity Work with a partner to identify two metaphors in "Sympathy." Create a graphic organizer like the one shown for each metaphor. You and your partner should each explain one metaphor and its use in the poem.

Metaphor	Explanation of Use
include text from poem and line number(s)	

Review

Metaphor: "And the river flows like a stream of glass," line 4.

Explanation of Use: At first glance, this figure of speech appears to be a simile. It is actually a metaphor embedded within a simile. The speaker uses the word *like* to compare the flowing river to a stream of glass, but *stream of glass* is a metaphor that in turn compares the shiny, glittering surface of the stream to glass in a liquid, flowing state. Dunbar asks the reader to imagine what liquid glass would look like when flowing like a river.

Metaphor: "And the faint perfume from its chalice steals," lines 7–8.

Explanation of Use: The speaker compares the opened bud of a flower to a chalice, or sacred drinking vessel. The caged bird can smell the "faint perfume" from the flower but is unable to drink the sweet-smelling nectar from the "chalice."

Reading Strategy Apply Background Knowledge

Writers often write about experiences from their own lives, and knowing something about an author's background can give the reader insight into the theme(s) of a particular work. Review the web diagram you made, and then answer the following questions.

1. Using what you know about the poet's life, what do you think is the theme of "Sympathy"?
2. List three details from Dunbar's life that correspond to the theme of the poem.

Vocabulary Practice

Practice with Analogies Choose the word that best completes the analogy.

1. ladle : spoon :: chalice :
   a. flower **c.** throne
   b. cup **d.** gilded
2. inspired : bland :: keen :
   a. moderate **c.** dull
   b. vivid **d.** moved

Academic Vocabulary

Dunbar uses the title "Sympathy" to ***unify*** *the poem and create a central theme.*

The academic word *unify* is closely related to the more familiar word *unite.* Authors can use elements such as title, setting, or imagery to **unify** any literary work. Using context clues, try to figure out the meaning of the word *unify.* Check your guess in a dictionary.

For more on academic vocabulary, see pages 54–55 and R79–R81.

LOG ON **Literature** Online

Selection Resources For Selection Quizzes, eFlashcards, and Reading-Writing Connection activities, go to glencoe.com and enter QuickPass code GL49787u3.

Write with Style

Apply Symbolism

Assignment If the caged bird's song had words, what do you imagine they would be? Use symbolism to express the caged bird's feelings in your own poetic version of the bird's song.

Get Ideas What would the bird in Dunbar's poem sing about? Think about what is important to the bird and choose a symbol to represent it.

Give It Structure Follow Dunbar's three-stanza structure, and use your symbol in a different way in each stanza. Create a chart like the one below to determine how you will develop the symbolism in each stanza. In the left box, write your chosen symbol. In the right boxes, briefly describe how you will use the symbol to express the bird's perspective in each stanza.

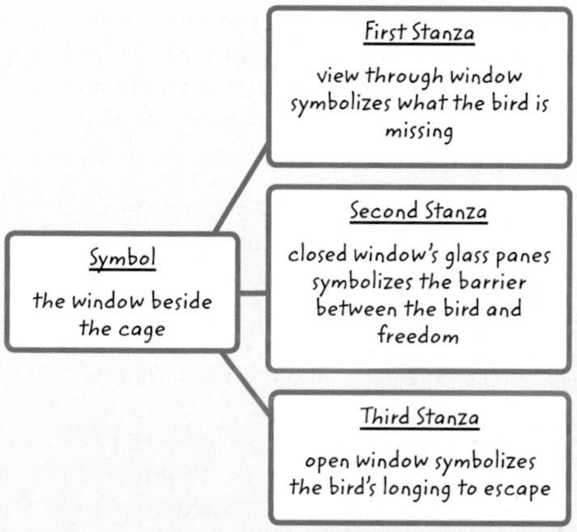

Symbol
the window beside the cage
First Stanza
view through window symbolizes what the bird is missing
Second Stanza
closed window's glass panes symbolizes the barrier between the bird and freedom
Third Stanza
open window symbolizes the bird's longing to escape

As you write, focus each stanza on the idea that is being expressed by the symbol in that stanza.

Look at Language Because readers infer the meaning of symbols based on the text, it is important that your descriptions of the symbol accurately express your meaning. Review your descriptions for precision and meaning.

EXAMPLE:

leaving me as they fly
My notes slip out the open window, ~~roaming free and flying~~ into pure blue air.

For additional assessment, see Assessment Resources, pp. 139–140.

To create custom assessments online, go to Progress Reporter Online Assessment.

To create custom assessments using software, use ExamView Assessment Suite.

After You Read

Assess

Reading Strategy

1. The pain caused by barriers to freedom and fulfillment
2. His enslaved parents, his battle with racism, his rejection by critics

Progress Check

Can students apply background knowledge?

If No → See Unit 3 Teaching Resources Book, p. 194.

Vocabulary Practice

1. b **2.** c

Academic Vocabulary

Sample answer: Based on context clues, *unify* means "to bring something together." Dunbar's title brought together the poem's messages and gathered them into a central theme.

Write with Style

Apply Symbolism

Students' poems should:

- provide the bird's point of view
- be presented like a song
- focus on a symbol that represents something to the bird
- include precise meaningful descriptions of the symbol
- follow the structure of Dunbar's poem

For grammar practice, see Unit 3 Teaching Resources Book, p. 196.

Before You Read

Focus

Bellringer Options

Selection Focus Transparency 25

Daily Language Practice Transparency 60

Or **write** on the board: What is your definition of family? Ask students to quickly jot down the names of their family members. Now ask them to reconsider their lists. Did they include any pets? Any distant or deceased relatives? Any friends? What about plants? Urge students to broaden their definition of *family* and consider to whom and what they are truly connected.

Before You Read

Remember

Meet **Joy Harjo**

(born 1951)

"I read a lot as a child," says poet Joy Harjo, "but I always felt that to read poetry I had to change *myself* to be inside the work. I had to think like a European or a white American."

An enrolled member of the Muscogee Creek Indian Tribe, Joy Harjo was born in Tulsa, Oklahoma. She embraced her American Indian heritage early in life. Harjo had family members who were painters, and they inspired her to study the visual arts. She left home at sixteen to attend the Institute of American Indian Arts in Arizona. She then attended the University of New Mexico, where she focused on painting and theater.

The Road to Poetry As a student at the University of New Mexico, Harjo attended a reading by the poet Simon Ortiz. Listening to Ortiz's poetry, Harjo realized that "poetry can include the experience of a person of the Southwest." This experience led her to seek out American Indian, African American, and Latin American writers. It also spurred her to begin writing poetry herself. In 1978, she earned a master's degree in creative writing from the University of Iowa. Harjo returned to the Institute of American Indian Arts as a creative writing instructor in 1978. Since then, she has taught at several universities, including the University of New Mexico, where she was a professor of creative writing.

> *"We are inventing our own poetic forms and these should take place alongside traditional European forms in the study of literature."*
>
> —Joy Harjo

Women Warriors Survival and gender play important roles in Harjo's depiction of the American Indian experience. "I believe those so-called 'womanly' traits are traits of the warrior," Harjo remarks. "They've been brave—not in the national headlines, but they've been true to themselves, and who they are, and to their families."

Artistic Goals Harjo's artistic goals focus on spreading awareness of the historical conditions in which Native Americans have lived. She urges her readers to examine their own worlds and to become aware of realities they may never have considered before. Her techniques reflect her intention to preserve memory. By repeating an idea or word, she guides the reader to focus on it.

LOG ON **Literature** Online

Author Search For more about Joy Harjo, go to glencoe.com and enter QuickPass code GL49787u3.

Selection Skills

Remember

Reading Skills
- Draw Conclusions About Author's Beliefs (SE pp. 537–539)

Listening/Speaking/Viewing Skills
- Respond to Literature (TE p. 538)

Literary Elements
- Repetition (SE pp. 537, 539)

Vocabulary Skills
- Academic Vocabulary (SE p. 539)

Writing Skills/Grammar
- Personal Essay (SE p. 539)

Literature and Reading Preview

Connect to the Poem

How does your life affect other living things? Discuss this question with a partner. Consider how your actions impact nature and those around you.

Build Background

From earliest times, American Indian cultures have believed in a deep spiritual connection between humans, animals, and forces of nature. Respect—for the past, for social traditions, and for the various processes of all life—is deeply embedded in American Indian cultural heritage.

Set Purposes for Reading

Big Idea Life Lessons

As you read "Remember," ask yourself, What life lesson might Harjo want readers to take away from this poem?

Literary Element Repetition

Repetition is the recurrence of sounds, words, phrases, lines, or stanzas in a literary work. Repetition increases the sense of unity in a work and can call attention to particular ideas. As you read, ask yourself, What is the purpose behind Harjo's use of repetition?

Reading Strategy Draw Conclusions About Author's Beliefs

Literature can often provide you with clues to an **author's beliefs.** In most works, you will need to piece together clues from the writing to identify those beliefs. As you read, ask yourself, What can I learn about Harjo's beliefs through the content, tone, and organization of her poem?

Tip: Pay Attention to Details When you read, remember that authors add details only when those details serve a particular purpose. Use a chart to organize the conclusions you draw from details in the poem.

Details	Conclusion
The speaker refers to the moon as "she."	Harjo gives nature human attributes, which means . . .

Learning Objectives

For pages 536–539

In studying this text, you will focus on the following objectives:

Literary Study: Analyzing repetition.

Reading: Drawing conclusions about author's beliefs.

Writing: Writing a personal essay.

Muscogee Creek pottery jar and mano with pestle grinding rock.

Before You Read

Focus

Summary

Joy Harjo urges readers to remember that they are part of nature. She stresses the unity of and interdependence of all peoples and cultures and suggests that the natural world is also a work of art.

For summaries in languages other than English, see Unit 3 Teaching Resources Book, pp. 199–204.

Interactive Read and Write

Other options for teaching this selection can be found in

- Interactive Read and Write for EL Students, pp. 127–132
- Interactive Read and Write for Approaching-Level Students, pp. 127–132
- Interactive Read and Write for On-Level Students, pp. 127–132

Approaching Level

DIFFERENTIATED INSTRUCTION

Established Ask: What important lessons have you learned that were important to you to remember? (Answers may vary.) Encourage students to explain why they chose to value such information.

Teach

Big Idea 1

Life Lessons **Answer:** *All generations are connected, and appreciating that connection is important to understanding one's heritage. Students may also note the importance of respecting one's mother.*

Reading Strategy 2

Draw Conclusions About Author's Beliefs

Answer: *She believes that all things in nature, including various peoples, are connected and are part of a whole.*

For additional practice using the reading skill or strategy, see Unit 3 Teaching Resources Book, p. 206.

View the Art ★

Native American artist Tim Nicola (1954–) considered becoming a painter but found that sculpture provided a better avenue for his artistic vision.

Say: A three-dimensional sculpture can often be appreciated through touch as well as sight. Consider how texture contributes to the mood of the work. How does this sculpture relate to the poem? *(Students may mention the sculpture's title or notice how the smooth curving shape suggests a sense of wholeness.)*

To check students' understanding of the selection, see Unit 3 Teaching Resources Book, p. 208.

Remember

Joy Harjo

Remember the sky that you were born under,
know each of the star's stories.
Remember the moon, know who she is.
Remember the sun's birth at dawn, that is the
strongest point of time. Remember sundown
and the giving away to night.
Remember your birth, how your mother struggled
to give you form and breath. You are evidence of
her life, and her mother's, and hers.
Remember your father. He is your life, also.
Remember the earth whose skin you are:
red earth, black earth, yellow earth, white earth
brown earth, we are earth.
Remember the plants, trees, animal life who all have their
tribes, their families, their histories, too. Talk to them,
listen to them. They are alive poems.
Remember the wind. Remember her voice. She knows the
origin of this universe.
Remember you are all people and all people
are you.
Remember you are this universe and this
universe is you.
Remember all is in motion, is growing, is you.
Remember language comes from this.
Remember the dance language is, that life is.
Remember.

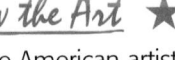

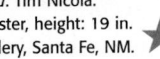

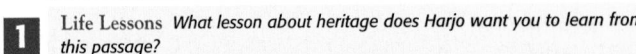

In the Wind. Tim Nicola. Utah alabaster, height: 19 in. Artistic Gallery, Santa Fe, NM. ★

1 Life Lessons *What lesson about heritage does Harjo want you to learn from this passage?*

2 Draw Conclusions About Author's Beliefs *What can you conclude about Harjo's beliefs from these two lines?*

Listening and Speaking Practice

PARTNERS SPIRAL REVIEW

Respond to Literature

Ask: Why does the speaker repeat the word "remember" throughout the poem? *(Students may point out that the speaker wants to emphasize important ideas.)* With a partner, have students read the poem and discuss the affect that repetition has on Harjo's poem. Ask students to answer the following questions:

- Does repetition improve the poem? Why or why not?
- How does repetition affect Harjo's poem?
- How is the use of repetition different in the two poems?

After You Read

Respond and Think Critically

Respond and Interpret

1. How did you feel after reading this poem? What did you find yourself thinking about? Explain.
2. (a)Give five examples of elements in nature that the speaker urges readers to remember. (b)Why are these things important?
3. (a)According to the speaker, what does the wind know? (b)What does this statement mean?

Analyze and Evaluate

4. **Personification** is giving human qualities or characteristics to an object, animal, force of nature, or idea. How does Harjo use personification in this poem?
5. (a)Harjo urges readers to remember "the plants, trees, animal life" because "they are alive poems." What does this statement mean? (b)Is it possible to learn from these parts of nature? Explain.
6. (a)In lines 19–22, what idea is Harjo trying to express? (b)Do you agree with this idea? Explain.

Connect

7. **Big Idea** Life Lessons (a)What lesson does Harjo share with the reader? (b)How do you think she learned this lesson?
8. **Connect to Today** Why might this poem be especially significant in our world today?

Literary Element Repetition

Repetition increases the sense of unity in a work and can call attention to particular ideas.

1. List two examples of repetition in this poem.
2. What is the effect of these instances of repetition?

Reading Strategy Draw Conclusions About Author's Beliefs

Review the chart you created while you read the poem. Then answer the following questions.

1. Based on this poem and the background knowledge you have of the poet, what do you think Harjo believes about people's relationships with one another and with the earth?
2. In support of your opinion, list three details from the poem.

LOG ON Literature Online

Selection Resources For Selection Quizzes, eFlashcards, and Reading-Writing Connection activities, go to glencoe.com and enter QuickPass code GL49787u3.

Academic Vocabulary

*In her poem, Harjo tries to **reinforce** the idea that we are connected to everything around us.*

Reinforce is an academic word. In more casual conversation, someone might suggest using nails to **reinforce** a weak spot in a fence. Using context clues, try to figure out the meaning of the word *reinforce.* Check your guess in a dictionary.

For more on academic vocabulary, see pages 54–55 and R79–R81.

Writing

Write a Personal Essay Recall a childhood moment when you felt closely connected with nature. Describe the setting as well as your thoughts and feelings. How does remembering this moment relate to your understanding of the poem? How does this moment shed light on the connections between humans and the natural world?

After You Read

Assess

1. Answers should focus on family connections and origins.
2. (a) Sky, stars, moon, sun, sundown, night, birth, parents, ancestors, earth, and so forth (b) To consider their lives within a broader perspective
3. (a) The "origin of the universe" (b) It was part of the world forever.
4. The stars having stories, the plants and animals having families and histories, and the wind having a voice
5. (a) Possible answer: They are living works of art with their own stories to tell. (b) Students should support their ideas.
6. (a) Our heritage and the essence of our being are shaped by everyone and everything around us. (b) Students should support their answers.
7. (a) That all lives are interconnected and united as part of the universe (b) Possibly from her family, Native Americans who revered their ancestors, nature, and the great mysteries of the universe
8. Sample answer: Today many environmental problems are worse than they've ever been. Perhaps Harjo's poem might encourage people to be more conscious of taking better care of the environment.

Literary Element

1. "Remember" and "earth"
2. Rhythm and emphasis

Progress Check

Can students analyze repetition?

If No → See Unit 3 Teaching Resources Book, p. 205.

Reading Strategy

1. All life forms have equal value.
2. Students should support their answers with appropriate details.

Writing

Students' personal essays should:

- recall a childhood moment
- use descriptive details

Academic Vocabulary

Sample answer: Based on context clues, reinforce means to support or to make stronger. Harjo's poem supported or strengthened the idea that we are connected to everything.

Before You Read

Focus

Bellringer Options

Selection Focus Transparency 26

Daily Language Practice Transparency 61

Or **ask:** How might you experience the road not taken? Suggest students jot down their regular, daily routines. Brainstorm ways they might deviate, such as taking a different way to class or eating lunch at a different table. Have them implement the changes and report on the results. Discuss what they've learned.

Before You Read

The Road Not Taken

Meet **Robert Frost**
(1874–1963)

According to poet Robert Frost, a good poem "begins in delight, and ends in wisdom." Frost is one of the most popular American poets of the twentieth century. He used both traditional and modern forms in his poems, which perhaps accounts for the wide appeal of his writing. Frost received numerous awards and honors for his works, including four Pulitzer Prizes for Literature.

A Rich Heritage Robert Frost was born in San Francisco, where his father was establishing a career in journalism. When Frost was eleven years old, his father died, and his mother moved the family back to New England. From his boyhood until his later years, Frost enjoyed long walks in the woods. Not surprisingly, references to nature and New England settings and speech patterns abound in Frost's poetry.

> *"[T]he ear does it. The ear is the only true writer and the only true reader."*
>
> —Robert Frost

Frost began writing poetry while in high school, a passion he shared with his co-valedictorian and future wife, Elinor Miriam White. After spending a year at college, Frost went to work as a teacher. He also worked as a factory laborer, a newspaper editor, and a lecturer at Amherst College and several other universities throughout his life.

A New England Poet In 1900 Frost and his family moved to a farm in Derry, New Hampshire. While Frost was ultimately unsuccessful as a farmer, he did write many of the poems during those years that would make up his first books. *A Boy's Will* (1913) and *North of Boston* (1914) were published by a London publishing house while Frost and his family were living in England. While in England, Frost wrote "The Road Not Taken."

Frost's first three books of poetry were well received by both critics and the public. His fourth book, *New Hampshire,* won a Pulitzer Prize in 1924. As a successful poet, Frost spent much of his time reading his poems to audiences around the country.

Frost's middle years were plagued by tragedy. Between 1934 and 1940, he lost his daughter, Marjorie; his wife, Elinor; and his son, Carol. In 1942 he published a book of poems titled *A Witness Tree,* which explored the themes of loss and sorrow.

LOG ON **Literature Online**

Author Search For more about Robert Frost, go to glencoe.com and enter QuickPass code GL49787u3.

Selection Skills

The Road Not Taken

Literary Elements
- Lyric Poetry (SE pp. 541, 544)
- Rhythm (SE p. 544)

Writing Skills/Grammar
- Expository Essay (SE p. 545)
- In-Text Quotations (SE p. 545)
- Respond to Literature (TE p. 542)

Reading Skills
- Make Inferences About Theme (SE pp. 541, 542, 544)

Vocabulary Skills
- Context Clues (SE pp. 541, 544)

Literature and Reading Preview

Connect to the Poem

What kinds of decisions are most difficult to make? Write a journal entry about a difficult decision you had to make and the outcome of that decision.

Build Background

"The Road Not Taken" is one of Frost's most famous poems. On the surface, this poem was meant as a friendly jest toward Frost's British friend, Edward Thomas, who used to guide Frost on walks in the English countryside. Thomas often stated that the well-worn path was not the best way to go. The poem's deeper meaning, however, has universal appeal.

Set Purposes for Reading

Big Idea Life Lessons

As you read "The Road Not Taken," ask yourself, How does Frost link making decisions and having second thoughts to the theme of life lessons?

Literary Element Lyric Poetry

A **lyric poem** expresses a speaker's personal thoughts and feelings. These types of poems are usually short and musical. As you read, ask yourself, How does the speaker express his thoughts and feelings?

Reading Strategy Make Inferences About Theme

The **theme** of a literary work is the work's main idea or message. A literary work may have more than one theme. Some themes are universal, meaning that they are widely held ideas about life. Sometimes, the reader has to **infer** the theme, or use reason and his or her experience to deduce a work's implied meaning. As you read "The Road Not Taken," ask yourself, What inferences can I make about the poem's theme?

Tip: Take Notes As you read, record the inferences you make about the theme.

Detail	Inference
"sorry I could not travel both"	I think the speaker is expressing regret here.

Learning Objectives

For pages 540–544

In studying this text, you will focus on the following objectives:

Literary Study: Analyzing lyric poetry.

Reading: Making inferences about theme.

Vocabulary

diverge (di vurj′) *v.* to lead in different directions away from a common starting point; p. 542 *The path diverged at the edge of the water and led in two directions around the lake.*

want (wont) *v.* to fail to possess; to lack; p. 542 *The old station wagon wanted a proper paint job.*

Tip: Context Clues To figure out the meaning of an unfamiliar word, look for context clues, or hints in the words and sentences around the unfamiliar word. Example: *The two friends thought they would always be close, but their lives diverged when one moved to California and the other moved to Boston.* The words *close, California,* and *Boston* tell you that to *diverge* is to go in different directions from a common point.

Before You Read

Focus

Summary

The speaker describes a day when he was walking in the woods and came to a fork in the path. He chose the less traveled path. Though he wonders about the other path, he states that taking the less traveled path has defined his life.

For summaries in languages other than English, see Unit 3 Teaching Resources Book, pp. 210–215.

Interactive Read and Write

Other options for teaching this selection can be found in

- Interactive Read and Write for EL Students, pp. 133–140
- Interactive Read and Write for Approaching-Level Students, pp. 133–140
- Interactive Read and Write for On-Level Students, pp. 133–140

Vocabulary

Use New Vocabulary To test vocabulary comprehension, have students write a paragraph using both vocabulary words at least twice. Ask students who have used the words in the best and most creative ways to share their paragraph with the rest of the class.

For additional vocabulary practice, see Unit 3 Teaching Resources Book, p. 218.

For additional context, see Glencoe Visual Vocabulary CD-ROM.

Approaching Level

DIFFERENTIATED INSTRUCTION

Established Have students read the information in the Build Background section. **Say:** Frost's friend Thomas felt that the "well-worn path was the best way to go," while Frost's poem expresses the opposite. **Ask:** Do you agree with Thomas or Frost about which is the best path to take? *(Answers will vary. Some students may agree with Thomas because a "well-worn" path is predictable. Others may agree with Frost and that it is important to take some risks in life.)*

Teach

Reading Strategy 1

Make Inferences About Theme **Answer:** *Students may suggest that the speaker wants to know where both roads lead.*

For additional practice using the reading skill or strategy, see Unit 3 Teaching Resources Book, p. 217.

Big Idea 2

Life Lessons **Answer:** *It suggests how one choice leads to another, gradually defining a person's life and making it harder to turn back or change direction.*

ADVANCED For advanced students, **ask:** What life lesson is Frost sharing with the reader? *(He seems to suggest that a person can take pride in making an unusual or less popular choice.)*

View the Art ★

Claude Monet (1840–1926) was the leader of the Impressionist movement in painting. A central goal of Impressionism was to realistically portray the colors and forms of objects in nature, rejecting the muted colors and conventional forms traditionally used in painting. Monet's many landscape paintings showcase this technique. **Ask:** Do you think the colors and forms in this painting display a realistic setting? *(Accept reasonable responses.)*

The Road Not Taken

Robert Frost

Sous-Bois, 1876. Claude Monet. Oil on canvas, 73 x 54 cm. London, Sotheby's. Lot 3, 28/6/99. ★

Two roads **diverged** in a yellow wood,
And sorry I could not travel both
And be one traveler, long I stood
And looked down one as far as I could
To where it bent in the undergrowth;

Then took the other, as just as fair,
And having perhaps the better claim,
Because it was grassy and **wanted** wear;
Though as for that the passing there
Had worn them really about the same,

And both that morning equally lay
In leaves no step had trodden black.
Oh, I kept the first for another day!
Yet knowing how way leads on to way,
I doubted if I should ever come back.

I shall be telling this with a sigh
Somewhere ages and ages hence:
Two roads diverged in a wood, and I—
I took the one less traveled by,
And that has made all the difference.

1 Make Inferences About Theme *Why might the speaker want to travel both roads?*

Vocabulary

diverge (di vurj′) *v.* to lead in different directions away from a common starting point

want (wont) *v.* to fail to possess; to lack

Life Lessons *What does Frost mean by this line?* 2

Writing Practice

Respond to Literature Robert Frost uses nature in many of his poems to discuss the twists and turns life takes. In *The Road Not Taken,* the roads in the woods represent life's choices. Show students other poems by Frost *(e.g. Birches, Nothing Gold Can Stay, A Tuft of Flowers)* that prominently feature nature. Have students write an essay about the role of nature in Frost's poetry. Students should explain how nature is represented in each of these poems. Students should also explain whether the poems appeal to them and provide support for their ideas.

After You Read

Respond and Think Critically

Respond and Interpret

1. Which road in the poem would you have taken?
2. (a)What clues tell you the season during which the poem takes place? (b)How is the season related to the theme?
3. (a)Does the speaker think that he will ever return to the fork in the road? (b)Do you think that he wants to return? Explain.

Analyze and Evaluate

4. Frost uses **contradiction,** or opposing ideas, in this poem. Explain how the descriptions of the paths include a contradiction. What does this contradiction reveal about the speaker?
5. How does Frost communicate the speaker's self-doubts? Give examples.
6. (a)What techniques does Frost use to create an emotional impact at the end of the poem? (b)Are these techniques effective? Explain.

Connect

7. **Big Idea** Life Lessons Is the speaker happy or regretful at the end of the poem? Explain.
8. **Connect to the Author** Frost was well known for his appreciation of nature and his curiosity about the natural world. Where in the poem are these feelings revealed?

Visual Literacy

Cartoon

A **parody** is a humorous imitation of a literary work that often aims to point out the work's shortcomings. A parody may imitate the plot, characters, or style of a work. As you read the cartoon, think about how the title and caption add to the humor of the parody.

Group Activity Discuss the following questions with classmates.

1. What does the cartoonist use in place of Frost's two roads?
2. Does this cartoon trivialize the emotions of the speaker in Frost's poem? Explain.

famous cat quotes
with deepest apologies to Robert Frost
TWO SLUGS SLITHERED ON A YELLOW WOOD AND SORRY I COULD NOT TRAMPLE BOTH, BEING ONE TRAMPLER. LONG I STOOD AND LOOKED THEM DOWN AS FIERCE AS I COULD TO WHERE THEY SAT IN THE UNDERGROWTH...
I WILL BE TELLING THIS WITH A SIGH SOMEWHERE SITTING UPON A FENCE: TWO SLUGS SLITHERED ON A YELLOW WOOD AND I--I ATE THE SLUG LESS TRAMPLED BY, AND THAT HAS MADE ALL THE DIFFERENCE.
12/12 ©2001 Darby Conley. Dist. by UFS, Inc. WWW.COMICS.COM
darb

GET FUZZY ©Darby Conley. Dist. by United Features Syndicate, Inc.

After You Read

Assess

1. (a) Accept reasonable answers.
2. (a) The yellow wood and leaves on the ground suggest autumn. (b) Autumn suggests a later stage of life, times when people look back and reflect on their choices.
3. (a) The speaker doubts that he will ever return. (b) Students should support their answers with details from the text.
4. They are described the same in terms of wear, but then one is described as less worn. It suggests that a person's memory of past circumstances may be inaccurate.
5. The speaker hesitates at the fork, wavers, and wonders about the forsaken path.
6. (a) Repetition of *I* in the last stanza evokes emotion: regret in the first line, faltering hesitation in the third line. The ambiguity of the final line lets readers draw their own conclusions. (b) Students should support their answers.
7. Possible answer: "With a sigh" suggests regret.
8. Students should support their responses with examples from the poem, such as wanting to explore both paths and describing the color of the wood and leaves.

Visual Literacy

1. The cartoonist uses two slugs in place of Frost's roads.
2. Possible answer: The comic makes the speaker's dilemma seem silly—that a person's life-changing decisions amount to no more than a cat's dilemma about which slug to eat.

After You Read

Assess

Literary Element

1. Second stanza: *cdccd;* third stanza: *efeef;* fourth stanza: *ghggh;* yes
2. Doubt, curiosity, pride; possible answers: musical flow conveys changing emotions and suggests a life journey; rigid rhyme scheme suggests conventionality and counters the speaker's claim to individuality

Progress Check

Can students interpret lyric poetry?

If No → See Unit 3 Teaching Resources Book, p. 216.

Review: Rhythm

Possible answer:

Line: And sor/ry I could/ not trav/el both
Rhythm: Irregular
Effect: Stresses the speaker's sense of regret

Line: And be/ one travel/er, long/ I stood
Rhythm: Irregular
Effect: Emphasizes that the speaker is only "one" person and can only take one road

Line: And looked/ down one/ as far/ as I could
Rhythm: Irregular
Effect: Continues to stress the idea of one person, one choice, one road

Line: To where/ it bent/ in the un/dergrowth;
Rhythm: Irregular
Effect: Sound enhances the image of a bending and obscured road

Literary Element Lyric Poetry

A **lyric poem** is an expression of the author's thoughts and feelings. It is a short, musical poem that has a concrete meter and rhyme scheme. Determining the rhyme scheme can help the reader better hear a poem's musical quality.

The method used to indicate a poem's rhyme scheme is to assign the same letter of the alphabet to the words at the ends of lines that rhyme. In the first stanza, the lines that end with *wood, stood,* and *could* can be labeled *a;* the lines that end with *both* and *undergrowth* can be labeled *b.* So, the rhyme scheme in the first stanza is *abaab.*

1. Using this standard poetic notation, identify the rhyme schemes of the second, third, and fourth stanzas of "The Road Not Taken." Is the rhyme scheme identical in each stanza?
2. What thoughts and feelings are expressed in this poem? How does the structure help express them?

Review: Rhythm

As you learned on page 462, **rhythm** is the pattern of beats created by the arrangement of stressed and unstressed syllables. Rhythm gives poetry a musical quality, adds emphasis to certain words, and may help convey the poem's meaning. Rhythm can be regular—with a predictable pattern or meter—or irregular.

Partner Activity With a classmate, analyze the rhythm of "The Road Not Taken." Working with your partner, create a graphic organizer like the one below. Mark the scansion for each line in the first stanza. Then list the type of rhythm—regular or irregular—and the effect of the rhythm.

Line	Rhythm	Effect
Two roads diverged in a yellow wood,	Irregular	Stresses the image of two roads, or two choices

Reading Strategy Make Inferences About Theme

SAT Skills Practice

1. Which statement best expresses the primary theme of "The Road Not Taken"?
   (A) It is wise not to follow the crowd.
   (B) You can never go back.
   (C) Some decisions are life-altering.
   (D) Memories are often melancholy.
   (E) Life is a journey.

Vocabulary Practice

Practice with Context Clues Look back at the poem to find context clues for the vocabulary words below. Record your findings in a chart like the one below.

diverge   want

Example:

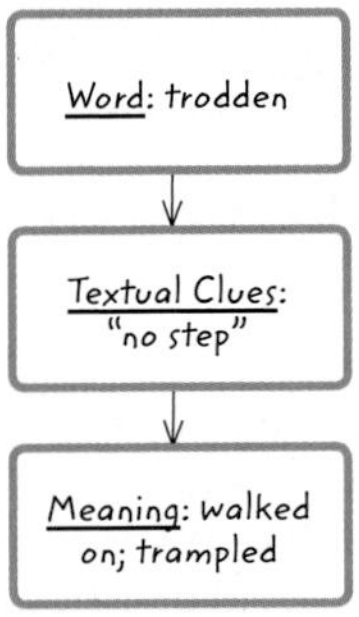

LOG ON Literature Online

Selection Resources For Selection Quizzes, eFlashcards, and Reading-Writing Connection activities, go to glencoe.com and enter QuickPass code GL49787u3.

Reading Strategy

1. C is the correct answer. The decision to follow a path takes one's life in a unique direction.

Vocabulary Practice

Sample answer:
Word: diverge
Textual Clues: "could not travel both"
Meaning: go in different directions
Word: want
Textual Clues: "Because it was grassy"
Meaning: to lack (wear)

Respond Through Writing

Expository Essay

Analyze Theme Write an essay in which you analyze the main theme of "The Road Not Taken." As you work, consider how Frost's use of language creates ambiguities of meaning.

Understand the Task **Ambiguity** is the state of having more than one meaning.

Prewrite Identify lines that relate to the poem's theme. Note the words or phrases in these lines that might create ambiguities of meaning. Use a series of diagrams like the one below to help you list the interpretations of the ambigious words or phrases. In the main oval, write an ambigous word or phrase. In the surrounding ovals, list possible interpretations.

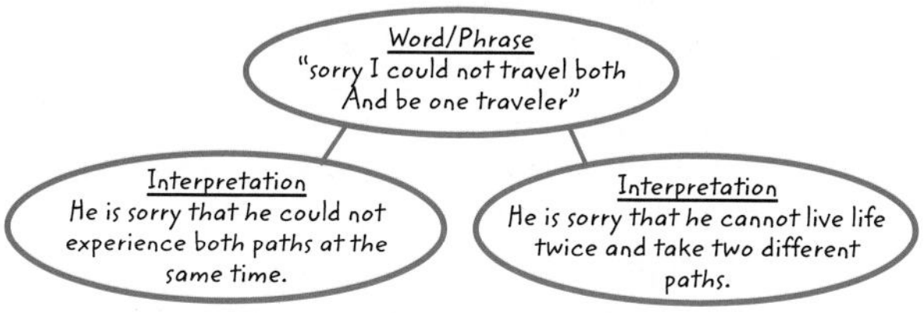

List the ways in which these ambiguities might affect how readers interpret the poem's theme. Highlight the strongest ideas from your list and the best examples from your web diagrams to use in your essay.

Draft In the opening of your essay, provide your interpretation of the poem's main theme. Your opening also should include a thesis stating how Frost's use of language creates ambiguities of meaning. As you write, refer to your diagrams and include the highlighted ideas and examples that support your thesis. Make sure you include an analysis of how the ambiguities might lead a reader to a different interpretion of the theme. Then explain why the theme you've chosen is stronger.

Revise As you revise your essay, identify places where it would be helpful to insert quotations from the poem that support or provide an example of an idea presented in your essay. After revising, exchange essays with a partner and provide constructive feedback for each other.

Edit and Proofread Proofread your paper, correcting any errors in grammar, spelling, and punctuation. Review the Grammar Tip in the side column to help you with in-text quotations from poems.

Learning Objectives

In this assignment, you will focus on the following objectives:

Writing: Writing an expository essay analyzing theme.

Grammar: Understanding how to punctuate in-text poetry quotations correctly.

Grammar Tip

In-text Quotations

When you include a direct quotation from a poem in the text of an essay or a report, the quotation must appear inside quotation marks. If the quote includes words from more than one line, show the line break with a slash.

The idea is made more ambiguous when Frost says "I could not travel both / And be one traveler."

After You Read

Assess

Respond Through Writing

Students' essays should

- provide their interpretation of the poem's theme
- include a thesis stating how Frost's use of language creates ambiguity
- provide direct quotations from the poem as supporting examples
- explain why the quoted words or phrases are ambiguous
- analyze how the ambiguities might affect how readers interpret the theme

For grammar practice, see Unit 3 Teaching Resources Book, p. 219.

For additional assessment, see Assessment Resources, pp. 143–144.

To create custom assessments online, go to Progress Reporter Online Assessment.

To create custom assessments using software, use ExamView Assessment Suite.

Before You Read

Focus

Bellringer Options

Daily Language Practice Transparency 62

Or ask students to think about how people can become overwhelmed with a busy schedule. **Ask:** How do most people respond to being busy? Do you ever feel as if you are being controlled by a busy schedule? What do you do when you feel this way?

Before You Read

Time

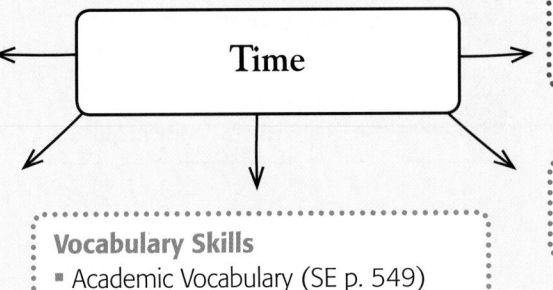

Meet **Joseph Bruchac**

(born 1942)

At the age of 24, after finishing his graduate studies in literature and writing, poet Joseph Bruchac traveled to West Africa to teach at a secondary school. During his three-year stay, Bruchac learned as much as he taught. Regarding his experience, Bruchac said, "It showed me many things. How much we have as Americans and take for granted. How much our eyes refuse to see because we are blinded to everything in a man's face except for color. And most importantly, how human people are everywhere—which may be the one grace that saves us all." Bruchac's writing, which is heavily influenced by his Native American roots, reflects his belief in our shared humanity.

> *"I think it is important to consider . . . storytelling in all its aspects from oral history to social commentary to spiritual awareness to humor."*
>
> —Joseph Bruchac

Connected to His Heritage Bruchac was born on October 16, 1942, in Saratoga Springs, New York. Although he has both Native American and European ancestors, Bruchac's childhood was more connected to his Native American heritage. He was raised by his grandparents in the foothills of the Adirondack Mountains in New York. His grandfather was an Abenaki Indian, and Bruchac learned to appreciate the tribal lore of his grandfather's people.

Bruchac attended college at Cornell University. He went on to attain his masters degree at Syracuse University and followed with his three-year stay in Africa. After returning to the United States, Bruchac continued teaching while he began to build his career as a writer. Early on, Bruchac succeeded primarily as a poet. His first book, a collection of poems, was published in 1971.

Sharing the Art of Storytelling In addition to his efforts as a poet, Bruchac continued his passion for teaching. While working toward his doctoral degree, he began teaching creative writing in prisons. In 1975, his efforts were rewarded with a prestigious National Endowment for the Arts grant.

As his career as a writer grew, Bruchac began sharing his Native American tales through award-winning short fiction, children's stories, and oral storytelling. He and his family are also heavily involved in projects preserving the Abenaki culture. Bruchac still lives and writes in the house that he grew up in—among the foothills of the Adirondacks and the shadows of his ancestors.

LOG ON **Literature** Online

Author Search For more about Joseph Bruchac, go to glencoe.com and enter QuickPass code GL49787u3.

Selection Skills

Time

Literary Elements
- Personification (547–549)

Reading Skills
- Identify Irony (SE pp. 547–549)

Vocabulary Skills
- Academic Vocabulary (SE p. 549)

Listening/Speaking/Viewing Skills
- Understand Irony (TE p. 548)

Writing Skills/Grammar
- Memo (SE p. 549)

Literature and Reading Preview

Connect to the Poem

When does time feel like it speeds up or slows down? Discuss this question with a small group. Share your experiences and talk about why it feels like time moves at different speeds.

Build Background

The mink, a type of thick-furred weasel, is a common character in Native American myths. The mythic Mink is a *trickster*, which is typically a small animal that uses skill and wit to overcome great forces. In this poem, Mink steals Time from the Europeans. In real life, Europeans introduced clocks to Native Americans, who had used the sun to mark time.

Set Purposes for Reading

Big Idea Life Lessons

As you read "Time," ask yourself, What can happen when you pay too much attention to time?

Literary Element Personification

Personification is a figure of speech in which an animal, object, force of nature, or idea is given human characteristics. Personification provides insight into the thoughts and feelings a thing might have if it were human. As you read, ask yourself, What instances of personification can I find in this poem?

Reading Strategy Identify Irony

Irony is a contrast between appearance and reality. To **identify irony** look for an unexpected result or event. By finding the contrast between the expected and what actually occurred, you can find what is ironic. As you read, ask yourself, How do the results of Mink's actions differ from what Mink intended?

Tip: Take Notes As you read the poem, use a three-column chart like the one below to note ironic elements.

Action action taken by a character	Appearance expected result of this action	Reality what actually occurred

Learning Objectives

For pages 546–549

In studying this text, you will focus on the following objectives:

Literary Study: Analyzing personification.

Reading: Identifying irony.

Writing: Writing a memo.

Before You Read

Focus

Summary

In this poem, Mink steals Time from the Europeans. In the end, he finds that instead of controlling Time, Time controls him.

For summaries in languages other than English, see Unit 3 Teaching Resources Book, pp. 222–227.

Interactive Read and Write

Other options for teaching this selection can be found in

- Interactive Read and Write for EL Students, pp. 141–146
- Interactive Read and Write for Approaching-Level Students, pp. 141–146
- Interactive Read and Write for On-Level Students, pp. 141–146

Approaching Level

DIFFERENTIATED INSTRUCTION

Established When students read the poem on page 548, they should realize that the main character, Mink, is an animal. **Say:** Many Native American tales, along with the stories of many other cultures, involve animals as characters. Often, these animals are personified, which means they take on human characteristics. **Ask:** How might this poem be different if the character was a person? *(Students may think that a person might not steal things, or might not become controlled by the clock.)* **Ask:** What other stories do you know are about animals doing amazing things? *(Students may think of any of hundreds of examples from classic or modern tales.)*

Teach

Literary Element 1

Personification Answer: *Because he is being personified; the Mink is being described using human actions (stealing).*

APPROACHING To assist approaching-level students, have a student reread the explanation of the Literary Element on page 547.

Reading Strategy 2

Identify Irony Answer: *Because he expected Time to be better than the Sun. Instead it was worse, and he wishes he still owned the Sun.*

ADVANCED For advanced learners, **ask:** What kind of irony is this? *(This is an example of situational irony because the opposite of what we expect happens. We expect Mink to own Time when he steals it, but instead Time ends up owning him.)*

For additional practice using the reading skill or strategy, see Unit 3 Teaching Resources Book, p. 229.

To check students' understanding of the selection, see Unit 3 Teaching Resources Book, p. 231.

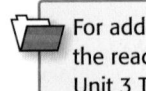

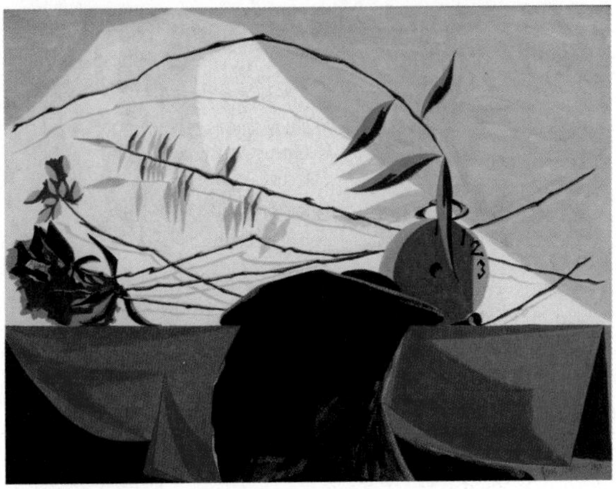

Time, 1955. Jacob Lawrence. Casein tempera on paper, 17⅞ x 23⅞ in. Private Collection, Chicago, IL. © ARS, NY.

TIME

Joseph Bruchac

Mink once stole the Sun
so the People could have light.

Then the Europeans came
and brought with them
a new thing called Time.

So Mink stole Time.
He carried it off—
a big metal clock.

But instead of owning it,
he soon found out that
it owned him.

To this day he sits
with three big keys
around his neck.

Each day he uses them
to wind up Time
which owns us all now
the way we once owned the Sun.

---

1 Personification *How can you tell that Mink is not intended to be seen as an actual animal?*

2 Identify Irony *Why is it ironic that Mink replaced the Sun with Time?*

Listening and Speaking Practice

SMALL GROUP **Understand Irony** Remind students that irony occurs when an unexpected event takes place. An example would be studying and preparing very hard for an English test and then realizing the upcoming test is in math. Have students explain the basic events in the poem. Then discuss with them how the poem is ironic. *(The main irony in the poem is that Mink wanted to own the clock but the clock came to own him.)*

When students understand the irony, put them into small groups and ask each group to think of three examples of irony, whether from real life or their imaginations.

After You Read

Respond and Think Critically

Respond and Interpret

1. How did the poem affect the way you view time?
2. (a)Why did Mink steal the Sun? (b)What does this tell you about Mink's relationship with the native people?
3. (a)Why was Mink unfamiliar with Time? (b)Why does this end up being a problem?
4. (a)How does Mink's appearance change after he steals Time? (b)What might this image symbolize about Mink's fate?

Analyze and Evaluate

5. How does Bruchac use the final lines to express how Native American life changed after the arrival of the Europeans?
6. A **universal theme** is a message commonly found in works of literature from a variety of cultures. Do you think this poem is effective in making its message universal and not just about the Native American experience? Explain.

Connect

7. **Big Idea** Life Lessons Based on this poem, do you think it is wise to worry about time? Explain.
8. **Connect to the Author** Joseph Bruchac has published many retellings of Native American myths. In what ways does this poem remind you of a myth?

Literary Element Personification

Many authors use **personification**. While readers recognize that nonhuman characters do not literally exhibit human qualities, personification can help readers see the author's point more vividly.

1. List two examples of personification in the poem.
2. What human behaviors are described in each of the examples you named?

Reading Strategy Identify Irony

To **identify irony,** locate the unexpected twists in a literary work. If the reality of a situation contrasts with what appeared to be true, it is often ironic. Use your chart to help answer the questions below.

1. What is the poem's main ironic twist?
2. Why is this twist ironic?

LOG ON **Literature** Online

Selection Resources For Selection Quizzes, eFlash-cards, and Reading-Writing Connection activities, go to glencoe.com and enter QuickPass code GL49787u3.

Academic Vocabulary

After Native Americans ***encountered*** *Europeans, their lives were not the same.*

Encounter is an academic word. In more casual conversation, someone might say that she **encountered** her friends at the library. Using context clues, try to figure out the meaning of the word in the sentence about Native Americans above. Check your guess in a dictionary.

For more on academic vocabulary, see pages 54–55 and R79–R81.

Writing

Write a Memo The ironic twists in trickster tales are often humorous. Write a memo that tells a lighter version of the story told in "Time." Your memo should be brief and humorous. Make sure to address your memo to a specific audience and note why the information is relevant to them. Write with a clear purpose and maintain a consistent tone.

After You Read

Assess

1. Answers may vary. Students should support their answers.
2. (a) To give light to the people (b) It tells you that he has a good relationship with the people and tries to help them.
3. (a) Because he had never seen it until the Europeans brought it with them (b) Because he doesn't know what to expect when he steals it and doesn't realize it will end up owning him
4. (a) He has a ring with three keys around his neck. (b) It might symbolize how the mink is trapped and controlled by Time from now on.
5. He talks about how the Native Americans are owned by time now instead of owning the Sun. This expresses how they used to control their own fate but now are controlled by others—the Europeans.
6. Students should support their answers.
7. Answers may vary. Students should support their answers.
8. Sample answer: It's a short tale with a lesson.

Literary Element

1. Mink and Time
2. The Mink takes human actions (such as stealing and trying to own something). Time "owns" people and the Mink.

Progress Check

Can students identify personification?

If No → See Unit 3 Teaching Resources Book, p. 228.

Reading Strategy

1. Time ends up owning the Mink
2. It is ironic because the Mink intended to own Time, but the unexpected happened and Time ended up owning the Mink instead.

For additional assessment, see Assessment Resources, pp. 145–146.

Academic Vocabulary

Students should use a dictionary to confirm their understanding of the word.

Writing

Students' memos should

- be addressed to a specific audience
- be humorous and brief
- retell the story told in the poem

Before You Read

Focus

Bellringer Options

Daily Language Practice Transparency 63

Or ask students to talk about a teacher, coach, or counselor who has influenced their lives in a positive way. **Ask:** In what ways have you been positively influenced by a teacher, coach, or counselor? What can teachers, counselors, and coaches learn from their students?

Before You Read

Theme for English B

Meet **Langston Hughes**

(1902–1967)

In his writing, Langston Hughes captured African American experiences and explored ideas that have resonated with generations of readers. His first big break came through a chance meeting. On a night in 1925, while he was working at his job as a busboy at a hotel restaurant, the famous poet Vachel Lindsay stopped in for dinner. Hughes recognized Lindsay and left three poems by his plate. Lindsay liked the poems, and when Hughes arrived at work the next day, reporters were waiting to interview the "busboy poet."

Crafting a Voice Hughes was born in Joplin, Missouri, in 1902. He spent much of his childhood living with his grandmother in Lawrence, Kansas. She died when he was thirteen and he eventually settled in Cleveland, Ohio, with his mother and stepfather. By the time he was in high school, Hughes had already begun writing poetry and he often published his work in the school's literary magazine.

A year after Hughes finished high school, he enrolled at Columbia University in New York City. However, before he began college, Hughes wrote what is now one of his most famous poems, "The Negro Speaks of Rivers." He composed the poem while on a train to Mexico to visit his father. Hughes's stay at Columbia lasted only a year, but his move to New York introduced him to Harlem, the place that would define his career as a writer.

Leading a Cultural Revival During the 1920s, Harlem was home to a large group of groundbreaking African American artists. Hughes mingled with these writers, musicians, and painters in the clubs and homes of Harlem. The young poet was particularly influenced by blues and jazz, the new musical styles that were being played in the Harlem clubs. As he developed his unique style, Hughes incorporated the rhythm of blues and jazz music into his poems. In 1926, Hughes published his first book of poems, *The Weary Blues.* By the end of the 1920s, Hughes had established himself as one of the leaders of the art movement known as the Harlem Renaissance.

> *"Droning a drowsy syncopated tune,*
> *Rocking back and forth to a mellow croon,*
> *I heard a Negro play."*
>
> —Langston Hughes, "The Weary Blues"

The Great Depression of the 1930s led to tough times in Harlem. As conditions declined and racism persisted, Hughes began writing more political poems, as well as plays and fiction. Throughout his life, he continued to explore and celebrate the African American experience through his writing.

LOG ON **Literature** Online

Author Search For more about Langston Hughes, go to glencoe.com and enter QuickPass code GL49787u3.

Selection Skills

Theme for English B

Literary Elements
- Voice (SE pp. 551, 552, 554)
- Lyric Poetry (SE p. 554)

Study Skills/Research Assessment
- Research (TE p. 552)

Reading Skills
- Analyze Skills (SE pp. 551, 552, 555)

Vocabulary Skills
- Academic Vocabulary (SE p. 555)

Writing Skills/Grammar
- Apply Tone (SE p. 555)

Literature and Reading Preview

Connect to the Text

How do you think other people see you? Freewrite for a few minutes about what you think defines you in other people's eyes.

Build Background

The Harlem Renaissance of the 1920s was a landmark time of creative and cultural growth for the African American community. Hughes's poems—such as "Theme for English B"—captured the concerns of African American communities across the United States, such as equality, cultural pride, and intellectual growth.

Set Purposes for Reading

Big Idea Life Lessons

As you read "Theme for English B," ask yourself, What might Hughes's instructor have learned from this poem?

Literary Element Voice

In poetry, **voice** refers to the personality of the speaker. Voice can be determined by word choice or by the speaker's attitude. In some cases, the voice captures the personality of the speaker at a specific time in his or her life. As you read, ask yourself, What is the speaker's attitude toward the reader?

Reading Strategy Analyze Style

A poem's style is defined by its language, structure, and tone. To **analyze style,** you need to examine the sound and rhythm of the lines, as well as the tone. As you read, ask yourself, How does Hughes use rhythm to create a distinct style of poetry?

Tip: Read First, Then Analyze Read a poem first to understand its main ideas. Then return to the poem and analyze it. You can use a diagram like the one below to help you analyze a poem's style. In each box, list examples of the different elements that help create the style.

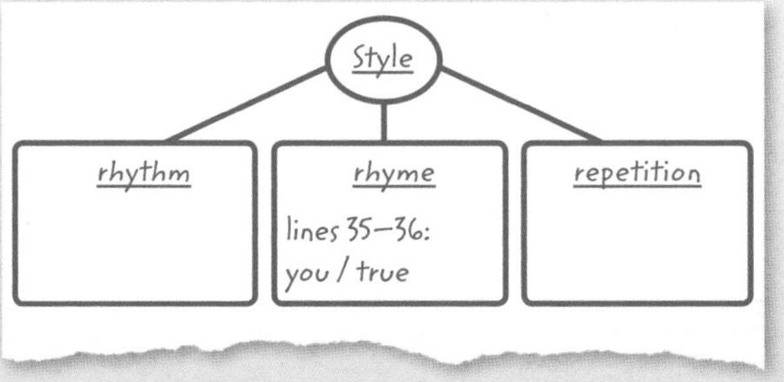

Learning Objectives

For pages 550–555

In studying this text, you will focus on the following objectives:

Literary Study: Analyzing voice.

Reading: Analyzing style.

Writing: Applying tone in an essay.

Approaching Level

DIFFERENTIATED INSTRUCTION

Established Explain that poetry gives writers the opportunity to play with identity in a way that other forms of writing can't. Have approaching-level students reread the biography of Langston Hughes on page 550. Have students summarize the important parts of Hughes's life that may have influenced him to write *Theme for English B*. Then hold a class discussion on whether or not they think that Hughes's life and influences will play a part in the characterization of the speaker. Remind students that speakers are not necessarily the author's voice but could be a character in the poem.

Before You Read

Focus

Summary

The African American speaker explains what makes him who he is. He realizes that although he is different in many ways from his white teacher, his teacher is a part of him and he is a part of his teacher. In his opinion, this is American.

For summaries in languages other than English, see Unit 3 Teaching Resources Book, pp. 233–238.

Interactive Read and Write

Other options for teaching this selection can be found in

- Interactive Read and Write for EL Students, pp. 149–152
- Interactive Read and Write for Approaching-Level Students, pp. 149–152
- Interactive Read and Write for On-Level Students, pp. 149–152

Vocabulary

Correct or Incorrect Write two sentences on the board using the word *unify.* One sentence should use the word correctly and the other should use the word incorrectly. Ask students which sentence is correct and which is incorrect. Tell students to choose a word that better completes the incorrect sentence. Then have students use a dictionary to find the definition of the word. Have students use the word in a sentence.

For additional context, see Glencoe Interactive Vocabulary CD-ROM.

Teach

Literary Element 1

Voice Answer: *It reveals that the speaker is not passive and that he is willing to question authority.*

ENGLISH LEARNERS Ask English learners to share some traditions or rules about authority that are practiced in their culture.

For additional literary element practice, see Unit 3 Teaching Resources Book, p. 239.

Reading Strategy 2

Analyze Style Answer: *He creates a rhythm by stringing together lists of short words creating a staccato effect and by using the same sentence structure for each line.*

For an audio recording of this selection, use Listening Library Audio CD-ROM.

THEME FOR ENGLISH B

Langston Hughes

The instructor said,

Go home and write
a page tonight.
And let that page come out of you—
Then, it will be true.

I wonder if it's that simple?
I am twenty-two, colored, born in Winston-Salem.
I went to school there, then Durham, then here
to this college on the hill above Harlem.
I am the only colored student in my class.
The steps from the hill lead down into Harlem,
through a park, then I cross St. Nicholas,
Eighth Avenue, Seventh, and I come to the Y,
the Harlem Branch Y, where I take the elevator
up to my room, sit down, and write this page:

It's not easy to know what is true for you or me
at twenty-two, my age. But I guess I'm what
I feel and see and hear, Harlem, I hear you.
hear you, hear me—we two—you, me, talk on this page.
(I hear New York, too.) Me—who?

Well, I like to eat, sleep, drink, and be in love.
I like to work, read, learn, and understand life.
I like a pipe for a Christmas present,
or records—Bessie, bop, or Bach.

1 Voice *What does this line reveal about the speaker's personality?*

2 Analyze Style *How does Hughes create rhythm in these two lines?*

Research Practice

PARTNERS SPIRAL REVIEW **Research the Harlem Renaissance Say:** *Renaissance* means rebirth. The Harlem Renaissance was considered a time when African American art and literature blossomed. It was a rebirth of the culture. Ask students to pair up and research the Harlem Renaissance.

Students should use the library and the Internet to find information about the movement as well as the artists, writers, and musicians of that time. Encourage students to share their findings in a class discussion.

Harlem Street Scene, 1942. Jacob Lawrence. Gouache on paper, 21 x 20¾ in. Private collection. © ARS NY.

I guess being colored doesn't make me *not* like
the same things other folks like who are other races.
So will my page be colored that I write?
Being me, it will not be white.
But it will be
a part of you, instructor.
You are white—
yet a part of me, as I am a part of you.
That's American.
Sometimes perhaps you don't want to be a part of me.
Nor do I often want to be a part of you.
But we are, that's true!
As I learn from you,
I guess you learn from me—
although you're older—and white—
and somewhat more free.

This is my page for English B.

---

3 **Life Lessons** *What do you think the speaker is trying to point out to his instructor?*

Teach

Big Idea 3

Life Lessons Answer: *He is trying to point out that—despite the instructor's age, race, and place in society—the instructor probably learns about life from him, just as he learns from the instructor.*

To check students' understanding of the selection, see Unit 3 Teaching Resources Book, p. 242.

Approaching Level

DIFFERENTIATED INSTRUCTION

Established Ask students to write answers to the following questions:

- How is Hughes' poem different from the other poems you have read? How is it similar? *(Answers will vary. Students might point out the lack of rhyme in the poem or comment on how the poem is punctuated.)*
- How does the poem make you feel? Explain your answer. *(Answers will vary.)*
- What lines of the poem do you find interesting and why? *(Students should provide detailed explanations to support their answers.)* Have student share their answers with the class during a class discussion.

After You Read

Assess

1. Answers will vary. Student should support their answers.
2. (a) His classmates are all white and he is the only "colored" student. (b) He mentions this because he is pointing out how he sometimes feels isolated in white society, which is the main topic of the poem.
3. (a) He "guesses" that he is what he feels, sees, and hears—and he says that he hears Harlem. (b) He i is the community, Harlem, and that he represents what he has learned from the community.
4. (a) Everyone being a part of one another is American. (b) If being American means that people are a part of one another, even if they do not want to be, then perhaps people will eventually focus on their similarities, rather than their differences.
5. It helps to create a straightforward, almost confrontational, tone.
6. Sample answer: It fulfills the assignment very effectively. The instructor asked him to reveal his true self and the poem does exactly that.
7. Answers may vary. Students should support their answers.
8. Possible answer: Hughes may have chosen a young speaker because young people, no matter what their race, often seek to understand where they fit into society, while older people are often more set in their roles and places.

After You Read

Respond and Think Critically

Respond and Interpret

1. What thoughts about race came to mind as you read this poem?
2. (a)How is the speaker different from his classmates? (b)Why do you think he mentions this?
3. (a)What does the speaker "guess" he is? (b)What does this tell you about his relationship to his community?
4. (a)According to the speaker, what is "American"? (b)Why might this definition be significant to the speaker?

Analyze and Evaluate

5. Throughout the poem, the poet directly addresses his instructor. What effect does this have on the tone of the poem?
6. How effectively does the poem fulfill the instructor's assignment? Explain your opinion.

Connect

7. **Big Idea** Life Lessons Do you think the poem is hopeful or pessimistic about relationships between people of different races? Explain.
8. **Connect to the Author** In this poem, the speaker seeks to understand his place in society and the ways in which other people view him. Why might Hughes have chosen to use a young speaker to convey these concerns? Explain.

Literary Element Voice

In poetry, **voice** influences how the audience perceives the speaker. Voice conveys the speaker's personality and helps define his or her perspective. For example, if the voice is wild and angry, the audience will likely feel that the speaker is out of control.

1. What is the attitude of the speaker in "Theme for English B"? How does it reflect the speaker's conflicting feelings?
2. The speaker in this poem is a young man. Do you think the voice seems wise or naïve for someone of his age? Explain your opinion.

Review: Lyric Poetry

As you learned on page 541, **lyric poetry** expresses a speaker's personal thoughts and feelings. While the subject of a lyric poem might be an object, a person, or an event, the emphasis of the poem is on the experience of emotion.

Partner Activity With a classmate, identify the main emotions that are expressed in "Theme for English B." Is there one emotion that seems dominant or does the poem move through a series of emotions? After analyzing the feelings expressed in the poem, prepare a joint reading in which you and your partner alternate stanzas. Make sure to express the appropriate emotions for each passage as you read.

Literary Element

1. The speaker is defiant, but thoughtful. His attitude reflects both controlled anger and openness to other people.
2. The voice seems wise. He seems to understand the issues of race and society better than his instructor. He also speaks with a lot of confidence, which makes him seem older.

Review: Lyric Poetry

Possible emotions might include the feelings of isolation and uncertainty. Students should use appropriate verbal techniques when reading the poem aloud.

Reading Strategy Analyze Style

When analyzing a poet's style, pay close attention to word choice. Hughes carefully selects language that reflects the sounds and rhythms of Harlem. Review the language you recorded in your style diagram, and then answer the questions below.

1. Identify the line that makes a direct reference to music. In what ways is the style of this line musical?
2. What is unique about Hughes's use of rhyme in this poem? How is his use of rhythm similar to his use of rhyme?
3. Why is the style appropriate for the voice of this poem?

Academic Vocabulary

In school, a teacher introduced Langston Hughes to the writings of two of his ***primary*** *literary influences.*

Primary is an academic word. More familiar words that are similar in meaning are *main* and *major.* To study this word further, fill out the graphic organizer below.

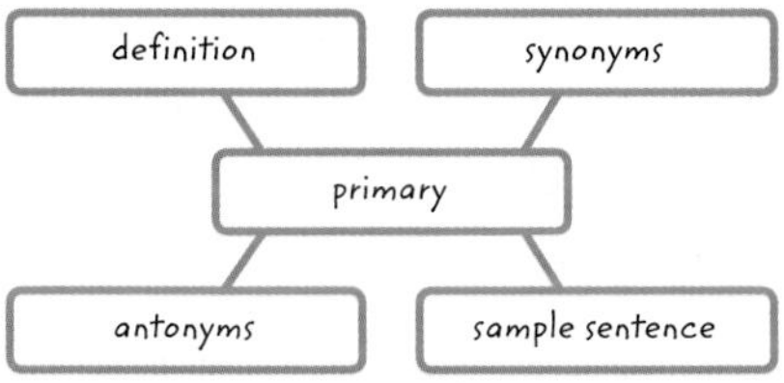

For more on academic vocabulary, see pages 54–55 and R79–R81.

LOG ON **Literature** Online

Selection Resources For Selection Quizzes, eFlashcards, and Reading-Writing Connection activities, go to glencoe.com and enter QuickPass code GL49787u3.

Write with Style

Apply Tone

Assignment Write an essay describing what you are and if you are what you "feel and see and hear." Compare your point of view on the topic with that of the speaker of Hughes's poem. Review the way Hughes uses tone in his poem and keep your tone consistent throughout your essay.

Get Ideas Use a Venn diagram to help you sort out what you are and what you "feel and see and hear." In one circle list words that you think describe you. In the other circle list words that describe what you "feel and see and hear." In the overlapping area list the words that describe both what you are and what you "feel and see and hear."

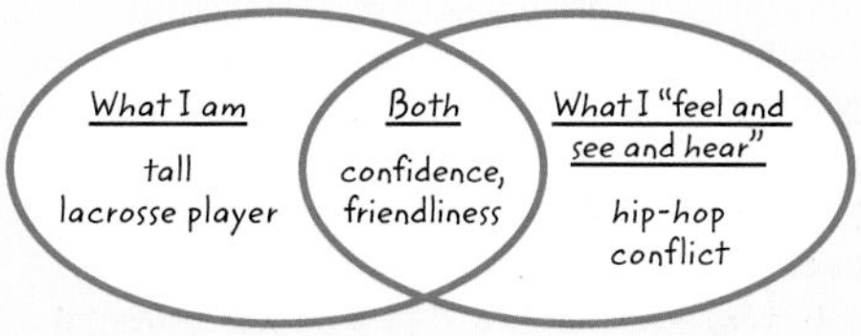

Give It Structure Focus your essay by beginning with a clear thesis statement. In the body of the essay, you can either compare your view and the speaker's view point-by-point, or discuss each view separately. Either way, be sure to organize your essay logically.

Look at Language As you review the language in your essay, remember that the tone reflects the author's attitude. Make sure that your tone consistently reflects your attitude toward the subject. Revise any language that creates the wrong tone. For example, the revision in the sample below is intended to make the tone less hostile.

EXAMPLE:

The notion that you are what you "see and hear"

misleading should not be taken seriously

is a ~~stupid~~ idea that ~~only a fool would believe~~.

In addition to reflecting the proper tone, the language should help to develop your personal style. Although it is a formal essay, the style should still express your personality or voice.

After You Read

Assess

Reading Strategy

1. (a) Line 24 is a direct reference, "or records—Bessie, bop, or Bach." (b) This line uses alliteration (Bessie, bop, Bach), and has a beat created through the use of punctuation and short words.
2. (a) He uses rhyme in the poem, but not in any regular patterns. The rhymes occur both within lines and at the end of lines, and many lines don't rhyme at all. (b) The rhythms are also irregular. Some lines have long flowing rhythms and others have short, fragmented rhythms.
3. The style feels young, fresh and urban, words that also describe the voice of the poem.

Progress Check

Can students analyze style?

If No → See Unit 3 Teaching Resources Book, p. 240.

Academic Vocabulary

definition: first in importance or value

synonyms: main, first, major

antonyms: minor, secondary

sentence: His primary goal was to finish college.

For grammar practice, see Unit 3 Teaching Resources Book, p. 241.

For additional assessment, see Assessment Resources, pp. 147–148.

To create custom assessments online, go to Progress Reporter Online Assessment.

To create custom assessments using software, use ExamView Assessment Suite.

Write with Style

Students' essays should:

- discuss the poem's idea that what you are is what you "feel and see and hear"
- compare the student's opinion with the point of view in the poem
- maintain a consistent, appropriate tone throughout
- begin with a clear thesis statement
- be organized logically

Before You Read

Focus

Bellringer Options

Selection Focus Transparency 27

Daily Language Practice Transparency 64

Or **write** on the board: Are songs the poems of the modern age? Discuss how song lyrics can inspire people now in the same way that poetry has throughout history. What are the similarities and differences? Invite students to share song lyrics they find inspiring.

Before You Read

World Literature
England

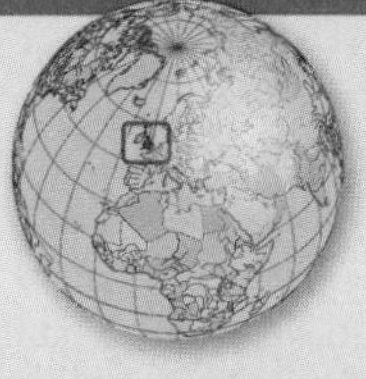

The Secret

Meet **Denise Levertov**
(1923–1997)

Poet Kenneth Rexroth once said that Denise Levertov was "the most subtly skillful poet of her generation, the most profound, the most modest, the most moving." Poet, educator, essayist, and political activist—Levertov has a voice that brims with imagination and vision.

Born in London, Levertov was raised by religious and artistic parents. When she decided to become a writer at age twelve, she sent some of her poems to writer T. S. Eliot. He responded with a letter encouraging Levertov to keep writing. At age seventeen, she was working as a World War II nurse in London when her work appeared in *Poetry Quarterly.* In 1946, her first book of poetry, *The Double Image,* was published.

> *"For me revelation in poetry always concerns the movement of the mind as it thinks and feels."*
>
> —Denise Levertov

Influences and Style After Levertov married American writer Mitchell Goodman, the two moved to New York. There she met the Black Mountain Poets—Robert Creeley, Charles Olson, and Robert Duncan. They introduced Levertov to open verse poetry that used direct description of nature, feeling, and human experience. Her poetry moved away from the formal structure of Romantic poetry and focused more on creating an emotional tone. Her second and third books of poetry, *Here and Now* (1957) and *Overland to the Islands* (1958), represented her change in style.

Social Consciousness Levertov wrote her first political poetry during the Vietnam War. In the 1960s, Levertov was caught up with the anti-war movement and began writing poetry that reflected her beliefs. She also organized a group called the Writers' and Artists' Protest Against the War in Vietnam. In the 1970s, Levertov's style shifted again. She moved away from political concerns to explore private thoughts and experiences.

From 1981 to 1994, Levertov taught at Stanford University. She published more than twenty volumes of poetry and won the Governor's Award from the Washington Commission for the Humanities.

LOG ON **Literature** Online

Author Search For more about Denise Levertov, go to glencoe.com and enter QuickPass code GL49787u3.

Selection Skills

The Secret

Literary Elements
- Paradox (SE pp. 557–559)

Listening/Speaking/Viewing Skills
- Literature Groups (SE p. 560)

Reading Skills
- Analyze Parallelism and Juxtaposition (SE pp. 557, 560)

Vocabulary Skills
- Academic Vocabulary (SE p. 560)

Writing Skills/Grammar
- Write Paradoxes (TE p. 558)

Literature and Reading Preview

Connect to the Poem

What is your favorite poem or line from a song? Why? Write a journal entry explaining how a single line of poetry can have a profound effect on a reader.

Build Background

Since ancient times, people around the world have enjoyed and respected poetry as a special form of communication. Today poetry remains a popular art form. By reading, writing, and reciting poetry, combining it with visual arts, music, and drama, and even posting it on the Internet, people of all ages continue to demonstrate their love of poetic expression.

Set Purposes for Reading

Big Idea Life Lessons

As you read "The Secret," ask yourself, How might the poem influence readers?

Literary Element Paradox

A **paradox** is a situation or statement that seems to be impossible or contradictory but is nevertheless true, literally or figuratively. Learning how to identify a paradox will help you understand hidden meanings. As you read, ask yourself, Where does Levertov use paradoxes within the text to express ideas?

Reading Strategy Analyze Parallelism and Juxtaposition

Parallelism uses a series of words, phrases, or sentences that have similar grammatical structures to show the relationship between ideas and help emphasize thoughts. **Juxtaposition** is the placement of two or more distinct things side by side in order to contrast or compare them. As you read, ask yourself, How does Levertov use these devices?

Tip: Chart Style Use a chart like the one below to record examples of parallelism and juxtaposition in Levertov's poem.

Examples of Parallelism	Examples of Juxtaposition
the secret, the line, the name of the poem	

Learning Objectives

For pages 556–560

In studying this text, you will focus on the following objectives:

Literary Study: Analyzing paradox.

Reading: Analyzing parallelism and juxtaposition.

Speaking and Listening: Participating in a group discussion.

In the 1950s, poets belonging to the Beat Movement began reciting their works in coffeehouses. The practice continues today.

Before You Read

Focus

Summary

Denise Levertov writes of two girls who claim they found the secret of life in a line of her poetry. She herself has no idea what the secret was. She suspects that the girls will forget everything about the secret, but that they will continue to find meaning in other writing. Levertov loves them for searching for truth and for finding it in poetry.

For summaries in languages other than English, see Unit 3 Teaching Resources Book, pp. 244–249.

English Learners

DIFFERENTIATED INSTRUCTION

Intermediate Tell students that the poem on page 558 is about two girls who are affected by a single line of poetry. Ask students to think about the texts they read in their everyday lives (newspapers, textbooks, e-mails, etc.). **Ask:** How do these texts affect your life? *(Students may say that newspapers keep them informed about world events, textbooks help them learn, e-mails help them stay connected to friends and family, etc.)* **Say:** Everything we read, from the back of a cereal box to a famous poem, can affect our lives in one way or another.

Teach

Literary Element 1

Paradox **Answer:** *The speaker wrote the line of poetry but does not know the secret the girls found in the line.*

ADVANCED For advanced students, **ask:** How does this paradox contribute to the tone? *(Students may find the line ironic or say that it contributes to the tone of affectionate humor.)*

For additional literary element practice, see Unit 3 Teaching Resources Book, p. 250.

For an audio recording of this selection, see Listening Library Audio CD-ROM.

To check students' understanding of the selection, see Unit 3 Teaching Resources Book, p. 251.

The Secret

Denise Levertov

Two Girls at a Window, 1937. Georg Schrimpf. Oil on canvas, 78.5 x 73 cm. Inv. A IV 92. Nationalgalerie, Staatliche Museen zu Berlin, Germany.

Two girls discover
the secret of life
in a sudden line of
poetry.

I who don't know the
secret wrote
the line. They
told me

(through a third person)
they had found it
but not what it was
not even

what line it was. No doubt
by now, more than a week
later, they have forgotten
the secret,

the line, the name of
the poem. I love them
for finding what
I can't find,

and for loving me
for the line I wrote,
and for forgetting it
so that

a thousand times, till death
finds them, they may
discover it again, in other
lines

in other
happenings. And for
wanting to know it,
for

assuming there is
such a secret, yes,
for that
most of all.

1 Paradox *How is this sentence paradoxical?*

Writing Practice

PARTNERS **Write Paradoxes** Have pairs of students work together to write paradoxical statements. Stress that although the statements should be contradictory, they must be true. **Write** this example on the board: I love you, but you make me crazy. Discuss how such statements can add irony and complexity to writing. Encourage students to share their statements with the class. Have the class analyze the statements for validity and contradiction.

After You Read

Respond and Think Critically

Respond and Interpret

1. Do you think the author knows, or will ever discover, the secret? Explain.
2. (a)In the first stanza, what adjective does Levertov use to describe the line of poetry? (b)Why do you think Levertov chose this particular word?
3. (a)Why don't the girls tell the poet what the secret was? (b)What does this say about the nature of the secret?
4. (a)The girls approach the secret in several different ways. For which approach does the poet most love the girls? (b)What is the metaphorical meaning of the word *secret* in this poem?

Analyze and Evaluate

5. What is the poet's tone, or attitude, toward her readers, and how does she convey this tone?
6. How does Levertov make the secret seem mysterious?

Connect

7. **Big Idea** Life Lessons What do you think Levertov wants the reader to learn about poetry and life from this poem?
8. **Connect to Today** Identify a traditional song that has inspired people over the years. What is it about the lyrics that continue to inspire or influence listeners today?

Literary Element Paradox

Although a **paradox** seems contradictory, it is true. It can be either literally true or figuratively true. Some writers use paradox to express conflicting ideas or emotions that work together to create a greater truth.

1. Is the paradox in lines 18–20 literally or figuratively true? Explain.
2. How could Levertov write the line but not know the secret?

Toroni-Nagy, 1969. Victor Vasarely. Private Collection

Review: Free Verse

Poetry is often written to follow a specific form. This form may include a well-defined rhyme scheme, highly metered lines, a prescribed line length, and a predetermined stanza arrangement. As you learned on page 466, **free verse** is poetry that has no fixed pattern of meter, rhyme, line length, or stanza arrangement. Free verse often imitates natural forms of speech and can be used to emphasize the relationship between form and meaning in a poem. Although poets who write free verse do not follow traditional rules of form, they use techniques such as repetition and alliteration to create musical patterns in their poems.

Partner Activity Pair up with a classmate and read lines 1–13 aloud. Then answer the questions below.

1. How would you describe the rhythm of these lines?
2. What tone does Levertov convey in these lines?

After You Read

Assess

1. Possible answers: She has discovered the secret before because she says it can be repeatedly forgotten and rediscovered; or, she has never found it because she says, "I love them for finding what I can't find."
2. (a) *Sudden* (b) It is surprising in this context and therefore imparts a sense of discovery.
3. (a) They forget the secret and even its location. (b) It is elusive and ever changing.
4. (a) For assuming there is meaning to be found in poetry and in life (b) It refers to meaning, purpose, or truth.
5. She loves her readers for engaging with her poetry. The overall tone is gentle, conversational, and direct. Simple words, short lines, and commas help create the conversational tone.
6. She talks about how and where it can be found, how it can be forgotten, and the importance of believing that it exists, but she never says what it is.
7. Students should support their answers.
8. Answers will vary. Sample answer: "The Star Spangled-Banner." The lyrics inspire American patriotism.

Literary Element

1. Figurative; the girls have not found the secret either.
2. She cannot know exactly what meaning the girls saw in the poem.

Review: Free Verse

1. Natural, not regular
2. Playful, a bit rueful

Progress Check

Can students analyze paradox?

If No → See Unit 3 Teaching Resources Book, p. 250.

After You Read

Assess

Reading Strategy

1. E is the correct answer. The repeated pattern of *for* plus a gerund (for finding, for loving, for forgetting, etc.) draws the poem's second half together.

Progress Check

Can students analyze parallelism and juxtaposition?

If No → See Unit 3 Teaching Resources Book, p. 251.

Academic Vocabulary

definition: to pull out; to get
synonyms: obtain, remove
antonyms: insert, add
sample sentence: I like the song because I can extract personal meaning from its complicated lyrics.

Speaking and Listening

Students' literature groups should:

- set a clear purpose for their discussion
- listen and respond appropriately during the discussion
- present their positions logically and support them with evidence
- create a list of themes proposed during the discussion and summaries of best ideas
- follow-up with a thorough evaluation of each group member's participation and skill

Reading Strategy Analyze Parallelism and Juxtaposition

SAT Skills Practice

1. The parallel structures in lines 18–36 have the effect of

(A) creating stanzas of four lines each
(B) emphasizing the speaker's bewilderment at what the girls found in her poem
(C) hinting at what the secret might be
(D) giving the poem a repetitive rhythmic structure
(E) unifying the second half of the poem

Academic Vocabulary

The speaker of the poem is grateful that the girls were able to ***extract*** *a secret meaning from the poem.*

Extract is an academic word. In more casual conversation, one might say that dentists often extract bad teeth. To study this word further, fill out the graphic organizer below.

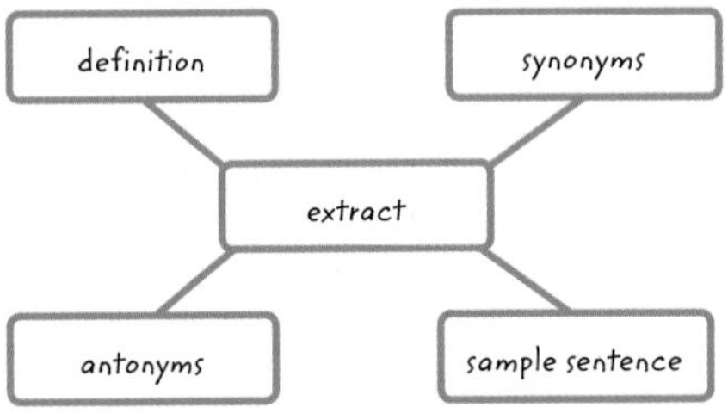

For more on academic vocabulary, see pages 54–55 and R79–R81.

Speaking and Listening

Literature Groups

Assignment In a small group, discuss the theme of "The Secret." How do you think the speaker in the poem would define poetry? What would she say is the purpose of poetry? Use evidence from "The Secret" to defend your position.

Prepare Before your group begins, work together to set a purpose for your discussion. Make a list of questions to answer and create a discussion format that will allow everyone a chance to present his or her opinions about "The Secret."

Discuss During the discussion, listen to others attentively. If you have a response, wait until the person is finished stating his or her full opinion. When presenting your position, structure it logically. For example, after presenting evidence from the poem, follow it up directly with a statement that explains why it is important. Use a statement like:

I bring this up because ______.

Report At the end of the discussion, create a list of all the themes that were proposed by the group and summarize the best ideas.

Evaluate Think about each of your classmate's contributions to the group discussion. Who had the most to say? Who discussed the poem most skillfully? Use the rubric on page 249 to create a checklist for evaluating the members of your group. For each group member, including yourself, go through the checklist and evaluate the person's performance during the discussion. Make sure to evaluate everyone's participation and communication skills. Conclude by writing a brief summary of the group's strengths and weaknesses.

LOG ON **Literature** Online

Selection Resources For Selection Quizzes, eFlashcards, and Reading-Writing Connection activities, go to glencoe.com and enter QuickPass code GL49787u3.

For additional assessment, see Assessment Resources, pp. 149–150.

To create custom assessments online, go to Progress Reporter Online Assessment.

To create custom assessments using software, use ExamView Assessment Suite.

PART 3

The Strength of Family

Circle of Love, 1996. Michael Escoffery. Private collection.

View the Art This piece of art by Michael Escoffery uses bright colors and unexpected shapes. Do you think the title, "Circle of Love," is a good title for the image? Why or why not? ★

BIG IDEA

Family members sometimes seem to give one another endless grief, but the real truth about families lies in their healing power. The poems in Part 3 explore the strength of families. As you read the poems, ask yourself, What about my family might others find inspiring?

UNIT THREE

PART 3

Analyze and Extend

Big Idea

The Strength of Family
Discuss what qualities lend a family strength.

Ask: How do you define *family?* Note that the concept of family can be broadened to include anyone who is close to them. Discuss what strengths these extended family members lend.

View the Art ★

Answer: *Students should support their answers.*

Originally from Kingston, Jamaica, Michael Escoffery came to the U.S. in his 20s. His work focuses on the strength of women in African American culture and often highlights the beauty of the female form. He has won many awards but says "awards are just icing on the cake. They point the direction I should go and remind me of where I've been."

English Learners

DIFFERENTIATED INSTRUCTION

Intermediate Have a student volunteer read the explanation of the Big Idea aloud. **Ask:** What do you think the author means by "endless grief"? *(Students may say that they criticize or harass one another.)* Then **ask:** What do you think the author means by the "healing power" of family? *(Students may say that family members help one another. They may say that being part of a group makes people feel better about themselves.)* Ask volunteers to explain what the Big Idea "The Strength of Family" means to them. Encourage students to look for these themes as they read the poems in this part.

For additional support for English Learners, see Unit 3 Teaching Resources Book, p. 255.

UNIT THREE

PART 3

Focus

Bellringer Options

Daily Language Practice Transparency 65

Or ask students to share a well-known poem or rhyme they remember from their childhood. Have students identify sound patterns that occur in these poems or rhymes.

Teach

Literary Element 1

Sound Devices Point out to students that sound devices can be used to make poems jarring and dissonant.

Ask: How could you use sound devices to create an unsettling mood? *(Answers will vary.)*

Learning Objectives

For pages 561–563

In studying this text, you will focus on the following objective:

Literary Study: Analyzing sound devices.

LITERARY FOCUS

Sound Devices

What does sound contribute to poetry?

A poem's impact depends not only on what it says but on how it sounds. Read this poem aloud or, if that is impractical, read each word so you hear it in your head. 1

from *The Bells*

by Edgar Allan Poe

2
Hear the sledges with the bells—
Silver bells!
What a world of merriment their melody foretells!
How they tinkle, tinkle, tinkle,
In the icy air of night!
While the stars that oversprinkle
All the heavens, seem to twinkle
With a crystalline delight;
Keeping time, time, time,
In a sort of Runic rhyme,
To the tintinnabulation that so musically wells 2
From the bells, bells, bells, bells,
Bells, bells, bells—
From the jingling and the tinkling of the bells.

Jingle Bells. George Harlow White.

Literary Practice

The Sound of Poetry Challenge students to a sound-device competition. Have students create small poems or parts of poems that incorporate the sound devices defined on page 563. Have students read their creations to the class. Then let the class vote on the best sound device usage. After each student reads aloud his or her verse, have other students name the sound device that is being used.

Sound Devices

Sound devices are the elements in poetry that appeal to the ear. Poets use them to establish mood, create rhythm, reinforce meaning, or add a musical quality. Examples of sound devices include alliteration, assonance, consonance, and onomatopoeia.

Alliteration The repetition of consonant sounds at the beginnings of words is called **alliteration.** Poets use alliteration as a way of emphasizing important words in the poem. Note the alliteration Poe uses in "The Bells":

What a world of merriment their melody foretells!

—Edgar Allan Poe, **from "The Bells"**

Assonance The repetition of similar vowel sounds within non-rhyming words is called **assonance.** Assonance is often used in place of end rhyme, especially in ballads and free verse. Like all sound devices, assonance helps unify a poem and emphasize important ideas.

They followed plows and bent to toil.
They moved through fields sowing seed.

—Margaret Walker, **from "Lineage"**

Consonance When two words have different vowel sounds but share a single consonant sound —such as *brick* and *clock*— they are said to have **consonance.** Like assonance, consonance can be used in place of rhyme or to supplement rhyme.

I can read regret in her fingers

—Chitra Banerjee Divakaruni, **from "My Mother Combs My Hair"**

Onomatopoeia Words such as "ping," "splash," and "knock" are examples of another sound device. **Onomatopoeia** is the use of words that imitate the sound of what they describe. Poe uses onomatopoeia in "The Bells":

From the jingling and the tinkling of the bells.

—Edgar Allan Poe, **from "The Bells"**

Repetition The **repetition** of a sound, word, phrase, line, or even an entire stanza is another frequently used poetic sound device. Repetition can occur anywhere in a poem, including within lines and from one stanza to another. Among other things, poets use repetition to create unity and mood and to enhance meaning. Notice how repetition affects the sound of the lines below:

They followed plows and bent to toil.
They moved through fields sowing seed.
They touched earth and grain grew.

—Margaret Walker, **from "Lineage"**

Quickwrite

Capture the Sounds Think about the sounds you hear in a given location, such as in a crowded room, on a bus or train, during a sporting event, or in the woods. Make a list of the sounds. How many examples of onomatopoeia can you use in your list? Write a short paragraph using words that capture the sounds in your chosen location.

LOG ON **Literature** Online

Literature and Reading For more about literary elements, go to glencoe.com and enter QuickPass code GL49787u3.

Approaching Level

DIFFERENTIATED INSTRUCTION

Emerging Explain to students that they can better understand the effect of sound devices by listening to someone use them. To practice **reading fluency,** have a student read aloud Poe's "The Bells." As the student reads, other students should note any sound devices. Encourage the reader to use effective verbal techniques to present the poem.

Teach

Reading Strategy 2

Test-Taking Tip In a testing situation, it isn't appropriate for students to read aloud or even whisper as they read. Suggest to students that they get into the habit of "hearing" the words as they read to themselves.

Ask: What does the speaker in your head sound like? Does your speaker have an accent? Is your speaker male or female? Have students experiment with "hearing" different kinds of speakers as they read.

View the Art ★

George Harlow White (1817–1887) came to Canada from England in the 1870s. He was known for his drawings and watercolors of Canadian pioneer life. He returned to England in 1878.

Ask: Is the scene in this painting similar to what you envision when you read the excerpt from Poe's poem? Explain. *(Answers will vary.)*

Before You Read

Focus

Bellringer Options

Daily Language Practice Transparency 66

Or display images associated with Memorial Day, such as a military cemetery with identical headstones, a veteran selling red paper poppies, parades, or picnics with flags and red, white, and blue bunting.

Ask: Has your family participated in any of these activities? How does your family celebrate Memorial Day?

Ask students to compare their Memorial Day practices with that described in this poem.

Before You Read

Grape Sherbet

Meet **Rita Dove**

(born 1952)

Perhaps you think of a poet as a person with his or her head buried in a notebook all day, struggling to create the perfect phrase. Not Rita Dove. She is serious about poetry, but she also finds joy in classical voice training, ballroom dancing, and playing the viola de gamba—a seventeenth-century instrument similar to the cello.

> *"One can be a poet, but you have to have a life."*
>
> —Rita Dove

An Unfamiliar Path Dove was born in Akron, Ohio, to a middle-class family. She began writing at an early age, but as a child, she never thought of writing as a possible career; her father wanted her to become a doctor or a lawyer. "[Poetry] simply wasn't in the stars," Dove has said. "It wasn't anything anyone I knew had ever done." Luckily, she had a high-school English teacher who noticed her talent and took her to a writer's conference. Soon Dove began to think of herself as a real writer. She went on to study poetry at the highly esteemed University of Iowa Writer's Workshop, where she met her husband, the German writer Fred Viebahn.

Family and Fame "Grape Sherbet" comes from a series of poems written about Dove's father, entitled "My Father's Telescope." She wrote these poems to better understand her brilliant but sometimes distant father. Many of Dove's poems seek an understanding of history, family, and a sense of place in the ever-changing landscape of America. Her most famous work, *Thomas and Beulah,* is a re-creation of her grandparents' lives from the 1920s to the 1960s. The book earned Dove the Pulitzer Prize in 1987, one of the highest honors a writer can achieve. Dove was the second African American poet to win the award, after Gwendolyn Brooks in 1950.

Dove's fame has allowed her to enter unusual worlds—she has read her poetry at a White House state dinner and has appeared on *Sesame Street.* In 1999 she published *On the Bus with Rosa Parks,* a collection in which several poems explore the life of civil-rights icon Rosa Parks. Dove currently teaches at the University of Virginia in Charlottesville.

LOG ON **Literature** Online

Author Search For more about Rita Dove, go to glencoe.com and enter QuickPass code GL49787u3.

Selection Skills

Grape Sherbet

Literary Elements
- Assonance and Consonance (SE pp. 565–567)
- Metaphor (SE p. 567)
- Exact Rhyme and Slant Rhyme (TE p. 566)

Reading Skills
- Make Inferences About Setting (SE pp. 565, 566, 568)

Writing Skills/Grammar
- Apply Diction (SE p. 568)

Vocabulary Skills
- Analogy (SE pp. 565, 568)
- Academic Vocabulary (SE p. 568)

Literature and Reading Preview

Connect to the Poem

What childhood memories do you have of holidays spent with family or friends? Create a list of special holiday memories. Then share your list with a small group. Explain why these memories are special to you.

Build Background

In 1868 General John Logan, the leader of a group of former Civil War soldiers, declared, "The 30th of May, 1868, is designated for the purpose of strewing with flowers, or otherwise decorating the graves of comrades who died in defense of their country during the late rebellion, and whose bodies now lie in almost every city, village, and hamlet churchyard in the land." Memorial Day is now observed on the last Monday in May.

Set Purposes for Reading

Big Idea The Strength of Family

As you read "Grape Sherbet," ask yourself, How does Dove describe her father and what does this description tell you about their relationship?

Literary Element Assonance and Consonance

Assonance is the repetition of the same or similar vowel sounds in poetry or other writing. **Consonance** is the repetition of consonant sounds, typically at the end of nonrhyming words and preceded by different vowel sounds. As you read, ask yourself, Where in the poem does Dove use assonance and consonance?

Reading Strategy Make Inferences About Setting

Setting is the time and place in which the events of a literary work occur. You can often determine the setting even if it is not directly stated. As you read, ask yourself, What clues can I find in "Grape Sherbet" from which I can infer the setting?

Tip: Categorize Details Create a chart like the one below to help you list and categorize details that define the setting in "Grape Sherbet."

Detail	What it tells about setting
The day? Memorial.	The events take place on Memorial Day.

Learning Objectives

For pages 564–568

In studying this text, you will focus on the following objectives:

Literary Study: Analyzing assonance and consonance.

Reading: Making inferences about setting.

Writing: Applying diction in a poem.

Vocabulary

gelled (jeld) *adj.* in a semisolid state after having been liquid; p. 566 *The treat was made of gelled lemonade.*

dollop (dol′əp) *n.* a glob of a soft, mushy substance; p. 566 *He spooned a dollop of whipped cream onto his pie.*

Tip: Analogies An analogy is a comparison that is based on the relationships between things or ideas. To finish an analogy, decide what relationship exists between the first two things or ideas. Then apply that relationship to another pair of words and see if it is the same.

Example:
gelled : mushy :: frozen : firm

Something that is *gelled* feels *mushy;* something that is *frozen* feels *firm.*

Before You Read

Focus

Summary

The speaker describes memories of her family's Memorial Day celebration, a day in which they visit a cemetery and her father makes a special dessert.

For summaries in languages other than English, see Unit 3 Teaching Resources Book, pp. 258–263.

Vocabulary

Using New Words To test vocabulary comprehension, have students write a paragraph using each of the vocabulary words at least once. Ask students who have used the words in the best and most creative ways to share their stories with the rest of the class.

For additional vocabulary practice, see Unit 3 Teaching Resources Book, p. 266.

For additional context, see Interactive Visual Vocabulary CD-ROM.

English Learners

DIFFERENTIATED INSTRUCTION

Early Advanced Tell students that this poem is set on Memorial Day. Ask students what they know about the holiday and its significance. *(Students should point out that it is a day to honor men and women who have died serving their country.)*

Approaching Level

DIFFERENTIATED INSTRUCTION

Established Ask: Why do you think the author wrote this poem? *(Possible answer: This poem is in memory of the narrator's father.)* Ask students to point out vivid images that the author uses in the poem. Discuss the use of images to describe the setting.

Teach

Reading Strategy 1

Make Inferences About Setting **Answer:** *She is describing a cemetery.*

APPROACHING Approaching-level learners may have difficulty making inferences about the setting. **Say:** The setting of the poem is in a cemetery. We can infer this from the "grassed-over mounds" and "stone," which are references to graves and headstones.

For additional practice using the reading skill or strategy, see Unit 1 Teaching Resources Book, p. 265.

Literary Element 2

Assonance and Consonance **Answer:** *The words* I've *and* trying *create assonance by repeating the long* i *sound. The words* it *and* exist *repeat the short* i *sound. The words* taste, but, it, doesn't, *and* exist *all contain the /t/ sound, which creates consonance.*

GRAPE SHERBET

Games We Played, 1992. Anne Belle Lee Washington. Oil on canvas.

Rita Dove

The day? Memorial.
After the grill
Dad appears with his masterpiece—
swirled snow, **gelled** light.
We cheer. The recipe's
a secret, and he fights
a smile, his cap turned up
so the bib[1] resembles a duck.

That morning we galloped
through the grassed-over mounds
and named each stone
for a lost milk tooth.[2] Each **dollop**
of sherbet, later,
is a miracle,
like salt on a melon that makes it sweeter.
Everyone agrees—it's wonderful!
It's just how we imagined lavender
would taste. The diabetic[3] grandmother
stares from the porch, a torch
of pure refusal.

We thought no one was lying
there under our feet,
we thought it
was a joke. I've been trying
to remember the taste,
but it doesn't exist.
Now I see why
you bothered,
father.

1. Here, *bib* means "the bill or visor of a cap."
2. *Milk tooth* is another term for a baby tooth that falls out during childhood and is replaced by a permanent tooth.
3. *Diabetic* means "affected by diabetes," a disease which prevents the body from metabolizing sugar properly.

1 Make Inferences About Setting *What place is the speaker describing in these lines?*

Vocabulary

gelled (jeld) *adj.* in a semisolid state after having been liquid

dollop (dol′ əp) *n.* a glob of a soft, mushy substance

Assonance and Consonance *Which words in these lines create assonance? Which create consonance?* **2**

Literary Practice

SPIRAL REVIEW

Exact Rhyme and Slant Rhyme

Tell students that *rhyme* refers to the sounds that are repeated at the ends of two or more lines of poetry. *Slant rhyme* refers to the words at the ends of lines whose sounds are similar but are not exact rhymes. Sometimes the vowel sounds are slightly different, as in *sweeter* and *better.* Sometimes the consonant sounds are slightly different, as in *lights* and *bright* or *pack* and *lacked.* In "Grape Sherbet," Rita Doves uses exact rhyme and slant rhyme. Have students identify the rhymes in each stanza, stating whether they are exact rhymes or slant rhymes.

After You Read

Respond and Think Critically

Respond and Interpret

1. How are the speaker's Memorial Day experiences the same as or different from your own?
2. (a)List two ways the speaker describes the grape sherbet. (b)What do you think is so special about this treat?
3. (a)What did the speaker of the poem do that morning? (b)Why does that experience make the sherbet seem like "a miracle"?

Analyze and Evaluate

4. In the first line of the poem, the speaker describes the day as "Memorial." Explain at least two different meanings the word might have within the context of the poem. Use a dictionary if you need help.
5. (a)What does line 2, "After the grill," mean? (b)Why does the poet use so few words to describe what is happening?
6. (a)Who is the speaker of this poem? Explain how you know. (b)To whom is she referring when she uses the pronoun *we*?

Connect

7. **Big Idea** **The Strength of Family** The last three lines of the poem read "Now I see why / you bothered, / father." What do those lines mean?
8. **Connect to the Author** Why do you think Dove wrote "Grape Sherbet"? Support your answer with information from Dove's biography on page 564.

Literary Element Assonance and Consonance

A poem that lacks regular meter or rhyme can be unified using other techniques, such as **assonance** and **consonance.** Words that do not quite rhyme but contain some variation of assonance or consonance—such as *owl* and *power,* or *jackal* and *buckle*—are called *slant rhymes.*

1. Identify three places in the first, second, or fourth stanzas of the poem where Dove uses slant rhyme.
2. Read through the third stanza of "Grape Sherbet." Focusing on the last word in each line, describe how assonance and consonance work to unify this stanza.

Games We Played, 1992 (detail). Anna Belle Lee Washington. Oil on canvas.

Review: Metaphor

As you learned on page 520, **metaphor** is a figure of speech that compares or equates two seemingly unlike things. In contrast to a simile, a metaphor implies the comparison rather than stating it directly, so there is no use of connective words such as *like* or *as.* Poet Carl Sandburg once used the metaphor: "The past is a bucket of ashes."

Partner Activity Pair up with a classmate and identify the metaphors in "Grape Sherbet." Create a chart similar to the one below and fill in the left column with the poem's metaphors and the right column with the effect each one has on the reader.

Metaphor	Effect on the Reader
Dad appears with his masterpiece—/ swirled snow, gelled light.	The sherbet seems almost magical, as though made from snow or light.

Literary Element

1. Possible answers: *up* and *duck; lavender* and *grandmother; bothered* and *father*
2. The consonance between *wonderful* and *refusal,* which end the first and last lines of the stanza, tie the stanza together. There is assonance and consonance between *lavender* and *grandmother* and rhyme between *porch* and *torch.*

Progress Check

Can students explain assonance and consonance?

If No → See Unit 3 Teaching Resources Book, p. 264.

Review: Metaphor

Check to see that explanations of the metaphors' effects are plausible.

After You Read

Assess

1. Students' answers will vary.
2. (a) "swirled snow, gelled light"; "a miracle" (b) The father makes it just for this holiday; it tastes different from anything else.
3. (a) The speaker played in the cemetery. (b) Eating the sherbet makes everyone glad to be alive, in contrast to the dead lying in the cemetery.
4. The literal meaning is the holiday set aside to remember the war dead. *Memorial* also means "a reminder of a person or of somebody's life and work."
5. (a) It means "after the meal prepared on the grill." (b) To suggest flashes of images or memories
6. (a) The speaker is an adult looking back on a childhood memory. The poem is in the present tense, as if the speaker were still a child, but in the last stanza we realize she is an adult because of the shift to past tense. (b) Everybody, as in lines 5 and 17, or the speaker and other children, as in lines 9 and 21
7. Students may say the lines refer to the father making the sherbet, because a day set aside to remember the dead calls for something to remind people of the joys of living.
8. Possible answers. Perhaps to show that she now understands her father's efforts to provide a simple, yet memorable pleasure during her childhood. Her biography says that she wrote many poems to help her understand her father.

After You Read

Assess

Reading Strategy

1. B is the correct answer. "After the grill" indicates a cookout. Father has been preparing sherbet, which he probably carries from the freezer to the back yard.

Vocabulary

1. b **2.** a

Academic Vocabulary

Sample answer: Images that support the meaning of the poem are usually considered to be an **integral** part of a poem.

For additional assessment, see Assessment Resources, pp. 151–152.

Reading Strategy Make Inferences About Setting

SAT Skills Practice

1. The setting in the opening stanza of the poem is most likely

(A) dinner time at a restaurant
(B) afternoon in the backyard
(C) evening at an ice cream parlor
(D) noon on Main Street for the Memorial Day parade
(E) late at night in the speaker's dreams

Vocabulary Practice

Practice with Analogies Choose the word that best completes each analogy.

1. liquid : gelled :: rainy :
a. stormy **b.** snowy **c.** sunny

2. dollop : spoonful :: expansion :
a. growth **b.** contraction **c.** size

Academic Vocabulary

*The images of the cemetery are an **integral** part of the poem "Grape Sherbet."*

Integral is an academic word. More familiar words that are similar in meaning are *necessary* and *essential*. Complete this sentence:

Images that _____ are usually considered to be an **integral** part of a poem.

For more on academic vocabulary, see pages 54–55 and R79–R81.

LOG ON **Literature** Online

Selection Resources For Selection Quizzes, eFlashcards, and Reading-Writing Connection activities, go to glencoe.com and enter QuickPass code GL49787u3.

Write with Style

Apply Diction

Assignment Write a poem about a memory. Before you start, freewrite pairs of words with interesting assonance and consonance. Use the pairs to develop sounds and ideas for your poem.

Get Ideas List some of your vivid childhood memories. Then freewrite about one memory that you would like to write a poem about. Once you have chosen the memory, list some words that you will likely use in the poem. For each word on your list, think of other words that share the same vowel or consonant sounds. Write these next to the appropriate word on your list. Review your completed list and highlight pairs of words with lively assonance or consonance that you want to use in your poem.

Give It Structure Use a chart like the one below to develop poetic language to describe your chosen memory. First, briefly summarize the memory in the center box. Then, fill in the other boxes with word pairs from your list that describe or support each aspect of the memory. Use any word pairs from your list that apply or create new ones.

Use words from the chart to help write the poem.

EXAMPLE:
Twinkling skies, golden air, autumn forest—it was a fine night for a first campfire.

Look at Language After completing your draft, review the poem's diction, or word choice. Make sure the poem's language works with your word pairs to create a consistent style and tone.

Write with Style

Students' poems should
- explore a family memory
- make use of assonance and consonance
- provide strong descriptive language
- maintain a consistent style and tone

For grammar practice, see Unit 3 Teaching Resources Book, p. 267.

Before You Read

"Good Night, Willie Lee, I'll See You in the Morning"

Meet **Alice Walker**
(born 1944)

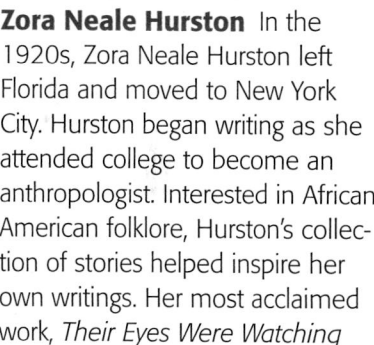

When Alice Walker was eight, her brother accidentally shot her with a BB gun, blinding her in the right eye. Believing that the scar tissue in her eye disfigured her, Walker became self-conscious and withdrawn. She began to spend much of her time alone, reading and writing poems. By the time she was fourteen and had undergone eye surgery to improve her appearance, she was hooked on literature. Her youthful passion for the written word would blossom into an impressive body of creative works.

> *"Not enough credit has been given to the black woman, who has been oppressed beyond recognition."*
>
> —Alice Walker

Early Years Born near Eatonton, Georgia, Walker's parents were poor sharecroppers who raised eight children. Walker left home to attend Spelman College in Atlanta, thus ending a troubled relationship with her father. After traveling to Africa, she attended Sarah Lawrence College in New York, graduating in 1965. During and after college, Walker actively participated in the civil rights movement.

☆ In 1970 Walker discovered the works of Zora Neale Hurston, a deceased and neglected Harlem Renaissance writer. Deeply moved by Hurston's books, especially *Mules and Men* (1935) and *Their Eyes Were Watching God* (1937), Walker dedicated herself to promoting Hurston's works, ensuring that they would receive the credit they deserved.

Walker's poetry, fiction, and essays explore African American history and culture. Much of her work focuses on personal and family relationships, portraying black women whose strength of spirit enables them to triumph over racism and other forms of oppression.

Literary Acclaim Walker is a prolific writer. Her collections of poetry include *Once* (1968), which relates her experiences working in the civil rights movement and living in Africa, and *Good Night, Willie Lee, I'll See You in the Morning* (1979). Her short stories about black women appear in the collections *In Love and Trouble* (1973) and *You Can't Keep a Good Woman Down* (1981). Walker's most famous work is *The Color Purple* (1982). This highly acclaimed novel won both the Pulitzer Prize and the American Book Award. It was adapted into a successful movie and later into a Broadway musical.

LOG ON **Literature** Online

Author Search For more about Alice Walker, go to glencoe.com and enter QuickPass code GL49787u3.

Before You Read

Focus

Bellringer Options

Selection Focus Transparency 28

Daily Language Practice Transparency 67

Or **ask:** What feelings might someone have after the death of a family member or close friend? How might a loved one's death cause a change of feelings about that person? Encourage students to keep these questions in mind as they read the following selections.

Literary History ☆

Zora Neale Hurston In the 1920s, Zora Neale Hurston left Florida and moved to New York City. Hurston began writing as she attended college to become an anthropologist. Interested in African American folklore, Hurston's collection of stories helped inspire her own writings. Her most acclaimed work, *Their Eyes Were Watching God,* was published in 1937.

Selection Skills

Good Night, Willie Lee, I'll See You in the Morning

Literary Elements
- Epiphany (SE pp. 570, 572)

Writing Skills/Grammar
- Journal Entry (SE p. 572)

Reading Skills
- Make Generalizations (SE pp. 570, 572)

Vocabulary Skills
- Academic Vocabulary (SE pp. 570, 572)

Before You Read

Focus

Summary

In "Good Night, Willie Lee, I'll See You in the Morning," the speaker reflects on the death of her father and on her mother's response to his death. Even though her mother seems to have no emotional response to his death, she treats him with "civility" in her last good-bye. The speaker recognizes that old wounds can be healed through forgiveness.

For summaries in languages other than English, see Unit 3 Teaching Resources Book, pp. 270–275.

Literature and Reading Preview

Learning Objectives

For pages 569–572

In studying this text, you will focus on the following objectives:

Literary Study: Analyzing epiphany.

Reading: Making generalizations.

Writing: Writing a journal entry.

Connect to the Poem

Have you ever felt forced to be civil as a courtesy? Discuss this question with a partner. Consider situations where you have felt compelled by society to be polite and civil.

Build Background

Alice Walker and her father, whose name was Willie Lee, were often at odds. Walker regrets that their relationship "did not improve until after his death." Besides writing poems about him, Walker has used her father's experiences in her novels. She states, "Writing about people helps us understand them, and understanding them helps us understand ourselves."

Set Purposes for Reading

Big Idea The Strength of Family

As you read, ask yourself, What does the poem reveal about the source of a family's strength?

Literary Element Epiphany

An **epiphany** is a moment of sudden revelation of the true meaning of a situation, person, or object. In a moment of epiphany, a character sees something in a new light. The character often gains insight into the essential meaning or nature of that thing as a result. As you read, ask yourself, What is the speaker's epiphany and what does it suggest?

Reading Strategy Make Generalizations

You **make generalizations** by formulating a statement that is supported by details in a work. For example, after reading a literary work, you might make a generalization that heroes control their fears instead of giving in to them. As you read, ask yourself, What generalizations can I make based on the poem?

Tip: Take Notes On a chart like the one below, write a generalization about death. Then, after reading the poem by Alice Walker, write a generalization supported by the poem.

Before Reading	After Reading
Grieving people long to relive good times with the deceased.	

Relatives Embracing. Jim Dandy.

Vocabulary Practice

SPIRAL REVIEW **Word Roots** Tell students that a root is a word part that conveys a basic meaning. Explain that a key word in the poem is *civility*. It contains that Latin word *civ*, which means "citizen." This root is found in many other English words. All of the following terms contain the root *civis*. Have students locate them in a dictionary and write their definitions. Then have students explain how each is related to the meaning of *civis*.

- civil rights
- civics
- civilization
- civil war
- civilized

Serenity, 1901. Alphonse Osbert. Oil on canvas, 22.5 x 51 cm. Private collection.

"Good Night, Willie Lee, I'll See You in the Morning"

Alice Walker

Looking down into my father's
dead face
for the last time
my mother said without
tears, without smiles
without regrets
but with *civility*
"Good night, Willie Lee, I'll see you
in the morning."

1 And it was then I knew that the healing
of all our wounds
is forgiveness
that permits a promise
of our return
at the end.

2 The Strength of Family *The mother speaks to Willie Lee, but the speaker of the poem does not. What does this suggest about their respective relationships with Willie Lee?*

Teach

Literary Element 1

Epiphany **Ask:** According to this line, when does the speaker's epiphany take place? *(The epiphany takes place when the mother speaks the words, "Good night, Willie Lee, I'll see you in the morning.")*

Big Idea 2

The Strength of Family
Answer: *It suggests that the mother and Willie Lee had a stronger bond and were better able to share their feelings.*

APPROACHING **Ask:** On the basis of these words, do you think the mother has forgiven the father? Explain. *(She seems to have forgiven him, since she says that she will see him "in the morning.")*

For additional literary element practice, see Unit 3 Teaching Resources Book, p. 276.

Progress Check

Can students make generalizations?

If No → See Unit 3 Teaching Resources Book, p. 265.

English Learners

DIFFERENTIATED INSTRUCTION

Intermediate Guide students to interpret the meaning of the poem. Explain that when the speaker's mother tells Willie Lee that she will see him in the morning, she means that she will one day see him again. Point out that the speaker does not say anything to her father; only her mother does, and she does this "without tears." **Ask:** What kind of person do you think Willie Lee was? *(Students may say that he may have been harsh and not loving.)* Then read aloud the last stanza of the poem. Help students paraphrase this stanza. **Ask:** What does the speaker mean here? *(Students may say that people feel better when they forgive someone and promise to see them again.)*

After You Read

Assess

1. Students' answers will vary.
2. (a) A wife says goodbye to her husband before he is buried. (b) In a funeral home
3. (a) The mother does not cry, smile, or show regret. (b) Her calm and dignity suggest that acceptance and faith keep her on an even keel.
4. Possible answer: to emphasize the speaker's surprise
5. She is a woman of great dignity and faith, and she has great emotional strength.
6. "Wounds" suggests that the marriage may have been stormy at times. Because the speaker is just learning about the healing power of forgiveness, she may not have forgiven her father for problems in their relationship.
7. Students may say that forgiveness allows families to put aside injuries and renew their loving commitment.
8. Most students will agree that the poem portrays the theme of strong women overcoming difficulties. Students should support their responses with examples from the poem.

Writing

Students' journal entries should

- be about a character's epiphany
- be from that character's point of view
- immediately establish the speaker

Reading Strategy

1. The relationship was conflicted but had its redeeming qualities.
2. The healing power of forgiveness brings people together, in life and in death.

After You Read

Respond and Think Critically

Respond and Interpret

1. What questions would you like to ask the speaker of this poem?
2. (a)What happens in this poem? (b)Where might the events be taking place?
3. (a)What is missing when the mother looks at her husband's face and speaks? (b)In your opinion, what does the absence of this convey?

Analyze and Evaluate

4. In your opinion, why did Walker write the word *civility* in italics?
5. What does the mother's statement make you think or feel about her?
6. What kind of relationships do you imagine the mother and the speaker each had with Willie Lee? Give evidence from the poem to support your interpretations.

Connect

7. **Big Idea** **The Strength of Family** How does forgiveness promote emotional healing?
8. **Connect to the Author** Walker often portrays women whose strength has helped them overcome difficulties. Does this poem include this theme? Explain.

Literary Element Epiphany

The word *epiphany* was first applied to literature by James Joyce, who used it to describe a new understanding of something commonplace. An epiphany can also mark a change in a character.

1. What life lesson does the speaker learn from her mother's words?
2. How do lines 10–15 relate to her interpretation?

Reading Strategy Make Generalizations

Review the chart you made before and after reading, and then answer the following questions.

1. What generalization can you make about the parents' relationship in this poem?
2. Based on the poem, what generalization can be made about the healing power of forgiveness?

LOG ON Literature Online

Selection Resources For Selection Quizzes, eFlashcards, and Reading-Writing Connection activities, go to glencoe.com and enter QuickPass code GL49787u3.

Academic Vocabulary

Walker's poem is a reminder that there is no standard ***protocol*** *for responding to a loved-one's death.*

Protocol is an academic word. In a more casual conversation, an official might describe the **protocol** for a fire drill. Complete the following sentence:

If someone is talking about the **protocol** for a school dress code, they are _____.

For more on academic vocabulary, see pages 54–55 and R79–R81.

Writing

Write a Journal Entry Walker establishes the characters of this short poem quickly and effectively. Write a journal entry from the point of view of a character who has just experienced an epiphany. Make it clear who the narrator is right away in order to bring the epiphany into dramatic focus.

Literary Element

1. Restraint, kindness, and forgiveness are necessary to a long-term relationship between human beings.
2. The speaker realizes that her parents hurt each other but also forgave each other, strengthening their relationship.

Academic Vocabulary

Answers will vary. Students answers should reflect the meaning of *protocol.* Sample answer: *referring to the rules and standards set for what should and should not be worn*

Before You Read

World Literature
Kenya

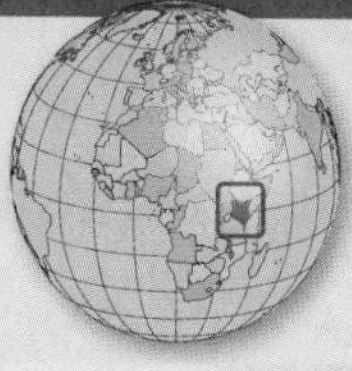

Where Are Those Songs?

Meet **Micere Githae Mugo**
(born 1942)

Micere Githae Mugo was born in Kenya when it was still under the rule of the British Empire. Under colonial rule, black Kenyans such as Mugo were not granted the same privileges as white citizens. In 1961 Mugo played a key role in her people's battle for equality when she became the first black citizen in Kenya to be admitted to the "white-only" Limuru Girls School. Her admission—which had been fought for by political activists—represented a victory in the struggle for African independence. The experience inspired her to continue to break down barriers throughout her life.

> *"The first slave to escape captivity was he/she who learned to read and write."*
>
> —Micere Githae Mugo

Singing Her Song Mugo's parents were teachers and committed political activists who instilled progressive beliefs in Mugo and her nine siblings. They taught their children to fight the racial and gender boundaries of the society around them. As a teenager, Mugo was already writing poetry. After she graduated from the Limuru Girls School, she went on to Makerere University, where she studied drama and continued to write.

When she finished school, Mugo pursued a career teaching and writing and also became active in politics. Her first collection of poems, *Daughter of My People, Sing!* was published in 1976. Although British colonial rule in Kenya had ended in the 1960s, Mugo's battle for progress and equality continued. In 1982 she was forced to leave Kenya because of her political beliefs. She now lives in the United States. A firm believer in the power of literacy, Mugo has taught in several universities, including in the African American Studies department at Syracuse University.

Mount Kenya, Kenya.

Creating New Traditions Whenever she reads the poem "Where Are Those Songs?," Mugo tries to involve her audience. The critical idea in the poem is what people remember and what has been forgotten. During readings, Mugo always becomes silent for a few moments after the line "What do you remember?" so that her audience can realize how many memories have been lost. The constant repetition throughout the poem, along with the mother's command to sing, emphasizes how important it is that people not forget their own songs. Even if the old songs have been lost, Mugo says, people should pass along their own, new traditions.

LOG ON **Literature** Online

Author Search For more about Micere Githae Mugo, go to glencoe.com and enter QuickPass code GL49787u3.

Before You Read

Focus

Bellringer Options

Daily Language Practice Transparency 68

Or ask students to name songs that hold an important meaning to them and to explain why.
Ask: Why might a song hold a significant meaning to people of certain cultural groups?

Selection Skills

Where Are Those Songs?

Literary Elements
- Rythm (SE pp. 574, 577, 578)

Listening/Speaking/Viewing Skills
- Speech (p. 579)

Reading Skills
- Analyze Structure (SE pp. 574, 577, 579)

Vocabulary Skills
- Academic Vocabulary (SE p. 579)

Writing Skills/Grammar
- Essay (SE p. 574)

Before You Read

Focus

Summary

The speaker talks about songs that were sung by women of her family. She cannot remember the words, but the thought of these songs bring back memories of her childhood and tell stories of her African history.

For summaries in languages other than English, see Unit 3 Teaching Resources Book, pp. 281–286.

Literature and Reading Preview

Connect to the Poem

What is a vivid memory of a song from your childhood? Write a journal entry about the memory and why it is important to you.

Build Background

Oral tradition is a valued and long-standing aspect of many African societies. Through it, stories, songs, and poems have been passed on verbally from generation to generation by storytellers and singers.

Set Purposes for Reading

Big Idea The Strength of Family

As you read the poem, ask yourself, What family values are passed along through the songs that the speaker remembers?

Literary Element Rhythm

In poetry, **rhythm** is the pattern of beats created by stressed and unstressed syllables. Patterns of rhythm can be regular or irregular. As you read, ask yourself, Does the rhythm in this poem follow a predictable pattern, or is it irregular?

Reading Strategy Analyze Structure

When you **analyze structure,** you examine the organization of a work to understand its meaning and effects. For example, the writer might have created repetitions within a stanza, across different stanzas, or from line to line. As you read, ask yourself, What is the effect of repetition in this poem?

Tip: Take Notes Use a chart to record repetition in the poem. Divide the examples into two categories: repetition that occurs in the poem's stanzas and repetition that occurs in specific lines.

Repetition in Stanza	Repetition in Line
Repetition of "What was" or "What did" to begin stanzas 2, 3, 4, and 6	lines 35–36, "child-birth"/"child-naming"

Learning Objectives

For pages 573–579

In studying this text, you will focus on the following objectives:

Literary Study: Analyzing rhythm.

Reading: Analyzing structure.

Speaking and Listening: Delivering a speech.

Writing Practice

SPIRAL REVIEW **Write About Family Traditions** **Ask:** What is a tradition? *(Students may say that a tradition is something that is done by all members of a group and carried on for generations.)* Tell students that Mugo's poem is about singing—a tradition in her family. **Ask:** What makes a tradition special? Why are traditions important? *(Students may say that traditions are special because they are unique to a certain group of people and that traditions are important because they are a link to the past.)* Have students write an essay about a tradition in their family. Have them share their essays with the class.

WHERE ARE THOSE SONGS?

Micere Githae Mugo

African Family & Boatman. Todd Davidson.

Teach

Big Idea

The Strength of Family
Ask students to share the names of songs that have special meaning within their families or cultures. Have students explain the meaning and significance of these songs.

Approaching Level

DIFFERENTIATED INSTRUCTION

Emerging Remind students that the songs the speaker is searching for are part of a family tradition. Her African ancestors sang songs throughout their daily lives—while caring for children, cooking, working in the fields, carrying wood through the forests, and at ceremonies. The speaker would like to share these songs with her daughter but she cannot remember them.

Ask: Why do you think the author has forgotten her mother's songs? *(Students may say that she is more contemporary and lives in a different world.)* **Ask:** Why do you think no one wrote down the songs? *(It is possible that the women's culture emphasized oral expression rather than written expression.)*

Teach

Reading Strategy 1

Analyze Structure

Answer: *Mugo creates rhythm by repeating the pattern of the -ing verb & object in the structure of the line.*

ENGLISH LEARNERS Unfamiliar words may cause English learners difficulty in answering questions about rhythm. Have students look up the definitions and pronunciations to maize, threshing, and millet. Then ask them to reconsider how the poet creates rhythm in this line.

Where are those songs
my mother and yours
always sang
fitting rhythms
to the whole
vast span of life?

What was it again
they sang
  harvesting maize, threshing millet,
    storing the grain . . .

What did they sing
bathing us, rocking us to sleep . . .
and the one they sang
stirring the pot
(swallowed in parts by choking smoke)?

What was it
the woods echoed
as in long file
my mother and yours and all the women
    on our ridge
beat out the rhythms

---

1 Analyze Structure *How does Mugo create rhythm in this line?*

To Market, 1954. Ellis Wilson. Oil with turpentine on panel, 22⅜ x 28⅞ in. North Carolina Museum of Art, Raleigh.

Reading Practice

SMALL GROUP SPIRAL REVIEW **Paraphrase to Understand** Break students into small groups and have them paraphrase lines 51–81. Point out the reference to "Mother" in line 52 and the reference to "daughter" in line 61. **Ask:** What is the speaker saying in these lines? *(Students may say that while the speaker cannot remember the songs she heard, she remembers her mother saying that she should sing and make her own songs using her own rhythms so that the song is soulful. Since the speaker remembers this, she passes this message on to her daughter and says that there is much to sing about all around her if she looks, listens, and takes it in. She tells her to bathe herself in life and sing about it.)* Ask students to write down any questions they might have. Allow students to ask their questions as part of the class discussion. Encourage other students to answer these questions if they can.

trudging gaily
as they carried
piles of wood
through those forests
miles from home
What song was it?

And the row of bending women
hoeing our fields
to what beat
did they
break the stubborn ground
as they weeded
our *shambas?*

What did they sing
at the ceremonies
child-birth
child-naming
second birth
initiation. . . ?
how did they trill the *ngemi*
what was
the warriors' song?
how did the wedding song go?
sing me
the funeral song.
What do you remember?
Sing
I have forgotten
my mother's song
my children
will never know.
This I remember:
Mother always said
sing child sing
make a song
and sing
beat out your own rhythms
the rhythms of your life
but make the song soulful
and make life
sing
Sing daughter sing
around you are
uncountable tunes
some sung
others unsung
sing them
to your rhythms
observe
listen
absorb
soak yourself
bathe
in the stream of life
and then sing
sing
simple songs
for the people
for all to hear
and learn
and sing
with you

2 Rhythm *How do lines 20–24 reflect the action mentioned in line 19?*

3 The Strength of Family *What does this line suggest about the role of family?*

Analyze Structure *What is the effect of the unique structure in these lines?* **4**

Teach

Literary Element 2

Rhythm **Answer:** *The clipped rhythms of lines 20–24 echo the actions of the women who "beat out the rhythms."*

For additional literary element practice, see Unit 3 Teaching Resources Book, p. 287.

Big Idea 3

The Strength of Family
Answer: *The line suggests that it is often through family that we learn the ideas we value deeply later in life.*

Reading Strategy 4

Analyze Structure
Answer: *This structure is built on one word per line, which emphasizes each individual word and the ideas it represents.*

English Learners

DIFFERENTIATED INSTRUCTION

Early Advanced Students may benefit from an explanation of uncommon words and phrases in the poem. Point out the following words and phrases in the poem and discuss their meaning:

- fitting rhythms *(appropriate rhythms)*
- beat out the rhythms *(sang loudly)*
- on our ridge *(where we lived or worked)*
- hoeing *(loosening the soil)*
- break the stubborn ground *(crack into hard soil)*
- weeded *(removed weeds)*
- second birth initiation *(a kind of baptism)*
- bathe in the stream of life *(take in your surroundings)*

After You Read

Assess

1. Answers may vary.
2. (a) They were carrying piles of wood back to their homes. (b) They probably sang because the journey was long and they were trying to entertain themselves.
3. (a) She advises her to sing her own song in life and to make sure it reflects who she is. (b) She wanted to give her daughter confidence to be her own person.
4. (a) She is told that there are songs all around her, some sung and some unsung. (b) Understanding this will help her to open herself up to the world around her and fully experience life.
5. Including several songs allows the poem to show the variety in life and the way in which music interacts with those different parts of our lives.
6. (a) The second line of the poem draws attention to the role of mothers. (b) This line might prompt the reader to reflect on his or her own memories and to become more engaged with the ideas in the poem.
7. They help her to remember and relive times that she has shared with her family in the past; they keep the values of her mother alive in her.
8. She has chosen to sing her songs through her poems and has therefore followed her mother's advice.

After You Read

Respond and Think Critically

Respond and Interpret

1. Now that you have read the poem, how would you answer the question posed in the title of the poem?
2. (a)What were the women doing out in the forests away from home? (b)Why do you think they sang while they were away from home?
3. (a)What advice does the speaker's mother give in lines 52–60? (b)In your opinion, why does she give this advice to her daughter?
4. (a)In the last stanza, what is the daughter told about the songs of life? (b)Why might this advice be important for the daughter to understand?

Analyze and Evaluate

5. Instead of focusing on one song, the poet chooses to include several different songs. What is the effect of this choice?
6. (a)What is the significance of line 2 in the poem? (b)What effect might this line have on the reader?

Connect

7. **Big Idea** **The Strength of Family** How do the songs in this poem connect the speaker to her family?
8. **Connect to the Author** Reread "Meet Micere Githae Mugo" on page 573. In what ways has Mugo taken the mother's advice expressed in this poem?

Literary Element Rhythm

Poems sometimes use **rhythm** to evoke the feeling of a certain type of music. In "Where Are Those Songs?," Mugo's rhythms echo the beats of the African songs about which she is writing.

To determine a line's rhythmic pattern, you need to identify which syllables are stressed and which are unstressed. It often helps to read the line aloud and listen to where the stresses naturally occur.

1. Does the rhythm of this poem generally follow a regular or irregular pattern? Explain.
2. What effect does line length have on the poem's rhythm?

Review: Assonance

As you learned on page 565, **assonance** is the repetition of vowel sounds. An example of assonance in "Where Are Those Songs?" is the repetition of the long *o* in "swallowed in parts by choking smoke." Poets often use such sound devices to emphasize certain words and underscore their meaning, to create or enhance rhythm, and to add musical quality to their work.

Partner Activity With a classmate, identify other examples of assonance in the poem. Choose three or four pairs of words from the poem that share a vowel sound. Working together, use the word pairs to create a short poem that features assonance in each line.

Literary Element

1. The poem has an irregular pattern of rhythm. The beats in each line do not follow a consistent pattern—they are more natural, like the rhythms of everyday language.
2. The shorter lines make the rhythms choppy rather than long and flowing.

For additional assessment, see Assessment Resources, pp. 155–156.

Review: Assonance

Poems should include examples of assonance.

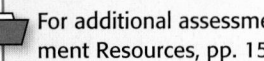

Reading Strategy Analyze Structure

Use the notes in your chart to review Mugo's use of repetition in the structure of the poem and answer the questions below.

1. (a)What kind of sentence is repeated throughout the first half of the poem? (b)How does this create a structure for that part of the poem?
2. What set of lines creates rhythm through a repeated sentence structure?

Academic Vocabulary

In this poem, the speaker is trying to recall the songs of the women from the generations that ***preceded*** *her.*

Precede is an academic word. In a more casual conversation, one might describe the women in the example as being from the generations that *came before* the speaker. To study this word further, fill out the graphic organizer below.

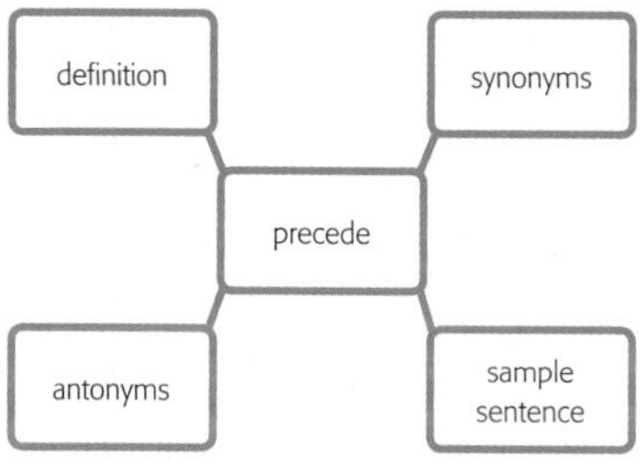

For more on academic vocabulary, see pages 54–55 and R79–R81.

LOG ON Literature Online

Selection Resources For Selection Quizzes, eFlashcards, and Reading-Writing Connection activities, go to glencoe.com and enter QuickPass code GL49787u3.

Speaking and Listening

Speech

Assignment Write and present a speech in which you discuss why it is important for people to understand their cultural heritage. In your speech, note the ways in which people can pass on their heritage to younger generations.

Prepare Begin by writing a clear thesis statement that expresses why it is important to understand one's heritage. The statement should be concise and should set up the rest of your speech. For example, you could structure your thesis like this:

I think that people should _____ because _____.

After you write your thesis, develop an engaging structure for the rest of your speech. Use smooth transitions and a logical organization—your ideas should build on one another as the speech progresses. In your conclusion, try to inspire your audience to take action.

Before you deliver your speech, create notecards outlining your speech. Do not write your entire speech on the cards or you run the risk of reading it without looking at your audience. Instead include main ideas and key phrases you want to discuss.

Deliver Try to express emotion in your delivery. To help connect with your audience, make eye contact as you talk. Speak loudly and clearly so that everyone can understand you. Maintain a strong, confident posture and use gestures where it feels natural.

Evaluate Use the checklist on page 1091 to review your performance. Then, write a paragraph evaluating your skills in the speech. As you evaluate your performance, try to consider it from the audience's point of view.

After You Read

Reading Strategy

1. (a) Questions are repeated throughout the first half. (b) These questions provide a framework for the first half of the poem—each stanza or passage is built around a question.
2. Lines 40–42; "what was/the warriors' song?/how did the wedding song go?"

Progress Check

Can students analyze structure?

If No → See Unit 3 Teaching Resources Book, p. 288.

Academic Vocabulary

definition—to go before
synonyms—come before, lead up to
antonyms—follow, trail
sentences—(b) When the graduation begins, the president of the university will precede the professors in line.

Speaking and Listening

Students' speeches should

- include a strong thesis statement in the introduction
- explain why people should understand their heritage
- discuss ways to pass on cultural heritage to younger generations
- be structured engagingly
- be delivered clearly and confidently

To create custom assessments online, go to Progress Reporter Online Assessment.

To create custom assessments using software, use ExamView Assessment Suite.

Before You Read

Focus

Bellringer Options

Daily Language Practice Transparency 69

Or show images of mothers and adult children. **Ask:** How do you think the relationship between mothers and their children changes as children mature? What behaviors remain the same? Discuss with students how their relationships with their parents are changing.

Before You Read

World Literature
India

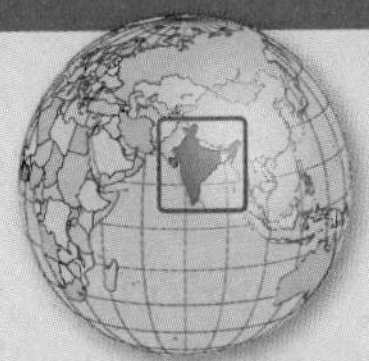

My Mother Combs My Hair

Meet **Chitra Banerjee Divakaruni**
(born 1956)

Imagine stepping off a plane to live in a land where the traditions and values are very different from anything you have ever known. That is what it was like for Chitra Banerjee Divakaruni. In 1976 she left her home in Calcutta, India, to live in the United States. She was nineteen years old. Since then, Divakaruni has straddled two worlds. As a poet and fiction writer, she gives a voice to immigrants who, like herself, struggle to create a new life while maintaining ties with their homeland. Divakaruni says the immigrant experience is often difficult, but it is also a source of inspiration.

"To me, the art of dissolving boundaries is what living is all about."

—Chitra Banerjee Divakaruni

Poetic Beginnings When Divakaruni first came to the United States, she worked various jobs to earn money for college. Divakaruni studied literature, but she did not write her own works until after her grandfather died. "I felt like I was forgetting things, forgetting him, and how things were in India and how people thought," she says. By 1990 she had published her first book of poems, *The Reason for Nasturtiums.*

Divakaruni's first poems were deeply personal. Soon she found additional inspiration. While working as a volunteer in a women's center, she witnessed the plight of battered women. To help these women, Divakaruni founded a nonprofit group, called Maitri, for Southeast Asian women. The women inspired Divakaruni, and she began writing short stories based on her experiences with them. Her first collection, *Arranged Marriages,* won the American Book Award.

Creating a New Tradition Divakaruni followed her early poems and short stories with a novel, *The Mistress of Spices.* It tells the story of a mystical figure who must choose between her heritage and her love for a non-Indian. Since then, Divakaruni has published numerous novels, short stories, and poems. Like the characters in her works, Divakaruni often crosses boundaries. She blends poetry and prose, fable and fiction, to bring together different traditions.

LOG ON **Literature** Online

Author Search For more about Chitra Banerjee Divakaruni, go to glencoe.com and enter QuickPass code GL49787u3.

Selection Skills

My Mother Combs My Hair

Literary Elements
- Simile (SE pp. 581, 583, 585)
- Form (SE p. 585)

Vocabulary Skills
- Analogies (SE pp. 581, 585)
- Academic Vocabulary (SE p. 585)

Reading Skills
- Visualize (SE pp. 581, 585)

Writing Skills/Grammar
- Character Traits (SE p. 582)

Literature and Reading Preview

Connect to the Poem

What traditions do you observe? Write a journal entry examining one or two household or family traditions. Consider what circumstances would cause you to break tradition.

Build Background

In India, many marriages are arranged by parents for their children. As part of a marriage agreement, the woman's family provides a *dowry,* a payment in money or property, to the husband. In some cultures, long hair is a symbol of beauty and, as such, a source of status and power.

Set Purposes for Reading

Big Idea The Strength of Family

As you read "My Mother Combs My Hair," ask yourself, How is the relationship between the mother and daughter revealed?

Literary Element Simile

A **simile** is a figure of speech that uses *like* or *as* to compare things that do not seem alike. As you read, ask yourself, What does Divakaruni compare using similes?

Reading Strategy Visualize

To **visualize** means to use your imagination to form mental pictures of the setting, characters, and action based on the details you read. When you visualize, ask yourself questions such as: How does the setting, character, or object look? Who is in the scene? Where are the characters in their surroundings? By visualizing, you can immerse yourself in the action that takes place. As you read, ask yourself, What descriptions and sensory details are in the poem that help me form a mental picture of the mother and daughter as well as of the setting?

Tip: Note Descriptive Details Descriptive details can help you visualize what is being described in writing. As you read, pick out descriptive phrases and words from the selection. Use a chart like the one below to help organize your details.

Descriptive Phrases/Words	Item Described
scent of crushed hibiscus	room, hair

Learning Objectives

For pages 580–585

In studying this text, you will focus on the following objectives:

Literary Study: Analyzing similes.

Reading: Visualizing.

Vocabulary

plait (plāt) *n.* a braid of material or hair; p. 583 *The woman's long hair was worked into an elaborate plait.*

brocade (brō kād′) *n.* a silk fabric with raised patterns embroidered on it; p. 583 *The shiny, patterned vest and jacket were made of a luxurious brocade.*

Tip: Analogies Analogies are comparisons based on the relationships between things or ideas. To complete an analogy, you must first decide what relationship exists between a pair of words. Then choose the word that creates the same relationship in a second pair of words.

brocade : textile :: frown : expression

Brocade is a type of *textile;* a *frown* is a type of *expression.*

Before You Read

Focus

Summary

"My Mother Combs My Hair" describes an incident involving a grown daughter and her mother, in which the mother combs and braids the daughter's hair. During the course of the poem, the relationship between the mother and the daughter is revealed, along with the values that the mother holds.

For summaries in languages other than English, see Unit 3 Teaching Resources Book, pp. 292–297.

Interactive Read and Write

Other options for teaching this selection can be found in

- Interactive Read and Write for EL Students, pp. 153–160
- Interactive Read and Write for Approaching-Level Students, pp. 153–160
- Interactive Read and Write for On-Level Students, pp. 153–160

Vocabulary

Have students read each word, its definition, and the sentence underneath the word. Ask students to write a sentence of their own on the board using the new vocabulary words.

For additional vocabulary practice, see Unit 3 Teaching Resources Book, p. 300.

For additional context, see Glencoe Visual Vocabulary CD-ROM.

English Learners

DIFFERENTIATED INSTRUCTION

Intermediate Read aloud the Build Background feature on this page. Explain that arranged marriages and long hair are Indian traditions. Ask English learners to share some interesting marriage traditions from their culture. Then, to help them understand American traditions, **ask:** What kind of traditions do Americans have today regarding marriage? *(Students may say that brides often wear white and that a father walks his daughter down the aisle.)*

Teach

View the Art ★

The woman in this image displays the traditional ornaments worn by Indian women for centuries. The arm bangles she wears could be made of gold, silver, glass, or other materials. Bangles are worn on important occasions and are considered a sign of good luck. The woman also wears anklets and toe rings. Silver beads are attached to the anklets, so that the tinkling sound of beads is heard as the woman walks. Toe rings, usually made of silver, are customary in some Hindu communities. In North India, toe rings symbolize marriage. The rings are placed on the bride's toes by the bridegroom during the wedding ceremony. Today, toe rings have become fashionable ornaments for women in other parts of the world.

My Mother Combs My Hair

Chitra Banerjee Divakaruni

Woman Dressing Her Hair, 18th century India. Private collection. ★

Reading Practice

PARTNERS SPIRAL REVIEW

Character Traits Remind students that readers can tell what a character is like by what the character says, does, and thinks. Pair up students and have them jot down character traits for both the speaker and her mother based on the poem. **Ask:** What can you tell about the speaker's mother from the poem? About the speaker? *(Students should note that the speaker's mother is conventional—she has long, beautiful hair when she marries—she is disappointed in her daugther's hair, she cares about her daughter's future, her husband has left her, and her hair is turning gray and wrinkles are forming on her face. Students should note that the daughter is aware that her mother disapproves of her hair because it is permed. She does not seem to be enjoying their time together.)*

The room is full
of the scent of crushed hibiscus,[1]
my mother's breath.
Our positions are of childhood,
I kneeling on the floor,
she crosslegged
on the chair behind.
She works the comb
through permed strands
rough as dry seaweed.
I can read regret in her fingers
untangling snarls,
rubbing red *jabakusum*[2] oil
into brittle ends.

When she was my age,
her hair reached her knees,
fell in a thick black rush
beyond the edges
of old photographs. In one,
my father has daringly
covered her hand with his
and made her smile.
At their marriage, she told me,
because of her hair
he did not ask for a dowry.

This afternoon I wait
for the old comments,
how you've ruined your hair,
this **plait's** *like a lizard's tail,*
or, *if you don't take better care*
of it, you'll never get married.
But the braiding is done,
each strand
in its neat place, shining,
the comb put away.

I turn to her, to the gray
snaking in at the temples,
the cracks growing
at the edges of her eyes
since father left.
We hold the silence
tight between us
like a live wire,
like a strip of gold
torn from a wedding **brocade.**

1. *Hibiscus* (hī bis′ kəs) is a showy red flower that grows in India and in many tropical climates.
2. *Jabakusum* is the brand name of expensive scented oil from the hibiscus flower.

1 The Strength of Family *How does this line reflect the relationship between the mother and daughter?*

Simile *Why does the poet use these images to describe the silence?* **2**

Vocabulary

plait (plāt) *n.* a braid of material or hair

brocade (brō kād′) *n.* a silk fabric with raised patterns embroidered on it

Teach

Big Idea 1

The Strength of Family

Answer: *The girl kneels on the floor in front of her mother, who sits in a chair. Their positions suggest the mother's elevated status over her daughter as well as the daughter's duty to be respectful to her mother.*

Literary Element 2

Simile **Answer:** *The silence, like "a live wire" and "a strip of gold," is difficult to ignore, but the two women ignore it, although they hold it between them. A live wire is dangerous if you touch it, and by comparing the silence to such a wire, the author creates tension between the women. The comparison between the silence and the strip of brocade suggests a wedding gone wrong, which creates tension between the mother and daughter.*

ADVANCED Ask advanced learners to think of other similes that might describe the tense silence between mother and daughter in the poem.

For additional literary element practice, see Unit 3 Teaching Resources Book, p. 298.

Approaching Level

DIFFERENTIATED INSTRUCTION

Emerging Draw students' attention to the painting on page 582 and read aloud the Viewing the Art anno in the side column of the Teacher Edition. Point out the similarity of using rings as a symbol of marriage in both the Indian and American cultures. Initiate a discussion of ornaments and clothing that are considered traditional today. Discuss how people may be treated differently when seen wearing certain kinds of traditional clothing. *(Students may point out the attire of a nun or priest.)*

After You Read

Assess

1. Students' answers will vary.
2. (a) She permed it. (b) Students may say the daughter permed her hair to rebel against family tradition.
3. (a) The speaker's hair is damaged and rough, whereas the mother's was thick and long. (b) For the mother, long hair symbolizes beauty and power. For the daughter, hair symbolizes the freedom to do as she likes.
4. (a) The mother's hair has become gray, and wrinkles have appeared around her eyes. (b) Time and sadness over the loss of her husband have aged her.
5. The mother believes that beautiful hair shows respect for traditional values. The daughter's modern hairstyle is symbolic of her desire for independence.
6. Students may say that the speaker is a single young woman at the age when traditionally she should be married. She is independent and probably lives on her own and supports herself.
7. (a) Answers will vary. (b) Similes help the reader visualize the scene. Divakaruni wants readers to use their senses and imagination.
8. Students may say that the relationship seems fairly typical. Mothers and daughters routinely have conflicts.
9. Students should support their responses with examples from the poem.

After You Read

Respond and Think Critically

Respond and Interpret

1. Which lines from this poem did you find the most memorable? Explain.
2. (a)What did the daughter do to her hair that causes the mother's regret? (b)Why did the daughter do it?
3. (a)How does the speaker's hair compare with the hair of her mother at the same age? (b)What does hair symbolize for the mother and daughter?
4. (a)What changes does the daughter notice in her mother? (b)Why have these changes occurred?

Analyze and Evaluate

5. Why has the daughter's hair been a source of conflict between the mother and daughter?
6. How would you describe the speaker in this poem? Consider her age and where she might live.
7. (a)In your opinion, what is the most effective simile in the poem? (b)Why do you think the author uses similes in the poem?

Connect

8. **Big Idea** **The Strength of Family** Is the relationship between the mother and daughter in the poem a typical mother-daughter relationship? Explain.
9. **Connect to the Author** Divakaruni often uses personal memories for inspiration in her poems. What do you think is the most personal idea that she uses in this poem? Explain.

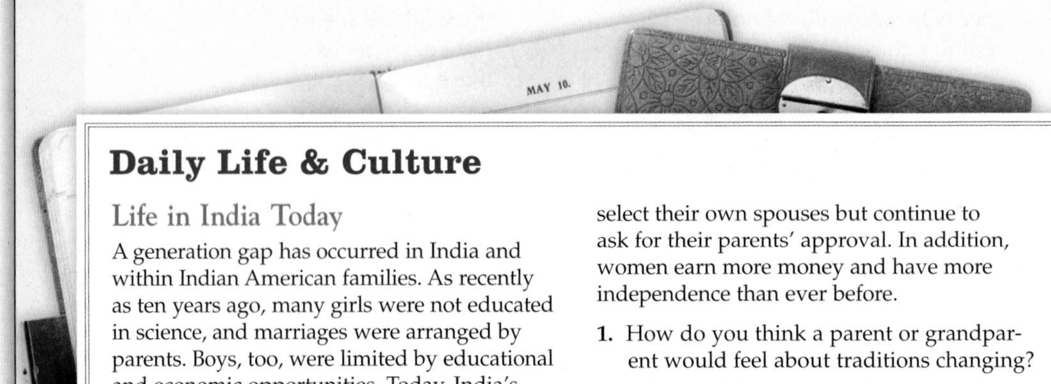

Daily Life & Culture

Life in India Today

A generation gap has occurred in India and within Indian American families. As recently as ten years ago, many girls were not educated in science, and marriages were arranged by parents. Boys, too, were limited by educational and economic opportunities. Today, India's youth are affected by the improvements in the country's economy and by the Internet and other technological advances.

Western television and products have influenced the youth culture in India as well. While the older generation in India tends to follow traditions, the younger generation is pursuing careers in fields such as technology and engineering and mixing Indian culture with Western traditions. Indian youth today more often select their own spouses but continue to ask for their parents' approval. In addition, women earn more money and have more independence than ever before.

1. How do you think a parent or grandparent would feel about traditions changing?
2. Why would young people want traditions to change?

A woman in Bangalore, India, uses a handheld computer.

Daily Life & Culture

1. A parent or grandparent may be worried about traditions changing or disappearing. They may be angry that their children do not respect their heritage.
2. Young people may not agree with the way their parents do things. Some traditions may be obstacles to pursuing careers and opportunities.

To create custom assessments online, go to Progress Reporter Online Assessment.

To create custom assessments using software, use ExamView Assessment Suite.

Literary Element Simile

A **simile** can be concrete or abstract. A concrete simile uses *like* or *as* to describe two tangible objects, such as "The wind was like a bulldozer." An abstract simile uses a tangible object to describe a concept or idea, for example, "Freedom was like a surprise gift."

1. Which image in "My Mother Combs My Hair" is an abstract simile?
2. How does this simile make the abstract concept more clear?
3. How well does the poet's use of the abstract simile convey the mother's and daughter's feelings? Explain.

Review: Form

As you learned on page 448, **form** refers to the external pattern of a poem, including the way lines and stanzas are organized. Form often dictates such elements as rhythm, meter, and rhyme. Free verse, which has no dictated form, often is arranged in verse paragraphs that, unlike stanzas, have no set number of lines. Many contemporary poems are made up of verse paragraphs, which help organize a poem into thoughts in much the same way that paragraphs help organize prose.

Partner Activity Meet with a classmate and discuss the use of free verse and verse paragraphs in "My Mother Combs My Hair." Working with your partner, rewrite the poem in stanzas with a regular rhyme scheme. Determine the effect this new form has on the sound and theme of the poem. Use a chart like the one below to list your ideas.

	Original Poem	Rewritten Poem
Sound		
Theme		

Reading Strategy Visualize

A poet sometimes will use descriptions or comparisons to help a reader form a mental image of a character. A poet may use similes, symbols, and deliberate word choice to help the reader **visualize** characters. Look back at the chart you made of descriptive details in the poem.

1. Which details help you visualize what the mother looked like in her youth? Which details help you imagine what she looks like now?
2. Which details help you see the mother in the poem combing the daughter's hair?

Vocabulary Practice

Practice with Analogies Choose the word that best completes each analogy.

1. ring : jewelry :: plait :
   - **a.** curl
   - **b.** dish
   - **c.** hairstyle
   - **d.** necklace
2. yarn : sweater :: brocade :
   - **a.** pattern
   - **b.** silk
   - **c.** vest
   - **d.** fabric

Academic Vocabulary

In this poem, the mother considers long hair an important ***commodity*** *that can help her daughter get married.*

Commodity is an academic word. In casual conversation, someone might say that the popular singer's musical talent was a real **commodity.** What is your most valuable **commodity** and why?

For more on academic vocabulary, see pages 54–55 and R79–R81.

LOG ON Literature Online

Selection Resources For Selection Quizzes, eFlashcards, and Reading-Writing Connection activities, go to glencoe.com and enter QuickPass code GL49787u3.

After You Read

Assess

Literary Element

1. An abstract simile is "silence/ tight between us/like a live wire."
2. Comparing silence to a live wire gives the impression that the mother and daughter want to speak to each other but are afraid of the tense current that runs between them.
3. Answers will vary.

Progress Check

Can students explain simile?

If No → See Unit 3 Teaching Resources Book, p. 298.

Review: Form

Students' poems may change words to regularize rhythm and add rhyme. However, their poems should include the same main ideas and maintain the same tone.

Reading Strategy

1. In her youth, the mother's hair "reached her knees." It "fell in a thick black rush / beyond the edges / of old photographs." The author also describes her smiling in a photo. Now, the mother has "gray / snaking in at the temples" and "cracks growing / at the edges of her eyes." There is no further mention of a smile.
2. The poet shows the speaker "kneeling on the floor" and the mother "crosslegged / on the chair behind." We can see the mother working the comb through the snarls in the daughter's hair and smell the flowery scent of the oil she applies to the hair's brittle ends.

Vocabulary

1. c **2.** c

For additional assessment, see Assessment Resources, pp. 157–158.

Academic Vocabulary

Sample answer: My determination is my most valuable commodity. It is a commodity because it helps me more than anything else I have.

After You Read

Assess

Respond Through Writing

Students' essays should

- provide a clear opinion of how well Divakaruni uses figurative language in the poem
- evaluate how well the figurative language supports the poem's meaning
- be organized in a logical, well-planned fashion
- include examples from the text that support the essay's position
- explore the figurative language in detail, explaining its effects and meaning

For grammar practice, see Unit 3 Teaching Resources Book, p. 301.

Respond Through Writing

Expository Essay

Evaluate Figurative Language Write an essay in which you evaluate how well Divakaruni uses figurative language in the poem. Consider how well her use of this stylistic device supports the poem's meaning.

Understand the Task **Figurative language** is language that uses figures of speech or expressions that are not literally true but express some truth beyond the literal level. Types of figurative language include hyperbole, metaphor, personification, simile, and understatement.

Prewrite Before writing, use an outline to plan the structure of your essay. Organize the body of the essay according to your main ideas or points. Below each main idea, list examples of figurative language that support the idea. Make sure the outline also includes details about your essay's introduction and conclusion.

Draft Use your outline as a guide as you write the draft of your essay. In order to expand upon each idea listed in your outline, you will need to develop your evaluation of the author's use of figurative language. Begin by fleshing out your introduction and thesis statement. The introduction should state the poem's meaning and how well you think the figurative language supports that meaning. Present your opinion directly, with a statement like:

My own view is that _____, because _____.

As you explore your main ideas in the body of the essay, focus on one example of figurative language at a time. For each example, explain how the example supports your point. Note the effects of the language and how well you think it expresses the poem's meaning. If there is ambiguous or complicated language in the poem, help clarify it for the reader. Include direct quotations from the poem throughout your essay.

Revise After completing your draft, exchange essays with a classmate. How clear is the essay's argument? Are the main ideas well supported with language from the text? Provide comments for your classmate and revise your own paper according to the comments you receive.

Edit and Proofread Proofread your paper, correcting any errors in spelling, grammar, and punctuation. Review the Grammar Tip in the side column to help you with paragraph development.

Learning Objectives

In this assignment, you will focus on the following objectives:

Writing: Writing an expository essay.

Grammar: Building logical structure by developing cohesive paragraphs.

Grammar Tip

Paragraphing

Focusing each paragraph on one main idea can help you build a logical structure. Set the focus of each paragraph in its opening sentence. For example:

The figurative language describing the daughter's hair also powerfully expresses the tension between mother and daughter.

The rest of the paragraph should only include evidence and reasoning that directly supports the main idea.

Writing Practice

Create an Editing Checklist Students can work in writing conferences with peer editors during the revising and editing stages. Students should check for correct use of grammar, punctuation, and mechanics. After students have edited their work, have students create an editing checklist to assist them in future writing assignments.

Winner of the Eisner Award

Jeff Smith

Learning Objectives

For pages 587–589

In studying this text, you will focus on the following objective:

Reading:
Interpreting graphic forms of literature.
Making connections across literature.

Set a Purpose for Reading

As you read, ask yourself, How do Fone Bone's adventures relate to the Big Idea? How do Ted and his big brother show strength of family?

Build Background

One of the most popular series of graphic novels in recent years is Jeff Smith's *Bone*, which appeared from 1991 to 2004. Smith has observed that his series, whose hero is an amiable Everyman character named Fone Bone, focuses on the theme of "growing up and leaving home for the first time." The story begins when Fone Bone and his two cousins are expelled from their hometown of Boneville. The three soon become separated in an uncharted desert, and each eventually finds his way into a forested valley filled with strange, menacing creatures. In the following excerpt from Bone: *Out from Boneville,* Fone Bone, just arrived in the valley, encounters two of its inhabitants.

Reading Strategy Interpret Graphic Forms of Literature

A graphic novel is a longer form of a comic book, often with more complex plot lines and aimed at a more mature audience. How is reading a graphic novel different from reading a conventional novel? Traditional novelists use imagery to evoke an emotional response in the reader. A graphic novelist can use actual pictures, along with words. Here are a few guidelines for reading and **interpreting graphic forms of literature:**

- Pay attention to visual details of characters, such as facial expressions, which are shown rather than described in words.
- Look for visual indications about the setting. Is the action taking place outdoors? Indoors? In the past?
- Typography cues show the emotions, speed, and sound level of dialogue. Capitalization, for example, usually means that the character is shouting. Boldface type means that a word is being stressed. Tiny type often indicates whispering.
- Scan the background of each panel. Graphic novelists sometimes like to insert clues or hidden details for the reader to discover.

Visual Perspective
on *The Strength of Family*

Focus

Summary

In searching for his cousins, Fone Bone nearly steps on Ted the bug. Fone Bone inadvertently offends Ted by telling him he looks like a leaf, so Ted calls his big brother, who is far bigger than Fone Bone. Big Brother lets Fone Bone go without harm but warns him to move quickly so he doesn't become trapped by impending winter. Ted takes Fone Bone to Thorn, who is very knowledgeable and may help Fone Bone find his cousins.

For activities related to this selection, see Unit 3 Teaching Resources Book, pp. 304–309.

For an audio recording of this selection, use Listening Library Audio CD-ROM.

For additional assessment, see Assessment Resources, pp. 159–160.

Advanced Learners

UNIVERSAL ACCESS

Graphic Novels Students may be unfamiliar with the concept of a graphic novel. Be sure to explain to students how to follow the dialogue bubbles to understand the conversations in the story. Explain that although graphic novels look like comic books, they are not always funny and do not always describe fictional or fantastical events. Inform students that the graphic novel *Maus,* tells the story of the Holocaust with characters depicted as mice and cats. **Ask:** Why might an author choose to tell a serious or unpleasant story in a graphic novel format? *(To make the subject matter more manageable for different readers; to explain an unpleasant topic in a way that is more appealing to readers)*

Ask: How does Jeff Smith's theme of growing up and leaving home for the first time relate to this idea? *(Growing up and finding yourself in an unfamiliar territory can be unpleasant and difficult.)*

Teach

Reading Strategy

Interpret Graphic Forms of Literature Have student volunteers read the different roles aloud once for comprehension. Then have the volunteers read the parts again, this time including some characterization. Encourage students to use the punctuation and the font type and size to help them in their readings. Encourage students to play with regional dialect or accent to add to the characterizations.

ENGLISH LEARNERS Inform English learners that authors sometimes use an apostrophe to indicate that they are a dropping a letter or letters from a word, in order to create the impression of a dialect. Point out the word "pickin'" is a shortened form of *picking.* Ask students to look for other words like this in the selection.

Listening, Speaking, and Viewing Practice

Personal Experience In the graphic novel *Bone: Out from Boneville,* author Jeff Smith presents a character who has left home and suddenly finds himself all alone in an unfamiliar land. Ask students to consider how Bone must feel in this situation. **Say:** The pictures in a graphic novel can help you discover how characters are feeling or what they are doing. Then ask students to consider a time when they may have felt alone or may have found themselves in an unfamiliar place. **Ask:** How did you feel in this situation? How do your feelings compare to how Bone might feel? *(Students may say that they were afraid of meeting new people or encountering new difficult situations. They may point out that Bone doesn't know how to act in the valley, which is a new place for him, and finds himself in a potentially dangerous situation when he accidentally insults a creature who lives there.)*

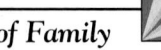

Respond and Think Critically

Respond and Interpret

1. Write a brief summary of the main events in the excerpt before you answer the following questions. For help on writing a summary, see page 42.
2. Have you ever been in a situation where a mistaken first impression got you in trouble? Explain.
3. (a)How does Ted react when Bone mistakes him for a leaf? (b)What is the effect of this reaction?
4. (a)How does Bone respond when Ted calls for his big brother? (b)Why does Bone react this way?

Analyze and Evaluate

5. (a)How do family ties shape this episode from *Bone*? (b)How are these family ties presented?
6. (a)What is the difference between the way Ted's big brother is presented in the first panels in which he appears and in the last panel in which he appears? (b)What is the effect of this last panel?

Connect

7. What other works have you read that remind you of *Bone*? What similarities do you see?

Visual Perspective
on *The Strength of Family*

Assess

1. Students' summaries should reflect the main ideas presented in the graphic story.
2. Answers will vary.
3. (a) Ted becomes furious. (b) The effect is humorous because Ted is so tiny.
4. (a) Bone cannot imagine that Ted's big brother could pose any threat. (b) Because he assumes that Ted's big brother will be another tiny insect
5. (a) Bone is searching for his lost cousins; Ted calls in his big brother to punish Bone for his "insulting" remark. (b) These family ties are presented as strong, binding, and protective.
6. (a) In the first panels, Ted's big brother is presented from the side and seems huge and monstrous; in the final panel, he is presented in silhouette from the rear and appears delicate. (b) The effect is both odd and funny.
7. Students might mention *Peanuts.* Both Smith's graphic depiction of Bone and the character's childlike personality are similar to Charles Schulz's Charlie Brown.

Approaching Level

DIFFERENTIATED INSTRUCTION

Early Advanced Point out to students that the theme of finding oneself alone in a new place has been highlighted in many different literary works. Discuss with students how this theme is explored in one or more of the following texts: *Alice in Wonderland, Pippi Longstocking, Charlotte's Web, Winnie the Pooh,* or *Great Expectations.* Ask students which stories they are most familiar with and choose the most popular text(s) to use as an example. Then ask students if they can think of any other examples of something else they have read that focuses on this theme.

Before You Read

Focus

Bellringer Options

Selection Focus Transparency 42

Daily Language Practice Transparency 70

Or display images of elderly women at work. **Say:** Think about how you remember or think about your grandmother. What qualities do you associate with her? What qualities does or did your grandmother possess that you wish you had?

Before You Read

Lineage

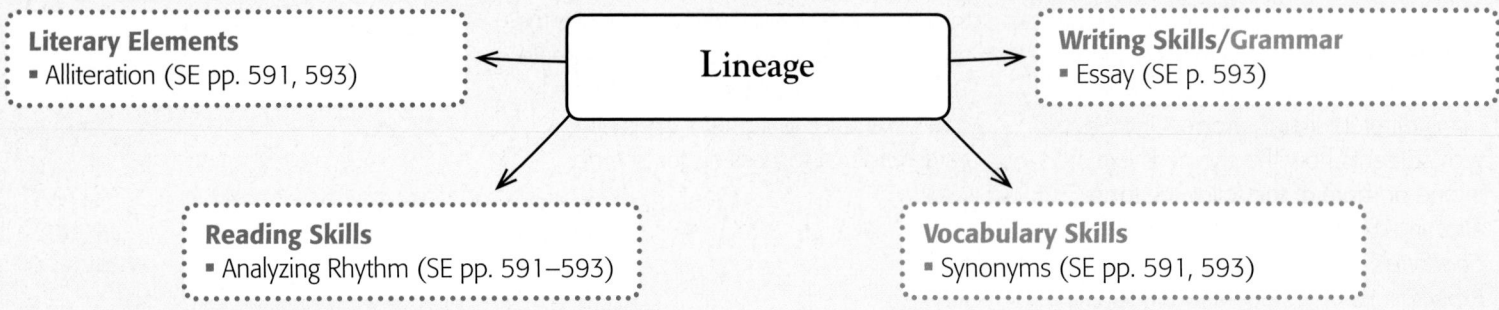

Meet **Margaret Walker**
(1915–1998)

Margaret Walker was born in Birmingham, Alabama, the daughter of a minister and a music teacher. The home was a nurturing environment full of poetry, philosophy, and music. Walker went to high school in New Orleans, and then attended New Orleans University (now Dillard University) for two years. During college, she met the renowned poet Langston Hughes at a reading. Hughes recognized her talent and urged her to study and hone her craft in the North. Walker transferred to Northwestern University in Illinois, where she received a bachelor's degree in English at the age of nineteen.

"Let a people loving freedom come to growth."

—Margaret Walker, from "For My People"

A Witness to History In 1936 Walker began work with the Federal Writers' Project in Chicago, funded by Franklin D. Roosevelt's Works Project Administration (WPA). Involvement in the Writers' Project provided Walker with firsthand knowledge of the Great Migration, a period of American history that resulted in hard times and broken dreams for many Southern blacks who moved north during the first half of the twentieth century.

After completing her tenure with the WPA in 1939, Walker returned to school, entering the creative writing program at the University of Iowa, where she earned a master's degree and a Ph.D. From 1949 to 1979 she taught English at Jackson State University in Mississippi.

Her Published Works In 1937 "For My People" appeared in *Poetry* magazine. It was Walker's first published poem and became the work for which she is best known. Walker's first book of poetry appeared in 1942. The volume garnered Walker the Yale Younger Poets Award. Her other creative works include *Jubilee* (1968), which was her first published novel, *Prophets for a New Day* (1970), and *October Journey* (1973). In 1988 Walker wrote *Richard Wright, Daemonic Genius: A Portrait of the Man, a Critical Look at His Work.* The book chronicled her friendship and professional collaboration with the great African American writer.

Throughout Walker's life, the art of writing was an integral part of her identity. A gifted poet and determined woman, Walker became a successful writer and scholar at a time when few African American women had the opportunity to purse a college education.

LOG ON **Literature** Online

Author Search For more about Margaret Walker, go to glencoe.com and enter QuickPass code GL49787u3.

Selection Skills

Lineage

Literary Elements
- Alliteration (SE pp. 591, 593)

Writing Skills/Grammar
- Essay (SE p. 593)

Reading Skills
- Analyzing Rhythm (SE pp. 591–593)

Vocabulary Skills
- Synonyms (SE pp. 591, 593)

Literature and Reading Preview

Connect to the Poem

What traits do you associate with your ancestors? Make a list of the traits and share your list with a small group. Provide examples or a brief anecdote to support the traits you've listed.

Build Background

Walker lived in Mississippi during a time of great inequality, when African Americans were seen as second-class citizens and treated with little respect. Segregation was still enforced through Jim Crow laws. The civil rights movement that began in the 1950s fought against these and other unjust laws.

Set Purposes for Reading

Big Idea The Strength of Family

As you read "Lineage," ask yourself, What traits does the speaker associate with her grandmothers?

Literary Element Alliteration

Alliteration is the repetition of consonant sounds at the beginnings of words. It can be used to reinforce meaning or create a musical effect. The phrase "the wild, wild West" is an example of alliteration. As you read "Lineage," ask yourself, Where does Walker provide examples of alliteration?

Reading Strategy Analyze Rhythm

Rhythm is the pattern of beats created by the arrangement of stressed and unstressed syllables in poetry. Rhythm can be regular, with a predictable pattern or meter, or irregular. As you read, ask yourself, How does Walker use rhythm to evoke an emotional response?

Tip: Read Aloud You may want to read this poem aloud to get a stronger impression of its rhythmic emphasis. As you read, use a chart like the one below to keep track of how rhythmic elements are used.

Place in the Poem	How Rhythm Is Used
First line	Simple sentence that gives rhythmic emphasis to the last word, "strong."

Learning Objectives

For pages 590–593

In studying this text, you will focus on the following objectives:

Literary Study: Analyzing alliteration.

Reading: Analyzing rhythm.

Writing: Writing a dialogue.

Vocabulary

toil (toil) *v.* to work very hard or for long hours; p. 592 *After the flood, we toiled for days trying to clean the mud out of the basement.*

sow (sō) v. to plant by scattering seeds; p. 592 *In the spring, the gardener will sow the seeds, walking the length of the garden several times as she scatters them.*

Tip: Synonyms Words that have similar meanings are called synonyms. Synonyms are always the same part of speech. For example, the verbs *toil* and *labor* are synonyms. Thinking of one or two synonyms for each vocabulary word can help you remember the meanings of the words.

English Learners

DIFFERENTIATED INSTRUCTION

Beginning/Early Intermediate Read the Building Background feature on page 591, and point out the word *unjust.* Explain to students that *just* is used to describe something that is considered to be correct, proper, or fair. Then point out that adding the prefix *un-* changes the word's meaning. **Ask:** What do you think the word *unjust* means? *(Students should discern that the prefix un-, meaning not, creates a word that means "not fair" or "not right.")* Have students think of words that include *un-* as a prefix. Ask students to use these words in a sentence.

Before You Read

Focus

Summary

In this poem, the speaker describes the qualities that her grandmothers possessed and her memories of them. She ends by wondering why she does not possess the same qualities.

For summaries in languages other than English, see Unit 3 Teaching Resources Book, pp. 313–318.

Interactive Read and Write

Other options for teaching this selection can be found in

- Interactive Read and Write for EL Students, pp. 161–166
- Interactive Read and Write for Approaching-Level Students, pp. 161–166
- Interactive Read and Write for On-Level Students, pp. 161–166

Vocabulary

Vocabulary Poster Review the vocabulary words with your students. Then have volunteers come up to the board and write a sentence using either word.

For additional vocabulary practice, see Unit 3 Teaching Resources Book, p. 321.

For additional context, see Glencoe Visual Vocabulary CD-ROM.

Teach

Reading Strategy

Analyze Rhythm Answer: *The line gives an impression of balance, solidity, and finality. The series of lines ending with periods creates a rhythm that reflects the sequence of planting a crop.*

APPROACHING Tell approaching level learners that a poet can use rhythm to evoke the sounds of what they are describing. **Say:** The author uses a series of lines ending in periods to create a rhythm that recreates the steady, repetitive sounds of planting a field

For additional practice using the reading skill or strategy, see Unit 3 Teaching Resources Book, p. 320.

Progress Check

Can students explain alliteration?

If No → See Unit 3 Teaching Resources Book, p. 319.

Woman Sowing. Robert Gwathmet. Watercolor and ink, $13\frac{7}{8}$ x $15\frac{3}{8}$ in. Gift of International Business Machines Corporation. Smithsonian American Art Museum, Washington, D.C.

Lineage

Margaret Walker

My grandmothers were strong.
They followed plows and bent to **toil.**
They moved through fields **sowing** seed.
They touched earth and grain grew.
They were full of sturdiness and singing.
My grandmothers were strong.

My grandmothers are full of memories
Smelling of soap and onions and wet clay
With veins rolling roughly over quick hands
They have many clean words to say.
My grandmothers were strong.
Why am I not as they?

Analyze Rhythm *What effect does the rhythm of this line have, both as one line and in the context of its stanza?*

Vocabulary

toil (toil) *v.* to work very hard or for long hours
sow (sō) *v.* to plant by scattering seeds

Listening and Speaking

SMALL GROUP SPIRAL REVIEW Ask students to think of someone in their family they admire and develop a list of characteristics that describe the person. Then have students share their lists within small groups. Students identify the person they chose and explain why they admire him or her.

After You Read

Respond and Think Critically

Respond and Interpret

1. Which sensory image from the poem appeals to you most? Why?
2. (a)What kind of work does the speaker say her grandmothers did? (b)What do the details suggest to you about the grandmothers?
3. (a)How are verb tenses different in the two stanzas of the poem? (b)What does the change in tense suggest about the grandmothers?
4. (a)How would you describe the speaker's attitude toward her grandmothers? (b)What details from the poem reveal this attitude?

Analyze and Evaluate

5. Why might the speaker describe herself as different from her grandmothers?
6. How do you think the speaker defines strength? Cite evidence from the poem.

Connect

7. **Big Idea** The Strength of Family What kind of relationship do you think the speaker has with her grandmothers? Cite evidence from the poem.
8. **Connect to the Author** Margaret Walker grew up during the time of enforced segregation. How might that have influenced her to write a poem paying tribute to her ancestors?

Literary Element Alliteration

Alliteration is often used in poetry, where it helps to emphasize words or phrases, create images, and establish an appealing sound and rhythm.

1. In lines 3 and 4, how does the emphasis created by alliteration support the meaning?
2. Identify another instance of alliteration. Why do you think the author chose to use it there?

Reading Strategy Analyze Rhythm

Review the chart you made while reading the poem and answer the following questions.

1. How does the rhythm in the first stanza differ from the rhythm in the second?
2. What rhythmic effect does the poet's repetition of the line "My grandmothers were strong" have on the poem?

LOG ON Literature Online

Selection Resources For Selection Quizzes, eFlashcards, and Reading-Writing Connection activities, go to glencoe.com and enter QuickPass code GL49787u3.

Vocabulary Practice

Practice with Synonyms A synonym is a word that has the same or nearly the same meaning as another word. With a partner, match each boldfaced vocabulary word below with its synonym. You will not use all the answer choices. Use a dictionary to check your answers.

1. toil	a. release
2. sow	b. labor
	c. plant
	d. attach

Writing

Write a Dialogue The speaker in "Lineage" looks back through generations to comment on the lives of her grandmothers. What do you think the grandmothers themselves would say? Write a dialogue between the speaker and her grandmothers, as the grandmothers explain their perspectives on their own lifetimes and the experiences of the speaker. Use quotation marks and dialogue tags.

After You Read

Assess

1. Students' answers will vary.
2. (a) They plowed and planted fields of grain by hand. (b) They were strong, hardworking, capable women.
3. (a) In the first stanza, the verbs are in the past tense. In the second, most are in the present tense. (b) It suggests that the grandmothers are no longer working in the fields. They are now "full of memories."
4. (a) She admires them for their ability to draw life from the earth. (b) "Sturdiness and singing" and "clean words"
5. She may not have experienced hard labor or lived in touch with the earth.
6. The first stanza focuses on the grandmothers' physical strength. The second emphasizes their mental and spiritual strength.
7. (a) "They have many clean words to say" suggests that the grandmothers talk frequently to the speaker.
8. Sample answer: During the time of segregation, African Americans were not treated as equal citizens in America. Walker corrects this and shows that her ancestors deserve respect for the strength with which they carried their hardships.

Literary Element

1. It draws attention to the cause/effect and time relationship described.
2. The /r/ sounds in "rolling roughly" parallel the image of distended veins moving on quick hands.

Reading Strategy

1. First-stanza lines have a regular meter; the others do not.
2. It frames the first stanza.

Vocabulary Practice

1. b 2. c

Writing

Students should

- express sentiments between the speaker and her grandmothers
- use dialogue tags
- use quotation marks correctly

Writing Workshop

Reflective Essay

Focus

Bellringer Options

Display images of daily life, such as photographs depicting work, family life, or recreation. **Ask:** What feelings or thoughts do these images evoke? Ask students to reflect on an important activity in their own life as a first step in writing a descriptive essay.

Summary

The process of writing a descriptive essay is presented in stages, beginning with prewriting activities such as brainstorming. Students are guided through drafting, revising, and editing their essays. Instruction on precise adjectives and dangling participles is included. Students will also present essays orally.

Learning Objectives

For pages 594–601

In this workshop, you will focus on the following objectives:

Writing:
Writing a reflective essay.
Using precise adjectives.

Grammar: Understanding how to correct misplaced modifiers.

Writing Process

At any stage of a writing process, you may think of new ideas. Feel free to return to earlier stages as you write.

- Prewrite
- Draft
- Revise
- Focus Lesson: Precise Adjectives
- Edit and Proofread
- Focus Lesson: Misplaced Modifiers
- Present

LOG ON Literature Online

Writing and Research
For prewriting, drafting, and revising tools, go to glencoe.com and enter QuickPass code GL49787u3.

Writing Workshop

Reflective Essay

Literature Connection In "who are you,little i," E. E. Cummings reflects on looking out a window at a November sunset as a child.

who are you,little i

(five or six years old)
peering from some high

window;at the gold

of november sunset

(and feeling:that if day
has to become night

this is a beautiful way)

Poets contemplate many experiences, from observations of nature to the meaning of life and death. Similarly, writers of essays reflect on their experiences. When you write a reflective essay, you describe something you observed or experienced and how it affected you. The purpose is to communicate your thoughts to others. To write a successful essay, follow the goals and strategies below.

Checklist:

Goals	Strategies
To narrate and describe a personal experience	☑ Relate a sequence of events in chronological order or use a flashback ☑ Set the experience in a specific time and place ☑ Use the first-person point of view
To express the meaning of the experience	☑ Create a clear, controlling idea of the experience ☑ Maintain a tone and focus consistent with the meaning of the experience
To engage your audience	☑ Use precise details, sensory language, action verbs, and the active voice ☑ Show your own or others' interior thoughts, emotions, gestures, and movements, as appropriate to your controlling idea

Workshop Resources

Print Materials

- Unit 3 Teaching Resources, pp. 326–328
- Writing Kit
- Success in Writing: Research and Reports

Transparencies

- Grammar and Language Transparency 70
- Writing Workshop Transparencies 16–20

Technology

- Literature Online: Writing Resources and Grammar Resources, www.glencoe.com
- Online Essay Grader, www.glencoe.com
- Student Presentation Builder on StudentWorks Plus CD-ROM
- Media Workshop DVD
- Online Student Edition

Assignment: Narrate and Reflect on a Personal Experience

Write a reflective essay of about 1,500 words about a meaningful experience. As you work, keep your audience and purpose in mind. ☆

Audience: peers, classmates, and teacher

Purpose: create a vivid impression of your experience for others

Real-World Connection

Give your essay to or read it aloud to someone who may have shared the experience with you or who would be especially interested in the way it changed you.

Analyze a Professional Model

Donald Hall writes about New England's bad weather. The comments in the margin point out features to include in your own reflective essay.

"Good Use for Bad Weather" by Donald Hall

My grandparents nailed two thermometers side by side on the porch of their New Hampshire farmhouse. One registered ten degrees cold, the other ten degrees hot, so that there was always something to brag about. Every morning when my grandmother sat in the rocker under Christopher the canary, writing three postcards to three daughters, she could say, "Thirty below this morning. Seems like it might get cold." Or, "Ninety already and the sun's not over the mountain."

In New England we take pride in our weather because it provides us with pain and suffering, necessities for the spirit, like food and clothing for the body. We never brag about good weather. Let Tucson display self-esteem over eighty-three days without rain. Let Sarasota newspapers go free for the asking when the sun doesn't shine. We smirk in the murk, superior. It's true that we have good weather; we just don't pay it any mind. When summer people flock north to the lakes and the mountains, they do not gather to enjoy our foggy rain. If they're from Boston, they don't come *for* bright sun and cool dry air; they migrate north *against* the soup-kettle mugginess of home. It seems more decent.

In good weather—apple days of October, brilliant noons

Time and Place

Use vivid details to create a sense of time and place.

Point of View

Use the first-person point of view in a reflective essay. Plural pronouns, such as *we, us,* and *our,* identify the writer as part of a group.

Audience Engagement

Use precise language, sensory details, and action verbs.

Descriptive Details

Use sensory details that show how things look, sound, feel, smell, and taste.

Writing Workshop

Reflective Essay

Teach

Writing Skills

Use Anecdotes Ask: What does the anecdote in the first paragraph show us about Hall's grandparents? *(They are rugged country people who like to show how tough they are.)* What makes the anecdote humorous? *(They make light of bad weather, but in fact the weather is never really so bad as their broken thermometers indicate.)*

Literary History ☆

Michel de Montaigne

One of the great thinkers of the Renaissance, Michel de Montaigne (1533–1592) popularized the essay form in a series of personal observations renowned for their wit, skepticism, and disarming honesty. Montaigne's *Essays* explores his own experiences and the customs and beliefs of his contemporaries to arrive at universal truths.

Advanced Learners

DIFFERENTIATED INSTRUCTION

Concrete Details Challenge students to enliven their writing with specific concrete details. Note, for instance, how much more effectively the reader's senses are engaged if the word *clothes* is replaced by the phrase *rustling red silk robes.* Encourage students to consider the kinds of details that will engage their target audience.

Write the words *food, boy,* and *loud noises* on the board. Have students create concrete examples of each of the words (e.g, crunchy corn on the cob, young red-headed ball players, and big banging booms). Ask volunteers to share their answers with the class.

Writing Workshop

Reflective Essay

Teach

Big Idea

Life Lessons Explain that in reflective essays writers gather their thoughts on a subject and, in the process, derive insights about life and human nature. Often, everyday events and experiences serve as their starting point.

Ask: What are some typical everyday activities? *(Students may mention school, jobs, hobbies, sports, recreation, commuting and doing chores.)*

Political History ☆

New Hampshire On June 21, 1788, New Hampshire became the ninth state to ratify the Constitution. The state motto, "Live Free or Die," was penned by the Revolutionary War general John Stark, hero of the Battle of Bennington. Robert Frost, who worked as a farmer and schoolteacher in Derry, celebrated New Hampshire's picturesque rural landscape in many of his poems.

and cool evenings of August—we remain comfortable despite our pleasure by talking about pleasure's brevity, forecasting what we're in for as soon as the good spell is done with. Winter is best for bragging. For a week or two in March, mud is almost as good. (Mud is weather as much as snow is; leaves are landscape.) "Tried to get the Buick up New Canada this morning. Have to wait for a dry spell to pull it out, I suppose. Of course, we'll have to dig to find it, first."

Characterization
Show your own or others' words, interior thoughts, and feelings.

Black ice is first rate, but most of us who cherish difficulty will settle for a good ten feet of snow. We get up about five-fifteen, make the coffee, check the thermometer: ten degrees above. The warmth must account for the snow. Highway department plows blunder down Route 4 in the dark outside. We get dressed, dragging on flannel-lined chinos, flannel shirt, sweater, down jacket, and boots. Then we broom one car, headlights and taillights, gun it in reverse over the hump of snow Forrest's plow left, swing it up Forrest's alley, and swoop it down to the road, scattering ridges of snow.

Tone and Focus
Maintain a consistent tone and focus throughout your essay.

Only two miles to the store. It's not adventurous driving, but it pays to be attentive, to start slowing for a turn a hundred yards early. The store opens at six. Because this is New Hampshire, somebody's bound to be there by five-forty-five. ☆ We park with the motor running and the heater on—it'll get warm while we pick up the *Globe*—to go inside. Bob's there with his cup of coffee, and Bill who owns garage and store, and Judy the manager who makes coffee and change. We grin at each other as I stamp my boots and slip my paper out of the pile. We say things like, "Nice weather!" "Bit of snow out there!" "Hear we're getting two feet more!" but what we're really saying is *It takes more than a couple of feet of snow to slow us down!*

Descriptive Details
Use details to describe people and places.

Controlling Idea
Be sure all your details support or create a single controlling idea.

Reading-Writing Connection Try the writing techniques that you have just encountered in your own reflective essay.

Writing Practice

SMALL GROUP

Write Descriptive Statements Say: Reread the last paragraph. Note Hall's use of specific details and actions. They show the hardiness of New Hampshire natives. Instead of simply stating that they are resilient, he paints a picture with words. Have students work with a partner to create descriptive statements. First, model the exercise by writing a descriptive sentence on the board. (Wind blows through the starry sky, past the icicles that dangle from the gutters, and right through my winter clothes.)

Prewrite

Manage Your Time Begin your prewriting now. Develop a schedule for completing all the stages of your writing process by the due date.

Choose a Subject Choose a subject that is important to you and will be meaningful to your readers.

- **Find a familiar subject.** Ask yourself questions such as the following: How do I feel about this place? What do I notice about the people who live in my neighborhood? What do I think about what happens here every morning/afternoon/evening?
- **Select a subject that is meaningful to others.** Choose a subject that others will find meaningful, either because it is familiar to them or because it gives them new insight. Ask yourself: Why do I think people are interested in this subject? How can I describe it so that it is meaningful to others?
- **Use a cluster diagram.** To gather your ideas before you begin to write, jot them down in an organizer. You might, for example, put "What Happened Last Year" in the center. Then add notes to help you decide on a memorable experience for your essay.

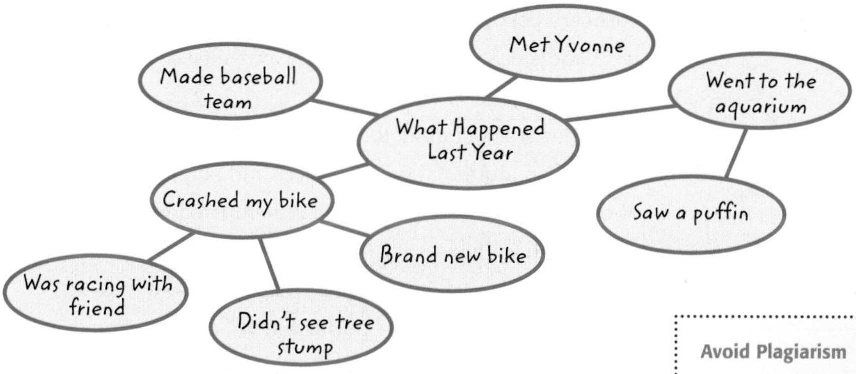

Reflect on Your Subject Before you begin drafting, think about why this event was important in your life and why others will want to read about it. Consider what you learned or how it changed your life.

Talk About Your Ideas To help develop your writing voice, describe your reflections to a partner. Ask your partner to suggest where you might add narrative details to help develop the story or sensory details to help your readers experience what you went through. Listen to your partner's reflections too. Ask questions to help your partner recall the details and conversations that took place.

Explore Sensory Details

Record sensory details about your experience or observation. Make a list of images. Describing one image may help you remember others.

bright orange beak
loud, growling calls
sturdy webbed feet
fake rocks
painted blue sky
plastic bucket

Avoid Plagiarism

Never download an essay from the Internet. Not only is this dishonest but it is likely to bring serious consequences. Remember that your teacher or anyone else can probably find the source just as easily as you did.

Teach

Writing Process

Prewrite Allow students time for brainstorming, and ask them to recall examples of meaningful people, places, or activities. Ask them to visualize and record as many memories, details, and impressions as possible.

Writing Skills

Observation Hall brought his essay to life through close observations of his subjects. Tell students to imagine watching their subjects in a movie or looking at them in photographs. Challenge them to capture these pictures in words, so that an audience can "see" them, too.

Approaching Level

DIFFERENTIATED INSTRUCTION

Emerging Read aloud a paragraph of the essay to help students grasp the rhythm and expressiveness of fluent reading. Pay special attention to enunciation, pacing, tone of voice, and emphasis. Then ask students what they noticed about your reading that made the writing easier for them to understand. Help students understand the techniques you used to make the meaning of the passage clearer. Invite volunteers to read aloud, using the techniques you demonstrated to work on their reading fluency.

Teach

Writing Process

Draft Encourage students to explore their hunches and inspirations in the early stages of writing. Stress the importance of generating a flow of ideas rather than struggling with word choices or sentence construction. Urge them to jot down ideas and then review them for unexpected insights or a fresh angle on their subject. Remind students that they can revise later.

Time and Place / Point of View

Answer: *The word* I *is a clue that the first-person point of view is being used. The description of the aquarium and the puffin help reveal the setting.*

Audience Engagement

Answer: *The writer uses a flashback to create interest.*

Narrative Details

Answer: *They provide the narrative structure, or "story," of the essay.*

Descriptive Details

Answer: *The details about the puffins' calls and appearance make the experience seem real.*

Writing Frames

As you read the workshop model, think about the writer's use of the following frames:

I remembered my first experience with ____.

Since then, I have ____.

I realized that ____.

Consider using frames like these in your own reflective essay.

Draft

Put Your Thoughts and Feelings into Words Retell your experience using chronological order, or begin with or include a flashback. Remember that your goal in this step is to let your ideas flow without being concerned about grammar and mechanics. Leave the evaluation of your writing for later.

Analyze a Workshop Model

Here is a final draft of a reflective essay. Read the essay and answer the questions in the margin. Use the answers to these questions to guide you as you write.

Time and Place/ Point of View

How does the opening paragraph reveal setting and point of view?

Audience Engagement

What narrative technique does the writer use to create interest?

Narrative Details

What do narrative details add to an essay?

Descriptive Details

How do sensory images help you visualize an experience?

Watching a Puffin Through Glass

I stood in front of the aquarium glass and watched a puffin. Not two inches away from my nose, the puffin gazed earnestly back at me. I thought, "How wonderful to be so close." I could see every detail of the feathers. I watched the sturdy webbed feet paddle beneath the water. For a long time, I had hoped to see a puffin up close.

Yet this was not quite the encounter that I had expected. As I looked around at the fake rocks and painted blue sky of the tiny place where it lived, I remembered my first experience with puffins.

It was on a vacation in Maine when I was six years old. My parents took me on a "puffin watch," an Audubon-sponsored boat trip to an island where puffins were being reintroduced. I can still remember leaning over the rail of the boat and looking through my father's binoculars to find the three or four real puffins among the decoys set to attract them. I remember their loud, growling calls and bright orange beaks. It was amazing to see in real life the birds that I had seen only in pictures. That boat trip sparked my interest in studying nature.

For a graphic organizer and rubric to use with this workshop, see Unit 3 Teaching Resources Book, pp. 332–334.

Since then, I have looked for activities that put me in touch with nature. The summer before my sophomore year, I took part in a program with other teenagers to help a biologist with her field research. We traveled around the lakes of New Hampshire for two weeks to record the behavior of loons. I was fascinated by the actions of these graceful birds. It was well worth the challenge of paddling across a large lake to watch a family of loons with two newborn chicks.

Looking through the aquarium glass, I realized that I was missing the satisfaction of observing puffins in their own habitat. I felt I got to know the loons better from fifty feet away than I could possibly get to know this puffin in its tiny enclosure. The puffin turned away from looking at me to take a morsel of food that a worker handed it from a plastic bucket. As I walked away from the puffin, I saw tanks of fish. The fish were swimming in endless circles. At that point I knew that I wanted to study animals in their natural habitats.

Narration / Description

Controlling Idea
How does the writer maintain a consistent tone and focus despite shifts in time and place?

Audience Engagement
What interior thoughts does the writer reveal?

Significance
How is the focus here consistent with the focus of the entire essay?

Writing Workshop

Reflective Essay

Teach

Writing Skills

Controlling Idea Answer: *The tone remains that of an interested observer. The focus remains on bird habitats.*

Audience Engagement
Answer: *The writer reveals his realization that he prefers to observes birds in their natural habitats. His perspective shifts between his current observations and his memories.*

Significance
Answer: *The focus is on animal habitats.*

Elaborate Explain that writing an effective reflective essay requires showing how a particular subject is relevant to your audience by elaborating, or expanding, on your main ideas. Stress the value of making connections between the main subject and related topics to flesh out an essay.

English Learners

DIFFERENTIATED INSTRUCTION

Beginning/Early Intermediate Developing an ear for tone can be challenging for English language learners. Reading their essays aloud will provide practice in listening and speaking and will build confidence. Have students practice reading their essay aloud, and meet independently with students who need to work on gaining fluency. Have students read excerpts from their essays to the class.

Writing Workshop

Reflective Essay

Teach

Writing Process

Revise Feedback from partners can provide students with a starting point for their revisions. You may want to have peer readers focus particularly on issues of clarity and completeness. **Ask:** Did any sections seem unclear? Are there any points or details you'd like to know more about? Encourage students to refer to the checklist on the student page to help them evaluate their partners' work.

Writing Skills

Punctuation Many students will have trouble punctuating quotations. **Write on the board:** I thought, "How wonderful to be so close." Note the placement of the comma after *thought,* which introduces the quotation. Point out that *How* is capitalized, even though it comes after a comma. Stress that in American English, periods and commas always go inside quotation marks.

Traits of Strong Writing

Include these traits of strong writing to express your ideas effectively.

Ideas

Organization

Voice

Word Choice

Sentence Fluency

Conventions

Presentation

For more information on using the Traits of Strong Writing, see pages R28–R30.

Word Choice

This academic vocabulary word appears in the student model:

encounter (en koun′ tər) *n.* 1. a chance meeting; 2. a violent or hostile clash; *Yet this was not quite the encounter that I had expected.* Using academic vocabulary may help strengthen your writing. Try to use one or two academic vocabulary words in your reflective essay. See the complete list on pages R79–R81.

LOG ON Literature Online

Writing and Research
For editing and publishing tools, go to glencoe.com and enter QuickPass code GL49787u3.

Revise

Peer Review Exchange drafts with a partner. Use the checklist below to evaluate and strengthen each other's essays.

Checklist

- ☑ Do you describe a personal experience that was meaningful to you?
- ☑ Do you use the first-person point of view?
- ☑ Do you set the experience in a specific time and place?
- ☑ Do you use precise language, sensory details, and the active voice?
- ☑ Do you present interior thoughts and emotions?
- ☑ Do you maintain a consistent tone and focus?
- ☑ Do you convey the meaning of the experience or its effect on you?

Focus Lesson

Precise Adjectives

Your essay will be more memorable if you use precise, descriptive adjectives. Adjectives modify nouns and pronouns by telling what kind, how many, which one, or how much. Phrases and clauses can act as adjectives. Remember that you can use a dictionary or thesaurus to select more precise language.

Draft:

The puffin turned away from looking at me to take a morsel.

Revision:

The puffin turned away from looking at me to take a morsel <u>of food</u>[1] <u>that a worker handed it</u>[2] from a <u>plastic</u>[3] bucket.

1: Adjective phrase describing morsel

2: Adjective clause telling which morsel of food

3: Adjective telling what kind of bucket

Writing Practice

SMALL GROUP **Give Feedback** Instruct peer reviewers to pay special attention to the student's descriptive writing. Write these questions on the board:

- Which descriptive details are most powerful? Why?
- Which details could use more explanation? Why?
- Which parts of the essay are the most interesting? Why?

Emphasize that writers need not accept every suggested change. They should use the comments as a basis for making improvements.

Edit and Proofread

Get It Right When you have completed the final draft of your essay, proofread for errors in grammar, usage, mechanics, and spelling. Refer to the Language Handbook, pages R40–R59, as a guide.

Focus Lesson

Misplaced Modifiers

Misplaced modifiers are words and phrases that modify, or seem to modify, the wrong word in a sentence. Dangling participles are one type of misplaced modifier. A participle is the form of a verb used to modify a noun or pronoun—for example, *diving* puffin. A participial phrase is made up of a participle and its objects and modifiers: All puffins *viewed on the tour* were part of an experiment. A participial phrase needs to be connected to the word it modifies. If it has no referent, it is called a dangling participle and the sentence should be revised. Below is an example of two ways to correct this problem.

Problem: Dangling Participle

Looking through the aquarium glass, the satisfaction of observing puffins in their own habitat was missing.

Solution A: To avoid a dangling participle, make sure that the participial phrase and the word it modifies appear next to each other.

Looking through the aquarium glass, I realized that I was missing the satisfaction of observing puffins in their own habitat.

Solution B: Rewrite the sentence.

I realized that I was missing the satisfaction of observing puffins in their own habitat because I was looking at them through the aquarium glass.

Present ☆

Check Details Before you submit your essay for others to read, you should check all the details. Make sure you have followed the assignment guidelines for placement of your title and name. Whether you type or handwrite your paper, it should have a neat appearance.

Peer Review Tips

A classmate may ask you to read his or her reflective essay. Take your time and jot down notes as you read so you can give constructive feedback. Use the following questions to get started:

Does the essay maintain a single controlling idea?

Does the writer create interest through word choice and sensory details, as well as through details about the people, time, and place?

Word-Processing Tip

Always remember that your words must create your emphasis—not italics, underlining, boldface, capital letters, or extra exclamation points. Even though word processing gives you many design options, only a few of them are appropriate for a formal essay.

Writer's Portfolio

Place a clean copy of your reflective essay in your portfolio to review later.

Teach

Writing Skills

Correct Dangling Participles
Students sometimes misplace modifiers in their sentences, resulting in unclear or inaccurate statements. Explain that in participles and participial phrases, verbs can act as adjectives: a *diving* puffin, all puffins *viewed on the tour.* Read the example sentences on this page. Note that the meaning of the problem sentence is less clear than that of the two correct alternatives.

Writer's Technique ☆

Blogs These days, one of the easiest and most popular ways of sharing personal reflections is through a Web log or "blog." Blogs can take the form of journals, editorials, informal essays, or any possible combination of these and other kinds of information. Often blogs focus on writers' major interests, such as movies, music, sports, or politics.

Approaching Level

DIFFERENTIATED INSTRUCTION

African American Vernacular English Students who use African American Vernacular English (AAVE) may have difficulty with the placement of an adverb of frequency (e.g., never, always, usually) after, rather than before, the helping verb in a sentence. Model the correct placement of adverbs. **Say:** Instead of writing "He always is complaining," you should write "He is always complaining."

Write a list of adverbs of frequency on the board: *usually, sometimes, always, never.* Have students copy the list into their notebooks and check their essays for any mistakes with adverbs of frequency.

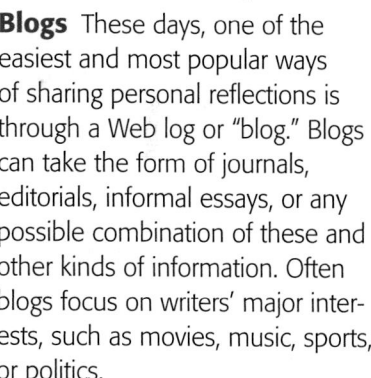

Speaking, Listening, and Viewing Workshop

Reflective Presentation

Focus

Summary

Students will plan and develop a descriptive presentation and will learn techniques for presenting it to an audience.

Teach

Speaking Skills

Address an Audience Some students will find the prospect of addressing an audience daunting. Explain that learning and practicing specific skills, such as preparing note cards and rehearsing their delivery, will build their confidence. Stress the importance of speaking slowly and clearly and of modulating their expression appropriately. Emphasize that these techniques will make it easier for listeners to process the content of their speeches.

For help with creating presentations, see Student Presentation Builder on StudentWorks Plus.

Learning Objectives

For pages 602–603

In this workshop, you will focus on the following objective:

Speaking and Listening: Delivering a reflective presentation.

Speaking, Listening, and Viewing Workshop

Reflective Presentation

Literature Connection Poet E. E. Cummings also wrote essays and a novel. The novel was based on his experiences in prison in France during World War I. As a young man, he joined an ambulance corps and served in France, but he and a friend were mistakenly held in a detention camp for about three months. After returning home, he reflected on the experience to write his first and only novel, *The Enormous Room.* In this workshop, you will learn to present a reflection on an observation or experience to an audience of listeners.

Assignment **Plan a reflective presentation and present it to the class.**

Plan Your Presentation

When you wrote your reflective essay, you used narrative techniques, descriptive details, and sensory images to tell why an experience was meaningful to you. Keep these strategies in mind as you prepare your reflective presentation.

- You can use your essay as a starting point, or you can choose another experience or observation.
- Discuss your options with a partner and choose one of them for your presentation.
- Write down descriptive details and sensory images to include.
- Write concise notes on cards to use in your presentation. Be sure to include a note about why the experience was meaningful in your life.

Choose Carefully

When you are presenting a reflection to others, you will want to choose a subject you are comfortable talking about and a subject that will be meaningful to others.

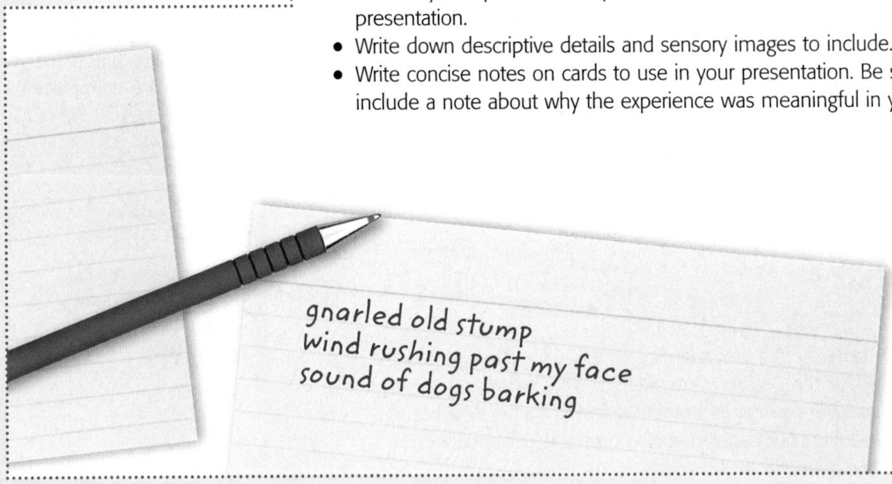

Speaking Practice

SMALL GROUP

Effective Oral Presentations Discuss with students the elements of good speech delivery, such as eye contact, expression, gestures, and body language. Have students watch a clip from famous speech, such as Martin Luther King's "I Have a Dream" speech. Then have students watch a clip from a forum discussion or debate.

As a supplement, you may also wish to include a clip from an infomercial or other commercial presentation. As students watch, have them point out different elements of good public speaking. **Ask:** What makes these speeches effective? *(Students should point out elements of body language, eye contact, inflection, volume, and other elements that make the presentations effective.)*

Develop Your Presentation

As you work on your presentation, choose an organizational method that makes sense for the subject you have chosen. You might order your presentation chronologically, by comparison and contrast, by cause and effect, or by order of importance. Include an introduction to grab your listeners' interest, a body in which you tell what happened, and a conclusion in which you explain the meaning of what happened.

Rehearse

Work with a partner to analyze the occasion and audience for your presentation. Decide which verbal and nonverbal techniques will be most effective. Draw ideas from the list below. Then rehearse your presentation several times. As you listen, evaluate how well the presentation will work for the intended audience. Also provide feedback on which techniques the speaker is using effectively, as well as suggestions for improvement for others.

Techniques for Delivering a Reflective Presentation

Verbal Techniques	Nonverbal Techniques
☑ **Volume** Speak loudly enough to be heard by everyone in your audience.	☑ **Eye Contact** Look from person to person in your audience, but focus on one individual at a time. Respond to the expressions you see.
☑ **Pace** Pause at appropriate places in your presentation to let your audience reflect on your words.	☑ **Body Language** Gesture with your hands to make important points. Use facial expressions to help communicate joy, sadness, surprise, fear, and other emotions.
☑ **Tone** Match your tone to the content. Some reflections are humorous, but others require a serious tone of voice.	☑ **Facial Expressions** Be sure to use facial expressions to show your own responses and reactions to events.
☑ **Pronunciation** Speak clearly, pronouncing all words.	☑ **Posture** Stand up tall with your head straight.

Speaking Frames

Consider using the following frames in your reflective presentation:

I experienced ____.

____ surrounded/enveloped/beckoned to me.

Looking back on it now, ____.

Presentation Tips

Use the following checklist to evaluate your reflective presentation:

☑ Did you create interest through sensory images and other descriptive details?

☑ Did you create interest at the beginning and end with your reflection?

☑ Did you use effective verbal and nonverbal techniques?

LOG ON **Literature** Online

Speaking, Listening, and Viewing For project ideas, templates, and presentation tips, go to glencoe.com and enter QuickPass code GL49787u3.

Teach

Speaking Skills

Voice Remind students of the importance of using their voice effectively when making a presentation. Point out that audiences become bored when a speaker speaks in a monotone. Encourage students to do the following:

- Practice changing pitch and tone to communicate emotions.
- Speak loudly enough so that every person in the room can hear clearly.
- Eliminate expressions such as *uh, um, you know,* and *okay.*

Listening Skills

Assess a Presentation

Encourage active listening by having students assess one another's speeches. Tell them to base their evaluations on the following questions:

- What feelings and ideas did the presentation reflect?
- What descriptive details do you remember?
- Did the presentation explain why the subject was important to the speaker?

English Learners

DIFFERENTIATED INSTRUCTION

Beginning/Early Intermediate

English Learners may feel especially uneasy about giving an oral presentation. Assign students to groups of two or three. Try to pair stronger students with those who need extra help with speaking and oral presentation skills. Allow students to practice delivering their descriptive presentations within their groups. Have students critique each other's presentations, and encourage students to practice delivering their presentations to others outside of the classroom (such as family members or friends outside of class or school) in order to receive more varied feedback on their performances.

Focus

Summary

Students are encouraged to explore a variety of poems and novels covering a range of themes, including the inspiring beauty of nature, life's lessons, and the value of family.

Teach

Literary History ☆

Favorite Poem Project
Started in 1997 by former poet laureate Robert Pinsky, the Favorite Poem Project is a series of print anthologies and documentaries in which Americans from every walk of life present their favorite poems. In its first year, 18,000 people volunteered. The videos became a popular feature on PBS's *The News Hour with Jim Lehrer* and can be viewed online at www.favoritepoem.org.

Independent Reading

Poetry and Novels

AS YOU HAVE SEEN IN THIS UNIT, POEMS DO EVERYTHING FROM ASKING questions of identity to celebrating nature. They can be short, playful, and lively or long, measured, and serious. They can take you deeper inside yourself or well beyond the world you know. For more poetry on a range of themes, try the three suggestions on these pages. For novels that address the Big Ideas of *Nature Inspires, Life Lessons,* and *The Strength of Family,* try the titles from the Glencoe Literature Library on the next page.

Poems for Life: Famous People Select Their Favorite Poem and Say Why It Inspires Them

compiled by the Grade 5 Classes from the Nightingale-Bamford School ☆

Determined to raise money for a good cause, a group of students in New York City mailed letters to a host of famous people. "We were wondering if you would like to send us a copy of your favorite poem with an explanation of why you chose it," they wrote. Fifty renowned writers, musicians, politicians, actors, and television personalities responded. The result is this fascinating collection.

This Same Sky: A Collection of Poems from around the World

selected by Naomi Shihab Nye

Nearly every culture has a poetic tradition, and, as this anthology reflects, all over the world, poets address similar subjects: childhood, family, and the beauty of the natural world. In addition to these topics, some poems in *This Same Sky* discuss the nature of poetry. Others explore political topics. As a whole, this collection of 129 poets from 68 countries celebrates both the diversity of their origins and the similarity of their feelings and aspirations.

Speaking Practice

Present a Poem Begin this activity with a class discussion about what makes a particular poet appealing to readers. Encourage students to consider which poem is their favorite poet and why they are drawn to this poet's work. Then ask students to choose a poem by their favorite poet and prepare a short presentation in which they will read the poem and explain to the class exactly what they like about the poet and the poem. Students should address the poetic elements of form and style employed by the poet, as well as the student's emotional response to the poem.

GLENCOE LITERATURE LIBRARY

High Elk's Treasure

by Virginia Driving Hawk Sneve

Nature inspires Joe as his love of horses leads him to a new understanding of the Lakota people.

The Chosen

by Chaim Potok

Two young Jewish men form an enduring friendship as they learn lessons from life.

The Glory Field

by Walter Dean Myers

Over 241 years, a family's strength is tested as they journey away from and back to a small plot of land.

CRITICS' CORNER

"[W]hat Ogden Nash does is take words apart to see what makes them tick, and put them together so that they click. And not necessarily in the condition in which he found them. [Nash] demonstrates that our mother tongue can be made to behave in a manner hardly becoming a mother, but irreproachably amusing. [In his work] the English language is not only flexible; it is double jointed, ambidextrous, telescopic, kaleidoscopic, and slightly demented."

—Lisle Bell, *New York Herald Tribune Books*

Under Water with Ogden Nash

by Ogden Nash ☆

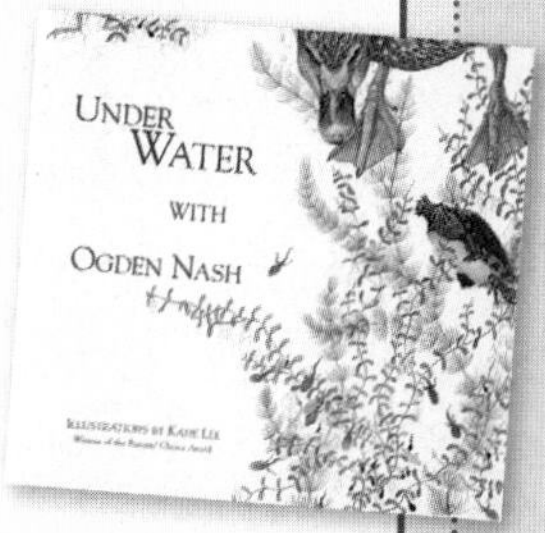

In this collection of 26 delightfully humorous poems, Ogden Nash writes about sea creatures such as the turtle, the jellyfish, the squid, and the shark. Each poem is sweetly surprising, slightly laughable, and utterly original. Detailed color drawings by award-winning zoological illustrator Katie Lee are paired with the poems.

Write a Review

Read one of the books listed on these pages and write a review of it for your classmates. Be sure to explain why other students might enjoy the book, or offer suggestions on how they might overcome difficulties in reading the book. Present your review to the class.

Teach

Literary History ☆

Ogden Nash Nash (1902–1971) was brought up in Savannah, Georgia, and several other eastern cities. He began his career as a book editor and children's author before going on to become one of the twentieth century's masters of light verse. Known for their whimsy and clever word play, his poems achieved great popular success.

Glencoe Literature Library

Glencoe Literature Library offers an extensive collection of hardcover books that help you encourage your students to read independently. Choose among the more than 120 full-length literary works—novels, novellas, plays, and nonfiction. Each book includes related readings from a broad range of genres. Go to www.glencoe.com for more information.

Writing Skills

Students' reviews should address one book mentioned in the Independent Reading feature and should include reasons why others might like the book as well as tips on how to overcome difficulties reading it.

For access to all study guides for the Glencoe Literature Library, see the Literature Library Teacher Resources CD-ROM.

To create customized reading lists from a database of more than 30,000 titles, use BookLink K–12 CD-ROM.

Approaching Level

DIFFERENTIATED INSTRUCTION

Established Encourage students to explore poetry from a culture of their choice. Students should conduct Internet or library research and choose one poem to discuss in a short paragraph. In their paragraphs, students should explain what elements of the poem reflect a certain culture and why they have chosen to highlight these elements of the poem.

Focus

Bellringer Options

Say: Test-taking strategies can be helpful on standardized tests, such as the SAT, or on subject-matter tests administered by your teachers. Learning test-taking strategies and applying them to any test that you encounter will help you be a more successful test taker. Have students discuss tests they have taken recently and the different test-taking strategies they have used to improve their scores.

Teach

Assessment Explain that the Assessment is intended to reinforce general test-taking strategies. Students will first read two selections and answer comprehension, context-clue, and inference questions. Then they answer ten paragraph-improvement questions. Finally, they will respond to an essay question.

Assessment

English Language Arts

Reading: Poetry, Fiction, Image

Carefully read the following passages. Use context clues to help define any words with which you are unfamiliar. Pay close attention to the author's main idea and use of literary devices. Then answer the questions on page 608.

"Possum Crossing" by Nikki Giovanni

Backing out the driveway
the car lights cast an eerie glow
in the morning fog centering
on movement in the rain slick street

Hitting brakes I anticipate a squirrel or a cat or sometimes
a little raccoon
I once braked for a blind little mole who try though he did
could not escape the cat toying with his life
Mother-to-be possum occasionally lopes home . . . being
naturally . . . slow her condition makes her even more ginger

We need a sign POSSUM CROSSING to warn coffee-gurgling neighbors:
we share the streets with more than trucks and vans and
railroad crossings

All birds being the living kin of dinosaurs
think themselves invincible and pay no heed
to the rolling wheels while they dine
on an unlucky rabbit

I hit brakes for the flutter of the lights hoping it's not a deer
or a skunk or a groundhog
coffee splashes over the cup which I quickly put away from me
and into the empty passenger seat
I look . . .
relieved and exasperated . . .
to discover I have just missed a big wet leaf
struggling . . . to lift itself into the wind
and live

Reading Practice

Visualize Encourage students to form mental pictures as they read. Instruct them to visualize, or try to see the settings, animals, and events described by Giovanni and Twain. **Say: As you read each detail, take a moment to add it to the picture in your mind.**

When students finish reading, **Ask: According to the text and your mental picture, what is the setting like? What do the animals look like? What do they do?** *(Responses will vary.)* Explain to students that visualizing is one way to help them understand what they read.

from *"The Laborious Ant"* by Mark Twain

Now and then, while we rested, we watched the laborious ant at his work. I found nothing new in him—certainly nothing to change my opinion of him. It seems to me that in the matter of intellect the ant must be a strangely overrated bird. During many summers, now, I have watched him, when I ought to have been in better business, and I have not yet come across a living ant that seemed to have any more sense than a dead one. I refer to the ordinary ant, of course; I have had no experience of those wonderful Swiss and African ones which vote, keep drilled armies, hold slaves, and dispute about religion. Those particular ants may be all that the naturalist paints them, but I am persuaded that the average ant is a sham. I admit his industry, of course; he is the hardest working creature in the world—when anybody is looking—but his leather-headedness is the point I make against him. He goes out foraging, he makes a capture, and then what does he do? Go home? No—he goes anywhere but home. He doesn't know where home is. His home may be only three feet away—no matter, he can't find it. He makes his capture, as I have said; it is generally something which can be of no sort of use to himself or anybody else; it is usually seven times bigger than it ought to be; he hunts out the awkwardest place to take hold of it; he lifts it bodily up in the air by main force, and starts: not toward home, but in the opposite direction; not calmly and wisely, but with a frantic haste which is wasteful of his strength; he fetches up against a pebble, and instead of going around it, he climbs over it backwards, dragging his booty after him, tumbles down on the other side, jumps up in a passion, kicks the dust off his clothes, moistens his hands, grabs his property viciously, yanks it this way then that, shoves it ahead of him a moment, turns tail and lugs it after him another moment, gets madder and madder, then presently hoists it into the air and goes tearing away in an entirely new direction; comes to a weed; it never occurs to him to go around it; no, he must climb it; and he does climb it, dragging his worthless property to the top—which is as bright a thing to do as it would be for me to carry a sack of flour from Heidelberg to Paris by way of Strasburg steeple; when he gets up there he finds that that is not the place; takes a cursory glance at the scenery and either climbs down again or tumbles down, and starts off once more—as usual, in a new direction. At the end of half an hour, he fetches up within six inches of the place he started from and lays his burden down; meantime he has been over all the ground for two yards around, and climbed all the weeds and pebbles he came across.

LOG ON Literature Online

Assessment For additional test practice, go to glencoe.com and enter QuickPass code GL49787u3.

Teach

Literary Element

Humor Point out that Mark Twain's humor, in most of his writing, focused on deflating pompous, self-important, and arrogant people. His sympathy was always for the lowly. The humor in "The Laborious Ant" does not rely on "punch lines," "slapstick" comedy, plays on words (puns), or insults. Encourage students to notice, as they read the essay, what makes it funny.

Approaching Level

DIFFERENTIATED INSTRUCTION

Established Help less proficient readers better understand the similarities and differences in the two selections by having them list details from both in a Venn diagram like the one shown. Remind students to also consider the theme presented in each selection. Students may work with partners to complete their diagrams.

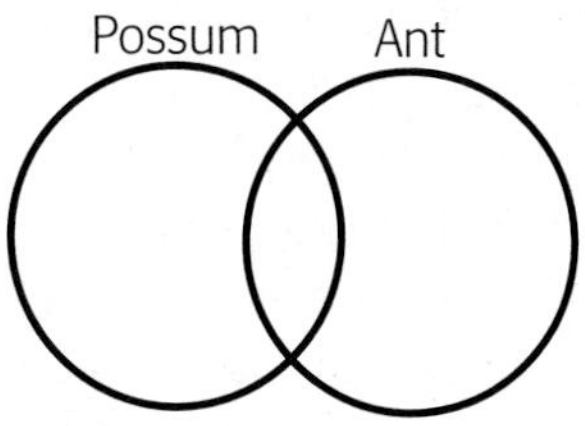

Assess

Reading

1. C is the correct answer because no symbol, simile, or end rhyme appears in this line. The car lights casting an eerie glow constitutes a vivid sensory detail, or image. DOK 2
2. H is the correct answer because the possum is described as "Mother-to-be" in line 9. DOK 1
3. D is the correct answer because the author clearly conveys concern for the safety of animals. DOK 3
4. F is the correct answer because the use of the pronoun *I* indicates the first-person point of view. DOK 3
5. D is the correct answer because the poem has no consistent rhyme, meter, or syllabic pattern. DOK 2
6. J is the correct answer. Since *drilled* refers to *armies,* this option makes the most sense. DOK 1
7. A is the correct answer. Twain disparages ants. DOK 2
8. F is the correct answer. Twain claims that the ants' rapid movement shows not industry but that they are lost. DOK 2
9. A is the correct answer. The author pokes fun at his subject. DOK 3
10. G is the correct answer. The author finds ants to have an overrated reputation. DOK 2
11. A is the correct answer. No other option reflects themes found in both works. DOK 4

Items 1–5 apply to "Possum Crossing."

1. What literary device is used in line 2?
   A. symbol
   B. simile
   C. imagery
   D. end rhyme

2. What is the "condition" referred to in line 10?
   F. danger
   G. travel
   H. pregnancy
   J. raining

3. Which word best describes the overall mood?
   A. fear
   B. hope
   C. sadness
   D. compassion

4. What is the point of view of this poem?
   F. first person
   G. second person
   H. third-person limited
   J. third-person omniscient

5. What is the form of this poem?
   A. haiku
   B. iambic pentameter
   C. sonnet
   D. free verse

Items 6–10 apply to "The Laborious Ant."

6. What do you think "drilled" in line 14 means?
   F. burrowed
   G. thrown
   H. beaten
   J. trained

7. What is the narrator's attitude toward the "average" ant, as expressed in line 18?
   A. disdainful
   B. hopeful
   C. respectful
   D. sorrowful

8. According to Twain, why does the ant move as it does?
   F. It cannot find its way.
   G. It follows the others.
   H. It protects its home.
   J. It always heads south.

9. What is the overall tone of this passage?
   A. comic
   B. angry
   C. sad
   D. sarcastic

10. What is the main idea of the selection?
    F. Ants are the most fascinating of all creatures.
    G. Ants appear to lack intelligence.
    H. People are really no more important than small creatures, such as ants.
    J. Life is a constant struggle between humankind and nature.

Items 11 and 12 apply to "Possum Crossing" and "The Laborious Ant."

11. Which of the following themes appears in both selections?
    A. fascination with living things
    B. love of all animals
    C. protecting endangered species
    D. the use of the environment

12. According to the selections, what belief about nature do Giovanni and Twain share?
    F. It should be tamed.
    G. It should be appreciated.
    H. It should be ignored.
    J. It should be defended.

Short Answer **To complete this item, refer to "Possum Crossing" and "The Laborious Ant."**

13. What themes and purposes do these two selections have in common? How do they differ? Be sure to present evidence from both selections to support your argument.

12. G is the correct answer. Both authors appreciate nature, though in different ways. DOK 4
13. Answers will vary but should include text to support the intentions of both authors to appreciate or increase awareness of living things. DOK 4

Vocabulary Skills: Sentence Completion

For each item in the Vocabulary Skills section, choose the word that best completes the sentence.

1. After studying abroad, Alex felt that everything back home was ______ and lacking in excitement.
   A. ceaseless
   B. dreary
   C. keen
   D. detached

2. The knight raised his ______ to toast the king.
   F. rosin
   G. chalice
   H. bog
   J. host

3. Geoff ______ on many hot summer days at his landscaping job.
   A. diverged
   B. isolated
   C. toiled
   D. gelled

4. Hiking the 2,174-mile Appalachian Trail takes ______ and planning.
   F. forethought
   G. calligraphy
   H. plait
   J. chalice

5. My mother wore ______ when she married my father.
   A. chalice
   B. supplicant
   C. brocade
   D. rosin

6. The speaker's anger was evident in his responses to the ______ accusations of the audience.
   F. detached
   G. archetypal
   H. belligerent
   J. isolated

7. As a life-long resident of New York City, Rob felt ______ when he moved to a remote town in Maine.
   A. reverent
   B. keen
   C. gelled
   D. isolated

8. The ______ prayed earnestly for forgiveness.
   F. supplicant
   G. brocade
   H. rosin
   J. host

9. After hosting a huge graduation party, Tom craved ______ and quiet.
   A. solitude
   B. bog
   C. gale
   D. brocade

10. When experiencing stress, students should not ______ themselves further by worrying.
    F. toil
    G. sow
    H. diverge
    J. tax

English Learners

DIFFERENTIATED INSTRUCTION

Early Advanced English language learners may have difficulty identifying and correcting misplaced or dangling modifiers. **Say:** **A word or phrase that makes the meaning of another word or phrase more specific is called a modifier. The position of a modifier in a sentence is very important. Unless a modifier is near the word or phrase it describes, the meaning of the sentence may be unclear or incorrect.**

Review the paragraphs on page 609 and point out sentences that have modifier errors. *(She barks and dances twirling through the foyer so glad to see me.)* Discuss some ways to correct the errors.

Assess

Vocabulary Skills

1. B is the correct answer. The phrase *lacking in excitement* implies no other option but *dreary.* DOK 1
2. G is the correct answer. One definition of *chalice* is "cup." No other option makes sense in this context. DOK 1
3. C is the correct answer. *Toiled* is a synonym for *worked.* DOK 1
4. F is the correct answer. The word *planning* indicates that this is the correct answer. DOK 1
5. C is the correct answer. None of the other options are something one would wear. DOK 1
6. H is the correct answer. The fact that the speaker is angry about accusations indicates that this is the correct answer. DOK 1
7. D is the correct answer. The contrast between a city and a remote area indicates that this is the correct answer. DOK 1
8. F is the correct answer. The verb *prayed* suggests no other option but *supplicant.* DOK 1
9. A is the correct answer. The key word here is *quiet.* Only *solitude* makes sense in this context. DOK 1
10. J is the correct answer. The word *worrying* indicates that this is the correct answer. DOK 1

Assess

Grammar and Writing Skills

1. B is the correct answer. A comma should never separate a verb from its object, in this case the noun clause *how much easier life might be if I were my dog.* DOK 1
2. H is the correct answer. The sentence should be *She has very few cares in life.* The verb must agree in number with the singular pronoun. DOK 1
3. B is the correct answer. The three items in the compound subject are in parallel form. DOK 1
4. G is the correct answer. A finite verb form is needed in the main clause, and the subjunctive mood of the verb is needed when a supposition or a hypothetical case is expressed. DOK 1
5. C is the correct answer. *Hurrying from one obligation to the next* should appear before *we,* not following *things,* to make the meaning clear. DOK 1

Grammar and Writing Skills: Paragraph Improvement

Read carefully through the following paragraphs from the first draft of a student's reflective essay. Pay close attention to the student's use of verb tense, commas, adjectives, and parallel construction, and watch for subject-verb agreement and dangling participles. Then answer the questions below.

(1) *I often think, how much easier life might be if I were my dog.* (2) *She have very few cares in life.* (3) *A full bowl of food, an open dog door, and a warm place to nap are all it takes to make her happy.* (4) *Life be much simpler if that was all we needed.* (5) *We often miss out on the little things hurrying from one obligation to the next.*

(6) *Without the pressures of work and paying bills, we might all be able to give the unconditional love that she does.* (7) *Every day she waits by the door when the car pulls into the driveway.* (8) *She barks and dances twirling through the foyer so glad to see me.* (9) *She doesn't mind if I haven't done a single thing right all day.* (10) *Wouldn't it be nice if everyone were so horribly happy to see you?*

1. Which would be the best way to revise sentence 1?
   - **A.** Insert a comma after *be.*
   - **B.** Delete the comma after *think.*
   - **C.** Change *were* to *was.*
   - **D.** No change is needed.

2. Which grammatical error appears in sentence 2?
   - **F.** a dangling participle
   - **G.** lack of parallel construction
   - **H.** lack of subject-verb agreement
   - **J.** a missing comma

3. Which grammar element appears in sentence 3?
   - **A.** principal and subordinate clauses
   - **B.** parallel structure
   - **C.** pronoun-antecedent agreement
   - **D.** adverbs

4. Which is the best revision of sentence 4?
   - **F.** Life would be much simpler, if that was all we needed.
   - **G.** Life would be much simpler if that were all we needed.
   - **H.** Life is much simpler, if that is all we need.
   - **J.** Life could be much simpler if that was all we needed.

5. Which grammar error appears in sentence 5?
   - **A.** lack of subject-verb agreement
   - **B.** omission of a comma
   - **C.** misplaced modifier
   - **D.** wrong verb tense

Writing Practice

Understanding the Essay Point out that the author of the essay on page 609 compares a dog's life to a human being's. Ask students to reread the paragraphs and to create a comparison chart like the one that follows, listing differences between the two lives, according to the writer.

A Dog's Life	A Human's Life
Few cares	Hurrying from one obligation to the next
Full bowl of food	Work
Nap	Paying bills
Unconditional love	
Chasing tail	

6. Which is the best revision of sentence 6?
   F. No change is needed.
   G. We might all be able to give the unconditional love she does without the pressures of work and paying bills.
   H. Without the pressure of work and paying bills, we all might give her unconditional love.
   J. Without the pressures of work and paying bills, we might all be able to give the unconditional love that she do.

7. Which is the best revision of sentence 7?
   A. Every day, she waits by the door when the car pulls into the driveway.
   B. The car pulls into the driveway every day; she waits by the door.
   C. Every day, when the car pulls into the driveway, she waits by the door.
   D. No change is needed.

8. Which is the best revision of sentence 8?
   F. So glad to see me, she barks and dances, twirling through the foyer.
   G. She barks and dances, twirling through the foyer so glad to see me.
   H. Twirling through the foyer, she barks and dances so glad to see me.
   J. No change is needed.

9. Which of the following is the best title for this essay?
   A. "Why My Dog Is Better Than Yours"
   B. "The Importance of Pet Rescue"
   C. "A Dog's Life"
   D. "Dancing and Twirling"

10. Which syntax error appears in sentence 10?
   F. improper connotation
   G. inappropriate adjective
   H. illogical construction
   J. offensive language

Assess

Grammar and Writing Skills

6. F is the correct answer. There is no error in this sentence. DOK 1

7. D is the correct answer. There is no error in this sentence. DOK 1

8. F is the correct answer. The meaning of the sentence is unclear without commas to set off the subordinate clause and with a misplaced modifier. DOK 1

9. C is the correct answer. No other option addresses the thesis of the essay. DOK 3

10. G is the correct answer. The intensifier *very* is more suitable than *horribly* for modifying a noun with a positive denotation. DOK 1

English Learners

DIFFERENTIATED INSTRUCTION

Intermediate Tell students that context can help them figure out the meaning of unfamiliar words. Encourage them to look for these types of context clues as they complete the items above:

- a synonym or an explanation of the unknown word
- a reference to what the word is or is not like
- a general topic associated with the word
- a description or action associated with the word

Write this sentence completion activity on the board:

Some people contend that teenagers are irresponsible, but in fact most are quite _____.

A polite
B reliable
C respectful
D intelligent

Students should choose the word that means the opposite of *irresponsible.* Explain that the words *irresponsible* and *but* offer clues.

UNIT FOUR

Skills Scope and Sequence

Readability Scores Key: Dale-Chall/DRP/Lexile

PART 1: The Power of Love

Selections and Features	Literary Elements
Unit Introduction pp. 612–618	Act and Scene **SE** p. 614 Stage Directions **SE** p. 614 Cast of Characters **SE** p. 614 Tragedy **SE** p. 615 Chorus **SE** p. 615 Comedy **SE** p. 615 Farce **TE** p. 617
Literary Focus pp. 620–621	Tragedy **TE** p. 620 Tragic Hero **SE** p. 621 Dramatic Devices **SE** p. 621
Literary History pp. 622–623	Shakespearean Drama SE pp. 622-623
Drama The Tragedy of Romeo and Juliet, Act 1, by William Shakespeare pp. 624–654	Foil **SE** p. 625 Oxymoron **TE** p. 635 Rhyming Couplet **TE** p. 644 Figurative Language **TE** p. 647
Drama The Tragedy of Romeo and Juliet, Act 2, by William Shakespeare pp. 655–678	Figurative Language **SE** p. 655 Stage Directions **TE** p. 656 Characterization **TE** p. 661 Similes **TE** p. 662 Puns **TE** p. 668 Foil **TE** p. 673
Drama The Tragedy of Romeo and Juliet, Act 3, by William Shakespeare pp. 679–706	Monologue, Soliloquy, and Aside **SE** p. 679 Tone **TE** p. 680 Oxymoron **TE** p. 688 Suspense **TE** p. 693 Tragedy **TE** p. 695 Symbol **TE** p. 696 Atmosphere **TE** p. 696

Reading Skills and Strategies	Vocabulary	Writing / Grammar	Speaking, Listening, and Viewing
Analyze Satire **SE** p. 616		Write a Scene **TE** p. 616 Note Taking **SE** p. 618 Write Dialogue **SE** p. 618 Write a Review **TE** p. 618	Staged Reading **TE** p. 614 Discussion **SE** p. 618
Analyze Plays **TE** p. 621	Word Origins **TE** p. 620		
Preview **TE** p. 622		Write an Essay **TE** p. 622	
Summarize **SE** p. 625 Visualize **TE** p. 627 Paraphrase **TE** p. 636 Connect **TE** p. 644 Visualize **TE** p. 646	Synonyms **SE** p. 654	Possessives **TE** p. 628 Subject-Verb Order **TE** p. 638 Write a Response **TE** p. 642 Write a Description **TE** p. 644 Complements **TE** p. 652 Write a Dialogue **SE** p. 654	Perform a Scene **TE** p. 630 Oral Interpretation **TE** p. 648
Make Inferences About Characters **SE** p. 655 Interpret **TE** p. 658 Question **TE** p. 666	Context Clues **SE** p. 678	Correlative Conjunctions **TE** p. 656 Intensive Pronouns **TE** p. 664 Write a Persuasive Essay **TE** p. 670 Interjections **TE** p. 674 Write an Annotation **SE** p. 678	Analyze Media **TE** p. 660 Readers Theater **TE** p. 672
Compare and Contrast Scenes **SE** p. 679 Predict **TE** p. 680 Interpret **TE** p. 681 Connect **TE** p. 684 Understand Sequence **TE** p. 700 Analyze Characterization **TE** p. 704	Analogies **SE** p. 706	Write a Response to Literature **TE** p. 682 Write a Research Report **TE** p. 684 Write Using Hyperbole **TE** p. 686 Appositive Phrases **TE** p. 688 Write a Poem or Journal Entry **TE** p. 690 Write a Persuasive Letter **TE** p. 698 Write an Essay **SE** p. 706	Dialogue **TE** p. 680 Discussion **TE** p. 692 Analyze Art **SE** p. 694

Readability Scores Key: Dale-Chall/DRP/Lexile

PART 1: The Power of Love *(continued)*

Selections and Features	Literary Elements
Drama The Tragedy of Romeo and Juliet, Act 4, by William Shakespeare pp. 707–723	Irony **SE** p. 707 Comic Relief **TE** p. 712 Tone **TE** p. 714 Figurative Language **TE** p. 719
Drama The Tragedy of Romeo and Juliet, Act 5, by William Shakespeare pp. 724–743	Tragedy **SE** p. 724 Irony **TE** p. 727 Theme **TE** p. 727 Style (review) **SE** p. 742
Informational Text TIME: A Long Overdue Encore, by Barry Hillenbrand pp. 744–747	
Grammar Workshop p. 748	
Comparing Literature **The Taxi** (poem), by Amy Lowell **Counting the Beats** (poem), by Robert Graves **The Princess and All the Kingdom** (fable), by Pär Lagerkvist **7.0/54/910** pp. 749–754	Theme **SE** p. 749 Mood **TE** p. 751

Reading Skills and Strategies	Vocabulary	Writing Grammar	Speaking, Listening, and Viewing
Interpret Imagery **SE** p. 707 Predict **TE** p. 708 Make Inferences **TE** p. 715	Context Clues **SE** p. 723	Write in the Active Voice **TE** p. 710 Prepositional Phrases **TE** p. 714 Write a Character Sketch **TE** p. 716 Write a Persuasive Essay **TE** p. 718 Linking Verbs **TE** p. 722 Write a Journal Entry **SE** p. 723	Dialogue **TE** p. 720
Make Inferences About Theme **SE** p. 724 Interpret **TE** p. 725 Draw Conclusions **TE** p. 730 Evaluate **TE** p. 737	Word Parts **SE** p. 742 Academic Vocabulary **SE** p. 742	Pronouns **TE** p. 728 Write a Research Report **TE** p. 732 Subject-Verb Agreement **TE** p. 734 Write a Description **TE** p. 736 Write an Editorial **SE** p. 743	Oral Reading **TE** p. 730
Preview **SE** p. 744 Identify Sequence **SE** p. 744		Write a Description **TE** p. 746 Write a Summary **SE** p. 747	
		Verb Tense **SE** p. 748	
Compare and Contrast **SE** p. 749	Multiple-Meaning Words **TE** p. 752	Write a Paragraph **SE** p. 753	Discussion **SE** p. 754

Readability Scores Key: Dale-Chall/DRP/Lexile

PART 2: Awkward Encounters

Selections and Features	Literary Elements
Literary Focus pp. 756–757	Comedy and Modern Drama **SE** pp. 756–757 Satire **TE** p. 756 Act and Scene **SE** p. 757 Dialogue **SE** p. 757 Stage Directions **SE** p. 757 Irony **SE** p. 757
Drama The Bear, by Anton Chekhov pp. 758–772	Farce **SE** p. 759 Repetition **TE** p. 762 Dialogue (review) **SE** p. 771
Drama The Hitchhiker, by Lucille Fletcher pp. 773–787	Idiom **SE** p. 774 Onomatopoeia **TE** p. 784
Vocabulary Workshop p. 788	
Drama The Leader, by Eugène Ionesco pp. 789–799	Stage Directions **SE** p. 790 Satire **TE** p. 793 Farce (review) **SE** p. 798
Literary Perspective How I Came to the Theater *from* **Conversations with Eugène Ionesco,** by Claude Bonnefoy **9.2/not scorable/1000** pp. 800–803	
Writing Workshop pp. 804–811	
Speaking, Listening, and Viewing Workshop p. 812–813	
Independent Reading pp. 814–815	
Assessment pp. 816–821	

Reading Skills and Strategies	Vocabulary	Writing Grammar	Speaking, Listening, and Viewing
Identify Elements **TE** p. 757		Define Comedy **SE** p. 757	
Analyze Cause-and-Effect Relationships **SE** p. 759 Make Predictions **TE** p. 768	Word Study **TE** p. 762 Antonyms **SE** p. 772 Academic Vocabulary **SE** p. 772	End Punctuation **TE** p. 766 Write a Dialogue **SE** p. 772	Analyze Art **SE** p. 765
Make and Verify Predictions **SE** p. 774 Analyze Motivation **TE** p. 780	Word Usage **SE** p. 787	Write a Character Sketch **TE** p. 778 Dashes **TE** p. 782 Write a Dramatic Scene **SE** p. 787	Presentation **SE** p. 774
	Denotation and Connotation **SE** p. 788	Keep a Word Journal **TE** p. 788	
Draw Conclusions About Author's Meaning **SE** p. 790 Interpret **TE** p. 792	Context Clues **SE** p. 799	Adverbs **TE** p. 790 Use Interjections **TE** p. 794	Performance **SE** p. 799
Identify Assumptions and Ambiguities **SE** p. 800 Sequence **TE** p. 801 Interpret **TE** p. 801		Write a Character Sketch **TE** p. 800	
		Write a Literary Criticism Essay **SE** p. 805 Prewrite **SE** p. 807 Draft **SE** p. 808 Revise **SE** p. 810	
			Oral Response to Literature **SE** p. 812
		Write a Short Essay **TE** p. 814 Write a Review **SE** p. 815	
		Use Apostrophes **TE** p. 820 Write an Essay **SE** p. 821	

UNIT FOUR

Focus

Bellringer Options

Literature Launchers Pre-Reading Videos DVD: Unit 4

Daily Language Practice Transparency 71

Or **ask:** What was the first role you played? Prompt students to remember plays they did in kindergarten or skits they did as children with their friends.

Ask: If you could play any character, who would it be? Why?

For school-to-home activities, see Unit 4 Teaching Resources Book, pp. 5–11.

For students who would profit from idependent novel study, see Novel Companion, pp. 163–230.

Comedia dell'Arte, 1991. Andre Rouillard. Acrylic on canvas, 73 x 100 cm. Private collection.

View the Art Commedia dell'arte, a type of theater performance that involves improvisation, began in Italy in the 1400s and remained popular through the 1700s. What emotions are expressed by the figures in this painting? ★

612

Unit Introduction Skills

Looking Ahead

Literary Elements
- Drama (SE pp. 614–615)
- Literary Analysis (SE pp. 616–617)

Reading Skills
- Guide to Reading Drama (SE p. 618)
- Choral Reading Drama (TE p. 615)
- Read Satire (TE p. 616)

Listening/Speaking/Viewing Skills
- Play Discussion (SE p. 618)
- Staged Reading (TE p. 614)

Writing Skills/Grammar
- Dialogue (SE p. 618)
- Write a Review (TE p. 618)

UNIT FOUR

Drama

Looking Ahead

What do horror movies, soap operas, sitcoms, and *Romeo and Juliet* have in common? They are all examples of drama—stories told mainly through dialogue and the actions of the characters. Drama differs from other genres in that it is written to be performed by actors in front of an audience. Although it shares some literary elements with other genres, it also has its own unique elements, including comedy, tragedy, and dramatic conventions such as stage directions, acts, and scenes.

Each part in Unit Four focuses on a Big Idea that can help you connect the selections to your life.

PREVIEW	Big Ideas	Literary Focus
PART 1	The Power of Love	Tragedy
PART 2	Awkward Encounters	Comedy and Modern Drama

613

UNIT FOUR

Focus

Summary

The unit discusses acts and scenes, dialogue, stage directions, tragedy, chorus, comedy, and irony in drama. It includes quotes from writers on reading drama as well as a literary analysis of *The Importance of Being Earnest.*

View the Art ★

Answer: *Sadness, rapture, excitement, longing*

Commedia dell'arte originated in Renaissance Italy, where roving bands of actors improvised performances for the public. The costumed figures in Rouillard's painting suggest the stereotyped roles that characterized this form of drama.

Ask: What do you think the figures represent? *(Roles such as the clown, the damsel, and the melancholy youth)*

For diagnostic and end-of-unit assessment, see Assessment Resources, pp. 19–24 and 231–232.

Unit Resources

Print Materials

- Unit 4 Teaching Resources, pp. 1–180
- Interactive Read and Write (On Level, Approaching, EL), pp. 167–226
- Novel Companion, pp. 163–230
- Bellringer Option Transparencies: Selection Focus 30; Daily Language Practice 71–80
- Literary Element Transparencies 28, 106
- Assessment Resources, Unit Assessment, pp. 231–232
- Assessment Resources, Selection Assessment, pp. 163–184

Technology

- TeacherWorks Plus CD
- StudentWorks Plus CD
- Literature Launchers: Pre-Reading Videos DVD, Unit 4
- Literature Online
- Interactive Vocabulary CD-ROM
- Listening Library CD-ROM
- ExamView CD-ROM
- Skill Level Up! CD-ROM

Teach

Literary Element 1

Stage Directions Discourage students from glossing over or skipping the stage directions when reading a play. Remind them that stage directions often contain crucial information and will help them visualize the action.

Cultural History ☆

Greek Drama Greek drama evolved out of the choral odes in religious festivals. Early Greek plots and characters were drawn from the Greek myths. Unlike modern theater, Greek drama was a core public activity, not a business enterprise.

Learning Objectives

For pages 612–618

In studying this text, you will focus on the following objectives:

Literary Study:
Analyzing literary genres.
Connecting to the literature.

Genre Focus: Drama

How does drama differ from other genres of literature?

What is your favorite television drama series, and why do you like to watch it? Perhaps you identify strongly with one of the characters. Maybe the plots are intriguing, or you find the dialogue funny. You'll find these elements—and others—in the dramas you read as well.

Elements of Drama

Acts and Scenes

In plays, **acts** and **scenes** are the major divisions, similar to paragraphs in a short story or stanzas in a poem. Most plays have two or more acts, but short plays often have only one. Acts are often further divided into scenes.

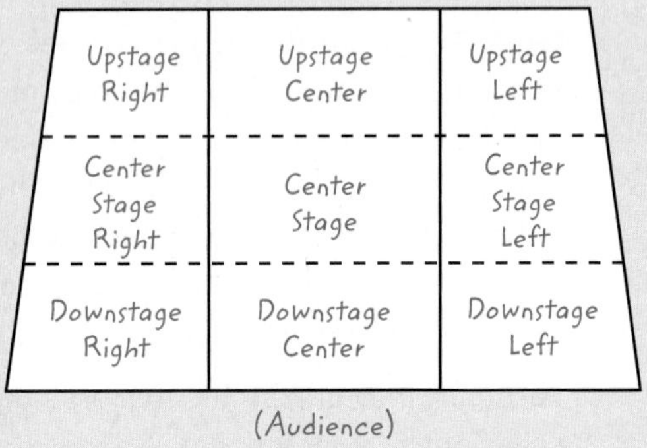

Stage Directions

Stage directions specify such things as the details of the setting and scenery; how the characters should look, speak, behave; and when and where actors should appear on stage. Stage directions describe locations on the stage from the perspective of the actor. Thus, "stage left" refers to the right side of the stage as you look at it from the audience. 1

Characters

The **cast** of characters is listed at the beginning of a play. Sometimes the cast list includes a brief description of one or more characters. As in other genres, a character's words and actions reveal further information about him or her.

YELÉNA IVÁNOVNA POPÓVA: a widow with dimples and a large estate

GRIGÓRY STEPÁNOVICH SMÍRNOFF: landowner, in his thirties

LUKÁ: an elderly servant

—Anton Chekhov, **from** ***The Bear***

Speaking Practice

SMALL GROUP **Staged Reading** Have small groups of students choose poems from Unit 3 to present to the class. Instruct students to design and perform a staged reading of their poem, using techniques specific to drama, including stage directions, costumes, and music. Students should write lines for a chorus as well as for individual speakers. Follow each presentation with a discussion.

Ask: Was that performance comedy or tragedy? Why? *(Answers will vary.)*

Tragedy

Tragedy

Tragedy is drama in which the main character, called the **tragic hero,** suffers a fall from good fortune. This usually occurs because of some **tragic flaw,** such as pride or indecisiveness. Well known tragedies include Sophocles' *Oedipus Rex* and William Shakespeare's *Hamlet* and *Macbeth.* In *Romeo and Juliet,* Friar Lawrence identifies Romeo's tragic flaw—irrationality and impulsive behavior.

FRIAR. Hold thy desperate hand.
Art thou a man? Thy form cries out thou art;
Thy tears are womanish, thy wild acts denote
The unreasonable fury of a beast.
Unseemly woman in a seeming man,
And ill-beseeming beast in seeming both.

—William Shakespeare, **from *Romeo and Juliet* Act 3, Scene 3**

☆ Chorus

The tragedy originated in Greece. The earliest productions included choral groups that sang hymns in praise of the gods. Soon Greek dramatists emerged and introduced other actors, as well as dialogue in early plays. As plays evolved, the actors became more significant to the plot than the chorus. During the Elizabethan era in England, the **chorus** was portrayed by one actor, who often spoke the prologue and epilogue to the play. Unlike the other actors, who engaged in dialogue, the chorus spoke directly to the audience.

[The Chorus enters and addresses the audience]

CHORUS. Now old desire doth in his deathbed
lie,
And young affection gapes to be his heir;
That fair for which love groan'd for and
would die,
With tender Juliet match'd, is now not fair.

—William Shakespeare, **from *Romeo and Juliet* Act 2, Prologue** **2**

Comedy and Modern Drama

Comedy

Comedy is drama that deals with light and amusing subjects or with serious subjects in a light, familiar, or satirical manner. A **satire** is a kind of comedy that ridicules people, practices, or institutions in order to reveal their failings. A **farce** is a kind of comedy that places flat, one-dimensional characters in ridiculous situations.

LOG ON **Literature** Online

Literature and Reading For more selections in this genre, go to glencoe.com and enter QuickPass code GL49787u4.

ANNOUNCER. The leader's coming. He approaches. He's bending. He's unbending. . . . Ah . . . ! He's signing autographs. The leader is stroking a hedgehog, a superb hedgehog! The crowd applauds. He's dancing, with the hedgehog in his hand. He's embracing his dancer. Hurrah! Hurrah!

—Eugène Ionesco, **from *The Leader***

Teach

Reading Strategy 2

Choral Reading Guide the class in a choral reading. First, have one student read the Shakespeare chorus excerpt, then have the class read it as a group.

Ask: How does having a group instead of an individual read affect the audience? Discuss the differences between the two readings.

APPROACHING **Ask:** In what way does reading drama aloud help you understand it? *(Reading aloud conveys emotion and creates mood and tone.)*

Approaching Level

DIFFERENTIATED INSTRUCTION

Established Auditory learners will benefit from hearing choral readings. Invite students to read the chorus excerpt several times, experimenting with volume, intensity, and the number of people reading each line. Discuss the impact of the different readings.

Emerging Students may be unfamiliar with words in the chorus. Have them find the meanings of unknown words and paraphrase the meaning of the chorus. After the students better understand the material, have a volunteer read the chorus aloud.

Teach

Reading Strategy 1

Read Satire Have a student read the blurb at the beginning of the excerpt aloud.

Ask: How does this information help prepare you to read the excerpt? *(It gives the background for the scene and the characters and reveals that the play is a satirical farce.)*

Writer's Technique ☆

Oscar Wilde Wilde's brilliant use of situational irony is a sly way of bringing the audience around to his way of thinking. His characters are so ridiculous that the audience can only concur that they are deserving of mockery.

Writing Practice

SMALL GROUP **Write a Scene** **Ask:** What does the term sitcom mean? *(Situation Comedy)* Note that a comic situation involves the complications that arise from a character's awkward dilemma. Have groups of students create characters and a predicament for a sitcom. Suggest that students write a scene for their sitcom and perform it for the class. Discuss which elements of the scenes and pitches work best and why.

Literary Analysis Model

How do literary elements create meaning in a play?

1 In this scene from *The Importance of Being Earnest,* Jack is interviewed by Lady Bracknell, the mother of the young woman he has fallen in love with.

Oscar Wilde, or Fingal O'Flahertie Wills, 1854–1900, Irish writer, poet, and playwright based in England, ca. 19th century.

APPLYING Literary Elements

Farce

Through Lady Bracknell and her pompous pronouncements, Wilde is able to mock the social attitudes of Victorian England.

from *The Importance of Being Earnest*

by Oscar Wilde ☆

CHARACTERS:

LADY BRACKNELL She is an elderly English woman. Her ideas about what makes a suitable husband are extremely rigid.

JACK Jack Worthing is superficial, flippant, flirtatious, dishonest, witty, charming, and entirely self-serving.

SETTING: a fashionable apartment in London

LADY BRACKNELL. Now to minor matters. Are your parents living?

JACK. I have lost both my parents.

LADY BRACKNELL. To lose one parent, Mr. Worthing, may be regarded as a misfortune; to lose both looks like carelessness. Who was your father? He was evidently a man of some wealth. Was he born in what the Radical papers call the purple of commerce, or did he rise from the ranks of the aristocracy?

JACK. I am afraid I really don't know. The fact is, Lady Bracknell, I said I had lost my parents. It would be nearer the truth to say that my parents seem to have lost me . . . I don't actually know who I am by birth. I was . . . well, I was found.

LADY BRACKNELL. Found!

JACK. The late Mr. Thomas Cardew, an old gentleman of a very charitable and kindly disposition, found me, and gave me the name Worthing, because he happened to have a first-class ticket for Worthing in his pocket at the time. Worthing is a place in Sussex. It is a seaside resort.

LADY BRACKNELL. Where did the charitable gentleman who had a first-class ticket for this seaside resort find you?

JACK. [*Gravely.*] In a handbag.

LADY BRACKNELL. A handbag?

Rupert Everett as Jack and Judi Dench as Lady Bracknell

JACK. [*Very seriously.*] Yes, Lady Bracknell. I was in a handbag—a somewhat large, black leather handbag, with handles to it—an ordinary handbag, in fact.

LADY BRACKNELL. In what locality did this Mr. James, or Thomas, Cardew come across this ordinary handbag?

JACK. In the cloakroom at Victoria Station. It was given to him in mistake for his own.

LADY BRACKNELL. The cloakroom at Victoria Station?

JACK. Yes. The Brighton line.

LADY BRACKNELL. The line is immaterial. Mr. Worthing, I confess I feel somewhat bewildered by what you have just told me. To be born, or at any rate bred, in a handbag, whether it had handles or not, seems to me to display a contempt for the ordinary decencies of family life that remind one of the worst excesses of the French Revolution. And I presume you know what that unfortunate movement led to? As for the particular locality in which the handbag was found, a cloakroom at a railway station might serve to conceal a social indiscretion—has probably, indeed, been used for that purpose before now—but, it could hardly be regarded as an assured basis for a recognized position in good society. ☆

Dialogue

Lady Bracknell's words reveal that Lady Bracknell is a pompous fool.

JACK. May I ask you then what you would advise me to do? I need hardly say I would do anything in the world to ensure Gwendolen's happiness.

LADY BRACKNELL. I would strongly advise you, Mr. Worthing, to try and acquire some relations as soon as possible, and make a definite effort to produce at any rate one parent, of either sex, before the season is quite over.

JACK. Well, I don't see how I could possibly manage to do that. I can produce the handbag at any moment. It is in my dressing room at home. I really think that should satisfy you, Lady Bracknell.

2 LADY BRACKNELL. Me, sir! What has it to do with me? You can hardly imagine that I and Lord Bracknell would dream of allowing our daughter—a girl brought up with the utmost care—to marry into a cloakroom, and form an alliance with a parcel? Good morning, Mr. Worthing! [*Lady Bracknell sweeps out in majestic indignation.*]

JACK. Good morning!

Stage Directions

Stage directions can describe clues about a character's tone, giving his or her state of mind.

Reading Check

Interpret What literary elements does Wilde use to create comic effect in this scene from *The Importance of Being Earnest?*

Teach

Reading Check

Answer: *Wilde uses situational irony, farce, and satire.*

Literary Element 2

Farce **Ask:** How is the character of Lady Bracknell farcical? *(She is a "one note" character in the ridiculous situation of interviewing a son-in-law.)*

ADVANCED **Ask:** Why do you think Wilde makes Lady Bracknell farcical? *(He wants to criticize the social attitudes of Victorian England.)*

Cultural History ☆

Victorian England Nineteenth-century English society in the era of Queen Victoria was characterized by concern with status, morality, manners, and hard work. Wilde's plays defied the rigid conventions of his time by pushing the limits of what was deemed acceptable.

English Learners

DIFFERENTIATED INSTRUCTION

Beginning / Early Intermediate English learners may have difficulty interpreting character traits through reading. To emphasize the various character traits of farcical characters, have more proficient readers read the scene from *The Importance of Being Earnest* aloud. Suggest that students use exaggerated voices that fit the characters. For example, have students read the part of Lady Bracknell in a highly pompous voice. Have students suggest appropriate voices for Jack and explain their choice. After the performance, ask English learners to describe the characters.

Assess

Guide to Reading Drama

Stress that students should take time to note visual details as well as other sensory details, such as sounds and smells.

Elements of Drama

Suggest students keep notes on which elements of each play they find most appealing. Do they relate to the characters or get wrapped up in the suspenseful plot? Is the dialogue insightful or witty?

Activities

1. **Speaking and Listening** If students feel that Wilde is making an important point, they should clearly state that point and how he makes it.
2. **Write** Have students consider what theme their dialogue expresses and why it is meaningful to them.
3. **Take Notes** Students' organizers should include notes on literary elements from selections in this unit.

FOLDABLES® Study Organizer

Have students jot down notes on each literary element in the sections of their organizer.

Wrap-Up:

Guide to Reading Drama

- Plays should not be read a few pages at a time, as you might read a novel. Try to read a play in its entirety in one sitting.
- Because drama is meant to be performed, you will need to use your imagination to visualize what is happening in each scene.
- Focus your attention on plot and character. Think about theme only after you finish reading.
- Read the stage directions and then try to visualize what the set stage would look like.

Elements of Drama

- **Drama** is written to be performed by actors in front of an audience.
- Most plays are divided into **acts** and **scenes.**
- Written drama is mostly **dialogue** and **stage directions.**
- In a **tragedy,** the **tragic hero** suffers a reversal of fortune.
- The **chorus** is an actor or a group of actors who speak directly to the audience.
- **Comedy** is drama that deals with light and amusing subjects or with serious subjects in a light or humorous way.

LOG ON **Literature** Online

Unit Resources For additional skills practice, go to glencoe.com and enter QuickPass code GL49787u4.

Activities

Use what you have learned about reading and analyzing drama to complete one of the following activities.

1. **Speaking and Listening** Discuss with a small group your opinion of the excerpt from *The Importance of Being Earnest.* Begin by reviewing Wilde's characters. Does Wilde successfully make a point in this scene? Why or why not?
2. **Write** Write out a bit of dialogue from your favorite movie or television show. Then write a brief explanation of what elements in the dialogue make it memorable.
3. **Take Notes** Try using this study organizer to keep track of the literary elements you learn in this unit. See pages R20–R21 for folding instructions.

FOLDABLES Study Organizer **THREE-TAB BOOK**

Writing Practice

Write a Review Have the class design a checklist based on the elements of drama and use it to write a review of a play or movie. Include the following:

- Is the dialogue effective?
- Do the scenes flow smoothly?
- Is there a tragic hero?
- Is there irony?
- Are the characters interesting?

Have the class add elements to the checklist, then instruct students to write their reviews.

PART 1

The Power of Love

Couple with a Dove, 2001. Suad Al-Attar. Oil on canvas, 24.02 x 18.11 in. Private collection.

View the Art The works of Iraqi artist Suad Al-Attar often have a strong dreamlike quality. What elements of this painting seem dreamlike? ★

BIG IDEA

Throughout history young lovers have spoken of the strength of their love and pledged that it would last forever. The selections in Part 1 focus on this universal subject. As you read the selections, ask yourself, What makes love so powerful? How does it drive the action of these works?

UNIT FOUR

PART 1

Analyze and Extend

Big Idea

The Power of Love **Ask:** What is powerful about love? *(Answers will vary.)* Discuss the various ways love can motivate people. Have students cite examples of the power of love in literature, music, movies, and other arts.

View the Art ★

Answer: *The blurred lines and blended colors make the painting seem like a scene from a dream.*

Suad Al-Attar (1942–) held the first solo exhibition by a female artist in Baghdad. She has degrees from universities in California, Baghdad, and London and has exhibited her work all over the world.

For additional support for English Learners, see Unit 4 Teaching Resources Book, p. 20.

English Learners

DIFFERENTIATED INSTRUCTION

Early Advanced Guide students to find the word *love* in a dictionary and note the different definitions. Explain that the topic of love, in all its forms, appears in every genre and culture. Ask students to name stories or plays that focus on love. Then ask them what kind of love is being explored in the stories. *(Possible answers: romance, friendship, humanitarian)*

Ask: What message do these stories send about love? *(Possible answers: Love conquers all; Love is both pain and pleasure.)*

UNIT FOUR

PART 1

Focus

Bellringer Options

Daily Language Practice Transparency 72

Or note that people use the word *tragedy* in reference to both major and minor catastrophes as well as to unfortunate circumstances that involve comic or absurd elements.

Write on the board: Major, Minor, Tragicomic. Ask what constitutes a major tragedy *(Death, war, natural disasters)*, a minor tragedy *(flat tire)*, and a comic tragedy *(fools who continually make the same mistakes)*, and list the results on the board. Discuss how these notions of tragedy compare with the definition of classical tragic drama.

Teach

Literary Element 1

Tragedy **Ask:** If tragedies are about bad things happening to good people, why does the audience enjoy them? Introduce students to the concept of catharsis—a purifying release of tension and emotion through art.

Learning Objectives

For pages 620–621

In studying this text, you will focus on the following objectives:

Literary Study: Analyzing tragedy, tragic flaws, and tragic heroes.

LITERARY FOCUS

Tragedy

What are the elements that define a tragedy?

1 According to the ancient Greek philosopher Aristotle, a tragedy is a play about a person of high social standing (a hero or a king) who suffers a fall from good fortune. Aristotle also outlined the Six Elements of Drama which many playwrights have used as a guide throughout history.

Aristotle's Six Elements

Element	Definition
Plot	What happens in a play
Diction/ Language/ Dialogue	The playwright's word choices and the actors' enunciation while delivering their lines
Music/ Rhythm	Not music as we think of it, but rather the sound, rhythm, and melody of the speeches
Theme	What a play means, as opposed to what happens
Spectacle	The scenery, costumes, and special effects in a play
Character	The person an actor represents in a play

In *Romeo and Juliet,* the plot centers on the young Romeo and Juliet, who fall in love at first sight at a masked ball. Since they belong to rival families—the Montagues and the Capulets—Romeo and Juliet must keep their love a secret. The rivalry of the Montague and Capulet families soon erupts into violence. In the following scene, Tybalt, a Capulet, vows revenge on Romeo.

TYBALT. This, by his voice, should be a Montague.
Fetch me my rapier, boy. What! Dares the slave
Come hither, cover'd with an antic face,
To fleer and scorn at our solemnity?
Now, by the stock and honor of my kin,
To strike him dead I hold it not a sin.

—from Act 1, Scene 5

Aristotle's elements of diction/language/dialogue and music/rhythm are apparent in Shakespeare's *Romeo and Juliet,* as most of his characters often speak in **blank verse,** or unrhymed iambic pentameter. (**Iambic pentameter** means that there are ten syllables per line, and every second syllable is stressed.) In order to deliver lines from Shakespearean text, an actor must develop an ear for the rhythm and musicality of the text, as well as be able to enunciate Shakespeare's often tongue-twisting phrases.

The elements of theme and spectacle also appear in Shakespearean tragedy. As you read the play, you will discover the main ideas that Shakespeare wants to convey to his audiences. In viewing the play, an audience member would witness such spectacles as sword fights, a masked ball, a secret exchange upon a balcony, and a tragic death scene.

LOG ON **Literature Online**

Literature and Reading For more about literary elements, go to glencoe.com and enter QuickPass code GL49787u4.

Vocabulary Practice

Tragedy Explain that the word *tragedy* comes from the Greek word *tragōidia,* which means "goat song." Philosophers still argue about the correct explanation of this name. Many believe the word evolved from early Greek rituals in which goats were worshipped. Others believe the mention of goats alludes to the Greek god Dionysus.

Have advanced students research the etymology of the word *tragedy.* Instruct them to think about the possible meaning as they progress through the chapter.

The final Aristotelian element is character. Characters' actions and words define their personalities. There are often many characters in plays, including the **protagonist,** or the central character; the **antagonist,** or the character who opposes the protagonist; and a number of supporting and minor characters. The protagonist is often a tragic hero.

Tragic Hero

The most important character in a tragedy is its **tragic hero.** He or she is a person born into nobility and responsible for his or her own fate. A tragic hero has the potential for greatness but is doomed to make one or more serious errors in judgment. In most cases, these errors are the result of a **tragic flaw** in the hero's character. Romeo's tragic flaw is that he is blinded by his love for Juliet; therefore, he behaves rashly. In these lines, he wills to lose his life for his love.

> **ROMEO.** Let me be ta'en, let me be put to death.
> I am content, so thou wilt have it so.
>
> **—from Act 3, Scene 5**

In most tragedies, the tragic hero eventually realizes his mistake and faces death with great honor and dignity.

2 Dramatic Devices

Playwrights cannot comment directly upon how a character is thinking or feeling, so they rely on three dramatic devices. The first is **monologue,** in which the character speaks directly to another character or to himself or herself. In a **soliloquy** a character speaks his or her innermost thoughts when no other characters are on stage. For example, in Act 1, Scene 4, of *Romeo and Juliet,* Mercutio, Romeo's best friend, in a monologue refers to Queen Mab, a mythological queen of fairies who takes the form of an evil spirit. Mercutio uses the metaphor to express his cynicism about love.

> **MERCUTIO.** O, then I see Queen Mab hath been with you.
> She is the fairies' midwife, and she comes
> In shape no bigger than an agate stone
> On the forefinger of an alderman. . . .
>
> **—from Act 1, Scene 4**

The third device playwrights rely on for revealing a character's thoughts or feelings is the **aside.** In an aside, a character says something to the audience that the other characters are not supposed to hear.

> **JULIET.** O Romeo, Romeo! Wherefore art thou Romeo?
> Deny thy father and refuse thy name;
> Or, if thou wilt not, be but sworn my love,
> And I'll no longer be a Capulet.
> **ROMEO.** [*Aside.*] Shall I hear more, or shall I speak at this?
>
> **—from Act 2, Scene 2**

Tragic mask from a mosaic in the House of the Fawn in Pompeii by Gustavo Tomsich. ★

Quickwrite

Define Tragedy In fifteen minutes or less, write a definition of *tragedy.* Consider how the elements of a tragedy help the author achieve his or her purpose. Your answer should be specific and include examples.

Teach

Reading Strategy 2

Analyze Plays Encourage students to jot down their first impressions of a play immediately after their initial reading. Then, they can go back to analyze the play for elements such as plot or dramatic devices.

View the Art ★

When drama was born in Greece, all actors were male. These actors played multiple roles, including those of women. There were only two types of plays—comedy and tragedy—so the two types of masks allowed actors to easily slip between multiple roles. Eventually the comedy and tragedy masks became the symbol of the theater.

Quickwrite

Answers will vary. Make sure students support their definitions with reasons and examples.

Approaching Level

DIFFERENTIATED INSTRUCTION

Established Have students create a graphic organizer like the one on page 620 that lists Aristotle's six elements. Instead of *definition,* they should write the title of a tragic play or movie with which they are familiar. In the right column, students should describe how the element listed on the left is present in the play. For example, in the block next to plot, students should summarize what happens in the play or movie. **Ask:** What do you think Aristotle would think about movies and plays produced today?

Focus

Bellringer Options

Daily Language Practice Transparency 73

Or note that in live theater the use of special effects is far more limited than in movies.

Ask: Do you think a stage play could ever be as exciting as one of today's movies? Encourage students who have seen live theater to participate in the discussion. Point out how compelling plots, dialogue, and characters can engage the imagination of the audience.

Teach

Reading Strategy 1

ADVANCED **Preview** Have students review the subheads and the illustrations on pages 622 and 623. Then read the introductory quotation and the first paragraph of the essay aloud. Encourage students to list any questions they have about the Elizabethan era. Students should be encouraged to research answers to their questions in a library or on the Internet and present them to the class.

Learning Objectives

For pages 622–623

In studying this text, you will focus on the following objectives:

Literary Study:
Analyzing literary periods.
Evaluating historical influences.

Shakespearean Drama

It is a summer afternoon in London, England, near the end of the reign of Queen Elizabeth I. People from all classes of London society—from laborers to the nobility—have crossed the Thames River to the suburb of Southwark to see a play. Groups of excited playgoers are arriving at a large round building—William Shakespeare's Globe Theatre. A fanfare of trumpets signals that the performance will soon begin. Because a black flag flies over the theater, everyone knows that today's play is a tragedy. The playgoers take their seats in the galleries, except for those "groundlings" who stand in the open courtyard around the stage.

> *"Theater in Elizabeth's day took the place now filled by the novel, the short story, the drama, the newspaper, motion pictures, radio, and television."*
>
> —Vera Mowry Roberts, *On Stage*

The Age of Shakespeare

Shakespeare was fortunate to begin his career in the late 1500s, when English theater was going through major changes. Professional actors had been performing in England for centuries. Called "players," they traveled from town to town, setting up makeshift stages in public halls, marketplaces, and the courtyards of inns. Often they met hostility from local authorities, who believed that crowds of playgoers were a magnet for crime and also contributed to the spread of disease.

Actor James Burbage built England's first permanent playhouse in 1576. Other open-air theaters sprang up during the next few decades. In 1599 Shakespeare's acting company, the Lord Chamberlain's Men, built their own playhouse, the Globe. This roughly circular building had three levels of covered galleries.

Portrait of William Shakespeare, 1849. Ford Madox Brown. Oil on canvas. Manchester Art Gallery, UK.

A platform stage about forty feet wide projected out into the open courtyard, where people who paid the lowest admission price could stand and watch the play. Wealthy people paid sixpence (what a skilled laborer earned in a day) to sit in the "lords' room," the part of the gallery directly over the stage. In all, the Globe could accommodate about 3,000 spectators.

Writing Practice

Write an Essay The original Globe Theatre opened in 1599 and closed in 1642. In June 1997, a new Globe Theatre was completed. The restoration faithfully replicated the original theater's materials and design. Tell groups of students to research the old and new Globe Theatres and write a short essay comparing and contrasting them. Then have them present their findings in class.

Shakespeare's Stagecraft

The stage at the Globe had trapdoors for the entrance and exit of actors playing ghosts or other supernatural characters. At the back of the main stage was a small, curtained inner stage used for indoor scenes. Above this stood a two-tiered gallery. The first tier was used to stage balcony and bedroom scenes; the second to house musicians. Sound effects, such as the booming of thunder, were produced in a hut on top of the stage roof.

2 All performances took place in the afternoon because there was no artificial lighting. The stage was mostly bare. There were few props and no movable scenery. Instead of relying on scenery, Shakespeare used descriptive language to help audiences visualize the settings of his plays. For example, his long descriptions of the moon are more than just beautiful writing—they reminded Elizabethan audiences that the characters were meeting at night.

What the Elizabethan stage lacked in scenery, it made up for in costumes. Shakespeare's audiences considered clothing an important indication of social rank, so they demanded extravagant—if not always historically accurate—costuming. Along with its playbooks, an elaborate wardrobe was an Elizabethan theater company's biggest expense and most important asset.

Boy actors had an important function in Elizabethan theater. Because it was considered immoral for women to appear onstage, adolescent males played the female parts. They used wigs, costumes, and their voices to create this illusion. Very popular with Elizabethan theatergoers, these boy actors must have been highly skilled performers who created convincing and moving portrayals of Shakespeare's great female roles, from Lady Macbeth and Cleopatra to Rosalind and Juliet.

Even though Shakespeare was a very popular dramatist in his time, the audiences at the Globe would have been surprised to learn that their era would be best known for his work. Shakespeare's contemporary Ben Jonson saw far into the future when he described his great rival as "not of an age, but for all time."

Aerial View of the Globe Theatre. Cyril Walter Hodges. Engraving. Private collection.

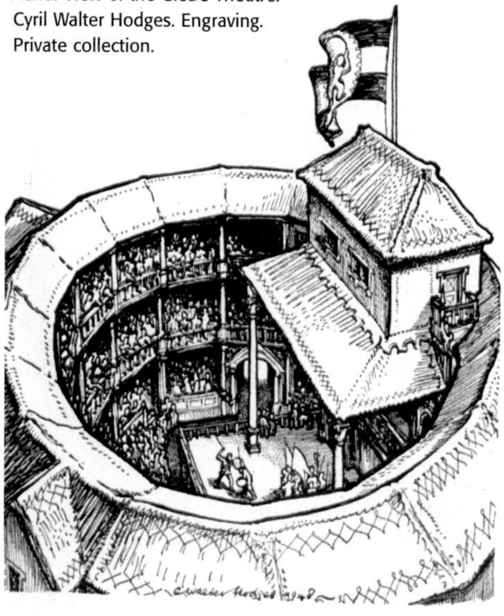

LOG ON **Literature** Online

Literature and History For more about Shakespearean drama, go to glencoe.com and enter QuickPass code GL49787u4.

Respond and Think Critically

1. If you had been a member of the audience at the Globe, what feature of the theater do you think would have most held your attention? Explain.
2. What event during Shakespeare's lifetime probably helped his career as a dramatist?
3. How do today's productions of plays differ from productions during Shakespeare's lifetime? Consider the use of scenery and props.

English Learners

DIFFERENTIATED INSTRUCTION

Early Advanced Write these words on the board: *playbills, theatergoers, playhouse*. Explain that a compound noun consists of two or more nouns that are written as one word or as separate or hyphenated words.

Have students offer examples of compound words while you list them on the board. Encourage English language learners to enter compound nouns and their definitions in their notebooks as they read. Explain that this is a great way to increase their vocabulary.

Literary History

Teach

Big Idea 2

The Power of Love **Ask:** How might the stage at the Globe lend itself to expressing a powerful love story like that of Romeo and Juliet? *(The size of the stage lends itself to bold expression of emotion. The semicircular seating allows the audience to see all the action and connect closely with the play. Also, the lack of scenery puts the focus strongly on the actors and the play.)*

Cultural History ☆

The Elizabethan Era

Queen Elizabeth I (1558–1603) was a notable writer, orator, and patron of the arts who loved theater. Through patronage and protection of theater companies, she helped support the great flowering of drama during her time.

Assess

1. Students may mention the elaborate costuming.
2. The construction of England's first permanent theaters
3. Women act in today's productions; today's theaters have elaborate props and can achieve dramatic effects with lighting.

Before You Read

Focus

Bellringer Options

Literature Launchers: Pre-Reading Videos DVD, Selection Launcher

Selection Focus Transparency 30

Daily Language Practice Transparency 74

Or students may have read stories about people who accomplished extraordinary feats on behalf of loved ones. **Ask:** What examples can you think of that illustrate the remarkable power of love? **Say:** Jot down some case studies. For example, how might love overcome hatred? Defeat prejudice? Strengthen—or shatter—the will to live?

Before You Read

World Literature
England

The Tragedy of Romeo and Juliet

Meet **William Shakespeare**
(1564–1616)

Few authors have proven as timeless as William Shakespeare. Nearly four centuries after his death, his plays are still read and performed around the world. Shakespeare's appeal is profound. Author Maya Angelou summed up the feelings of many people toward Shakespeare when she said, "I know it was written for me."

> *"All the world's a stage,*
> *And all the men and women*
> *merely players:*
> *They have their exits and their entrances."*
>
> —William Shakespeare

From Stratford to London Shakespeare was born in Stratford-upon-Avon, a market town about one hundred miles from London. His father was a glove maker, tradesman, and bailiff (the equivalent of a mayor). His mother came from a prosperous farming family. Because of his family's status, Shakespeare almost certainly attended the town's grammar school, considered one of the best in England. There he would have learned Latin and read classical literature. At eighteen, he married Anne Hathaway and started a family.

Sometime between 1585 and the early 1590s, Shakespeare moved to London to pursue a career in theater. He worked as an actor and playwright, quickly gaining attention for his comedies and historical plays. By 1594 he had joined a theater group called the Lord Chamberlain's Men (renamed the King's Men during the reign of James I). This remained his professional home for the rest of his career.

Playwrights of that time did not earn much money, but Shakespeare made substantial earnings from his share in the company's profits. He bought an estate for his family in Stratford and retired there in 1610. He died in 1616. Seven years later, a group of friends published a collected edition of his works, ensuring their preservation for future generations.

A Master of His Craft Shakespeare wrote thirty-seven plays, including such tragic masterpieces as *Hamlet, Macbeth,* and *Romeo and Juliet.* Shakespeare's plays are complex and full of poetic language. Shakespeare's friend and rival playwright Ben Jonson declared that Shakespeare was "not of an age, but for all time," and Shakespeare continues to inspire writers, filmmakers, and other artists.

LOG ON **Literature** Online

Author Search For more about William Shakespeare, go to glencoe.com and enter QuickPass code GL49787u4.

Selection Skills

The Tragedy of Romeo and Juliet, Act 1

Listening/Speaking/Viewing Skills
- Analyze Art (SE pp. 629, 634, 643, 648)
- Comic/Dramatic Speeches (TE p. 630)
- Oral Interpretation (TE p. 648)

Writing Skills/Grammar
- Possessives (TE p. 628)
- Subject-Verb Order (TE p. 638)
- Vivid Description (TE p. 644)
- Complements (TE p. 652)

Vocabulary Skills
- Synonyms (SE pp. 625, 654)

Reading Skills
- Summarize (SE pp. 625–654)
- Paraphrase (TE p. 636)

Literary Elements
- Foil (SE pp. 625–654)

Literature and Reading Preview

Connect to the Drama

Do you believe that young teenagers can fall as deeply in love as adults can? Discuss this question with a partner.

Build Background

Shakespeare borrowed the story of Romeo and Juliet from an old tale. The events in the play take place during the summer in Verona and Mantua, two cities in northern Italy, in the 1300s. The characters Romeo and Juliet come from two distinguished families who are embroiled in a bitter feud. In Italy during the 1300s, such feuds between families were common. Italian families were extended to include brothers, sisters, aunts, uncles, nieces, nephews, cousins, and even servants. All these members of a family might become involved in a *vendetta,* a feud between two families often ignited by a murder and perpetuated by acts of revenge.

Set Purposes for Reading

Big Idea The Power of Love

As you read Act 1, ask yourself, How are the characters' attitudes toward love similar and different?

Literary Element Foil

A **foil** is a character who provides a strong contrast to another character. A foil may emphasize another character's distinctive traits or may make another character look better by comparison. As you read, ask yourself, Which characters exhibit contrasting personalities?

Reading Strategy Summarize

Summarizing means stating the main ideas of a work or passage in your own words and in a logical sequence. A summary is much shorter than the original. As you read, ask yourself, How would I summarize the events so far?

Tip: **Answer the 5 Ws** When reading a Shakespeare play, it is helpful to summarize eventful or difficult passages. For each passage you summarize, make a list answering *who, what, when, where,* and *why* questions about the passage. Use the list to help create your summary.

Learning Objectives

For pages 624–654

In studying this text, you will focus on the following objectives:

Literary Study: Analyzing foils.

Reading: Summarizing.

Writing: Writing a dialogue.

Vocabulary

pernicious (pər nish′ əs) *adj.* destructive; deadly; p. 632 *The false rumor had a pernicious effect on our friendship.*

posterity (pos ter′ ə tē) *n.* future generations; p. 637 *We must protect the environment for posterity.*

anguish (ang′ gwish) *n.* extreme suffering; agony; p. 639 *The hurricane victim described the anguish of losing everything he owned.*

profane (prō fān′) *v.* to degrade or disrespect something holy or important; p. 651 *Do not profane the sanctuary with loud noise.*

Tip: **Synonyms** Words that have the same or similar meanings are called synonyms. Words can only be synonyms if they are the same part of speech. For example, the noun *suffering* is a synonym for the noun *anguish.* Noting the part of speech can help you distinguish synonyms from words that merely have related meanings.

Approaching Level

DIFFERENTIATED INSTRUCTION

Emerging Explain that *The Tragedy of Romeo and Juliet* is one of the most popular plays about love that has ever been written. The play has influenced movies, books, and even modern language and culture. **Ask:** What does it mean if we call someone a Romeo? *(The person is a ladies' man.)* **Ask:** What does it mean if we say a couple is like Romeo and Juliet? *(The couple is very much in love.)* Have students offer other examples of ways the play has become part of mainstream culture. (*many film versions* of Romeo and Juliet, *rap star Lil' Romeo, many adaptations* of Romeo and Juliet—*for example,* West Side Story)

Before You Read

Focus

Summary

Two prominent families, the Montagues and the Capulets, are locked in a bitter feud. After a street fight between their servants, the Prince of Verona bans further violence. That night, the Capulet patriarch holds a ball, where his teenaged daughter Juliet meets a young stranger in disguise, unaware that he is Romeo, the son of her father's sworn enemy. Romeo is forced to flee the ball to avoid a skirmish with Juliet's cousin, Tybalt. When Romeo and Juliet learn each other's identity, both feel torn between romantic attraction and family loyalty.

For summaries in languages other than English, see Unit 4 Teaching Resources Book, pp. 24–29.

Vocabulary

Synonyms Ask students to find a synonym for each vocabulary word, other than the ones used in the definition. *(pernicious: evil; posterity: offspring; anguish: torment; profane: abuse (v))*

For additional vocabulary practice, see Unit 4 Teaching Resources Book, p. 32.

Teach

Big Idea 1

The Power of Love

Say: Keep these questions in mind as you read: How does Shakespeare juxtapose loyalty and love with conflict in Act I? *(By alternating between themes of love and conflict in the dialogue)* What is the effect of this technique? *(It creates contrast and builds dramatic tension.)*

View the Art ★

Although created in the twentieth century, *Juliet on the Balcony* recalls the illuminated manuscripts popular during the Middle Ages and the Renaissance. Illumination is the art of embellishing parchment book pages with ornately drawn letters and designs using colored inks and gold leaf.

Interactive Read and Write

Other options for teaching this selection can be found in

- Interactive Read and Write for EL Students, pp. 167–186
- Interactive Read and Write for Approaching-Level Students, pp. 167–186
- Interactive Read and Write for On-Level Students, pp. 167–186

The Tragedy of Romeo and Juliet

William Shakespeare

Juliet on the Balcony. Illumination from text *The Tragedy of Romeo and Juliet,* 1920. Sangorski and Sutcliffe, binders, calligraphers, and illuminators. Private collection. ★

Viewing Practice

SPIRAL REVIEW **Study Graphics** Explain to students that previewing illustrations before reading a text can be helpful. Artwork helps set the mood and provides clues about the tone, content, and theme. Guide students to preview the artwork in Act 1. Then, discuss students' impressions. **Ask:** Based on what you have seen, what do you predict will be the tone of the story? *(The story might be sad and serious because the pictures use muted colors.)* Have students write a descriptive paragraph about one of the paintings in Act 1.

CHARACTERS

The Montagues

LORD MONTAGUE: wealthy nobleman of Verona and enemy to Lord Capulet

LADY MONTAGUE: his wife

ROMEO: their son

BENVOLIO: Lord Montague's nephew, Romeo's cousin and friend

BALTHASAR: Romeo's servant

ABRAM: a servant

The Capulets

LORD CAPULET: wealthy nobleman of Verona and enemy to Lord Montague

LADY CAPULET: his wife

JULIET: their daughter, who is thirteen years old

TYBALT: Lady Capulet's nephew, Juliet's cousin

OLD MAN: elderly relative of the family

NURSE: servant who has cared for Juliet since infancy

PETER: the Nurse's servant

SAMPSON: servant

GREGORY: servant

Others

☆ CHORUS: actor who speaks directly to the audience to introduce the play

PRINCE ESCALUS: ruler of Verona

COUNT PARIS: relative of the Prince and suitor to Juliet

MERCUTIO: relative of the Prince and Romeo's friend

FRIAR LAWRENCE: Catholic priest of the order of Franciscans and a pharmacist

APOTHECARY: pharmacist in Mantua

FRIAR JOHN: Franciscan priest

PAGE: servant to Paris

OFFICERS AND CITIZENS OF VERONA, RELATIVES OF BOTH FAMILIES, MASKERS, OFFICERS, GUARDS, WATCHMEN, SERVANTS, AND ATTENDANTS

SETTING

2 SCENE: *Italy—the cities of Verona and Mantua. The fourteenth century.*

Teach

Reading Strategy 2

Visualize Discuss what fourteenth-century Verona and Mantua might have looked like. Encourage students to picture the buildings, streets, and methods of transportation. Have them describe the appearance of the cities' inhabitants.

APPROACHING Have students locate Verona and Mantua on a map to help them visualize the setting.

Cultural History ☆

Theatrical Chorus The chorus has its roots in ancient Greek tragedy. Groups of twelve to fifteen performers would chant an entrance song and then sing and dance during the play. The group's leader would engage in dialogue with the characters. In Shakespeare's plays, the chorus is usually one individual whose role ranges from introducing the play to helping the audience visualize the unfolding drama.

English Learners

DIFFERENTIATED INSTRUCTION

Intermediate Explain to students that many words and expressions that Shakespeare used are now obsolete or have changed in meaning. The word, *doth,* for instance, is a shortened form of *doeth,* and both words are archaic forms of the verb *do*. English language has changed considerably since this play was written; therefore, some people find Shakespeare's work difficult to understand. Encourage students to use context clues while reading the play.

Teach

Reading Strategy 1

Summarize Ask: Why do you think Shakespeare begins the play with a rowdy, action-packed street fight? *(To capture the audience's attention and to introduce the main conflict)*

APPROACHING Explain to students that authors often begin their stories in the middle of the action, instead of starting from the very beginning, in order to immediately grab the attention of their audience.

For additional practice using the reading skill or strategy, see Unit 4 Teaching Resources Book, p. 31.

Literary Element 2

Foil Answer: *Sampson seems rash and eager to fight the Montagues. Gregory pokes fun at his friend's boasts to steer him away from a confrontation.*

Writer's Technique ☆

The Prologue is in the form of a fourteen-line sonnet with the following rhyme scheme: *abab, cdcd, efef, gg.* Shakespeare often uses sonnets and rhymed couplets to emphasize crucial speeches.

Act 1

Prologue ☆

CHORUS.° Two households, both alike in dignity,°
In fair Verona, where we lay our scene,
From ancient grudge break to new mutiny,°
Where civil blood makes civil hands unclean.°
From forth the fatal° loins of these two foes
A pair of star-cross'd° lovers take their life;
Whose misadventur'd° piteous overthrows°
Doth with their death bury their parents' strife.
The fearful passage of their death-mark'd love,
And the continuance of their parents' rage,
Which, but° their children's end, nought could remove,
Is now the two hours' traffic of our stage;°
The which if you with patient ears attend,
What here shall miss, our toil shall strive to mend.°

[*The* CHORUS *exits.*]

1 Chorus: Elizabethan dramatists sometimes used a figure known as the chorus to comment on a play's action and describe events not shown on stage. In this prologue, or introduction, the chorus explains what the play is about. **dignity:** social status.
3 mutiny (mū ′ tə nē): violence.
4 civil blood . . . unclean: citizens soil their hands with each other's blood.
5 fatal: ill-fated.
6 star-cross'd: doomed because of the positions of the planets when they were born.
7 misadventur'd: unfortunate. **overthrows:** ruin.
11 but: except for.
12 two hours' . . . stage: subject of our play.
14 What here . . . mend: We will try to clarify in our performance whatever is unclear in this prologue.

SCENE 1. Early morning. A public square in Verona.

1 [*SAMPSON and GREGORY, servants of the Capulets, enter. Because of the feud between the powerful Capulet and Montague families, they are armed with swords and bucklers, or small shields.*]

SAMPSON. Gregory, on my word, we'll not carry coals.°

GREGORY. No, for then we should be colliers.°

SAMPSON. I mean, and we be in choler, we'll draw.°

GREGORY. Ay, while you live, draw your neck out of collar.°

SAMPSON. I strike quickly,° being mov'd.°

GREGORY. But thou art not quickly° mov'd to strike.

SAMPSON. A dog of the house of Montague moves me.

GREGORY. To move is to stir, and to be valiant is to stand. Therefore, if thou art mov'd, thou run'st away.

SAMPSON. A dog of that house shall move me to stand. I will take the wall° of any man or maid of Montague's.

GREGORY. That shows thee a weak slave, for the weakest goes to the wall.°

SAMPSON. 'Tis true, and therefore women, being the weaker vessels, are ever thrust to the wall;° therefore I will push

1 carry coals: put up with insults (an Elizabethan expression).
2 colliers (kol ′ yərz): coal vendors.
3 and . . . draw: if we are angry, or **in choler** (kol ′ ər), we will draw our swords.
4 collar: the hangman's noose. (Gregory extends the pun with *collier* and *choler.*)
5 quickly: vigorously. **mov'd:** roused.
6 quickly: speedily.
11 take the wall: walk on the side of the path closest to the walls of houses. (Since this was the cleaner side, Sampson is asserting his superiority over any of the Montague servants.)
12–13 weakest . . . wall: the weakest are pushed to the rear.
15 thrust to the wall: assaulted.

2 Foil *What contrasts do you see between Gregory and Sampson?*

Grammar Practice

Exceptional Posessives

Instruct students to write these examples in their notebooks. **Write:** "the heads of the maids" on the board. **Ask:** How else could you say this? *(the maids' heads)* Point out "maid of Montague's" in line 11. **Ask:** Is this posessive form an error? *(No, when one of several is implied, this usage is fine. Note that we typically say "a friend of mine" (possessive pronoun) as opposed to "a friend of me.")*

Write: (a) Romeo and Juliet's love and (b) Romeo's and Juliet's love on the board. **Ask:** Which is correct? *(a; When something is possessed equally by two closely linked nouns, only the second noun takes the possessive form.)*

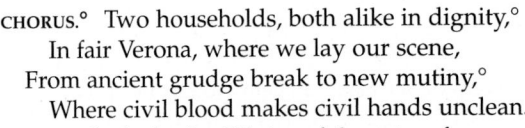

Teach

View the Art ★

Answer: *Clothing shows nobles' lavish lifestyle; ornate carvings and domed arches show architectural style; figure groupings suggest sexes didn't mingle as freely as today.*

This detail from *The Wedding Chamber* by Andrea Mantegna (1431–1506) is a small segment of a famous *trompe l'oeil* (French for "trick of the eye") fresco. Painted on the walls and ceiling of a tiny windowless room, the mural's masterly use of perspective creates the illusion of a pavilion topped with a dome opening to the sky.

Camera degli Sposi (The Wedding Chamber), 1474 (detail). Andrea Mantegna. Fresco. Palazzo Ducale, Mantua, Italy.

View the Art Which details in this fresco help you visualize what life was like in northern Italy in the fourteenth and fifteenth centuries? ★

English Learners

DIFFERENTIATED INSTRUCTION

Beginning / Early Intermediate To help students struggling to understand the play's language, discuss the stage directions. Have students summarize the first set of stage directions. Then, invite volunteers to act out the stage directions and read the accompanying dialogue. Instruct the rest of the class to write a summary of the performance. *(Students should write that the servants of two dueling families entered a public square and began a fight.)*

Teach

Reading Strategy 1

Summarize Answer: *The long-standing hostility between the families is so intense and unyielding that even their servants are at war.*

Have students review the dialogue between Sampson and Gregory and describe its subject, mood, and language. *(Their crude talk about their master's feud is alternately hostile and jesting.)*

Montague's men from the wall, and thrust his maids to the wall.

GREGORY. The quarrel is between our masters and us their men.

SAMPSON. 'Tis all one.° I will show myself a tyrant. When I have fought with the men, I will be civil with the maids; I will cut off their heads.

GREGORY. The heads of the maids?

SAMPSON. Ay, the heads of the maids, or their maidenheads, take it in what sense thou wilt.

GREGORY. They must take it in sense° that feel it.

SAMPSON. Me they shall feel while I am able to stand, and 'tis known I am a pretty piece of flesh.

GREGORY. 'Tis well thou art not fish; if thou hadst, thou hadst been poor-John.° Draw thy tool,° here comes two of the house of Montagues.

[*ABRAM and BALTHASAR, servants of the Montagues, enter.*]

SAMPSON. My naked weapon is out. Quarrel! I will back thee.

GREGORY. How? Turn thy back and run?

SAMPSON. Fear me not.

GREGORY. No, marry.° I fear thee!

SAMPSON. Let us take the law of our sides; let them begin.°

GREGORY. I will frown as I pass by, and let them take it as they list.°

SAMPSON. Nay, as they dare. I will bite my thumb° at them, which is disgrace to them if they bear it.

ABRAM. Do you bite your thumb at us, sir?

SAMPSON. I do bite my thumb, sir.

ABRAM. Do you bite your thumb at us, sir?

SAMPSON. [*Aside to GREGORY.*] Is the law of our side if I say ay?

GREGORY. [*Aside to SAMPSON.*] No.

SAMPSON. No, sir, I do not bite my thumb at you, sir; but I bite my thumb, sir.

GREGORY. Do you quarrel, sir?

ABRAM. Quarrel, sir? No, sir.

19 one: the same.

25 Gregory plays on two meanings of **sense**, "feeling" and "meaning."

29 poor-John: salted fish (considered a poor man's dish).
tool: sword.

34 marry: by the Virgin Mary (a mild oath similar to *indeed*).
35 Let us . . . begin: Sampson wants to let them begin the fight so that he and Gregory can claim to have fought in self-defense.
37 list: please.
38 bite my thumb: an insulting gesture.

1 Summarize *What have you learned so far about the grudge between the Capulets and Montagues?*

Speaking Practice

SMALL GROUP

Comic vs. Dramatic Speeches This scene quickly shifts from a comic exchange of words to violent action. Reading the scene aloud will help students understand this sudden shift. Assign each role in the scene to a student. Then, discuss character and motivation to determine each speaker's delivery, including tone of voice, gestures, and body language. Have the student actors perform the scene and instruct the rest of the class to write a review of their performance.

SAMPSON. But if you do, sir, I am for you.° I serve as good a man as you.

ABRAM. No better?

SAMPSON. Well, sir.

[*Enter* BENVOLIO, LORD MONTAGUE'*s nephew.*]

GREGORY. Say "better." Here comes one of my master's kinsmen.

SAMPSON. Yes, better, sir.

ABRAM. You lie.

SAMPSON. Draw, if you be men. Gregory, remember thy washing° blow.

[*They fight.*]

BENVOLIO. Part, fools!
Put up your swords. You know not what you do. [*Beats down their swords.*]

[TYBALT, LADY CAPULET'*s nephew, enters with his sword drawn. He speaks first to* BENVOLIO.]

TYBALT. What, art thou drawn among these heartless hinds?°
Turn thee, Benvolio; look upon thy death.

BENVOLIO. I do but keep the peace. Put up thy sword,
Or manage it to part these men with me.

TYBALT. What, drawn, and talk of peace? I hate the word
As I hate hell, all Montagues, and thee.
Have at thee, coward!

[BENVOLIO *and* TYBALT *fight as men of both families enter and join the brawl. Then an* OFFICER *of the town and several* CITIZENS *enter. They carry clubs, battle-axes (bills), and spears (partisans).*]

CITIZENS. Clubs, bills and partisans! Strike! Beat them down!
Down with the Capulets! Down with the Montagues!

[LORD CAPULET, *in his dressing gown, and* LADY CAPULET *enter.*]

CAPULET. What noise is this? Give me my long sword, ho!

LADY CAPULET. A crutch, a crutch! Why call you for a sword?

49 I am for you: I accept your challenge.

58 washing: slashing.

61 heartless hinds: cowardly servants. Tybalt, assuming that Benvolio is involved in the servants' quarrel, challenges him to fight someone of his own rank.

2 Summarize *Summarize what has happened thus far in Scene 1.*

3 Foil *What does this comment indicate about the difference between Benvolio and Tybalt?*

Teach

Reading Strategy 2

Summarize Answer: *The Capulets' servants Gregory and Sampson encounter Abram and Balthasar, Montague servants. After Sampson and Gregory banter about whether to pick a fight, Sampson goads their enemies into a skirmish.*

Say: Shakespeare doesn't reveal the cause of the feud. What do you think it might be? *(Students may propose issues serious enough to cause deep and lasting hatred. Note that the omission of a specific cause might also imply that the feud's origin is too trivial to recall.)*

ADVANCED Challenge students to come up with their own origin of the feud and share it with the rest of the class.

Literary Element 3

Foil Answer: *Benvolio is more restrained and conciliatory than the hotheaded Tybalt.*

Approaching Level

DIFFERENTIATED INSTRUCTION

SMALL GROUP

Emerging Closer study of Shakespeare's use of punctuation in long passages such as the prince's speech may be helpful. Have students reread the passage silently, noting pauses, line endings, and apostrophes. Point out that the passage resembles a poem and remind students that a line break does not neccesarily indicate the end of a sentence. Small groups should take turns reading the speech aloud and paraphrasing its meaning. Once groups have a firm understanding of the speech, invite volunteers to perform the speech for the class.

Teach

Reading Strategy 1

Summarize **Answer:** *He condemns the families for disturbing the peace, bans further fighting, and warns that violators will be executed.*

Cultural History ☆

Melancholy In sixteenth-century England, four cardinal "humors," or fluids—choler, phlegm, blood, and melancholy—were thought to control personality, mood, and health. An imbalance in these humors was believed to cause sickness or even death. *The Anatomy of Melancholy,* a famous treatise on depression published by Robert Burton in 1621, recognized the melancholy of lovers, such as that suffered by Romeo, as a serious disease.

CAPULET. My sword, I say! Old Montague is come
And flourishes his blade in spite° of me.

[LORD MONTAGUE and LADY MONTAGUE enter. LADY MONTAGUE tries to hold back her husband.]

MONTAGUE. Thou villain Capulet!—Hold me not; let me go.

LADY MONTAGUE. Thou shalt not stir one foot to seek a foe.

[PRINCE ESCALUS enters with his TRAIN.]

PRINCE. Rebellious subjects, enemies to peace,
Profaners of this neighbor-stained steel°—
Will they not hear? What, ho! You men, you beasts,
That quench the fire of your **pernicious** rage
With purple fountains issuing from your veins!
On pain of torture, from those bloody hands
Throw your mistemper'd° weapons to the ground
And hear the sentence of your moved° prince.
Three civil brawls, bred of an airy word
By thee, old Capulet, and Montague,
Have thrice disturb'd the quiet of our streets
And made Verona's ancient citizens
Cast by their grave beseeming ornaments°
To wield old partisans, in hands as old,
Cank'red with peace,° to part your cank'red hate.°
If ever you disturb our streets again,
Your lives shall pay the forfeit of the peace.°
For this time all the rest depart away.
You, Capulet, shall go along with me;
And, Montague, come you this afternoon,
To know our farther pleasure in this case,
To old Freetown, our common judgment place.
Once more, on pain of death, all men depart.

[Everyone leaves except MONTAGUE, LADY MONTAGUE, and their nephew BENVOLIO.]

MONTAGUE. Who set this ancient quarrel new abroach?°
Speak, nephew, were you by when it began?

BENVOLIO. Here were the servants of your adversary
And yours, close fighting ere I did approach.

73 spite: defiance.

77 Profaners . . . steel: Those who disrespect the law by staining their weapons with neighbors' blood.

82 mistemper'd: "poorly made" or "put to bad use."
83 moved: angry.

88 Cast by . . . ornaments: put aside the dignified clothing appropriate for their age.
90 Cank'red with peace: rusty from disuse. **cank'red hate:** dangerous feud.
92 Your lives . . . peace: You will pay with your lives for disturbing the peace.

99 Who . . . abroach: Who reopened this old feud?

1 Summarize *Summarize the prince's words to the crowd. What is his attitude toward the brawls between the Capulets and Montagues?*

Vocabulary

pernicious (pər nish′ əs) *adj.* destructive; deadly

Reading Practice

SPIRAL REVIEW **Construct a Flow Chart** Have students create a flow chart to map the progression of the plot. They can mark the page numbers where a scene occurs next to each box for easy reference later. Students can arrange events in either sequential or cause-and-effect order, or they can draw two flow charts: (1) the conflict between the Capulets and Montagues and (2) Romeo and Juliet's dilemma. Challenge them to connect the charts when events overlap.

I drew to part them. In the instant came
The fiery Tybalt, with his sword prepar'd;
Which, as he breath'd° defiance to my ears,
He swung about his head and cut the winds,
Who, nothing hurt withal,° hiss'd him in scorn.
While we were interchanging thrusts and blows,
Came more and more, and fought on part and part,°
Till the Prince came, who parted either part.

LADY MONTAGUE. O, where is Romeo? Saw you him today?
Right glad I am he was not at this fray.

BENVOLIO. Madam, an hour before the worship'd sun
Peer'd forth° the golden window of the east,
A troubl'd mind drive° me to walk abroad;
Where, underneath the grove of sycamore
That westward rooteth from° this city side,
So early walking did I see your son.
Towards him I made, but he was ware° of me
And stole into the covert of the wood.°
I, measuring his affections,° by my own,
Which then most sought where most might not be found,°
Being one too many by my weary self,
Pursued my humor not pursuing his,°
And gladly shunn'd who gladly fled from me.

MONTAGUE. Many a morning hath he there been seen,
With tears augmenting the fresh morning's dew,
Adding to clouds more clouds with his deep sighs;
But all so soon as the all-cheering sun
Should in the farthest east begin to draw
The shady curtains from Aurora's° bed,
Away from light steals home my heavy° son
And private in his chamber pens himself,
Shuts up his windows, locks fair daylight out,
And makes himself an artificial night.
Black and portentous must this humor prove
Unless good counsel may the cause remove.°

BENVOLIO. My noble uncle, do you know the cause?

MONTAGUE. I neither know it nor can learn of him.

BENVOLIO. Have you importun'd° him by any means?

MONTAGUE. Both by myself and many other friends;
But he, his own affections' counselor,

105 breath'd: uttered.

107 nothing hurt withal: not hurt by this.

109 Came more . . . part: More and more men arrived and fought on one side or the other.

114 forth: out from.

115 drive: drove.

117 westward rooteth from: grows to the west of.

119 ware: aware.

120 covert of the wood: concealment of the forest.

121 affections: feelings.

122 most sought . . . found: wanted to find a solitary place.

124 Pursued my . . . his: followed my own mood **(humor)** by not following him.

131 Aurora (ə rôr ʹ ə)**:** the goddess of the dawn in classical mythology.

132 heavy: sad.

136–137 Black and . . . remove: Montague fears that this mood will lead to trouble if allowed to continue.

140 importun'd: questioned.

2 The Power of Love *From Montague's description of Romeo's behavior, what ideas are you forming about Romeo?*

Teach

Big Idea 2

The Power of Love

Answer: *Students may say that Romeo seems romantic, emotional, or impulsive.* Invite two volunteers to read the parts of Benvolio and Montague (lines 113–139) aloud. **Ask:** Why might Benvolio have decided not to pursue Romeo into the woods? *(Perhaps he sensed Romeo's desire to be alone or had too much on his mind to deal with Romeo's distress.)*

APPROACHING To help students understand the scene, direct them to think about a time when they wanted to be left alone or when they knew that a friend wanted to be left alone.

English Learners

DIFFERENTIATED INSTRUCTION

Intermediate Students may be distracted by constantly checking the definitions in the right column as they read. Suggest that students begin each page by reviewing the side-column information. Have them locate the sentence in which the word or phrase appears, review the definition, and then read the sentence. This preparation will not only improve their comprehension but also increase their enjoyment of the play.

Teach

View the Art ★

Answer: *His fine clothes suggest a young aristocratic hero. His expression is pensive, suggesting Romeo's melancholy.*

Known for religious paintings, Italian painter Biagio d'Antonio (1446–1516) assisted with work on the Sistine Chapel.

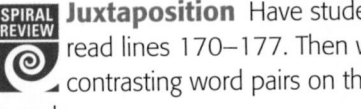

Portrait of a Young Man, ca. 1470. Biagio d'Antonio.

View the Art Biagio d'Antonio often incorporated saturated colors to capture faces, costumes, and landscapes. In what ways does the young man in the painting remind you of Romeo? ★

Reading Practice

SPIRAL REVIEW **Juxtaposition** Have students read lines 170–177. Then write contrasting word pairs on the board:

- brawling
- loving
- love
- hate

Note how the use of parallel construction—using two participles with opposite meanings to modify two nouns with opposite meanings—weighs one idea against the other in a way that is pleasing to the ear. Have students write similarly constructed sentences that balance related ideas.

Is to himself—I will not say how true°—
But to himself so secret and so close,°
So far from sounding and discovery,°
As is the bud bit with an envious worm
Ere he can spread his sweet leaves to the air
Or dedicate his beauty to the sun.°
Could we but learn from whence his sorrows grow,
We would as willingly give cure as know.

[*ROMEO enters. He appears distracted and does not notice the others on stage.*]

BENVOLIO. See where he comes. So please you step aside;
I'll know his grievance, or be much denied.

MONTAGUE. I would thou wert so happy by thy stay
To hear true shrift.° Come, madam, let's away.

[*MONTAGUE and LADY MONTAGUE leave.*]

BENVOLIO. Good morrow,° cousin.

ROMEO. Is the day so young?

BENVOLIO. But new° struck nine.

ROMEO. Ay me! Sad hours seem long.
Was that my father that went hence so fast?

BENVOLIO. It was. What sadness lengthens Romeo's hours?

ROMEO. Not having that which having makes them short.

BENVOLIO. In love?

ROMEO. Out—

BENVOLIO. Of love?

ROMEO. Out of her favor where I am in love.

BENVOLIO. Alas that love, so gentle in his view,
Should be so tyrannous and rough in proof!°

ROMEO. Alas that love, whose view is muffled still,
Should without eyes see pathways to his will!°
Where shall we dine? O me! What fray was here?°
Yet tell me not, for I have heard it all.
Here's much to do with hate, but more with love.
3 Why then, O brawling love, O loving hate,
O any thing, of nothing first create!°

143 how true: how trustworthy (a counselor Romeo is to himself).
144 close: secretive, reticent.
145 far from . . . discovery: unwilling to let others question and come to understand him.
146–148 As is the bud . . . the sun: Montague compares Romeo to a bud that is destroyed by a malicious caterpillar before it can open its petals.

153–154 I would . . . shrift: I hope that by waiting (for Romeo) you will be lucky enough to hear a true confession.

155 morrow: morning.

156 But new: only just.

164–165 love . . . proof: love appears so gentle but proves to be a rough tyrant.
166–167 Alas that . . . will: Romeo regrets that love, although blind, is still able to hit its target. (Cupid, the god of love, is often portrayed wearing a blindfold.)
168 What fray was here: Romeo only now notices blood or some other sign of the fighting.
172 of nothing first create: Romeo refers to the idea that God created the universe from nothing.

---

1 Summarizing *What information has Benvolio just extracted from Romeo?*

2 The Power of Love *What details in Romeo's dialogue help illustrate love's power?*

Teach

Reading Strategy 1

Summarize **Answer:** *Romeo is in love, but his love is not returned.*

Big Idea 2

The Power of Love
Answer: *Love is blind ("love, whose view is muffled still"); love of family can lead to feuds ("O brawling love, O loving hate").*

Literary Element 3

Oxymoron Remind students that an oxymoron combines opposite or contradictory terms. Invite a volunteer to identify the oxymorons in Romeo's speech and explain how they are true. *(Example: "brawling love . . . loving hate." Family loyalty demands that Montagues hate Capulets; Romeo loves, but his love has not brought happiness.)*

ADVANCED Encourage students to come up with their own oxymorons and share them with the class.

Approaching Level

DIFFERENTIATED INSTRUCTION

Emerging Invite students to explain why Romeo is depressed. **Ask:** **Can you relate to Romeo and Benvolio?** Have them explain what Benvolio senses about Romeo's predicament and evaluate how well Benvolio consoles Romeo.

Established Have students write a letter that a modern-day Romeo might send to an advice columnist. Then, have students read their letters to the class. Follow each reading with a short discussion.

Teach

Cultural History ☆

Women's Place In Shakespeare's time, marriage and childbearing were considered a woman's destiny. While Elizabeth I managed to remain unmarried without damaging her immense popularity, single women were generally regarded with suspicion. The choice of a mate was usually dictated by a woman's father and generally involved complicated negotiations in pursuit of financial or political gain or to cement alliances.

O heavy lightness, serious vanity,
Misshapen chaos of well-seeming forms,
3 Feather of lead, bright smoke, cold fire, sick health,
Still-waking sleep, that is not what it is!°
This love feel I, that feel no love in this.°
Dost thou not laugh?

BENVOLIO. No, coz,° I rather weep.

ROMEO. Good heart, at what?

BENVOLIO. At thy good heart's oppression.

ROMEO. Why, such is love's transgression.
Griefs of mine own lie heavy in my breast,
Which thou wilt propagate, to have it press'd
With more of thine.° This love that thou hast shown
Doth add more grief to too much of mine own.
Love is a smoke made with the fume of sighs;
Being purg'd,° a fire sparkling in lovers' eyes;
Being vex'd, a sea nourish'd with loving tears.
What is it else? A madness most discreet,°
A choking gall,° and a preserving sweet.
Farewell, my coz.

BENVOLIO. Soft!° I will go along.
And if you leave me so, you do me wrong.

ROMEO. Tut! I have lost myself; I am not here;
This is not Romeo, he's some other where.

BENVOLIO. Tell me in sadness,° who is that you love?

ROMEO. What, shall I groan and tell thee?

BENVOLIO. Groan? Why, no;
But sadly tell me who.

ROMEO. Bid a sick man in sadness make his will.
A word ill urg'd to one that is so ill!
In sadness, cousin, I do love a woman.

BENVOLIO. I aim'd so near when I suppos'd you lov'd.

ROMEO. A right good markman. And she's fair I love.

BENVOLIO. A right fair mark,° fair coz, is soonest hit.

ROMEO. Well, in that hit you miss. She'll not be hit
With Cupid's arrow. She hath Dian's wit,°
And, in strong proof° of chastity well arm'd,
From Love's weak childish bow she lives uncharm'd.
She will not stay the siege of loving terms,°
☆ Nor bide° th' encounter of assailing eyes,
Nor ope her lap to saint-seducing gold.°

170–176 Here's much . . . it is: Romeo says that the feud involves love (of fighting and devotion to family) as well as hatred. He then suggests the paradoxical nature of love.
177 that feel no love in this: who feels no happiness from this sort of love.
178 coz: cousin. (Any relative might be addressed as cousin.)

182–183 Which thou . . . thine: Your concern over my grief only increases the burden of my sorrow.

186 Being purg'd: when the smoke has cleared.

188 discreet: discriminating.

189 gall: bitterness.

190 Soft: Wait a minute!

194 in sadness: seriously.

202 right fair mark: easily seen target.

204 Dian's wit: the cleverness of Diana, Roman goddess of chastity.
205 proof: armor.

207 stay . . . terms: submit to courtship.
208 bide: tolerate.
209 Nor ope . . . gold: Nor can she be seduced by expensive gifts.

Reading Practice

SPIRAL REVIEW **Paraphrase** Explain that paraphrasing means restating the events of a story in one's own words. **Say:** The ability to paraphrase will be essential to understanding this play. Explain that each time students fill in their flow charts, they are paraphrasing what happened in the play. Have volunteers read aloud passages such as Capulet's speech (lines 13–34, Scene 2). Pause to read explanatory notes. Then invite volunteers to paraphrase the passage, and ask the class to discuss each version until they arrive at the correct meaning.

O, she is rich in beauty; only poor
That, when she dies, with beauty dies her store.°

BENVOLIO. Then she hath sworn that she will still° live chaste?

ROMEO. She hath, and in that sparing makes huge waste;
For beauty starv'd with her severity
Cuts beauty off from all **posterity.**°
She is too fair,° too wise, wisely too fair,
To merit bliss° by making me despair.
She hath forsworn to° love, and in that vow
Do I live dead that live to tell it now.

BENVOLIO. Be ruled by me; forget to think of her.

ROMEO. O, teach me how I should forget to think!

BENVOLIO. By giving liberty unto thine eyes.
Examine other beauties.

ROMEO. 'Tis the way
To call hers, exquisite, in question more.°
These happy° masks° that kiss fair ladies' brows,
Being black puts us in mind they hide the fair.
He that is strucken blind cannot forget
The precious treasure of his eyesight lost.
Show me a mistress that is passing° fair:
What doth her beauty serve but as a note
Where I may read who pass'd° that passing fair?
Farewell. Thou canst not teach me to forget.

BENVOLIO. I'll pay that doctrine, or else die in debt.°

[*They exit.*]

SCENE 2. Later that afternoon. A street near CAPULET's house in Verona.

[*CAPULET enters with COUNT PARIS, a young relative of the PRINCE, and with a SERVANT.*]

CAPULET. But Montague is bound as well as I,
In penalty alike; and 'tis not hard, I think,
For men so old as we to keep the peace.

211 when she . . . store: When she dies, all her wealth will die with her beauty (because she will have no children to inherit her beauty).

212 still: always.

213–215 In that sparing . . . posterity: Romeo says that her thriftiness is really wasteful, because no children will be born to perpetuate her beauty.

216 fair: "beautiful" or "just."

217 To merit bliss: to win heavenly bliss.

218 forsworn to: sworn not to.

223–224 'Tis . . . more: Examining other women will only make me dwell more upon her exquisite beauty.

225 happy: fortunate. **masks:** worn by fashionable Elizabethan women to protect fair complexions from the sun.

229 passing: surpassingly.

231 pass'd: surpassed.

233 I'll pay . . . debt: I'll teach you to forget, or never give up trying until I die.

1 Summarize *What do we learn about the woman Romeo loves in this speech?*

2 Summarize *How would you summarize Romeo and Benvolio's conversation?*

Vocabulary

posterity (pos ter′ ə tē) *n.* future generations

Teach

Reading Strategy 1

Summarize Answer: *She vows to remain chaste, refuses to be courted, and accepts no presents.*

Reading Strategy 2

Summarize Answer: *Romeo claims that nothing can cure him of his love. Benvolio vows to keep trying.*

Cultural History ☆

Velvet Masks Women of the Elizabethan era often carried or wore black velvet masks that covered their entire faces to protect their complexions from the sun. Sometimes viewed as an expression of modesty, the mask would also hide women's faces from undesirable acquaintances.

Approaching Level

DIFFERENTIATED INSTRUCTION

African American Vernacular English Approaching level students who use African American vernacular English may have difficulty eliminating the -*s* in the third person singular and using the -*s* in third person plural. **Write on the board:** I see; You see; He, she, or it sees; We see; You see; They see. Have students repeat the sentences several times.

Teach

Literary Element 1

Foil Answer: *The servant provides contrast in that he is from a lower class, is less knowledgeable, and provides comic relief.*

ADVANCED **Ask:** What technique does Shakespeare use to distinguish the servant from nobility like Romeo? *(The servant's dialogue is written in prose instead of verse.)*

PARIS. Of honorable reckoning° are you both,
And pity 'tis you liv'd at odds so long.
But now, my lord, what say you to my suit?

CAPULET. But saying o'er what I have said before:
My child is yet a stranger in the world,
She hath not seen the change of fourteen years;
Let two more summers wither in their pride
Ere we may think her ripe to be a bride.

PARIS. Younger than she are happy mothers made.

CAPULET. And too soon marr'd are those so early made.
Earth hath swallowed all my hopes but she;°
She is the hopeful lady of my earth.°
But woo her, gentle Paris, get her heart;
My will to her consent is but a part.
And she agreed within her scope of choice
Lies my consent and fair according voice.°
This night I hold an old accustom'd° feast,
Whereto I have invited many a guest,
Such as I love; and you among the store,
One more, most welcome, makes my number more.
At my poor house look to behold this night
Earth-treading stars° that make dark heaven light.
Such comfort as do lusty young men feel
When well-apparel'd April on the heel
Of limping Winter treads, even such delight
Among fresh fennel buds shall you this night
Inherit at my house.° Hear all, all see,
And like her most whose merit most shall be;
Which, on more view of many, mine, being one,
May stand in number, though in reck'ning none.°
Come, go with me.

[CAPULET speaks to his SERVANT and hands him a piece of paper that contains the names of the people he is inviting to his party.]

Go, sirrah,° trudge about
Through fair Verona; find those persons out
Whose names are written there, and to them say
My house and welcome on their pleasure stay.°

[CAPULET and PARIS exit. The SERVANT, who cannot read, looks at the paper.]

SERVANT. Find them out whose names are written here! It is written that the shoemaker should meddle with his yard and the tailor with his last, the fisher with his pencil and the painter with his nets; but I am sent to find those persons whose names are here writ, and can never find

4 reckoning: reputation.

14 Earth hath . . . she: She is my only surviving child.

15 She is . . . earth: "She will inherit all my property," or "She is the woman in whom all my hopes lie."

18–19 And she . . . voice: As long as she chooses appropriately, I will let her marry whomever she chooses.

20 old accustom'd: long established.

25 Earth-treading stars: young women.

26–30 Such comfort . . . house: Tonight the pleasure you will take at my house is like the joy that young men feel when spring replaces winter.

30–33 Hear all . . . none: Capulet suggests that after Paris has compared Juliet to the others, she may strike him as merely one woman among many, not worth special consideration.

34 sirrah (sir′ ə): a term of address used when speaking to someone inferior in rank.

37 stay: wait.

Grammar Practice

Subject-Verb Order

Explain that in most English sentences, the subject precedes the verb, but in verse this order is sometimes reversed (e.g., lines 81–82). Have students reverse the subject-verb order in each sentence. Point out the following sentences on page 639:

- ". . . in that crystal scales let there be weigh'd / Your lady's love against some other maid." (lines 95 and 96) *((You) Let your lady's love be weighed . . . in that crystal scale.)*
- "Come Lammas Eve at night shall she be fourteen." (line 17) *(She shall be fourteen come . . . night.)*

what names the writing person hath here writ.° I must to the learned. In good time!°

[*ROMEO and BENVOLIO enter, still talking about ROMEO's unhappiness in love.*]

BENVOLIO. Tut, man, one fire burns out another's burning;
One pain is less'ned by another's **anguish;**
Turn giddy, and be holp by backward turning;°
One desperate grief cures with another's languish.
Take thou some new infection to thy eye,
And the rank poison of the old will die.

ROMEO. Your plantan° leaf is excellent for that.

BENVOLIO. For what, I pray thee?

ROMEO. For your broken° shin.

BENVOLIO. Why, Romeo, art thou mad?

ROMEO. Not mad, but bound more than a madman is;
3 Shut up in prison, kept without my food,
Whipt and tormented and—God-den,° good fellow.

SERVANT. God gi'° god-den. I pray, sir, can you read?

ROMEO. Ay, mine own fortune in my misery.

SERVANT. Perhaps you have learn'd it without book.
But, I pray, can you read anything you see?

ROMEO. Ay, if I know the letters and the language.

SERVANT. Ye say honestly. Rest you merry.°

ROMEO. Stay, fellow; I can read. [*He reads.*]
"Signior Martino and his wife and daughters; County° Anselm and his beauteous sisters; the lady widow of Vitruvio; Signior Placentio and his lovely nieces; Mercutio and his brother Valentine; mine uncle Capulet, his wife and daughters; my fair niece Rosaline; Livia; Signior Valentio and his cousin Tybalt; Lucio and the lively Helena."
A fair assembly. Whither should they come?

SERVANT. Up.

ROMEO. Whither? To supper?

---

1 Foil *How does the character of the servant provide contrast to the characters who have just been talking?*

2 The Power of Love *What cure does Benvolio suggest for Romeo's lovesickness?*

Vocabulary

anguish (ang′ gwish) *n.* extreme suffering; agony

38–43 Find them . . . writ: The illiterate servant means to say that people should stick to what they know how to do, but he comically mixes up the types of workers and their tools.

43 In good time: Just in time! (He sees men who appear to be educated.)

47 Turn giddy . . . turning: Become dizzy, and be helped by turning in the opposite direction.

51 plantan: plantain (a type of leaf used to stop bleeding).

52 broken: scraped.

56 God-den: good afternoon; good evening.

57 God gi': God give you.

62 Rest you merry: The servant misunderstands Romeo's reply and bids him farewell.

64 County: Count.

Teach

Big Idea 2

The Power of Love

Answer: *Exposing Romeo to other beautiful women will extinguish his excessive love.*

Invite a volunteer to read aloud lines 45–50. **Ask:** What point is Benvolio trying to make in this passage? *(He is trying to convince Romeo that there is a way out of his lovesickness, only if he would be willing to listen and consider what Benvolio has to say.)*

Big Idea 3

The Power of Love

Say: Explain Romeo's metaphor in line 55 when he says, "Shut up in prison, kept without my food." *(The prison is his own lovesick heart, and his food—which he lacks—is Rosaline's love.)*

APPROACHING **Ask:** Why does Romeo speak in metaphor instead of saying exactly what he means? *(Metaphor gives a more vivid impression of Romeo's emotions than literal language would.)*

English Learners

DIFFERENTIATED INSTRUCTION

Intermediate Students may benefit from reading along while listening to a recording of the play. Select one scene for students to read while listening to an audio version of the same scene. After students have finished reading, have them work in small groups to answer the following questions:

- Who was in the scene?
- Which words best describe the characters' moods?
- What happened in the scene?
- Why did it happen?
- Which words best describe the tone of the scene?

Teach

Reading Strategy 1

Summarize Answer: *They learn that the Capulets are holding a big party. Since Rosaline will be there, Benvolio proposes that he and Romeo attend the party so Romeo can see that other women there are as fair as Rosaline.*

Big Idea 2

The Power of Love Have students identify and analyze the comparison Romeo makes here.

Ask: How does the comparison characterize Romeo? *(Romeo's lofty, extravagant comparison of love to a fiercely demanding religion suggests an impetuous nature and a highly romantic view of love.)*

SERVANT. To our house.

ROMEO. Whose house?

SERVANT. My master's.

ROMEO. Indeed I should have ask'd thee that before.

SERVANT. Now I'll tell you without asking. My master is the great rich Capulet; and if you be not of the house of Montagues, I pray come and crush a cup° of wine. Rest you merry.

[*The* SERVANT *exits.*]

BENVOLIO. At this same ancient° feast of Capulet's
Sups the fair Rosaline whom thou so loves;
With all the admired beauties of Verona.
Go thither,° and with unattainted° eye
Compare her face with some that I shall show,
And I will make thee think thy swan a crow.

2 ROMEO. When the devout religion of mine eye
Maintains such falsehood, then turn tears to fires;
And these, who, often drown'd, could never die,
Transparent heretics,° be burnt for liars!°
One fairer than my love? The all-seeing sun
Ne'er saw her match since first the world begun.

BENVOLIO. Tut! you saw her fair, none else being by,
Herself pois'd° with herself in either eye;
But in that crystal scales° let there be weigh'd
Your lady's love against some other maid
That I will show you shining at this feast,
And she shall scant show well that now seems best.

ROMEO. I'll go along, no such sight to be shown,
But to rejoice in splendor of mine own.°

[*They exit.*]

SCENE 3. Later that evening, before the party. A room in CAPULET's house.

[*LADY CAPULET and the Capulets' NURSE enter.*]

LADY CAPULET. Nurse, where's my daughter? Call her forth to me.

NURSE. Now by my maidenhead at twelve year old,
I bade her come. What, lamb! What, ladybird!
God forbid! Where's this girl? What, Juliet!

79 crush a cup: have a drink.

81 ancient: traditional.

84 thither: there. **unattainted:** impartial.

87–90 When the . . . liars: Romeo says that if he accepted such a falsehood, his tearful eyes would be heretics for having broken faith with Rosaline, and he would wish the tears turned to fire so that his eyes could be burned like heretics.

90 heretics: People who maintain a religious belief contrary to accepted doctrine.

94 pois'd: weighed; compared.

95 crystal scales: That is, Romeo's eyes.

100 in splendor of mine own: in the splendor of my own lady (Rosaline).

1 Summarize *What do Benvolio and Romeo learn from the servant? What does Benvolio propose to do with the information?*

Reading Practice

SPIRAL REVIEW

Self-Monitor Comprehension

Explain that the natural divisions of a play—acts and scenes—are good places for readers to pause and think about what they have read. They also might want to reread the character descriptions and paraphrase the previous act or scene. Encourage students to note unresolved questions in their notebooks and to reflect on their questions later to see if they have been addressed.

[*JULIET enters.*]

JULIET. How now? Who calls?

NURSE. Your mother.

JULIET. Madam, I am here.
What is your will?

LADY CAPULET. This is the matter—Nurse, give leave° awhile;
We must talk in secret. Nurse, come back again.
I have remembʼred me; thouʼs hear our counsel.°
Thou knowest my daughter's of a pretty age.

NURSE. Faith, I can tell her age unto an hour.

LADY CAPULET. She's not fourteen.

NURSE. I'll lay fourteen of my teeth—
And yet, to my teen° be it spoken, I have but four—
She's not fourteen. How long is it now
To Lammastide?°

LADY CAPULET. A fortnight and odd days.°

NURSE. Even or odd, of all days in the year,
Come Lammas Eve at night shall she be fourteen.
Susan and she (God rest all Christian souls!)
Were of an age.° Well, Susan is with God;
She was too good for me. But, as I said,
On Lammas Eve at night shall she be fourteen;
That shall she, marry;° I remember it well.
ʼTis since the earthquake now eleven years;
And she was weanʼd—I shall never forget it—
Of all the days of the year, upon that day;
For I had then laid wormwood° to my dug,°
Sitting in the sun under the dove-house wall.
My lord and you were then at Mantua—
Nay, I do bear a brain°—but as I said,
When it did taste the wormwood on the nipple
Of my dug and felt it bitter, pretty fool,
To see it teachy° and fall out wiʼ thʼ dug!
Shake, quoth the dove-house;° ʼtwas no need, I trow,
To bid me trudge.°
And since that time it is eleven years,
For then she could stand high-lone;° nay, by thʼ rood,°
She could have run and waddled all about;
For even the day before, she broke her brow,
And then my husband—God be with his soul!

3 Foil *How do the Nurse and Lady Capulet differ? How do their characters contrast?*

8 give leave: leave us alone.

9 thouʼs hear our counsel: You shall hear our conversation.

13 teen: sorrow.

15 Lammastide: August 1, a religious feast day. **A fortnight and odd days:** two weeks plus a few days.

19 of an age: the same age. (The Nurse's daughter, now dead, was born around the same time as Juliet.)

22 marry: indeed.

26 wormwood: a bitter oil from the leaves of a plant. **dug:** breast.

29 I do bear a brain: My mind is still sharp.

32 teachy: tetchy; irritably or peevishly sensitive.

33 Shake . . . dove-house: The dove-house began to shake from the earthquake.

33–34 ʼtwas . . . trudge: I didn't need any urging to get away.

37 high-lone: upright without support. **rood:** cross.

Teach

Literary Element 3

Foil **Answer:** *One is the biological mother; the other, the foster mother. The coarse Nurse is warm and intimate with Juliet. Lady Capulet is refined and reserved.*

Ask: How does Shakespeare temper the humor of the dialogue and engage our sympathy for the Nurse? *(In lines 18–20, the Nurse remembers her dead daughter, who would now be Juliet's age had she lived.)*

Advanced Learners

DIFFERENTIATED INSTRUCTION

Evaluate Reason Ask students what persuasive techniques they would use to get a friend to agree to a blind date. What evidence would they provide to support their arguments? Have students list and evaluate the reasons Lady Capulet and the Nurse give for accepting Paris's proposal. *(Lady Capulet says that she was already married with children when she was Juliet's age and that Paris has wealth and position; the Nurse points out that Paris is attractive.)* **Ask:** Are they based on logic or emotion? *(They are more logical than emotional)* What arguments might work better? *(Because Juliet is young, she might be more moved by romantic arguments that appeal to her emotions.)*

Teach

Literary Element 1

Foil **Answer:** *She seems stiff and unamused.*

ADVANCED Note that this long speech establishes the Nurse as a fully rounded character: humorous, affectionate, self-aware, and observant. **Ask:** Why do you think Shakespeare features the Nurse so prominently in the scene that introduces Juliet? *(Because the Nurse serves as a surrogate mother to Juliet, it's possible she'll play an important role in the relationship between Romeo and Juliet.)*

Literary Element 2

Foil **Answer:** *Although both women approve of the match, the Nurse's emphasis on the physical aspects of marriage contrast with Lady Capulet's focus on wealth and status. The Nurse seems concerned primarily with Juliet's happiness, while the more distant Lady Capulet wants to ensure Juleit's financial securtiy and social status.*

'A° was a merry man—took up the child.
"Yea," quoth he, "dost thou fall upon thy face?
Thou wilt fall backward when thou hast more wit,°
Wilt thou not, Jule?" and by my holidam,°
The pretty wretch left crying and said, "Ay."
To see now how a jest shall come about!
I warrant, and I should live a thousand years,
I never should forget it: "Wilt thou not, Jule?" quoth he;
And, pretty fool, it stinted° and said, "Ay."

LADY CAPULET. Enough of this, I pray thee hold thy peace.

NURSE. Yes, madam, yet I cannot choose but laugh
To think it should leave crying and say, "Ay."
And yet I warrant it had upon its brow
A bump as big as a young cock'rel's stone—
A perilous knock—and it cried bitterly.
"Yea," quoth my husband, "fall'st upon thy face?
Thou wilt fall backward when thou comest to age,
Wilt thou not, Jule?" It stinted and said, "Ay."

JULIET. And stint thou too, I pray thee, nurse, say I.

NURSE. Peace, I have done. God mark thee to his grace!
Thou wast the prettiest babe that e'er I nurs'd.
And I might live to see thee married once,
I have my wish.

LADY CAPULET. Marry, that "marry" is the very theme
I came to talk of. Tell me, daughter Juliet,
How stands your disposition to be married?

JULIET. It is an honor that I dream not of.

NURSE. An honor! were not I thine only nurse,
I would say thou hadst suck'd wisdom from thy teat.

LADY CAPULET. Well, think of marriage now. Younger than you,
Here in Verona, ladies of esteem,
Are made already mothers. By my count,
I was your mother much upon these years°
That you are now a maid. Thus then in brief:
The valiant Paris seeks you for his love.

NURSE. A man, young lady! Lady, such a man
As all the world—Why, he's a man of wax.°

40 'A: he.

42 wit: knowledge.

43 by my holidam: by my holiness (an oath).

48 stinted: stopped.

72 much upon these years: at about the same age.

76 man of wax: a model man, as perfect as a wax statue.

1 Foil *How would you characterize Lady Capulet's response to the Nurse's funny story?*

2 Foil *Compare and contrast the reactions of the Nurse and Lady Capulet in this scene. What is the focus and principal concern of each character?*

Writing Practice

Respond to the Play

Encourage students to express their reactions to the play in a journal as they read. Provide these questions as a starting point:

- What impresses you about the drama?
- What bothers you about it?
- What questions, if any, do you have about it?

Encourage students to support their views with examples from the text.

Invite volunteers to use questions and observations from their journals during class discussions.

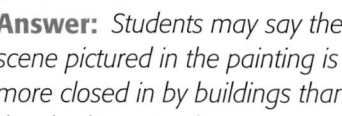

Italian Palace, 1623. Hendrik Steenwyck the Younger. Oil on copper, 54.5 x 80 cm. Hermitage, St. Petersburg, Russia.

View the Art Hendrik Steenwyck the Younger specialized in painting buildings. How does this scene compare to how you imagine the setting in Scene 4? ★

LADY CAPULET. Verona's summer hath not such a flower.

☆ NURSE. Nay, he's a flower, in faith—a very flower.

LADY CAPULET. What say you? Can you love the gentleman?
This night you shall behold him at our feast.
Read o'er the volume° of young Paris' face,
And find delight writ there with beauty's pen;
Examine every married lineament,°
And see how one another lends content;
And what obscur'd in this fair volume lies
Find written in the margent° of his eyes.
This precious book of love, this unbound lover,
To beautify him only lacks a cover.°
The fish lives in the sea, and 'tis much pride
For fair without the fair within to hide.°
That book in many's eyes doth share the glory,
That in gold clasps locks in the golden story;
So shall you share all that he doth possess,
By having him making yourself no less.

81 volume: book. (This metaphor is extended in lines 82–92.)

83 every married lineament (lin′ ē ə mənt): all the harmonious features of his face.

86 margent (mär′ jənt): margin (which, like the marginal notes in a book, reveal whatever is not clear in the rest of his face).

88 cover: binding (that is, a wife).

89–90 The fish . . . hide: The fair sea is made even more beautiful by the fair fish hiding within it.

Teach

Cultural History ☆

Men in Women's Roles

Because English law barred Elizabethan women from appearing onstage, male actors played all the female roles. Most scholars believe that the majority of these actors were teenagers who, because of the less nutritious diet of those times, tended to be frailer and less physically mature than today's adolescents.

View the Art ★

Answer: *Students may say the scene pictured in the painting is more closed in by buildings than they had imagined.*

Flemish painter Hendrik Steenwyck the Younger (1580–1649) and his father, the Elder, specialized in painting architectural views. Both the Younger and the Elder are known for their paintings of churches.

Advanced Learners

DIFFERENTIATED INSTRUCTION

Song Lyrics Four centuries ago, lovesick suitors wrote poems; today, they write songs. Ask students to bring in song lyrics that illustrate Romeo's feelings. Discuss how the lyrics reflect Romeo's state of mind. Have students write song lyrics from the point of view of one of the characters. The song should describe the character's feeling and situation. Have students read their lyrics with the class.

Teach

Reading Strategy 1

Summarize **Answer:** *She notes Paris's good looks and fine character as well as the economic advantages to be gained. Juliet seems neutral on the proposal but dutifully agrees to consider it.*

Literary Element 2

Rhyming Couplet **Ask:** How does Shakespeare end Scene 3? *(He ends it with a pair of rhyming couplets.)*

Reading Strategy 3

Connect **Ask:** What are Benvolio and Mercutio doing in the opening of Scene 4? *(Students should note that Romeo is being morose and his friends, Benvolio and Mercutio, are trying to shake him out of his bad mood.)*

NURSE. No less! nay, bigger: women grow° by men.

LADY CAPULET. Speak briefly, can you like of Paris' love?

JULIET. I'll look to like, if looking liking move;
But no more deep will I endart mine eye
Than your consent gives strength to make it fly.°

[*A* SERVANT *enters.*]

SERVINGMAN. Madam, the guests are come, supper served up, you call'd, my young lady ask'd for, the nurse curs'd° in the pantry, and everything in extremity. I must hence to wait. I beseech you follow straight.°

2

[*The* SERVANT *exits.*]

LADY CAPULET. We follow thee. Juliet, the County stays.°

NURSE. Go, girl, seek happy nights to happy days.

[*They exit.*]

SCENE 4. Later that night. A street in Verona.

[*ROMEO enters with his friends MERCUTIO and BENVOLIO. They are on their way to CAPULET'S party; they wear masks to conceal their identities because ROMEO and BENVOLIO are Montagues. Several other MASKERS and TORCHBEARERS accompany them.*]

ROMEO. What, shall this speech be spoke for our excuse?
Or shall we on without apology?°

BENVOLIO. The date is out of such prolixity:°
We'll have no Cupid hoodwink'd° with a scarf,
Bearing a Tartar's painted bow of lath,°
Scaring the ladies like a crow-keeper,°
Nor no without-book prologue,° faintly spoke
After the prompter, for our entrance;
But let them measure us by what they will,
We'll measure them a measure° and be gone.

3

ROMEO. Give me a torch. I am not for this ambling.
Being but heavy,° I will bear the light.

MERCUTIO. Nay, gentle Romeo, we must have you dance.

ROMEO. Not I, believe me. You have dancing shoes
With nimble soles; I have a soul of lead
So stakes me to the ground I cannot move.

MERCUTIO. You are a lover. Borrow Cupid's wings
And soar with them above a common bound.°

1 Summarize *Summarize Lady Capulet's attempt to persuade her daughter. How does Juliet respond?*

95 grow: become pregnant.

97–99 I'll look . . . fly: I am prepared to look favorably on him, if looking can persuade me, but I won't give him encouraging glances beyond your approval.

101 curs'd: The Nurse is cursed because she is not helping.

103 straight: immediately.

104 the County stays: Count Paris is waiting.

1–2 What, shall . . . apology: Maskers would arrive uninvited to a festival or celebration and expect hospitality. Romeo wonders if they should deliver a customary speech greeting the host and apologizing for their intrusion.

3 The date . . . prolixity: Such wordiness is out of fashion.

4 hoodwink'd: blindfolded.

5 Tartar's . . . lath: a short bow made of thin wood.

6 crow-keeper: scarecrow holding a bow.

7 without-book prologue: memorized speech.

10 measure them a measure: stay for a dance.

12 heavy: sad.

18 bound: leap (in a dance).

Writing Practice

Vivid Description Stress the importance of specific concrete sensory details in writing. Write these sentences on the board:

- She drives around in a nutshell with an insect for a driver.
- Her chariot is an empty hazelnut, her wagoner, a small gray-coated gnat.

Ask students to compare the specificity of the nouns and adjectives. **Ask:** What sense do the details appeal to? *(sight)* Discuss how these words paint a picture and create a mood. Have students write a vivid description of one of the settings in the play.

3

ROMEO. I am too sore empiercèd with his shaft°
To soar with his light feathers; and so bound
I cannot bound a pitch° above dull woe.
Under love's heavy burden do I sink.

MERCUTIO. And, to sink in it, should you burden love—
Too great oppression for a tender thing.

ROMEO. Is love a tender thing? It is too rough,
Too rude, too boist'rous and it pricks like thorn.

MERCUTIO. If love be rough with you, be rough with love.
Prick love for pricking, and you beat love down.
Give me a case° to put my visage° in. [*Puts on a mask.*]
A visor° for a visor! What care I
What curious eye doth quote° deformities?
Here are the beetle brows° shall blush for me.

BENVOLIO. Come, knock and enter; and no sooner in
But every man betake him to his legs.°

ROMEO. A torch for me! Let wantons light of heart
Tickle the senseless rushes° with their heels;
For I am proverb'd with a grandsire phrase,°
I'll be a candleholder° and look on;
The game was ne'er so fair, and I am done.

MERCUTIO. Tut, dun's the mouse,° the constable's own word.
If thou art Dun, we'll draw thee from the mire
Of this sir-reverence° love, wherein thou stickest
Up to the ears. Come, we burn daylight,° ho!

ROMEO. Nay, that's not so.

MERCUTIO. I mean, sir, in delay
We waste our lights in vain, like lights by day!
Take our good meaning, for our judgment sits
Five times in that ere once in our five wits.°

ROMEO. And we mean well in going to this mask,
But 'tis no wit to go.

MERCUTIO. Why, may one ask?

ROMEO. I dreamt a dream tonight.°

MERCUTIO. And so did I.

ROMEO. Well, what was yours?

19 enpierced . . . shaft: wounded with Cupid's arrow.

21 a pitch: any height.

29 case: cover. **visage:** face.

30 visor: mask.

31 quote: make note of.

32 beetle brows: bushy eyebrows.

34 betake . . . legs: begin to dance.

36 rushes: straw floor covering.

37 proverb'd . . . phrase: guided by an old saying.

38 candleholder: spectator. The proverb advises leaving a gambling table when you are ahead.

40 dun's the mouse: an expression meaning, "Keep quiet and hidden." (Mercutio plays off the word *done* with *dun,* meaning "dark.")

42 sir-reverence: an apologetic expression used to introduce something thought indecent (but Mercutio ironically uses it to introduce the word *love*).

43 burn daylight: waste time.

46–47 Take our . . . wits: Accept our intended **(good)** meaning, for true understanding is five times as likely to be found there as in cleverness.

50 tonight: last night.

4 Foil *How does Mercutio's attitude and energy level differ from Romeo's? What does the contrast between the two characters lend to the scene?*

5 Summarize *Reread lines 35–47. Also read the margin notes. How would you summarize this exchange?*

Teach

Literary Element 4

Foil **Answer:** *Mercutio is energetic and upbeat. Romeo is weary and morose because of unrequited love. The contrast lends drama and humor to the scene.*

Point out that Mercutio is trying to cajole Romeo out of his bleak mood. Invite two volunteers to assume the parts of Romeo and Mercutio and read lines 11–26 aloud. Encourage them to express the mood of each character through voice inflection.

ENGLISH LEARNERS Help students build confidence for this activity by pairing them up with other students and allowing them time to practice with partners before performing in front of the class.

Reading Strategy 5

Summarize **Answer:** *Mercutio encourages Romeo to go to the party. Romeo insists he has wearied of love and the enjoyments of youth. Mercutio makes light of Romeo's lovesickness and urges him to cheer up and have fun.*

Ask: What does Romeo's persistent refusal to join in the fun suggest about his personality? *(He seems stubborn and self-involved, preferring to wallow in his suffering.)*

Approaching Level

DIFFERENTIATED INSTRUCTION

Established Show students pictures of the typical costumes worn by actors who play Romeo and Juliet. **Ask:** How do the costumes help tell the story of Romeo and Juliet? *(The Montagues wear one color and the Capulets another; this shows they have differences. The clothes help show the time when the story occurs.)* Remind students that every choice, even the characters' costumes, is telling the story of the play. Ask students how they would dress each character in a modern production of the play.

Teach

Reading Strategy 1

Visualize Note that the Queen Mab speech is famous for its inventive language. Have students describe the impressions created by its images and details. Have students compare this speech with the Nurse's in Scene 3 and describe what each speech reveals about the speaker. *(Nurse: bumbling, affectionate, talkative; Mercutio clever, imaginative, cynical about women.)*

MERCUTIO. That dreamers often lie.

ROMEO. In bed asleep, while they do dream things true.

[*As* ROMEO *speaks with his friends, the* MASKERS *and* TORCHBEARERS *march about the stage.* MERCUTIO *continues trying to cheer* ROMEO.]

MERCUTIO. O, then I see Queen Mab° hath been with you.
She is the fairies' midwife,° and she comes
In shape no bigger than an agate stone°
On the forefinger of an alderman,
Drawn with a team of little atomi°
Over men's noses as they lie asleep;
Her chariot is an empty hazelnut,
Made by the joiner° squirrel or old grub,
Time out o' mind the fairies' coachmakers.
Her wagon spokes made of long spinners'° legs,
The cover, of the wings of grasshoppers;
Her traces,° of the smallest spider web;
Her collars, of the moonshine's wat'ry beams;
Her whip, of cricket's bone; the lash, of film;°
Her wagoner,° a small gray-coated gnat,
Not half so big as a round little worm
Pricked from the lazy finger of a maid;°
And in this state° she gallops night by night
Through lovers' brains, and then they dream of love;
O'er courtiers' knees, that dream on curtsies straight;°
O'er lawyers' fingers, who straight dream on fees;
O'er ladies' lips, who straight on kisses dream,
Which oft the angry Mab with blisters plagues,
Because their breath with sweetmeats° tainted are.
Sometime she gallops o'er a courtier's nose,
And then dreams he of smelling out a suit;°
And sometime comes she with a tithe pig's° tail
Tickling a parson's nose as 'a lies asleep,
Then he dreams of another benefice.°
Sometime she driveth o'er a soldier's neck,
And then dreams he of cutting foreign throats,
Of breaches, ambuscadoes,° Spanish blades,
Of healths° five fathom deep; and then anon°
Drums in his ear, at which he starts and wakes,
And being thus frighted, swears a prayer or two
And sleeps again. This is that very Mab
That plats° the manes of horses in the night,
And bakes the elf-locks° in foul sluttish hairs,
Which, once untangled, much misfortune bodes.
This is the hag, when maids lie on their backs,

53 Queen Mab: queen of the fairies.
54 fairies' midwife: the fairy who helps sleepers give birth to dreams.
55 agate stone: gem set in a ring.
57 little atomi: tiny creatures.
60 joiner: carpenter.
62 spinners': spiders'.
64 traces: harnesses.
66 film: cobweb.
67 wagoner: driver.
68–69 worm . . . maid: Worms were said to grow in the fingers of lazy maids.
70 state: majestic style.
72 that dream . . . straight: who immediately dream of respectful bows.
76 sweetmeats: sweets.
78 smelling out a suit: having someone pay him for his influence with the king.
79 tithe (tīth) **pig:** a pig that a parishioner gives to a parson as a customary contribution to the church.
81 benefice (ben′ ə fis): church appointment with an assured income.
84 ambuscadoes (am′ bus kä′ dōz): ambushes.
85 healths: drinking toasts. **anon:** at once.
89 plats: tangles.
90 elf-locks: hair that is matted from lack of grooming.

Reading Practice

SPIRAL REVIEW **Set a Purpose** Remind students that establishing a goal for their reading will improve their focus and help them understand the material. Note that Scene 5 culminates in the first meeting of Romeo and Juliet. Have students write down three questions they hope to answer by reading Scene 5. Compile a list of commonly asked student questions on the board and address them as you read through the scene.

1 That presses them and learns them first to bear,
Making them women of good carriage.
This is she—

ROMEO. Peace, peace Mercutio, peace!
Thou talk'st of nothing.

MERCUTIO. True, I talk of dreams;
Which are the children of an idle brain,
Begot of nothing but vain fantasy;
Which is as thin of substance as the air,
3 And more inconstant° than the wind, who woos
Even now the frozen bosom of the north
And, being anger'd, puffs away from thence,
Turning his side to the dew-dropping south.

BENVOLIO. This wind you talk of blows us from ourselves.
Supper is done, and we shall come too late.

ROMEO. I fear, too early; for my mind misgives
Some consequence yet hanging in the stars
Shall bitterly begin his fearful date
With this night's revels and expire the term
Of a despised life, clos'd in my breast,
By some vile forfeit of untimely death.°
But He that hath the steerage of my course
Direct my sail! On, lusty gentlemen!

BENVOLIO. Strike, drum.

[*They march about the stage and exit.*]

SCENE 5. Immediately following the previous scene. A hall in CAPULET's house.

[*SERVANTS enter carrying napkins. They are clearing away the tables from dinner and making the hall ready for dancing.*]

FIRST SERVINGMAN. Where's Potpan, that he helps not to take away?° He shift a trencher!° He scrape a trencher!

SECOND SERVINGMAN. When good manners° shall lie all in one or two men's hands, and they unwash'd too, 'tis a foul thing.

FIRST SERVINGMAN. Away with the join-stools,° remove the court cupboard,° look to the plate.° Good thou, save me a

100 inconstant: fickle, changing.

106–111 I fear . . . death: Romeo says that he has a premonition that some event **(consequence)** being worked out by fate will occur at the festivities and lead to his premature death, like a loan that comes due early.

1–2 take away: clean up after dinner.
2 trencher: wooden platter.
3 manners: a pun on the Latin root for "hands."

5 join-stools: sturdy stools made by a joiner, or carpenter.
6 court cupboard: cabinet that holds linen, silver, and china. **plate:** silverware.

2 The Power of Love *What connection is Mercutio making here between dreams and Romeo's love?*

4 Summarize *What does Romeo reveal in lines 106–111?*

Teach

Big Idea 2

The Power of Love

Answer: *Romeo's love is as unreal and insubstantial as his dreams.*

Literary Element 3

Figurative Language

Ask: What examples of simile, metaphor, and personification do you find in Mercutio's speech in lines 98–103?
(Metaphor: dreams are the "children of an idle brain"; Simile: fantasy "as thin of substance as the air"; Personification: "the wind, who woos . . . puffs away from thence.")

Reading Strategy 4

Summarize

Answer: *Romeo reveals his premonition that an event at the festivities will lead to his premature death.*

APPROACHING **Ask:** What literary technique is Shakespeare using by telling the audience that Romeo has a premonition? *(Foreshadowing)*

Approaching Level

DIFFERENTIATED INSTRUCTION

Emerging Have students visualize the characters at the ball. Draw a stage on the board and have students place the characters (Capulet, Tybalt, the serving man, Romeo, and Juliet) in locations where they might appear at different points in the action. Discuss how the movement of the characters changes the focus of the audience's attention as the scene unfolds.

Established Watch a video of the ball scene to help students comprehend the scene. Have students identify differences between their interpretation and the film version.

Teach

View the Art ★

Answer: *Sir Dicksee might have chosen to use the en grisaille style so that the viewer's attention is drawn to Romeo and Juliet's body language rather than to their outfits or to the festivities. Additionally, the somber tones foreshadow the tragedy to come.*

The work of English illustrator and painter Sir Frank Dicksee (1853–1928) combines poetic sentiment with realistic detail. *Gouache*—an opaque watercolor paint—and a technique for achieving varied tones known as *en grisaille* were used to create this intricately detailed scene.

The Ball Scene from Romeo and Juliet, 1882. Sir Frank Dicksee. Gouache, en grisaille. Private collection.

View the Art The term *en grisaille* refers to a style of painting in which the artist uses only various tones of a single color. Why might Sir Dicksee have chosen this style to portray Romeo and Juliet? ★

Speaking and Listening Practice

SPIRAL REVIEW **Oral Interpretation** Have pairs of students present oral interpretations of dialogues between Tybalt and Romeo or Romeo and Juliet. Allow them time to practice and provide the following guidelines:

- Decide where pauses go.
- Vary pitch and tone appropriately.
- Experiment with phrasings and emphases.
- Rehearse until confident.

Have volunteers perform their dialogues in front of the class.

piece of marchpane,° and, as thou loves me, let the porter
let in Susan Grindstone and Nell. Anthony, and Potpan!

[*ANTHONY and POTPAN enter. SECOND SERVANT exits.*]

ANTHONY. Ay, boy, ready.

FIRST SERVINGMAN. You are look'd for and call'd for, ask'd
for and sought for, in the great chamber.

POTPAN. We cannot be here and there too. Cheerly, boys!
Be brisk awhile, and the longer liver take all.°

[*The SERVANTS retire to the back. CAPULET enters with LADY CAPULET, JULIET, TYBALT, and other CAPULETS, the NURSE, and all the GUESTS. The MASKERS join the group.*]

CAPULET. Welcome, gentlemen! Ladies that have their toes
Unplagu'd with corns will walk a bout° with you.
Ah, my mistresses, which of you all
Will now deny to dance? She that makes dainty,°
She I'll swear hath corns. Am I come near ye now?°

[*CAPULET notices the MASKERS and speaks to them.*]

Welcome, gentlemen! I have seen the day
That I have worn a visor and could tell
A whispering tale in a fair lady's ear,
Such as would please. 'Tis gone, 'tis gone, 'tis gone.
You are welcome, gentlemen! Come, musicians, play.

[*Music plays, and the GUESTS dance.*]

A hall, a hall! Give room!° And foot it, girls.
More light, you knaves, and turn the tables up,
And quench the fire; the room is grown too hot.
Ah, sirrah, this unlook'd-for sport° comes well.
Nay, sit; nay, sit, good cousin Capulet;
For you and I are past our dancing days.
How long is't now since last yourself and I
Were in a mask?

SECOND CAPULET. By'r Lady, thirty years.

CAPULET. What, man? 'Tis not so much, 'tis not so much;
'Tis since the nuptial° of Lucentio,
Come Pentecost° as quickly as it will,
Some five-and-twenty years, and then we mask'd.

SECOND CAPULET. 'Tis more, 'tis more. His son is elder, sir;
His son is thirty.

7 marchpane: marzipan, a sweet made of sugar and almonds.

13 the longer . . . all: The one who outlives the rest of us takes everything.

15 walk a bout: dance.

17 makes dainty: coyly hesitates.

18 Am I . . . now: Have I struck close to home?

24 A hall . . . room: Clear the hall and make room for dancing!

27 unlook'd-for sport: unexpected entertainment (referring to the arrival of the maskers).

33 nuptial (nup′ shəl): wedding.

34 Pentecost (pen′ tə kôst): seventh Sunday after Easter.

Summarize *Summarize the dialogue in lines 14–37.*

Teach

Reading Strategy

Summarize Answer: *Capulet welcomes his guests and urges the women to dance. He sees the masked guests and welcomes them, remembering the days when he and his friends wore masks and crashed parties. He and his cousin disagree about when they last did this.*

Cultural History

Renaissance Dance

Dancing was a popular pastime among the privileged classes of the Renaissance. Capulet's guests probably engaged in a simple line or circle dance. Because of constrictive clothing styles, most dances of that period relied more on footwork than on upper body movement.

Approaching Level

DIFFERENTIATED INSTRUCTION

Emerging Have volunteers read aloud the exchange between Tybalt and Capulet. **Ask:** What exactly do the two disagree about? *(Students should indicate that Tybalt wants to fight, but Capulet does not want a fight at his party.)* **Ask:** Has Tybalt ever acted similarly? *(Students may remember when Benvolio wanted peace, but Tybalt said he hated the word.)*

Ask: What can you tell about Tybalt from these two scenes? *(Tybalt has a violent streak that is hard to control.)*

Teach

Big Idea 1

The Power of Love
Answer: *Romeo is awed by Juliet's beauty; his dramatic shift in mood and his immediate infatuation with Juliet make him seem fickle and impetuous.*

Reading Strategy 2

Summarize **Ask:** What is the purpose of Tybalt's speech? *(It reminds the audience that the feud poses a dangerous obstacle to the young lovers.)*

APPROACHING Help students answer the question by asking them who Tybalt threatens, with what, and what implications his threat could have on the rest of the story.

CAPULET. Will you tell me that?
His son was but a ward° two years ago.

[*ROMEO has been watching JULIET and stops a SERVANT to ask about her.*]

ROMEO. [*To a SERVINGMAN.*] What lady's that which doth
enrich the hand
Of yonder knight?

SERVINGMAN. I know not, sir.

ROMEO. O, she doth teach the torches to burn bright!
It seems she hangs upon the cheek of night
As a rich jewel in an Ethiop's ear—
Beauty too rich for use, for earth too dear!
So shows° a snowy dove trooping with crows
As yonder lady o'er her fellows shows.
The measure done, I'll watch her place of stand°
And, touching hers, make blessed my rude° hand.
Did my heart love till now? Forswear° it, sight!
For I ne'er saw true beauty till this night.

2

TYBALT. This, by his voice, should be a Montague.
Fetch me my rapier,° boy. What! Dares the slave
Come hither, cover'd with an antic face,°
To fleer and scorn at our solemnity?°
Now, by the stock and honor of my kin,
To strike him dead I hold it not a sin.

CAPULET. Why, how now, kinsman? Wherefore° storm you so?

TYBALT. Uncle, this is a Montague, our foe,
A villain, that is hither come in spite
To scorn at our solemnity this night.

CAPULET. Young Romeo is it?

TYBALT. 'Tis he, that villain Romeo.

CAPULET. Content thee, gentle coz,° let him alone.
'A bears him like a portly gentleman,°
And, to say truth, Verona brags of him
To be a virtuous and well-govern'd youth.
I would not for the wealth of all this town
Here in my house do him disparagement.°
Therefore be patient; take no note of him.
It is my will, the which if thou respect,

38 but a ward: only a minor (under twenty-one).

46 shows: appears.

48 The measure . . . stand: After this dance I will see where she goes to stand.

49 rude: "rough" or "unmannerly."

50 Forswear: deny.

53 rapier (rā′ pē ər): sword.

54 antic face: grotesque mask.

55 fleer . . . solemnity: mock our celebration.

58 Wherefore: why.

63 Content . . . coz: Be calm, noble cousin.

64 'A bears . . . gentleman: He bears himself like a well-mannered gentleman.

68 do him disparagement: insult him.

1 **The Power of Love** *What has just happened? From this speech, how would you characterize Romeo?*

Research Practice

SPIRAL REVIEW **Changing Times** Instruct students to consult an almanac for statistics about the average age at which couples marry today and factors that affect this statistic. Invite volunteers to discuss their research and compare and contrast Romeo and Juliet's situation with that of today's brides and grooms.

Show a fair presence and put off these frowns,
An ill-beseeming semblance° for a feast.

TYBALT. It fits when such a villain is a guest.
I'll not endure him.

CAPULET. He shall be endured.
What, goodman boy! I say he shall. Go to!°
Am I the master here, or you? Go to!
You'll not endure him, God shall mend my soul!°
You'll make a mutiny among my guests!
You will set cock-a-hoop!° You'll be the man!

TYBALT. Why, uncle, 'tis a shame.

CAPULET. Go to, go to!
You are a saucy boy. Is't so, indeed?
This trick may chance to scathe you.° I know what.
You must contrary me! Marry, 'tis time—
Well said, my hearts°—You are a princox°—go!
Be quiet, or—More light, more light!—For shame!
I'll make you quiet. What!—Cheerly, my hearts!

TYBALT. Patience perforce° with willful choler° meeting
Makes my flesh tremble in their different greeting.°
I will withdraw; but this intrusion shall,
Now seeming sweet, convert to bitt'rest gall.

[*Trembling with anger,* TYBALT *exits. At the same time,* ROMEO *walks over to* JULIET *and speaks to her.*]

ROMEO. If I **profane** with my unworthiest hand
This holy shrine,° the gentle sin is this:
My lips, two blushing pilgrims, ready stand
To smooth that rough touch with a tender kiss.

JULIET. Good pilgrim, you do wrong your hand too much,
Which mannerly devotion shows in this;
For saints° have hands that pilgrims' hands do touch,
And palm to palm is holy palmers'° kiss.

ROMEO. Have not saints lips, and holy palmers too?

JULIET. Ay, pilgrim, lips that they must use in pray'r.

72 ill-beseeming semblance: inappropriate appearance.

75 Go to: an expression of impatience. Capulet rebukes Tybalt by calling him a boy and using a term of address **(goodman)** appropriate for someone below the rank of gentleman.
77 God . . . soul: God save me!
79 set cock-a-hoop: abandon all restraint.

82 This trick . . . you: This mischief may come to harm you.

84 Well said, my hearts: Well done, my friends (addressed to the dancers). **princox:** conceited youngster.

87 Patience perforce: enforced restraint. **choler** (kol′ ər): anger.
88 different greeting: opposition.

92 holy shrine: referring to Juliet's hand, which Romeo has taken.

97 saints: statues of saints.

98 palmers: pilgrims who visited the Holy Sepulcher in Jerusalem. (The term is derived from their practice of wearing palm leaves as a sign of devotion.)

3 Foil *What differences in attitude and tone do you see between Tybalt and Capulet? Why do they respond so differently to the maskers?*

Vocabulary

profane (prō fān′) *v.* to degrade or disrespect something holy or important

Teach

Literary Element 3

Foil Answer: *Proud and impulsive, the youthful Tybalt is fiercely eager to defend the family honor. Capulet refuses to see his guests treated rudely. He is a mature gentleman who values courtesy and respects Romeo's good reputation.*

Encourage volunteers to act out the argument between Capulet and Tybalt to help the class understand the differences between the two men.

Advanced Learners

DIFFERENTIATED INSTRUCTION

Author's Purpose Guide students to reread lines 91–104 while a volunteer reads the lines aloud. Point out that the words at the ends of the lines rhyme and have them determine the rhyme scheme *(abab, cdcd, efef, gg).* Explain that this section of the play is a sonnet, a poem with fourteen lines and a fixed rhyme scheme, and that Shakespeare is as famous for his sonnets as for his plays.

Ask: Why do you think Shakespeare made Romeo and Juliet's first words to each other a perfectly rhymed poem? *(The poem helps show that Romeo and Juliet complement each other and belong together.)* Have students work with a partner to paraphrase the passage line by line, and create an original sonnet with the same rhyme scheme.

Teach

Big Idea 1

The Power of Love
Answer: *Students may express anticipation or dread about the situation of two people from feuding families falling in love.*

ROMEO. O, then, dear saint, let lips do what hands do!
They pray; grant thou, lest faith turn to despair.

JULIET. Saints do not move, though grant for prayers' sake.°

ROMEO. Then move not while my prayer's effect I take.
Thus from my lips, by thine my sin is purg'd.

[*He kisses her.*]

JULIET. Then have my lips the sin that they have took.

ROMEO. Sin from my lips? O trespass sweetly urg'd!°
Give me my sin again.

[*He kisses her again.*]

JULIET. You kiss by th' book.°

[*The* NURSE *joins* JULIET.]

NURSE. Madam, your mother craves a word with you.

[JULIET *goes to speak with her mother.*]

ROMEO. What is her mother?

NURSE. Marry, bachelor,°
Her mother is the lady of the house,
And a good lady, and a wise and virtuous.
I nurs'd her daughter that you talk'd withal.°
I tell you, he that can lay hold of her
Shall have the chinks.°

ROMEO. Is she a Capulet?
O dear account! My life is my foe's debt.°

BENVOLIO. Away, be gone; the sport is at the best.°

ROMEO. Ay, so I fear; the more is my unrest.

CAPULET. Nay, gentlemen, prepare not to be gone;
We have a trifling foolish banquet towards.°
[*They whisper in his ear.*]
Is it e'en so?° Why then, I thank you all.
I thank you, honest gentlemen. Good night.
More torches here! Come on then; let's to bed.
Ah, sirrah, by my fay,° it waxes° late;
I'll to my rest.

103 Saints . . . sake: Statues of saints cannot move, although saints may help people if they are moved by prayer.

107 urg'd: argued.

108 kiss by th' book: "kiss as if you've studied books of etiquette" or "use poetry and rhetoric to gain kisses from me."

111 bachelor: young man.

113 withal: with.

115 the chinks: plenty of money.

116 O dear . . . debt: O costly transaction! My life now belongs to my enemy.

117 the sport is at the best: The fun has already reached its peak.

120 banquet towards: light refreshment in preparation.

121 Is it e'en so: Do you insist (on leaving)?

124 fay: faith. **waxes:** grows.

1 The Power of Love *What is your response to this interchange?*

Grammar Practice

SPIRAL REVIEW **Complements** Write the following sentences on the board:

- Your mother craves a word with you.
- Is she a Capulet?

Say: In the first sentence, *word* is a direct object; it tells what the mother craves. In the second, *Capulet* is a subject complement renaming the subject *she*. Have students identify other examples of each type of complement in the selection and write them in their notebooks.

[*JULIET returns to the NURSE as everyone else starts to leave. JULIET disguises her interest in ROMEO by asking about other men first.*]

JULIET. Come hither, nurse. What is yond gentleman?

NURSE. The son and heir of old Tiberio.

JULIET. What's he that now is going out of door?

NURSE. Marry, that, I think, be young Petruchio.

JULIET. What's he that follows here, that would not dance?

NURSE. I know not.

JULIET. Go ask his name.

[*The NURSE goes to ask ROMEO'S name.*]

—If he be married,
My grave is like to be my wedding bed.

[*The NURSE returns.*]

NURSE. His name is Romeo, and a Montague,
The only son of your great enemy.

JULIET. My only love, sprung from my only hate!
Too early seen unknown, and known too late!
Prodigious° birth of love it is to me
That I must love a loathed enemy.

NURSE. What's this? What's this?

JULIET. A rhyme I learnt even now
Of one I danc'd withal.

[*Someone calls from another room, "Juliet."*]

NURSE. Anon,° anon!
Come, let's away; the strangers all are gone.

3 [*They exit.*]

138 Prodigious (prə dij ′ əs): unnatural and ominous.

141 Anon: at once.

2 The Power of Love *What is the meaning of Juliet's remark?*

Teach

Big Idea 2

The Power of Love

Answer: *Her love for Romeo is the only love she has ever experienced, but it is connected to her only hate, her hate for his family.*

Big Idea 3

The Power of Love Ask: How does love affect Romeo throughout Act 1? *(Romeo is incapacitated by love, just as one can be incapacitated by an illness.)* Have students evaluate the connection of love and violence in the play.

Ask: Which seems more powerful? *(Accept thoughtful and well-supported answers.)*

To check students' understanding of the selection, see Unit 4 Teaching Resources Book, p. 35.

Progress Check

Can students identify foil?

If No → See Unit 4 Teaching Resources Book, p. 30.

English Learners

DIFFERENTIATED INSTRUCTION

Intermediate Have pairs of students work together to paraphrase the last page of Act 1. **Ask:** What words describe Romeo and Juliet's reactions to finding out each other's names? *(hopeless, damned)* **Ask:** Why do they feel this way? *(They have just realized that their families are enemies.)* Have students speculate on what will happen in Act 2. As students make suggestions, ask them to support their ideas with evidence from the text.

After You Read

Assess

1. Accept reasonable answers.
2. (a) A Capulet servant makes a rude gesture at the Montague servants. (b) Servants' identities are closely tied to their masters'.
3. (a) Rosaline has rejected him. (b) Concerned
4. (a) Her father's ball (b) Her beauty; his gallant manner
5. Answers will vary.
6. (a) Both love Juliet; Nurse is closer to Juliet than the mother. (b) Students should explain their answers.
7. Answers will vary. Most students would probably not be happy about it.
8. Answers will vary. Students will likely say that people today do continue to hold grudges, but it is still possible for them to be honorable, so long as they do not resort to violence or cruelty.

Literary Element

1. The Nurse offsets Lady Capulet's refinement with her bawdy humor.
2. Benvolio serves as the foil to Tybalt. Tybalt is ruled by his temper, which leads to his downfall. Benvolio controls his temper and is much happier. The contrast shows the dangers of an unruly temper and the benefits of moderation.

Reading Strategy

1. Juliet agrees to consider Paris's proposal but seems indifferent. She respects her mother but confides in the Nurse. The mother seems ambivalent toward the Nurse; she's condescending but close to Juliet.

After You Read

Respond and Think Critically

Respond and Interpret

1. What are your thoughts about the first encounter between Romeo and Juliet?
2. (a)What causes members of the Capulet and Montague households to fight in the streets of Verona? (b)What might the quarrel reveal about Verona's society?
3. (a)Why is Romeo depressed at the beginning of the play? (b)How would you characterize Benvolio's attitude toward Romeo?
4. (a)Describe the circumstances that lead to Romeo meeting Juliet. (b)What seems to be the basis for their attraction to each other?

Analyze and Evaluate

5. Is Benvolio and Mercutio's plan to cure Romeo of his lovesickness a good idea? Explain.
6. (a)Compare and contrast the Nurse and Lady Capulet. (b)Whom do you prefer? Why?

Connect

7. **Big Idea** The Power of Love How would you feel about being asked to marry at age thirteen? Explain.
8. **Connect to Today** Do people in contemporary society hold grudges? Can people who hold grudges be considered "honorable"? Explain.

Literary Element Foil

In drama, the purpose of a **foil** is to highlight the particular qualities of another character.

1. Which character serves as a foil to Lady Capulet? Explain the contrast between the two characters.
2. Which character serves as a foil to Tybalt? What does the contrast between the two characters tell you about each of them?

Reading Strategy Summarize

A **summary** is a brief restatement of the main ideas and events in a literary work.

1. How would you summarize Juliet's discussion with Lady Capulet and the Nurse? What did you learn about their relationships with each other?
2. Briefly summarize the main events of Act 1. What questions did you have as the act closed?

LOG ON Literature Online

Selection Resources For Selection Quizzes, eFlashcards, and Reading-Writing Connection activities, go to glencoe.com and enter QuickPass code GL49787u4.

Vocabulary Practice

Practice with Synonyms With a partner, match each boldfaced vocabulary word below with its synonym. You will not use all the answer choices. Use a thesaurus or dictionary to check your answers.

1. pernicious	**a.** painful
2. posterity	**b.** dishonor
3. anguish	**c.** future
4. profane	**d.** destroy
	e. misery
	f. harmful

Writing

Write a Dialogue Imagine that Juliet speaks to Rosaline after the party. Write a scene in which they discuss Romeo and what they think of him. Use modern speech, but keep Juliet's dialogue consistent with her character in the play. Base Rosaline's dialogue on Romeo's descriptions of her behavior.

2. Prince bans brawling between feuding Montagues and Capulets. Romeo and his friends crash Lord Capulet's ball. Romeo spots Juliet; it's love at first sight. Capulet defuses a quarrel. Romeo and Juliet learn each other's true identities. Accept reasonable answers.

Vocabulary

1. f **2.** c **3.** e **4.** b

Writing

Students' dialogues should reflect an understanding of Juliet's character and should use proper grammar and punctuation.

For additional selection assessment, see Assessment Resources, pp. 163–164.

Before You Read

Romeo and Juliet, Act 2

Connect to the Drama

To what groups or ideals are people today expected to show loyalty? Write a journal entry in which you examine loyalties.

Build Background

During the Renaissance, young people needed permission from their parents or guardians to get married. In practice, parents from upper-class households frequently chose partners for their children. Such arranged marriages usually required the bride's consent. Girls could legally marry at age twelve, but fifteen or sixteen was a more customary age. Juliet, at age thirteen, would have been considered a young bride.

Set Purposes for Reading

Big Idea The Power of Love

As you read Act 2, ask yourself, What actions do Romeo and Juliet take because of love?

Literary Element Figurative Language

Figurative language includes **similes,** which compare seemingly unlike things using the word *like* or *as;* **metaphors,** which compare seemingly unlike things without using the word *like* or *as;* and **personification,** in which an animal, object, or idea is given human characteristics. As you read, ask yourself, What is the effect of figurative language on the mood of each scene?

Reading Strategy Make Inferences About Characters

A character's motivations, or reasons for acting in a certain way, are not always clear. To find out what drives characters to think, act, or speak the way they do, readers often have to **make inferences,** or use reason and knowledge to form ideas about characters' motivations. As you read, ask yourself, Based on what I know, what can I infer about the characters involved?

Tip: Examine the Evidence Use a 2-column chart to record details about characters and your inferences. In one column, list what you know about the situation or characters. It may be helpful to write out relevant passages from the text. In the other column, list what you infer about the characters.

Learning Objectives

For pages 655–678

In studying this text, you will focus on the following objectives:

Literary Study: Analyzing figurative language.

Reading: Making inferences about characters.

Writing: Writing annotations to explain puns.

Vocabulary

adjacent (ə jā′ sənt) *adj.* next to or close to; neighboring; p. 657 *His office is adjacent to mine, so I know who visits him.*

retain (ri tān′) *v.* to keep possession of; p. 659 *The children retain good memories of the holidays.*

perverse (pər vurs′) *adj.* deliberately unreasonable or wrong; stubborn; p. 661 *She seems to take a perverse delight in teasing me.*

rancor (rang′ kər) *n.* bitter resentment against someone; long-lasting spite; p. 667 *There was rancor between the feuding families.*

Before You Read

Focus

Summary

Romeo and Juliet declare their love and make plans to meet secretly and marry. Romeo's spiritual advisor, Friar Lawrence, agrees to marry them, hoping the union will end the feud between the families.

For summaries in languages other than English, see Unit 4 Teaching Resources Book, pp. 37–42.

Vocabulary

Analogies Tell students that antonyms often appear in word analogies, or groups of words that are related in the same ways. For example: cold : hot :: insidious : honest **Ask:** Which vocabulary word best completes this analogy: up : down :: distant : ____? *(adjacent)* Which vocabulary word best completes this analogy: back : reverse :: preserve: ____? *(retain)*

For additional vocabulary practice, see Unit 4 Teaching Resources Book, p. 45.

Selection Skills

The Tragedy of Romeo and Juliet, Act 2

Literary Elements
- Figurative Language (SE pp. 655–678)

Writing Skills/Grammar
- Correlative Conjunctions (TE p. 656)
- Intensive Pronouns (TE p. 664)
- Persuasive Writing (TE p. 670)
- Interjections (TE p. 674)

Reading Skills
- Make Inferences About Characters (SE pp. 655–678)

Vocabulary Skills
- Context Clues (SE p. 678)

Listening/Speaking/Viewing Skills
- Analyze Art (SE pp. 660, 665, 670, 674; TE pp. 677)

Teach

Big Idea 1

The Power of Love
Answer: *Romeo's love for Rosaline has died; he is now in love with Juliet, and Juliet returns his love. Though their love is made difficult by the feud, the difficulties are tempered by the sweetness of love; they will still attempt to meet.*

Literary Element 2

Stage Directions Point out that stage directions are an important component of a play's text. Stage directions provide information about the setting and about the movements, appearance, gestures, and motivation of the characters.

Ask: What do we learn from the stage directions here about Romeo's motivation? *(He avoids his friends and does not want to reveal his new love interest.)*

APPROACHING **Ask:** Why do you think Shakespeare chose to describe Romeo's actions through stage directions rather than dialogue? *(Plays rely on visual as well as auditory elements. Describing actions in dialogue would not be as effective as showing them on stage.)*

Act 2

Prologue

[*The* CHORUS *enters and addresses the audience.*]

CHORUS. Now old desire° doth in his deathbed lie,
  And young affection gapes° to be his heir;
That fair for which love groan'd for and would die,
  With tender Juliet match'd, is now not fair.
Now Romeo is belov'd and loves again,°
  Alike bewitched by the charm of looks;
But to his foe suppos'd he must complain,°
  And she steal love's sweet bait from fearful hooks.
Being held a foe, he may not have access
  To breathe such vows as lovers use° to swear,
And she as much in love, her means much less
  To meet her new beloved anywhere;
But passion lends them power, time means, to meet,
Temp'ring extremities with extreme sweet.°

[*The* CHORUS *exits.*]

1 old desire: Romeo's love for Rosaline.

2 young affection gapes: new love is eager.

5 is belov'd . . . again: is loved and loves in return.

7 to his foe . . . complain: he must express his love to a supposed enemy.

10 use: are accustomed.

14 Temp'ring . . . sweet: mixing difficulties with great delights.

SCENE 1. Later the same night. Outside the wall that surrounds CAPULET's orchard.

[ROMEO *enters. He is walking alone after the party.*]

ROMEO. Can I go forward when my heart is here?
  Turn back, dull earth,° and find thy center° out.

2 [BENVOLIO *and* MERCUTIO *enter; they are looking for* ROMEO. *Because he wishes to remain near* JULIET *and because he prefers to be alone,* ROMEO *avoids his friends and climbs the wall into* CAPULET'S *orchard.*]

BENVOLIO. Romeo! My cousin Romeo! Romeo!

MERCUTIO.   He is wise
  And, on my life, hath stol'n him home to bed.

BENVOLIO. He ran this way and leapt this orchard wall.
  Call, good Mercutio.

MERCUTIO.   Nay, I'll conjure° too.
  Romeo! Humors! Madman! Passion! Lover!
  Appear thou in the likeness of a sigh;
  Speak but one rhyme, and I am satisfied!

2 dull earth: Romeo's body. **center:** heart (that is, Juliet).

6 conjure (kon′ jər): summon a spirit. (In the conjuring that follows, Mercutio mocks Romeo's lovesickness.)

---

1 The Power of Love *How would you restate what the Chorus explains here?*

Grammar Practice

SMALL GROUP

Correlative Conjunctions Write this list of correlative conjunctions on the board: *both / and, either / or, neither / nor, not only / but also.* Explain that correlative conjunctions join pairs of words to frame parallel terms. Have students write sentences about relationships between characters, such as Romeo and Benvolio or Benvolio and Mercutio, using each of the correlative conjunctions on the board. Then have partners exchange papers and evaluate each other's use of parallel terms.

10 Cry but "Ay me!" pronounce but "love" and "dove."
 Speak to my gossip Venus one fair word,
 One nickname for her purblind° son and heir,
☆ Young Abraham Cupid, he that shot so trim
 When King Cophetua lov'd the beggar-maid!°
15 He heareth not, he stirreth not, he moveth not;
 The ape is dead,° and I must conjure him.
 I conjure thee by Rosaline's bright eyes,
 By her high forehead and her scarlet lip,
 By her fine foot, straight leg, and quivering thigh,
20 And the demesnes° that there **adjacent** lie,
 That in thy likeness thou appear to us!

 BENVOLIO. And if he hear thee, thou wilt anger him.

 MERCUTIO. This cannot anger him; 'twould anger him
 To raise a spirit in his mistress' circle,
25 Of some strange nature, letting it there stand
 Till she had laid it and conjur'd it down.°
 That were° some spite. My invocation
 Is fair and honest:° in his mistress' name,
 I conjure only but to raise up him.

30 BENVOLIO. Come, he hath hid himself among these trees
 To be consorted with° the humorous° night.
 Blind is his love and best befits the dark.

 MERCUTIO. If love be blind, love cannot hit the mark.
 Now will he sit under a medlar tree,
35 And wish his mistress were that kind of fruit
 As maids call medlars, when they laugh alone.
 O, Romeo, that she were, O that she were
 An open-arse, thou a pop'rin pear!
 Romeo, good night. I'll to my truckle bed;°
40 This field bed° is too cold for me to sleep.
 Come, shall we go?

 BENVOLIO. Go then, for 'tis in vain
 To seek him here that means not to be found.

 [*They exit.*]

12 purblind: completely blind.
13–14 Young . . . beggar-maid: Mercutio refers to an old ballad about a king who falls in love with a beggar-maid after being wounded by Cupid's arrow.
16 The ape is dead: Romeo is playing dead, like a trained ape.

20 demesnes (di mānz´): regions.

23–26 This . . . down: Mercutio says that his conjuring would anger Romeo only if it led to someone else romancing Rosaline.
27 were: would be.
28 honest: honorable.

31 consorted with: in the company of. **humorous:** damp.

39 truckle bed: a small rollaway bed for a child or servant.
40 field bed: portable bed used by soldiers during a campaign.

3 Make Inferences About Characters *What is Mercutio's attitude toward Romeo's lovesickness?*

Vocabulary

adjacent (ə jā´ sənt) *adj.* next to or close to; neighboring

ROMEO AND JULIET, ACT 2, SCENE 1 **657**

Teach

| **Reading Strategy** | **3** |

Make Inferences About Characters Answer: *He finds Romeo's lovesickness foolish and amusing. He does not take love so seriously.*

 For additional practice using the reading skill or strategy, see Unit 4 Teaching Resources Book, p. 44.

Cultural History ☆

Cupid Shakespeare's plays contain numerous allusions to Greek and Roman mythology and history. Here, the reference to Cupid is to the god of love, son of the goddess Venus. Cupid was often depicted as a mischievous boy who used arrows to incite the pangs of love.

Interactive Read and Write

Other options for teaching this selection can be found in

- Interactive Read and Write for EL Students, pp. 187–206
- Interactive Read and Write for Approaching-Level Students, pp. 187–206
- Interactive Read and Write for On-Level Students, pp. 187–206

English Learners

DIFFERENTIATED INSTRUCTION

Early Advanced Explain to English learners that summarizing passages can help them understand and remember what they have read. To summarize effectively, they should omit details and condense main events and ideas. A summary gives a general idea of characters, setting, and plot. Have students write a short summary of Act 2, Scene 1. Ask volunteers to share their summaries with the class. Follow each summary with a short discusssion.

Teach

Literary Element 1

Figurative Language
Answer: *The wound of love, inflicted by Cupid's arrow*

Reading Strategy 2

Interpret Have students compare these lines to Romeo's speech about Rosaline in Act 1, Scene 2, lines 86–91.

Ask: What do these two speeches suggest about Romeo? *(Comparing both girls to the sun suggests he sees them as idealized images rather than as individuals.)*

ENGLISH LEARNERS English learners may have difficulty understanding the figurative language throughout the play. Aid their understanding by helping them to identify all of the figures of speech on this page.

Literary Element 3

Figurative Language **Say:** Romeo compares Juliet's eyes to stars. Why might Shakespeare use heavenly bodies to express passion here? *(Stars suggest the otherworldly idealism of Romeo's devotion. Juliet's perfection and the joy and lightness of spirit she brings Romeo make their love heavenly in his eyes.)*

SCENE 2. Immediately following the previous scene. CAPULET's orchard.

[*ROMEO, alone, comments on MERCUTIO's joking.*]

ROMEO. He jests at scars that never felt a wound. **1**

[*JULIET enters at a window above and stands on a balcony. She does not know that ROMEO is nearby.*]

2
But soft!° What light through yonder window breaks?
It is the East, and Juliet is the sun!
Arise, fair sun, and kill the envious moon,
Who is already sick and pale with grief
That thou her maid art far more fair than she.
Be not her maid, since she is envious.
Her vestal livery is but sick and green,
And none but fools do wear it. Cast it off.°
It is my lady! O, it is my love!
O, that she knew she were!
She speaks, yet she says nothing. What of that?
Her eye discourses; I will answer it.
I am too bold; 'tis not to me she speaks.

3
Two of the fairest stars in all the heaven,
Having some business, do entreat her eyes
To twinkle in their spheres till they return.
What if her eyes were there, they in her head?
The brightness of her cheek would shame those stars
As daylight doth a lamp; her eyes in heaven
Would through the airy region stream so bright°
That birds would sing and think it were not night.
See how she leans her cheek upon her hand!
O, that I were a glove upon that hand,
That I might touch that cheek!

JULIET. Ay me!

ROMEO. [*Aside.*] She speaks.
O, speak again, bright angel, for thou art
As glorious to this night, being o'er my head,
As is a winged messenger of heaven
Unto the white-upturned wond'ring eyes
Of mortals that fall back to gaze on him
When he bestrides the lazy puffing clouds
And sails upon the bosom of the air.

2 **soft:** wait!

4–9 **Arise . . . off:** The moon is associated with Diana, Roman goddess of chastity. Romeo urges Juliet to cast off the virginal uniform **(vestal livery)** she wears as one of the moon's maids, since the moon is envious of her beauty.

21 **stream so bright:** shine so brightly.

1 Figurative Language *What "wound" does Romeo suggest that Mercutio has never felt?*

Writing Practice

SMALL GROUP

Make Inferences

Explain that authors build their characters detail by detail. Each detail is a clue to the character's personality. For example, Mercutio's words in Acts 1 and 2 suggest that he is a cynic in regard to romantic love. Divide the class into groups and assign each a character from the play. Groups should list their characters' actions and statements and then write a description of the character's personality.

JULIET. O Romeo, Romeo! Wherefore art thou Romeo?°
Deny thy father and refuse thy name;
Or, if thou wilt not, be but sworn my love,
And I'll no longer be a Capulet.

ROMEO. [*Aside.*] Shall I hear more, or shall I speak at this?

JULIET. 'Tis but thy name that is my enemy.
Thou art thyself, though not° a Montague.
What's Montague? It is nor hand, nor foot,°
Nor arm, nor face, nor any other part
Belonging to a man. O, be some other name!
What's in a name? That which we call a rose
By any other word would smell as sweet.
So Romeo would, were he not Romeo call'd,
Retain that dear perfection which he owes°
Without that title. Romeo, doff° thy name;
And for thy name, which is no part of thee,
Take all myself.

[*ROMEO speaks aloud so that JULIET can hear him for the first time.*]

ROMEO. I take thee at thy word.
Call me but love, and I'll be new baptiz'd;°
Henceforth I never will be Romeo.

JULIET. What man art thou, that, thus bescreen'd° in night,
So stumblest on my counsel?°

ROMEO. By a name
I know not how to tell thee who I am.
My name, dear saint, is hateful to myself
Because it is an enemy to thee.
Had I it written, I would tear the word.

JULIET. My ears have yet not drunk a hundred words
Of thy tongue's uttering, yet I know the sound.
Art thou not Romeo, and a Montague?

ROMEO. Neither, fair maid, if either thee dislike.

5

JULIET. How camest thou hither, tell me, and wherefore?
The orchard walls are high and hard to climb,
And the place death, considering who thou art,
If any of my kinsmen find thee here.

33 Wherefore . . . Romeo: Why are you Romeo (a Montague)?

39 though not: even if you were not.

40 nor hand, nor foot: neither hand nor foot.

46 owes: owns.

47 doff: remove.

50 Call . . . baptiz'd: Romeo says that if she only calls him her love, he will take ***love*** for his new name (as infants are given their Christian names when they are baptized).

52 bescreen'd: hidden.

53 counsel: secret thoughts.

4

Figurative Language *What figure of speech does Juliet use here? What words does Shakespeare use to suggest the strength of Juliet's love?*

Vocabulary

retain (ri tān′) *v.* to keep possession of

Teach

Literary Element 4

Figurative Language

Answer: *Personification; she suggests her ears can drink;* ears *and* tongue, *her use of concrete imagery shows courage and certainty.*

Big Idea 5

The Power of Love Invite volunteers to read the dialogue of Romeo and Juliet on this page. Note that despite the risks Romeo has taken to see her, Juliet hesitates to promise her love to Romeo.

Ask: What else does she ask of Romeo? *(She wants him to swear he loves her faithfully.)*

English Learners

DIFFERENTIATED INSTRUCTION

Early Intermediate English learners may have trouble with dated language. Note that dictionaries label such words and definitions as archaic. Have students list unfamiliar words from Scene 2. Then have small groups of students define the words, using context clues and dictionaries. Have students note which words are obsolete, which words have changed meaning, and which words haven't changed. For words that are obsolete, have students suggest modern words that have taken their place.

Teach

View the Art ★

Answer: *Many students may say he captures it well—pointing out the intense emotion shown between the couple and the darkness of the sky. Others may argue that Romeo and Juliet appear too old.*

Emphasizing the importance of technique, German artist Anselm Feuerbach (1829–1880) painted in a classic style reminiscent of the style favored in ancient Greek and Roman art.

Romeo and Juliet, 1864. Anselm Feuerbach. Oil on canvas, 200 x 115 cm. Thueringer Museum, Eisenach, Germany.

View the Art This painting depicts Romeo and Juliet on her balcony. How well does this image capture Scene 2? Explain. ★

ROMEO. With love's light wings did I o'erperch° these walls;
For stony limits cannot hold love out,
And what love can do, that dares love attempt.
Therefore thy kinsmen are no stop° to me.

JULIET. If they do see thee, they will murder thee.

ROMEO. Alack, there lies more peril in thine eye
Than twenty of their swords! Look thou but sweet,
And I am proof against° their enmity.

5

JULIET. I would not for the world they saw thee here.

ROMEO. I have night's cloak to hide me from their eyes;
And but° thou love me, let them find me here.
My life were better ended by their hate
Than death prorogued,° wanting of° thy love.

JULIET. By whose direction foundst thou out this place?

ROMEO. By love, that first did prompt me to inquire.
He lent me counsel,° and I lent him eyes.
I am no pilot; yet, wert thou as far

66 o'erperch: fly over.

69 stop: obstacle.

73 proof against: protected from.

76 but: unless.

78 prorogued (prō rōgd′): postponed. **wanting of:** lacking.

81 counsel: advice.

Speaking and Listening Practice

SPIRAL REVIEW **Analyze Media** Show the class a movie or TV adaptation of *Romeo and Juliet,* such as Franco Zeffirelli's 1968 film (rated PG) starring Leonard Whiting and Olivia Hussey. If time is short, consider showing only the famous balcony scene. After students have viewed the adaptation, **ask:** How did your experience viewing the adaptation of the play differ from your experience reading the actual play? *(Students may say that they were able to follow the action of the play better while viewing the adaptation.)* **Ask:** How did the director make the play appeal to a general audience? *(Students may say there is an emphasis on the intense feelings of the characters.)* Conclude with a class discussion of what students liked most and least about the adaptation. Encourage them to provide support for their opinions.

As that vast shore wash'd with the farthest sea,
I should adventure° for such merchandise.

JULIET. Thou knowest the mask of night is on my face;
Else would a maiden blush bepaint my cheek
For that which thou hast heard me speak tonight.
Fain would I dwell on form°—fain, fain deny
What I have spoke; but farewell compliment!°
Dost thou love me? I know thou wilt say "Ay";
And I will take thy word. Yet, if thou swear'st,
Thou mayst prove false. At lovers' perjuries,
They say Jove° laughs. O gentle Romeo,
If thou dost love, pronounce it faithfully.
Or if thou thinkest I am too quickly won,
I'll frown and be **perverse** and say thee nay,
So thou wilt woo;° but else,° not for the world.
In truth, fair Montague, I am too fond,°
And therefore thou mayst think my behavior light;°
But trust me, gentleman, I'll prove more true
Than those that have more coying to be strange.°
I should have been more strange, I must confess,
But that thou overheard'st, ere I was ware,°
My truelove passion. Therefore pardon me,
And not impute this yielding° to light love,
Which the dark night hath so discovered.°

ROMEO. Lady, by yonder blessed moon I vow,
That tips with silver all these fruit-tree tops—

JULIET. O, swear not by the moon, th' inconstant moon,
That monthly changes in her circle orb,
Lest that thy love prove likewise variable.

ROMEO. What shall I swear by?

JULIET. Do not swear at all;
Or if thou wilt, swear by thy gracious self,
Which is the god of my idolatry,°
And I'll believe thee.

ROMEO. If my heart's dear love—

JULIET. Well, do not swear. Although I joy in thee,
I have no joy of this contract° tonight.

84 adventure: risk a journey.

88 Fain . . . form: Gladly would I show concern for decorum.
89 compliment: formal manners.

93 Jove: the most powerful god in Roman mythology.

97 So thou wilt woo: so you will have to woo me. **else:** otherwise.
98 fond: loving, infatuated.
99 light: frivolous, unmaidenly.

101 coying to be strange: ability to appear distant.

103 ere I was ware: before I was aware (of your presence).

105 not impute this yielding: do not attribute this giving in so easily.
106 discovered: revealed.

114 idolatry (ī dol′ ə trē): blind devotion.

117 contract: exchange of vows.

2 Make Inferences About Characters *In this passage, what worries does Juliet express?*

Vocabulary

perverse (pər vurs′) *adj.* deliberately unreasonable or wrong; stubborn

Teach

Literary Element 1

Characterization Ask: What does this speech reveal about Juliet's character? *(She is intelligent and thoughtful and seems more mature and cautious than Romeo but remains vulnerable to Romeo's attentions.)*

Reading Strategy 2

Make Inferences About Characters Answer: *She worries that she might seem too easily won and that their feelings arose too suddenly to last.*

Approaching Level

DIFFERENTIATED INSTRUCTION

Emerging Have students draw a map of the Capulet orchard where the balcony scene takes place. Encourage students to study Scene 2 for details about the setting and to incorporate those details into their map. After allowing students time to work, have volunteers show their maps to the class and explain how the map was based on details in the play.

Established Ask: How do you think the orchard setting is created on a stage? Show some photos of stage versions of the balcony scene and encourage students to critique the sets.

Ask: What do you think Shakespeare intended when he wrote the play?

Teach

Literary Element 1

Figurative Language
Answer: *She worries that their love is like lightning, which comes and goes in a flash. The metaphor of the flower expresses a wish that their love will grow and blossom.*

ADVANCED Ask students to analyze Romeo and Juliet's relationship thus far and discuss whether they think the couple's love is a lasting one, or if it will fizzle out like Romeo's previous relationships with women.

Literary Element 2

Figurative Language Ask students to characterize the tone of Romeo's and Juliet's speeches. *(Joyous, loving)*

Ask: How does Shakespeare communicate this tone? *(With imagery involving vast surroundings—the sea and the sky—and exclamations and vows.)*

Cultural History ☆

West Side Story In this modern (1957) musical adaptation of *Romeo and Juliet,* the main characters, Tony and Maria, are affiliated with rival gangs in New York City. Their love blooms amid ethnic tensions that lead to a deadly rumble. In *West Side Story,* the balcony scene occurs on the fire escape of Maria's apartment.

It is too rash, too unadvis'd, too sudden;
Too like the lightning, which doth cease to be
Ere one can say it lightens. Sweet, good night!
This bud of love, by summer's ripening breath,
☆ May prove a beauteous flow'r when next we meet.
Good night, good night! As sweet repose and rest
Come to thy heart as that within my breast!

ROMEO. O, wilt thou leave me so unsatisfied?

JULIET. What satisfaction canst thou have tonight?

ROMEO. Th' exchange of thy love's faithful vow for mine.

JULIET. I gave thee mine before thou didst request it;
And yet I would it were to give again.°

ROMEO. Wouldst thou withdraw it? For what purpose, love?

JULIET. But to be frank° and give it thee again.
And yet I wish but for the thing I have.
My bounty is as boundless as the sea,
My love as deep; the more I give to thee,
The more I have, for both are infinite. [*The* NURSE *calls from within the house.*]
I hear some noise within. Dear love, adieu!
Anon,° good nurse! Sweet Montague, be true.
Stay but a little, I will come again.

[*JULIET goes into the house.*]

2 ROMEO. O blessed, blessed night! I am afeard,
Being in night, all this is but a dream,
Too flattering-sweet to be substantial.°

[*JULIET reappears on the balcony.*]

JULIET. Three words, dear Romeo, and good night indeed.
If that thy bent° of love be honorable,
Thy purpose marriage, send me word tomorrow,
By one that I'll procure° to come to thee,
Where and what time thou wilt perform the rite;°
And all my fortunes at thy foot I'll lay
And follow thee my lord throughout the world.

NURSE. [*She calls from within the house.*] Madam!

JULIET. [*To the* NURSE.] I come anon. [*To* ROMEO.]—But if thou meanest not well,
I do beseech° thee—

129 I would . . . again: I wish I had it back.

131 frank: generous.

137 Anon: right away.

141 substantial: real.

143 bent: intention.

145 procure (prə kyoor′): obtain.

146 rite: marriage ceremony.

151 beseech (bi sēch′): beg.
By and by: in a moment.

1 Figurative Language *Why does Juliet compare her and Romeo's declarations of love to lightning in lines 119–120? What is the point of the metaphor in lines 121–122?*

Literary Element Practice

Similes in Character Description
Juliet calls her love "as boundless as the sea." Note that with just a few words, this simile vividly conveys the idea of a love that is vast, overwhelming, and all-encompassing. After students have finished reading the scene, have them skim it for two other similes and describe the impression each creates. *(Possible answers: [1] lines 26–28—"for thou art . . . as is a winged messenger of heaven"; [2] lines 165–166—"How silver-sweet . . . night, / Like softest music to attending ears!")*

NURSE. [*From within again.*] Madam!

JULIET. [*To the* NURSE.] By and by° I come.—
[*To* ROMEO.] To cease thy strife° and leave me to my grief.
Tomorrow will I send.

ROMEO. So thrive my soul—

JULIET. A thousand times good night!

[*JULIET goes into the house.*]

ROMEO. A thousand times the worse, to want° thy light!
Love goes toward love as schoolboys from their books;
But love from love, toward school with heavy looks.

[*JULIET returns to the balcony.*]

JULIET. Hist! Romeo, hist! O for a falc'ner's voice
To lure this tassel gentle back again!°
Bondage is hoarse and may not speak aloud,°
Else would I tear the cave where Echo° lies
And make her airy tongue more hoarse than mine
With repetition of my Romeo's name. Romeo!

ROMEO. It is my soul that calls upon my name.
How silver-sweet sound lovers' tongues by night,
Like softest music to attending ears!

JULIET. Romeo!

ROMEO. My niesse?°

JULIET. What o'clock tomorrow
Shall I send to thee?

ROMEO. By the hour of nine.

JULIET. I will not fail. 'Tis twenty year till then.
I have forgot why I did call thee back.

ROMEO. Let me stand here till thou remember it.

JULIET. I shall forget, to have thee still stand there,
Remembr'ring how I love thy company.

ROMEO. And I'll still stay, to have thee still forget,
Forgetting any other home but this.

JULIET. 'Tis almost morning. I would have thee gone—
And yet no farther than a wanton's° bird,
That lets it hop a little from his hand,
Like a poor prisoner in his twisted gyves,°

152 strife: efforts.

155 want: be deprived of.

158–159 Hist! . . . again: Juliet refers to the special call that a falcon master **(falc'ner)** uses to lure back a male falcon **(tassel gentle).**

160 Bondage . . . aloud: Juliet compares being under her family's control to hoarseness, since it prevents her from speaking loudly.

161 Echo: a wood nymph in classical mythology. After being rejected in love, she retired to a cave and wasted away until only her voice was left.

167 niesse (nē es′): a young hawk ready to leave the nest.

177 wanton's: spoiled child's.

179 gyves (jīvz): shackles.

3 Figurative Language *What idea is communicated by the simile in lines 156–157? Restate it in your own words.*

Teach

Literary Element 3

Figurative Language

Answer: *The simile conveys the reluctance of lovers to part. People in love rush as eagerly toward their beloved as children rush out of school and part as reluctantly as children drag into class.*

Advanced Learners

DIFFERENTIATED INSTRUCTION

Graph Emotions Have students graph the lovers' shifting emotions, using the scene's events (e.g., the ball, the balcony scene) as the x-axis and a "barometer" of emotions (e.g., joy, anxiety) as the y-axis. They should graph each character's emotions individually. Allow volunteers to explain their graphs to the class.

Teach

Literary Element 1

Figurative Language

Answer: *It suggests she wants to nurture and protect him, while at the same time implying that her possessiveness might "smother" a creature that by nature wants freedom.*

Students should appreciate the ironic truth in Juliet's "sweet sorrow." (line 184) **Ask:** How is this phrase appropriate to the lovers' dilemma? *(It suggests that joy and sorrow in love are closely connected and foreshadows the tragedy to come.)*

APPROACHING Help students understand how a positive emotion like love could cause sorrow by asking students to think of examples in which loving someone has caused sadness.

Cultural History ☆

Friars Friars (from *frater*, the Latin word for "brother") of Shakespeare's time spent much of their time traveling from town to town, preaching to the poor. Pledged to a strict vow of poverty, they survived on charity and lived and served in the secular world rather than secluded in monasteries.

And with a silken thread plucks it back again,
So loving-jealous of his liberty.

ROMEO. I would I were thy bird.

JULIET. Sweet, so would I.
Yet I should kill thee with much cherishing.
Good night, good night! Parting is such sweet sorrow
That I shall say good night till it be morrow.

[*JULIET goes into the house.*]

ROMEO. Sleep dwell upon thine eyes, peace in thy breast!
Would I were sleep and peace, so sweet to rest!
Hence will I to my ghostly sire's° close cell,°
His help to crave and my dear hap° to tell.

[*ROMEO exits to find the FRIAR.*]

188 ghostly sire's: spiritual advisor's. **close cell:** small private room.
189 hap: good fortune.

SCENE 3. Early the next morning. FRIAR LAWRENCE's **cell.**

☆ [*FRIAR LAWRENCE, ROMEO's spiritual advisor, enters alone carrying a basket full of herbs.*]

FRIAR. The gray-ey'd morn smiles on the frowning night,
Check'ring the eastern clouds with streaks of light;
And flecked° darkness like a drunkard reels
From forth day's path and Titan's fiery wheels.°
Now, ere the sun advance his burning eye
The day to cheer and night's dank dew to dry,
I must upfill this osier cage° of ours
With baleful° weeds and precious-juiced flowers.
The earth that's nature's mother is her tomb;
What is her burying grave, that is her womb;
And from her womb children of divers° kind
We sucking on her natural bosom find:
Many for many virtues° excellent,
None but for some,° and yet all different.
O, mickle° is the powerful grace° that lies
In plants, herbs, stones, and their true qualities;
For naught° so vile that on the earth doth live
But to the earth some special good doth give;
Nor aught so good but, strained from that fair use,°
Revolts from true birth, stumbling on abuse.°
Virtue itself turns vice, being misapplied,
And vice sometime by action dignified.

3 flecked: spotted.
4 From . . . wheels: out of the path of the sun god (who was said to drive a fiery chariot across the sky).
7 upfill this osier cage: fill up this willow basket.
8 baleful: harmful.
11 divers (dī´ vərz): varied.
13 virtues: healing properties.
14 None but for some: None that are not good for some use.
15 mickle: great. **grace:** divine goodness.
17 naught (nôt): there is nothing.
19 strained from that fair use: diverted from its proper use.
20 Revolts . . . abuse: rebels against its natural state and becomes harmful.

1 Figurative Language *In an extended metaphor, Juliet compares Romeo to a bird. What idea about her love is communicated by this comparison?*

Grammar Practice

Intensive Pronouns

Write this statement on the board: *Virtue itself turns vice.* Note that *itself* is placed right after the noun *virtue* to emphasize it. The pronouns *himself, herself, themselves,* or *itself* used this way are called intensive pronouns. Have students add an intensive pronoun to each of these sentences. *(Answers appear in parentheses.)*

- Romeo *(himself)* visited the friar to arrange the wedding.
- The lovers *(themselves)* cannot change their destiny.
- I find the story *(itself)* sad but fascinating.

Studies of the Heads of Two Men, 1517. Raphael (Raffaello Sanzio). Chalk on gray paper. Ashmolean Museum, Oxford, England.

View the Art ★ This drawing reflects the influence of classical Greek and Roman art on Raphael's work. Yet, the natural poses of the men also convey specific attitudes and emotions. What emotions are conveyed by the men? What parallels can you draw between these men and Romeo and the Friar?

[ROMEO *enters. The* FRIAR *does not see him and continues speaking until* ROMEO *interrupts him.*]

Within the infant rind° of this weak flower
Poison hath residence and medicine power;°
For this, being smelt, with that part cheers each part;
Being tasted, stays all senses with the heart.°
Two such opposed kings encamp them still
In man as well as herbs—grace and rude will;°
And where the worser is predominant,
Full soon the canker° death eats up that plant.

ROMEO. Good morrow, father.

FRIAR. *Benedicite!*°
What early tongue so sweet saluteth me?
Young son, it argues a distempered head°
So soon to bid good morrow to thy bed.
Care keeps his watch in every old man's eye,
And where care lodges, sleep will never lie;
But where unbruised youth with unstuff'd brain
Doth couch° his limbs, there golden sleep doth reign.
Therefore thy earliness doth me assure
Thou art uprous'd with some distemp'rature;°

23 infant rind: tender skin.

24 Poison . . . power: there dwells poison and medicinal power.

25–26 For this . . . heart: When the flower is smelled, it stimulates every part of the body, but when tasted it causes the heart to stop beating.

27–28 Two such . . . will: Two such opposing qualities are always present in man as well as in herbs—goodness and a tendency toward violence.

30 canker: cankerworm, a larva that feeds on buds.

31 *Benedicite* (ben′ ə dis′ ə tē): God bless you!

33 argues a distempered head: suggests a disturbed mind.

38 couch: lay down.

40 uprous'd . . . distemp'rature: awakened by some emotional or mental disturbance.

2 Figurative Language *In lines 7–30, how does the Friar describe herbs and their nature? How are people like herbs?*

Teach

Literary Element 2

Figurative Language

Answer: *Herbs are diverse, and people are as well. None are so bad that they are worthless, and none are so good that they can't be put to bad use if they deviate from their true nature.*

View the Art ★

Answer: *Romeo confides in the Friar and seeks his help. The young man looks earnest and troubled. The older man's compassionate expression and upraised hands suggest he's sympathetic while advising Romeo to be careful.*

One of the most influential artists of the Italian Renaissance, Raphael (1483–1520) was famed for his portraits and use of perspective.

English Learners

DIFFERENTIATED INSTRUCTION

Early Advanced To improve reading fluency, invite volunteers to recite Friar's opening speech (lines 1–30). Have each volunteer read four lines, pausing only where punctuation indicates a break in the flow. After these individual readings, organize a choral reading to reinforce students' understanding of the rhythm of Shakespeare's verse.

Teach

Reading Strategy 1

Make Inferences About Characters **Answer:** *Friar Lawrence is wise and kindly; he has a fatherly attitude toward Romeo.*

Reading Strategy 2

Interpret Friar Lawrence's reactions to Romeo provide an adult's insights into his character.

Ask: Why might Shakespeare have chosen to insert the Friar's viewpoint here? *(It deepens the audience's understanding of Romeo, highlighting the tragic flaw of youthful impetuousness that will lead to his downfall.)*

APPROACHING **Ask:** What tone does Friar Lawrence take with Romeo? *(exasperated and admonishing)* Ask for a volunteer to read the Friar's dialogue in lines 65–80 and challenge them to interpret his tone.

Or if not so, then here I hit it right—
Our Romeo hath not been in bed tonight.

ROMEO. That last is true. The sweeter rest was mine.

FRIAR. God pardon sin! Wast thou with Rosaline?

ROMEO. With Rosaline, my ghostly father? No.
I have forgot that name and that name's woe.

FRIAR. That's my good son! But where hast thou been then?

ROMEO. I'll tell thee ere thou ask it me again.
I have been feasting with mine enemy,
Where on a sudden one hath wounded° me
That's by me wounded. Both our remedies
Within thy help and holy physic° lies.
I bear no hatred, blessed man, for, lo,
My intercession° likewise steads° my foe.

FRIAR. Be plain, good son, and homely in thy drift.
Riddling confession finds but riddling shrift.°

ROMEO. Then plainly know my heart's dear love is set
On the fair daughter of rich Capulet;
As mine on hers, so hers is set on mine,
And all combin'd,° save what thou must combine
By holy marriage. When and where and how
We met, we wooed, and made exchange of vow,
I'll tell thee as we pass; but this I pray,
That thou consent to marry us today.

FRIAR. Holy Saint Francis! What a change is here!
Is Rosaline, that thou didst love so dear,
So soon forsaken? Young men's love then lies
Not truly in their hearts, but in their eyes.
Jesu Maria! What a deal of brine°
Hath washed thy sallow° cheeks for Rosaline!
How much salt water thrown away in waste
To season love, that of it doth not taste!
The sun not yet thy sighs from heaven clears,
Thy old groans yet ringing in mine ancient ears.
Lo, here upon thy cheek the stain doth sit
Of an old tear that is not wash'd off yet.
If e'er thou wast thyself, and these woes thine,
Thou and these woes were all for Rosaline.
And art thou chang'd? Pronounce this sentence° then:
Women may fall when there's no strength in men.°

50 wounded: That is, wounded with Cupid's arrow.

52 physic: medicine; healing power.

54 intercession: petition. **steads:** benefits.

55–56 Be plain . . . shrift: Speak plainly and directly. A confusing confession only leads to confusing forgiveness.

60 all combin'd: We are completely united.

69 brine: salt water (tears).

70 sallow: sickly yellow.

79 sentence: saying; general truth.

80 Women . . . men: Women can be expected to be unfaithful when men are so fickle.

1 Make Inferences About Characters *What can you infer about Friar Lawrence's character and his attitude toward Romeo from these lines?*

Reading Practice

SMALL GROUP

Generate Questions Having students generate questions at the end of each scene can help to monitor their level of understanding.

- Literal questions ask readers to recall facts stated in the text and require remembering information. *(What does Romeo ask Friar Lawrence to do?)*
- Interpretive questions ask readers to explain the meaning of the words and require readers to draw inferences. *(When Friar says, "Young men's love then lies / Not truly in their hearts, but in their eyes," is he suggesting that Romeo does not truly love Juliet?)*
- Evaluative questions ask readers to go beyond the text by making outside connections or offering personal opinions or ideas which cannot be supported by the text. *(Why do you think Romeo is in such a hurry to get marrried?)*

Have students work in groups to write one of each type of question for Act 2, Scene 3. When each group has finished, redistribute the questions to new groups to answer the questions. Solicit examples of questions from the class and discuss both the questions and answers.

2

ROMEO. Thou chidst° me oft for loving Rosaline.

FRIAR. For doting, not for loving, pupil mine.

ROMEO. And badst me° bury love.

FRIAR. Not in a grave
To lay one in, another out to have.

ROMEO. I pray thee chide me not. Her I love now
Doth grace for grace and love for love allow.°
The other did not so.

FRIAR. O, she knew well
Thy love did read by rote, that could not spell.°
But come, young waverer, come go with me.
In one respect I'll thy assistant be;
For this alliance may so happy prove
To turn your households' **rancor** to pure love.

ROMEO. O, let us hence! I stand° on sudden haste.

FRIAR. Wisely and slow. They stumble that run fast.

[They exit.]

81 chidst (chīdst): scolded.

83 badst (bādst) **me:** urged me to.

85–86 Her I love . . . allow: I love her because she gives back or exchanges favor for favor and love for love.

88 read . . . spell: read by memorizing words, without understanding their meaning.

93 stand: insist.

SCENE 4. Approximately nine o'clock in the morning, the time at which JULIET was to send a messenger to ROMEO. A street in Verona.

[BENVOLIO and MERCUTIO enter; they are still concerned about ROMEO's disappearance the night before.]

MERCUTIO. Where the devil should this Romeo be?
Came he not home tonight?

BENVOLIO. Not to his father's. I spoke with his man.

MERCUTIO. Why, that same pale hardhearted wench, that Rosaline,
Torments him so that he will sure run mad.

BENVOLIO. Tybalt, the kinsman to old Capulet,
Hath sent a letter to his father's house.

MERCUTIO. A challenge, on my life.

BENVOLIO. Romeo will answer it.°

MERCUTIO. Any man that can write may answer a letter.

10 answer it: accept the challenge to a duel.

3

The Power of Love *This section of the play permits the audience to hear an adult's view of Romeo and his passions. How does this help to show Romeo in a new light? Explain.*

Vocabulary

rancor (rang′ kər) *n.* bitter resentment against someone; long-lasting spite

Teach

Big Idea 3

The Power of Love

Answer: *From the Friar's perspective, Romeo appears rash and immature and does not really understand the difference between infatuation and love.*

Approaching Level

DIFFERENTIATED INSTRUCTION

Established Help students generate questions about the play by explaining the purpose of each type of question and how to begin writing different levels of questions. **Say:** Literal questions ask about what happened or how something happened. They can start with "What . . ." or "How . . ." Have students work together to write several literal questions. **Say:** Interpretive questions take a quote directly from the text and ask about what it means. They can start with "What does Shakespeare mean when he says . . ." Have students work together to write several interpretive questions. Encourage students to focus their interpretive questions on quotes they do not understand or that could have more than one interpretation. **Say:** Evaluative questions ask about how the reader connects or relates to the themes or ideas in the text. They can start with "What do you think . . ." or "How did you feel when . . ." Have students work together to write several evaluative questions. After writing the questions, have students discuss the answers and review the important elements of Act 2, Scene 3.

Teach

Reading Strategy 1

Make Inferences About Characters **Ask:** What do Mercutio's words suggest about his attitude toward romantic love? *(Love weakens a man and will prove to be his downfall.)*

Reading Strategy 2

Make Inferences About Characters **Answer:** *Tybalt is an experienced duelist, and Mercutio seems concerned that Romeo is in no shape to face him in a fight.*

ENGLISH LEARNERS Mercutio's description of Tybalt can be challenging to English learners. Help them monitor their comprehension by going over the side column notes and explaining the figurative language.

BENVOLIO. Nay, he will answer the letter's master, how he dares, being dared.

MERCUTIO. Alas, poor Romeo, he is already dead: stabbed with a white wench's black eye; run through the ear with a love song; the very pin° of his heart cleft with the blind bow-boy's butt-shaft;° and is he a man to encounter Tybalt?

BENVOLIO. Why, what is Tybalt?

MERCUTIO. More than Prince of Cats.° O, he's the courageous captain of compliments.° He fights as you sing prick-song,° keeps time, distance, and proportion;° he rests his minim rests;° one, two, and the third in your bosom: the very butcher of a silk button, a duelist, a duelist! A gentleman of the very first house,° of the first and second cause.° Ah, the immortal *passado!*° The *punto reverso!*° The *hay!*°

BENVOLIO. The what?

MERCUTIO. The pox of such antic, lisping, affecting phantasimes, these new tuners of accent! "By Jesu, a very good blade! a very tall man! a very good whore!" Why, is not this a lamentable thing, grand-sire, that we should be thus afflicted with these strange flies, these fashion-mongers, these pardon-me's who stand so much on the new form, that they cannot sit at ease on the old bench? O, their bones, their bones!°

[ROMEO enters. He seems much happier than he was at the beginning of the play.]

BENVOLIO. Here comes Romeo! Here comes Romeo!

MERCUTIO. Without his roe,° like a dried herring: O flesh, flesh, how art thou fishified! Now is he for the numbers° that Petrarch° flow'd in. Laura° to his lady was a kitchen wench (marry, she had a better love to berhyme her), Dido a dowdy, Cleopatra a gipsy, Helen and Hero hildings and harlots, Thisby a gray eye or so, but not to the purpose.° Signior Romeo, *bonjour!* there's a French salutation to your French slop!° You gave us the counterfeit° fairly last night.

ROMEO. Good morrow to you both. What counterfeit did I give you?

MERCUTIO. The slip, sir, the slip. Can you not conceive?°

ROMEO. Pardon, good Mercutio. My business was great, and in such a case as mine a man may strain courtesy.

16 pin: peg in the center of an archery target.
16–17 blind . . . shaft: Cupid's blunt practice arrow.
19 Prince of Cats: a pun on Tybalt's name. In a popular fable, the Prince of Cats was called Tybert.
20 captain of compliments: master of all the formal rules of dueling. **prick-song:** from printed music (as opposed to the less accurate singing from memory).
21 proportion: rhythm.
21–22 minim rests: shortest possible musical pauses.
23–24 very first house: best fencing school.
24 cause: excuse for challenging a man to a duel.
25 *passado* (pə sä′ dō): forward sword thrust. ***punto reverso*** (poon′ tō rə ver′ sō): back-handed thrust. ***hay:*** a fencing term signaling a hit.
27–34 The pox . . . bones: Mercutio mimics an old traditionalist complaining about the younger fencers who use newfangled and foreign terminology.
36 roe: fish eggs. Mercutio makes a pun on Romeo's name (without "Ro" he is all sighs—"meo" or "oh me!").
37 numbers: verses; poems.
38 Petrarch (pē′ trärk): an influential Italian poet who composed love sonnets to his chaste love, **Laura.**
38–41 Laura . . . purpose: Mercutio refers to famous women from classical mythology and ancient history. He suggests these women are good-for-nothings **(hildings)** and not worth mentioning **(to the purpose)** in Romeo's eyes.
43 French slop: loose breeches, or pants. **counterfeit:** A counterfeit coin was called a *slip,* a word that also means "escape."
46 conceive: understand (my pun).

2 Make Inferences About Characters *What points does Mercutio make about Tybalt's skill at dueling? Why does Mercutio make these points?*

Cultural History ☆

Cleopatra and Helen

Mercutio refers to two famously bewitching but faithless women whose great loves ended in disaster. Cleopatra, queen of Egypt from 51 to 30 B.C., killed herself when a plan to help Marc Antony regain control of Rome failed. Helen of Troy, wife to Menelaus of Sparta, fell in love with her abductor, Paris, sparking the Trojan War.

Literary Element Practice

Puns Explain that a pun is a way to play with words. A pun relies on a word having multiple meanings or sounding a lot like another word. Point out that Mercutio uses a pun in line 43 *(You gave us the counterfeit fairly last night),* but Romeo does not understand. *(Romeo does not intepret "counterfeit" to mean "slip," but thinks Mercutio is referring to a fake coin.)* Share the following puns with students and have them explain their meanings:

- The book is a novel idea.
- A boiled egg is hard to beat.
- A backward poet writes inverse.

Allow students to suggest some of their own puns or identify more puns from the play in a class discussion.

MERCUTIO. That's as much as to say, such a case as yours constrains a man to bow in the hams.

ROMEO. Meaning to cur'sy.°

MERCUTIO. Thou hast most kindly hit it.°

ROMEO. A most courteous exposition.

MERCUTIO. Nay, I am the very pink° of courtesy.

ROMEO. Pink for flower.

MERCUTIO. Right.

ROMEO. Why then is my pump° well flower'd.°

MERCUTIO. Sure wit! Follow me this jest now, till thou hast worn out thy pump, that when the single sole of it is worn, the jest may remain, after the wearing, soly singular.

ROMEO. O single-sol'd jest, soly singular for the singleness!°

MERCUTIO. Come between us, good Benvolio, my wits faints.

ROMEO. Swits and spurs,° swits and spurs, or I'll cry a match.°

MERCUTIO. Nay, if our wits run the wild-goose chase,° I am done; for thou hast more of the wild goose° in one of thy wits than, I am sure, I have in my whole five. Was I with you° there for the goose?°

ROMEO. Thou wast never with me for anything when thou wast not there for the goose.

MERCUTIO. I will bite thee by the ear for that jest.

ROMEO. Nay, good goose, bite not.

MERCUTIO. Thy wit is a very bitter sweeting, it is a most sharp sauce.

ROMEO. And is it not then well serv'd in to a sweet goose?°

MERCUTIO. O, here's a wit of cheverel,° that stretches from an inch narrow to an ell° broad!

ROMEO. I stretch it out for that word "broad,"° which, added to the goose, proves thee far and wide a broad goose.

MERCUTIO. Why, is not this better now than groaning for love? Now art thou sociable, now art thou Romeo; now art thou what thou art, by art as well as by nature, for this drivelling love is like a great natural that runs lolling up and down to hide his bable in a hole.°

BENVOLIO. Stop there, stop there.

51 cur'sy: curtsy, a slight lowering of the body with bending of the knees, usually done by women.
52 most kindly hit it: put it most graciously.

54 pink: perfection.
55–57 Pink . . . flower'd: Romeo plays on two other meanings of *pink:* "flower" and "decorative perforations," which might be found on a shoe **(pump).**
58–61 Sure . . . singleness: Mercutio and Romeo play on the words **sole** ("solitary" or "bottom of a shoe"), **soly** ("only" or "uniquely"), **single-sol'd** ("shoddy"), **singular** ("unique"), and **singleness** ("silliness").

63 Swits and spurs: spur on your horse (keep going). **cry a match:** claim victory.
64 wild-goose chase: a game of "follow the leader" on horseback.
65 goose: fool.
67 with you: even with you. **for the goose:** to chase women.

74 is it not . . . goose: doesn't my wit (a sharp sauce) go well with you (its sweet victim).
75 cheverel (shev′ ər el′): kid leather (which stretches easily).
76 ell: forty-five inches.
77 broad: "obvious" or "indecent."

80–83 Now art . . . hole: Mercutio compares love to a drooling idiot **(natural)** running around with his fool's wand **(bable),** a stick with an inflated bladder, or balloon, on one end.

3 Make Inferences About Characters *From their banter, what inferences can you make about the relationship between Romeo and Mercutio?*

Teach

Reading Strategy 3

Make Inferences About Characters **Answer:** *Romeo and Mercutio tease each other and compete in witty wordplay in the same way two brothers might.*

APPROACHING **Ask:** Why do you think Romeo is in such a good mood? *(He is happy because Juliet has requited his love.)*

English Learners

DIFFERENTIATED INSTRUCTION

Intermediate English learners may have difficulty understanding the exchange between Romeo and Mercutio. Have small groups paraphrase Romeo and Mercutio's wordplay and update the exchange to modern language. Invite volunteers to illustrate the banter (good-natured teasing and joking) in the scene by reading their dialogues for the class.

Teach

Literary Element 1

Figurative Language

Answer: *Romeo maintains a playful mood, joking about the servants' clothing, suggesting they are comically overdressed.*

View the Art ★

Answer: *The close figure groupings suggest intimate conversations such as those that occur in the scene.*

The sunny, romantic scenes of Venice painted by Francesco Guardi (1712–1793) typically display sparkling colors and intricate details.

A Capriccio with Figures Conversing Under an Archway, a Courtyard Beyond. Francesco Guardi. Oil on canvas, 24.2 x 17.7 cm. Private collection.

View the Art Guardi's famous landscapes were influenced by the Rococo artists of France, who sought to move away from the dramatic art that had been favored by Louis XIV and toward lighter, more decorative styles. In what ways might the scene depicted in this painting reflect the setting of Act 2, Scene 4? ★

MERCUTIO. Thou desirest me to stop in my tale against the hair.

BENVOLIO. Thou wouldst else have made thy tale large.

MERCUTIO. O, thou art deceiv'd; I would have made it short, for I was come to the whole depth of my tale and meant indeed to occupy the argument no longer.

ROMEO. Here's goodly gear!°

[*The* NURSE *enters with* PETER, *a servant.*]

A sail,° a sail!

MERCUTIO. Two, two! A shirt and a smock.°

NURSE. Peter!

PETER. Anon.

NURSE. My fan, Peter.

MERCUTIO. Good Peter, to hide her face; for her fan's the fairer face.

NURSE. God ye° good morrow, gentlemen.

90 goodly gear: fine stuff (an inappropriate reference to the Nurse's appearance or outfit that is meant to be funny).
91 A sail: an expression used when a sailor sees another ship.
92 A shirt and a smock: a man and a woman.

98 God ye: God give you.

1 Figurative Language *Why does Romeo compare the sight of the Nurse and Peter to the sight of ships coming into view?*

Writing Practice

Persuasive Writing

Explain that persuasive writing tries to influence readers to accept an idea, adopt a position, or take a particular action. Have students write an essay advising Romeo and Juliet on how to proceed. The essay should define romantic love and, based on their definition, develop either an argument for Romeo and Juliet to take their time and wait for marriage or to trust that they have found true love at first sight and begin their marriage as soon as possible. Remind students to support their argument with examples from the text and to conclude by suggesting the actions that Romeo and Juliet should take.

MERCUTIO. God ye good den,° fair gentlewoman.

NURSE. Is it good den?

MERCUTIO. 'Tis no less, I tell ye, for the bawdy hand of the dial is now upon the prick° of noon.

NURSE. Out upon you, what a man are you?

2

ROMEO. One, gentlewoman, that God hath made, himself to mar.°

NURSE. By my troth, it is well said; "for himself to mar," quoth 'a! Gentlemen, can any of you tell me where I may find the young Romeo?

ROMEO. I can tell you; but young Romeo will be older when you have found him than he was when you sought him. I am the youngest of that name, for fault of a worse.°

NURSE. You say well.

MERCUTIO. Yea, is the worst well? Very well took, i' faith! Wisely, wisely.

NURSE. If you be he, sir, I desire some confidence with you.

BENVOLIO. She will indite him to some supper.°

MERCUTIO. A bawd, a bawd, a bawd! So ho!°

ROMEO. What hast thou found?

MERCUTIO. No hare, sir, unless a hare, sir, in a lenten pie, that is something stale and hoar° ere it be spent.°

[*MERCUTIO walks by them and sings.*]

An old hare hoar,
And an old hare hoar,
Is very good meat in Lent;
But a hare that is hoar
Is too much for a score,
When it hoars ere it be spent.

Romeo, will you come to your father's? We'll to dinner thither.

ROMEO. I will follow you.

MERCUTIO. Farewell, ancient lady. Farewell. [*Singing.*] "lady, lady, lady."

[*BENVOLIO and MERCUTIO exit.*]

NURSE. I pray you, sir, what saucy merchant° was this that was so full of his ropery?°

99 good den: good afternoon.

102 prick: mark on a clock.

103–105 Out upon . . . mar: The Nurse indignantly asks Mercutio what sort of a man he is. Romeo responds that Mercutio was made in God's image but marred by himself.

111 fault of a worse: Romeo plays on the expression "for want of a better." **fault:** lack.

115–116 If you . . . supper: Benvolio deliberately misuses **indite** to mean "invite" as a way of mocking the Nurse's use of **confidence** to mean "private conversation."

117 So ho: The cry a hunter makes upon spotting prey.

119–120 No hare . . . spent: Mercutio compares the Nurse to meat hidden in a pie for Lent (when it is forbidden to eat meat) and kept long after it has become stale and moldy.

120 hoar: gray or white from age.

132 saucy merchant: rude fellow.

133 ropery: lewd jesting.

3 Make Inferences About Characters *What can you guess about the Nurse's reasons for looking for Romeo?*

Teach

Reading Strategy 2

Make Inferences About Characters Invite volunteers to read the parts of Mercutio and the Nurse. **Ask:** Which phrases in Mercutio's speech demonstrate his rudeness? *("Hide her face; for her fan's the fairer face." ". . . for the bawdy hand of the dial . . .")*

Reading Strategy 3

Make Inferences About Characters Answer: *She probably brings a message from Juliet.*

APPROACHING Check to make sure that students are making inferences based on clues from the text and not just guessing. **Ask:** What information helped you make your inference? *(Juliet told Romeo she would send a message to him in Scene 2.)*

Advanced Learners

DIFFERENTIATED INSTRUCTION

Wordplay Discuss the techniques Shakespeare uses to make his dialogue lively and revealing. Invite students to give examples of ways they use wordplay. Have partners write a skit about two friends having a disagreement. Instruct them to begin by writing a summary of the situation. Their dialogue should employ wordplay to reveal personality traits. Invite partners to perform their skits for the class.

Teach

Reading Strategy 1

Make Inferences About Characters **Answer:** *Romeo behaves with courtesy and gentleness. Students may infer that he is decent and kind.*

Language History ☆

Scurvy Knave The derivations of *scurvy* and *knave* shed light on the Nurse's insults. The Middle English word *skurfr* referred to scaly skin or dandruff; *scurfy* meant "vile, contemptible." *Knave,* spelled *knaue* in Middle English, originally meant "serving boy" but came to mean "a low deceitful person."

ROMEO. A gentleman, nurse, that loves to hear himself talk and will speak more in a minute than he will stand to° in a month.

NURSE. And 'a° speak anything against me, I'll take him down, and 'a were lustier than he is, and twenty such Jacks; and if I cannot, I'll find those that shall. Scurvy knave, I am none of his flirt-gills,° I am none of his skains-mates.° [*She turns to* PETER, *her man.*] And thou must stand by too and suffer every knave to use me at his pleasure!

PETER. I saw no man use you at his pleasure; if I had, my weapon should quickly have been out. I warrant you, I dare draw as soon as another man, if I see occasion in a good quarrel, and the law on my side.

NURSE. Now, afore God, I am so vex'd that every part about me quivers. Scurvy Knave! Pray you, sir, a word; and, as I told you, my young lady bid me inquire you out. What she bid me say, I will keep to myself; but first let me tell ye, if ye should lead her in a fool's paradise, as they say, it were a very gross kind of behavior, as they say; for the gentlewoman is young; and therefore, if you should deal double with her, truly it were an ill thing to be off'red to any gentlewoman, and very weak° dealing.

ROMEO. Nurse, commend me° to thy lady and mistress.
I protest° unto thee—

NURSE. Good heart, and i' faith I will tell her as much. Lord, Lord, she will be a joyful woman.

ROMEO. What wilt thou tell her, nurse? Thou dost not mark° me.

NURSE. I will tell her, sir, that you do protest, which, as I take it, is a gentlemanlike offer.

ROMEO. Bid her devise
Some means to come to shrift° this afternoon;
And there she shall at Friar Lawrence' cell
Be shriv'd° and married. Here is for thy pains.

[*He puts money into her hand.*]

NURSE. No, truly, sir; not a penny.

ROMEO. Go to! I say you shall.

NURSE. This afternoon, sir? Well, she shall be there.

135 stand to: carry out.

137 And 'a: if he.

140 flirt-gills: loose women. **skains-mates:** cutthroats' companions.

155 weak: contemptible.

156 commend me: send my regards.

157 protest: swear.

161 mark: pay attention to.

165 shrift: confession.

167 shriv'd: forgiven of her sins.

1 Make Inferences About Characters *Mercutio teased and mocked the Nurse. In contrast, how does Romeo behave toward her? What do you infer about Romeo?*

Speaking Practice

SPIRAL REVIEW **Readers Theater** Explain that readers theater involves speaking the characters' lines without physically performing the parts. Note that effective interpretation requires a careful study of the script. Remind students that actors in readers theater cannot rely on sets, costumes, and actions to help tell the story. Readers must use tone of voice, facial expressions, body language, and gestures to convey the characters' feelings. Invite volunteers to interpret Romeo's exchange with the nurse. Assign every student one or two lines to read, beginning with line 132 and ending with line 199. Have students practice delivering their line or lines. Then conduct a class reading of the scene. Ask students how the reading helped their understanding of the characters.

ROMEO. And stay, good nurse, behind the abbey wall.
Within this hour my man shall be with thee
And bring thee cords made like a tackled stair,°
Which to the high topgallant° of my joy
Must be my convoy° in the secret night.
Farewell. Be trusty, and I'll quit thy pains.°
Farewell. Commend me to thy mistress.

NURSE. Now God in heaven bless thee! Hark you, sir.

ROMEO. What say'st thou, my dear nurse?

NURSE. Is your man secret? Did you ne'er hear say,
"Two may keep counsel, putting one away?"°

ROMEO. Warrant thee my man's as true as steel.

NURSE. Well, sir, my mistress is the sweetest lady. Lord, Lord! When 'twas a little prating° thing—O, there is a nobleman in town, one Paris, that would fain lay knife aboard;° but she, good soul, had as lieve° see a toad, a very toad, as see him. I anger her sometimes, and tell her that Paris is the properer man; but I'll warrant you, when I say so, she looks as pale as any clout in the versal world.° Doth not rosemary and Romeo begin both with a letter?°

ROMEO. Ay, nurse; what of that? Both with an *R*.

NURSE. Ah, mocker! That's the dog's name.° *R* is for the—No; I know it begins with some other letter; and she hath the prettiest sententious° of it, of you and rosemary, that it would do you good to hear it.

ROMEO. Commend me to thy lady.

NURSE. Ay, a thousand times. [*ROMEO exits.*] Peter!

PETER. Anon.

NURSE. Before, and apace.°

3 [*PETER exits, followed by the NURSE.*]

SCENE 5. Later that day. CAPULET's orchard.

[*JULIET, waiting for the NURSE to return from the meeting with ROMEO, paces impatiently.*]

JULIET. The clock struck nine when I did send the nurse;
In half an hour she promised to return.
Perchance she cannot meet him. That's not so.
O, she is lame! Love's heralds should be thoughts,
Which ten times faster glides than the sun's beams

173 tackled stair: rope ladder.

174 topgallant: a platform atop a ship's mast.

175 convoy: means of conveyance.

176 quit thy pains: reward your trouble.

181 Two . . . away: A secret cannot be kept by more than one person.

184 prating: chattering.

185 lay knife aboard: claim her for himself.

186 had as lieve (lēv): would as willingly.

189 any clout in the versal world: any cloth in the whole world.

190 a letter: the same letter.

192 dog's name: The letter *R* sounds like a dog's growl.

194 sententious (sen ten′ shəs): The Nurse means to say *sentences,* or "pithy sayings."

199 Before, and apace: Go before me, and hurry.

---

2 Make Inferences About Characters ***Why does the Nurse give Romeo this information?***

Teach

Reading Strategy 2

Make Inferences About Characters Answer: *She seems to be looking after Juliet's interests, enhancing Juliet's value in Romeo's eyes by revealing that she's sought after and implying he may have to fight for her affections.*

Literary Element 3

Foil Ask: How do the Nurse and Mercutio function as foils to Juliet and Romeo? *(The Nurse and Mercutio, in refusing to take Romeo and Juliet as seriously as they take themselves, provide the audience with a realistic view of the lovers' immaturity and impetuosity.)*

Approaching Level

DIFFERENTIATED INSTRUCTION

Established Point out Shakespeare's repeated use of simile. Have a volunteer read lines 16–17 as an example. **Ask:** What is Juliet saying about the Nurse here? *(old people are boring, slow, and might as well be dead)* **Ask:** What do these thoughts reveal about Juliet? *(She is impatient and immature.)*

Have students write similes about three different characters in the play. Then, have students share their similes with the class. In a discussion, ask students to interpret each other's similes.

Teach

View the Art ★

Answer: *Lines 38–44—in which the Nurse looks earnest and Juliet looks distracted—seem to fit the painting best.*

English painter John Roddam Spencer Stanhope (1829–1908) was a captain in the militia before becoming an artist. Known for his use of color, Stanhope tended to paint allegorical and mythical subjects. He moved to Florence in 1880 to help cure his asthma.

Driving back shadows over low'ring° hills.
Therefore do nimble-pinion'd doves draw Love,°
And therefore hath the wind-swift Cupid wings.
Now is the sun upon the highmost hill
Of this day's journey, and from nine till twelve
Is three long hours; yet she is not come.
Had she affections and warm youthful blood,
She would be as swift in motion as a ball;
My words would bandy° her to my sweet love,
And his to me.
But old folks, many feign as they were dead—
Unwieldy, slow, heavy and pale as lead.

[*The* NURSE *enters, with* PETER.]

O God, she comes! O honey nurse, what news?
Hast thou met with him? Send thy man away.

NURSE. Peter, stay at the gate. [PETER *exits.*]

JULIET. Now, good sweet nurse—O Lord, why lookest thou sad?

6 low'ring: dark, threatening.

7 Therefore . . . Love: Venus, the goddess of love, was often portrayed riding a chariot drawn by nimble-winged (**nimble-pinion'd**) doves.

14 bandy: toss back and forth.

Juliet and her Nurse. John Roddam Spencer Stanhope. Oil on canvas. Private collection.

View the Art Stanhope's decision to become an artist went against the wishes of his wealthy parents—a decision reminiscent of Romeo and Juliet's rebellion. Which lines in this scene are reflected in the mood of Stanhope's painting? ★

Grammar Practice

SPIRAL REVIEW **Interjections** Explain that interjections—words or phrases that express emotion—emphasize a character's reaction. Ask for examples. *(Wow! No kidding! Hey!)* Have students find interjections in the dialogue on pages 674 and 675 and write modern expressions to replace them. *(Fie: Oh man!; Jesu, what haste: Slow down! Cool it!; I'faith: Really)*

Though news be sad, yet tell them merrily;
If good, thou shamest the music of sweet news
By playing it to me with so sour a face.

NURSE. I am aweary, give me leave° awhile.
Fie, how my bones ache! What a jaunce° have I!

JULIET. I would thou hadst my bones, and I thy news.
Nay, come, I pray thee speak. Good, good nurse, speak.

NURSE. Jesu, what haste! Can you not stay awhile?
Do you not see that I am out of breath?

JULIET. How art thou out of breath when thou hast breath
To say to me that thou art out of breath?
The excuse that thou dost make in this delay
Is longer than the tale thou dost excuse.
Is thy news good or bad? Answer to that.
Say either, and I'll stay the circumstance.°
Let me be satisfied, is't good or bad?

NURSE. Well, you have made a simple° choice; you know not how to choose a man. Romeo? No, not he. Though his face be better than any man's, yet his leg excels all men's; and for a hand and a foot, and a body, though they be not to be talk'd on,° yet they are past compare. He is not the flower of courtesy, but, I'll warrant him, as gentle as a lamb. Go thy ways,° wench; serve God. What, have you din'd at home?

JULIET. No, no. But all this did I know before.
What says he of our marriage? What of that?

NURSE. Lord, how my head aches! What a head have I!
It beats as it would fall in twenty pieces.
My back a t'other side—ah, my back, my back!
Beshrew° your heart for sending me about
To catch my death with jauncing up and down!

JULIET. I'faith, I am sorry that thou art not well.
Sweet, sweet, sweet nurse, tell me, what says my love?

NURSE. Your love says, like an honest° gentleman,
And a courteous, and a kind, and a handsome,
And, I warrant, a virtuous— Where is your mother?

JULIET. Where is my mother? Why, she is within.
Where should she be? How oddly thou repliest!
"Your love says, like an honest gentleman,
'Where is your mother?'"

25 give me leave: let me alone.

26 jaunce (jôns): rough walk.

36 stay the circumstance: wait for the details.

38 simple: foolish.

41–42 not to be talk'd on: not worth mentioning.

43–44 Go thy ways: off you go.

50 Beshrew: curse.

54 honest: honorable.

Make Inferences About Characters *What details suggest that the Nurse is deliberately delaying the telling of her message? Why is she doing this?*

Teach

Reading Strategy

Make Inferences About Characters **Answer:** *She complains of weariness. She seems to enjoy teasing Juliet, perhaps to heighten the excitement of the moment or to prolong her own pleasure in the power she enjoys as the messenger of such important news.*

Approaching Level

DIFFERENTIATED INSTRUCTION

Established Have students paraphrase Juliet's soliloquy at the beginning of Scene 5 to understand Juliet's state of mind. If possible, reproduce lines 1–17 on a separate handout on which students can write. Read through the passage, one line at a time, discussing and clarifying meaning. For example, direct students to line 1 and **say:** "The clock struck nine when I did send the nurse;" **Ask:** What does this line mean? *(at 9:00 Juliet sent her nurse)* **Ask:** Where did she send the nurse? *(to meet Romeo)* **Ask:** Is it morning or evening? *(morning)* Have students write on the handout next to line 1: *At 9:00 a.m., Juliet sent her nurse to meet Romeo.* Work through the rest of the passage one line at a time, emphasizing how Juliet's impatience is revealed and having students write their paraphrases next to each line.

Teach

Literary Element 1

Figurative Language

Answer: *He compares Juliet and Romeo's love to fire touched to gunpowder—consuming one another as they unite. This simile injects a note of volatility and danger into the atmosphere.*

APPROACHING **Ask:** What is the Friar trying to warn Romeo of with this metaphor? *(He is trying to tell Romeo that intense love never lasts and that Romeo will be hurt or disappointed if he does not temper his passion with reason.)*

Cultural History ☆

Monks' Cells In keeping with a Franciscan monk's vow of poverty, Friar Lawrence's cell would have been a tiny, unadorned room or cubicle in a larger building or a freestanding mud hut.

NURSE. O God's Lady dear!
Are you so hot?° Marry come up, I trow.°
Is this the poultice for my aching bones?
Henceforward do your messages yourself.

JULIET. Here's such a coil!° Come, what says Romeo?

NURSE. Have you got leave to go to shrift today?

JULIET. I have.

NURSE. Then hie you hence° to Friar Lawrence' cell;
There stays a husband to make you a wife.
Now comes the wanton° blood up in your cheeks:
They'll be in scarlet straight° at any news.
Hie you to church; I must another way,
To fetch a ladder, by the which your love
Must climb a bird's nest soon when it is dark.
I am the drudge, and toil in your delight;
But you shall bear the burthen soon at night.
Go; I'll to dinner; hie you to the cell.

JULIET. Hie to high fortune! Honest nurse, farewell.

[*They exit in separate directions.*]

61 hot: impatient. **Marry . . . trow:** Come on now, I declare.

64 coil: fuss.

67 hie you hence: hurry from here.

69 wanton (wont′ ən): unrestrained.

70 They'll . . . straight: They will turn red immediately.

☆ SCENE 6. Later that afternoon. FRIAR LAWRENCE's cell.

[*ROMEO and FRIAR LAWRENCE are waiting for JULIET so that the wedding can take place.*]

FRIAR. So smile the heavens upon this holy act
That after hours with sorrow chide us not!°

ROMEO. Amen, amen! But come what sorrow can,
It cannot countervail the exchange of joy°
That one short minute gives me in her sight.
Do thou but close our hands with holy words,
Then love-devouring death do what he dare—
It is enough I may but call her mine.

FRIAR. These violent delights have violent ends
And, in their triumph die, like fire and powder,
Which, as they kiss, consume.° The sweetest honey
Is loathsome in his own deliciousness
And in the taste confounds the appetite.°
Therefore love moderately: long love doth so;
Too swift arrives as tardy as too slow.

[*JULIET enters.*]

2 That after . . . not: and not punish us for it later.

4 countervail the exchange of joy: outweigh the joy I receive.

9–11 These violent . . . consume: Like lighted gunpowder, these extreme joys destroy themselves as they reach their high point.

12–13 Is loathsome . . . appetite: becomes cloying and destroys our appetite for it.

1 Figurative Language *Identify the simile in the Friar's warning. What does this simile add to the drama of the scene?*

Reading Practice

SMALL GROUP **Elaboration** Explain that elaboration develops and supports an important point in the text. For example, the many times Juliet begs the nurse to reveal Romeo's message emphasizes Juliet's fixation on the young man.

Have partners compose a general statement about Romeo's character; for example, "Romeo acts without thinking about the consequences." Then have students locate and list details that elaborate on this point of character.

Romeo and Juliet silhouette from Shakespeare's play as performed by the Footsbarn Traveling Theatre at Brighton on 07/05/93. ★

Here comes the lady. O, so light a foot
Will ne'er wear out the everlasting flint.°
A lover may bestride the gossamers°
That idles in the wanton° summer air,
And yet not fall; so light is vanity.°

JULIET. Good even to my ghostly confessor.

FRIAR. Romeo shall thank thee, daughter, for us both.

JULIET. As much to° him, else is his thanks too much.

ROMEO. Ah, Juliet, if the measure of thy joy
Be heap'd like mine, and that thy skill be more
To blazon it,° then sweeten with thy breath
This neighbor air, and let rich music's tongue
Unfold the imagin'd happiness that both
Receive in either by this dear encounter.

JULIET. Conceit, more rich in matter than in words,
Brags of his substance, not of ornament.°
They are but beggars that can count their worth;
But my true love is grown to such excess
I cannot sum up sum of° half my wealth.

FRIAR. Come, come with me, and we will make short work;
For, by your leaves, you shall not stay alone
Till Holy Church incorporate two in one.

[*They exit to perform the wedding ceremony.*]

16–17 Here . . . flint: In observing Juliet's light footsteps, the Friar alludes to a saying that small drops of water can wear away stones.
18 bestride the gossamers: walk on the cobwebs.
19 wanton: Here, it means "playful."
20 vanity: the temporary pleasures of this world.
23 As much to: the same to.

25–26 that thy . . . blazon it: if you are better able to proclaim it.

30–31 Conceit . . . ornament: True understanding does not need to be elaborated in words.

34 sum up sum of: add up the total of.

2 The Power of Love *How would you describe the mood, or feeling, of this scene? Why did Shakespeare create such a mood?*

Teach

Big Idea 2

The Power of Love

Answer: *The mood is solemn, reflecting the irrevocable nature of what Romeo and Juliet are doing.*

View the Art ★

The Footsbarn Traveling Theatre is an international company based in France, which tours the world, like the wandering storytellers of old. The multinational group has performed on all six continents. The company repertoire tends toward classics such as plays by Shakespeare and Molière.

To check students' understanding of the selection, see Unit 4 Teaching Resources Book, p. 48.

Progress Check

Can students identify figurative language?

If No → See Unit 4 Teaching Resources Book, p. 43.

Approaching Level

DIFFERENTIATED INSTRUCTION

Emerging Have a student volunteer read aloud lines 9–15. **Ask:** What is the Friar trying to say? *(He worries that the couple's love is too extreme and will fade.)* **Ask:** What might make the Friar have such thoughts? *(He knows that Romeo was just as in love with Rosaline as he is with Juliet.)*

Ask: Which words best describe how the Friar feels about marrying Romeo and Juliet? *(scared, concerned)* **Ask:** Why do you think the Friar feels this way? *(He worries what the consequences will be since their families are feuding.)*

After You Read

Assess

1. Accept reasonable answers.
2. (a) He thinks Romeo is silly for mooning over Rosaline. (b) Romeo has forgotten about Rosaline.
3. (a) From her speech on the balcony (b) Romeo's safety
4. (a) Juliet pretends she's going to confession and meets Romeo in the friar's cell. (b) Passion and fear of discovery
5. Juliet is more mature in considering the realities of their situation.
6. Students should support their answers.
7. Accept reasonable answers.
8. Answers will vary. Students may say that teenagers are likely to confide in adults, such as their parents, coaches, counselors, when they need advice or help that their friends cannot give them.

Literary Element

1. To the sun; asks her to rise and kill her mistress, the moon
2. Juliet wishes the news from Romeo would come faster—rushing to her in the winged chariot of the goddess of love. She compares the Nurse to lead—heavy, cold, and slow. A younger messenger would bounce between the lovers like a ball. The lines convey impatience.

Writing

Examples in Act 2, Scene 4 include *slip* (2.4.43–46), *pink* (54–57), *single* and *sole* (58–61), and *goose* (64–69). Examples in Act 1, Scene 1 include *collier, collar,* and *choler* (2.1.1–4)

After You Read

Respond and Think Critically

Respond and Interpret

1. Do you approve of Romeo and Juliet's quick actions? Why or why not?
2. (a)Why does Mercutio make fun of Romeo after they leave the party? (b)What makes this incident ironic?
3. (a)How does Romeo find out that Juliet shares his feelings? (b)What does Juliet seem most concerned about during the balcony scene?
4. (a)How do Romeo and Juliet carry out their plan to marry? (b)Why do they want to act so quickly?

Analyze and Evaluate

5. Who seems more mature to you, Romeo or Juliet? Why?
6. Which moments in this act did you consider especially amusing or humorous? Why?

Connect

7. **Big Idea** The Power of Love In this act, Shakespeare presents several views of love. With which view do you most identify? Explain.
8. **Connect to Today** Are modern teenagers likely to disclose their secrets to adults to whom they are close, as Romeo and Juliet do? Explain.

Literary Element Figurative Language

At times, Shakespeare may extend a metaphor over several lines, elaborating on its meaning.

1. To what does Romeo compare Juliet when he first sees her on the balcony in Scene 2? How does he extend this metaphor?
2. Identify the type of figurative language used by Juliet in Scene 5, lines 1–17. What do these lines convey?

Reading Strategy Make Inferences About Characters

A character's motivations are his or her reasons for acting in a certain way.

1. In your opinion, what motivates the Nurse and Friar Lawrence to help Romeo and Juliet?
2. Are these characters wise, irresponsible, or a mixture of the two? Explain.

LOG ON **Literature** Online

Selection Resources For Selection Quizzes, eFlashcards, and Reading-Writing Connection activities, go to glencoe.com and enter QuickPass code GL49787u4.

Vocabulary Practice

Practice with Context Clues Identify the context clues in the following sentences that help you determine the meaning of each boldfaced vocabulary word.

1. His property is **adjacent** to mine, and because it is adjoining, we need to decide on the fence together.
2. Even after moving across town, she wanted to **retain** most of her old friends, because she did not want to lose their friendship.
3. His demands were **perverse**—deliberately stubborn and unreasonable.
4. The long-time enemies felt nothing toward each other but **rancor.**

Writing

Write an Annotation A pun is a humorous play on different meanings of a word or on words that sound alike but have different meanings. Find a pun in Act 2, Scene 4 that plays on different meanings of a word and write a footnote explaining it.

Vocabulary Practice

1. *adjoining*
2. "she did not want to lose" her friendships
3. "deliberately stubborn and unreasonable"
4. *enemies* and *suffering*

Reading Strategy

1. They both care about the lovers; they get caught up in the excitement. The friar hopes to end the feud.
2. Students should explain their answers.

For additional selection assessment, see Assessment Resources, pp. 165–166.

Before You Read

Romeo and Juliet, Act 3

Connect to the Drama

How is your attitude toward the world different from that of adults you know? Freewrite for a few minutes about these different viewpoints.

Build Background

Seven hundred years ago northern Italy was a patchwork of independent city-states, each with its own government. Two such city-states were Verona and Mantua. Only twenty-four miles apart, they were completely independent of each other, akin to independent countries in our own time.

Set Purposes for Reading

Big Idea The Power of Love

As you read, ask yourself, How do societal expectations affect the love between friends or family members?

Literary Element Monologue, Soliloquy, and Aside

In a play, a **monologue** is a long speech by a character. A **soliloquy** is a special type of monologue delivered by a character who is alone onstage. An **aside** is a comment made by a character that is heard by the audience or another character but not by the other characters onstage. Both soliloquies and asides are used to provide information to the audience and to reveal the private thoughts of characters. As you read, ask yourself, What information do I learn from soliloquies and asides?

Reading Strategy Compare and Contrast Scenes

Playwrights carefully craft the scenes within an act to further plot and to create artful parallels and contrasts. As you read Act 3, ask yourself, How does each scene compare with the ones that come after and/or before?

Tip: Make a Web Diagram Use a web diagram to record the details of each scene. List the scene number in the center, and details about setting, plot, mood, and characterization in surrounding circles. Then review your web diagrams to compare and contrast the details.

Learning Objectives

For pages 679–706

In studying this text, you will focus on the following objectives:

Literary Study: Analyzing soliloquies, asides, and monologues.

Reading: Comparing and contrasting scenes.

Writing: Writing a compare-and-contrast essay.

Vocabulary

eloquence (el′ ə kwəns) *n.* the quality of persuasive, inspirational speech; p. 687 *The defense lawyer's eloquence brought tears to the jurors' eyes.*

adversity (ad vur′ sə tē) *n.* hardship; p. 692 *She remains upbeat despite adversity.*

predicament (pri dik′ ə mənt) *n.* a difficult or tricky situation; p. 693 *When a skunk started a family in our cellar, we were in quite a predicament.*

fickle (fik′ əl) *adj.* given to frequent changes of thought or mood; unreliable; inconstant; p. 700 *The ups and downs of life prove that fate is fickle.*

Tip: Analogies Analogies express the relationship between words or sets of words. For example, in the analogy *adversity : hardship :: prosperity : success*, the relationship is that the words in each set have similar meanings.

Before You Read

Focus

Summary

Tybalt challenges Romeo to a duel. Mercutio fights Tybalt and is killed. Enraged, Romeo kills Tybalt and is banished. The friar urges Romeo to wait in Mantua until the situation cools down. Although horrified by Romeo's crime, Juliet remains loyal to her new husband, and they spend the night together before Romeo leaves. Juliet's father commands her to wed Paris.

For summaries in languages other than English, see Unit 4 Teaching Resources Book, pp. 50–55.

Vocabulary

Context Clues Remind students that they sometimes can figure out unfamiliar words by looking at more familiar words in the text. Have them find the words in the selection using the page numbers in the definiton.

For additional vocabulary practice, see Unit 4 Teaching Resources Book, p. 58.

Selection Skills

The Tragedy of Romeo and Juliet, Act 3

Literary Elements
- Monologue, Soliloquy, and Aside (SE pp. 679–706)

Listening/Speaking/Viewing Skills
- Analyze Art (SE pp. 683, 689, 694, 699)

Reading Skills
- Compare and Contrast Scenes (SE pp. 679–706)

Writing Skills/Grammar
- Write Reports (TE p. 684)
- Hyperbole (TE p. 686)
- Appositives (TE p. 688)
- Persuasion (TE p. 698)

Vocabulary Skills
- Analogies (SE pp. 679, 706)

Teach

Reading Strategy 1

Compare and Contrast Scenes **Answer:** *The audience learns that he has a quick temper.*

For additional practice using the reading skill or strategy, see Unit 4 Teaching Resources Book, p. 57.

Reading Strategy 2

Predict Have students read Benvolio's first lines and recall the challenge Tybalt sent to Romeo. **Ask:** What do you predict might happen? *(Benvolio's words establish that the time is ripe for a confrontation. Students know that Tybalt is looking for one. There may be a duel.)*

Literary Element 3

Tone Point out that Mercutio's speech mingles a number of different tones: humorous wordplay; ironic teasing; and hyperbole, or exaggeration.

Ask: What makes Mercutio a round character? *(He has a mixture of conflicting, believable personality traits, which are revealed in his dialogue.)*

ADVANCED **Ask:** Why do you think Mercutio's dialogue is written in prose here? *(prose suggests that he is speaking quickly and without his usual rhythm because he is angry with Benvolio)*

Act 3

SCENE 1. The same afternoon. A street in Verona.

[BENVOLIO and MERCUTIO enter with some of their SERVANTS.]

2

BENVOLIO. I pray thee, good Mercutio, let's retire.
The day is hot, the Capels° are abroad,
And, if we meet, we shall not 'scape a brawl,
For now, these hot days, is the mad blood stirring.

MERCUTIO. Thou art like one of these fellows that, when he enters the confines of a tavern, claps me his sword upon the table and says, "God send me no need of thee!" and by the operation of the second cup draws him on the drawer,° when indeed there is no need.

BENVOLIO. Am I like such a fellow?

MERCUTIO. Come, come, thou art as hot a Jack° in thy mood as any in Italy; and as soon mov'd to be moody, and as soon moody to be mov'd.°

BENVOLIO. And what to?

3

MERCUTIO. Nay, and° there were two such, we should have none shortly, for one would kill the other. Thou! Why, thou wilt quarrel with a man that hath a hair more or a hair less in his beard than thou hast. Thou wilt quarrel with a man for cracking nuts, having no other reason but because thou hast hazel eyes. What eye but such an eye would spy out such a quarrel? Thy head is as full of quarrels as an egg is full of meat;° and yet thy head hath been beaten as addle° as an egg for quarreling. Thou hast quarreled with a man for coughing in the street, because he hath wakened thy dog that hath lain asleep in the sun. Didst thou not fall out with a tailor for wearing his new doublet° before Easter? With another for tying his new shoes with old riband?° And yet thou wilt tutor me from quarreling!°

BENVOLIO. And I were so apt to quarrel as thou art, any man should buy the fee simple of my life for an hour and a quarter.°

MERCUTIO. The fee simple? O simple!°

2 Capels: Capulets.

7–8 by the . . . drawer: when the second cup has had its effect, draws his sword on the waiter.

11 Jack: fellow.

12–13 and as soon mov'd . . . mov'd: as easily provoked to be angry as you are angry at being provoked.

15 and: if.

22 meat: food. **addle:** confused; rotten.

26 doublet: jacket. (New fashions were traditionally not supposed to be worn before Easter.)

27 riband: ribbon.

28 tutor me from quarreling: teach me not to quarrel.

31 buy . . . quarter: buy complete ownership of my life for a fraction of its value (since I would not live long).

32 O simple: Oh, how stupid!

---

1 Compare and Contrast Scenes *What new information about Benvolio does the audience learn here?*

Reading Practice

SPIRAL REVIEW **Read Dialogue** Break students into groups of three. Assign each student a role: Tybalt, Mercutio, or Romeo. Have students practice reading the dialogue on these pages. Explain that mastering Shakespeare's language takes practice. Encourage students to use expression and to follow stage directions. Have three students memorize their lines and act out the confrontation on these pages for the class.

[*TYBALT, JULIET's cousin, enters with other CAPULETS. He has not been able to find ROMEO since sending him a challenge earlier that day.*]

BENVOLIO. By my head, here comes the Capulets.

MERCUTIO. By my heel, I care not.

TYBALT. [*To his companions.*] Follow me close, for I will speak to them. [*To BENVOLIO and MERCUTIO.*] Gentlemen, good-den. A word with one of you.

MERCUTIO. And but one word with one of us? Couple it with something; make it a word and a blow.

4 TYBALT. You shall find me apt enough to that, sir, and you will give me occasion.

MERCUTIO. Could you not take some occasion without giving?

TYBALT. Mercutio, thou consortest with Romeo.

MERCUTIO. Consort? What, dost thou make us minstrels?° And thou make minstrels of us, look to hear nothing but discords. [*He places his hand on the hilt of his sword.*] Here's my fiddlestick;° here's that shall make you dance. 'Zounds,° consort!

BENVOLIO. We talk here in the public haunt of men.
Either withdraw unto some private place,
Or reason coldly of your grievances,
Or else depart. Here all eyes gaze on us.

MERCUTIO. Men's eyes were made to look, and let them gaze.
I will not budge for no man's pleasure, I.

[*ROMEO enters. He is calm and happy after his secret marriage to JULIET.*]

TYBALT. Well, peace be with you, sir. Here comes my man.°

MERCUTIO. But I'll be hang'd, sir, if he wear your livery.°
Marry, go before to field,° he'll be your follower!°
Your worship in that sense may call him man.

6 TYBALT. Romeo, the love I bear thee can afford
No better term than this: thou art a villain.

ROMEO. Tybalt, the reason that I have to love thee
Doth much excuse the appertaining rage°
To such a greeting. Villain am I none.
Therefore farewell. I see thou knowest me not.

43–44 Mercutio . . . minstrels: Mercutio plays on the word consort, which can refer to a group of musicians (minstrels). Here, consortest means "keep company."
47 fiddlestick: violin bow. **'Zounds:** an exclamation of surprise or anger.

55 my man: the man I am looking for.
56 But . . . livery: Mercutio then plays on another meaning of my man, which is "servant," declaring that Romeo shall never wear the servant's uniform (**livery**) of Tybalt's household.
57 field: dueling field. **follower:** servant (but Mercutio means that Romeo will follow him to fight).
62 the appertaining rage: the appropriate angry response.

---

5 Compare and Contrast Scenes *What plot complications are developing in this scene?*

7 The Power of Love *To what does Romeo allude in line 61?*

Teach

Reading Strategy 4

Interpret Have students describe Tybalt's character.
Ask: What effect do you imagine Tybalt and Mercutio have on each other? With what result? *(Mercutio's biting wit and Tybalt's temper are likely to clash.)*

Reading Strategy 5

Compare and Contrast Scenes **Answer:** *Mercutio, Tybalt, and Benvolio have encountered one another and seem on the verge of fighting.*

Literary Element 6

Foil Note that compared with Romeo and Mercutio, Tybalt is a flat character. Tybalt's driving motivation is resentment toward the Montagues. Under the circumstances, Romeo shows considerable restraint, counting Tybalt a relative by marriage now that Romeo is married to Juliet—although, ironically, Romeo cannot reveal this fact.

Big Idea 7

The Power of Love
Answer: *Romeo alludes to his marriage to Tybalt's kinswoman, Juliet.*

Approaching Level

DIFFERENTIATED INSTRUCTION

Emerging Students may benefit from listening to lines 15–28 read aloud.
Ask: What can you tell about Benvolio from what Mercutio says here? What point is Mercutio trying to make? *(Students may say that Mercutio implies that Benvolio frequently quarrels, sometimes unnecessarily.)*

Established Point out clues in the relationship between Mercutio and Benvolio—they are friends, so their tone is sometimes playful. Draw students' attention to lines 29–32. Guide them to use the notes in the margin to determine meaning.

Teach

Reading Strategy 1

Listen Ask students to imagine the emotions of Tybalt, Mercutio, and Romeo in this situation. What tone of voice does each character use? What volume? Invite volunteers to demonstrate by reading selected lines of each character aloud.

6

TYBALT. Boy, this shall not excuse the injuries
That thou hast done me; therefore turn and draw.

ROMEO. I do protest I never injured thee,
But love thee better than thou canst devise°
Till thou shalt know the reason of my love;
And so, good Capulet, which name I tender°
As dearly as mine own, be satisfied.

MERCUTIO. O calm, dishonorable, vile submission!
Alla stoccata° carries it away.

[*MERCUTIO, upset at TYBALT's insults and at ROMEO's refusal to fight, draws his sword.*]

Tybalt, you ratcatcher, will you walk?°

TYBALT. What wouldst thou have with me?

MERCUTIO. Good King of Cats, nothing but one of your nine lives. That I mean to make bold withal,° and, as you shall use me hereafter, dry-beat the rest of the eight.° Will you pluck your sword out of his pilcher° by the ears?° Make haste, lest mine be about your ears ere it be out.

TYBALT. I am for you. [*TYBALT draws his sword.*]

ROMEO. Gentle Mercutio, put thy rapier up.

MERCUTIO. Come sir, your *passado!*°

1

[*MERCUTIO and TYBALT fight. ROMEO, trying to stop the fight, turns to BENVOLIO for help.*]

ROMEO. Draw, Benvolio; beat down their weapons.
Gentlemen, for shame! Forbear this outrage!
Tybalt, Mercutio, the Prince expressly hath
Forbid this bandying in Verona streets.
Hold, Tybalt! Good Mercutio!

[*ROMEO, trying to separate the two men, steps between them and blocks MERCUTIO's sword arm. At that moment TYBALT thrusts his sword under ROMEO's arm and stabs MERCUTIO. TYBALT flees with his followers.*]

MERCUTIO. I am hurt.
A plague a' both houses!° I am sped.°
Is he gone and hath nothing?

BENVOLIO. What, art thou hurt?

MERCUTIO. Ay, ay, a scratch, a scratch. Marry, 'tis enough.
Where is my page? Go, villain, fetch a surgeon.

[*The PAGE, a servant, exits.*]

ROMEO. Courage, man. The hurt cannot be much.

68 devise: imagine.

70 tender: value.

73 *Alla stoccata* (ä′ lä stə kä tə): Italian fencing term that means "at the thrust." Mercutio may be using this as a contemptuous nickname for Tybalt, or he may mean that his sword thrust will erase Romeo's "vile submission."

74 walk: withdraw (to fight).

77 make bold withal: take.

77–78 as you shall . . . eight: According to how you treat me from now on, I will either spare your other lives or thrash them.

79 pilcher: scabbard, sheath. **by the ears:** as one would pull out a coward from hiding.

83 *passado:* Italian fencing term meaning "pass" or "lunge."

89 a' both houses: on the Montagues and Capulets. **sped:** done for.

Writing Practice

SPIRAL REVIEW **Respond to Literature** Explain that writing one's response to a work of literature creates a lasting tribute that gives personal meaning to the work. Ask students to decide which character—either Benvolio, Mercurio, or Romeo—they most identify with, and have them write a letter to that character. The letter should express and explain the sympathy or other emotion prompted by the character's situation or actions on this page.

Rival Factions from Romeo & Juliet, 1882. Sir Frank Dicksee. Gouache, en grisaille. Private collection.

View the Art Sir Dicksee painted a number of scenes from Romeo and Juliet, including this one and the one on page 648. Does his vision of the fight scene fit your idea of it? Explain. ★

MERCUTIO. No, 'tis not so deep as a well, nor so wide as a church door; but 'tis enough, 'twill serve. **3** Ask for me tomorrow, and you shall find me a grave° man. I am pepper'd,° I warrant, for this world. A plague a' both your houses! 'Zounds, a dog, a rat, a mouse, a cat, to scratch a man to death! A braggart, a rogue, a villain, that fights by the book of arithmetic!° Why the devil came you between us? I was hurt under your arm.

ROMEO. I thought all for the best.

MERCUTIO. Help me into some house, Benvolio.
Or I shall faint. A plague a' both your houses!
They have made worms' meat of me. I have it,
And soundly too. Your houses!

[*MERCUTIO exits, supported by* BENVOLIO *and his men.*]

ROMEO. This gentleman, the Prince's near ally,°
My very friend, hath got this mortal hurt
In my behalf—my reputation stain'd
With Tybalt's slander—Tybalt, that an hour
Hath been my cousin. O sweet Juliet,

96 grave: "serious" or "dead."

97 pepper'd: finished.

100 book of arithmetic: fencing manual.

107 near ally: close relative.

2 Compare and Contrast Scenes *How does the mood, or feeling, suddenly shift as the scene progresses?*

Teach

Reading Strategy 2

Compare and Contrast Scenes Answer: *As the fight escalated, the scene was tense, exciting, and full of action. Now that Mercutio has been stabbed, the mood becomes intensely poignant and tragic.*

Literary Element 3

Pun Point out that Mercutio puns with his dying breath. Have students explain the pun. *(Grave means both "serious" and "a place for the dead." Mercutio is being dead serious: he will soon be in the grave.)*

APPROACHING Ask students to think of other examples of puns to help them understand how this figure of speech works.

View the Art ★

Answer: *The dress, architecture, and fierce, angry energy of the fight scene are true to Scene 1. While the painting shows many people involved in the melee, only Tybalt and Mercutio fight in the play, with Romeo trying to separate them.*

Sir Frank Dicksee (1853–1928) was an English painter and illustrator renowned for expressing poetic sentiments in a realistic style.

English Learners

DIFFERENTIATED INSTRUCTION

Beginning/Early Intermediate
Students may be unfamiliar with the style of art in the selection. Tell students that European artists painted what they believed to be realistic interpretations of events. The artwork by Dicksee on page 683, for example, uses color and line to re-create a violent scene from this play. Dicksee was known for painting subjects in lavish costumes using rich colors.

Teach

Literary Element 1

Monologue, Soliloquy, and Aside **Answer:** *Romeo laments that Mercutio died protecting Romeo's honor from Tybalt's slurs. Romeo regrets that because he was softened toward Tybalt by Juliet's love, he tried to intervene in the duel, inadvertently giving Tybalt a fatal advantage.*

APPROACHING **Ask:** What benefit does Romeo's soliloquy give to the audience? *(Knowing Romeo's inner thoughts helps the audience understand the character and his motivations.)*

Reading Strategy 2

Connect Mercutio and Romeo were the best of friends. Have students consider how they would respond to Mercutio's death if they were Romeo.

Cultural History ☆

Revenge In Shakespeare's time, intense friendships between men were considered a higher form of love than the romantic bond between men and women. Mercutio fights Tybalt to defend Romeo's honor, and Romeo puts aside his feelings for Juliet to avenge his friend's death. Although complicated by Christianity's emphasis on forgiveness, Elizabethan attitudes toward revenge included the expectation that men were honor-bound to avenge the murder of a friend or relative.

Thy beauty hath made me effeminate
And in my temper soft'ned valor's steel!°

[*BENVOLIO returns.*]

BENVOLIO. O Romeo, Romeo, brave Mercutio is dead!
That gallant spirit hath aspir'd° the clouds,
Which too untimely here did scorn the earth.

ROMEO. This day's black fate on moe days doth depend;°
This but begins the woe others must end.

[*TYBALT returns.*]

BENVOLIO. Here comes the furious Tybalt back again.

2

ROMEO. He gone in triumph, and Mercutio slain?
Away to heaven, respective lenity,°
And fire-ey'd fury be my conduct° now!
Now, Tybalt, take the "villain" back again
That late thou gavest me; for Mercutio's soul
Is but a little way above our heads,
Staying for thine to keep him company.
Either thou or I, or both, must go with him.

TYBALT. Thou, wretched boy, that didst consort him here,
Shalt with him hence.

ROMEO. This shall determine that.

☆ [*ROMEO draws his sword; TYBALT draws his in response. They fight until ROMEO stabs TYBALT, who falls.*]

BENVOLIO. Romeo, away, be gone!
The citizens are up, and Tybalt slain.
Stand not amazed. The Prince will doom thee death
If thou art taken. Hence, be gone, away!

ROMEO. O, I am fortune's fool!

BENVOLIO. Why dost thou stay?

[*ROMEO flees just before a group of angry CITIZENS enters.*]

CITIZEN. Which way ran he that kill'd Mercutio?
Tybalt, that murderer, which way ran he?

BENVOLIO. There lies that Tybalt.

CITIZEN. Up, sir, go with me.
I charge thee in the Prince's name obey.

113 in my . . . steel: softened the courage in my character.

115 aspir'd (əs pīrd′): risen to.

117 This day's . . . depend: Today's fatal event will darken future days.

121 respective lenity (len′ə tē): careful leniency.

122 conduct: guide.

1 Monologue, Soliloquy, and Aside *What inner thoughts does Romeo reveal in this soliloquy?*

Research Practice

SPIRAL REVIEW **Reports** Note that sword fights such as the one at the beginning of Act 3 added excitement to many Shakespearean plays and were a popular aspect of his productions. Have students research various types of swords used during Shakespeare's time, including rapiers, broadswords, and épées. Students should begin by learning the shapes and dimensions of the weapons and then include other interesting facts about their histories and uses. Encourage them to illustrate their reports.

[*PRINCE ESCALUS, LORD MONTAGUE, LADY MONTAGUE, LORD CAPULET, and* LADY CAPULET *enter with various followers.*]

PRINCE. Where are the vile beginners of this fray?

BENVOLIO. O noble Prince, I can discover° all
The unlucky manage° of this fatal brawl.
There lies the man, slain by young Romeo,
That slew thy kinsman, brave Mercutio.

LADY CAPULET. Tybalt, my cousin! O my brother's child!
O Prince! O husband! O, the blood is spill'd
Of my dear kinsman! Prince, as thou art true,
For blood of ours shed blood of Montague.
O cousin, cousin!

PRINCE. Benvolio, who began this bloody fray?

BENVOLIO. Tybalt, here slain, whom Romeo's hand did slay.
Romeo, that spoke him fair, bid him bethink
How nice the quarrel was, and urg'd withal
Your high displeasure.° All this—uttered
With gentle breath, calm look, knees humbly bowed—
Could not take truce with the unruly spleen
Of Tybalt deaf to peace, but that he tilts°
With piercing steel at bold Mercutio's breast;
Who, all as hot,° turns deadly point to point,
And, with a martial scorn, with one hand beats
Cold death aside and with the other sends
It back to Tybalt, whose dexterity
Retorts it.° Romeo he cries aloud,
"Hold, friends! Friends, part!" and swifter than his tongue,
His agile arm beats down their fatal points,
And 'twixt them rushes; underneath whose arm
An envious° thrust from Tybalt hit the life
Of stout Mercutio, and then Tybalt fled;
But by and by comes back to Romeo,
Who had but newly entertain'd revenge,
And to't they go like lightning; for, ere I
Could draw to part them, was stout Tybalt slain;
And, as he fell, did Romeo turn and fly.
This is the truth, or let Benvolio die.

LADY CAPULET. He is a kinsman to the Montague;
Affection makes him false, he speaks not true.
Some twenty of them fought in this black strife,

140 discover: disclose.

141 manage: course.

151–153 Romeo . . . displeasure: Romeo, who spoke courteously to him, asked him to consider how trivial the quarrel was, and also argued that it would greatly displease you.

156 tilts: points.

158 all as hot: just as angry.

159–162 And, with . . . Retorts it: This description suggests that both Mercutio and Tybalt ward off the other's jabs with a dagger held in one hand and return **(Retorts)** the jabs with a sword held in the other hand.

166 envious (en′ vē əs): hateful.

3 The Power of Love *From this scene, what do you infer about common beliefs about love, obligation, and revenge in Italy in the 1300s?*

Teach

Big Idea 3

The Power of Love

Answer: *Family obligations seem paramount. Any insult to the family required an immediate forceful response.*

Approaching Level

DIFFERENTIATED INSTRUCTION

Emerging Remind students that when you paraphrase writing, you state its meaning in your own words. Pair up students and help them understand the action on these pages by having them paraphrase what each character says. Model this process by reading aloud lines 150–153. Then **say:** Romeo killed Tybalt. Romeo spoke courteously to Tybalt and made him think the quarrel was minor and would displease the Prince. Assign pairs of students two or three lines to paraphrase and read to the class.

Teach

Literary Element 1

Characterization Discuss the major personality traits of Benvolio, the Prince, Lady Capulet, and Lord Montague. Note that the Prince becomes the fulcrum of their interaction by demanding an explanation for the fray. **Ask:** What traits does the Prince display? *(Sternness, sorrow over bloodshed, moderation in determining Romeo's punishment by death)*

Reading Strategy 2

Compare and Contrast Scenes **Answer:** *Juliet's happy anticipation of her reunion with Romeo poses a jarring contrast to the fatal fight in the previous scene. Her obliviousness to the disastrous complications in Scene 1 is poignant.*

And all those twenty could but kill one life.
I beg for justice, which thou, Prince, must give.
Romeo slew Tybalt; Romeo must not live.

PRINCE. Romeo slew him; he slew Mercutio.
Who now the price of his dear blood doth owe?

MONTAGUE. Not Romeo, Prince; he was Mercutio's friend;
His fault concludes but what the law should end,
The life of Tybalt.°

PRINCE. And for that offense
Immediately we do exile him hence.
I have an interest in your heart's proceeding,
My blood° for your rude brawls doth lie a-bleeding;
But I'll amerce° you with so strong a fine
That you shall all repent the loss of mine.
I will be deaf to pleading and excuses;
Nor tears nor prayers shall purchase out abuses.°
Therefore use none. Let Romeo hence in haste,
Else, when he is found, that hour is his last.
Bear hence this body and attend our will.°
Mercy but murders, pardoning those that kill.

1 [*They all exit.*]

SCENE 2. Later that day. CAPULET's orchard.

[*JULIET, unaware of what has happened, waits impatiently for the night so that she can see ROMEO again.*]

JULIET. Gallop apace, you fiery-footed steeds,
Towards Phoebus' lodging! Such a wagoner
As Phaëton would whip you to the west
And bring in cloudy night immediately.°
Spread thy close° curtain, love-performing night,
That th' runaway's eyes may wink,° and Romeo
Leap to these arms untalk'd of and unseen!
Lovers can see to do their amorous rites
By their own beauties, or, if love be blind,
It best agrees with night. Come, civil° night,
Thou sober-suited matron all in black,
And learn me how to lose a winning match,
Play'd for a pair of stainless maidenhoods.
Hood my unmann'd blood, bating in my cheeks,
With thy black mantle; till strange love grows bold,

183–184 His fault . . . Tybalt: His only offense was that he killed Tybalt, which the law should have done anyway.

187 blood: relative.

188 amerce (ə murs'): penalize.

191 purchase out abuses: buy forgiveness for crimes.

194 attend our will: obey my wishes.

1–4 Gallop . . . immediately: Juliet urges the horses that drive **Phoebus** (fē' bus) the sun god's chariot across the sky to hurry home. **Phaëton** (fā' ət ən), a son of the sun god, was known for recklessly driving the chariot.
5 close: concealing.
6 That . . . wink: so that the eyes of wandering observers may close.
10 civil: solemn.

---

2 Compare and Contrast Scenes *How does the situation of Scene 2 contrast with that of Scene 1? What is the effect?*

Writing Practice

SPIRAL REVIEW **Use Hyperbole for Effect** Discuss the effect of using hyperbole—extravagant, overstated language—in Juliet's soliloquy to describe her mood and emotions. Note how her words help the reader imagine the thrill of a teenager's first love. Have students write about a personal experience that caused overwhelming excitement *(e.g., seeing their favorite singer perform, winning a big game, or traveling to a new place for the first time)* using extravagant figures of speech.

Think true love acted simple modesty.°
Come, night, come, Romeo, come, thou day in night,
For thou wilt lie upon the wings of night,
Whiter than new snow upon a raven's back.
Come, gentle night; come, loving, black-brow'd night;
Give me my Romeo; and, when I shall die,
Take him and cut him out in little stars,
And he will make the face of heaven so fine
That all the world will be in love with night
And pay no worship to the garish sun.
O, I have bought the mansion of a love,
But not possess'd it, and though I am sold,
Not yet enjoy'd. So tedious is this day
As is the night before some festival
To an impatient child that hath new robes
And may not wear them. O, here comes my nurse,

[*The* NURSE *enters carrying a rope ladder.*]

And she brings news; and every tongue that speaks
But Romeo's name speaks heavenly **eloquence.**
5 Now, nurse, what news? What hast thou there, the cords
That Romeo bid thee fetch?

NURSE. Ay, ay, the cords.

[*She throws down the ladder.*]

JULIET. Ay me! What news? Why dost thou wring thy hands?

NURSE. Ah, weraday!° He's dead, he's dead, he's dead!
We are undone, lady, we are undone!
Alack the day! He's gone, he's kill'd, he's dead!

JULIET. Can heaven be so envious?

NURSE. Romeo can,
Though heaven cannot. O Romeo, Romeo!
Who ever would have thought it? Romeo!

JULIET. What devil art thou that dost torment me thus?
This torture should be roar'd in dismal hell.
Hath Romeo slain himself? Say thou but ay,

14–16 Hood . . . modesty: Falconers would place a hood on an untamed **(unmanned)** falcon to prevent it from fluttering **(bating)** its wings. Juliet asks the night to conceal her blushing until she overcomes her innocent modesty.

37 weraday: welladay (alas!).

3 Monologue, Soliloquy, and Aside *What emotions and concerns does Juliet reveal here?*

4 Monologue, Soliloquy, and Aside *What makes Juliet's impatience particularly touching?*

Vocabulary

eloquence (el′ ə kwens) *n.* the quality of persuasive, inspirational speech

Teach

Literary Element 3

Monologue, Soliloquy, and Aside **Answer:** *Juliet anticipates but also worries about her first night with her husband.*

Literary Element 4

Monologue, Soliloquy, and Aside **Answer:** *Her ignorance of Romeo's banishment for the murder of her cousin makes her eagerness to see him particularly touching.*

Reading Strategy 5

Connect Students will be able to empathize with Juliet's impatience and the perception that time is creeping. Have them recall a meeting, date, or event they looked forward to anxiously and describe how their anticipation affected their mood and perception of time.

Advanced Learners

DIFFERENTIATED INSTRUCTION

Allusions Encourage students to delve deeper into the play's allusions to Greek mythology. Have them find the meaning of the names *Phoebus* and *Phaëton* in a dictionary *("shining" and "bright one," respectively).* Direct them to research Phoebus and Phaëton at a library or on the Internet. Then have them summarize their findings for the class and explain why Juliet's allusion foreshadows calamity. *(Phaëton's recklessness almost set the world on fire.)*

Teach

Literary Element 1

Pun Have students identify Juliet's pun. *(I and eye sound like ay, which means "yes.")* Juliet now has the sinking feeling that her self, which now is defined by her relationship to Romeo, is taken from her.

Literary Element 2

Monologue, Soliloquy, and Aside **Answer:** *Juliet expresses outrage at Romeo's deceit. He appeared to be "beautiful" and "divine," but was in fact a "villain" and "vile."*

Literary Element 3

Oxymoron Have students locate the oxymorons—abruptly paradoxical or contradictory phrases or statements—that Juliet uses in this speech. *(beautiful tyrant, fiend angelical, damned saint, honorable villain)*

Ask: Why does she combine these opposites to describe Romeo? *(To express the conflict she feels and the two conflicting images of her husband: gentle lover and raging murderer)*

And that bare vowel *I* shall poison more
Than the death-darting eye of cockatrice.°
I am not I, if there be such an ay,
Or those eyes shut, that makes thee answer ay.
If he be slain, say ay, or if not, no.
Brief sounds determine my weal° or woe.

NURSE. I saw the wound, I saw it with mine eyes,
(God save the mark!)° here on his manly breast.
A piteous corse, a bloody piteous corse;°
Pale, pale as ashes, all bedaub'd in blood,
All in gore-blood. I sounded° at the sight.

JULIET. O, break, my heart! Poor bankrout,° break at once!
To prison, eyes; ne'er look on liberty!
Vile earth, to earth resign;° end motion here,
And thou and Romeo press one heavy bier!°

NURSE. O Tybalt, Tybalt, the best friend I had!
O courteous Tybalt! Honest gentleman!
That ever I should live to see thee dead!

JULIET. What storm is this that blows so contrary?
Is Romeo slaught'red, and is Tybalt dead?
My dearest cousin, and my dearer lord?
Then, dreadful trumpet, sound the general doom!
For who is living, if those two are gone?

NURSE. Tybalt is gone, and Romeo banished;
Romeo that kill'd him, he is banished.

JULIET. O God! Did Romeo's hand shed Tybalt's blood?

NURSE. It did, it did! Alas the day, it did!

JULIET. O serpent heart, hid with a flow'ring face!°
Did ever dragon keep° so fair a cave?
Beautiful tyrant! fiend angelical!
Dove-feather'd raven! wolvish ravening lamb!
Despised substance of divinest show!°
Just opposite to what thou justly seem'st,
A damned saint, an honorable villain!
O nature, what hadst thou to do in hell
When thou didst bower° the spirit of a fiend
In mortal paradise of such sweet flesh?
Was ever book containing such vile matter
So fairly bound? O, that deceit should dwell
In such a gorgeous palace!

47 cockatrice (kok' ə tris'): a mythical serpent that was thought to kill with a glance.

51 weal: happiness.

53 God save the mark: an expression uttered to ward off bad luck when something unpleasant is mentioned.
54 corse: corpse.
56 sounded: swooned, fainted.
57 bankrout: bankrupt (because it has lost everything it values).

59 Vile earth, to earth resign: Miserable body, give yourself back to the earth.
60 bier (bēr): a platform on which corpses are displayed before burial.

73 hid with a flow'ring face: hidden by a flower-like face. (Similar images throughout this speech express Juliet's shock that evil can dwell within one she finds so attractive.)
74 keep: guard.
77 show: appearance.

81 bower: enclose, conceal.

2 Monologue, Soliloquy, and Aside *How would you describe the emotions Juliet expresses over the course of this monologue?*

Grammar Practice

SPIRAL REVIEW **Appositive Phrases** Explain that an appositive is a noun or pronoun that follows and identifies another noun or pronoun. An appositive phrase includes the appositive and its modifiers, as in line 61: "O Tybalt, Tybalt, the best friend I ever had!" Point out how the appositive phrase "the best friend I ever had" identifies the noun Tybalt.

Explain that an appositive phrase not essential to the meaning of the sentence is set off by commas. Have students correctly punctuate and underline the appositive phrase in each sentence:

- The Prince a kinsman of Mercutio must pass judgment on Romeo. *(Commas should be placed before and after* a kinsman of Mercutio.*)*
- Juliet grieves for Tybalt her dear cousin. *(A comma should be placed before the phrase* her dear cousin.*)*

Verona, Italy, ca. 1722–1788. Francesco Zuccarelli.

View the Art Zuccarelli was known for painting idyllic country scenes—his work had a large influence on the 18th century English landscape painters. How is Verona depicted in his painting? Is this how you envision the setting of the play? ★

NURSE. There's no trust,
No faith, no honesty in men; all perjur'd,
All forsworn, all naught,° all dissemblers.°
Ah, where's my man? Give me some aqua vitae.°
These griefs, these woes, these sorrows make me old.
Shame come to Romeo!

JULIET. Blister'd be thy tongue
For such a wish! He was not born to shame.
Upon his brow shame is asham'd to sit;
For 'tis a throne where honor may be crown'd
Sole monarch of the universal earth.
O, what a beast was I to chide at him!

NURSE. Will you speak well of him that kill'd your cousin?

JULIET. Shall I speak ill of him that is my husband?
Ah, poor my lord, what tongue shall smooth° thy name
When I, thy three-hours wife, have mangled it?
But wherefore, villain, didst thou kill my cousin?
That villain cousin would have kill'd my husband.
☆ Back, foolish tears, back to your native spring!
Your tributary drops° belong to woe,
Which you, mistaking, offer up to joy.
My husband lives, that Tybalt would have slain;
And Tybalt's dead, that would have slain my husband.

87 naught: wicked. **dissemblers:** liars.
88 aqua vitae (ak′ wə vī′ tē): brandy.

98 smooth: speak well of.

103 Your tributary drops: the drops you have contributed.

Teach

View the Art ★

Answer: *Verona is depicted as peaceful, semi-rural, and beautiful. Students may say that the calmness reflected in the painting does not fit with their image of Verona, which Shakespeare portrays as a place of intrigue—involving feuds, parties, and secret meetings—in addition to the romantic setting of a love story.*

Italian painter Francesco Zuccarelli (1702–1788) was one of the most popular landscape painters of his time. His landscapes focus more on lyricism than realism.

Writer's Technique ☆

Metaphor Shakespeare is famous for his use of extended metaphor. Here he refers to "native spring" and "tributary drops." Both the spring and the tributary are parts of a river. In this case, Shakespeare is using the terminology of an actual river to refer to the flow of Juliet's "river" of tears.

English Learners

DIFFERENTIATED INSTRUCTION

Beginning/Early Intermediate Help students decipher Juliet's speech by working line by line. Have student volunteers read a line aloud, then have the class paraphrase the line. Model the process by reading line 43. Then, **say:** Why do you torment me? Ask students to point out words that give them clues as to how Juliet is feeling. **Ask:** Why do you think she is so emotional? *(Students may say that this is characteristic of teenagers and because she is in love.)* Assign students short phrases or sentences to paraphrase and read aloud to the class.

Teach

Big Idea 1

The Power of Love
Answer: *As Juliet reflects, she remembers her love for her husband and that Tybalt wanted to kill him. Her anger toward Romeo rapidly changes to despair over his banishment.*

Reading Strategy 2

Compare and Contrast Scenes **Answer:** *Since Scene 1, many fresh obstacles to Romeo and Juliet's happiness have developed. Tybalt and Mercutio have been killed, and Romeo has been banished.*

All this is comfort; wherefore weep I then?
Some word there was, worser than Tybalt's death,
That murd'red me. I would forget it fain;°
But O, it presses to my memory
Like damned guilty deeds to sinners' minds!
"Tybalt is dead, and Romeo—banished."
That "banished," that one word "banished,"
Hath slain ten thousand Tybalts. Tybalt's death
Was woe enough, if it had ended there;
Or, if sour woe delights in fellowship
And needly will be rank'd with° other griefs,
Why followed not, when she said "Tybalt's dead,"
Thy father, or thy mother, nay, or both,
Which modern lamentation might have moved?°
But with a rearward° following Tybalt's death,
"Romeo is banished"—to speak that word
Is father, mother, Tybalt, Romeo, Juliet,
All slain, all dead. "Romeo is banished"—
There is no end, no limit, measure, bound,
In that word's death; no words can that woe sound.°
Where is my father and my mother, nurse?

NURSE. Weeping and wailing over Tybalt's corse.
Will you go to them? I will bring you thither.

JULIET. Wash they his wounds with tears? Mine shall be spent,
When theirs are dry, for Romeo's banishment.
Take up those cords. Poor ropes, you are beguil'd,°
Both you and I, for Romeo is exil'd.
He made you for a highway to my bed,
But I, a maid, die maiden-widowed.
Come, cords, come, nurse, I'll to my wedding-bed,
And death, not Romeo, take my maidenhead!

NURSE. Hie to your chamber. I'll find Romeo
To comfort you. I wot° well where he is.
Hark ye, your Romeo will be here at night.
I'll to him; he is hid at Lawrence' cell.

JULIET. O, find him! Give this ring to my true knight
And bid him come to take his last farewell.

[*They exit.*]

109 fain: gladly.

117 needly . . . with: must be accompanied by.

120 modern . . . moved: might have roused ordinary grief.
121 rearward: rear guard.

126 no words can that woe sound: no words can express the depth of that misery.

132 beguil'd: cheated.

139 wot: know.

---

1 The Power of Love *Describe the rapid changes Juliet's ideas undergo as she comes to understand the situation. Why does she say, ". . . wherefore weep I then"?*

2 Compare and Contrast Scenes *How have events developed since Scene 1?*

Writing Practice

SPIRAL REVIEW **Point of View** In her speech about banishment, Juliet speaks from the point of view of a young woman with almost no power to act independently. Have students write a poem or journal entry describing how Juliet feels and why. They may use a logical explanation or expressive language to communicate their understanding. Then direct the students to share their poem or journal entry with the class.

SCENE 3. Later. FRIAR LAWRENCE's cell.

[*FRIAR LAWRENCE enters and notices that ROMEO is hiding in the room.*]

FRIAR. Romeo, come forth; come forth, thou fearful man.
Affliction is enamor'd of thy parts,°
And thou art wedded to calamity.

[*ROMEO steps forward.*]

ROMEO. Father, what news? What is the Prince's doom?°
What sorrow craves acquaintance at my hand
That I yet know not?

FRIAR. Too familiar
Is my dear son with such sour company.
I bring thee tidings of the Prince's doom.

ROMEO. What less than doomsday° is the Prince's doom?

FRIAR. A gentler judgment vanish'd° from his lips—
Not body's death, but body's banishment.

ROMEO. Ha, banishment? Be merciful, say "death";
For exile hath more terror in his look,
Much more than death. Do not say "banishment."

FRIAR. Here from Verona art thou banished.
Be patient, for the world is broad and wide.

ROMEO. There is no world without° Verona walls,
But purgatory, torture, hell itself.
Hence "banished" is banish'd from the world,
And world's exile is death. Then "banished"
Is death misterm'd. Calling death "banished,"
Thou cut'st my head off with a golden ax
And smilest upon the stroke that murders me.

FRIAR. O deadly sin! O rude unthankfulness!
Thy fault our law calls death;° but the kind Prince,
Taking thy part, hath rush'd° aside the law,
And turn'd that black word "death" to "banishment."
This is dear° mercy, and thou seest it not.

ROMEO. 'Tis torture, and not mercy. Heaven is here,
Where Juliet lives; and every cat and dog
And little mouse, every unworthy thing,
Live here in heaven and may look on her;
But Romeo may not. More validity,°
More honorable state, more courtship lives

2 Affliction . . . parts: Misfortune has fallen in love with your attractive qualities.

4 doom: judgment.

9 doomsday: my death.

10 vanish'd: escaped.

17 without: outside.

25 our law calls death: is punishable by death.
26 rush'd: brushed.

28 dear: uncommon.

33 validity: value.

3 The Power of Love *How would you evaluate Romeo's claim that the Friar is downplaying the severity of banishment?*

Teach

Big Idea 3

The Power of Love

Answer: *Some students may say that because of his immaturity, impetuousness, and passion for Juliet, Romeo overreacts to the Friar's sensible advice, although as adolescents, some may sympathize and recall experiencing similar feelings.*

APPROACHING **Ask:** What kind of figurative language is Romeo using in this scene? Explain. *(Romeo is using hyperbole—he is using exaggeration to communicate the severity of his situation.)*

English Learners

DIFFERENTIATED INSTRUCTION

Intermediate Students may be confused by Shakespeare's use of hyperbole. Point out examples of hyperbole in Juliet's speech (lines 113–114 and 123–124). Explain that he is exaggerating the truth because she is very upset. Ask students to recall stories they have heard in which people exaggerated. **Ask:** How did you react to these overstatements? *(Students may say that they laughed or that they tried to calm the person.)*

Teach

Literary Element 1

Monologue, Soliloquy, and Aside **Answer:** *His extreme descriptions of his situation and his melodramatic assertions of his own doom suggest that he is juvenile, inexperienced, and out of control.*

Reading Strategy 2

Compare and Contrast Scenes **Answer:** *In both cases, young people turn to adults for help.*

Cultural History ☆

Christian Hell Explain that to Renaissance Christians, hell represented a state or place to which the spirits of unrepentant sinners were condemned to suffer for eternity after death. Purgatory was the state or place in which those who had died in a state of God's grace atoned by suffering. Hell was permanent; purgatory was temporary.

In carrion flies than Romeo. They may seize
On the white wonder of dear Juliet's hand
And steal immortal blessing from her lips.
Who, even in pure and vestal° modesty,
Still° blush, as thinking their own kisses sin;°
But Romeo may not, he is banished.
Flies may do this but I from this must fly;
They are free men, but I am banished.
And sayest thou yet that exile is not death?
Hadst thou no poison mix'd, no sharp-ground knife,
No sudden mean° of death, though ne'er so mean,°
But "banished" to kill me—"banished"?
☆ O friar, the damned use that word in hell;
Howling attends it! How hast thou the heart,
Being a divine, a ghostly confessor,
A sin-absolver, and my friend profess'd,
To mangle me with that word "banished"?

FRIAR. Thou fond° mad man, hear me a little speak.

ROMEO. O, thou wilt speak again of banishment.

FRIAR. I'll give thee armor to keep off that word;
Adversity's sweet milk, philosophy,
To comfort thee, though thou art banished.

ROMEO. Yet "banished"? Hang up° philosophy!
Unless philosophy can make a Juliet,
Displant° a town, reverse a prince's doom,
It helps not, it prevails not. Talk no more.

FRIAR. O, then I see that madmen have no ears.

ROMEO. How should they, when that wise men have no eyes?

FRIAR. Let me dispute with thee of thy estate.°

ROMEO. Thou canst not speak of that thou dost not feel.
Wert thou as young as I, Juliet thy love,
An hour but married, Tybalt murdered,
Doting like me,° and like me banished,

38 vestal (vest′ əl): virginal.

39 Still: always. **thinking . . . sin:** believing it is sinful for them to touch when her mouth closes.

45 mean: means. **mean:** lowly.

52 fond: foolish.

57 Hang up: forget about.

59 Displant: transplant.

63 dispute . . . estate: discuss your situation with you.

67 Doting like me: as obsessively in love as I am.

1 Monologue, Soliloquy, and Aside *What details in this monologue suggest Romeo's youth?*

2 Compare and Contrast Scenes *What echoes do you see between this conversation and Juliet's conversation with the Nurse in Scene 2?*

Vocabulary

adversity (ad vur′ sə tē) *n.* hardship

Speaking Practice

SMALL GROUP

Respond to Literature Break students into groups to discuss whether they think the Prince's decision to exile Romeo was fair. Have students take into account Romeo's reaction on this page to being exiled and the Friar's response. **Ask:** Do you think the Prince was biased? Do you think he would have awarded the same punishment to Tybalt if he had killed Romeo? *(Some students may say that the Prince was likely biased, since the prince refers to Tybalt as "My blood." Other students may contend that he was fair; he could have had Romeo killed and that he had warned the townspeople that he would no longer tolerate fighting.)* Have students discuss these questions in their groups. Encourage them to use quotes from the selection to support their assertions.

Then mightst thou speak, then mightst thou tear thy hair,
And fall upon the ground, as I do now,

[ROMEO throws himself on the floor.]

Taking the measure of an unmade grave.°

[There is a knock at the door to the cell.]

FRIAR. Arise, one knocks. Good Romeo, hide thyself.

ROMEO. Not I; unless the breath of heartsick groans
Mistlike infold me° from the search of eyes.

[Another knock.]

FRIAR. Hark, how they knock! Who's there? Romeo, arise;
Thou wilt be taken.—Stay° awhile!—Stand up;

[The knocking continues more loudly than before.]

Run to my study.—By and by!°—God's will,
What simpleness° is this.—I come, I come!

[There is a very loud knock. The FRIAR goes to the door.]

Who knocks so hard? Whence come you? What's your will?

NURSE. Let me come in, and you shall know my errand.
I come from Lady Juliet.

FRIAR. Welcome then.

[The NURSE enters.]

NURSE. O holy friar, O, tell me, holy friar,
Where is my lady's lord, where's Romeo?

FRIAR. There on the ground, with his own tears made drunk.

NURSE. O, he is even in my mistress' case,°
Just in her case! O woeful sympathy!
Piteous **predicament!** Even so lies she,
Blubb'ring and weeping, weeping and blubb'ring.
Stand up, stand up! Stand, and you be a man.
For Juliet's sake, for her sake, rise and stand!
Why should you fall into so deep an O?°

ROMEO. *[He rises.]* Nurse—

NURSE. Ah sir, ah sir! Death's the end of all.

ROMEO. Spakest thou of Juliet? How is it with her?
Doth not she think me an old° murderer,
Now I have stain'd the childhood of our joy

69–70 And fall . . . grave: Romeo makes his gesture of throwing himself to the ground even more melodramatic by suggesting that he is seeing how large a grave he will need.

73 Mistlike infold me: forms a mist to hide me.

75 Stay: wait.

76 By and by: in a moment. The Friar interrupts his pleading with Romeo to address the person knocking at the door.

77 simpleness: foolishness.

84 even in my mistress' case: exactly in Juliet's condition.

90 so deep an O: so heavy a cry of grief.

94 old: hardened.

Vocabulary

predicament (pri dik′ e ment) *n.* a difficult or tricky situation

Teach

Literary Element 3

Suspense Note how Shakespeare capitalizes on the suspense created by the Nurse's knocking. **Ask:** How would you describe the effect when the Nurse finally enters? *(Anticlimactic, humorous)*

APPROACHING **Ask:** Whom do you expect was knocking? *(The Prince's men out to arrest Romeo or the Capulets out for revenge)*

English Learners

DIFFERENTIATED INSTRUCTION

Early Intermediate Before students read each scene, read a prose summary of it aloud. (Charles and Mary Lamb's *Tales from Shakespeare*, available on the Internet, contains a prose version of *Romeo and Juliet.*) After students finish reading silently, read selected passages aloud, explaining language and clarifying meaning. Encourage students to connect to the play and take time after reading each scene to record notes in a journal on events, actions, and feelings similar to those in their own lives.

Teach

Big Idea 1

The Power of Love
Answer: *Knowing that Juliet has probably heard that he killed Tybalt, Romeo is anxious to know if Juliet is well and if she still loves him.*

View the Art ★

Answer: *Students may say that the Friar and the Nurse look frightened or concerned. Romeo looks distraught, heartbroken, or exhausted.*

This picture is one of twenty-two watercolors that illustrator and painter William Hatherell (1855–1928) created for *Romeo and Juliet.* Hatherell worked as an illustrator for numerous Victorian magazines and had a reputation for refusing to rush his work.

Romeo in Friar Laurence's Cell, Illustration to "Romeo and Juliet" Act III, Scene 3. William Hatherell. Watercolor over pencil on board, 37.1 x 27 cm. Birmingham Museums and Art Gallery, UK.

View the Art In this painting, Romeo is in the foreground, but his cloak blends with the rug. Each of the three characters has a distinct stance and facial expression—what words would you use to describe their individual emotions as depicted in the painting? ★

With blood removed but little from her own?
Where is she? And how doth she! And what says
My conceal'd lady° to our cancel'd° love?

NURSE. O, she says nothing, sir, but weeps and weeps;
And now falls on her bed, and then starts up,
And Tybalt calls; and then on Romeo cries,
And then down falls again.

98 **conceal'd lady:** secret bride. **cancel'd:** nullified.

1 The Power of Love *Why does Romeo ask these questions?*

Viewing Practice

SPIRAL REVIEW **Analyze the Painting** Ask students to write an interpretive analysis of the painting in relation to the scene. Have students interpret the following:

- color
- positioning of the characters
- setting
- facial expressions

Ask students to read their interpretations to the class. Hold a class discussion to compare the details in the paintings with those in the scene. Encourage students to give their own perceptions of the characters.

ROMEO. As if that name,
Shot from the deadly level of a gun,
Did murder her; as that name's cursed hand
Murder'd her kinsman. O, tell me, friar, tell me,
In what vile part of this anatomy
Doth my name lodge? Tell me, that I may sack°
The hateful mansion.

[*ROMEO takes out his dagger and offers to stab himself. The NURSE snatches the dagger away.*]

FRIAR. Hold thy desperate hand.
Art thou a man? Thy form cries out thou art;
Thy tears are womanish, thy wild acts denote
The unreasonable fury of a beast.
2 Unseemly woman in a seeming man,
And ill-beseeming beast in seeming both,°
Thou hast amaz'd me. By my holy order,
I thought thy disposition better temper'd.
Hast thou slain Tybalt? Wilt thou slay thyself?
And slay thy lady that in thy life lives,
By doing damned hate upon thyself?
Why railest thou on° thy birth? the heaven and earth?
Since birth,° and heaven,° and earth,° all three do meet
In thee at once, which thou at once wouldst lose.
Fie, fie, thou shamest thy shape, thy love, thy wit,
Which like a usurer abound'st in all,
And usest none in that true use indeed
Which should bedeck thy shape, thy love, thy wit.°
Thy noble shape is but a form of wax,
Digressing from the valor of a man;°
Thy dear love sworn but hollow perjury,
Killing that love which thou hast vow'd to cherish;
Thy wit, that ornament to shape and love,
Misshapen in the conduct° of them both,
Like powder in a skilless soldier's flask,
Is set afire by thine own ignorance,
And thou dismemb'red with thine own defense.°
What, rouse thee, man! Thy Juliet is alive,
For whose dear sake thou wast but lately dead.°
There art thou happy. Tybalt would kill thee,
But thou slewest Tybalt. There art thou happy.

107 sack: plunder.

110–113 Thy tears . . . both: The Friar scolds Romeo for grieving like a woman and expressing fury inappropriate **(ill-beseeming)** even for a beast.

119 Why railest thou on: why do you complain bitterly about.
120 birth: family origin. **heaven:** soul. **earth:** body.
122–125 thou shamest . . . thy wit: Like a moneylender who misuses his wealth, you are misusing the appearance **(shape)**, love, and intelligence **(wit)** you have been blessed with.

126–127 Thy noble . . . man: You are nothing but a waxwork figure, straying from a real man's courage.

131 Misshapen in the conduct: badly flawed in the guidance.
132–134 Like powder . . . defense: Just as a clumsy soldier might accidentally set off his container of gunpowder, you have ignored good reason and let yourself be blown apart by your intelligence, which should have been your defense.
136 but lately dead: only just now declaring yourself dead.

3 Monologue, Soliloquy, and Aside *Consider the effect of the repeated sentence "There art thou happy." How does the Friar try to reassure Romeo?*

Teach

Literary Element 2

Tragedy Note that in tragedies, the main characters, though admirable in many ways, have one or more tragic flaws that bring about their downfall. Have a student read aloud the Friar's speech (lines 109–121).

Ask: What tragic flaws does the Friar see in Romeo? *(He is too emotional and impetuous; he fails to consider the consequences of his actions.)*

APPROACHING Help students understand the concept of a tragic flaw by giving them examples from other stories. *(In the fable of the Gingerbread Man, the Gingerbread Man's excessive pride leads to his destruction.)*

Literary Element 3

Monologue, Soliloquy, and Aside **Answer:** *The repetition has an upbeat rhythm and a persuasive effect. The Friar reminds Romeo that he has many reasons to be grateful: Juliet is still alive; Tybalt is dead and no longer a threat; and Romeo has been allowed to live.*

Approaching Level

DIFFERENTIATED INSTRUCTION

Emerging Emphasize the difficult situation Juliet is in. Explain that the man she loves has killed her beloved cousin. Point out that in line 101, the nurse says that she falls on her bed, gets up, "And Tybalt calls; and then on Romeo cries." Juliet at first blames and condemns Romeo for taking the life of a member of her family. Over time, however, she stops blaming him and begins defending him. Have students trace this change in Juliet's behavior as they read.

Teach

Literary Element 1

Symbol **Ask:** What might the ring the Nurse hands Romeo symbolize? *(Love, the lovers' wedding, or their eternal devotion to one another)*

Literary Element 2

Atmosphere **Ask:** What is the atmosphere at the end of this scene? Ask students to support their interpretations with references to the text. *(The mood at the end of the scene is hopeful. Romeo has agreed to the Friar's plan. The ring from Juliet raises Romeo's spirits.)*

The law, that threat'ned death, becomes thy friend
And turns it to exile. There art thou happy.
A pack of blessings light° upon thy back;
Happiness courts thee in her best array;°
But, like a mishaved° and sullen wench,
Thou pouts upon thy fortune and thy love.
Take heed, take heed, for such die miserable.
Go get thee to thy love, as was decreed,
Ascend her chamber, hence and comfort her.
But look thou stay not till the watch be set,°
For then thou canst not pass to Mantua,
Where thou shalt live till we can find a time
To blaze° your marriage, reconcile your friends,
Beg pardon of the Prince, and call thee back
With twenty hundred thousand times more joy
Than thou went'st forth in lamentation.°
Go before, nurse. Commend me to thy lady,
And bid her hasten all the house to bed,
Which heavy sorrow makes them apt unto.°
Romeo is coming.

NURSE. O Lord, I could have stay'd here all the night
To hear good counsel. O, what learning is!
My lord, I'll tell my lady you will come.

ROMEO. Do so, and bid my sweet prepare to chide.°

1 [*The* NURSE *begins to exit but turns again to* ROMEO *handing him a ring.*]

NURSE. Here, sir, a ring she bid me give you, sir.
Hie you,° make haste, for it grows very late.

ROMEO. How well my comfort is reviv'd by this!

[NURSE *exits.*]

2

FRIAR. Go hence; good night; and here stands all your state:°
Either be gone before the watch be set,
Or by the break of day disguis'd from hence.
Sojourn in Mantua. I'll find out your man,
And he shall signify from time to time
Every good hap to you that chances here.°
Give me thy hand. 'Tis late. Farewell; good night.

ROMEO. But that a joy past joy calls out on me,
It were a grief so brief to part with thee.
Farewell.

[ROMEO *and* FRIAR LAWRENCE *clasp hands and then exit in opposite directions.*]

141 light: alight, set down lightly.

142 array (ə rā′): outfit.

143 mishaved: misbehaved.

148 look . . . set: See that you do not remain with her until the watchmen go on duty at the city gates.

151 blaze: make public.

154 lamentation: sorrowful outcry.

157 apt unto: inclined to.

162 prepare to chide: to be ready to scold.

164 Hie you: hurry.

166 here . . . state: this is your situation.

169–171 Sojourn . . . here: The Friar asks Romeo to stay temporarily **(sojourn)** in Mantua, a city near Verona. He will send Romeo's servant there occasionally to bring news of favorable events.

Reading Practice

SMALL GROUP

Understand Foils Have students create a character web for Friar Lawrence. Then read aloud lines 145–158. **Ask:** What can you tell about the Friar from these lines? *(Students may say that he is fatherly, calm, and rational.)* Tell students to fill in their web with the Friar's character traits. Then break students into groups and have them discuss how the Friar is a foil to Romeo. Have groups present their findings to the class. Lead a discussion as to why Shakespeare may have included the Friar in the play.

SCENE 4. Late that night. A room in CAPULET's house.

[*PARIS, LORD CAPULET, and LADY CAPULET enter.*]

CAPULET. Things have fall'n out, sir, so unluckily
That we have had no time to move° our daughter.
Look you, she lov'd her kinsman Tybalt dearly,
And so did I. Well, we were born to die.
'Tis very late; she'll not come down tonight.
I promise you, but for your company,
I would have been abed an hour ago.

PARIS. These times of woe afford no times to woo.
Madam, good night. Commend me to your daughter.

LADY. I will, and know her mind early tomorrow;
Tonight she's mewed up to her heaviness.°

CAPULET. Sir Paris, I will make a desperate tender°
Of my child's love. I think she will be rul'd
In all respects by me; nay more, I doubt it not.
Wife, go you to her ere you go to bed;
Acquaint her here of my son Paris' love
And bid her (mark you me?) on Wednesday next—
But soft! What day is this?

PARIS. Monday, my lord.

CAPULET. Monday! Ha, ha! Well, Wednesday is too soon.
3 A'° Thursday let it be—a' Thursday, tell her,
She shall be married to this noble earl.
Will you be ready? Do you like this haste?
We'll keep no great ado°—a friend or two;
For hark you, Tybalt being slain so late,
It may be thought we held him carelessly,°
Being our kinsman, if we revel much.
Therefore we'll have some half a dozen friends,
And there an end. But what say you to Thursday?

PARIS. My lord, I would that Thursday were tomorrow.

CAPULET. Well, get you gone. A' Thursday be it then.
[*To his wife.*] Go you to Juliet ere you go to bed;
Prepare her, wife, against° this wedding day.
Farewell, my lord.—Light to my chamber, ho!
Afore me,° it is so very late that we
May call it early by and by. Good night.

[*They exit.*]

2 move: persuade.

11 mewed up to her heaviness: confined to her sadness. (Hawks were housed in structures called *mews.*)

12 desperate tender: bold offer.

20 A': on.

23 keep no great ado: not make a big fuss.

25 held him carelessly: had little regard for him.

32 against: for.

34 Afore me: indeed.

---

4 Compare and Contrast Scenes *How does this scene contrast with the one that comes before? Taken together, what mood or feeling do the scenes evoke?*

Teach

Literary Element 3

Conflict Ask: What conflict will Juliet have with her parents soon as a result of this action? *(Juliet cannot marry Paris because she's already married to Romeo.)*

Reading Strategy 4

Compare and Contrast Scenes Answer: *In this scene, Romeo and Juliet share loving and hopeful conversation. They are completely unaware of the new obstacles to their union presented in the previous scene. The contrast evokes tension and sadness.*

Approaching Level

DIFFERENTIATED INSTRUCTION

Established Help students understand that when the Friar tells Romeo "I'll find out your man" *(line 169)*, he means he will summon his servant. Explain that servants were common during Shakespeare's time and while the word has a negative connotation, many people in England worked as servants at some point during their lives. It was not uncommon for someone who wanted to be an actor, for example, to work as a household servant for an actor to learn the trade.

Teach

Reading Strategy 1

Compare and Contrast Scenes **Answer:** *In Scene 4, Capulet, Lady Capulet, and Paris converse in the Capulet house. In Scene 5, Romeo and Juliet converse on Juliet's balcony. In the same house, quite different scenes are being played out. The contrast helps to create tension and to reinforce the dangerous nature of the arrangements the characters are making.*

Big Idea 2

The Power of Love **Answer:** *Romeo's remark implies that he is willing to die for Juliet's sake.*

Reading Strategy 3

Listen Discuss how Romeo and Juliet must feel as their night together draws to a close. Students should be sensitive to the mood changes both undergo throughout this scene.

SCENE 5. Later that night, just before daybreak. CAPULET's orchard and, above, JULIET's room and balcony.

[*ROMEO and JULIET are on the balcony. The rope ladder hangs down from the balcony into the garden.*]

JULIET. Wilt thou be gone? It is not yet near day.
It was the nightingale, and not the lark,
That pierc'd the fearful hollow of thine ear.
Nightly she sings on yond pomegranate tree.
Believe me, love, it was the nightingale.

ROMEO. It was the lark, the herald of the morn;
No nightingale. Look, love, what envious streaks
Do lace the severing° clouds in yonder east.
Night's candles° are burnt out, and jocund° day
Stands tiptoe on the misty mountaintops.
I must be gone and live, or stay and die.

JULIET. Yond light is not daylight; I know it, I.
It is some meteor° that the sun exhal'd
To be to thee this night a torchbearer
And light thee on thy way to Mantua.
Therefore stay yet; thou need'st not to be gone.

ROMEO. Let me be ta'en, let me be put to death.
I am content, so thou wilt have it so.
I'll say yon gray is not the morning's eye,°
'Tis but the pale reflex° of Cynthia's brow;°
Nor that is not the lark whose notes do beat
The vaulty heaven so high above our heads.
I have more care to stay than will to go.
Come, death, and welcome! Juliet wills it so.
How is't, my soul! Let's talk; it is not day.

3

JULIET. It is, it is! Hie hence, be gone, away!
It is the lark that sings so out of tune,
Straining harsh discords and unpleasing sharps.°
Some say the lark makes sweet division;°
This doth not so, for she divideth us.
Some say the lark and loathed toad change° eyes;
O, now I would they had chang'd voices too,
Since arm from arm that voice doth us affray,°

8 severing: dispersing.
9 Night's candles: the stars. **jocund** (jok′ənd): cheerful.

13 meteor: thought to be gasses that the sun ignited.

19 morning's eye: sunrise.

20 reflex: reflection. **Cynthia's brow:** the forehead of Cynthia, the moon goddess.

28 Straining . . . sharps: singing harsh sounds and unpleasant high notes.
29 division: melody.
31 change: exchange. (The lark has a beautiful body and ugly eyes, while the toad has an ugly body and beautiful eyes.)
33 affray: frighten.

---

1 Compare and Contrast Scenes *How do Scenes 4 and 5 contrast in terms of characters and setting? What points are reinforced by the contrast?*

2 The Power of Love *How does Romeo show his love for Juliet?*

Writing Practice

SPIRAL REVIEW **Use Evidence to Persuade** Remind students that persuasion requires arguments and evidence as support. Have students summarize the arguments the Friar uses to convince Romeo not to end his life. *(His conduct is unmanly, he has been spared death, and he and Juliet can be reunited.)* Have students write a letter to the Prince, urging him to pardon Romeo by using arguments that appeal to logic and feelings and by presenting evidence.

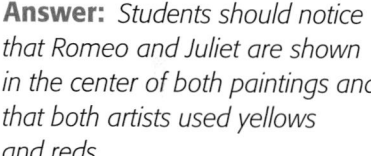

Romeo and Juliet, 1884. Frank Dicksee. Oil on canvas. Southampton City Art Gallery, Hampshire, UK.

View the Art Compare the painting of this balcony scene with the painting by Anselm Feuerbach on page 660. What choices about color and composition are similar in the two works? ★

3 Hunting thee hence with hunt's-up° to the day.
O, now be gone! More light and light it grows.

ROMEO. More light and light—more dark and dark our woes.

[*The* NURSE *enters* JULIET'*s room.*]

4 NURSE. Madam!

JULIET. Nurse?

NURSE. Your lady mother is coming to your chamber.
The day is broke; be wary, look about.

[*She exits.*]

JULIET. Then, window, let day in, and let life out.

ROMEO. Farewell, farewell! One kiss, and I'll descend.

[*They kiss. Then* ROMEO *climbs down the rope ladder to the garden below.*]

JULIET. Art thou gone so, love, lord, ay husband, friend?
I must hear from thee every day in the hour,

34 hunt's-up: a morning song to awaken hunters.

Teach

Literary Element 4

Imagery Ask: How have the mood and meaning of Shakespeare's light and dark imagery changed over the course of the play? *(At the start of the play the love scenes included images of stars, the sun, and heavenly light. Here, light is dim (pre-dawn), and darkness has become a heavy gloom, blotting out the lovers' happiness.)*

View the Art ★

Answer: *Students should notice that Romeo and Juliet are shown in the center of both paintings and that both artists used yellows and reds.*

Early in his career, English artist Sir Frank Dicksee (1853–1928) illustrated books and magazines. With his painting *Harmony,* Dicksee became a noted painter, known for using figures from history and legend as subjects. Dicksee is also famous for his portraits of beautiful women.

Advanced Learners

DIFFERENTIATED INSTRUCTION

Descriptive Language Challenge pairs of students to present a dramatic reading of the dialogue between Romeo and Juliet on page 698. Have the students practice their lines until they can say them fluently and with expression. Encourage them to add their own interpretation of tone and expression. Have them present this reading to the class. Have other students note instances of descriptive language in this scene.

Teach

Reading Strategy 1

Compare and Contrast Scenes **Answer:** *Students should support their answers.*

ENGLISH LEARNERS Help English learners express their responses by pairing them up with students to discuss their ideas.

For in a minute there are many days.
O, by this count I shall be much in years
Ere I again behold my Romeo!

ROMEO. Farewell!
I will omit no opportunity
That may convey my greetings, love, to thee.

JULIET. O, think'st thou we shall ever meet again?

ROMEO. I doubt it not; and all these woes shall serve
For sweet discourses° in our times to come.

JULIET. O God, I have an ill-divining soul!°
Methinks I see thee, now thou art so low,
As one dead in the bottom of a tomb.
Either my eyesight fails, or thou lookest pale.

ROMEO. And trust me, love, in my eye so do you.
Dry° sorrow drinks our blood. Adieu, adieu!

[*ROMEO leaves.*]

JULIET. O Fortune, Fortune! All men call thee **fickle.**
If thou art fickle, what dost thou with him
That is renown'd for faith?° Be fickle, Fortune,
For then I hope thou wilt not keep him long
But send him back.

[*LADY CAPULET enters JULIET's room.*]

LADY CAPULET. Ho, daughter! Are you up?

JULIET. Who is't that calls? It is my lady mother.
Is she not down° so late, or up so early?
What unaccustom'd cause procures her hither?°

[*JULIET returns to her room from the balcony.*]

LADY CAPULET. Why, how now, Juliet?

JULIET. Madam, I am not well.

LADY CAPULET. Evermore weeping for your cousin's death?
What, wilt thou wash him from his grave with tears?

53 discourses: conversations.

54 ill-divining soul: soul that foresees misfortune.

59 Dry: thirsty. (Romeo refers to a belief that each sigh draws a drop of blood from the heart.)

61–62 If thou . . . faith: If you are unfaithful, why are you involved with a man known for his faithfulness?

66 down: going to bed.

67 What . . . hither: What unusual reason brings her here?

1 Compare and Contrast Scenes *In this act, Shakespeare develops the plot rapidly, raising the conflict level along several fronts. As tension rises and falls and the mood changes from moment to moment, what responses do you have?*

Vocabulary

fickle (fik′əl) *adj.* given to frequent changes of thought or mood; unreliable; inconstant

Reading Practice

SMALL GROUP

Understand Sequence

The characters move to and from several settings in Act 3. Students will benefit from creating a sequence chart to keep track of the time and sequence in this act. Break students into small groups and have them create a sequence chart for each scene to use to outline the different settings. Have them discuss their sequence charts as a class to clear up any ambiguities.

And if thou couldst, thou couldst not make him live.
Therefore have done. Some grief shows much of love;
But much of grief shows still some want of wit.°

JULIET. Yet let me weep for such a feeling loss.

LADY CAPULET. So shall you feel the loss, but not the friend°
Which you weep for.

JULIET. Feeling so the loss,
I cannot choose but ever weep the friend.

LADY CAPULET. Well, girl, thou weep'st not so much for his death
As that the villain lives which slaughter'd him.

JULIET. What villain, madam?

LADY CAPULET. That same villain Romeo.

JULIET. [*Aside.*] Villain and he be many miles asunder.°—
[*To* LADY CAPULET.] God pardon him! I do, with all my heart;
And yet no man like he doth grieve my heart.

LADY CAPULET. That is because the traitor murderer lives.

JULIET. Ay, madam, from the reach of these my hands.
Would none but I might venge my cousin's death!

LADY CAPULET. We will have vengeance for it, fear thou not.
☆ Then weep no more. I'll send to one in Mantua,
Where that same banish'd runagate° doth live,
Shall give him such an unaccustom'd dram°
That he shall soon keep Tybalt company;
And then I hope thou wilt be satisfied.

JULIET. Indeed I never shall be satisfied
With Romeo till I behold him—dead°—
Is my poor heart so for a kinsman vex'd.
Madam, if you could find out but a man
To bear a poison, I would temper° it;
That Romeo should, upon receipt thereof,
Soon sleep in quiet. O, how my heart abhors
To hear him nam'd and cannot come to him,
To wreak° the love I bore my cousin
Upon his body that hath slaughter'd him!

LADY CAPULET. Find thou the means, and I'll find such a man.
But now I'll tell thee joyful tidings, girl.

73 shows . . . wit: always shows lack of judgment.

75 friend: "cousin" or "lover."

81 asunder: apart.

89 runagate: renegade; runaway.
90 unaccustom'd dram: unexpected dose (of poison).

94 Here, as elsewhere in this dialogue, Juliet communicates one thing to her mother and something else to the audience. The word ***dead*** can be understood to complete this line ("till I behold him dead") or to begin the next line ("Dead is my poor heart").
97 temper: "mix" or "dilute."

101 wreak (rēk): "avenge" or "express."

2 Monologue, Soliloquy, and Aside ***In your opinion, why does Shakespeare include this aside?***

3 The Power of Love ***What double meaning can be read into lines 93–102?***

Teach

Literary Element 2

Monologue, Soliloquy, and Aside **Answer:** *It alerts the audience to Juliet's true feelings about Romeo. She does not consider him a villain.*

Big Idea 3

The Power of Love
Answer: *Juliet's words suggest that she will never be happy until she sees Romeo dead, but the audience realizes she means that she will never be happy until she sees Romeo. She would like to "wreak" the love she bore her cousin upon Romeo's body; the audience realizes that these words imply love for Romeo.*

Historical Note ☆

Mantua, Italy Considered one of the great Renaissance Court cities, Mantua was the city to which Romeo was exiled. At the time *Romeo and Juliet* was written, Mantua was under the control of the powerful Gonzaga family, who ruled from 1328 to 1707.

Approaching Level

DIFFERENTIATED INSTRUCTION

Established Tell students that Juliet's father is arranging for her to marry someone other than Romeo. Explain that a woman during Shakespeare's time had little say in who her husband would be. Marriages were arranged to bring wealth and status to both families. It was not uncommon for a couple to meet for the first time on their wedding day. Point out that Capulet wants Juliet to marry a noble earl. Discuss arranged marriages versus love matches.

Teach

Reading Strategy 1

Compare and Contrast Scenes **Answer:** *In Act 1, Scene 3, Juliet appears open to taking her mother's advice regarding Paris. Now she is resolutely against marrying him.*

Literary Element 2

Irony Note that in line 140, Lady Capulet, out of impatience, wishes her daughter dead. Ironically, her wish will soon come true—twice.

JULIET. And joy comes well in such a needy time.
What are they, beseech your ladyship?

LADY CAPULET. Well, well, thou hast a careful° father, child;
One who, to put thee from thy heaviness,°
Hath sorted out° a sudden day of joy
That thou expects not nor I look'd not for.

JULIET. Madam, in happy time! What day is that?

LADY CAPULET. Marry, my child, early next Thursday morn
The gallant, young, and noble gentleman,
The County Paris, at Saint Peter's Church,
Shall happily make thee there a joyful bride.

JULIET. Now by Saint Peter's Church, and Peter too,
He shall not make me there a joyful bride!
I wonder at this haste, that I must wed
Ere he that should be husband comes to woo.
I pray you tell my lord and father, madam,
I will not marry yet; and when I do, I swear
It shall be Romeo, whom you know I hate,
Rather than Paris. These are news indeed!

LADY CAPULET. Here comes your father. Tell him so yourself,
And see how he will take it at your hands.

[*CAPULET and the NURSE enter.*]

CAPULET. When the sun sets the earth doth drizzle dew,
But for the sunset of my brother's son
It rains downright.
How now? A conduit,° girl? What, still in tears?
Evermore show'ring? In one little body
Thou counterfeits° a bark,° a sea, a wind:
For still thy eyes, which I may call the sea,
Do ebb and flow with tears; the bark thy body is,
Sailing in this salt flood; the winds, thy sighs,
Who, raging with thy tears and they with them,
Without a sudden calm will overset°
Thy tempest-tossed body. How now, wife?
Have you delivered to her our decree?

LADY CAPULET. Ay, sir; but she will none, she gives you thanks.
2 I would the fool were married to her grave!

CAPULET. Soft! Take me with you, take me with you,° wife.
How? Will she none? Doth she not give us thanks?

107 careful: considerate.
108 put . . . heaviness: remove you from sorrow.
109 sorted out: chosen.
129 conduit (kon′ do͞o it): fountain.
131 counterfeits: resemble. **bark:** small sailing vessel.
136 overset: upset, capsize.
141 Soft! . . . you: Wait, let me understand you.

1 Compare and Contrast Scenes *How has Juliet's attitude toward Paris changed since the first conversation she and her mother had about him?*

Writing Practice

SMALL GROUP

Sequence Point out that the plot develops rapidly in Act 3. Assess students' grasp of the plot by having them create a timeline. Have partners first list the events that occur from the end of Act 2 (Scene 5) to the end of Act 3. Then have them place each event in order of occurrence on a timeline. Explain that the entire play happens in less than a week's time. Encourage students to compare their work with the work of other students and discuss any discrepancies.

Is she not proud? Doth she not count her blest,
Unworthy as she is, that we have wrought°
So worthy a gentleman to be her bride?°

JULIET. Not proud you have, but thankful that you have.
Proud can I never be of what I hate,
But thankful even for hate that is meant love.

CAPULET. How, how, how, how, chopp'd-logic?° What is this?
"Proud"—and "I thank you"—and "I thank you not"—
And yet "not proud"? Mistress minion° you,
Thank me no thankings, nor proud me no prouds,
But fettle your fine joints 'gainst° Thursday next
☆ To go with Paris to Saint Peter's Church,
Or I will drag thee on a hurdle° thither.
Out, you green-sickness carrion!° Out, you baggage!°
You tallow-face!°

LADY CAPULET. [*To* CAPULET.] Fie, fie! What, are you mad?

JULIET. [*She kneels before her father.*] Good father, I beseech you on my knees,
Hear me with patience but to speak a word.

CAPULET. Hang thee, young baggage! Disobedient wretch!
I tell thee what—get thee to church a' Thursday
Or never after look me in the face.
Speak not, reply not, do not answer me!
My fingers itch. Wife, we scarce thought us blest
That God had lent us but this only child;
But now I see this one is one too much,
And that we have a curse in having her.
Out on her, hilding!°

NURSE. God in heaven bless her!
You are to blame, my lord, to rate° her so.

CAPULET. And why, my Lady Wisdom? Hold your tongue,
Good Prudence. Smatter with your gossips, go!°

NURSE. I speak no treason.°

CAPULET. O, God-i-god-en!°

NURSE. May not one speak?

CAPULET. Peace, you mumbling fool!
Utter your gravity° o'er a gossip's bowl,°
For here we need it not.

144 wrought (rôt): arranged for.
145 bride: bridegroom.

149 chopp'd-logic: clever but false argument.

151 Mistress minion: spoiled miss.

153 fettle your fine joints 'gainst: prepare your fine limbs for.

155 hurdle: a sled used to bring prisoners to their executions.
156 green-sickness carrion: anemic flesh. **baggage:** shameless girl.
157 tallow-face: pale face.

168 hilding: worthless person.

169 rate: scold angrily.

171 Smatter with your gossips, go: Go chatter with your old pals.
172 treason: disloyalty. **God-i-god-en:** God give you good evening (used here as a mild oath).

174 gravity: wisdom. **gossip's bowl:** cup of hot punch.

3 Compare and Contrast Scenes *Are you surprised by the way characters are behaving in this scene? Why or why not?*

Teach

Reading Strategy 3

Compare and Contrast Scenes Answer: *Students may be surprised at the change in Capulet's behavior. Previously, he seemed gentle, sympathetic, and civilized. He now seems brutal and unjust.*

Historical Note ☆

St. Peter's The most famous St. Peter's Church is St. Peter's Basilica. Located in Vatican City, within the city of Rome, the basilica was named for the apostle Peter. Verona, however, had its own saint named Peter. St. Peter of Verona (1206–1252) was canonized in 1253.

English Learners

DIFFERENTIATED INSTRUCTION

Intermediate Direct students' attention to the marginal notes giving meanings for the words *careful, heaviness,* and *sorted out* in lines 107–110 and the word *soft, wrought,* and *bride* in lines 141–145. Remind students that some words in Shakespeare's time had different meanings from their meanings today. Have students look up these words in a dictionary and copy down the current meanings for each word.

Teach

Literary Element 1

Monologue, Soliloquy, and Aside **Answer:** *The words are in quotation marks because Capulet is quoting Juliet's words to him. He might mimic her voice as he says her words.*

APPROACHING Ask for a volunteer to read Capulet's rant and challenge him or her to capture the tone implied by the quotation marks to demonstrate how they affect the monologue.

Big Idea 2

The Power of Love
Answer: *Some students may consider Capulet a tyrant. Others may point out that his fury results from great love. Juliet is his only daughter, and Paris is a perfect match. He is baffled by her disobedience.*

LADY CAPULET. You are too hot.

CAPULET. God's bread! It makes me mad. Day, night; work, play;
Alone, in company; still my care hath been
To have her match'd; and having now provided
A gentleman of noble parentage,
Of fair demesnes,° youthful, and nobly lien'd,°
Stuff'd, as they say, with honorable parts,°
Proportion'd as one's thought would wish a man—
And then to have a wretched puling° fool,
A whining mammet,° in her fortune's tender,°
To answer, "I'll not wed, I cannot love;
I am too young, I pray you pardon me"!
But, and° you will not wed, I'll pardon you!°
Graze where you will, you shall not house with me.
Look to't, think on't; I do not use° to jest.
Thursday is near; lay hand on heart, advise:°
And you be mine, I'll give you to my friend;
And you be not, hang, beg, starve, die in the streets,
For, by my soul, I'll ne'er acknowledge thee,
Nor what is mine shall never do thee good.°
Trust to't. Bethink you. I'll not be forsworn.°

[*CAPULET exits. JULIET rises and speaks to her mother.*]

JULIET. Is there no pity sitting in the clouds
That sees into the bottom of my grief?
O sweet my mother, cast me not away!
Delay this marriage for a month, a week;
Or if you do not, make the bridal bed
In that dim monument where Tybalt lies.

LADY CAPULET. Talk not to me, for I'll not speak a word.
Do as thou wilt, for I have done with thee.

[*LADY CAPULET exits.*]

JULIET. O God!—O nurse, how shall this be prevented?
My husband is on earth, my faith in heaven.°
How shall that faith return again to earth
Unless that husband send it me from heaven
By leaving earth?° Comfort me, counsel me.

180 demesnes (di mānz′): property. **lien'd:** descended.
181 parts: qualities.

183 puling (pūl′ing): whimpering.

184 mammet: puppet. **in her fortune's tender:** when good fortune is offered her.

187 and: if. **pardon you:** excuse you (from this house).

189 I do not use: it is not my custom.
190 advise: consider.

193–194 I'll ne'er . . . good: Capulet threatens to disown Juliet and cut off any family support.
195 be forsworn: break my vow.

205 my faith in heaven: my marriage vow is recorded in heaven.
206–208 How . . . earth: How can I be free to pledge myself again unless by Romeo's death?

1 Monologue, Soliloquy, and Aside ***Why is this passage in quotation marks? How might Capulet say these lines?***

2 The Power of Love ***Why does Capulet make this threat?***

Reading Practice

SPIRAL REVIEW **Characterization** Ask students if they expected Juliet's response to her parents or if they were surprised. As students offer their answers, invite them to explain why they were or were not surprised. **Ask:** Was this behavior typical of Juliet? *(Yes, she is very emotional.)* Explain that good writers describe their characters so that readers do not feel surprised when the characters act. The actions should seem likely.

If students are not surprised by Juliet's behavior, have them identify which details prepared them for this behavior. *(Possible answers: how fast she fell in love with Romeo, how impatient she is with her nurse)*

Alack, alack, that heaven should practice stratagems°
Upon so soft a subject as myself!
What say'st thou? Hast thou not a word of joy?
Some comfort, nurse.

NURSE. Faith, here it is.
Romeo is banished; and all the world to nothing
That he dares ne'er come back to challenge you;°
Or if he do, it needs must be by stealth.
Then, since the case so stands as now it doth,
I think it best you married with the County.
O, he's a lovely gentleman!
Romeo's a dishclout to him.° An eagle, madam,
Hath not so green, so quick, so fair an eye
As Paris hath. Beshrew° my very heart,
I think you are happy in this second match,
For it excels your first; or if it did not,
Your first is dead—or 'twere as good he were
As living here and you no use of him.

JULIET. Speak'st thou from thy heart?

NURSE. And from my soul too; else beshrew them both.

JULIET. Amen!

NURSE. What?

JULIET. Well, thou has comforted me marvelous much.
Go in; and tell my lady I am gone,
Having displeas'd my father, to Lawrence' cell,
To make confession and to be absolv'd.°

NURSE. Marry, I will; and this is wisely done.

[The NURSE exits to find LADY CAPULET.]

JULIET. Ancient damnation!° O most wicked fiend!
Is it more sin to wish me thus forsworn,
Or to dispraise my lord with that same tongue
Which she hath prais'd him with above compare
So many thousand times? Go, counselor!
Thou and my bosom henceforth shall be twain.°
I'll to the friar to know his remedy.
If all else fail, myself have power to die.

[JULIET exits.]

209 stratagems (strat′ ə jəmz): tricks.

213–214 all the world . . . you: The odds are greatly against his ever coming back to claim you.

219 dishclout to him: dish cloth compared to him.

221 Beshrew (bi shro͞o′): curse (used in mild oaths).

233 absolv'd: forgiven.

235 Ancient damnation: wicked old woman.

240 Thou and . . . twain: From now on I'll keep my secrets from you.

3 Monologue, Soliloquy, and Aside *In this soliloquy, what mood does Juliet express?*

Teach

Literary Element 3

Monologue, Soliloquy, and Aside **Answer:** *She expresses determination and unwillingness to obey her father.*

To check students' understanding of the selection, see Unit 4 Teaching Resources Book, p. 61.

Progress Check

Can students identify monologue, soliloquy, and aside?

If No → See Unit 4 Teaching Resources Book, p. 56.

Approaching Level

DIFFERENTIATED INSTRUCTION

Established Kinesthetic learners will benefit from staging the scene and exploring the relationships between characters. Have students write detailed descriptions of Juliet, the Nurse, Lady Capulet, and Lord Capulet. Then have students use these details in staging the scene. Encourage students to incorporate body positioning, facial expressions, and gestures into the subtext of the scene. After their performance, have other students discuss their portrayals of the characters.

After You Read

Assess

1. Accept reasonable answers.
2. (a) By trying to step between them, blocking Mercutio's sword arm (b) Fate has tricked him into making fatal mistakes.
3. (a) Going to confession (b) She is desperate.
4. The inevitability of conflict between the generations.
5. (a) She feels betrayed when the Nurse advises her to marry Paris. (b) The loss of her one confidante increases her desperation; the plan seems like her only hope.
6. Their ideal love is now tainted by family conflict, exile, and death.
7. Answers will vary. Students may say that modern American views on grief are similar to Lady Capulet's—people are expected to grieve quickly or to see a counselor if they cannot do so. This might reveal that our culture places high value on the appearance of happiness and well-being, even if it is a facade.

Literary Element

1. Example: Scene 2, lines 1–31; Juliet expresses longing and impatience to see Romeo.
2. Example: Scene 3, lines 29–51; Romeo despairs over his exile.

For additional selection assessment, see Assessment Resources, pp. 167–168.

After You Read

Respond and Think Critically

Respond and Interpret

1. What would you do if you were Juliet?
2. (a)How does Romeo accidentally help cause Mercutio's death? (b)How do you interpret Romeo's description of himself as "fortune's fool"?
3. (a)What excuse does Juliet use to leave her house? (b)How would you describe her state of mind at this point?

Analyze and Evaluate

4. What insight or truth might Shakespeare be expressing through the character of Capulet?
5. (a)How does Juliet's relationship with the Nurse change during this act? (b)How do you think this change affects Juliet's state of mind and faith in her plan?

Connect

6. **Big Idea** The Power of Love How does Act 3 suggest a dark side to love?
7. **Connect to Today** Lady Capulet opines that too much grief shows "want of wit." How are people encouraged to grieve in modern American society? What might this reveal about our culture?

Literary Element Monologue, Soliloquy, and Aside

Monologues, soliloquies, and asides reveal information about characters' thoughts and feelings.

1. Identify a soliloquy in Act 3. What thoughts or feelings does it reveal?
2. What was your favorite monologue in Act 3? Explain.

Reading Strategy Compare and Contrast Scenes

Review the web diagrams you created as you read, and then answer the following questions.

1. How does the mood change from scene to scene in Act 3, and what is the overall effect?
2. Explain how your understanding of one character is enriched over the course of Act 3.

LOG ON Literature Online

Selection Resources For Selection Quizzes, eFlashcards, and Reading-Writing Connection activities, go to glencoe.com and enter QuickPass code GL49787u4.

Vocabulary Practice

Practice with Analogies Find the word that best completes each analogy.

1. speech : eloquence :: appearance : ____
   a. persuasion b. laughter c. beauty
2. wealth : riches :: adversity : _____
   a. hardship b. happiness c. health
3. tragedy : sad :: predicament : _____
   a. documentary b. triumph c. difficult
4. fickle : reliable :: satisfaction : _____
   a. displeasure b. mutable c. joy

Writing

Write an Essay Lord Capulet orders Juliet to marry Paris. Can you imagine your parents ordering you into a relationship? Write a brief essay in which you compare and contrast the roles of parents today and parents in 14th-century Italy as portrayed by Shakespeare. Discuss how children in both time periods rebel against that authority.

Reading Strategy

1. The mood varies from gentle love scenes between Romeo and Juliet to violence between Tybalt, Mercutio, and Romeo. There are also various complications involving the Friar, the Nurse, and the Capulets. These shifting moods increase the suspense.
2. Students should support their answers.

Vocabulary

1. c **2.** a **3.** c **4.** a

Writing

Students should support their comparisons with evidence from the text. Their essays should be well-organized and should incorporate correct grammar and spelling.

Before You Read

Romeo and Juliet, Act 4

Connect to the Drama

Have you heard or read about people who have taken desperate measures? Discuss these stories with a partner.

Build Background

In fifteenth-century Italy, the evergreen herb called *rosemary* was regarded as a symbol of immortality. It was also prized for its fragrance. When a person died, he or she was often strewn with rosemary, which was also carried by mourners.

Set Purposes for Reading

Big Idea The Power of Love

As you read this act, ask yourself, Can love make us act in ways that are reckless or even unethical?

Literary Element Irony

Irony refers to a contrast or discrepancy between appearance and reality. There are three main types of irony. **Situational irony** exists when an occurrence is the opposite of what is expected. **Verbal irony** occurs when a person says one thing and means another. **Dramatic irony** exists when the reader or audience knows something a character does not know. As you read Act 4, ask yourself, Where can I find examples of irony?

Reading Strategy Interpret Imagery

The word pictures in a work of literature are called **imagery.** In creating effective imagery, authors use sensory details, or descriptions that appeal to one or more of the five senses: sight, sound, touch, taste, or smell. As you read, ask yourself, What emotional response does the imagery evoke in me?

Tip: Take Notes Keep a record of your responses to Shakespeare's imagery in a chart like the one below.

Image	My Response
Scene 1, line 29: Juliet's face is "much abus'd with tears."	Her eyes must be red and swollen. She's miserable.

Learning Objectives

For pages 707–723

In studying this text, you will focus on the following objectives:

Literary Study: Analyzing irony.

Reading: Interpreting imagery.

Writing: Writing a fictional journal entry.

Vocabulary

lurk (lurk) *v.* to conceal oneself; to move about in a sneaky manner; p. 711 *Foxes lurk in the woods, awaiting their prey.*

stifle (stī′ fəl) *v.* to smother for lack of air; to prevent from developing properly; p. 715 *We felt stifled by the obstacles in our path.*

revive (ri vīv′) *v.* to bring back to life; to give new strength; p. 718 *A bit of fresh air will revive me.*

lament (lə ment′) *v.* to express deep sorrow; p. 721 *Many old friends gathered at the funeral to lament his passing.*

Tip: Context Clues You can often determine the meaning of an unfamiliar word by using context clues in the surrounding text. For example, in the sentence *Do not stifle me, I want to grow,* you can determine that *stifle* probably means the opposite of *grow.*

Before You Read

Focus

Summary

Friar Lawrence learns from Paris of the intended wedding. He advises Juliet to take a potion that will simulate death on the night before the ceremony. When she revives in 42 hours, Romeo and the Friar will rescue her from the Capulet vault. Despite misgivings, she drinks the potion and is borne to the vault by her grieving parents.

Vocabulary

Descriptive Verbs Using descriptive verbs creates writing which is more specific and interesting. Each of the vocabulary words in the list are descriptive verbs. Have students identify more commonly used synonyms for each of the verbs. *(lurk: walk; stifle: cover; revive: refresh; lament: mourn)* Have students write sentences using both the vocabulary word and its counterpart to illustrate the effects of descriptive verbs.

Selection Skills

The Tragedy of Romeo and Juliet, Act 4

Literary Elements
- Irony (SE pp. 704–723)

Listening/Speaking/Viewing Skills
- Read Dialogue (TE p. 720)
- Analyze Art (SE pp. 710, 716, 720)

Reading Skills
- Interpret Imagery (SE pp. 704–723)

Vocabulary Skills
- Context Clues (SE pp. 707, 723)

Writing Skills/Grammar
- Write a Journal Entry (SE p. 723)
- Active Voice (TE p. 710)
- Prepositional Phrases (TE p. 714)
- Persuasive Essays (TE p. 718)
- Linking Verbs (TE p. 722)

Teach

Reading Strategy 1

Predict Have students read the setting details and stage directions on page 708 and name the characters brought together. Ask them to predict what Juliet and Paris will say to each other.

Ask: What problem does Juliet have as she greets Paris? *(She has to pretend that she is content to marry Paris, and not show her grief and concern about Romeo.)*

Literary Element 2

Irony Answer: *Juliet has come to the Friar's cell to discuss her reunion with Romeo, but Paris believes that Juliet will soon be his wife.*

Act 4

SCENE 1. Later that morning. FRIAR LAWRENCE's cell.

[FRIAR LAWRENCE and PARIS enter. PARIS has just explained to the confused FRIAR that he will marry JULIET.]

FRIAR. On Thursday, sir? The time is very short.

PARIS. My father° Capulet will have it so,
And I am nothing slow to slack his haste.°

FRIAR. You say you do not know the lady's mind.
Uneven is the course;° I like it not.

PARIS. Immoderately she weeps for Tybalt's death,
And therefore have I little talk'd of love;
For Venus smiles not in a house of tears.
Now, sir, her father counts it dangerous
That she do give her sorrow so much sway,
And in his wisdom hastes our marriage
To stop the inundation of her tears,
Which, too much minded° by herself alone,
May be put from her by society.
Now do you know the reason of this haste.

FRIAR. *[Aside.]* I would I knew not why it should be slowed.—
Look, sir, here comes the lady toward my cell.

1 *[JULIET enters. Surprised to see PARIS there, she pretends to be in good spirits.]*

PARIS. Happily met, my lady and my wife!

JULIET. That may be, sir, when I may be a wife.

PARIS. That "may be" must be, love, on Thursday next.

JULIET. What must be shall be.

FRIAR. That's a certain text.°

PARIS. Come you to make confession to this father?

JULIET. To answer that, I should confess to you.

PARIS. Do not deny to him that you love me.

JULIET. I will confess to you that I love him.

PARIS. So will ye, I am sure, that you love me.

JULIET. If I do so, it will be of more price,°
Being spoke behind your back, than to your face.

2 change Irony *What is ironic about this situation?*

2 father: father-in-law.

3 I am . . . haste: I will not delay him.

5 Uneven is the course: The plan is irregular.

13 minded: brooded over.

21 That's a certain text: That's an indisputable saying.

27 price: value.

Literary Element Practice

Irony Remind students that in literature irony is the discrepancy between what a character says and what the character really means. Read aloud the Literary Element question on this page and discuss how Juliet is being ironic. *(She tells Paris that she will confess to Friar her love for "him." She leads Paris to believe that she is referring to him, but she is actually referring to Romeo.)*

Pair up students and have them find other instances of irony on these pages. Have them write down these instances to share with the class.

PARIS. Poor soul, thy face is much abus'd with tears.

JULIET. The tears have got small victory by that,
For it was bad enough before their spite.°

PARIS. Thou wrong'st it more than tears with that report.

JULIET. That is no slander, sir, which is a truth;
3 And what I spake, I spake it to my face.°

PARIS. Thy face is mine, and thou hast sland'red it.

JULIET. It may be so, for it is not mine own.°
[*To* FRIAR LAWRENCE.] Are you at leisure, holy father, now,
Or shall I come to you at evening mass?

FRIAR. My leisure serves me, pensive daughter, now.
[*To* PARIS.] My lord, we must entreat the time alone.

PARIS. God shield I should disturb devotion!
Juliet, on Thursday early will I rouse ye.
Till then, adieu, and keep this holy kiss.

[*PARIS exits.*]

JULIET. O, shut the door, and when thou hast done so,
Come weep with me—past hope, past cure, past help!

FRIAR. O Juliet, I already know thy grief;
It strains me past the compass of my wits.°
I hear thou must, and nothing may prorogue° it,
On Thursday next be married to this County.

JULIET. Tell me not, friar, that thou hearest of this,
Unless thou tell me how I may prevent it.
If in thy wisdom thou canst give no help,
Do thou but call my resolution wise
And with this knife I'll help it presently.°
God join'd my heart and Romeo's, thou our hands;
And ere this hand, by thee to Romeo's seal'd,
Shall be the label to another deed,°
Or my true heart with treacherous revolt
Turn to another, this shall slay them both.
Therefore, out of thy long-experienc'd time,
Give me some present counsel;° or, behold,
'Twixt my extremes and me this bloody knife
Shall play the umpire, arbitrating that
Which the commission of thy years and art
Could to no issue of true honor bring.°

31 it was . . . spite: my face was bad enough before the tears marred it.

34 to my face: openly (not behind my back).

36 It may . . . own: Juliet's reply suggests that her face belongs to Romeo or that she is presenting a false face to Paris.

47 strains me past the compass of my wits: forces me beyond the limits of my understanding.

48 prorogue (prō rōg′): postpone.

53–54 Do thou . . . presently: Juliet asks the Friar to approve of her resolution to kill herself, a mortal sin.

57 be the . . . deed: confirm another marriage.

61 present counsel: immediate advice.

62–65 'Twixt my . . . bring: Juliet threatens that her knife will settle the dispute between herself and her great difficulties, which the Friar's wisdom and learning could not bring to an honorable outcome.

4 Irony *What information about this private meeting is known to the audience, but not to Paris?*

Teach

Reading Strategy 3

Interpret Have students examine Juliet's responses to Paris and explain the double meaning.

Ask: How does she avoid lying? *("What must be shall be" [page 708, line 21] could refer to the wedding, but in fact refers to her joining Romeo or dying. She uses words that introduce doubt without contradicting Paris ["If I do so"—page 708, line 27]. She says her face is not [her] own [page 709, line 36]—meaning she shows Paris a false face, which is true.)*

ENGLISH LEARNERS English learners will likely have difficulty understanding the double meanings in this scene. Take time to go over the examples given and explain how double meanings affect the overall meaning of the passage.

Literary Element 4

Irony **Answer:** *Juliet does not wish to confess to the Friar; she wishes instead to discuss her plans for reuniting with Romeo.*

Approaching Level

DIFFERENTIATED INSTRUCTION

Emerging Tell students that when authors give hints of what is to come, it is called foreshadowing. Read aloud lines 68–70. **Ask:** What could Shakespeare be foreshadowing here?

(Students may say that he says he sees a sign of hope in a desperate act; Shakespeare may be foreshadowing something risky or dangerous.)

Emerging Students may have trouble understanding what Juliet is saying in lines 50–67. Read aloud these lines and explain that Juliet would rather kill herself than marry Paris because she loves Romeo.

Teach

View the Art ★

Answer: *Some may say he looks kind, comforting, and compassionate, as they imagined. Others may imagine the Friar as younger and less stern looking.*

The work of Scottish artist John Pettie (1839–1893) focuses on historical scenes and themes. He is best known for his scenes of the English Civil Wars (1642–1651) and the Jacobite Rebellion (1689).

Friar Lawrence and Juliet, exhibited 1874. John Pettie. Oil on canvas, 110.5 x 76.5 cm. Royal Shakespeare Theatre Collection, Stratford-upon-Avon, England.

View the Art In this painting, John Pettie meticulously re-creates the traditional cowl of the Franciscan Friars. This rough wool cloak is worn to symbolize their vow of poverty. Does this portrayal of Friar Lawrence match your own image of him? Why or why not? ★

Writing Practice

SPIRAL REVIEW **Active Voice** Note that writers may frame sentences so that the subject performs the action: Romeo *married* Juliet (active voice) or so that the action is performed on the subject: They *were married* by the Friar (passive voice). The active voice is generally preferable in standard English usage.

Have students write a paragraph describing the scene in the painting using the active voice as much as possible.

Be not so long to speak. I long to die
If what thou speak'st speak not of remedy.

FRIAR. Hold, daughter. I do spy a kind of hope,
Which craves° as desperate an execution°
As that is desperate which we would prevent.
If, rather than to marry County Paris,
Thou hast the strength of will to slay thyself,
Then is it likely thou wilt undertake
A thing like death to chide away this shame,
That cop'st with death himself to scape from it;°
And, if thou darest, I'll give thee remedy.

2

JULIET. O, bid me leap, rather than marry Paris,
From off the battlements of any tower,
Or walk in thievish ways,° or bid me **lurk**
Where serpents are; chain me with roaring bears,
Or hide me nightly in a charnel house,°
O'ercover'd quite with dead men's rattling bones,
With reeky shanks° and yellow chapless° skulls;
Or bid me go into a new-made grave
And hide me with a dead man in his shroud—
Things that, to hear them told, have made me tremble—
And I will do it without fear or doubt,
To live an unstain'd wife to my sweet love.

FRIAR. Hold, then. Go home, be merry, give consent
To marry Paris. Wednesday is tomorrow.
Tomorrow night look that thou lie alone;
Let not the nurse lie with thee in thy chamber.
Take thou this vial, being then in bed,
And this distilling liquor° drink thou off;
When presently through all thy veins shall run
A cold and drowsy humor;° for no pulse
Shall keep his native progress,° but surcease;°
No warmth, no breath, shall testify thou livest;
The roses in thy lips and cheeks shall fade
To wanny ashes,° thy eyes' windows° fall
Like death when he shuts up the day of life;
Each part, depriv'd of supple government,°

69 **craves:** requires. **execution:** act.

71–75 **If, rather . . . from it:** The Friar says that since Juliet is willing to face **(cop'st)** death itself to avoid the shame of marrying Paris, then she probably would go through something similar to death to achieve the same result.

79 **in thievish ways:** on roads where thieves lurk.

81 **charnel** (chärn′ əl) **house:** a vault where skulls and bones were stored.

83 **reeky shanks:** foul-smelling limbs. **chapless:** jawless.

94 **distilling liquor:** liquid medicine that permeates the body.

96 **cold and drowsy humor:** a fluid that will make your body cold and put you to sleep.

97 **his native progress:** its natural movement. **surcease:** stop.

100 **To wanny ashes:** to the paleness of ashes. **eyes' windows:** eyelids.

102 **supple government:** the ability to move.

1 Interpret Imagery *To what senses do the details in this passage appeal? What do the images help Juliet to convey?*

Vocabulary

lurk (lurk) *v.* to conceal oneself; to move about in a sneaky manner

Teach

Reading Strategy 1

Interpret Imagery
Answer: *They appeal to all five senses and emphasize her willingness to sacrifice for Romeo and her fidelity to him.*

For additional practice using the reading skill or strategy, see Unit 4 Teaching Resources Book, p. 70.

Literary Element 2

Irony Note that while Juliet is making a point about her determination to remain faithful to Romeo, she is also describing an ordeal like the one she will have to endure.

English Learners

DIFFERENTIATED INSTRUCTION

Intermediate Students may have difficulty understanding what the Friar is suggesting in the dialogue on this page. Read aloud lines 89–108, stopping every few lines to explain what the Friar has said. Tell students that the Friar wants Juliet to agree to marry Paris and then drink a poison before she goes to bed that will make her appear to be dead for 42 hours—long enough for her family and Paris to grieve. Then she will awaken.

Teach

Reading Strategy 1

Interpret Imagery
Answer: *The disturbing images create a grim, desperate mood.*

Big Idea 2

The Power of Love
Answer: *To avoid marrying Paris, Juliet will fake her death by taking a sleeping potion. Her family will bury her in the vault. In the meantime, the Friar will notify Romeo of the plan. When Juliet revives, Romeo will rescue her from the vault and take her to Mantua.*

Ask: Do you think the Friar's plan will be successful? Why or why not? *(Responses will vary)* Students should provide evidence to support their answers.

Literary Element 3

Comic Relief **Ask:** How would you describe the change in mood and tone in the opening lines of Scene 2? *(This bustling, comical scene contrasts sharply with the dark mood of the previous one.)*

Shall, stiff and stark and cold, appear like death;
And in this borrowed likeness of shrunk death
Thou shalt continue two-and-forty hours,
And then awake as from a pleasant sleep.
Now, when the bridegroom in the morning comes
To rouse thee from thy bed, there art thou dead.
Then, as the manner of our country is,
In thy best robes uncovered on the bier
Thou shalt be borne to that same ancient vault
Where all the kindred of the Capulets lie.
In the meantime, against° thou shalt awake,
Shall Romeo by my letters know our drift;°
And hither shall he come; and he and I
Will watch thy waking, and that very night
Shall Romeo bear thee hence to Mantua.
And this shall free thee from this present shame,
If no inconstant toy° nor womanish fear
Abate thy valor° in the acting it.

[*JULIET takes the vial.*]

JULIET. Give me, give me! O, tell not me of fear!

FRIAR. Hold! Get you gone, be strong and prosperous°
In this resolve. I'll send a friar with speed
To Mantua, with my letters to thy lord.

JULIET. Love give me strength, and strength shall help afford.°
Farewell, dear father.

[*They exit.*]

113 against: in preparation for when.
114 drift: intentions.
119 inconstant toy: whim.
120 Abate thy valor: lessen your courage.
122 prosperous: successful.
125 afford: carry out.

SCENE 2. Later that day. A hall in CAPULET's house.

[*LORD CAPULET, LADY CAPULET, and the NURSE enter with several SERVANTS. They are making arrangements for the wedding that will be held in just two days.*]

CAPULET. So many guests invite as here are writ.

[*CAPULET hands a SERVANT a guest list, and the SERVANT exits to invite the wedding guests.*]

3

Sirrah, go hire me twenty cunning° cooks.

SERVINGMAN. You shall have none ill, sir; for I'll try° if they can lick their fingers.

2 cunning: skilled.
3 try: test.

1 Interpret Imagery *What mood does this imagery establish?*

2 The Power of Love *How would you summarize the Friar's plan to save Juliet from marrying Paris?*

Grammar Practice

SPIRAL REVIEW **Exclamation Points** Point out the use of the exclamation point on this page. Tell students that exclamation points should be used sparingly in writing—and never in business communications. An exclamation point is used to show strong emotion, to give a strong command, or after an interjection. **Write:**

- I can't believe your behavior! *(strong emotion)*
- Return my book now! *(strong command)*
- Wow! *(interjection)*

Explain that in dialogue, the exclamation point goes inside quotation marks only if it is part of the quotation. Otherwise, it goes outside the quotation marks. **Write:**

- Mary shouted, "Get out now!"
- I cannot stand it when she says "Puh-leez"!

Have students write three sentences in which they use the exclamation point correctly.

CAPULET. How canst thou try them so?

3 SERVINGMAN. Marry, sir, 'tis an ill cook that cannot lick his
own fingers.° Therefore he that cannot lick his fingers goes
not with me.

[The second SERVANT exits to hire more cooks.]

CAPULET. Go begone.
We shall be much unfurnish'd° for this time.
What, is my daughter gone to Friar Lawrence?

NURSE. Ay, forsooth.°

CAPULET. Well, he may chance to do some good on her.
A peevish self-will'd harlotry it is.°

[JULIET enters, returning from FRIAR LAWRENCE's cell.]

NURSE. See where she comes from shrift with merry look.

CAPULET. How now, my headstrong? Where have you been
gadding?

JULIET. Where I have learnt me to repent the sin
Of disobedient opposition
4 To you and your behests,° and am enjoin'd°
By holy Lawrence to fall prostrate° here
To beg your pardon.

[She kneels before her father.]

Pardon, I beseech you!
Henceforward I am ever rul'd by you.

CAPULET. Send for the County. Go tell him of this.
I'll have this knot knit up tomorrow morning.°

JULIET. I met the youthful lord at Lawrence' cell
And gave him what becomed° love I might,
Not stepping o'er the bounds of modesty.

CAPULET. Why, I am glad on't. This is well. Stand up.

[JULIET rises.]

This is as't should be. Let me see the County.
Ay, marry, go, I say, and fetch him hither.
Now, afore God, this reverend holy friar,
All our whole city is much bound° to him.

6–7 'tis an ill . . . fingers: a proverbial expression for cooks who lack faith in their cooking.

10 unfurnish'd: unprepared.

12 forsooth: in truth.

14 A peevish . . . is: She is a quarrelsome, stubborn good-for-nothing.

19 behests (bi hests´): requests. **enjoin'd:** directed.
20 fall prostrate: kneel down in humility.

23–24 Send for . . . morning: Juliet's apparent change of heart moves Capulet to change the wedding day to Wednesday.
26 becomed: becoming; proper.

32 bound: indebted.

5 The Power of Love *Capulet decides to move the wedding from Thursday to Wednesday. What problems could this cause for Juliet and the Friar?*

6 Irony *Why is Capulet's statement ironic?*

Teach

Reading Strategy 4

Interpret In this speech, Juliet comes nearer to outright lying than at any other point.

Ask: Is she justified in pretending to repent? Why or why not? *(Encourage students to support their opinions with reasons.)*

Big Idea 5

The Power of Love
Answer: *His decision throws the Friar's plan off schedule. Juliet will awaken from her induced sleep sooner than anticipated.*

Literary Element 6

Irony **Answer:** *Capulet is relieved that Juliet's future is settled, unaware that she has agreed to a dangerous plan to avoid marrying Paris.*

English Learners

DIFFERENTIATED INSTRUCTION

Beginning/Early Intermediate Invite students to share helpful techniques for understanding Shakespeare's language. Stress that paraphrasing, or putting a passage into one's own words, can help them monitor their comprehension. Have partners orally paraphrase the conversation between Capulet, Lady Capulet, and Juliet in Scene 2.

Intermediate Guide students to use a dictionary to look up unfamiliar words that are not defined in the marginal notes. Have them write these words in their notebooks and use each in a sentence.

Teach

Vocabulary Activity 1

Multiple Meanings Direct students' attention to the following words in this passage: *stir, warrant, deck, forth,* and *light.* Note that they all have multiple meanings. Have small groups of students look up the words in a dictionary and then determine the correct meaning for the context.

Literary Element 2

Tone Have students discuss the overall tone of Scene 2. Note that the scene contains some complex ironies; for example, Capulet's fussy attention to detail, his ignorance of Friar Lawrence's true role, and Juliet's feigned submission.

Ask: How might these elements affect a live audience? *(The audience would probably laugh uneasily because of the tension from knowing the situation is not what it seems.)*

APPROACHING Call on volunteers to perform a dramatic reading of Scene 2 to aid the class in understanding the effects of irony in this scene.

JULIET. Nurse, will you go with me into my closet°
To help me sort such needful ornaments°
As you think fit to furnish me tomorrow?

LADY CAPULET. No, not till Thursday. There is time enough.

CAPULET. Go, nurse, go with her. We'll to church tomorrow.

[*JULIET and the NURSE exit.*]

LADY CAPULET. We shall be short in our provision.
'Tis now near night.

CAPULET. Tush, I will stir about,
And all things shall be well, I warrant thee, wife.
Go thou to Juliet, help to deck up her.°
I'll not to bed tonight; let me alone.
1 I'll play the housewife for this once. What, ho!
They are all forth; well, I will walk myself°
To County Paris, to prepare up him
Against tomorrow. My heart is wondrous light,
Since this same wayward girl is so reclaim'd.

2 [*CAPULET and LADY CAPULET exit.*]

33 **closet:** private room.

34 **sort such needful ornaments:** select the necessary clothing.

41 **deck up her:** dress her.

43–44 **I'll play . . . walk myself:** Capulet calls for a servant but realizes that he has already sent them all on errands.

SCENE 3. The evening of the same day, the night before the wedding. JULIET's room.

[*JULIET and the NURSE have been preparing JULIET's clothing for the wedding.*]

JULIET. Ay, those attires are best; but, gentle nurse,
I pray thee leave me to myself tonight;
For I have need of many orisons°
To move the heavens to smile upon my state,
Which, well thou knowest, is cross° and full of sin.

[*LADY CAPULET enters.*]

LADY CAPULET. What, are you busy, ho? Need you my help?

JULIET. No, madam; we have cull'd° such necessaries
As are behoveful for our state° tomorrow.
So please you, let me now be left alone,
And let the nurse this night sit up with you;
For I am sure you have your hands full all
In this so sudden business.

LADY CAPULET. Good night.
Get thee to bed, and rest; for thou hast need.

[*LADY CAPULET and the NURSE exit.*]

JULIET. Farewell! God knows when we shall meet again.
I have a faint cold fear thrills through my veins

3 **orisons** (ôr′ i zənz): prayers.

5 **cross:** wrong; perverse.

7 **cull'd:** selected.

8 **behoveful for our state:** appropriate for our ceremony.

Grammar Practice

SPIRAL REVIEW **Prepositional Phrases** Explain that a prepositional phrase includes a preposition and the object of a preposition (a noun or pronoun) as well as any modifiers related to either. Note the prepositional phrase in line 2: "I pray thee leave me <u>to myself</u> tonight;"

Point out the preposition in this phrase (to) and the object of the preposition (myself).

Write these prepositional phrases on the board and have students identify the preposition, the object of the preposition, and any modifiers.

- upon my state *(preposition: upon; object: state; modifier: my)*
- through my veins *(preposition: through; object: veins; modifier: my)*
- in this marriage *(preposition: in; object: marriage; modifier: this)*
- into the tomb *(preposition: into; object: tomb; modifier: the)*

That almost freezes up the heat of life.
I'll call them back again to comfort me.
Nurse!—What should she do here?
My dismal scene I needs must act alone.
Come, vial.
What if this mixture do not work at all?
Shall I be married then tomorrow morning?
No, no! This shall forbid it. Lie thou there.

3 *[She places a dagger beside the bed.]*

What if it be a poison which the friar
Subtly hath minist'red to have me dead,
Lest in this marriage he should be dishonor'd
Because he married me before to Romeo?
I fear it is; and yet methinks it should not,
For he hath still been tried° a holy man.
How if, when I am laid into the tomb,
I wake before the time that Romeo
Come to redeem° me? There's a fearful point!
Shall I not then be **stifled** in the vault,
To whose foul mouth no healthsome air breathes in,
And there die strangled ere my Romeo comes?
Or, if I live, is it not very like°
The horrible conceit° of death and night,
Together with the terror of the place—
As in a vault, an ancient receptacle
Where for this many hundred years the bones
Of all my buried ancestors are pack'd;
Where bloody Tybalt, yet but green in earth,°
Lies fest'ring° in his shroud; where, as they say,
At some hours in the night spirits resort°—
Alack, alack, is it not like that I,
So early waking—what with loathsome smells,
And shrieks like mandrakes° torn out of the earth,
That living mortals, hearing them, run mad—
O, if I wake, shall I not be distraught,°
Environed° with all these hideous fears,
And madly play with my forefathers' joints,
And pluck the mangled Tybalt from his shroud,
And, in this rage, with some great kinsman's bone

29 still been tried: always proven to be.

32 redeem: rescue.

36 like: likely.

37 conceit: thought.

42 green in earth: newly buried.

43 fest'ring: decaying.

44 resort: gather.

47 mandrakes: plants with thick forked roots. (Many people in Shakespeare's time believed that mandrakes shrieked when pulled up and that anyone who heard the sound would become insane.)

49 distraught (dis trôt′): crazed.

50 Environed: surrounded.

Vocabulary

stifle (stī′ fəl) *v.* to smother for lack of air; to prevent from developing properly

Teach

Reading Strategy 3

Make Inferences Ask students if they are surprised that Juliet has a knife in her bedroom. Have them recall preceding scenes and decide when and how Juliet might have armed herself. You may wish to share the following model for drawing inferences.

MODEL: Right after her parents insist she marry Paris, Juliet says, "If all else fail, myself have power to die." In the next scene, she says, "'Twixt me and my extremes this bloody knife shall . . ." I can infer from these remarks that she's been considering suicide as an option.

Approaching Level

DIFFERENTIATED INSTRUCTION

Established Help students understand Juliet's terror at the thought of being locked in the burial vault by reading lines 33–58 aloud. As you read, list her fears on the board. *(not enough air, bones of buried ancestors, Tybalt's body, the smells, plants that might make her insane, Tybalt's ghost)* **Ask:** Would you be afraid in her situation? Why or why not? *(Most students will likely say that they would be afraid for many of the same reasons; some may say that she will be asleep, so she will not notice these things.)*

Teach

Reading Strategy 1

Interpret Imagery
Answer: *Juliet imagines the burial vault to be a ghoulish, nightmarish place. Students may react with dismay at the thought of her waking up there.*

View the Art ★

Answer: *As in the text, people bustle around, carrying various items for the wedding. There is a feast and servants. It differs because the bride and groom in the painting seem happy and engaged with one another.*

Tempera, a fast-drying paint that contains egg yolk and water, dates back to ancient times. Much of the panel painting done between the twelfth and fifteenth centuries was done in tempera, which allows the artist to use extremely delicate brushwork to show fine detail.

Story of Alatiel Tavoli (detail), 15th century. Master of the Jarves Cassoni. Tempera on panel. Museo Correr, Venice.

View the Art This painting was created to decorate a *cassoni,* an intricately decorated marriage chest used to hold the bride's dowry in Renaissance times. How does this painting reflect the preparations for Juliet's wedding? How does it differ? ★

As with a club dash out my desp'rate brains?
O, look! Methinks I see my cousin's ghost
Seeking out Romeo, that did spit° his body
Upon a rapier's point. Stay,° Tybalt, stay!
Romeo, Romeo, Romeo! Here's drink—I drink to thee.

[*JULIET drinks the contents of the vial and falls onto her bed, which is surrounded with curtains.*]

56 spit: impale.
57 Stay: Remain where you are.

SCENE 4. During the night. A hall in CAPULET's house.

[*Preparations for the wedding continue. LADY CAPULET and the NURSE enter.*]

LADY CAPULET. Hold, take these keys and fetch more spices, nurse.

NURSE. They call for dates and quinces° in the pastry.°

[*LORD CAPULET enters.*]

CAPULET. Come, stir, stir, stir! The second cock hath crowed,
The curfew bell° hath rung, 'tis three o'clock.

2 quinces (kwin′ səz): a golden, apple-shaped fruit. **pastry:** place where baking is done.
4 curfew bell: rung in the morning at daybreak as well as in the evening.

1 Interpret Imagery *How does Juliet imagine the burial vault? How does the imagery in this passage make you feel about Juliet waking up in such a place?*

Writing Practice

SMALL GROUP
Character Traits
Break students into small groups and have them reread the conversation between the Nurse, Capulet, and Lady Capulet on these pages. **Ask:** What have you learned about Capulet? About Lady Capulet? And what can you tell about the Nurse? *(Students may say that Capulet is impatient and was a womanizer when he was younger. They may say that Lady Capulet is jealous but seems to have a sense of humor. Nurse is funny and loves Juliet.)* Have students write a character sketch for one of these characters using the traits on these pages and what they have learned about the character from the rest of the story.

Look to the bak'd meats, good Angelica;
Spare not for cost.

NURSE. Go, you cotquean,° go,
Get you to bed! Faith, you'll be sick tomorrow
For this night's watching.°

CAPULET. No, not a whit. What, I have watch'd ere now
All night for lesser cause, and ne'er been sick.

LADY CAPULET. Ay, you have been a mouse hunt° in your time;
But I will watch you from such watching now.

[*LADY CAPULET and the NURSE exit.*]

CAPULET. A jealous hood,° a jealous hood!

[*Several SERVANTS enter with spits, logs, and baskets for preparing the wedding feast.*]

Now, fellow, what is there?

FIRST FELLOW. Things for the cook, sir; but I know not what.

CAPULET. Make haste, make haste.

[*One SERVANT exits.*]

Sirrah, fetch drier logs.
Call Peter; he will show thee where they are.

SECOND FELLOW. I have a head, sir, that will find out logs
And never trouble Peter for the matter.

CAPULET. Mass,° and well said; a merry whoreson,° ha!
Thou shalt be loggerhead.°

[*The SERVANTS exit.*]

Good faith, 'tis day.
The County will be here with music straight,°
For so he said he would.

[*Music plays from offstage. PARIS is outside the house with musicians.*]

I hear him near.
Nurse! Wife! What, ho! What, nurse, I say!

[*The NURSE enters.*]

Go waken Juliet; go and trim her up.
I'll go and chat with Paris. Hie, make haste,
Make haste! The bridegroom he is come already:
Make haste, I say.

[*They exit.*]

6 cotquean (kät′ kwēn): a man who does housework.

8 watching: staying awake.

11 mouse hunt: woman chaser.

13 jealous hood: "jealousy" or "jealous woman."

20 Mass: by the mass (a mild oath). **whoreson** (hor′ sən): rascal.
21 loggerhead: blockhead.

22 straight: immediately.

2 Irony *What ironies do you see in this scene?*

Teach

Literary Element 2

Irony **Answer:** *The family happily fusses over preparations for a wedding that the audience knows will never happen. Students may feel a sense of impending doom that conflicts with Capulet's joy.*

English Learners

DIFFERENTIATED INSTRUCTION

Beginning/Early Intermediate Draw students' attention to the many exclamation points on page 718. Explain that Shakespeare uses them to show the Nurse's extreme emotion because she thinks that Juliet has actually died. Show students that the Nurse first expresses excitement over the wedding and then shock and anguish upon discovering Juliet. The Nurse speaks in short sentences ("My lord! My lady!") because she is likely shouting.

Intermediate Point out the words *aqua vitae* in line 16. Explain that *aqua* is the Latin word for *water* and *vitae* is the Latin word for *life.* The Nurse is asking the Capulets to bring some "water of life" for Juliet.

Teach

Literary Element 1

Irony Answer: *The audience knows Juliet is only sleeping; the Nurse does not. This may help to create suspense about what reaction the Nurse will have to Juliet's state.*

Reading Strategy 2

Listen Say: Describe how the Nurse delivers these lines. Have students read lines 1–16 aloud, noting how phrasing suits the situation. *(The speech consists of abrupt, exclamatory verse, spoken in a loud voice and interrupted often by pauses. Its uneven, jarring rhythm suits the emotional bomb about to go off.)*

SCENE 5. Immediately after the previous scene. JULIET's room.

[*JULIET is behind the curtain that surrounds her bed. The NURSE enters.*]

NURSE. Mistress! What, mistress! Juliet! Fast,° I warrant her, she.
Why, lamb! Why, lady! Fie, you slugabed.
Why, love, I say! Madam; Sweetheart! Why, bride!
What, not a word? You take your pennyworths° now;
Sleep for a week, for the next night, I warrant,
The County Paris hath set up his rest°
That you shall rest but little, God forgive me!
Marry and amen! How sound is she asleep!
I needs must wake her. Madam, madam, madam!
Ay, let the County take you° in your bed,
He'll fright you up, i' faith. Will it not be?

[*The NURSE pulls open the bed curtain.*]

What, dress'd, and in your clothes, and down again?°
I must needs wake you. Lady! Lady! Lady!
Alas, alas! Help, help! My lady's dead!
O weraday that ever I was born!
Some aqua vitae, ho! My lord! My lady!

[*LADY CAPULET enters.*]

LADY CAPULET. What noise is here?

NURSE. O lamentable day!

LADY CAPULET. What is the matter?

NURSE. Look, look! O heavy day!

LADY CAPULET. O me, O me! My child, my only life!
Revive, look up, or I will die with thee!
Help, help! Call help.

[*LORD CAPULET enters.*]

CAPULET. For shame, bring Juliet forth; her lord is come.

NURSE. She's dead, deceas'd; she's dead, alack the day!

LADY CAPULET. Alack the day, she's dead, she's dead, she's dead!

CAPULET. Ha! Let me see her. Out alas! She's cold,
Her blood is settled, and her joints are stiff;
Life and these lips have long been separated.

1 **Fast:** fast asleep.

4 **pennyworths:** small amounts (of rest).

6 **set up his rest:** resolved.

10 **take you:** catch you.

12 **down again:** gone back to bed.

---

1 Irony *What information does the audience have that the Nurse lacks? How does this irony help to create tension?*

Vocabulary

revive (ri vīv′) *v.* to bring back to life; to give new strength

Writing Practice

SMALL GROUP **Persuasive Essays** Have students reread Capulet's reaction to Juliet's death. Break students into groups. **Ask:** Do you think Capulet now regrets trying to force Juliet into marrying Paris? *(Some students may say yes because he has now lost his daughter; others will note that he gives no indication that he believes she has killed herself; he only knows that she has died.)* Have students look for evidence in the play to support both sides of this argument. Then have them individually write a persuasive composition in response to the question.

Death lies on her like an untimely frost
Upon the sweetest flower of all the field.

NURSE. O lamentable day!

LADY CAPULET. O woeful time!

CAPULET. Death, that hath ta'en her hence to make me wail,
Ties up my tongue and will not let me speak.

4

[*FRIAR LAWRENCE and PARIS enter.*]

FRIAR. Come, is the bride ready to go to church?

CAPULET. Ready to go, but never to return.
O son, the night before thy wedding day
Hath Death lain with thy wife. There she lies,
Flower as she was, deflowered by him.
Death is my son-in-law, Death is my heir;
My daughter he hath wedded. I will die
And leave him all. Life, living, all is Death's.

PARIS. Have I thought long to see this morning's face,
And doth it give me such a sight as this?

LADY CAPULET. Accurs'd, unhappy, wretched, hateful day!
Most miserable hour that e'er time saw
In lasting labor of his pilgrimage!
But one, poor one, one poor and loving child,
But one thing to rejoice and solace° in,
And cruel Death hath catch'd it from my sight.

NURSE. O woe! O woeful, woeful, woeful day!
Most lamentable day, most woeful day
That ever ever I did yet behold!
O day, O day, O day! O hateful day!
Never was seen so black a day as this.
O woeful day! O woeful day!

PARIS. Beguil'd,° divorced, wronged, spited, slain!
Most detestable Death, by thee beguil'd,

6

By cruel, cruel thee quite overthrown.
O love! O life!—not life, but love in death!

CAPULET. Despis'd, distressed, hated, martyr'd, kill'd!
Uncomfortable° time, why cam'st thou now
To murder, murder our solemnity?°

47 solace (sol′ is): take comfort.

55 Beguil'd (bi gīld′): cheated.

60 Uncomfortable: bringing no comfort.
61 solemnity (sə lem′ nə tē): celebration.

3 Interpret Imagery *Why does Capulet compare death to an "untimely frost" and Juliet to "the sweetest flower of all the field"?*

5 The Power of Love *What details in this scene reveal how much Capulet, Lady Capulet, and the Nurse love Juliet?*

English Learners

DIFFERENTIATED INSTRUCTION

Beginning/Early Intermediate
Shakespeare uses several different literary elements and techniques on these pages. Help students identify and understand the following:

- "Death lies on her like an untimely frost" *(simile comparing death to frost, which kills flowers)*
- "Death is my son-in-law, Death is my heir; My daughter he hath wedded." *(personification making death a husband who will spend eternity with Juliet)*
- "O day, O day, O day! O hateful day!" *(repetition for emphasis)*
- "In lasting labor of his pilgrimage!" *(alliteration to make the language more poetic)*

Encourage students to look for other literary elements on these pages.

Teach

Reading Strategy 3

Interpret Imagery
Answer: *The comparison expresses his feeling that Juliet was beautiful and precious, and that death has taken her too soon.*

Literary Element 4

Figurative Language Have students identify the similes and metaphors Capulet uses for death. *(Death as killing frost on a flower; as bridegroom and heir)*

Ask: What makes them apt? *(Frost kills delicate young plants. In place of all that Capulet hoped to achieve—his daughter's marriage, a son-in-law, grandchildren—there is only death.)*

Big Idea 5

The Power of Love
Answer: *Their dramatic exclamations of grief: "all is death's"; "wretched, hateful day!"; "O woe!"*

Big Idea 6

The Power of Love Note that Shakespeare portrays Romeo and Juliet's love as sincere and beautiful. At the same time, he shows how passion leads both characters into acts that violate the rules of their families and society and put themselves at risk. Have students summarize these acts. Discuss the paradoxical nature of love in the play.

APPROACHING Assist students in their discussion by reminding them that a paradox is a self-contradicting idea. Love is a paradox because it is a joyful, positive emotion that can bring great sorrow.

Teach

Big Idea

The Power of Love
Answer: *Juliet is in heaven.*

The feigned death of Juliet, 1856–1858. Frederic Leighton. Britain. Oil on canvas, 44¾ x 69 in. Art Gallery of South Australia.

View the Art In this depiction of Juliet's death, Leighton contrasts the somber mood in her bedroom with the flurry of activity outside the window. In your opinion, do the emotions portrayed in the painting reflect the emotions of Scene 5? Explain. ★

O child, O child! My soul, and not my child!
Dead art thou—alack, my child is dead,
And with my child my joys are buried!

FRIAR. Peace, ho, for shame! Confusion's cure lives not
In these confusions.° Heaven and yourself
Had part° in this fair maid—now heaven hath all,
And all the better is it for the maid.
Your part° in her you could not keep from death,
But heaven keeps his part in eternal life.
The most you sought was her promotion,°
For 'twas your heaven she should be advanc'd;°
And weep ye now, seeing she is advanc'd
Above the clouds, as high as heaven itself?
O, in this love, you love your child so ill
That you run mad, seeing that she is well.°

65–66 Confusion's . . . confusions: The healing of this calamity does not lie in your uncontrolled outbursts.
67 Had part: shared.
69 Your part: that is, Juliet's mortal self.
71 promotion: social advancement (from marrying Paris).
72 For 'twas . . . advanc'd: For the greatest joy you could imagine was to see her elevated to a higher station in life.
76 well: in heaven.

The Power of Love *According to the Friar, why should Juliet's parents feel comforted?*

Speaking Practice

SPIRAL REVIEW **Read Dialogue** Have students work in groups of three to act out the conversation between Peter and the first and second musicians. Point out the many marginal notes for this scene. Tell students that they must understand the action and the words before they can determine the tone and effectively act out the scene. After students have had time to prepare, randomly select one group to perform for the class. Allow the students to use props if they are available. Afterward, ask the other students what they have learned about the conversation from the performance.

She's not well married that lives married long,
But she's best married that dies married young.
Dry up your tears and stick your rosemary°
On this fair corse, and, as the custom is,
And in her best array bear her to church;
For though fond nature bids us all **lament,**
Yet nature's tears are reason's merriment.°

CAPULET. All things that we ordained festival°
Turn from their office° to black funeral—
Our instruments to melancholy bells,
Our wedding cheer to a sad burial feast;
Our solemn hymns to sullen dirges° change;
Our bridal flowers serve for a buried corse;
And all things change them to the contrary.

FRIAR. Sir, go you in; and, madam, go with him;
And go, Sir Paris. Everyone prepare
To follow this fair corse unto her grave.
The heavens do low'r° upon you for some ill;°
Move them no more by crossing their high will.

[They all cast rosemary leaves on JULIET. *All but the* NURSE *and the* MUSICIANS *exit.]*

FIRST MUSICIAN. Faith, we may put up our pipes and be gone.

NURSE. Honest good fellows, ah, put up, put up,
For well you know this is a pitiful case.°

[NURSE exits.]

FIRST MUSICIAN. Ay, by my troth, the case° may be amended.°

[PETER enters.]

PETER. Musicians, O musicians, "Heart's ease,"° "Heart's ease"! O, and you will have me live, play "Heart's ease."

FIRST MUSICIAN. Why "Heart's ease"?

PETER. O musicians, because my heart itself plays "My heart is full." O, play me some merry dump° to comfort me.

FIRST MUSICIAN. Not a dump we, 'tis no time to play now.

PETER. You will not then?

FIRST MUSICIAN. No.

PETER. I will then give it you soundly.°

79 rosemary: an herb used in funerals as a symbol of remembrance.

82–83 For though . . . merriment: Although foolish human nature commands us to grieve, reason finds cause for rejoicing (because Juliet is in heaven).

84 ordained festival: ordered for festive purposes.

85 office: function.

88 sullen dirges (dur′ jəz): gloomy funeral music.

94 low'r: frown. **ill:** sin.

98 case: situation.

99 the case: my instrument's case. **amended:** repaired. (This may be a pun, or the First Musician might have misunderstood the Nurse.)

100 "Heart's ease": a popular song.

104 dump: sad tune.

108 give it you soundly: let you have it thoroughly.

Vocabulary

lament (lə ment′) *v.* to express deep sorrow

Teach

View the Art ★

Answer: *Students may say that the emotions shown by the people in the painting seem more restrained and decorous than the emotions expressed by the characters in the text.*

Frederick Leighton (1830–1896) was known for works with classical themes. His earlier works, like the one on this page, reflect the influence of the Florentine masters.

English Learners

DIFFERENTIATED INSTRUCTION

Beginning/Early Intermediate Direct students' attention to the marginal notes which provide meanings for the words *well, case, dump,* and *sound* on these pages. Remind students that some words in Shakespeare's time had different meanings from their meanings today. Have students look up these words in a dictionary and copy down the current meanings for each word.

Teach

Big Idea

The Power of Love

Answer: *The hired musicians are indifferent to the family's grief and focused on their own pleasures. This glimpse into human nature shows how grief and gaiety, sorrow and self-interest are intermingled in life.*

Cultural History ☆

Minstrel Wandering minstrels and troubadours provided the precursors to modern drama. Performers would travel, sharing songs, stories, and news. Eventually, stable groups formed, sponsored by wealthy patrons or by the towns. Even the Catholic Church sometimes used minstrels to spread stories from the Bible as plays.

To check students' understanding of the selection, see Unit 4 Teaching Resources Book, p. 74.

Progress Check

Can students identify irony?

If No → See Unit 4 Teaching Resources Book, p. 69.

FIRST MUSICIAN. What will you give us?

☆ PETER. No money, on my faith, but the gleek;° I will give you the minstrel.°

FIRST MUSICIAN. Then will I give you the serving-creature.

PETER. Then will I lay the serving-creature's dagger on your pate.° I will carry° no crotchets,° I'll *re*° you, I'll *fa*° you. Do you note° me?

FIRST MUSICIAN. And you *re* us and *fa* us, you note us.

SECOND MUSICIAN. Pray you put up your dagger, and put out° your wit.

PETER. Then have at you with my wit! I will drybeat° you with an iron wit, and put up my iron dagger. Answer me like men:

"When griping° griefs the heart doth wound,
And doleful dumps the mind oppress,
Then music with her silver sound"—

why "silver sound"? Why "music with her silver sound"? What say you, Simon Catling?°

FIRST MUSICIAN. Marry, sir, because silver hath a sweet sound.

PETER. Pretty! What say you, Hugh Rebeck?°

SECOND MUSICIAN. I say, "silver sound," because musicians sound° for silver.

PETER. Pretty too! What say you, James Soundpost?°

THIRD MUSICIAN. Faith, I know not what to say.

PETER. O, I cry you mercy, you are the singer;° I will say for you; it is "music with her silver sound," because musicians have no gold for sounding:

"Then music with her silver sound
With speedy help doth lend redress."

[*PETER exits.*]

FIRST MUSICIAN. What a pestilent knave is this same!

SECOND MUSICIAN. Hang him, Jack! Come, we'll in here, tarry for the mourners, and stay° dinner.

[*MUSICIANS exit.*]

110–111 gleek: insulting jest. **give you the minstrel:** call you a minstrel (an insult).

114 pate: head. **carry:** put up with. **crotchets** (kroch′ itz): "whims" or "quarter notes in music." **Re** and **fa** are musical notes, which Peter uses threateningly.

115 note: understand.

117 put out: display.

119 drybeat: thrash.

122 griping: distressing. (Peter is reciting lines from a poem.)

126 Catling (kat′ ling): a lute string.

128 Rebeck (rē′ bek): a three-stringed fiddle.

130 sound: play.

131 Soundpost: a small peg beneath the bridge of a stringed instrument.

133 you are the singer: that is, you can only sing, not say.

140 stay: wait for.

The Power of Love *What does this final dialogue suggest about human nature?*

Grammar Practice

SMALL GROUP

Linking Verbs

Write:

- *This* is a *pitiful* case.
- *Never* was seen *so black a day.*

In the first example, *is* links a noun in the predicate with a pronoun in the subject. Explain that *was seen* is a verb phrase using *was* as an auxiliary, or helping, verb.

Have students underline and identify the verbs as linking verbs or verb phrases.

1. Everyone in the Capulet household is greiving for Juliet. *(verb phrase)*
2. The musicians are opportunists. *(linking verb)*
3. Peter's puns and wisecracks are crass under the circumstances. *(linking verb)*

After You Read

Respond and Think Critically

Respond and Interpret

1. What do you think of Friar Lawrence's plan and its consequences?
2. (a)What plan does the Friar suggest to Juliet? (b)Why does he suggest this plan?
3. (a)What does Capulet decide when Juliet agrees to marry Paris? (b)Why do you think he makes this decision, and how might it cause problems for Juliet?
4. (a)What does Juliet fear most about carrying out the Friar's plan? (b)What does her resolution to go ahead with the plan indicate about her?

Analyze and Evaluate

5. Do you think the Friar's plan is realistic? Why or why not?
6. After Juliet's body is found, do you think Capulet regrets his earlier harshness toward her? Explain.

Connect

7. **Big Idea** The Power of Love What would you have done in Juliet's situation? Explain.
8. **Connect to Today** In what instances in the modern world do people lie or trick others to get out of obligations? How is such behavior viewed?

Literary Element Irony

Irony is a contrast between appearance and reality.

1. What is one example of situational irony in Act 4? What effect does it help create? Explain.
2. What is one example of dramatic irony? Explain.

Reading Strategy Interpret Imagery

In creating effective **imagery,** writers use descriptions that appeal to the senses—sight, sound, touch, taste, and smell.

1. Which image in this act struck you as the most vivid or effective? Explain.
2. Find two other examples of imagery in Act 4. (a)What senses do they appeal to? (b)What effect do they have on you?

Vocabulary Practice

Practice with Context Clues Look back at pages 708–722 to find context clues for the vocabulary words below. Record your findings in a chart like the one below.

lurk stifle revive lament

Example:

Word: haste

↓

Textual Clues: "I knew not why it should be slowed"

↓

Meaning: speed

LOG ON Literature Online

Selection Resources For Selection Quizzes, eFlashcards, and Reading-Writing Connection activities, go to glencoe.com and enter QuickPass code GL49787u4.

Writing

Write a Journal Entry Write a journal entry from the point of view of either Friar Lawrence or the Nurse. Describe the young lovers' dilemma, the advice you have offered, and your hopes and fears about their future. Include details from the play.

After You Read

Assess

1. Accept well-reasoned answers.
2. (a) He gives her a potion that will make her appear dead for 42 hours. Romeo can then be summoned to rescue her from the burial vault. (b) Juliet has spoken of suicide so desperate measures seem justified.
3. (a) He moves the wedding up a day, hoping to dispel the gloom caused by Tybalt's death. (b) There may not be time to summon Romeo back to Verona.
4. (a) Wakening alone in the gruesome tomb (b) Desperation to be with Romeo
5. Accept reasonable answers.
6. He does not mention regret, but perhaps his guilt is too painful to acknowledge.
7. Accept reasonable answers.
8. Answers will vary—one example might be students who fake illness to get out of school. Such behavior is not overly criticized unless it is done frequently.

Literary Element

1. Capulet's decision to have the wedding sooner so Juliet will be safely and happily married is situational irony. Although his intentions are good, his act causes the lovers' plan to go awry. The irony creates tension and arouses pity for Capulet.
2. The Capulets' grief over Juliet's apparent death is a dramatic irony because the audience knows she's alive.

Reading Strategy

1. Students should support their answers.
2. Students should support their answers.

Vocabulary

Word: lurk
Textual Clues: "walk in thievish ways"
Meaning: to conceal oneself

Word: stifle
Textual Clues: "no healthsome air breathes in"
Meaning: to smother for lack of air

Word: revive
Textual Clues: "or will die with thee"
Meaning: to bring back to life

Word: lament
Textual Clues: "nature's tears"
Meaning: to express deep sorrow

Writing

Journal entries should include descriptions of the advice offered to Romeo and Juliet by either the Friar or the Nurse and reflect accurate details from the play.

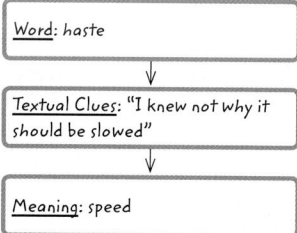

Before You Read

Focus

Summary

Balthasar reports to Romeo that Juliet is dead. Romeo decides to join her and persuades a pharmacist to sell him poison. Paris confronts Romeo; they fight and Romeo kills Paris. Romeo takes the poison and dies just before the arrival of Friar Lawrence, who has learned that his letter never reached Romeo. Juliet wakes and refuses to leave; the Friar flees, and Juliet stabs herself with Romeo's dagger. The various witnesses confess to the Prince, and Montague and Capulet express remorse.

Vocabulary

"A Rose by Any Other Name . . ." Shakespeare chose many of the names in his plays for specific reasons. For instance, the character Paris was named for the Trojan prince that kidnapped Helen and started the Trojan War. Have students select a character from the play and research the name.

Before You Read

Romeo and Juliet, Act 5

Connect to the Drama

Do children wind up paying a price for the ill deeds of their parents? Freewrite for a few minutes exploring this question.

Build Background

In Act 5, a character is suspected by the authorities of having been exposed to infectious disease. Called the Black Death, the bubonic plague was among the most feared diseases in Europe. Dirt and overcrowding in cities encouraged rats, which carried fleas infected with the disease.

Set Purposes for Reading

Big Idea The Power of Love

As you read, ask yourself, Are Romeo and Juliet's misfortunes due to an excess of love, or to the failures of other people?

Literary Element Tragedy

A **tragedy** is a play in which a main character, called the **tragic hero,** suffers a downfall. The downfall may result from outside forces or from a weakness within the character, which is known as a **tragic flaw.** *Romeo and Juliet* is an unusual tragedy because it has two tragic heroes. As you read, ask yourself, What tragic flaws lead to the downfall of the tragic heroes?

Reading Strategy Make Inferences About Theme

The **theme** of a piece of literature is the dominant idea—often a universal message about life. A work may have more than one theme. As you read, ask yourself, What insights is Shakespeare expressing through plot and dialogue?

Tip: Take Notes Use a chart like the one shown (based on Act 3) to record inferences you draw from the details in Act 5.

Detail	Inference About Theme
Romeo accidentally causes Mercutio's death.	The source of one's death is fated, yet cannot be predicted.

Learning Objectives

For pages 724–742

In studying this text, you will focus on the following objectives:

Literary Study: Analyzing tragedy.

Reading: Making inferences about theme.

Vocabulary

misadventure (mis′ əd ven′ chər) *n.* a mishap; an unfortunate event; p. 725 *Mark had a misadventure with a flat bike tire.*

haughty (hô′ tē) *adj.* very proud and scornful of others; p. 730 *Maria talked down to people and acted rudely; I thought she was haughty.*

unsavory (un sā′ vər ē) *adj.* unpleasant in character; disagreeable to the taste; p. 732 *Because of dishonest dealings, Greg has an unsavory reputation.*

tedious (tē′ dē əs) *adj.* tiresome; boring; p. 737 *I found the long bus ride tedious and uncomfortable.*

Tip: Word Parts When you encounter a difficult word, look for familiar prefixes or suffixes and remove them to determine the root word. For example, in the vocabulary word *misadventure,* you can identify the common prefix *mis-* and the root word *adventure.* Breaking down the meaning of the root word and affixes can help you to understand difficult words.

Selection Skills

The Tragedy of Romeo and Juliet, Act 5

Literary Elements
- Tragedy (SE pp. 724–743)
- Style (SE p. 742)

Reading Skills
- Make Inferences About Theme (SE pp. 724–743)

Vocabulary Skills
- Word Parts (SE p. 742)
- Academic Vocabulary (SE p. 742)

Writing Skills/Grammar
- Editorial (SE p. 743)
- Pronouns (TE, p. 728)
- Descriptive Paragraph (TE p. 736)
- Subject-Verb Agreement (TE p. 736)
- Indefinite Pronouns (TE p. 740)

Listening/Speaking/Viewing Skills
- Analyze Art (SE pp. 730, 734, 738)
- Oral Reading and Response (TE p. 730)

Act 5

SCENE 1. The next day. A street in Mantua, the city where ROMEO lives in exile.

[*ROMEO enters; he is waiting for his servant,* BALTHASAR, *to return from Verona with news of* JULIET.]

ROMEO. If I may trust the flattering truth of sleep,
My dreams presage,° some joyful news at hand.
My bosom's lord° sits lightly in his throne,
And all this day an unaccustom'd spirit
Lifts me above the ground with cheerful thoughts.
I dreamt my lady came and found me dead
(Strange dream that gives a dead man leave to think!)
And breath'd such life with kisses in my lips
That I reviv'd and was an emperor.
Ah me! How sweet is love itself possess'd,
When but love's shadows° are so rich in joy!

[*ROMEO's servant,* BALTHASAR, *enters.*]

News from Verona! How now, Balthasar?
Dost thou not bring me letters from the friar?
How doth my lady? Is my father well?
How fares my Juliet? That I ask again,
For nothing can be ill if she be well.

BALTHASAR. Then she is well, and nothing can be ill.
Her body sleeps in Capel's monument,°
And her immortal part with angels lives.
I saw her laid low in her kindred's vault
And presently took post° to tell it you.
O, pardon me for bringing these ill news,
Since you did leave it for my office,° sir.

ROMEO. Is it e'en so? Then I defy you, stars!
Thou knowest my lodging. Get me ink and paper
And hire post horses. I will hence° tonight.

BALTHASAR. I do beseech you, sir, have patience.
Your looks are pale and wild and do import
Some **misadventure.**°

2 presage (pres′ ij): predict.

3 bosom's lord: heart.

11 but love's shadows: only dreams of love.

18 Capel's monument: the Capulet tomb.

21 presently took post: immediately set out on post horses.

23 office: duty.

26 hence: leave here.

28–29 and do . . . misadventure: suggest that some misfortune will occur.

Vocabulary

misadventure (mis′ əd ven′ chər) *n.* a mishap; an unfortunate event

Teach

Reading Strategy

Interpret How would students describe Romeo's mood after reading this opening soliloquy in Act 5? *(He has had a strange dream about being brought back to life by the kisses of his beloved. He takes it as a positive sign that joyful news is on its way, and he is hopeful and excited.)*

APPROACHING Have students form small groups. Then ask them to choose one confusing sentence and work together to look up any unknown words, then paraphrase the sentence into contemporary, everyday language.

English Learners

DIFFERENTIATED INSTRUCTION

Beginning/Early Intermediate Students may need extra practice with pronunciation and vocabulary. Make dictionaries available and help students understand how to use the pronunciation key. Have groups of students choose a scene, discuss the meanings of unfamiliar vocabulary and phrases in the scene, and work together to look up pronunciations.

Early Advanced Have more proficient students use the unfamiliar words in sentences after they study the pronunciations. Then, allow each student to read aloud the sentences to the class.

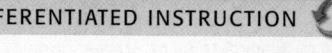

Teach

Literary Element 1

Tragedy **Answer:** *Romeo decides to return to Verona because he believes Juliet is dead. Students may consider Romeo's decision to be a rash one.*

Literary Element 2

Tragedy **Answer:** *Balthasar, like Friar Lawrence, urges Romeo to stop and think, but Romeo is ruled by impatience.*

Literary Element 3

Tragedy With this decision, the final stage of the tragedy is set in motion. Romeo and Juliet must die, as we have known from the prologue. This miscommunication, though well intended, is deadly. Encourage students to consider Romeo's response to the news.

Ask: What evidence of unthinking behavior do you see in his response? *(He never asks what happened or how it happened.* He also neglects to wonder much that the Friar did not inform him, simply saying "No matter." All of this points to unreasonable impulsiveness.)

Cultural History ☆

Known as the Black Death, the bubonic plague was among the most feared diseases in Europe. An estimated one third to one half of Europe's population died from the disease during the Middle Ages and the Renaissance.

ROMEO. Tush, thou art deceiv'd.
Leave me and do the thing I bid thee do.
Hast thou no letters to me from the friar?

BALTHASAR. No, my good lord.

ROMEO. No matter. Get thee gone.
And hire those horses. I'll be with thee straight.

[*BALTHASAR exits. ROMEO, grief stricken, begins to walk aimlessly.*]

Well, Juliet, I will lie with thee tonight.
3 Let's see for means. O mischief, thou art swift
To enter in the thoughts of desperate men!
I do remember an apothecary,°
And hereabouts 'a dwells, which late I noted
In tatt'red weeds,° with overwhelming° brows,
Culling of simples.° Meager were his looks,
Sharp misery had worn him to the bones;
And in his needy shop a tortoise hung,
An alligator stuff'd, and other skins
Of ill-shap'd fishes; and about his shelves
A beggarly account° of empty boxes,
Green earthen pots, bladders, and musty seeds.
Remnants of packthread,° and old cakes of roses°
Were thinly scattered, to make up a show.
Noting this penury,° to myself I said,
"An' if a man did need a poison now
Whose sale is present death° in Mantua,
Here lives a caitiff° wretch would sell it him."
O, this same thought did but forerun my need,
And this same needy man must sell it me.
As I remember, this should be the house.
Being holiday, the beggar's shop is shut.
What, ho! Apothecary!

[*APOTHECARY enters.*]

APOTHECARY. Who calls so loud?

ROMEO. Come hither, man. I see that thou art poor.
Hold, there is forty ducats.° Let me have
A dram of poison, such soon-speeding gear°
As will disperse itself through all the veins

37 apothecary (ə poth′ ə ker′ ē): one who prepares and sells drugs.

39 tatt'red weeds: torn clothing. **overwhelming:** overhanging.
40 Culling of simples: sorting medicinal herbs.

45 beggarly account: small number.

47 packthread: twine for tying packages. **cakes of roses:** rose petals pressed into cakes and used for perfume.
49 penury (pen′ yər ē): poverty.

51 Whose sale . . . death: the sale of which is punishable by immediate execution.
52 caitiff (kā′ tif): miserable.

59 ducats (duk′ ətz): gold coins.

60 soon-speeding gear: fast-working stuff.

1 Tragedy *Why does Romeo decide to return to Verona? What is your response to his decision?*

2 Tragedy *Think about Balthasar's caution and Romeo's response. What consistent flaw in Romeo is revealed again here?*

Reading Practice

SPIRAL REVIEW **Set a Purpose** Remind students to set a purpose for reading. Have a volunteer summarize the play up to Act 5. **Ask:** What is Romeo's state of mind in Act 5, Scene 1? *(desperate, frantic, hopeless)* **Say:** What do you think might happen as the play proceeds? Why? Have students write their responses in their notebooks. Then, ask volunteers to share their predictions with the class. Encourage students to jot down whether their predictions were correct as they progress through Act 5.

That the life-weary taker may fall dead.
And that the trunk° may be discharg'd of breath
As violently as hasty powder fir'd
Doth hurry from the fatal cannon's womb.

APOTHECARY. Such mortal° drugs I have; but Mantua's law
Is death to any he that utters° them.

ROMEO. Art thou so bare and full of wretchedness
And fearest to die? Famine is in thy cheeks,
Need and oppression starveth in thy eyes,
Contempt and beggary hangs upon thy back:
The world is not thy friend, nor the world's law;
The world affords no law to make thee rich;
Then be not poor, but break it and take this.

APOTHECARY. My poverty but not my will consents.

ROMEO. I pay thy poverty and not thy will.

APOTHECARY. Put this in any liquid thing you will
And drink it off, and if you had the strength
Of twenty men, it would dispatch you straight.

4 ROMEO. There is thy gold—worse poison to men's souls,
Doing more murder in this loathsome world,
Than these poor compounds that thou mayst not sell.
I sell thee poison; thou hast sold me none.
Farewell. Buy food and get thyself in flesh.

[*APOTHECARY exits.*]

Come, cordial° and not poison, go with me
To Juliet's grave; for there must I use thee.

[*ROMEO exits.*]

63 **trunk:** body.

66 **mortal:** deadly.

67 **any he that utters:** any man who dispenses.

85 **cordial** (kôr′ jəl): tonic, restoring drink.

SCENE 2. The same afternoon. FRIAR LAWRENCE's cell in Verona.

[*FRIAR JOHN enters. Sent by FRIAR LAWRENCE to Mantua with a letter for ROMEO, he has just returned.*]

JOHN. Holy Franciscan friar, brother, ho!

[*FRIAR LAWRENCE enters.*]

LAWRENCE. This same should be the voice of Friar John.
Welcome from Mantua. What says Romeo?
Or, if his mind be writ,° give me his letter.

5 JOHN. Going to find a barefoot brother° out,
One of our order, to associate° me
Here in this city visiting the sick,
And finding him, the searchers° of the town,
Suspecting that we both were in a house
☆ Where the infectious pestilence° did reign,

4 **if his mind be writ:** if his message is written.

5 **barefoot brother:** Franciscan friar.

6 **associate:** accompany.

8 **searchers:** health officials who searched houses for victims of the plague and quarantined, or isolated, them.

10 **infectious pestilence:** plague.

Teach

Literary Element 4

Irony Ask students to explain the irony of Romeo's lines. *(To Romeo, the poison is like medicine that will cure his longing because it allows him to rejoin Juliet.)* Have students scan Act 2, Scene 3 (page 665, lines 23–24) to recall words that foreshadow this action. ("Within the infant rind of this weak flower / Poison hath residence and medicine power.") *(The point is that even a good thing taken to an extreme is harmful; here the extreme has become the only remedy for Romeo.)*

Literary Element 5

Theme Once again, unforeseeable bad luck thwarts the lovers. Have students relate this incident to the prologue's statement about "star-cross'd" lovers bound for "misadventur'd piteous" ruin. *(They might have been reunited if the letter had arrived on time, but a chance incident prevents the letter from being delivered.)*

English Learners

DIFFERENTIATED INSTRUCTION

Beginning/Early Intermediate Write *unaccustomed, joyful, misadventure, discharged,* and *wretchedness* on the board. Explain that the underlined letters are prefixes and suffixes added to words to change their form and meaning. Help students use dictionaries to analyze meanings of prefixes and suffixes and how they alter the words to which they are added. Have students list common suffixes and prefixes and their meanings in their notebooks. Suggest that students scan the play for additonal examples. Encourage students to share the words and meanings they find with the class.

Teach

Reading Strategy 1

Make Inferences About Theme **Answer:** *The courier was quarantined because of possible exposure to the plague. Romeo's repeated misfortunes suggest that a person's destiny is fixed.*

Seal'd up the doors, and would not let us forth,
So that my speed to Mantua there was stay'd.°

LAWRENCE. Who bare° my letter, then, to Romeo?

JOHN. I could not send it—here it is again—
Nor get a messenger to bring it thee,
So fearful were they of infection.

5

LAWRENCE. Unhappy fortune! By my brotherhood,
The letter was not nice, but full of charge,°
Of dear import;° and the neglecting it
May do much danger. Friar John, go hence,
Get me an iron crow° and bring it straight
Unto my cell.

JOHN. Brother, I'll go and bring it thee.

[*FRIAR JOHN exits.*]

LAWRENCE. Now must I to the monument alone.
Within this three hours will fair Juliet wake.
She will beshrew° me much that Romeo
Hath had no notice of these accidents,°
But I will write again to Mantua,
And keep her at my cell till Romeo come—
Poor living corse, clos'd in a dead man's tomb!

[*He exits.*]

SCENE 3. Late that night. The churchyard that contains the Capulets' tomb.

[*PARIS enters with his PAGE who carries a torch and flowers.*]

PARIS. Give me thy torch, boy. Hence, and stand aloof.
Yet put it out, for I would not be seen.
Under yond yew trees lay thee all along,°
Holding thy ear close to the hollow ground.
So shall no foot upon the churchyard tread
(Being loose, unfirm, with digging up of graves)
But thou shalt hear it. Whistle then to me,
As signal that thou hearest something approach.
Give me those flowers. Do as I bid thee, go.

PAGE. [*Aside.*] I am almost afraid to stand alone
Here in the churchyard; yet I will adventure.°

[*The PAGE retires to a watching place while PARIS sprinkles the tomb with flowers.*]

12 stay'd: stopped.

13 bare: bore; carried.

18 not nice, but full of charge: not trivial, but full of importance.

19 dear import: serious consequence.

21 crow: crowbar.

25 beshrew: blame; scold.

26 accidents: occurrences.

3 lay thee all along: lie flat on the ground.

11 adventure: risk it.

---

1 Make Inferences About Theme *Why did Romeo not receive Friar Lawrence's letter? What do these repeated misfortunes suggest about destiny or fate?*

Grammar Practice

SPIRAL REVIEW **Pronouns** Explain that pronouns are used in place of nouns. Also explain that antecedents are what the pronoun refers to. Review the following:

Personal: singular—*I, me, you, he, him, she, her, it;* **plural**—*we, us, you, they, them*

Possessive: singular—*my, mine, your, yours, his, her, hers, its;* **plural**—*our, ours, your, yours, their, theirs*

Have students explain what Elizabethan pronouns replace *you* and *your* in Shakespeare's writing. *(thee, thou, thy)* Have students scan Scene 3 to identify at least one example of each personal and possessive pronoun on the list and to name its antecedent.

PARIS. Sweet flower, with flowers thy bridal bed I strew
(O woe! thy canopy is dust and stones)
Which with sweet° water nightly I will dew;°
Or, wanting that, with tears distill'd by moans.
The obsequies° that I for thee will keep
Nightly shall be to strew thy grave and weep.

[The PAGE *whistles, his signal that someone is coming.]*

The boy gives warning something doth approach.
What cursed foot wanders this way tonight
To cross° my obsequies and true love's rite?
What, with a torch? Muffle° me, night, awhile.

*[*PARIS *hides as* ROMEO *and* BALTHASAR *enter.]*

ROMEO. Give me that mattock° and the wrenching iron.°
Hold, take this letter. Early in the morning
See thou deliver it to my lord and father.
Give me the light. Upon thy life I charge° thee,
Whate'er thou hearest or seest, stand all aloof
And do not interrupt me in my course.
Why I descend into this bed of death
Is partly to behold my lady's face,
But chiefly to take thence from her dead finger
A precious ring—a ring that I must use
In dear employment.° Therefore hence, be gone.
But if thou, jealous,° dost return to pry
In what I farther shall intend to do,
By heaven, I will tear thee joint by joint
And strew this hungry churchyard with thy limbs.
The time and my intents are savage-wild,
More fierce and more inexorable far°
Than empty° tigers or the roaring sea.

BALTHASAR. I will be gone, sir, and not trouble ye.

ROMEO. So shalt thou show me friendship. Take thou that.

[He hands BALTHASAR *money.]*

Live, and be prosperous; and farewell, good fellow.

BALTHASAR. *[Aside.]* For all this same, I'll hide me hereabout.
His looks I fear, and his intents I doubt.

*[*BALTHASAR *hides.]*

14 sweet: perfumed. **dew:** sprinkle.

16 obsequies (ob′ sə kwēz): funeral rites.

20 cross: interrupt.

21 Muffle: hide.

22 mattock (mat′ ək): pickaxe. **wrenching iron:** crowbar.

25 charge: command.

32 In dear employment: for an important purpose.

33 jealous: suspicious.

38 More . . . far: far more fierce and determined.

39 empty: hungry.

2 The Power of Love *What does Shakespeare reveal about Paris in this scene?*

3 The Power of Love *Why does Shakespeare put such harsh and angry words in Romeo's mouth?*

Teach

Big Idea 2

The Power of Love

Answer: *The scene reveals Paris's love for Juliet.*

Big Idea 3

The Power of Love

Answer: *The angry words suggest Romeo's grim determination to die.*

Approaching Level

DIFFERENTIATED INSTRUCTION

Emerging Help students understand Act 5 by having them review what each of the involved characters has at stake. Have students review their notebooks—flow charts, summaries, and notes—to create character sketches of Romeo and Paris. **Ask:** What is the motivation of each character to be at the tombs? *(Romeo: to join his love in death; Paris: to punish Romeo)* After students have an understanding of the characters' feelings, have volunteers read a section of the play. Instruct the volunteers to incorporate the characters' emotions into their readings. Then, have students critique the volunteers' acting.

Teach

Reading Strategy 1

Draw Conclusions Using the following model, guide students to compare and contrast Romeo and Paris, noting how Romeo has grown as a character.

MODEL: Romeo and Paris are both young men of the same class and background who love Juliet. Romeo is the one whose love is returned. Juliet's love opens Romeo's heart, enabling him to look beyond the feud. Paris, however, remains stuck in the world of the feud and views Romeo only as his enemy. When they meet, only Paris wants vengeance. Paris lacks the deeper perspective on life that Romeo has gained through love.

Romeo Slaying Paris at the Bier of Juliet, 1809. Henry Fuseli. Folger Shakespeare Library, Washington, DC.

View the Art Why might the figure of Juliet seem to radiate light? What does the lighting tell you about Juliet's importance in this scene? ★

ROMEO. Thou detestable maw,° thou womb of death,
Gorg'd° with the dearest morsel of the earth,
Thus I enforce thy rotten jaws to open,
And in despite° I'll cram thee with more food.

[*As* ROMEO *forces open the tomb,* PARIS *watches from his hiding place.*]

PARIS. This is that banish'd **haughty** Montague
That murd'red my love's cousin—with which grief
It is supposed the fair creature died—

45 maw: the mouth, jaws, or stomach of a flesh-eating animal.
46 Gorg'd (gôrjd): stuffed.

48 in despite: to spite you.

Vocabulary

haughty (hô′ tē) *adj.* very proud and scornful of others

View the Art ★

Answer: *Juliet, although presumed dead, remains the only light of their lives. She is the central figure.*
Swiss-born Henry Fuseli (1741–1825), a leading painter of the Romantic Movement, emulated the grand style of Renaissance master Michelangelo.

Skills Practice

SPIRAL REVIEW **Oral Reading and Response** Lines 74–119 convey Romeo's anguished struggle with guilt and despair. Play the audio CD of these lines, pausing to discuss how Romeo's tone of voice helps listeners understand his meaning. Then have groups of four to six students take turns reading this speech aloud, using tone, pace, and expression to communicate their understanding of his state of mind. Have students discuss the professional reading compared to the reading students performed.

And here is come to do some villainous shame
To the dead bodies. I will apprehend° him.

[*PARIS comes forward and speaks to ROMEO.*]

Stop thy unhallowed° toil, vile Montague!
Can vengeance be pursued further than death?
Condemned villain, I do apprehend thee.
Obey, and go with me; for thou must die.

ROMEO. I must indeed; and therefore came I hither.
Good gentle youth, tempt not a desp'rate man.
Fly hence and leave me. Think upon these gone;
Let them affright thee. I beseech thee, youth,
Put not another sin upon my head
By urging me to fury. O, be gone!
By heaven, I love thee better than myself,
For I come hither arm'd against myself.
Stay not, be gone. Live, and hereafter say
A madman's mercy bid thee run away.

PARIS. I do defy thy conjurations.°
1 And apprehend thee for a felon here.

ROMEO. Wilt thou provoke me? Then have at thee, boy!

[*They draw swords and fight.*]

PAGE. O Lord, they fight! I will go call the watch.

[*The PAGE runs off to call the WATCHMEN. PARIS is wounded and falls.*]

PARIS. O, I am slain! If thou be merciful,
Open the tomb, lay me with Juliet.

[*PARIS dies.*]

ROMEO. In faith, I will. Let me peruse° this face.
Mercutio's kinsman, noble County Paris!
What said my man when my betossed° soul
Did not attend° him as we rode? I think
He told me Paris should have married Juliet.
Said he not so, or did I dream it so?
Or am I mad, hearing him talk of Juliet,
To think it was so? O, give me thy hand,
One writ with me in sour misfortune's book!

53 **apprehend:** arrest.

54 **unhallowed:** unholy.

68 **conjurations:** appeals.

74 **peruse** (pə ro͞oz′): examine.

76 **betossed:** upset.

77 **attend:** pay attention to.

---

2 Tragedy *Shakespeare is bringing together characters who are in extreme emotional turmoil. What do you think will happen next?*

3 Make Inferences About Theme *Why is Romeo so reluctant to fight Paris?*

Teach

Literary Element 2

Tragedy Answer: *Students may anticipate that something bad is about to happen.*

ADVANCED Students may enjoy the opportunity to play with language. Have students try writing their own sentence in the style of Shakespeare that foreshadows a tragic event.

Reading Strategy 3

Make Inferences About Theme Answer: *Romeo has wearied of the pain and death caused by the feud.*

Approaching Level

DIFFERENTIATED INSTRUCTION

Emerging Writing about the text will reinforce students' reading skills and allow you to monitor their comprehension. Have students review Act 5 and write down lines of dialogue that reveal joy, anger, fear, or despair. Tell them to identify the emotion each line expresses.

Teach

Literary Element

Tragedy **Answer:** *The suffering Romeo expresses as he mourns for Juliet and ponders suicide seems unbearably tragic because it rests on the mistaken idea that Juliet is dead. The audience is gripped by suspense because they know that all is lost unless Juliet awakens in time.*

APPROACHING **Ask:** What device does Shakespeare use in this section to increase suspense? *(Foreshadowing; by showing that Juliet still has color in her face, he foreshadows her revival)*

I'll bury thee in a triumphant grave.
A grave? O, no, a lanthorn,° slaught'red youth,
For here lies Juliet, and her beauty makes
This vault a feasting presence,° full of light.
Death, lie thou there, by a dead man interr'd.

[*ROMEO carries PARIS into the tomb and lays him there. Then he walks to JULIET's body.*]

How oft when men are at the point of death
Have they been merry! Which their keepers call
A lightning before death.° O, how may I
Call this a lightning? O my love, my wife!
Death, that hath suck'd the honey of thy breath,
Hath had no power yet upon thy beauty.
Thou art not conquer'd. Beauty's ensign° yet
Is crimson in thy lips and in thy cheeks,
And death's pale flag is not advanced there.
Tybalt, liest thou there in thy bloody sheet?
O, what more favor can I do to thee
Than with that hand that cut thy youth in twain
To sunder his that was° thine enemy?
Forgive me, cousin! Ah, dear Juliet,
Why art thou yet so fair? Shall I believe
That unsubstantial° Death is amorous,°
And that the lean abhorred monster keeps
Thee here in dark to be his paramour?°
For fear of that I still will stay with thee
And never from his pallet° of dim night
Depart again. Here, here will I remain
With worms that are thy chambermaids. O, here
Will I set up my everlasting rest
And shake the yoke of inauspicious stars°
From this world-wearied flesh. Eyes, look your last!
Arms, take your last embrace! And, lips, O you
The doors of breath, seal with a righteous kiss
A dateless° bargain to engrossing death!°
Come, bitter conduct; come, **unsavory** guide!
Thou desperate pilot, now at once run on

84 lanthorn (lan′ tərn): a dome with windows that let sunlight into a church or palace.
86 feasting presence: a hall lit brightly for celebration.

90 lightning before death: a proverbial phrase based on the idea that people's spirits revive just before death.

94 ensign (en′ sīn): flag.

100 sunder his that was: cut off the youth of the man who was.

103 unsubstantial: without a body. **amorous:** in love.

105 paramour (par′ ə moor′): mistress.

107 pallet: bed.

111 inauspicious (in′ ôs pish′ əs) **stars:** ill fate.

115 dateless: eternal. **engrossing death:** death who buys up everything.

Tragedy *How does Romeo's speech heighten the audience's sense of tragedy and of suspense?*

Vocabulary

unsavory (un sā′ vər ē) *adj.* unpleasant in character; disagreeable to the taste

Research Practice

SPIRAL REVIEW **Dreams** Discuss Balthazar's dream of a fight between Romeo and Paris. Note that modern research indicates that external sounds are often incorporated into our dreams. **Ask:** How might this fact explain Balthazar's dream? *(His sleeping mind may have heard the fight.)* Discuss the implications of this detail. **Ask:** Do you think it suggests that Shakespeare was observant of how the dreaming mind functions? Have students research theories about dreams and write a report on their findings.

The dashing rocks thy seasick weary bark!°
Here's to my love!

[*He takes out the poison and drinks it.*]

O true apothecary!
Thy drugs are quick. Thus with a kiss I die.

[*ROMEO kisses JULIET and falls. Outside the tomb, FRIAR LAWRENCE enters the churchyard carrying a lantern, crowbar, and spade.*]

☆ **FRIAR.** Saint Francis be my speed! How oft tonight
Have my old feet stumbled at graves! Who's there?

[*BALTHASAR steps out from his hiding place.*]

BALTHASAR. Here's one, a friend, and one that knows you well.

FRIAR. Bliss be upon you! Tell me, good my friend,
What torch is yond that vainly lends his light
To grubs° and eyeless skulls? As I discern,°
It burneth in the Capels' monument.

BALTHASAR. It doth so, holy sir; and there's my master,
One that you love.

FRIAR. Who is it?

BALTHASAR. Romeo.

FRIAR. How long hath he been there?

BALTHASAR. Full half an hour.

FRIAR. Go with me to the vault.

BALTHASAR. I dare not, sir.
My master knows not but I am gone hence,
And fearfully° did menace me with death
If I did stay to look on his intents.

FRIAR. Stay then; I'll go alone. Fear comes upon me.
O, much I fear some ill unthrifty° thing.

BALTHASAR. As I did sleep under this yew tree here,
I dreamt my master and another fought,
And that my master slew him.

FRIAR. Romeo!
Alack, alack, what blood is this which stains
The stony entrance of this sepulcher?
What mean these masterless and gory swords
To lie discolor'd by this place of peace?

[*He enters the tomb.*]

Romeo! O, pale! Who else? What, Paris too?
And steep'd in blood? Ah, what an unkind hour

116–118 Come . . . bark: Romeo addresses the poison as a guide **(conduct)** who, like a navigator that runs a ship **(bark)** into the rocks, will lead him to destruction.

126 grubs: worms. **discern:** make out.

133 fearfully: fearsomely.

136 unthrifty: unfortunate.

Teach

Cultural Note ☆

St. Francis Founder of the Franciscan Order of monks, St. Francis of Assisi (1181 or 1182–1226) is the Catholic patron saint of animals and the environment. St. Francis followed the Bible literally, doing as Jesus said and emulating Jesus as much as possible. St. Francis was canonized in 1228.

Approaching Level

DIFFERENTIATED INSTRUCTION

Emerging The final scene moves rapidly and involves a great deal of action. Students who process knowledge through body movement will grasp the significance of actions more easily if they act them out. Have students visualize the movements of characters in each part of the scene to improve their comprehension. Invite volunteers to pantomime segments as other classmates summarize the action.

Teach

Reading Strategy 1

Make Inferences About Theme **Answer:** *Students may put the blame on fate, the characters' own natures, the feud, or a combination of circumstances.*

APPROACHING Make sure students are following the twists of the plot. **Ask:** What does the Friar refer to when he says, "our intents?" *(He refers to the plan he had made with Juliet to reunite her with Romeo using the sleeping potion.)*

View the Art ★

Answer: *Students should notice that the darkness reflects the somber mood of the scene. Juliet seems to be holding her arm up against the light coming into the room, and the shadow of someone coming toward her seems ominous.*

This work by Joseph Wright (1734–1797) reflects the English Romantic painter's skill as a portraitist as well as his fascination with the effects of light and atmosphere.

Romeo and Juliet: The Tomb Scene, exhibited 1790. Joseph Wright of Derby. Oil on canvas, 177.8 x 241 cm. Derby Museum & Art Gallery, England.

View the Art Joseph Wright was fascinated by the effects of light. How does lighting in this painting reflect the mood of the scene pictured? ★

Is guilty of this lamentable chance!°
The lady stirs.

[JULIET *wakes.*]

JULIET. O comfortable friar! Where is my lord?
I do remember well where I should be,
And there I am. Where is my Romeo?

FRIAR. I hear some noise. Lady, come from that nest
Of death, contagion, and unnatural sleep.
A greater power than we can contradict
Hath thwarted our intents.° Come, come away.

146 chance: event.

154 thwarted our intents: ruined our plans.

1 Make Inferences About Theme *What power has thwarted Romeo and Juliet, in your opinion?*

Grammar Practice

SPIRAL REVIEW **Subject-Verb Agreement** Stress that subjects and verbs must agree in number. Recommend that students isolate the subject and verb of a sentence to check the agreement. Write this sentence on the board: "Poison, I see, hath been his timeless end." Circle the words *Poison, hath,* and *been.*
Ask: Would you replace *hath* with *has* or *have*? Why? *(*has, *because* poison *is singular)* Have students determine agreement in these verb phrases:

- Her body sleeps in Capel's monument and her immortal part with angels (live, *lives*).
- My poverty but not my will (*consents,* consent).
- A greater power than we can contradict (*has,* have) thwarted our intents.

Thy husband in thy bosom there lies dead;
And Paris too. Come, I'll dispose of thee
Among a sisterhood of holy nuns.
Stay not to question, for the watch is coming.
Come, go, good Juliet. I dare no longer stay.

JULIET. Go, get thee hence, for I will not away.

[Hearing the approaching WATCHMAN, FRIAR LAWRENCE *hurries off.]*

What's here? A cup, clos'd in my true love's hand?
Poison, I see, hath been his timeless° end.
O churl!° Drunk all, and left no friendly drop
To help me after? I will kiss thy lips.
Haply° some poison yet doth hang on them
To make me die with a restorative.°

[She kisses ROMEO'S *lips.]*

Thy lips are warm!

CHIEF WATCHMAN. *[He calls from off stage.]*
Lead, boy. Which way?

JULIET. Yea, noise? Then I'll be brief. O happy dagger!

[She snatches ROMEO'S *dagger.]*

This is thy sheath; there rust, and let me die.

[She stabs herself, falls, and dies. PARIS' PAGE *enters the churchyard with a troop of* WATCHMEN.*]*

PAGE. This is the place. There, where the torch doth burn.

CHIEF WATCHMAN. The ground is bloody. Search about the churchyard.
Go, some of you; whoe'er you find attach.°

[Some of the WATCHMEN *exit to search the churchyard. The remainder of the* WATCHMEN, *with the* PAGE, *enter the tomb.]*

Pitiful sight! Here lies the County slain;
And Juliet bleeding, warm, and newly dead,
Who here hath lain this two days buried.
Go, tell the Prince; run to the Capulets;
Raise up the Montagues; some others search.

[Other WATCHMEN *exit.]*

We see the ground° whereon these woes do lie,
But the true ground of all these piteous woes
We cannot without circumstance descry.°

162 timeless: untimely.

163 churl: miser.

165 Haply: perhaps.

166 restorative: a medicine or other substance that restores health or consciousness. (However, Juliet wants the kiss to restore her to Romeo by killing her.)

173 attach: arrest.

179 ground: cause.

181 without circumstance descry (di skrī´): understand without more information.

2 Tragedy *What common human traits and weaknesses are displayed by Juliet?*

Teach

Literary Element 2

Tragedy Answer: *Juliet is naïve and impulsive and subject to extremes of emotion.*

ADVANCED **Ask:** Why would Shakespeare want Juliet to be a flawed character? *(He wanted Juliet to have flaws so that audience members could see her as a real person and relate to her, thus heightening the emotional effect of the tragedy.)*

Approaching Level

DIFFERENTIATED INSTRUCTION

Emerging Note that a play's action builds to a climax and then must be resolved. Thus, the surviving characters must discover and respond to the climactic events and grasp whatever truth can be learned from the tragedy. Have students create a graphic organizer to map the events that resolve the action. They should include the following:

- Who provides what information to the Prince
- Which characters have died and why
- How the survivors react

Teach

Reading Strategy 1

Make Inferences About Theme **Answer:** *The feud is the original source of all the misfortunes and misunderstandings that ultimately lead to these deaths.*

Cultural Note ☆

Herbal Medicine

Historically, the science and art of herbal medicine was often the province of monks. In Europe, writings about herbs by Catholic monks date to the eighth century. Monks tended to be well educated and were able to translate older herbal texts from Latin and Greek and then to build on that knowledge.

[Some WATCHMEN *return with* BALTHASAR.*]*

SECOND WATCHMAN. Here's Romeo's man. We found him in
the churchyard.

CHIEF WATCHMAN. Hold him in safety till the Prince come hither.

[Another WATCHMAN *returns with* FRIAR LAWRENCE.*]*

THIRD WATCHMAN. Here is a friar that trembles, sighs, and weeps.
We took this mattock and this spade from him
As he was coming from this churchyard's side.

CHIEF WATCHMAN. A great suspicion! Stay the friar too.

*[*PRINCE ESCALUS *enters with his* ATTENDANTS.*]*

PRINCE. What misadventure is so early up,
That calls our person from our morning rest?

*[*LORD CAPULET *and* LADY CAPULET *enter with others.]*

CAPULET. What should it be, that is so shriek'd abroad?

LADY CAPULET. O, the people in the street cry "Romeo,"
Some "Juliet," and some "Paris"; and all run
With open outcry toward our monument.

PRINCE. What fear is this which startles in your ears?

CHIEF WATCHMAN. Sovereign,

[He calls them to the entrance of the tomb.]

here lies the County Paris slain;
And Romeo dead; and Juliet, dead before,
Warm and new kill'd.

PRINCE. Search, seek, and know how this foul murder comes.

CHIEF WATCHMAN. Here is a friar, and slaughter'd Romeo's man,
With instruments upon them fit to open
These dead men's tombs.

CAPULET. O heavens! O wife, look how our daughter bleeds!
This dagger hath mista'en,° for, lo, his house°
Is empty on the back of Montague,
And it missheathed in my daughter's bosom!

LADY CAPULET. O me, this sight of death is as a bell
That warns° my old age to a sepulcher.

*[*LORD MONTAGUE *enters with others. The* PRINCE *calls them to the entrance of the tomb.]*

203 mista'en: missed its proper target. **his house:** its sheath.

207 warns: summons; calls.

1 Make Inferences About Theme *Lady Capulet predicts her coming death. How are this prediction and the murders and suicides in this scene related to the feud?*

Writing Practice

SPIRAL REVIEW **Description** Have students recall a vivid scene from the play and explain its dominant impression. Have them explain how figures of speech, word choice, and punctuation contributed to creating this impression. *(Specific, concrete details that appeal to the senses)* Provide these guidelines for writing descriptions:

- Decide what overall impression to create.
- List details that contribute to the impression.
- Organize details so that the eye moves logically over the scene or the object.

Have students write a descriptive paragraph about a setting from the play. Have volunteers share their paragraphs with the class.

PRINCE. Come, Montague; for thou art early up
To see thy son and heir now early down.

MONTAGUE. Alas, my liege,° my wife is dead tonight!
Grief of my son's exile hath stopp'd her breath.
What further woe conspires against mine age?

PRINCE. Look, and thou shalt see.

MONTAGUE. O thou untaught!° What manners is in this,
To press before thy father to a grave?

PRINCE. Seal up the mouth of outrage° for a while,
Till we can clear these ambiguities°
And know their spring,° their head, their true descent;
And then will I be general of your woes°
And lead you even to death. Meantime forbear,
And let mischance be slave to patience.°
Bring forth the parties of suspicion.

FRIAR. I am the greatest,° able to do least,
Yet most suspected, as the time and place
Doth make against me, of this direful murder;
And here I stand, both to impeach and purge°
Myself condemned and myself excus'd.

PRINCE. Then say at once what thou dost know in this.

FRIAR. I will be brief, for my short date of breath°
Is not so long as is a **tedious** tale.
Romeo, there dead, was husband to that Juliet;
And she, there dead, that's Romeo's faithful wife.
I married them; and their stol'n marriage day
Was Tybalt's doomsday, whose untimely death
Banish'd the new-made bridegroom from this city;
3 For whom, and not for Tybalt, Juliet pin'd.
You, to remove that siege of grief from her,
Betroth'd and would have married her perforce°
To County Paris. Then comes she to me
And with wild looks bid me devise some mean
To rid her from this second marriage,
Or in my cell there would she kill herself.
Then gave I her (so tutor'd by my art)°
☆ A sleeping potion; which so took effect

210 liege (lēj): lord.

214 untaught: one who is unschooled in manners.

216 Seal up the mouth of outrage: hold off your emotional outcry.

217 ambiguities: mysteries.

218 spring: source.

219 general of your woes: chief mourner.

221 let mischance be slave to patience: let your response to misfortune be governed by restraint.

223 greatest: most suspect.

226 impeach and purge: blame and clear from blame.

229 date of breath: time I have left to live.

238 perforce: forcibly.

243 so tutor'd by my art: which I learned to do from my studies.

2 Tragedy *Why does the Prince say this? What might he be helping Montague to understand?*

Vocabulary

tedious (tē′ dē′ əs) *adj.* tiresome; boring

Teach

Literary Element 2

Tragedy **Answer:** *The Prince's remark suggests that Montague has been blind to the consequences of the feud. He wants Montague to open his eyes to the high price of hatred and violence.*

Reading Strategy 3

Evaluate **Ask:** Why might Shakespeare have inserted this summary even though the audience already knows this information? *(The passage serves to inform the remaining characters and also to provide the vehicle for their remorse and reconciliation.)* Have students note how economically the lines summarize the complex plot.

Approaching Level

DIFFERENTIATED INSTRUCTION

Established Explain that *Romeo and Juliet* is one of the most performed plays ever written. Show stills from the many different film versions of *Romeo and Juliet* and explain that the play has been made into many widely varying films. Show two different film versions of the same scene. Ask students which version they prefer and why. Also ask what they would have done differently if they were directing. Then, have students write a paragraph that compares and contrasts the films.

Teach

View the Art ★

Answer: *He is probably overcome with remorse and regret that his plan has ended in tragedy. Students may imagine similar feelings.*

Frederick Leighton (1830–1896) tended to lose the freshness of his sketches and studies in the elaboration of the finished piece.

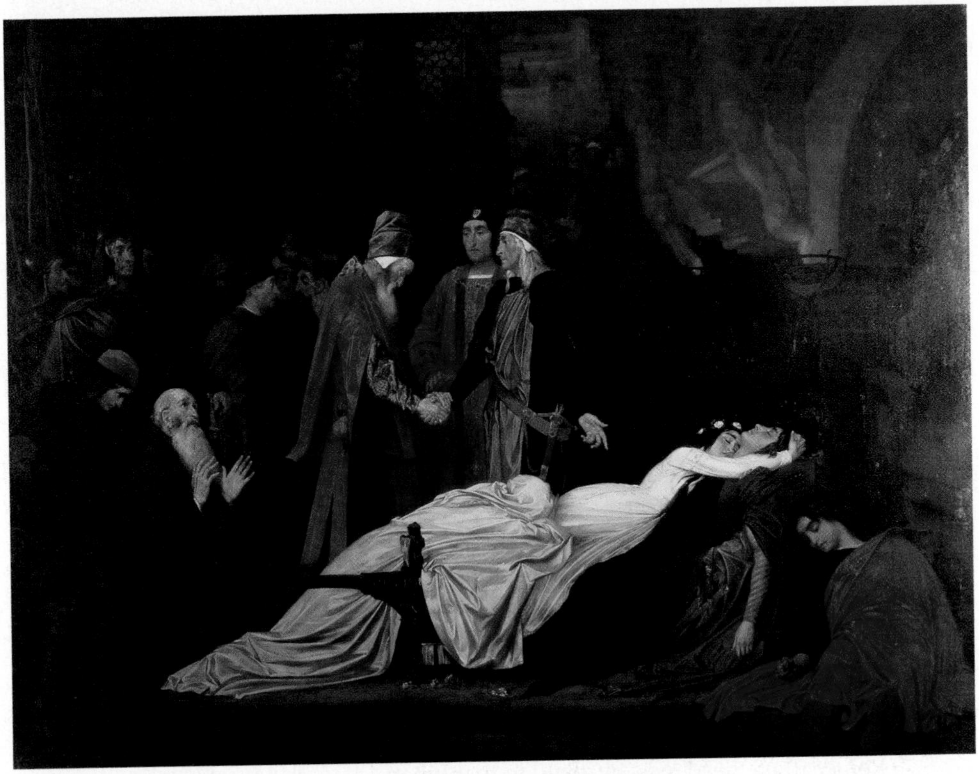

The Reconciliation of the Montagues and Capulets Over the Dead Bodies of Romeo and Juliet, 1853–1855. Frederick Leighton. Oil on canvas, 70 x 91 in. Agnes Scott College, Decatur, GA.

View the Art The lines of Juliet's dress in this painting draw the viewer's eyes to the friar. What do you suppose the friar is thinking? What would you be thinking? ★

As I intended, for it wrought on her
The form of death. Meantime I writ to Romeo
That he should hither come as this° dire night
To help to take her from her borrowed° grave,
Being the time the potion's force should cease.
But he which bore my letter, Friar John,
Was stayed by accident,° and yesternight
3 Return'd my letter back. Then all alone
At the prefixed hour of her waking
Came I to take her from her kindred's vault;
Meaning to keep her closely° at my cell
Till I conveniently could send to Romeo.
But when I came, some minute ere the time
Of her awakening, here untimely lay

247 as this: this.

248 borrowed: temporary.

251 stayed by accident: prevented from going by circumstances.

255 closely: secretly.

Research Practice

SPIRAL REVIEW **Critical Perspective** Note that the meaning of *Romeo and Juliet* has been debated for more than 400 years. **Ask:** What themes can you identify in this play? List students' responses on the board. Have students perform a search in a library or on the Internet for critical essays about *Romeo and Juliet.* Tell them to write a paragraph about two or three interpretations of the play as a whole or of parts of the play that have not been discussed in class. Begin a class discussion with students' discoveries and compare with students' understanding of the play.

The noble Paris and true Romeo dead.
She wakes; and I entreated her come forth
And bear this work of heaven with patience;
But then a noise did scare me from the tomb,
And she, too desperate, would not go with me,
3 But, as it seems, did violence on herself.
All this I know, and to the marriage
Her nurse is privy;° and if aught in this
Miscarried by my fault, let my old life
Be sacrific'd some hour before his time
Unto the rigor of severest law.

PRINCE. We still° have known thee for a holy man.
Where's Romeo's man? What can he say to this?

BALTHASAR. I brought my master news of Juliet's death;
And then in post he came from Mantua
To this same place, to this same monument.
This letter he early bid me give his father,
And threat'ned me with death, going in the vault,
If I departed not and left him there.

PRINCE. Give me the letter. I will look on it.

[*BALTHASAR hands the letter to the PRINCE.*]

Where is the County's page that rais'd the watch?
Sirrah, what made your master in this place?°

PAGE. He came with flowers to strew his lady's grave;
And bid me stand aloof, and so I did.
Anon° comes one with light to ope the tomb;
And by and by my master drew on him;
And then I ran away to call the watch.

PRINCE. [*He is reading ROMEO's letter.*] This letter doth make good the friar's words,
Their course of love, the tidings of her death;
And here he writes that he did buy a poison
Of a poor pothecary and therewithal°
Came to this vault to die and lie with Juliet.
Where be these enemies? Capulet, Montague,
See what a scourge is laid upon your hate,
That heaven finds means to kill your joys with love.

266 is privy: shares the secret.

270 still: always.

280 what . . . place: What was your master doing here?

283 Anon: shortly.

289 therewithal: with this.

Tragedy *In your opinion, how much blame does Friar Lawrence deserve for the deaths of Romeo and Juliet?*

Approaching Level

DIFFERENTIATED INSTRUCTION

African American Vernacular English Approaching-level students who use African American Vernacular English may have difficulty with words that begin with a th- sound. These students might pronounce the word *this* as *dis*, for example. Model the correct pronunciation of words such as *this, that,* and *there.* Then, have a volunteer read aloud lines 305–310.

Teach

Literary Element

Tragedy **Answer:** *Some students may argue that he has been a loyal and resourceful friend to the young lovers. Others may point out that he has been reckless and weak when put to the test.*

ADVANCED Have students discuss their ideas about how much control other people have over their lives. **Ask:** Did anyone in this play have control over what happened? *(Answers will vary, as some students may be more in favor of free will, others of fate.)*

Teach

Literary Element 1

Tragedy **Answer:** *He regrets not dealing more severely with the warring families. If he had taken stronger measures, Romeo and Juliet might still be alive.*

Reading Strategy 2

Make Inferences About Theme **Answer:** *Violence and hatred don't pay off for anybody. A person who acts violently winds up experiencing violence.*

ADVANCED **Ask:** Could the deaths of Romeo, Juliet, and Paris have been avoided? Would the families have learned anything if they had? *(The events might have been avoided if they had been able to communicate their messages to each other, but the play would not have been a tragedy. Even if they had been avoided, the families might have continued to feud, leading to other deaths.)*

To check students' understanding of the selection, see Unit 4 Teaching Resources Book, p. 87.

And I, for winking at your discords too,
Have lost a brace of kinsmen.° All are punish'd.

CAPULET. O brother Montague, give me thy hand.
This is my daughter's jointure,° for no more
Can I demand.

MONTAGUE. But I can give thee more;
For I will raise her statue in pure gold,
That whiles Verona by that name is known,
There shall no figure at such rate° be set
As that of true and faithful Juliet.

CAPULET. As rich shall Romeo's by his lady's lie—
Poor sacrifices of our enmity!

PRINCE. A glooming° peace this morning with it brings.
The sun for sorrow will not show his head.
Go hence, to have more talk of these sad things;
Some shall be pardon'd, and some punished;
For never was a story of more woe
Than this of Juliet and her Romeo.

[*Everyone exits.*]

295 brace of kinsmen: pair of relatives (Mercutio and Paris).

297 jointure (join′chər): marriage settlement.

301 rate: value.

305 glooming: cloudy; gloomy.

1 Tragedy *What does the Prince mean when he tells Capulet and Montague, "See what a scourge is laid upon your hate"? Why does the Prince regret "winking" at their discords?*

2 Make Inferences About Theme *What did Capulet and Montague learn from their children's deaths?*

Grammar Practice

SPIRAL REVIEW **Indefinite Pronouns** Explain that indefinite pronouns such as *one* and *all* refer to people or things in a general way. Help students make a list of other indefinite pronouns, such as *all, another, any, anybody, anyone, anything, both, each, either, everybody, everyone, everything, few, little, many, more, most, much, neither, nobody, no one, none, nothing, one, other(s), several, some, somebody, someone,* and *something.*

Have students find examples of indefinite pronouns of the play. As they find them in the text, write them on the board along with the page and line numbers where they appear.

After You Read

Respond and Think Critically

Respond and Interpret

1. What was your reaction to the end of the play?
2. (a)While in Mantua, what news does Romeo hear about Juliet? (b)Why does he choose such a drastic course of action upon hearing it?
3. (a)What prevents Romeo from finding out the truth about Juliet? (b)What happens when he arrives at the Capulet's tomb?
4. (a)As a result of events at the tomb, what do Capulet, Montague, and the Prince say they will do? (b)Describe the mood in lines 229–310.

Analyze and Evaluate

5. When Paris tries to apprehend Romeo at the tomb, why does Romeo refuse to surrender and accept his punishment? Explain.
6. How does Romeo and Juliet's need for secrecy shape the action of the play?

Connect

7. **Big Idea** The Power of Love Do the deaths of Romeo and Juliet prove or disprove the idea that love is powerful? Explain.
8. **Connect to Today** Can you imagine a situation in today's world in which a young couple might resort to such drastic actions? Explain.

Daily Life & Culture

The Two Worlds of the Renaissance

What was life like in Verona when the Italian Renaissance was at its height? For some, it was a time and place of luxury. Paintings from the period show beautifully clothed men and women in grand palaces. For the noble and the very wealthy, life sometimes resembled these images.

But just outside the doors of the nobility was a world of poverty. Cities were disorganized, dirty, and densely crowded. People and animals jostled for space on narrow, unpaved roads. A poor family typically slept in one room. At a time when half the population did not live to the age of thirty, there were few gray hairs among the poor.

1. What evidence do you see in the play of the two worlds of the Renaissance?
2. (a)What insights do you gain about the lives of servants through this play? (b)Do you think Shakespeare portrayed servants and other commoners sympathetically? Explain.

The Benevolence of St. Elizabeth, 1529. Nikolaus Glockendon. Painting. Collection of Kassel, Murhard'sche und landesbibliothek.

After You Read

Assess

1. Students should explain their reactions.
2. (a) Juliet is dead. (b) He can't bear living without her.
3. (a) The Friar's courier is delayed, and Romeo never learns that Juliet is alive. (b) Romeo kills Paris, takes the poison, and dies just before Friar Lawrence appears. Juliet awakens and refuses to leave with the Friar. She stabs herself with Romeo's knife as watchmen approach.
4. (a) They will make peace and erect statues to the lovers. (b) The sorrowful mood is balanced by a sense of harmony and resolution.
5. He wants to control his own destiny; he can't wait to join Juliet.
6. It leads to fatal misunderstandings; the characters act on the basis of wrong or incomplete information.
7. Students should explain their answers.
8. Students might mention young couples from feuding gangs or religions.

For additional selection assessment, see Assessment Resources, pp. 171–172.

Daily Life & Culture

1. Mention of the plague; the poverty of the apothecary; the families have servants and hold lavish celebrations.
2. (a) The servants' lives are controlled by their masters; their masters' interests and loyalties dictate their own. (b) Accept reasonable answers.

After You Read

Assess

Literary Element

1. Romeo and Juliet share the tragic flaw of allowing themselves to be ruled by passion and despair, which causes them both to act impetuously. The uncompromising quality of their love is itself a tragic flaw—it results in their suicides.
2. They are doomed by a combination of bad luck, social and family circumstances, and their own youthful impetuousness and passion.

Progress Check

Can students identify tragedy?

If No → See Unit 4 Teaching Resources Book, p. 82.

Review: Style

Make sure students' webs contain examples of figurative language, imagery, sound devices, and wordplay.

Reading Strategy

1. **C** is the correct answer. Possessed by the power of love, Romeo and Juliet show courage in defying their families but act irrationally in their suicides.

Progress Check

Can students make inferences about theme?

If No → See Unit 4 Teaching Resources Book, p. 83.

Literary Element Tragedy

In a **tragedy** the main character, or **tragic hero,** is usually a respected person whose personality is marred by a fatal weakness or tragic flaw. Fate may work against this tragic hero, but usually his or her downfall is also brought about by a character flaw. Even if flawed, most tragic heroes are admirable individuals, and the audience regrets their loss.

1. Does Romeo have a tragic flaw? Does Juliet? If so, what are they?
2. Do you think that Romeo and Juliet are destroyed by fate, by their own character flaws, by the flaws of others, or by a combination of factors? Explain your answer.

Review: Style

As you learned on page 230, **style** is the distinctive way in which an author uses language. Elements that are important to Shakespeare's style include:

- **figurative language,** descriptive language used to imply ideas, including metaphor, simile, and personification.
- **imagery,** "word pictures" that appeal to the five senses.
- **sound devices,** elements that appeal to the ear, enhance rhythm, and create a musical quality.
- **wordplay,** puns or other instances of language that rely on double meanings.

Group Activity In a small group choose a favorite scene or passage from the play and discuss how Shakespeare uses the elements listed above. Create a web diagram to record examples of Shakespeare's style that you find striking. List the Act and Scene numbers in the central circle. In the surrounding circles, list examples of figurative language, imagery, sound devices, and wordplay.

LOG ON Literature Online

Selection Resources For Selection Quizzes, eFlashcards, and Reading-Writing Connection activities, go to glencoe.com and enter QuickPass code GL49787u4.

Reading Strategy Make Inferences About Theme

SAT Skills Practice

1. Which sentence best states one important theme of *The Tragedy of Romeo and Juliet*?
   (A) Tragedy is always the result of secrecy.
   (B) There can be no meaningful communication between different generations.
   (C) Love is a powerful force that can make people act without reason or fear.
   (D) Violence is the only consequence of rash decision making.
   (E) In a struggle of wills, the family always prevails over the individual.

Vocabulary Practice

Practice with Word Parts For each boldfaced vocabulary word in the left column, identify the related word with a shared root in the right column. Write each word and underline the part they have in common. Use a printed or online dictionary to look up the meaning of the related word. Then explain how it is related to the vocabulary word.

1. misadventure	a. savoring
2. unsavory	b. haute
3. tedious	c. unadventurous
4. haughty	d. tedium

Academic Vocabulary

*In this play, Capulet attempts to **restrict** Juliet's freedom and keep her from doing what she wants.*

Restrict is an academic word. More familiar words that have a similar meaning are *limit* and *control.* In what ways do parents sometimes **restrict** their children's freedom?

For more on academic vocabulary, see pages 54–55 and R79–R81.

Vocabulary

1. **mis<u>adventure</u>,** un<u>adventur</u>ous
Unadventurous means "careful or boring." An unadventurous person is trying to avoid a misadventure.
2. **un<u>savor</u>y,** <u>savor</u>ing
Unsavory relates to the noun *savor*; someone unsavory is lacking in pleasant characteristics.
3. **<u>tedi</u>ous,** <u>tedi</u>um
Tedium is the state of being tedious.
4. **<u>haut</u>y,** <u>haute</u>
Someone who is haughty thinks they are better than others; *haute* means "high-class."

Academic Vocabulary

Sample answer: Parents can ground their children or make them come straight home after school.

Respond Through Writing

Editorial

Offer a Solution Write an editorial about relationships of a couple that cause disapproval from friends or family. Offer suggestions for how both sides can deal with the tension. Incorporate an allusion to *The Tragedy of Romeo and Juliet,* including advice that might be gained from the play.

Understand the Task An **editorial** presents an opinion on a current news event or issue. An **allusion** is a reference to a well-known character, place, or situation from history, music, art, or literature.

Prewrite Before writing, use a Venn diagram to organize your ideas. In the left circle, list advice for the couple. In the right circle, list advice for disapproving family and friends. In the overlapping area, list advice for everyone. Plan to direct your editorial toward all of the people involved.

Advice for Couple
Don't let other people get you down.
Advice for Both
Spend time together and get to know each other better.
Advice for Family and Friends
Don't tell the couple what they should do.

Draft Use ideas from the diagram to create your draft. As you present your suggestions, include an allusion to *Romeo and Juliet* as part of your supporting evidence. When responding to opposing arguments, use persuasive techniques to promote your point of view. Appeal to the audience's emotions, ethics, or logic.

Revise Review your editorial and make sure that it is structured logically. For example, you might want to address general suggestions first and suggestions for individuals later. When revising, you can help support your editorial's logic by adding transitions that smoothly lead from one idea to another. For example, after explaining an opposing argument, you can transition to your counter-argument with a statement such as:

While it is true that _____, it does not necessarily mean that _____.

You might also want to review the checklist for an editorial on p. 1082.

Edit and Proofread Proofread your paper, correcting any errors in grammar, spelling, and punctuation. Use the Grammar Tip in the side column to help you with apostrophes.

Learning Objectives

In this assignment, you will focus on the following objectives:

Writing: Writing an editorial.

Grammar: Understanding how to use apostrophes in forming contractions.

Grammar Tip

Apostrophe

When creating contractions, an **apostrophe** is used in place of the letters that are omitted.

That is why…

That's why…

By using an **apostrophe** to create a contraction, you can make a sentence sound more informal and relaxed. In an editorial, if you are trying to make an emotional appeal, an informal, personal tone can sometimes be more persuasive.

After You Read

Assess

Respond Through Writing

Students' editorials should:

- discuss relationships that cause disapproval from friends and family
- provide advice to the couples, family, and friends about how to ease the tension
- include an allusion and a lesson from *Romeo and Juliet* as supporting evidence
- be organized logically
- make use of persuasive techniques

For grammar practice, see Unit 4 Teaching Resources Book, p. 86.

To create custom assessments online, go to Progress Reporter Online Assessment.

To create custom assessments using software, use ExamView Assessment Suite.

Approaching Level

DIFFERENTIATED INSTRUCTION

Emerging Lead a discussion in which students reveal which images in the play were the most striking and memorable. Then allow students to flip through old magazines to find and tear out images that represent scenes from *Romeo and Juliet*—for instance, a student might collect a picture of two young lovers in an embrace. After students have collected several photos, have them construct collages that represent the play. Allow each student to show and explain their collage to the class.

TIME

Focus

Summary

This article describes the construction of a replica of Shakespeare's Globe Theatre in London, England. The new theater stages the plays to resemble the productions of the original 1599 playhouse.

Teach

Reading Strategy

Identify Sequence Note that three common forms of sequencing are chronological order, spatial order, and order of importance.

APPROACHING Remind approaching-level students that are struggling with this activity that their graphic organizer should be in chronological order, or the order in which things happen.

Readability Scores

Dale-Chall: 8.7
DRP: 64
Lexile: 1170

Reading Practice

Analyze Structure and Format Have students analyze the structure and format of the text before they read. Have them read the title and introductory notes and scan headings, pictures, marked text, and quotations. Students should then write a skeleton outline:

I. Historical Overview
II. To Build or Not to Build
III. Close to the Action

Learning Objectives

For pages 744–747

In studying this text, you will focus on the following objectives:

Reading:
Analyzing informational text.
Identifying sequence.

Set a Purpose for Reading

Read to learn about the history of Shakespeare's Globe Theatre in London, England.

Preview the Article

1. Skim the first three paragraphs. What part of the Globe Theatre's history do you think this article focuses on?
2. Scan the article's subheadings. What topics do you think this article will discuss?

Reading Strategy Identify Sequence

Identifying sequence involves recognizing the order in which thoughts are arranged. Identifying sequence will help you remember ideas better. As you read "A Long-Overdue Encore," ask yourself, What is the sequence of events? Use a graphic organizer like the one below.

TIME

A LONG-OVERDUE ENCORE

In a reproduction of the theater where Shakespeare's plays were first performed, actors put on shows the way they were done in the Bard's day.

By BARRY HILLENBRAND

THE OPENING LINES OF WILLIAM SHAKESPEARE'S *Henry V* have a seductive charm. Using the humble voice of the narrator, the playwright asks the audience to suspend disbelief. It is a bit much to ask, he admits, but might the audience transform "this unworthy scaffold" of the stage into the "vasty fields of France? Or may we cram / Within this wooden O the very casques / That did affright the air at Agincourt?" For nearly four centuries, audiences have readily joined in this theatrical pretense. After all, who can refuse the Bard a favor?

When those famous lines were spoken at the opening of a contemporary London production of *Henry V,* they were more irresistible—and relevant—than ever before. For they were delivered from the stage of Shakespeare's Globe Theatre, a remarkably faithful reconstruction of Shakespeare's original "wooden *O*." The first Globe, which Shakespeare called a "wooden *O*" because it was an open-air, round building, was built in 1599. Shakespeare worked there for many years, and wrote many of his greatest plays for its company of actors. In 1613, a cannon used in a production of *Henry VIII* set the thatched roof on fire, and the theater burned to the ground. A new playhouse was built on the original foundation and continued to operate until 1642, when the Puritans closed down all theaters. Two years later, the Globe was torn down, and more than 350 years passed before the new Globe opened its doors in 1997.

Located on the south bank of the River Thames and only a stone's throw from where the original once stood, the

TIME

THE PLAY'S THE THING
A group of students at the Globe.

new Globe Theatre is an accurate replica of Shakespeare's playhouse. The structure has a brick foundation and oak beams, and its roof is open to the sky in the center, letting in sunshine or rain just as the original Globe did. But the new Globe is more than the ultimate theme park for Shakespeare fanatics: It is also the arena for a fresh and fascinating style of Shakespearean performances. **1**

To Build or Not To Build

Much to the dismay of some tradition-minded British theater fans, the new Globe owes its existence to a U.S. actor named ☆ Sam Wanamaker, who came to England in 1949 to shoot a movie. During his stay, he learned that a government committee led by U.S. Senator Joseph McCarthy was investigating him for his leftist political views. Like many others in the movie industry, Wanamaker was blacklisted. No longer able to work in Hollywood, he decided to pursue a stage career in England. It would be years before his film career took off again.

When Wanamaker first arrived in London, he searched for the site of Shakespeare's playhouse. He was shocked to discover that the only acknowledgment of the original Globe was a plaque attached to the front of a brewery. In 1970, he began a long and difficult campaign to build a modern version of the theater. There were many ups and downs along the way, and sometimes it seemed as if the new Globe would never get built. But Wanamaker was a determined man, and by 1993, after 23 years of fund-raising, he had squeezed enough money ($20.5 million) from corporations and individual donors to start construction. First, however, he and his building team had to struggle to come up with the right design.

Few details about the original theater had survived, but the

Teach

Big Idea 1

The Power of Love Ask: What might have motivated Sam Wanamaker to spend more than twenty years on this project? *(His love of theater and history)*

Cultural Note ☆

Sam Wanamaker

Wanamaker's parents came to the United States in 1905 from Russia. His early encounters with anti-Semitic persecution prompted him to consider a career as a boxer, but he settled instead on law and later went on to pursue his true passion, acting, at Chicago's Goodman Theatre School. His distinguished career has also included television and movie acting.

English Learners

DIFFERENTIATED INSTRUCTION

Intermediate Help English language learners understand the features of the magazine article. Draw their attention to the title. **Ask:** What does the word *encore* mean? *(a repeat performance)* Explain that the Globe is an encore because it is modeled after Shakespeare's original globe. Have students read the headings and first sentence in each section. Then, have them predict the section's topic. Read the article aloud, pausing after each section to check students' predictions.

TIME

Teach

Big Idea 1

The Power of Love **Ask:** Why do you think Shakespeare's works have stood the test of time? *(Students may note his eloquent language and his timeless, powerful themes.)* Is it possible for people to love something like the Globe Theatre? *(Students may say that if someone's time, energy, and life are put into a place, they may grow to love it. Others may say that most people do not love something inanimate such as a building.)*

Cultural History ☆

Today's Globe Since the Globe Theatre is open air, plays are performed there only from May to September. The theater also stages modern dramas and works by other Elizabethan playwrights.

team found designs for two other theaters, the Rose and the Fortune, that had stood near the old Globe. Since both theaters were built by the same master carpenter who constructed the Globe, the building team relied on those designs to guide them. But many of the most basic questions remained unanswered. For example, no one could agree on how many sides the polygon structure should have. In 1992, a group of experts met to settle the controversy. The scholars voted—14 to 6—for 20 sides.

Workmen used traditional building methods and materials. "I am proud that the general way we constructed the whole structure is entirely consistent with the practices of 1595," says Peter McCurdy, the meticulous master carpenter who directed the construction project. Still, some compromises had to be made. For example, goat hair had to be used to give body to the plaster because no cow hair of the proper—and authentic—length could be found.

FOUNDER Wanamaker, who died in 1993, views a design model in 1986. ★

Close to the Action 1

Wanamaker died in 1993, too soon to see the completion of his grand project. He would not have been surprised that the Globe's productions reveal a style of Shakespearean performances different from what is offered in the darkened theaters of the modern world. For one thing, performances take place during the day, in natural light. Sometimes women's roles are played by men, as they were in Shakespeare's day. And because the 900 seats curve around the stage in tiered galleries, everyone in the audience sees the action from a different angle. Some views are blocked by pillars, but the sense of intimacy makes up for any obstructions. No audience member is farther than 50 feet from the stage. In fact, some of the hundreds of people who stand in the central yard, where the "groundlings" stood in Shakespeare's day, even rest their arms on the edge of the stage. They may have to stand, but many of these modern-day groundlings say they have the best "seats" in the house. They're close to the stage, and the atmosphere in the yard is casual and fun.

"I was so close I felt I was part of the action," says Katie Marshall, a U.S. college student who stood during a performance of *The Winter's*

Writing Practice

Connect Ideas Point out the description of the Globe on page 746. Draw students' attention to the photograph on this page. **Ask:** What was the Globe like? *(Students may say that the Globe had 900 seats curved around the stage in tiered galleries, which you can clearly see in the picture. This design ensured that no audience member was more than 50 feet from the stage. Hundreds of people also stood in the central yard to watch the performance.)*

Have students write a description of the Globe based on the text and their photograph.

TIME

Drawing of William Shakespeare

Tale. As in Elizabethan times, audience members tend to be vocal, and some even join in the proceedings. Mentions of the French are often hissed, and when a French officer in *Henry V* proclaimed that "England shall couch down in fear and yield," an English patriot in the audience shouted back, "Never!"

Still, performances of Shakespeare's plays at the Globe are not for everyone. Purists are annoyed by the distractions during performances: small children who sometimes roam around in the central yard, vendors who circulate selling drinks and sandwiches, and elderly tourists defeated by the hard seats who flee in the middle of an act. "This is nothing like the film [starring Kenneth Branagh]," complained a disappointed woman from New York City after viewing a performance of *Henry V.* But that, of course, is exactly the point. Seeing Shakespeare's works at the Globe is not like seeing them anywhere else in the world.

—Updated 2005, from TIME, June 23, 1997

Respond and Think Critically

Respond and Interpret

1. Write a brief summary of the main ideas in this article before you answer the following questions. For help with writing a summary, see page 421.
2. Would you like to visit the Globe Theatre? Why or why not?
3. (a)What is the purpose of the opening lines of *Henry V*? (b)Why do you think Shakespeare used this device?
4. (a)What makes the performances in the modern Globe Theatre similar to those in Shakespeare's day? (b)Do you think the Globe audiences are disrespectful to the actors on stage? Why or why not?

Analyze and Evaluate

5. Consider the article's organization. What details does the writer use to maintain the reader's interest?
6. (a)What is Hillenbrand's opinion of his subject? (b)How does his opinion influence his tone?
7. Is this article an example of an informative essay or a persuasive essay? Explain.

Connect

8. Recall the ball scene from *Romeo and Juliet,* Act 1, Scene 5. How would you stage this scene at the Globe Theatre?

Assess

1. Students' summaries should reflect the main idea of the selection.
2. Students should explain their answers.
3. (a) The purpose is to tell the audience that an imaginative work is going to take place. (b) Shakespeare used this device to suggest how the audience should view the play.
4. (a) Performances take place in the daytime; some audience members stand near the stage; male actors sometimes play female roles; there are vendors; the audience tends to be boisterous. (b) Students should explain their answers. Some may feel that the theater encourages boisterous behavior. Others may feel that audiences should always be quiet when watching a theatrical performance.
5. Hillenbrand begins with a comment on *Henry V*. He then tells an anecdote about a cannon destroying the original theater and the story of Wanamaker's blacklisting. To maintain interest, he mentions the plaque on the brewery where the original theater stood, describes details about the workmanship, and includes quotes.
6. (a) He is enthusiastic about Shakespeare and the story of the Globe. (b) His tone is engaging because he is excited about his subject.
7. Students may suggest that the article seems more persuasive than informative. However, the primary purpose is to be informative. While statements such as "seeing Shakespeare's works at the Globe is not like seeing it anywhere else in the world" reflect the bias of the author, the article's main purpose is to provide a history of the project.
8. Accept reasonable answers.

Focus

Use Correct Verb Tenses

Write this sentence on the board: The Capulets and Montagues have fighted each other for a long time.

Discuss what makes this sentence incorrect. Remind students that incorrect verb tense is a common mistake that can adversely affect their writing.

Teach

Use Verbs Ask students to explain how to use verbs to show time. Review rules for forming the simple tenses, and have students list the tenses of several irregular verbs. Also remind students that when two or more verbs in a sentence describe events that occur at the same time, the verbs must be parallel.

Assess

1. A feud had gone on for a long time.
2. One night, Capulet gave a ball.
3. Romeo saw Juliet there.
4. Soon, she had stolen his heart.

For additional grammar practice, see Unit 4 Teaching Resources Book, p. 98.

Learning Objectives

In this workshop, you will focus on the following objective:

Grammar: Understanding how to correct verb tense.

Grammar Workshop

Verb Tense

Literature Connection The perfection of Shakespeare's line below—

> *"For I ne'er saw true beauty till this night."*
>
> —William Shakespeare, from *Romeo and Juliet*

—would be lost if it were *For I never seen true beauty till this night.* The poet used the past tense (*saw*) of the verb *see,* not the incorrect past participle (*seen*).

Check your sentences for the correct verb forms and tenses.

Problem 1 An incorrect form of an irregular verb is used.

Romeo and Juliet <u>falled</u> deeply in love.

Solution Remember that the past tense and the past participle of some verbs are formed irregularly.

Romeo and Juliet <u>fell</u> deeply in love.

Problem 2 The past tense is used when the past participle is needed.

What light has <u>broke</u> through the window?

Solution Use the past participle, not the past tense, in a sentence with any form of the helping, or auxiliary, verbs *have* or *be.*

What light has <u>broken</u> through the window?

Problem 3 The past participle is used incorrectly.

Romeo <u>taken</u> a potion.

Solution A Add a helping or auxiliary verb.

Romeo <u>had taken</u> a potion.

Solution B Replace the past participle with the past tense of the verb.

Romeo <u>took</u> a potion.

Linking Verbs

A **linking verb** connects a subject to its complement by expressing a relationship between the two. The chief linking verbs are *be, become, seem,* and *appear.*

She seems very happy today.

Tip

Auxiliary verbs (*have, shall, be, will, may, can, should, do,* and *must*) join participles to form tenses and moods.

Ian should study for his vocabulary test.

Language Handbook

For more about verb tense, see Language Handbook, pp. R50–R51.

Revise Rewrite each sentence, correcting the underlined verb.

1. A feud had <u>went</u> on for a long time.
2. One night, Capulet <u>gived</u> a ball.
3. Romeo <u>seen</u> Juliet there.
4. Soon, she had <u>stole</u> his heart.

LOG ON Literature Online

Grammar For more grammar practice, go to glencoe.com and enter QuickPass code GL49787u4.

Grammar Practice

Sequence of Tenses Discuss the sequence of tenses: Juliet <u>woke</u>, but Romeo <u>had</u> already <u>killed</u> himself. *(The action in the second clause occurred **before** the action in the first clause, so its verb is in the **past perfect** tense.)*

When the Capulets <u>saw</u> Juliet, they <u>wept</u>. *(The actions are simultaneous; both verbs are in the **simple past**.)* Have students correct the following:

- Juliet *(had)* already threatened to kill herself when the Friar suggested the potion.
- Because Romeo *(had)* killed Tybalt, he had been *(was)* banished.
- Tybalt still wanted to fight after Benvolio *(had)* asked for peace.

Comparing Literature

Across Genres

Learning Objectives

For pages 749–754

In studying these texts, you will focus on the following objectives:

Literary Study:
Comparing themes.
Comparing genres.

Compare Literature About Love

Literature of every age and culture abounds with love stories. Throughout the centuries, works of poetry and prose describe the happiness, heartache, worry, and delight of love. The following works explore the many sides of love, an all-consuming passion that has the power to depress and the power to elate.

COMPARE THE **Big Idea** The Power of Love

Love is unpredictable. It can come upon us suddenly, and it can change our lives in ways we never anticipated. As you read, ask yourself, What does each author featured here suggest about love's power?

COMPARE Theme

The **theme** of a literary work is its central insight or message. Each of these selections expresses an insight about the dark or difficult side of love. As you read, ask yourself, What is the theme of each selection?

COMPARE Ideas

When reading a literary work, you may make inferences about the ideas of the author. As you read, ask yourself, What can I infer about the ideas of William Shakespeare, Amy Lowell, Robert Graves, and Pär Lagerkvist?

LOG ON **Literature Online**

Author Search For more about the authors, go to glencoe.com and enter QuickPass code GL49787u4.

Comparing Literature

Across Genres

Focus

Bellringer Options

Daily Language Practice Transparency 75

Or display images of loving couples of different ages and from a variety of cultures.

Ask: What do you think these people are feeling? How do people generally show that they are in love? What effects can lost love have on a person?

Connect to the Reading Selections

Allow students to share responses to the opening statements about love. Then have students discuss what they already know about William Shakespeare, Amy Lowell, Robert Graves, and Pär Lagerkvist.

Selection Skills

Comparing Literature

Literary Elements
- Compare Theme (SE pp. 749, 754)

Listening/Speaking/Viewing Skills
- Discussion Starter (SE p. 751)

Reading Skills
- Compare Ideas (SE pp. 749, 754)
- Compare and Contrast (TE p. 754)

Writing Skills/Grammar
- Quickwrite (SE pp. 750, 753)
- Compare-and-Contrast Essay (SE p. 754)
- Create an Impression (TE p. 750)

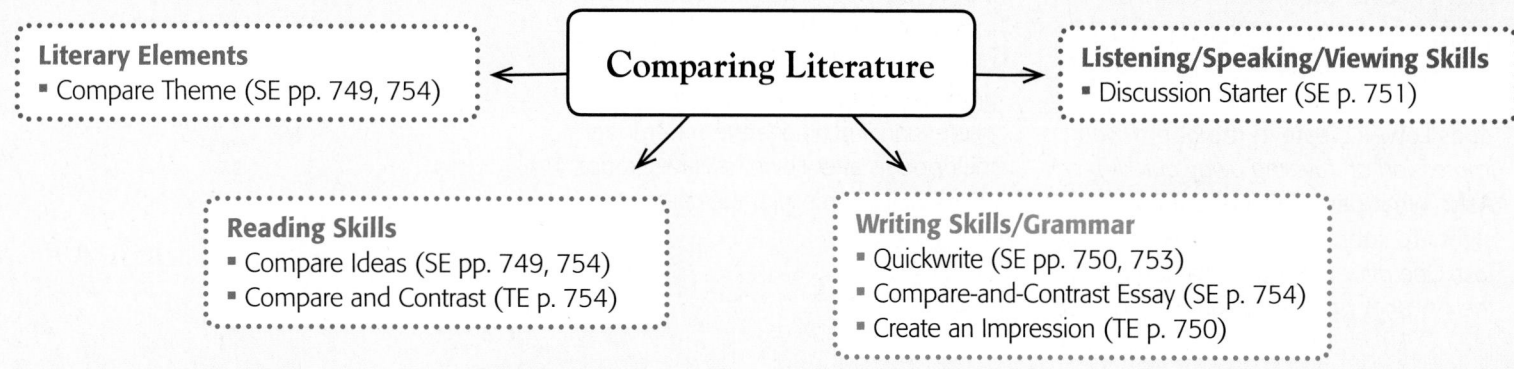

Focus

Summary

This poem is about the speaker's sadness over parting with someone he or she loves.

Teach

Quickwrite

Students may say that the drum and the shout appeal to hearing, the stars and the lamps appeal to sight, and wedging and wounding appeal to touch.

Comparing Literature

Build Background

Amy Lowell was a controversial, uncompromising woman, and one of the most important poets of the Imagist movement. The Imagists were a group of American poets in the early twentieth century whose goal was to produce poems that create vivid pictures in the reader's mind. Imagist poetry uses straightforward, everyday language and makes a radical break with traditional poetic rhythms. Lowell is known for both her literary contributions and her promotion of Imagism.

East 72nd Street Snow, 1992. Max Furguson. Oil on canvas. Private collection.

The Taxi

Amy Lowell

When I go away from you
The world beats dead
Like a slackened drum.
I call out for you against the jutted stars
And shout into the ridges of the wind.
Streets coming fast,
One after the other,
Wedge you away from me,
And the lamps of the city prick my eyes
So that I can no longer see your face.
Why should I leave you,
To wound myself upon the sharp edges of the night?

Quickwrite

What senses does Lowell appeal to in this poem? Write a paragraph describing details that appeal to your senses of sight, sound, smell, taste, and/or touch.

Writing Practice

SPIRAL REVIEW **Create an Impression** Ask students to note the impression Lowell creates in the poem as you read it aloud. **Ask:** What impression does Lowell create in the poem? *(an impression of traveling away quickly)* **Ask:** What part of the poem appeals to sight? To sound? *(sight: "Streets coming fast/One after the other" "the lamps of the city prick my eyes" sound: "slackened drum" "call out")* Encourage students to look for parts of the poem that appeal to other senses. Have students work in small groups to write a poem that creates an impression. Encourage them to model their poems after Lowell's. Have groups share their poems with the class.

Build Background

Robert Graves was fifteen when he decided to become a poet. In Graves's life, as well as in his poetry, romantic love was of vital importance. He regarded the women he loved as muses who inspired him. This poem is about two people who believe that their love will last until death.

Counting the Beats

Robert Graves

1

You, love, and I,
(He whispers) you and I,
And if no more than only you and I
What care you or I?

Counting the beats,
Counting the slow heart beats,
The bleeding to death of time in slow heart beats,
Wakeful they lie.

Cloudless day,
Night, and a cloudless day,
Yet the huge storm will burst upon their heads one day
From a bitter sky.

Where shall we be,
(She whispers) where shall we be,
When death strikes home, O where then shall we be
Who were you and I?

Not there but here,
(He whispers) only here,
As we are, here, together, now and here,
Always you and I.

Counting the beats,
Counting the slow heart beats,
The bleeding to death of time in slow heart beats,
Wakeful they lie.

Discussion Starter

Robert Graves once said that he wrote about "the practical impossibility, transcended only by a belief in miracle, of absolute love between man and woman." Discuss how this quotation applies to "Counting the Beats."

Focus

Summary

This poem is about two people who believe their love can be ended only by death.

Teach

Literary Element 1

Mood Have students read the first two stanzas and describe the mood. **Ask:** Which words and connotations help build this feeling? *(The man's whisper and the slow heartbeats build a mood of intimacy; the couple's wakefulness and the comparison of heartbeats as time "bleeding to death" tinge it with dread.)*

Discussion Starter

Students should support their points with evidence from the selection. Remind students to be respectful to one another during their discussions.

Approaching Level

DIFFERENTIATED INSTRUCTION

Established Encourage less proficient readers to read through the poem several times. First have them read the poem silently. Then have students take turns reading aloud to a partner. **Ask:** What does the punctuation tell you? *(when to pause)* Then point out the repetition of words at the end of each line and at the end of each stanza. Read the poem aloud to students. Tell them to think about the subject of the poem. **Ask:** What does the rhythm of the poem remind you of? *(a beating heart)*

Focus

Summary

This fable is about a prince who conquers a kingdom to win the love of a beautiful princess. The chancellor of the kingdom informs the prince, much to the prince's dismay, that he has not only won the princess but also the responsibilities of king.

Teach

Big Idea 1

The Power of Love

Ask: How does the prince prove his love for the princess? *(He fights bravely and risks his life.)* Why would the prince suffer for his love? *(His desire for the princess is so strong that he would endure any trial to win her love.)*

Readability Scores

Dale-Chall: 7.0
DRP: 54
Lexile: 910

Comparing Literature

Build Background

Swedish-born Pär Lagerkvist may be best remembered as one of the creators of Swedish Expressionism, which emphasized the use of experimental styles of writing. The works of Expressionists, whether in painting, drama, or poetry, frequently contain dark and terrifying images that evoke a dreamlike state. Lagerkvist said that as a writer, he was interested in "the enigma of our life which makes human destiny at once so great and so hard."

Pär Lagerkvist
Translated by Alan Blair

Once upon a time there was a prince, who went out to fight in order to win the princess whose beauty was greater than all others' and whom he loved above everything. He dared his life, he battled his way step by step through the country, ravaging it; nothing could stop him. **1**

He bled from his wounds but merely cast himself from one fight to the next, the most valiant nobleman to be seen and with a shield as pure as his own young features. At last he stood outside the city where the princess lived in her royal castle. It could not hold out against him and

Vocabulary Practice

SPIRAL REVIEW **Words with Multiple Meanings** Tell students that many words in the fable have more than one meaning. Have students jot down words with more than one meaning as they read. When they finish, write these words on the board and discuss their meaning. Have students use the word in a new sentence, so that its definition is the same as in the story. Model this process.

Write: "He bled from his wounds but merely cast himself from one fight to the next . . ."

The tall trees cast a long shadow when the sun is overhead.

Guide students to use a dictionary when needed.

had to beg for mercy. The gates were thrown open; he rode in as conqueror.

When the princess saw how proud and handsome he was and thought of how he had dared his life for her sake, she could not withstand his power but gave him her hand. He knelt and covered it with ardent kisses. "Look, my bride, now I have won you!" he exclaimed, radiant with happiness. "Look, everything I have fought for, now I have won it!"

And he commanded that their wedding should take place this same day. The whole city decked itself out for the festival and the wedding was celebrated with rejoicing, pomp, and splendor.

When in the evening he went to enter the princess's bedchamber, he was met outside by the aged chancellor, a venerable man. Bowing his snow-white head, he tendered the keys of the kingdom and the crown of gold and precious stones to the young conqueror.

"Lord, here are the keys of the kingdom which open the treasuries where everything that now belongs to you is kept."

The prince frowned.

"What is that you say, old man? I do not want your keys. I have not fought for sordid gain. I have fought merely to win her whom I love, to win that which for me is the only costly thing on earth."

The old man replied, "This, too, you have won, lord. And you cannot set it aside. Now you must administer and look after it."

"Do you not understand what I say? Do you not understand that one can fight, can conquer, without asking any reward other than one's happiness—not fame and gold, not land and power on earth? Well, then, I have conquered but ask for nothing, only to live happily with what, for me, is the only thing of value in life."

"Yes, lord, you have conquered. You have fought your way forward as the bravest of the brave, you have shrunk from nothing, the land lies ravaged where you have passed by. You have won your happiness. But, lord, others have been robbed of theirs. You have conquered, and therefore everything now belongs to you. It is a big land, fertile and impoverished, mighty and laid waste, full of riches and need, full of joy and sorrow, and all is now yours. For he who has won the princess and happiness, to him also belongs this land where she was born; he shall govern and cherish it."

The prince stood there glowering and fingering the hilt of his sword uneasily.

"I am the prince of happiness, nothing else!" he burst out. "Don't want to be anything else. If you get in my way, then I have my trusty sword."

But the old man put out his hand soothingly and the young man's arm sank. He looked at him searchingly, with a wise man's calm. 2

"Lord, you are no longer a prince," he said gently. "You are a king."

And lifting the crown with his aged hands, he put it on the other's head.

When the young ruler felt it on his brow he stood silent and moved, more erect than before. And gravely, with his head crowned for power on earth, he went in to his beloved to share her bed.

Quickwrite

What difficulties does the prince suffer in his effort to reach the princess? What surprises occur when he reaches his destination? How does the mood, or feeling, of the story shift as the story progresses? Write a paragraph in which you address these questions.

Comparing Literature

Teach

Big Idea 2

The Power of Love **Ask:** Why is the prince angry about having the responsibility of king? *(His desire was only for love, not responsibility.)* Why does the prince accept the responsibility of king in the end? *(Out of love for the princess)*

ADVANCED Advanced students may choose to write an alternate ending to the story. Have students read their revised ending to the class. **Ask:** Which ending do you think is more effective, Lagerkvist's or yours? *(Responses will vary.)*

Quickwrite

Students should mention that the prince has to fight battles and has to lay siege to a castle. Students may be surprised that the prince at first refuses the land's riches. The mood shifts as the prince realizes that he is responsible for the land and not just the princess.

Approaching Level

DIFFERENTIATED INSTRUCTION

Emerging Help students understand the irony of the prince's situation. Explain that he has entered into many battles to get to the royal castle and win over the princess. Remind students that the princess is proud of his actions and agrees to marry him. **Ask:** How does the prince feel then? *(Students will likely say that he is very happy.)* **Ask:** What upsets him after this? *(Students may say that he learned now that he has married the princess he must rule the kingdom and he does not want to do this. He wants only to be married to the princess.)*

Wrap-Up: Comparing Literature

Across Genres

Assess

Writing

Remind students to support their arguments with details from the selections.

Group Activity

Student discussions should focus on the nature of the problems or hardships love poses in each of the selections as well as on the outcome of the various complications that ensue.

Speaking and Listening

Students' charts should include examples of imagery, dialogue, and plot events that reveal the authors' beliefs about love. Students' oral reports should explain which aspects of love are presented in each selection.

For additional selection assessment, see Assessment Resources, pp. 175–176.

Wrap-Up: Comparing Literature

Across Genres

- ***The Tragedy of Romeo and Juliet*** by William Shakespeare
- ***The Taxi*** by Amy Lowell
- ***Counting the Beats*** by Robert Graves
- ***The Princess and All the Kingdom*** by Pär Lagerkvist

COMPARE THE **Big Idea** The Power of Love

Writing How does love affect a person? In "The Taxi" and "Counting the Beats," the speakers are dramatically affected by love. In *Romeo and Juliet* and "The Princess and All the Kingdom," the main characters are strongly influenced by love. Write a short-response essay comparing and contrasting the way these four literary works represent love's power over a person.

Red Heart. Joe Baker.

COMPARE Theme

Group Activity With a group of classmates, answer the following questions as you compare and contrast the messages about love, responsibility, and parting that these works convey.

1. What is similar about the themes of the four works?
2. How do the themes differ?
3. In your opinion, which work conveys its theme or themes most effectively? Why do you think so?

COMPARE Ideas

Speaking and Listening What do Shakespeare, Lowell, Graves, and Lagerkvist believe about love's role in a person's life? How can you tell? With a partner, go back through the selections and look for details that may reveal each author's ideas about love. Discuss which aspects of love each author seems to consider especially important, taking notes about your ideas. Then, prepare a formal report to share your ideas with the class.

LOG ON **Literature** Online

Selection Resources For Selection Quizzes, eFlashcards, and Reading-Writing Connection activities, go to glencoe.com and enter QuickPass code GL49787u4.

Reading Practice

Compare and Contrast Help students begin the Writing activity on this page. Break students into small groups. Have them discuss and write a response to each of these questions:

- How does love affect the speaker in "The Taxi"? In "Counting the Beats"? *(Students may say that the speaker in "The Taxi" is hurt because she is moving away from the person she loves; the speaker in "Counting the Beats" seems to enjoy being in love but worries what will happen when either he or his love dies.)*
- What lesson does the prince in the fable learn about love? *(that it comes with responsibilities)*

Awkward Encounters

Midsummer's Dream, 1986. Charles Bell.

View the Art As a photorealist, Charles Bell used fine details to make the objects in his paintings look real, as if the painting were a photograph. Consider the title of this painting. How does the photorealist technique add to or take away from the subject of the painting? ★

BIG IDEA

Being asked a question you do not know the answer to, slipping and falling in front of a group of friends, having to lead your class in a song—any of these moments may make you feel awkward. The plays in Part 2 present characters who face awkward moments. As you read these selections, ask yourself, How would I handle these awkward moments?

UNIT FOUR

PART 2

Analyze and Extend

Big Idea

Awkward Encounters

Ask: How do you react in an awkward situation? Discuss various strategies. Do students walk away, try to be diplomatic, or ignore the situation? Have them point out any correlations between how they react and how the characters in the painting are reacting.

APPROACHING Ask approaching-level students to work in groups to compose a list of tips for dealing with an awkward situation. *(Lists should address situations students may encounter in daily life, as well as possible solutions for resolving the situation.)*

View the Art ★

Answer: *Students may say the realism of the painting makes it seem less dream-like, but the subjects do seem dream-like.*

American photorealist Charles Bell (1935–1995) painted ordinary objects such as toys and gumball machines in exacting detail. Photorealism reacted against the fantastical elements of surrealism and Pop Art with paintings of mundane subjects that resembled photographic images.

English Learners

DIFFERENTIATED INSTRUCTION

Beginning/Early Intermediate English learners may have difficulty understanding the concept of an awkward encounter. Define the word *awkward* as "lacking ease, grace, harmony, or skill," and provide students with examples of how awkward conversation and body language can create an overall awkward encounter in a social setting. Ask students to offer examples of times when they have found themselves in awkward situations. **Ask:** Was this a positive or negative experience in the end? What did you learn from this situation?

For additional support for English Learners, see Unit 4 Teaching Resources Book, p. 101.

UNIT FOUR

PART 2

Focus

Bellringer Options

Daily Language Practice Transparency 77

Or **list** students' favorite movies on the board. Sort them by category into drama and comedy. Discuss what makes these movies special and memorable.

Teach

View the Art ★

Mikhail Larionov (1881–1964) and his wife, Natalya Gonchoarova, founded an artistic movement known as "Rayonism." Larionov was one of Russia's first artists to experiment with styles that would later become known as "abstract art." In 1914, Larionov and Gonchoarova moved to Paris, where they designed magnificent sets for the renowned Ballets Russes dance company, as well as for other productions.

Ask: What dramatic elements do you see in this set? *(Students may mention the distorted figures of the dancers and the fantastically large set elements, such as the trees and the sun.)*

Learning Objectives

For pages 755–757

In studying this text, you will focus on the following objectives:

Literary Study: Analyzing comedy and modern drama. Connecting to literature.

LITERARY FOCUS

Comedy and Modern Drama

What are the elements of comedy and modern drama?

Traditionally, drama is separated into two main categories: comedy and tragedy. **Tragedy** is drama in which the main character suffers a fall from good fortune. **Comedy,** on the other hand, is drama that deals with light and amusing subjects or with serious subjects in a light, familiar, or satirical manner. Traditional tragedies and comedies follow a set of prescribed rules. **Modern drama** can be either comedy or tragedy. However, these plays generally do not follow the rules of the traditional forms.

Stage design for the ballet *The Midnight Sun* by Rimski-Korsakov, from the opera *Snow Maiden,* 1915. Mikhali Larionov. Watercolor. Private collection. ★

Reading Practice

SPIRAL REVIEW **Understand Satire** Define *satire* as writing that uses humor or wit to ridicule the vices or follies of people and societies, often to bring about change or improvement. Then **write** on the board and explain the meanings of the words wit *(clever humor),* ridicule *(to mock or make fun of),* vice *(a moral defect or weakness),* and folly *(a foolish act or idea).* **Ask:** Where have you seen these elements of satire used to entertain an audience? *(Students may respond that these elements appear in drama, on television shows, in literature, and in interactions with peers.)*

Elements of Drama

Acts and Scenes Plays usually contain two or more acts, which are major divisions in the action. In some plays, acts are further divided into scenes. Usually, an act or scene change means that the characters and setting will change.

Dialogue Dialogue is the conversation between characters in a play or other literary work. Dialogue reveals the personalities, feelings, and thoughts of the characters. It also advances the plot.

Stage Directions A play's written instructions, or stage directions, explain how to perform the play, including how the characters should look, speak, move, and behave. Stage directions are also used to establish the time and place of the play, as well as the sets, costumes, lighting, props, and sound effects.

Lucille Fletcher's *The Hitchhiker* was written to be performed on the radio. Because the audience would only hear, and not see, the action of the play, she included directions for such things as sound effects and music in addition to the more usual directions for characters' tone of voice.

> SOUND. *Automobile wheels humming over concrete road.*
> MUSIC. *Something weird and shuddery.*
> **ADAMS.** [*Narrating.*] I am in an auto camp on Route Sixty-Six just west of Gallup, New Mexico. If I tell it, perhaps it will help me.
>
> —Lucille Fletcher, **from *The Hitchhiker***

Elements of Comedy

Comedy is a type of drama that deals with light and amusing subjects—or with serious subjects in a light or satirical manner. Comedies typically have happy endings, and they entertain audiences with verbal wit, physical humor, ridicule, or irony.

Irony Irony is a contrast between what appears to be and what really is. Playwrights use three types of irony as the basis for humor in a comedy:

- **Situational irony** exists when the outcome of the situation is the opposite of what is expected.
- **Dramatic irony** occurs when the audience knows something that the characters do not. While watching Eugène Ionesco's *The Leader,* the audience realizes there is nothing truly exceptional about the Leader, yet all of the characters onstage cheer for him.

> **ANNOUNCER.** Long live the leader! [*Wildly enthusiastic.*] Hurrah! Hurrah! He's changing his shirt. He disappears behind a red screen. He reappears! [*The applause intensifies.*] Bravo! Bravo!
>
> —Eugène Ionesco, **from *The Leader***

- **Verbal irony** occurs when a character says one thing and means another. Sarcasm, hyperbole, and understatement are forms of verbal irony.

> **SMÍRNOFF.** This is why I don't like women and hate talking to them. I'd rather light a campfire on a powder keg than talk to a woman.
>
> —Anton Chekhov, **from *The Bear***

Quickwrite

Define Comedy Write for two to three minutes finishing this statement: "For comedy to be funny, it should . . ." Support your opinion with examples from movies and plays you have seen.

LOG ON Literature Online

Literature and Reading For more about literary elements, go to glencoe.com and enter QuickPass code GL49787u4.

UNIT FOUR

PART 2

Teach

Reading Strategy

Identify Elements Invite volunteers to read the excerpts aloud. Ask students what stands out about each of the excerpts. Is there important information in the stage directions? Is the dialogue humorous? Instruct students to read the descriptions of the elements of comedy and drama. Discuss how focusing on these new elements improved their comprehension.

Quickwrite

Answers will vary. Make sure students support their responses.

Approaching Level

DIFFERENTIATED INSTRUCTION

Emerging Auditory learners may find it useful to think of tone in musical terms. Have students write the musical description that would accompany these storylines:

- A separated couple in love finally reunite *(happy, triumphant music)*
- An animal hides its babies from a predator *(fast, suspenseful music)*
- A pilot flies troops home from war *(patriotic music)*

Suggest that students think of the writer's words as his or her instrument for expressing attitudes and emotions and creating moods.

Before You Read

Focus

Bellringer Options

Literature Launchers: Pre-Reading Videos DVD: Unit 4

Daily Language Practice Transparency 78

Or have students brainstorm a list of promises people often make. **Write** their ideas on the board. Ask students to consider which of these promises are usually kept and which are generally broken.

Say: The drama you are about to read is about a woman who makes a promise she plans to keep for the rest of her life. As students read, have them predict if Popóva will keep her promise.

Before You Read

World Literature
Russia

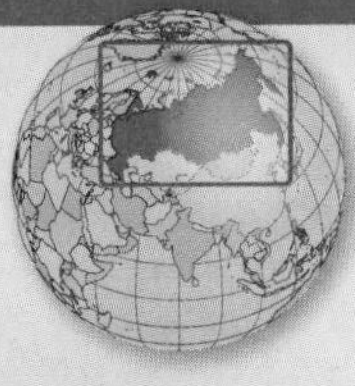

The Bear

Meet **Anton Chekhov**
(1860–1904)

In 1886 in Moscow, Russia, a young doctor and writer wrote, "All my hope is pinned to the future. I am only twenty-six. Perhaps I shall succeed in achieving something, though time flies fast." Little did that writer, Anton Chekhov, know that one day he would be considered the father of the modern short story and the modern drama.

A Russian Childhood Anton Pavlovich Chekhov was born in Taganrog, a Russian seaport near the Black Sea, in 1860. Chekhov had very few positive things to say about his childhood. He was particularly critical of his father, Pavel, who was a grocer. His mother, Yevgeniya, however, taught Chekhov how to read and write. She was an excellent storyteller and passed that gift on to her son. The Chekhov family faced many financial difficulties. In 1875, his father's store failed. The family left Taganrog, but Chekhov stayed behind to finish his schooling.

> *"It is time for writers, particularly artists, to confess that in this world you cannot make head or tail of anything."*
>
> —Anton Chekhov

Chekhov started writing as a way to earn money, not for artistic expression. While studying medicine at Moscow University, Chekhov published many short sketches, humorous stories, jokes, and trivia in popular magazines. After graduating from medical school in 1884, Chekhov continued to write. By 1886, he had become a well-known writer.

Gaining Momentum Between 1888 and 1893, Chekhov began writing longer narratives. He included contrasting themes, such as life and death. Many of his characters were challenged by isolation, missed opportunities, and class barriers. During this time, Chekhov also produced several one-act plays, such as *The Bear,* as well as full-length dramas.

The years between 1894 and 1904 proved to be the most artistically productive. Chekhov's short stories began to have more complex plots. He also wrote some of his more acclaimed plays during this period, including *The Three Sisters* and *The Cherry Orchard.*

Chekhov first noticed signs of tuberculosis in 1884. However, the disease went largely untreated, an irony given his medical background. He finally agreed to treatment in 1897, but, in 1904, he died of the disease.

LOG ON **Literature** Online

Author Search For more about Anton Chekhov, go to glencoe.com and enter QuickPass code GL49787u4.

Selection Skills

The Bear

Literary Elements
- Farce (SE pp. 759–771)
- Dialogue (SE p. 771)

Listening/Speaking/Viewing Skills
- Analyze Art (SE pp. 765, 768; TE p. 760)
- Acting (TE p. 770)

Reading Skills
- Analyze Cause-and-Effect Relationships (SE pp. 759–772)

Vocabulary Skills
- Antonyms (SE pp. 759, 772)
- Academic Vocabulary (SE p. 772)

Writing Skills/Grammar
- Apply Dialogue (SE p. 772)
- Write a Prediction (TE p. 760)

Literature and Reading Preview

Connect to the Drama

Have you ever promised yourself that you would act a certain way or do something specific? List several reasons you might have to make a promise to yourself.

Build Background

A mortgage is a loan from a bank that allows a person to buy a house or property on a payment plan. Instead of paying the full price at once, the person can make periodic payments until the loan is paid off. If the person cannot make the payments when they are due, however, the bank can foreclose on the loan, or require full payment immediately. If the person cannot pay the entire amount, the bank can take possession of the property and the person would lose not only the property but also all of the money he or she has paid until then.

Set Purposes for Reading

Big Idea Awkward Encounters

As you read *The Bear,* ask yourself, How do the characters' actions and reactions create awkward moments?

Literary Element Farce

Farce is a type of comedy that incorporates ridiculous situations, characters, or events. Most farce includes exaggerated speech and action. As you read, ask yourself, How does Chekhov use exaggeration to create humor?

Reading Strategy Analyze Cause-and-Effect Relationships

A cause is an event that makes something happen, and the effect is the result of the cause. You can see **cause-and-effect relationships** in a work of literature by identifying what leads to each event. As you read *The Bear,* ask yourself, Where can I find cause-and-effect relationships?

Tip: Take Notes As you read *The Bear,* take careful notes on the play's action. Use a series of cause-and-effect charts like the one below to record your thoughts.

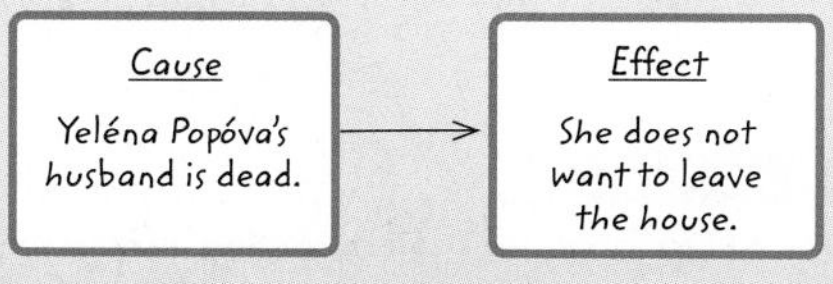

Learning Objectives

For pages 758–772

In studying this text, you will focus on the following objectives:

Literary Study: Analyzing farce.

Reading: Analyzing cause-and-effect relationships.

Writing: Applying dialogue to a scene.

Vocabulary

mourn (môrn) *v.* to feel or express grief or sorrow; p. 760 *She needed to mourn after experiencing such a great loss.*

logic (loj′ ik) *n.* a method of reasoning; p. 763 *To solve the problem, you must use logic.*

pretentious (pri ten′ shəs) *adj.* expressing exaggerated importance or worth; p. 766 *At first they thought she seemed pretentious, but later they realized she had just been nervous.*

monopoly (mə nop′ ə lē) *n.* exclusive possession or control; p. 766 *He has a monopoly on good restaurants in our town.*

Tip: Antonyms Antonyms are words with opposite meanings. Sometimes you can form a word's antonym by adding a prefix like *un-* or *non-* to the beginning of the word. For example, by adding the prefix *un-* to the vocabulary word *pretentious,* you can create its antonym, *unpretentious.*

Advanced Learners

DIFFERENTIATED INSTRUCTION

Russian Culture Have students research the Russian government, under the czars or communism. Ask them to focus on how the Russian government differs from the U.S. government. Have students share their findings in a class discussion comparing the governments. Suggest that students keep these differences in mind as they read *The Bear.* Tell students to consider how these differences might affect culture in Russia. Encourage interested students to study how Russian culture is evident in *The Bear.*

Before You Read

Focus

Summary

After the death of her husband, Yeléna Ivánovna Popóva vows to wear black and remain inside her house until she dies. When Smírnoff shows up to collect on a debt owed by Popóva's late husband, Popóva tells him she cannot pay until the day after tomorrow. The two argue until Smírnoff falls in love with Popóva.

For summaries in languages other than English, see Unit 4 Teaching Resources Book, pp. 102–107.

Interactive Read and Write

Other options for teaching this selection can be found in

- Interactive Read and Write for EL Students, pp. 207–226
- Interactive Read and Write for Approaching-Level Students, pp. 207–226
- Interactive Read and Write for On-Level Students, pp. 207–226

Vocabulary

Write with Vocabulary

Have students read the vocabulary words and their definitions. Then have them write a paragraph about a recent event in their lives. Students must use all of the vocabulary words from the list.

For additional vocabulary practice, see Unit 4 Teaching Resources Book, p. 110.

Teach

Literary Element 1

Farce Answer: *The drama will probably not be realistic since a person would not spend a whole year in the house. There will probably be other exaggerations.*

Big Idea 2

Awkward Encounters Ask: Why is the exchange between Popóva and Luká awkward? *(Luká is a servant and would not speak to his mistress this way.)* Ask students to find additional dialogue that creates an awkward encounter.

ADVANCED Have more proficient students write a short scene, with dialogue, that contains an awkward situation and characters reacting to it.

View the Art ★

British painter Edmund Blair Leighton (1853–1922) painted primarily historical people and scenes. At first, he focused on medieval scenes. Later, many of his paintings, such as *Olivia,* depicted elegant, upper-class women.

Ask: What qualities and details in the painting create a sense of richness? *(Students might note the ornate gold-colored background or the woman's dress.)*

For an audio recording of this selection, use Listening Library Audio CD-ROM.

Olivia. Edmund Blair Leighton. ★

The Bear

A Comic Sketch in One Act

Anton Chekhov

CHARACTERS

YELÉNA IVÁNOVNA POPÓVA: a widow with dimples and a large estate

GRIGÓRY STEPÁNOVICH SMÍRNOFF: landowner, in his thirties

LUKÁ: an elderly servant

The action takes place in Popóva's living room.

POPÓVA'S living room. POPÓVA, dressed completely in black, sits staring at a photograph. LUKÁ, her old servant, tries to talk sense to her.

LUKÁ. It's just not right, missus. You're letting yourself fall to pieces. Cook and the maid have gone berry picking, every living thing is out enjoying the sunshine, even your cat, now, he's out there trying to catch himself a bird, and here you sit, shut up in the house all day long, like some kind of nun. That's no fun. You listen to what I'm saying, now! It's been a whole year since you left the house!

POPÓVA. I shall never leave this house. Why should I? My life is over. He's dead and buried, and so am I, buried here within these four walls. We're both dead.

LUKÁ. I never heard the like! Your husband's dead. Well, God rest him, he's not 2
coming back. You **mourned** him good and proper; now it's time to move on. You can't sit here wearing black and crying for the rest of your life. I lost my old woman, too, a while back, I cried for a month, and that was that. No need to sit around for years singing hymns; she wasn't worth it. [*Sighs.*]

1 Farce *From Luká's comments, how realistic do you think this drama will be? Explain.*

Vocabulary

mourn (môrn) *v.* to feel or express grief or sorrow

Writing Practice

Write a Prediction Stop students at the end of page 761 and ask them to think about what they know about the characters so far. *(Students may say that Popóva is dramatic, Luká is encouraging, and Smírnoff is pushy.)* Then have students write a short summary of what they think will happen in the play based on what they know about the characters and what has happened so far. **Say:** Remember that this play contains elements of satire. *(Students' predictions will vary. Students may predict that Popóva will be tricked into leaving the house and enjoying her life again. Some may write that Popóva's hate for her husband will overcome her desire to show him what real love means.)*

You haven't seen your neighbors in months, you don't go out, and you tell us not to let anybody in. We're all living like spiders in the dark here, if you'll excuse the expression. My livery jacket's[1] got moth holes. Fine, if there was nobody around worth seeing, but the whole country's crawling with eligible young men. There's a regiment in the next town, all those good-looking officers, melt in your mouth, most of them, and they have a dance every Friday night, and the band gives a concert every afternoon. Oh, missus, take a look at yourself—you're still a juicy young thing, you're still beautiful, you can go out and enjoy life. But a beautiful face won't last forever, you know. You wait—ten years from now you're going to want to go swanning[2] after those officers, and it'll be too late.

POPÓVA. [*Firmly.*] I must ask you never to talk to me like this again! When my husband died, life lost all meaning for me. You know that. I may look like I'm alive, but I'm not. I swore I'd wear black and shut myself up here until the day I die, didn't I? And I will. He'll see how much I loved him. . . . Oh, I know he treated me badly—I don't have to tell you about it. He was mean and . . . and even unfaithful. But I intend to be faithful to the grave and show him *what* real love means.

LUKÁ. That's just a lot of talk. You'd do better to go out and take a walk, or have me hitch up Toby and go visit the neighbors.

POPÓVA. Oh! [*Bursts into hysterical tears.*]

LUKÁ. Missus! What is it? For God's sake, what's the matter?

POPÓVA. Toby! He used to love Toby so! He'd ride all over the neighborhood on him. What a horseman! Remember how grand he looked in the saddle? Oh, Toby, Toby! Go tell them he gets extra oats today.

LUKÁ. [*Sighs.*] Don't worry, I will.

[*The doorbell rings. And keeps ringing.*]

POPÓVA. [*Exasperated.*] Now who's that? Go tell whoever it is I am not at home! To anyone!

LUKÁ. Whatever you say, missus. [*Goes out.*]

POPÓVA. [*To the photograph.*] You see what real love means, Nicky? My love will last as long as I do, right to my last heartbeat. [*Laughs, almost crying.*] And I hope you're ashamed of yourself! You see what a good girl I am, what a faithful wife? I locked myself up here and will be faithful to you till the day I die, while you . . . I hope you're ashamed, you little pig. You were mean to me, you cheated on me, you left me alone for weeks at a time—

[*Enter* LUKÁ; *he's upset.*]

LUKÁ. Missus, there's someone wants to see you. Says it can't wait.

POPÓVA. Didn't you tell him that my husband is dead and that I see no one?

LUKÁ. I did, but he doesn't want to listen, says it's very important.

POPÓVA. And I said I see no one!

LUKÁ. That's what I told him, but he's . . . he's kind of a wild man—he started shouting and pushed his way into the house. He's in the dining room right now.

POPÓVA. All right, all right, tell him all right. Really! The nerve of some people!

[LUKÁ *goes out.*]

Why must people be so difficult? Why can't they just leave me alone? [*Sighs.*]

1. *Livery* is the feeding, stabling, and care of horses for pay. Here, Luká refers to the jacket he wears when he drives Popóva in a horse carriage.
2. Here, *swanning* means wandering aimlessly or idly.

Analyze Cause-and-Effect Relationships *What causes Popóva to imprison herself at home?* **3**

Teach

Reading Strategy 3

Analyze Cause-and-Effect Relationships **Answer:** *She wants to show she is more faithful than her late husband was during their marriage by remaining in a state of mourning.*

Approaching Level

DIFFERENTIATED INSTRUCTION

Emerging Approaching-level students may have difficulty understanding the concept of satire. Directing their attention to examples of satire in the text may enhance their comprehension. **Say:** Chekhov uses exaggeration when Popóva says that she will wear black and stay in the house until she dies. This is an example of satire because it is a silly, nonsensical idea. **Ask:** What other examples of satire do you see on pages 760 and 761? *(Students may recognize the folly in Popóva's desire to lock herself away from the world in order to teach her dead husband—who treated her badly—a lesson in true love.)*

Teach

Literary Element 1

Farce **Answer:** *His language is silly and exaggerated, which creates an atmosphere in which ridiculous things might be possible.*

Ask: Why is it ridiculous for Popóva to say she will join a nunnery? *(This is an extreme measure for her to take.)*

Big Idea 2

Awkward Encounters
Answer: *He has intruded upon her and won't take "No" for an answer.*

Ask: Why is this awkward? (It was customary at that time to greet a person with a handshake.)

Literary Element 3

Repetition Have two students read the dialogue in the first column between Popóva and Smírnoff. **Ask:** What effect does the repetition of the two characters' positions have on the audience? *(Students may feel it creates an absurd circular argument that stresses the farcical quality of the scene.)*

Oh, I may have to go join a nunnery[3] after all. [*Thinks.*] I wonder what kind of nun I'd make. . . .

[*Enter* SMÍRNOFF, *trailed by* LUKÁ.]

SMÍRNOFF. [*To* LUKÁ.] You dingbat, stop trying to talk me out of here! Idiot! [*Sees* POPÓVA; *suddenly very dignified.*] Ah, madam. Let me introduce myself: Grigóry Stepánovich Smírnoff, Field Artillery,[4] retired. I own a place over in the next county. Sorry to disturb you, but this is important—

POPÓVA. [*Doesn't offer him her hand.*] What can I do for you?

SMÍRNOFF. I had the pleasure of knowing your late husband, and as it happens, he left me two IOUs—the total comes to twelve hundred rubles.[5] Now, I have a mortgage payment due tomorrow, so I have to ask you, madam, to pay up. And I'm afraid I need the money today.

POPÓVA. Twelve hundred? What did my husband owe you the money for?

SMÍRNOFF. I sold him a couple of loads of oats.

3 POPÓVA. [*With a sigh, to* LUKÁ.] Now don't forget what I told you, Luká. You make sure Toby gets his extra oats.

[LUKÁ *goes out.*]

[*To* SMÍRNOFF.] If my husband owed you the money, then of course I'll pay it, but you'll have to excuse me—I don't have any cash on me today. My manager will be back from town the day after tomorrow, and he'll see that you get paid. But today, I'm afraid, I cannot help you. It's exactly seven months today that my husband died, and I'm in a sad mood. I'm in no condition to talk about money.

SMÍRNOFF. [*Annoyed.*] And I'm in a sad mood too, because if I don't meet my mortgage payment tomorrow, they'll foreclose on my property! I'll lose my shirt!

POPÓVA. You'll have your money the day after tomorrow.

SMÍRNOFF. I need the money today, not the day after tomorrow.

POPÓVA. Excuse me; I've already said I cannot pay you today.

SMÍRNOFF. And I've already said I can't wait till the day after tomorrow.

POPÓVA. What can I do? I don't *have* the money!

SMÍRNOFF. That means you won't pay me?

POPÓVA. It means *I can't* pay you!

SMÍRNOFF. I see. Is that your final word?

POPÓVA. That is my final word.

SMÍRNOFF. You've made up your mind?

POPÓVA. I've made up my mind.

SMÍRNOFF. Thank you very much. I won't forget this. [*Shrugs.*] Am I supposed to take all this lying down? On my way here, I met my accountant. "Why are you always so down in the dumps?" he asks me. Well, excuse me, he should know! I'm desperate for money! I got up at dawn yesterday and rode around to everyone I know who owes me money, and not a one of them came across! I ran in more circles than a hunting dog, spent the night in some godforsaken fleabag[6] hotel, and finally I get here, fifty miles from home, expect to get paid, and what do I get?

3. A *nunnery* is a convent of nuns.
4. *Artillery* refers to firearms or guns.
5. A *ruble* is Russian currency.

6. A *fleabag* is an inferior hotel or rooming house.

1 Farce *How does Smírnoff's language help define the play as farce?*

2 Awkward Encounters *Why does Popóva refuse to shake his hand?*

Vocabulary Practice

Word Study Ask students to look up the word *petticoat* in a dictionary. Then have students research on the Internet to find additional information about the origin and history of the garment. Each student should write a short essay explaining the meaning of the phrase "petticoat logic." *(Smirnoff uses the term "petticoat logic" to represent what he believes to be a woman's foolish way of thinking.)*

"A sad mood"! What kind of mood do you think that puts *me* in?

POPÓVA. I think I made myself perfectly clear: I'll pay you as soon as my manager gets back from town.

SMÍRNOFF. I came to see you, not your manager! What the hell—excuse my language—do I want with your manager?

POPÓVA. My dear sir, I will not have such language in my house, nor will I tolerate that tone of voice! I refuse to listen to any more of this! [*Storms out.*]

SMÍRNOFF. I don't believe this! "It's seven months today my husband died, and I'm in a sad mood. . . ." What's that got to do with me? I have to make a mortgage payment! Fine, your husband's dead, your manager's gone to town, you're in a mood or whatever—what do you expect me to do? Flap my wings and fly away from my creditors?[7] Run around banging my head into a brick wall? I go see Grúzdeff, he's not home. I go see Yarosévich, he hides. I go see Kurítsyn, we get into a fight; I nearly threw him out his own window. I go see Mazútov, he's sick. And now this one has "a sad mood." Not a one of them paid me! What a bunch of deadbeats![8] And it's all because I'm such a soft touch, I'm a sucker for a hard-luck story! I'm too nice for my own good! Well, it's time to get a little tough. Nobody's going to fool around with me like this! I'm not moving; I'm staying put until she pays up! Oh, boy, am I mad! Look at me—I'm quivering mad! Mad through and through! Mad enough to get nasty! [*Shouts.*] Hey, you!

[*Enter* LUKÁ.]

LUKÁ. What do you want?

SMÍRNOFF. A glass of water. Or better yet, a beer.

[*LUKÁ goes out.*]

What kind of **logic** is that? Here's a man so desperate for money he's ready to hang himself, and she can't pay him because—excuse me very much—she's "in no condition to talk about money." Talk about petticoat logic! This is why I don't like women and hate talking to them. I'd rather light a campfire on a powder keg[9] than talk to a woman. Makes my skin crawl, they make me so mad! All I have to do is see one of those romantic creatures coming, my leg muscles start cramping up. I want to start shouting for help.

[*Enter* LUKÁ.]

LUKÁ. [*Brings* SMÍRNOFF *a glass of water.*] The missus is sick; she says she can't see anybody!

SMÍRNOFF. Get out of here!

[*LUKÁ goes out.*]

She's sick and she can't see anybody! That's fine; she doesn't have to see me. I'll just stay right here until I get my money, that's all. She stays sick for a week, I stay here for a week. She's sick for a year, I stay here for a year. I want my money, lady! Your black dress and your dimples don't impress me. I've seen plenty of dimples before! [*Goes to the window and shouts.*] Hey, Semyón, unhitch the horses! We're not leaving just yet! I'm staying right here! Tell them in the stable to give my horses some oats! And watch it, you nitwit—

7. *Creditors* are people to whom money is owed.
8. A *deadbeat* is someone who does not pay his or her debts.

9. A *powder keg* is a small, usually metal, cask for holding gunpowder or blasting powder.

4 Analyze Cause-and-Effect Relationships *Why does Popóva's explanation provoke Smírnoff?*

Farce *Is the play humorous at this point? Why or why not?* **5**

Vocabulary

logic (loj′ik) *n.* a method of reasoning

Teach

Reading Strategy 4

Analyze Cause-and-Effect Relationships Answer: *He thinks her reasoning is poor and that she does not understand his situation and is self-absorbed.*

APPROACHING For approaching-level students, **ask:** Why can't Popóva pay Smírnoff? *(Her manager is out of town, and she has no money.)*

Literary Element 5

Farce Answer: *Some students will find the situation comical, based on the language and Smírnoff's exaggerated reaction. Others may say the situation is frightening.*

Approaching Level

DIFFERENTIATED INSTRUCTION

Established Writers often create characters who are unable to handle situations in a rational or logical manner, which can add to the humor or drama of a work. Here, Smírnoff shows up without warning to tell Popóva about her husband's debt and then becomes uncontrollably angry when she cannot pay it at once. Ask students to discuss how they might have handled the situation differently. *(Students might say they would have tried to contact Popóva ahead of time to make sure she had the money when they got there, or they would have been more sympathetic to Popóva's grief.)* **Ask:** How would the play be different if Smírnoff handled this situation logically? *(The play would not be farcical because Smírnoff's reaction would not be exaggerated and would not cause a humorous situation to unfold.)*

Teach

Reading Strategy 1

Analyze Cause-and-Effect Relationships **Answer:**

Smírnoff notices his rough appearance. He needs a shave, his hair is uncombed, and he has dirt on his boots.

ENGLISH LEARNERS For English learners, **say:** We know that Smírnoff looks this way because he describes himself in a soliloquy. What visual clues would an audience watching the play have? Have students describe how the scene might appear. *(An audience would be able to see his dirty clothes and rough mannerisms.)*

you've got the trace horse[10] tangled again! You just wait till I get . . . oh, forget it. [*Moves away from the window.*] What a mess. Hottest day of the year, nobody wants to pay me, couldn't sleep the whole night, and now I've got to deal with some wacky widow and her moods. It's enough to give a man a headache. I need a drink, that's what I need. [*Yells.*] Hey, you!

[*Enter* LUKÁ.]

LUKÁ. What do you want?

SMÍRNOFF. A shot of vodka!

[LUKÁ *goes out;* SMÍRNOFF *falls into a chair and looks himself over.*]

Oof, I'm a mess. Dirt, mud on my boots, I need a shave, my hair needs combing, straw sticking out of my pockets. The lady must have thought I was out to rob her. [*Yawns.*] Not too polite, I guess, showing up like this, but what the hell . . . I'm not a guest, I'm a bill collector; nobody says I have to dress right. . . .

[*Enter* LUKÁ; *he gives* SMÍRNOFF *a glass of vodka.*]

LUKÁ. You take too many liberties, you know that . . . ?

SMÍRNOFF. [*Angry.*] What?

LUKÁ. Oh, nothing. I just . . . Nothing.

SMÍRNOFF. Who do you think you're talking to? Just shut up, will you?

LUKÁ. [*Aside, as he goes out.*] How're we going to get rid of him. . . ?

SMÍRNOFF. Oh, I'm mad! I am so mad! Mad enough to blow up the world! Mad enough to get nasty! [*Shouts.*] Hey, you!

[*Enter* POPÓVA.]

POPÓVA. [*Not looking at him.*] My dear sir, I have lived so long in retirement I have grown unused to the human voice. I cannot stand shouting. I must earnestly beg you to respect my solitude.[11]

SMÍRNOFF. Pay me my money and I'll go.

POPÓVA. I have told you in no uncertain terms that I have no money here at the moment and you will have to wait until the day after tomorrow.

SMÍRNOFF. And I also told you in no uncertain terms that I need the money today, not the day after tomorrow. If you don't pay me today, I might as well hang myself by the day after tomorrow.

POPÓVA. But what can I do, since I don't have the money?

SMÍRNOFF. You mean you're not going to pay me? Is that what you mean?

POPÓVA. I can't!

SMÍRNOFF. In that case, I stay right here until I get it. [*Sits down.*] You're going to pay me the day after tomorrow? Fine. I'll be sitting right here! [*Jumps up.*] Look, don't you believe I have a mortgage payment due tomorrow? You think I'm joking?

POPÓVA. I asked you not to shout! You're not in a stable.

SMÍRNOFF. I didn't ask you about a stable! What I asked you was, Don't you believe I have a mortgage payment due tomorrow?

POPÓVA. You haven't the faintest idea of how to behave in a lady's presence.

SMÍRNOFF. I do so know how to behave in a lady's presence!

POPÓVA. No, you do not! You are ill-mannered and vulgar![12] No gentleman would speak like this in front of a lady!

10. A *trace horse* is a horse that is harnessed for pulling a load or a wagon.

11. *Solitude* refers to being alone.

12. *Vulgar* means "lacking in cultivation, perception, or taste."

1 Analyze Cause-and-Effect Relationships *Why does Smírnoff think Popóva might have suspected he was a robber?*

Reading Practice

PARTNERS SPIRAL REVIEW **Analyze Drama** Have students pair off and read the exchange between Popóva and Smírnoff on pages 764 and 765. Point out the elements of ridicule in this exchange *(Smírnoff mocks Popóva by speaking in a French accent; he mimics her insults; Popóva mocks his statements about men being faithful and true).* Then ask students to discuss why the focus of the argument changes from money to gender differences. *(Students may recognize that Smírnoff has had troubles with love in the past, and that though he claims to be unaffected by Popóva, her presence has caused him to fixate on women rather than on collecting the debt. Advanced students may point out that Smírnoff knows he will not get his money right away, but won't leave because he enjoys arguing with Popóva.)*

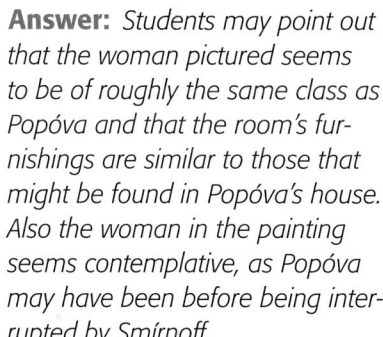

A Woman In An Interior, c. 1878. Luisa Rovn Hansen. Oil on canvas.

View the Art What similarities might the woman in this painting have with Popóva? Explain. ★

SMÍRNOFF. Oh, well, excuse me! Just how would he speak in front of a lady? In French? [*With a nasty lisp.*] *Madame, je vous prie* . . . How charmed I am to know that you reject to pay me my money! Ah, *pardon,* I seem to be upsetting you! Lovely weather we're having! And my, my, don't you look lovely in black! [*Makes a fake bow.*]

POPÓVA. You're being very stupid and not funny.

SMÍRNOFF. [*Mocking.*] Stupid and not funny! I don't know how to behave in a lady's presence! Woman, I have seen more ladies in my time than you have seen sparrows in yours! I have fought three duels[13] because of ladies, I have walked out on twelve ladies, and nine ladies have walked out on me! So there! Oh, I used to be an idiot, got crushes on them, sweet-talked, cast my pearls before— Well . . . Bow, click my heels, fall in love, suffer, sigh in the moonlight, freeze up, melt into puddles—I did it all. I could rattle on for hours about women's rights: I spent half my life hanging around women, but not anymore! No, thank you very much! No more wool over my eyes! I've had it! Dark eyes, red lips, dimples in the cheeks, moonlight, sighs—no, sir, I wouldn't give you two cents for any of it now. Present company excepted,

2 Awkward Encounters *Do you think Popóva is enjoying her conversation with Smírnoff at this point? Explain.*

13. *Duels* are combats between two persons, usually men, using pistols or swords.

Teach

Big Idea 2

Awkward Encounters

Answer: *She and Smírnoff may be flirting, so it is possible that she is enjoying the conversation.*

ADVANCED For advanced students, **ask:** When does it become clear that Smírnoff may be enjoying the conversation? Note the lines. *(He may be starting to indicate it with "Dark eyes, red lips . . . Present company excepted, of course . . .")*

View the Art ★

Answer: *Students may point out that the woman pictured seems to be of roughly the same class as Popóva and that the room's furnishings are similar to those that might be found in Popóva's house. Also the woman in the painting seems contemplative, as Popóva may have been before being interrupted by Smírnoff.*

English Learners

DIFFERENTIATED INSTRUCTION

Beginning/Early Intermediate Point out the use of contractions in the text. Have students scan pages 764 and 765 for contractions and call them out as you **write** them on the board. *(How're, I'm, I'll, you're, don't, can't, didn't, haven't, we're, I've, wouldn't, she's)* Then ask students to provide the full words used to form each contraction. If necessary, clarify the difference between an apostrophe used in a contraction and an apostrophe used to show possession.

Teach

Literary Element 1

Farce Answer: *This detail is funny and ridiculous. The chair breaking reminds the audience that this play is taking place in an exaggerated version of reality.*

Reading Strategy 2

Analyze Cause-and-Effect Relationships Answer: *She experienced her husband's unfaithfulness.*

Ask: What evidence does Popóva give to support her claim that men are not faithful? *(She says that she loved her husband, but he cheated on her, left her for weeks at a time, flirted with other women in front of her, and spent all of her money.)*

of course, but all women are **pretentious,** affected,[14] gossipy, hateful, liars to the marrow[15] of their bones, vain,[16] petty,[17] merciless, they can't think straight, and as for this part here [*Slaps his forehead.*] . . . well—excuse my frankness—a sparrow has ten times more brains than any philosopher in skirts. Take a good look at anyone of these romantic creatures: petticoats and hot air, divine transports, the whole works; then take a look at her soul. Pure crocodile. [*Grabs the back of a chair; the chair cracks and breaks.*] And the worst part is, this crocodile thinks she has a **monopoly** on the tender emotion of love! Has any woman ever known how to love anything except her lapdog? She's in love, all she can do is snivel[18] and whine. A man in love, now, he suffers and sacrifices, but a woman, her love shows up how? She swishes her skirt and gets a firm grip on your nose. You're a woman, unfortunately, but at least you know what I mean, what woman's nature is like. Tell me honestly: have you ever seen a woman who was faithful and true? No, you haven't! The only honest and faithful women are old or ugly.

POPÓVA. Excuse me, but would you mind telling me just who you think *is* faithful and true? Men?

SMÍRNOFF. Well, of course, men.

POPÓVA. Men! [*A mean laugh.*] Men are faithful and true in love! Well, spread the good news! [*Hotly.*] How dare you say that? Men faithful and true? Let me tell you a thing or two! Of all the men I know or have ever known, my dear departed husband was the best. I loved him passionately, with all my heart and soul, the way only a young and sensitive girl can love; I gave him my youth, my happiness, my life, my money; I lived and breathed for him, I worshiped him, he was my idol, and . . . and what do you think he did? This best of all possible men betrayed me in the worst possible way: he cheated on me every chance he got. After he died I found boxes and boxes of love letters in his desk! And when he was alive he'd leave me alone for weeks on end. And he flirted with other women right in front of me, he deceived me, he spent all my money, he laughed at me when I objected. And despite everything, I loved him, and I will be faithful to his memory. Even though he's dead, I am faithful and unshakable. I have buried myself within these four walls, where I shall mourn him forever. I shall wear black until the day I die.

SMÍRNOFF. [*A sneering laugh.*] Black? Don't make me laugh! How dumb do you think I am? I know exactly why you go around in that Mardi Gras[19] outfit and why you've buried yourself within these walls! Of course! It's all so romantic, so mysterious! You're waiting for some shavetail[20] army lieutenant to come riding by, or some sentimental schoolboy with a bad complexion,

14. Here, *affected* means "fake" or "cultivated."
15. *Marrow* is the tissue that fills the inner hollow part of most bones.
16. *Vain* means "having no real value."
17. *Petty* means "small-minded."
18. To *snivel* is to speak or act in a whining, sniffling, tearful, or overly emotional manner.
19. *Mardi Gras* is a festival of carnivals, masquerade balls, costumes, and revelry that culminates on Shrove Tuesday (the day before Ash Wednesday) on the Christian calendar.
20. A *shavetail* is a pack mule. Here, it is used to mean a second lieutenant.

1 Farce *How does this stage direction add to the element of farce in this play?*

Vocabulary

pretentious (pri ten′ shəs) *adj.* expressing exaggerated importance or worth

monopoly (mə nop′ ə lē) *n.* exclusive possession or control

Analyze Cause-and-Effect Relationships *Why does Popóva doubt Smírnoff's statement about the faithfulness of men?* 2

Grammar Practice

SPIRAL REVIEW **End Punctuation Say:** Chekhov has carefully chosen the punctuation at the end of many of the sentences at this point in the play. Ask students to read the dialogue on these pages. **Ask:** How does Chekhov use the question mark to show conflict? *(The characters "question" each other's words to show disbelief and shock at what the other has said [i.e., "Black?" "What?" "You dare sit down?" "No?"].)* **Ask:** How are exclamation points used in this conversation? *(Chekhov uses exclamation points to show that the characters are shouting at each other. When Smírnoff asks Popóva to stop shouting, his speech ends in periods. Chekhov shows here that Smírnoff is trying to provoke Popóva to become even more emotionally involved in the argument.)*

and he'll look up at your window and think: Ah! There dwells the mysterious Tamara, who loved her husband so much she buried herself within four walls. . . . I know all about your little games.

POPÓVA. [*Flares up.*] What? How dare you even suggest anything of the kind!

SMÍRNOFF. You buried yourself alive, but you didn't forget to powder your nose!

POPÓVA. How dare you!! How dare you speak to me like this!

SMÍRNOFF. Don't yell at me—I'm not your manager. But I'm a man, not a woman, and I'm used to calling a spade a spade. And please stop shouting.

POPÓVA. I'm not shouting—you are! Will you please go away and leave me alone!

SMÍRNOFF. Pay me my money and I'll go!

POPÓVA. I will not give you any money!

SMÍRNOFF. You will too!

POPÓVA. I will not! You won't get one red cent from me! Now please go away!

SMÍRNOFF. I do not have the pleasure of being either your husband or your fiancé,[21] so please stop making scenes for my benefit. [*Sits down.*] I hate that.

POPÓVA. [*Snorting with anger.*] You dare sit down?

SMÍRNOFF. Exactly.

POPÓVA. Will you please go!

SMÍRNOFF. Just give me my money! [*Aside.*] Oh, am I mad! Am I *mad*!

POPÓVA. Of all the nerve! I want nothing more to do with you! Please leave!

[*Pause.*]

You're still here? You haven't left?

SMÍRNOFF. No.

POPÓVA. No?

SMÍRNOFF. No.

POPÓVA. All right! [*Rings.*]

[*Enter* LUKÁ.]

Luká, will you please show this gentleman out?

LUKÁ. [*Goes over to* SMÍRNOFF.] Please leave, sir. The lady asked you to. She doesn't want you here.

SMÍRNOFF. [*Leaps to his feet.*] And you shut up! Who do you think you're talking to? I'll make a tossed salad out of you!

LUKÁ. [*Clutches his heart.*] Oh, my God! Oh, mother of God! [*Falls into an armchair.*] I'm dying! I'm dying! I can't breathe!

POPÓVA. Dásha! Where's Dásha? [*Screams.*] Dásha! Pelégea! Dásha! [*Rings frantically.*]

LUKÁ. They all went off berry picking. There's nobody else in the house! Oh, I'm dying! Water!

POPÓVA. Will you get out of here?

SMÍRNOFF. Can't you be a little more polite?

POPÓVA. [*Makes a fist and stamps her foot.*] You peasant! You bear! You vulgar bear! Monster! You . . . *radical!*

SMÍRNOFF. What? What did you call me?

POPÓVA. I said you were a bear!

SMÍRNOFF. [*Moves toward her.*] And just who said you could insult me like that?

POPÓVA. You're right, I am insulting you! What about it? You think I'm afraid of you?

SMÍRNOFF. You think, just because you're some kind of romantic heroine, that gives you the right to insult me with impunity?[22] Is that it? Oh, no! This is a matter for the field of honor!

LUKÁ. Oh, my God! Oh, my God! Water!

21. *Fiancé* is a man engaged to be married.

22. *Impunity* is freedom from punishment, harm, or loss.

Farce *How does the word choice here communicate an element of farce?* **3**

Teach

Literary Element 3

Farce Answer: *The language, especially the phrase "tossed salad," exaggerates Smírnoff's behavior. The words show his frustration, but are humorous in nature.*

Ask: How does Luká's response to Smírnoff add to the farce? *(Luká's heart attack is greatly exaggerated and ridiculous. His reaction is more comical than realistic.)*

English Learners

DIFFERENTIATED INSTRUCTION

Early Advanced English learners may have different cultural ideas of gender roles. Discuss with students Smírnoff's idea of a "real woman." Ask students to describe characteristics that Smírnoff admires in Popóva and **write** these on the board. *(Students should say that Popóva is not a "sissy" and is "all flint and firepower," meaning that she is strong; she is not "wishy-washy," meaning she is determined and unyielding.)* **Ask:** Why do you think Smírnoff suddenly admires these things about her? *(Students may suggest that he thinks these are manly qualities and admires them in a woman. They may also point out that she is the first woman he has met who exhibits these qualities.)*

Teach

Literary Element 1

Farce Answer: *He is suggesting that equal rights for women means the right to die in a duel, as men do. But fighting does not really signify equality. Smírnoff does not seem to understand the concept of equality between men and women. He thinks women are weaker than men.*

ENGLISH LEARNERS Ask English learners what equality means to them. Discuss the idea of being able to live in equality—as opposed to dying with "equality." **Ask:** Do you think women and men have equality today? *(Students will probably say that women and men do not have equality today, although their definitions of what this means will vary.)*

Reading Strategy 2

Analyze Cause-and-Effect Relationships Answer: *At first, he seems happy to kill her and calls her the weaker sex, but then he realizes that he is attracted to her. The irony is that it is Popóva's strength and personality that Smírnoff are attracted to, not her alleged "weakness."*

View the Art ★

Answer: *Students may say the painting focuses on emotion, and point to elements such as the horse being set away from the others and looking forlorn.*

Anglo-Arabian Stallion In The Imperial Stables At Versailles. Theodore Gericault.

View the Art The Romantic movement emphasized emotion over reason. Does this painting focus on emotion? Why or why not? ★

SMÍRNOFF. Time to choose weapons!

POPÓVA. And just because you've got big fists and a bull neck, you think I'm afraid of you? You . . . you bear!

SMÍRNOFF. To the field of honor! Nobody insults me like that, not even a woman!

POPÓVA. [*Trying to shout him down.*] Bear! Bear! Bear!

SMÍRNOFF. It's about time we got rid of old prejudices about only men needing to defend themselves on the field of honor! If it's equality you want, then it's equality you get! 1 I challenge you to a duel!

POPÓVA. You want to fight a duel! Good! Let's fight!

SMÍRNOFF. Right this minute!

POPÓVA. Right this minute! My husband had a set of pistols; wait here, I'll go get them. [*Starts out and immediately returns.*] You have no idea what a pleasure it will be for me to put a bullet through your thick head! [*Goes out.*]

SMÍRNOFF. I'll shoot her like a sitting duck! I'm not a schoolboy anymore, I'm no sentimental puppy—I don't care if she *is* the weaker sex!

LUKÁ. Oh, please, sir! [*Falls to his knees.*] Please don't do this, please just leave, please. I'm an old man, my heart won't stand all the excitement! Please don't shoot her!

SMÍRNOFF. [*Pays no attention to him.*] I'll shoot her—that's real equality; that'll emancipate her! Equality of the sexes at last! But what a woman! [*Imitates her.*] "You have no idea what a pleasure it will be to put a bullet through your thick head!" Yes, what a woman! 2 She got all flushed; her eyes were flashing fire; she accepted my challenge without even thinking! That's the first time this has ever happened to me!

LUKÁ. Oh, please, sir, please go! Just go away!

SMÍRNOFF. Now, that's a woman I understand! That's a real woman! She's not one of your sissies, nothing wishy-washy about her; she's all flint and firepower! I'm almost sorry to have to kill her!

1 Farce *What makes Smírnoff's remark here ridiculous?*

2 Analyze Cause-and-Effect Relationships *How does Smírnoff react to Popóva's acceptance to a duel?*

Reading Practice

SMALL GROUP SPIRAL REVIEW

Make Predictions The drama's ending hints that Popóva and Smírnoff have fallen in love. Ask students to predict what will happen to the couple in the future. They should write down their predictions and support them with examples and quotations from the drama. Tell students to form small groups to discuss their conclusions. Each group should choose a prediction to discuss with the rest of the class.

LUKÁ. [*Cries.*] Please, sir, please, just go! Please!

SMÍRNOFF. I definitely like this woman! Definitely! So she has dimples—I still like her. I'm almost ready to tell her to forget about the money. And I'm not mad anymore. . . . What an astonishing woman!

[*Enter* POPÓVA; *she carries a pair of dueling pistols.*]

POPÓVA. Here's the pistols. But before we have our duel, will you please show me how to use the things? I've never even touched one before.

LUKÁ. Oh, God have mercy on us all! I'm going to get the gardener and the coachman. . . . Why did this have to happen to us. . . ? [*Goes out.*]

SMÍRNOFF. [*Looks over the pistols with a professional eye.*] You see, there are several different makes of weapon. You've got your Mortimer,[23] now—that's a special dueling pistol, percussion[24] action. But what you have here are Smith and Wesson revolvers, triple action, with an extractor[25] and central sights. Beautiful pieces! Must have cost at least ninety rubles the pair. Now look, you hold the pistol like this. . . . [*Aside.*] What amazing eyes she's got! What a little spitfire!

POPÓVA. Like this?

SMÍRNOFF. That's it, that's the way. Next you cock the piece, like this . . . and you take aim. . . . Move your head back a little. Stretch out your arm . . . that's the way. Then you press your finger on this little thing here, and that's all there is to it. Main thing is, keep your cool and take slow, careful aim. Try not to let your hand shake.

POPÓVA. Right. . . . We shouldn't shoot indoors—let's go outside.

SMÍRNOFF. All right, let's go outside. Only I warn you, I intend to shoot into the air.

POPÓVA. Oh, that's the last straw! Why?

SMÍRNOFF. Because . . . because . . . It's none of your business why!

POPÓVA. Are you getting scared? Is that it? Aha, that's it! Oh no, you won't get out of this so easily! Come on, we're going outside! I won't rest until I put a bullet through that head of yours—that head I hate so! What's the matter, are you a coward?

SMÍRNOFF. That's it, I'm a coward.

POPÓVA. You're lying! Why don't you want to fight?

SMÍRNOFF. Because . . . because . . . because I like you.

POPÓVA. [*Sarcastic laugh.*] He likes me! He dares to tell me he likes me! [*Points to the door.*] Just go.

SMÍRNOFF. [*Puts down the pistol in silence, takes his hat, and starts out; at the door, he stops and turns. They look at each other in silence for a moment; then he goes hesitantly toward* POPÓVA.] Listen . . . are you still mad? I was crazy myself until just a minute ago, but you know . . . how can I put it? Well, the fact is, I . . . you see, the fact is, nothing like this ever happened to me before. . . . [*Shouts.*] Well, is it my fault I like you? [*Grabs a chair behind his back; the chair cracks and breaks.*] Why do you have such fragile furniture! I like you! You understand? I . . . I think I'm in love with you!

23. *Mortimer* and *Smith and Wesson* are manufacturers of firearms.
24. *Percussion* is the striking of a cap in a way to set off the charge in a firearm.
25. The *extractor* is the mechanism in a firearm that dislodges a used cartridge from the chamber.

Analyze Cause-and-Effect Relationships *What result does Smírnoff hope to achieve by saying he's a coward?* **3**

Awkward Encounters *Why do you think Smírnoff is having trouble expressing himself?* **4**

Teach

Reading Strategy 3

Analyze Cause-and-Effect Relationships **Answer:** *He wants to end the proposed duel with Popóva. He no longer wants to harm her.*

Ask: What has caused Smírnoff to change his attitude toward Popóva? *(He likes her bravery in accepting his challenge.)*

Big Idea 4

Awkward Encounters
Answer: *His feelings for Popóva are changing and he is tongue-tied. He hesitates to admit his new feelings.*

Ask: How might Smírnoff's words, tone, and actions make the situation more awkward? *(Smírnoff is stuttering, shouting, and breaking furniture, which might cause Popóva to feel more uncomfortable.)*

Approaching Level

DIFFERENTIATED INSTRUCTION

Emerging Point out that sarcasm plays a large part in this play. Direct students' attention to Popóva's reaction to Smírnoff admitting his feelings that he likes her, *"He likes me! He dares to tell me he likes me!"*. Read this dialogue aloud to the class. **Ask:** Why do you think Chekhov chose to write her dialogue this way? *(The disbelief and sarcasm here introduce more humor into the scene.)*

Teach

Literary Element 1

Farce Answer: *It is not a literal statement. It is exaggerated. Smírnoff thinks that because of Popóva's temperament, a romance might be challenging. Yet, her spark is attractive.*

Ask: What aspects of this scene add to the farce? *(The indecisiveness of Popóva, her exaggerated distress over what Smírnoff is saying and doing, and his list of things to do the next day make the scene ridiculous.)*

ENGLISH LEARNERS Explain to English learners that the expression "I'll never forgive myself" is an exaggeration, indicating that Smirnoff expects to regret his actions.

Reading Strategy 2

Analyze Cause-and-Effect Relationships Answer: *Feeding Toby extra oats was meant to show loyalty to her late husband. Her loyalty to him is replaced with her feelings for Smírnoff.*

Ask: What causes Popóva to change her mind about Smírnoff? *(Students may say the kiss did, but others may say Popóva was lonely and did not really want to mourn her dead husband for the rest of her life.)*

To check students' understanding of the selection, see Unit 4 Teaching Resources Book, p. 113.

POPÓVA. Get away from me! I hate you!

SMÍRNOFF. What a woman! I've never seen anything like her in my entire life! I'm done for! I'm caught in her mousetrap!

POPÓVA. Get away from me, or I'll shoot!

SMÍRNOFF. Go ahead, shoot! You don't know how happy that will make me, to die with your beautiful eyes upon me, die from a gun in your silky little hand. . . . Oh, I'm out of my mind! Look, you'd better think this over fast and decide right away. Once I leave here, we'll never see each other again. Make up your mind. I own a lot of land, I'm from a good family, I've got an income of ten thousand a year. . . . I can put a bullet through a coin in the air at twenty paces. . . . I've got the best horses you'll ever see. . . . Will you marry me?

POPÓVA. [*Angry, she waves the pistol.*] Marry you? I intend to shoot you! On the field of honor!

SMÍRNOFF. I'm out of my mind! I don't understand what's happening. . . .

POPÓVA. On the field of honor!

SMÍRNOFF. I'm out of my mind! I'm in love! I'm behaving like an idiot schoolboy! [*Grabs her hand; she shrieks with pain.*] I love you! [*Falls to his knees.*] I love you, the way I've never loved anyone before! I walked out on twelve women, nine walked out on me, but I never loved one of them the way I do you! My mind has turned to jelly, my joints have turned to sugar, I'm on my knees like a dope, and I'm asking for your hand. . . . Oh, the shame, the shame! I haven't been in love for six years, I swore I never would again, and all of a sudden I'm head over heels! I'm asking you to marry me! Yes or no? Will you? Yes or no? No? Fine! [*Gets up and heads quickly toward the door.*]

POPÓVA. Wait a minute . . .

SMÍRNOFF. [*Stops.*] Well?

POPÓVA. Nothing, just go! No, I mean, wait. . . . No, go away! Go away! I hate you! I mean, no, don't go! Oh, you make me so mad! [*Throws the pistol on the floor.*] My finger's all swollen up from that thing! [*Starts tearing her handkerchief.*] Well, what are you waiting for? Just get out of here!

SMÍRNOFF. All right then. Good-bye.

POPÓVA. Yes, yes, just go! [*Screams.*] Where are you going? Wait a minute. . . . Oh, come on back. Oh, I'm so mad! Stay away from me! Stay away from me!

SMÍRNOFF. [*Crosses to her.*] *You're* mad? *I'm* mad. I fell in love like a schoolboy, got down on my knees, I even got goose bumps. . . . [*Roughly.*] I love you! That's all I needed, to fall in love with you! Tomorrow I've got to pay the mortgage, start cutting hay, and now you— [*Grabs her around the waist.*] I'll never forgive myself for this—

POPÓVA. Get away from me! Get your hands off me! I . . . I hate you! I want to fight the d-d-duel!

[*A long kiss. Enter* LUKÁ *with a shovel, the gardener with a rake, the coachman with a pitchfork, some farmworkers with sticks.*]

LUKÁ. [*Sees the couple kissing.*] Oh, my. . . .

[*Pause.*]

POPÓVA. [*Shyly.*] Luká, go out to the stable and tell them Toby doesn't get extra oats anymore.

CURTAIN.

Farce *Would you interpret Smírnoff's comments literally? Explain.* **1**

Analyze Cause-and-Effect Relationships *Why does Popóva change her mind about feeding Toby the extra oats?* **2**

Speaking Practice

SMALL GROUP **Acting** Brainstorm ways in which students can bring the drama alive. Encourage them to use the stage directions in parentheses to help them act out a scene in the play. In addition, their pitch, tone of voice, eye contact, and posture should contribute to their portrayal of the characters. Invite students to form groups of three, and choose to portray Popóva, Smírnoff, or Luká. Each group should choose one scene, plan how they will perform it, and practice. Allow each group to perform their scene in front of the class.

After You Read

Respond and Think Critically

Respond and Interpret

1. (a)What was your first reaction to *The Bear*? (b)How do the characters' actions over the course of the play verify or challenge your initial reaction?
2. (a)What does Luká encourage Popóva to do at the beginning of the play? (b)What is his reasoning?
3. (a)What tactics does Smírnoff use to get into the house? (b)How do these tactics influence the way Popóva views him?
4. (a)Why is Smírnoff eager to see Popóva? (b)What will happen if he cannot accomplish his goal?

Analyze and Evaluate

5. How do Smírnoff's feelings for Popóva change over the course of the play? Explain.
6. What does Popóva's change of heart toward Smírnoff reveal about her period of mourning?

Connect

7. **Big Idea** **Awkward Encounters** Describe a similar awkward encounter you have experienced or heard about. Identify some ways in which it was similar to the encounter described in *The Bear.*
8. **Connect to Today** Would audiences today still enjoy this play? Can you think of any recent movies in which two people who instantly dislike each other end up falling in love?

Literary Element Farce

A **comedy** is a type of play that is humorous and that often has a happy ending. A **farce** is a specific type of comedy. In a farce, you can expect to find situations, characters, or events that are absurd or ridiculous, as well as funny.

1. In a play, the characters' words and actions tell you about the story. Identify the first line of dialogue in *The Bear* that tells you the play might be a farce.
2. Why do you think Chekhov might have chosen to write *The Bear* as a farce?

Review: Dialogue

As you learned on page 757, **dialogue** is the conversation between two characters in a literary work. Dialogue can help to create mood, develop the plot, and convey theme. It is also an excellent way for a writer to reveal a character's personality.

Partner Activity Use a graphic organizer like the one below to help you think about how the characters in *The Bear* are developed through dialogue. Then pair up with a classmate and write one page of dialogue that Smírnoff and Popóva might speak after the play's end. Present the dialogue to the rest of the class and give a brief analysis of how the dialogue shows that Smírnoff and Popóva have either changed or stayed the same.

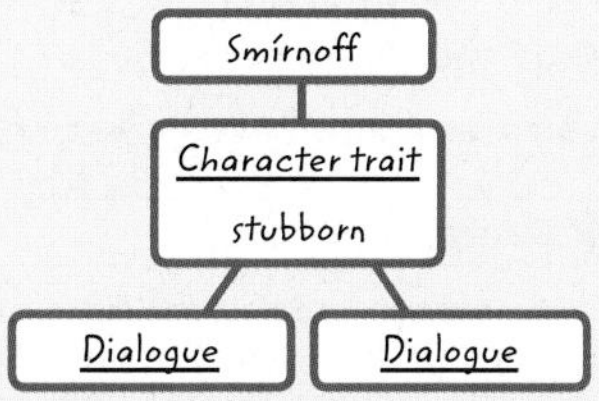

After You Read

Assess

1. (a) Answers will vary and may reflect students' difficulty in comprehending the play at the first reading. (b) Students may conclude that Popóva or Smírnoff surprised them in the course of the play's events.
2. (a) He thinks she has mourned long enough and encourages her to begin socializing again. (b) He feels she has a chance at new love before she ages.
3. (a) He shouts and pushes his way in. (b) She is put off by his forceful and loud behavior.
4. (a) He wants her to repay her husband's debt to him. (b) He will lose his property.
5. In the beginning, he is angry with her and dislikes her; at the end, he is in love with her.
6. Her quick change of heart reveals that she was not sincerely sorrowful. She was mourning to prove a point.
7. Students should identify a personal story about an awkward encounter.
8. Students should recognize that the story of *The Bear* is common to many romantic comedies. Encourage students to list recent movies, books, and television shows.

For additional selection assessment, see Assessment Resources, pp. 177–178.

Literary Element

1. Possible answer: "He was mean and…even unfaithful. But I intend to be faithful to the grave and show him what real love means."
2. By creating a farce, Chekhov could make statements about society and about members of the military, as well as about relationships and customs.

Review: Dialogue

Responses should indicate students' understanding of how dialogue helps to create characters and enables the audience to understand the action and the play's intent.

Progress Check

Can students identify farce?

If No → See Unit 4 Teaching Resources Book, p. 108.

After You Read

Assess

Reading Strategy

1. D is the correct answer. Without the business request to pay a debt, the initial tension of the play would be lost.

Progress Check

Can students analyze cause-and-effect relationships?

If No → See Unit 4 Teaching Resources Book, p. 109.

Vocabulary

1. b **2.** e **3.** f **4.** a

Academic Vocabulary

Sample answer: To determine someone's status in the community you would need to know what role the person plays in the community and what people think of the person.

To create custom assessments online, go to Progress Reporter Online Assessment.

To create custom assessments using software, use ExamView Assessment Suite.

Reading Strategy Analyze Cause-and-Effect Relationships

ACT Skills Practice

1. Much of the conflict in the play begins with:
   - **A.** an interfering servant.
   - **B.** an unexpected romance.
   - **C.** an unfaithful husband.
   - **D.** an unpaid debt.

Vocabulary Practice

Practice with Antonyms An **antonym** is a word that has a meaning opposite to that of another word. With a partner, match each boldfaced vocabulary word below with its antonym. Use a thesaurus or dictionary to check your answers. You will not use all the answer choices.

1. mourn	a. community
2. logic	b. celebrate
3. pretentious	c. reason
4. monopoly	d. overbearing
	e. nonsense
	f. humble

Academic Vocabulary

Even before writing his most famous works, Chekhov had achieved the ***status*** *of a well-known writer.*

Status is an academic word. More familiar words that have a similar meaning are *standing* and *position*. Complete the following sentence:

To determine someone's **status** in the community you would need to know _____.

For more on academic vocabulary, see pages 54–55 and R79–R81.

LOG ON **Literature** Online

Selection Resources For Selection Quizzes, eFlashcards, and Reading-Writing Connection activities, go to glencoe.com and enter QuickPass code GL49787u4.

Write with Style

Apply Dialogue

Assignment Write a dialogue between two characters. Include stage directions.

Get Ideas To help make your dialogue more dynamic, create a premise in which there is conflict between the characters. Determine the characters' opposing purposes or points of view.

Give It Structure Build your dialogue around the characters' responses to each other's statements or actions. Use a graphic organizer to determine the scene's structure and to lay out how the character interaction moves the dialogue forward.

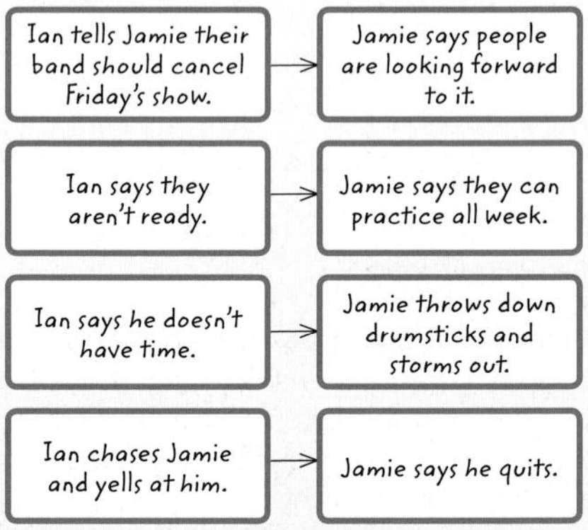

Look at Language When revising the scene, make the dialogue more colorful by including words, expressions, and figurative language that fits with the character's personality. Use the dialogue to make each of the characters seem like real people.

EXAMPLE:

~~*Ian: I don't think we're ready to play in front of people yet!*~~

Ian: You've got to be kidding—there's no way we're ready! You think I want to make a fool of myself in front of the entire school?

Also rewrite any stage directions that are not clear and specific. Make the characters' actions distinctive and the directions precise.

Write with Style

Students' dialogues should:
- be written in the format of a written drama
- present a scene involving tension or conflict
- have a logical structure
- use the dialogue to express the characters' personalities
- include specific stage directions

For grammar practice, see Unit 4 Teaching Resources Book, p. 112.

Before You Read

The Hitchhiker

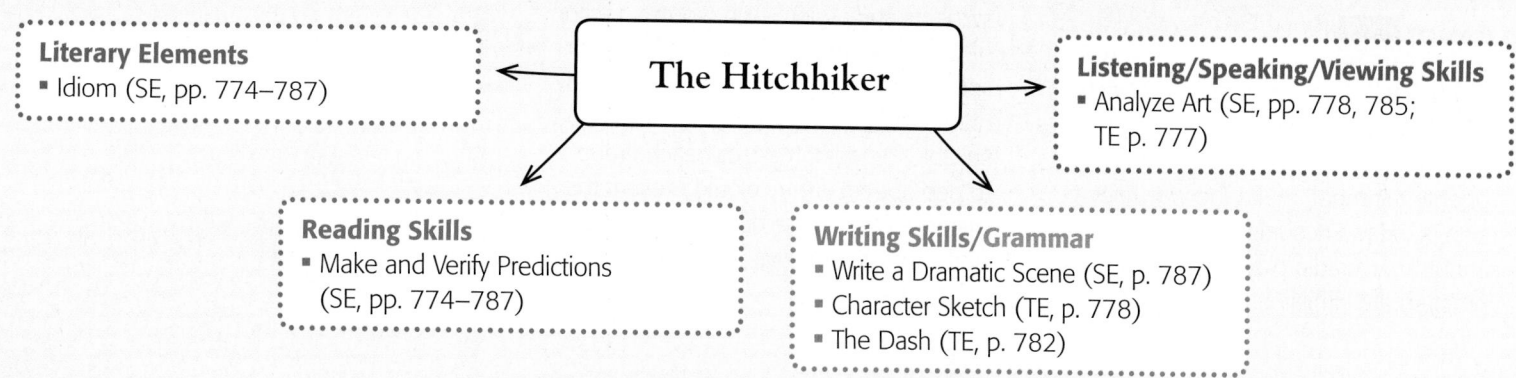

Meet **Lucille Fletcher**
(1912–2000)

At CBS radio in 1940, radio writer and producer Norman Corwin was handed an unpublished short story about a celebrity caterpillar titled "My Client Curly." The story was written by a woman who worked in the publicity department—an unknown 28-year-old writer named Lucille Fletcher. Corwin was charmed by the story and decided to turn it into a script for his radio program. By 1944, "My Client Curly" was being used as the basis for the Cary Grant film *Once Upon a Time* and Fletcher's long career as a fiction, radio, television and film writer was well under way.

> *"Sometimes you want your spine to tingle."*
>
> — Lucille Fletcher, from *The Hitchhiker*

Master of Suspense Fletcher was born in Brooklyn, New York, in 1912. Even as a child, Fletcher knew that she wanted to be a writer. She attended Vassar College, graduating in 1933 with a degree in English. After college, Fletcher got a job as a typist at CBS, which was the largest broadcast company in America at the time. At CBS, she met conductor and composer Bernard Hermann and married him in 1939. Soon thereafter, Corwin discovered Fletcher while she was working in CBS's publicity department.

After having "My Client Curly" turned into a radio play, Fletcher sought to build on her success. She found inspiration in a strange encounter on the highway. While driving on a trip with her husband, Fletcher twice saw the same odd-looking man hitchhiking. The story became the basis of one of Fletcher's most famous stories, the classic suspense tale *The Hitchhiker.* Her short story was turned into a popular radio play in 1941. She followed that up two years later with her most acclaimed work, a chilling suspense tale titled *Sorry, Wrong Number.*

From the Page to the Screen Although *The Hitchhiker* and *Sorry, Wrong Number,* were first broadcast on radio, they were both later remade. *The Hitchhiker* was eventually used for an episode of the television show *The Twilight Zone; Sorry, Wrong Number* was turned into a film in 1948. That same year, Fletcher and Hermann divorced, and a year later she married John Douglass Wallop. In the 1950s she began writing novels, one of which was made into a suspense film starring Rock Hudson. Fletcher's writing career spanned six decades, and she continued to write stories, novels, stage plays, and film scripts until she was in her seventies. She died in Pennsylvania in August of 2000.

LOG ON **Literature** Online

Author Search For more about Lucille Fletcher, go to glencoe.com and enter QuickPass code GL49787u4.

Before You Read

Focus

Bellringer Options

Daily Language Transparency 79

Or show students pictures of the headlines of mass panic following the War of the Worlds broadcast of 1938. **Say:** Orson Welles performed this play so well that several people took the story as fact and thought the world was being invaded by aliens. Play an excerpt of the broadcast. Explain that "The Hitchhiker" was also performed by Welles. **Ask:** Do people still mistake fact and fiction today? What are some examples? *(Possible answers: urban legends, rumors, tabloids)*

Selection Skills

The Hitchhiker

Literary Elements
- Idiom (SE, pp. 774–787)

Listening/Speaking/Viewing Skills
- Analyze Art (SE, pp. 778, 785; TE p. 777)

Reading Skills
- Make and Verify Predictions (SE, pp. 774–787)

Writing Skills/Grammar
- Write a Dramatic Scene (SE, p. 787)
- Character Sketch (TE, p. 778)
- The Dash (TE, p. 782)

Before You Read

Focus

Summary

In Lucille Fletcher's *The Hitchhiker,* Ronald Adams sets out alone on a cross-country drive despite his mother's warnings that the trip is dangerous. Adams spots a hitchhiker after beginning his trip—the first of many strange sightings leading to a chilling ending.

For summaries in languages other than English, see Unit 4 Teaching Resources Book, pp. 115–120.

Vocabulary

Writing with Vocabulary

Have students read the vocabulary words and their definitions. Then have them write a paragraph about a recent event in their lives. Students must use all of the vocabulary words from the list.

For additional vocabulary practice, see Unit 4 Teaching Resources Book, p. 123.

Literature and Reading Preview

Connect to the Drama

What kind of settings do you find spooky or scary? With a partner, discuss a situation in which the location or conditions created an eerie setting.

Build Background

The Hitchhiker was originally performed on the radio in 1941 as an installment of Orson Welles' "Mercury Theater on the Air." Welles was a pioneering radio and film star who had a reputation for producing compelling radio dramas. At the time, television was just beginning to develop an audience and radio was still a major source of dramatic entertainment. Although Fletcher's drama is mainly dialogue, the broadcast also used music and sound effects to develop the story's atmosphere.

Set Purposes for Reading

Big Idea Awkward Encounters

As you read, ask yourself, How does the situation in which you meet someone affect your impression of the person?

Literary Element Idiom

An **idiom** is an expression whose meaning is different from its literal meaning. Although idioms may be easily understood by a region's local speakers, they can be puzzling to outsiders. In *The Hitchhiker,* many of the characters use idioms when they speak. As you read, ask yourself, How do the idioms add realism to the story?

Reading Strategy Make and Verify Predictions

When reading a drama, you can use what you read about characters and events to **make and verify predictions** about the plot. As you read, ask yourself, How does the writer hint at what is going to happen to the main character?

Tip: Take Notes Use a two-column chart like the one below to list and verify your predictions.

Prediction	What happened
Adams will encounter something strange along his drive.	As soon as he begins his journey, Adams sees a mysterious man.

Learning Objectives

For pages 773–787

In studying this text, you will focus on the following objectives:

Literary Study: Analyzing idioms.

Reading: Making and verifying predictions.

Writing: Writing a dramatic scene.

Vocabulary

ominous (om′ ə nəs) *adj.* like an evil omen; threatening; p. 778 *The sudden appearance of clouds and thunder was an ominous sign.*

beckoning (bek′ ən ing) *v.* signaling or summoning; p. 782 *They could see their mother on the shore waving her hands and beckoning them for dinner.*

arid (ar′ id) *adj.* dry; parched; p. 784 *After two months of drought, the land was completely arid.*

prostrated (pros′ trāt id) *adj.* completely exhausted; helpless; overcome; p. 786 *After hearing the shocking news, she was prostrated and couldn't do anything for days.*

Tip: Word Usage When you encounter a new word, asking yourself a specific question about the word can help you to understand it. For example, when encountering the word *ominous,* you might ask yourself: *How could I make a scary setting seem less ominous?*

Reading Practice

SMALL GROUP SPIRAL REVIEW **Read Different Mediums** Explain to students that *The Hitchhiker* was written for presentation on radio. Radio was once a popular medium of entertainment, much the way television is today. Encourage students to think about how a radio play and a television program are similar and different. Group students and assign each group a section of text. Give students time to study their lines. Then, ask each group to present a dramatically spoken version, as would be suitable for radio. Next, ask each group to describe how they would present the material if they were developing a television program or movie about it.

The Hitchhiker

Lucille Fletcher

CHARACTERS

ORSON WELLES, NARRATOR
RONALD ADAMS
MOTHER
VOICE
MECHANIC
HENRY
WOMAN
GIRL
GALLUP OPERATOR
LONG DISTANCE OPERATOR
ALBUQUERQUE OPERATOR
NEW YORK OPERATOR
MRS. WHITNEY

WELLES. [*Narrating.*] Good evening, this is Orson Welles. . . .

MUSIC. *In.*

WELLES. Personally I've never met anybody who didn't like a good ghost story, but I know a lot of people who think there are a lot of people who don't like a good ghost story. For the benefit of these, at least, I go on record at the outset of this evening's entertainment with the sober assurance that, although blood may be curdled on the program, none will be spilt. There's no shooting, knifing, throttling, axing, or poisoning here. No clanking chains, no cobwebs, no bony and/or hairy hands appearing from secret panels or, better yet, bedroom curtains. If it's any part of that dear old phosphorescent[1] foolishness that people who don't like ghost stories don't like, then again, I promise you we haven't got it. What we do have is a thriller. If it's half as good as we think it is, you can call it a shocker, and we present it proudly and without apologies. After all, a story doesn't have to appeal to the heart—it can also appeal to the spine. Sometimes you want your heart to be warmed—sometimes you want your spine to tingle. The tingling, it's to be hoped, will be quite audible as you listen tonight to *The Hitchhiker*—That's the name of our story, *The Hitchhiker*—

1. *Phosphorescent* describes something that is *emitting light.*

Idiom *Review the definition of* idiom *on page 774. Why would this phrase be considered an idiom?* **1**

Teach

Literary Element 1

Idiom Answer: *Because he is really saying that people want to feel scared, not that they literally want something to happen to their spines.*

English Learners

DIFFERENTIATED INSTRUCTION

Intermediate Explain to English learners that in contemporary plays, actors rarely address the audience. **Ask:** What role does Welles play in this passage? *(the narrator, person who tells the story)* **Ask:** What is this role similar to in *Romeo and Juliet*? *(the chorus)*

Ask: What do you think is the purpose of the narrator in this story? *(to get the audience in the mood to enjoy a spooky story, to set the tone.)*

Teach

Reading Strategy 1

Make and Verify Predictions **Answer:** *We know that he will reach New Mexico.*

Reading Strategy 2

Make and Verify Predictions **Sample answer:** *Adams will encounter a hitchhiker and may pick him up. Many students will predict that the hitchhiker will cause problems.*

For additional practice using the reading skill or strategy, see Unit 4 Teaching Resources Book, p. 122.

SOUND. *Automobile wheels humming over concrete road.*

MUSIC. *Something weird and shuddery.*

ADAMS. [*Narrating.*] I am in an auto camp[2] on Route Sixty-Six just west of Gallup, New Mexico. If I tell it, perhaps it will help me. It will keep me from going mad. But I must tell this quickly. I am not mad now. I feel perfectly well, except that I am running a slight temperature. My name is Ronald Adams. I am thirty-six years of age, unmarried, tall, dark, with a black mustache. I drive a 1940 Ford V-8, license number 6V-7989. I was born in Brooklyn.[3] All this I know. I know that I am, at this moment, perfectly sane. That it is not I who has gone mad—but something else—something utterly beyond my control. But I must speak quickly . . . very quickly. At any moment the link with life may break. This may be the last thing I ever tell on earth . . . the last night I ever see the stars. . . .

MUSIC. *In.*

ADAMS. [*Narrating.*] Six days ago I left Brooklyn to drive to California. . . .

MOTHER. Good-bye, son. Good luck to you, my boy. . . .

ADAMS. Good-bye, mother. Here—give me a kiss, and then I'll go. . . .

MOTHER. I'll come out with you to the car.

ADAMS. No. It's raining. Stay here at the door. Hey—what is this? Tears? I thought you promised me you wouldn't cry.

MOTHER. I know dear. I'm sorry. But I—do hate to see you go.

ADAMS. I'll be back. I'll only be on the coast three months.

MOTHER. Oh—it isn't that. It's just—the trip. Ronald—I really wish you weren't driving.

ADAMS. Oh—mother. There you go again. People do it every day.

MOTHER. I know. But you'll be careful, won't you. Promise me you'll be extra careful. Don't fall asleep—or drive fast—or pick up any strangers on the road. . . .

ADAMS. Lord, no. You'd think I was still seventeen to hear you talk—

MOTHER. And wire me as soon as you get to Hollywood, won't you, son?

ADAMS. Of course I will. Now don't you worry. There isn't anything going to happen. It's just eight days of perfectly simple driving on smooth, decent, civilized roads, with a hotdog or a hamburger stand every ten miles. . . . *[Fade.]*

SOUND. *Auto hum.*

MUSIC. *In.*

ADAMS. [*Narrating.*] I was in excellent spirits. The drive ahead of me, even the loneliness, seemed like a lark. But I reckoned without *him.*

MUSIC. *Changes to something weird and empty.*

ADAMS. [*Narrating.*] Crossing Brooklyn Bridge that morning in the rain, I saw a man leaning against the cables. He seemed to be waiting for a lift. There were spots of fresh rain on his shoulders. He was carrying a cheap overnight bag in one hand. He was thin, nondescript, with a cap pulled down over his eyes. He stepped off the walk right in front of me and, if I hadn't swerved hard, I'd have hit him.

SOUND. *Terrific skidding.*

MUSIC. *In.*

2. An *auto camp* is a rest area for cars along the highway.
3. *Brooklyn* is one of New York City's five boroughs.

1 Make and Verify Predictions *What do you already know about what will happen on his drive?*

2 Make and Verify Predictions *Based on this line of dialogue and the title, what do you predict will happen?*

Literary Element Practice

SPIRAL REVIEW **Characteristics of Drama** Talk with students about the difference between radio theater and a play performed on stage in front of a live audience. Students may have an easier time understanding a stage play, because of the visual clues that are lacking in a radio play. **Ask:** What do you think might be the differences between radio theater and a play performed on stage? *(Radio theater must rely more on sound and dialogue than visual action and props.)* Encourage students to look for these differences as they read *The Hitchhiker.* Ask them to jot down places where a visual clue could be added to help comprehension.

Teach

View the Photograph ★

Have students analyze the mood of the photograph and relate it to the mood of the selection. **Ask:** What mood does this photograph create? *(ominous, foreboding)* Which elements create this mood? *(The blurred, dark image and the dark figure of a person standing alone on a street)* Does the mood in the photograph effectively reflect the mood of the play? *(Answers will vary. Most students will agree that both moods are dark and mysterious.)*

English Learners

DIFFERENTIATED INSTRUCTION

Early Advanced English learners may have a hard time determining what a given pronoun refers to. Have a student read Adams's first five lines in the play. **Ask:** What is the "it" and the "this" to which Adams refers? *(the story that he is about to tell)* **Ask:** Why do you think the author used these pronouns without providing an explanation? *(The author is trying to set a tone of mystery. The narrator seems to be asking, Is this a story? What is this?)*

Teach

Big Idea 1

Awkward Encounters
Answer: *Because he thinks it is strange that he was able to get ahead of him and it makes him suspicious.*

Literary Element 2

Idiom **Answer:** *Adams is spooked or nervous.*

View the Photograph ★
Answer: *Students may feel this photo adequately represents the scene. Some may think the photo should be more ominous.*

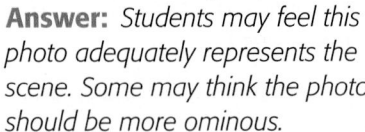

View the Photograph In your opinion, how well does this photo capture the scene in which Adams talks to the mechanic? ★

ADAMS. [*Narrating.*] I would have forgotten him completely, except that just an hour later, while crossing the Pulaski Skyway[4] over the Jersey flats, I saw him again. At least, he looked like the same person. He was standing now, with one thumb pointing west. I couldn't figure out how he'd got there, but I thought probably one of those fast trucks had picked him up, beaten me to the Skyway, and let him off. I didn't stop for him. Then—late that night, I saw him again.

MUSIC. *Changing.*

ADAMS. [*Narrating.*] It was on the New Pennsylvania Turnpike between Harrisburg and Pittsburgh. It's two hundred and sixty-five miles long, with a very high speed limit. I was just slowing down for one of the tunnels—when I saw him—standing under an arc light by the side of the road. I could see him quite distinctly. The bag, the cap, even the spots of fresh rain spattered over his shoulders. He hailed me this time. . . .

VOICE. [*Very spooky and faint.*] Hall-ooo. . . . [*It echoes as though coming through the tunnel.*] Hall-ooo. . . !

ADAMS. [*Narrating.*] I stepped on the gas like a shot. That's lonely country through the Alleghenies,[5] and I had no intention of stopping. Besides, the coincidence, or whatever it was, gave me the willies. I stopped at the next gas station.

SOUND. *Auto tires screeching to stop . . . horn honk.*

4. The *Pulaski Skyway* is a highway overpass in New Jersey.
5. The *Alleghenies* are a mountain range extending from north central Pennsylvania through western Maryland, eastern West Virginia and western Virginia.

1 Awkward Encounters *Why do you think Adams chooses not to pick up the hitchhiker here?*

Idiom *What does this phrase mean?* **2**

Writing Practice

Character Sketch Explain that literature's most treasured characters are those with whom readers can relate despite differences in sex, age, culture, and so on. Readers live vicariously through characters, so writers attempt to include redeemable qualities—reasons for readers to like characters. **Ask:** Can you relate to Ronald Adams? Have students write a short character sketch of Ronald. They should describe his appearance, his personality, and his strengths and weaknesses. Explain that knowing the characters well will help them understand the story.

MECHANIC. Yes, sir.

ADAMS. Fill her up.

MECHANIC. Certainly, sir. Check your oil, sir?

ADAMS. No, thanks.

SOUND. *Gas being put into car.*

MECHANIC. Nice night, isn't it?

ADAMS. Yes. It—hasn't been raining here recently, has it?

MECHANIC. Not a drop of rain all week.

ADAMS. I suppose that hasn't done your business any harm.

MECHANIC. Oh—people drive through here all kinds of weather. Mostly business, you know. There aren't many pleasure cars out on the Turnpike this season of the year.

ADAMS. I suppose not. [*Casually.*] What about hitchhikers?

MECHANIC. [*Laughing.*] Hitchhikers here?

ADAMS. What's the matter? Don't you ever see any?

MECHANIC. Not much. If we did, it'd be a sight for sore eyes.

ADAMS. Why?

MECHANIC. A guy'd be a fool who started out to hitch rides on this road. Look at it. It's two hundred and sixty-five miles long, there's practically no speed limit, and it's a straightaway. Now what car is going to stop to pick up a guy under those conditions? Would you stop?

ADAMS. No. [*He answers slowly, with puzzled emphasis.*] Then you've never seen anybody?

MECHANIC. Nope. Mebbe they get the lift before the Turnpike starts—I mean, you know—just before the toll house—but then it'd be a mighty long ride. Most cars wouldn't want to pick up a guy for that long a ride. And you know—this is pretty lonesome country here—mountains, and woods. . . . You ain't seen anybody like that, have you?

ADAMS. No. [*Quickly.*] Oh no, not at all. It was—just a—technical question.

MECHANIC. I see. Well—that'll be just a dollar forty-nine—with the tax.

. . . [*Fade.*]

SOUND. *Auto hum up.*

MUSIC. *Changing.*

ADAMS. [*Narrating.*] The thing gradually passed from my mind, as sheer coincidence. I had a good night's sleep in Pittsburgh. I did not think about the man all next day—until just outside of Zanesville, Ohio, I saw him again.

MUSIC. *Dark,* ***ominous*** *note.*

ADAMS. [*Narrating.*] It was a bright sunshiny afternoon. The peaceful Ohio fields, brown with the autumn stubble, lay dreaming in the golden light. I was driving slowly, drinking it in, when the road suddenly ended in a detour. In front of the barrier, he was standing.

MUSIC. *In.*

ADAMS. [*Narrating.*] Let me explain about his appearance before I go on. I repeat. There was nothing sinister about him. He was as drab as a mud fence. Nor was his attitude menacing. He merely stood there, waiting, almost drooping a little, the cheap overnight bag in his hand. He looked as though he had been waiting there for hours. Then he looked up. He hailed me. He started to walk forward.

VOICE. [*Far off.*] Hall-ooo . . . Hall-ooo. . . .

Awkward Encounters *Why do you think Adams lies to the mechanic?* **3**

Make and Verify Predictions *Do you think Adams will pick him up this time?* **4**

Vocabulary

ominous (om′ ə nəs) *adj.* like an evil omen; threatening.

Teach

Big Idea 3

Awkward Encounters
Answer: *Because he is afraid that the mechanic will think that he's crazy.*

Reading Strategy 4

Make and Verify Predictions **Sample answer:** *No, I don't think he'll pick him up because he is even more scared of him now than before.*

Approaching Level

DIFFERENTIATED INSTRUCTION

Emerging Have students go back and scan Adams's first sightings of the hitchhiker. **Ask:** What detail does Fletcher repeatedly point out to the reader? *(Fletcher repeats that the hitchhiker has drops of rain on his jacket.)* **Ask:** Why is this detail worth pointing out? *(Adams talks about the golden light of Ohio, so this is probably morning. The character is still wet from last night's rain, which is odd. This detail also helps readers see that this is the same hitchhiker as the one who appeared on the Brooklyn Bridge.)*

Teach

Reading Strategy 1

Make and Verify Predictions **Sample answer:** *I don't think the man will help him because he is already cranky and it's the middle of the night..*

ADAMS. [*Narrating.*] I had stopped the car, of course, for the detour. And for a few moments, I couldn't seem to find the new road. I knew he must be thinking that I had stopped for him.

VOICE. [*Sounding closer now.*] Hall-ooo . . . Hallll . . . ooo. . . .

SOUND. *Gears jamming . . . sound of motor turning over hard . . . nervous accelerator.*

VOICE. [*Closer.*] Hall . . . oooo. . . .

ADAMS. [*With panic in his voice.*] No. Not just now. Sorry. . . .

VOICE. [*Closer.*] Going to California?

SOUND. *Starter starting . . . gears jamming.*

ADAMS. [*As though sweating blood.*] No. Not today. The other way. Going to New York. Sorry . . . sorry. . . .

SOUND. *Car starts with squeal of wheels on dirt . . . into auto hum.*

MUSIC. *In.*

ADAMS. [*Narrating.*] After I got the car back onto the road again, I felt like a fool. Yet the thought of picking him up, of having him sit beside me was somehow unbearable. Yet, at the same time, I felt, more than ever, unspeakably alone.

SOUND. *Auto hum up.*

ADAMS. [*Narrating.*] Hour after hour went by. The fields, the towns ticked off, one by one. The lights changed. I knew now that I was going to see him again. And though I dreaded the sight, I caught myself searching the side of the road, waiting for him to appear.

SOUND. *Auto hum up . . . car screeches to a halt . . . impatient honk two or three times . . . door being unbolted.*

SLEEPY MAN'S VOICE. Yep? What is it? What do you want?

ADAMS. [*Breathless.*] You sell sandwiches and pop here, don't you?

VOICE. [*Cranky.*] Yep. We do. In the daytime. But we're closed up now for the night.

ADAMS. I know. But—I was wondering if you could possibly let me have a cup of coffee—black coffee.

VOICE. Not at this time of night, mister. My wife's the cook and she's in bed. Mebbe further down the road—at the Honeysuckle Rest. . . .

SOUND. *Door squeaking on hinges as though being closed.*

ADAMS. No—no. Don't shut the door. [*Shakily.*] Listen—just a minute ago, there was a man standing here—right beside this stand—a suspicious looking man. . . .

WOMAN'S VOICE. [*From distance.*] Henry? Who is it, Henry?

HENRY. It's nobuddy, mother. Just a feller thinks he wants a cup of coffee. Go back into bed.

ADAMS. I don't mean to disturb you. But you see, I was driving along—when I just happened to look—and there he was. . . .

HENRY. What was he doing?

ADAMS. Nothing. He ran off—when I stopped the car.

HENRY. Then what of it? That's nothing to wake a man in the middle of his sleep about. [*Sternly.*] Young man, I've got a good mind to turn you over to the local sheriff.

ADAMS. But—I—

HENRY. You've been taking a nip, that's what you've been doing. And you haven't got anything better to do than to wake decent folk out of their hard-earned sleep. Get going. Go on.

Make and Verify Predictions *Do you think the man will help Adams? Why?* **1**

Reading Practice

SPIRAL REVIEW **Motivation** Explain that characters' actions should seem natural for a character; they should not seem forced or unlikely. Analyze the scene between Adams and the voice (Henry). **Ask:** What reason does Adams give to the man for stopping his car? *(He wanted coffee.)* What was the real reason that Adams stopped? *(He was afraid of the "suspicious looking man.")* Have students support their answers with evidence from the text. Have students reflect on their character sketches.

Ask: Is Adams's behavior erratic or unpredictable based on your character sketches? *(Answers will vary. Most students will note that Adams's fear of the strange man fits his character.)*

ADAMS. But—he looked as though he were going to rob you.

HENRY. I ain't got nothin' in this stand to lose. Now—on your way before I call out Sheriff Oakes. [*Fade.*]

SOUND. *Auto hum up.*

ADAMS. [*Narrating.*] I got into the car again, and drove on slowly. I was beginning to hate the car. If I could have found a place to stop . . . to rest a little. But I was in the Ozark Mountains of Missouri now. The few resort places there were closed. Only an occasional log cabin, seemingly deserted, broke the monotony of the wild wooded landscape. I had seen him at that roadside stand; I knew I would see him again—perhaps at the next turn of the road. I knew that when I saw him next, I would run him down. . . .

SOUND. *Auto hum up.*

ADAMS. But I did not see him again until late next afternoon. . . .

SOUND. *Warning system at train crossing.*

ADAMS. [*Narrating.*] I had stopped the car at a sleepy little junction just across the border into Oklahoma—to let a train pass by—when he appeared, across the tracks, leaning against a telephone pole.

SOUND. *Distant sound of train chugging . . . bell ringing steadily.*

2 Awkward Encounters *Why does Adams talk to Henry for such a long time even though Henry clearly wants Adams to leave?*

Teach

Big Idea 2

Awkward Encounters

Answer: *He is beginning to get desperate and wants someone else to be worried about the suspicious hitchhiker.*

English Learners

DIFFERENTIATED INSTRUCTION

Beginning/Early Intermediate

English language learners may find the slang in *The Hitchhiker* confusing. Have a proficient English speaker read Henry's lines on pages 780–781. Knowing the tone of what is said will help English language learners interpret unknown slang.

Ask: What is the tone of Henry's voice as he speaks to Adams? *(distressed, annoyed)*

As a class, decipher the meaning of these phrases from the passage:

- Mebbe further down the road *(Try somewhere else)*
- I've got a good mind to . . . *(I should probably . . .)*
- You've been taking a nip . . . *(You've been drinking)*

Encourage students to share interesting examples of slang from other languages.

Teach

Reading Strategy 1

Make and Verify Predictions **Sample answer:** *I think he is going to turn out to be a ghost in the end.*

Literary Element 2

Idiom **Answer:** *Context clues from the previous sentence ("Mind if I take off my shoes") suggest that she means her feet hurt.*

ADAMS. [*Narrating, very tensely.*] It was a perfectly airless, dry day. The red clay of Oklahoma was baking under the southwestern sun. Yet there were spots of fresh rain on his shoulders. I couldn't stand that. Without thinking, blindly, I started the car across the tracks.

SOUND. *Train chugging closer.*

ADAMS. [*Narrating.*] He didn't even look up at me. He was staring at the ground. I stepped on the gas hard, veering the wheel sharply toward him. I could hear the train in the distance now, but I didn't care. Then something went wrong with the car. It stalled right on the tracks.

SOUND. *Train chugging closer. Above this, sound of car stalling.*

ADAMS. [*Narrating.*] The train was coming closer. I could hear its bell ringing, and the cry of its whistle. Still he stood there. And now—I knew that he was **beckoning**—beckoning me to my death.

SOUND. *Train chugging close. Whistle blows wildly. Then train rushes up and by with pistons going.*

ADAMS. [*Narrating.*] Well—I frustrated him that time. The starter had worked at last. I managed to back up. But when the train passed, he was gone. I was all alone in the hot dry afternoon.

SOUND. *Train retreating. Crickets begin to sing in background.*

MUSIC. *In.*

ADAMS. [*Narrating.*] After that, I knew I had to do something. I didn't know who this man was or what he wanted of me. I only knew that from now on, I must not let myself be alone on the road for one single moment.

SOUND. *Auto hum up. Slow down. Stop. Door opening.*

ADAMS. Hello, there. Like a ride?

GIRL. Well, what do you think? How far you going?

ADAMS. Amarillo . . . I'll take you all the way to Amarillo.

GIRL. Amarillo, Texas?

ADAMS. I'll drive you there.

GIRL. Gee!

SOUND. *Door closes—car starts.*

MUSIC. *In.*

GIRL. Mind if I take off my shoes? My dogs are killing me.

ADAMS. Go right ahead.

GIRL. Gee, what a break this is. A swell car, a decent guy, and driving all the way to Amarillo. All I been getting so far is trucks.

ADAMS. Hitchhike much?

GIRL. Sure. Only it's tough sometimes, in these great open spaces, to get the breaks.

ADAMS. I should think it would be. Though I'll bet if you get a good pick-up in a fast car, you can get to places faster than—say, another person, in another car?

GIRL. I don't get you.

ADAMS. Well, take me, for instance. Suppose I'm driving across the country, say, at a nice steady clip of about forty-five miles an hour. Couldn't a girl like you, just standing beside the road, waiting for lifts, beat me to town after town—provided she got picked up every time in a car doing from sixty-five to seventy miles an hour?

1 Make and Verify Predictions *In the end, who do you think the hitchhiker is going to turn out to be?*

Vocabulary

beckoning (bek′ ən ing) *v.* signaling or summoning

Idiom *What does the girl mean by "dogs"? How do you know?* 2

Grammar Practice

SPIRAL REVIEW **The Dash** Point out that Fletcher uses the dash often in this play. Explain that the dash can be effective if used correctly and not overused. Model the main uses of the dash in writing:

- to show a sudden change of thought
- to indicate a break in a sentence
- in place of parentheses

Have students write three sentences, each using the dash in a different way. Invite volunteers to share their sentences with the class.

GIRL. I dunno. Maybe and maybe not. What difference does it make?

ADAMS. Oh—no difference. It's just a—crazy idea I had sitting here in the car.

GIRL. [*Laughing*.] Imagine spending your time in a swell car thinking of things like that!

ADAMS. What would you do instead?

GIRL. [*Admiringly*.] What would I do? If I was a good-looking fellow like yourself? Why—I'd just enjoy myself—every minute of the time. I'd sit back, and relax, and if I saw a good-looking girl along the side of the road . . . [*sharply*] Hey! Look out!

ADAMS. [*Breathlessly*.] Did you see him too?

GIRL. See who?

ADAMS. That man. Standing beside the barbed wire fence.

GIRL. I didn't see—anybody. There wasn't nothing but a bunch of steers[6]—and the barbed wire fence. What did you think you was doing? Trying to run into the barbed wire fence?

ADAMS. There was a man there, I tell you . . . a thin gray man, with an overnight bag in his hand. And I was trying to—run him down.

GIRL. Run him down? You mean—kill him?

ADAMS. He's a sort of—phantom. I'm trying to get rid of him—or else prove that he's real. But [*Desperately*.] you say you didn't see him back there? You're sure?

GIRL. [*Queerly*.] I didn't see a soul. And as far as that's concerned, mister . . .

ADAMS. Watch for him the next time, then. Keep watching. Keep your eyes peeled on the road. He'll turn up again—maybe any minute now. [*Excitedly*.] There. Look there—

SOUND. *Auto sharply veering and skidding. Girl screams.*

SOUND. *Crash of car going into barbed wire fence. Frightened lowing of steer.*

GIRL. How does this door work? I—I'm gettin' outta here.

ADAMS. Did you see him that time?

GIRL. [*Sharply*.] No. I didn't see him that time. And personally, mister, I don't expect never to see him. All I want to do is to go on living—and I don't see how I will very long driving with you—

ADAMS. I'm sorry. I—I don't know what came over me. [*Frightened*.] Please—don't go. . . .

GIRL. So if you'll excuse me, mister—

ADAMS. You can't go. Listen, how would you like to go to California? I'll drive you to California.

GIRL. Seeing pink elephants all the way? No thanks.

ADAMS. [*Desperately*.] I could get you a job there. You wouldn't have to be a waitress. I have friends there—my name is Ronald Adams—You can check up.

SOUND. *Door opens.*

GIRL. Uhn-hunh. Thanks just the same.

ADAMS. Listen. Please. For just one minute. Maybe you think I am half cracked. But this man. You see, I've been seeing this man all the way across the country. He's been following me. And if you could only help me—stay with me—until I reach the coast—

6. *Steers* are bulls that are raised for beef.

3 Awkward Encounters *How do you think the girl views Adams at this point?*

Make and Verify Predictions *Do you think he is going to make it all the way to California? Why?* 4

Awkward Encounters *What would you do if you were in the girl's situation?* 5

Teach

Big Idea 3

Awkward Encounters
Answer: *She thinks he is a little strange or not quite right.*

Reading Strategy 4

Make and Verify Predictions **Sample answer:** *No, because I think he'll go crazy before he reaches California.*

Big Idea 5

Awkward Encounters
Answer: *I would definitely not go with him and I would get out of his car right away.*

Approaching Level

DIFFERENTIATED INSTRUCTION

AAVE Approaching-level learners who use African American Vernacular English (AAVE) may have difficulty with double negatives. Point out this sentence from page 783: ". . . I don't expect never to see him." Have students point out the two negative words in the sentence. (*don't* and *never*) Explain that this construction actually says the opposite of what was intended. Have a student rewrite this sentence on the board, using Standard Academic English.

Teach

Big Idea 1

Awkward Encounters
Sample answer: *Yes, he should just pick him up because he should finally find out what he wants.*

GIRL. You know what I think you need, big boy? Not a girl friend. Just a good dose of sleep. . . . There, I got it now.

SOUND. *Door opens . . . slams.*

ADAMS. No. You can't go.

GIRL. [*Screams.*] Leave your hands offa me, do you hear! Leave your—

ADAMS. Come back here, please, come back.

SOUND. *Struggle . . . slap . . . footsteps running away on gravel . . . lowing of steer.*

ADAMS. [*Narrating.*] She ran from me, as though I were a monster. A few minutes later, I saw a passing truck pick her up. I knew then that I was utterly alone.

SOUND. *Lowing of steer up.*

ADAMS. [*Narrating.*] I was in the heart of the great Texas prairies. There wasn't a car on the road after the truck went by. I tried to figure out what to do, how to get hold of myself. If I could find a place to rest. Or even, if I could sleep right here in the car for a few hours, along the side of the road . . . I was getting my winter overcoat out of the back seat to use as a blanket, [Hall-ooo], when I saw him coming toward me [Hall-ooo], emerging from the herd of moving steer. . .

VOICE. Hall-ooo . . . Hall-oooo . . .

SOUND. *Auto starting violently. . . up to steady hum.*

MUSIC. *In.*

ADAMS. [*Narrating.*] I didn't wait for him to come any closer. Perhaps I should have spoken to him then, fought it out then and there. For now he began to be everywhere. Whenever I stopped, even for a moment—for gas, for oil, for a drink of pop, a cup of coffee, a sandwich—he was there.

MUSIC. *Faster.*

ADAMS. [*Narrating.*] I saw him standing outside the auto camp in Amarillo that night, when I dared to slow down. He was sitting near the drinking fountain in a little camping spot just inside the border of New Mexico.

MUSIC. *Faster.*

ADAMS. [*Narrating.*] He was waiting for me outside the Navajo Reservation,[7] where I stopped to check my tires. I saw him in Albuquerque where I bought twelve gallons of gas . . . I was afraid now, afraid to stop. I began to drive faster and faster. I was in lunar landscape now—the great **arid** mesa[8] country of New Mexico. I drove through it with the indifference of a fly crawling over the face of the moon.

MUSIC. *Faster.*

ADAMS. [*Narrating.*] But now he didn't even wait for me to stop. Unless I drove at eighty-five miles an hour over those endless roads—he waited for me at every other mile. I would see his figure, shadowless, flitting before me, still in its same attitude, over the cold and lifeless ground, flitting over dried-up rivers, over broken stones cast up by old glacial upheavals, flitting in the pure and cloudless air. . . .

MUSIC. *Strikes sinister note of finality.*

ADAMS. [*Narrating.*] I was beside myself when I finally reached Gallup, New Mexico, this morning. There is an auto camp here—cold, almost deserted at this

7. A *Navajo Reservation* is a tract of land set aside by the United States government for the Native American Navajo tribe to live on.
8. A *mesa* is a flat-topped hill or mountain with steep sides descending to the plain below.

1 Awkward Encounters *After encountering the hitchhiker this many times, do you think Adams should finally pick him up? Why?*

Vocabulary
arid (ar′ id) *adj.* dry; parched

Literary Element Practice

SPIRAL REVIEW **Onomatopoeia** Explain that onomatopoeia is when a word or group of words imitate the sound they describe. Point out the word *slap* on this page as an example. Have students list examples of onomatopoeia as you **write** them on the board. You can start with these examples:

- splat
- boom
- crash
- twinkle

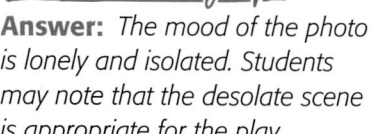

View the Photograph How would you describe the overall mood of this photo? Is this photo appropriate for *The Hitchhiker?* Why or why not? ★

time of year. I went inside, and asked if there was a telephone. I had the feeling that if only I could speak to someone familiar, someone I loved, I could pull myself together.

SOUND. *Nickel put in slot.*

OPERATOR. Number, please?

ADAMS. Long distance.

SOUND. *Return of nickel: buzz.*

LONG DISTANCE. This is long distance.[9]

ADAMS. I'd like to put in a call to my home in Brooklyn, New York. My name is Ronald Adams. The number there is Beechwood 2-0828.

LONG DISTANCE. Thank you. What is your number?

ADAMS. 312.

ALBUQUERQUE OPR. Albuquerque.

LONG DISTANCE. New York for Gallup. [*Pause.*]

NEW YORK OPR. New York.

LONG DISTANCE. Gallup, New Mexico, calling Beechwood 2-0828. [*Fade.*]

9. At the time of this story—around 1940—long distance calls needed to be connected by operators. A local operator would contact an operator on the other end and they would connect the two long distance parties.

Make and Verify Predictions *What do you predict will happen on this phone call?* **2**

Teach

Reading Strategy 2

Make and Verify Predictions **Sample answer:** *I think he is going to find out that someone he loves has just died.*

View the Photograph ★

Answer: *The mood of the photo is lonely and isolated. Students may note that the desolate scene is appropriate for the play.*

Advanced Learners

DIFFERENTIATED INSTRUCTION

Mapping the Story One way Fletcher helps readers know where they are in the story is by reminding them how far Adams has traveled on his cross-country trip. Have more proficient students trace Adams's progression on a U.S. map. They can create a point-to-point outline of Adams's trip on an individual map, marking the page number on which Fletcher mentions each new location.

Teach

Reading Strategy 1

Make and Verify Predictions **Sample answer:** *I thought the hitchhiker was a ghost, but I didn't think Adams was dead.*

To check students' understanding of the selection, see Unit 4 Teaching Resources Book, p. 126.

ADAMS. I had read somewhere that love could banish demons. It was the middle of the morning. I knew Mother would be home. I pictured her, tall, white-haired, in her crisp house dress, going about her tasks. It would be enough, I thought, merely to hear the even calmness of her voice. . . .

LONG DISTANCE. Will you please deposit three dollars and eighty-five cents for the first three minutes? When you have deposited a dollar and a half, will you please wait until I have collected the money?

SOUND. *Clunk of six coins.*

LONG DISTANCE. All right, deposit another dollar and a half.

SOUND. *Clunk of six coins.*

LONG DISTANCE. Will you please deposit the remaining twelve cents?

SOUND. *Clunk of four coins.*

LONG DISTANCE. Ready with Brooklyn—go ahead, please.

ADAMS. Hello.

MRS. WHITNEY. Mrs. Adams's residence.

ADAMS. Hello. Hello—Mother?

MRS. WHITNEY. [*Very flat and rather proper . . . dumb, too, in a flighty sort of way.*] This is Mrs. Adams's residence. Who is it you wished to speak to, please?

ADAMS. Why—who's this?

MRS. WHITNEY This is Mrs. Whitney.

ADAMS. Whitney? I don't know any Mrs. Whitney. Is this Beechwood 2-0828?

MRS. WHITNEY. Yes.

ADAMS. Where's my mother? Where's Mrs. Adams?

MRS. WHITNEY. Mrs. Adams is not at home. She is still in the hospital.

ADAMS. The hospital!

MRS. WHITNEY. Yes. Who is this calling please? Is it a member of the family?

ADAMS. What's she in the hospital for?

MRS. WHITNEY. She's been **prostrated** for five days. Nervous breakdown. But who is this calling?

ADAMS. Nervous breakdown? But—my mother was never nervous . . .

MRS. WHITNEY. It's all taken place since the death of her oldest son, Ronald.

ADAMS. The death of her oldest son, Ronald. Hey—what is this? What number is this?

MRS. WHITNEY. This is Beechwood 2-0828. It's all been very sudden. He was killed just six days ago in an automobile accident on the Brooklyn Bridge.

OPERATOR. [*Breaking in.*] Your three minutes are up, sir. [*Silence.*]

OPERATOR. Your three minutes are up, sir. [*Pause.*] Your three minutes are up, sir. [*Fade.*] Sir, your three minutes are up. Your three minutes are up, sir.

ADAMS. [*Narrating in a strange voice.*] And so, I am sitting here in this deserted auto camp in Gallup, New Mexico. I am trying to think. I am trying to get hold of myself. Otherwise, I shall go mad . . . Outside it is night—the vast, soulless night of New Mexico. A million stars are in the sky. Ahead of me stretch a thousand miles of empty mesa, mountains, prairies—desert. Somewhere among them, he is waiting for me. Somewhere I shall know who he is, and who . . . I . . . am. . . .

MUSIC. *Up.*

Make and Verify Predictions *Did you predict this ending? Explain.* **1**

Vocabulary

prostrated (pros′ trāt id) *adj.* completely exhausted; helpless; overcome

Reading Practice

SPIRAL REVIEW **Repetition** Have readers find examples of repetition on this page. Most students will point to the operator's eerie repetition of the words "Your three minutes are up, sir." **Ask:** What effect does this use of repetition have on the reader? *(The repetition reinforces Adams's disbelief and surprise at what he has just learned. It also adds a feeling of madness to the story.)*

After You Read

Respond and Think Critically

Respond and Interpret

1. What part of the drama did you find most suspenseful or frightening? Explain.
2. (a)What is Adams's mother worried about at the beginning? (b)Why is this important to the story?
3. (a)What does Adams decide to do about the hitchhiker when he sees him at the railroad tracks? (b)What does this decision tell you about Adams's state of mind?

Analyze and Evaluate

4. How does Fletcher slow down the action and build suspense in the moments before the drama's final climax?
5. Fletcher builds her drama around the repeated appearances of the hitchhiker. Do you think this repetition lessens the suspense or adds to it? Explain.

Connect

6. **Big Idea** Awkward Encounters How do the other characters' reactions to Adams's behavior change as the story progresses?
7. **Connect to the Author** In addition to radio plays, Lucille Fletcher also wrote short stories, novels, and screenplays. Why do you think "The Hitchhiker" was performed as a radio drama?

Literary Element Idiom

An **idiom** is colorful language that expresses something in a figurative way. Idioms can be used in dialogue to help reveal a character's personality.

1. List two examples of idioms in the drama and explain what they mean.
2. What do the idioms in this drama reveal about the characters that Adams encounters?
3. How do the idioms add to the realism?

Reading Strategy Make and Verify Predictions

Review the predictions you recorded in your chart, and then answer these questions.

1. When Adams first picks up the girl, what did you think was going to happen? Why?
2. What clues about the end were provided at the beginning of the drama?

LOG ON **Literature** Online

Selection Resources For Selection Quizzes, eFlash-cards, and Reading-Writing Connection activities, go to glencoe.com and enter QuickPass code GL49787u4.

Vocabulary Practice

Practice with Word Usage Answer these questions to help you explore the meanings of vocabulary words from the selection.

1. What is the difference between an annoying situation and an **ominous** one?
2. If someone is **beckoning** you, what kind of a response does that person want?
3. Why would an **arid** season probably be harmful to a farm?
4. What kind of event might cause someone to become **prostrated?**

Writing

Write a Dramatic Scene What do you think would happen if Adams were to make it to California? Write a dramatic scene about his arrival in Hollywood. In your scene, show how Adams's state of mind and his understanding of his situation have progressed since the auto camp in New Mexico. Follow Fletcher's example and write the scene for a radio broadcast, including directions for sound effects and music.

After You Read

Assess

1. Answers will vary.
2. (a) She is worried that something will happen to Adams while driving. (b) This is important because it sets up the ending of the story and foreshadows what happens to Adams.
3. (a) He asks if it has rained recently. (b) It leads him to suspect that there is something "unreal" about the hitchhiker; because he had rain on his shoulders even though it hadn't rained recently.
4. *Sample answer:* She plays out the entire sequence in which he places the call with the operator and deposits the change. With each step of the process, the suspense builds.
5. Answers will vary.
6. As the story progresses, the characters seem more alarmed by Adams's behavior. The mechanic in the beginning is merely puzzled by Adams, and the girl is terrified by him.
7. Answers will vary.

Literary Element

1. *Sample answer:* When Adams says, "keep your eyes peeled on the road," he means keep your eyes open and look carefully. The phrase "taking a nip" means he has been drinking.
2. The idioms reveal that these are simple, rural, small-town people.
3. The idioms help the dialogue mimic the way people talk.

Reading Strategy

1. Answers will vary.
2. His mother's tears and warning about not picking up any strangers are clues to the ominous nature of the hitchhiker. Also, in Adams's beginning narration, he says "At any moment the link with life may break" suggesting that his life is ending.

Vocabulary Practice

1. An annoying situation would only present a small problem, but an ominous situation could be serious.
2. The person is looking for you to come over to them right away.
3. It would be harmful because it might be too dry for the crops to grow.
4. A sad or shocking event, like the loss of a loved one

Writing

Students' scenes should

- depict what happens when Adams arrives in Hollywood
- reflect how Adams's state of mind has changed

Vocabulary Workshop

Denotation and Connotation

Focus

Brainstorm a list of words that carry an association beyond their definition. Have students list synonyms for the noun *smell (scent, odor, stench, fragrance, stink,* and *aroma).* Discuss the connotation of each word.

Teach

Denotation and Connotation

Remind students that a denotation indicates the exact meaning of a word. Connotation refers to an underlying emotion or value beyond a word's dictionary meaning.

Assess

Practice

Possible answers:

1. **finality:** *(denotation)* end, finish, completeness, entirety; *(connotation)* ominous terminality **lonely:** *(denotation)* alone; *(connotation)* uncomfortably desolate

   Fletcher may have chosen the word *finality*, rather than *ending* or *completeness* to convey an ominous connotation.
2. Answers will vary. Sample answer: *drab*; synonyms: *dull, dingy. Dingy* gives a sense of dirtiness; *dull* suggests not only uninteresting, but also worn out; and *drab* indicates something depressingly uninteresting.

For additional vocabulary practice, see Glencoe Interactive Vocabulary CD-ROM.

Learning Objectives

In this workshop, you will focus on the following objective:

Vocabulary: Understanding denotation and connotation.

Vocabulary Workshop

Denotation and Connotation

Literature Connection In the following quotation, Lucille Fletcher conveys more than the **denotation** (or the literal meaning) of the words; she also conveys the **connotation** (or the feelings suggested) by them.

> *"He merely stood there, waiting, almost drooping a little, the cheap overnight bag in his hand."*
>
> —Lucille Fletcher, from "The Hitchhiker"

The description of the hitchhiker provides the reader with an image of a pathetic man. Even his overnight bag is "cheap." The denotation of the word *cheap* is "inexpensive," and Fletcher could have used another word, such as *low-priced,* to convey that meaning. However, the connotative sense of the word *cheap*—"shabby" or "of poor quality"—adds to the sad and dismal image of the hitchhiker.

A semantic chart like the one below can help you analyze connotations.

- In the first column of the chart, write the words you will analyze.
- Find the definition of each word in a dictionary and record it in the denotation column.
- In the third column of the chart, record each word's connotations. For example, if one of the words were *frightful,* you might associate it with events in a horror movie or with the screeching sound some people make when something frightful occurs.

	Denotation	Connotation
cheap	inexpensive	shabby
finality		
lonely		

Denotation and Connotation

The **denotation** of a word is its literal meaning; the **connotation** of a word is its implied meanings and associations.

Tip

If you are asked for the denotation of a word, do your best to supply its dictionary definition. If asked for connotations, think of your own associations with the word, especially positive and negative feelings. Also consider situations in which you might use the word and images the word brings to mind.

Practice

1. Complete the chart above on a separate sheet of paper. Discuss the denotations and connotations of the three words. Explain why Fletcher chose *finality* instead of *ending* or *completeness.*
2. Find another word in "The Hitchhiker" for which you can name two or three synonyms. Explain how the connotations help convey shades of meaning.

LOG ON Literature Online

Vocabulary For more vocabulary practice, go to glencoe.com and enter QuickPass code GL49787u4.

Vocabulary Practice

SPIRAL REVIEW **Word Journal** Encourage students to keep a word journal in which they list new words as they learn them. Students should define these words and identify each word's connotations. Encourage them to categorize the journal in a way that is meaningful and helpful for them.

A student might categorize the journal by words that are difficult to spell, words that have more than one meaning, or parts of speech. Ask students if they can come up with any other ways to divide their journals and to share their ideas with the class.

Before You Read

World Literature
Romania/France

The Leader

Meet **Eugène Ionesco**
(1909–1994)

Eugène Ionesco's first play, *The Bald Soprano* (1949), sprang from an idea he had while learning English. The English language textbook he was reading featured empty clichés and pointless dialogue. With this type of language, he wondered how people managed to communicate at all. In *The Bald Soprano,* conversation between characters becomes more and more meaningless as they continue to talk.

This was like no comedy ever written before. Audiences used to traditional drama booed the actors on stage. Audiences for Ionesco's second play, *The Lesson,* chased the lead actor off the stage and demanded their money back. Even though most theater critics also ridiculed Ionesco's early work, *The Bald Soprano* and *The Lesson* established Ionesco as an avant-garde artist.

> *"It's not a certain society that seems ridiculous to me—it's mankind."*
>
> —Eugène Ionesco

Trouble at Home Eugène Ionesco was born in Slatina, Romania. His father was Romanian and his mother was French, and in 1911, his family moved to Paris. His parents were not happy together and his father soon returned to Romania. In 1925, Ionesco's mother returned to Bucharest, Romania, to reunite with her husband. When she arrived, she found that he had secretly divorced her, remarried, and gained custody of the children. From then on Ionesco lived unhappily with his father, whom he described as controlling and violent. Ionesco escaped his troubled home when he went to college. There he studied literature and French and began writing poems and literary criticism.

Stampeding Rhinoceroses Once Ionesco began to write plays, he wrote many of them in the space of just a few years. His first popular success came with the play *Rhinoceros* (1959), which contains the following exchange between an elderly man and a logician, a person with special training in logic:

> LOGICIAN [to the Old Gentleman]: Here is an example of a syllogism. The cat has four paws. Isidore and Fricot both have four paws. Therefore Isidore and Fricot are cats.
>
> OLD GENTLEMAN [to the Logician]: My dog has got four paws.
>
> LOGICIAN [to the Old Gentleman]: Then it's a cat.

Such is the humor and wit of Ionesco.

LOG ON **Literature** Online

Author Search For more about Eugène Ionesco, go to glencoe.com and enter QuickPass code GL49787u4.

Before You Read

Focus

Bellringer Options

Daily Language Practice Transparency 80

Or display images of fans at a sports event or pep rally and images of people rioting.

Ask: How are these scenes alike and how are they different?

As they read, students should think about how people lose control of their behavior when drawn into emotionally charged situations.

Selection Skills

The Leader

Literary Elements
- Stage Directions (SE pp. 790–798)
- Farce (SE p. 798)

Listening/Speaking/Viewing Skills
- Perform (SE p. 799)
- Verbal Techniques (TE p. 792)

Reading Skills
- Draw Conclusions About Author's Meaning (SE pp. 790–799)

Vocabulary Skills
- Context Clues (SE p. 799)

Writing Skills/Grammar
- Understand Adverbs (TE p. 790)
- Use Interjections (TE p. 794)

Before You Read

Focus

Summary

The characters in this play are citizens anxiously awaiting the arrival of their leader. They are encouraged and admonished by the announcer, who is the only one able to see the approaching leader. The announcer gives a running commentary on the leader's activities until the leader finally arrives on stage. The characters are shocked and then accept the fact that their leader has no head.

For summaries in languages other than English, see Unit 4 Teaching Resources Book, pp. 128–133.

Vocabulary

Brief Narrative Have students form pairs. Each pair should write a brief narrative that incorporates all five vocabulary words. Narratives should be at least a few sentences to demonstrate understanding of the vocabulary.

For additional vocabulary practice, see Unit 4 Teaching Resources Book, p. 136.

Literature and Reading Preview

Connect to the Drama

Have you ever found yourself going along with something even though you thought it was silly or wrong? Freewrite about a time when you went along with what others were doing.

Build Background

Ionesco's plays are classified as Theatre of the Absurd, a style of drama that first appeared in the 1950s. Plays of this style include ridiculous and surreal settings, and the characters reveal the profound nonsense of human action and interaction.

Set Purposes for Reading

Big Idea Awkward Encounters

As you read *The Leader,* ask yourself, Why does Ionesco create awkward encounters between his characters?

Literary Element Stage Directions

The instructions written by a playwright to describe the actions and appearance of characters are called **stage directions.** Stage directions can also describe sets, costumes, and lighting. When you watch a play, you hear the dialogue and see the visual details. When you read a play, however, you must rely on the stage directions. As you read, ask yourself, How do the stage directions help me interpret the meaning of the play?

Reading Strategy Draw Conclusions About Author's Meaning

In literary works, an author's meaning is usually implied rather than stated directly. You **draw conclusions about an author's meaning** when you determine the author's meaning based on evidence from the text. As you read, ask yourself, How do the details in this play suggest Ionesco's meaning?

Tip Create a Chart As you read, use a chart like the one below to note details that strike you as important or compelling. Then identify the underlying idea the details support.

Compelling Detail	Underlying Idea
The admirers stay pressed against the wall.	They are trying to remain unseen.

Learning Objectives

For pages 789–799

In studying this text, you will focus on the following objectives:

Literary Study: Analyzing stage directions.

Reading: Drawing conclusions about author's meaning.

Speaking and Listening: Presenting an oral interpretation.

Vocabulary

riveted (riv′ it əd) *adj.* fixed or secured firmly; p. 791 *In his fear, he felt as though his feet were riveted to the floor.*

itinerary (ī tin′ ər er′ ē) *n.* the planned route for a journey; p. 793 *Using the map, they planned the itinerary for their cross-country vacation.*

exalted (eg′ zōl təd) *adj.* noble; exaggerated; p. 793 *The scientist had an exalted commitment to finding a cure for cancer.*

vanquished (vang′ kwishd) *n.* people who have been defeated in battle; p. 795 *The vanquished surrendered their arms.*

apparition (ap′ ə rish′ ən) *n.* an unexpected or unusual sight; p. 797 *When bubbles appeared to be coming from the magician's hand, the audience gasped at the apparition.*

Grammar Practice

SPIRAL REVIEW **Understand Adverbs**

Explain to students that adverbs modify verbs, adjectives, or other adverbs by telling *when, where, how,* and *to what degree.* **Write** the following lines on the board: "Glen studied the itinerary closely."

Discuss ways adverbs add meaning to sentences. Show how the adverb answers a question: How did Glen study the itinerary? *(closely)*

Ask: What other adverbs would make sense in place of *closely*? *(possible answers: secretly, excitedly)* Have students find adverbs in the selection and write them in their notebook, along with the words they modify. Then ask students to choose two adverbs and use each in a sentence of their own.

French Print of a Man in an Overcoat, 1811.

The Leader

Eugène Ionesco

CHARACTERS

1

THE ANNOUNCER	THE FEMALE ADMIRER	THE GIRLFRIEND
THE MALE ADMIRER	THE BOYFRIEND	THE LEADER

[*Standing with his back to the public, center-stage, and with his eyes fixed on the up-stage exit, the* ANNOUNCER *waits for the arrival of the* LEADER. *To right and left,* **riveted** *to the walls, two of the* LEADER'S ADMIRERS, *a man and a woman, also wait for his arrival.*]

ANNOUNCER. [*After a few tense moments in the same position.*] There he is! There he is! At the end of the street! [*Shouts of "Hurrah!" etc., are heard.*] There's the leader! He's coming, he's coming nearer! [*Cries of acclaim and applause are heard from the wings.*] It's better if he doesn't see us . . . [*The* TWO ADMIRERS *hug the wall even closer.*] Watch out! [*The* ANNOUNCER *gives vent to a brief display of enthusiasm.*] Hurrah! Hurrah! The leader! The leader! Long live the leader! [*The* TWO ADMIRERS, *with their bodies rigid and flattened against the wall, thrust their necks and heads as far forward as they can to get a glimpse of the* LEADER.] The leader! The leader! [*The* TWO ADMIRERS *in unison:*] Hurrah! Hurrah! [*Other "Hurrahs!" mingled with "Hurrah! Bravo!" come from the wings and gradually die down.*] Hurrah! Bravo!

Vocabulary

riveted (riv′ it əd) *adj.* fixed or secured firmly

Awkward Encounters *What does the admirers' response tell you about the relationship between them and the announcer?* **2**

Teach

Big Idea 1

Awkward Encounters Have students keep these questions in mind as they read.

Ask: Why does Ionesco have the announcer give a running commentary on the leader's actions? *(In a society, few people have direct contact with their leaders. They must rely on the observations of others, such as news reporters.)* Why are the characters willing to accept a headless leader? *(Ionesco sees most people as mindless members of a group, capable only of a "herd" mentality.)*

Big Idea 2

Awkward Encounters

Answer: *The announcer is in charge of the situation. The admirers do as he says, even though what he is telling them does not make sense.*

APPROACHING For approaching-level students, explain the concept of absurdism. Ask them to look for three examples of absurd events in the first few pages of the selection.

English Learners

DIFFERENTIATED INSTRUCTION

Beginning/Early Intermediate English learners may have difficulty understanding Ionesco's dialogue because it is constantly interrupted with stage directions for actors both on and off the stage. As a class, go over the lines on this page. Make sure students are clear who is speaking each line. Then, have students perform these lines. Some students will have to stay out of view of the audience to read the lines for offstage actors. Hearing the dialogue performed aloud will help students understand the writer's intention.

Teach

Reading Strategy 1

Interpret **Ask:** What does the stage direction, "echoes . . . like a bleating cry" tell you about the author's purpose? *(Ionesco may want the audience to associate his characters with sheep.)*

Big Idea 2

Awkward Encounters
Answer: *He finds common ground on which to build a future in the fact that they are strangers.*

Literary Element 3

Stage Directions **Answer:** *They mimic the actions of the crowd. Also, the TWO ADMIRERS believe everything the announcer reports to them.*

[The ANNOUNCER takes a step up-stage, stops, then up-stage, followed by the TWO ADMIRERS, saying as he goes: "Ah! Too bad! He's going away! He's going away! Follow me quickly! After him!" The ANNOUNCER and the TWO ADMIRERS leave, crying: "Leader! Leeeeader! Lee-ee-eader!" (This last "Lee-ee-eader!" echoes in the wings like a bleating cry.)] **1**

[Silence. The stage is empty for a few brief moments. The BOYFRIEND enters right, and his GIRLFRIEND left; they meet center-stage.]

BOYFRIEND. Forgive me, Madame, or should I say Mademoiselle?

GIRLFRIEND. I beg your pardon, I'm afraid I don't happen to know you!

BOYFRIEND. And I'm afraid I don't know you either!

GIRLFRIEND. Then neither of us knows each other.

BOYFRIEND. Exactly. We have something in common. It means that between us there is a basis of understanding on which we can build the edifice[1] of our future.

GIRLFRIEND. That leaves me cold, I'm afraid.

[She makes as if to go.]

BOYFRIEND. Oh, my darling, I adore you.

GIRLFRIEND. Darling, so do I!

[They embrace.]

BOYFRIEND. I'm taking you with me, darling. We'll get married straightaway.

[They leave left. The stage is empty for a brief moment.]

ANNOUNCER. *[Enters up-stage followed by the TWO ADMIRERS.]* But the leader swore that he'd be passing here.

MALE ADMIRER. Are you absolutely sure of that?

ANNOUNCER. Yes, yes, of course.

FEMALE ADMIRER. Was it really on his way?

ANNOUNCER. Yes, yes. He should have passed by here, it was marked on the Festival program . . .

MALE ADMIRER. Did you actually see it yourself and hear it with your own eyes and ears?

ANNOUNCER. He told someone. Someone else!

MALE ADMIRER. But who? Who was this someone else?

FEMALE ADMIRER. Was it a reliable person? A friend of yours?

ANNOUNCER. A friend of mine who I know very well. *[Suddenly in the background one hears renewed cries of "Hurrah!" and "Long live the leader!"]* That's him now! There he is! Hip! Hip! Hurrah! There he is! Hide yourselves. Hide yourselves!

[The TWO ADMIRERS flatten themselves as before against the wall, stretching their necks out towards the wings from where the shouts of acclamation come; the ANNOUNCER watches fixedly up-stage his back to the public.]

ANNOUNCER. The leader's coming. He approaches. He's bending. He's unbending. *[At each of the ANNOUNCER'S words, the ADMIRERS give a start and stretch their necks even farther; they shudder.]* He's jumping. He's crossed the river. They're shaking his hand. He sticks out his thumb. Can you hear? They're laughing. *[The ANNOUNCER and the TWO ADMIRERS also laugh.]* Ah . . . ! they're giving him a box of tools. What's he going to do with them? Ah . . . ! he's signing autographs. The leader is stroking a hedgehog, a superb hedgehog! The crowd applauds. He's dancing, with the hedgehog in his hand. He's embracing his dancer. Hurrah! Hurrah! *[Cries are heard in*

1. An *edifice* is a building or a complex structure of ideas.

2 Awkward Encounters *How does the boyfriend respond to his awkward encounter with the girlfriend?*

Stage Directions *What does this stage direction tell you about the reactions of the Announcer and the Two Admirers?* **3**

Listening Practice

SPIRAL REVIEW **Identify Verbal Techniques**

Actors give clues when they speak. For instance, on page 792, the announcer says, "That's him now! There he is! Hip! Hip! Hurrah!" The stage directions don't tell if the character shouts his dialogue or speaks softly. The audience must rely on the actor to interpret the words.

- Have students think of situations in which their voices convey meaning, such as winning a prize or apologizing.
- Have students write dialogue to go with each situation.

Allow volunteers to read some of the dialogues to the class.

the wings.] He's being photographed, with his dancer on one hand and the hedgehog on the other . . . He greets the crowd . . . He spits a tremendous distance.

FEMALE ADMIRER. Is he coming past here? Is he coming in our direction?

MALE ADMIRER. Are we really on his route?

ANNOUNCER. [*Turns his head to the* TWO ADMIRERS.] Quiet, and don't move, you're spoiling everything . . .

FEMALE ADMIRER. But even so . . .

ANNOUNCER. Keep quiet, I tell you! Didn't I tell you he'd promised, that he had fixed his **itinerary** himself. . . . [*He turns back up-stage and cries.*] Hurrah! Hurrah! Long live the leader! [*Silence.*] Long live, long live, the leader! [*Silence.*] Long live, long live, long live the lead-er! [*The* TWO ADMIRERS, *unable to contain themselves, also give a sudden cry of:*] Hurrah! Long live the leader!

ANNOUNCER. [*to the* ADMIRERS] Quiet, you two! Calm down! You're spoiling everything! [*Then, once more looking up-stage, with the* ADMIRERS *silenced.*] Long live the leader! [*Wildly enthusiastic.*] Hurrah! Hurrah! He's changing his shirt. He disappears behind a red screen. He reappears! [*The applause intensifies.*] Bravo! Bravo! [*The* ADMIRERS *also long to cry "Bravo" and applaud; they put their hands to their mouths to stop themselves.*] He's putting his tie on! He's reading his newspaper and drinking his morning coffee! He's still got his hedgehog . . . He's leaning on the edge of the parapet.[2] The parapet breaks. He gets up . . . he gets up unaided! [*Applause, shouts of "Hurrah!"*] Bravo! Well done! He brushes his soiled clothes.

2. A *parapet* is a low wall or railing.

Vocabulary

itinerary (ī tin′ ər er′ ē) *n.* the planned route for a journey

TWO ADMIRERS. [*Stamping their feet.*] Oh! Ah! Oh! Oh! Ah! Ah!

ANNOUNCER. He's mounting the stool! He's climbing piggy-back, they're offering him a thin-ended wedge, he knows it's meant as a joke, and he doesn't mind, he's laughing. **4**

[*Applause and enormous acclaim.*]

MALE ADMIRER. [*To the* FEMALE ADMIRER.] You hear that? You hear? Oh! If I were king . . .

FEMALE ADMIRER. Ah . . . ! the leader! [*This is said in an* **exalted** *tone.*]

ANNOUNCER. [*Still with his back to the public.*] He's mounting the stool. No. He's getting down. A little girl offers him a bouquet of flowers . . . What's he going to do? He takes the flowers . . . He embraces the little girl . . . calls her "my child" . . .

MALE ADMIRER. He embraces the little girl . . . calls her "my child" . . .

FEMALE ADMIRER. He embraces the little girl . . . calls her "my child" . . .

ANNOUNCER. He gives her the hedgehog. The little girl's crying . . . Long live the leader! Long live the leead-er!

MALE ADMIRER. Is he coming past here?

FEMALE ADMIRER. Is he coming past here?

ANNOUNCER. [*With a sudden run, dashes out up-stage.*] He's going away! Hurry! Come on!

[*He disappears, followed by the* TWO ADMIRERS, *all crying "Hurrah! Hurrah!"*]

5 Stage Directions *What do you think Ionesco is implying by having the Announcer spend most of the play with his back turned toward the audience?*

6 Draw Conclusions About Author's Meaning *What technique does the author use in this and the previous few lines? What conclusions can you draw about the author's meaning?*

Vocabulary

exalted (eg′ zôl təd) *adj.* noble; exaggerated

Teach

Literary Element 4

Satire **Ask:** What is being satirized in this dialogue? *(The author is satirizing how some people praise their leader regardless of the leader's actions.)*

Literary Element 5

Stage Directions **Answer:** *The announcer is ostensibly watching and reporting the leader's words and actions to the public, but Ionesco is implying that the news media serve the ruling class rather than the public.*

Reading Strategy 6

Draw Conclusions About Author's Meaning
Answer: *The author uses repetition here. The admirers repeat what the announcer has said about the leader embracing the little girl. Conclusions will vary but might include the fact that the repetition seems hypnotic and that the author is drawing attention to the way in which people are hypnotized into following a leader, whether or not he or she is worthy of admiration.*

English Learners

DIFFERENTIATED INSTRUCTION

PARTNERS

Beginning/Early Intermediate English language learners are often challenged by idioms. **Ask:** What idioms are you familiar with? *(If students have trouble thinking of idioms, offer these examples to help them get started: "a bad hair day," "apple of my eye," "go out on a limb")* Have students work in pairs with proficient English speakers to decode these idioms and other idioms generated by the class.

- GIRLFRIEND: That leaves me cold, I'm afraid. *(disinterested)*
- ANNOUNCER: You're spoiling everything! *(ruining)*

Encourage students to find more idioms as they progress through the story and to share them with the class.

Teach

Reading Strategy 1

Interpret Ask: How can the boyfriend and girlfriend be oblivious to the excitement surrounding them? *(They are so in love that they are unaware of anything else.)*

Expectation (Erwartung), 1935–1936. Richard Oelze. Oil on canvas, 32⅛ x 39⅝ in. The Museum of Modern Art, NY.

[The stage is empty for a few moments. The BOYFRIEND *and* GIRLFRIEND *enter, entwined*[3] *in an embrace; they halt center-stage and separate; she carries a basket on her arm.]*

GIRLFRIEND. Let's go to the market and get some eggs!

BOYFRIEND. Oh! I love them as much as you do!

[She takes his arm. From the right the ANNOUNCER *arrives running, quickly regaining his place, back to the public, followed closely by the* TWO ADMIRERS, *arriving one from the left and the other from the right; the* TWO ADMIRERS *knock into the* BOYFRIEND *and* GIRLFRIEND *who were about to leave right.]*

MALE ADMIRER. Sorry!

BOYFRIEND. Oh! Sorry!

FEMALE ADMIRER. Sorry! Oh! Sorry!

GIRLFRIEND. Oh! Sorry, sorry, sorry, so sorry!

MALE ADMIRER. Sorry, sorry, sorry, oh! sorry, sorry, so sorry!

BOYFRIEND. Oh, oh, oh, oh, oh, oh! So sorry, everyone!

GIRLFRIEND. [*To her* BOYFRIEND.] Come along, Adolphe! [*To the* TWO ADMIRERS:] No harm done! 1

[She leaves, leading her BOYFRIEND *by the hand.]*

3. *Entwined* means "coiled or twisted together."

Grammar Practice

SPIRAL REVIEW

Use Interjections

Explain that an interjection is a word or phrase that expresses emotion. It has no grammatical connection to other words in a sentence. Point out the interjections in these examples:

- Ha! That is a funny story!
- Oh, look at the sky!
- Great! You are on time for once.

Have students complete each statement with an interjection.

______, the cake is ruined.

______! Stop that.

______, what happened?

______! I lost my wallet.

Then ask them to write down an original sentence that contains an interjection.

ANNOUNCER. [*Watching up-stage.*] The leader is being pressed forward, and pressed back, and now they're pressing[4] his trousers! [*The* TWO ADMIRERS *regain their places.*] The leader is smiling. Whilst they're pressing his trousers, he walks about. He tastes the flowers and the fruits growing in the stream. He's also tasting the roots of the trees. He suffers the little children to come unto him. He has confidence in everybody. He inaugurates the police force. He pays tribute to justice. He salutes the great victors and the great **vanquished.** Finally he recites a poem. The people are very moved.

TWO ADMIRERS. Bravo! Bravo! [*Then, sobbing:*] Boo! Boo! Boo!

ANNOUNCER. All the people are weeping. [*Loud cries are heard from the wings; the* ANNOUNCER *and the* ADMIRERS *also start to bellow.*] Silence! [*The* TWO ADMIRERS *fall silent; and there is silence from the wings.*] They've given the leader's trousers back. The leader puts them on. He looks happy. Hurrah! [*"Bravos," and acclaim from the wings. The* TWO ADMIRERS *also shout their acclaim, jump about, without being able to see anything of what is presumed to be happening in the wings.*] The leader's sucking his thumb! [*To the* TWO ADMIRERS*:*] Back, back to your places, you two, don't move, behave yourselves and shout: "Long live the leader!"

TWO ADMIRERS. [*Flattened against the wall, shouting.*] Long live, long live the leader!

ANNOUNCER. Be quiet, I tell you, you'll spoil everything! Look out, the leader's coming!

4. Here, *pressing* means "ironing."

2 Draw Conclusions About Author's Meaning *From this monologue, what conclusion can you draw about the author's attitude toward the leader's actions?*

Vocabulary

vanquished (vang′ kwishd) *n.* people who have been defeated in battle

MALE ADMIRER. [*In the same position.*] The leader's coming!

FEMALE ADMIRER. The leader's coming!

ANNOUNCER. Watch out! And keep quiet! Oh! The leader's going away! Follow him! Follow me!

[*The* ANNOUNCER *goes out up-stage, running; the* TWO ADMIRERS *leave right and left, whilst in the wings the acclaim mounts, then fades. The stage is momentarily empty. The* BOYFRIEND, *followed by his* GIRLFRIEND, *appear left running across the stage right.*]

BOYFRIEND. [*Running.*] You won't catch me! You won't catch me! 3

[*Goes out.*]

GIRLFRIEND. [*Running.*] Wait a moment! Wait a moment!

[*She goes out. The stage is empty for a moment; then once more the* BOYFRIEND *and* GIRLFRIEND *cross the stage at a run, and leave.*]

BOYFRIEND. You won't catch me!

GIRLFRIEND. Wait a moment!

[*They leave right. The stage is empty. The* ANNOUNCER *reappears up-stage, the* MALE ADMIRER *from the right, the* FEMALE ADMIRER *from the left. They meet center.*]

MALE ADMIRER. We missed him!

FEMALE ADMIRER. Rotten luck!

ANNOUNCER. It was your fault!

MALE ADMIRER. That's not true!

FEMALE ADMIRER. No, that's not true!

ANNOUNCER. Are you suggesting it was mine?

MALE ADMIRER. No, we didn't mean that!

FEMALE ADMIRER. No, we didn't mean that!

[*Noise of acclaim and "Hurrahs" from the wings.*]

Awkward Encounters *Why is the conversation here between the admirers and the announcer so awkward?* 4

Approaching Level

DIFFERENTIATED INSTRUCTION

Established Encourage students to discuss how the characters relate to each other and the Leader. **Ask:** Which words best describe how the characters feel about their leader? *(fascinated, interested, complimentary)* **Ask:** How does the behavior of the characters toward their leader compare with how real people act toward their leaders? *(Possible answer: Like the characters in the play, real people seem interested in every aspect of their leaders' lives.)*

Teach

Reading Strategy 2

Draw Conclusions About Author's Meaning

Answer: *The author is showing how the leader's image is delivered to the public. The announcer helps with this delivery. According to this image, the leader is a man in tune with nature, children, and the public. He cares about people and is sensitive. Because the author's tone is ironic, we know that the author does not really believe the leader embodies these traits.*

Reading Strategy 3

Interpret **Ask:** Why is the boyfriend running from the girlfriend? *(The author is reversing traditional courtship roles to add to the absurdity of the dramatic action.)*

Big Idea 4

Awkward Encounters

Answer: *They have missed the leader. The admirers blame bad luck, but the announcer blames them. When they refuse to take the blame, he assumes they are blaming him.*

APPROACHING **Ask:** What does Ionesco use to make the dialogue even more absurd? *(Repetition)*

Teach

Literary Element 1

Stage Directions Answer: *The stage directions suggest that the characters are suffering mass hysteria. Their fanatical hero worship derives from unquestioning allegiance to authority.*

View the Art ★

Answer: *The people in the painting show a variety of expressions including awe, rapture, sternness, and boredom.*

Ilja Efimovic Repin (1844–1930) was a famous Russian artist. He created realistic paintings that often criticized faults he saw in society.

Procession of the Cross in the Kursk Region (detail), 1880–1883. Ilja Efimovic Repin. Oil on canvas. Tretykov Gallery, Moscow, Russia.

View the Art Ilja Efimovic Repin's paintings often criticized faults he saw in society. How would you describe the expressions on the faces of the people in this painting? ★

ANNOUNCER. Hurrah!

FEMALE ADMIRER. It's from over there! [*She points up-stage.*]

MALE ADMIRER. Yes, it's from over there! [*He points left.*]

ANNOUNCER. Very well. Follow me! Long live the leader!

[*He runs out right, followed by the* TWO ADMIRERS, *also shouting.*]

TWO ADMIRERS. Long live the leader!

[*They leave. The stage is empty for a moment. The* BOYFRIEND *and his* GIRLFRIEND *appear left; the* BOYFRIEND *exits up-stage; the* GIRLFRIEND, *after saying "I'll get you!", runs out right. The* ANNOUNCER *and the* TWO ADMIRERS *appear from up-stage. The* ANNOUNCER *says to the* ADMIRERS:] Long live the leader! [*This is repeated by the* ADMIRERS. *Then, still talking to the* ADMIRERS, *he says:*] Follow me! Follow the leader! [*He leaves up-stage, still running and shouting:*] Follow him!

[*The* MALE ADMIRER *exits right, the* FEMALE ADMIRER *left into the wings. During the whole of this, the acclaim is heard louder or fainter according to the rhythm of the stage action; the stage is empty for a moment, then the* BOYFRIEND *and* GIRLFRIEND *appear from right and left, crying:*]

BOYFRIEND. I'll get you!

GIRLFRIEND. You won't get me!

[*They leave at a run, shouting:*] *Long live the leader!* [*The* ANNOUNCER *and the* TWO ADMIRERS *emerge from up-stage, also shouting: "Long live the leader", followed by the* BOYFRIEND *and* GIRLFRIEND. *They all leave right, in single file, crying as they run: "The leader! Long live the leader! We'll get him! It's from over here! You won't get me!"*]

[*They enter and leave, employing all the exits; finally, entering from left, from right, and from up-stage they all meet center, whilst the acclaim and the applause from the wings becomes a fearful din.*[5] *They embrace each other feverishly, crying at the tops of their voices:*] *Long live the leader! Long live the leader! Long live the leader!*

[*Then, abruptly, silence falls.*]

5. *Din* means "a jumble of loud, confused sounds."

Stage Directions *What do these stage directions suggest about the behavior of the characters in the play?* 1

Writing Practice

SPIRAL REVIEW **Identify Author's Purpose** Give examples of ways in which students can determine author's purpose:

- Locate a direct statement.
- Infer from tone.
- Compare the work with other work by the same author.
- Analyze how the author treats his or her subject.

When students finish reading the play, have them write a paragraph about the author's purpose for writing the play. They should also explain how they arrived at their conclusions. Students should support their ideas with examples from the text. They may also refer to the author's background and his opinions and analysis of society.

ANNOUNCER. The leader is arriving. Here's the leader. To your places! Attention!

[*The* MALE ADMIRER *and the* GIRLFRIEND *flatten themselves against the wall right; the* FEMALE ADMIRER *and the* BOYFRIEND *against the wall left; the two couples are in each other's arms, embracing.*]

MALE ADMIRER AND GIRLFRIEND. My dear, my darling!

FEMALE ADMIRER AND BOYFRIEND. My dear, my darling!

[*Meanwhile the* ANNOUNCER *has taken up his place, back to the audience, looking fixedly up-stage; a lull in the applause.*]

ANNOUNCER. Silence. The leader has eaten his soup. He is coming. He is nigh.[6]

2 [*The acclaim redoubles its intensity; the* TWO ADMIRERS *and the* BOYFRIEND *and* GIRLFRIEND *shout:*]

ALL. Hurrah! Hurrah! Long live the leader!

[*They throw confetti before he arrives. Then the* ANNOUNCER *hurls himself suddenly to one side to allow the* LEADER *to pass; the other four characters freeze with outstretched arms holding confetti; but still say:*] Hurrah! [*The* LEADER *enters from up-stage, advances down-stage to center; to the footlights, hesitates, makes a step to left, then takes a decision and leaves with great, energetic strides by right, to the enthusiastic "Hurrahs!" of the* ANNOUNCER *and the feeble, somewhat astonished "Hurrahs!" of the other four; these, in fact, have some reason to be surprised, as the* LEADER *is headless, though wearing a hat. This is simple to effect: the actor playing the* LEADER *needing only to wear an overcoat with the collar turned up round his forehead and topped with a hat. The-man-in-an-overcoat-with-a-hat-without-a-head is a somewhat surprising* **apparition** *and will doubtless produce a certain sensation. After the* LEADER'S *disappearance, the* FEMALE ADMIRER *says:*]

FEMALE ADMIRER. But . . . but . . . the leader hasn't got a head!

ANNOUNCER. What's he need a head for when he's got genius!

BOYFRIEND. That's true! [*To the* GIRLFRIEND:] What's your name?

[*The* BOYFRIEND *to the* FEMALE ADMIRER, *the* FEMALE ADMIRER *to the* ANNOUNCER, *the* ANNOUNCER *to the* GIRLFRIEND, *the* GIRLFRIEND *to the* BOYFRIEND:] *What's yours? What's yours? What's yours?* [*Then, all together, one to the other:*] What's your name?

6. *Nigh* means "near."

Awkward Encounters *Consider Ionesco's attitude toward his subject so far. How do you think the Admirers and the Boyfriend and Girlfriend will react to their encounter with the headless leader?* 3

Draw Conclusions About Author's Meaning *What theme does the end of the play convey? Why do you think Ionesco chose to end the play this way?* 4

Vocabulary

apparition (ap′ ə rish′ ən) *n.* an unexpected or unusual sight

Teach

Reading Strategy 2

Draw Conclusions About Author's Purpose

Ask: What is the author's purpose for these stage directions? *(The author shows how the boyfriend and the girlfriend, previously unaware of the leader, are drawn into the general excitement; they begin shouting because everyone else is.)*

Big Idea 3

Awkward Encounters

Answer: *Evidence in the play supports conformity. The characters will still find the leader "admirable."*

Reading Strategy 4

Draw Conclusions About Author's Meaning

Answer: *The theme is that people—even people in love—are anonymous or unidentifiable to each other. Leaders, as well as lovers, are interchangeable and do not need to be present to be admired. People project leadership traits onto a leader, rather than finding out who the leader actually is.*

To check students' understanding of the selection, see Unit 4 Teaching Resources Book, p. 139.

Approaching Level

DIFFERENTIATED INSTRUCTION

Emerging Approaching-level students may benefit from taking part in a choral reading, which will help students understand the relationship between the written and spoken word.

Assign students to read sections of the play together. At first, read a section of the play aloud as students follow along silently. Later, assign parts and have students join in as you read aloud. Make the most of the dramatic elements of the play.

After You Read

Assess

1. Many students will find the play humorous.
2. (a) He tells them to follow him, to be quiet, and to stand still or hide. (b) He will take them to the leader if they obey him.
3. (a) The leader falls down, signs autographs, dances with a hedgehog, and recites a poem. (b) To show how we dramatize trivial activities of powerful people
4. (a) He says, "What's he need a head for when he's got genius?" (b) That people may follow a leader because others do, not because they have informed opinions.
5. The effect is rhythmic and hypnotic.
6. (a) At first, they are strangers, but they quickly declare their love. (b) They shift their affections to the admirers.
7. (a) It is humorous, with a bit of anxiety. (b) Details: Descriptions of the leader's activities, and the lines of the boyfriend and girlfriend are humorous. The announcer's bullying creates anxiety.
8. Students may mention the leader without his trousers and the boyfriend and girlfriend embracing the admirers. People behave inappropriately, but are unaware of this.
9. Answers will vary. Students should realize that people throughout time have criticized their leaders.

Literary Element

1. They see themselves as so insignificant that they are afraid to take up space.
2. It occurs after frenetic activity on stage. The emptiness functions as an interlude during which the audience can reflect upon the absurdity of the actions.

Progress Check

Can students identify stage directions?

If No → See Unit 4 Teaching Resources Book, p. 134.

Review: Farce

Farce: Boyfriend and girlfriend fall in love immediately; characters run around the stage; characters have exaggerated characteristics

Both Use humor and irony

Satire: Leader has no head; ridicules love; equates characters' actions with the game Follow the Leader

After You Read

Respond and Think Critically

Respond and Interpret

1. What was your overall reaction to the play? Explain.
2. (a)What does the announcer repeatedly instruct the admirers to do? (b)Why do they follow his directions?
3. (a)What types of activities is the leader involved in throughout the play? (b)Why does the announcer narrate these activities?
4. (a)How does the announcer respond when the female admirer points out that the leader has no head? (b)What theme is the author emphasizing here?

Analyze and Evaluate

5. The sentence "Long live the leader!" appears many times in Ionesco's play. What is the effect of such repetition on the audience?
6. (a)How does the relationship of the boyfriend and girlfriend change as the play progresses? (b)Evaluate the significance of their relationship at the end of the play.
7. (a)Describe the atmosphere the play conveys. (b)List three details that help to create this atmosphere.

Connect

8. **Big Idea** **Awkward Encounters** Describe a scene in the play in which you would have felt awkward but the characters did not seem to. What comment about human behavior is Ionesco making?
9. **Connect to Today** Would an audience in the United States today find this play relevant? Explain.

Literary Element Stage Directions

Stage directions can supply clues and bits of information that influence a reader's interpretation of the play. If that reader is the director, the stage directions are likely to affect his or her choices in staging the play.

1. Throughout the play, the stage directions tell the reader that the Two Admirers flatten themselves against the wall while trying to get a glimpse of the Leader. What does this behavior suggest about the roles of common people in the play?
2. A recurring stage direction in the play is *The stage is empty for a brief moment.* How might the repetition of this direction contribute to the meaning of the play?

Review: Farce

As you learned on page 759, **farce** is a type of comedy that uses ridiculous situations, characters, or events. Another type of comedy is satire. **Satire** often uses an ironic tone and ridicule to communicate its themes. An ironic tone is one that conveys the feeling that the author's attitude is the opposite of his characters. Ridicule is a type of humor that mocks its subject scornfully.

Partner Activity Where do the characteristics of farce and satire overlap? Discuss with a classmate which aspects of *The Leader* could be categorized as farce and which could be categorized as satire. Use a Venn diagram similar to the one below.

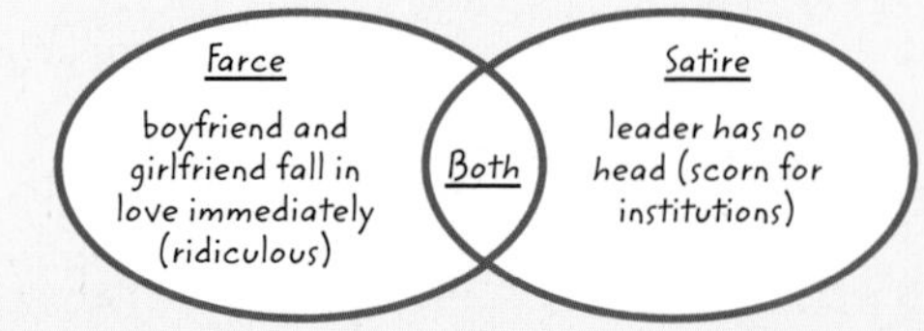

Reading Strategy Draw Conclusions About Author's Meaning

ACT Skills Practice

1. What does Ionesco suggest about the nature of leadership?

   A. Leadership creates a following.

   B. Leadership may be good or bad.

   C. Even mindless leadership is better than no leadership.

   D. Leaders come and go.

Vocabulary Practice

Practice with Context Clues Identify the context clues in the following sentences that help you determine the meaning of each boldfaced word.

1. He promised her that he wouldn't move from the spot where he was standing, that he would be **riveted** to that spot until she returned.
2. Their friends wanted a specific day-by-day schedule of where they were going on their family vacation, so Nathaniel and Emma created a detailed **itinerary.**
3. The king returned from battle an **exalted** and noble hero.
4. The conquering army surrounded the **vanquished** warriors and ordered them to lay down their weapons.
5. The house was so dark and spooky that they feared an **apparition** might appear in their room.

Speaking and Listening

Perform

Assignment With a group of classmates, choose a favorite section of Ionesco's *The Leader* and stage it for your class, following the stage directions. Incorporate appropriate movements into your interpretation. After performing your scene, discuss with the class how the physical movement of the actors can reinforce the theme of the play.

Prepare As a group, choose a section from *The Leader* for your performance. Begin your rehearsal by reading through the text. Then, rehearse the section several times with the proper staging. As you rehearse, focus on developing the appropriate tone of voice and body language for each character.

Perform After rehearsing together, perform your chosen section from *The Leader* for your class. Focus on speaking the lines with appropriate expression. Adding the proper emotion to your delivery will help the audience to understand the meaning behind the lines. Make sure you follow the written stage directions, and remember that the body language of the characters should reflect their emotions.

At the conclusion of your performance, lead the class in a discussion about how the physical movement of the actors can reinforce the theme of the play. As an example, analyze your performance. You can build your discussion around these questions:

- Which physical movements did the audience notice most?
- How did these movements relate to the theme of the play?
- Why did the actors choose those movements?

Evaluate As a group, review your performance and the discussion that you led. List things that you did well, and things that could have been improved.

LOG ON **Literature** Online

Selection Resources For Selection Quizzes, eFlashcards, and Reading-Writing Connection activities, go to glencoe.com and enter QuickPass code GL49787u4.

After You Read

Assess

Reading Strategy

1. A is the correct answer. This is the only conclusion that can be drawn from those suggested. The people are followers simply because there is a leader.

Progress Check

Can students draw conclusions about author's meaning?

If No → See Unit 4 Teaching Resources Book, p. 135.

Vocabulary Practice

1. "he wouldn't move from the spot where he was standing"
2. "a specific day-by-day schedule of where they were going"
3. noble
4. conquering warriors
5. dark and spooky, appear

For additional selection assessment, see Assessment Resources, pp. 181–182.

To create custom assessments online, go to Progress Reporter Online Assessment.

To create custom assessments using software, use ExamView Assessment Suite.

Speaking and Listening

Students' performances should:

- stage a section of *The Leader* as it is described in the script
- incorporate appropriate movements
- demonstrate appropriate expression in the delivery of their lines
- be followed by a group discussion about how movement reinforces theme

Focus

Summary

During his conversation with Eugène Ionesco, Claude Bonnefoy asks Ionesco to share a personal analysis of his writing. The author shares his experiences as a poet, novelist, and playwright.

For summaries in languages other than English, see Unit 4 Teaching Resources Book, pp. 141–147.

Teach

Reading Strategy

Identify Assumptions and Ambiguities Before students read the excerpt, tell them Bonnefoy makes assumptions about Ionesco's work and motivation. Ionesco's responses reflect an honest ambiguity as he tries to analyze himself and his work.

For an audio recording of this selection, use Listening Library Audio CD-ROM.

Readability Scores

Dale-Chall: 9.2
DRP: interview format not scorable
Lexile: 1000

How I Came *to the* THEATER

Claude Bonnefoy

Learning Objectives

For pages 800–803

In studying this text, you will focus on the following objectives:

Reading:
Analyzing informational text.
Identifying assumptions and ambiguities.

Set a Purpose for Reading

Read to discover contrasting ideas about Eugène Ionesco and his plays.

Build Background

Eugène Ionesco's plays are categorized as part of the Theatre of the Absurd, a style of drama that emphasizes the absurdity of humanity. Absurdists often use unrealistic, illogical structure. Dialogue may include repetition, plays on words, and a random sequence of ideas.

Reading Strategy

Identify Assumptions and Ambiguities

Identifying assumptions involves looking at assumptions an author makes based on his or her experiences, observations, and knowledge in order to understand why an author has drawn certain conclusions. **Identifying ambiguities** involves looking at how a text can support two or more contrasting interpretations. As you read, ask yourself, What assumptions and ambiguities are present in the text? Use a graphic organizer like the one below.

Assumption or Ambiguity	Interpretation

CLAUDE BONNEFOY. I can't help wondering how and why you happened to become a playwright.

EUGÈNE IONESCO. It puzzles me as well. You'd do better to ask a psychologist about it. Why *did* I write my first play? Perhaps it was to prove that nothing had any real importance, that everything was unlivable—literature, drama, life, human values, they were all unlivable.

C.B. But you could have chosen to express this in another literary form—a poem, a novel, or an essay. Certain of your plays like *The Killer, Victims of Duty, Rhinoceros,* and *A Stroll in the Air* were originally short stories that you've now published in a single volume called *The Colonel's Photograph.* Wasn't your vocation originally more that of a storyteller?

E.I. I started by writing literary criticism. And poems, very bad poems.

C.B. Should I contradict you?

E.I. Oh, they're really pitiful, full of a primitive anthropomorphism:[1] flowers weeping and bleeding and dreaming of meadows and springtime and heaven knows what

1. *Anthropomorphism* means "the assigning of human characteristics or behavior to inanimate objects, animals, or nature."

Writing Practice

SMALL GROUP

Write a Character Sketch Break students into small groups and have them discuss what they have learned about Ionesco so far. **Ask:** What can you tell about him from the conversation on these pages? *(Students may say that he criticizes himself and his work in a humorous way, that he is very intelligent, and that he began writing at a young age.)* Have each group write a character sketch about Ionesco to share with the class.

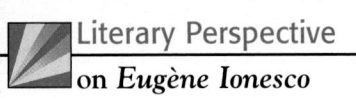

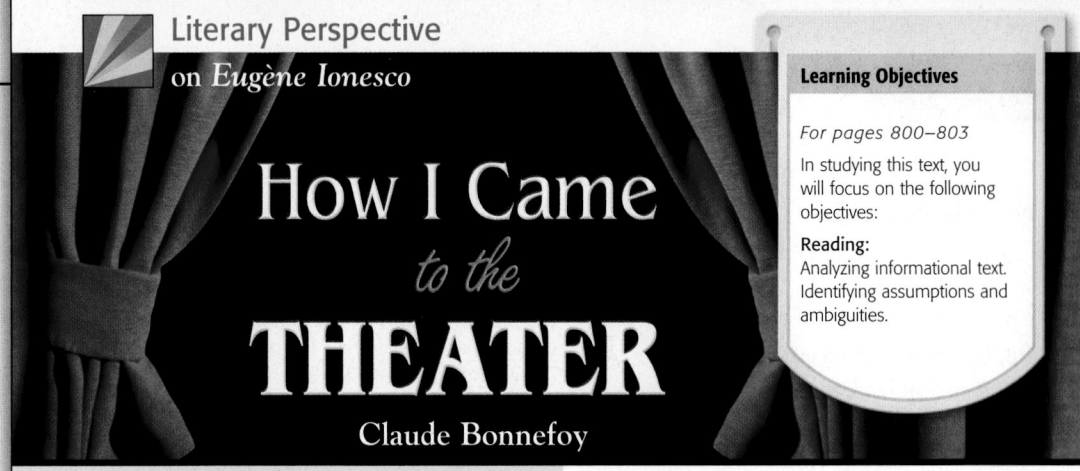

1 else. I was only seventeen. It wasn't all my fault, Maeterlinck[2] and Francis Jammes[3] were partly to blame. Anyway, after I'd written some very bad poems, I started writing extremely harsh criticism, as though I was trying to punish myself by punishing other people. After that, I tried to write a novel. It was all a long, long time ago.

C.B. What was the novel about?

E.I. About me, of course.

C.B. So you started out in the classic adolescent way by writing poems?

E.I. No, I'd already written some plays before that.

C.B. Already?

2 E.I. Well, let me see . . . first of all, when I was about ten or eleven, I started to write my *Memoirs.* I wrote two pages, but I've now lost them both. I can still remember the first page, the first sentences. I described how I'd had my photograph taken at the age of three. Now, of course, I've forgotten what it was like having my photo taken at the age of three. I can only remember being ten and writing down what it was like. And when I was eleven, I wrote poetry and some patriotic plays. *French* patriotic plays. When I was thirteen, I moved to Romania and learned Romanian, and when I was fourteen, I translated my patriotic play and turned it into a Romanian patriotic play.

C.B. One could say you were doubly patriotic.

E.I. Actually, I was very confused as a child. At primary school, in France, I'd been taught that French—which was my language—was the most beautiful language in the world, that the French were the bravest people in the world, that they'd always defeated their enemies, that if they had on occasion been defeated themselves, it was because the odds had been ten-to-one against them or because of a few individuals like Grouchy at Waterloo[4] and Bazaine in the Franco-Prussian War.[5] When I got to Bucharest, my teachers explained that my language was Romanian, that the most beautiful language in the world was not French but Romanian, that the Romanians had always defeated their enemies, that if they hadn't always been victorious it was because they'd had people like Grouchy and Bazaine—I can't even remember their names—on their side. So I learned that it was not the French but the Romanians who were the best people, superior to everyone else. It's a good thing I didn't move to Japan the year after that. . . . So, I began by writing a patriotic play. And I also wrote a comic play at the same time.

C.B. You were always drawn towards comedy, then?

E.I. Yes. But my memory of the play is very hazy. I was eleven or twelve years old at the time and it was set in Paris, on the Rue de l'Avre. A child, one of my schoolfriends, 3 had told me that he could make a film because he had a camera, which in fact wasn't true. He was a little mythomaniac. He's asked me to write a script for him. What I do remember is that it ended with the characters smashing everything in the

2. *Maurice Maeterlinck* (1862–1949) was a Belgian poet, playwright, and essayist. His work was considered part of the symbolist movement, which used symbols and myth to convey universal truths.
3. *Francis Jammes* (1868–1938) was a French poet and novelist. His work emphasized nature and simplicity.
4. *Grouchy at Waterloo* refers to Emmanuel Grouchy, one of Napoléon's marshals during the Battle of Waterloo in 1815. Grouchy's leadership was considered weak.
5. *Bazaine in the Franco-Prussian War* refers to Achille Bazaine (1811–1888), a French marshal sentenced to death for withdrawing his forces in battle on October 27, 1870, during the Franco-Prussian War.

English Learners

DIFFERENTIATED INSTRUCTION

Beginning/Early Intermediate English learners may have trouble understanding Ionesco's use of sarcasm and irony on these pages. Point out instances where he seems to be serious but is really making a joke. Read aloud the paragraph on this page beginning with "Well, let me see . . ." **Ask:** What does Ionesco say that is ironic? *(Students may say that he began writing his Memoirs when he was about ten or eleven—this is too young to recount your life story. They may also say that he easily transformed his French patriotic play into a Romanian patriotic play—this would be very difficult to do well.)*

Teach

Reading Strategy 1

Interpret Ask: Why does Ionesco blame Maeterlinck and Jammes for his work? *(Both men influenced the literary style of their time and, therefore, Ionesco's writing.)*

Reading Strategy 2

Sequence Ask: What sequence of events does Ionesco describe in this passage? *(He describes the stages of his growth as a writer from the age of ten until he was fourteen.)*

ENGLISH LEARNERS Ask English learners to draw a timeline and fill in the events to aid their comprehension.

Reading Strategy 3

Identify Assumptions and Ambiguities Ask: Which statement is an assumption? Which statement is ambiguous? *(Bonnefoy's statement is an assumption. Ionesco's statement is ambiguous because it is contradictory.)*

Literary Perspective
on *Eugène Ionesco*

Teach

Reading Strategy 1

Identify Assumptions and Ambiguities **Ask:** Is Bonnefoy's statement an assumption or an ambiguity? *(An assumption)*

Reading Strategy 2

Interpret **Ask:** What is Ionesco's concern about the analyses of his writing by others? *(People assume that his writing is an expression of his innermost thoughts. He does not believe that is necessarily the case.)*

ADVANCED Invite advanced students to have a discussion about what a piece of writing reveals about its author. Have them look at Ionesco's list, on pages 802–803, of what his characters may represent, and discuss whether they can think of examples from other literary works of characters that might fit each description.

Romanian-born French playwright Eugène Ionesco speaks to an interviewer at home. Ionesco was elected to the Académie Française in 1970.

house. Seven or eight children were sitting having their tea together, and afterwards they smashed their cups, they smashed all the crockery, they smashed up all the furniture, and threw their parents out of the windows.

1 C.B. I suppose it couldn't have ended with an atom bomb, like *Anger.*[6] But it's curious to discover in this childhood script the same patterns and themes that one finds in *Anger:* acceleration, proliferation, and destruction.

E.I. Perhaps I've always thought along the same lines. You get the same thing in Feydeau[7] too, the same acceleration and proliferation; maybe it goes back to his childhood as well. Acceleration and proliferation are probably a part of my personal rhythm, of the way I see things.

C.B. Were they also present in the novel that you'd started?

E.I. No. Definitely not.

C.B. Was it a fear of exposing yourself, a fear of being recognized that made you stop work on this novel, whose subject, you say, was yourself?

E.I. Possibly.

C.B. In the theater, on the other hand, because of the characters, you can wear a mask even when you're talking about yourself.

E.I. What irritates me is that, increasingly, when I write anything new, everyone—academics, psychologists and so on—ferrets[8] about to find evidence that it's me who's talking. Every day it's brought home to me more and more clearly that my plays can be seen as a series of confessions in which I give voice to my most unspeakable thoughts. People send me doctoral theses,[9] they send me 2 unpublished books about myself and I am absolutely terrified. Did I really have all these hidden meanings? Did I really hope that people wouldn't understand or that they'd put all the blame on my characters? I also realize that I've said certain things without intending to. And it's other people who discover all the things that I wasn't really aware of: it's insane. For the sake of clarity, I ought to say that my characters are not always "alter-egos"; they're other people, as well, imaginary people; they're

6. Ionesco's play *Anger* casts a scene of an ordinary day with three happy couples sitting down to eat dinner. Tension ensues, and the husbands and wives attack one another.
7. *Georges Feydeau* (1862–1921) was a French playwright of popular farces during World War I.

8. Here, *ferrets* means "hunts or searches."
9. *Doctoral theses* are lengthy and formal treatises written by graduate students at a university.

Reading Practice

SPIRAL REVIEW **Generate Questions** Give students practice generating questions about writing that can be researched by having them jot down questions as they read. Model the process by reading aloud the second column on this page. **Say:** Ionesco says that people find evidence that it's he who is talking in his work. **Write:** What do critics say about his plays? **Say:** He says that his characters are not always alter-egos of himself. **Write:** What are his characters like? Encourage students to continue writing down relevant questions as they read. Add students' questions to the list on the board.

also caricatures of myself, of what I've been frightened of becoming, of what I could have—but fortunately didn't—become; or else they're simply enlargements of different facets of myself; or else—and I'm repeating myself deliberately—they're other people, people I pity, people I laugh at, people I hate or love; sometimes, but more rarely, they are people I should have liked to be. They are also the personifications of a kind of anguish. And quite often, too, they are characters from my dreams.

C.B. If writing was a way of liberating yourself from certain things, didn't it upset you to rediscover these things in the distorting mirrors of other people's criticism?

E.I. Yes, it did.

C.B. So there's the danger that what starts out as a liberation can cease to be one as a result of this mirror of criticism.

E.I. Yes, in fact, you could say that everything shared this danger, but only if everyone were a poet or an artist, or else a psychiatrist or a priest. But as most people have the mentality of a concierge,[10] or else are society people, which is to say, simply concierges further up the social ladder, literature is constantly being undressed. The whole of literary history as we know it is just back-stairs snooping. Journalists and readers don't understand what a man says in the same way an artist would, or a priest, or a doctor or a psychologist. They don't see the meaning of these confessions, they don't understand the deepest or most universal truth of an individual confession. What interests them isn't the universal truth but the personal confession—looking through the keyhole, in other words. What interests people is not what's universal or general in a writer's work, but knowing about his private life. In other words, everything but the work itself. Of course, it's interesting to study sources, but it's more interesting to study the work itself. A work is more than the sum of its causes, it goes beyond them.

C.B. What I find interesting is the reverse—I want to find out how and why you came to put on the mask of playwright.

E.I. How I came to the theater? Quite simply, I don't know.

10. Here, *concierge* refers to a person who lives in a building and acts as its janitor.

Respond and Think Critically

Respond and Interpret

1. Write a brief summary of the main ideas in this interview before you answer the following questions. For help on writing a summary, see page 421.
2. Why do you think Ionesco does not give clear-cut answers to Bonnefoy's questions?
3. (a)In what genre does Ionesco say he began writing? (b)How does he contradict himself when answering questions about the genre of his early writings?

Analyze and Evaluate

4. Ionesco says his characters are many things. Why do you think he does not make one specific statement about his characters?
5. Ionesco says that "A work is more than the sum of its causes, it goes beyond them." What do you think he means by this statement?

Connect

6. How does Ionesco use "acceleration" (the act of increasing speed) and "proliferation" (the act of rapid growth) in *The Leader*?

English Learners

DIFFERENTIATED INSTRUCTION

PARTNERS **Intermediate** Ionesco uses elaborate language toward the end of the interview. To facilitate comprehension for English learners, suggest that they break the selection into smaller parts, such as one question and its response. Pair proficient English speakers with English learners and have them paraphrase the main idea of each section. Help students understand ambiguities and ironies. Guide them to use a dictionary to look up unfamiliar words.

Assess

1. Students' summaries should include Ionesco's journey through writing and his opinions on how others view his writing.
2. Responses will vary. Some students may think that Ionesco avoids giving answers because he feels it is up to readers to interpret his work. Others may say that he is trying to answer Bonnefoy's questions, but in the end, he realizes that he doesn't know why.
3. (a) Literary criticism and poetry (b) At first, he says he wrote poetry, criticism, and a novel. Then, he says that when he was eleven, he wrote a memoir, poetry, and a play.
4. It would limit readers' interpretations of his characters.
5. He means that a work comments on more than its writer, the time period when it was written, and its subject matter. The work makes a broader statement about the human condition.
6. Dialogue happens in short, quick bursts. The characters enter and exit many times. Growth occurs when all the characters are entering and exiting the stage simultaneously. There is the climax of the Leader entering without a head. The play accelerates again with all the characters asking, "What's your name?"

For additional assessment, see Assessment Resources, pp. 183–184.

Writing Workshop

Literary Criticism Essay

Focus

Bellringer Options

Write on the board: revenge, justice, friendship, love

Go around the room and ask students which of these four words they find most powerful.

Ask: Which do you think would make the best subject for

- a play or a story?
- a reflective essay?
- an analytical essay about Shakespeare's Romeo and Juliet?

Summary

In this workshop, students will write a literary criticism essay. Students will follow the stages of the writing process, including prewriting, drafting, revising, and editing. In addition, the workshop includes two focus lessons on supporting a thesis statement and quoting from a play.

Learning Objectives

For pages 804–811

In this workshop, you will focus on the following objectives:

Writing:
Writing a literary analysis using a writing process.
Supporting a thesis statement.
Citing quotations.

Writing Workshop

Literary Analysis Essay

Literature Connection One reason William Shakespeare's dramas have stood the test of time is their universal themes which are still relevant today, hundreds of years after the plays were written.

> *"My only love, sprung from my only hate!*
> *Too early seen unknown, and known too late!*
> *Prodigious birth of love it is to me*
> *That I must love a loathed enemy."*

A literary analysis essay about *The Tragedy of Romeo and Juliet* might discuss the theme of "star-crossed" lovers as introduced in the quote above, or it might discuss and evaluate one or more elements in the play, such as a character, the plot, the setting, or the portrayal of romantic love. The rubric below provides an overview of what you must do to write an effective literary analysis essay about a drama.

Writing Process

At any stage of a writing process, you may think of new ideas. Feel free to return to earlier stages as you write.

- Prewrite
- Draft
- Revise
- Focus Lesson: Thesis Statement Support
- Edit and Proofread
- Focus Lesson: Quotations and In-Text Citations
- Present

Checklist

Goals	Strategies
To analyze a drama	☑ Develop an understanding of the play as a whole ☑ Find a single, narrow aspect of the play to focus on
To state a strong, clear, insightful thesis	☑ State your own perspective on one aspect of the work ☑ Maintain a consistent focus on that perspective throughout your essay
To support your thesis	☑ Quote the play (and cite it correctly) to support your main ideas ☑ Make accurate and detailed references to the drama
To reflect a careful, thoughtful reading	☑ Make inferences; explain subtle details ☑ Show your understanding of shades of meaning and complex aspects of the work

LOG ON Literature Online

Writing and Research
For prewriting, drafting, and revising tools, go to glencoe.com and enter QuickPass code GL49787u4.

Workshop Resources

Print Materials

- Unit 4 Teaching Resources, pp. 151–153
- Writing Kit
- Success in Writing: Research and Reports

Transparencies

- Grammar and Language Transparency 4
- Writing Workshop Transparencies 21, 22, 23, 24, 25

Technology

- Literature Online: Writing Resources and Grammar Resources, www.glencoe.com
- Online Essay Grader, www.glencoe.com
- Student Presentation Builder on Student-Works Plus CD-ROM
- Media Workshop DVD
- Online Student Edition

Assignment: Analyze a Drama

Write a literary analysis essay of at least 1,500 words in which you support your thesis about a drama. As you work, keep your audience and purpose in mind.

Audience: your classmates and teacher

Purpose: to analyze a drama by presenting a viewpoint and supporting it with examples and quotations

Real-World Connection

Submit your essay to your high school literary magazine or e-zine, or look for reputable publishers of student work on the Web. A reference librarian can help you identify trustworthy publications.

Analyze a Professional Model

In the following selection, Marchette Chute analyzes *Romeo and Juliet* by showing how Shakespeare took an ordinary plot and used it to create a remarkable play. As you read, pay close attention to the comments in the margin. They point out features to include in your literary analysis.

From *An Introduction to Shakespeare* by Marchette Chute

It is part of Shakespeare's great strength as a writer that he never felt superior to anyone, and he kept a gentle courtesy in his point of view even towards fools.

Introduction

Introduce your subject in an interesting way and provide a bit of background.

This same gentleness on Shakespeare's part shows in his attitude towards the earlier writers from whom he took the plots of some of his plays. He could pick up a rather foolish play or poem, read it with great care, ignore its foolishness for the little of value there might be in it, and then transform it into a masterpiece.

Thesis Statement

Include a statement that presents your position or makes an argument.

For instance, at about this time [before he wrote *The Tragedy of Romeo and Juliet*], Shakespeare read a popular poem by Arthur Brooke on the tragedy of two young lovers named Romeus and Juliet. Brooke was retelling an old Italian story, and he used an extraordinary style. This, according to Brooke, is Juliet's behavior in the potion scene:

Her dainty tender parts gan shiver all for dread,
Her golden hairs did stand upright upon her chillish head

Support and Citations

A quotation is one form of support that strengthens your argument. Note that when you quote a play, you should include a citation that lists the act number, the scene number, and, if available, the line number.

Approaching Level

DIFFERENTIATED INSTRUCTION

Emerging Students who have trouble reading Shakespeare's language may benefit from seeing and hearing the play performed. Encourage them to watch a film version of the play. Note that a film's visual elements—costumes, close-ups, set designs—help shape the audience's reactions to the story. Similarly, a film's musical score gives the viewer important clues about the story's turning points and the characters' emotions.

Teach

Big Idea

The Power of Love **Ask:** Why is *Romeo and Juliet* such a popular love story? *(Students may say that Romeo and Juliet's struggle to be together constitutes a powerful drama. The failure of their love to triumph over circumstances is profoundly moving.)*

Writing Skills

Introduce a Thesis

Refer students to Chute's essay. **Say:** Paraphrase this essay's thesis statement. *(Shakespeare could transform another writer's inferior work into a masterpiece.)* Explain how Chute first argues that Shakespeare "never felt superior to anyone." Then she shows how this generous view of others allowed Shakespeare to find value even in inferior literature.

Cultural History ☆

Film Adaptations A famous film adaptation of *Romeo and Juliet* by the Italian director Franco Zeffirelli was shot on location in northern Italy's medieval villages in 1968. It was the first movie version to cast teenagers—Leonard Whiting and Olivia Hussey—in the title roles. Baz Luhrmann's 1996 *Romeo + Juliet,* stars Leonardo DiCaprio and Claire Danes.

Teach

Cultural History ☆

Shakespeare's Sources
Although Shakespeare was one of the most original and gifted dramatists of all time, he rarely invented the plots of his plays. Instead, he often adapted well-known stories by writers such as Giovanni Boccaccio or historical writings by authors such as Plutarch or Holinshed. What makes Shakespeare a genius is the way he transformed these stories into something wholly his own.

Example
Support your thesis statement with examples.

Elaboration
Explain and clarify your example. The writer explains that Shakespeare made *Romeo and Juliet* a story of "haste" to provide a reason for the tragedy.

Analysis
Reflect a careful reading through insights into subtle details or complexities, such as a sober nurse who is funny.

Shakespeare took Brooke's stuffed characters and transformed them into real people, he took the pretentious verse and transmuted it into golden poetry, and he made *Romeo and Juliet* into one of the most loved plays ever written. Brooke's tragedy was meaningless because there was no special reason why it should have happened, but Shakespeare made it into a tragedy of haste. He emphasizes the sense of hurry by making Juliet younger than she was in the original version and condensing the action into less than a week. Even the weather is hot, and an atmosphere of quick-flowering beauty and early death is the background that is created for the story of the immortal and tragic lovers.

A lesser writer than Shakespeare might have tried to keep the play to a single note of lyric love. But Shakespeare, who had thrust a weaver into fairyland, had no hesitation about putting a couple of cheerful realists into *Romeo and Juliet*. Mercutio and Juliet's nurse do not weaken the tragedy; they enrich it, in the usual astonishing fashion of Shakespeare's comedians. Mercutio is a humorist by intention; he is a subtle and intelligent young man who knows exactly how entertaining he is, and the fact that he "loves to hear himself talk" is only proof of his good judgment. The Nurse, on the other hand, does not mean to be funny. She feels she is a very sober, sensible, practical woman and she has no idea what actually happens every time she opens her mouth. Shakespeare had no objection to laughter in his tragedies. The two elements combine in real life and they were free to combine in his plays also.

Reading-Writing Connection Try out the writing techniques you have just encountered in the literary analysis essay you write.

Reading Practice

SPIRAL REVIEW **Supporting Examples** In her second-to-last paragraph, Chute uses examples and elaboration to support her claim that Shakespeare transformed Brooke's mediocre poem into a masterpiece. Have students reread the paragraph. **Ask:** In what ways did Shakespeare improve on Brooke? *(He created more realistic characters and better poetry, added haste as a factor in the tragedy, made Juliet younger, compressed the action, and intensified the dramatic atmosphere by introducing hot weather.)*

Prewrite

Choose a Focus As you plan your literary criticism essay, consider the points you want to discuss. Examine how a particular element such as character, setting, plot, or theme contributes to the effect of the play as a whole. For example, compare and contrast two characters, describe a technique the playwright uses to develop the plot, or analyze how the theme develops throughout the play.

Read the Drama Carefully As you plan, reread important parts of the drama as necessary. Use the following criteria to help you plan your thesis and analysis:

- **Begin with Your Opinion** Base your analysis on your own opinion. Do you have a strong opinion about the playwright's work? What do you think about a character, the plot, the setting, or the theme? It is easier to write convincingly when you believe in your position.
- **Choose a Position** Think about the argument you will develop to be sure it can be easily supported with evidence. What examples and details can you draw on for evidence? Are there quotations you can use to support your thesis?
- **Narrow Your Focus** You may have so many ideas about a drama that you want to cover everything. If your focus is too broad, though, your analysis will not be thorough. Narrow your focus so that your analysis is specific and well developed.

Organize Details Organize your ideas in a cluster diagram like the one below. This will help you decide which ideas to include and how to present your argument.

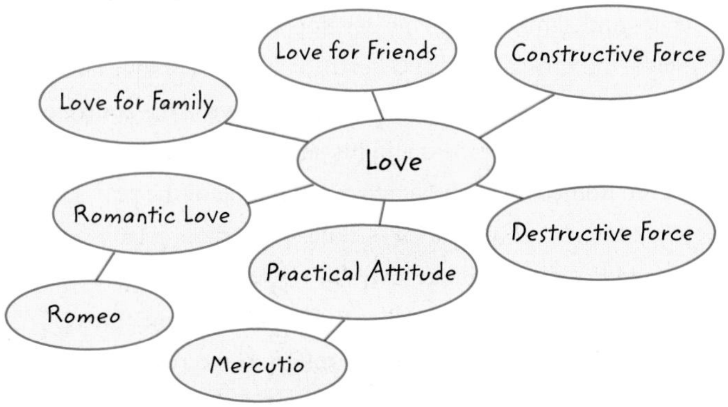

Discuss Your Ideas Develop a formal writing voice to use when you write a literary analysis. Ask a partner to help you develop a thesis statement with the appropriate tone for a formal essay.

Literary Analysis

When you analyze a literary work, you examine the specific parts of a work in order to understand the work as a whole. Ask yourself questions such as these:

How are the characters revealed—through their own words, actions, and thoughts (in a monologue), or through the words of other characters?

How does the plot progress, and what is the central conflict?

Is there a theme of universal interest? How is it developed throughout the work?

How does the setting contribute to your understanding of the work?

Avoid Plagiarism

It is not necessary to use outside sources to complete this assignment, but, if you do, remember that both honesty and the law require you to acknowledge them in citations.

Writing Workshop

Literary Criticism Essay

Teach

Writing Skills

Organize Ideas Remind students that the writing process always involves shifting between brainstorming and organization. Ways of organizing ideas include

- looking for connections between two or more ideas
- looking for a broader concept that incorporates two or more ideas

APPROACHING For approaching-level students, **say:** Before you begin to organize your essay, be sure you completely understand the selection. List any sections that are confusing, and break them down into smaller parts.

Writer's Technique ☆

Persuasive Language

An effective persuasive argument requires not only good ideas but also the ability to express them in clear and powerful language. Discourage students from using bland phrases such as "in my opinion" and "it could be argued." Explain that such phrases weaken the impact of a statement by introducing a note of hesitation or doubt. Persuasive writing uses concise language to state ideas boldly and directly.

Approaching Level

DIFFERENTIATED INSTRUCTION

Emerging Help students choose a topic and form an opinion. Encourage them to analyze an aspect of the play that interests them. Have them consider these questions:

- What impressed you most about the play?
- The setting?
- The plot?
- The language?
- The characters?
- Something else?

Guide students to be more specific. For example, if some students say that the setting impressed them, ask them what they liked most about the setting. Then guide students to form an opinion.

Teach

Writing Skills

Introduction

Answer: *They summarize part of the plot of* Romeo and Juliet *and point out that attitudes toward love are important in the play.*

Thesis Statement

Answer: *It flows smoothly from the preceding sentence and clearly states that positive and negative aspects of love are a major theme of the play.*

APPROACHING For approaching-level students, **ask:** What makes a good thesis statement? *(A thesis should let the reader know what the paper will be about, and should tell them why they should read it.)*

Support

Answer: *The quotation reflects the destructive side of love presented in the thesis statement.*

Draft

Be Open Many writers find that an argument becomes clearer as they examine the evidence and draft their essays. As you write your draft, occasionally check that the evidence you provide supports your thesis statement. Feel free to adjust your thesis as necessary.

Analyze a Workshop Model

Here is a final draft of a literary analysis essay. Read the essay and answer the questions in the margin. Use the answers to these questions to guide you as you write your own essay.

Writing Frames

As you read the workshop model, think about the writer's use of the following frames:

____ have similar attitudes about ____, but they have different attitudes about ____.

This scene shows how ____.

The ____ help develop a major theme of ____.

Consider using frames like these in your own literary analysis essay.

Love in *Romeo and Juliet*

The two main characters in William Shakespeare's play *The Tragedy of Romeo and Juliet* are young lovers whose families are involved in a bitter feud. After Romeo and Juliet declare their love for each other, they agree to meet the next day. Later in the afternoon of that day, they are secretly married.

Introduction
In what way do the first paragraph and this sentence introduce the essay?

Mercutio is Romeo's best friend. Romeo and Mercutio have different attitudes toward romantic love, but they have similar attitudes about love and loyalty toward their friends and family. Shakespeare's portrayal of the friends' differences and similarities helps develop a major theme of the play—the constructive and destructive forces of love.

Thesis Statement
What makes this a strong, insightful thesis statement?

From the very beginning of the play, love is the source of both Romeo's happiness and his suffering. For example, before Romeo meets Juliet at the beginning of the play, he tells Mercutio about his lovesickness for a young lady named Rosaline. "Under love's heavy burden do I sink" (1.4.22). Romeo then describes the emotional pain of love: "Is love a tender thing? It is too rough, / Too rude, too boist'rous and it pricks like thorn" (1.4.25–26). In contrast, Mercutio has a more practical attitude toward romantic love. He offers Romeo sensible advice: "If love be rough with you, be rough with love" (1.4.27). In matters of romance,

Support
How does this quotation relate to the thesis? How does the entire paragraph make accurate, specific, and detailed references to the drama?

Writing Practice

SPIRAL REVIEW **Introductions** A good introduction grabs the reader's attention and leads smoothly into the thesis statement. Have students review the introduction and thesis on this page. Point out the strong thesis in the second paragraph. As students draft their own essays, ask them to consider the following questions:

- How does my thesis statement connect to the play in general?
- What information do I need to provide so that my thesis statement makes sense?

Ask students to share their introductions with the class and discuss ways to improve them.

Mercutio does not believe in playing the helpless victim.

Romeo and Mercutio, however, do share similar views about love and loyalty between friends and family. In Act 3, Scene 1, the strength of their friendship is put to the test. Tybalt challenges Romeo to a duel, but Romeo refuses to fight. Tybalt does not know that Romeo has secretly married Juliet and become Tybalt's cousin by marriage. Mercutio, seeing Romeo's refusal to fight as a threat to Romeo's reputation, feels compelled to save Romeo's honor and fights Tybalt in Romeo's place. As Romeo tries to stop the duel, Tybalt stabs and kills Mercutio. Romeo declares, "My very friend, hath got this mortal hurt / In my behalf—my reputation stain'd / With Tybalt's slander. . . . " (3.1.108–110). Romeo then rises to defend Mercutio's honor by slaying Tybalt. This scene shows how both Romeo and Mercutio are willing to sacrifice their lives for the sake of their friendship.

Out of love for Juliet, Romeo tries to end the feud between his family and Juliet's. Initially, he responds to Tybalt's challenge with love. When Tybalt challenges Romeo in Act 3, Romeo says to him, "[I] love thee better than thou canst devise" (3.1.68). This shows that love can conquer hatred and bring about peace. However, love can also be destructive. Out of love and loyalty, Mercutio fights Tybalt, but Mercutio's duel with Tybalt intensifies the conflict between the feuding families and leads to a series of senseless deaths.

The idea of love in *Romeo and Juliet* is more complicated than it first appears. As one might expect in a love story, love is shown to be wonderful, but it is also shown as something that encourages destructive behavior. The differences and similarities between Romeo's and Mercutio's attitudes toward love serve a dramatic purpose. The views and actions of these two friends help develop a major theme of the play—that love can be both a constructive and a destructive force.

Exposition

Support
How do detailed references to the text and quoted details work together to support the thesis? Where and why is a citation used?

Analysis/Focus
How does the writer show insight into the complexities of the drama? How does the writer maintain a consistent focus?

Conclusion
How does it help to summarize and restate the thesis in the conclusion?

Writing Workshop

Literary Criticism Essay

Teach

Writing Skills

Support

Answer: *They show examples of ways in which the theme of love is carried out in the play. The citation is used to show which lines from the play are being cited.*

Precise Language

Answer: *Action verbs include* responds, conquer, fights, *and* intensifies. *The subject is presented first and performs the action on the verb.*

Analysis/Criticism

Answer: *The writer provides an insight and interpretation of evidence from the play.*

Conclusion

Answer: *It sums up all that has been written in the essay and reminds readers of the thesis.*

English Learners

DIFFERENTIATED INSTRUCTION

Beginning/Early Intermediate

Students new to the English language may struggle with the formal vocabulary used in essays, particularly transitional expressions. Go over the workshop model essay, defining words and phrases such as *for example, in contrast,* and *however.* Explain that their function is to connect ideas in an essay and to create a sense of flow.

Teach

Writing Skills

Support As students revise their drafts, have them go back to make sure their arguments are supported properly. If their arguments are weak, students may need to elaborate on their ideas.

Say: Supporting information must be related to your main idea. As you elaborate on the points in your arguments, make sure the information you have added truly explains, clarifies, or extends your points instead of making new points.

APPROACHING For approaching-level students who have trouble constructing a strong argument, draw on the board a graphic organizer that illustrates the organization of a basic five-paragraph essay.

Writer's Technique ☆

Revise Revising is a way of enhancing and clarifying the arguments made in an essay. Referring to the checklist on this page, point out to students that the goal of an essay is to communicate as clearly as possible.

Say: When answering the questions, remember that your essay is addressed to another person. Would they share your viewpoint?

Revise

Traits of Strong Writing

Include these traits of strong writing to effectively express your ideas.

Ideas

Organization

Voice

Word Choice

Sentence Fluency

Conventions

Presentation

For more information on using the Traits of Strong Writing, see pages R28–R30.

Word Choice

This academic vocabulary word appears in the student model:

respond (ri spond′) *v.* 1. to say something as an answer 2. to react to; *Initially, he responds to Tybalt's challenge with love.* Using academic vocabulary may help strengthen your writing. Try to use one or two academic vocabulary words in your literary analysis essay. See the complete list on pages R79–R81.

Peer Review Exchange your finished draft with a partner. Use this checklist to evaluate and strengthen your writing.

Checklist

- ☑ Do you present a strong, insightful thesis in your introduction?
- ☑ Do you support your thesis with direct quotations that are cited?
- ☑ Do you maintain a consistent tone and focus?
- ☑ Do you explain subtle details and shades of meaning?

Focus Lesson

Thesis Statement Support

The effectiveness of your essay depends on strong support for your thesis statement. See the example below.

Draft:

Shakespeare's portrayal of the friends' differences and similarities helps develop a major theme of the play—the constructive and destructive forces of love.

Revision:

Shakespeare's portrayal of the friends' differences and similarities helps develop a major theme of the play—the constructive and destructive forces of love. From the very beginning of the play, love is Romeo's entire motivation and the source of both his happiness and his suffering.[1] For example, before Romeo meets Juliet at the beginning of the play, he tells Mercutio about his lovesickness[2] for a young lady named Rosaline. . . . In contrast, Mercutio has a more practical attitude toward romantic love.[3]

1: Description of Romeo's attitude **2:** Example shows Romeo's attitude **3:** Explanation of how Mercutio's attitude differs

LOG ON Literature Online

Writing and Research
For editing and publishing tools, go to glencoe.com and enter QuickPass code GL49787u4.

Listening and Speaking Practice

SMALL GROUP **Getting Feedback** Break students into groups and have them read each other's essays. Have them consider specific questions, such as,

- Does the introduction grab the reader's attention?
- Is the thesis solid?
- Is the thesis proven in the essay?
- Which evidence is most convincing?
- What further evidence could be added?
- Are there opposing arguments that should be addressed?

Emphasize that writers do not have to accept every suggested change. They should listen to all comments and choose the ideas they think will improve their essays.

Edit and Proofread

Get It Right When you have completed the final draft of your essay, proofread for errors in grammar, usage, mechanics, and spelling. Refer to the Language Handbook, pages R40–R59, as a guide.

Focus Lesson

Quotations and In-Text Citations

Quotations from the drama provide clear, convincing support for your thesis. Any time you include the exact words from a play, these words should be enclosed in quotation marks. If the play is written in lines in the form of poetry, as Shakespeare's plays are, line breaks should be indicated by slashes (/). Cite the location of the words in the play by listing the act number, scene number, and, if available, line number(s) so that your readers can look up and read the quotation in context.

Problem: Quotation marks and slashes are omitted in quoting lines from a play. The location of the quotation in the text is not identified.

Is love a tender thing? It is too rough, Too rude, too boist'rous and it pricks like thorn

Solution: Enclose the exact words from a play in quotation marks and use slashes to show line breaks. Use an in-text citation to identify where the quote occurs in the play.

"Is love a tender thing? It is too rough, / Too rude, too boist'rous and it pricks like thorn" (1.4.25–26)

Present

Make It Readable After you correct errors, make sure your paper looks neat. Make your handwriting consistently legible, or type your essay. Double-check that you have followed your teacher's general guidelines regarding length, spacing, font size, and margins.

Peer Review Tips

A classmate may ask you to read his or her literary analysis essay. Take your time and jot down notes as you read so you can give constructive feedback. Use the following questions to get started:

Does the writer prove the thesis? Where is the support most substantial and convincing?

Does the writer organize ideas effectively by means of a clear introduction, focused body paragraphs, and an effective conclusion?

Word-Processing Tip

An essay is a formal writing assignment, so always print using black ink. Choose a readable 12-point font that looks like one you would find in a textbook and not in a comic book or an ad.

Writer's Portfolio

Place a clean copy of your literary analysis essay in your portfolio to review later.

Writing Workshop

Literary Criticism Essay

Teach

Writing Skills

Quoting/In-Text Citations

Many students have difficulty remembering the proper mechanics when using quotations. Help students practice. **Write** on the board a few quotations from *Romeo and Juliet,* leaving out the punctuation and citation information. Then ask students to come up to the board and fill in the missing details.

Writer's Technique ☆

Presentation The first impression an essay makes has nothing to do with its ideas or the way they're supported. A reader's first response is to the physical appearance of the essay. Emphasize the importance of a neat manuscript, free of typographical errors and sloppy writing.

Approaching Level

DIFFERENTIATED INSTRUCTION

AAVE For approaching-level students who are users of African American Vernacular English (AAVE), explain the difference between the active and passive voice.

Write:

- The girl hit the ball with the bat. *(active voice)*
- The ball was hit by the girl with the bat. *(passive voice)*

Encourage students to use the active voice in their writing.

Oral Response to Literature

Focus

Summary

In this workshop, students will learn techniques for planning, rehearsing, presenting, and listening to a literary analysis.

Teach

Speaking Skills

Recite Passages One of the challenges of presenting an oral response to literature is reciting quotations from a play or other source. As practice, choose a few of the most famous or important speeches from *Romeo and Juliet* and ask students to recite them. It may spark enthusiasm to turn this into a contest, having a series of students recite the same passage and then polling the class about whose performance was best.

ENGLISH LEARNERS English learners and some other students may find this very intimidating. For students who won't benefit from reading to the whole class, invite them to form small groups and practice, encouraging each other rather than competing.

For help with creating presentations, see Student Presentation Builder on StudentWorks Plus.

Learning Objectives

For pages 812–813

In this workshop, you will focus on the following objectives:

Speaking and Listening: Delivering a literary analysis. Listening to and evaluating a presentation.

Select Passages
To support your literary analysis of a drama, choose lines from the play to illustrate the points you want to make. Make sure the lines accurately represent the context in which they appear. To capture the attention of your audience, look for dramatic quotes and familiar passages with universal meaning.

Speaking, Listening, and Viewing Workshop

Literary Analysis

Literature Connection Marchette Chute retold thirty-six of William Shakespeare's plays as narratives. Although her book of retellings was first published almost fifty years ago, it is still available and widely used today. Chute is known for her critical analyses of the works of some of the best-loved English writers, including Shakespeare.

Literary critics often present their ideas by speaking to large or small groups. In this workshop, you will learn to present your literary analysis of a drama.

Assignment Plan and present a literary analysis.

Plan Your Presentation

Review these content requirements for an effective literary analysis:

- State a thesis or make a judgment that shows your understanding of the play.
- Support your thesis with specific and substantial references to the play.

To turn your essay into an effective oral presentation, follow these guidelines.

- Select your thesis and the best evidence for presentation.
- Think of ways to make your opening and conclusion more exciting or memorable for your audience of listeners, perhaps by selecting a quotation or telling a brief story.
- Select figurative language from your essay, or find ways to incorporate it in your oral presentation to create interest and reinforce your thesis or main points.
- Make note cards or cue cards that you can use during your presentation to recall the main ideas and details of your presentation. Use them to jot down your thesis, main ideas, figurative language, and other details, as well as your best quoted evidence from the play.

Listening and Speaking Practice

Organization Strategies After students have decided on the topic of their oral response to literature, they should select an organizational pattern that will help them effectively communicate their thesis to the audience. Explain that good oral communication is organized. Students need to plan out what they are going to say. Encourage students to think about their topic in terms of how they want to present it to the class. What sort of organizational stategy best fits the topic the student has chosen? The students should also consider how or if they want their audience to participate in the discussion. Mapping out parts of the speech where the student might want to present visual material is also a good idea.

Communicate Your Ideas

When you give a presentation with quotes from a drama, use your voice to communicate the meaning of the lines. Speak as if you were an actor: the examples and quotations you use for support will capture your listeners' attention if they are presented expressively rather than in a monotone. If possible, memorize quotations so that you can make eye contact with your audience while speaking.

Consider the following two quotations. How would you say each line in order to show the contrast between Romeo's attitude toward romantic love and that of Mercutio?

- "Under love's heavy burden do I sink" (Act 1, Scene 4, line 22).
- "If love be rough with you, be rough with love" (Act 1, Scene 4, line 27).

Rehearse

With a partner, practice saying each quotation as you would for an audience. Give your partner constructive suggestions for using tone of voice, pitch, and volume. Listen to your partner's ideas for your interpretation and incorporate the suggestions to make your presentation stronger.

Techniques for Presenting a Literary Analysis

Verbal Techniques	Nonverbal Techniques
☑ **Volume** Use loudness or softness to help express the meaning of the quoted lines.	☑ **Facial Expressions** Use facial expressions to emphasize the feelings of the characters you quote.
☑ **Pitch** Speak in a high or low voice when appropriate.	☑ **Gestures** Use gestures to highlight the drama in the examples you provide.
☑ **Tone** Adjust your tone to reflect your attitude toward the drama, or to reflect the attitude of a character you are quoting.	☑ **Posture** Modify your posture as necessary to reveal the mood or personality of characters when quoting them.
☑ **Enunciation** Pronounce your words clearly. This is especially important when quoted lines include words that are no longer common.	☑ **Eye Contact** As you speak, make eye contact with your audience.

Speaking Frames

Consider using the following frames in your literary analysis:

Notice how ____ uses this image/metaphor/word choice ____ to show ____.

This is shown when ____ says, ____.

Presentation Tips

Use the following checklist to evaluate your literary analysis.

☑ Did you present and support a clear, insightful thesis?

☑ Did you begin and end memorably?

☑ Did you use verbal and nonverbal techniques to engage your audience?

LOG ON Literature Online

Speaking, Listening, and Viewing For project ideas, templates, and presentation tips, go to glencoe.com and enter QuickPass code GL49787u4.

Teach

Speaking Skills

Address an Audience

As students rehearse their presentations, remind them that it is important to remember the audience. Encourage students to:

- speak at an appropriate pace and not rush
- make eye contact with individuals in the audience to make a stronger connection
- enunciate clearly and speak loudly enough for all to hear

Listening Skills

Pay Attention Remind students that listening to a presentation is not passive but requires active engagement with the speaker. As they listen to the presentations of other students, encourage students to:

- make a mental note of what each speaker's thesis is
- assess how the speaker's argument is supported
- look for patterns in the presentation
- reflect on the speaker's conclusion

English Learners

DIFFERENTIATED INSTRUCTION

Early Advanced English learners might have a hard time understanding how tone affects speech. In some languages, changes in tone indicate different words rather than different emotions or sentence constructions. **Ask:** What might *Romeo and Juliet* be like if it were read in an unchanging tone?

(Students may say that the play might seem silly if all of the lines were only read in one way. Others might point out that the play would lose its passion if the speaker's tone of voice did not change.) Encourage students to look at the way Shakespeare uses punctuation to indicate tone. **Ask:** What clues does the author give readers to let them know that the line should be read a certain way? *(Students might point out exclamation points or line breaks that help convey emotion in the dialogue.)*

Independent Reading

Focus

Summary

In this section, students will read summaries of dramas from a variety of cultures and time periods. They will also be introduced to two novels that address the themes of the power of love and awkward encounters.

Teach

Literary History ☆

Gary Soto Born in Fresno, California, in 1952, Gary Soto is recognized as one of the most important voices in Mexican American literature. Acclaimed as a poet, essayist, and fiction writer, Soto was a finalist for the National Book Award for his *New and Selected Poems* (1995). His memoir *Living up the Street* (1985) won the American Book Award. Soto lives in Northern California.

Independent Reading

Drama and Novels

DRAMA IS THE ONE TYPE OF LITERATURE THAT IS ALWAYS WRITTEN to be performed rather than just read. More than any other genre, drama requires a reader to see, hear, and feel the action. Therefore, readers who want to experience the life and impact of drama should pay careful attention to stage directions. For more drama on a range of themes, try the three suggestions on these pages. For novels that address the Big Ideas of the *Power of Love* and *Awkward Encounters,* try the titles from the Glencoe Literature Library on the next page.

Novio Boy: A Play

by Gary Soto

This play begins with Rudy asking his friend Alex for advice about girls. Rudy, a ninth grader, has finally gotten a date with Patricia, who is two years older than he is. He eventually takes her to a restaurant in their Mexican American community. When Rudy's best friend, his "crazy" guitar-playing uncle, and his mother show up, he worries that they might embarrass him and pretends not to know them. The play includes performance notes, a Spanish-English glossary, and plenty of humor.

Plays of America from American Folklore for Young Actors Grades 7–12

by L. E. McCullough

The ten plays that form this collection draw on subjects ranging from Native American myths to traditional European, African, and Asian stories and include pioneer-era heroes as well as more recent cultural figures such as Elvis Presley. Each play includes notes about the setting, as well as tips on costumes, casting, and special effects. Many plays have contemporary narrators, even though they deal with past events.

Writing Practice

SPIRAL REVIEW **Respond to Literature** Ask students to think about how reading a drama compares to reading a novel or a short story. In a short essay, ask students to explain the differences they encounter reading a drama.

- Is a drama easier or more difficult to understand than a novel?
- Which genre do they prefer reading and why?

Encourage students to share their responses in a class discussion about the differences in the two genres. What are the advantages and disadvantages of both? How might a play be different if it were written as a novel? What would be lost or gained by performing a novel as a play?

GLENCOE LITERATURE LIBRARY

Missing May

by Cynthia Rylant

This is a touching story of change, loss, and the power of love.

Heart of Darkness

by Joseph Conrad

The interior of Africa is the setting for this tale of psychological unraveling and a disturbing and awkward encounter.

CRITICS' CORNER

"Our Town is popular, in part at least, because it is not tragic. The American public has approved of it because of its charming, folksy presentation of simple, 'good' people, its sentimentally idealized account of the small town. It projects a vision of a time and place which have vanished from the American scene, which never existed in fact. . . ."

—George D. Stephens, from *Modern Drama*

Our Town

by Thornton Wilder

In Grover's Corners, New Hampshire, in the first days of the twentieth century, two neighbor children fall in love and grow up. The town is meant to represent a typical American town; the characters are meant to be typical middle-class Americans. Each of the play's three acts takes place at a different point in the characters' lives, providing snapshots of life and death in a small town. Generations of readers have been moved by this Pulitzer Prize–winning play.

Write a Review

Read one of the books listed on these pages and write a review of it for your classmates. Be sure to explain why other students might enjoy the book, or offer suggestions on how they might overcome difficulties in reading the book. Present your review to the class.

Teach

Literary History ☆

Thornton Wilder American playwright and novelist Thornton Wilder (1897–1975) spent his early years in China, where his father was a diplomat. His most famous play, *Our Town,* won a Pulitzer Prize.

Assess

Glencoe Literature Library

Glencoe Literature Library offers an extensive collection of hardcover books that help you encourage your students to read independently. Choose among the more than 120 full-length literary works—novels, novellas, plays, and nonfiction. Each book includes related readings from a broad range of genres.

For access to all study guides for the Glencoe Literature Library, see the Literature Library Teacher Resources CD-ROM.

To create customized reading lists from a database of more than 30,000 titles, use BookLink K–12 CD-ROM.

Write a Review

Students' reviews should address one book mentioned in the Independent Reading feature and should include reasons why others might like the book as well as tips on how to overcome difficulties reading it.

Approaching Level

DIFFERENTIATED INSTRUCTION

Established Help students understand why literary criticism is important. **Ask:** What do we gain from reading what critics think about literary work? *(Students may say that critics let people know if something is worth reading. Others might observe that critics point out many important details that a casual reader might miss.)* Explain that literary criticism allows us to look at a work from different perspectives. By doing this, we can derive multiple meanings from a text. Explain that by asking questions, literary critics find new ways to explore classics.

Assessment

English Language Arts

Focus

Bellringer Options

Say: Some of you may experience stress and anxiety when faced with a test. Knowing and using test-taking strategies will help to minimize that stress. Have half the students brainstorm reasons why taking a test might cause anxiety and have the other half brainstorm strategies to reduce test anxiety.

Teach

Assessment Explain to students that Assessment is intended to reinforce general test-taking strategies as well as test the skills and vocabulary covered in the unit. They will first be asked to read an excerpt from a drama and a poem and answer comprehension, context-clue, and inference questions. Then they will be asked to answer ten paragraph-improvement questions and to write a short essay.

Listening and Speaking

Test Directions Explain to students that instructors often give test directions orally. Ask students to listen carefully as you read aloud the test directions at the top of the page. Ask students who clearly understand the directions to restate them. Tell students that restating or paraphrasing information is a listening strategy for checking comprehension.

Assessment

English Language Arts

Reading: Drama and Poetry

Carefully read the following two selections. Use context clues to help you define any words with which you are unfamiliar. In each selection, pay close attention to dramatic conventions, the main idea, and the use of literary or rhetorical devices. Then, on a separate sheet of paper, answer the questions on pages 817–818.

from *In the Bear's House* by N. Scott Momaday

One: You are, Urset. I AM, Yahweh

[UNDEFINED SPACE. ***Two chairs under a light, perhaps a street lamp or a Chinese lantern in a tree. YAHWEH, the Creator, is slouched in one of the chairs, dozing. Enter URSET, the bear, very softly, warily. He stands for a moment beside the empty chair, tentative, ill at ease. He sits.]***

URSET. Ah, ahem. Pardon, Great Mystery. Beg pardon.

[YAHWEH *stirs, stretches, looks up.]*

It is only I, Urset.

YAHWEH. Yes? What? Oh, yes, it is you, Urset. How are you?

URSET. Do you know me, then?

YAHWEH. Know you? How could I not know you, Urset. I created you.

URSET. Yes, yes, I have dreamed of that. I have dreamed that I came very small from your hands.

YAHWEH. So small. You were scarcely larger than a rat. I thought, when I saw you in your new corporeal being, that I had made some mistake, for I meant you to be formidable, and there you were, a wet rat. And yes, you did indeed come from these hands. These very fingers, these palms, the heels of these hands. I made a little ball of fur, wet fur—from something floating on the waters, as I recall—a knot of hair, a bit of drift. It was you! And, behold, you became formidable. I don't mind telling you, Urset, you are one of my showpieces. I am proud of you.

URSET. I was accomplished at your hands. I was wonderful, therefore, was I not? Am I not?

YAHWEH. The accomplishment was realized on time, according to plan. It was a simple thing, really—child's play.

The Traveling Bear by Amy Lowell

Grass-blades push up between the cobblestones
And catch the sun on their flat sides
Shooting it back,
Gold and emerald,
Into the eyes of passers-by.

And over the cobblestones,
Square-footed and heavy,
Dances the trained bear.
The cobbles cut his feet,
And he has a ring in his nose
Which hurts him;
But still he dances,
For the keeper pricks him with a sharp stick,
Under his fur.

Now the crowd gapes and chuckles,
And boys and young women shuffle their feet in time to the dancing bear.
They see him wobbling
Against a dust of emerald and gold,
And they are greatly delighted.

The legs of the bear shake with fatigue,
And his back aches,
And the shining grass-blades dazzle and confuse him.
But still he dances,
Because of the little, pointed stick.

Items 1–10 apply to "In the Bear's House."

1. What can you infer from the stage directions at the beginning of the selection?
   A. Urset and Yahweh are in a natural setting.
   B. Urset has come to see Yahweh.
   C. Yahweh is unhappy with Urset.
   D. Yahweh knows Urset well.

2. What is not provided specifically in the selection?
   A. characters
   B. directions
   C. setting
   D. dialogue

Assess

Reading

1. B is the correct answer because the stage directions state that Urset enters the area where Yahweh is sleeping. **DOK 2**

2. C is the correct answer because the stage directions describe the place as "undefined space." **DOK 1**

English Learners

DIFFERENTIATED INSTRUCTION

Advanced English learners may have difficulty understanding the dramatic passage and poem included in this section. Have volunteers read the selections aloud, or read the selections for them. Encourage them to visualize the imagery in each passage. Point out that both selections have to do with bears. Tell students to think about the tone and message in each and note how they are different.

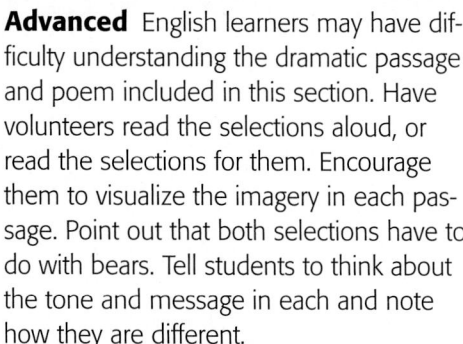

Assess

3. D is the correct answer because Yahweh is describing Urset as he appeared at birth. DOK 1

4. A is the correct answer because Yahweh says in lines 14–15, "I made a little ball of fur. . . . It was you!" DOK 1

5. B is the correct answer because *corporeal* means "having physical form." DOK 1

6. A is the correct answer because the only option that contrasts with something small and insignificant is *formidable*. DOK 1

7. D is the correct answer. Yahweh is central to the story. DOK 2

8. B is the correct answer. In the paragraph ending on line 17, Yahweh explains that he is proud that Urset has become formidable. DOK 1

9. C is the correct answer. Only dialogue, an exchange between characters, appears here. DOK 2

10. A is the correct answer. Urset shows no character development or varied personality traits in this selection. DOK 2

11. C is the correct answer. The author uses descriptive terms to evoke images. No other literary device is found here. DOK 2

12. A is the correct answer. A stick is used to urge the bear to dance. DOK 1

13. C is the correct answer. The meaning of line 17 is incomplete without line 18. No other literary or sound device appears here. DOK 2

14. D is the correct answer. The poem deals with a painfully serious subject. DOK 3

15. A is the correct answer. Both selections explore the feelings of animals. DOK 3

---

3. What is the "rat" Yahweh speaks of in line 11?
   A. Urset's creator
   B. Urset in a past life
   C. Urset's own offspring
   D. Urset as a cub

4. How does Yahweh know Urset?
   A. He created Urset.
   B. He spoke to Urset earlier.
   C. He has observed Urset.
   D. He is related to Urset.

5. From the context, what do you think the word *corporeal,* in line 12, means?
   A. replaceable
   B. bodily
   C. improved
   D. permanent

6. From the context, what do you think the word *formidable,* in lines 12 and 16, means?
   A. awesome
   B. early
   C. hateful
   D. shrinking

7. How do you know that Yahweh is a main character in the play?
   A. He is fully developed.
   B. He reveals many traits.
   C. He changes during the story.
   D. He is central to the story.

8. Why is Yahweh proud of Urset?
   A. because of what Urset did
   B. because of what Urset has become
   C. because Urset was always impressive
   D. because Urset is powerful

9. Which term best describes the characters' lines in this selection?
   A. soliloquy
   B. monologue
   C. dialogue
   D. asides

10. Which terms best describe the character of Urset in the selection?
   A. flat and static
   B. flat and dynamic
   C. round and dynamic
   D. round and static

Items 11–15 apply to "The Traveling Bear."

11. What literary device does Lowell use in line 2?
   A. meter
   B. simile
   C. imagery
   D. personification

12. Why does the bear dance?
   A. He is forced to do so.
   B. He loves children.
   C. He is popular.
   D. He is hungry.

13. What literary device appears in lines 17–18?
   A. metaphor
   B. alliteration
   C. enjambment
   D. paradox

14. What is the overall mood of this poem?
   A. comic
   B. hopeful
   C. mysterious
   D. somber

15. Which of the following themes do "In the Bear's House" and "The Traveling Bear" share?
   A. Animals have feelings.
   B. Animals are mysterious.
   C. Animals are treated badly.
   D. Animals are spiritual.

LOG ON **Literature** Online

Assessment For additional test practice, go to glencoe.com and enter QuickPass code GL49787u4.

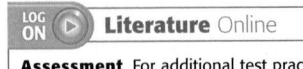

Vocabulary Skills: Sentence Completion

For each item in the Vocabulary Skills section, choose the word that best completes the sentence.

1. Long periods of captivity can ______ an animal's development.
   A. contrive
   B. lament
   C. sanction
   D. stifle

2. In ______ regions, landscapers recommend using plants that do not require a lot of rain.
   A. arid
   B. haughty
   C. profane
   D. riveted

3. The child was drawn to the ______ call of his mother.
   A. beckoning
   B. prostrated
   C. imposing
   D. incriminating

4. Dina chose the scenic ______ for her trip, even though it would take her twice as long to get to her final destination.
   A. apparition
   B. itinerary
   C. misadventure
   D. predicament

5. The deer was ______ by fright and did not run away.
   A. nonchalant
   B. furled
   C. riveted
   D. exalted

6. Some predators ______ quietly, waiting for the right moment to attack.
   A. profane
   B. mourn
   C. lurk
   D. retain

7. Many people consider humankind a more ______ threat to wild animals than any force of nature.
   A. fickle
   B. perverse
   C. effusive
   D. pernicious

8. He thought at first that the ______ was a ghost, but he soon realized that it was just a shadow.
   A. apparition
   B. diffidence
   C. vanquished
   D. adversity

9. Even though the dog owner spoke with great ______, the town council denied her petition for the development of a dog park.
   A. adversity
   B. rancor
   C. monotony
   D. eloquence

10. Having spent so much time close together, the animals in ______ cages became familiar with one another.
    A. exalted
    B. adjacent
    C. imperious
    D. baleful

English Learners

DIFFERENTIATED INSTRUCTION

Beginner/Early Intermediate

English language learners may have difficulty understanding the context clues provided in the sentence-completion questions. Have students read only the stem of a question and, without looking at the answer choices, try to identify the correct answer from the unit vocabulary words. Once students identify what they think is the correct answer, have them look at the four answer choices to see if their answer is there. If students cannot identify the correct vocabulary words, have them work with partners to find the answers.

Assess

Vocabulary Skills

1. D is the correct answer. Because the sentence relates to an animal's development, this is the only answer choice that makes sense. DOK 1
2. A is the correct answer. The fact that the region does not get much rain indicates that this is the correct answer. DOK 1
3. A is the correct answer. The fact that the child was drawn to the call indicates that this is the correct answer. DOK 1
4. B is the correct answer. Trips involve itineraries. DOK 1
5. C is the correct answer. The deer does not run away, which indicates that this is the correct answer. DOK 1
6. C is the correct answer. Because the predators wait to attack, *lurk* is the only word that makes sense in the context. DOK 1
7. D is the correct answer. The context suggests that the correct word is something threatening. DOK 1
8. A is the correct answer. *Apparition* is a synonym for *ghost.* DOK 1
9. D is the correct answer. The words *even though* signal a contrast between the speaker's tone and the end result. DOK 1
10. B is the correct answer. The key phrase here is *close together.* No other option makes sense in this context. DOK 1

Assess

Grammar and Writing Skills

1. C is the correct answer. The sentence is simply declarative, not exclamatory, so it requires no exclamation point. DOK 1

2. C is the correct answer. The pronoun *them* does not agree in number with its antecedent, *Ursa Major.* DOK 1

3. C is the correct answer. The phrase *because of its northern latitudes* modifies *Classical Age,* whereas it should modify *constellation.* DOK 1

4. A is the correct answer. The sentence lacks a verb. DOK 1

Grammar and Writing Skills: Paragraph Improvement

Read carefully through the following passage from the first draft of a student's essay. Pay close attention to verb tense, use of apostrophes, and sentence structure. Then, on a separate sheet of paper, answer the questions on pages 820–821.

[1] The constellation Ursa Major has fascinated people since the dawn of time! [2] Many cultures have noticed Ursa Major, also known as the "Great Bear," and have attached great significance to them. [3] The bear has been associated with the constellation since the Classical Age, because of its northern latitudes. [4] Only an extraordinary bear could live so far north. [5] Throughout the ages, the Great Bear with the gods and royalty.

[6] To the ancient Greeks, Ursa Major represent Callisto, a follower of the goddess Artemis. [7] Zeus, king of the gods, fell in love with Callisto, and they had a child named Arcas. [8] Hera, Zeus wife, became intensely jealous and changed Callisto into a bear. [9] One day, when Arcas came upon Callisto in the forest, Callisto stood on her hind leg's to greet him. [10] Feeling threatened, Arcas readied his bow. [11] Zeus, seeing what was about to happen, turned Arcas into a small bear. [12] He then hurled them into the sky, where they remain as Ursa Major and Ursa Minor. [13] Some North American tribes, including the Algonquin and Iroquois, also associated the constellation with a gigantic bear.

1. Which of the following is the best way to revise sentence 1?
   A. Insert a comma after *people.*
   B. Lowercase *Ursa Major.*
   C. Change the exclamation mark to a period.
   D. Make no change.

2. Which error appears in sentence 2?
   A. sentence fragment
   B. run-on sentence
   C. lack of pronoun-antecedent agreement
   D. lack of subject-verb agreement

3. Which error appears in sentence 3?
   A. fragment
   B. incorrect verb tense
   C. misplaced modifier
   D. run-on sentence

4. Which of the following is the best way to revise sentence 5?
   A. Insert *has been connected* after *Bear.*
   B. Insert a comma after *Bear.*
   C. Delete *the* before *gods.*
   D. Lowercase *Great Bear.*

Grammar Practice

Use Apostrophes
Remind students that the apostrophe has only four uses:

- to create a possesive form *(Tom's wallet, students' essays)*
- to express amounts of money or time that modify a noun *(twenty dollars' savings, ten weeks' study)*
- to replace omitted letters or numerals *(isn't [is not], the '70s)*
- with *s* to form the plural of a letter, numeral, symbol, or word used as a word *(8's, A's and B's, #'s, many uh's in his speech)*

Have students write a paragraph that uses two of the four possible uses of apostrophes.

5. Which of the following is the best revision of sentence 6?
   A. To the ancient Greeks, Ursa Major represented Callisto, a follower of the goddess Artemis.
   B. To the ancient Greeks, Ursa Major represents Callisto, a follower of the goddess Artemis.
   C. To the ancient Greeks Ursa Major represents Callisto, a follower of the goddess Artemis.
   D. To the ancient Greeks, Ursa Major represented Callisto a follower of the goddess Artemis.

6. Which of the following is the best revision of sentence 8?
   A. Hera, Zeus's wife and—queen of the gods—became intensely jealous and changed Callisto into a bear.
   B. Hera, Zeus's wife, became intensely jealous and changed Callisto into a bear.
   C. Hera, Zeus's wife became intensely jealous and changed Callisto into a bear.
   D. Hera, Zeus's wife, became intensely jealous, and changed Callisto into a bear.

7. Which error appears in sentence 9?
   A. run-on sentence
   B. split infinitive
   C. misspelling
   D. lack of parallelism

8. Which sentence is not related to the main idea of the second paragraph?
   A. 9
   B. 11
   C. 12
   D. 13

9. What is most notably missing from this essay?
   A. supporting arguments
   B. historical quotations
   C. a concluding paragraph
   D. an introductory paragraph

10. Which of the following titles would best suit this essay?
   A. "The Mythology of a Constellation"
   B. "The History of the Bear"
   C. "How Ursa the Bear Got Her Name"
   D. "A Guide to Greek Astronomy"

Essay

The playwright Vaclav Havel wrote, "Drama assumes an order, if only so that it might have—by disrupting that order—a way of surprising." Write an essay in which you consider two works from this unit in light of Havel's idea. Include a thoughtful and logical interpretation of his statement, your opinion of the validity of this statement, and an explanation of how this statement is refuted or supported by the works that you examine. Include an introduction, several paragraphs explaining your position, and a conclusion. As you write, keep in mind that your essay will be checked for **ideas, organization, voice, word choice, sentence fluency, conventions,** and **presentation.**

Essay

Evaluate essays for the following:

- a clearly stated interpretation and evaluation of Havel's statement and an explanation of how it relates to the two works
- support of interpretation and evaluation by quotations, examples, and details from the selections
- effective voice, word choice, and sentence variety
- effective presentation, with attention to grammar and spelling conventions DOK 4

Assess

5. A is the correct answer. The verb here does not agree in number with the subject. Nor is it in the past tense, as it should be. Options **B** and **C** agree in number but contain the incorrect tense. Option **D** lacks the comma needed to set off the nonessential appositive. DOK 1

6. B is the correct answer. The possessive form of *Zeus* must appear here. No other option corrects this error without introducing other errors. DOK 1

7. C is the correct answer. The apostrophe in *leg's* makes the word possessive instead of plural. DOK 1

8. D is the correct answer. Sentence 13 relates not to Greek, but to Native American, myths. DOK 3

9. C is the correct answer. This passage ends abruptly. Supporting arguments or quotations are not needed in a historical essay, so options **A** and **B** are incorrect. The essay already has an introductory paragraph, so option **D** is incorrect. DOK 3

10. A is the correct answer. No other title is related to the main idea of the essay. DOK 3

Skills Scope and Sequence

Readability Scores Key: Dale-Chall/DRP/Lexile

PART 1: Journeys

Selections and Features	Literary Elements
Unit Introduction pp. 822–828	Epic and Myth **SE** p. 824 Archetype **SE** p. 825
Literary Focus pp. 830–831	Hero **SE** p. 830
Literary History pp. 832–833	Epic Poetry **SE** p. 832
Epic The Odyssey, Part 1, by Homer pp. 834–856	Epic and Epic Hero **SE** p. 835
Epic The Odyssey, Part 2, by Homer pp. 857–870	Conflict **SE** p. 857
Epic The Odyssey, Part 3, by Homer pp. 871–884	Characterization **SE** p. 871, **TE** pp. 874, 876
Epic The Odyssey, Part 4, by Homer pp. 885–898	Plot **SE** p. 885 Narrator (review) **SE** p. 897

Reading Skills and Strategies	Vocabulary	Writing / Grammar	Speaking, Listening, and Viewing
		Write an Adventure **TE** p. 824 Write a Graphic Novel **TE** p. 826 Write a Comparison-Contrast Essay **SE** p. 828	Dialogue **SE** p. 828 Visual Presentation **TE** p. 828
		Write a Research Report **TE** p. 830 Write a Description **SE** p. 831	
		Write a Research Report **TE** p. 832	
Analyze Figurative Language **SE** p. 835 Identify Author's Purpose **TE** p. 840 Identify Cause-and-Effect Relationships **TE** p. 850	Synonyms **SE** p. 856	Write a Journal Entry **TE** p. 836 Write a Description **TE** p. 844 Dashes **TE** p. 846 Write a Story **TE** p. 848 Simple and Compound Sentences **TE** p. 854 Write an Interior Monologue **SE** p. 856	Oral Presentation **TE** p. 838 Oral Report **TE** p. 852
Identify Sequence **SE** p. 857 Identify Problem and Solution **TE** p. 858 Summarize **TE** p. 866	Context Clues **SE** p. 870	Write a Monologue **TE** p. 860 Adverb Clauses **TE** p. 862 Participles and Participle Phrases **TE** p. 868 Write a Summary **SE** p. 870	Oral Interpretation **TE** p. 864
Make Inferences about Theme **SE** p. 871 Predict **TE** p. 880	Analogies **SE** p. 884	Write a Persuasive Letter **TE** p. 872 Compound Predicates **TE** p. 882 Write an Interior Monologue **SE** p. 884	Performance **TE** p. 878
Analyze Cause-and-Effect Relationships **SE** p. 885 Connect to Contemporary Issues **TE** p. 888	Word Origins **SE** p. 897	Write a Comparison-Contrast Essay **TE** p. 890 Write a Journal Entry **TE** p. 892 Noun Clauses **TE** p. 894 Write a Review **SE** p. 898	Oral Report **TE** p. 886 Discussion **SE** p. 896

Readability Scores Key: **Dale-Chall/DRP/Lexile**

PART 1: Journeys *(continued)*

Selections and Features	Literary Elements
Vocabulary Workshop p. 899	
Comparing Literature **Ithaca (poem),** by C. P. Cavafy **An Ancient Gesture (poem),** by Edna St. Vincent Millay **Waiting** *from* **The Penelopiad (novel),** by Margaret Atwood **7.9/59/910** pp. 900–906	Symbol **TE** p. 902 Point of View **TE** p. 904
Informational Text TIME: Leaving It All Behind, by Susan Jakes **7.9/58/920** pp. 907–911	
Novel Over Hill and Under Hill *from* **The Hobbit,** by J. R. R. Tolkien **7.3/59/1080** pp. 912–925	Motif **SE** p. 913 Narrator (review) **SE** p. 924
Visual Perspective *from* **The Hobbit,** adapted by Charles Dixon and illustrated by David Wenzel pp. 926–930	Text Features **TE** p. 928

PART 2: Courage and Cleverness

Literary Focus pp. 932–933	Archetype **SE** p. 932
Myth Perseus, by Edith Hamilton **6.9/54/1030** pp. 934–944	Plot Pattern Archetype **SE** p. 935 Hero (review) **SE** p. 943
Grammar Workshop p. 945	
Myth The Fenris Wolf, by Olivia Coolidge **9.4/57/1120** pp. 946–952	Theme Archetype **SE** p. 947 Plot Pattern Archetype (review) **SE** p. 951
Vocabulary Workshop p. 953	

Reading Skills and Strategies	Vocabulary	Writing Grammar	Speaking, Listening, and Viewing
	Word Origins **SE** p. 899		
Compare Theme and Author's Meaning **SE** p. 900		Write a Comparison-Contrast Essay **SE** p. 906	Discussion **SE** p. 906
Respond to Events **SE** p. 907 Preview **SE** p. 907 Question **TE** p. 908		Write an Expository Essay **TE** p. 910 Write a Summary **SE** p. 911	
Compare and Contrast Characters **SE** p. 913 Analyze Figurative Language **TE** p. 920 Connect to Contemporary Issues **TE** p. 922	Context Clues **SE** p. 924 Academic Vocabulary **SE** p. 924	Write a Character Sketch **TE** p. 914 Write an Expository Essay **SE** p. 925	Analyze Images **TE** p. 916 Performance **TE** p. 918 Discussion **SE** p. 923
Compare and Contrast Versions of a Story **SE** p. 926 Predict **TE** p. 930		Create a Graphic Novel **TE** p. 926 Write a Summary **SE** p. 930	
		Write a Description **SE** p. 933	Oral Report **TE** p. 932
Identify Genre **SE** p. 935	Antonyms **SE** p. 943	Write a Character Sketch **TE** p. 936 Write a Research Report **TE** p. 938 Write an Expository Essay **SE** p. 944 Active and Passive Voice **SE** p. 944	Discussion **TE** p. 940
		Transitional Expressions **SE** p. 945	
Interpret Imagery **SE** p. 947	Connotation **TE** p. 948 Context Clues **SE** p. 952	Write a Description **SE** p. 952	
	Word Origins **SE** p. 953		

Readability Scores Key: Dale-Chall/DRP/Lexile

PART 2: Courage and Cleverness *(continued)*

Selections and Features	Literary Elements
Legend Coyote and Crow, by Ella Clark **3.8/42/510** pp. 954–957	Character Archetype **SE** p. 955
Ballad Sweet Betsy from Pike, traditional pp. 958–961	Ballad **SE** p. 958 Meter and Rhythm (review) **SE** p. 960
Writing Workshop pp. 962–971	
Speaking, Listening, and Viewing Workshop pp. 972–975	
Independent Reading pp. 976–977	
Assessment pp. 978–983	

Reading Skills and Strategies	Vocabulary	Writing / Grammar	Speaking, Listening, and Viewing
Activate Prior Knowledge **SE** p. 955	Academic Vocabulary **SE** p. 957	Write a Story **SE** p. 957	
Analyze Archetypes **SE** p. 958	Academic Vocabulary **SE** p. 961	Write a Self-Evaluation **SE** p. 961	Oral Presentation **SE** p. 961
		Prewrite **SE** p. 963 Write Research Questions **TE** p. 964 Draft **SE** p. 966 Write an Introduction **TE** p. 966 Verb Tense **TE** p. 968 Revise **SE** p. 970 Write a Research Report **SE** p. 971	
Compare and Contrast **TE** p. 972 Visualize **TE** p. 974		Create a Story Board **SE** p. 974	Multimedia Presentation **SE** p. 975
		Write a Review **SE** p. 977	
		Write a Reflective Essay **SE** p. 983	

UNIT FIVE

Focus

Bellringer Options

Literature Launcher Pre-Reading Video Unit 5

Daily Language Practice Transparency 81

Or **write on the board:** Name as many modern epics as you can. *(Possible answers could include* The Lord of the Rings, Star Wars, *and the Harry Potter books.)* **Encourage students to consider multiple media, including movies, TV, books, and computer and video games. Discuss what makes these stories epic.**

For school-to-home activities, see Unit 5 Teaching Resources Book, pp. 5–11.

For students who would profit from independent novel study, see Novel Companion, pp. 231–298.

The Burning of Troy, 1606. Pieter Schoubroeck.

View the Art Pieter Schoubroeck belonged to the Flemish school of painting, a style that included painstaking attention to detail. What details in this painting contribute to the larger-than-life quality of the event shown?

Unit Introduction Skills

Epic and Myth

Literary Elements
- The Epic (SE p. 824)
- Structure (SE p. 824)
- Myth and Archetype (SE p. 825)
- Symbol (SE p. 826)
- Literary Analysis (SE pp. 826–827)

Listening/Speaking/Viewing Skills
- Epic Ad Presentation (TE p. 828)

Writing Skills/Grammar
- Choose Your Own Adventure (TE p. 824)
- Graphic Novel (TE p. 826)

Reading Skills
- Read Epics (SE p. 828)

UNIT FIVE

Epic and Myth

Looking Ahead

Many centuries ago, before books, magazines, paper, and pencils were invented, people recited their stories. Some of the stories they told offered explanations of natural phenomena, such as thunder and lightning, or the culture's customs or beliefs. Other stories were meant for entertainment. Taken together, these stories—these myths, epics, and legends—tell a history of loyalty and betrayal, heroism and cowardice, love and rejection. In this unit, you will explore the literary elements that make them unique.

Each part in Unit Five focuses on a Big Idea that can help you connect the selections to your life.

PREVIEW	Big Idea	Literary Focus
PART 1	Journeys	Hero
PART 2	Courage and Cleverness	Archetype

823

UNIT FIVE

Focus

Summary

The unit defines literary structure, myth, archetype, and symbol and gives examples of their use in epics and myths. Quotes from writers on reading Homer and an analysis of "The Wedding" from the Hindu epic *The Ramayana* are included.

View the Art ★

Answer: *Students may point to the large numbers of people shown and the gruesome details among the people as they flee.*

Dutch artist Pieter Schoubroeck (c. 1570–1607) belonged to the Flemish school of painting, a style that arose in the Middle Ages in Flanders, an area now divided between Belgium, the Netherlands, and France. The influence of manuscript illumination on the Flemish style is visible in the attention to detail, rich colors, and highly developed technique of artists such as Schoubroeck.

For diagnostic and end-of-unit assessment, see Assessment Resources, pp. 25–32.

Unit Resources

Print Materials

- Unit 5 Teaching Resources, pp. 1–192
- Interactive Read and Write (On Level/ Approaching, EL), pp. 227–286
- Novel Companion, pp. 231–298
- Bellringer Option Transparencies: Selection Focus 44, , 48; Daily Language Practice 81–91
- Literary Element Transparencies 1, 34, 57
- Assessment Resources, Unit Assessment, pp. 233–234
- Assessment Resources, Selection Assessment, pp. 185–208

Technology

- TeacherWorks Plus CD
- StudentWorks Plus CD
- Literature Launchers: Pre-Reading Videos DVD, Unit 5
- Literature Online
- Interactive Vocabulary CD-ROM
- Listening Library CD-ROM
- ExamView CD-ROM
- Skill Level Up! CD-ROM

UNIT FIVE

Teach

Reading Strategy 1

Connect Have a student read aloud the paragraph at the top of the page.

Ask: Do you agree with Jung that in order for us to understand ourselves today, we must understand the past? Have students consider the impact of the past on their lives. What beliefs, knowledge, or traditions have their families handed down through the generations? How have they been affected by various historical events? Instruct students to keep this interconnectedness in mind while reading.

Cultural History ☆

Poseidon The god Poseidon was believed by the Greeks to be the cause of violent, unpredictable movement. He ruled over the sea, earthquakes, and horses and was the son of Gaia (Earth) and Kronos (Time), brother to Zeus, Hera, Hades, and Demeter. The equivalent Roman god was called Neptune. His symbol is the trident, a three-pronged fishing spear.

Learning Objectives

For pages 822–828

In studying this text, you will focus on the following objectives:

Literary Study:
Analyzing literary genres.
Connecting to literature.

Genre Focus: Epic and Myth

What is unique about epics and myths?

Why do we read stories from the distant past? Why should we care about heroes and villains long dead? About cities and palaces that were destroyed centuries before our time? The noted psychologist and psychiatrist Carl Jung thought he knew the answer. He thought that in order for us to understand the people we are today, we have to learn about those who came before us. One way to do that, Jung believed, was to read the myths and epics of long ago. 1

Epic

Illustrated page with Battle Scene from the *Shahnameh*, 10th century. Ferdowsi. Decorative Museum, Tehran. Epics often include descriptions of huge battles or wars.

The Epic

An **epic** is a long narrative poem about a serious subject. The purpose of an epic poem is threefold: to entertain, to teach, and to inspire with examples of how people can succeed against great odds.

Epic Heroes and Gods The action in an epic centers on the **epic hero,** whose primary goal is usually to save his nation or its people during a time of crisis. Gods may take part in the action or at least take an interest in what happens, sometimes intervening to affect the course of events.

Yet all the gods had pitied Lord Odysseus, ☆
all but Poseidon, raging cold and rough
against the brave king till he came ashore
at last on his own land.

—Homer, **from the *Odyssey***

Structure The way an author organizes images, ideas, words, and lines is called **structure.** Like many epics, the *Odyssey* begins with an **invocation,** a request to a muse to provide inspiration. In Greek mythology, the **muses** are nine goddesses who preside over the arts and sciences and inspire those who show talent in these areas.

Sing in me, Muse, and through me tell the story
of that man skilled in all ways of contending,
the wanderer, harried for years on end,
after he plundered the stronghold
on the proud height of Troy.

—Homer, **from the *Odyssey***

Writing Practice

SMALL GROUP

Choose Your Own Adventure Have students sharpen their writing skills by creating an adventure. Have the class work together to develop a hero, a setting, and a tricky situation. Then, split the class into groups. Invite each group to determine how the hero handles the situation and wins the day. Have each group present its finished story to the class. Then, have the class vote on the best adventure.

Myth and the Archetype

Myth

A **myth** is a traditional story of anonymous origin. Many myths are about the creation of earth; others are about love, adventure, trickery, or revenge. In many myths, human action is controlled or guided by gods and other supernatural beings. Many myths began as a part of the **oral tradition,** or literature that passes by word of mouth from one generation to the next. Oral literature was a way of recording the past, glorifying leaders, and teaching morals and traditions to young people.

For a time she kept his birth secret from her father, but it became increasingly difficult to do so in the narrow limits of that bronze house and finally one day the little boy—his name was Perseus—was discovered by his grandfather. "Your child!" Acrisius cried in great anger. "Who is his father?" But when Danaë answered proudly, "Zeus," he would not believe her.

—Edith Hamilton, **from "Perseus"**

Archetype

2 An **archetype** is a thing, person, or pattern of circumstances that appears repeatedly in literature. Most ancient myths, folktales, fables, ballads, and legends contain archetypal characters, such as the evil villain, the lovesick suitor, and the fool. They also may contain archetypal themes, such as the hidden treasure or the rite of passage.

When the gods first saw the Fenris Wolf, he was so young that they thought they could tame him. They took him to Asgard, therefore, and brave Tyr undertook to feed and train him. Presently, however, the black monster grew so enormous that his open jaws would stretch from heaven to earth, showing teeth as large as the trunks of oak trees and as sharply pointed as knives.

—Olivia Coolidge, **from "The Fenris Wolf"**

LOG ON **Literature** Online

Literature and Reading For more selections in this genre, go to glencoe.com and enter QuickPass code GL49787u5.

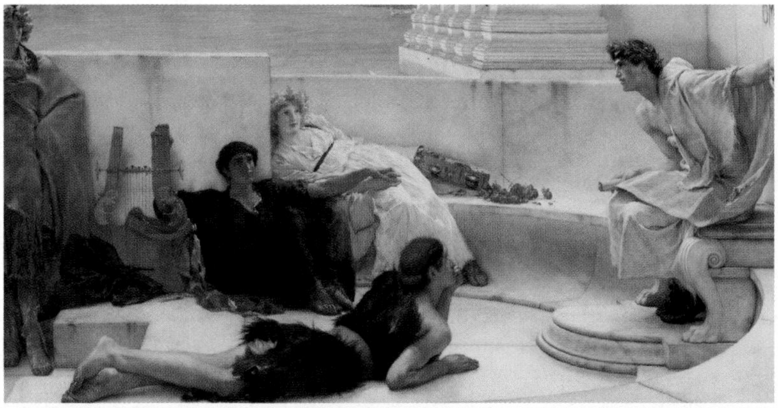

A Reading from Homer, 1885. Lawrence Alma-Tadema. Oil on canvas, 91.8 x 183.5 cm. Philadelphia Museum of Art, PA.

UNIT FIVE

Teach

Literary Element 2

Archetype Note that the character of the evil villain is a familiar example of an archetype.

Ask: Who would you consider to be an archetypal villain in modern films? *(Possible answers: Sauron from* Lord of the Rings, *Voldemort from the Harry Potter books, Darth Vader from* Star Wars*)*

Advanced Learners

DIFFERENTIATED INSTRUCTION

Myth Makers Suggest that students try their hand at creating a myth. Instruct them to begin with an outline that includes:

- plot events
- characterization of the hero, including background and character traits
- archetypes and symbols

Encourage students to include drawings, paintings, or collages of their settings and characters to illustrate their stories. Have them share their work with the class.

UNIT FIVE

Teach

Reading Strategy 1

Set a Purpose Remind students that setting a purpose before reading a passage will improve their reading speed and comprehension. Suggest that students read with the purpose of being able to summarize the plot concisely. After they've read the story, have them write a one-paragraph summary and then compare it with their classmates' to determine if they missed any important plot points or characters.

Writing Practice

SMALL GROUP

Graphic Novel Challenge students to create a graphic novel of *The Wedding.* Assign groups of students various sections of the story. Remind them to include plot, dialogue, and characters. Students may use clippings from magazines or their own drawings for visuals. When all the sections have been combined, have students review the story for completeness.

Literary Analysis Model

How do literary elements help us enjoy epics and myths?

1 The *Ramayana*, which was written by a man named Maharishi Valmiki, is a Hindu epic of 24,000 verses divided into seven chapters, or books. It tells the story of Prince Rama of Ayodhya (an ancient city of India), his wife, Sita, and his close companion and brother, Lakshmana. The *Ramayana* is thought to contain the teachings of ancient Hindu sages.

APPLYING Literary Elements

Symbol

Here, as in many myths and epics, the bow is a symbol of war and vengeance. This bow belonged to Shira, a Hindu god also known as the "Destroyer."

The Wedding from the *Ramayana*

translated by R. K. Narayan

King Janaka had in his possession an enormous bow which at one time belonged to Shiva, who had abandoned it and left it in the custody of an early ancestor of Janaka's, and it had remained an heirloom. Sita, as a baby girl, was a gift of Mother Earth to Janaka, being found in a furrow when a field was ploughed. Janaka adopted the child, tended her, and she grew up into a beauty, so much so that several princes who considered themselves eligible thronged Janaka's palace and contended for Sita's hand. Unable to favor anyone in particular, and in order to ward them off, King Janaka made it a condition that whoever could lift, bend, and string Shiva's bow would be considered fit to become Sita's husband. When her suitors took a look at the bow, they realized that it was a hopeless and unacceptable condition. . . . As time passed Janaka became anxious whether he would ever see his daughter married and settled—since the condition once made could not be withdrawn. No one on earth seemed worthy of approaching Shiva's bow. Janaka sighed. "I tremble when I think of Sita's future, and question my own judgment in linking her fate with this mighty, divine heirloom in our house."

. . . Janaka said, "I'll have it brought here. It has lain in its shed too long. . . . Who knows, moving it out may change all our fates." He called on his attendants to fetch the bow. . . .

The bow was placed in a carriage on eight pairs of wheels and arrived drawn by a vast number of men. During its passage from its shed through the streets, a crowd followed it. It was so huge that no one could comprehend it at one glance. . . .

The marriage of Rama and his brothers from the Sangri Ramayana, ca. 1760–1765. Pahari School. National Museum, New Delhi, India.

Rama looked at his master. Viswamithra nodded as if to say, "Try it." As Rama approached the bow with slow dignity, the onlookers held their breath and watched. Some prayed silently for him. Some commented, "How cruel! This supposed sage is not ashamed to put the delicate, marvelous youth to this harsh trial!" "The King is perverse and cruel to place this godlike youth in this predicament. . . . If he was serious about it, he should have just placed Sita's hand in his instead of demanding all this acrobatic feat. . . ." "The King's aim is to keep Sita with him forever—this is one way of never facing separation!"

Archetype The handsome suitor forced to earn the trust and admiration of the bride's father is a thematic archetype.

2 While they were speculating thus, Rama approached the bow. Some of the onlookers, unable to bear the suspense, closed their eyes and prayed for his success, saying, "If he fails to bring the ends of this bow together, what is to happen to the maiden?" What they missed, because they had shut their eyes, was to note how swiftly Rama picked up the bow, tugged the string taut, and brought the tips together. They were startled when they heard a deafening report, caused by the cracking of the bow at its arch, which could not stand the pressure of Rama's grip.

The atmosphere was suddenly relaxed. The gods showered down flowers and blessings, clouds parted and precipitated rains, the oceans tossed up in the air all the rare treasures from their depths. The sages cried, "Janaka's tribulations and trials are ended." Music filled the air.

Epic ☆ Gods, goddesses, and other supernatural beings are important characters in most myths and epics.

Reading Check

Interpret Why does Janaka worry that his daughter, Sita, will never be married?

UNIT FIVE

Teach

Reading Check

Answer: *The task he set for the suitors proved too difficult.*

Literary Element 2

Hero Ask: Who is the hero in this story? How do you know he is the hero? *(Rama; He faces a difficult challenge and overcomes it against great odds.)*

APPROACHING To help approaching level students, **ask:** What qualities make a good hero? *(Courage and ingenuity: these qualities help the hero solve problems.)*

Writer's Technique ☆

Epic Style The grand writing style characteristic of epics is evident in the formal tone of the dialogue in *The Wedding.* The highly proper language sharply contrasts with the colloquial style that modern readers expect in realistic dialogue.

English Learners

DIFFERENTIATED INSTRUCTION

Beginning/Early Intermediate Students may find the unusual names difficult to remember. Have them keep a list in their notebooks with the following heads:

- Name
- Description and character traits
- Role (include who the person is related to and how; for example, Viswamithra is Rama's master)

Encourage students to make a similar list in their notebooks when they are reading the *Odyssey.* Explain that there are many unusually named characters in epic stories.

Assess

Guide to Reading Epics and Myths

Suggest that students take notes on these points:

- What insight into human nature does the story provide?
- What emotions are explored?

Elements of Epics and Myths

Suggest that students create a chart that includes *myth, epic hero, symbol,* and *archetype.* As they read, have students add specifics to their charts.

Activities

1. **Speaking/Listening** Have students consider whether they wish to use formal or colloquial language.
2. **Write** Have students brainstorm a list of epics and myths to use as examples.
3. **Take Notes** Encourage students to use the organizer with each selection.

FOLDABLES® Study Organizer

Have students make and label the Tab Book. Their notes on people, places, and events can be written on each tab.

Wrap-Up:

Guide to Reading Epics and Myths

- Epics and myths give us insight into human nature.
- Most epics and myths explore a range of human emotions, including anger, love, jealousy, rage, and vengeance.
- Epics and myths are timeless because they have the characteristics of a good story. They are imaginative, interesting, inspiring, and completely authentic.

Elements of Epics and Myths

- An **epic** is a long narrative poem written about a serious subject.
- A **myth** is a traditional story of anonymous origin that deals with gods, goddesses, heroes, and supernatural events.
- The **epic hero** is the central character in an epic. He is driven by his desire to save his country or its people during a time of crisis.
- An **archetype** is a thing, person, or pattern of circumstances that appears repeatedly in literature.

LOG ON Literature Online

Unit Resources For additional skills practice, go to glencoe.com and enter QuickPass code GL49787u5.

Activities

Use what you have learned about reading and analyzing epics and myths to complete one of the following activities.

1. **Speaking and Listening** With a partner, invent a conversation between two characters mentioned in the Unit Introduction. Write your dialogue, rehearse it, and then present it to the class.
2. **Write** Create a bulleted list that details the characteristics of a myth and another that details the characteristics of an epic. Use your lists to write a brief compare-and-contrast essay about the two genres.
3. **Take Notes** Try using this study organizer to take notes on the people, places, and events you read about in this unit. See pages R20–R21 for folding instructions.

FOLDABLES Study Organizer **TAB BOOK**

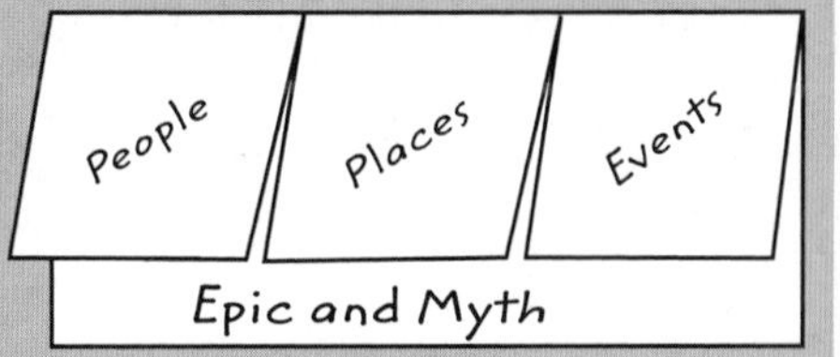

Viewing Practice

SMALL GROUP **Epic Ad Presentation** Invite students to create an advertisement for the *Odyssey.* Divide the class into groups. Have them decide on a form for the epic, such as a novel, movie, or TV miniseries. Instruct them to use elements from the Introduction, such as quotes and adjectives, to help them "sell" their concepts. Stress the importance of including strong visuals. Have students present (or perform) their completed ads to the class.

PART 1

Journeys

Captain Desse of Bordeaux saves the crew of the Dutch ship "Columbus", ca. 19th century. J. A. Theodore Gudin. Musée des Beaux-Arts, Bordeaux, France.

View the Art J. A. Theodore Gudin was well-known for his depictions of ships at sea. Does this painting seem realistic to you? Why or why not? ★

BIG IDEA

Journeys have long been important in literature and in history. Travelers encounter new cultures, new sights, new experiences, and sometimes grave dangers. The literature in Part 1 includes the epic tale of a legendary hero of ancient Greece, Odysseus. As you read the epic, ask yourself, What actions or traits make a person heroic?

Approaching Level

DIFFERENTIATED INSTRUCTION

Established Explain that journeys can be both literal and figurative. While a story may be about an actual journey, the author may also be writing about the emotional or spiritual journeys of the characters. Have students name the different kinds of journeys they have taken. Encourage them to think carefully by offering a personal journey, such as becoming a teacher. As they read, have students identify the different kinds of journeys.

UNIT FIVE

PART 1

Analyze and Extend

Big Idea

Journeys Encourage students to connect with the idea of the journey by considering their own travels.

Write on the board: Sights, Experiences, Challenges. Have students recall a trip and list their impressions under each category. Invite students to share their impressions.

ENGLISH LEARNERS To help English learners, **say:** A popular American expression is that "Life is a journey." **Ask:** What do you think that means? *(Life is a learning experience in which we never know where we are headed.)*

View the Art ★

Answer: *Students should refer to specific details from the painting in their responses.*

French painter Jean-Antoine Theodore Gudin (1802–1880) was renowned for his marine paintings. French King Louis-Philippe commissioned Gudin to paint pictures of the French navy for the palace of Versailles.

For additional support for English Learners, see Unit 5 Teaching Resources Book, p. 18.

UNIT FIVE

PART 1

Focus

Bellringer Options

Daily Language Practice Transparency 82

Or **write on the board:** How many heroes and heroines can you think of? List the examples on the board and prompt students to consider other categories of heroes they had overlooked, such as real-life or imaginary heroes. Discuss what makes a character heroic.

ADVANCED Ask advanced level students to name heroes from real life or literature. Explain the concept of anti-heroes *(heroes who lack common heroic traits)* and ask students for examples *(Holden Caulfield from* Catcher in the Rye, *Satan from* Paradise Lost*)*.

Teach

Literary Element 1

Hero **Ask:** What qualities do you consider heroic? *(Students may mention courage, honesty, or compassion.)*

Learning Objectives

For pages 829–831

In studying this text, you will focus on the following objectives:

Literary Study:
Analyzing epics and epic heroes.
Connecting to the literature.

LITERARY FOCUS

Hero

What qualities make a hero? 1

In this passage below from Margaret Atwood's *The Penelopiad,* Odysseus's wife, Penelope, tells how she learned of her husband's exploits while he was away at war. Minstrels sang ballads that passed history from one man to the next and one town to the next, tailoring their performance to each audience. Penelope hears the tales that make her husband seem heroic. Does this make him a hero to her?

> They always sang the noblest versions in my presence—the ones in which Odysseus was clever, brave, and resourceful, and battling supernatural monsters, and beloved of goddesses.
>
> —Margaret Atwood, ***Waiting* from *The Penelopiad***

Heroes

The **hero** is the main character in a literary work. His or her admirable character or noble actions arouse the admiration of the reader. While epic heroes are traditionally male, women can also be heroes. Heroes appear in epic literature as well as in other literary genres and in film. Modern heroes include comic book superheroes such as Superman.

> At that he woke up with a horrible start, and found that part of his dream was true. A crack had opened at the back of the cave, and was already a wide passage. He was just in time to see the last of the ponies' tails disappearing into it. Of course he gave a very loud yell, as loud a yell as a hobbit can give, which is surprising for their size.
>
> —J. R. R. Tolkien, **from *The Hobbit***

King Arthur, 1903. Charles Ernest Butler. Oil on canvas, 123.2 x 73.7 cm. Private Collection.

Writing Practice

SMALL GROUP **Create a Hero** Have students work in groups to create their own hero or heroine. Students should create a list of character traits that make their characters heroic. Students should write a short adventure detailing an exploit of their heroic character. The adventure should show how the character demonstrates the heroic traits. Invite students to create a visual representation of their character in the medium of their choice. Have students explain their heroes to the class, display their images, and read the heroic character's adventure to the class.

The Tragic Hero

As you learned in Unit 4, a **tragic hero** is a person of great ability who comes to grief because of a fault within his or her character. This fault, the **tragic flaw,** is often a characteristic that has helped him or her achieve success: pride, ambition, anger. Sometimes the human weakness that defeats the hero is an excess of virtue, such as the pursuit of duty.

The Epic Hero

An **epic** is a long narrative poem that recounts the actions, adventures, and travels of a heroic figure, called the **epic hero.** The epic hero—whose typical goal is to save his nation or its people—embarks on a journey over the expanse of continents or even the entire universe. Along the way, natural and supernatural beings test the hero's bravery, wits, and battle skills.

Characteristics of Most Epics

- Written in the style of a long poem
- Language is formal, lofty
- Mood is serious
- Protagonist undergoes many adventures
- Gods and monsters intervene in action
- Poet uses extended similes, called epic similes
- Poem begins in the middle of the action *(in medias res)*

The traditional epic hero is a strong, courageous, noble, and confident man with a thirst for glory. Most epic heroes, Odysseus included, are known for their intelligence, quick thinking, and tremendous self-confidence.

2 I am Laertes' son, Odysseus.
Men hold me
formidable for guile in peace and war:
this fame has gone abroad to the sky's rim.

—Homer, **from the *Odyssey***

LOG ON **Literature** Online

Literature and Reading For more about literary elements, go to glencoe.com and enter QuickPass code GL49787u5.

As a result of their keen intelligence, most epic heroes are articulate speakers and can win over an audience with ease. They are deeply admired for their ability to use both brains and brawn to defeat an enemy or to deal with any other challenge that arises.

Odysseus in one motion strung the bow.
Then slid his right hand down the cord and
plucked it,
so the taut gut vibrating hummed and sang
a swallow's note.

—Homer, **from the *Odyssey***

Gods and Monsters Epics often feature gods and monsters that hold power over the human world. Monsters like Typhon with its one hundred heads kill without mercy and wreak general havoc. Gods have the power to create and destroy, and they use that power at will. Often it is the task of the epic hero to subdue a monster or appease the gods. Perseus does this, as does Odysseus.

I happened to glance aft at ship and oarsmen and caught sight of their arms and legs, dangling high overhead. Voices came down to me in anguish, calling my name for the last time. . . . [Scylla] ate them as they shrieked there, in her den.

—Homer, **from the *Odyssey***

Quickwrite

Describe Monsters If you could create an epic monster, would it have seventy eyes, wings made of fire, or a voice so beautiful it could lure humans to their deaths? Write a description of your monster and its powers or abilities. Then ask a partner to read your description and draw a picture of your monster.

UNIT FIVE

PART 1

Teach

Literary Element 2

Character Have volunteers read each section aloud. Pause after each section and ask students for examples of the type of character described.

Assess

Quickwrite

Students' descriptions should include features that are frightening, grotesque, and dangerous.

Approaching Level

DIFFERENTIATED INSTRUCTION

Established Instruct students to copy the characteristics of epics and myths into their notebooks. They should also write a short definition of each characteristic by paraphrasing the information on page 831. Encourage them to refer to the list as they read the *Odyssey*. Instruct students to write examples of how the *Odyssey* employs each characteristic. They should use the list as a guide as they read.

Focus

Bellringer Options

Daily Language Practice Transparency 83

Or **have students discuss this question:** What personal challenges have you faced that you were unsure you could meet? How did you manage to meet the challenge?

Teach

Reading Strategy 1

Preview Have students examine the subheads and the illustrations on pages 832–833. Then read aloud the introductory quotation and the first paragraph of the essay. Explain that American scholar Milman Parry pioneered the field of oral literature studies in the 1920s and 1930s. Parry's research proved that Homer's epics were intended to be presented orally.

APPROACHING To help approaching level students, **ask:** What details about poetry make it particularly nice to listen to rather than to read? *(rhyme, rhythm)*

Learning Objectives

For pages 832–833

In studying this text, you will focus on the following objective:

Literary Study: Recognizing the characteristics of an epic poem.

Literary History

Homer and the Epic

LIKE THE FICTIONAL BARD DEMODOCUS IN the *Odyssey,* ancient Greek oral poets composed narratives and chanted them to musical accompaniment. The greatest of these Greek oral poets was Homer. Little is certain about him—even his name. We know that his works include two of the earliest surviving epic poems—the *Iliad* and the *Odyssey*. The precise dates are unknown, but most experts believe that Homer composed his epics around 750 B.C.

1 *"We will have Demodocus to sing to us; for there is no bard like him whatever he may choose to sing about."*

—Homer, the *Odyssey*

The Art of the Bard

How did an oral poet such as Homer compose his poems? In some ways, he was like a jazz musician who starts with a well-known tune and plays different variations on it every time he performs. Just as a musician plays to a steady rhythm, so Homer had a steady rhythm in his words. The Greek singers recited their poems so that long syllables and short syllables alternated in a regular pattern.

Composing poetry in front of an audience without hesitating or "drawing a blank" may sound like an impossible task, but the fact that Homer performed to a rhythm simplified the job. It meant that certain phrases worked better than others because they would fit rhythmically into a line of poetry. So Homer used them again and again. When describing people or things, he often used verbal "formulas." For example, he repeatedly refers to the goddess Athena as "gray-eyed Athena," and mentions dawn's "fingertips of rose." Homer would also recycle longer passages of description. These passages often concerned routine actions, such as a character's way of entering a room, putting on his armor, going to bed, or saying good-bye to his host.

This use of repetition helped Homer and pleased his audience. The poet did not have to memorize or make up every word. Most of his story was a little different each time it was told, but the repeated phrases remained like handles for the poet to grip. Homer's audience looked forward to these repetitions, as listeners look forward to the repeated chorus of a song.

A book illustration depicts Homer reciting one of his epic poems.

Epic Poetry

Homer's most famous compositions, the *Iliad* and the *Odyssey*, have been read for centuries as **epic poems.** Since Homer's time, epic poetry has been considered a genre, or type of

Research Practice

Oral Literature Point out that in addition to the epic, there are many other types of oral literature. These include riddles, folk tales, myths, legends, ballads, nursery rhymes, hymns, and spirituals. Have students select an oral form of literature (other than epic) and use encyclopedias and Internet resources to research and write a short report. Students' reports should include the characteristics of the form, the specific ways in which this oral tradition conveys the content from generation to generation, and geographic regions in which this particular oral form has flourished.

literature, just as nonfiction, fiction, and drama are genres. The epic poem has the following characteristics:

- It is a long narrative poem.
- The speaker is a narrator who tells a story.
- The setting is expansive. It may be a sea, a region, the world, or a universe.
- There is a main character, who is a hero or is capable of being heroic.
- The action includes extraordinary or superhuman deeds. Typically, the epic hero has a goal and has embarked upon a long journey. In this journey, he struggles with natural and supernatural obstacles and antagonists—gods, monsters, and humans—which test his bravery, wits, and physical prowess.
- 2 Gods or supernatural beings take a part, or an interest, in the action.
- The purpose of an epic poem is not only to entertain but also to teach and inspire the listener or reader with examples of how people can strive and succeed against great odds.

Epic Narration

An epic poem is narrated in predictable ways:

- In an invocation, the poet-narrator begins by stating the tale's subject and asking for poetic inspiration from a guiding spirit.
- The narrator begins telling the tale in the "middle of things," describing what is happening after certain important events have already occurred.

Hercules fighting Cerberus, the monsterous three-headed dog that guards the entrance to Hades. 530–525 B.C. Terra-cotta. Louvre Museum, Paris.

- The narrative includes speeches by principal characters—including gods and antagonists of the epic hero—which reveal their personalities.
- The narrative's tone and style are formal 2 rather than conversational.
- The use of figurative language makes the narrative vivid and exciting for listeners and readers.

The epic you are about to read, the *Odyssey*, is a celebration of the human spirit and of ordinary life. It is for this timeless appeal to our common humanity that the *Odyssey* is still read and enjoyed nearly three thousand years after its creation.

LOG ON **Literature** Online

Literature and Reading For more about Homer and the epic, go to glencoe.com and enter QuickPass code GL49787u5.

Respond and Think Critically

1. Why do you think the works of Homer are still enjoyed today?
2. How does the composition method of ancient Greek oral poets resemble that of a jazz musician?
3. What different purposes did Homer's epics serve for the ancient Greeks?

English Learners

DIFFERENTIATED INSTRUCTION

Early Advanced Ask students to name some of the epic poets in different cultures and to talk about the subjects and sources of their poems. Make sure students understand that the term "epic poetry" is applied to an entire genre of literature and that epic poems were originally long oral stories—hence the use of formulas and repetition. Have students compare the list of characteristics on page 833 to epic poems in their native languages.

Teach

Reading Strategy 2

Monitor Comprehension

Prepare a checklist of the elements in epic poetry and epic narration, and give each student a copy. Have students check off each element as they identify it in the *Odyssey.* Next to each element, leave a space in which students can write the example.

Literary History ☆

Translations of Homer

Since the English Renaissance in the 1500s, every age has produced distinctive translations of Homer's epics. The first notable translation in English was by George Chapman (c. 1559–1634). Robert Fitzgerald was widely praised for his version of the *Odyssey.*

Assess

1. They tell exciting stories and provide a glimpse into ancient life.
2. Like a jazz musician, the ancient Greek poets took a familiar theme and used it as the basis for improvisation.
3. His epics provided entertainment and instruction.

Before You Read

Focus

Bellringer Options

Selection Focus Transparency 44

Daily Language Practice Transparency 84

Or tell students that in reading these selections from the *Odyssey,* they will meet a man who journeys through lands and seas of mythical proportions to get to that most elusive desti nation of all—home. Students will also meet a woman who represents another facet of travel—learning how to plan and how to wait.

Ask: Is there a place you dream of visiting? What do you hope to find there? What obstacles might you encounter along the way?

Before You Read

World Literature
Ancient Greece

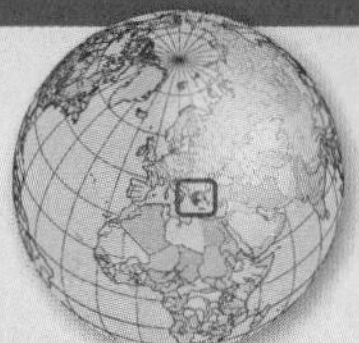

from the *Odyssey*

Meet **Homer**

(circa 9th century B.C.)

Homer is one of the great mysteries of literature. His poems are among the most famous in the world, but it is unlikely that he ever "wrote" a word. His name is as well known as Shakespeare's, but no one has found any convincing evidence to indicate who he was or exactly when and where he lived. Legend has it that he was a blind man who lived on the rocky Greek island of Chios, but legends are impossible to prove. Although Homer was one of the greatest poets of the ancient world, he composed his works orally and recited or sang them aloud. Like most people in his day, Homer could probably neither read nor write.

The Few Facts What we do know for certain is that Homer's works include two of the earliest surviving epic poems, the *Iliad* and the *Odyssey*. Although the precise dates are uncertain, most experts believe that Homer composed and recited his poems over 2,700 years ago, sometime before the year 700 B.C. This was the period when speakers of Greek were emerging from illiteracy—developing an alphabet and learning the benefits of recording things on a kind of paper called papyrus. However, in those days people were still accustomed to hearing, rather than reading, their literature. Homer's great poems were written down only long after his death.

Homer's poetic tales describe famous people and events from history as well as from legends, myths, and folktales—characters and events that people had been describing for centuries. The *Iliad* and the *Odyssey*, which are set during and after the siege of Troy, include all of these ingredients. To this mix of fact and fiction, Homer added his insights into human experience, his imaginative plots, and his expert storytelling style.

> *"Where shall a man find sweetness to surpass his own home and his parents?"*
>
> —Homer, from the *Odyssey*

Action and Adventure Homer's repertoire probably included hundreds of tales by the time he was a mature artist. Audiences would call for certain ones—the "action-adventure" stories of the day—again and again: the legend of Theseus, Jason and the Golden Fleece, the twelve labors of Hercules, and the many love affairs of Zeus. Homer's audiences believed the stories were true. To appreciate Homer's gift, modern readers must suspend their disbelief.

LOG ON **Literature** Online

Author Search For more about Homer, go to glencoe.com and enter QuickPass code GL49787u5.

Selection Skills

***from the* Odyssey, Part 1**

Reading Skills
- Analyze Figurative Language (SE pp. 835–856)
- Use Pronunciation Guides (TE p. 838)

Literary Elements
- Epic (SE pp. 835–856)

Vocabulary Skills
- Synonyms (SE pp. 835, 856)

Study Skills/Research/Assessment
- Research (TE p. 965)

Listening/Speaking/Viewing Skills
- Analyze Art (SE pp. 840, 842, 851)
- Listening Techniques (TE p. 842)
- Storytelling (TE p. 848)

Writing Skills/Grammar
- Spatial Order (TE p. 844)
- The Dash (TE p. 846)
- Simple and Compound Sentences (TE p. 854)

Literature and Reading Preview

Connect to the Epic

Why do people love hearing about the triumphs of a hero? Take a few minutes to freewrite about why people enjoy stories about heroes.

Build Background

The *Odyssey* describes the wanderings of the Greek general Odysseus on his return from the city of Troy in what is now northwest Turkey to his home island of Ithaca, off the west coast of Greece. The events take place shortly before the year 1200 B.C.

Set Purposes for Reading

Big Idea Journeys

As you read the *Odyssey,* Part 1, ask yourself, How is Odysseus's journey home interrupted?

Literary Element Epic and Epic Hero

An **epic** is a long narrative poem that traces the adventures of a larger-than-life hero, called an **epic hero.** Epics intertwine myths, legends, and history, reflecting the values of the societies in which they originate. As you read, ask yourself, Where does Homer use elements of mythical stories to create drama?

Reading Strategy Analyze Figurative Language

Like most poets, Homer intensifies his images and descriptions through **figurative language,** or language that uses figures of speech such as metaphors, similes, and personification. An **epic simile** extends a comparison with elaborate details that can fill several lines of verse. As you read, ask yourself, How does the language add to the storytelling?

Tip: Take Notes Use a chart to record striking figures of speech in Part 1.

Figure of Speech	Analysis
lines 82–83 "but he seemed rather a shaggy mountain reared in solitude"	metaphor capturing the size, roughness, and antisocial behavior of the Cyclops

Learning Objectives

For pages 834–856

In studying this text, you will focus on the following objectives:

Literary Study: Analyzing epic and epic hero.

Reading: Analyzing figurative language.

Writing: Writing an interior monologue.

Vocabulary

plunder (plun′ dər) *v.* to take (property) by force, especially in warfare; p. 839 *The victorious army plundered the defenseless city.*

valor (val′ ər) *n.* great courage, especially in battle; p. 839 *The medal was awarded to the soldier for valor in combat.*

guile (gīl) *n.* slyness; craftiness; skillful deception; p. 841 *The con man relied on quick thinking and guile to fool his clients.*

ponderous (pon′ dər əs) *adj.* having great weight or bulk; heavy; p. 847 *The workers tried to lift the ponderous stone with their hands but finally had to use a pulley.*

Tip: Synonyms Words that have the same or similar meanings are called synonyms. When you encounter a new word in a difficult sentence, try replacing the word with a more familiar synonym. For example, if you came across the vocabulary word *valor* in a difficult sentence, you could replace it with the synonym *courage.*

Before You Read

Focus

Summary

In the invocation, the poet summarizes some of Odysseus's major adventures. Odysseus begins recounting his travels to the Phaeacian king, Alcinous. In the land of the Cyclopes, Odysseus and twelve of his men explore the cave of Polyphemus and become trapped. The giant eats six of Odysseus's men before the hero contrives an escape plan. They get the giant drunk, and when he falls asleep, they blind him with a sharpened tree trunk. In the morning, the adventurers tie themselves to the bellies of sheep and escape.

For summaries in languages other than English, see Unit 5 Teaching Resources Book, pp. 23–28.

Vocabulary

Write a Vocab-Story Have students copy the vocabulary words and their definitions into their notebooks. Instruct students to look at the words and determine what kind of story could best be written using the words. *(Possible Answer: adventure)* Have students write a brief story using the words. Encourage volunteers to share their stories with the class.

For additional vocabulary practice, see Unit 5 Teaching Resources Book, p. 31.

Approaching Level

DIFFERENTIATED INSTRUCTION

Established Point out that a Homeric simile is similar to an extended metaphor. Both use figurative language to describe something. Explain that a simple simile might be "My daughter is as sneaky as a cat." An extended or Homeric simile might say, "My daughter is as sneaky as a black cat. She hides in shadows, and occasionally crosses my path, warning me she's about to be bad." Point out that a simple simile compares only one detail, whereas a Homeric simile compares a whole situation. Have students create their own Homeric similes and share them with the class.

Teach

Big Idea

Journeys **Say:** Look at the photograph on pages 836–837, and then imagine spending many months on a sailboat on the open sea.

Ask: How would you feel, knowing that you would be out on the ocean for many months before returning home? *(Students' responses will vary but should reflect some of the fears and joys associated with a long journey.)* How might the natural elements affect you? *(Students may suggest feelings of insignificance and helplessness against such powerful forces.)*

from the Odyssey ☆

Homer

Translated by Robert Fitzgerald

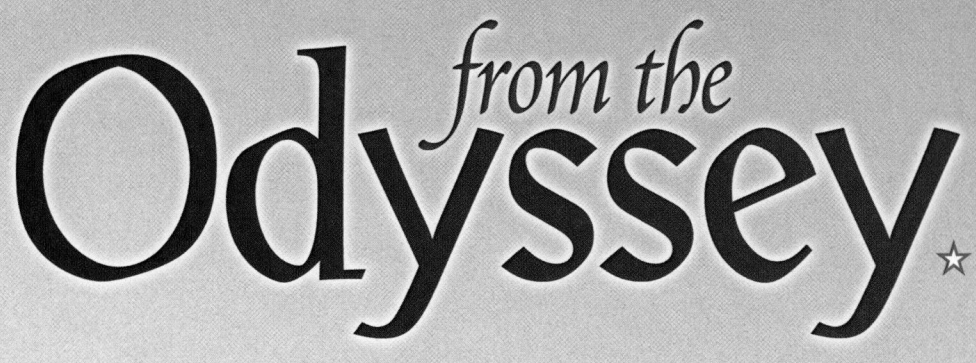

Writing Practice

Imagine a Journey

Explain that when the Odyssey begins, the main character Odysseus has been traveling for about twenty years. Instruct students to close their eyes. **Say:** Pretend you leave today on a journey and will not return to your home and family for twenty years. What would coming back be like? What sort of difficulties might you have? Have students write a journal entry about their first day back after their twenty-year journey.

Teach

Cultural History ☆

Ancient Greece The geography of Ancient Greece caused people to be isolated. The sea and the mountainous terrain hindered travel between communities. The simple, herding lifestyle and the warlike characteristics of the Achaeans prevented alliances between city-states, which began developing in the seventh century B.C.

Ancient Greece never became a united nation. Ancient Greeks felt loyalty only to their cities, whose populations were tiny by today's standards. Only Athens, the largest city-state, had more than 20,000 inhabitants.

Interactive Read and Write

Other options for teaching this selection can be found in

- Interactive Read and Write for EL Students, pp. 227–266
- Interactive Read and Write for Approaching-Level Students, pp. 227–266
- Interactive Read and Write for On-Level Students, pp. 227–266

Approaching Level

DIFFERENTIATED INSTRUCTION

Emerging Encourage students with little or no knowledge of Greek mythology to refer to handbooks of mythology as they read. Have students research Zeus, Calypso, Helios, Poseidon, and other figures they encounter as they read these excerpts from the *Odyssey.* Encourage students to keep a list of the gods, jotting down descriptive attributes or drawing illustrations to accompany each one. When discussing these figures in class, have students share their findings.

Teach

Literary Element 1

Epic Explain that the *Odyssey* is an epic poem, with elements that may remind students of poetry, fiction, and drama. It uses meter and poetic devices, but it also tells an adventure story, filled with dramatic action and graphic details. The list of characters helps the reader keep the many characters and their relationships straight.

APPROACHING Have approaching level students review the list of characters. **Ask:** Have you ever heard of these characters before? What do you know about them? *(Students with some knowledge of Greek mythology may be familiar with the gods.)*

1 PRINCIPAL CHARACTERS IN THE ODYSSEY

HUMANS

AGAMEMNON (ag′ ə mem′ non): king and leader of Greek forces during the Trojan war

ALCINOUS (al sin′ ō əs): king of the Phaeacians and person to whom Odysseus relates his story

AMPHINOMUS (am fin′ ə məs): one of Penelope's suitors

ANTINOUS (an tin′ ō əs): rudest of Penelope's suitors

EUMAEUS (yoo mē′ əs): Odysseus's loyal swineherd

EURYCLEIA (yoó ri klē′ ə): Odysseus's faithful old nurse

EURYLOCHUS (yoo ri′ ə kəs): one of Odysseus's crew

EURYMACHUS (yoo rim′ ə kəs): one of Penelope's suitors

EURYNOME (yoo rin′ ə mē): Penelope's housekeeper

LAERTES (lā ur′ tēz): Odysseus's father

MARON (mār′ on): priest of Apollo who gives Odysseus a gift of powerful wine

ODYSSEUS (ō dis′ ē əs): king of Ithaca and hero of the Trojan war

PENELOPE (pə nel′ ə pē): Odysseus's wife

PERIMEDES (per′ i mē′ dēz): one of Odysseus's crew

TELEMACHUS (tə lem′ ə kəs): Odysseus and Penelope's son

TIRESIAS (tī rē′ sē əs): blind prophet from the underworld

GODS AND IMMORTALS

APOLLO (ə pol′ ō): god of sunlight, music, poetry, medicine, law, and the tending of flocks and herds

ATHENA (ə thē′ nə): daughter of Zeus and goddess of wisdom, skills, and warfare who helps her chosen heroes

CALYPSO (kə lip′ sō): immortal sea nymph who holds Odysseus captive for many years

CHARYBDIS (kə rib′ dis): dangerous whirlpool personified as a female monster

CIRCE (sur′ sē): enchantress who lives on the island of Aeaea

CYCLOPES (sī klō′ pēz): race of one-eyed giants; an individual member of the race is a Cyclops (sī klops)

HELIOS (hē′ lē os′): god of the sun; another name for Apollo

LOTUS (lō′ təs) EATERS: inhabitants of a land visited by Odysseus and his crew

POLYPHEMUS (pol′ i fē′ məs): a Cyclops and son of Poseidon

POSEIDON (pə sīd′ ən): god of the sea and earthquakes

SCYLLA (sil′ ə): six-headed female sea monster

SIRENS (sī′ rənz): sea nymphs who sing songs that lure men to their death

ZEUS (zo͞os): king of the gods

Reading Practice

SMALL GROUP

Use Pronunciation Guides Explain to students that they will become more comfortable with the unfamiliar Greek names if they can pronounce them properly. Before students read through the list of names, review pronunciation clues, such as stress marks and vowel marks. To help students with the correct pronunciations of the names, have them work with a partner to read through the lists of humans and gods and immortals. Tell students to read the names aloud with their partners. Then ask volunteers to read the names aloud to the class. Correct pronunciations as needed.

Part 1

An Invocation

2 *Poets in Homer's day believed that the gods inspired their storytelling and singing. According to custom, Homer begins his performance with an invocation, calling upon the Muse, the goddess of epic poetry, for help and inspiration. The invocation serves a second purpose: to capture the audience's attention with highlights of heroic adventures that the poet will later describe in detail.*

Sing in me, Muse, and through me tell the story
of that man skilled in all ways of contending,°
the wanderer, harried° for years on end,
after he **plundered** the stronghold
on the proud height of Troy.

He saw the townlands
and learned the minds of many distant men,
and weathered° many bitter nights and days
in his deep heart at sea, while he fought only
to save his life, to bring his shipmates home.
But not by will nor **valor** could he save them,
for their own recklessness destroyed them all—
children and fools, they killed and feasted on
the cattle of Lord Helios,° the Sun,
and he who moves all day through heaven
took from their eyes the dawn of their return.

Of these adventures, Muse, daughter of Zeus,°
tell us in our time, lift the great song again.
Begin when all the rest who left behind them
headlong death in battle or at sea
had long ago returned, while he alone still hungered
for home and wife. Her ladyship Calypso°
clung to him in her sea-hollowed caves—
a nymph,° immortal° and most beautiful,
who craved him for her own.

2 contending: fighting or dealing with difficulty.
3 harried: constantly tormented or troubled.

8 weathered: got through safely; survived.

14 Helios (hē′ lē os′): the god of the sun.

17 Zeus (zōōs): The most powerful of the gods, Zeus is the father of countless major and minor gods.

22 Calypso (kə lip′ sō)

24 nymph: a young, beautiful spirit, or minor goddess, representing the divine power of a place or of something in nature, such as a tree, cave, or body of water.
immortal: living forever; eternal.

3 Epic and Epic Hero ***How does the reader quickly learn that the story about to unfold recounts the deeds of an epic hero?***

Vocabulary

plunder (plun′ dər) *v.* to take (property) by force, especially in warfare
valor (val′ ər) *n.* great courage, especially in battle

Teach

Reading Strategy 2

Clarify Point out that the paragraphs in italics give essential background or summarize omitted sections of the epic. After students read the paragraph, ask them to explain the significance of the invocation. *(It honors the gods and creates interest in the audience.)*

Literary Element 3

Epic and Epic Hero
Answer: *The reader immediately learns that Odysseus has triumphed over many hardships after leaving Troy and is determined to make it home. This opening passage establishes that his adventures are intertwined with history and mythology.*

Approaching Level

DIFFERENTIATED INSTRUCTION

Established Tell students that many English words are derived from Latin. The word *invocation,* for example, comes from the Latin verb *invocare,* meaning "to call on." **Ask:** Who is Homer calling on? *(the Muse, the goddess of epic poetry)* Having some background in Latin, Greek, or Anglo-Saxon roots can be a useful vocabulary tool. Help students to understand that knowing root words in several languages can help them determine meanings of English words.

Teach

Reading Strategy 1

Clarify Explain to students that the paraphrased summary in italics covers the first eight books of the original epic (which contains 24 books in all). Also, be sure students understand the handling of time. Odysseus is entertaining his hosts, the Phaeacians, by telling the story of his earlier adventures at sea. In fact, "the present" is ten years after Odysseus set out from Troy.

Reading Strategy 2

Analyze Figurative Language **Answer:** *By describing the passage of time as "wheeling," Homer draws attention to the fact that a year is like a circle, always coming back to where it started.*

Progress Check

Can students analyze figurative language?

If No → See Unit 5 Teaching Resources Book, p. 30.

And when long years and seasons
wheeling brought around that point of time
ordained° for him to make his passage homeward,
trials and dangers, even so, attended him
even in Ithaca, near those he loved.
Yet all the gods had pitied Lord Odysseus,
all but Poseidon, raging cold and rough°
against the brave king° till he came ashore
at last on his own land.

28 ordained: set or determined by an authority—in this case, fate, or the gods.

31–33 Odysseus (ō dis′ ē əs) . . . **the brave king:** Odysseus is the king of Ithaca.

32 Poseidon (pə sīd′ ən), **raging cold and rough:** Poseidon, brother of Zeus, governs the oceans as well as earthquakes. In the next section, you will find clues to his anger at Odysseus.

New Coasts and Poseidon's Son

The gods are worried. Nearly ten years have passed since the end of the war against Troy, but one of the greatest Greek generals has not yet returned home. Odysseus has encountered a series of disasters on his voyage and is now the prisoner of a nymph named Calypso. He has also angered Poseidon, who has prevented him from returning to his wife, Penelope (pə nel′ ə pē), *and his son, Telemachus* (tə lem′ ə kəs), *on the island of Ithaca. But Poseidon is visiting Africa, and the other gods agree to act behind his back.*

1 *The poet now tells of Odysseus, who is miserable after seven years on his island prison. Calypso loves her handsome captive and will not let him go, but she is forced to reconsider her position when she receives a strongly worded order from Mount Olympus. Giving in, Calypso helps Odysseus make a raft, and he thankfully departs. But he does not have smooth sailing. Poseidon, returning from Africa, spots his old enemy at sea and shipwrecks him in an instant with a fierce storm.*

Zeus's daughter Athena intervenes. She casts Odysseus, naked and near death, ashore on the island of Phaeacia (fē ā′ she). *There a beautiful princess discovers him and takes him home to the palace of her father, King Alcinous* (al sin′ ō əs). *The Phaeacians treat Odysseus as a noble guest and urge him to reveal his identity. At last he relents and uncertainly begins to tell his gripping story.*

Calliope, Muse of epic poetry. Marble. Ludovisi collection.

View the Art Calliope is the muse of epic poetry. In Greek mythology, muses were believed to inspire the creation of the arts. Poets, musicians, and artisans often looked to them as the source of their creativity. What about this sculpture suggests that the woman might be involved with the creation of epic poetry? ★

2 Analyze Figurative Language *Why might the poet have used the verb* wheeling *to describe the passing of years and seasons?*

View the Art ★

Answer: *In the sculpture, Calliope is holding a pencil and pad of paper.*

Ask: Why might Greek mythology include a character whose primary purpose is to help writers find inspiration? *(Students may note that the Greek epics were long inspiring stories and anyone setting out to write an epic must have felt a desire for help from the gods.)*

Reading Practice

SPIRAL REVIEW **Identify Author's Purpose** Explain that there are several ways to determine an author's purpose: (1) locate a direct statement of purpose; (2) infer from the tone and indirect statements; (3) recall similar readings and their purposes. After students read the invocation, ask them to summarize the speaker's purpose for telling the Odyssey and explain how they determined it. *(Students should use methods 1 and 2 to decide that the purpose is to describe the adventures of Odysseus and to inspire listeners with his feats and the interactions of gods with men.)*

"What shall I
say first? What shall I keep until the end?
The gods have tried° me in a thousand ways.
But first my name: let that be known to you,
and if I pull away from pitiless death,
friendship will bind us, though my land lies far.
I am Laertes' son, Odysseus.
Men hold° me
formidable° for **guile** in peace and war:
this fame has gone abroad to the sky's rim.
My home is on the peaked sea-mark of Ithaca
under Mount Neion's° wind-blown robe of leaves,
in sight of other islands—Dulichium,°
Same,° wooded Zacynthus°—Ithaca
being most lofty in that coastal sea,
and northwest, while the rest lie east and south.
A rocky isle, but good for a boy's training;
I shall not see on earth a place more dear,
though I have been detained long by Calypso,
loveliest among goddesses, who held me
in her smooth caves, to be her heart's delight,
as Circe of Aeaea, the enchantress,°
desired me, and detained me in her hall.
But in my heart I never gave consent.
Where shall a man find sweetness to surpass
his own home and his parents? In far lands
he shall not, though he find a house of gold.
What of my sailing, then, from Troy?
What of those years
of rough adventure, weathered under Zeus?"°

3

Odysseus relates his first adventure. He and his fleet of twelve ships attacked and plundered the coastal settlement of the Cicones (si kō′ nēz). *The raid was a success, but the overconfident men became drunk and mutinous (unresponsive to Odysseus's orders to retreat). The Cicones's army surprised Odysseus and his men at dawn, and drove them back to sea with heavy losses.*

"I might have made it safely home, that time,
but as I came round Malea° the current

3 tried: tested.

8 hold: regard; consider.

9 formidable: causing fear, dread, awe, or admiration as a result of size, strength, power, or some other impressive quality.

12 Neion (nē′ on)

13 Dulichium (do͞o lik′ ē əm)

14 Same (sā′ mē). **Zacynthus** (zə sin′ thəs)

22 Circe (sur′ sē). . . **the enchantress:** Circe is a goddess capable of enchanting, or working magic upon, men. **Aeaea** (ē ē′ ə) is her island.

30 weathered under Zeus: Odysseus uses words craftily. Here, he appears to give respectful credit to Zeus for getting him safely through danger; but he also is making a pun on the word *weathered.* Zeus governs the heavens and the weather and is well known for sending people storms, lightning, and thunder when he is displeased.

32 Malea (mə lē′ ə)

4 Journeys *How has Odysseus proved to his audience that he is determined to achieve his journey's end?*

Vocabulary

guile (gīl) n. slyness; craftiness; skillful deception

Teach

Reading Strategy 3

Evaluate **Ask:** How would you describe Odysseus's feelings about Ithaca, his home? *(He calls it "lofty," indicating that he has fond feelings for Ithaca. He cherishes it, as expressed in the line "I shall not see on earth a place more dear.")*

Big Idea 4

Journeys **Answer:** *Even the love of two beautiful goddesses has failed to tempt him from his objective of reaching home. Odysseus is eager to return to his home and parents, whose sweetness cannot be surpassed by far lands, even those where he finds a house of gold.*

APPROACHING To help approaching level students, **ask:** In what other stories has the idea of home played an important part? *(Possible answers: The Wizard of Oz, Gone With the Wind, The House on Mango Street)* Explain that home is a common topic in literature.

Advanced Learners

DIFFERENTIATED INSTRUCTION

Research Students can use a library and the Internet to learn more about some of the places referred to in the *Odyssey.* Have them research some of the places mentioned up to this point, such as Troy and Ithaca. If students find information on the Internet, have them evaluate the source. Emphasize that not everything on the Internet comes from a reputable and authoritative source. Have students compare the information they find. Then encourage students to share the information that they found with the class.

Teach

Reading Strategy 1

Draw Conclusions

Odysseus's perspective and behavior allow students to recognize some traits that set him apart from his men. **Say:** Odysseus reports that the Lotus Eaters did not coerce his men and that the lotus is sweet and drains one of desire for real action and real life. I think that the sailors easily gave in to temptation, but Odysseus did not.

Ask: What can you tell about Odysseus's character from the way he treats his men? *(Since Odysseus drove his men back to the ship, I can conclude that he looked on them as weaker beings for whom he was responsible.)*

View the Art ★

Answer: *Students may point out the use of sharp lines throughout, the repeated angular oars, and the horizontal lines indicating wind.*

Swiss-born artist Francois-Louis Schmied (1873–1941) was an engraver well-known for his collaborations with binders and publishers on illustrated books.

The Ship of Odysseus with Oars and a Furled Sail, 1930–1933. Francois-Louis Schmied. Stapleton Collection.

View the Art The Art Deco movement expressed modernity in art through the use of angular, geometric figures. How does this work by Francois-Louis Schmied reflect the Art Deco movement? ★

took me out to sea, and from the north
a fresh gale drove me on, past Cythera.°
Nine days I drifted on the teeming sea
before dangerous high winds. Upon the tenth
we came to the coastline of the Lotus Eaters,
who live upon that flower. We landed there
to take on water. All ships' companies
mustered° alongside for the mid-day meal.
Then I sent out two picked men and a runner
to learn what race of men that land sustained.°
They fell in, soon enough, with Lotus Eaters,
who showed no will to do us harm, only
offering the sweet Lotus to our friends—
1 but those who ate this honeyed plant, the Lotus,
never cared to report, nor to return:
they longed to stay forever, browsing on
that native bloom, forgetful of their homeland.

34 Cythera (sith′ ə rə)

40 mustered: gathered together.

42 sustained: kept alive; supported.

Listening Practice

SPIRAL REVIEW **Listening Techniques** Explain that most listeners remember only a fraction of what they hear. Discuss techniques that can help students become better listeners:

- Listen actively and think about what you hear.
- Jot down important ideas.
- Concentrate on the speaker.

Have students close their books and listen as you read aloud part of the passage on pages 842–843. Then ask them to list what they remember on a sheet of paper. After you finish a reading, have them check their lists against the text.

I drove them, all three wailing, to the ships,
tied them down under their rowing benches,
1 and called the rest: 'All hands aboard;
come, clear the beach and no one taste
the Lotus, or you lose your hope of home.'
Filing in to their places by the rowlocks
my oarsmen dipped their long oars in the surf,
and we moved out again on our sea faring.

In the next land we found were Cyclopes,°
giants, louts,° without a law to bless them.
In ignorance leaving the fruitage of the earth in mystery
to the immortal gods, they neither plow
nor sow by hand, nor till the ground, though grain—
wild wheat and barley—grows untended, and
wine-grapes, in clusters, ripen in heaven's rain.
Cyclopes have no muster and no meeting,
no consultation or old tribal ways,
but each one dwells in his own mountain cave
dealing out rough justice to wife and child,
indifferent to what the others do."

Just offshore from the land of the Cyclopes is a deserted island with a fine natural harbor. Odysseus and his men spend two comfortable nights there. On the second day, overcome by curiosity, Odysseus sails with one ship and a crew to the mainland. He wants to see just what sort of creatures these Cyclopes are.

"As we rowed on, and nearer to the mainland,
at one end of the bay, we saw a cavern
yawning above the water, screened with laurel,°
and many rams and goats about the place
inside a sheepfold°—made from slabs of stone
earthfast between tall trunks of pine and rugged
towering oak trees.
A prodigious° man
slept in this cave alone, and took his flocks
to graze afield—remote from all companions,
knowing none but savage ways, a brute
so huge, he seemed no man at all of those
who eat good wheaten bread; but he seemed rather
2 a shaggy mountain reared in solitude.
We beached there, and I told the crew
to stand by and keep watch over the ship;

58 Cyclopes (sī klō' pēz): a race of one-eyed giants.
59 louts: stupid beings.

72 screened with laurel: partly hidden behind laurel trees.

74 sheepfold: an enclosure, or pen, for holding sheep.

77 prodigious: huge; enormous.

---

3 Epic and Epic Hero ***What traits does Odysseus reveal in this episode that set him apart from his men?***

Teach

Literary Element 2

Figurative Language

Have students explain the metaphor here and explain why it is appropriate to the Cyclops. *(The giant is compared to a "shaggy mountain": the comparison accurately captures his size, roughness, and antisocial behavior.)*

Literary Element 3

Epic and Epic Hero

Answer: *In making his men return to their ships, he proves that he is a true leader, responsible for the welfare of his crew and determined to attain his goal.*

Approaching Level

DIFFERENTIATED INSTRUCTION

Established Remind students that appositives are nouns placed next to other nouns or pronouns to identify or give more information. **Write:** I had a goatskin full of that sweet liquor that Euanthes' son, Maron, had given me. Explain that *Maron* is an appositive identifying *Euanthes'* son. Tell students to find three other examples of appositives in the text so far. Then ask students to write three original sentences that contain appositives.

Teach

Reading Strategy 1

Visualize Ask students to describe their impressions of the Cyclops's cave—how it looks, sounds, smells, and feels. Encourage students to use vivid, concrete details.

ADVANCED Have students draw the Cyclops's cave and share their work with the class.

Big Idea 2

Journeys **Answer:** *He is curious to find out more about the people who live on these islands. Students may conclude that epic journeys are rarely direct; they often include other travels and adventures.*

APPROACHING To help approaching level students, **ask:** Do you think stories today are more direct than this epic? *(Many current stories involve characters who want one thing, but are sidetracked by other situations)* Encourage students to offer examples.

as for myself I took my twelve best fighters
and went ahead. I had a goatskin full
of that sweet liquor that Euanthes' son,
Maron, had given me. He kept Apollo's
holy grove at Ismarus;° for kindness
we showed him there, and showed his wife and child,
he gave me seven shining golden talents°
perfectly formed, a solid silver winebowl,
and then this liquor—twelve two-handled jars
of brandy, pure and fiery. Not a slave
in Maron's household knew this drink; only
he, his wife and the storeroom mistress knew;
and they would put one cupful—ruby-colored,
honey-smooth—in twenty more of water,
but still the sweet scent hovered like a fume
over the winebowl. No man turned away
when cups of this came round.

A wineskin full
I brought along, and victuals° in a bag,
for in my bones I knew some towering brute
would be upon us soon—all outward power,
a wild man, ignorant of civility.°

We climbed, then, briskly to the cave. But Cyclops°
had gone afield, to pasture his fat sheep,
so we looked round at everything inside:
a drying rack that sagged with cheeses, pens
crowded with lambs and kids, each in its class:
firstlings apart from middlings, and the 'dewdrops,'
or newborn lambkins, penned apart from both.°
And vessels full of whey° were brimming there—
bowls of earthenware and pails for milking.
My men came pressing round me, pleading:

'Why not
take these cheeses, get them stowed, come back,
throw open all the pens, and make a run for it?
We'll drive the kids and lambs aboard. We say
put out again on good salt water!'

Ah,
how sound° that was! Yet I refused. I wished
to see the caveman, what he had to offer—
no pretty sight, it turned out, for my friends.

88–90 Euanthes' (yoo an′ thēz) **son, . . . Ismarus** (iz mär′ əs): In ancient Greece, worshippers of certain gods built shrines to them, surrounded by woods, or "groves," that were considered sacred sanctuaries. Priests oversaw the planting and tending of the groves. **Maron** (mär′ on) is a priest of **Apollo** (ə pol′ ō), an important god associated with music, medicine, law, and the tending of flocks and herds.

92 talents: bars of gold used as money in ancient Greece.

104 victuals (vit′ əls): food.

107 civility: polite and courteous behavior.

108 Cyclops (sī′ klops): Note the different spelling and pronunciation of this reference to a single one-eyed giant.

111–114 pens . . . both: The lambs are grouped by age.

115 whey: the watery part of milk that separates from the curd, or solid part, during the cheese-making process.

2 Journeys *Why is Odysseus making this expedition? What does this side trip suggest about epic journeys?*

Writing Practice

Spatial Order

Read aloud lines 110–117 on page 844. Have students use those lines to jot down how the cave might be arranged. Explain that when describing places, writers often use spatial order, meaning that they describe things in a sequence that the eye can follow. Have students write a paragraph describing a room at home. They should use spatial order to organize the description. Remind them to try to establish an overall impression of the place through their word choices.

We lit a fire, burnt an offering,°
and took some cheese to eat; then sat in silence
around the embers, waiting. When he came
he had a load of dry boughs on his shoulder
to stoke his fire at suppertime. He dumped it
with a great crash into that hollow cave,
and we all scattered fast to the far wall.
Then over the broad cavern floor he ushered
the ewes he meant to milk. He left his rams
and he-goats in the yard outside, and swung
high overhead a slab of solid rock
to close the cave. Two dozen four-wheeled wagons,
with heaving wagon teams, could not have stirred
the tonnage of that rock from where he wedged it
over the doorsill. Next he took his seat
and milked his bleating ewes. A practiced job
he made of it, giving each ewe her suckling;
thickened his milk, then, into curds and whey,
sieved out the curds to drip in withy baskets,°
and poured the whey to stand in bowls
cooling until he drank it for his supper.
When all these chores were done, he poked the fire,
heaping on brushwood. In the glare he saw us.

'Strangers,' he said, 'who are you? And where from?
What brings you here by sea ways—a fair traffic?
Or are you wandering rogues, who cast your lives
like dice, and ravage other folk by sea?'°

We felt a pressure on our hearts, in dread
of that deep rumble and that mighty man.
But all the same I spoke up in reply:

3

'We are from Troy, Achaeans,° blown off course
by shifting gales on the Great South Sea;
homeward bound, but taking routes and ways
uncommon; so the will of Zeus would have it.
We served under Agamemnon, son of Atreus°—
the whole world knows what city
he laid waste, what armies he destroyed.
It was our luck to come here; here we stand,
beholden for your help, or any gifts

127 burnt an offering: The men burned some food as a gift to the gods in the hope of winning their support.

144–145 thickened . . . baskets: The milk is curdled **(thickened)** by adding fig juice, and the whey is drained off through wicker **(withy)** baskets.

151–153 What brings . . . by sea: What brings you here from the sea—honest trade? Or are you wandering scoundrels who carelessly risk your lives and steal from others?

157 Achaeans (ə kē′ əns): Greeks.

161 Agamemnon (ag′ ə mem′ non), **son of Atreus** (ā′ trē əs): king of Argos, in southern Greece, who led the war against Troy.

4 Epic and Epic Hero *Epics include a mixture of the everyday and the supernatural. How does the Cyclops embody both of these states?*

5 Journeys *What is Odysseus suggesting about misfortunes that occur on a journey?*

Teach

Reading Strategy 3

Question Odysseus hopes to lessen the giant's anger as he introduces himself and his men.

Ask: What are three pieces of information that Odysseus gives in order to accomplish his purpose? *(He says that they are able soldiers; he reminds the Cyclops of the code of hospitality; and he warns of Zeus's anger.)* What has Odysseus assumed about the Cyclops's beliefs? *(that he respects soldiers, honors societal codes, and fears the gods)*

Literary Element 4

Epic and Epic Hero
Answer: *The Cyclops is an enormous, supernatural creature. He also carries on the domestic tasks of shepherding and milking.*

Big Idea 5

Journeys **Answer:** *He is suggesting that misfortunes are orchestrated by the gods.*

English Learners

DIFFERENTIATED INSTRUCTION

Intermediate Students may find the language in the *Odyssey* difficult to understand. Explain to students that the side notes are aids to comprehension: the degree symbol (°) in the text indicates a corresponding note in the margin, defining difficult words or paraphrasing difficult passages. As they read, students should use a dictionary to jot down additional definitions of challenging words or phrases. Tell them to note the corresponding line numbers and page numbers for each entry.

Teach

Reading Strategy 1

Analyze Figurative Language **Answer:** *The Cyclops caught two men "like squirming puppies." Then he made a meal of them, crunching "like a mountain lion."*

Cultural History ☆

Greek Ships The ancient Greeks were primarily seafaring people, relying on their ships for trade, warfare, and food. When winds were contrary, ships were propelled by physical labor, and so they were equipped with oars and benches for twenty rowers on either side. Gear and supplies were stored beneath the benches.

you give—as custom is to honor strangers.
We would entreat you, great Sir, have a care
for the gods' courtesy; Zeus will avenge
the unoffending guest.'°
He answered this
from his brute chest, unmoved:
'You are a ninny,°
or else you come from the other end of nowhere,
telling me, mind the gods! We Cyclopes
care not a whistle for your thundering Zeus
or all the gods in bliss; we have more force by far.
I would not let you go for fear of Zeus—
you or your friends—unless I had a whim to.
Tell me, where was it, now, you left your ship—
around the point, or down the shore, I wonder?'

He thought he'd find out, but I saw through this,
and answered with a ready lie:
☆ 'My ship?
Poseidon Lord, who sets the earth a-tremble,
broke it up on the rocks at your land's end.
A wind from seaward served him, drove us there.
We are survivors, these good men and I.'

Neither reply nor pity came from him,
but in one stride he clutched at my companions
and caught two in his hands like squirming puppies
to beat their brains out, spattering the floor.
Then he dismembered them and made his meal,
gaping and crunching like a mountain lion—
everything: innards, flesh, and marrow bones.
We cried aloud, lifting our hands to Zeus,
powerless, looking on at this, appalled;°
but Cyclops went on filling up his belly
with manflesh and great gulps of whey,
then lay down like a mast among his sheep.
My heart beat high now at the chance of action,
and drawing the sharp sword from my hip I went
along his flank to stab him where the midriff
holds the liver. I had touched the spot
when sudden fear stayed me: if I killed him
we perished there as well, for we could never

167–169 We would . . . guest: Odysseus earnestly asks or begs **(entreat)** for the Cyclops's hospitality and warns him that Zeus punishes anyone who mistreats a harmless guest.
172 ninny: fool.

196 appalled: horrified; shocked; terrified.

1 Analyze Figurative Language *The poet uses two similes in this grisly description of the Cyclops's dinner. What are they?*

Grammar Practice

SPIRAL REVIEW **The Dash** Point out the use of dashes on pages 846–847. Explain that dashes signal an abrupt break, a change of thought, or information added to a thought. For example, in line 193, the dash sets off added information. Have students explain why dashes are used in the folllowing places and their effect on meaning:

- line 215 *(To signal a break; suggesting first hope at the door's opening, then disappointment at its closing)*
- line 239–240 *(Added information; it emphasizes why Odysseus would have chosen the men.)*

Have students write three sentences that include dashes. Have volunteers share their sentences with the class.

move his **ponderous** doorway slab aside.
So we were left to groan and wait for morning.

When the young Dawn with fingertips of rose
lit up the world, the Cyclops built a fire
and milked his handsome ewes, all in due order,
putting the sucklings to the mothers. Then,
his chores being all dispatched,° he caught
another brace° of men to make his breakfast,
and whisked away his great door slab
to let his sheep go through—but he, behind,
reset the stone as one would cap a quiver.°
There was a din of whistling as the Cyclops
rounded his flock to higher ground, then stillness.
And now I pondered how to hurt him worst,
if but Athena° granted what I prayed for.
Here are the means I thought would serve my turn:

a club, or staff, lay there along the fold—
an olive tree, felled green and left to season
for Cyclops's hand. And it was like a mast
a lugger of twenty oars, broad in the beam—
a deep-sea-going craft—might carry:°
so long, so big around, it seemed. Now I
chopped out a six foot section of this pole
and set it down before my men, who scraped it;
and when they had it smooth, I hewed° again
to make a stake with pointed end. I held this
in the fire's heart and turned it, toughening it,
then hid it, well back in the cavern, under
2 one of the dung piles in profusion there.
Now came the time to toss for it: who ventured
along with me? whose hand could bear to thrust
and grind that spike in Cyclops's eye, when mild
sleep had mastered him? As luck would have it,
the men I would have chosen won the toss—
four strong men, and I made five as captain.

At evening came the shepherd with his flock,
his woolly flock. The rams as well, this time,
entered the cave: by some sheep-herding whim—
or a god's bidding—none were left outside.

212 dispatched: finished.

213 brace: pair.

216 cap a quiver: put the cap on a case for holding arrows.

220 Athena: Odysseus prays for the support of Athena, his patron goddess who guides and protects him. Among other things, Athena is a warrior goddess who directly helps her chosen heroes.

221–226 Here are . . . carry: Odysseus spies the trunk of an olive tree, which the Cyclops cut down **(felled)** when the wood was green and left to dry **(season)** before carving it into a club or staff. Odysseus compares its size to that of a mast on a seafaring ship **(lugger)** that is wide in the middle **(broad in the beam)**.
230 hewed: chopped or hacked.

3 Journeys *What hint is Odysseus dropping here about the future of his journey?*

Vocabulary

ponderous (pon′dər əs) *adj.* having great weight or bulk; heavy

Teach

Vocabulary 2

Context Clues Ask: What details about the cave suggest that *profusion* in line 234 means "abundance"? *(Homer has described the many sheep in the cave. It is logical to assume that their droppings would be everywhere.)*

ENGLISH LEARNERS To help English learners, **ask:** What are some synonyms of the word *profusion*? *(bounty, plenty, a lot)*

Big Idea 3

Journeys Answer: *He is alerting his audience to the importance of the Cyclops's rams in this adventure. He is also suggesting that a god may be taking an interest in the hero's journey.*

Approaching Level

DIFFERENTIATED INSTRUCTION

Established Odysseus approaches the problem of escaping from the Cyclops's cave by carrying out a series of steps. Guide students through Odysseus's thinking process.

- Decide how to impair the giant without diminishing his strength.
- Find raw materials for the spear.
- Set up a way and a time to make the spear without being seen.
- Think of a way to dull the giant's senses and make him sleep soundly.

Have students work in small groups to solve a modern problem—such as how to help someone anonymously. Have them create a list of steps like the ones listed here.

Teach

Cultural History ☆

Ambrosia In Greek mythology, ambrosia, which means "immortal," was the food of the gods; nectar was their drink, which was brought by the cupbearer Ganymede.

He hefted his great boulder into place
and sat him down to milk the bleating ewes
in proper order, put the lambs to suck,
and swiftly ran through all his evening chores.
Then he caught two more men and feasted on them.
My moment was at hand, and I went forward
holding an ivy bowl of my dark drink,°
looking up, saying:
'Cyclops, try some wine.
Here's liquor to wash down your scraps of men.
Taste it, and see the kind of drink we carried
under our planks. I meant it for an offering
if you would help us home. But you are mad,
unbearable, a bloody monster! After this,
will any other traveler come to see you?'

He seized and drained the bowl, and it went down
so fiery and smooth he called for more:

'Give me another, thank you kindly. Tell me,
how are you called? I'll make a gift will please you.
Even Cyclopes know the wine-grapes grow
out of grassland and loam in heaven's rain,
☆ but here's a bit of nectar and ambrosia!'°

Three bowls I brought him, and he poured them down.
I saw the fuddle and flush° cover over him,
then I sang out in cordial tones:
'Cyclops,
you ask my honorable name? Remember
the gift you promised me, and I shall tell you.
My name is Nohbdy: mother, father, and friends,
everyone calls me Nohbdy.'
And he said:
'Nohbdy's my meat, then, after I eat his friends.
Others come first. There's a noble gift, now.'

Even as he spoke, he reeled and tumbled backward,
his great head lolling to one side; and sleep
took him like any creature. Drunk, hiccuping,
he dribbled streams of liquor and bits of men.

Now, by the gods, I drove my big hand spike
deep in the embers, charring it again,
and cheered my men along with battle talk
to keep their courage up: no quitting now.
The pike of olive,° green though it had been,
reddened and glowed as if about to catch.
I drew it from the coals and my four fellows

251 dark drink: This is the liquor Odysseus described in lines 94–102.

266 nectar and ambrosia: the foods of the gods, causing immortality. The Cyclops suggests that any wine is a gift from heaven, but this one is like the gods' own drink.

268 fuddle and flush: the confused mental state and reddish complexion caused by drinking alcohol.

286 pike of olive: the sharpened stake made from the olive tree.

Speaking Practice

SMALL GROUP

Storytelling

Point out that Homer uses imagery and concrete language to bring action to life. Point out the simple syntax he uses for reporting what happens (for example, "straight forward they sprinted, lifted it, and rammed it deep in his crater eye"). He focuses on sight, touch, and hearing. Point out that simple language and vivid details are vital to good storytelling. Have partners make up a story about Polyphemus fighting a monstrous beast. Students should practice telling their stories, focusing on creating vivid pictures in listeners' minds. Instruct one student to read the story aloud while his or her partner listens, attempting to picture the story. Then, the students should edit the stories together. Encourage volunteers to read their stories to the class.

Ulysses and Polyphemos, 1560. Alessandro Allori. Fresco. Collection of Banca Toscana (Palazzo Salviati), Florence, Italy. ★

gave me a hand, lugging it near the Cyclops
as more than natural force nerved them; straight
forward they sprinted, lifted it, and rammed it
deep in his crater eye, and I leaned on it
turning it as a shipwright turns a drill
in planking, having men below to swing
the two-handled strap that spins it in the groove.
So with our brand° we bored that great eye socket
while blood ran out around the red hot bar.
Eyelid and lash were seared; the pierced ball
hissed broiling, and the roots popped.
                                                                      In a smithy
one sees a white-hot axehead or an adze°
plunged and wrung in a cold tub, screeching steam—
the way they make soft iron hale° and hard—:
just so that eyeball hissed around the spike.
The Cyclops bellowed and the rock roared round him,
and we fell back in fear. Clawing his face

296 brand: the piece of burning hot wood.

301 adze: an axe-like tool with a curved blade.

303 hale: strong.

1 Analyze Figurative Language *To what action does Homer compare the blinding of the Cyclops? Why might he have chosen this comparison?*

Teach

Reading Strategy 1

Analyze Figurative Language **Answer:** *He compares driving the stake into the Cyclops's eye to boring a hole with a shipwright's drill. This action was most likely a familiar image to Homer's audience.*

APPROACHING To help approaching level students, **ask:** Is this comparison a simile or a metaphor? *(simile because it uses the word* as*)*

View the Art ★

Alessandro Allori (1535–1607) painted in late-sixteenth-century Florence. On a visit to Rome, Allori was influenced by the artwork of Michelangelo. He returned to Florence, where he painted for the ruling Medici family. In the mid-1570s, Allori became director of the Florentine tapestry workshop. In his painting, Allori depicted the human body in complicated twisting poses.

English Learners

DIFFERENTIATED INSTRUCTION

Beginning/Early Intermediate Explain that translations of the *Odyssey* often use words that are difficult or use words in unusual ways. Have English language learners identify difficult words on this page. Then, have them write what they think the words mean by studying the context. Have them research each word in the dictionary to clarify meaning.

Teach

Literary Element 1

Epic and Epic Hero **Answer:** *Odysseus uses a false name to deceive the Cyclops's neighbors into thinking that nobody has hurt him. Odysseus's plan has served him well, but he will find that he has made a powerful enemy in Poseidon, Polyphemus's father.*

APPROACHING To help approaching level students, **ask:** If Odysseus is the protagonist in this situation, what or whom is the antagonist? *(Death is the antagonist; Odysseus vs. death)*

Reading Strategy 2

Analyze Figurative Language **Answer:** *Death is made human to emphasize the life-and-death struggle. Homer describes it as a game Odysseus is playing with the personified character "Death," with wit and courage as his tools.*

APPROACHING To help approaching level students, **ask:** What other words in this section show readers that this is a game? *(laughter, silly, fool, wit, trick)*

he tugged the bloody spike out of his eye,
threw it away, and his wild hands went groping;
then he set up a howl for Cyclopes
who lived in caves on windy peaks nearby.
Some heard him; and they came by divers° ways
to clump around outside and call:
'What ails you,
Polyphemus?° Why do you cry so sore
in the starry night? You will not let us sleep.
Sure no man's driving off your flock? No man
has tricked you, ruined you?'
Out of the cave
the mammoth Polyphemus roared in answer:
'Nohbdy, Nohbdy's tricked me, Nohbdy's ruined me!'
To this rough shout they made a sage° reply:
'Ah well, if nobody has played you foul
there in your lonely bed, we are no use in pain
given by great Zeus. Let it be your father,
Poseidon Lord, to whom you pray.'
So saying
they trailed away. And I was filled with laughter
to see how like a charm the name deceived them.
Now Cyclops, wheezing as the pain came on him,
fumbled to wrench away the great doorstone
and squatted in the breach° with arms thrown wide
for any silly beast or man who bolted°—
hoping somehow I might be such a fool.
But I kept thinking how to win the game:
death sat there huge; how could we slip away?
I drew on all my wits, and ran through tactics,
reasoning as a man will for dear life,
until a trick came—and it pleased me well.
The Cyclops' rams were handsome, fat, with heavy
fleeces, a dark violet.
Three abreast
I tied them silently together, twining
cords of willow from the ogre's° bed;
then slung a man under each middle one

311 divers: several different; various.

314 Polyphemus (pol´ i fē´ məs): the blinded Cyclops's name.

321 sage: wise.

331 breach: a gap or opening.

332 bolted: broke away.

343 ogre: monster; fearsome giant.

1 Epic and Epic Hero *Why did Odysseus tell the Cyclops his name was Nohbdy? How well has Odysseus's plan worked?*

2 Analyze Figurative Language *Why do you think the poet chose to personify death in this passage?*

Reading Practice

SPIRAL REVIEW **Identify Cause-and-Effect Relationships** Ask students to recall what happened because Odysseus wanted to see the Cyclops. *(He and his men were trapped in the cave; some men were devoured.)* Point out that Odysseus's impulsive actions cause many of his troubles. Have students make a list of cause-and-effect relationships. Instruct students to list Odysseus's impulsive actions in Part 1. Then, have students list the results or effects of those actions. Ask volunteers to share their lists with the class.

Odysseus. Jacob Jordaens. Oil on canvas, 61 x 97 cm. Pushkin Museum, Moscow.

View the Art Jacob Jordaens's paintings often portrayed scenes from mythological, Biblical, or historical stories. What might the Cyclops be thinking and feeling in this scene? ★

to ride there safely, shielded left and right.
So three sheep could convey each man. I took
the woolliest ram, the choicest of the flock,
and hung myself under his kinky belly,
pulled up tight, with fingers twisted deep
in sheepskin ringlets for an iron grip.
So, breathing hard, we waited until morning.

When Dawn spread out her fingertips of rose
the rams began to stir, moving for pasture,
and peals of bleating echoed round the pens
where dams with udders full called for a milking.
Blinded, and sick with pain from his head wound,
the master stroked each ram, then let it pass,
but my men riding on the pectoral fleece°
the giant's blind hands blundering never found.
Last of them all my ram, the leader, came,
weighted by wool and me with my meditations.
The Cyclops patted him, and then he said:

358 pectoral fleece: the wool on the rams' chests.

Teach

View the Art ★

Answer: *Students may say the Cyclops is as determined to destroy the men as they are to escape.*

Jacob Jordaens (1593–1678) was a Flemish painter who was famous for large canvases, often featuring scenes of revelry. *Odysseus* is typical in its sensuous use of color, deep red tones, and focus on a dramatic moment.

Approaching Level

DIFFERENTIATED INSTRUCTION

Emerging The vivid descriptions and suspenseful action may motivate students who struggle with reading. Play the audiotape as students read along. Pause to answer students' questions and to have them paraphrase the action. Use dramatic activities to reinforce students' comprehension. Play the audiotape of students' favorite scenes a second time, having volunteers pantomime actions, such as tying the men under the rams, and character reactions, such as Odysseus's fury and exhilaration after he escapes.

Teach

Literary Element 1

Irony Remind students that a situation is ironic when its outcome is the opposite of what is expected to happen. Invite a volunteer to explain the irony of Polyphemus's words in this passage. *(He thinks the ram lags behind out of grief for the Cyclops's eye and that the animal would tell its master where Odysseus is if it could speak. In fact, the ram is giving Odysseus a way out.)*

Literary Element 2

Epic and Epic Hero
Answer: *The Cyclops expresses self-pity and rage. Odysseus, in contrast, is always using his intelligence and cunning.*

View the Art ★

Ask: In your opinion, how well does this picture illustrate the scene described in lines 395–401? *Explain. (Students may say the picture accurately shows the events but lacks emotion.)*

Odysseus and Polyphem, 1910. After L. du Bois-Reymond. Color print. Collection of Karl Becker, Sagen des klassischen Altertums, Berlin (Verlag Jugendhort). ★

'Sweet cousin ram, why lag behind the rest
in the night cave? You never linger so,
but graze before them all, and go afar
to crop sweet grass, and take your stately way
leading along the streams, until at evening
you run to be the first one in the fold.
1 Why, now, so far behind? Can you be grieving
over your Master's eye? That carrion° rogue
and his accurst companions burnt it out
when he had conquered all my wits with wine.
Nohbdy will not get out alive, I swear.
Oh, had you brain and voice to tell
where he may be now, dodging all my fury!
Bashed by this hand and bashed on this rock wall
his brains would strew the floor, and I should have
rest from the outrage Nohbdy worked upon me.'

370 **carrion:** rotten, filthy.

2 Epic and Epic Hero *What emotions does the Cyclops express in this passage? Contrast his character with that of Odysseus.*

Research Practice

Causes of Earthquakes The ancient Greeks explained earthquakes as the handiwork of the god Poseidon. Today, geologists believe that earthquake tremors result from the shifting tectonic plates on which the continents of Earth's crust ride. Have students break into groups and use an earth science text, encyclopedia, or the Internet to learn more about the causes of earthquakes and the technology used to monitor and measure them. Have the students compile their findings in a presentation for the class. Suggest that students include illustrations and graphic organizers in their presentations.

He sent us into the open, then. Close by,
I dropped and rolled clear of the ram's belly,
going this way and that to untie the men.
With many glances back, we rounded up
his fat, stiff-legged sheep to take aboard,
and drove them down to where the good ship lay.
We saw, as we came near, our fellows' faces
shining; then we saw them turn to grief
tallying those who had not fled from death.
I hushed them, jerking head and eyebrows up,
and in a low voice told them: 'Load this herd;
move fast, and put the ship's head toward the breakers.'°
They all pitched in at loading, then embarked°
and struck their oars into the sea. Far out,
as far off shore as shouted words would carry,
I sent a few back to the adversary:

3

'O Cyclops! Would you feast on my companions?
Puny, am I, in a Caveman's hands?
How do you like the beating that we gave you,
you damned cannibal? Eater of guests
under your roof! Zeus and the gods have paid you!'
The blind thing in his doubled fury broke
a hilltop in his hands and heaved it after us.
Ahead of our black prow it struck and sank
whelmed in a spuming geyser, a giant wave
that washed the ship stern foremost back to shore.
I got the longest boathook out and stood
fending us off, with furious nods to all
to put their backs into a racing stroke—
row, row, or perish. So the long oars bent
kicking the foam sternward, making head
until we drew away, and twice as far.°
Now when I cupped my hands I heard the crew
in low voices protesting:

'Godsake, Captain!
Why bait the beast again? Let him alone!'
'That tidal wave he made on the first throw
all but beached us.'

'All but stove us in!'

'Give him our bearing with your trumpeting,
he'll get the range and lob a boulder.'°

390 put . . . breakers: turn the ship around, toward the open sea.
391 embarked: got on board.

402–410 Ahead . . . twice as far: The sinking hilltop creates a wave at the ship's front end **(prow)** that washes the boat backwards **(stern foremost)** to the shore.

415–419 That tidal . . . boulder: The men complain, reasonably enough, that Polyphemus nearly smashed the ship **(All but stove us in)** and that Odysseus's shouting will give away their position **(bearing)**.

4 Epic and Epic Hero *Why does Odysseus behave in this way?*

Teach

Reading Strategy 3

Oral Reading Ask: What is Odysseus feeling after the narrow escape? Have students suggest the tone with which Odysseus delivers these lines. Invite students to read them aloud with suitable expressions and gestures.

Literary Element 4

Epic and Epic Hero
Answer: *Odysseus is furious with the Cyclops and proud that his trick has worked. Students may point out that he is drawing attention to himself, exactly what he had told his men not to do a few moments earlier.*

English Learners

DIFFERENTIATED INSTRUCTION

Beginning/Early Intermediate
Extensive use of pronouns in the selection may prove confusing for English learners, especially for students who have difficulty with the he/she distinction. As students read the selection, ask them to pause to identify antecedents for the pronouns, including subject and object pronouns, posessives, and indefinite pronouns such as *one.* Remind students that *it* does not always have an antecedent. Have them list the pronouns and antecedents in their notebooks. Then, ask volunteers to share what they have found.

Teach

Literary Element 1

Epic and Epic Hero

Answer: *Odysseus's judgment is clouded by his pride and his desire for fame. He reveals who he is and where he lives, allowing the Cyclops to have him pursued and punished.*

ADVANCED To challenge advanced level students, **ask:** Letting pride cloud one's judgment is a common theme. What other stories share this theme? *(Possible Answer: Lord of the Rings)*

'Aye
He'll smash our timbers and our heads together!'

I would not heed them in my glorying spirit,
but let my anger flare and yelled:

'Cyclops,
if ever mortal man inquire
how you were put to shame and blinded, tell him
Odysseus, raider of cities, took your eye:
Laertes' son, whose home's on Ithaca!'

At this he gave a mighty sob and rumbled:

'Now comes the weird° upon me, spoken of old.
A wizard, grand and wondrous, lived here—Telemus,°
a son of Eurymus;° great length of days
he had in wizardry among the Cyclopes,
and these things he foretold for time to come:
my great eye lost, and at Odysseus' hands.
Always I had in mind some giant, armed
in giant force, would come against me here.
But this, but you—small, pitiful and twiggy—
you put me down with wine, you blinded me.
Come back, Odysseus, and I'll treat you well,
praying the god of earthquake° to befriend you—
his son I am, for he by his avowal
fathered me, and, if he will, he may
heal me of this black wound—he and no other
of all the happy gods or mortal men.'

Few words I shouted in reply to him:

'If I could take your life I would and take
your time away, and hurl you down to hell!
The god of earthquake could not heal you there!'

At this he stretched his hands out in his darkness
toward the sky of stars, and prayed Poseidon:

'O hear me, lord, blue girdler of the islands,
if I am thine indeed, and thou art father:
grant that Odysseus, raider of cities, never
see his home: Laertes' son, I mean,
who kept his hall on Ithaca. Should destiny
intend that he shall see his roof again
among his family in his father land,
far be that day, and dark the years between.

430 the weird: the strange fate.
431 Telemus (tel'ə məs)
432 Eurymus (yoo ri'məs)

441 god of earthquake: Poseidon

1 Epic and Epic Hero *How would you characterize Odysseus's judgment?*

Grammar Practice

SPIRAL REVIEW **Simple and Compound Sentences** Write these sentences on the board:

- In these words he prayed, and the god heard him.
- We beached her, grinding keel in the soft sand, and waded in.

Explain that the first item is a compound sentence, and the second is a simple sentence with two verbs. Have students identify subjects and verbs and label the sentence to the right as simple or compound.

- He raged at Polyphemus, and the giant nearly beached their boat. *(compound)*

Let him lose all companions, and return
under strange sail to bitter days at home.'°

In these words he prayed, and the god heard him.
Now he laid hands upon a bigger stone
and wheeled around, titanic for the cast,°
to let it fly in the black-prowed vessel's track.
But it fell short, just aft° the steering oar,
and whelming seas rose giant above the stone
to bear us onward toward the island.°

There
as we ran in we saw the squadron waiting,
the trim° ships drawn up side by side, and all
our troubled friends who waited, looking seaward.
We beached her, grinding keel in the soft sand,
and waded in, ourselves, on the sandy beach.
Then we unloaded all the Cyclops's flock
to make division, share and share alike,
only my fighters voted that my ram,
the prize of all, should go to me. I slew him
by the seaside and burnt his long thighbones
to Zeus beyond the stormcloud, Cronus'° son,
who rules the world. But Zeus disdained° my offering;
destruction for my ships he had in store
and death for those who sailed them, my companions.
Now all day long until the sun went down
we made our feast on mutton and sweet wine,
till after sunset in the gathering dark
we went to sleep above the wash of ripples.

2

When the young Dawn with fingertips of rose
touched the world, I roused the men, gave orders
to man the ships, cast off the mooring lines;
and filing in to sit beside the rowlocks
oarsmen in line dipped oars in the gray sea.
So we moved out, sad in the vast offing,°
having our precious lives, but not our friends."

3 Journeys *What does this passage suggest about Odysseus's return journey to Ithaca?*

4 Analyze Figurative Language *Where have you encountered this figure of speech before? Why might the poet have repeated it?*

452–461 O hear . . . home: In ancient cultures, curses were neither made nor taken lightly. Homer's audience would have believed in their power. In his curse upon Odysseus, Polyphemus begs Poseidon to make his enemy suffer, using every detail he knows about Odysseus to make sure the god's punishment will be directed toward the right person.
464 titanic for the cast: drawing upon his great size and strength in preparation for the throw.
466 aft: behind.
468 the island: the deserted island where the other eleven ships and their crews have remained while Odysseus and his handpicked men explored the Cyclops's mainland.
471 trim: in good condition and ready to sail.

480 Cronus (krō′ nəs): Heaven and Earth, the first gods, had been dethroned by their son Cronus, who was in turn overthrown by his son Zeus.
481 disdained: rejected.

493 vast offing: the visible expanse of open sea.

Teach

Big Idea 2

Journeys Ask students to name other stories they know that tell of a hero's adventures while on a journey. How is this story similar to and different from the *Odyssey*?

ENGLISH LEARNERS Encourage English language learners to compare Odysseus with heroes from their culture.

Big Idea 3

Journeys **Answer:** *This passage suggests that Odysseus's journey home will be long and difficult.*

Reading Strategy 4

Analyze Figurative Language **Answer:** *It also appears in lines 208 and 352. Note that repetition aids the memory of both poet and audience. Also, each mention of the dawn signals the arrival of a new day, so each reference serves as a transition.*

Approaching Level

DIFFERENTIATED INSTRUCTION

African American Vernacular English Approaching level students who use African American vernacular English may have difficulty with the pronunciation of past tense verbs. Emphasize the need to pronounce the second consonant sound so that a past tense verb does not sound like the present tense verb. Model the correct pronunciation of these past tense verbs:

- We unloaded all the Cyclops's flock . . .
- Zeus disdained my offering . . .
- Fingertips of rose touched the world . . .
- I roused the men . . .
- So we moved out . . .

Have students find these sentences on page 855 and pronounce the sentence correctly.

After You Read

Assess

1. Answers will vary.
2. (a) They lose all desire to leave the island. (b) Odysseus is determined to reach his home.
3. (a) The Cyclops eats six men. Odysseus and his men get the giant drunk and blind him. They tie themselves beneath sheep to escape. (b) Courage and cunning
4. By criticizing their crude way of life, he builds up tension.
5. (a) Odysseus is both a strong, caring leader and a reckless adventurer. (b) The crew respects and trusts Odysseus, but may feel that his inconsistent behavior puts them at risk.
6. The story's appeal lies in what happens along the way, not in how the journey ends.
7. Students should compare elements of the *Odyssey* to science-fiction stories and movies of today.

Literary Element

1. Odysseus is clever at solving problems. His pride and anger make him ordinary.
2. The fight with the Cyclops is entertaining. Odysseus's love of his home is inspirational. His leadership in escaping from the Lotus Eaters is instructive.

Progress Check

Can students identify epic and epic hero?

If No → See Unit 5 Teaching Resources Book, p. 29.

For additional selection assessment, see Assessment Resources, pp. 185–186.

After You Read

Respond and Think Critically

Respond and Interpret

1. How did you respond to Part 1? Explain.
2. (a)What happens to the men who go ashore in the land of the Lotus Eaters? (b)Why might Odysseus be so opposed to the eating of lotus?
3. (a)Summarize what happens inside the Cyclops's cave. (b)What personality traits does Odysseus reveal in leading his men to safety?

Analyze and Evaluate

4. Why might Odysseus have commented on the Cyclopes's way of life before describing his adventures in their land? Was it effective? Explain.
5. (a)Find supporting evidence for the following statement: "There are two distinct sides to Odysseus's personality." (b)How do you think his crew regards him, given these aspects of his personality?

Connect

6. **Big Idea** Journeys The Invocation reveals what happens to Odysseus and his men. How did knowing the outcome affect your reading of Part 1?
7. **Connect to Today** Identify story elements in the *Odyssey* that you might find in modern-day science-fiction or action stories and movies.

Literary Element Epic and Epic Hero

Epics were intended to entertain, to inspire, and to instruct listeners. The **epic hero** has recognizable human characteristics—including human faults.

1. Give an example of how Odysseus is extraordinary and an example of how he is ordinary.
2. How could the *Odyssey* serve to entertain, to inspire, and to teach? Explain.

Reading Strategy Analyze Figurative Language

An **epic simile** extends a comparison with elaborate description that can fill several lines of verse.

1. The scene describing the blinding of the Cyclops contains two epic similes. Identify the lines of each simile and tell what is being compared.
2. Why might Homer have used more than one epic simile to describe this event?

LOG ON **Literature** Online

Selection Resources For Selection Quizzes, eFlashcards, and Reading-Writing Connection activities, go to glencoe.com and enter QuickPass code GL49787u5.

Vocabulary Practice

Practice with Synonyms With a partner, match each boldfaced vocabulary word below with its synonym. You will not use all the answer choices. Use a thesaurus or dictionary to check your answers.

1. **plunder**	a. bravery
2. **valor**	b. revenge
3. **guile**	c. genius
4. **ponderous**	d. rob
	e. hefty
	f. deviousness

Writing

Write an Interior Monologue If you were one of Odysseus's men, what would you think about his actions and leadership? Has Odysseus made any mistakes? Write an interior monologue from the point of view of one of the men. Your monologue should reveal the man's thoughts about events described in Part 1 of the *Odyssey.*

Reading Strategy

1. Lines 293–295: Boring the spike into the eye is like a shipbuilder drilling into a plank. Lines 300–304: The hissing of the eyeball is like the sound of hot metal plunged into a tub of cold water.
2. The emphasis is appropriate, as the act avenges the deaths of Odysseus's men.

Vocabulary Practice

1. d **2.** a **3.** f **4.** e

Writing

Students' interior monologues should draw from the events of Part 1 of the *Odyssey* and reveal the thoughts of one of Odysseus's men.

from the *Odyssey*, Part 2

Connect to the Epic

When have you had to choose between two equally unpleasant alternatives? Write a journal entry explaining how you made your decision and describing how it all turned out.

Build Background

The ancient Greeks frequently attributed disaster or good fortune to the influence of the gods. They believed that all the gods had magical powers and were immortal, but that they also possessed human foibles and failings. For example, the gods were believed to hold grudges and behave vengefully.

Set Purposes for Reading

Big Idea Journeys

As you read Part 2 of the *Odyssey,* ask yourself, What tests must Odysseus pass as he makes his way home?

Literary Element Conflict

Conflict is the central struggle between two opposing forces in a story. **External conflict** exists when a character struggles against some outside force. An **internal conflict** takes place within the mind of a character. As you read, ask yourself, Between whom or what does conflict arise?

Reading Strategy Identify Sequence

Identifying the sequence means understanding the correct order of events in a literary work. Stopping to summarize the story periodically—using words such as *then, next, later,* and *finally*—is one way to identify sequence. As you read, ask yourself, How would I summarize this event?

Tip: Take Notes Use a graphic organizer to keep a record of the sequence of events.

SEQUENCE OF EVENTS

Odysseus and men leave Circe's island. → Odysseus is lashed to mast. Only he can hear sirens. → Ship sails between Scylla and Charybdis. Six men are lost.

Learning Objectives

For pages 857–870

In studying this text, you will focus on the following objectives:

Literary Study: Analyzing conflict.

Reading: Identifying sequence.

Writing: Writing a summary.

Vocabulary

shun (shun) *v.* to keep away from; avoid; p. 859 *Do not shun people for their ideas.*

ardor (är′dər) *n.* passion; intensity of emotion; enthusiasm; p. 860 *Jon's ardor for video games waned as he grew interested in skiing.*

tumult (to͞o′məlt) *n.* commotion; uproar; p. 860 *The escaped horse caused a scene of tumult on the crowded city street.*

shroud (shroud) *v.* to cover, as with a veil or burial cloth; conceal; p. 865 *The contents of the will were shrouded in secrecy.*

Tip: Context Clues Often you can unlock the meaning of unfamiliar words by examining context clues. For example, sometimes you can find a synonym or a definition of an unfamiliar word in the surrounding text. Example: *The people of the town* shunned *him. Wherever he went, the townsfolk* avoided *him.*

Before You Read

Focus

Summary

Odysseus and his crew set sail from Circe's island. Odysseus uses wax to plug his men's ears so they cannot hear the irresistible song of the Sirens, and he tells the men to tie him to the mast. As they pass Scylla and Charybdis, Scylla devours six men. They travel near Helios's island, and Odysseus lets the men go ashore. The desperate crew members kill some cattle for food. In revenge, Zeus sends a squall to destroy the ship. Odysseus is the only man to survive, and after nine days adrift, he lands on the island of Ogygia, where the nymph Calypso detains him.

Vocabulary

Mnemonic Devices Explain that mnemonic devices help students remember definitions. **Write:** Like a shroud, the cloud concealed the sun. Point out how the sentence helps to define the word. Also explain that the rhyming words help students remember the sentences. Have students create their own mnemonic devices for the vocabulary words.

Selection Skills

from the Odyssey, Part 2

Listening/Speaking/Viewing Skills
- Analyze Art (SE p. 860, 862, 864)
- Oral Interpretation (TE p. 864)

Vocabulary Skills
- Context Clues (SE pp. 857, 870)

Reading Skills
- Identify Sequence (SE pp. 857–870)
- Problem and Solution (TE p. 858)
- Sequence of Events (TE p. 866)

Literary Elements
- Conflict (SE pp. 857–870)

Writing Skills/Grammar
- Write a Summary (SE p. 870)
- Monologue Using Jargon (TE p. 860)
- Adverb Clauses (TE p. 862)
- Participles and Participial Phrases (TE p. 868)

Teach

Reading Strategy 1

Review Have students read the interpolation and note Odysseus's problems with his crew and with the gods.

Ask: Why might the gods and goddesses inform Odysseus of what is ahead and warn him about certain actions? *(They mean to test him, not to kill him.)*

Literary Element 2

Personification Remind students that personification is a figure of speech in which human qualities are given to something inanimate. Ask students to identify the personification in line 1 on page 858. *(Dawn is a queen rising to her throne.)*

Big Idea 3

Journeys Answer: *The men feel delighted to be starting for home again after a year of captivity. Odysseus must feel less cheerful, knowing that there are serious hardships ahead.*

Part 2

Sea Perils and Defeat

Odysseus and his men traveled to the floating islands of Aeolus (ē′ ə ləs), *god of the winds, who then gave Odysseus a bag containing all of the unfavorable winds. With only the good west wind behind them, Odysseus and his crew made rapid progress. Odysseus fell asleep when Ithaca was in sight, but his men, believing that Odysseus was not sharing valuable treasures with them, opened the bag. Instantly, the winds rushed out, blowing them back to Aeolus, who refused to help them a second time.*

After several days back at sea, they reached the land of the Laestrygonians, monstrous cannibals. Only Odysseus's ship and crew escaped destruction.

Next stop: a thickly forested island. When Odysseus sent half of his remaining men to explore the interior, only a single breathless survivor returned. He told Odysseus that the goddess Circe had lured the rest of the men to her house with food and wine and then turned them into pigs. Odysseus rescued them, forcing Circe to restore his men to their original forms with a magical herb provided by the messenger god Hermes (hur′ mēz).

1 *Before Circe allowed Odysseus to leave a year later, he had to journey to the land of the dead. There he learned from the blind prophet, Tiresias, that he would eventually return home, but that he must not injure the cattle of the sun god Helios. Upon Odysseus's return from the land of the dead, Circe repeated this warning and described the dangers that Odysseus would encounter. First, he'd meet the sirens, who lure sailors to their deaths with a beautiful song; then, the many-headed Scylla, who lurks in a cave on a high cliff above a ship-devouring whirlpool named Charybdis. She instructed him to steer toward Scylla and not try to fight back.*

Odysseus continues telling his host about his adventures.

2 "As Circe spoke, Dawn mounted her golden throne,
and on the first rays Circe left me, taking
her way like a great goddess up the island.
I made straight for the ship, roused up the men
to get aboard and cast off at the stern.
They scrambled to their places by the rowlocks
and all in line dipped oars in the gray sea.
But soon an off-shore breeze blew to our liking—
a canvas-bellying breeze, a lusty shipmate
sent by the singing nymph with sunbright hair.°

8–10 But soon . . . hair: The goddess Calypso has sent the breeze.

3 **Journeys** *Assess how Odysseus's men must be feeling at the beginning of this journey. Why might Odysseus feel differently?*

Reading Practice

SMALL GROUP

Problem and Solution Odysseus faces many problems and is clever at solving most of them. Point out that problem solving requires the ability to carry out several tasks:

- To define the problem clearly
- To analyze options and select the best option
- To plan steps and carry them out

Ask: What was Odysseus's problem-solving strategy for getting by the Sirens? *(putting wax in his men's ears and being tied up)* What steps does it involve? *(1. Carve beeswax into ear plugs 2. Cover each man's ears with wax 3. Have men tie Odysseus to the ship)* Have groups suggest other ways he might have solved the conflict and create a detailed step-by-step list that Odysseus could have followed.

So we made fast the braces,° and we rested,
letting the wind and steersman work the ship.
The crew being now silent before me, I
addressed them, sore at heart:
'Dear friends,
more than one man, or two, should know those things
Circe foresaw for us and shared with me,
so let me tell her forecast: then we die
with our eyes open, if we are going to die,
☆ or know what death we baffle if we can. Sirens
weaving a haunting song over the sea
we are to **shun**, she said, and their green shore
all sweet with clover; yet she urged that I
alone should listen to their song. Therefore
4 you are to tie me up, tight as a splint,
erect along the mast, lashed to the mast,
and if I shout and beg to be untied,
take more turns of the rope to muffle me.'

I rather dwelt on this part of the forecast,
while our good ship made time, bound outward down
the wind for the strange island of Sirens.
Then all at once the wind fell, and a calm
came over all the sea, as though some power
lulled the swell.
The crew were on their feet
briskly, to furl the sail, and stow it; then,
each in place, they poised the smooth oar blades
and sent the white foam scudding° by. I carved
a massive cake of beeswax into bits
and rolled them in my hands until they softened—
no long task, for a burning heat came down
from Helios, lord of high noon. Going forward
I carried wax along the line, and laid it
thick on their ears. They tied me up, then, plumb
amidships,° back to the mast, lashed to the mast,
and took themselves again to rowing. Soon,
as we came smartly° within hailing distance,°
the two Sirens, noting our fast ship
off their point, made ready, and they sang. . . .

11 made fast the braces: tied down the ropes used to maneuver the sails.

38 scudding: moving swiftly.

44–45 plumb amidships: at the exact center of the ship.

47 smartly: proudly; insultingly. **hailing distance:** earshot.

---

5 Identify Sequence *How has a change in the weather influenced the actions of the men?*

Vocabulary

shun (shun) *v.* to keep away from; avoid

Teach

Reading Strategy 4

Evaluate Ask: Is this a sound plan? What danger is there in leaving Odysseus's ears unplugged? *(With his powerful, persuasive ability, Odysseus might convince the men to untie him; a crewman might unplug his ears and succumb to the Sirens' voices.)* What is implied by his being the only man to hear the Sirens' song? *(As a hero, Odysseus is made of stronger stuff than his men, and he should experience adventures to the fullest.)*

Reading Strategy 5

Identify Sequence Answer: *The wind has suddenly fallen still. The men stow the sail and begin to row.*

Progress Check

Can students identify sequence?

If No → See Unit 5 Teaching Resources Book, p. 43.

Cultural History ☆

Sirens The Sirens were three sea nymphs, part bird and part woman, whose singing was so seductive that sailors were either lured to their deaths on rocky coasts or forgot to eat and starved. According to myth, when the Sirens failed to lure Odysseus, they threw themselves into the sea and perished.

English Learners

DIFFERENTIATED INSTRUCTION

Beginning/Early Intermediate

Because students may be unfamiliar with the Greek myths, provide brief introductions to Circe, the Sirens, Helios, Scylla, and Charybdis, who figure in this part of the *Odyssey*. Encourage students to describe similar mythic figures with which they are familiar. Have pairs of students select one of the gods or monsters in the *Odyssey* and read further stories and summaries about it. Have students compile their research into a few brief paragraphs. Have each pair present their findings to the class.

Teach

Literary Element 1

Conflict **Answer:** *They disobey him here in order to obey his prior order. Otherwise, their ship would be destroyed.*

View the Art ★

Answer: *Many students will say they imagined the sirens as having the bodies of women, not the bodies of birds.*

English painter John William Waterhouse (1849–1917) was influenced by the Pre-Raphaelites but used paint in his own unique, rich way. *Ulysses and the Sirens* reflects Waterhouse's shift in the 1880s from Greek and Roman pictures to literary subjects, using a romantic style.

Ulysses and the Sirens, 1891. John William Waterhouse. Oil on canvas, 100 x 201.7 cm. Collection of National Gallery of Victoria, Melbourne, Australia.

View the Art The subject of many of John William Waterhouse's paintings was female characters from literature, such as the sirens, seen here. Is this how you imagined the sirens to look? Compare and contrast your vision of the sirens with Waterhouse's. ★

The lovely voices in **ardor** appealing over the water
made me crave to listen, and I tried to say
'Untie me!' to the crew, jerking my brows;
but they bent steady to the oars. Then Perimedes°
got to his feet, he and Eurylochus,°
and passed more line about, to hold me still.
So all rowed on, until the Sirens
dropped under the sea rim,° and their singing
dwindled° away.
My faithful company
rested on their oars now, peeling off
the wax that I had laid thick on their ears;
then set me free.
But scarcely had that island
faded in blue air than I saw smoke
and white water, with sound of waves in **tumult**—
a sound the men heard, and it terrified them.
Oars flew from their hands; the blades went knocking
wild alongside till the ship lost way,
with no oarblades to drive her through the water.

53 Perimedes (per′ i mē′ dēz)

54 Eurylochus (yoo ril′ ə kəs)

57 sea rim: horizon.

58 dwindled: gradually lessened; diminished.

1 Conflict *Why are the men disobeying Odysseus? What would happen if they obeyed him?*

Vocabulary

ardor (är′ dər) *n.* passion; intensity of emotion; enthusiasm

tumult (to͞o′ məlt) *n.* commotion; uproar

Writing Practice

SMALL GROUP

Monologue Using Jargon Odysseus's speech to the sailors in lines 73–91 is filled with sailing jargon. Explain that jargon is the special vocabulary of a group or profession. Ask students who play a sport to explain some of its jargon. **Say:** For example, people on the track team use the jargon terms *legs, heats,* and *shotput.* Point out that jargon makes prose sound more realistic. Form small groups of students who have knowledge of a specific hobby or sport. Have them write a brief monologue that uses jargon. Volunteers can take turns delivering their monologue to the class.

Well, I walked up and down from bow to stern,
trying to put heart into them, standing over
every oarsman, saying gently,
'Friends,
have we never been in danger before this?
More fearsome, is it now, than when the Cyclops
penned us in his cave? What power he had!
Did I not keep my nerve, and use my wits
to find a way out for us?
Now I say
by hook or crook this peril° too shall be
something that we remember.
Heads up, lads!
We must obey the orders as I give them.
Get the oarshafts in your hands, and lay back
hard on your benches; hit these breaking seas.
Zeus help us pull away before we founder.
You at the tiller, listen, and take in
all that I say—the rudders are your duty;
keep her out of the combers and the smoke;
steer for that headland; watch the drift, or we
fetch up in the smother, and you drown us.'

2

That was all, and it brought them round to action.
But as I sent them on toward Scylla,° I
told them nothing, as they could do nothing.
They would have dropped their oars again, in panic,
to roll for cover under the decking. Circe's
bidding against arms had slipped my mind,
so I tied on my cuirass° and took up
two heavy spears, then made my way along
to the foredeck—thinking to see her first from there,
the monster of the gray rock, harboring
torment for my friends. I strained my eyes
upon that cliffside veiled in cloud, but nowhere
could I catch sight of her.
And all this time,
in travail,° sobbing, gaining on the current,
we rowed into the strait—Scylla to port
and on our starboard beam Charybdis, dire
gorge of the salt sea tide. By heaven! when she
vomited, all the sea was like a cauldron

80 peril: danger; risk; something that may cause injury or destruction.

93 Scylla (sil ʹ ə): an immortal monster with twelve tentacled arms, six heads, and three rows of teeth in each of her six mouths.

98 cuirass: armor.

106 travail: exhausting, painful labor.

3 Conflict *What potential conflict is Odysseus trying to avoid here? Do you think he is being wise?*

Teach

Reading Strategy 2

Connect Have students reread lines 73–91, in which Odysseus gives heart to the panicked crew. Students may be able to relate to the leader's urgency and tone of voice through their own experience. Ask a volunteer to describe the manner in which a coach delivers a pep talk to players or to describe another similar situation with which they are familiar.

APPROACHING Have a student read lines 73–91 as if he or she was Odysseus. Encourage the student to show emotion through tone and gestures.

Literary Element 3

Conflict **Answer:** *Odysseus is avoiding having his men disobey orders. Students may argue that Odysseus knows his men well enough to predict how they will behave.*

Approaching Level

DIFFERENTIATED INSTRUCTION

Established Visual learners may be particularly interested in the vivid descriptions and action in this part. Discuss how students would direct the scenes with the sirens for a film. Have students prepare storyboards for a film summary of a scene. Explain that the product should look like a comic book, with an abbreviated version of what happens and what is said. Ask students to present their materials as if to persuade a producer to finance the film. Explain that this type of presentation is called a *pitch*.

Teach

Literary Element 1

Conflict **Answer:** *One is a monster that can kill six men at a time. The other is a whirlpool that can destroy the whole ship.*

View the Art ★

Answer: *Students should point to specific details from the paintings as they compare and contrast the styles.*

Contemporary author and artist Peter Connolly has written many books about the ancient world.

Scylla Devours Odyssesus' Companions. Peter Connolly. Watercolor.

View the Art Peter Connolly wrote and illustrated a book about the legend of Odysseus. Compare and contrast the contemporary style of this painting with the style of the other paintings in this part. ★

seething over intense fire, when the mixture
suddenly heaves and rises.
The shot spume
soared to the landside heights, and fell like rain.°
But when she swallowed the sea water down
we saw the funnel of the maelstrom,° heard
the rock bellowing all around, and dark
sand raged on the bottom far below.
My men all blanched° against the gloom, our eyes
were fixed upon that yawning mouth in fear
of being devoured.
Then Scylla made her strike,
whisking six of my best men from the ship.
I happened to glance aft at ship and oarsmen
and caught sight of their arms and legs, dangling
high overhead. Voices came down to me
in anguish, calling my name for the last time.

A man surfcasting on a point of rock
for bass or mackerel, whipping his long rod
to drop the sinker and the bait far out,
will hook a fish and rip it from the surface
to dangle wriggling through the air:
so these
were borne aloft in spasms° toward the cliff.

107–114 we rowed . . . rain: The ship enters a narrow channel **(strait)** between Scylla on the left and **Charybdis** (kə rib′ dis) on the right. Rising and falling with the surge of tidal currents, the whirlpool sucks water down her dreadful throat **(dire gorge)**, then spews it into the air as a geyser.

116 maelstrom: violent whirlpool.

119 blanched: turned pale.

134 borne aloft in spasms: carried high while struggling furiously.

1 Conflict *The men are in conflict with both Scylla and Charybdis. Why are the two a particularly dangerous combination?*

Grammar Practice

SPIRAL REVIEW **Adverb Clauses** Remind students that a subordinate clause must be joined to a main clause because it cannot stand alone. Give students this sentence: *More fearsome, is it now, than when the Cyclops penned us in his cave?* Explain that the underlined clause functions as an adverb telling when. Write this sentence on the board. Have students underline the adverb clause and identify its subject and verb.

When **she** vomited, all the sea was like a cauldron seething . . .

She ate them as they shrieked there, in her den,
in the dire grapple,° reaching still for me—
and deathly pity ran me through
at that sight—far the worst I ever suffered,
questing° the passes of the strange sea.
We rowed on.
☆ The Rocks were now behind; Charybdis, too,
and Scylla dropped astern.
Then we were coasting
the noble island of the god, where grazed
those cattle with wide brows, and bounteous flocks
of Helios,° lord of noon, who rides high heaven.

From the black ship, far still at sea, I heard
the lowing of the cattle winding home
and sheep bleating; and heard, too, in my heart
the words of blind Tiresias of Thebes
and Circe of Aeaea: both forbade me
the island of the world's delight, the Sun.
So I spoke out in gloom to my companions:

'Shipmates, grieving and weary though you are,
listen: I had forewarning from Tiresias
and Circe, too; both told me I must shun
this island of the Sun, the world's delight.
Nothing but fatal trouble shall we find here.
Pull away, then, and put the land astern.'
That strained them to the breaking point, and, cursing,
Eurylochus cried out in bitterness:

3 'Are you flesh and blood, Odysseus, to endure
more than a man can? Do you never tire?
God, look at you, iron is what you're made of.
Here we all are, half dead with weariness,
falling asleep over the oars, and you
say "No landing"—no firm island earth
1 where we could make a quiet supper. No:
pull out to sea, you say, with night upon us—
just as before, but wandering now, and lost.
Sudden storms can rise at night and swamp
ships without a trace.
Where is your shelter
if some stiff gale blows up from south or west—
the winds that break up shipping every time

136 dire grapple: desperate struggle.

139 questing: seeking; searching or pursuing in order to find something or achieve a goal.

146 Helios: the Greek god of the sun. Odysseus's ship is nearing the island where Helios lives.

2 Identify Sequence *How can you tell that Odysseus's ship has successfully navigated Scylla and Charybdis?*

Teach

Reading Strategy 2

Identify Sequence

Answer: *Odysseus and his men are rowing on, leaving behind the rocks, Scylla, and Charybdis.*

APPROACHING To help approaching-level students, **ask:** How does Odysseus feel as his ship rows away? How do you know? *(Odysseus feels guilty because some of the men serving him have died.)*

Reading Strategy 3

Make Judgments Students should note that these lines provide further evidence that Odysseus is made of tougher stuff than his crew. You may want to discuss the implications of a saga in which a mortal reaches godlike stature and gods stoop to human behavior.

Cultural History ☆

Scylla Myth has it that Circe fell in love with a god who loved Scylla. To get rid of her rival, Circe poisoned the waters where Scylla bathed. This changed Scylla into a frightful monster, and she threw herself into the sea. She was changed into rocks, which still bear her name and continue to pose danger to sailors.

Approaching Level

DIFFERENTIATED INSTRUCTION

Established Say: In the *Odyssey,* Odysseus has to lead his team through many obstacles. **Ask:** What qualities make a good leader? *(understands people with whom he/she works; knows when and how much information to give; is a good listener; sees the big picture and the larger goal)* Have students discuss whether Odysseus has these qualities and whether he is a good leader. Encourage them to identify areas in the story where Odysseus should have acted differently than he did, and to explain what he should have done differently.

Teach

Reading Strategy 1

Evaluate Eurylochus wants to persuade Odysseus to land the ship for the night. Help students evaluate his argument.

Say: First, Eurylochus points out two undeniable facts. The men are exhausted and unfit to cope with a night storm. Without food and rest, they face death at sea. Second, he suggests that they will stay only one night. He also suggests that Odysseus is heartless, reminding him of what he owes to the men. The argument is persuasive.

Big Idea 2

Journeys Answer: *It was unusual to sail at night.*

View the Art ★

Answer: *It suggests both terror and desperation. The men fear for their lives, but since they are starving, they will risk the wrath of Helios.*

Pellegrino Tibaldi (1527–1596) is noted for his "inspired" work. His use of color and bold perspectives added a sense of three-dimensionality, a quality that earlier art had lacked.

The Companions of Ulysses Slaying the Cattle of the Sun God Helios, 16th century. Pellegrino Tibaldi. Fresco. Palazzo Poggi, Bologna, Italy.

View the Art Pellegrino Tibaldi used the story of Odysseus as the subject for a series of frescoes. A fresco is a painting made directly on freshly spread plaster, so the paint is absorbed into the wet plaster. What does the expression and body language of the man in the lower left corner of the painting suggest to you? Consider the warning Odysseus has given his crew. ★

when seamen flout° the lord gods' will? I say
1 do as the hour demands and go ashore
before black night comes down.
We'll make our supper
alongside, and at dawn put out to sea.'

Now when the rest said 'Aye' to this, I saw
the power of destiny devising ill.
Sharply I answered, without hesitation:

'Eurylochus, they are with you to a man.
I am alone, outmatched.
Let this whole company
swear me a great oath: Any herd of cattle
or flock of sheep here found shall go unharmed;
no one shall slaughter out of wantonness°
ram or heifer; all shall be content
with what the goddess Circe put aboard.'

They fell at once to swearing as I ordered,
and when the round of oaths had ceased, we found
a halfmoon bay to beach and moor the ship in,

176 flout: defy; ignore; scoff at.

189 wantonness: recklessness or lack of restraint.

2 **Journeys** *What does this passage suggest about sea journeys in Homer's time?*

Speaking Practice

SMALL GROUP

Oral Interpretation

Present these guidelines for oral interpretation:

- Use a clear voice and enunciate.
- Use posture, gestures, and movements to suggest mood and character.
- Vary expression, eye contact, and use stress and pauses to convey meaning and mood.

Have students work in small groups to prepare an oral interpretation of one section of the *Odyssey*. After assigning roles, have students practice several times before delivering their presentations.

with a fresh spring nearby. All hands ashore
went about skillfully getting up a meal.
3 Then, after thirst and hunger, those besiegers,
were turned away, they mourned for their companions
plucked from the ship by Scylla and devoured,
and sleep came soft upon them as they mourned.

In the small hours of the third watch, when stars
that shone out in the first dusk of evening
had gone down to their setting, a giant wind
blew from heaven, and clouds driven by Zeus
shrouded land and sea in a night of storm;
so, just as Dawn with fingertips of rose
touched the windy world, we dragged our ship
to cover in a grotto, a sea cave
where nymphs had chairs of rock and sanded floors.
I mustered all the crew and said:

'Old shipmates,
our stores are in the ship's hold, food and drink;
the cattle here are not for our provision,
or we pay dearly for it.

Fierce the god is
who cherishes these heifers and these sheep:
☆ Helios; and no man avoids his eye.'

To this my fighters nodded. Yes. But now
we had a month of onshore gales, blowing
day in, day out—south winds, or south by east.
As long as bread and good red wine remained
to keep the men up, and appease their craving,
they would not touch the cattle. But in the end,
when all the barley in the ship was gone,
hunger drove them to scour the wild shore
with angling hooks, for fishes and sea fowl,
whatever fell into their hands; and lean days
wore their bellies thin.

The storms continued.
So one day I withdrew to the interior
to pray the gods in solitude, for hope
that one might show me some way of salvation.
Slipping away, I struck across the island

4 Identify Sequence *What sequence of events is described in lines 218–232?*

Vocabulary

shroud (shroud) *v.* to cover, as with a veil or burial cloth; conceal

Teach

Literary Element 3

Personification **Ask:** How are hunger and thirst given human qualities? *(They are compared to besiegers.)* Why is this comparison appropriate? *(The men are fighters. To them, hunger and thirst are enemies who have threatened the men just as human besiegers would have.)*

Reading Strategy 4

Identify Sequence
Answer: *The men experience a month of wind storms, during which they eat bread and drink red wine. After they eat all the barley, the men fish and hunt. Many men become thin. Then Odysseus prays to the gods for help.*

Literary History ☆

Helios Helios belonged to the race of Titans. Ancient Greek artists pictured him as a vigorous young man with a beardless face, his head crowned by sunbeams, racing his chariot from India to the Atlantic Ocean. At the close of each day, he was thought to return to a large bowl, from which he would rise again the next morning.

Approaching Level

DIFFERENTIATED INSTRUCTION

Established Explain that a word's history can provide clues to its meaning. Provide this history for the word *supplication*: Latin *supplicare* to kneel down, pray <*sub-* under, below + *plicare*, to fold double up. Point out that the word originally described the posture of someone "folded up" in prayer. Explain how this word relates to *supplicant (names a person)* and *pliable (something foldable)*. Have students use a dictionary to learn about the following word: **insidious.** *(Latin* insidiae, *an ambush, plot* <insidiere *to sit in or on, lie in wait for* <in- *in* + sidere *to sit)* Then, have students share their answers with the class.

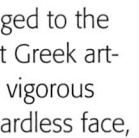

Teach

Literary Element 1

Conflict Answer: *There is a conflict between what Odysseus has told them—not to kill Helios's cattle—and their own natures, which tell them to do anything to survive.*

to a sheltered spot, out of the driving gale.
I washed my hands there, and made supplication
to the gods who own Olympus, all the gods—
but they, for answer, only closed my eyes
under slow drops of sleep.
Now on the shore Eurylochus
made his insidious° plea:
'Comrades,' he said,
'You've gone through everything; listen to what I say.
All deaths are hateful to us, mortal wretches,
but famine is the most pitiful, the worst
end that a man can come to.
Will you fight it?
Come, we'll cut out the noblest of these cattle
for sacrifice to the gods who own the sky;
and once at home, in the old country of Ithaca,
if ever that day comes—
we'll build a costly temple and adorn° it
with every beauty for the Lord of Noon.
But if he flares up over his heifers lost,
wishing our ship destroyed, and if the gods
make cause with him, why, then I say: Better
open your lungs to a big sea once for all
than waste to skin and bones on a lonely island!'

Thus Eurylochus; and they murmured 'Aye!'
trooping away at once to round up heifers.
Now, that day tranquil cattle with broad brows
were grazing near, and soon the men drew up
around their chosen beasts in ceremony.
They plucked the leaves that shone on a tall oak—
having no barley meal—to strew the victims,°
performed the prayers and ritual, knifed the kine°
and flayed° each carcass, cutting thighbones free
to wrap in double folds of fat. These offerings,
with strips of meat, were laid upon the fire.
Then, as they had no wine, they made libation°
with clear spring water, broiling the entrails° first;
and when the bones were burnt and tripes° shared,
they spitted° the carved meat.
Just then my slumber
left me in a rush, my eyes opened,
and I went down the seaward path. No sooner

240 insidious: slyly treacherous or deceitful; scheming.

251 adorn: to decorate; add beauty, honor, or distinction.

263–264 They . . . victims: Usually, in preparing a burnt offering, fruit or grain was spread over and around the animal's carcass.
265 kine: cattle.
266 flayed: stripped off the skin of.
269 libation: a ritual pouring of wine or another liquid as part of an offering.
270–271 entrails, tripes: internal organs.
272 spitted: threaded pieces onto a spit, or rod, for roasting over a fire.

1 Conflict *With whom, or what, are Eurylochus and the other men in conflict?*

Reading Practice

SPIRAL REVIEW **Sequence of Events and Summarizing** Epics are action-driven. Assess students' grasp of Part 2 with a review exercise. Have students summarize the significant events that have occurred up to this point. Have students close their books and list, in chronological order, the events they can recall from Part 2. Ask volunteers to read their lists as you compile a master list on the board. Then have students check the text for forgotten or out-of-order incidents. When finished, have the class copy the completed summary into their notebooks.

had I caught sight of our black hull, than savory
odors of burnt fat eddied° around me;
grief took hold of me, and I cried aloud:

2 'O Father Zeus and gods in bliss forever,
you made me sleep away this day of mischief!
O cruel drowsing, in the evil hour!
Here they sat, and a great work they contrived.'°

Lampetia° in her long gown meanwhile
had borne swift word to the Overlord of Noon:

'They have killed your kine.'

And the Lord Helios
burst into angry speech amid the immortals:

'O Father Zeus and gods in bliss forever,
punish Odysseus' men! So overweening,°
now they have killed my peaceful kine, my joy
at morning when I climbed the sky of stars,
and evening, when I bore westward from heaven.
Restitution or penalty they shall pay—
and pay in full—or I go down forever
to light the dead men in the underworld.'°

Then Zeus who drives the stormcloud made reply:

'Peace, Helios: shine on among the gods,
shine over mortals in the fields of grain.
Let me throw down one white-hot bolt, and make
splinters of their ship in the winedark sea.'°

—Calypso later told me of this exchange,
as she declared that Hermes° had told her.
Well, when I reached the sea cave and the ship,
I faced each man, and had it out;° but where
could any remedy be found? There was none.
The silken beeves° of Helios were dead.
4 The gods, moreover, made queer signs appear:
cowhides began to crawl, and beef, both raw
and roasted, lowed like kine upon the spits.

Now six full days my gallant crew could feast
upon the prime beef they had marked for slaughter
from Helios' herd; and Zeus, the son of Cronus,
added one fine morning.

All the gales
had ceased, blown out, and with an offshore breeze

276 eddied: swirled.

281 contrived: schemed; plotted.

282 Lampetia (lam pē ′ shə): a guardian of the island and animals. Her father is Helios; her mother is a human woman.

288 overweening: arrogant; self-important; not humble enough.

292–294 Restitution . . . underworld: Helios threatens to abandon the sky and shine, instead, on the land of the dead if the gods do not punish Odysseus's men.

296–299 Peace . . . winedark sea: Zeus coolly silences Helios, offering to set matters straight with a single thunderbolt.

301 Hermes (hur ′ mēz): the messenger god.

303 I faced each man, and had it out: Odysseus confronts each crewman.

305 beeves: cattle.

3 Conflict *Why has Zeus entered the conflict?*

Teach

Reading Strategy 2

Respond **Ask:** Do you agree with Odysseus? Have the bad weather and his sleep been caused by the gods to force Odysseus's men to kill the cattle? *(Students should recall Poseidon's fury against Odysseus and Polyphemus's prayer that Odysseus be doomed to wander long and alone.)*

APPROACHING Have approaching-level students find the section of text that foreshadows this treatment. *(lines 450–461 on page 853)*

Literary Element 3

Conflict **Answer:** *Helios has threatened to stop shining on the earth if Odysseus and his men are not punished. Zeus is not personally angry with Odysseus but agrees to Helios's demand in order to keep the sun in the sky.*

Reading Strategy 4

Visualize Call attention to the grim picture of the dead cattle being reanimated. This is not only horrifying to the men but also a ghostly foreboding that they will pay with their lives.

Approaching Level

DIFFERENTIATED INSTRUCTION

Emerging Intrapersonal learners have a capacity for self-knowledge and understanding. They are able to accurately assess their feelings, motivations, and needs. Ask students to imagine that they are members of Odysseus's crew. Have them choose one of the incidents described in the *Odyssey* so far and write a paragraph in which they examine how they would react in that situation. What would they do? How would their actions differ from those of Odysseus? How would they feel? What strengths do they have that would help them?

Teach

Literary Element 1

Similes As students read this page, tell them to look for comparisons. *(Example: The doomed men bob in the ocean "like petrels on the waves" at line 335.)* **Ask:** How does this simile make the men appear? *(They are reduced to helpless animals, fighting for survival.)*

Literary Element 2

Personification Have students note the personification of the whirlpool. **Ask:** What is the effect of giving it the human capacity to drink the tide? *(It seems more terrifying, as if it were striving with an evil intent.)*

Big Idea 3

Journeys **Answer:** *Since the men were forewarned, Zeus's action is just. Or students may say that the gods made it impossible to leave the island, thereby practically assuring the slaughter of the cattle. This manipulation is not really fair.*

we launched again stepping° the mast and sail,
to make for the open sea. Astern of us
the island coastline faded, and no land
showed anywhere, but only sea and heaven,
when Zeus Cronion° piled a thunderhead
above the ship, while gloom spread on the ocean.
We held our course, but briefly. Then the squall
struck whining from the west, with gale force, breaking
both forestays,° and the mast came toppling aft
along the ship's length, so the running rigging°
showered into the bilge.°
On the afterdeck
the mast had hit the steersman a slant blow
bashing the skull in, knocking him overside,
as the brave soul fled the body, like a diver.
With crack on crack of thunder, Zeus let fly
a bolt against the ship, a direct hit,
so that she bucked, in reeking fumes of sulphur,
and all the men were flung into the sea.
They came up 'round the wreck, bobbing awhile
like petrels° on the waves.
No more seafaring
homeward for these, no sweet day of return;
the god had turned his face from them.
I clambered
fore and aft my hulk until a comber
split her, keel from ribs, and the big timber
floated free; the mast, too, broke away.
A backstay floated dangling from it, stout
rawhide rope, and I used this for lashing
mast and keel together. These I straddled,
riding the frightful storm.°
Nor had I yet
seen the worst of it: for now the west wind
dropped, and a southeast gale came on—one more
twist of the knife—taking me north again,
straight for Charybdis. All that night I drifted,
and in the sunrise, sure enough, I lay
off Scylla mountain and Charybdis deep.
There, as the whirlpool drank the tide, a billow°
tossed me, and I sprang for the great fig tree,
catching on like a bat under a bough.

315 stepping: fixing into position.

319 Cronion: a name that identifies Zeus as Cronus's son.

323 forestays: the ropes that support the main mast.
324 running rigging: the ropes that support all masts and sails.
325 bilge: the lowest interior part of a ship.

335 petrels: sea birds.

339–346 I clambered . . . storm: Before the ship is broken in two by a long breaking wave **(comber)**, Odysseus scrambles from front to back **(fore and aft)**; afterwards, he grabs a mast rope **(backstay)** and pieces together a crude raft.

354 billow: a great, swelling wave.

---

3 Journeys *Is Zeus's action just? Why or why not?*

Grammar Practice

SPIRAL REVIEW **Participles and Participle Phrases** Explain that a participle is an *-ing* or *-ed* verb form used as an adjective. Point out these examples: *These I straddled, <u>riding</u> the frightful storm* (lines 345–346). Point out that *riding the frightful* storm is a participial phrase describing the subject.

Ask students to find two other participial phrases on pages 868 and 869.

- I sprang for the great fig tree, *catching on like a bat under a bough.* (lines 355–356)
- Now I let go with hands and feet, *plunging straight into the foam . . .* (lines 368–369)

Nowhere had I to stand, no way of climbing,
the root and bole° being far below, and far
above my head the branches and their leaves,
massed, overshadowing Charybdis pool.
But I clung grimly, thinking my mast and keel
would come back to the surface when she spouted.
And ah! how long, with what desire, I waited!
till, at the twilight hour, when one who hears
and judges pleas in the marketplace all day
between contentious men, goes home to supper,
the long poles at last reared from the sea.

Now I let go with hands and feet, plunging
straight into the foam beside the timbers,
pulled astride, and rowed hard with my hands
to pass by Scylla. Never could I have passed her
had not the Father of gods and men, this time,
kept me from her eyes. Once through the strait,
nine days I drifted in the open sea
before I made shore, buoyed up by the gods,
upon Ogygia° Isle. The dangerous nymph
Calypso lives and sings there, in her beauty,
and she received me, loved me.

But why tell
the same tale that I told last night in hall
to you and to your lady? Those adventures
made a long evening, and I do not hold
with° tiresome repetition of a story."

358 bole: trunk.

376 Ogygia (o gij′ yə)

382–383 hold with: approve of; have patience for.

4 Identify Sequence *Odysseus has been telling his story to the Phaeacians. When did this narrative begin?*

Scylla. 5th century B.C. Melos, Greece. Terra-cotta relief. British Museum, London. ★

Teach

Reading Strategy 4

Identify Sequence

Answer: *After the Invocation, all of Parts 1 and 2 have been a retelling.*

View the Art ★

Ask: How does this relief of Scylla differ from the illustration on page 862? In your opinion, which piece of art gives a better sense of Scylla? Why? *(The illustration, though not true to the description of Scylla, gives a greater sense of horror and monstrosity.)*

To check students' understanding of the selection, see Unit 5 Teaching Resources Book, p. 47.

Progress Check

Can students identify conflict?

If No → See Unit 5 Teaching Resources Book, p. 42.

Advanced Learners

DIFFERENTIATED INSTRUCTION

Research Point out that one of Odysseus's most impressive skills is his tactful adaptability in almost any situation. Encourage advanced learners to research the skills and duties of diplomats. Challenge students to research a topic related to the subject of diplomacy. They might choose an ambassador and learn about his or her background, qualifications, and duties. They could find out what skills are required to become a diplomat. They could interview someone who works at a consulate. They might also research the written and unwritten rules of diplomacy. Have students report their results to the class.

After You Read

Assess

1. Odysseus is unlucky because he has lost all of his men. He is lucky because his life has been spared.
2. (a) Plugs their ears with wax (b) Tie him to the mast
3. (a) Scylla is a six-headed monster that lives in a cliff. Charybdis is a whirlpool. (b) He knows they will be terrified.
4. (a) A month of fierce gales prevents them from leaving. When supplies run out, the men kill some of Helios's cattle. (b) Starvation makes the men want to do as Eurylochus says.
5. (a) Desire and weakness (b) These are believable responses.
6. Odysseus. Some students may find Zeus guilty of unjust punishment. Others may argue that he must keep the sun happy.
7. Any journey can have delays caused by weather and equipment failures.
8. Students might mention that a leader may not share everything to avoid widespread panic.

Literary Element

1. (a) Getting past the sirens and Scylla and Charybdis; Odysseus's attempts at keeping his men from killing the sun god's cattle (b) Odysseus seems stronger than his men and more able to resist temptation.
2. (a) Odysseus's men know that killing the cattle will lead to punishment, but they can see no other way to survive. (b) That humans have a conscience

Writing

Students' summaries should briefly describe all of the key events in part 2.

Reading Strategy

1. Examples: But *soon* an off-shore breeze blew to our liking (line 8); *Then all at once* the wind fell (line 32); *Then, after* thirst and hunger, those besiegers were turned away (lines 197–198); *All that night* I drifted (line 351).
2. Example: *First,* the men moored the ship; *then* they prepared a meal; *next,* they mourned for their companions. *At last,* they slept.

Vocabulary

1. "After betraying everyone" "no friends"
2. "passion"
3. "had been calm and peaceful"
4. "kept it hidden from us"

After You Read

Respond and Think Critically

Respond and Interpret

1. At the end of Part 2, is Odysseus very lucky, very unlucky, or a combination of both? Explain.
2. (a)How does Odysseus protect his men from the song of the Sirens? (b)How do his men protect him?
3. (a)What are Scylla and Charybdis? (b)Why does Odysseus not tell his men about Scylla?
4. (a)Why do Odysseus and his men stay longer than planned on the island of Helios, and what are the consequences of this delay? (b)Why does Eurylochus prove to be a more persuasive leader in this episode than Odysseus?

Analyze and Evaluate

5. (a)What character traits do the events in Part 2 expose in Odysseus and his men? (b)Do you find these traits believable? Why or why not?
6. In your opinion, who is responsible for Odysseus's survival, Zeus or Odysseus? Explain.

Connect

7. **Big Idea** Journeys Which circumstances of Odysseus's journey so far might happen on real-life journeys? Explain.
8. **Connect to Today** Why might a leader today choose not to tell his or her people everything about a potentially dangerous situation?

Literary Element Conflict

In the *Odyssey,* **external conflict** takes center stage. Look a little closer, however, and you will also see evidence of **internal conflict.**

1. (a)Identify three examples of external conflict in Part 2. (b)What did these conflicts reveal about the characters involved in them?
2. (a)What is an example of an internal conflict in Part 2? (b)What did this internal conflict suggest about life or about human nature?

Reading Strategy Identify Sequence

Review the sequence chain you made. Then answer the following questions.

1. List four sequence signal words or phrases used in Part 2. What did they signal?
2. Summarize the events on Helios's island. Use a different signal word for each event.

LOG ON Literature Online

Selection Resources For Selection Quizzes, eFlashcards, and Reading-Writing Connection activities, go to glencoe.com and enter QuickPass code GL49787u5.

Vocabulary Practice

Practice with Context Clues Identify the context clues in the following sentences that help you determine the meaning of each boldfaced vocabulary word.

1. After betraying everyone, he had no friends and the whole community **shunned** him.
2. She was impressed by his **ardor** for painting—she thought his passion was inspiring.
3. Yesterday the town had been calm and peaceful, but today it was unending **tumult.**
4. The truth was **shrouded** by confusion. All of the mystery kept it hidden from us.

Writing

Write a Summary Summarizing the plot of a complex literary work can help you understand it better. Write a summary of Part 2 of the *Odyssey.* Remember that a summary should be shorter than the original. For help writing a plot summary, see page 42.

Before You Read

from the *Odyssey*, Part 3

Connect to the Epic

Recall an occasion when you met someone after a long absence. Write a journal entry describing the experience.

Build Background

Strangers were important figures in Greek culture during Homer's time. In a society divided into tiny kingdoms that were often at war, a stranger was a potential threat. On the other hand, kindness to strangers could lead to valuable alliances. And what if a stranger was a god, wandering the earth in disguise? Strangers expected—and generally received—hospitality.

Set Purposes for Reading

Big Idea Journeys

At the beginning of Part 3, Odysseus arrives on the shores of Ithaca after an absence of twenty years. As you read Part 3 of the *Odyssey,* ask yourself, How does the arrival of a stranger play a major role in the end of Odysseus's journey?

Literary Element Characterization

Characterization refers to the methods a writer uses to reveal the personality of a character. In **direct characterization,** explicit statements are made about a character. In **indirect characterization,** the writer reveals a character's personality through his or her words, thoughts, and actions and through what other characters think and say about that individual. As you read, ask yourself, What actions and words help to reveal the personality and character of Odysseus?

Reading Strategy Make Inferences About Theme

The **theme** in a literary work is its main idea or message about life. Sometimes a work's theme is implied rather than directly stated. When you **make inferences about theme,** you make educated guesses about the implied theme based on such literary elements as plot, dialogue, characterization, and voice. As you read, ask yourself, Based on the details of Part 3, what can I infer about the theme of this part of the *Odyssey*?

Tip: **Take Notes** List details and the inferences you make based on them. Then read through your list to see how they build to your understanding of the implied theme.

Learning Objectives

For pages 871–884

In studying this text, you will focus on the following objectives:

Literary Study: Analyzing characterization.

Reading: Making inferences about theme.

Writing: Writing an interior monologue.

Vocabulary

cower (kou′ ər) *v.* to crouch or shrink back, as in fear or shame; p. 872 *The mouse cowered in the corner as the cat moved toward it.*

impudence (im′ pyə dəns) *n.* speech or behavior that is aggressively forward or rude; p. 876 *We were amazed at our guests' impudence in requesting special privileges.*

guise (gīz) *n.* outward appearance; false appearance; p. 877 *He worked for his own interests under the guise of compassion toward others.*

renowned (ri nound′) *adj.* famous; widely known; p. 879 *Many people attended the talk by the renowned scientist.*

Before You Read

Focus

Summary

Odysseus reveals his identity to Telemachus. Then, disguised as a beggar, Odysseus returns to the manor. Penelope sends for the beggar to discover if he has news of Odysseus. She reveals problems she has had during her husband's absence. She sets the suitors to a test and promises to marry the winner. When the beggar succeeds, his identity is revealed.

For summaries in languages other than English, see Unit 5 Teaching Resources Book, pp. 49–54 .

Vocabulary

Analogies Explain that an analogy is a type of comparison. **Write:** Cower is to fear as smile is to happiness. Show students how the words relate to each other. Then, erase the words *smile* and *happiness,* and have students fill in two other words to complete the analogy. Have students create analogies for each vocabulary word. Encourage volunteers to share their analogies with the class.

Selection Skills

from the Odyssey, *Part 3*

Reading Skills
- Make Inferences About Theme (SE pp. 871–884)
- Analyze Interactions (TE p. 874)

Listening/Speaking/Viewing Skills
- Analyze Art (SE pp. 878, 880, 883)
- Performance (TE p. 878)

Vocabulary Skills
- Analogies (SE pp. 871, 884)

Writing Skills/Grammar
- Write an Interior Monologue (SE p. 884)

Literary Elements
- Characterization (SE pp. 871–884)

Teach

Reading Strategy 1

Respond After students read the interpolation, have them discuss how Odysseus feels about the suitors. **Ask:** How have they betrayed him? *(They intend to take his wife and squander his assets.)*

APPROACHING To help approaching level students, **ask:** Why does Athena most likely disguise Odysseus as a beggar? *(so no one will recognize the well-known man)*

Big Idea 2

Journeys **Answer:** *Odysseus was pursued by the gods and helpless among strangers. Now he is back in Ithaca, reunited with his son and befriended by a powerful goddess.*

Part 3

Father and Son

The kindly Phaeacians load Odysseus with gifts and take him home, leaving him fast asleep on the shores of Ithaca. On their return journey, Poseidon turns their ship into a lump of stone for daring to assist Odysseus.

1 *Odysseus is disoriented after twenty years away from home, but the goddess Athena meets him and tells him what happened: during his long absence, a number of young men from Ithaca and neighboring islands have moved into Odysseus's great house. Thinking Odysseus is dead, the suitors, as they are called, eat his food, drink his wine, and insist that Odysseus's wife Penelope choose one of them as her husband. Penelope, who still loves Odysseus and prays for his safe return, has put off a decision as long as she can, but the situation has become very tense.*

Athena disguises Odysseus as an old beggar and promises to help him. She tells him to seek shelter with a swineherd named Eumaeus (yoo mē′ əs)*. Meanwhile, Odysseus's son, Telemachus* (tə lem′ ə kəs)*, who had set out on a journey to discover the fate of his father, escapes an ambush planned by the suitors and secretly lands on Ithaca. Following Athena's instructions, he also goes to Eumaeus's hut. While the loyal swineherd is informing Penelope of her son's return, Athena appears to the disguised Odysseus.*

Helmeted Athena. c. 420-410 BC. Roman copy of a greek original attributed to Alkamenes or Cresilas. Louvre, Paris.

From the air
she walked, taking the form of a tall woman,
handsome and clever at her craft, and stood
beyond the gate in plain sight of Odysseus,
unseen, though, by Telemachus, unguessed,
for not to everyone will gods appear.°
Odysseus noticed her; so did the dogs,
who **cowered** whimpering away from her. She only
nodded, signing to him with her brows,
a sign he recognized. Crossing the yard,
he passed out through the gate in the stockade
to face the goddess. There she said to him:

1–6 From . . . appear: Athena's "craft" includes the ability to disguise herself or others and to make herself visible or invisible. She has already made Odysseus appear to be an old beggar. Now she makes herself visible to Odysseus and, at the same time, invisible to his son **Telemachus.**

2 Journeys *What has happened to Odysseus since he left Helios's island? What is happening now?*

Vocabulary

cower (kou′ ər) *v.* to crouch or shrink back, as in fear or shame

Writing Practice

Persuasive Writing

After students read these pages, **ask:** What could Odysseus do to convince Telemachus that he is his father? *(Students may say that he could say something that only Telemachus's father would know or that he could explain what Athena had done and why.)* Have students write a letter from Odysseus to Telemachus to persuade him that he is his father even though his appearance has changed. Have students use details from the selection to support this claim. Ask volunteers to share their letters with the class.

"Son of Laertes and the gods of old,
Odysseus, master of land ways and sea ways,
dissemble° to your son no longer now.
The time has come: tell him how you together
will bring doom on the suitors in the town.
I shall not be far distant then, for I
myself desire battle."
Saying no more,
she tipped her golden wand upon the man,
making his cloak pure white, and the knit tunic
fresh around him. Lithe and young she made him,
ruddy° with sun, his jawline clean, the beard
no longer gray upon his chin. And she
withdrew when she had done.
Then Lord Odysseus
reappeared—and his son was thunderstruck.°
☆ Fear in his eyes, he looked down and away
as though it were a god, and whispered:
"Stranger,
you are no longer what you were just now!
Your cloak is new; even your skin! You are
one of the gods who rule the sweep of heaven!
Be kind to us, we'll make you fair oblation°
and gifts of hammered gold. Have mercy on us!"

The noble and enduring man replied:

"No god. Why take me for a god? No, no.
I am that father whom your boyhood lacked
and suffered pain for lack of. I am he."

Held back too long, the tears ran down his cheeks
as he embraced his son.
Only Telemachus,
uncomprehending,° wild
with incredulity,° cried out:
"You cannot
be my father Odysseus! Meddling spirits
conceived this trick to twist the knife in me!°
No man of woman born could work these wonders
by his own craft, unless a god came into it
with ease to turn him young or old at will.
I swear you were in rags and old,

15 dissemble: pretend.

24 ruddy: tanned.

28 thunderstruck: astonished. The word is carefully chosen for its additional association with the works of one of the gods (Zeus).

35 make you fair oblation: offer you good sacrifices and proper worship.

44 uncomprehending: not understanding.
45 incredulity: disbelief.

47–48 Meddling . . . me: Telemachus assumes that interfering gods **(Meddling spirits)** thought up **(conceived)** this astonishing transformation to intensify his pain **(twist the knife)** over his father's long absence and possible death.

3 Make Inferences About Theme *What can the reader infer about the theme of Part 3 from these words of Odysseus?*

Teach

Reading Strategy 3

Make Inferences About Theme **Answer:** *The reader can infer that the theme will involve identity, honor, and the importance of family bonds. Odysseus feels sorrow that his twenty-year absence from home has deprived Telemachus of a father and himself of fatherhood.*

Progress Check

Can students make inferences about theme?

If No → See Unit 5 Teaching Resources Book, p. 56.

Writer's Technique ☆

Abstract vs. Concrete Language Help students identify language that communicates the emotion of this scene and also reminds readers of the involvement of the gods. The passage combines concrete descriptions with abstract emotion. For example, the abstract word *thunderstruck* reminds us of Zeus, while "looked down and away" creates an image of fear and humility. Encourage students to note how instances of abstract and concrete language support one another.

Approaching Level

DIFFERENTIATED INSTRUCTION

Emerging Help students understand Athena's character traits. **Ask:** What does the author say about Athena on these pages? *(Students may say that she gives signs, desires battle, and makes Odysseus young and handsome.)* Write these details on the board. Guide students to come up with character traits for Athena based on these details. For example, students may say that she is intelligent, powerful, and clever.

Teach

Literary Element 1

Characterization Ask students to find details in this scene that reveal Telemachus's character. *(He is at first disbelieving and then weeps for joy, suggesting that he steels himself against further disappointment and has strong feelings about his father.)* Tell students to look for the further development of Telemachus and Penelope.

Literary Element 2

Characterization Answer: *Telemachus has not seen his father since he was a little boy and did not recognize him or trust him. Telemachus has strong feelings for Odysseus but wants to shield himself against disappointment.*

APPROACHING To help approaching level students, **ask:** What does this scene show readers about heroes? *(Heroes have feelings. They love people. They are not always strong)*

and here you stand like one of the immortals!"°
Odysseus brought his ranging mind to bear°
and said:
"This is not princely, to be swept
away by wonder at your father's presence.
No other Odysseus will ever come,
for he and I are one, the same; his bitter
fortune and his wanderings are mine.
Twenty years gone, and I am back again
on my own island.
As for my change of skin,
that is a charm Athena, Hope of Soldiers,°
uses as she will; she has the knack
to make me seem a beggar man sometimes
and sometimes young, with finer clothes about me.
It is no hard thing for the gods of heaven
to glorify a man or bring him low."°
When he had spoken, down he sat.
Then, throwing
his arms around this marvel of a father
Telemachus began to weep. Salt tears
rose from the wells of longing in both men,
and cries burst from both as keen and fluttering
as those of the great taloned hawk,
whose nestlings farmers take before they fly.
So helplessly they cried, pouring out tears,
and might have gone on weeping so till sundown,
had not Telemachus said:
"Dear father! Tell me
what kind of vessel put you here ashore
on Ithaca? Your sailors, who were they?
I doubt you made it, walking on the sea!"
Then said Odysseus, who had borne the barren sea:°
"Only plain truth shall I tell you, child.
Great seafarers, the Phaeacians, gave me passage
as they give other wanderers. By night
over the open ocean, while I slept,
they brought me in their cutter,° set me down
on Ithaca, with gifts of bronze and gold
and stores of woven things. By the gods' will

53 the immortals: a common reference to the gods, who never die.
54 Odysseus . . . bear: Odysseus focuses his thoughts.

64 Hope of Soldiers: When she chooses to be, Athena is a fierce battle-goddess, defending Greece—and favored Greeks—from outside enemies.

68–69 It is . . . low: It is not difficult for the gods to make a man appear great or humble.

85 borne the barren sea: endured the hardships of the sea.

90 cutter: a single-masted sailboat.

2 Characterization *Why did Telemachus not believe his father at first? What are your impressions of Telemachus?*

Reading Practice

Analyze Interactions Read aloud the interaction between Odysseus and Telemachus on these pages. **Ask:** What can you tell about Odysseus from this scene? *(Students may say that he is honest and loves his son.)* **Ask:** What can you tell about Telemachus? *(Students may say that he is trusting and curious and that he loves his father and has missed him.)* Break students into small groups. Have them analyze the interaction between the characters to determine additional traits for each character. Have them share their findings with the class.

Odysseus, title page of "Homer: The Odyssey," 1830–1833. Francois-Louis Schmied. Color lithograph. Private collection. ★

these lie all hidden in a cave. I came
to this wild place, directed by Athena,
so that we might lay plans to kill our enemies.
Count up the suitors for me, let me know
what men at arms are there, how many men.
I must put all my mind to it, to see
if we two by ourselves can take them on
or if we should look round for help."

The Beggar at the Manor

3 *The next morning Telemachus returns home and tells Penelope about his travels but not about his father's homecoming. Odysseus, disguised again as a beggar, also returns to his own house. No one recognizes him except his faithful old dog, which lifts up its head, wags its tail, and dies. In the great hall, Telemachus permits the "beggar" to ask for food. The suitors give him bread and meat, as is the custom, but one of their leaders, a man named Antinous* (an tin′ ō əs), *is particularly insulting. He refuses to offer any food, and while Odysseus is talking, he angrily interrupts.*

But here Antinous broke in, shouting:
"God!
What evil wind blew in this pest?
Get over,
stand in the passage! Nudge my table, will you?
Egyptian whips are sweet
to what you'll come to here, you nosing rat,

4 Journeys *In what sense is Odysseus's journey far from over?*

Teach

Reading Strategy 3

Logical Reasoning After students read the interpolation, have them consider the logic behind not telling Penelope about Odysseus's return.

Say: The situation at the manor is treacherous. There are many suitors; they have ill intentions (they intend to consume or take everything) and willingness to kill (they plotted against Telemachus). It is logical that they would try to kill the king and prince if forewarned. These two need the element of surprise if they are to succeed. It might be impossible for Penelope to hide her feelings if she knew her husband had returned. Therefore, Odysseus and Telemachus must keep their secret for now.

Big Idea 4

Journeys **Answer:** *Although he is home, Odysseus's journey is far from over. He now faces the huge task of ridding his halls of the suitors.*

View the Art ★

Francois-Louis Schmied (1873–1941) is considered one of the finest wood-block engravers of the early 1900s. He was known for his meticulous attention to detail.

English Learners

DIFFERENTIATED INSTRUCTION

Beginning/Early Intermediate
Remind students that an idiom is an expression that is not meant to be taken literally. Guide students to determine the meaning of idioms and unfamiliar words and phrases on these pages by reviewing the text line by line. For example, **ask:** What does it mean to be "swept away"? *(to get caught up)* What does Odysseus mean when he says "Twenty years gone"? *(twenty years have passed)* What does the word "charm" mean in line 64? *(trick)*

Teach

Literary Element 1

Characterization Answer: *Antinous is arrogant, selfish, and cruel.*

Reading Strategy 2

Clarify Odysseus's words to Antinous are powerful and dignified. Their rhythm illustrates the meter of epic verse. Have a strong reader read aloud Odysseus's response in lines 31–42. **Ask:** Why do the suitors suspect they are not dealing with a simple beggar? *(Odysseus has shown strength, eloquence, poise, and dignity—qualities that all suggest nobility.)*

Cultural History ☆

Hospitality The ancient Greeks revered the tradition of hospitality. In fact, they took it so seriously that Zeus was considered to be the protector of strangers, as well as the defender of oaths and the patron of suppliants. Thus, Antinous's violation of hospitality is particularly shocking. Students may compare the Cyclops's behavior in Part 1, in which the monster rejects Odysseus's argument that strangers should be given a hospitable reception.

making your pitch to everyone!
These men have bread to throw away on you
because it is not theirs. Who cares? Who spares
another's food, when he has more than plenty?"

With guile Odysseus drew away,° then said:

"A pity that you have more looks than heart.
You'd grudge a pinch of salt from your own larder
to your own handy man. You sit here, fat
on others' meat, and cannot bring yourself
☆ to rummage out a crust of bread for me!"

Then anger made Antinous' heart beat hard,
and, glowering° under his brows, he answered:
"Now!
You think you'll shuffle off and get away
after that **impudence**? Oh, no you don't!"

The stool he let fly hit the man's right shoulder
on the packed muscle under the shoulder blade—
like solid rock, for all the effect one saw.
Odysseus only shook his head, containing
thoughts of bloody work,° as he walked on,
then sat, and dropped his loaded bag again
upon the door sill. Facing the whole crowd
he said, and eyed them all:
"One word only,
my lords, and suitors of the famous queen.
One thing I have to say.
There is no pain, no burden for the heart
when blows come to a man, and he defending
his own cattle—his own cows and lambs.
Here it was otherwise. Antinous
hit me for being driven on by hunger—
how many bitter seas men cross for hunger!
If beggars interest the gods, if there are Furies
pent in the dark to avenge a poor man's wrong, then may
Antinous meet his death before his wedding day!"°

Then said Eupeithes'° son, Antinous:
"Enough.

12 With guile . . . away: Odysseus is slyly provoking Antinous.

19 glowering: scowling; looking at angrily.

26–27 containing thoughts of bloody work: keeping murderous thoughts under control. Odysseus imagines killing Antinous, but holds his temper.

34–42 There is . . . wedding day: A man is not really hurt, the beggar says, when he is injured defending his property; but when he is attacked for being hungry, that's another matter. Odysseus's curse upon Antinous calls upon the **Furies**—three female spirits who punish wrongdoers—to bring about his death.

43 Eupeithes (yoo pē′ thēz)

1 Characterization *What have you learned about Antinous so far?*

Vocabulary

impudence (im′ pyə dəns) n. speech or behavior that is aggressively forward or rude

Reading Practice

SPIRAL REVIEW **Understand Foils** Remind students that a foil is a secondary character who contrasts with a main character. Begin by reading the Literary Element on this page. Have students brainstorm Antinous's characteristics. Write their responses on the board. **Ask:** How is Antinous a foil to Odysseus? *(Students may say that Antinous is cruel and violent, while Odysseus is calm and thoughtful.)* Have students write a paragraph in response to this question.

Eat and be quiet where you are, or shamble elsewhere,
unless you want these lads to stop your mouth
pulling you by the heels, or hands and feet,
over the whole floor, till your back is peeled!"

But now the rest were mortified,° and someone
spoke from the crowd of young bucks to rebuke° him:

"A poor show, that—hitting this famished tramp—
bad business, if he happened to be a god.
You know they go in foreign **guise**, the gods do,
looking like strangers, turning up
in towns and settlements to keep an eye
on manners, good or bad."

But at this notion
Antinous only shrugged.

Telemachus,
after the blow his father bore, sat still
without a tear, though his heart felt the blow.
Slowly he shook his head from side to side,
containing murderous thoughts.

Penelope
on the higher level of her room had heard
the blow, and knew who gave it. Now she murmured:

"Would god you could be hit yourself, Antinous—
hit by Apollo's bowshot!"°

And Eurynome°
her housekeeper, put in:

"He and no other?
If all we pray for came to pass, not one
would live till dawn!"

Her gentle mistress said:
"Oh, Nan, they are a bad lot; they intend
ruin for all of us; but Antinous
appears a blacker-hearted hound than any.

49 mortified: deeply embarrassed, shamed, or humiliated.
50 rebuke: to scold sharply; criticize.

68 Apollo's bowshot: Among other things, Apollo is the archer god and the god of truth. His sacred silver bow can kill literally with an arrow and figuratively with the truth.
69 Eurynome (yoo rin′ ə mē)

2

3 Make Inferences About Theme *What do these thoughts of Telemachus tell you about the implied theme of Part 3?*

4 Characterization *From what you have read so far, how would you describe Penelope?*

Vocabulary

guise (gīz) *n.* outward appearance; false appearance

Teach

Reading Strategy 3

Make Inferences About Theme Answer: *Telemachus knows that the abused beggar is his father Odysseus in disguise. His feelings of sorrow and humiliation cause him to contemplate revenge on the suitors.*

Literary Element 4

Characterization Answer: *She seems kind because she chastises Antinous for his treatment of the beggar. Homer describes her as gentle. From her speech, it is clear that she has strong opinions about the suitors, especially Antinous.*

Approaching Level

DIFFERENTIATED INSTRUCTION

Established Point out the verb tenses in lines 5–19. Note that when Odysseus is telling the story he uses past tense, but as characters speak and bring the past to life, present tense is used. Point out that within each kind of narrative, the tense is consistent. **Write:** "With guile Odysseus drew away, then said:" *(past tense—Odysseus is telling the story)* "'You sit here, fat on others' meat, and cannot bring yourself to rummage out a crust of bread for me.'" *(present tense—Odysseus is speaking)*

Teach

View the Art ★

Answer: *Students should support their responses by pointing to details from the text.*

Odysseus Reunited with Penelope. Terra-cotta relief. Louvre Museum, Paris.

View the Art The artwork shown here is made of terra cotta. Terra cotta is porous clay that has been used over time to make pottery, sculptures, tiles, and other building materials. Why do you think Penelope is looking down, away from Odysseus? ★

Here is a poor man come, a wanderer,
driven by want to beg his bread, and everyone
in hall gave bits, to cram his bag—only
Antinous threw a stool, and banged his shoulder!"

So she described it, sitting in her chamber
among her maids—while her true lord was eating.
Then she called in the forester and said:

"Go to that man on my behalf, Eumaeus,°
and send him here, so I can greet and question him.
Abroad in the great world, he may have heard
rumors about Odysseus—may have known him!"

85 Eumaeus (yoo mē´ əs)

Lively action continues in the great hall, where another beggar attempts to bully Odysseus. Antinous mockingly arranges a boxing match between the two, which Odysseus wins. Telemachus orders the disorderly crowd to leave for the evening. Surprised by his authority, the suitors obey, giving Odysseus and Telemachus time to remove all weapons from the hall as part of their preparation for battle. Then Odysseus goes to meet his wife for the first time in nearly twenty years.

Carefully Penelope began:
"Friend, let me ask you first of all:

Speaking Practice

SMALL GROUP

Performance Have students work in groups to plan and perform a scene from this section of the epic. Help students understand Odysseus's emotions as he confronts the wife he has not seen in twenty years. *(He cannot yet reveal his identity.)* Ask students to consider how Penelope and Odysseus are alike. *(They are both loyal and kind.)*

Have groups of students prepare a scene, cast parts, and deliver oral interpretations. After rehearsing, students can perform their dialogue for the class as a whole.

who are you, where do you come from, of what nation
and parents were you born?"

And he replied:

"My lady, never a man in the wide world
should have a fault to find with you. Your name
has gone out under heaven like the sweet
honor of some god-fearing king, who rules
1 in equity° over the strong: his black lands bear
both wheat and barley, fruit trees laden bright,
new lambs at lambing time—and the deep sea
gives great hauls of fish by his good strategy,
so that his folk fare well.

O my dear lady,

this being so, let it suffice° to ask me
of other matters—not my blood, my homeland.
Do not enforce me to recall my pain.
My heart is sore; but I must not be found
sitting in tears here, in another's house:
it is not well forever to be grieving.
One of the maids might say—or you might think—
I had got maudlin° over cups of wine."
And Penelope replied:

"Stranger, my looks,

my face, my carriage,° were soon lost or faded
when the Achaeans crossed the sea to Troy,
Odysseus my lord among the rest.
If he returned, if he were here to care for me,
I might be happily **renowned!**
But grief instead heaven sent me—years of pain.
Sons of the noblest families on the islands,
Dulichium, Same, wooded Zacynthus,
with native Ithacans, are here to court me,
against my wish; and they consume this house.
Can I give proper heed to guest or suppliant°
or herald° on the realm's affairs?

How could I?

wasted with longing for Odysseus, while here
they press for marriage.

98 equity: fairness and justice.

104 suffice: be enough.

111 maudlin: excessively and foolishly emotional.

114 carriage: manner of moving or holding the head and body.

124 suppliant (sup′ lē ənt): one who humbly begs or requests something.
125 herald: court messenger.

---

2 Make Inferences About Theme *Why might Odysseus say this to his wife, Penelope?*

Vocabulary

renowned (ri nound′) *adj.* famous; widely known

Approaching Level

DIFFERENTIATED INSTRUCTION

Emerging Some students may have trouble understanding what is happening during this scene. Explain that Odysseus has come to the home he once lived in disguised as a beggar, and he has been attacked by Antinous, one of the men who has invaded his home. Penelope feels badly for this harsh treatment and asks to see him. She speaks of her devotion and love for her deceased husband—Odysseus—but Odysseus cannot yet reveal his identity and tell her that he is alive.

Teach

Literary Element 1

Simile Make sure students understand the basis for comparison in this extended simile. *(The disguised Odysseus compares Penelope to a good king, whose justice and benevolent rule result in prosperity for his kingdom.)* Point out that the simile, in some respects, inverts the situation. In actuality, it is Odysseus who is the "good king" and Penelope who is his consort. Is he hinting at his own identity by using this comparison? Ask students to speculate.

Reading Strategy 2

Make Inferences About Theme **Answer:** *Penelope assumes that Odysseus is dead and does not yet know that she is talking to her husband. Odysseus hints to her that soon her grieving for him will come to an end.*

APPROACHING To help approaching level students, **ask:** How is this scene an example of dramatic irony? *(Readers know the beggar is Odysseus, but Penelope does not.)*

Teach

Literary Element 1

Characterization Continue to have students analyze Penelope's actions in order to add to their portrait of her character. What new traits appear? What traits are developed further? *(She speaks honestly and without fear. She has set a task that requires her potential future husband to be the equal of Odysseus. Her intelligence and dignity are further developed.)*

Literary Element 2

Characterization Answer: *They are both crafty, using their wits to defeat their opponents.*

View the Art ★

Answer: *The ship outside the window suggests that Odysseus has returned, and yet suitors are still approaching Penelope.*

Bernardino Pintoricchio (1454–1513), also known as Bernardino di Betto, was a prolific painter. He worked for five popes and several cardinals. The Metropolitan Museum of Art in New York City owns several of his paintings that represent mythological scenes. The National Gallery in Washington, D.C., has several of his religious paintings.

Scenes From the Odyssey, ca. 1509. Bernardino Pintoricchio. National Gallery Collection, London.

View the Art Bernardino Pintoricchio was one of the artists who worked on the Sistine Chapel. How does the scene through the window create a sense of tension in this image? ★

Ruses° served my turn
to draw the time out—first a close-grained web
I had the happy thought to set up weaving
on my big loom in hall. I said, that day:
'Young men—my suitors, now my lord is dead,
let me finish my weaving before I marry,
1 or else my thread will have been spun in vain.
It is a shroud I weave for Lord Laertes°
when cold Death comes to lay him on his bier.°
The country wives would hold me in dishonor
if he, with all his fortune, lay unshrouded.'
I reached their hearts that way, and they agreed.
So every day I wove on the great loom,
but every night by torchlight I unwove it;

129 Ruses: tricks; schemes.

136 It is . . . Laertes: Penelope has claimed to be weaving a burial cloth **(shroud)** for Odysseus's father.

137 bier: a platform on which a corpse or coffin is placed before burial.

2 Characterization *What characteristic do Odysseus and Penelope share?*

Reading Practice

SPIRAL REVIEW **Predict Outcomes** Expand on the Big Idea on page 881. Guide students to see that this was the perfect time for Odysseus to arrive home because his wife was just about to give in and marry one of the men. **Ask:** What do you think would have happened if Odysseus had come back a month later? *(Students will likely say that Penelope would have remarried; the marriage may not have been valid, however.)* Have students freewrite a paragraph on what might have happened if Odysseus had returned home at a later date.

and so for three years I deceived the Achaeans.
But when the seasons brought a fourth year on,
as long months waned,° and the long days were spent,
through impudent folly in the slinking maids
they caught me—clamored up to me at night;°
I had no choice then but to finish it.
And now, as matters stand at last,
I have no strength left to evade a marriage,
cannot find any further way; my parents
urge it upon me, and my son
will not stand by while they eat up his property.
He comprehends it, being a man full grown,
able to oversee the kind of house
Zeus would endow° with honor.

The Test of the Bow

Resigned to ending the suitors' reign over her home, Penelope cries herself to sleep that night, dreaming of the husband she believes is lost forever. The next day the suitors return to the hall, more unruly than ever. Penelope appears, carrying the huge bow that belongs to Odysseus. Her maids follow, bearing twelve iron ax heads. Penelope has a proposition for the suitors.

"My lords, hear me:
suitors indeed, you commandeered° this house
to feast and drink in, day and night, my husband
being long gone, long out of mind. You found
no justification° for yourselves—none
except your lust to marry me. Stand up, then:
we now declare a contest for that prize.
3 Here is my lord Odysseus' hunting bow.
Bend and string it if you can. Who sends an arrow
through iron axe-helve sockets, twelve in line?°
I join my life with his, and leave this place, my home,
my rich and beautiful bridal house, forever
to be remembered, though I dream it only."

One by one the suitors try to string the bow, and all fail. Only Antinous delays his attempt. In the meantime, Odysseus steps outside with the swineherd Eumaeus and Philoetius (fi loi′ tē əs), *another faithful herdsman, and reveals his identity to them. Odysseus returns to the hall and asks to try his hand at stringing the bow. Antinous sneers at this idea,*

4 Journeys *Why was this the perfect time for Odysseus to arrive home?*

145 waned: drew to an end.

146–147 through . . . night: After outwitting the suitors for more than three years, Penelope is finally betrayed by some of her own sneaky **(slinking)** maids, who crept into her room at night and caught her in the act of undoing her weaving.

156 endow: provide or equip.

2 commandeered: seized by force or threats.

5 justification: a reason for an action that shows it to be just, right, or reasonable.

9–10 Bend . . . line: The challenge has two parts: First, a suitor must bend and string the heavy bow—a task requiring strength and skill. Second, he must shoot an arrow through the narrow holes of twelve ax-heads set in a row.

Teach

Reading Strategy 3

Evaluate Guide students in evaluating Penelope's choice of contest. Remind them that they will need to review her history with the suitors.

Big Idea 4

Journeys Answer: *Penelope has run out of time. A few days later, and she might have remarried.*

Approaching Level

DIFFERENTIATED INSTRUCTION

Established Help students understand why Penelope wanted to test the men by having them use the bow. The bow was heavy, so she wanted to see which man was strongest; it was also difficult to use, so she wanted to see which man was most skilled. The man who was strongest and the most skilled would be the man most like her husband. **Ask:** Why do you think Antinous delays his attempt to use the bow? *(Students may say that he is sneaky and may be looking for a way to cheat to win.)*

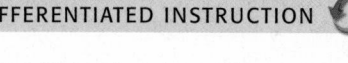

Teach

Reading Strategy 1

Identify Bias **Ask:** What slanted thinking does the suitors' reaction show? *(Students should deduce from their laughter and sarcasm that the suitors look down on the beggar and dismiss him as a threat. Their class bias is so great that they do not even consider the fact that the "beggar" has already shown great strength and prowess.)*

ENGLISH LEARNERS To help English learners, **ask:** According to the text, what does Odysseus do right before he shoots the bow? *(He examines it to see if it has changed since the last time he held it.)*

Literary Element 2

Characterization **Answer:** *Odysseus is compared to a poet and musician. He handles the bow like a musical instrument. These comparisons emphasize his skill—almost an artistic talent—at warfare.*

but Penelope and Telemachus both insist he proceed. Telemachus orders the women to leave, Philoetius locks the gates of the hall, and Eumaeus presents to Odysseus the great bow he has not held for twenty years.

And Odysseus took his time,
turning the bow, tapping it, every inch,
for borings that termites might have made
while the master of the weapon was abroad.
1 The suitors were now watching him, and some
jested among themselves:
"A bow lover!"
"Dealer in old bows!"
"Maybe he has one like it
at home!"
"Or has an itch to make one for himself."
"See how he handles it, the sly old buzzard!"°
And one disdainful suitor added this:
"May his fortune grow an inch for every inch he bends it!"
But the man skilled in all ways of contending,
satisfied by the great bow's look and heft,°
like a musician, like a harper, when
with quiet hand upon his instrument
he draws between his thumb and forefinger
a sweet new string upon a peg: so effortlessly
Odysseus in one motion strung the bow.
Then slid his right hand down the cord and plucked it,
so the taut gut° vibrating hummed and sang
a swallow's note.
In the hushed hall it smote° the suitors
and all their faces changed. Then Zeus thundered
overhead, one loud crack for a sign.
And Odysseus laughed within him that the son
of crooked-minded Cronus had flung that omen° down.°
He picked one ready arrow from his table
where it lay bare: the rest were waiting still
in the quiver for the young men's turn to come.°
He nocked it,° let it rest across the handgrip,
and drew the string and grooved butt of the arrow,
aiming from where he sat upon the stool.
Now flashed
arrow from twanging bow clean as a whistle

14–25 And Odysseus . . . old buzzard: As Odysseus examines the old bow for termite holes **(borings)** that might have weakened the wood since he last used it, the suitors take the chance to make fun of the "beggar."

29 heft: weight.

36 taut gut: tightly drawn bowstring (made of animal "gut" or intestine).

38 smote: struck, as though from a hard blow; affected suddenly with a powerful and unexpected feeling, such as fear.

39–42 Then Zeus . . . down: Odysseus recognizes the crack of thunder as a sign that Zeus is on his side.

42 omen: a sign or event thought to foretell good or bad fortune; forewarning.

44–45 the rest . . . come: The remaining arrows will be used by the contestants who follow Odysseus.

46 nocked it: fitted the nock, or notched end, of the arrow into the string.

---

2 Characterization *To what is Homer comparing Odysseus in lines 28–34? What do these comparisons contribute to his characterization?*

Grammar Practice

SPIRAL REVIEW **Compound Predicates** Explain that a compound predicate has two or more verbs joined by a conjunction. The verbs share the same subject. Write the following sentence on the board, and have students identify each verb: He <u>notched</u> it, <u>let</u> it rest against the handgrip, and <u>drew</u> the string. *(Verbs are underlined.)*

Have students scan these pages for other examples and write each compound predicate they identify.

1. dropped/nodded *(line 63)*
2. belted/clapped/stood *(lines 65–67)*

Odysseus Competes with the Suitors (detail). 5th century BC, Greek. Attic red-figured skyphos. Staatliche Museum, Antikensammlung, Berlin, Germany.

View the Art A form of pottery, a *skyphos* is a deep, two-handled wine cup. This image of Odysseus appears on a skyphos dating back to 5th century B.C. What do you suppose Odysseus is thinking as he takes aim? ★

through every socket ring, and grazed° not one,
to thud with heavy brazen head° beyond.
Then quietly
Odysseus said:
"Telemachus, the stranger
you welcomed in your hall has not disgraced you.
I did not miss, neither did I take all day
stringing the bow. My hand and eye are sound,
not so contemptible as the young men say.
The hour has come to cook their lordships' mutton°—
supper by daylight. Other amusements later,
with song and harping that adorn a feast."

He dropped his eyes and nodded, and the prince
Telemachus, true son of King Odysseus,
belted his sword on, clapped hand to his spear,
and with a clink and glitter of keen bronze
stood by his chair, in the forefront near his father. ∾

51 grazed: touched.

52 brazen head: brass arrowhead.

60 cook their lordships' mutton: literally, cook their sheep meat. But Odysseus is using a phrase that Telemachus can take metaphorically, like the phrase *cook their goose* ("get even").

3 Journeys *Do you think that Odysseus's long journey is finally over? Why or why not?*

Teach

Big Idea 3

Journeys Answer: *Odysseus's journey—a long, exhausting, and trying adventure designed by the gods to test him—has ended, but his struggles have not.*

View the Art ★

Answer: *Odysseus may be thinking that he must make the shot so that he can win the contest.*

The art appears on a skyphos, an ancient Greek drinking vessel. A skyphos had a deep body, a flat bottom, and two horizontal handles near the rim.

To check students' understanding of the selection, see Unit 5 Teaching Resources Book, p. 61.

Progress Check

Can students identify characterization?

If No → See Unit 5 Teaching Resources Book, p. 55.

English Learners

DIFFERENTIATED INSTRUCTION

Early Advanced Tell students that a simile is a comparison of two things using the words *like* or *as.* Point out and explain the meaning of these similes on page 882:

- "like a musician, like a harper" *(line 30; shows that Odysseus is very skilled at using the bow)*
- "clean as a whistle" *(line 50; shows that the shot was a very good one)*

After You Read

Assess

1. Students may be surprised at his tears, his keeping his identity secret from his wife, and his boasting.
2. (a) Athena directs both men to Eumaeus's hut. She first disguises Odysseus as a beggar but then transforms him so he can convince his son of his identity. (b) Telemachus had not seen his father since he was young; a beggar looks nothing like a king.
3. (a) She hopes the beggar has some word of Odysseus. (b) He shows self-restraint and inner strength.
4. (a) The winner must string Odysseus's bow and shoot an arrow through twelve axe-helve sockets. (b) In creating a test that none of the suitors is likely to pass, she has found an effective delaying tactic.
5. (a) Antinous is arrogant, selfish, and cruel. The other suitors are shocked by his behavior. (b) To show that he deserves Odysseus's revenge
6. Students' responses will vary.
7. Students' responses will vary.
8. Answers may vary. Students should support their answers.

Literary Element

1. Odysseus's words about her "sweet honor" directly reveal her virtue and beauty. She indirectly reveals both compassion and cunning when she talks to the "beggar."
2. Answers will vary. One example is Antinous. He rants and throws a stool at the beggar. He shows bad temper and contempt. He reveals these qualities through his actions.

After You Read

Respond and Think Critically

Respond and Interpret

1. Did any aspects of Odysseus's behavior surprise you in Part 3? Explain, telling what you might have done if you were in his place.
2. (a)What role does Athena play in reuniting Odysseus with his son, Telemachus? (b)Give two reasons why Telemachus might have trouble identifying his father at first.
3. (a)Why does Penelope summon the beggar? (b)How does Odysseus behave, and what does this say about his character?
4. (a)What is "the test of the bow"? (b)Why might Penelope have given it?

Analyze and Evaluate

5. (a)How does Antinous stand apart from the rest of the suitors? (b)Why do you think Homer develops Antinous's character in this way?
6. Which scene in this part did you consider the most interesting or effective? Explain.

Connect

7. **Big Idea** Journeys Now that Odysseus's journey seems to be over, what do you think might happen next? Explain.
8. **Connect to the Author** What may have been Homer's purpose for writing the *Odyssey*?

Literary Element Characterization

Authors may describe their characters both directly and indirectly.

1. What method of characterization does Homer use to reveal Penelope's personality? Support your ideas with examples.
2. For another character in Part 3, find an action, a line or two of dialogue, or another clue to that character's personality. Explain what insight the detail gave you about the character.

Reading Strategy Make Inferences About Theme

Refer to the inference chart you made while reading to help you answer the following questions.

1. How would you state another implied theme in Part 3 of the *Odyssey*?
2. Cite details from the text that helped you infer this theme.

LOG ON **Literature** Online

Selection Resources For Selection Quizzes, eFlashcards, and Reading-Writing Connection activities, go to glencoe.com and enter QuickPass code GL49787u5.

Vocabulary Practice

Practice with Analogies Complete each analogy.

1. guise : mask :: omen :
   a. prayer **b.** forewarning **c.** gift
2. cower : fear :: cringe :
   a. happiness **b.** sadness
   c. embarrassment
3. healthful : unwholesome :: renowned :
   a. unknown **b.** knowing
   c. unknowable
4. impudence : politeness :: reluctance :
   a. cheerfulness **b.** eagerness
   c. intelligence

Writing

Write an Interior Monologue When Antinous throws a stool at the disguised Odysseus, Odysseus restrains himself from committing murder. Write an interior monologue that reveals Odysseus's state of mind at that moment. Apply what you have learned so far about Odysseus's character.

Reading Strategy

1. One possible theme is that familial love can be strong enough to survive hardships and prolonged absence.
2. Telemachus lovingly embraces his father; Telemachus is saddened and angered by the insults the suitors heap upon Odysseus; Penelope remains faithful to Odysseus.

Vocabulary

1. b **2.** c **3.** a **4.** b

Writing

Students' monologues should

- reveal Odysseus's thoughts
- explain Odysseus's behavior
- reflect events from the *Odyssey*

from the *Odyssey*, Part 4

Learning Objectives

For pages 885–897

In studying this text, you will focus on the following objectives:

Literary Study: Analyzing plot.

Reading: Analyzing cause-and-effect relationships.

Connect to the Epic

What do you miss most when you are away from home? List several items that you miss and rank them.

Build Background

The *Odyssey* is set during the Mycenaean period, long before Homer wrote it. Throughout the epic, Homer offers his audience glimpses of the government, social classes, customs, and values of Mycenaean culture, which he collected from the myths and legends that had been passed on orally from that time.

Set Purposes for Reading

Big Idea Journeys

As you read Part 4, ask yourself, How does Homer resolve questions about Odysseus's homecoming?

Literary Element Plot

The sequence of events in a narrative work is its **plot.** The point of greatest emotional intensity, interest, or suspense is the plot's **climax.** As you read, ask yourself, Which event is the moment of greatest intensity?

Reading Strategy Analyze Cause-and-Effect Relationships

One event frequently causes another. For example, Odysseus offends Poseidon (cause) and spends much of the epic paying for his behavior (effect). **Analyzing cause-and-effect relationships** in a work of literature will help you understand the plot. As you read, ask yourself, How are the events related?

Tip: Take Notes Use a graphic organizer to help you track cause-and-effect relationships.

Cause	Effect(s)
Odysseus disguised as beggar	Telemachus does not recognize him.
	Antinous thinks he can abuse him.

Vocabulary

jostle (jos′əl) *v.* to bump, push, or shove roughly, as with elbows in a crowd; p. 886 *I was jostled in the crowd.*

implacable (im plak′ə bəl) *adj.* impossible to satisfy or soothe; unyielding; p. 888 *The general was implacable and refused to admit defeat.*

lavish (lav′ish) *v.* to give generously; provide in abundance; p. 893 *Ben's grandparents lavished gifts upon him when he graduated.*

aloof (ə lo͞of′) *adj.* emotionally distant; uninvolved; disinterested; standoffish; p. 893 *Rather than interfere, I tried to remain aloof.*

Tip: Word Origins The origin or history of a word is called its etymology. It is not always obvious how the history of a word is tied to its present day meaning. For example, the vocabulary word *aloof* is derived from the Dutch word *te loef,* meaning "to windward." In a more broad sense, being *aloof* is like being lost in the wind, distant from others.

Before You Read

Focus

Summary

Odysseus kills Antinous with an arrow. The suitors react angrily. Odysseus insists on revenge; the suitors decide to "go down fighting." Odysseus, Telemachus and two herdsmen kill all the suitors. Penelope sets a secret test for Odysseus. When he proves that he is Odysseus, the two are joyfully reunited.

For summaries in languages other than English, see Unit 5 Teaching Resources Book, pp. 62–67.

Vocabulary

Mix and Match Point out that there are two verbs and two adjectives in the vocabulary list. Have students write two sentences. Each sentence should use one verb and one adjective from the list. **Say:** For example, you may write, "She aloofly jostled the people around her as if only her own safety mattered." Encourage students to share their sentences with the class.

Selection Skills

***from the* Odyssey, Part 4**

Literary Elements
- Plot (SE pp. 885–897)
- Narrator (SE p. 897)

Listening/Speaking/Viewing Skills
- Analyze Art (SE p. 887, 895)

Reading Skills
- Analyze Cause-and-Effect Relationships (SE pp. 885–897)

Vocabulary Skills
- Word Origins (SE pp. 885, 897)

Writing Skills/Grammar
- Review (SE p. 898)
- Noun Clauses (TE p. 894)

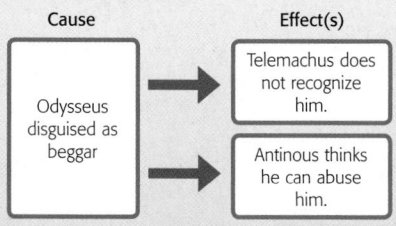

Teach

Big Idea **1**

Journeys **Ask:** Do you think it was inevitable that Odysseus's journey led to his confrontation with Antinous? *(Answers will vary. Some will feel that Antinous's behavior combined with Odysseus's personality made the conflict inevitable. Others may feel that regardless of Antinous's behavior, Odysseus could have chosen a different path.)*

Literary Element **2**

Plot **Answer:** *Most students will agree that Odysseus will take his bloody revenge on the suitors. Any suspense lies in exactly when and how this will happen.*

Part 4

Death in the Great Hall

Now shrugging off his rags the wiliest fighter of the islands
leapt and stood on the broad door sill, his own bow in his hand.
He poured out at his feet a rain of arrows from the quiver
and spoke to the crowd:

"So much for that. Your clean-cut game is over.
Now watch me hit a target that no man has hit before,
if I can make this shot. Help me, Apollo."

1
He drew to his fist the cruel head of an arrow for Antinous
just as the young man leaned to lift his beautiful drinking cup,
embossed,° two-handled, golden: the cup was in his fingers:
the wine was even at his lips: and did he dream of death?
How could he? In that revelry° amid his throng of friends
who would imagine a single foe—though a strong foe indeed—
could dare to bring death's pain on him and darkness on his eyes?
Odysseus' arrow hit him under the chin
and punched up to the feathers° through his throat.

Backward and down he went, letting the winecup fall
from his shocked hand. Like pipes his nostrils jetted
crimson runnels,° a river of mortal red,
and one last kick upset his table
knocking the bread and meat to soak in dusty blood.
Now as they craned to see their champion where he lay
the suitors **jostled** in uproar down the hall,
everyone on his feet. Wildly they turned and scanned
the walls in the long room for arms; but not a shield,
not a good ashen spear was there for a man to take and throw.°
All they could do was yell in outrage at Odysseus:

"Foul! to shoot at a man! That was your last shot!"

"Your own throat will be slit for this!"

10 embossed: decorated with designs that are slightly raised from the surface.
12 revelry: noisy festivity; merrymaking.

16 punched up to the feathers: The arrow goes clear through the throat so that only the arrow's feathers remain visible in front.

19 runnels: streams.

24–26 Wildly . . . throw: Odysseus and Telemachus had removed all weapons and armor from the room on the previous night.

2 Plot *How would you describe the level of suspense at this point in the story? Explain.*

Vocabulary

jostle (jos′ əl) *v.* to bump, push, or shove roughly, as with elbows in a crowd

Research Practice

SMALL GROUP

Greek Gods Point out that before Odysseus begins to fight, he asks for help from Apollo, a Greek god. Tell students that Apollo is the son of Zeus.

Break students into small groups and have them use library resources or the Internet to answer these questions: Why did Odysseus ask Apollo for help? How are Odysseus and Apollo alike? Encourage groups to research other Greek gods referenced in the selection such as Athena and Zeus. Have groups share their findings with the class.

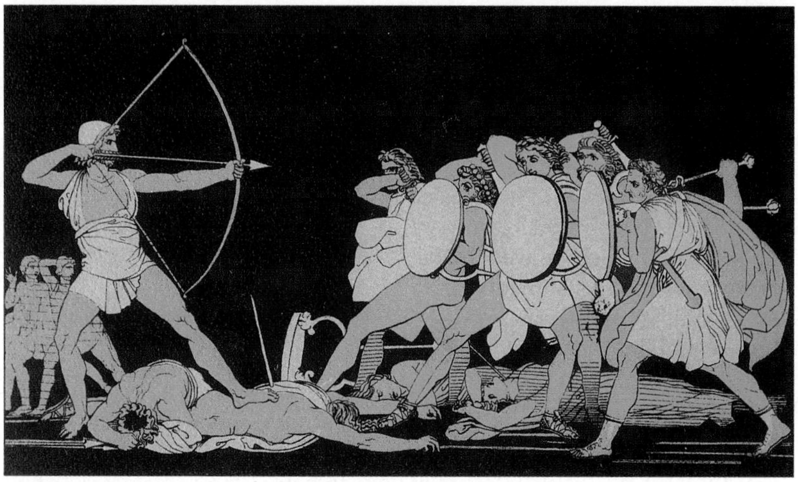

Odysseus Slaying the Suitors, 19th century. Flaxman.

View the Art Study the posture and body language of the figures in this image. What does the image suggest to you about Odysseus's standing among other men? ★

"Our finest lad is down!
You killed the best on Ithaca."
"Buzzards will tear your eyes out!"
For they imagined as they wished—that it was a wild shot,
an unintended killing—fools, not to comprehend
they were already in the grip of death.°
But glaring under his brows Odysseus answered:
"You yellow dogs, you thought I'd never make it
home from the land of Troy. You took my house to plunder,
twisted my maids to serve your beds. You dared
bid for my wife while I was still alive.
Contempt was all you had for the gods who rule wide heaven,
contempt for what men say of you hereafter.
Your last hour has come. You die in blood."
As they all took this in, sickly green fear
pulled at their entrails, and their eyes flickered
looking for some hatch or hideaway from death.
Eurymachus alone could speak. He said:
"If you are Odysseus of Ithaca come back,
all that you say these men have done is true.

33–35 For they . . . death: The suitors still do not realize that their opponent is Odysseus and that he has killed Antinous intentionally.

3 Analyze Cause-and-Effect Relationships *What has caused Odysseus to decide to kill the suitors? Explain.*

Teach

Reading Strategy 3

Analyze Cause-and-Effect Relationships Answer: *Odysseus is enraged by what has gone on in his own house while he was away.*

Ask: Why does Eurymachus request that Odysseus spare the other suitors? *(Antinous was the leader and chief instigator of the suitors. With the leader dead, Eurymachus reasons that the rest of the suitors will disband. He also offers restitution.)*

View the Art ★

Answer: *Odysseus is larger than life and stands alone. The men cower behind their shields. Odysseus is feared and respected for his strength and skill in battle.*

Odysseus and his bow are alone on the left side. They are balanced against the group of men who are huddled and appear to be hiding more than attacking. Point out that contrasting posture, bearing, and lines give Odysseus power while diminishing the others.

Approaching Level

DIFFERENTIATED INSTRUCTION

Emerging Direct students' attention to the art on this page. **Ask:** What can you tell about Odysseus from the art? What can you tell about the other men? *(He is larger and confident. He is stepping on the back of a slain man. They are smaller and hide behind their shields. Even though there are several of them, they seem afraid.)* Tell students to look at Odysseus's bow and arrow. **Ask:** What can you tell about his bow and arrow from the art? *(It is very large and the arrow is pointing down at the men.)*

Teach

Big Idea 1

Journeys **Ask:** How do the suitors choose to face the end of their lives' journeys? *(Students should point to Eurymachus encouraging the suitors to remember the joy of fighting. Some may say the suitors are brave, while others may feel that they are desperate.)*

Reading Strategy 2

Analyze Cause-and-Effect Relationships **Answer:** *The suitors have seen Odysseus's extraordinary skill with the bow, they have no armor or heavy weapons themselves, and Odysseus and Telemachus are blocking the door.*

ENGLISH LEARNERS To help English learners, **Ask:** What are some antonyms of the word *implacable*? *(Possible answers: content, satisfied)*

Rash actions, many here, more in the countryside.
But here he lies, the man who caused them all.
Antinous was the ringleader, he whipped us on°
to do these things. He cared less for a marriage
than for the power Cronion° has denied him
as king of Ithaca. For that
he tried to trap your son and would have killed him.
He is dead now and has his portion.° Spare
your own people. As for ourselves, we'll make
restitution of wine and meat consumed,
and add, each one, a tithe° of twenty oxen
with gifts of bronze and gold to warm your heart.
Meanwhile we cannot blame you for your anger."

Odysseus glowered under his black brows
and said:

"Not for the whole treasure of your fathers,
all you enjoy, lands, flocks, or any gold
put up by others, would I hold my hand.
There will be killing till the score is paid.
You forced yourselves upon this house. Fight your way out,
or run for it, if you think you'll escape death.
I doubt one man of you skins by."°

They felt their knees fail, and their hearts—but heard
Eurymachus for the last time rallying them.

"Friends," he said, "the man is **implacable**.
Now that he's got his hands on bow and quiver
he'll shoot from the big door stone there
until he kills us to the last man.

Fight, I say,
1 let's remember the joy of it. Swords out!
Hold up your tables to deflect° his arrows.
After me, everyone: rush him where he stands.
If we can budge him from the door, if we can pass
into the town, we'll call out men to chase him.
This fellow with his bow will shoot no more."

He drew his own sword as he spoke, a broadsword of fine
bronze,

52 whipped us on: encouraged us; drove us.

54 Cronion: Zeus.

57 his portion: what he deserved; what fate had in store for him.

60 tithe (tīth): payment; tax.

71 skins by: gets out alive.

80 deflect: to cause to go off course; turn aside.

2 Analyze Cause-and-Effect Relationships *The suitors vastly outnumber Odysseus and Telemachus. Why are they so alarmed?*

Vocabulary

implacable (im plak′ ə bəl) *adj.* impossible to satisfy or soothe; unyielding

Reading Practice

SMALL GROUP **Analyze Issues** Discuss Odysseus's actions on these pages with students. Remind them that prior to this, he and Telemachus have taken weapons off the walls. Odysseus kills Antinous and the other men are outraged. Eurymachus pleads for his life and the lives of the other men and offers to give Odysseus gifts and start anew, but Odysseus slays him. **Ask:** Were Odysseus's actions fair? *(Most students will say no, that he should have given the men a second chance.)* Do you think people during Homer's time would consider them fair? *(yes)* What about people today? *(no)* Initiate a discussion in which students contemplate what might have happened to Odysseus if he had killed the men today.

1 honed like a razor on either edge. Then crying hoarse and loud
he hurled himself at Odysseus. But the kingly man let fly
an arrow at that instant, and the quivering feathered butt°
sprang to the nipple of his breast as the barb° stuck in his liver.
The bright broadsword clanged down. He lurched and fell
aside,
pitching across his table. His cup, his bread and meat,
were spilt and scattered far and wide, and his head slammed
on the ground.
Revulsion,° anguish in his heart, with both feet kicking out,
he downed his chair, while the shrouding wave of mist° closed
on his eyes.

Amphinomus° now came running at Odysseus,
broadsword naked in his hand. He thought to make
the great soldier give way at the door.
But with a spear throw from behind Telemachus hit him
3 between the shoulders, and the lancehead drove
clear through his chest. He left his feet and fell
forward, thudding, forehead against the ground.
Telemachus swerved around him, leaving the long dark spear
planted in Amphinomus. If he paused to yank it out
someone might jump him from behind or cut him down with
a sword
at the moment he bent over. So he ran—ran from the tables
to his father's side and halted, panting, saying:

"Father let me bring you a shield and spear,
a pair of spears, a helmet.
I can arm on the run myself; I'll give
outfits to Eumaeus and this cowherd.
Better to have equipment."

Said Odysseus:

"Run then, while I hold them off with arrows
as long as the arrows last. When all are gone
if I'm alone they can dislodge° me."

Quick

upon his father's word Telemachus
ran to the room where spears and armor lay.
4 He caught up four light shields, four pairs of spears,
four helms of war high-plumed with flowing manes,°
and ran back, loaded down, to his father's side.

88 butt: end.
89 barb: arrowhead; point.
93 revulsion: intense dislike, disgust, or horror.
94 shrouding wave of mist: death.
95 Amphinomus (am fin ′ ə məs)
115 dislodge: force back; kill.
120 helms . . . manes: war helmets decorated from front to back with a crest or ridge of long feathers resembling horses' manes.

5 Plot *Is tension rising or falling at this point? Explain.*

6 Journeys *How is Telemachus responding to the challenges of the fight?*

Approaching Level

DIFFERENTIATED INSTRUCTION

Emerging Help students gain insight into Telemachus's character. **Ask:** In what way is Telemachus like this father? *(He is brave and risks his life in battle; he is intelligent.)*

Established Ensure that students understand the action in this part of the story. Tell them that Telemachus has just saved his father's life and wants to leave the room to get weapons and shields for Eumaeus and a cowherd so that they can assist them in battle.

Teach

Reading Strategy 3

Analyze Cause-and-Effect Relationships Ask: When Telemachus slays Amphinomus and saves Odysseus, how does this differ from the typical father-son relationship? *(Students should note that typically it is the father who protects the son. In this case, it is the son who is protecting the father.)*

Literary Element 4

Plot Ask: Why does Telemachus leave the battle? *(to get spears, shields, and helmets to aid Odysseus)* Do you think this was an act of bravery? *(Some may feel that Telemachus is being brave in volunteering to fetch the armor by himself. Others may feel he shouldn't leave Odysseus's side.)*

For additional literary element practice, see Unit 5 Teaching Resources Book, p. 69.

Literary Element 5

Plot Answer: *This is the high point of tension in the scene. Negotiation has failed. The battle has begun in earnest; the characters must kill or be killed.*

Big Idea 6

Journeys Answer: *He is aiding Odysseus as an equal in battle.*

Teach

Literary Element 1

Ask: If the outcome of the battle is a foregone conclusion, is the battle truly climactic? *(Some students may feel that the battle is so intense and action-packed that it concludes a portion of Odysseus's journey, and therefore it is climactic. Others may say that knowing the outcome makes the battle anticlimactic.)*

Reading Strategy 2

Analyze Cause-and-Effect Relationships **Answer:** *Eurymachus encourages the suitors to fight; then he draws his sword and hurls himself toward Odysseus. That action causes Odysseus to shoot an arrow at Eurymachus. Amphinomus runs toward Odysseus, causing Odysseus to throw a spear at him. That action causes Telemachus to help his father. After Telemachus brings weapons to his father, Odysseus, Telemachus, and their allies kill all the suitors.*

He was the first to pull a helmet on
and slide his bare arm in a buckler strap.°
The servants armed themselves, and all three took their stand
beside the master of battle.°
While he had arrows
1 he aimed and shot, and every shot brought down
one of his huddling enemies.
But when all barbs had flown from the bowman's fist,
he leaned his bow in the bright entry way
beside the door, and armed: a four-ply shield
hard on his shoulder, and a crested helm,
horsetailed, nodding stormy upon his head,
then took his tough and bronze-shod spears.

Odysseus and Telemachus, along with their two allies, cut down all the suitors. Athena also makes an appearance, rallying their spirits and ensuring that none of her favorites is injured. Finally the great hall is quiet.

In blood and dust
he saw that crowd all fallen, many and many slain.
Think of a catch that fishermen haul in to a halfmoon bay
in a fine-meshed net from the whitecaps of the sea:
how all are poured out on the sand, in throes for° the salt sea,
twitching their cold lives away in Helios' fiery air:
so lay the suitors heaped on one another.

123 slide . . . strap: The Greeks' small, round shield **(buckler)** had a strap in back through which the warrior slid his arm.
125 master of battle: Odysseus.

139 in throes for: in pain or struggle to return to.

The Trunk of the Olive Tree

Penelope's old nurse hurries upstairs to tell her mistress that Odysseus has returned and that all the suitors are dead. Penelope is amazed but refuses to admit that the stranger could be her husband. Instead, she believes that he must be a god.

The old nurse sighed:
"How queer, the way you talk!
Here he is, large as life, by his own fire,
and you deny he ever will get home!
Child, you always were mistrustful!
But there is one sure mark that I can tell you:
that scar left by the boar's tusk long ago.
I recognized it when I bathed his feet

Statuette of Ulysses. Roman. Bronze. Bibliotheque Nationale, Paris.

2 Analyze Cause-and-Effect Relationships *What causes and effects did you notice in this scene?*

Writing Practice

SMALL GROUP **Character Traits** Discuss with students the traits that Homer gives to Odysseus and whether Homer considers Odysseus the ideal Greek man. Then discuss the traits that Homer gives to Penelope and whether Homer considers her to be the ideal Greek woman. Have students write a brief comparison of Odysseus and Penelope. Have them consider how the two characters demonstrate the ideals of Greek manhood and womanhood and how they differ. Remind students to support their opinions with evidence from the poem.

and would have told you, but he stopped my mouth,
forbade me, in his craftiness.
Come down,
I stake my life on it, he's here!
Let me die in agony if I lie!"
Penelope said:
"Nurse dear, though you have your wits about you,
still it is hard not to be taken in
by the immortals. Let us join my son, though,
and see the dead and that strange one who killed them."
She turned then to descend the stair, her heart
in tumult. Had she better keep her distance
and question him, her husband? Should she run
up to him, take his hands, kiss him now?°
Crossing the door sill she sat down at once
in firelight, against the nearest wall,
across the room from the lord Odysseus.
There
leaning against a pillar, sat the man
and never lifted up his eyes, but only waited
for what his wife would say when she had seen him.
And she, for a long time, sat deathly still
in wonderment—for sometimes as she gazed
she found him—yes, clearly—like her husband,
but sometimes blood and rags were all she saw.°
Telemachus's voice came to her ears:
"Mother,
cruel mother, do you feel nothing,
drawing yourself apart this way from Father?
Will you not sit with him and talk and question him?
What other woman could remain so cold?
Who shuns her lord, and he come back to her
from wars and wandering, after twenty years?
Your heart is hard as flint and never changes!"
Penelope answered:
"I am stunned, child.
I cannot speak to him. I cannot question him.
I cannot keep my eyes upon his face.
If really he is Odysseus, truly home,
beyond all doubt we two shall know each other
better than you or anyone. There are
secret signs we know, we two."°

19–22 She turned . . . now: Penelope's thoughts reveal that she is not so uncertain of "that strange one" as she has let on.

33 blood . . . saw: Odysseus is again disguised as the old beggar.

50 secret . . . two: Eurynome has already said that she recognized Odysseus's scar; but Penelope is thinking of signs that are a secret strictly between her and Odysseus.

3 Journeys *Why does Penelope hesitate to accept her husband?*

Teach

Big Idea 3

Journeys Answer: *She still suspects that the stranger might be a trick played by the gods. She is not ready to let her guard down and accept him.*

ADVANCED **Ask:** If you were Penelope, what criteria would you set to satisfy yourself that the beggar is Odysseus? Have students brainstorm a list of criteria. Write the list on the board. Include criteria that the beggar has already passed, such as his being able to string Odysseus's bow, something no one else could do. As students read, have them compare what they read to what they have listed on the board.

Approaching Level

DIFFERENTIATED INSTRUCTION

Emerging Students may have trouble understanding why Penelope hesitates in accepting Odysseus as her husband. Point out that Odysseus has changed—Athena has made him larger and stronger. Penelope believes that Odysseus has changed from a beggar to a young soldier and then back to a beggar again—his behavior is very god-like. Penelope was certain that her husband was dead and may think that this man is really a god in disguise.

Teach

Literary Element 1

Plot **Ask:** Why does Odysseus smile when he hears Penelope's speech? *(Penelope needs proof, and he realizes he can give it. He also knows that he'll be more recognizable when he's clean.)*

Reading Strategy 2

Analyze Cause-and-Effect Relationships **Answer:** *He fears that he must once again leave home when the people of Ithaca come to avenge the loss of the suitors.*

APPROACHING Have approaching level students take a minute to write about a time when they had to make a hard decision. This will help them empathize with Odysseus.

Literary Element 3

Plot **Answer:** *A battle is looming between Odysseus and the families and friends of the slaughtered suitors.*

View the Art ★

The kithara was a musical instrument of the lyre family with two hollow arms, a wooden box, seven strings, and often a flat base. Larger than a typical lyre, the kithara was held by a standing musician who strummed the strings to produce music.

A smile
1 came now to the lips of the patient hero, Odysseus,
who turned to Telemachus and said:

"Peace: let your mother test me at her leisure.
Before long she will see and know me best.
These tatters, dirt—all that I'm caked with now—
make her look hard at me and doubt me still.
As to this massacre, we must see the end.
Whoever kills one citizen, you know,
and has no force of armed men at his back,
had better take himself abroad by night
and leave his kin. Well, we cut down the flower of Ithaca,
the mainstay of the town. Consider that."

Telemachus replied respectfully:

"Dear Father,
enough that you yourself study the danger,
foresighted in combat as you are,
they say you have no rival.

We three stand
ready to follow you and fight. I say
for what our strength avails,° we have the courage."

And the great tactician,° Odysseus, answered:

"Good.
Here is our best maneuver, as I see it:
bathe, you three,° and put fresh clothing on,
order the women to adorn themselves,
and let our admirable harper choose a tune
for dancing, some lighthearted air, and strum it.
Anyone going by, or any neighbor,
will think it is a wedding feast he hears.
These deaths must not be cried about the town
till we can slip away to our own woods. We'll see
what weapon, then, Zeus puts into our hands."°

They listened attentively, and did his bidding,
bathed and dressed afresh; and all the maids
adorned themselves. Then Phemius° the harper
took his polished shell° and plucked the strings,
moving the company to desire

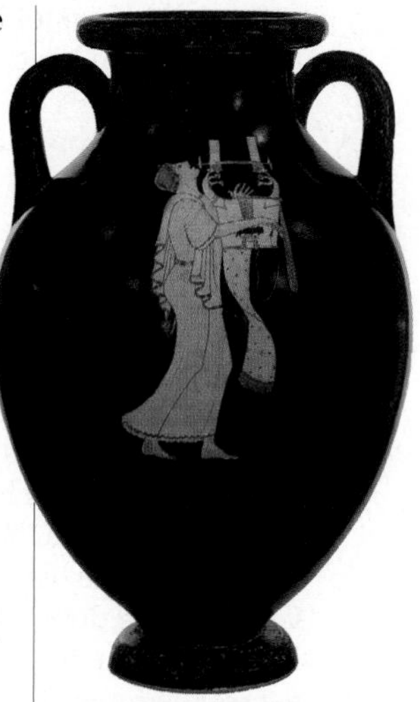

Youth Singing and Playing the Kithara, c. 490 B.C. Terracotta, height: 16⅜ in. The Metropolitan Museum of Art, NY. ★

71 avails: is worth; helps.
72 tactician: one skilled in forming and carrying out (military) tactics or plans.
75 you three: Telemachus, Eumaeus, and Philoetius.

74–83 Here . . . hands: Odysseus's plan is this: First, stall for time by making people think that Penelope's wedding feast is in progress. Then escape to the woods, and trust in Zeus.
86 Phemius (fē′ mē əs)
87 polished shell: harp.

2 Analyze Cause-and-Effect Relationships *What does Odysseus fear will be the effect of his slaughter of the suitors?*

3 Plot *How is Homer introducing rising tension?*

Writing Practice

SMALL GROUP **Point of View** Pair up students and have them reread the conversation between Odysseus and Penelope on these pages. Explain that Penelope is not sure that Odysseus is the husband she once loved. While he feels she is cold-hearted, she is wisely cautious. Explain that Penelope hides her reactions and thought processes beneath her formality. Have students write a journal entry from Penelope's point of view about her internal conflicts as she keeps "aloof" from Odysseus. Students might write their entries in the form of a dialogue between her head and her heart.

for singing, for the sway and beat of dancing,
until they made the manor hall resound
with gaiety of men and grace of women.
Anyone passing on the road would say:

"Married at last, I see—the queen so many courted.
Sly, cattish wife! She would not keep—not she!—
the lord's estate until he came."

So travelers'
thoughts might run—but no one guessed the truth.
Greathearted Odysseus, home at last,
was being bathed now by Eurynome
and rubbed with golden oil, and clothed again
in a fresh tunic and a cloak. Athena
lent him beauty, head to foot. She made him
taller, and massive, too, with crisping hair
in curls like petals of wild hyacinth
4 but all red-golden. Think of gold infused
on silver by a craftsman, whose fine art
Hephaestus° taught him, or Athena:° one
whose work moves to delight: just so she **lavished**
beauty over Odysseus' head and shoulders.
He sat then in the same chair by the pillar,
facing his silent wife, and said:

"Strange woman,
the immortals of Olympus made you hard,
harder than any. Who else in the world
would keep **aloof** as you do from her husband
if he returned to her from years of trouble,
cast on his own land in the twentieth year?°

Nurse, make up a bed for me to sleep on.
Her heart is iron in her breast."

Penelope
spoke to Odysseus now. She said:

5 "Strange man,
if man you are . . . This is no pride on my part
nor scorn for you—not even wonder, merely.

6 Analyze Cause-and-Effect Relationships *What is Athena doing? Why?*

Vocabulary

lavish (lav′ ish) *v.* to give generously; provide in abundance
aloof (ə lo͞of′) *adj.* emotionally distant; uninvolved; disinterested; standoffish

107 Hephaestus (hi fes′ təs): the god of fire and metalworking. **Athena:** In addition to all her other roles, she was the goddess of arts and crafts.

112–117 Strange . . . year: Finally, after all his other battles have been won, Odysseus must win back his wife. Now he questions and criticizes her with uncharacteristic directness.

Teach

Big Idea 4

Journeys **Ask:** How might Odysseus's appearance have changed since the last time Penelope saw him? *(Twenty years have passed since Penelope last saw Odysseus. Students may say that he will be older. They may also say that he will be hardened from his adventures and possibly scarred from battle.)*

Reading Strategy 5

Analyze Cause-and-Effect Relationships **Ask:** How do you think Penelope's unwillingness to accept Odysseus reflects on her character? *(Students may say that Penelope is a reflection of the Greek ideal of womanhood. She's exceedingly loyal to her husband and very careful not to betray that loyalty.)*

Reading Strategy 6

Analyze Cause-and-Effect Relationships **Answer:** *Athena is having Odysseus bathed and clothed in hopes that Penelope might finally recognize him as the husband she last saw twenty years earlier.*

English Learners

DIFFERENTIATED INSTRUCTION

Early Intermediate Students may have trouble understanding the idioms in the poem as well as figurative and elaborate language. Guide students through these pages by explaining the meaning of the following words and phrases:

- "foresighted in combat" *(line 68; can see what is going to happen ahead of time in battle)*
- "some lighthearted air" *(line 78; happy tune)*
- "did his bidding" *(line 84; did as he said)*
- "made you hard, harder than any" *(lines 113–114; made you meaner than anyone else)*
- "Her heart is iron in her breast." *(line 119; her heart is as hard as iron)*

Teach

Literary Element 1

Plot **Answer:** *Odysseus is outraged that Penelope would have his bed moved outside their bedchamber.*

Ask: How is this scene climactic? *(Students should recognize that tension is at its height while Odysseus waits for Penelope to recognize him. He is home, yet his home and wife are still being denied to him. When he explodes at Penelope, it shows his distress and the action takes a new turn.)*

Big Idea 2

Journeys **Answer:** *She is passionate now, whereas before she had been guarded; she expresses joy and relief from long suffering.*

I know so well how you—how he—appeared
boarding the ship for Troy. But all the same . . .

Make up his bed for him, Eurycleia.°
Place it outside the bedchamber my lord
built with his own hands. Pile the big bed
with fleeces, rugs, and sheets of purest linen."°

With this she tried him to the breaking point,
and he turned on her in a flash raging:

"Woman, by heaven you've stung me now!
Who dared to move my bed?
No builder had the skill for that—unless
a god came down to turn the trick. No mortal
in his best days could budge it with a crowbar.
There is our pact and pledge, our secret sign,
built into that bed—my handiwork
and no one else's!

An old trunk of olive
grew like a pillar on the building plot,
and I laid out our bedroom round that tree,
lined up the stone walls, built the walls and roof,
gave it a doorway and smooth-fitting doors.
Then I lopped off the silvery leaves and branches,
hewed and shaped that stump from the roots up
into a bedpost, drilled it, let it serve
as model for the rest. I planed them all,
inlaid them all with silver, gold and ivory,
and stretched a bed between—a pliant web
of oxhide thongs dyed crimson.

There's our sign!
I know no more. Could someone else's hand
have sawn that trunk and dragged the frame away?"°

Their secret! as she heard it told, her knees
grew tremulous° and weak, her heart failed her.
With eyes brimming tears she ran to him,
throwing her arms around his neck, and kissed him,
murmuring:

"Do not rage at me, Odysseus!
No one ever matched your caution! Think
what difficulty the gods gave: they denied us

127 **Eurycleia** (yoo´ ri klē´ ə)

127–130 **Make up . . . linen:** Sounding sweetly hospitable, Penelope now tests the man who says he is her husband. She proposes that her maid move Odysseus's big bed out of the bedchamber and make it up.

133–155 **Woman, . . . away:** The original bed could not be moved. One bedpost was a tree trunk rooted in the ground, a secret known only by Penelope, a servant, and Odysseus, who built the bed with his own hands. Furious and hurt, Odysseus thinks Penelope has allowed someone to saw the bed frame from the tree.

157 **tremulous:** characterized by trembling; shaky.

1 Plot *How does Odysseus respond to Penelope's suggestion that the maid move the bed outside the bedchamber?*

2 Journeys *How has Penelope's tone shifted? Why?*

Grammar Practice

SMALL GROUP

Noun Clauses Explain to students that a clause (a word group with a subject and verb) can act as a noun. As an example, **write:** Odysseus values whatever shows respect for the gods. Identify the underlined words as a clause; have students replace it with a single noun, such as *honor*.

Explain that like *honor*, the clause *whatever shows respect for the gods* is a direct object telling what Odysseus values. Have students identify two noun clauses in Part 4 and explain whether they function as an object of a preposition, a subject, or a direct object.

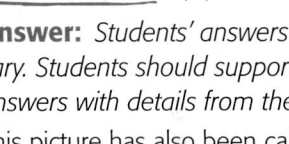

Ulysses and Penelope Embracing, 19th century. Flaxman.

View the Art In ancient Roman tellings of the Trojan War, Odysseus was called Ulysses. How well do you think this image captures the end of the epic? ★

life together in our prime and flowering years,
kept us from crossing into age together.
Forgive me, don't be angry. I could not
welcome you with love on sight! I armed myself
long ago against the frauds of men,
impostors who might come—and all those many
whose underhanded ways bring evil on! . . .
But here and now, what sign could be so clear
as this of our own bed?
No other man has ever laid eyes on it—
only my own slave, Actoris,° that my father
sent with me as a gift—she kept our door.
You make my stiff heart know that I am yours."

Now from his breast into his eyes the ache
of longing mounted, and he wept at last,
his dear wife, clear and faithful, in his arms,
longed for
as the sunwarmed earth is longed for by a swimmer
spent in rough water where his ship went down
under Poseidon's blows, gale winds and tons of sea.
Few men can keep alive through a big surf
to crawl, clotted with brine, on kindly beaches
in joy, in joy, knowing the abyss behind:°
and so she too rejoiced, her gaze upon her husband,
her white arms round him pressed as though forever.

3 *The next day, Odysseus is reunited with his father, Laertes, as news of the death of the suitors passes through town. Families go to Odysseus's manor to gather the bodies for burial. There, Antinous's father rallies the families to avenge the deaths of their sons and brothers. As battle begins, however, Athena appears and calls the island to peace.*

174 Actoris (ak tôr′ is)

181–186 a swimmer . . . behind: Odysseus is compared to someone who swims to shore after a shipwreck. Coated with sea salt (**clotted with brine**), he rejoices that his wife is in his arms and his hellish experience (**the abyss**) is over.

Teach

Big Idea 3

Journeys At last Odysseus's homecoming is complete.

Ask: What do you think the future holds for Odysseus, Penelope, and Telemachus? What role might his past journeys play in Odysseus's future? Do you believe he is home for good? *(Students' answers will vary. They should support their answers with details from the text.)*

View the Art ★

Answer: *Students' answers will vary. Students should support their answers with details from the text.*

This picture has also been called *The Meeting of Ulysses and Penelope*. When the Romans told the story of the Trojan War, they referred to Odysseus as Ulysses. "Ulysses" is a Latin form of Odysseus's name.

To check students' understanding of the selection, see Unit 5 Teaching Resources Book, p. 73.

Approaching Level

DIFFERENTIATED INSTRUCTION

Emerging Help students understand that Odysseus's reaction to his bed being moved out of the bedroom was the "secret sign" (line 50) that Penelope needed to believe that the man standing before her was her husband. Because one bedpost of the tree was rooted in the ground, the bed could not be moved. This detail was known only by Penelope, Odysseus, and a servant. Odysseus thinks that Penelope let someone saw the bed from the trunk in order to move it, and he is deeply hurt and angry. His reaction shows Penelope that he is indeed the husband she lost twenty years ago.

After You Read

Assess

1. Some students will think it savage; others will think it just.
2. (a) Eurymachus asks Odysseus to spare his people. (b) Odysseus feels that their crimes cannot be repaid with material wealth; he is determined to even the score.
3. (a) The nurse sees a familiar scar. Telemachus urges Penelope to talk with him to be convinced. (b) After so many years, it is hard for her to accept him as real; she thinks the gods are meddling.
4. (a) He cannot use strength or cunning to win her. He must earn her trust. (b) Remembering the secret of how their bedpost was rooted in the ground
5. (a) His first speech is diplomatic, reasonable; he pledges to reimburse Odysseus. His second speech urges the suitors to join him in attacking Odysseus. (b) Most students will say that the second plea represents the "real" Eurymachus.
6. (a) He is a young man who has grown up without a father and is eager to please him. (b) He is a brave fighter, but he has a long way to go before acquiring Odysseus's abilities.
7. He proves to be a courageous, curious, cunning, and resourceful survivor.
8. Most students might agree that people still take revenge but in forms such as litigation. Odysseus's revenge is savage and gory by today's standards.

After You Read

Respond and Think Critically

Respond and Interpret

1. What do you think of the way in which Odysseus deals with the suitors?
2. (a)How does Eurymachus attempt to avert bloodshed? (b)How does Odysseus respond?
3. (a)How do the nurse and Telemachus try to convince Penelope that the stranger is Odysseus? (b)Why might Penelope be unclear about what to do?
4. (a)How is proving himself to his wife different from the other challenges Odysseus has faced? (b)What enables him to meet this challenge?

Analyze and Evaluate

5. (a)Compare Eurymachus's first speech to Odysseus with his second plea to the suitors. (b)Which do you think represents the "real" Eurymachus?
6. (a)What kind of person is Telemachus? (b)How does he compare with his father?

Connect

7. **Big Idea** **Journeys** How have Odysseus's adventures shaped his character?
8. **Connect to Today** Do you believe that Odysseus's desire for revenge is common in society today? Explain.

Daily Life & Culture

Ancient Greece and Family Roles

The geography of ancient Greece created isolation. The sea and the mountainous terrain hindered travel between city-states. The simple herding lifestyle and warlike character of the Achaeans (who comprise the characters of the *Odyssey*) prevented permanent alliances between the independent city-states. Although the *Iliad* tells how Greeks from many city-states joined to fight a common foe, citizens felt loyalty only to their city or kingdom.

The households of aristocratic families included husband, wife, and children as well as members of the extended family and servants and slaves. All men, including the noblemen, were familiar with the physical tasks of daily life, including plowing and caring for animals. An important chieftain such as Odysseus, however, would have rarely spent time in such lowly occupations.

Women in ancient Greece were not considered equal to men. Marriages were arranged by men for political or social reasons. A woman had little say in the matter. A noblewoman might spend her days managing her household or working at crafts such as weaving or embroidery.

Discuss the following questions with your classmates.

1. Why might geographical and political isolation have made a journey like Odysseus's difficult?
2. What evidence do you find in the *Odyssey* to confirm that women were not considered of equal status to men?

Daily Life & Culture

1. Many of the people on islands and in the cities might never have heard of his homeland or might have been at war with it. As a result, people might send a traveler in the wrong direction or hinder his return.
2. Although Penelope is an important woman—the wife of a king—there is no question that she must marry one of the suitors. She does not have the power simply to refuse.

For additional selection assessment, see Assessment Resources, pp. 191–192.

Literary Element Plot

In a story or epic narrative, the **climax** is the moment when the events of the plot reach an emotional high point and the action takes a new turn. Very often this is also the moment of greatest interest or excitement for the reader. In a long work such as the *Odyssey,* there may be more than one climax.

1. What is the climax of "Death in the Great Hall"? What is the climax of "The Trunk of the Olive Tree"?
2. Which of these climaxes could be considered the climax of the epic as a whole? Explain your answer.

Review: Narrator

As you learned on pages 184–185, a **narrator** is the person who tells a story. An epic poem is narrated in predictable ways. For example, a poet-narrator may start out with an invocation that states the tale's subject and asks for inspiration from a guiding spirit. The narration may begin in the "middle of things," describing what is happening after certain important events have already occurred. The *Odyssey* has two principal narrators: Odysseus and the poet.

Partner Activity Meet with a classmate and go through the text to decide which events are narrated by Odysseus and which by the poet. Then designate one of you to be Odysseus and one to be the poet. Take turns narrating the sections assigned to you in your own words. Use note cards to help you recall details.

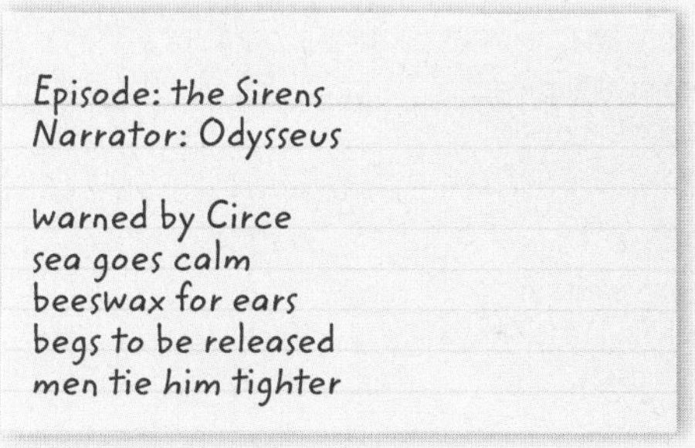

Reading Strategy Analyze Cause-and-Effect Relationships

ACT Skills Practice

1. By unraveling her shroud every evening, Penelope:
   I. initiates the massacre in the Great Hall.
   II. postpones having to choose a husband.
   III. devises a scheme to recognize Odysseus.

   A. I only
   B. II only
   C. I and II only
   D. II and III only

Vocabulary Practice

Practice with Word Origins Studying the etymology, or origin and history, of a word can help you better understand and explore its meaning. Create a word map, like the one below, for each of these vocabulary words from the selection. Use a dictionary for help.

jostle **implacable** **lavish** **aloof**

Example:

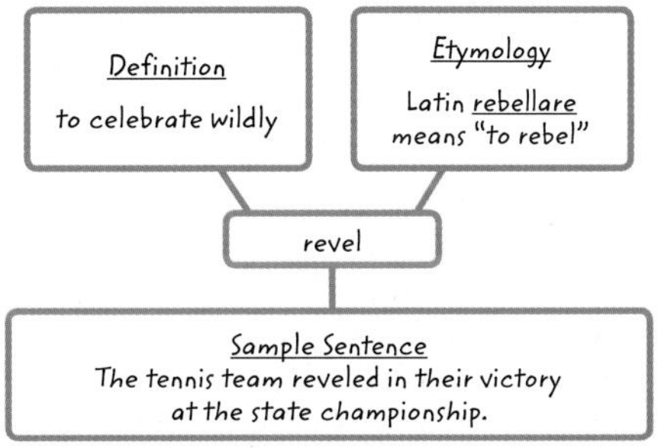

LOG ON **Literature** Online

Selection Resources For Selection Quizzes, eFlashcards, and Reading-Writing Connection activities, go to glencoe.com and enter QuickPass code GL49787u5.

After You Read

Assess

Literary Element

1. "Death in the Great Hall": line 85, when the battle begins in earnest; "The Trunk of the Olive Tree": line 133, when Odysseus rages against Penelope
2. The conflict that results in Odysseus's acceptance by Penelope and brings the whole epic to a successful close, for it restores home and hearth—the things he sought and has come to value most.

Progress Check

Can students identify plot?

If No → See Unit 5 Teaching Resources Book, p. 68.

Review: Narrator

Challenge students to explore how the passages spoken by Odysseus differ in tone from those retold by the narrator.

Reading Strategy

1. B is the correct answer. Penelope has told the suitors that she will choose a husband only when her shroud is complete.

Vocabulary

jostle definition: to bump or shove roughly; etymology: Latin juxta "near"

implacable definition: impossible to satisfy; etymology: Latin implacabilis "not placable"

lavish definition: to give in abundance; etymology: Middle French laver "to wash"

aloof definition: standoffish; etymology: Dutch te loef "to windward"

Progress Check

Can students analyze cause-and-effect relationships?

If No → See Unit 5 Teaching Resources Book, p. 69.

After You Read

Assess

Respond Through Writing

Students' essays should

- identify the major themes in the *Odyssey*
- note how the themes are addressed through the plot
- argue whether or not the *Odyssey* is relevant reading for students today
- support their position with evidence
- use persuasive techniques in presenting their position
- be written for a student Internet audience

For grammar practice, see Unit 5 Teaching Resources Book, p. 72.

To create custom assessments online, go to Progress Reporter Online Assessment.

To create custom assessments using software, use ExamView Assessment Suite.

Respond Through Writing

Review

Convince an Audience Do the major themes in the *Odyssey* apply to life today? Write a review for a Web site that lists recommended reading for students. In your review, answer the question above and support your opinion.

Understand the Task A **theme** is the main idea or message of a story, poem, novel, or play often expressed as a general statement about life.

Prewrite What are the larger or more universal ideas explored in the *Odyssey*? Brainstorm notes about the various themes in the epic. Which of these themes are most important to the epic poem? From your notes, identify the poem's main themes. Then, list the ways these main themes are addressed through the plot. How do the plot's major events relate to the poem's main themes? How do Odysseus's actions reflect the main themes?

After making your own notes on theme and plot, discuss your ideas with a partner. Talk about whether the themes you have listed apply to life today. Are the lessons learned by Odysseus still relevant? Share your opinions and use the discussion to test and explore your ideas.

Using your notes and what you learned in your discussion, make a plan for writing your essay. Write a clear thesis statement addressing the question of whether the *Odyssey* is relevant reading for students. Choose the themes and plot events that you will use to support your position.

Draft Structure your draft around your plan. Make sure to support your argument with evidence of the poem's relevance or irrelevance to students today. Present your arguments and evidence using persuasive techniques that appeal to readers emotions, logic, or ethics.

Revise Review your essay. Does it respond to the opposing arguments that came up in your partner discussion? If necessary, revise the essay to ensure that readers' concerns and opposing arguments are directly addressed.

Edit and Proofread Proofread your paper, correcting any errors in grammar, spelling, and punctuation. Review the Grammar Tip in the side column on sentence fragments before you proofread your essay.

Learning Objectives

In this assignment, you will focus on the following objectives:

Writing: Writing a review.

Grammar: Understanding how and when to use sentence fragments for effect.

Grammar Tip

Sentence Fragments

Sentence fragments are incomplete sentences that are punctuated as if they are complete. Fragments are often missing either a subject or a verb.

Example:

Ran down the hall.
The tall vase from my mom.

Although it is best to avoid fragments when writing, fragments can sometimes be used by writers to create a special effect. For example, fragments can be used in dialogue for dramatic effect.

Example:

"In his own home?!"
"Yes! Just walked right in!"

Grammar Practice

SMALL GROUP

Subordinate Clauses Remind students that subordinate clauses begin with a subordinate conjunction *(e.g., although, because, since, wherever, while)*. A subordinate clause must be attached to an independent clause—otherwise it is a sentence fragment.

Write: Because the play is this evening, our principal dismissed school early today. Explain that "Because the play is this evening" is a subordinate clause and "our principal dismissed school early today" is an independent clause. Have students write an independent clause to go with each of these subordinate clauses.

- While we were waiting . . .
- Since I was a child . . .
- . . . although I will never forget it.

Vocabulary Workshop

Word Origins: Words from Greek and Roman Mythology

Learning Objectives

In this workshop, you will focus on the following objective:

Vocabulary: Understanding word origins.

Literature Connection In Homer's story, Sirens are creatures who lure sailors off their course and onto dangerous rocks by singing.

"Soon,
as we came smartly within hailing distance,
the two Sirens, noting our fast ship
off their point, made ready, and they sang. . . ."

—Homer, the *Odyssey*

Today we use the word *siren* to refer to a type of alarm. Although its meaning has changed, the word *siren,* like many English words, originated in Greek and Roman myth.

This chart shows the Greek or Roman origin of five adjectives in the English language.

Word	Origin	Meaning Today
herculean	from Hercules, the Greek hero, whose twelve labors demonstrated his strength	demonstrating great strength, perseverance, or determination
jovial	from Jove or Jupiter, the Roman god of light, the sky, and weather	good humored; jolly
martial	from Mars, the Roman god of war	warlike; relating to war
mercurial	from Mercury, the Roman god of business and travel, known for his shrewdness	characterized by unpredictable and quickly changing moods
narcissistic	from Narcissus, the Greek youth who fell in love with his reflection	self-loving; egocentric

Etymology
The *etymology* of a word is its origin. Etymologies can usually be found in brackets in a dictionary entry.

Tip
Always apply your knowledge of word history when you encounter unfamiliar words while reading passages or when you have to choose a correct meaning on a multiple-choice test.

Practice Answer the following questions.

1. Write one modern English word that comes from or is related to each of the following words from the *Odyssey: muse, Olympus, Chronus*. Use a dictionary if you need help.
2. Find the etymology for each of these words from Greek or Roman myth. Write the word's meaning and its origin.
   a. atlas **b.** cereal **c.** mentor

LOG ON **Literature Online**

Vocabulary For more vocabulary practice, go to glencoe.com and enter QuickPass code GL49787u5.

English Learners

DIFFERENTIATED INSTRUCTION

Intermediate Explain to students that a word's etymology can be found in a dictionary beside the word. Have students use dictionaries to look up the etymology of words. For example, have students look up the etymology of the word *volcano*. The dictionary states that *volcano* comes from Vulcan. Explain to students the the word *volcano* originates from Vulcan, the Roman god of fire and metalworking. Today, a volcano is more commonly known as a vent in the Earth's crust that issues molten rock, steam, and lava. *Volcanic* means "relating to or produced by a volcano."

Ask: How are these words derived from the Roman word Vulcan? *(Students may answer that volcanoes are vents to hot lava, which relates to the god of fire.)*

Focus

Write on the board:

Word: Siren; Word Origin: Sirens of Greek myth; Meaning Today: alarm. Ask students to consider how the Sirens of Greek mythology evolved into today's meaning.

Teach

Word Origins

Have students add the word origin chart on page 899 to their vocabulary lists. Suggest that students organize all their *Odyssey* vocabulary in this manner.

Assess

1. muse—museum, music; Olympus—Olympics, Olympian; Chronus—chronology, chronometer
2. **a.** atlas—a bound book of maps; from Atlas, a Titan, who supports the world on his shoulders
   b. cereal—a grain; from Ceres, the Roman goddess of agriculture
   c. mentor—coach or tutor; from Mentor, Odysseus's friend who was to educate his son, Telemachus

Focus

Bellringer Options

Selection Focus Transparency 35

Daily Language Practice Transparency 85

Or **write on the board:** Do you think it's harder to be the person who leaves for a journey or the person who is left behind? Discuss times when students have been away from home and what it felt like to leave. Then, discuss what it was like to stay when someone they knew left. Prompt students to consider the benefits and drawbacks of both experiences.

Connect to the Reading Selections

Allow students to share their responses to the opening question. Then have students discuss what they already know about C. P. Cavafy, Edna St. Vincent Millay, and Margaret Atwood.

Comparing Literature

Across Genres

Learning Objectives

For pages 900–906

In studying these texts, you will focus on the following objectives:

Reading: Comparing theme. Comparing author's meaning.

Compare Literature About a Classic Story

Have you ever found a character or setting from a literary work particularly inspiring? C. P. Cavafy, Edna St. Vincent Millay, and Margaret Atwood use characters and settings from Homer's classic epic, the *Odyssey*, in their works. Different aspects of the *Odyssey* have inspired these writers to give their own twist to this classic story.

COMPARE THE Big Idea Journeys

The first two selections present the journey from the viewpoint of the traveler, while the other two relate to the person awaiting the traveler's return. As you read, ask yourself, In what ways are journeys important to each of these selections?

COMPARE Theme

Although the writers of the following selections draw their subject matter from the same source, each work has its own theme. As you read, ask yourself, How does each writer illustrate his or her understanding of life?

COMPARE Author's Meaning

In the selections that follow, Edna St. Vincent Millay, C. P. Cavafy, and Margaret Atwood allude to the characters, places, and events in the *Odyssey*. As you read, ask yourself, What is the underlying meaning behind each author's references to the *Odyssey*?

Statuette of Ulysses. Roman. Bronze. Bibliotheque Nationale, Paris.

LOG ON **Literature** Online

Author Search For more about the authors, go to glencoe.com and enter QuickPass code GL49787u5.

Selection Skills

Comparing Literature

Literary Elements
- Compare Theme (SE pp. 900, 906)
- Allusion (TE pp. 903, 904)

Writing Skills/Grammar
- Use Symbols (TE p. 902)
- Point of View (TE p. 904)

Reading Skills
- Analyze Cause and Effect (TE p. 905)

Listening/Speaking/Viewing Skills
- Discuss Author's Meaning (SE p. 906)

Build Background

Through her poetry and her life, Edna St. Vincent Millay came to represent the rebellious, independent, youthful spirit of the 1920s. She is known for her lyrical poems as well as for her striking imagery. Her poetry expresses personal joys and sorrows in strict verse form.

An Ancient Gesture

Edna St. Vincent Millay

I thought, as I wiped my eyes on the corner of my apron:
Penelope did this too.
And more than once: you can't keep weaving all day
And undoing it all through the night;
Your arms get tired, and the back of your neck gets tight;
And along towards morning, when you think it will never be light,
And your husband has been gone, and you don't know where, for years,
Suddenly you burst into tears;
There is simply nothing else to do.

And I thought, as I wiped my eyes on the corner of my apron:
This is an ancient gesture, authentic, antique,
In the very best tradition, classic, Greek;
Ulysses[1] did this too.
But only as a gesture,—a gesture which implied
To the assembled throng that he was much too moved to speak.
He learned it from Penelope . . .
Penelope, who really cried.

1. Ulysses (ū lis′ ēz) was the Roman name for the Greek hero Odysseus.

Quickwrite

Think of a gesture or other action that has special significance for you. Write a paragraph describing this gesture and its meanings and associations.

Comparing Literature

Teach

Reading Strategy

Predict Have students read the first two lines of the poem. Ask them to predict what they think the poem will be about. Discuss with students how the allusion to Penelope influences their predictions.

APPROACHING Have approaching-level students note their predictions so they can check their accuracy when they are done reading the poem.

Quickwrite

Students' responses should demonstrate an understanding of the concept of gestures as physical movements that communicate meaning or emotion.

Approaching Level

DIFFERENTIATED INSTRUCTION

Emerging Point out that students will be able to compare themes, meanings, and journeys, as explained on this page. Tell students to write down comparisons they can make to the *Odyssey* and to the other poems.

Established Have a student read the paragraph under "Compare Literature About a Classic Story." The poets on the following pages have used characters from Homer's *Odyssey.* Encourage students to discuss ways in which they have been inspired by characters and settings from the *Odyssey.*

Comparing Literature

Teach

Big Idea 1

Journeys **Ask:** If the journey to Ithaca is a metaphor, what journey might it represent? *(Answers will vary. Students may say that it's about enjoying the larger journey of life and not focusing just on the end goal.)*

Literary Element 2

Allusion **Ask:** What do the allusions to the "journey to Ithaca" and to the giants and god of the sea bring to mind? *(Odysseus's disastrous encounters with beings and gods)*

Ask: How do they affect the view of the journey the speaker describes? *(They suggest that difficulty will come to those who stop appreciating the beauty life offers or whose thoughts do not "remain lofty.")*

Build Background

Constantine Cavafy (1863–1933) was a Greek poet who spent most of his life in the Egyptian city of Alexandria, where he was born. During his lifetime he published few poems and received little literary acclaim, but he is now regarded as the finest Greek poet of the twentieth century. In his writing, Cavafy reintroduced literary forms that had rarely been used since the time of the ancient Greeks. With its classical themes and subjects, much of Cavafy's poetry reflects his interest in ancient Greek and Roman culture.

ITHACA

C. P. Cavafy
Translated by Rae Dalven

Ulysses Returns Chryseis to Her Father. Claude Lorrain. Collection of Louvre, Paris.

1 When you start on your journey to Ithaca,
then pray that the road is long,
full of adventure, full of knowledge.
2 Do not fear the Lestrygonians
and the Cyclopes and the angry Poseidon.
You will never meet such as these on your path,

Writing Practice

Use Symbols Explain to students that in "Ithaca," the author has created a number of symbols for everyday life. Ithaca itself is a symbol for life. The Cyclopes and angry Poseidon are symbols for internal struggles and obstacles. **Ask:** What might you use as a symbol for your own life? How might you create a poem around that symbol? *(Students may answer that they would use books in progress, a journey, or a year with season changes.)* Tell students to come up with a symbol for life. Then, have them write a paragraph about their symbol for life.

if your thoughts remain lofty, if a fine
emotion touches your body and your spirit.
You will never meet the Lestrygonians,
the Cyclopes and the fierce Poseidon,
if you do not carry them within your soul,
if your soul does not raise them up before you.

Then pray that the road is long.
That the summer mornings are many,
that you will enter ports seen for the first time
with such pleasure, with such joy!
Stop at Phoenician markets, ☆
and purchase fine merchandise,
mother-of-pearl and corals, amber and ebony,
and pleasurable perfumes of all kinds,
buy as many pleasurable perfumes as you can;
visit hosts of Egyptian cities,
to learn and learn from those who have knowledge.

Always keep Ithaca fixed in your mind.
To arrive there is your ultimate goal.
But do not hurry the voyage at all.
It is better to let it last for long years;
and even to anchor at the isle when you are old,
rich with all that you have gained on the way,
not expecting that Ithaca will offer you riches.

Ithaca has given you the beautiful voyage.
Without her you would never have taken the road.
But she has nothing more to give you.

And if you find her poor, Ithaca has not defrauded you.
With the great wisdom you have gained, with so much experience,
you must surely have understood by then what Ithacas mean.

Quickwrite

Cavafy uses many symbols in this poem. Symbols are objects, places, or experiences that represent something other than what they mean literally. Write a paragraph in which you discuss the symbols you find most important in the poem. What do you think they stand for? How do they contribute to the overall message of the poem?

Comparing Literature

Teach

Cultural History ☆

Phoenicians The Phoenicians had a large impact on many societies. The Phoenicians were traders and sailors who dominated the Mediterranean area for centuries. Although most of their writings were lost when they were conquered, the Phoenicians were responsible for creation of the modern alphabet.

Quickwrite

Students should discuss two or more symbols from "Ithaca." Students might discuss how Cavafy gives the Lestrygonians, the Cyclopes, and Poseidon new meaning by indicating that they are symbols of internal enemies, enemies in a person's soul.

English Learners

DIFFERENTIATED INSTRUCTION

Intermediate Some of the language and symbolism found in these poems can be overwhelming for students who are learning the English language. Remind students that it can help them to read a poem twice: first for meaning and then for rhythm and literary techniques. Have students read through the poems carefully and take notes about difficult words and symbols. Students may struggle with the last stanza of "Ithaca." Have a student read the last stanza aloud. **Ask:** What does *Ithaca* mean? What is Ithaca a symbol for? *(Students may answer that Ithaca is a symbol for life, life experience, or old age.)* Explain to students that this is shown in lines such as "It is better to let it last for long years."

Teach

Literary Element 1

Allusion The speaker alludes to the chariot of Helios and the silver boat of Artemis. **Ask:** What does the speaker reveal about herself with these allusions? *(Answers will vary, but students should note that the speaker believes in Greek mythology and probably lives in a time and place where that belief was prevalent.)*

ADVANCED Have advanced level students research these elements of Greek mythology and present their findings to the class.

Readability Scores

Dale-Chall: 7.9
DRP: 59
Lexile: 910

Build Background

In *The Penelopiad*, Margaret Atwood retells the story of the *Odyssey* from Penelope's point of view. Atwood writes, "Homer's *Odyssey* is not the only version of the story." The tale of Odysseus, she explains, came out of Greek oral tradition, which means that the myth would have been told differently by different storytellers. In the role of storyteller, she provides a new version of the tale.

WAITING from The Penelopiad

Margaret Atwood

Penelope. Sir Frank Dicksee. Watercolour on paper. Private collection.

What can I tell you about the next ten years? Odysseus sailed away to Troy. I stayed in Ithaca. The sun rose, traveled across the sky, set. Only sometimes did I think of it as the flaming chariot of Helios.[1] The moon did the same, changing from phase to phase. Only sometimes did I think of it as the silver boat of Artemis.[2] Spring, summer, fall, and winter followed one another in their appointed rounds. Quite often the wind blew. Telemachus grew from year to year, eating a lot of meat, indulged by all.

We had news of how the war with Troy was going: sometimes well, sometimes badly. Minstrels sang songs about the notable heroes—Achilles, Ajax, Agamemnon, Menelaus, Hector, Aeneas,[3] and the rest. I didn't care about them: I waited only for news of Odysseus. When would he come back and relieve my boredom? He too appeared in the songs, and I relished those moments. There he was making an inspiring speech, there he was uniting the quarreling factions,[4] there he was inventing an astonishing falsehood, there he was delivering sage advice, there he was disguising himself as a runaway slave and sneaking into Troy and speaking with Helen[5] herself, who—the song proclaimed—had bathed him and anointed him with her very own hands.

I wasn't so fond of that part.

Finally, there he was, concocting the stratagem of the wooden horse filled with

1. *Helios* is the Greek god of the sun.
2. *Artemis* is the Greek goddess of the Moon.
3. These men were the heroes of Homer's *Iliad*, his account of the battle of Troy.
4. A *faction* is a small group within a larger group.
5. *Helen* refers to Helen of Troy, who was, according to myth, the most beautiful woman in Greece and the cause of the Trojan war.

Writing Practice

Point of View Tell students that writing stories from the *Odyssey* from Penelope's point of view drastically changes the events. Because the reader knows what happened in the *Odyssey* from Odysseus's point of view, some of the things that are said from Penelope's point of view are humorous. Break students into pairs, and have each pair think of a story. They can use something that happened in their lives or something from the *Odyssey.* Each student in the pair should describe the events of the story from a different point of view.

soldiers.[6] And then—the news flashed from beacon to beacon—Troy had fallen. There were reports of a great slaughtering and looting in the city. The streets ran red with blood, the sky above the palace turned to fire; innocent boy children were thrown off a cliff, and the Trojan women were parceled out as plunder, King Priam's daughters among them. And then, finally, the hoped-for news arrived: the Greek ships had set sail for home.

And then, nothing.

Day after day I would climb up to the top floor of the palace and look out over the harbor. Day after day there was no sign. Sometimes there were ships, but never the ship I longed to see.

Rumors came, carried by other ships. Odysseus and his men had got drunk at their first port of call and the men had mutinied, said some; no, said others, they'd eaten a magic plant that had caused them to lose their memories, and Odysseus had saved them by having them tied up and carried onto the ships. Odysseus had been in a fight with a giant one-eyed Cyclops, said some; no, it was only a one-eyed tavern keeper, said another, and the fight was over non-payment of the bill. Some of the men had been eaten by cannibals, said some; no, it was just a brawl of the usual kind, said others, with ear-bitings and nosebleeds and stabbings and eviscerations.[7] Odysseus was the guest of a goddess on an enchanted isle, said some; she'd turned his men into pigs—not a hard job in my view—but had turned them back into men because she'd fallen in love with him and was feeding him unheard-of delicacies prepared by her own immortal hands; no, said others, he was sponging off[8] the woman.

Needless to say, the minstrels took up these themes and embroidered them considerably. They always sang the noblest versions in my presence—the ones in which Odysseus was clever, brave, and resourceful, and battling supernatural monsters, and beloved of goddesses. The only reason he hadn't come back home was that a god—the sea-god Poseidon, according to some—was against him, because a Cyclops crippled by Odysseus was his son. Or several gods were against him. Or the Fates. Or something. For surely—the minstrels implied, by way of praising me—only a strong divine power could keep my husband from rushing back as quickly as possible into my loving—and lovely—wifely arms. **2**

The more thickly they laid it on, the more costly were the gifts they expected from me. I always complied. Even an obvious fabrication[9] is some comfort when you have few others. **3**

6. The *wooden horse* refers to Odysseus's successful plan to get inside the fortress at Troy by building a gigantic wooden horse and offering it as a gift of peace. The Trojans accepted the gift, not knowing that Greek soldiers were hiding inside it.
7. *Evisceration* means "the removal of internal organs."
8. Here, *sponging off* means "living at the expense of."
9. A *fabrication* is a lie or a made-up story.

Quickwrite

What impression do you have of Penelope's character after reading this selection? Write a paragraph addressing how Atwood's version of Penelope's point of view affects your impression of the events and characters in the *Odyssey*.

Teach

Big Idea 2

Journeys Ask: How does the speaker handle the rumors about what has been delaying Odysseus? *(The speaker points out the contradictions in the rumors. She makes humorous asides. Students should infer that she doesn't take any of the rumors very seriously.)*

Reading Strategy 3

Analyze Cause-and-Effect Relationships Instruct students to read the last sentence of the story. **Ask:** What effect has Odysseus's absence had on the speaker? *(Students may say that despite the humor, the speaker despairs because of Odysseus's absence. Others may feel that she has grown stronger as a result of his absence.)*

Quickwrite

Students should cite the differences in the story of the *Odyssey* as told from different viewpoints. For example, when told with Odysseus as the central figure, the story is an epic tale of heroism. When told from Penelope's point of view, Odysseus's adventures can be exaggerated to make them seem dangerous.

English Learners

DIFFERENTIATED INSTRUCTION

Intermediate Have a student read aloud the paragraph that begins "Rumors came, carried by other ships." Explain to students that the author is using events that happened in the *Odyssey* to make a statement about what Penelope may have heard. **Say:** Recall the sequence of events that happened during the *Odyssey*. **Ask:** What from this paragraph do you remember from the *Odyssey?* *(Students may answer that they remember Circe turning the men into pigs or Odysseus fighting Polyphemus.)* Point out that without understanding that these events are from the *Odyssey,* it would be difficult to understand this story told from Penelope's point of view.

Wrap-Up: Comparing Literature

Across Genres

Assess

Compare the Big Idea

Possible student answers:

"An Ancient Gesture"—Who: wife's husband; Purpose: fame and recognition; Attitude: sorrowful, lonely. "Ithaca"—Who: reader; Purpose: self-discovery; Attitude: welcoming. "Waiting"—Who: Odysseus; Purpose: to get home; Attitude: skeptical, doubtful.

Compare Theme

The theme of "Ithaca" is that life is an exciting journey and should be enjoyed, since much of our fate is shaped by our own decisions. The message of "An Ancient Gesture" is that a common expressive gesture in times of hardship draws people together in an ancient tradition. A theme of "Waiting" is that those long anticipating a traveler's return accept tall tales and false comfort to escape boredom and worry.

Wrap-Up: Comparing Literature

Across Genres

- from the *Odyssey* by Homer
- *An Ancient Gesture* by Edna St. Vincent Millay
- *Ithaca* by C. P. Cavafy
- *Waiting* from *The Penelopiad* by Margaret Atwood

Julia at Start Point, Devon, 1992. Robert O'Rorke. Oil on canvas, 17 x 21 in. London.

COMPARE THE Big Idea Journeys

Writing What role do journeys play in each of these selections? In what ways are the journeys similar? In what ways are they different? Create a chart to organize your ideas about the ways journeys are important to each of these selections. Then write a short essay comparing and contrasting the role of the Big Idea in the selections.

Selection	Who is Traveling?	Purpose of Journey	Speaker's Attitude
Odyssey	Odysseus	to return home	
An Ancient Gesture			
Ithaca			
Waiting			

COMPARE Theme

Speaking and Listening With a partner, discuss the themes of each of the selections. In your discussion, address the following questions, referring to specific places in the texts to support your answers:

1. What attitudes about life and human nature does each work convey?
2. How are these attitudes similar or different?

Then present a formal report to share your ideas with the rest of the class.

COMPARE Author's Meaning

Group Activity In a small group, discuss the author's overall meaning in each selection. Then work separately, each looking closely at the action or actions of one character in one of the selections. What do you think the author means to tell the reader by describing this action in the way he or she does? Meet with your group to share your ideas.

LOG ON **Literature** Online

Selection Resources For Selection Quizzes, eFlashcards, and Reading-Writing Connection activities, go to glencoe.com and enter QuickPass code GL49787u5.

Compare Author's Meaning

Cavafy develops the symbolic journey in the poem and imbues it with vivid historical associations. Millay bestows a sense of timelessness and expressive power upon a traditional feminine gesture. Atwood brings to life the world of the *Odyssey* from Penelope's point of view. As students examine one character, they should support their conclusions with examples.

Learning Objectives

For pages 907–911

In studying this text, you will focus on the following objectives:

Reading:
Analyzing informational text.
Responding to events.

Set a Purpose for Reading

Read to discover the purpose and outcome of one woman's journey.

Preview the Article

1. Read the *deck,* or the sentence in large type that appears below the title. What do you predict the outcome of this article will be?
2. Scan the captions to the photographs. In your opinion, what do they reveal about the girl in the photographs?

Reading Strategy Respond to Events

Responding to events involves telling what you like, dislike, or find interesting or surprising about the events in a selection. As you read "Leaving it All Behind," ask yourself, What is my response to the events described in the article? Use a graphic organizer like the one below to take notes on the events that occur and how you respond to them.

Events	Response

TIME

Leaving it All Behind

With $100 in her pocket, a teenage girl bids farewell to life in rural China and heads to the big city in search of work.

By SUSAN JAKES

FOR THE FIRST 20 MINUTES OF HER NEW LIFE IN Shenzhen, Mo Yunxiu stood perfectly still. Behind her, sleeper coaches rolled, groaning into the city's crowded bus depot. Ahead stretched a tangle of freeways, already teeming at 10 a.m. on a Sunday. A plastic bag containing a package of sour plums, a water bottle, and the remains of a loaf of sliced bread—snacks left over from the overnight ride—hung from her left wrist. Her right hand gripped the handle of a small suitcase on wheels, and she leaned against it stiffly, as if for support.

The Promise of the City

Mo said nothing, but it was clear that she had a lot on her mind. She was 17 years old, and farther from her farm in Guangxi province than she'd ever been. She knew no one in Shenzhen, and had nowhere specific to go. This was a place she'd dreamed about. She had seen pictures of Shenzhen's high-tech factories on television, and she pictured herself working in one, wearing a smart uniform and making a good salary. But her dream had left out the scenes between the arrival of her bus and her arrival in paradise.

At last, for no discernible reason, Mo moved. She walked uncertainly, and very quietly asked a policeman for directions to the nearest bus stop. There, she stood silently again for 20 minutes, looking at the buses come and go. Finally, she asked a stranger where to find a cheap place to stay. Within minutes Mo was back on a bus, pressing her face to the window, watching the sprawl of her

TIME

Focus

Summary

Susan Jakes tells the story of a Chinese country girl immigrating to the city. Seventeen-year-old Mo wants to find a factory job in the city of Shenzhen. However, she is overwhelmed by the number of factories. Finally, she takes a job as a waitress. As soon as she gets paid, Mo plans to go home and work two jobs.

For summaries in languages other than English, see Unit 5 Teaching Resources Book, pp. 76–81.

Teach

Reading Strategy

Respond to Events Author Susan Jakes says Mo leaned against her suitcase "as if for support." **Ask:** What can you infer about Mo from this? *(Students may say she's nervous.)* How does this detail help you relate to her? *(Students may say that knowing Mo is nervous helps them feel empathy for her right from the beginning.)*

English Learners

DIFFERENTIATED INSTRUCTION

Intermediate Students may understand Mo's feelings of alienation. To interest them in this article, discuss her sense of alienation. **Ask:** Why did Mo stand motionless for 20 minutes? What might Mo have been feeling? *(Students may answer that Mo was in awe of the big city or that she was afraid. She was feeling excited, scared, and overwhelmed.)* Have students discuss how they felt the first time they arrived at a new place, like a big city or a high school. Encourage students to note how they have overcome their own fears about new situations and challenges. Ask students to compare their stories with what they know of Mo's story so far.

Readability Scores

Dale-Chall: 7.9
DRP: 58
Lexile: 920

TIME

Teach

Big Idea 1

Journeys **Ask:** Do you think Mo's decision to leave home with only $100 was brave? Why or why not? *(Some students will say that Mo is from a poor area and this was all she could afford, so she was brave. Others will feel she was foolish not to save more money before attempting such a journey.)*

Cultural History ☆

Shenzhen Shenzhen is located in the Guangdong province in China and borders Hong Kong. In 1979, Shenzhen gained prefecture status, allowing it to be directly governed by the province. This paved the way for the 1980 promotion to China's first "special economic zone (SEZ)." SEZ status allows a province to have different economic laws than are typical for the country. As a result, Shenzhen has become a thriving economic hub.

new home slip by. Our arrival in Shenzhen had been fraught with anticipation: for Mo because she had so much riding on this journey; for me because I was writing about what would happen to her.

I'd told Chinese friends that I wanted to find a country girl lured from her home by the promise of the city. Mo had been introduced to me by her cousin, a tour guide in Yangshuo, a vacation spot on the Li River about 400 miles from Shenzhen. When I met Mo, I thought she was all wrong. I wanted a typical migrant—whatever that meant—and Mo had tinted hair and stylish, bleach-striped jeans. After a three-month stay with her cousin, she already seemed a bit worldly.

Mo had been one of the best students in her middle school, but high school cost $500 a year—nearly seven times her farmer family's annual income. If she got a decent job in ☆ Shenzhen, she figured, she could save enough money in a year or two to attend a vocational school and learn a skill, like computer programming or English, which in turn could get her a better job. She wanted to build a new house for her parents and treat herself to "one of those tape recorders, the kind with the earphones that you can listen to in bed before you fall asleep." She believed Shenzhen had the power to change her life.

I was impressed by Mo's determination—and by her courage. She had only $100 when she boarded the bus in Yangshuo. It seemed to me an incredibly risky proposition, but when I'd pressed her to tell me how she would manage, she just shrugged her shoulders. She'd work it out when she got there. "Bu yaojin," Mo would often say: "It's not serious." **1**

But now that she'd arrived in Shenzhen, it all felt very serious. I started to worry that the trip had been a mistake. Mark Leong, the photographer, and I had agreed to try our best to observe Mo without interfering in her decisions; we'd agreed to intercede only if we thought she was putting herself in danger. Now we wondered if we'd been irresponsible to put so much faith in the dreams of a 17-year-old who'd never been more than three hours away from home.

NO PLACE LIKE HOME
Mo (in jeans and sneakers) spent one last day at the family farm before joining China's vast migrant workforce.

Saying Good-bye

Two days before leaving Yangshuo for Shenzhen, Mo had returned to her parents' farm to say good-bye. Mo's father, Li Simin, had come to the village of Matou in 1972 to marry. His wife's family had lived in Matou, a village of about 50 households, for generations. Neither of Mo's parents had ever traveled outside Guangxi province. "Being a farmer is relatively difficult," Li told me, but he sounded modestly satisfied with what he'd achieved. The family ate the rice he grew, raised pigs, and grew oranges and pomelos for cash—about $75 most years—and could now afford to eat meat a few times a month.

The mud-brick house was comfortably cool and airy. Its four rooms were clean and furnished with the barest of necessities. The only decorations

Reading Practice

SPIRAL REVIEW **Ask Questions** Tell students that it is common to have questions about articles and stories that deal with other cultures. Explain that when dealing with different cultures, students should generate a list of researchable questions to help them understand what they are reading. Break students into groups. Have each group form a question. **Ask:** What is difficult to understand? What confuses you? *(Possible answers include why school costs $500 yearly, why the family earns $75 yearly, or why Mo has never traveled more than three hours from home.)* Tell students to use the Internet and books to research their question. Have each group share its answer with the class. Answers may include exchange rates, information about farms in China, and information about public schools in China.

INTO THE URBAN JUNGLE
After arriving in Shenzhen, Mo wandered its streets seeking a cheap but safe place to live.

were some calendars tacked to one wall, and a row of Mo's certificates of academic merit hung neatly on another. In the corner sat a television the family bought for about $120 in 2000, its edges still cushioned in blocks of Styrofoam.

Li clearly had a soft spot for his only daughter. But he had no reservations about her decision to move to Shenzhen. "I couldn't leave," he explained, "I didn't have the right requirements. But now things are better. If kids want to go, they can just go." Besides, he added with a small laugh, Mo was stubborn. When she was little she'd once refused to go to school for a whole year.

In the afternoon, Mo took a walk through the fields, showing off the rosebush and the two geraniums she had planted when she was a student. Ever since she could remember, Mo said, she had been told that she lived in one of the world's most beautiful places. Not having ever seen other places, she had been skeptical. But the grandeur of the landscape was unmistakable. The expanse of limestone hills and rice fields made me wonder if she would feel bereft when she left it behind.

Now it was time to leave. I expected an emotional farewell. Instead, Mo simply told her parents that she was leaving, tousled her young niece's hair, and walked toward the road without looking back.

The Job Search

The local Shenzhen bus dropped us off close to the center of downtown. The buildings were more than 20 stories high. When an alley plastered with signs for boardinghouses came into view, I heaved a sigh of relief. The neighborhood looked promising: crowded and poor, but not seedy. Mo's eyes were fixed on the ground. There were people all around, but Mo didn't ask anyone for advice. Once or twice I asked her where she was going: she said she didn't know. Eventually we wound up where we had begun. Mo slipped into the first boardinghouse we'd seen and emerged a few minutes later with her first smile of the day. She'd found a room. It was just big enough to hold a single bed, an electric fan, and a plastic basin for washing clothes. It looked safe. It cost $3 a night.

After lunch, Mo started to look for work. We walked all afternoon along wide roads lined with skyscrapers. I recognized them as luxury apartments, and could tell that we wouldn't find factories in this neighborhood. But Mo couldn't discern this, and I reminded myself that people aren't born with an understanding of how cities work.

Even here, though, Shenzhen revealed itself as a city thriving on migrant labor. At one intersection, we came across a bulletin board full of job announcements, mostly for hotel workers and security guards. The salaries were high—up to $200 per month—and most employers wanted applicants under the age of 30. While Mo studied the board, a couple of men walked up and offered unsolicited advice. "Don't believe these ads," they told her. "They're fakes. They trick you into paying deposits, and then they disappear."

That night, Mo washed one of her three sets of clothes and hung them in my room to dry—hers was too small. "Tomorrow," she said, spreading a Shenzhen map on my bed, "we'll go to Longhua." Earlier this year, a woman from her village had come home and said that she'd worked in a factory in this industrial, Shenzhen satellite town, but that was all Mo knew. "I think Longhua has a lot of factories," said Mo, "but I guess they don't put them on the map." She was wearing a nightgown with a teddy bear **2**
on it, and she looked exhausted and very young.

The next morning, Mo got on the wrong bus and found herself heading in the opposite direction from Longhua. She had wasted a 3-yuan fare, about 40¢. We crossed the street, paid

TIME

Teach

Reading Strategy 2

Respond to Events The author includes the detail (on page 909) that Mo's nightgown has a teddy bear on it. **Ask:** How do you think this detail is intended to help you relate to Mo? *(Students may say that the teddy bear reinforces that Mo is young and makes her seem vulnerable, eliciting sympathy from the reader. Students may also note that this detail reminds them that Mo is near their own age.)*

APPROACHING To help approaching level students, **ask:** Why do you think the author wants readers to sympathize with Mo? *(When readers sympathize with an article's subject, they want to keep reading.)*

Approaching Level

DIFFERENTIATED INSTRUCTION

Emerging Susan Jakes reminds herself that "People aren't born with an understanding of how cities work." **Ask:** Keeping in mind that all cities are different, what does the author mean? *(Students may answer that the author means people have to learn where things are in cities. Even though it seems obvious to the author, Mo has never been in a city before.)*

Established Tell students that Mo took $100 with her to the city. Explain that, although that does not sound like much, her family's salary was $75 a year. Mo saved quite a bit of money before she left on her trip. Her room will cost $3 a night, which means Mo has enough money to pay her rent for about a month.

TIME

Teach

Reading Strategy 1

Respond to Events **Ask:** Why do you think Mo doesn't see the Star River Talent Market sign? *(Students may say that Mo is too carsick, frightened, or overwhelmed to see what's going on around her.)*

APPROACHING To help approaching level students, **ask:** Why do you think the author pointed out that Mo was sitting right in front of the sign and did not see it? *(to show that coming to the city is more confusing than it seems)*

To check students' understanding of the selection, see Unit 5 Teaching Resources Book, p. 83.

another fare, and Mo spent the hour-long ride with her head in her hands, feeling carsick. At the Longhua stop, Mo squatted on the sidewalk for nearly half an hour. Behind her was a giant sign for the Star River Talent Market, an employment agency. For a long time she seemed not
1 to see it.

The Star River office had a giant bulletin board cluttered with hand-painted and computer-printed job listings. Mo wrote down the address of a factory looking for "ordinary workers," and we tried to find it. The search for the Meiyu Electric Works ate up the rest of the day. First we walked, passing factory upon factory with signs on their doors advertising vacancies. Then we took a bus in the wrong direction. We reached Meiyu four hours later on motorcycle taxis. By the time we arrived, the job Mo wanted had been filled.

JOB SEARCH
Mo visited an employment agency, took a motorcycle taxi to a factory, and got lost on buses.

Looking for the bus stop to get back to Shenzhen, Mo got lost again. Eventually, in desperation, she overcame her aversion to asking directions, and we boarded our last bus of the day. By then Mo had spent more than $2 on bus fares. She hadn't had lunch. "Longhua isn't what I'd expected," she said. "I thought it would be smaller and the factories would be easier to find. It's a bad place." Tomorrow, she said, she would stay closer to her base. "There was a moment today," she whispered, "when I didn't think I'd find my way back."

That night, I left Mo and went to find an Internet café. When I called the boardinghouse to say I was on my way back, Mo sounded giddy: "Can I tell you something? While you were out, I found a job." The next morning, she bounced in her chair as she related the story. On the bus back from Longhua, she had spotted a restaurant with a "Help Wanted" sign in the window. Later, she retraced the route, found the restaurant, and waited an hour for the manager. He offered her a waitressing job on the spot. The salary was only 500 yuan, or $60, a month, but the job came with free room and board. "I was so happy last night," said Mo, "I thought I was going to die."

Working Girl

I walked with her to the restaurant, which was on a bustling, tree-lined street. While Mo went inside to put down a 260-yuan ($30) deposit for her uniform, I noticed that the restaurant was open 24 hours a day. There were grandparents playing with babies right outside, and the neighborhood seemed safe. A cab driver said the restaurant was known for 24-hour dim sum, a brunch or light meal.

Mo emerged a few hours later with a shiny tag stamped with her employee number—and an enormous smile. That afternoon, we shopped for necessities. Mo weighed each purchase heavily. She bought a ceramic mug for 3 yuan instead of a 5-yuan plastic mug with a cartoon character. After buying a towel to use as a blanket (22 yuan), she decided she could live without a pillow. A blue plastic bowl to wash her clothes cost 4 yuan—twice as much as it would have been at home, she said. Her one extravagance was a fork. It cost more than a pair of chopsticks, but for some reason she wanted it badly. Her bill for the day came to $5—the most money Mo had ever spent.

Writing Practice

SPIRAL REVIEW **Form an Opinion** Explain to students that after reading this article, some people may think Mo's trip was a failure, while others may feel that it was a success. Ask students to form an opinion about whether they think Mo's trip was successful. Have students write a short essay explaining what they think. Tell students that they must include evidence in their essays. Evidence may include quotes from the story or research.

Ask: What caused you to form your opinion? *(Possible answers for success include that Mo found a job and that she learned about a better way to live and work. Possible answers for failure include that Mo could not make it living in the city and that she worked very hard for a very small salary.)*

After her first day at the restaurant, Mo and I parted ways. A week later, I returned to watch her on the job. She was working up to 11 hours a day, seven days a week. Her feet were sore from standing in the flimsy cloth shoes she had to wear with her uniform; her wrists ached from carrying heavy trays. The older waitresses didn't talk to her except to order her around. She was tired, but it wasn't serious, she said.

As the weeks wore on, her stamina grew but her enthusiasm dimmed. After a solid month of work, she still hadn't received a cent of her salary. She'd decided she wanted to work elsewhere, or just head back to Yangshuo. But, to prevent her leaving, her boss wouldn't pay her and refused to refund the 260-yuan deposit she'd paid him for her uniform. She had no contract. She was trapped.

Just before the end of her second month, we met again. I was shocked at how different Mo looked. Her smile was just as broad, but the ruddiness in her cheeks had gone. She was so pale that her skin had an almost greenish cast. She was now on the night shift, walking the empty streets with a friend after she finished work at 2:30 a.m., then sleeping during the day. But she had a new plan. Her boss—who still had yet to pay her salary—told her he wasn't letting her quit because she was a hard worker. Flattered, Mo reckoned she could take it a little longer until he found someone to replace her. With her usual optimism, she assured me the money would come eventually and that for now she was fine without it. As soon as she was paid, she'd decided, she would head home. **2**

LANDING ON HER FEET
After only two days of searching, Mo found a job—waitressing in a 24-hour dim-sum restaurant.

No Place Like Home

"I've figured it out," she told me exuberantly. "I'll go back to Yangshuo and work two jobs. At night I'll waitress at a café and practice speaking English with the customers, and during the day I'll try to find people to let me be their tour guide." The money, she admitted, might not be as good but at least she would be near her family. She could always return to Shenzhen if she changed her mind, knowing now that she could make it on her own. "Shenzhen was fine," she said, "but home will be better."

—Updated 2005, from TIME Asia, July 26/August 2, 2004

Respond and Think Critically

Respond and Interpret

1. Write a brief summary of the main events in this article before you answer the following questions. For help on writing a summary, see page 42.
2. How do you feel about the journalist Susan Jakes's decision to follow Mo and observe her life?
3. (a)Why did Mo get lost so often? (b)How might she have better prepared for her journey?
4. (a)What happened at Mo's job after two months? (b)Why do you think she reacted the way she did?

Analyze and Evaluate

5. (a)What preconceptions did the writer have about migrant workers? (b)Do you think her preconceptions of migrants interfered with her portrayal of Mo? Why or why not?
6. What details does the writer use to illustrate Mo's youthful and energetic demeanor?

Connect

7. Jakes wrote that Mo "believed Shenzhen had the power to change her life." Based on the outcome of the article, what do you think Mo may have learned from her journey?

For additional selection assessment, see Assessment Resources, pp. 195–196.

TIME

Teach

Big Idea 2

Journeys **Ask:** What is the result of Mo's journey? *(She gets a job as a waitress but doesn't get paid. She plans to go home.)*

Assess

1. Students' summaries should reflect the main idea of the selection.
2. Answers will vary. Some will think it was a good choice.
3. (a) She never asked for directions. (b) She could have learned more about the layout of the city.
4. (a) She still had not been paid. (b) She did not know how to stand up for herself.
5. (a) She has some preconceptions about how they are supposed to behave. (b) Some may feel the author made Mo sound naïve. Others may feel she was objective.
6. She describes Mo's reaction to getting a job as "giddy." She writes that Mo considered buying a "plastic mug with a cartoon character."
7. She may have learned that when you set out to do something, there are a number of unexpected factors that may get in the way of success. She learned the importance of family and that city life may not be for everyone.

Before You Read

Focus

Bellringer Options

Daily Language Practice Transparency 86

Or **ask:** If you could live in a fictional world, where would you live? Prompt students to consider multiple fictional settings, such as the *Star Wars* and Harry Potter worlds. Have students discuss what the allure is of these places and why they chose their particular setting.

Before You Read

Over Hill and Under Hill from *The Hobbit*

World Literature
England

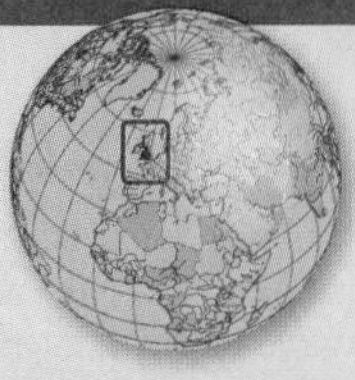

Meet **J. R. R. Tolkien**

(1892–1973)

The Lord of the Rings is probably the most well-known fantasy story ever written and undoubtedly the most important. Even before the award-winning movies were produced, the popular trilogy sold millions of copies. *The Lord of the Rings* trilogy, however, is a sequel to one of J. R. R. Tolkien's most successful works, *The Hobbit*.

A Young Orphan Born in South Africa, Tolkien returned to his parents' birthplace, England, when he was three and a half years old. Tolkien was four when his father died. His mother died a few years later, and a Roman Catholic priest became Tolkien's guardian.

As a young student, Tolkien developed a passion for languages. He studied Latin and Greek and taught himself Welsh, Old and Middle English, Old Norse, Gothic, and Finnish. Eventually, Tolkien became a professor of language and literature at Oxford University. His knowledge and love of languages would help to inspire all of his work. Drawing upon his familiarity with various literatures, he invented entire languages and used them in his stories. In fact, he created a complete world of his own, with a distinctive history and a variety of civilizations.

A Hobbit Is Born One hot summer day while Tolkien was correcting papers at Oxford, his mind began to wander. Soon, he was scribbling in an examination book. He wrote: "In a hole in the ground there lived a hobbit." In Tolkien's imagination, the hobbit was a little creature, reminiscent of a rustic human being, but much smaller, and very fond of his or her comforts and meals.

"I always in writing start with a name. Give me a name and it produces a story, not the other way about normally."

—J. R. R. Tolkien

Fame and Fortune The name *hobbit* went on to inspire first, the imaginary creature, and later, the adventures. Tolkien developed his ideas about the hobbit into a book, which he published in 1937. At first it was popular among children, but Tolkien insisted that children were not the intended audience. Seventeen years later, he published the first volume of *The Lord of the Rings*. By the late 1960s, his fame was widespread. Tolkien fan clubs sprang up all over America and elsewhere.

LOG ON **Literature** Online

Author Search For more about J. R. R. Tolkien, go to glencoe.com and enter QuickPass code GL49787u5.

Selection Skills

Over Hill and Under Hill

Literary Elements
- Motif (SE pp. 913–924)
- Narrator (SE p. 924)

Reading Skills
- Compare and Contrast Characters (SE pp. 913–924)

Vocabulary Skills
- Context Clues (SE p. 924)

Listening/Speaking/Viewing Skills
- Analyze Art (SE pp. 916, 919)
- Visual Literacy (SE p. 923)
- Make Judgments (TE p. 918)

Writing Skills/Grammar
- Expository Essay (SE p. 925)
- Adverbs (SE p. 925)
- Character Development (TE p. 914)

Literature and Reading Preview

Connect to the Story

Why do you think writers and artists create fantastical, imaginary worlds? Discuss the question with a partner.

Build Background

In the book *The Hobbit,* Bilbo Baggins is a hobbit: a small, human-like creature who lives in a hobbit hole. One day, Gandalf, a wise old wizard, asks Bilbo to join him and thirteen dwarves on a great adventure to reclaim the dwarves' treasure. Bilbo, an unlikely hero, does not want to leave his comfortable home, but he sets out with the group on a long journey. In this excerpt, which occurs early in the novel, the group has just left Elrond, the leader of the elves at Rivendell. Elrond has given the group ponies and helpful advice.

Set Purposes for Reading

Big Idea Journeys

As you read, ask yourself, How can a journey be both an adventure and a test?

Literary Element Motif

A **motif** is a significant word, phrase, image, idea, or other element repeated throughout a literary work and related to the theme. Common motifs in hero stories include good and evil and light and darkness. As you read, ask yourself, Are any characters or places associated with light or darkness? Good or evil?

Reading Strategy Compare and Contrast Characters

When you **compare and contrast characters,** you look for similarities and differences in the way characters think, look, and act. You can also compare and contrast the way characters are presented: with great detail or with only a few words. As you read, ask yourself, What similarities and differences do I notice among the characters?

Tip: Make a Chart As you read, use a chart to record the names of main characters and minor characters.

Main Characters	Minor Characters
Gandalf	Elrond

Learning Objectives

For pages 912–924

In studying this text, you will focus on the following objectives:

Literary Study: Analyzing motif.

Reading: Comparing and contrasting characters.

Vocabulary

uncanny (un kan′ē) *adj.* not normal or natural; seemingly supernatural in origin; p. 914 *Ruth could predict the outcome of every football game with uncanny precision.*

paraphernalia (par′ ə fər nāl′ yə) *n.* personal items or equipment; p. 917 *Amanda laid out all her hiking and climbing paraphernalia before deciding what to pack for the expedition.*

ingenious (in jēn′ yəs) *adj.* especially clever, inventive, or original; p. 920 *His solution to their problem was ingenious.*

horde (hôrd) *n.* crowd, throng, or swarm; p. 922 *The horde of angry Vikings swept through the English town, pillaging and destroying houses.*

Before You Read

Focus

Summary

Bilbo the hobbit is traveling with Gandalf the wizard and some dwarves on a quest to retrieve treasure from a dragon. While sheltering in a mountain cave from a massive storm, Bilbo and company are captured by goblins. Gandalf escapes capture and rescues the company, killing the Great Goblin in the process. As they retreat through the goblin tunnels, the company is overtaken by more goblins. Bilbo falls, hits his head, and blacks out.

For summaries in languages other than English, see Unit 5 Teaching Resources Book, pp. 85–90.

Vocabulary

Matching Write a list of classroom vocabulary words (for the selection, for the week, for the unit, etc.) on the backs of index cards and pass them out to the class. Then read the definition of each word and ask the students to turn in their card when the definition for their word is read aloud.

For additional vocabulary practice, see Unit 5 Teaching Resources Book, p. 93.

English Learners

DIFFERENTIATED INSTRUCTION

Intermediate This story contains some difficult words. Direct students to read the vocabulary list on this page. Help explain the words and meanings if they are still hard to grasp. Then, encourage students to make their own lists of unknown words as they read the story. The students may find some old-fashioned words and terms, like "haymaking" (p. 914) or "tinder and flint" (p. 918), unfamiliar. Explain that *haymaking* is preparing hay on a farm, and *tinder and flint* are simple tools for starting fires.

Teach

Big Idea 1

Journeys Answer: *The journey is long, dangerous, and confusing. It is guided by Gandalf's memory and Elrond's advice.*

Ask: Do you think the journey will be successful? *(Students may feel that the ominous imagery bodes ill for the journey. Others will feel that with Gandalf and Elrond aiding the company, they will succeed.)*

Over Hill and Under Hill

J. R. R. Tolkien

from The Hobbit

There were many paths that led up into those mountains, and many passes over them. But most of the paths were cheats and deceptions and led nowhere or to bad ends; and most of the passes were infested by evil things and dreadful dangers. The dwarves and the hobbit, helped by the wise advice of Elrond and the knowledge and memory of Gandalf, took the right road to the right pass.

Long days after they had climbed out of the valley and left the Last Homely House[1] miles behind, they were still going up and up. It was a hard path and a dangerous path, a crooked way and a lonely and a long. Now they could look back over the lands they had left, laid out behind them far below. Far, far away in the West, where things were blue and faint, Bilbo knew there lay his own country of safe and comfortable things, and his little hobbit-hole. He shivered. It was getting bitter cold up here, and the wind came shrill among the rocks. Boulders, too, at times came galloping down the mountain-sides, let loose by mid-day sun upon the snow, and passed among them (which was lucky), or over their heads (which was alarming). The nights were comfortless and chill, and they did not dare to sing or talk too loud, for the echoes were **uncanny**, and the silence seemed to dislike being broken—except by the noise of water and the wail of wind and the crack of stone.

"The summer is getting on down below," thought Bilbo, "and haymaking is going on

1. The *Last Homely House* is the name of Elrond's home in Rivendell.

1 Journeys *How would you describe this journey?*

Vocabulary

uncanny (un kan′ ē) *adj.* not normal or natural; seemingly supernatural in origin

Writing Practice

Character Development Although the author tells this story from the third-person point of view, he takes care to give readers insights into the characters' thoughts and feelings. On the first page of the story, the author shares Bilbo's emotions with readers. Bilbo is feeling lonely and distant from all comforting and familiar places. Ask students to write a paragraph about how Bilbo shows readers how he is feeling. *(Bilbo looked far into the distance to think about his home. Then, he shivered in the bitter cold of the mountain.)* Explain to students that the author gives us this information so we can understand what Bilbo is going through.

and picnics. They will be harvesting and blackberrying, before we even begin to go down the other side at this rate." And the others were thinking equally gloomy thoughts, although when they had said good-bye to Elrond in the high hope of a midsummer morning, they had spoken gaily of the passage of the mountains, and of riding swift across the lands beyond. They had thought of coming to the secret door in the Lonely Mountain,[2] perhaps that very next first moon of Autumn—"and perhaps it will be Durin's Day"[3] they had said. Only Gandalf had shaken his head and said nothing. Dwarves had not passed that way for many years, but Gandalf had, and he knew how evil and danger had grown and thriven[4] in the Wild, since the dragons had driven men from the lands, and the goblins had spread in secret after the battle of the Mines of Moria.[5] Even the good plans of wise wizards like Gandalf and of good friends like Elrond go astray sometimes when you are off on dangerous adventures over the Edge of the Wild; and Gandalf was a wise enough wizard to know it.

He knew that something unexpected might happen, and he hardly dared to hope that they would pass without fearful adventure over those great tall mountains with lonely peaks and valleys where no king ruled. They did not. All was well, until one day they met a thunderstorm—more than a thunderstorm, a thunder-battle. You know how terrific a really big thunderstorm can be down in the land and in a river-valley; especially at times when two great thunderstorms meet and clash. More terrible still are thunder and lightning in the mountains at night, when storms come up from East and West and make war. The lightning splinters on the peaks, and rocks shiver, and great crashes split the air and go rolling and tumbling into every cave and hollow; and the darkness is filled with overwhelming noise and sudden light.

Bilbo had never seen or imagined anything of the kind. They were high up in a narrow place, with a dreadful fall into a dim valley at one side of them. There they were sheltering under a hanging rock for the night, and he lay beneath a blanket and shook from head to toe. When he peeped out in the lightning-flashes, he saw that across the valley the stone-giants were out, and were hurling rocks at one another for a game, and catching them, and tossing them down into the darkness where they smashed among the trees far below, or splintered into little bits with a bang. Then came a wind and a rain, and the wind whipped the rain and the hail about in every direction, so that an overhanging rock was no protection at all. Soon they were getting drenched and their ponies were standing with their heads down and their tails between their legs, and some of them were whinnying with fright. They could hear the giants guffawing[6] and shouting all over the mountainsides. **2**

"This won't do at all!" said Thorin, "If we don't get blown off, or drowned, or struck by lightning, we shall be picked up by some giant and kicked sky-high for a football."

2. *Lonely Mountain* is the dwarves' ultimate destination.
3. *Durin's Day* is the dwarf new year.
4. *Thriven* means "prospered" or "increased."
5. The battle at the *Mines of Moria* occurred before *The Hobbit* begins and involved the ancestors of Thorin, the dwarf who is leading the journey described here.
6. *Guffawing* means "laughing loudly."

3 Compare and Contrast Characters *How does Gandalf's knowledge of what lies ahead compare with Bilbo's and the dwarves' knowledge?*

4 Motif *How does this description of the dark thunderstorm help illustrate the danger that surrounds Bilbo and his friends?*

Teach

Reading Strategy 2

Compare and Contrast Characters Ask: How do the giants react to the storm as compared to Bilbo and his friends? *(The storm makes Bilbo and his friends terrified and miserable. The giants are laughing.)*

Reading Strategy 3

Compare and Contrast Characters Answer: *Gandalf is aware of the dangers and difficulties that lie ahead. He has traveled through the Wild and seen its evil firsthand. The dwarves have not traveled that way for a long time. Both Bilbo and the dwarves are more optimistic and think that the journey might be easy.*

For additional practice using the reading skill or strategy, see Unit 5 Teaching Resources Book, p. 92.

Literary Element 4

Motif Answer: *The darkness and the storm are frightening and foreboding. The storm, which is compared to war, causes the rocks to shiver. The darkness threatens to overwhelm the company. Even the lightning only illuminates the vicious giants below.*

Approaching Level

DIFFERENTIATED INSTRUCTION

Emerging In this section of the story, Bilbo is thinking about the pleasures of home. He feels sorry that he is stuck in the mountains, missing his quiet, comfortable lifestyle. Group students and instruct them to list the ways in which Bilbo's current situation differs from his life at home. Next, ask students to imagine they were in the mountains with Bilbo. Instruct them to write a paragraph or a poem about the things about their current lives that they would miss. Some students might say they would miss their families and friends; others might focus more on the comforts of safe homes or soft beds.

Teach

Big Idea 1

Journeys **Ask:** How does the comment "So it proved on this occasion" foreshadow the next part of the journey? *(Students may say that the line foreshadows that the journey is about to take an unexpected turn.)*

View the Art ★

Answer: *The journey appears equally long and dangerous, but the weather is clear in the painting.*

Belgian painter Joos de Momper (1564–1635) was a pioneer in landscape painting. His work is marked by the use of dark colors in the foreground and blue or green for mountains and background.

Mountain Landscape with Firtrees in the Torrent, after 1591. Joos de Momper. Oil on oak, 53 x 71.5 cm. Collection of Gemäldegalerie, Alte Meister, Dresden, Germany.

View the Art How does the journey pictured here compare with the journey Bilbo, Gandalf, and the dwarves are on? ★

"Well, if you know of anywhere better, take us there!" said Gandalf, who was feeling very grumpy, and was far from happy about the giants himself.

The end of their argument was that they sent Fili and Kili to look for a better shelter. They had very sharp eyes, and being the youngest of the dwarves by some fifty years they usually got these sort of jobs (when everybody could see that it was absolutely no use sending Bilbo). There is nothing like looking, if you want to find something (or so Thorin said to the young dwarves). You certainly usually find something, if you look, but it is not always quite the something you
1 were after. So it proved on this occasion.

Soon Fili and Kili came crawling back, holding on to the rocks in the wind. "We have found a dry cave," they said, "not far round the next corner; and ponies and all could get inside."

"Have you *thoroughly* explored it?" said the wizard, who knew that caves up in the mountains were seldom unoccupied.

"Yes, yes!" they said, though everybody knew they could not have been long about it; they had come back too quick. "It isn't all that big, and it does not go far back."

That, of course, is the dangerous part about caves: you don't know how far they go back, sometimes, or where a passage behind may lead to, or what is waiting for

Viewing Practice

SPIRAL REVIEW **Study Graphics** The painting of the mountain on this page was painted long before the story of the hobbits was written. However, the picture helps emphasize the setting of the story. Instruct students to look carefully at the picture for a minute or two, and then write at least five words or phrases to describe it. The students' replies may vary. Some students may take a negative point of view. They may think the mountain appears chilly, dangerous, distant, or unforgiving. Other students, however, will likely take another perspective. These students may think the mountain is beautiful, challenging, or colorful.

you inside. But now Fili and Kili's news seemed good enough. So they all got up and prepared to move. The wind was howling and the thunder still growling, and they had a business getting themselves and their ponies along. Still it was not very far to go, and before long they came to a big rock standing out into the path. If you stepped behind, you found a low arch in the side of the mountain. There was just room to get the ponies through with a squeeze, when they had been unpacked and unsaddled. As they passed under the arch, it was good to hear the wind and the rain outside instead of all about them, and to feel safe from the giants and their rocks. But the wizard was taking no risks. He lit up his wand—as he did that day in Bilbo's dining-room that seemed so long ago, if you remember—and by its light they explored the cave from end to end.

> "When he did sleep, he had very nasty dreams."

It seemed quite a fair size, but not too large and mysterious. It had a dry floor and some comfortable nooks.[7] At one end there was room for the ponies; and there they stood (mighty glad of the change) steaming, and champing in their nosebags. Oin and Gloin wanted to light a fire at the door to dry their clothes, but Gandalf would not hear of it. So they spread out their wet things on the floor, and got dry ones out of their bundles; then they made their blankets comfortable, got out their pipes and blew smoke rings, which Gandalf turned into different colors and set dancing up by the roof to amuse them. They talked and talked, and forgot about the storm, and discussed what each would do with his share of the treasure (when they got it, which at the moment did not seem so impossible); and so they dropped off to sleep one by one. And that was the last time that they used the ponies, packages, baggages, tools, and **paraphernalia** that they had brought with them.

It turned out a good thing that night that they had brought little Bilbo with them, after all. For, somehow, he could not go to sleep for a long while; and when he did sleep, he had very nasty dreams. He dreamed that a crack in the wall at the back of the cave got bigger and bigger, and opened wider and wider, and he was very afraid but could not call out or do anything but lie and look. Then he dreamed that the floor of the cave was giving way, and he was slipping—beginning to fall down, down, goodness knows where to.

At that he woke up with a horrible start, and found that part of his dream was true. A crack had opened at the back of the cave, and was already a wide passage. He was just in time to see the last of the ponies' tails disappearing into it. Of course he gave a very loud yell, as loud a yell as a hobbit can give, which is surprising for their size.

7. *Nooks* are small areas of a room.

2 Compare and Contrast Characters *Do either Fili or Kili exhibit character traits that set them apart from each other or the other dwarves? Explain.*

3 Motif *How is the cave lit? What is the connection between light and awareness in this passage?*

Vocabulary

paraphernalia (par′ ə fər nāl′ yə) *n.* personal items or equipment

Teach

Reading Strategy 2

Compare and Contrast Characters Answer: *Fili and Kili are the youngest dwarves. Neither exhibits any trait that would distinguish him from the other or from the other dwarves.*

APPROACHING **Ask:** How are Fili and Kili different from Gandalf? *(Students may say that Fili and Kili are dwarves, whereas Gandalf is a wizard. Fili and Kili are young and seem eager to go to the cave, whereas Gandalf is older and more cautious about entering the cave.)*

Literary Element 3

Motif Answer: *Light is equated with knowledge. Gandalf uses his wand to light the cave. The light allows the company to investigate the cave and see their surroundings.*

Approaching Level

DIFFERENTIATED INSTRUCTION

Emerging Students may wonder about the author's frequent use of parentheses in the story. For example, on page 917, a note in parentheses tells us that the ponies were "mighty glad of the change" when they found a place to stop. Students may find many other examples of parenthetical notes. Encourage students to consider the uses of parentheses. **Ask:** Why does the author include parentheses in the story? What effect do they have? *(Answer: The author uses parentheses primarily to offer the reader extra bits of information that do not necessarily fit in the main part of the text.)*

Teach

Literary Element 1

Motif Answer: *The image of lightning or light is repeated here.*

ADVANCED **Ask:** How does this reinforce the motif of good versus evil? *(Students may say that the lightning flash allows Gandalf to escape the goblins, allowing good to triumph over evil.)*

Big Idea 2

Journeys Answer: *Bilbo is a reluctant traveler. This is the second time he has wished for his hobbit-hole. At this point, students who are unfamiliar with the story may say Bilbo was a bad choice because his heart is not in the journey.* Point out that the narrator says this isn't the last time Bilbo wishes for his hobbit-hole. **Ask:** What does that foretell about the rest of his journey? *(Students may say that the journey will continue to be filled with danger and that Bilbo will remain a reluctant traveler.)* How does the foreshadowing of danger encourage the reader? *(By alerting the reader to further drama and adventure, Tolkien entices the reader to continue on.)*

Literary Element 3

Motif Answer: *Gandalf's light is generally white or blue rather than red. His light defends or helps the travelers, while this light reveals the threatening goblins.*

Out jumped the goblins, big goblins, great ugly-looking goblins, lots of goblins, before you could say *rocks and blocks*. There were six to each dwarf, at least, and two even for Bilbo; and they were all grabbed and carried through the crack, before you could say *tinder and flint*. But not Gandalf. Bilbo's yell had done that much good. It had wakened him up wide in a splintered second, and when goblins came to grab him, there was a terrific flash like lightning in the cave, a smell like gunpowder, and several of them fell dead.

The crack closed with a snap, and Bilbo and the dwarves were on the wrong side of it! Where was Gandalf? Of that neither they nor the goblins had any idea, and the goblins did not wait to find out. They seized Bilbo and the dwarves and hurried them along. It was deep, deep, dark, such as only goblins that have taken to living in the heart of the mountains can see through. The passages there were crossed and tangled in all directions, but the goblins knew their way, as well as you do to the nearest post-office; and the way went down and down, and it was most horribly stuffy. The goblins were very rough, and pinched unmercifully, and chuckled and laughed in their horrible stony voices; and Bilbo was more unhappy even than when the troll had picked him up by his toes. He wished again and again for his nice bright hobbit-hole. Not for the last time.

Now there came a glimmer of a red light before them. The goblins began to sing, or croak, keeping time with the flap of their flat feet on the stone, and shaking their prisoners as well.

Clap! Snap! the black crack!
Grip, grab! Pinch, nab!
And down down to Goblin-town
You go, my lad!

Clash, crash! Crush, smash!
Hammer and tongs! Knocker and gongs!
Pound, pound, far underground!
Ho, ho! my lad!

Swish, smack! Whip crack!
Batter and beat! Yammer and bleat![8]
Work, work! Nor dare to shirk,[9]
While Goblins quaff,[10] *and Goblins laugh,*
Round and round far underground
Below, my lad!

It sounded truly terrifying. The walls echoed to the *clap, snap!* and the *crush, smash!* and to the ugly laughter of their *ho, ho! my lad!* The general meaning of the song was only too plain; for now the goblins took out whips and whipped them with a *swish, smack!*, and set them running as fast as they could in front of them; and more than one of the dwarves were already yammering and bleating like anything, when they stumbled into a big cavern.

It was lit by a great red fire in the middle, and by torches along the walls, and it was full of goblins. They all laughed and stamped and clapped their hands, when the dwarves (with poor little Bilbo at the back and nearest to the whips) came running in, while the goblin-drivers whooped and cracked their whips behind. The ponies were already there huddled in a corner; and there were all the baggages and packages lying broken open, and being rummaged by goblins, and smelt by goblins, and fingered by goblins, and quarreled over by goblins.

1 Motif *What image or motif is repeated here?*

2 Journeys *Gandalf chose Bilbo to join this journey. Based on what you have read here, do you think it was a good choice? Explain.*

8. To *yammer* is to talk loudly on and on. To *bleat* is to cry out in complaint.
9. To *shirk* is to avoid responsibility for a task.
10. To *quaff* is to drink deeply.

Motif *How does this light differ from Gandalf's light?* **3**

Listening Practice

SPIRAL REVIEW **Make Judgments** Tolkien was well known for his use of invented languages and lively songs within his stories. He added these devices to bring great depth to his characters and the world they live in. Page 918 gives an example of one of the author's famous and rousing songs. Ask students to read lines of the song aloud—singing them might help, but is not necessary. **Ask:** What effect does this song and its words have on the story? *(Students may answer that the song's angry tone shows the goblins' violent ways. Also, the song adds sound and energy to the text.)*

The Posillipo Cave at Naples. Hubert Robert. Oil on canvas. Collection of Musée Jeanne d'Aboville, La Fere, France.

View the Art Hubert Robert was nicknamed "Robert des Ruines," French for "Robert of the ruins," because he often painted old crumbling buildings. What mood does the single source of light in this painting help create? ★

I am afraid that was the last they ever saw of those excellent little ponies, including a jolly sturdy little white fellow that Elrond had lent to Gandalf, since his horse was not suitable for the mountain-paths. For goblins eat horses and ponies and donkeys (and other much more dreadful things), and they are always hungry. Just now, however, the prisoners were thinking only of themselves. The goblins chained their hands behind their backs and linked them all together in a line, and dragged them to the far end of the cavern with little Bilbo tugging at the end of the row.

There in the shadows on a large flat stone sat a tremendous goblin with a huge head, and armed goblins were standing round him carrying the axes and the bent swords that they use. Now goblins are cruel, wicked, and bad-hearted. They make no beautiful things, but they make many clever ones. They can tunnel and mine as well as any but the most skilled dwarves, when they take the trouble, though they are usually untidy and dirty. Hammers, axes, swords, daggers, pickaxes, tongs, and also instruments of torture, they make very well, or get other people to make to their design, prisoners and slaves that have to work till they die for want of air and light. It is not unlikely that they invented some of the machines that have since troubled the

Teach

View the Art ★

Answer: *The single source of light creates an ominous mood. The people are walking toward something they can't see.*

English Learners

DIFFERENTIATED INSTRUCTION

Beginning/Early Intermediate Explain to students that even in fictional stories background information is often needed. In this story, for example, the author stops to explain the ways goblins feel about dwarves and other creatures. **Ask:** What do you learn about goblins and dwarves from the author's note? *(Students may answer that goblins hate every kind of creature, including dwarves. However, they especially hated dwarves of Thorin's line.)* Although all of this information is fictional, this extra background on the characters and situations makes the story much broader and more interesting.

Teach

Literary Element 1

Motif **Answer:** *The goblins come secretly in the darkness and seize Bilbo and the dwarves. They live deep underground, where there is little air or light. They are associated with shadows; they need torches and a "great red fire" to light their world. The goblins represent evil and deception; they make instruments of torture, take joy in hurting others, capture people secretly, and enslave them.*

Reading Strategy 2

Compare and Contrast Characters **Answer:** *Thorin is the leader of the dwarves. He is not a fully developed character, but he is presented in much greater detail than the other dwarves. Some of Thorin's inner thoughts are revealed by the narrator.*

world, especially the **ingenious** devices for killing large numbers of people at once, for wheels and engines and explosions always delighted them, and also not working with their own hands more than they could help; but in those days and those wild parts they had not advanced (as it is called) so far. They did not hate dwarves especially, no more than they hated everybody and everything, and particularly the orderly and prosperous; in some parts wicked dwarves had even made alliances with them. But they had a special grudge against Thorin's people, because of the war which you have heard mentioned, but which does not come into this tale; and anyway goblins don't care who they catch, as long as it is done smart and secret, and the prisoners are not able to defend themselves.

"Who are these miserable persons?" said the Great Goblin.

"Dwarves, and this!" said one of the drivers, pulling at Bilbo's chain so that he fell forward onto his knees. "We found them sheltering in our Front Porch."

"What do you mean by it?" said the Great Goblin turning to Thorin. "Up to no good, I'll warrant![11] Spying on the private business of my people, I guess! Thieves, I shouldn't be surprised to learn! Murderers and friends of Elves, not unlikely! Come! What have you got to say?"

"Thorin the dwarf at your service!" he replied—it was merely a polite nothing. "Of the things which you suspect and imagine we had no idea at all. We sheltered from a storm in what seemed a convenient cave and unused; nothing was further from our thoughts than inconveniencing goblins in any way whatever." That was true enough!

"Um!" said the Great Goblin. "So you say! Might I ask what you were doing up in the mountains at all, and where you were coming from, and where you were going to? In fact I should like to know all about you. Not that it will do you much good, Thorin Oakenshield, I know too much about your folk already; but let's have the truth, or I will prepare something particularly uncomfortable for you!"

"We were on a journey to visit our relatives, our nephews and nieces, and first, second, and third cousins, and the other descendants of our grandfathers, who live on the East side of these truly hospitable mountains," said Thorin, not quite knowing what to say all at once in a moment, when obviously the exact truth would not do at all.

"He is a liar, O truly tremendous one!" said one of the drivers. "Several of our people were struck by lightning in the cave, when we invited these creatures to come below; and they are as dead as stones. Also he has not explained this!" He held out the sword which Thorin had worn, the sword which came from the Trolls' lair.[12]

The Great Goblin gave a truly awful howl of rage when he looked at it, and all his soldiers gnashed their teeth, clashed their shields, and stamped. They knew the sword at once. It had killed hundreds of goblins in its time, when the fair elves of Gondolin hunted them in the hills or did

11. Here, *warrant* means "declare."

12. In an earlier chapter, hungry trolls capture the group, but Gandalf tricks the trolls, and they are turned to stone. Gandalf and Thorin take their magic swords.

1 Motif *In what ways are the goblins associated with darkness? How do the goblins represent deception and evil?*

Vocabulary

ingenious (in jēn′ yəs) *adj.* especially clever, inventive, or original

Compare and Contrast Characters *How is Thorin presented differently from the other dwarves?* **2**

Vocabulary Practice

SPIRAL REVIEW **Figurative Language** The author uses very expressive language in this story. Many of his words deal with sounds. Instruct students to scan the page and pick out words that describe sounds. On page 921, words such as "yells," "yammering," "croaking," "jibbering," and "jammering" all fit this criteria. Ask students to consider what effect these words have on the story. Some students may say that the words create the impression of many loud noises. Other students may elaborate that these noises seem to be filled with fear, pain, and confusion. Challenge students to consider other kinds of sound words.

battle before their walls. They had called it Orcrist, Goblin-cleaver, but the goblins called it simply Biter. They hated it and hated worse any one that carried it.

"Murderers and elf-friends!" the Great Goblin shouted. "Slash them! Beat them! Bite them! Gnash them! Take them away to dark holes full of snakes, and never let them see the light again!" He was in such a rage that he jumped off his seat and himself rushed at Thorin with his mouth open.

Just at that moment all the lights in the cavern went out, and the great fire went off poof! into a tower of blue glowing smoke, right up to the roof, that scattered piercing white sparks all among the goblins.

The yells and yammering, croaking, jibbering and jabbering; howls, growls and curses; shrieking and skriking, that followed were beyond description. Several hundred wild cats and wolves being roasted slowly alive together would not have compared with it. The sparks were burning holes in the goblins, and the smoke that now fell from the roof made the air too thick for even their eyes to see through. Soon they were falling over one another and rolling in heaps on the floor, biting and kicking and fighting as if they had all gone mad.

Suddenly a sword flashed in its own light. Bilbo saw it go right through the Great Goblin as he stood dumbfounded in the middle of his rage. He fell dead, and the goblin soldiers fled before the sword shrieking into the darkness.

The sword went back into its sheath. "Follow me quick!" said a voice fierce and quiet; and before Bilbo understood what had happened he was trotting along again, as fast as he could trot, at the end of the line, down more dark passages with the yells of the goblin-hall growing fainter behind him. A pale light was leading them on.

"Quicker, quicker!" said the voice. "The torches will soon be relit."

"Half a minute!" said Dori, who was at the back next to Bilbo, and a decent fellow. He made the hobbit scramble on his shoulders as best he could with his tied hands, and then off they all went at a run, with a clink-clink of chains, and many a stumble, since they had no hands to steady themselves with. Not for a long while did they stop, and by that time they must have been right down in the very mountain's heart.

Then Gandalf lit up his wand. Of course it was Gandalf; but just then they were too busy to ask how he got there. He took out his sword again, and again it flashed in the dark by itself. It burned with a rage that made it gleam if goblins were about; now it was bright as blue flame for delight in the killing of the great lord of the cave. It made no trouble whatever of cutting through the goblin-chains and setting all the prisoners free as quickly as possible. This sword's name was Glamdring the Foe-hammer, if you remember.[13] The goblins just called it Beater, and hated it worse than Biter if possible. Orcrist, too, had been saved; for Gandalf had brought it along as well, snatching it from one of the terrified guards. Gandalf thought of most things; and though he could not do everything, he could do a great deal for friends in a tight corner.

"Are we all here?" said he, handing his sword back to Thorin with a bow. "Let me see: one—that's Thorin; two, three, four, five, six, seven, eight, nine, ten, eleven;

13. Elrond explains the history of *Glamdring* to Gandalf in a previous chapter.

3 Compare and Contrast Characters *How does the leader of the goblins compare with Gandalf?*

4 Motif *How does this image relate to the group's dangerous position?*

5 Motif *How does Gandalf represent awareness?*

Teach

Reading Strategy 3

Compare and Contrast Characters **Answer:** *Gandalf knows what is going on; he takes action to protect the dwarves and to fight evil. The Great Goblin is unaware; even at the moment of his death, he does not know what is happening.*

Literary Element 4

Motif **Answer:** *The companions are following a pale light, but they are still surrounded by darkness. There is hope of escape from the goblins, but they are not yet safe.*

APPROACHING To help approaching-level students, **ask:** What do light and darkness often mean to people? *(Students may say that light represents warmth and safety, while darkness often shows cold and danger.)*

Literary Element 5

Motif **Answer:** *Gandalf "thought of most things"; he knows what to do to protect and save the dwarves. He also knows enough to save the sword, which will probably be needed later. He is also the source of "safe" light throughout the story.*

Approaching Level

DIFFERENTIATED INSTRUCTION

Established As the story progresses, encourage students to pay attention to the author's tone, or the mood, of his "voice." Ask students to try to describe the tone. Students may feel it is conversational and casual, but also descriptive and exciting. They may note that it is an excellent tone for a storyteller. One of the most striking aspects of the author's tone is the humor he uses. Even amid the tense and often scary situations in the story, the author keeps a sense of humor. On page 921, for example, Bilbo and Bombur trade amusing complaints as they flee the tunnel.

Teach

Big Idea 1

Journeys **Ask:** How might you relate the ups and downs of Bilbo's journey with life's journey? *(Answers will vary. Students may say that real life is filled with dangers and unexpected events, just like Bilbo's journey.)*

Big Idea 2

Journeys **Answer:** *The struggle between good and evil is ongoing; different characters play their parts, and while the journey eventually ends for everyone, the fight continues.*

ADVANCED Have advanced students research other examples of artwork that are representative of this story. Have them share the art with the class and explain the connection.

To check students' understanding of the selection, see Unit 5 Teaching Resources Book, p. 96.

where are Fili and Kili? Here they are! twelve, thirteen—and here's Mr. Baggins:[14] fourteen! Well, well! it might be worse, and then again it might be a good deal better. No ponies, and no food, and no knowing quite where we are, and **hordes** of angry goblins just behind! On we go!"

On they went. Gandalf was quite right: they began to hear goblin noises and horrible cries far behind in the passages they had come through. That sent them on faster than ever, and as poor Bilbo could not possibly go half as fast—for dwarves can roll along at a tremendous pace, I can tell you, when they have to—they took it in turn to carry him on their backs.

Still goblins go faster than dwarves, and these goblins knew the way better (they had made the paths themselves), and were madly angry; so that do what they could the dwarves heard the cries and howls getting closer and closer. Soon they could hear even the flap of the goblin feet, many many feet which seemed only just round the last corner. The blink of red torches could be seen behind them in the tunnel they were following; and they were getting deadly tired.

"Why, O why did I ever leave my hobbit-hole!" said poor Mr. Baggins bumping up and down on Bombur's back.

"Why, O why did I ever bring a wretched little hobbit on a treasure hunt!" said poor Bombur, who was fat, and staggered along with the sweat dripping down his nose in his heat and terror.

At this point Gandalf fell behind, and Thorin with him. They turned a sharp corner. "About turn!"[15] he shouted. "Draw your sword Thorin!"

There was nothing else to be done; and the goblins did not like it. They came scurrying round the corner in full cry, and found Goblin-cleaver, and Foe-hammer shining cold and bright right in their astonished eyes. The ones in front dropped their torches and gave one yell before they were killed. The ones behind yelled still more, and leaped back knocking over those that were running after them. "Biter and Beater!" they shrieked; and soon they were all in confusion, and most of them were hustling back the way they had come.

It was quite a long while before any of them dared to turn that corner. By that time the dwarves had gone on again, a long, long, way on into the dark tunnels of the goblins' realm.[16] When the goblins discovered that, they put out their torches and they slipped on soft shoes, and they chose out their very quickest runners with the sharpest ears and eyes. These ran forward, as swift as weasels in the dark, and with hardly any more noise than bats.

That is why neither Bilbo, nor the dwarves, nor even Gandalf heard them coming. Nor did they see them. But they were seen by the goblins that ran silently up behind, for Gandalf was letting his wand give out a faint light to help the dwarves as they went along.

Quite suddenly Dori, now at the back again carrying Bilbo, was grabbed from behind in the dark. He shouted and fell; and the hobbit rolled off his shoulders into the blackness, bumped his head on hard rock, and remembered nothing more. 1

14. *Mr. Baggins* is Bilbo.
15. *About turn* is a command meaning "turn around 180 degrees" or "about face."
16. Here, *realm* means "domain" or "own area."

Vocabulary

horde (hôrd) *n.* crowd, throng, or swarm

Journeys *The goblins know the ancient history surrounding Biter and Beater. What does this say about the struggle between good and evil?* 2

Writing Practice

SPIRAL REVIEW **Enduring Stories** Explain that the events and characters of *The Hobbit* continue to interest readers to this day. Have students write a paragraph considering the factors that have made *The Hobbit* appeal to so many people over the years. **Ask:** What parts of the story may have special meaning to many people? What makes this story stay in our imaginations? *(Students may reply that the story is an exciting adventure that many people find entertaining. Other students may point to the richness of the story which allows readers to constantly discover new details in the text. Still other students may suggest that readers can relate to the characters and feel connected to them.)*

After You Read

Respond and Think Critically

Respond and Interpret

1. What do you think is the most otherworldly or fantastical element of this story? Explain.
2. (a)Who is traveling on this adventure? (b)Describe the setting in your own words.
3. (a)How do the goblins capture the adventurers? (b)How does Tolkien characterize the goblins?
4. (a)What happens to Bilbo and his companions? (b)What do you predict will happen next? Why?

Analyze and Evaluate

5. Bilbo's journey is full of twists and turns. How is the plot of this excerpt full of ups and downs?
6. How would you describe Gandalf? Cite examples from the text to support your answer.
7. Do you think Bilbo is a hero? Explain.

Connect

8. **Big Idea** **Journeys** Jot down three words that you think characterize this journey. Explain your choices to a classmate.
9. **Connect to the Author** J. R. R. Tolkien himself acknowledged that he would probably be remembered as the author of *The Lord of the Rings,* even though he accomplished a great deal more. Why do you think this fantastical world continues to capture audiences?

Visual Literacy

Fine Art

In his novels, Tolkien creates an entirely new world populated with distinctive creatures. Generations of readers, filmmakers, and artists have enjoyed visualizing and re-creating *The Hobbit*. One of the many visual delights and challenges for artists has been capturing the appearance and personality of the characters.

Group Activity Study the illustration of Bilbo, and discuss these questions with classmates.

1. How well does this illustration reflect Bilbo's appearance as he is described in this excerpt from *The Hobbit*? How well does it capture Bilbo's personality? Cite details from the text and the illustration that support your opinion.
2. What does the artist bring to the illustration that is not mentioned in the story?

Bilbo on His Pony. Mikhail Belomlinsky. Engraving. Private collection.

After You Read

Assess

1. Students' responses will vary.
2. (a) Bilbo Baggins, Gandalf the wizard, Thorin the dwarf leader, and twelve other dwarves (six other dwarves are given names). (b) Mountains with dangerous paths, rolling boulders, treacherous thunderstorms, and dark caverns
3. (a) While everyone is sleeping, they open a crack at the back of the cave. (b) They live deep underground in the darkness; they do evil things.
4. (a) They are about to be killed when Gandalf kills the Great Goblin and rescues them. (b) Gandalf will rescue Bilbo.
5. They face the dangers of the mountains in a thunderstorm; they finally find shelter and are attacked by goblins; Gandalf rescues them; the goblins attack again and hurt Bilbo.
6. He is wise and brave. Example of his wisdom: the dwarves take the right road because of Gandalf's memory. He demonstrates courage when he saves the others.
7. Students cannot call Bilbo a hero based on the information in this excerpt.
8. Students' answers will vary. Possible answers: *perilous, unpredictable, fantastic, determined,* and *adventurous.*
9. Students should support their responses with specific examples from the text.

For additional selection assessment, see Assessment Resources, pp. 197–198.

Visual Literacy

1. Answers will vary. Students may say that the illustration captures Bilbo's physical likeness. Students may say the expression captures Bilbo's sweetness.
2. Answers will vary. Students may point to Bilbo's thinning hair in the illustration, which the artist uses to show age.

After You Read

Assess

Literary Element

1. The most obvious use is the thunderstorm.
2. (a) The dwarves, Bilbo, and especially Gandalf (b) The goblins (c) Students' responses may vary. Examples may include the Goblin's dark cavernous home and Gandalf's lighted sword.

Progress Check

Can students identify motif?

If No → See Unit 5 Teaching Resources Book, p. 91.

Review: Narrator

1. The reader
2. The narrator comments on events.
3. Examples include: "Even the good plans of wise wizards . . . the Wild" and "The sword's name was . . . if you remember."

Reading Strategy

1. A is the correct answer. Bilbo is a hobbit, but he is a fully developed character.

Literary Element Motif

Good and evil, light and darkness, and awareness and deception can all be viewed as two sides of the same idea. In *The Hobbit,* Tolkien uses these **motifs** to advance the plot, foreshadow events, create suspense, reveal character traits, and convey themes.

1. Explain how Tolkien uses one or more of these motifs to create suspense. Cite specific passages.
2. (a)Which characters are associated with goodness and awareness? (b)Which characters are associated with evil and deception? (c)How does Tolkien's use of light and dark imagery support your observations? Cite specific examples in your response.

Review: Narrator

As you learned on pages 184–185, the **narrator** is the person who tells a story. If the narrator is a character inside the story then the story is told from the **first-person point of view.** If the narrator is outside the story then the story is told from the **third-person point of view.** Sometimes a story is told by an **intrusive narrator**—a narrator who openly comments on and evaluates characters, decisions, and actions in a story.

Partner Activity Meet with a partner to study the following passage and determine whether the narrator is inside or outside the story.

> "You certainly usually find something, if you look, but it is not always quite the something you were after. So it proved on this occasion."

1. In this passage, who is the narrator addressing?
2. Describe the narrator's role in telling the story.
3. Find two more examples in the story where the narrator intrudes, or comments upon the story itself.

Reading Strategy Compare and Contrast Characters

ACT Skills Practice

1. In which of the following ways is the Great Goblin similar to Bilbo Baggins?

   I. He is not a human being.
   II. He is a stock character, embodying a stereotype.
   III. He is motivated by evil.

   A. I only
   B. II only
   C. I and II only
   D. I, II, and III

Vocabulary Practice

Practice with Context Clues Identify the context clues in the following sentences that help you determine the meaning of each boldface vocabulary word.

1. The fortune-teller's predictions were nothing special and often wrong. She did not possess **uncanny** abilities.
2. The closet was filled with keyboards, monitors, printers, and modems—almost every kind of computer **paraphernalia** you can imagine.
3. Her teacher said that her lyrics were **ingenious.** He told her that they were incredibly clever and inventive.
4. He saw the **horde** approaching from a distance. It was not a small or quiet group.

LOG ON **Literature** Online

Selection Resources For Selection Quizzes, eFlashcards, and Reading-Writing Connection activities, go to glencoe.com and enter QuickPass code GL49787u5.

Vocabulary

1. "nothing special and often wrong" "did not possess **uncanny** abilities"
2. "keyboards, monitors, printers, and modems" "every kind of computer **paraphernalia**"
3. "incredibly clever and inventive"
4. "not a small or quiet group"

Respond Through Writing

Expository Essay

Analyze Theme Review the names that Tolkien gives his characters. How do the names align with the motifs of good and evil that support the theme of the story? Write an essay answering this question and using examples from the text as support.

Prewrite Prepare for writing by using a graphic organizer to record the characters' names and their alignment with good or evil. You might want to use a chart like the one shown below.

Character Name	Aligned with Good or Evil?	Good or Evil Character Trait
Elrond	Good	Provides wise advice

Draft Use the characters and examples from your chart to create your draft. In your essay, discuss how these examples support the motifs of good and evil. Explore the motifs in depth by identifying complexities in Tolkien's themes and noting how his style reflects those complexities.

Revise Review your essay. How well are your ideas about Tolkien's motifs supported by examples from the text? Strengthen your essay by inserting one or two longer passages that support your main idea. Use these detailed examples to replace more general ones. When inserting a longer passage from the story, precede the quote with a colon. If the quoted text is longer than four lines, start a new line and indent the entire quote.

Make sure your examples and quotes are used with statements that explain their significance. For example, you might introduce a quoted passage with a statement such as:

The author implies ____ by saying ____:

After you have inserted your examples and revised the related text, check the essay against the checklist on page 805 and make any final changes.

Edit and Proofread Proofread your paper, correcting any errors in spelling, grammar, and punctuation. Review the Grammar Tip in the side column for information about adverbs.

Learning Objectives

In this assignment, you will focus on the following objectives:

Writing: Writing an expository essay.

Grammar: Understanding the use and formation of comparative and superlative forms of adverbs.

Grammar Tip

Adverbs

Some adverbs have different forms to indicate their degree of comparison. The comparative form of an adverb compares two actions.

*Manuel runs **faster** than Jose does.*

For most adverbs of only one syllable, you add *-er* to make the comparative form and *-est* to make the superlative form. The superlative form compares more than two actions.

*Out of everyone on the team, Philippe runs **fastest**.*

In your essay, you can use these types of adverbs to compare the characters' degrees of good and evil.

After You Read

Assess

Respond Through Writing

Students' essays should

- discuss how the characters' names align with the motifs of good and evil
- analyze how the motifs support the themes
- support the analysis with examples from the text
- include one or two longer passages that provide detailed examples in support of the essay's main ideas
- clearly explain how the examples support the themes

For grammar practice, see Unit 5 Teaching Resources Book, p. 95.

To create custom assessments online, go to Progress Reporter Online Assessment.

To create custom assessments using software, use ExamView Assessment Suite.

English Learners

DIFFERENTIATED INSTRUCTION

Beginning/Early Intermediate Encourage students to pay attention to the behavior of the characters in this story. As page 925 explains, some characters seem to be evil and act with meanness and cruelty. Other characters display good behaviors, such as kindness and courage. Still other characters have a mixture of these behaviors. Good versus evil is an important theme in this story. It is also one of the most basic conflicts in world literature. **Ask:** What other conflicts are often dealt with in stories? *(Students may say that characters in a story may have conflicts with each other, with nature, with ideas, or even with themselves.)*

Focus

Summary

While resting in a cave on their journey through the mountains, Bilbo and a company of dwarves are captured by goblins. Gandalf the wizard escapes capture. The Goblin King is infuriated by Thorin the dwarf's sword Orcrist, the goblin-cleaver. As he sentences the company to torment, Gandalf appears to rescue them. A battle ensues and the company flees.

For summaries in languages other than English, see Unit 5 Teaching Resources Book, pp. 98–103.

Teach

Literary Element 1

Dialogue Engage students in a classroom discussion of the graphic novel dialogue. Have them note such elements as length, diction, punctuation, and dialect. Discuss whether students find the dialogue realistic and effective.

Visual Perspective
on *The Hobbit*

Learning Objectives

For pages 926–930

In studying this text, you will focus on the following objectives:

Reading: Making connections across literature. Comparing and contrasting versions of a story.

from The Hobbit

Adapted by Charles Dixon
Illustrated by David Wenzel

Set a Purpose for Reading

Read to discover the similarities and differences between the graphic novel version of *The Hobbit* and the original text.

Build Background

Graphic novels are longer versions of comic books and are more complex and literary in nature. Will Eisner, who wrote what is considered to be the first modern graphic novel in 1978, popularized the term "graphic novel." In 1992 Art Spiegelman received the Pulitzer Prize for his graphic novel, *Maus: A Survivor's Tale*. Other graphic novels that have achieved success include *Ghost World* by Daniel Clowes and *American Splendor* by Harvey Pekar; both have been adapted into films. In this graphic novel version of *The Hobbit*, Charles Dixon uses dia-
1 logue and David Wenzel illustrates the characters from the novel by J. R. R. Tolkien.

Reading Strategy Compare and Contrast Versions of a Story

When you **compare and contrast,** you identify the similarities and differences between two works of literature. Many elements of different works can be compared and contrasted, including theme, imagery, use of language, characterization, and setting. As you read, take notes on the images in the graphic novel version of *The Hobbit.* Ask yourself, How are the images similar to and different from images evoked by the original text?

Images	Similarities	Differences
"There in the shadows on a large flat stone sat a tremendous goblin with a huge head, and armed goblins were standing round him carrying the axes and the bent swords that they use."	There is one large goblin. Goblins are holding axes and swords, and they surround the dwarves.	More defined facial characteristics of goblins in the graphic novel. Dialogue is also different from the original.

Writing Practice

SMALL GROUP

Graphic Novels Students are about to read a graphic novel, an interesting mix of words and pictures. Explain to students that graphic novels are similar to comic books, but tell a longer, more detailed, and often more serious story. Encourage students to think about stories they know that might make good graphic novels. Group students and challenge each group to create one page of a graphic novel. They can use stories that they've read elsewhere or their own stories. If students feel they cannot draw well, encourage them to use simple sketches or stick figures. Be sure they are focusing on words and ideas, not just artwork.

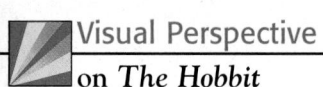

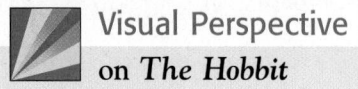

2

Teach

Literary Element 2

Motif **Ask:** How does the graphic representation of the goblins and dwarves reflect the motif of darkness and light, and good and evil? *(Answers will vary. Students may point to the color palette used by the artist or the repulsive appearance of the goblins as examples of darkness and evil. They should contrast the dwarves' appearance as more representative of the light and good.)*

APPROACHING To help approaching level students, **ask:** What other colors in this painting show you about the scene? *(Students may feel that the green skin of the goblins shows that they are disgusting creatures.)*

Approaching Level

DIFFERENTIATED INSTRUCTION

Emerging In this lesson, students will experience literature that involves both words and images. They may be unused to seeing such materials used in academic settings. Explain that images can often be used to enhance the presentation of great stories. Each frame in this story, for example, is very carefully crafted. Challenge students to study this page carefully and list at least five details they notice. Ask students to consider the colors of the setting, the arrangement of the figures, and the expressions of the characters. All of these features are designed to create a sense of tension and danger.

Teach

Literary Element 1

Motif **Ask:** How does the artist visually express that Thorin and Orcrist are forces of good? *(Students should note the use of color, specifically of white for purity and truth. They may also note that the dwarf and the sword are prettier than their surroundings.)*

Reading Strategy 2

Interpret Meaning Have students look at the pictures of the goblins. **Ask:** How would you describe the Goblin King's expression? *(Students may note the anger, disgust, and hatred.)* Point out to students the importance of incorporating the visual information when reading the dialogue.

1 2

Reading Practice

SPIRAL REVIEW **Textual Features** Students may notice that the text in this graphic novel varies from the text of most books. Most notably, the graphic novel uses many bold and italic words. These specially written words are meant to add extra meaning to the dialogue. They can help to show the speaker's tone, attitude, and speech patterns. Notice the bold and italic words on this page, such as "Thorin Oakenshield," "Liar," and "The Goblin-Cleaver!" **Ask:** How do these textual features enhance the story? *(The bold style is intended to add emphasis to the word, as though it is spoken more loudly or harshly. The italics indicate excitement to the tone of the speaker.)*

Teach

Reading Strategy 3

Sound Effects **Ask:** How does the author use sound to illustrate plot? *(Students should note the use of the words* foosh, pfff, *and* kroooshh *to indicate actions that are taking place.)* Point out to students that the use of sound to indicate action and plot is a common attribute of the comic book and graphic novel.

APPROACHING To help approaching level students, **ask:** In which other ways are comic books and graphic novels different from regular text-based books? *(Students may point out that text-based books tend to have fewer graphics and rely on words alone to convey meaning.)*

To check students' understanding of the selection, see Unit 5 Teaching Resources Book, p. 105.

English Learners

DIFFERENTIATED INSTRUCTION

Beginning/Early Intermediate
Graphic novels often deal with adventure and action. Authors want to convey this action in their work. They do so with both their text and visual art, but some use auditory words as well. On this page, auditory words include "FOOSH," "PFFF," "YAAA," and "KROOOSHHH." Challenge students to read these words aloud in tones that suggest the words' meanings. The words represent fire, fires going out, screaming goblins, and a great crash in the cave. Work with the class to think of other auditory words that might work for these scenarios.

Visual Perspective
on *The Hobbit*

Assess

1. Student summaries will vary.
2. Answers will vary.
3. (a) They are surrounded by goblins and accused of being murderers and the friends of elves. (b) The dwarves represent peace, and the goblins represent unrest.
4. (a) The illustrations show the physical characteristics of goblins, who appear lizard and rat-like in nature. They are also dark to emphasize the idea of darkness and evil. (b) The illustrations stress that the goblins are dark and evil.
5. (a) Students may say that he wanted to make the dialogue more active. (b) Many students will say that adaptation is a way to pass stories on in a variety of artistic and literary mediums.
6. Dialogue changes the tone of the piece into more of an action-adventure than a tale.
7. Answers will vary. Some may argue that it is exciting to create your own images of what you read. Others may feel the graphic novel helps them understand the plot more easily.

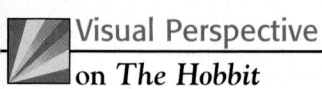

Respond and Think Critically

Respond and Interpret

1. Write a brief summary of the main events in this excerpt before you answer the following questions. For help on writing a summary, see page 42.
2. Does the graphic novel version of *The Hobbit* enhance your understanding of the original text? Why or why not?
3. (a)What happens to the dwarves in this selection? (b)What do you think the dwarves and the goblins represent?
4. (a)What aspects of direct characterization, or statements about character, do Wenzel's illustrations convey? (b)Are the illustrations effective? Why or why not?

Analyze and Evaluate

5. (a)Why do you think Dixon did not use many direct quotes from the original text of *The Hobbit*? (b)Do you think there is value in adapting literary works to other mediums? Why or why not?
6. Why do you think Dixon used dialogue instead of narration for his adaptation of *The Hobbit*?

Connect

7. Which do you prefer, imagining the characters from *The Hobbit*, or seeing illustrations of them? Why?

Writing Practice

Interpretation

This block of images finishes the graphic novel excerpt, but does not show exactly what happens to the characters. It appears that someone with a magical sword appears, fends off the goblins, and saves the heroes. It may be interesting to learn how students interpret this sudden twist in the narrative. Ask students to write paragraphs describing what they think happened on this page, and what happens to the characters next. Students familiar with the story may recount the later adventures of the hobbit and his companions. Students unfamiliar with the story may create new tales all their own.

PART 2

Courage and Cleverness

Siegfried killing Fafner, illustration from "Puissances Secretes," c. 1935. S. Schroeter. Color lithograph.

View the Art This image depicts a scene from an opera by Richard Wagner. The opera is a retelling of a Norse myth about Siegfried, who killed a dragon. How does this image show Siegfried's courage and cleverness? ★

BIG IDEA

Almost every culture has its stories of humans who triumph over fate, the gods, or natural disaster. They do so not always by great strength, but often by their personal attributes, which may include courage or cleverness. The selections in Part 2 relate some of these tales. As you read them, ask yourself, Why do these stories remain popular through time?

931

Approaching Level

DIFFERENTIATED INSTRUCTION

Emerging To practice *reading fluency* have a student read the the explanation of Big Idea on this page. To help students connect to the myth they are about to read, **ask:** What are some movies in which a human being triumphs over fate, the gods, or a natural disaster? *(Answers will vary, but students may say the* Lord of the Rings *and* Harry Potter *movies,* Clash of the Titans, *and* The Day After Tomorrow.*)* *Ask students to compare these works and their themes.*

UNIT FIVE

PART 2

Analyze and Extend

Big Idea

Courage and Cleverness

Ask: How do you define courage and cleverness? *(Answers will vary.)* Discuss with students how the painting shows courage and cleverness. Students may find the act of fighting courageous or the means of fighting clever.

APPROACHING Have approaching-level students name a character from a story or movie who shows courage and cleverness. Ask them to explain how he or she does so. *(Answers will vary.)*

View the Art ★

Answer: *Students may say it shows his courage for killing a large monster and his cleverness for managing it without getting killed himself.*

"Siegfried Killing Fafner" is a reference to Richard Wagner's (1813–1883) Ring Cycle, which consists of four operas: *Das Rheingold (The Rhinegold), Die Walküre (The Valkyrie), Siegfried, and Götterdämmerung (Twilight of the Gods).* In the opera *Siegfried,* the character of Siegfried is the hero.

UNIT FIVE

PART 2

Focus

Bellringer Options

Daily Language Practice Transparency 87

Or **write:** What are your favorite myths? **List** examples on the board. Then have students point out the heroes, villains, and other characters associated with each myth. Discuss what makes these myths and characters memorable.

Teach

Literary Element 1

Characteristics of Myth

Ask: Why do you think the myth of Perseus has stood the test of time? *(Students may mention Perseus's heroic acts and the inclusion of a monster in the myth.)*

View the Art ★

Ask: What kinds of archetypes do you see in this image? *(Students may mention the heroic knight or the terrifying monster.)*

Learning Objectives

For pages 931–933

In studying this text, you will focus on the following objectives:

Literary Study:
Analyzing archetypes, myths, and ballads.
Connecting to the literature.

LITERARY FOCUS

Archetypes

What kinds of stories endure over thousands of years?

In the myth of Perseus, Danaë and her son Perseus live with a kind fisherman, Dictys. Dictys's brother, Polydectes, ruler of the island, falls in love with Danaë, but he wants to get rid of Perseus. To do so, Polydectes convinces Perseus to bring him the head of a Gorgon.

Medusa was one of the Gorgons,
And they are three, the Gorgons, each with wings
And snaky hair, most horrible to mortals.
Whom no man shall behold and draw again
1 The breath of life,
for the reason that whoever looked at them turned instantly into stone. It seemed that Perseus had been led by his angry pride into making an empty boast. No man unaided could kill Medusa.

—Edith Hamilton, **from "Perseus"**

Knight on Horse Battling Dragon. Steven Noble. ★

Archetypes

An **archetype** is a character, thing, or pattern of events that appears repeatedly in myth, folk tales, and other literature and is something that has concerned humans deeply throughout history. For example, you may have noticed several familiar character types in the summary of the Perseus myth, such as the brave young hero. The Perseus myth also involves some familiar situations: The hero undertakes a seemingly impossible task.

Character Archetype A **character archetype** is a familiar individual such as the wise leader, the rebel, the damsel in distress, and the traitor. In Native American folklore, the trickster Coyote is a common character archetype.

Coyote looked at Crow with this fat and thought how good it would taste. Becoming hungrier and hungrier, he wondered how he could get the fat for himself. He thought hard. Then he laughed.

—retold by Ella Clark, **from "Coyote and Crow"**

Research Practice

Oral Report Invite students to connect to mythology by researching a myth of their choosing and presenting an oral report. Students' oral reports should include the following:

- a summary of the myth
- a character synopses
- a visual or graphic organizer

Encourage them to talk about retellings of the myth over time (e.g., the myth of Helen of Troy has been used in books, poetry, and movies).

Image Archetype An object or a place that has a universal symbolism is called an **image archetype.** For example, a circle often represents the continuation of life.

2 In the early days Loki, though a god, had wedded a monstrous giantess, and the union of these two evil beings produced a fearful brood. The first was the great world serpent, whom Odin cast into the sea, and who became so large that he completely encircled the earth, his tail touching his mouth.

—retold by Olivia Coolidge, **from "The Fenris Wolf"**

Plot Pattern Archetype Sometimes the same basic story is told in many cultures. Details such as the setting and character names may change, but the basic plot is the same. These plot lines are called **plot pattern archetypes.** For example, in "Perseus," the King is told that his daughter will have a son who will kill him. He tries to avoid this fate by locking her away.

Acrisius did not dare slay his daughter. Instead, he had a house built all of bronze and sunk underground, but with part of the roof open to the sky so that light and air could come through. Here he shut her up and guarded her.

—Edith Hamilton, **from "Perseus"**

Theme Archetype A **theme archetype** is an idea that occurs wherever people tell stories. The ideas that good can overcome evil, that people can redeem themselves, and that an underworld exists are all archetypal themes.

Stock Characters A **stock character** is a common character type, such as the tough-guy detective, the faithful friend of the hero, or the damsel in distress whom the hero rescues. Stock characters do not have the same universal quality as archetypes, however. They may be limited to a specific culture or time period.

Myth

The word *myth* comes from the Greek *mythos,* meaning "word" or "story." Ancient people told one another stories to interpret natural events and to explain the nature of the universe and humanity. These stories, which have been passed down from one generation to another for thousands of years, are today's myths. Virtually all ancient cultures had myths that were particular to that culture, although many of these stories had certain elements in common.

Characteristics of Most Myths

- Sought to explain things people could not otherwise understand
- Served to bind a group of people together
- Were used to set examples for both virtuous behavior and flawed behavior
- Contained supernatural elements

Ballad

A **ballad** is a song or poem that tells a story. Folk ballads typically tell the saga of thrilling, dramatic—and often catastrophic—events. Like epics and myths, they were passed on by word of mouth for generations before being written down.

LOG ON **Literature** Online

Literature and Reading For more about literary elements, go to glencoe.com and enter QuickPass code GL49787u5.

Quickwrite

Write a Description Choose an archetype such as the quest or the unwilling hero. Write a description of who and what comes to mind when you think about your chosen archetype. Give a modern example of your chosen archetype. (For example, *the hero*: Superman.)

UNIT FIVE
PART 2

Teach

Literary Element 2

Characteristics of Myth

Have volunteers read the descriptions and quotations aloud. After each quote is read, **ask:** How is this quote a good example? Discuss how the quotes relate to the section topic.

Assess

Quickwrite

Descriptions and examples of the chosen archetype should reflect an understanding of its universal significance.

For additional support for English Learners, see Unit 5 Teaching Resources Book, p. 109.

English Learners

DIFFERENTIATED INSTRUCTION

Emerging Help students understand the difference between an archetype and a stock character. Explain that an archetype is a universal character that transcends language barriers. An archetype is a well-rounded character. A stock character is much more narrowly defined and is often a flat character. Stock characters rely heavily on cultural stereotypes for their personalities. Ask students to identify an archetype or stock character from a well-known story or film and explain how the character's actions affect the plot.

Before You Read

Focus

Bellringer Options

Daily Language Practice Transparency 88

Or **display** images of characters from ancient Greek mythology.

Ask: What do you know about the ancient Greeks? Why do you think their myths and stories are still studied today? Ask students to consider as they read what the story of Perseus has to teach modern readers.

Before You Read

Perseus

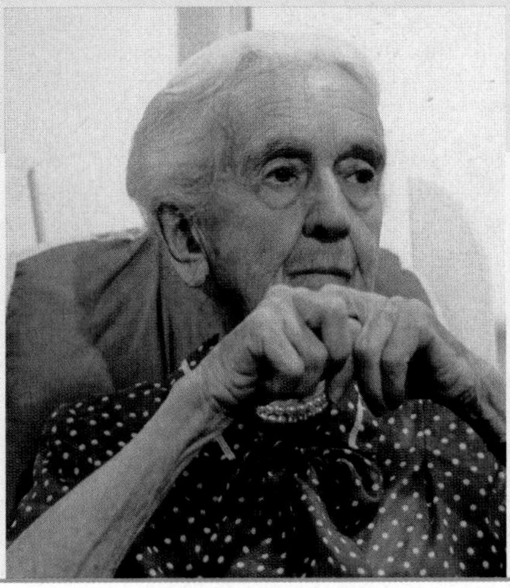

Meet **Edith Hamilton**
(1867–1963)

Students who enjoy reading Greek and Roman mythology as part of their English classes have Edith Hamilton to thank. At the age of sixty-three, Hamilton began a second career retelling the ancient myths of Greece and Rome. Hamilton's scholarly work single-handedly renewed an interest in the classical world in American schools.

Edith Hamilton was born in 1867 in Dresden, Germany. Her father was the son of a prominent Fort Wayne, Indiana, family, and the family eventually moved back to Fort Wayne.

A Classical Education As girls, Hamilton and her sisters were educated at home by their parents and private tutors. From 1884 to 1886, Hamilton attended Miss Porter's School for Young Ladies in Connecticut. In 1891 she entered Bryn Mawr College, where she studied Greek and Latin languages and literature.

Headmistress In 1896 Hamilton accepted an offer from M. Carey Thomas, the President of Bryn Mawr College, to head Bryn Mawr School. It was the first private high school that focused on college preparation for young women. Hamilton's theories of education were based on the Greek ideals of individualism, academic freedom, and intellectual exploration. She remained headmistress at Bryn Mawr School for twenty-six years.

The Greek Way After her retirement, Hamilton turned to writing about her favorite subject: the Greek and Roman classics. In 1930 she published her first book, *The Greek Way*. Several other books followed, including her most famous work, *Mythology* (1942).

"Ideals have tremendous power. When ideals are low they fade out and are forgotten; great ideals have had power of persistent life."

—Edith Hamilton

In her books, Hamilton made ancient cultures accessible to a wide range of readers. She also idealized Greek culture over all others. In *Mythology* she wrote, "In Greece man first realized what mankind was." She believed that the Greeks maintained a balance of mind, body, and spirit superior to other cultures. Some critics have called her portrayal of the Greeks simplistic. However, her work in classical studies proved instrumental in reviving the study of the classics in America in the mid-twentieth century.

LOG ON Literature Online

Author Search For more about Edith Hamilton, go to glencoe.com and enter QuickPass code GL49787u5.

Selection Skills

Perseus

Literary Elements
- Plot Pattern Archetype (SE pp. 935–943)
- Hero (SE p. 943)

Listening/Speaking/Viewing Skills
- Analyze Art (SE pp. 936, 941)

Reading Skills
- Identify Genre (SE pp. 935–943)

Vocabulary Skills
- Antonyms (SE pp. 935, 943)
- Academic Vocabulary (SE p. 943)

Writing Skills/Grammar
- Expository Essay (SE p. 944)
- Describe Character Traits (TE p. 936)

Literature and Reading Preview

Connect to the Myth

What does the word *hero* mean to you? Write a journal entry explaining your personal definition of *hero.*

Build Background

In Greek mythology, Hermes is known as the messenger god and the bringer of good fortune and is also thought to offer protection to travelers. Athena is identified with wisdom and is described as an expert in war and strategy.

Set Purposes for Reading

Big Idea Courage and Cleverness

As you read "Perseus," ask yourself, Where can I find examples of Perseus's bravery and intelligence?

Literary Element Plot Pattern Archetype

A **plot pattern archetype** is a sequence of events that is familiar because it appears repeatedly in stories told across cultures, all over the world. One plot pattern archetype, for example, involves a hero guided by magical beings or gods. As you read, ask yourself, How many plot pattern archetypes can I identify?

Reading Strategy Identify Genre

Genre refers to a category of literature. Each genre has its own conventions, or standards, that give readers certain expectations. When reading a story categorized as a mystery, for example, the reader expects a mysterious event to occur. The reader also expects a suspenseful tone, twists and turns in the plot, and a final resolution in which the mystery is solved. "Perseus" is a myth. As you read, ask yourself, What are the characteristics of the myth genre?

Tip: List Characteristics As you read, it may help you to list the characteristics that make "Perseus" different from fiction that describes everyday life in the present. List the characteristics of each in a chart like the one below.

Myth	Contemporary Realistic Fiction
Set in the distant past	Set in the present

Learning Objectives

For pages 934–943

In studying this text, you will focus on the following objectives:

Literary Study: Analyzing plot pattern archetype.

Reading: Identifying genre.

Vocabulary

kindred (kin′ drid) *n.* people who are related; family; p. 936 *My brothers, parents, aunts, and uncles are my kindred.*

shrill (shril) *adj.* loud; piercing; p. 937 *The shrill cry of the neighbor's cat keeps us up at night.*

withered (with′ ərd) *adj.* shriveled or dried up; p. 938 *He looked out on his withered fields and cursed the drought.*

Tip: Antonyms Antonyms are words with opposite meanings. Words can only be antonyms if they are both the same part of speech. For example, the vocabulary word *shrill* is an antonym of *quiet,* but not of the word *whisper.* Even though *whisper* and *quiet* have related meanings, *quiet* and *shrill* are both adjectives but *whisper* is a verb.

Before You Read

Focus

Summary

A prophecy foretells the killing of King Acrisius by his grandson. After his daughter gives birth to Perseus, the king tries to kill the mother and child, but both survive. As a young man, Perseus offers to kill the monster Medusa for King Polydectes. With the help of the gods Hermes and Athena, he accomplishes his quest.

For summaries in languages other than English, see Unit 5 Teaching Resources Book, pp. 110–115.

Interactive Read and Write

Other options for teaching this selection can be found in

- Interactive Read and Write for EL Students, pp. 267–280
- Interactive Read and Write for Approaching-Level Students, pp. 267–280
- Interactive Read and Write for On-Level Students, pp. 267–280

Vocabulary

Word Origins Have students research each word to find its language origin. Then have students use each word in a sentence.

For additional vocabulary practice, see Unit 5 Teaching Resources Book, p. 118.

For additional context, see Interactive Visual Vocabulary CD-ROM.

Approaching Level

DIFFERENTIATED INSTRUCTION

Emerging Help students understand and identify genre. Write the following genres on the board:

- Mystery
- Science fiction
- Romance
- Fairy tales

Ask students to think of books or movies that fit into these genres. Ask students to explain why the book or movie fits the genre they have chosen. Students should explain characteristics of the book or movie that lead them to categorize it within the genre they chose. Write students' responses on the board. Explain that myth is a genre. Myths involve the supernatural—forces that don't exist in real life. People created myths to explain events in nature that they did not understand.

Teach

Reading Strategy 1

Identify Genre Answer: *It is common in myth for humans to consult gods.*

APPROACHING **Say:** Another convention of myth is for humans to try to avoid fate. Ask approaching-level students to predict how the king will respond.

Literary Element 2

Plot Pattern Archetype Note that many folk and fairy tales use elements of myths.

Possible Answers: *"Rapunzel," "Rumplestiltskin"*

For additional literary element practice, see Unit 5 Teaching Resources Book, p. 116.

View the Art ★

Xavier Cortada was born in New York in 1964 but was raised in Miami. He is well known for his public art projects, including several murals, and has been commissioned to create works for the White House and many cultural institutions.

For an audio recording of this selection, use Listening Library Audio CD-ROM.

Readability Scores

Dale-Chall: 6.9

DRP: 54

Lexile: 1030

Perseus

Retold by Edith Hamilton

King Acrisius of Argos[1] had only one child, a daughter, Danaë. She was beautiful above all the other women of the land, but this was small comfort to the King for not having a son. He journeyed to Delphi[2] to ask the god if there was any hope that some day he would be the father of a boy. The priestess told him no, and added what was far worse: that his daughter would have a son who would kill him.

The only sure way to escape that fate was for the King to have Danaë instantly put to death—taking no chances, but seeing to it himself. This Acrisius would not do. His fatherly affection was not strong, as events proved, but his fear of the gods was. They visited with terrible punishment those who shed the blood of **kindred.** Acrisius did not dare slay his daughter. Instead, he had a house built all of bronze and sunk underground, but with part of the roof open to the sky so that light and air could come through. Here he shut her up and guarded her.

1. *Argos* was a powerful city in southeastern Greece during the seventh century B.C.
2. *Delphi* was an ancient Greek town to the south of Mount Parnassus. It was the site of an oracle, or shrine, where a priestess supposedly channeled predictions of the god Apollo.

1 Identify Genre *What do the details of the story so far tell you about the characteristics of myth?*

2 Plot Pattern Archetype *What other stories, fairy tales, or myths do you know that include a woman shut up alone?*

Vocabulary

kindred (kin′ drid) *n.* people who are related; family

Perseus, 1998. Xavier Cortada. Acrylic on canvas, 121.9 x 91.4 cm. Private collection. ★

So Danaë endured, the beautiful,
To change the glad daylight for brass-
  bound walls,
And in that chamber secret as the grave
She lived a prisoner. Yet to her came
Zeus in the golden rain. ☆

As she sat there through the long days and hours with nothing to do, nothing to see except the clouds moving by overhead, a mysterious thing happened, a shower of gold fell from the sky and filled her chamber. How it was revealed to her that it was Zeus who had visited her in this shape we are not told, but she knew that the child she bore was his son.

For a time she kept his birth secret from her father, but it became increasingly difficult to do so in the narrow limits of that bronze house and finally one day the little boy—his name was Perseus—was discovered by his grandfather. "Your child!" Acrisius cried in great anger. "Who is his father?" But when Danaë answered proudly, "Zeus," he would not believe her. One thing

Writing Practice

SPIRAL REVIEW **Describe Character Traits** Have students read pages 936 and 937 aloud. **Ask:** What can you tell about Danaë from what you have read? **Write** responses on the board. *(Students may say that she is exceptionally beautiful. They may say that she does not seem to complain even when she is kept prisoner in an underground chamber. Students should note that she is honest—she tells her father that Zeus is the father of her child. She also loves her son.)*

Have students write a paragraph describing Danaë based on the details in the story. Encourage them to speculate how she felt in each situation.

only he was sure of, that the boy's life was a terrible danger to his own. He was afraid to kill him for the same reason that had kept him from killing her, fear of Zeus and the Furies[3] who pursue such murderers. But if he could not kill them outright, he could put them in the way of tolerably certain death. He had a great chest made, and the two placed in it. Then it was taken out to sea and cast into the water.

In that strange boat Danaë sat with her little son. The daylight faded and she was alone on the sea.

> When in the carven chest the winds and waves
> Struck fear into her heart she put her arms,
> Not without tears, round Perseus tenderly
> She said, "O son, what grief is mine.
> But you sleep softly, little child,
> Sunk deep in rest within your cheerless home,
> Only a box, brass-bound. The night, this darkness visible,
> The scudding[4] waves so near to your soft curls,
> The **shrill** voice of the wind, you do not heed,
> Nestled in your red cloak, fair little face."

Through the night in the tossing chest she listened to the waters that seemed always about to wash over them. The dawn came, but with no comfort to her for she could not see it. Neither could she see that around them there were islands rising high above the sea, many islands. All she knew was that presently a wave seemed to lift them and carry them swiftly on and then, retreating, leave them on something solid and motionless. They had made land; they were safe from the sea, but they were still in the chest with no way to get out.

Fate willed it—or perhaps Zeus, who up to now had done little for his love and his child—that they should be discovered by a good man, a fisherman named Dictys. He came upon the great box and broke it open and took the pitiful cargo home to his wife who was as kind as he. They had no children and they cared for Danaë and Perseus as if they were their own. The two lived there many years, Danaë content to let her son follow the fisherman's humble trade, out of harm's way. But in the end more trouble came. Polydectes, the ruler of the little island, was the brother of Dictys, but he was a cruel and ruthless man. He seems to have taken no notice of the mother and son for a long time, but at last Danaë attracted his attention. She was still radiantly beautiful even though Perseus by now was full grown, and Polydectes fell in love with her. He wanted her, but he did not want her son, and he set himself to think out a way of getting rid of him.

There were some fearsome monsters called Gorgons who lived on an island and were known far and wide because of their deadly power. Polydectes evidently talked to Perseus about them; he probably told him that he would rather have the head of one of them than anything else in the world. This seems practically certain from the plan he devised for killing Perseus. He announced that he was about to be married and he called his friends together for a celebration, including Perseus in the invitation. Each guest, as was customary, brought a gift for the bride-to-be, except Perseus alone. He had nothing he could

3. The *Furies* were female snake-haired goddesses who carried out revenge on humans for their wrongdoings.
4. *Scudding* means "moving along at a fast pace."

3 Plot Pattern Archetype *Does this turn of events seem familiar or surprising to you? Explain.*

Vocabulary

shrill (shril) *adj.* loud; piercing

Teach

Literary Element 3

Plot Pattern Archetype

Answer: *Students may say that mythical characters often are placed in dangerous situations with little hope of survival.* Ask students for examples of other stories (including film and television shows) in which characters are in similar situations.

ENGLISH LEARNERS Have English language learners offer examples of stories from their own culture in which characters are thrown into hopeless situations.

Literary History ☆

Zeus and Cronus Like Perseus, Zeus was fated to kill his father, Cronus. Cronus, too, tried to kill his children, but his wife escaped with Zeus, who later replaced Cronus as king of the gods.

English Learners

DIFFERENTIATED INSTRUCTION

Beginning/Early Intermediate English language learners may have trouble keeping track of the many different characters in this selection. Have students list the names of the characters as they read. Next to each character's name, students should jot down basic characterizations, such as *Acrisius: king, evil.* Have them continue to add to their list as they read the rest of the story.

Teach

Big Idea 1

Courage and Cleverness

Answer: *Although he knows that the Gorgons are fierce monsters, he goes after them anyway in order to keep his promise.*

Remind students that ancient Greek culture celebrated individuals with courage and intelligence.

Reading Strategy 2

Identify Genre **Answer:** *The presence of the gods indicates that the story is a myth, which generally includes supernatural forces like gods and goddesses. The god or goddess aiding a mortal is also a common myth archetype.*

Literary History ☆

The Quest A hero's quest, or attempt to claim a prize or meet a challenge, is one of the most common plot patterns in mythology and literature. The hero's encounters with daunting obstacles make quest stories exciting and suspenseful. Readers identify with the hero as he or she rises to each task required.

give. He was young and proud and keenly mortified. He stood up before them all and did exactly what the King had hoped he would do, declared that he would give him a present better than any there. He would go off and kill Medusa and bring back her head as his gift. Nothing could have suited the King better. No one in his senses would have made such a proposal. Medusa was one of the Gorgons,

> And they are three, the Gorgons, each with wings
> And snaky hair, most horrible to mortals.
> Whom no man shall behold and draw again
> The breath of life,

for the reason that whoever looked at them was turned instantly into stone. It seemed that Perseus had been led by his angry pride into making an empty boast. No man unaided could kill Medusa.

But Perseus was saved from his folly. Two great gods were watching over him. He took ship as soon as he left the King's hall, not daring to see his mother first and tell her what he intended, and he sailed to Greece to learn where the three monsters were to be found. He went to Delphi, but all the priestess would say was to bid him seek the land where men eat not Demeter's golden grain,[5] but only acorns. So he went to Dodona,[6] in the land of oak trees, where the talking oaks were which declared Zeus's will and where the Selli[7] lived who made their bread from acorns. They could tell him, however, no more than this, that he was under the protection of the gods. They did not know where the Gorgons lived.

When and how Hermes and Athena came to his help is not told in any story, but he must have known despair before they did so. At last, however, as he wandered on, he met a strange and beautiful person. We know what he looked like from many a poem, a young man with the first down upon his cheek when youth is loveliest, carrying, as no other young man ever did, a wand of gold with wings at one end, wearing a winged hat, too, and winged sandals. At sight of him hope must have entered Perseus' heart, for he would know that this could be none other than Hermes, the guide and the giver of good.

This radiant personage[8] told him that before he attacked Medusa he must first be properly equipped, and that what he needed was in the possession of the nymphs[9] of the North. To find the nymphs' abode,[10] they must go to the Gray Women who alone could tell them the way. These women dwelt in a land where all was dim and shrouded in twilight. No ray of sun looked ever on that country, nor the moon by night. In that gray place the three women lived, all gray themselves and **withered** as in extreme old age. They were strange creatures, indeed, most of all because they had but one eye for the three, which it was their custom to take turns with, each removing it from her forehead when she had had it for a time and handing it to another.

5. *Demeter's golden grain* refers to Demeter, the Greek goddess of agriculture.
6. *Dodona,* in northwestern Greece, was the site of an oracle dedicated to Zeus.
7. The *Selli* were a tribe of people who lived in the northwestern part of ancient Greece.
8. *Personage* means "an important person."
9. *Nymphs* are female nature spirits in Greek mythology.
10. An *abode* is a home or place of residence.

1 Courage and Cleverness *Does Perseus show courage here? Why or why not?*

Identify Genre *Why do you think the Greeks created this and other stories about humans aided by gods?* **2**

Vocabulary

withered (with′ ərd) *adj.* shriveled or dried up

Research Practice

SPIRAL REVIEW **Answer Questions** Have students conduct research using library resources or the internet to answer the following questions about Medusa:

- Why did Medusa have snakes for hair? *(She was ravaged by Poseidon in Athena's temple. Athena was outraged that her sacred temple had been violated, so she turned Medusa's beautiful tresses into snakes.)*
- How was Medusa different from the other Gorgons? *(She was mortal and her gaze could turn people into stone.)* Encourage students to bring in images of Medusa to share with the class.

All this Hermes told Perseus and then he unfolded his plan. He would himself guide Perseus to them. Once there Perseus must keep hidden until he saw one of them take the eye out of her forehead to pass it on. At that moment, when none of the three could see, he must rush forward and seize the eye and refuse to give it back until they told him how to reach the nymphs of the North.

He himself, Hermes said, would give him a sword to attack Medusa with—which could not be bent or broken by the Gorgon's scales, no matter how hard they were. This was a wonderful gift, no doubt, and yet of what use was a sword when the creature to be struck by it could turn the swordsman into stone before he was within striking distance? But another great deity[11] was at hand to help. Pallas[12] Athena stood beside Perseus. She took off the shield of polished bronze which covered her breast and held it out to him. "Look into this when you attack the Gorgon," she said. "You will be able to see her in it as in a mirror, and so avoid her deadly power."

Now, indeed, Perseus had good reason to hope. The journey to the twilight land was long, over the stream of Ocean and on to the very border of the black country where the Cimmerians[13] dwell, but Hermes was his guide and he could not go astray. They found the Gray Women at last, looking in the wavering light like gray birds, for they had the shape of swans. But their heads were human and beneath their wings they had arms and hands. Perseus did just as Hermes had said, he held back until he saw one of them take the eye out of her forehead. Then before she could give it to her sister, he snatched it out of her hand. It was a moment or two before the three realized they had lost it. Each thought one of the others had it. But Perseus spoke out and told them he had taken it and that it would be theirs again only when they showed him how to find the nymphs of the North. They gave him full directions at once; they would have done anything to get their eye back. He returned it to them and went on the way they had pointed out to him. He was bound, although he did not know it, to the blessed country of the Hyperboreans,[14] at the back of the North Wind, of which it is said: "Neither by ship nor yet by land shall one find the wondrous road to the gathering place of the Hyperboreans." But Perseus had Hermes with him, so that the road lay open to him, and he reached that host of happy people who are always banqueting and holding joyful revelry.[15] They showed him great kindness: they welcomed him to their feast, and the maidens dancing to the sound of flute and lyre[16] paused to get for him the gifts he sought. These were three: winged sandals, a magic wallet[17] which would always become the right size for whatever was to be carried in it, and, most important of all, a cap which made the wearer invisible. With these and Athena's shield and Hermes' sword

11. A *deity* is a god or goddess.
12. *Pallas* is another name for Athena and is sometimes used as part of her regular name. One myth claims Pallas was a friend of Athena's whom she killed accidentally. She added his name to her own so that he would not be forgotten.
13. *Cimmerians* were a race of people living in what is now Russia and Ukraine.
14. *Hyperboreans* were a mythical group of people living in the northern parts of Asia and Europe. Their land was supposed to be perfect.
15. *Revelry* means "loud, boisterous celebrating."
16. A *lyre* is a stringed instrument similar to a harp.
17. Here, *wallet* is used in its Middle English sense and means "knapsack."

3 Identify Genre *How does the description of this sword fit the characteristics of a myth?*

4 Identify Genre *Would these three items be found in a realistic story set in the present? Explain.*

Teach

Reading Strategy 3

Identify Genre Answer: *Magical elements like this sword are common in myth. This sword is magical or fantastic because it cannot be bent or broken. In some cases, swords can represent an archetype.*

ADVANCED For advanced students, **ask:** What other stories can you think of that include a weapon that cannot be broken? *(The Legend of King Arthur)*

Reading Strategy 4

Identify Genre Answer: *No; in a realistic story set in the present, people do not rely on magic or supernatural powers to solve their problems.*

Approaching Level

DIFFERENTIATED INSTRUCTION

Emerging Students may have trouble comprehending the sequence of events leading Perseus to Medusa. Reread these events beginning in the second column on page 938. Stop reading to write each of the following events on the board or have students write them in a sequence chart:

- Perseus goes to Delphi, where a priestess tells him to go to the land of talking oaks.
- Perseus goes to Dodona, where the talking oaks tell him he is under the protection of the gods.
- Perseus wanders and meets Hermes, who tells him he needs to be properly equipped to fight Medusa and must find the nymphs of the North.
- Perseus must find the three women who share one eye and take the eye to make them tell him where the nymphs live.

Teach

Big Idea 1

Courage and Cleverness

Answer: *Because Medusa could turn a person to stone with one look, Perseus cleverly avoids her gaze.*

APPROACHING For approaching-level students, **ask:** Do you think Athena helping Perseus makes him less clever or brave? *(Students should support their opinions with logical arguments.)*

Big Idea 2

Courage and Cleverness

Say: Quest myths always circle back to the place or the conflict that started the quest.

ADVANCED For advanced students, **ask:** How is Perseus better equipped to realize his destiny after defeating the Gorgons? *(He has completed his quest. He has not only done the impossible, but also has the tools to kill his enemies.)*

Perseus was ready for the Gorgons. Hermes knew where they lived, and leaving the happy land the two flew back across Ocean and over the sea to the Terrible Sisters' island.

By great good fortune they were all asleep when Perseus found them. In the mirror of the bright shield he could see them clearly, creatures with great wings and bodies covered with golden scales and hair a mass of twisting snakes. Athena was beside him now as well as Hermes. They told him which one was Medusa and that was important, for she alone of the three could be killed; the other two were immortal. Perseus on his winged sandals hovered above them, looking, however, only at the shield. Then he aimed a stroke down at Medusa's throat and Athena guided his hand. With a single sweep of his sword he cut through her neck and, his eyes still fixed on the shield with never a glance at her, he swooped low enough to seize the head. He dropped it into the wallet which closed around it. He had nothing to fear from it now. But the two other Gorgons had awakened and, horrified at the sight of their sister slain, tried to pursue the slayer. Perseus was safe; he had on the cap of darkness and they could not find him.

So over the sea rich-haired Danaë's son,
Perseus, on his winged sandals sped,
Flying swift as thought.
In a wallet of silver,
A wonder to behold,
He bore the head of the monster,
While Hermes, the son of Maia,
The messenger of Zeus,
Kept ever at his side.

On his way back he came to Ethiopia[18] and alighted there. By this time Hermes had left him. Perseus found, as Hercules was later to find, that a lovely maiden had been given up to be devoured by a horrible sea serpent. Her name was Andromeda and she was the daughter of a silly vain woman,

That starred Ethiop queen who strove
To set her beauty's praise above
The sea-nymphs, and their power
offended.

She had boasted that she was more beautiful than the daughters of Nereus, the Sea-god. An absolutely certain way in those days to draw down on one a wretched fate was to claim superiority in anything over any deity; nevertheless people were perpetually doing so. In this case the punishment for the arrogance the gods detested fell not on Queen Cassiopeia, Andromeda's mother, but on her daughter. The Ethiopians were being devoured in numbers by the serpent; and, learning from the oracle that they could be freed from the pest only if Andromeda were offered up to it, they forced Cepheus, her father, to consent. When Perseus arrived the maiden was on a rocky ledge by the sea, chained there to wait for the coming of the monster. Perseus saw her and on the instant loved her. He waited beside her until the great snake came for its prey; then he cut its head off just as he had the Gorgon's. The headless body dropped back into the water; Perseus took Andromeda to her parents and asked for her hand, which they gladly gave him.

With her he sailed back to the island and **2** his mother, but in the house where he had lived so long he found no one. The fisherman Dictys' wife was long since dead, and the two others, Danaë and the man who had been like a father to Perseus, had had to fly and hide themselves from Polydectes, who was furious at Danaë's refusal to marry him. They had taken refuge in a temple, Perseus was told. He learned also that the King was holding a banquet in the palace and all the men who favored him were gathered there.

18. *Ethiopia* is a coastal country in northeastern Africa.

1 Courage and Cleverness *What is clever about Perseus's method of killing Medusa?*

Reading Practice

SMALL GROUP SPIRAL REVIEW **Characteristics of Genre** Remind students that supernatural forces are a characteristic of myth. Break students into small groups and have them reread Perseus' slaying of Medusa and of the sea serpent.
Ask: How did supernatural forces help Perseus overcome Medusa and the sea serpent? *(Students may say that Perseus would not have been able to kill Medusa without help from Hermes and Athena—Hermes gave him a sword that could not be bent or broken and a shield he could use as a mirror to see her indirectly, in order to avoid her deadly powers. Students may say that he used the same sword to kill the sea serpent.)* Then have them discuss the role of supernatural forces in the story. Students should take notes during their discussion.

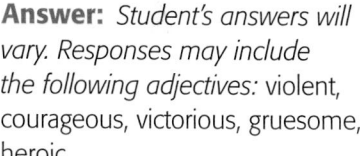

Perseus assisted by Minerva, presents the head of Medusa to Phineus and his companions. Jean Marc Nattier. Musee des Beaux-Arts, Tours, France.

View the Art What adjectives would you use to describe this scene? ★

Perseus instantly saw his opportunity. He went straight to the palace and entered the hall. As he stood at the entrance, Athena's shining buckler[19] on his breast, the silver wallet at his side, he drew the eyes of every man there. Then before any could look away he held up the Gorgon's head; and at the sight one and all, the cruel King and his servile courtiers,[20] were turned into stone. There they sat, a row of statues, each, as it were, frozen stiff in the attitude he had struck when he first saw Perseus.

When the islanders knew themselves freed from the tyrant it was easy for Perseus to find Danaë and Dictys. He made Dictys king of the island, but he and his mother decided that they would go back with Andromeda to Greece and try to be reconciled to Acrisius, to see if the many years that had passed since he had put them in the chest had not softened him so that he would be glad to receive his daughter and grandson. When they reached Argos, however, they found that Acrisius had been driven away from the city, and where he was no one could say. It happened that soon after their arrival Perseus heard that the King of Larissa,[21] in the North, was holding a great athletic contest, and he journeyed there to take part. In the discus-throwing[22] when his turn came and he hurled the heavy missile, it swerved and fell among the spectators. Acrisius was there on a visit to the King, and the discus struck him. The blow was fatal and he died at once.

So Apollo's[23] oracle was again proved true. If Perseus felt any grief, at least he knew that his grandfather had done his best to kill him and his mother. With his death their troubles came to an end. Perseus and Andromeda lived happily ever after. Their son, Electryon, was the grandfather of Hercules.[24]

Medusa's head was given to Athena, who bore it always upon the aegis, Zeus's shield, which she carried for him. ❧

19. A *buckler* is a type of shield.
20. The term *servile courtiers* refers to the submissive people who advised the king.
21. *Larissa* is a city in eastern Greece.
22. A *discus* is a heavy round disk that is thrown in track and field competitions.
23. *Apollo* is a Greek god known for healing, prophesy, and music.
24. *Hercules* is the Roman name for the Greek hero Heracles, who was the son of Zeus and a human woman named Alcemene. Hercules successfully completed twelve tasks in order to become a god.

Plot Pattern Archetype *How does this event complete one archetypal pattern in the story?* **3**

Teach

Literary Element 3

Plot Pattern Archetype

Answer: *With this event, the prophesy is fulfilled. Even though Acrisius does everything possible to stop the prophecy from coming true, he fails. Perseus kills him just as was prophesied, but by accident rather than intent.*

ENGLISH LEARNERS For English learners, **ask:** Did the story of Perseus end the way you expected? Explain. *(Students may say that they knew that in Greek myths, the fates never lie.)*

View the Art ★

Answer: *Student's answers will vary. Responses may include the following adjectives:* violent, courageous, victorious, gruesome, heroic.

To check students' understanding of the selection, see Unit 5 Teaching Resources Book, p. 121.

English Learners

DIFFERENTIATED INSTRUCTION

Beginning/Early Intermediate Tell students that *missile,* as used in this myth, means "an object thrown at a target" and does not refer to a weapon or ballistic missile. Explain that this is a good example of a situation where context clues can help you determine meaning. *(Perseus is throwing a discus, which is referred to as a missile.)*

Ask students to find other examples of multiple-meaning words in the selection. *(Students might identify* oracle, *which in this case means the response of a prophetic person. Another example is* bore, *which here means "wore" and not "gave birth to.")*

After You Read

Assess

1. Accept reasonable answers.
2. (a) He sets them adrift in the sea. (b) A prophecy said his daughter's son would kill him. (c) He loves himself more than he loves his family and stubbornly rebels against fate.
3. (a) Hermes helps him find his way. Both Athena and Hermes give him magical tools. (b) They consider him worthy; he is Zeus's son—and their brother.
4. Fate is unchangeable.
5. Both Andromeda and Perseus were placed in life-threatening situations by their family members.
6. His relationship with her shows his bravery and also allows him to become an adult with a family of his own.
7. Students should support their answers.
8. Students should point to specific details from the myth in their answers.

After You Read

Respond and Think Critically

Respond and Interpret

1. What event in the story surprised you the most? Why?
2. (a)What does King Acrisius do to Danaë and Perseus? (b)Why does Acrisius take such drastic measures? (c)What does this tell you about his character?
3. (a)How do the gods help Perseus achieve his goal of killing Medusa and cutting off her head? (b)Why are they willing to help him?

Analyze and Evaluate

4. What does Acrisius's death in this myth reveal about the Ancient Greeks' beliefs about fate?
5. How are Andromeda and Perseus similar? Consider the nature of the situations they find themselves in.
6. Why is Perseus's relationship with Andromeda important to the story?

Connect

7. **Big Idea** Courage and Cleverness How courageous and clever is Perseus? Support your answer with details from the story.
8. **Connect to the Author** Edith Hamilton believed the ancient Greek culture was superior to all others. What elements of that culture seem worthy of high praise? Explain.

Visual Literacy

Graphic Organizer

Sometimes when you are reading, it can be helpful to create a flowchart showing what is happening in the plot. The flowchart allows you to define the major plot events and character decisions in a story. Use the flowchart shown as the beginning of your own flowchart, charting the major events of the myth of Perseus.

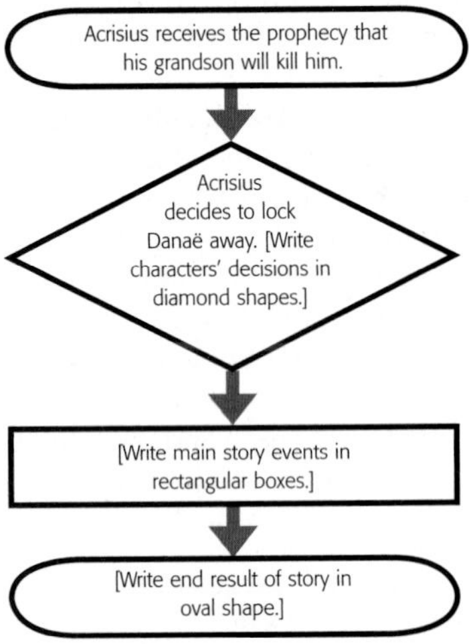

Acrisius receives the prophecy that his grandson will kill him.
Acrisius decides to lock Danaë away. [Write characters' decisions in diamond shapes.]
[Write main story events in rectangular boxes.]
[Write end result of story in oval shape.]

Partner Activity When you have completed your flowchart, meet with a classmate to answer the following questions.

1. At what point does Perseus decide to kill Medusa? Why does he make this decision?
2. At what point in the story do the gods intervene and help Perseus?

Visual Literacy

Students' charts should summarize the main events and decisions.

1. At the wedding announcement dinner of Polydectes and Danaë; To make up for the embarrassment of having no gift
2. The text states that it is not known when they came to his aid, but suggests that it was after he became discouraged.

Literary Element Plot Pattern Archetype

Certain plot patterns are characterized as archetypal when they are common across cultures. Most cultures, for example, have created myths about how Earth and its people were created. Similarly, many cultures have stories in which humans are helped by gods.

1. List some plot patterns from this story that you have come across in other stories, books, plays, or movies.
2. Choose one plot pattern from this story and explain why it might be meaningful to readers around the world.

Review: Hero

As you learned on pages 830–831, the **hero** in a literary work is the main character. In myths, the hero usually has traits or abilities that exceed those of a normal person. These traits or abilities allow the hero to accomplish great deeds.

Partner Activity With a partner, create a chart like the one below listing the actions and personality traits that make Perseus a hero. In the second column of your chart, explain why each element demonstrates heroism.

Heroic Action or Trait	Heroic Explanation
Perseus does not give up his quest even before the gods help him.	His actions show that he is willing to persevere even when things look hopeless.

LOG ON Literature Online

Selection Resources For Selection Quizzes, eFlashcards, and Reading-Writing Connection activities, go to glencoe.com and enter QuickPass code GL49787u5.

Reading Strategy Identify Genre

Knowing a story's genre can help you understand what to expect. Myths like "Perseus" are traditional stories that involve gods, goddesses, heroes, and supernatural forces. Myths may explain beliefs, customs, or forces of nature. Review the chart you made as you read, and answer these questions.

1. What elements of "Perseus" fit the description of a myth?
2. How do supernatural events in a story affect your expectations as a reader?

Vocabulary Practice

Practice with Antonyms With a partner, match each boldface vocabulary word below with its antonym. You will not use all the answer choices. Use a thesaurus or dictionary to check your answers.

1. **kindred**	a. silent
2. **shrill**	b. piercing
3. **withered**	c. known
	d. strangers
	e. wrinkled
	f. thriving

Academic Vocabulary

In this story, Perseus's quest is ***voluntary*** *and nobody forces him to undertake it.*

Voluntary is an academic word. A word that shares a similar meaning is *optional.* To study this word further, fill out the graphic organizer below.

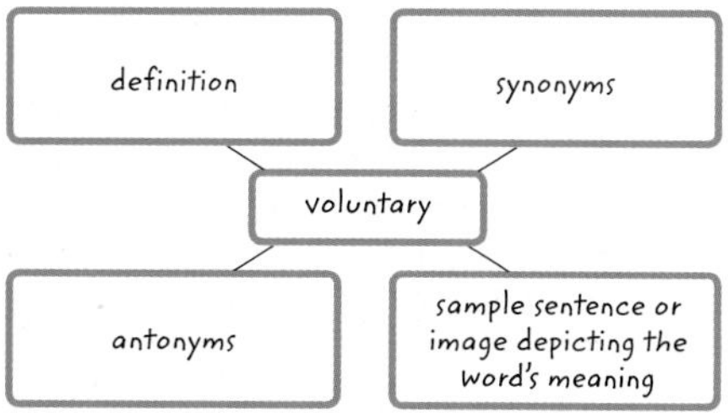

For more on academic vocabulary, see pages 54–55 and R79–R81.

After You Read

Assess

Literary Element

1. Students' answers should refer to patterns from quest stories, such as a hero slaying monsters or winning a beautiful maiden; they may also refer to stories in which evil parents try to kill their heirs or in which fate triumphs.
2. People enjoy the suspense and adventure of a quest story. Tales of people meeting seemingly impossible challenges are instructive and uplifting.

Review: Hero

Remind students that while heroes need not be perfect, they possess qualities that are considered extraordinary. Stress the importance of including specific evidence from the text in their charts.

Reading Strategy

1. Inclusion of supernatural elements, prophecy, and fate; involvement of heroes and rulers
2. The reader knows that anything can happen. The laws of science do not apply.

Progress Check

Can students identify genre?

If No → See Unit 5 Teaching Resources Book, p. 117.

Vocabulary Practice

1. d **2.** a **3.** f

Academic Vocabulary

GO should include the following:

definition—done by choice

synonyms—elective, noncompulsory

antonyms—obligatory, compulsory

sentence/image—(sample sentence) The homework was not voluntary, so everyone had to do it.

After You Read

Assess

Respond Through Writing

Students' essays should

- include a strong thesis statement in the introduction
- discuss each of the questions listed in the writing task
- use the answers to the questions to analyze how cause-and-effect relationships advance the plot
- contain multiple examples from the text to support the essay's ideas
- contain a cause-and-effect chain tracking the major plot points

A student who meets all of these criteria should receive the equivalent of a 5-point response.

A student who fully meets four or partially meets three of these criteria should receive the equivalent of a 4-point response.

A student who fully meets three or partially meets two of these criteria should receive the equivalent of a 3-point response.

A student who meets two of these criteria should receive the equivalent of a 2-point response.

A student who partially meets one of these criteria should receive the equivalent of a 1-point response.

Respond Through Writing

Expository Essay

Analyze Cause and Effect In *Perseus* how much do the actions of the gods and goddesses affect the outcome of the story? How do their actions affect Perseus, the hero? Do they cause him to be any more or less heroic? Analyze how cause-and-effect relationships affect the plot.

Understand the Task A **cause** is that which makes something happen. An **effect** is what happens as a result of the cause. You also may find that an effect can in turn become the cause of the next effect.

Prewrite Before beginning your draft, think about the questions listed in the writing task above. Brainstorm answers for each question and record them in your notebook. Using these brainstorming notes, create a list of examples from the text that support your answers. Then discuss your ideas with a partner. During the discussion, identify the strongest ideas in your notes, eliminate the weaker ones, and record new ideas.

After choosing ideas to build your essay around, develop a thesis that expresses the essay's main idea. The thesis should state something about how the story's cause-and-effect relationships move the plot along. Make sure your thesis also states the general conclusion of your analysis. You may want to use a sentence like this for your thesis statement:

The author uses ______ to ______.

Draft When writing your draft, fill it with the evidence that you gathered and prepared during prewriting. Convey your ideas about cause-and-effect relationships that you developed through brainstorming and partner discussion. Focus the essay on the most important ideas and the strongest examples.

Revise Create a graphic organizer to insert into your final essay. The organizer should track the story's major plot points, showing how one effect causes the next effect. You may want to use a cause-and-effect chain: a cause is listed in a box and an arrow points from it to the effect. The effect box may also have an arrow pointing to an effect caused by the first effect, and so on. Exchange essays with your discussion partner and address any problems with the evidence that your partner notes.

Edit and Proofread Proofread your paper, correcting any errors in spelling, grammar, and punctuation. Use the Grammar Tip in the side column to help you with active and passive voice.

Learning Objectives

In this assignment, you will focus on the following objectives:

Writing: Writing an expository essay.

Grammar: Understanding how and when to use active voice.

Grammar Tip

Active and Passive Voice

A verb is in the **active voice** if the subject of the sentence performs the action.

The cat chased the squirrel.
The receiver caught the ball.

A verb is in the **passive voice** if the subject of the sentence receives the action of the verb.

The squirrel was chased by the cat.
The ball was caught by the receiver.

The active voice is usually preferred, because it is generally considered stronger. When talking about the characters' actions in the story, try to use the active voice.

For grammar practice, see Unit 5 Teaching Resources Book, p. 120.

To create custom assessments online, go to Progress Reporter Online Assessment.

For additional assessment, see Assessment Resources, pp. 201–202.

To create custom assessments using software, use ExamView Assessment Suite.

Grammar Workshop

Transitional Expressions

Literature Connection In Edith Hamilton's retelling of the story of Perseus, transitions function as they do in every good story: they hold sentences, paragraphs, and story parts together so that they all make sense.

> *It happened that soon after their arrival Perseus heard that the King of Larissa, in the North, was holding a great athletic contest, and he journeyed there to take part.*
>
> —Edith Hamilton, from "Perseus"

In the quotation above, the transitional expressions include *soon* and *after their arrival,* which both tell when; *in the North,* which tells where; and *and,* which connects similar sentence elements. They all show how ideas are related.

This chart shows some relationships and transitional expressions.

Relationship	Transitional Words and Phrases
Time	*after, before, finally, meanwhile, then, today, when*
Location	*above, along, beneath, inside, next to, throughout*
Importance	*above all, first, in fact, mainly, to begin with*
Contrast	*although, but, in spite of, nevertheless, on the other hand, instead*
Cause and Effect	*as a result, because, for, so, so that, therefore, thus*

Examples

- Instead, he had a house built of bronze and sunk underground.
  [*Instead* shows a relationship of contrast.]
- But Perseus had Hermes with him, so the road lay open to him.
  [*So* shows a cause-and-effect relationship.]

Revise Add a transitional word or phrase to show a relationship between each pair of sentences. Underline the transitional expression and tell what relationship it shows.

1. The Gray Women looked like birds. They had the shape of swans.
2. He could attack Medusa. He must first be properly equipped.
3. He rushed forward and seized the eye. None of them could see.

Learning Objectives

In this workshop, you will focus on the following objective:

Grammar: Understanding how to use transitional expressions.

Transitional Expressions

Transitional expressions show how ideas are related and help story parts make sense.

Tip

Coordinating conjunctions (*and, but, or, nor, for, so, yet*) can serve as transitions but do not usually begin a sentence. In three instances, however, a coordinating conjunction can be used that way: (1) when it completes not the sentence that immediately precedes it but what comes *before* the preceding sentence that acts as an interrupter; (2) when it completes the sentence that immediately precedes it *as well as* at least one other sentence; and (3) when it begins a paragraph.

LOG ON **Literature Online**

Grammar For more grammar practice, go to glencoe.com and enter QuickPass code GL49787u5.

English Learners

DIFFERENTIATED INSTRUCTION

Intermediate Have students develop a story using transitional words and phrases. Each student should provide one sentence that includes a transitional word or phrase. Students should continue until all students have had a chance to add a sentence to the story.

Focus

Activity

Write: Many princes wished to marry the princess, but the king was in no hurry. When the time was right, the king sent out messengers.

Discuss with students what purpose the underlined word and phrase are serving.

Teach

Transitional Expressions

Explain that transitional expressions show the relationship between ideas in sentences.

Assess

Note that there is more than one possible answer to each item in the exercise.

Possible answers:

1. The Gray Women looked like birds, **because** they had the shape of swans. (cause-and-effect relationship)
2. He could attack Medusa, **but** he must first be properly equipped. (contrast relationship)
3. He must rush forward and seized the eye **when** none of them could see. (time relationship)

For additional grammar practice, see Unit 5 Teaching Resources Book, p. 147.

Before You Read

Focus

Bellringer Options

Daily Language Practice Transparency 89

Or **display** photographs and images of wolves. **Ask:** What characteristics do you associate with wolves? Why do you think they are often portrayed as villains? Encourage students to consider the relationship between people and wolves as they read.

Before You Read

World Literature
England

The Fenris Wolf

Meet **Olivia Coolidge**
(born 1908)

Nothing interests Olivia Coolidge like history, biography, ancient legends, and myths—and when Coolidge is interested in something, she explores it thoroughly. She has written about the Trojan War, imperial Romans, Revolutionary War heroes, the British, Mahatma Gandhi, Abraham Lincoln, and the struggle for women's rights. She has retold myths and tales from a variety of cultures.

An Early Interest in Stories Coolidge was born in England, the daughter of Sir Robert Charles Kirkwood, a journalist and historian who taught at Oxford University. She grew up in a house without gas, electricity, central heating, or a hot-water system. Stories were an early amusement, and she and her sister spent hours creating fairy tales to tell each other before bedtime.

When she was older, Coolidge attended Oxford and went on to become a teacher. She moved to the United States just before World War II, and her experiences as a teacher in American schools inspired her to write her first book for young adults, a collection called *Greek Myths.* Soon after, she published *Legends of the North,* which includes "The Fenris Wolf." Since then, Coolidge has published more than two dozen other works.

The Norse god, Thor, with a hammer, statuette found in Iceland. Bronze. National Museum of Iceland, Reykjavik.

Her Own Voice Coolidge is a voracious reader and a stylish writer. In her work, she provides fascinating insights into the minds of characters. Above all, she believes that it is important for young people to read work that excites and entertains them.

> *"A good book should excite, amuse and interest. It should give a sense of seeing as a movie does."*
>
> —Olivia Coolidge

Coolidge explains that she focuses on history, biography, and legends because she is interested in "values that always have been of concern to people." According to her, the experiences of the past have a lot to teach people of the present day about their own humanity. Many experiences, emotions, and values are universal, known to all cultures and eras.

Recent Work One recent book of Coolidge's tells the story of a colonial businessman in Maine at the time of the American Revolution. In this work, she invites readers into a world of lumber camps, immigrants, and harsh winters. Coolidge remains best known, however, for mythological retellings based on careful research and for her extraordinary ability to bring more well-known chapters of the past to life. Her work teaches valuable lessons to people of all ages.

LOG ON **Literature** Online

Author Search For more about Olivia Coolidge, go to glencoe.com and enter QuickPass code GL49787u5.

Selection Skills

The Fenris Wolf

Literary Elements
- Theme Archetype (SE pp. 947–951)
- Plot Pattern Archetype (SE p. 951)

Listening/Speaking/Viewing Skills
- Analyze Art (SE p. 950)
- Tell a Tale (TE p. 950)

Reading Skills
- Interpret Imagery (SE pp. 947, 949, 952)

Vocabulary Skills
- Context Clues (SE pp. 947, 952)

Writing Skills/Grammar
- Apply Imagery/Sensory Details (SE p. 952)

Literature and Reading Preview

Connect to the Myth

Have you ever outsmarted someone? Freewrite for a few minutes about a time, real or fictional, when you outsmarted someone, or thought you had.

Build Background

"The Fenris Wolf" is a Norse tale, or a tale that comes from the pre-Christian religion of the Scandinavian peoples. In Norse mythology, Asgard is the home of the warrior gods, including Odin, the chief of all gods. Loki, Tyr, and Thor are other great gods. Thor is both the god of thunder and a blacksmith. Smiths are often powerful figures in myths and tales because they can control fire and make tools, chains, and weapons out of metal.

Set Purposes for Reading

Big Idea Courage and Cleverness

As you read, ask yourself, How do the characters demonstrate cleverness and courage?

Literary Element Theme Archetype

The **theme** is the central idea or message about life or human nature in a literary work. A **theme archetype** is a theme that recurs in myths, stories, and tales all over the world. Examples of theme archetypes include the victory of good over evil and the importance of courage and loyalty. As you read, ask yourself, What theme archetypes are present in Coolidge's retelling of "The Fenris Wolf"?

Reading Strategy Interpret Imagery

To **interpret imagery,** notice details in the text that appeal to your senses. As you read, ask yourself, How do these details affect my emotions and influence my understanding of the text?

Tip: Take Notes As you read, make a list of images and record your emotional responses to them.

Image	My Emotional Response
Huge serpent that completely encircles the earth so that its head meets its tail.	This image seems horrifying and repulsive to me.

Learning Objectives

For pages 946–952

In studying this text, you will focus on the following objectives:

Literary Study: Analyzing theme archetype.

Reading: Interpreting imagery.

Writing: Applying imagery and sensory details in a descriptive paragraph.

Vocabulary

brood (brōōd) *n.* the young of a family; p. 948 *The cat gave birth to a large brood of kittens.*

fetter (fet′ ər) *v.* to chain; p. 949 *The animal control officer fettered the dangerous animal.*

forge (fôrj) *v.* to form or make, especially by heating or hammering; p. 949 *The smith forged a large metal tool over the fire.*

writhe (rīth) *v.* to twist in pain; p. 950 *The wounded elephant was writhing in pain when the explorers discovered him.*

Tip: Context Clues You can use context clues to help you determine the meaning of an unfamiliar word. Examine the surrounding text to figure out what the passage is describing. Then try to figure out how the unfamiliar word is being used in the description. Example: *He was in so much pain that he was **writhing** back and forth on the ground.* In this sentence you can determine that *writhing* is a word that is describing his response to pain and his action on the ground.

Before You Read

Focus

Summary

The Fenris Wolf is the offspring of Loki, the fire god, and a giantess. Odin and the other gods think they can tame the young wolf, but it soon grows out of control. The gods forge two chains, but the wolf breaks free. Then the gods tie the wolf with a magical thread, and it holds—but only until the end of the world.

For summaries in languages other than English, see Unit 5 Teaching Resources Book, pp. 123–128.

Vocabulary

Using New Vocabulary

To test vocabulary comprehension, have students write a paragraph using each of the vocabulary words at least once. Ask students who have used the words in the best and most creative ways to share their stories with the rest of the class.

For additional vocabulary practice, see Unit 5 Teaching Resources Book, p. 131.

For additional context, see Interactive Visual Vocabulary CD-ROM.

Approaching Level

DIFFERENTIATED INSTRUCTION

Established Point out the Reading Strategy on this page. Remind students that imagery appeals to the senses—what they can see, hear, touch, taste, and smell. Have students write a few sentences that describe an event related to one of the topics below.

- a day at the beach
- a sunrise on a spring day
- an exciting sporting event
- the last day of school for the year
- a walk outdoors on a dark night

Encourage students to use descriptive language and imagery to enhance their description. Encourage volunteers to share their writing with the class.

Teach

Big Idea **1**

Courage and Cleverness

Ask: Why are the gods so afraid of the brood? *(The serpent encircles the earth, Hel rules the underworld, and the wolf is huge and ferocious.)*

Literary History ☆

Odin Odin, the king of the Norse gods, was the god of sky, wind, and war. Scholars believe that his name meant "wild or furious." Norse mythology tells stories of his triumphs over frost giants and his fall during an ending of the world. Odin could also take human form, appearing in our world as an old, one-eyed man wearing a floppy hat.

For an audio recording of this selection, use Listening Library Audio CD-ROM.

Readability Scores

Dale-Chall: 9.4
DRP: 57
Lexile: 1120

The Fenris Wolf

Retold by Olivia Coolidge

Three standing figures identified as Odin, Thor and Frey. From a Viking tapestry, 12th c. Statens Historiska Museet, Stockholm, Sweden.

Though Loki, the fire god, was handsome and ready-witted, his nature was really evil. He was, indeed, the cause of most of the misfortunes which befell the gods. He was constantly in trouble, yet often forgiven because the gods valued his cleverness. It was he who found ways out of difficulty for them, so that for a long time they felt that they could not do without him.

In the early days Loki, though a god, had wedded a monstrous giantess, and the union of these two evil beings produced a fearful **brood.** The first was the great **1** world serpent, whom Odin cast into the ☆ sea, and who became so large that he completely encircled the earth, his tail touching his mouth. The second was Hel, the grisly goddess of the underworld, who reigned in the horrible land of the dead. The third was the most dreadful of all, a huge monster called the Fenris Wolf.

Vocabulary

brood (bro͞od) n. the young of a family

Vocabulary Practice

SMALL GROUP WHOLE GROUP **Connotation** Remind students that denotation is the dictionary definition of a word. Connotation, on the other hand, refers to the emotions or associations a word evokes. Have students discuss the connotations of the words used to describe the Fenris Wolf on pages 948 and 949. **Ask:** What do words such as *monster, howl, beast, dreadful,* and *violently* suggest about the wolf? *(Students may say that he was dangerous and terrifying.)* Break students into small groups and have them list five words that have positive conotations and five words that have negative connotations. Have students share their lists with the class.

When the gods first saw the Fenris Wolf, he was so young that they thought they could tame him. They took him to Asgard, therefore, and brave Tyr undertook to feed and train him. Presently, however, the black monster grew so enormous that his open jaws would stretch from heaven to earth, showing teeth as large as the trunks of oak trees and as sharply pointed as knives. The howls of the beast were so dreadful as he tore his vast meals of raw meat that the gods, save for Tyr, dared not go near him, lest[1] he devour them.

At last all were agreed that the Fenris Wolf must be **fettered** if they were to save their very lives, for the monster grew more ferocious towards them every day. They **forged** a huge chain, but since none was strong enough to bind him, they challenged him to a trial of strength. "Let us tie you with this to see if you can snap the links," said they.

The Fenris Wolf took a look at the chain and showed all his huge white teeth in a dreadful grin. "Bind me if you wish," he growled, and he actually shut his eyes as he lay down at ease to let them put it on.

The gods stepped back, and the wolf gave a little shake. There was a loud cracking sound, and the heavy links lay scattered around him in pieces. The wolf howled in triumph until the sun and moon in heaven trembled at the noise.

Thor, the smith, called other gods to his aid, and they labored day and night at the second chain. This was half as strong again[2] as the first, and so heavy that no one of the gods could drag it across the ground. "This is by far the largest chain that was ever made," said they. "Even the Fenris Wolf will not be able to snap fetters such as these."

Once more they brought the chain to the wolf, and he let them put it on, though this time it was clear that he somewhat doubted his strength. When they had chained him, he shook himself violently, but the fetters held. His great, red eyes burned with fury, the black hair bristled[3] on his back, and he gnashed his teeth until the foam flew. He strained heavily against the iron until the vast links flattened and lengthened, but did not break. Finally with a great bound and a howl he dashed himself against the ground, and suddenly the chain sprang apart so violently that broken pieces were hurled about the heads of the watching gods.

Now the gods realized in despair that all their strength and skill would not avail[4] to bind the wolf. Therefore Odin sent a messenger to the dwarf people under the earth, bidding them forge him a chain. The messenger returned with a little rope, smooth and soft as a silken string, which was hammered on dwarfish anvils[5] out of strange materials which have never been seen or heard. The sound of a cat's footfall, the breath of a fish, the flowing beard of a woman, and the roots of a mountain made the metal from which it was forged.

The gods took the tiny rope to the Fenris Wolf. "See what an easy task we have for you this time," they said.

1. Here, *lest* means "for fear that."
2. *Half as strong again* means one and one-half times as strong.

3. Here, *bristle* means "to raise the hairs on the back, as in fear, anger, or excitement."
4. Here, *avail* means "be sufficient."
5. *Anvils* are blocks on which blacksmiths pound hot metal into shapes.

Vocabulary

fetter (fet′ ər) *v.* to chain
forge (fôrj) *v.* to form or make, especially by heating or hammering

Theme Archetype *What is significant about the gods turning to the dwarfs for help?* **2**

Interpret Imagery *What do these images suggest about the chain and the dwarves who made it?* **3**

Teach

Literary Element 2

Theme Archetype Answer: *Odin himself is the chief of all gods, and yet he cannot control the Fenris Wolf. Even the gods themselves sometimes need help from others.*

For additional literary element practice, see Unit 5 Teaching Resources Book, p. 129.

Reading Strategy 3

Interpret Imagery
Answer: *Students should recognize that these unusual items could only be acquired and used in a magical world by magical beings.*

ADVANCED For advanced students, **ask:** What quality is suggested by each of the rope's ingredients? *(They all are immaterial and insubstantial, suggesting a spiritual quality.)*

English Learners

DIFFERENTIATED INSTRUCTION

Intermediate Students may benefit from visualizing the description of Loki and the great world serpent.
Ask: What details does the author give about Loki? *(He was evil but clever.)*
Ask: What details does the author give about the great world serpent? *(She was a monstrous giant who was also evil.)* Encourage students to consider what they might look like.

Teach

Big Idea 1

Courage and Cleverness
Answer: *He senses the magical power of the rope and tries to protect himself by demanding a terrible sacrifice.*

ENGLISH LEARNERS For English learners, **ask:** Why does the wolf become suspicious? *(The clever wolf realizes that the tiny rope must have special powers or the gods would not use it.)*

Literary Element 2

Theme Archetype **Answer:** *The mythic hero—in this case, a god—is willing to risk life and limb to subdue an evil monster.*

View the Art ★

Answer: *Students' answers will vary. Many will have imagined Fenris Wolf as more fearsome.*

To check students' understanding of the selection, see Unit 5 Teaching Resources Book, p. 134.

The Norse god Tyr losing his hand to the bound wolf, Fenris. Manuscript. Royal Library, Copenhagen, Denmark.

View the Art In what ways does this illustration correspond with or differ from your mental image of the Fenris Wolf and Tyr? ★

"Why should I bother myself with a silken string?" asked the wolf sullenly. "I have broken your mightiest chain. What use is this foolish thing?"

"The rope is stronger than it looks," answered they. "We are not able to break it, but it will be a small matter to you."

"If this rope is strong by enchantment," said the wolf in slow suspicion, "how can I tell that you will loosen me if I cannot snap it after all? On one condition you may bind me: You must give me a hostage from among yourselves."

"How can we do this?" they asked.

The Fenris Wolf stretched himself and yawned until the sun hid behind clouds at the sight of his great, red throat. "I will let you bind me with this rope," he said, "if one of you gods will hold his hand between my teeth while I do it."

The gods looked at one another in silence. The wolf grinned from ear to ear. Without a word Tyr walked forward and laid his bare hand inside the open mouth.

The gods bound the great wolf, and he stretched himself and heaved as before. This time, however, he did not break his bonds. He gnashed his jaws together, and Tyr cried out in pain as he lost his hand. Nevertheless, the great black wolf lay howling and **writhing** and helplessly biting the ground. There he lay in the bonds of the silken rope as long as the reign of Odin endured. The Fates declared, however, that in the last days, when the demons of ice and fire should come marching against the gods to the battlefield, the great sea would give up the serpent, and the Fenris Wolf would break his bonds. The wolf would swallow Odin, and the gods would go down in defeat. Sun and moon would be devoured, and the whole earth would perish utterly.

1 Courage and Cleverness *How is the Fenris Wolf clever?*

Theme Archetype *What archetypal theme is demonstrated in this passage?* **2**

Vocabulary

writhe (rīth) *v.* to twist in pain

Speaking Practice

PARTNERS **Oral Interpretation** Have students analyze how Coolidge's use of imagery and concrete and figurative language bring the myth to life. Have pairs of students prepare an oral interpretation of various paragraphs in the selection. Stress the importance of using tone of voice and expression to reflect the content and the mood of the text. Students should rehearse before presenting to the class.

After You Read

Respond and Think Critically

Respond and Interpret

1. What did you find most fearful about the Fenris Wolf? Explain.
2. (a)How does the Fenris Wolf come to be? (b)What is evil about the Fenris Wolf's family?
3. (a)Why do the gods feel that they must control the Fenris Wolf? (b)Why are the gods unsuccessful at first?
4. (a)To whom does Odin turn for help in defeating the Fenris Wolf? (b)What is surprising about his solution to the problem?

Analyze and Evaluate

5. What characteristics does the Fenris Wolf display?
6. What qualities or character traits does this tale seem to promote?
7. (a)Do you think that Tyr and the gods betray the Fenris Wolf? (b)Do you think that the Fenris Wolf betrays Tyr? Explain.

Connect

8. **Big Idea** Courage and Cleverness How do Tyr's courage and the Fenris Wolf's cleverness affect the outcome of this story?
9. **Connect to Today** What insights into the Norse culture does the myth provide? What similarities do you see between the Norse culture and today's culture? Explain.

Literary Element Image Archetype

Time, setting, and characters may vary in world myths, but **theme archetypes** tend to be universal. Many of the main ideas, messages, or lessons about life remain constant from place to place, people to people, and age to age. "The Fenris Wolf" is a distinctively Norse version of the archetypal struggle between the forces of good and evil.

1. One characteristic of world myths is that evil is passed down from one generation to the next. How does this archetypal theme manifest itself in "The Fenris Wolf"?
2. Stories about the end of the world, known as apocalyptic tales, are one type of archetypal theme. How does the ending of "The Fenris Wolf" qualify it as an apocalyptic myth?

Review: Plot Pattern Archetype

As you learned on page 935, a **plot pattern archetype** is a sequence of events in a narrative work that is familiar because it appears repeatedly in stories and myths from many different cultures and time periods around the world. One plot pattern archetype, for example, is the quest story, in which a hero strives against great odds to achieve a desirable goal.

Partner Activity With a partner, track the plot pattern archetype in "The Fenris Wolf." Use a sequence diagram similar to the one below.

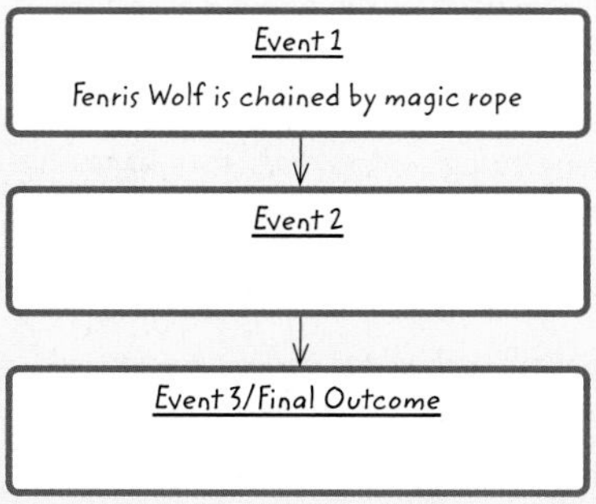

LOG ON Literature Online

Selection Resources For Selection Quizzes, eFlashcards, and Reading-Writing Connection activities, go to glencoe.com and enter QuickPass code GL49787u5.

After You Read

Assess

1. Accept reasonable answers.
2. (a) He is born of Loki and a giantess. (b) All are monsters or associated with misfortune or death.
3. (a) He is huge and destructive. (b) He is too strong.
4. (a) The underground dwarves (b) He turns to tiny beings to solve a problem too big for the gods; the solution is an insubstantial rope.
5. He is crafty, powerful, and destructive.
6. Courage, self-sacrifice, and restraint
7. (a) Accept reasonable answers. (b) Accept reasonable answers.
8. Tyr's courage allows a temporary solution. The Fenris wolf is bound despite his cleverness.
9. Students should point to specific details from the myth to support their answers.

Literary Element

1. Loki is described in the first paragraph as having an evil nature. He "wedded a monstrous giantess, and the union of these two evil beings produced a fearful brood." The third, and most dreadful, member of this evil brood is the Fenris Wolf.
2. At the end of the story, we are told that the victory over the Fenris Wolf will last only until the end of Odin's reign. It is prophesied by the Fates that the demons of fire and ice will free the Fenris Wolf, who will swallow Odin, as well as the sun and moon, and that the earth will "perish utterly."

To create custom assessments online, go to Progress Reporter Online Assessment.

To create custom assessments using software, use ExamView Assessment Suite.

For additional assessment, see Assessment Resources, pp. 203–204.

Review: Plot Pattern Archetype

Event 2: The god Tyr sacrifices his hand to help subdue the Fenris Wolf.

Event 3/Final Outcome: The fates prophesy the death of the gods and the end of the world.

After You Read

Reading Strategy

1. **Possible answer:** Tearing "vast meals of raw meat" (visual); "teeth as large as oak trees" (visual); growling and gnashing (auditory)
2. Proposing that one of the gods hold his hand between the wolf's teeth

Progress Check

Can students interpret imagery?

If No → See Unit 5 Teaching Resources Book, p. 130.

Vocabulary Practice

Answers will vary. Sample responses:

Word: *brood*
Textual Clues: Used to describe something that Loki and his wife's "union . . . produced."
Meaning: the young of a family

Word: *fetter*
Textual Clues: Used to describe how the gods tied the Fenris Wolf with a "huge chain" in order to "save their very lives."
Meaning: to chain

Word: *forge*
Textual Clues: Used to describe how the gods and dwarfs make a strong chain. "They forged a huge chain" and "labored day and night" and "hammered on dwarfish anvils."
Meaning: to form or make, especially by heating or hammering.

Word: *writhe*
Textual Clues: While the Fenris Wolf was writhing he was also "laying howling" and "helplessly biting the ground" so it must be an action that involves moving around on the ground helplessly.
Meaning: to twist in pain

Reading Strategy Interpret Imagery

Review the chart you created as you read, and then answer the following questions.

1. List three or more images that demonstrate the enormous strength and power of the Fenris Wolf. Explain how each image appeals to your senses.
2. Name one image that shows the Fenris Wolf's cleverness.

Vocabulary Practice

Practice with Context Clues Look back at pages 948–950 to find context clues for the vocabulary words below. Record your findings in a chart like the one here.

brood fetter forge writhe

Example:

Word:
grisly

↓

Textual Clues:
Used to describe the "goddess of the underworld," who lives in "the horrible land of the dead."

↓

Meaning:
causing one to feel horror

Academic Vocabulary

The Norse gods tried to find a ***device*** *that would be strong enough to hold the wolf.*

Device is a word that has more than one meaning. Using context clues, try to figure out the meaning of *device* in the sentence above and the sentence below. Then explain the difference between the meanings:

Symbolism, such as the snake biting its own tail, is a common literary ***device*** *in myths.*

For more on academic vocabulary, see pages 54–55 and R79–R81.

Write with Style

Apply Imagery/Sensory Details

Assignment Create and describe a character that could be used to represent evil in a myth or story.

Get Ideas Brainstorm a list of traits that would imply your character is evil. Make sure to include details about both appearance and behavior. You can use a chart like the one below to organize your ideas.

Appearance	Behavior
Dark circles around eyes	Takes advantage of the weak

Give It Structure Begin your description by briefly explaining why the character is evil. Use your list of behaviors to create this part of the description. Then use your appearance list to develop a detailed description of what it would be like to meet the character in person.

Look at Language Make the character's physical appearance the heart of your character sketch. Fill the description with strong imagery that provides a full range of sensory details. Replace any general details with language that expresses your own style. Also, write in an active voice.

EXAMPLE:

~~The beast has dark circles around its eyes.~~

Heavy, black rings surround the narrow slits of the beast's eyes.

To help the flow of your description, check the sentence variety throughout your piece. If there is a passage with too much repetition in the sentence construction, restructure one of the sentences.

EXAMPLE:

Surrounding the narrow slits of its eyes are heavy, black rings.

^ ~~Heavy, black rings surround the narrow slits of its eyes.~~ Long, snake-like hair covers the tops of the beast's shoulders.

Academic Vocabulary

The first sentence refers to a tool or mechanism. The second sentence refers to a technique used to achieve an effect.

For grammar practice, see Unit 5 Teaching Resources Book, p. 133.

Write with Style

Students' character descriptions should:

- depict a character that represents evil
- describe the character's appearance and key behaviors
- include strong imagery with specific sensory details
- use language and sentence structure to create a personal style

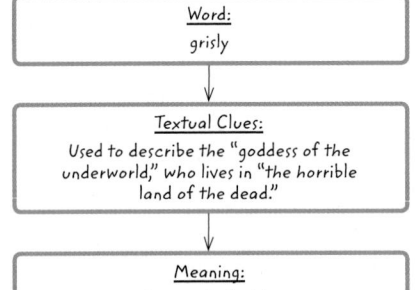

Vocabulary Workshop

Word Origins: Words from Norse Mythology

Learning Objectives

In this workshop, you will focus on the following objective:

Vocabulary: Understanding word origins.

Literature Connection In Norse mythology, Tyr is the bravest and noblest of gods—which may be one reason why we might have a day of the week named after him.

> *"They took him to Asgard, therefore, and brave Tyr undertook to feed and train him."*
>
> —Olivia Coolidge, from "The Fenris Wolf"

Tyr, whose name can also be spelled *Tiu,* may be the source of our word *Tuesday.* Many words from Old Norse are difficult to trace, however, because the Old Norse language was so similar to Old English.

This chart shows the origins of the names of three other weekdays.

Day of the Week	Origin
Wednesday	From the greatest of the Norse gods, Odin, + *daeg*, or "day" (Odin's Day)
Thursday	From the Norse god Thor, or from the Old English word *thunor* (both meaning "thunder"), + *daeg*, or "day" (Thor's Day)
Friday	From Old English or from the Norse goddess Frigga, wife of Odin, + *daeg*, or "day" (Frigga's Day)

Practice Answer the following questions.

1. There are approximately nine hundred words of Scandinavian origin in the English language. Several of them have just one syllable and begin with *sk.* Find one of them in a dictionary.
2. Identify the words, other than *Tyr* and *Fenris Wolf,* that come from Old Norse in each of these sentences. Use a dictionary for help.
   a. Loki was the husband of a monstrous giantess.
   b. To good gods, such as Tyr, it was wrong not to preserve the world.
   c. The teeth of the Fenris Wolf were sharper than a knife.
   d. No chain, rule, or law could bind the powerful Fenris Wolf.
   e. Could the gods get something strong enough to hold him?

Norse Origins

What we call **Norse** words and myths, which relate to the Scandinavian countries (Sweden, Denmark, Norway, and Iceland), sprang from the Icelandic *Eddas,* or heroic epic poems. However, much of Norse mythology, including parts of myths which were told in Scandinavia a thousand years ago, originally came from Germanic Europe.

Tip

Always apply your knowledge of word history when you encounter unfamiliar words in reading passages or have to choose a correct meaning on a multiple-choice test.

LOG ON **Literature** Online

Vocabulary For more vocabulary practice, go to glencoe.com and enter QuickPass code GL49787u5.

Approaching Level

DIFFERENTIATED INSTRUCTION

Established Have approaching-level students use an unabridged dictionary to look up the meaning of each of these Norse words. Have students write each new word in a sentence in their notebooks.

- brigg *(bridge)*
- crake *(crow)*
- dollop *(lump of something)*
- glocken *(to start to thaw)*
- lop *(flea)*

Vocabulary Workshop

Word Origins: Words from Norse Mythology

Focus

Word Origins

Explain that letter combinations can serve as clues to a word's origin. Words of Old Norse origin tend to sound harsh because they include combined consonants, such as *g* and *t.* Have students look for short words with combined consonants as they complete the second activity.

Teach

Old Norse Old Norse is the medieval language in which the literature of Norway, Iceland, Denmark, and Sweden was first recorded. It is a North Germanic language. The Norwegian and Icelandic languages spoken today come from Old Norse.

Assess

1. Possible answers: *scald, skate, skeet, ski, skid, skill, skin, skirt, sky*
2. (a) husband (b) wrong (c) knife (d) law (e) get

For additional vocabulary practice, see Interactive Visual Vocabulary CD-ROM.

Before You Read

Focus

Bellringer Options

Daily Language Practice Transparency 90

Or **display** photos and other images of coyotes and crows. **Ask:** What characteristics do we often associate with these animals? Why do you think people attribute human characteristics to animals? Have students consider as they read how the coyote and the crow illustrate human strengths and weaknesses.

Before You Read

Coyote and Crow

Meet **Ella Clark**
(1896–1984)

Ella Clark taught English for most of her life; however, once Native American literature and culture captured her attention, she devoted herself to preserving its legacy in myth and folktale collections.

English Teacher Ella Clark's teaching career began in 1917, and she continued teaching high school English and dramatics while completing a bachelor's degree at Northwestern University. From 1927 to 1961, Clark taught in the English department at Washington State University in Pullman, Washington. In the 1930s, Clark began to travel around the Pacific Northwest, Alaska, and Canada. While living in Washington state, she began to collect Native American myths and stories, laying the foundation for her later books.

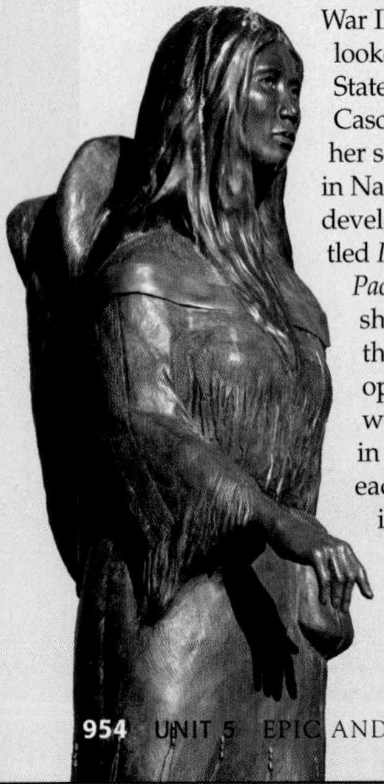
Sacagawea

Fire Lookout During World War II, Clark served as a fire lookout for the United States Forest Service in the Cascade Mountains. During her service there, her interest in Native American stories developed into a book entitled *Indian Legends of the Pacific Northwest* (1953). As she collected material for the book, Clark developed clear goals. She writes, "My two criteria in the consideration of each tale have been inseparable: Is it authentic? And is it interesting?"

Clark's first collection of Native American stories is diverse in its sources—she found bits and pieces from government documents, anthropological reports, manuscripts of pioneers, old periodicals, and published histories. Clark also included interviews with Native Americans. Using these varied sources, she produced a written history of what was once an exclusively oral tradition. Some of the stories she included had not previously been published.

> *"Until modern civilization changed family life, the telling of stories was one of the most satisfying pastimes for the entire family."*
>
> —Ella Clark

Storyteller Clark did not consider herself an anthropologist or sociologist. She considered herself an anthologist of literature. In 1979 Clark co-authored the book *Sacagawea of the Lewis and Clark Expedition* with Margo Edmonds. This work stands as one of the first attempts at a realistic biography of Sacagawea.

Ella Clark died in San Diego County, California. She left behind a rich collection of Native American stories and myths, now considered an integral part of American literature.

LOG ON **Literature** Online

Author Search For more about Ella Clark, go to glencoe.com and enter QuickPass code GL49787u5.

Selection Skills

Coyote and Crow

Literary Elements
- Character Archetype (SE pp. 955–957)

Listening/Speaking/Viewing Skills
- Tell a Tale (TE p. 956)

Reading Skills
- Activate Prior Knowledge (SE pp. 955–957)

Writing Skills/Grammar
- Write a Short Story (SE p. 957)

Literature and Reading Preview

Connect to the Legend

Why do you think many myths and legends include animals as characters? Discuss this question with a partner. Create a list of possible answers to share with the rest of the class.

Build Background

"Coyote and Crow" is a Yakama legend. The Yakama were part of a larger group of Native Americans known as the Sahaptians, who lived in the northwestern part of the United States. Some myths and legends include stories about a trickster. Tricksters are often comical characters whose sly plans can either reveal flaws or backfire on themselves.

Set Purposes for Reading

Big Idea Courage and Cleverness

As you read "Coyote and Crow," ask yourself, How does each character display cleverness?

Literary Element Character Archetype

A **character archetype** is a type of character who appears repeatedly in literature across cultures. Some character archetypes include the hero, the poor person who wishes to be rich, and the mysterious stranger. As you read, ask yourself, What are the characteristics of the trickster archetype in this story?

Reading Strategy Activate Prior Knowledge

When you read a story or other text for the first time, you **activate prior knowledge** to make sense of the information. Prior knowledge is what you already know. It includes ideas and information you have learned from reading, listening, observing, or acting. Prior knowledge influences how you understand the material you read. As you read, ask yourself, What details seem familiar or spark connections in my mind?

Tip: Brainstorm From the title of the story you are about to read, you know that it will include at least two characters: a coyote and a crow. Like many other animals, coyotes and crows represent common character traits. For example, owls and elephants are often associated with wisdom. Before you read "Coyote and Crow," use your prior knowledge of these animals to make a list of the characteristics you associate with them.

Learning Objectives

For pages 954–957

In studying this text, you will focus on the following objectives:

Literary Study: Analyzing character archetype.

Reading: Activating prior knowledge.

Writing: Writing a short story about a trickster.

Native American ceremonial dance regalia

Before You Read

Focus

Summary

After traveling across the country, Coyote is hungry when he meets Crow, who has a mouthful of food. Coyote flatters Crow into singing, and Crow drops the food. Coyote eats the food and tells Crow he is foolish.

For summaries in languages other than English, see Unit 5 Teaching Resources Book, pp. 136–141.

Interactive Read and Write

Other options for teaching this selection can be found in

- Interactive Read and Write for EL Students, pp. 282–286
- Interactive Read and Write for Approaching-Level Students, pp. 282–286
- Interactive Read and Write for On-Level Students, pp. 282–286

Approaching Level

DIFFERENTIATED INSTRUCTION

Established Explain that you can determine a character's traits by what the character says and does or by what other characters say about him or her. Ask students to think of examples of characters representing each character archetype mentioned above in the Literary Element feature on page 955. Give them the following additional archetypes.

- rebel
- gentle giant
- mentor

Ask them to name characters who represent these character archetypes. They may be characters from books, movies, or television. Students should then explain the character's traits that support this archetype.

Teach

Reading Strategy 1

Activate Prior Knowledge

Answer: *Coyote will probably figure out how to get the deer fat from Crow, because coyotes are considered cunning.* Have students read and summarize the first paragraph.

ENGLISH LEARNERS For English learners, **ask:** Does this story sound familiar to you? What other tales does it remind you of? *(Students may suggest that the story sounds like other folktales that they have read.)*

Literary Element 2

Character Archetype

Answer: *Coyote: cunning, tricky, sly; Crow: foolish, gullible, proud*

Literary History ☆

Coyote The Coyote is an important figure in the mythology of North American Indians. In many tales of the Native Americans of the Great Plains, California, and the Southwest, Coyote is a creature who introduces humans to fire and daylight.

For an audio recording of this selection, use Listening Library Audio CD-ROM.

Readability Scores

Dale-Chall: 3.8
DRP: 42
Lexile: 510

To check students' understanding of the selection, see Unit 5 Teaching Resources Book, p. 145.

Coyote and Crow

Retold by
Ella Clark

Prairie Wolf, 1848.
John James Audubon.

☆ Coyote traveled through the country, fighting monsters and making the world ready for the people who were to follow. He crossed the Cascade Mountains[1] and came into the Puget Sound[2] country. He was hungry, very hungry.

He saw Crow sitting on the peak of a high cliff, with a ball of deer fat in his mouth. Coyote looked at Crow with this fat and thought how good it would taste. Becoming hungrier and hungrier, he wondered how he could get the fat for himself. He thought hard. Then he laughed.

"I know what to do. I know how I can get the fat from Crow."

Then Coyote came close to the base of the cliff and called, "Oh, Chief! I hear that you can make a good noise, a pleasing noise with your voice. You are a big chief, I know. You are a wise chief, I have heard. Let me hear your voice, Chief. I want to hear you, Chief Crow."

Crow was pleased to be called chief. So he answered, "Caw!"

"Oh, Chief Crow," called Coyote, "that wasn't much. You can sing better than that. Sing a good song for me, Chief. I want to hear you sing loud."

Crow was pleased again. So he opened his mouth wide and called from the cliff in a loud voice, "C-a-a-w!"

Of course the ball of deer fat fell down from Crow's open mouth.

Coyote grabbed it quickly. Then he laughed.

"You are not a wise chief," said Coyote. "You are not a chief at all. I called you 'Chief' just to fool you. I wanted your deer fat. I am hungry. Now you can go hungry because of your foolishness." ∾

1. The *Cascade Mountains* cut across Oregon, Washington, and northern California.
2. *Puget Sound* is a large bay off the Pacific Ocean. It is located in northwestern Washington state.

1 Activate Prior Knowledge *Make a prediction about what will happen in the story based on your prior knowledge of such tales.*

Character Archetype *What adjectives would you use to describe Coyote and Crow?* 2

Speaking Practice

PARTNERS **Tell a Tale** Students may enjoy creating and telling their own version of a trickster tale. Have pairs of students devise a trickster character, a situation and an outcome. They may use "Coyote an Crow" as a model or read other trickster tales for more background. Their tricksters should be animals with human traits. Invite volunteers to tell their stories to the class.

After You Read

Respond and Think Critically

Respond and Interpret

1. What is your opinion of Coyote? Explain.
2. (a)What was Coyote doing before he encountered Crow? (b)Why is this information important to the story?
3. (a)What does Coyote call Crow in order to trick him? (b)In your opinion, what is the significance of this particular name?

Analyze and Evaluate

4. Based on what you know about Coyote and Crow, why do you think Coyote is confident that his plan will work?
5. (a)How would you describe the personalities of Coyote and Crow? (b)Have you encountered characters like them in other stories? Explain.
6. (a)Why does Coyote say Crow is foolish? (b)Do you think Crow behaved foolishly? Explain.

Connect

7. **Big Idea** Courage and Cleverness Was Coyote clever in the story? Explain.
8. **Connect to Today** What lesson can be learned from the legend "Coyote and Crow"? Is it a relevant lesson in today's world?

Literary Element Character Archetype

In this story, one of the **character archetypes** is the trickster. A trickster is a mischievous character. He or she deceives or plays pranks on other characters. Readers usually like trickster characters because they are entertaining.

1. Which character is the trickster in this story?
2. Support your answer with two examples from the story.

Reading Strategy Activate Prior Knowledge

Review the list you created before reading "Coyote and Crow." Then answer the following questions.

1. Before you read the story, what role did you think the coyote would play? Explain.
2. Were your initial ideas about Crow's character correct? Explain.

LOG ON **Literature** Online

Selection Resources For Selection Quizzes, eFlashcards, and Reading-Writing Connection activities, go to glencoe.com and enter QuickPass code GL49787u5.

Academic Vocabulary

Coyote knows that if he can convince Crow to ***respond*** *to him, he will be able to get the deer fat.*

Respond is an academic word. In a more casual conversation, someone might try to prompt your answer by asking, "Would you please **respond** to the question I just asked?" Using context clues, try to figure out the meaning of the word. Check your guess in a dictionary.

For more on academic vocabulary, see pages 54–55 and R79–R81.

Writing

Write a Story Trickster characters have appeared in stories told in many cultures for thousands of years. Tricksters may be portrayed as heroes, fools, or cunning predators, but they all share a disregard for accepted standards of behavior. Using "Coyote and Crow" as an example, write a short story that incorporates a trickster character.

Literary Element

1. Coyote is the trickster.
2. Coyote easily gets what he wants, and he outsmarts Crow.

Progress Check

Can students identify character archetype?

If No → See Unit 5 Teaching Resources Book, p. 142.

Reading Strategy

1. Answers will vary.
2. Students should explain their answers.

Progress Check

Can students activate prior knowledge?

If No → See Unit 5 Teaching Resources Book, p. 143.

After You Read

Assess

1. Students should explain their answers.
2. (a) He was killing monsters and making the world safe for people. (b) It shows that Coyote is the hero of the story.
3. (a) Chief (b) It suggests a respected leader, and this appeals to Crow's vanity.
4. The wily Coyote knows the vain Crow will fall for his flattery.
5. (a) Coyote is smart and tricky; Crow is foolishly vain. (b) Students should explain their answers.
6. (a) It was obvious what would happen when Crow opened his mouth. (b) Students should support their answers.
7. Yes; he showed keen insight into Crow's nature.
8. Flattery is not always sincere and often comes with a price. Answers will vary.

Writing

Student's short stories should: include a trickster character, give the character the trait of having a disregard for accepted standards of behavior, and reflect "Coyote and Crow" as an example.

Academic Vocabulary

Based on the context clues, *respond* means to answer or reply or react to something.

For additional assessment, see Assessment Resources, pp. 205–206.

Before You Read

Focus

Bellringer Options

Daily Language Practice Transparency 91

Or **display** images of the Old West. **Ask:** Why do tales about people who sought a new life in the West remain fascinating today?

Summary

The ballad describes Betsy and Ike's long and perilous journey to California. As they cross deserts and mountains, they face hunger, thirst, and deep discouragement.

For summaries in languages other than English, see Unit 5 Teaching Resources Book, pp. 148–153.

Before You Read

Learning Objectives

For pages 958–961

In studying this text, you will focus on the following objectives:

Literary Study: Analyzing ballads.

Reading: Analyzing archetypes.

Speaking and Listening: Presenting an oral report about a song.

Connect to the Ballad

Do you have a goal that you would travel a long way and overcome many obstacles to reach? Freewrite for a few minutes describing what accomplishing that goal would require.

Build Background

During the 1800s the desire for gold, land, adventure, and greater opportunity led women and men to undertake the dangerous journey westward across the United States. Mountains, rivers, harsh weather, and disease were some of the obstacles encountered by these determined adventurers.

Set Purposes for Reading

Big Idea Courage and Cleverness

As you read, ask yourself, How do the characters use courage and cleverness to deal with their circumstances?

Literary Element Ballad

A **ballad** is a song or poem that tells a story. A **folk ballad** usually tells of an exciting or dramatic event. Folk ballads have no known author and were passed along orally—usually as songs—over generations before being written down. A **literary ballad** is written in imitation of a folk ballad and has at least one known author. As you read, ask yourself, Why might this story have been told in the form of a ballad?

Reading Strategy Analyze Archetypes

An **archetype** is a model, or a perfect example of something. An archetypal hero, for example, has all the characteristics readers would expect a hero to have: bravery, intelligence, strength, and wit. As you read, ask yourself, What archetypes are these characters based on?

Tip: Create Character Webs As you read, use a character web to describe the main character in "Sweet Betsy from Pike."

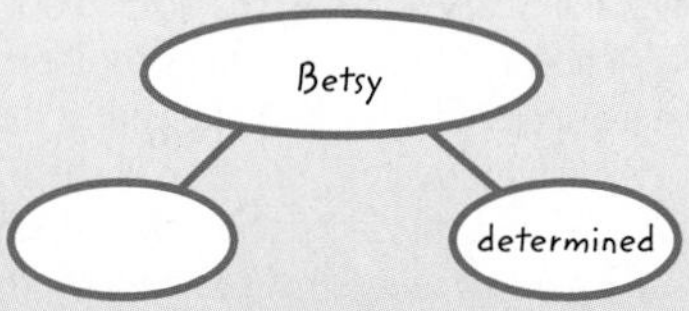

The Oregon Trail, 1869. Albert Bierstadt. Oil on canvas, 78.7 x 124.5 cm. Butler Institute of American Art, Youngstown, OH.

Selection Skills

Sweet Betsy from Pike

Literary Elements
- Ballad (SE pp. 958, 960)
- Meter and Rhythm (SE p. 960)

Listening/Speaking/Viewing Skills
- Oral Report (SE p. 961)

Reading Skills
- Analyze Archetypes (SE pp. 958, 959, 961)

Vocabulary Skills
- Academic Vocabulary (SE p. 961)

Sweet Betsy from Pike

Traditional

Encampment in the Valley of the Sacramento (from *California: Its Past, Present & Future*), 1850. Newberry Library, Chicago, IL. ☆

Oh, do you remember sweet Betsy from Pike,
Who crossed the wide prairies with her husband Ike?
With two yoke[1] of oxen, a big yaller dog,
A tall Shanghai rooster,[2] and one spotted hog.

Chorus:
Hoodle dang, fol dee dye do,
Hoodle dang, fol dee day.

The rooster ran off and the oxen all died;
The last piece of bacon that morning was fried.
Poor Ike got discouraged and Betsy got mad;
The dog wagged his tail and looked wonderfully sad.

Chorus

The alkali[3] desert was burning and hot,
And Ike, he decided to leave on the spot:
"My dear old Pike County, I'll go back to you."
Said Betsy, "You'll go by yourself if you do."

Chorus

They swam the wide rivers, they crossed the tall peaks,
They camped out on prairies for weeks and for weeks,
Fought off starvation and big storms of dust,
Determined to reach California or bust.

Chorus

They passed the Sierras[4] through mountains of snow,
'Til old California was sighted below.
Sweet Betsy, she hollered, and Ike gave a cheer,
Said, "Betsy, my darlin', I'm a made millioneer."

Chorus

1. A *yoke* is a pair of animals joined together for working.
2. A *Shanghai rooster* is a breed of rooster that originated in East Asia. *Shanghai* is an ancient city in China.
3. Here, *alkali* means "composed of soil that contains a mineral salt that prevents or stunts plant growth."
4. The *Sierras* refers to the Sierra Nevadas, a mountain range in the western United States.

Analyze Archetypes *What characteristics of Betsy's seem familiar? Explain.* **1**

Teach

Reading Strategy 1

Analyze Archetypes

Answer: *Her determination and toughness are reminiscent of the archetypal pioneer.*

APPROACHING For approaching-level students, **ask:** Why are these important traits for a pioneer? *(Life on the frontier was hard and tough, so to survive pioneers needed these traits..)*

For additional practice using the reading skill or strategy, see Unit 5 Teaching Resources Book, p. 155.

Cultural History ☆

California Gold Rush

After a sawmill builder discovered gold near Sacramento in 1848, thousands of prospectors flooded into the region. By 1853, more than a quarter of a million people had moved to California in search of wealth, and the value of the gold mined from its rivers and hills amounted to almost $2 billion.

To check students' understanding of the selection, see Unit 5 Teaching Resources Book, p. 157.

Approaching Level

DIFFERENTIATED INSTRUCTION

Emerging Students may benefit from some historical background. Explain that the Oregon Trail, which began in Independence, Missouri, and ended in Oregon City, Oregon, was a two-thousand-mile pathway leading to the West. Beginning in 1843 and for the next 25 years, about 50,000 pioneers traveled the Oregon Trail. While some journeyed west for farmland in Oregon, many, like Betsy and Ike, headed to California in search of gold. Traveling the Oregon Trail was difficult and dangerous; many people died from diseases caused by poor sanitation, injuries, and lack of food.

After You Read

Assess

1. (a) Answers should show an understanding of that era's challenges. (b) Students should include their view of today's challenges.
2. (a) Seven (b) Their journey took them through isolated territory with few places to get provisions.
3. (a)The rooster runs off, the oxen dies, and the food runs out. (b) Everything has gone wrong, and the journey looks hopeless.
4. (a) Home to Pike County (b) She's going to California with or without him.
5. Accept reasonable answers.
6. The regular rhythm and rhyme scheme make the ballad easy to remember.
7. Betsy seems representative of the many strong, resourceful women who journeyed west in those times.
8. (a) They are adventurous, courageous, clever, and determined. (b) Accept reasonable answers.

After You Read

Respond and Think Critically

Respond and Interpret

1. (a)Do you think Betsy would have been a good role model for people in the 1800s? Explain. (b)Describe a fictional character who you think would be a good role model for people today.
2. (a)How many animals do Betsy and Ike take with them on their trip? (b)What does the fact that Betsy and Ike are traveling with these animals tell you about their journey?
3. (a)What happens on the day the last piece of bacon is fried? (b)Explain why Ike may become discouraged at that time.
4. (a)To what place does Ike want to return? (b)Explain what Betsy means by saying, "You'll go by yourself if you do."

Analyze and Evaluate

5. Which of the two characters—Betsy or Ike—is more memorable? Why?
6. Would this ballad be easy or difficult to memorize? Explain.

Connect

7. **Big Idea** Courage and Cleverness Why do you think a woman is the central character in this ballad about courage and cleverness?
8. **Connect to Today** (a)What qualities do Betsy and Ike exhibit that would make them successful in the present day? (b)What do you think Betsy and Ike would be doing if they were living in the present day?

Literary Element Ballad

Ballads are poems or songs that tell a story. They generally fall into one of two types: folk or literary.

1. Is "Sweet Betsy from Pike" a folk ballad or a literary ballad? How do you know?
2. What is the main action taking place in "Sweet Betsy from Pike"? How does the main action help define it as a ballad?
3. What feature or features of this ballad tell you that it may have originated as a song?

LOG ON Literature Online

Selection Resources For Selection Quizzes, eFlashcards, and Reading-Writing Connection activities, go to glencoe.com and enter QuickPass code GL49787u5.

Review: Meter and Rhythm

As you learned on page 462, meter and rhythm are elements in poetic expression. **Meter** is a regular pattern of stressed and unstressed syllables that gives a line of poetry or a song a predictable rhythm. **Rhythm** is the sound pattern created by the arrangement of stressed and unstressed syllables that gives poetry a musical quality. You can analyze the rhythm in poetry by scanning it. To scan a line, write out the words and use symbols to indicate stressed and unstressed syllables. A ˘ above a syllable indicates that it is unstressed, and a ´ indicates that it is stressed. An example is given below.

> I wandered lonely as a cloud
> That floats on high o'er vales and hills.

Partner Activity With a classmate, discuss the meter and rhythm in "Sweet Betsy from Pike." Scan the lines in the first verse to determine the number of beats in each line and to decide which syllables are stressed.

Progress Check

Can students identify ballads?

If No → See Unit 5 Teaching Resources Book, p. 154.

Literary Element

1. Folk ballad; no author is listed; the song is labeled "Traditional."
2. The ballad tells of Betsy and Ike's journey to California. The events constitute a story, or narrative.
3. Its rhythm and a rhyme scheme, the chorus

Review: Meter and Rhythm

Students should indicate four beats in each line with the following syllables stressed:

˘ ´ ˘ ˘ ´ ˘ ˘ ´ ˘
(Oh, do you remember sweet Betsy
˘ ´
from Pike,
˘ ´ ˘ ˘ ´ ˘ ˘
Who, crossed the wide prairies with
´ ˘ ˘ ´
her husband Ike?

Reading Strategy Analyze Archetypes

Archetypal characters occur often in folklore—the traditional beliefs, customs, stories, and songs belonging to a culture that are passed down by word of mouth. These characters are universally recognized "types," such as heroes or villains. The stubborn wife and henpecked husband on a quest for riches while battling hunger and the elements are character archetypes typical to folklore.

1. Describe Betsy and Ike. Why might Betsy be considered an archetypal wife?
2. Do you think the journey of Betsy and Ike could be considered archetypal? Explain.

Academic Vocabulary

For pioneers like "Sweet Betsy from Pike," survival was their main ***priority*** *during the difficult journey west.*

Priority is an academic word. In a more casual conversation, a person might try to express how badly they need something by saying it is their top **priority.** Using context clues, try to figure out the meaning of the word in the sentence about pioneers above. Check your guess in a dictionary.

For more on academic vocabulary, see pages 54–55 and R79–R81.

A wagoner drives his horses along the eastern section of the Union Pacific Railroad.

Speaking and Listening

Oral Report

Assignment Research a song linked to a particular historical event or period. Give an oral presentation about the song; include a recording of the song, if possible.

Prepare Choose a historical event or period and do your initial research of the topic. Use the information to narrow your musical search and find a song. Once you've chosen a song, do further research on the song itself, such as learning more about the writer/composer or finding a recording.

Report Support your oral presentation with visual aids and media from the historical period. Use photographs or posters from the era, and incorporate a recording of the song into your report. If you cannot find a recording, create a visual aid that features the song's lyrics or sheet music.

Evaluate After you have given the report, evaluate your presentation. If possible, have someone record your presentation on audio or video for your critique. If not, evaluate the oral report based on your memory.

Review your oral report according to the checklist below. Note areas where you were weak, and suggest ways to improve.

- ☑ Speak loudly enough so everyone can hear you.
- ☑ Speak at a moderate speed, but vary the rate and use pauses.
- ☑ Speak with confidence.
- ☑ Vary your facial expressions to reflect what you are saying.

Summarize the information and notes from the checklist into a paragraph that provides a brief overall critique of your presentation. Highlight your main strengths and weaknesses, and include suggestions for how you might improve future oral presentations.

After You Read

Assess

Reading Strategy

1. Betsy is tougher than her discouraged husband. She is ready to go on without him if she has to. She is the archetype of the stubborn wife who pushes her husband for the sake of her own goals.
2. It seems typical of stories about pursuing a goal. There is usually a point in such journeys when the long, hard struggle seems hopeless.

Academic Vocabulary

Sample Answer: A priority is something that is the most important focus, such as staying alive was to the pioneers during their hardships.

Speaking and Listening

Students' oral reports should:

- present a song linked to a particular historical event or period
- provide background information about the song
- include visual support depicting the song's historical era
- include a recording of the song, if possible
- be followed by a thorough self-evaluation that is summarized in writing

To create custom assessments online, go to Progress Reporter Online Assessment.

For additional assessment, see Assessment Resources, pp. 207–208.

To create custom assessments using software, use ExamView Assessment Suite.

Writing Workshop

Research Report

Focus

Bellringer Options

Display pictures showing different kinds of heroes, including celebrities, such as athletes, and noncelebrities, such as firemen.

Ask: What makes these people heroes? Which one do you find most heroic? Is it possible to be a hero without being famous?

Have students freewrite about aspects of heroism that interest them or about people they have known who have acted heroically.

Summary

In this workshop, students will write a research paper and give an expository presentation of it. Students will follow the stages of the writing process, including prewriting, drafting, revising, and editing. In addition, the workshop includes two focus lessons, on building paragraph unity and using quotation marks correctly.

Learning Objectives

For pages 962–971

In this workshop, you will focus on the following objectives:

Writing: Writing a research paper using the writing process.
Understanding how to build paragraph unity.

Grammar: Understanding how to punctuate in-text citations.

Writing Process

At any stage of a writing process, you may think of new ideas. Feel free to return to earlier stages as you write.

- Prewrite
- Draft
- Revise
- Focus Lesson: Paragraph Unity
- Edit and Proofread
- Focus Lesson: Quotation Marks and In-Text Citations
- Present

Writing Workshop

Research Report

Literature Connection In Homer's *Odyssey,* the outsized hero Odysseus boasts of feats that seem to have no possible basis in fact:

> *"Cyclops,*
> *if ever mortal man inquire*
> *how you were put to shame and blinded, tell him*
> *Odysseus, raider of cities, took your eye:*
> *Laertes' son, whose home's on Ithaca!"*

Could such adventures contain a grain of truth? Researchers have used vast supplies of ink and paper on facts in the *Odyssey.* In a research report, you uncover and merge the facts of history, literature, or other content areas to answer a central question. Read the following goals and strategies for writing your own research report.

Checklist

Goals	Strategies
To provide a clear answer to a research question	☑ Draw a central conclusion from your research and state it clearly as your thesis
To explain and support the thesis	☑ Read and take notes from a variety of primary and secondary sources ☑ Synthesize information from many sources and perspectives ☑ Support main ideas with substantial, relevant evidence ☑ Explain why some evidence is more valuable, convincing, or significant
To anticipate and answer your reader's questions and concerns	☑ Clearly relate all evidence to your thesis ☑ Define terms as needed ☑ Use precise language and the active voice
To use sources honestly and credit them correctly	☑ Credit all your sources ☑ Use a standardized method of documentation

Workshop Resources

Print Materials

- Unit 5 Teaching Resources, pp. 160–162
- Writing Kit
- Success in Writing: Research and Reports

Transparencies

- Grammar and Language Transparency 4
- Writing Workshop Transparencies 26, 27, 28, 29, 30

Technology

- Literature Online: Writing Resources and Grammar Resources, www.glencoe.com
- Online Essay Grader, www.glencoe.com
- Student Presentation Builder on StudentWorks Plus CD-ROM
- Media Workshop DVD
- Online Student Edition

Assignment: Write a research report

Write a research report of at least 1,500 words about an everyday hero or historical figure who has character traits similar to those of an epic hero. Keep your audience and purpose in mind.

Audience: classmates and teacher

Purpose: to research a topic and present your conclusions supported by evidence

Prewrite

Make a Schedule Create a time frame for completing each step in your writing process.

▶ **Choose a Topic and Narrow the Focus** Do research to refine and shape your topic. If your topic is too narrow, you will not be able to find the information you need. If it is too broad, you will have difficulty organizing the details and making a clear point. The chart shows examples of topics that are too broad, too narrow, and just right.

Too Broad	Too Narrow	Just Right
The soldiers in World War II, Red Cross workers, and Rosie the Riveter are heroes who share character traits with epic heroes.	Rosie Bonavita was a real riveter who fastened a record number of rivets in six hours.	Rosie the Riveter symbolizes the American women who became everyday heroes during World War II.

Gather Information Begin by writing four or five questions to research. Start with the basics: *who, what, why, when, where,* and *how.*

Student Model

Who was Rosie the Riveter?
What kind of work did women do during World War II?
When and where did women start working?

Look for answers on reliable Web sites and in encyclopedias, books, and magazines. Try to use primary sources such as letters, diaries, and interviews as well as secondary sources, such as books and articles about the topic. Think of visual aids, such as maps or graphs, that you could use both to record information now and to display in your paper later.

Real World Connection

Research skills are important in many jobs, from patient care to engineering. As you present ideas and options to team members and managers in your working life, you will need to synthesize information, make judgments about it, explain it effectively, and provide any necessary background information.

Quote Versus Paraphrase

The exact words from a reliable authority give credibility to research, so you should include some direct quotations in your paper. On the other hand, when the exact words from another source are not memorable, it is better to put the idea in your own words, or paraphrase. Paraphrasing helps maintain the flow of your writing.

LOG ON Literature Online

Writing and Research For prewriting, drafting, and revising tools, go to glencoe.com and enter QuickPass code GL49787u5.

English Learners

DIFFERENTIATED INSTRUCTION

PARTNERS **Beginning/Early Intermediate** Encourage English learners to select a hero from their native culture. They may be able to research resources in their native language. After they organize information, pair them with a more proficient English speaker to help translate notes into English.

Intermediate Remind English learners to use the library and its resources to research their topic. Encourage them to take advantage of school and public librarians, who are very willing to help with research projects. Students should not feel shy in asking questions.

Writing Workshop

Research Report

Teach

Big Idea

Courage and Cleverness

At first glance, students may be puzzled by the idea of "everyday" heroics. Remind them that even in everyday life we have opportunities to display our courage and our cleverness. **Ask:** What are some examples of courage or cleverness that you remember from your own life? What are some examples that you've heard of from the news? *(In answer to the second question, students may mention humanitarian relief workers, rescue workers, or other vivid "human interest" stories.)*

Writing Skills

Narrow the Focus Use the chart on page 963 to help students understand how to determine the proper scope of a topic. **Ask:** Why is the example cited under the first subhead too broad? *(Each of the three examples could be the subject of a whole essay on their own.)* Why is the example cited under the second subhead too narrow? *(This statement is a detail that could best be used to support a more general thesis.)*

Teach

Political History ☆

Rosie the Riveter Memorial
Dedicated in October of 2000, the Rosie the Riveter Memorial is a large outdoor sculpture set in the former Kaiser Shipyards of Richmond, California, where many women worked to assemble ships used in World War II. The large stainless steel structure was designed by visual artist Susan Schwartzberg and landscape architect/environmental sculptor Cheryl Barton. It commemorates the important labor done by women during the war.

Take Notes As you find sources, take notes on index cards. Keep track of your sources as you research so you can list them on a Works Cited page at the end of your paper. Copy direct quotations if you think you will be able to use them to support your thesis. Other information can be paraphrased or summarized.

▶ **Bibliography Note Card**

Source number	④
	Online Interview
Author	Harvey, Sheridan.
Title	"Rosie the Riveter: Real Women Workers in World War II."
Web site information	Rosie the Riveter Transcript (Journeys and Crossings)
Sponsoring organization	Library of Congress Digital Reference Team.
Date of access	Dec. 19, 2008
URL	http://www.loc.gov/rr/program/journey/rosie-transcript.html

▶ **Paraphrase Note Card**

Source number: ③
Main idea group: Norman Rockwell's Rosie

☆ Rosie the Riveter appears on a cover that Norman Rockwell illustrated for the Saturday Evening Post in May 1943. She is a big, strong woman, and she has a smudge on her face. Rosie wears overalls, loafers, and a leather strap around her arm. There is a riveter gun in her lap.

▶ **Direct Quotation Note Card**

Source number: ②
Main idea group: Norman Rockwell's Rosie

"Rosie is powerful, competent, and womanly. But there are contradictions in the image. She's masculine: look at the size of her arms, which are a real focus of the cover. . . . Yet she's feminine: She's wearing rouge and lipstick. Makeup is essential to women's mental health, according to some articles of the time. Her compact and handkerchief peek out of her pocket; she has nail polish on; her curly red hair and upturned nose feminize her; her visor almost looks like a halo, providing an angelic side to this strong woman."

Using Ellipses
Use ellipsis points (. . .) to show that a word or words are omitted from an original quotation.

Research Practice

Research Methods
One of the challenges of researching a paper is deciding what information is worth including. As students begin to research their papers, offer them the following advice:

- Use a variety of consumer, workplace, and public documents.
- Start with a general source that will give you just the basics, such as an encyclopedia or a reliable website.
- When selecting sources to use as research, read for big ideas, rather than for details. Have students make a list of questions that will help guide them in their research.
- Be sure to record from your sources all of the information that you will need to prepare a standard bibliography.

Organize Your Information An outline is an excellent way to organize the data you collect from various sources. Begin with a working outline that you can revise as you draft your paper. Below are some tips.

- **Groupings** Group note cards and use the groupings to develop the main topics in your outline.
- **Topic Groups** Form subtopics in the main topic groups and use these as secondary heads in your outline.
- **Order** Put your main topics in the most logical order.

Sample Outline

Rosie the Riveter: A Symbol for Everyday Heroes During World War II

I. Posters of Rosie the Riveter
   A. Famous in the 1940s
      1. A made-up character
      2. Based on a real woman, maybe Rosie Bonavita
   B. All women with men's jobs came to be known as Rosie the Riveter
II. Men left jobs to join the military
   A. Workers needed to keep the country running
   B. OWI created in 1942
      1. Ran advertising campaign
      2. Posters challenged women to join the war effort

Develop Your Thesis Statement After you have chosen the main ideas, draft a thesis statement that covers them. You may revise the statement as you write, but it helps to get something down on paper.

Sample Thesis Statement

During World War II, Rosie the Riveter was a symbol for the women who became everyday heroes when they accepted the challenge and showed strength and courage in doing jobs that they had never done before.

In-Text Citations

In the body of your paper, use parentheses to credit your sources briefly by giving the last name of the author and the page reference. Include a separate page, titled Works Cited, at the end of your paper to give a full description of each source.

Avoid Plagiarism

Avoiding plagiarism begins at the note-taking stage. The more careful you are to summarize and paraphrase (instead of just copy), as well as to attribute the source of each idea, the more likely you are to avoid using someone else's words and ideas without crediting them. Remember that plagiarism can have consequences that range from failing grades to legal action against you.

Teach

Writing Skills

Take Notes To help students take effective notes while researching their papers, emphasize the following strategies:

- Make sure that the information is relevant to your topic.
- For each subject, use a separate note card.
- Be sure to carefully note your sources for your bibliography.
- When you're finished taking notes, organize your note cards according to subject.

Create an Outline Tell students that all of the information they have gathered in their research should fit somewhere in their outline. If something doesn't fit, students should consider whether to eliminate the bit of information or adapt any of the topics or subtopics to incorporate it. Creating an outline may also bring to light any gaps in the gathered information, and more research may be required.

Approaching Level

DIFFERENTIATED INSTRUCTION

Emerging Students who reason logically will excel at organizing their note cards. Have some of these students bring in their note cards, so they can model this process for the class. Have these students divide their note cards into subtopics. Then initiate a class discussion in which you ask volunteers to name logical ways to organize them. Use the board or an overhead projector to demonstrate how to use the note cards to create an outline.

Teach

Writing Skills

Introduction

Answer: *The subject is Rosie the Riveter.*

Thesis Statement

Answer: *During World War II, Rosie the Riveter symbolized the possibility that women can do jobs they have never done before and become everyday heroes.*

Main Idea

Answer: *Right away the reader understands that the idea of Rosie the Riveter and what she symbolized was well-known.*

Support

Answer: *The details present facts and information about the woman upon whom the poster character is believed to be based, reinforcing the message that women can be everyday heroes.*

Draft

Getting Started As with any writing, it is best to start writing your research report immediately. Begin with the ideas in your notes and outline. As you draft, keep your thesis in mind, and do not stray too far from it. Be sure to include examples and details to support your topic sentences and main ideas. Visual aids are also an option for support.

Analyze a Workshop Model

Here is a final draft of a research report. Answer the questions in the margin, and use the answers to guide you as you write your own draft.

Introduction
Begin by letting your readers know the subject. What will this research paper be about?

Thesis Statement
State your point of view in a thesis statement. What viewpoint will be presented?

Main Idea
Use the main ideas from your outline to develop your body paragraphs. Why is this a good main idea to put at the beginning of a body paragraph?

Support
Use facts, examples, statistics, quotations, and reasons to support your main idea. How do these details support the main idea of the paragraph?

Rosie the Riveter: Everyday Hero

If you had been alive during World War II, you would have seen posters on the walls of banks, post offices, and other public places of a young American woman wearing overalls and carrying a wrench or a rivet gun in her hand. Who was this woman, and why was her image all over town? She was known as Rosie the Riveter, and during World War II, she was a symbol for all of the women who became everyday heroes when they showed strength and courage in doing jobs that they had never done before.

Rosie the Riveter was one of the most famous women in the United States in the early 1940s. She was a made-up character, but she may have been based on a real woman named Rosina D. Bonavita who, in one shift with her partner, drove a record 3,345 rivets to assemble the wing of a torpedo bomber (Ambrose 42). Even though the Rosie in the posters was not a real person, she set a powerful example for women during the war. She called on them to serve their country by doing jobs they had never done before.

Millions of men left their jobs to fight in World War II. While they were away, somebody had to fill their jobs to keep the country running. Who could do peacetime jobs

Writing Practice

PARTNERS

Write Effective Introductions

Say: Your introduction should grab the reader's attention. **List** the following ideas on the board:

- Begin with an unusual fact or detail.
- Ask a question that the paper will answer.
- State your thesis.
- Begin with an anecdote.
- Begin with an interesting fact.
- Give a quotation that you can tie into your paper.
- Explain a term that is relevant to your topic.

Using two of the techniques provided, have students draft two versions of an introduction. Then have them exchange papers with a partner to discuss which introduction is the strongest and why.

such as driving buses? Who could do wartime jobs such as making weapons? Around 1942, an artist named J. Howard Miller worked for a company that probably wanted to encourage women to work there. According to Library of Congress women's studies specialist Sheridan Harvey, Miller created an image of a woman rolling up her sleeve as if getting ready to work. The poster is titled "We Can Do It!" However, Rosie was not connected to this poster (Harvey 1).

Then, on May 29, 1943, Norman Rockwell's picture of a confident woman in overalls illustrated the cover of the *Saturday Evening Post*. One hand rests on a lunch box that is labeled "Rosie" and the other holds a ham sandwich. A huge riveter lies across her lap.

> Rosie is powerful, competent, and womanly. But there are contradictions in the image. She's masculine: look at the size of her arms, which are a real focus of the cover. . . . Yet she's feminine: She's wearing rouge and lipstick. Makeup is essential to women's mental health, according to some articles of the time (Harvey 2).

The country needed women to go to work, and that is where Rosie and the Office of War Information, or OWI, came in. The OWI was created in 1942, and it was an important U.S. government agency during World War II. One of the OWI's many tasks was to run an advertising campaign. They were not selling a product, though. They were selling an idea: All able-bodied citizens, including women, should go to work in jobs that would help the war effort. Until then, some women had worked but not in jobs usually held by men. For example, they worked in clothing factories (Appleby, Brinkley, and McPherson 308–09). Posters of Rosie that were created by the OWI challenged women to do their patriotic duty and participate in the war effort. They helped convince women that they could do men's work, and they could do it well.

More than six million women met the challenge

Exposition

Audience

Engage and inform your reader by using precise language. What makes this language precise?

Direct Quotations

Use direct quotations when the exact words of your sources are particularly memorable or difficult to restate effectively. If a quotation is long, indent it and do not use quotation marks. Why do you think the writer used this quotation?

Anticipate Your Reader's Questions

Remember to fill in likely gaps in the reader's knowledge. How does the writer anticipate the reader's questions here?

Use Sources Honestly

Even when you put information in your own words, be sure to identify your source. Why are there no quotation marks for this information even though a source is cited?

Support

Statistics and specific details support your argument. How do these facts and examples support the idea that women met the challenge and joined the workforce?

Teach

Writing Skills

Audience

Answer: *The use of descriptive words and specific names makes the language precise.*

Direct Quotations

Answer: *The quotation supports the idea that women were strong and capable of filling what were traditionally men's roles at home while the men were fighting for our country.*

Anticipate Your Reader's Questions

Answer: *The writer provides a connection between Rosie and the OWI.*

Use Sources Honestly

Answer: *Paraphrased information is not a direct quotation, so quotation marks are unnecessary.*

Support

Answer: *The facts and examples provide specific information about the kinds of work women did.*

English Learners

DIFFERENTIATED INSTRUCTION

Intermediate English learners may have trouble distinguishing between higher-level and lower-level words. Although a research paper uses relatively formal language, remind students that a simple friendly style is best. Point out the warm, friendly style of writing on these pages. Draw students' attention to the opening sentence, which speaks to the reader. Point out the phrase "She may have been a made-up character" and the sentence "While they were away, somebody had to fill their jobs to keep the country running." Remind students to use language appropriate for their audience and revise their writing for appropriate word choice.

Teach

Writing Skills

Primary Sources

Answer: *The quotations come from women who actually filled men's roles during the war.*

Secondary Sources

Answer: *Encyclopedias compile information from many primary sources to provide general background and factual information.*

Restate Thesis

Answer: *Restating the thesis reinforces its impact.*

Draw Conclusions

Answer: *Rosie the Riveter not only was a symbol during World War II but remains an inspiration for women to join the work force.*

(Colman 16). Women worked in factories and shipyards. They served in the military or worked in hospitals overseas. Some were farmworkers. Women learned new skills, such as welding, hammering, and—of course—riveting. Posters let them know they could help the war effort by working as typists, waitresses, salespeople, and conductors ("Powers").

Primary Sources

Try to include the words of someone who experienced the event. What makes this quotation a primary source? How does the writer integrate it smoothly and attribute it correctly? How does it help show varying perspectives?

Joining the workforce during the war changed many women's lives. One of these women, Jane Ward Mayta, said, "I learned a lot in those years. . . . I learned to look for a job. I learned to get along with and mingle with people from different backgrounds" (Wise and Wise 12).

On October 19, 1942, *Time* magazine reported on the "striking evidence" of the social changes brought by World War II. The reason given was that women were working in new occupations. "Northwest lumber yards now have 4,000 women whistle punks, talleymen, flunkies, bull cooks. . . . In Marshfield, Ore., gaffers watched incredulously as a woman maneuvered a State Highway Commission steam roller down the main street" ("Women").

Secondary Sources

A secondary source is the interpretation of someone who studied primary sources. Why is an encyclopedia a secondary source?

In 1945 World War II came to an end, and the work opportunities for women closed. Many women were not happy to be out of work, but most of them returned to lives focused on homemaking and raising children. By 1960 fewer women were employed as professionals than in 1930 ("Feminism").

Restate Thesis

Restate your viewpoint. Why is it a good idea to restate your thesis in your conclusion?

Yet the example set by Rosie the Riveter would continue to inspire women in the years that followed. Her name remained a symbol for women's strength, courage, and ability to perform a variety of jobs. To this day, the symbol of Rosie the Riveter hard at work remains a real inspiration for generations of women.

Draw Conclusions

End by drawing your own conclusions. What idea does this writer want to leave with readers?

Grammar Practice

SPIRAL REVIEW **Verb Tense** Many students have trouble remaining in the past tense when writing an essay about a historical event. Explain that it is important to keep the verb tense consistent.

Write: Women work in lumberyards and on highways. They prove that in a time of crisis people can do extraordinary things. Have students rewrite these sentences in the past tense. *(Women worked in lumberyards and on highways. They proved that in a time of crisis people could do extraordinary things.)*

Write: In 1945, World War II came to an end, and men who return from the war expect to return to their old jobs.

Point out that the verb tense is inconsistent and ask students to fix the error. *(In 1945, World War II came to an end, and men who returned from the war expected to return to their old jobs.)*

Works Cited

Ambrose, Stephen E. The Good Fight: How World War II Was Won. New York: Atheneum, 2001.

Appleby, Joyce Oldham, Alan Brinkley, and James M. McPherson. The American Journey. New York: Glencoe/McGraw-Hill, 2003.

Colman, Penny. Rosie the Riveter: Women Working on the Home Front in World War II. New York: Crown, 1995.

"Feminism." Encyclopaedia Britannica Online. 2005. Encyclopaedia Britannica Premium Service. 19 Dec. 2005. <http://www.britannica.com/eb/article-216009>.

Fried, Ellen. "From Pearl Harbor to Elvis: Images That Endure." Prologue 36.4, Winter 2004.

Harvey, Sheridan. "Rosie the Riveter: Real Women Workers in World War II." Journeys and Crossings, Library of Congress, Transcript. <http://www.loc.gov/rr/program/journey/rosie-transcript.html>.

"Powers of Persuasion: Poster Art from World War II." National Archives. <http://www.archives.gov/exhibits/powers_of_persuasion/its_a_womans_war_too.html>.

"Rosie the Riveter: Women Working During World War II."<http://www.nps.gov/pwro/collection/website/rosie.htm>.

Wise, Nancy Baker, and Christy Wise. A Mouthful of Rivets: Women at Work in World War II. San Francisco: Jossey-Bass, 1994.

"Women, Women Everywhere." Time Archive Online. XL.16, October 19, 1942. <http://www.time.com/time/archive/preview/0,10987,850057,00.html>.

Exposition

Citing Sources

Books and textbooks are usually reliable sources. What information should be included in the citation for a book?

Reliable Sources

Web sites often have interviews or documents that are primary sources. Why do you have to be careful when you use the Internet as a resource?

Internet Research

Back issues of some magazines are found in archives on the Internet. Why might you want to use information from an old magazine article?

Teach

Writing Skills

Citing Sources

Answer: *The information included in a book citation is the author, article title (if there is one), book title, publisher and its location, and publication year.*

Reliable Sources

Answer: *Internet sources are not always reliable. It's a good idea to check two or three sources to be sure Internet information is accurate.*

Internet Research

Answer: *Issues of old magazines can provide interesting and appropriate historical or background information that may be difficult to find in other sources or otherwise unavailable.*

Advanced Learners

DIFFERENTIATED INSTRUCTION

Critiquing Challenge students to suggest ways to improve the Workshop Model. Have them consider these questions:

- Where could subheads be added in the essay to break up information?
- What evidence could be added to make the essay more convincing?
- What changes could be made to the language to make it more professional while still keeping a friendly tone?
- What other improvement would you make to the essay?

Teach

Writing Skills

Paragraph Unity Explain that the sentences in a paragraph work like a team: Each sentence is a "player" contributing to the overall good. Refer to the focus lesson. **Ask:** Why should the sentence about Norman Rockwell be omitted? *(Because the paragraph is about women joining the workforce, not about Norman Rockwell.)*

Writer's Technique ☆

Gurganus on Revision The novelist Allan Gurganus (1947–) wrote, "The first impulse in writing is to flood it out, let as much run freely as you possibly can. Then to take a walk or go to the bank . . . and come back in a day or six months later. To read it with a cold eye and say, 'This is good. This is not. That sentence works. This is magical. This is crummy.'"

Traits of Strong Writing

Include these traits of strong writing to express your ideas effectively.

Ideas

Organization

Voice

Word Choice

Sentence Fluency

Conventions

Presentation

For more information on using the Traits of Strong Writing, see pages R28–R30.

Word Choice

This academic vocabulary appears in the student model:

participate (pär tis′ ə pāt′) *v.* 1. to take part in; 2. to have a part or share in; *The OWI challenged women to do their patriotic duty and participate in the war effort.* Using academic vocabulary may help strengthen your writing. Try to use one or two academic vocabulary words in your research report. See the complete list on pages R79–R81.

LOG ON Literature Online

Writing and Research
For editing and publishing tools, go to glencoe.com and enter QuickPass code GL49787u5.

Revise

Peer Review Exchange drafts with a partner. Note problems in the ☆ organization or the lack of a conclusion. Use the checklist below to evaluate and strengthen each other's essay.

Checklist

- ☑ Do you clearly state your thesis in your introduction?
- ☑ Do you anticipate your reader's questions?
- ☑ Do you include and fully explain supporting details from a range of sources and perspectives, including primary and secondary sources?
- ☑ Do you correctly cite all your sources?
- ☑ Do you use precise language?

Focus Lesson

Paragraph Unity

To build paragraph unity, use a topic sentence with related supporting details. The topic sentence is often the first sentence, but it can be anywhere in the paragraph. See the example below.

Draft:

Women worked in factories and shipyards. They served in the military or worked in hospitals overseas. Some were farmworkers. In the 1940s, Norman Rockwell was a popular illustrator. Women learned new skills.

Revision:

More than six million women met the challenge and joined the workforce[1] (Colman 16). Women worked in factories and shipyards. They served in the military or worked in hospitals overseas. Some were farmworkers. ~~In the 1940s, Norman Rockwell was a popular illustrator.~~[2] Women learned many new skills, such as welding, hammering, and—of course—riveting.[3]

1: Begin with a topic sentence.
2: Omit sentences that do not relate to the topic.
3: Add specific details.

Writing Practice

PARTNERS

Precise Language Remind students of the importance of using precise language, descriptive details, and active verbs to engage the reader. Have students exchange papers with a partner. Partners should point out sentences that can be revised using precise language, more descriptive synonyms, and sensory details.

Edit and Proofread

Get It Right When you have completed the final draft of your research paper, proofread for errors in grammar, usage, mechanics, and spelling. Refer to the Language Handbook, pages R40–R59, as a guide.

Focus Lesson

Quotation Marks and In-Text Citations

When you quote from a source, use double quotation marks before the first word you quote and after the last word. Begin the quotation with a capital letter unless you begin in the middle of a sentence. Place the citation after the quotation and before the period. Long quotations are indented and need no quotation marks.

Original: Quoted information is not in quotation marks; there is no citation.

Jane Ward Mayta said, I learned a lot in those years. . . . I learned to look for a job. I learned to get along with and mingle with people from different backgrounds.

Improved: Add quotation marks and a citation.

Jane Ward Mayta said, "I learned a lot in those years. . . . I learned to look for a job. I learned to get along with and mingle with people from different backgrounds" (Wise and Wise 12).

Original: Quotation marks are used with words that are paraphrased.

"More than six million women met the challenge" (Colman 16).

Improved: Omit the quotation marks around the paraphrase.

More than six million women met the challenge (Colman 16).

Present

Finish Your Research Report Before you turn the paper in, make sure it is neat. Review the assignment guidelines to see if you have forgotten anything. Check your use of quotation marks, identification of sources, and Works Cited page for accuracy and format.

Exposition

Peer Review Tips

A classmate may ask you to read his or her research report. Take your time and jot down notes as you read so you can give constructive feedback. Use the following questions to get started:

Can you identify the thesis and the main points that support it?

Does the writer introduce and fully explain all quoted evidence?

Does the writer define unfamiliar terms and otherwise address the audience?

Word-Processing Tip

Begin each entry in a Works Cited list at the far left and indent any lines that follow. Show book titles in italic type. In the body of the paper, follow all quoted, paraphrased, and summarized material by parenthetical references. Usually, these references require only the author's name and page number; however, if you must cite a book title, italicize it.

Writer's Portfolio

Place a clean copy of your research report in your portfolio to review later.

Writing Workshop

Research Report

Teach

Writing Process

Edit and Proofread

After students proofread their own papers, have them exchange papers with a partner, each of them proofreading the other's. Instruct them to pay special attention to quotations and citations. Have them keep these questions in mind as they work:

- Is the punctuation correct?
- Are all the sources cited?

Remind students to be respectful while proofreading their partners' manuscripts.

Use Quotation Marks

Students are often confused by the mechanics of quotations. As practice, **write** on the board some sample quotations, such as the ones in the focus lesson, leaving out the quotation marks and punctuation. Ask students to come up to the board and correct the mistakes. Review the placement of quotation marks, commas, and periods, as well as the rules for capitalization.

Approaching Level

DIFFERENTIATED INSTRUCTION

PARTNERS

Emerging Less-proficient students may need extra time editing and proofreading their papers. Pair them with proficient students and have the pairs work together throughout the editing and proofreading process. Have the proficient students check papers for spelling, grammar, and usage problems. Encourage students to reread the Workshop Model as needed for clues about how to construct an effective research paper.

Speaking, Listening, and Viewing Workshop

Multimedia Presentation

Focus

Summary

Students will plan and develop a multimedia presentation based on their historical investigation reports and will learn techniques for presenting it to an audience.

Teach

Speaking Skills

Presentation Some students may not understand how planning a multimedia presentation is very different from planning a standard oral presentation. Discuss with students the reasons why some presenters incorporate different types of media into their presentations. Explain that these elements can increase the audience's interest in a presentation, as well as improve the accuracy of the information being presented.

Learning Objectives

For pages 972–975

In this workshop, you will focus on the following objective:

Speaking and Listening: Delivering a multimedia presentation.

Workshop Model
In this workshop, note the examples used from a multimedia presentation titled "Rosie the Riveter: Everyday Hero." You might try out some of the techniques shown in the multimedia presentation that you create.

Real-World Connection
History museums often present multimedia exhibits. Try visiting a virtual or online museum for ideas and inspiration before you begin your presentation.

LOG ON Literature Online

Speaking, Listening, and Viewing For project ideas, templates, and presentation tips, go to glencoe.com and enter QuickPass code GL49787u5.

Speaking, Listening, and Viewing Workshop

Multimedia Presentation

Literature Connection Sounds and images have long been used to translate the bold actions and exotic settings of ages-old epics and myths to television, movie, and computer screens. Media producers take ancient spoken and written works and re-create them as new works of art and popular culture. In this workshop, you will learn how to re-create your historical investigation report as a multimedia presentation.

Assignment **Plan and deliver a multimedia presentation of your historical investigation report. As you develop your presentation, keep your audience and purpose in mind.**

Audience: classmates and teacher

Purpose: to inform and describe; to engage

Plan Your Presentation

A multimedia presentation combines text, sound, and images (art, photos, video clips, animation, and print). Multimedia presentations include narrated slide or transparency presentations, Web sites, and Web casts.

Begin your planning by finding out what kind of equipment is available at your school. For example, consider these issues:

- Does your school have digital or video cameras, screens, or projectors? Are they available for student use?
- Do you have to apply to use equipment or reserve it in advance?
- Are there computers available to you? Do they have enough memory for video or large graphics programs?
- What kinds of software are available to you? For example, are there photo, animation, or multimedia authorship programs?

The chart on the next page shows some options for your presentation and the types of equipment each requires.

Listening, Speaking, and Viewing Practice

SPIRAL REVIEW **Compare and Contrast Presentations** Read students a short writing on a historical topic. Then, read the same writing again, but this time include music and visual aids such as photographs, video clips, and props. As you are reading, ask students to compare and contrast the two readings and assess how these added elements can enhance the effectiveness of a presentation. Ask students to assess how language, tone, delivery, and multimedia elements can affect a presentation and impact the mood of the audience.

Ways to Create a Multimedia Presentation

	Equipment	Application
Low-tech	Camera, slide or overhead projector, and tape recorder	Use 35-mm slides or overhead transparencies for the visuals—images or text, or images with text
↓	Computer with speakers, monitor, and microphone	Use presentation software to create a computer-based slide show combining text, graphics, images, and sound
High-tech	Computer with speakers, monitor, a microphone plus a digital camera, video camera, and scanner	Use a hypertext program to combine text, graphics, images, and sounds to create a series of "cards" containing hyperlinks that make different sequences possible

Choose Your Media

Once you decide on a type of presentation, reread your historical investigation report. Decide how you can add sounds and images to the ideas there. You can do this by returning to your outline and highlighting or annotating key ideas and details, as this sample shows.

I. Introduction and Thesis
  Sound clip of riveting, factory motors?
  WWII song "Rosie the Riveter" by Redd Evans
II. Rosie the Riveter
  A. made-up character: maybe Rosie Bonavita
    Pictures of Rosie
  B. all women factory workers known as "Rosie"
III. Workers needed; OWI campaign created
  A. advertising/propaganda
    WWII posters/photos of "Rosie"
  B. Norman Rockwell
    Fine art of Norman Rockwell print of Rosie
IV. Changes in Women's Lives
  A. new experiences
  B. change in status for women
    Dramatic reading of Jane Ward Mayta quotation
    Image of paycheck of female factory worker
    Part of an oral history interview with a "Rosie"
  C. lost jobs at end of war
V. Conclusion

You can use search engines to find your sounds and images. You may also be able to use databases. Remember that your school and public library may offer some subscription databases that are free to you.

Select Appropriate Media
To write your historical investigation report, you looked carefully at your sources. You determined how objective, reliable, and valid they were. Evaluate the media you select in the same way. Ask yourself whether the writer or sponsor is an authority. Ask why the work was created. Also ask how the work might have been checked or edited before publication or release.

Edit the Media
Choose carefully. Decide which media explain or support your thesis and will engage your audience. Use your narration to help your audience understand what the images and sounds convey.

Teach

Speaking Skills

Speaking Practice Tell students that the rate and tone at which they speak can effect the overall impression of the audience and how they receive the information in the presentation. Explain that talking very quickly can sometimes make it hard for an audience to hear and understand everything that is being said. Also, point out that speaking too slowly can cause an audience to lose interest in what you are saying. Suggest that they practice reading aloud to get a sense of rate of speech and engaging tone of voice.

For help with creating presentations, see Student Presentation Builder on StudentWorks Plus.

Reading Skills

Technical Directions Have students work together to understand technical directions for software programs or to access guides to World Wide Web Sites on the Internet.

Approaching Level

DIFFERENTIATED INSTRUCTION

Emerging Have students look over each other's historical investigation reports and think about what media techniques could be incorporated into the other students' presentations. Students should also consider props, visual aids, and graphs. Ask students to make a list of all possibilities, and then have students narrow down the list until only the best two or three techniques are left. Remind students to use the information and techniques that they have learned so far to narrow down their presentation choices. Students should consider using these suggestions to enhance their presentation.

Speaking, Listening, and Viewing Workshop

Multimedia Presentation

Teach

Speaking Skills

Organization Remind students that their job as presenters is to keep their audience interested in the topic. Point out that good organization and varied media elements will help students accomplish this goal. Encourage students to think about what techniques are successful in their favorite books, magazines, television shows, and so forth, as well as how they might incorporate those elements into their own presentations.

Develop Your Presentation

Your main purpose is to pull together the information from both your primary and secondary sources in order to inform your audience accurately. Follow these steps:

- ***Create your narration.*** You must also be as clear as possible, so create a narration that helps your audience make links between the different parts of your presentation.
- ***Emphasize your thesis.*** Because your thesis is the most important idea you will present, be sure to display it or repeat it.
- ***Focus on your purpose.*** Your purpose is also to show how you drew ideas from different sources with different facts and ideas. To help your audience see how your sources varied, you might display their title pages, along with examples. Then your listeners can focus on the information as you explain how your sources treated different ideas. Re-create these pages by scanning them or by photocopying and enlarging them.
- ***Remember the audience and occasion.*** Think about other possible problems your audience might have in understanding or following your presentation. Be sure to explain any unfamiliar or technical terms. Consider using maps, graphs, or charts to display unfamiliar concepts, and use software to create them. Also, address biases your audience may have, such as believing that all women went to work during World War II.
- ***Edit.*** Use only well-supported, reliable information. Stay focused on your thesis.

Avoid Plagiarism
Correctly credit each image, video clip, and sound, along with all your print sources, in a Works Cited slide at the end of your presentation. (See pages R35–R37 for standardized citation styles.)

Organize Your Presentation

Next, create a storyboard. Make a frame for each slide, card, or transparency you will use. Begin with a title and author frame. End with a Works Cited frame. Be sure you credit all your research sources, as well as all your visual and sound sources. In each frame, list the ideas for the images, sounds, and text you will use.

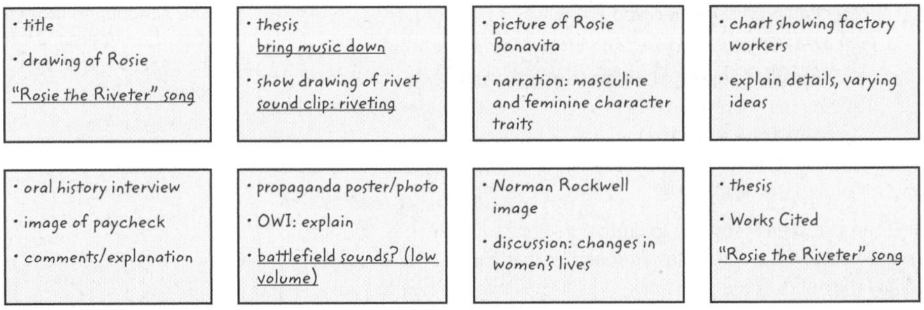

· title
· drawing of Rosie
"Rosie the Riveter" song
· thesis
bring music down
· show drawing of rivet
sound clip: riveting
· picture of Rosie Bonavita
· narration: masculine and feminine character traits
· chart showing factory workers
· explain details, varying ideas
· oral history interview
· image of paycheck
· comments/explanation
· propaganda poster/photo
· OWI: explain
· battlefield sounds? (low volume)
· Norman Rockwell image
· discussion: changes in women's lives
· thesis
· Works Cited
"Rosie the Riveter" song

Listening, Speaking, and Viewing Practice

Visuals Tell students that a picture sometimes tells a story or expresses an idea. Ask students to look in a magazine or on the Internet to find a historical picture that tells a story. Have students find a picture that relates to the topic of their historical investigation report to incorporate into their presentations. **Ask:** What is happening in the picture? What message does the picture convey? Why do you think the photographer took the picture? How does the picture enhance your presentation?

Note these two examples of slides based on ideas mapped out in the model storyboard.

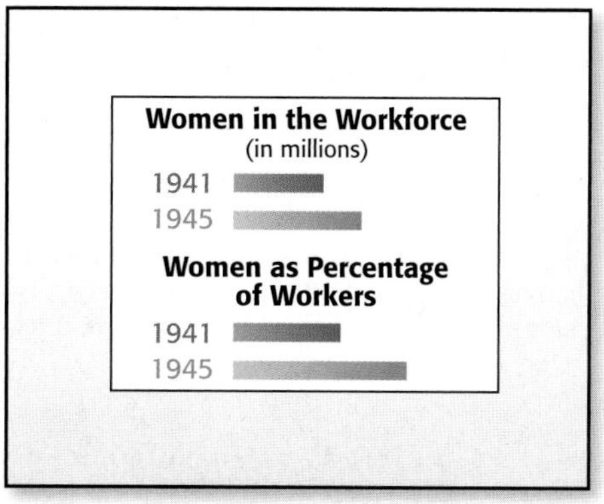

Rehearse and Deliver Your Presentation

Timing is an important—and a tricky—part of a multimedia presentation. You will need to rehearse your presentation many times in order to be sure that all your images, sound, and narration are working smoothly together. Once these parts are well balanced, rehearse the presentation in front of a small audience of classmates, family members, or friends. Ask them to tell you what is or is not clear to them. Also ask them to explain which sounds and images are most effective for them and why.

As you rehearse and deliver your presentation, keep the presentation techniques below in mind. When you are an audience member, keep the listening and viewing techniques in mind.

Techniques for Delivering a Multimedia Presentation

Presentation Techniques	Listening and Viewing Techniques
☑ **Pace** Your audience is not familiar with your research or images, so do not rush.	☑ **Body Language** Sit upright. Keep your head up. Do not tap or fidget.
☑ **Volume** Make sure everyone can hear you. Ask people to raise their hands if they cannot hear.	☑ **Facial Expression** Keep an interested look on your face. For example, show surprise or nod.
☑ **Eye Contact** Make as much eye contact with your audience as possible.	☑ **Focus** Look only at the presenter or at the images.

Evaluation Checklist

- ☑ Is the thesis clear?
- ☑ Do the text, images, and sounds clearly support the thesis and main ideas?
- ☑ Does the presentation flow smoothly from beginning to end?
- ☑ Does the presentation reflect careful editing and rehearsal?

Teach

Speaking Skills

Address the Audience Remind students of the importance of maintaining a good demeanor throughout a presentation. Explain that a presenter should speak clearly and be courteous to his or her audience. Note the ways to incorporate an audience into a presentation, such as by asking questions or by directly addressing the audience.

Approaching Level

DIFFERENTIATED INSTRUCTION

AAVE Encourage approaching-level students who use African American Vernacular English (AAVE) to remember the following pronunciation tips when speaking.

- Avoid dropping the /ng/ sound in words ending in *-ing.* (*wedding* instead of *weddin', thinking* instead of *thinkin'*)
- Pronounce the /k/ sound in words ending is *-sk.* (*desk* instead of *des, mask* instead of *mass*)
- Pronounce the /s/ and /k/ sounds when saying *ask.* Do not use the pronunciation of *ax* for *ask.*

Independent Reading

Focus

Summary

In this section, students will be introduced to epics and myths from cultures around the world, as well as two novels related to the Big Ideas of journeys and courage and cleverness. Encourage students to read these works, which are related to the themes they learned about in this unit.

Teach

Literary History ☆

Edith Hamilton The author of many popular books on ancient Greece and Rome, Edith Hamilton (1867–1963) grew up in Fort Wayne, Indiana. After graduating from Bryn Mawr College, she and her sister Alice went on to further studies at universities in Leipzig and Munich, Germany. Hamilton then spent 26 years as the headmistress of a school for girls, before retiring in 1922 to devote herself to classical studies. In honor of her achievements, the city of Athens, Greece, made her an honorary citizen in 1957.

Independent Reading

Epics, Myths, and Novels

EPICS AND MYTHS ARE TRADITIONAL TALES. WHILE MYTHS OFTEN FEATURE creatures whose traits are linked to supernatural powers, epics usually feature human or superhuman heroes. Both epics and myths take place long ago and far away and are told in a dignified, grave, or awe-filled tone. For more epics and myths covering a range of themes, try the suggestions on these pages. For novels that treat the Big Ideas of *Journeys* and *Courage and Cleverness,* try the titles from the Glencoe Literature Library on the next page.

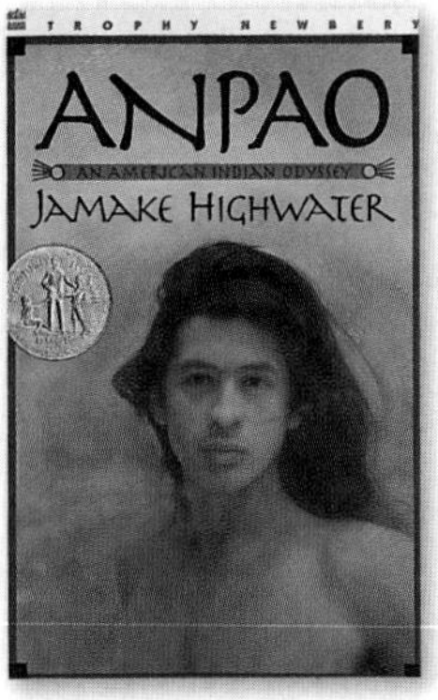

Anpao: An American Indian Odyssey

by Jamake Highwater

This book incorporates the folklore of Plains and Southwest Native Americans to tell the story of Anpao, a poor but brave young man who falls in love with the daughter of a chief. She agrees to marry him, but only after he gets the permission of the Sun. Anpao undertakes a dramatic journey across mountains, deserts, and prairies to reach back in time to the dawn of the world. He must relive his own creation and do battle with mythological forces before he can achieve his goal.

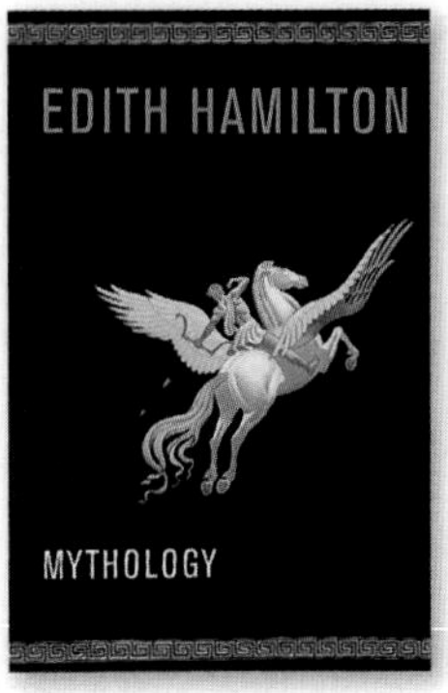

Mythology

by Edith Hamilton ☆

Zeus and Odysseus, Cupid and Psyche, Hercules and the Titans—these and other Greek gods and heroes have inspired, frightened, enlightened, and entertained generations of readers around the world. This collection includes the stories that are an important part of Western culture. For example, in one story, Midas turns everything to gold. In another, Arachne is turned into a spider for being too proud.

Writing Practice

Write a Book Review Students interested in the recommended literature should be encouraged to write a book review. Explain that a book review includes the following:

- a brief summary or overview of the book
- a description of notable highlights
- opinions on the writer's style and technique
- a recommendation to read the book (or not), supported by sound reasons

GLENCOE LITERATURE LIBRARY

The Call of the Wild

by Jack London

Told from the perspective of a dog, this journey of change and discovery has universal meaning.

The Adventures of Tom Sawyer

by Mark Twain

The clever pranks and narrow escapes of a boy growing up along the Mississippi River in the 1840s have entertained generations of readers.

CRITICS' CORNER

"Seasons of Splendour *simply and playfully reveals to the Western reader the heart and soul of traditional Indian society, where order and continuity are still preferred to the pursuit of [illusory] progress. . . . In all these stories the surfaces ripple, shimmer, change, but the center holds."*

—Barbara Thompson, *The New York Times Book Review*

Seasons of Splendour: Tales, Myths, and Legends of India

by Madhur Jaffrey ☆

This collection of myths and folklore from India is arranged in chronological sequence, starting with tales that might be told at the beginning of the Hindu calendar year in April. The author introduces each tale with a recollection from her childhood. Many of the stories come from Hindu epics. There are stories from the life of Krishna and episodes in Ram's defeat over the demon king Ravan. There are also origin tales, such as how Ganesh got his elephant's head.

Write a Review

Read one of the books listed on these pages and write a review of it for your classmates. Be sure to explain why other students might enjoy the book, or offer suggestions on how they might overcome difficulties in reading the book. Present your review to the class.

Approaching Level

DIFFERENTIATED INSTRUCTION

Emerging Point out the book by Madhur Jaffrey on this page. Tell students that Jaffrey was born in India but spent most of her life living in Britain and the United States. A famous actress, Jaffrey starred in many films in which she incorporated her Indian heritage into the many characters she played. Jaffrey also achieved fame as the author of cookbooks on authentic Indian cuisine. Point out that Jaffrey includes stories from the life of Krishna in *Seasons of Splendour: Tales, Myths, and Legends of India.* Explain that Krishna is one of the most popular Hindu gods, and is known for his bravery as well as his divinity.

Teach

Cultural History ☆

Madhur Jaffrey Born in Delhi, India, she later emigrated to England. In 1973, her book *An Invitation to Indian Cooking* made her famous around the world. Subsequent books have included a memoir, *Climbing the Mango Trees* (2006).

Glencoe Literature Library

Glencoe Literature Library offers an extensive collection of hardcover books that help you encourage your students to read independently. Choose among the more than 120 full-length literary works—novels, novellas, plays, and nonfiction. Each book includes related readings from a broad range of genres. Go to glencoe.com for more information.

For access to all study guides for the Glencoe Literature Library, see the Literature Library Teacher Resources CD-ROM.

To create customized reading lists from a database of more than 30,000 titles, use BookLink K–12 CD-ROM.

Assess

Write a Review

Students' reviews should explain the likes and dislikes of the book and suggest strategies for reading difficult sections of the book.

Assessment
English Language Arts

Focus

Bellringer Options

Say: A multiple-choice test like this one is different from essay tests and short answer tests. In a multiple-choice test, each answer is provided for you along with several incorrect answer choices. To identify the correct answer, you sometimes need to identify the incorrect answers first. Have students discuss which type of test they prefer and why.

Teach

Assessment Explain to students that Assessment is intended to reinforce general test-taking strategies and test the skills and vocabulary covered in the unit.

Assessment

English Language Arts

Reading: Fiction

Carefully read the following passage. Use context clues to help you define any words with which you are unfamiliar. Pay close attention to the theme, the use of literary devices, and the tone. Then, on a separate sheet of paper, answer questions 1–9 on page 980.

from *The Apple of Discord* by Thomas Bulfinch

Athena was the goddess of wisdom, but on one occasion she did a very foolish thing: she entered into competition with Hera, the queen of the gods, and Aphrodite, the goddess of beauty, for the prize of beauty.

It happened thus: At the wedding of Peleus and Thetis all the gods were invited with the exception of Eris, or Discord. Enraged at her exclusion, the goddess threw a golden apple among the guests, with the inscription, "For the fairest." Hera, Aphrodite, and Athena each claimed the apple. Zeus, not willing to decide in so delicate a matter, sent the goddesses to Mount Ida, where the beautiful shepherd Paris was tending his flocks, and to him was committed the decision. The goddesses accordingly appeared before him. Hera promised him power and riches, Athena glory and renown in war, and Aphrodite the fairest of women for his wife, each attempting to bias his decision in her own
1 favor. Paris decided in favor of Aphrodite and gave her the golden apple, thus making the two other goddesses his enemies. Under the protection of Aphrodite, Paris sailed to Greece, and was hospitably received by Menelaus, king of Sparta.

Now Helen, the wife of Menelaus, was the fairest of her sex and the very woman whom Aphrodite had destined for Paris. She had been sought as a bride by numerous suitors, and before her decision was made known, they all, at the suggestion of Odysseus, one of their number, took an oath that they would defend her from all injury and avenge her cause if necessary. She chose Menelaus, and was living with him happily when Paris became their guest. Paris, aided by Aphrodite, persuaded her to elope with him, and carried her to Troy, whence arose the famous Trojan War, the theme of the greatest poems of antiquity, those of Homer and Virgil.

Reading Practice

Purpose for Reading For this test practice, students will be reading two different types of text. When students are reading from varied types of materials, it is important that they establish a purpose for reading to get the greatest benefit from the material. Have students preview each the selection. **Ask: If you were reading this information on your own and not for a test, what might be your purpose for reading each selection?** *(Students may say that the first selection might be read for enjoyment and the second selection might be read to find information.)*

Informational Reading Carefully read the following announcement, paying close attention to details and specific instructions. Then answer questions 10–12 on page 980.

Real-world reading

File Edit View Favorites Tools Help

Address Auditions Announcement

- Home
- About Woodlawn Theater
- Calendar
- Directors
- Tryouts
- Callbacks
- Casting
- Rehearsals
- Tech Crews

Tryouts!

Auditions for *Trojan Women, Our Town,* and *Arsenic and Old Lace*

You will need to memorize a short monologue for your audition or to check the bulletin board for information on improvisational auditions. The sign-up sheet is on our bulletin board in Blaine Hall. Everyone will be heard. If you have any problems, **let us know!**

Schedule

Monday, March 3
Monologue auditions: 1:00 PM–6:30 PM
In Blaine Hall

Tuesday, March 4
Callbacks: noon–3:00 PM
Improvisational auditions: 2:00 PM–4:00 PM
Voice and dance auditions: 3:00 PM–6:00 PM

Wednesday, March 5
Miscellaneous callbacks: 2:30 PM–5:30 PM

Thursday, March 6
Casting announcements: Check the bulletin board or our Web site.

Friday, March 7
Rehearsals: 3:00 PM–5:00 PM

LOG ON **Literature** Online

Assessment For additional test practice, go to glencoe.com and enter QuickPass code GL49787u5.

Teach

Reading Strategy 1

Summarize To help students better understand "The Apple of Discord," have them summarize the passage.

To assist approaching-level students, **say: When you summarize, you relate the main ideas of a selection in your own words. To create a good summary, include all the main ideas. Do not include anything that is not important.**

English Learners

DIFFERENTIATED INSTRUCTION

Intermediate Have English language learners paraphrase each selection to ensure that they understand it. Encourage them to use a dictionary to look up unfamiliar words. Give them the following additional tips for monitoring their comprehension:

- Reread each selection.
- Make a graphic organizer to help sort out your thoughts.
- Write comments or questions on another piece of paper for later review or discussion.

Encourage students to try one or more of these tips as they read.

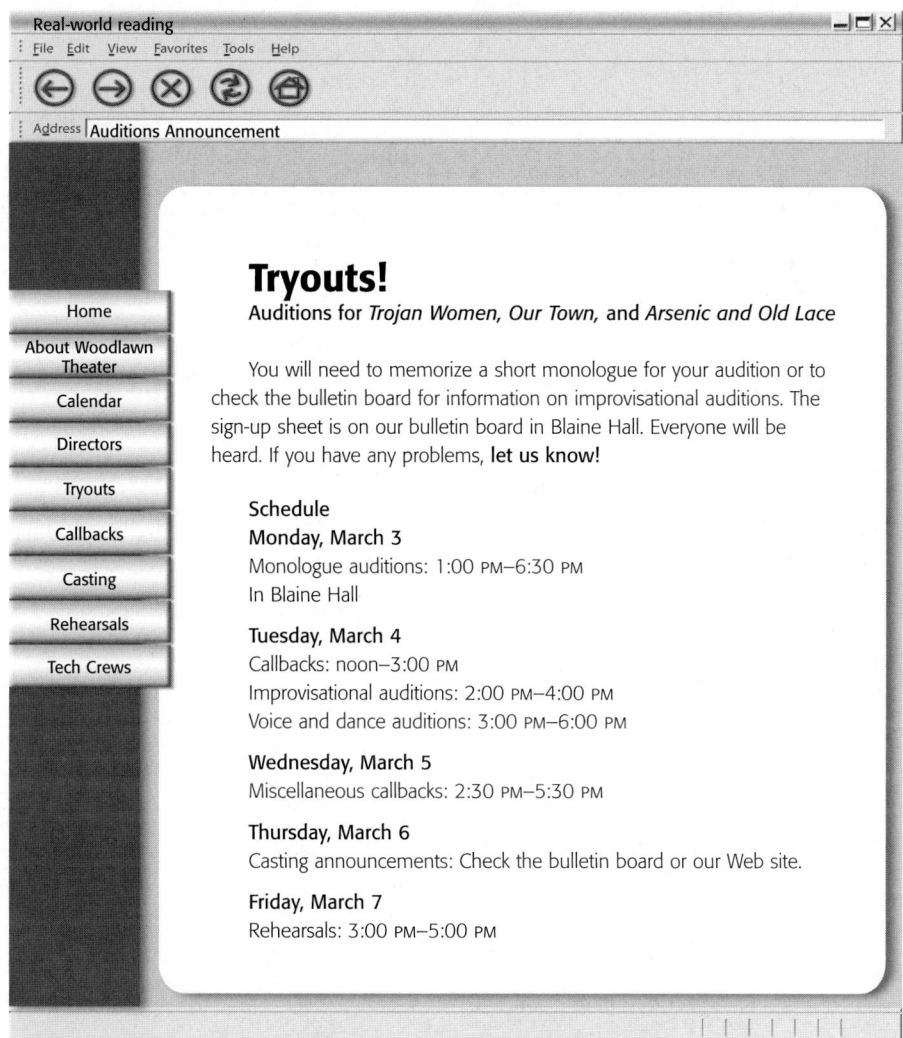

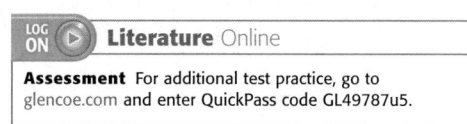

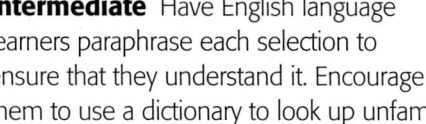

Assess

Reading

1. D is the correct answer because introducing the apple creates the conflict. DOK 2
2. H is the correct answer because three parallel clauses are used as the subject of the sentence. DOK 2
3. C is the correct answer because the apple serves as a symbol of beauty. DOK 2
4. G is the correct answer because *hospitably* means "in a generous and cordial manner." DOK 1
5. A is the correct answer because the sentence introduces one character and develops another. DOK 2
6. J is the correct answer because Zeus sent the goddesses to Paris so he could "decide in so delicate a matter." DOK 1
7. B is the correct answer because "who is fairest" is a recurring theme, or motif in the passage. DOK 2
8. H is the correct answer because Aphrodite had promised to find Paris "the fairest of women for his wife" if he selected her. DOK 2
9. A is the correct answer because the dispute among the goddesses led to the Trojan War. DOK 3
10. H is the correct answer because those auditioning will learn the results when the casting is announced on Thursday. DOK 1

Items 1–9 apply to "The Apple of Discord."

1. To what element of the story does the sentence beginning on line 5 contribute?
   A. characters
   B. setting
   C. theme
   D. conflict

2. What literary element is most evident in the sentence beginning in line 10?
   F. allusion
   G. imagery
   H. parallelism
   J. simile

3. What literary element is used in connection with the golden apple in the second paragraph?
   A. metaphor
   B. simile
   C. symbolism
   D. idiom

4. From the context, what do you think that the word *hospitably,* in line 16, means?
   F. dangerously
   G. warmly
   H. quickly
   J. greedily

5. To what element of the story does the first sentence of the last paragraph contribute?
   A. characters
   B. setting
   C. plot
   D. conflict

6. What did Hera, Aphrodite, and Athena expect Paris to do?
   F. to choose one of the goddesses to marry
   G. to take Helen away to Troy
   H. to travel from Mount Ida to Sparta
   J. to decide which goddess was the fairest

7. The word *fairest* is used as what kind of literary device in this passage?
   A. metaphor
   B. motif
   C. symbol
   D. idiom

8. What can you infer about Paris's reason for making his selection?
   F. He wanted great riches.
   G. He wanted to leave Mount Ida.
   H. He wanted to marry a beautiful woman.
   J. He wanted great wisdom.

9. What is the main idea of the passage?
   A. A fight among the goddesses led to a large war.
   B. The gods continually fought wars with people.
   C. Paris was loved dearly by all of the gods.
   D. Helen did something that angered the gods.

Items 10–12 apply to Auditions Announcement.

10. According to the information on the Web page, when will those who audition learn whether they were chosen for a role?
    F. Tuesday
    G. Wednesday
    H. Thursday
    J. Friday

11. How can people sign up to audition?
    A. They can send an e-mail message.
    B. They can go to the bulletin board.
    C. They can attend a callback.
    D. They can use the Web site.

12. Who will audition for the first time on March 3?
    F. those who are to memorize lines
    G. those who are to do improvisation
    H. those who sing
    J. those who dance

11. B is the correct answer because the Web site states that there is a sign-up sheet on the bulletin board. DOK 1
12. F is the correct answer because the announcement says "You will need to memorize a short monologue." Monologue auditions will be held on March 3. DOK 1

Vocabulary Skills: Sentence Completion

For each item in the Vocabulary Skills section, choose the word that best completes the sentence.

1. Murphy's first novel was clever, but the plot of his second novel was even more ______.
   A. aloof
   B. withered
   C. ingenious
   D. implacable

2. By the time they had loaded all their ______ into the van, there was no room left for the passengers.
   F. paraphernalia
   G. staff
   H. fetter
   J. brood

3. The dog trembled and ______ at the mere sight of a cane.
   A. fettered
   B. cowered
   C. lavished
   D. renowned

4. After the invaders defeated the enemy, they ______ the town.
   F. shunned
   G. withered
   H. jostled
   J. plundered

5. The body was wrapped in a ______ and buried at sea.
   A. tumult
   B. fetter
   C. shroud
   D. guise

6. After speaking rudely to his elders, the child was accused of ______.
   F. ardor
   G. impudence
   H. guile
   J. valor

7. Brian's teacher would often ______ him with praise for his hard work.
   A. horde
   B. plunder
   C. writhe
   D. lavish

8. Under the ______ of concern, the spy gathered information from unsuspecting people.
   F. guise
   G. stead
   H. staff
   J. fetter

9. We took care not to ______ the delicate clock as we carried it to the antique fair.
   A. jostle
   B. shun
   C. horde
   D. tumult

10. Ancient legends tell of powerful beings with the ______ ability to foretell the future.
   F. lavish
   G. kindred
   H. uncanny
   J. implacable

Assess

Vocabulary Skills

1. C is the correct answer. The words *even more* indicate that the answer should be a more extreme meaning of *clever.* DOK 1

2. F is the correct answer. The context of the sentence indicates that they were loading things, not people. DOK 1

3. B is the correct answer. *Trembled* indicates that this is the correct answer. DOK 1

4. J is the correct answer. The fact that the invaders defeated the enemy indicates that this is the correct answer. DOK 1

5. C is the correct answer. None of the other answer choices is something one could be wrapped in. DOK 1

6. G is the correct answer. The fact that the child spoke rudely indicates that this is the correct answer. DOK 1

7. D is the correct answer. None of the other options make sense in the context of praising someone. DOK 1

8. F is the correct answer. The fact that the people were unsuspecting indicates that the spy was not being forthright. DOK 1

9. A is the correct answer. The fact that the clock was delicate indicates that it should not have been jostled. DOK 1

10. H is the correct answer. *Uncanny* is the only word that describes an ability to tell the future. DOK 1

Assessment

English Language Arts

Assess

Grammar and Writing Skills

1. **B** is the correct answer. The "sentence" is a fragment. No other option corrects this error without introducing another error. **DOK 1**
2. **H** is the correct answer. The comma is unnecessary. **DOK 1**

Grammar and Writing Skills: Paragraph Improvement

In the following excerpt from a student's first draft of a persuasive essay, numbers appear beneath underlined parts. The numbers correspond to items below that provide options for replacing, or ask questions about, those parts. On a separate sheet of paper, record the letter of the best option in each item. If you think that the original should not be changed, choose "NO CHANGE."

Boxed numbers refer to questions about specific paragraphs or to the essay as a whole.

Read the passage through once before you begin to answer the questions. As you read, pay close attention to the writer's use of main and subordinate clauses, commas, and organization.

The Iliad *and the* Odyssey*, two of the greatest epic poems ever written.* (1) *They are extremely long works involving many characters and tales. Homer is credited, by most scholars with writing both of these poems.* (2) *However, there was a period when most of them questioned this. In the nineteenth century, people debated this "Homeric question": was he really the author of both of these works, and did he write them alone?*

[3] *Many who doubted that Homer wrote the* Iliad *and the* Odyssey *pointed to older, shorter poems.* (4) *These works, not written by Homer, tell many of the same tales. This led scholars to believe that the* Iliad *and the* Odyssey *were actually just a collection of such poems. That were woven together into the great epics.* (5)

[6] *There is abundant evidence to suggest that Homer was in fact the author of both poems. The* Iliad*, along with many other similar poems, have been analyzed carefully.* (7) *This analysis suggests that the* Iliad *was written by a single person. Moreover, considerable historical evidence suggests that a poet named Homer did actually live before 700* B.C. *His home was probably in Asia Minor, where the city of Troy once stood.* (8) *Troy was the site of the Trojan War, the subject of the* Iliad. *Finally, careful examination of both poems suggest that they were written by the same poet after all.* (9) *So we can conclude that there really was a Homer; he is not a legend.* (10) *He deserves his legendary reputation, though, for writing two of the greatest works of literature in the history of civilization.*

1. **A.** NO CHANGE
   B. The *Iliad* and the *Odyssey* are two of the greatest epic poems ever written.
   C. The *Iliad* and the *Odyssey*, are two of the greatest epic poems ever written.
   D. The *Iliad* and the *Odyssey* two of the great epic poems ever written.

2. **F.** NO CHANGE
   G. Insert a comma after *writing.*
   H. Delete the comma after *credited.*
   J. Insert a comma after *scholars.*

3. Which of the following should the writer include when writing an introductory paragraph?
   A. information not related to the rest of the essay
   B. responses to opposing viewpoints
   C. detailed discussion of examples
   D. a clear statement of the thesis

4. **F.** NO CHANGE
   G. Many who doubt that Homer wrote the *Iliad* and the *Odyssey,* pointed to older, shorter poems.
   H. Many who were doubting that Homer wrote the *Iliad* and the *Odyssey* point to older, shorter poems.
   J. Many who doubt that Homer wrote the *Iliad* and the *Odyssey* and point to older, shorter poems.

5. **A.** NO CHANGE
   B. That are woven together into epics.
   C. They were woven together into the great epics.
   D. They were woven together, into the great epics.

6. Which of the following, if inserted at this point, would provide the most effective transition in this paragraph?
   F. The two epics are similar in many ways.
   G. However, it now seems likely that the scholars were wrong.
   H. Therefore, it is possible that Homer did not write the *Iliad.*
   J. The *Odyssey* is about the voyages of Odysseus, a great hero.

7. **A.** NO CHANGE
   B. The *Iliad,* along with many other similar poems, were analyzed carefully.
   C. The *Iliad,* along with many other similar poems, has been analyzed carefully.
   D. Scholars analyzed the *Iliad* along with many other similar poems, carefully.

8. **F.** NO CHANGE
   G. He probably lived in Asia Minor, where the city of Troy, stands.
   H. He probably lived in Asia Minor, the location of the city of Troy.
   J. He probably lived at Asia Minor where the city of Troy once stood.

9. **A.** NO CHANGE
   B. Finally, careful examination suggests that they had been written by the same poet.
   C. Finally, careful examination of both poems suggests that they were written by the same poet.
   D. Finally, carefully examination suggest that they were both written by the same poet.

10. **F.** NO CHANGE
   G. So we concluded that their really was a Homer; he is not just a legend.
   H. So we can conclude that there was a Homer, really; he was not a legend.
   J. So we conclude that there really was a Homer; and he is not just a legend.

Essay

President John F. Kennedy firmly believed that "Mythology distracts us everywhere. The great enemy of the truth is very often not the lie—deliberate, contrived, and dishonest—but the myth—persistent, persuasive, and unrealistic." Describe an example from your own life in which you witnessed Kennedy's principle in action. As you write, keep in mind that your essay will be checked for **ideas, organization, voice, word choice, sentence fluency, conventions,** and **presentation.**

Assess

Grammar and Writing Skills

3. D is the correct answer. An introduction to a persuasive essay should state a thesis. None of the other options is essential to a persuasive essay. DOK 3

4. F is the correct answer. This sentence contains no error. DOK 1

5. C is the correct answer. This "sentence" is a fragment. No other option corrects this error without introducing additional errors. DOK 1

6. G is the correct answer. This sentence connects the topic of the previous paragraph to that of the current paragraph. DOK 2

7. C is the correct answer. The verb must agree in number with its subject, *Iliad.* The phrase beginning "along with . . ." is not part of the subject. DOK 1

8. F is the correct answer. This sentence contains no error. DOK 1

9. C is the correct answer. The verb must agree in number with *examination,* its subject, not with *poems,* part of the modifying phrase. DOK 1

10. F is the correct answer. This sentence contains no error. DOK 1

Essay

Evaluate essays for the following:

- a clearly stated description of the relationship between a personal experience and Kennedy's belief about myth supported by details from the experience
- effective voice, word choice, and sentence variety
- effective presentation, with attention to grammar and spelling conventions DOK 4

Skills Scope and Sequence

Readability Scores Key: Dale-Chall/DRP/Lexile

Our World and Beyond

Selections and Features	Literary Elements
Unit Introduction pp. 984–990	Style and Description **SE** p. 987
Literary Focus pp. 992–993	Description and Style SE pp. 992-993
Short Story The Sentinel, by Arthur C. Clarke **8.3/63/1240** pp. 994–1007	Suspense **SE** p. 995 Foreshadowing **TE** p. 1000 Description (review) **SE** p. 1006
Historical Perspective 2001: A Space Odyssey, by Roger Ebert **6.8/62/940** pp. 1008–1010	
Grammar Workshop p. 1011	
Short Story He—y, Come on Ou—t!, by Shinichi Hoshi **7.7/55/890** pp. 1012–1019	Moral **SE** p. 1013 Character (review) **SE** p. 1018
Comparing Literature **In Memoriam** (short story) **4.8/54/650**, by Nancy Kress **Purchase** (poem), by Naomi Long Madgett **The Gift** (poem), by Li-Young Lee pp. 1020–1033	Dialogue **SE** p. 1022
Short Story The Golden Kite, the Silver Wind, by Ray Bradbury **7.1/55/1030** pp. 1034–1041	Allegory **SE** p. 1035 Moral (review) **SE** p. 1040
Vocabulary Workshop p. 1042	
Short Story The Red-Headed League, by Sir Arthur Conan Doyle **7.2/61/1110** pp. 1043–1067	Foreshadowing **SE** p. 1044 Figurative Language **TE** p. 1058 Character Archetype **TE** p. 1062, **SE** p. 1066

Reading Skills and Strategies	Vocabulary	Writing Grammar	Speaking, Listening, and Viewing
Analyze Literary Genres **SE** p. 986 Analyze Point of View **TE** p. 988		Write a Description **TE** p. 990	Performance **SE** p. 990 Oral Presentation **TE** p. 986
Analyze Description and Style **SE** p. 992		Write a Journal Entry **SE** p. 993	
Analyze Motivation **SE** p. 995 Identify Author's Purpose **TE** p. 996	Analogies **SE** p. 1006 Academic Vocabulary **SE** p. 1006	Write a Summary **TE** p. 998 Write a Research Report **SE** p. 1007	Research Report **TE** p. 1002 Discussion **TE** p. 1004
Evaluate Argument **SE** p. 1008 Connect to Historical Documents **SE** p. 1008		Write a Summary **SE** p. 1010	Discussion **TE** p. 1008
		Commas with Items in a Series **SE** p. 1011	
Connect to Contemporary Issues **SE** p. 1013	Word Origins **TE** p. 1014 Antonyms **SE** p. 1019	Write a Research Report **TE** p. 1016	Speech **SE** p. 1019
Compare and Contrast Characters **SE** p. 1022	Word Usage **TE** p. 1026, **SE** p. 1029	Write a Journal Entry **TE** p. 1024 Write a Summary **TE** p. 1028 Write a Description **TE** p. 1030 Write a Comparison-Contrast Essay **SE** p. 1033	Discussion **TE** p. 1022, **SE** pp. 1031, 1033 Visual Presentation **SE** p. 1033
Evaluate Figures of Speech **SE** p. 1035 Identify Problem and Solution **TE** p. 1038	Word Usage **TE** p. 1036 Synonyms **SE** p. 1041	Apply Symbolism **SE** p. 1041	
	Loaded Words **SE** p. 1042		
Make Inferences about Characters **SE** p. 1044 Analyze Tone **TE** p. 1048 Synthesize **TE** p. 1052	Word Usage **TE** p. 1054 Synonyms **SE** p. 1066 Academic Vocabulary **SE** p. 1066	Write a Character Sketch **TE** p. 1046 Pronouns **TE** p. 1050 Write a Literary Analysis **TE** p. 1056 Revise **TE** p. 1060 Write an Expository Essay **SE** p. 1067	Discussion **TE** p. 1064, **SE** p. 1065

Readability Scores Key: Dale-Chall/DRP/Lexile

Our World and Beyond *(continued)*

Selections and Features	Literary Elements
Informational Text TIME: Lost Apes of the Congo, by Stephan Faris **8.8/61/1020** pp. 1068–1070	
Short Story The Stolen Cigar Case, by Bret Harte **9.4/58/1020** pp. 1071–1081	Parody **SE** p. 1072 Character **TE** p. 1074
Writing Workshop pp. 1082–1089	
Speaking, Listening, and Viewing Workshop pp. 1090–1091	
Independent Reading pp. 1092–1093	
Assessment pp. 1094–1099	

Reading Skills and Strategies	Vocabulary	Writing / Grammar	Speaking, Listening, and Viewing
Evaluate Credibility **SE** p. 1068 Preview **SE** p. 1068		Write an Evaluation **TE** p. 1068 Write a Summary **SE** p. 1070	
Evaluate Details **SE** p. 1082 Compare and Contrast **TE** p. 1072 Analyze Plot **TE** p. 1076	Connotation and Denotation **SE** p. 1081	Revise **TE** p. 1080 Write a Parody **SE** p. 1081	Performance **TE** p. 1078
		Prewrite **SE** p. 1085 Draft **SE** p. 1086 Revise **SE** p. 1088 Reasonable Tone **SE** p. 1088 Write a Bibliography **TE** p. 1088 Parallelism **SE** p. 1089 Write an Editorial **SE** p. 1089	Provide Feedback **TE** p. 1086
Analyze Persuasion **TE** p. 1090		Revise **SE** p. 1090	Persuasive Presentation **SE** p. 1090
		Write an Adaptation **TE** p. 1092 Write a Review **SE** p. 1093	
		Write a Reflective Essay **SE** p. 1099	

Focus

Bellringer Options

Literature Launcher
Pre-Reading Video Unit 6
Daily Language Practice Transparency 92

Or **write on the board:** What is your favorite movie genre? Literary genre? Would you rather read a newspaper or watch a television newscast? Discuss with students why a genre appeals to them more in one medium than in another.

For school-to-home activities, see Unit 6 Teaching Resources Book, pp. 5–11.

For students who would profit from independent novel study, see Novel Companion, pp. 299–342.

Government Office, George Tooker. Metropolitan Museum of Art, New York.

View the Art George Tooker's paintings often combine elements of stark realism with an unsettling surreal quality. What elements of this painting are realistic? What elements are surreal? ★

984

Unit Introduction Skills

Genre Fiction

Literary Elements
- Genre Fiction (SE pp. 986–987)
- Description and Imagery (SE p. 987)
- Style and Tone (SE p. 987)

Reading Skills
- Literary Analysis Model (SE pp. 988–989)
- Point of View (TE p. 988)

Study Skills/Research/Assessment
- Foldables (SE p. 990)

Writing Skills/Grammar
- Imagery (TE p. 990)

Listening/Speaking/Viewing Skills
- Create a Genre (TE p. 986)

UNIT SIX

Genre Fiction

Looking Ahead

Genre fiction is a flexible term used to group works of fiction that have similar characters, plots, or settings. Bookstores and libraries often shelve their fiction by genre categories—such as romance, mystery, science fiction, and fantasy—for the convenience of readers who prefer particular kinds of stories. You know the conventions—the requirements of character, plot, or setting—that distinguish many genres of fiction. Westerns, for example, have a particular setting—the U.S. frontier during the second half of the 1800s—and often particular character types—rugged, individualistic cowboys—as heroes. You have been studying genres, or types, of literature. This unit presents a few genres specific to fiction.

Each literary work in Unit 6 focuses on a Big Idea that can help you make connections to your life.

PREVIEW	Big Ideas	Literary Focus
	Our World and Beyond	Description and Style

UNIT SIX

Focus

Summary

The unit introduction begins with the Genre Focus, which identifies the characteristics of science fiction, modern fable, and mystery. An analysis of a science fiction story, *Buy Jupiter,* is provided.

View the Art ★

Answer: *Realistic elements include the drab, depressing colors of the office, as well as the long lines of people waiting. Surreal elements of the painting are the repetition of figures in line and of the generic figure of the government worker peering through the cutout in the glass.*

Brooklyn-born artist George Tooker (1920–) often paints figures that reflect the alienation and disaffection of Americans in the Cold War era.

For diagnostic and end-of-unit assessment, see Assessment Resources, pp. 33–40 and 235–236.

Unit Resources

Print Materials

- Unit 6 Teaching Resources, pp. 1–155
- Interactive Read and Write (On Level/Approaching, EL), pp. 287–312
- Novel Companion, pp. 299–342
- Bellringer Option Transparencies: Selection Focus 36, 37; Daily Language Practice 92–99
- Literary Element Transparencies 24, 98
- Assessment Resources, Unit Assessment, pp. 33–40
- Assessment Resources, Selection Assessment, pp. 209–224

Technology

- TeacherWorks Plus CD
- StudentWorks Plus CD
- Literature Launchers: Pre-Reading Videos DVD, Unit 6
- Literature Online
- Interactive Vocabulary CD-ROM
- Listening Library CD-ROM
- ExamView CD-ROM
- Skill Level Up! CD-ROM

UNIT SIX

Teach

Reading Strategy 1

Summarize Instruct students to copy the genre headings on these two pages in their notebooks. Under each heading, have them write brief notes summarizing the elements of the different genres.

Cultural History ☆

Aesop One famous fable writer is Aesop. While Aesop's exact birthplace remains a matter of debate, historians believe he was born a slave in the sixth century B.C. After earning his freedom, he traveled and became involved in public affairs. King Croesus was so impressed by Aesop that he gave him a position in his court.

Learning Objectives

For pages 984–990

In studying this text, you will focus on the following objectives:

Literary Study:
Analyzing literary genres.
Connecting to the literature.

Genre Focus: Genre Fiction

What are some genres of fiction?

This unit includes several kinds, or genres, of fiction: fantasy, mysteries, modern fables, and science fiction. In each genre, the world can be as familiar as a city street at twilight or as strange as an island that speaks to its inhabitants. Part of the fun in reading these types of fiction is discovering what these wonderful worlds are like and understanding the elements the author used to create them.

Science Fiction, Fable, and Mystery

Science Fiction 1

A setting in the future or away from Earth is often a major element of **science fiction.** Writers of the genre also address the impact of science and technology—real or imagined—on society and on individuals. Many critics argue that the best science fiction reveals an underlying truth about our own world. These truths are uncovered by reflecting on common themes in uncommon settings.

We had begun our journey early in the slow lunar dawn, and still had almost a week of Earth-time before nightfall. Half a dozen times a day we would leave our vehicle and go outside in the space suits to hunt for interesting minerals, or to place markers for the guidance of future travelers. It was an uneventful routine.

—Arthur C. Clarke, **from "The Sentinel"**

Modern Fable

A **fable** is a brief, usually simple story intended to teach a lesson about human behavior or to give advice about how to behave. Modern fables also focus on themes relating to human behavior, with little development of individual characters. In "The Golden Kite, The Silver Wind," Ray Bradbury tells a simple tale that points out the destructiveness of political rivalry. ☆

"I have called you here," said the Mandarin aloud, "because our city is shaped like an orange, and the vile city of Kwan-Si has this day shaped theirs like a ravenous pig—"

—Ray Bradbury, **from "The Golden Kite, The Silver Wind"**

Speaking Practice

SMALL GROUP **Create a Genre** Instruct groups of students to combine several existing literary genres to create a new one. Students should discuss characteristics of their new genre and make a list of these characteristics and features of the genre. Students should decide upon what kind of characters, imagery, style, and tone typify their genre. Have them explain how their new genre differs from others. Students should take notes during their discussion and present their new genre to the class.

Mystery

Mysteries or detective stories follow a particular plot pattern: a crime is committed and a detective gathers clues to identify the criminal. The detective may be a tough, street-smart character—often called the hard-boiled detective—or a brilliant eccentric with keen powers of observation and reasoning, like Sherlock Holmes.

"Beyond the obvious facts that he has at some time done manual labor, that he takes snuff, that he is a Freemason, that he has been in China, and that he has done a considerable amount of writing lately, I can deduce nothing else."

—Sir Arthur Conan Doyle, **from "The Red-Headed League"**

Style and Description

Style and Tone

Style is the expressive qualities that distinguish an author's work, including word choice, sentence structure, and figures of speech. **Tone** is the author's attitude toward the audience or the subject of the work. Style and tone help create the mood of a story, such as the mysterious mood at the beginning of "He—y, Come on Ou—t!"

Where they had all gathered there was a hole about a meter in diameter. They peered in, but it was so dark nothing could be seen. However, it gave one the feeling that it was so deep it went clear through to the center of the earth.

There was even one person who said, "I wonder if it's a fox's hole."

—Shinichi Hoshi, **from "He—y, Come on Ou—t!"**

2 Description and Imagery

In fiction set in unfamiliar places or imaginary worlds, description becomes especially important. **Description** is a detailed portrayal of a person, place, thing, or event. Good description allows a reader to understand what he or she has never encountered. **Imagery** is descriptive language that appeals to one or more of the five senses (sight, hearing, touch, taste, and smell). The use of these sensory details helps to create an emotional response in the reader.

All those memories: the shade of blue of a dress worn fifty years ago, the tilt of the head of someone long dead, the sudden sharp smell of a grandmother's cabbage soup mingled with the dusty scent of an apartment razed for two decades.

—Nancy Kress, **from "In Memoriam"**

LOG ON **Literature** Online

Literature and Reading For more selections in these genres, go to glencoe.com and enter QuickPass code GL49787u6.

Teach

Literary Element 2

Description and Imagery
Suggest students organize their notes on description and imagery by listing images under the appropriate senses. Have them write the heads "Seeing," "Hearing," "Tasting," "Touching," and "Smelling" in their notebooks and add examples to the categories as they read.

English Learners

DIFFERENTIATED INSTRUCTION

Early Advanced Explain to students that each literary genre has a style, theme, tone, and imagery specific to it. Less proficient students might have difficulty understanding genre fiction, particularly how to read the tone of the work. Explain that once students become familiar with different genres, understanding the content becomes less difficult.

Ask: What elements do you expect to find in a mystery? *(Possible answers: an unsolved crime, a mysterious plot, a detective)* **Ask:** What elements do you expect to find in a science fiction story? *(Possible answers: unusual technology, life on another planet, unreal creatures)* Students should support their answers with references to other works.

UNIT SIX

Teach

Reading Strategy 1

Set a Purpose Have a volunteer read the introductory paragraph aloud. Instruct students to consider the goals of the science fiction writer as they read the excerpt from *Buy Jupiter.*

- Does the story entertain?
- Does it inspire wonder?
- Does the story force the reader to ask "What if?"

View the Photograph ★

Contemporary photographer Douglas Kirkland has photographed icons including Marilyn Monroe and Elizabeth Taylor. In addition to his work on more than 100 movies, Kirkland also has exhibited fine art photography and published several books.

Literary Analysis Model

How do literary elements impact genre fiction?

In Isaac Asimov's short story "Buy Jupiter" a simulacron representing the people of Mizzarett meets with government officials on Earth. The Mizzarett people want to buy Jupiter, which is on their new trade route. The simulacron wants to hide the deal from the Lamberj people, which arouses the suspicion of some Earth officials. Are the two peoples at war? In this scene, Earth's Secretary of Science reveals the truth. **1**

APPLYING Literary Elements

Description
The description of how the Secretary *looks* clues us in to how he *feels.*

Science Fiction
References to the "Mizzarett-Lamberj war" and the planet Jupiter are clues that this story is science fiction.

from *Buy Jupiter*

by Isaac Asimov

The Secretary of Science emerged, mopping his forehead and looking ten years younger. He said softly, "I told him his people could have it as soon as I obtained the President's formal approval. I don't think he'll object, or Congress, either. Good Lord, gentlemen, think of it; free power at our fingertips in return for a planet we could never use in any case."

The Secretary of Defense, growing purplish with objection, said, "But we had agreed that only a Mizzarett-Lamberj war could explain their need for Jupiter. Under those circumstances, and comparing their military potential with ours, a strict neutrality is essential."

"But there is no war, sir," said the Secretary of Science, "The simulacron presented an alternate explanation of their need for Jupiter so rational and plausible that I accepted at once. I think the President will agree with me, and you gentlemen, too, when you understand. In fact, I have here their plans for the new Jupiter, as it will soon appear."

The others rose from their seats, clamoring. "A new Jupiter?" gasped the Secretary of Defense.

"Not so different from the old, gentlemen," said the Secretary of Science. "Here are the sketches provided in form suitable for observation by matter beings such as ourselves."

He laid them down. The familiar banded planet was there before them on one of the sketches: yellow, pale green, and light brown with curled white streaks here and there and all against the speckled velvet background of

Author and scientist Isaac Asimov, ca. 1989. Douglas Kirkland. ★

Reading Practice

SMALL GROUP

Point of View Ask: Do you think the simulacron in the story was telling the truth about the reason for buying Jupiter? Have students explain how the story might be rewritten. Students should answer the following questions.

- What kind of ethics would an advanced race have?
- What alternative motives might they have for buying Jupiter?
- How might an advanced race like the Mizzaretts view humanity?

Have volunteers share their answers with the class.

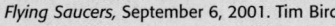

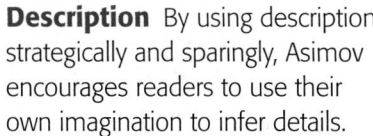

Flying Saucers, September 6, 2001. Tim Bird.

space. But across the bands were streaks of blackness as velvet as the background, arranged in a curious pattern.

"That," said the Secretary of Science, "is the day side of the planet. The night side is shown in this sketch." (There, Jupiter was a thin crescent enclosing darkness, and within that darkness were the same thin streaks arranged in similar pattern, but in a phosphorescent glowing orange this time.) ☆

"The marks," said the Secretary of Science, "are a purely optical phenomenon, I am told, which will not rotate with the planet, but will remain static in its atmospheric fringe."

"But what is it?" asked the Secretary of Commerce.

"You see," said the Secretary of Science, "our solar system is now on one of their major trade routes. As many as seven of their ships pass within a few hundred million miles of the system in a single day, and each ship has the major planets under telescopic observation as they pass. Tourist curiosity, you know. Solid planets of any size are a marvel to them."

"What has that to do with these marks?"

"That is one form of their writing. Translated, those marks read: 'Use Mizzarett Ergone Vertices For Health and Glowing Heat.'"

"You mean Jupiter is to be an advertising billboard?"
2 exploded the Secretary of Defense.

"Right. The Lamberj people, it seems, produce a competing ergone tablet, which accounts for the Mizzarett anxiety to establish full legal ownership of Jupiter—in case of Lamberj lawsuits. Fortunately, the Mizzaretts are novices at the advertising game, it appears."

"Why do you say that?" asked the Secretary of the Interior.

"Why, they neglected to set up a series of options on the other planets. The Jupiter billboard will be advertising our system, as well as their own product. And when the competing Lamberj people come storming in to check on the Mizzarett title to Jupiter, we will have Saturn to sell to *them. With* its rings. As we will be easily able to explain to them, the rings will make Saturn much the better spectacle."

"And therefore," said the Secretary of the Treasury, suddenly beaming, "worth a *much* better price."

And they all suddenly looked very cheerful.

Description
The comparison to velvet helps the reader "see" and even "touch" the absolute darkness of the streaks on the bands.

Tone
The Secretary of Science projects a calm, objective tone, which makes him sound reliable and authoritative.

Style
Asimov uses italics to indicate emphasized words in dialogue.

Reading Check
Interpret Why is the committee pleased with the Secretary of Science's deal with the simulacron?

Teach

Reading Check

Answer: *They will be able to use the Jupiter billboard to advertise their own system.*

Literary Element 2

Description **Ask:** How does the author characterize the Secretary of Defense? Does this characterization make him seem more or less reliable than the Secretary of Science? *(Words such as "gasped" and "exploding" suggest the Secretary of Defense is overly emotional and therefore less reliable than the Secretary of Science.)*

APPROACHING **Ask:** Which words describe the Secretary of Science? *(intelligent, rational)*

Writer's Technique ☆

Description By using description strategically and sparingly, Asimov encourages readers to use their own imagination to infer details.

English Learners

DIFFERENTIATED INSTRUCTION

Beginning/Early Intermediate English language learners may feel overwhelmed by the odd names and places in "Buy Jupiter." Explain that this difficulty is not a language issue. Since the names and places are imaginary, all readers have to visualize them from the writer's description. Assign the roles, including a narrator, to student volunteers and have them read the story aloud while role-playing the characters. To help them interpret the characters, have students imitate the facial expressions and hand gestures indicated by Asimov.

Assess

Guide to Genre Fiction

Go through each bullet point with the class. **Ask:** What elements of this genre entertain you?

Elements of Genre Fiction

Go through each bullet point with the class and have them volunteer examples. To demonstrate diction, have several different students describe the same thing, noting how the various word choices of the students result in different styles.

Activities

1. **Visual Literacy** Suggest that students make note of word choices that catch their attention.
2. **Speaking and Listening** Encourage students to include sounds, such as footsteps or traffic.
3. **Take Notes** Ask students to note particular elements of each text (e.g., sensory detail, subject matter, literary form) that evoke a personal response to what they are reading.

FOLDABLES® Study Organizer

Have students make the Bound Book. Their notes on the literary elements can be written on the pages.

Wrap-Up:

Guide to Genre Fiction

- Like all fiction, **genre fiction** is usually meant to teach, to entertain, or to do both.
- **Mystery** deals with the unknown. Thrillers, horror stories, and detective stories are types of mysteries.
- **Fables** teach a lesson, or moral, about human behavior.
- **Science fiction** frequently deals with the interplay between science or technology and human nature.
- **Fantasy** fiction is usually set in an imaginary world and includes supernatural creatures and forces.

Elements of Genre Fiction

- **Description** makes readers feel that they are part of the action.
- **Imagery** makes description more vivid by appealing to the reader's five senses.
- **Style** is the distinctive way an author uses language. **Diction** and **word choice** contribute to a writer's style.
- **Tone** is the writer's attitude toward the subject or the audience.

LOG ON **Literature** Online

Unit Resources For additional skills practice, go to glencoe.com and enter QuickPass code GL49787u6.

Activities

Use what you have learned about reading and analyzing genre fiction to complete one of the following activities.

1. **Visual Literacy** Create a three-column chart that you can use to compare and contrast the tone and style of three different selections from the unit.
2. **Speaking and Listening** In a small group, prepare a dramatic reading of an important scene from one of the stories in the unit. Pretend your reading is being recorded for a radio program. Assign one student in the group to provide background music for the show.
3. **Take Notes** You might try using this study organizer to explore your personal response to genre fiction you read in this unit. See pages R20–R21 for folding instructions.

FOLDABLES® Study Organizer **BOUND BOOK**

Writing Practice

Imagery In small groups, have students practice using imagery. Assign each group an event to describe.

- a day at the beach
- a baseball game
- an afternoon at the mall

Students should try to describe the event, using imagery and sensory details.

Have them create a chart with "Hear," "See," "Taste," "Touch," and "Smell" as column headers. Students should fill in their charts during their discussion. Invite students to share some of their descriptions with the class.

Our World and Beyond

The Rimfall. Jonathan Barry. Oil on canvas. Private collection.

View the Art The title of this painting is a reference to Terry Pratchett's fantasy series Discworld. How well does this painting reflect the Big Idea Our World and Beyond? ★

BIG IDEA

Imagine that time can move backward, that space has more than three dimensions, or that fantastic creatures share the universe with us. The stories in this unit will engage your imagination. As you read them, ask yourself, What can we gain from thinking about realities different from our own?

Approaching Level

DIFFERENTIATED INSTRUCTION

Emerging Visual learners will benefit from engaging with the artwork. Have students study the picture and then read the Big Idea note on page 991. **Ask:** In what ways is the picture different from our usual view of reality? Have students interpret the elements in the picture.

UNIT SIX

Analyze and Extend

Big Idea

Ask: What is your definition of "reality"? What makes something "real"? Discuss differences between fantasy and reality and examples of fantasies of the past, for instance space travel, that have become realities.

APPROACHING **Ask:** What current fantasies do you think will one day become reality? *(Possible answers: time travel, living on the moon)*

View the Art ★

Answer: *Answers may vary. Students should support their answers with a detailed explanation.*

Contemporary Irish artist and illustrator Jonathan Barry specializes in painting scenes from literature, including such classics as *Alice in Wonderland, The Wind in the Willows,* and *Peter Pan.*

For additional support for English Learners, see Unit 6 Teaching Resources Book, p. 20.

Focus

Bellringer Options

Daily Language Practice Transparency 93

Or **say:** Imagine an unusual creature or character. Instruct students to write a detailed description of this character. Encourage them to include as many sensory details as possible. Have them share their descriptions with the class.

Teach

Literary Element 1

Description Instruct students to describe a common object, such as an orange. Write the descriptions on the board.

Ask: What's missing? Have students add sensory details and figurative language to the descriptions.

View the Art ★

Contemporary American artist Ellen Schuster combines her talents as a photographer, computer illustrator, and graphic artist to create her unique artwork.

Learning Objectives

For pages 991–993

In studying this text, you will focus on the following objectives:

Literary Study:
Analyzing description and imagery.
Connecting to the literature.

LITERARY FOCUS

Description and Style

How do description and style contribute to genre fiction?

Writers of genre fiction sometimes face unique challenges, such as describing something that no one has ever seen or heard of, or providing clues to lead readers to both correct and false conclusions about a mystery. In his detective stories, Sir Arthur Conan Doyle uses description and style to create Dr. Watson's moderately acute sense of observation.

I did not gain very much, however, by my inspection. Our visitor bore every mark of being an average, commonplace British tradesman, obese, pompous, and slow. He wore rather baggy gray shepherd's check trousers, a not overclean black frock coat, unbuttoned in the front, and a drab waistcoat with a heavy, brassy Albert chain, and a square pierced bit of metal dangling down as an ornament. A frayed top hat and a faded brown overcoat with a wrinkled velvet collar lay upon a chair beside him. Altogether, look as I would, there was nothing remarkable about the man save his blazing red head, and the expression of extreme chagrin and discontent upon his features.

—Sir Arthur Conan Doyle,
from "The Red-Headed League"

See Past and Future with Eyes in Back of Head. Ellen Schuster. ★

Speaking and Listening Practice

SMALL GROUP **Description** Divide the class into two groups. Assign each group several objects to describe. Have one group begin by asking the other a question about the object, such as "What color is it?" or "What does it smell like?" Each group may ask only one question per sense in each round. If students haven't guessed the object by the fifth sense, they start over again by asking another question in the category of the first sense (for example, if they started with a visual question, they can now ask another visual question). The groups continue asking questions using each sense until they guess the object.

The group to guess the most objects with the fewest questions wins.

Description

Description is a detailed portrayal of a person, a place, an object, or an event. Good description can help a reader see, hear, smell, taste, or

1 feel a person, place, creature, or object. There are many literary techniques a writer can use to describe something. Figurative language and imagery are two.

Figurative Language Language that uses expressions that are not literally true but express some truth beyond the literal level is called **figurative language. Figures of speech,** such as similes, metaphors, and personification, are specific devices or kinds of figurative language. Nancy Kress uses a simile in the passage below.

2 The crows' feet at the corners of his eyes were still tentative, like lines scratched in soft sand.

—Nancy Kress, **from "In Memoriam"**

Imagery Language that appeals to one or more of the five senses—sight, hearing, touch, taste, and smell—is called **imagery.** Writers use imagery to help create effective descriptions that will engage the reader.

The whole southern curve of the Mare Crisium is a vast delta where a score of rivers once found their way into the ocean, fed perhaps by the torrential rains that must have lashed the mountains in the brief volcanic age when the Moon was young.

—Arthur C. Clarke, **from "The Sentinel"**

Style

The distinctive way a writer uses language is called **style.** Diction, use of literary devices, and tone all contribute to an author's style.

The words a writer chooses and the arrangement of those words into phrases and sentences is **diction.** The author's diction conveys meaning, suggests attitude, and creates **mood,** or the emotional quality of a story. For example, in Bret Harte's parody, he immediately sets a comic mood by using a contrast in style and characterization: the narrator of the story has a precise and analytical style, but his character is ridiculous.

I found Hemlock Jones in the old Brook Street lodgings, musing before the fire. With the freedom of an old friend I at once threw myself in my usual familiar attitude at his feet, and gently caressed his boot. I was induced to do this for two reasons: one, that it enabled me to get a good look at his bent, concentrated face, and the other, that it seemed to indicate my reverence for his superhuman insight. So absorbed was he even then, in tracking some mysterious clue, that he did not seem to notice me.

—Bret Harte, **from "The Stolen Cigar Case"**

Quickwrite

Describe a Process Write a journal entry describing a real or imagined time you prepared a special food. For example, you might tell about the time you made a birthday cake or the time you created a feast for the birds outside your window. Describe the steps involved in the process and what you saw, heard, smelled, tasted, and touched as you worked. Use diction and other elements of style to create a specific mood.

LOG ON **Literature** Online

Literature and Reading For more about literary elements, go to glencoe.com and enter QuickPass code GL49787u6.

Teach

Reading Strategy 2

Visualize Explain that authors use description and style to help readers experience and understand characters and the world the authors have created. Have students read each displayed quotation aloud. **Ask:** What does the language make you understand about the stories? *(Answers will vary.)*

Quickwrite

Students' descriptions should include details from each of the five senses.

Approaching Level

DIFFERENTIATED INSTRUCTION

Emerging Visual learners will benefit from clearly "seeing" the descriptions. Have students choose one of the excerpts on the page and create an illustration based on the description. Instruct students to use the author's description to imagine as many details as possible, and then to translate those details into an image. When students are finished, have them present their art to the class. The class should ask the artists questions about their choices.

Before You Read

Focus

Bellringer Options

Literature Launchers: Pre-Reading Videos DVD, Selection Launcher

Selection Focus Transparency 36

Daily Language Practice Transparency 94

Or display images of outer space and space travel.

Ask: Why do people dream of exploring the stars? What do people hope to discover in space?

As they read, tell students to consider what the story says about the human desire to explore the universe.

Before You Read

World Literature
England

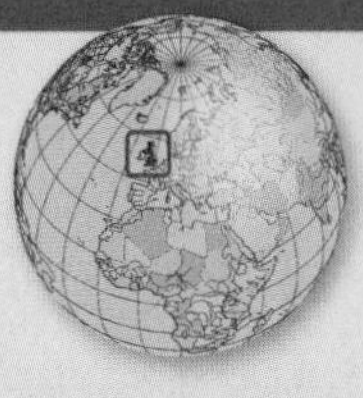

The Sentinel

Meet **Arthur C. Clarke**
(1917–2008)

"I've seen far more than I ever imagined would happen. I mean, I never dreamed we would have explored the solar system as we have."

—Arthur C. Clarke

Unlike many science fiction authors, Arthur C. Clarke is truly a scientist. In fact, in 1945, when he was only 28 years old, he developed the idea for orbital communication satellites, which are indispensable to global communications today.

Imagining the Future Clarke was born in Minehead, England. He was the son of an English farming family and attended schools in his home county until moving to London at the age of nineteen. In London, Clarke pursued his interest in space sciences by joining the British Interplanetary Society and by beginning to write science fiction. When World War II started in 1939, Clarke joined the Royal Air Force, eventually becoming an officer in charge of the first radar talk-down equipment, which was used to help pilots land.

In 1945 Clarke initiated a new era of communication when he published a technical paper entitled "Extra-terrestrial Relays" in the British magazine *Wireless World*. The paper introduced his idea of orbital communication satellites.

Milestones in Science Fiction After the war, Clarke resumed his formal studies, obtaining a Fellowship at King's College London. He began publishing stories and he quickly emerged as a renowned science fiction writer. His works have been credited with inspiring space exploration and missions such as NASA's Apollo moon landings. His short story "The Sentinel" inspired filmmaker Stanley Kubrick, and the two men worked together to expand the story into the screenplay for the film *2001: A Space Odyssey*. The movie stands as a milestone in science fiction filmmaking and earned Clarke and Kubrick Academy Award nominations.

The Future Is Now Clarke has written more than eighty science fiction books, many of which describe "fantastic" elements that have since become realities, such as orbiting space stations and computers with artificial intelligence. He has received numerous honors for his work, including a nomination for the Nobel Peace Prize. Since 1956 Clarke has lived in Sri Lanka, keeping in touch with his international friends and colleagues by satellite, fax, and e-mail, all of which he predicted in his early science fiction.

LOG ON **Literature** Online

Author Search For more about Arthur C. Clarke, go to glencoe.com and enter QuickPass code GL49787u6.

Selection Skills

The Sentinel

Literary Elements
- Suspense (SE pp. 995–1006)
- Description (SE p. 1006)

Reading Skills
- Analyze Motivations (SE pp. 995–1006)

Writing Skills/Grammar
- Research Report (SE p. 1007)
- Ellipses (SE p. 1007)
- Write a Summary (TE p. 998)

Listening/Speaking/Viewing Skills
- Analyze Art (SE pp. 997; TE p. 999)
- Visual Literacy (SE p. 1005)

Vocabulary Skills
- Analogies (SE pp. 995, 1006)
- Academic Vocabulary (SE p. 1006)

Literature and Reading Preview

Connect to the Story

Have you ever decided to do something based on your own instincts or intuition? Write a journal article about a time when you took a risk and were surprised by the outcome.

Build Background

A sentinel is a person or object stationed to guard against and warn of danger. First published in 1951, Clarke's "The Sentinel" looks ahead to the "future." It takes place on the surface of the Moon during the late summer of 1996. The story's ideas about ancient water formations and basic life are similar to some currently developing hypotheses about the surface of Mars.

Set Purposes for Reading

Big Idea Our World and Beyond

As you read, ask yourself, How does the narrator compare living on the Moon with living on Earth?

Literary Element Suspense

Suspense is the growing interest and excitement readers experience while reading a work of literature. To build suspense, a writer may provide just enough information to keep the reader wondering: "What will happen next?" As you read, ask yourself, How does Clarke use suspense in this story?

Reading Strategy Analyze Motivations

When you **analyze motivations,** you figure out why characters in a story act the way they do. The reasons for a character's actions may be external, such as a reaction to other characters and events, or internal, based on the character's psychology and beliefs. As you read, ask yourself, How is the plot of "The Sentinel" affected by the motivations of the characters?

Tip: Chart Motivations Use a three-column chart similar to the one below to chart characters' motivations.

Character	Action	Motivation
narrator	trains telescope on shining object	curiosity about the "elusive symmetry" of shining object

Learning Objectives

For pages 994–1006

In studying this text, you will focus on the following objectives:

Literary Study: Analyzing suspense.

Reading: Analyzing motivations.

Vocabulary

tantalize (tant′ əl īz′) *v.* to torment or tease by tempting with something and then withholding it; p. 999 *She tantalized the horse by keeping its hay just out of reach.*

enigma (i nig′ mə) *n.* a mystery; a baffling person or thing; p. 999 *The stranger kept to himself and remained an enigma to everyone.*

ebb (eb) *v.* to become less or weaker; decline; fail; p. 1002 *As the battery died, the device's power slowly ebbed.*

irrevocably (i rev′ ə kə blē) *adv.* in a way that cannot be revoked or undone; p. 1003 *As a result of the fire, the church was irrevocably damaged.*

Tip: Analogies An analogy is a type of comparison based on the relationships between things or ideas. For example, the word *enigma* has the same relationship to *solution* as *ebb* has to *grow.*

ARTHUR C. CLARKE **995**

Before You Read

Focus

Summary

The story is set in 1996. A team of scientists is living on and exploring the surface of the moon. One morning, the narrator sees a bright metallic flash on the horizon, and he and a fellow scientist go in search of its source. What they find is a mysterious structure that changes their ideas about the moon, the human race, and the universe.

 For summaries in languages other than English, see Unit 6 Teaching Resources Book, pp. 21–26.

Vocabulary

Vocabulary Word Toss

Write the selection vocabulary words on the board and stand at the front of the classroom with a foam ball. Explain that each student to catch the ball will have to correctly use one of the vocabulary words in a sentence. The student must then pass the ball to another student.

 For additional vocabulary practice, see Unit 6 Teaching Resources Book, p. 29.

Approaching Level

DIFFERENTIATED INSTRUCTION

Established Explain that "The Sentinel" is a story about astronauts in space, but it was written long before any astronauts actually traveled to space. Encourage students to pay close attention to how Clarke uses his imagination to speculate about outer space and the future.

Have students suggest situations that would make a good science fiction story.

(Possible answers: Going to camp on the moon, dogs and cats becoming as intelligent as humans)

Teach

Big Idea **1**

Our World and Beyond
Answer: *Clarke begins by looking at the moon from far away and then zooms in to the moon's surface, where the action begins.*
Remind students that the story was written in 1951, when space travel and exploration were still a distant possibility. For Clarke's original readers, moon exploration was an idea possible only in stories.

For an audio recording of this selection, use Listening Library Audio CD-ROM.

Readability Scores
Dale-Chall: 8.3
DRP: 63
Lexile: 1240

The Sentinel

Arthur C. Clarke

The next time you see the full moon high in the south, look carefully at its right-hand edge and let your eye travel upward along the curve of the disk. Round about two o'clock you will notice a small, dark oval: anyone with normal eyesight can find it quite easily. It is the great walled plain, one of the finest on the Moon, known as the Mare Crisium[1]—the Sea of Crises. Three hundred miles in diameter, and almost completely surrounded by a ring of magnificent mountains, it had never been explored until we entered it in the late summer of 1996.

Our expedition was a large one. We had two heavy freighters which had flown our supplies and equipment from the main lunar base in the Mare Serenitatis,[2] five hundred miles away. There were also three small rockets which were intended for short-range transport over regions which our surface vehicles couldn't cross. Luckily, most of the Mare Crisium is very flat. There are none of the great crevasses[3] so common and so dangerous elsewhere, and very few craters or mountains of any size. As far as we could tell, our powerful caterpillar tractors would have no difficulty in taking us wherever we wished to go.

I was geologist—or selenologist, if you want to be pedantic[4]—in charge of the group exploring the southern region of the Mare. We had crossed a hundred miles of it in a week, skirting the foothills of the mountains along the shore of what was once the ancient sea, some thousand million years before. When life was beginning on Earth, it was already dying here. The waters were retreating down the flanks of those stupendous cliffs, retreating into the empty heart of the Moon. Over the land which we were crossing, the tideless ocean had once been half a mile deep, and now the only trace of moisture was the hoarfrost one could sometimes find in caves which the searing sunlight never penetrated.

1. *[Mare Crisium]* In 1609, when Italian scientist Galileo Galilei first viewed the moon's dark patches through an early telescope, he called them "seas." *Mare* (mär′ ā) is Latin for "sea." Today, these dark areas are known to be broad, lowland plains, but the Latin names given them in the 1600s are still used.
2. *[Mare Serenitatis]* In the early 1970s, Apollo astronauts landed near the Sea of Serenity ("calmness").
3. A *crevasse* (kri vas′) is a deep, narrow crack.
4. One who is *pedantic* (pi dan′ tik) pays excessive attention to minor details and formal rules. Such a person would insist that a *geologist* studies the structure and history of Earth, while a *selenologist* studies the Moon.

1 Our World and Beyond *How does this opening paragraph create the effect of transporting the reader to the moon?*

Reading Practice

SPIRAL REVIEW **Identify Author's Purpose** Most fiction is meant to entertain readers. Science fiction writers, however, may have other purposes in mind. One thing many science fiction writers try to do is answer questions that are beyond the scope of human knowledge. Ask students what purpose, besides entertaining his readers, Clarke may have had as he wrote the story. As students read, ask them to look for clues that suggest Clarke's purpose. Challenge students to write a few sentences explaining Clarke's purpose or purposes.

Man Gazing at a Dark Moon. Paul Anderson.

View the Art What do you think the man pictured is thinking? Why? ★

We had begun our journey early in the slow lunar dawn, and still had almost a week of Earth-time before nightfall. Half a dozen times a day we would leave our vehicle and go outside in the space suits to hunt for interesting minerals, or to place markers for the guidance of future travelers. It was an uneventful routine. There is nothing hazardous or even particularly exciting about lunar exploration. We could live comfortably for a month in our pressurized tractors, and if we ran into trouble, we could always radio for help and sit tight until one of the spaceships came to our rescue.

I said just now that there was nothing exciting about lunar exploration, but of course that isn't true. One could never grow tired of those incredible mountains, so much more rugged than the gentle hills of Earth. We never knew, as we rounded the capes and promontories[5] of that vanished sea, what new splendors would be revealed to us. The whole southern curve

5. Points of land that project out into a body of water, *capes* are usually low and flat, whereas *promontories* are elevated.

Analyze Motivations *What motivation of the narrator is revealed in this passage?* **2**

Teach

Reading Strategy 2

Analyze Motivations

Answer: *The narrator is motivated to explore the moon because he derives aesthetic pleasure from a contemplation of its physical beauty.*

View the Art ★

Answer: *Answers will vary. Students may note the prominence of the planet and the sky and conclude that the figure is dreaming about space.*

In addition to his artwork, Paul Anderson takes historical, news, sports, and entertainment photographs. Anderson's artwork is often characterized by a dreamlike quality.

Interactive Read and Write

Other options for teaching this selection can be found in

- Interactive Read and Write for EL Students, pp. 287–302
- Interactive Read and Write for Approaching-Level Students, pp. 287–302
- Interactive Read and Write for On-Level Students, pp. 287–302

English Learners

DIFFERENTIATED INSTRUCTION

Intermediate Suggest that readers pretend they are casting a movie of the story. Have them form well-rounded mental images of the characters' appearances and personalities. Then have them think of actors and actresses who might play the characters in a film version of the story.

Advanced Learners

DIFFERENTIATED INSTRUCTION

Direct the Story Have creative students discuss what choices they would make when creating the film version of the story. Ask the following questions:

- How would you re-create the scenery in the story?
- What sort of special effects would you use?

Teach

Big Idea 1

Our World and Beyond
Answer: *Students may say that the explorers find comfort in a daily routine kept on an Earth timetable.* Point out Clarke's realism here—explorers and settlers always bring their culture and traditions with them when they go to new places.

Literary Element 2

Suspense **Answer:** *He points out a moment he still remembers. Readers don't yet know what happened. This creates suspense.*

Say: Authors may build suspense by emphasizing the normal and then disrupting it.

of the Mare Crisium is a vast delta where a score of rivers once found their way into the ocean, fed perhaps by the torrential rains that must have lashed the mountains in the brief volcanic age when the Moon was young. Each of these ancient valleys was an invitation, challenging us to climb into the unknown uplands beyond. But we had a hundred miles still to cover, and could only look longingly at the heights which others must scale.

We kept Earth-time aboard the tractor, and precisely at 2200 hours the final radio message would be sent out to Base and we would close down for the day. Outside, the rocks would still be burning beneath the almost vertical sun, but to us it would be night until we awoke again eight hours later. Then one of us would prepare breakfast, there would be a great buzzing of electric razors, and someone would switch on the short-wave radio from Earth. Indeed, when the smell of frying sausages began to fill the cabin, it was sometimes hard to believe that we were not back on our own world—everything was so normal and homely, apart from the feeling of decreased weight and the unnatural slowness with which objects fell.

It was my turn to prepare breakfast in the corner of the main cabin that served as a galley. I can remember that moment quite vividly after all these years, for the radio had just played one of my favorite melodies, the old Welsh air "David of the White Rock." Our driver was already outside in his space suit, inspecting our caterpillar treads. My assistant, Louis Garnett, was up forward in the control position, making some belated entries in yesterday's log.

As I stood by the frying pan, waiting, like any terrestrial[6] housewife, for the sausages to brown, I let my gaze wander idly over the mountain walls which covered the whole of the southern horizon, marching out of sight to east and west below the curve of the Moon. They seemed only a mile or two from the tractor, but I knew that the nearest was twenty miles away. On the Moon, of course, there is no loss of detail with distance—none of that almost imperceptible[7] haziness which softens and sometimes transfigures[8] all far-off things on Earth.

On the Moon, of course, there is no loss of detail with distance . . .

Those mountains were ten thousand feet high, and they climbed steeply out of the plain as if ages ago some subterranean eruption had smashed them skyward through the molten crust. The base of even the nearest was hidden from sight by a steeply curving surface of the plain, for the Moon is a very little world, and from where I was standing the horizon was only two miles away.

I lifted my eyes toward the peaks which no man had ever climbed, the peaks which, before the coming of terrestrial life, had watched the retreating oceans sink sullenly into their graves, taking with them the hope and the morning promise of a world. The sunlight was beating against those ramparts[9]

1 Our World and Beyond *Why do you think the lunar explorers live much as they would on Earth?*

2 Suspense *What does this comment suggest about the moment the narrator is about to describe?*

6. *Terrestrial* means "of the earth; earthly."
7. *Imperceptible* means "not noticeable."
8. To *transfigure* a thing is to change its outward appearance, often into something glorious.
9. *Ramparts* are walls or embankments built for protection, as around a castle. Here, metaphorically, the ramparts are the mountain walls.

Writing Practice

Write a Summary Explain that because the story was written before astronauts actually explored space, Clarke was free to imagine space explorers' daily routines. Students may be interested in learning about how real astronauts eat, cook, groom themselves, and exercise. Suggest that students use the Internet and other reference sources to research astronauts' routines. Then have students write a summary of their findings.

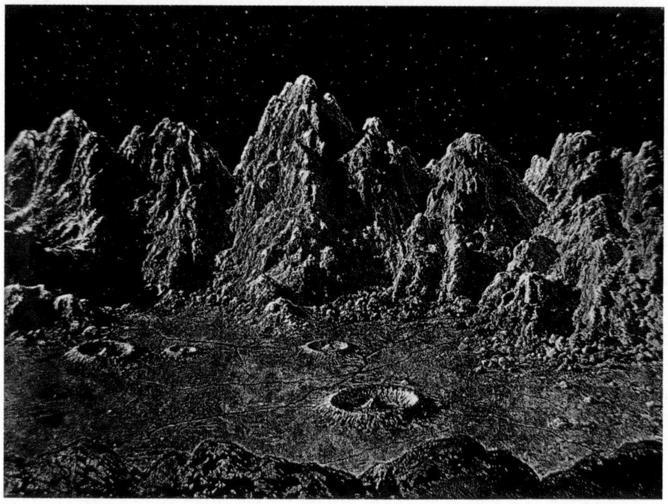

A group of lunar mountains stands on the surface of the moon, creating the ideal lunar landscape. ★

with a glare that hurt the eyes, yet only a little way above them the stars were shining steadily in a sky blacker than a winter midnight on Earth.

I was turning away when my eye caught a metallic glitter high on the ridge of a great promontory thrusting out into the sea thirty miles to the west. It was a dimensionless point of light, as if a star had been clawed from the sky by one of those cruel peaks, and I imagined that some smooth rock surface was catching the sunlight and heliographing[10] it straight into my eyes. Such things were not uncommon. When the Moon is in her second quarter, observers on Earth can sometimes see the great ranges in the Oceanus Procellarum[11] burning with a blue-white iridescence[12] as the sunlight flashes from their slopes and leaps again from world to world. But I was curious to know what kind of rock could be shining so brightly up there, and I climbed into the observation turret and swung our four-inch telescope round to the west.

I could see just enough to **tantalize** me. Clear and sharp in the field of vision, the mountain peaks seemed only half a mile away, but whatever was catching the sunlight was still too small to be resolved.[13] Yet it seemed to have an elusive[14] symmetry, and the summit upon which it rested was curiously flat. I stared for a long time at the glittering **enigma,** straining my eyes into space, until presently a smell of burning from the galley told me that our breakfast

10. Here, *heliographing* means "reflecting." A *heliograph* is a signaling device that uses mirrors to reflect light from the sun.
11. *Oceanis Procellarum* is the (waterless) Ocean of Storms.
12. *Iridescence* is a display of shimmering and changing colors.

3 Analyze Motivations *How does the narrator's motivation derive from his profession?*

13. Here, *resolved* means "made clearly visible."
14. The precise shape of the object was difficult to identify or grasp (*elusive*).

Suspense *What descriptive phrases in this passage help build suspense?* 4

Vocabulary

tantalize (tant′ əl īz′) *v.* to torment or tease by tempting with something and then withholding it

enigma (i nig′ mə) *n.* a mystery; a baffling person or thing

Teach

Reading Strategy 3

Analyze Motivations
Answer: *All scientists are driven by curiosity about the natural world. The narrator describes himself as a selentologist, one who specializes in the study of the moon. Consequently, he cannot resist investigating the source of the shining "rock" on top of the mountain.*

Literary Element 4

Suspense **Answer:** *Students may suggest these phrases:* elusive symmetry, curiously flat, *and* glittering enigma.

Say: The writer builds suspense and then undercuts it with humor when the narrator lets breakfast burn.

View the Art ★

Lunar mountains, also called mons or montes, can be viewed from Earth with simple telescopes. By measuring the shadows of the mountains, their heights can be determined.

Advanced Learners

DIFFERENTIATED INSTRUCTION

Solve Math Problems Students who have strong math and logic skills may enjoy solving math problems related to the story. Have them complete the following calculations. **Ask:** If the mountain is 12,000 feet high and the narrator can scale it in twenty hours, how many feet will he climb per hour? *(600)*

Ask: If a person's weight on the moon is one-sixth of his or her normal weight on earth, how much would a 120-pound man weigh on the moon? (20 pounds) Challenge students to create their own story-related math problems and share them with the class.

Teach

Vocabulary 1

Words with Prefixes

Remind students that the prefixes *un-* and *in-* mean "not" or "the reverse of." Point out several words on pages 1100 and 1101 that contain these prefixes—*unscalable, unaccustomed, incorruptible, unchanging,* and *unusual.* The narrator's choice of words suggests that he is succinct.

Language History ☆

Goose Chase The origin of the expression "a wild goose chase" is unknown, but it first appeared in print in Shakespeare's 1592 tragedy *Romeo and Juliet.* The expression is a vivid one that connotes a foolish and unproductive pursuit.

sausages had made their quarter-million-mile journey in vain.

All that morning we argued our way across the Mare Crisium while the western mountains reared higher in the sky. Even when we were out prospecting in the space suits, the discussion would continue over the radio. It was absolutely certain, my companions argued, that there had never been any form of intelligent life on the Moon. The only living things that had ever existed there were a few primitive plants and their slightly less degenerate[15] ancestors. I knew that as well as anyone, but there are times when a scientist must not be afraid to make a fool of himself.

The real danger in lunar mountaineering lies in overconfidence.

"Listen," I said at last, "I'm going up there, if only for my own peace of mind. That mountain's less than twelve thousand feet high—that's only two thousand under Earth gravity—and I can make the trip in twenty hours at the outside. I've always wanted to go up into those hills, anyway, and this gives me an excellent excuse."

"If you don't break your neck," said Garnett, "you'll be the laughingstock of the expedition when we get back to Base. That mountain will probably be called Wilson's Folly from now on."

"I won't break my neck," I said firmly. "Who was the first man to climb Pico and Helicon?"[16]

"But weren't you rather younger in those days?" asked Louis gently.

"That," I said with great dignity, "is as good a reason as any for going."

We went to bed early that night, after driving the tractor to within half a mile of the promontory. Garnett was coming with me in the morning; he was a good climber, and had often been with me on such exploits[17] before. Our driver was only too glad to be left in charge of the machine.

At first sight, those cliffs seemed completely unscalable, but to anyone with a 1 good head for heights, climbing is easy on a world where all weights are only a sixth of their normal value. The real danger in lunar mountaineering lies in overconfidence; a six-hundred-foot drop on the Moon can kill you just as thoroughly as a hundred-foot fall on Earth.

We made our first halt on a wide ledge about four thousand feet above the plain. Climbing had not been very difficult, but my limbs were stiff with the unaccustomed effort, and I was glad of the rest. We could still see the tractor as a tiny metal insect far down at the foot of the cliff, and we reported our progress to the driver before starting on the next ascent.

Inside our suits it was comfortably cool, for the refrigeration units were fighting the sun and carrying away the body heat of our exertions. We seldom spoke to each other, except to pass climbing instructions and to discuss our best plan of ascent. I do not know what Garnett was thinking, probably that this was the craziest goose chase he had ever embarked upon. I more ☆ than half agreed with him, but the joy of

15. Here, *degenerate* (di jen′ er it) means "having sunk below a former condition." The idea is that as water vanished, the moon's plant life gradually deteriorated in quality and finally died out.
16. Moon mountains are commonly named after Earth mountains. *Pico* is a mountain in the Azores, a group of islands in the northern Atlantic, and *Helicon* is a peak in Greece.
17. An *exploit* is a bold, daring deed.

Literary Element Practice

SMALL GROUP

Foreshadow Events

Explain that Clarke uses several techniques to create suspense. He piques readers' interest by giving just enough information to keep them guessing what will happen next. He also uses foreshadowing to give clues about future events. Have students use these techniques in their own story-telling.

Ask each student to think of a story and tell it to a classmate. Students should use foreshadowing and reveal only enough information to keep listeners interested. Afterward, listeners should tell storytellers whether their stories were effective.

climbing, the knowledge that no man had ever gone this way before, and the exhilaration of the steadily widening landscape gave me all the reward I needed.

I don't think I was particularly excited when I saw in front of us the wall of rock I had first inspected through the telescope from thirty miles away. It would level off about fifty feet above our heads, and there on the plateau would be the thing that had lured me over these barren wastes. It would be, almost certainly, nothing more than a boulder splintered ages ago by a falling meteor, and with its cleavage planes[18] still fresh and bright in this incorruptible, unchanging silence.

There were no handholds on the rock face, and we had to use a grapnel. My tired arms seemed to gain new strength as I swung the three-pronged metal anchor round my head and sent it sailing up toward the stars. The first time it broke loose and came falling slowly back when we pulled the rope. On the third attempt, the prongs gripped firmly and our combined weights could not shift it.

Garnett looked at me anxiously. I could tell that he wanted to go first, but I smiled back at him through the glass of my helmet and shook my head. Slowly, taking my time, I began the final ascent.

Even with my space suit, I weighed only forty pounds here, so I pulled myself up hand over hand without bothering to use my feet. At the rim I paused and waved to my companion, then I scrambled over the edge and stood upright, staring ahead of me.

You must understand that until this very moment I had been almost completely convinced that there could be nothing strange or unusual for me to find here. Almost, but not quite; it was that haunting doubt that had driven me forward. Well, it was a doubt no longer, but the haunting had scarcely begun.

I was standing on a plateau perhaps a hundred feet across. It had once been smooth—too smooth to be natural—but falling meteors had pitted and scored its surface through immeasurable eons.[19] It had been leveled to support a glittering, roughly pyramidal structure, twice as high as a man, that was set in the rock like a gigantic, many-faceted jewel.

Probably no emotion at all filled my head in those first few seconds. Then I felt a great lifting of my heart, and a strange, inexpressible joy. For I loved the Moon, and now I knew that the creeping moss of Aristarchus and Eratosthenes[20] was not the ☆ only life she had brought forth in her youth. The old, discredited dream of the first explorers was true. There had, after all, been a lunar civilization—and I was the first to find it. That I had come perhaps a hundred million years too late did not distress me; it was enough to have come at all.

My mind was beginning to function normally, to analyze and to ask questions. Was this a building, a shrine—or something for which my language had no name? If a building, then why was it erected in so uniquely inaccessible a spot? I wondered

18. Here, *planes* are rock surfaces, exposed as a result of the boulder's splitting, or *cleavage*.

19. An *eon* (ē ən′) is an indefinitely long period of time.

20. Most moon craters are named for scientists and philosophers, such as these Greek astronomers of the third century B.C. *Aristarchus* was among the first to say that Earth moves around the Sun; *Eratosthenes* accurately calculated Earth's circumference.

2 Suspense *How does the narrator's uncertainty help build suspense as he climbs toward the plateau?*

Analyze Motivations *How does this statement illustrate a common motivation among all dedicated scientists?* **3**

Our World and Beyond *Why do you think the narrator is thrilled to have made this discovery?* **4**

English Learners

DIFFERENTIATED INSTRUCTION

Intermediate Like the scientists in the story, students from different cultures often make discoveries. Ask English learners to share a discovery they have made about American culture.

Teach

Literary Element 2

Suspense **Answer:** *The narrator doesn't know what he is about to discover, and neither does the reader.*

APPROACHING **Ask:** What do you think the narrator will discover? Why? *(Students should support their answers with evidence from the text.)*

Reading Strategy 3

Analyze Motivations
Answer: *Scientists are dedicated to uncovering the truth about the natural world. They will gather and evaluate evidence until all doubts have been eliminated.*

Big Idea 4

Our World and Beyond
Answer: *He is the first person to make the discovery. Also, humans have long wondered about life elsewhere in the universe; this discovery supports that hypothesis.*

Literary History ☆

Eratosthenes A poet, librarian, and astronomer, Eratosthenes (276–194 B.C.) calculated Earth's circumference and the tilt of its axis. His calculations were not accurate by modern standards, but his work was groundbreaking.

Teach

Reading Strategy 1

Analyze Motivations

Answer: *The narrator falsely assumes that any evidence of life on the moon must be the product of a civilization inferior to that on Earth. This pride delays his realization that the "sentinel" was erected on the moon by a superior civilization of beings much more highly evolved than humans.*

Lunar Phenomenon, November 24 1893.

if it might be a temple, and I could picture the adepts[21] of some strange priesthood calling on their gods to preserve them as the life of the Moon **ebbed** with the dying oceans, and calling on their gods in vain.

I took a dozen steps forward to examine the thing more closely, but some sense of caution kept me from going too near. I knew a little of archaeology, and tried to guess the cultural level of the civilization that must have smoothed this mountain and raised the glittering mirror surfaces that still dazzled my eyes.

The Egyptians could have done it, I thought, if their workmen had possessed whatever strange materials these far more ancient architects had used. Because of the thing's smallness, it did not occur to me that I might be looking at the handiwork of a race more advanced than my own. The idea that the Moon had possessed intelligence at all was still almost too tremendous to grasp, and my pride would not let me take the final, humiliating plunge.

And then I noticed something that set the scalp crawling at the back of my neck—something so trivial and so innocent that many would never have noticed it at all. I have said that the plateau was scarred by meteors; it was also coated inches deep with the cosmic dust that is always filtering down upon the surface of any world where there are no winds to disturb it. Yet the dust and the meteor scratches ended quite abruptly in a wide circle enclosing the little pyramid, as though an invisible wall was protecting it from the ravages of time and the slow but ceaseless bombardment from space.

There was someone shouting in my earphones, and I realized that Garnett had been calling me for some time. I walked unsteadily to the edge of the cliff and signaled him to join me, not trusting myself to speak. Then I went back toward the circle in the dust. I picked up a fragment of splintered rock and tossed it gently toward the shining enigma. If the pebble had vanished at that invisible barrier, I should not have been surprised, but it seemed to hit a smooth, hemispheric surface and slide gently to the ground.

I knew then that I was looking at nothing that could be matched in the antiquity of my own race. This was not a building, but a machine, protecting itself with forces that had challenged Eternity. Those forces, whatever they might be, were still operat-

21. *Adepts* are experts; here, they are priests.

Vocabulary

ebb (eb) *v.* to become less or weaker; decline; fail

Analyze Motivations *How is the narrator's pride a negative motivating factor?* 1

Research Practice

SPIRAL REVIEW **Investigate Radiation** Explain that a nuclear reactor throws off both radioactive neutrons and gamma rays. Therefore, a reactor must be surrounded by a shield that absorbs the radiation and protects the people who work with it, as well as those who live near it. Have students research a topic related to radiation, such as how nuclear reactors work, how nuclear waste is created and disposed of, or the dangers that radioactivity poses to humans. Have students prepare a brief report in which they share their findings.

ing, and perhaps I had already come too close. I thought of all the radiations man had trapped and tamed in the past century. For all I knew, I might be as **irrevocably** doomed as if I had stepped into the deadly, silent aura of an unshielded atomic pile.[22]

I remember turning then toward Garnett, who had joined me and was now standing motionless at my side. He seemed quite oblivious to me, so I did not disturb him but walked to the edge of the cliff in an effort to marshal my thoughts.[23] There below me lay the Mare Crisium—Sea of Crises, indeed—strange and weird to most men, but reassuringly familiar to me. I lifted my eyes toward the crescent Earth, lying in her cradle of stars, and I wondered what her clouds had covered when these unknown builders had finished their work. Was it the steaming jungle of the Carboniferous,[24] the bleak shoreline over which the first amphibians must crawl to conquer the land—or, earlier still, the long loneliness before the coming of life?

Do not ask me why I did not guess the truth sooner—the truth that seems so obvious now. In the first excitement of my discovery, I had assumed without question that this crystalline apparition[25] had been built by some race belonging to the Moon's remote past, but suddenly, and with overwhelming force, the belief came to me that it was as alien to the Moon as I myself.

In twenty years we had found no trace of life but a few degenerate plants. No lunar civilization, whatever its doom, could have left but a single token of its existence.

I looked at the shining pyramid again, and the more I looked, the more remote it seemed from anything that had to do with the Moon. And suddenly I felt myself shaking with a foolish, hysterical laughter, brought on by excitement and overexertion: For I had imagined that the little pyramid was speaking to me and was saying, "Sorry, I'm a stranger here myself."

It has taken us twenty years to crack that invisible shield and reach the machine inside those crystal walls. What we could not understand, we broke at last with the savage might of atomic power and now I have seen the fragments of the lovely, glittering thing I found up there on the mountain.

They are meaningless. The mechanisms—☆ if indeed they are mechanisms—of the pyramid belong to a technology that lies far beyond our horizon, perhaps to the technology of paraphysical forces.[26]

The mystery haunts us all the more now that the other planets have been reached and we know that only Earth has ever been the home of intelligent life in our Universe. Nor could any lost civilization of our own world have built that machine, for the thickness of the meteoric dust on the plateau has enabled us to measure its age. It was set there upon its mountain before life had emerged from the seas of Earth.

When our world was half its present age, *something* from the stars swept

---

22. *Atomic pile* is another term for a nuclear reactor.
23. Garnett seemed *oblivious to,* or unaware of, the narrator. *To marshal one's thoughts* is to organize and make sense of them.
24. In geologic time, earth's *Carboniferous* (kär′ bə nif′ ər əs) Period was between 280 million and 345 million years ago, when land was covered with lush vegetation and swamps.
25. An *apparition* is a ghost or ghostly vision.
26. *Paraphysical forces* produce ordinary physical effects without using recognizable physical causes. Such effects might include the ability to float in midair, to materialize and dematerialize, and to move objects with the mind.

2 Suspense *How is suspense built in this passage?*

Vocabulary

irrevocably (i rev′ ə kə blē) *adv.* in a way that cannot be revoked or undone

Teach

Literary Element 2

Suspense Answer: *The narrator's own fear helps build suspense.*

ADVANCED **Ask:** What techniques does the narrator use to build suspense? *(He withholds information and uses foreshadowing.)*

Writer's Technique ☆

Sentence Variety Point out that most of the sentences in the story are long, often compound or complex, with interrupters or asides. Then direct students to the three-word sentence "They are meaningless." Stylistically, the sentence is like hitting the brakes. After paragraphs of long, winding sentences, the sentence pulls readers up short and makes them pay attention.

Approaching Level

DIFFERENTIATED INSTRUCTION

Emerging The story contains several descriptions of the lunar landscape. Have students choose a favorite passage from the story to share and read aloud. Remind students to use their voices to convey emotion and to build suspense.

Teach

Big Idea 1

Our World and Beyond
Answer: *Answers will vary. Based on the title of the story, students may predict that the machine was created to watch for something.*

Literary Element 2

Suspense **Answer:** *He implies that a major event involving the aliens will happen soon.*

Ask: How does this last sentence make you feel? *(Students may say that the ending is not reassuring; they may feel uneasy or worried.)*

Ask: Is the ending appropriate to what you expected in a science fiction story? *(Students may say that they do not expect a science fiction story to have such an open or ominous ending.)*

To check students' understanding of the selection, see Unit 6 Teaching Resources Book, p. 32.

through the Solar System, left this token of its passage, and went again upon its way. Until we destroyed it, that machine was still fulfilling the purpose of its builders; and as to that purpose, here is my guess.

Nearly a hundred thousand million stars are turning in the circle of the Milky Way, and long ago other races on the worlds of other suns must have scaled and passed the heights that we have reached. Think of such civilizations, far back in time against the fading afterglow of Creation, masters of a universe so young that life as yet had come only to a handful of worlds. Theirs would have been a loneliness we cannot imagine, the loneliness of gods looking out across infinity and finding none to share their thoughts.

They must have searched the star clusters as we have searched the planets. Everywhere there would be worlds, but they would be empty or peopled with crawling, mindless things. Such was our own Earth, the smoke of the great volcanoes still staining the skies, when that first ship of the peoples of the dawn came sliding in from the abyss[27] beyond Pluto. It passed the frozen outer worlds, knowing that life could play no part in their destinies. It came to rest among the inner planets, warming themselves around the fire of the Sun and waiting for their stories to begin.

Those wanderers must have looked on Earth, circling safely in the narrow zone between fire and ice, and must have guessed that it was the favorite of the Sun's children. Here, in the distant future, would be intelligence; but there were countless stars before them still, and they might never come this way again.

So they left a sentinel, one of millions they scattered throughout the Universe, watching over all worlds with the promise of life. It was a beacon that down the ages patiently signaled the fact that no one had discovered it.

Perhaps you understand now why that crystal pyramid was set upon the Moon instead of on the Earth. Its builders were not concerned with races still struggling up from savagery. They would be interested in our civilization only if we proved our fitness to survive—by crossing space and so escaping from the Earth, our cradle. That is the challenge that all intelligent races must meet, sooner or later. It is a double challenge, for it depends in turn upon the conquest of atomic energy and the last choice between life and death.

. . . we have set off the fire alarm . . .

Once we had passed that crisis, it was only a matter of time before we found the pyramid and forced it open. Now its signals have ceased, and those whose duty it is will be turning their minds upon Earth. Perhaps they wish to help our infant civilization. But they must be very, very old, and the old are often insanely jealous of the young.

I can never look now at the Milky Way without wondering from which of those banked clouds of stars the emissaries[28] are coming. If you will pardon so commonplace a simile, we have set off the fire alarm and have nothing to do but wait.

I do not think we will have to wait for long. ∾

27. Here, *abyss* (ə bis′) refers to the immeasurably vast reaches of space.

28. An *emissary* is a person or agent sent, often in secret, on an official mission.

1 Our World and Beyond *What purpose do you think the machine was fulfilling?*

Suspense *Why does Clarke end the story on a suspenseful note?* **2**

Listening and Speaking Practice

SMALL GROUP

Group Discussion Have students find newspaper, magazine, or online articles about space exploration. Divide the class into small groups to discuss the articles. Students should answer questions such as these:

- What is the topic of the article?
- What problems are addressed?
- What discoveries have been made?

Students should notice similarities and differences in the ways scientific topics are reported. Ask volunteers to take notes while groups are speaking and then summarize the discussions.

After You Read

Respond and Think Critically

Respond and Interpret

1. What would you leave on a distant world to be found by an alien civilization? Why?

2. (a)Describe the setting of the story. Include details about daily life, as well as about people's ideas and values at the time. (b)What can you infer about life on the Moon from the setting's details?

3. (a)Why did the narrator experience "a strange, inexpressible joy" upon making his discovery? (b)Early in the story, the narrator states, "There is nothing hazardous or even particularly exciting about lunar exploration." Given the outcome of the story, what do you make of this statement?

Analyze and Evaluate

4. Why did the scientists try for twenty years to crack the shield surrounding the machine?

5. Why do you think Clarke chose not to give any definitive answers about the machine's origins or purpose?

6. In your opinion, was the use of atomic power against "the sentinel" appropriate, or should the scientists have left it intact? Explain.

Connect

7. **Big Idea** Our World and Beyond The narrator guesses that beings from other worlds left sentinels "watching over all worlds with the promise of life." Does this seem like a reasonable hypothesis? Explain.

8. **Connect to the Author** Many of the science-based ideas that Clarke wrote about have become realities. What concepts from this story have come true since it was published in 1951?

Visual Literacy

Timeline of a Mystery

As the mystery of "The Sentinel" unfolds, we slowly learn the narrator's hypothesis about the origin and purpose of the machine. The narrator describes his hypothesis in relationship to events in Earth's history. The timeline below marks events as described in the story. After studying the timeline, answer the following questions.

1. Roughly how much time passes between the formation of Earth and the aliens leaving "the sentinel" on the Moon?

2. In what year do humans discover "the sentinel"?

3. If you were going to add the date of the destruction of "the sentinel" to this timeline, where would you place it? Explain.

Story Timeline

Earth and Moon form.	Aliens leave "the sentinel" on the Moon.		First humans appear on Earth.		Humans discover "the sentinel."	
4.5 BYA	**2.5 BYA**	**1 BYA**	**2 MYA**	**A.D. 1**	**1996**	

BYA = billion years ago **MYA** = million years ago

Visual Literacy

1. About two billion years passed between the formation of Earth and the aliens' leaving of "the sentinel" on the Moon.

2. Humans discovered the sentinel in 1996.

3. Students' answers will vary.

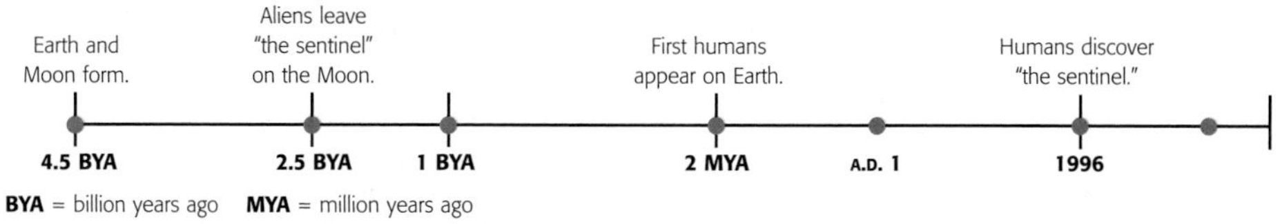

After You Read

Assess

1. Students should explain their choices.

2. (a) The story is set in an imaginary 1996 on the Moon. It is daytime and will remain light for "almost a week of Earth-time." The scientists assume that earthlings are the only intelligent beings there. When not exploring the Moon's surface, they live in their tractor. (b) The Moon seems silent, bleak, and lifeless.

3. (a) He loves the Moon and is glad it hosted an earlier civilization. He is happy to be the first to discover that fact. (b) Something exciting happens to a man who felt lunar exploration was unexciting.

4. They thought that by cracking the shield, they would release the machine's mysteries.

5. It adds to the mystery of the story and allows readers to use their own imaginations.

6. Students may think the use of atomic power was destructive and cowardly or that it was an appropriate action.

7. Students should provide support for their opinions.

8. Answers may vary. Students should support their answers with details from the text.

 For additional selection assessment, see Assessment Resources, pp. 209–210.

After You Read

Assess

Literary Element

1. Students' answers may include that the narrator says the glitter captivated him so thoroughly that he let breakfast burn.
2. The narrator's belief that he will find nothing makes the actual discovery more exciting. The fact that the narrator pursues his search despite his beliefs also builds suspense. His actions cause readers to ask, "What is going to happen?"

Progress Check

Can students identify suspense?

If No → See Unit 6 Teaching Resources Book, p. 27.

Review: Description

Students should fill their web diagrams with details from the story. Encourage students to select appropriate details and quotations from the story.

Reading Strategy

1. (a) The narrator's main motivation is scientific curiosity. He feels compelled to investigate it. (b) Without scientific curiosity, the narrator would not have made his unexpected and momentous discovery.
2. (a) The "sentinel" was erected on the Earth's moon in the hope that intelligent life would eventually evolve on Earth. (b) It ends the story with the intriguing expectation of an impending visit to Earth by an alien.

Literary Element Suspense

Authors use a variety of techniques to create **suspense** in their work. One technique is the use of foreshadowing, which provides clues to future events and allows readers to make guesses about the outcome.

1. The narrator is cooking breakfast on the morning of his discovery. What specific events and details in this scene add to the suspense of the story?
2. Several times in the story, the narrator says that he and others believed that nothing "strange or unusual" would be found on top of the mountain and that intelligent life had never existed on the Moon. Why might these statements be considered foreshadowing of discoveries to come? What do they add to the overall suspensefulness of the story?

Review: Description

As you learned on page 993, **description** is writing that helps readers picture settings, events, and characters. In "The Sentinel," Clarke provides vivid descriptions of elements such as the moonscape, the mysterious pyramid, and the actions of the astronauts. Strong description is especially important in science fiction and fantasy, which may have characters, settings, and actions that are totally unfamiliar to the reader.

Partner Activity With a classmate, choose a story element that Clarke describes in detail, such as the machine he finds. Create a web diagram like the one below, and record the details Clarke uses to describe the element.

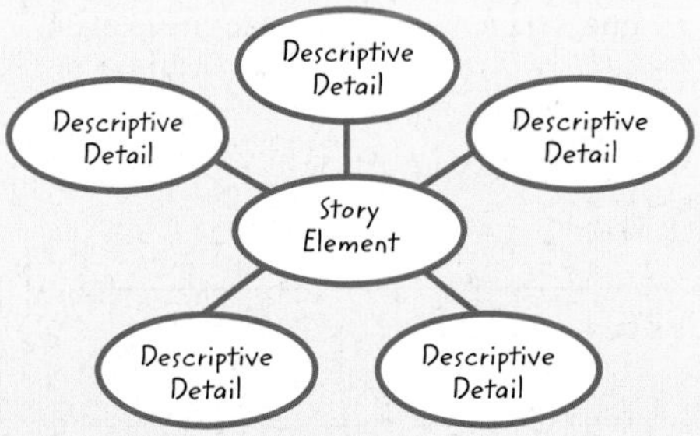

Reading Strategy Analyze Motivations

Refer to the chart you made while reading to help you answer the following questions.

1. At one point, the narrator says, "I'm going up there, if only for my own piece of mind." (a)How does this statement sum up the narrator's main motivation in the story? (b)How does this motivation set up the climax, or turning point, of the story?
2. (a)According to the narrator, what motivated the visitors from a distant galaxy to erect "the sentinel" on the Moon? (b)How does the narrator's speculation serve as an appropriate resolution to the plot of the story?

Vocabulary Practice

Practice with Analogies Choose the word that best completes each analogy.

1. tantalize : discourage :: pull :
   a. yank **b.** drop **c.** push
2. enigma : mystery :: answer :
   a. question **b.** solution **c.** maybe
3. work : relax :: ebb :
   a. flatten **b.** struggle **c.** increase
4. irrevocably : firmly :: similarly :
   a. identically **b.** differently **c.** closely

Academic Vocabulary

*Arthur C. Clarke combined imagination, **logic,** and science to create his visions of the future.*

Logic is an academic word. More familiar words with the same or similar meanings are *reason* and *sense.* Why would using **logic** help Clarke to make his futuristic stories more realistic?

For more on academic vocabulary, see pages 54–55 and R79–R81.

LOG ON **Literature** Online

Selection Resources For Selection Quizzes, eFlashcards, and Reading-Writing Connection activities, go to glencoe.com and enter QuickPass code GL49787u6.

Progress Check

Can students analyze motivations?

If No → See Unit 6 Teaching Resources Book, p. 28.

Vocabulary

1. c **2.** b **3.** c **4.** a

Academic Vocabulary

Sample answer: Because logic would help him to determine what the future would most likely be like—based on his knowledge of science and common sense.

Respond Through Writing

Research Report

Investigate Space Technology Research new technology that is being developed to help us better understand the universe. Then write a report of at least 1,500 words in which you describe the technology and discuss its potential uses. Use quotations to support your information.

Understand the Task When you **discuss** a topic in an essay or report, you present information on a variety of different aspects of the topic. Strong discussions present details and evidence that explore the topic.

Prewrite Begin by doing general research on space technology. Then choose one kind of technology and do further research on how it will help us better understand the universe. Organize your research and lay out a structure for your draft by creating an outline of the report. The outline should group information according to the report's main topics.

Draft Begin your draft with a thesis statement that summarizes the technology and its potential uses. Using your outline as a guide, present evidence from your research that supports and illustrates the thesis. As you introduce new evidence, note how it relates to the technology you are discussing.

When including evidence from your sources, it is important that it is accurately and clearly conveyed. If you need to convey an especially complicated idea, try using a longer quotation from one of your sources and inserting it directly into the text. In addition to quotations, use visual aids, such as diagrams or charts, to help explain complex ideas.

You should also discuss any fears or concerns that readers might have about the technology. Try to address misperceptions in a way that shows an understanding of conflicting views. Try using statements like this:

Some might object that ______, but I would reply that ______.

Revise Review your draft and make sure that all of the information you included directly supports or is relevant to your thesis. Even if a fact is interesting, do not include it if it does not relate to the thesis. During your revision, also make sure that all specific technical terms are correctly defined and used.

Edit and Proofread Proofread your paper, correcting any errors in spelling, grammar, and punctuation. Use the Grammar Tip in the side column to help you use ellipses correctly.

Learning Objectives

In this assignment, you will focus on the following objectives:

Writing: Writing a research report.

Grammar: Understanding how and when to use ellipses.

Grammar Tip

Ellipses

When inserting a long quotation from a source, start a new line and indent the quoted text. This is called a block quote. In the case of very long quotes, you can also use ellipses to conserve space and feature only the most relevant part of the quote. Ellipses (. . .) are inserted in place of text that has been omitted.

"The Phoenix Mars Lander . . . was launched by NASA in August 2007."

After You Read

Assess

Respond Through Writing

Students' reports should

- describe a space technology and discuss its potential uses
- present evidence to support discussion
- include direct quotes from source material
- use visual aids to explain complex ideas
- address concerns or fears regarding the technology
- be at least 1,500 words

For grammar practice, see Unit 6 Teaching Resources Book, p. 31.

To create custom assessments online, go to Progress Reporter Online Assessment.

To create custom assessments using software, use ExamView Assessment Suite.

Approaching Level

DIFFERENTIATED INSTRUCTION

Established Say: This story follows a man through an imaginary adventure. The author had to include concrete sensory details to help readers believe in his fictional world as they read the story. Have students identify sensory details and examples of imagery present in the selection. Students should explain how each example helps to enhance the story.

Focus

Summary

Roger Ebert reviews Stanley Kubrick's 1968 film *2001: A Space Odyssey.* Ebert considers the film's visual style, lack of action, and message.

Teach

Reading Strategy 1

Evaluate Argument Recall that an effective argument expresses an opinion and then supports it with reasons and evidence. Review the different kinds of evidence—facts, statistics, anecdotes, and personal experiences.

Cultural History ☆

Stanley Kubrick American filmmaker Stanley Kubrick (1928–1999) focused on detail and portrayed an ironic view. His films included political satire, works of literature, and antiwar statements.

For activities related to this selection, see Unit 6 Teaching Resources Book, pp. 34–42.

Readability Scores

Dale-Chall: 6.8
DRP: 62
Lexile: 940

Historical Perspective
on *The Sentinel*

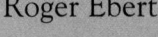

2001: A Space Odyssey

Roger Ebert

Learning Objectives

For pages 1008–1010

In studying this text, you will focus on the following objectives:

Reading:
Evaluating argument.
Connecting to historical documents.

Pulitzer Prize Winner

Set a Purpose for Reading

Read to discover how Roger Ebert supports his opinion of the film *2001: A Space Odyssey.*

Build Background

☆ The innovative film director Stanley Kubrick based many of his films on literary works. The screenplay for his movie *2001: A Space Odyssey* was based on Arthur C. Clarke's short story "The Sentinel." In fact, Kubrick collaborated with the science fiction writer on the project. The following selection is a review of the film by Roger Ebert.

Reading Strategy Evaluate Argument

Evaluating argument requires you to make a judgment about an author's opinion and how it is supported. Consider the evidence used by the author to support his or her opinion, as well as the author's chain of reasoning. As you read, ask yourself, Are the author's claims fully supported? Do I agree? Use a graphic organizer like the one below to take notes on Ebert's opinions and the support he provides for them. 1

Opinion	Support
the space ships are "out of scale with human concerns."	Ebert says the focus is on machines, not people.

1008 UNIT 6 GENRE FICTION

Listening and Speaking Practice

Evaluate a Review If students are not familiar with Kubrick's film *2001: A Space Odyssey,* they may benefit from viewing scenes that are described in Ebert's review. Show students excerpts from the film, including the scene of the apes as they encounter the monolith and a scene that highlights the movie's special effects, such as the final sequence. Invite students to jot down their responses. In a class discussion, have them compare their reactions to Ebert's.

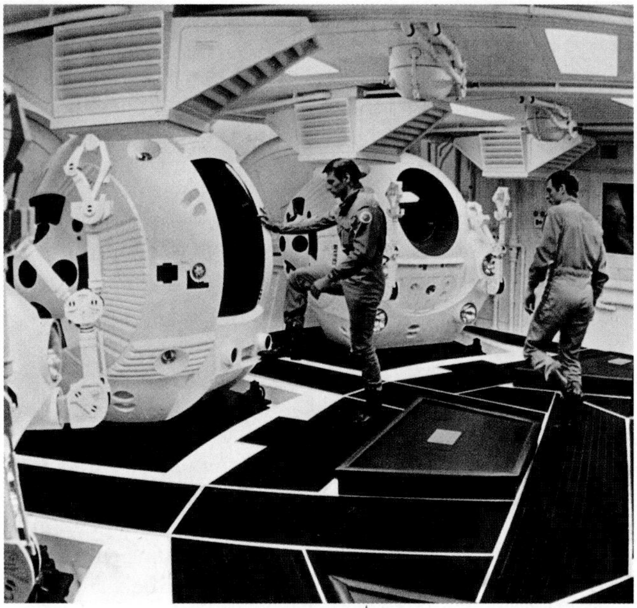

Scene from the film: *2001: A Space Odyssey.* ★

Chicago Sun-Times

April 12, 1968

It was e. e. cummings, the poet, who said he'd rather learn from one bird how to sing than teach 10,000 stars how not to dance. I imagine cummings would not have enjoyed Stanley Kubrick's *2001: A Space Odyssey,* in which stars dance but birds do not sing. The fascinating thing about this film is that it fails on the human level but succeeds magnificently on a cosmic scale.

Kubrick's universe, and the space ships he constructed to explore it, are simply out of scale with human concerns. The ships are perfect, impersonal machines which venture from one planet to another, and if men are tucked away somewhere inside them, then they get there too.

But the achievement belongs to the machine. And Kubrick's actors seem to sense this; they are lifelike but without emotion, like figures in a wax museum. Yet the machines are necessary because man himself is so helpless in the face of the universe.

Kubrick begins his film with a sequence in which one tribe of apes discovers how splendid it is to be able to hit the members of another tribe over the head. Thus do man's ancestors become tool-using animals.

At the same time, a strange monolith[1] appears on Earth. Until this moment in the film, we have seen only natural shapes: earth and sky and arms and legs. The shock of the monolith's straight edges and square corners among the weathered rocks is one of the most effective moments in the film. Here, you see, is perfection. The apes circle it warily, reaching out to touch, then jerking away. In a million years, man will reach for the stars with the same tentative motion.

Who put the monolith there? Kubrick never answers, for which I suppose we must be thankful. The action advances to
the year 2001, when explorers on the moon 2
find another of the monoliths. This one beams signals toward Jupiter. And man, confident of his machines, brashly follows the trail.

Only at this point does a plot develop. The ship is manned by two pilots, Keir Dullea and Gary Lockwood. Three scientists are put on board in suspended animation to conserve supplies. The pilots grow suspicious of the computer, "Hal," which runs the ship. But they behave so strangely—

1. *Monolith* means a large stone block.

English Learners

DIFFERENTIATED INSTRUCTION

Beginning Ebert's discursive style and cultural references may confuse less proficient readers. Have students identify the main idea in each paragraph of the review. Ask students to paraphrase the main ideas and to share their paraphrases with the class. If students disagree on the main idea of a paragraph, they should compare their ideas and come to an agreement.

Historical Perspective

on *The Sentinel*

Teach

Literary Element 2

Tone Point out that Ebert writes in a conversational tone. Draw students' attention to the second-to-last paragraph on page 1009, which begins with a question. Discuss how Ebert writes almost as if he's having a conversation with the reader. This highly readable style engages readers and is especially effective for a movie critic, whose job is not only to give opinions but also to inform readers about the content of the movie.

APPROACHING **Ask:** What other types of writing often use a conversational tone? *(Possible answers: informal articles, newspaper feature stories)*

View the Photograph ★

Stanley Kubrick's 1968 film *2001: A Space Odyssey* was loosely based upon Arthur C. Clarke's short story "The Sentinel." The movie was a collaboration between Kubrick and Clarke; Kubrick wrote the screenplay as Clarke wrote the novel *2001*.

Assess

1. Students' summaries should reflect the main ideas presented in the selection.
2. Students' answers will vary. Some may say that the review makes the film sound unappealing. Others may be interested in seeing how Clarke's short story was made into a film.
3. (a) Ebert thinks the movie lacks character development and suspense but keeps viewers' interest with fantastic special effects. (b) He supports his opinion by describing the dull way in which the characters speak and the convincing special effects: "The stars look like stars and outer space is bold and bleak."
4. (a) Ebert does not see any significance in the monolith. (b) He may be unfamiliar with the story. The monolith in the story was a pyramid that may have been built by intelligent life forms other than human beings.
5. The introductory paragraph is effective because Ebert captures the reader's attention with an intriguing quotation from e. e. cummings and ends the paragraph with a mix of criticism and praise.
6. Ebert says that "Kubrick's universe, and the space ships he constructed to explore it, are simply out of scale with human concerns." Today there are space stations. Ebert might now applaud Kubrick's imagination.
7. Students should support their answers with information from the selection.

talking in monotones like characters from *Dragnet*[2]—that we're hardly interested.

There is hardly any character development in the plot, then, and as a result little suspense. What remains fascinating is the fanatic care with which Kubrick has built his machines and achieved his special effects. There is not a single moment, in this long film, when the audience can see through the props. The stars look like stars and outer space is bold and bleak.

Some of Kubrick's effects have been criticized as tedious. Perhaps they are, but I can understand his motives. If his space vehicles move with agonizing precision, wouldn't we have laughed if they'd zipped around like props on *Captain Video*?[3] This is how it would really be, you find yourself believing.

In any event, all the machines and computers are forgotten in the astonishing last half-hour of this film, and man somehow comes back into his own. Another monolith is found beyond Jupiter, pointing to the stars. It apparently draws the spaceship into a universe where time and space are twisted.

Man will eventually outgrow his machines . . .

What Kubrick is saying, in the final sequence, apparently, is that man will eventually outgrow his machines, or be drawn beyond them by some cosmic awareness. He will then become a child again, but a child of an infinitely more advanced, more ancient race, just as apes once became, to their own dismay, the infant stage of man.

And the monoliths? Just road markers, I suppose, each one pointing to a destination so awesome that the traveler cannot imagine it without being transfigured. Or as cummings wrote on another occasion, "listen—there's a good universe next door; let's go."

2. *Dragnet* was a television police drama that aired from 1952 to 1959, and received high television ratings. The actors read from a teleprompter, contributing to their terse speech.
3. *Captain Video* is credited with being the first science fiction program aired on television. The series aired from 1949 to 1955.

Respond and Think Critically

Respond and Interpret

1. Write a brief summary of the main ideas in this review before you answer the following questions. For help on writing a summary, see page 421.
2. After reading this review, are you interested in seeing the film *2001: A Space Odyssey*? Why or why not?
3. (a)How does Ebert feel about the interest level of the film? (b)Does he support his opinion well? Explain.
4. (a)What does Ebert think of the monolith? (b)Do you think Ebert understood the context provided by Clarke's short story "The Sentinel"? Explain.

Analyze and Evaluate

5. Is Ebert's introductory paragraph effective? Explain.
6. Ebert wrote his review in 1968. Do you think his opinion of the film would be different today?
7. How well does Ebert support his opinion of the movie? What evidence does he point to? Is he persuasive?

Connect

8. Ebert says that there is "little suspense" in the film. Why might the use of suspense have been more effective in the story than in the film? Explain.

8. When Clarke wrote "The Sentinel," he wanted to captivate readers with the element of suspense, and so he wrote the story in such a way that readers would want to keep reading. Kubrick, on the other hand, was more interested in special effects than character development, and so he wasn't concerned with creating a suspenseful movie.

For additional selection assessment, see Assessment Resources, pp. 211–212.

Grammar Workshop

Commas with Items in a Series

Literature Connection This sentence includes items in a series.

> *"When our world was half its present age, something from the stars swept through the Solar System, left this token of its passage, and went again upon its way."*
>
> —Arthur C. Clarke, "The Sentinel"

The phrases that make up the series, "swept through the Solar System," "left this token of its passage," and "went again upon its way," are verb phrases. A verb phrase is a verb followed by a direct object and/or prepositional phrases. Notice how a comma follows each phrase; the comma separates one phrase in the series from the next. A series can consist of single words, phrases, or clauses.

Review these problems with commas in a series and their solutions.

Problem 1 There are no commas separating words in a series.

The narrator is curious daring and energetic.

Solution Use a comma after each word in the series that precedes the coordinating conjunction.

The narrator is curious, daring, and energetic.

Problem 2 There are no commas separating clauses in a series.

Each morning the lunar explorers awake at 0600 hours they prepare breakfast and they switch on the shortwave radio.

Solution Use a comma after each clause in the series that precedes the coordinating conjunction.

Each morning the lunar explorers awake at 0600 hours, they prepare breakfast, and they switch on the shortwave radio.

Revise Rewrite each sentence, adding commas and conjunctions as needed.

1. The freighters delivered supplies equipment and personnel.
2. The explorers left their vehicle to examine the landscape to hunt for interesting minerals and to place markers for future travelers.
3. The narrator was inquisitive he was brave and he was unprepared for what he discovered.

Learning Objectives

In this workshop, you will focus on the following objective:

Grammar: Understanding how to use commas with items in a series.

Vocabulary Terms

A **series** is a group of parallel items, such as three adjectives, four infinitive phrases, or three independent clauses in a row.

Tip

When proofreading your writing, check for commas that separate items in a series. If these commas are missing, the sentence may be unclear to your reader.

Language Handbook

For more about commas, see Language Handbook, pp. R52 and R54.

LOG ON Literature Online

Grammar For more grammar practice, go to glencoe.com and enter QuickPass code GL49787u6.

Approaching Level

DIFFERENTIATED INSTRUCTION

Established Write: *It had been leveled to support a glittering, pyramidal structure, twice as high as a man, that was set in the rock like a gigantic, many-faceted jewel.* Ask students to point out which commas separate words in a series. *(glittering, pyramidal structure; gigantic, many-faceted jewel)*

Focus

Write the following sentence on the board: The narrator sees the shiny glittering object decides to discover it and reaches a disturbing conclusion. Discuss why the lack of commas makes the sentence hard to understand.

Teach

Using Commas in a Series

Offer this strategy for placing commas.

Say: Try saying *and* between words, phrases, or clauses in a series. If the word *and* makes sense, then insert a comma between the words, phrases, or clauses.

Assess

1. The freighters delivered supplies, equipment, and personnel.
2. The explorers left their vehicle to examine the landscape, to hunt for interesting minerals, and to place markers for future travelers.
3. The narrator was inquisitive, he was brave, and he was unprepared for what he discovered.

For additional grammar practice, see Unit 6 Teaching Resources Book, p. 43.

Before You Read

Focus

Bellringer Options

Literature Launchers: Pre-Reading Videos DVD, Selection Launcher

Selection Focus Transparency 37

Daily Language Practice Transparency 95

Or show images of trash (such as trash bins or landfills). **Say:** Each generation hopes that the following generation will solve the problem of how to get rid of waste. **Ask:** How do you think your generation will solve problems it inherits, such as landfills and nuclear waste?

As they read, have students consider whether the people in the village make the right decision about the hole.

Before You Read

World Literature
Japan

He—y, Come on Ou—t!

Meet **Shinichi Hoshi**
(1926–1997)

Shinichi Hoshi is considered the grandfather of Japanese science fiction. As a result of the U.S. post–World War II occupation of Japan, American science fiction paperbacks circulated throughout Japan. By the late 1940s, the genre was amazingly popular. However, while there were numerous translations of American writers, there was a noticeable lack of original Japanese science fiction. When Hoshi began publishing his short stories in the late 1950s, he helped usher in a new era of original Japanese science fiction.

> *"Everyone disliked thinking about the eventual consequences."*
>
> —Shinichi Hoshi, from "*He—y, Come on Ou—t!*"

Short-Short Stories Hoshi was born in Tokyo and grew up in the house of his grandparents, Koganei Yoshikiyo, an anthropologist, and Kimiko. He studied agricultural chemistry at Tokyo University and, at the age of twenty-three, took over as president of his family's pharmaceutical company when his father died. After selling the company, Hoshi joined the Japan Flying Saucer Research Club and began writing science fiction. Hoshi published his first story in 1957, when "Sekisutora" was selected for inclusion in the magazine *Hôseki* (The Jewel).

Hoshi focused on writing short-short stories and made them his specialty. His distinctive short-shorts were usually more abstract, focusing mainly on the story line and minimizing description. His prose has been described as uniquely Japanese and his stories have been likened to haiku—sparse, simple, and indispensable. His work became known for combining a deep human understanding and social criticism with strange, surprising, and twisting tales.

1,001 Tales His first collection, *Jinzô bijîn* (An Artificial Beauty, 1961), was nominated for the Naoki Prize, and his collection *Môsô ginkô* (The Delusion Bank, 1968) won the Japan Mystery Writers Award. After finishing his 1,001st story in 1983, Hoshi put down his pen, saying, "One thousand and one stories are enough."

Hoshi also wrote several highly regarded longer works. These included the science fiction novel *Koe no ami* (A Net of Voices, 1971) and the biographies *Jinmin wa yowashi, kanri wa tsuyoshi* (The People Are Weak, Bureaucracy Is Strong, 1968), about Hoshi's father, and *Sôfu: Koganei Yoshikiyo no ki* (My Grandfather: An Account of Koganei Yoshikiyo, 1975).

LOG ON **Literature** Online

Author Search For more about Shinichi Hoshi, go to glencoe.com and enter QuickPass code GL49787u6.

Selection Skills

He—y, Come on Ou—t!

Literary Elements
- Moral (SE pp. 1013–1018)
- Character (SE p. 1018)

Listening/Speaking/Viewing Skills
- Analyze Art (SE p. 1017; TE p. 1014)
- Speech (SE p. 1019)

Reading Skills
- Connect to Contemporary Issues (SE pp. 1013–1019)

Vocabulary Skills
- Antonyms (SE pp. 1013, 1019)

Study Skills/Research/Assessment
- Track Society's Waste (TE p. 1016)

Literature and Reading Preview

Connect to the Story

What is your first reaction when you encounter something that you know nothing about? Write a journal entry describing a time when you encountered something unknown to you.

Build Background

"He—y, Come on Ou—t!" provides a unique perspective on a growing environmental issue: the disposal of waste materials. Unrecyclable solid wastes are incinerated (burned), buried in landfills, or sometimes illegally dumped in oceans or rivers. All of these disposal methods, however, contribute to air, water, and soil pollution, and many landfills are nearing their capacity.

Set Purposes for Reading

Big Idea Our World and Beyond

As you read, ask yourself, What are realistic elements and what are fantastic elements in this story?

Literary Element Moral

A **moral** is a practical lesson about right and wrong conduct, often found in fables and parables. A **parable** is a simple story that is intended to teach a lesson about human behavior or society. As you read, ask yourself, What are the smaller moral lessons or social commentary within the story that support the larger or overall moral?

Reading Strategy Connect to Contemporary Issues

Connecting a story to events and issues in today's world can help you understand the author's message. As you read, ask yourself, How do the events in the story relate to issues in the real world today?

Tip: Make the Link As you read, use a chart to record at least three significant issues or problems that the story raises. After you read, note issues from today's world that relate to each issue in the story.

Issue from Story	Related Issue from Today
Human greed	

Learning Objectives

For pages 1012–1019

In studying this text, you will focus on the following objectives:

Literary Study: Analyzing moral.

Reading: Connecting to contemporary issues.

Speaking and Listening: Presenting an explanatory speech.

Vocabulary

plausible (plô′ zə bəl) *adj.* apparently true or acceptable; likely; p. 1015 *The scientist had the most experience and his explanation was the most plausible.*

disperse (dis purs′) *v.* to go off in different directions; to scatter; p. 1015 *When the police arrived, the unruly crowd began to disperse.*

cohort (kō′ hôrt) *n.* a companion, associate, or member of the same group; p. 1016 *Even if it meant that she would be caught and sent to jail, Evelyn promised that she wouldn't leave her cohort behind.*

reverie (rev′ ər ē) *n.* fanciful thinking, especially of pleasant things; a daydream; p. 1017 *He tried to get her attention, but she was lost in reverie.*

Tip: Antonyms Like synonyms, antonyms must also be the same part of speech. For example, the vocabulary word *plausible* can only be an antonym to another adjective, such as *ridiculous.*

Approaching Level

DIFFERENTIATED INSTRUCTION

Emerging To prepare students to read the story, **ask:** Has anyone ever offered you an easy solution to a big problem? What sort of trouble do people encounter when they take the easy way out of their problems? *(Possible answer: Easy solutions are often only temporary.)*

Established Ask students to provide an example of a moral presented in a story. Students should briefly summarize a story and then reveal the moral of the story.

Before You Read

Focus

Summary

In the aftermath of a typhoon, the people of a small Japanese village discover a mysterious hole at the site of a destroyed shrine. The hole seems endlessly deep, and the people decide to use it for waste disposal—a decision they will live to regret.

For summaries in languages other than English, see Unit 6 Teaching Resources Book, pp. 44–49.

Vocabulary

Word Clues Explain that word puzzles are so popular that they appear daily in most American newspapers. Read a few clues from the crossword puzzle in your local paper and have students guess the correct answers. Then have students create their own crossword clues for the vocabulary words. Encourage volunteers to share their clues, and ask other students to guess the answers.

For additional vocabulary practice, see Unit 6 Teaching Resources Book, p. 52.

Teach

Big Idea 1

Our World and Beyond

Answer: *The story is set in a village in modern times, but the mysterious hole seems to come from another world.*

Say: Science fiction is often set in the real world, but the events that take place would be impossible in the world as we know it.

Readability Scores

Dale-Chall: 7.7
DRP: 55
Lexile: 890

He—y, Come on Ou—t!

In the Pit II, 1987. Evelyn Williams. Charcoal & chalks on paper. Private collection.

Shinichi Hoshi
translated by Stanleigh H. Jones

The typhoon had passed and the sky was a gorgeous blue. Even a certain village not far from the city had suffered damage. A little distance from the village and near the mountains, a small shrine[1] had been swept away by a landslide.

"I wonder how long that shrine's been here."

"Well, in any case, it must have been here since an awfully long time ago."

"We've got to rebuild it right away."

While the villagers exchanged views, several more of their number came over.

"It sure was wrecked."

"I think it used to be right here."

"No, looks like it was a little more over there."

Just then one of them raised his voice. "Hey, what in the world is this hole?"

Where they had all gathered there was a hole about a meter in diameter. They peered in, but it was so dark nothing could be seen. However, it gave one the feeling

1. A *shrine* is any site or structure used in worship or devotion.

1 Our World and Beyond *What does the setting of this story have in common with the world you know? What is different?*

Vocabulary Practice

SPIRAL REVIEW **Latin Roots** **Say:** The word *parable* comes from the Latin *parabola* and the Greek *parabole,* both of which mean "a comparison." Explain that a parable teaches a lesson that readers can apply to their lives. In other words, readers can compare the problems of the story with problems in their own lives. Give small groups of students a Latin or Greek root to research. Instruct them to identify the meaning of the root and identify three English words using the root. Have each group share their findings with the class.

that it was so deep it went clear through to the center of the earth.

There was even one person who said, "I wonder if it's a fox's hole."

"He—y, come on ou—t!" shouted a young man into the hole. There was no echo from the bottom. Next he picked up a pebble and was about to throw it in.

"You might bring down a curse on us. Lay off," warned an old man, but the younger one energetically threw the pebble in. As before, however, there was no answering response from the bottom. The villagers cut down some trees, tied them with rope and made a fence which they put around the hole. Then they repaired[2] to the village.

"What do you suppose we ought to do?"

"Shouldn't we build the shrine up just as it was over the hole?"

A day passed with no agreement. The news traveled fast, and a car from the newspaper company rushed over. In no time a scientist came out, and with an all-knowing expression on his face he went over to the hole. Next, a bunch of gawking curiosity seekers showed up; one could also pick out here and there men of shifty glances who appeared to be concessionaires.[3] Concerned that someone might fall into the hole, a policeman from the local substation kept a careful watch.

One newspaper reporter tied a weight to the end of a long cord and lowered it into the hole. A long way down it went. The cord ran out, however, and he tried to pull it out, but it would not come back up. Two or three people helped out, but when they all pulled too hard, the cord parted at the edge of the hole. Another reporter, a camera in hand, who had been watching all of this, quietly untied a stout rope that had been wound around his waist. ☆

The scientist contacted people at his laboratory and had them bring out a high-powered bullhorn, with which he was going to check out the echo from the hole's bottom. He tried switching through various sounds, but there was no echo. The scientist was puzzled, but he could not very well give up with everyone watching him so intently. He put the bullhorn right up to the hole, turned it to its highest volume, and let it sound continuously for a long time. It was a noise that would have carried several dozen kilometers above ground. But the hole just calmly swallowed up the sound.

Visual Vocabulary
A *bullhorn* is a handheld microphone combined with a speaker that is used to communicate to a large group of people.

In his own mind the scientist was at a loss, but with a look of apparent composure he cut off the sound and, in a manner suggesting that the whole thing had a perfectly **plausible** explanation, said simply, "Fill it in."

Safer to get rid of something one didn't understand.

The onlookers, disappointed that this was all that was going to happen, prepared to **disperse.** Just then one of the concession-

2. In this context, *repaired* means simply "went."
3. *Concessionaires* (kən sesh′ ə nārz′) are business owners or operators.

2 Connect to Contemporary Issues *In what ways does this paragraph reflect how modern events unfold in the real world?*

Vocabulary

plausible (plô′ zə bəl) *adj.* apparently true or acceptable; likely

disperse (dis purs′) *v.* to go off in different directions; to scatter

Teach

Reading Strategy 2

Connect to Contemporary Issues **Answer:** *News spreads quickly in the modern world; just one day after the discovery of the hole, the media arrived, as well as a scientist and a group of curiosity seekers.*

Writer's Technique ☆

Understatement Hoshi's subtle use of detail and understatement creates humor. The first part of the paragraph shows how people discover that the hole is extremely deep and that objects cannot be retrieved from it. The last detail of a reporter removing a rope from his waist implies that he has changed his mind about being lowered into the hole.

Interactive Read and Write

Other options for teaching this selection can be found in

- Interactive Read and Write for EL Students, pp. 303–312
- Interactive Read and Write for Approaching-Level Students, pp. 303–312
- Interactive Read and Write for On-Level Students, pp. 303–312

English Learners

DIFFERENTIATED INSTRUCTION

Early Advanced Write the following words on the board: *scientists, officials, functionaries, authorities, concessionaires, mayor, citizens, police officers, vagrants, students,* and *criminals*. While some of these words will be familiar to English learners, others will not. As they read the story, students should look for the words and write down the sentences in which the words first appear. Instruct them to also note the page number. Students should use context clues and their knowledge of affixes and roots to figure out the meanings of unfamiliar words.

Teach

Literary Element 1

Moral **Answer:** *Students may be surprised by the concessionaire's decision to get rid of nuclear waste at a site so close to a shrine.*

Reading Strategy 2

Connect to Contemporary Issues **Answer:** *The hole provides the perfect answer to the community's waste disposal problems. Landfills play a similar role in the real world. Garbage is put in landfills and forgotten. People don't think about garbage once it has been dumped.*

aires, having broken through the throng and come forward, made a proposal.

"Let me have that hole. I'll fill it in for you."

"We'd be grateful to you for filling it in," replied the mayor of the village, "but we can't very well give you the hole. We have to build a shrine there."

"If it's a shrine you want, I'll build you a fine one later. Shall I make it with an attached meeting hall?"

Before the mayor could answer, the people of the village all shouted out.

"Really? Well, in that case, we ought to have it closer to the village."

"It's just an old hole. We'll give it to you!"

So it was settled. And the mayor, of course, had no objection.

The concessionaire was true to his promise. It was small, but closer to the village he did build for them a shrine and an attached meeting hall.

About the time the autumn festival was held at the new shrine, the hole-filling company established by the concessionaire hung out its small shingle at a shack near the hole.

The concessionaire had his **cohorts** mount a loud campaign in the city. "We've got a fabulously deep hole! Scientists say it's at least five thousand meters deep! Perfect for the disposal of such things as waste from nuclear reactors."

Government authorities granted permission. Nuclear power plants fought for contracts. The people of the village were a bit worried about this, but they consented when it was explained that there would be absolutely no above-ground contamination for several thousand years and that they would share in the profits. Into the bargain, very shortly a magnificent road was built from the city to the village.

Trucks rolled in over the road, transporting lead boxes. Above the hole the lids were opened, and the wastes from nuclear reactors tumbled away into the hole.

From the Foreign Ministry and the Defense Agency boxes of unnecessary classified documents were brought for disposal. Officials who came to supervise the disposal held discussions on golf. The lesser functionaries,[4] as they threw in the papers, chatted about pinball.

The hole showed no signs of filling up. It was awfully deep, thought some; or else it might be very spacious at the bottom. Little by little the hole-filling company expanded its business.

Bodies of animals used in contagious disease experiments at the universities were brought out, and to these were added the unclaimed corpses of vagrants.[5] Better than dumping all of its garbage in the ocean, went the thinking in the city, and plans were made for a long pipe to carry it to the hole.

The hole gave peace of mind to the dwellers of the city. They concentrated solely on producing one thing after another. Everyone disliked thinking about the eventual consequences. People wanted only to work for production companies and sales corporations; they had no interest in becoming junk dealers. But, it was thought, these problems too would gradually be resolved by the hole.

1 Moral *Is this how you expected the concessionaire to fill the hole? Explain.*

Vocabulary

cohort (kō′ hôrt) *n.* a companion, associate, or member of the same group

4. *Functionaries* are also officials.
5. *Vagrants* (vā′ grənts) are people who, whether by choice or by circumstance, are without homes and jobs and who wander from place to place, often supporting themselves by begging.

Connect to Contemporary Issues *What role does the hole come to play in this community? What plays a similar role in the real world?* **2**

Research Practice

SPIRAL REVIEW **Track Society's Waste** Students may be interested in learning more about the garbage their community makes and throws out. Encourage students to use a search engine to find information on waste-related Web sites by typing in the word *garbage, trash,* or *waste.* Challenge students to use the sites and other sources of information to find out more about where local waste products and trash go. Ask students to share their findings in an oral report or visual presentation. Follow up the presentations with a discussion on how well their community handles waste.

The Messenger. René Magritte. Private collection. ©ARS, NY.

View the Art What might the objects in this sphere represent? In light of this story, what might the sphere itself symbolize? What connection can you draw between the title of the painting and the story's ending? ★

Young girls whose betrothals[6] had been arranged discarded old diaries in the hole. There were also those who were inaugurating new love affairs and threw into the hole old photographs of themselves taken with former sweethearts. The police felt comforted as they used the hole to get rid of accumulations of expertly done counterfeit bills. Criminals breathed easier after throwing material evidence[7] into the hole.

Whatever one wished to discard, the hole accepted it all. The hole cleansed the city of its filth; the sea and sky seemed to have become a bit clearer than before.

Aiming at the heavens, new buildings went on being constructed one after the other. One day, atop the high steel frame of a new building under construction, a workman was taking a break. Above his head he heard a voice shout:

"He—y, come on ou—t!"

But, in the sky to which he lifted his gaze there was nothing at all. A clear blue sky merely spread over all. He thought it must be his imagination. Then, as he resumed his former position, from the direction where the voice had come, a small pebble skimmed by him and fell on past.

The man, however, was gazing in idle[8] **reverie** at the city's skyline growing ever more beautiful, and he failed to notice. ❧

6. Their parents had arranged the girls' *betrothals* (bi trō′ thəlz), or engagements to be married.
7. *Material evidence* would be any object that could directly connect a criminal to a crime.

8. Here, *idle* means "useless."

Moral *How might this ending be seen as a warning?* **3**

Vocabulary

reverie (rev′ ər ē) *n.* fanciful thinking, especially of pleasant things; a daydream

Teach

Literary Element 3

Moral **Answer:** *It warns that actions have consequences that will force us to take notice eventually.*

View the Art ★

Answer: *The objects might represent society's garbage. The sphere might symbolize the earth buried in trash. Both might warn about controlling our wastes. The garbage sphere is like the pebble in the story's ending.*

René Magritte (1898–1967) was a prominent Surrealist painter. His art blends fantasy, horror, humor, and danger.

To check students' understanding of the selection, see Unit 6 Teaching Resources Book, p. 55.

Approaching Level

DIFFERENTIATED INSTRUCTION

Emerging Students may benefit from listing, in order, the things thrown into the hole. Suggest that students use the list to get a sense of the sequence and significance of disposed items. At the end of the story, have students consult their list to predict what may happen next.

Established Have students paraphrase the Hoshi's message in this story. *(We cannot escape our past. If we don't solve problems but rather sweep them under the rug, they wil come back to haunt us.)* **Ask:** Is this message still relevant today?

After You Read

Assess

1. Most students will be surprised by the shout and the pebble falling from the sky.
2. (a) They are afraid and want to fill it in or fence it off. (b) They want to know more about the hole.
3. (a) He promises them a new shrine and meeting hall. (b) He knows the hole will be more valuable than the shrine.
4. The pebble is the first thing thrown into the hole and the first to fall from the sky at the end. Its appearance at the end recalls the old man's warning at the start.
5. Students may not have expected the pebble to fall out of the sky; the hole defies the laws of physics.
6. People from all walks of life put things into the hole.
7. The setting helps connect the story's problems to the real-world problem of waste.
8. Hoshi combines the understanding that humans wish to find easy solutions to their problems with the social criticism that easy solutions are not the best solutions.

Literary Element

1. A is the correct answer. The story suggests that all of the waste thrown into the hole will return to bury civilization.
2. G is the correct answer. The pebble reminds the reader of the very first object thrown into the hole. The remaining waste will almost certainly follow.

After You Read

Respond and Think Critically

Respond and Interpret

1. Were you surprised by the ending? Why or why not?
2. (a)What is the villagers' first reaction to the hole? (b)Why do the villagers try to measure the hole?
3. (a)How does the concessionaire convince the villagers to let him have the hole? (b)Why is the concessionaire willing to make this offer?

Analyze and Evaluate

4. How does Hoshi use the pebble to connect the beginning of the story to the end of the story?
5. How effective is Hoshi in creating unexpected twists in the story? Explain.
6. How does Hoshi show us that all of society is responsible for what happened to the hole?

Connect

7. **Big Idea** **Our World and Beyond** Why do you think Hoshi chose to place the story in a contemporary setting instead of a more unusual science fiction setting?
8. **Connect to the Author** Hoshi was known for combining human understanding and social criticism. What is his main combination of understanding and criticism in this story?

Literary Element Moral

ACT Skills Practice

1. What is the implied moral of "He—y, Come on Ou—t!"?
   - A. Every action has a consequence.
   - B. Hard work has its rewards.
   - C. Some things are better left unexplored.
   - D. Everything has a purpose.
2. What event from the story leads the reader to understand the moral?
   - F. The sea and sky become cleaner than before.
   - G. A pebble whizzes past the head of a construction worker.
   - H. A concessionaire purchases the hole.
   - J. A weight lowered into the hole does not come back up.

Review: Character

As you learned on pages 96–97, a **character** is a person portrayed in a literary work. In fables and parables, characters are typically flat or one-dimensional because they are intended to represent a type of person or part of society.

Partner Activity With a partner, identify the characters in the story. Together, examine what part of society each character might represent. Using a chart like the one below, record the characters and what part of society they represent.

Character	Part of Society

LOG ON Literature Online

Selection Resources For Selection Quizzes, eFlashcards, and Reading-Writing Connection activities, go to glencoe.com and enter QuickPass code GL49787u6.

Progress Check

Can students identify moral?

If No → See Unit 6 Teaching Resources Book, p. 50.

Review: Character

young man, old man, worker	ordinary citizens
scientist and reporter	educated authorities
concessionaire	money maker
mayor	local authority

Reading Strategy Connect to Contemporary Issues

After identifying the **contemporary issues connected** to the story, you can determine what the author's message is in regard to those issues. The author usually reveals his or her criticism or opinion through the events of the story. For example, if a story about people and technology ends with the technology saving the people, the author probably thinks that technology is good for society. Refer to the chart you made while reading, and then answer the following questions.

1. In "He—y, Come on Ou—t!" the pebble does not drop from the sky until long after it is thrown into the hole. (a)What is Hoshi's criticism in regard to waste disposal and protecting the environment? (b)Do you agree or disagree with Hoshi's commentary?
2. Based on what happens in the story, what action do you think Hoshi would want us to take in order to prevent the catastrophe created by the villagers in the story?

Vocabulary Practice

Practice with Antonyms An **antonym** is a word that has a meaning opposite to that of another word. With a partner, match each boldface vocabulary word below with its antonym. You will not use all the answer choices. Use a thesaurus or dictionary to check your answers.

1. plausible	a. united
2. disperse	b. enemy
3. cohort	c. gather
4. reverie	d. excuse
	e. unlikely
	f. concentration
	g. scatter

Speaking and Listening

Speech

Assignment Imagine that the construction worker does *not* fail to notice the amazing occurrence at the end of the story. Instead, he reports to a scientist exactly what happened. As the scientist, develop a theory about what happened and explain it in a speech to the class.

Prepare Develop your theory about what happened and divide it into three parts for your speech:

- First, identify the signs of trouble and what the problem is.
- Second, explain why it is happening and what future problems it could cause.
- Third, present a possible response to the problem.

Develop the first part of your speech into an engaging introduction that immediately grabs listeners. Use strong transitions between the three main sections of your speech. Transitions should smoothly and logically lead into the next section and help to maintain listeners' interest.

Create visual aids that support or illustrate your theory. For example, you could create a large diagram that shows where the garbage is going in and where it is coming out.

Deliver Engage your audience by making eye contact and using gestures to emphasize important points. Make sure to speak loudly and clearly so the audience can understand you.

Evaluate While your performance is still fresh in your mind, write a paragraph evaluating your speech. Was it engaging? Did you present your ideas clearly? Was your delivery strong?

After You Read

Assess

Reading Strategy

1. (a) We should be cautious because we may not know what consequences will result from things we do now. (b) Students' responses should be based on their understanding of real events.
2. People today should produce less waste and learn more about the effects of the waste that we are disposing.

Progress Check

Can students connect to contemporary issues?

If No → See Unit 6 Teaching Resources Book, p. 51.

Vocabulary Practice

1. e **2.** c **3.** b **4.** f

For additional selection assessment, see Assessment Resources, pp. 213–214.

To create custom assessments online, go to Progress Reporter Online Assessment.

To create custom assessments using software, use ExamView Assessment Suite.

Speaking and Listening

Students' speeches should

- present a theory about what happened at the end of the story
- present their theory in three parts
- use an engaging introduction and transitions
- use visual aids to support their theory
- be delivered in a clear, confident, engaging manner

Focus

Bellringer Options

Daily Language Practice Transparency 96

Or **ask:** What are some of the biggest changes you have gone through? How did you feel about these changes? How do these changes affect your future? Tell students that the characters in the following selections face changes in their lives. As students read, encourage them to compare their feelings about change with those of the characters in the selections.

Connect to the Reading Selections

Allow students to share their responses to the opening questions. Then have students discuss what they already know about Nancy Kress, Naomi Long Madgett, and Alan Lightman.

Comparing Literature

Across Genres

Learning Objectives

For pages 1020–1033

In studying these texts, you will focus on the following objectives:

Literary Study: Analyzing dialogue.

Reading: Comparing and contrasting characters. Comparing description. Comparing ideas.

Writing: Writing a pamphlet.

Compare Literature About Time and Memory

What memories do you cherish? Which ones would you like to forget? To some degree, our memories influence who we are and what we do. The three works compared here—a science fiction story and two poems by American writers—explore connections, strong and subtle, between past and present.

COMPARE THE Big Idea Our World and Beyond

The past is important in each of these selections, whether the characters are living in a world we find familiar or a world with different rules. As you read, ask yourself, How would you describe the world that each author creates?

COMPARE Description

Description is an author's portrayal of characters, places, objects, or events. Good descriptive writing helps the reader imagine what the characters are experiencing in a story or poem. As you read, ask yourself, What sensory images in the works by Kress, Lee, and Madgett create new worlds for the reader to explore?

COMPARE Ideas

You can infer an author's ideas about a subject by analyzing the tone, mood, and theme of a literary work. As you read "In Memoriam," "The Gift," and "Purchase," ask yourself, How would you compare these authors' ideas about memory and time?

LOG ON **Literature** Online

Author Search For more about the authors, go to glencoe.com and enter QuickPass code GL49787u6.

Reading Practice

Compare Selections Have students develop a graphic organizer to aid in comparing the selections. Instruct students to make a chart with four columns labeled as follows: *Selection Title, Familiar or Different World, Description,* and *Theme*. Students should include specific details in their organizers and page numbers for reference.

Before You Read

In Memoriam

Meet **Nancy Kress**
(born 1948)

Nancy Kress never read science fiction as a child or even took high school chemistry. But when she decided to ☆ pick up writing as a hobby, "it came out science fiction."

A shy child, Kress loved reading, telling stories, and playing in the woods near her family's home in East Aurora, New York. As a teenager, she read Nancy Drew, Zane Grey, and Jane Austen, who would later influence her writing style. Kress chose teaching as a profession. She taught fourth grade for several years before leaving the profession to marry and raise children.

From Fantasy to Sci-Fi While at home with her sons during the day, Kress turned to writing as a way to relax and "explore reality." Her first novel, *Prince of the Morning Bells* (1981), was a lighthearted fantasy about a young princess and an enchanted dog. Kress never gave up trying to find a publisher for her manuscript, even though five years passed before it was accepted for publication.

By 1990 Kress was working full-time as a writer. Her first major success was the novella *Beggars in Spain* (1991), which explores a world of genetically modified humans who never need sleep. According to Kress, who requires nine hours of sleep a night, the idea for the book came from her "sheer jealousy" of people who get by on much less. Later, Kress expanded the novella into a novel and then into a trilogy that includes the novels *Beggars and Choosers* (1994) and *Beggars Ride* (1996).

Making Her Mark For the novella *Beggars in Spain,* Kress won a Nebula Award and a Hugo Award. These awards honor groundbreaking work in science fiction and fantasy. She also won two Nebula awards for short fiction in 1985 and 1997. Kress remains one of the leading science fiction writers of the day.
The topics of her novels and stories include genetic engineering, biological weapons, poverty, and alien life forms.

> *"[In science fiction,] the setting can be specifically chosen to throw into sharp relief those aspects of human nature which concern the writer."*
>
> —Nancy Kress

In 2002, Kress lost her second husband, fellow science fiction writer Charles Sheffield. She moved back to Rochester, New York, to live near her grown children. When she is not writing fiction, she writes a monthly fiction column for *Writer's Digest* magazine and teaches at the Clarion Science Fiction and Fantasy Writers' Workshop at Michigan State University.

Comparing Literature

Before You Read

Focus

Writer's Technique ☆

Kress's Hobby Kress began writing as a hobby because she was not good at needlework. Even though her writing began as a hobby, it turned into a highly successful career. Kress has more than 70 short stories and 18 books to her credit.

Selection Skills

Comparing Literature

Literary Elements
- Dialogue (SE pp. 1022–1029)

Listening/Speaking/Viewing Skills
- Analyze Art (SE pp. 1027)
- Visual Display (SE p. 1033)

Reading Skills
- Compare and Contrast Characters (SE pp. 1022–1029)

Vocabulary Skills
- Word Usage (SE pp. 1022, 1029)

Writing Skills/Grammar
- Write a Pamphlet (SE p. 1029)
- Write a Summary (TE p. 1028)

Comparing Literature

Before You Read

Focus

Summary

This story is set in the future, at a time when people's memories can be wiped away so that they can live longer. Mrs. Kinnian argues with her son Aaron because he wants her to have her memory erased so that she will not die. Mrs. Kinnian believes that having her memory wiped would be a death in itself. Aaron plans to have his own memory wiped so that he can continue living.

For summaries in languages other than English, see Unit 6 Teaching Resources Book, pp. 58–63.

Vocabulary

Flash Cards Have students write each of the vocabulary words on a separate index card, with the definition on the other side. Pair up students and have them quiz each other using the cards. Then quiz students on the meaning of each vocabulary word.

Literature and Reading Preview

Connect to the Story

How much does your past define who you are? Write a journal entry about an event that has had a lasting impact on your life.

Build Background

The phrase *in memoriam* means "in memory of." It is a phrase often found on gravestones. Stories from many cultures tell of quests to be rejuvenated, or made youthful and vigorous again. Research continues for processes and products that will slow the signs and effects of aging.

Set Purposes for Reading

Big Idea Our World and Beyond

As you read, ask yourself, How is the future world of this story different from the world we know today?

Literary Element Dialogue

Dialogue is the conversation between characters in a literary work. It can contribute to characterization, create a mood, advance the plot, and develop the theme. As you read, ask yourself, What does the dialogue reveal about each character and his or her relationships with the other characters?

Reading Strategy Compare and Contrast Characters

Characters are the people who appear in a literary work. A **main character** is central to the work, while a **minor character** may appear only to help develop the story or act as a contrast to the main character. As you read, ask yourself, How is each character similar to or different from other characters?

Tip: Take Notes Use a Venn diagram to help you recognize important similarities and differences between the characters.

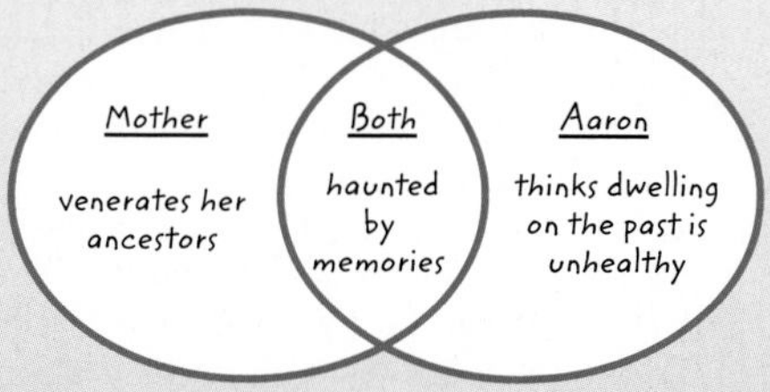

Vocabulary

acquiescence (ak′ wē es′ əns) *n.* passive acceptance; compliance; p. 1024 *Although she did not agree with the plan, she announced her acquiescence without arguing.*

meticulous (mi tik′ yə ləs) *adj.* characterized by extreme or excessive care in the treatment of details; p. 1025 *He was meticulous about the organization of his books, arranging them by date.*

repulsive (ri pul′ siv) *adj.* arousing aversion or disgust; p. 1027 *Her mother considered rats repulsive and would not let her keep one as a pet.*

bewildered (bi wil′ dərd) *adj.* perplexed or confused; p. 1028 *The hikers became bewildered when they discovered they had taken the wrong path.*

Tip: Word Usage When you encounter an unfamiliar word, ask yourself, How is the word being used? Example: *We left the room because the smell was **repulsive.*** In this sentence, the vocabulary word *repulsive* is being used to describe the smell. This tells you that *repulsive* is an adjective, which can help you determine its meaning.

Listening and Speaking Practice

SPIRAL REVIEW **Group Discussion** Divide students into groups and instruct them to have a brief discussion. **Ask:** If our society discovered memories could kill us, what effect would that knowledge have on the way we live? Write on the board the following rules for effective group discussion:

- Listen to other group members as they speak. Don't interrupt.
- Help members stay on track if the discussion starts to wander.
- Challenge ideas, not people.
- Accept criticism gracefully.
- Encourage quiet members to partipate.

Students should take notes during their discussion. After allowing students time to discuss the subject, have a volunteer summarize the group's discussion.

In Memoriam

Nancy Kress

As soon as Aaron followed me into the garden, I knew he was angry. He pursed his mouth, that sweet exaggerated fullness of lips that hadn't changed since he was two years old and that looked silly on the middle-aged man he had become. But he said nothing—in itself a sign of trouble. Oh, I knew him through and through. As well as I knew his father, as well as his father had known me.

Aaron closed the door behind us and walked to the lawn chairs, skirting the tiny shrine as if it weren't there. He lowered himself gingerly into a chair.

"Be careful," I said, pointlessly. "Your back again?"

He waved this remark away; even as a little boy he had hated to have attention called to any physical problem. A skinned knee, a stiff neck, a broken wrist. I remembered. I remembered everything.

"Coffee? A splash?"

"Coffee. Come closer, I don't want to shout. You don't have your hearing field on, do you?"

I didn't. I poured him his coffee from the lawn bar and floated my chair close enough to hand it to him. Next door, Todd came out of his house, dressed in shorts and carrying a trowel. He waved cheerfully.

"I know you don't want to hear this," Aaron began—he had never been one for small talk, never one for subtlety—"but I have to say it one more time. Listen to Dr. Lorsky about the operation."

"Sugar?"

Our World and Beyond *What impression do you have so far about the kind of world these characters live in?* **1**

Comparing Literature

Teach

Big Idea 1

Our World and Beyond

Answer: *The characters live in the future, at a time when new inventions and technologies have been created to make life easier.*

Ask: How do the details of this world differ from our own? *(Our world does not have floating chairs or lawn bars in people's homes.)* As students continue reading, encourage them to look for additional details that make the world in the story different from our own world.

Readability Scores

Dale-Chall: 4.8
DRP: 54
Lexile: 650

English Learners

DIFFERENTIATED INSTRUCTION

Intermediate Less proficient readers will increase their comprehension by recording information about the characters, setting, and plot in a chart or diagram. Demonstrate how to create cluster diagrams for recording basic information about the literary elements of character, plot, and setting. Tell students to add information to their diagrams as they read. Suggest that they use a separate sheet of paper for each cluster.

Comparing Literature

Teach

Literary Element 1

Dialogue **Answer:** *He has strong feelings, but he is logical and methodical. He tries to appeal to his mother's sense of reason to convince her to see things his way.*

Big Idea 2

Our World and Beyond
Answer: *A wirehead may be a device worn on the head and used for viewing images. The author is emphasizing the fact that these characters live in a different world from ours, where things are possible that we have not even imagined.*

Literary Element 3

Dialogue **Ask:** Why does Aaron ask his mother what she does? *(Students may say that he does not want the conversation to move toward what the shrine means to his mother, perhaps because it makes him feel uncomfortable or simply because he does not want to be diverted from his argument.)*

"Black. Mom—"

"Be quiet," I said, and he looked startled enough, but his surprise wasn't followed by a scowl. Aaron, who always reacted to a direct order as if to assault. I sat up straighter and peered at him. No scowl.

He took a long, deliberate sip of coffee, which was too hot for long sips. "Is there a reason you won't listen to Dr. Lorsky? A real, rational reason?" He didn't look at the shrine.

"You know the reason," I said. Thirty feet away in his side yard, Todd began to weed his flower beds, digging out the most stubborn weeds with the trowel, pulling the rest by hand. He never used a power hoe. The flowers, snapdragons and yarrow and azaleas and lemondrop marigolds, crowded together in the brief hot riot of midsummer.

"That's not a reason!"

Aaron waggled his fingers at the shrine he still wouldn't see. "That's not a reason!"

He was right, of course—the shrine was effect, not cause. I smiled at his perceptiveness, unable to help the sly, silly glow of a maternal pride thirty years out of date. But Aaron took the smile for something else: **acquiescence**, perhaps, or weakening. He put his cup on the grass and leaned forward. Earnestly[1]—he had been such an earnest little boy, unsmiling in the face of jokes he didn't understand, putting his toys away in the exact same spots each night, presenting his teenage demands in carefully numbered lists, lecturing the other boys on their routine childish brutality.

A prig,[2] actually.

"Mom, listen to me. I'm asking you to reconsider. That's all. For three reasons. First, because it's getting dangerous for you to live out here all alone. Despite the electronic surveillance. What if you were robbed?"

"Robbed," I said dryly. Aaron didn't catch it; I didn't really expect him to. He knew why I had bought this house, why I stayed in it. I said gently, "Your coffee's getting cold." He ignored me, pressing doggedly on, his hands gripping the arms of his chair. On the back of the left hand were two liver spots. When had that happened?

"*Second,* this business of ancestor worship or whatever it's supposed to be. This shrine. You never believed in this nonsense before. You raised me to think rationally, without superstition, and here you are planting flowers to your dead forebears unto the nth generation and meditating to them like you were some teenaged wirehead split-brain."

"We used to meditate a lot when I was a girl, before wireheads were invented," I said, to annoy him. His intensity was scaring me. "But Aaron, darling, that's not what I do here."

"What do you do?" he said, and immediately, I could see, regretted it. The shrine 3
shone lustrous in the sunlight. It was a triptych[3] of black slabs two feet high. In the late afternoon heat, the black

1. *Earnestly* means "in a very serious manner."

2. A *prig* is someone who is irritatingly proper.

3. A *triptych* is a painting or altar made up of three hinged panels.

Vocabulary

acquiescence (ak´ wē es´ əns) *n.* passive acceptance; compliance

Dialogue *What does Aaron's comment reveal about his character?* 1

Our World and Beyond *What do you think a* wirehead *is? Why does the author use it without explanation?* 2

Writing Practice

Connect to the Story

Encourage students to connect to the characters in this story on a personal level. They might ask themselves if certain exchanges remind them of relationships in their own lives. Also, they might try to put themselves into a character's shoes and imagine what they would do in that character's situation. As students read, have them consider this question: *Is there some aspect of Mrs. Kinnian and Aaron's relationship that reminds you of your relationship with one of your parents? If so, what is it?* Have students write a short journal entry explaining their answers.

neo-nitonol[4] had softened into featurelessness, but when night fell, the names would again spring into hard-etched clarity. Hundreds of tiny names, engraved close together in **meticulous** script, linked with the lines of generation. At the base of the triptych bloomed low flowers: violets and forget-me-nots and rosemary.

"'There's rosemary, that's for remembrance,'" I said, but Aaron, being Aaron, didn't recognize Ophelia's line.[5] Not a reader, my Aaron. Bytes not books. Oh, I remembered.

In the other yard, Todd's trowel clunked as it hit a buried stone.

"It isn't healthy," Aaron said. "Shrines. Ancestor worship! And in the third place, time is running out for you to have the operation. I spoke to Dr. Lorsky yesterday—"

"You spoke to my doctor without my permission—"

"—and he said your temporal lobes[6] still scan well but he can't say how much longer that will be true. There's that cut-off point where the body just can't handle it anymore. And then the brain wipe wouldn't do you any good. It would be too late. Mom—you *know*."

I knew. The sheer weight of memory reached some critical mass. All those memories: the shade of blue of a dress worn fifty years ago, the tilt of the head of someone long dead, the sudden sharp smell of a grandmother's cabbage soup mingled with the dusty scent of an apartment razed for two decades. And each memory bringing on others, a rush of them, till the grandmother was there before you, whole. The burden and bulk of all those minute sensations over days and years and decades, triggering chemical changes in the brain which in turn trigger cellular changes, until the body cannot bear any more and breakdown accelerates. The cut-off point. It is our memories that kill us.

Man Digging. Bror Julius Olsson Nordfeldt. Watercolour on paper. Private collection.

4. *Nitonol* is a metal made of titanium and nickel.
5. *Ophelia* is a character in William Shakespeare's *Hamlet*.
6. The *temporal lobes* are the sensory part of the brain.

4 Dialogue *What does this comment tell you about Aaron's attitude toward his mother and toward the past?*

Vocabulary

meticulous (mi tik ʹ yə ləs) *adj.* characterized by extreme or excessive care in the treatment of details

Our World and Beyond *What effect do you think this would have on the way people see themselves and think about the world?* 5

Comparing Literature

Teach

Literary Element 4

Dialogue Answer: *Aaron seems to have no use for the past; he fears and scorns it. He seems to think it is a sign of his mother's approaching senility that she values her memory.*

Big Idea 5

Our World and Beyond

Answer: *People would fear memory and try to forget the past as much as possible. These people might try to see the world as if it existed solely in the present, and not consider their past as part of their identity.*

APPROACHING **Ask:** How might not having any memories help people? *(Many people suffer because of their traumatic memories. If they could erase those memories, they wouldn't have to relive them.)*

Approaching Level

DIFFERENTIATED INSTRUCTION

Established Explain to students that good writers know that dialogue is an important device in writing. The best dialogue not only conveys information important to the plot, but also teaches readers about the personalities of the characters speaking.

Say: The dialogue in "In Memoriam" is very sparse and disjointed, meaning that the conversation doesn't flow easily. Instruct students as they read to pay close attention to the dialogue in this story and to think about what it shows them about the relationship between the characters.

Teach

Big Idea 1

Our World and Beyond
Answer: *Students should explain their varied opinions.*

Reading Strategy 2

Compare and Contrast Characters **Answer:** *Aaron prefers wiping his memory clean to growing old and dying. However, his mother sees the loss of memory as far too great a sacrifice to make simply in order to live longer.*

For additional practice using the reading skill or strategy, see Unit 6 Teaching Resources Book, p. 65.

Aaron groped with one hand for his coffee cup, beside his chair on the grass. The crows' feet at the corners of his eyes were still tentative, like lines scratched in soft sand. He ducked his head and mumbled. "I just . . . I just don't want you to die, Mom."

I looked away. It is always, somehow, a surprise to find that an adult child still loves you.

Next door, Todd straightened from one flower bed and moved to the next. He pulled his shirt over his head and tossed it to the ground. Sweat gleamed on the muscles of his back, still hard and taut in his mid-thirties body. The shirt made a dark patch on the bright grass.

A bee buzzed up from the flowers around the black triptych and circled by my ear. Glad of the distraction, I waved it away.

"Aaron . . . I *can't.* I just can't. Be wiped."

"Even if you die for it? What point is there to that?"

I stayed silent. We had discussed it before, all of it, the whole dreary topic. But Aaron had never before looked like that. And he had never begged.

"Please, Mom. Please. You already get confused. Last week you thought that woman in the park was your dead sister. I know you're going to say it was just for a second, but that's the way it starts. Just for a second, then more and more, and then it's too late for the wipe. You say you wouldn't be 'you' anymore with a wipe—but if your memory goes and the body follows it, are you 'you' anyway? Feeble and senile? Are you still 'you' if you're dead?"

"That isn't the point," I began, but he must have seen on my face something which he thought was a softening, a wavering. He reached for my hand. His fingers were dry and hot.

"It *is* the point! Death is the point! Your body can't be made any younger, but it doesn't have to become any older. You *don't.* And you have the bodily strength, still, you have the money—it isn't as if you would be a vegetable. You'd still remember language, routines—and you'd make new memories, start over. A new life. *Life,* not death!" **1**

I said nothing to that. Aaron could see the years of my life stretching behind me, years he wanted me to cut off as casually as paring a fingernail. He could not see the other, greater loss. **2**

It is our memories that kill us.

"You're wrong," I said, as gently as I could, and took my fingers from his. "I'm not refusing the wipe because I want death. I'm refusing it because too much of me has already died."

He stared at me with incomprehension. The bee I had waved away buzzed around his left ear. I saw his blue eyes flick to it and then back to me, refusing to be distracted. Linear thinking, always: was it growing up with all those computers? Such blue eyes, such a handsome man, still.

Next door Todd began to whistle. Aaron stiffened and half-turned to look for the first time over his shoulder; he had not

---

1 Our World and Beyond *Does this possibility sound attractive to you? Why or why not?*

2 Compare and Contrast Characters *What fundamental difference between the characters becomes apparent here?*

Vocabulary Practice

Unfamiliar Vocabulary
Tell students that rereading a passage will help them clarify meaning. Suggest that students write down any words or phrases with which they are unfamiliar. Then tell them to refer to a dictionary to look up these words and terms. For example, students might want to clarify the meaning of the term "linear thinking." Once students have defined the words, have them write three sentences using the new words or phrases they have learned. Encourage volunteers to share their sentences with the class.

Song from a Distant Land. Ferdinand Hodler. Oil on canvas, 180 x 125 cm. Collection of Hamburger Kunsthalle, Hamburg, Germany.

View the Art Ferdinand Hodler developed a style of painting that he called Parallelism. These paintings consist mainly of groups of figures arranged in dancelike poses. How would you describe the attitude of the woman pictured? In what ways is she like the narrator of the story? ★

realized Todd was there. He looked back at me. His eyes shadowed and dropped, and in that tiny sideways slide—not at all linear—I knew. I suddenly knew.

He saw it. "Mom . . . Mother . . ."

"You're going to have the wipe."

He raised the coffee cup to his mouth and drank: an automatic covering gesture, the coffee must have been cold. **Repulsive.** Cold coffee is repulsive.

I folded my arms across my belly and leaned forward.

He said quietly, "My back is getting worse. The migraines are back, once or twice every week. Lorsky says I'm an old forty-two, you know how much people vary. I'm not the easy-living type who forgets easily. I take things hard, I don't forget, and I don't want to die."

I said nothing.

"Mom?"

I said nothing.

"Please understand . . . please." It came out in a whisper. I said nothing. Aaron put his cup on the table and eased himself from the chair, leaning heavily on its arm and webbed back. The movement attracted Todd's attention. I saw, past the bulk of Aaron's body, the moment Todd decided to walk over and be neighborly.

"Hello, Mrs. Kinnian. Aaron."

I watched Aaron's face clench. He turned slowly.

Todd said, "Hot, isn't it? I was away for a week and my weeds just ambushed everything."

"Sailing," Aaron said carefully.

"Yes, sailing." Todd said, faintly surprised. He wiped the sweat from his eyes. "Do you sail?" 4

"I did. Once. When I was a kid. My father used to take me."

"You should have kept it up. Great sport. Mrs. Kinnian, can I weed those flowers for you?"

He pointed to the black triptych.

I said, "No, thank you, Todd. The gardener will be around tomorrow."

3 Compare and Contrast Characters *What is Aaron's attitude toward his own memories?*

Vocabulary

repulsive (ri pul′ siv) *adj.* arousing aversion or disgust

Comparing Literature

Teach

Reading Strategy 3

Compare and Contrast Characters Answer: *Aaron wishes he could forget his memories, but the fact that he cannot shows that they are very powerful for him. He makes his memories sound like a disease that will kill him in the end if he does not get rid of them.*

ENGLISH LEARNERS Have students write a short journal entry on the question: Is there any memory that you wish you could forget? Can you relate to Aaron's view?

Reading Strategy 4

Predict Ask: What role do you think Todd may play in this story? Support your prediction with clues from the text on page 1027. *(Some students may guess that Todd is a family member by references to both men's blue eyes and sailing and from Aaron's reaction when he notices Todd. Students may not realize Todd is Aaron's father because he seems younger than Aaron.)*

Advanced Learners

DIFFERENTIATED INSTRUCTION

Read Dialogue Some gifted and talented students excel at dramatic reading. Allow students to read the dialogue between Mrs. Kinnian and Aaron on page 1026 aloud. Assign speaking parts and encourage students to read only the words of the characters they have been assigned. Students should use verbal techniques for effects and to convey underlying meanings.

View the Art ★

Answer: *The woman in the painting appears to be self-confident and in control of her body and mind. Like the narrator, she is in control of herself.*

Comparing Literature

Teach

Literary Element 1

Dialogue Answer: *The mother's comment implies that she will be deeply affected by her son's choice to erase her from his memory. Aaron's answer emphasizes his concern for himself and the present, not acknowledging that his past is intertwined with others.*

APPROACHING **Ask:** How does your past make you who you are today? *(Possible answer: Our experiences help shape our personalities.)*

Reading Strategy 2

Compare and Contrast Characters Answer: *The mother's comment implies that if Aaron had been less caught up in abstract things, he would not be afraid of death or eager to erase his memories.*

Big Idea 3

Our World and Beyond Answer: *The fervor with which these old people hold on to their memories*

"Well, if you . . . all right. Take care."

He smiled at us: a handsome blue-eyed man in his prime, ruddy with health and exercise, his face as open and clear as a child's. Beside him, Aaron looked puffy, stiff, out of shape. The skin at the back of Aaron's neck formed ridges that worked up and down above his collar.

"Take care," I said to Todd. He walked back to his weeding. Aaron turned to me. I saw his eyes.

"I'm sorry, Mom. I am . . . sorry. But I'm going to have the wipe. I'm going to do it."

"To me."

"For me."

After that there was nothing else to say. I watched Aaron walk around the flowered shrine, open the door to the house, disappear in the cool interior. There was a brief hum from the air conditioner, cut off the moment the door closed. A second door slammed; Todd, too, had gone inside his house.

I realized that I had not asked Aaron when Dr. Lorsky would do the wipe. He might not have told me. He had already been stretched as far as he would go, pulled off center by emotion and imagination, neither of which he wanted. He had never been an imaginative child, only a practical one. Coming to me in the garden with his math homework, worried about fractions, unconcerned with the flowers blooming and dying around him. I remembered.

But *he* would not.

Todd came back outside, carrying a cold drink, and returned to weeding. I watched him a while. I watched him an hour, two. I watched him after he had left and dusk began to fall over the garden. Then I struggled out of my chair—everything ached, I had been sitting too long—and picked some snapdragons. Purple, deepened by the shadows. I laid them in front of the black triptych.

When Todd and I had been married, I had carried roses: white with pink undertones at the tips of the petals, deep pink at the heart. I hadn't seen such roses in years. Maybe the strain wasn't grown anymore.

The script on the shrine had sprung out clear and hard. I touched it with one finger, tracing the names. Then I went into the house to watch TV. A brain-wipe clinic had been bombed. Elderly activists crowded in front of the camera, yelling and waving gnarled fists. They were led away by police, strong youthful men and women trying to get the old people to *behave* like old people. The unlined faces beneath their helmets looked **bewildered.** They *were* bewildered. Misunderstanding everything; believing that remembrance is death; getting it all backwards. Trying to make us go away as if we didn't exist. As if we never had.

---

1 Dialogue *What does this simple exchange reveal about the different viewpoints of these characters?*

2 Compare and Contrast Characters *What is the significance of Aaron's indifference to the flowers?*

Our World and Beyond *What is it that these young police officers cannot understand?* 3

Vocabulary

bewildered (bi wil′ dərd) *adj.* perplexed or confused

Writing Practice

Write a Summary
Tell students that summarizing a short story can help ensure comprehension. Ask students to summarize the events in "In Memoriam." Remind them to answer who, what, where, when, and why questions in their summaries. Instruct them to write the summary as concisely as possible. After allowing students time to finish, ask volunteers to read aloud their summaries to the class. Ask other students to critique the summary.

After You Read

Respond and Think Critically

Respond and Interpret

1. What is your opinion of the "brain wipe"? Explain.
2. (a)What does Aaron want to convince his mother to do? (b)What are his motivations for wanting her to do it?
3. (a)Who is Todd and how has he changed? (b)What effect do you think Todd's presence has had on the narrator of the story?

Analyze and Evaluate

4. What is the effect of the mother's description and characterization of Aaron and Todd?
5. Why does the mother choose not to have the brain wipe? Cite passages from the story to support your response.

Connect

6. **Big Idea** **Our World and Beyond** How would you feel if someone you loved decided to have a brain wipe?
7. **Connect to Today** Imagine that the technology were available to perform brain wipes. How do you think the existence of such a possibility would affect our society?

Literary Element Dialogue

Dialogue reveals characters' personalities through their words. It can also serve to increase the drama of a story and call attention to important themes.

1. What impression do you get of Aaron from his dialogue? How does this impression compare with the way he is described by his mother?
2. At what point in the story does the dialogue create a moment of drama or high tension? Explain.

Reading Strategy Compare and Contrast Characters

Even characters who are very different often have similarities. Review your Venn diagram and answer the following questions.

1. What do Aaron and his mother have in common?
2. How do the characters' ways of expressing themselves differ?

LOG ON **Literature** Online

Selection Resources For Selection Quizzes, eFlashcards, and Reading-Writing Connection activities, go to glencoe.com and enter QuickPass code GL49787u6.

Vocabulary Practice

Practice with Word Usage Respond to these statements to help you explore the meaning of each boldface vocabulary word.

1. Why might someone's **acquiescence** be seen as "giving in"?
2. What kind of job would a **meticulous** person probably be good at?
3. What is someone likely to do when they encounter something **repulsive?**
4. How would a lost person probably act if they are **bewildered?**?

Writing

Write a Pamphlet The story's characters are divided over the morality of the brain-wipe procedure. Choose one side of the debate and write a pamphlet in support of that viewpoint. Explain the debate under one heading and your arguments under another. Refute potential counter-arguments under another heading. Fold the pamphlet so that your explanation of the debate is on the front flap.

Comparing Literature

After You Read

Assess

1. Answers will vary.
2. (a) To have a "memory wipe" (b) He does not want her to die.
3. (a) Todd, Aaron's father, has had a memory wipe. (b) Todd's action may have influenced her decision.
4. They emphasize the power of the past.
5. At the end of the story, the mother comments that people like her son live their lives "believing that remembrance is death; getting it all backwards." To her, memory is life—people live in the memories of others.
6. People would become more isolated and self-centered.
7. Answers will vary. People might never learn from their mistakes because they wouldn't remember any of them.

Literary Element

1. Aaron seems stubborn and logical. She makes him seem more human.
2. Students should refer to story details and dialogue.

Progress Check

Can students identify dialogue?

If No → See Unit 6 Teaching Resources Book, p. 64.

Reading Strategy

1. They know memory is powerful.
2. He is direct; she tries to avoid the discussion. Aaron's urgent tone reflects his underlying fear; she appears wise.

Vocabulary Practice

1. Because they agreed without protest and just quietly went along.
2. Any job that was very detail oriented, like an accountant.
3. They are likely to look away from it or move away from it.
4. They would probably seem disorganized or confused.

Writing

Students' pamphlets should support a viewpoint and refute counter-arguments.

Focus

Summary

Li-Young Lee reflects on an intimate moment that he shared with his father during his childhood. He then connects that moment to who he is today.

Teach

Big Idea 1

Our World and Beyond

ADVANCED Help students see that writers often compare the past to the present. **Ask:** How is the past like a fantasy? *(Answers will vary.)*

Build Background

The poems of Li-Young Lee reflect the influence of classic Chinese poets. Writing with simplicity and lyrical passion, Lee often recalls memories of his childhood in which his father, portrayed as both strict and tender, was a strong presence. **1**

Study of Hands, 1859–1860. Edgar Degas. Oil on canvas. Musee d'Orsay, Paris.

The Gift

Li-Young Lee

To pull the metal splinter from my palm
my father recited a story in a low voice.
I watched his lovely face and not the blade.
Before the story ended, he'd removed
the iron sliver I thought I'd die from.

Writing Practice

SPIRAL REVIEW **Imagery** Lee uses several images of his father to describe his memories. Ask students to identify the different images that Lee mentions in the poem. *(the father taking the sliver from the young boy's hand; the father putting his hands on the young boy's face).* Then have students reflect on their own life and identify an image that tells a story about their past. Have students describe the image in a poetic style like Lee's. **Say:** The details that you choose to describe should tell a story about your past. Students should use precise language, action verbs, and sensory details.

I can't remember the tale,
but hear his voice still, a well
of dark water, a prayer.
And I recall his hands,
two measures of tenderness
he laid against my face,
the flames of discipline
he raised above my head.

Had you entered that afternoon
you would have thought you saw a man
planting something in a boy's palm,
a silver tear, a tiny flame.
Had you followed that boy
you would have arrived here,
where I bend over my wife's right hand.

Look how I shave her thumbnail down
so carefully she feels no pain.
Watch as I lift the splinter out.
I was seven when my father
took my hand like this,
and I did not hold that shard[1]
between my fingers and think,
Metal that will bury me,
christen it Little Assassin,
Ore Going Deep for My Heart.
And I did not lift up my wound and cry,
Death visited here!
I did what a child does
when he's given something to keep.
I kissed my father.

1. *Shard* means "a piece or fragment."

Discussion Starter

What images in this poem impress you the most? What do they suggest about the power of memory? What is "the gift" mentioned in the title? Use details from the poem to support your responses.

Teach

Literary Element 2

Description APPROACHING

Ask: Why does Lee describe this act as "a man planting something in a boy's palm"? *(The father is putting his ability to take care of others into his boy.)*

Discussion Starter

Students' responses will vary. Students should support their answers with explanations and details from the poem.

Approaching Level

DIFFERENTIATED INSTRUCTION

Emerging In "The Gift," Lee connects the past to the present by showing how as a child he learned certain qualities that he still has today. Have students locate the moment in the poem where Lee shifts from the past to the present. *(the third stanza)* Point out that Lee shows how an incident in his past influenced a specific moment in the present.

Have students recall a memory in their own lives and connect it to something in their present lives. For example, a student might say that watching his mother cook taught him to multitask, a skill that helps him participate in several different activities in high school. Encourage students to share their connections with the class.

Comparing Literature

Focus

Summary

The poem's narrator tells how new clothes make her feel like a new person because no memories are connected with them.

Teach

Quickwrite

Students' paragraphs should explain what new clothes symbolize. Students should support their writings with details from the poem.

Build Background

For more than sixty years, Naomi Long Madgett, an African American writer, teacher, and editor, has written poems that celebrate her own and her people's experiences. In "Purchase," she creates a speaker who explores the symbolic meaning of clothing.

PURCHASE

Naomi Long Madgett

I like the smell of new clothes,
The novel[1] aroma of challenge.
This dress has no past
Linked with regretful memories
To taint[2] it,
Only a future as hopeful
As my own.
I can say of an old garment
Laid away in a trunk:
"This lace I wore on that day when. . . ."
But I prefer the new scent
Of a garment unworn,
Untainted like the new self
That I become
When I first wear it.

1. Here, *novel* means "new."
2. To *taint* something is to spoil it.

Quickwrite

Why does the speaker like to wear new clothes? Write a paragraph in which you explain what new clothes might symbolize in this poem. Use details from the poem to support your views.

Listening, Speaking, and Viewing Practice

Oral Presentation Ask students to bring in a unique piece of jewelry or item of clothing. Have students present their item. Students should explain what makes the item special to them and what they like about the item. Have students discuss how an item of clothing or jewelry can reflect a person's personality and beliefs.

Wrap-Up: Comparing Literature

Across Genres

- ***In Memoriam*** by Nancy Kress
- ***The Gift*** by Li-Young Lee
- ***Purchase*** by Naomi Long Madgett

COMPARE THE Big Idea Our World and Beyond

Writing How would you characterize the worlds in these selections? What elements do you find familiar? What elements are very different from those of your world? Write a brief essay exploring the worlds in the selections. Before you begin writing, make a chart like the one below to organize your ideas.

Selection	Familiar Aspects	Unfamiliar Aspects
Im Memoriam		
The Gift		
Purchase		

Song from a Distant Land. Ferdinand Hodler. Oil on canvas, 180 x 125 cm. Collection of Hamburger Kunsthalle, Hamburg, Germany.

COMPARE Description

Visual Display Kress describes the garden setting in her story "In Memoriam" as a "hot riot of midsummer." Vivid description also helps us imagine the worlds of Lee's "The Gift" and Madgett's "Purchase." Create a triptych, or three related panels, of collages or paintings based on the descriptions in each of these three works. Each of the three artworks should reflect the world as it is described in the story or poem. Then display your triptych to the class and explain your choice of images in an oral presentation.

COMPARE Ideas

Group Activity Kress, Madgett, and Lee all explore the subjects of time and memory. Discuss the following questions with a small group. Support your answers with specific evidence from the texts.

1. What attitudes do the characters in "In Memoriam" and the speakers in "The Gift" and "Purchase" have toward time and memory?
2. In your opinion, what does each author believe about time and memory?

LOG ON Literature Online

Selection Resources For Selection Quizzes, eFlashcards, and Reading-Writing Connection activities, go to glencoe.com and enter QuickPass code GL49787u6.

Wrap-Up: Comparing Literature

Across Genres

Assess

Compare the Big Idea

Students' essays should
- show an understanding of the concepts in the selections
- show an ability to compare and contrast fictional and realistic aspects of the worlds in the selections

Compare Description

Provide students with a wide variety of materials, and encourage them to bring materials from home. Create an exhibit of the finished work.

Compare Ideas

1. In "In Memoriam," Aaron wants a brain wipe. His mother feels that the wipe would be a form of suicide. In "The Gift," the speaker explores fond memories of his father. In "Purchase," the speaker prefers to put the past aside.
2. Each author views time differently. Kress and Madgett both believe that time is a problem, while Lee seems to have benefited from the passing of time. Kress seems to want others to learn that our identity is inseparable from our memory. Lee's memories are mostly warm and have helped him treat his wife with the same tenderness his father once exhibited toward him. Madgett seems gently critical of the speaker of her poem, who has the naïve belief that new clothes will create a new beginning.

For additional selection assessment, see Assessment Resources, pp. 215–216.

Before You Read

Focus

Bellringer Options

Daily Language Practice Transparency 97

Or display images of Chinese culture (such as parades, landscapes, villages, and the Great Wall).

Ask: What seems familiar in these pictures? How is this culture similar to our own? How is this culture different?

Say: The story you will read takes place in two fictional Chinese cities a long time ago.

As they read, have students think about how life in the story is similar to and different from their own.

Before You Read

The Golden Kite, the Silver Wind

Meet **Ray Bradbury**
(born 1920)

"I've never doubted myself," celebrated author Ray Bradbury remarked on his eighty-second birthday. A childhood spent attending movies and magic shows, as well as reading the magazine *Amazing Stories,* fired his imagination. At age eleven, he wrote his first stories.

A Fantasy Writer Bradbury, who had no formal education beyond high school, did not follow any formulas for writing success. Instead, he simply wrote and wrote—and then wrote some more. He had written many stories before *The Martian Chronicles* was published in 1950, but that was the book that made his reputation. Many of Bradbury's signature themes appear in it. They include the longing for a simpler world and the fear of nuclear war.

> *"The act of writing is, for me, like a fever—something I must do."*
>
> —Ray Bradbury

The novel *Fahrenheit 451,* often hailed as Bradbury's greatest work, was published in 1953. Set in a future world where firefighters are considered heroes for burning books, *Fahrenheit 451* is Bradbury's only science fiction work—at least according to the author. Bradbury says all his other work is fantasy, because fantasy is about things that cannot happen. Science fiction, he explains, is about things that can happen.

In addition to fantasy, Bradbury has written horror stories. In the 1950s, he wrote for two television series, *Alfred Hitchcock* and *The Twilight Zone.* He also adapted many stories for his namesake television show, *Ray Bradbury Theater.* His work includes plays, nonfiction, and children's stories.

Economical Style "The Golden Kite, the Silver Wind" was first published in 1953. In a 2002 interview, Bradbury explained that he had gotten the idea for the story when he was thirteen years old. At the time, he "hung around" various movie studios. There he saw sets being built and destroyed in a seemingly endless cycle. He wrote the story based on the destruction of those sets, he said, "and they were metaphorically representative of the world."

Bradbury has received many awards, including the O. Henry Memorial Award, the 1988 Nebula Grand Master Award, and the 1989 Bram Stoker Award. In 2004 he was awarded the National Medal of the Arts.

LOG ON **Literature** Online

Author Search For more about Ray Bradbury, go to glencoe.com and enter QuickPass code GL49787u6.

Selection Skills

The Golden Kite, the Silver Wind

Reading Skills
- Evaluate Figures of Speech (SE pp. 1035–1041)
- Problem and Solution (TE p. 1038)

Listening/Speaking/Viewing Skills
- Analyze Art (SE p. 1039; TE p. 1036)

Literary Elements
- Allegory (SE pp. 1035–1040)
- Moral (SE p. 1040)

Writing Skills/Grammar
- Apply Symbolism (SE p. 1041)

Vocabulary Skills
- Synonyms (SE pp. 1035, 1041)

Literature and Reading Preview

Connect to the Story

Have you ever known of a competition that got out of hand? Discuss this question with a partner.

Build Background

"The Golden Kite, the Silver Wind" is set in a long-ago time in China. Mandarins, or public officials, rule autocratically, and walls surrounding cities are built laboriously by hand, at the whim of the ruler. In this world, women have no official power.

Set Purposes for Reading

Big Idea Our World and Beyond

As you read, ask yourself, What are the realistic elements and what are the fantastic elements in this story?

Literary Element Allegory

An **allegory** is a literary work in which all or most of the characters, settings, and events stand for ideas, qualities, or figures beyond themselves. The overall purpose of an allegory is to teach a moral lesson. As you read "The Golden Kite, the Silver Wind," ask yourself, What lesson does the story convey about competition and cooperation?

Reading Strategy Evaluate Figures of Speech

Figurative language is language or expressions that are not literally true but convey some truth beyond the literal level. **Evaluating figures of speech** is making judgments about the originality and expressive effect of the various similes, metaphors, and personifications in a literary work. As you read, ask yourself, How effective is Bradbury's use of figures of speech?

Tip: Take Notes As you read, use a chart to record how well figures of speech convey ideas or emotions.

Figure of speech	Evaluation
p. 1036 "Death swam in the wetness of an eye"	effectively shows how horrible some "symbols and omens" can be

Learning Objectives

For pages 1034–1041

In studying this text, you will focus on the following objectives:

Literary Study: Analyzing allegory.

Reading: Evaluating figures of speech.

Writing: Applying symbolism in a short story.

Vocabulary

portent (pôr′ tent) *n.* something that foreshadows a coming event; p. 1036 *The problems with the car turned out to be a portent of the miserable evening ahead.*

ravenous (rav′ ə nəs) *adj.* extremely hungry; p. 1037 *The ravenous dog had not eaten for two days.*

spurn (spurn) *v.* to reject with disdain or contempt; p. 1037 *The fashion model spurns the same clothes she wore only one year ago.*

monotony (mə not′ ən ē) *n.* undesirable sameness; p. 1039 *Sara hated the monotony of eating the same lunch every day of the week.*

Tip: Synonyms Words that share the same or similar meaning are called synonyms. Note that synonyms are always the same part of speech. For example, because the vocabulary word *spurn* is a verb, a word that is a synonym for *spurn* must also be a verb, like *reject.*

Before You Read

Focus

Summary

This story tells of two cities that compete with each other by rebuilding their walls over and over again. They do nothing but rebuild their walls until the people are almost dead. Finally, at the advice of the Mandarin's daughter, one city's wall is built like the wind and the other city's wall is built like a kite so that instead of competing, they support and sustain each other.

For summaries in languages other than English, see Unit 6 Teaching Resources Book, pp. 71–76.

Vocabulary

Complete the Sentence

Have students write sentences using words from the vocabulary list. Then ask volunteers to write three of their sentences on the board, leaving a blank line in place of the vocabulary word. Have students come to the board and complete a sentence with the correct vocabulary word.

Approaching Level

DIFFERENTIATED INSTRUCTION

Established Say: We all need support in our lives to accomplish great things. Explain to students that througout history, people have provided each other with support in many different ways in order to help each other accomplish goals. Give examples of this idea, such as volunteer organizations that work to prevent poverty and hunger in Africa, or government-provided grants and scholarships for students and researchers, or the formation of the United Nations to assist international cooperation on laws, economic development, and other issues. **Ask:** How have you been supported in your goals? Who has supported you? *(Students' answers will vary. Students may say that their teachers have helped them prepare for a successful life beyond school, or that their neighbors planted a community garden to improve the area for all who live there.)*

Teach

Literary Element 1

Allegory **Answer:** *The shape of the wall represents the strength or character of each city.*

ENGLISH LEARNERS **Ask:** What is a symbol in literature? *(A symbol is something that stands for or represents something else. It is another way of getting an idea across without directly stating it.)*

View the Art ★

Giandomenico Tiepolo (1727–1802) was born into an artistic Venetian family, and he took up the family occupation in his youth. His art depicts Venetian street scenes of his time, as well as exotic images of foreign places.

Readability Scores

Dale-Chall: 7.1
DRP: 55
Lexile: 1030

The Golden Kite, the Silver Wind

Ray Bradbury

The Walk of the Mandarins. Giandomenico Tiepolo. Villa Valmarana, Vicenza, Italy. ★

"In the shape of a *pig*?" cried the Mandarin.

"In the shape of a pig," said the messenger, and departed.

"Oh, what an evil day in an evil year," cried the Mandarin. "The town of Kwan-Si, beyond the hill, was very small in my childhood. Now it has grown so large that at last they are building a wall."

"But why should a wall two miles away make my good father sad and angry all within the hour?" asked his daughter quietly.

"They build their wall," said the Mandarin, "in the shape of a pig! Do you see? Our own city wall is built in the shape of an orange. That pig will devour us, greedily!"

"Ah."

They both sat thinking.

Life was full of symbols and omens. Demons lurked everywhere. Death swam in the wetness of an eye, the turn of a gull's wing meant rain, a fan held *so,* the tilt of a roof, and, yes, even a city wall was of immense importance. Travelers and tourists, caravans, musicians, artists, coming upon these two towns, equally judging the **portents,** would say, "The city shaped like an orange? No! I will enter the city shaped like a pig and prosper, eating all, growing fat with good luck and prosperity!"

The Mandarin wept. "All is lost! These symbols and signs terrify. Our city will come on evil days."

"Then," said the daughter, "call in your stonemasons and temple builders. I will whisper from behind the silken screen[1] and you will know the words."

The old man clapped his hands despairingly. "Ho,[2] stonemasons! Ho, builders of towns and palaces!"

1 **Allegory** *The city walls are more than just walls in this story. What do you think they might represent?*

1. Movable wall-like *screens* often provide privacy in Chinese and other homes.
2. *Ho* is an interjection used to get somebody's attention.

Vocabulary

portent (pôr′ tent) *n.* something that foreshadows a coming event

Vocabulary Practice

SMALL GROUP **Science Fiction and Fantasy** Remind students that Ray Bradbury is also known for writing science fiction. Have students conduct Internet research on the genre of science fiction and create a list of common terms and phrases related to the genre. Students should compile a list of terms and provide a definition for each term. *(Students may present words such as "cyborg, forcefield, tractor beam, robot, outerspace, teleport, android, terraforming" and many other words.)*

The men who knew marble and granite and onyx and quartz came quickly. The Mandarin faced them most uneasily, himself waiting for a whisper from the silken screen behind his throne. At last the whisper came.

"I have called you here," said the whisper.

"I have called you here," said the Mandarin aloud, "because our city is shaped like an orange, and the vile city of Kwan-Si has this day shaped theirs like a **ravenous** pig—"

Here the stonemasons groaned and wept. Death rattled his cane in the outer courtyard. Poverty made a sound like a wet cough in the shadows of the room.

"And so," said the whisper, said the Mandarin, "you raisers of walls must go bearing trowels and rocks and change the shape of *our* city!"

The architects and masons gasped. The Mandarin himself gasped at what he had said. The whisper whispered. The Mandarin went on: "And you will change our walls into a club which may beat the pig and drive it off!"

The stonemasons rose up, shouting. Even the Mandarin, delighted at the words from his mouth, applauded, stood down from his throne. "Quick!" he cried. "To work!"

When his men had gone, smiling and bustling, the Mandarin turned with great love to the silken screen. "Daughter," he whispered, "I will embrace you." There was no reply. He stepped around the screen, and she was gone.

Such modesty, he thought. She has slipped away and left me with a triumph, as if it were mine.

The news spread through the city; the Mandarin was acclaimed. Everyone carried stone to the walls. Fireworks were set off and the demons of death and poverty did not linger, as all worked together. At the end of the month the wall had been changed. It was now a mighty bludgeon[3] with which to drive pigs, boars, even lions, far away. The Mandarin slept like a happy fox every night.

"I would like to see the Mandarin of Kwan-Si when the news is learned. Such pandemonium and hysteria; he will likely throw himself from a mountain! A little more of that wine, oh Daughter-who-thinks-like-a-son."

But the pleasure was like a winter flower; it died swiftly. That very afternoon the messenger rushed into the courtroom. "Oh, Mandarin, disease, early sorrow, avalanches, grasshopper plagues, and poisoned well water!"

The Mandarin trembled.

"The town of Kwan-Si," said the messenger, "which was built like a pig and which animal we drove away by changing our walls to a mighty stick, has now turned triumph to winter ashes. They have built their city's walls like a great bonfire to burn our stick!"

The Mandarin's heart sickened within him, like an autumn fruit upon an ancient tree. "Oh, gods! Travelers will **spurn** us. Tradesmen, reading the symbols, will turn from the stick, so easily destroyed, to the fire, which conquers all!"

"No," said a whisper like a snowflake from behind the silken screen.

"No," said the startled Mandarin.

3. A *bludgeon* is a short stick used as a weapon.

2 Our World and Beyond *How are the Mandarin and his followers similar to leaders and followers everywhere?*

3 Evaluate Figures of Speech *Why is the simile in this sentence particularly effective?*

Vocabulary

ravenous (rav′ ə nəs) *adj.* extremely hungry

Vocabulary

spurn (spurn) *v.* to reject with disdain or contempt

Teach

Big Idea 2

Our World and Beyond

Answer: *Even when a leader asks for something absurd, there will always be those who applaud the leader for his or her wisdom.*

Reading Strategy 3

Evaluate Figures of Speech

Answer: *A fox is typically regarded as a sly animal. In this case, the Mandarin feels as if he has just done something clever and has solved his problems at the same time, so he sleeps as contentedly as a sly fox.*

English Learners

DIFFERENTIATED INSTRUCTION

Beginning/Early Intermediate English learners may have difficulty understanding the many similies used in this story. **Say:** A simile uses the word "like" to compare two things that, at first, might not seem to be alike. On the board, draw a chart with the word "Simile" on one side and "Meaning" on the other. Under the first heading, **write:** "The pleasure was like a winter flower." Under the second, **write:** "Neither lasts for a long time." Ask students to pick out other similes in the story and attempt to determine their meaning. *("The Mandarin's heart sickened within him, like an autumn fruit upon an ancient vine" means "Both have lived for a long time and are now rotting"; "a whisper like a snowflake" means "Both are soft and delicate.")*

Teach

Big Idea 1

Our World and Beyond
Answer: *Students may answer generally that peasants, slaves, and other laborers have often been worked to death for the grand aims of rulers. They may cite the Egyptian pyramids or the Great Wall of China as examples.*

Reading Strategy 2

Evaluate Figures of Speech
Answer: *The mandarins are "very ill and withered away," so their breath is like the winter wind, that is, cold like death. The wind flutters, as if the mandarins can just barely breathe. The descriptive language is expressive of their near-death state.*

"Tell my stonemasons," said the whisper that was a falling drop of rain, "to build our walls in the shape of a shining lake."

The Mandarin said this aloud, his heart warmed.

"And with this lake of water," said the whisper and the old man, "we will quench the fire and put it out forever!"

The city turned out in joy to learn that once again they had been saved by the magnificent Emperor of ideas. They ran to the walls and built them nearer to this new vision, singing, not as loudly as before, of course, for they were tired, and not as quickly, for since it had taken a month to build the wall the first time, they had had to neglect business and crops and therefore were somewhat weaker and poorer.

There then followed a succession of horrible and wonderful days, one in another like a nest of frightening boxes.

"Oh, Emperor," cried the messenger, "Kwan-Si has rebuilt their walls to resemble a mouth with which to drink all our lake!"

"Then," said the Emperor, standing very close to his silken screen, "build our walls like a needle to sew up that mouth!"

"Emperor!" screamed the messenger. "They make their walls like a sword to break your needle!"

The Emperor held, trembling, to the silken screen. "Then shift the stones to form a scabbard to sheathe that sword!"

"Mercy," wept the messenger the following morn, "they have worked all night and shaped the walls like lightning which will explode and destroy that sheath!"

Sickness spread in the city like a pack of evil dogs. Shops closed. The population, working now steadily for endless months upon the changing of the walls, resembled Death himself, clattering his white bones like musical instruments in the wind. Funerals began to appear in the streets, though it was the middle of summer, a time when all should be tending and harvesting. The Mandarin fell so ill that he had his bed drawn up by the silken screen and there he lay, miserably giving his architectural orders. The voice behind the screen was weak now, too, and faint, like the wind in the eaves.

"Kwan-Si is an eagle. Then our walls must be a net for that eagle. They are a sun to burn our net. Then we build a moon to eclipse their sun!"

Like a rusted machine, the city ground to a halt.

At last the whisper behind the screen cried out:

"In the name of the gods, send for Kwan-Si!"

Upon the last day of summer the Mandarin Kwan-Si, very ill and withered away, was carried into our Mandarin's courtroom by four starving footmen. The two mandarins were propped up, facing each other. Their breaths fluttered like winter winds in their mouths. A voice said:

"Let us put an end to this."

The old men nodded.

"This cannot go on," said the faint voice. "Our people do nothing but rebuild our cities to a different shape every day, every hour. They have no time to hunt, to fish, to love, to be good to their ancestors and their ancestors' children."

"This I admit," said the mandarins of the towns of the Cage, the Moon, the Spear, the Fire, the Sword and this, that, and other things.

"Carry us into the sunlight," said the voice.

---

1 Our World and Beyond *How does this outcome echo political events in world history?*

Evaluate Figures of Speech *How well does descriptive language capture the condition of the two mandarins?* **2**

Reading Practice

SPIRAL REVIEW **Problem and Solution** Explain that one strategy for reading stories is to think of them as a series of problems and solutions. A character has a problem, the character tries different solutions to the problem, and the problem may or may not be solved. Have small groups of students write three problems and solutions from the story, indicating whether the solutions worked. Have the groups take turns offering their problems and solutions.

The old men were borne out under the sun and up a little hill. In the late summer breeze a few very thin children were flying dragon kites in all the colors of the sun, and frogs and grass, the color of the sea and the color of coins and wheat.

The first Mandarin's daughter stood by his bed.

"See," she said.

"Those are nothing but kites," said the two old men.

"But what is a kite on the ground?" she said. "It is nothing. What does it need to sustain it and make it beautiful and truly spiritual?"

"The wind, of course!" said the others.

"And what do the sky and the wind need to make *them* beautiful?"

"A kite, of course—many kites, to break the **monotony**, the sameness of the sky. Colored kites, flying!"

"So," said the Mandarin's daughter. "You, Kwan-Si, will make a last rebuilding of your town to resemble nothing more nor less than the wind. And we shall build like a golden kite. The wind will beautify the kite and carry it to wondrous heights. And the kite will break the sameness of the wind's existence and give it purpose and meaning. One without the other is nothing. Together, all will be beauty and cooperation and a long and enduring life."

Whereupon the two mandarins were so overjoyed that they took their first nourishment in days, momentarily were given strength, embraced, and lavished praise upon each other, called the Mandarin's daughter a boy, a man, a stone pillar, a warrior, and a true and unforgettable son. Almost immediately they parted and hurried to their towns, calling out and singing, weakly but happily.

Vocabulary

monotony (mə not′ ən ē) *n.* undesirable sameness

Tea Manufacture, Ming dynasty. Vase decoration. Collection of Golestan Palace, Tehran, Iran.

View the Art In what ways are the people in this image similar to and different from the villagers in the story? ★

And so, in time, the towns became the Town of the Golden Kite and the Town of the Silver Wind. And harvestings were harvested and business tended again, and the flesh returned, and disease ran off like a frightened jackal.[4] And on every night of the year the inhabitants in the Town of the Kite could hear the good clear wind sustaining them. And those in the Town of the Wind could hear the kite singing, whispering, rising, and beautifying them.

"So be it," said the Mandarin in front of his silken screen.

4. A *jackal* is a small doglike animal. The jackal has long been connected with superstitions about death and evil spirits.

Allegory *What do the golden kite and the silver wind represent?* **3**

Teach

Literary Element 3

Allegory **Answer:** *Together they represent harmony, beauty, and a natural order marked by cooperation rather than competition.*

APPROACHING **Ask:** How might the Mandarin and his daughter relate to these symbols? *(The daughter lifts her father up and sustains him by giving him advice, and the Mandarin appears before the people as a symbol of strength and wisdom. They work together to help their people.)*

View the Art ★

Answer: *Like the villagers, the people in the image work hard and are doing construction tasks. Unlike the story characters, they look happy, healthy, content, and rested.*

The Chinese first drank tea more than 5,000 years ago. The first book about tea, written in A.D. 800, described how ancient China grew and prepared it. Tea is made by processing the leaves of the flowering plant *Camellia Sinensis.*

Approaching Level

DIFFERENTIATED INSTRUCTION

Emerging Explain that The Great Wall of China was originally constructed as a defense fortification to protect Chinese states against outside forces attempting to overtake them, and that it was expanded for over 2,000 years until it eventually stretched for about 4,000 miles and was manned by one million armed soldiers. Explain that almost two million people were forced to build the wall, and that many of them died during its construction. **Ask:** How is the history of The Great Wall similar to that of the walls in the story? How is it different? *(Students may say that walls resulted from the hard work and sacrifices of many people, and that while The Great Wall was built for protection of a culture, the walls in the story were built for vanity and pride. Some may argue that the fictional walls were also built for protection—to sustain the economy of one city or the other by drawing people to it.)*

After You Read

Assess

1. Students may say that they like the clever daughter or that they dislike the excessive figurative language.
2. (a) Kwan-Si has built its walls in the shape of a pig. (b) This gives Kwan-Si greater symbolic power: the pig shape over the orange shape.
3. (a) His daughter (b) He never acknowledges her role, but he values her advice.
4. (a) Each city wants to be more powerful than its neighbor. (b) Bradbury clearly shows how groups compete at great cost.
5. Competition carried to extremes is destructive; cooperation is positive.
6. (a) She makes the Mandarin look more foolish, for he cannot think for himself. (b) The story would have lacked as many problems and a solution.
7. Competition can still lead to destruction, while cooperation can be a good solution.
8. Student responses will vary but should reflect examples from current political attitudes and personal observation.

Literary Element

1. Cities rebuild walls to outdo each other. When people die, each city builds its wall to complement the other's.
2. The rebuilding represents a drive for supremacy. The final walls represent harmony and cooperation.
3. Students may cite stadiums, theme parks, and other attractions.

After You Read

Respond and Think Critically

Respond and Interpret

1. What did you like best or least about this story? Explain.
2. (a)What news does the Mandarin learn about Kwan-Si at the beginning of the story? (b)Why is this bad news?
3. (a)Who advises the Mandarin to rebuild his city walls in the shape of a club? (b)Describe the relationship between the Mandarin and his advisor.

Analyze and Evaluate

4. (a)Why does each city keep rebuilding its walls? (b)How well does this wall-building activity represent the competition that has occurred throughout history between city-states, nations, or political alliances?
5. What message does the story express about competition? About cooperation?
6. (a)Why do you think the daughter is a character in the story? (b)Explain what the story would have lacked without her.

Connect

7. **Big Idea** Our World and Beyond Bradbury has said that he did not write this story as a political fable. However, are there lessons in the story for leaders of the modern world? Explain your answer.
8. **Connect to Today** How might a modern-day woman advise a family member who was involved in politics?

Literary Element Allegory

An **allegory** has two levels of meaning. There is a literal level, which is the story, or the events of the plot. There is also a symbolic level, which is what the events mean. In an allegory, the story is less important than the message it conveys.

1. What happens on the literal level of this story? In other words, summarize the main events of the plot.
2. What happens on the symbolic level of the story? In other words, tell what the major events of the plot symbolize, or represent.
3. The Mandarin worries that tourists will go to his rival's city because it appears more prosperous. Do modern cities have symbols of prosperity that might sway tourists? Explain.

Review: Moral

As you learned on page 1013, a **moral** is a practical lesson about right and wrong conduct. Morals often are stated at the end of a fable. In most stories, however, the moral is not stated directly. The reader must infer the moral by thinking about the events of the story and by examining what the characters do, say, and think.

Partner Activity Work with a partner to identify the moral in "The Golden Kite, the Silver Wind." Complete an organizer like the one below to show how story events support the moral.

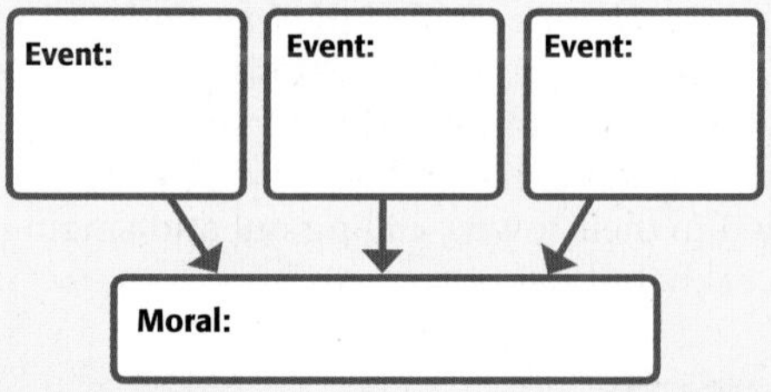

LOG ON Literature Online

Selection Resources For Selection Quizzes, eFlashcards, and Reading-Writing Connection activities, go to glencoe.com and ender QuickPass code GL49787u6.

Progress Check

Can students identify allegory?

If No → See Unit 6 Teaching Resources Book, p. 77.

Review: Moral

Students may list these story events:

- Wall building is repeated.
- People grow weak from overwork.
- Prosperity returns when people cooperate.

Students might write this moral:
It is wiser to cooperate than to compete.

Reading Strategy Evaluate Figures of Speech

Bradbury is known for his poetic and figurative language. In "The Golden Kite, the Silver Wind," readers get the first taste of descriptive language in the title and encounter additional examples in nearly every paragraph.

1. What is descriptive about the story's title? Explain how the title conveys ideas and emotions. Consider connotations as well as images. How well does the title fit the story?
2. Return to the chart you created as you read the story. Choose two of the most effective uses of figurative language that you recorded. Explain what makes each of them memorably descriptive or aptly expressive of the emotion in the story.

Vocabulary Practice

Practice with Synonyms A synonym is a word that has the same or nearly the same meaning as another word. With a partner, match each boldface vocabulary word below with its synonym. You will not use all the answer choices. Use a thesaurus or dictionary to check your answers.

1. portent	a. starving
2. ravenous	b. sameness
3. spurn	c. sharp
4. monotony	d. value
	e. scorn
	f. sign
	g. full

Write with Style

Apply Symbolism

Assignment Write a short story built around a symbolic event or object. Use a comparison matrix to organize the event or object's literal and symbolic meaning in the story.

Get Ideas Brainstorm characters and a setting for your story. Then briefly outline a plot that involves a symbolic event or object. The symbol should play a significant role in the plot.

Give It Structure Use your symbolic event or object to reflect the story's main idea or message. As you move through the story, the meaning of the symbol may grow or change as it reflects the development of the main idea or message. Use a comparison matrix to organize the event or object's literal and symbolic meaning throughout the story. Structure the symbol's development in three basic phases: beginning, middle, and end.

Symbolic Event: a tornado striking		
	Literal meaning	Symbolic meaning
Beginning	need to prepare house, get family to safety	fear of unknown, nature's unpredictability
Middle	need to keep calm and stay sheltered while tornado strikes	nature's power, human determination
End	cleaning up aftermath	the fragile relationship between humans and nature

Build the story's details around the backbone of the symbol's development.

Look at Language Make sure your descriptions of the symbol emphasize its qualities that support the story's meaning.

EXAMPLE:

The tornado ~~landed~~ *slammed down* in the pasture and ~~quickly cut a path~~ *roared* toward the house, *like a freight train,* tearing up the ground as it went.

Write with Style

Students' short stories should:

- be built around a symbolic event or object
- use the symbol to reflect the meaning of the story
- work the symbol into the beginning, middle, and end of the plot
- use language that supports the story's meaning

After You Read

Assess

Reading Strategy

1. The gold and silver suggest precious things; the two objects suggest two things balanced in harmony. The title fits the ending of the story, in which balance and beauty are achieved through cooperation.
2. Students may include "a whisper like a snowflake," which suggests the softness and gentleness of the daughter's voice; or "disease ran off like a frightened jackal," which provides a strong visual image of how quickly disease disappears and helps convey the mood of harmony at the end of the story.

Progress Check

Can students evaluate figures of speech?

If No → See Unit 6 Teaching Resources Book, p. 78.

Vocabulary Practice

1. f **2.** a **3.** e **4.** b

For additional selection assessment, see Assessment Resources, pp. 217–218.

To create custom assessments online, go to Progress Reporter Online Assessment.

To create custom assessments using sofware, use ExamView Assessment Suite.

Loaded Words

Focus

Write this sentence on the board: The basketball player towers over his teammates.
Say: Towers are tall structures, but the word connotes an awesome height that can be intimidating. What would change if instead you say "The boy is tall"? How does the word *tower* affect the sentence? *(Students may say that someone who towers over others shows strength and power as well as great height.)*

Teach

Denotation and Connotation
Say: The literal meaning of a word is its *denotation.* A word may also have another meaning associated with it, called its *connotation.* For example, you may describe someone as *slim* or *scrawny.* The first has a positive connotation and the second a negative one. Both have the denotation "thin."

Assess

1. b **2.** c **3.** a **4.** b

For additional vocabulary practice, see Glencoe Interactive Vocabulary CD-ROM.

Learning Objectives

In this workshop, you will focus on the following objective:

Vocabulary: Understanding denotation and connotation.

Vocabulary Workshop

Loaded Words

Literature Connection In Bradbury's story, when a messenger utters the following words to the Mandarin, the Mandarin's heart sinks.

> *"They have built their city's walls like a great bonfire to burn our stick!"*
>
> —Ray Bradbury, from "The Golden Kite, the Silver Wind"

The Mandarin responds to the loaded words in the message. First, the phrase "great bonfire" makes the fire sound like no ordinary flame, but a huge conflagration. On the other hand, the word *stick* makes the wall, previously referred to as a *club,* seem like less than it is—insignificant and easily burned. Loaded words, which are powerful tools in the art of fiction, can also be used to drive home a point in persuasive writing.

There are different kinds of loaded words.

- **Bias** is language that demonstrates a prejudgment about people and events that is not necessarily accurate or truthful. Try substituting *avoid* for *spurn* in the sentence below. *Spurn* conveys an especially negative bias about what will occur.
  Travelers will spurn us.
- **Hyperbole,** or exaggerated language, is used to make a point.
  We will face disease, early sorrow, avalanches, grasshopper plagues, and poisoned well water.
- **Propaganda** is language that distorts the truth in order to influence others.
  The evil Kwan-Si will destroy our city if you don't change our walls.

Loaded Words

Loaded words are words that express strong opinions or emotions. Some reveal **bias,** or prejudice. Others express **hyperbole,** or exaggeration. Some are used as **propaganda,** or language that distorts the truth for persuasive purposes.

Tip

When you are asked to uncover bias, propaganda, or hyperbole, read the whole passage first to learn the writer's purpose. Then think about individual word choices the writer made to express and support that purpose.

Practice From the words and phrases listed below, select those that convey the greatest bias or hyperbole.

As the greatest, **1.** ______ nation on earth, only we have the right to **2.** ______ space. If life exists in space, it can only be **3.** ______ or degenerate. We will be the explorers who challenge **4.** ______ itself: that is our mighty nation's destiny.

1. a. biggest	**b.** most powerful	**c.** friendliest
2. a. visit	**b.** explore	**c.** colonize
3. a. primitive	**b.** unimportant	**c.** small
4. a. space	**b.** eternity	**c.** purpose

LOG ON **Literature Online**

Vocabulary For more vocabulary practice, go to glencoe.com and enter QuickPass code GL49787u6.

Vocabulary Practice

Understand Hyperbole
Conduct a classroom exercise to help students understand the exaggerated elements of hyperbole. **Write:** I quickly went home from school and checked my mailbox for an expected package. Ask students to rewrite this sentence using hyperbole. *(I raced home from school at the speed of light and looked into my mailbox with eyes as wide as saucers, hoping to find it bursting with a package I'd been expecting forever.)* Ask volunteers to share their sentences with the class. Then ask students to write four sentences of their own using hyperbole.

Before You Read

World Literature
United Kingdom

The Red-Headed League

Meet **Sir Arthur Conan Doyle**
(1859–1930)

What if you were a doctor with little money but plenty of free time due to a shortage of patients? That is what happened to Arthur Conan Doyle. His medical training did not go to waste, however. While a student at Edinburgh University, Doyle was impressed with an instructor, Dr. Bell, who combined keen observations with brilliant deductions to help diagnose diseases. Doyle modeled his fictional detective Sherlock Holmes on Dr. Bell.

Early Career In 1886 Doyle wrote a mystery novel featuring Sherlock Holmes and his colleague John H. Watson. At first, few readers seemed to like it. About a year later, however, the story began to stir interest, prompting an American editor to ask Doyle to write another novel featuring the same detective. Doyle responded by writing *The Sign of Four.* Doyle then wrote six more Sherlock Holmes stories for a magazine, and his life was never the same. The public demanded more and more stories, and Doyle could barely keep up.

> *"Letters of abuse . . . showered upon me when it was thought that I had killed [Holmes]. 'You brute!' was the promising opening of one lady's epistle."*
>
> —Sir Arthur Conan Doyle

Killing Off His Detective Doyle prided himself on both his nonfiction writing and his historical fiction. With readers clamoring for more Sherlock Holmes stories, however, Doyle could not interest editors in publishing anything else. Frustrated, in 1893 Doyle killed off Holmes in a short story called "The Final Solution." Doyle's readers were outraged.

Withstanding the criticism, Doyle went on to write other books on different topics. In 1901, however, after a friend related the story of a ghostly hound, Doyle began writing the mystery that would become *The Hound of the Baskervilles* and resurrect Sherlock Holmes.

Sir Arthur Doyle was knighted in 1902 for his pamphlet defending the British during the Boer War in South Africa. Still, the creation of Sherlock Holmes was Doyle's crowning achievement. To this day, the Baker Street Irregulars, an organization of avid readers of Sherlock Holmes stories, meet regularly to honor the world's best-known detective.

LOG ON **Literature** Online

Author Search For more about Sir Arthur Conan Doyle, go to glencoe.com and enter QuickPass code GL49787u6.

Before You Read

Focus

Bellringer Options

Daily Language Practice Transparency 98

Or display images of the classic fictional detectives, such as Sherlock Holmes, Charlie Chan, Hercule Poirot, and Ellery Queen. Discuss how these sleuths solved crimes through the power of their intellect.

Ask: What do these detectives have in common? How do they compare with today's fictional detectives? Have students consider as they read how Doyle reveals the deductive reasoning powers that are the signature talent of Holmes.

Selection Skills

The Red-Headed League

Literary Elements
- Foreshadowing (SE pp. 1044–1066)
- Character Archetype (SE p. 1066)

Reading Skills
- Make Inferences About Characters (SE pp. 1044–1066)

Vocabulary Skills
- Synonyms (SE pp. 1044, 1066)
- Academic Vocabulary (SE p. 1066)

Listening/Speaking/Viewing Skills
- Analyze Art (SE pp. 1047, 1052, 1055, 1063)

Writing Skills/Grammar
- Expository Essay (SE p. 1067)
- Diction (SE p. 1067)

Before You Read

Focus

Summary

Jabez Wilson, a London pawnbroker, goes to work for an employer that hires only redheads. When the employer mysteriously vanishes, Wilson consults Holmes and Watson. Holmes's investigation uncovers a serious crime masterminded by the infamous John Clay.

For summaries in languages other than English, see Unit 6 Teaching Resources Book, pp. 84–89.

Vocabulary

Make a Synonym Chain

Have groups of students create a synonym chain by instructing one student to write one of the vocabulary words on a sheet of paper and then pass the sheet to the student on his or her right. That student should write a synonym of the word underneath the original word and then pass the sheet to the right. Instruct the students to keep the chain going for as long as possible.

Literature and Reading Preview

Connect to the Story

Who are your favorite detectives on television? Freewrite for a few minutes explaining why you enjoy watching them.

Build Background

The narrator of "The Red-Headed League" is Dr. Watson, whom Holmes refers to as his "partner" and "helper." Always one step behind Holmes, Watson takes the reader's place in the story. He comments on Holmes's observational and deductive powers, thereby shedding light on the detective's character.

Set Purposes for Reading

Big Idea Our World and Beyond

As you read, ask yourself, What important details are hidden at first and later revealed in this story?

Literary Element Foreshadowing

Foreshadowing is an author's use of clues to prepare readers for later developments in the plot. This technique involves a reader in a story by generating a feeling of suspense, dread, or eager anticipation. As you read, ask yourself, What clues does Doyle use that foreshadow events in the story?

Reading Strategy Make Inferences About Characters

Making inferences involves using your reason and experience to make educated guesses based on what an author implies or suggests. Writers do not always directly state what they want readers to know, so you must infer a character's motivations, relationships, and personality traits. As you read, ask yourself, What inferences can I make about the characters in this story?

Tip: Take Notes As you read, use a chart to record your inferences about the characters in this story.

Details	Inferences
Holmes deduces facts about Mr. Wilson.	Holmes is very observant and has excellent powers of reasoning and deduction.

Learning Objectives

For pages 1043–1066

In studying this text, you will focus on the following objectives:

Literary Study: Analyzing foreshadowing.

Reading: Making inferences about characters.

Vocabulary

singular (sing′ gyə lər) *adj.* unusual or out of the ordinary; odd; p. 1046 *Jenna remembered the suspect because of his singular appearance.*

nominal (nom′ ən əl) *adj.* insignificant; p. 1048 *Writing an e-mail message to a friend often requires only nominal effort.*

languid (lang′ gwid) *adj.* drooping; weak and listless; p. 1057 *He was feeling languid after a day of heavy physical work.*

formidable (fôr′ mi də bəl) *adj.* impressive; awe-inspiring; p. 1058 *The tennis champion was a formidable opponent to the other players in the tournament.*

Tip: Synonyms Words that have the same or nearly the same meaning are called **synonyms.** When encountering a difficult word, replacing it with a more familiar synonym can help you determine how the difficult word is being used. For example, you might replace *formidable* with a synonym like *impressive.*

Vocabulary Practice

SMALL GROUP

Modifiers Point out that the vocabulary words on this page are adjectives—a type of modifier that modifies nouns and pronouns. Explain that adjectives answer the questions,

- "Which one?"
- "What kind?"
- "How much?"

Have students read the sample sentences for each word. Explain that the word *singular* modifies the noun *appearance,* the word *nominal* modifies the noun *effort,* and the word *formidable* modifies the noun *opponent.* Tell students that the word *languid* is used in a different way—as a predicate adjective. Explain that since the predicate in the sentence *(was feeling)* is a linking verb, the word *languid* is a predicate adjective.

Break students into small groups. Have them use each vocabulary word in a sentence as an adjective and as a predicate adjective.

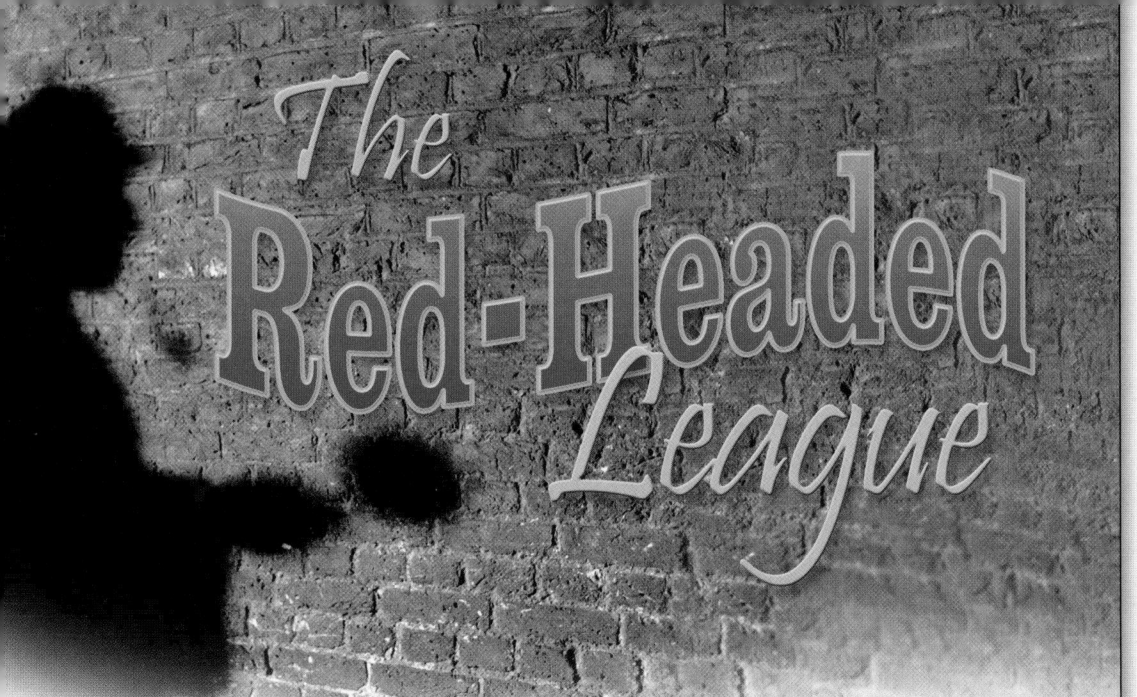

The Red-Headed League

Sir Arthur Conan Doyle

I had called upon my friend, Mr. Sherlock Holmes, one day in the autumn of last year, and found him in deep conversation with a very stout, florid-faced, elderly gentleman, with fiery red hair. With an apology for my intrusion, I was about to withdraw, when Holmes pulled me abruptly into the room and closed the door behind me. "You could not possibly have come at a better time, my dear Watson," he said, cordially.

"I was afraid that you were engaged."

"So I am. Very much so."

"Then I can wait in the next room."

"Not at all, Watson. Mr. Wilson, I would like you to meet Dr. Watson, my partner, friend, and helper in many of my most successful cases."

1 Make Inferences About Characters *Based on what you have read so far, how would you describe Watson's relationship with Holmes?*

The stout gentleman half rose from his chair and gave a bob of greeting, with a quick, little, questioning glance from his small, fat-encircled eyes.

"Try the settee,"[1] said Holmes, relapsing into his armchair, and putting his finger tips together, as was his custom when in judicial moods. "I know, my dear Watson, that you share my love of all that is bizarre and outside the conventions and humdrum routine of everyday life. You have shown your relish for it by the enthusiasm which has prompted you to chronicle, and, if you will excuse my saying so, somewhat to embellish so many of my own little adventures."

"Your cases have indeed been of the greatest interest to me," I observed.

"You will remember that I remarked the other day, just before we went into the very

1. A *settee* (se tē´) is a medium-sized sofa.

Teach

Reading Strategy 1

Make Inferences About Characters **Answer:** *They are close friends with shared interests and mutual respect, as well as a good professional team.*

For an audio recording of this selection, use Listening Library Audio CD-ROM.

Readability Scores

Dale-Chall: 7.2
DRP: 61
Lexile: 1110

Approaching Level

DIFFERENTIATED INSTRUCTION

Emerging Write: "Do you want to go to the movies on Friday?" asked Dion. Explain that "asked Dion" is a dialogue tag. Point out the dialogue on this page. Explain that Doyle often omits dialogue tags. Omitting tags speeds up the conversation for the reader, but can also cause confusion as to who is speaking. Pair up students and have them identify the speakers on this page.

Established Remind students that they can better understand an author's words by paraphrasing them. Encourage students to work together to paraphrase parts of the selection where Doyle's language is difficult to comprehend. Guide them to use a dictionary to look up new words.

Teach

Literary Element 1

Foreshadowing Answer: *Holmes's remark that life is more extraordinary than imagination suggests that Wilson's case will be unusual.*

APPROACHING To guide approaching-level students, **ask:** Do you think this is true? Why or why not? *(Students may say that this is not true, because they can imagine much more extraordinary things than they can dream in day-to-day life.)*

Literary Element 2

Foreshadowing Answer: *It is another hint that the case will be strange and makes the reader want to find out more about it.*

Cultural History ☆

Freemasons An international secret society that espouses brotherhood and charity, the Freemasons is thought to have roots in the trade guilds of medieval Europe. (The term *freemason* originally referred to a master stonemason, who was privileged to work where he wanted unrestrained by the guild.) As the Freemasons evolved over the centuries, its members were often subjected to persecution. Even today the organization remains a favorite target of conspiracy theorists—as it was in Doyle's time.

simple problem presented by Miss Mary Sutherland, that for strange effects and extraordinary combinations we must go to life itself, which is always far more daring than any effort of the imagination."

"A proposition which I took the liberty of doubting."

"You did, doctor, but nonetheless you must come round to my view, for otherwise I shall keep on piling fact upon fact on you, until your reason breaks down under them and acknowledges me to be right. Now, Mr. Jabez[2] Wilson here has been good enough to call upon me this morning, and to begin a narrative which promises to be one of the most **singular** which I have listened to for some time. You have heard me remark that the strangest and most unique things are very often connected not with the larger but with the smaller crimes, and occasionally, indeed, where there is room for doubt whether any positive crime has been committed. As far as I have heard, it is impossible for me to say whether the present case is an instance of crime or not, but the course of events is certainly among the most singular that I have ever listened to. Perhaps, Mr. Wilson, you would have the great kindness to recommence your narrative. I ask you, not merely because my friend, Dr. Watson, has not heard the opening part, but also because the peculiar nature of the story makes me anxious to have every possible detail from your lips. As a rule, when I have heard some slight indication of the course of events, I am able to guide myself by the thousands of other similar cases, which occur to my memory. In the present instance I am forced to admit that the facts are, to the best of my belief, unique."

The portly client puffed out his chest with an appearance of some little pride, and pulled a dirty and wrinkled newspaper from the inside pocket of his greatcoat. As he glanced down the advertisement column, with his head thrust forward, and the paper flattened out upon his knee, I took a good look at the man, and endeavored, after the fashion of my companion, to read the indications which might be presented by his dress or appearance.

I did not gain very much, however, by my inspection. Our visitor bore every mark of being an average, commonplace British tradesman, obese, pompous, and slow. He wore rather baggy gray shepherd's check trousers, a not overclean black frock coat, unbuttoned in the front, and a drab waistcoat with a heavy, brassy Albert chain,[3] and a square pierced bit of metal dangling down as an ornament. A frayed top hat and a faded brown overcoat with a wrinkled velvet collar lay upon a chair beside him. Altogether, look as I would, there was nothing remarkable about the man save his blazing red head, and the expression of extreme chagrin[4] and discontent upon his features.

Sherlock Holmes's quick eye took in my occupation, and he shook his head with a smile as he noticed my questioning glances. "Beyond the obvious facts that he has at some time done manual labor, that

2. *Jabez* (jā′ bez) is Wilson's first name.

1 Foreshadowing *What might Holmes's remark foreshadow about Wilson's case?*

Vocabulary

singular (sing′ gyə lər) *adj.* unusual or out of the ordinary; odd

3. An *Albert chain* is a watch chain named after Prince Albert (1819–1861), the husband of England's Queen Victoria (1819–1901).

4. *Chagrin* is distress caused by disappointment.

Foreshadowing *How does this statement build suspense?* 2

Writing Practice

Character Traits Remind students that you can tell a lot about characters from what they say about themselves and from what others say about them. Point out that Watson and Holmes draw very different conclusions about Wilson's appearance based on the same evidence. **Ask:** What can you tell about Watson? About Holmes? *(Watson inspects Wilson, but cannot tell much about him from his appearance; Holmes, on the other hand, gains great insight into Wilson's character from his appearance. This shows that Holmes reads people better and is perhaps more experienced at doing so.)* Have students write a character sketch of Wilson based on the details in the story.

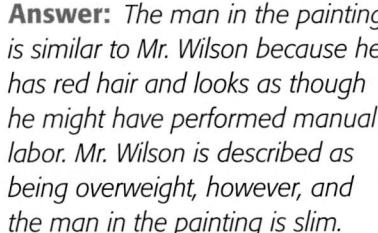

Head of Red Moore, 1933. Eugene E. Speicher. Albright-Knox Art Gallery.

View the Art In 1936 *Esquire* magazine named Eugene E. Speicher the "most important living artist." In what ways is the man in this painting similar to and different from Mr. Jabez Wilson? ★

☆ he takes snuff, that he is a Freemason,[5] that he has been in China, and that he has done a considerable amount of writing lately, I can deduce nothing else."

Mr. Jabez Wilson started up in his chair, with his forefinger upon the paper, but with his eyes upon my companion. "How, in the name of good fortune, did you know all that, Mr. Holmes?" he asked. "How did you know, for example, that I did manual labor? It's as true as gospel, for I began as a ship's carpenter."

"Your hands, my dear sir. Your right hand is quite a size larger than your left. You have worked with it, and the muscles are more developed."

"Well, the snuff, then, and the Freemasonry?"

"I won't insult your intelligence by telling you how I read that, especially as, rather against the strict rules of your order, you use an arc-and-compass breastpin."

"Ah, of course, I forgot that. But the writing?"

"What else can be indicated by that right cuff so very shiny for five inches, and the left one with the smooth patch near the elbow where you rest it upon the desk?"

"Well, but China?"

"The fish that you have tattooed immediately above your right wrist could only have been done in China. I have made a

5. A *Freemason* is a member of a secret fraternal order. The emblem of the group is the arc and compass, which, as Holmes notes, should always be concealed.

Teach

View the Art ★

Answer: *The man in the painting is similar to Mr. Wilson because he has red hair and looks as though he might have performed manual labor. Mr. Wilson is described as being overweight, however, and the man in the painting is slim.*

English Learners

DIFFERENTIATED INSTRUCTION

Beginning/Early Intermediate Students may have trouble understanding Doyle's use of idioms and unfamiliar language on these pages. Write the following on the board:

- "come round to my view" *(see what I see)*
- "recommence" *(begin again)*
- "save his blazing red head" *(except for his bright red hair)*
- "how I read that" *(how I discovered that)*
- "off the beaten track" *(uncommon)*

Encourage them to add words and phrases to this list as they read. Then discuss the meanings of these words and phrases.

Teach

Reading Strategy 1

Make Inferences About Characters **Answer:** *He seems too dense to appreciate Holmes's intelligence.*

Reading Strategy 2

Make Inferences About Characters **Answer:** *Watson is confused, but Holmes's behavior conveys his amusement and suggests that he has already begun to solve the case.*

APPROACHING To help approaching-level students, **ask:** How are the two characters alike? *(They are both dedicated to solving mysteries.)*

small study of tattoo marks, and have even contributed to the literature of the subject. That trick of staining the fishes' scales of a delicate pink is quite peculiar to China. When, in addition, I see a Chinese coin hanging from your watch chain, the matter becomes even more simple."

Mr. Jabez Wilson laughed heavily. "Well, I never!" said he. "I thought at first that you had done something clever, but I see that there was nothing in it, after all."

"I begin to think, Watson," said Holmes, "that I make a mistake in explaining. *'Omne ignotum pro magnifico,'*[6] you know, and my poor little reputation, such as it is, will suffer shipwreck if I am so candid. Can you not find the advertisement, Mr. Wilson?"

"Yes, I have got it now," he answered, with his thick, red finger planted halfway down the column. "Here it is. This is what began it all. You just read it for yourself, sir."

I took the paper from him, and read as follows:

> To the Red-Headed League:
>
> On account of the bequest[7] of the late Ezekiah[8] Hopkins, of Lebanon, Pa., U.S.A., there is now another vacancy open which entitles a member of the League to a salary of four pounds a week for purely **nominal** services. All red-headed men who are sound in body and mind, and above the age of twenty-one years, are eligible. Apply in person on Monday, at eleven o'clock, to Duncan Ross, at the offices of the League, 7 Pope's Court, Fleet Street.

"What on earth does this mean?" I ejaculated, after I had twice read over the extraordinary announcement.

Holmes chuckled, and wriggled in his chair, as was his habit when in high spirits. "It is a little off the beaten track, isn't it?" said he. "And now, Mr. Wilson, off you go at scratch,[9] and tell us all about yourself, your household, and the effect which this advertisement had upon your fortunes. You will first make a note, doctor, of the paper and the date."

"It is *The Morning Chronicle* of April 27, 1890. Just two months ago."

"Very good. Now, Mr. Wilson?"

"Well it is just as I have been telling you, Mr. Sherlock Holmes," said Jabez Wilson, mopping his forehead; "I have a small pawnbroker's business at Coburg Square, near the City.[10] It's not a very large affair, and of late years it has not done more than just give me a living. I used to be able to keep two assistants, but now I only keep one; and I would have a job to pay him, but that he is willing to come for half wages, so as to learn the business."

"What is the name of this obliging youth?" asked Sherlock Holmes.

"His name is Vincent Spaulding, and he's not such a youth, either. It's hard to say his age. I should not wish a smarter assistant, Mr. Holmes; and I know very well that he could better himself, and earn twice what I am able to give him. But, after all, if he is satisfied, why should I put ideas in his head?"

"Why indeed? You seem most fortunate in having an employee who comes under

6. *Omne ignotum pro magnifico* is Latin for "Every mysterious thing seems greater than it really is."
7. A *bequest* is something given in a will.
8. *Ezekiah* (ez′ ə kī′ ə) is a first name that was more common in the 1800s than it is now.
9. *At scratch* means "from the beginning."
10. The *City* refers to the center of downtown London.

1 Make Inferences About Characters *What are your impressions of Mr. Wilson?*

2 Make Inferences About Characters *How would you contrast Watson and Holmes?*

Vocabulary

nominal (nom′ ən əl) *adj.* insignificant

Reading Practice

SMALL GROUP

Tone Tell students that the tone of Doyle's stories is often suspenseful. Break students into groups and have them look for examples of suspense on these pages. Have students consider how Doyle's choice of a narrator contributes to this suspense. **Ask:** Would the story be more or less suspenseful if it were written from Holmes's point of view? *(Students should note that the story would likely be less suspenseful; since Holmes has such a keen eye for detail, he might have told the reader what was happening and eliminated the suspense.)*

the full market price. It is not a common experience among employers in this age. I don't know that your assistant is not as remarkable as your advertisement."

"Oh, he has his faults, too," said Mr. Wilson. "Never was such a fellow for photography. Snapping away with a camera when he ought to be improving his mind, and then diving down into the cellar like a rabbit into its hole to develop his pictures. That is his main fault; but, on the whole, he's a good worker. There's no vice in him."

"He is still with you, I presume?"

"Yes, sir. He and a girl of fourteen, who does a bit of simple cooking, and keeps the place clean—that's all I have in the house, for I am a widower, and never had any family. We live very quietly, sir, the three of us; and we keep a roof over our heads, and pay our debts, if we do nothing more.

"The first thing that put us out was that advertisement. Spaulding, he came down into the office just this day eight weeks, with this very paper in his hand, and he says:

"'I wish to the Lord, Mr. Wilson, that I was a red-headed man.'

"'Why that?' I asks.

"'Why,' says he, 'here's another vacancy on the League of the Red-Headed Men. It's worth quite a little fortune to any man who gets it, and I understand that there are more vacancies than there are men, so that the trustees are at their wits' end what to do with the money. If my hair would only change color, here's a nice little crib[11] all ready for me to step into.'

"'Why, what is it, then?' I asked. You see, Mr. Holmes, I am a very stay-at-home man, and as my business came to me instead of my having to go to it, I was often weeks on end without putting my foot over the door-mat. In that way I didn't know much of what was going on outside, and I was always glad of a bit of news.

"'Have you never heard of the League of the Red-Headed Men?' he asked, with his eyes open.

"'Never.'

"'Why, I wonder at that, for you are eligible yourself for one of the vacancies.'

"'And what are they worth?' I asked.

"'Oh, merely a couple of hundred a year, but the work is slight, and it need not interfere very much with one's other occupations.'

"Well, you can easily think that that made me prick up my ears, for the business has not been over-good for some years, and an extra couple of hundred would have been very handy. **5**

"'Tell me all about it,' said I.

"'Well,' said he, showing me the advertisement, 'you can see for yourself that the League has a vacancy, and there is the address where you should apply for particulars. As far as I can make out, the League was founded by an American millionaire, Ezekiah Hopkins, who was very peculiar in his ways. He was himself red-headed, and he had a great sympathy for all red-headed men; so, when he died, it was found that he had left his enormous fortune in the hands of trustees, with instructions to apply the interest to the providing of easy berths to men whose hair is of that color. From all I hear it is splendid pay, and very little to do.'

"'But,' said I, 'there would be millions of red-headed men who would apply.'

"'Not so many as you might think,' he answered. 'You see it is really confined to Londoners, and to grown men. This

11. A *crib* is an easy job or position.

3 Foreshadowing *What might Spaulding's willingness to work for half wages foreshadow?*

Make Inferences About Characters *What does Wilson's admission suggest about him?* **4**

Teach

Literary Element 3

Foreshadowing Answer: *It might foreshadow that Spaulding's real motive is to gain access to Wilson's shop.*

ADVANCED To challenge advanced students, **ask:** How does Wilson view Spaulding's attitude? What does that suggest about Wilson? *(Wilson is puzzled by Spaulding's attitude, but thinks it is harmless. He is very trusting and naïve.)*

Reading Strategy 4

Make Inferences About Characters Answer: *He is not very curious about or engaged in the world.*

Reading Strategy 5

Analyze Dialogue

Ask: Based on its context in the paragraph, what do you think the expression "prick up my ears" means? *(To pay close attention to what has been said)* Why was Wilson so interested in the league? *(It was an easy way to make money.)*

Approaching Level

DIFFERENTIATED INSTRUCTION

Emerging Explain that Wilson's revelations about himself on these pages show that he is naive. Point out that his employee works for only half of what he should be paid, that Wilson stays in his house for weeks without going outside, and that he does not suspect foul play when the man at the office of the Red-Headed League is nicer to him than he is to the others. **Ask:** Do you think it would be easy to trick Wilson? Why or why not? *(Students should say that it would be easy because Wilson seems to believe what others tell him and is cut off from most of the world.)*

Teach

Reading Strategy 1

Make Inferences About Characters **Answer:** *Spaulding's determination to get Wilson through the crowd is a clue that the assistant has an interest in making sure Wilson joins the league.*

Literary Element 2

Foreshadowing **Answer:** *The "office" contains little furniture, as though it had recently been set up, and each candidate before Wilson is disqualified on the basis of "some fault."*

Literary History ☆

Fleet Street Fleet Street was the journalistic center of London for more than 250 years. The first London daily newspaper, *The Courant,* came from Fleet Street in 1702. Fleet Street also attracted numerous literary figures, including Shakespeare. Fleet Street is named for the Fleet River, which runs under London.

American had started from London when he was young, and he wanted to do the old town a good turn. Then, again, I have heard it is no use applying if your hair is light red, or dark red, or anything but real bright, blazing, fiery red. Now, if you cared to apply, Mr. Wilson, you would just walk in; but perhaps it would hardly be worth your while to put yourself out of the way for the sake of a few hundred pounds.'

"Now, it is a fact, gentlemen, as you may see for yourself, that my hair is of a very full and rich tint, so that it seemed to me that, if there was to be any competition in the matter, I stood as good a chance as any man that I had ever met. Vincent Spaulding seemed to know so much about it that I thought he might prove useful, so I ordered him to put up the shutters for the day, and to come right away with me. He was very willing to have a holiday, so we shut the business up, and started off for the address that was given us in the advertisement.

"I never hope to see such a sight as that again, Mr. Holmes. From north, south, east, and west every man who had a shade of red in his hair had tramped into the City to answer the advertisement. Fleet ☆ Street was choked with red-headed folk, and Pope's Court looked like a coster's orange barrow.[12] I should not have thought there were so many in the whole country as were brought together by that single advertisement. Every shade of color they were—straw, lemon, orange, brick, Irish setter, liver, clay; but, as Spaulding said there were not many who had the real vivid flame-colored tint. When I saw how many were waiting I would have given it up in despair; but Spaulding would not hear of it. How he did it I could not imagine, but he pushed and pulled and butted until he got me through the crowd, and right up the steps which led to the office. There was a double stream upon the stair, some going up in hope, and some coming back dejected; but we wedged in as well as we could, and soon found ourselves in the office."

"Your experience has been a most entertaining one," remarked Holmes, as his client paused and refreshed his memory with a huge pinch of snuff. "Pray continue your very interesting statement."

"There was nothing in the office but a couple of wooden chairs and a deal table, behind which sat a small man, with a head that was even redder than mine. He said a few words to each candidate as he came up, and then he always managed to find some fault in them which would disqualify them. Getting a vacancy did not seem to be such a very easy matter, after all. However, when our turn came, the little man was much more favorable to me than to any of the others, and he closed the door as we entered, so that he might have a private word with us.

"'This is Mr. Jabez Wilson,' said my assistant, 'and he is willing to fill a vacancy in the League.'

"'And he is admirably suited for it,' the other answered. 'He has every requirement. I cannot recall when I have seen anything so fine.' He took a step backward, cocked his head on one side, and gazed at my hair until I felt quite bashful. Then suddenly he plunged forward, wrung my hand, and congratulated me warmly on my success.

Make Inferences About Characters *Why do you think it is so important to Spaulding to see Wilson get through the crowd?* **1**

Foreshadowing *What details in this paragraph hint that things are not what they seem?* **2**

12. A *coster's orange barrow* is a fruit vendor's bin of oranges.

Grammar Practice

SMALL GROUP

Pronouns Students may sometimes be confused by the use of personal pronouns in fiction. Explain to students that personal pronouns refer to certain people or things. **Say:** These pronouns may refer to the person telling the story, the person the story is about, or the person hearing the story. Divide the class into small groups. Assign each group a paragraph from this page. Then, challenge the groups to rewrite the paragraph by changing the point of view to third person and then adjusting all pronouns. For example, the line "I never hope to see such a sight," would become "He never hopes to see such a sight."

"'It would be injustice to hesitate,' said he. 'You will, however, I am sure, excuse me for taking an obvious precaution.' With that he seized my hair in both his hands, and tugged until I yelled with the pain. 'There is water in your eyes,' said he, as he released me, 'I perceive that all is as it should be. But we have to be careful, for we have twice been deceived by wigs and once by paint. I could tell you tales of cobbler's wax[13] which would disgust you with human nature.'

"He stepped over to the window, and shouted through it at the top of his voice that the vacancy was filled. A groan of disappointment came up from below, and the folk all trooped away in different directions, until there was not a red head to be seen except my own and that of the manager.

"'My name,' said he, 'is Mr. Duncan Ross, and I am myself one of the pensioners upon the fund left by our noble benefactor. Are you a married man, Mr. Wilson? Have you a family?'

"I answered that I had not.

"His face fell immediately.

3 "'Dear me!' he said, gravely, 'that is very serious indeed! I am sorry to hear you say that. The fund was, of course, for the propagation and spread of the redheads as well as for their maintenance. It is exceedingly unfortunate that you should be a bachelor.'

"My face lengthened at this, Mr. Holmes, for I thought that I was not to have the vacancy after all; but, after thinking it over for a few minutes, he said that it would be all right.

"'In the case of another,' said he, 'the objection might be fatal, but we must stretch a point in favor of a man with such a head of hair as yours. When shall you be able to enter upon your new duties?'

"'Well, it is a little awkward, for I have a business already,' said I.

"'Oh, never mind about that, Mr. Wilson!' said Vincent Spaulding. 'I shall be able to look after that for you.'

"'What would be the hours?' I asked.

"'Ten to two.'

"Now a pawnbroker's business is mostly done of an evening, Mr. Holmes, especially Thursday and Friday evenings, which is just before payday, so it would suit me very well to earn a little in the mornings. Besides, I knew that my assistant was a good man, and that he would see to anything that turned up.

"'That would suit me very well,' said I. 'And the pay?'

Man reading under the lamplight, 1814. Georg Friedrich Kersting. Canvas, 47.5 x 37 cm. Coll. Oskar Reinhart, Winterthur, Switzerland.

13. *Cobbler's wax* is a sticky substance with which shoemakers treat thread.

Teach

Reading Strategy 3

Review and Summarize

Say: In spite of not having a family, Wilson is accepted into the league. **Ask:** Why do you think an exception was made? *(Possible answer: They may have some reason besides his hair for wanting to hire him.)*

English Learners

DIFFERENTIATED INSTRUCTION

Beginning/Early Intermediate Point out the use of single and double quotation marks in the selection. **Write:** "'It would be injustice to hesitate,' said he." Explain that double quotation marks are used to indicate that someone is speaking. In this case, however, a character is quoting another character—it is a quotation within a quotation. When a character quotes another character, double quotes are used around the first character's words and single quotes are used around the second character's words. Point out that the double quotes are repeated at the beginning of each paragraph to show that the first character is still speaking.

Teach

Literary Element 1

Foreshadowing Answer: *It adds to the aura of strangeness and mystery surrounding the unusual job.*

Big Idea 2

Our World and Beyond

Answer: *Wilson must copy the* Encyclopedia Britannica, *though no reason is given for this task. He must remain in the office for a set time every day. It does not matter how much Wilson accomplishes or how well he does his "busy work."*

View the Art ★

Answer: *Answers will vary. Students may note that the man's posture looks tentative, as if he's prepared to leave quickly.*

English illustrator Sidney Paget (1860–1908) illustrated Doyle's Sherlock Holmes series that appeared in the *Strand Magazine.*

Mr. Jabez Wilson reading a sign that says, "THE RED-HEADED LEAGUE IS DISSOLVED OCTOBER 9, 1890." Sidney Paget.

View the Art How does the man's posture in this illustration reveal his attitude at the moment? ★

"'Is four pounds a week.'

"'And the work?'

"'Is purely nominal.'

"'What do you call purely nominal?'

"'Well, you have to be in the office, or at least in the building, the whole time. If you leave, you forfeit your whole position forever. The will is very clear upon that point. You don't comply with the conditions if you budge from the office during that time.'

"'It's only four hours a day, and I should not think of leaving,' said I.

"'No excuse will avail,' said Mr. Duncan Ross. 'Neither sickness nor business nor anything else. There you must stay, or you lose your billet.'[14]

"'And the work?'

"'Is to copy out the *Encyclopedia Britannica.* There is the first volume of it in that press.[15] You must find your own ink, pens, and chair. Will you be ready tomorrow?'

"'Certainly,' I answered.

"'Then, good-bye, Mr. Jabez Wilson, and let me congratulate you once more on the important position which you have been fortunate enough to gain.' He bowed me out of the room, and I went home with my assistant, hardly knowing what to say or do, I was so pleased at my own good fortune.

"Well, I thought over the matter all day, and by evening I was in low spirits again for I had quite persuaded myself that the whole affair must be some great hoax or fraud, though what its object might be I could not imagine. It seemed altogether past belief that anyone could make such a will, or that they would pay such a sum for doing anything so simple as copying out the *Encyclopedia Britannica.* Vincent Spaulding did what he could to cheer me up, but by bedtime I had reasoned myself out of the whole thing. However, in the morning I determined to have a look at it anyhow, so I bought a penny bottle of ink, and with a quill pen and seven sheets of foolscap paper,[16] I started off for Pope's Court.

14. A *billet* is a job.
15. A *press* is a cupboard.
16. *Foolscap paper* is writing paper.

Foreshadowing *What effect does Ross's emphatic order create?* **1**

Our World and Beyond *What unusual details about this position does Mr. Wilson overlook?* **2**

Writing Practice

Synthesize Ideas Have students read Wilson's account of his job coming to an end on page 1053. Have students write a paragraph in the third person describing how Wilson looked and felt when he discovered that the Red-Headed League had dissolved. Encourage students to use their own imagination as well as details in the text and the art. **Ask:** What did Wilson probably do right after he saw the sign on the door? *(Students may say that he may have read the sign several times and leaned against the wall or sat down in disbelief.)*

"Well, to my surprise and delight, everything was as right as possible. The table was set out ready for me, and Mr. Duncan Ross was there to see that I got fairly to work. He started me off upon the letter A, then he left me; but he would drop in from time to time to see that all was right with me. At two o'clock he bade me good-day, complimented me upon the amount that I had written, and locked the door of the office after me.

"This went on day after day, Mr. Holmes, and on Saturday the manager came in and planked down four golden sovereigns[17] for my week's work. It was the same next week, and the same the week after. Every morning I was there at ten, and every afternoon I left at two. By degrees Mr. Duncan Ross took to coming in only once of a morning, and then, after a time, he did not come in at all. Still, of course, I never dared to leave the room for an instant, for I was not sure when he might come, and the billet was such a good one, and suited me so well, that I would not risk the loss of it.

"Eight weeks passed away like this, and I had written about Abbots and Archery and Armor and Architecture and Attica, and hoped with diligence that I might get on to the B's before very long. It cost me something in foolscap, and I had pretty nearly filled a shelf with my writings. And then suddenly the whole business came to an end."

"To an end?"

"Yes, sir. And no later than this morning. I went to my work as usual at ten o'clock, but the door was shut and locked, with a little square of cardboard hammered on to the middle of the panel with a tack. Here it is, and you can read for yourself."

He held up a piece of white cardboard about the size of a sheet of note paper. It read in this fashion:

THE RED-HEADED LEAGUE
IS DISSOLVED
OCTOBER 9, 1890

Sherlock Holmes and I surveyed this curt[18] announcement and the rueful[19] face behind it, until the comical side of the affair so completely overtopped every other consideration that we both burst out into a roar of laughter.

"I cannot see that there is anything very funny," cried our client, flushing up to the roots of his flaming head. "If you can do nothing better than laugh at me, I can go elsewhere."

"No, no," cried Holmes, shoving him back into the chair from which he had half risen. "I really wouldn't miss your case for the world. It is most refreshingly unusual. But there is, if you will excuse my saying so, something just a little funny about it. Pray, what steps did you take when you found the card upon the door?"

"I was staggered, sir. I did not know what to do. Then I called at the offices round, but none of them seemed to know anything about it. Finally, I went to the landlord, who is an accountant living on the ground floor, and I asked him if he could tell me what had become of the Red-Headed League. He said that he had never heard of any such body. Then I asked him who Mr. Duncan Ross was. He answered that the name was new to him.

"'Well,' said I, 'the gentleman at No. 4.'

"'What, the red-headed man?'

17. *Sovereigns* (sov′ rənz) are gold coins worth one pound each at the time of the story.

18. *Curt* means "so short as to seem impolite."

19. *Rueful* refers to Wilson's pitiably disappointed face.

3 Make Inferences About Characters *What can you infer about Mr. Wilson?*

Our World and Beyond *How would you respond to seeing this sign?* **4**

Teach

Reading Strategy 3

Make Inferences About Characters Answer: *Wilson is not only gullible but also mercenary. He would rather be paid well than question the value of his work.*

APPROACHING For approaching-level students, **ask:** Do you think you would have taken the job Mr. Wilson takes? *(Some students may say that they would not have taken a job that seemed too good to be true or that sounded so unlikely.)*

Big Idea 4

Our World and Beyond
Answer: *Students may say that they would be surprised, confused, or angry.*

English Learners

DIFFERENTIATED INSTRUCTION

Beginning/Early Intermediate Students will likely have some trouble with the vocabulary in this story. Many words are difficult or old-fashioned. Encourage students to keep a list of unfamiliar words for later research. You may ask students to look up the words in a dictionary or discuss them in groups. Here are some words students may find difficult:

- "sleuth" *(detective)*
- "astuteness" *(cleverness)*
- "contemplative" *(thoughtful)*
- "languor" *(weakness)*
- "intuition" *(insight)*

Teach

Reading Strategy 1

Predict **Ask:** What do you think Mr. Wilson will find out? *(That the league is a fraud)*

Reading Strategy 2

Draw Conclusions **Ask:** Do you agree with the assistant's advice to Wilson? *(Possible answer: No; Wilson has been too passive and trusting; by now he should realize something suspicious is going on.)*

Reading Strategy 3

Make Inferences About Characters **Ask:** What does this remark reveal about Mr. Wilson? *(His only interest seems to be money.)*

Reading Strategy 4

Make Inferences About Characters **Answer:** *Holmes observes keenly and has excellent recall of details. He surmises Vincent Spaulding's real identity.*

"'Yes.'

"'Oh,' said he, 'his name was William Morris. He was a solicitor,[20] and was using my room as a temporary convenience until his new premises were ready. He moved out yesterday.'

"'Where could I find him?'

Visual Vocabulary
St. Paul's is a famous cathedral in London.

"'Oh, at his new offices. He did tell me the address. Yes, 17 King Edward Street, near St. Paul's.'

1 "I started off, Mr. Holmes, but when I got to that address it was a manufactory of artificial kneecaps, and no one in it had ever heard of either Mr. William Morris or Mr. Duncan Ross."

"And what did you do then?" asked Holmes.

"I went home to Saxe-Coburg Square, and I took the advice of my assistant. But
2 he could not help me in any way. He could only say that if I waited I should hear by post. But that was not quite good enough, Mr. Holmes. I did not wish to lose such a place without a struggle; so, as I have heard that you were good enough to give advice to poor folk who were in need of it, I came right away to you."

"And you did very wisely," said Holmes. "Your case is an exceedingly remarkable one, and I shall be happy to look into it. From what you have told me I think that it is possible that graver issues hang from it than might at first sight appear."

"Grave enough!" said Mr. Jabez Wilson.
3 "Why I have lost four pounds a week."

"As far as you are personally concerned," remarked Holmes, "I do not see that you have any grievance against this remarkable league. On the contrary, you are, as I understand, richer by some thirty pounds, to say nothing of the minute[21] knowledge which you have gained on every subject that comes under the letter A. You have lost nothing by them."

"No, sir. But I want to find out about them, and who they are, and what their object was in playing this prank—if it was a prank—upon me. It was a pretty expensive joke for them, for it cost them two-and-thirty pounds."

"We shall endeavor to clear up these points for you. And, first, one or two questions, Mr. Wilson. This assistant of yours who first called your attention to the advertisement—how long had he been with you?"

"About a month then."

"How did he come?"

"In answer to an advertisement."

"Was he the only applicant?"

"No, I had a dozen."

"Why did you pick him?"

"Because he was handy, and would come cheap."

"At half wages, in fact?"

"Yes."

"What is he like, this Vincent Spaulding?"

"Small, stout-built, very quick in his ways, no hair on his face, though he's not short of thirty. Has a white splash of acid upon his forehead."

Holmes sat up in his chair in considerable excitement. "I thought as much," said he. "Have you ever observed that his ears are pierced for earrings?"

20. *Solicitor* is the British term for an attorney who handles legal matters but does not appear in court.

21. Here, minute (mī no͞ot′) means "detailed."

Make Inferences About Characters *What can you conclude about Holmes?* 4

Vocabulary Practice

SPIRAL REVIEW **Word Detective** Have students play a game of Word Detective. Instruct students to look through these two pages to find a word that is unfamiliar to them or one that might be unfamiliar to other students in the class. Make sure to tell them to keep their words secret. Have students look up the word in the dictionary to verify the definition and the part of speech. Ask a volunteer to come to the front of the class and give the page number where the word can be found. Then have the student provide word clues such as the definition, part of speech, synonyms and antonyms, and other word clues. Instruct the class to guess the secret word. Then invite another student to the front of the class to provide word clues for his or her secret word.

William Gillette, 1903. Unattributed illustration.

View the Art William Gillette was an American actor who was well-known for his portrayal of Sherlock Holmes in stage productions. This portrait shows him in character. Do you think Gillette made a good Sherlock Holmes? Why or why not? ★

"Yes sir. He told me that a gypsy had done it for him when he was a lad."

"Hum!" said Holmes, sinking back in deep thought. "He is still with you?"

"Oh, yes, sir; I have only just left him."

"And has your business been attended to in your absence?"

"Nothing to complain of, sir. There's never very much to do of a morning."

"That will do, Mr. Wilson. I shall be happy to give you an opinion upon the subject in the course of a day or two. Today is Saturday, and I hope that by Monday we may come to a conclusion."

"Well, Watson," said Holmes, when our visitor had left us, "what do you make of it all?"

"I make nothing of it," I answered, frankly. "It is a most mysterious business."

"As a rule," said Holmes, "the more bizarre a thing is, the less mysterious it proves to be. It is your commonplace, featureless crimes which are really puzzling,

Teach

View the Art ★

Answer: *Answers will vary. Students will probably say Gillette portrayed Holmes as they imagine him. He looks contemplative and dapper, as Holmes is described..*

Approaching Level

DIFFERENTIATED INSTRUCTION

Emerging Read out loud the description of Sherlock Holmes sitting in his chair to think. This unusual description may have taken students by surprise. Note that the author compares Sherlock's appearance to that of a bird. **Ask:** In what ways does the author tell us Sherlock looks like a bird? *(The author tells us that Sherlock has a "hawk-like nose" and smokes a pipe that looks "like the bill of some strange bird." Students may also note that he has thin knees, which may seem like bird legs.)* Ask students to consider reasons why Sherlock might seem like a bird. *(Students may feel that birds are wise creatures.)*

Teach

Reading Strategy 1

Make Inferences About Characters Answer: *He is contemplating the evidence.*

APPROACHING For approaching-level students, **ask:** How is this another example of the two men's differences? *(Watson actually did doze off, while Holmes was actually deep in thought.)*

Reading Strategy 2

Visualize Ask: How do you visualize the neighborhood based on the writer's description? *(It is a seedy but respectable neighborhood, where the smoky air makes everything look dirty.)*

Big Idea 3

Our World and Beyond
Answer: *He is checking whether the area beneath the pavement is solid or hollow.*

Reading Strategy 4

Predict Ask students what they think Holmes has deduced from this clue. Have them revisit their predictions as more information is revealed.

just as a commonplace face is the most difficult to identify. But I must be prompt over this matter."

"What are you going to do, then?" I asked.

"To smoke," he answered. "It is quite a three-pipe problem, and I beg that you won't speak to me for fifty minutes." He curled himself up in his chair, with his thin knees drawn up to his hawk-like nose, and there he sat with his eyes closed and his black clay pipe thrusting out like the bill of some strange bird. I had come to the conclusion that he had dropped asleep, and indeed was nodding myself, when he suddenly sprang out of his chair with the gesture of a man who has made up his mind, and put his pipe down upon the mantelpiece.

"Sarasate[22] plays at the St. James's Hall this afternoon," he remarked. "What do you think, Watson? Could your patients spare you for a few hours?"

"I have nothing to do today. My practice is never very absorbing."

"Then put on your hat and come. I am going through the City first, and we can have some lunch on the way. I observe that there is a good deal of German music on the program, which is rather more to my taste than Italian or French. It is introspective,[23] and I want to introspect. Come along!"

We traveled by the Underground[24] as far as Aldersgate; and a short walk took us to Saxe-Coburg Square, the scene of the singular story which we had listened to in the morning. **2** It was a poky, little, shabby-genteel place, where four lines of dingy, two-storied brick houses looked out into a small railed-in enclosure, where a lawn of weedy grass and a few clumps of faded laurel-bushes made a hard fight against a smoke-laden and uncongenial atmosphere. **2** Three gilt balls[25] and a brown board with JABEZ WILSON in white letters, upon a corner house, announced the place where our red-headed client carried on his business. Sherlock Holmes stopped in front of it with his head on one side, and looked it all over, with his eyes shining brightly between puckered lids. Then he walked slowly up the street, and then down again to the corner, still looking keenly at the houses. Finally he returned to the pawnbroker's, and, having thumped vigorously upon the pavement with his stick two or three times, he went up to the door and knocked. It was instantly opened by a bright-looking, clean-shaven young fellow, who asked him to step in.

"Thank you," said Holmes, "I only wished to ask you how you would go from here to the Strand."[26]

"Third right, fourth left," answered the assistant, promptly, closing the door.

"Smart fellow, that," observed Holmes, as we walked away. "He is, in my judgment, the fourth smartest man in London, and for daring, I am not sure that he has not a claim to be third. I have known something of him before."

"Evidently," said I, "Mr. Wilson's assistant counts for a good deal in this mystery of the Red-Headed League. I am sure that you inquired your way merely in order that you might see him."

"Not him."

"What then?"

"The knees of his trousers." **4**

22. *Sarasate* (sa′ rə sa′ tē) is Pablo de Sarasate (1844–1908), a Spanish violinist.
23. *Introspective* means "inward looking."
24. The *Underground* is the London subway system.
25. *Three gilt,* or gold-colored, *balls* signify a pawnbroker's shop.
26. *The Strand* is a major London street.

1 Make Inferences About Characters *What was Holmes really doing instead of resting?*

Our World and Beyond *Why might Holmes do such an odd thing?* **3**

Writing Practice

Solving a Mystery A mystery story is unlike most other works of fiction because it offers the reader a growing puzzle of clues. In a Sherlock Holmes story, a reader must be very alert to notice and understand these clues. Ask students to write a paragraph answering the question: How does Sherlock find clues, and what does he find on this page? *(Students may reply that Sherlock searches for clues in odd ways, such as by tapping on the pavement or looking at a man's knees. On this page, he sees that there is something unusual about the knees of Jabez Wilson's trousers. Perhaps students will begin to suspect Wilson of working underground.)*

"And what did you see?"

"What I expected to see."

"Why did you beat the pavement?"

"My dear doctor, this is a time for observation, not for talk. We are spies in an enemy's country. We know something of Saxe-Coburg Square. Let us now explore the parts which lie behind it."

The road in which we found ourselves as we turned round the corner from the retired Saxe-Coburg Square presented as great a contrast to it as the front of a picture does to the back. It was one of the main arteries which convey the traffic of the City to the north and west. The roadway was blocked with the immense stream of commerce flowing in a double tide inward and outward, while the footpaths were black with the hurrying swarm of pedestrians. It was difficult to realize, as we looked at the line of fine shops and stately business premises, that they really abutted[27] on the other side upon the faded and stagnant square which we had just quitted.

"Let me see," said Holmes, standing at the corner, and glancing along the line, "I should like just to remember the order of the houses here. It is a hobby of mine to have an exact knowledge of London. There is Mortimer's, the tobacconist, the little newspaper shop, the Coburg branch of the City and Suburban Bank, the Vegetarian Restaurant, and McFarlane's carriage-building depot. That carries us right on to the other block. And now, doctor, we've done our work, so it's time we had some play. A sandwich and a cup of coffee, and then off to violinland, where all is sweetness and delicacy and harmony, and there are no red-headed clients to vex us with their conundrums."[28]

27. Here, *abutted* means "bordered."
28. *Conundrums* are puzzling problems.

5 Foreshadowing *What does Holmes's attention to detail suggest about the street?*

My friend was an enthusiastic musician, being himself not only a very capable performer, but a composer of no ordinary merit. All the afternoon he sat in the stalls[29] wrapped in the most perfect happiness, gently waving his long, thin fingers in time to the music, while his gently smiling face and his **languid,** dreamy eyes were as unlike those of Holmes, the sleuth-hound, Holmes, the relentless, keen-witted, ready-handed criminal agent, as it was possible to conceive. In his singular character the dual nature alternately asserted itself, and his extreme exactness and astuteness represented, as I have often thought, the reaction against the poetic and contemplative mood which occasionally predominated in him. The swing of his nature took him from extreme languor to devouring energy; and, as I knew well, he was never so truly formidable as when, for days on end, he had been lounging in his armchair amid his improvisations and his black-letter editions. Then it was that the lust of the chase would suddenly come upon him, and that his brilliant reasoning power would rise to the level of intuition, until those who were unacquainted with his methods would look askance at him as on a man whose knowledge was not that of other mortals. When I saw him that afternoon so enwrapped in the music at St. James's Hall, I felt that an evil time might be coming upon those whom he had set himself to hunt down.

"You want to go home, no doubt, doctor," he remarked, as we emerged.

"Yes, it would be as well."

29. Here, *stalls* are theater seats located on the ground floor close to the stage.

Make Inferences About Characters *What effect does Watson's view of Holmes have on the reader?* **6**

Vocabulary

languid (lang′ gwid) *adj.* drooping; weak and listless

Teach

Literary Element 5

Foreshadowing Answer: *The street will play an important role in the solution to the mystery.*

Reading Strategy 6

Make Inferences About Characters Answer: *His remark bolsters the reader's admiration for and confidence in the detective's abilities.*

English Learners

DIFFERENTIATED INSTRUCTION

Beginning/Early Intermediate As students read, have them record all the difficult words they encountered. Create a list of these words on the blackboard. Then work with the class to define the words. Some examples of difficult vocabulary:

- "ingenious" *(brilliant)*
- "hunting crop" *(whip)*
- "incites" *(causes)*
- "lurid" *(horrible)*
- "protruded" *(stuck out)*

Teach

Literary Element 1

Foreshadowing Answer: *His request hints that there may be serious danger ahead.*

APPROACHING To help approaching-level students, **say:** The foreshadowing in this story helps set the unique mood. **Ask:** What factors do you know of that have foreshadowed events in real life? *(Students may explain that cold wind and shorter days foreshadow winter, or that a sore throat and a stuffy nose might foreshadow the flu.)*

Reading Strategy 2

Make Inferences About Characters Ask: Based on Watson's description, what kind of personality would this character most likely have? *(He sounds gloomy, uptight, and conventional.)*

Cultural History ☆

Scotland Yard Scotland Yard is officially known as the Metropolitan Police Service. When British Home Secretary Sir Robert Peel founded the police force in 1829, the first police headquarters opened onto a courtyard that was once owned by the Kings of Scotland. Thus, came the name Scotland Yard.

"And I have some business to do which will take some hours. This business at Coburg Square is serious."

"Why serious?"

"A considerable crime is in contemplation.[30] I have every reason to believe that we shall be in time to stop it. But today being Saturday rather complicates matters. I shall want your help tonight."

"At what time?"

"Ten will be early enough."

"I shall be at Baker Street[31] at ten."

"Very well. And, I say, doctor, there may be some little danger, so kindly put your army revolver in your pocket." He waved his hand, turned on his heel, and disappeared in an instant among the crowd.

I trust that I am not more dense than my neighbors, but I was always oppressed with a sense of my own stupidity in my dealings with Sherlock Holmes. Here I had heard what he had heard, I had seen what he had seen, and yet from his words it was evident that he saw clearly not only what had happened, but what was about to happen, while to me the whole business was still confused and grotesque. As I drove home to my house in Kensington I thought over it all from the extraordinary story of the red-headed copier of the *Encyclopedia* down to the visit to Saxe-Coburg Square, and the ominous words with which he had parted from me. What was this nocturnal expedition, and why should I go armed? Where were we going, and what were we to do? I had the hint from Holmes that this smooth-faced pawnbroker's assistant was a **formidable** man—a man who might play a deep game. I tried to puzzle it out, but gave it up in despair, and set the matter aside until night should bring an explanation.

It was a quarter past nine when I started from home and made my way across the Park, and so through Oxford Street to Baker Street. Two hansoms were standing at the door, and, as I entered the passage, I heard the sound of voices from above. On entering his room I found Holmes in animated conversation with two men, one of whom I recognized as Peter Jones, the official police agent, while the other was a long, thin, sad-faced man, with a very shiny hat and oppressively respectable frock coat. 2

Visual Vocabulary Hansoms are two-wheeled horse carriages.

"Ha! our party is complete," said Holmes, buttoning up his pea jacket, and taking his heavy hunting crop from the rack. "Watson, I think you know Mr. Jones, of Scotland Yard?[32] Let me introduce you to Mr. Merryweather, who is to be our companion in tonight's adventure." ☆

"We're hunting in couples again, doctor, you see," said Jones, in his consequential way. "Our friend here is a wonderful man for starting a chase. All he wants is an old dog to help him do the running down."

"I hope a wild goose may not prove to be the end of our chase," observed Mr. Merryweather, gloomily.

"You may place considerable confidence in Mr. Holmes, sir," said the police agent,

30. *In contemplation* means "being planned."
31. *Baker Street* is the London street where Holmes lives.
32. *Scotland Yard* is the headquarters of the London police.

1 Foreshadowing *How does this request build suspense?*

Vocabulary
formidable (fôr′ mi də bəl) *adj.* impressive; awe-inspiring

Literary Element Practice

SPIRAL REVIEW **Figurative Language** Sir Arthur Conan Doyle uses many examples of figurative language in his narration and dialogue. Many of these literary devices deal with different kinds of animals. On this page, Peter Jones says that Mr. Merryweather wants "an old dog." Mr. Merryweather then says he hopes to avoid "a wild goose." Challenge students to consider the meanings of these terms.

Say: The characters are not really talking about animals. They're using animal names for people and events. The "old dog" refers to the use of dogs for hunting. As students may already know, a "wild goose" is a symbol of a fruitless chase.

"I think you will find," said Sherlock Holmes, "that you will play for a higher stake tonight than you have ever done yet, and that the play will be more exciting. For you, Mr. Merryweather, the stake will be some thirty thousand pounds; and for you, Jones, it will be the man upon whom you wish to lay your hands."

"John Clay, the murderer, thief, smasher,[34] and forger. He's a young man, Mr. Merryweather, but he is at the head of his profession, and I would rather have my bracelets[35] on him than on any criminal in London. He's a remarkable man, is young John Clay. His grandfather was a royal duke, and he himself has been to Eton and Oxford.[36] His brain is as cunning as his fingers, and though we meet signs of him at every turn, we never know where to find the man himself. He'll crack a crib[37] in Scotland one week, and be raising money to build an orphanage in Cornwall the next. I've been on his track for years, and have never set eyes on him yet."

"I hope that I may have the pleasure of introducing you tonight. I've had one or

loftily. "He has his own little methods, which are, if he won't mind my saying so, just a little too theoretical and fantastic, but he has the makings of a detective in him. It is not too much to say that once or twice, as in that business of the Sholto murder and the Agra treasure,[33] he has been more nearly correct than the official force."

"Oh, if you say so, Mr. Jones, it is all right," said the stranger, with deference. "Still, I confess that I miss my bridge games. It is the first Saturday night for seven-and-twenty years that I have not had my bridge."

33. *The Sholto murder and the Agra treasure* are references to an earlier Holmes novel, *The Sign of Four.*

34. A *smasher* is a person who passes counterfeit money.
35. Here, *bracelets* are handcuffs.
36. *Eton* is an exclusive private preparatory school near London; *Oxford* is one of England's most famous universities.
37. To *crack a crib* is to break into a building.

Make Inferences About Characters *What can you infer about Mr. Merryweather?* **3**

Teach

Reading Strategy 3

Make Inferences About Characters **Answer:** *Mr. Merryweather probably has a lot of money or may be a bank official because his "stake" in the events is so high.*

Approaching Level

DIFFERENTIATED INSTRUCTION

Emerging Explain to students that fiction stories usually have a climax, or a passage near the end where the action rises. In a mystery story, the climax might come in the form of an "ah-ha!" moment in which the characters or readers begin to realize the solution to the mystery. **Ask:** How does this page give the characters or readers an "ah-ha!" moment? What do the characters learn that makes the mystery begin to unfold? *(Students may say that Sherlock Holmes has led his team into a bank cellar and he realizes that thieves are tunneling in to steal a shipment of French gold.)*

Teach

Reading Strategy 1

Analyze Dialogue **Ask:** What does Holmes mean? *(He has had dealings with the criminal and acknowledges that the man is clever.)*

Literary Element 2

Foreshadowing **Answer:** *His decision to bring someone who is "brave as a bulldog" and "tenacious as a lobster" suggests that catching and holding the culprit will be dangerous and difficult.*

APPROACHING To guide approaching-level students, **ask:** Why might Jones have been thought of as a "bulldog" or a "lobster"? What ideas do many people have about these animals? *(People often think of bulldogs as tough and mean dogs. Meanwhile, lobsters are thought to be persistent creatures.)*

Reading Strategy 3

Draw Conclusions **Ask:** What has been the ultimate goal of the criminals who devised the ruse of the Red-Headed League? *(To rob a London bank)*

1 two little turns also with Mr. John Clay, and I agree with you that he is at the head of his profession. It is past ten, however, and quite time that we started. If you two will take the first hansom, Watson and I will follow in the second."

Sherlock Holmes was not very communicative during the long drive, and lay back in the cab humming the tunes which he had heard in the afternoon. We rattled through an endless labyrinth[38] of gas-lit streets until we emerged into Farringdon Street.

"We are close there now," my friend remarked. "This fellow Merryweather is a bank director, and personally interested in the matter. I thought it as well to have Jones with us also. He is not a bad fellow, though an absolute imbecile in his profession. He has one positive virtue. He is as brave as a bulldog, and as tenacious as a lobster if he gets his claws upon anyone. Here we are, and they are waiting for us."

We had reached the same crowded thoroughfare in which we had found ourselves in the morning. Our cabs were dismissed, and, following the guidance of Mr. Merryweather, we passed down a narrow passage and through a side door, which he opened for us. Within, there was a small corridor, which ended in a very massive iron gate. This also was opened, and led down a flight of winding stone steps, which terminated at another formidable gate. Mr. Merryweather stopped to light a lantern, and then conducted us down a dark, earth-smelling passage, and so, after opening a third door, into a huge vault, or cellar, which was piled all round with crates and massive boxes.

"You are not very vulnerable from above," Holmes remarked, as he held up the lantern and gazed about him.

"Nor from below," said Mr. Merryweather, striking his stick upon the flags which lined the floor. "Why, dear me, it sounds quite hollow!" he remarked, looking up in surprise.

"I must really ask you to be a little more quiet," said Holmes, severely. "You have already imperiled the whole success of our expedition. Might I beg that you would have the goodness to sit down upon one of those boxes, and not to interfere?"

The solemn Mr. Merryweather perched himself upon a crate, with a very injured expression upon his face, while Holmes fell upon his knees upon the floor, and, with the lantern and a magnifying lens, began to examine minutely the cracks between the stones. A few seconds sufficed to satisfy him, for he sprang to his feet again, and put his glass in his pocket.

"We have at least an hour before us," he remarked; "for they can hardly take any steps until the good pawnbroker is safely in bed. Then they will not lose a minute, for the sooner they do their work the longer time they will have for their escape. We are at present, doctor—as no doubt you have divined[39]—in the cellar of the City branch of one of the principal London banks. Mr. Merryweather is the chairman of directors, and he will explain to you that 3
there are reasons why the more daring criminals of London should take a considerable interest in this cellar at present."

"It is our French gold," whispered the director. "We have had several warnings that an attempt might be made upon it."

"Your French gold?"

"Yes. We had occasion some months ago to strengthen our resources and borrowed,

38. Here, a *labyrinth* suggests an area of winding, twisting streets.

2 Foreshadowing *What might Holmes's decision to bring Jones along foreshadow?*

39. Here, to *divine* means "to perceive."

Writing Practice

Word Flow A writer can change a story by altering the flow of the words. By combining sentences or moving punctuation, an author can make a reader read faster or slower, or completely change the tone of the story. Read out loud the paragraph beginning with "What a time it seemed!" **Ask:** What makes the flow of words in this paragraph unusual? *(Students may say that many phrases seem bunched into long sentences.)* Explain that this style of writing demonstrates the nervous tension that Watson feels. Challenge students to rewrite the paragraph to make the tone more relaxed.

for that purpose, thirty thousand napoleons[40] from the Bank of France. It has become known that we have never had occasion to unpack the money, and that it is still lying in our cellar. The crate upon which I sit contains two thousand napoleons packed between layers of lead foil. Our reserve of bullion[41] is much larger at present than is usually kept in a single branch office, and the directors have had misgivings upon the subject."

"Which were very well justified," observed Holmes. "And now it is time that we arranged our little plans. I expect that within an hour matters will come to a head. In the meantime, Mr. Merryweather, we must put the screen over that dark lantern."

"And sit in the dark?"

"I am afraid so. I had brought a pack of cards in my pocket, and I thought that, as we were a *partie carrée*,[42] you might have your bridge games after all. But I see that the enemy's preparations have gone so far that we cannot risk the presence of a light. And, first of all, we must choose our positions. These are daring men, and though we shall take them at a disadvantage, they may do us some harm unless we are careful. I shall stand behind this crate, and do you conceal yourself behind those. Then when I flash a light upon them, close in swiftly. If they fire, Watson, have no compunction about shooting them down."

I placed my revolver, cocked, upon the top of the wooden case behind which I crouched. Holmes shot the slide across the front of his lantern, and left us in pitch darkness—such an absolute darkness as I have never before experienced. The smell of hot metal remained to assure us that the light was still there, ready to flash out at a moment's notice. To me, with my nerves worked up to a pitch of expectancy, there was something depressing and subduing in the sudden gloom, and in the cold, dank air of the vault. 5

"They have but one retreat," whispered Holmes. "That is back through the house into Saxe-Coburg Square. I hope that you have done what I asked you, Jones?"

"I have an inspector and two officers waiting at the front door."

"Then we have stopped all the holes. And now we must be silent and wait."

What a time it seemed! From comparing notes afterwards it was but an hour and a quarter, yet it appeared to me that the night must have almost gone, and the dawn be breaking above us. My limbs were weary and stiff, for I feared to change my position; yet my nerves were worked up to the highest pitch of tension, and my hearing was so acute that I could not only hear the gentle breathing of my companions, but I could distinguish the deeper, heavier in-breath of the bulky Jones from the thin, sighing note of the bank director. From my position I could look over the case in the direction of the floor. Suddenly my eyes caught the glint of a light.

At first it was but a lurid spark upon the stone pavement. Then it lengthened out until it became a yellow line, and then, without any warning or sound, a gash seemed to open and a hand appeared; a white, almost womanly hand, which felt about in the center of the little area of light. For a minute or more the hand, with its writhing fingers, protruded out of the floor. Then it was withdrawn as suddenly as it appeared, and all was dark again save the single lurid spark which marked a chink between the stones.

Its disappearance, however, was but momentary. With a rending, tearing sound,

40. *Napoleons* are French gold coins; thirty thousand napoleons are worth about $1,200,000 today.
41. Here, *bullion* is gold.
42. *Partie carrée* (pär tē′ ka rā′) is French for "party of four," the number needed to play some card games.

4 Foreshadowing *How does this comment build suspense?*

Teach

Literary Element 4

Foreshadowing Answer: *It suggests that the criminals are armed and desperate and ready to kill for the money.*

Reading Strategy 5

Interpret Ask: Who is speaking? What does he feel? *(Watson is speaking; he feels great anxiety about what might happen.)*

English Learners

DIFFERENTIATED INSTRUCTION

Early Intermediate Say: Many authors show their characters in similar ways. For example, readers often come to expect heroes to be brave, smart, strong characters. Sometimes authors provide unexpected personalities for their characters. **Ask:** Does John Clay fit most people's ideas of a thief? *(Students will most likely say he does not.)* Begin a class discussion of the behavior of John Clay and the behavior readers normally expect of a thief in a story. John Clay is unlike most literary thieves because he is smart, handsome, and highborn. Next, talk about other literary characters and discuss their usual traits.

Teach

Reading Strategy 1

Predict **Ask:** What do you think will happen next? *(Possible answer: Once the criminals climb out of the hole, Holmes will spring his trap and capture them.)*

Reading Strategy 2

Make Inferences About Characters **Answer:** *He seems sophisticated, gentlemanly and well bred, even giving credit to Holmes for his skill. On the surface, he is similar to Holmes.*

ENGLISH LEARNERS To guide English learners, **Say:** Sherlock Holmes and John Clay are alike in some ways. **Ask:** What makes these interesting and brilliant characters different? *(Despite their several similarities, John Clay and Sherlock Holmes are essentially different in that Clay uses his genius for crime and Holmes uses his genius to solve crimes.)*

Language History ☆

Great Scott The origin of "Great Scott" is under some debate. One popular theory is that it refers to an actual person: American General Winfield Scott (1786–1866). His heroism in the Mexican War in addition to his 300-pound weight later in life make him a good candidate for the expression's origin, figuratively and literally.

1 one of the broad, white stones turned over upon its side, and left a square, gaping hole, through which streamed the light of a lantern. Over the edge there peeped a clean-cut, boyish face, which looked keenly about it, and then, with a hand on either side of the aperture,[43] drew itself shoulder-high and waist-high, until one knee rested upon the edge. In another instant he stood at the side of the hole, and was hauling after him a companion, lithe and small like himself, with a pale face and a shock of very red hair.

☆ "It's all clear," he whispered. "Have you the chisel and the bags? Great Scott! Jump, Archie, jump, and I'll swing for it!"

"Great Scott! Jump, Archie, jump, and I'll swing for it!"

Sherlock Holmes had sprung out and seized the intruder by the collar. The other dived down the hole, and I heard the sound of rending cloth as Jones clutched at his skirts.[44] The light flashed upon the barrel of a revolver, but Holmes's hunting crop came down on the man's wrist, and the pistol clinked upon the stone floor.

"It's no use, John Clay," said Holmes blandly. "You have no chance at all."

"So I see," the other answered, with the utmost coolness. "I fancy that my pal is all right, though I see you have got his coattails."

"There are three men waiting for him at the door," said Holmes.

"Oh, indeed! You seem to have done the thing very completely. I must compliment you."

43. An *aperture* is an opening.

44. Here, *skirts* refers to any clothing that hangs freely below the waist.

2 Make Inferences About Characters *What are your impressions of Clay?*

"And I you," Holmes answered. "Your red-headed idea was very new and effective."

"You'll see your pal again presently," said Jones. "He's quicker at climbing down holes than I am. Just hold out while I fix the derbies."[45]

"I beg that you will not touch me with your filthy hands," remarked our prisoner, as the handcuffs clattered upon his wrists. "You may not be aware that I have royal blood in my veins. Have the goodness, also, when you address me always to say 'sir' and 'please.'"

"All right," said Jones, with a stare and a snigger. "Well, would you please, sir, march upstairs, where we can get a cab to carry your highness to the police station?"

"That is better," said John Clay, serenely. He made a sweeping bow to the three of us, and walked quietly off in the custody of the detective.

"Really, Mr. Holmes," said Mr. Merryweather, as we followed them from the cellar, "I do not know how the bank can thank you or repay you. There is no doubt that you have detected and defeated in the most complete manner one of the most determined attempts at bank robbery that has ever come within my experience."

"I have had one or two little scores of my own to settle with Mr. John Clay," said Holmes. "I have been at some small expense over this matter, which I shall expect the bank to refund, but beyond that I am amply repaid by having had an experience which is in many ways unique, and by hearing the very remarkable narrative of the Red-Headed League."

45. *Derbies* are handcuffs.

Literary Element Practice

Character By the end of this story, the reader should have a good idea of what kind of person Sherlock Holmes is. Challenge students, either individually or as a class, to develop a list of personality traits that are shown by Holmes in this tale. You may also want to develop similar lists for Watson, Clay, or other characters. Holmes is famous for being clever and observant, characteristics he needs to crack difficult cases like this one. However, some readers may also notice more subtle aspects of his behavior. Some students may note that he is forceful, easily bored, and sometimes direct to the point of rudeness.

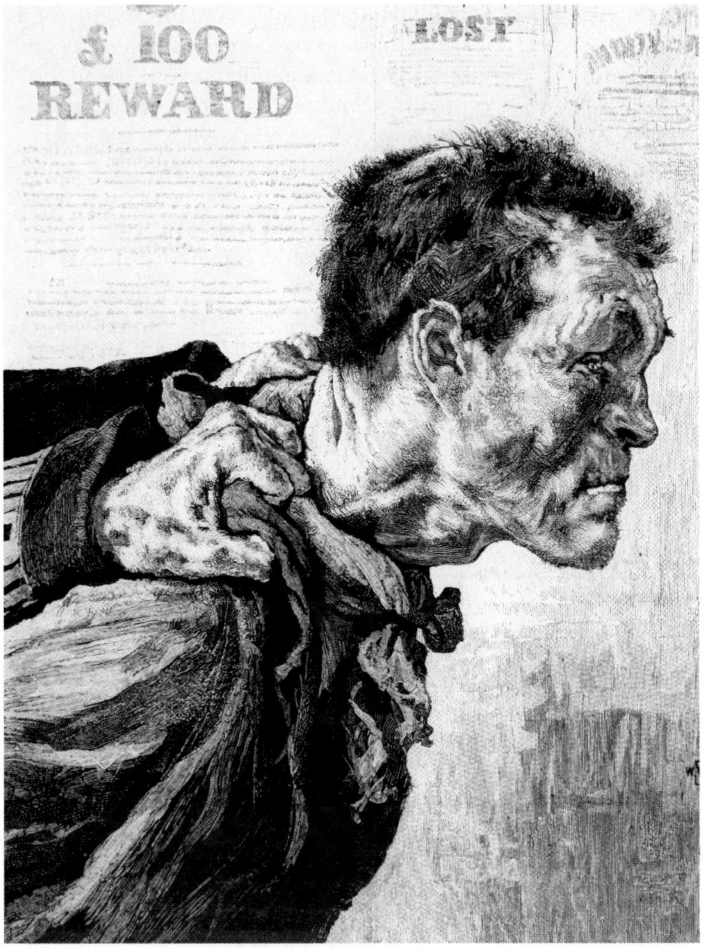

English Street Thief Being Apprehended by Authority, ca 1800.

View the Art This illustration is from the 1800s. In your opinion, how well does it capture the scene of John Clay's arrest? Explain. ★

"You see, Watson," he explained, in the early hours of the morning, "it was perfectly obvious from the first that the only possible object of this rather fantastic business of the advertisement of the League, and the copying of the *Encyclopedia,* must be to get this not over-bright pawnbroker out of the way for a number of hours every day. It was a curious way of managing it, but, really, it would be difficult to suggest a better. The method was no doubt suggested to Clay's ingenious mind by the color of his accomplice's hair. The four pounds a week was a lure which must draw him, and what was it to them, who were playing for thousands? They put in the advertisement, one rogue[46] has the temporary office, the other rogue incites the man to apply for it, and together they manage to secure his absence every morning in the week. From the time that I heard of the assistant having come for half wages, it was obvious to me that

46. Here, a *rogue* is a dishonest or worthless person.

Teach

View the Art ★

Answer: *Students may say the thief in the illustration looks more rough and tumble than Clay seems to be.*

English Learners

DIFFERENTIATED INSTRUCTION

Strategic By the end of the story, students should understand that the job offered to Jabez Wilson, and the entire premise of the Red-Headed League, was simply a cover for an elaborate crime. John Clay created the league with the specific intent of getting Wilson's attention and distracting him for hours a day. **Ask:** What are some other examples of leagues or jobs that could have covered up a crime like John Clay's? *(Students may reply that a Left-Handed League or a Freckle-Nose League would serve the same purpose.)* Give students the opportunity to use their imagination while they are gaining understanding of the plot.

Teach

Reading Strategy 1

Make Inferences About Characters **Answer:** *Holmes makes deductions about people based on his insights into human nature.*

Reading Strategy 2

Make Inferences About Characters **Answer:** *Watson is clearly impressed by Holmes's reasoning abilities. He seems to regard him as infallible.*

APPROACHING To guide approaching-level students, **ask:** How do you feel about Sherlock Holmes? Do you think he is a good detective? Do you think he is a good person? *(Students will likely feel that Holmes is a very good detective, although their opinions on his personality may vary widely. Some may feel he is good because he fights crime, while others may think he is a rather cold or rude person.)*

To check students' understanding of the selection, see Unit 6 Teaching Resources Book, p. 95.

he had some strong motive for securing the situation."

"But how could you guess what the motive was?"

"Had there been women in the house, I should have suspected a mere vulgar intrigue. That, however, was out of the question. The man's business was a small one, and there was nothing in his house which could account for such elaborate preparations and such an expenditure as they were at. It must, then, be something out of the house. What could it be? I thought of the assistant's fondness for photography, and his trick of vanishing into the cellar. The cellar! There was the end of this tangled clue. Then I made inquiries as to this mysterious assistant, and found that I had to deal with one of the coolest and most daring criminals in London. He was doing something in the cellar—something which took many hours a day for months on end. What could it be, once more? I could think of nothing save that he was running a tunnel to some other building.

"So far I had got when we went to visit the scene of action. I surprised you by beating upon the pavement with my stick. I was ascertaining whether the cellar stretched out in front or behind. It was not in front. Then I rang the bell, and, as I hoped, the assistant answered it. We have had some skirmishes, but we had never set eyes upon each other before. I hardly looked at his face. His knees were what I wished to see. You must yourself have remarked how worn, wrinkled, and stained they were. They spoke of those hours of burrowing. The only remaining point was what they were burrowing for. I walked round the corner, saw the City and Suburban Bank abutted on our friend's premises, and felt that I had solved my problem. When you drove home after the concert, I called upon Scotland Yard, and upon the chairman of the bank directors, with the result that you have seen."

"And how could you tell that they would make their attempt tonight?"

"Well, when they closed their League offices, that was a sign that they cared no longer about Mr. Jabez Wilson's presence—in other words, that they had completed their tunnel. But it was essential that they should use it soon, as it might be discovered, or the bullion might be removed. Saturday would suit them better than any other day, as it would give them two days for their escape. For all these reasons I expected them to come tonight."

"You reasoned it out beautifully," I exclaimed, in unfeigned admiration. "It is so long a chain, and yet every link rings true."

"It saved me from ennui,"[47] he answered, yawning. "Alas! I already feel it closing in upon me. My life is spent in one long effort to escape from the commonplaces of existence. These little problems help me to do so."

"And you are a benefactor of the race," said I.

He shrugged his shoulders. "Well, perhaps, after all, it is of some little use," he remarked. "'*L'homme c'est rien—l'oeuvre c'est tout,*'[48] as Gustave Flaubert wrote to George Sand."[49]

47. *Ennui* (än wē′) is boredom.
48. *L'homme . . . tout* (lôm sā rē en′ loov′ rə sā too) is French for "Man is nothing; his work is everything."
49. *Gustave Flaubert* (goos täv flō bār′) (1821–1880) and *George Sand* (1804–1876) were French novelists.

1 Make Inferences About Characters *What does this explanation reveal about Holmes?*

2 Make Inferences About Characters *How does Watson regard Holmes?*

Reading Practice

SMALL GROUP **Reader Expectations** Explain to students that when reading, they may often feel involved in the story. In a story like this, with a mystery unfolding, they may begin to expect certain outcomes. Sometimes the results they might expect from a mystery are very different from what actually occurs in the book. Discuss with students how they feel about the end of the mystery in this story. Was it like or unlike their expectations? Do they like their ideas or the author's ideas more? Arrange students in small groups and ask them to create an alternate ending to the mystery.

After You Read

Respond and Think Critically

Respond and Interpret

1. If you were to meet Sherlock Holmes, do you think you would like him? Explain why or why not.
2. (a)What conclusions does Holmes draw about Jabez Wilson's past activities? Upon what evidence does Holmes base these conclusions? (b)What evidence supports Holmes's conclusion that Wilson is "not over-bright"?
3. (a)List the clues that enable Holmes to solve the mystery. (b)What does Holmes do to foil the bank robbers' plan?

Analyze and Evaluate

4. Why is Holmes a better observer than Watson? In what other ways are they different?
5. Would you have liked the story better if Holmes had explained his reasoning at each stage of the investigation? Why or why not?
6. Why do you think Sherlock Holmes became so enormously popular with readers? Use evidence from this story to support your answer.

Connect

7. **Big Idea** **Our World and Beyond** How is Sherlock Holmes's way of viewing the world similar to and different from your way of viewing the world? Explain.
8. **Connect to the Author** Doyle often uses the narrator, Dr. Watson, to shed light upon Holmes's character. Where is this technique used in this story? Explain.

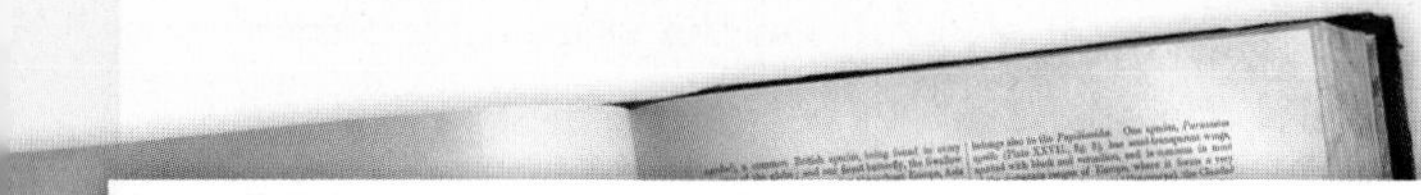

You're the Critic

Different Viewpoints

Read the two excerpts of literary criticism. As you read, notice the difference in emphasis between the two critics.

> *"Doyle was a master storyteller. Even his weaker fictional efforts hold reader interest; when his plots are hackneyed and contain no real surprises—which is sometimes the case, even though Doyle prided himself on his ability to devise ingenious plots—the reader is carried away by the sheer power of the storyteller's art."*
>
> —*Contemporary Authors Online*

> *"In the stories the logic can sometimes be found wanting; occasionally the end hardly lives up to the beginning; we are not invariably given the clues Holmes has seen. . . . But none of these matter. Doyle's gifts for storytelling . . . sweep away all criticism."*
>
> —H. R. F. Keating

Group Activity Discuss the following questions with your classmates. Refer to the quotations and cite evidence from "The Red-Headed League" to support your responses.

1. Does the comment that some of Doyle's stories "contain no real surprises" apply to "The Red-Headed League"? Explain.
2. Are the flaws that Keating notices in some of Doyle's stories also found in "The Red-Headed League"? Explain.

After You Read

Assess

1. Students should explain their answers.
2. (a) He's a Freemason, has been to China, has done manual labor and, recently, much writing. He has a Freemason's pin, a fish tattoo, a muscular right hand, and a shiny cuff. (b) He accepts the obviously bizarre and shady circumstances of his employment at face value.
3. (a) Wilson's gullibility, the league's sudden dissolution, and the description of Spaulding (b) He hides in the vault with Watson, Jones, and Merryweather and catches Clay.
4. Holmes notes the smallest details. He's more learned, imaginative, and sophisticated.
5. Students should explain their answers.
6. Students should support their answers.
7. Students should confirm the cleverness of Clay's elaborate scheme. In recognizing Clay, discerning his plan, and foiling his robbery attempt, Holmes seems almost unbelievably clever.
8. Students should support their responses with examples from the text.

For additional selection assessment, see Assessment Resources, pp. 219–220.

You're the Critic

1. Possible answer: No; the league's true purpose would probably surprise most readers.
2. Possible answer: Holmes's logic is portrayed as impeccable, but his inferences about Wilson seem elaborately contrived by the author. The details of his appearance could have simpler explanations. There aren't enough clues to identify Clay. The answers are less strange and intriguing than the puzzle at the outset.

After You Read

Assess

Literary Element

1. The absurd requirements for membership in the league suggest it is a trick or a front. Wilson is too easily hired, as if he were singled out ahead of time, foreshadowing the forthcoming sinister plan.
2. He works for half wages, snaps pictures and then goes into the cellar to develop them, and seems overly interested in the ad. These details foreshadow Spaulding's hidden motives and his involvement in a plot.

Progress Check

Can students identify foreshadowing?

If No → See Unit 6 Teaching Resources Book, p. 90.

Review: Character Archetype

Encourage students to recall other fictional detectives. What qualities do they and Holmes share?

Reading Strategy

1. C is the correct answer. From his behavior and the casual references to previous cases, it is clear that Watson is Holmes's loyal friend.

Progress Check

Can students make inferences about character?

If No → See Unit 6 Teaching Resources Book, p. 91.

Literary Element Foreshadowing

Foreshadowing can take the form of minor incidents or statements that suggest later developments. Foreshadowing increases the reader's involvement in any story, but it is particularly effective in a mystery like "The Red-Headed League." Such clues enable the reader to feel like the detective who eventually solves the mystery.

1. What is unusual about the Red-Headed League? How do its requirements for the open position foreshadow a strange outcome? How does Wilson's interview with "Mr. Duncan Ross" provide foreshadowing?
2. What is suspicious about Vincent Spaulding as a worker? About his interest in the ad for the Red-Headed League? What do these details foreshadow?

Review: Character Archetype

As you learned on page 955, a **character archetype** is the prime or foremost example of a type of character that recurs in different times and places. Sherlock Holmes is the archetype of the detective hero who uses his wits and keen powers of observation to foil criminals.

Partner Activity Meet with a classmate to discuss your ideas about Holmes as the archetypal detective. Working with your partner, create a web like the one below and fill it in with details for each category listed.

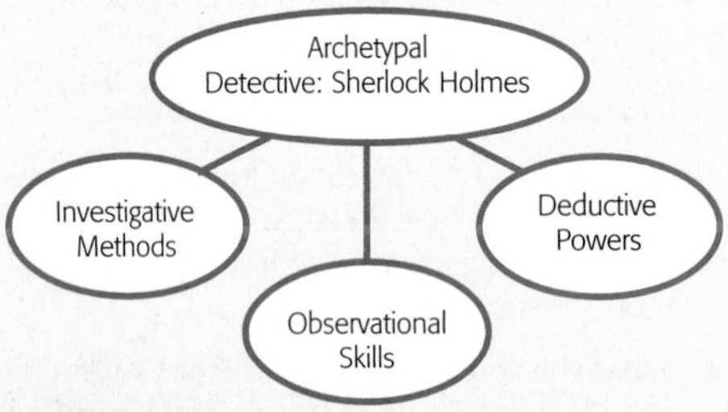

LOG ON Literature Online

Selection Resources For Selection Quizzes, eFlashcards, and Reading-Writing Connection activities, go to glencoe.com and enter QuickPass code GL49787u6.

Reading Strategy Make Inferences About Characters

SAT Skills Practice

1. In agreeing to accompany Holmes on the Saturday night excursion, Dr. Watson
   (A) seeks to prove that his theory about the crime is correct
   (B) reveals that he too has "a score to settle" with Mr. John Clay
   (C) shows himself to be a loyal friend of Sherlock Holmes
   (D) acts in a manner out of character with his usual personality
   (E) exhibits a reckless side to his nature

Vocabulary Practice

Practice with Synonyms With a partner, match each boldface vocabulary word below with its synonym. You will not use all the answer choices. Use a thesaurus or dictionary to check your answers.

1. singular	a. strong
2. nominal	b. weak
3. languid	c. asleep
4. formidable	d. round
	e. unusual
	f. slight

Academic Vocabulary

*In this story, Spaulding's plan **involves** the use of a pawnbroker's shop.*

Involve is an academic word. A word that shares a similar meaning is *include*. To study this word further, fill out the graphic organizer below.

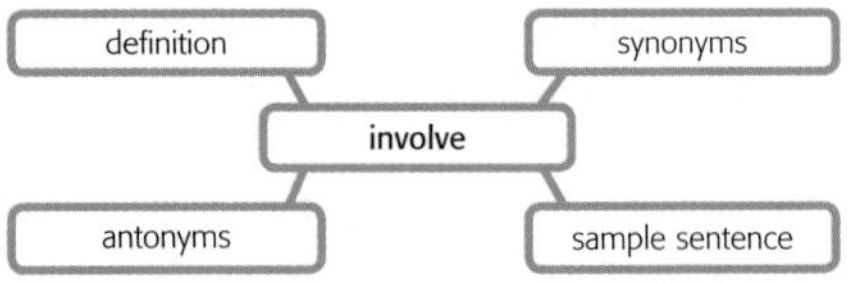

For more on academic vocabulary, see pages 54–55 and R79–R81.

Vocabulary

1. e **2.** f **3.** b **4.** a

Students may observe that Doyle's language choices are more formal than contemporary usage.

Academic Vocabulary

definition—to include; to relate to closely
synonyms—require, entail
antonyms—preclude, prohibit
sample sentence—Camping involves a lot of preparations.

Respond Through Writing

Expository Essay

Analyze Genre Classic mysteries usually begin with a strange event and include foreshadowing, a series of clues or puzzling events, an exciting climax, and a skillful detective who unravels the mystery and captures the villain. Write an essay in which you explain how "The Red-Headed League" reflects, or does not reflect, the elements of the mystery genre.

Prewrite Identify the elements in the story that are common to the mystery genre. Use a chart to note examples of the genre elements listed in the task above. After reviewing the story, develop your essay's main idea, or thesis, stating why the story is or is not a classic mystery.

strange event triggering plot	foreshadowing	clues	climax	detective details
Red-Headed League ad				

Draft When drafting your essay, build the introductory paragraph around your thesis statement, and build the body around the examples from your chart. Make sure the examples that you include support your thesis.

As you present your evidence, highlight the examples that provide the strongest evidence. You can introduce these examples with a sentence such as:

Some of the best examples of ____ in the story are ____ and ____.

After introducing these examples, explain each one in detail. When referring to the different genre elements, use literary terms, such as plot, foreshadowing, and climax, accurately. If necessary, look up these terms in the *Literary Terms Handbook* to review their meanings.

Revise When you review your draft, revise any passages that might be confusing or easily misunderstood. After revising the text, make a chart based on the one you created earlier to accompany your essay. In this chart, include the examples that you reference in your essay.

Edit and Proofread Proofread your paper, correcting any errors in spelling, grammar, and punctuation. Use the Grammar Tip in the side column to help you use formal diction.

Learning Objectives

In this assignment, you will focus on the following objectives:

Writing: Writing an expository essay.

Grammar: Understanding word choice.

Grammar Tip

Diction

Essays should be written using formal language. The formality of the language is reflected in both diction, or word choice, and syntax, or the order of words. Although Doyle's story is not an essay, it also uses formal diction. For example:

"I did not gain very much, however, by my inspection."

Using informal language, you might express the same thing by saying:

I didn't see anything new.

When reviewing your essay, note places where using formal language would make your writing clearer and more refined. This does not mean you should use language from Doyle's time or make extremely formal word choices, but you should use correct grammar and omit slang expressions and contractions.

After You Read

Assess

Respond Through Writing

Students' essays should

- include a strong thesis stating why the story is a classic mystery
- support the thesis with examples of a strange event-triggering plot, foreshadowing, clues, climax, and detective
- highlight the strongest examples of supporting evidence
- be written using formal diction and syntax
- be accompanied with a chart noting key genre elements

For grammar practice, see Unit 6 Teaching Resources Book, p. 94.

To create custom assessments online, go to Progress Reporter Online Assessment.

To create custom assessments using software, use ExamView Assessment Suite.

Approaching Level

DIFFERENTIATED INSTRUCTION

Emerging Some students enjoy a mystery story; others prefer their fiction to be more straightforward. Poll students on their reaction to this classic mystery tale. Ask them whether they like having to follow and interpret clues, or if they like to be told exactly what is happening to the characters. Follow up with a discussion about whether the story was interesting, exciting, or believable. **Ask:** Would you have enjoyed the story more if Holmes had explained his discoveries as they occurred, instead of waiting until the end? *(Students may respond in many ways; encourage them to be honest and expressive.)*

TIME

Focus

Summary

The writer presents both sides of a debate between scientists regarding a mysterious primate living in the jungles of the Congo. Is it a chimpanzee? A gorilla? An entirely new species? The article offers observations and opinions but no conclusions, leaving readers to consider the evidence and decide for themselves.

For activities related to this selection, see Unit 6 Teaching Resources Book, pp. 97–105.

Teach

Reading Strategy 1

Evaluate Credibility Point out that students should keep track of the writer's sources as they read the article so that they can determine how credible the information in the article is.

Ask: Who do you think might be qualified to provide readers with information about apes living in the jungles of the Congo? *(Answers may vary. Students should support their answers.)*

Learning Objectives

For pages 1068–1070

In studying this text, you will focus on the following objectives:

Reading:
Evaluating credibility.
Analyzing and evaluating informational text.

Set a Purpose for Reading

Read to learn about researchers' efforts to reveal the truth about a mysterious primate species.

Preview the Article

1. Scan the article's title and its subheadings. What do you think it is going to be about?
2. Read the *deck,* or the sentence in large type that appears under the title. What tone do you think the article might have?

Reading Strategy Evaluate Credibility

Evaluating is making a judgment or forming an opinion about something. When you **evaluate the credibility** of a text, you must consider who wrote it, if the sources referenced are reliable, and if the publication in which the article appears is a valid one. As you read, ask yourself, Is the writer a reliable source? Why or why not? To examine the credibility of "Lost Apes of the Congo," take notes about the writer and the scientists.

1

Writer: Stephan Faris
Credible?
Why or why not?

TIME

Lost Apes of the Congo

A TIME reporter travels deep into the African jungle in search of a mysterious chimp called "the lion killer."

By STEPHAN FARIS

RON PONTIER WAS FLYING LIGHT AND LOW ABOVE the northern wilds of the Democratic Republic of the Congo when he saw a dark shape racing between two patches of tropical forest. "It was huge," says Pontier, a pilot. "It was black. The skin was kind of bouncing up and down on it." From its bulk and color, Pontier thought it was a buffalo until he circled down for another look. "I saw it again just before it went into the forest," he says. "It was an ape—and a big one." Not buffalo size, but big.

What Pontier saw is a piece of a primate puzzle; it is another splinter of evidence for a mysterious ape with characteristics of gorillas and chimpanzees. It is an animal that has scientists in a furious debate over what it might be.

Bili is a geographic region in Congo's far north, where deep tropical forests break up into patches of savanna, or flat, treeless grasslands. Civil war and neglect have left the region nearly untouched by humans. Overgrown dirt roads with bridges of roughly-cut logs string together thatched-roofed villages. Nearly all goods are carried in by bicycle. Local residents hunt with homemade shotguns and crossbows that seem to be based on 16th-century Portuguese designs. "This area is the last part of Africa where there are still wild animals," says Pontier, who grew up in the region. "It's not a game park. It's not a reserve. The animals are really wild."

A Surprising Animal

When Karl Ammann, a Swiss photographer who works to

Writing Practice

Write an Evaluation
Have students conduct Internet research on the mysterious apes of the Congo to find out more about the supporting information in the article. Then ask students to write a short essay in which they evaluate the credibility of the information in the TIME article. Students should support these beliefs with information gathered during their research. Remind students to document their Internet sources and explain, in detail, what specific information they found to confirm or refute the information in the TIME article.

stop the killing of wild animals for meat, first visited the region in 1996, he was looking for gorillas. He had hoped that the great apes still roamed its jungles. What he found surprised him. Locals had two names for the apes in their forests: the "tree beaters" and the "lion killers." The tree beaters stayed safe in the tree branches. The lion killers were bigger, darker, and so strong that they were unaffected by the poison arrows used by local hunters.

Ammann discovered a strange skull with the dimensions of a chimpanzee's but with an odd, prominent crest like a gorilla's. Motion-detecting cameras in the forest caught images of what looked like huge chimpanzees, and a photograph bought from hunters showed the men posing with an animal estimated
2 to be twice the size of an ordinary chimp. Ammann measured an animal dropping three times as large as a chimp's and footprints as large as, or larger than, a gorilla's.

Most unusual were the gorilla-like ground nests found in the swamps. Chimps normally make their nests in the high safety of trees. Why would they build their beds of branches and shoots on the ground? And why here, of all places? At night Cleve Hicks, 32, a graduate student who observes the animals, regularly hears the laughs of hyenas and the low, throaty cries of leopards. Recently, his trackers filmed the footprints of a lion crossing a river. But the apes here—at least some of them—pulled together branches and shoots to make beds on the ground. "We know [the apes] are a perfect target for leopards," says Hicks. "So how can they get away with that?"

A New Species?

The first scientist to see the Bili apes was Shelly Williams, a gorilla expert who visited the region in the summers of 2002 and 2003. She says that she documented separate groups of relatives of East and West African chimpanzees and what she calls the "mystery ape." The larger animal turned gray early in life and had a much flatter face and a straight-across brow like a gorilla. Two or three would nest on the ground, with others low in nearby branches. They made a distinct sound like a howl and were louder when the full moon rose and set. "The unique characteristics they exhibit just don't fit into the other groups of great apes," says Williams. The apes, she argues, could be a new species unknown to science. They might be a new close relative of the chimpanzee, or a cross between the gorilla and the chimp. "At the very least, we have a unique, isolated chimp culture that's unlike any that's been studied," she says.

That last, least dramatic theory is the one which most scientists who have visited the region 3
believe, including Harvard ape expert Richard Wrangham. He thinks that the ground nests are built by chimps looking to escape dampness during the day.

When Hicks and Ammann describe the animal that they are studying, they use the term "mystery ape" only with irony. Ammann is worried that 4
Williams's incredible ideas have brought ridicule to his project. "If there's scientific data, that's one thing," he says. But he believes that there isn't enough proof yet. Recently, Ammann was emailed

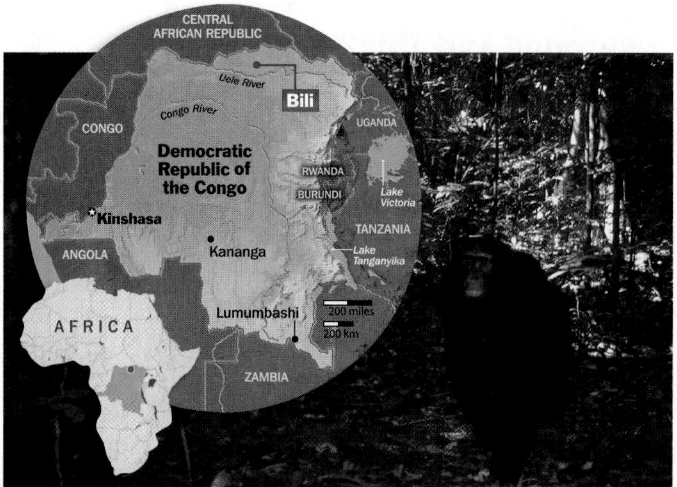

CAUGHT ON FILM A rare shot of the elusive ape taken from a camera trap near the bamboo-lined track to Bili (top).

TIME

Teach

Big Idea 2

Our World and Beyond
Ask: What proof of the animals' existence did Ammann gather? *(A strange skull; an image from a motion-detecting camera; a photo taken by hunters; droppings; ground nests)*

Reading Strategy 3

Interpret **Ask:** Which of Shelly Williams's theories are most scientists who visited the area willing to accept? *(The animals may belong to a previously unobserved chimp culture.)*

Reading Strategy 4

Evaluate Credibility **Ask:** Which observer would you consider least credible? *(Possible answer: Ammann—he isn't a scientist.)*

Approaching Level

DIFFERENTIATED INSTRUCTION

Emerging Some of the language in this article may be difficult for approaching-level students to comprehend. Tell students that not all phrases in the article are used to convey a literal meaning. Direct students' attention to the second paragraph, where the writer uses phrases such as "piece of a primate puzzle," "splinter of evidence," and "furious debate." Encourage students to decode the text to uncover the figurative meanings of these and other phrases in the article.

Assess

1. Students' summaries should reflect the main ideas presented in the selection.
2. To deepen scientists' understanding of genes, evolution, and/or animal behavior.
3. Large size, flat face, straight-across eyebrow, black fur that turns gray early
4. (a) She believes they may be a new species. (b) No; the animal's DNA suggests she is wrong.
5. No; he discusses both sides in neutral language.
6. The initial sighting of the creature, mention of the "strange" skull, introducing evidence in the form of clues, and his closing statement
7. To see the importance of preserving wild species and their habitats
8. Hicks: points to the animals' ground nests and use of tools as evidence of behavioral, rather than biological, difference; Williams: offers theories unsupported by evidence

pictures of a chimp with a pug-dog's head and a seal with a gorilla's face. "Clearly, someone thinks we're a joke," he says. A study of hairs found in the ground nests identified their mitochondrial DNA (mtDNA) as that of the East African chimpanzee. Williams has three arguments concerning that finding: The DNA could have been contaminated, the use of human genetic markers might hide differences, and mtDNA would not show variation in the paternal line. "Until we know the father's lineage, we can't say if it's a new species or not," Williams insists. Williams says she will return to the area in March to set up her own project.

What's in the Forest?

"I think people are going to be disappointed with the yeti in the forest," warns Hicks, referring to the rumored oversize mix of human and ape. Hicks says that the apes that he has seen are clearly chimps, although some are strangely oversize. "The evidence doesn't point to [a new species]." Hicks thinks that more attention has to be paid to the differences in how the apes and chimps live. In addition to building ground nests, the apes fish for ants with tools that are several times longer than those used by other chimps. For now, Hicks is concentrating on living near the animals, getting them used to the noisy, nosy presence of researchers. The science—and the videotapes—will come later.

"Genetically, they're not even a subspecies," says Hicks. But he thinks that behaviorally, they may be different. "We could actually be catching evolution in the act. That is, if they're allowed to survive."

That's an open question. The forests here have been hit hard by commercial hunting. Machine gun-carrying hunters stage raids from the Central African Republic and central Congo. Pontier, the pilot, used to see herds of a hundred elephants when he first flew over the region in 1983. Now seeing three together is a rare sighting. And with the big animals disappearing, Ammann, who has set up a conservation project in the area, says that the illegal hunters are turning to hogs, antelopes, monkeys, and chimpanzees. "The pressure on smaller game is increasing now that the elephants are gone," he says.

If there's one thing that all the scientists can agree on, it's that if this part of the Congo goes the way of other African wild lands, the great apes could soon disappear. All that will be left of the Bili ape will be the mystery.

—From TIME, January 17, 2005

Respond and Think Critically

Respond and Interpret

1. Write a brief summary of the main ideas in this article before you answer the following questions. For help on writing a summary, see page 421.
2. Why is it important for researchers to understand the Bili ape?
3. What are some physical characteristics of the Bili apes?
4. (a)What does Shelly Williams, a gorilla expert, believe to be true about the Bili apes? (b)Does she have substantial evidence to support her theory? Why or why not?

Analyze and Evaluate

5. Is the writer's opinion about whether the Bili apes are a new species evident in the article? Explain.
6. How does the writer use the idea of mystery to capture the reader's interest?
7. Based on the last paragraph, what overall reaction to the article do you think Faris wants the reader to have?

Connect

8. Cleve Hicks and Shelly Williams have differing opinions about the Bili apes. Who has more clues to support his or her opinion? Explain.

For additional selection assessment, see Assessment Resources, pp. 221–222.

Before You Read

The Stolen Cigar Case

Meet **Bret Harte**
(1836–1902)

Bret Harte grew up in the eastern United States, but in his stories, he effortlessly captured the sights and sounds of places all over the world. Harte was a pioneer of the local color movement—a movement of writers who used vivid details to create portrayals of the customs and speech of particular places.

From New York to California Harte was born in Albany, New York, but ventured west in 1854, when he was only eighteen. In California he tried prospecting, rode "shotgun" on a stagecoach, and then found work in journalism.

> *"One big vice in a man is apt to keep out a great many smaller ones."*
>
> —Bret Harte

In the 1850s, California was a booming, turbulent, and exciting frontier. The discovery of gold in 1848 had drawn prospectors and adventurers from all over the United States and the rest of the world. Mining towns had sprung up; small towns had turned into cities; fortunes had been made and lost; and people from all walks of life had been thrown together in rough, sometimes violent circumstances. History was being made, and a whole new way of life was being forged. The colorful incidents of western life and vivid anecdotes of "old-timers" fired Harte's imagination, and he began to turn this material into fiction.

Literary Fame While serving as the editor of a literary magazine, Harte began writing stories that made him famous all over the United States. His fame soon spread to Great Britain, where readers were eager for Harte's descriptions of California and the Wild West. Harte became acquainted with many of the leading writers of his day. In his short stories, he parodied some of them with great wit.

Among Harte's friends was American humorist Mark Twain. Harte helped mentor the young Twain, who later acknowledged his help. Twain said that Harte had changed him from "an awkward utterer of coarse grotesqueness to a writer of paragraphs and chapters."

Harte spent many of his last years abroad, while continuing to write and working as a diplomat. When Harte died, his greatest legacy was his stories. Many of his characters, such as John Oakhurst, an outlaw with nerves of steel, have become fixtures in American literature.

LOG ON **Literature** Online

Author Search For more about Bret Harte, go to glencoe.com and enter QuickPass code GL49787u6.

Before You Read

Focus

Bellringer Options

Daily Language Practice Transparency 99

Or display images of Peter Sellers as Inspector Clouseau or of Tony Shaloub as Adrian Monk. If students are unfamiliar with these characters, explain that both are detectives with comic foibles: Clouseau is bumbling; Monk has an obsessive-compulsive personality.

Ask: Why might Sherlock Holmes be a good subject for parody? *(He's never wrong and seems rather full of himself.)* Have students consider as they read how Harte's characters and plot parallel Doyle's.

Selection Skills

The Stolen Cigar Case

Literary Elements
- Parody (SE pp. 1072–1081)

Listening/Speaking/Viewing Skills
- Analyze Art (SE p. 1076; TE p. 1079)

Reading Skills
- Evaluate Details (SE pp. 1072–1081)
- Understand Plot (TE p. 1076)

Vocabulary Skills
- Connotation and Denotation (SE pp. 1072, 1081)

Writing Skills/Grammar
- Write a Story (SE p. 1081)
- Freewrite (TE p. 1074)

Before You Read

Focus

Summary

The faithful and adoring sidekick of detective Hemlock Jones joins forces with his friend in the hunt for a stolen cigar case. Jones is a paranoid narcissist whose bizarrely convoluted logic makes him the perfect takeoff on Sherlock Holmes.

For summaries in languages other than English, see Unit 6 Teaching Resources Book, pp. 106–111.

Vocabulary

Synonyms and Antonyms

Organize students into pairs, and have them look up synonyms and antonyms for each new vocabulary word. Then have the students test one another to guess the vocabulary word by its synonym or antonym. Students can present their synonyms and antonyms to the class to allow other students to guess the vocabulary word for each.

For additional vocabulary practice, see Unit 6 Teaching Resources Book, p. 114.

Literature and Reading Preview

Connect to the Story

What errors in logic or reasoning do you notice yourself and others making? Freewrite for a few minutes about an amusing error in reasoning you or someone you know has made.

Build Background

In the story you are about to read, Bret Harte parodies the Sherlock Holmes stories of Sir Arthur Conan Doyle. In "The Stolen Cigar Case," Doyle's ingenious detective, Sherlock Holmes, is transformed into the detective Hemlock Jones. The story's narrator is modeled after Dr. Watson, Holmes's sidekick and the narrator of the Sherlock Holmes stories.

Set Purposes for Reading

Big Idea Our World and Beyond

As you read, ask yourself, How does this story reverse the conventions of most detective stories?

Literary Element Parody

A **parody** is a work that imitates the style of some other work in a satirical or humorous way. As you read, ask yourself, How do the characters and events in this story resemble those in a Sherlock Holmes story? How does the style in which it is written resemble that of Sir Arthur Conan Doyle?

Reading Strategy Evaluate Details

When you **evaluate details** in a literary work, you assess how well the author has supported his or her themes and generalizations with specific, concrete examples. Harte's main purpose in "The Stolen Cigar Case" is to amuse the reader. As you read, ask yourself, How well does Harte use details to create humor in his story?

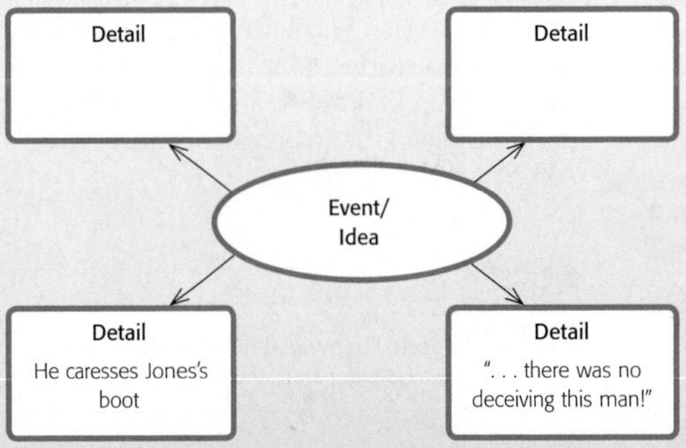

Learning Objectives

For pages 1071–1081

In studying this text, you will focus on the following objectives:

Literary Study: Analyzing parody.

Reading: Evaluating details.

Writing: Writing a parody.

Vocabulary

inscrutable (in skrōō′ tə bəl) *adj.* not readily understood or interpreted; p. 1074 *Mr. Serkin was a quiet man who kept his intentions to himself; I found him inscrutable.*

trifle (trī′ fəl) *n.* something of little value or importance; p. 1074 *He didn't want to buy a trifle, but he hoped to give a generous gift.*

perspicacity (pur′ spə kas′ ə tē) *n.* acute mental powers or perception; p. 1076 *The detective's perspicacity resulted in a swift solution to the crime.*

infallibility (in fal′ ə bil′ ə tē) *n.* state of being incapable of error; p. 1080 *Do not credit experts with infallibility; they too can make mistakes.*

Tip: Connotation and Denotation A word's denotation is its dictionary meaning. Its connotations are ideas and meanings associated with the word. For example, the words *trifle* and *trinket* have a similar denotation "something of little value," but they have different connotations. *Trinket* is more positive, and *trifle* is more negative or neutral.

Viewing Practice

View an Episode Explain to students that Harte's story is a parody of Doyle's Sherlock Holmes stories. **Say:** A parody is a humorous imitation of a literary work that aims to point out the work's shortcomings. A parody may imitate the style, characters, or plot of another work. Allow students to watch an episode of "The Adventures of Sherlock Holmes." As students watch, encourage them to take notes on the plot, characters, and style of the story. Have students explain how the works are similar and how they are different. Students should also explain which elements are being imitated.

The Stolen Cigar Case

Bret Harte

I found Hemlock Jones in the old Brook Street lodgings, musing before the fire. With the freedom of an old friend I at once threw myself in my usual familiar attitude at his feet, and gently caressed his boot. I was induced to do this for two reasons: one, that it enabled me to get a good look at his bent, concentrated face, and the other, that it seemed to indicate my reverence for his superhuman insight. So absorbed was he even then, in tracking some mysterious clue, that he did not seem to notice me. But therein I was wrong—as I always was in my attempt to understand that powerful intellect.

"It is raining," he said, without lifting his head.

"You have been out, then?" I said quickly.

"No. But I see that your umbrella is wet, and that your overcoat has drops of water on it."

I sat aghast at his penetration. After a pause he said carelessly, as if dismissing the subject: "Besides, I hear the rain on the window. Listen."

I listened. I could scarcely credit my ears, but there was the soft pattering of drops on the panes. It was evident there was no deceiving this man!

"Have you been busy lately?" I asked, changing the subject. "What new problem—given up by Scotland Yard[1] as

1. *Scotland Yard* is the detective division of the British metropolitan police force.

1 Parody *What qualities of the narrator's are exaggerated or humorous?*

Evaluate Details *How do the details of Jones's deduction in this passage create a humorous effect?* **2**

Teach

Literary Element 1

Parody **Answer:** *The narrator's slavish worship of Jones and his exaggerated ideas about Jones's brilliance*

APPROACHING **Ask:** Why does the narrator mention Scotland Yard, the London police? *(to highlight Jones's skills and reputation by showing that the police come to him for help when they cannot solve a crime)*

Reading Strategy 2

Evaluate Details **Answer:** *The details of Jones's deduction that it is raining—the narrator's wet coat and umbrella, as well as the sound of rain on the window—are so obvious that they contradict the narrator's claim that Jones possesses a "powerful intellect."*

For additional practice using the reading skill or strategy, see Unit 6 Teaching Resources Book, p. 113.

Readability Scores

Dale-Chall: 9.4
DRP: 58
Lexile: 1020

Approaching Level

DIFFERENTIATED INSTRUCTION

Emerging Remind students that a parody is a humorous imitation of a literary work that aims to point out the work's shortcomings. Then ask students to think of other parodies they may have seen and to share these with the class. *(Students may mention television parodies such as the newscast and gameshow sketches of* Saturday Night Live *or cinematic parodies such as* Scary Movie *or* Spaceballs.*)*

Teach

Literary Element 1

Parody **Answer:** *Apparently he has lost everything.*

inscrutable—has occupied that gigantic intellect?"

He drew back his foot slightly, and seemed to hesitate ere he returned it to its original position. Then he answered wearily: "Mere **trifles**—nothing to speak of. The Prince Kupoli has been here to get my advice regarding the disappearance of certain rubies from the Kremlin; the Rajah of Pootibad, after vainly beheading his entire bodyguard, has been obliged to seek my assistance to recover a jeweled sword. The Grand Duchess of Pretzel-Brauntswig is desirous of discovering where her husband was on the night of February 14; and last night"—he lowered his voice slightly—"a lodger in this very house, meeting me on the stairs, wanted to know why they didn't answer his bell."

I could not help smiling—until I saw a frown gathering on his inscrutable forehead.

"Pray remember," he said coldly, "that it was through such an apparently trivial question that I found out Why Paul Ferroll Killed His Wife, and What Happened to Jones!"

I became dumb[2] at once. He paused for a moment, and then suddenly changing back to his usual pitiless, analytical style, he said: "When I say these are trifles, they are so in comparison to an affair that is now before me. A crime has been committed—and, singularly enough, against myself. You start," he said. "You wonder who would have dared to attempt it. So did I; nevertheless, it has been done. *I* have been *robbed!*"

"*You* robbed! You, Hemlock Jones, the Terror of Peculators!"[3] I gasped in amazement, arising and gripping the table as I faced him.

"Yes! Listen. I would confess it to no other. But *you* who have followed my career, who know my methods; you, for whom I have partly lifted the veil that conceals my plans from ordinary humanity,—you, who have for years rapturously accepted my confidences, passionately admired my inductions and inferences, placed yourself at my beck and call, become my slave, groveled at my feet, given up your practice except those few unremunerative and rapidly decreasing patients to whom, in moments of abstraction over *my* problems, you have administered strychnine for quinine and arsenic for Epsom salts;[4] you, who have sacrificed anything and everybody to me—*you* I make my confidant!"

I arose and embraced him warmly, yet he was already so engrossed in thought that at the same moment he mechanically placed his hand upon his watch chain as if to consult the time. "Sit down," he said. "Have a cigar?"

"I have given up cigar smoking," I said.

"Why?" he asked.

I hesitated, and perhaps colored. I had really given it up because, with my diminished practice, it was too expensive. I could afford only a pipe. "I prefer a pipe," I said laughingly. "But tell me of this robbery. What have you lost?"

He arose, and planting himself before the fire with his hands under his coat-tails, looked down upon me reflectively for a

2. Here, *dumb* means "speechless."

Vocabulary

inscrutable (in skrōō′ tə bəl) *adj.* not readily understood or interpreted

trifle (trī′ fəl) *n.* something of little value or importance

3. *Peculator* is a term for an embezzler.

4. A doctor who administers *strychnine for quinine and arsenic for Epsom salts* would kill his or her patients.

Parody *What has happened to the narrator as a result of his devotion to Jones?* **1**

Writing Practice

Freewrite About Characters' Traits

Ask students to notice how the dialogue and narration reveal personality traits of each character. **Ask:** What can you tell about Hemlock Jones from what he says to the narrator? What can you tell about the narrator from what he says to Jones and to readers? Have students freewrite about each character's traits and how they affect a reader's involvement in the story. *(Students may point out that Jones is rude and condescending to the narrator; he is conceited, mysterious, and believes himself to be infallible. The narrator is oblivious, foolishly adoring, trusting, kind, and helpful. Readers may find that they strongly dislike Jones and feel bad for the narrator. Other readers may grow annoyed with the narrator's blind adoration.)*

moment. "Do you remember the cigar case presented to me by the Turkish Ambassador for discovering the missing favorite of the Grand Vizier[5] in the fifth chorus girl at the Hilarity Theater? It was that one. I mean the cigar case. It was incrusted with diamonds."

"And the largest one had been supplanted by paste,"[6] I said.

"Ah," he said, with a reflective smile, "you know that?"

"You told me yourself. I remember considering it a proof of your extraordinary perception. But, by Jove, you don't mean to say you have lost it?"

He was silent for a moment. "No; it has been stolen, it is true, but I shall still find it. And by myself alone! In your profession, my dear fellow, when a member is seriously ill, he does not prescribe for himself, but calls in a brother doctor. Therein we differ. I shall take this matter in my own hands."

"And where could you find better?" I said enthusiastically. "I should say the cigar case is as good as recovered already."

"I shall remind you of that again," he said lightly. "And now, to show you my confidence in your judgment, in spite of my determination to pursue this alone, I am willing to listen to any suggestions from you."

He drew a memorandum book from his pocket and, with a grave smile, took up his pencil.

I could scarcely believe my senses. He, the great Hemlock Jones, accepting suggestions from a humble individual like myself! I kissed his hand reverently, and began in a joyous tone:

"First, I should advertise, offering a reward; I should give the same intimation in hand-bills, distributed at the pubs and the pastry-cooks'. I should next visit the different pawnbrokers; I should give notice at the police station. I should examine the servants. I should thoroughly search the house and my own pockets. I speak relatively," I added, with a laugh. "Of course I mean *your* own."

He gravely made an entry of these details.

"Perhaps," I added, "you have already done this?"

"Perhaps," he returned enigmatically. "Now, my dear friend," he continued, putting the notebook in his pocket and rising, "would you excuse me for a few moments? Make yourself perfectly at home until I return; there may be some things," he added with a sweep of his hand toward his heterogeneously[7] filled shelves, "that may interest you and wile away the time. There are pipes and tobacco in that corner."

Then nodding to me with the same inscrutable face he left the room. I was too well accustomed to his methods to think much of his unceremonious withdrawal, and made no doubt he was off to investigate some clue which had suddenly occurred to his active intelligence. **3**

Left to myself I cast a cursory glance over his shelves. There were a number of small glass jars containing earthy substances, labeled "Pavement and Road Sweepings," from the principal thoroughfares and suburbs of London, with the subdirections "for identifying foot-tracks." There were several other jars, labeled "Fluff from Omnibus[8] and Road Car Seats," "Cocoanut Fibre and Rope Strands

5. A *Grand Vizier* is a high-ranking political adviser.
6. Here, *paste* refers to a type of fake gemstone.

2 Parody *What elements in this passage resemble the elements of a Sherlock Holmes story?*

7. Jones's *heterogeneously* filled shelves include a wide variety of items.
8. *Omnibus* is a term for *bus* that is no longer in use.

Teach

Literary Element 2

Parody **Answer:** *Holmes often solicits ideas and advice from his sidekick Watson.*

ADVANCED **Ask:** What elements here are an apparent exaggeration of the relationship between Sherlock Holmes and Dr. Watson? *(the narrator's shock at Jones's request for his advice; the narrator's extreme adoration of Jones, which leads him to kiss his hand)*

Reading Strategy 3

Recognize Author's Purpose **Ask:** Why does Harte have Jones nod with an inscrutable face? *(Jones maintains an aura of mystery; everything has a secret or double meaning for him. He likes to imply he knows more than he's willing to reveal.)*

English Learners

DIFFERENTIATED INSTRUCTION

Strategic Explain to students the medical terms used on page 1074. Tell them that strychnine and arsenic are poisons, while quinine is a drug used to treat malaria, and Epsom salt is a mineral primarily used as an anti-inflammatory.

Teach

Reading Strategy 1

Evaluate Details Answer: *The trivial bits of information that Jones collects reveal him to be obsessive rather than systematic.*

Big Idea 2

Our World and Beyond
Answer: *A mysterious intruder enters Jones's apartment. The narrator notices a strange stickiness in one of Jones's drawers. The narrator hints at exciting events to come.*

View the Art ★
Answer: *Answers will vary. Some students may say that the cartoon-like feel of the picture captures the mood of a parody. Others may feel that the picture isn't comic enough to capture the mood of a parody.*

Detective Looking for Clues. Todd Davidson.

★ *View the Art* In your opinion, does this illustration capture the mood of a parody? Why or why not?

from Mattings in Public Places," "Cigarette Stumps and Match Ends from Floor of Palace Theater, Row A, 1 to 50." Everywhere were evidences of this wonderful man's system and **perspicacity.**

I was thus engaged when I heard the slight creaking of a door, and I looked up as a stranger entered. He was a rough-looking man, with a shabby overcoat and a still more disreputable muffler around his throat and the lower part of his face. Considerably annoyed at his intrusion, I turned upon him rather sharply, when, with a mumbled, growling apology for mistaking the room, he shuffled out again and closed the door. I followed him quickly to the landing and saw that he disappeared down the stairs. With my mind full of the robbery, the incident made a singular impression upon me. I knew my friend's habit of hasty absences from his room in his moments of deep inspiration; it was only too probable that, with his powerful intellect and magnificent perceptive genius concentrated on one subject, he should be careless of his own belongings, and no doubt even forget to take the ordinary precaution of locking up his drawers. I tried one or two and found that I was right, although for some reason I was unable to open one to its fullest extent. The handles were sticky, as if some one had opened them with dirty fingers. Knowing Hemlock's fastidious[9] cleanliness, I resolved to inform him of this circumstance, but I forgot it, alas! until—but I am anticipating my story.

His absence was strangely prolonged. I at last seated myself by the fire, and lulled

1 Evaluate Details *How do the details in this paragraph poke fun at Jones's methods of detection?*

Vocabulary

perspicacity (pur´ spə kas´ tē) *n.* acute mental powers or perception

9. *Fastidious* means "excessively careful" or "difficult to please."

Our World and Beyond *What new complications to the mystery are introduced in this passage?* **2**

Reading Practice

SPIRAL REVIEW **Understand Plot** Draw a two-column chart on the board with the following elements on the left side:

- **Exposition** (introduction of conflict)
- **Rising action** (builds suspense; adds complications)
- **Climax** (turning point)
- **Falling action** (leads to the conclusion)
- **Conclusion** (logical results of the climax)

Ask students to copy the chart in their notebooks. Have students complete the chart as they read to help them understand the plot of the story.

*(Answers: **Exposition:** Jones tells the narrator that the cigar case is missing. **Rising action:** The narrator's adoration of Jones becomes clear; the narrator helps Jones look for the case; a mysterious stranger enters the office. **Climax:** Jones accuses the narrator of being the thief. **Falling action:** Jones explains his reasoning; the narrator finds the case; Jones sticks to his convictions. **Conclusion:** The narrator never sees Jones again; questions whether he might have stolen the case after all.)*

by warmth and the patter of the rain on the window, I fell asleep. I may have dreamt, for during my sleep I had a vague semi-consciousness as of hands being softly pressed on my pockets—no doubt induced by the story of the robbery. When I came fully to my senses, I found Hemlock Jones sitting on the other side of the hearth, his deeply concentrated gaze fixed on the fire.

"I found you so comfortably asleep that I could not bear to awaken you," he said, with a smile.

I rubbed my eyes. "And what news?" I asked. "How have you succeeded?"

"Better than I expected," he said, "and I think," he added, tapping his notebook. "I owe much to *you.*"

Deeply gratified, I awaited more. But in vain. I ought to have remembered that in his moods Hemlock Jones was reticence itself, I told him simply of the strange intrusion, but he only laughed.

Later, when I arose to go, he looked at me playfully.

"If you were a married man," he said, "I would advise you not to go home until you had brushed your sleeve. There are a few short brown sealskin hairs on the inner side of your forearm, just where they would have adhered if your arm had encircled a sealskin coat with some pressure!"

"For once you are at fault," I said triumphantly; "the hair is my own, as you will perceive; I have just had it cut at the hairdresser's, and no doubt this arm projected beyond the apron."

He frowned slightly, yet, nevertheless, on my turning to go he embraced me warmly—a rare exhibition in that man of ice. He even helped me on with my overcoat and pulled out and smoothed down the flaps of my pockets. He was particular, too, in fitting my arm in my overcoat sleeve, shaking the sleeve down from the armhole to the cuff with his deft fingers. "Come again soon!" he said, clapping me on the back.

"At any and all times," I said enthusiastically; "I only ask ten minutes twice a day to eat a crust at my office, and four hours' sleep at night, and the rest of my time is devoted to you always, as you know."

"It is indeed," he said, with his impenetrable smile.

Nevertheless, I did not find him at home when I next called. One afternoon, when nearing my own home, I met him in one of his favorite disguises—a long blue swallow-tailed coat, striped cotton trousers, large turn-over collar, and white hat, carrying a tambourine. Of course to others the disguise was perfect, although it was known to myself, and I passed him—according to an old understanding between us—without the slightest recognition, trusting to a later explanation. At another time, as I was making a professional visit to the wife of a publican[10] at the East End, I saw him, in the disguise of a broken-down artisan, looking into the window of an adjacent pawnshop. I was delighted to see that he was evidently following my suggestions, and in my joy I ventured to tip him a wink; it was abstractedly returned. ☆

Two days later I received a note appointing a meeting at his lodgings that night. That meeting, alas! was the one memorable occurrence of my life, and the last meeting I ever had with Hemlock Jones! I will try to set it down calmly, though my pulses still throb with the recollection of it.

I found him standing before the fire, with that look upon his face which I had seen only once or twice in our acquaintance—a look which I may call an absolute concatenation of inductive and deductive

10. A *publican* is the operator of a British public house, or pub.

Parody *So far, how has this story resembled a Sherlock Holmes mystery story? How has it differed, and what is the effect of the difference?* **3**

Teach

Literary Element 3

Parody **Answer:** *Jones is presented as a master detective like Holmes, and the twists and turns of the mystery resemble the complications in Doyle's stories. Through exaggeration and bizarre details, Harte makes the characters and their situation seem absurd.*

Cultural History ☆

The East End "The East End" is a popular designation for the area of London roughly east of the City of London, south of the Thames, and bordered by the River Lea. Historically a poor section of London, the East End is home to the Tower of London and was often visited by Jack the Ripper.

Approaching Level

DIFFERENTIATED INSTRUCTION

Emerging Ask students to imagine themselves in the narrator's situation. **Ask:** Can you think of a time when you struggled to win approval or attention from someone? How did you feel? Would you act this way again in the future? *(Answers may vary.)* **Say:** Think about these questions as you continue reading the story. Think about how the narrator handles situations with Jones, and whether you might handle things differently if you were in his situation.

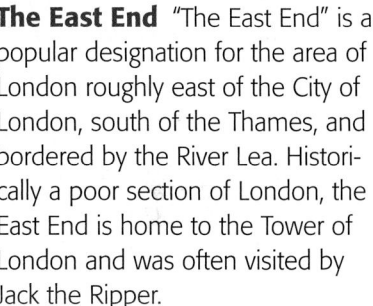

Teach

Big Idea 1

Our World and Beyond
Answer: *Answers may vary. Students should support their answers.*

Reading Strategy 2

Evaluate Details **Answer:** *Jones makes the ridiculous assumption that the narrator's fondness for cigars is the clinching motive for his theft of the cigar case, even though the diamond-studded case itself is the main attraction.*

ratiocination[11]—from which all that was human, tender, or sympathetic was absolutely discharged. He was simply an icy algebraic symbol! Indeed, his whole being was concentrated to that extent that his clothes fitted loosely, and his head was absolutely so much reduced in size by his mental compression that his hat tipped back from his forehead and literally hung on his massive ears.

After I had entered he locked the doors, fastened the windows, and even placed a chair before the chimney. As I watched these significant precautions with absorbing interest, he suddenly drew a revolver and, presenting it to my temple, said in low, icy tones:

"Hand over that cigar case!"

Even in my bewilderment my reply was truthful, spontaneous, and involuntary. "I haven't got it," I said.

He smiled bitterly, and threw down his revolver. "I expected that reply! Then let me now confront you with something more awful, more deadly, more relentless and convincing than that mere lethal weapon—the damning inductive and deductive proofs of your guilt!" He drew from his pocket a roll of paper and a notebook.

"But surely," I gasped, "you are joking! You could not for a moment believe"—

"Silence! Sit down!" I obeyed.

"You have condemned yourself," he went on pitilessly. "Condemned yourself on my processes—processes familiar to you, applauded by you, accepted by you for years! We will go back to the time when you first saw the cigar case. Your expressions," he said in cold, deliberate tones, consulting his paper, "were, 'How beautiful! I wish it were mine.' This was your first step in crime—and my first indication. From 'I *wish* it were mine' to 'I *will* have it mine,' and the mere detail, '*How can* I make it mine?' the advance was obvious. Silence! But as in my methods it was necessary that there should be an overwhelming inducement to the crime, that unholy admiration of yours for the mere trinket itself was not enough. You are a smoker of cigars."

"But," I burst out passionately, "I told you I had given up smoking cigars."

"Fool!" he said coldly, "that is the *second* time you have committed yourself. Of course you told me! What more natural than for you to blazon forth that prepared and unsolicited statement to *prevent* accusation. Yet, as I said before, even that wretched attempt to cover up your tracks was not enough. I still had to find that overwhelming, impelling motive necessary to affect a man like you. That motive I found in the strongest of all impulses—Love, I suppose you would call it," he added bitterly, "that night you called! You had brought the most conclusive proofs of it on your sleeve."

"But—" I almost screamed.

"Silence!" he thundered. "I know what you would say. You would say that even if you had embraced some Young Person in a sealskin coat, what had that to do with the robbery? Let me tell you, then, that that sealskin coat represented the quality and character of your fatal entanglement! You bartered your honor for it—that stolen cigar case was the purchaser of the sealskin coat!

"Silence! Having thoroughly established your motive, I now proceed to the commission of the crime itself. Ordinary people would have begun with that—with an

11. A *concatenation* is a series of things linked together in a chain. *Ratiocination* is reasoning.

1 Our World and Beyond *Are you surprised by this development? Why or why not?*

Evaluate Details *How does this final detail of Jones's accusation ridicule his faulty logic?* **2**

Speaking Practice

PARTNERS **Re-create Comic Effect** Ask students to work with a partner to act out a scene from the story. Explain to students that they should choose a scene that best captures the comedy of the story, and then re-create their own interpretation of that scene. Students should consider how to use comedic delivery techniques. Encourage students to create rough props for use in their presentations. Have students present their scene to the class.

Eye With Magnifying Glass. Bob Commander. ★

attempt to discover the whereabouts of the missing object. These are not *my* methods."

So overpowering was his penetration that, although I knew myself innocent, I licked my lips with avidity to hear the further details of this lucid exposition of my crime.

"You committed that theft the night I showed you the cigar case, and after I had carelessly thrown it in that drawer. You were sitting in that chair, and I had arisen to take something from that shelf. In that instant you secured your booty without rising. Silence! Do you remember when I helped you on with your overcoat the other night? I was particular about fitting your arm in. While doing so I measured your arms with a spring tape measure, from the shoulder to the cuff. A later visit to your tailor confirmed that measurement. It proved to be *the exact distance between your chair and that drawer!*"

I sat stunned.

Parody *What is your response to this passage?* **3**

Teach

Literary Element **3**

Parody **Answer:** *Students should support their answers with examples from the selection.*

View the Art ★

Contemporary illustrator Bob Commander has illustrated for corporations, ad agencies, publishers, and design firms. Commander combines drawing and painting with oil, acrylic, and watercolor with computer design using programs such as Photoshop, Illustrator, Flash, and 3D animation.

English Learners

DIFFERENTIATED INSTRUCTION

Intermediate English learners may be confused by some of the British English words used throughout the story. Have them list any words they do not understand and the page number where the words are found. Encourage students to use context clues and a dictionary to find the meaning of these unfamiliar words.

Approaching Level

DIFFERENTIATED INSTRUCTION

Emerging Discuss with students the dangers of making a false accusation. **Ask:** Have you ever accused someone of something, only to find out later that you were wrong? How did you handle the situation? Did the person forgive you? *(Student responses will vary.)* Then discuss how it might feel to be the falsely accused.

Teach

Reading Strategy 1

Evaluate Details Answer: *He wanted to show that the bumbling Jones is so incompetent that he requires two attempts to throw the narrator out of the house.*

APPROACHING **Ask:** Do you think Jones will ever regret this decision? *(Students may say that Jones will never believe that he was wrong about the narrator and will therefore never regret kicking him out of his life forever.)*

To check students' understanding of the selection, see Unit 6 Teaching Resources Book, p. 117.

Progress Check

Can students identify parody?

If No → See Unit 6 Teaching Resources Book, p. 112.

"The rest are mere corroborative details! You were again tampering with the drawer when I discovered you doing so! Do not start! The stranger that blundered into the room with a muffler on—was myself! More, I had placed a little soap on the drawer handles when I purposely left you alone. The soap was on your hand when I shook it at parting. I softly felt your pockets, when you were asleep, for further developments. I embraced you when you left—that I might feel if you had the cigar case or any other articles hidden on your body. This confirmed me in the belief that you had already disposed of it in the manner and for the purpose I have shown you. As I still believed you capable of remorse and confession, I twice allowed you to see I was on your track: once in the garb of an itinerant minstrel, and the second time as a workman looking in the window of the pawnshop where you pledged your booty."

"But," I burst out, "if you had asked the pawnbroker, you would have seen how unjust"—

"Fool!" he hissed, "that was one of *your* suggestions—to search the pawnshops! Do you suppose I followed any of your suggestions, the suggestions of the thief? On the contrary, they told me what to avoid."

"And I suppose," I said bitterly, "you have not even searched your drawer?"

"No," he said calmly.

I was for the first time really vexed. I went to the nearest drawer and pulled it out sharply. It stuck as it had before, leaving a part of the drawer unopened. By working it, however, I discovered that it was impeded by some obstacle that had slipped to the upper part of the drawer, and held it firmly fast. Inserting my hand, I pulled out the impeding object. It was the missing cigar case! I turned to him with a cry of joy.

But I was appalled at his expression. A look of contempt was now added to his acute, penetrating gaze. "I have been mistaken," he said slowly; "I had not allowed for your weakness and cowardice! I thought too highly of you even in your guilt! But I see now why you tampered with that drawer the other night. By some inexplicable means—possibly another theft—you took the cigar case out of pawn and, like a whipped hound, restored it to me in this feeble, clumsy fashion. You thought to deceive me, Hemlock Jones! More, you thought to destroy my **infallibility.** Go! I give you your liberty. I shall not summon the three policemen who wait in the adjoining room—but out of my sight forever!"

As I stood once more dazed and petrified, he took me firmly by the ear and led me into the hall, closing the door behind him. This reopened presently, wide enough to permit him to thrust out my hat, overcoat, umbrella, and overshoes, and then closed against me forever!

I never saw him again. I am bound to say, however, that thereafter my business increased, I recovered much of my old practice, and a few of my patients recovered also. I became rich. I had a brougham and a house in the West End.[12] But I often wondered, pondering on that wonderful man's penetration and insight, if, in some lapse of consciousness, I had not really stolen his cigar case!

12. A *brougham* is a horse-drawn carriage with a driver. At the time of the story, the *West End* was a fashionable residential area of London.

Evaluate Details *Why do you think Harte included these details?* 1

Vocabulary

infallibility (in fal′ ə bil′ ə tē) *n.* state of being incapable of error

Speaking Practice

SPIRAL REVIEW **Create Alternate Endings** Ask students to think about other ways the story might have ended. **Ask:** What might the characters have done differently? What other characters might have been introduced? How might the plot have changed? Have students discuss ideas for an alternate ending to the story. Students should take notes during their discussion and write a short summary of their new ending. Have a representative from each group present their ending to the class. *(In their alternate endings, students may have Jones realize his mistake when the narrator finds the case; they may introduce an actual thief; they may have Jones falsely accuse someone else of taking the case.)*

After You Read

Respond and Think Critically

Respond and Interpret

1. What did you enjoy most about "The Stolen Cigar Case"?
2. (a)What mystery does Hemlock Jones set out to solve? (b)What advice does the narrator provide?
3. (a)What steps does Jones take to solve the mystery? (b)How successful are Jones's methods and way of thinking?

Analyze and Evaluate

4. **Irony** is a discrepancy between appearance and reality, or between what is expected and what actually happens. How does irony add humor to this story? Explain.
5. On a humor scale of one to ten, evaluate the level of humor of this story. Explain.

Connect

6. **Big Idea** **Our World and Beyond** In what way does the ending of the story reverse the usual conclusion to a detective story?
7. **Connect to Today** How might a detective go about solving a similar crime today?

Literary Element Parody

Parody imitates the style of another work or author in a humorous way.

1. How does Harte hold up the conventions of detective stories for ridicule? Include details from the story in your answer.
2. What details make Jones and the narrator especially funny or ridiculous? Explain.

Reading Strategy Evaluate Details

Refer to the web diagram you created as you read the story. Then answer the following questions.

1. When Jones accuses the narrator of stealing the cigar case, what significant detail of the narrator's reaction identifies the narrator as a comic character? Explain.
2. Evaluate the humorous details in the last paragraph of the story. How effective are the details in achieving an ironic ending? Explain.

LOG ON **Literature Online**

Selection Resources For Selection Quizzes, eFlashcards, and Reading-Writing Connection activities, go to glencoe.com and enter QuickPass code GL49787u6.

Vocabulary Practice

Practice with Connotation and Denotation Each of the vocabulary words is listed with a word that has a similar denotation. Choose the word that has a more negative connotation.

1. inscrutable	mysterious
2. trifle	toy
3. perspicacity	genius
4. infallibility	competence

Writing

Write a Story Write your own parody in the style of a familiar genre or of a favorite author. Approach your subject in a humorous manner while maintaining the style of the genre or author you are parodying. Trade stories with a classmate and see if you can guess the subject of each other's parody.

Reading Strategy

1. The significant detail occurs when the narrator displays his undiminished admiration for Jones even though he knows that the accusation is false. The narrator's reaction is comic because he praises Jones's explanation as being lucid but untrue.
2. Answers will vary. Students must support their answers with information from the text.

Vocabulary Practice

1. inscrutable
2. trifle
3. perspicacity
4. competence

For additional selection assessment, see Assessment Resources, pp. 223–224.

After You Read

Assess

1. Students should support their answers.
2. (a) To find his missing cigar case (b) To post notices, call police and check pawnbrokers, the help and his house
3. (a) Jones accuses the narrator. He tries to search the narrator's clothes and to trap him into revealing his guilt. (b) They are unsuccessful.
4. The huge gap between Jones and the archetypal sleuth is what makes this story funny.
5. Students should support their answers.
6. The sidekick solves the mystery. Both the mystery and its solution are mundane.
7. Answers will vary. Possible answers include using the Internet, a telephone, and a surveillance camera.

Literary Element

1. Most detective stories hinge on a serious crime and feature a brilliantly logical sleuth; Harte's story revolves around a misplaced cigar box and involves a detective who's wrong about everything.
2. Students should support their answers.

Writing

Students' stories should

- be a parody of a genre or author's style
- have a theme and subject
- be told in a humorous manner
- maintain the style of chosen genre or author

Writing Workshop

Persuasion: Editorial

Focus

Bellringer Options

Have the class brainstorm aspects of space exploration and list their ideas on the board.

Ask: What are some benefits of exploring space? Do you think governments should spend money on space programs, or on education, health care, the environment, or other issues? Why? Have students freewrite on questions related to space exploration.

Learning Objectives

For pages 1082–1089

In this workshop, you will focus on the following objectives:

Writing:
Writing an editorial.
Using a reasonable tone.

Grammar: Understanding parallelism.

Writing Process

At any stage of a writing process, you may think of new ideas. Feel free to return to earlier stages as you write.

- Prewrite
- Draft
- Revise
- Focus Lesson: Reasonable Tone
- Edit and Proofread
- Focus Lesson: Parallelism
- Present

LOG ON Literature Online

Writing and Research
For prewriting, drafting, and revising tools, go to glencoe.com and enter QuickPass code GL49787u6.

Writing Workshop

Persuasion: Editorial

Literature Connection As a science fiction writer, Arthur C. Clarke has made startling proposals about the future. He wrote "The Sentinel" in 1948, and although experts of the time dismissed space travel as impossible, Neil Armstrong and Buzz Aldrin set foot on the moon in 1969—just over twenty years later. In "The Sentinel," the main character makes a discovery that has enormous implications for the future of people on Earth.

> *"There had, after all, been a lunar civilization—and I was the first to find it. That I had come perhaps a hundred million years too late did not distress me; it was enough to have come at all."*
>
> —Arthur C. Clarke, from "The Sentinel"

Whether or not humans *should* explore space is still a matter of debate. Is space exploration worth the cost in money and possible danger to human lives? Issues such as these are the subjects of editorials.

Checklist

Goals	Strategies
To express an opinion on a current event or issue	☑ Clearly state your position or claim ☑ Maintain a clear focus on your position or claim throughout your editorial
To support your opinion, claim, or thesis	☑ Present evidence, examples, and reasoning
To persuade an audience	☑ Address opposing arguments ☑ Use persuasive techniques such as emotional appeals, repetition, hyperbole, irony, word choice, or bandwagon

Workshop Resources

Print Materials

- Unit 6 Teaching Resources, pp. 159–161
- Writing Kit
- Success in Writing: Research and Reports

Technology

- Literature Online: Writing Resources and Grammar Resources, www.glencoe.com
- Online Essay Grader, www.glencoe.com
- Student Presentation Builder on StudentWorks Plus CD-ROM
- Media Workshop DVD
- Online Student Edition

Assignment: Write an Editorial

Write an editorial of at least 1,500 words supporting your opinion about an issue affecting the future of the world.

Audience: peers, classmates, and teacher

Purpose: present an opinion and provide support for your opinion

Real-World Connection

Does your editorial address an issue in your school? If so, submit it to your school newspaper. Does it address a community issue? Submit it to your local newspaper.

Analyze a Professional Model

Scott Sheppard, who studies solar systems, argues that robots should be used to explore space in the future. Pay close attention to the comments in the margin. They point out features to include in your own editorial.

from *"Decision Time for Space Exploration"*
by Scott Sheppard
San Francisco Chronicle, October 10, 2005

Ever since the race to the Moon ended, the question of where to send humans next has yet to be answered. The plan now is to slowly build out, by completing the International Space Station and then going back to the Moon and eventually on to Mars. There is an explanation as to why this has been the general plan for more than 30 years but yet very little has been done to make it reality.

Audience/Purpose/Tone

Provide background on the subject as preparation for your opinion/argument. Create a tone that will encourage your reader to read on.

The simple fact is that there is no real reason to do any of this. There is no Cold War to propel us to the Moon again, and even if the space race with China heats up it will not last. There is no major economic benefit for humans going to the Moon or any of the inhospitable planets. Space tourism may one day find a niche, but unlike air travel, there are no major capitalistic reasons to have human space travel, and it seems very unlikely to ever become a major enterprise. What little there is to do in space is far easier and cheaper to do with robotic spacecraft. . . .

Reasoning

Your audience is more likely to consider your opinion if you provide logical reasons for it.

Position or Claim

State your position or claim clearly and concisely.

Imagine if there were a habitable planet or moon in our Solar System. If Mars, Venus, our Moon, or even one of

Writing Workshop

Persuasion: Editorial

Teach

Big Idea

Our World and Beyond

Help students make a connection between the editorial and issues affecting our planet. Explain that in editorials writers express their views about important issues, from politics to humanity's place in the cosmos.

Ask: What are some issues that may affect the future of the world? (Students may mention war, infectious diseases, climate change, energy supplies, or other issues.)

English Learners

DIFFERENTIATED INSTRUCTION

Benchmark English learners struggle with the meaning of words as well as pronunciation. Have students look up words from the model, such as *inhospitable* and *niche*. Then show them how to use the pronunciation guide in a dictionary to find the correct pronunciation for each word.

Writing Workshop

Persuasion: Editorial

Big Idea 1

Our World and Beyond **Ask:** What does the author feel would be the best motive for human exploration of space? *(The author feels that economic benefit is the best motivator.)*

APPROACHING **Ask:** What is the current motivator for space travel? *(scientific curiosity)*

Literary Element 2

Description **Ask:** Do you feel the author does a good job of describing the challenges of purely scientific space exploration? Why or why not? *(Some students may feel that the author presents a succinct description that clarifies the argument. Other students may feel that more concrete descriptive examples would better the argument.)*

Cultural History ☆

NASA After the Soviet Union launched the Sputnik satellite in 1957, the U.S. government established the National Aeronautics and Space Administration, or NASA. Its mission is to research and develop technologies for space exploration, to broaden our understanding of space, and to establish a human presence there. Famous achievements include the Apollo moon mission, the space shuttle, and the Hubble Space Telescope.

Jupiter's larger moons could host tenants, the question of where do we go next would not be debatable. We would be on the verge of colonizing these places right now. Imagine what that would do for our technology. It would be similar to the discovery of the Americas by the Europeans in the fifteenth century. . . .

Unfortunately, we don't have these habitable areas anywhere near us. Our exploration through curiosity will continue to drive us scientifically, but with no real economic benefits to our society from humans being in space, it will be a much slower process. It is hoped that conditions for civilization on the Earth will improve with increasing technology, but our expansion into outer space is now stunted, because there is no obvious answer to the question "Where do we send humans next?" . . . **1**

Audience/Focus
Point out the problems of any alternative viewpoints. Here the question brings readers back to the focus of the editorial.

Robotic, instead of human, space missions should be used to satisfy our curiosity. The new mobile robots unveiled at the NASA Ames research center last week are a step in the right direction. ☆ Robotic exploration is a much cheaper and more productive way to explore our hostile space environment. Robotic spacecraft will soon be able to accomplish most of the science a human would on the Moon or Mars.

Robotic exploration of these environments would cost a few billion dollars, whereas human exploration is expected to cost a few hundred billion dollars. The human Moon-Mars initiative was not proposed or even backed by the vast majority of scientists, because they understand that more science for our money is obtained through robotic missions. It's time our space program put its money where it counts—in the robotic spacecraft that are rolling around right under our noses. **2**

Evidence
Use facts to support your opinion. A fact is a statement that can be proven.

Conclusion
In your conclusion, restate your opinion on the issue and your proposed solution.

Reading-Writing Connection Try out the writing techniques that you have just encountered in the editorial you write.

Writing Practice

SMALL GROUP **Prewriting** Writing questions related to their topics can help students clarify their ideas and focus their research. Have students write questions about their chosen topic. When they are finished, have them exchange papers with a partner. Partners should review the questions and make additional suggestions. Encourage students to use the information from their prewritng session to help them write their editorial.

Prewrite

Read Published Editorials Read a newspaper published in your city or area, paying attention to the different subjects of the editorials over a period of several days. How do you respond to the different issues raised?

Choose an Issue Choose an issue about which you feel strongly. If you are invested in your subject, then you will likely communicate your enthusiasm and effectively express your opinion.

Use a Graphic Organizer Create an organizer like the one shown to help you plan your editorial.

Issue or Problem
Destruction of rain forests

↓

My Opinion
We must stop destroying rain forests because they provide many benefits and treasures, including medicines, foods, and animal life.

↓

Other Viewpoints
Timber from rain forests is needed for building new homes and burning as fuel.

↓

My Proposed Solution
Avoid using paper products made from trees. Conserve energy and fuel.

Discuss Your Ideas Meet with a partner to express ideas about your issue. Explain your opinion, talk about other viewpoints, and provide support for your conclusion. Ask your partner for suggestions on how to match your writing style to your purpose and audience.

- Remember, your style should sound natural but professional.
- Keep your tone calm and reasonable.
- Finally, have your partner restate your opinion. This will test whether or not you have presented it clearly.

Use Persuasive Techniques

Try out one or more of these persuasive techniques in your editorial:

Emotional Appeal Present ideas that create strong feelings.

Repetition Repeat your thesis, key words, or ideas.

Word Choice Use words with especially positive or negative connotations.

Irony Say one thing when you mean the opposite.

Hyperbole Overstate your case or exaggerate the results of doing nothing.

Bandwagon Suggest that everyone else will see your logic and follow your advice.

Avoid Plagiarism

Almost any print publication on your topic, as well as many Internet publications, is likely to be copyrighted, which means that only the author has the right to reuse it. If you use either the words or ideas of someone else, be sure to credit your sources.

Writing Workshop

Persuasion: Editorial

Teach

Writing Process

Prewriting Remind students to keep an open mind during the prewriting phase of their editorials. Tell them to keep in mind these questions as they work:

- Why does this subject interest me?
- What facts will I need to support my position?
- Based on my research, do I need to modify my opinions?
- What is the most effective way to convince others?

Writing Skill

Use a Graphic Organizer

The graphic organizer on page 1085 provides an effective template for students to use in constructing their editorials. Tell students to focus on these four points as they develop their essays. Information that does not fit easily under these four headings may be irrelevant. Remind students to be sure that the last three headings are supported by evidence.

English Learners

DIFFERENTIATED INSTRUCTION

Intermediate English learners may have difficulty organizing their thoughts in a logical structure for their essays. Encourage students to create a rough outline to help them organize main ideas and supporting details. If they are struggling, encourage them to mimic the example editorial. Have students exchange graphic organizers at an early stage in the process and offer each other feedback.

Students should check for the following:

- The writer's opinion should be clearly stated.
- Each argument should be well supported with evidence.
- The information in each rectangle should be related to the topic in the label.

Teach

Writing Skills

Audience/Persuasive Language

Answer: *The writer poses questions about discoveries that might result from exploring other worlds.*

Opinion

Answer: *The rain forests are being destroyed and we should take action to ensure its benefits will not be lost.*

Support

Answer: *This support consists of concrete examples of the most important reasons for destroying the rain forest.*

Audience

Answer: *Acknowledging more than one side shows you are fair and logical, and it provides a stronger basis for your argument.*

Draft

Get Going Using your graphic organizer as a guide, begin drafting your editorial. Start with background information about your issue. State your opinion clearly, address other viewpoints, and include strong support for your opinion and proposed solution. Remember that you can revise your plan at any time in the process, so if your research turns up a new example or fact, add it in the appropriate place.

Writing Frames

As you read the workshop model, think about the writer's use of the following frames:

The problem is that ____, and it is necessary to take action now to ensure that ____.

Some argue that ____.

Yet, these reasons don't justify ____.

What can be done to ____?

Consider using frames like these in your own editorial.

Analyze a Workshop Model

Here is a final draft of an editorial. Read it and answer the questions in the margin. Use the answers to these questions to guide you as you write.

The Future of the Rain Forest

Do you ever wonder what incredible discoveries might result from exploring other worlds? Are there miraculous cures for healing the sick and delicious foods for improving our diets? Are there animals too beautiful to imagine? This promising but unknown world is right here on Earth. It's the rain forest: a warm, lush, and soggy region located mostly in countries near the equator.

Audience/Persuasive Technique
What technique does this writer use to provide background on the subject?

We have only begun to uncover the treasure of the rain forest and to recognize its many benefits. The problem is that the rain forests of the world are being destroyed rapidly, and it is necessary to take action now to ensure that these benefits will not disappear in the future.

Claim
What is the writer's position or claim?

Let's take a look at how rain forests are being destroyed and what we can do today to save them. Trees are being cut down for a number of purposes: they supply wood, fuel, and products made from paper. Burning forests creates land that can be used for farming by people who have no other way to grow the food they need. Population growth has led some cities to take over land that once was rain forest.

Examples/Reasoning
How do these examples help the audience understand the issue?

Some argue that homes are needed because of the growth in population, and wood is needed for new construction. Timber

Audience
Why give an opposing view?

Reading Practice

Counterarguments To help students anticipate counterarguments to their opinions, suggest that they work with partners who will review their graphic organizers. Reading partners will have objective viewpoints and can help provide ideas for counterarguments. Have partners work together to come up with ideas that can be substantiated. Encourage writers to make notes during this meeting, and then address the rebuttals in their essays.

is used for fuel to heat the new homes and to make products that people are demanding in today's world. Moreover, logging companies provide jobs and help the economy.

Yet these reasons don't justify the long-term consequences of destroying rain forests. First, we know that many rain-forest plants provide substances helpful in treating illnesses. For example, the bark of a plant found in Latin America contains a chemical used to treat multiple sclerosis and Parkinson's disease. This same chemical is used during certain kinds of surgery to reduce pain.

Second, we know that the rain forest is a source of countless foods that taste great or help keep you healthy. Favorite snack foods containing ingredients originally from the rain forest include chocolate, popcorn, peanuts, cashews, cola drinks, and salsa. Fruits from the rain forest include bananas, pineapples, lemons, coconuts, and avocados.

Finally, we know that as many as 50 million different kinds of animals live in various rain forests. Millions of these animals have no names because scientists haven't identified them yet. This number includes animals so tiny you can see them only with a microscope. Brilliantly colored butterflies and birds, jaguars, gorillas, and boas are just some of the animals you would see if you explored rain forests around the world.

What can be done to save the treasures of the rain forest? For one thing, it is impractical not to reduce the amount of paper we use and throw away. We can all avoid or cut back on using products made from trees, such as paper plates and cups. Most of us can sometimes walk or ride a bike, but we often choose the easy way and ride in cars, resulting in wasted fuel. Cutting back on electricity also helps.

Saving the rain forest is crucial to the people who live in and near rain forests as well as to everyone in the world who needs to rely on the resources of rain forests in the future.

Persuasion

Audience
How does disputing an opposing view help the writer's argument?

Reasoning
What is the purpose of providing facts?

Persuasive Techniques
What persuasive techniques does the writer use here?

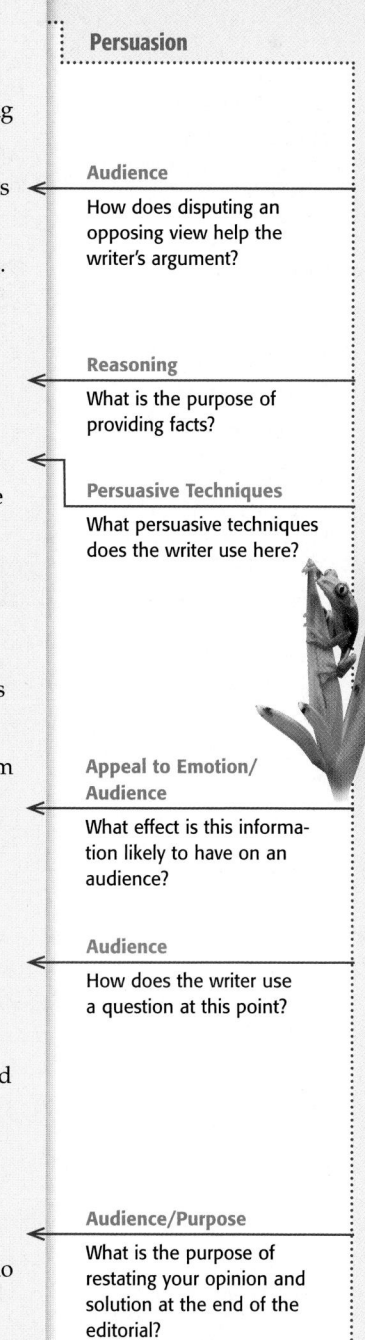

Appeal to Emotion/ Audience
What effect is this information likely to have on an audience?

Audience
How does the writer use a question at this point?

Audience/Purpose
What is the purpose of restating your opinion and solution at the end of the editorial?

Writing Workshop

Persuasion: Editorial

Teach

Writing Skills

Audience

Answer: *Showing the weaknesses of other arguments strengthens the writer's argument.*

Appeal to Logic

Answer: *Facts provide evidence for your opinion.*

Purpose/Tone/Focus

Answer: *The writer uses a positive tone to appeal to something people are interested in—their favorite foods. The entire paragraph focuses on foods that come from the rain forest.*

Organization

Answer: *The writer explains the problem, offers three reasons the audience should take action, and suggests several ways to help solve the problem.*

Audience/Purpose

Answer: *Restating your opinion and solution summarizes the argument and leaves readers with the main point of the editorial.*

Approaching Level

DIFFERENTIATED INSTRUCTION

Established Students can build reading fluency and glean feedback by reading their essay drafts aloud to partners. **Say:** While one student reads, the other student should listen attentively and take notes. Have listening partners provide suggestions for improving the essays' organization, flow, and strength of argument.

English Learners

DIFFERENTIATED INSTRUCTION

Early Advanced English language learners will benefit from hearing their essays read aloud. Have partners read aloud each other's essay. Instruct writers to listen closely. If writers notice misreads, they should work with their partners to clarify meaning.

Teach

Writing Process

Revise Remind students that all writers must constantly revise their work to

- say what they really mean
- present their messages in the most effective way

After students exchange papers and critique each other's work, refer them to the Checklist on this page. Challenge them to take another look at their essays and find at least one or two ways to improve them.

Writing Skill

Reasonable Tone A calm, rational tone gives a dignified quality to an editorial. Explain to students that a rational argument is more difficult to refute than an emotional one. Refer to the focus lesson.

Ask: Why is it more effective to say "We can all avoid products made of paper" than it is to say "Only greedy, careless people use products made from trees"? *(The first statement is hard to refute, while the second statement sounds extremist. Since most people use products made from trees, the second statement is insulting. This will alienate the audience, rather than win them over.)*

Traits of Strong Writing

Include these traits of strong writing to express your ideas effectively.

Ideas

Organization

Voice

Word Choice

Sentence Fluency

Conventions

Presentation

For more information on using the Traits of Strong Writing, see pages R28–R30.

Word Choice

This academic vocabulary word appears in the student model:

economy (i kon′ə mē) *n.* 1. the system of exchange of labor, resources, goods, and services; 2. thriftiness. *Moreover, logging companies provide jobs and help the economy.* Using academic vocabulary may help strengthen your writing. Try to use one or two academic vocabulary words in your editorial. See the complete list on pages R79–R81.

LOG ON Literature Online

Writing and Research
For editing and publishing tools, go to glencoe.com and enter QuickPass code GL49787u6.

Revise

Peer Review Exchange completed drafts with a partner. Ask your partner to evaluate how effectively your editorial convinces others. Use the checklist below to evaluate and strengthen each other's editorials.

Checklist

- ☑ Do you clearly state your position or claim?
- ☑ Do you maintain a clear focus throughout your editorial?
- ☑ Do you support your claim with evidence, examples, and reasoning?
- ☑ Do you address opposing arguments?
- ☑ Do you use persuasive techniques such as emotional appeals, repetition, hyperbole, irony, word choice, or bandwagon?

Focus Lesson

Reasonable Tone

Tone is the writer's attitude toward the subject of the written work. It is communicated through the choice of words and details. You should use a reasonable, unbiased tone to convince readers that your argument is fair, logical, and worth considering.

Draft:

It is insane not to reduce the amount of paper we use and throw away. Only greedy, careless people use products made from trees, such as paper plates and cups. Everyone can ride a bike or walk, but lazy people choose the easy way and ride in cars.

Revision:

It is impractical[1] not to reduce the amount of paper we use and throw away. We can all avoid or cut back on using products made from trees,[2] such as paper plates and cups. Most of us can sometimes walk or ride a bike, but we often choose the easy way and ride in cars, resulting in wasted fuel.[3]

1: Avoid emotionally charged words, such as insane. **2: Soften your language so that you do not insult your readers.** **3: Do not make sweeping statements that may not be true.**

Research Practice

Bibliography Consider requiring students to supply a bibliography along with their editorial to cite sources where they found factual information. Students should use a variety of consumer, workplace, and public documents to find facts to back up their arguments. Have students generate a list of these sources as they write so they will be prepared to compile a bibliography when they are done writing.

Edit and Proofread

Get It Right When you have completed the final draft of your editorial, proofread for errors in grammar, usage, mechanics, and spelling. Refer to the Language Handbook, pages R40–R59, as a guide.

Focus Lesson

Parallelism

Parallelism is created by a series of words, phrases, or sentences that have a similar grammatical structure. Using parallel structures creates unity in writing, emphasizes certain ideas, and gives rhythm to the words.

Original: The grammatical structure is not the same in both phrases.

We have only begun to uncover the treasure of the rain forest and recognizing its many benefits.

Improved: Make both verbals grammatically alike.

We have only begun to uncover the treasure of the rain forest and to recognize its many benefits.

Original: Groups of words with the same function in the sentence are expressed as a phrase and a clause.

Are there miraculous cures for healing the sick and delicious foods that could improve our diets?

Improved: Give both groups the same grammatical structure.

Are there miraculous cures for healing the sick and delicious foods for improving our diets?

Present

Make a Good Impression The purpose of an editorial is to convince others to take a side on an issue. Making a good case includes making a good impression by taking care with the writing you present. Do not forget to double-check the length of your editorial. Ask yourself if it is the correct number of words for the assignment or an appropriate length to be printed in a newspaper.

Peer Review Tips

A classmate may ask you to read his or her editorial. Take your time and jot down notes as you read so you can give constructive feedback. Use the following questions to get started:

Does the writer present convincing, well-supported reasons for the thesis or claim?

Does the writer persuade you? What persuasive techniques do you identify?

Word-Processing Tip

Use the header or footer option for numbering your pages. If you select the header, place the page number in the upper right-hand corner. If you select the footer, center the page number. It is not necessary to add any extra formatting, such as hyphens, slashes, boldface, italics, or the word *page*.

Writer's Portfolio

Place a clean copy of your editorial in your portfolio to review later.

Approaching Level

DIFFERENTIATED INSTRUCTION

Established Remind students that most past tense verbs end in *-ed,* but past tense forms of irregular verbs vary. Also suggest that students use a checklist to ensure that they have checked for common errors.

Write on the board:

- Subject and verbs agree in person and number.
- Sentences end with proper punctuation.
- Proper names and places are capitalized.
- All words are spelled correctly.

Teach

Writing Skill

Parallelism Parallelism is a way of giving coherence and flow to a passage of writing. Refer to the focus lesson. **Say:** The problem with the first example is the verbs "to uncover" and "recognizing." To improve the sentence, make the verbs match: Either use "to uncover" and "to recognize," or use "uncovering" and "recognizing." Point out that the original sentence is confusing to read, as if the writer were saying "We have only begun to recognizing its benefits."

Writing Process

Present Small errors in grammar, punctuation, usage, mechanics, and spelling make a negative impression on the reader. Write on the board a few examples of opening sentences that contain errors of this kind and point out the way these errors cause the reader to mistrust the author. It may be helpful to have students switch papers with partners in order to proofread each other's work.

Speaking, Listening, and Viewing Workshop

Persuasive Presentation

Focus

Summary

In this workshop, students will learn techniques for planning, developing, and delivering a persuasive presentation.

Teach

Speaking Skills

Voice and Tone Discuss the importance of speaking clearly and using a tone that appeals to the audience. Remind students to use a voice that conveys meaning and is convincing to listeners.

For help with creating presentations, see Student Presentation Builder on StudentWorks Plus.

Learning Objectives

For pages 1090–1091

In this workshop, you will focus on the following objective:

Speaking and Listening: Delivering a persuasive presentation.

Persuasive Appeals

Appeal to the emotions of your audience to encourage responses to feelings and sentiments, such as joy, fear, horror, and love. Appeal to logic when you want your audience to consider serious matters. You can also appeal to authority by referring to an expert on the subject.

Speaking, Listening, and Viewing Workshop

Persuasive Presentation

Literature Connection Arthur C. Clarke wrote "The Sentinel" and later received an Oscar nomination for co-writing the screenplay for the movie *2001: A Space Odyssey,* based on his story. He has appeared on television shows and hosted a Japanese television series based on one of his books. In this workshop, you will re-create your written editorial as a presentation for television or radio.

Assignment **Deliver a persuasive presentation on the issue you chose for your editorial.**

Plan Your Persuasive Presentation

In your editorial, you chose an issue of importance and presented your opinion on it. You stated your opinion, acknowledged the concerns of others on the issue, and supplied examples and facts to support your proposed solution. Look to your editorial for ideas as you plan your persuasive presentation. Remember that your purpose is to win support for your opinion. To do this, supply convincing arguments and evidence.

- Begin by knowing the issue well. Read articles and reports, and make sure you have solid reasons for your opinion.
- Know your audience. Will your presentation be for a radio or television broadcast? How will the medium affect your planning and delivery?
- Choose one or two significant points to give focus to your presentation. It is not necessary to cover every aspect of the issue.
- Propose a solution for the issue.

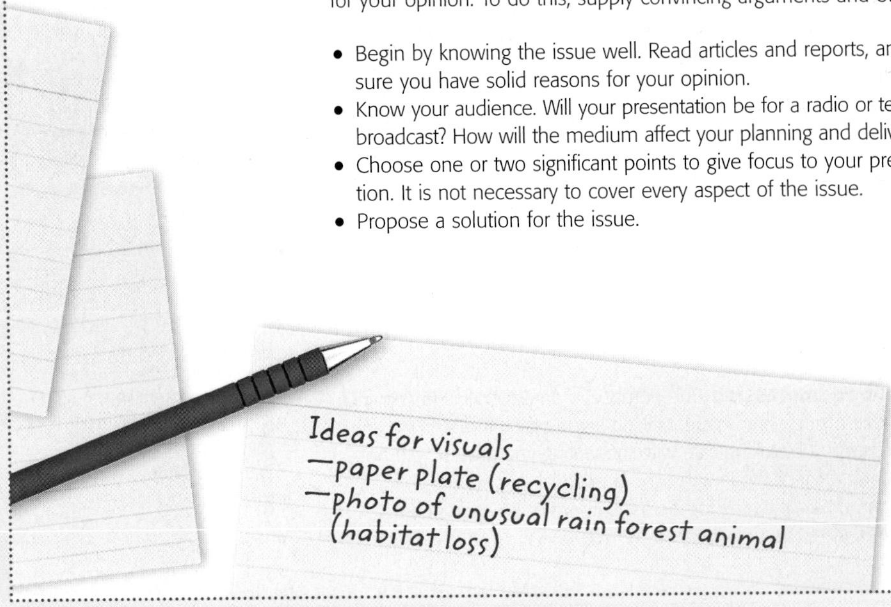

Ideas for visuals
—paper plate (recycling)
—photo of unusual rain forest animal
(habitat loss)

Listening, Speaking, and Viewing Practice

Persuasive Appeals An effective persuasive presentation is anchored by a logical argument but also makes emotional appeals. Have students listen to or watch a persuasive speech. Suggest that students keep in mind the following questions as they listen or watch.

Write on the board:

- What logical arguments does the speaker present?
- How does the speaker appeal to the audience's emotions?
- Which word best describes the emotion the writer is trying to inspire in readers?

Then have small groups present their responses.

Use a Cause-and-Effect Chart As you think about your solution for the issue, you could jot your ideas in a cause-and-effect chart to clarify the connection between the problem and the solution.

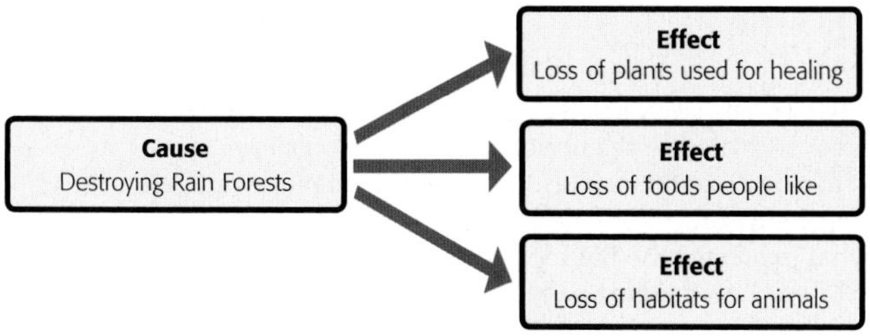

Develop Your Presentation

Adjust Your Format to the Medium If you are planning a television broadcast, consider using visuals. You could use props that are symbolic of your issue. You could also prepare a graph or chart to illustrate a statistic that supports your view. In contrast, a radio broadcast has no need for visuals. You will have to rely on effective word choice and tone of voice to communicate.

Develop Your Argument As in your editorial, include background information, a statement of your opinion, supporting evidence, audience concerns, and a proposed solution. End with your conclusion.

The "Hook" Ask yourself what will immediately interest your audience. Begin with a statement to grab their attention. End memorably, too.

Use the chart below to practice and deliver your persuasive presentation. Try not to rely on notes.

Goals	Strategies
☑ To speak convincingly	☑ Give facts and details. Acknowledge and challenge opposing views.
☑ To keep the attention of your audience	☑ Vary the speed at which you speak.
☑ To match your presentation format to a radio or television broadcast	☑ Rely on your tone of voice for a radio broadcast. Use facial expressions and visuals for a television broadcast.
☑ To persuade your audience	☑ Use appeals to emotion, logic, or authority.

Variety Is the Key

Using your voice is important in delivering a presentation, especially during a radio broadcast. Vary the tone and pitch of your voice to keep your listeners interested. If you speak in a flat, monotonous voice, you will lose your audience quickly. Raise your voice to show enthusiasm and lower it to show a more objective view.

Speaking Frames

Consider using the following frames in your persuasive presentation:

My own view is that ____ because ____.

Of course, some may disagree with my claim and say that ____.

For these reasons, ____ should be ____.

Presentation Tips

Use the following checklist to evaluate your persuasive presentation.

☑ Did you organize your ideas effectively?

☑ Was your presentation appropriate for the audience, occasion, and purpose?

Teach

Speaking Skills

Persuade an Audience The first step in persuading an audience is developing a powerful argument. Remind students to

- grab the audience's attention with a bold statement or surprising piece of information
- focus on their most important points
- propose a solution in clear, convincing language

Listening Skills

Active Listening Encourage students to listen to presentations with a critical and attentive ear. Have them take notes during the presentations of other students and write down objections, counterarguments, questions, or further thoughts they have on the issues presented. Allow time for a question-and-answer period after each presentation, in which students can further discuss and explore the important themes.

English Learners

DIFFERENTIATED INSTRUCTION

Intermediate Some English learners may struggle with identifying different tones in writing. Bring in samples of different forms of writing, such as an op-ed piece from a newspaper, an editorial written by a scholar or an expert, and a magazine article directed to teenagers. Have students read these different kinds of writings and discuss their effects. Ask them to identify words and phrases that convey particular tones. It may be helpful for students to read the article aloud.

Focus

Summary

In this lesson, students will be introduced to a variety of genre fiction, including mysteries and science fiction. They will also be introduced to two novels relating to the Big Idea of Our World and Beyond. Encourage students to read these works, which are related to themes they learned about in this unit.

Teach

Literary History ☆

Du Maurier and Hitchcock Both born in London, England, Daphne du Maurier (1907–1989) and Alfred Hitchcock (1899–1980) became legends of the modern suspense story, she in literature, he in film. Hitchcock's first American film, *Rebecca* (1940), was based on du Maurier's 1938 novel. His masterpiece *The Birds* (1963) was based on a du Maurier short story. Her macabre, imaginative stories were the perfect prototypes for Hitchcock's films.

For access to all study guides for the Glencoe Literature Library, see the Literature Library Teacher Resources CD-ROM.

To create customized reading lists from a database of more than 30,000 titles, use BookLink K–12 CD-ROM.

Independent Reading

Genre Fiction

THERE ARE MANY VARIETIES OF FICTION. ONE OF THEM IS SCIENCE FICTION, which presents imagined events related to science or technology. Mysteries, in which characters use clues to puzzle out the solution to a problem, make up another well-known fiction category. For genre fiction on a range of themes, consider the suggestions on these pages. For genre fiction that expresses the Big Idea of *Our World and Beyond,* try the titles from the Glencoe Literature Library on the next page.

Rebecca

by Daphne du Maurier

This novel combines the haunting setting of a remote seacoast estate with jealousy, suspense, and mystery. As the novel opens, a young wife finds herself overshadowed by a former wife's reputation for beauty and grace. Yet the new wife can learn nothing about the mysterious death of the first wife. A formal and secretive husband and a forbidding housekeeper add layers of suspense and mystery. This tale is so full of ☆ psychological tension that Alfred Hitchcock turned it into a thriller movie.

The Beekeeper's Apprentice

by Laurie R. King

When Sir Arthur Conan Doyle retired mystery detective Sherlock Holmes, he left him in Sussex raising bees. It is there that fifteen-year-old American Mary Russell finds him. In this feminist tale, the bright, clever, self-confident Mary represents a dramatic shift from Holmes's previous assistant Dr. Watson. As the story unfolds, she and Holmes match wits with great criminal minds. One of them turns out to be the evil daughter of Holmes's old archrival, Professor Moriarty. The book combines mystery, humor, and history for an exciting and original read.

Viewing Practice

Watch an Adaptation Have students read excerpts from *Frankenstein,* and then watch a film adaptation of the novel. Then ask them to consider the following questions:

- What might a director take into consideration when making a film adaptation of a short story or novel?
- What are some reasons for reading the novel instead of watching the film?

Have small groups discuss their views on these questions. Invite a volunteer from each group to present an oral statement to the class.

GLENCOE LITERATURE LIBRARY

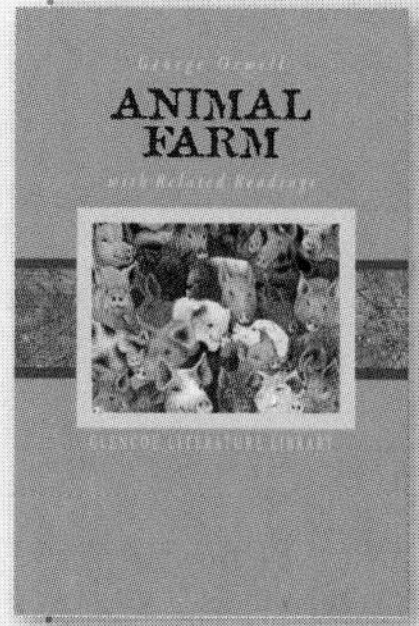

Animal Farm

by George Orwell

In this modern fable set in a world different from our own, animals who are a lot like humans revolt against the owner who mistreats them.

Frankenstein

by Mary Shelley

This early science fiction story explores the idea of creating life by scientific means and reveals something about what it means to be human.

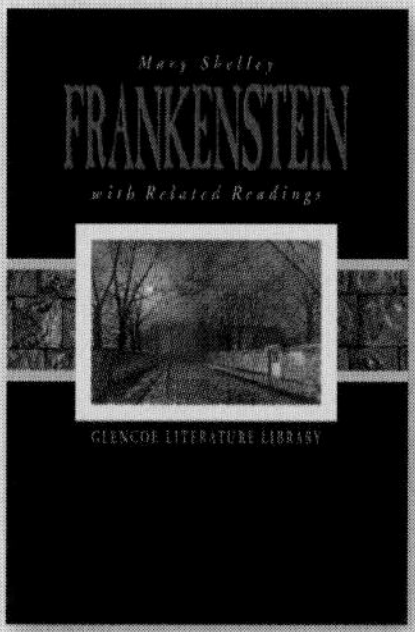

CRITICS' CORNER

"The end of Fahrenheit 451 is essentially optimistic, despite the horrifying vision of an apocalyptic near-future presented earlier in the novel. Even though machines have produced the situation whereby books are banned and men and women are hunted for reading them, Bradbury is never simplistically antimachine and never illustrates a blind . . . prejudice when writing of the impediments of science or technology."

—Willis E. McNelly, *Science Fiction Writers*

Fahrenheit 451 ☆

by Ray Bradbury

This novel begins with the sentence, "It was a pleasure to burn." This is what the main character, a fireman, is thinking as he routinely carries out his job of setting fire to the homes of people who illegally have books. Set in an unspecified time in the future, the novel has many themes. One of them is a celebration of books and readers. Another theme is the increasing isolation of humans in the modern world and their separation from nature.

Write a Review

Read one of the books listed on these pages and write a review of it for your classmates. Be sure to explain why other students might enjoy the book, or offer suggestions on how they might overcome difficulties in reading the book. Present your review to the class.

Approaching Level

DIFFERENTIATED INSTRUCTION

Established Many of the novels described in this lesson address serious philosophical and political questions. **Ask:** Do you think a story can change the way people think? Have you ever read a book that changed the way you thought about the world?

Teach

Cultural History ☆

Totalitarianism The word *totalitarianism* refers to a government so repressive that it has total control over all political and cultural opposition. The twentieth century saw the emergence of totalitarian or near-totalitarian states across Europe and Asia, notably Nazi Germany, Joseph Stalin's Soviet Union, and Mao Zedong's China. Both *Fahrenheit 451* and *Animal Farm* address the consequences of such government repression.

Glencoe Literature Library

Glencoe Literature Library offers an extensive collection of hardcover books that help you encourage your students to read independently. Choose among the more than 120 full-length literary works—novels, novellas, plays, and nonfiction. Each book includes related readings from a broad range of genres. Go to www.Glencoe.com for more information.

Write a Review

Students' reviews should address one book mentioned in the Independent Reading feature and should include reasons why others might like the book as well as tips on how to overcome difficulties reading it.

Focus

Bellringer Options

Ask: Do you experience anxiety before taking a test? Your feelings are normal and common to many. The best solution for test anxiety is preparation. Have students brainstorm lists of ways they can prepare for tests. Encourage them to list things like getting a good night's sleep or specific study techniques.

Teach

Assessment Explain to students that Assessment is intended to reinforce general test-taking strategies as well as to test the skills and vocabulary covered in the unit. They will first be asked to read a fiction selection and answer comprehension, context-clue, and inference questions. Then they will be asked to answer ten paragraph-improvement questions and to write a short reflective essay.

Assessment

English Language Arts

Reading: Fiction

Carefully read the following passage. Use context clues to help you define any words with which you are unfamiliar. Pay close attention to the author's main idea and use of rhetorical devices. Then, on a separate sheet of paper, answer the questions on pages 1095–1096.

from *"Wasps' Nest"* by Agatha Christie

"So I shall find Harrison on the terrace," murmured Poirot. "I wonder." He went in through the garden door and up the path. Harrison was sitting in a chair by the table. He sat motionless and did not even turn his head as Poirot came up to him.

"Ah! *Mon ami,*" said Poirot. "You are all right, eh?"

There was a long pause and then Harrison said in a queer, dazed voice, "What did you say?"

"I said—are you all right?"

"All right? Yes, I'm all right. Why not?"

"You feel no ill effects? That is good."

"Ill effects? From what?"

"Washing soda."

Harrison roused himself suddenly. "Washing soda? What do you mean?"

Poirot made an apologetic gesture. "I infinitely regret the necessity, but I put some in your pocket."

"You put some in my pocket? What on earth for?"

Harrison stared at him. Poirot spoke quietly and impersonally like a lecturer coming down to the level of a small child.

"You see, one of the advantages, or disadvantages, of being a detective is that it brings you into contact with the criminal classes. And the criminal classes, they can teach you some very interesting and curious things. There was a pickpocket once—I interested myself in him because for once in a way he has not done what they say he has done—and so I get him off. And because he is grateful he pays me in the only way he can think of—which is to show me the tricks of his trade.

"And it so happens that I can pick a man's pocket if I choose without his ever suspecting the fact. I lay one hand on his shoulder, I excite myself, and he feels nothing. But all the same I have managed to transfer what is in his pocket to my pocket and leave washing soda in its place.

"You see," continued Poirot dreamily, "if a man wants to get at some poison quickly to put in a glass, unobserved, he positively must keep it in his right-hand coat pocket; there is nowhere else. I knew it would be there."

He dropped his hand into his pocket and brought out a few white, lumpy crystals. "Exceedingly dangerous," he murmured, "to carry it like that—loose."

Writing Practice

Punctuate Dialogue Point out to students that Christie has correctly punctuated the lines of dialogue in this excerpt from "Wasps' Nest." Quotation marks enclose the spoken words, and commas set off the speaker tags. Have students take a portion of this excerpt and copy the story exactly as it was published but without the punctuation. Then tell students to exchange papers with a partner and use proofreading marks to indicate where the quotation marks and other punctuation should be inserted without looking at the original.

Calmly and without hurrying himself, he took from another pocket a wide-mouthed bottle. He slipped in the crystals, stepped to the table and filled up the bottle with plain water. Then carefully corking it, he shook it until all the crystals were dissolved. Harrison watched him as though fascinated.

Satisfied with his solution, Poirot stepped across to the nest. He uncorked the bottle, turned his head aside, and poured the solution into the wasps' nest, then stood back a pace or two watching.

Some wasps that were returning alighted, quivered a little and then lay still. Other wasps crawled out of the hole only to die. Poirot watched for a minute or two and then nodded his head and came back to the veranda.

"A quick death," he said. "A very quick death."

Harrison found his voice. "How much do you know?"

1. To what element of the story does the first paragraph contribute?
   A. characters
   B. point of view
   C. setting
   D. all of the above

2. From the context, what do you think that the word *roused,* on line 11, means?
   F. delayed
   G. angered
   H. replied
   J. stirred

3. What literary device does Christie use in the sentence beginning on line 15?
   A. parallelism
   B. irony
   C. analogy
   D. metaphor

4. What plot element is developed in this excerpt?
   F. exposition
   G. rising action
   H. conflict
   J. climax

5. Why did Poirot pick Harrison's pocket?
   A. to switch its contents
   B. to remove a knife
   C. to take Harrison's money
   D. to save the wasps

6. What kind of character is Poirot?
   F. minor
   G. flat
   H. round
   J. dynamic

7. What is the genre of this story?
   A. farce
   B. mystery
   C. fantasy
   D. science fiction

8. From the context, what do you think that the word *impersonally,* on line 15, means?
   F. coldly
   G. shyly
   H. kindly
   J. artificially

LOG ON **Literature** Online

Assessment For additional test practice, go to glencoe.com and enter QuickPass code GL49787u6.

Assess

Reading

1. D is the correct answer because the first paragraph introduces all the literary elements. DOK 2

2. J is the correct answer because no other option makes sense in this context. DOK 1

3. C is the correct answer because Christie uses the word *like* in comparing Poirot to someone lecturing a child. DOK 2

4. J is the correct answer because the suspense level of the scene is very high. DOK 2

5. A is the correct answer because Poirot says he took what was in Harrison's pocket and left washing soda in its place. DOK 1

6. H is the correct answer because Poirot shows many character traits in the excerpt. DOK 2

7. B is the correct answer because the story involves many elements of mystery and none of the other genres. DOK 2

8. F is the correct answer because no other option makes sense in this context. DOK 1

English Learners

DIFFERENTIATED INSTRUCTION

Intermediate English learners may have difficulty reading a long passage silently. Encourage students to use the following strategies:

- Highlight or underline important information.
- Use a story map or other graphic organizer to help you stay focused on the important details of the story.
- Vary your reading rate with the demands of the text.

For students who have a hard time comprehending what they read, recommend that they stop reading occasionally to summarize what they have read. **Say: If you can't put what you've read into your own words, reread the material.**

Assess

Reading

9. B is the correct answer because Christie uses imagery to describe the dying wasps. DOK 2

10. F is the correct answer because Poirot says he helped a man who was falsely accused of a crime. DOK 1

11. D is the correct answer because the story isn't told from the point of view of any specific character. DOK 3

12. G is the correct answer because the expression *found his voice* has the figurative meaning of recovering from surprise. DOK 2

13. B is the correct answer because Poirot says he "poured the solution into the wasps' nest." DOK 1

14. J is the correct answer because the reader is kept in suspense about why Poirot put washing soda in the pocket. DOK 3

9. What literary device does Christie use in the paragraph beginning on line 35?
   A. parallelism
   B. imagery
   C. hyperbole
   D. metaphor

10. Why did a criminal agree to teach Poirot?
   F. Poirot helped him.
   G. Poirot threatened him.
   H. Poirot captured him.
   J. Poirot paid him.

11. From what point of view is this excerpt written?
   A. first-person limited
   B. first-person omniscient
   C. second person
   D. third-person omniscient

12. What literary device is used in the sentence on line 39?
   F. literal language
   G. idiomatic language
   H. connotative language
   J. symbolic language

13. How did Poirot prove that the white crystals were poisonous?
   A. He mixed them with wine.
   B. He poured them into a wasps' nest.
   C. He put them into Harrison's pocket.
   D. He gave them to a criminal.

14. What is the overall tone of this passage?
   F. gloomy
   G. humorous
   H. formal
   J. suspenseful

Reading Practice

Create a Graphic Organizer After students have read the story, have them create a graphic organizer to outline the plot and improve their understanding of the events in the story. Show students examples of a flow chart and a timeline. Then allow them to choose which graphic organizer will help them best organize the events of the story.

Vocabulary Skills: Sentence Completion

For each item in the Vocabulary Skills section, choose the word that best completes the sentence.

1. In a parliamentary democracy, the king or queen is only the ______ head of government.
   A. ravenous
   B. nominal
   C. expedient
   D. prodigal

2. The results of the experiment were a/an ______, because they were contrary to those reported by all previous researchers.
   F. enigma
   G. trifle
   H. cohort
   J. imputation

3. Although the television miniseries had been running for 18 weeks, viewers' interest showed no signs of ______.
   A. spurning
   B. ebbing
   C. tantalizing
   D. fulfilling

4. When the dog was rescued from the mine shaft, it was ______ and ate every bit of food that was offered to it.
   F. hyperactive
   G. nominal
   H. perfidious
   J. ravenous

5. Although his explanation was ______, it proved to be incorrect.
   A. plausible
   B. prodigal
   C. bewildered
   D. singular

6. A good mystery story can ______ the reader by serving up clues but keeping the solution out of reach.
   F. ebb
   G. spew
   H. disperse
   J. tantalize

7. After reading the latest best-selling novel, I was totally ______ by its popularity.
   A. ravenous
   B. bewildered
   C. meticulous
   D. profound

8. The speaker was so persuasive that the audience gave him their unanimous ______.
   F. rancor
   G. nostalgia
   H. itinerary
   J. acquiescence

9. A mystery writer must be ______ in presenting the details of the story.
   A. veritable
   B. languid
   C. meticulous
   D. singular

10. Although seemingly an insignificant detail, the candlestick was a ______ of the story's ending.
    F. portent
    G. cataract
    H. trifle
    J. reverie

Approaching Level

DIFFERENTIATED INSTRUCTION

Established Remind students that multiple-choice questions will ask them to answer a question or complete a sentence. Students will encounter these kind of questions most often on standardized tests. **Say:** Keep these tips in mind.

Write on the board:

- Read the question carefully.
- Read all the answers before selecting one.
- Eliminate responses that are clearly incorrect.

Ask students to identify other important tips for taking multiple-choice tests.

Assess

Vocabulary Skills

1. **B** is the correct answer. The words *is only* indicates that this is the correct answer. DOK 1
2. **F** is the correct answer. Being contrary to expectation suggests that the correct answer is something puzzling, or an enigma. DOK 1
3. **B** is the correct answer. The context suggests that the correct answer is an antonym for "running for a long time." DOK 1
4. **J** is the correct answer. The fact that the dog was so hungry indicates that this is the correct answer. DOK 1
5. **A** is the correct answer. Although *formidable* might fit here, *plausible* is more appropriate in this context. DOK 1
6. **J** is the correct answer. The context suggests that the correct answer might be a synonym of *tease.* DOK 1
7. **B** is the correct answer. None of the other options make sense in the context of reading. DOK 1
8. **J** is the correct answer. The fact that the speaker was so persuasive and the support was unanimous indicates that this is the correct answer. DOK 1
9. **C** is the correct answer. The context suggests that the correct answer should mean "precise" or "careful." DOK 1
10. **F** is the correct answer. The words *seemingly insignificant* indicate that the answer should be in contrast to this. DOK 1

Assessment
English Language Arts

Assess

Grammar and Writing Skills

1. D is the correct answer. Sentence 2 is a fragment. No option corrects this problem so efficiently without introducing new errors. DOK 2
2. H is the correct answer. Ellipsis points are the device used for shortening borrowed text. DOK 2
3. B is the correct answer. Combining this sentence with sentence 6 would join the related clauses: *I felt sorry for the family, so I really wanted to help.* DOK 1

Grammar Practice

Fragments Remind students that a sentence should express a complete thought. If a group of words does not have a subject and a verb, it is usually a fragment. To correct a fragment, identify what is missing. Have students rewrite these fragments as complete sentences.

- The rubber bands on her legs.
- Outside her building.
- The men carrying off the furniture.
- That he was afraid.

Grammar and Writing Skills: Paragraph Improvement

Read carefully through the following paragraphs from the first draft of a student's reflective essay. Pay close attention to the writer's use of grammar, parallel construction, modifiers, and adjectives. Then, on a separate piece of paper, answer the questions on pages 1098–1099.

(1) *I remember the first time I got to be a detective, when I was just nine years old.* (2) *A family living a few doors down.* (3) *Their daughter couldn't find her dog.* (4) *She looked everywhere, and so had her parents.*

(5) *Soon, the neighbors were helping out too.* (6) *I felt sorry for the family.* (7) *So I really wanted to help.* (8) *My mom said that I was great at finding things.*

(9) *As I was looking around a nearby house, I noticed that a cat was in the tree.* (10) *I wondered whether something could have scared it up there.* (11) *I walked around the outside of the house, expect to find more clues.* (12) *Some dirt had been dug away at the base of the porch.* (13) *It definitely looks like the work of an animal.* (14) *I looked underneath, and—sure enough—there was the dog!* (15) *He must have gotten stuck there when he was chasing the poor cat.*

(16) *This case gave me reason to think that I would a good detective.* (17) *I spotted clues that no one else had noticed.* (18) *Even parents and other adults.* (19) *They say that to be taught to be perceptive cannot be done.*

1. Which of the following is the best way to rewrite sentences 2 and 3?
   - **A.** A family living a few doors down whose daughter couldn't find her dog.
   - **B.** Their was a family living a few doors down. Their daughter couldn't find her dog.
   - **C.** A family lived a few doors down; their daughter couldn't find her dog.
   - **D.** The daughter in a family living a few doors down couldn't find her dog.

2. What punctuation could be used to shorten a long quotation so that it could be included in the first paragraph?
   - **F.** an exclamation mark
   - **G.** a semicolon
   - **H.** ellipsis points
   - **J.** parentheses

3. Which would be the best way to revise sentence 7?
   - **A.** Combine it with the sentence that follows.
   - **B.** Combine it with the previous sentence.
   - **C.** Delete it.
   - **D.** Make no change.

4. Which of the following could the writer add to the end of the second paragraph to develop the point made there?
   F. quotations
   G. an example
   H. vivid imagery
   J. a rhetorical question

5. Which of the following is the best revision of sentence 11?
   A. I walked around the outside of the house to expect to find more clues.
   B. I walked around the outside of the house, expecting finding more clues.
   C. I walked around the outside of the house, expect that to find more clues.
   D. Expecting to find more clues, I walked around the outside of the house.

6. Which of the following errors appears in sentence 13?
   F. a run-on sentence
   G. a sentence fragment
   H. an incorrect verb tense
   J. a misplaced modifier

7. Which of the following idioms could effectively be added to the end of the third paragraph?
   A. It was a sad sight to behold.
   B. That dog had really gotten in over his head.
   C. That was a surprising discovery.
   D. This was how Little Bo Peep must have felt.

8. Which of the following is the best way to rewrite sentences 17 and 18?
   F. I spotted clues that no one else, even parents and other adults, had noticed.
   G. I spotted clues that no one else had noticed. Not even parents and other adults.
   H. I spotted clues that no one else had noticed, even parents and other adults.
   J. I spotted clues that no one else have noticed, not even parents and other adults.

9. Which of the following is the best revision of sentence 19?
   A. I don't think that to be perceptive can be taught.
   B. Being perceptive is what parents do not know how to teach.
   C. Clearly, perceptiveness cannot be taught.
   D. Most people say that you can't teach someone in being perceptive.

10. In the concluding paragraphs of this draft, what information should the writer include to develop the essay's point?
   F. advice on how to locate a lost dog
   G. lessons on how to keep from losing things
   H. examples of other things the "detective" found
   J. facts about how the case affected his life

Essay

Agatha Christie said, "Evil is not something superhuman; it's something less than human." Do you agree with this statement? Write a short reflective essay that discusses your ideas about evil and Christie's opinion. As you write, keep in mind that your essay will be checked for **ideas, organization, voice, word choice, sentence fluency, conventions,** and **presentation.**

Assessment

English Language Arts

Assess

Grammar and Writing Skills

4. G is the correct answer because an example would explain the writer's ability to find things. DOK 3

5. D is the correct answer because the modifying phrase requires a participle. DOK 1

6. H is the correct answer. The verb *looks* is in the past tense, which is not consistent with the rest of the essay. DOK 1

7. B is the correct answer because no other option includes an idiom. DOK 3

8. F is the correct answer because no other option corrects the fragment in sentence 18 without introducing other errors. DOK 2

9. C is the correct answer because no other option clarifies the intent of the awkward sentence without introducing other errors. DOK 1

10. J is the correct answer because the passage seems to suggest that the writer continued to apply his sleuthing skills. DOK 4

Essay

Evaluate essays for

- a clearly stated reaction to Christie's statement and explanation of the writer's concept of evil supported by examples and details
- clearly expressed statement of students' agreement or disagreement with the statement
- effective voice, word choice, and sentence variety
- effective presentation, with attention to grammar and spelling conventions DOK 4

UNIT SEVEN

Skills Scope and Sequence

Readability Scores Key: Dale-Chall/DRP/Lexile

Selections and Features	Literary Elements
Unit Introduction pp. 1100–1103	
Lesson 1 **Agenda, Meeting Minutes, Warranty, License Agreement, Installation Guide** pp. 1104–1110	
Lesson 2 **Memo, Train Schedule, Meeting Schedule, Travel Directions, Map** pp. 1111–1117	
Lesson 3 **Contract, Press Release, Web site** pp. 1118–1122	
Lesson 4 **Inquiry E-mail, Application, Cover Letter** pp. 1123–1127	

Reading Skills and Strategies	Vocabulary	Writing Grammar	Speaking, Listening, and Viewing
Analyze Functional and Workplace Documents **SE** p. 1102	Word Usage **TE** p. 1102		
Identify Sequence **SE** p. 1104 Summarize **SE** p. 1104		Note Taking **TE** p. 1104 Take Minutes **TE** p. 1106 Write a Description **TE** p. 1108 Write a Summary **SE** p. 1109 Write an Agenda **SE** p. 1110	
Review **SE** p. 1111 Visualize **SE** p. 1111 Identify Sequence **SE** p. 1114		Write a Schedule **TE** p. 1114 Write Travel Directions **SE** p. 1117	Interview **TE** p. 1112 Discussion **TE** p. 1116
Determine Main Idea **SE** p. 1118 Identify Cause-and-Effect Relationships **SE** p. 1118		Write a Contract **TE** p. 1118 Write a Press Release **TE** p. 1120 Write an Annotated Bibliography **SE** p. 1122	Discussion **TE** p. 1122
Make Generalizations **SE** p. 1123 Distinguish Fact and Opinion **SE** p. 1123		Create an E-Mail **TE** p. 1124 Write a Business Letter **SE** p. 1127	

UNIT SEVEN

Focus

Bellringer Options

Daily Language Practice Transparency 100

Or **ask:** How does an installation guide differ from a novel? How does travel directions differ from a poem? Explain the difference between consumer and workplace documents and traditional forms of literature such as a poem, novel, or autobiography.

Unit Introduction Skills

Functional Documents

Writing Skills/Grammar
- Write an Agenda (SE p. 1110)
- Write Travel Directions (SE p. 1117)
- Write an Annotated Bibliography (SE p. 1122)
- Write a Business Letter (SE p. 1127)

Reading Skills
- Identify Sequence (SE pp. 1104–1109, 1113, 1114)
- Summarize (SE pp. 1104–1109, 1120)
- Review (SE pp. 1111–1116)
- Visualize (SE pp. 1111–1113, 1115–1116)
- Determine Main Idea (SE pp. 1118–1121)
- Analyze Cause-and-Effect Relationships (SE pp. 1118–1121)
- Make Generalizations (SE pp. 1123–1126)
- Distinguish Fact and Opinion (SE pp. 1123–1126)

Listening/Speaking/Viewing Skills
- Interview Techniques (TE p. 1112)
- Group Discussions (TE p. 1122)

UNIT SEVEN

CONSUMER AND WORKPLACE

DOCUMENTS

UNIT SEVEN

Focus

Summary

Unit Seven explores functional documents and provides several examples including an agenda, a warranty, a train schedule, a memo, and a contract. Students will learn how to understand the information presented in these materials.

For additional resources, see Unit 6 and 7 Teaching Resources Book, pp. 127–135.

Interactive Read and Write

Other options for teaching this selection can be found in

- Interactive Read and Write for EL Students, pp. 313–323
- Interactive Read and Write for Approaching-Level Students, pp. 313–323
- Interactive Read and Write for On-Level Students, pp. 313–323

Workshop Resources

Print Materials

- Unit Teaching Resources, pp. 127–135
- Writing Kit
- Success in Writing: Research and Reports

Technology

- Literature Online: Writing Resources and Grammar Resources, www.glencoe.com
- Online Essay Grader, www.glencoe.com
- Student Presentation Builder on Student-Works Plus CD-ROM
- Media Workshop DVD
- Online Student Edition

UNIT SEVEN

Teach

Functional Documents

Information Ask: What resources will help you learn specific details about a new electronic gadget you recently purchased? *(the owner's manual)* Have students talk about times when they had to use an owner's manual. **Ask:** What information did you need to find? Was your experience positive or negative? What would have made the experience better? Students should support their answers.

Learning Objectives

For pages 1102–1103

In studying this text, you will focus on the following objective:

Reading: Analyzing and evaluating functional and workplace documents.

FOCUS ON FUNCTIONAL DOCUMENTS

Why Read Functional Documents?

The term *functional documents* might suggest something you would find in the workplace. But would you go to the airport not knowing the flight schedule or set out on a lengthy journey without checking a map? Every day you rely on functional documents. Though they differ in content, these documents all share a purpose—to communicate information.

Examples of Functional Documents		
TV or movie listings	menus	flyers
instructions	e-mails	posters
applications	maps	memos
schedules	rules or handbooks	warranties

Evaluating Functional Documents

Critique the Logic

Most functional documents use a logical plan—a text structure—to help you find, follow, and understand the information you need. Here are some text structures, or patterns of organization, that you will find in functional documents.

Functional Document	Text Structure
Application or form to fill out	Questions and write-on lines
Schedule	Time order
Map or seating plan	Space order
Directions for a process	Sequence, or step-by-step order

Vocabulary Practice

SPIRAL REVIEW **Vocabulary List** Ask students to review the examples of functional documents in the chart above. Then have them provide a definition for each example and explain how each functional document is used. Students should write these definitions and explanations in their notebooks. Students may choose to refer to this list of terms throughout the unit.

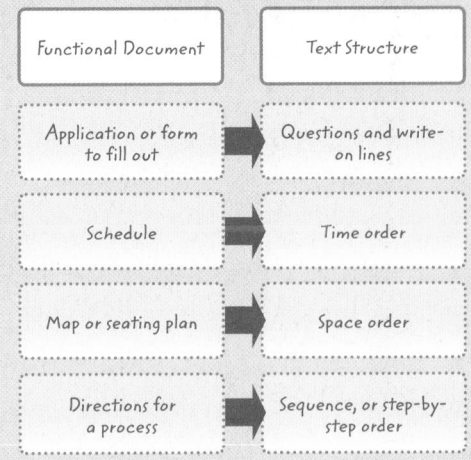

Critique the Credibility

Would you take a publicity flyer for a new vitamin seriously if it claimed that the vitamin would prolong your life? Would you believe a promotional poster for a movie if it stated the film was among the best ever made? When you read functional documents, it is important to determine the credibility of an argument or claim. Here are a few tips for evaluating credibility:

- **Look at the statements the writer makes. Do they fit with your own experience?**

  If the writer of a product information document states that a particular clock-radio will last you a lifetime, you might not find this statement credible because of your experiences with electronic products. If, on the other hand, the writer states that the clock-radio will bring you years of listening pleasure, you might accept that statement.

- **Look at the evidence the writer uses to support the statements.**

  For example, are there enough facts to indicate the statements are true? Are there testimonials or statements from current users of the product or from certified product testers?

- **Consider the possible motivation of the writer.**

  For example, if a writer of an ad or brochure is trying to sell a product, you might question the accuracy of the statements. The writer might be slanting information about the product so that it is more appealing or sounds more effective than it might actually be.

Using Functional Documents

Making a Film

In this unit, you will encounter different functional documents as you follow the progress of a young filmmaker named Jane Stevens, who is making a documentary about nuclear energy. You will join Jane's creative journey at the point when she has a basic idea of the film and is ready to share it with her film crew. As you accompany Jane through the filmmaking process, you will gain knowledge of a variety of functional documents.

By the final lesson, you will know how to get the most out of a functional document. You will also understand what it takes to make a compelling documentary film.

As you read the functional documents in this unit, be sure to

- Examine text structures to understand how information is organized
- Form opinions and make judgments about what you are reading

Teach

Critique the Credibility

Evidence Say: To support their ideas and opinions, authors present evidence—details that prove an idea or position is true. A manufacturer might provide evidence such as statistics, expert opinions, and results of studies to prove that a product is reliable.

Making a Film

Build Background If students are unfamiliar with Jane's topic, ask each student to bring in a source of information about nuclear energy. Encourage students to choose from a variety of consumer, workplace, and public documents. Then work as a class to compile a bibliography of these sources.

English Learners

DIFFERENTIATED INSTRUCTION

Intermediate Explain that functional documents are used in everyday situations for a variety of purposes. Learning how to read functional documents will help students understand the world around them. Have students identify features of various functional documents, such as maps, instructions, or schedules. *(Students may say that these documents often include diagrams and headings to help readers easily identify information.)* Point out some of the functional documents in your classroom (i.e., schedules, maps, posters).

Before You Read

Focus

Bellringer Options

Daily Language Practice Transparency 101

Or display a warranty, an instruction guide, or a license agreement. **Ask:** Have you ever taken the time to read one of these documents? What kind of information do you think might be included in these documents?

Vocabulary

Write Sentences Have students discuss the meaning of each vocabulary word. Then ask students to write two sentences in their notebooks using each of these words. Ask for volunteers to read their sentences aloud.

Before You Read

Learning Objectives

For pages 1104–1110

In studying these texts, you will focus on the following objectives:

Reading: Identifying sequence. Summarizing.

Writing: Writing a meeting agenda.

Build Background

Once Jane had a clear vision for her film, she decided to meet with crew members to share her ideas and plan the production. Before the meeting, Jane created a meeting agenda and distributed copies of it to all participants so they could prepare. After completing the agenda, Jane asked her film editor, Dare Vaillant, to take notes during the meeting and write minutes.

Reading Preview

Identify Sequence In an effective **sequence,** information is arranged in a logical way. Here are two common forms of logical sequences:

- **Chronological order** (such as the instruction guide for installing video editing software on page 1109)
- **Order of importance** (such as the warranty and the license agreement on pages 1107 and 1108)

To identify the type of sequence in a document, look carefully at its features. For example, does the document contain numbered lists or blank space between lines? These types of elements provide clues about the sequence of the document.

Summarize As you read, try to **summarize,** or briefly state the main ideas of a passage in a logical sequence and in your own words. To create a good summary, include only important information. If you are not sure if an idea is a main idea or a detail, try taking it out of your summary. Does your summary still sound complete?

Workplace Vocabulary

agenda a list of things to be accomplished in a meeting

minutes the record of a meeting

warranty an agreement that describes a customer's rights and a company's obligations if a product is defective

license agreement an agreement that specifies how a product may and may not be used

instruction guide a manual that explains how to install or operate a product

Reading Practice

SPIRAL REVIEW **Take Notes** Have students review the Before You Read page and select key words that will help them remember the information they have read. Students should record these words in their notebooks, along with a brief note such as a definition, example, or explanation. Using their notes, ask volunteers to summarize the information on page. Encourage students to use this technique in their everyday reading.

Read an Agenda

On Monday, April 16, Jane distributed the following agenda to members of her film crew.

Planning the film **"Nuclear Energy: A Viable Alternative?"**

Wednesday, April 18, 2007
4:00 P.M.–6:15 P.M.
Lakeview High School, Room 201 ❶

❷

Overview of documentary by the filmmaker	4:00 P.M.
Discussion: Share ideas about footage[1] and interviews	4:15 P.M.
Create a list of shots[2]	5:00 P.M.
Establish a schedule and budget	5:15 P.M. ❸
Assign duties	5:45 P.M.
Wrap-up, plans for next stage	6:00 P.M.

1

❶ The purpose of the meeting is clearly stated in the title. The date, time, and place of the meeting follow the title.

❷ The items are listed in the order in which they will be discussed. In informal meetings, the most important items are typically listed first on the agenda.

❸ A time limit is established for each of the topics to be discussed.

1. **footage:** any sequence, or length, of motion picture film
2. **shot:** a single piece of motion picture film recording a continuous action

Reading Check

Identify Sequence What features of the agenda indicate that it uses a chronological sequence?

Summarize Based on the agenda, briefly summarize Jane's main purposes for the meeting.

Draw Conclusions Meeting planners often plan to spend the most time on the most important issues. Would you conclude that Jane followed that pattern in preparing this agenda?

Approaching Level

DIFFERENTIATED INSTRUCTION

Emerging Ask: Why do you think agendas typically list the most important items first? *(To ensure that those items are complete by the end of the meeting, they are given priority and put at the top of the list. When time runs out, the more important work is already finished.)* Have students offer suggestions on how to develop a useful agenda.

Teach

Reading Strategy 1

Identify Sequence

Ask: Why is it important to list the topics of discussion in chronological order? *(Chronological order works best to show the sequence of time order. It also makes it easier for readers to identify what will happen first, next, and so on.)*

Assess

Reading Check

Identify Sequence Answer: *The notation of time in the left column.*

Summarize Answer: *Jane wants to describe her plans for the film, to identify potential footage and interview subjects, to create a list of shots to include in the film, to determine a workable budget and schedule, and to assign responsibilities to group members.*

Draw Conclusions Answer: *Answers will vary. Students should support their answers with reasonable explanations.*

Teach

Reading Strategy 1

Identify Sequence

APPROACHING **Ask:** Why is it important to include follow-up activities in meeting minutes? *(so people know what actions they should take after the meeting)*

Assess

Reading Check

Identify Sequence Answer: *Transition words and phrases that relate to time, such as "at the beginning," "then," and "after" indicate chronological order .*

Summarize Answer: *The meeting covered Jane's plans for the film, viewing possible footage, planning shots and interviews, a fundraising idea, and discussion of assignments.*

Identifying the Main Idea Answer: *The main idea: The group decided interviews would be at the heart of the film. Additional information: The interviews will be with people who both support and oppose nuclear energy use. They will be interspersed with existing footage.*

Read Meeting Minutes

After the meeting, Jane distributed these meeting minutes to participants.

1. The name of the group holding the meeting, the reason for the meeting, and date are given.
2. The time and place of the meeting are stated.
3. The names of the participants and of the author of the minutes are listed.
4. The essential facts of the meeting are described in the body of the summary.
5. The final paragraph describes any follow-up that will be accomplished after the meeting.

Film Crew
Planning **"Nuclear Energy: A Viable Alternative?"** ❶
Minutes
Wednesday, April 18, 2007

TIME AND PLACE: 4:00 P.M.–6:15 P.M.
Lakeview High School, Room 201 ❷

PRESENT: Dare Vaillant, Ryan Michaels, Lourdes Trent, Jane Stevens, Aiden Smith

PREPARED BY: Dare Vaillant ❸

❹ At the beginning of the meeting, Jane shared her ideas about how she would like the film to look and feel. She noted that she wanted the film to begin with a voice detailing the pros and cons of nuclear energy use and then cut[1] to interviews with individuals on all sides of the issue. She also passed around copies of her script.

Ryan and Lourdes then presented existing footage they had found relating to nuclear energy. After their presentation, the group came up with lists of potential shots and interview subjects for the film. The group decided the interviews would be at the heart of the film.

1 Discussion was then held about the amount of money available for the film. Aiden suggested that the group hold a car wash to raise additional money and everyone agreed this was a good idea. The meeting then ended with a brief talk about crew assignments. Ryan will work on nailing down these assignments before the next meeting. ❺

1. **cut:** a sudden change from one scene to another

Reading Check

Identify Sequence What clues indicate that the minutes are organized chronologically?

Summarize The essential facts of the meeting are described in the body of the minutes. Summarize those facts in your own words.

Identifying the Main Idea Read the minutes carefully. What sentence states the main idea of the minutes? What additional information about the main idea do the supporting details provide?

Writing Practice

SPIRAL REVIEW **Take Minutes** Point out that meeting minutes are a more formal version of the class notes that students take every day. Have students choose a day's notes from their notebooks to convert into a formal document like the one on page 1106. Ask that they include definitions to aid comprehension. Allow students time at a computer to properly format their document and edit it when they are done.

Read A Warranty

After the meeting, Jane identified a camcorder that met her needs. Before purchasing the camcorder, however, she decided to compare warranties. Here is one of the warranties.

Morishito Vanguard Camcorder

Full One-Year Warranty ❶

Please read the following information and save these instructions in the unlikely event the camcorder malfunctions.

Activation: This warranty will become active after you fill out the enclosed card and mail it to the address below.

Coverage: This warranty covers any defects in material and workmanship under normal use for a period of one year from the date of purchase. ❷

Claims: If your camcorder has any mechanical defects during the warranty period, pack the camcorder carefully to prevent damage in transport and ship it to the address below. Be sure to include in your package proof of purchase, your name and address, and a clear description of the problem. ❸

Morishito Corporation ❹

2 Repair Service
552 Main Street
Ann Arbor, MI 48103

Our trained technicians will inspect the camcorder and repair or replace it free of charge. However, if they discover product defects resulting from improper use or storage, you will be billed for the repair or replacement. After we receive your payment, we will return the camcorder to you.

Exceptions: This warranty does not cover Morishito products purchased outside of the United States.

Additional Information: This warranty gives you specific legal rights; you may have other rights, which vary from state to state. Contact your state attorney general's office for further information. ❺

❶ A good title includes a phrase specifying the period of coverage. It also tells whether a warranty is full or limited (restricted in coverage).

❷ The types of problems the warranty covers are specified in this section.

❸ This section describes what steps to take if a problem arises.

❹ The contact information is set off so that it can be easily found.

❺ The final section tells you how to find out about other rights you may have.

Reading Check

Identify Sequence In what order does the warranty present information?

Summarize In your own words, tell what the warranty says.

Questioning Reread the section under the heading "Claims." What exactly is the writer saying in this section?

English Learners

DIFFERENTIATED INSTRUCTION

Intermediate Explain that functional documents often have a vocabulary of their own. Like other words, these unfamiliar words can be searched in dictionaries or online. Share these definitions with the class:

- **end user**—the person who uses a product after it has been developed and marketed
- **license agreement**—a document which outlines the rules an end user must follow to use a product legally

Have students identify other technical words often found in functional documents. *(activation, coverage, claims)* Have students explain the meanings of these words.

Teach

Reading Strategy 2

Summarize Have students discuss why each section of information is important to the warranty. They should summarize what each section says and explain why it is important.

Assess

Reading Check

Identify Sequence Answer: *Information is presented in the order of importance. After dealing with preliminary concerns of how to activate the warranty and how long it lasts, the warranty presents the main point: what to do if the product fails.*

Summarize Answer: *Possible answer: If the camcorder doesn't work during the first year after purchase, return it to the manufacturer. If the problem is caused by a manufacturing failure, the company will repair or replace the camcorder for free. If the owner damaged the camera, he or she will have to pay the cost of repairing or replacing it.*

Questioning Answer: *The writer provides specific instructions about shipping the camcorder, if it becomes defective during the warranty period.*

Teach

Reading Strategy 1

Summarize Have students summarize sections of the document.

ENGLISH LEARNERS To assist English learners, ask them to identify words they do not understand. Encourage other students to explain the definitions of these words or have students use a dictionary to define these words.

Assess

Reading Check

Identify Sequence Answer: *The list follows order of importance to present the most important first.*

Summarize Answer: *If you violate this agreement, you lose your right to use the software.*

Paraphrase Answer: *A customer can use one copy of the software on his or her computer, can make one additional copy, and can contact the Morishito Corporation for a troubleshooting guidance. A customer can't give the software, or a copy of it, to anyone else, nor can a customer tamper with the software.*

Read a License Agreement and an Installation Guide

In order to turn her footage into a work of art, Jane purchased video editing software. The software came with two functional documents: an **end user license agreement** and an **installation guide.**

1. The first section explains the reasons for reading the document.
2. All of the text is flush left, except for the numbered lists.
3. The customer's rights are clearly stated in the numbered list.
4. The numbered list in this section specifies how the software may not be used.
5. The document includes an explanation of the consequences of failing to comply with the agreement's terms.

End User License Agreement

(1) **Important:** Carefully read the terms of this end user license agreement (EULA) before installing or using the software product. By installing or using the software, you agree to abide by all of these terms.

License The software product is owned by the Morishito Corporation and is protected by copyright laws and international treaties. It is licensed to you by (2) the Morishito Corporation, which grants you the following rights:

1. You may use one copy of the software product on a single computer at a time.
2. You may make one copy of the software exclusively for backup purposes.
3. You may use the support services that the Corporation provides for the software. (3)

1 **License Restrictions** The following restrictions apply to the software product:

1. You may not sell, loan, or lease the software to any third party.
2. You may not make or distribute copies of the software, or transmit the software over a network or from one computer to another.
3. You may not translate, alter, adapt, or disassemble the software. (4)

Termination If you fail to comply with the terms set forth in this agreement, your rights under this license will automatically terminate. (5)

Limitation of Liability Under no circumstances shall the Morishito Corporation be legally responsible for any damages whatsoever resulting from the use of, or inability to use, the software product.

Reading Check

Identify Sequence The numbered list in the paragraph labeled "License" states the customer's rights. Why do you think these rights are listed in this particular order?

Summarize In your own words, summarize the paragraph labeled "Termination."

Paraphrase Describe in your own words how a customer can and can not use the video editing software.

Writing Practice

SPIRAL REVIEW **Provide Examples** Ask students to create examples that will help readers to comprehend more easily the license agreement on this page. For example, students might describe a person using the software correctly and another person using it incorrectly. Suggest that their examples cover material in the lists under both the License subhead and the License Restrictions subhead. To help students get started, ask if they can provide examples orally of other software's having been used in a way that would not follow the terms of this agreement.

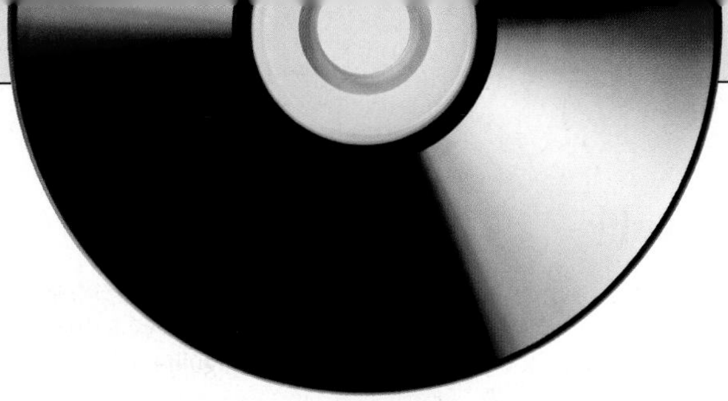

Morishito Premiere Video Quick Start Guide ❶

1. Insert the Premiere Video disc into your computer's DVD-ROM drive.

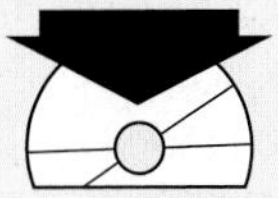

2. To start the installation, double-click the Install Premiere Video icon and follow the on-screen prompts. If the installation doesn't proceed smoothly, refer to page 9 of the Premiere Video's User Guide for troubleshooting information. ❷

3. After completing the installation, register your copy of Premiere Video. Enter the serial number found at the bottom of this document in the serial number field and click OK.

4. Once you have completed the registration process, click exit. ❸

❶ The information is arranged in a step-by-step sequence.

❷ The most important information is included in steps 1 and 2.

❸ All of the steps must be performed in the order presented.

Reading Check

Identify Sequence In what order does the installation guide present information?

Summarize Briefly summarize how to install the software.

Analyze Why does the reader need to perform the steps in this guide in the order in which they are presented?

Assess

Reading Check

Identify Sequence Answer: *The guide presents information in chronological order. The guide describes the steps of installing the program in the order they must be taken.*

Summarize Answer: *Insert the disk into the computer drive, click the install icon, register the software, and click the exit icon.*

Analyze Answer: *The installation might not be successful if the reader tried to perform the steps in a different order.*

Approaching Level

DIFFERENTIATED INSTRUCTION

Emerging Explain that an important aspect of functional documents is their ease of use. Writers must find ways to easily convey information because readers of functional documents are often performing an action while reading. Have students study the Quick Start Guide on page 1109. **Say:** Identify organizational features of the document that help you to read and understand the information. *(Possible answers: the bold heading, the numbered steps, the large icon to the right of each step)*

After You Read

Assess

1. C is the correct answer. The group will first discuss footage and interview subjects to be included in the film.
2. D is the correct answer. The warranty already covers defects resulting from a malfunction of the camcorder.
3. D is the correct answer. You would find this information under the heading "License," which specifies the customer's rights.
4. C is the correct answer. You should refer to the User Guide for troubleshooting information.

Writing

Students' agendas should

- list items in a logical order
- use an appropriate style of writing
- follow the format of a meeting

After You Read

Respond and Think Critically

Directions Read the questions about functional documents below and select the best answer.

1. According to the meeting agenda, what will the group discuss FIRST?
   - **A.** their vision for the final product
   - **B.** a list of potential shots
   - **C.** potential footage and interview subjects
   - **D.** crew assignments
2. Customers are dissatisfied with the warranty on page 1107. The Morishito Corporation could make the warranty better by doing any of the following, EXCEPT
   - **A.** offering longer coverage
   - **B.** covering camcorders purchased outside the United States
   - **C.** reimbursing the customer for the cost of postage
   - **D.** covering defects resulting from malfunction of the camcorder
3. Under which heading in the license agreement would you find information related to how you may use the video editing software?
   - **A.** Termination
   - **B.** Limitation of Liability
   - **C.** License Restrictions
   - **D.** License
4. According to the installation guide, what should you do if the installation is not successful?
   - **A.** start from the beginning
   - **B.** contact the Morishito Corporation's service center
   - **C.** refer to the User Guide for troubleshooting information
   - **D.** remove the installation disc from your DVD-ROM drive

Write an Agenda

Assignment Imagine that you are planning a school event or project with a few other students. Create an agenda for an informal planning meeting that you will distribute before the meeting. The purpose of the meeting is to plan those aspects of the upcoming event or project that are most important to a successful outcome.

Draft Writing an effective meeting agenda is crucial to the success of a meeting. To write a good agenda, try to do the following:

- List agenda items in a logical order.
- Use a style of writing appropriate for your audience.
- Follow the standard format and structure of a meeting agenda. Use the agenda on page 1105 as a guide.

Give It Structure As you begin structuring your agenda, think carefully about the order in which you present items. Do you want to list the most important items first? Or at the end of the agenda? In most informal meetings, the important items are usually listed first, so that if time is limited, participants will at least have the opportunity to discuss these essential topics.

Informal meeting agenda

Most important item

Less important item

Less important item

Least important item

Reading Practice

PARTNERS SPIRAL REVIEW **Functional Documents** Have students bring to class an example of one of the functional documents covered in the lesson. Allow students to work with a partner to compare and contrast their documents. Students should identify the purpose of each document. Students should also discuss how each document is organized and evaluate whether the information is presented clearly and effectively. Have volunteers share highlights of their discussion with the rest of the class.

Before You Read

Build Background

Following the format of her favorite documentary films, Jane decided to give interviews a prominent role in her film. To prepare for the interviews, Jane first figured out what she wanted to find out and the best people to ask. She then contacted these individuals. Once a person had agreed to be interviewed, Jane sent him or her an envelope containing the following documents: a memo specifying the date, time, and location of the interview; bus, train, or airplane schedules listing departure and arrival times; a meeting schedule describing the plan for the interview; and a map to Lakeview High School.

Learning Objectives

For pages 1111–1117

In studying these texts, you will focus on the following objectives:

Reading:
Reviewing.
Visualizing.

Writing: Writing travel directions.

Reading Preview

Review When you pause to think about or summarize what you have just read, you are **reviewing.** The process of reviewing includes activities such as

- scanning, or glancing over a passage to find information
- putting difficult language into your own words
- looking for the main idea of a passage
- identifying details that support the main idea
- determining the writer's purpose

Visualize To **visualize,** use the details the writer gives you to form a mental picture of a place or object or to see the steps in a process. Pay attention to concrete nouns and active verbs. These details will help you see how one step relates to another or how to get from one place to another.

Workplace Vocabulary

memo a short, informal note that conveys important information

transportation schedule a list of times of departures and arrivals

meeting schedule a detailed plan for an event

directions instructions about how to get from one place to another

interview a meeting in which one person questions another person

Before You Read

Bellringer Options

Daily Language Practice Transparency 102

Say: Lesson Two covers several functional documents you might use on a daily basis—a train schedule, travel directions, and a map. Provide students with copies of these kinds of functional documents. Have students identify features that help make these documents easy to follow.

Vocabulary

Fill in the Blanks Using the words from the vocabulary list, have students create a fill-in-the-blank exercise. When students finish, collect the exercises and randomly hand them out to the class. Creating the exercise will teach the vocabulary. Completing the exercise will measure how much students have learned.

Approaching Level

DIFFERENTIATED INSTRUCTION

Emerging Say: Creating pictures in your mind as you read is called visualizing. Visualizing is a powerful aid to understanding. As you read directions or maps, try to imagine city streets, landmarks, and points of directions such as east and west or left and right. Visualize the steps in a process to help you remember what happens first, next, and last. Ask students to talk about a time when they used this strategy to remember information. Students should explain how the strategy helped them.

Teach

Reading Strategy 1

Review **Say:** Review the memo to understand what participants should expect to receive a week after getting the memo. *(a list of topics to help them prepare for the interview)*

ENGLISH LEARNERS To help English learners understand unfamiliar words, ask students to scan the memo for any difficult language or unfamiliar terms. Then have a student define the word, using a dictionary.

Assess

Reading Check

Review **Answer:** *The interview is at 1:00 on June 15 at Lakeview High School.*

Visualize **Answer:** *clothing with muted colors and no patterns; little or no jewelry*

Make Inferences **Answer:** *You can infer that Jane wants the interviewees to arrive on time, so the filming of the interviews is not delayed.*

Read a Memo

When Jane was ready to conduct the interviews, she sent participants a memo to inform them of filming times and location. Here is one of the memos she mailed.

1. The topic of the memo is stated clearly in the subject line.
2. The memo indicates when and where the interview will take place.
3. Additional practical details are provided in the second paragraph.
4. The contact information is succinctly summarized here.

TO: Phoebe Wilson, President, American Nuclear Association

FROM: Jane Stevens

(1) SUBJECT: Filming schedule and location for **"Nuclear Energy: A Viable Alternative?"**

DATE: May 1, 2007

This is just a reminder that your interview is scheduled for Saturday, June 15, between 1:00 and 2:00 P.M. in Room 201 of Lakeview High School in Woodstock, Michigan. (2) Please arrive 30 minutes before the interview is scheduled to begin so that we can briefly describe our vision for the shoot and answer any questions you may have.

Also, please try to wear to the interview clothes that work well on camera. We ask, for instance, that you refrain from wearing plaids, checks, stripes, and bright, vibrant colors and that you keep accessories to a minimum. (3)

[1] Next week, I will send you a list of topics we plan to cover to help you prepare for the interview. If you have any questions in the meantime, you can contact me at (734) 555-1234 or send an e-mail to JStevens@dkvworld.net. (4)

Reading Check

Review What is the main idea of the first paragraph of the memo?

Visualize Use details from the second paragraph to visualize how an interviewee should dress. Describe your mental picture.

Make Inferences From the clues given in the first paragraph, what inference can you draw about Jane's main purpose for writing the memo?

Speaking Practice

PARTNERS SPIRAL REVIEW **Interview Techniques** Explain that some interviews have a conversational style, but in a more formal interview, students should never speak in the same manner they would talk to friends. With a partner, have students conduct their own interviews. Each student should write a list of interview questions that an employer might ask during a job interview. One student should play the role of the employer while the other student plays the role of the potential employee. Students should take turns interviewing each other. Encourage students to note the language they use during the interview.

Read a Train Schedule

To help interviewees plan their trips to Woodstock, Michigan, Jane sent them various bus, train, and plane schedules. On May 7, an interviewee living in Chicago, Illinois, received a large envelope containing information including the following train schedule.

Chicago-Detroit Service ❶

Train Name		Michigan Robin	Michigan Robin	White Pine	❷
Train Number		S252	S254	S256	
Days of Operation		Monday–Friday	Monday–Friday	Daily	
Station	Miles				
Chicago, IL	0	9:30a*	1:15p*	3:10p*	❸
Gary, IN	51	10:21a*	2:06p*	-----	
Kalamazoo, MI	138	12:55p	4:40p	6:30p	
Battle Creek, MI	160	1:20p	-----	-----	❹
Jackson, MI	208	1:56p	-----	-----	
Woodstock, MI	243	2:48p	6:23p	8:13p	
Ann Arbor, MI	256	3:20p	6:55p	8:45p	
Detroit, MI	281	4:00p	7:35p	9:25p	

* Times for Chicago and Gary are central time. All other stations observe eastern time.

❶ The title indicates the train's point of departure and final destination.

❷ Both the name and number of each train are provided.

❸ The information is organized in rows and columns.

❹ The writer uses hyphens to indicate stations where a train does not stop.

Reading Check

Review Scan the train schedule to determine which train gets from Chicago to Woodstock most quickly.

Visualize Notice when the three trains arrive in Woodstock. Which would you prefer to travel on?

Identify Sequence In what **sequence,** or order, is the information in this schedule presented?

Assess

Reading Check

Review Answer: *the White Pine S256*

Visualize Answer: *Answers will vary. Students should support their answers.*

Identify Sequence Answer: *The information is presented in chronological order.*

English Learners

DIFFERENTIATED INSTRUCTION

Benchmark Say: Reviewing is going back over what you have read to remember important ideas. Reviewing is especially important when you have new ideas and a lot of informaton to remember. Encourage students to take time to pause and think about important information and ideas, so they can recall them later. Ask students to talk about a time when they used this reading strategy to recall information. Students should explain how the strategy helped them.

Teach

Reading Strategy 1

Review **Ask:** What is the author's purpose for creating this meeting schedule? *(Possible answers: Students may point out that the schedule will help keep the filmmaker and her team organized throughout the day.)*

Assess

Reading Check

Review Answer: *They will be in the cafeteria having dinner.*

Identify Logical Sequence Answer: *The time that each activity begins is the most important piece of information in the itinerary.*

Read a Meeting Schedule

Jane also included the following meeting schedule in each packet she sent to participants.

1. The date is set off in a separate line.
2. The schedule indicates the timeframe for each event.
3. The schedule includes a brief description of each event.
4. The location for each event is given.

1

Saturday, June 15 ❶	
❷ 9:00–9:30 A.M.	Check-in—*Entrance to Lakeview High School*
9:30–10:00 A.M.	Breakfast—*Cafeteria*
10:00–10:30 A.M.	Overview of Film—*Cafeteria*
10:30 A.M.–1:00 P.M.	Film interviews—*Room 201*
1:00–1:30 P.M.	Lunch—*Teacher's lounge*
1:30–5:00 P.M.	Film interviews—*Room 201*
5:30–7:00 P.M.	Group dinner—*Cafeteria*
7:15–8:55 P.M.	View "An Inconvenient Truth"—*Melinda Jones Auditorium* ❸
Sunday, June 16	
9:00–10:00 A.M.	Breakfast—*Cafeteria*
10:00–11:30 A.M.	Film additional interviews—*Room 201*
12:00–1:00 P.M.	Lunch—*Teacher's lounge*
1:00–3:30 P.M.	Reshoot problematic scenes—*Room 201* ❹
4:00 P.M.	Meet outside school for taxi ride to airport, bus terminal, or train station

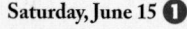

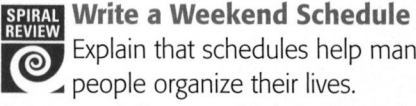

Reading Check

Review Scan the meeting schedule to determine where the group will be at 6:00 Saturday evening.

Identify Logical Sequence Why does the writer list the timeframe for each activity before listing its location?

Writing Practice

SPIRAL REVIEW **Write a Weekend Schedule** Explain that schedules help many people organize their lives.

Say: You follow a schedule every day in school. You go to class, eat, and play at certain times during the day. Ask students to think about the activities they do each day, from the time they wake until they go to sleep. Have students draft a daily schedule for themselves for the upcoming weekend. The schedule should include Friday, Saturday, and Sunday. Remind them that important information, such as who, what, when, and where, needs to be clear. The schedule should include their activities from 7:00 A.M. to 11:00 P.M.

Read Travel Directions

One of Jane's subjects lives in Woodstock but does not know how to get to Lakeview High School. To help this person find her way, Jane sent her the following set of directions.

Directions to Lakeview High School by Car ❶

1. Turn right out of your driveway onto Wells Hill Road. After a quarter-mile, turn left onto East Common Road and go a half mile to US-49. ❷
2. Merge onto eastbound US-49 in the direction of Toledo.
3. After 3 miles, merge onto southbound I-95 in the direction of Chicago.
4. Once you exit I-95, follow Redding Road south for 2 miles.
5. Turn right onto Martin Luther King Boulevard and go straight for 1 mile.
6. ❸ Lakeview High School will be on your left, between a gas station and GL Carpets.
7. Enter the school driveway and follow the signs to the visitor parking lot.

❶ The purpose of the directions is stated in the title.

2 ❷ The information is presented in chronological order to help the reader visualize each step and how it relates to the next step.

❸ The writer uses a numbered list to make the document easy to read.

Reading Check

Review Scan the directions to determine what direction the interviewee will travel on US-49.

Visualize What landmarks do the directions use to help a reader visualize where Lakeview High School is?

Evaluate To avoid possible reader misunderstandings, where in the directions should the following additional step be inserted? Take the Redding Road exit, or Exit 12.

Teach

Reading Strategy 2

Identify Sequence

Say: When providing travel directions, it is essential to present information in chronological order. What other kinds of information is best presented best in chronological order? *(Possible answers: a recipe, instructions for assembling furniture)*

APPROACHING Ask students to provide words that indicate sequential order. *(Possible answers: first, second, then, finally)*

Assess

Reading Check

Review Answer: *Step 2 states that the interviewee should go south on US-49.*

Visualize Answer: *Landmarks include a gas station and a carpet store.*

Evaluate Answer: *The added step should be inserted between steps 3 and 4.*

Advanced Learners

DIFFERENTIATED INSTRUCTION

Organize and Lead Say: Imagine you have been asked to lead a group project at school. Organize a time and place for the members of your group to meet and work on the project. Have students write a memo to the members of his or her group. The memo should include all of the important information about what will take place at the meeting and what the members of the group should bring.

Remind students that although they will be writing the memo to their classmates, the tone and language should be appropriate and formal. Encourage students to peer review their memos once they have finished.

Assess

Reading Check

Visualize Answer: *Answers will vary. Students should support their answers.*

Review Answer: *From Wells Hill Road, go west on one of the three unlabeled streets immediately south of East Common Road. When the street ends at West Park, turn left (south) and go to Redding Road. Turn right (west) on Redding Road, turn right (north) on Martin Luther King Boulevard, and look for Lakeview High School on the left, between a gas station and GL Carpets.*

Evaluate Answer: *Answers will vary. Some people operate better with directions; others prefer to follow a map.*

Read a Map

Jane included the following map with her written directions.

1. Physical features of the area, such as parks, are shown.
2. The unnamed lines represent streets found in the area.
3. Streets mentioned in the set of directions are named.
4. The two highways mentioned in the set of directions are displayed.

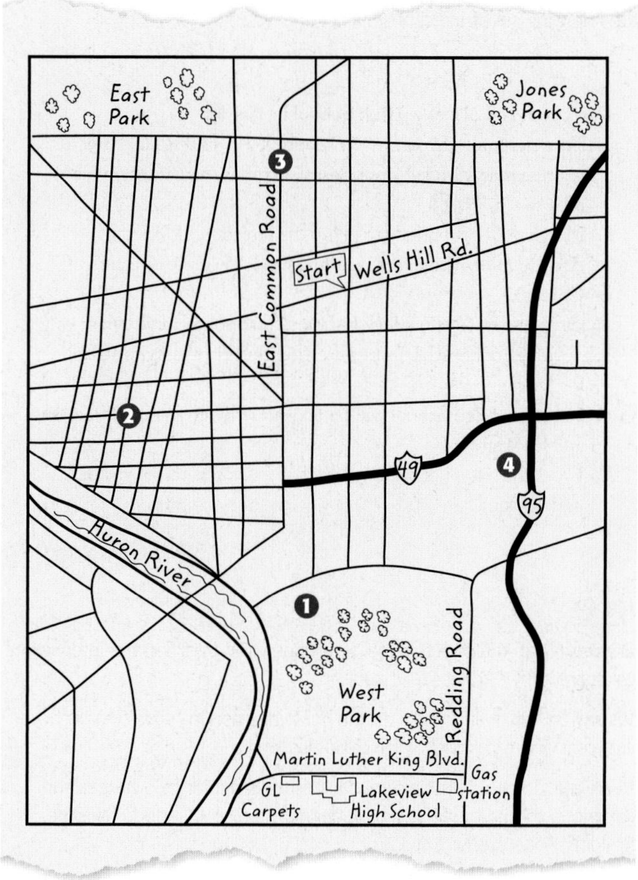

Reading Check

Visualize Follow the directions step by step and trace the route on the map. Which document better helps you visualize the route to Lakeview High School?

Review Look again at the map. Could you tell the interviewee how to reach the high school without using highways 49 or 95?

Evaluate Which is more likely to help the interviewee find her way to the school, the written directions or the map? Why?

Reading Practice

SMALL GROUP SPIRAL REVIEW

Expository Critique

Say: Maps can be difficult to understand. Carefully look at the map on this page. **Ask:** Is this map easy to read? What parts are difficult to understand? Encourage students to share their ideas in a class discusssion. Break students into small groups and have them develop ways to improve the map. Have groups decide which parts to save and which parts to discard. Ask them to think about the look of the map and write these questions on the board:

- Would you make anything larger?
- Would you change the color or highlight anything?
- What additional information would you provide?

Have the groups share their answers in a group discussion.

After You Read

Respond and Think Critically

Directions Read the questions about workplace and consumer documents below and select the best answer.

1. The memo provides the MOST information on
   - **A.** how to dress for the interview
   - **B.** the topics to be covered in the interview
   - **C.** the date, time, and location of the interview
   - **D.** the contact information of the interviewer
2. Based on information in the train schedule, which statement is accurate?
   - **A.** Three trains travel from Chicago to Woodstock every day.
   - **B.** The distance from Chicago to Woodstock is 243 miles.
   - **C.** The number of all three trains is S252.
   - **D.** The trip from Chicago to Woodstock takes about 4 hours.
3. The meeting schedule provides the LEAST information about
   - **A.** meal times
   - **B.** check-in time
   - **C.** when interviews will be filmed
   - **D.** when interviews will be edited
4. What is the purpose of the map?
   - **A.** to help an interviewee visualize how to get to the school
   - **B.** to show the physical features of Woodstock
   - **C.** to provide an interviewee with a clear set of directions
   - **D.** to locate the town of Woodstock in the state of Michigan

Write Travel Directions

Assignment On a map showing the streets in your hometown, find the location of your home and of your school. Then use the map to write a clear set of directions to tell how to get from your school to your home. You might set the directions in a scenario of inviting friends to your home to study after school. Be sure to include street, route, and highway names as well as local landmarks.

Draft To create directions that are effective, make sure you

- use verbs that command.
- provide accurate and detailed instructions. For example, if you tell your friends to turn left when you mean right, they might get lost.
- put your directions into the right order. If you do not get the sequence right, your friends could end up far from your home.
- include graphics that facilitate comprehension.

Create a Graphic Graphic elements can be vital to good directions, since they can often explain a step better than words can. Create a map to go with your written travel directions. Mark which direction on your map is north and include landmarks, street and highway numbers, and distances between points, where appropriate.

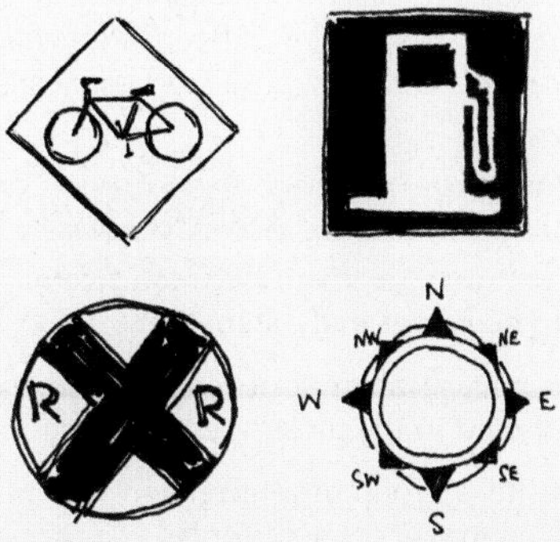

After You Read

Assess

1. C is the correct answer. The memo provides the most information on the date, time, and location of the interview, since this information is the most important.
2. B is the correct answer. The second column of the schedule shows that the distance from Chicago to Woodstock is 243 miles.
3. D is the correct answer. The itinerary doesn't cover the editing phase of production.
4. A is the correct answer. The map helps an interviewee visualize how to get to the school.

Writing

Students' directions should

- use verbs that command
- provide detailed instructions
- provide directions in sequential order
- include a graphic

English Learners

DIFFERENTIATED INSTRUCTION

Beginning/Early Intermediate Say: **Learning how to read functional documents will help you understand the world around you.** Explain that functional documents are used in everyday situations for a variety of purposes. Ask English learners to explain how they might use functional documents in traveling from one country to another. *(Students might point out the use of a road map, a train schedule, a car rental agreement, a luggage insurance policy, a hotel confirmation, etc.)*

Before You Read

Focus

Bellringer Options

Daily Language Practice Transparency 103

Or **ask:** Why are contracts necessary? *(Possible answer: Contracts are often used between two or more parties to ensure that the responsibilities of an agreement are met.)* Encourage students to think of other instances in which a person would have to sign a contract.

Vocabulary

Using New Vocabulary

To test vocabulary comprehension, have students write a paragraph using each of the vocabulary words at least once. Ask students who have used the words in the best and most creative ways to share their stories with the rest of the class.

Before You Read

Learning Objectives

For pages 1118–1122

In studying these texts, you will focus on the following objectives:

Reading:
Determining main idea.
Analyzing cause-and-effect relationships.

Writing: Writing an annotated bibliography.

Build Background

Jane screened the finished film before the entire film crew. She also sent copies to independent movie theaters in the area to see if they were interested in showing the film. A week later, Jane received a letter from the director of the Woodstock Film Center expressing his keen interest in the film. Jane met with the director and signed a contract, or legal agreement, that laid out the rights and obligations of both the filmmaker and the Woodstock Film Center. Signing the contract was an important step for Jane to take to prevent future misunderstandings with the Film Center. If she had made a verbal agreement instead, she might have become entangled in a "he said/she said" situation at some later date.

Reading Preview

Determine Main Idea To increase your understanding of a document, look for the **main idea** in each paragraph or passage. Often, you can identify this idea by zeroing in on the important points the writer is making. In a single paragraph, the main idea will often be the thought around which all other sentences are built. While the main idea is often stated in a topic sentence, it may also be implied with clues. Once you have identified the main idea, you can use the supporting details to learn additional information about it.

Analyze Cause-and-Effect Relationships A **cause-and-effect relationship** exists when one event causes another to happen. If you can answer *why* something happened, you know its cause. If you can answer *what happened as a result of* something, you know the effect. Words and phrases such as *because, as a result,* and *consequently* often signal cause-and-effect relationships. Writers of legal documents often choose to use a cause-and-effect structure to present information.

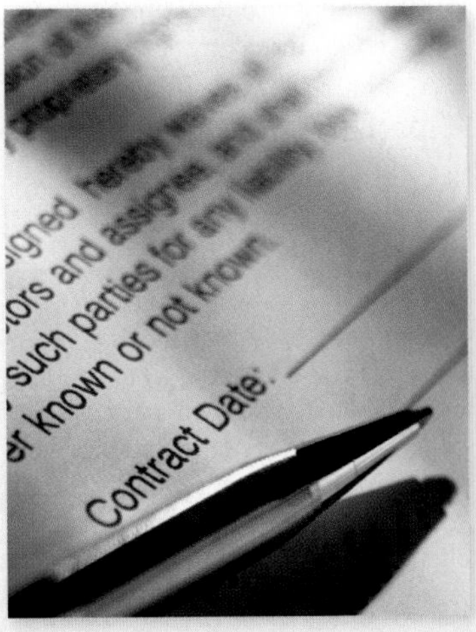

Workplace Vocabulary

contract an agreement between two or more parties to do or not to do something

press release an announcement of an event that is distributed to the press

Web site a group of interrelated web pages devoted to one or more topics

Skills Practice

SPIRAL REVIEW **Write a Contract** Ask students to imagine they have been given an assignment that requires them to work with a partner. In pairs, ask students to create a contract that divides the workload for this imaginary assignment. The contract should include information about the work that each student is responsible for completing, a deadline for each phase of the project, and the consequences each student faces for not completing their work on time. Each student should carefully read over the terms and conditions of the contract before agreeing to the imaginary terms. Have students present their contracts to the class.

Read a Contract

Here is the contract that Jane and the director of the Woodstock Film Center signed.

BOOKING CONTRACT

THIS AGREEMENT, made and entered into this 15th day of July, 20 09, by and between Jane Stevens (hereafter referred to as the "Filmmaker," and the Woodstock Film Center (hereafter referred to as the "Film Center"), provides as follows:

1. The Filmmaker hereby grants the Film Center the right to show the film *Nuclear Energy: A Viable Alternative?* at the following dates and location and under the following conditions.
   Place of Screening: The Woodstock Film Center
   Dates of Screening: September 1-7, 2009 ❶
2. The Film Center shall receive 60% of net profits from the showing of the film and the Filmmaker shall receive the other 40%. ❷
3. Box office receipts shall be deposited in a Bank Five account the day after the final screening of the film. A check shall then be issued to the Filmmaker for his/her share of the profits no later than October 30, 2009. ❸
4. The print shall not be used for any purpose other than that of the screenings at the Film Center ❹
5. The film shall be featured on the flyers printed and distributed by the Film Center. Any additional publicity is the responsibility of the Filmmaker. ❺
6. The Film Center may cancel a screening in the event that its equipment malfunctions or its projectionist is unavailable.
7. This contract shall be governed by and interpreted in compliance with the laws of the State of Michigan.
8. The two parties have read and agree to the terms laid out in this contract.

____
Filmmaker

____
Film Center ❻

❶ The introduction identifies the two parties involved, the title of the film, and the dates and location of the screenings.

❷ The contract spells out how the profits from the screening will be split.

❸ The contract clearly states when Jane will receive her share of the net profits.

❹ The contract explains how the print of the film may and may not be used.

❺ The contract lays out the Film Center's responsibility for marketing the film.

❻ Lines are provided for the signatures of the two parties.

Reading Check

Determine Main Idea What is the main idea of number 4?

Analyze Cause and Effect What events can cause the Film Center to cancel a screening?

Focus

Teach

Reading Strategy 1

Identify Purpose **Ask:** What is the purpose of the contract on page 1119? *(Possible answers: The purpose of the contract is to establish an agreement between Jane Stevens and the film center concerning the rights to show the film* Nuclear Energy: A Viable Alternative?*)*

Assess

Reading Check

Determine Main Idea
Answer: *The print of the film may be used only for screening at the Film Center.*

Analyze Cause and Effect
Answer: *The causes are mentioned in paragraph 6: malfunctioning equipment or the lack of a projectionist.*

Approaching Level

DIFFERENTIATED INSTRUCTION

Emerging Ask students to explain reasons why a person might break a contract. *(Possible answers: Sometimes contracts are broken when people have to move, as with rental agreements.)* **Ask:** What may happen if someone decides to break a contract? *(Possible answers: The person who breaks the contract may have to pay a fine. He or she may not be entitled to certain rights originally agreed to in the contract. The opposite party may choose to file a lawsuit against the person who broke the contract. It often depends on the stipulations stated in the contract.)*

Teach

Reading Strategy 1

Analyze Cause and Effect Relationships **Ask:** What is the intended effect of the press release? *(Possible answer: The press release is intended to get people interested in the movie and to promote a screening of the movie.)*

APPROACHING To guide approaching-level students **ask:** In the description of the film, what words are used to attract the interest of the reader? *(The words "provocative" and "deeply informative" are used to grab the reader's attention.)*

Assess

Reading Check

Analyze Cause and Effect
Answer: *skyrocketing oil prices and the threat of global warming*

Determine Main Idea and Supporting Details
Answer: *that it investigates behind the rhetoric, that it explores the risks and benefits of nuclear energy, and that it includes interviews with experts on all sides of the issue*

Summarize Answer: *The film* Nuclear Energy: A Viable Alternative? *explores all sides of the debate about nuclear energy.*

Read a Press Release

Jane wrote the following press release to get the news about her film into local newspapers and on local radio broadcasts.

1. The heading includes all of the major facts about the event—the date, time, location, and price. It also gives the name of a contact person.
2. The press release provides a brief description of the film.
3. The press release is written in an engaging style.
4. The press release refers to an event related to the screening.

EVENT: Screening of "Nuclear Energy: A Viable Alternative?"
DATE: September 1–7, 2009
TIME: 7–9 P.M.
PLACE: Woodstock Film Center, 406 N. Main Street
PRICE: $8.00
CONTACT: Jane Stevens, 555-1234 ❶

1 In recent years, Americans have grown increasingly alarmed over skyrocketing oil prices and the threat of global warming. As the world has heated up, so too has the debate over whether to use nuclear power to meet the country's energy needs. In "Nuclear Energy: A Viable Alternative?," Jane Stevens gives an in-depth look at the nuclear option. She investigates behind the rhetoric to explore the real risks and benefits associated with nuclear energy use. The film includes illuminating interviews with scientists, experts, and politicians on all sides of the issue. ❷ Provocative and deeply informative, "Nuclear Energy: A Viable Alternative?" will arm citizens with the knowledge they need to make up their own minds about this controversial issue. ❸

An opening reception will be held at the Woodstock Film Center following the September lst screening at 9 P.M. The filmmaker and members of the film crew will be on hand to answer questions. For information about the Film Center, call 555-9877. ❹

Reading Check

Analyze Cause and Effect According to the press release, what has caused Americans to grow increasingly alarmed?

Determine Main Idea and Supporting Details What details support the idea that the film gives an in-depth look at the nuclear option?

Summarize In your own words, state the main idea of the press release.

Writing Practice

SPIRAL REVIEW **Write a Press Release** Have students write a press release for a school's spring musical. The press release should include all necessary information about the performance schedule including dates, times, locations, and the price of admission. Students should also list a contact person who can answer further questions about the musical. They should also use engaging language that encourages people to see the film.

Read a Web Site

Jane and her film crew worked together to build a Web site to promote the film. Here is the home page.

HOME ❶
ABOUT THE FILM ❷
CLIPS
SCREENINGS
THE SCIENCE
REVIEWS AND BLOGS
PRESS MATERIALS
EDUCATIONAL RESOURCES
PEOPLE IN THE FILM

"Nuclear Energy: A Viable Alternative?"

a film by Jane Stevens

Oil fuels our modern way of life, but we are quickly running out of this precious resource. And if the world's climate scientists are right, the burning of oil and other fossil fuels causes serious environmental problems. ❸ **2** In her first documentary feature, director Jane Stevens provides an eye-opening look at one of the possible alternatives to oil: nuclear energy. Through interviews with climate scientists, energy experts, and policy makers, the film uncovers the facts and myths that surround the nuclear option, and it spells out the real risks and benefits. In addition, it challenges viewers to take action to solve the global warming and oil-supply crises while there's still time.

Comments? Questions? Contact the filmmaker at JStevens@dkvworld.net. ❹

❶ The home page provides users with a brief overview of what they can find on the site.

❷ The page includes the basic links for users to click on to reach the pages in the site.

❸ The page provides a few basic sentences about the film, so readers will know they have found the right site.

❹ Contact information appears at the bottom of the home page.

Reading Check

Analyze Cause and Effect According to the Web page, what are the effects of using oil to meet our energy needs?

Determine Main Idea Which sentence contains the main idea of the Web page?

Compare and Contrast Reread the press release on page 1120 and this Web site page. Which document presents the more persuasive argument for seeing the film? Why did you find that document more convincing?

Teach

Reading Strategy 2

Analyze Cause and Effect Relationships **Ask:** According to the Web page, what causes environmental problems? *(the burning of oil and other fossil fuels.)*

ENGLISH LEARNERS To ensure English language learners comprehend the scientific terms on this page, have a student define *fossil fuels, climate,* and *nuclear energy,* using a dictionary.

Assess

Reading Check

Analyze Cause and Effect
Answer: *We are running out of the resource, and we are contributing to global warming.*

Determine Main Idea
Answer: *"Through interviews with climate scientists, energy experts, and policy makers, the film uncovers the facts and myths that surround the nuclear option, and it spells out the real risks and benefits."*

Compare and Contrast
Answer: *Answers will vary. Students should support their answers with reasonable explanations.*

English Learners

DIFFERENTIATED INSTRUCTION

Beginning/Early Intermediate Ask students to think about Web sites they have visited at school or at home. Encourage them to reflect on the organization of the page. **Ask:** Was the site easy to navigate? Could you find what you were looking for? What problems did you have while using the website? Ask students to identify common problems they sometimes encounter when using Web sites. *(Students may have difficulty finding current contact information, or they may experience broken links.)*

After You Read

Assess

1. D is the correct answer. Press materials are included.
2. B is the correct answer. Both documents state that the film explores the pros and cons of nuclear energy use.
3. C is the correct answer. The information is organized in order of importance.
4. A is the correct answer. The main purpose of the press release is to get the word out regarding the screening.

Writing

Students' annotated bibliographies should

- use simple and concise language
- use language appropriat e for the audience
- list links in a logical order
- include information about the validity of the site

After You Read

Respond and Think Critically

Directions Read the questions about functional documents below and select the best answer.

1. Which of the following is NOT included on the home page of Jane's Web site?
   A. Links to other pages
   B. A brief explanation of the purpose of the Web site
   C. Easy-to-read text
   D. Press materials
2. According to both the press release and the Web site, the film explores
   A. the production of oil
   B. the limitations of nuclear energy use
   C. the science behind global warming
   D. the advantages of solar and wind energy
3. In the contract, the information is organized in which logical sequence?
   A. Chronological order
   B. Spatial order
   C. Order of importance
   D. Alphabetical order
4. The main purpose of the press release is
   A. to publicize the screening of "Nuclear Energy: A Viable Alternative?"
   B. to provide information about the film
   C. to explain how to get to the Woodstock Film Center
   D. to invite the public to the post-screening reception

Write an Annotated Bibliography

Assignment Create an annotated bibliography of Web sites. First think of a topic that will be of interest to other students. Then search for related Web sites. Choose the best five sites you find and, for each site, write an annotation, or a brief note explaining why your audience might be interested in it. Keep your comments concise and clear, and check for spelling, punctuation, and grammar errors.

Draft Below are a few guidelines for writing annotations that will help other students find the information they are looking for easily and quickly.

- Keep your language simple and concise. Complicated words or constructions will confuse the reader, causing him or her to move on.
- Use language that conveys the central idea, or organizing thought, of the site.
- Write text that is appropriate for your intended audience. Do not, for instance, use technical words to describe a site about romance novels.
- List the links in a logical order. For example, you may wish to list the best sites first.
- Include information about the validity and reliability of the site. For example, if you notice that the site has not been updated in a long time, mention that information in your annotation.

Highlight the Main Idea When writing annotations for the sites on your list, it is important to highlight the main ideas of the sites. To determine the main idea of each site, look carefully at its home page. Can you find a sentence that states the main idea? If not, use the clues the writer gives to identify the main idea. Once you have done so, you can begin to write your note about the site. After writing, read over your text to make sure it captures the essence of the site.

Listening and Speaking Practice

SPIRAL REVIEW **Group Discussion** This section shows that events can be promoted in a number of ways.
Ask: If you were promoting an event in your town, would you send a press release or set up a Web site? In small groups, have students make a decision about what kind of event they want to have. They should then discuss various methods of promotion—posters, television commercials, Web pages, press releases, etc. Students should decide which two methods would be most useful in spreading the word about their event and discuss why. Remind students that they need to carefully consider their audience before making a decision. Students should take notes during their discussion. Once they have finished, encourage a representative from each group to share their discussion with the class.

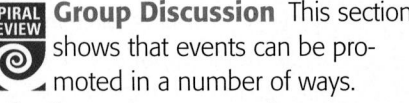

Before You Read

Build Background

Inspired by her recent success at the Woodstock Film Center, Jane decided to submit her film to a national film festival. To determine the right niche for her film, Jane surfed the Web to locate festivals that focus on real-world issues and documentaries. She then identified the festival with which she shared the most common ground—the Chelsea Film Festival.

Reading Preview

Make Generalizations When you **make a generalization,** you apply details or facts from specific situations to more general circumstances. As you read, identify and analyze key details, looking for patterns among them. Then use your analysis to make general statements about a particular subject or type of document. Beware of inaccurate generalizations, such as "all documentaries aim to change the world."

Distinguish Fact and Opinion The documents in this lesson contain both **facts**—statements that can be proved—and **opinions**—statements that express personal views, interpretations, or attitudes. Because opinions can sometimes be faulty or incorrect, it is important to be able to distinguish opinions and facts. To help differentiate the two, use the tips below.

- Determine if the statement can be proved. For instance, the statement "Jane Stevens has made a documentary film" can be proved, whereas the statement "Jane Stevens is an accomplished filmmaker" cannot.
- Look at the author's wording. Phrases such as *I think, I believe,* and *it appears* often indicate opinions, as do words such as *belief, view, feeling, always,* and *never.*
- Examine the evidence. Does the author supply enough to prove that a statement is accurate?

Workplace Vocabulary

e-mail a message or messages sent and received electronically over a computer network

application a written form to be completed by an applicant

cover letter a letter sent along with other documents to give additional information

Learning Objectives

For pages 1123–1127

In studying these texts, you will focus on the following objectives:

Reading: Making generalizations. Distinguishing fact and opinion.

Writing: Writing a business letter.

Before You Read

Focus

Bellringer Options

Daily Language Practice Transparency 104

Or **ask:** What is the difference between a fact and an opinion? *(An opinion explains what someone thinks or feels, while a fact is true information.)* **Ask:** What resources rely heavily on factual information? *(newspapers, encyclopedias, almanacs)* What resources usually offer opinions? *(blogs)*

Vocabulary

Using New Vocabulary

To test vocabulary comprehension, have students write a paragraph using each of the vocabulary words at least once. Ask students who have used the words in the best and most creative ways to share their stories with the rest of the class.

Approaching Level

DIFFERENTIATED INSTRUCTION

Emerging Ask students to think of an opinion. For example, they might think that their city is a wonderful place to live. Then **ask:** How you would defend that opinion to someone who disagreed? Have students write a paragraph that defends their opinion.

Established **Ask:** How can a difference of opinion be a good thing? Why might a difference of opinion be problematic? Can you think of any real-life situations where a difference of opinions has led to a positive outcome? Encourage students to share their answers with the class.

Teach

Reading Strategy 1

Distinguish Fact and Opinion Have students identify several facts about the e-mail. (Possible answers: The e-mail is dated September 15, 2009. It is from Jane Stevens. She is requesting information about the Chelsea Film Festival.)

Assess

Reading Check

Distinguish Fact and Opinion
Answer: *The heading provides facts.*

Make Generalizations
Answer: *It begins with a heading that identifies the recipient, the sender, the date, and the subject; it states the main purpose of the e-mail in the opening paragraph, and it ends by thanking the recipient.*

Paraphrase Answer: *Possible answers: Jane is asking for earlier festival programs and for information on how to apply to the festival.*

Read an Inquiry E-mail

After a successful screening of her film at the Woodstock Film Center, Jane was emboldened to submit her documentary to a national film festival. Here is the e-mail she sent to request information about the festival.

1. The heading identifies the recipient of the e-mail, the sender, the date, and the subject.
2. The purpose of the e-mail is stated immediately and in an appropriate tone.
3. The writer specifies the type of information she is looking for.
4. Contact information is included in the final sentence.
5. The writer expresses her thanks.

1

TO: info@chelseafilmfest.org
From: JStevens@dkvworld.net
Date: September 15, 2009
Subject: Chelsea Film Festival ❶

To Whom It May Concern,

❷ I am writing to request information regarding the Chelsea Film Festival. Specifically, I would like to learn more about how to apply for festival consideration and about upcoming deadlines. ❸

In addition, I would appreciate receiving copies of programs from past festivals. Please address all materials to me at: 224 Wells Hill Road, Woodstock, Michigan, 48103. ❹

Thank you in advance for your prompt attention to my request. ❺

Jane Stevens

Reading Check

Distinguish Fact and Opinion Does the heading of this e-mail present facts or opinions?

Make Generalizations How is the structure of this e-mail similar to other e-mails you have seen?

Paraphrase In your own words, state what Jane is asking for in this e-mail.

Writing Practice

SPIRAL REVIEW **Create an E-mail** Explain that although e-mail is a fairly relaxed form of communication, any correspondence with a potential employer, business associate, or professional should be more formal. Have students compose an e-mail to a college admissions counselor asking for information about the school's academic programs and extacurricular activities. Explain that although this e-mail is not as formal as a business letter, it should still contain similar elements. A proper greeting and salutation should be used, and necessary contact information should be provided. Have students send their e-mails to you or print out a saved copy of their e-mail to hand in during class.

Read an Application

At the end of September, Jane received a package from the Chelsea Film Festival. Inside the package, she found this application form.

2

2009
Chelsea Film Festival
Official Entry Form

Name: Jane Stevens ❶
Address: 224 Wells Hill Road, Woodstock, MI 48103
Home Phone: (734) 555-1234 Work Phone: none
E-mail: JStevens@dkvworld.net

Film ❷

Title: Nuclear Energy: A Viable Alternative?
Director(s): Jane Stevens
Writer(s): Jane Stevens
Editor(s): Dare Vaillant
Cast: Interviewed climate scientists, energy experts, and policy makers.

Category: ☐ Drama ☐ Comedy ☒ Documentary ☐ Animation ❸
☐ Short subject ☐ Other (specify) ______
Running Time: 90 minutes Date of Completion: 2009
Shooting format: VHS Screening format: DVD
Is this your first film? ☒ Yes ☐ No
A brief synopsis: ______

Please send this entry form, a videotape or DVD, and a check for $30 to the following address by October 30, 2009: ❹
Chelsea Film Festival, 330 Main Street, Chelsea, MI 48118

❶ Contact information appears at the top of the application.

❷ The application requests information related to the film.

❸ The application is designed so that it is easy to fill out.

❹ Specific instructions are given at the bottom of the application.

Reading Check

Distinguish Fact and Opinion Does this application form ask for opinions or facts?

Make Generalizations What information do you think all event applications require?

Analyze Based on the information requested, what do you think is the main purpose of the application?

Teach

Reading Strategy 2

Distinguish Fact and Opinion **Ask:** What facts can you identify about the film, based on the application? *(Possible answers: The director and writer is Jane Stevens. The running time is ninety minutes.)*

Assess

Reading Check

Distinguish Fact and Opinion
Answer: *It asks for facts about the filmmaker and the film, but it does not call for opinions.*

Making Generalizations
Answer: *the name and contact information of the person applying for consideratio; information relating to the application process*

Analyze **Answer:** *The main purpose of the application is to gather information about the film.*

Advanced Learners

DIFFERENTIATED INSTRUCTION

Electronic Versus Paper In the past, many applications were filled out on paper. Today, people apply for services, loans, and even jobs online. **Ask:** Do you think all applications should be available online? Are there some applications that should be filled out in person? *(Possible answer: Many applications require a signature and should be filled out in person.)*

Have students compare filling out applications electronically and filling them out in person. Point out that one of the benefits of filling out online applications is convenience. Ask students to give clear and specific reasons why they believe that one form is better than the other.

Teach

Reading Strategy 1

Evaluate **Ask:** Does Jane's letter provide sufficient information? Explain why or why not. *(Answers will vary. Students should support their answers.)*

Assess

Reading Check

Distinguish Fact and Opinion
Answer: *The statement that the filmmaking course gave Jane the skills she needs to make compelling films is opinionated. The first clause of the sentence, stating that Jane took a filmmaking class, is a fact because it can be proven or disproved.*

Make Generalizations
Answer: *This format enables the reader to find information quickly and easily. It also increases the likelihood that the reader will comprehend the information.*

Evaluate Answer: *Answers will vary. Students should support their answers with reasonable explanations.*

Read a Cover Letter

Jane returned the application and other materials with this cover letter.

1

1 The writer uses a block format. With this type of format, the text is justified left, and one line of space separates each paragraph.

2 The writer states her purpose directly and immediately.

3 The writer provides a brief description of her qualifications.

4 Convenient contact information is included.

5 The writer inserts four lines of space to leave adequate room for her signature.

224 Wells Hill Road
Woodstock, MI 48103
October 1, 2009

Chelsea Film Festival
330 Main Street
Chelsea, MI 48118

To Whom It May Concern: 1

2 I am submitting my film for consideration in the 2009 Chelsea Film Festival. As an avid fan of the socially conscious films you screen, I would be thrilled to have my film included in this year's festival.

Though "Nuclear Energy: A Viable Alternative?" is my first feature-length film, I have written and produced a short film that explores the hard times of the American car industry. Last year, this film won the Michigan Arts Center award for the best short documentary. In addition, I have completed a year-long filmmaking course at a local community college, which gave me the skills I need to make compelling films. 3

I have enclosed an entry form, a check for $30, and a DVD of my film. If you have any questions regarding the film or my experiences, feel free to contact me by phone (734-555-1234) or e-mail (JStevens@dkvworld.net). 4

I hope you enjoy "Nuclear Energy: A Viable Alternative?" I look forward to hearing from you in the near future.

Sincerely,

5

Jane Stevens

Reading Check

Distinguish Fact and Opinion Reread the last sentence of the second paragraph. What information is based more on opinion than fact?

Make Generalizations Why do you think the writer used a block format to present information?

Evaluate Do you think the author includes enough evidence to prove she is capable of making a strong feature-length documentary?

Writing Practice

SPIRAL REVIEW **Write a Business Letter** Explain that a cover letter is a way of introducing yourself to potential employers. Cover letters will often accompany a résumé. Explain that a cover letter should be brief and to the point. It should give the employer a sense of the applicant's personality and explain the person's interest in a specific position or organization. Have students write a cover letter explaining why they are interested in a job. Explain that because a cover letter is often the first contact a potential employer has with an applicant, it is important that the cover letter gives a good impression.

After You Read

Respond and Think Critically

Directions Read the questions about workplace and consumer documents below and select the best answer.

1. The main purpose of the e-mail is
   A. to request information concerning the film festival
   B. to request past festival programs
   C. to request information concerning the festival's application process
   D. to request directions to the festival
2. The application form includes all of the following elements *except*
   A. bold type
   B. sections
   C. space between sections
   D. artwork
3. The application form requests the MOST information about
   A. the director of the film
   B. the content of the film
   C. the film festival
   D. the application process
4. According to the cover letter, which of the following summarizes the main reason the film should be considered for the festival?
   A. The filmmaker is an avid fan of the festival.
   B. The filmmaker has produced a socially conscious film.
   C. The filmmaker has the qualifications needed to make a strong film.
   D. The filmmaker has won a prestigious award.

Write a Business Letter

Assignment Think of a situation in which writing a business letter might help you achieve one of your goals. Perhaps you want to be considered for an internship, require help with a community project, or need information about an after-school program. Write a letter in which you briefly explain your purpose in writing and convincingly describe your qualifications.

Draft For the best results, you should make a favorable impression on your reader. Therefore, when writing your letter, pay close attention to details of spelling, grammar, and punctuation. Also make sure you follow the conventions of a proper business letter, as described below. Anything positive that makes your letter stand out will help your cause. On the other hand, anything negative, even a single misspelling, may hurt your chances.

- Include the standard parts of a business letter: a return address, the date, an inside address, a salutation, the text of the letter, a complimentary close, a signature, and a printed name.
- Use the block-style format: all parts of the letter are aligned on the left margin (see page R22). Choose a businesslike font that is easy to read.
- Keep to the major points. Including inconsequential details will not impress your reader.
- Arrange information in a logical order. In the opening paragraph of your letter, clearly state your purpose for writing. In the second paragraph, briefly describe your qualifications. In the third paragraph, express your interest in the job, organization, program, and/or project. Finally, thank your reader for their time.

Consider Your Audience Before you begin writing, form a clear picture of your audience. Who will read your letter? What does this person need and want to know? Once you have a clear idea of your audience, choose a writing style and tone that will help you communicate your message to that audience. In the majority of business letters, the style is formal, but not so stilted or boring that it turns away readers. To write in a formal style, use standard punctuation, spelling, and grammar and avoid using slang or sentence fragments.

English Learners

DIFFERENTIATED INSTRUCTION

Intermediate Help English learners understand additional business terms often related to functional documents. Discuss the following: correspondence, block style, RSVP, memo, salutation. As you discuss each word or phrase, have a student read its definition from a dictionary.

After You Read

Assess

1. C is the correct answer. The main purpose is to learn more about how to apply for festival consideration.
2. D is the correct answer. The application includes all of the elements mentioned above except artwork.
3. B is the correct answer. The application form requests the most information about the content of the film.
4. C is the correct answer. The filmmaker has the skills and background needed to make a compelling film.

Writing

Students' business letters should

- include standard parts of a business letter
- use block-style format
- keep to major points
- be arranged in a logical order

Reference Section

Literary Terms Handbook

A

Abstract language Language that expresses an idea or intangible reality, as opposed to a specific object or occurrence or a concrete reality. Words such as *dog* and *sky* are concrete, whereas words such as *truth* and *evil* are abstract.

See also *CONCRETE LANGUAGE.*

Absurd, Theater of the See *THEATER OF THE ABSURD.*

Act A major unit of a drama, or play. Modern dramas generally have one, two, or three acts. Older dramas often have five acts. Although Shakespeare did not separate his plays into acts, each play was later divided into five acts. Acts may be divided into one or more scenes.

See page 614.

See also *DRAMA, SCENE.*

Allegory A literary work in which all or most of the characters, settings, and events stand for ideas, qualities, or figures beyond themselves. The overall purpose of an allegory is to teach a moral lesson.

See page 1035.

See also *SYMBOL.*

Alliteration The repetition of consonant sounds, generally at the beginnings of words. Alliteration can be used to emphasize words, reinforce meaning, or create a musical effect. Note the repeated *s* and *f* sounds in the following line from Mary Oliver's poem "The Black Snake":

> It is what sent the snake coiling and
> flowing forward . . .

See pages 443 and 591.

See also *SOUND DEVICES.*

Allusion A reference to a well-known character, place, or situation from history, music, art, or another work of literature. Discovering the meaning of an allusion can often be essential to understanding a work. Edna St. Vincent Millay alludes to Penelope, Odysseus's wife in Homer's *Odyssey*, in her poem "An Ancient Gesture":

> I thought, as I wiped my eyes on the
> corner of my apron:
>
> Penelope did this too.

Ambiguity The state of having more than one meaning. The richness of literary language lies in its ability to evoke multiple layers of meaning.

See also *CONNOTATION.*

Analogy A comparison that shows similarities between two things that are otherwise dissimilar. A writer may use an analogy to explain something unfamiliar by comparing it to something familiar. Chitra Banerjee Divakaruni makes the following analogies in these lines from her poem "My Mother Combs My Hair":

> We hold the silence
> tight between us
> like a live wire,
> like a strip of gold
> torn from a wedding brocade.

See also *METAPHOR, RHETORICAL DEVICES, SIMILE.*

Anecdote A short written or oral account of an event from a person's life. Essayists often use anecdotes to support their opinions, clarify their ideas, grab the reader's attention, or entertain. In "Field Trip," Naomi Shihab Nye's story about her time at camp is an anecdote.

See page 298.

Antagonist A person or a force in society or nature that opposes the *protagonist*, or central character, in a story or drama. The reader is generally meant not to sympathize with the antagonist. Polyphemus, the Cyclops, is Odysseus's antagonist in one episode of Homer's *Odyssey*.

See page 99.

See also *CHARACTER, CONFLICT, PROTAGONIST.*

Anthropomorphism The assignment of human characteristics to gods, animals, or inanimate objects. It is a key element in fables and folktales, in which the main characters are often animals. The animals in "Baker's Bluejay Yarn" have human characteristics.

See also *FABLE.*

Antithesis The technique of putting opposite ideas side by side in order to point out their differences or to draw attention to the superiority of one. Antithesis is often used in logical argument. Michel de Montaigne makes frequent use of antithesis in his essay "That One Man's Profit Is Another's Loss," as when he writes, "No profit can be made except at another's expense."

See page 387.

See also *ARGUMENT, PERSUASION.*

Aphorism A short, pointed statement that expresses a wise or clever observation about human experience. Naomi Shihab Nye concludes her essay "Field Trip" with an aphorism:

> The things we worry about are never the things that happen. And the things that happen are the things we never could have dreamed.

Apostrophe A literary device in which a speaker addresses an inanimate object, an idea, or an absent person. In Act 3, Scene 2, of *The Tragedy of Romeo and Juliet*, Juliet addresses the night:

> Spread thy close curtain, love-performing night,
> That th' runaway's eyes may wink, and Romeo
> Leap to these arms untalk'd of and unseen!

See also *PERSONIFICATION.*

Archetype An idea, a character, a story, or an image that is common to human experience across cultures and throughout the world. In their purest form, archetypes occur in oral tradition, but they also appear in written works of literature. They can be divided into the following categories:

Character archetype: Includes familiar individuals such as the wise leader, the rebel, the damsel in distress, and the traitor. Coyote, the trickster of Native American folklore, is a character archetype.

Image archetype: An object or a place that has a universal symbolism. For example, a rose symbolizes love.

Plot pattern archetype: A story that occurs in many cultures. Making the long journey home, completing the "impossible" task, and outwitting the formidable enemy are all archetypal plots.

Theme archetype: An idea that occurs wherever people tell stories. The ideas that good can overcome evil, that people can redeem themselves, and that an underworld exists are all archetypal themes.

See pages 825, 935, and 954.

See also *FOLKLORE, MYTH, ORAL TRADITION, STOCK CHARACTER, SYMBOL.*

Argument A type of persuasive writing in which logic or reason is used to try to influence a reader's ideas or actions. Anna Quindlen presents an argument against being perfect in "Put Down the Backpack."

See page 261.

See also *PERSUASION.*

Aside In a play, a comment that a character makes to the audience, which other characters onstage do not hear. The speaker turns to one side—or "aside"—away from the action onstage. Asides, which are rare in modern drama, reveal what a character is thinking or feeling. For example, in Act 2, Scene 2, of Shakespeare's *Romeo and Juliet*, Romeo makes two asides to the audience as he decides whether to make his presence known to Juliet, who is standing on the balcony above him.

See page 679.

See also *SOLILOQUY.*

Assonance The repetition of same or similar vowel sounds within nonrhyming words. In the following lines from Rita Dove's poem "Grape Sherbet," the long *i* sound is repeated in *I've* and *trying,* and the short *i* sound is repeated in *it* and *exist.*

> I've been trying / to remember the taste, /
> but it doesn't exist.

See page 565.

See also *SOUND DEVICES.*

Atmosphere The dominant emotional feeling of a literary work that contributes to the mood. Authors create atmosphere primarily through details of setting, such as time, place, and weather. In "The Cask of Amontillado," Edgar Allan Poe creates atmosphere by describing the eerie setting:

> We had passed through walls of piled
> bones, with casks and puncheons
> intermingling, into the inmost recesses
> of the catacombs.

See also *MOOD.*

Author's purpose An author's intent in writing a literary work. For example, the author may want to persuade, inform, describe a process, entertain, or express an opinion. Anna Quindlen's purpose in "Put Down the Backpack" is to persuade and inspire.

See pages 269 and 413.

See also *DICTION, STYLE, THEME.*

Autobiography A person's account of his or her life. The author typically focuses on the most significant events in his or her life. Autobiographies can give insights into the author's view or himself or herself and of the society in which he or she lived. For example, in *The Story of My Life,* Helen Keller traces the importance of education in her life.

See page 260.

See also *BIOGRAPHY, MEMOIR, NONFICTION.*

B

Ballad A musical narrative song or poem that in most cases recounts a single exciting or dramatic episode. Folk ballads were passed down by word of mouth for generations before being written down. Literary ballads are written in imitation of folk ballads and have a known author. Many ballads include elements of plot, such as exposition, conflict, climax, and resolution. "Sweet Betsy from Pike" is a folk ballad.

See page 958.

See also *FOLKLORE, NARRATIVE POETRY, ORAL TRADITION, PLOT.*

Bias An inclination toward a certain opinion or position on a topic, possibly stemming from prejudice.

See also *NONFICTION.*

Biography A nonfiction account of a person's life written by another person. Biographies can vary in length, from brief encyclopedia entries to works that span several volumes. James Cross Giblin's "A Brother's Crime" is an excerpt from a biography of John Wilkes Booth's brother Edwin.

See page 260.

See also *AUTOBIOGRAPHY, JOURNAL, MEMOIR.*

Blank verse Unrhymed poetry or dramatic verse written in a meter known as *iambic pentameter.* Each line of iambic pentameter has five units, or feet; each foot is made up of an unstressed syllable followed by a stressed syllable. Much of Shakespeare's work is written in blank verse. The following line from *Romeo and Juliet*, spoken by Friar Lawrence, is an example of blank verse.

> ˘ ´ ˘ ´ ˘ ´ ˘ ´ ˘
> Be pa / tient, for / the world / is broad / and
>
> ´
> wide.

See also *FOOT, IAMB, METER, RHYTHM.*

C

Cadence The rhythmic rise and fall of language when it is spoken or read aloud.

See also *FREE VERSE, METER.*

Catalog The listing of images, details, people, or events in a literary work. In "The Drums of Washington," Arthur M. Schlesinger Jr. catalogs the responses of world leaders and artists on hearing that President Kennedy had been assassinated.

Character An individual in a literary work. *Main characters* are central to the story and are typically fully developed. *Minor characters* display few personality traits and are used to help develop the story. In James Hurst's "The Scarlet Ibis," Brother and Doodle are main characters, and Mama, Daddy, and Aunt Nicey are minor characters. A character who shows varied and sometimes contradictory traits, such as Walter Mitty in James Thurber's "The Secret Life of Walter Mitty," is a *round character*. A character who reveals only one personality trait, such as the vengeful murderer in Edgar Allan Poe's "The Cask of Amontillado," is a *flat character.* A *stock character* is a flat character of a familiar and often-repeated type, such as the hard-boiled detective. A *dynamic character* changes during the story. A *static character*—such as the king in Frank R. Stockton's "The Lady, or the Tiger?"—remains the same throughout the story.

See pages 2 and 614.

See also *ANTAGONIST, CHARACTERIZATION, FOIL, PROTAGONIST, STEREOTYPE, STOCK CHARACTER.*

Character archetype See *ARCHETYPE.*

Characterization The methods a writer uses to reveal the personality of a character. In *direct characterization,* the writer makes explicit statements about a character. In *indirect characterization,* the writer reveals a character through that individual's words, thoughts, and actions and through what other characters think and say about that character. In his play *The Bear,* Anton Chekhov uses indirect characterization to create Smírnoff, a bold, brazen egotist who becomes sentimental when he falls in love with Popóva.

See pages 115 and 871.

See also *CHARACTER.*

Climax The point of greatest emotional intensity, interest, or suspense in the plot of a literary work. Also called the *turning point,* the climax usually comes near the end of a story or drama. For example, in Amy Tan's "Rules of the Game," the climax occurs when Meimei and her mother exchange harsh words and Meimei runs away.

See also *CONFLICT, PLOT.*

Colloquialism Informal language used in everyday conversation but not in formal writing or speech. The narrator's speech in Mark Twain's short story "Baker's Bluejay Yarn" is peppered with colloquialisms, as when he says:

> **He glances up perfectly joyful, this time; winks his wings and his tail both, and says, 'Oh, no, this ain't no fat thing, I reckon! If I ain't in luck!—why it's a perfectly elegant hole!'**

See also *DIALECT.*

Comedy A type of drama that is humorous and typically has a happy ending. Comedy can be divided into two categories: high and low. *High comedy* makes fun of human behavior in a witty, sophisticated manner. *Low comedy* involves physical humor and simple, often vulgar, wordplay. Eudora Welty's play *Bye-Bye Brevoort* is an example of high comedy.

See page 615.

See also *DRAMA, FARCE, HUMOR, PARODY, SATIRE.*

Comic relief A humorous scene, event, or speech in an otherwise serious drama. It provides relief from emotional intensity while at the same time highlighting the seriousness of the story. In Paddy Chayefsky's *Marty,* there is a moment of comic relief when Marty's mother uses the slang word *tomatoes* to describe the young women who will be at the Waverly Ballroom.

> **MOTHER. I say, why don't you go to the Waverly Ballroom? It's loaded with tomatoes.**

Conceit An elaborate figure of speech that makes a comparison between two significantly different things. The conceit draws an analogy between some object from nature or everyday life and the subject or theme of a poem. Emily Dickinson's poem "'Hope' is the thing with feathers—" is a conceit.

See also *ANALOGY, EXTENDED METAPHOR.*

Concrete language Specific language about actual things or occurrences. Words such as *dog* and *sky* are concrete, while words such as *truth* and *evil* are abstract.

See also *ABSTRACT LANGUAGE.*

Conflict The struggle between opposing forces in a story or drama. An *external conflict* exists when a character struggles against some outside force, such as another person, nature, society, or fate. In Homer's *Odyssey*, for example, Odysseus is involved in external conflicts with Polyphemus, Scylla and Charbydis, and the suitors. An *internal conflict* is a struggle that takes place within the mind of a character who is torn between opposing feelings or goals. In W. D. Wetherell's "The Bass, the River, and Sheila Mant," the narrator is torn between reeling in the fish (and losing the potential affections of Sheila) and letting it go (and losing the catch of a lifetime).

See pages 2, 11 and 857.

See also *ANTAGONIST, PLOT, PROTAGONIST.*

Connotation The suggested or implied meanings associated with a word beyond its dictionary definition, or *denotation.* A word can have a positive or negative connotation, or no connotation.

See also *AMBIGUITY, DENOTATION, FIGURATIVE LANGUAGE.*

Consonance The repetition of consonant sounds, typically within or at the end of words that do not rhyme and preceded by different vowel sounds.

See page 565.

See also *SOUND DEVICES.*

Couplet Two consecutive lines of rhymed verse that work together as a unit to make a point or to express an idea. Paul Laurence Dunbar's poem "Sympathy" contains many couplets, such as:

> **And the faint perfume from its chalice**
> **steals—**
> **I know what the caged bird feels!**

See also *RHYME, SONNET, STANZA.*

D

Denotation The literal, or dictionary, meaning of a word.

See also *CONNOTATION.*

Denouement The resolution of a story. *Denouement* is a French word meaning "unknotting." The denouement comes after the climax of a story and often ties in with the falling action.

See also *FALLING ACTION, PLOT, RESOLUTION.*

Description A detailed portrayal of a person, a place, an object, or an event. Good descriptive writing helps readers to see, hear, smell, taste, or feel the subject. The opening paragraph of James Hurst's "The Scarlet Ibis" contains this rich description:

> **The last graveyard flowers were blooming, and their smell drifted across the cotton field and through every room of our house, speaking softly the names of our dead.**

See pages 70 and 987.

See also *FIGURATIVE LANGUAGE, IMAGERY.*

Descriptive essay See *ESSAY.*

Dialect A variation of a language spoken by a group of people, often within a particular region. Dialects may differ from the standard form of a language in vocabulary, pronunciation, or grammatical form. For example, the following lines from Robert Burns's "A Red, Red Rose" make use of Scottish dialect:

> **Till a' the seas gang dry, my dear,**
> **And the rocks melt wi' the sun!**

See page 3.

Dialogue Conversation between characters in a literary work. Dialogue brings characters to life by revealing their personalities and by showing what they are thinking and feeling as they react to other characters. Dialogue can also create mood, advance the plot, and develop theme. Plays are composed almost completely of dialogue. This dialogue takes place between Friar Lawrence and Romeo in Act 3, Scene 3 of *Romeo and Juliet*:

> FRIAR. O, then I see that madmen have no ears.
>
> ROMEO. How should they, when that wise men have no eyes?
>
> FRIAR. Let me dispute with thee of thy estate.

See pages 173 and 1021.

See also *MONOLOGUE.*

Diction A writer's choice of words; an important element in the writer's voice or style. Skilled writers choose their words carefully to convey a particular meaning or feeling.

See page 187.

See also *AUTHOR'S PURPOSE, CONNOTATION, STYLE, TONE, VOICE.*

Drama A story written to be performed by actors before an audience. The script of a dramatic work, or play, often includes the author's instructions to the actors and director, known as stage directions. A drama may be divided into acts, which may also be broken up into scenes, indicating changes in location or the passage of time.

See pages 613-615.

See also *ACT, COMEDY, DIALOGUE, SCENE, STAGE DIRECTIONS, TRAGEDY.*

Dramatic irony See *IRONY.*

Dynamic character See *CHARACTER.*

E

End rhyme The rhyming of words at the ends of lines as in William Wordsworth's "I Wandered Lonely as a Cloud."

End-stopped line A line of poetry that ends in a punctuation mark. An end-stopped line usually contains a complete thought or image. Emily Dickinson's "I'm Nobody! Who are you?" contains the following end-stopped lines:

> I'm Nobody! Who are you?
> Are you—Nobody—Too?

See also *ENJAMBMENT.*

Enjambment The continuation of a sentence or phrase from one line of a poem to the next, without a pause between the lines. The following lines from William Wordsworth's "I Wandered Lonely as a Cloud" are an example of enjambment:

> The waves beside them danced; but they
> Outdid the sparkling waves in glee . . .

See page 492.

See also *END-STOPPED LINE.*

Epic A long narrative poem that recounts, in formal language, the exploits of a larger-than-life figure. This *epic hero* is usually a person of high social status who embodies the ideals of his or her people. He or she is often of historical or legendary importance. Epic plots typically involve supernatural events, long time periods, distant journeys, and life-and-death struggles between good and evil. *Folk epics* have no known author and usually arise through storytelling and collective experiences. *Literary epics* are written by known authors.

See pages 823-825 and 835.

See also *FOLKLORE, HERO, MYTH, NARRATIVE POETRY, ORAL TRADITION.*

Epic hero See *EPIC, HERO.*

Epic simile A long, elaborate comparison that continues for several lines. It is a feature of epic poems but occurs in other poems as well. In the *Odyssey*, for example, Homer compares Scylla plucking her victims from Odysseus's ship to an angler catching fish.

See also *EPIC, SIMILE.*

Epiphany A sudden understanding of the meaning or essence of something. In William Wordsworth's "I Wandered Lonely as a Cloud," the speaker has an epiphany when he sees a field of wild daffodils and recognizes nature's power to bring joy.

See page 570.

Epithet A brief phrase used to characterize a person, place, or thing. A *Homeric epithet* is a formulaic or stock phrase specific to epic poetry. Homeric epithets fit the meter of the poem and appear throughout. Before poems were written, these epithets functioned as mnemonic devices, helping the poet remember the lines during his or her performance. For example, in the *Odyssey*, Homer repeatedly uses "bleating ewes" to describe the Cyclops's flock and "fingertips of rose" to describe the dawn.

Essay A short work of nonfiction on a single topic. *Descriptive essays* describe a person, place, or thing. *Narrative essays* relate true stories. *Persuasive essays* promote an opinion. *Reflective essays* reveal an author's observations on a subject. All of these types of essays fall into two general categories, according to their style. A *formal essay* is serious and impersonal, often with the purpose of instructing or persuading. Typically, the author strikes a serious tone and develops a main idea, or *thesis,* in a logical, highly organized way. An *informal* or *personal essay* entertains while it informs, usually in light, conversational style.

See pages 261, 329 and 341.

See also *NONFICTION.*

Exaggeration See *HYPERBOLE.*

Exposition An author's introduction of the characters, setting, and situation at the beginning of a story, novel, or play.

See page 4.

See also *PLOT.*

Extended metaphor A metaphor that compares two unlike things in various ways throughout a paragraph, a stanza, or an entire selection. Emily Dickinson uses an extended metaphor in "'Hope' is the thing with feathers—."

See also *CONCEIT, METAPHOR.*

F

Fable A short, usually simple tale that teaches a moral and sometimes uses animal characters. Themes in fables are often directly stated. Pär Lagerkvist's "The Princess and All the Kingdom" is a modern fable.

See page 986.

See also *LEGEND, MORAL, PARABLE, THEME.*

Falling action In a play or story, the action that follows the climax. The falling action may show the results of the climax. It may also include the *denouement,* a French word meaning "unknotting." The denouement, or *resolution,* explains the plot or unravels the mystery.

See also *CLIMAX, PLOT.*

Fantasy A highly imaginative genre of fiction, usually set in an unfamiliar world or a distant, heroic past. Fantasy stories commonly take place in imaginary worlds and may include gnomes, elves, or other fantastical beings and forces. The use of some type of magic is common in fantasy stories.

See also *SCIENCE FICTION.*

Farce A type of comedy with stereotyped characters in ridiculous situations. Anton Chekhov's play *The Bear* contains many farcical situations, such as when Smírnoff challenges Popóva to a duel.

See pages 615 and 759.

See also *COMEDY, HUMOR, PARODY, SATIRE.*

Fiction Literature in which situations and characters are invented by the writer. Fiction includes both short stories, such as James Thurber's "The Secret Life of Walter Mitty," and novels, such as Willa Cather's *My Ántonia*. Aspects of a fictional work may be based on fact or experience.

See also *DRAMA, NONFICTION, NOVEL, SHORT STORY.*

Figurative language Language that uses figures of speech, or expressions that are not literally true but express some truth beyond the literal level. Types of figurative language include hyperbole, metaphor, personification, simile, and understatement.

See pages 443 and 655.

See also *HYPERBOLE, IMAGERY, METAPHOR, OXYMORON, PERSONSIFICATION, SIMILE, SYMBOL, UNDERSTATEMENT.*

Figures of speech See *FIGURATIVE LANGUAGE.*

Flashback An interruption in the chronological order of a narrative to describe an event that happened earlier. A flashback gives readers information that may help explain the main events of the story. There are examples of flashback in Louise Erdrich's "The Leap," a story that is told from the point of view of a woman who is remembering various events in her life and her mother's life.

See page 44.

Flat character See *CHARACTER.*

Foil A character who provides a strong contrast to another character, usually a main character. By using a foil, a writer calls attention to the strengths or weaknesses of a character. In *Romeo and Juliet*, the fun-loving Mercutio is a foil to the love-struck Romeo.

See page 625.

See also *CHARACTER.*

Folklore The traditional beliefs, customs, stories, songs, and dances of a culture. Folklore is based on the concerns of ordinary people and is passed down through oral tradition.

See also *BALLAD, EPIC, FOLKTALE, MYTH, ORAL TRADITION, TALL TALE.*

Folktale An anonymous traditional story passed down orally long before being written down. Folktales include animal stories, trickster stories, fairy tales, myths, legends, and tall tales.

See also *EPIC, FOLKLORE, LEGEND, MYTH, ORAL TRADITION, TALL TALE.*

Foot The basic unit in the measurement of rhythm in poetry. A foot usually contains one stressed syllable (´) and one or more unstressed syllables (˘).

See also *METER, RHYTHM, SCANSION.*

Foreshadowing An author's use of clues to prepare readers for events that will happen later in a story. The pistol shots and jarring cries that Rainsford hears at the beginning of Richard Connell's short story "The Most Dangerous Game" foreshadow Rainsford's fate: he will be hunted on the island.

See page 1044.

See also *PLOT, RISING ACTION, SUSPENSE.*

Form The structure of a poem. Many modern writers use loosely structured poetic forms instead of following traditional or formal patterns. These poets vary the lengths of lines and stanzas, relying on emphasis, rhythm, pattern, or the placement of words and phrases to convey meaning.

See pages 442 and 456.

See also *RHYTHM, STANZA, STRUCTURE.*

Formal essay See *ESSAY.*

Frame story A plot structure that includes the telling of a story within a story. The frame is the outer story, which usually precedes and follows the inner, more important story. Twain uses a frame in "Baker's Bluejay Yarn." Some literary works have frames that bind together many different stories.

Free verse Poetry that has no fixed pattern of meter, rhyme, line length, or stanza arrangement. Alma Luz Villanueva's poem "I Was a Skinny Tomboy Kid" is composed in free verse.

See pages 466 and 511.

See also *POETRY, RHYTHM.*

G

Genre A category or type of literature. Examples of genres are poetry, drama, fiction, nonfiction, essay, and epic. The term also refers to subcategories of literary work. For example, fantasy, magical realism, mystery, romance, and science fiction are genres of fiction. Ursula K. Le Guin's short story "The Rule of Names," for example, belongs to both the fiction and fantasy genres.

H

Haiku A traditional Japanese form of poetry that has three lines and seventeen syllables. The first and third lines have five syllables each; the second line has seven syllables. The purpose of traditional haiku is to capture a flash of insight that occurs during an observation of nature.

See page 497.

Hero The main character in a literary work, typically a character whose admirable qualities or noble deeds arouse admiration. For example, Ivan is the hero in the Russian tale "Vasilisa of the Golden Braid and Ivan the Pea." In contemporary usage, the term can refer to either a female or male.

See also *EPIC, MYTH, PROTAGONIST, TRAGEDY.*

High comedy See *COMEDY.*

Historical narrative A work of nonfiction that tells the story of important historical events or developments. James Cross Giblin's "A Brother's Crime" is an example of a historical narrative.

See page 283.

Homeric epithet See *EPITHET.*

Humor The quality of a literary work that makes the characters and their situations seem funny, amusing, or ludicrous. Humor often points out human failings and the irony found in many situations. Humorous language includes sarcasm, exaggeration, and verbal irony. Humorous writing can be equally effective in fiction and nonfiction.

See page 391.

See also *COMEDY, FARCE, PARODY, PUN, SATIRE.*

Hyperbole A figure of speech that uses exaggeration to express strong emotion, make a point, or evoke humor. "You've asked me a million times" is an example of hyperbole.

See also *FIGURATIVE LANGUAGE, UNDERSTATEMENT.*

I

Iamb A two-syllable metrical foot consisting of one unstressed syllable (˘) followed by one stressed syllable (ʹ), as in the word *divide.*

Iambic pentameter A specific poetic meter in which each line has five metric units, or feet, and each foot consists of an unstressed syllable (˘) followed by a stressed syllable (ʹ). The rhythm of a line of iambic pentameter would be indicated as shown in this example from Shakespeare's *Romeo and Juliet*:

˘ ʹ ˘ ʹ ˘ ʹ ˘ ʹ ˘
Be pa / tient, for / the world / is broad / and

ʹ
wide.

See also *BLANK VERSE, METER, SCANSION.*

Idiom An expression whose meaning is different from its literal meaning. Idioms are readily understood by native speakers but are often puzzling to nonnative speakers. Phrases such as "catch his eye," "turn the tables," "over the hill," and "keep tabs on" are idiomatic expressions in English. Idioms can add realism to dialogue in a story and contribute to characterization.

See page 774.

See also *COLLOQUIALISM, DIALECT.*

Image archetype See *ARCHETYPE.*

Imagery Descriptive language that appeals to one or more of the five senses: sight, hearing, touch, taste, and smell. This use of sensory detail helps create an emotional response in the reader. For example, the following lines from Chitra Banerjee Divakaruni's "My Mother Combs My Hair" use imagery to make *silence* concrete:

We hold the silence
tight between us
like a live wire,
like a strip of gold
torn from a wedding brocade.

See pages 443, 507, and 987.

See also *FIGURATIVE LANGUAGE.*

Informal essay See *ESSAY.*

In medias res Latin phrase meaning "in the middle of things." A work of literature is said to start in medias res when the story begins in the middle of the action. A work of literature that starts in medias res skips the exposition and moves directly to the rising action.

Internal conflict See *CONFLICT.*

Inversion The reversal of the usual word order in a prose sentence or line of poetry. Writers use inversion to maintain rhyme scheme or meter, or to emphasize certain words or phrases. The following line from Shakespeare's *Romeo and Juliet* contains an example of inversion:

> **JULIET. So Romeo would, were he not**
> **Romeo call'd.**

See also *STYLE.*

Irony A contrast or discrepancy between appearance and reality, or between what is expected and what actually happens. In *situational irony,* the actual outcome of a situation is the opposite of what is expected—as in the ending of O. Henry's "The Gift of the Magi." In *verbal irony,* a person says one thing and means another. For example, in Poe's "The Cask of Amontillado," as Montresor leads Fortunato to his doom in the vaults, he says, "Come, we will go back ere it is too late. Your cough—," as if he were genuinely concerned about Fortunato.

In *dramatic irony,* the audience or reader knows information that characters do not. In Shakespeare's *Romeo and Juliet*, for example, the audience knows that Juliet is alive, while Romeo is convinced that she is dead.

See pages 80 and 707.

See also *PARADOX.*

J

Journal A daily record of events kept by a participant in those events or a witness to them. A journal is usually less intimate than a diary and often emphasizes events rather than emotions. Patricia Hampl's "North Shore Mornings" is an example of a journal.

See also NONFICTION.

Juxtaposition The placement of two or more distinct elements side by side in order to contrast or compare them. It is commonly used to evoke an emotional response in the reader. In her essay *"Sayonara,"* Anne Morrow Lindbergh juxtaposes the way to say "good-bye" in several languages to prove that *Sayonara* is the most eloquent.

> **For *Sayonara,* literally translated, "Since it must be so," of all the good-byes I have heard is the most beautiful. Unlike the *Auf Wiedersehens* and *Au revoirs,* it does not try to cheat itself by any bravado "Till we meet again . . ."**

L

Language See *DICTION, FIGURATIVE LANGUAGE, IMAGERY, SENSORY DETAILS.*

Legend A traditional story handed down from past generations and believed to be based on real people and events. Legends usually celebrate the heroic qualities of a national or cultural leader. Because legends are the stories of the people, they are often expressions of the values or character of a nation.

See also *EPIC, FABLE, FOLKLORE, HERO, MYTH, ORAL TRADITION.*

Line The basic unit of poetry. A line consists of a word or a row of words. In metered poems, lines are measured by the number of feet they contain.

See page 476.

See also *FOOT, STANZA.*

Literal language Language that is simple, straightforward, and free of embellishment. It is the opposite of figurative language, which conveys ideas indirectly.

See also *DENOTATION.*

Local color The use of specific details to re-create the language, customs, geography, and habits of a particular area. Isaac Bashevis Singer's short story "The Son from America" has many examples of local color.

> **The more prosperous villagers had kerosene lamps, but Berl and his wife did not believe in newfangled gadgets. What was wrong with a wick in a dish of oil? Only for the Sabbath would Berlcha buy three tallow candles at the store.**

See also *DIALECT.*

Low comedy See *COMEDY.*

Lyric poetry Poetry that expresses a speaker's personal thoughts and feelings. Lyric poems are usually short and musical. While the subject of a lyric poem might be an object, a person, or an event, the emphasis of the poem is on the experience of emotion. William Wordsworth's "I Wandered Lonely as a Cloud" is an example of a lyric poem.

See page 541.

See also *POETRY.*

M

Magical realism Fiction that combines fantasy and realism. Magical realism inserts fantastic, sometimes humorous, events and details into a believable reality. Diana García's "The Flat of the Land" is an example of magical realism.

See also *GENRE.*

Memoir A type of narrative nonfiction that presents an author's personal experience of an event or a period in the writer's life. A memoir is usually written from the first-person point of view. It often emphasizes the person's thoughts and feelings, his or her relationships with other people, or the impact of significant historical events on his or her life. James Herriot's "A Case of Cruelty" is an example of a memoir.

See page 277.

See also *AUTOBIOGRAPHY.*

Metaphor A figure of speech that makes a comparison between two seemingly unlike things. Unlike a *simile,* a metaphor implies an underlying similarity between the two and does not use the word *like* or *as.* In the following lines from Shakespeare's *Romeo and Juliet*, Romeo uses a metaphor to compare his lips to religious pilgrims:

> **My lips, two blushing pilgrims, ready stand**
> **To smooth that rough touch with a tender**
> **kiss.**

See pages 443, 520, and 527.

See also *ANALOGY, FIGURATIVE LANGUAGE, SIMILE.*

Meter A regular pattern of stressed and unstressed syllables that gives a line of poetry a predictable rhythm. The unit of meter within a line is the *foot.* Each type of foot has a unique pattern of stressed (´) and unstressed (˘) syllables:

- iamb (˘´) as in *complete*
- trochee (/´) as in *trouble*
- anapest (˘˘´) as *intervene*
- dactyl (´˘˘) as in *majesty*
- spondee (´ ´) as in *blue-green*

A particular meter is named for the type of foot and the number of feet per line. For example, *trimeter* has three feet per line, *tetrameter* has four feet, *pentameter* has five feet, and *hexameter* has six feet. William Wordsworth wrote "I Wandered Lonely as a Cloud" in iambic tetrameter:

> ˘ ´ ˘ ´ ˘ ´ ˘ ´
> **I wan / dered lone / ly as / a cloud**
>
> ˘ ´ ˘ ´ ˘ ´ ˘ ´
> **That floats / on high / o'er vales / and hills**

See pages 442 and 462.

See also *FOOT, IAMBIC PENTAMETER, RHYTHM, SCANSION.*

Monologue A long speech or written expression of thoughts by a character in a literary work. Friar Lawrence's summary of events in the final scene of Shakespeare's *Romeo and Juliet* is a monologue.

See page 679.

See also *DIALOGUE, SOLILOQUY.*

Mood The emotional quality of a literary work. A writer's choice of language, subject matter, setting, diction, and tone, as well as sound devices such as rhyme and rhythm, contributes to mood. Richard Connell sustains a tense, eerie mood throughout much of his short story "The Most Dangerous Game":

> **An apprehensive night crawled slowly by like a wounded snake, and sleep did not visit Rainsford, although the silence of a dead world was on the jungle.**

See page 57.

See also *ATMOSPHERE, SETTING, TONE.*

Moral A practical lesson about right and wrong conduct. In fables, the moral is stated directly; in other literary forms, it is often implied.

See page 1013.

See also *FABLE, PARABLE, THEME.*

Motif A significant word, phrase, image, description, idea, or other element that is repeated throughout a literary work and is related to the theme. Fishing is a motif in W. D. Wetherell's "The Bass, the River, and Sheila Mant."

See page 913.

Motivation The stated or implied reason a character acts, thinks, or feels a certain way. Motivation may be an external circumstance or an internal moral or emotional impulse. In O. Henry's "The Gift of the Magi," Della is motivated to sell her hair by the desire to buy her husband a beautiful gift.

See page 128.

Mystery A genre of fiction that follows a standard plot pattern—a crime is committed, and a detective searches for clues that will lead him or her to the criminal. Any story that relies on the unknown or the terrifying can be considered a mystery. "The Mystery of Hunter's Lodge" is an example of a mystery.

See page 987.

See also *FICTION, GENRE.*

Myth A traditional story that deals with goddesses, gods, heroes, and supernatural forces. A myth may explain a belief, a custom, or a force of nature. Homer's *Odyssey* incorporates some of the most famous traditional myths of ancient Greece, such as the myth of the Sirens.

See pages 823-825.

See also *EPIC, FOLKLORE, LEGEND, ORAL TRADITION.*

N

Narrative Writing or speech that tells a story. Driven by a *conflict,* or problem, a narrative unfolds event by event and leads to a *resolution.* The story is narrated, or told, by a *narrator* and can take the form of a novel, an essay, a poem, or a short story.

See also *NARRATIVE POETRY, NARRATOR, PLOT.*

Narrative essay See *ESSAY.*

Narrative poetry Verse that tells a story. Narrative poems are usually contrasted with *lyric poetry. Ballads, epics,* and *romances* are all types of narrative poetry. Robert Frost's "The Road Not Taken" is a narrative poem.

See also *BALLAD, EPIC, LYRIC POETRY, NARRATIVE.*

Narrator The person who tells a story. The narrator may be a character in the story, as in Truman Capote's "A Christmas Memory," or a character outside the story, as in Frank R. Stockton's "The Lady, or the Tiger?" Narrators are not always truthful. A narrator in a work of literature may be *reliable* or *unreliable.* Some unreliable narrators intentionally mislead readers. Others fail to understand the true meaning of the events they describe. Most stories with unreliable narrators are written in the first person.

See page 3.

See also *NARRATIVE, POINT OF VIEW, SPEAKER.*

Nonfiction Literature about real people, places, and events. Among the categories of nonfiction are biographies, autobiographies, and essays. Maya Angelou's *All God's Children Need Traveling Shoes* is an example of nonfiction.

See pages 259-261.

See also *AUTOBIOGRAPHY, BIOGRAPHY, ESSAY, FICTION, MEMOIR.*

Novel A book-length fictional prose narrative. Because of its length, a novel has greater potential to develop plot, character, setting, and theme than does a short story.

See also *FICTION, PLOT, SHORT STORY.*

O

Onomatopoeia The use of a word or phrase that imitates or suggests the sound of what it describes. Some examples are *mew, hiss, crack, swish, murmur,* and *buzz.*

See also *SOUND DEVICES.*

Oral tradition Literature that passes by word of mouth from one generation to the next. Oral literature was a way of recording the past, glorifying leaders, and teaching morals and traditions to young people. Epics such as Homer's *Odyssey* were originally passed on in this manner.

See also *BALLAD, EPIC, FOLKLORE, LEGEND, MYTH.*

Oxymoron A figure of speech in which opposite ideas are combined. For example, the following line from Act 1, Scene 1 of Shakespeare's *Romeo and Juliet* contains two oxymorons:

> **Why then, O brawling love, O loving hate . . .**

See also *FIGURATIVE LANGUAGE, PARADOX.*

P

Parable A simple story pointing to a moral or religious lesson. It differs from a fable in that the characters are usually people instead of animals. Shinichi Hoshi's "He—y, Come on Ou—t!" is a modern parable.

See also *FABLE, MORAL.*

Paradox A situation or statement that appears to be contradictory but is actually true, either in fact or in a figurative sense. These lines from Denise Levertov's "The Secret" contain a paradox:

> **I who don't know the**
> **secret wrote**
> **the line.**

See page 557.

See also *OXYMORON.*

Parallelism The use of a series of words, phrases, or sentences that have similar grammatical form. Parallelism shows the relationship between ideas and helps emphasize thoughts. In his inaugural address, John F. Kennedy used many fine examples of parallelism, including the famous line:

> **And so, my fellow Americans, ask not**
> **what your country can do for you—ask**
> **what you can do for your country.**

See page 487.

See also *REPETITION.*

Parody A humorous imitation of a literary work that aims to point out the work's shortcomings. A parody may imitate the plot, characters, or style of another work, usually through exaggeration. Bret Harte's "The Stolen Cigar Case" is a parody of Sherlock Holmes stories.

See page 1072.

See also *COMEDY, FARCE, HUMOR, SATIRE.*

Persona The person who is understood to be speaking or telling a story or another work. Whether the story is told by an omniscient narrator, as in Guy de Maupassant's "The Necklace," or by one of the characters, as in Amy Tan's "Rules of the Game," the narrator is not the author. The attitudes and beliefs of the persona may not be the same as those of the author.

See page 226.

See also *NARRATOR, POINT OF VIEW.*

Personification A figure of speech in which an animal, an object, a force of nature, or an idea is given human characteristics. Juliet personifies night in this line from Act 3, Scene 2 of Shakespeare's *Romeo and Juliet*:

> **Come, gentle night; come, loving, black-**
> **brow'd night**

See pages 443 and 547.

See also *APOSTROPHE, FIGURATIVE LANGUAGE.*

Persuasion A type of writing, usually nonfiction, that attempts to convince readers to think or act in a particular way. Writers of persuasive works use appeals to logic, emotion, morality, and authority to sway their readers. John Dos Passos's "The American Cause" is an example of persuasive writing.

See also *ARGUMENT.*

Persuasive essay See *ESSAY.*

Play A literary work of any length intended for performance onstage with actors assuming the roles of the characters and speaking the lines from a playwright's script.

See also *DRAMA.*

Plot The sequence of events in a narrative work. *Conflicts* are introduced in the *exposition,* the first stage of the plot. As the work progresses, *rising action* builds suspense and adds complications, which lead to the *climax,* or turning point. After the climax, which is the moment of highest emotional pitch or greatest suspense, come *the falling action* and *resolution,* sometimes called the *denouement,* which reveal the logical results of the climax.

See pages 2 and 885.

See also *CLIMAX, CONFLICT, DENOUEMENT, EXPOSITION, FALLING ACTION, FORESHADOWING, RESOLUTION, RISING ACTION.*

Plot pattern archetype See *ARCHETYPE.*

Poetry A form of literary expression that differs from prose in emphasizing the line, rather than the sentence, as the unit of composition. Many other traditional characteristics of poetry apply to some poems but not to others. Some of these characteristics are emotional, imaginative language; use of figures of speech; division into stanzas; and the use of rhyme and regular meter.

See pages 441-443.

See also *FIGURATIVE LANGUAGE, METER, PROSE, RHYME, STANZA.*

Point of view The perspective from which a story is told. In a story with *first-person* point of view, the narrator is a character in the story, referred to as "I." The reader sees everything through that character's eyes. Truman Capote's "A Christmas Memory" is told from the first-person point of view. In a story with *third-person limited* point of view, the narrator reveals the thoughts, feelings, and observations of only one character, referring to that character as "he" or "she," as in Diana García's "The Flat of the Land." In a story with *third-person omniscient,* or all-knowing, point of view, the narrator is not a character in the story but rather someone who stands outside the story and comments on the action. A third-person omniscient narrator knows everything about the characters and the events and may reveal details that the characters themselves could not reveal. Guy de Maupassant's "The Necklace" is told from the third-person omniscient point of view. Occasionally an author uses *second-person* point of view, addressing the reader or a character as "you."

See pages 3, 197, and 209.

See also *NARRATOR, SPEAKER.*

Prologue An introductory section of a play, a speech, or another literary work. Shakespeare's *Romeo and Juliet* begins with a prologue.

Propaganda Written or spoken material designed to bring about a change or to damage a cause through use of emotionally charged words, name-calling, or other techniques.

Props A theater term (a shortened form of *properties*) for objects and elements of the scenery used in a stage play, movie, or television show.

See also *STAGE DIRECTIONS.*

Prose Literature that is written in sentence and paragraph form (as distinguished from poetry, which is arranged in lines and stanzas). Essays, short stories, novels, magazine articles, and most plays are examples of prose.

See also *POETRY.*

Protagonist The central character in a literary work, around whom the main conflict revolves. During the course of the literary work, the protagonist undergoes a conflict that is crucial to the plot. Generally, the reader or audience is meant to sympathize with the protagonist. Walter Mitty is the protagonist in James Thurber's story "The Secret Life of Walter Mitty."

See page 99.

See also *ANTAGONIST, CHARACTER, CONFLICT, HERO.*

Pun A humorous play on words. Puns usually involve words that are similar in sound (*merry* and *marry*) or a word that has several meanings. In Act 3, Scene 1 of Shakespeare's *Romeo and Juliet*, when Mercutio is fatally wounded, he says, "Ask for me tomorrow, and you shall find me a grave man," meaning both serious and dead.

See also *HUMOR.*

Q

Quatrain A four-line stanza. The quatrain is the most common stanza form in English poetry. It may be unrhymed or have a variety of rhyme schemes.

See also *COUPLET, SONNET, STANZA.*

R

Refrain A line or lines repeated at intervals in a poem or song, usually at the end of a stanza. In Paul Laurence Dunbar's "I Know Why the Caged Bird Sings," the line "I know why the caged bird sings" serves as a refrain.

See also *REPETITION.*

Reliable narrator See *NARRATOR.*

Repetition The recurrence of sounds, words, phrases, lines, or stanzas in a speech or literary work. Writers use repetition to emphasize an important point, to expand upon an idea, to help create rhythm, and to increase the feeling of unity in a work. In her poem "Remember," Joy Harjo uses repetition to emphasize the importance of remembering where one comes from.

See pages 443 and 537.

See also *PARALLELISM, RHETORICAL DEVICES, RHYME.*

Resolution Also called the *denouement,* a French word meaning "unknotting," the resolution is the part of a plot that concludes the falling action by revealing or suggesting the outcome of the conflict.

See also *CONFLICT, FALLING ACTION, PLOT.*

Rhetorical devices Persuasive techniques used by public speakers and writers of literary works, especially those written to persuade. Rhetorical devices include repetition, parallelism, analogy, logic, and the skillful use of connotation and anecdote. Effective rhetoric often appeals to logic, emotion, morality, or authority.

See page 379.

See also *ANALOGY, ANECDOTE, ARGUMENT, CONNOTATION, PARALLELISM, PERSUASION, REPETITION.*

Rhyme The repetition of the same stressed vowel sounds and any succeeding sounds in two or more words. *End rhyme* occurs at the ends of lines of poetry. *Internal rhyme* occurs within a single line. *Slant rhyme* occurs when words include sounds that are similar but not identical (*jackal* and *buckle*). Slant rhyme typically involves some variation of *consonance* (the repetition of similar consonant sounds) or *assonance* (the repetition of similar vowel sounds).

See pages 442 and 451.

See also *ASSONANCE, CONSONANCE, RHYME SCHEME, SOUND DEVICES.*

Rhyme scheme The pattern that end rhymes form in a stanza or poem. Rhyme scheme is designated by the assignment of a different letter of the alphabet to each new rhyme. William Wordsworth used the following rhyme scheme for his six-line stanzas in "I Wandered Lonely as a Cloud":

I wandered lonely as a cloud	a
That floats on high o'er vales and hills,	b
When all at once I saw a crowd,	a
A host, of golden daffodils;	b
Beside the lake, beneath the trees,	c
Fluttering and dancing in the breeze.	c

See page 451.

See also *RHYME.*

Rhythm The pattern of beats created by the arrangement of stressed and unstressed syllables, especially in poetry. Rhythm gives poetry a musical quality. It can also emphasize certain words or ideas to help convey meaning. Rhythm can be *regular,* with a predictable pattern or meter, or *irregular.*

See pages 442, 462, and 574.

See also *BLANK VERSE, FOOT, IAMBIC PENTAMETER, METER, SCANSION.*

Rising action The part of a plot where complications to the conflict develop and increase reader interest.

See also *PLOT.*

Round character See *CHARACTER.*

S

Satire Writing that uses humor or wit to ridicule the vices or follies of people or societies, often to bring about change or improvement. Satire uses devices such as *exaggeration, understatement,* and *irony.* Eugène Ionesco's play *The Leader* is a satire.

See also *COMEDY, FARCE, HUMOR, PARODY, SARCASM, WIT.*

Scansion The analysis of the meter of a line of verse. To scan a line of poetry means to note the stressed (ˊ) and unstressed (˘) syllables and to divide the line into its feet, or rhythmic units. Note the scansion of these lines from William Wordsworth's "I Wandered Lonely as a Cloud":

˘ ˊ ˘ ˊ ˘ ˊ ˘ ˊ
I wan / dered lone / ly as / a cloud

˘ ˊ ˘ ˊ ˘ ˊ ˘ ˊ
That floats / on high / o'er vales / and hills

See also *FOOT, METER, RHYTHM.*

Scene A subdivision of an act in a play. Each scene usually takes place in a specific setting and time.

See page 614.

See also *ACT, DRAMA.*

Science fiction Fiction that deals with the impact of science and technology—real or imagined—on society and on individuals. Sometimes occurring in the future, science fiction commonly portrays space travel, exploration of other planets, and future societies. Arthur C. Clarke's short story "The Sentinel" is an example of science fiction.

See page 986.

See also *FANTASY, GENRE.*

Sensory details Evocative words or phrases that convey sensory experiences—seeing, hearing, tasting, touching, and smelling. Sensory details make writing come alive by helping readers experience what is being described.

See also *IMAGERY.*

Setting The time and place in which the events of a literary work occur. Setting includes not only the physical surroundings but also the ideas, customs, values, and beliefs of a particular time and place. Setting often helps create an atmosphere or a mood. Judith Ortiz Cofer's "American History" is set in Paterson, New Jersey, on November 22, 1963, the day John F. Kennedy was assassinated.

See page 2.

See also *ATMOSPHERE, MOOD.*

Short story A brief fictional narrative in prose. A short story usually focuses on a single event and has only a few characters. Elements of the short story include *setting, characters, plot, point of view,* and *theme.*

See pages 2-5.

See also *FICTION, NOVEL, PLOT.*

Simile A figure of speech that uses *like* or *as* to compare seemingly unlike things. For example, this simile appears in Truman Capote's "A Christmas Memory":

> **She is small and sprightly, like a bantam hen.**

See pages 443, 527, and 581.

See also *ANALOGY, EPIC SIMILE, FIGURATIVE LANGUAGE, METAPHOR.*

Situational irony See *IRONY.*

Slant rhyme See *RHYME.*

Soliloquy A dramatic device in which a character, alone onstage (or while under the impression of being alone), reveals his or her private thoughts and feelings as if thinking aloud. An example of a soliloquy may be found in Act 2, Scene 2 of Shakespeare's *Romeo and Juliet,* in the speech by Romeo that begins: "But soft! What light through yonder window breaks?"

See page 679.

See also *ASIDE, MONOLOGUE.*

Sonnet A lyric poem of fourteen lines, typically written in iambic pentameter and usually following strict patterns of stanza division and rhyme.

The *Shakespearean sonnet,* also called the *English sonnet,* consists of three *quatrains,* or four-line stanzas, followed by a *couplet,* or pair of rhyming lines. The rhyme scheme is typically *abab cdcd efef gg.* The couplet often presents a conclusion to the issues or questions presented in the three quatrains.

In the *Petrarchan sonnet,* also called the *Italian sonnet,* fourteen lines are divided into two stanzas, the eight-line *octave* and the six-line *sestet.* The sestet usually responds to a question or situation posed by the octave. The rhyme scheme is typically *abbaabba cdcdcd* or *abbaabba cdecde.*

See also *COUPLET, LYRIC POETRY, RHYME SCHEME, STANZA.*

Sound devices Techniques used to emphasize particular sounds in writing. Writers use sound devices, such as *alliteration* or *rhyme,* to underscore the meaning of certain words, to enhance rhythm, and to add to the musical quality of the work.

See page 443.

See also *ALLITERATION, ASSONANCE, CONSONANCE, ONOMATOPOEIA, RHYME, RHYTHM.*

Speaker The voice that communicates with the reader of a poem, similar to the narrator in a work of prose. Sometimes the speaker's voice is that of the poet, sometimes that of a fictional person or even a thing. The speaker's words communicate a particular tone, or attitude, toward the subject of the poem. One should never assume that the speaker and the writer are the same. The speaker in Margaret Walker's poem "Lineage" is a granddaughter who is in awe of the strength of her grandmothers.

See page 516.

See also *NARRATOR, TONE.*

Stage directions Instructions written by a playwright that describe the appearance and actions of characters, as well as the sets, props, costumes, sound effects, and lighting for a play.

See pages 614 and 790.

See also *DRAMA, PROPS.*

Stanza A group of lines forming a unit in a poem or song. A stanza in a poem is similar to a paragraph in prose. Typically, stanzas in a poem are separated by a line of space.

See pages 442 and 476.

See also *COUPLET, QUATRAIN, SONNET.*

Stereotype A generalization about a group of people that is made without regard for individual differences. In literature, this term is often used to describe a conventional or flat character who conforms to an expected, fixed pattern of behavior. The rebellious teenager is a stereotype.

See also *CHARACTER.*

Stock character A character who represents a type that is recognizable as belonging to a particular genre. For example, a cruel stepmother or charming prince is often found in fairy tales. Valiant knights and heroes are found in legends and myths. The hard-boiled detective is found in detective stories. Stock characters have conventional traits and mannerisms shared by all members of their type. Gandalf in J. R. R. Tolkien's *The Hobbit* is an example of a stock character: the wise wizard.

See also *ARCHETYPE, CHARACTER, STEREOTYPE.*

Stream of consciousness The literary representation of an author's or a character's free-flowing thoughts, feelings, and memories. Stream-of-consciousness writing does not always employ conventional sentence structure or other rules of grammar and usage.

Structure The particular order or pattern a writer uses to present ideas. For example, narratives sometimes follow a chronological order. Listing detailed information, comparing and contrasting, analyzing cause-and-effect relationships, or describing a problem and then offering a solution are some other ways a writer can structure a text. Poetic structure—or *form*—refers to the organization of words, lines, and images, as well as of ideas.

See pages 356 and 442.

See also *FORM.*

Style The expressive qualities that distinguish an author's work, including word choice, sentence structure, and figures of speech.

See pages 2, 230, and 987.

See also *AUTHOR'S PURPOSE, DICTION, IMAGERY, TONE, VOICE.*

Subject The topic of a literary work.

Surprise ending An unexpected plot twist at the end of a story. The ending might surprise readers because the author provided misleading clues or withheld important information. O. Henry's "The Gift of the Magi" and Richard Connell's "The Most Dangerous Game" both have surprise endings.

Suspense A feeling of curiosity, uncertainty, or even dread about what is going to happen next in a story. To build suspense, an author may create a threat to the central character or use *foreshadowing*. Suspense is especially important in the plot of an adventure or a mystery story. Edgar Allan Poe's "The Cask of Amontillado" is an example of a suspenseful story. The reader, like Fortunato, is led through the catacombs and is kept "in the dark" until the very end about what sort of revenge the narrator will take.

See pages 21 and 995.

See also *FORESHADOWING, MOOD.*

Symbol Any person, animal, place, object, or event that exists on a literal level within a work but also represents something on a figurative level. In O. Henry's story "The Gift of the Magi," Della's hair is the symbol of her beauty.

See pages 156 and 532.

See also *ALLEGORY, FIGURATIVE LANGUAGE.*

T

Tall tale A wildly imaginative story, usually passed down orally, about the fantastic adventures or amazing feats of folk heroes in realistic local settings. Mark Twain's "Baker's Bluejay Yarn" is an example of a tall tale.

See also *FOLKLORE.*

Teleplay The script of a drama written for television, which, in addition to dialogue and stage directions, usually contains detailed instructions about camera shots and angles. Paddy Chayefsky wrote *Marty* for television, so the script contains instructions about how the play should be filmed.

> *Dissolve to: Live shot—a row of stags along a wall. Camera is looking lengthwise down the row.*

See also *STAGE DIRECTIONS.*

Theater of the absurd Drama, primarily of the 1950s and 1960s, that does not contain a plot but instead presents a series of scenes in which the characters speak in meaningless conversations or perform actions with little purpose. The central concern of this drama is to show that people are helpless or confused in an alienating world. French playwright Eugène Ionesco was a leading writer of this type of drama.

See also *DRAMA*.

Theme The main idea or message of a story, poem, novel, or play often expressed as a general statement about life. Some works have a *stated theme,* which is expressed directly. More commonly, works have an *implied theme,* which is revealed gradually through other elements such as plot, character, setting, point of view, and symbol. A literary work may have more than one theme. Themes and subjects are different. The subject of a work might be love;

the theme would be what the writer says about love—for example, love is cruel; love is wonderful; or love is fleeting.

See pages 3, 142, and 946.

See also *AUTHOR'S PURPOSE, FABLE, MORAL.*

Theme archetype See *ARCHETYPE*.

Thesis The main idea of an essay or another work of nonfiction. The thesis may be implied but is commonly stated directly.

See page 349.

See also *ESSAY, NONFICTION.*

Title The name given to a literary work. The title can help explain the setting, provide insight into the theme, or describe the action that will take place in the work.

Tone An author's attitude toward his or her subject matter. Tone is conveyed through elements such as word choice, rhythm, sentence structure, and figures of speech. A writer's tone may convey a variety of attitudes, such as sympathy, objectivity, seriousness, irony, sadness, bitterness, or humor. James Thurber's amused, affectionate tone in "The Secret Life of Walter Mitty" contrasts with Margaret Atwood's ironic tone in "Waiting."

See pages 308 and 987.

See also *ATMOSPHERE, AUTHOR'S PURPOSE, DICTION, MOOD, NARRATOR, SPEAKER, STYLE, VOICE.*

Tragedy A play in which a main character suffers a downfall. That character, the *tragic hero*, is typically a person of dignified or heroic stature. The downfall may result from outside forces or from a weakness within the character, which is known as a *tragic flaw.* In Shakespeare's *Romeo and Juliet,* the two young lovers—joint heroes of the play—meet their fates in part because of their own uncontrolled passions.

See pages 615 and 724.

See also *DRAMA, HERO.*

Tragic Hero See *TRAGEDY.*

U

Understatement Language that makes something seem less important than it really is. Understatement may be used to add humor or to focus the reader's attention on something the author wants to emphasize. In "Field Trip," Naomi Shihab Nye uses understatement when she says that the woman who cut off her finger was "distracted."

See also *HYPERBOLE.*

Unreliable narrator See *NARRATOR*.

V

Verbal irony See *IRONY.*

Verse paragraph A group of lines in a poem that form a unit. Unlike a stanza, a verse paragraph does not have a fixed number of lines. While poems written before the twentieth century usually contain stanzas, many contemporary poems are made up of verse paragraphs. Verse paragraphs help to organize a poem into thoughts, as paragraphs help to organize prose.

See also *FREE VERSE, STANZA.*

Voice The distinctive use of language that conveys the author's or narrator's personality to the reader. Voice is determined by elements of style such as word choice and tone.

See pages 3 and 551.

See also *DICTION, NARRATOR, STYLE, TONE.*

W

Word choice See *DICTION.*

Reading and Thinking with Foldables®

by Dinah Zike, M.Ed., Creator of Foldables®

Using Foldables® Makes Learning Easy and Enjoyable

Anyone who has paper, scissors, and maybe a stapler or some glue can use Foldables in the classroom. Just follow the illustrated step-by-step directions. Check out the following sample:

Reading Objective: to understand how one character's actions affect other characters in a short story

Use this Foldable to keep track of what the main character does and how his or her actions affect the other characters.

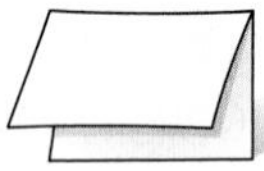

Step 1 Place a sheet of paper in front of you so that the short side is at the top. Fold the paper in half from top to bottom.

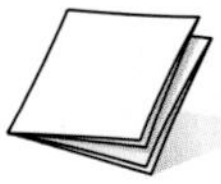

Step 2 Fold in half again, from side to side, to divide the paper into two columns. Unfold the paper so that the two columns show.

Step 3 Draw a line along the column crease. Then, through the top layer of paper, cut along the line you drew, forming two tabs.

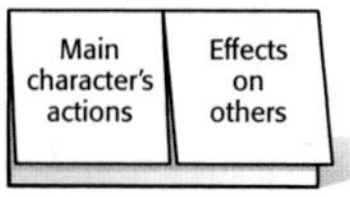

Step 4 Label the tabs ***Main character's actions*** and ***Effectson others.***

Step 5 As you read, record the main character's actions under the first tab. Record how each of those actions affects other characters under the second tab.

Short Story

Reading Objective: to analyze a short story on the basis of its literary elements

As you read, use the following Foldable to keep track of five literary elements in the short story.

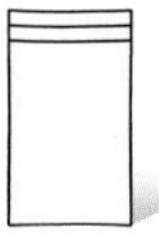

Step 1 Stack three sheets of paper with their top edges about a half-inch apart. Be sure to keep the side edges straight.

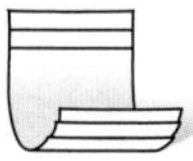

Step 2 Fold up the bottom edges of the paper to form six tabs, five of which will be the same size.

Step 3 Crease the paper to hold the tabs in place and staple the sheets together along the crease.

Step 4 Turn the sheets so that the stapled side is at the top. Write the title of the story on the top tab. Label the five remaining tabs *Setting, Characters, Plot, Point of View,* and *Theme.*

Step 5 Use your Foldable as you read the short story. Under each labeled tab, jot down notes about the story in terms of that element.

You may adapt this simple Foldable in several ways.

- Use it with dramas, longer works of fiction, and some narrative poems—wherever five literary elements are present in the story.
- Change the labels to focus on something different. For example, if a story or a play has several settings, characters, acts, or scenes, you could devote a tab to each one.

Drama

Reading Objective: to understand conflict and plot in a drama

As you read the drama, use the following Foldable to keep track of conflicts that arise and ways that those conflicts are resolved.

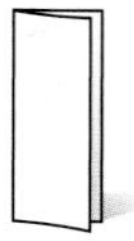

Step 1 Place a sheet of paper in front of you so that the short side is at the top. Fold the paper in half from side to side.

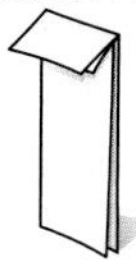

Step 2 Fold the paper again, one inch from the top as shown here.

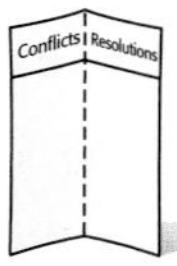

Step 3 Unfold the paper and draw lines along all of the folds. This will be your chart.

Step 4 At the top, label the left column *Conflicts* and the right column *Resolutions.*

Step 5 As you read, record in the left column the various conflicts that arise in the drama. In the right column, explain how each conflict is resolved by the end of the drama.

You may adapt this simple Foldable in several ways.

- Use it with short stories, longer works of fiction, and many poems—wherever conflicts and their resolutions are important.
- Change the labels to focus on something different. For example, you could record the actions of two characters, or you could record the thoughts and feelings of a character before and after the story's climax.

Lyric Poem

Reading Objective: to interpret the poet's message by understanding the speaker's thoughts and feelings

As you read the poem, use the following Foldable to help you distinguish between what the speaker *says* and what the poet *means.*

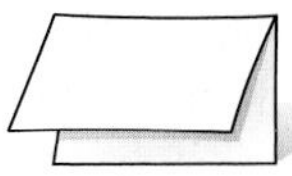

Step 1 Place a sheet of paper in front of you so that the short side is at the top. Fold the paper in half from top to bottom.

Step 2 Fold the paper in half again from left to right.

Step 3 Unfold and cut through the top layer of paper along the fold line. This will make two tabs.

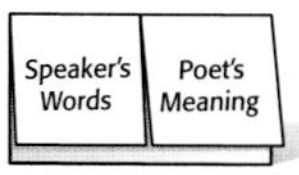

Step 4 Label the left tab *Speaker's Words.* Label the right tab *Poet's Meaning.*

Step 5 Use your Foldable to jot down notes on as you read the poem. Under the left tab, write down key things the speaker says. Under the right tab, write down what you think the poet means by having the speaker say those things.

You may adapt this simple Foldable in several ways.

- Use it to help you visualize the images in a poem. Just replace *Speaker's Words* with *Imagery* and replace *Poet's Meaning* with *What I See.*
- Replace the label *Speaker's Words* with *Speaker's Tone* and under the tab write adjectives that describe the tone of the speaker's words.
- If the poem you are reading has two stanzas, you might devote each tab to notes about one stanza.

Functional Documents

Functional documents are specialized forms of expository writing that serve specifc purposes. Functional documents are an every day part of business, school, and even home life. They must be clear, concise, accurate, and correct in style and usage.

Letter of Application

A letter of application is a form of business writing. It can be used when applying for a job, an internship, or a scholarship. In most cases, the letter is intended to accompany a résumé or an application. Because detailed information is usually included in the accompanying form, a letter of application should provide a general overview of your qualifications and the reasons you are submitting an application. A letter of application should be concise. You should clearly state which position you are applying for and then explain why you are interested and what makes you qualified. The accompanying material should speak for itself.

32 South Street
Austin, Texas 78746
May 6, 2009

Melissa Reyes
City Life magazine
2301 Davis Avenue
Austin, Texas 78764

❶ Re: Internship

❷ Dear Ms. Reyes:

I am a junior at City High School and editor of the City High Herald. I am ❸ writing to apply for your summer internship at City Life magazine. As a journalism student and a longtime fan of your magazine, I feel that an internship with your magazine would provide me with valuable experience in the field of journalism. I believe that my role with the City High Herald has ❹ given me the skills necessary to be a useful contributor to your magazine this summer. In addition, my enclosed application shows that I am also a ❺ diligent worker.

I thank you for considering my application for your summer internship, and I hope to be working with you in the coming months.

Sincerely,
Anne Moris
Anne Moris

❶ The optional subject line indicates the topic of the letter.

❷ In a business letter, the greeting is followed by a colon.

❸ The writer states her purpose directly and immediately.

❹ The writer comments briefly on her qualifications.

❺ The writer makes reference to the accompanying material.

Activity

Choose a local business where you might like to work. Write a letter of application for an internship at that business. Assume that you will be submitting this letter along with a résumé or an internship application that details your experience and qualifications.

Résumé

The purpose of a résumé is to provide the employer with a comprehensive record of your background information, related experience, and qualifications. Although a résumé is intended to provide a great deal of information, the format is designed to provide this information in the most efficient way possible.

❶ Jane Wiley
909 West Main Street, Apt. #1
Urbana, Illinois 61802
(217) 555-0489 • jane@internet.edu

Goal

Seeking position in television news production

❷ **Education**

Junior standing in the College of Communications at the University of Illinois, Urbana-Champaign
2005 Graduate of City High School

Honors

Member of National Honor Society

Activities

❸ Member, Asian American Association: 2005–Present
Environmental Committee Chairperson, Asian American Association: August 2006–May 2007

Work Experience

❹ Radio Reporter, WPGU, 107.1 FM, Champaign, Illinois: May 2007–Present
❺ • Rewrote and read stories for afternoon newscasts
• Served as field reporter for general assignments

Cashier, Del's Restaurant, Champaign, Illinois: May 2006–August 2006
• Responsible for taking phone orders
• Cashier for pickup orders

Assistant Secretary, Office of Dr. George Wright, Woodstock, Illinois: May 2005–August 2005
• Answered phones
• Made appointments

❶ Header includes all important contact information.

❷ All important education background is included.

❸ Related dates are included for all listed activities.

❹ Job title is included along with the place of employment.

❺ Job responsibilities are briefly listed, with a parallel structure used in each bulleted item.

Activity

Create an outline that lists the information that you would want to include in a résumé. Use a word processor to help format your outline.

Job Application

When applying for a job, you usually need to fill out a job application. When you fill out the application, read the instructions carefully. Examine the entire form before beginning to fill it out. If you fill out the form by hand, make sure that your handwriting is neat and legible. Fill out the form completely, providing all information directly and honestly. If a question does not apply to you, indicate that by writing *n/a,* short for "not applicable." Keep in mind that you will have the opportunity to provide additional information in your résumé, in your letter of application, or during the interview process.

❶ **Please type or print neatly in blue or black ink.**

❷ **Name:** ______________________ **Today's date:** ______
Address: ______________________________
Phone #: ________ **Birth date:** ____ **Sex:** __ **Soc. Sec. #:** ___

* *

❸ **Job History** (List each job held, starting with the most recent job.)

1. Employer: ______________________ Phone #: __________
Dates of employment: ______________________________
Position held: ______________________________
❹ Duties: ______________________________

2. Employer: ______________________ Phone #: __________
Dates of employment: ______________________________
Position held: ______________________________
Duties: ______________________________

* *

Education (List the most recent level of education completed.)

____

* *

Personal References:

1. Name: ______________________ Phone #: __________
Relationship: ______________________________

2. Name: ______________________ Phone #: __________
Relationship: ______________________________

❶ The application provides specific instructions.

❷ All of the information requested should be provided in its entirety.

❸ The information should be provided legibly and succinctly.

❹ Experience should be stated accurately and without embellishment.

Activity

Pick up a job application from a local business or use the sample application shown. Complete the application thoroughly. Fill out the application as if you were actually applying for the job. Be sure to pay close attention to the guidelines mentioned above.

Memos

A memorandum (memo) conveys precise information to another person or a group of people. A memo begins with a leading block. It is followed by the text of the message. A memo does not have a formal closing.

TO: All Employees
FROM: Jordan Tyne, Human Resources Manager
❶ SUBJECT: New Human Resources Assistant Director
DATE: November 3, 2009

❷ Please join me in congratulating Daphne Rudy on her appointment as assistant director in the Human Resources Department. Daphne comes to our company with five years of experience in the field. Daphne begins ❸ work on Monday, November 10. All future general human resource inquiries should be directed to Daphne.

Please welcome Daphne when she arrives next week.

❶ The topic of the memo is stated clearly in the subject line.

❷ The announcement is made in the first sentence.

❸ All of the important information is included briefly in the memo.

Business E-mail

E-mail is quickly becoming the most common form of business communication. While e-mail may be the least formal and most conversational method of business writing, it shouldn't be written carelessly or too casually. The conventions of business writing—clarity, attention to your audience, proper grammar, and the inclusion of relevant information—apply to e-mail.

An accurate subject line should state your purpose briefly and directly. Use concise language and avoid rambling sentences.

To: LiamS@internet.com
From: LisaB@internet.com
CC: EricC@internet.com
Date: January 7, 8:13 a.m.
❶ Subject: New Product Conference Call

Liam,

❷ I just wanted to make sure that arrangements have been made for next week's conference call to discuss our new product. The East Coast sales team has already scheduled three sales meetings at the end of the month with potential buyers, so it's important that our sales team is prepared to talk about the product. Please schedule the call when the manufacturing director ❸ is available, since he will have important information for the sales team.

Lisa

❶ Subject line clearly states the topic.

❷ The purpose is stated immediately and in a conversational tone.

❸ Important details are included in a brief, direct fashion.

Activity

Write an e-mail to your coworkers. Inform them of a change in company procedure that will affect them.

Travel Directions

When planning an event or a social occasion, it is often necessary to provide people with detailed directions to the location. These directions must be clear enough that anyone who is unfamiliar with the surrounding area can easily find their way. Creating a map that shows the route with clearly labeled streets can also be a great help.

Directions to Darien High School's Graduation Ceremony

From I-95 North, take Exit 11. ❶

Turn Left onto Post Road (Route 1).

At the first light, turn Left onto Samuel Avenue. Travel 2.5 miles. ❷

Turn Right onto Cherry Hill Road.

Turn Left onto High School Lane. ❸

Follow signs to Visitor Parking.

❶ Begins at a point from which most people will be coming

❷ Offers travel distances to help travelers locate streets

❸ Gives the name of each street along the route

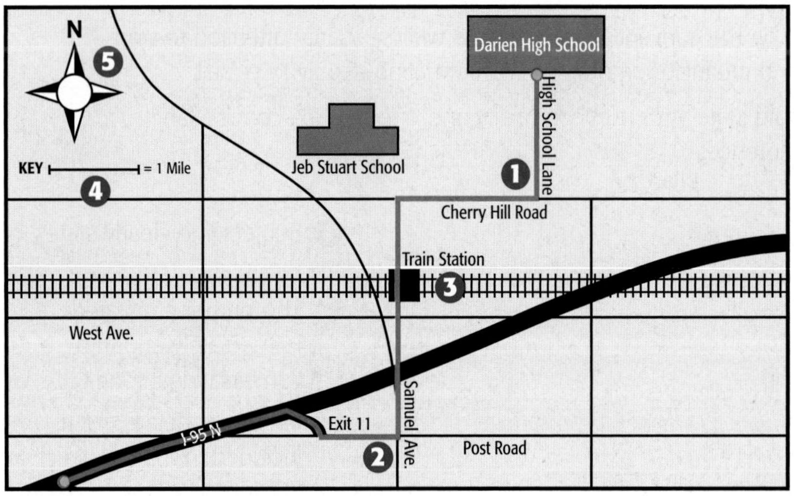

❶ Clearly labels all streets to be traveled

❷ Labels major cross streets so the traveler can keep better track of his or her progress

❸ Includes landmarks to help identify the area

❹ Includes legend to show scale

❺ Includes compass rose to help orientate the traveler

Activity

Write directions and draw an accompanying map to a location in your town. Be sure to include enough details and give enough clear directions so that even someone who is unfamiliar with the area could find the destination.

Technical Writing

Technical writing involves the use of very specific vocabulary and a special attention to detail. The purpose of technical writing is to describe a process clearly enough so that the reader can perform the steps and reach the intended goal, such as installing software, connecting a piece of equipment, or programming a device.

Instructions for Connecting DVD Player to HDTV

❶ Your DVD player can be connected to an HDTV using RCA cables or, for best picture quality, an HDMI cable.

Connecting with RCA Cables:

❷ **Step 1:** Insert the ends of the red, white, and yellow cables into the jacks labeled "AUDIO/VIDEO OUT." Be sure to match the colors of the cable with the color of the jack.

Step 2: Insert the other ends of the RCA cables into the jacks labeled "AUDIO/VIDEO IN" on your HDTV. These are usually located on the side or the back of the television. Again, be sure to match the colors of the cables with the colors of the jacks.

Connecting with HDMI Cable:

Step 1: Insert one end of the HDMI cable into the HDMI port located on the back of the DVD player.

Step 2: Insert the other end of the HDMI cable into the HDMI port on your HDTV.

❸ **Note:** Your HDTV may have more than one HDMI port. If so, be sure that you set your HDTV to the correct input when viewing.

❶ Uses specific language to clearly describe the process

❷ Lists each step individually

❸ Directs attention to possible variations the reader may encounter

Activity

Choose a device that you own or have access to, such as an mp3 player or a cell phone. Write brief step-by-step directions on how to perform a specific function on the device, so that someone else can follow your instructions and perform the function successfully.

Writing Handbook

Using the Traits of Strong Writing

What are some basic terms you can use to discuss your writing with your teacher or classmates? What should you focus on as you revise and edit your compositions? Check out the following terms, or traits, that describe the qualities of strong writing. Learn the meaning of each trait and find out how using the traits can improve your writing.

Ideas

The message or the theme and the details that develop it

Writing is clear when readers can grasp the meaning of your ideas right away. Check to see whether you're getting your message across.

- ☑ Does the title suggest the theme of the composition?
- ☑ Does the composition focus on a single narrow topic?
- ☑ Is the thesis—the main point or central idea—clearly stated?
- ☑ Do well-chosen details elaborate your main point?

Organization

The arrangement of main ideas and supporting details

An effective plan of organization points your readers in the right direction and guides them easily through your composition from start to finish. Find a structure, or order, that best suits your topic and writing purpose. Check to see whether you've ordered your key ideas and details in a way that keeps your readers on track.

- ☑ Are the beginning, middle, and end clearly linked?
- ☑ Is the internal order of ideas easy to follow?
- ☑ Does the introduction capture your readers' attention?
- ☑ Do sentences and paragraphs flow from one to the next in a way that makes sense?
- ☑ Does the conclusion wrap up the composition?

Voice

A writer's unique way of using tone and style

Your writing voice comes through when your readers sense that a real person is communicating with them. Readers will respond to the **tone** (or attitude) that you express toward a topic and to the **style** (the way that you use language and shape your sentences). Read your work aloud to see whether your writing voice comes through.

☑ Does your writing sound interesting?

☑ Does your writing reveal your attitude toward your topic?

☑ Does your writing sound like you—or does it sound like you're imitating someone else?

Word Choice

The vocabulary a writer uses to convey meaning

Words work hard. They carry the weight of your meaning, so make sure you choose them carefully. Check to see whether the words you choose are doing their jobs well.

☑ Do you use lively verbs to show action?

☑ Do you use vivid words to create word pictures in your readers' minds?

☑ Do you use precise words to explain your ideas simply and clearly?

Sentence Fluency

The smooth rhythm and flow of sentences that vary in length and style

The best writing is made up of sentences that flow smoothly from one sentence to the next. Writing that is graceful also sounds musical—rhythmical rather than choppy. Check for sentence fluency by reading your writing aloud.

☑ Do your sentences vary in length and structure?

☑ Do transition words and phrases show connections between ideas and sentences?

☑ Does parallelism help balance and unify related ideas?

Conventions

Correct spelling, grammar, usage, and mechanics

A composition free of errors makes a good impression on your readers. Mistakes can be distracting, and they can blur your message. Try working with a partner to spot errors and correct them. Use this checklist to help you.

☑ Are all words spelled correctly?

☑ Are all proper nouns—as well as the first word of every sentence—capitalized?

☑ Is your composition free of sentence fragments?

☑ Is your composition free of run-on sentences?

☑ Are punctuation marks—such as apostrophes, commas, and end marks—inserted in the right places?

Presenting and Publishing

The formatting of writing for various purposes

For many writers, the writing process is not complete until they present their work to an audience. This can mean submitting your writing for publication in a school paper or a national magazine, or it can simply mean preparing your writing in a neat and presentable format. For readers to fully appreciate your writing, it is very important that you present it neatly, effectively, and according to professional standards.

Format

- The standard typeface setting for most writing submissions is Courier 12 point.
- Double-space your work so that it is easy to read.
- Leave one-inch margins on all sides of every page.
- Italicize titles or when using terms from other languages. You may also italicize words to add emphasis, but do this only when it is necessary to make your point clear. (If you are submitting your writing to a professional publication, underline words that should appear in italics.)
- Most word processing programs make it easy to set the page number to appear in the upper right-hand corner of each page. Include your last name before each page number after the first page.
- If you are including charts, graphs, maps, or other visual aids, consider setting them on their own page. This will allow you to show the graphic at a full size that is easy to read.

Organization

- On a separate sheet of paper, center your name under the title of your work. If you are submitting your writing for publication, include the total number of words in the upper right-hand corner, and your name and address in the upper left-hand corner.
- The body of your work follows immediately.
- End your presentation with you list of works cited.

Research Paper Writing

More than any other type of paper, research papers are the product of a search—a search for data, for facts, for informed opinions, for insights, and for new information.

Selecting a topic

- If a specific topic is not assigned, choose a topic. Begin with the assigned subject or a subject that interests you. Read general sources of information about that subject and narrow your focus to some aspect of it that interests you. Good places to start are encyclopedia articles and the tables of contents of books on the subject. A computerized library catalog will also display many subheads related to general topics. Find out if sufficient information about your topic is available.
- As you read about the topic, develop your paper's central idea, which is the purpose of your research. Even though this idea might change as you do more research, it can begin to guide your efforts. For example, if you were assigned the subject of the Civil War, you might find that you're interested in women's roles during that war. As you read, you might narrow your topic down to women who went to war, women who served as nurses for the Union, or women who took over farms and plantations in the South.

Conducting a broad search for information

- Generate a series of researchable questions about your chosen topic. Then research to find answers to your questions.
- Among the many sources you might use are the card catalog, the computer catalog, the *Reader's Guide to Periodical Literature* (or an electronic equivalent), newspaper indexes, and specialized references such as biographical encyclopedias.
- If possible, use primary sources as well as secondary sources. A **primary source** is a firsthand account of an event—for example, the diary of a woman who served in the army in the Civil War is a primary source. **Secondary sources** are sources written by people who did not experience or influence the event. Locate specific information efficiently by using the table of contents, indexes, chapter headings, and graphic aids.

Developing a working bibliography

If a work seems useful, write a **bibliography card** for it. On an index card, write down the author, title, city of publication, publisher, date of publication, and any other information you will need to identify the source. Number your cards in the upper right-hand corner so you can keep them in order.

Following are model bibliography, or source, cards.

Book

❶ Settle, Mary Lee ❷ 6
❸ All the Brave Promises.
❹ Columbia: University of
South Carolina
❺ Press, 1995.

❻ Evanston Public Library D810.W754

❶ Author
❷ Source number
❸ Title
❹ City of publication/Publisher
❺ Date of publication
❻ Location of source
❼ Library call number

Periodicals

(1) Chelminski. R.	(2) 2
(3) "The Maginot Line"	
(4) *Smithsonian*, June 1997: 90–99	

(1) Author
(2) Source number
(3) Title
(4) Title of magazine/date/page number(s)

Online Source

(1) "Job Hunting Resources"	(2) 6
(3) The Career Building Network	
(4) CareerBuilder	
(5) 14 Feb. 2002	
(6) http://www.careerbuilder.com	

(1) Title
(2) Source number
(3) Title of database
(4) Sponsoring organization
(5) Date of access
(6) URL

Evaluating your sources

Your sources should be **a**uthoritative, **r**eliable, **t**imely, and **s**uitable **(arts)**.

- The source should be **authoritative.** The author should be well-known in the field. An author who has written several books or articles about a subject or who is frequently quoted may be considered an authority. You might also consult *Book Review Index* and *Book Review Digest* to find out how other experts in the field have evaluated a book or an article.
- The source should be **reliable.** If possible, avoid material from popular magazines in favor of that from more scholarly journals. Be especially careful to evaluate material from online sources. For example, the Web site of a well-known university is more reliable than that of an individual. (You might also consult a librarian or your instructor for guidance in selecting reliable online sources.)
- The source should be **timely.** Use the most recent material available, particularly for subjects of current importance. Check the publication date of books as well as the month and year of periodicals.
- The source should be **suitable,** or **appropriate.** Consider only material that is relevant to the purpose of your paper. Do not waste time on books or articles that have little bearing on your topic. If you are writing on a controversial topic, you should include material that represents more than one point of view.

Compiling and organizing note cards

Careful notes will help you to organize the material for your paper.

- As you reread and study sources, write useful information on index cards. Be sure that each note card identifies the source (use the number of the bibliography card that corresponds to each source).
- In the lower right-hand corner of the card, write the page number on which you found the information. If one card contains several notes, write the page number in parentheses after the relevant material.
- Three helpful ways to take notes are paraphrasing, summarizing, and quoting directly.
  1. **Paraphrase** important details that you want to remember; that is, use your own words to restate specific information.
  2. **Summarize** main ideas that an author presents. When you summarize several pages, be sure to note the page on which the material begins and the page on which it ends—for example, 213–221.
  3. **Quote** the exact words of an author only when the actual wording is important. Be careful about placing the author's words in quotation marks.
- Identify the subject of each note card with a short phrase written in the upper left.

See the sample note card below, which includes information about careers and goals from three pages.

> Careers and goals 12
> Many people "crave work that will spark . . . excitement and energy." (5) Sher recognizes that a career does not necessarily satisfy a person's aim in life. (24) She also offers ads on how to overcome obstacles that people experience in defining their goals. (101)

- Organize your note cards to develop a **working outline.** Begin by sorting them into piles of related cards. Try putting the piles together in different ways that suggest an organizational pattern. (If, at this point, you discover that you do not have enough information, go back and do further research.) Many methods of organization are possible. You might also combine methods of organization.

Developing a thesis statement

A thesis statement tells what your topic is and what you intend to say about it—for example, "World War II changed the lives of African Americans and contributed to the rise of the civil rights movement."

- Start by examining your central idea.
- Refine it to reflect the information that you gathered in your research.
- Next, consider your approach to the topic. What is the purpose of your research? Are you proving or disproving something? illustrating a cause-and-effect relationship? offering a solution to a problem? examining one aspect of the topic thoroughly? predicting an outcome?
- Revise your central idea to reflect your approach.
- Be prepared to revise your thesis statement if necessary.

Drafting your paper

Consult your working outline and your notes as you start to draft your paper.

- Concentrate on getting your ideas down in a complete and logical order.
- Write an introduction and a conclusion. An effective introduction creates interest, perhaps by beginning with a question or a controversial quotation; it should also contain your thesis statement. An effective conclusion will summarize main points, restate your thesis, explain how the research points to important new questions to explore, and bring closure to the paper.

Avoiding Plagiarism

Plagiarism is the act of presenting an author's words or ideas as if they were your own. This is not only illegal, it is also unethical. You must credit the source not only for material directly quoted but also for any facts or ideas obtained from the source.

Consider this example:

From the original SparkNotes study guide by Melissa and Stephanie Martin

> Throughout the novel, Twain depicts the society that surrounds Huck as little more than a collection of degraded rules and precepts that defy logic. This faulty logic appears early in the novel, when the new judge in town allows Pap to keep custody of Huck.

Plagiarized usage

> Twain's depiction of society is as a collection of illogical rules and principles. A good example of this is when Pap is awarded custody of Huck.

Simply rewording the original passage is not enough. In order to legally and ethically use the words or ideas of another writer you must credit the writer of the original or rework the original into your own new idea.

Using Material Without Plagiarizing

1. **Quote the original directly and credit the author.**
   As Melissa and Stephanie Martin note in their SparkNotes study guide, Huck lives in a society that is "little more than a collection of degraded rules and precepts that defy logic." They offer the example of Pap being awarded custody of Huck.
2. **Paraphrase the original and credit the author.**
   In their SparkNotes study guide, Melissa and Stephanie Martin note that Twain's depiction of society is as a collection of illogical rules and principles. A good example of this is when Pap is awarded custody of Huck.
3. **Use the information in the original to create your own idea.**
   It is hard to blame Huck for wanting to escape from a world where he is forced to follow arbitrary rules, and where he is forced to live with an abusive father.

Crediting your source is not only fair to the writer of the original source, it is also the law. Plagiarism is a serious offence and can result in failing grades, expulsion, and even legal action.

- In addition to citing books and periodicals from which you take information, cite song lyrics, letters, and excerpts from literature.
- Also credit original ideas that are expressed graphically in tables, charts, and diagrams, as well as the sources of any visual aids you may include, such as photographs.
- You do not need to cite the source of any information that is common knowledge, such as "John F. Kennedy was assassinated in 1963 in Dallas, Texas."

In-text citations The most common method of crediting sources is with parenthetical documentation within the text. Generally a reference to the source and page number is included in parentheses at the end of each quotation, paraphrase, or summary of information borrowed from a source. An in-text citation points readers to a corresponding entry in your **works-cited list**—a list of all your sources, complete with publication information, that will appear as the final page of your paper. The Modern Language Association (MLA) recommends the following guidelines for crediting sources in text. You may wish to refer to the *MLA Handbook for Writers of Research Papers* by Joseph Gibaldi for more information and examples.

- Put in parentheses the author's last name and the page number where you found the information. An art historian has noted, "In Wood's idyllic farmscapes, man lives in complete harmony with Nature; he is the earth's caretaker" (Corn 90).
- If the author's name is mentioned in the sentence, put only the page number in parentheses. Art historian Wanda Corn has noted, "In Wood's idyllic farmscapes, man lives in complete harmony with Nature; he is the earth's caretaker" (90).
- If no author is listed, put the title or a shortened version of the title in parentheses. Include a page number if you have one. Some critics believe that Grant Wood's famous painting *American Gothic* pokes fun at small-town life and traditional American values ("Gothic").

Compiling a list of works cited

At the end of your text, provide an alphabetized list of published works or other sources cited.

- Include complete publishing information for each source.
- For magazine and newspaper articles, include the page numbers. If an article is continued on a different page, use + after the first page number.
- For online sources, include the date accessed.
- Cite only those sources from which you actually use information.
- Arrange entries in alphabetical order according to the author's last name. Write the last name first. If no author is given, alphabetize by title.
- For long entries, indent five spaces every line after the first.

How to cite sources

On the next three pages, you'll find sample style sheets that can help you prepare your list of sources—the final page of the research paper. Use the one your teacher prefers.

MLA Style

MLA style is most often used in English and social studies classes. Center the title *Works Cited* at the top of your list.

Source	Style
Book with one author	Isaacson, Walter. *Einstein: His Life and Universe.* New York: Simon & Schuster, 2007.
Book with two or three authors	Mortenson, Greg and Relin, David Oliver. *Three Cups of Tea: One Man's Mission to Promote Peace…One School at a Time.* New York: Penguin Books, 2006. [If a book has more than three authors, name only the first author and then write "et al." (Latin abbreviation for "and others")]
Book with editor(s)	Lehman, David and McHugh, Heather, eds. The Best American Poetry 2007. New York: Scribner, 2007.
Book with an organization or a group as author or editor	Adobe Creative Team. *Adobe Photoshop CS3 Classroom in a Book.* Berkeley: Adobe Press, 2007.
Work from an anthology	Kilmer, Joyce. "Trees." *The Poetry Anthology, 1912–2002.* Ed. Joseph Parisi. Chicago: Ivan R. Dee, 2004. 7
Introduction in a published book	Jackson, Peter. Introduction. *The Making of* Star Wars*: The Definitive Story Behind the Original Film.* By. J.W. Rinzler. New York: Del Rey, 2007. iii.
Encyclopedia article	"Jazz." *Encyclopedia Britannica.* 15th ed. 2007.
Weekly magazine article	Sacks, Oliver. "A Bolt from the Blue." *The New Yorker.* 23 July 2007: 38–42.
Monthly magazine article	Plotnikoff, David. "Hungry Man." *Saveur.* July 2007: 35–36.
Newspaper article	Long, Ray and Meitrodt, Jeffrey. "Some Budget Progress Made." *Chicago Tribune.* 26 July 2007: B3. [If no author is named, begin the entry with the title of the article.]
Internet	"Americans Embracing 'Green' Cleaning." *ABC News.* 30 January 2006. ABC News Internet Ventures. 1 August 2007 <http://abcnews.go.com/Technology/Business/story?id=1544322>.
Online magazine article	Parks, Bob. "Robot Buses Pull In to San Diego's Fastest Lane." *Wired Magazine.* 15.08 (July 2007). 25. Oct. 2007 <http://www.wired.com/cars/futuretransport/magazine/15-08/st_robot>.
Radio or TV program	"Jungles." *Planet Earth.* Animal Planet. Discovery Channel. 25 July. 2007.
Videotape or DVD	Guggenheim, David, dir. *An Inconvenient Truth.* DVD. Paramount, 2006. [For a videotape (VHS) version, replace "DVD" with "Videocassette."]
Interview	Campeche, Tanya. E-mail interview. 25 Feb. 2004. [If an interview takes place in person, replace "E-mail" with "Personal"; if it takes place on the telephone, use "Telephone."]

CMS Style

CMS style was created by the University of Chicago Press to meet its publishing needs. This style, which is detailed in *The Chicago Manual of Style* (CMS), is used in a number of subject areas. Center the title *Bibliography* at the top of your list.

Source	Style
Book with one author	Isaacson, Walter. *Einstein: His Life and Universe.* New York: Simon & Schuster, 2007.
Book with two or three authors	Mortenson, Greg and Relin, David Oliver. *Three Cups of Tea: One Man's Mission to Promote Peace…One School at a Time.* New York: Penguin Books, 2006. [If a book has more than ten authors, name only the first seven and then write "et al." (Latin abbreviation for "and others")].
Book with editor(s)	Lehman, David and McHugh, Heather, eds. *The Best American Poetry 2007.* New York: Scribner, 2007.
Book with an organization or a group as author or editor	Adobe Creative Team. *Adobe Photoshop CS3 Classroom in a Book.* Berkeley: Adobe Press, 2007.
Work from an anthology	Kilmer, Joyce. "Trees." *The Poetry Anthology, 1912–2002.* Ed. Joseph Parisi, 7. Chicago: Ivan R. Dee, 2004.
Introduction in a published book	Rinzler, J.W. *The Making of* Star Wars: *The Definitive Story Behind the Original Film.* Introduction by Peter Jackson. New York: Del Rey, 2007.
Encyclopedia article	[Credit for encyclopedia articles goes in your text, not in your bibliography.]
Weekly magazine article	Sacks, Oliver. "A Bolt from the Blue." *The New Yorker,* July 23, 2007, 38–42.
Monthly magazine article	Plotnikoff, David. "Hungry Man." *Saveur.* July 2007, 35–36.
Newspaper article	Long, Ray and Meitrodt, Jeffrey. "Some Budget Progress Made." *Chicago Tribune.* July 26, 2007, B3. [Credit for unsigned newspaper articles goes in your text, not in your bibliography.]
Internet	ABC News Internet Ventures. "Americans Embracing 'Green' Cleaning." *ABC News.* http://abcnews.go.com/Technology/Business/story?id=1544322.
Online magazine article	Parks, Bob. "Robot Buses Pull In to San Diego's Fastest Lane." *Wired Magazine.* 15.08 (July 2007). http://www.wired.com/cars/futuretransport/magazine/15-08/st_robot.
Radio or TV program	[Credit for radio and TV programs goes in your text, not in your bibliography.]
Videotape or DVD	Guggenheim, David, dir. *An Inconvenient Truth.* Paramount, 2006. DVD. [For a videotape (VHS) version, replace "DVD" with "Videocassette."]
Interview	[Credit for interviews goes in your text, not in your bibliography.]

APA Style

The American Psychological Association (APA) style is commonly used in the sciences. Center the title References at the top of your list.

Source	Style
Book with one author	Isaacson, Walter. (2007). *Einstein: His life and universe.* New York: Simon & Schuster.
Book with two or three authors	Mortenson, Greg and Relin, David Oliver. *Three cups of tea: One man's mission to promote peace...One school at a time.* New York: Penguin Books, 2006. [If a book has more than ten authors, name only the first seven and then write "et al." (Latin abbreviation for "and others")].
Book with editor(s)	Lehman, David and McHugh, Heather. (Eds.). (2007). The best American poetry 2007. New York: Scribner.
Book with an organization or a group as author or editor	Adobe Creative Team. (2007). *Adobe Photoshop CS3 Classroom in a Book.* Berkeley: Adobe Press.
Work from an anthology	Kilmer, Joyce. "Trees." *The Poetry Anthology, 1912–2002.* Ed. Joseph Parisi, 7. Chicago: Ivan R. Dee, 2004.
Introduction in a published book	[Credit for introductions goes in your text, not in your references.]
Encyclopedia article	Jazz. (2007). In *Encyclopedia Britannica.* (Vol. 6, pp. 519). Chicago: Encyclopedia Britannica.
Weekly magazine article	Sacks, Oliver. (2007, July 23).A bolt from the blue. *The New Yorker,* 38–42.
Monthly magazine article	Plotnikoff, David. (2007, July). Hungry man. *Saveur,* 103, 35–36.
Newspaper article	Long, Ray and Meitrodt, Jeffrey. (2007, July 26). Some budget progress made. *Chicago Tribune,* p. B3. [If no author is named, begin the entry with the title of the article.]
Internet	ABC News Internet Ventures. (2006, January 30). *ABC News.* "Americans Embracing 'Green' Cleaning." Retrieved August 1, 2007, from http://abcnews.go.com/Technology/Business/story?id=1544322.
Online magazine article	Parks, Bob. (2007, July). Robot buses pull in to San Diego's fastest lane." *Wired Magazine.* 15.08.Retreived July 25, 2007, from http://www.wired.com/cars/futuretransport/magazine/15-08/st_robot.
Radio or TV program	Jungles. (2007, July 25). *Planet Earth* [Television series episode]. Animal Planet. Silver Spring, MD: Discovery Channel.
Videotape or DVD	Guggenheim, David (Director). (2006). *An inconvenient truth.* DVD. Paramount, 2006. [For a videotape (VHS) version, replace "DVD" with "Videocassette."]
Interview	[Credit for interviews goes in your text, not in your bibliography.]

Reading Handbook

Being an active reader is a crucial part of being a lifelong learner. It is also an ongoing task. Good reading skills are recursive; that is, they build on each other, providing the tools you'll need to understand text, to interpret ideas and themes, and to read critically.

Understanding Text Structure

To follow the logic and message of a selection and to remember it, analyze the **text structure,** or organization of ideas, within a writer's work. Recognizing the pattern of organization can help you discover the writer's purpose and will focus your attention on important ideas in the selection. **Look for signal words** to point you to the structure.

- **Spatial sequence** uses words or phrases such as *nearby, to the left, above,* and *behind* to show the physical arrangement of people and objects in an area.
- **Order of importance** will use words such as *most important* and *least necessary* to compare the importance of things or ideas.
- **Chronological order** often uses such words as *first, then, after, later,* and *finally* to show a sequence of events in time.
- **Cause-and-effect order** discusses chains of events using words or phrases such as *therefore, because, subsequently,* or *as a result.*
- **Comparison-contrast order** may use words or phrases such as *similarly, in contrast, likewise,* or *on the other hand.*
- **Problem-solution order** presents a problem and then offers one or more solutions. A problem-solution structure may incorporate other structures such as order of importance, chronological order, or comparison-contrast order.

Comprehension Strategies

Because understanding is the most critical reading task, lifelong learners use a wide variety of reading strategies before, during, and after reading to ensure their comprehension.

Determining the Main Idea

The **main idea** of a selection is the writer's purpose in writing the selection. As you read, it will be helpful to determine the main idea not only of the entire piece, but also of each paragraph. After identifying the important details in each paragraph, pause and ask yourself

- What is the main point of this selection?
- What do these details add up to?
- What is the writer trying to communicate?

Summarizing

A summary is a short restatement of the main ideas and important details of a selection. Summarizing what you have read is an excellent tool for understanding and remembering a passage. To summarize a selection:

- Identify the **main ideas.**
- Determine the essential **supporting details.**
- Relate all the main ideas and essential details in a **logical sequence.**
- **Paraphrase**—that is, restate the selection in your own words.
- Answer **who, what, where, when,** and **why** questions.

The best summaries can easily be understood by someone who has not read the selection. If you're not sure whether an idea is a main idea or a supporting detail, try taking it out of your summary. Does your summary still sound complete?

Distinguishing between fact and opinion

It is always important to be able to tell whether the ideas in a selection are facts or the writer's opinions.

- **Facts** can be proven or measured; you can verify them in reference materials. Sometimes you can observe or test them yourself.

  Example: Chicago is about 800 miles from New York City.

- **Opinions** are often open to interpretation and contain phrases such as "I believe" or "from my point of view."

  Example: Chicago to New York is too far to drive.

As you read a selection, evaluate any facts as well as any opinions you find. Ask yourself:

- Are the facts relevant? Are they actually true?
- Are the opinions well informed and based on verifiable facts? Are they persuasive?

Drawing inferences and supporting them

An **inference** involves using your reason and experience to come up with an idea based on what a writer implies or suggests but does not directly state.

- **Drawing a conclusion** is making a general statement you can explain with reason or with supporting details from the text.
- **Making a generalization** is generating a statement that can apply to more than one item or group.

What is most important when inferring is to be sure that you have accurately based your thoughts on supporting details from the text as well as on your own knowledge.

Making a prediction

A **prediction** is an educated guess about what a text will be about based on initial clues a writer provides. You can also make predictions about what will happen next in a story as you read.

- Take breaks during your reading and **ask yourself questions** about what will happen next, such as, "How will this character react to this news?"
- **Answer these questions for yourself,** supporting your answers with evidence from the text. For example, "Sam will be jealous when he hears the news, because he is in love with Antonia."
- As you continue reading, **verify** your predictions.

Reading silently for sustained periods

When you read for long periods of time, your task is to avoid distractions. Check your comprehension regularly by summarizing what you've read so far. Using study guides or graphic organizers can help you get through difficult passages. Take regular breaks when you need them and vary your reading rate with the demands of the task.

Keep in mind:

Whichever strategies you choose to use while reading, it will always be helpful to:

- Read slowly and carefully.
- Reread difficult passages.
- Take careful notes.

Also, when reading more difficult material, consider these steps to modify or change your reading strategies when you don't understand what you've read.

- Reread the passage.
- Consult other sources, including text resources, teachers, and other students.
- Write comments or questions on another piece of paper for later review or discussion.

Language Handbook

Grammar Glossary

This glossary will help you quickly locate information on parts of speech and sentence structure.

A

Absolute phrase. *See* Phrase.

Abstract noun. *See* Noun chart.

Action verb. *See* Verb.

Active voice. *See* Voice.

Adjective A word that modifies a noun or pronoun by limiting its meaning. Adjectives appear in various positions in a sentence. **(The *gray* cat purred. The cat is *gray*.)**

Many adjectives have different forms to indicate degree of comparison. **(short, shorter, shortest)**

The positive degree is the simple form of the adjective. **(easy, interesting, good)**

The comparative degree compares two persons, places, things, or ideas. **(easier, more interesting, better)**

The superlative degree compares more than two persons, places, things, or ideas. **(easiest, most interesting, best)**

A predicate adjective follows a linking verb and further identifies or describes the subject. **(The child is happy.)**

A proper adjective is formed from a proper noun and begins with a capital letter. Many proper adjectives are created by adding these suffixes: -*an*, *-ian*, *-n*, *-ese*, and *-ish*. **(Chinese, African)**

Adjective clause. *See* Clause chart.

Adverb A word that modifies a verb, an adjective, or another adverb by making its meaning more specific. When modifying a verb, an adverb may appear in various positions in a sentence. **(Cats *generally* eat less than dogs. *Generally,* cats eat less than dogs.)** When modifying an adjective or another adverb, an adverb appears directly before the modified word. **(I was *quite* pleased that they got along so well.)** The word *not* and the contraction *-n't* are adverbs. **(Mike *wasn't* ready for the test today.)** Certain adverbs of time, place, and degree also have a negative meaning. **(He's *never* ready.)**

Some adverbs have different forms to indicate degree of comparison. **(soon, sooner, soonest)**

The comparative degree compares two actions. **(better, more quickly)**

The superlative degree compares three or more actions. **(fastest, most patiently, least rapidly)**

Adverb clause. *See* Clause chart.

Antecedent. *See* Pronoun.

Appositive A noun or a pronoun that further identifies another noun or pronoun. **(My friend *Julie* lives next door.)**

Appositive phrase. *See* Phrase.

Article The adjective *a, an,* or *the.*

Indefinite articles **(*a* and *an*)** refer to one of a general group of persons, places, or things. **(I eat *an* apple *a* day.)**

The definite article **(the)** indicates that the noun is a specific person, place, or thing. **(*The* alarm woke me up.)**

Auxiliary verb. *See* Verb.

B

Base form. *See* Verb tense.

C

Clause A group of words that has a subject and a predicate and that is used as part of a sentence. Clauses fall into two categories: *main clauses,* which are also called *independent clauses,* and *subordinate clauses,* which are also called *dependent clauses.*

A main clause can stand alone as a sentence.

Types of Subordinate Clauses			
Clause	**Function**	**Example**	**Begins with . . .**
Adjective clause	Modifies a noun or a pronoun	Songs *that have a strong beat* make me want to dance.	A relative pronoun such as *which, who, whom, whose,* or *that*
Adverb clause	Modifies a verb, an adjective, or an adverb	*Whenever Al calls me,* he asks to borrow my bike.	A subordinating conjuction such as *after, although, because, if, since, when,* or *where*
Noun clause	Serves as a subject, an object, or a predicate nominative	*What Philip did* surprised us.	Words such as *how, that, what, whatever, when, where, which, who, whom, whoever, whose,* or *why*

There must be at least one main clause in every sentence. (***The rooster crowed,* and *the dog barked.***)

A subordinate clause cannot stand alone as a sentence. A subordinate clause needs a main clause to complete its meaning. Many subordinate clauses begin with subordinating conjunctions or relative pronouns. (***When Geri sang her solo,* the audience became quiet.**) The chart on the next page shows the main types of subordinate clauses.

Collective noun. *See* Noun chart.

Common noun. *See* Noun chart.

Comparative degree. *See* Adjective; Adverb.

Complement A word or phrase that completes the meaning of a verb. The four basic kinds of complements are *direct objects, indirect objects, object complements,* and *subject complements.*

A direct object answers the question *What?* or *Whom?* after an action verb. (**Kari found a *dollar.* Larry saw *Denise.***)

An indirect object answers the question *To whom? For whom? To what?* or *For what?* after an action verb. (**Do *me* a favor. She gave the *child* a toy.**)

An object complement answers the question *What?* after a direct object. An object complement is a noun, a pronoun, or an adjective that completes the meaning of a direct object by identifying or describing it. (**The director made me the *understudy* for the role. The little girl called the puppy *hers.***)

A subject complement follows a subject and a linking verb. It identifies or describes a subject. The two kinds of subject complements are *predicate nominatives* and *predicate adjectives.*

A predicate nominative is a noun or pronoun that follows a linking verb and tells more about the subject. (**The author of "The Raven" is *Poe.***)

A predicate adjective is an adjective that follows a linking verb and gives more information about the subject. (**Ian became *angry* at the bully.**)

Complex sentence. *See* Sentence.

Compound preposition. *See* Preposition.

Compound sentence. *See* Sentence.

Compound-complex sentence. *See* Sentence.

Conjunction A word that joins single words or groups of words.

A coordinating conjunction ***(and, but, or, nor, for, yet, so)*** joins words or groups of words that are equal in grammatical importance. (**David *and* Ruth are twins. I was bored, *so* I left.**)

Correlative conjunctions ***(both . . . and, just as . . . so, not only . . . but also, either . . . or, neither . . . nor, whether . . . or)*** work in pairs to join words and groups of words of equal importance.

(Choose *either* the muffin *or* the bagel.)

A subordinating conjunction ***(after, although, as if, because, before, if, since, so that, than, though, until, when, while)*** joins a dependent idea or clause to a main clause. **(Beth acted *as if* she felt ill.)**

Conjunctive adverb An adverb used to clarify the relationship between clauses of equal weight in a sentence. Conjunctive adverbs are used to replace *and* ***(also, besides, furthermore, moreover)***; to replace *but* ***(however, nevertheless, still)***; to state a result ***(consequently, therefore, so, thus)***; or to state equality ***(equally, likewise, similarly).*** **(Ana was determined to get an A; *therefore,* she studied often.)**

Coordinating conjunction. *See* Conjunction.

Correlative conjunction. *See* Conjunction.

D

Declarative sentence. *See* Sentence.

Definite article. *See* Article.

Demonstrative pronoun. *See* Pronoun.

Direct object. *See* Complement.

E

Emphatic form. *See* Verb tense.

F

Future tense. *See* Verb tense.

G

Gerund A verb form that ends in *-ing* and is used as a noun. A gerund may function as a subject, the object of a verb, or the object of a preposition. **(*Smiling* uses fewer muscles than *frowning.* Marie enjoys *walking.*)**

Gerund phrase. *See* Phrase.

I

Imperative mood. *See* Mood of verb.

Imperative sentence. *See* Sentence chart.

Indicative mood. *See* Mood of verb.

Indirect object. *See* Complement.

Infinitive A verb form that begins with the word *to* and functions as a noun, an adjective, or an adverb. **(No one wanted *to answer.*)** Note: When *to* precedes a verb, it is not a preposition but instead signals an infinitive.

Infinitive phrase. *See* Phrase.

Intensive pronoun. *See* Pronoun.

Interjection A word or phrase that expresses emotion or exclamation. An interjection has no grammatical connection to other words. Commas follow mild ones; exclamation points follow stronger ones. **(*Well,* have a good day. *Wow!*)**

Interrogative pronoun. *See* Pronoun.

Intransitive verb. *See* Verb.

Inverted order In a sentence written in *inverted order,* the predicate comes before the subject. Some sentences are written in inverted order for variety or special emphasis. **(Up the beanstalk *scampered Jack.*)** The subject also generally follows the predicate in a sentence that begins with *here* or *there.* **(*Here* was the solution to his problem.)** Questions, or interrogative sentences, are generally written in inverted order. In many questions, an auxiliary verb precedes the subject, and the main verb follows it. **(*Has* anyone *seen* Susan?)** Questions that begin with *who* or *what* follow normal word order.

Irregular verb. *See* Verb tense.

L

Linking verb. *See* Verb.

M

Main clause. *See* Clause.

Mood of verb A verb expresses one of three moods: indicative, imperative, or subjunctive.

The indicative mood is the most common. It makes a statement or asks a question. **(We *are* out of bread. *Will* you *buy* it?)**

The imperative mood expresses a command or makes a request. **(*Stop* acting like a child! Please *return* my sweater.)**

Types of Nouns		
Noun	Function	Examples
Abstract noun	Names an idea, a quality, or a characteristic	capitalism, terror
Collective noun	Names a group of things or persons	herd, troop
Common noun	Names a general type of person, place, thing, or idea	city, building
Compound noun	Is made up of two or more words	checkerboard, globe-trotter
Noun of direct addrress	Identifies the person or persons being spoken to	*Maria,* please stand.
Possessive noun	Shows possession, ownership, or the relationship between two nouns	my *sister's* room
Proper noun	Names a particular person, place, thing, or idea	Cleopatra, Italy, Christianity

The subjunctive mood is used to express, indirectly, a demand, suggestion, or statement of necessity **(I demand that he *stop* acting like a child. It's necessary that she *buy* more bread.)** The subjunctive is also used to state a condition or wish that is contrary to fact. This use of the subjunctive requires the past tense. **(If you *were* a nice person, you *would return* my sweater.)**

N

Nominative pronoun. *See* Pronoun.

Noun A word that names a person, a place, a thing, or an idea. The chart on this page shows the main types of nouns.

Noun clause. *See* Clause chart.

Noun of direct address. *See* Noun chart.

Number A noun, pronoun, or verb is *singular* in number if it refers to one; *plural* if it refers to more than one.

O

Object. *See* Complement.

P

Participle A verb form that can function as an adjective. Present participles always end in *-ing.* **(The woman comforted the *crying* child.)** Many past participles end in *-ed.* **(We bought the beautifully *painted* chair.)** However, irregular verbs form their past participles in some other way. **(Cato was Caesar's *sworn* enemy.)**

Passive voice. *See* Voice.

Past tense. *See* Verb tense.

Perfect tense. *See* Verb tense.

Personal pronoun. *See* Pronoun, Pronoun chart.

Phrase A group of words that acts in a sentence as a single part of speech.

An absolute phrase consists of a noun or pronoun that is modified by a participle or participial phrase but has no grammatical relation to the complete subject or predicate. **(*The vegetables being done,* we finally sat down to eat dinner.)**

An appositive phrase is an appositive along with any modifiers. If not essential to the meaning of the sentence, an appositive phrase is set off by commas. **(Jack plans to go to the jazz concert, *an important musical event.*)**

A gerund phrase includes a gerund plus its complements and modifiers. **(*Playing the flute* is her hobby.)**

An infinitive phrase contains the infinitive plus its complements and modifiers. **(It is time *to leave for school.*)**

A participial phrase contains a participle and any modifiers necessary to complete its meaning. **(The woman *sitting over there* is my grandmother.)**

A prepositional phrase consists of a preposition, its object, and any modifiers of the object. A prepositional phrase can function as an adjective, modifying a noun or a pronoun. **(The dog *in the yard* is very gentle.)** A prepositional phrase may also function as an adverb when it modifies a verb, an adverb, or an adjective. **(The baby slept *on my lap.*)**

A verb phrase consists of one or more auxiliary verbs followed by a main verb. **(The job *will have been completed* by noon tomorrow.)**

Positive degree. *See* Adjective.

Possessive noun. *See* Noun chart.

Predicate The verb or verb phrase and any objects, complements, or modifiers that express the essential thought about the subject of a sentence.

A simple predicate is a verb or verb phrase that tells something about the subject. **(We *ran*.)**

A complete predicate includes the simple predicate and any words that modify or complete it. **(We *solved the problem in a short time.*)**

A compound predicate has two or more verbs or verb phrases that are joined by a conjunction and share the same subject. **(We *ran to the park and began to play baseball.*)**

Predicate adjective. *See* Adjective; Complement.

Predicate nominative. *See* Complement.

Preposition A word that shows the relationship of a noun or pronoun to some other word in the sentence. Prepositions include *about, above, across, among, as, behind, below, beyond, but, by, down, during, except, for, from, into, like, near, of, on, outside, over, since, through, to, under, until, with.* **(I usually eat breakfast *before* school.)**

A compound preposition is made up of more than one word. **(according to, ahead of, as to, because of, by means of, in addition to, in spite of, on account of) (We played the game *in spite of* the snow.)**

Prepositional phrase. *See* Phrase.

Present tense. *See* Verb tense.

Progressive form. *See* Verb tense.

Pronoun A word that takes the place of a noun, a group of words acting as a noun, or another pronoun. The word or group of words that a pronoun refers to is called its antecedent. **(In the following sentence, *Mari* is the antecedent of *she. Mari likes Mexican food, but she doesn't like Italian food.*)**

A demonstrative pronoun points out specific persons, places, things, or ideas. ***(this, that, these, those)***

An indefinite pronoun refers to persons, places, or things in a more general way than a noun does. ***(all, another, any, both, each, either, enough, everything, few, many, most, much, neither, nobody, none, one, other, others, plenty, several, some)***

An intensive pronoun adds emphasis to another noun or pronoun. If an intensive pronoun is omitted, the meaning of the sentence will be the same. **(Rebecca *herself* decided to look for a part-time job.)**

An interrogative pronoun is used to form questions. ***(who? whom? whose? what? which?)***

A personal pronoun refers to a specific person or thing. Personal pronouns have three cases: nominative, possessive, and objective. The case depends upon the function of the pronoun in a sentence. The first chart on this page shows the case forms of personal pronouns.

A reflexive pronoun reflects back to a noun or pronoun used earlier in the sentence, indicating that the same person or thing is involved. **(We told *ourselves* to be patient.)**

A relative pronoun is used to begin a subordinate clause. ***(who, whose, that, what, whom, whoever, whomever, whichever, whatever)***

Proper adjective. *See* Adjective.

Proper noun. *See* Noun chart.

R

Reflexive pronoun. *See* Pronoun.

Relative pronoun. *See* Pronoun.

S

Sentence A group of words expressing a complete thought. Every sentence has a subject and a predicate. Sentences can be classified by function or by structure. The second chart on this page shows the categories by function; the following subentries describe the categories by structure. *See also* Subject; Predicate; Clause.

A simple sentence has only one main clause and no subordinate clauses. ***(Alan found an old violin.)*** A simple sentence may contain a compound subject or a compound predicate or both. ***(Alan and Teri found an old violin. Alan found an old violin and tried to play it. Alan and Teri found an old violin and tried to play it.)*** The subject and the predicate can be expanded with adjectives, adverbs, prepositional phrases, appositives, and verbal phrases. As long as the sentence has only one main clause, however, it remains a simple sentence. ***(Alan, rummaging in the attic, found an old violin.)***

A compound sentence has two or more main clauses. Each main clause has its own subject and predicate, and these main clauses are usually joined by a comma and a coordinating conjunction. ***(Cats meow, and dogs bark, but ducks quack.)*** Semicolons may also be used to join the main clauses in a compound sentence. ***(The helicopter landed; the pilot had saved four passengers.)***

A complex sentence has one main clause and one or more subordinate clauses. ***(Since the movie starts at eight, we should leave here by seven-thirty.)***

A compound-complex sentence has two or more main clauses and at least one subordinate clause. ***(If we leave any later, we may miss the previews, and I want to see them.)***

Simple predicate. *See* Predicate.

Simple subject. *See* Subject.

Subject The part of a sentence that tells what the sentence is about.

A simple subject is the main noun or pronoun in the subject. **(*Babies* crawl.)**

A complete subject includes the simple subject and any words that modify it. **(*The man from New Jersey* won the race.)** In some sentences, the simple subject and the complete subject are the same. **(*Birds* fly.)**

Personal Pronouns			
Clause	**Singular Pronouns**	**Plural Pronouns**	**Function in Sentence**
Nominative	I, you, she, he, it	we, you, they	subject or predicate nominative
Objective	me, you, her, him, it	us, you, them	direct object, indirect object, or object of a preposition

Types of Sentences			
Sentence Type	**Function**	**Ends with . . .**	**Examples**
Declarative sentence	Makes a statement	A period	I did not enjoy the movie.
Exclamatory sentence	Expresses strong emotion	*An exclamation point*	*What a good writer Consuela is!*
Imperative sentence	Makes a request or gives a command	A period or an exclamation point	*Please come to the party. Stop!*
Interrogative sentence	Asks a question	*A question mark*	*Is the composition due?*

A compound subject has two or more simple subjects joined by a conjunction. The subjects share the same verb. (***Firefighters* and *police officers* protect the community.**)

Subjunctive mood. *See* Mood of verb.

Subordinate clause. *See* Clause.

Subordinating conjunction. *See* Conjunction.

Superlative degree. *See* Adjective; Adverb.

T

Tense. *See* Verb tense.

Transitive verb. *See* Verb.

V

Verb A word that expresses action or a state of being. ***(cooks, seem, laughed)***

An action verb tells what someone or something does. Action verbs can express either physical or mental action. (**Crystal *decided* to *change* the tire herself.**)

A transitive verb is an action verb that is followed by a word or words that answer the question *What?* or *Whom?* (**I *held* the baby.**)

An intransitive verb is an action verb that is not followed by a word that answers the question *What?* or *Whom?* (**The baby *laughed.***)

A linking verb expresses a state of being by linking the subject of a sentence with a word or an expression that identifies or describes the subject. (**The lemonade *tastes* sweet. He *is* our new principal.**) The most commonly used linking verb is be in all its forms ***(am, is, are, was, were, will be, been, being).*** Other linking verbs include *appear, become, feel, grow, look, remain, seem, sound, smell, stay, taste.*

An auxiliary verb, or helping verb, is a verb that accompanies the main verb to form a verb phrase. (**I *have been* swimming.**) The forms of *be* and *have* are the most common auxiliary verbs: ***(am, is, are, was, were, being, been; has, have, had, having).*** Other auxiliaries include *can, could, do, does, did, may, might, must, shall, should, will, would.*

Verbal A verb form that functions in a sentence as a noun, an adjective, or an adverb. The three kinds of verbals are gerunds, infinitives, and participles. *See* Gerund; Infinitive; Participle.

Verb tense The tense of a verb indicates when the action or state of being occurs. All the verb tenses are formed from the four principal parts of a verb: a base form ***(talk),*** a present participle ***(talking),*** a simple past form ***(talked),*** and a past participle ***(talked).*** A regular verb forms its simple past and past participle by adding *-ed* to the base form. ***(climb, climbed)*** An irregular verb forms its past and past participle in some other way. ***(get, got, gotten)***

In addition to present, past, and future tenses, there are three perfect tenses.

The present perfect tense expresses an action or a condition that occurred at some indefinite time in the past. This tense also shows an action or a condition that began in the past and continues into the present. (**She *has played* the piano for four years.**)

The past perfect tense indicates that one past action or condition began *and* ended before another past action started. (**Andy *had finished* his homework before I even began mine.**)

The future perfect tense indicates that one future action or condition will begin *and* end before another future event starts. Use *will have* or *shall have* with the past participle of a verb. (**By tomorrow, I *will have finished* my homework, too.**)

The progressive form of a verb expresses a continuing action with any of the six tenses. To make the progressive forms, use the appropriate tense of the verb *be* with the present participle of the main verb. (**She *is swimming.* She *has been swimming.***)

The emphatic form adds special force, or emphasis, to the present and past tense of a verb. For the emphatic form, use *do, does,* or *did* with the base form. (**Toshi *did want* that camera.**)

Voice The voice of a verb shows whether the subject performs the action or receives the action of the verb.

A verb is in the active voice if the subject of the sentence performs the action. (**The referee *blew* the whistle.**)

A verb is in the passive voice if the subject of the sentence receives the action of the verb. (**The whistle *was blown* by the referee.**)

Troubleshooter

The Troubleshooter will help you recognize and correct errors that you might make in your writing.

Sentence Fragment

Problem: A fragment that lacks a subject

The grass is wet. Can't be mowed now.

Solution: Add a subject to the fragment to make it a complete sentence.

The grass is wet. It can't be mowed now.

Problem: A fragment that lacks a complete verb

We enjoyed our dinner. Beans, rice, and salad.
The storm was fierce. The wind blowing hard.

Solution A: Add either a complete verb or a helping verb to make the sentence complete.

We enjoyed our dinner. Beans, rice, and salad make a good meal.
The storm was fierce. The wind was blowing hard.

Solution B: Combine the fragment with another sentence.

We enjoyed our dinner of beans, rice, and salad.
The storm was fierce with the wind blowing hard.

Problem: A fragment that is a subordinate clause

We went to the park. Where we had often gone before.
Jan won the swimming medal. Which she gave to her parents.

Solution A: Combine the fragment with another sentence.

We went to the park, where we had often gone before.
Jan won the swimming medal, which she gave to her parents.

Solution B: Rewrite the fragment as a complete sentence, eliminating the subordinating conjunction or the relative pronoun and adding a subject or other words necessary to make a complete thought.

We went to the park. We had often gone there before.
Jan won the swimming medal. She gave it to her parents.

Problem: A fragment that lacks both a subject and a verb

The birds woke us with their songs. At six in the morning.

Solution: Combine the fragment with another sentence.

The birds woke us with their songs at six in the morning.

Rule of Thumb: Sentence fragments can make your writing hard to understand. Make sure every sentence has a subject and a verb.

Note: In almost all of the writing you do, especially for school, you should avoid sentence fragments. However, sentence fragments can be used to create special effects, such as adding emphasis or conveying realistic dialogue.

"Not again!" she cried.
The pizza was gone. All of it.

Run-On Sentence

Problem: Comma splice—two main clauses separated only by a comma

The sky is pitch black, there is no moon.

Solution A: Replace the comma with an end mark of punctuation, such as a period or a question mark, and begin the new sentence with a capital letter.

The sky is pitch black. There is no moon.

Solution B: Place a semicolon between the two main clauses.

The sky is pitch black; there is no moon.

Solution C: Add a coordinating conjunction after the comma.

The sky is pitch black, and there is no moon.

Problem: Two main clauses with no punctuation between them.

We picked the apples then we made pies.

Solution A: Separate the main clauses with an end mark of punctuation, such as a period or question mark, and begin the second sentence with a capital letter.

We picked the apples. Then we made pies.

Solution B: Separate the main clauses with a semicolon.

We picked the apples; then we made pies.

Solution C: Add a comma and a coordinating conjunction between the main clauses.

We picked the apples, and then we made pies.

Problem: The main clauses with no comma before the coordinating conjunction

Elephants still live in the wild but they are endangered.

Solution: Add a comma before the coordinating conjunction to separate the two main clauses.

Elephants still live in the wild, but they are endangered.

Rule of Thumb: It often helps to have someone else read your longer sentences to see if they are clear. Since you know what the sentences are supposed to mean, you might miss the need for punctuation.

Lack of Subject-Verb Agreement

Problem: A subject that is separated from the verb by an intervening prepositional phrase

Ten pieces of the puzzle is on the floor.
The shoe department in each of our stores are closing.

Solution: Make the verb agree with the subject, which is never the object of a preposition.

Ten pieces of the puzzle are on the floor.
The shoe department in each of our stores is closing.

Problem: A predicate nominative that differs in number from the subject

Hamburgers is tonight's dinner.
Tonight's dinner are hamburgers.

Solution: Ignore the predicate nominative, and make the verb agree with the subject of the sentence.

Hamburgers are tonight's dinner.
Tonight's dinner is hamburgers.

Problem: A subject that follows the verb

On my desk is two letters from my dad.
Here is my answers to them both.

Solution: In an inverted sentence look for the subject after the verb. Then make sure the verb agrees with the subject.

On my desk are two letters from my dad.
Here are my answers to them both.

Rule of Thumb: Reversing the order of an inverted sentence may help you decide on the verb form to use: "My answers to them both are here."

Problem: A collective noun as the subject

The cross country team are in first place.
The team gathers at the captain's house after each meet.

Solution A: If the collective noun refers to a group as a whole, use a singular verb.

The cross country team is in first place.

Solution B: If the collective noun refers to each member of a group individually, use a plural verb.

The team gather at the captain's house after each meet.

Problem: A noun of amount as the subject

Five bushels are a great many tomatoes.
Three marbles is in my pocket.

Solution: Determine whether the noun of amount refers to one unit and is therefore singular or whether it refers to a number of individual unites and is therefore plural.

Five bushels is a great many tomatoes.
Three marbles are in my pocket.

Problem: A compound subject that is joined by *and*

The hill and the lake makes a lovely setting for a picnic.
Spaghetti and meatballs are her favorite dinner.

Solution A: If the parts of the compound subject do not belong to one unit or if they refer to different people of things, use a plural verb.

The hill and the lake make a lovely setting for a picnic.

Solution B: If the parts of the compound subject belong to one unit or if both parts refer to the same person or thing, use a singular verb.

Spaghetti and meatballs is her favorite dinner.

Problem: A compound subject that is joined by *or* or *nor*

Neither those trees nor that shrub are healthy.

Solution: Make the verb agree with the subject that is closer to it.

Neither those trees nor that shrub is healthy.

Problem: **A compound subject that is preceded by *many a, every,* or *each***
Many a dog and cat ends up in an animal shelter or a pound.

Solution: When *many a, every,* or *each* precedes a compound subject, the subject is considered singular. Use a singular verb.
Many a dog and cat ends up in an animal shelter or a pound.

Problem: **A subject that is separated from the verb by an intervening expression**
That issue, as well as several others, are bothering me.

Solution: Certain expressions, such as these beginning with *as well as, in addition to,* and *together with,* do not change the number of the subject. Ignore an intervening expression between a subject and its verb, and make the verb agree with the subject.
That issue, along with several others, is bothering me.

Problem: **An indefinite pronoun as the subject**
Neither of the boys are on time.

Solution: Determine whether the indefinite pronoun is singular or plural, and make the verb agree. Some indefinite pronouns are singular—*another, anyone, everyone, one, each, either, neither, anything, everything, something,* and *somebody.* Some are plural—*both, many, few, several,* and *others.* Some can be singular or plural—*some, all, any, more, most,* and *none.* In these cases, find the noun to which the pronoun refers to determine which verb form to use.
Neither of the boys is on time.

Lack of Pronoun-Antecedent Agreement

Problem: **A singular antecedent that can be either male or female.**
A climber must check his equipment carefully.

Solution A: Traditionally, a masculine pronoun has been used to refer to an antecedent that may be either male or female. This usage ignores or excludes females. Reword the sentence to use *he or she, him or her,* and so on.
A climber must check his or her equipment carefully.

Solution B: Reword the sentence so that both the antecedent and the pronoun are plural.
Climbers must check their equipment carefully.

Solution C: Reword the sentence to eliminate the pronoun.
A climber must check the equipment carefully.

Rule of Thumb: Although you may see the masculine forms used exclusively in older literature, they are not acceptable in contemporary writing.

Problem: **A second-person pronoun that refers to a third-person antecedent**
Juan likes sitcoms that make you think as well as laugh.

Solution A: Use the appropriate third-person pronoun.
Juan likes sitcoms that make him think as well as laugh.

Solution B: Use an appropriate noun instead of a pronoun.
Juan likes sitcoms that make people think as well as laugh.

Problem: **A singular indefinite pronoun as an antecedent**
Each of the volumes has their own index.

Solution: *Each, every, either, neither,* and *one* are singular and therefore require singular personal pronouns even when followed by a prepositional phrase that contains a plural noun.
Each of the volumes has its own index.

Rule of Thumb: To help you remember that *each, either,* and *neither* are singular, think *each one, either one,* and *neither one.*

Lack of Clear Pronoun Reference [Unclear Antecedent]

Problem: **A pronoun reference that is weak or vague**
We spent several weeks at the farm this summer, and it was exciting.
The label says to shake it before pouring a serving.

Solution A: Rewrite the sentence, adding a clear antecedent for the pronoun.
We spent our vacation at the farm this summer, and it was exciting.

Solution B: Rewrite the sentence, substituting a noun for the pronoun.
The label says to shake the bottle of salad dressing before pouring a serving.

Problem: A pronoun that could refer to more than one antecedent
Lauren and Abby wrote six songs, and she recorded them all.
Don't buy a car from that dealership: it will let you down.

Solution A: Rewrite the sentence, substituting a noun for the pronoun.
Lauren and Abby wrote six songs, and Abby recorded them all.

Solution B: Rewrite the sentence, making the antecedent of the pronoun clear.
A car from that dealership will let you down; don't buy one there.

Problem: The indefinite use of *you* or *they*
You just have to laugh at that scene in the movie.
They say the weather will be clear tomorrow.

Solution A: Rewrite the sentence, substituting a noun for the pronoun.
The audience just has to laugh at that scene in the movie.

Solution B: Rewrite the sentence, eliminating the pronoun entirely.
According to the forecast, the weather will be clear tomorrow.

Shift in Pronoun

Problem: An incorrect shift in person between two pronouns
Lynn likes the front seat, where you are most comfortable.
The Chins planted a maple on the south side of the house, where you need shade the most.

Solution A: Replace the incorrect pronoun with a pronoun that agrees with its a antecedent.
Lynn likes the front seat, where she is most comfortable.

Solution B: Replace the incorrect pronoun with an appropriate noun.
The Chins plants a maple on the south side of the house, where the house needs shade the most.

Shift in Verb Tense

Problem: An unnecessary shift in tense.
The children will give their mother flowers, and they kiss her.
After the party ended, we go home.

Solution: When two or more events occur at the same time, be sure to use the same verb tense to describe each event.
The children will give their mother flowers, and they will kiss her.
After the party ended, we went home.

Problem: A lack of correct shift in tenses to show that one event precedes or follows another
By the time the concert ended, we sat for four hours.

Solution: When two past events being described have occurred at different times, shift from the past tense to the past perfect tense to indicate that one action began and ended before another past action began. Use the past perfect tense for the earlier of the two actions.
By the time the concert ended, we had sat for four hours.

Rule of Thumb: When you need to use several verb tenses in your writing, it may help to first jot down the sequence of events you're writing about. Be clear in your mind what happened first, next, last.

Incorrect Verb Tense or Form

Problem: An incorrect or missing verb ending
When I began taking lessons, I learn about quarter, half, and whole notes.
I had start the lessons two months ago.

Solution: Add –ed to a regular verb to form the past tense and the past participle.
When I began taking lessons, I learned about quarter, half, and whole notes.
I had started the lessons two months ago.

Problem: An improperly formed irregular verb
James brung the book back to the library.
Catherine has writed six pages on that topic.

Solution: Irregular verbs form their past and past participles in some way other than by adding –ed. Memorize these forms, or look them up.
James brought the book back to the library.
Catherine has written six pages on that topic.

Problem: Confusion between the past form and the past participle
We have ate too many apples.
She had swam the Chesapeake last July.

Solution: Use the past participle form of an irregular verb, not the past form, when you use the auxiliary verb *have*.
We have eaten too many apples.
She had swum the Chesapeake last July.

Problem: Improper use of the past participle
The catcher thrown several runners out.
The DiCaprios done a fine job rearing those children.

Solution A: The past participle of an irregular verb cannot stand alone as a verb. Add a form of the auxiliary verb *have* to the past participle to form a complete verb.
The catcher had thrown several runners out.
The DiCaprios have done a fine job rearing those children.

Solution B: Replace the past participle with the past form of the verb.
The catcher threw several runners out.
The DiCaprios did a fine job rearing those children.

Misplaced or Dangling Modifier

Problem: A misplaced modifier
The children were swimming in the photograph.
Swooping down on a fish, I spotted the gull.
I saw a man at the movies eating popcorn.

Solution: Modifiers that modify the wrong word or seem to modify more than own word in a sentence are called misplaced modifiers. Move the misplaced phrase as close as possible to the word or words it modifies.
The children in the photograph were swimming.
I spotted the gull swooping down on a fish.
I saw a man eating popcorn at the movies.

Problem: Incorrect placement of the adverb *only*
Tricia only has enough money to buy a pencil.

Solution: Place the adverb only immediately before the word or group of words it modifies.
Only Tricia has enough money to buy a pencil.
Tricia has enough money to buy only a pencil.
Tricia has only enough money to buy a pencil.

Rule of Thumb: Note that each time *only* is moved, the meaning of the sentence changes. Check to be sure your sentence says what you mean.

Problem: A dangling modifier
Croaking loudly, I listened to the sounds of the frogs in the bog.
Stealing home, the game was won for the Pirates.

Solution: Dangling modifiers do not seem to logically modify any word in the sentence. Rewrite the sentence, adding a noun to which the dangling phrase clearly refers. Often you will have to add other words too.
I listened to the sounds of the frogs croaking loudly in the bog.
Stealing home, Layla won the game for the Pirates.

Missing or Misplaced Possessive Apostrophe

Problem: Singular nouns
The womans child loved the circus trapeze artists.

Solution: Use an apostrophe and –s to form the possessive of a singular noun, even one that ends in *s*.
The woman's child loved the circus's trapeze artist.

Problem: Plural nouns ending in – s
The hikers cars were parked at the base of the trail.

Solution: Use an apostrophe alone to form the possessive of a plural noun that ends in –s.
The hikers' cars were parked at the base of the trail.

Problem: Plural nouns not ending in –s
Did Brian join the mens group?

Solution: Use an apostrophe and –s to form the possessive of a plural noun that does not end in –s.
Did Brian join the men's group?

Problem: Pronouns
Everyones contribution helps.
These pencils are your's, and those pencils are their's.

Solution A: Use an apostrophe and –s to form the possessive of a singular indefinite pronoun.
Everyone's contribution helps.

Solution B: Do not use an apostrophe with any of the possessive personal pronouns.
These pencils are yours, and those pencils are theirs.

Problem: Confusion between *its* and *it's*
Will you tell me when its ten o'clock?
The cat licked it's fur.

Solution: Do not use an apostrophe to form the possessive of *it.* Use an apostrophe to form the contraction of *it is.*
Will you tell me when it's ten o'clock?
The cat licked its fur.

Missing Commas with Nonessential Element

Problem: Missing commas with nonessential participles, infinitives, and their phrases
Pounding hard on the roof the rain awakened me.
The whole set of cups chipped from many years of use was discarded.
To answer you question this software package is worth the price.

Solution: Determine whether the participle, infinitive, or phrase is essential to the meaning of the sentence. If it is not essential, set off the phrase with commas.
Pounding hard on the roof, the rain awakened me.
The whole set of cups, chipped from many years of use, was discarded.
To answer your question, this software package is worth the price.

Problem: Missing commas with nonessential adjective clauses
My mother who is a very generous woman gave us investment tips.

Solution: Determine whether the clause is essential to the meaning of the sentence. If it is not essential, set off the clause with commas.
My mother, who is a very generous woman, gave us investment tips.

Problem: Missing comas with nonessential appositives
John the lead-off batter singles on a line drive

Solution: Determine whether the appositive is essential to the meaning of the sentence. If it is not essential, set off the appositive with commas.
John, the lead-off batter, singled on a line drive.

Rule of Thumb: To determine whether a word or phrase is essential, try reading the sentence without it.

Problem: Missing commas with interjections and parenthetical expressions
Wow what a great cat that is
On Saturdays as a rule we sleep late.

Solution: Set off the interjection or parenthetical expression with commas.
Wow, what a great cat that is!
On Saturdays, as a rule, we sleep late.

Missing Commas in a Series

Problem: Missing commas in a series of words, phrases, or clauses
Alicia Nirupam and Matt made the honor roll.
Mark made the dough kneaded it and left it to rise
The firefighter carries the child out of the apartment down the stairs and into the arms of her mother.
Joe pitched the tent Meg gathered firewood and Bud unloaded the truck.

Solution: When there are three or more elements in a series, use a comma after each element that precedes the conjunction
Alicia, Nirupam, and Matt made the honor roll.
Mark made the dough, kneaded it, and left it to rise.
The firefighter carries the child out of the apartment, down the stairs, and into the arms of her mother.
Joe pitched the tent, Meg gathered firewood, and Bud unloaded the truck.

Rule of Thumb: When you're having difficulty with a rule of usage, try rewriting the rule in your own words. Then check with your teacher to be sure you have grasped the concept.

Mechanics

This section will help you use correct capitalization, punctuation, and abbreviations in your writing.

Capitalization

This section will help you recognize and use correct capitalization in sentences.

Rule: Capitalize the first word in any sentence, including direct quotations and sentences in parentheses unless they are included in another sentence.

Example: *She said, "Come back soon."*

Example: *Emily Dickinson became famous only after her death. (She published only six poems during her lifetime.)*

Rule: Always capitalize the pronoun ***I*** no matter where it appears in the sentence.

Example: *Some of my relatives think that I should become a doctor.*

Rule: Capitalize proper nouns, including

a. names of individuals and titles used in direct address preceding a name or describing a relationship.
Example: *George Washington; Dr. Morgan; Aunt Margaret*

b. names of ethnic groups, national groups, political parties and their members, and languages.
Example: *Italian Americans; Aztec; the Republican Party; a Democrat; Spanish*

c. names of organizations, institutions, firms, monuments, bridges, buildings, and other structures.
Example: *Red Cross; Stanford University; General Electric; Lincoln Memorial; Tappan Zee Bridge; Chrysler Building; Museum of Natural History*

d. trade names and names of documents, awards, and laws.
Example: *Microsoft; Declaration of Independence; Pulitzer Prize; Sixteenth Amendment*

e. geographical terms and regions or localities.
Example: *Hudson River; Pennsylvania Avenue; Grand Canyon; Texas; the Midwest*

f. names of planets and other heavenly bodies.
Example: *Venus; Earth; the Milky Way*

g. names of ships, planes, trains, and spacecraft.
Example: *USS* Constitution; Spirit of St. Louis; Apollo 11

h. names of most historical events, eras, calendar items, and religious names and items.
Example: *World War II; Age of Enlightenment; June; Christianity; Buddhists; Bible; Easter; God*

i. titles of literary works, works of art, and musical compositions.
Example: *"Why I Live at the P.O.";* The Starry Night; Rhapsody in Blue

j. names of specific school courses.
Example: *Advanced Physics; American History*

Rule: Capitalize proper adjectives (adjectives formed from proper nouns).

Example: *Christmas tree; Hanukkah candles; Freudian psychology; American flag*

Punctuation

This section will help you use these elements of punctuation correctly.

Rule: Use a period at the end of a declarative sentence or a polite command.

Example: *I'm thirsty.*
Example: *Please bring me a glass of water.*

Rule: Use an exclamation point to show strong feeling or after a forceful command.

Example: *I can't believe my eyes!*
Example: *Watch your step!*

Rule: Use a question mark to indicate a direct question.

Example: *Who is in charge here?*

Rule: Use a colon

a. to introduce a list (especially after words such as these, the following, or as follows) and to introduce material that explains, restates, or illustrates previous material.

Example: *The following states voted for the amendment: Texas, California, Georgia, and Florida.*
Example: *The sunset was colorful: purple, orange, and red lit up the sky.*

b. to introduce a long or formal quotation.
Example: *It was Mark Twain who stated the following proverb: "Man is the only animal that blushes. Or needs to."*

c. in precise time measurements, biblical chapter and verse references, and business letter salutations.

Example:	*3:35 P.M.*	*7:50 A.M.*
	Gen. 1:10–11	*Matt. 2:23*
	Dear Ms. Samuels:	*Dear Sir:*

Rule: Use a semicolon
a. to separate main clauses that are not joined by a coordinating conjunction.
Example: *There were two speakers at Gettysburg that day; only Lincoln's speech is remembered.*

b. to separate main clauses joined by a conjunctive adverb or by *for example* or *that is.*
Example: *Because of the ice storm, most students could not get to school; consequently, the principal canceled all classes for the day.*

c. to separate the items in a series when these items contain commas.
Example: *The students at the rally came from Senn High School, in Chicago, Illinois; Niles Township High School, in Skokie, Illinois; and Evanston Township High School, in Evanston, Illinois.*

d. to separate two main clauses joined by a coordinating conjunction when such clauses already contain several commas.
Example: *The designer combined the blue silk, brown linen, and beige cotton into a suit; but she decided to use the yellow chiffon, yellow silk, and white lace for an evening gown.*

Rule: Use a comma
a. between the main clauses of a compound sentence.
Example: *Ryan was late getting to study hall, and his footsteps echoed in the empty corridor.*

b. to separate three or more words, phrases, or clauses in a series.
Example: *Mel bought carrots, beans, pears, and onions.*

c. between coordinate modifiers.
Example: *That is a lyrical, moving poem.*

d. to set off parenthetical expressions, interjections, and conjunctive adverbs.
Example: *Well, we missed the bus again.*
Example: *The weather is beautiful today; however, it is supposed to rain this weekend.*

e. to set off nonessential words, clauses, and phrases, such as:

—**adverbial clauses**

Example: *Since Ellen is so tall, the coach assumed she would be a good basketball player.*

—**adjective clauses**

Example: *Scott, who had been sleeping, finally woke up.*

—**participles and participial phrases**

Example: *Having found what he was looking for, he left.*

—**prepositional phrases**

Example: *On Saturdays during the fall, I rake leaves.*

—**infinitive phrases**

Example: *To be honest, I'd like to stay awhile longer.*

—**appositives and appositive phrases**

Example: *Ms. Kwan, a soft-spoken woman, ran into the street to hail a cab.*

f. to set off direct quotations.
Example: *"My concert," Molly replied, "is tonight."*

g. to set off an antithetical phrase.
Example: *Unlike Tom, Rob enjoys skiing.*

h. to set off a title after a person's name.
Example: *Margaret Thomas, Ph.D., was the guest speaker.*

i. to separate the various parts of an address, a geographical term, or a date.
Example: *My new address is 324 Indian School Road, Albuquerque, New Mexico 85350.*

I moved on March 13, 1998.

j. after the salutation of an informal letter and after the closing of all letters.
Example: *Dear Helen,*   *Sincerely,*

k. to set off parts of a reference that direct the reader to the exact source.
Example: *You can find the article in the* Washington Post, *April 4, 1997, pages 33–34.*

l. to set off words or names used in direct address and in tag questions.
Example: *Yuri, will you bring me my calculator?*
Lottie became a lawyer, didn't she?

Rule: Use a dash to signal a change in thought or to emphasize parenthetical material.

Example: *During the play, Maureen—and she'd be the first to admit it—forgot her lines.*

Example: *There are only two juniors attending—Mike Ramos and Ron Kim.*

Rule: Use parentheses to set off supplemental material. Punctuate within the parentheses only if the punctuation is part of the parenthetical expression.

Example: *If you like jazz (and I assume you do), you will like this CD. (The soloist is Miles Davis.)*
Example: *The upper Midwest (which states does that include?) was hit by terrible floods last year.*

Rule: Use brackets to enclose information that you insert into a quotation for clarity or to enclose a parenthetical phrase that already appears within parentheses.

Example: *"He serves his [political] party best who serves the country best."—Rutherford B. Hayes*
Example: *The staircase (which was designed by a famous architect [Frank Lloyd Wright]) was inlaid with ceramic tile.*

Rule: Use ellipsis points to indicate the omission of material from a quotation.

Example: *". . . Neither an individual nor a nation can commit the least act of injustice against the obscurest individual. . . ." —Henry David Thoreau*

Rule: Use quotation marks
a. to enclose a direct quotation, as follows:
Example: *"Hurry up!" shouted Lisa.*

When a quotation is interrupted, use two sets of quotation marks.

Example: *"A cynic," wrote Oscar Wilde, "is someone who knows the price of everything and the value of nothing."*

Use single quotation marks for a quotation within a quotation.

Example: *"Did you say 'turn left' or 'turn right'?" asked Leon.*

In writing dialogue, begin a new paragraph and use a new set of quotation marks every time the speaker changes.

Example: *"Do you really think the spaceship can take off?" asked the first officer.*
"Our engineer assures me that we have enough power," the captain replied.

b. o enclose titles of short works, such as stories, poems, essays, articles, chapters, and songs.
Example: *"The Lottery" [short story]*
"Provide, Provide" [poem]
"Civil Disobedience" [essay]

c. to enclose unfamiliar slang terms and unusual expressions.
Example: *The man called his grandson a "rapscallion."*

d. to enclose a definition that is stated directly.
Example: Gauche *is a French word meaning "left."*

Rule: Use italics
a. for titles of books, lengthy poems, plays, films, television series, paintings and sculptures, long musical compositions, court cases, names of newspapers and magazines, ships, trains, airplanes, and spacecraft. Italicize and capitalize articles *(a, an, the)* at the beginning of a title only when they are part of the title.
Example: E.T. *[film];* The Piano Lesson *[play]*
The Starry Night *[painting]*
the New Yorker *[magazine]*
Challenger *[spacecraft]*
The Great Gatsby *[book]*
the Chicago Tribune *[newspaper]*

b. for foreign words and expressions that are not used frequently in English.
Example: *Luciano waved good-bye, saying, "Arrivederci."*

c. for words, letters, and numerals used to represent themselves.
Example: *There is no* Q *on the telephone keypad.*
Example: *Number your paper from* 1 *through* 10.

Rule: Use an apostrophe

a. for a possessive form, as follows:

Add an apostrophe and *s* to all singular nouns, plural nouns not ending in *s*, singular indefinite pronouns, and compound nouns. Add only an apostrophe to a plural noun that ends in *s*.

Example: *the tree's leaves*
the man's belt
the bus's tires
the children's pets
everyone's favorite
my mother-in-law's job
the attorney general's decision
the baseball player's error
the cats' bowls

If two or more persons possess something jointly, use the possessive form for the last person named. If they possess it individually, use the possessive form for each one's name.

Example: *Ted and Harriet's family*
Ted's and Harriet's bosses
Lewis and Clark's expedition
Lewis's and Clark's clothes

b. to express amounts of money or time that modify a noun.

Example: *two cents' worth*
Example: *three days' drive (You can use a hyphenated adjective instead: a three-day drive.)*

c. in place of omitted letters or numerals.

Example: *haven't [have not]* *the winter of '95*

d. to form the plural of letters, numerals, symbols, and words used to represent themselves. Use an apostrophe and *s*.

Example: *You wrote two 5's instead of one.*
Example: *How many s's are there in Mississippi?*
Example: *Why did he use three !'s at the end of the sentence?*

Rule: Use a hyphen

a. after any prefix joined to a proper noun or proper adjective.

Example: *all-American* *pre-Columbian*

b. after the prefixes *all-*, *ex-*, and *self-* joined to any noun or adjective, after the prefix *anti-* when it joins a word beginning with *i*, after the prefix *vice-* (except in some instances such as *vice president*), and to avoid confusion between words that begin with *re-* and look like another word.

Example: *ex-president*
self-important
anti-inflammatory
vice-principal
re-creation of the event
recreation time
re-pair the socks
repair the computer

c. in a compound adjective that precedes a noun.

Example: *a bitter-tasting liquid*

d. in any spelled-out cardinal or ordinal numbers up to *ninety-nine* or *ninety-ninth*, and with a fraction used as an adjective.

Example: *twenty-three* *eighty-fifth*
one-half cup

e. to divide a word at the end of a line between syllables.

Example: *air-port* *scis-sors*
fill-ing *fin-est*

Abbreviations

Abbreviations are shortened forms of words.

Rule: Use only one period if an abbreviation occurs at the end of a sentence. If the sentence ends with a question mark or an exclamation point, use the period and the second mark of punctuation.

Example: *We didn't get home until 3:30 A.M.*
Example: *Did you get home before 4:00 A.M.?*
Example: *I can't believe you didn't get home until 3:30 A.M.!*

Rule: Capitalize abbreviations of proper nouns and abbreviations related to historical dates.

Example: *John Kennedy Jr.* *P.O. Box 333*
800 B.C. *A.D. 456* *1066 C.E.*

Use all capital letters and no periods for most abbreviations of organizations and government agencies.

Example: *CBS* *CIA* *PIN*
CPA *IBM* *NFL*
MADD *GE* *FBI*

Spelling

The following basic rules, examples, and exceptions will help you master the spellings of many words.

Forming plurals

English words form plurals in many ways. Most nouns simply add *s.* The following chart shows other ways of forming plural nouns and some common exceptions to the pattern.

General Rules for Forming Plurals		
if the word ends in	**Rule**	**Example**
ch, s, sh, x, z	add *es*	glass, glasses
a consonant + *y*	change *y* to *i* and add *es*	caddy, caddies
a vowel + *y* or *o*	add only *s*	cameo, cameos monkey, monkeys
a consonant + *o* common exceptions	generally add *es* but sometimes add only *s*	potato, potatoes cello, cellos
f or *ff* common exceptions	add *s* change *f* to *v* and add *es*	cliff, cliffs hoof, hooves
lf	change *f* to *v* and add *es*	half, halves

A few plurals are exceptions to the rules in the previous chart, but they are easy to remember. The following chart lists these plurals and some examples.

Special Rules for Forming Plurals	
Rule	**Example**
To form the plural of most proper names and one-word compound nouns, follow the general rules for plurals.	Cruz, Cruzes Mancuso, Mancusos crossroad, crossroads
To form the plural of hyphenated compound nouns or compound nouns of more than one word, make the most important word plural.	sister-in-law, sisters-in-law motion picture, motion pictures
Some nouns have unusual plural forms.	goose, geese child, children
Some nouns have the same singular and plural forms.	moose scissors pants

Adding prefixes

When adding a prefix to a word, keep the original spelling of the word. Use a hyphen only when the original word is capitalized or with prefixes such as *all-*, *ex-*, and *self-* joined to a noun or adjective.

co + operative = cooperative
inter + change = interchange
pro + African = pro-African
ex + partner = ex-partner

Suffixes and the silent *e*

Many English words end in a silent letter *e*. Sometimes the *e* is dropped when a suffix is added. When adding a suffix that begins with a consonant to a word that ends in silent *e*, keep the *e*.

like + ness = likenesssure + ly = surely
COMMON EXCEPTIONS awe + ful = awful;
judge + ment = judgment

When adding a suffix that begins with a vowel to a word that ends in silent *e*, usually drop the *e*.

believe + able = believable
expense + ive = expensive
COMMON EXCEPTION mile + age = mileage

When adding a suffix that begins with *a* or *o* to a word that ends in *ce* or *ge*, keep the *e* so the word will retain the soft *c* or *g* sound.

notice + able = noticeable
courage + ous = courageous

When adding a suffix that begins with a vowel to a word that ends in *ee* or *oe*, keep the final *e*.

see + ing = seeing   toe + ing = toeing

Drop the final silent *e* after the letters *u* or *w*.

argue + ment = argument
owe + ing = owing

Keep the final silent *e* before the suffix *-ing* when necessary to avoid ambiguity.

singe + ing = singeing

Suffixes and the final *y*

When adding a suffix to a word that ends in a consonant + *y*, change the *y* to *i* unless the suffix begins with *i*. Keep the *y* in a word that ends in a vowel + *y*.

try + ed = tried   fry + ed = fried
stay + ing = staying   display + ed = displayed
copy + ing = copying joy + ous = joyous

Adding *ly* and *ness*

When adding *ly* to a word that ends in a single *l*, keep the *l*, but when the word ends in a double *l*, drop one *l*. When the word ends in a consonant + *le*, drop the *le*. When adding -ness to a word that ends in *n*, keep the *n*.

casual + ly = casually
practical + ly = practically
dull + ly = dully
probable + ly = probably
open + ness = openness
mean + ness = meanness

Doubling the final consonant

Double the final consonant in words that end in a consonant preceded by a single vowel if the word is one syllable, if it has an accent on the last syllable that remains there even after the suffix is added, or if it is a word made up of a prefix and a one-syllable word.

stop + ing = stopping
admit + ed = admitted
replan + ed = replanned

Do not double the final consonant if the accent is not on the last syllable, or if the accent shifts when the suffix is added. Also do not double the final consonant if the final consonant is *x* or *w*. If the word ends in a consonant and the suffix begins with a consonant, do not double the final consonant.

benefit + ed = benefited
similar + ly = similarly
raw + er = rawer
box + like = boxlike
friend + less = friendless
rest + ful = restful

Forming Compound Words

When joining a word that ends in a consonant to a word that begins with a consonant, keep both consonants.

> out + line = outline
> after + noon = afternoon
> post + card = postcard
> pepper + mint = peppermint

ie and *ei*

Learning this rhyme can save you many misspellings: "Write *i* before *e* except after *c,* or when sounded like *a* as in *neighbor* and *weigh.*" There are many exceptions to this rule, including *seize, seizure, leisure, weird, height, either, neither, forfeit.*

-cede, -ceed, and *-sede*

Because of the relatively few words with *sēd* sounds, these words are worth memorizing.

> These words use *-cede:* **accede, precede, secede.**
> One word uses *-sede:* **supersede.**
> Three words use *-ceed:* **exceed, proceed, succeed.**

Logic and Persuasion Handbook

Persuasion

Propositions

One of the main reasons people write and talk is to persuade each other. Persuasive writing and speaking attempts to convince someone of the truth of a **proposition,** that is, a statement or claim. There are four basic types of proposition:

- A proposition of **fact** is a claim that certain information is correct.
  Candidate Wilkins comes from Illinois.
- A proposition of **value** is a statement that a feeling or judgment is valid.
  Candidate Wilkins is a friendly woman.
- A proposition about a **problem** combines fact and judgment.
  Candidate Wilkins is not qualified to run.
- A proposition of **policy** is a claim that someone should do something.
  Everyone should vote for candidate Wilkins.

A proposition may be **true** or **false.** In evaluating persuasive speaking and writing, you need to know which type of proposition is being made so that you can decide whether it is true or false.

Evidence and Arguments

Persuasive writing and speaking usually includes **evidence,** that is, reasons why someone should accept a proposition. Together, a proposition and a reason for accepting it make up an **argument.**

Everyone should vote for candidate Wilkins, because she is the most qualified.

An argument may be **valid** or **invalid,** that is, reasonable or unreasonable.

Appeals

Arguments are meant to appeal to certain beliefs, values, or feelings belonging to the reader or listener. Most reasons given in support of a proposition make at least one of four types of **appeal:**

- An **appeal to logic** is a claim based on fact and reason.
  Wilkins is unqualified, because she does not meet the age requirement.
- An **appeal to ethics or values** is a claim based on shared values or judgments.
  Wilkins is best, because she is the most honest and caring.
- An **appeal to authority** is a claim based on sources believed to be reliable.
  Wilkins is best, because the Metropolitan Bar Association supports her.
- An **appeal to emotion** is a claim based on shared feelings.
  Wilkins is best, because she has overcome hardship.

In evaluating arguments, you need to know which type of appeal is being made so that you can decide whether it is valid or invalid. Note that an argument may involve more than one type of appeal.

Exercise: Analyzing an Argument

Read the following statements. For each statement, identify the type of proposition made and the type of appeal used to support it..

1. If we want clean beaches, then we need to provide trash cans and arrange for garbage removal in the summer.
2. It is our responsibility as human beings to keep ocean ecosystems healthy by polluting them as little as possible or not at all.
3. According to eminent marine biologists, we have a lot to learn about the animals that live in the ocean depths.
4. Restricting owners of beachfront property from building wherever they want to on their property is highly unfair.

Statement	Proposition	Appeal
1	about a problem	
2		
3		
4		to ethics or values

Logic

Inductive Reasoning

Inductive reasoning involves putting facts together to come up with a generalized statement as a conclusion.

Specific facts:

Fact 1. *Star Wars* is the second-biggest money maker of all time.

Fact 2. The number one movie at the box office in 2004 was *Shrek 2.*

Fact 3. *Spider-man* broke many box office records in 2002.

Generalization: Science fiction and fantasy films do very well at the box office.

Errors In Inductive Reasoning

To avoid errors in inductive reasoning, be sure you use a large enough sample of specific facts, and of course, make sure your facts are accurate. Assuming you have a large enough sample of accurate facts, make sure that your generalization is logical.

For example, it would be illogical to conclude from the facts above that movies whose titles begin with the letter *S* do well at the box office.

Deductive Reasoning

Deductive reasoning is essentially the opposite of inductive reasoning. With deductive reasoning you start with a generalization to come to a conclusion about a specific case.

Generalization: Paul can only eat vegetarian food.

Specific fact: The Glory Diner offers vegetarian food.

Conclusion: Paul can eat at the Glory Diner.

Syllogisms

A syllogism is a formal statement of a deductive argument. It consists of a **major premise,** or general statement; a **minor premise,** or related fact; and a **conclusion** based on the two.

Major premise: People who travel between countries need a passport.

Minor premise: Jody is flying from the United States to Spain.

Conclusion: Jody needs a passport.

Errors In Deductive Reasoning

Errors in deductive reasoning result from faulty construction of the argument. Make sure the major premise is a universal statement, that both premises are true, and that the conclusion follows logically from the premises.

Note: A syllogism is *valid* if it follows the rules of deductive reasoning. A syllogism is *true* if the statements are factually accurate. Therefore, a perfectly valid syllogism can be untrue. For example:

Major premise: All voters are good citizens. [There is more to good citizenship than voting.]

Minor premise: My parents are voters.

Conclusion: Therefore, my parents are good citizens.

This conclusion is valid according to the premises; however, it isn't necessarily true because the major premise is flawed.

Exercise: Analyzing Logical Reasoning

For each argument below, identify whether inductive or deductive reasoning is used. Evaluate whether the conclusion is valid or invalid and explain your evaluation.

1. An epic poem is a serious, long narrative poem centered on the life of a cultural or national hero or heroine. *El Cid* is an epic poem. In more than 30,000 lines, it celebrates the life and accomplishments of a Spanish military and political leader who lived in the eleventh century.

2. If a computer can play compact discs, the computer must have been built before 1985. This computer can play CDs. This computer must have been built before 1985.

3. Many humorists use puns. Mark Twain used puns in his writing and his speeches. Ogden Nash used puns in his poems. Woody Allen uses puns in his movies.

Exercise: Using Logical Reasoning

Write a short essay arguing a proposition. In your argument, use at least two examples each of valid inductive and deductive reasoning.

Logical Fallacies

A **logical fallacy** is a particular type of faulty reasoning. Fallacies often seem reasonable at face value, so they are often used, both intentionally and unintentionally. Some fallacies are so common that they have names.

To identify fallacies in the writing and speaking of others and to avoid it in your own persuasive communication, you need to be able to identify fallacies and to understand why they are illogical.

- **Ad Hominem**
  Don't listen to what Smyth says about the election; he spent time in prison.
  An ad hominem argument (literally, an argument "against the person") implies that a defect in a person's character or behavior is evidence that what he says is unreliable. Note that the ad hominem fallacy contains a hidden premise: *People who have spent time in prison cannot have valid opinions.* Because this premise is untrue, the argument about Smyth is untrue also.
- **Non Sequitur or False Causality**
  This shirt is unlucky: every time I wear it, something bad happens.
  Non sequitur literally means "it doesn't follow." Just because two events occur together, it doesn't follow logically that one caused the other.
- **Glittering Generalities**
  If you love freedom, vote for Jack.
  Glittering generalities are words with overwhelmingly positive connotations, used to make it seem impossible to disagree with an idea. How can you argue against the idea of freedom? A listener's initial reaction to this statement might be, "Freedom is a good thing, so I must vote for Jack."
- **Overgeneralization and Stereotype**
  Tall people make excellent basketball players.
  An overgeneralization is any conclusion that may be accurate about a small group, but is inaccurate when applied to a much larger group. An overgeneralization about a group of people is called a stereotype.
- **Argument from Authority and Celebrity Endorsement**
  Four out of five doctors recommend Pumpidox for most heart conditions.
  Argument from authority is the quoting of an alleged expert on a certain topic. As a logical fallacy, arguments from authority rely solely on the mention of the word "expert," and give no clear facts from the expert. Companies often hire celebrities to appear in commercials for their products in the hope that audiences will respond to the likability of the famous person, even if that person has no real expert knowledge about the product.
- **The Bandwagon Effect**
  Choose America's favorite toothpaste!
  The term "jumping on the bandwagon" means doing or thinking something because everyone else is doing it or thinking it. This type of reasoning provides no evidence to support a decision or viewpoint.
- **Card Stacking**
  Senator Porter voted against childcare laws and recycling programs. It's time for new leadership!
  Card stacking involves piling on evidence that supports one side of an argument while ignoring or suppressing valid evidence supporting the other side. Saying that a politician voted against positive-sounding programs does not mean that he or she didn't have good reason to, or that the opposition has a better record.

Ethical Reasoning and Propaganda

Propaganda

Propaganda is the process of persuading by deliberately misleading or confusing an audience. Through the use of combinations of logical fallacies, propaganda can appeal to ethics or values, authority, or emotion, but they do so in a way that is unsupported or inappropriate.

Political propaganda

A vote for Marmelard is a vote for the enemy!

America: You're with us or against us!

Advertising

Be the best parent you can be: Serve your kids Super Goody cereal.

The most successful people shop at Blorland's Department Store.

Ethical Reasoning

Reasoning that persuades by helping its intended audience make informed decisions is called **ethical reasoning.** As a writer or speaker, you have the responsibility to use ethical reasoning and avoid propaganda. This means that you must gather complete information about a topic, check your facts for accuracy, and make sure that your reasoning includes no errors in logic or false conclusions. You should address opposing evidence with clear and accurate argumentation. Using ethical reasoning in your persuasive writing or speeches will strengthen your positions as your audience sees that you have logically addressed all sides of an idea.

Identifying Unethical Persuasive Techniques

The following essay contains several examples of faulty reasoning. Read through the entire text once, then go back and look for logical fallacies, invalid arguments, and manipulative appeals. For each example you find, make an entry in a chart like the one shown. Then write a paragraph evaluating the essay's argument.

Passage	Type(s) of Appeals	Why Invalid
"Principal Spaly"	Appeal to logic	Card stacking

Don't Take Away Our Freedom

The school board recently announced plans to remove all vending machines from our schools' cafeterias. They say that candy, snacks, and cola are bad for students. But is starvation good for students? Is taking away freedom to choose good for students?

Every expert on nutrition agrees that it is not healthy for kids to go for hours between meals without some sort of snack in between to tide them over. If the school board has its way, students will be passing out at their desks from hunger and dehydration. Principal Spaly claims that students are more likely to pass out from a "sugar crash." This is the same Principal Spaly who recently showed what he thought of students when he denied sophomores the right to park at the high school.

We are taught in these very schools that America is a land of democracy, freedom, and liberty. It is clear that the school board has forgotten this. Any student who loves his or her school will write to the school board and let them know how we feel.

Glossary/Glosario

This glossary lists the vocabulary words found in the selections in this book. The definition given is for the word as it is used in the selection; you may wish to consult a dictionary for other meanings of these words. The key below is a guide to the pronunciation symbols used in each entry.

Pronunciation Key					
a	**a**t	ō	h**o**pe	ng	si**ng**
ā	**a**pe	ô	f**o**rk, **a**ll	th	**th**in
ä	f**a**ther	oo	w**oo**d, p**u**t	t͟h	**th**is
e	**e**nd	o͞o	f**oo**l	zh	trea**s**ure
ē	m**e**	oi	**oi**l	ə	**a**go, tak**e**n, penc**i**l,
i	**i**t	ou	**ou**t		lem**o**n, circ**u**s
ī	**i**ce	u	**u**p	′	indicates primary stress
o	h**o**t	ū	**u**se	′	indicates secondary

English

A

abash (ə bash′) *v.* to make ashamed or uneasy; to embarrass; **p. 521**

accost (ə kôst′) *v.* to approach and speak to, especially in an aggressive manner; **p. 59**

acquiesce (ak′ wē es′) *v.* to consent or agree to without protest; **p. 81**

acquiescence (ak′ wē es′ əns) *n.* passive acceptance; compliance; **p. 1024**

adjacent (ə jā′ sənt) *adj.* next to or close to; neighboring; **p. 657**

admonition (ad′ mə nish′ ən) *n.* cautionary advice; warning; **p. 132**

adversary (ad′ vər ser ē) *n.* an opponent or enemy; **p. 104**

adversity (ad vur′ sə tē) *n.* hardship; **p. 692**

aghast (ə gast′) *adj.* filled with fear, horror, or amazement; **p. 202**

Español

A

abash/avergonzar(se) *v.* producir vergüenza; abochornar; **p. 521**

accost/abordar *v.* acercarse a alguien para hablar, especialmente en una manera agresiva; **p. 59**

acquiesce/acceder *v.* mostrarse de acuerdo en lo que alguien solicita o quiere; **p. 81**

acquiescence/aquiescencia *s.* la acomodación a las opiniones o a los gustos ajenos; sumisión; **p. 1024**

adjacent/adyacente *adj.* situado en las proximidades; contiguo; **p. 657**

admonition/advertencia *s.* llamarle a alguien la atención sobre algo; amonestación; **p. 132**

adversary/adversario(a) *s.* enemigo; persona o grupo que están en contra; **p. 104**

adversity/adversidad *s.* infortunio; penalidad; **p. 692**

aghast/espantado(a) *adj.* lleno de miedo, horror, o asombro; **p. 202**

aloof (ə lo͞of′) *adj.* emotionally distant; uninvolved; disinterested; standoffish; **p. 893**

anguish (ang′ gwish) *n.* extreme suffering; agony; **p. 639**

anthology (an thol′ ə jē) *n.* a collection of written works, such as poems, stories, or essays, in a single book or set; **p. 278**

antiquity (an tik′ wə tē) *n.* an ancient time or times; **p. 145**

apparition (ap′ ə rish′ ən) *n.* an unexpected or unusual sight; **p. 797**

archetypal (är′ kə tī′ pəl) *adj.* serving as an ideal model or perfect example; **p. 528**

ardor (är′ dər) *n.* passion; intensity of emotion; enthusiasm; **p. 860**

arid (ar′ id) *adj.* dry; parched; **p. 784**

articulate (är tik′ yə lit) *adj.* able to express oneself well or effectively; **p. 303**

audible (ô′də bəl) *adj.* loud enough to be heard; **p. 343**

B

beckoning (bek′ən ing) *v.* signaling or summoning; **p. 781**

belligerent (be lij′ ər ənt) *adj.* inclined or eager to fight; **p. 508**

benediction (ben′ ə dik′ shən) *n.* short prayer used as a blessing; **p. 235**

benevolently (bə nev′ ə lənt lē) *adv.* kindly; **p. 105**

bestow (bi sto′) *v.* to give as a gift; **p. 237**

bewildered (bi wil′ dərd) *adj.* perplexed or confused; **p. 1028**

blighted (blīt′ əd) *adj.* damaged or spoiled; **p. 163**

bog (bog) *n.* a wetland ecosystem where shrubs and peat moss grow and various animals live; **p. 522**

bravado (brə vä′ dō) *n.* pretended courage or confidence; **p. 352**

brocade (brō kād′) *n.* a silk fabric with raised patterns embroidered on it; **p. 583**

aloof/apartado(a) *adj.* distante emocionalmente; desinteresado; retraído; **p. 893**

anguish/angustia *s.* sufrimiento extremo; agonía; **p. 639**

anthology/antología *s.* una colección de obras escritas, como poemas, historias, o ensayos, en un libro singular; **p. 278**

antiquity/antigüedad *s.* un tiempo o un época antigua; **p. 145**

apparition/aparición *s.* manifestación de algo que antes no estaba o era desconocido; **p. 797**

archetypal/arquetípico(a) *adj.* que sirve como modelo o forma ideal; **p. 528**

ardor/ardor *s.* pasión; intensidad de emoción; entusiasmo; **p. 860**

arid/árido *adj.* seco; parched; **p. 784**

articulate/articulado *adj.* capaz de expresarse bien o eficazmente; **p. 303**

audible/audible *adj.* bastante alto para ser oído; **p. 343**

B

beckoning/haciendo venir por señas *v.* señalando o llamando; **p. 781**

belligerent/belicoso(a) *adj.* que tiende a la violencia; que está impaciente luchar; **p. 508**

benediction/bendición *s.* petición de la protección divina; **p. 235**

benevolently/benévolamente *adv.* con cariño; **p. 105**

bestow/conceder *v.* dar regalos; **p. 237**

bewildered/perplejo(a) *adj.* confundido, confuso; **p. 1028**

blighted/marchitado(a) *adj.* dañado o estropeado; **p. 163**

bog/pantano *s.* ecosistema de tierra húmeda en que crece arbustos y musgo de pantano y donde animales varios viven; **p. 522**

bravado/bravuconada *s.* hecho con lo que parece valentía pero no lo es; **p. 352**

brocade/brocado *s.* tejido de seda con dibujos entretejidos; **p. 583**

brood (bro͞od) *n.* the young of a family; **p. 947**

brood/cría *s.* los jóvenes de una familia; **p. 947**

C

calamity (kə lam′ ə tē) *n.* a disastrous event; **p. 286**

calamity/calamidad *s.* situación desastrosa; **p. 286**

calligraphy (kə lig′ re fē) *n.* artistic, decorative, or stylized writing or lettering; **p. 498**

calligraphy/caligrafía *s.* técnica de escribir con letra bella según diferentes estilos; **p. 498**

campaign (kam pān′) *n.* a series of related actions with the purpose of a specific goal, such as an election campaign; **p. 72**

campaign/campaña *s.* serie de actividades que se aplican para conseguir un fin, como una campaña electoral; **p. 72**

careen (kə ren′) *v.* to tilt or sway while moving, as if out of control; **p. 159**

careen/carenar *v.* inclinar o oscilar cuando está moviendo, como si no tiene control; **p. 159**

cathedral (ke thē′ drəl) *n.* a large, important church; sometimes used to describe something of great importance; **p. 401**

cathedral/catedral *s.* iglesia principal de una zona que es sede de una diócesis; **p. 401**

ceaselessly (sēs′ lis lē) *adv.* without stopping; continually; **p. 534**

ceaselessly/incesantemente *adv.* sin parar; continuamente; **p. 534**

chalice (chal′ is) *n.* drinking cup; a cup-shaped interior of a flower; **p. 533**

chalice/cáliz *s.* copa o vaso; parte exterior de una flor formada por varias hojas, comúnmente verdes, que se unen al tallo (bot.); **p. 533**

chide (chīd) *v.* to express disapproval; **p. 315**

chide/regañar *v.* reprender o llamar la atención; comunicar desaprobación; **p. 315**

cohort (kō′ hôrt) *n.* a companion, an associate, or a member of the same group; **p. 1016**

cohort/cohorte *s.* compañero o miembro del mismo grupo; **p. 1016**

collective (kə lek′ tiv) *adj.* having to do with a group of persons or things; common; shared; **p. 145**

collective/colectivo(a) *adj.* de un grupo de personas o cosas; común; repartido; **p. 145**

commemorate (kə mem′ ə rāt′) *v.* to preserve the memory of; **p. 46**

commemorate/conmemorar *v.* guardar la memoria de; **p. 46**

communal (kə mūn′əl) *adj.* belonging to a community, society, or group; common; shared; **p. 343**

communal/comunal *adj.* perteneciente a una comunidad, sociedad o grupo; común; compartido; **p 343**

condemn (kən dem′) *v.* to declare to be wrong; to pronounce guilty; **p. 388**

condemn/condenar *v.* desaprobar; decir que es malo; imponer un castigo; **p. 388**

condone (kən dōn′) *v.* to excuse or overlook an offense, usually a serious one, without criticism; **p. 30**

condone/perdonar *v.* olvidar una ofensa, usualmente alguna seria, sin crítica; **p. 30**

confidant (kon′ fə dant′) *n.* a person to whom secrets are entrusted; **p. 271**

confidant/confidente *s.* una persona quien reciba secretos; **p. 271**

conglomerate (kən glom′ ər it) *adj.* made up of separate parts collected together as one; **p. 350**

conglomerate/conglomerado *s.* compuesto de partes distintos congregados junto como uno; **p. 350**

conspiratorial (kən spir´ ə tôr´ ē əl) *adj.* suggesting a secret plot or plan; **p. 917**

constricting (kən strikt´ ing) *adj.* restricting; limiting; **p. 49**

contention (kən tən´ shən) *n.* a point advanced in a debate or an argument; **p. 388**

contour (kon´ toor) *n.* outline or general shape; **p. 235**

conviction (kən vik´shən) *n.* a firmly established opinion or belief; **p. 300**

cower (kou´ ər) *v.* to crouch or shrink back, as in fear or shame; **p. 872**

craven (krā´ vən) *adj.* extremely cowardly; **p. 190**

D

denigrate (den´ ə grāt´) *v.* to criticize or belittle; **p. 418**

depreciate (di prē´ shē āt´) *v.* to lessen the price or value of; **p. 117**

detached (di tacht´) *adj.* separated; apart; **p. 534**

detachment (di tach´ mənt) *n.* indifference; a state of being apart from; **p. 365**

dire (dīr) *adj.* dreadful; terrible; **p. 13**

discern (di surn´) *v.* to detect or recognize; to make out; **p. 25**

disconsolate (dis kon´ sə lit) *adj.* so unhappy that nothing can comfort; hopeless and depressed; **p. 199**

discreet (dis krēt´) *adj.* showing good judgment; cautious; **p. 212**

disdainful (dis dān´ fəl) *adj.* showing scorn for something or someone regarded as unworthy; **p. 192**

disperse (dis purs´) *v.* to go off in different directions; to scatter; **p. 1015**

distracted (dis trakt´ əd) *adj.* unable to pay attention; agitated; **p. 130**

distraught (dis trôt´) *adj.* very upset; confused; **p. 189**

conspiratorial/clandestino(a) *adj.* que sugiere una conspiración o un plan secreto; **p. 917**

constricting/constreñido(a) *adj.* restrictido; limitador; **p. 49**

contention/argumento *s.* razonamiento que se usa para provar o demostrar algo; **p. 388**

contour/contorno *s.* líneas generales; perfil; **p. 235**

conviction/convicción *n.* opinión o creencia firmemente establecida; **p. 300**

cower/agacharse *v.* agazaparse o retroceder, como si tiene miedo o vergüenza; **p. 872**

craven/acobardado(n) *adj.* cobardísmo; **p. 190**

D

denigrate/denigrar *v.* ofender la reputación o la buena fama; menospreciar; **p. 418**

depreciate/depreciar *v.* aminorar el precio o el valor de algo; **p. 117**

detached/separado(a) *adj.* aislado; suelto; **p. 534**

detachment/aislamiento *s.* separación de algo; indiferencia; **p. 365**

dire/espantoso(a) *adj.* que causa terror, asombro, consternación; **p. 13**

discern/discernir *v.* detectar o reconocir, redactar; **p. 25**

disconsolate/desconsolado(a) *adj.* tan infeliz que mada puede confortar; sin esperanza; deprimido; **p. 199**

discreet/discreto(a) *adj.* juicioso; prudente; que muestra buen juicio; **p. 212**

disdainful/desdeñoso(a) *adj.* que muestra desdén para algo o a alguien indignol o con una reputación sin valor; **p. 192**

disperse/dispersar *v.* ir por direcciones diferentes; poner en fuga; **p. 1015**

distracted/distraído(a) *adj.* que no presta atención a lo que sucede a su alrededor; **p. 130**

distraught/consternado(a) *adj.* conturbado y abatido; **p. 189**

diverge (di vurj′) *v.* to lead in different directions away from a common starting point; **p. 542**

diverse (di vurs′) *adj.* markedly different; varied; **p. 342**

dollop (dol′ əp) *n.* a glob of a soft, mushy substance; **p. 566**

dreary (drēr′ ē) *adj.* sad; depressing; dull; uninteresting; **p. 522**

dubious (do͞o′ bē əs) *adj.* skeptical; feeling doubt; **p. 177**

E

ebb (eb) *v.* to become less or weaker; decline; fail; **p. 1002**

elation (i lā′ shən) *n.* a feeling of great joy; ecstasy; **p. 215**

elemental (el′ ə ment′ el) *adj.* of or like the forces of nature; ancient and powerful; **p. 342**

eloquence (el′ ə kwəns) *n.* the quality of persuasive, inspirational speech; **p. 687**

emanate (em′ ə nāt′) *v.* to come forth; **p. 13**

embroider (em broi′ dər) *v.* to make a story more interesting with imaginary details or exaggerations; **p. 278**

endeavor (en dev′ ər) *n.* a serious or strenuous attempt to accomplish something; **p. 84**

enigma (i nig′ mə) *n.* a mystery; a baffling person or thing; **p. 999**

enthrall (en thrôl′) *v.* to hold spellbound; fascinate; **p. 214**

eradicate (i rad′ ə kāt′) *v.* to get rid of completely; **p. 382**

evade (i vād′) *v.* to escape or avoid, often by cleverness; **p. 343**

exacerbate (ig zas′ ər bāt′) *v.* to make worse, more violent, or more bitter; **p. 361**

exalted (eg zôl′ təd) *adj.* noble; exaggerated; **p. 793**

exhilarated (ig zil′ ə rāt′ əd) *adj.* cheerful, lively, or excited; **p. 272**

diverge/divergir *v.* llevar en direcciones diferentes lejos de un punto de partida común; **p. 542**

diverse/diverso *adj.* marcadamente diferente; variado; **p. 342**

dollop/porción (de masa) *s.* cantidad separada de otra mayor; **p. 566**

dreary/lóbrego(a) *adj.* triste; melancólico; sombrío; **p. 522**

dubious/dudoso(a) *adj.* escéptico; que siente incertidumbre; **p. 177**

E

ebb/disminuir *v.* hacerse menos poderoso; decaer; faltar; **p. 1002**

elation/elación *s.* un sentimiento de alegría intensa; éxtasis; **p. 215**

elemental/elemental *adj.* perteneciente a las fuerzas de la naturaleza; antiguo o poderoso; **p. 342**

eloquence/elocuencia *s.* la facultad de persuadir, conmover o delitar con palabras habladas o escritas; **p. 687**

emanate/emanar *v.* desprenderse o salir de algo; **p. 13**

embroider/embellecer *v.* hacerun cuento más interesante con detalles imaginarios o exageraciones; **p. 278**

endeavor/empeño *s.* esfuerzo en lo que se hace; **p. 84**

enigma/enigma *s.* un misterio; una persona o cosa desconcertante; **p. 999**

enthrall/esclavizar *v.* fascinar; tener encantado; **p. 214**

eradicate/erradicar *v.* eliminar por completo; **p. 382**

evade/evadir *v.* escapar o evitar, muchas veces por ingenio; **p. 343**

exacerbate/exacerbar *v.* causar gran enfado o enojo, irritar; **p. 361**

exalted/exaltado(a) *adj.* noble; elevado; digno de admiración y respeto; **p. 793**

exhilarated/animado(a) *adj.* alegre, vivo, o excitado; **p. 272**

explicit (eks plis′ it) *adj.* definitely stated; clearly expressed; **p. 60**

extricate (eks′ trə kāt′) *v.* to release from entanglement or difficulty; to set free; **p. 48**

F

fervent (fur′ vənt) *adj.* having or showing great intensity of feeling; passionate; **p. 14**

fetter (fet′ ər) *v.* to chain; **p. 948**

fickle (fik′ əl) *adj.* given to frequent changes of thought or mood; unreliable; inconstant; **p. 700**

forethought (for′ thôt′) *n.* thinking or planning beforehand; **p. 493**

forge (fôrj) *v.* to form or make, especially by heating or hammering; **p. 948**

formidable (fôr′ mi də bəl) *adj.* impressive; awe-inspiring; **p. 1058**

fulfill (fo͞ol fil′) *v.* to measure up to, or satisfy; to bring to pass; **p. 279**

futilely (fū′ til ē) *adv.* uselessly; vainly; hopelessly; **p. 146**

G

gale (gāl) *n.* a very strong wind; **p. 521**

gamut (gam′ ət) *n.* the entire range or series of something; **p. 203**

gelled (jeld) *adj.* in a semisolid state after having been liquid; **p. 566**

guile (gīl) *n.* slyness; craftiness; skillful deception; **p. 841**

guise (gīz) *n.* outward appearance; false appearance; **p. 877**

H

haggard (hag′ ərd) *adj.* having a worn and tired look; **p. 189**

haughty (hô′ tē) *adj.* very proud; scornful of others; **p. 730**

horde (hôrd) *n.* crowd, throng, or swarm; **p. 922**

explicit/explícito(a) *adj.* claro; expresado definitivamente; **p. 60**

extricate/desembarazar *v.* liberar de enredo o dificultad; hacer libre; **p. 48**

F

fervent/ardiente *adj.* que muestra una intensidad de sentimiento; apasionado; **p. 14**

fetter/encadenar *v.* poner en cadenas; **p. 948**

fickle/caprichoso(a) *adj.* que obra arbitrariamente, según el humor o por antojo; inconstante; **p. 700**

forethought/providencia *s.* cuidado que se pone al hacer algo para evitar problemas; precaución; **p. 493**

forge/forjar *v.* formar o hacer, especialmente por califacción o martilleo; **p. 948**

formidable/formidable *adj.* que infunde asombro y miedo; que causa respeto y tenor; **p. 1058**

fulfill/cumplir *v.* realizar; satisfacer; **p. 279**

futilely/vanamente *adv.* desperadamente; inútilmente; **p. 146**

G

gale/vendaval *s.* viento muy fuerte; **p. 521**

gamut/gama *s.* la escala entera o una serie de algo; **p. 203**

gelled/en estado de gel frase *adj.* que la parte líquida está coagulada; **p. 566**

guile/astucia *s.* travesura; artería; engaño hábil; **p. 841**

guise/guisa *s.* apariencía física; apariencia falsa; **p. 877**

H

haggard/macilento(a) *adj.* que tiene una apariencia cansada y usada; **p. 189**

haughty/orgulloso(a) *adj.* desdeñoso de los otros y con demasiado orgullo; **p. 730**

horde/horda *n.* multitude, muchedumbre, o enjambre; **p. 922**

host (hōst) *n.* a great number; a multitude; **p. 452**

hyperactive (hī′ pər ak′ tiv) *adj.* overly energetic; very lively; **p. 130**

I

impart (im pärt′) *v.* to make known; to tell; **p. 100**

impartial (im pär′ shəl) *adj.* not favoring one side more than another; fair; **p. 13**

imperative (im per′ ə tiv) *adj.* absolutely necessary; **p. 35**

impervious (im pur′ vē əs) *adj.* incapable of being passed through, affected, or disturbed; **p. 333**

implacable (im plak′ ə bəl) *adj.* impossible to satisfy or soothe; unyielding; **p. 888**

implore (im plôr′) *v.* to ask earnestly; to beg; **p. 63**

imposing (im pō′ zing) *adj.* impressive in appearance or manner; **p. 271**

impudence (im′ pyə dəns) *n.* speech or behavior that is aggressively forward or rude; **p. 876**

impunity (im pū′ nə tē) *n.* freedom from punishment, harm, or bad consequences; **p. 58**

imputation (im′ pyə tā′ shən) *n.* an accusation; **p. 116**

incessantly (in ses′ ənt lē) *adv.* endlessly; constantly; **p. 198**

inconsolable (in kən sō′ lə bəl) *adj.* heartbroken; impossible to comfort; **p. 133**

incriminating (in krim′ ə nāt′ ing) *adj.* showing involvement in a crime; **p. 287**

infallibility (in fal′ ə bil′ ə tē) *n.* state of being incapable of error; **p. 180**

ingenious (in jēn′ yəs) *adj.* especially clever, inventive, or original; **p. 1041**

inhibition (in′ i bish′ ən) *n.* a restraint on one's natural impulses; **p. 178**

inscrutable (in skrōō′ tə bəl) *adj.* not readily understood or interpreted; **p. 1074**

host/multitud *s.* gran cantidad de personas, animales o cosas; **p. 452**

hyperactive/hiperactivo(a) *adj.* que tiene exceso de actividad; **p. 130**

I

impart/impartir *v.* dar a conocer; decir; **p. 100**

impartial/imparcial *adj.* que no favorece un lado más que el otro; justo; **p. 13**

imperative/imperativo *adj.* absolutamente necesario; **p. 35**

impervious/ impenetrable *adj.* incapaz de ser permeado, afectado, o perturbado; **p. 333**

implacable/implacable *adj.* imposible de satisfacer o aliviar; inflexible; **p. 888**

implore/implorar *v.* preguntar seriamente; rogar; **p. 63**

imposing/imponente *adj.* impresivo por la apararencia o la manera; **p. 271**

impudence/aplomo *s.* dicho o comportamiento que es grosero o agresivamente delantero; **p. 876**

impunity/impunidad *s.* libertad de castigo, daño, o consequencias malas; **p. 58**

imputation/imputación *s.* una acusación; **p. 116**

incessantly/incesantemente *adv.* que se repite con mucha frecuencia; **p. 198**

inconsolable/inconsolable *adj.* doloroso; imposible de consolar; **p. 133**

incriminating/inculpatorio(a) *adj.* que muestra que ha actuado en un delito; **p. 287**

infallibility/infalibilidad *s.* estado de ser incapaz de hacer errores; **p. 180**

ingenious/ingenioso(a) *adj.* especialmente listo, inventivo, u original; **p. 1041**

inhibition/prohibición *s.* una restricción sobre los impulsos naturales; **p. 178**

inscrutable/inescrutable *adj.* que no se puede entender o interpretar fácilmente; **p. 1074** intimation (in′ tə mā′ shən) *n.* a suggestion or hint; **p. 285**

intuitive (in tōō′ ə tiv) *adj.* rising from an impulse or natural tendency; instinctive; not learned **p. 299**

invincible (in vin′ sə bəl) *adj.* not able to be beaten or overcome; **p. 361**

irreverent (i rev′ ər ənt) *adj.* showing a lack of proper respect; **p. 273**

irrevocably (i rev′ ə kə blē) *adv.* in a way that cannot be revoked or undone; **p. 1003**

isolated (ī′ sə lāt′ əd) *adj.* alone; cut off from others; **p. 534**

itinerary (ī tin′ ər er′ ē) *n.* the planned route for a journey; **p. 793**

J

jostle (jos′ əl) *v.* to bump, push, or shove roughly, as with elbows in a crowd; **p. 886**

K

keen (kēn) *adj.* sharp; intense; **p. 533**

kindred (kin′ drid) *n.* people who are related; family; **p. 936**

L

lament (lə ment′) *v.* to express deep sorrow; **p. 721**

languid (lang′ gwid) *adj.* drooping; weak and listless; **p. 1057**

languor (lang′ gər) *n.* weakness; fatigue; **p. 85**

lavish (lav′ ish) *v.* to give generously; provide in abundance; **p. 893**

lithe (līth) *adj.* limber; bending easily; **p. 180**

livelong (liv′ lông′) *adj.* complete; whole; used to emphasize the length of a period of time; **p. 522**

logic (loj′ ik) *n.* a method of reasoning; **p. 763**

intimation/insinuación *s.* hecho que permite suponer algo; **p. 285**

intuitive/intuitivo *adj.* que surge de una tendencia o impulso natural; instintivo; no aprendido **p. 299**

invincible/invencible *adj.* que no puede ser vencido; **p. 361**

irreverent/irreverente *adj.* que muestra una falta de respeto; **p. 273**

irrevocably/irrevocablemente *adv.* en una manera que no se puede revocar; **p. 1003**

isolated/aislado(a) *adj.* solitario; separado de otros; **p. 534**

itinerary/itinerario *s.* la ruta planeada por un viaje; **p. 793**

J

jostle/empujar *v.* empellar mientras se camina, como en una multitud; **p. 886**

K

keen/penetrante *adj.* agudo, intenso; **p. 533**

kindred/pariente *s.* de la familia ya sea por consanguinidad o afinidad; **p. 936**

L

lament/lamentar *v.* expresar dolor profundo; **p. 721**

languid/lánguido(a) *adj.* débil o sin fuerzas; **p. 1057**

languor/languidez *s.* debilidad o falta de fuerza; falta de ánimo; **p. 85**

lavish/prodigar *v.* dar en gran cantidad o abundancia; **p. 893**

lithe/flexible *adj.* ágil; que dobla fácilmente; **p. 180**

livelong/todo(a) *adj.* enteramente o completamente; usado para dar énfasis a la duración de un tiempo; **p. 522**

logic/lógica *s.* razonamiento, método o sentido común; **p. 763**

lurk (lurk) *v.* to conceal oneself; to move about in a sneaky manner; **p. 711**

M

magnitude (mag′ nə to͞od′) *n.* great size, volume, or extent; importance; significance; **p. 409**

malodorous (mal ō′ dər əs) *adj.* bad-smelling; stinky; **p. 107**

meticulous (mi tik′ yə ləs) *adj.* characterized by extreme or excessive care in the treatment of details; **p. 1025**

misadventure (mis′ əd ven′ chər) *n.* a mishap; an unfortunate event; **p. 725**

mock (mok) *v.* to make fun of or ridicule; **p. 231**

molasses (mə las′ iz) *n.* a thick, dark brown syrup created by boiling down raw sugar; **p. 76**

monogrammed (mon′ ə gramd) *adj.* decorated with a design of one or more letters, usually the initials of a name; **p. 414**

monopoly (mə nop′ ə lē) *n.* exclusive possession or control; **p. 766**

monotony (mə not′ ən ē) *n.* undesirable sameness; **p. 1039**

mortal (môrt′ əl) *adj.* deadly; **p. 73**

mourn (môrn) *v.* to feel or express grief or sorrow; **p. 760**

N

naïve (nä ēv′) *adj.* innocent; unsophisticated; **p. 303**

negligently (neg′ li jənt lē) *adv.* in a carelessly inattentive manner; **p. 392**

negotiate (ni gō′ shē āt′) *v.* to discuss or compromise; **p. 381**

nominal (nom′ ən əl) *adj.* insignificant; **p. 1048**

lurk/acechar *v.* observar o esperar cautelosamente con algún propósito; merodear; **p. 711**

M

magnitude/magnitud *s.* tamaño o importancia; **p. 409**

malodorous/maloliente *adj.* férido; que ole malo; **p. 107**

meticulous/meticuloso(a) *adj.* muy puntual, escrupuloso o concienzudo; **p. 1025**

misadventure/desgracia *s.* un contratiempo; un suceso infortunado; **p. 725**

mock/burlar(se) *v.* reírse de algo o poner en ridículo; **p. 231**

molasses/melaza *s.* jarabe saturado obtenido entre dos cristalizaciones o cocciones sucesivas en la fabricación del azúcar; **p. 76**

monogrammed/con monograma *frase prep adj.* decorado con las letras de un nombre, generalmente las iniciales; **p. 414**

monopoly/monopolio *s.* ejercicio exclusivo de una actividad; **p. 766**

monotony/monotonía *s.* falta de variedad; **p. 1039**

mortal/mortal *adj.* que puede producir la muerte; que tiene que morir; muy fuerte o muy grande; **p. 73**

mourn/deplorar *v.* sentir o expresar pena o dolor; **p. 760**

N

naïve/ingénuo *adj.* inocente; poco sofisticado; **p. 303**

negligently/negligentemente *adv.* en una manera sin atencíon o cuidado; **p. 392**

negotiate/negociar *v.* referido a un asunto tratarlo o resolverlo; **p. 381**

nominal/nominal *adj.* pequeño y de poca importancia; insignificante; **p. 1048**

nostalgia (nos tal′ jə) *n.* a feeling of longing experienced when remembering the past; an overly sentimental feeling; **p. 402**

novel (nov′ əl) *adj.* new and unusual; **p. 14**

O

obstinately (ob′ stə nit lē) *adv.* stubbornly; in spite of reason or persuasion; **p. 394**

ominous (om′ ə nəs) *adj.* like an evil omen; threatening; **p. 778**

P

pandemonium (pan′ də mō′ nē əm) *n.* wild uproar; **p. 191**

pang (pang) *n.* a sudden sharp feeling of pain or distress; **p. 331**

pantry (pan′ trē) *n.* room or closet in which food and articles for preparing and serving food are kept; **p. 227**

paperweight (pāp′ ər wāt′) *n.* a heavy, often decorative object traditionally used to hold down loose papers; **p. 71**

paraphernalia (par′ ə fər nāl′ yə) *n.* personal items or equipment; **p. 917**

parsimony (pär′ sə mō′ nē) *n.* stinginess; **p. 116**

pensive (pen′ siv) *adj.* thinking deeply, often sadly; **p. 174**

pernicious (pər nish′ əs) *adj.* destructive; deadly; **p. 632**

perpetrator (pur′ pə trā′ tər) *n.* one who commits a crime or another similar act; **p. 286**

perpetually (pər pech′ o͞o əl ē) *adv.* constantly; unceasingly; **p. 49**

perspicacity (pur′ spə kas′ ə tē) *n.* acute mental powers or perception; **p. 1076**

pervade (pər vād′) *v.* to go through or fill every part of; **p. 311**

perverse (pər vurs′) *adj.* deliberately unreasonable or wrong; stubborn; **p. 661**

nostalgia/nostalgia *s.* un sentimiento de añoranza cuando estaba recordando el pasado; un sentimiento demasiado sentimental; **p. 402**

novel/nuevo(a) *adj.* raro o lo que no conocido antes; **p. 14**

O

obstinately/obstinadamente *adv.* de forma perseverante o firme y decidida; **p. 394**

ominous/ominoso *adj.* como un agüero malo; amenazante; **p. 778**

P

pandemonium/pandemónium *s.* lugar en el que hay mucho ruido y confusión; **p. 191**

pang/punzada *s.* un sentimiento súbito y afilado, de daño o dolor; **p. 331**

pantry/despensa *n.* habitación o armario en que se guardan comida o artículos para preparar; **p. 227**

paperweight/pisapapeles *s.* objeto pesado que se coloca sobre los papeles para que no se muevan; **p. 71**

paraphernalia/bienes parafernales *s.* utensilios, herramientas o instrumentos de un oficio o arte; **p. 917**

parsimony/parsimonia *s.* tacañería; avaricia; **p. 116**

pensive/pensativo(a) *adj.* que piensa profundamente, muchas veces con tristeza; **p. 174**

pernicious/pernicioso(a) *adj.* extremadamente malo o perjudicial; **p. 632**

perpetrator/perpetrador(a) *s.* que comete o consume un delito; **p. 286**

perpetually/perpetuamente *adv.* constantamente; incesantemente; **p. 49**

perspicacity/perspicacia *s.* agudeza mental, penetración o entendimiento; **p. 1076**

pervade/difundir(se) *v.* propagar, esparcir, extender; **p. 311**

perverse/obstinado(a) *adj.* perseverante y porfiado; **p. 661**

pious (pī′ əs) *adj.* having either genuine or pretended religious devotion; **p. 83**

plait (plāt) *n.* a braid of material or hair; **p. 583**

plausible (plô′ zə bəl) *adj.* apparently true or acceptable; likely; **p. 1015**

plunder (plun′ dər) *v.* to take (property) by force, especially in warfare; **p. 839**

ponderous (pon′ dər əs) *adj.* having great weight or bulk; heavy; **p. 847**

portent (pôr′ tent) *n.* something that foreshadows a coming event; **p. 1036**

posterity (pos ter′ ə tē) *n.* future generations; **p. 637**

precariously (pri kār′ ē əs lē) *adv.* dangerously; insecurely; **p. 165**

preclude (pri klo͞od′) *v.* to prevent; to make impossible; **p. 58**

predicament (pri dik′ ə mənt) *n.* a difficult or tricky situation; **p. 693**

premonition (prē mə nish′ ən) *n.* anticipation of an event without outside warning or reason; **p. 284**

pretentious (pri ten′ shəs) *adj.* expressing exaggerated importance or worth; **p. 766**

privation (prī vā′ shən) *n.* the lack of the comforts or basic necessities of life; **p. 203**

profane (prō fān′) *v.* to degrade or disrespect something holy or important; **p. 651**

prostrated (pros′ trāt id) *v.* completely exhausted; helpless; overcome; **p. 786**

prudence (pro͞od′ əns) *n.* caution, good judgment; **p. 119**

prudent (pro͞od′ ənt) *adj.* showing wisdom and good judgment; **p. 395**

putrid (pū′ trid) *adj.* very nasty; disgusting; **p. 131**

pious/piadoso(a) *adj.* religioso, devoto; **p. 83**

plait/trenza *s.* conjunto de tres o más mechones que se cruzan entre sí alternativamente; de cabello u otra matera; **p. 583**

plausible/creíble *adj.* alparecer es verdad o aceptable; probable; **p. 1015**

plunder/saquear *v.* apoderarse por la fuerza de lo que se encuentra en un lugar, especialmente en la guerra; **p. 839**

ponderous/ponderoso(a) *adj.* que tiene peso grandre o bulto; pesado; **p. 847**

portent/presagio *s.* adivinación o conocimiento de las cosas futuras; **p. 1036**

posterity/posteridad *s.* generaciones futuras; **p. 637**

precariously/precariamente *adv.* peligrosamente; inseguramente; **p. 165**

preclude/impedir *v.* prevenir; hacer imposible; **p. 58**

predicament/apuro *s.* aprieto o situación difícil; **p. 693**

premonition/premonición *s.* presentimiento de que algo va a ocurrir; **p. 284**

pretentious/pretencioso(a) *adj.* que pretende ser más que lo que en realidad es; **p. 766**

privation/privación *s.* la falta de comodidades o necesidades basicas de vivir; **p. 203**

profane/profanar *v.* referido a algo sagrado o importante tratarlo sin respeto o deshonrarlo; **p. 651**

prostrated/prostrado *adj.* completamente agotado; sin ayuda; vencido; **p. 786**

prudence/prudencia *s.* aviso; buen juicio; **p. 119**

prudent/prudente *adj.* que actúa con cautela y tiene sensatez y buen juicio; **p. 395**

putrid/pútrido(a) *adj.* podrido, dañado, echado a perder; **p. 131**

Q

quandary (kwon′ drē) *n.* state of indecision or doubt; **p. 309**

R

rancor (rang′ kər) *n.* bitter resentment against someone; long-lasting spite; **p. 667**

ravenous (rav′ ə nəs) *adj.* extremely hungry; **p. 1037**

reconciliation (rek′ ən sil ē ā′ shən) *n.* a settlement of a controversy or disagreement; **p. 86**

redundant (ri dun′ dənt) *adj.* unnecessarily repetitive; without a purpose; **p. 416**

reiterate (rē it′ ə rāt′) *v.* to say again or do again; repeat; **p. 165**

relent (ri lent′) *v.* to become less harsh or strict; to yield; **p. 104**

renowned (ri nound′) *adj.* famous; widely known; **p. 879**

repulsive (ri pul′ siv) *adj.* arousing aversion or disgust; **p. 1027**

résumé (rez′ o͞o mā′) *n.* a listing of one's accomplishments; a summary; **p. 919**

retain (ri tān′) *v.* to keep possession of; **p. 659**

retrospect (ret′ rə spekt′) *n.* the act of looking back or thinking about the past; **p. 279**

reverberate (ri vur′ bə rāt′) *v.* to echo; resound; **p. 336**

reverent (rev′ ər ənt) *adj.* feeling or expressing respect or courtesy; **p. 528**

reverie (rev′ ər ē) *n.* fanciful thinking, especially of pleasant things; a daydream; **p. 1017**

revive (ri vīv′) *v.* to bring back to life; to give new strength; **p. 718**

riveted (riv′ it əd) *adj.* fixed or secured firmly; **p. 791**

rosin (roz′ in) *n.* a resin made from the sap of various pine trees and used to increase sliding friction on the bows of certain stringed instruments; **p. 508**

Q

quandary/incertidumbre *s.* estado de duda o con temor de errar; **p. 309**

R

rancor/rencor *s.* resentimiento arraigado y que resulta difícil de quitar; **p. 667**

ravenous/famélico(a) *adj.* hambriento; **p. 1037**

reconciliation/reconciliación *s.* restablecimiento de buenas relaciones; **p. 86**

redundant/redundante *adj.* que sobra; que se repite innecesariamente; **p. 416**

reiterate/reiterar *v.* decir otravez o hacer otra vez; repetir; **p. 165**

relent/ceder *v.* hacerse menos áspero o estricto; rendir; **p. 104**

renowned/renombrado(a) *adj.* famoso; conocido extensamente; **p. 879**

repulsive/repulsivo(a) *adj.* que produce asco o rechazo; **p. 1027**

résumé/resumen *n.* una lista o inscripción de sus logros o éxitos; un sumario; **p. 919**

retain/retener *v.* conservar en la memoria; conservar; **p. 659**

retrospect/mirada retrospectiva *s.* el acto de reflexionar sobre el pasado; **p. 279**

reverberate/reflejar *v.* hacer un eco; resonar; **p. 336**

reverent/reverente *adj.* que muestra o expresa respeto; **p. 528**

reverie/ensueño *s.* pensamiento imaginativo, especialmente de cosas agradables; fantasía; **p. 1017**

revive/revivir *v.* resucitar; recuperar la vitalidad; **p. 718**

riveted/remachado(a) *adj.* sujeto con remaches; **p. 791**

rosin/colofonia *s.* resina obtenida en la destilación de la trementina de pinos y otros árboles; **p. 508**

S

sashay (sa shā′) *v.* to walk or move in a way that shows indifference or a lack of interest; **p. 227**

serene (sə rēn′) *adj.* calm; peaceful; undisturbed; **p. 162**

shrill (shril) *adj.* loud; piercing; **p. 937**

shroud (shroud) *v.* to cover, as with a veil or burial cloth; conceal; **p. 865**

shun (shun) *v.* to keep away from; avoid; **p. 859**

singular (sing′ gyə lər) *adj.* unusual or out of the ordinary; odd; **p. 1046**

solitude (sol′ ə to͞od′) *n.* isolation; the state of being alone; **p. 452**

sow (sō) *v.* to plant by scattering seeds; **p. 592**

spurn (spurn) *v.* to reject with disdain or contempt; **p. 1037**

staggering (stag′ ər ing) *adj.* shocking; overwhelming; **p. 404**

stifle (stī′ fəl) *v.* to smother for lack of air; to prevent from developing properly; **p. 715**

stoke (stōk) *v.* to stir up; to cause to increase; **p. 312**

subsequent (sub′ sə kwənt) *adj.* following in time, order, or place; **p. 393**

suffuse (sə fūz′) *v.* to spread through or over; **p. 331**

supplicant (sup′ lə kənt) *n.* one who asks humbly and earnestly; **p. 529**

surge (surj) *v.* to move suddenly in a wave; **p. 311**

surreptitiously (sur′ əp tish′ əs lē) *adv.* secretly or slyly; **p. 178**

T

tangible (tan′ jə bəl) *adj.* capable of being touched or felt; **p. 23**

tantalize (tant′ əl īz′) *v.* to torment or tease by tempting with something and then withholding it; **p. 999**

S

sashay/pavonearse *v.* andar o moverse de manera que muestra indiferencia o una falta de interés; **p. 227**

serene/sereno(a) *adj.* tranquilo; pacífico; quieto; **p. 162**

shrill/chillón(ona) *adj.* sonido con una frecuencia de vibración grande; **p. 937**

shroud/amortajar *v.* cubrir, como con un velo o tela de entierro; ocultar; **p. 865**

shun/eludir *v.* apartarse de; evitar; **p. 859**

singular/singular *adj.* raro, excelente o extraordinario; peculiar; **p. 1046**

solitude/soledad *s.* falta de compañía, estar solo; **p. 452**

sow/sembrar *v.* arrojar, esparcir o colocar la semilla en la tierra para que crezca; **p. 592**

spurn/rechazar *v.* mostrar oposición o desprecio; **p. 1037**

staggering/asombroso(a) *adj.* que causa admiración, susto o espanto; **p. 404**

stifle/sofocar *v.* impedir la respiración; **p. 715**

stoke/avivar *v.* aumentar la fuerza de algo; animar, excitar; **p. 312**

subsequent/subsiguiente *adj.* que sigue inmediatamente; en tiempo, orden o lugar; **p. 393**

suffuse/esparcir *v.* extender o bañar; diseminar; **p. 331**

supplicant/suplicante *s.* persona que pide con humildad y sumisión; **p. 529**

surge/levantar(se) *v.* empezar a producirse como un oleaje; **p. 311**

surreptitiously/subrepticiamente *adv.* secretamente o furtivamente; **p. 178**

T

tangible/tangible *adj.* capaz de ser tocado o sentido; **p. 23**

tantalize/atormentar *v.* tortutar o fastidiar por temptar con algo (y entonces lo detener); **p. 999**

tax (taks) *v.* to place a heavy burden on; to strain; **p. 493**

tedious (tē′ dē əs) *adj.* tiresome; boring; **p. 737**

template (tem′ plāt) *n.* a pattern that serves as a guide to making something accurately; **p. 415**

tenuously (ten′ ū əs lē) *adv.* uncertainly; shakily; **p. 360**

terrain (tə rān′) *n.* the physical features of the land; **p. 363**

testimony (tes′ tə mō′ nē) *n.* a solemn declaration; **p. 382**

throng (thrông) *n.* a large number of people or things crowded together; **p. 330**

toil (toil) *v.* to work very hard or for long hours; **p. 592**

tread (tred) *n.* step or footstep; **p. 237**

trifle (trī′ fəl) *n.* something of little value or importance; **p. 1074**

tumult (to͞o′ məlt) *n.* commotion; uproar; **p. 860**

twine (twīn) *v.* to coil around; **p. 498**

U

ubiquitous (ū bik′ wə təs) *adj.* seeming to be everywhere at once; **p. 146**

uncanny (un kan′ ē) *adj.* not normal or natural; seemingly supernatural in origin; **p. 914**

unintelligible (un′ in tel′ ə jə bəl) *adj.* not able to be understood; **p. 352**

unsavory (un sā′ vər ē) *adj.* unpleasant in character; disagreeable to the taste; **p. 732**

V

valor (val′ ər) *n.* great courage, especially in battle; **p. 839**

vanquished (vang′ kwishd) *n.* people who have been defeated in battle; **p. 795**

tax/fatigar *v.* someter a un esfuerzo; **p. 493**

tedious/tedioso(a) *adj.* cansado; aburrido; **p. 737**

template/plantilla *s.* pieza que se coloca sobre otra y que sirve como guía para cortar o dibujar; **p. 415**

tenuously/débilmente *adv.* con poco vigor con poca fuerza; **p. 360**

terrain/terreno *s.* características físicas de la tierra; **p. 363**

testimony/testimonio *s.* declaración o explicación de alguien que afirma o asegura algo; prueba de la verdad de algo; **p. 382**

throng/muchedumbre *s.* un gran número de gente o cosas; una peña; **p. 330**

toil/trabajar duro *frase verbal* trabajar con gran esfuerza; **p. 592**

tread/pisada *s.* paso, golpe dado con el pie; **p. 237**

trifle/bagatela *s.* de poco valor o importancia; **p. 1074**

tumult/tumulto *s.* conmoción; alboroto; **p. 860**

twine/enroscar *v.* colocar en forma de rosca; **p. 498**

U

ubiquitous/obicuo(a) *adj.* que parecer estar por todas partes ahora mismo; **p. 146**

uncanny/extraño(a) *adj.* que es raro o distinto de lo normal; **p. 914**

unintelligible/ininteligible *adj.* que no se puede entender; **p. 352**

unsavory/insípido(a) *adj.* desagradable en carácter; desagradable en sabor; **p. 732**

V

valor/valor *s.* valería, especialmente en batalla; **p. 839**

vanquished/vencido(a) *adj.* pueblo o individuo que ha sido derrotado; **p. 795**

venture (ven′ chər) *n.* an undertaking involving chance, risk, or danger; **p. 381**

vice (vīs) *n.* a moral fault or failing; **p. 388**

vigilant (vij′ əl ənt) *adj.* alert and watchful for danger or trouble; **p. 213**

W

want (wont) *v.* to fail to possess; to lack; **p. 542**

withered (wit͟h′ ərd) *adj.* shriveled or dried up; **p. 938**

writhe (rīt͟h) *v.* to twist in pain; **p. 949**

Z

zealous (zel′ əs) *adj.* very eager; enthusiastic; **p. 35**

venture/empresa *s.* acción o tarea que conlleva dificultad o riesgo; **p. 381**

vice/vicio *s.* mal hábito que se repite con frecuencia; costumbre gusto o necesidad censurable, especialmente en sentido moral; **p. 388**

viligant/vigilante *adj.* alerta y en vela por peligro o problemas; **p. 213**

W

want/carecer de *v.* no tener algo; **p. 542**

withered/marchito(a) *adj.* falto de frescura, vigor o vitalidad; **p. 938**

writhe/torcer *v.* retorcer a causa de dolor; **p. 949**

Z

zealous/fervoroso(a) *adj.* entusiasta; muy ávido; **p. 35**

Academic Word List

To succeed academically in high school and prepare for college, it is important to know academic vocabulary–special terms used in classroom discussion, assignments, and tests. These words are also used in the workplace and among friends to share information, exchange ideas, make decisions, and build relationships. Research has shown that the words listed below, compiled by Averil Coxhead in 2000, are the ones most commonly used in these ways. You will encounter many of them in the Glencoe Language Arts program. You will also focus on specific terms in connection with particular reading selections.

Note: The lists are ordered by frequency of use from most frequent to least frequent.

List One

analysis
approach
area
assessment
assume
authority
available
benefit
concept
consistent
constitutional
context
contract
create
data
definition
derived
distribution
economic
environment
established
estimate
evidence
export
factors
financial
formula
function
identified
income
indicate
individual
interpretation
involved
issues
labor
legal
legislation
major
method
occur
percent
period
policy
principle
procedure
process
required
research
response
role
section
sector
significant
similar
source
specific
structure
theory
variables

List Two

achieve
acquisition
administration
affect
appropriate
aspects
assistance
categories
chapter
commission
community
complex
computer
conclusion
conduct
consequences
construction
consumer
credit
cultural
design
distinction
elements
equation
evaluation
features
final
focus
impact
injury
institute
investment
items
journal
maintenance
normal
obtained
participation
perceived
positive
potential
previous
primary
purchase
range
region
regulations
relevant
resident
resources
restricted
security
select
site
sought
strategies
survey
text
traditional
transfer

List Three

alternative
circumstances
comments
compensation
components
consent
considerable
constant
constraints
contribution
convention
coordination
core
corporate
corresponding
criteria
deduction
demonstrate
document
dominant
emphasis
ensure
excluded
framework
funds
illustrated
immigration
implies
initial

instance
interaction
justification
layer
link
location
maximum
minorities
negative
outcomes
partnership
philosophy
physical
proportion
published
reaction
registered
reliance
removed
scheme
sequence
sex
shift
specified
sufficient
task
technical
techniques
technology
validity
volume

List Four

access
adequate
annual
apparent
approximated
attitudes
attributed
civil
code
commitment
communication
concentration
conference
contrast
cycle
debate
despite
dimensions
domestic
emerged
error
ethnic
goals
granted
hence
hypothesis
implementation
implications
imposed
integration
internal
investigation
job
label
mechanism
obvious
occupational
option
output
overall
parallel
parameters
phase
predicted
principal
prior
professional
project
promote
regime
resolution
retained
series
statistics
status
stress
subsequent
sum
summary
undertaken

List Five

academic
adjustment
alter
amendment
aware
capacity
challenge
clause
compounds
conflict
consultation
contact
decline
discretion
draft
enable
energy
enforcement
entities
equivalent
evolution
expansion
exposure
external
facilitate
fundamental
generated
generation
image
liberal
license
logic
marginal
medical
mental
modified
monitoring
network
notion
objective
orientation
perspective
precise
prime
psychology
pursue
ratio
rejected
revenue
stability
styles
substitution
sustainable
symbolic
target
transition
trend
version
welfare
whereas

List Six

abstract
accurate
acknowledged
aggregate
allocation
assigned
attached
author
bond
brief
capable
cited
cooperative
discrimination
display
diversity
domain
edition
enhanced
estate
exceed
expert
explicit
federal
fees
flexibility
furthermore
gender
ignored
incentive
incidence
incorporated
index
inhibition
initiatives
input
instructions
intelligence
interval
lecture
migration
minimum
ministry
motivation
neutral
nevertheless
overseas
preceding
presumption
rational
recovery
revealed
scope
subsidiary
tapes
trace
transformation
transport
underlying
utility

List Seven

adaptation
adults
advocate
aid
channel
chemical
classical
comprehensive
comprise
confirmed
contrary
converted
couple
decades
definite
deny
differentiation
disposal
dynamic
eliminate
empirical
equipment
extract
file
finite
foundation
global
grade
guarantee
hierarchical
identical
ideology
inferred
innovation
insert
intervention
isolated
media
mode
paradigm
phenomenon
priority
prohibited
publication
quotation
release
reverse
simulation
solely
somewhat
submitted
successive
survive
thesis
topic
transmission
ultimately
unique
visible
voluntary

List Eight

abandon
accompanied
accumulation
ambiguous
appendix
appreciation
arbitrary
automatically
bias
chart
clarity
conformity
commodity
complement
contemporary
contradiction
crucial
currency
denote
detected
deviation
displacement
dramatic
eventually
exhibit
exploitation
fluctuations
guidelines
highlighted
implicit
induced
inevitably
infrastructure
inspection
intensity
manipulation
minimized
nuclear
offset
paragraph
plus
practitioners
predominantly
prospect
radical
random
reinforced
restore
revision
schedule
tension
termination
theme
thereby
uniform
vehicle
via
virtually
visual
widespread

List Nine

accommodation
analogous
anticipated
assurance
attained
behalf
bulk
ceases
coherence
coincide
commenced
concurrent
confined
controversy
conversely
device
devoted
diminished
distorted
duration
erosion
ethical
format
founded
incompatible
inherent
insights
integral
intermediate
manual
mature
mediation
medium
military
minimal
mutual
norms
overlap
passive
portion
preliminary
protocol
qualitative
refine
relaxed
restraints
revolution
rigid
route
scenario
sphere
subordinate
supplementary
suspended
team
temporary
trigger
unified
violation
vision

List Ten

adjacent
albeit
assembly
collapse
colleagues
compiled
conceived
convinced
depression
encountered
enormous
forthcoming
inclination
integrity
intrinsic
invoked
levy
likewise
nonetheless
notwithstanding
odd
ongoing
panel
persistent
posed
reluctant
so-called
straightforward
undergo
whereby

Index of Skills

References beginning with **R** refer to handbook pages.

Literary Concepts

Reading and Critical Thinking

Writing

Grammar

Vocabulary

Speaking, Listening, and Viewing

Research, Test-taking, and Study Skills

Interdisciplinary Activities

Index of Authors and Titles

Acknowledgments

Unit 1

"The Most Dangerous Game" by Richard Connell. Copyright © 1924 by Richard Connell. Copyright renewed © 1952 by Louise Fox Connell. Used by permission of Brandt & Hochman Literary Agents, Inc. Any electronic copying or distribution of this text is expressly forbidden.

"The Leap" by Louise Erdrich. First published in *Harper's* magazine, March 1990. Later adapted for inclusion in *Tales of Burning Love* (HarperCollins, 1996). Copyright © 1990 and 1996 by Louise Erdrich, reprinted by permission of The Wylie Agency.

"Blues Ain't No Mockin Bird", copyright © 1971 by Toni Cade Bambara, from *Gorilla, My Love* by Toni Cade Bambara. Used by permission of Random House, Inc.

"Rules of the Game" from *The Joy Luck Club* by Amy Tan. Copyright © 1989 by Amy Tan. Used by permission of G. P. Putnam's Sons, a division of Penguin Group (USA) Inc.

"Liberty" by Julia Alvarez. Copyright © 1996 by Julia Alvarez. First published in *Writer's Harvest 2,* edited by Ethan Canin, published by Harcourt Brace and Company, 1996. Reprinted by permission of Susan Bergholz Literary Services, New York. All rights reserved.

"The Struggle to Be an All-American Girl" by Elizabeth Wong. Reprinted by permission of the author, www.elizabethwong.net.

"Legal Alien" is reprinted with permission from the publisher of Chants by Pat Mora (© 1985 Arte publico Press- University of Houston)

"Sweet Potato Pie" by Eugenia Collier. Reprinted by permission of the author.

"The Scarlet Ibis" by James Hurst. Reprinted by permission of the author.

"The Bass, the River, and Sheila Mant" is from *The Man Who Loved Levittown,* by W. D. Wetherell, © 1985. Used by permission of the University of Pittsburgh Press.

"The Secret Life of Walter Mitty" from *My World—And Welcome to It* © 1942 by James Thurber. Copyright renewed 1971 by James Thurber. Reprinted by permission of Rosemary A. Thurber and The Barbara Hogenson Agency. All rights reserved.

"American History" from *The Latin Deli: Prose and Poetry* by Judith Ortiz Cofer. Copyright © 1993 by Judith Ortiz Cofer. Reprinted by permission of The University of Georgia Press.

"The Drums of Washington" from *A Thousand Days: John F. Kennedy in the White House* by Arthur M. Schlesinger, Jr. Copyright © 1965, and renewed 1993 by Arthur M. Schlesinger, Jr. Reprinted by permission of Houghton Mifflin Company. All rights reserved.

Oscar, Hijuelos, "On 'The Aleph'" from *You've Got to Read This* by Ron Hansen and Jim Shepard (New York: Harper, 1994). Copyright © 1994 by Oscar Hijuelos. Used by permission of The Jennifer Lyons Literary Agency, LLC

Unit 2

Copyright © 1995 by Julia Alvarez. From "On Finding a Latino Voice," first published in Washington Post Book World, May 14, 1995, and later published in *Something to Declare,* by Plume, an imprint of Penguin Group (USA), in 1999 and originally in hardcover by Algonquin Books of Chapel Hill. Reprinted by permission of Susan Bergholz Literary Services, New York. All rights reserved.

"Of Dry Goods and Black Bow Ties" by Yoshiko Uchida, courtesy of the Bancroft Library, University of California, Berkeley.

"Only Daughter" by Sandra Cisneros. Copyright © 1990 by Sandra Cisneros. First published in *Glamour,* November 1990. Reprinted by permission of Susan Bergholz Literary Services, New York. All rights reserved.

"A Brother's Crime" from *Good Brother, Bad Brother: The Story of Edwin Booth and John Wilkes Booth* by James Cross Giblin. Copyright © 2005 by James Cross Giblin. Reprinted by permission of Clarion Books, an imprint of Houghton Mifflin Company. All rights reserved.

From *Black Boy* by Richard wright. Copyright 1937, 1942, 1944, 1945 by Richard Wright; renewed © 1973 by Ellen Wright. Repritned by permission of HarperCollins Publishers.

Reprinted with the permission of Simon Spotlight Entertainment, an imprint of Simon & Schuster, from *The Story of My Life: An Afghan Girl on the Other Side of the Sky* by Farah Ahmedi with Tamim Ansary. Text copyright © 2005 Nestegg Productions LLC.

From *All God's Children Need Traveling Shoes* by Maya Angelou, copyright © 1986 by Maya Angelou. Used by permission of Random House, Inc.

"Walking," copyright © 1990 by Linda Hogan, from *Dwellings: A Spiritual History of the Living World* by Linda Hogan. Used by permission of W.W. Norton & Company, Inc.

"Sayonara" from *North to the Orient,* copyright 1935 and renewed 1963 by Anne Morrow Lindbergh, reprinted by permission of Harcourt, Inc.

From *Into Thin Air* by Jon Krakauer, copyright © 1997 by Jon Krakauer. Used by permission of Villard Books, a division of Random House, Inc.

"That One Man's Profit Is Another's Loss" from *Essays* by Michel de Montaigne, translated with an introduction by J. M. Cohen (Penguin Classics, 1958). Copyright © J. M. Cohen, 1958. Reprinted by permission of Penguin Group (UK).

From "Thoughts on Fenway Park," by Jayson Stark. ESPN.com. Copyright © 2005 ESPN Internet Ventures. Reprinted by permission.

From "Being Perfect" by Anna Quindlen. Copyright © 1999 by Anna Quindlen. Reprinted by permission of International Creative Management, Inc.

Unit 3

"who are you,little i" copyright © 1963, 1991 by the Trustees for the E. E. Cummings Trust, from *Complete Poems: 1904–1962* by E. E. Cummings. Edited by George J. Firmage. Used by permission of Liveright Publishing Corporation.

"l(a" Copyright © 1958, 1986, 1991 by the Trustees for the E.E. Cummings Trust, from *Complete Poems: 1904-1962* by E.E. Cummings, edited by George J. Firmage. Used by permission of Liveright Publishing Corporation.

"The Monument" from *Native Guard: Poems* by Natasha Trethewey. Copyright © 2006 by Natasha Threthewey. Reprinted by permission of Houghton Mifflin Company. All rights reserved.

"The Black Snake" from *Twelve Moons* by Mary Oliver. Copyright © 1972, 1973, 1974, 1976, 1978, 1979 by Mary Oliver. By permission of Little, Brown and Co., Inc.

"The Peace of Wild Things" from *Openings,* copyright © 1968 and renewed 1996 by Wendell Berry, reprinted by permission of Harcourt Brace & Company.

From *The Devil in the White City* by Erik Larson, copyright © 2003 by Erik Larson. Used by permission of Crown Publishers, a division of Random House, Inc.

Haiku by Bashō and haiku by Chiyo, from *Zen Art for Meditation* by Stewart W. Holmes and Chimyo Horioko. Reprinted by permission of Charles E. Tuttle Co., Inc.

"Haiku" by Katy Peake, from *Shared Sightings,* copyright © 1995 by Sheila Golburgh Johnson. Reprinted by permission of Daniel & Daniel Publishers, Inc.

"Peace" by Paula Yup. Reprinted by permission of the author.

"How Things Work" from *A Fire In My Hands,* copyright © 2006, 1999 by Gary Soto, reprinted by permission of Harcourt, Inc.

"I Was a Skinny Tomboy Kid" by Alma Luz Villanueva. Reprinted by permission of the author.

"Choices" from *Cotton Candy on a Rainy Day* by Nikki Giovanni. Copyright © 1978 by Nikki Giovanni. Reprinted by permission of HarperCollins Publishers.

"Hope is the thing with feathers" and "I'm Nobody! Who are you?" reprinted by permission of the publishers, and the Trustees of Amherst College from *The Poems of Emily Dickinson,* Thomas H. Johnson, ed., Cambridge, Mass: The Belknap Press of Harvard University Press, copyright © 1951, 1955, 1979, 1983 by the President and Fellows of Harvard College.

"Defining the Grateful Gesture" by Yvonne Sapia. Reprinted by permission of the author.

"Remember" by Joy Harjo, from the book *She Had Some Horses.* Copyright © 1983. Appears by permission of the publisher, Thunder's Mouth Press, A Division of Avalon Publishing Group, Inc.

"The Road Not Taken" from *The Poetry of Robert Frost,* edited by Edward Connery Latham. Copyright 1916, 1969 by Henry Holt and Company. Copyright 1944 by Robert Frost. Reprinted by permission of Henry Holt and Company, LLC.

"Time," from *Translator's Son* by Joseph Bruchac. Repritned by permission of Barbara S. Kouts, literary Agent.

"The Secret" by Denise Levertov, from *Poems 1960–1967,* copyright © 1964 by Denise Levertov. Reprinted by permission of New Directions Publishing Corp.

"Grape Sherbet" from *Museum,* Carnegie Mellon University Press, © 1983 by Rita Dove. Reprinted by permission of the author.

"Goodnight Willie Lee, I'll See You in the Morning," copyright © 1975 by Alice Walker, from *Goodnight Willie Lee, I'll See You in the Morning* by Alice Walker. Used by permission of Doubleday, a division of Random House, Inc.

"Where are Those Songs" by Micere Mugo. Reprinted by permission of the author.

"My Mother Combs My Hair" by Chitra Banerjee Divakaruni, from *Black Candle,* copyright © 1991 by Chitra Banerjee Divakaruni. Reprinted by permission of CALYX Books.

"Lineage" from *This Is My Century: New and Collected Poems* by Margaret Walker Alexander. Copyright © 1989 by Margaret Walker Alexander. Reprinted by permission of The University of Georgia Press.

"Good Use for Bad Weather" from *Here at Eagle Pond* by Donald Hall. Copyright © 1990 by Donald Hall. Reprinted by permission of Houghton Mifflin Company. All rights reserved.

"Possum Crossing" from *Quilting the Black-Eyed Pea* by Nikki Giovanni. Copyright © 2002 by Nikki Giovanni. Reprinted by permission of HarperCollins Publishers.

Unit 4

"The Taxi" from *The Complete Poetical Works of Amy Lowell.* Copyright © 1955 by Houghton Mifflin Company. Copyright © renewed 1983 by Houghton Mifflin Company, Brinton P. Roberts, and G. D'Andelot Belin, Esquire. Reprinted by permission of Houghton Mifflin Company. All rights reserved.

"Counting the Beats" from *Complete Poems in One Volume* by Robert Graves. Reprinted by permission of Carcanet Press Ltd.

"The Bear" from *The Plays of Anton Chekhov* by Paul Schmidt. Copyright © 1997 by Paul Schmidt. Reprinted by permission of HarperCollins Publishers.

From ***Introduction to Shakespeare*** by Marchette Chute, copyright 1951, renewed © 1979 by Marchette Chute. Used by permission of Dutton, A Division of Penguin Young Readers Group, A Member of Penguin Group (USA) Inc., 345 Hudson Street, New York, NY 10014. All rights reserved.

"The Traveling Bear" from *The Complete Poetical Works of Amy Lowell.* Copyright © 1955 by Houghton Mifflin Company. Copyright © renewed 1983 by Houghton Mifflin Company, Brinton P. Roberts, and G. D'Andelot Belin, Esquire. Reprinted by permission of Houghton Mifflin Company. All rights reserved.

Unit 5

From *The Ramayana: A Shortened Modern Prose Version of the Indian Epic* by R. K. Narayan (First published by Viking Penguin Inc. 1972, Penguin Books 1977). Copyright © R. K. Narayan, 1972. Reprinted by permission of Penguin Group (UK) and Viking Penguin, a division of Penguin Group (USA) Inc.

"Ithaca" from *The Complete Poems of Cavafy,* copyright © 1961 and renewed 1989 by Rae Dalven, reprinted by permission of Harcourt, Inc.

"An Ancient Gesture" by Edna St. Vincent Millay. From *Collected Poems,* HarperCollins. Copyright © 1954, 1982 by Edna St. Vincent Millay and Norma Millay Ellis. All rights reserved. Used by permission of Elizabeth Barnett, literary executor.

"Waiting" from *The Penelopiad* by Margaret Atwood. Copyright © 2005 by O. W. Toad Ltd. Used by permission of Grove/Atlantic, Inc.

"Over Hill and Under Hill" from *The Hobbit* by J. R. R. Tolkien. Copyright © 1966 by J. R. R. Tolkien. Copyright © renewed 1994 by Christopher R. Tolkien, John F. R. Tolkien and Priscilla M. A. R. Tolkien. Reprinted by permission of Houghton Mifflin Company. All rights reserved.

"Perseus" from *Mythology* by Edith Hamilton. Copyright © 1942 by Edith Hamilton; copyright © renewed 1969 by Dorian Fielding Reid and Doris Fielding Reid. By permission of Little, Brown and Co., Inc.

"The Fenris Wolf" from *Legends of the North* by Olivia E. Coolidge. Copyright © 1951, renewed 1979 by Olivia E. Coolidge. Reprinted by permission of Houghton Mifflin Company. All rights reserved.

"Coyote and Crow" from *Indian Legends of the Pacific Northwest,* by Ella Clark. Copyright © 1953 The Regents of the University of California; © renewed 1981 by Ella E. Clark. Reprinted by permission of the University of California Press.

Unit 6

From "Buy Jupiter" by Isaac Asimov. Published by permission of The Estate of Isaac Asimov c/o Ralph M. Vicinanza Ltd.

"The Sentinel" by Arthur C. Clarke. Reprinted by permission of the author and the author's agents, Scovil Chichak Galen Literary Agency, Inc.

"2001: A Space Odyssey" by Roger Ebert. Copyright © The Ebert Co. Ltd. Reprinted by permission.

"He-y, Come on Ou-t!" by Sinichi Hoshi. Reprinted by permission of the translator, Stanleigh H. Jones.

"In Memoriam" by Nancy Kress. Reprinted by permission of the author.

"The Gift," copyright © 1990 by Li-Young Lee. Reprinted from *Rose* with the permission of BOA editions, Ltd., www.boaeditions.org.

"Purchase" by Naomi Long Madgett, from *Remembrances of Spring: Collected Early Poems* (Michigan State University Press, 1993). Reprinted by permission of the author.

"The Golden Kite, the Silver Wind" by Ray Bradbury. Copyright © 1953 by Epoch Associates, renewed 1981 by Ray Bradbury. Reprinted by permission of Don Congdon Associates, Inc.

"Wasps' Nest" from *Double Sin and Other Stories* by Agatha Christie, copyright 1925, 1926, 1929, 1954 © 1957, 1958, 1960, 1961 by Agatha Christie Ltd., copyright renewed. Used by permission of G.P. Putnam's sons, a division of Penguin Group (USA) Inc.

Reference Section

Martin, Melissa and Stephanie. *SparkNote on The Adventures of Huckleberry Finn.* 10 Dec. 2007 <http://www.sparknotes.com/lit/huckfinn/>.

Content from The Academic Word List, developed at the School of Linguistics and Applied Language Studies at Victoria University of Wellington, New Zealand, is reprinted by permission of Averil Coxhead.

http://language.massey.ac.nz/staff/awl/index.shtml.

Maps

Mapping Specialists Inc.

Photography

0 Private Collection/Bridgeman Art Library; **5** HIP/Art Resource, NY; **7** Private Collection/Bridgeman Art Library; **8** David David Gallery/SuperStock; **10** Brown Brothers; **11** St. Nicholas Center, www.stnicholascenter.org.; **12** Vanni/Art Resource, NY; **15** Tate Gallery, London/Art Resource, NY; **16** Gavin Graham Gallery, London/Bridgeman Art Library; **16** The Newark Museum/Art Resource, NY; **20** New York Times Pictures; **22** Private Collection, Photo ©Christie's Images/Bridgeman Art Library; **25** Stockbyte/SuperStock; **26** The Museum of Modern Art/Licensed by SCALA/Art Resource, NY; **28** Getty Images; **32** Bo Zaunders/CORBIS; **33** Aaron Haupt Photography; **35** Erich Lessing/Art Resource, NY; **37** Aaron Haupt Photography; **38** The Butler Institute of American Art, Youngstown, OH; **40** Getty Images; **43** Nancy Crampton; **45** Christie's Images. ©1998 Artists Rights Society, New York/ADAGP, Paris.; **46** Creatas/PunchStock; **48** Réunion des Musées Nationaux/Art Resource, NY; **50** (t)Christie's Images/SuperStock. ©1998 Estate of Pablo Picasso/Artists Rights Society, NY, (b)George Hall/CORBIS; **56** Library of Congress; **58** Erich Lessing/Art Resource, NY; **60** State Russian Museum, St. Petersburg/Bridgeman Art Library; **61** Getty Images; **62** Seamas Culligan/ZUMA/CORBIS; **64** North Wind Picture Archives; **65** (t)Getty Images, (b)Blue Lantern Studio/CORBIS; **69** 1998 Bill Gaskins; **71** Royalty-Free/CORBIS; **72** Hampton University Art Museum, Hampton, VA./Elizabeth Catlett/VAGA; **74** Private Collection/Jessie Coates/SuperStock; **75** Robert Franz/CORBIS; **76** Anthony Bannister/CORBIS; **79** E.O. Hoppe/Time Life Pictures/Getty Images; **81** Nationalmuseum 1992/E. Cornelius ©Estate of Bruno Liljefors/Licensed by VAGA, NY; **82** (l)Musee d'Orsay, Paris/Bridgeman Art Library; **82** (br)Heinz Wohner/Getty Images; **84** Christie's Images/SuperStock; **86** Tom Brakefield/SuperStock; **87** Getty Images; **91 92** Rick Farrell/TIME; **95** Private Collection/Bridgeman Art Library; **96** Calvin and Hobbes ©1986 Watterson. Dist. By Universal Press Syndicate. Reprinted with permission. All rights reserved.; **98** Frank Capri/Getty Images; **100** Royalty-Free/CORBIS; **101** Getty Images; **102** Private Collection/Bridgeman Art Library; **107** Bettmann/CORBIS; **108** CNAC/MNAM/Dist. Réunion des Musées Nationaux/Art Resource, NY; **114** Bettmann/CORBIS; **118** (t)Scala/Art Resource, NY, (b)Michael Rutherford/SuperStock; **120** Brooklyn Museum/CORBIS; **121** Fred Partridge/Cheltenham Art Gallery & Museums, Glouchestershire, UK/Bridgeman Art Library; **122** (tl tc)Getty Images, (tr)Dorling Kindersley/Getty Images, (b)The Art Archive/Victoria and Albert Museum London/Sally Chappell; **127** Theo Westernberger; **129** T. F. Chen Cultural Center/SuperStock; **133** Bridgeman Art Library; **134** AP Images; **136** Art Explosion; **138** Visual Arts Library/Art Resource, NY; **140** T. F. Chen Cultural Center/SuperStock; **143** Patti Mollica/SuperStock; **144** Smithsonian American Art Museum, Washington, DC/Art Resource, NY; **146** N. Carter/North Wind Picture Archives; **149** Hirshhorn Museum and Sculpture Garden, Smithsonian Institution. Gift of Joseph W. Hirshhorn, 1966. Photographer; Lee Stalsworth; **151** Getty Images; **155** MedioImages/Punchstock; **157** Burstein Collection/CORBIS; **158** Getty Images; **160** Fine Art Photographic Library, London/Art Resource, NY; **162** Mark Steinmetz; **163** Private Collection/Christie's Images; **164** Getty Images; **166** CORBIS; **167** Christie's Images/SuperStock; **168** Getty Images; **172** Courtesy of W.D. Wetherell; **176** Ed Labadie/Stock Illustration Source; **179** Winslow Homer/SuperStock; **183** The Museum of Modern Art/Licensed by SCALA/Art Resource, NY; **184** Private Collection, ©Agnew's, London/Bridgeman Art Library; **186** Time & Life Pictures/Getty Images; **188** The Art Archive/Imperial War Museum; **191** Edward Hopper/Indianapolis Museum of Art/Bridgeman Art Library; **196** Library of Congress; **198** Victoria & Albert Museum, London/Art Resource, NY; **199** P. Hussenot/photocuisine/CORBIS; **201** Julius L. Stewart/SuperStock; **203** Georges Stein/Gavin Graham Gallery, London/Bridgeman Art Library; **205** Getty Images; **208** University of Georgia, Peter Frey; **210** The Newark Museum/Art Resource, NY; **213** Patti Mollica/CORBIS; **217** ©The Andy Warhol Foundation, Inc./Art Resource, NY; **220** (t)AP Images, (b)Bettmann/CORBIS; **221** Carl Mydans/Time Life Pictures/Getty Images; **222** CORBIS; **225** Jerry Bauer; **227** Valerie Spain/Stock Illustration Source; **229** Nancy R. Schiff/Getty Images; **231** National Museum in Cracow, Poland/Bridgeman Art Library; **234** The State Russian Museum/CORBIS; **237** Erich Lessing/Art Resource, NY; **242** The Fleming-Wyfold Art Foundation/Bridgeman Art Library; **245** Images.com/CORBIS; **248** The McGraw-Hill Companies; **258** Private Collection/David Findlay, Jr. Fine Art, NYC/Bridgeman Art Library; **261** Private Collection/Bridgeman Art Library; **262** Theo Westernberger; **265** Private Collection/Bridgeman Art Library; **266** Foxtrot ©2006 Bill Amend. Reprinted with permission of Universal Press Syndicate. All rights reserved.; **267** Fine Art Photographic Library/CORBIS; **268** Photograph by George Fry; **270** Museum of History and Industry, Seattle, Washington; **273** California Historical Society; **274** E.O. Hoppe/CORBIS; **276** Dana Tynan/AP Images; **278** Kactus Foto, Santiago, Chile/SuperStock; **282** Photo of James Cross Giblin courtesy of the author; **284** Mary Evans Picture Library/The Image Works; **286** CORBIS; **288** Library of Congress; **289** Getty Images; **292-296** Excerpt from The Murder of Abraham Lincoln, ©2005 Rick Geary, published by permission from NBM Publishing.; **297** Hulton Archive/Getty Images; **299** Jerry Archieri/CORBIS; **301** Smith College Museum of Art, Northampton, Massachusetts. Purchased 1942. Licensed by VAGA, NY.; **307** David

Bartolomi Photography; **309** Shepard Sherbell/CORBIS; **310** (inset)Art Explosion, Map Art; **313** Michael S. Yamashita/CORBIS; **320** "Minefield surrounding Kuito, Angola" photo by Tim Grant (www.iinet.net.au/~pictim). National Geographic/Getty Images; **321** Giovanni Diffidenti/International Committee of the Red Cross; **322** Darren McCollester/Getty Images; **325** Smithsonian American Art Museum, Washington, DC/Art Resource, NY; **326** Elizabeth Barakah Hodges/SuperStock; **327** Pam Ingalls/CORBIS; **328** Nancy Robinson/AP Images; **331** John Shaw/Tom Stack & Associates; **332** Rosemary Woods/Getty Images; **334** Tilly Willis/Getty Images; **337** (l c)Getty Images; (b)Dennis Stock/Magnum Photos; **0340** Douglas Kentall; **342** Getty Images; **344** Christie's Images/CORBIS; **348** Bettmann/CORBIS; **350** The Art Archive/Private Collection/Chris Deakes; **355** Time Life Pictures/Getty Images; **357** Neal Beidleman/Woodfin Camp & Associates; **359** Scott Fischer/Woodfin Camp and Associates; **360** Neal Beidleman/Woodfin Camp & Associates; **363** Scott Fischer/Woodfin Camp & Associates; **366** Time Life Pictures/Getty Images; **369-373** Onne Van Der Wal/TIME; **375** Schalkwijk/Art Resource, NY; **376** National Portrait Gallery, Smithsonian Institution/Art Resource, NY; **378 380** Bettmann/CORBIS; **383** (l c)Getty Images; (b)Bettmann/CORBIS; **388** akg-images; **390** The Corcoran Gallery of Art/CORBIS; **392** Pam Ingalls/CORBIS; **395** Erich Lessing/Art Resource, NY; **396** Comstock Images/Alamy Images; **401** CORBIS; **403** Ed Quinn/CORBIS; **404** Ezra Shaw/Getty Images; **405** Jed Jacobsohn/Getty Images; **407** Mike Segar/Reuters/CORBIS; **409** Icon SMI/CORBIS; **412** AP Images; **417** Giraudon/Art Resource, NY; **418** Images.com/CORBIS; **419** Getty Images; **424** Christie's Images Ltd.; **432** (l r)Aaron Haupt Photography; **433** (cr)Underwood and Underwood/CORBIS; **440** Vincent van Gogh. Rijksmuseum Kroeller-Mueller, Otterio, The Netherlands/Art Resource, NY; **441** Scala/Art Resource, NY; **442** Calvin and Hobbes © 1995 Watterson. Dist. By Universal Press Syndicate. Reprinted with permission. All rights reserved.; **444** Mary Evans Picture Library; **445** The Art Archive/National Archives Washington DC; **450** Library of Congress; **452** John Newcomb/SuperStock; **455** AP/World Wide Photos; **457** Leslie Hinrichs/SuperStock; **458** Scala/Art Resource, NY; **461** Library of Congress; **462** FOXTROT ©Bill Amend. Reprinted with permission of UNIVERSAL PRESS SYNDICATE. All rights reserved.; **463** Private Collection/Bridgeman Art Library; **465** The National Portrait Gallery, Smithsonian Institution/Art Resource, NY; **471-473** Brian Doben/TIME; **475** Library of Congress; **476** Julian Novorol/Bridgeman Art Library/Getty Images; **477** Getty Images; **479** Smithsonian American Art Museum, Washington, DC/Art Resource, NY; **481** Fred Jones Jr. Museum of Art, University of Oklahoma, Purchase, U.S. State Department Collection, 1948/Bridgeman Art Library; **482** Dea Picture Library/Getty Images; **485** Scala/Art Resource, NY; **486** Mark Lennihan/AP Images; **487** Charles & Josette Lenars/CORBIS; **488** Academy of Natural Sciences of Philadelphia/CORBIS; **491** Amy Wollot/The State Journal/AP Images; **493** Fine Art Photographic Library, London/Art Resource, NY; **496** Snark/Art Resource, NY; **498** Asian Art & Archaeology, Inc./CORBIS; **499** (tl tr)Getty Images, (b)Yoshitoshi/Asian Art & Archaeology, Inc./CORBIS; **503** Private Collection/Bridgeman Art Library; **504** Non Sequitur ©Wiley Miller. Dist. By Universal Press Syndicate. Reprinted with permission. All rights reserved.; **506** Courtesy Gary Soto; **508** Erich Lessing/Art Resource, NY; **510** Leon Canerot; **511** Brand X/SuperStock; **513** Bridgeman Art Library; **515** Steve Helber/AP Images; **517** Banque d'Images, ADAGP, Art Resource, NY; **519** Hulton Archive/Getty Images; **521** Mimmo Jodice/CORBIS; **522** Diana Ong/SuperStock; **523** Getty Images; **524** Erich Lessing/Art Resource, NY; **526** Joan Fetchen; **529** SuperStock; **531** Library of Congress; **533** Bridgeman Art Library; **534** Giraudon/Art Resource, NY; **536** Paul Abdoo/MPI/Getty; **537** Marilyn Angel Wynn/Native Stock; **538** Tim Nicola courtesy Artistic Gallery, Santa Fe. Photography by Jerry Jacka.; **540** Eric Schaal/Getty Images; **542** Sotheby's/akg-images; **543** (t)Getty Images, (b)GET FUZZY: ©Darby Conley/Dist. by United Feature Syndicate, Inc.; **546** Martin Benjamin; **548** The Jacob and Gwendolyn Lawrence Foundation/Art Resource, NY; **550** Library of Congress; **553** The Jacob and Gwendolyn Lawrence Foundation/Art Resource, NY; **556** Christopher Felver/CORBIS; **557** Bettmann/CORBIS; **558** Bildarchiv Preussischer Kulturbesitz/Art Resource, NY; **559** Erich Lessing/Art Resource, NY; **561** Michael Escoffery/Art Resource, NY; **562** Fine Art Photographic Library/CORBIS; **564** Dan Addison/U.Va. Public Affairs; **566-567** Anna Belle Lee Washington/SuperStock; **569** Adam Scull/Globe Photos, Inc. 200; **570** Images.com/CORBIS; **571** Erich Lessing/Art Resource, NY; **573** Charlotte Thege/Alamy Images; **575** Todd Davidson/Getty Images; **576** North Carolina Museum of Art, Raleigh. Purchased with funds from the State of North Carolina; **580** Neela Banerjee; **582** Private collection/Bridgeman Art Library; **584** (tl tr)Getty Images; (b)AFP/Getty Images; **588–589** From BONE ®: OUT FROM BONEVILLE by Jeff Smith. Published by Graphix, an imprint of Scholastic Inc. Copyright ©2005, 1992, 1991 by Jeff Smith. Reprinted by permission. **590** Nancy Crampton; **592** Smithsonian American Art Museum, Washington, DC/Art Resource, NY; **599** CORBIS; **604** (l r cl)Aaron Haupt Photography; **612** Andre Rouillard/SuperStock; **616** The Art Archive; **617** Miramax/Dimension Films/The Kobal Collection/Paul Chedlow; **619** Private Collection/Bridgeman Art Library; **621** Gustavo Tomsich/CORBIS; **622** Manchester Art Gallery, UK/Bridgeman Art Library; **623** Private Collection/Bridgeman Art Library; **624** Erich Lessing/Art Resource, NY; **626** Private Collection/Christie's Images; **629** Palazzo Ducale, Mantua, Italy/SuperStock; **634** Geoffrey Clements/CORBIS; **643** Hermitage, St. Petersburg, Russia/Bridgeman Art Library; **648** Private collection/Christie's Images; **660** akg-images; **665** Ashmolean Museum, Oxford; **670** Private collection/Christie's Images; **674** Courtesy of Julian Hartnoll/Bridgeman Art Library; **677** ArenaPal/Topham/The Image Works; **683** Private Collection/Christie's Images; **689** Fine Art Photographic Library/CORBIS; **694** Birmingham Museums and Art Gallery/Bridgeman Art Library; **699** Bridgeman Art Library/SuperStock; **710** From the RSC Collection with the permission of the Govenors of the Royal Shakespeare Theatre. Photo by Brian Glover.; **716** Master of the Jarves Cassonie/SuperStock; **720** Art Gallery of South Australia, Adelaide. Elder Bequest Fund 1899.; **730** Art Resource, NY; **734** Derby Museum & Art Gallery, England/Bridgeman Art Library; **738** Frederick Leighton/From the collection of Agnes Scott College; **741** (tl tr)Getty Images; (b)akg-images; **750** Max Furguson/Bridgeman Art Library/Getty Images; **752** Illustration Works; **754** Joe Baker/Stock Illustration Source; **755** Louis K. Meisel Gallery, Inc./CORBIS; **756** Erich Lessing/Art Resource, NY; **758** Topham/The Image Works; **760** Christie's Images/CORBIS; **765 768** Christie's Images Ltd; **773** UCSB/Writer Pictures; **775** Bettmann/CORBIS; **776** Workbook Stock/Bruce Brown/Jupiter Images; **779 782** Bettmann/CORBIS; **785** Peter Sickles/SuperStock; **789** Getty Images; **791** Historical Picture Archive/CORBIS; **794** The Museum of Modern Art/Licensed by SCALA/Art Resource, NY; **795** SuperStock, Inc.; **800** Photodisc/Alamy Images; **802** Sophie Bassouls/CORBIS SYGMA; **806** Paramount Pictures/Hulton Archive/Getty Images; **809** Ed Bradshaw/TIME; **810** Kaveh Golestan/TIME; **811** The Granger Collection; **814** (l r)Aaron Haupt Photography; **815** (l)Jonathan Magee/Trinity University, (cr br)Aaron Haupt Photography; **822** Archivo Iconografico, S.A./CORBIS; **824** CORBIS; **825** (t)The Philadelphia Museum of Art/Art Resource, NY; **827** Art Resource, NY; **829** Erich Lessing/Art Resource, NY; **830** Private Collection/Bridgeman Art Library; **832** SuperStock; **833** Erich Lessing/Art Resource, NY; **834** SEF/Art Resource, NY; **836-0837** Kevin Fleming; **840** The Art Archive/Dagli Orti; **842** Stapleton Collection/CORBIS; **849** Erich Lessing/Art Resource, NY; **851** Pushkin Museum, Moscow/Bridgeman Art Library; **852** akg-images; **860** National Gallery of Victoria, Melbourne/Bridgeman Art Library; **862** akg-images/Peter Connolly; **864** Scala/Art Resource, NY; **869** Erich Lessing/Art Resource, NY; **872** SuperStock; **875** Private Collection, The Stapleton Collection/Bridgeman Art Library; **880** National Gallery Collection; By kind permission of the Trustees of the National Gallery, London/CORBIS; **883** Erich Lessing/Art Resource, NY; **887** Ancient Art & Architecture Collection; **890** Erich Lessing/Art Resource, NY; **892** The Metropolitan Museum of Art, Fletcher Fund,

1956 (56.171.38). Photograph ©1986 The Metropolitan Museum of Art; **895** Bettmann/CORBIS; **896** (l c)Getty Images; David Lees/ CORBIS; **902** Scala/Art Resource, NY; **904** Private Collection, The Maas Gallery, London/Bridgeman Art Library; **906** The Art Archive/Private Collection London; **908-911** Mark Leong/TIME; **912** Haywood Magee/ Getty Images; **914** The McGraw-Hill Companies; **916** akg-images; **918** Musée Jeanne d'Aboville, La Fere, France, Lauros/Giraudon/ Bridgeman Art Library; **923** (t)Getty Images, (b)Mikhail Belomlinsky/ Private Collection/Bridgeman Art Library; **927-930** Reprinted by permission of HarperCollins Publishers Ltd. ©1937 JRR Tolkien; **931** Private Collection/Bridgeman Art Library; **932** Images.com/ CORBIS; **934** Gjon Mili/Getty Images; **936** Bridgeman Art Library; **941** Giraudon/Art Resource, NY; **942** Getty Images; **946** National Museum of Iceland, Reykjavik/Bridgeman Art Library; **947** Werner Forman/Art Resource, NY; **949** Royal Library, Copenhagen, Denmark/ Bridgeman Art Library; **953** Connie Ricca/CORBIS; **955** Academy of Natural Sciences of Philadelphia/CORBIS; **958** Butler Institute of American Art, Youngstown, OH/Bridgeman Art Library; **959** Newberry Library/SuperStock; **961** Alexander Gardner/CORBIS; **969** J. Howard Miller/CORBIS; **976** (l)Aaron Haupt Photography; **977** (tr)Barnabas Bosshart/CORBIS; **984** George Tooker/Metropolitan Museum of Art, New York/Bridgeman Art Library; **988** Douglas Kirkland/CORBIS; **989** Tim Bird/CORBIS; **991** Private Collection/Bridgeman Art Library; **992** Ellen Schuster/Getty Images; **994** William Coupon/CORBIS; **997** Paul Anderson/Images.com/CORBIS; **999** Sean Sexton Collection/CORBIS; **1001** Erich Lessing/Art Resource, NY; **1002** Mary Evans Picture Library; **1005** Getty Images; **1008** AP Images; **1008** SUNSET BOULEVARD/CORBIS SYGMA; **1009** akg-images; **1012** ©Shinchosha; **1015** Bob Daemmrich/Stock Boston; **1017** Christie's Images/Bridgeman Art Library. ©1998 Charly Herscovici, Brussels/Artists Rights Society, New York.; **1021** Henry Koningisor; **1023** A. Belov/CORBIS; **1025** Private Collection, Phillips, Fine Art Auctioneers, New York/Bridgeman Art Library; **1030** Réunion des Musées Nationaux/Art Resource, NY; **1032** Caroline Burrows/ Illustration Works/Getty Images; **1033** Bildarchiv Preussischer Kulturbesitz/Art Resource, NY; **1034** Vince Bucci/Getty Images; **1036** Scala/Art Resource, NY; **1039** SEF/Art Resource, NY; **1043** Keystone/Getty Images; **1045** Peter Ruck/BIPs/Getty Images; **1047** Albright-Knox Art Gallery/CORBIS; **1051** Erich Lessing/Art Resource, NY; **1052** Time Life Pictures/Mansell//Getty Images; **1054** ImageGap/Alamy Images; **1055** Mary Evan Picture Library; **1058** Bettmann/CORBIS; **1059** Alinari/Art Resource, NY; **1063** Bettmann/CORBIS; **1065** Getty Images; **1068** Karl Ammann/ TIME; **1071** W. and D. Downey/Getty Images; **1073 1076 1079** Images.com/CORBIS; **1084** (tl)Brand X Pictures/PunchStock; **1087** Keren Su/CORBIS; **1093** (cr b)Aaron Haupt Photography; **1100** mediablitzimages (uk) Limited/Alamy Images; **1103** Digital Vision/Alamy Images; **1104** Frank Chmura/Alamy Images; **1105** Terence Mendoza/Alamy Images; **1109** bobo/Alamy Images; **1111** tine eelman/Alamy Images; **1114** Michael Newman/PhotoEdit; **1118** Photodisc/Alamy Images; **1121** Sean Justice/CORBIS; **1225** Mark Leong/TIME.